THE

HOLY BIBLE

CONTAINING THE

OLD AND NEW TESTAMENTS

THE TEXT CAREFULLY PRINTED FROM THE MOST CORRECT COPIES OF THE PRESENT AUTHORIZED TRANSLATION, INCLUDING THE MARGINAL READINGS AND PARALLEL TEXTS

WITH

A COMMENTARY AND CRITICAL NOTES

DESIGNED AS A HELP TO A BETTER UNDERSTANDING OF THE SACRED WRITINGS

BY ADAM CLARKE, LL.D., F.S.A., &c.

A NEW EDITION, WITH THE AUTHOR'S FINAL CORRECTIONS

For whatsoever things were written aforetime were written for our learning, that we through patience and comfort of the Scriptures might have hope.—Rom. xv. 4.

THE OLD TESTAMENT

VOLUME IV.—ISAIAH TO MALACHI

ABINGDON PRESS
NASHVILLE • NEW YORK

ISBN 0-687-09126-8

Printed in the United States of America

INTRODUCTION

TO THE

BOOK OF THE PROPHET ISAIAH

ON the term *prophet,* and on the nature and several kinds of prophecy, I have already discoursed in different parts of this work. See the notes on Gen. xv. 1, xx. 7, and the preface to the four Gospels, and Acts of the Apostles. A few things only require to be recapitulated. נבא *naba* signifies not only to *foretell future events,* but also to *pray* and *supplicate;* and נביא *nabi,* the *prophet,* was by office not only a *declarer of events still future,* but the general *preacher* of the day; and as he frequently foresaw the approach of disastrous times, such was the wickedness of the people, he employed his time in counselling sinners to turn from the error of their ways, and in making strong prayer and supplication to God to avert the threatened judgments: for such predictions, however apparently *positive* in their *terms,* were generally *conditional;* strange as this may appear to some who, through their general ignorance of every thing but the peculiarities of their own creed, suppose that every occurrence is impelled by an *irresistible necessity.*

To his own conduct, in reference to such matters, God has been pleased to give us a *key* (see Jer. xviii.) which opens all difficulties, and furnishes us with a general comment on his own providence. God is absolute master of his own ways; and as he has made man a *free agent,* whatever concerns him in reference to futurity, on which God is pleased to express his mind in the way of *prophecy,* there is a *condition* generally implied or expressed. As this is but seldom attended to by partial interpreters, who wish by their doctrine of *fatalism* to bind even God himself, many contradictory sentiments are put in the mouths of his prophets.

In ancient times those who were afterwards called PROPHETS were termed SEERS; 1 Sam. ix. 9. הראה *haroeh,* the *seeing person;* he who *perceives mentally* what the design of God is. Sometimes called also חזה *chozeh,* the man who has *visions,* or supernatural *revelations;* 1 Kings xxii. 17; 2 Kings xvii. 13. Both these terms are translated *seer* in our common Version. They were sometimes called *men of God,* and *messengers* or *angels of God.* In their case it was ever understood that all God's prophets had an extraordinary commission and had their message given them by immediate inspiration.

In this the heathen copied after the people of God. They also had their *prophets* and *seers;* and hence their *augurs* and *auguries,* their *haruspices,* and *priestesses,* and their *oracles;* all pretending to be divinely inspired, and to declare nothing but the *truth;* for what was *truth* and *fact* among the *former,* was *affected* and *pretended* among the *latter.*

Many *prophets* and *seers* are mentioned in the sacred writings; but, *fragments* and *insulated prophecies* excepted, we have the works of only SIXTEEN; *four* of whom are termed the *former* or *larger* prophets, and *twelve,* the *latter* or *minor* prophets. They have these epithets, not from *priority of time,* or from *minor importance,* but merely from the places they occupy in the present arrangement of the books in the Bible, and from the relative *size* of their productions.

The Jews reckon *forty-eight prophets,* and *seven prophetesses;* and *Epiphanius,* in a fragment preserved by *Cotelerius,* reckons not fewer than *seventy-three prophets,* and *ten prophetesses;* but in both collections there are many which have no Scriptural pretensions to such a distinguished rank.

The *succession* of prophets in the Jewish Church is well worthy of note, because it not only manifests the merciful regards of God towards that people, but also the uninterrupted succession of the *prophetic influence*, at least from Moses to Malachi, if not before; for this gift was not withheld under the *patriarchal* dispensation; indeed we might boldly ask any man to show when the time was in which God left himself without a witness of this kind.

To show this succession, I shall endeavour to give the different prophets in order of time.

1. The first man, ADAM, has an undoubted right to stand at the *head of the prophets*, as he does at the head of the *human race*. His declaration concerning marriage, "For this cause shall a man leave his father and mother, and cleave to his wife," is so truly *prophetic*, that no doubt can be formed on the subject. There was then nothing in *nature* or *experience* to justify such an assertion; and he could have it only by Divine inspiration. The millions of instances which have since occurred, and the numerous laws which have been founded on this principle among all the nations of the earth, show with what precision the declaration was conceived, and with what truth it was published to the world. Add to this, his correct *knowledge of the nature of the different animals*, so that he could impose on them names expressive of their respective natures or *propensities;* which proves that he must have acted under a Divine inspiration; for known only to God are all his works from the beginning.

2. ENOCH, the seventh from Adam, is expressly called a *prophet;* and St. Jude, ver. 14, 15, has preserved a fragment of one of his prophecies, relative to the corruption of the antediluvian world, and the approaching judgments of God.

3. NOAH was a *prophet* and *preacher of righteousness*, and predicted the general deluge, and the time of respite which God in his mercy had granted to the offenders of that age.

4. ABRAHAM is expressly called a *prophet* also, Gen. xx. 7; and it appears from Psa. cv. 15, that he partook of the Divine anointing.

5. ISAAC, Gen. xxvii. 27, predicted the future greatness of his son Jacob, and of the race that was to spring from him.

6. JACOB was so especially favoured with the prophetic gift, that he distinctly foretold what should happen to each of his sons. See Gen. xlix.

7. JOSEPH was favoured with several prophetic visions, and had the gift of interpreting dreams which portended *future occurrences;* (see Gen. xxvii., xl., xli.;) and *foretold* the redemption of the Israelites from Egypt; Gen. l. 25. Thus far the prophetic influence extended through the patriarchal dispensation for about *two thousand three hundred and seventy* years from the creation.

With the Jewish dispensation the prophetic gift revived; and,

8. MOSES became one of the most eminent prophets that had ever appeared. He not only enjoyed the continual prophetic afflatus, but had such visions of and intercourse with God as no other person either before or since was favoured with; and by which he was highly qualified to perform the arduous work which God had given him to do, and to frame that *Code of Laws* which had no equal before the promulgation of the *Gospel.* See Deut. xxiv. 10. He predicted expressly the coming of the Messiah. See Deut. xviii. 18.

9. AARON, the brother of Moses, his prime minister and God's high priest, was also a partaker of his Divine influence, and declared the will of God to Pharaoh and the Israelites, not merely from information received from Moses, but also by immediate communication from God. See Exod. iv. 15.

10. MIRIAM, the sister of Moses and Aaron, is expressly called a prophetess, Exod. xv. 20; Num. xii. 2.

11. JOSHUA, who succeeded Moses, was a partaker of the same grace. He was appointed by Moses under the especial direction of God; Num. xxvii. 18–23; Deut. xxxiv. 9; and has always been reckoned among the Jews as one of the prophets. See Ecclus. xlvi. 1–6.

Though I cannot place them in the same rank, yet it is necessary to state that, by the

Jews, several of the *judges* are classed among the prophets; such as *Othniel, Ehud, Samson,* and *Barak.*

12. DEBORAH, the coadjutor of Barak, is called a *prophetess,* Judg. iv. 4. During her time, and down to the days of Eli the high priest, prophecy had been very scarce, there having been very few on whom the Spirit of the Lord had rested; for "the word of the Lord was scarce in those days, and there was no open vision;" 1 Sam. iii. 1.

13. HANNAH, the wife of Elkanah, is supposed to have partaken of the spirit of prophecy; and to have foretold, at least indirectly, the advent of the Messiah, and the glory that should be revealed under the Gospel. See her Song, 1 Sam. ii. 1–10. And what renders this more likely is, that it is on the *model,* and with many of the *expressions,* of this song, that the blessed Virgin composed her *Magnificat,* Luke i. 46–55.

14. SAMUEL, her son, was one of the most eminent of the Jewish prophets, and was the last, and indeed the *greatest,* of the *judges* of Israel. In his time the prophetic influence seems to have rested upon *many;* so that we find even *whole schools* or *colleges* of *prophets* which were under his direction. See 1 Sam. x. 5, 10, xix. 20, and elsewhere.

15. DAVID united in himself the character of *prophet* and king, in the most eminent manner; and from his reign down to the *captivity* the succession was not only *not interrupted,* but these extraordinary messengers of God became very *numerous.*

16. GAD flourished under his reign, and was emphatically called David's *Seer,* 2 Sam. xxiv. 11; 1 Chron. xxi. 9, 19, 20; and it appears that he had written a Book of Prophecies, which is now lost, 1 Chron. xxix. 29.

17. NATHAN lived also under the same reign, 2 Sam. vii. 2; and, in conjunction with *Gad,* composed a book of the acts of David, 1 Chron. xxix. 29.

18. To SOLOMON also, son of David, the prophetic gift has been attributed. This might be implied in the extraordinary wisdom with which God had endowed him, 1 Kings iii. 5–9; 2 Chron. i. 7, vii. 12; and in his writings several prophetic declarations may be found, even independently of the *supposed* reference to *Christ and his Church* in the *Canticles.*

19. IDDO is termed a *Seer,* 2 Chron. xii. 15, xiii. 22; and was one of Solomon's biographers.

20. SHEMAIAH lived under *Rehoboam;* he is called *a man of God,* and to him the word of prophecy came relative to Judah and Benjamin, 1 Kings xii. 22–24. Some think this was the same person who was sent to *Jeroboam* relative to his idolatry; see 1 Kings xiii. 1, &c.

21. AHIJAH, the Shilonite, prophesied to Jeroboam, 1 Kings xi. 29–39.

22. HANANI the *Seer* prophesied under *Azariah* and Asa, 2 Chron. xvi. 7.

23. JEHU, son of Hanani, prophesied under Jehoshaphat, 1 Kings xvi. 1, 7; 2 Chron. xvi. 7, xix. 2, and xx. 34.

24. AZARIAH, the son of *Oded,* prophesied under *Asa,* 2 Chron. xv. 1.

25. ELIJAH prophesied under the reign of *Ahab* and *Jezebel.*

26. ELISHA succeeded Elijah under the same reigns. And these eminent men had many disciples on whom the spirit of prophecy rested. *They,* and their *masters,* Elijah and Elisha, prophesied in the kingdoms both of Israel and Judah. Their histories make a prominent part of the first and second Books of Kings; and are well known.

27. MICAIAH, the son of Imlah, prophesied under the same reign, 1 Kings xxi. 9.

28. HOSEA prophesied under *Jeroboam* the second, king of Israel, and under the reign of *Uzziah,* king of Judah.

29. ISAIAH was contemporary with Hosea, but probably began to prophesy a little later than he did.

30. AMOS prophesied about the same time.

31. JONAH, son of Amittai, is supposed to have been contemporary with the above.

32. ELIEZER, the son of Dodavah, prophesied against *Jehoshaphat* and *Ahaziah,* 2 Chron. xx. 37.

33. Jahaziel, son of Zechariah, prophesied against Judah and Israel under the same reign, 2 Chron. xx. 14.

34. Micah prophesied against Samaria and Jerusalem, in the reigns of *Jotham, Ahaz,* and *Hezekiah.*

35. Oded, father of Azariah, prophesied against *Asa,* 2 Chron. xv. 8.

36. Nahum prophesied under *Hezekiah.*

37. Joel, under *Josiah.*

38. Jeremiah, about the same time.

39. Zephaniah, under the same reign. See their prophecies.

40. Huldah, the prophetess, was contemporary with the above.

41. Igdaliah, called *a man of God,* and probably a prophet, was contemporary with Jeremiah, Jer. xxxv. 4.

42. Habakkuk lived about the end of the reign of *Josiah,* or the beginning of that of *Jehoiakim.*

43. Ezekiel lived under the captivity; and prophesied in Mesopotamia, about the time that Jeremiah prophesied in Jerusalem.

44. Obadiah lived in Judea, after the capture of Jerusalem and before the desolation of Idumea by Nebuchadnezzar.

45. Daniel prophesied in Babylon during the captivity.

46. Haggai prophesied during and after the captivity.

47. Urijah, the son of Shemaiah, prophesied under *Jehoiakim.* See Jer. xxvi. 20, 21.

48. Zechariah, son of Barachiah, flourished in the second year of *Darius,* after the captivity.

49. Malachi lived under *Nehemiah,* and some time after Haggai and Zechariah.

Here is a succession of divinely inspired men, by whom God at sundry times and in divers manners spake unto the fathers, from the beginning of the world down to the restoration from the Babylonish captivity, a period of *three thousand six hundred* years. From the time of Malachi, who was the last of the prophets, till the advent of Christ, a period of nearly *four hundred* years elapsed without vision or prophecy: but during the whole of that interval the Jews had the *law* and *the prophetical writings,* to which, till the time of Christ, there was no necessity to add any thing; for God had with the writings of the last mentioned prophet completed the *canon of the Old Testament,* nothing being farther necessary, till he should, in the fulness of time, superadd the Gospel; and this having taken place, vision and prophecy are now for ever sealed up, and the temple of God is established among all genuine believers in Christ Jesus.

It is not easy to ascertain the *order* in which the *sixteen prophets,* whose writings are preserved, have succeeded to each other. There are *chronological notes* prefixed to several of their prophecies, which assist to settle generally the times of the whole. Several were contemporary, as the reader has already seen in the preceding list. The major and minor prophets may be thus arranged:—

1. Jonah, under the reign of Jeroboam the second.
2. Hosea, under Uzziah, Jotham, Ahaz, &c.
3. Joel, contemporary with Hosea.
4. Amos, under Uzziah and Jeroboam the second.
5. Isaiah, under Uzziah, Jotham, Ahaz, and Hezekiah.
6. Micah, contemporary with Isaiah.
7. Nahum, under the reign of Hezekiah.
8. Habakkuk, under the reign of Manasseh or Josiah.
9. Zephaniah, under Josiah.
10. Jeremiah, from Josiah to Zedekiah.
11. Daniel, under the captivity, after Zedekiah.

12. EZEKIEL, at the same time.
13. OBADIAH, during the captivity.
14. HAGGAI began to prophecy in the second year of Darius.
15. ZECHARIAH, about the same time. See Zech. i. 1, vii. 1.
16. MALACHI, under Nehemiah. The last of all the prophets.

The works of these prophets constitute the principal and most important part of what is called THE BIBLE or *Old Testament.*

ON the *style of the prophets* much has been said by several learned men; particularly *Calmet, Lowth,* Bishop *Newton, Vitringa, Michaelis,* and *Houbigant.* Their chief observations, and especially those most within the reach of the common people, have been selected and abridged with great care and industry by the *Rev. Dr. John Smith,* of Cambleton, in his little Tract entitled "A Summary View and Explanation of the Writings of the Prophets," to which it forms *preliminary observations,* drawn up at the desire of the Scottish Society for propagating Christian Knowledge, in a small 8vo. 1804. From this work I thankfully borrow what concerns the present subject; taking occasion at the same time to recommend the whole to all Christian ministers, to private persons, and to all families who wish to read the prophets to their edification.

"The writings of the prophets, the most sublime and beautiful in the world, lose much of that usefulness and effect which they are so well calculated to produce on the souls of men, from their not being more generally understood. Many prophecies are somewhat dark, till events explain them. They are, besides, delivered in such lofty and figurative terms, and with such frequent allusions to the customs and manners of times and places the most remote, that ordinary readers cannot, without some help, be supposed capable of understanding them. It must therefore be of use to make the language of prophecy as intelligible as may be, by explaining those images and figures of speech in which it most frequently abounds; and this may be done generally, even when the prophecies themselves are obscure.

"Some prophecies seem as if it were not intended that they should be clearly understood before they are fulfilled. As they relate to different periods, they may have been intended for exciting the attention of mankind from time to time both to providence and to Scripture and to furnish every age with new evidence of Divine revelation; by which means they serve the same purpose to the last ages of the world that miracles did to the first. Whereas, if they had been in every respect clear and obvious from the beginning, this wise purpose had been in a great measure defeated. Curiosity, industry, and attention would at once be at an end, or, by being too easily gratified, would be little exercised.

"Besides, a great degree of obscurity is necessary to some prophecies before they can be fulfilled; and if not fulfilled, the consequence would not be so beneficial to mankind. Thus many of the ancient prophecies concerning the destruction of Jerusalem had a manifest relation to the remoter destruction by the Romans, as well as to the nearer one by the Chaldeans. Had the Jews perceived this, which was not indeed clear enough till the event explained it, they would probably have wished to have remained for ever in their captivity at Babylon, rather than expose themselves or their offspring a second time to a destruction so dreadful as that which they had already experienced.

"With respect to our times, by far the greatest number of prophecies relate to events which are now past; and therefore a sufficient acquaintance with history, and with the language and style of prophecy, is all that is requisite to understand them. Some prophecies, however, relate to events still future; and these too may be understood in general, although some particular circumstances connected with them may remain obscure till they are fulfilled. If prophecies were not capable of being understood in general, we should not find the Jews so often blamed in this respect for their ignorance and want of discernment. That they did actually understand many of them when they chose to search the Scriptures we know. Daniel understood, from the prophecies of Jeremiah, the time at which the captivity in Babylon was to be at an end; and the scribes knew from Micah, and told Herod, where the Messiah was to be born. A very little attention might have enabled them in the same manner to understand others, as they probably did; such as the seventy weeks of Daniel; the destruction of the Babylonian empire, and of the other three that were to succeed; and also of the ruin of the people and places around them, Moab, Ammon, Tyre, Sidon, Philistia, Egypt, and Idumea. Perhaps, indeed, a few enigmatical circumstances might have been annexed, which could not be understood till they were accomplished; but the general tenor of the prophecies they could be at no loss to understand. With regard to prophecies still future, we are in a similar situation. It is understood in general, that the Jews will be gathered from their dispersions, restored to their own land, and converted to Christianity; that the fulness of the Gentiles will likewise come in; that Antichrist, Gog and Magog, and all the enemies of the Church will be destroyed; after which the Gospel will remarkably flourish, and be more than ever glorified. But several circumstances connected with those general events must probably remain in the dark till their accomplishment shall clearly explain them.

"But this degree of obscurity which sometimes attends prophecy does not always proceed from the circumstances or subject; it frequently proceeds from the highly poetical and figurative style, in which prophecy is for the most part conveyed, and of which it will be proper to give some account. To speak of all the rhetorical figures with which the prophets adorn their style would lead us into a field too wide, and would be more the province of the rhetorician than of the commentator. It will be sufficient for our purpose at present to attend to the most common of them, consisting of *allegory, parable,* and *metaphor,* and then to consider the *sources* from which the prophets most frequently borrow their images in those figures, and the sense which they wish to convey by them.

"By *allegory,* the first of the figures mentioned, is meant that mode of speech in which the writer or speaker means to convey a different idea from what the words in their obvious and primary signification bear. Thus, 'Break up your fallow ground, and sow not among thorns,' (Jer. iv. 3,) is to be understood, not of *tillage,* but of *repentance.* And these words, 'Thy rowers have brought thee into great waters, the east wind hath broken thee in the midst of the seas,' Ezek. xxvii. 26, allude not to the fate of a *ship,* but of a *city.*

"To this figure the *parable,* in which the prophets frequently speak, is nearly allied. It consists in the application of some feigned narrative to some real truth, which might have been less striking or more disagreeable if expressed in plain terms. Such is the following one of Isaiah, v. 1, 2: 'My well-beloved hath a vineyard in a very fruitful hill. And he fenced it, and gathered out the stones thereof, and planted it with the choicest vine, and built a tower in the midst of it, and also made a wine-press therein; and he looked that it should bring forth grapes, and it brought forth wild grapes.' The seventh verse tells us that this *vineyard* was the *house of Israel,* which had so ill requited the favour which God had shown it. On this subject see the dissertation at the end of the notes on Matt. xiii.

"There is, besides, another kind of allegory not uncommon with the prophets, called *mystical allegory* or *double prophecy.* Thus it is said of Eliakim, Isa. xxii. 22: 'And the key of the house of David will I lay upon his shoulder; and he shall open, and none shall shut; and he shall shut, and none shall open.' In the first and obvious sense, the words relate to Eliakim; but in the secondary or mystical sense, to the Messiah. Instances of the same kind are frequent in those prophecies that relate to David, Zerubbabel, Cyrus, and other types of Christ. In the first sense the words relate to the type; in the second, to the antitype. The use of this allegory, however, is not so frequent as that of the former. It is generally confined to things most nearly connected with the Jewish religion; with Israel, Sion, Jerusalem, and its kings and rulers; or such as were most opposite to these, Assyria, Babylon, Egypt, Idumea, and the like. In the former kind of allegory the primitive meaning is dropped, and the figurative only is retained; in this, both the one and the other are preserved, and this is what constitutes the difference.

"But of all the figures used by the prophets the most frequent is the *metaphor,* by which words are transferred from their primitive and plain to a secondary meaning. This figure, common in all poetry and in all languages, is of indispensable necessity in Scripture, which, having occasion to speak of Divine and spiritual matters, could do it only by terms borrowed from sensible and material objects. Hence it is that the sentiments, actions, and corporeal parts, not only of man, but also of inferior creatures, are ascribed to God himself; it being otherwise impossible for us to form any conceptions of his pure essence and incommunicable attributes. But though the prophets, partly from necessity and partly from choice, are thus profuse in the use of metaphors, they do not appear, like other writers, to have the liberty of using them as fancy directed. The same set of images, however diversified in the manner of applying them, is always used, both in allegory and metaphor, to denote the same subjects, to which they are in a manner appropriated. This peculiar characteristic of the Hebrew poetry might perhaps be owing to some rules taught in the prophetic schools, which did not allow the same latitude in this respect as other poetry. Whatever it may be owing to, the uniform manner in which the prophets apply these images tends greatly to illustrate the prophetic style; and therefore it will be proper now to consider the *sources* from which those images are most frequently derived, and the *subjects* and *ideas* which they severally denote. These sources may be classed under four heads; *natural, artificial, religious,* and *historical.*

"I. The first and most copious, as well as the most pleasing source of images in the prophetic writings, as in all other poetry, is *nature;* and the principal images drawn from nature, together with their application, are the following:—

"The *sun, moon,* and *stars,* the highest objects in the natural world, figuratively represent *kings, queens,* and *princes* or *rulers;* the highest in the world politic. 'The moon shall be confounded, and the sun ashamed;' Isa. xxiv. 23. 'I will cover the heavens, and make the stars thereof dark: I will cover the sun with a cloud, and the moon shall not give her light;' Ezek. xxxii. 7.

"*Light* and *darkness* are used figuratively for *joy* and *sorrow,* prosperity and adversity. 'We wait for *light,* but behold *obscurity;* for *brightness,* but we walk in *darkness;*' chap. lix. 9. An uncommon degree of light denotes an uncommon degree of joy and prosperity, and *vice versa.* 'The light of the *moon* shall be as the light of the *sun,* and the light of the sun shall be *sevenfold;*' chap. xxx. 26. The same metaphors are likewise used to denote *knowledge* and *ignorance.* 'If they speak not according to this word, it is because there is no *light* in them;' chap. viii. 20. 'The people that walked in darkness have seen a great *light;*' chap. ix. 2.

"*Dew, moderate rains, gentle streams,* and *running waters* denote the *blessings of the Gospel.* 'Thy *dew* is as the dew of herbs;' chap. xxvi. 19. 'He shall come unto us as the rain;' Hosea vi. 3. 'I will *water* it every moment;' chap. xxvii. 3. 'I will pour *water* on him that is thirsty;' chap. xliv. 3.

"*Immoderate rains* on the other hand, *hail, floods, deep waters, torrents,* and *inundations,* denote *judgments* and *destruction.* 'I will rain upon him an *overflowing rain,* and *great hailstones,*' Ezek. xxxviii. 22. 'Waters rise up out of the north, and shall overflow the land,' Jer. xlvii. 2.

"*Fire* also, and the *east wind,* parching and hurtful, frequently denote the same. 'They shall cast thy choice cedars into the *fire,*' Jer. xxii. 7. 'He stayeth his *rough wind* in the day of the *east wind,*' Isa. xxvii. 8.

"*Wind* in general is often taken in the same sense. 'The *wind* shall eat up all thy pastures,' Jer. xxii. 22. Sometimes it is put for any thing *empty* or *fallacious,* as well as hurtful. 'The prophets shall become *wind,*' Jer. v. 13. 'They have sown the *wind,* and they shall reap the *whirlwind,*' Hos. viii. 7.

"*Lebanon* and *Carmel;* the one remarkable for its *height* and stately *cedars,* was the image of *majesty, strength,* or anything very *great* or *noble.* 'He shall cut down the thickets of the *forest* with iron, and *Lebanon* shall fall by a mighty one,' Isa. x. 34. 'The Assyrian was a *cedar* in Lebanon,' Ezek. xxxi. 3. The other mountain (*Carmel*) being fruitful, and abounding in vines and olives, denoted *beauty* and *fertility.* 'The glory of Lebanon shall be given it, the excellency of *Carmel,*' Isa. xxxv. 2. The vine alone is a frequent image of the Jewish Church. 'I had planted thee a noble *vine,*' Jer. ii. 21.

"*Rams* and *bullocks of Bashan, lions, eagles, sea-monsters,* or any *animals of prey,* are figures frequently used for cruel and oppressive *tyrants* and *conquerors.* 'Hear this word, ye *kine* of *Bashan,* which oppress the poor,' Amos iv. 1. 'The *lion* is come up from his thicket,' Jer. iv. 7. 'A great *eagle* came unto Lebanon, and took the *highest branch* of the cedar,' Ezek. xvii. 3. 'Thou art as a *whale* in the seas,' Ezek. xxxii. 2. 'The *unicorns* shall come down, and their land shall be soaked with blood,' Isa. xxxiv. 7.

"II. The ordinary *occupations* and *customs* of life, with the few *arts* practised at the time, were another source from which the prophets derived many of their figures, particularly,

"From *husbandry* in all its parts, and from its *implements.* 'Sow to yourselves in righteousness, reap in mercy: break up your fallow ground,' Hos. x. 12. 'Put in the *sickle,* for the harvest is ripe,' Joel iii. 13. 'I am pressed under you, as a *wain* under a load of sheaves,' Amos ii. 13. *Threshing* was performed in various ways, (mentioned Isa. xxviii. 24, &c.,) which furnish a variety of images denoting punishment. 'Arise and thresh, O daughter of Zion; for I will make thine *horn* iron, and thy *hoofs* brass,' &c., Micah iv. 13. The operation was performed on rising grounds, where the *chaff* was driven away by the wind, while the *grain* remained; a fit emblem of the *fate of the wicked,* and of the *salvation of the just.* 'Behold, I will make thee a new *threshing-instrument* having teeth; thou shalt thresh the mountains, and beat them small, and thou shalt make the hills as *chaff*. Thou shalt *fan* them, and the wind shall carry them away, and the *whirlwind* shall scatter them,' Isa. xli. 15, 16.

"The *vintage* and *winepress* also furnish many images, obvious enough in their application. 'The *press* is full, the *fats* overflow, for their wickedness is great,' Joel iii. 13. 'I have trod the *winepress* alone. I will tread down the people in mine anger,' Isa. lxiii. 3, &c. As the *vintage* was gathered with *shouting* and *rejoicing*, the ceasing of the vintage-shouting is frequently one of the figures that denote *misery* and *desolation*. 'None shall *tread* with *shouting*; their *shouting* shall be no *shouting*,' Jer. xlviii. 33.

"From the occupation of *tending cattle* we have many images. 'Wo unto the *pastors* that destroy and scatter the *sheep* of my pasture,' Jer. xxiii. 1. The people are the *flock*; *teachers* and *rulers* the *pastors*. 'Israel is a *scattered sheep*, the lions have driven him away.' 'As a *shepherd* taketh out of the mouth of the lion two legs, or a piece of an ear,' &c., Amos iii. 12. Some of the images derived from *husbandry*, *tending cattle*, &c., may perhaps appear mean to us; though not to the Jews, whose manner of life was simple and plain, and whose greatest men (such as Moses, David, Gideon, &c.) were often *husbandmen* and *shepherds*. Accordingly, the Messiah himself is frequently described under the character of a *shepherd*. [See *Fleury's* Manners of the Israelites.]

"It was customary in deep mournings to *shave* the *head* and *beard*, to retire to the *house-tops*, which in those countries were flat, and furnished with little chambers adapted to the purposes of devotion or of sequestered grief; also to sing dirges at funerals, and to accompany them with a mournful sort of music; and from these and the like circumstances images are frequently borrowed by the prophets to denote the *greatest danger*, and the *deepest distress*. 'Mine heart shall sound for Moab like pipes.' 'Every head shall be *bald*, and every *beard clipt*—there shall be lamentation on all the *house-tops* of Moab,' Jer. xlviii. 36–38; Isa. xv. 2, 3.

"The mode of *burying in the Jewish sepulchres*, or 'sides of the pit,' and their *Hades*, or state of the dead, supplied many images of the same kind. See observations on Isa. xiv., and Ezek. xxvi. 20.

"According to the barbarous custom of those times, conquerors *drove their captives before them* almost *naked*, and exposed to the intolerable heat of the sun, and the inclemencies of the weather. They afterwards employed them frequently in *grinding at the handmill*, (watermills not being then invented;) hence *nakedness*, and *grinding at the mill*, and *sitting on the ground* (the posture in which they wrought) express captivity. 'Descend and sit in the dust, O virgin daughter of Babylon; take the *millstones*—thy *nakedness* shall be uncovered,' Isa. xlvii. 1–3.

"The *marriage relation* supplied metaphors to express the relation or covenant between God and his people. On the other hand *adultery*, *infidelity* to the *marriage bed*, &c., denoted any breach of covenant with God, particularly the *love and worship of idols*. 'Turn, O backsliding children, saith the Lord, for I am married unto you,' Jer. iii. 14. 'There were two women, the daughters of one mother, and they committed whoredoms—with their idols have they committed adultery,' &c., Ezek. xxiii. 2–37.

"The *debility* and *stupefaction* caused by *intoxicating liquors* suggested very apt images to express the terrible effects of the Divine judgments on those who are the unhappy objects of them. 'Thou shalt be filled with drunkenness, with the cup of thy sister Samaria,' Ezek. xxiii. 33.

"From the method of *refining metals in the furnace* images are often borrowed to denote the *judgments* inflicted by God on his people, with a view to cleanse them from their sins, as metal from its dross. 'Israel is dross in the midst of the furnace,' Ezek. xxii. 18. 'He shall sit as a refiner and purifier of silver,' Mal. iii. 3.

"Among the other few arts from which the Hebrew poets derive some of their images, are those of the *fuller* and *potter*, Mal. iii. 2, &c.; Jer. xviii. 1, &c.; of which the application is obvious. No less so is that of images derived from *fishing*, *fowling*, and the *implements* belonging to them; the *hook*, *net*, *pit*, *snare*, &c., which generally denote *captivity* or *destruction*. 'I will send for many fishers, and they shall fish them; and for many hunters, and they shall hunt them; for their iniquity is not hid from mine eyes,' Jer. xvi. 16, 17. 'I will put hooks to thy jaws,' Ezek. xxix. 4. 'Fear, and the pit, and the snare, are upon thee, O inhabitant of the earth,' Isa. xxiv. 17.

"A few images are derived from *building*, as when the Messiah is denoted by a *foundation* and *corner-stone*, Isa. xxviii. 16. The next verse describes the *rectitude* of *judgment* by metaphors borrowed from the *line* and *plummet*; and by *building with precious stones* is denoted a very high degree of *prosperity*, whether applied to church or state, Isa. liv. 11, 12.

"III. Religion, and things connected with it, furnished many images to the sacred poets.

"From the *temple* and its pompous service, from the *tabernacle, shechinah, mercy-seat,* &c., are derived a variety of images, chiefly serving to denote the glory of the Christian Church, the excellency of its worship, God's favour towards it, and his constant presence with it; the prophets speaking to the Jews in terms accommodated to their own ideas. 'And the Lord will create upon every dwelling-place of Mount Zion, and upon her assemblies, a cloud and smoke by day, and the shining of a flaming fire by night; for upon all the glory shall be a covering,' Isa. iv. 5. 'Then will I sprinkle clean water upon you, and ye shall be clean,' Ezek. xxxvi. 25.

"The *ceremonial law,* and especially its distinctions between things *clean* and *unclean,* furnished a number of images, all obvious in their application. 'Wash ye, make you clean, put away the evil of your doings,' Isa. i. 16. 'Their way was before me as the uncleanness of a removed woman,' Ezek. xxxvi. 17.

"The *killing of sacrifices* and *feasting upon them,* serve as metaphors for *slaughter.* 'The Lord hath a sacrifice in Bozrah,' Isa. xxxiv. 6; Ezek. xxxix. 17.

"The *pontifical robes,* which were very splendid, suggested several images expressive of the *glory* of both the Jewish and Christian Church. 'I clothed thee with broidered work,' &c., Ezek. xvi. 10. 'He clothed me with the garments of salvation,' Isa. lxi. 10. The prophets wore a *rough upper garment;* false prophets wore the like, in imitation of true ones; and to this there are frequent allusions. 'Neither shall they wear a rough garment to deceive,' Zech. xiii. 4.

"From the *pots,* and other *vessels* and *utensils* of the temple, are likewise borrowed a few metaphors obvious enough without explanation: 'Every pot in Jerusalem and in Judah shall be holiness,' Zech. xiv. 21.

"The prophets have likewise many images that allude to the *idolatrous rites* of the neighbouring nations, to their *groves* and *high places,* Isa. xxvii. 9, and to the worship paid to their idols, *Baal, Molech, Chemosh, Gad, Meni, Ashtaroth, Tammuz,* &c., Ezek. viii. 10–14.

"IV. Many of the metaphors and images used by the prophets are likewise borrowed from *history,* especially sacred.

"From the *fall of angels:* 'How art thou fallen from heaven, O Lucifer, son of the morning;' Isa. xiv. 12. 'Thou art the anointed cherub,—thou wast upon the holy mountain of God;' Ezek. xxviii. 14. And from *the fall of man:* 'Thou hast been in Eden, the garden of God;' ver. 13.

"From *chaos:* 'I beheld the earth, and, lo! it was without form, and void; and the heavens, and they had no light;' Jer. iv. 23. 'He shall stretch over it the line of devastation, and the plummet of emptiness;' Isa. xxxiv. 11.

"From the *deluge:* 'The windows from on high are open, and the foundations of the earth do shake;' Isa. xxiv. 18.

"From the *destruction of Sodom and Gomorrah:* 'And the streams thereof shall be turned into pitch, and the dust thereof into brimstone, and the land thereof shall become burning pitch;' Isa. xxxiv. 9. Also from the destruction of the Hivites and Amorites, &c., Isa. xvii. 9.

"The *exodus* and *deliverance from Egypt,* is frequently used to shadow forth other great deliverances: 'Thus saith the Lord, who maketh a way in the sea, and a path in the mighty waters,' &c.; Isa. xi. 15, 16; xliii. 16–19; li. 9, 10, &c.

"From the *descent on Sinai:* 'Behold, the Lord cometh forth out of his place, and will come down and tread on the high places of the earth; and the mountains shall be molten under him;' Micah i. 3, 4.

"From the *resurrection,* the *end of the world,* and the *last judgment,* are derived many images, of which the application is natural and obvious: 'Thy dead men shall live, with my dead body shall they arise,—awake and sing, ye that dwell in the dust,' &c.; Isa. xxvi. 19. 'And all the host of heaven shall be dissolved, and the heavens shall be rolled together as a scroll; and all their host shall fall down as a leaf falleth from the vine, and as a falling fig from the fig-tree;' Isa. xxxiv. 4.

"The foregoing account of the images which most frequently occur in the writings of the prophets may be of considerable use in studying their style; but as a thorough knowledge of this must be allowed to be of the highest importance, a few *general remarks* are farther added, although some part of them may appear to be superseded by what has been already observed.

"1. Although the prophets use words so frequently in a figurative or metaphorical meaning; yet we ought not, without necessity, to depart from the primitive and original sense of language; and such a necessity there is, when the plain and original sense is less proper, less suitable to the subject and context, or contrary to other scriptures.

"2. By images borrowed from the world natural the prophets frequently understand something analogous in the world politic. Thus, the *sun, moon, stars,* and *heavenly bodies* denote *kings, queens, rulers,* and *persons* in *great power;* their *increase of splendour* denotes *increase of prosperity;* their *darkening, setting,* or *falling* denotes a *reverse of fortune,* or the entire ceasing of that power or kingdom to which they refer. *Great earthquakes,* and the *shaking of heaven and earth,* denote the *commotion* and *overthrow of kingdoms;* and the *beginning* or *end of the world,* their *rise* or *ruin.*

"3. The *cedars of Lebanon, oaks of Bashan, fir-trees,* and other *stately* trees of the forest, denote *kings, princes, potentates,* and *persons of the highest rank; briers* and *thorns,* the *common people,* or those of the meanest order.

"4. *High mountains* and *lofty hills,* in like manner, denote *kingdoms, republics, states,* and *cities; towers* and *fortresses* signify *defenders* and *protectors; ships of Tarshish,* merchants or commercial people; and the *daughter* of any capital or mother city, the *lesser cities* or *suburbs* around it. *Cities never conquered* are farther styled *virgins.*

"5. The prophets likewise describe *kings* and *kingdoms* by their *ensigns;* as *Cyrus* and the *Romans* by an *eagle,* the *king of Macedon* by a *goat,* and the *king of Persia* by a *ram;* these being the figures on their respective standards, or in the ornaments of their architecture.

"6. The prophets in like manner borrow some of their images from *ancient hieroglyphics,* which they take in their usual acceptation: thus, a *star* was the emblem of a *god* or *hero;* a *horn,* the emblem of *great power* or *strength;* and a *rod,* the emblem of *royalty;* and they signify the same in the prophets.

"7. The same prophecies have frequently a *double meaning;* and refer to different events, the one *near,* the other *remote;* the one *temporal,* the other *spiritual,* or perhaps *eternal.* The prophets having thus several events in their eye, their expressions may be partly applicable to one, and partly to another; and it is not always easy to mark the transitions. Thus, the prophecies relating to the *first* and *second restoration* of the *Jews,* and *first* and *second coming of our Lord,* are often interwoven together; like our Saviour's own prediction (Matt. xxiv.) concerning the *destruction of Jerusalem* and the *end of the world.* What has not been fulfilled in the first, we must apply to the second; and what has been already fulfilled may often be considered as typical of what still remains to be accomplished.

"8. Almost all the prophecies of the *Old Testament,* whatever view they may have to nearer events, are ultimately to be referred to the *New,* where only we are to look for their full completion. Thus *Babylon,* under the *Old Testament,* was a type of *mystical Babylon* under the *New;* and the *king of Syria,* (Antiochus Epiphanes,) a type of *Antichrist;* the *temporal enemies* of the *Jews,* types and figures of the *spiritual enemies* of *Christians.* We must not, however, expect to find always a mystical meaning in prophecy; and when the near and most obvious meaning is plain, and gives a good sense, we need not depart from it, nor be over-curious to look beyond it.

"9. In prophecies, as in parables, we are chiefly to consider the *scope* and *design,* without attempting too minute an explication of all the poetical images and figures which the sacred writers use to adorn their style.

"10. Prophecies of a general nature are applicable *by accommodation* to individuals; most of the things that are spoken of the Church in general being no less applicable to its individual members.

"11. Prophecies of a particular nature, on the other hand, admit, and often require, to be extended. Thus, Edom, Moab, or any of the enemies of God's people, is often put for the whole; what is said of one being generally applicable to the rest.

"12. In like manner, what is said to or of any of God's people, on any particular occasion, is of general application and use; all that stand in the same relation to God having an interest in the same promises.

"13. A *cup of intoxicating liquor* is frequently used to denote the *indignation of God;* and the effects of such a cup, the effects of his displeasure.

"14. As the *covenant of God* with his people is represented under the figure of *marriage;* so their *breach of that covenant,* especially their idolatry, is represented by *whoredom, adultery,* and *infidelity to the marriage bed;* on which the prophets sometimes enlarge, to excite detestation of the crime. The epithet *strange* does likewise, almost always, relate to something connected with *idolatry.*

"15. Persons or nations are frequently said in Scripture to be related to those whom they resemble in their life and conduct. In the same manner, men are denoted by *animals* whose qualities they resemble. A definite number, such as *three, four, seven, ten,* &c., is sometimes used by the prophets for an *indefinite,* and commonly denotes a *great many.*

"16. In the reckoning of time, a *day* is used by the prophets to denote a *year;* and things *still future,* to denote their certainty, are spoken of as *already past.*

"17. When the prophets speak of the *last* or *latter days,* they always mean the *days of the Messiah,* or the time of the Gospel dispensation. *That day* means often the same, and always some period at a distance.

"18. When places are mentioned as lying *north, south, east,* or *west,* it is generally to be understood of their situation with respect to *Judea* or *Jerusalem,* when the context does not plainly restrict the scene to some other place.

"19. By the *earth,* or the word so translated, the prophets frequently mean the *land of Judea;* and sometimes, says Sir Isaac Newton, the great continent of all Asia and Africa, to which they had access by land. By the *isles of the sea,* on the other hand, they understood the places to which they sailed, particularly all Europe, and probably the islands and seacoasts of the Mediterranean.

"20. The greatest part of the prophetic writings was first composed in *verse,* and still retains, notwithstanding all the disadvantages of a literal prose translation, much of the air and cast of the original, particularly in the division of the lines, and in that peculiarity of Hebrew poetry by which the sense of one line or couplet so frequently corresponds with that of the other. Thus:—

> I will greatly rejoice in the Lord,
> My soul shall be joyful in my God;
> For he hath clothed me with the garments of salvation,
> He hath covered me with the robe of righteousness:
> As a bridegroom decketh himself with ornaments,
> And as a bride adorneth herself with her jewels.
>
> Isa. lxi. 10.

"Attention to this peculiarity in sacred poetry will frequently lead to the meaning of many passages in the poetical parts of Scripture, in which it perpetually occurs, as the one line of a couplet, or member of a sentence, is generally a commentary on the other. Thus:—

> The Lord hath a sacrifice in Bozrah,
> And a great slaughter in the land of Idumea.
>
> Isa. xxxiv. 6.

"Here the metaphor in the first line is expressed in plain terms in the next: the *sacrifice in Bozrah* means the *great slaughter in Idumea,* of which Bozrah was the capital.

"It must be observed that the *parallelism* is frequently more extended. Thus:—

> For I will pour out waters on the thirsty,
> And flowing streams upon the dry ground;
> I will pour out my Spirit on thy seed,
> And my blessing on thine offspring.
>
> Isa. xliv. 3.

"Here the two last lines explain the metaphor in the two preceding."

As the *gift of prophecy* was the greatest which God gave to men upon earth, so the *prophet,* as being the immediate instrument of revealing the will of God to the people, was the greatest, the most important, the most august, venerable, and useful person in the land of Israel. Ipsi eis exeant, says St. Augustine, philosophi ipsi sapientes, ipsi theologi, ipsi prophetæ, ipsi doctores probitatis ac pietatis; "They were to the people the philosophers, the wise men, the divines, the prophets, and the teachers of truth and godliness." By their intercourse with God, they were his mediators with the people; and their *persons,* as well as their *office,* were considered as peculiarly sacred. They did not mix with the people, and only appeared in public when they came to announce the will of God. They were also a kind of typical persons—whatever occurred to them was instructive, so that they were for signs, metaphors, and portents.

Most of the ancient prophets were *extraordinary* messengers. They were not bred up to the prophetic function; as the office was immediately from God, as well as the message they were to deliver to the people, so they had no previous education, in reference to such an office, for no man knew whom the God of Israel might please to call to announce his righteousness to the people. Several of them were taken out of the walks of *common life. Jonah* appears to have been a private person at Gath-heper, in Galilee, before God called him to prophesy against Nineveh. *Elisha* was a ploughman at Abel-meholah (1 Kings xix. 16) when called to the prophetic function. *Zechariah* appears to have been a husbandman, and a keeper of cattle, Zech. xiii. 5. *Amos* was a herdsman of Tekoa, and a gatherer of sycamore fruit; (Amos i. 1, vii. 14, 15;) and no doubt several others of the ancient prophets had an equally mean origin; but the office and the calling *dignified* the man. We know that our blessed Lord called not his disciples from the higher walks or offices of life; but out of fishermen, tax-gatherers, and tent-makers, he formed *evangelists* and *apostles.*

The prophets appear to have gone in mean clothing; either *sack-cloth, hair-cloth,* or *coats of skin* appear to have been their ordinary clothing. They spoke against the pride and vain-glory of man; and their very garb and manner gave additional weight to the solemn words they delivered. They lived in a retired manner; and, when not sent on special errands, they employed their vacant time in the instruction of youth; as this is probably what we are to understand by the *schools of the prophets,* such as those over which Elijah, Elisha, and Samuel presided; though no doubt there were some of their disciples that were made partakers of the prophetic gift.

The prophets do not appear to have been called to a life of *celibacy. Isaiah* was a married man, chap. viii. 3; and so was *Hosea,* chap. i. 2; unless we are to understand the latter case enigmatically. And that the sons of the prophets had *wives,* we learn from 2 Kings iv. 1, &c.; and from this, as well as from the case of the *apostles,* we learn that the matrimonial state was never considered, either by Moses or the prophets, Christ or his apostles, as disqualifying men from officiating in the most holy offices; as we find Moses, Aaron, Isaiah, Zechariah, and Peter, all married men, and yet the most eminent of their order.

Of Isaiah, the writer of this book, very little is known. He is supposed to have been of the *tribe of Judah,* and of the *royal family of David.* Himself says that he was *son of Amoz;* and others tell us that this *Amoz* was the son of *Joash,* and brother of *Amaziah,* king of Judah. "Of his family and tribe we know nothing," says *R. D. Kimchi,* "only our rabbins, of blessed memory, have received the tradition that Amoz and Amaziah were brothers;" and it is on this ground that he has been called the *royal prophet.* It has been also said that Isaiah gave his daughter in marriage to Manasseh, son of Hezekiah, king of Judah; and that himself was put to death by Manasseh, being sawn asunder with a wooden saw. But all these traditions stand on very slender authority, and are worthy of very little regard. Several commentators have thought that his prophecies afford presumptive evidence of his *high descent* and *elegant education:* 1. Because his *style* is more *correct* and *majestic* than any of the other prophets. 2. That his frequent use of *images* taken from *royalty* is a proof that this state was familiar to him, being much at court, as he must have been, had he been the brother of the king. These things are spoken by many with much confidence; for my own part, I had rather look to his *inspiration* for the correctness of his language and the dignity of his sentiments, than to those very inferior helps. On the other hypothesis nothing is left to the Divine Spirit, except the mere *matter* of his prophecies. Suppositions of this kind are not creditable to Divine revelation.

Isaiah appears to have had *two sons,* who were typical in their names; one, *Shear-jashub,* "a remnant shall return," chap. vii. 3; and the other *Maher-shalal-hash-baz,* "haste to the spoil; quick to the prey;" chap. viii. 3; and it is remarkable, that his wife is called a *prophetess.* Other matters relative to his character will appear in the notes on his prophecies.

In the notes on this book I have consulted throughout the commentary of *Rabbi David Kimchi,* and have made much use of *Bishop Lowth,* as the reader will perceive. His *various readings* I have re-collated with Dr. *Kennicott,* and *B. De Rossi;* in consequence of which I have been enabled in many cases to add double weight to the authorities by which the learned bishop was supported in the readings which he has either mentioned, or *received into the text*. Bishop *Lowth* could avail himself only of the *collections* of Dr. *Kennicott*—the sheets of Isaiah in the doctor's edition of the Hebrew Bible, as they passed through the press, were sent by him to the Bishop; but the Collections of *De Rossi*, more numerous and more accurate than those of Dr. *Kennicott*, were not published till *six* years after the doctor had published his Bible, and about *one* year before this most learned and pious prelate went to his reward. I have also consulted some excellent Hebrew MSS. in my own library, from *six* to *eight hundred* years old, which have afforded me additional help in estimating the worth and importance of the various readings in the above Collections of *Kennicott* and *De Rossi*, as far as they are employed in the illustration of this prophet. From the ancient English MS. Version of this prophet I have extracted several curious translations of select parts, which I have no doubt will meet with every reader's approbation. Though I have followed Bishop *Lowth* chiefly, yet I have consulted the best commentators within my reach, in order to remove doubts and clear up difficult passages, but have studied to be as brief as possible, that the sacred text might not be encumbered either with the multitude or length of the notes, nor the reader's time occupied with any thing not essentially necessary; besides, I wish to bring my work to as speedy a close as possible.

This book, according to Vitringa, is *twofold* in its *matter:* 1. *Prophetical;* 2. *Historical.*

1. The *prophetical* is divided into *five* parts: Part I. From chap. i. to chap. xiii. is directed to the Jews and Ephraimites, and contains *five* prophetic discourses. Part II. From chap. xiii. to chap. xxiv. declares the fate of the Babylonians, Philistines, Moabites, Syrians, Egyptians, Tyrians, and others; and contains *eight* prophetic discourses. Part III. From chap. xxiv. to chap. xxxvi. denounces judgments on the disobedient Jews, and consoles the true followers of God. This contains *three* discourses. Part IV. From chap. xl. to chap. xlix. refers to the Messiah and the deliverance of the Jews from the Babylonians; and contains *four* discourses. Part V. From chap. xlix. to the *end*, points out the passion, crucifixion, and glory of the Messiah, and contains *five* discourses.

2. The *historical* part begins with chap. xxxvi., and ends with chap. xxxix., and relates some of the transactions of the prophet's own times. On this analysis *Vitringa* explains the whole prophecy. For my own part I have little or no confidence in such *technical arrangements*.

Calmet takes a different view of it. He divides it into *eight* parts, viz.: Part I. he supposes to relate to Jotham, son of Uzziah, king of Judah: this is included in the first *six* chapters. The prophet inveighs against the crimes of the Jews; declares the judgments of God against them; predicts a more auspicious time, which took place under Hezekiah, who was a type of Christ. Part II. concerns the reign of Ahaz, and comprehends the six following chapters, in which he speaks of the siege of Jerusalem by Pekah and Rezin; of the birth of Immanuel, as a proof of the approaching deliverance of Judah; predicts the calamities that were to fall on the kingdoms of Syria and Israel, &c. Part III. contains many prophecies against Babylon, the Philistines, Moabites, &c. Part IV. contains prophecies against Egypt, Babylon, Kedar, Arabia, &c. Part V. concerns the reign of Hezekiah, and especially the war of Sennacherib against the Jews, &c. The *four historical chapters* inserted here contain the account of the fulfilment of the preceding prophecy. Part VI., included in chap. xl. to xlv. inclusive, contains the prophet's discourses on the existence of God, the truth and perfection of the Jewish religion, the vanity of idolatry, the return of the people from captivity, and the coming of Christ. Part VII. from chap. xlix. to chap. lvi., the prophet, personifying the Messiah, speaks of his sufferings, death, and burial; predicts the return from the Babylonish captivity, and the glory of the latter days. Part VIII. speaks of the coming of the Messiah, and the vocation of the Gentiles; the disgrace and confusion of all false prophets and teachers; and the establishment of a pure and holy Church, &c.

I might give other analyses of this book, but it is needless; from what is before the reader he will at once see how vain all attempts of this kind are, and how foolish to make divisions and subdivisions, partitions and classifications, where the Spirit of God has given no intimations of the kind, and where even the most learned men differ in their arrangement.

"God never left his work for man to mend." The prophecies were given as they were necessary, and no classification was ever intended. We should take them up as we find them; and humbly endeavour to find out their objects and meaning, and how far ourselves are interested in these denunciations of Divine wrath; and in those glorious promises of mercy and salvation through Him who was once the hope of Israel, and now is salvation to the ends of the earth.

Bishop Lowth's translation is by far the best that has ever been made of this sublime prophet: as he thoroughly understood his *language*, so he entered deeply into his spirit. Were it allowable, I should be glad to supersede what is called the *authorized version*, and put that of the learned bishop, with a few genuine alterations, in its place, as being abundantly more correct and nervous, rendering the sacred text more clearly, and consequently more intelligibly, so that the common reader can understand this text better without a comment, than he can the authorized version even with one. His *notes*, which are a treasure of learning and sound criticism, I have almost universally preserved, intermingling them with my own; but large quotations from his notes I have distinguished by the letter L.; and I have often adopted his *text*, as being vastly superior to that in common use; the catch words from which follow those from the authorized version. Should a *new translation* of the Bible be ever published by authority, I have no doubt but, with a few alterations, that of Bishop Lowth would be adopted as the standard.

A. C.

Millbrook, Sept. 24, 1823.

THE BOOK

OF THE

PROPHET ISAIAH

Chronological Notes relative to the commencement of Isaiah's prophecy

Year from the Creation of the World, according to the computation of Archbishop Usher, 3244.—Year from the Deluge, according to the generally received Hebrew text, 1588.—Year from the vocation of Abram, 1161.—Year from the foundation of Solomon's Temple, 251.—First year of the fifth Olympiad.—Year before the building of Rome, according to the Varronian computation, 7.—Fifteenth year of the reign of Thurimas, king of Macedon.—Eleventh year of the reign of Theopompus, king of Lacedæmon.—Second year of the reign of Alyattes, king of Lydia.—Eighteenth year of Æschylus, perpetual archon of the Athenians.—Second year of the reign of Pekahiah, king of Israel.—Fifty-first year of the reign of Azariah, or Uzziah, king of Judah.—Epoch of the establishment of the Ephori at Lacedæmon by Theopompus.

CHAPTER I

The prophet, with a boldness and majesty becoming the herald of the Most High, begins with calling on the whole creation to attend while Jehovah speaks, 2. *A charge of gross insensibility and ingratitude is then brought against the Jews, by contrasting their conduct with that of the* ox *and* ass, *the most stupid of animals,* 3. *This leads to an amplification of their guilt,* 4; *highly aggravated by their slighting the chastisements and judgments of God, though repeated till they had been left almost like* Sodom *and* Gomorrah, 5–9. *The incidental mention of those places leads to an address to the rulers and people of the Jews, under the character of* princes of Sodom, *and* people of Gomorrah, *which is no less spirited and severe than elegant and unexpected,* 10. *The vanity of trusting to the performance of the outward rites and ceremonies of religion is then exposed,* 11–15; *and the necessity of repentance and reformation is strongly enjoined,* 16, 17, *and urged by the most encouraging promises as well as by the most awful threatenings,* 18–20. *But neither of these producing the proper effect on that people who were the prophet's charge, he bitterly laments their degeneracy,* 21–23; *and concludes with introducing God, declaring his purpose of inflicting such heavy judgments as would entirely cut off the wicked, and excite in the righteous, who should also pass through the furnace, an everlasting shame and abhorrence of every thing connected with idolatry, the source of their misery,* 24–31.

A. M. cir. 3244
B. C. cir. 760
Anno Olymp. Quintæ I.
Ante Urbem Conditam 7

THE [a]vision of Isaiah the son of Amoz, which he saw concerning Judah and Jerusalem in the days of Uzziah, Jotham, Ahaz, *and* Hezekiah, kings of Judah.

[a]Numbers, chap. xii. 6

Isaiah exercised the prophetical office during a long period of time, if he lived to the reign of Manasseh; for the lowest computation, beginning from the year in which Uzziah died, when some suppose him to have received his first appointment to that office, brings it to sixty-one years. But the tradition of the Jews, that he was put to death by Manasseh, is very uncertain; and one of their principal rabbins, *Aben Ezra*, Com. in Isa. i. 1, seems rather to think that he died before Hezekiah, which is indeed more probable. It is however certain that he lived at least to the fifteenth or sixteenth year of Hezekiah; this makes the least possible term of the duration of his prophetical office about forty-eight years. The time of the delivery of some of his prophecies is either expressly marked, or sufficiently clear from the history to which they relate; that of a few others may with some probability be deduced from internal marks; from expressions, descriptions, and circumstances interwoven. It may therefore be of some use in this respect, and for the better understanding of his prophecies in general, to give here a summary view of the history of his time.

The kingdom of Judah seems to have been in a more flourishing condition during the reigns of Uzziah and Jotham, than at any other time after the revolt of the ten tribes. The former recovered the port of Elath on the Red Sea, which the Edomites had taken in the reign of Joram. He was successful in his wars with the Philistines, and took from them several cities,

A. M. cir. 3244 B. C. cir. 760 Anno Olymp. Quintæ I. Ante Urbem Conditam 7

2 [b]Hear, O heavens, and give
ear, O earth; for the LORD
hath spoken: [c]I have nourished and brought up children,
and they have rebelled against
me.
3 [d]The ox knoweth his owner,
and the ass his master's crib:

[b]Deut. xxxii. 1; Jer. ii. 12; vi. 19; xxii. 29; Ezek. xxxvi. 4; Mic. i. 2; vi. 1, 2——[c]Chap. v. 1, 2——[d]Jer. viii. 7

Gath, Jabneh, Ashdod; as likewise against some people of Arabia Deserta, and against the Ammonites, whom he compelled to pay him tribute. He repaired and improved the fortifications of Jerusalem; and had a great army, well appointed and disciplined. He was no less attentive to the arts of peace; and very much encouraged agriculture, and the breeding of cattle. Jotham maintained the establishments and improvements made by his father; added to what Uzziah had done in strengthening the frontier places; conquered the Ammonites, who had revolted; and exacted from them a more stated and probably a larger tribute. However, at the latter end of his time, the league between Pekah, king of Israel, and Retsin, king of Syria, was formed against Judah; and they began to carry their designs into execution.

But in the reign of Ahaz his son not only all these advantages were lost, but the kingdom of Judah was brought to the brink of destruction. Pekah king of Israel overthrew the army of Ahaz, who lost in battle *one hundred and twenty thousand* men; and the Israelites carried away captives *two hundred thousand* women and children, who however were released and sent home again upon the remonstrance of the prophet Oded. After this, as it should seem, (see *Vitringa* on chap. vii. 2,) the two kings of Israel and Syria, joining their forces, laid siege to Jerusalem; but in this attempt they failed of success. In this distress Ahaz called in the assistance of Tiglath-pileser, king of Assyria, who invaded the kingdoms of Israel and Syria, and slew Rezin; but he was more in danger than ever from his too powerful ally; to purchase whose forbearance, as he had before bought his assistance, he was forced to strip himself and his people of all the wealth he could possibly raise from his own treasury, from the temple, and from the country. About the time of the siege of Jerusalem the Syrians took Elath, which was never after recovered. The Edomites likewise, taking advantage of the distress of Ahaz, ravaged Judea, and carried away many captives. The Philistines recovered what they had before lost; and took many places in Judea, and maintained themselves there. Idolatry was established by the command of the king in Jerusalem, and throughout Judea; and the service of the temple was either intermitted, or converted into an idolatrous worship.

Hezekiah, his son, on his accession to the throne, immediately set about the restoration of the legal worship of God, both in Jerusalem and through Judea. He cleansed and repaired the temple, and held a solemn passover. He improved the city, repaired the fortification, erected magazines of all sorts, and built a new aqueduct. In the fourth year of his reign Shalmaneser, king of Assyria, invaded the kingdom of Israel, took Samaria, and carried away the Israelites into captivity, and replaced them by different people sent from his own country; and this was the final destruction of that kingdom, in the sixth year of the reign of Hezekiah. Hezekiah was not deterred by this alarming example from refusing to pay the tribute to the king of Assyria, which had been imposed on Ahaz: this brought on the invasion of Sennacherib in the fourteenth year of his reign, an account of which is inserted among the prophecies of Isaiah. After a great and miraculous deliverance from so powerful an enemy, Hezekiah continued his reign in peace. He prospered in all his works, and left his kingdom in a flourishing state to his son Manasseh—a son in every respect unworthy of such a father. See *Lowth.*

NOTES ON CHAP. I

Verse 1. *The vision of Isaiah*] It seems doubtful whether this title belongs to the whole book, or only to the prophecy contained in this chapter. The former part of the title seems properly to belong to this particular prophecy; the latter part, which enumerates the kings of Judah under whom Isaiah exercised his prophetical office, seems to extend it to the whole collection of prophecies delivered in the course of his ministry. *Vitringa*—to whom the world is greatly indebted for his learned labours on this prophet and to whom we should have owed much more if he had not so totally devoted himself to Masoretic authority—has, I think, very judiciously resolved this doubt. He supposes that the former part of the title was originally prefixed to this single prophecy; and that, when the collection of all Isaiah's prophecies was made, the enumeration of the kings of Judah was added, to make it at the same time a proper title to the whole book. As such it is plainly taken in 2 Chron. xxxii. 32, where the book of Isaiah is cited by this title: "The vision of Isaiah the prophet, the son of Amoz."

The prophecy contained in this first chapter stands single and unconnected, making an entire piece of itself. It contains a severe remonstrance against the corruptions prevailing among the Jews of that time, powerful exhortations to repentance, grievous threatenings to the impenitent, and gracious promises of better times, when the nation shall have been reformed by the just judgments of God. The expression, upon the whole, is clear; the connection of the several parts easy; and in regard to the images, sentiments, and style, it gives a beautiful example of the prophet's elegant manner of writing; though perhaps it may not be equal in these respects to many of the following prophecies.

Verse 2. *Hear, O heavens*—"Hear, O ye heavens"] God is introduced as entering into a public action, or pleading, before the whole world, against his disobedient people. The prophet, as herald or officer to proclaim the summons to the court, calls upon all created beings, celestial and terrestrial, to attend and bear witness to the truth of his plea and the justice of his cause. The same scene is more fully displayed in the noble exordium of Psa. l., where God summons all mankind, from east to west, to

A. M. cir. 3244
B. C. cir. 760
Anno Olymp.
Quintæ I.
Ante Urbem
Conditam 7

but Israel [e]doth not know, my
people [f]doth not consider.
4 Ah sinful nation, a people
[g]laden with iniquity, [h]a seed of
evil doers, children that are corrupters! They have forsaken
the LORD, they have provoked
the Holy One of Israel unto

[e]Jer. ix. 3, 6——[f]Chap. v. 12——[g]Heb. *of heaviness*——[h]Chap. lvii. 3, 4; Matt. iii. 7

be present to hear his appeal; and the solemnity is held on Sion, where he is attended with the same terrible pomp that accompanied him on Mount Sinai:—

"A consuming fire goes before him,
And round him rages a violent tempest:
He calleth the heavens from above.
And the earth, that he may contend in judgment with his people." Psa. l. 3, 4.

By the same bold figure, Micah calls upon the mountains, that is, the whole country of Judea, to attend to him, chap. vi. 1, 2:—

"Arise, plead thou before the mountains,
And let the hills hear thy voice.
Hear, O ye mountains, the controversy of JEHOVAH;
And ye, O ye strong foundations of the earth:
For JEHOVAH hath a controversy with his people,
And he will plead his cause against Israel."

With the like invocation, Moses introduces his sublime song, the design of which was the same as that of this prophecy, "to testify as a witness, against the Israelites," for their disobedience, Deut. xxxi. 21:—

"Give ear, O ye heavens, and I will speak;
And let the earth hear the words of my mouth." Deut. xxxii. 1.

This, in the simple yet strong oratorical style of Moses, is, "I call heaven and earth to witness against thee this day; life and death have I set before thee; the blessing and the curse: choose now life, that thou mayest live, thou and thy seed." Deut. xxx. 19. The poetical style, by an apostrophe, sets the personification in a much stronger light.

Hath spoken—"That speaketh"] I render it in the present time, pointing it דבר *dober.* There seems to be an impropriety in demanding attention to a speech already delivered. But the present reading may stand, as the prophet may be here understood to declare to the people what the Lord *had* first spoken to him.

I have nourished] The *Septuagint* have εγεννησα, "I have begotten." Instead of גדלתי *giddalti,* they read ילדתי *yaladti;* the word little differing from the other, and perhaps more proper; which the Chaldee likewise seems to favour; "vocavi eos filios." See Exod. iv. 22; Jer. xxxi. 9.

Verse 3. *The ox knoweth*] An amplification of the gross insensibility of the disobedient Jews, by comparing them with the most heavy and stupid of all animals, yet not so insensible as they. Bochart has well illustrated the comparison, and shown the peculiar force of it. "He sets them lower than the beasts, and even than the most stupid of all beasts, for there is scarcely any more so than the ox and the ass. Yet these acknowledge their master; they know the manger of their lord; by whom they are fed, not for their own, but for his good; neither are they looked upon as children, but as beasts of burden; neither are they advanced to honours, but oppressed with great and daily labours. While the Israelites, chosen by the mere favour of God, adopted as sons, promoted to the highest dignity, yet acknowledged not their Lord and their God; but despised his commandments, though in the highest degree equitable and just." Hieroz. i., col. 409.

Jeremiah's comparison to the same purpose is equally elegant, but has not so much spirit and severity as this of Isaiah.

"Even the stork in the heavens knoweth her season;
And the turtle, and the swallow, and the crane, observe the time of their coming:
But my people doth not know the judgment of JEHOVAH." Jer. viii. 7.

Hosea has given a very elegant turn to the same image, in the way of metaphor or allegory:—

"I drew them with human cords, with the bands of love:
And I was to them as he that lifteth up the yoke upon their cheek;
And I laid down their fodder before them."
Hos. xi. 4.

Salomo ben Melech thus explains the middle part of the verse, which is somewhat obscure: "I was to them at their desire as they that have compassion on a heifer, lest she be overworked in ploughing; and that lift up the yoke from off her neck, and rest it upon her cheek that she may not still draw, but rest from her labour an hour or two in the day."

But *Israel*] The *Septuagint, Syriac, Aquila, Theodotion,* and *Vulgate,* read וישראל *veyisrael,* BUT *Israel,* adding the *conjunction,* which being rendered as an adversative, sets the opposition in a stronger light.

Doth not know] The same ancient versions agree in adding ME, which very properly answers, and indeed is almost necessarily required to answer, the words *possessor* and *lord* preceding. Ισραηλ δε ΜΕ ουκ εγνω; *Sept.* "Israel *autem* ME *non cognovit;*" *Vulg.* Ισραηλ δε ΜΟΥ ουκ εγνω; *Aquil., Theod.* The testimony of so scrupulous an interpreter as *Aquila* is of great weight in this case. And both his and *Theodotion's* rendering is such as shows plainly that they did not add the word ΜΟΥ to help out the sense, for it only embarrasses it. It also clearly determines what was the original reading in the old copies from which they translated. It could not be ידעני *yedani,* which most obviously answers to the version of the *Septuagint* and *Vulgate,* for it does not accord with that of *Aquila* and *Theodotion.* The version of these latter interpreters, however injudicious, clearly ascertains both the phrase, and the order of the words of the original Hebrew; it was וישראל אותי לא ידע *veyisrael*

A. M. cir. 3244
B. C. cir. 760
Anno Olymp.
Quintæ I.
Ante Urbem
Conditam 7

anger, they are [l]gone away
backward.
5 [k]Why should ye be stricken
any more? ye will [l]revolt more
and more: the whole head is sick, and the
whole heart faint.

6 From the sole of the foot
even unto the head *there is* no
soundness in it; *but* wounds,
and bruises, and putrefying
sores; [m]they have not been closed, neither
bound up, neither mollified with [n]ointment.

A. M. cir. 3244
B. C. cir. 760
Anno Olymp.
Quintæ I.
Ante Urbem
Conditam 7

---

[i]Heb. *alienated,* or *separated;* Psa. lviii. 3——[k]Chap. ix. 13; Jer. ii. 30; v. 3

[l]Hebrew, *increase revolt*——[m]Jeremiah viii. 22
[n]Or, *oil*

---

othi lo yada. The word אותי *othi has been* lost out of the text. The very same phrase is used by Jeremiah, chap. iv. 22, עמי אותי לא ידעו *ammi othi lo yadau.* And the order of the words must have been as above represented; for they have joined ישראל *yisrael,* with אותי *othi,* as *in regimine;* they could not have taken it in this sense, *Israel* MEUS *non cognovit,* had either this phrase or the order of the words been different. I have endeavoured to set this matter in a clear light, as it is the first example of a *whole word* lost out of the text, of which the reader will find many other plain examples in the course of these notes. But *Rosenmüller* contends that this is unnecessary, as the pasage may be translated, "Israel knows nothing: my people have no understanding."

The *Septuagint, Syriac,* and *Vulgate,* read ועמי *veammi,* "*and* my people;" and so likewise sixteen MSS. of *Kennicott,* and fourteen of *De Rossi.*

Verse 4. *Ah sinful nation*—"Degenerate"] Five MSS., one of them ancient, read משחתים *moschathim,* without the first י *yod,* in *hophal corrupted,* not *corrupters.* See the same word in the same form, and in the same sense, Prov. xxv. 26.

Are corrupters—"Are estranged"] Thirty-two MSS., five ancient, and two editions, read נזורו *nazoru;* which reading determines the word to be from the root זור *zur, to alienate,* not from נזר *nazar, to separate;* so *Kimchi* understands it. See also *Annotat.* in *Noldium,* 68.

They are gone away backward—"They have turned their backs upon him."] So *Kimchi* explains it: "they have turned unto him the back, and not the face." See Jer. ii. 27; vii. 24. I have been forced to render this line paraphrastically; as the verbal translation, "they are estranged backward," would have been unintelligible.

Verse 5. *Why should ye be stricken any more*—"On what part," &c.?] The *Vulgate* renders על מה *al meh, super quo,* (see Job xxxviii. 6; 2 Chron, xxxii. 10,) *upon what* part. And so *Abendana* on *Sal. ben Melech:* "There are some who explain it thus: Upon what limb shall you be smitten, if you add defection? for already for your sins have you been smitten upon all of them; so that there is not to be found in you a whole limb on which you can be smitten." Which agrees with what follows: "From the sole of the foot even unto the head, there is no soundness in it:" and the sentiment and image is exactly the same with that of *Ovid, Pont.* ii. 7, 42:—

Vix habet in nobis jam nova plaga locum.

There is no place on you for a new stripe.

Or that still more expressive line of *Euripides;* the great force and effect of which *Longinus* ascribes to its close and compressed structure, analogous to the sense which it expresses:—

Γεμω κακων δη· κ' ουκετ' εσθ' ὁπη τιθῃ.

I am full of miseries: there's no room for more.

Herc. Fur. 1245, *Long.* sec. 40.

"On what part will ye strike again? will ye add correction?" This is addressed to the instruments of God's vengeance; those that inflicted the punishment, who or whatsoever they were. Ad verbum certæ personæ intelligendæ sunt, quibus ista actio quæ per verbum exprimitur competit; "The words are addressed to the persons who were the agents employed in the work expressed by the original word," as Glassius says in a similar case, *Phil. Sacr.* i. 3, 22. See chap. vii. 4.

As from ידע *yada,* דעה *deah,* knowledge; from יעץ *yaats,* עצה *etsah,* counsel; from ישן *yashan,* שנה *shenah,* sleep, &c.; so from יסר *yasar* is regularly derived סרה *sarah,* correction.

Verse 5. *The whole head is sick*] The king and the priests are equally gone away from truth and righteousness. Or, The state is oppressed by its enemies, and the Church corrupted in its rulers and in its members.

Verse 6. *They have not been closed, &c.*—"It hath not been pressed," &c.] The pharmaceutical art in the East consists chiefly in external applications: accordingly the prophet's images in this place are all taken from surgery. Sir John Chardin, in his note on Prov. iii. 8, "It shall be health to thy navel, and marrow to thy bones," observes that "the comparison is taken from the plasters, ointments, oils, and frictions, which are made use of in the East upon the belly and stomach in most maladies. Being ignorant in the villages of the art of making decoctions and potions, and of the proper doses of such things, they generally make use of external medicines."—*Harmer's Observations on Scripture,* vol. ii. p. 488. And in surgery their *materia medica* is extremely simple, oil making the principal part of it. "In India," says *Tavernier,* "they have a certain preparation of oil and melted grease, which they commonly use for the healing of wounds." Voyage Ind. So the good Samaritan poured oil and wine on the wounds of the distressed Jew: wine, cleansing and somewhat astringent, proper for a fresh wound; oil, mollifying and healing, Luke x. 34. Kimchi has a judicious remark here: "When various medicines are applied, and no healing takes place, that disorder is considered as coming immediately from God."

Of the three verbs in this sentence, one is in the singular number in the text; another is

A. M. cir. 3244
B. C. cir. 760
Anno Olymp.
Quintæ I.
Ante Urbem
Conditam 7

7 °Your country *is* desolate,
your cities *are* burned with fire:
your land, strangers devour it in
your presence, and *it is* desolate,
[p]as overthrown by strangers.

8 And the daughter of Zion
is left [q]as a cottage in a vineyard, as a lodge in a garden
of cucumbers, [r]as a besieged
city.

A. M. cir. 3244
B. C. cir. 760
Anno Olymp.
Quintæ I.
Ante Urbem
Conditam 7

°Deut. xxviii. 51, 52——[p]Heb. *as the overthrow of strangers*——[q]Job xxvii. 18; Lam. ii. 6——[r]Jer. iv. 17

singular in two MSS., (one of them ancient,) חבשה *chubbeshah;* and the *Syriac* and *Vulgate* render all of them in the singular number.

Verses 7-9. *Your country* is *desolate*] The description of the ruined and desolate state of the country in these verses does not suit with any part of the prosperous times of Uzziah and Jotham. It very well agrees with the time of Ahaz, when Judea was ravaged by the joint invasion of the Israelites and Syrians, and by the incursions of the Philistines and Edomites. The date of this prophecy is therefore generally fixed to the time of Ahaz. But on the other hand it may be considered whether those instances of idoltary which are urged in ver. 29—the worshipping in groves and gardens—having been at all times too commonly practised, can be supposed to be the only ones which the prophet would insist upon in the time of Ahaz; who spread the grossest idolatry through the whole country, and introduced it even into the temple; and, to complete his abominations, made his son pass through the fire to Molech. It is said, 2 Kings xv. 37, that in Jotham's time "the Lord began to send against Judah Rezin—and Pekah." If we may suppose any invasion from that quarter to have been actually made at the latter end of Jotham's reign, I should choose to refer this prophecy to that time.

And *your cities* are *burned.—Nineteen* of Dr. *Kennicott's* MSS. and *twenty-two* of *De Rossi's*, some of my own, with the *Syriac* and *Arabic*, add the conjunction which makes the hemistich more complete.

Verse 7. זרים *zarim* at the end of the verse. This reading, though confirmed by all the ancient versions, gives us no good sense; for "your land is devoured by strangers; and is desolate, as if overthrown by *strangers*," is a mere tautology, or, what is as bad, an identical comparison. *Aben Ezra* thought that the word in its present form might be taken for the same with זרם *zerem, an inundation: Schultens* is of the same opinion; (see *Taylor's* Concord.;) and *Schindler* in his Lexicon explains it in the same manner: and so, says *Kimchi*, some explain it. *Abendana* endeavours to reconcile it to grammatical analogy in the following manner: "זרים *zarim* is the same with זרם *zerem;* that is, as overthrown by *an inundation of waters:* and these two words have the same analogy as קדם *kedem* and קדים *kadim.* Or it may be a concrete of the same form with שכיר *shechir;* and the meaning will be: as overthrown by rain pouring down violently, and causing a flood." On *Sal. ben Melech, in loc.* But I rather suppose the true reading to be זרם *zerem*, and have translated it accordingly: the word זרים *zerim*, in the line above, seems to have caught the transcriber's eye, and to have led him into this mistake. But this conjecture of the learned prelate is not confirmed by any MS. yet discovered.

Verse 8. *As a cottage in a vineyard*—"As a shed in a vineyard"] A little temporary hut covered with boughs, straw, turf, or the like materials, for a shelter from the heat by day, and the cold and dews by night, for the watchman that kept the garden or vineyard during the short season the fruit was ripening, (see Job xxvii. 18,) and presently removed when it had served that purpose. See *Harmer's* Observ. i. 454. They were probably obliged to have such a constant watch to defend the fruit from the jackals. "The jackal," (*chical* of the Turks,) says *Hasselquist*, (Travels, p. 227,) "is a species of mustela which is very common in Palestine, especially during the vintage; and often destroys whole vineyards, and gardens of cucumbers." "There is also plenty of the *canis vulpes*, the fox, near the convent of St. John in the desert, about vintage time; for they destroy all the vines unless they are strictly watched." Ibid. p. 184. See Cant. ii. 15.

Fruits of the gourd kind, melons, watermelons, cucumbers, &c., are much used and in great request in the Levant, on account of their cooling quality. The Israelites in the wilderness regretted the loss of the cucumbers and melons among the other good things of Egypt, Num. xi. 5. In Egypt the season of *watermelons*, which are most in request, and which the common people then chiefly live upon, lasts but three weeks. See *Hasselquist*, p. 256. *Tavernier* makes it of longer continuance: L'on y void de grands carreaux de melons et de concombres, mais beaucoup plus de derniers, dont les Levantins font leur delices. Le plus souvent, ils les mangent sans les peler, après quoi ils vont boire une verre d'eau. Dans toute l'Asie c'est la nourriture ordinaire du petit peuple pendant trois ou quatre mois; toute la famille en vit; et quand un enfant demand à manger, au lieu qu'en France ou aillieurs nous luy donnerions du pain, dans le Levant on luy presente un concombre, qu'il mange cru comme on le vient de cueillir. Les concombres dans le Levant ont une bontè particuliere; et quoiqu' on les mange crus, ils ne font jamais de mal; "There are to be seen great beds of melons and cucumbers, but a greater number of the latter, of which the Levantines are particularly fond. In general they eat them without taking off the rind, after which they drink a glass of water. In every part of Asia this is the aliment of the common people for three or four months; the whole family live on them; and when a child asks something to eat, instead of giving it a piece of bread, as is done in France and other countries, they present it with a cucumber, which it eats raw, as gathered. Cucumbers in the Levant are peculiarly excellent; and although eaten raw, they are seldom injurious." *Tavernier*, Relat. du Serrail, cap. xix.

As a lodge, &c.] That is, after the fruit was gathered; the lodge being then permitted to fall into decay. Such was the desolate, ruined state of the city.

As a lodge, &c.] That is, after the fruit was So the ὡς πολις πολιορκουμενη; *Septuagint:* see also the *Vulgate.*

A. M. cir. 3244
B. C. cir. 760
Anno Olymp. Quintæ I.
Ante Urbem Conditam 7

9 [s]Except the LORD of hosts had left unto us a very small remnant, we should have been as [t]Sodom, *and* we should have been like unto Gomorrah.

10 Hear the word of the LORD, ye rulers [u]of Sodom; give ear unto the law of our God, ye people of Gomorrah.

11 To what purpose *is* the multitude of your [v]sacrifices unto me? saith the LORD: I am full of the burnt-offerings of rams, and the fat of fed beasts; and I delight not in the blood of bullocks, or of lambs, or of [w]he-goats.

12 When ye come [x]to [y]appear before me, who hath required this at your hand, to tread my courts?

13 Bring no more [z]vain oblations; incense is an abomination unto me; the new moons and Sabbaths, [a]the calling of assemblies, I

[s]Lam. iii. 22; Rom. ix. 29——[t]Gen. xix. 24——[u]Deut. xxxii. 32; Ezek. xvi. 46——[v]1 Sam. xv. 22; Psa. l. 8, 9; li. 16; Prov. xv. 8; xxi. 27; chap. lxvi. 3; Jer. vi. 20; vii. 21; Amos v. 21, 22; Mic. vi. 7——[w]Heb. *great he-goats*——[x]Heb. *to be seen*——[y]Exod. xxiii. 17; xxxiv. 23——[z]Matt. xv. 9——[a]Joel i. 14; ii. 15

Verse 9. *The Lord of hosts*—"JEHOVAH God of hosts"] As this title of God, יהוה צבאות *Yehovah tsebaoth,* "JEHOVAH of hosts, occurs here for the first time, I think it proper to note, that I translate it always, as in this place, "JEHOVAH God of hosts;" taking it as an elliptical expression for יהוה אלהי צבאות *Yehovah Elohey tsebaoth.* This title imports that JEHOVAH is the God or Lord of hosts or armies; as he is the Creator and Supreme Governor of all beings in heaven and earth, and disposeth and ruleth them all in their several orders and stations; the almighty, universal Lord.

We should have been as Sodom] As completely and finally ruined as *that* and the cities of the plain were, no vestige of which remains at this day.

Verse 10. *Ye rulers of Sodom*—"Ye princes of Sodom"] The incidental mention of Sodom and Gomorrah in the preceding verse suggested to the prophet this spirited address to the rulers and inhabitants of Jerusalem, under the character of princes of Sodom and people of Gomorrah. Two examples of a sort of elegant turn of the like kind may be observed in St. Paul's Epistle to the Romans, chap. xv. 4, 5, 12, 13. See Locke on the place; and see ver. 29, 30, of this chapter, which gives another example of the same.

AND—*like unto Gomorrah.—The* ו *vau* is added by *thirty-one* of *Kennicott's* MSS., *twenty-nine* of *De Rossi's* and one, very ancient, of my own. See on ver. 6.

Verse 11. *To what purpose, &c.*—"What have I to do."] The prophet Amos has expressed the same sentiments with great elegance:—

"I hate, I despise your feasts;
And I will not delight in the odour of your solemnities:
Though ye offer unto me burnt-offerings
And your meat-offerings, I will not accept:
Neither will I regard the peace-offerings of your fatlings.
Take away from me the noise of your songs;
And the melody of your viols I will not hear.
But let judgment roll down like waters;
And righteousness like a mighty stream."
Amos v. 21-24.

So has Persius; see Sat. ii. v. 71-75:—

"Quin damus id Superis, de magna quod dare lanæ," &c.

The two or three last pages of Plato's *Euthyphro* contain the same idea. Sacrifices and prayers are not profitable to the offerer, nor acceptable to the gods, unless accompanied with an upright life.

Verse 11. *The fat of fed beasts, &c.*] The fat and the blood are particularly mentioned, because these were in all sacrifices set apart to God. The fat was always burnt upon the altar, and the blood was partly sprinkled, differently on different occasions, and partly poured out at the bottom of the altar. See Lev. iv.

Verse 12. *When ye come to appear*] Instead of לראות *leraoth,* to *appear,* one MS. has לִראות *liroth,* to *see.* See *De Rossi.* The appearing before God here refers chiefly to the three solemn annual festivals. See Exod. xxiii. 14.

Tread my courts (no more)] So the *Septuagint* divide the sentence, joining the end of this verse to the beginning of the next: Πατειν την αυλην μου, ου προσθησεσθε; "To tread my court ye shall not add—ye shall not be again accepted in worship."

Verse 13. *The new moons and Sabbaths*—"The fast and the day of restraint"] און ועצרה *aven vaatsarah.* These words are rendered in many different manners by different interpreters, to a good and probable sense by all; but I think by none in such a sense as can arise from the phrase itself, agreeably to the idiom of the Hebrew language. Instead of און *aven,* the *Septuagint* manifestly read צום *tsom,* νηστειαν, "the fast." This *Houbigant* has adopted. The prophet could not well have omitted the *fast* in the enumeration of their *solemnities,* nor the *abuse* of it among the instances of their *hyprocrisy,* which he has treated at large with such force and elegance in his *fifty-eighth chapter.* Observe, also, that the prophet Joel, (chap. i. 14, and ii. 15,) twice joins together the fast and the day of restraint:—

קדשו צום קראו אצרה
atsarah kiru tsom kaddeshu

"Sanctify a fast; proclaim a day of restraint:"

which shows how properly they are here joined together. עצרה *atsarah,* "the restraint," is rendered, both here and in other places of our English translation, "the solemn assembly." Certain holy days ordained by the law were distinguished by a particular charge that "no servile work should be done therein;" Lev. xxviii. 36; Num. xxix. 35; Deut. xvi. 8. This circumstance clearly explains the reason of the

A. M. cir. 3244
B. C. cir. 760
Anno Olymp. Quintæ I.
Ante Urbem Conditam 7

cannot away with; *it is* [b]iniqui-
ty, even the solemn meeting.
14 Your [c]new moons and your
[d]appointed feasts my soul hateth: they are a trouble unto me; [e]I am
weary to bear *them.*
15 And [f]when ye spread forth your hands,
I will hide mine eyes from you: [g]yea, when
ye [h]make many prayers, I will not hear:
your hands are full of [i]blood.[k]
16 [l]Wash you, make you clean; put away
the evil of your doings from before mine eyes;
[m]cease to do evil;
17 Learn to do well; [n]seek judgment, [o]re-
lieve the oppressed, judge the fatherless, plead
for the widow.
18 Come now, and [p]let us reason together, saith the LORD:
though your sins be as scarlet,
[q]they shall be as white as snow;
though they be red like crimson, they shall be
as wool.
19 If ye be willing and obedient, ye shall eat
the good of the land:
20 But if ye refuse and rebel, ye shall be
devoured with the sword: [r]for the mouth of
the LORD hath spoken *it.*
21 [s]How is the faithful city become a
harlot! it was full of judgment; righteousness lodged in it; but now murderers.
22 [t]Thy silver is become dross, thy wine
mixed with water:

A. M. cir. 3244
B. C. cir. 760
Anno Olymp. Quintæ I.
Ante Urbem Conditam 7

---

[b]Or, *grief*——[c]Num. xxviii. 11——[d]Lev. xxiii. 2, &c.; Lam. ii. 6——[e]Ch. xliii. 24——[f]Job xxvii. 29; Psa. cxxxiv. 2; Prov. i. 28; ch. lix. 2; Jer. xiv. 12; Mic. iii. 4 [g]Psa. lxvi. 18; 1 Tim. ii. 8——[h]Heb *multiply prayer* [i]Ch. lix. 3——[k]Heb. *bloods*——[l]Jer. iv. 14

[m]Psa. xxxiv. 14; xxxvii. 27; Amos v. 15; Rom. xii. 9; 1 Pet. iii. 11——[n]Jer. xxii. 3, 16; Mic. vi. 8; Zech. vii. 9; viii. 16——[o]Or, *righten*——[p]Ch. xliii. 26; Mic. vi. 2 [q]Psa. li. 7; Rev. vii. 14——[r]Num. xxiii. 19; Tit. i. 2 [s]Jer. ii. 20, 21——[t]Jer. vi. 28, 30; Ezek. xxii. 18, 19

---

name, *the restraint*, or *the day of restraint*, given to those days.

If I could approve of any translation of these two words which I have met with, it should be that of the Spanish version of the Old Testament, made for the use of the Spanish Jews: *Tortura y detenimento*, "it is a pain and a constraint unto me." But I still think that the reading of the *Septuagint* is more probably the truth.

Verse 15. *When ye spread*] The *Syriac*, *Septuagint*, and a MS., read בפרשכם *beparshecem*, without the conjunction ו *vau*.

Your hands—"For your hands"] Αἱ γαρ χειρες—*Sept.* *Manus* enim *vestræ*—*Vulg.* They seem to have read כי ידיכם *ki yedeychem.*

Verse 16. *Wash you*] Referring to the preceding verse, "your hands are full of blood;" and alluding to the legal washing commanded on several occasions. See Lev. xiv. 8, 9, 47.

Verse 17. *Relieve the oppressed*—"Amend *that which is corrupted*"] אשרו חמוץ *asheru chamots.* In rendering this obscure phrase I follow *Bochart*, (*Hieroz.* Part i., lib. ii., cap. 7.,) though I am not perfectly satisfied with this explication of it.

Verse 18. *Though your sins be as scarlet*] שני *shani*, "scarlet or crimson," *dibaphum*, *twice dipped*, or *double dyed;* from שנה *shanah*, *iterare*, *to double*, or *to do a thing twice.* This derivation seems much more probable than that which *Salmasius* prefers from שנן *shanan*, *acuere*, to *whet*, from the *sharpness* and strength of the colour, οξυφοινικον; תלע *tela*, the same; properly the *worm*, *vermiculus*, (from whence *vermeil*,) for this colour was produced from a worm or insect which grew in a coccus or excrescence of a shrub of the ilex kind, (see Plin. Nat. Hist. xvi. 8,) like the cochineal worm in the opuntia of America. See Ulloa's Voyage, book v., chap. ii., note to page 342. There is a shrub of this kind that grows in Provence and Languedoc, and produces the like insect, called the *kermes oak*, (see Miller, Dict. *Quercus*,) from *kermez*, the Arabic word for this colour, whence our word *crimson* is derived.

> "Neque amissos colores
> Lana refert medicata fuco,"

says the poet, applying the same image to a different purpose. To discharge these strong colours is impossible to human art or power; but to the grace and power of God all things, even much more difficult, are possible and easy. Some copies have כשנים *keshanim*, "like crimson garments."

Though they be red, &c.] But the conjunction ו *vau* is added by *twenty-one* of *Kennicott's*, and by *forty-two* of *De Rossi's* MSS., by some early editions, with the *Septuagint*, *Syriac*, *Vulgate*, and *Arabic*. It makes a fuller and more emphatic sense. "AND *though they be red as crimson*," &c.

Verse 19. *Ye shall eat the good of the land*] Referring to ver. 7: it shall not be "devoured by strangers."

Verse 20. *Ye shall be devoured with the sword*—"Ye shall be food for the sword"] The *Septuagint* and *Vulgate* read תאכלכם *tochalchem*, "the sword *shall devour you;*" which is of much more easy construction than the present reading of the text.

The Chaldee seems to read בחרב אויב תאכלו *bechereb oyeb teachelu*, "ye shall be consumed *by* the sword *of the enemy.*" The *Syriac* also reads בחרב *bechereb* and renders the verb passively. And the rhythmus seems to require this addition.—Dr. JUBB.

Verse 21.—*Become a harlot*] See before, the Discourse on the Prophetic Style; and see Lowth's Comment on the place, and De Sacr. Poës. Hebr. Præl. xxxi.

Verse 22. *Wine mixed with water*] An image used for the *adulteration* of wines, with more propriety than may at first appear, if what *Thevenot* says of the people of the Levant of late times were true of them formerly. He says, "They never mingle water with their wine

A. M. cir. 3244
B. C. cir. 760
Anno Olymp.
Quintæ I.
Ante Urbem
Conditam 7

23 [u]Thy princes *are* rebellious,
and [v]companions of thieves:
[w]every one loveth gifts, and followeth after rewards: they
[x]judge not the fatherless, neither
doth the cause of the widow come
unto them.
24 Therefore saith the LORD,

[u]Hosea ix. 15——[v]Proverbs xxix. 24——[w]Jeremiah xxii. 17; Ezekiel xxii. 12; Hosea iv. 18; Micah iii. 11; vii. 3——[x]Jeremiah v. 28; Zechariah vii. 10

to drink; but drink by itself what water they think proper for abating the strength of the wine." "Lorsque les Persans boivent du vin, ils le prennent tout pur, à la facon des Levantins, qui ne le mêlent jamais avec de l'eua; mais en beuvant du vin, de temps en temps ils prennent un pot d'eau, et en boivent de grand traits." Voyage, part ii., liv. ii., chap. 10. "Ils (les Turcs) n'y meslent jamais d'eau, et se moquent des Chrètiens qui en mettent, ce qui leur semble tout à fait ridicule." Ibid. part i., chap. 24. "The Turks never mingle water with their wine, and laugh at the Christians for doing it, which they consider altogether ridiculous."

It is remarkable that whereas the Greeks and Latins by *mixed* wine always understood wine diluted and lowered with water, the Hebrews on the contrary generally mean by it wine made stronger and more inebriating by the addition of higher and more powerful ingredients, such as honey, spices, defrutum, (or wine inspissated by boiling it down to two-thirds or one-half of the quantity,) myrrh, mandragora, opiates, and other strong drugs. Such were the exhilarating, or rather stupifying, ingredients which Helen mixed in the bowl together with the wine for her guests oppressed with grief to raise their spirits, the composition of which she had learned in Egypt:—

Αυτικ' αρ' εις οινον βαλε φαρμακον, ενθεν επινον,
Νηπενθες τ' αχολον τε, κακων επιληθον ἁπαντων.
HOMER. *Odyss.* lib. iv., ver. 220.

"Meanwhile, with genial joy to warm the soul,
Bright Helen mix'd a mirth-inspiring bowl;
Temper'd with drugs of sovereign use, to assuage
The boiling bosom of tumultuous rage:
Charm'd with that virtuous draught, the exalted mind
All sense of wo delivers to the wind."
POPE.

Such was the "spiced wine and the juice of pomegranates," mentioned Cant. viii. 2. And how much the Eastern people to this day deal in artificial liquors of prodigious strength, the use of wine being forbidden, may be seen in a curious chapter of Kempfer upon that subject. Amœn. Exot. Fasc. iii., Obs. 15.

Thus the drunkard is properly described, Prov. xxiii. 30, as one "that seeketh *mixed* wine," and "is mighty to *mingle* strong drink," Isa. v. 22. And hence the poet took that highly poetical and sublime image of the cup of God's wrath, called by Isaiah li. 17, the "cup of trembling," causing intoxication and stupefaction, (see Chappelow's note on Hariri, p. 33,) containing, as St. John expresses in Greek the Hebrew idea with the utmost precision, though with a seeming contradiction in terms, κεκερασμενον ακρατον, *merum mixtum*, pure wine made yet stronger by a mixture of powerful ingredients; Rev. xiv. 10. "In the hand of JEHOVAH," saith the psalmist, Psa. lxxv. 8, "there is a cup, and the wine is turbid: it is full of a mixed liquor, and he poureth out of it;" or rather, "he poureth it out of one vessel into another," to mix it perfectly, according to the reading expressed by the ancient versions, ויגר מזה אל זה *vaiyagger mizzeh al zeh*, and he pours it from this to that, "verily the dregs thereof," the thickest sediment of the strong ingredients mingled with it, "all the ungodly of the earth shall wring them out, and drink them."

R. D. Kimchi says, "The current coin was adulterated with brass, tin, and other metals, and yet was circulated as good money. The wine also was adulterated with water in the taverns, and sold notwithstanding for pure wine."

Verse 23. *Companions of thieves*—"Associates"] The *Septuagint*, *Vulgate*, and four MSS., read חברי *chabrey* without the conjunction ו *vau*.

Verse 24. *Ah, I will ease me*—"Aha! I will be eased"] Anger, arising from a sense of injury and affront, especially from those who, from every consideration of duty and gratitude, ought to have behaved far otherwise, is an uneasy and painful sensation: and revenge, executed to the full on the offenders, removes that uneasiness, and consequently is pleasing and quieting, at least for the present. Ezekiel, chap. v. 13, introduces God expressing himself in the same manner:—

"And mine anger shall be fully accomplished;
And I will make my fury rest upon them;
And I will give myself ease."

This is a strong instance of the metaphor called anthropopathia, by which, throughout the Scriptures, as well the historical as the poetical parts, the sentiments, sensations, and affections, the bodily faculties, qualities, and members, of men, and even of brute animals, are attributed to God, and that with the utmost liberty and latitude of application. The foundation of this is obvious; it arises from necessity; we have no idea of the natural attributes of God, of his pure essence, of his manner of existence, of his manner of acting: when therefore we would treat on these subjects, we find ourselves forced to express them by sensible images. But necessity leads to beauty; this is true of metaphor in general, and in particular of this kind of metaphor, which is used with great elegance and sublimity in the sacred poetry; and what is very remarkable, in the grossest instances of the application of it, it is generally the most striking and the most sublime. The reason seems to be this: when the images are taken from the superior faculties of the human nature, from the purer and more generous affections, and applied to God, we are apt to acquiesce in the notion; we overlook the metaphor, and take it as a proper attribute; but when the idea is gross and offensive, as in this passage of Isaiah, where the impatience of anger and the pleasure of revenge is attributed to God, we are immediately shocked at the application; the impropriety

A. M. cir. 3244
B. C. cir. 760
Anno Olymp. Quintæ I.
Ante Urbem Conditam 7

the LORD of hosts, the mighty
one of Israel, Ah, [y]I will ease
me of mine adversaries, and
avenge me of mine enemies:
25 And I will turn my hand upon thee, and
[z]purely [a]purge away thy dross, and take away
all thy tin:
26 And I will restore thy judges [b]as at the
first, and thy counsellors as at the beginning:
afterward [c]thou shalt be called, The city
of righteousness, the faithful
city.
27 Zion shall be redeemed
with judgments, and [d]her converts with righteousness.
28 And the [e]destruction [f]of the transgressors and of the sinners *shall be* together, and
they that forsake the LORD shall be consumed.
29 For they shall be ashamed of [g]the oaks

[y]Deut. xxviii. 63; Ezek. v. 13——[z]Heb. *according to pureness*——[a]Jer. vi. 29; ix. 7; Mal. iii. 3——[b]Jer. xxxiii. 7——[c]Zech. viii. 3

[d]Or, *they that return of her*——[e]Job xxxi. 3; Psa. i. 6; v. 6; lxxiii. 27; xcii. 9; civ. 35——[f]Heb. *breaking* [g]Chap. lvii. 5.

strikes us at once; and the mind, casting about for something in the Divine nature analogous to the image, lays hold on some great, obscure, vague idea, which she endeavours to comprehend, and is lost in immensity and astonishment. See De Sacr. Poesi. Hebr. Præel. xvi. *sub. fin.*, where this matter is treated and illustrated by examples.

Verse 25. *I will turn my hand upon thee*] So the common version; and this seems to be a metaphor taken from the custom of those who, when the metal is melted, strike off the scoriæ with their hand previously to its being poured out into the mould. I have seen this done with the naked hand, and no injury whatever sustained.

Purge away thy dross—"In the furnace"] The text has כבר *cabbor*, which some render "as with soap;" as if it were the same with כברית *keborith;* so *Kimchi;* but soap can have nothing to do with the purifying of metals. Others, "according to purity," or "purely," as our version. *Le Clerc* conjectured that the true reading is כבור *kechur*, "as in the furnace;" see Ezek. xxii. 18, 20. Dr. *Durell* proposes only a transposition of letters כבר to the same sense; and so likewise Archbishop *Secker*. That this is the true reading is highly probable.

Verse 26. *I will restore*] "This," says *Kimchi*, "shall be in the days of the Messiah, in which all the wicked shall cease, and the remnant of Israel shall neither do iniquity, nor speak lies." What a change must this be among *Jews!*

Afterward—"And after this"] The *Septuagint*, *Syriac*, *Chaldee*, and *eighteen* MSS., and one of my own, very ancient, add the *conjunction* ו *vau*, AND.

Verse 27. *With judgment*—"In judgment"] By the exercise of God's strict justice in destroying the obdurate, (see ver. 28,) and delivering the penitent *in righteousness;* by the truth and faithfulness of God in performing his promises."

Verse 29. *For they shall be ashamed of the oaks*—"For ye shall be ashamed of the ilexes"] Sacred groves were a very ancient and favourite appendage of idolatry. They were furnished with the temple of the god to whom they were dedicated, with altars, images, and every thing necessary for performing the various rites of worship offered there; and were the scenes of many impure ceremonies, and of much abominable superstition. They made a principal part of the religion of the old inhabitants of Canaan; and the Israelites were commanded to destroy their groves, among other monuments of their false worship. The Israelites themselves became afterwards very much addicted to this species of idolatry.

"When I had brought them into the land,
Which I swore that I would give unto them;
Then they saw every high hill and every thick tree;
And there they slew their victims;
And there they presented the provocation of their offerings;
And there they placed their sweet savour;
And there they poured out their libations."
Ezek. xx. 28.

"On the tops of the mountains they sacrifice;
And on the hills they burn incense;
Under the oak and the poplar;
And the ilex, because her shade is pleasant."
Hos. iv. 13.

Of what particular kinds the trees here mentioned are, cannot be determined with certainty. In regard to אלה *ellah*, in this place of Isaiah, as well as in Hosea, *Celsius* (Hierobot.) understands it of the terebinth, because the most ancient interpreters render it so; in the first place the *Septuagint*. He quotes eight places; but in three of these eight places the copies vary, some having δρυς, *the oak*, instead of τερεβινθος, the *terebinth* or *turpentine tree*. And he should have told us, that these same *seventy* render it in sixteen other places by δρυς, *the oak;* so that their authority is really against him; and the *Septuagint*, "stant pro quercu," contrary to what he says at first setting out. Add to this that *Symmachus*, *Theodotion*, and *Aquila*, generally render it by δρυς, *the oak;* the latter only once rendering it by τερεβινθος, *the terebinth*. His other arguments seem to me not very conclusive; he says, that all the qualities of אלה *ellah* agree to the terebinth, that it grows in mountainous countries, that it is a strong tree, long-lived, large and high, and deciduous. All these qualities agree just as well to the *oak*, against which he contends; and he actually attributes them to the oak in the very next section. But I think neither the oak nor the terebinth will do in this place of Isaiah, from the last circumstance which he mentions, their being deciduous, where the prophet's design seems to me to require an evergreen, otherwise the casting of its leaves would be nothing out of the common established course of nature, and no proper

A. M. cir. 3244
B. C. cir. 760
Anno Olymp.
Quintæ I.
Ante Urbem
Conditam 7

which ye have desired, [h]and
ye shall be confounded for the
gardens that ye have chosen.
30 For ye shall be as an oak
whose leaf fadeth, and as a garden that hath
no water.
31 [i]And the strong shall be
[k]as tow, [l]and the maker of it as
a spark, and they shall both burn
together, and none shall quench
them.

A. M. cir. 3244
B. C. cir. 760
Anno Olymp.
Quintæ I.
Ante Urbem
Conditam 7

[h]Chap. lxv. 3; lxvi. 17——[i]Ezek. xxxii. 21

[k]Chap. xliii. 17——[l]Or, *and his work*

image of extreme distress and total desolation, parallel to that of a garden without water, that is, wholly burnt up and destroyed. An ancient, who was an inhabitant and a native of this country, understands it in like manner of a tree blasted with uncommon and immoderate heat; *velut arbores, cum frondes æstu torrente decusserunt. Ephrem Syr.* in loc., edit. Assemani. Compare Psa. i. 4; Jer. xvii. 8. Upon the whole I have chosen to make it the ilex, which word *Vossius*, Etymolog., derives from the Hebrew אלה *ellah*, that whether the word itself be rightly rendered or not, I might at least preserve the propriety of the poetic image.—L.

By the *ilex* the learned prelate means the *holly*, which, though it generally appears as a sort of shrub, grows, in a good soil, where it is unmolested, to a considerable height. I have one in my own garden, rising *three* stems from the root, and between *twenty* and *thirty* feet in height. It is an evergreen.

Verse 29. *For they shall be ashamed*—"For ye shall be ashamed"] תבושו *teboshu*, in the second person, *Vulgate, Chaldee, three* MSS., one of my own, ancient, and one edition; and in agreement with the rest of the sentence.

Verse 30. *Whose leaf*—"Whose leaves"] *Twenty-six* of *Kennicott's, twenty-four* of *De Rossi's*, one ancient, of my own, and *seven* editions, read אליה *aleyha*, in its full and regular form. This is worth remarking, as it accounts for a great number of anomalies of the like kind, which want only the same authority to rectify them.

As a garden that hath no water—"A garden wherein is no water."] In the hotter parts of the Eastern countries, a constant supply of water is so absolutely necessary for the cultivation and even for the preservation and existence of a garden, that should it want water but for a few days, every thing in it would be burnt up with the heat, and totally destroyed. There is therefore no garden whatever in those countries but what has such a certain supply, either from some neighbouring river, or from a reservoir of water collected from springs, or filled with rain water in the proper season, in sufficient quantity to afford ample provision for the rest of the year.

Moses, having described the habitation of man newly created as a garden planted with every tree pleasant to the sight and good for food, adds, as a circumstance necessary to complete the idea of a garden, that it was well supplied with water, "And a river went out of Eden to water the garden;" Gen. ii. 10: see also xiii. 10.

That the reader may have a clear notion of this matter, it will be necessary to give some account of the management of their gardens in this respect.

"Damascus," says *Maundrell*, p. 122, "is encompassed with gardens, extending no less, according to common estimation, than thirty miles round; which makes it look like a city in a vast wood. The gardens are thick set with fruit trees of all kinds, kept fresh and verdant by the waters of the Barrady, (the Chrysorrhoas of the ancients,) which supply both the gardens and city in great abundance. This river, as soon as it issues out from between the cleft of the mountain before mentioned into the plain, is immediately divided into three streams; of which the middlemost and biggest runs directly to Damascus, and is distributed to all the cisterns and fountains of the city. The other two (which I take to be the work of art) are drawn round, one to the right hand, and the other to the left, on the borders of the gardens, into which they are let as they pass, by little currents, and so dispersed all over the vast wood, insomuch that there is not a garden but has a fine quick stream running through it. The Barrady is almost wholly drunk up by the city and gardens. What small part of it escapes is united, as I was informed, in one channel again on the southeast side of the city; and, after about three or four hours' course finally loses itself in a bog there, without ever arriving at the sea." This was likewise the case in former times, as *Strabo*, lib. xvi., Pliny, lib. v. 18, testify; who say, "that this river was expended in canals, and drunk up by watering the place."

"The best sight," says the same *Maundrell*, p. 39, "that the palace of the emir of Beroot, anciently Berytus, affords, and the worthiest to be remembered, is the orange garden. It contains a large quadrangular plat of ground, divided into sixteen lesser squares, four in a row, with walks between them. The walks are shaded with orange trees of a large spreading size. Every one of these sixteen lesser squares in the garden was bordered with stone; and in the stone work were troughs, very artificially contrived, for conveying the water all over the garden; there being little outlets cut at every tree for the stream as it passed by to flow out and water it." The royal gardens at Ispahan are watered just in the same manner, according to *Kempfer's* description, Amœn. Exot., p. 193.

This gives us a clear idea of the פלגי מים *palgey mayim*, mentioned in the first Psalm, and other places of Scripture, "the divisions of waters," the waters distributed in artificial canals; for so the phrase properly signifies. The prophet Jeremith, chap. xvii. 8, has imitated, and elegantly amplified, the passage of the psalmist above referred to:—

"He shall be like a tree planted by the water side,
And which sendeth forth her roots to the aqueduct.
She shall not fear, when the heat cometh;
But her leaf shall be green;
And in the year of drought she shall not be anxious,
Neither shall she cease from bearing fruit."

From this image the son of Sirach, Ecclus. xxiv. 30, 31, has most beautifully illustrated the influence and the increase of religious wisdom in a well prepared heart.

"I also come forth as a canal from a river,
And as a conduit flowing into a paradise.
I said, I will water my garden,
And I will abundantly moisten my border:
And, lo! my canal became a river,
And my river became a sea."

This gives us the true meaning of the following elegant proverb, Prov. xxi. 1:—

"The heart of the king is like the canals of waters in the hand of JEHOVAH;
Whithersoever it pleaseth him, he inclineth it."

The direction of it is in the hand of JEHOVAH, as the distribution of the water of the reservoir through the garden by different canals is at the will of the gardener.

"Et, cum exustus ager morientibus æstuat herbis,
Ecce supercilio clivosi tramitis undam
Elicit: illa cadens raucum per levia murmur
Saxa ciet, scatebrisque arentia temperat arva."
Virg., Georg. i. 107.

"Then, when the fiery suns too fiercely play,
And shrivelled herbs on withering stems decay,
The wary ploughman on the mountain's brow
Undams his watery stores; huge torrents flow;
And, rattling down the rocks, large moisture yield,
Tempering the thirsty fever of the field."
DRYDEN.

Solomon, Eccles. ii. 5, 6, mentions his own works of this kind:—

"I made me gardens, and paradises;
And I planted in them all kinds of fruit trees.
I made me pools of water,
To water with them the grove flourishing with trees."

Maundrell, p. 88, has given a description of the remains, as they are said to be, of these very pools made by Solomon, for the reception and preservation of the waters of a spring, rising at a little distance from them; which will give us a perfect notion of the contrivance and design of such reservoirs. "As for the pools, they are three in number, lying in a row above each other; being so disposed that the waters of the uppermost may descend into the second, and those of the second into the third. Their figure is quadrangular, the breadth is the same in all, amounting to about ninety paces. In their length there is some difference between them; the first being about *one hundred and sixty* paces long, the second, *two hundred*, and the third, *two hundred and twenty*. They are all lined with wall and plastered; and contain a great depth of water."

The immense works which were made by the ancient kings of Egypt for recovering the waters of the Nile, when it overflowed, for such uses, are well known. But there never was a more stupendous work of this kind than the reservoir of Saba, or Merab, in Arabia Felix. According to the tradition of the country, it was the work of Balkis, that queen of Sheba who visited Solomon. It was a vast lake formed by the collection of the waters of a torrent in a valley, where, at a narrow pass between two mountains, a very high mole or dam was built. The water of the lake so formed had near *twenty* fathoms depth; and there were *three* sluices at different heights, by which, at whatever height the lake stood, the plain below might be watered. By conduits and canals from these sluices the water was constantly distributed in due proportion to the several lands; so that the whole country for many miles became a perfect paradise. The city of Saba, or Merab, was situated immediately below the great dam; a great flood came, and raised the lake above its usual height; the dam gave way in the middle of the night; the waters burst forth at once, and overwhelmed the whole city, with the neighbouring towns and people. The remains of eight tribes were forced to abandon their dwellings, and the beautiful valley became a morass and a desert. This fatal catastrophe happened long before the time of Mohammed, who mentions it in the Koran, chap. xxxiv. ver. 15. See also *Sale*, Prelim. s. i. p. 10, and *Michaelis*, Quest. aux Voyag. Dan. No. 94. *Niebuhr*, Descrip. de l'Arabie. p. 240.—L.

CHAPTER II

Prophecy concerning the kingdom of the Messiah, and the conversion of the Gentile world, 1–5. *Great wickedness and idolatry of the unbelieving Jews,* 6–9. *Terrible consternation that will seize the wicked, who shall in vain seek for rocks and mountains to hide them from the face of God in the day of his judgments,* 10–17. *Total destruction of idolatry in consequence of the establishment of Messiah's kingdom,* 18–21. *An exhortation to put no confidence in man,* 22.

A. M. cir. 3244
B. C. cir. 760
Anno Olymp. Quintæ I.
Ante Urbem Conditam 7

THE word that Isaiah the son of Amoz saw concerning Judah and Jerusalem.

2 And [a]it shall come to pass [b]in the last days [c]*that* the mountain of the LORD's house shall [d]be established in the top of the mountains, and shall be exalted

[a]Mic. iv. 1, &c.——[b]Gen. xlix. 1; Jer. xxiii. 30

[c]Psa. lxviii. 15, 16——[d]Or, *prepared*

The prophecy contained in the second, third, and fourth chapters, makes one continued discourse. The first five verses of chap. ii. foretell the kingdom of Messiah, the conversion of the Gentiles, and their admission into it. From the sixth verse to the end of the second chapter is foretold the punishment of the unbelieving Jews for their idolatrous practices, their confidence in their own strength, and distrust of God's protection; and moreover the destruction of idolatry, in consequence of the establishment of Messiah's kingdom. The whole of the third chapter, with the first verse of the fourth, is a prophecy of the calamities of the Babylonian invasion and captivity; with a particular amplification of the distress of the proud

A. M. cir. 3244 B. C. cir. 760 Anno Olymp. Quintæ I. Ante Urbem Conditam 7

above the hills; [e]and all nations shall flow unto it.

3 And many people shall go and say, [f]Come ye and let us go up to the mountain of the LORD, to the house of the God of Jacob; and he will teach us of his ways, and we will walk in his paths:

[e]Psa. lxxii. 8; chap. xxvii. 13

[f]Jer. xxxi. 6; l. 5; Zech. viii. 21, 23

and luxurious daughters of Sion; chap. iv. 2-6 promises to the remnant, which shall have escaped this severe purgation, a future restoration to the favour and protection of God.

This prophecy was probably delivered in the time of Jotham, or perhaps in that of Uzziah, as Isaiah is said to have prophesied in his reign; to which time not any of his prophecies is so applicable as that of these chapters. The seventh verse of the second, and the latter part of the third chapter, plainly point out times in which riches abounded, and luxury and delicacy prevailed. Plenty of silver and gold could only arise from their commerce; particularly from that part of it which was carried on by the Red Sea. This circumstance seems to confine the prophecy within the limits above mentioned, while the port of Elath was in their hands: it was lost under Ahaz, and never recovered.

NOTES ON CHAP. II

Verse 2. *In the last days*—"In the latter days"] "Wherever the latter times are mentioned in Scripture, the days of the Messiah are always meant," says *Kimchi* on this place: and, in regard to this place, nothing can be more clear and certain. And *the mountain of the Lord's house*, says the same author, is Mount *Moriah*, on which the temple was built. The prophet Micah, chap. iv. 1-4, has repeated this prophecy of the establishment of the kingdom of Christ, and of its progress to universality and perfection, in the same words, with little and hardly any material variation: for as he did not begin to prophesy till Jotham's time, and this seems to be one of the first of Isaiah's prophecies, I suppose Micah to have taken it from hence. The variations, as I said, are of no great importance. Ver. 2. הוא *hu*, after ונשא *venissa*, a word of some emphasis, may be supplied from Micah, if dropped in Isaiah. An ancient MS. has it here in the margin. It has in like manner been lost in chap. liii. 4, (see note on the place,) and in Psa. xxii. 29, where it is supplied by the *Syriac* and *Septuagint*. Instead of כל הגוים *col haggoyim, all the nations*, Micah has only עמים *ammim, peoples;* where the *Syriac* has כל עמים *col ammim, all peoples*, as probably it ought to be. Ver. 3. For the second אל *el*, read ואל *veel*, seventeen MSS., one of my own, ancient, two editions, the *Septuagint*, *Vulgate*, *Syriac*, *Chaldee*, and so Micah, iv. 2. Ver. 4. Micah adds עד רחק *ad rachok, afar off*, which the *Syriac* also reads in this parallel place of Isaiah. It is also to be observed that Micah has improved the passage by adding a verse, or sentence, for imagery and expression worthy even of the elegance of Isaiah:—

"And they shall sit every man under his vine,
And under his fig tree, and none shall affright them:
For the mouth of JEHOVAH, God of hosts, hath spoken it."

The description of well established peace, by the image of "beating their swords into ploughshares, and their spears into pruninghooks," is very poetical. The Roman poets have employed the same image, *Martial*, xiv. 34. "Falx ex ense."

"Pax me certa ducis placidos curvavit in usus:
Agricolæ nunc sum; militis ante fui."

"Sweet peace has transformed me. I was once the property of the soldier, and am now the property of the husbandman."

The prophet Joel, chap. iii. 10, hath reversed it, and applied it to war prevailing over peace:—

"Beat your ploughshares into swords,
And your pruning-hooks into spears."

And so likewise the Roman poets:—

——————— Non ullus aratro
Dignus honos: squalent abductis arva colonis,
Et curvæ rigidum falces conflantur in ensem.
Virg., Georg. i. 506.

"Agriculture has now no honour: the husbandmen being taken away to the wars, the fields are overgrown with weeds, and the crooked sickles are straightened into swords."

Bella diu tenuere viros: erat aptior ensis
Vomere: cedebat taurus arator equo
Sarcula cessabant; versique in pila ligones;
Factaque de rastri pondere cassis erat.
Ovid, Fast. i. 697.

"War has lasted long, and the sword is preferred to the plough. The bull has given place to the war-horse; the weeding-hooks to pikes; and the harrow-pins have been manufactured into helmets."

The prophet Ezekiel, chap. xvii. 22-24, has presignified the same great event with equal clearness, though in a more abstruse form, in an allegory; from an image, suggested by the former part of the prophecy, happily introduced, and well pursued:—

"Thus saith the Lord JEHOVAH:
I myself will take from the shoot of the lofty cedar,
Even a tender scion from the top of his scions will I pluck off:
And I myself will plant it on a mountain high and eminent.
On the lofty mountain of Israel will I plant it;
And it shall exalt its branch, and bring forth fruit,
And it shall become a majestic cedar:
And under it shall dwell all fowl of every wing;
In the shadow of its branches shall they dwell:
And all the trees of the field shall know,
That I JEHOVAH have brought low the high tree;

A. M. cir. 3244 B. C. cir. 760 Anno Olymp. Quintæ I. Ante Urbem Conditam 7

[g]for out of Zion shall go forth
the law, and the word of the
LORD from Jerusalem.
4 And he shall judge among
the nations, and shall rebuke many people:
and [h]they shall beat their swords into plow-
shares, and their spears into [i]pruning-hooks:
nation shall not lift up sword against nation,
[k]neither shall they learn war any more.

5 O house of Jacob, come ye,
and let us [l]walk in the light of
the LORD.
6 Therefore thou hast forsaken
thy people the house of Jacob, because they be
replenished [m]from [n]the east, and [o]*are* soothsayers like the Philistines, [p]and they [q]please
themselves in the children of strangers.
7 [r]Their land also is full of silver and gold,

[g]Luke xxiv. 47——[h]Psa. xlvi. 9; Hos. ii. 18; Zech. ix. 10——[i]Or, *scythes*——[k]Psa. lxii. 3, 7——[l]Eph. v. 8 [m]Or, *more than the east*

[n]Num. xxiii. 7——[o]Deut. xviii. 14——[p]Psa. cvi. 35; Jer. x. 2——[q]Or, *abound with the children*, &c. [r]Deut. xvii. 16, 17

Have exalted the low tree;
Have dried up the green tree;
And have made the dry tree to flourish:
I JEHOVAH have spoken it, and will do it."

The word ונתתי *venathatti*, in this passage, ver. 22, as the sentence now stands, appears incapable of being reduced to any proper construction or sense. None of the ancient versions acknowledge it, except *Theodotion*, and the *Vulgate;* and all but the latter vary very much from the present reading of this clause. *Houbigant's* correction of the passage, by reading instead of ונתתי *venathatti*, ויונקת *veyoneketh, and a tender scion*—which is not very unlike it, perhaps better ויונק *veyonek*, with which the adjective רך *rach* will agree without alteration—is ingenious and probable; and I have adopted it in the above translation.—L.

Verse 3. *To the house*] The conjunction ו *vau* is added by nineteen of *Kennicott's*, thirteen of *De Rossi's* MSS., one of my own, and two editions, the *Septuagint*, *Syriac*, *Vulgate*, *Arabic*, and some copies of the *Targum;* AND *to the house.* It makes the sentence more emphatic.

He will teach us of his ways] Unless God grant a revelation of his will, what can we know?

We will walk in his paths] Unless we purpose to walk in the light, of what use can that light be to us?

For out of Zion shall go forth the law] In the house of God, and in his ordinances only, can we expect to hear the pure doctrines of revelation preached. 1. God alone can give a revelation of his own will. 2. We must use the proper means in order to know this will. 3. We should *know* it in order to *do* it. 4. We should *do* it in order to profit by it. 5. He who will not walk in the light when God vouchsafes it, shall be shut up in everlasting darkness. 6. Every man should help his neighbour to attain that light, life, and felicity: "Come ye, and let us walk in the light of the Lord."

Verse 4. *Neither shall they learn war any more.*] If wars are *necessary*, how deep must that *fall* be that renders them so! But what a reproach to humanity is the *trade of war!* Men are regularly instructed in it, as in any of the necessary arts.

"How to dislodge most souls from their frail
shrines
By bomb, sword, ball, and bayonet, is the art
Which some call great and glorious!"

And is this a necessary part of a finished education in civilized society? O Earth! Earth! Earth!

Verse 6. *They be replenished*—"And they multiply"] Seven MSS. and one edition, for ישפיקו *yaspiku*, read יספיחו *yaspichu*, "and have joined themselves to the children of strangers;" that is, in marriage or worship.—Dr. JUBB. So *Vulg.*, *adhæserunt.* Compare chap. xiv. 1. But the very learned professor Chevalier *Michaelis* has explained the word יספחו *yesupachu*, Job xxx. 7, (German translation, note on the place,) in another manner; which perfectly well agrees with that place, and perhaps will be found to give as good a sense here. ספיח *saphiach*, the noun, means corn springing up, not from the seed regularly sown on cultivated land, but in the untilled field, from the scattered grains of the former harvest. This, by an easy metaphor, is applied to a spurious brood of children irregularly and casually begotten. The *Septuagint* seem to have understood the verb here in this sense, reading it as the *Vulgate* seems to have done. This justifies their version, which it is hard to account for in any other manner: *και τεκνα πολλα αλλοφυλα εγεννηθη αυτοις.* Compare Hos. v. 7, and the *Septuagint* there. But instead of ובילדי *ubeyaldey*, "and in the children," two of *Kennicott's* and eight of *De Rossi's* MSS. have וכילדי *ucheyaldey*, "and as the children." And they sin impudently as the children of strangers. See *De Rossi.*

And are *soothsayers*—"They are filled with diviners"] Heb. "They are filled from the east;" or "more than the east." The sentence is manifestly imperfect. The *Septuagint*, *Vulgate*, and *Chaldee*, seem to have read כמקדם *kemikkedem;* and the latter, with another word before it, signifying *idols;* "they are filled with idols as from of old." *Houbigant*, for מקדם *mikkedem*, reads מקסם *mikkesem*, as *Brentius* had proposed long ago. I rather think that both words together give us the true reading: מקדם *mikkedem*, מקסם *mikkesem*, "with divination from the east;" and that the first word has been by mistake omitted, from its similitude to the second.

Verse 7. *Their land is also full of horses*—"And his land is filled with horses"] This was in direct contradiction to God's command in the law: "But he (the king) shall not multiply horses to himself; nor cause the people to return to Egypt, to the end that he should multiply horses; neither shall he greatly multiply to himself silver and gold," Deut. xvii. 16, 17. Uzziah seems to have followed the

A. M. cir. 3244
B. C. cir. 760
Anno Olymp.
Quintæ I.
Ante Urbem
Conditam 7

neither *is there any* end of their treasures; their land is also full of horses, neither *is there any* end of their chariots:

8 [s]Their land also is full of idols; they worship the work of their own hands, that which their own fingers have made:

9 And the mean man boweth down, and the great man humbleth himself: therefore forgive them not.

10 [t]Enter into the rock, and hide thee in the dust, for fear of the LORD, and for the glory of his majesty.

11 The [u]lofty looks of man shall be humbled, and the haughtiness of men shall be bowed down, and the LORD alone shall be exalted [v]in that day.

12 For the day of the LORD of hosts *shall be* upon every *one that is* proud and lofty, and upon every *one that is* lifted up; and he shall be brought low:

13 And upon all [w]the cedars of Lebanon, *that are* high and lifted up, and upon all the oaks of Bashan,

14 And [x]upon all the high mountains, and upon all the hills *that are* lifted up,

15 And upon every high tower, and upon every fenced wall,

16 [y]And upon all the ships of Tarshish, and upon all [z]pleasant pictures.

A. M. cir. 3244
B. C. cir. 760
Anno Olymp.
Quintæ I.
Ante Urbem
Conditam 7

[s]Jer. ii. 28——[t]Ver. 19, 21; Rev. vi. 15——[u]Ver. 17; chap. v. 15, 16; xiii. 11——[v]Chap. iv. 1; xi. 10, 11; xii. 1, 4; xxiv. 21; xxv. 9; xxvi. 1; xxvii. 1, 2, 12, 13; xxviii. 5; xxix. 18; xxx. 23; lii. 6; Jer. xxx. 7, 8; Ezek. xxxviii. 14, 19; xxxix. 11, 22; Hos. ii. 16, 18, 21; Joel iii. 18; Amos ix. 11; Obad. 8; Mic. iv. 6; v. 10; vii. 11, 12; Zeph. iii. 11, 16; Zech. ix. 16——[w]Chap. xiv. 8; xxxvii. 24; Ezek. xxx. i. 3; Zech. xi. 1, 2 [x]Chap. xxx. 25——[y]1 Kings x. 22——[z]Heb. *pictures of desire*

example of Solomon, see 1 Kings x. 26-29, who first transgressed in these particulars; he recovered the port of Elath on the Red Sea, and with it that commerce which in Solomon's days had "made silver and gold as plenteous at Jerusalem as stones," 2 Chron. i. 15. He had an army of 307,500 men, in which, as we may infer from the testimony of Isaiah, the chariots and horse made a considerable part. "The law above mentioned was to be a standing trial of prince and people, whether they had trust and confidence in God their deliverer." See *Bp. Sherlock's* Discourses on Prophecy. Dissert. iv., where he has excellently explained the reason and effect of the law, and the influence which the observance or neglect of it had on the affairs of the Israelites.

Verse 8. *Their land also is full of idols*—"And his land is filled with idols"] Uzziah and Jotham are both said, 2 Kings xv. 3, 4, 34, 35, "to have done that which was right in the sight of the Lord;" that is, to have adhered to and maintained the legal worship of God, in opposition to idolatry and all irregular worship; for to this sense the meaning of that phrase is commonly to be restrained; "save that the high places were not removed where the people still sacrificed and burned incense." There was hardly any time when they were quite free from this irregular and unlawful practice, which they seem to have looked upon as very consistent with the true worship of God; and which seems in some measure to have been tolerated, while the tabernacle was removed from place to place, and before the temple was built. Even after the conversion of Manasseh, when he had removed the strange gods, commanded Judah to serve JEHOVAH the God of Israel, it is added, "Nevertheless the people did sacrifice still on the high places, yet unto JEHOVAH their God only," 2 Chron, xxxiii. 17. The worshipping on the high places therefore does not necessarily imply idolatry; and from what is said of these two kings, Uzziah and Jotham, we may presume that the public exercise of idolatrous worship was not permitted in their time. The idols therefore here spoken of must have been such as were designed for a private and secret use. Such probably were the teraphim so often mentioned in Scripture; a kind of household gods, of human form, as it should seem, (see 1 Sam. xix. 13, and compare Gen. xxxi. 34,) of different magnitude, used for idolatrous and superstitious purposes, particularly for divination, and as oracles, which they consulted for direction in their affairs.

Verse 9. *Boweth down*—"Shall he bowed down"] This has reference to the preceding verse. They bowed themselves down to their idols, therefore shall they be bowed down and brought low under the avenging hand of God.

Therefore forgive them not.] "And thou wilt not forgive them."—L.

Verse 10. "When he ariseth to strike the earth with terror."] On the authority of the *Septuagint*, confirmed by the *Arabic* and an ancient MS., I have added here to the text a line, which in the 19th and 21st verses is repeated together with the preceding line, and has, I think, evidently been omitted by mistake in this place. The MS. here varies only in one letter from the reading of the other two verses; it has בארץ *baarets,* instead of הארץ *haarets.* None of *De Rossi's* MSS. confirm this addition. The line added is, *When he ariseth to strike the earth with terror.*

Verse 11. *Be humbled*] "שפל ושח *shaphel veshach,* read שפלו שח *shaphelu shach.*"—Dr. *Durell.* Which rectifies the grammatical construction. No MS. or version confirms this reading.

Verses 13-16. *And upon all the cedars*—"Even against all the cedars"] Princes, potentates, rulers, captains, rich men, &c.—So *Kimchi.* These verses afford us a striking example of that peculiar way of writing, which makes a principal characteristic of the parabolical or poetical style of the Hebrews, and in which the prophets deal so largely, namely, their manner of exhibiting things Divine, spiritual, moral, and political, by a set of images taken from things natural, artificial, religious, historical,

A. M. cir. 3244
B. C. cir. 760
Anno Olymp. Quintæ I.
Ante Urbem Conditam 7

17 [a]And the loftiness of man
shall be bowed down, and the
haughtiness of men shall be made
low: and the LORD alone shall
be exalted [b]in that day.
18 And [c]the idols he shall utterly abolish.
19 And they shall go into the [d]holes of the
rocks, and into the caves of [e]the earth, [f]for
fear of the LORD, and for the glory of his majesty, when he ariseth [g]to shake terribly the
earth.
20 [h]In that day a man shall
cast [i]his idols of silver, and his
idols of gold, [k]which they made
each one for himself to worship,
to the moles and to the bats;
21 [l]To go into the clefts of the rocks, and
into the tops of the ragged rocks, [m]for fear of
the LORD, and for the glory of his majesty,
when he ariseth to shake terribly the earth.
22 [n]Cease ye from man, whose [o]breath *is* in his
nostrils: for wherein is he to be accounted of?

A. M. cir. 3244
B. C. cir. 760
Anno Olymp. Quintæ I.
Ante Urbem Conditam 7

[a]Ver. 11——[b]Ver. 11——[c]Or, *the idols shall utterly pass away*——[d]Ver. 10; Hos. x. 8; Luke xxiii. 30; Rev. vi. 16; ix. 6——[e]Heb. *the dust*——[f]2 Thess. i. 9——[g]Chap. xxx. 32; Hag. ii. 6, 21; Heb. xii. 26

[h]Chap. xxx. 22; xxxi. 27——[i]Heb. *the idols of his silver*, &c.——[k]Or, *which they made for him*——[l]Ver. 19——[m]Ver. 10, 19——[n]Psa. cxlvi. 3; Jer. xvii. 5——[o]Job xxvii. 3

in the way of metaphor or allegory. Of these nature furnishes much the largest and the most pleasing share; and all poetry has chiefly recourse to natural images, as the richest and most powerful source of illustration. But it may be observed of the Hebrew poetry in particular, that in the use of such images, and in the application of them in the way of illustration and ornament, it is more regular and constant than any other poetry whatever; that it has for the most part a set of images appropriated in a manner to the explication of certain subjects. Thus you will find, in many other places besides this before us, that *cedars of Lebanon* and *oaks of Bashan*, are used in the way of metaphor and allegory for kings, princes, potentates of the highest rank; *high mountains* and *lofty hills*, for kingdoms, republics, states, cities; towers and fortresses, for defenders and protectors, whether by counsel or strength, in peace or war; *ships of Tarshish* and works of art, and invention employed in adorning them, for merchants, men enriched by commerce, and abounding in all the luxuries and elegances of life, such as those of Tyre and Sidon; for it appears from the course of the whole passage, and from the train of ideas, that the fortresses and the ships are to be taken metaphorically, as well as the high trees and the lofty mountains.

Ships of Tarshish] Are in Scripture frequently used by a metonymy for ships in general, especially such as are employed in carrying on traffic between distant countries, as Tarshish was the most celebrated mart of those times, frequented of old by the Phœnicians, and the principal source of wealth to Judea and the neighbouring countries. The learned seem now to be perfectly well agreed that Tarshish is Tartessus, a city of Spain, at the mouth of the river Bætis, whence the Phœnicians, who first opened this trade, brought silver and gold, (Jer. x. 9; Ezek. xxvii. 12,) in which that country then abounded; and, pursuing their voyage still farther to the Cassiterides, (*Bochart*, Canaan, i. c. 39; *Huet*, Hist. de Commerce, p. 194,) the islands of Scilly and Cornwall, they brought from thence lead and tin.

Tarshish is celebrated in Scripture, 2 Chron, viii. 17, 18, ix. 21, for the trade which Solomon carried on thither, in conjunction with the Tyrians. Jehoshaphat, 1 Kings xxii. 48, 2 Chron. xx. 36, attempted afterwards to renew their trade. And from the account given of his attempt it appears that his fleet was to sail to Ezion-geber on the Red Sea; they must therefore have designed to sail round Africa, as Solomon's fleet had done before, (see *Huet*, Histoire de Commerce, p. 32,) for it was a three years' voyage, (2 Chron. ix. 21,) and they brought gold from Ophir, probably on the coast of Arabia; silver from Tartessus; and ivory, apes, and peacocks, from Africa. "אופרי *Afri*, Africa, the Roman termination, *Africa terra*. תרשיש *Tarshish*, some city or country in Africa. So the *Chaldee* on 1 Kings xxii. 49, where it renders תרשיש *Tarshish* by אפריקה *Aphricah;* and compare 2 Chron. xx. 36, from whence it appears, to go to Ophir and to Tarshish is one and the same thing."—Dr. *Jubb*. It is certain that under Pharaoh Necho, about *two hundred* years afterwards, this voyage was made by the Egyptians; *Herodot*. iv. 42. They sailed from the Red Sea, and returned by the Mediterranean, and they performed it in three years, just the same time that the voyage under Solomon had taken up. It appears likewise from *Pliny*, Nat. Hist., ii. 67, that the passage round the Cape of Good Hope was known and frequently practised before his time, by Hanno the Carthaginian, when Carthage was in its glory; by one Eudoxus, in the time of Ptolemy Lathyrus, king of Egypt; and *Cœlus Antipater*, a historian of good credit, somewhat earlier than *Pliny*, testifies that he had seen a merchant who had made the voyage from Gades to Ethiopia. The Portuguese under Vasco de Gama, near *three hundred* years ago, recovered this navigation, after it had been intermitted and lost for many centuries.—L.

Verse 18. *Shall utterly abolish*—"Shall disappear"] The ancient versions and an ancient MS. read יחלפו *yachalpu*, plural. One of my MSS. reads יחלוף *yachaloph*, probably a mistake for יחלפו *yachalpu*.

Verses 19-21. *Into the holes of the rocks*—"Into caverns of rocks"] The country of Judea being mountainous and rocky, is full of caverns, as appears from the history of David's persecution under Saul. At En-gedi, in particular, there was a cave so large that David with *six hundred* men hid themselves in the sides of it; and Saul entered the mouth of the cave without perceiving that any one was there, 1 Sam. xxiv. *Josephus*, Antiq., lib. xiv., c. 15, and Bell. Jud., lib. 1, c. 16, tells us of a numerous gang of banditti, who. having infested the country, and being pursued by Herod with his army, retired into certain caverns almost inaccessible, near Arbela in Galilee, where they were with great difficulty subdued. Some of these were natural, others artificial. "Beyond Damascus," says *Strabo*, lib. xvi., "are two mountains called Trachones; from which the country has the name of Trachonitis; and from hence towards Arabia and Iturea, are certain rugged mountains, in which there are deep caverns, one of which will hold *four thousand* men." *Tavernier*, Voyage de Perse, part ii., chap. 4, speaks of a grot, between Aleppo and Bir, that would hold near *three thousand* horse. "*Three* hours distant from Sidon, about a mile from the sea, there runs along a high rocky mountain, in the sides of which are hewn a multitude of grots, all very little differing from each other. They have entrances about two feet square: on the inside you find in most or all of them a room of about four yards square. There are of these subterraneous caverns *two hundred* in number. It may, with probability at least, be concluded that these places were contrived for the use of the living, and not of the dead. *Strabo* describes the habitations of the Troglodytæ to have been somewhat of this kind."—*Maundrell*, p. 118. The Horites, who dwelt in Mount Seir, were Troglodytæ, as their name הרים *horim*, imports. But those mentioned by *Strabo* were on each side of the Arabian gulf. Mohammed (Koran, chap. xv. xxvi.) speaks of a tribe of Arabians, the tribe of Thamud, "who hewed houses out of the mountains, to secure themselves." Thus, "because of the Midianites, the children of Israel made them the dens which are in the mountains, and caves and strong holds," Judg. vi. 2. To these they betook themselves for refuge in times of distress and hostile invasion: "When the men of Israel saw that they were in a strait, for the people were distressed, then the people did hide themselves in caves, and in thickets, and in rocks, and in high places, and in pits," 1 Sam. xiii. 6, and see Jer. xli. 9. Therefore "to enter into the rock, to go into the holes of the rocks, and into the caves of the earth," was to them a very proper and familiar image to express terror and consternation. The prophet Hosea, chap. x. 8, hath carried the same image farther, and added great strength and spirit to it:

"They shall say to the mountains, Cover us;
And to the hills, Fall on us;"

which image, together with these of Isaiah, is adopted by the sublime author of the Revelation, chap. vi. 15, 16, who frequently borrows his imagery from our prophet.—L.

Verse 20. *Which they made* each one *for himself to worship*—"Which they have made to worship"] The word לו *lo, for himself*, is omitted by two ancient MSS., and is unnecessary. It does not appear that any copy of the *Septuagint* has it, except MS. *Pachom*, and MS. I. D. II., and they have ἑαυτοις, להם *lahem, to themselves*.

To the moles] They shall carry their idols with them into the dark caverns, old ruins, or desolate places, to which they shall flee for refuge; and so shall give them up, and relinquish them to the filthy animals that frequent such places, and have taken possession of them as their proper habitation. *Bellonius*, *Greaves*, *P. Lucas*, and many other travellers, speak of bats of an enormous size, as inhabiting the Great Pyramid. See *Harmer*, Obs., vol. ii., 455. Three MSS. express חפרפרות *chapharperoth*, *the moles*, as one word.

Verse 22. *Cease ye from man*] Trust neither in him, nor in the gods that he has invented. Neither he, nor they, can either save or destroy.

CHAPTER III

The whole of this chapter, with the first verse of the next, is a prophecy of those calamities that should be occasioned by the Babylonish invasion and captivity. These calamities are represented as so great and so general, that even royal honours, in such a state, are so far from being desirable, that hardly any can be got to accept them, 1–7. *This visitation is declared to be the consequence of their profanity and guilt; for which the prophet farther reproves and threatens them,* 8–15. *Particular amplification of the distress of the delicate and luxurious daughters of Zion; whose deplorable situation is finely contrasted with their former prosperity and ease,* 16–26.

A. M. cir. 3244
B. C. cir. 760
Anno Olymp. Quintæ I.
Ante Urbem Conditam 7

FOR, behold, the Lord, the
LORD of hosts, [a]doth take
away from Jerusalem and from
Judah [b]the stay and the staff, the
whole stay of bread, and the
whole stay of water,
2 [c]The mighty man, and the
man of war, the judge, and the

[a]Jer. xxxvii. 21; xxxviii. 9——[b]Lev. xxvi. 26

[c]See 2 Kings xxiv. 14; Psa. xxiv. 8; xxix. 1

NOTES ON CHAP. III

Verse 1. *The stay and the staff*—"Every stay and support"] *Hebrew*, "the support masculine, and the support feminine:" that is, every kind of support, whether great or small, strong or weak. "*Al Kanitz, wal-kanitzah;* the wild beasts, male and female. Proverbially applied both to fishing and hunting: i. e., I seized the prey, great or little, good or bad. From hence, as *Schultens* observes, is explained Isa. iii. 1, literally, the *male and female stay:* i. e., the strong and weak, the great and small."—*Chappelow*, note on *Hariri*, Assembly I. Compare Eccles. ii. 8.

The Hebrew words משען ומשענה *mashen umashenah* come from the same root שען *shaan*, to lean against, to incline, to support; and here, being masculine and feminine, they may signify all things necessary for the support both of *man* and *woman*. My old MS. understands the staff and stay as meaning particular persons, and translates the verse thus:—**Lo forsoth, the Lordschip Lord of Hoostis schal don awey fro Jerusalem and fro Juda the stalworth and the stronge.**

A. M. cir. 3244
B. C. cir. 760
Anno Olymp.
Quintæ I.
Ante Urbem
Conditam 7

prophet, and the prudent, and
the ancient.
3 The captain of fifty, and the
[d]honourable man, and the coun-
sellor, and the cunning artificer, and the [e]elo-
quent orator.
4 And I will give [f]children *to be* their
princes, and babes shall rule over them.
5 And the people shall be oppressed, every
one by another, and every one by his neighbour: the child shall behave himself proudly
against the ancient, and the base
against the honourable.
6 When a man shall take hold
of his brother of the house of his
father, *saying,* Thou hast clothing, be thou
our ruler, and *let* this ruin *be* under thy hand:
7 In that day shall he [g]swear, saying, I will
not be a [h]healer; for in my house *is* neither
bread nor clothing: make me not a ruler of
the people.
8 For Jerusalem [i]is ruined, and Judah is

[d]Heb. *a man eminent in countenance*——[e]Or, *skilful of speech*——[f]Eccles. x. 16

[g]Heb. *lift up* the hand; Gen. xiv. 22——[h]Heb. *binder up*
[i]Mic. iii. 12

The two following verses, 2, 3, are very clearly explained by the sacred historian's account of the event, the captivity of Jehoiachin by Nebuchadnezzar king of Babylon: "And he carried away all Jerusalem, and all the princes, and all the mighty men of valour, even ten thousand captives, and all the craftsmen and smiths; none remained save the poorest sort of the people of the land," 2 Kings xxiv. 14. Which is supplied by our version.

Verse 4. *I will give children to be their princes*—"I will make boys their princes"] This also was fully accomplished in the succession of weak and wicked princes, from the death of Josiah to the destruction of the city and temple, and the taking of Zedekiah, the last of them, by Nebuchadnezzar.

Babes shall rule over them.] **Wymennysche men schul lordschipen to hem.**—Old MS. Bible.

Verse 6. *Of the house of his father*—"Of his father's house"] For בית *beith, the house*, the ancient interpreters seem to have read מבית *mibbeith, from the house;* του οικειου του πατρος αυτου, *Septuagint; domesticum patris sui, Vulgate;* which gives no good sense. But the *Septuagint* MS. I. D. II. for οικειου has οικου. And, *his brother, of his father's house*, is little better than a tautology. The case seems to require that the man should apply to a person of some sort of rank and eminence; one that was the head of his father's house, (see Josh. xii. 14,) whether of the house of him who applies to him, or of any other; ראש בית אביו *rosh beith abaiv*, the chief, or head of his father's house. I cannot help suspecting, therefore, that the word ראש *rosh, head, chief*, has been lost out of the text.

Saying] Before שמלה *simlah, garment*, two MSS., one ancient, and the Babylonish *Talmud* have the word לאמר *lemor*, saying; and so the *Septuagint, Vulgate, Syriac* and *Chaldee.* I place it with *Houbigant, after* שמלה *simlah.*

Thou hast clothing—"Take by the garment"] That is, shall entreat him in an humble and supplicating manner. "Ten men shall take hold of the skirt of him that is a Jew, saying, Let us go with you; for we have heard that God is with you," Zech. viii. 23. And so in Isa. iv. 1, the same gesture is used to express earnest and humble entreaty. The behaviour of Saul towards Samuel was of the same kind, when he laid hold on the skirt of his raiment, 1 Sam. xv. 27. The preceding and following verses show, that his whole deportment, in regard to the prophet, was full of submission and humility.

And let this ruin be under thy hand—"And let thy hand support"] Before תחת ידך *tachath yadecha*, a MS. adds תהיה *tihyeh*, "let it be;" another MS. adds in the same place, תקח בידך *takach beyadecha*, which latter seems to be a various reading of the two preceding words, making a very good sense: "Take into thy hand our ruinous state." *Twenty-one* MSS. of *Kennicott's, thirteen* of *De Rossi's*, one of my own, ancient, and *three* editions of the *Babylonish Talmud* have ידיך *yadeycha*, plural, "thy hands."

Verse 7. *In that day shall he swear*—"Then shall he openly declare"] The *Septuagint, Syriac* and *Jerome*, read וישא *veyissa*, adding the conjunction, which seems necessary in this place.

I will not be a healer] **I am not a leche.**—Old MS. Bible. *Leech* was the ancient English word for a *physician.*

For in my house is neither bread nor clothing—"For in my house is neither bread nor raiment"] "It is customary through all the East," says Sir *J. Chardin*, "to gather together an immense quantity of furniture and clothes; for their fashions never alter." Princes and great men are obliged to have a great stock of such things in readiness for presents upon all occasions. "The kings of Persia," says the same author, "have great wardrobes, where there are always many hundreds of habits ready, designed for presents, and sorted," *Harmer*, Observ., II. 11 and 88. A great quantity of provision for the table was equally necessary. The daily provision for Solomon's household, whose attendants were exceedingly numerous, was proportionately great, 1 Kings iv. 22, 23. Even Nehemiah, in his strait circumstances, had a large supply daily for his table; at which he received a *hundred and fifty* of the Jews and rulers, besides those that came from among the neighbouring heathen, Neh. v. 17, 18.

This explains the meaning of the excuse made by him that is desired to undertake the government. He alleges that he has not wherewithal to support the dignity of the station, by such acts of liberality and hospitality as the law of custom required of persons of superior rank. See *Harmer's* Observations, I. 340, II. 88.

Verse 8. *The eyes*—"The cloud"] This word appears to be of very doubtful form, from the printed editions, the MSS., and the ancient versions. The first yod in עיני *eyney*, which is

A. M. cir. 3244 B. C. cir. 760 Anno Olymp. Quintæ I. Ante Urbem Conditam 7

fallen: because their tongue and their doings *are* against the LORD, to provoke the eyes of his glory.

9 The show of their countenance doth witness against them; and they declare their sin as [k]Sodom, they hide *it* not. Wo unto their soul! for they have rewarded evil unto themselves.

10 Say ye to the righteous, [l]that *it shall be* well *with him:* [m]for they shall eat the fruit of their doings:

11 Wo unto the wicked! [n]*it shall be* ill *with him:* for the reward of his hands shall be [o]given him.

12 *As for* my people, [p]children *are* their oppressors, and women rule over them. O my people, [q]they [r]which lead thee cause *thee* to err, and [s]destroy the way of thy paths.

13 The LORD standeth up [t]to plead, and standeth to judge the people.

14 The LORD will enter into judgment with the ancients of his people, and the princes thereof: for ye have [u]eaten [v]up the vineyard; the spoil of the poor *is* in your houses.

[k]Gen. xiii. 13; xviii. 20, 21; xix. 5——[l]Eccles. viii. 12 ——[m]Psa. cxxviii. 2——[n]Psa. xi. 6; Eccles. viii. 13——[o]Heb. *done to him*——[p]Ver. 4——[q]Chap. ix. 16——[r]Or, *they which call thee blessed*——[s]Heb. *swallow up*——[t]Mic. vi. 2——[u]Or, *burnt*——[v]Chap. v. 7; Matt. xxi. 33

necessary according to the common interpretation, is in many of them omitted; the two last letters are upon a rasure in *two* MSS. I think it should be ענן *anan*, "a cloud," as the *Syriac* reads; and the allusion is to the cloud in in which the glory of the Lord appeared above the tabernacle; see Exod. xvi. 9, 10; xl. 34-38; Num. xvi. 41, 42.

Either of the readings gives a very good sense. The allusion may be to the cloud of the Divine presence in the wilderness: or the *eyes of the Lord* may be meant, as they *are in every place beholding the evil and the good.* And he cannot look upon iniquity but with abhorrence; therefore, *the eyes of his glory* might be well provoked by their crimes.

Verse 9. *The show of their countenance*] Bishop Lowth has it *the steadfastness of their countenance*—they appear to be bent on iniquity, their eyes tell the wickedness of their hearts. The *eye* is the index of the mind. Envy, hatred, malice, malevolence, concupiscence, and murder, when in the heart, look most intelligently out at the eye. They tell the innocent to be on their guard; and serve the same purpose as the *sonorous rings* in the tail of the *rattlesnake*—they announce the presence of the destroyer.

They declare their sin as Sodom] Impure propensities are particularly legible in the eyes: whoever has beheld the face of a *debauchee* or a *prostitute* knows this; of these it may be said, they wish to appear what they really are. They glory in their iniquity. This is the highest pitch of ungodliness.

They have rewarded evil unto themselves.] Every man's sin is against his own soul. Evil awaiteth sinners—and he that offends his God injures himself.

Verse 10. *Say ye to the righteous*] לצדיק *letsaddik;* the ל *lamed* is added here by one MS. and the *Chaldee*. The righteous is the person, 1. Who fears God. 2. Departs from evil. 3. Walks according to the testimony of God. 4. And expects and prepares for a glorious immortality.

"Pronounce ye."—The reading of this verse is very dubious. The *Septuagint* for אמרו *imru* read נאסר *neasor*, or both, אמרו נאסר *imru neasor*, and כי לא טוב לנו *ki lo tob lanu.* Δησωμεν τον δικαιον, ὁτι δυσχρηστος ἡμιν εστι. Perhaps, for אמרו *imru*, the true reading may be אשרו *ashsheru*, "bless you;" or אמרו אשרי *imru ashrey*, "say ye, blessed is." The *Vulgate* and an ancient MS. read in the singular number, יאכל *yochel, comedat*, "he shall eat."

"It shall be *well* with him:"—כי טוב *ki tob*, "that good." Say nothing to such but *good.* He is a *good man*, he does nothing but *good*, and has a *good* God to deal with, from whom he expects nothing but *goodness.* It shall be well with such in all circumstances of life. 1. In prosperity. 2. In adversity. 3. In sickness. 4. In health. 5. In death. 6. In judgment. And, 7. Through eternity. In every case, occurrence, and circumstance, he *shall eat the fruit of his doings*—he shall derive benefit from being a righteous man, and walking in a righteous way.

Verse 11. *Wo unto the wicked*] לרשע *lerasha*, the man who is, 1. Evil in his heart. 2. Evil in his purposes. 3. Evil in his life. As he is *wicked*, he does that which is *wicked;* and is influenced by the *wicked one*, of whom he is the *servant* and the *son.* It shall be *ill* with him, רע *ra;* in a single word say to him—*evil! Of* him you can speak no good; and *to* him you can speak no good—all is *evil, in* him —*before* him—*after* him—*round about* him—*above* him—*below* him. Evil in *time*—evil through *eternity!*

The reward of his hands.] What he has deserved he shall get. He shall be paid that for which he has laboured, and his reward shall be in proportion to his work. O, what a lot is that of the wicked! Cursed in time, and accursed through eternity!

Verse 12. *Err*—"Pervert"] בלעו *billeu*, "swallow." Among many unsatisfactory methods of accounting for the unusual meaning of this word in this place, I choose Jarchi's explication, as making the best sense. "Read בללו *billalu*, 'confound.' *Syriac.*"—Dr. *Judd.* "Read בהלו *beholu*, 'disturb or trouble.'"—*Secker.* So *Septuagint.*

This verse might be read, "The collectors of grapes shall be their oppressors; and usurers (*noshim*, instead of *nashim*, women) shall rule over them."

Verse 13. *The people*—"His people"] עמו *ammo, Septuagint.*

Verse 14. *The vineyard.*—"My vineyard"] כרמי *carmi, Septuagint, Chaldee, Jerome.*

A. M. cir. 3244
B. C. cir. 760
Anno Olymp.
Quintæ I.
Ante Urbem
Conditam 7

15 What mean ye *that* ye
[w]beat my people to pieces, and
grind the faces of the poor? saith
the Lord GOD of hosts.
16 Moreover the LORD saith, Because the
daughters of Zion are haughty,
and walk with stretched forth
necks and [x]wanton eyes, walking and [y]mincing *as* they go,
and making a tinkling with their feet:

A. M. cir. 3244
B. C. cir. 760
Anno Olymp.
Quintæ I.
Ante Urbem
Conditam 7

[w]Chap. lviii. 4; Mic. iii. 2, 3

[x]Heb. *deceiving with their eyes*——[y]Or, *tripping nicely*

Verse 15. *And grind the faces*] The expression and the image is strong, to denote grievous oppression but is exceeded by the prophet Micah, chap. iii. 1-3:—

"Hear, I pray you, ye chiefs of Jacob,
And ye princes of the house of Israel:
Is it not yours to know what is right?
Ye that hate good and love evil:
Who tear their skins from off them,
And their flesh from off their bones;
Who devour the flesh of my people;
And flay from off them their skin;
And their bones they dash in pieces;
And chop them asunder, as morsels for the pot:
And as flesh thrown into the midst of the caldron."

In the last line but one, for כאשר *keasher*, read, by the transposition of a letter, כשאר *kisher*, with the *Septuagint* and *Chaldee*.

Verse 16. *And wanton eyes*—"And falsely setting off their eyes with paint"] Hebrew, *falsifying* their eyes. I take this to be the true meaning and literal rendering of the word; from שקר *shakar*. The Masoretes have pointed it, as if it were from שקר *sakar*, a different word. This arose, as I imagine, from their supposing that the word was the same with סקר *sakar*, *Chaldee*, "intueri, innuere oculis;" or that it had an affinity with the noun סיקרא *sikra*, which the Chaldeans, or the rabbins at least, use for *stibium*, the mineral which was commonly used in colouring the eyes. See *Jarchi's* comment on the place. Though the colouring of the eyes with stibium be not particularly here expressed, yet I suppose it to be implied; and so the Chaldee paraphrase explains it; stibio linitis oculis, "with eyes dressed with stibium." This fashion seems to have prevailed very generally among the Eastern people in ancient times; and they retain the very same to this day.

Pietro della Valle, giving a description of his wife, an Assyrian lady born in Mesopotamia, and educated at Bagdad, whom he married in that country, (*Viaggi*, Tom. I., Lettera 17,) says, "Her eyelashes, which are long, and, according to the custom of the East, dressed with stibium, (as we often read in the Holy Scriptures of the Hebrew women of old, Jer. iv. 30; Ezek. xxiii. 40; and in Xenophon, of Astyages the grandfather of Cyrus, and of the Medes of that time, *Cyropæd.* lib. i.,) give a dark, and at the same time a majestic, shade to the eyes." "Great eyes," says *Sandys*, Travels, p. 67, speaking of the Turkish women, "they have in principal repute; and of those the blacker they be the more amiable; insomuch that they put between the eyelids and the eye a certain black powder, with a fine long pencil, made of a mineral, brought from the kingdom of Fez, and called *Alcohole;* which by the not disagreeable staining of the lids doth better set forth the whiteness of the eye; and though it be troublesome for a time, yet it comforteth the sight, and repelleth ill humours." Vis ejus (stibii) astringe ac refrigerare, principalis autem circa oculos; namque ideo etiam plerique Platyophthalmon id appellavere, quoniam in calliblepharis mulierum dilatat oculos; et fluxiones inhibet oculorum exulcerationesque. "It is astringent in its virtue, and refrigerant, and to be chiefly employed about the eyes, and it is called *Platyophthalmon,* for being put into those ointments with which women *beautify their eyes,* it dilates them, removes defluxions, and heals any ulcerations that may be about the eyelids."—*Pliny,* Nat. Hist. xxxiii. 6.

Ille supercilium madida fuligine tactum
Obliqua producit acu, pingitque trementes
Attollens oculos Juv. Sat. ii. 93.

One his eyebrows, tinged with black soot,
Lengthens with an oblique bodkin, and paints,
Lifting up his winking eyes.

"But none of those [Moorish] ladies," says Dr. *Shaw,* Travels, p. 294, fol., "take themselves to be completely dressed, till they have tinged the hair and edges of their eyelids with *alkahol,* the powder of lead ore. This operation is performed by dipping first into the powder a small wooden bodkin of the thickness of a quill; and then drawing it afterwards through the eyelids, over the ball of the eye." Ezekiel, chap. xxiii. 40, uses the same word in the form of a verb, כחלת עיניך *cachalt eynayik,* "thou didst dress thine eyes with *alcahol;*" which the *Septuagint* render εστιβιζου τους οφθαλμους σου, "thou didst dress thine eyes with *stibium;*" just as they do when the word פוך *phuch* is employed: compare 2 Kings ix. 30; Jer. iv. 30. They supposed, therefore, that פוך *phuch* and כחל *cachal,* or in the Arabic form, *alcahol,* meant the same thing; and probably the mineral used of old for this purpose was the same that is used now; which Dr. *Shaw* (*ibid.* note) says is "a rich lead ore, pounded into an impalpable powder." *Alcoholados;* the word משקרות *meshakkeroth* in this place is thus rendered in an old Spanish translation.—*Sanctius.* See also *Russell's* Nat. Hist. of Aleppo, p. 102.

The following inventory, as one may call it, of the wardrobe of a Hebrew lady, must, from its antiquity, and the nature of the subject, have been very obscure even to the most ancient interpreters which we have of it; and from its obscurity must have been also peculiarly liable to the mistakes of transcribers. However, it is rather matter of curiosity than of importance; and is indeed, upon the whole, more intelligible and less corrupted than one might have reasonably expected. *Clemens Alexandrinus,* Pædag. lib. ii., c. 12, and *Julius Pollux,* lib. vii., c 22, have each of them preserved from a comedy of *Aristophanes,* now lost, a similar catalogue of the several parts of the dress and ornaments of a Grecian lady; which, though much more capable of illustration from other writers, though of

A. M. cir. 3244
B. C. cir. 760
Anno Olymp.
Quintæ I.
Ante Urbem
Conditam 7

17 Therefore the LORD will
smite with [z]a scab the crown of
the head of the daughters of
Zion, and the LORD will [a]discover
[b]their secret parts.

18 In that day the LORD will
take away the bravery of *their*
tinkling ornaments *about their*
feet, and *their* [c]cauls, and *their*
[d]round tires like the moon,

A. M. cir. 3244
B. C. cir. 760
Anno Olymp.
Quintæ I.
Ante Urbem
Conditam 7

[z]Deuteronomy xxviii. 24——[a]Hebrew, *make naked*——[b]Chapter xlvii. 2, 3; Jeremiah xiii. 22; Nahum ii. 5——[c]Or, *net-works*——[d]Judges viii. 21

later date, and quoted and transmitted down to us by two different authors, yet seems to be much less intelligible, and considerably more corrupted, than this passage of Isaiah. *Salmasius* has endeavoured, by comparing the two quotations, and by much critical conjecture and learned disquisition, to restore the true reading, and to explain the particulars; with what success, I leave to the determination of the learned reader, whose curiosity shall lead him to compare the passage of the comedian with this of the prophet, and to examine the critic's learned labours upon it. *Exercit. Plinian*, p. 1148; or see *Clem. Alex.* as cited above, edit. Potter, where the passage, as corrected by *Salmasius*, is given.

Nich. Guel. Schroederus, professor of oriental languages in the University of Marpurg, has published a very learned and judicious treatise upon this passage of Isaiah. The title of it is, "Commentarius Philologico-Criticus de Vestitu Mulierum Hebræarum ad Iesai iii. ver. 16-24. Lugd. Bat. 1745." 4to. As I think no one has handled this subject with so much judgment and ability as this author, I have for the most part followed him, in giving the explanation of the several terms denoting the different parts of dress, of which this passage consists; signifying the reasons of my dissent, where he does not give me full satisfaction.

Bishop Lowth's translation of these verses is the following:—

18. In that day will the Lord take from them the ornaments,
Of the feet-rings, and the net-works, and the crescents;
19. The pendants, and the bracelets, and the veils;
20. The tires, and the fetters, and the zones,
And the perfume-boxes, and the amulets;
21. The rings, and the jewels of the nostrils;
22. The embroidered robes, and the tunics,
And the cloaks, and the little purses,
23. The transparent garments, and the fine linen vests,
And the turbans, and the mantles.
24. And there shall be instead of perfume, a putrid ulcer;
And instead of well-girt raiment, rags;
And instead of high-dressed hair, baldness;
And instead of a zone, a girdle of sackcloth;
And sun-burnt skin, instead of beauty.

The daughters of Zion—walk] What is meant by these several kinds of action and articles of dress cannot be well conjectured. How our ancestors understood them will appear from the following, which is the translation of these verses in my old MS. Bible:—

16. **The doughteris of Syon wenten with stright out necks, and in beckes** (winking) **of eegen, geeden and flappeden with hondis for joye, and geeden; and with theire feet in curyous goying geeden;**—17. **the Lord schall fully make ballid the top of the doughtris of Syon: and the Lord the her of hem schal naken. And for ournemente schal be schenschip.**

18. **In that day, the Lord schal don awey the ournement of Schoon and hoosis;** 19. **and beegis, and brochis, and armeerclis, and mytris;** 20. **and coombis, and rybanys and reversis at the hemmys, and oynment boris and ereringis;** 21. **and ryngis and jemmys in the frount hongynge;** 22. **and chaunginge clothis, and litil pallis, and scheetis, and prynys;** 23. **and scheweris, and necke kercheuys, and fyletis, and roketis;** 24. **and ther schal be for swot smel, stynke, and for gyrdil, a litil coord; and for crisp her, ballidnesse; and for brest boond and heyr.**

Some of these things are hard to be understood, though I think this version as good as that of the very learned bishop: but there is little doubt that articles of clothing and dress bore these names in the fourteenth century.

Verse 17. *The Lord will smite*—"Will the Lord humble"] ταπεινωσει, *Septuagint;* and so *Syriac* and *Chaldee*. For שפח *sippach* they read שפל *shaphal*. Instead of יהוה *Yehovah*, many MSS. have אדני *Adonai*.

Will discover their secret parts—"Expose their nakedness"] It was the barbarous custom of the conquerors of those times to strip their captives naked, and to make them travel in that condition, exposed to the inclemency of the weather; and the worst of all, to the intolerable heat of the sun. But this to the women was the height of cruelty and indignity; and especially to such as those here described, who had indulged themselves in all manner of delicacies of living, and all the superfluities of ornamental dress; and even whose faces had hardly ever been exposed to the sight of man. This is always mentioned as the hardest part of the lot of captives. Nahum, chap. iii. 5, 6, denouncing the fate of Nineveh, paints it in very strong colours:—

"Behold, I am against thee, saith JEHOVAH, God of hosts:
And I will discover thy skirts upon thy face;
And I will expose thy nakedness to the nations;
And to the kingdoms thy shame.
And I will throw ordures upon thee;
And I will make thee vile, and set thee as a gazing-stock."

Verse 18. *Ornaments* about their feet—"The ornaments of the feet rings"] The late learned Dr. *Hunt*, professor of Hebrew and Arabic in the University of Oxford, has very well explained the word עכס both verb and noun, in his very ingenious Dissertation on Prov. vii. 22, 23. The verb means to *skip*, to *bound*, to *dance along;* and the noun, those *ornaments* of the *feet* which the Eastern ladies wore; *chains* or *rings*, which made a tinkling sound as they moved nimbly in walking. *Eugene Roger*, Description de la Terre Sainte, Liv. ii. ch. 2,

A. M. cir. 3244 B. C. cir. 760 Anno Olymp. Quintæ I. Ante Urbem Conditam 7

19 The [e]chains, and the bracelets, and the [f]mufflers,
20 The bonnets, and the ornaments of the legs, and the head-
bands, and the [g]tablets, and the ear-rings,
21 The rings, and nose-
jewels,
22 The changeable suits of
apparel, [h]and the mantles, and
the wimples, and the crisping-pins,

[e]Or, *sweet balls*——[f]Or, *spangled ornaments*

[g]Heb. *houses of the soul*——[h]Dan. iii. 21, in the margin

speaking of the Arabian women, of the first rank in Palestine, says,—"Au lieu de brasselets elles ont de menottes d'argent, qu'elles portent aux poignets et aux pieds; où sont attachez quantitè de petits annelets d'argent, qui font un cliquetis comme d'une cymbale, lorsqu'elles cheminent ou se mouvent quelque peu." See Dr. *Hunt's Dissertation;* where he produces other testimonies to the same purpose from authors of travels. Hindoo women of ill fame wear loose ornaments one above another on their ankles, which at every motion make a tinkling noise. See WARD.

And their *cauls*—"the net-works"] I am obliged to differ from the learned *Schroederus* almost at first setting out. He renders the word שביסים *shebisim* by *soliculi*, little ornaments, bullæ, or studs, in shape representing the *sun*, and so answering to the following word שהרנים *saharonim*, *lunulæ*, crescents. He supposes the word to be the same with שמישים *shemishim*, the י *yod* in the second syllable making the word diminutive, and the letter מ *mem* being changed for ב *beth*, a letter of the same organ. How just and well founded his authorities for the transmutation of these letters in the Arabic language are, I cannot pretend to judge; but as I know of no such instance in Hebrew, it seems to me a very forced etymology. Being dissatisfied with this account of the matter, I applied to my good friend above mentioned, the late Dr. *Hunt*, who very kindly returned the following answer to my inquiries:—

"I have consulted the Arabic Lexicons, as well MS. as printed, but cannot find שביסים *shebisim* in any of them, nor any thing belonging to it; so that no help is to be had from that language towards clearing up the meaning of this difficult word. But what the *Arabic* denies, the *Syriac* perhaps may afford; in which I find the verb שבש *shabas*, to *entangle* or *interweave*, an etymology which is equally favourable to our marginal translation, *net-works*, with שבץ *shabats, to make chequer work*, or *embroider*, (the word by which *Kimchi* and others have explained שבים *shabis;*) and has moreover this advantage over it, that the letters ש *sin* and ס *samech* are very frequently put for each other, but צ *tsaddi* and ס *samech* scarcely ever. Aben Ezra joins שביסים *shebisim* and עכסים *achasim*, which immediately precedes it, together; and says that שבים *shabis* was *the ornament of the legs*, as עכס *eches* was *of the feet.* His words are, שבים תכשיט של שוקים כמו עכס של רגלים—L."

Verse 20. *The tablets*] The words בתי הנפש *bottey hannephesh*, which we translate *tablets*, and Bishop *Lowth*, *perfume boxes*, literally signify *houses of the soul;* and may refer to strong-scented bottles used for pleasure and against fainting; similar to bottles with *otto of roses*, worn by the ladies of the East to the present time.

Verse 21. *Nose-jewels*—"The jewels of the nostril."] נזמי האף *nizmey haaph. Schroederus* explains this, as many others do, of jewels, or strings of pearl hanging from the forehead, and reaching to the upper part of the nose; than which nothing can be more ridiculous, as such are seldom seen on an Asiatic face. But it appears from many passages of Holy Scripture that the phrase is to be literally and properly understood of nose-jewels, rings set with jewels hanging from the nostrils, as ear-rings from the ears, by holes bored to receive them.

Ezekiel, enumerating the common ornaments of women of the first rank, has not omitted this particular, and is to be understood in the same manner, chap. xvi. 11, 12. See also Gen. xxiv. 47:—

"And I decked thee with ornaments;
And I put bracelets upon thine hands,
And a chain on thy neck:
And I put a jewel on thy nose,
And ear-rings on thine ears,
And a splendid crown upon thine head."

And in an elegant proverb of Solomon, Prov. xi. 22, there is a manifest allusion to this kind of ornament, which shows it to have been used in his time:—

"As a jewel of gold in the snout of a swine;
So is a woman beautiful, but wanting discretion."

This fashion, however strange it may appear to us, was formerly and is still common in many parts of the East, among women of all ranks. *Paul Lucas*, speaking of a village or clan of wandering people, a little on this side of the Euphrates, says, (2d Voyage du Levant, tom. i., art. 24,) "The women, almost all of them, travel on foot; I saw none handsome among them. They have almost all of them the nose bored; and wear in it a great ring, which makes them still more deformed." But in regard to this custom, better authority cannot be produced than that of *Pietro della Valle*, in the account which he gives of the lady before mentioned, Signora Maani Gioerida, his own wife. The description of her dress, as to the ornamental parts of it, with which he introduces the mention of this particular, will give us some notion of the taste of the Eastern ladies for finery. "The ornaments of gold and of jewels for the head, for the neck, for the arms, for the legs, and for the feet (for they wear rings even on their toes) are indeed, unlike those of the Turks, carried to great excess, but not of great value: for in Bagdad jewels of high price are either not to be had, or are not used; and they wear such only as are of little value, as turquoises, small rubies, emeralds, carbuncles, garnets, pearls, and the like. My spouse dresses herself with all of them according to their fashion; with exception, however, of certain ugly rings of very large size, set with jewels, which, in truth, very absurdly, it is the custom to wear fastened to one of their nostrils, like buffaloes: an ancient custom, however, in the

A. M. cir. 3244
B. C. cir. 760
Anno Olymp. Quintæ I.
Ante Urbem Conditam 7

23 The glasses, [i]and the fine
linen, and the hoods, and the
veils.
24 And it shall come to pass,
that instead of sweet smell there shall be
stink: and instead of a girdle a rent; and instead of well-set hair [k]baldness; and instead
of a stomacher a girding of sack-
cloth; *and* burning instead of
beauty.
25 Thy men shall fall by the
sword, and thy [l]mighty in the war.
26 [m]And her gates shall lament and mourn; and
she *being* [n]desolate [o]shall [p]sit upon the ground.

[i]Gen. xli. 42——[k]Chap. xxii. 12; Mic. i. 16——[l]Heb. *might*

[m]Jer. xiv. 2; Lam. i. 4——[n]Or, *emptied*——[o]Heb. *cleansed*——[p]Lam. ii. 10

East, which, as we find in the Holy Scriptures, prevailed among the Hebrew ladies even in the time of Solomon, Prov. xi. 22. These nose-rings, in complaisance to me, she has left off; but I have not yet been able to prevail with her cousin and her sisters to do the same; so fond are they of an old custom, be it ever so absurd, who have been long habituated to it." *Viaggi*, Tom. i., Let. 17.

It is the left nostril that is bored and ornamented with rings and jewels. More than *one hundred* drawings from life of Eastern ladies lie now before me, and scarcely *one* is without the nose-jewel: both the arms and wrists are covered with bracelets, arm-circles, &c., as also their legs and feet; the soles of their feet and palms of their hands coloured beautifully red with *henna*, and their hair plaited and ornamented superbly. These beautiful drawings are a fine comment on this chapter.

Verse 23. *The glasses*] The conjunction ו *vau, and*—AND *the glasses*, is added here by *forty-three* of *Kennicott's* and *thirty-four* of *De Rossi's* MSS., and one of my own, ancient, as well as by many *editions*.

And the veils.—"*The transparent garments.*"] Τα διαφανη Λακωνικα, *Sept.* A kind of silken dress, transparent, like gauze; worn only by the most elegant women, and such as dressed themselves elegantius quam necesse esset probis, "more elegantly than modest women should." Such garments are worn to the present day; garments that not only show the shape of every part of the body, but the very colour of the skin. This is evidently the case in some scores of drawings of Asiatic females now before me. This sort of garments was afterwards in use among the Greeks. *Prodicus*, in his celebrated fable (Xenoph. Memorab. Socr. lib. ii.) exhibits the personage of Sloth in this dress: Εσθητα δε, εξ ἡς αν μαλιστα ὡρα διαλαμποι:—

"Her robe betray'd
Through the clear texture every tender limb,
Height'ning the charms it only seem'd to shade;
And as it flow'd adown so loose and thin,
Her stature show'd more tall, more snowy white
her skin."

They were called *multitia* and *coa* (*scil, vestimenta*) by the Romans, from their being invented, or rather introduced into Greece, by one *Pamphila* of the island of Cos. This, like other Grecian fashions, was received at Rome, when luxury began to prevail under the emperors. It was sometimes worn even by the men, but looked upon as a mark of extreme effeminacy. See Juvenal, Sat. ii., 65, &c. *Publius Syrus*, who lived when the fashion was first introduced, has given a humorous satirical description of it in two lines, which by chance have been preserved:—

"Æquum est, induere nuptam ventum textilem?
Palam prostare nudam in nebula linea?"

Verse 24. *Instead of sweet smell*—"perfume."] A principal part of the delicacy of the Asiatic ladies consists in the use of baths, and of the richest oils and perfumes; an attention to which is in some degree necessary in those hot countries. Frequent mention is made of the rich ointments of the spouse in the Song of Solomon, Cant. iv. 10, 11:—

"How beautiful are thy breasts, my sister, my
spouse!
How much more excellent than wine;
And the odour of thine ointments than all perfumes!
Thy lips drop as the honey-comb, my spouse!
Honey and milk are under thy tongue:
And the odour of thy garments is as the odour
of Lebanon."

The preparation for Esther's being introduced to King Ahasuerus was a course of bathing and perfuming for a whole year; "six months with oil of myrrh, and six months with sweet odours;" Esth. ii. 12. See the notes on this place. A diseased and loathsome habit of body, instead of a beautiful skin, softened and made agreeable with all that art could devise, and all that nature, so prodigal in those countries of the richest perfumes, could supply, must have been a punishment the most severe and the most mortifying to the delicacy of these haughty daughters of Sion.

Burning instead of beauty—"A sunburnt skin."] *Gaspar Sanctius* thinks the words כי תחת *ki thachath* an interpolation, because the *Vulgate* has omitted them. The clause כי תחת יפי *ki thachath yophi* seems to me rather to be imperfect at the end. Not to mention that כי *ki*, taken as a noun for *adustio, burning*, is without example, and very improbable. The passage ends abruptly, and seems to want a fuller conclusion.

In agreement with which opinion, of the defect of the Hebrew text in this place, the *Septuagint*, according to MSS. Pachom. and 1 D. ii., and Marchal., which are of the best authority, express it with the same evident marks of imperfection at the end of the sentence; thus: ταυτα σοι αντι καλλωπισμου— The two latter add δου. This chasm in the text, from the loss probably of three or four words, seems therefore to be of long standing.

Taking כי *ki* in its usual sense, as a particle, and supplying לך *lech* from the σοι of the *Septuagint*, it might possibly have been originally somewhat in this form:—

כי תחת יפי תהיה לך רעת מראה

marah raath lech thihyeh yophi thachath ki

"Yea, instead of beauty thou shalt have an ill-favoured countenance."

כי תחת יפי *ki thachath yophi* (q. יחת *yachath,*) "for beauty *shall be destroyed.*" *Syr.* חתת *chathath* or נחת *nachath.*—Dr. DURELL.

"May it not be כהי *cohey, 'wrinkles* instead of beauty?' as from יפה *yaphah* is formed יפי *yephi, yophi;* from מרה *marah,* מרי *meri,* &c.; so from כהה *cahah, to be wrinkled,* כהי *cohey.*" —Dr. JUBB. The כי *ki* is wanting in one MS., and has been omitted by several of the ancients.

Verse 25. *Thy mighty men.*] For גבורתך *geburathech* an ancient MS. has גבורך *gibborech.* The true reading, from the *Septuagint, Vulgate, Syriac,* and *Chaldee,* seems to be גבוריך *gibborayich.*

Verse 26. *Sit upon the ground.*] Sitting on the ground was a posture that denoted mourning and deep distress. The prophet Jeremiah (Lam. ii. 8) has given it the first place among many indications of sorrow, in the following elegant description of the same state of distress of his country:—

"The elders of the daughter of Sion sit on the ground, they are silent:
They have cast up dust on their heads; they have girded themselves with sackcloth;
The virgins of Jerusalem have bowed down their heads to the ground."

"We find Judea," says Mr. Addison, (on Medals, Dial. ii,) "on several coins of Vespasian and Titus, in a posture that denotes sorrow and captivity. I need not mention her sitting on the ground, because we have already spoken of the aptness of such a posture to represent an extreme affliction. I fancy the Romans might have an eye on the customs of the Jewish nation, as well as those of their country, in the several marks of sorrow they have set on this figure. The psalmist describes the Jews lamenting their captivity in the same pensive posture: 'By the waters of Babylon we sat down and wept, when we remembered thee, O Zion.' But what is more remarkable, we find Judea represented as a woman in sorrow sitting on the ground, in a passage of the prophet, that foretells the very captivity recorded on this medal." Mr. *Addison,* I presume, refers to this place of Isaiah; and therefore must have understood it as foretelling the destruction of Jerusalem and the Jewish nation by the Romans: whereas it seems plainly to relate, in its first and more immediate view at least, to the destruction of the city by Nebuchadnezzar, and the dissolution of the Jewish state under the captivity at Babylon.—L.

Several of the coins mentioned here by Mr. *Addison* are in my own collection: and to such I have already referred in this work. I shall describe one here. On the obverse a fine head of the emperor *Vespasian* with this legend, *Imperator Julius Cæsar Vespasianus Augustus, Pontifex Maximus, Tribunitia Potestate Pater Patriæ, Consul* VIII.

On the reverse a tall palm tree, emblem of the land of *Palestine,* the emperor standing on the left, close to the tree, with a trophy behind him; on the right, Judea under the figure of a female captive sitting on the ground, with her head resting on her hand, the elbow on her knee, weeping. Around is this legend, *Judea Capta. Senatus Consulto.* However this prediction may refer proximately to the destruction of Jerusalem by Nebuchadnezzar, I am fully of opinion that it ultimately refers to the final ruin of the Jewish state by the *Romans.* And so it has been understood by the general run of the best and most learned interpreters and critics.

CHAPTER IV

The havoc occasioned by war, and those other calamities which the prophet had been describing in the preceding chapter, are represented as so terribly great that seven women should be left to one man, 1. *Great blessedness of the remnant that shall be accounted worthy to escape these judgments,* 2–4. *The privileges of the Gospel set forth by allusions to the glory and pomp of the Mosaic dispensation,* 5, 6.

A. M. cir. 3244
B. C. cir. 760
Anno Olymp. Quintæ I.
Ante Urbem Conditam 7

AND [a]in that day seven women
shall take hold of one man,
Saying, We will [b]eat our own
bread, and wear our own apparel:
only [c]let us be called by thy
name, [d]to take away [e]our reproach.
2 In that day shall [f]the branch

[a]Chap. ii. 11, 17——[b]2 Thess. iii. 12——[c]Heb. *let thy name be called upon us*

[d]Or, *take thou away*——[e]Luke i. 25——[f]Jer. xxiii. 5; Zech. iii. 8; vi. 12

NOTES ON CHAP. IV

Verse 1. *And seven women*] The division of the chapters has interrupted the prophet's discourse, and broken it off almost in the midst of the sentence. "The numbers slain in battle shall be so great, that seven women shall be left to one man." The prophet has described the greatness of this distress by images and adjuncts the most expressive and forcible. The young women, contrary to their natural modesty, shall become suitors to the men: they will take hold of them, and use the most pressing importunity to be married. In spite of the natural suggestions of jealousy, they will be content with a share only of the rights of marriage in common with several others; and that on hard conditions, renouncing the legal demands of the wife on the husband, (see Exod. xxi. 10,) and begging only the name and credit of wedlock, and to be freed from the reproach of celibacy. See chap. liv. 4, 5. Like Marcia,

A. M. cir. 3244
B. C. cir. 760
Anno Olymp. Quintæ I.
Ante Urbem Conditam 7

of the LORD be [g]beautiful and
glorious, and the fruit of the earth
shall be excellent and comely [h]for
them that are escaped of Israel.
3 And it shall come to pass *that he that*
is left in Zion, and *he that* remaineth in
Jerusalem, [i]shall be called holy, *even* every
one that is [k]written [l]among the living in
Jerusalem.
4 When [m]the LORD shall have washed away
the filth of the daughters of Zion, and shall
have purged the blood of Jerusalem from the
midst thereof by the spirit of
judgment, and by the spirit of
burning.
5 And the LORD will create upon
every dwelling place of Mount Zion, and
upon her assemblies, [n]a cloud and smoke by
day, and [o]the shining of a flaming fire by night:
for [p]upon all the glory *shall be* [q]a defence.
6 And there shall be a tabernacle for a shadow in the day-time from the heat, and [r]for
a place of refuge, and for a covert from storm
and from rain.

[g]Heb. *beauty and glory*——[h]Heb. *for the escaping of Israel*——Chap. lx. 21——[k]Phil. iv. 3; Rev. iii. 5 [l]Or, *to life*

[m]Mal. iii. 2, 3——[n]Exod. xiii. 21——[o]Zech. ii. 5 [p]Or, *above*——[q]Heb. *a covering;* chap viii. 14——[r]Chap. xxv. 4

on a different occasion, and in other circumstances:—

> Da tantum nomen inane
> Connubii: liceat tumulo scripsisse, Catonis
> Marcia. LUCAN, ii. 342.

"This happened," says *Kimchi*, "in the days of Ahaz, when Pekah the son of Remaliah slew in Judea *one hundred and twenty thousand* men in one day; see 2 Chron. xviii. 6. The widows which were left were so numerous that the prophet said, 'They are multiplied beyond the sand of the sea,'" Jer. xv. 8.

In that day] These words are omitted in the *Septuagint*, and MSS.

Verse 2. *The branch of the Lord*—"the branch of JEHOVAH"] The Messiah of JEHOVAH, says the *Chaldee*. And *Kimchi* says, *The Messiah, the Son of David.* The branch is an appropriate title of the Messiah; and the fruit of the land means the great Person to spring from the house of Judah, and is only a parallel expression signifying the same; or perhaps the blessings consequent upon the redemption procured by him. Compare chap. xlv. 8, where the same great event is set forth under similar images, and see the note there.

Them that are escaped of Israel—"the escaped of the house of Israel."] A MS. has בית ישראל *beith yisrael*, the house of Israel.

Verse 3. *Written among the living*] That is, whose name stands in the enrolment or register of the people; or every man living, who is a citizen of Jerusalem. See Ezek. xiii. 9, where, "they shall not be written in the writing of the house of Israel," is the same with what immediately goes before, "they shall not be in the assembly of my people." Compare Psa. lxix. 28; lxxxvii. 6; Exod. xxxii. 32. To number and register the people was agreeable to the law of Moses, and probably was always practised; being, in sound policy, useful, and even necessary. David's design of numbering the people was of another kind; it was to enrol them for his army. *Michaelis Mosaisches Recht*, Part iii., p. 227. See also his *Dissert. de Censibus Hebræorum.*

Verse 4. *The spirit of burning*] Means the fire of God's wrath, by which he will prove and purify his people; gathering them into his furnace, in order to separate the dross from the silver, the bad from the good. The severity of God's judgments, the fiery trial of his servants, Ezekiel (chap. xxii. 18-22) has set forth at large, after his manner, with great boldness of imagery and force of expression. God threatens to gather them into the midst of Jerusalem, as into the furnace; to blow the fire upon them, and to melt them. Malachi, chap. iii. 2, 3, treats the same subject, and represents the same event, under the like images:—

> "But who may abide the day of his coming?
> And who shall stand when he appeareth?
> For he is like the fire of the refiner,
> And like the soap of the fullers.
> And he shall sit refining and purifying the silver;
> And he shall purify the sons of Levi;
> And cleanse them like gold, and like silver;
> That they may be JEHOVAH'S ministers,
> Presenting unto him an offering in righteousness."

This is an allusion to a chemist purifying metals. He *first judges* of the state of the ore or adulterated metal. *Secondly*, he kindles the proper degree of *fire*, and applies the requisite test; and thus *separates* the *precious* from the *vile*.

Verse 5. *And the Lord will create*—One MS., the *Septuagint*, and the *Arabic*, have יביא *yabi, He shall bring:* the cloud already exists; the Lord will bring it over. This is a blessed promise of the presence of God in all the assemblies of his people.

Every dwelling place—"the station"] The Hebrew text has, *every station:* but four MSS. (one ancient) omit כל *col, all;* very rightly, as it should seem: for the station was Mount Zion itself, and no other. See Exod. xv. 17. And the *Septuagint*, *Arabic*, and MSS., add the same word כל *col*, before מקראה *mikraeha*, probably right: the word has only changed its place by mistake. מקראיה *mikrayeh*, "the place where they were gathered together in their holy assemblies," says *Sal ben Melech.* But *twenty-five* of *Kennicott's* MSS., and *twenty-two* of *De Rossi's fifty-three* editions, besides the *Septuagint*, *Syriac*, and *Arabic*, have the word in the plural number.

A cloud and smoke by day] This is a manifest allusion to the pillar of a cloud and of fire which attended the Israelites in their passage out of Egypt, and to the glory that rested on the tabernacle, Exod. xiii. 21, xl. 38. The prophet Zechariah, chap. ii. 5, applies the same image to the same purpose:—

"And I will be unto her a wall of fire round about;
And a glory will I be in the midst of her."

That is, the visible presence of God shall protect her. Which explains the conclusion of this verse of Isaiah; where the *makkaph* between כל *col*, and כבוד *cabod*, connecting the two words in construction, which ought not to be connected, has thrown an obscurity upon the sentence, and misled most of the translators.

For upon all the glory shall be *a defence.*] Whatever God creates, he must uphold, or it will fail. Every degree of grace brings with it a degree of power to maintain itself in the soul.

Verse 6. *A tabernacle*] In countries subject to violent tempests, as well as to intolerable heat, a portable tent is a necessary part of a traveller's baggage, for defence and shelter. And to such tents the words of the text make evident allusion. They are to be met with in every part of Arabia and Egypt, and in various other places in the East.

CHAPTER V

This chapter begins with representing, in a beautiful parable, the tender care of God for his people, and their unworthy returns for his goodness, 1–7. *The parable or allegory is then dropped; and the prophet, in plain terms, reproves and threatens them for their wickedness; particularly for their covetousness,* 8–10; *intemperance,* 11; *and inattention to the warnings of Providence,* 12. *Then follows an enumeration of judgments as the necessary consequence. Captivity and famine appear with all their horrors,* 13. *Hades, or the grave, like a ravenous monster, opens wide its jaws, and swallows down its myriads,* 14. *Distress lays hold on all ranks,* 15; *and God is glorified in the execution of his judgments,* 16; *till the whole place is left desolate, a place for the flocks to range in,* 17. *The prophet then pauses; and again resumes his subject, reproving them for several other sins, and threatening them with woes and vengeance,* 18–24; *after which he sums up the whole of his awful denunciation in a very lofty and spirited* epiphonema *or conclusion. The God of armies, having hitherto corrected to no purpose, is represented with inimitable majesty, as only giving a hist, and a swarm of nations hasten to his standard,* 25–27. *Upon a guilty race, unpitied by heaven or by earth, they execute their commission; and leave the land desolate and dark, without one ray of comfort to cheer the horrid gloom,* 28–30.

A. M. cir. 3244
B. C. cir. 760
Anno Olymp. Quintæ I.
Ante Urbem Conditam 7

NOW will I sing to my well-beloved a song of my beloved touching [a]his vineyard. My well-beloved hath a vineyard in [b]a very fruitful hill.

2 And he [c]fenced it, and gathered out the stones thereof, and planted it with the choicest vine, and built a tower in the midst of it, and also [d]made a wine press therein: [e]and

[a]Psa. lxxx. 8; Cant. viii. 12; chap. xxvii. 2; Jer. ii. 21; Matt. xxi. 33; Mark xii. 1; Luke xx. 9

[b]Heb. *the horn of the son of oil*——[c]Or, *made a wall about it*——[d]Heb. *hewed*——[e]Deut. xxxii. 6; chap. i. 2, 3

This chapter likewise stands single and alone, unconnected with the preceding or following. The subject of it is nearly the same with that of the first chapter. It is a general reproof of the Jews for their wickedness; but it exceeds that chapter in force, in severity, in variety, and elegance; and it adds a more express declaration of vengeance by the Babylonian invasion.

NOTES ON CHAP. V

Verse 1. *Now will I sing to my well-beloved a song of my beloved*—"Let me sing now a song," &c.] A MS., respectable for its antiquity, adds the word שיר *shir, a song*, after נא *na;* which gives so elegant a turn to the sentence by the repetition of it in the next member, and by distinguishing the members so exactly in the style and manner in the Hebrew poetical composition, that I am much inclined to think it genuine.

A song of my beloved—"A song of loves"] דודי *dodey*, for דודים *dodim; status constructus pro absoluto*, as the grammarians say, as Mic. vi. 16; Lam. iii. 14, 66, so Archbishop *Secker*. Or rather, in all these and the like cases, a mistake of the transcribers, by not observing a small stroke, which in many MSS., is made to supply the ם *mem*, of the plural, thus, דודי׳ *dodi*. שירת דודים *shirath dodim* is the same with שיר ידידת *shir yedidoth*, Psa. xlv. 1. In this way of understanding it we avoid the great impropriety of making the author of the song, and the person to whom it is addressed, to be the same.

In a very fruitful hill—"On a high and fruitful hill."] Heb. בקרן בן שמן *bekeren ben shamen*, "on a horn the son of oil." The expression is highly descriptive and poetical. "He calls the land of Israel a horn, because it is higher than all lands; as the horn is higher than the whole body; and the son of oil, because it is said to be a land flowing with milk and honey."—*Kimchi* on the place. The parts of animals are, by an easy metaphor, applied to parts of the earth, both in common and poetical language. A promontory is called a cape or head; the Turks call it a nose. "Dorsum immane mari summo;" *Virgil*, a back, or ridge of rocks:—

"Hanc latus angustum jam se cogentis in arctum
Hesperiæ tenuem producit in æquora *linguam*,
Adriacas flexis claudit quæ *cornibus* undas."

A. M. cir. 3244
B. C. cir. 760
Anno Olymp.
Quintæ I.
Ante Urbem
Conditam 7

he looked that it should bring
forth grapes, and it brought
forth wild grapes.
3 And now, O inhabitants of
Jerusalem, and men of Judah,
[f]judge, I pray you, betwixt me
and my vineyard.
4 What could have been done

[f]Romans, chap. iii. 4

Lucan, ii. 612, of *Brundusium*, i. e., Βρεντεσιον, which, in the ancient language of that country, signifies stag's head, says *Strabo*. A horn is a proper and obvious image for a mountain or mountainous country. *Solinus*, cap. viii., says, "Italiam, ubi longius processerit, in *cornua* duo scindi;" that is, the high ridge of the Alps, which runs through the whole length of it, divides at last into two ridges, one going through Calabria, the other through the country of the Brutii. "Cornwall is called by the inhabitants in the British tongue *Kernaw*, as lessening by degrees like a horn, running out into promontories like so many horns. For the Britons call a horn *corn*, in the plural *kern*."—*Camden*. "And *Sammes* is of opinion, that the country had this name originally from the Phœnicians, who traded hither for tin; *keren*, in their language, being a *horn*."—*Gibson*.

Here the precise idea seems to be that of a high mountain standing by itself; "vertex montis, aut pars montis ad aliis divisa;" which signification, says *I. H. Michaelis*, Bibl. *Hallens.*, Not. in loc., the word has in Arabic.

Judea was in general a mountainous country, whence Moses sometimes calls it The Mountain, "Thou shalt plant them in the mountain of thine inheritance;" Exod. xv. 17. "I pray thee, let me go over, and see the good land beyond Jordan; that goodly mountain, and Lebanon;" Deut. iii. 25. And in a political and religious view it was detached and separated from all the nations round it. Whoever has considered the descriptions given of Mount Tabor, (see *Reland*, Palæstin.; *Eugene Roger*, Terre Sainte, p. 64,) and the views of it which are to be seen in books of travels, (*Maundrell*, p. 114; *Egmont* and *Heyman*, vol. ii., p. 25; *Thevenot*, vol. i., p. 429,) its regular conic form rising singly in a plain to a great height, from a base small in proportion, and its beauty and fertility to the very top, will have a good idea of "a horn the son of oil;" and will perhaps be induced to think that the prophet took his image from that mountain.

Verse 2. *And gathered out the stones*—"And he cleared it from the stones"] This was agreeable to the husbandry: "Saxa, summa parte terræ, et vites et arbores lædunt; ima parte refrigerant;" *Columell.* de arb. iii. "Saxosum facile est expedire lectione lapidum;" *Id.* ii. 2. "Lapides, qui supersunt, [al. insuper sunt,] hieme rigent, æstate fervescunt; idcirco satis, arbustis, et vitibus nocent;" *Pallad.* i. 6. A piece of ground thus cleared of the stones *Persius*, in his hard way of metaphor, calls "exossatus ager," *an unboned field;* Sat. vi. 52.

The choicest vine—"Sorek"] Many of the ancient interpreters, the *Septuagint*, *Aquila*, and *Theod.*, have retained this word as a proper name; I think very rightly. Sorek was a valley lying between Ascalon and Gaza, and running far up eastward in the tribe of Judah. Both Ascalon and Gaza were anciently famous for wine; the former is mentioned as such by *Alexander Trallianus;* the latter by several authors, quoted by *Reland*, Palæst., p. 589 and 986. And it seems that the upper part of the valley of Sorek, and that of Eshcol, where the spies gathered the single cluster of grapes, which they were obliged to bear between two upon a staff, being both near to Hebron were in the same neighbourhood, and that all this part of the country abounded with rich vineyards. Compare Num. xiii. 22, 23; Judg. xvi. 3, 4. *P. Nau* supposes Eshcol and Sorek to be only different names for the same valley. Voyage Noveau de la Terre Sainte, lib. iv., chap. 18. See likewise *De Lisle's* posthumous map of the Holy Land. Paris, 1763. See *Bochart*, Hieroz. ii., col. 725. *Thevenot*, i, p. 406. *Michaelis* (note on Judg. xvi. 4, German translation) thinks it probable, from some circumstances of the history there given, that Sorek was in the tribe of Judah, not in the country of the Philistines.

The vine of Sorek was known to the Israelites, being mentioned by Moses, Gen. xlix. 11, before their coming out of Egypt. Egypt was not a wine country. "Throughout this country there are no wines;" *Sandys*, p. 101. At least in very ancient times they had none. *Herodotus*, ii. 77, says it had no vines and therefore used an artificial wine made of barley. That is not strictly true, for the vines of Egypt are spoken of in Scripture, Psa. lxxviii. 47; cv. 33; and see Gen. xl. 11, by which it should seem that they drank only the fresh juice pressed from the grape, which was called οινος αμπελινος; *Herodot.*, ii. 37. But they had no large vineyards, nor was the country proper for them, being little more than one large plain, annually overflowed by the Nile. The Mareotic in later times is, I think, the only celebrated Egyptian wine which we meet with in history. The vine was formerly, as *Hasselquist* tells us it is now, "cultivated in Egypt for the sake of eating the grapes, not for wine, which is brought from Candia," &c. "They were supplied with wine from Greece, and likewise from Phœnicia," *Herodot.*, iii. 6. The vine and the wine of Sorek therefore, which lay near at hand for importation into Egypt, must in all probability have been well known to the Israelites, when they sojourned there. There is something remarkable in the manner in which Moses, Gen. xlix. 11, makes mention of it, which, for want of considering this matter, has not been attended to; it is in Jacob's prophecy of the future prosperity of the tribe of Judah:—

"Binding his foal to the vine,
And his ass's colt to his own sorek;
He washeth his raiment in wine,
And his cloak in the blood of grapes."

I take the liberty of rendering שרקה *sorekah*, for שרקו *soreko*, his sorek, as the Masoretes *do by pointing* עירה *iroh*, for עירו *iro*, his foal. עיר *ir*, might naturally enough appear in the feminine form; but it is not at all probable that שרק *sorek* ever should. By naming particularly the vine of Sorek, and as the vine

A. M. cir. 3244
B. C. cir. 760
Anno Olymp.
Quintæ I.
Ante Urbem
Conditam 7

more to my [g]vineyard, that I have not done in it? wherefore, when I looked that it should bring forth grapes, brought it forth wild grapes?

5 And now go to; I will tell you what I will do to my vineyard: [h]I will take away the hedge thereof, and it shall be eaten up; *and* break down [i]the wall

A. M. cir. 3244
B. C. cir. 760
Anno Olymp.
Quintæ I.
Ante Urbem
Conditam 7

[g]Luke xiii. 6, 7, 8, 9, 10

[h]Psa. lxxx. 12——[i]Lam. ii. 8

belonging to Judah, the prophecy intimates the very part of the country which was to fall to the lot of that tribe. Sir *John Chardin* says, "that at Casbin, a city of Persia, they turn their cattle into the vineyards after the vintage, to browse on the vines." He speaks also of vines in that country so large that he could hardly compass the trunks of them with his arms. Voyages, tom. iii., p. 12, 12mo. This shows that the ass might be securely bound to the vine, and without danger of damaging the tree by browsing on it.

And built a tower in the midst of it] Our Saviour, who has taken the general idea of one of his parables, Matt. xxi. 33, Mark xii. 1, from this of Isaiah, has likewise inserted this circumstance of building a tower; which is generally explained by commentators as designed for the keeper of the vineyard to watch and defend the fruits. But for this purpose it was usual to make a little temporary hut, (Isa. i. 8,) which might serve for the short season while the fruit was ripening, and which was removed afterwards. The tower therefore should rather mean a building of a more permanent nature and use; the farm, as we may call it, of the vineyard, containing all the offices and implements, and the whole apparatus necessary for the culture of the vineyard, and the making of the wine. To which image in the allegory, the situation, the manner of building, the use, and the whole service of the temple, exactly answered. And so the *Chaldee* paraphrast very rightly expounds it: Et statui eos (Israelitas) ut plantam vineæ selectæ et ædificavi *Sanctuarium* meum in medio illorum. "And I have appointed the Israelites as a plant of a chosen vine, and I have built my *sanctuary* in the midst of them." So also *Hieron.* in loc. Ædificavit quoque turrim in medio ejus; templum videlicet in media civitate. "He built also a tower in the midst of it, viz., his *own temple* in the midst of the city." That they have still such towers or buildings for use or pleasure, in their gardens in the East, see *Harmer's* Observations, ii. p. 241.

And also made a wine-press therein.—"And hewed out a lake therein."] This image also our Saviour has preserved in his parable. יקב *yekeb;* the *Septuagint* render it here προληνιον, and in four other places ὑποληνιον, Isa. xvi. 10; Joel iii. 13; Hag. ii. 17; Zech. xiv. 10, I think more properly; and this latter word St. Mark uses. It means not the wine-press itself, or *calcatorium*, which is called גת *gath*, or פורה *purah;* but what the Romans called *lacus*, the *lake;* the large open place or vessel, which by a conduit or spout received the *must* from the wine-press. In very hot countries it was perhaps necessary, or at least very convenient, to have the lake under ground, or in a cave hewed out of the side of the rock, for coolness, that the heat might not cause too great a fermentation, and sour the must. Vini confectio instituitur in cella, vel intimæ domus camera quadam a ventorum ingressu remota. *Kempfer*, of Shiras wine. *Amœn. Exot.* p. 376. For the wind, to which that country is subject, would injure the wine. "The wine-presses in Persia," says Sir *John Chardin*, "are formed by making hollow places in the ground, lined with masons' work." *Harmer's* Observations, i., p. 392. See a print of one in *Kempfer*, p. 377. *Nonnus* describes at large Bacchus hollowing the inside of a rock, and hewing out a place for the wine-press, or rather the lake:—

Και σκοπελους ελαχηνε· πεδοσκαφεος δε σιδηρου
Θηγαλεῃ γλωχινι μυχον κοιληνατο πετρης·
Λειηνας δε μετωπα βαθυνομενων κενεωνων
Αφρον [f. ακρον] εὐστραφυλοιο τυπον ποιησατο λενου.
DIONYSIAC. lib. xii., l. 331.

"He pierced the rock; and with the sharpen'd tool
Of steel well-temper'd scoop'd its inmost depth:
Then smooth'd the front, and form'd the dark recess
In just dimensions for the foaming lake."

And he looked—"And he expected"] Jeremiah, chap. ii. 21, uses the same image, and applies it to the same purpose, in an elegant paraphrase of this part of Isaiah's parable, in his flowing and plaintive manner:—

"But I planted thee a sorek, a scion perfectly genuine:
How then art thou changed, and become to me the degenerate shoots of the strange vine!"

Wild grapes—"poisonous berries."] באשים *beushim*, not merely useless, unprofitable grapes, such as wild grapes; but grapes offensive to the smell, noxious, poisonous. By the force and intent of the allegory, to good grapes ought to be opposed fruit of a dangerous and pernicious quality; as, in the explication of it, to judgment is opposed tyranny, and to righteousness, oppression. גפן *gephen*, the vine, is a common name or genus, including several species under it; and Moses, to distinguish the true vine, or that from which wine is made, from the rest, calls it, Num. vi. 4, גפן היין *gephen haiyayin*, the wine-vine. Some of the other sorts were of a poisonous quality, as appears from the story related among the miraculous acts of Elisha, 2 Kings iv. 39-41. "And one went out into the field to gather potherbs; and he found a field vine, and he gathered from it wild fruit, his lapful; and he went and shred them into the pot of pottage, for they knew them not. And they poured it out for the men to eat: and it came to pass, as they were eating of the pottage, that they cried out and said, There is death in the pot, O man of God; and they could not eat of it. And he said, Bring meal, (leg. קחו *kechu*, *nine* MSS., *one* edition,) and he threw it into the pot. And he said, Pour out for the people,

A. M. cir. 3244
B. C. cir. 760
Anno Olymp. Quintæ I.
Ante Urbem Conditam 7

thereof, and it shall be [k]trodden
down.
6 And I will lay it waste: it
shall not be pruned nor digged;
but there shall come up briers and thorns: I
will also command the clouds that they
rain no rain upon it.
7 For the vineyard of the LORD of hosts *is*
the house of Israel, and the men of Judah
[l]his pleasant plant: and he looked for judgment, but behold [m]oppression; for righteousness, but behold a cry.
8 Wo unto them that join [n]house to house,
that lay field to field, till *there be* no place,
that [o]they may be placed alone in the midst
of the earth!
9 [p]In [q]mine ears, *said* the
LORD of hosts, [r]Of a truth many
houses shall be desolate, *even*
great and fair, without inhabitant.
10 Yea, ten acres of vineyard shall yield
one [s]bath, and the seed of a homer shall yield
an ephah.
11 [t]Wo unto them that rise up early in the
morning, *that* they may follow strong drink;
that continue until night, *till* wine [u]inflame
them!
12 And [v]the harp, and the viol, the tabret,
and pipe, and wine, are in their feasts: but
[w]they regard not the work of the LORD,
neither consider the operation of his hands.

---

[k]Heb. *for a trading*——[l]Heb. *plant of his pleasures*——[m]Heb. *a scab*——[n]Mic. ii. 2——[o]Heb. *ye*——[p]Chap. xxii. 14——[q]Or, *This* is *in mine ears,* saith *the LORD,* &c.——[r]Heb. *If not,* &c.——[s]See Ezek. xlv. 11——[t]Prov. xxiii. 29, 30; Eccles. x. 16; ver. 22——[u]Or, *pursue them*——[v]Amos vi. 5, 6——[w]Job xxxiv. 27; Psalm xxviii. 5

---

that they may eat. And there was nothing hurtful in the pot."

From some such sorts of poisonous fruits of the grape kind Moses has taken these strong and highly poetical images, with which he has set forth the future corruption and extreme degeneracy of the Israelites, in an allegory which has a near relation, both in its subject and imagery, to this of Isaiah: Deut. xxxii. 32, 33.

"Their vine is from the vine of Sodom,
And from the fields of Gomorrah:
Their grapes are grapes of gall;
Their clusters are bitter:
Their wine is the poison of dragons,
And the cruel venom of aspics."

"I am inclined to believe," says *Hasselquist*, "that the prophet here, Isa. v. 2-4, means the hoary nightshade, *solanum incanum;* because it is common in Egypt, Palestine, and the East; and the Arabian name agrees well with it. The Arabs call it *anab el dib*, i. e., *wolf grapes.* The באושים *beushim*, says Rab. *Chai.*, is a well known species of the vine, and the worst of all sorts. The prophet could not have found a plant more opposite to the vine than this; for it grows much in the vineyards, and is very pernicious to them; wherefore they root it out: it likewise resembles a vine by its shrubby stalk;" Travels, p. 289. See also *Michaelis*, Questions aux Voyageurs Danois, No. 64.

Verse 3. *Inhabitants*] ישבי *yoshebey*, in the plural number; *three* MSS., (*two* ancient,) and so likewise the *Septuagint* and *Vulgate.*

Verse 6. *There shall come up briers and thorns*—"The thorn shall spring up in it"] *One* MS. has בשמיר *beshamir.* The true reading seems to be בו שמיר *bo shamir*, which is confirmed by the *Septuagint, Syriac*, and *Vulgate.*

Verse 7. *And he looked for judgment*] The *paronomasia*, or play on the words, in this place, is very remarkable; *mishpat, mishpach, tsedakah, tseakah.* There are many examples of it in the other prophets, but Isaiah seems peculiarly fond of it. See chap. xiii. 6, xxiv. 17, xxxii. 7, xxviii. 1, lvii. 6, lxi. 3, lxv. 11, 12. Rabbi *David Kimchi* has noticed the *paronomasia* here: he expected משפט *mishpat, judgment*, but behold משפח *mishpach, oppression;* he expected צדקה *tsedakah, righteousness*, but behold צעקה *tseakah, a cry.* The rabbins esteem it a great beauty; their term for it is צחות הלשון *tsachoth hallashon, elegance of language.*

Oppression—"tyranny."] משפח *mishpach*, from שפח *shaphach*, servum fecit, *Arab. Houbigant:* שפחה *shiphchah* is *serva*, a handmaid, or female slave. משפח *mispach*, eighteen MSS.

Verse 8. *Wo unto them that—lay field to field*—"You who lay field unto field"] Read תקריבו *takribu*, in the second person; to answer to the verb following. So *Vulgate.*

Verse 9. *In mine ears.*—"To mine ear"] The sentence in the Hebrew text seems to be imperfect in this place; as likewise in chap. xxii. 14, where the very same sense seems to be required as here. See the note there; and compare 1 Sam. ix. 15. In this place the *Septuagint* supply the word ηκουσθη, and the *Syriac* אשתמע *eshtama*, auditus est JEHOVAH in auribus meis, i. e., נגלה *niglah*, as in chap. xxii. 14.

Many houses] This has reference to what was said in the preceding verse: "In vain are ye so intent upon joining house to house, and field to field; your houses shall be left uninhabited, and your fields shall become desolate and barren; so that a vineyard of ten acres shall produce but one bath (not eight gallons) of wine, and the husbandman shall reap but a tenth part of the seed which he has sown." *Kimchi* says this means such an extent of vineyard as would require ten yoke of oxen to plough in one day.

Verse 11. *Wo unto them that rise up early*] There is a likeness between this and the following passage of the prophet Amos, chap. vi. 3-6, who probably wrote before Isaiah. If the latter be the copier, he seems hardly to have equalled the elegance of the original:—

A. M. cir. 3244
B. C. cir. 760
Anno Olymp.
Quintæ I.
Ante Urbem
Conditam 7

13 [x]Therefore my people are
gone into captivity, [y]because
they have no knowledge: and
[z]their honourable men *are* famished, and their multitude dried up with
thirst.
14 Therefore hell hath enlarged herself, and
opened her mouth without measure: and their
glory, and their multitude, and their pomp,
and he that rejoiceth, shall descend into it.
15 And [a]the mean man shall be brought
down, and the mighty man shall be humbled,
and the eyes of the lofty shall
be humbled:
16 But the LORD of hosts
shall be exalted in judgment,
and [b]God [c]that is holy shall be sanctified
in righteousness.
17 Then shall the lambs feed after their
manner, and the waste places of [d]the fat ones
shall strangers eat.
18 Wo unto them that draw iniquity with
cords of vanity, and sin as it were with a cart-
rope:

[x]Hos. iv. 6——[y]Chap. i. 3; Luke xix. 44——[z]Heb. *their glory* are *men of famine*

[a]Chap. ii. 9, 11, 17——[b]Or, *the holy God*——[c]Heb. *the God the holy*——[d]Chap. x. 16

"Ye that put far away the evil day,
And affect the seat of violence;
Who lie upon beds of ivory,
And stretch yourselves upon your couches;
And eat the lambs from the flock,
And calves from the midst of the stall;
Who chant to the sound of the viol,
And like David invent for yourselves instruments of music;
Who quaff wine in large bowls,
And are anointed with the choicest ointments:
But are not grieved for the affliction of Joseph."

Kimchi says, "they consider not the heavens nor their hosts: they pray not the morning nor the evening prayer unto the Lord."

Follow strong drink] *Theodoret* and *Chrysostom* on this place, both Syrians, and unexceptionable witnesses in what belongs to their own country, inform us that שכר *shechar* (σικερα in the Greek of both Testaments, rendered by us by the general term *strong drink*) meant properly *palm wine*, or date wine, which was and is still much in use in the Eastern countries. Judea was famous for the abundance and excellence of its palm trees; and consequently had plenty of this wine. "Fiunt (vina) et e pomis; primumque e palmis, quo Parthi et Indi utuntur, et oriens totus: maturarum modio in aquæ congiis tribus macerato expressoque." Plin. lib. xiv. 19. "Ab his *cariotæ* [palmæ] maxime celebrantur; et cibo quidem, sed et succo, uberrimæ. Ex quibus præcipua vina orienti; iniqua *capiti*, unde pomo nomen." Id. xiii. 9. Καρος signifies *stupefaction:* and in Hebrew likewise the wine has its name from its remarkably *inebriating* quality.

Verse 13. *And their honourable men*—"And the nobles"] These verses have likewise a reference to the two preceding. They that indulged in feasting and drinking shall perish with hunger and thirst; and Hades shall indulge his appetite as much as they had done, and devour them all. The image is strong and expressive in the highest degree. Habakkuk, chap. ii. 5, uses the same image with great force:—the ambitious and avaricious conqueror.

"Enlargeth his appetite like Hades;
And he is like Death, and will never be satisfied."

But, in Isaiah, Hades is introduced to much greater advantage, in person; and placed before our eyes in the form of a ravenous monster, opening wide his immeasurable jaws, and swallowing them all together: "Therefore Shoel hath dilated her soul, she hath opened her mouth beyond limit." Destruction expects more than a common meal, when God visits Jerusalem for her iniquities. This seems to refer to the ruin brought on the Jews by the Romans. Our blessed Lord repeats this parable, and applies it to this very transaction, Matt. xxi. 33.

Verse 17. *The lambs*—"And the kids"] גרים *gerim*, "strangers." The *Septuagint* read, more agreeably to the design of the prophet, כרים *carim*, αρνες, "the lambs." ודים *gedayim*, "the kids," Dr. *Durell;* nearer to the present reading: and so Archbishop *Secker*. The meaning is, their luxurious habitations shall be so entirely destroyed as to become a pasture for flocks.

After their manner—"Without restraint"] כדברם *kedobram*, secundum ductum eorum; i. e., suo ipsorum ductu; as their own will shall lead them.

Verse 18. *With a cart-rope*—"As a long cable"] The *Septuagint*, *Aquila*, *Sym.*, and *Theod.*, for בחבלי *bechabley*, read כחבלי *kechabley*, ὡς σχοινιῳ, or σχοινιοις; and the *Septuagint*, instead of שוא *shav*, read some other word signifying *long;* ὡς σχοινιῳ μακρῳ; and so likewise the *Syriac*, אריכא *arecha*. *Houbigant* conjectures that the word which the *Septuagint* had in their copies was שרוע *sarua*, which is used Lev. xxi. 18, xxii. 23, for something in an animal body superfluous, lengthened beyond its natural measure. And he explains it of sin added to sin, and one sin drawing on another, till the whole comes to an enormous length and magnitude; compared to the work of a rope-maker still increasing and lengthening his rope, with the continued addition of new materials. "Eos propheta similes facit homini restiario, qui funem torquet, cannabe addita et contorta, eadem iterans, donec funem in longum duxerit, neque eum liceat protrahi longius." "An evil inclination," says *Kimchi* on this place, from the ancient rabbins, "is at the beginning like a fine hair-string, but at the finishing like a thick cart-rope." By a long progression in iniquity, and a continued accumulation of sin, men arrive at length to the highest degree of wickedness; bidding open defiance to God, and scoffing at his threatened judgments, as it is finely expressed in the next verse. The *Chaldee* paraphrast explains it in the same manner, of

A. M. cir. 3244
B. C. cir. 760
Anno Olymp. Quintæ I.
Ante Urbem Conditam 7

19 [e]That say, Let him make
speed, *and* hasten his work, that
we may see *it:* and let the
counsel of the Holy One of
Israel draw nigh and come, that we may
know *it!*
20 Wo unto them [f]that call evil good, and
good evil; that put darkness for light, and
light for darkness; that put bitter for sweet,
and sweet for bitter!
21 Wo unto *them that are* [g]wise in their
own eyes, and prudent [h]in their own sight!
22 [i]Wo unto *them that are* mighty to drink
wine, and men of strength to mingle strong
drink:
23 Which [k]justify the wicked for reward,
and take away the righteousness
of the righteous from him!
24 Therefore [l]as [m]the fire
devoureth the stubble, and the
flame consumeth the chaff, *so* [n]their root shall
be as rottenness, and their blossom shall go
up as dust: because they have cast away the
law of the LORD of hosts, and despised the
word of the Holy One of Israel.
25 [o]Therefore is the anger of the LORD
kindled against his people, and he hath
stretched forth his hand against them, and
hath smitten them: and [p]the hills did tremble,
and their carcasses *were* [q]torn in the midst of
the streets. [r]For all this his anger is not
turned away, but his hand *is* stretched out still.

[e]Chap. lxvi. 5; Jer. xvii. 15; Amos v. 18; 2 Pet. iii. 3, 4 [f]Heb. *that say concerning evil,* It is *good,* &c.——[g]Prov. iii. 7; Rom. i. 22; xii. 16——[h]Heb. *before their face* [i]Verse 11——[k]Prov. xvii. 15; xxiv. 24

[l]Exod. xv. 7——[m]Heb. *the tongue of fire*——[n]Job xviii. 16; Hos. ix. 16; Amos ii. 9——[o]2 Kings xxii. 13, 17 [p]Jer. iv. 24——[q]Or, *as dung*——[r]Lev. xxvi. 14, &c.; chap. ix. 12, 17, 21; x. 4

wickedness increasing from small beginnings, till it arrives to a great magnitude.—L.

I believe neither the rabbins nor Bishop *Lowth* have hit on the true meaning of this place; the prophet seems to refer to *idol sacrifices.* The victims they offered were splendidly decked out for the sacrifice. Their horns and hoofs were often gilded, and their heads dressed out with fillets and garlands. The *cords of vanity* may refer to the silken strings by which they were led to the altar, some of which were unusually thick. The offering for iniquity was adorned with fillets and garlands; the sin-offering with silken cords, like unto cart-ropes. *Pride,* in their acts of *humiliation,* had the upper hand.

Verse 19. *Let the counsel of the Holy One*] *Tryphiodorus* has an expression something like this:—

—— επει Διος ηλυθε βουλη.

TRYPH. *Il Excid.* 239.

Because the counsel of Jupiter was come.

"This expression, ηλυθε βουλη, is, I believe, something uncommon; but it is exactly paralleled and explained by a passage in Isaiah, chap. v. 19. The *Septuagint* has expressed it in the very same words with *Tryphiodorus:* και ελθοι ἡ βουλ η του ἁγιου Ισραηλ, ἱνα γνωμεν."—*Merrick's note, ad loc.*

Verse 22. *Mighty to drink wine*] "They show not," says *Kimchi,* "their strength in combating their enemies, but in drunkenness and debauchery."

Verse 23. *The righteous*] צדיק *tsaddik,* singular, *Sept., Vulg.,* and two editions.

Verse 24. *The flame*—"The tongue of fire"] "The flame, because it is in the shape of a tongue; and so it is called metaphorically." *Sal. ben Melec.* The metaphor is so exceedingly obvious, as well as beautiful, that one may wonder that it has not been more frequently used. Virgil very elegantly intimates, rather than expresses, the image:—

Ecce levis summo de vertice visus Iüli
Fundere lumen apex; tactuque innoxia molli
Lambere flamma comas, et circum tempora pasci.

Æn. ii. 682.

"Strange to relate! from young Iulus' head
A *lambent flame* arose, which gently spread
Around his brows, and on his temples fed."

And more boldly of Ætna darting out flames from its top:—

Interdumque atram prorumpit ad æthera nubem,
Turbine fumantem piceo, et candente favilla:
Attollitque globos flammarum, et sidera *lambit.*

Æn. iii. 574.

"By turns a pitchy cloud she rolls on high,
By turns hot embers from her entrails fly,
And flakes of mountain flames, that *lick* the sky."

The disparted tongues, as it were of fire, Acts ii. 3, which appeared at the descent of the Holy Spirit, on the apostles, give the same idea; that is, of flames shooting diversely into pyramidal forms, or points, like tongues. It may be farther observed that the prophet in this place has given the metaphor its full force, in applying it to the action of fire in eating up and devouring whatever comes in its way, like a ravenous animal whose tongue is principally employed in taking in his food or prey; which image Moses has strongly exhibited in an expressive comparison: "And Moab said to the elders of Midian, Now shall this collection of people lick up all that are around about us, as the ox licketh up the grass of the field," Num. xxii. 4. See also 1 Kings xviii. 38.

Their root shall be as rottenness] כמק *cammak, like mak;* whence probably our word *muck,* dung, was derived.

Verse 25. *The hills did tremble*—"And the mountains trembled"] Probably referring to the great earthquakes in the days of Uzziah

A. M. cir. 3244
B. C. cir. 760
Anno Olymp.
Quintæ I.
Ante Urbem
Conditam 7

26 [s]And he will lift up an
ensign to the nations from far,
and will [t]hiss unto them from
[u]the end of the earth: and,
behold, [v]they shall come with speed
swiftly:
27 None shall be weary nor stumble among
them; none shall slumber nor sleep; neither
[w]shall the girdle of their loins be loosed, nor
the latchet of their shoes be broken:
28 [x]Whose arrows *are* sharp, and all their
bows bent, their horses' hoofs shall be counted
like flint, and their wheels like
a whirlwind:
29 Their roaring *shall be* like
a lion, they shall roar like young
lions: yea, they shall roar, and lay hold of the
prey, and shall carry *it* away safe, and none
shall deliver *it*.
30 And in that day they shall roar against
them like the roaring of the sea: and if *one*
[y]look unto the land, behold darkness *and*
[z]sorrow, [a]and the [b]light is darkened in the
heavens thereof.

[s]Chap. xi. 12——[t]Chap. vii. 18——[u]Deut. xxviii. 49; Psa. lxxii. 8; Mal. i. 11——[v]Joel ii. 7——[w]Dan. v. 6
[x]Jer. v. 16

[y]Chap. viii. 22; Jer. iv. 23; Lam. iii. 2; Ezek. xxxii. 7, 8
[z]Or, *distress*——[a]Or, *when it is light it shall be dark in the destructions thereof*——[b]Ezek. xxxii. 8, in the margin

king of Judah, in or not long before the time of the prophet himself, recorded as a remarkable era in the title of the prophecies of Amos., chap. i. 1, and by Zechariah, chap. xiv. 5.

Verse 26. *He will—hiss*—"He will hist"] "The metaphor is taken from the practice of those that keep bees, who draw them out of their hives into the fields, and lead them back again, *συρισμασι*, by a hiss or a whistle."—*Cyril*, on this place; and to the same purpose *Theodoret*, ib. In chap. vii. 18, the metaphor is more apparent, by being carried farther, where the hostile armies are expressed by the fly and the bee:—

"JEHOVAH shall hist the fly
That is in the utmost parts of Egypt;
And the bee, that is in the land of Assyria."

On which place see Deut. i. 44; Psa. cxviii. 12; and God calls the locusts his great army, Joel ii. 25; Exod. xxiii. 28. See Huet, Quest. Alnet. ii. 12. שרק *sharak* or *shrak*, he shall *whistle* for them, call loud and *shrill;* he shall *shriek*, and they (their enemies) shall come at his call.

With speed] This refers to the *nineteenth* verse. As the scoffers had challenged God to make speed, and to hasten his work of vengeance, so now God assures them that with speed and swiftly it shall come.

Verse 27. *None—among them*] *Kimchi* has well illustrated this continued exaggeration or hyperbole, as he rightly calls it, to the following effect: "Through the greatness of their courage, they shall not be fatigued with their march; nor shall they stumble though they march with the utmost speed: they shall not slumber by day, nor sleep by night; neither shall they ungird their armour, or put off their sandals to take their rest. Their arms shall be always in readiness, their arrows sharpened, and their bows bent. The hoofs of their horses are hard as a rock. They shall not fail, or need to be shod with iron: the wheels of their carriages shall move as rapidly as a whirlwind."

Neither shall the girdle] The Eastern people, wearing long and loose garments, were unfit for action or business of any kind, without girding their clothes about them. When their business was finished they took off their girdles. A girdle therefore denotes strength and activity; and to unloose the girdle is to deprive of strength, to render unfit for action. God promises to unloose the loins of kings before Cyrus, chap. xlv. 1. The girdle is so essential a part of a soldier's accoutrement, being the last that he puts on to make himself ready for action, that *to be girded*, *ζωννυσθαι*, with the Greeks means to be completely armed and ready for battle:—

Ατρειδης δ εβοησεν, ιδε ζωννυσθαι ανωγεν
Αργειους. Iliad, xi. 15.

Το *δε ενδυναι τα ὁπλα εκαλουν οἱ παλαιοι ζωννυσθαι.* Pausan. Bœot. It is used in the same manner by the Hebrews: "Let not him that girdeth himself boast as he that unlooseth his girdle," 1 Kings xx. 11; that is, triumph not before the war is finished.

Verse 28. *Their horses' hoofs shall be counted like flint*—"The hoofs of their horses shall be counted as adamant"] The shoeing of horses with iron plates nailed to the hoof is quite a modern practice, and was unknown to the ancients, as appears from the silence of the Greek and Roman writers, especially those that treat of horse medicine, who could not have passed over a matter so obvious and of such importance that now the whole science takes its name from it, being called by us farriery. The horseshoes of leather and iron which are mentioned; the silver and gold shoes with which Nero and Poppæa shod their mules, used occasionally to preserve the hoofs of delicate cattle, or for vanity, were of a very different kind; they enclosed the whole hoof as in a case, or as a shoe does a man's foot, and were bound or tied on. For this reason the strength, firmness and solidity of a horse's hoof was of much greater importance with them than with us, and was esteemed one of the first praises of a fine horse. Xenophon says that a good horse's hoof is hard, hollow, and sounds upon the ground like a cymbal. Hence the *χαλκοποδες ἱπποι*, of Homer, and Virgil's *solido graviter sonat ungula cornu.* And Xenophon gives directions for hardening the horses' hoofs by making the pavement on which he stands in the stable with round-headed stones. For want of this artificial defence to the foot which our horses have Amos, chap. vi. 12, speaks of it as a thing as much impracticable to make horses run upon a hard rock as to plough up the same rock with oxen:—

"Shall horses run upon a rock?
Shall one plough it up with oxen?"

These circumstances must be taken into consideration in order to give us a full notion of the propriety and force of the image by which the prophet sets forth the strength and excellence of the Babylonish cavalry, which made a great part of the strength of the Assyrian army. Xenop. Cyrop. lib. ii.

Like a whirlwind] כסופה *cassuphah, like the stormy blast.* Here *sense* and *sound* are well connected.

Verse 30. *If one look unto the land, &c.*—"And these shall look to the heaven upward, and down to the earth"] ונבט לארץ *venibbat laarets.* Και εμβλεψονται εις την γην. So the *Septuagint*, according to the Vatican and Alexandrian copies; but the Complutensian and Aldine editions have it more fully, thus:—Και εμβλεψονται εις τον ουρανον ανω, και κατω; and the *Arabic* from the *Septuagint*, as if it had stood thus:—Και εμβλεψονται εις τον ουρανον, και εις την γην κατω, both of which are plainly defective; the words εις την γην, *unto the earth*, being wanted in the former, and the word ανω, *above*, in the latter. But an ancient *Coptic* version from the *Septuagint*, supposed to be of the second century, some fragments of which are preserved in the library of St. Germain des Prez at Paris, completes the sentence; for, according to this version, it stood thus in the *Septuagint:*—Και εμβλεψονται εις τον ουρανον ανω, και εις την γην κατω; "And they shall look unto the heavens above and unto the earth beneath," and so it stands in the *Septuagint* MSS., Pachom. and I. D. II., according to which they must have read their Hebrew text in this manner:—ונבט לשמים למעלה ולארץ למטה. This is probably the true reading, with which I have made the translation agree. Compare chap. viii. 22; where the same sense is expressed in regard to both particulars, which are here equally and highly proper, the looking *upwards*, as well as *down to the earth:* but the form of expression is varied. I believe the Hebrew text in that place to be right, though not so full as I suppose it was originally here; and that of the *Septuagint* there to be redundant, being as full as the *Coptic* version and MSS. Pachom. and I. D. II. represent it in this place, from which I suppose it has been interpolated.

Darkness—"The gloomy vapour"] The *Syriac* and *Vulgate* seem to have read בערפלח *bearphalach;* but *Jarchi* explains the present reading as signifying *darkness;* and possibly the *Syriac* and *Vulgate* may have understood it in the same manner.

CHAPTER VI

This chapter, by a particular designation of Isaiah to the prophetic office, 1–8, *introduces, with great solemnity, a declaration of the whole tenor of the Divine conduct in reference to his people, who, on account of their unbelief and impenitence, should for a very long period be given up to a judicial blindness and hardness of heart,* 9, 10; *and visited with such calamities as would issue in the total desolation of their country, and their general dispersion,* 11, 12. *The prophet adds, however, that under their repeated dispersions, (by the Chaldeans, Romans, &c.,) a small remnant would be preserved as a seed from which will be raised a people, in whom will be fulfilled all the Divine promises,* 13.

A. M. 3245
B. C. 759
Anno Olymp. Quintæ 2
Ante Urbem Conditam 6

1 IN the year that [a]King Uzziah died I [b]saw also the Lord sitting upon a throne, high and lifted up, and [c]his train filled the temple.

2 Above it stood the seraphims; each one had six wings; with twain he covered his face, and [d]with twain he covered his feet, and with twain he did fly.

A. M. 3245
B. C. 759
Anno Olymp. Quintæ 2
Ante Urbem Conditam 6

[a]2 Kings xv. 7——[b]1 Kings xxii. 19; John xii. 41; Rev. iv. 2——[c]Or, *the skirts thereof*——[d]Ezek. i. 11

As this vision seems to contain a solemn designation of Isaiah to the prophetic office, it is by most interpreters thought to be the first in order of his prophecies. But this perhaps may not be so; for Isaiah is said, in the general title of his prophecies, to have prophesied in the time of Uzziah, whose acts, first and last, he wrote, 2 Chron. xxvi. 22; which is usually done by a contemporary prophet; and the phrase, *in the year that Uzziah died*, probably means after the death of Uzziah; as the same phrase (chap. xiv. 28) means after the death of Ahaz. Not that Isaiah's prophecies are placed in exact order of time. Chapters ii., iii., iv., v., seem by internal marks to be antecedent to chap. i.; they suit the time of Uzziah, or the former part of Jotham's reign; whereas chap. i. can hardly be earlier than the last years of Jotham. See note on chap. i. 7, and ii. 1. This might be a new designation, to introduce more solemnly a general dedication of the whole course of God's dispensations in regard to his people and the fates of the nation; which are even now still depending, and will not be fully accomplished till the final restoration of Israel.

In this vision the ideas are taken in general from royal majesty, as displayed by the monarchs of the East; for the prophet could not represent the ineffable presence of God by any other than sensible and earthly images. The particular scenery of it is taken from the temple. God is represented as seated on his throne above the ark, in the most holy place, where the glory appeared above the cherubim, surrounded by his attendant ministers. This is called by God himself "the place of his throne, and the place of the soles of his feet," Ezek. xliii. 7. "A glorious throne exalted of old, is the place of our sanctuary," saith the prophet Jeremiah, chap, xvii. 12. The very posture of sitting is a mark of state and solemnity: Sed et ipsum verbum *sedere* regni significat potestatem, saith *Jerome*, Comment. in Eph. i. 20. See note on chap. iii. 2. St. John, who has taken

A. M. 3245
B. C. 759
Anno Olymp.
Quintæ 2
Ante Urbem
Conditam 6

3 And [e]one cried unto another, and said, [f]Holy, holy, holy, *is* the LORD of hosts: [g]the [h]whole earth *is* full of his glory.

4 And the posts of the [i]door moved at the voice of him that cried, and [k]the house was filled with smoke.
5 [l]Then said I, Wo *is* me! for I am

[e]Heb. *this cried to this*——[f]Rev. iv. 8——[g]Heb. *his glory* is *the fulness of the whole earth*——[h]Psa. lxxii. 19

[i]Heb. *thresholds*——[k]Exod. xl. 34; 1 Kings viii. 10——[l]Exod. iv. 10; vi. 30; Judg. vi. 22; xiii. 22; Jer. i. 6

many sublime images from the prophets of the Old Testament, and in particular from Isaiah, hath exhibited the same scenery, drawn out into a greater number of particulars; Rev. iv.

The veil, separating the most holy place from the holy or outermost part of the temple, is here supposed to be taken away; for the prophet, to whom the whole is exhibited, is manifestly placed by the altar of burnt-offering, at the entrance of the temple, (compare Ezek. xliii. 5, 6,) which was filled with the train of the robe, the spreading and overflowing of the Divine glory. The Lord upon the throne, according to St. John (chap. xii. 41,) was Christ; and the vision related to his future kingdom, when the veil of separation was to be removed, and the whole earth was to be filled with the glory of God, revealed to all mankind: which is likewise implied in the hymn of the seraphim, the design of which is, saith *Jerome* on the place, Ut mysterium Trinitatis in una Divinitate demonstrent; et nequaquam templum Judaicum, sicut prius, sed omnem terram illius gloria plenam esse testentur; "That they may point out the mystery of the Trinity in one Godhead; and that the Jewish temple alone should not be, as formerly, the place of the Divine glory, for the whole earth should be filled with it." It relates, indeed, primarily to the prophet's own time, and the obduration of the Jews of that age, and their punishment by the Babylonish captivity; but extends in its full attitude to the age of Messiah, and the blindness of the Jews to the Gospel, (see Matt. xiii. 14; John xii. 40; Acts xxviii. 26; Rom. xi. 8,) the desolation of their country by the Romans, and their being rejected by God. That nevertheless a holy seed—a remnant, should be preserved; and that the nation should spread out and flourish again from the old stock.—L.

NOTES ON CHAP. VI

Verse 1. *The Lord*] *Fifty-one* MSS. of *Kennicott's*, and *fifty-four* of *De Rossi's*, and *one* edition; in the 8th verse, *forty-four* MSS. of *Kennicott's*, and *forty-six* of *De Rossi's*, and *one* edition; and in the 11th verse *thirty-three* MSS. of *Kennicott's*, and many of *De Rossi's*, and *one* edition, for אדני *Adonai*, "the Lord" read יהוה "JEHOVAH," which is probably the true reading; (compare ver. 6;) as in many other places, in which the superstition of the Jews has substituted אדני *Adonai* for יהוה *Yehovah*. One of my own MSS., a very ancient and large folio, to which the points and the masora have been added by a later hand, has יהוה *Yehovah* in the 1st and 8th verses, in the teeth of the masora, which orders it in both places to be read אדני *Adonai*.

Verse 2. *Above it stood the seraphim*] שרפים *seraphim*, from שרף *seraph*, to *burn*. He saw says *Kimchi*, the angels as flames of fire, that the depravity of that generation might be exhibited, which was worthy of being totally burnt up.

He covered his feet—"He covereth his feet"] By the *feet* the Hebrews mean all the lower parts of the body. But the people of the East generally wearing long robes, reaching to the ground, and covering the lower parts of the body down to the feet, it may hence have been thought want of respect and decency to appear in public and on solemn occasions with even the feet themselves uncovered. *Kempfer*, speaking of the king of Persia giving audience, says, Rex in medio supremi atrii cruribus more patrio inflexis sedebat: corpus tunica investiebat flava, ad suras cum staret protensa; discumbentis vero *pedes discalceatos pro urbanitate patria operiens.*—Amœn. Exot. p. 227. "The king sat on the floor cross-legged, as is the custom of the country. He was covered with a yellow garment, which reached down to the feet when standing, but covered the feet for decency when sitting with his slippers off." Sir *John Chardin's* MS. note on this place of Isaiah is as follows: Grande marque de respect en orient de se cacher les pieds, quand on est assis, et de baisser le visage. Quand le souvrain se monstre en Chine et à Japon, chacun se jette le visage contre terre, et il n'est pas permis de regarder le roi; "It is a great mark of respect in the East to cover the feet, and to bow down the head in the presence of the king."

Verse 3. *Holy, holy, holy*] This hymn, performed by the seraphim, divided into two choirs, the one singing responsively to the other, which *Gregory Nazian.*, Carm. 18, very elegantly calls Συμφωνον, αντιφωνον, αγγελων στασιν, is formed upon the practice of alternate singing, which prevailed in the Jewish Church from the time of Moses, whose ode at the Red Sea was thus performed, (see Exod. xv. 20, 21,) to that of Ezra, under whom the priests and Levites sung alternately,

"O praise JEHOVAH, for he is gracious;
For his mercy endureth for ever;"

Ezra iii. 11. See De Sac. Poes. Hebr. Præl. xix., at the beginning.

Verse 5. *Wo* is *me! for I am undone*] נדמיתי *nidmeythi*, I am become dumb. There is something exceedingly affecting in this complaint. I am a man of unclean lips; I cannot say, Holy, holy, holy! which the seraphs exclaim. They are holy; I am not so: they see God, and live; I have seen him, and must die, because I am unholy. Only the pure in heart shall see God; and they only can live in his presence for ever. Reader, lay this to heart; and instead of boasting of thy excellence, and trusting in thy might, or comforting thyself in thy comparative innocence, thou wilt also be dumb before him, because thou hast been a man of unclean lips, and because thou hast still an unclean heart.

I am undone—"I am struck dumb"] נדמיתי

A. M. 3245
B. C. 759
Anno Olymp. Quintæ 2
Ante Urbem Conditam 6

[m]undone; because I *am* a man of unclean lips, and I dwell in the midst of a people of unclean lips; for mine eyes have seen the King, the LORD of hosts.

6 Then flew one of the seraphims unto me, [n]having a live coal in his hand, *which* he had taken with the tongs from off [o]the altar:

7 And he [p]laid [q]*it* upon my mouth, and said, Lo, this hath touched thy lips; and thine iniquity is taken away, and thy sin purged.

8 Also I heard the voice of the Lord, saying, Whom shall I send, and who will go for [r]us? Then said I, [s]Here *am* I; send me.

9 And he said, Go, and tell this people, [t]Hear ye [u]indeed, [v]but understand not; and see ye [w]indeed, but perceive not.

10 Make [x]the heart of this people fat, and make their ears heavy, and shut their eyes; [y]lest they see with their eyes, and hear with their ears, and understand with their heart, and convert, and be healed.

11 Then said I, Lord, how long? And he answered, [z]Until the cities be wasted without inhabitant, and the houses without man, and the land be [a]utterly desolate,

A. M. 3245
B. C. 759
Anno Olymp. Quintæ 2
Ante Urbem Conditam 6

[m]Heb. *cut off*——[n]Heb. *and in his hand a live coal* [o]Rev. viii. 3——[p]Heb. *caused* it *to touch*——[q]See Jer. i. 9; Dan. x. 16——[r]Gen. i. 26; iii. 22; xi. 7——[s]Heb. *Behold me*——[t]Chap. xliii. 8; Matt. xiii. 14; Mark iv. 12; Luke viii. 10; John xii. 40; Acts xxviii. 26; Romans xi. 8——[u]Or, *without ceasing*, &c.——[v]Hebrew, *hear ye in hearing*, &c.——[w]Hebrew, *in seeing*——[x]Psalm cxix. 70; chapter lxiii. 17——[y]Jeremiah v. 21——[z]Micah iii. 12——[a]Hebrew, *desolate with desolation*

nidmeythi, twenty-eight MSS. (*five* ancient) and *three* editions.——I understand it as from דום *dum* or דמם *damam, silere*, "to be silent;" and so it is rendered by the *Syriac, Vulgate, Symmachus*, and by some of the Jewish interpreters, *apud* Sal. b. Melec. The rendering of the Syriac is תויר אני *tavir ani, stupens, attonitus sum*, "I am amazed." He immediately gives the reason why he was struck dumb: because he was a man of polluted lips, and dwelt among a people of polluted lips; and was unworthy, either to join the seraphim in singing praises to God, or to be the messenger of God to his people. Compare Exod. iv. 10; vi. 12; Jer. i. 6.

Verse 6. *A live coal*] The word of prophecy, which was put into the mouth of the prophet.

From off the altar] That is, from the altar of burnt-offerings, before the door of the temple, on which the fire that came down at first from heaven (Lev. ix. 24; 2 Chron. vii. 1) was perpetually burning. It was never to be extinguished, Lev. vi. 12, 13.

Verse 9. *And he said*] לי *li, to me, two* MSS. and the *Syriac. Thirteen* MSS. have ראה *raah*, in the regular form.

Verse 10. *Make the heart of this people fat*—"Gross"] The prophet speaks of the event, the fact as it would actually happen, not of God's purpose and act by his ministry. The prophets are in other places said to perform the thing which they only foretell:—

"Lo! I have given thee a charge this day
Over the nations, and over the kingdoms;
To pluck up, and to pull down;
To destroy, and to demolish;
To build, and to plant." Jer. i. 10.

And Ezekiel says, "When I came to destroy the city;" that is, as it is rendered in the margin of our version, "when I came to prophesy that the city should be destroyed;" chap. xliii. 3. To hear, and not understand; to see, and not perceive; is a common saying in many languages. *Demosthenes* uses it, and expressly calls it a proverb: *ὡστε το της παροιμιας ὁρωντας μη ὁρᾳν, και ακουοντας μη ακουειν; Contra Aristogit.* I., *sub fin.* The prophet, by the bold figure in the sentiment above mentioned, and the elegant form and construction of the sentence, has raised it from a common proverb into a beautiful *mashal*, and given it the sublime air of poetry.

Or the words may be understood thus, according to the Hebrew idiom: "Ye certainly hear, but do not understand; ye certainly see, but do not acknowledge." Seeing this is the case, make the heart of this people fat—declare it to be stupid and senseless; and remove from them the means of salvation, which they have so long abused.

There is a saying precisely like this in *Æschylus*:—

——————— *βλεποντες εβλεπον ματην,*
Κλυοντες ουκ ηκουον. ÆSCH. *Prom. Vinct.* 456.

"Seeing, they saw in vain; and hearing, they did not understand."

And shut—"Close up"] השע *hasha*. This word *Sal. ben Melec* explains to this sense, in which it is hardly used elsewhere, on the authority of *Onkelos*. He says it means closing up the eyes, so that one cannot see; that the root is שוע *shava*, by which word the *Targum* has rendered the word טח *tach*, Lev. xiv. 42, וטח את בית *vetach eth beith*, "and shall plaster the house." And the word טח *tach* is used in the same sense, Isa. xliv. 18. So that it signifies to close up the eyes by some matter spread upon the lids. Mr. *Harmer* very ingeniously applies to this passage a practice of sealing up the eyes as a ceremony, or as a kind of punishment used in the East, from which the image may possibly be taken. Observ. ii. 278.

With their heart—"With their hearts"] ובלבבו *ubilebabo, fifteen* MSS. of *Kennicott's* and *fourteen* of *De Rossi's*, and *two* editions, with the *Septuagint, Syriac, Chaldee*, and *Vulgate*.

And be healed—"And I should heal"] ואר פא *veer pa, Septuagint, Vulgate*. So likewise Matt. xiii. 14; John xii. 40; Acts xxviii. 27.

Verse 11. *Be utterly desolate*—"Be left"] For תשאה *tishaeh*, the *Septuagint* and *Vulgate* read תשאר *tishshaer*.

A. M. 3245
B. C. 759
Anno Olymp. Quintæ 2
Ante Urbem Conditam 6

12 [b]And the LORD have removed men far away, and *there be* a great forsaking in the midst of the land.

13 But yet in it *shall be* a tenth, [c]and *it* shall return, and shall be eaten: as a teil tree, and as an oak, whose [d]substance *is* in them, when they cast *their leaves: so* [e]the holy seed *shall be* the substance thereof.

[b]2 Kings xxv. 21——[c]Or, *when it is returned, and hath been broused*

[d]Or, *stock* or *stem*——[e]Ezra ix. 2; Mal. ii. 15; Romans xi. 5

Verse 13. *A tenth*] This passage, though somewhat obscure, and variously explained by various interpreters, has, I think, been made so clear by the accomplishment of the prophecy, that there remains little room to doubt of the sense of it. When Nebuchadnezzar had carried away the greater and better part of the people into captivity, there was yet a *tenth* remaining in the land, the poorer sort left to be vinedressers and husbandmen, under Gedaliah, 2 Kings xxv. 12, 22, and the dispersed Jews gathered themselves together, and returned to him, Jer. xl. 12; yet even these, fleeing into Egypt after the death of Gedaliah, contrary to the warning of God given by the prophet Jeremiah, miserably perished there. Again, in the subsequent and more remarkable completion of the prophecy in the destruction of Jerusalem, and the dissolution of the commonwealth by the Romans, when the Jews, after the loss of above a million of men, had increased from the scanty residue that was left of them, and had become very numerous again in their country; Hadrian, provoked by their rebellious behaviour, slew above half a million more of them, and a second time almost extirpated the nation. Yet after these signal and almost universal destructions of that nation, and after so many other repeated exterminations and massacres of them in different times and on various occasions since, we yet see, with astonishment, that the stock still remains, from which God, according to his promise frequently given by his prophets, will cause his people to shoot forth again, and to flourish.—L.

A tenth, עשיריה *asiriyah.* The meaning, says *Kimchi*, of this word is, there shall yet be in the land *ten kings* from the time of declaring this prophecy. The names of the ten kings are *Jotham, Ahaz, Hezekiah, Manasseh, Amon, Josiah, Jehoahaz, Jehoiachin, Jehoiakim,* and *Zedekiah;* then there shall be a general consumption, the people shall be carried into captivity, and Jerusalem shall b- destroyed.

For בם *bam, in them*, above seventy MSS., *eleven* of *Kennicott's*, and *thirty-four* of *De Rossi's*, read בה *bah, in it;* and so the *Septuagint.*

CHAPTER VII

The king of Judah and the royal family being in the utmost consternation on receiving accounts of the invasion of the kings of Syria and Israel, the prophet is sent to assure them that God would make good his promises to David and his house; so that, although they might be corrected, *they could not be* destroyed, *while these prophecies remained to be accomplished,* 1–9. *The Lord gives Ahaz a sign that the confederacy against Judah shall be broken, which sign strikingly points out the miraculous conception of the Messiah, who was to spring from the tribe of Judah,* 10–16. *Prediction of very heavy calamities which the Assyrians would inflict upon the land of Judea,* 17–25.

A. M. cir. 3262
B. C. cir. 742
Anno Olymp. Nonæ 3
Ante Urbem Conditam 12

AND it came to pass in the days of [a]Ahaz the son of Jotham, the son of Uzziah, king of Judah, *that* Rezin the king of Syria, and [b]Pekah the son of Remaliah, king of Israel, went up toward Jerusalem to war against it, but could not prevail against it.

[a]2 Kings xvi. 5; 2 Chron. xxiii. 5, 6

[b]2 Kings xv. 25, 30, 37

The confederacy of *Rezin*, king of Syria, and *Pekah*, king of Israel, against the kingdom of Judah, was formed in the time of Jotham; and perhaps the effects of it were felt in the latter part of his *reign;* see 2 Kings xv. 37, and note on chap. i. 7-9. However, in the very beginning of the reign of *Ahaz*, they jointly invaded Judah with a powerful army, and threatened to destroy or to dethrone the house of David. The king and royal family being in the utmost consternation on receiving advices of their designs, Isaiah is sent to them to support and comfort them in their present distress, by assuring them that God would make good his promises to David and his house. This makes the subject of this, and the following, and the beginning of the ninth chapters, in which there are many and great difficulties.

Chap. vii. begins with an historical account of the occasion of this prophecy; and then follows, ver. 4-16, a prediction of the ill success of the designs of the Israelites and Syrians against Judah; and from thence to the end of the chapter, a denunciation of the calamities to be brought upon the king and people of Judah by the Assyrians, whom they had now hired to assist them. Chap. viii. has a pretty close connection with the foregoing; it contains a con-

A. M. cir. 3262
B. C. cir. 742
Anno Olymp. Nonæ 3
Ante Urbem Conditam 12

2 And it was told the house of
David, saying, Syria [c]is confederate with Ephraim. And his
heart was moved, and the heart
of his people, as the trees of the wood are
moved with the wind.
3 Then said the LORD unto Isaiah, Go forth
now to meet Ahaz, thou, [d]and [e]Shearjashub
thy son, at the end of the [f]conduit of the
upper pool in the [g]highway of the fuller's field;
4 And say unto him, Take heed and be
quiet; fear not, [h]neither be faint-hearted for
the two tails of these smoking firebrands, for
the fierce anger of Rezin with Syria, and of
the son of Remaliah.
5 Because Syria, Ephraim, and the son of
Remaliah, have taken evil counsel against thee, saying,
6 Let us go up against Judah,
and [i]vex it, and let us make a
breach therein for us, and set a king in the
midst of it, *even* the son of Tabeal;
7 Thus saith the Lord GOD, [k]It shall not
stand, neither shall it come to pass.
8 [l]For the head of Syria *is* Damascus, and
the head of Damascus *is* Rezin: and within
threescore and five years shall Ephraim be
broken, [m]that it be not a people.
9 And the head of Ephraim *is* Samaria, and
the head of Samaria *is* Remaliah's son. [n]If
[o]ye will not believe, surely ye shall not be
established.

A. M. cir. 3262
B. C. cir. 742
Anno Olymp. Nonæ 3
Ante Urbem Conditam 12

---

[c]Heb. *resteth on Ephraim*——[d]Chap. x. 21——[e]That is, *The remnant shall return;* see chap. vi. 13; x. 21——[f]2 Kings xviii. 17; chap. xxxvi. 2——[g]Or, *causeway*——[h]Hebrew, *let not thy heart be tender*——[i]Or, *waken*

[k]Proverbs xxi. 30; chapter viii. 10——[l]2 Samuel viii. 6——[m]Hebrew, *from a people*——[n]See 2 Chronicles xx. 20——[o]Or, *Do ye not believe?* it is *because ye are not stable*

---

firmation of the prophecy before given of the approaching destruction of the kingdoms of Israel and Syria by the Assyrians, of the denunciation of the invasion of Judah by the same Assyrians. Verses 9, 10, give a repeated general assurance, that all the designs of the enemies of God's people shall be in the end disappointed, and brought to naught; ver. 11, &c., admonitions and threatenings, (I do not attempt a more particular explanation of this very difficult part,) concluding with an illustrious prophecy, chap. ix. 1-6, of the manifestation of Messiah, the transcendent dignity of his character, and the universality and eternal duration of his kingdom.

NOTES ON CHAP. VII

Verse 3. *Now*] נא *na*, is omitted by *two* MSS., the *Septuagint*, *Syriac*, *Arabic*, and *Vulgate*.

Verse 4. The *Syriac* omits וארם *vearam*, "and Syria;" the *Vulgate* reads מלך ארם *melech aram*, "king of Syria:" one or the other seems to be the true reading. I prefer the former: or, instead of וארם ובן *vearam uben*, read ופקח בן *vepekach ben, and pekah son*, MS.

Verse 5. *Because—Remaliah*] All these words are omitted by one MS. and the *Syriac;* a part of them also by the *Septuagint*.

Verses 8, 9. *For the head of Syria, &c.*]

"Though the head of Syria be Damascus,
And the head of Damascus Retsin;
Yet within *threescore* and *five* years
Ephraim shall be broken, that he be no more a people:
And the head of Ephraim be Samaria;
And the head of Samaria Remaliah's son.

"Here are *six* lines, or *three* distichs, the order of which seems to have been disturbed by a transposition, occasioned by three of the lines beginning with the same word וראש *verosh*, "and the head," which three lines ought not to have been separated by any other line intervening; but a copyist, having written the first of them, and casting his eye on the *third*, might easily proceed to write after the *first* line beginning with וראש *verosh*, that which ought to have followed the third line beginning with וראש *verosh*. Then finding his mistake, to preserve the beauty of his copy, added at the end the distich which should have been in the middle; making that the second distich, which ought to have been the third. For the order as it now stands is preposterous: the destruction of Ephraim is denounced, and then their grandeur is set forth; whereas naturally the representation of the grandeur of Ephraim should precede that of their destruction. And the destruction of Ephraim has no coherence with the grandeur of Syria, simply as such, which it now follows: but it naturally and properly follows the grandeur of Ephraim, joined to that of Syria their ally.

"The arrangement then of the whole sentence seems originally to have been thus:—

Though the head of Syria be Damascus,
And the head of Damascus Retsin;
And the head of Ephraim be Samaria;
And the head of Samaria Remaliah's son:
Yet within *threescore* and *five* years
Ephraim shall be broken that he be no more a people." DR. JUBB.

Threescore and five years] It was *sixty-five* years from the beginning of the reign of Ahaz, when this prophecy was delivered, to the total depopulation of the kingdom of Israel by Esarhaddon, who carried away the remains of the *ten* tribes which had been left by Tiglath-pileser, and Shalmaneser, and who planted the country with new inhabitants. That the country was not wholly stripped of its inhabitants by Shalmaneser appears from many passages of the history of Josiah, where Israelites are mentioned as still remaining there, 2 Chron. xxxiv. 6, 7, 33; xxxv. 18; 2 Kings xxiii. 19, 20. This seems to be the best explanation of the chronological difficulty in this place, which has much embarrassed the commentators: see *Usserii*

A. M. cir. 3262
B. C. cir. 742
Anno Olymp.
Nonæ 3
Ante Urbem
Conditam 12

10 [p]Moreover the LORD spake again unto Ahaz, saying,

11 [q]Ask thee a sign of the LORD thy God; [r]ask it either in the depth, or in the height above.

12 But Ahaz said, I will not ask, neither will I tempt the LORD.

13 And he said, Hear ye now, O house of David, *Is it* a small thing for you to weary men, but will ye weary my God also?

14 Therefore the LORD himself shall give you a sign; [s]Behold, a virgin shall conceive, and bear [t]a son, and [u]shall call his name [v]Immanuel.

15 Butter and honey shall he eat, that he may know to refuse the evil, and choose the good.

[p]Heb. *And the LORD added to speak*——[q]Judg. vi. 36, &c.; Matt. xii. 33——[r]Or, *make* thy *petition deep* [s]Matt. i. 23; Luke i. 31, 34

[t]Chap. ix. 6——[u]Or, *thou*, O virgin, *shalt call;* see Genesis iv. 1, 25; xvi. 11; xxix. 32; xxx. 6, 8; 1 Sam. iv. 21——[v]Chap. viii. 8

Annal. V. T. *ad an.* 3327, and Sir *I. Newton*, Chronol. p. 283.

"That the last deportation of Israel by Esarhaddon was in the *sixty-fifth* year after the *second* of Ahaz, is probable for the following reasons: The Jews, in *Seder Olam Rabba*, and the Talmudists, in *D. Kimchi* on Ezek. iv., say, that Manasseh king of Judah was carried to Babylon by the king of Assyria's captains, 2 Chron. xxxiii. 11, in the *twenty-second* year of his reign; that is, before Christ 676, according to Dr. *Blair's* tables. And they are probably right in this. It could not be much earlier; as the king of Assyria was not king of Babylon till 680, ibid. As Esarhaddon was then in the neighbourhood of Samaria, it is highly probable that he did then carry away the last remains of Israel, and brought those strangers thither who mention him as their founder, Ezra iv. 2. But this year is just the *sixty-fifth* from the *second* of Ahaz, which was 740 before Christ. Now the carrying away the remains of Israel, who, till then, though their kingdom was destroyed *forty-five* years before, and though small in number, might yet keep up some form of being a people, by living according to their own laws, entirely put an end to the people of Israel, as a people separate from all others: for from this time they never returned to their own country in a body, but were confounded with the people of Judah in the captivity; and the whole people, the *ten tribes* included, were called Jews."—DR. JUBB. *Two* MSS. have *twenty-five* instead of *sixty-five;* and *two* others omit the word *five*, reading only *sixty*.

If ye will not believe—"If ye believe not"] "This clause is very much illustrated by considering the captivity of Manasseh as happening at the same time with this predicted final ruin of Ephraim as a people. The near connection of the *two* facts makes the prediction of the one naturally to cohere with the prediction of the other. And the words are well suited to this event in the history of the people of Judah: 'If ye believe not, ye shall not be established;' that is, unless ye believe this prophecy of the destruction of Israel, ye Jews also, as well as the people of Israel, shall not remain established as a kingdom and people; ye also shall be visited with punishment at the same time: as our Saviour told the Jews in his time, 'Unless ye repent, ye shall all likewise perish;' intimating their destruction by the Romans; to which also, as well as to the captivity of Manasseh, and to the Babylonish captivity, the views of the prophet might here extend. The close connection of this threat to the Jews with the prophecy of the destruction of Israel, is another strong proof that the order of the preceding lines above proposed is right."—DR. JUBB.

"If ye believe not in me."—The exhortation of Jehoshaphat, 2 Chron. xx. 20, to his people, when God had promised to them, by the prophet Jahaziel, victory over the Moabites and Ammonites, is very like this both in sense and expression, and seems to be delivered in verse:

"Hear me, O Judah; and ye inhabitants of Jerusalem;
Believe in JEHOVAH your God, and ye shall be established:
Believe his prophets, and ye shall prosper."

Where both the sense and construction render very probable a conjecture of Archbishop *Secker* on this place; that instead of כי *ki*, we should read בי *bi*. "If ye will not believe *in me*, ye shall not be established." So likewise Dr. *Durell*. The *Chaldee* has, "If ye will not believe in the words of the prophet;" which seems to be a paraphrase of the reading here proposed. In favour of which it may be farther observed, that in one MS. כי *ki* is upon a rasure; and another for the last לא *lo* reads ולא *velo*, which would properly follow בי *bi*, but could not follow כי *ki*.

Some translate thus, and paraphrase thus: If ye will not believe, surely ye shall not be established. Or, If ye do not give credit, it is because ye are unfaithful. Ye have not been faithful to the grace already given: therefore ye are now incapable of crediting my promises.

Verse 11. *In the depth*—"Go deep to the grave"] So *Aquila*, *Symmachus*, *Theodotion*, and the *Vulgate*.

Verse. 14. *The Lord*—"JEHOVAH"] For אדני *Adonai*, *twenty-five* of *Kennicott's* MSS., *nine* ancient, and *fourteen* of *De Rossi's*, read יהוה *Yehovah*. And so ver. 20, *eighteen* MSS.

Immanuel.] For עמנואל *Immanuel*, many MSS. and editions have עמנו אל *immanu El*, God with us.

Verse 15. *That he may know*—"When he shall know"] "Though so much has been written on this important passage, there is an obscurity and inconsequence which still attends it, in the general run of all the interpretations given to it by the most learned. And this obscure incoherence is given to it by the false rendering of a Hebrew particle, viz., ל *le*, in לדעתו *ledato*. This has been generally rendered, either 'that he may know,' or 'till he know.' It

A. M. cir. 3262
B. C. cir. 742
Anno Olymp. Nonæ 3
Ante Urbem Conditam 12

16 [w]For before the child shall know to refuse the evil, and choose the good, the land that thou abhorrest shall be forsaken of [x]both her kings.

17 [y]The LORD shall bring upon thee, and upon thy people, and upon thy father's house, days that have not come from the day that [z]Ephraim departed from

[w]See chap. viii. 4——[x]2 Kings xv. 30; xvi. 9

[y]2 Chron. xxviii. 19——[z]1 Kings xii. 16

is capable of either version, without doubt; but either of these versions makes ver. 15 incoherent and inconsistent with ver. 16. For ver. 16 plainly means to give a reason for the assertion in ver. 15, because it is subjoined to it by the particle כי *ki, for.* But it is no reason why a child should eat butter and honey *till* he was at an age to distinguish, that *before* that time the land of his nativity should be free from its enemies. This latter supposition indeed implies, what is inconsistent with the preceding assertion. For it implies, that in part of that time of the infancy spoken of the land should not be free from enemies, and consequently these species of delicate food could not be attainable, as they are in times of peace. The other version, 'that he may know,' has no meaning at all; for what sense is there in asserting, that a child shall eat butter and honey *that* he may know to refuse evil and choose good? Is there any such effect in this food? Surely not. Besides, the child is thus represented to eat those things, which only a state of peace produces, during its whole infancy, inconsistently with ver. 16, which promises a relief from enemies only before the *end* of this infancy: implying plainly, that part of it would be passed in distressful times of war and siege, which was the state of things when the prophecy was delivered.

"But all these objections are cut off, and a clear, coherent sense is given to this passage, by giving another sense to the particle ל *le*, which never occurred to me till I saw it in *Harmer's* Observat., vol. i., p. 299. See how coherent the words of the prophet run, with how natural a connection one clause follows another, by properly rendering this one particle: 'Behold this Virgin shall conceive and bear a Son, and thou shalt call his name Immanuel; butter and honey, shall he eat, *when* he shall know to refuse evil, and choose good. For before this child shall know to refuse evil and choose good, the land shall be desolate, by whose two kings thou art distressed.' Thus ver. 16 subjoins a plain reason why the child should eat butter and honey, the food of plentiful times, *when* he came to a distinguishing age; viz., because before that time the country of the two kings, who now distressed Judea, should be desolated; and so Judea should recover that plenty which attends peace. That this rendering, which gives perspicuity and rational connection to the passage, is according to the use of the Hebrew particle, is certain. Thus לפנות בקר *liphnoth boker*, '*at* the appearing of morning, or *when* morning appeared,' Exod. xiv. 27; לעת האכל *leeth haochel*, '*at* mealtime, or *when* it was time to eat,' Ruth ii. 14. In the same manner, לדעתו *ledato*, '*at* his knowing, that is, *when* he knows.'

"*Harmer* (*ibid.*) has clearly shown that these articles of food are delicacies in the East, and, as such, denote a state of plenty. See also Josh. v. 6. They therefore naturally express the plenty of the country, as a mark of peace restored to it. Indeed, in ver. 22 it expresses a plenty arising from the thinness of the people; but that it signifies, ver. 15, a plenty arising from deliverance from war then present, is evident; because otherwise there is no expression of this deliverance. And that a deliverance was intended to be here expressed is plain, from calling the child which should be born *Immanuel*, God with us. It is plain, also, because it is before given to the prophet in charge to make a declaration of the deliverance, ver. 3-7; and it is there made; and this prophecy must **undoubtedly** be conformable to that in this matter."—Dr. *Jubb.*

The circumstance of the child's eating butter and honey is explained by *Jarchi*, as denoting a state of plenty: "Butter and honey shall this child eat, because our land shall be full of all good." *Comment in locum.* The infant Jupiter, says *Callimachus*, was tenderly nursed with goat's milk and honey. Hymn, in Jov. 48. *Homer*, of the orphan daughters of Pandareus:—

Κομισσε δε δι' Αφροδιτη
Τυρῳ και μελιτι γλυκερῳ, και ἡδει οινῳ.
ODYSS. XX., 68.

"Venus in tender delicacy rears
With honey, milk, and wine, their infant years." POPE.

Τρυφης εστιν ενδειξις; "This is a description of delicate food," says *Eustathius* on the place.

Agreeably to the observations communicated by the learned person above mentioned, which perfectly well explain the historical sense of this much disputed passage, not excluding a higher secondary sense, the obvious and literal meaning of the prophecy is this: "that within the time that a young woman, now a virgin, should conceive and bring forth a child, and that child should arrive at such an age as to distinguish between good and evil, that is, within a few years, (compare chap. viii. 4,) the enemies of Judah should be destroyed." But the prophecy is introduced in so solemn a manner; the sign is so marked, as a sign selected and given by God himself, after Ahaz had rejected the offer of any sign of his own choosing out of the whole compass of nature; the terms of the prophecy are so peculiar, and the name of the child so expressive, containing in them much more than the circumstances of the birth of a common child required, or even admitted; that we may easily suppose that, in minds prepared by the general expectation of a great Deliverer to spring from the house of David, they raised hopes far beyond what the present occasion suggested; especially when it was found, that in the subsequent prophecy, delivered immediately afterward, this child, called Immanuel, is treated as the Lord and

A. M. cir. 3262
B. C. cir. 742
Anno Olymp.
Nonæ 3
Ante Urbem
Conditam 12

Judah; *even* the king of Assyria.
18 And it shall come to pass in that day, *that* the LORD [a]shall hiss for the fly that *is* in the uttermost part of the rivers of Egypt, and for the bee that *is* in the land of Assyria.

[a]Isaiah, chap. v. 26

Prince of the land of Judah. Who could this be, other than the heir of the throne of David; under which character a great and even a Divine person had been promised? No one of that age answered to this character except Hezekiah; but he was certainly born nine or ten years before the delivery of this prophecy. That this was so understood at that time is collected, I think, with great probability, from a passage of Micah, a prophet contemporary with Isaiah, but who began to prophesy after him; and who, as I have already observed, imitated him, and sometimes used his expressions. Micah, having delivered that remarkable prophecy which determines the place of the birth of Messiah, "the Ruler of God's people, whose goings forth have been of old, from everlasting;" that it should be Bethlehem Ephratah; adds immediately, that nevertheless, in the mean time, God would deliver his people into the hands of their enemies: "He will give them up, till she, who is to bear a child, shall bring forth," Mic. v. 3. This obviously and plainly refers to some known prophecy concerning a woman to bring forth a child; and seems much more properly applicable to this passage of Isaiah than to any others of the same prophet, to which some interpreters have applied it. St. Matthew, therefore, in applying this prophecy to the birth of Christ, does it, not merely in the way of accommodating the words of the prophet to a suitable case not in the prophet's view, but takes it in its strictest, clearest, and most important sense; and applies it according to the original design and principal intention of the prophet.—L.

After all this learned criticism, I think something is still wanting to diffuse the proper light over this important prophecy. On Matt. i. 23 I have given what I judge to be the true meaning and right application of the whole passage, as there quoted by the evangelist, the substance of which it will be necessary to repeat here:—

At the time referred to, the kingdom of Judah, under the government of Ahaz, was reduced very low. *Pekah*, king of Israel, had slain in Judea *one hundred and twenty thousand* persons in one day; and carried away captives *two hundred thousand*, including women and children, together with much spoil. To add to their distress, *Rezin*, king of Syria, being confederate with *Pekah*, had taken *Elath*, a fortified city of Judah, and carried the inhabitants away captive to Damascus. In this critical conjuncture, need we wonder that Ahaz was afraid that the enemies who were now united against him must prevail, destroy Jerusalem, end the kingdom of Judah, and annihilate the family of David? To meet and remove this fear, apparently well grounded, Isaiah is sent from the Lord to Ahaz, swallowed up now both by sorrow and by unbelief, in order to assure him that the counsels of his enemies should not stand; and that they should be utterly discomfited. To encourage Ahaz, he commands him to *ask a sign* or *miracle*, which should be a pledge in hand, that God should, in due time, fulfill the predictions of his servant, as related in the context. On Ahaz humbly refusing to ask any sign, it is immediately added, "Therefore the Lord himself shall give you a sign; Behold, a virgin shall conceive and bear a son; and shall call his name Immanuel. Butter and honey shall he eat," &c. Both the *Divine* and *human* nature of our Lord, as well as the miraculous conception, appear to be pointed out in the prophecy quoted here by the evangelist: He shall be called עמנו־אל IMMANU-EL; literally, *The* STRONG GOD WITH US: similar to those words in the New Testament: *The word* which *was God—was made flesh, and dwelt among us, full of grace and truth;* John i. 1, 14. And *God was manifested in the flesh*, 1 Tim. iii. 16. So that we are to understand *God with us* to imply, God *incarnated*—God in *human nature*. This seems farther evident from the words of the prophet, ver. 15: *Butter and honey shall he eat*—he shall be truly *man*—grow up and be nourished in a *human natural way;* which refers to his being WITH US, i. e., incarnated. To which the prophet adds, *That he may know to refuse the evil, and choose the good;* or rather, *According to his knowledge*, לדעתו *ledato, reprobating the evil, and choosing the good;* this refers to him as GOD, and is the same idea given by this prophet, chap. liii. 11: *By* (or in) *his knowledge*, בדעתו *bedato*, (the knowledge of Christ crucified,) *shall my righteous servant justify many; for he shall bear their offences.* Now this *union* of the Divine and human nature is termed a *sign* or *miracle*, אות *oth*, i. e., something which exceeds the power of nature to produce. And this *miraculous union* was to be brought about in a *miraculous way: Behold, a* VIRGIN *shall conceive:* the word is very emphatic, העלמה *haalmah*, THE *virgin;* the only one that ever was, or ever shall be, a *mother* in this way. But the *Jews*, and some called *Christians*, who have espoused their desperate cause, assert that "the word עלמה *almah* does not signify a VIRGIN *only;* for it is applied Prov. xxx. 19 to signify a young *married* woman." I answer, that this latter text is no proof of the contrary doctrine: the words דרך גבר בעלמה *derech geber bealmah, the way of a man with a maid*, cannot be proved to mean *that* for which it is produced. Besides, one of De Rossi's MSS. reads בעלמיו *bealmaiv*, the *way of a strong* or stout *man* (גבר *geber*) IN HIS YOUTH; and in this reading the *Syriac*, *Septuagint*, *Vulgate*, and *Arabic* agree; which are followed by the *first version* in the *English* language, as it stands in a MS. in my own possession: **the weie of a man in his waxing youth**: so that this place, the only one that can with any *probability* of *success* be produced, were the interpretation contended for correct, which I am by no means disposed to admit, proves nothing. Besides, the consent of so many *versions* in the opposite meaning deprives it of much of its influence in this question.

A. M. cir. 3262
B. C. cir. 742
Anno Olymp.
Nonæ 3
Ante Urbem
Conditam 12

19 And they shall come, and
shall rest all of them in the
desolate valleys, and in [b]the
holes of the rocks, and upon
all thorns, and upon all
[c]bushes.
20 In the same day shall the
Lord shave with a [d]razor that is

[b]Chap. ii. 19; Jer. xvi. 16——[c]Or, *commendable trees*

[d]2 Kings xvi. 7, 8; 2 Chron. xxviii. 20, 21; see Ezek. v. 1

The word עלמה *almah,* comes from עלם *alam,* to *lie hid,* be *concealed:* and we are told, that "virgins were so called, because they were *concealed* or *closely kept up* in their father's houses till the time of their marriage." This is not correct: see the case of Rebecca, Gen. xxiv. 43, and my note there; that of Rachel, Gen. xxix. 6, 9, and the note there also; and see the case of Miriam, the sister of Moses, Exod. ii. 8, and also the Chaldee paraphrase on Lam. i. 4, where the *virgins* are represented as *going out* in the dance. And see also the whole history of *Ruth.* This being *concealed* or *kept at home,* on which so much stress is laid, is purely fanciful; for we find that young *unmarried* women drew water, kept sheep, gleaned publicly in the fields, &c., &c., and the same works they perform among the Turcomans to the present day. This reason, therefore, does not account for the radical meaning of the word; and we must seek it elsewhere. Another well-known and often-used root in the Hebrew tongue will cast light on this subject. This is גלה *galah,* which signifies to *reveal, make manifest,* or *uncover;* and is often applied to matrimonial connections in different parts of the Mosaic law: עלם *alam,* therefore, may be considered as implying the *concealment* of the *virgin,* as *such,* till lawful, marriage had taken place. A virgin was not called עלמה *almah,* because she was concealed by being kept at home in her father's house, which is not true; but, *literally* and *physically,* because as a *woman* she had not been *uncovered* —she had not known man. This fully applies to the blessed virgin, see Luke i. 34. "How can this be, seeing *I know no man?*" And this text throws much light on the subject before us. This also is in perfect agreement with the ancient prophecy, "The seed of the woman shall bruise the head of the serpent," Gen. iii. 15; for the person who was to destroy the work of the devil was to be the progeny of the *woman,* without any concurrence of the *man.* And hence the text in Genesis speaks as fully of the *virgin state* of the person from whom *Christ,* according to the flesh, should come, as that in the *prophet,* or this in the *evangelist.* According to the original promise there was to be a *seed,* a *human being,* who should destroy sin: but this *seed* or *human being,* must come from the *woman* ALONE; and no *woman* ALONE could produce such a human being without being a *virgin.* Hence, *A virgin shall bear a son,* is the very spirit and meaning of the original text, independently of the *illustration* given by the prophet; and the *fact* recorded by the evangelist is the proof of the whole. But how could that be a *sign* to *Ahaz,* which was to take place so many hundreds of years after? I answer, the meaning of the prophet is plain: not only Rezin and Pekah should be unsuccessful against Jerusalem at *that time,* which was the fact; but Jerusalem, Judea, and the house of David should be both preserved, notwithstanding their depressed state, and the multitude of their adversaries, till the time should come when a VIRGIN *should bear a son.* This is a most remarkable circumstance—the house of David could never fail, till a virgin should conceive and bear a son—nor did it: but when that incredible and miraculous fact did take place, the kingdom and house of David became extinct! This is an irrefragable confutation of every argument a Jew can offer in vindication of his opposition to the Gospel of Christ. Either the prophecy in Isaiah has been fulfilled, or the kingdom and house of David are yet standing. But the kingdom of David, we know, is destroyed: and where is the man, Jew or Gentile, that can show us a single descendant of David on the face of the earth? The prophecy could not fail: the kingdom and house of David have failed; the *virgin,* therefore, must have brought forth her son, and this son is Jesus, the Christ. Thus Moses, Isaiah, and Matthew concur; and facts the most unequivocal have confirmed the whole! Behold the wisdom and providence of God!

Notwithstanding what has been said above, it may be asked, In what sense could this name, *Immanuel,* be applied to Jesus Christ, if he be not truly and properly GOD? Could the Spirit of truth ever design that Christians should receive him as an *angel* or a *mere man;* and yet, in the very beginning of the Gospel history, apply a character to him which belongs only to the most high God? Surely *no.* In what sense, then, is Christ God with us? Jesus is called Immanuel, or *God with us,* in his *incarnation;* God united to our nature; *God with man,* God *in* man; *God with us,* by his continual *protection; God with us,* by the *influences* of his *Holy Spirit,* in the *holy sacrament,* in the *preaching* of his *word,* in *private prayer.* And *God with us,* through every *action* of our life, that we begin, continue, and end in his name. He is *God with us,* to *comfort, enlighten, protect,* and *defend* us, in every time of *temptation* and *trial,* in the hour of *death,* in the day of *judgment;* and *God with us* and *in* us, and we *with* and *in* him, to all eternity.

Verse 17. *The Lord shall bring*—"But Jehovah will bring"] *Houbigant* reads יביא *vaiyabi,* from the *Septuagint,* αλλα επαξει ὁ Θεος, to mark the transition to a new subject.

Even *the king of Assyria.*] *Houbigant* supposes these words to have been a marginal gloss, brought into the text by mistake; and so likewise Archbishop *Secker.* Besides their having no force or effect here, they do not join well in construction with the words preceding, as may be seen by the strange manner in which the ancient interpreters have taken them; and they very inelegantly forestall the mention of the king of Assyria, which comes in with great propriety in the 20th verse. I have therefore taken the liberty of omitting them in the translation.

Verse 18. *Hiss for the fly*—"Hist the fly"] See note on chap. v. 26.

Egypt, and—Assyria.] Sennacherib, Esar-

A. M. cir. 3262
B. C. cir. 742
Anno Olymp.
Nonæ 3
Ante Urbem
Conditam 12

hired, *namely,* by them beyond
the river, by the king of Assyria,
the head, and the hair of the
feet: and it shall also consume the beard.
21 And it shall come to pass in that day,
that a man shall nourish a young cow, and
two sheep:
22 And it shall come to pass, for the abundance of milk *that* they shall give that he shall
eat [e]butter: for butter and honey shall every
one eat that is left [f]in the land.
23 And it shall come to pass in that day,
that every place shall be, where
there were a thousand vines
at a thousand silverlings, [g]it
shall *even* be for briers and
thorns.
24 With [h]arrows and with bows shall *men*
come thither; because all the land shall become briers and thorns.
25 And *on* all hills that shall be digged with
the mattock, there shall not come thither the
fear of briers and thorns: but it shall be for
the sending forth of oxen, and for the treading of lesser cattle.

[e]Deut. xxxii. 14——[f]Heb. *in the midst of the land*

[g]Chap. v. 6——[h]Jer. l. 14

haddon, Pharaoh-necho, and Nebuchadnezzar, who one after another desolated Judea.

Verse 19. *Holes of the rocks*—"Caverns"] So the *Septuagint, Syriac,* and *Vulgate,* whence *Houbigant* supposes the true reading to be הנחללים *hannachalolim.* One of my oldest MSS. reads הנחלולים *hannachalolim.*

Verse 20. *The river*] That is, the Euphrates: הנהר *hanahar.* So read the *Septuagint* and two MSS.

Shall the Lord shave with a razor that is hired—"Jehovah shall shave by the hired razor"] To shave with the hired razor the head, the feet, and the beard, is an expression highly parabolical, to denote the utter devastation of the country from one end to the other; and the plundering of the people, from the highest to the lowest, by the Assyrians, whom God employed as his instrument to punish the Jews. Ahaz himself, in the first place, hired the king of Assyria to come to help him against the Syrians, by a present made to him of all the treasures of the temple, as well as his own. And God himself considered the great nations, whom he thus employed as his mercenaries; and paid them their wages. Thus he paid Nebuchadnezzar for his services against Tyre, by the conquest of Egypt, Ezek. xxix. 18-20. The hairs of the head are those of the highest order in the state; those of the feet, or the lower parts, are the common people; the beard is the king, the high priest, the very supreme in dignity and majesty. The Eastern people have always held the beard in the highest veneration, and have been extremely jealous of its honour. To pluck a man's beard is an instance of the greatest indignity that can be offered. See Isa. l. 6. The king of the Ammonites, to show the utmost contempt of David, "cut off half the beards of his servants, and the men were greatly ashamed; and David bade them tarry at Jericho till their beards were grown," 2 Sam. x. 4, 5. *Niebuhr,* Arabie, p. 275, gives a modern instance of the very same kind of insult. "The Turks," says *Thevenot,* "greatly esteem a man who has a fine beard; it is a very great affront to take a man by his beard, unless it be to kiss it; they swear by the beard." Voyages, i., p. 57. *D'Arvieux* gives a remarkable instance of an Arab, who, having received a wound in his jaw, chose to hazard his life, rather than suffer his surgeon to take off his beard. Memoires, tom. iii., p. 214. See also *Niebuhr,* Arabie, p. 61.

The remaining verses of this chapter, 21-25, contain an elegant and very expressive description of a country depopulated, and left to run wild, from its adjuncts and circumstances: the vineyards and cornfields, before well cultivated, now overrun with briers and thorns; much grass, so that the few cattle that are left, a young cow and two sheep, have their full range, and abundant pasture, so as to yield milk in plenty to the scanty family of the owner; the thinly scattered people living, not on corn, wine, and oil, the produce of cultivation; but on milk and honey, the gifts of nature; and the whole land given up to the wild beasts, so that the miserable inhabitants are forced to go out armed with bows and arrows, either to defend themselves against the wild beasts, or to supply themselves with necessary food by hunting.

A very judicious friend has sent me the following observations on the preceding prophecy, which I think worthy of being laid before the reader; though they are in some respects different from my own view of the subject.

"To establish the primary and literal meaning of a passage of Scripture is evidently laying the true foundation for any subsequent views or improvements from it.

"The kingdom of Judah, under the government of Ahaz, was reduced very low. Pekah, king of Israel, had slain in Judea *one hundred and twenty thousand* in one day; and carried away captive *two hundred thousand,* including women and children, with much spoil. To add to this distress, Rezin, king of Syria, being confederate with Pekah, had taken Elath, a fortified city of Judah, and carried the inhabitants to Damascus. I think it may also be gathered from the *sixth* verse of chap. viii., that the kings of Syria and Israel had a considerable party in the land of Judea, who, regardless of the Divine appointment and promises, were disposed to favour the elevation of Tabeal, a stranger, to the throne of David.

"In this critical conjuncture of affairs, Isaiah was sent with a message of mercy, and a promise of deliverance, to Ahaz. He was commanded to take with him *Shearjashub,* his son, whose *name* contained a *promise* respecting the captives lately made by Pekah, whose *return* from Samaria, effected by the expostulation of the prophet Oded and the concurrence of the princes of Ephraim, was now promised as a pledge of the Divine interposition offered to Ahaz in favour of the house of David. And as a farther token of this preservation, notwithstanding the incredulity of Ahaz, Isaiah was directed to predict the birth of *another* son which should be born to him within the space of a year, and to be named *Immanuel*, signifying thereby the protection of God to the land of Judah and family of David at this present conjuncture, with reference to the promise of the Messiah who was to spring from that family, and be born in that land. Compare chap. viii. 8. Hence Isaiah testifies, chap. viii. 18: 'Behold, I and the children whom the Lord hath given me are for signs and for *types* in Israel.' Compare Zech. iii. 8: 'Thy companions are men of sign and type:' see Dr. *Lowth* on this verse. The message of Divine displeasure against Israel is in like manner expressed by the *names* the prophet Hosea was directed to give *his* children; see Hos. i. and ii.

"Concerning *this child*, who was to be named Immanuel, the prophet was commissioned to declare, that notwithstanding the present scarcity prevailing in the land from its being harassed by war, yet within the space of time wherein this child should be of age to discern good and evil, both these hostile kings, viz., of Israel and Syria, should be cut off; and the country enjoy such plenty, that butter and honey, food accounted of peculiar delicacy, should be a *common* repast. See *Harmer's* Observations, p. 299.

"To this it may be objected that Isaiah's son was *not* named Immanuel, but *Maher-shalal-hash-baz;* the signification of which bore a threatening aspect, instead of a consolatory one. To this I think a satisfactory answer may be given. Ahaz, by his unbelief and disregard of the message of mercy sent to him from God, (for instead of depending upon it he sent and made a treaty with the king of Assyria,) drew upon himself the Divine displeasure, which was expressed by the *change of the child's name*, and the declaration that *though* Damascus and Samaria should, according to the former prediction, fall before the king of Assyria, yet that this very power, i. e., Assyria, in whom Ahaz trusted for deliverance, (see 2 Kings xvi. 7, &c.,) should afterwards come against *Judah*, and 'fill the breadth of the land,' which was accomplished in the following reign, when Jerusalem was so endangered as to be delivered only by miracle. The *sixth* and *seventh* verses of chap. viii. indicate, I think, as I before observed, that the kings of Syria and Israel had many adherents in Judah, who are said to *refuse* the peaceful waters of Shiloah or Siloam, *him that is to be sent*, who ought to have been their confidence, typified by the fountain at the foot of Mount Zion, whose stream watered the city of Jerusalem; and therefore, since the splendour of victory, rather than the blessings of peace, was the object of their admiration, compared to a swelling river which overflowed its banks, God threatens to chastise them by the victorious armies of Ashur. The prophet at the same time addresses words of consolation to such of the people who yet feared and trusted in Jehovah, whom he instructs and comforts with the assurance (ver. 10) that they shall prove the fulfilment of the promise contained in the name Immanuel.

"But it may still be objected, that according to this interpretation of the *fourteenth* verse of chap. vii. nothing *miraculous* occurs, which is readily admitted; but the objection rests upon the supposition that something miraculous was intended; whereas the word אות *oth*, 'sign,' does by no means generally imply a miracle, but most commonly an *emblematic representation*, (see Ezek. iv. 3-12; xi.; xx. 20; Zech. vi. 14,) either by actions or names, of some future event either promised or threatened. Exod. iii. 12; 1 Sam. ii. 34; 2 Kings xix. 29; Jer. xliv. 29, 30, are all examples of a *future event* given as a sign or token of something else which is also future. The birth of Isaiah's son was indeed typical of him whose name he was, at first, appointed to bear, viz., Immanuel, even as Oshea the son of Nun had his name changed to Jehoshua, the same with Jesus, of whom *he* was an eminent type. Hence the prophet, in the *ninth* chapter, breaks forth into a strain of exultation: 'To us a child is born;' after which follow denunciations against Rezin and the kingdom of Israel, which are succeeded by declarations, that when *Assyria* had completed the appointed chastisement upon Judah and Jerusalem, that empire should be destroyed. The whole of the *tenth* chapter is a very remarkable prophecy, and was probably delivered about the time of Sennacherib's invasion.

"But still it will be urged, that St. Matthew, when relating the miraculous conception of our Lord, says, 'Now all this was done that it might be fulfilled which was spoken of the Lord by the prophet,' &c. To this it may readily be answered, that what was spoken by the prophet was indeed now fulfilled in a higher, more important, and also in a more literal sense, than the primary fulfilment could afford, which derived all its value from its connection with this event, to which it ultimately referred.

"In like manner the prophecy of Isaiah, contained in the *second* chapter, received a *complete* fulfilment in our Saviour's honouring Capernaum with his residence, and preaching throughout Galilee; though there appears reason to interpret the passage as having a primary respect to the reformation wrought by Hezekiah and which, at the eve of the dissolution of the kingdom of Israel by the captivity of the ten tribes, extended to the tribes of Asher and Zebulun, and many of the inhabitants of Ephraim and Manasseh, who were hereby stirred up to destroy idolatry in their country. See 2 Chron. xxxi. 1. And without doubt the great deliverance wrought afterwards for Judah by the miraculous destruction of Sennacherib's army, and the recovery of Hezekiah in so critical a conjuncture from a sickness which had been declared to be unto death, contributed not a little to revive the fear of God in that part of Israel which, through their defection from the house of David, had grievously departed from the temple and worship of the true God; and as Galilee lay contiguous to countries inhabited by Gentiles, they had probably sunk deeper into idolatry than the southern part of Israel.

"In several passages of St. Matthew's Gospel, our translation conveys the idea of things being done *in order to fulfil certain prophecies;* but I apprehend that if the words *ἱνα και ὁπως* were rendered as simply denoting the event, *so that* and *thus* was fulfilled, the sense would be much clearer. For it is obvious that our Lord did not speak in parables or ride into Jerusalem previously to his last passover, simply for the purpose of fulfilling the predictions recorded, but also from other motives; and in chap. ii. the evangelist only remarks that the circumstance of our Lord's *return from Egypt* corresponded with the prophet Hosea's relation of that part of the history of the Israelites. So in the *twenty-third* verse Joseph dwelt at Nazareth *because* he was directed so to do by God himself; and the sacred historian, having respect to the effect afterwards produced, (see John vii. 41, 42, 52,) remarks that this abode in Nazareth was a means of fulfilling those predictions of the prophets which indicate the contempt and neglect with which by many the Messiah should be treated. Galilee was considered by the inhabitants of Judea as a degraded place, chiefly from its vicinity to the Gentiles; and Nazareth seems to have been *proverbially contemptible;* and from the account given of the spirit and conduct of the inhabitants by the evangelists, not without reason."—E. M. B.

To my correspondent, as well as to many learned men, there appears some difficulty in the text; but I really think this is quite done away by that mode of interpretation which I have already adopted; and as far as the miraculous conception is concerned, the whole is set in the clearest and strongest light, and the objections and cavils of the Jews entirely destroyed.

CHAPTER VIII

Prediction respecting the conquest of Syria and Israel by the Assyrians, 1–4. *Israel, for rejecting the* gentle stream *of Shiloah, near Jerusalem, is threatened to be overflowed by the* great river *of Assyria, manifestly alluding by this strong figure to the conquests of Tiglath-pileser and Shalmaneser over that kingdom,* 5–7. *The invasion of the kingdom of Judah by the Assyrians under Sennacherib foretold,* 8. *The prophet assures the Israelites and Syrians that their hostile attempts against Judah shall be frustrated,* 9, 10. *Exhortation not to be afraid of the wrath of man, but to fear the displeasure of God,* 11–13. *Judgments which shall overtake those who put no confidence in Jehovah,* 14, 15. *The prophet proceeds to warn his countrymen against idolatry, divination, and the like sinful practices, exhorting them to seek direction from the word of God, professing in a beautiful apostrophe that this was his own pious resolution. And to enforce this counsel, and strengthen their faith, he points to his children, whose symbolic names were signs or pledges of the Divine promises,* 16–20. *Judgments of God against the finally impenitent,* 21, 22.

A. M. cir. 3262
B. C. cir. 742
Anno Olymp. Nonæ 3
A. U. C. 12

MOREOVER the LORD said unto me, Take thee a great roll, and [a]write in it with a man's pen concerning [b]Maher-shalal-hash-baz.

2 And I took unto me faithful

[a]Chap. xxx. 8; Hab. ii. 2——[b]Heb. *in making speed to the spoil he hasteneth the prey*, or *make speed*, &c.

The prophecy of the foregoing chapter relates directly to the kingdom of Judah only: the first part of it promises them deliverance from the united invasion of the Israelites and Syrians; the latter part, from ver. 17, denounces the desolation to be brought upon the kingdom of Judah by the Assyrians. The *sixth, seventh,* and *eighth* verses of this chapter seem to take in both the kingdoms of Israel and Judah. "This people that refuseth the waters of Shiloah," may be meant of both: the Israelites despised the kingdom of Judah, which they had deserted, and now attempted to destroy; the people of Judah, from a consideration of their own weakness, and a distrust of God's promises, being reduced to despair, applied to the Assyrians for assistance against the two confederate kings. But how could it be said of Judah, that they rejoiced in Rezin, and the son of Remaliah, the enemies confederated against them? If some of the people were inclined to revolt to the enemy, (which however does not clearly appear from any part of the history or the prophecy,) yet there was nothing like a tendency to a general defection. This, therefore, must be understood of Israel. The prophet denounces the Assyrian invasion, which should overwhelm the whole kingdom of Israel under Tiglath-pileser, and Shalmaneser; and the subsequent invasion of Judah by the same power under Sennacherib, which would bring them into the most imminent danger, like a flood reaching to the neck, in which a man can but just keep his head above water. The two next verses, 9 and 10, are addressed by the prophet, as a subject of the kingdom of Judah, to the Israelites and Syrians, and perhaps to all the enemies of God's people; assuring them that their attempts against that kingdom shall be fruitless; for that the promised Immanuel, to whom he alludes by using his name to express the signification of it, *for God is with us*, shall be the defence of the house of David, and deliver the kingdom of Judah out of their hands. He then proceeds to warn the people of Judah against idolatry, divination, and the like forbidden practices; to which they were much inclined, and which would soon bring down God's judgments upon Israel. The prophecy concludes at the *sixth* verse of chap. ix. with promises of blessings in future times by the coming of the great deliverer already pointed out by the name of Immanuel, whose person and character is set forth in terms the most ample and magnificent.

And here it may be observed that it is almost the constant practice of the prophet to connect in like manner deliverances temporal with spiritual. Thus the *eleventh* chapter, setting forth the kingdom of Messiah, is closely connected with the *tenth*, which foretells the destruction of Sennacherib. So likewise the destruction of nations, enemies to God, in the *thirty-fourth*

A. M. cir. 3262 B. C. cir. 742 Anno Olymp. Nonæ 3 Ante Urbem Conditam 12

witnesses to record, [c]Uriah the priest, and Zechariah the son of Jeberechiah.

3 And I [d]went unto the prophetess; and she conceived, and bare a son. Then said the LORD to me, Call his name Maher-shalal-hash-baz.

4 [e]For before the child shall have knowledge to cry, My father and my mother, [f]the [g]riches of Damascus and the spoil of Samaria shall be taken away before the king of Assyria.

A. M. cir. 3263 B. C. cir. 741 Olymp. IX. 4 cir. annum Romuli, Regis Roman., 13

5 The LORD spake also unto me again, saying,

6 Forasmuch as this people refuseth the waters of [h]Shiloah that go softly, and rejoice [i]in Rezin and Remaliah's son;

7 Now therefore, behold, the LORD bringeth up upon them the waters of the river, strong and many, *even* [k]the king of Assyria, and all his glory: and he shall come up over all his channels, and go over all his banks:

[c]2 Kings xvi. 10——[d]Hebrew, *approached unto*——[e]See chap. vii. 16——[f]Or, he that is *before the king of Assyria shall take away the riches*, &c.——[g]2 Kings xv. 29; xvi. 9; chapter xvii. 3——[h]Nehemiah iii. 15; John ix. 7——[i]Chapter vii. 1, 2, 6——[k]Chapter x. 12

chapter, introduces the flourishing state of the kingdom of Christ in the *thirty-fifth*. And thus the chapters from xl. to xlix. inclusive, plainly relating to the deliverance from the captivity of Babylon, do in some parts plainly relate to the greater deliverance by Christ.

NOTES ON CHAP. VIII

Verse 1. *Take thee a great roll*—"Take unto thee a large mirror"] The word גליון *gillayon* is not regularly formed from גלל *galal, to roll,* but from גלה *galah,* as פדיון *pidyon* from פדה *padah,* כליון *killayon* from כלה *calah,* נקיון *nikkayon* from נקה *nakah,* עליון *elyon* from עלה *alah,* &c., the י *yod* supplying the place of the radical ה *he.* גלה *galah* signifies to *show, to reveal;* properly, as *Schroederus* says, (De Vestitu Mulier. Hebr. p. 294,) *to render clear and bright by rubbing; to polish.* גליון *gillayon,* therefore, according to this derivation, is not a roll or volume: but may very well signify *a polished tablet of metal,* such as was anciently used for a *mirror.* The *Chaldee* paraphrast renders it by לוח *luach, a tablet,* and the same word, though somewhat differently pointed, the Chaldee paraphrast and the rabbins render *a mirror,* chap. iii. 23. The mirrors of the Israelitish women were made of brass finely polished, Exod. xxxviii. 8, from which place it likewise appears that what they used were little hand mirrors which they carried with them even when they assembled at the door of the tabernacle. I have a metalline mirror found in Herculaneum, which is not above three inches square. The prophet is commanded to take a mirror, or brazen polished tablet, not like these little hand mirrors, but a large one; large enough for him to engrave upon it in deep and lasting characters, בחרט אנוש *becheret enosh,* with a workman's graving tool, the prophecy which he was to deliver. חרט *cheret* in this place certainly signifies an *instrument* to *write* or *engrave* with: but חריט *charit,* the same word, only differing a little in the form, means something belonging to a lady's dress, chap. iii. 22, (where however *five* MSS. leave out the י *yod,* whereby only it differs from the word in this place,) either a crisping-pin, which might be not unlike a graving tool, as some will have it, or a purse, as others infer from 2 Kings v. 23. It may therefore be called here חרט אנוש *cheret enosh, a workman's instrument,* to distinguish it from חרט אשה *cheret ishshah, an instrument* of the same name, *used by the women.* In this manner he was to record the prophecy of the destruction of Damascus and Samaria by the Assyrians; the subject and sum of which prophecy is here expressed with great brevity in four words, מהר שלל חש בז *maher shalal hash baz;* i. e., *to hasten the spoil, to take quickly the prey;* which are afterwards applied as the name of the prophet's son, who was made a sign of the speedy completion of it; Maher-shalal-hash-baz; *Haste-to-the-spoil, Quick-to-the-prey.* And that it might be done with the greater solemnity, and to preclude all doubt of the real delivery of the prophecy before the event, he calls witnesses to attest the recording of it.

The prophet is commanded to take a great roll, and yet *four words* only are to be written in it, מהר שלל חש בז *maher shalal hash baz, Make haste to the spoil; fall upon the prey.* The great volume points out the land of Judea; and the few words the small number of inhabitants, after the *ten* tribes were carried into captivity.

The words were to be written with a *man's pen;* i. e., though the prophecy be given in the *visions* of God, yet the writing must be real; the words must be transcribed on the great roll, that they may be read and publicly consulted. Or, חרט אנוש *cherot enosh, the pen* or *graver* of the weak miserable man, may refer to the already condemned Assyrians, who though they should be the instruments of chastening Damascus and Samaria, should themselves shortly be overthrown. The four words may be considered as the commission given to the Assyrians to destroy and spoil the cities. *Make haste to the spoil; Fall upon the prey,* &c.

Verse 4. *For before the child*] For *my father and my mother,* one MS. and the *Vulgate* have *his father and his mother.* The prophecy was accordingly accomplished within three years; when Tiglath-pileser, king of Assyria, went up against Damascus and took it, and carried the people of it captive to Kir, and slew Rezin, and also took the Reubenites and the Gadites, and the half-tribe of Manasseh, and carried them captive to Assyria, 2 Kings xv. 29; xvi. 9; 1 Chron. v. 26.

Verse 6. *Forasmuch as this people refuseth*—

A. M. cir. 3263
B. C. cir. 741
Olymp. IX. 4
cir. annum
Romuli, Regis
Roman., 13

8 And he shall pass through Judah; he shall overflow and go over, [l]he shall reach *even* to the neck; and [m]the stretching out of his wings shall fill the breadth of thy land, O [n]Immanuel.

9 [o]Associate yourselves, O ye people, [p]and ye shall be broken in pieces; and give ear, all ye of far countries: gird yourselves, and ye shall be broken in pieces; gird yourselves, and ye shall be broken in pieces.

10 [q]Take counsel together, and it shall come to naught; speak the word, [r]and it shall not stand: [s]for God *is* with us.

11 For the LORD spake thus to me [t]with a strong hand, and instructed me that I should not walk in the way of this people, saying,

12 Say ye not, A confederacy, to all *them to* whom [u]this people shall say, A confederacy; [v]neither fear ye their fear, nor be afraid.

[l]Chap. xxx. 28——[m]Heb. *the fulness of the breadth of thy land shall be the stretchings out of his wings*——[n]Chapter viii. 14——[o]Joel iii. 9, 11——[p]Or, *yet*

[q]Job v. 12——[r]Chap. vii. 7——[s]Chap. vii. 14; Acts v. 38, 39; Rom. viii. 13——[t]Heb. *in strength of hand*——[u]Chap. vii. 2——[v]1 Pet. iii. 14, 15

"Because this people have rejected"] The gentle waters of Shiloah, a small fountain and brook just without Jerusalem, which supplied a pool within the city for the use of the inhabitants, is an apt emblem of the state of the kingdom and house of David, much reduced in its apparent strength, yet supported by the blessing of God; and is finely contrasted with the waters of the Euphrates, great, rapid, and impetuous; the image of the Babylonian empire, which God threatens to bring down like a mighty flood upon all these apostates of both kingdoms, as punishment for their manifold iniquities, and their contemptuous disregard of his promises. The brook and the river are put for the kingdoms to which they belong, and the different states of which respectively they most aptly represent. *Juvenal*, inveighing against the corruption of Rome by the importation of Asiatic manners, says, with great elegance, that "the Orontes has been long discharging itself into the Tiber:"—

Jampridem Syrus in Tiberim defluxit Orontes.

And *Virgil*, to express the submission of some of the Eastern countries to the Roman arms, says:—

Euphrates ibat jam mollior undis.
Æn. viii. 726.

"The waters of the Euphrates now flowed more humbly and gently."

But the happy contrast between the brook and the river gives a peculiar beauty to this passage of the prophet, with which the simple figure in the Roman poets, however beautiful, yet uncontrasted, cannot contend.

Verse 8. *He shall reach even to the neck*] He compares Jerusalem, says *Kimchi*, to the head of the human body. As when the waters come up to a man's neck, he is very near drowning, (for a little increase of them would go over his head,) so the king of Assyria coming up to Jerusalem was like a flood reaching to the neck—the whole country was overflowed, and the capital was in imminent danger. Accordingly the *Chaldee* renders *reaching to the neck* by *reaching to Jerusalem.*

Verse 9. *Associate yourselves*—"Know ye this"] God by his prophet plainly declares to the confederate adversaries of Judah, and bids them regard and attend to his declaration, that all their efforts shall be in vain. The present reading, רעו *rou*, is subject to many difficulties; I follow that of the *Septuagint*, דעו *deu*, γνωτε. Archbishop *Secker* approves this reading. דעו *deu, know ye this*, is parallel and synonymous to האזינו *haazinu, give ear to it*, in the next line. The *Septuagint* have likewise very well paraphrased the conclusion of this verse: "*When ye have strengthened yourselves, ye shall be broken; and though ye again strengthen yourselves, again shall ye be broken;*" taking חתו *chottu* as meaning the same with נשברו, *ye shall be broken.*

Verse 11. *With a strong hand*—"As taking me by the hand"] *Eleven* MSS., (*two* ancient,) of *Kennicott's*, *thirty-four* of *De Rossi's*, and *seven* editions, read כחזקת *kechezkath;* and so *Symmachus*, the *Syriac*, and *Vulgate*. Or rather *with a strong hand*, that is, with a strong and powerful influence of the prophetic Spirit.

Verse 12. *Say ye not, A confederacy*—"Say ye not, It is holy"] קשר *kesher*. Both the reading and the sense of this word are doubtful. The *Septuagint* manifestly read קשה *kashah;* for they render it by σκληρον, *hard*. The *Syriac* and *Chaldee* render it מרדא *merda*, and מרוד *merod, rebellion*. How they came by this sense of the word, or what they read in their copies, is not so clear. But the worst of it is, that neither of these readings or renderings gives any clear sense in this place. For why should God forbid his faithful servants to say with the unbelieving Jews, It is *hard;* or, There is a *rebellion;* or, as our translators render it, a *confederacy?* And how can this be called "walking in the way of this people?" ver. 11, which usually means, following their example, joining with them in religious worship. Or what confederacy do they mean? The union of the kingdoms of Syria and Israel against Judah? That was properly a league between two independent states, not an unlawful conspiracy of one part against another in the same state; this is the meaning of the word קשר *kesher*. For want of any satisfactory interpretation of this place that I can meet with, I adopt a conjecture of Archbishop *Secker*, which he proposes with great diffidence, and even seems immediately to give up, as being destitute of any authority to support it. I will give it in his own words:—"Videri potest ex cap. v. 16, et hujus cap. 13, 14, 19, legendum קדש vel קדוש *kadosh*, eadem sententia, qua אלהינו *Eloheynu*, Hos. xiv. 3. Sed nihil necesse est. Vide enim Jer. xi. 9; Ezek. xxii. 25. Optime tamen sic responderent huic

A. M. cir. 3263 B. C. cir. 741 Olymp. IX. 4 cir. annum Romuli, Regis Roman., 13

13 [w]Sanctify the LORD of hosts himself; and [x]*let* him *be* your fear, and *let* him *be* your dread.

14 And [y]he shall be for a sanctuary; but for [z]a stone of stumbling and for a rock of offence to both the houses of Israel, for a gin and for a snare to the inhabitants of Jerusalem.

15 And many among them shall [a]stumble, and fall, and be broken, and be snared, and be taken.

16 Bind up the testimony, seal the law among my disciples.

17 And I will wait upon the LORD, that [b]hideth his face from the house of Jacob, and I [c]will look for him.

18 [d]Behold, I and the children whom the LORD hath given me [e]*are* for signs and for wonders in Israel from the LORD of hosts, which dwelleth in Mount Zion.

19 And when they shall say unto you, [f]Seek unto them that have familiar spirits, and unto wizards [g]that peep, and that mutter: should not a people seek unto their God? for the living [h]to the dead?

20 [i]To the law and to the testimony: if they speak not according to this word, *it is* because [k]*there is* [l]no light in them.

[w]Num. xx. 12——[x]Psa. lxxvi. 7; Luke xii. 5——[y]Ezek. xi. 16——[z]Chap. xxviii. 16; Luke ii. 34; Rom. ix. 33; 1 Pet. ii. 8——[a]Matt. xxi. 44; Luke xx. 18; Rom. ix. 32; xi. 25——[b]Chap. liv. 8

[c]Hab. ii. 3; Luke ii. 25, 38——[d]Heb. ii. 13——[e]Psa. lxxi. 7; Zech. iii. 8——[f]1 Sam. xxviii. 8; chap. xix. 3——[g]Chap. xxix. 4——[h]Psa. cvi. 28——[i]Luke xvi. 29——[k]Mic. iii. 6——[l]Heb. *no morning*

versiculo versiculi 13, 14." The passages of Jeremiah and Ezekiel above referred to seem to me not at all to clear up the sense of the word קשר *kesher* in this place. But the context greatly favours the conjecture here given, and makes it highly probable: "Walk not in the way of this people; call not their idols holy, nor fear ye the object of their fear:" (that is, the *σεβασματα*, or *gods* of the idolaters; for so *fear* here signifies, to wit, the thing feared. So God is called "The fear of Isaac," Gen. xxxi. 42, 53:) "but look up to JEHOVAH as your Holy One; and let him be your fear, and let him be your dread; and he shall be a holy Refuge unto you." Here there is a harmony and consistency running through the whole sentence; and the latter part naturally arises out of the former, and answers to it. Idolatry, however, is full of *fears*. The superstitious fears of the Hindoos are very numerous. They fear death, bad spirits generally, and *hobgoblins* of all descriptions. They fear also the cries of *jackalls, owls, crows, cats, asses, vultures, dogs, lizards*, &c. They also dread different *sights* in the air, and are alarmed at various dreams. See WARD'S Customs. Observe that the difference between קשר *kesher* and קדש *kadosh* is chiefly in the transposition of the two last letters, for the letters ר *resh* and ד *daleth* are hardly distinguishable in some copies, printed as well as MS.; so that the mistake, in respect of the letters themselves, is a very easy and a very common one.—L.

Verse 14. *And he shall be for a sanctuary*—"And he shall be unto you a sanctuary"] The word לכם *lachem, unto you*, absolutely necessary, as I conceive, to the sense, is lost in this place: it is preserved by the *Vulgate*, "et erit *vobis* in sanctificationem." The *Septuagint* have it in the singular number: *εσται σοι εις ἁγιασμον, it shall be to* THEE. Or else, instead of מקדש *mikdash, a sanctuary*, we must read מוקש *mokesh, a snare*, which would then be repeated without any propriety or elegance, at the end of the verse. The *Chaldee* reads instead of it משפט *mishpat, judgment;* for he renders it by פורען *purean*, which word frequently answers to משפט *mishpat* in his paraphrase. *One* MS. has instead of מקדש ולאבן *mikdash uleeben*, להם לאבן *lahem leeben*, which clears the sense and construction. But the reading of the *Vulgate* is, I think, the best remedy to this difficulty; and is in some degree authorized by להם *lahem*, the reading of the MS. above mentioned.

Verse 16. *Among my disciples.*] בלמדי *belimmudai.* The *Septuagint* render it *του μη μαθειν*. Bishop *Chandler*, Defence of Christianity, p. 308, thinks they read מלמד, *that it be not understood*, and approves of this reading.—Abp. *Secker.*

Verse 18. *Lord of hosts*] *One* MS. reads אלהי צבאות *Elohey tsebaoth, God of hosts.*

Verse 19. *Should not a people seek*—"Should they seek"] After ידרש *yidrosh*, the *Septuagint*, repeating the word, read הידרש *hayidrosh: Ουκ εθνος προς Θεον αυτου εκζητησουσι; τι εκζητησουσι περι των ζωντων τους νεκρους; Should not a nation seek unto its God? Why should you seek unto the dead concerning the living?* and this repetition of the verb seems necessary to the sense; and, as *Procopius* on the place observes, it strongly expresses the prophet's indignation at their folly.

Verse 20. *To the law and to the testimony*—"Unto the command, and unto the testimony."] "Is not תעודה *teudah* here the attested prophecy, ver. 1-4? and perhaps תורה *torah* the command, ver. 11-15? for it means sometimes a particular, and even a human, command; see Prov. vi. 20, and vii. 1, 2, where it is ordered to be hid, that is, secretly kept."—Abp. *Secker.* So *Deschamps*, in his translation, or rather paraphrase, understands it: "Tenons nous à l'instrument authentique mis en dèpôt par ordre du Seigneur," "Let us stick to the authentic instrument, laid up by the command of the Lord." If this be right, the *sixteenth* verse must be understood in the same manner.

Because there is *no light in them*—"In which there is no obscurity."] שחר *shachor*, as an adjective, frequently signifies *dark, obscure;* and the noun שחר *shachar* signifies *darkness, gloominess*, Joel ii. 2, if we may judge by the context:—

A. M. cir. 3263 B. C. cir. 741 Olymp. IX. 4 cir. annum Romuli, Regis Roman., 13

21 And they shall pass through it, hardly bestead and hungry: and it shall come to pass, that when they shall be hungry, they shall fret themselves, and [m]curse their king and their God, and look upward.

22 And [n]they shall look unto the earth; and behold trouble and darkness, [o]dimness of anguish; and *they shall be* driven to darkness.

[m]Rev. xvi. 11

[n]Chap. v. 30——[o]Chap. ix. 1

"A day of darkness and obscurity;
Of cloud, and of thick vapour;
As the gloom spread upon the mountains:
A people mighty and numerous."

Where the *gloom*, שחר *shachar*, seems to be the same with the cloud and thick vapour mentioned in the line prceding. See Lam. iv. 8, and Job xxx. 30. See this meaning of the word שחר *shachar* well supported in *Christ. Muller.* Sat. Observat. Phil. p. 53, Lugd. Bat. 1752. The *morning* seems to have been an idea wholly incongruous in the passage of Joel; and in this of Isaiah the words *in which there is no morning* (for so it ought to be rendered if שחר *shachar* in this place signifies, according to its usual sense, *morning*) seem to give no meaning at all. "It is because there is no light in them," says our translation. If there be any sense in these words, it is not the sense of the original; which cannot justly be so translated. *Qui n'a rien d'obscur*, "which has no obscurity."—*Deschamps.* The reading of the *Septuagint* and *Syriac*, שחד *shochad, gift*, affords no assistance towards the clearing up of any of this difficult place. *R. D. Kimchi* says this was the form of an oath: "By the law and by the testimony such and such things are so." Now if they had sworn this falsely, it is because there is no *light*, no *illumination*, שחר *shachar*, no scruple of conscience, in them.

Ver. 21. *Hardly bestead*—"Distressed"] Instead of נקשה *niksheh, distressed*, the *Vulgate, Chaldee*, and *Symmachus* manifestly read נכשל *nichshal, stumbling, tottering through weakness, ready to fall;* a sense which suits very well with the place.

And look upward—"And he shall cast his eyes upward."] The learned professor *Michaelis*, treating of this place (Not. in de Sacr. Poës. Hebr. Præl. ix.) refers to a passage in the Koran which is similar to it. As it is a very celebrated passage, and on many accounts remarkable, I shall give it here at large, with the same author's farther remarks upon it in another place of his writings. It must be noted here that the learned professor renders נבט *nibbat*, הביט *hibbit*, in this and the parallel place, chap. v. 30, which I translate *he looketh*, by *it thundereth*, from *Schultens*, Orig. Ling. Hebr. Lib. i. cap. 2, of the justness of which rendering I much doubt. This brings the image of Isaiah more near in one circumstance to that of *Mohammed* than it appears to be in my translation:—

"*Labid*, contemporary with *Mohammed*, the last of the seven Arabian poets who had the honour of having their poems, one of each, hung up in the entrance of the temple of Mecca, struck with the sublimity of a passage in the Koran, became a convert to Mohammedism; for he concluded that no man could write in such a manner unless he were Divinely inspired.

"One must have a curiosity to examine a passage which had so great an effect upon *Labid*, It is, I must own, the finest that I know in the whole Koran: but I do not think it will have a second time the like effect, so as to tempt any one of my readers to submit to circumcision. It is in the second chapter, where he is speaking of certain apostates from the faith. 'They are like,' saith he, 'to a man who kindles a light. As soon as it begins to shine, God takes from them the light, and leaves them in darkness that they see nothing. They are deaf, dumb, and blind; and return not into the right way. Or they fare as when a cloud, full of darkness, thunder, and lightning, covers the heaven. When it bursteth, they stop their ears with their fingers, with deadly fear; and God hath the unbelievers in his power. The lightning almost robbeth them of their eyes: as often as it flasheth they go on by its light; and when it vanisheth in darkness, they stand still. If God pleased, they would retain neither hearing nor sight.' That the thought is beautiful, no one will deny; and *Labid*, who had probably a mind to flatter *Mohammed*, was lucky in finding a passage in the Koran so little abounding in poetical beauties, to which his conversion might with any propriety be ascribed. It was well that he went no farther; otherwise his taste for poetry might have made him again an infidel." *Michaelis*, Erpenii Arabische Grammatik abgekurzt, Vorrede, s. 32.

CHAPTER IX

This chapter contains an illustrious prophecy of the Messiah. He is represented under the glorious figure of the sun, or light, rising on a benighted world, and diffusing joy and gladness wherever he sheds his beams, 1–3. *His conquests are astonishing and miraculous, as in the day of Midian; and the peace which they procure is to be permanent, as denoted by the burning of all the implements of war,* 4, 5. *The person and character of this great Deliverer are then set forth in the most magnificent terms which the language of mankind could furnish,* 6. *The extent of his kingdom is declared to be universal, and the duration of it eternal,* 7. *The prophet foretells most awful calamities which were ready to fall upon the Israelites on account of their manifold impieties,* 8–21.

A. M. cir. 3264 B. C. cir. 740 Olymp. X. 1 cir. annum Romuli, Regis Roman., 14

NEVERTHELESS [a]the dimness *shall* not *be* such as *was* in her vexation, when at the [b]first he lightly afflicted the land of Zebulun, and the land of Naphtali, and [c]afterward did more grievously afflict *her by* the way of the sea, beyond Jordan, in Galilee [d]of the nations.

2 [e]The people that walked in darkness have seen a great light: they that dwell in the land of the shadow of death, upon them hath the light shined.

3 Thou hast multiplied the nation, *and* [f]not increased the joy: they joy before thee according to the joy in harvest, *and* as *men* rejoice [g]when they divide the spoil.

A. M. cir. 3264 B. C. cir. 740 Olymp. X. 1 cir. annum Romuli, Regis Roman., 14

4 [h]For thou hast broken the yoke of his burden, and the [i]staff of his shoulder, the rod of his oppressor, as in the day of [k]Midian.

5 [l]For every battle of the warrior *is* with confused noise, and garments rolled in blood; [m]but [n]*this* shall be with burning *and* [o]fuel of fire.

[a]Chap. viii. 22——[b]2 Kings xv. 29; 2 Chron. xvi. 4——[c]Lev. xxvi. 24; 2 Kings xvii. 5, 6; 1 Chron. v. 26——[d]Or, *populous*——[e]Matt. iv. 16; Eph. v. 8, 14——[f]Or, *to him*——[g]Judg. v. 30

[h]Or, *When thou brakest*——[i]Chap. x. 5; xiv. 5——[k]Judg. vii. 22; Psa. lxxxiii. 9; chap. x. 26——[l]Or, *When the whole battle of the warrior was, &c.*——[m]Chap. lxvi. 15, 16——[n]Or, *and it was, &c.*——[o]Heb. *meat*

NOTES ON CHAP. IX

Verse 1. *Dimness*—"Accumulated darkness"] Either מנדחה *menuddechah*, fem. to agree with אפלה *aphelah;* or אפל המנדח *aphel hammenuddach*, alluding perhaps to the palpable Egyptian darkness, Exod. x. 21.

The land of Zebulun] Zebulun, Naphtali, Manasseh, that is, the country of Galilee all round the sea of Gennesareth, were the parts that principally suffered in the first Assyrian invasion under Tiglath-pileser; see 2 Kings xv. 29; 1 Chron. v. 26. And they were the first that enjoyed the blessings of Christ's preaching the Gospel, and exhibiting his miraculous works among them. See *Mede's* Works, p. 101, and 457. This, which makes the *twenty-third* verse of chap. viii. in the Hebrew, is the *first* verse in chap. ix. in our authorized version. Bishop *Lowth* follows the division in the Hebrew.

Verse 3. And *not increased the joy*—"Thou hast increased their joy"] *Eleven* MSS. of *Kennicott's* and *six* of *De Rossi's*, *two* ancient, read לו *lo, it*, according to the Masoretical correction, instead of לא *lo, not.* To the same purpose the *Targum* and *Syriac.*

The joy in harvest] כשמחת בקציר *kesimchath bakkatsir.* For בקציר *bakkatsir one* MS. of *Kennicott's* and *one* of *De Rossi's* have קציר *katsir*, and another הקציר *hakkatsir*, "the harvest;" one of which seems to be the true, reading, as the noun preceding is *in regimine.*

Verse 5. *Every battle of the warrior*—"The greaves of the armed warrior"] סאון סאן *seon soen.* This word, occurring only in this place, is of very doubtful signification. *Schindler* fairly tells us that we may guess at it by the context. The Jews have explained it, by guess I believe, as signifying *battle, conflict:* the *Vulgate* renders it *violenta prædatio.* But it seems as if something was rather meant which was capable of becoming fuel for the fire, together with the garments mentioned in the same sentence. In *Syriac* the word, as a noun, signifies a *shoe*, or a *sandal*, as a learned friend suggested to me some years ago. See Luke xv. 22; Acts xii. 8. I take it, therefore, to mean that part of the armour which covered the legs and feet; and I would render the two words in Latin by *caliga caligati.* The burning of heaps of armour, gathered from the field of battle, as an offering made to the god supposed to be the giver of victory, was a custom that prevailed among some heathen nations; and the Romans used it as an emblem of peace, which perfectly well suits with the design of the prophet in this place. A medal struck by *Vespasian* on finishing his wars both at home and abroad represents the goddess Peace holding an olive branch in one hand, and, with a lighted torch in the other, setting fire to a heap of armour. *Virgil* mentions the custom:—

"—Cum primam aciem Præneste sub ipsa
Stravi, scutorumque incendi victor acervos."
Æn. lib. viii., ver. 561.

"Would heaven, (said he,) my strength and youth recall,
Such as I was beneath Præneste's wall—
Then when I made the foremost foes retire,
And set *whole heaps of conquered shields on fire.*"
DRYDEN.

See *Addison* on Medals, Series ii. 18. And there are notices of some such practice among the Israelites, and other nations of the most early times. God promises to Joshua victory over the kings of Canaan. "To-morrow I will deliver them up all slain before Israel: thou shalt hough their horses, and burn their chariots with fire," Josh. xi. 6. See also Nahum ii. 13. And the psalmist employs this image to express complete victory, and the perfect establishment of peace:—

"He maketh wars to cease, even to the end of the land:
He breaketh the bow, and cutteth the spear in sunder;
And burneth the chariots in the fire."
—Psa. xlvi. 9.

עגלות *agaloth*, properly *plaustra, impedimenta*, the *baggage-wagons:* which however the *Septuagint* and *Vulgate* render *scuta*, "shields;" and the *Chaldee*, "round shields," to show the propriety of that sense of the word from the etymology; which, if admitted, makes the image the same with that used by the Romans.

Ezekiel, chap xxxix. 8-10, in his bold manner, has carried this image to a degree of amplification which I think hardly any other of the Hebrew poets would have attempted. He describes the burning of the arms of the enemy,

A. M. cir. 3264 B. C. cir. 740 Olymp. X. 1 cir. annum Romuli, Regis Roman., 14

6 [p]For unto us a child is born,
unto us a [q]son is given: and
[r]the government shall be upon
his shoulder: and his name shall
be called [s]Wonderful, Counsellor, [t]The
mighty God, The everlasting Father, The
[u]Prince of Peace.

7 Of the increase of *his* government and peace [v]*there shall be* no
end, upon the throne of David,
and upon his kingdom, to order
it, and to establish it with judgment and with
justice from henceforth even for ever. The
[w]zeal of the LORD of hosts will perform this.

A. M. cir. 3264 B. C. cir. 740 Olymp. X. 1 cir. annum Romuli, Regis Roman., 14

[p]Chap. vii. 14; Luke ii. 11——[q]John iii. 16——[r]Matt. xxviii. 18; 1 Cor. xv. 25——[s]Judg. xiii. 18

[t]Tit. ii. 13——[u]Eph. ii. 14——[v]Dan. ii. 44; Luke i. 32, 33——[w]2 Kings xix. 31; chap. xxxvii. 32

in consequence of the complete victory to be obtained by the Israelites over Gog and Magog:—

"Behold, it is come to pass, and it is done,
Saith the Lord JEHOVAH.
This is the day of which I spoke:
And the inhabitants of the cities of Israel shall go forth.
And shall set on fire the armour, and the shield,
And the buckler, and the bow, and the arrows,
And the clubs, and the lances;
And they shall set them on fire for seven years.
And they shall not bear wood from the field;
Neither shall they hew from the forest:
For of the armour shall they make their fires;
And they shall spoil their spoilers,
And they shall plunder their plunderers."

R. D. Kimchi, on this verse says this refers simply to the destruction of the Assyrians. Other battles are fought man against man, and spear against spear; and the garments are rolled in blood through the wounds given and received: but this was with burning, for the angel of the Lord smote them by night, and there was neither sword nor violent commotion, nor blood; they were food for the fire, for the angel of the Lord consumed them.

Verse 6. The government shall *be upon his shoulder*] That is, the ensign of government; the sceptre, the sword, the key, or the like, which was borne upon or hung from the shoulder. See note on chap. xxii. 22.

And his name shall be called] אל גבור *El gibbor*, the prevailing or conquering God.

The everlasting Father—"The Father of the everlasting age"] Or אבי עד *Abi ad*, the Father of eternity. The *Septuagint* have μεγαλης βουλης Αγγελος, "the Messenger of the Great Counsel." But instead of אבי עד *Abi ad*, a MS. of *De Rossi* has אבעזר *Abezer*, the *helping Father;* evidently the corruption of some Jew, who did not like such an evidence in favour of the Christian Messiah.

Prince of Peace] שר שלום *sar shalom*, the Prince of prosperity, the Giver of all blessings.

A MS. of the *thirteenth* century in *Kennicott's* collection has a remarkable addition here. "He shall be a *stumbling-block*, המכשלה; the government is on his shoulder." This reading is nowhere else acknowledged, as far as I know.

Verse 7. *Of the increase*] In the common *Hebrew* Bibles, and in many MSS., this word is written with the *close* or final ם לםרבה. But in *twelve* of *Kennicott's* MSS., and *twelve* of *De Rossi's*, it is written with the open מ *mem;* but here it is supposed to contain mysteries, viz., that Jerusalem shall be *shut up, closed*, and *confined*, till the days of the Messiah.

This is an illustrious prophecy of the *incarnation* of Christ, with an enumeration of those *characters* in which he stands most nearly related to mankind as their Saviour; and of others by which his infinite *majesty* and *Godhead* are shown. He shall appear as a *child, born of a woman*, born as a Jew, *under the law*, but not in the way of ordinary generation. He is a *Son given*—the human nature, in which the fulness of the Godhead was to dwell, being produced by the creative energy of the Holy Ghost in the womb of the Virgin. See Matt. i. 20, 21, 23, 25, and Luke i. 35, and Isa. vii. 14, and the notes on those passages. As being *God manifested in the flesh*, he was *wonderful* in his conception, birth, preaching, miracles, sufferings, death, resurrection, and ascension; *wonderful* in his person, and *wonderful* in his working. He is the *Counsellor* that expounds the law; shows its origin, nature, and claims; instructs, pleads for the guilty; and ever appears in the presence of God for men. He is the *mighty God;* God essentially and *efficiently prevailing* against his enemies, and destroying ours. He is the *Father of eternity;* the Origin of all being, and the Cause of the existence, and particularly the Father, of the spirits of all flesh. The *Prince of peace*—not only the *Author* of peace, and the Dispenser of peace, but also he that *rules* by *peace*, whose rule tends always to *perfection*, and produces *prosperity. Of the increase of his government*—this Prince has a *government*, for he has all power both in heaven and in earth: and his government *increases*, and is daily more and more *extended*, and will continue till all things are put under his feet. His kingdom is *ordered*—every act of government regulated according to wisdom and goodness; is *established* so securely as not to be overthrown; and administered in *judgment* and *justice*, so as to manifest his wisdom, righteousness, goodness, and truth. Reader, *such* is that Jesus who came into the world to save sinners! Trust in HIM!

Chap. ix. 8-chap. x. 4. This whole passage reduced to its proper and entire form, and healed of the dislocation which it suffers by the absurd division of the chapters, makes a distinct prophecy, and a just poem, remarkable for the regularity of its disposition and the elegance of its plan. It has no relation to the preceding or following prophecy; though the parts, violently torn asunder, have been, on the one side and the other, patched on to them. Those relate principally to the kingdom of Judah; this is addressed exclusively to the kingdom of Israel. The subject of it is a denunciation of vengeance awaiting their crimes. It is divided

A. M. cir. 3266
B. C. cir. 738
Olymp. X. 3
cir. annum
Romuli, Regis
Roman., 16

8 The Lord sent a word into
Jacob, and it hath lighted upon
Israel.
9 And all the people shall
know, *even* Ephraim and the inhabitant of
Samaria, that say in the pride and stoutness
of heart,
10 The bricks are fallen down, but we will
build with hewn stones: the sycamores are
cut down, but we will change *them into* cedars.
11 Therefore the LORD shall set up the
adversaries of Rezin against him,
and [x]join his enemies together;
12 The Syrians before and the
Philistines behind; and they
shall devour Israel [y]with open mouth. [z]For
all this his anger is not turned away, but his
hand *is* stretched out still.
13 For [a]the people turneth not unto him
that smiteth them, neither do they seek the
LORD of hosts.
14 Therefore the LORD will cut off from

[x]Heb. *mingle*——[y]Heb. *with whole mouth*

[z]Chap. v. 25; x. 4; Jer. iv. 8——[a]Jer. v. 3; Hos. vii. 10

into *four* parts, each threatening the particular punishment of some grievous offence—of their pride, of their perseverance in their vices, of their impiety, and of their injustice. To which is added a general denunciation of a farther reserve of Divine wrath, contained in a distich, before used by the prophet on a like occasion, chap. v. 25, and here repeated after each part. This makes the intercalary verse of the poem; or, as we call it, the burden of the song.

"Post hoc comma (cap. ix. 4) interponitur spatium unius lineæ, in Cod. 2 et 3: idemque observatur in 245. in quo nullum est spatium ad finem capitis ix." *Kennicott*, Var. Lect.

"After this clause (chap. ix. 4) is interposed the space of one line in Cod. 2 and 3. The same is likewise observed in Cod. 245, in which no space exists at the end of chap. ix."

Verse 8. *Lord*—"JEHOVAH"] For אדני *Adonai*, *thirty* MSS. of *Kennicott's*, and many of *De Rossi's*, and *three* editions, read יהוה *Yehovah*.

Verse 9. *Pride and stoutness of heart*—"Carry themselves haughtily"] וידעו *veyadeu*, "and they shall know;" so ours and the Versions in general. But what is it that they shall know? The verb stands destitute of its object; and the sense is imperfect. The *Chaldee* is the only one, as far as I can find, that expresses it otherwise. He renders the verb in this place by ואתרברבו *veithrabrabu*, "they exalt themselves, or carry themselves haughtily; the same word by which he renders גבהו *gabehu*, chap. iii. 16. He seems, therefore, in this place to have read ויגבהו *vaiyigbehu*, which agrees perfectly well with what follows, and clears up the difficulty. Archbishop *Secker* conjectured וידברו *vayedabberu*, referring it to לאמר *lemor*, in the next verse, which shows that he was not satisfied with the present reading. *Houbigant* reads וירעו *vaiyereu, et pravi facti sunt*, they are become wicked, which is found in a MS.; but I prefer the reading of the *Chaldee*, which suits much better with the context.

Houbigant approves of this reading; but it is utterly unsupported by any evidence from antiquity: it is a mere mistake of ר *resh* for ד *daleth;* and I am surprised that it should be favoured by *Houbigant*.

Verse 10. *The bricks*] "The eastern bricks," says Sir *John Chardin*, (see *Harmer's* Observ. I., p. 176,) "are only clay well moistened with water, and mixed with straw, and dried in the sun." So that their walls are commonly no better than our mud walls; see *Maundrell*, p. 124. That straw was a necessary part in the composition of this sort of bricks, to make the parts of the clay adhere together, appears from Exod. v. These bricks are properly opposed to hewn stone, so greatly superior in beauty and durableness. The sycamores, which, as *Jerome* on the place says, are timber of little worth, with equal propriety are opposed to the cedars. "As the grain and texture of the sycamore is remarkably coarse and spongy, it could therefore stand in no competition at all (as it is observed, Isa. ix. 10) with the cedar, for beauty and ornament."—*Shaw*, Supplement to Travels, p. 96. We meet with the same opposition of cedars to sycamores, 1 Kings x. 27, where Solomon is said to have made silver as the stones, and cedars as the sycamores in the vale for abundance. By this *mashal*, or figurative and sententious speech, they boast that they shall easily be able to repair their present losses, suffered perhaps by the first Assyrian invasion under Tiglath-pileser; and to bring their affairs to a more flourishing condition than ever.

Some of the *bricks* mentioned above lie before me. They were brought from the site of ancient Babylon. The *straw* is *visible, kneaded with the clay;* they are very *hard*, and evidently were *dried in the sun;* for they are very easily *dissolved* in *water*.

Verse 11. *The adversaries of Rezin against him*—"The princes of Retsin against him"] For צרי *tsarey, enemies, Houbigant*, by conjecture, reads שרי *sarey, princes;* which is confirmed by *thirty* of *Kennicott's* and *De Rossi's* MSS., (two ancient,) one of my own, ancient; and *nine* more have צ *tsaddi*, upon a rasure, and therefore had probably at first שרי *sarey*. The princes of Retsin, the late ally of Israel, that is, the Syrians, expressly named in the next verse, shall now be excited against Israel.

The *Septuagint* in this place give us another variation; for רצין *Retsin*, they read הר ציון *har tsiyon*, ορος Σιων, *Mount Sion*, of which this may be the sense; but JEHOVAH shall set up the adversaries of Mount Sion against him, (i. e., against Israel,) and will *strengthen* his enemies together; the Syrians, the Philistines, who are called the adversaries of Mount Sion. See *Simonis* Lex. in voce סכך *sachach*.

Verse 12. *With open mouth*—"On every side"] בכל פה *bechol peh*, in every corner, in every part of their country, pursuing them to the remotest extremities, and the most retired parts. So the *Chaldee* בכל אתר *bechol athar*, in every place.

Verse 14. *In one day.*] *Thirteen* MSS. of

A. M. cir. 3266
B. C. cir. 738
Olymp. X. 3
cir. annum
Romuli, Regis
Roman., 16

Israel head and tail, branch and
rush, [b]in one day.
15 The ancient and honourable, he *is* the head; and the prophet that teacheth lies, he *is* the tail.
16 For [c]the [d]leaders of this people cause
them to err; and [e]*they that are* led of them
are [f]destroyed.
17 Therefore the Lord [g]shall have no joy
in their young men, neither shall have mercy
on their fatherless and widows: [h]for every one
is a hypocrite and an evil doer, and every
mouth speaketh [i]folly. [k]For all this his
anger is not turned away, but his hand *is*
stretched out still.
18 For wickedness [l]burneth as the fire: it
shall devour the briers and thorns,
and shall kindle in the thickets of
the forest, and they shall mount
up *like* the lifting up of smoke.
19 Through the wrath of the LORD of hosts
is [m]the land darkened, and the people shall
be as the [n]fuel of the fire: [o]no man shall
spare his brother.
20 And he shall [p]snatch on the right hand,
and be hungry; and he shall eat on the left
hand, [q]and they shall not be satisfied: [r]they
shall eat every man the flesh of his own arm:
21 Manasseh, Ephraim; and Ephraim, Manasseh: *and* they together *shall be* against
Judah. [s]For all this his anger is not turned
away, but his hand *is* stretched out still.

[b]Chap. x. 17; Rev. xviii. 8——[c]Chap. iii. 12——[d]Or, *they that call them blessed*——[e]Or, *they that are called blessed of them*——[f]Heb. *swallowed up*——[g]Psa. cxlvii. 10, 11——[h]Mic. vii. 2——[i]Or, *villany*

[k]Ver. 12, 21; chap. v. 25; x. 4——[l]Chap. x. 17; Mal. iv. 1——[m]Chap. viii. 22——[n]Heb. *meat*——[o]Mic. vii. 2, 6——[p]Heb. *cut*——[q]Lev. xxvi. 26——[r]Chap. xlix. 26; Jer. xix. 9——[s]Ver. 12, 17; chap. v. 25; x. 4

Kennicott and *De Rossi* read ביום *beyom*, in a day; and another has a rasure in the place of the letter ב *beth*.

Verse 17. *The Lord*—"JEHOVAH"] For אדני *Adonai*, a great number of MSS. read יהוה *Yehovah*.

Verse 18. *For wickedness*] Wickedness rageth like a fire, destroying and laying waste the nation: but it shall be its own destruction, by bringing down the fire of God's wrath, which shall burn up the briers and the thorns; that is, the wicked themselves. Briers and thorns are an image frequently applied in Scripture, when set on fire, to the rage of the wicked; violent, yet impotent, and of no long continuance. "They are extinct as the fire of thorns," Psa. cxviii. 12. To the wicked themselves, as useless and unprofitable, proper objects of God's wrath, to be burned up, or driven away by the wind. "As thorns cut up they shall be consumed in the fire," Isa. xxxiii. 12. Both these ideas seem to be joined in Psa. lviii. 9:—

"Before your pots shall feel the thorn,
As well the green as the dry, the tempest shall bear them away."

The green and the dry is a proverbial expression, meaning all sorts of them, good and bad, great and small, &c. So Ezekiel: "Behold, I will kindle a fire, and it shall devour every green tree, and every dry tree," chap. xx. 47. *D'Herbelot* quotes a Persian poet describing a pestilence under the image of a conflagration: "This was a lightning that, falling upon a forest, consumed there the green wood with the dry." See *Harmer's* Observations, Vol. II., p. 187.

Verse 20. *The flesh of his own arm*—"The flesh of his neighbour"] "Του βραχιονος του αδελφου αυτου, the *Septuagint Alexand. Duplex versio, quarum altera legit* רעו *reo, quæ vox extat*, Jer. vi. 21. *Nam* רע *rea*, αδελφος, Gen. xliii. 33. *Recte ni fallor*."—SECKER. I add to this excellent remark, that the *Chaldee* manifestly reads רעו *reo, his neighbour*, not זרעו *zeroo, his arm;* for he renders it by קריביה *karibeyh, his neighbour*. And Jeremiah has the very same expression: ואיש בשר רעהו יאכלו *veish besar reehu yochelu*, "and every one shall eat the flesh of his neighbour," chap. xix. 9. This observation, I think, gives the true reading and sense of this place: and the context strongly confirms it by explaining the general idea by particular instances, in the following verse: "Every man shall devour the flesh of his neighbour;" that is, they shall harass and destroy one another. "Manasseh shall destroy Ephraim, and Ephraim, Manasseh;" which two tribes were most closely connected both in blood and situation as brothers and neighbours; "and both of them in the midst of their own dissensions shall agree in preying upon Judah." The common reading, "shall devour the flesh of his own *arm*," in connexion with what follows, seems to make either an inconsistency, or an anticlimax; whereas by this correction the following verse becomes an elegant illustration of the foregoing.—L.

CHAPTER X

God's judgments against oppressive rulers, 1–4. *The prophet foretells the invasion of Sennacherib, and the destruction of his army. That mighty monarch is represented as a rod in the hand of God to correct his people for their sins; and his ambitious purposes, contrary to his own intentions, are made subservient to the great designs of Providence,* 5–11. *Having accomplished this work, the Almighty takes account of his impious vauntings,* 12–14; *and threatens utter destruction to the small and great of his army, represented by the thorns, and the glory of the forest,* 15–19. *This leads the prophet to comfort his countrymen with the promise of this signal interposition of God in their favour,* 20–27. *Brief description of the march of Sennacherib towards*

Jerusalem, and of the alarm and terror which he spread every where as he hastened forward, 28–32. *The spirit and rapidity of the description is admirably suited to the subject. The affrighted people are seen fleeing, and the eager invader pursuing; the cries of one city are heard by those of another; and groan swiftly succeeds to groan, till at length the rod is lifted over the last citadel. In this critical situation, however, the promise of a Divine interposition is seasonably renewed. The scene instantly changes; the uplifted arm of this mighty conqueror is at once arrested and laid low by the hand of heaven; the forest of Lebanon, (a figure by which the immense Assyrian host is elegantly pointed out, is hewn down by the axe of the Divine vengeance; and the mind is equally pleased with the equity of the judgment, and the beauty and majesty of the description,* 33, 34.

A. M. cir. 3291
B. C. cir. 713
Olymp. XVI. 4
cir. annum
NumæPompilii,
R. Roman., 3

WO unto them that [a]decree unrighteous decrees, and [b]that write grievousness *which* they have prescribed;

2 To turn aside the needy from judgment, and to take away the right from the poor of my people, that widows may be their prey, and *that* they may rob the fatherless!

3 And [c]what will ye do in [d]the day of visitation, and in the desolation *which* shall come from far? to whom will ye flee for help? and where will ye leave your glory?

4 Without me they shall bow down under the prisoners, and they shall fall under the slain. [e]For all this his anger is not turned away, but his hand *is* stretched out still.

5 [f]O [g]Assyrian, [h]the rod of mine anger, [i]and the staff in their hand is mine indignation.

6 I will send him against [k]a hypocritical nation, and against the people of my wrath will I [l]give him a charge, to take the spoil, and to take the prey, and [m]to tread them down like the mire of the streets.

7 [n]Howbeit he meaneth not so, neither doth his heart think so; but *it is* in his heart to destroy and cut off nations not a few.

A. M. cir. 3291
B. C. cir. 713
Olymp. XVI. 4
cir. annum
NumæPompilii,
R. Roman., 3

8 [o]For he saith, *Are* not my princes altogether kings?

9 *Is* not [p]Calno [q]as Carchemish? *is* not Hamath as Arpad? *is* not Samaria as [r]Damascus?

10 As my hand hath found the kingdoms of the idols, and whose graven images did excel them of Jerusalem and of Samaria;

11 Shall I not, as I have done unto Samaria and her idols, so do to Jerusalem and her idols?

12 Wherefore it shall come to pass, *that* when the Lord hath performed his whole work [s]upon Mount Zion, and on Jerusalem, [t]I will [u]punish the fruit [v]of the stout heart of the king of Assyria, and the glory of his high looks.

13 [w]For he saith, By the strength of my hand I have done *it*, and by my wisdom; for

[a]Psa. lviii. 2; xciv. 20——[b]Or, *to the writers that write grievousness*——[c]Job xxxi. 14——[d]Hos. ix. 7; Luke xix. 44——[e]Chap. v. 25; ix. 12, 17, 21——[f]Or, *Wo to the Assyrian*——[g]Heb. *Asshur*——[h]Jer. li. 20——[i]Or, *though*——[k]Chap. xix. 17——[l]Jer. xxxiv. 22——[m]Heb. *to lay them a treading*

[n]Gen. l. 20; Mic. iv. 12——[o]2 Kings xviii. 24, 33, &c.; xix. 10, &c.——[p]Amos vi. 2——[q]2 Chron. xxxv. 20——[r]2 Kings xvi. 9——[s]2 Kings xix. 31——[t]Jer. l. 18——[u]Heb. *visit upon*——[v]Heb. *of the greatness of the heart*——[w]Isa. xxxvii. 24; Ezek. xxviii. 4, &c.; Dan. iv. 30

NOTES ON CHAP. X

Verse 2. *My people*] Instead of עמי *ammi*, my people, many MSS., and one of my own, ancient, read עמו *ammo*, his people. But this is manifestly a corruption.

Verse 4. *Without me*] That is, without my aid: they shall be taken captive even by the captives, and shall be subdued even by the vanquished. "The י *yod* in בלתי *bilti* is a pronoun, as in Hos. xiii. 4."—*Kimchi* on the place. One MS. has לבלתי *lebilti*.

As the people had hitherto lived *without God* in worship and obedience; so they should now be *without* his help, and should perish in their transgressions.

Verse 5. *O Assyrian*—"Ho to the Assyrian"] Here begins a new and distinct prophecy, continued to the end of the *twelfth* chapter: and it appears from ver. 9-11 of this chapter, that this prophecy was delivered after the taking of Samaria by Shalmaneser; which was in the sixth year of the reign of Hezekiah: and as the former part of it foretells the invasion of Sennacherib, and the destruction of his army, which makes the whole subject of this chapter, it must have been delivered before the *fourteenth* of the same reign.

The staff in their hand—"The staff in whose hand"] The word הוא *hu*, the staff *itself*, in this place seems to embarrass the sentence. I omit it on the authority of the Alexandrine copy of the *Septuagint: nine* MSS., (*two* ancient,) and one of my own, ancient, for ומטה הוא *umatteh hu*, read מטהו *mattehu, his staff.* Archbishop *Secker* was not satisfied with the present reading. He proposes another method of clearing up the sense, by reading ביום *beyom, in the day*, instead of בידם *beyadam, in their hand:* "And he is a staff *in the day* of mine indignation."

Verse 12. *The Lord*—"JEHOVAH"] For אדני *Adonai, fourteen* MSS. and *three editions* read יהוה *Yehovah.*

The fruit—"The effect"] "פרי *peri*, f. צבי *tsebi*, vid. xiii. 19, *sed confer*, Prov. i. 31; xxxi. 16, 31."—SECKER. The *Chaldee* renders the word פרי *peri* by עיבדי *obadey, works;* which seems to be the true sense; and I have followed it.—L.

Verse 13. *Like a valiant* man—"Strongly

A. M. cir. 3291 B. C. cir. 713 Olymp. XVI. 4 cir. annum NumæPompilii, R. Roman., 3

I am prudent: and I have removed the bounds of the people,
and have robbed their treasures,
and I have put down the inhabitants [x]like a valiant *man:*
14 And [y]my hand hath found as a nest the
riches of the people: and as one gathereth
eggs *that are* left, have I gathered all the
earth; and there was none that moved the
wing, or opened the mouth, or peeped.
15 Shall [z]the axe boast itself against him
that heweth therewith? *or* shall the saw magnify itself against him that shaketh it? [a]as if
the rod should shake *itself* against them that
lift it up, *or* as if the staff should lift up
[b]*itself, as if it were* no wood.
16 Therefore shall the Lord, the Lord of
hosts, send among his [c]fat ones leanness; and
under his glory he shall kindle a burning like
the burning of a fire.
17 And the light of Israel
shall be for a fire, and his Holy
One for a flame: [d]and it shall
burn and devour his thorns and
his briers in one day;
18 And shall consume the glory of his forest,
and of [e]his fruitful field, [f]both soul and body;
and they shall be as when a standard bearer
fainteth.
19 And the rest of the trees of his forest
shall be [g]few, that a child may write them.
20 And it shall come to pass in that day,
that the remnant of Israel, and such as are
escaped of the house of Jacob, [h]shall no more
again stay upon him that smote them; but
shall stay upon the LORD, the Holy One of
Israel, in truth.
21 [i]The remnant shall return, *even* the remnant of Jacob, unto the mighty God.
22 [k]For though thy people Israel be as the

[x]Or, *like many people*——[y]Job xxxi. 25——[z]Jer. li. 20 [a]Or, *as if a rod should shake them that lift it up*——[b]Or, that which is *not wood*——[c]Chap. v. 17——[d]Chap. ix. 18; xxvii. 4

[e]2 Kings xix. 23——[f]Heb. *from the soul, and even to the flesh*——[g]Heb. *number*——[h]See 2 Kings xvi. 7; 2 Chronicles xxviii. 20——[i]Chapter vii. 3——[k]Rom. ix. 27

seated." *Twelve* MSS. agree with the Keri in reading כביר *kabbir*, without the א *aleph.* And *Sal. ben Melec* and *Kimchi* thus explain it: "them who dwelled in a great and strong place I have brought down to the ground."

Verse 15. *No wood*—"Its master."] I have here given the meaning, without attempting to keep to the expression of the original, לא עץ *lo ets*, "the no-wood;" that which is not wood like itself, but of a quite different and superior nature. The Hebrews have a peculiar way of joining the negative particle לא *lo* to a noun, to signify in a strong manner a total negation of the thing expressed by the noun.

"How hast thou given help (ללא כח *lelo choach*) to the no-strength?
And saved the arm (לא עז *lo oz*) of the no-power?
How hast, thou given counsel (ללא חכמה *lelo chochmah*) to the no-wisdom?"
Job xxvi. 2, 3.

That is, to the man totally deprived of strength, power, and wisdom.

"Ye that rejoice (ללא דבר *lelo dabar*) in nothing." Amos vi. 13.

That is, in your fancied strength, which is none at all, a mere nonentity.

"For I am God, (ולא איש *velo ish,*) and no-man;
The Holy One in the midst of thee, yet do not frequent cities." Hos. xi. 9.

"And the Assyrian shall fall by a sword (לא איש *lo ish*) of no-man;
And a sword of (לא אדם *lo adam*) no-mortal, shall devour him." Isa. xxxi. 8.

"Wherefore do ye weigh out your silver (בלוא לחם *belo lechem*) for the no-bread."
Isa. lv. 2.

So here לא עץ *lo ets* means him who is far from being an inert piece of wood, but is an animated and active being; not an instrument, but an agent.

Verse 16. *The Lord*—"JEHOVAH."] For אדני *Adonai, fifty-two* MSS., *eleven* editions, and two of my own, ancient, read יהוה *Yehovah,* as in other cases.

And under his glory] That is, all that he could boast of as great and strong in his army, (*Sal. ben Melec in loc.,*) expressed afterwards, ver. 18, by the glory of his forest, and of his fruitful field.

Verse 17. *And it shall burn and devour his thorns*—"And he shall burn and consume his thorn."] The briers and thorns are the common people; the glory of his forest are the nobles and those of highest rank and importance. See note on chap. ix. 17, and compare Ezek. xx. 47. The fire of God's wrath shall destroy them, both great and small; it shall consume them *from the soul to the flesh;* a proverbial expression; *soul and body,* as we say; it shall consume them entirely and altogether; and the few that escape shall be looked upon as having escaped from the most imminent danger; "as a firebrand plucked out of the fire," Amos iv. 11; ὡς δια πυρος, *so as by fire,* 1 Cor. iii. 15; as a man when a house is burning is forced to make his escape by running through the midst of the fire.

I follow here the reading of the *Septuagint,* כמאש נסס *kemash noses,* ὡς ὁ φευγων απω φλογος χαιομενης, *as he who flees from the burning flame. Symmachus* also renders the latter word by φευγων, *flying.*

Verse 21. *The remnant shall return—unto*

A. M. cir. 3291 B. C. cir. 713 Olymp. XVI. 4 cir. annum NumæPompilii, R. Roman., 3

sand of the sea, [l]*yet* a remnant
[m]of them shall return: [n]the consumption decreed shall overflow
[o]with righteousness.

23 [p]For the Lord GOD of hosts shall make
a consumption, even determined, in the midst
of all the land.

24 Therefore thus saith the Lord GOD of
hosts, O my people that dwellest in Zion, [q]be
not afraid of the Assyrian: he shall smite
thee with a rod, [r]and shall lift up his staff
against thee, after the manner of [s]Egypt.

25 [t]For yet a very little while, [u]and the indignation shall cease, and mine
anger in their destruction.

26 And the LORD of hosts shall
stir up [v]a scourge for him according to the slaughter of [w]Midian at the
rock of Oreb: and [x]*as* his rod *was* upon
the sea, so shall he lift it up after the manner of Egypt.

27 And it shall come to pass in that day,
that [y]his burden [z]shall be taken away from
off thy shoulder, and his yoke from off thy
neck, and the yoke shall be destroyed because of [a]the anointing.

[l]Chap. vi. 13——[m]Heb. *in* or *among*——[n]Chap. xxviii. 22——[o]Or, *in*——[p]Chap. xxviii. 22; Dan. ix. 27; Rom. ix. 28——[q]Chap. xxxvii. 6——[r]Or, *but he shall lift up his staff for thee*——[s]Exod. xiv

[t]Chap. liv. 7——[u]Dan. xi. 36——[v]2 Kings xix. 35 [w]Judg. vii. 25; chap. ix. 4——[x]Exod. xiv. 26, 27 [y]Chap. xiv. 25——[z]Heb. *shall remove*——[a]Psa. cv. 15; Dan. ix. 24; 1 John ii. 20

the mighty God.] אל גבור *El gibbor*, the *mighty* or *conquering God;* the Messiah, the same person mentioned in ver. 6 of the preceding chapter.

Verse 22. *For though thy people Israel*] I have endeavoured to keep to the letter of the text as nearly as I can in this obscure passage; but it is remarkable that neither the *Septuagint*, nor St. *Paul*, Rom. ix. 28, who, except in a few words of no great importance, follows them nearly in this place, nor any one of the ancient Versions, take any notice of the word שוטף *shoteph, overflowing;* which seems to give an idea not easily reconcilable with those with which it is here joined. *I. S. Mœrlius* (Schol. Philolog. ad Selecta S. Cod. loca) conjectures that the two last letters of this word are by mistake transposed, and that the true reading is שפט *shophet, judging*, with strict justice. The *Septuagint* might think this sufficiently expressed by *εν δικαιοσυνῃ*, *in righteousness.* One MS., with St. *Paul* and *Septuagint Alex.*, omits בו *bo* in ver. 22; *sixty-nine* of *Kennicott's* and *seventeen* of *De Rossi's* MSS. and *eight* editions, omit כל *col, all*, in ver. 23; and so St. *Paul*, Rom. ix. 28.

The learned Dr. *Bagot*, dean of Christ Church, Oxford, afterwards Bishop of Bristol and Norwich, in some observations on this place, which he has been so kind as to communicate to me, and which will appear in their proper light when he himself shall give them to the public, renders the word כליון *kilayon* by *accomplishment*, and makes it refer to the predictions of Moses; the blessing and the curse which he laid before the people; both conditional, and depending on their future conduct. They had by their disobedience incurred those judgments which were now to be fully executed upon them. His translation is, *The accomplishment determined overflows with justice; for it is accomplished, and that which is determined the Lord God of hosts doeth in the midst of the land.*—L. Some think that the words might be paraphrased thus: The determined destruction of the Jews shall overflow with righteousness, (צדקה *tsedakah,*) justification, the consequence of the Gospel of Christ being preached and believed on in the world. After the destruction of Jerusalem this word or doctrine of the Lord had free course,—did *run*, and was glorified.

Verse 24. *After the manner of Egypt*—"In the way of Egypt."] I think there is a designed ambiguity in these words. Sennacherib, soon after his return from his Egyptian expedition, which, I imagine, took him up three years, invested Jerusalem. He is represented by the prophet as lifting up his rod in his march from Egypt, and threatening the people of God, as Pharaoh and the Egyptians had done when they pursued them to the Red Sea. But God in his turn will lift up his rod over the sea, as he did at that time, in the way, or after the manner, of Egypt; and as Sennacherib has imitated the Egyptians in his threats, and came full of rage against them from the same quarter; so God will act over again the same part that he had taken formerly in Egypt, and overthrow their enemies in as signal a manner. It was all to be, both the attack and the deliverance, בדרך *bederech*, or כדרך *kederech*, as a MS. has it in each place, *in the way*, or *after the manner*, of Egypt.

Verse 25. *The indignation*—"Mine indignation."] *Indignatio mea, Vulg.* *ἡ οργη, Sept.* *Μου ἡ οργη ἡ κατα σου*, MS. *Pachom.* *Μου ἡ οργη κατα σου*, MS. I. D. II. So that זעמי *zaami*, or הזעם *hazzaam*, as one MS. has it, seems to be the true reading.

Verse 26. *And* as *his rod* was *upon the sea*—"And like his rod which he lifted up over the sea"] The Jewish interpreters suppose here an ellipsis of כ *ke*, the particle of similitude, before מטהו *mattehu*, to be supplied from the line above; so that here are two similitudes, one comparing the destruction of the Assyrians to the slaughter of the Midianites at the rock of Oreb; the other to that of the Egyptians at the Red Sea. *Aben Ezra, Kimchi, Sal. ben Melec.*

Verse 27. *From off thy shoulder*] Bishop *Lowth* translates the whole verse thus:—

"And it shall come to pass in that day,
His burden shall be removed from off thy shoulder;
And his yoke off thy neck:
Yea, the yoke shall perish from off your shoulders."

A. M. cir. 3291
B. C. cir. 713
Olymp. XVI. 4
cir. annum
NumæPompilii,
R. Roman., 3

28 He is come to Aiath, he is
passed to Migron; at Michmash
he hath laid up his carriages:
29 They are gone over the
[b]passage: they have taken up their lodging at
Geba; Ramah is afraid; [c]Gibeah of Saul
is fled.
30 [d]Lift up thy voice, O daughter [e]of Gallim: cause it to be heard unto [f]Laish, [g]O
poor Anathoth.
31 [h]Madmenah is removed; the inhabitants
of Gebim gather themselves to flee.
32 As yet shall he remain [i]at
Nob that day: he shall [k]shake
his hand *against* the mount of
[l]the daughter of Zion, the hill
of Jerusalem.
33 Behold, the Lord, the LORD of hosts,
shall lop the bough with terror: and [m]the
high ones of stature *shall be* hewn down, and
the haughty shall be humbled.
34 And he shall cut down the thickets of
the forest with iron, and Lebanon shall fall
[n]by a mighty one.

[b]1 Sam. xiii. 23——[c]1 Sam. xi. 4——[d]Heb. *cry shrill with thy voice*——[e]1 Sam. xxv. 44——[f]Judg. xviii. 7 [g]Josh. xxi. 18

[h]Josh. xv. 31——[i]1 Sam. xxi. 1; xxii. 19; Neh. xi. 32 [k]Chap. xiii. 2——[l]Chap. xxxvii. 22——[m]See Amos ii. 9——[n]Or, *mightily*

On which he gives us the following note: I follow here the *Septuagint*, who for מפני שמן *mippeney shamen* read משכמיכם *mishshichmeychem*, *απο των ωμων ὑμων*, *from your shoulders*, not being able to make any good sense out of the present reading. I will add here the marginal conjectures of Archbishop *Secker*, who appears, like all others, to have been at a loss for a probable interpretation of the text as it now stands. "δ. *leg.* שכם shakam; *forte legend.* מבני שמן mibbeney shamen, *vide* cap. v. 1. Zech. iv. 14: *Et possunt intelligi Judœi uncti Dei*, Psa. cv. 15, *vel Assyrii*, משמנים mishmannim, *hic* ver. 16, *ut dicat propheta depulsum iri jugum ab his impositum: sed hoc durius. Vel potest legi* מפני שמי mippeney shami."

Verse 28. *He is come to Aiath*] A description of the march of Sennacherib's army approaching Jerusalem in order to invest it, and of the terror and confusion spreading and increasing through the several places as he advanced; expressed with great brevity, but finely diversified. The places here mentioned are all in the neighbourhood of Jerusalem; from *Ai* northward, to *Nob* westward of it; from which last place he might probably have a prospect of Mount *Sion*. *Anathoth* was within three Roman miles of Jerusalem, according to *Eusebius*, *Jerome* and *Josephus*. Onomast. Loc. Hebr. et Antiq. Jud. x. 7, 3. *Nob* was probably still nearer. And it should seem from this passage of Isaiah that Sennacherib's army was destroyed near the latter of these places. In coming out of Egypt he might perhaps join the rest of his army at *Ashdod*, after the taking of that place, which happened about that time, (see chap. xx.;) and march from thence near the coast by *Lachish* and *Libnah*, which lay in his way from south to north, and both which he invested till he came to the north-west of Jerusalem, crossing over to the north of it, perhaps by *Joppa* and *Lydda;* or still more north through the plain of *Esdraelon.*

Verse 29. *They are gone over the passage*—"They have passed the strait"] The strait here mentioned is that of Michmas, a very narrow passage between two sharp hills or rocks, (see 1 Sam. xiv. 4, 5,) where a great army might have been opposed with advantage by a very inferior force. The author of the Book of Judith might perhaps mean this pass, at least among others: "Charging them to keep the passages of the hill country, for by them there was an entrance into Judea; and it was easy to stop them that would come up, because the passage was strait for two men at the most," Judith iv. 7. The enemies having passed the strait without opposition, shows that all thoughts of making a stand in the open country were given up, and that their only resource was in the strength of the city.

Their lodging] The sense seems necessarily to require that we read למו *lamo, to them*, instead of לנו *lanu, to us*. These two words are in other places mistaken one for the other. Thus chap. xliv. 7, for למו *lamo*, read לנו *lanu*. with the *Chaldee;* and in the same manner Psa. lxiv. 6, with the *Syriac*, and Psa. lxxx. 7, on the authority of the *Septuagint* and *Syriac*, besides the necessity of the sense.

Verse 30. *Cause it to be heard unto Laish, O poor Anathoth*—"Hearken unto her, O Laish; answer her, O Anathoth!"] I follow in this the *Syriac* Version. The prophet plainly alludes to the name of the place, and with a peculiar propriety, if it had its name from its remarkable echo. "ענתות anathoth, *responsiones: eadem ratio nominis, quœ in* בית ענת beith anath, *locus echus; nam hodienum ejus rudera ostenduntur in valle, scil. in medio montium, ut referunt Robertus in Itiner.* p. 70, *et Monconnysius*, p. 301." *Simonis Onomasticon Vet. Test.*—L. *Anathoth*—Answers, replies; for the same reason that Bethany, בית ענת *beith anath*, had its name, *the house of echo;* the remains of which are still shown in the valley, i. e., among the mountains.

Verse 33. *Shall lop the bough with terror*] פארה *purah;* but פורה *purah, wine-press*, is the reading of *twenty-six* of *Kennicott's* and *twenty-three* of *De Rossi's* MSS., *four* ancient editions, with *Symmachus*, *Theodotion*, and the *Chaldee.*

Verse 34. *Lebanon shall fall by a mighty one*] באדיר *beaddir*, the angel of the Lord, who smote them, *Kimchi*. And so *Vitringa* understands it. Others translate, "The high cedars of Lebanon shall fall:" but the king of Assyria is the person who shall be overthrown.

CHAPTER XI

The Messiah represented as a slender twig shooting up from the root of an old withered stem, which tender plant, so extremely weak in its first appearance, should nevertheless become fruitful and mighty, 1–4. *Great equity of the Messiah's government,* 5. *Beautiful assemblages of images by which the great peace and happiness of his kingdom are set forth,* 6–8. *The extent of his dominion shall be ultimately that of the whole habitable globe,* 9. *The prophet, borrowing his imagery from the exodus from Egypt, predicts, with great majesty of language, the future restoration* of the outcasts of Israel and the dispersed of Judah, (*viz., the whole of the* twelve *tribes of Israel,*) *from their several dispersions, and also that blessed period when both* Jews *and* Gentiles *shall assemble under the banner of Jesus, and zealously unite in extending the limits of his kingdom,* 10–16.

A. M. cir. 3291
B. C. cir. 713
Olymp. XVI. 4
cir. annum
NumæPompilii,
R. Roman., 3

AND [a]there shall come forth
a rod out of the stem of
[b]Jesse, and [c]a Branch shall grow
out of his roots:
2 [d]And the Spirit of the LORD shall rest
upon him, the spirit of wisdom and understanding, the spirit of counsel and might, the
spirit of knowledge and of the fear of the
LORD;
3 And shall make him of quick [e]under-
standing in the fear of the LORD: and he shall
not judge after the sight of his eyes, neither
reprove after the hearing of his ears;
4 But [f]with righteousness shall
he judge the poor, and [g]reprove
with equity for the meek of the
earth: and he shall [h]smite the
earth with the rod of his mouth, and with
the breath of his lips shall he slay the
wicked.
5 And [i]righteousness shall be the girdle of
his loins, and faithfulness the girdle of his reins.
6 [k]The wolf also shall dwell with the lamb,
and the leopard shall lie down with the kid;
and the calf and the young lion and the fatling
together; and a little child shall lead them.

[a]Chap. liii. 2; Zech. vi. 12; Rev. v. 5——[b]Acts xiii. 23; ver. 10——[c]Chap. iv. 2; Jer. xxiii. 5——[d]Chap. lxi. 1; Matt. iii. 16; John i. 32, 33; iii. 34——[e]Heb. *scent* or *smell*

[f]Psa. lxxii. 2, 4; Rev. xix. 11——[g]Or, *argue*——[h]Job iv. 9; Mal. iv. 6; 2 Thess. ii. 8; Rev. i. 16; ii. 16; xix. 15
[i]See Psa. xi. 9; li. 14; lxv. 5; lxxii. 19; Eph. vi. 14
[k]Chap. lxv. 25; Ezek. xxxiv. 25; Hos. ii. 18

NOTES ON CHAP. XI

The prophet had described the destruction of the Assyrian army under the image of a mighty forest, consisting of flourishing trees growing thick together, and of a great height; of Lebanon itself crowned with lofty cedars, but cut down and laid level with the ground by the axe wielded by the hand of some powerful and illustrious agent. In opposition to this image he represents the great Person who makes the subject of this chapter as a slender twig shooting out from the trunk of an old tree, cut down, lopped to the very root, and decayed; which tender plant, so weak in appearance, should nevertheless become fruitful and prosper. This contrast shows plainly the connexion between this and the preceding chapter, which is moreover expressed by the connecting particle; and we have here a remarkable instance of that method so common with the prophets, and particularly with Isaiah, of taking occasion, from the mention of some great temporal deliverance, to launch out into the display of the spiritual deliverance of God's people by the Messiah; for that this prophecy relates to the Messiah we have the express authority of St. Paul, Rom. xv. 12. "He joins this paragraph, with respect to the days of the Messiah, with the fidelity that was in the days of Hezekiah."—*Kimchi,* in ver. 1. Thus in the latter part of Isaiah's prophecies the subject of the great redemption, and of the glories of the Messiah's kingdom, arises out of the restoration of Judah by the deliverance from the captivity of Babylon, and is all along connected and intermixed with it.

Verse 4. *With the rod of his mouth*—"By the blast of his mouth"] For בשבט *beshebet,* by the *rod, Houbigant* reads בשבת *beshebeth,* by the *blast* of his mouth, from נשב *nashab, to blow.* The conjecture is ingenious and probable; and seems to be confirmed by the *Septuagint* and *Chaldee,* who render it by the *word* of his mouth, which answers much better to the correction than to the present reading. Add to this, that the *blast of his mouth* is perfectly parallel to *the breath of his lips* in the next line.

Verse 5. *The girdle*—"The cincture"] All the ancient Versions, except that of *Symmachus,* have two different words for *girdle* in the two hemistichs. It is not probable that Isaiah would have repeated אזור *azer,* when a synonymous word so obvious as חגור *chagor* occurred. The tautology seems to have arisen from the mistake of some transcriber. The meaning of this verse is, that a zeal for justice and truth shall make him active and strong in executing the great work which he shall undertake. See note on chap. v. 27.

Verse 6. *The wolf also shall, &c.*—"Then shall the wolf," &c.] The idea of the renewal of the golden age, as it is called, is much the same in the Oriental writers with that of the Greeks and Romans:—the wild beasts grow tame; serpents and poisonous herbs become harmless; all is peace and harmony, plenty and happiness:—

> Occidet et serpens, et fallax herba veneni
> Occidet. VIRG. *Eclog.* iv. 24.

> "The serpent's brood shall die. The sacred ground
> Shall weeds and noxious plants refuse to bear."

A. M. cir. 3291 B. C. cir. 713 Olymp. XVI. 4 cir. annum NumæPompilii, R. Roman., 3

7 And the cow and the bear
shall feed; their young ones
shall lie down together: and the
lion shall eat straw like the ox.
8 And the sucking child shall play on the
hole of the asp, and the weaned child shall put
his hand on the [l]cockatrice' den.
9 [m]They shall not hurt nor destroy in all
my holy mountain: for [n]the earth shall be full
of the knowledge of the LORD,
as the waters cover the sea.
10 [o]And in that day [p]there
shall be a root of Jesse, which
shall stand for an ensign of the people; to
it shall the [q]Gentiles seek: and [r]his rest
shall be [s]glorious.
11 And it shall come to pass [t]in that day,
that the LORD shall set his hand again the

[l]Or, *adder's*——[m]Job v. 23; ch. ii. 4; xxxv. 9——[n]Hab. ii. 14——[o]Chap. ii. 11

[p]Ver. 1; Rom. xv. 12——[q]Rom. xv. 10——[r]Heb. iv. 1, &c.——[s]Heb. *glory*——[t]Chap. ii. 11

——Nec magnos metuent armenta leones.
VIRG. *Eclog.* iv. 22.

"Nor shall the flocks fear the great lions."

Non lupus insidias explorat ovilia circum,
Nec gregibus nocturnus obambulat: acrior illum
Cura domat: timidæ damæ cervique fugaces
Nunc interque canes, et circum tecta vagantur.
VIRG. *Georg.* iii. 537.

"The nightly wolf that round the enclosure prowled,
To leap the fence, now plots not on the fold:
Tamed with a sharper pain, the fearful doe
And flying stag amidst the greyhounds go;
And round the dwellings roam, of man, their former foe."
DRYDEN.

Nec vespertinus circumgemit ursus ovile,
Nec intumescit alta viperis humus.
HOR. *Epod.* xvi. 51.

"Nor evening bears the sheepfold growl around,
Nor mining vipers heave the tainted ground."
DRYDEN.

Εσται δη τουτ' αμαρ, ὁπηνικα νεβρον εν ευνᾳ
Καρχαροδων δινεσθαι ιδων λυκος ουκ εθελησει.
THEOC. *Idyl.* xxiv. 84.

There shall be a time when the ravenous wolf shall see the kid lying at ease, and shall feel no desire to do it an injury.

I have laid before the reader these common passages from the most elegant of the ancient poets, that he may see how greatly the prophet on the same subject has the advantage upon the comparison; how much the former fall short of that beauty and elegance, and variety of imagery, with which Isaiah has set forth the very same ideas. Tho wolf and the leopard not only forbear to destroy the lamb and the kid, but even take their abode and lie down together with them. The calf, and the young lion, and the fatling, not only come together, but are led quietly in the same band, and that by a little child. The heifer and the she-bear not only feed together, but even lodge their young ones, for whom they used to be most jealously fearful, in the same place. All the serpent kind is so perfectly harmless, that the sucking infant and the newly weaned child puts his hand on the basilisk's den, and plays upon the hole of the aspic. The lion not only abstains from preying on the weaker animals, but becomes tame and domestic, and feeds on straw like the ox. These are all beautiful circumstances, not one of which has been touched upon by the ancient poets. The Arabian and Persian poets elegantly apply the same ideas to show the effects of justice impartially administered, and firmly supported, by a great and good king:—

"Mahmoud the powerful king, the ruler of the world,
To whose tank the wolf and the lamb come together to drink."
FERDUSI.

"Through the influence of righteousness, the hungry wolf
Becomes mild, though in the presence of the white kid."
IBN ONEIN.

JONES, *Poes. Asiat. Comment.*, p. 380.

The application is extremely ingenious and beautiful: but the exquisite imagery of Isaiah is not equalled.

Verse 7. In this verse a word is omitted in the text, יחדו *yachdav, together;* which ought to be repeated in the second hemistich, being quite necessary to the sense. It is accordingly twice expressed by the *Septuagint* and *Syriac.*

Verse 8. *The cockatrice' den.*] This is supposed, both by the *Targum* and by *Kimchi*, to mean the pupil of this serpent's eye. "When," says *Kimchi*, "he is in the mouth of his den, in an obscure place, then his eyes *sparkle* exceedingly: the child, seeing this, and supposing it to be a piece of *crystal*, or *precious stone*, puts forth his hand to take it. What would be very dangerous at another time, shall be safe in the days of the Messiah; for the serpent will not hurt the child."

Verse 10. *A root of Jesse, which shall stand*, &c.—"The root of Jesse, which standeth," &c.] St. John hath taken this expression from Isaiah, Rev. v. 5, and xxii. 16, where Christ hath twice applied it to himself. Seven MSS. have עומד *omed, standing*, the present participle. Radix Isæi dicitur jam stare, et aliquantum stetisse, in signum populorum.—VITRINGA. "The root of Jesse is said to *stand*, and for some time to *have stood*, for an ensign to the people." Which rightly explains either of the two readings. The *one hundred and tenth* psalm is a good comment on this verse. See the notes there.

Verse 11. *And it shall come to pass in that day*] This part of the chapter contains a prophecy which certainly remains yet to be accomplished.

The Lord—"JEHOVAH"] For אדני *Adonai*, thirty-three MSS. of *Kennicott's*, and many of *De Rossi's*, and two editions, read יהוה *Yehovah.*

The islands of the sea.] The Roman and Turkish empires, say *Kimchi.*

A. M. cir. 3291 B. C. cir. 713 Olymp. XVI. 4 cir. annum NumæPompilii, R. Roman., 3
second time to recover the remnant of his people, which shall
be left, [u]from Assyria, and from
Egypt, and from Pathros, and
from Cush, and from Elam, and from Shinar,
and from Hamath, and from the islands of
the sea.

12 And he shall set up an ensign for the
nations, and shall assemble the outcasts of
Israel, and gather together [v]the dispersed of
Judah from the four [w]corners of the earth.

13 [x]The envy also of Ephraim shall depart,
and the adversaries of Judah shall be cut off:
Ephraim shall not envy Judah, and Judah
shall not vex Ephraim.

14 But they shall fly upon the shoulders of
the Philistines toward the west; A. M. cir. 3291 B. C. cir. 713
they shall spoil [y]them of the Olymp. XVI. 4
east together: [z]they [a]shall lay cir. annum NumæPompilii,
their hand upon Edom and R. Roman., 3
Moab; [b]and the children of Ammon [c]shall
obey them.

15 And the Lord [d]shall utterly destroy the
tongue of the Egyptian Sea; and with his
mighty wind shall he shake his hand over the
river, and shall smite it in the seven streams
[e]and make *men* go over [f]dry shod.

16 [g]And there shall be a highway for the
remnant of his people, which shall be left,
from Assyria; [h]like as it was to Israel in the
day that he came up out of the land of
Egypt.

---

[u]Zech. x. 10——[v]John vii. 35; James i. 1——[w]Heb. *wings*——[x]Jer. iii. 18; Ezek. xxxvii. 16, 17, 22; Hos. i. 11 [y]Heb. *the children of the east*——[z]Dan. xi. 41——[a]Heb. *Edom and Moab* shall be *the laying on of their hand*

[b]Heb. *the children of Ammon their obedience*——[c]Chap. lx. 14——[d]Zech. x. 11——[e]Rev. xvi. 12——[f]Heb. *in shoes*——[g]Chap. xix. 23——[h]Exod. xiv. 29; chap. li. 10; lxiii. 12, 13

Verse 13. *The adversaries of Judah*—"And the enmity of Judah"] צוררים *tsorerim.* Postulat pars posterior versus, ut intelligantur *inimicitiæ* Judæ in Ephraimum: et potest (צררים *tsorerim*) inimicitiam notare, ut (נחומים *nichumim*) pœnitentiam, Hos. xi. 8.—Secker.

Verse 15. *The Lord—shall smite it in the seven streams*—"Smite with a drought"] The *Chaldee* reads החריב *hecherib;* and so perhaps the *Septuagint,* who have ερημωσει, the word by which they commonly render it. Vulg. *desolabit;* "shall desolate." The *Septuagint, Vulgate,* and *Chaldee* read הדריכהו *hidrichahu,* "shall make *it* passable," adding the pronoun, which is necessary: but this reading is not confirmed by any MS.

Here is a plain allusion to the passage of the Red Sea. And the Lord's shaking his hand over the river with his vehement wind, refers to a particular circumstance of the same miracle: for "he caused the sea to go back by a strong east wind all that night, and made the sea dry land," Exod. xiv. 21. The *tongue;* a very apposite and descriptive expression for a bay such as that of the Red Sea. It is used in the same sense, Josh. xv. 2, 5; xviii. 19. The Latins gave the same name to a narrow strip of land running into the sea: *tenuem producit in æquora linguam.* Lucan. ii. 613. *He shall smite the river in its seven streams.* This has been supposed to refer to the *Nile,* because it falls into the Mediterranean Sea by *seven mouths:* but *R. Kimchi* understands it of the *Euphrates,* which is the opinion of some good judges. See the *Targum.* See below.

Herodotus, lib. i. 189, tells a story of his Cyrus, (a very different character from that of the Cyrus of the Scriptures and Xenophon,) which may somewhat illustrate this passage, in which it is said that God would inflict a kind of punishment and judgment on the Euphrates, and render it fordable by dividing it into seven streams. "Cyrus, being impeded in his march to Babylon by the Gyndes, a deep and rapid river which falls into the Tigris, and having lost one of his sacred white horses that attempted to pass it, was so enraged against the river that he threatened to reduce it, and make it so shallow that it should be easily fordable even by women, who should not be up to their knees in passing it. Accordingly he set his whole army to work, and cutting three hundred and sixty trenches, from both sides of the river, turned the waters into them, and drained them off."

CHAPTER XII

Prophetic hymn of praise for the great mercies vouchsafed to the children of Israel in their deliverance from the great Babylonish captivity, and for redemption by the Messiah, 1–6.

A. M. cir. 3291 B. C. cir. 713 Olymp. XVI. 4 cir. annum NumæPompilii, R. Roman., 3
AND [a]in that day thou shalt
say, O Lord, I will praise
thee: though thou wast angry
with me, thine anger is turned
away, and thou comfortedst A. M. cir. 3291 B. C. cir. 713
me. Olymp. XVI. 4
2 Behold, God *is* my salvation; cir. annum NumæPompilii,
I will trust, and not be afraid: for R. Roman., 3

---

[a]Isaiah, chap. ii. 11

This hymn seems, by its whole tenor, and by many expressions in it, much better calculated for the use of the Christian Church than for the Jewish, in any circumstances, or at any

A. M. cir. 3291 B. C. cir. 713 Olymp. XVI. 4 cir. annum NumæPompilii, R. Roman., 3

the LORD [b]JEHOVAH *is* my
[c]strength and *my* song; he also
is become my salvation.
3 Therefore with joy shall
ye draw [d]water out of the wells of salvation.
4 And in that day shall ye say, [e]Praise the
LORD, [f]call upon his name, [g]declare his
doings among the people, make
mention that his [h]name is exalted.
5 [i]Sing unto the LORD; for he
hath done excellent things: this
is known in all the earth.
6 [k]Cry out and shout, thou [l]inhabitant of
Zion: for great *is* [m]the Holy One of Israel in
the midst of thee.

A. M. cir. 3291 B. C. cir. 713 Olymp. XVI. 4 cir. annum NumæPompilii, R. Roman., 3

[b]Psa. lxxxiii. 18——[c]Exod. xv. 2——[d]John iv. 10, 14; vii. 37, 38——[e]1 Chron. xvi. 8; Psa. cv. 1——[f]Or, *proclaim his name*——[g]Psa. cxlv. 4, 5, 6——[h]Psa. xxxiv. 3

[i]Exod. xv. 1, 21; Psa. lxviii. 32; xcviii. 1——[k]Chap. liv. 1; Zeph. iii. 14——[l]Heb. *inhabitress*——[m]Psa. lxxi. 22; lxxxix. 18; chap. xli. 14, 16

time that can be assigned. The Jews themselves seem to have applied it to the times of Messiah. On the last day of the feast of tabernacles they fetched water in a golden pitcher from the fountain of Shiloah, springing at the foot of Mount Sion without the city: they brought it through the water-gate into the temple, and poured it, mixed with wine, on the sacrifice as it lay upon the altar, with great rejoicing. They seem to have taken up this custom, for it is not ordained in the law of Moses, as an emblem of future blessings, in allusion to this passage of Isaiah, "Ye shall draw waters with joy from the fountains of salvation," expressions that can hardly be understood of any benefits afforded by the Mosaic dispensation. Our Saviour applied the ceremony, and the intention of it, to himself, and the effusion of the Holy Spirit, promised, and to be given, by him. The sense of the Jews in this matter is plainly shown by the following passage of the Jerusalem Talmud: "Why is it called the place or house of drawing?" (for that was the term for this ceremony, or for the place where the water was taken up) "Because from thence they draw the Holy Spirit; as it is written, And ye shall draw water with joy from the fountains of salvation." See Wolf. Curæ Philol. in N. T. on John vii. 37, 39.—L. The *water* is Divine knowledge, says *Kimchi*, and the *wells* the teachers of righteousness. The *Targum* renders this in a very remarkable manner: "Ye shall receive with joy (אולפן חדת *ulephan chadath*) a new doctrine from the chosen among the righteous." Does not this mean the *Gospel*, the *new covenant?* And did not the Targumist speak as a *prophet?*

NOTES ON CHAP. XII

Verse 1. *Though thou wast angry*—"For though thou hast been angry"] The Hebrew phrase, to which the *Septuagint* and *Vulgate* have too closely adhered, is exactly the same with that of St. Paul, Rom. vi. 17: "But thanks be to God, that ye were the slaves of sin; but have obeyed from the heart;" that is, "that whereas, or though, ye were the slaves of sin, yet ye have now obeyed from the heart the doctrine on the model of which ye were formed."

Verse 2. *The Lord JEHOVAH*] The word יה *Yah* read here is probably a mistake; and arose originally from the custom of the Jewish scribes, who, when they found a line too short for the word, wrote as many letters as filled it, and then began the next line with the whole word. In writing the word יהוה *Yehovah*, the line might terminate with יה *Yah*, the two first letters; and then at the beginning of the next line the whole word יהוה *Yehovah* would be written. This might give rise to יה יהוה *Yah Yehovah*. The *Yah* is wanting here in two of Dr. *Kennicott's* MSS., in one ancient MS. of my own, and in the *Septuagint*, *Vulgate*, *Syriac*, and *Arabic*. See *Houbigant* and *De Rossi*.

My *song*] The pronoun is here necessary; and it is added by the *Septuagint*, *Vulgate*, and *Syriac*, who read ומרתי *zimrathi*, as it is in a MS. Two MSS. omit יה *Yah*, see *Houbigant*, not. in loc. Another MS. has it in one word, זמרתיה *zimrathyah*. Seven others omit יהוה *Yehovah*. See Exod. xv. 2, with Var. Lect. *Kennicott*.

Verse 4. *Call upon his name*] קראו בשמו *kiru bishmo*, *invoke his name*. Make him your *Mediator*, or *call* the people *in his name*. Preach him who is the *Root of Jesse*, and *who stands as an ensign for the nations*. Call on the people to believe in him; as in him alone salvation is to be found.

Verse 6. *Thou inhabitant of Zion*] Not only the *Jewish people*, to whom his word of salvation was to be sent first; but also all members of the Church of Christ: as in *them*, and in his *Church*, the Holy One of Israel *dwells*. St. Paul, speaking of the *mystery* which had been proclaimed among the Gentiles, sums it up in these words: "which is CHRIST IN YOU, the hope of glory; whom we preach, warning every man, and teaching every man in all wisdom, that we may present every man perfect in Christ Jesus;" Col. i. 27, 28. Well, therefore, may the inhabitant of Zion *cry out and shout*, and proclaim the greatness of her Redeemer.

CHAPTER XIII

God mustereth the armies of his wrath against the inhabitants of Babylon, 1–6. *The dreadful consequences of this visitation, and the terror and dismay of those who are the objects of it,* 7–16. *The horrid cruelties that shall be inflicted upon the Babylonians by the Medes,* 17, 18. *Total and irrecoverable desolation of Babylon,* 19–22.

A. M. cir. 3292
B. C. cir. 712
Olymp. XVII. 1
cir. annum
NumæPompilii,
R. Roman., 4

THE [a]burden of Babylon,
which Isaiah the son of
Amoz did see.
2 [b]Lift ye up a banner [c]upon
the high mountain, exalt the
voice unto them, [d]shake the hand,
that they may go into the gates
of the nobles.

[a]Chap. xxi. 1; xlvii. 1; Jer. l., li——[b]Ch. v. 26; xviii. 3; Jer. l. 2——[c]Jer. li. 25——[d]Ch. x. 32

This and the following chapter,—striking off the *five* last verses of the latter, which belong to a quite different subject,—contain one entire prophecy, foretelling the destruction of Babylon by the Medes and Persians; delivered probably in the reign of Ahaz, (see *Vitringa*, i. 380,) about *two hundred* years before its accomplishment. The captivity itself of the Jews at Babylon, which the prophet does not expressly foretell, but supposes, in the spirit of prophecy, as what was actually to be effected, did not fully take place till about *one hundred and thirty* years after the delivery of this prophecy: and the Medes, who are expressly mentioned chap. xiii. 17, as the principal agents in the overthrow of the Babylonian monarchy, by which the Jews were released from that captivity, were at this time an inconsiderable people; having been in a state of anarchy ever since the fall of the great Assyrian empire, of which they had made a part, under Sardanapalus; and did not become a kingdom under Deioces till about the *seventeenth* of Hezekiah.

The former part of this prophecy is one of the most beautiful examples that can be given of elegance of composition, variety of imagery, and sublimity of sentiment and diction, in the prophetic style; and the latter part consists of an ode of supreme and singular excellence.

The prophecy opens with the command of God to gather together the forces which he had destined to this service, ver. 2, 3. Upon which the prophet immediately hears the tumultuous noise of the different nations crowding together to his standard; he sees them advancing, prepared to execute the Divine wrath, ver. 4, 5. He proceeds to describe the dreadful consequences of this visitation, the consternation which will seize those who are the objects of it; and, transferring unawares the speech from himself to God, ver. 11, sets forth, under a variety of the most striking images, the dreadful destruction of the inhabitants of Babylon which will follow, ver. 11-16, and the everlasting desolation to which that great city is doomed, ver. 17-22.

The deliverance of Judah from captivity, the immediate consequence of this great revolution, is then set forth, without being much enlarged upon, or greatly amplified, chap. xiv. 1, 2. This introduces, with the greatest ease and the utmost propriety, the triumphant song on that subject, ver. 4-28. The beauties of which, the various images, scenes, persons introduced, and the elegant transitions from one to another, I shall here endeavour to point out in their order, leaving a few remarks upon particular passages of these two chapters to be given after these general observations on the whole.

A chorus of Jews is introduced, expressing their surprise and astonishment at the sudden downfall of Babylon; and the great reverse of fortune that had befallen the tyrant, who, like his predecessors, had oppressed his own, and harassed the neighbouring kingdoms. These oppressed kingdoms, or their rulers, are represented under the image of the fir trees and the cedars of Libanus, frequently used to express any thing in the political or religious world that is super-eminently great and majestic: the whole earth shouteth for joy; the cedars of Libanus utter a severe taunt over the fallen tyrant, and boast their security now he is no more.

The scene is immediately changed, and a new set of persons is introduced. The regions of the dead are laid open, and Hades is represented as rousing up the shades of the departed monarchs: they rise from their thrones to meet the king of Babylon at his coming; and insult him on his being reduced to the same low estate of impotence and dissolution with themselves. This is one of the boldest prosopopœias that ever was attempted in poetry; and is executed with astonishing brevity and perspicuity, and with that peculiar force which in a great subject naturally results from both. The image of the state of the dead, or the *infernum poeticum* of the Hebrews, is taken from their custom of burying, those at least of the higher rank, in large sepulchral vaults hewn in the rock. Of this kind of sepulchres there are remains at Jerusalem now extant; and some that are said to be the sepulchres of the kings of Judah. See *Maundrell*, p. 76. You are to form to yourself an idea of an immense subterranean vault, a vast gloomy cavern, all round the sides of which there are cells to receive the dead bodies; here the deceased monarchs lie in a distinguished sort of state, suitable to their former rank, each on his own couch, with his arms beside him, his sword at his head, and the bodies of his chiefs and companions round about him. See Ezek. xxxii. 27. On which place Sir John Chardin's MS. note is as follows: "En Mingrelie ils dorment tous leurs epées sous leurs têtes, et leurs autres armes à leur cotè; et on les enterre de mesme, leurs armes posées de cette façon." In Mingrelia they always sleep with their swords under their heads, and their other arms by their sides; and they bury their dead with their arms placed in the same manner. These illustrious shades rise at once from their couches, as from their thrones; and advance to the entrance of the cavern to meet the king of Babylon, and to receive him with insults on his fall.

The Jews now resume the speech; they address the king of Babylon as the morning-star fallen from heaven, as the first in splendour and dignity in the political world, fallen from his high state; they introduce him as uttering the most extravagant vaunts of his power and ambitious designs in his former glory. These are strongly contrasted in the close with his present low and abject condition.

Immediately follows a different scene, and a most happy image, to diversify the same subject, to give it a new turn, and an additional force. Certain persons are introduced who light upon the corpse of the king of Babylon, cast out and lying naked on the bare ground, among the com-

A. M. cir. 3292 B. C. cir. 712 Olymp. XVII. 1 cir. annum Numæ Pompilii, R. Roman., 4

3 I have commanded my sanctified ones, I have also called
[e]my mighty ones for mine anger,
even them that [f]rejoice in my
highness.
4 The noise of a multitude in the mountains [g]like as of a great people; a tumultuous
noise of the kingdoms of nations gathered together; the LORD of hosts mustereth the host
of the battle.
5 They come from a far country, from the
end of heaven, *even* the LORD, and the weapons
of his indignation, to destroy the whole land.
6 Howl ye; [h]for the day of the LORD *is* at
hand; [i]it shall come as a destruction from the
Almighty.

[e]Joel iii. 11——[f]Psa. cxlix. 2, 5, 6——[g]Heb. *the likeness of*——[h]Zeph. i. 7; Rev. vi. 17——[i]Job xxxi. 23; Joel i. 15——[k]Or, *fall down*——[l]Psa. xlviii. 6; chap. xxi. 3——[m]Heb. *wonder*

A. M. cir. 3292 B. C. cir. 712 Olymp. XVII. 1 cir. annum Numæ Pompilii, R. Roman., 4

7 Therefore shall all hands [k]be
faint, and every man's heart
shall melt.
8 And they shall be afraid;
[l]pangs and sorrows shall take hold of them;
they shall be in pain as a woman that travaileth: they shall [m]be amazed [n]one at
another; their faces *shall be as* [o]flames.
9 Behold, [p]the day of the LORD cometh,
cruel both with wrath and fierce anger, to lay
the land desolate: and he shall destroy [q]the
sinners thereof out of it.
10 For the stars of heaven and the constellations thereof shall not give their light:
the sun shall be [r]darkened in his going forth,
and the moon shall not cause her light to shine.

[n]Heb. *every man at his neighbour*——[o]Heb. *faces of the flames*——[p]Mal. iv. 1——[q]Psa. civ. 35; Prov. ii. 22 [r]Chap. xxiv. 21, 23; Ezek. xxxii. 7; Joel ii. 31; iii. 15; Matt. xxiv. 29; Mark xiii. 24; Luke xxi. 25

mon slain, just after the taking of the city; covered with wounds, and so disfigured, that it is some time before they know him. They accost him with the severest taunts; and bitterly reproach him with his destructive ambition, and his cruel usage of the conquered; which have deservedly brought him this ignominious treatment, so different from that which those of his rank usually meet with, and which shall cover his posterity with disgrace.

To complete the whole, God is introduced, declaring the fate of Babylon, the utter extirpation of the royal family, and the total desolation of the city; the deliverance of his people, and the destruction of their enemies; confirming the irreversible decree by the awful sanction of his oath.

I believe it may with truth be affirmed, that there is no poem of its kind extant in any language, in which the subject is so well laid out, and so happily conducted, with such a richness of invention, with such variety of images, persons, and distinct actions, with such rapidity and ease of transition, in so small a compass, as in this ode of Isaiah. For beauty of disposition, strength of colouring, greatness of sentiment, brevity, perspicuity, and force of expression, it stands, among all the monuments of antiquity, unrivalled.—L.

NOTES ON CHAP. XIII.

Verse 1. *The burden of Babylon*] The prophecy that foretells its destruction by the Medes and Persians: see the preceding observations.

Verse 2. *Exalt the voice*] The word להם *lahem*, "to them," which is of no use, and rather weakens the sentence, is omitted by an ancient MS., and the *Vulgate*.

Verse 3. *I have commanded my sanctified ones*] מקדשי *mekuddashai*, the persons *consecrated* to this very purpose. Nothing can be plainer than that the verb קדש *kadash*, "to make holy," signifies also to *consecrate* or *appoint* to a particular purpose. Bishop *Lowth* translates, "my enrolled warriors." This is the *sense*.

Verse 4. *Of the battle*—"For the battle."] The *Bodleian* MS. has למלחמה *lemilchamah*. Cyrus's army was made up of many different nations. Jeremiah calls it an "assembly of great nations from the north country," chap. l. 9. And afterwards mentions the kingdoms of "Ararat, Minni, and Ashchenaz, (i. e. Armenia, Corduene, Pontus or Phrygia, Vitring.,) with the kings of the Medes," chap. li. 27, 28. See Xenophon. Cyrop.

Verse 5. *They come from a far country*] The word מארץ *meerets* is wanting in *one* MS. and in the *Syriac*: "They come from afar."

From the end of heaven] *Kimchi* says, *Media*, "the end of heaven," in Scripture phrase, means, the EAST.

Verse 8. *And they shall be afraid*—"And they shall be terrified"] I join this verb, ונבהלו *venibhalu*, to the preceding verse, with the *Syriac* and *Vulgate*.

Pangs and sorrows shall take hold of them—"Pangs shall seize them"] The *Septuagint*, *Syriac*, and *Chaldee* read יאחזום *yochezum*, instead of יאחזון *yochezun*, which does not express the pronoun *them*, necessary to the sense.

Verse 10. *For the stars of heaven*—"Yea, the stars of heaven"] The Hebrew poets, to express happiness, prosperity, the instauration and advancement of states, kingdoms, and potentates, make use of images taken from the most striking parts of nature, from the heavenly bodies, from the sun, moon, and stars: which they describe as shining with increased splendour, and never setting. The moon becomes like the meridian sun, and the sun's light is augmented sevenfold; (see Isa. xxx. 26;) new heavens and a new earth are created, and a brighter age commences. On the contrary, the overflow and destruction of kingdoms is represented by opposite images. The stars are obscured, the moon withdraws her light, and the sun shines no more! The earth quakes, and the heavens tremble; and all things seem tending to their original chaos. See Joel ii. 10, iii. 15,

A. M. cir. 3292 B. C. cir. 712 Olymp. XVII. 1 cir. annum Numæ Pompilii, R. Roman., 4

11 And I will punish the world
for *their* evil, and the wicked for
their iniquity; [s]and I will cause
the arrogancy of the proud to
cease, and will lay low the haughtiness of
the terrible.
12 I will make a man more precious than
fine gold; even a man than the golden wedge
of Ophir.
13 [t]Therefore I will shake the heavens, and
the earth shall remove out of her place, in the
wrath of the LORD of hosts, and in [u]the day
of his fierce anger.
14 And it shall be as the chased roe, and as
a sheep that no man taketh up:
[v]they shall every man turn to his
own people, and flee every one
into his own land.
15 Every one that is found shall be thrust
through; and every one that is joined *unto*
them shall fall by the sword.
16 Their children also shall be [w]dashed to
pieces before their eyes; their houses shall
be spoiled, and their wives ravished.
17 [x]Behold, I will stir up the Medes
against them, which shall not regard silver;
and *as for* gold, they shall not delight
in it.

A. M. cir. 3292 B. C. cir. 712 Olymp. XVII. 1 cir. annum Numæ Pompilii, R. Roman., 4

---

[s]Chap. ii. 17——[t]Hag. ii. 6——[u]Psa. cx. 5; Lam. i. 12 [v]Jer. l. 16; li. 9

[w]Psa. cxxxvii. 9; Nah. iii. 10; Zech. xiv. 2——[x]Chap. xxi. 2; Jer. li. 11, 28; Dan. v. 28, 31

16; Amos viii. 9; Matt. xxiv. 29; and De S. Poës. Herb. Præl. VI. et IX.

And the moon shall not cause her light to shine] This in its farther reference may belong to the Jewish polity, both in Church and state, which should be totally eclipsed, and perhaps shine no more in its distinct state for ever.

Verse 11. *I will punish the world*—"I will visit the world"] That is, the Babylonish empire; as *η οικουμενη*, for the Roman empire, or for Judea, Luke ii. 1; Acts xi. 28. So the *universus orbis Romanus*, for the Roman empire; *Salvian.* lib. v. *Minos* calls Crete his world: "Creten, quæ meus est orbis;" *Ovid. Metamorph.* viii. 9.

Verse 12. *I will make a man more precious than fine gold—wedge of Ophir.*] The Medes and Persians will not be satisfied with the *spoils* of the Babylonians. They seek either to destroy or enslave them; and they will accept no *ransom* for any man—either for אנוש *enosh*, the poor man, or for אדם *adam*, the more honourable person. All must fall by the sword, or go into captivity together; for *the Medes*, (ver. 17,) *regard not silver, and delight not in gold.*

Verse 14. "And the remnant"] Here is plainly a defect in this sentence, as it stands in the *Hebrew* text; the subject of the proposition is lost. What is it that shall be like a roe chased? The *Septuagint* happily supply it, *οἱ καταλελειμμενοι*, שאר *shear, the remnant.* A MS. here supplies the word יושב *yosheb, the inhabitant;* which makes a tolerably good sense; but I much prefer the reading of the *Septuagint.*

They shall—turn—"They shall look"] That is, the forces of the king of Babylon, destitute of their leader, and all his auxiliaries, collected from Asia Minor, and other distant countries, shall disperse and flee to their respective homes.

Verse 15. *Every one that is found*—"Every one that is overtaken"] That is, none shall escape from the slaughter; neither they who flee singly, dispersed and in confusion; nor they who endeavour to make their retreat in a more regular manner, by forming compact bodies: they shall all be equally cut off by the sword of the enemy. The *Septuagint* have understood it in this sense, which they have well expressed:—

Ὁς γαρ αν ἁλῳ ἡττηθησεται,
Και οἱτινες συνηγμενοι εισι πεσουνται μαχαιρα.

"Whosoever is caught shall be overthrown,
And all that are collected together shall fall by the sword."

Where, for *ἡττηθησεται*, MS. Pachom has *εκκενθησεται*, et *οἱ* Γ Cod. Marchal. in margine, et MS. I. D. II. *εκκεντηθησεται*, which seems to be right, being properly expressive of the *Hebrew*.

Verse 17. *Which shall not regard silver*—"Who shall hold silver of no account"] That is, who shall not be induced, by large offers of gold and silver for ransom, to spare the lives of those whom they have subdued in battle; their rage and cruelty will get the better of all such motives. We have many examples in the Iliad and in the Æneid of addresses of the vanquished to the pity and avarice of the vanquishers, to induce them to spare their lives.

Est domus alta: jacent penitus defossa talenta
Cælati argenti: sunt auri pondera facti
Infectique mihi: non hic victoria Teucrum
Vertitur; aut anima una dabit discrimina tanta.
Dixerat: Æneas contra cui talia reddit:
Argenti atque auri memoras quæ multa talenta
Gnatis parce tuis. Æn. x. 526.

"High in my dome are silver talents rolled,
With piles of laboured and unlaboured gold.
These, to procure my ransom, I resign;
The war depends not on a life like mine:
One, one poor life can no such difference yield,
Nor turn the mighty balance of the field.
Thy talents, (cried the prince,) thy treasured store
Keep for thy sons." *Pitt.*

It is remarkable that Xenophon makes Cyrus open a speech to his army, and in particular to the Medes, who made the principal part of it, with praising them for their disregard of riches. *Ανδρες Μηδοι, και παντες οἱ παροντες, εγω ὑμας οιδα σαφως, ὁτι ουτε χρηματων δεομενοι συν εμοι εξελθετε·* "Ye Medes, and others who now hear me, I well know that you have not accompanied me in this

A. M. cir. 3292 B. C. cir. 712 Olymp.XVII. 1 cir. annum NumæPompilii, R. Roman., 4

18 *Their* bows also shall dash
the young men to pieces; and
they shall have no pity on the
fruit of the womb; their eye shall
not spare children.
19 [y]And Babylon, the glory of kingdoms,
the beauty of the Chaldees' excellency, shall
be [z]as when God overthrew
[a]Sodom and Gomorrah.
20 [b]It shall never be inhabited,
neither shall it be dwelt in from
generation to generation: neither shall the
Arabian pitch tent there; neither shall the
shepherds make their fold there.

A. M. cir. 3292 B. C. cir. 712 Olymp.XVII. 1 cir. annum NumæPompilii, R. Roman., 4

---

[y]Chapter xiv. 4, 22——[z]Hebrew *as the overthrowing*——[a]Genesis xix. 24, 26; Deuteronomy xxix. 23; Jeremiah xlix. 18; l. 40——[b]Jeremiah l. 3, 39; li. 29, 62

---

expedition with a view of acquiring wealth."—*Cyrop.* lib. v.

Verse 18. Their *bows also shall dash*—"Their bows shall dash"] Both Herodotus, i. 61, and Xenophon, Anab. iii., mention, that the Persians used large bows τοξα μεγαλα: and the latter says particularly that their bows were *three* cubits long, Anab. iv. They were celebrated for their archers, see chap xxii. 6; Jer. xlix. 35. Probably their neighours and allies, the Medes, dealt much in the same sort of arms. In Psa. xviii. 34, and Job xx. 24, mention is made of a bow of steel; if the Persian bows were of metal, we may easily conceive that with a metalline bow of *three* cubits' length, and proportionably strong, the soldiers might dash and slay the young men, the weaker and unresisting of the inhabitants (for they are joined with the fruit of the womb and the children) in the general carnage on taking the city. תרתשנה *terattashnah*, shall be broken or shivered to pieces. This seems to refer, not to נערים *nearim*, young *men*, but to קשתות *keshathoth*, their *bows*. *The bows of the young men shall be broken to pieces.*

On the fruit, &c.—"And on the fruit," &c.] A MS. of Dr. *Kennicott's* reads ועל פרי *veal peri, and on the fruit.* And *nine* MSS. (*three* ancient) and *two* editions, with the *Septuagint*, *Vulgate*, and *Syriac*, add likewise the conjunction ו *vau, and,* to על *al, upon*, afterwards.

Verse 19. *And Babylon*] The great city of Babylon was at this time rising to its height of glory, while the Prophet Isaiah was repeatedly denouncing its utter destruction. From the first of Hezekiah to the first of Nebuchadnezzar, under whom it was brought to the highest degree of strength and splendour, are about *one hundred and twenty years.* I will here very briefly mention some particulars of the greatness of the place, and note the several steps by which this remarkable prophecy was at length accomplished in the total ruin of it.

It was, according to the lowest account given of it by ancient historians, a regular square, *forty-five* miles in compass, inclosed by a wall *two hundred* feet high and *fifty* broad; in which there were a *hundred* gates of brass. Its principal ornaments were the temple of Belus, in the middle of which was a tower of *eight* stories of building, upon a base of a quarter of a mile square, a most magnificent palace, and the famous hanging gardens, which were an artificial mountain, raised upon arches, and planted with trees of the largest as well as the most beautiful sorts.

Cyrus took the city by diverting the waters of the Euphrates which ran through the midst of it, and entering the place at night by the dry channel. The river being never restored afterward to its proper course, overflowed the whole country, and made it little better than a great morass; this and the great slaughter of the inhabitants, with other bad consequences of the taking of the city, was the first step to the ruin of the place. The Persian monarchs ever regarded it with a jealous eye; they kept it under, and took care to prevent its recovering its former greatness. Darius Hystaspes not long afterward most severely punished it for a revolt, greatly depopulated the place, lowered the walls, and demolished the gates. Xerxes destroyed the temples, and with the rest the great temple of Belus, Herod. iii. 159, Arrian, Exp. Alexandri, lib. vii. The building of Seleucia on the Tigris exhausted Babylon by its neighbourhood, as well as by the immediate loss of inhabitants taken away by Seleucus to people his new city, *Strabo*, lib. xvi. A king of the Parthians soon after carried away into slavery a great number of the inhabitants, and burned and destroyed the most beautiful parts of the city, *Valesii Excerpt. Diodori*, p. 377. Strabo (ibid.) says that in his time great part of it was a mere desert; that the Persians had partly destroyed it; and that time and the neglect of the Macedonians, while they were masters of it, had nearly completed its destruction. Jerome (*in loc.*) says that in his time it was quite in ruins, and that the walls served only for the inclosure for a park or forest for the king's hunting. Modern travellers, who have endeavoured to find the remains of it, have given but a very unsatisfactory account of their success. What Benjamin of Tudela and Pietro della Valle supposed to have been some of its ruins, Tavernier thinks are the remains of some late Arabian building. Upon the whole, Babylon is so utterly annihilated, that even the place where this wonder of the world stood cannot now be determined with any certainty! See also note on chap. xliii. 14.

We are astonished at the accounts which ancient historians of the best credit give of the immense extent, height, and thickness of the walls of Nineveh and Babylon; nor are we less astonished when we are assured, by the concurrent testimony of modern travellers, that no remains, not the least traces, of these prodigious works are now to be found. Scattered fragments of its *tiles* and *bricks* are yet to be found. Proud Babylon reduced now to a few brick-bats! Our wonder will, I think, be moderated in both respects, if we consider the fabric of these celebrated walls, and the nature of the materials of which they consisted. Buildings in the east have always been, and are to this day, made of earth or clay, mixed or beat up with straw to make the parts cohere, and dried only in the sun. This is their method of making bricks; see on chap. ix. 9. The walls of the city were built of the earth digged out on the spot, and

A. M. cir. 3292
B. C. cir. 712
Olymp. XVII. 1
cir. annum
NumæPompilii,
R. Roman., 4

21 [c]But [d]wild beasts of the desert shall lie there; and their houses shall be full of [e]doleful creatures; [f]and [g]owls shall dwell there, and satyrs shall dance there.

22 And [h]the wild beasts of the islands shall cry in their [i]desolate houses, and dragons in *their* pleasant palaces: [k]and her time *is* near to come, and her days shall not be prolonged.

[c]Chap. xxxiv. 11–15; Rev. xviii. 2——[d]Heb. *Ziim*——[e]Heb. *Ochim*——[f]Or, *ostriches*——[g]Heb. *daughters of the owl*——[h]Heb. *Iim*——[i]Or, *palaces*——[k]Jer. li. 33

dried upon the place, by which means both the ditch and the wall were at once formed, the former furnishing materials for the latter. That the walls of Babylon were of this kind is well known; and *Berosus* expressly says, (*apud Joseph.* Antiq. x. 11,) that Nebuchadnezzar added three new walls both to the old and new city, partly of brick and bitumen, and partly of brick alone. A wall of this sort must have a great thickness in proportion to its height, otherwise it cannot stand. The thickness of the walls of Babylon is said to have been one-fourth of their height, which seems to have been no more than was absolutely necessary. *Maundrell*, speaking of the garden walls of Damascus, says, "They are of a very singular structure. They are built of great pieces of earth, made in the fashion of brick, and hardened in the sun. In their dimensions they are two yards long each, and somewhat more than one broad, and half a yard thick." And afterward, speaking of the walls of the houses, he says, "From this dirty way of building they have this amongst other inconveniences, that upon any violent rain the whole city becomes, by the washing of the houses, as it were a quagmire;" p. 124. And see note on chap. xxx. 13. When a wall of this sort comes to be out of repair, and is neglected, it is easy to conceive the necessary consequences, namely, that in no long course of ages it must be totally destroyed by the heavy rains, and at length washed away, and reduced to its original earth.—L.

Verse 21. *Satyrs*] A kind of beast like to man, which is called מרמוטין *marmots, a monkey.*—*Rabbi Parchon.*

Verse 22. *In their pleasant palaces*—"In their palaces"] באלמנותיו *bealmenothaiv;* a plain mistake, I presume, for בארמנתיו *bearmenothaiv.* It is so corrected in *two* MSS., the *Syriac*, *Chaldee*, and *Vulgate*.

> *Πουλυποδες δ' εν εμοι θαλαμασ φωκαι τε μελαιναι*
> *Οικια ποιησονται ακηδεα, χητεϊ λαων.*
>
> Hom. *Hymn. in Apol.* 77.

Of which the following passage of *Milton* may be taken for a translation, though not so designed:—

> "And in their palaces,
> Where luxury late reigned, sea monsters whelped,
> And stabled." *Par. Lost*, xi. 750.

This image of desolation is handled with great propriety and force by some of the Persian poets:—

پرده داري ميكند در قصر قيصر عنكبوت
بومي نوبت ميزند بر گنبد افراسياب

> "The spider holds the veil in the palace of Cæsar;
> The owl stands centinel on the watch-tower of Afrasiab."

On this quotation Sir *W. Jones* observes, نوبت *noubet* is an Arabic word, signifying a *turn*, a *change*, a *watch;* hence نوبت زدن *noubet zudun* in Persian signifies to *relieve the guards by the sounds of drums and trumpets.* Their office is given by the poet to the *owl;* as that of پرده دار *purdeh dar*, or chamberlain, is elegantly assigned to the *spider*.

CHAPTER XIV

Deliverance of Israel from captivity, which shall follow the downfall of the great Babylonish empire, 1, 2. *Triumphant ode or song of the children of Jacob, for the signal manifestation of Divine vengeance against their oppressors,* 3–23. *Prophecy against the Assyrians,* 24, 25. *Certainty of the prophecy, and immutability of the Divine counsels,* 26, 27. *Palestine severely threatened,* 28–31. *God shall establish Zion in these troublous times,* 32.

A. M. cir. 3292
B. C. cir. 712
Olymp. XVII. 1
cir. annum
NumæPompilii,
R. Roman., 4

FOR the Lord [a]will have mercy on Jacob, and [b]will yet choose Israel, and set them in their own land: [c]and the strangers shall be joined with them, and they shall cleave to the house of Jacob.

2 And the people shall take

[a]Psa. cii. 13——[b]Zech. i. 17; ii. 12——[c]Chap. lx. 4, 5, 10; Eph. ii. 12, 13, &c.

NOTES ON CHAP. XIV

Verse 1. *And will yet choose Israel.*] That is, will still regard Israel as his chosen people; however he may seem to desert them, by giving them up to their enemies, and scattering them among the nations. Judah is sometimes called Israel; see Ezek. xiii. 16; Mal. i. 1; ii. 11: but the name of Jacob and of Israel, used apparently with design in this place, each of which names

A. M. cir. 3292 them, [d]and bring them to their
B. C. cir. 712
Olymp. XVII.1 place: and the house of Israel
cir. annum
NumæPompilii, shall possess them in the land
R. Roman., 4 of the LORD for servants and
handmaids: and they shall take them captives, [e]whose captives they were; [f]and they
shall rule over their oppressors.
3 And it shall come to pass in the day that
the LORD shall give thee rest from thy sorrow,
and from thy fear, and from the hard bondage
wherein thou wast made to serve,
4 That thou [g]shalt take up this [h]proverb
against the king of Babylon, and say, How
hath the oppressor ceased! and [i]golden [k]city
ceased!
5 The LORD hath broken [l]the staff of the
wicked, *and* the sceptre of the rulers.
6 He who smote the people in A. M. cir. 3292
B. C. cir. 712
wrath with [m]a continual stroke, Olymp. XVII.1
cir. annum
he that ruled the nations in anger, NumæPompilii,
is persecuted, *and* none hindereth. R. Roman., 4
7 The whole earth is at rest, *and* is quiet:
they break forth into singing.
8 [n]Yea, the fir trees rejoice at thee, *and* the
cedars of Lebanon, *saying,* Since thou art laid
down, no feller is come up against us.
9 [o]Hell [p]from beneath is moved for thee to
meet *thee* at thy coming: it stirreth up the
dead for thee, *even* all the [q]chief [r]ones of the
earth; it hath raised up from their thrones
all the kings of the nations.
10 All they shall speak and say unto thee,
Art thou also become weak as we? art thou
become like unto us?

[d]Chap. xlix. 22; lx. 9; lxvi. 20——[e]Heb. *that had taken them captives*——[f]Chap. lx. 14——[g]Chap. xiii. 19; Hab. ii. 6——[h]Or, *taunting speech*——[i]Or, *exactress of gold*

[k]Rev. xviii. 16——[l]Psa. cxxv. 3——[m]Heb. *a stroke without removing*——[n]Chap. lv. 12; Ezek. xxxi. 16——[o]Ezek. xxxii. 21——[p]Or, *The grave*——[q]Heb. *leaders*——[r]Or, *great goats*

includes the twelve tribes, and the other circumstances mentioned in this and the next verse, which did not in any complete sense accompany the return from the captivity of Babylon, seem to intimate that this whole prophecy extends its views beyond that event.

Verse 2. *For servants and handmaids*] **For thrallis and thrallesses.**—OLD BIBLE. Male and female slaves.

Verse 3. *In the day*—"In that day"] ביום ההוא *bayom hahu.* The word ההוא *hahu* is added in *two* MSS. of *Kennicott's*, and was in the copies from which the *Septuagint* and *Vulgate* translated: εν τῃ ἡμερᾳ εκεινῃ, *in die illa*, (ῇ αναπαυσει, MS. Pachom. adding ῇ,) in that day. This is a matter of no great consequence: however, it restores the text to the common form, almost constantly used on such occasions; and is one among many instances of a word apparently lost out of the printed copies.

Verse 4. *This proverb*—"This parable"] משל *mashal.* I take this to be the general name for poetic style among the Hebrews, including every sort of it, as ranging under one or other, or all of the characters, of sententious, figurative, and sublime; which are all contained in the original notion, or in the use and application of the word *mashal.* Parables or proverbs, such as those of Solomon, are always expressed in short pointed sentences; frequently figurative, being formed on some comparison; generally forcible and authoritative, both in the matter and the form. And such in general is the style of the Hebrew poetry. The verb *mashal* signifies to rule; to exercise authority; to make equal; to compare one thing with another; to utter parables, or acute, weighty, and powerful speeches, in the form and manner of parables, though not properly such. Thus Balaam's first prophecy, (Num. xxiii. 7-10,) is called his *mashal;* though it has hardly any thing figurative in it: but it is beautifully sententious, and, from the very form and manner of it, has great spirit, force, and energy. Thus Job's last speeches, in answer to his three friends, chap. xxvii.-xxxi., are called *mashals;* from no one particular character, which discriminates them from the rest of the poem, but from the sublime, the figurative, the sententious manner which equally prevails through the whole poem, and makes it one of the first and most eminent examples extant of the truly great and beautiful in poetic style. See the note on Prov. i. 1.

The *Septuagint* in this place render the word by θρηνος, *a lamentation.* They plainly consider the speech here introduced as a piece of poetry, and of that species of poetry which we call the elegiac; either from the subject, it being a poem on the fall and death of the king of Babylon, or from the form of the composition, which is of the longer sort of Hebrew verse, in which the Lamentations of Jeremiah, called by the *Septuagint* Θρηνοι, are written.

The golden city ceased] מדהבה *madhebah*, which is here translated *golden city*, is a Chaldee word. Probably it means that *golden coin* or *ingot* which was given to the Babylonians by way of tribute. So the word is understood by the *Vulgate*, where it is rendered *tributum;* and by Montanus, who translates it *aurea pensio*, the golden pension. *Kimchi* seems to have understood the word in the same sense. *De Rossi* translates it *auri dives*, rich in gold, or *auri exactrix*, the exactor of gold; the same as the exactor of tribute.

Verse 9. *Hell from beneath is moved for thee to meet* thee] That is, *Nebuchadnezzar.* "*It* (hell) hath raised up from their thrones all the kings of the earth;—the *ghosts* (*rephaim*) of all the *mighty ones*, or *goats*, (עתודי *attudey*,) of the earth—all the oppressors of mankind." What a most terrible idea is here! Tyrannical kings who have oppressed and spoiled mankind, are here represented as *enthroned in hell;* and as taking a Satanic pleasure in seeing others of the same description enter those abodes of misery!

A. M. cir. 3292
B. C. cir. 712
Olymp. XVII. 1
cir. annum
NumæPompilii,
R. Roman., 4

11 Thy pomp is brought down
to the grave, *and* the noise of
thy viols: the worm is spread
under thee and the worms
cover thee.
12 [s]How art thou fallen from heaven, [t]O
Lucifer, son of the morning! *how* art thou
cut down to the ground, which didst weaken
the nations!
13 For thou hast said in thine heart, [u]I will
ascend into heaven, [v]I will exalt my throne
above the stars of God: I will sit also upon
the mount of the congregation, [w]in the sides
of the north:
14 I will ascend above the heights of the
clouds; [x]I will be like the Most High.
15 Yet thou [y]shalt be brought
down to hell, to the sides of
the pit.
16 They that see thee shall nar-
rowly look upon thee, *and* consider thee, *say-*
ing, Is this the man that made the earth to
tremble, that did shake kingdoms?
17 *That* made the world as a wilderness,
and destroyed the cities thereof; *that* [z]opened
not the house of his prisoners.
18 All the kings of the nations, *even* all
of them, lie in glory, every one in his own
house.
19 But thou art cast out of thy grave like
an abominable branch, *and as* the raiment of
those that are slain, thrust through with a

[s]Chap. xxxiv. 4——[t]Or, *O day star*——[u]Matt. xi. 23——[v]Dan. viii. 10——[w]Psa. xlviii. 2——[x]Chap. xlvii. 8; 2 Thess. ii. 4——[y]Matt. xi. 23——[z]Or, *did not let his prisoners loose homeward*

Verse 11. *Cover thee*—"Thy covering."] *Twenty-eight* MSS. (*ten* ancient) of *Kennicott's*, *thirty-nine* of *De Rossi's*, *twelve* editions, with the *Septuagint* and *Vulgate*, read ומכסך *umechassecha*, in the singular number.

Verse 12. *O Lucifer, son of the morning*] The *Versions* in general agree in this translation, and render הילל *heilel* as signifying *Lucifer*, Φωσφωρος, the *morning star*, whether *Jupiter* or *Venus;* as these are both *bringers of the morning light*, or *morning stars*, annually in their turn. And although the context speaks explicitly concerning Nebuchadnezzar, yet this has been, I know not why, applied to the chief of the fallen angels, who is most incongruously denominated *Lucifer*, (the bringer of light!) an epithet as common to him as those of *Satan* and *Devil*. That the Holy Spirit by his prophets should call this arch-enemy of God and man the *light-bringer*, would be strange indeed. But the truth is, the text speaks nothing at all concerning *Satan* nor his *fall*, nor the *occasion* of that fall, which many divines have with great confidence deduced from this text. O how necessary it is to understand the literal meaning of Scripture, that preposterous comments may be prevented! Besides, I doubt much whether our translation be correct. הילל *heilel*, which we translate *Lucifer*, comes from ילל *yalal, yell, howl*, or *shriek*, and should be translated, "Howl, son of the morning;" and so the *Syriac* has understood it; and for this meaning *Michaelis* contends: see his reasons in *Parkhurst*, under הלל *halal*.

Verse 13. *I will ascend into heaven*] I will get the empire of the whole world. *I will exalt my throne above the stars of God*—above the Israelites, who are here termed the stars of God. So the *Targum* of Jonathan, and *R. D. Kimchi*. This chapter speaks not of the ambition and fall of Satan, but of the pride, arrogance, and fall of Nebuchadnezzar.

The mount of the congregation—"The mount of the Divine Presence"] It appears plainly from Exod. xxv. 22, and xxix. 42, 43, where God appoints the place of meeting with Moses, and promises to meet with him before the ark to commune with him, and to speak unto him; and to meet the children of Israel at the door of the tabernacle; that the tabernacle, and afterwards the door of the tabernacle, and Mount Zion, (or Moriah, which is reckoned a part of Mount Zion,) whereon it stood, was called the tabernacle, and the mount of convention or of appointment; not from the people's assembling there to perform the services of their religion, (which is what our translation expresses by calling it the tabernacle of the congregation,) but because God appointed that for the place where he himself would meet with Moses, and commune with him, and would meet with the people. Therefore הר מועד *har moed*, the "mountain of the assembly," or אהל מועד *ohel moed*, the "tabernacle of the assembly," means the place appointed by God, where he would present himself; agreeably to which I have rendered it in this place, *the mount of the Divine Presence*.

Verse 19. *Like an abominable branch*—"Like the tree abominated"] That is, as an object of abomination and detestation; such as the tree is on which a malefactor has been hanged. "It is written," saith St. Paul, Gal. iii. 13, "Cursed is every man that hangeth on a tree," from Deut. xxi. 23. The Jews therefore held also as accursed and polluted the tree itself on which a malefactor had been executed, or on which he had been hanged after having been put to death by stoning. "Non suspendunt super arbore, quæ radicibus solo adhæreat; sed super ligno eradicato, ut ne sit excisio molesta: nam lignum, super quo fuit aliquis suspensus, cum suspendioso sepelitur; ne maneat illi malum nomen, et dicant homines, Istud est lignum, in quo suspensus est ille, ὁ δεινα. Sic lapis, quo aliquis fuit lapidatus; et gladius, quo fuit occisus is qui est occisus; et sudarium sive mantile, quo fuit aliquis strangulatus; omnia hæc cum iis, qui perierunt, sepeliuntur." *Maimonides, apud Casaub. in Baron. Exercitat.* xvi. An. 34, Num. 134. "Cum itaque homo suspensu maximæ esset abominationi,—Judæi quoque præ cæteris abominabantur lignum

A. M. cir. 3292
B. C. cir. 712
Olymp. XVII.1
cir. annum
NumæPompilii,
R. Roman, 4

sword, that go down to the stones of the pit; as a carcass trodden under feet.

20 Thou shalt not be joined with them in burial, because thou hast destroyed thy land *and* slain thy people: [a]the seed of evil-doers shall never be renowned.

21 Prepare slaughter for his children [b]for the iniquity of their fathers; that they do not rise, nor possess the land, nor fill the face of the world with cities.

22 For I will rise up against them, saith the LORD of hosts, and cut off from Babylon [c]the name, and [d]remnant, [e]and son, and nephew, saith the LORD.

23 [f]I will also make it a possession for the bittern, and pools of water: and I will sweep it with the besom of destruction, saith the LORD of hosts.

24 The LORD of hosts hath sworn, saying, Surely as I have thought, so shall it come to pass; and as I have purposed, *so* shall it stand:

A. M. cir. 3292
B. C. cir. 712
Olymp. XVII.1
cir. annum
NumæPompilii,
R. Roman., 4

25 That I will break the Assyrian in my land, and upon my mountains tread him under foot: then shall [g]his yoke depart from off them, and his burden depart from off their shoulders.

26 This *is* the purpose that is purposed upon the whole earth: and this *is* the hand that is stretched out upon all the nations.

27 For the LORD of hosts hath [h]purposed, and who shall disannul *it?* and his hand *is* stretched out, and who shall turn it back?

A. M. cir. 3278
B. C. cir. 726
Olymp. XIII. 3
cir. annum
Romuli,
R. Roman., 28

28 In the year that [i]king Ahaz died was this burden.

[a]Job xviii. 19; Psa. xxi. 10; xxxvii. 28; cix. 13 —— [b]Exod. xx. 5; Matt. xxiii. 35 —— [c]Prov. x. 7; Jer. li 62 —— [d]1 Kings xiv. 10 —— [e]Job xviii. 19 —— [f]Chap. xxxiv. 11; Zeph. ii. 14

[g]Chapter x. 27 —— [h]2 Chronicles xx. 6; Job ix. 12; xxiii. 13; Psalm xxxiii. 11; Proverbs xix. 21; xxi. 30; chapter xliii. 13; Daniel iv. 31, 35 —— [i]2 Kings xvi. 20

quo fuerat suspensus, ita ut illud quoque terra tegerent, tanquam rem abominabilem. Unde interpres Chaldæus hæc verba transtulit כחת טמיר *kechat temir*, sicut virgultum absconditum, sive sepultum." *Kalinski, Vaticinia Observationibus Illustrata*, p. 342.

"The Jews never hang any malefactor upon a tree that is *growing in the earth*, but upon a post fixed in the ground, that it might never be said, 'That is the tree on which such a one was hanged;' for custom required that the tree should be *buried* with the *malefactor*. In like manner the *stone* by which a criminal was *stoned to death*, or the *sword* by which he was *beheaded*, or the *napkin* or *handkerchief* by which he was *strangled*, should be buried with him in the same grave." "For as the hanged man was considered the *greatest abomination*, so the very *post* or *wood* on which he was hanged was deemed a most abominable thing, and therefore buried under the earth."

Agreeably to which *Theodoret, Hist. Ecclesiast.* i. 17, 18, in his account of the finding of the cross by Helena, says, "That the three crosses were buried in the earth near the place of our Lord's sepulchre." And this circumstance seems to confirm the relation of the discovery of the cross of Christ. The crosses were found where the custom required they should be buried.

The raiment of those that are slain—"Clothed with the slain"] *Thirty-five* MSS., (*ten* ancient,) and *three* editions, have the word fully written, לבוש *lebush*. It is not a noun, but the participle passive; thrown out among the common slain, and covered with the dead bodies. So ver. 11, the earth-worm is said to be his bed-covering. This reading is confirmed by two ancient MSS. in my own collection.

Verse 20. *Because thou hast destroyed thy land*, &c.—"Because thou hast destroyed thy country; thou hast slain thy people"] Xenophon gives an instance of this king's wanton cruelty in killing the son of Gobrias, on no other provocation than that, in hunting, he struck a boar and a lion which the king had missed. *Cyrop.* iv. 309.

Verse 23. *I will sweep it with the besom of destruction*—"I will plunge it in the miry gulf of destruction"] I have here very nearly followed the Version of the *Septuagint;* the reasons for which see in the last note on De Poësi Hebr. Prælect. xxviii.

The besom of destruction, as our Version renders it. במטאטא *bematate*. This, says *Kimchi*, is a *Chaldee* word: and it is worthy of remark that the prophet, writing to the *Chaldeans*, uses several words peculiar to their own language to point out the *nature* of the Divine judgments, and the *causes* of them. See the note on Jer. x. 11. *Sixteen* of *Kennicott's* MSS., and *seventeen* of *De Rossi's*, and *one* ancient of my own, have the word במטאטי *bematatey*, in the plural. "I will sweep her with the besoms of destruction."

Verse 25. *I will break the Assyrian—upon my mountains*—"To crush the Assyrian—on my mountains"] The Assyrians and Babylonians are the same people, Herod. i. 199, 200. Babylon is reckoned the principal city in Assyria, *ibid.* 178. Strabo says the same thing, lib. xvi. *sub init.* The circumstance of this judgment being to be executed on God's mountains is of importance; it may mean the destruction of Sennacherib's army near Jerusalem, and have a still farther view: compare Ezek. xxxix. 4; and see Lowth on this place of Isaiah.

Verse 28. *In the year that king Ahaz died was this burden*] Uzziah had subdued the Philistines, 2 Chron. xxvi. 6, 7; but, taking advantage of the weak reign of Ahaz, they invaded Judea, and took, and held in possession, some cities in the southern part of the kingdom. On

A. M. cir. 3278
B. C. cir. 726
Olymp. XIII. 3
cir annum Romuli,
R. Roman., 28

29 Rejoice not thou, whole Palestina, [k]because the rod of him that smote thee is broken: for out of the serpent's root shall come forth a [l]cockatrice, [m]and his fruit *shall be* a fiery flying serpent.

30 And the first-born of the poor shall feed, and the needy shall lie down in safety: and I will kill thy root with famine, and he shall slay thy remnant.

A. M. cir. 3278
B. C. cir. 726
Olymp. XIII. 3
cir. annum Romuli,
R. Roman., 28

31 Howl, O gate; cry, O city; thou, whole Palestina, *art* dissolved: for there shall come from the north a smoke, and [n]none *shall be* alone in his [o]appointed times.

32 What shall *one* then answer the messengers of the nation? that [p]the LORD hath founded Zion, and [q]the poor of his people shall [r]trust in it.

[k]2 Chron. xxvi. 6——[l]Or, *adder*——[m]2 Kings xviii. 8——[n]Or, he shall *not* be *alone*——[o]Or, *assemblies*——[p]Psa. lxxxvii. 1, 5; cii. 16——[q]Zeph. iii. 12; Zech. xi. 11——[r]Or, *betake themselves unto it*

the death of Ahaz, Isaiah delivers this prophecy, threatening them with the destruction that Hezekiah, his son, and great-grandson of Uzziah, should bring upon them: which he effected; for "he smote the Philistines, even unto Gaza, and the borders thereof," 2 Kings xviii. 8. Uzziah, therefore, must be meant by the rod that smote them, and by the serpent from whom should spring the flying fiery serpent, ver. 29, that is, Hezekiah, a much more terrible enemy than even Uzziah had been.

The *Targum* renders the *twenty-ninth* verse in a singular way. "For, from the sons of Jesse shall come forth the Messiah; and his works among you shall be as the flying serpent."

Verse 30. *And the first-born of the poor*, &c.] The *Targum* goes on applying all to the *Messiah*. "And the poor of the people shall he feed, and the humble shall dwell securely in his days: and he shall kill thy children with famine, and the remnant of thy people shall he slay."

I will kill—"He will slay"] The *Septuagint* reads המית *hemith, in the third person*, ανελει; and so the *Chaldee*. The *Vulgate* remedies the confusion of persons in the present text, by reading both the verbs in the first person.

Verse 31. *There shall come from the north a smoke*—"From the north cometh a smoke"] That is, a cloud of dust raised by the march of Hezekiah's army against Philistia; which lay to the south-west from Jerusalem. A great dust raised has, at a distance, the appearance of smoke: *Fumantes pulvere campi;* "The fields *smoking* with dust."—VIRG. Æn. xi. 908.

Verse 32. *The messengers of the nation*—"The ambassadors of the nations"] The *Septuagint* read גוים *goyim*, εθνων, plural; and so the *Chaldee*, and one MS. The ambassadors of the neighbouring nations, that send to congratulate Hezekiah on his success; which in his answer he will ascribe to the protection of God. See 2 Chron. xxxii. 23. Or, if גוי *goi singular*, the reading of the text, be preferred, the ambassadors sent by the Philistines to demand peace. —L.

The Lord hath founded Zion] *Kimchi* refers this to the state of *Zion* under Hezekiah, when the rest of the cities of Judea had been taken, and this only was left for a *hope* to the poor of God's people: and God so defended it that Rabshakeh could not prevail against it.

The true Church of God is a place of safety; for as all its members are devoted to God, and walk in his testimonies, so they are continually defended and supported by him. In the congregations of his people, God dispenses his light and salvation; hence his *poor* or humble ones expect in his ordinances the blessings they need.

CHAPTER XV

Prediction of very heavy calamities about to fall upon the Moabites, 1–9.

A. M. cir. 3278
B. C. cir. 726
Olymp. XIII. 3
cir. annum Romuli,
R. Roman., 28

THE [a]burden of Moab. Because in the night [b]Ar of Moab is laid waste *and* [c]brought to silence; because in the night Kir of Moab is laid waste, *and* brought to silence:

2 [d]He is gone to Bajith, and to Dibon, the high places, to

[a]Jer. xlviii. 1, &c.; Ezek. xxv. 8–11; Amos ii. 1——[b]Num. xxi. 28——[c]Or, *cut off*——[d]Chap. xvi. 12

This and the following chapter, taken together, make one entire prophecy, very improperly divided into two parts. The time of its delivery, and consequently of its accomplishment, which was to be in three years from that time, is uncertain; the former not being marked in the prophecy itself, nor the latter recorded in history. But the most probable account is, that it was delivered soon after the foregoing, in the first year of Hezekiah; and that it was accomplished in his fourth year, when Shalmaneser invaded the kingdom of Israel. He might probably march through Moab; and to secure every thing behind him, possess himself of the whole country, by taking their principal strong places, Ar and Kirhares.—L. The authorized Version, which we have followed in the margin, places the prophecy in this chapter *fourteen* years earlier than that contained in the *two* preceding.

A. M. cir. 3278 B. C. cir. 726 Olymp. XIII. 3 cir. annum Romuli, R. Roman., 28

weep: Moab shall howl over
Nebo, and over Medeba: [e]on
all their heads *shall be* baldness,
and every beard cut off.
3 In their streets they shall gird themselves
with sackcloth: [f]on the tops of their houses,
and in their streets, every one shall howl,
[g]weeping abundantly.
4 And Heshbon shall cry, [h]and Elealeh:
their voice shall be heard *even* unto Jahaz:
therefore the armed soldiers
of Moab shall cry out; his
life shall be grievous unto
him.
5 [i]My heart shall cry out for Moab; [k]his
fugitives *shall flee* unto Zoar, a [l]heifer of
three years old: for [m]by the mounting up of
Luhith with weeping shall they go it up; for
in the way of Horonaim they shall raise up a
cry of [n]destruction.

[e]See Lev. xxi. 5; chap. iii. 24; xxii. 12; Jer. xlvii. 5; xlviii. 1, 37, 38; Ezek. vii. 18——[f]Jer. xlviii. 38——[g]Heb. *descending into weeping*, or *coming down with weeping*

[h]Chap. xvi. 9——[i]Chap. xvi. 11; Jer. xlviii. 31——[k]Or, *to the borders thereof, even as a heifer*——[l]Chap. xvi. 14; Jer. xlviii. 34——[m]Jer. xlviii. 5——[n]Heb. *breaking*

Jeremiah has happily introduced much of this prophecy of Isaiah into his own larger prophecy against the same people in his *forty-eighth* chapter, denouncing God's judgment on Moab, subsequent to the calamity here foretold, and to be executed by Nebuchadnezzar; by which means several mistakes of transcribers in the present text of both prophets may be rectified.

NOTES ON CHAP. XV

Verse 1. *Because in the night*] בליל *beleil.* That both these cities should be taken in the *night* is a circumstance somewhat unusual; but not so material as to deserve to be so strongly insisted upon. *Vitringa*, by his remark on this word, shows that he was dissatisfied with it in its plain and obvious meaning, and is forced to have recourse to a very hard metaphorical interpretation of it. Noctu vel nocturno impetu; vel metaphorice, repente, subito, inexpectata destructione: placet posterius. *Calmet* conjectures, and I think it probable, that the true reading is כליל *keleil, as the night.* There are many mistakes in the *Hebrew* text arising from the very great similitude of the letters ב *beth*, and כ *caph*, which in many MSS., and some printed editions, are hardly distinguishable. Admitting this reading, the translation will be,—

"Because Ar is utterly destroyed, Moab is undone!
Because Kir is utterly destroyed, Moab is undone!"

Verse 2. *He is gone to Bajith, and to Dibon*] עלה הבית *alah habbayith*, should be rendered, *he is gone to the* HOUSE, i. e., to their chief temple, where they practised idolatry. Dibon was the name of a tower where also was an idolatrous temple; thither they went to weep and pray before their idols, that they might interpose and save them from their calamities. So *R. D. Kimchi. He is gone to Bajith and to Dibon:* but Bishop *Lowth* reads *Beth Dibon;* this is the name of *one* place; and the two words are to be joined together, without the ו *vau* intervening. So the *Chaldee* and *Syriac.* This reading is not supported by any MS. or Version: but some MSS., instead of ער *ar*, have עיר *ir, a city*, others have עד *ad, unto*, and some editions have על *al, upon.* But all these help little, though they show that the place puzzled both the *scribes* and the *editors.*

On all their heads shall be *baldness*, &c.—"On every head there is baldness," &c.] Herodotus, ii. 36, speaks of it as a general practice among all men, except the Egyptians, to cut off their hair as a token of mourning. "Cut off thy hair, and cast it away," says Jeremiah, vii. 29, "and take up a lamentation."

> Τουτο νυ και γερας οιον οιζυροισι βροτοισι
> Κειρασθαι τε κομην, βαλεειν τ᾽ απο δακρυ παρειων.
> HOM. *Odyss.* iv. 197.

> "The rites of wo
> Are all, alas! the living can bestow;
> O'er the congenial dust enjoined to shear
> The graceful curl, and drop the tender tear."
> POPE.

On every head.—For ראשיו *roshaiv*, read ראש *rosh.* So the parallel place, Jer. xlviii. 37, and so *three* MSS., *one* ancient. An ancient MS. reads על כל ראש *al col rosh. Five* read בכל ראש *bechol rosh, on every head*, with the *Septuagint* and *Arabic.* AND *every head.* The ו *vau, and*, is found in *thirty* MSS., in *three* editions, and in the *Syriac, Vulgate*, and *Chaldee.*

Cut off—"Shorn."] The printed editions, as well as the MSS., are divided on the reading of this word. Some have גדועה *geduah, shorn*, others גרעה *geruah, diminished.* The similitude of the letters ד *daleth* and ר *resh* has likewise occasioned many mistakes. In the present case, the sense is pretty much the same with either reading. The text of Jer. xlviii. 37 has the latter, *diminished.* The former reading is found in *twelve* of Dr. *Kennicott's* MSS., *forty* of *De Rossi's*, and *two* of my own. A great number of *editions* have the same reading.

Verse 3. *With sackcloth*] שק *sak.* The word is in the plural שקים *sakkim, sacks*, in one of *De Rossi's* MSS.

Verse 4. *The armed soldiers*—"The very loins"] So the *Septuagint*, ἡ οσφυς, and the *Syriac.* They cry out violently, with their utmost force.

Verse 5. *My heart shall cry out for Moab*—"The heart of Moab crieth within her"] For לבי *libbi, my heart*, the *Septuagint* reads לבו *libbo, his heart*, or לב *leb;* the *Chaldee*, לבו *libbo.* For בריחיה *bericheyha*, the *Syriac* reads ברוחה *berocheh;* and so likewise the *Septuagint*, rendering it εν αυτῃ, *Edit. Vat:* or εν ἑαυτῃ, *Edit. Alex.* and MSS. I. D. II.

A heifer of three years old—"A young heifer."] *Hebrew*, a heifer *three years* old, in full strength; as *Horace* uses *equa trima*, for a

A. M. cir. 3278
B. C. cir. 726
Olymp. XIII. 3
cir. annum
Romuli,
R. Roman., 28

6 For the waters °of Nimrim
shall be ᵖdesolate: for the hay
is withered away, the grass faileth, there is no green thing.
7 Therefore the abundance they have gotten,
and that which they have laid up, shall they
carry away to the ᵍbrook of the willows.
8 For the cry is gone round about the borders of Moab; the howling
thereof unto Eglaim, and the
howling thereof unto Beer-
elim.
9 For the waters of Dimon shall be full of
blood: for I will bring ʳmore upon Dimon,
ˢlions upon him that escapeth of Moab, and
upon the remnant of the land.

A. M. cir. 3278
B. C. cir. 726
Olymp. XIII. 3
cir. annum
Romuli,
R. Roman., 28

°Num. xxxii. 36——ᵖHeb. *desolations*——ᵍOr, *valley of the Arabians*——ʳHeb. *additions*——ˢ2 Kings xvii. 25

young mare just coming to her prime. *Bochart* observes, from *Aristotle*, Hist. Animal. lib. iv., that in this kind of animals alone the voice of the female is deeper than that of the male; therefore the lowing of the heifer, rather than of the bullock, is chosen by the prophet, as the more proper image to express the mourning of Moab. But I must add that the expression here is very short and obscure; and the opinions of interpreters are various in regard to the meaning. Compare Jer. xlviii. 34.

Shall they go it up—"They shall ascend"] For יעלה *yaaleh*, the *Septuagint* and a MS. read in the plural, יעלו *yaalu*. And from this passage the parallel place in Jer. xlviii. 5 must be corrected; where, for יעלה בכי *yaaleh bechi*, which gives no good sense, read יעלה בו *yaaleh bo*.

Verse 7. "Shall perish"] אבדו *abadu or* אבדה *abadeh*. This word seems to have been lost out of the text: it is supplied by the parallel place, Jer. xlviii. 36. The *Syriac* expresses it by עבר *aber*, *præteriit*, "he hath passed;" and the *Chaldee* by יתבוזון *yithbazezun*, *diripientur*.

To the brook of the willows—"To the valley of willows"] That is, to Babylon. *Hieron.* and *Jarchi in loc.;* both referring to Psa. cxxxvii. 2. So likewise *Prideaux*, *Le Clerc*, &c.

Verse 9. *The waters of Dimon*] Some have *Dibon*, others have *Ribon* and *Rimon*. *St. Jerome* observes that the same town was called both *Dibon* and *Dimon*. The reading is therefore indifferent.

Upon him that escapeth of Moab, &c.—"Upon the escaped of Moab, and Ariel, and the remnant of Admah."] The *Septuagint* for עריה *aryeh* read אריאל *ariel*. Ar Moab was called also Ariel or Areopolis, *Hieron.* and *Theodoret*. See *Cellarius*. They make אדמה *Admah* also a proper name. Michaelis thinks that the Moabites might be called the remnant of Admah, as sprung from Lot and his daughters, escaped from the destruction of that and the other cities; or, metaphorically, as the Jews are called princes of Sodom, and people of Gomorrah, chap. i. 10. Bibliotheque Orient. Part v., p. 195. The reading of this verse is very doubtful; and the sense, in every way in which it can be read, very obscure.—L. *Calmet* thinks there may be a reference to 1 Chron. xi. 22, where it is said, "Benaiah slew two lion-like men of Moab," or the *two Ariels* of Moab, and would therefore translate, "I will bring down the remnant of Moab like Ariel, (which Benaiah smote,) and them that are escaped like Adamah." They shall be exterminated, as were the inhabitants of those two cities. Ariel was a double city—the river Arnon dividing it in two. This is the two Ariels of Moab—not *two lion-like men*, much less *two lions*. See *Calmet* on this place.

CHAPTER XVI

The distress of Moab pathetically described by the son of the prince, or ruler of the land, being forced to flee for his life through the desert, that he may escape to Judea; and the young women, like young birds scared from their nest, wade helpless through the fords of Arnon, the boundary of their country, to seek protection in some foreign land, 1, 2. *The prophet addresses Sion, exhorting her to show mercy to her enemies in their distress, that her throne may be established in righteousness,* 3–5. *Exceeding great pride of Moab,* 6. *The terrible calamities about to fall upon Moab farther described by the languishing of the vine, the ceasing of the vintage, the sound of the prophet's bowels quivering like a harp, &c.,* 7–13. *Awful nearness of the full accomplishment of the prophecy,* 14.

A. M. cir. 3278
B. C. cir. 726
Olymp. XIII. 3
cir. annum
Romuli,
R. Roman., 28

SEND ᵃye the lamb to the
ruler of the land ᵇfrom
ᶜSelaᵈ to the wilderness, unto the
mount of the daughter of Zion.
2 For it shall be, *that,* as a
wandering bird ᵉcast out of the
nest, *so* the daughters of Moab
shall be at the fords of ᶠArnon.

A. M. cir. 3278
B. C. cir. 726
Olymp. XIII. 3
cir. annum
Romuli,
R. Roman., 28

ᵃ2 Kings iii. 4——ᵇ2 Kings xiv. 7——ᶜOr, *Petra*——ᵈHeb. *a rock*——ᵉOr, *a nest forsaken*——ᶠNum. xxi. 13

NOTES ON CHAP. XVI

Verse 1. *Send ye the lamb, &c.*—"I will send forth the son, &c."] Both the reading and meaning of this verse are still more doubtful than those of the preceding. The *Septuagint* and *Syriac* read אשלח *eshlach*, *I will send*, in the first person singular, future tense: the *Vulgate* and *Talmud Babylon.*, read שלח *shelach*,

A. M. cir. 3278
B. C. cir. 726
Olymp. XIII. 3
cir. annum
Romuli,
R. Roman., 28

3 [g]Take counsel, execute judgment; make thy shadow as the night in the midst of the noonday; hide the outcasts; bewray not him that wandereth.

4 Let mine outcasts dwell with thee, Moab; be thou a covert to them from the face of the spoiler: for the [h]extortioner is at an end, the spoiler ceaseth, [i]the oppressors are consumed out of the land.

5 And in mercy [k]shall the throne be [l]established; and he shall sit upon it in truth in the tabernacle of David, [m]judging, and seeking judgment, and hasting righteousness.

6 We have heard of the [n]pride of Moab; *he is* very proud; *even* of his haughtiness, and his pride, and his wrath; [o]*but* his lies *shall* not *be* so.

7 Therefore shall Moab [p]howl for Moab,

[g]Heb. *Bring*——[h]Heb. *wringer*——[i]Heb. *the treaders down*——[k]Dan. vii. 14, 27; Mic. iv. 7; Luke i. 33 [l]Or, *prepared*

[m]Psa. lxxii. 2; xcvi. 13; xcviii. 9——[n]Jer. xlviii 29; Zeph. ii. 10——[o]Chapter xxviii. 15——[p]Jeremiah xlviii. 20

send, singular imperative: some read שלחו *shilchu, send ye forth*, or *shalechu, they send forth*. The *Syriac*, for כר *car, a lamb*, reads בר *bar, a son*, which is confirmed by five MSS. of *Kennicott* and *De Rossi*. The two first verses describe the distress of Moab on the Assyrian invasion; in which even the son of the prince of the country is represented as forced to flee for his life through the desert, that he may escape to Judea; and the young women are driven forth like young birds cast out of the nest, and endeavouring to wade through the fords of the river Arnon. Perhaps there is not so much difficulty in this verse as appears at first view. "Send the lamb to the ruler of the land," may receive light from 2 Kings iii. 4, 5: "And Mesha, king of Moab, was a sheepmaster, and rendered unto the king of Israel *one hundred thousand* lambs with their wool, and *one hundred thousand* rams: but when Ahab was dead, the king of Moab rebelled against Israel." Now the prophet exhorts them to begin paying the tribute as formerly, that their punishment might be averted or mitigated.

Verse 3. *Take counsel*—"Impart counsel"] The *Vulgate* renders the verbs in the beginning of this verse in the singular number. So the *Keri;* and so likewise *sixty-one* MSS. of *Kennicott's* and *De Rossi's* have it, and *nineteen* editions, and the *Syriac*. The verbs throughout the verse are also in the feminine gender; agreeing with Zion, which I suppose to be understood.

Verse 4. *Let mine outcasts dwell with thee, Moab*—"Let the outcasts of Moab sojourn with thee, O Zion"] Setting the points aside, this is by much the most obvious construction of the *Hebrew*, as well as most agreeable to the context, and the design of the prophet. And it is confirmed by the *Septuagint* οἱ φυγαδες Μωαβ, and *Syriac*.

The oppressors—"The oppressor"] Perhaps the Israelites, who in the time of Ahaz invaded Judah, defeated his army, slaying *one hundred and twenty thousand* men, and brought the kingdom to the brink of destruction. Judah, being now in a more prosperous condition, is represented as able to receive and to protect the fugitive Moabites. And with those former times of distress the security and flourishing state of the kingdom under the government of Hezekiah is contrasted.

Verse 5. *In mercy shall the throne be established*] May not this refer to the throne of Hezekiah? Here we have the character of such a king as cannot fail to be a blessing to the people. 1. "He sitteth on the throne in truth"—He does not merely *profess* to be the *father* and protector of his people: but he is actually such. 2. He is *judging.* He is not a man of war or blood, who wastes his subjects' lives and treasures in contentions with neighbouring nations, in order to satisfy his ambition by the extension of his territory. On the contrary, his whole life is occupied in the distribution of justice. 3. *He seeketh judgment.* He seeks out the poor distressed ones who cannot make their way to him, and avenges them on their oppressors. 4. *He hastens righteousness.* He does not suffer any of the courts of justice to delay the determination of the causes brought before them: he so orders that the point in litigation be fairly, fully, and speedily heard; and then judgment pronounced. *Delays* in the execution of justice answer little end but the enriching of unprincipled lawyers.

Verse 6. *We have heard of the pride of Moab*—"We have heard the pride of Moab"] For גא *ge*, read גאה *geah;* two MSS., one ancient, and Jer. xlviii. 29. Zephaniah, chap. ii. 8-10, in his prophecy against Moab, the subject of which is the same with that of Jeremiah in his *forty-eighth* chapter, (see the note on chap. xv. 1,) enlarges much on the pride of Moab, and their insolent behaviour towards the Jews:—

"I have heard the reproach of Moab;
And the revilings of the sons of Ammon:
Who have reproached my people;
And have magnified themselves against their borders.
Therefore, as I live, saith Jehovah God of hosts, the God of Israel:
Surely Moab shall be as Sodom,
And the sons of Ammon as Gomorrah:
A possession of nettles, and pits of salt,
And a desolation for ever.
The residue of my people shall spoil them,
And the remnant of my nation shall dispossess them:
This shall they have for their pride;
Because they have raised a reproach, and have magnified themselves
Against the people of Jehovah God of hosts."

Verse 7. *For the foundations of Kir-hareseth*—"For the men of Kirhares."] A palpable mistake in this place is happily corrected by the parallel text of Jer. xlviii. 31, where, instead of אשישי *ashishey, foundations* or *flagons*, we read אנשי *anshey, men.* In the same place of Jeremiah, and in ver. 36, and here in ver. 11, the name of the city is Kirhares, not Kirhareseth.

A. M. cir. 3278
B. C. cir. 726
Olymp. XIII. 3
cir. annum
Romuli,
R. Roman., 28

every one shall howl: for the foundations [q]of Kir-hareseth shall ye [r]mourn; surely *they are* stricken.

8 For [s]the fields of Heshbon languish, *and* [t]the vine of Shibmah: the lords of the heathen have broken down the principal plants thereof, they are come *even* unto Jazer, they wandered *through* the wilderness: her branches are [u]stretched out, they are gone over the sea.

9 Therefore [v]I will bewail with the weeping of Jazer the vine of Sibmah: I will water thee with my tears, [w]O Heshbon, and Elealeh: for [x]the shouting for thy summer fruits and for thy harvest is fallen.

10 And [y]gladness is taken away, and joy out of the plentiful field; and in the vineyards there shall be no singing, neither shall there be shouting: the treaders shall tread out no wine in *their* presses; I have made *their vintage*-shouting to cease.

11 Wherefore [z]my bowels shall sound like a harp for Moab, and mine inward parts for Kir-haresh.

12 And it shall come to pass, when it is seen that Moab is weary on [a]the high place, that

[q]2 Kings iii. 25——[r]Or, *mutter*——[s]Chap. xxiv. 7 [t]Ver. 9——[u]Or, *plucked up*——[v]Jer. xlviii. 32——[w]Ch. xv. 4

[x]Or, *the alarm is fallen upon*, &c.——[y]Chap. xxiv. 8; Jer. xlviii. 33——[z]Chap. xv. 5; lxiii. 15; Jer. xlviii. 36 [a]Chap. xv. 2

Verse 8. *Languish*—"Are put to shame"] Here the text of Jeremiah leaves us much at a loss, in a place that seems to be greatly corrupted. The *Septuagint* join the two last words of this verse with the beginning of the following. Their rendering is: *και ουκ εντραπησῃ, τα πεδια Εσεβων*. For אך *ach* they must have read אל *al;* otherwise, how came they by the negative, which seems not to belong to this place? Neither is it easy to make sense of the rest without a small alteration, by reading, instead of *εντραπησῃ τα*, *εντραπησεται*. In a word, the *Arabic* version, taken from the *Septuagint*, plainly authorizes this reading of the *Septuagint*, and without the negative; and it is fully confirmed by MSS. *Pachom.* and I. D. II., which have both of them *εντραπησεται πεδια Εσεβων*, without the negative; which makes an excellent sense, and, I think, gives us the true reading of the *Hebrew* text; אך נכלמו שדמות חשבון *ak nichlemu shadmoth cheshbon.* They frequently render the verb נכלם *nichlam* by *εντρεπομαι*. And נכלמו *nichlemu* answers perfectly well to אמלל *umlal*, the parallel word in the next line. The MSS. vary in expressing the word נכאים *nechaim*, which gives no tolerable sense in this place; one reads נוכאים *nochaim;* two others בכאים *bechaim;* in another the כ *caph* is upon a rasure of two letters; and the *Vulgate* instead of it reads מכותם *mecotham, plagas suas.*—L.

For the men of Kirhares ye shall make a moan. For the fields of Heshbon are put to shame. This is Bp. *Lowth's* sense of the passage.

Her branches are stretched out—"Her branches extended themselves."] For נטשו *nitteshu*, a MS. has נגשו *niggeshu;* which may perhaps be right. Compare Jer. xlviii. 32, which has in this part of the sentence the synonymous word נגעו *nagau.*

The meaning of this verse is, that the wines of Sibmah and Heshbon were greatly celebrated, and in high repute with all the great men and princes of that and the neighbouring countries; who indulged themselves even to intemperance in the use of them. So that their vines were so much in request as not only to be propagated all over the country of Moab to the sea of Sodom, but to have scions of them sent even beyond the sea into foreign countries. הלמו *halemu, knocked down, demolished;* that is overpowered, intoxicated. The drunkards of Ephraim are called by the prophet, chap. xxviii. 1, הלומי יין *halumey yayin, drinkers of wine.* See Schultens on Prov. xxiii. 25. Gratius, speaking of the Mareotic wine, says of it,

Pharios quæ fregit noxia reges. CYNEG. 312.

Verse 9. *With the weeping*—"As with the weeping"] For בבכי *bibechi*, a MS. reads בכי *bechi.* In Jer. xlviii. 32, it is מבכי *mibbechi.* The *Septuagint* read כבכי *kibeki, as with weeping*, which I follow.

For thy summer fruits and for thy harvest is fallen—"And upon thy vintage the destroyer hath fallen."] ועל קצירך הידד נפל *veal ketsirech heidad naphal.* In these few words there are two great mistakes, which the text of Jer. xviii. 32 rectifies. For קצירך *ketsirech*, it has בצירך *betsirech;* and for הידד *heidad*, שדד *shoded;* both which corrections the *Chaldee* in this place confirms. As to the first,

"Hesebon and Eleale, and
The flowery dale of Sibmah, clad with vines,"

were never celebrated for their *harvests;* it was the *vintage* that suffered by the irruption of the enemy; and so read the *Septuagint* and *Syriac.* הידד *heidad* is the noisy acclamation of the treaders of the grapes. And see what sense this makes in the literal rendering of the *Vulgate:* super messem tuam *vox calcantium irruit*, "upon thy harvest the voice of the treaders rushes." The reading in Jer. xlviii. 32 is certainly right, שדד נפל *shoded naphal*, "the destroyer hath fallen." The shout of the treaders does not come in till the next verse; in which the text of Isaiah in its turn mends that of Jeremiah, xlviii. 33, where instead of the first הידד *heidad*, "the shout," we ought undoubtedly to read, as here, הדרך *haddorech*, "the treader."

Verse 10. *Neither shall there be shouting*—"An end is put to the shouting"] The *Septuagint* read השבת *hishbeth*, passive, and in the third person; rightly, for God is not the speaker in this place. The rendering of the *Septuagint* is *πεπαυται γαρ κελευσμα*, "the cry ceaseth;" which last word, necessary to the rendering of the

A. M. cir. 3278
B. C. cir. 726
Olymp. XIII. 3
cir. annum Romuli,
R. Roman., 28

he shall come to his sanctuary to pray; but he shall not prevail.
13 This *is* the word that the LORD hath spoken concerning Moab since that time.
14 But now the LORD hath spoken, saying, Within three years, [b]as the years of a hireling, and the glory of Moab shall be contemned, with all that great multitude; and the remnant *shall be* very small *and* [c]feeble.

[b]Chap. xxi. 16 —— [c]Or, *not many*

Hebrew and to the sense, is supplied by MSS. *Pachom.* and I. D. II., having been lost out of the other copies.

Verse 12. *When it is seen that Moab, &c.*—"When Moab shall see," &c.] For נראה *nirah*, a MS. reads ראה *raah*, and so the *Syriac* and *Chaldee*. "Perhaps כי נראה *ki nirah* is only a various reading of כי נלאה *ki nilah*." SECKER. A very probable conjecture.

Verse 14. *Within three years*] בשליש *beshalish* כשליש *keshalish, according*, or *in or about three years*, is the reading of nine of *Kennicott's* and *De Rossi's* MSS., and *two* ancient editions.

But the *present reading* may well stand: "Now, the Lord hath spoken, saying, Within three years, as the years of a hireling." It seems as if this prophecy had been delivered before, without any time specified for its fulfilment; but now the time is determined—"in three years, as the years of a hireling"—for, as a *hireling* counts even to a single day, and will not abide with his employer an hour beyond the time agreed on; so, in *three years*, even to a day, from the delivery of this prophecy, shall destruction come upon Moab. This is the import of the present text; but if we take כשליש *keshalish*, AS in three years, or *in about three years' time*, the prophecy is not so definite.

These three years, says *Calmet*, are mentioned from the death of Ahaz, see chap. xiv. 28, and end the third year of Hezekiah, three years before the taking of Samaria by Shalmaneser. This conquerer did not ruin Moab so completely as not to leave a man in the land; the final desolation of Moab was reserved for Nebuchadnezzar, five years after the taking of Jerusalem.

Feeble—"And without strength."] An ancient MS., with the *Septuagint*, reads ולא *velo*, "and not."

CHAPTER XVII

Judgments of God upon Damascus, 1–3; *and upon Israel,* 4–6. *Good effects of these judgments on the small remnant or gleaning that should escape them,* 7, 8. *The same judgments represented in other but stronger terms, and imputed to irreligion and neglect of God,* 9–11. *The remaining verses are a distinct prophecy, a beautiful detached piece, worked up with the greatest elegance, sublimity, and propriety; and forming a noble description of the formidable invasion and sudden overthrow of Sennacherib, exactly suitable to the event,* 12–14.

A. M. cir. 3263
B. C. cir. 741
Olymp. IX. 4
cir. annum Romuli,
R. Roman., 13

THE [a]burden of Damascus. Behold, Damascus is taken away from *being* a city, and it shall be a ruinous heap.
2 The cities of Aroer *are* forsaken: they shall be for flocks, which shall lie down, and [b]none shall make *them* afraid.

[a]Jer. xlix 23; Amos i. 3; Zech. ix. 1; 2 Kings xvi. 9—— [b]Jer. vii. 33

This prophecy by its title should relate only to Damascus; but it full as much concerns, and more largely treats of, the kingdom of Samaria and the Israelites, confederated with Damascus and the Syrians against the kingdom of Judah. It was delivered probably soon after the prophecies of the seventh and eighth chapters, in the beginning of the reign of Ahaz; and was fulfilled by Tiglath-pileser's taking Damascus, and carrying the people captives to Kir, (2 Kings xvi. 9,) and overrunning great part of the kingdom of Israel, and carrying a great number of the Israelites also captives to Assyria; and still more fully in regard to Israel, by the conquest of the kingdom, and the captivity of the people, effected a few years after by Shalmaneser.—L.

NOTES ON CHAP. XVII

Verse 1. *The burden of Damascus.*] Which is, according to the common version, *The cities of Aroer are forsaken.* It has already been observed by the learned prelate that the prophecy, as it relates to Damascus, was executed in the beginning of the reign of Ahaz, probably about the *third* year. If we credit *Midrash*, the *Damascenes* were the most *extensive* and flagrant of all idolaters. "There were in Damascus *three hundred and sixty-five* streets, in each of these was an idol, and each idol had his peculiar day of worship; so that the whole were worshipped in the course of the year." This, or any thing like this, was a sufficient reason for this city's destruction.

A ruinous heap] For מעי *mei*, "a ruinous heap," the *Septuagint* reads לעי *lei*, "for a ruin," the *Vulgate* כעי *kei*, "as a ruin." I follow the former.

Verse 2. *The cities of Aroer* are *forsaken*—"The cities are deserted for ever"] What has Aroer on the river Arnon to do with Damascus? and if there be another Aroer on the northern border of the tribe of Gad, as Reland seems to

A. M. cir. 3263
B. C. cir. 741
Olymp. IX. 4
cir. annum
Romuli,
R. Roman., 13

3 [c]The fortress also shall cease
from Ephraim, and the kingdom
from Damascus, and the remnant of Syria: they shall be as
the glory of the children of Israel, saith the
LORD of hosts.
4 And in that day it shall come to pass, *that*
the glory of Jacob shall be made thin, and
[d]the fatness of his flesh shall wax lean.
5 [e]And it shall be as when the harvestman
gathereth the corn, and reapeth the ears with
his arm; and it shall be as he that gathereth
ears in the valley of Rephaim.
6 [f]Yet gleaning grapes shall be left in it, as
the shaking of an olive tree, two *or* three
berries in the top of the uppermost bough,
four *or* five in the outmost fruitful branches
thereof, saith the LORD God of Israel.
7 At that day shall a man [g]look to his
Maker, and his eyes shall have
respect to the Holy One of
Israel.
8 And he shall not look to the
altars, the work of his hands, neither shall
respect *that* which his fingers have made,
either the groves, or the [h]images.
9 In that day shall his strong cities be as a
forsaken bough, and an uppermost branch,
which they left because of the children of
Israel: and there shall be desolation.
10 Because thou hast forgotten [i]the God of
thy salvation, and hast not been mindful of
the rock of thy strength, therefore shalt thou
plant pleasant plants, and shalt set it with
strange slips:
11 In the day shalt thou make thy plant to
grow, and in the morning shalt thou make thy
seed to flourish: *but* the harvest *shall be*

A. M. cir. 3263
B. C. cir. 741
Olymp. IX. 4
cir. annum
Romuli,
R. Roman., 13

[c]Chap. vii. 16; viii. 4——[d]Chap. x. 16——[e]Jer. li. 33
[f]Chap. xxiv. 13
[g]Micah vii. 7——[h]Or, *sun images*——[i]Psalm lxviii. 19

think there might be, this is not much more to the purpose. Besides, *the cities of Aroer*, if Aroer itself is a city, makes no good sense. The *Septuagint*, for ערער *aroer*, read עדי עד *adey ad*, εις τον αιωνα, *for ever*, or for a long duration. The *Chaldee* takes the word for a verb from ערה *arah*, translating it חרבו *cherebu*, devastabuntur, "they shall be wasted." The *Syriac* read עדועיר *adoeir*. So that the reading is very doubtful. I follow the *Septuagint* as making the plainest sense.

Verse 3. *The remnant of Syria*—"The pride of Syria."] For שאר *shear*, "remnant," *Houbigant* reads שאת *seeth*, "pride," answering, as the sentence seems evidently to require, to כבוד *cabod*, "the glory of Israel." The conjecture is so very probable that I venture to follow it.

As the glory] בכבוד *bichbod*, "IN the glory," is the reading of *eight* MSS., and *ten* editions.

Verse 4. *In that day*] That is, says *Kimchi*, the time when the ten tribes of Israel, which were *the glory of Jacob*, should be carried into captivity.

Verse 5. *As when the harvestman gathereth*—"As when one gathereth"] That is, the king of Assyria shall sweep away the whole body of the people, as the reaper strippeth off the whole crop of corn; and the remnant shall be no more in proportion than the scattered ears left to the gleaner. The valley of Rephaim near Jerusalem was celebrated for its plentiful harvest; it is here used poetically for any fruitful country. *One* MS., and *one* ancient edition, has באסף *beesoph*, "IN gathering," instead of כאסף *keesoph*, "AS the gathering."

Verse 8. *The altars, the work of his hands*—"The altars dedicated to the work of his hands"] The construction of the words, and the meaning of the sentence, in this place, are not obvious; all the ancient Versions, and most of the modern, have mistaken it. The word מעשה *maaseh*, "the work," stands *in regimine* with מזבחות *mizbechoth*, "altars," not in opposition to it; it means the altars *of* the work of their hand; that is *of* the idols, which *are* the work of their hands. Thus *Kimchi* has explained it, and *Le Clerc* has followed him.

Verse 9. *As a forsaken bough, and an uppermost branch*—"the Hivites and the Amorites"] החרש והאמיר *hachoresh vehaamir*. No one has ever yet been able to make any tolerable sense of these words. The translation of the *Septuagint* has happily preserved what seems to be the true reading of the text, as it stood in the copies of their time; though the words are now transposed, either in the text or in their Version; οἱ Αμαρραιοι και οἱ Ευαιοι, "the Amorites and the Hivites." It is remarkable that many commentators, who never thought of admitting the reading of the *Septuagint*, understand the passage as referring to that very event which their Version expresses; so that it is plain that nothing can be more suitable to the context. "My father," says Bishop Lowth, "saw the necessity of admitting this variation at a time when it was not usual to make so free with the Hebrew text." Mr. Parkhurst is not satisfied with the prelate's adoption of the reading of the *Septuagint*, "the Hivites and the Amorites." He thinks the difficult words should be thus rendered; he takes the whole verse: "And his fortified cities shall be like the leaving, or what is left כעזובת *caazubath*, of or in a ploughed field, החרש *hachoresh*, or on a branch which they leave *coram*, before, the children of Israel." Which he considers a plain reference to the Mosaic laws relative to the *not gleaning of their ploughed fields, vineyards, and oliveyards*, but *leaving* עזב *ozeb*, somewhat of the fruits, for the poor of the land; Lev. ix. 9, 10; Deut. xxiv. 19-21, in the *Hebrew*. I fear that the text is taken by storm on both interpretations. One MS. has כל ערי *col arey*, "all the cities;" and instead of החלש *hachalash*, "of the branch," six MSS. have החדש *hachodesh*, "of the month." But this is probably a mistake.

Verse 10. *Strange slips*—"Shoots from a for-

A. M. cir. 3263
B. C. cir. 741
Olymp. IX. 4
cir. annum Romuli,
R. Roman., 13

[k]a heap in the day of grief and
of desperate sorrow.
12 Wo to the [l]multitude of
many people, *which* make a noise
[m]like the noise of the seas; and to the rushing of nations, *that* make a rushing like the
rushing of [n]mighty waters!
13 The nations shall rush like the rushing
of many waters: but *God* shall [o]rebuke them,
and they shall flee far off, and
[p]shall be chased as the chaff of
the mountains before the wind,
and like [q]a rolling thing before
the whirlwind.
14 And behold at evening-tide trouble; *and*
before the morning he *is* not. This *is* the
portion of them that spoil us, and the lot of
them that rob us.

[k]Or, *removed in the day of inheritance, and* there shall be *deadly sorrow*——[l]Or, *noise*——[m]Jer. vi. 23

[n]Or, *many*——[o]Psa. ix. 5——[p]Psa. lxxxiii. 13; Hos. xiii. 3——[q]Or, *thistle down*

eign soil."] The pleasant plants, and shoots from a foreign soil, are allegorical expressions for strange and idolatrous worship; vicious and abominable practices connected with it; reliance on human aid, and on alliances entered into with the neighbouring nations, especially Egypt; to all which the Israelites were greatly addicted, and in their expectations from which they should be grievously disappointed.

Verse 12. *Wo to the multitude*] The three last verses of this chapter seem to have no relation to the foregoing prophecy, to which they are joined. It is a beautiful piece, standing singly and by itself; for neither has it any connexion with what follows: whether it stands in its right place, or not, I cannot say. It is a noble description of the formidable invasion and the sudden overthrow of Sennacherib; which is intimated in the strongest terms and the most expressive images, exactly suitable to the event.

Like the rushing of mighty waters!] Five words, three at the end of the *twelfth* verse, and two at the beginning of the *thirteenth*, are omitted in eight MSS., with the *Syriac;* that is, in effect, the repetition contained in the first line of ver. 13 in this translation, is not made. After having observed that it is equally easy to account for the omission of these words by a transcriber if they are genuine, or their insertion if they are not genuine, occasioned by his carrying his eye backwards to the word לאמים *leammim*, or forwards to ישאון *yeshaon*, I shall leave it to the reader's judgment to determine whether they are genuine or not. Instead of כהמות *cahamoth*, "as the roaring," five MSS. and the *Vulgate* have כהמון *kehamon*, "as the multitude."

Verse 14. *He is not*—"He is no more."] For איננו *einennu* ten MSS. of Dr. *Kennicott's*, (three ancient,) ten of *De Rossi's*, and two editions, and the *Septuagint*, *Syriac*, *Chaldee*, *Vulgate*, and *Arabic*, have ואיננו *veeinenno*. This particle, authenticated by so many good vouchers, restores the sentence to its true poetical form, implying a repetition of some part of the parallel line preceding, thus:—

"At the season of evening, behold terror!
Before the morning, and [behold] he is no more!"

That spoil us] For שוסינו *shoseynu, them* that spoil us, fifteen MSS., one edition, and the *Syriac* have שוסנו *shosenu, him* that spoileth us. And for לבוזינו *lebozezeynu, them* that rob us, six MSS. and the *Syriac* have לבוזנו *lebozzeno, him* that robbeth us: and these readings make the place answer better to *Sennacherib*, according to Lowth's conjecture. Though God may permit the wicked to prevail for a time against his people, yet in the end those shall be overthrown, and the glory of the Lord shall shine brightly on them that fear him; for the earth shall be subdued, and the universe filled with his glory. Amen, and Amen!

CHAPTER XVIII

This chapter contains a very obscure prophecy; possibly designed to give the Jews, and perhaps the Egyptians, whose country is supposed to be meant, 1, 2, *and with whom many Jews resided, an intimation of God's interposition in favour of Sion,* 3, 4; *and of his counsels in regard to the destruction of their common enemy, Sennacherib, whose vast army, just as he thought his projects ripe, and ready to be crowned with success,* 5, *should become a prey to the beasts of the field, and to the fowls of heaven,* 6; *and that Egypt should be grateful to God for the deliverance vouchsafed her,* 7.

A. M. cir. 3290
B. C. cir. 714
Olymp. XVI. 3
cir. annum NumæPompilii,
R. Roman., 2

WO [a]to the land shadowing
with wings, which *is* beyond the rivers of Ethiopia:
2 That sendeth ambassadors by
the sea, even in vessels of bulrushes upon the waters, *saying,*
Go, ye swift messengers, to [b]a
nation [c]scattered and peeled, to

[a]Chap. xx. 4, 5; Ezek. xxx. 4, 5, 9; Zeph. ii. 12; iii. 10

[b]Ver. 7——[c]Or, *outspread and polished*

This is one of the most obscure prophecies in the whole Book of Isaiah. The *subject* of it, the *end* and *design* of it, the *people* to whom it is addressed, the *history* to which it belongs, the

A. M. cir. 3290
B. C. cir. 714
Olymp. XVI. 3
cir. annum
NumæPompilii,
R. Roman., 2

a people terrible from their beginning hitherto; [d]a [e]nation meted
out and trodden down, [f]whose
land the rivers have spoiled!

3 All ye [g]inhabitants of the
world, and dwellers on the earth,
see ye, [h]when he lifteth up an
ensign on the mountains; and

A. M. cir. 3290
B. C. cir. 714
Olymp. XVI. 3
cir. annum
NumæPompilii,
R. Roman., 2

[d]Or, *a nation that meteth out, and treadeth down*——[e]Heb. *a nation of line, and treading under foot*

[f]Or, *whose land the rivers despise*——[g]Jer. i. 14; x. 18; xlvii. 2; Hos. iv. 1; Joel ii. 1; Zech. xi. 6——[h]Ch. v. 26

person who sends the messengers, and the *nation* to whom the messengers are sent, are all obscure and doubtful.—L.

NOTES ON CHAP. XVIII

Verse 1. *Wo to the land*] הוי ארץ *hoi arets!* This interjection should be translated *ho!* for it is properly a particle of calling: Ho, land! Attend! Give ear!

Shadowing with wings—"The winged cymbal] צלצל כנפים *tsiltsal kenaphayim.* I adopt this as the most probable of the many interpretations that have been given of these words. It is *Bochart's:* see Phaleg, iv. 2. The Egyptian sistrum is expressed by a periphrasis; the Hebrews had no name for it in their language, not having in use the instrument itself. The cymbal they had was an instrument in its use and sound not much unlike the sistrum; and to distinguish it from the sistrum, they called it the cymbal with wings. The cymbal was a round hollow piece of metal, which, being struck against another, gave a ringing sound: the sistrum was a *round* instrument, consisting of a broad rim of metal, through which from side to side ran several loose laminæ or small rods of metal, which being shaken, gave a like sound. These, projecting on each side, had somewhat the appearance of wings; or might be very properly expressed by the same word which the Hebrews used for wings, or for the extremity, or a part of any thing projecting. The sistrum is given in a medal of Adrian, as the proper attribute of Egypt. See *Addison* on Medals, Series iii. No. 4; where the figure of it may be seen. The frame of the sistrum was in shape rather like the ancient *lyre;* it was not *round.*

If we translate *shadowing with wings*, it may allude to the multitude of its vessels, whose *sails* may be represented under the notion of *wings.* The *second* verse seems to support this interpretation. Vessels of bulrushes, גמא *gome,* or rather the flag *papyrus*, so much celebrated as the substance on which people *wrote* in ancient times, and from which our *paper* is denominated. The sails might have been made of this flag: but whole *canoes* were constructed from it. *Mat* sails are used to the present day in China. The *Vulgate* fully understood the meaning of the word, and has accordingly translated, *in vasis papyri,* "in vessels of papyrus." **Reshi vesselis.**—Old MS. Bib. This interpretation does not please Bp. *Lowth*, and for his dissent he gives the following reasons:—

In opposition to other interpretations of these words which have prevailed, it may be briefly observed that צלצל *tsiltsel* is never used to signify *shadow*, nor is כנף *canaph* applied to the sails of ships. If, therefore, the words are rightly interpreted *the winged cymbal*, meaning the sistrum, Egypt must be the country to which the prophecy is addressed. And upon this hypothesis the version and explanation must proceed. I farther suppose, that the prophecy was delivered before Sennacherib's return from his Egyptian expedition, which took up three years; and that it was designed to give to the Jews, and perhaps likewise to the Egyptians, an intimation of God's counsels in regard to the destruction of their great and powerful enemy.

Which is beyond the rivers of Ethiopia—"Which borders on the rivers of Cush"] What are the rivers of Cush? whether the eastern branches of the lower Nile, the boundary of Egypt towards Arabia, or the parts of the upper Nile towards Ethiopia, it is not easy to determine. The word מעבר *meeber* signifies either *on this side* or *on the farther side:* I have made use of the same kind of ambiguous expression in the translation.

Verse 2. *In vessels of bulrushes*—"In vessels of papyrus"] This circumstance agrees perfectly well with Egypt. It is well known that the Egyptians commonly used on the Nile a light sort of ships, or boats, made of the reed papyrus. Ex ipso quidem papyro navigia texunt. PLINY, xiii. 11.

Conseritur bibula Memphitis cymba papyro.
LUCAN, iv. 136.

Go, ye swift messengers] To this nation before mentioned, who, by the Nile, and by their numerous canals, have the means of spreading the report in the most expeditious manner through the whole country: go, ye swift messengers, and carry this notice of God's designs in regard to them. By the swift messengers are meant, not any particular persons specially appointed to this office, but any of the usual conveyers of news whatsoever, travellers, merchants, and the like, the instruments and agents of common fame. These are ordered to publish this declaration made by the prophet throughout Egypt, and to all the world; and to excite their attention to the promised visible interposition of God.

Scattered—"Stretched out in length"] Egypt, that is, the fruitful part, exclusive of the deserts on each side, is one long vale, through the middle of which runs the Nile, bounded on each side to the east and west by a chain of mountains seven hundred and fifty miles in length; in breadth from one to two or three days' journey: even at the widest part of the Delta, from Pelusium to Alexandria, not above two hundred and fifty miles broad. *Egmont* and *Hayman*, and *Pococke.*

Peeled—"Smoothed"] Either relating to the practice of the Egyptian priests, who made their bodies smooth by shaving off their hair, (see *Herod.* ii. 37;) or rather to their country's being made smooth, perfectly plain and level, by the overflowing of the Nile.

Meted out—"Meted out by line"] It is generally referred to the frequent necessity of having recourse to mensuration in Egypt, in order to determine the boundaries after the inundations of the Nile; to which even the origin of the science of geometry is by some ascribed. *Strabo*, lib. xvii. *sub init.*

Trodden down] Supposed to allude to a

A. M. cir. 3290
B. C. cir. 714
Olymp. XVI. 3
cir. annum
NumæPompilii,
R. Roman., 2

when he bloweth a trumpet, hear ye.

4 For so the LORD said unto me, I will take my rest, and I will [i]consider in my dwelling place like a clear heat [k]upon herbs, *and* like a cloud of dew in the heat of harvest.

[i]Or, *regard my set dwelling*

[k]Or, *after rain*

peculiar method of tillage in use among the Egyptians. Both Herodotus, (lib. ii.,) and Diodorus, (lib. i.,) say that when the Nile had retired within its banks, and the ground became somewhat dry, they sowed their land, and then sent in their cattle, (their hogs, says the former,) to tread in the seed; and without any farther care expected the harvest.

The rivers have spoiled—"The rivers have nourished"] The word בזאו *bazeu* is generally taken to be an irregular form for בזזו *bazezu*, "have spoiled," as four MSS. have it in this place; and so most of the Versions, both ancient and modern, understand it. On which Schultens, Gram. Heb. p. 491, has the following remark:—"Ne minimam quidem speciem veri habet בזאו *bazau*, Esai. xviii. 2, elatum pro בזזו *bazazu*, *deripiunt*. Hæc esset anomalia, cui nihil simile in toto linguæ ambitu. In talibus nil finire, vel fateri ex mera agi conjectura, tutius justiusque. Radicem בזא *baza* olim extare potuisse, quis neget? Si cognatum quid sectandum erat, ad בזה *bazah*, contemsit, potius decurrendum fuisset; ut בזאו *bazeu*, pro בזו *bazu*, sit enuntiatum, vel בזיו *baziv*. Digna phrasis, flumina contemmunt terram, i. e., inundant." "בזא *baza*, Arab. extulit se superbius, *item* subjecit sibi: *unde præt. pl.* בזאו *bazeu*, subjecerunt sibi, i. e., inundarunt."—*Simonis'* Lexic. Heb.

A learned friend has suggested to me another explanation of the word. בזא *baza*, *Syr.*, and ביזא *beiza*, *Chald.*, signifies *uber*, "a dug," *mamma*, "a breast;" agreeably to which the verb signifies *to nourish*. This would perfectly well suit with the Nile: whereas nothing can be more discordant than the idea of spoiling and plundering; for to the inundation of the Nile Egypt owed every thing; the fertility of the soil, and the very soil itself. Besides, the overflowing of the Nile came on by gentle degrees, covering without laying waste the country: "Mira æque natura fluminis, quod cum cæteri omnes abluant terras et eviscerent, Nilus tanto cæteris major adeo nihil exedit, nec abradit, ut contra adjiciat vires; minimumque in eo sit, quod solum temperet. Illato enim limo arenas saturat ac jungit; debetque illi Ægyptus non tantum fertilitatem terrarum, sed ipsas.—*Seneca*, Nat. Quæst., iv. 2. I take the liberty, therefore, which Schultens seems to think allowable in this place, of hazarding a conjectural interpretation. It is a fact that the *Ganges* changes its course, and overruns and lays barren whole districts, from which it was a few years back several miles distant. Such changes do not *nourish* but *spoil* the ground.

Verse 3. *When he lifteth up an ensign*—"When the standard is lifted up"] I take God to be the Agent in this verse; and that by the standard and the trumpet are meant the meteors, the thunder, the lightning, the storm, earthquake, and tempest, by which Sennacherib's army shall be destroyed, or by which at least the destruction of it shall be accompanied; as it is described in chap. x. 16, 17, xxix. 6, and xxx. 30, 31. See also Psa. lxxvi., and the title of it, according to the *Septuagint*, *Vulgate* and *Æthiopic*. They are called, by a bold metaphor, the standard lifted up, and the trumpet sounded. The latter is used by Homer, I think with great force, in his introduction to the battle of the gods; though I find it has disgusted some of the minor critics:—

Βραχε δ' ευρεια χθων,
Αμφι δε σαλπιγξεν μεγας ουρανος.
Il. xxi. 388.

"Heaven in loud thunders bids the trumpet sound,
And wide beneath them groans the rending ground." POPE.

Verse 4. *For so the Lord said unto me*—"For thus hath JEHOVAH said unto me"] The subject of the remaining part of this chapter is, that God would comfort and support his own people, though threatened with immediate destruction by the Assyrians; that Sennacherib's great designs and mighty efforts against them should be frustrated; and that his vast expectations should be rendered abortive, when he thought them mature, and just ready to be crowned with success; that the chief part of his army should be made a prey for the beasts of the field and the fowls of the air, (for this is the meaning of the allegory continued through the *fifth* and *sixth* verses;) and that Egypt, being delivered from his oppression, and avenged by the hand of God of the wrongs which she had suffered, should return thanks for the wonderful deliverance, both of herself and of the Jews, from this most powerful adversary.

Like a clear heat—"Like the clear heat"] The same images are employed by an Arabian poet:—

Solis more fervens, dum frigus; quumque ardet
Sirius, tum vero frigus ipse et umbra.

Which is illustrated in the note by a like passage from another Arabian poet:—

Calor est hyeme, refrigerium æstate.

Excerpta ex Hamasa; published by Schultens, at the end of Erpenius's Arabic Grammar, p. 425.

Upon herbs—"After rain"] "אור *aur* here signifies *rain*, according to what is said Job xxxvi. 11: 'The cloud scatters his rain.'"—*Kimchi*. In which place of Job the *Chaldee* paraphrast does indeed explain אורו *auro* by מטריה *matereyh;* and so again ver. 21 and chap. xxxvi. 30. This meaning of the word seems to make the best sense in this place; it is to be wished that it were better supported.

In the heat of harvest—"In the day of harvest."] For בחם *bechom*, *in the heat*, *fourteen* MSS., (several ancient,) the *Septuagint*, *Syriac*, *Arabic*, and *Vulgate* read ביום *beyom*, *in the day*. The mistake seems to have arisen from כחם *kechom* in the line above.

A. M. cir. 3290 B. C. cir. 714 Olymp. XVI. 3 cir. annum NumæPompilii, R. Roman., 2

5 For afore the harvest,
when the bud is perfect,
and the sour grape is ripening in the flower, he shall
both cut off the sprigs with pruning
hooks, and take away *and* cut down the
branches.
6 They shall be left together unto the fowls
of the mountains, and to the beasts of the
earth: and the fowls shall summer upon them,
and all the beasts of the earth
shall winter upon them.
7 In that time [l]shall the present
be brought unto the LORD of hosts
of a people [m]scattered and peeled, and from a
people terrible from their beginning hitherto;
a nation meted out and trodden under foot,
whose land the rivers have spoiled, to the place
of the name of the LORD of hosts, the mount
Zion.

[l]See Psa. lxviii. 31; lxxii. 10; chap. xvi. 1; Zeph. iii. 10; Mal. i. 11——[m]Or, *outspread and polished;* see ver. 2

Verse 5. *The flower*—"The blossom"] Heb. *her* blossom; נצה *nitstsah,* that is, *the blossom of the vine,* גפן *gephen, vine,* understood, which is of the common gender. See Gen. xl. 10. Note, that by the defective punctuation of this word, many interpreters, and our translators among the rest, have been led into a grievous mistake, (for how can the swelling grape become a blossom?) taking the word נצה *nitstsah* for the predicate; whereas it is the subject of the proposition, or the nominative case to the verb.

Verse 7. *The present*—"A gift"] The Egyptians were in alliance with the kingdom of Judah, and were fellow-sufferers with the Jews under the invasion of their common enemy Sennacherib; and so were very nearly interested in the great and miraculous deliverance of that kingdom, by the destruction of the Assyrian army. Upon which wonderful event it is said, 2 Chron. xxxii. 23, that "many brought gifts unto Jehovah to Jerusalem, and presents to Hezekiah king of Judah; so that he was magnified of all nations from henceforth." It is not to be doubted, that among these the Egyptians distinguished themselves in their acknowledgments on this occasion.

Of a people—"From a people"] Instead of עם *am, a people,* the *Septuagint* and *Vulgate* read מעם *meam, from a people,* which is confirmed by the repetition of it in the next line. The difference is of importance; for if this be the true reading, the prediction of the admission of Egypt into the true Church of God is not so explicit as it might otherwise seem to be. However, that event is clearly foretold at the end of the next chapter.—L.

CHAPTER XIX

Prophecy concerning Egypt, in which her lamentable condition under the Babylonians, Persians, &c., is forcibly pointed out, 1–17. *The true religion shall be propagated in Egypt; referring primarily to the great spread of Judaism in that country in the reign of the Ptolemies, and ultimately to its reception of the Gospel in the latter days,* 18–22. *Profound peace between Egypt, Assyria, and Israel, and their blessed condition under the Gospel,* 23–25.

A. M. cir. 3290 B. C. cir. 714 Olymp. XVI. 3 cir. annum NumæPompilii, R. Roman., 2

THE [a]burden of Egypt. Behold, the LORD [b]rideth upon
a swift cloud, and shall come
into Egypt: and [c]the idols
of Egypt shall be moved at
his presence, and the heart
of Egypt shall melt in the midst
of it.

[a]Jer. xlvi. 13; Ezek. xxix., xxx——[b]Psa. xviii. 10; civ. 3——[c]Exod. xii. 12; Jer. xliii. 12

Not many years after the destruction of Sennacherib's army before Jerusalem, by which the Egyptians were freed from the yoke with which they were threatened by so powerful an enemy, who had carried on a successful war of three years' continuance against them; the affairs of Egypt were again thrown into confusion by intestine broils among themselves, which ended in a perfect anarchy, that lasted some few years. This was followed by an aristocracy, or rather tyranny, of twelve princes, who divided the country between them, and at last by the sole dominion of Psammitichus, which he held for fifty-four years. Not long after that followed the invasion and conquest of Egypt by Nebuchadnezzar, and then by the Persians under Cambyses, the son of Cyrus. The yoke of the Persians was so grievous, that the conquest of the Persians by Alexander may well be considered as a deliverance to Egypt; especially as he and his successors greatly favoured the people and improved the country. To all these events the prophet seems to have had a view in this chapter; and in particular, from ver. 18, the prophecy of the propagation of the true religion in Egypt seems to point to the flourishing state of Judaism in that country, in consequence of the great favour shown to the Jews by the Ptolemies. Alexander himself settled a great many Jews in his new city Alexandria, granting them privileges equal to those of the Macedonians. The first Ptolemy, called Soter, carried great numbers of them thither, and gave them such encouragement that still more of them were collected there from different parts; so that Philo reckons that in his

A. M. cir. 3290
B. C. cir. 714
Olymp. XVI. 3
cir. annum
NumæPompilii,
R. Roman., 2

2 And I will [d]set [e]the Egyptians against the Egyptians:
and [f]they shall fight every one
against his brother, and every
one against his neighbour; city against city,
and kingdom against kingdom.
3 And the spirit of Egypt [g]shall fail in the
midst thereof; and I will [h]destroy the counsel
thereof: and they shall [i]seek to the idols, and
to the charmers, and to them that have familiar spirits, and to the wizards.
4 And the Egyptians will I [k]give over [l]into
the hand of a cruel lord; and a fierce king
shall rule over them, saith the Lord, the LORD
of hosts.
5 [m]And the waters shall fail from the sea,
and the river shall be wasted and dried up.
6 And they shall turn the rivers far away;
and the brooks [n]of defence shall
be emptied and dried up: the
reeds and flags shall wither.
7 The paper reeds by the
brooks, by the mouth of the brooks, and every
thing sown by the brooks, shall wither, be
driven away, [o]and be no *more.*
8 The fishers also shall mourn, and all they
that cast angle into the brooks shall lament,
and they that spread nets upon the waters
shall languish.
9 Moreover they that work in [p]fine flax,
and they that weave [q]networks, shall be confounded.
10 And they shall be broken in the [r]purposes thereof, all that make sluices *and* ponds
[s]for fish.
11 Surely the princes of [t]Zoan *are* fools,

[d]Heb. *mingle*——[e]Judg. vii. 22; 1 Sam. xiv. 16, 20; 2 Chron. xx. 23——[f]Ezek. xxxix. 21——[g]Heb. *shall be emptied*——[h]Heb. *swallow up*——[i]Chap. viii. 19; xlvii. 12——[k]Or, *shut up*——[l]Chap. xx. 4; Jer. xlvi. 26; Ezek. xxix. 19

[m]Jeremiah li. 36; Ezekiel xxx. 12——[n]2 Kings xix. 24——[o]Hebrew, *and shall not be*——[p]1 Kings x. 28; Proverbs vii. 16——[q]Or, *white works*——[r]Hebrew, *foundations*——[s]Hebrew, *of living things*——[t]Num. xiii. 22

time there were a million of Jews in that country. These worshipped the God of their fathers; and their example and influence must have had a great effect in spreading the knowledge and worship of the true God through the whole country. See Bp. *Newton* on the Prophecies, Dissert. xii.

NOTES ON CHAP. XIX

Verse 1. *The burden of Egypt.*] That is, the prophet's declaration concerning Egypt.

Verse 3. *They shall seek to the idols, and to the charmers, and to them that have familiar spirits, and to the wizards.*] **And thei schul asken their symulacres, and their devynouris, and their devyl clepers, and their devyl sacristers.**—Old Bible. The import of the original words has already been given where they occur in the Pentateuch. See Deut. xviii. 10, &c.

Verse 4. *A cruel lord*—"Cruel lords"] Nebuchadnezzar in the first place, and afterwards the whole succession of Persian kings, who in general were hard masters, and grievously oppressed the country. Note, that for קשה *kasheh, lord,* a MS. reads קשים *kashim, lords,* agreeable to which is the rendering of the *Septuagint, Syriac,* and *Vulgate.*

Verse 5. *The river shall be wasted and dried up.*] The Nile shall not overflow its banks; and if no inundation, the land must become barren. For, as there is little or no rain in Egypt, its fertility depends on the *overflowing* of the Nile.

Verse 6. *Shall turn the rivers far away*—"Shall become putrid"] האזניחו *heeznichu.* This sense of the word, which Simonis gives in his Lexicon, from the meaning of it in Arabic, suits the place much better than any other interpretation hitherto given; and that the word in Hebrew had some such signification, is probable from 2 Chron. xxix. 19, where the *Vulgate* renders it by *polluit, polluted,* and the *Targum,* by *profaned,* and *made abominable,* which the context in that place seems plainly to require. The form of the verb here is very irregular; and the rabbins and grammarians seem to give no probable account of it.

Verse 8. *The fishers also*—"And the fishers"] There was great plenty of fish in Egypt; see Num. xi. 5. "The Nile," says *Diodorus,* lib. i., "abounds with incredible numbers of all sorts of fish." And much more the lakes. So *Egmont, Pococke,* &c.

Verse 9. *They that work in fine flax*] פשתים שריקות *pishtim sericoth, heckled flax,* i. e., flax dressed on the heckle, or comb used for that purpose. The *Vulgate* uses the word *pectentes,* combing.

They that weave networks shall be confounded—**And confounden schul ben that wrogten flax, plattinge and wevynge sotel thingis.**—Old MS. Bible.

Verse 10. *And they shall be broken,* &c.—"Her stores"] שתתיה *shathotheyha,* αποθηκαι, *granaries.—Aquila.*

All that make sluices and *ponds for fish*—"All that make a gain of pools for fish."] This obscure line is rendered by different interpreters in very different manners. *Kimchi* explains אגמי *agmey* as if it were the same with אגמה *agemah,* from Job xxx. 25, in which he is followed by some of the rabbins, and supported by the *Septuagint:* and שכר *secher,* which I translate *gain,* and which some take for *nets* or *inclosures,* the *Septuagint* render by ζυθον, *strong drink* or *beer,* which it is well known was much used in Egypt; and so likewise the *Syriac,* retaining the Hebrew word שכרא *sekra.* I submit these very different interpretations to the reader's judgment. The Version of the *Septuagint* is as follows: Και παντες οἱ ποιουντες τον ζυθον λυπηθησονται, και τας ψυχας πονεσουσι· "And all they that make barley wine shall mourn, and be grieved in soul."

Verse 11. *The counsel of the wise counsellors of Pharaoh is become brutish*—"Have coun-

A. M. cir. 3290
B. C. cir. 714
Olymp. XVI. 3
cir. annum
NumæPompilii,
R. Roman., 2

the counsel of the wise counsellors of Pharaoh is become brutish: how say ye unto Pharaoh, I *am* the son of the wise, the son of ancient kings?

12 [u]Where *are* they? where *are* thy wise *men?* and let them tell thee now, and let them know what the LORD of hosts hath purposed upon Egypt.

13 The princes of Zoan are become fools, [v]the princes of Noph are deceived; they have also seduced Egypt, *even* [w]*they* [x]*that are* the stay of the tribes thereof.

14 The LORD hath mingled [y]a [z]perverse spirit in the midst thereof: and they have caused Egypt to err in every work thereof, as a drunken *man* staggereth in his vomit.

15 Neither shall there be *any* work for Egypt, which [a]the head or tail, branch or rush, may do.

A. M. cir. 3290
B. C. cir. 714
Olymp. XVI. 3
cir. annum
NumæPompilii,
R. Roman., 2

16 In that day shall Egypt [b]be like unto women: and it shall be afraid and fear because of the shaking of the hand of the LORD of hosts, [c]which he shaketh over it.

17 And the land of Judah shall be a terror unto Egypt, every one that maketh mention thereof shall be afraid in himself, because of the counsel of the LORD of hosts, which he hath determined against it.

18 In that day shall five cities in the land of Egypt [d]speak [e]the language of Canaan, and swear to the LORD of hosts; one shall be called, The city [f]of destruction.

[u]1 Cor. i. 20——[v]Jer. ii. 16——[w]Or, *governors*——[x]Heb. *corners*——[y]Heb. *a spirit of perverseness*——[z]1 Kings xxii. 22; chap. xxix. 10

[a]Chap. ix. 14——[b]Jer. li. 30; Nah. iii. 13——[c]Chap. xi. 15——[d]Zeph. iii. 9——[e]Heb. *the lip*——[f]Or, *of Heres*, or *of the sun*

selled a brutish counsel"] The sentence as it now stands in the Hebrew, is imperfect: it wants the verb. Archbishop *Secker* conjectures that the words יועצי פרעה *yoatsey pharoh* should be transposed; which would in some degree remove the difficulty. But it is to be observed, that the translator of the *Vulgate* seems to have found in his copy the verb יעצו *yaatsu* added after פרעה *pharoh:* Sapientes consiliarii Pharaonis *dederunt* consilium insipiens, "The wise counsellors of Pharaoh gave unwise counsel." This is probably the true reading: it is perfectly agreeable to the Hebrew idiom, makes the construction of the sentence clear, and renders the transposition of the words above mentioned unnecessary.—L.

Verse 12. "Let them come"] Here too a word seems to have been left out of the text. After חכמיך *chachameycha, thy wise men, two* MSS., *one* ancient, add יבאו *yibu, let them come;* which, if we consider the form and construction of the sentence, has very much the appearance of being genuine: otherwise the connective conjunction at the beginning of the next member is not only superfluous but embarrassing. See also the Version of the *Septuagint*, in which the same deficiency is manifest.

Let them tell thee now—"And let them declare"] For ידעו *yidu, let them know*, perhaps we ought to read יודיעו *yodiu, let them make known.—Secker.* The *Septuagint* and *Vulgate* favour this reading, ειπατωσαν, *let them declare.*

Verse 13. *Are deceived*—"They have caused," &c.] The text has והתעו *vehithu*, AND *they have caused to err. Fifty* of *Kennicott's* MSS., *fifty-three* of *De Rossi's*, and *one* of my own, ancient, *thirty-two* editions, and the *Vulgate* and *Chaldee*, omit the ו *vau, and.*

Stay—"Pillars"] פנת *pinnath*, to be pointed as plural *pinnoth*, without doubt. So *Grotius*, and so the *Chaldee.*

Verse 14. *In the midst thereof*] "בקרבם *bekirbam;* so the *Septuagint*, and perhaps more correctly."—*Secker.* So likewise the *Chaldee.*

Verse 15. *The head or tail, branch or rush*] *R. D. Kimchi* says, there are some who suppose that these words mean the dragon's head and tail; and refer to all those who are conversant in astronomy, astrology, &c.

Verse 16. *Shall Egypt be*—"The Egyptians shall be"] יהיו *yihyu, they shall be*, plural, MS. Bodl. *Septuagint*, and *Chaldee*. This is not proposed as an emendation, for either form is proper.

Verse 17. *And the land of Judah*] The threatening hand of God will be held out and shaken over Egypt, from the side of Judea; through which the Assyrians will march to invade it. It signifies that kind of terror that drives one to his wit's end, that causes him to *reel* like a drunken man, to be giddy through astonishment. Such is the import of חג *chag*, and חגה *chagah. Five* MSS. and *two* editions have לחגה *lechagah.*

Verse 18. *The city of destruction*—"The city of the sun"] עיר החרס *ir hacheres*. This passage is attended with much difficulty and obscurity. First, in regard to the true reading. It is well known that Onias applied it to his own views, either to procure from the king of Egypt permission to build his temple in the Hieropolitan Nome, or to gain credit and authority to it when built; from the notion which he industriously propagated, that Isaiah had in this place prophesied of the building of such a temple. He pretended that the very place where it should be built was expressly named by the prophet, עיר החרס *ir hacheres, the city of the sun.* This possibly may have been the original reading. The present text has עיר ההרס *ir haheres, the city of destruction;* which some suppose to have been introduced into the text by the Jews of Palestine afterwards, to express their detestation of the place, being much offended with this schismatical temple in Egypt. Some think the latter to have been the true reading; and that the prophet himself gave this turn to the name out of contempt, and to inti-

A. M. cir. 3290 B. C. cir. 714 Olymp. XVI. 3 cir. annum NumæPompilii, R. Roman., 2

19 In that day [g]shall there be
an altar to the LORD in the midst
of the land of Egypt, and a pillar
at the border thereof to the LORD.

20 And [h]it shall be for a sign and for a witness unto the LORD of hosts in the land of Egypt: for they shall cry unto the LORD because of the oppressors, and he shall send them a Saviour, and a great one, and he shall deliver them.

21 And the LORD shall be known to Egypt, and the Egyptians shall know the LORD in that day, and [i]shall do sacrifice and oblation; yea, they shall vow a vow unto the LORD, and perform *it*.

22 And the LORD shall smite Egypt: he
shall smite and heal *it:* and they
shall return *even* to the LORD,
and he shall be intreated of
them, and shall heal them.

A. M. cir. 3290 B. C. cir. 714 Olymp. XVI. 3 cir. annum NumæPompilii, R. Roman., 2

23 In that day [k]shall there be a highway out of Egypt to Assyria, and the Assyrian shall come into Egypt, and the Egyptian into Assyria, and the Egyptians shall serve with the Assyrians.

24 In that day shall Israel be the third with Egypt and with Assyria, *even* a blessing in the midst of the land:

25 Whom the LORD of hosts shall bless, saying, Blessed *be* Egypt my people, and Assyria [l]the work of my hands, and Israel mine inheritance.

---

[g]Gen. xxviii. 18; Exod. xxiv. 4; Josh. xxii. 10, 26, 27 — [h]See Josh. iv. 20; xxii. 27

[i]Mal. i. 11 — [k]Chap. xi. 16 — [l]Psa. c. 3; chap. xxix. 23; Hos. ii. 23; Eph. ii. 10

---

mate the demolition of this Hieropolitan temple; which in effect was destroyed by Vespasian's orders, after that of Jerusalem, "Videtur propheta consulto scripsisse הרס *heres, pro* חרס *cheres*, ut alibi scribitur בית און *beith aven* pro בית אל *beith El:* איש בשת *ish bosheth* pro איש בעל *ish baal*, &c. Vide *Lowth* in loc."—*Secker*. "It seems that the prophet designedly wrote הרס *heres, destruction*, for חרס *cheres, the sun:* as elsewhere בית און *beith aven, the house of iniquity*, is written for בית אל *beith El, the house of God;* איש בשת *ish bosheth* for איש בעל *ish baal*," &c. But on the supposition that עיר ההרס *air haheres* is the true reading, others understand it differently. The word הרס *heres* in Arabic signifies *a lion;* and Conrad Ikenius has written a dissertation (Dissert. Philol. Theol. XVI.) to prove that the place here mentioned is not Heliopolis, as it is commonly supposed to be, but Leontopolis in the Heliopolitan Nome, as it is indeed called in the letter, whether real or pretended, of Onias to Ptolemy, which Josephus has inserted in his Jewish Antiquities, lib. xiii. c. 3. And I find that several persons of great learning and judgment think that Ikenius has proved the point beyond contradiction. See *Christian. Muller*. Satura Observ. Philolog. *Michaelis* Bibliotheque Oriental, Part v., p. 171. But, after all, I believe that neither Onias, Heliopolis, nor Leontopolis has any thing to do with this subject. The application of this place of Isaiah to Onias's purpose seems to have been a mere invention, and in consequence of it there may perhaps have been some unfair management to accommodate the text to that purpose; which has been carried even farther than the Hebrew text; for the Greek version has here been either translated from a corrupted text, or wilfully mistranslated or corrupted, to serve the same cause. The place is there called πολις Ασεδεκ, *the city of righteousness;* a name apparently contrived by Onias's party to give credit to their temple, which was to rival that of Jerusalem. Upon the whole, the true reading of the Hebrew text in this place is very uncertain; *fifteen* MSS. and *seven* editions have חרס *cheres, the city of Hacheres*, or, *of the sun*. So likewise *Symmachus*, the *Vulgate*, *Arabic*, *Septuagint*, and *Complutensian*. On the other hand, *Aquila*, *Theodotion*, and the *Syriac* read הרס *heres, destruction;* the *Chaldee* paraphrase takes in both readings.

The reading of the text being so uncertain, no one can pretend to determine what the city was that is here mentioned by name; much less to determine what the four other cities were which the prophet does not name. I take the whole passage from the 18th verse to the end of the chapter, to contain a general intimation of the future propagation of the knowledge of the true God in Egypt and Syria, under the successors of Alexander; and, in consequence of this propagation, of the early reception of the Gospel in the same countries, when it should be published to the world. See more on this subject in *Prideaux's* Connect. An. 145; Dr. *Owen's* Inquiry into the present state of the *Septuagint* Version, p. 41; and *Bryant's* Observations on Ancient History, p. 124.—L.

Verse 19. *An altar to the Lord*] צבאות *tsebaoth*, "of hosts," or *Yehovah tsebaoth*, is added by *eight* MSS. of good repute, and the *Syriac* Version.

Verse 23. *Shall there be a highway*] Under the latter kings of Persia, and under Alexander, Egypt, Judea, and Assyria lived peaceably under the same government, and were on such friendly terms that there was a regular, uninterrupted intercourse between them, so that the Assyrian came into Egypt and the Egyptian into Assyria, and *Israel* became *the third*, i. e., was in strict union with the other two; and was a *blessing* to both, as affording them some knowledge of the true God, ver. 24.

Verse 25. *Blessed* be *Egypt—Assyria—and Israel*] All these countries shall be converted to the Lord. Concerning Egypt, it was said, chap. xviii. 7, that it should bring gifts to the Lord at Jerusalem. Here it is predicted, ver. 19, that there shall be an altar to the Lord in Egypt itself; and that they, with the Assyrians, shall become the people of God with the Israelites. This remains partly to be fulfilled. These countries shall be all, and perhaps at no very distant time from this, converted to the faith of our Lord Jesus Christ.

CHAPTER XX

The Prophet Isaiah a sign to Egypt and Cush or Ethiopia, that the captives and exiles of these countries shall be indignantly treated by the king of Assyria, 1–6.

A. M. cir. 3290
B. C. cir. 714
Olymp. XVI. 3
cir. annum
NumæPompilii,
R. Roman., 2

IN the year that [a]Tartan came unto Ashdod, (when Sargon the king of Assyria sent him,) and fought against Ashdod, and took it;

2 At the same time spake the LORD [b]by Isaiah the son of Amoz, saying, Go and loose the [c]sackcloth from off thy loins, and put off thy shoe from thy foot. And he did so, [d]walking naked and barefoot.

3 And the LORD said, Like as my servant Isaiah hath walked naked and barefoot three years [e]*for* a sign and wonder upon Egypt and upon Ethiopia;

4 So shall the king of Assyria lead away [f]the Egyptians prisoners, and the Ethiopians captives, young and old, naked and barefoot, [g]even with *their* buttocks uncovered, to the [h]shame of Egypt.

A. M. cir. 3290
B. C. cir. 714
Olymp. XVI. 3
cir. annum
NumæPompilii,
R. Roman., 2

5 [i]And they shall be afraid and ashamed of Ethiopia their expectation, and of Egypt their glory.

6 And the inhabitant of this [k]isle shall say in that day, Behold, such *is* our expectation, whither we flee for help to be delivered from the king of Assyria: and how shall we escape?

---

[a]2 Kings xviii. 17——[b]Heb. *by the hand of Isaiah*——[c]Zech. xiii. 4——[d]1 Sam. xix. 24; Mic. i. 8, 11——[e]Ch. viii. 18——[f]Heb. *the captivity of Egypt*

[g]2 Sam. x. 4; chap. iii. 17; Jer. xiii. 22, 26; Mic. i. 11——[h]Heb. *nakedness*——[i]2 Kings xviii. 21; chap. xxx. 3, 5, 7; xxxvi. 6——[k]Or, *country;* Jer. xlvii. 4

NOTES ON CHAP. XX

Tartan besieged Ashdod or Azotus, which probably belonged at this time to Hezekiah's dominions; see 2 Kings xviii. 8. The people expected to be relieved by the Cushites of Arabia and by the Egyptians. Isaiah was ordered to go uncovered, that is, without his upper garment, the rough mantle commonly worn by the prophets, (see Zech. xiii. 4,) probably three days to show that within three years the town should be taken, after the defeat of the Cushites and Egyptians by the king of Assyria, which event should make their case desperate, and induce them to surrender. Azotus was a strong place; it afterwards held out twenty-nine years against Psammitichus, king of Egypt, *Herod.* ii. 157. Tartan was one of Sennacherib's generals, 2 Kings xviii. 17, and Tirhakah, king of the Cushites, was in alliance with the king of Egypt against Sennacherib. These circumstances make it probable that by Sargon is meant Sennacherib. It might be one of the seven names by which Jerome, on this place, says he was called. He is called Sacherdonus and Sacherdan in the book of Tobit. The taking of Azotus must have happened before Sennacherib's attempt on Jerusalem; when he boasted of his late conquests, chap. xxxvii. 25. And the warning of the prophet had a principal respect to the Jews also, who were too much inclined to depend upon the assistance of Egypt. As to the rest history and chronology affording us no light, it may be impossible to clear either this or any other hypothesis, which takes Sargon to be Shalmaneser or Asarhaddon, &c., from all difficulties.—L. *Kimchi* says, this happened in the *fourteenth* year of Hezekiah.

Verse 2. *Walking naked and barefoot.*] It is not probable that the prophet walked uncovered and barefoot for three years; his appearing in that manner was a sign that within three years the Egyptians and Cushites should be in the same condition, being conquered and made captives by the king of Assyria. The time was denoted as well as the event; but his appearing in that manner for three whole years could give no premonition of the time at all. It is probable, therefore, that the prophet was ordered to walk so for *three days* to denote the accomplishment of the event in *three years;* a *day* for a *year*, according to the prophetical rule, Num. xiv. 34; Ezek. iv. 6. The words שלש ימים *shalosh yamim, three days*, may possibly have been lost out of the text, at the end of the second verse, after יחף *yacheph, barefoot;* or after the same word in the third verse, where, in the Alexandrine and Vatican copies of the *Septuagint*, and in MSS. *Pachom.* and I. D. II. the words τρια ετη, *three years*, are twice expressed. Perhaps, instead of שלש ימים *shalosh yamim, three days*, the Greek translator might read שלש שנים *shalosh shanim, three years*, by his own mistake, or by that of his copy, after יחף *yacheph* in the third verse, for which stands the first τρια ετη, *three years*, in the Alexandrine and Vatican *Septuagint*, and in the two MSS. above mentioned. It is most likely that Isaiah's walking naked and barefoot was done in a *vision;* as was probably that of the Prophet Hosea taking a *wife of whoredoms.* None of these things can well be taken *literally.*

From thy foot] רגליך *ragleycha*, thy *feet*, is the reading of *thirty-four* of *Kennicott's* and *De Rossi's* MSS., *four* ancient editions, with the *Septuagint, Syriac, Vulgate,* and *Arabic*

CHAPTER XXI

Prediction of the taking of Babylon by the Medes and Persians at the time of a great festival, 1–9. *Short application of the prophecy to the Jews, partly in the person of God, and partly in his own,* 10. *Obscure prophecy respecting Dumah,* 11, 12. *Prophecy concerning the Arabians to be fulfilled in a very short time after its delivery,* 13–17.

A. M. cir. 3290
B. C. cir. 714
Olymp. XVI. 3
cir. annum
NumæPompilii,
R. Roman., 2

THE burden of the desert of
the sea. As [a]whirlwinds in
the south pass through; *so* it
cometh from the desert, from a
terrible land.
2 A [b]grievous vision is declared unto me;
[c]the treacherous dealer dealeth treacherously,
and the spoiler spoileth. [d]Go
up, O Elam: besiege, O Media;
all the sighing thereof have I
made to cease.
3 Therefore are [e]my loins filled with pain:
[f]pangs have taken hold upon me, as the pangs
of a woman that travaileth: I was bowed down

[a]Zech. ix. 14——[b]Heb. *hard*——[c]Ch. xxxiii. 1——[d]Ch. xiii. 17; Jer. xlix. 34——[e]Ch. xv. 5; xvi. 11——[f]Ch. xiii. 8

The first *ten* verses of this chapter contain a prediction of the taking of Babylon by the Medes and Persians. It is a passage singular in its kind for its brevity and force, for the variety and rapidity of the movements, and for the strength and energy of colouring with which the action and event are painted. It opens with the prophet's seeing at a distance the dreadful storm that is gathering and ready to burst upon Babylon. The event is intimated in general terms, and God's orders are issued to the Persians and Medes to set forth upon the expedition which he has given them in charge. Upon this the prophet enters into the midst of the action; and in the person of Babylon expresses, in the strongest terms, the astonishment and horror that seizes her on the sudden surprise of the city at the very season dedicated to pleasure and festivity, ver. 3, 4. Then, in his own person, describes the situation of things there, the security of the Babylonians, and in the midst of their feasting the sudden alarm of war, ver. 5. The event is then declared in a very singular manner. God orders the prophet to set a watchman to look out, and to report what he sees; he sees two companies marching onward, representing by their appearance the two nations that were to execute God's orders, who declare that Babylon is fallen, ver. 6-9.

But what is this to the prophet, and to the Jews, the object of his ministry? The application, the end, and design of the prophecy are admirably given in a short, expressive address to the Jews, partly in the person of God, partly in that of the prophet: "O my threshing—" "O my people, whom for your punishment I shall make subject to the Babylonians, to try and to prove you, and to separate the chaff from the corn, the bad from the good, among you; hear this for your consolation: your punishment, your slavery, and oppression will have an end in the destruction of your oppressors."—L.

NOTES ON CHAP. XXI

Verse 1. *The desert of the sea*] This plainly means Babylon, which is the subject of the prophecy. The country about Babylon, and especially below it towards the sea, was a great flat morass, overflowed by the Euphrates and Tigris. It became habitable by being drained by the many canals that were made in it.

Herodotus, lib. i. 184, says that "Semiramis confined the Euphrates within its channel by raising great dams against it; for before it overflowed the whole country like a sea." And Abydenus, (quoting Megasthenes, *apud Euseb.* Præp. Evang. IX. 41,) speaking of the building of Babylon by Nebuchadonosor, says, "it is reported that all this part was covered with water, and was called the sea; and that Belus drew off the waters, conveying them into proper receptacles, and surrounded Babylon with a wall." When the Euphrates was turned out of its channel by Cyrus, it was suffered still to drown the neighbouring country; and, the Persian government, which did not favour the place, taking no care to remedy this inconvenience, it became in time a great barren morassy desert, which event the title of the prophecy may perhaps intimate. Such it was originally; such it became after the taking of the city by Cyrus; and such it continues to this day.

As whirlwinds in the south—"Like the southern tempests"] The most vehement storms to which Judea was subject came from the desert country to the south of it. "Out of the south cometh the whirlwind," Job xxxvii. 9. "And there came a great wind from the wilderness, and smote the four corners of the house," Job i. 19. For the situation of Idumea, the country (as I suppose) of Job, see Lam. iv. 21 compared with Job i. 1, was the same in this respect with that of Judea:—

"And JEHOVAH shall appear over them,
And his arrow shall go forth as the lightning;
And the Lord JEHOVAH shall sound the trumpet;
And shall march in the whirlwinds of the south." Zech. ix. 14.

Verse 2. *The treacherous dealer dealeth treacherously, and the spoiler spoileth*—"The plunderer is plundered, and the destroyer is destroyed."] הבוגד בוגד והשודד שודד *habboged boged vehashshoded shoded.* The MSS. vary in expressing or omitting the ו *vau,* in these four words. *Ten* MSS. of *Kennicott* are without the ו *vau* in the *second* word, and *eight* MSS. are without the ו *vau* in the *fourth* word; which justifies *Symmachus*, who has rendered them passively: ὁ αθετων αθετειται και ὁ ταλαιπωριζων ταλαιπωρει. He read בגוד שדוד *bagud shadud. Cocceius* (Lexicon *in voce*) observes that the *Chaldee* very often renders the verb בגד *bagad*, by בזז *bazaz, he spoiled;* and in this place, and in xxxiii. 1, by the equivalent word אנס *anas, to press, give trouble;* and in chap. xxiv. 16 both by אנס *anas* and בזז *bazaz;* and the *Syriac* in this place renders it by טלם *talam, he oppressed.*

All the sighing thereof have I made to cease—

A. M. cir. 3290 B. C. cir. 714 Olymp. XVI. 3 cir. annum NumæPompilii, R. Roman., 2

at the hearing *of it;* I was dismayed at the seeing *of it.*
4 [g]My heart panted, fearful-
ness affrighted me: [h]the night
of my pleasure hath he [i]turned into fear
unto me.

5 [k]Prepare the table, watch in the watchtower, eat, drink: arise, ye princes, *and*
anoint the shield.

6 For thus hath the LORD said unto me, Go,
set a watchman, let him declare what he
seeth.

7 [l]And he saw a chariot *with* a couple of
horsemen, a chariot of asses, *and* a chariot of
camels; and he hearkened diligently with
much heed:

8 And [m]he cried, a lion: My
lord, I stand continually upon the
[n]watchtower in the day-time, and
I am set in my ward [o]whole nights:

A. M. cir. 3290 B. C. cir. 714 Olymp. XVI. 3 cir. annum NumæPompilii, R. Roman., 2

9 And, behold, here cometh a chariot of men,
with a couple of horsemen. And he answered
and said, [p]Babylon is fallen, is fallen; and
[q]all the graven images of her gods he hath
broken unto the ground.

10 [r]O my threshing, and the [s]corn of my
floor: that which I have heard of the LORD of
hosts, the God of Israel, have I declared unto
you.

11 [t]The burden of Dumah. He calleth to
me out of Seir, Watchman, what of the night?
Watchman, what of the night?

[g]Or, *my mind wandered*——[h]Deut. xxviii. 67——[i]Heb. *put*——[k]Dan. v. 5——[l]Ver. 9——[m]Or, *cried as a lion*——[n]2 Chron. xx. 24; ver. 5; Hab. ii. 1——[o]Or, *every night*

[p]Jer. li. 8; Rev. xiv. 8; xviii. 2——[q]Chap. xlvi. 1; Jer. l. 2; li. 44——[r]Jer. li. 33——[s]Heb. *son*——[t]1 Chron. i. 30; Jer. xlix. 7, 8; Ezek. xxxv. 2; Obad. 1

"I have put an end to all her vexations"] *Heb.* "Her sighing; that is, the sighing caused by her." So *Kimchi* on the place: "It means those who groaned through fear of him: for the suffixes of the nouns refer both to the agent and the patient. All those who groaned before the face of the king of Babylon he caused to rest;" *Chald.* And so likewise *Ephrem Syr.* in loc., edit. Assemani: "His groans, viz., the grief and tears which the Chaldeans occasioned through the rest of the nations."

Verse 5. *Prepare the table*—"The table is prepared"] In *Hebrew* the verbs are in the infinitive mood absolute, as in Ezek. i. 14: "And the animals ran and returned, רצוא ושוב *ratso veshob*, like the appearance of the lightning;" just as the Latins say, *currere et reverti*, for *currebant et revertebantur.* See chap. xxxii. 11, and the note there.

Arise, ye princes, and *anoint the shield.*] *Kimchi* observes that several of the rabbins understood this of Belshazzar's impious feast and death. The king of a people is termed *the shield*, because he is their *defence.* The command, *Anoint the shield,* is the same with *Anoint a new king.* Belshazzar being now suddenly slain, while they were all eating and drinking, he advises the princes, whose business it was, to make speed and anoint another in his stead.

Verse 7. *And he saw a chariot, &c.*—"And he saw a chariot with two riders; a rider on an ass, a rider on a camel"] This passage is extremely obscure from the ambiguity of the term רכב *recheb*, which is used three times, and which signifies a chariot, or any other vehicle, or the rider in it; or a rider on a horse, or any other animal; or a company of chariots, or riders. The prophet may possibly mean a cavalry in two parts, with two sorts of riders; riders on asses or mules, and riders on camels; or led on by two riders, one on an ass, and one on a camel. However, so far it is pretty clear, that Darius and Cyrus, the Medes and the Persians, are intended to be distinguished by the two riders on the two sorts of cattle. It appears from *Herodotus,* i. 80, that the baggage of Cyrus' army was carried on camels. In his engagement with Crœsus, he took off the baggage from the camels, and mounted his horsemen upon them; the enemy's horses, offended with the smell of the camels, turned back and fled.—L.

Verse 8. *And he cried, A lion*—"He that looked out on the watch"] The present reading, אריה *aryeh, a lion*, is so unintelligible, and the mistake so obvious, that I make no doubt that the true reading is הראה *haroeh, the seer;* as the *Syriac* translator manifestly found it in his copy, who renders it by דוקא *duka, a watchman.*

Verse 9. *Here cometh a chariot of men, &c.*—"A man, one of the two riders"] So the *Syriac* understands it, and Ephrem Syr.

Verse 10. *O my threshing*] "O thou, the object upon which I shall exercise the severity of my discipline; that shalt lie under my afflicting hand, like corn spread upon the floor to be threshed out and winnowed, to separate the chaff from the wheat!" The image of threshing is frequently used by the Hebrew poets, with great elegance and force, to express the punishment of the wicked and the trial of the good, or the utter dispersion and destruction of God's enemies. Of the different ways of threshing in use among the Hebrews, and the manner of performing them, see the note on chap. xxviii. 27.

Our translators have taken the liberty of using the word *threshing* in a passive sense, to express the object or matter that is threshed; in which I have followed them, not being able to express it more properly, without departing too much from the form and letter of the original. "*Son* of my floor," *Heb.* It is an idiom of the *Hebrew* language to call the effect, the object, the adjunct, any thing that belongs in almost any way to another, the *son* of it. "O my threshing." The prophet abruptly breaks off the speech of God; and instead of continuing it in the form in which he had begun, and in the person of God, "This I declare unto you by my prophet," he changes the form of address, and adds, in his own person, "This I declare unto you from God."

Verse 11. *The burden of Dumah*—"The oracle

A. M. cir. 3290
B. C. cir. 714
Olymp. XVI. 3
cir. annum
NumæPompilii,
R. Roman., 2

12 The watchman said, The
morning cometh, and also the
night: if ye will inquire, inquire
ye: return, come.
13 [u]The burden upon Arabia. In the forest
in Arabia shall ye lodge, O ye
travelling companies [v]of De-
danim.
14 The inhabitants of the land
of Tema [w]brought water to him that was

[u]Jer. xlix. 28——[v]1 Chron. i. 9, 32

[w]Or, *bring ye*

concerning Dumah."] Pro דומה *Dumah*, Codex R. Meiri habet אדום *Edom;* and so the *Septuagint*, Vid. *Kimchi* ad h. l. Biblia Michaelis, Halæ, 1720, not. ad l. See also *De Rossi*. Bishop *Lowth* translates the prophecy thus:—

11. The oracle concerning Dumah.
A voice crieth to me from Seir:
Watchman, what from the night?
Watchman, what from the night?
12. The watchman replieth:—
The morning cometh, and also the night.
If ye will inquire, inquire ye: come again.

This differs very little from our common Version. One of *Kennicott's* MSS., and one of my own, omit the repetition, "Watchman, what from the night?"

This prophecy, from the uncertainty of the occasion on which it was uttered, and from the brevity of the expression, is extremely obscure. The Edomites as well as the Jews were subdued by the Babylonians. They inquire of the prophet how long their subjection is to last: he intimates that the Jews should be delivered from their captivity; not so the Edomites. Thus far the interpretation seems to carry with it some degree of probability. What the meaning of the last line may be, I cannot pretend to divine. In this difficulty the *Hebrew* MSS. give no assistance. The MSS. of the *Septuagint*, and the fragments of the other *Greek* Versions, give some variations, but no light. This being the case, I thought it best to give an exact literal translation of the whole two verses, which may serve to enable the English reader to judge in some measure of the foundation of the various interpretations that have been given of them.

The burden of Dumah.—R. D. Kimchi says, "His father understood this of the destruction of *Dumah* (one of the cities of the Ishmaelites) by the inhabitants of *Seir;* and that they inquired of the prophet to know the particular time in which God had given them a commission against it. The prophet answered: The *morning*—the time of *success* to you, cometh, is just at hand; and the *night*—the time of *utter destruction* to the inhabitants of Dumah, is also ready."

I have heard the words applied in the way of general exhortation. 1. Every minister of God is a *watchman*. He is continually *watching* for the *safety* and *interests* of his people, and looking for the counsel of God that he may be properly qualified to *warn* and to *comfort*. 2. Such are often called to denounce *heavy judgments;* they have the *burden* of the word of the Lord to denounce against the impenitent, the backslider, the lukewarm, and the careless. 3. When the watchman threatens judgments, some are *awakened*, and some *mock: Watchman, what of the night? "What* are the judgments thou threatenest, and *when* are they to take place?" 4. To this question, whether *seriously* or *tauntingly* proposed, the watchman answers: 1. *The morning cometh*—there is a *time of repentance* granted; a *morning* of God's *long-suffering kindness* now appears: and *also the night*—the time in which God will no longer wait to be gracious, but will cut you off as cumberers of the ground. 2. But *if you will inquire* seriously how you are to escape God's judgments, *inquire ye*. 3. There is still a door of hope; *continue* to pray for mercy. 4. *Return* from your iniquities. 5. *Come* to God, through Christ, that ye may obtain salvation.

Verse 13. *The burden upon Arabia*—"The oracle concerning Arabia"] This title is of doubtful authority. In the first place, because it is not in many of the MSS. of the *Septuagint;* it is in MSS. *Pachom.* and I. D. II. only, as far as I can find with certainty. Secondly, from the singularity of the phraseology; for משא *massa* is generally prefixed to its object without a preposition, as משא בבל *massa babel;* and never but in this place with the preposition ב *beth*. Besides, as the word בערב *baarab* occurs at the very beginning of the prophecy itself, the first word but one, it is much to be suspected that some one, taking it for a proper name and the object of the prophecy, might note it as such by the words משא בערב *massa baarab* written in the margin, which he might easily transfer to the text. The *Septuagint* did not take it for a proper name, but render it εν τῳ δρυμῳ ἑσπερας, "in the forest, in the evening," and so the *Chaldee*, which I follow; for otherwise, the forest *in Arabia* is so indeterminate and vague a description, that in effect it means nothing at all. This observation might have been of good use in clearing up the foregoing very obscure prophecy, if any light had arisen from joining the two together by removing the separating title; but I see no connexion between them. The *Arabic* Version has, "The prophecy concerning the Arabians, and the children of Chedar."

This prophecy was to have been fulfilled within a year of the time of its delivery, see ver. 16; and it was probably delivered about the same time with the rest in this part of the book, that is, soon before or after the 14th of Hezekiah, the year of Sennacherib's invasion. In his first march into Judea, or in his return from the Egyptian expedition, he might perhaps overrun these several clans of Arabians; their distress on some such occasion is the subject of this prophecy.—L.

Verse 14. *The land of Tema*—"The southern country"] Θαιμαν, *Sept.;* Austri, *Vulg.* They read תימן *teiman*, which seems to be right; for probably the inhabitants of Tema might be involved in the same calamity with their brethren and neighbours of Kedar, and not in a condition to give them assistance, and to relieve them, in their flight before the enemy, with bread and water. To bring forth bread and water is an instance of common humanity in such cases of distress; especially in those desert countries in which the common necessaries of life, more particularly water, are not easily to be met with or procured. Moses forbids the Ammonite and Moabite to be admitted into the congregation of the Lord to the tenth generation. One reason

A. M. cir. 3290
B. C. cir. 714
Olymp. XVI. 3
cir. annum
NumæPompilii,
R. Roman., 2

thirsty, they prevented with
their bread him that fled.
15 For they fled [x]from [y]the
swords, from the drawn sword,
and from the bent bow, and from the grievousness of war.
16 For thus hath the LORD said unto me,
Within a year, [z]according to the
years of a hireling, and all the
glory of [a]Kedar shall fail:
17 And the residue of the
number of [b]archers, the mighty men of the
children of Kedar, shall be diminished: for
the LORD God of Israel hath spoken *it*.

[x]Or, *for fear*——[y]Heb. *from the face*——[z]Chap. xvi. 14

[a]Psa. cxx. 5; chap. lx. 7——[b]Heb. *bows*

which he gives for this reprobation is their omission of the common offices of humanity towards the Israelites; "because they met them not with bread and water in the way, when they came forth out of Egypt," Deut. xxiii. 4.

Verse 17. *The archers, the mighty men of the children of Kedar*—"The mighty bowmen of the sons of Kedar"] *Sagittariorum fortium, Vulg.;* transposing the two words, and reading גבורי קשת *gibborey kesheth;* which seems to be right. The strong men of the bow, the most excellent archers.

For the Lord—hath spoken it—"For JEHOVAH hath spoken it."] The prophetic Carmina of Marcius, foretelling the battle of Cannæ, lib. xxv. 12, conclude with the same kind of solemn form: *Nam mihi ita Jupiter fatus est;* "Thus hath Jupiter spoken to me." Observe that the word נאם *naam, to pronounce, to declare,* is the solemn word appropriated to the delivering of prophecies: "Behold, I am against the prophets, saith (נאם *naam, pronounceth*) JEHOVAH, who use their tongues, וינאמו נאם *vaiyinamu neum, and solemnly pronounce,* He hath pronounced it;" Jer. xxiii. 31. What God says shall most assuredly come to pass; he cannot be deceived.

CHAPTER XXII

Prophecy concerning Jerusalem, 1–14. *Sentence against Shebna, who was over the household,* 15–19. *Prophecy concerning Eliakim, the son of Hilkiah,* 20, 21. *From Eliakim, Isaiah,* (*agreeably to the mode universally adopted in the prophetical writings, of making the things then present, or which were shortly to be accomplished,* types *or* representations *of things to be fulfilled upon a larger scale in distant futurity,*) *makes a transition to the Messiah, of whom Eliakim was a type, to whom the words will best apply, and to whom some passages in the prophecy must be solely restrained,* 20–24. *The sentence against Shebna again confirmed,* 25.

A. M. cir. 3292
B. C. cir. 712
Olymp. XVII. 1
cir. annum
NumæPompilii,
R. Roman., 4

THE burden of the valley of
vision. What aileth thee
now, that thou art wholly gone
up to the housetops?
2 Thou that art full of stirs, a
tumultuous city, [a]a joyous city:
thy slain *men are* not slain with
the sword, nor dead in battle.

[a]Isaiah, chap. xxxii. 13

This prophecy, ending with the *fourteenth* verse of this chapter, is entitled, "The oracle concerning the valley of vision," by which is meant Jerusalem, because, says *Sal. ben Melech,* it was the place of prophecy. Jerusalem, according to Josephus, was built upon two opposite hills, Sion and Acra, separated by a valley in the midst. He speaks of another broad valley between Acra and Moriah, *Bell. Jud.* v. 13, vi. 6. It was the seat of Divine revelation; the place where chiefly prophetic vision was given, and where God manifested himself visibly in the holy place. The prophecy foretells the invasion of Jerusalem by the Assyrians under Sennacherib; or by the Chaldeans under Nebuchadnezzar. *Vitringa* is of opinion that the prophet has both in view: that of the Chaldeans in the first part, ver. 1-5, which he thinks relates to the flight of Zedekiah, 2 Kings xxv. 4, 5; and that of the Assyrians in the latter part, which agrees with the circumstances of that time, and particularly describes the preparations made by Hezekiah for the defence of the city, ver. 8-11. Compare 2 Chron. xxxii. 2-5.—L.

NOTES ON CHAP. XXII

Verse 1. *Art—gone up to the house-tops*—"Are gone up to the house-tops"] The houses in the east were in ancient times, as they are still, generally, built in one and the same uniform manner. The roof or top of the house is always flat, covered with broad stones, or a strong plaster of terrace, and guarded on every side with a low parapet wall; see Deut. xxii. 8. The terrace is frequented as much as any part of the house. On this, as the season favours, they walk, they eat, they sleep, they transact business, (1 Sam. ix. 25, see also the *Septuagint* in that place,) they perform their devotions, Acts x. 9. The house is built with a court within, into which chiefly the windows open: those that open to the street are so obstructed with lattice-work that no one either without or within can see through them. Whenever, therefore, any thing is to be seen or heard in the

A. M. cir. 3292
B. C. cir. 712
Olymp. XVII. 1
cir. annum
NumæPompilii,
R. Roman., 4

3 All thy rulers are fled together, they are bound [b]by the archers: all that are found in thee, are bound together, *which* have fled from far.

4 Therefore, said I, Look away from me; [c]I [d]will weep bitterly, labour not to comfort me, because of the spoiling of the daughter of my people.

5 [e]For *it is* a day of trouble, and of treading down, and of perplexity [f]by the Lord GOD of hosts in the valley of vision, breaking down the walls, and of crying to the mountains.

6 [g]And Elam bare the quiver with chariots of men *and* horsemen, and [h]Kir [i]uncovered the shield.

7 And it shall come to pass, *that* [k]thy choicest valleys shall be full of chariots, and the horsemen shall set themselves in array [l]at the gate.

8 And he discovered the covering of Judah, and thou didst look in that day to the armour [m]of the house of the forest.

9 [n]Ye have seen also the breaches of the city of David, that they are many: and ye gathered together the waters of the lower pool.

10 And ye have numbered the houses of Jerusalem, and the houses have ye broken down, to fortify the wall.

11 [o]Ye made also a ditch between the two

[b]Heb. *of the bow*——[c]Jer. iv. 19; ix. 1——[d]Heb. *I will be bitter in weeping*——[e]Chap. xxxvii. 3——[f]Lam. i. 5; ii. 2——[g]Jer. xlix. 35——[h]Chap. xv. 1

[i]Heb. *made naked*——[k]Heb. *the choice of thy valleys* [l]Or, *toward*——[m]1 Kings vii. 2; x. 17——[n]2 Kings xx. 20; 2 Chron. xxxii. 4, 5, 30——[o]Neh. iii. 16

streets, any public spectacle, any alarm of a public nature, every one immediately goes up to the house-top to satisfy his curiosity. In the same manner, when any one has occasion to make any thing public, the readiest and most effectual way of doing it is to proclaim it from the house-tops to the people in the streets. "What ye hear in the ear, that publish ye on the house-top," saith our Saviour, Matt. x. 27. The people running all to the tops of their houses gives a lively image of a sudden general alarm. Sir *John Chardin's* MS. note on this place is as follows: "Dans les festes pour voir passer quelque chose, et dans les maladies pour les annoncer aux voisins en allumant des lumieres, le peuple monte sur les terrasses." "In festivals, in order to see what is going forward, and in times of sickness, in order to indicate them to neighbours by lighting of candles, the people go up to the house-tops."

Verse 3. *All thy rulers—are bound by the archers*—"All thy leaders—are fled from the bow"] There seems to be somewhat of an inconsistency in the sense according to the present reading. If the leaders were bound, אסרו *usseru*, how could they flee away? for their being bound, according to the obvious construction and course of the sentence, is a circumstance prior to their flight. I therefore follow *Houbigant*, who reads הסרו *huseru, remoti sunt*, "they are gone off." גלו *galu, transmigraverunt, Chaldee;* which seems to confirm this emendation.

Verse 6. *Chariots of men*—"The Syrian"] It is not easy to say what רכב אדם *recheb adam*, a *chariot of men*, can mean. It seems by the form of the sentence, which consists of three members, the first and the third mentioning a particular people, that the second should do so likewise. Thus ברכב ארם ופרשים *berecheb aram uparashim*, "with chariots the Syrian, and with horsemen:" the similitude of the letters ד *daleth* and ר *resh* is so great, and the mistakes arising from it are so frequent, that I readily adopt the correction of *Houbigant*, ארם *aram*, *Syria*, instead of אדם *adam, man;* which seems to me extremely probable. The conjunction ו *vau, and*, prefixed to פרשים *parashim, horsemen*, seems necessary in whatever way the sentence may be taken; and it is confirmed by *five* MSS., (one ancient,) *four* of *De Rossi's*, and two ancient of my own; one by correction of Dr. *Kennicott's*, and *three* editions. Kir was a city belonging to the Medes. The Medes were subject to the Assyrians in Hezekiah's time, (see 2 Kings xvi. 9, and xvii. 6;) and so perhaps might Elam (the Persians) likewise be, or auxiliaries to them.

Verse 8. *The armour*—"The arsenal"] Built by Solomon within the city, and called the house of the forest of Lebanon; probably from the great quantity of cedar from Lebanon which was employed in the building. See 1 Kings vii. 2, 3.

Verse 9. *Ye gathered together the waters*—"And ye shall collect the waters"] There were two pools in or near Jerusalem, supplied by springs: the upper pool, or the old pool, supplied by the spring called Gihon, 2 Chron. xxxii. 30, towards the higher part of the city, near Sion, or the city of David, and the lower pool, probably supplied by Siloam, towards the lower part. When Hezekiah was threatened with a siege by Sennacherib, he stopped up all the waters of the fountains without the city; and brought them into the city by a conduit, or subterranean passage cut through the rock; those of the old pool, to the place where he had a double wall, so that the pool was between the two walls. This he did in order to distress the enemy, and to supply the city during the siege. This was so great a work that not only the historians have made particular mention of it, 2 Kings xx. 20; 2 Chron. xxxii. 2, 3, 5, 30; but the son of Sirach also has celebrated it in his encomium on Hezekiah. "Hezekiah fortified his city, and brought in water into the midst thereof: he digged the hard rock with iron, and made wells for water," Ecclus. xlviii.

Verse 11. *Unto the maker thereof*—"To him that hath disposed this"] That is, to God the Author and Disposer of this visitation, the invasion with which he now threatens you. The

A. M. cir. 3292
B. C. cir. 712
Olymp. XVII. 1
cir. annum
NumæPompilii,
R. Roman., 4

walls for the water of the old
pool: but ye have not looked
unto [p]the maker thereof, neither
had respect unto him that
fashioned it long ago.
12 And in that day did the Lord GOD of
hosts [q]call to weeping, and to mourning, and
[r]to baldness, and to girding with sackcloth:
13 And behold joy and gladness, slaying
oxen, and killing sheep, eating flesh, and
drinking wine; [s]let us eat and
drink, for to-morrow we shall
die.
14 [t]And it was revealed in
mine ears by the LORD of hosts, Surely this
iniquity [u]shall not be purged from you till
ye die, saith the Lord GOD of hosts.
15 Thus saith the Lord GOD of Hosts, Go,
get thee unto this treasurer, *even* unto [v]Shebna,
[w]which *is* over the house, *and say,*

[p]See ch. xxxvii. 26——[q]Joel i. 13——[r]See Ezra ix. 3; ch. xv. 2; Mic. i. 16——[s]Ch. lvi. 12; Wisd. ii. 6; 1 Cor, xv. 32——[t]Ch. v. 9——[u]1 Sam. iii. 14; Ezek. xxiv. 13 [v]2 Kings xviii. 37; ch. xxxvi. 3——[w]1 Kings iv. 6

very same expressions are applied to God, and upon the same occasion, chap. xxxvii. 26:—

"Hast thou not heard of old, that I have disposed it;
And of ancient times, that I have formed it?"

Verse 13. *Let us eat and drink, for to-morrow we shall die.*] This has been the language of all those who have sought their portion in this life, since the foundation of the world. So the poet:—

Heu, heu nos miseri! quam totus homuncio nil est!
Sic erimus cuncti, postquam nos auferet orcus.
Ergo vivamus, dum licet esse, bene.

Alas, alas! what miserable creatures are we, only the semblances of men! And so shall we be all when we come to die. Therefore let us live joyfully while we may.

Domitian had an image of death hung up in his dining-room, to show his guests that as life was uncertain, they should make the best of it by indulging themselves. On this *Martial*, to flatter the emperor, whom he styles *god*, wrote the following epigram:—

Frange thoros, pete vina, tingere nardo.
Ipse jubet mortis te meminisse Deus.

Sit down to table—drink heartily—anoint thyself with spikenard; for God himself commands thee to remember death.

So the *adage:—*

Ede, bibe, lude: post mortem nulla voluptas.

"Eat, drink, and play, while here ye may:
No revelry after your dying day."

St. Paul quotes the same heathen sentiment, 1 Cor. xv. 32: "Let us eat and drink, for to-morrow we die."

Anacreon is full in point, and from him nothing better can be expected:—

Ὡς ουν ετ' ευδι' εστιν,
Και πινε και κυβευε
Και σπενδε τῳ Λυαιῳ·
Μη νουσος, ην τις ελθῃ,
Λεγῃ, σε μη δει πινειν.
ANAC. *Od.* xv., l. 11.

"While no tempest blots your sky,
Drink, and throw the sportful dye:
But to Bacchus drench the ground,
Ere you push the goblet round;
Lest some fatal illness cry,
'Drink no more the cup of joy.'"
ADDISON.

Verse 14. *It was revealed in mine ears*—"The voice of Jehovah"] The *Vulgate* has *vox Domini;* as if in his copy he had read קול יהוה *kol Yehovah;* and in truth, without the word קול *kol, voice,* it is not easy to make out the sense of the passage; as appears from the strange versions which the rest of the ancients, (except the *Chaldee,*) and many of the moderns, have given of it; as if the matter were revealed in or to the ears of JEHOVAH: *εν τοις ωσι Κυριου, in the ears of the Lord,* Septuagint. *Vitringa* translates it, Revelatus est in auribus meis JEHOVAH, "JEHOVAH hath revealed it in mine ears;" and refers to 1 Sam. ii. 27; iii. 21: but the construction in those places is different, and there is no speech of God added; which here seems to want something more than the verb נגלה *nigleh* to introduce it. Compare chap. v. 9, where the text is still more imperfect.

The Lord God of hosts] אדני יהוה צבאות *Adonai Yehovah tsebaoth.* But אדני *Adonai, Lord,* is omitted by *two* of *Kennicott's* and *De Rossi's* MSS., and by *two* of my own; by *three* editions, and the *Septuagint, Syriac* and *Arabic.*

Verse 15. *Go—unto Shebna*] The following prophecy concerning Shebna seems to have very little relation to the foregoing, except that it might have been delivered about the same time; and Shebna might be a principal person among those whose luxury and profaneness is severely reprehended by the prophet in the conclusion of that prophecy, ver. 11-14.

Shebna the scribe, mentioned in the history of Hezekiah, chap. xxxvi., seems to have been a different person from this Shebna, the treasurer or steward of the household, to whom this prophecy relates. The Eliakim here mentioned was probably the person who, at the time of Sennacherib's invasion, was actually treasurer, the son of Hilkiah. If so, this prophecy was delivered, as the preceding, (which makes the former part of the chapter,) plainly was, some time before the invasion of Sennacherib. As to the rest, history affords us no information.

"And say unto him"] Here are two words lost out of the text, which are supplied by *two* of Dr. *Kennicott's* MSS., *one* ancient, which read ואמרת אליו *veamarta elaiv, and thou shalt say unto him;* by the *Septuagint, και ειπον αυτῳ,* and in the same manner by all the ancient versions. It is to be observed that this passage is

A. M. cir. 3292
B. C. cir. 712
Olymp. XVII. 1
cir. annum
NumæPompilii,
R. Roman., 4

16 What hast thou here? and
whom hast thou here, that thou
hast hewed thee out a sepulchre
here, [x]*as* he [y]that heweth him
out a sepulchre on high, *and* that graveth a
habitation for himself in a rock?
17 Behold, [z]the LORD will carry thee away
with [a]a mighty captivity, [b]and will surely
cover thee.
18 He will surely violently turn and toss
thee *like* a ball into a [c]large country: there
shalt thou die, and there the chariots of thy
glory *shall be* the shame of thy lord's house.
19 And I will drive thee from thy station,
and from thy state shall he pull
thee down.

A. M. cir. 3292
B. C. cir. 712
Olymp. XVII. 1
cir. annum
NumæPompilii,
R. Roman., 4

20 And it shall come to pass
in that day, that I will call my
servant [d]Eliakim the son of Hilkiah:
21 And I will clothe him with thy robe, and
strengthen him with thy girdle, and I will
commit thy government into his hand: and
he shall be a father to the inhabitants of Jerusalem, and to the house of Judah.
22 And the key of the house of David will
I lay upon his shoulder; so he shall [e]open,
and none shall shut: and he shall shut, and
none shall open.

---

[x]Or, *O he*——[y]2 Sam. xviii. 18; Matt. xxvii. 60
[z]Or, *the LORD who covered thee with an excellent covering, and clothed thee gorgeously, shall surely,* &c.; ver. 18

[a]Heb. *the captivity of a man*——[b]Esth. vii. 8——[c]Heb. *large of spaces*——[d]2 Kings xviii. 18——[e]Job xii. 14; Rev. iii. 7

---

merely historical, and does not admit of that sort of ellipsis by which in the poetical parts a person is frequently introduced speaking, without the usual notice, that what follows was delivered by him.

Verse 16. *A sepulchre on high—in a rock*] It has been observed before, on chap. xiv., that persons of high rank in Judea, and in most parts of the east, were generally buried in large sepulchral vaults, hewn out in the rock for the use of themselves and their families. The vanity of Shebna is set forth by his being so studious and careful to have his sepulchre on high—in a lofty vault; and that probably in a high situation, that it might be more conspicuous. Hezekiah was buried, למעלה *lemalah*, *εν αναβασει*, *Sept.*: in the chiefest, says our translation; rather, in the highest part of the sepulchres of the sons of David, to do him the more honour, 2 Chron. xxxii. 33. There are some monuments still remaining in Persia of great antiquity, called *Naksi Rustam*, which give one a clear idea of Shebna's pompous design for his sepulchre. They consist of several sepulchres, each of them hewn in a high rock near the top; the front of the rock to the valley below is adorned with carved work in relievo, being the outside of the sepulchre. Some of these sepulchres are about thirty feet in the perpendicular from the valley, which is itself perhaps raised above half as much by the accumulation of the earth since they were made. See the description of them in Chardin, Pietro della Valle, Thevenot, and Kempfer. Diodorus Siculus, lib. xvii., mentions these ancient monuments, and calls them the sepulchres of the kings of Persia.—L.

Verse 17. *Cover thee*] That is, thy face. This was the condition of mourners in general, and particularly of condemned persons. See Esther vi. 12; vii. 8.

Verse 19. *I will drive thee*] אהרסך *ehersecha*, in the first person, *Syr. Vulg.*

Verse 21. *To the inhabitants*] ליושבי *leyoshebey*, in the plural number, four of Dr. *Kennicott's* MSS., (two ancient,) and two of *De Rossi's*, with the *Septuagint*, *Syriac*, and *Vulgate*.

Verse 22. *And the key of the house of David will I lay upon his shoulder*] As the robe and the baldric, mentioned in the preceding verse, were the ensigns of power and authority, so likewise was the key the mark of office, either sacred or civil. The priestess of Juno is said to be the key-bearer of the goddess, *κλειδουχος Ἡρας· Æschyl.* Suppl. 299. A female high in office under a great queen has the same title:—

Καλλιθοη κλειδουχος Ολυμπιαδος βασιλειης.

"Callithoe was the key-bearer of the Olympian queen."

Auctor Phoronidis ap. Clem. Alex. p. 418, edit. Potter. This mark of office was likewise among the Greeks, as here in Isaiah, borne on the shoulder; the priestess of Ceres, *κατωμαδιαν εχε κλαιδα*, *had the key on her shoulder. Callim.* Ceres, ver. 45. To comprehend how the key could be borne on the shoulder, it will be necessary to say something of the form of it: but without entering into a long disquisition, and a great deal of obscure learning, concerning the locks and keys of the ancients, it will be sufficient to observe, that one sort of keys, and that probably the most ancient, was of considerable magnitude, and as to the shape, very much bent and crooked. *Aratus*, to give his reader an idea of the form of the constellation Cassiopeia, compares it to a *key*. It must be owned that the passage is very obscure; but the learned Huetius has bestowed a great deal of pains in explaining it, Animadvers. in Manilii, lib. i. 355; and I think has succeeded very well in it. *Homer*, Odyss. xxi. 6, describes the key of Ulysses' storehouse as *ευκαμπτης*, of a large curvature; which Eustathius explains by saying it was *δρεπανοειδης*, in shape like a *reaphook*. Huetius says the constellation Cassiopeia answers to this description; the stars to the north making the curve part, that is, the principal part of the key; the southern stars, the handle. The curve part was introduced into the key-hole; and, being properly directed by the handle, took hold of the bolts within, and moved them from their places. We may easily collect from this account, that such a key would lie very well upon the shoulder; that it must be of some considerable size and weight, and could hardly be commodiously carried otherwise.

A. M. cir. 3292 B. C. cir. 712 Olymp. XVII. 1 cir. annum NumæPompilii, R. Roman., 4

23 And I will fasten him *as* [f]a nail in a sure place; and he shall be for a glorious throne to his father's house.

24 And they shall hang upon him all the glory of his father's house, the offspring and the issue, all vessels of small quantity, from the vessels of cups, even to all the [g]vessels of flagons.

25 In that day, saith the LORD of hosts, shall the [h]nail that is fastened in the sure place be removed, and be cut down, and fall; and the burden that *was* upon it shall be cut off: for the LORD hath spoken *it*.

[f]Ezra ix. 8 —— [g]Or, *instruments of viols* —— [h]Ver. 23

Ulysses' key was of brass, and the handle of ivory: but this was a royal key. The more common ones were probably of wood. In Egypt they have no other than wooden locks and keys to this day; even the gates of Cairo have no better. *Baumgarten*, Peregr. i. 18. *Thevenot*, part ii., chap. 10. But was it not the *representation* of a *key*, either cut out in *cloth* and *sewed* on the *shoulder* of the garment, or *embroidered* on that part of the garment itself? The idea of a *huge* key of a gate, in any kind of *metal*, laid across the shoulder, is to me very ridiculous.

In allusion to the image of the key as the ensign of power, the unlimited extent of that power is expressed with great clearness as well as force by the sole and exclusive authority to open and shut. Our Saviour, therefore, has upon a similar occasion made use of a like manner of expression, Matt. xvi. 19; and in Rev. iii. 7 has applied to himself the very words of the prophet.

Verse 23. *A nail*] In ancient times, and in the eastern countries, as the way of life, so the houses, were much more simple than ours at present. They had not that quantity and variety of furniture, nor those accommodations of all sorts, with which we abound. It was convenient and even necessary for them, and it made an essential part in the building of a house, to furnish the inside of the several apartments with sets of spikes, nails, or large pegs, upon which to dispose of and hang up the several movables and utensils in common use, and proper to the apartment. These spikes they worked into the walls at the first erection of them, the walls being of such materials that they could not bear their being driven in afterwards; and they were contrived so as to strengthen the walls by binding the parts together, as well as to serve for convenience. Sir John Chardin's account of this matter is this:—"They do not drive with a hammer the nails that are put into the eastern walls. The walls are too hard, being of brick; or, if they are of clay, too mouldering: but they fix them in the brick-work as they are building. They are large nails, with square heads like dice, well made, the ends being bent so as to make them cramp-irons. They commonly place them at the windows and doors, in order to hang upon them, when they like, veils and curtains." *Harmer's* Observ. i. p. 191. And we may add, that they were put in other places too, in order to hang up other things of various kinds; as appears from this place of Isaiah, and from Ezek. xv. 3, who speaks of a pin or nail, "to hang any vessel thereon." The word used here for a nail of this sort is the same by which they express that instrument, the stake, or large pin of iron, with which they fastened down to the ground the cords of their tents. We see, therefore, that these nails were of necessary and common use, and of no small importance in all their apartments; conspicuous, and much exposed to observation: and if they seem to us mean and insignificant, it is because we are not acquainted with the thing itself, and have no name to express it but by what conveys to us a low and contemptible idea. "Grace hath been showed from the Lord our God," saith Ezra, chap. ix. 8, "to leave us a remnant to escape, and to give us a nail in his holy place:" that is, as the margin of our Bible explains it, "a constant and sure abode."

"He that doth lodge near her (Wisdom's) house,
Shall also fasten a pin in her walls."
Ecclus. xiv. 24.

The dignity and propriety of the metaphor appears from the Prophet Zechariah's use of it:—

"From him shall be the corner-stone, from him the nail,
From him the battle-bow,
From him every ruler together." Zech. x. 4.

And Mohammed, using the same word, calls Pharaoh the lord or master of the *nails*, that is, well attended by nobles and officers capable of administering his affairs. Koran, Sur. xxxviii. 11, and lxxxix. 9. So some understand this passage of the Koran. Mr. Sale seems to prefer another interpretation.

Taylor, in his Concordance, thinks יתד *yathed* means the *pillar* or *post* that stands in the middle, and supports the tent, in which such pegs are fixed to hang their arms, &c., upon; referring to *Shaw's* Travels, p. 287. But יתד *yathed* is never used, as far as appears to me, in that sense. It was indeed necessary that the pillar of the tent should have such pegs on it for that purpose; but the hanging of such things in this manner upon this pillar does not prove that יתד *yathed* was the pillar itself.

A glorious throne—"A glorious seat"] That is, his father's house and all his own family shall be gloriously seated, shall flourish in honour and prosperity; and shall depend upon him, and be supported by him.

Verse 24. *All the glory*] One considerable part of the magnificence of the eastern princes consisted in the great quantity of gold and silver vessels which they had for various uses. "Solomon's drinking vessels were of gold, and all the vessels of the house of the forest of Lebanon were of pure gold; none were of silver; it was nothing accounted of in Solomon's days;" 1 Kings x. 21. "The vessels in the house of the forest of Lebanon," the armoury of Jerusalem so called, "were two hundred targets, and three hundred shields of beaten gold." Ibid. ver. 16, 17. These were ranged in order upon the walls of the armoury, (see Cant. iv. 4,) upon pins worked into the walls on purpose, as above mentioned. Eliakim is considered as a principal stake of this sort, immovably fastened in the wall for the support of all vessels destined for common or sacred uses; that is, as the principal support of the whole civil and ecclesiastical polity. And the consequence of his continued power will be the promotion and flourishing condition of his family and dependants, from the highest to the lowest.

Vessels of flagons—"Meaner vessels"] נבלים *nebalim* seems to mean earthen vessels of common use, brittle, and of little value, (see Lam. iv. 2; Jer. xlviii. 12,) in opposition to אגנות *aganoth*, goblets of gold and silver used in the sacrifices. Exod. xxiv. 6.

Verse 25. *The nail that is fastened*] This must be understood of Shebna, as a repetition and confirmation of the sentence above denounced against him.

What is said of Eliakim the son of Hilkiah, ver. 20-24, is very remarkable; and the literal meaning is not easy to be understood. From chap. ix. 6, and from Rev. iii. 7, it seems to belong to our Lord alone. The *removal* of *Shebna* from being *over the treasure* of the *Lord's house*, ver. 19, and the *investiture of Eliakim* with his *robe, girdle, office*, and *government*, ver. 20, &c., probably point out the *change* of the Jewish priesthood, and the proclaiming of the unchangeable priesthood of Christ. See Psa. cx. 4. *Eliakim* signifies *The resurrection of the Lord;* or, *My God, he shall arise. Hilkiah* signifies *The Lord my portion* or *lot.* The *key of David, shutting and opening*, &c., may intend the way of salvation through Christ alone. For the hope of salvation and eternal *life* comes only through *Eliakim*, the *resurrection* of Jesus Christ from the *dead.*

It is said, ver. 24, "They shall hang upon him all the glory of his father's house"—for, in Jesus Christ *dwells all the fulness of the Godhead bodily; and the offspring and the issue*, הצאצאים *hatstseetsaim* from יצא *yatsa, to go out*,—the *suckers from the root;* the *sideshoots*, the *apostles* and *primitive ministers* of his word. The *issue*, הצפיעות *hatstsephioth*, probably means the *issue's issue;* so the Targum. The *grandchildren*, all those who believe on the Lord Jesus through their word.

"The nail that is fastened in the sure place shall be removed," ver. 25, *Kimchi* refers not to *Eliakim*, but to *Shebna*, ver. 17-19. By, "They shall hang upon him all vessels of small quantity and large quantity," has been understood the *dependence* of *all souls*, of *all capacities*, from the *lowest* in *intellect* to the most *exalted*, on the Lord Jesus, as the only Saviour of all lost human spirits.

As the literal interpretation of this prophecy has not been found out, we are justified from *parallel texts* to consider the whole as referring to Jesus Christ, and the government of the Church, and the redemption of the world by him. Nor are there many prophecies which relate to him more clearly than this, taken in the above sense.

CHAPTER XXIII

Prophecy denouncing the destruction of Tyre by Nebuchadnezzar, delivered upwards of one hundred and twenty *years before its accomplishment, at a period when the Tyrians were in great prosperity, and the Babylonians in abject subjection to the Assyrian empire; and, consequently, when an event of so great magnitude was improbable in the highest degree,* 1–14. *Tyre shall recover its splendour at the termination of* seventy years, the days of ONE king, *or kingdom, by which must be meant the time allotted for the duration of the Babylonish empire, as otherwise the prophecy cannot be accommodated to the event,* 15–17. *Supposed reference to the early conversion of Tyre to Christianity,* 18.

A. M. cir. 3289 THE [a]burden of Tyre. Howl,
B. C. cir. 715 ye ships of Tarshish; for it
Olymp. XVI. 2 is laid waste, so that there is no
cir. annum NumæPompilii, house, no entering in: [b]from the
R. Roman., 1 land of Chittim it is revealed
to them.

2 Be [c]still, ye inhabitants of
the isle; thou whom the mer-

[a]Jer. xxv. 22; xlvii. 4; Ezek. xxvi., xxvii., xxviii; Amos i. 9; Zech. ix. 2, 4——[b]Ver. 12——[c]Heb. *silent*

NOTES ON CHAP. XXIII

Verse 1. *The burden of Tyre*] Tyre, a city on the coast of Syria, about lat. 32° N. was built *two thousand seven hundred and sixty* years before Christ. There were *two* cities of this name; *one* on the *continent*, and the other on an *island*, about half a mile from the shore; the city on the island was about four miles in circumference. *Old* Tyre resisted Nebuchadnezzar for thirteen years; then the inhabitants carried, so to speak, the city to the forementioned island, ver. 4. This *new* city held out against Alexander the Great for seven months; who, in order to take it, was obliged to fill up the channel which separated it from the main land. In A. D. 1289 it was totally destroyed by the sultan of Egypt; and now contains only a few huts, in which about fifty or sixty wretched families exist. This desolation was foretold by this prophet and by Ezekiel, *one thousand nine hundred* years before it took place!

Howl, ye ships of Tarshish] This prophecy denounces the destruction of Tyre by Nebuchadnezzar. It opens with an address to the Tyrian negotiators and sailors at Tarshish, (Tartessus, in Spain,) a place which, in the course of their trade, they greatly frequented. The news of the destruction of Tyre by Nebuchadnezzar is said to be brought to them from Chittim, the islands

A. M. cir. 3289 B. C. cir. 715 Olymp. XVI. 2 cir. annum NumæPompilii, R. Roman., 1

chants of Zidon, that pass over
the sea, have replenished.
3 And by great waters the seed
of Sihor, the harvest of the river,
is her revenue; and [d]she is a mart of nations.
4 Be thou ashamed, O Zidon: for the sea
hath spoken, *even* the strength of the sea,
saying, I travail not, nor bring forth children,
neither do I nourish up young men, *nor* bring
up virgins.
5 [e]As at the report concerning Egypt, *so*
shall they be sorely pained at the report of
Tyre.
6 Pass ye over to Tarshish; howl, ye inhabitants of the isle.
7 *Is* this your [f]joyous *city,*
whose antiquity *is* of ancient
days? her own feet shall carry
her [g]afar off to sojourn.

A. M. cir. 3289 B. C. cir. 715 Olymp. XVI. 2 cir. annum NumæPompilii, R. Roman., 1

8 Who hath taken this counsel against Tyre,
[h]the crowning *city,* whose merchants *are*
princes, whose traffickers *are* the honourable
of the earth.
9 The LORD of hosts hath purposed it, [i]to
stain the pride of all glory, *and* to bring into
contempt all the honourable of the earth.
10 Pass through thy land as a river, O
daughter of Tarshish: *there is* no more
[k]strength.
11 He stretched out his hand over the sea,

[d]Ezek. xxvii. 3——[e]Chap. xix. 16——[f]Chap. xxii. 2——[g]Heb. *from afar off*

[h]See Ezek. xxviii. 2, 12——[i]Heb. *to pollute*——[k]Heb. *girdle*

and coasts of the Mediterranean; "for the Tyrians," says Jerome on ver. 6, "when they saw they had no other means of escaping, fled in their ships, and took refuge in Carthage and in the islands of the Ionian and Ægean sea." From whence the news would spread and reach Tarshish; so also *Jarchi* on the same place. This seems to be the most probable interpretation of this verse.

Verse 2. *Be still*—"Be silent"] Silence is a mark of grief and consternation. See chap. xlvii. 5. Jeremiah has finely expressed this image:—

"The elders of the daughter of Zion sit on the ground, they are silent:
They have cast up dust on their heads, they have girded themselves with sackcloth.
The virgins of Jerusalem hang down their heads to the ground." Lam. ii. 10.

Verse 3. *The seed of Sihor*—"The seed of the Nile"] The Nile is called here *Shichor,* as it is Jer. ii. 18, and 1 Chron. xiii. 5. It had this name from the *blackness* of its waters, charged with the mud which it brings down from Ethiopia when it overflows, *Et viridem Ægyptum nigra fecundat arena;* as it was called by the Greeks *Melas,* and by the Latins *Melo,* for the same reason. See *Servius* on the above line of Virgil, Georg. iv. 291. It was called *Siris* by the Ethiopians, by some supposed to be the same with *Shichor.* Egypt by its extraordinary fertility, caused by the overflowing of the Nile, supplied the neighbouring nations with corn, by which branch of trade the Tyrians gained great wealth.

Verse 4. *Be thou ashamed, O Zidon*] Tyre is called ver. 12, the daughter of Sidon. "The Sidonians," says *Justin,* xviii. 3, "when their city was taken by the king of Ascalon, betook themselves to their ships, and landed, and built by Tyre." Sidon, as the mother city is supposed to be deeply affected with the calamity of her daughter.

Nor *bring up virgins*—"*Nor* educated virgins."] ורוממתי *veromamti;* so an ancient MS. of Dr. *Kennicott's* prefixing the ו *vau,* which refers to the negative preceding, and is equivalent to ולא *velo.* See Deut. xxiii. 6; Prov. xxx. 3. Two of my own MSS. have ו *vau* in the margin.

Verse 7. *Whose antiquity* is *of ancient days*—"Whose antiquity is of the earliest date"] Justin, in the passage above quoted, had dated the building of Tyre at a certain number of years before the taking of Troy; but the number is lost in the present copies. Tyre, though not so old as Sidon, was yet of very high antiquity: it was a strong city even in the time of Joshua. It is called עיר מבצר צר *ir mibtsar tsor,* "the city of the fortress of Sor," Josh. xix. 29. Interpreters raise difficulties in regard to this passage, and will not allow it to have been so ancient; with what good reason I do not see, for it is called by the same name, "the fortress of Sor," in the history of David, 2 Sam. xxiv. 7, and the circumstances of the history determine the place to be the very same. See on ver. 1.

Whose antiquity is of ancient days, may refer to *Palætyrus,* or *Old Tyre.*

Her own feet shall carry her afar off to sojourn.] This may belong to the *new* or insular *Tyre; her own feet,* that is, her own inhabitants, *shall carry her*—shall transport the city, from the continent to the island. "But the text says, it shall be carried *far off;* and the new city was founded only half a mile distant from the other." I answer, מרחוק *merachok* does not always signify a *great distance,* but distance or interval in general; for in Josh. iii. 4 רחוק *rachok* is used to express the *space* between the camp and the ark, which we know to have been only *two thousand* cubits. Some refer the *sojourning afar off* to the extent of the commercial voyages undertaken by the Tyrians and their foreign connexions.

Verse 10. *O daughter of Tarshish*] Tyre is called the daughter of Tarshish; perhaps because, Tyre being ruined, Tarshish was become the superior city, and might be considered as the metropolis of the Tyrian people; or rather because of the close connexion and perpetual intercourse between them, according to that latitude of signification in which the Hebrews use the words *son* and *daughter* to express any sort of conjunction and dependence whatever. מזח *mezach, a girdle,* which collects, binds, and keeps together the loose raiment, when applied

A. M. cir. 3289
B. C. cir. 715
Olymp. XVI. 2
cir. annum
NumæPompilii,
R. Roman., 1

he shook the kingdoms: the LORD hath given a commandment [l]against [m]the merchant *city,* to destroy the [n]strong holds thereof.
12 And he said, [o]Thou shalt no more rejoice, O thou oppressed virgin, daughter of Zidon: arise, [p]pass over to Chittim; there also shalt thou have no rest.
13 Behold the land of the Chaldeans; this people was not, *till* the Assyrian founded it for [q]them that dwell in the wilderness: they set up the towers thereof, they raised up the palaces thereof; *and* he brought it to ruin.
14 [r]Howl, ye ships of Tarshish: for your strength is laid waste.
15 And it shall come to pass in that day,

[l]Or, *concerning a merchantman*——[m]Heb. *Canaan* [n]Or, *strengths*

[o]Rev. xviii. 22——[p]Ver. 1——[q]Psa. lxxii. 9——[r]Ver. 1; Ezek. xxvii. 25, 30

to a river, may mean a mound, mole, or artificial dam, which contains the waters, and prevents them from spreading abroad. A city taken by siege and destroyed, whose walls are demolished, whose policy is dissolved, whose wealth is dissipated, whose people is scattered over the wide country, is compared to a river whose banks are broken down, and whose waters, let loose and overflowing all the neighbouring plains, are wasted and lost. This may possibly be the meaning of this very obscure verse, of which I can find no other interpretation that is at all satisfactory.—L.

Verse 13. *Behold the land of the Chaldeans*] This verse is extremely obscure; the obscurity arises from the ambiguity of the agents, which belong to the verbs, and of the objects expressed by the pronouns; from the change of number of the verbs, and of gender in the pronouns. The MSS. give us no assistance, and the ancient Versions very little. The *Chaldee* and *Vulgate* read שמוה *samoah,* in the plural number. I have followed the interpretation which, among many different ones, seemed to be most probable, that of Perizonius and Vitringa.

The Chaldeans, *Chasdim,* are supposed to have had their origin, and to have taken their name, from *Chesed,* the son of Nachor, the brother of Abraham. They were known by that name in the time of Moses, who calls Ur in Mesopotamia, from whence Abraham came, to distinguish it from other places of the same name, *Ur* of the *Chaldeans.* And Jeremiah calls them an ancient nation. This is not inconsistent with what Isaiah here says of them: "This people was not," that is, they were of no account, (see Deut. xxxii. 21;) they were not reckoned among the great and potent nations of the world till of later times; they were a rude, uncivilized, barbarous people, without laws, without settled habitations; wandering in a wide desert country (ציים *tsiyim*) and addicted to rapine like the wild Arabians. Such they are represented to have been in the time of Job, chap. i. 17, and such they continued to be till Assur, some powerful king of Assyria, gathered them together, and settled them in Babylon in the neighbouring country. This probably was Ninus, whom I suppose to have lived in the time of the Judges. In this, with many eminent chronologers, I follow the authority of Herodotus, who says that the Assyrian monarchy lasted but *five hundred and twenty* years. Ninus got possession of Babylon from the Cuthean Arabians; the successors of Nimrod in that empire collected the Chaldeans, and settled a colony of them there to secure the possession of the city, which he and his successors greatly enlarged and ornamented. They had perhaps been useful to him in his wars, and might be likely to be farther useful in keeping under the old inhabitants of that city, and of the country belonging to it; according to the policy of the Assyrian kings, who generally brought new people into the conquered countries; see Isa. xxxvi. 17; 2 Kings xvii. 6, 24. The testimony of Dicæarchus, a Greek historian contemporary with Alexander, (*apud.* Steph. de Urbibus, in voc. Χαλδαιος,) in regard to the fact is remarkable, though he is mistaken in the name of the king he speaks of. He says that "a certain king of Assyria, the *fourteenth* in succession from Ninus, (as he might be, if Ninus is placed, as in the common chronology, *eight hundred* years higher than we have above set him,) named, as it is said, *Chaldæus,* having gathered together and united all the people called Chaldeans, built the famous city, Babylon, upon the Euphrates."—L.

Verse 14. *Howl, ye ships*] The Prophet Ezekiel hath enlarged upon this part of the same subject with great force and elegance:—

"Thus saith the Lord JEHOVAH concerning Tyre:—
At the sound of thy fall, at the cry of the wounded,
At the great slaughter in the midst of thee, shall not the islands tremble?
And shall not all the princes of the sea descend from their thrones,
And lay aside their robes, and strip off their embroidered garments?
They shall clothe themselves with trembling, they shall sit on the ground;
They shall tremble every moment, they shall be astonished at thee.
And they shall utter a lamentation over thee, and shall say unto thee:
How art thou lost, thou that wast inhabited from the seas!
The renowned city, that was strong in the sea, she and her inhabitants!
That struck with terror all her neighbours!
Now shall the coasts tremble in the day of thy fall,
And the isles that are in the sea shall be troubled at thy departure."
Ezek. xxvi. 15-18.

Verse 15. *According to the days of one king*] That is, of one *kingdom;* see Dan. vii. 17, viii. 20. Nebuchadnezzar began his conquests in the first year of his reign; from thence to the taking of Babylon by Cyrus are *seventy* years, at which time the nations subdued by Nebuchadnezzar were to be restored to liberty. These

A. M. cir. 3289 B. C. cir. 715 that Tyre shall be forgotten
Olymp. XVI. 2 seventy years, according to the
cir. annum NumæPompilii, days of one king: after the end
R. Roman., 1 of seventy years [s]shall Tyre
sing as a harlot.

16 Take a harp, go about the city, thou
harlot that hast been forgotten; make sweet
melody, sing many songs, that thou mayest be
remembered.

17 And it shall come to pass after the end
of seventy years, that the LORD A. M. cir. 3289 B. C. cir. 715
will visit Tyre, and she shall turn Olymp. XVI. 2
to her hire, and [t]shall commit cir. annum NumæPompilii,
fornication with all the king- R. Roman., 1
doms of the world upon the face of the earth.

18 And her merchandise and her hire [u]shall
be holiness to the LORD: it shall not be treasured nor laid up; for her merchandise shall
be for them that dwell before the LORD, to
eat sufficiently, and for [v]durable clothing.

[s]Heb. *it shall be unto Tyre as the song of a harlot*

[t]Rev. xvii. 2——[u]Zech. xiv. 20, 21——[v]Heb. *old*

seventy years limit the duration of the Babylonish monarchy. Tyre was taken by him towards the middle of that period; so did not serve the king of Babylon during the whole period, but only for the remaining part of it. This seems to be the meaning of Isaiah; the days allotted to the one king or kingdom, are seventy years; Tyre, with the rest of the conquered nations, shall continue in a state of subjection and desolation to the end of that period. Not from the beginning and through the whole of the period; for, by being one of the latest conquests, the duration of that state of subjection in regard to her, was not much more than half of it. "All these nations," saith Jeremiah, xxv. 11, "shall serve the king of Babylon seventy years." Some of them were conquered sooner, some later; but the end of this period was the common term for the deliverance of them *all.*

There is another way of computing the *seventy years*, from the year in which Tyre was actually taken to the nineteenth of Darius Hystaspis; whom the Phœnicians, or Tyrians, assisted against the Ionians, and probably on that account might then be restored to their former liberties and privileges. But I think the former the more probable interpretation.—L.

Sing as a harlot] Fidicinam esse meretricum est, says *Donatus* in Terent. Eunuch. iii. 2, 4.

> Nec meretrix tibicina, cujus
> Ad strepitum salias.
>
> HOR. I. Epist. xiv. 25.

> "Nor harlot minstrel sings, when the rude sound
> Tempts you with heavy heels to thump the ground."
>
> FRANCIS.

Sir John Chardin, in his MS. note on this place, says:—C'est que les vielles prostituées,—ne font que chanter quand les jeunes dancent, et les animer par l'instrument et par la voix. "The old prostitutes do nothing but sing, while the young ones dance; and animate them both by vocal and instrumental music."

Verse 17. *After the end of seventy years*] Tyre, after its destruction by Nebuchadnezzar, recovered, as it is here foretold, its ancient trade, wealth, and grandeur; as it did likewise after a second destruction by Alexander. It became Christian early with the rest of the neighbouring countries. St. Paul himself found many Christians there, Acts xxi. 4. It suffered much in the Diocletian persecution. It was an archbishopric under the patriarchate of Jerusalem, with fourteen bishoprics under its jurisdiction. It continued Christian till it was taken by the Saracens in 639; was recovered by the Christians in 1124; but in 1280 was conquered by the Mamelukes, and afterwards taken from them by the Turks in 1517. Since that time it has sunk into utter decay; is now a mere ruin, a bare rock, "a place to spread nets upon," as the Prophet Ezekiel foretold it should be, chap. xxvi. 14. See *Sandy's* Travels; *Vitringa* on the place; Bp. *Newton* on the Prophecies, Dissert. xi.

CHAPTER XXIV

Dreadful judgments impending over the people of God, 1–4. *Particular enumeration of the horrid impieties which provoked the Divine vengeance,* 5, 6. *Great political wretchedness of the transgressors,* 7–12. *The calamities shall be so great that only a small remnant shall be left in the land, as it were the gleanings of the vintage,* 13. *The rest, scattered over the different countries, spread there the knowledge of God,* 14–16. *Strong figures by which the great distress and long captivity of the transgressors are set forth,* 17–22. *Gracious promise of a redemption from captivity; and of an extension of the kingdom of God in the latter days, attended with such glorious circumstances as totally to eclipse the light and splendour of the previous dispensation,* 23.

A. M. cir. 3292 B. C. cir. 712 BEHOLD, the LORD maketh
Olymp. XVII. 1 the earth empty, and mak-
cir. annum NumæPompilii, eth it waste, and [a]turneth
R. Roman., 4 it upside down, and scatter-
eth abroad the inhabitants A. M. cir. 3292 B. C. cir. 712
thereof. Olymp. XVII. 1

2 And it shall be, as with the cir. annum NumæPompilii,
people, so with the [b]priest; [c]as R. Roman., 4

[a]Heb. *perverteth the face thereof*

[b]Or, *prince*——[c]Hos. iv. 9

From the thirteenth chapter to the twenty-third inclusive, the fate of several cities and nations is denounced: of Babylon, of the Philistines, Moab, Damascus, Egypt, Tyre. After having foretold the destruction of the foreign nations, enemies of Judah, the prophet declares

A. M. cir. 3292 B. C. cir. 712 Olymp. XVII. 1 cir. annum NumæPompilii, R. Roman., 4
with the servant, so with his mas-
ter; as with the maid, so with
her mistress; [d]as with the buyer,
so with the seller; as with the
lender, so with the borrower; as with the taker
of usury, so with the giver of usury to him.
3 The land shall be utterly emptied, and
utterly spoiled: for the LORD hath spoken
this word.
4 The earth mourneth *and* fadeth away,
the world languisheth *and* fadeth away, [e]the
haughty people of the earth do languish.
5 [f]The earth also is defiled under the inhabitants thereof; because they have transgressed the laws, changed the ordinance,
broken the everlasting covenant.
6 Therefore hath [g]the curse devoured the
earth, and they that dwell therein are desolate: therefore the inhabitants of the earth are
burned, and few men left.
7 [h]The new wine mourneth, the vine languisheth, all the merry-hearted do sigh.
8 The mirth [i]of tabrets ceas- A. M. cir. 3292 B. C. cir. 712 Olymp. XVII. 1 cir. annum NumæPompilii, R. Roman., 4
eth, the noise of them that re-
joice endeth, the joy of the harp
ceaseth.
9 They shall not drink wine with a song;
strong drink shall be bitter to them that
drink it.
10 The city of confusion is broken down:
every house is shut up, that no man may
come in.
11 *There is* a crying for wine in the streets;
all joy is darkened, the mirth of the land is
gone.
12 In the city is left desolation, and the gate
is smitten with destruction.
13 When thus it shall be in the midst of
the land among the people, [k]*there shall be* as
the shaking of an olive tree, *and* as the gleaning grapes when the vintage is done.
14 They shall lift up their voice, they shall
sing for the majesty of the LORD, they shall
cry aloud from the sea.

[d]Ezek. vii. 12, 13——[e]Heb. *the height of the people*——[f]Gen. iii. 17; Num. xxxi. 35——[g]Mal. iv. 6——[h]Ch. xvi. 8, 9; Joel i. 10, 12——[i]Jer. vii. 34; xvi. 9; xxv. 10; Ezek. xxvi. 13; Hos. ii. 11; Rev. xviii. 22——[k]Ch. xvii. 5, 6

the judgments impending on the people of God themselves for their wickedness and apostasy, and the desolation that shall be brought on their whole country.

The twenty-fourth and the three following chapters seem to have been delivered about the same time: before the destruction of Moab by Shalmaneser; see chap. xxv. 10, consequently, before the destruction of Samaria; probably in the beginning of Hezekiah's reign. But concerning the particular subject of the twenty-fourth chapter interpreters are not at all agreed: some refer it to the desolation caused by the invasion of Shalmaneser; others to the invasion of Nebuchadnezzar; and others to the destruction of the city and nation by the Romans. Vitringa is singular in his opinion, who applies it to the persecution of Antiochus Epiphanes. Perhaps it may have a view to all of the three great desolations of the country, by Shalmaneser, by Nebuchadnezzar, and by the Romans; especially the last, to which some parts of it may seem more peculiarly applicable. However, the prophet chiefly employs general images; such as set forth the greatness and universality of the ruin and desolation that is to be brought upon the country by these great revolutions, involving all orders and degrees of men, changing entirely the face of things, and destroying the whole polity, both religious and civil; without entering into minute circumstances, or necessarily restraining it by particular marks to one great event, exclusive of others of the same kind.—L.

NOTES ON CHAP. XXIV

Verse 4. *The world languisheth*] The world is the same with the land; that is, the kingdoms of Judah and Israel; *orbis Israeliticus*. See note on chap. xiii. 11.

Verse 5. *The laws*—"The law"] תורה *torah*. singular: so read the *Septuagint*, *Syriac*, and *Chaldee*.

Verse 6. *Are burned*—"Are destroyed"] For חרו *charu*, read חרבו *charebu*. See the *Septuagint*, *Syriac*, *Chaldee*, and *Symmachus*.

Verse 8. *The mirth*, &c.] שאון *sheon*, *the noise*. גאון *geon*, *the pride*, is the reading of *three* of *De Rossi's* MSS., with the *Septuagint* and *Arabic*.

Verse 9. *Strong drink*—"Palm wine"] This is the proper meaning of the word שכר *shechar*, σικερα. See note on chap. v. 11. All enjoyment shall cease: the sweetest wine shall become bitter to their taste.

Verse 11. *All joy is darkened*—"All gladness is passed away"] For ערבה *arebah*, *darkened*, read עברה *aberah*, *passed away*, transposing a letter. *Houbigant*, *Secker*. *Five* of *Dr. Kennicott's* and *five* of *De Rossi's* MSS., several ancient, add כל *col*, *all*, after משוש *mesos*: the *Septuagint* adds the same word before it.

Verse 14. *They shall lift up their voice*—"But these shall lift up their voice"] That is, they that escaped out of these calamities. The great distresses brought upon Israel and Judah drove the people away, and dispersed them all over the neighbouring countries: they fled to Egypt, to Asia Minor, to the islands and the coasts of Greece. They were to be found in great numbers in most of the principal cities of these countries. Alexandria was in a great measure peopled by them. They had synagogues for their worship in many places, and were greatly instrumental in propagating the knowledge of the true God among these heathen nations, and

A. M. cir. 3292
B. C. cir. 712
Olymp. XVII. 1
cir. annum
NumæPompilii,
R. Roman., 4

15 Wherefore glorify ye the
LORD in the [l]fires *even* [m]the
name of the LORD God of Israel
in the isles of the sea.
16 From the [n]uttermost part of the earth
have we heard songs, *even* glory to the righteous. But I said, [o]My leanness, my leanness,
wo unto me! [p]the treacherous
dealers have dealt treacherously;
yea, the treacherous dealers have
dealt very treacherously.
17 [q]Fear, and the pit, and the [r]snare, *are*
upon thee, O inhabitant of the earth.
18 And it shall come to pass, *that* he who

[l]Or, *valleys*——[m]Mal. i. 11——[n]Heb. *wing*——[o]Heb. *Leanness to me*, or *My secret to me*

[p]Jer. v. 11——[q]See 1 Kings xix. 17; Jer. xlviii. 43, 44; Amos v. 19——[r]Psa. lxix. 22

preparing them for the reception of Christianity. This it what the prophet seems to mean by the celebration of the name of JEHOVAH in the waters, in the distant coasts, and in the uttermost parts of the land. מים *mayim, the waters;* ὑδωρ, *Sept.;* ὑδατα, *Theod.;* not מים *miyam from the sea.*

Verse 15. *In the isles of the sea*—"In the distant coasts of the sea."] For בארים *beurim, in the valleys*, I suppose we ought to read באיים *beiyim, in the isles*, which is in a great degree justified by the repetition of the word in the next member of the sentence, with the addition of הים *haiyam, the sea,* to vary the phrase, exactly in the manner of the prophet. איים *iyim* is a word chiefly applied to any distant countries, especially those lying on the Mediterranean Sea. Others conjecture ביארים *biorim*. בהרים *beharim*, באמים *beummim*, בעמים *beammim*, בחורים .*bechorim*, באורים *beurim*, a באר *bar*, illustrati.—*Le Clerc*. *Twenty-three* MSS. of *Kennicott's*, many of *De Rossi's*, and some of my own, read באורים *beorim, in the valleys*. The *Septuagint* do not acknowledge the reading of the text, expressing here only the word איים *iyim*. εν ταις νησοις, *in the islands*, and that not repeated. But MSS. Pachom. and I. D. II. supply in this place the defect in the other copies of the *Septuagint* thus, Δια τουτο ἡ δοξα Κυριου εσται εν ταις νησοις της θαλασσης· εν ταις νησοις το ονομα του Κυριου Θεου Ισραηλ ενδοξον εσται· "Therefore the glory of the Lord shall be in the isles of the sea: in the islands shall the name of the Lord God of Israel be glorified." *Kimchi* says, that by באורים *beurim, in the valleys*, is meant *the cities*, because they were generally built *in valleys*. The *Vulgate* has *in doctrinis*, and so my old MS., **in techingis**. *Coverdale* translates, *Praise the name of the Lord God of Israel* in the *valleys and in the floodis*. It should not be rendered *in the fires;* none of the ancient Versions understood it thus. According to which the *Septuagint* had in their Hebrew copy באיים *beiyim*, repeated afterwards, not בארים *beurim*.

Verse 16. *But I said*] The prophet speaks in the person of the inhabitants of the land still remaining there, who should be pursued by Divine vengeance, and suffer repeated distresses from the inroads and depredations of their powerful enemies. Agreeably to what he said before in a general denunciation of these calamities:—

"Though there be a tenth part remaining in it;
Even this shall undergo a repeated destruction."
Chap. vi. 13. See the note there.—L.

My leanness, my leanness—Or, *my secret;* so the *Vulgate, Montanus*, and my old MS. רזן *razan* has this meaning in *Chaldee;* but in *Hebrew* it signifies to *make lean*, to *waste*. This sentence in the *Hebrew* has a strange connexion of uncouth sounds: ואמר רזי לי רזי לי אוי לי בוגדים בגדו ובגד בגדים בגדו *Vaomer, razi li razi li, oi li, bogedim bagadu, ubeged bogedim bagadu.* This may be equalled by the translation in my Old MS. Bible: **And I seide, my priveye thinge to me: my priveye thinge to me: woo to me: The lawe brekynge thei breken: and in lawe brekynge of the overdon thingis, they breken the lawe.**

The treacherous dealers have dealt treacherously—"The plunderers plunder"] See note on chap. xxi. 2.

Verse 17. *Fear, and the pit*—"The terror, the pit"] If they escape one calamity, another shall overtake them.

"As if a man should flee from a lion, and a bear should overtake him:
Or should betake himself to his house, and lean his hand on the wall,
And a serpent should bite him."
Amos v. 19.

"For," as our Saviour expressed it in a like parabolical manner, "wheresoever the carcass is, there shall the eagles be gathered together," Matt. xxiv. 28. The images are taken from the different methods of hunting and taking wild beasts, which were anciently in use. The *terror* was a line strung with feathers of all colours, which fluttering in the air scared and frightened the beasts into the toils, or into the pit which was prepared for them. Nec est mirum, cum maximos ferarum greges linea pennis distincta contineat, et in insidias agat, ab ipso effectu dicta *formido*. *Seneca* de Ira, ii. 12. The *pit* or pitfall, *fovea;* digged deep in the ground, and covered over with green boughs, turf, &c., in order to deceive them, that they might fall into it unawares. The *snare*, or toils, *indago;* a series of nets, inclosing at first a great space of ground, in which the wild beasts were known to be; and then drawn in by degrees into a narrower compass, till they were at last closely shut up, and entangled in them.—L.

For מכול *mikkol*, a MS. reads מפני *mippeney*, as it is in Jer. xlviii. 44, and so the *Vulgate* and *Chaldee*. But perhaps it is only, like the latter, a *Hebraism*, and means no more than the simple preposition מ *mem*. See Psa. cii. 6. For it does not appear that the terror was intended to scare the wild beasts by its noise. The paronomasia is very remarkable; פחד *pachad*, פחת *pachath*, פח *pach:* and that it was a common proverbial form, appears from Jeremiah's repeating it in the same words, chap. xlviii. 43, 44.

Verse 18. *Out of the midst of the pit*—"From the pit"] For מתוך *mittoch, from the midst of*, a MS. reads מן *min, from*, as it is in Jer. xlviii.

A. M. cir. 3292 B. C. cir. 712 Olymp. XVII. 1 cir. annum NumæPompilii, R. Roman., 4

fleeth from the noise of the fear
shall fall into the pit; and he
that cometh up out of the midst
of the pit shall be taken in the
snare: for [s]the windows from on high are open,
and [t]the foundations of the earth do shake.
19 [u]The earth is utterly broken down, the
earth is clean dissolved, the earth is moved
exceedingly.
20 The earth shall [v]reel to and fro like a
drunkard, and shall be removed like a cottage;
and the transgression thereof shall be heavy
upon it; and it shall fall, and not rise again.
21 And it shall come to pass
in that day, *that* the LORD shall
[w]punish the host of the high
ones *that are* on high, [x]and the
kings of the earth upon the earth.

A. M. cir. 3292 B. C., cir. 712 Olymp. XVII. 1 cir. annum NumæPompilii, R. Roman., 4

22 And they shall be gathered together,
[y]*as* prisoners are gathered in the [z]pit, and
shall be shut up in the prison, and after many
days shall they be [a]visited.
23 Then the [b]moon shall be confounded,
and the sun ashamed, when the LORD of hosts
shall [c]reign [d]in Mount Zion, and in Jerusalem, and [e]before his ancients gloriously.

---

[s]Gen. vii. 11——[t]Psa. xviii. 7——[u]Jer. iv. 23 [v]Chap. xix. 14——[w]Heb. *visit upon*——[x]Psa. lxxvi. 12 [y]Heb. *with the gathering of prisoners*——[z]Or, *dungeon*

[a]Or, *found wanting*——[b]Chap. xiii. 10; lx. 19; Ezek. xxxii. 7; Joel ii. 31; iii. 15——[c]Rev. xix. 4, 6——[d]Heb. xii. 22——[e]Or, there shall be *glory before his ancients*

44; and so likewise the *Septuagint*, *Syriac*, and *Vulgate*.

Verse 19. *The earth*—"The land"] הארץ *haarets, forte delendum* ה *he, ut ex præcedente ortum.* Vid. seqq.—*Secker.* "Probably the ה *he*, in הארץ *haarets*, should be blotted out, as having arisen from the preceding."

Verse 20. *Like a cottage*—"Like a lodge for a night"] See note on chap. i. 8.

Verse 21. *On high—upon the earth.*] That is, the ecclesiastical and civil polity of the Jews, which shall be destroyed. The nation shall continue in a state of depression and dereliction for a long time. The image seems to be taken from the practice of the great monarchs of that time; who, when they had thrown their wretched captives into a dungeon, never gave themselves the trouble of inquiring about them; but let them lie a long time in that miserable condition, wholly destitute of relief, and disregarded. God shall at length revisit and restore his people in the last age: and then the kingdom of God shall be established in such perfection, as wholly to obscure and eclipse the glory of the temporary, typical, preparative kingdom now subsisting.

Verse 23. *Before his ancients gloriously*] **In the sigt of their olde men he schal ben glorified.** Old MS. BIBLE.

"The figurative language of the prophets is taken from the analogy between the *world natural* and an empire or kingdom considered as a *world politic*. Accordingly the whole world natural, consisting of *heaven* and *earth*, signifies the whole world politic, consisting of thrones and people; or so much of it as is considered in prophecy: and the things in that world signify the analogous things in this. For the *heavens* and the *things therein* signify *thrones* and *dignities*, and *those* who *enjoy them;* and the *earth* with the *things thereon*, the *inferior people;* and the *lowest parts* of the *earth*, called *hades* or *hell*, the *lowest* or most *miserable part of them*. Great *earthquakes*, and the *shaking of heaven* and *earth*, are put for the *shaking of kingdoms*, so as to *distract* and *overthrow* them; the *creating a new heaven* and *earth*, and the *passing away of an old one*, or the *beginning and end of a world*, for the *rise* and *ruin* of a *body politic* signified thereby. The *sun*, for the whole species and race of *kings*, in the kingdoms of the world politic; the *moon*, for the body of the common people, considered as the king's wife; the *stars*, for subordinate princes and great men; or for bishops and rulers of the people of God, when the sun is Christ: *setting* of the *sun*, *moon*, and *stars*, *darkening* the *sun*, turning the *moon* into *blood*, and *falling* of the *stars*, for the ceasing of a kingdom." Sir *I. Newton's* Observations on the Prophecies, Part I., chap. 2.

These observations are of great consequence and use, in explaining the phraseology of the prophets.

CHAPTER XXV

The short glance which the prophet gave at the promised restoration of the people of God and the Messiah's kingdom, in the close of the preceding chapter, makes him break out into a rapturous song of praise in this, where although he alludes to temporal mercies, such as the destruction of the cities which had been at war with Zion, the ruin of Moab, and other signal interpositions of Divine Providence in behalf of the Jews; yet he is evidently impressed with a more lively sense of future and much higher blessings under the Gospel dispensation, in the plenitude of its revelation, of which the temporal deliverances vouchsafed at various times to the primitive kingdoms of Israel and Judah were the prototypes, 1–5. *These blessings are described under the figure of a feast made for all nations,* 6; *the removing of a veil from their faces,* 7; *the total extinction of the empire of death by the resurrection from the dead, the exclusion of all sorrow, and the final overthrow of all the enemies of the people of God,* 8–12.

A. M. cir. 3292
B. C. cir. 712
Olymp. XVII. 1
cir. annum
NumæPompilii,
R. Roman., 4

O LORD, thou *art* my God; [a]I will exalt thee, I will praise thy name; [b]for thou hast done wonderful *things;* [c]*thy* counsels of old *are* faithfulness *and* truth.

2 For thou hast made [d]of a city a heap; *of* a defenced city a ruin: a palace of strangers to be no city; it shall never be built.

3 Therefore shall the strong people [e]glorify thee, the city of the terrible nations shall fear thee.

4 For thou hast been a strength to the poor, a strength to the needy in his distress, [f]a refuge from the storm, a shadow from the heat, when the blast of the terrible one *is* as a storm *against* the wall.

A. M. cir. 3292
B. C. cir. 712
Olymp. XVII. 1
cir. annum
NumæPompilii,
R. Roman., 4

5 Thou shalt bring down the noise of strangers, as the heat in a dry place; *even* the heat with the shadow of a cloud: the branch of the terrible ones shall be brought low.

6 And in [g]this mountain shall [h]the LORD of hosts make unto [i]all people a feast of fat things, a feast of wines on the lees, of fat things full of marrow, of wines on the lees well refined.

---

[a]Exod. xv. 2; Psalm cxviii. 28——[b]Psalm xcviii. 1——[c]Num. xxiii. 19——[d]Chap. xxi. 9; xxiii. 13; Jer. li. 37

[e]Rev. xi. 13——[f]Chap. iv. 6——[g]Chap. ii. 2, 3 [h]Prov. ix. 2; Matt. xxii. 4——[i]Dan. vii. 14; Matt. viii. 11

It does not appear to me that this chapter has any close and particular connexion with the chapter immediately preceding, taken separately, and by itself. The subject of that was the desolation of the land of Israel and Judah, by the just judgment of God, for the wickedness and disobedience of the people: which, taken by itself, seems not with any propriety to introduce a hymn of thanksgiving to God for his mercies to his people in delivering them from their enemies. But taking the whole course of prophecies, from the *thirteenth* to the *twenty-fourth* chapter inclusive, in which the prophet foretells the destruction of several cities and nations, enemies to the Jews, and of the land of Judah itself, yet with intimations of a remnant to be saved, and a restoration to be at length effected by a glorious establishment of the kingdom of God: with a view to this extensive scene of God's providence in all its parts, and in all its consequences, the prophet may well be supposed to break out into this song of praise; in which his mind seems to be more possessed with the prospect of future mercies than with the recollection of the past.—L.

NOTES ON CHAP. XXV

Verse 1. Thy *counsels of old* are *faithfulness* and *truth.*] That is, All thy past declarations by the prophets shall be fulfilled in their proper time.

Verse 2. *A city*—"The city"] Nineveh, Babylon, Ar, Moab, or any other strong fortress possessed by the enemies of the people of God.

For the first מעיר *meir, of a city,* the *Syriac* and *Vulgate* read העיר *hair, the city;* the *Septuagint* and *Chaldee* read ערים *arim, cities,* in the plural, transposing the letters. After the second מעיר *meir,* a MS. adds לגל *lagol, for a heap.*

A palace of strangers—"The palace of the proud ones"] For זרים *zarim, strangers,* MS. *Bodl.* and another read זדים *zedim, the proud:* so likewise the *Septuagint;* for they render it ασεβων here, and in ver. 5, as they do in some other places: see Deut. xviii. 20, 22. Another MS. reads צרים *tsarim, adversaries;* which also makes a good sense. But זרים *zarim, strangers,* and זדים *zedim, the proud,* are often confounded by the great similitude of the letters ד *daleth* and ר *resh.* See Mal. iii. 15, iv. 1; Psa. xix. 14, in the *Septuagint;* and Psa. liv. 5, where the *Chaldee* reads זדים *zedim,* compared with Psa. lxxxvi. 16.

Verse 4. *As a storm* against *the wall*—"Like a winter-storm."] For קיר *kir,* read קור *kor:* or, as עיר *ir* from ערר *arar,* so קיר *kir* from קרר *karar.*—Capellus.

Verse 5. *Of strangers*—"Of the proud"] The same mistake here as in ver. 2: see the note there. Here זדים *zedim, the proud,* is parallel to עריצים *aritsim, the formidable:* as in Psa. liv. 5, and lxxxvi. 14.

The heat with the shadow of a cloud—"As the heat by a thick cloud"] For חרב *choreb,* the *Syriac, Chaldee, Vulgate,* and two MSS. read כחרב *kechoreb;* which is a repetition of the beginning of the foregoing parallel line; and the verse taken out of the parallel form, and more fully expressed, would run thus: "As a thick cloud interposing tempers the heat of the sun on the burnt soil; so shalt thou, by the interposition of thy power, bring low and abate the tumult of the proud, and the triumph of the formidable."

Verse 6. *In this mountain*] Zion, at Jerusalem. In his Church.

Shall the Lord of hosts make unto all people a feast] Salvation by Jesus Christ. A feast is a proper and usual expression of joy in consequence of victory, or any other great success. The feast here spoken of is to be celebrated on Mount Sion; and all people, without distinction, are to be invited to it. This can be no other than the celebration of the establishment of Christ's kingdom, which is frequently represented in the Gospel under the image of a feast; "where many shall come from the east and west, and shall sit down at table with Abraham, Isaac, and Jacob, in the kingdom of heaven;" Matt. viii. 11. See also Luke xiv. 16; xxiv. 29, 30. This sense is fully confirmed by the concomitants of this feast expressed in the next verse; the removing of the veil from the face of the nations, and the abolition of death: the first of which is obviously and clearly explained of the preaching of the Gospel; and the second must mean the blessing of immortality procured for us by Christ, "who hath abolished death, and through death hath destroyed him that had the power of death."

Of wines on the lees—"Of old wines"] Heb. *lees;* that is, of wines kept long on the lees.

A. M. cir. 3292
B. C. cir. 712
Olymp. XVII. 1
cir. annum
NumæPompilii,
R. Roman., 4

7 And he will [k]destroy in this
mountain the face of the covering
[l]cast over all people, and [m]the
vail that is spread over all nations.
8 He will [n]swallow up death in victory; and
the Lord GOD will [o]wipe away tears from off
all faces; and the rebuke of his
people shall he take away from
off all the earth: for the LORD
hath spoken *it*.
9 And it shall be said in that day, Lo,
this *is* our God; [p]we have waited for him,

[k]Heb. *swallow up*——[l]Heb. *covered*——[m]2 Cor. iii. 15; Eph. iv. 18——[n]Hos. xiii. 14; 1 Cor. xv. 54; Rev. xx. 14; xxi. 4——[o]Rev. vii. 17; xxi. 4——[p]Gen. xlix. 18; Tit. ii. 13

The word used to express the lees in the original signifies the *preservers;* because they preserve the strength and flavour of the wine. "All recent wines, after the fermentation has ceased, ought to be kept on their lees for a certain time, which greatly contributes to increase their strength and flavour. Whenever this first fermentation has been deficient, they will retain a more rich and sweet taste than is natural to them in a recent true vinous state; and unless farther fermentation is promoted by their lying longer on their own lees, they will never attain their genuine strength and flavour, but run into repeated and ineffectual fermentations, and soon degenerate into a liquor of an acetous kind.—All wines of a light and austere kind, by a fermentation too great, or too long continued, certainly degenerate into a weak sort of vinegar; while the stronger not only require, but will safely bear a stronger and often-repeated fermentation; and are more apt to degenerate from a defect than excess of fermentation into a vapid, ropy, and at length into a putrescent state." Sir *Edward Barry*, Observations on the Wines of the Ancients, p. 9, 10.

Thevenot observes particularly of the Shiras wine, that, after it is refined from the lees, it is apt to grow sour. "Il a beaucoup de lie; c'est pourquoi il donne puissemment dans la teste; et pour le rendre plus traitable on le passe par un chausse d'hypocras; après quoi il est fort clair, et moins fumeux. Ils mettent ce vin dans des grandes jarres de terres qui tiennent dix ou douze jusqu'à quatorze carabas: mais quand l'on a entamé une jarre, il faut la vuider au plutost, et mettre le vin qu'on en tire dans des bouteilles ou carabas; car si l'on y manque en le laissant quelque tems après que la jarre est entamée il se gâte et s'aigrit." Voyages, Tom. ii. p. 245.—"It has much sediment, and therefore is intoxicating. In order to make it more mellow, they strain it through a hypocrates' sleeve, after which it is very clear and less heady. They lay up this wine in great earthen jars, which hold from ten to fourteen *carabas:* but when a jar is unstopped, it is necessary to empty it immediately, and put the wine into bottles, or carabas; for if it be left thus in the jar, it will spoil and become acid."

The *caraba*, or *girba*, is a goat's skin drawn off from the animal, having no apertures but those occasioned by the *tail*, the *feet*, and the *neck*. One opening is left, to pour in and draw off the liquor. This skin goes through a sort of tanning process, and is often beautifully ornamented, as is the case with one of these girbas now lying before me.

This clearly explains the very elegant comparison, or rather allegory, of Jeremiah, chap. xlviii. 11; where the reader will find a remarkable example of the mixture of the proper with the allegorical, not uncommon with the Hebrew poets:—

"Moab hath been at ease from his youth,
And he hath settled upon his lees;
Nor hath he been drawn off from vessel to vessel,
Neither hath he gone into captivity:
Wherefore his taste remaineth in him,
And his flavour is not changed."

Sir *John Chardin's* MS. note on this place of Jeremiah is as follows: "On change ainsi le vin de coupe en coupe en Orient; et quand on en entame une, il faut la vuider en petites coupes ou bouteilles, sans quoy il s'aigrit. "They change the wine from vessel to vessel in the east; and when they unstop a large one, it is necessary to empty it into small vessels, as otherwise it will grow sour."

Verse 7. *The face of the covering cast over all people*—"The covering that covered the face of all the peoples"] MS. *Bodl.* reads על פני כל *al peney chol.* The word פני *peney, face,* has been removed from its right place into the line above, where it makes no sense; as *Houbigant* conjectured. "The face of the covering," &c. He will unveil all the Mosaic ritual, and show by his apostles that it referred to, and was accomplished in, the sacrificial offering of Jesus Christ.

Verse 8. *He will swallow up death*] He, by the grace of God, will taste death for every man. Heb. ii. 9. Probably, *swallow up death*, and *taste death*, in both these verses, refer to the same thing: Jesus dying instead of a guilty world. These forms of speech may refer to the punishment of certain criminals; they were obliged to drink a cup of poison. That *cup* which every criminal in the world must have drunk, Jesus Christ drank for them; and thus he *swallowed up death:* but as he rose again from the dead, complete *victory* was gained.

From these *three* verses we learn:—

I. That the Gospel is a plenteous provision "I will make a feast for all people."

II. That it is a source of light and salvation "I will destroy the veil. I will abolish death, and bring life and immortality to light."

III. That it is a source of comfort and happiness: "I will wipe away all tears from off all faces."

As in the Arabic countries a *covering* was put over the face of him who was condemned to suffer death, it is probable that the words in ver. 7 may refer to this. The whole world was condemned to death, and about to be led out to execution, when the gracious Lord interposed, and, by a glorious sacrifice, procured a general pardon.

Verse 9. *It shall be said*—"Shall they say"] So the *Septuagint* and *Vulgate*, in the plural number. They read ואמרו *veameru*, the *Syriac* reads ואמרת *veamarta, thou shalt say. They shall say*, i. e., the Jews and the Gentiles—Lo,

A. M. cir. 3292
B. C. cir. 712
Olymp. XVII. 1
cir. annum
NumæPompilii,
R. Roman., 4

and he will save us: this *is* the
LORD; we have waited for him,
[q]we will be glad and rejoice in
his salvation:
10 For in this mountain shall the hand of
the LORD rest, and Moab shall be [r]trodden
down under him, even as straw is [s]trodden
down for the dunghill.
11 And he shall spread forth his hands in
the midst of them, as he
that swimmeth spreadeth forth
his hands to swim: and he
shall bring down their pride
together with the spoils of their hands.
12 And the [t]fortress of the high fort
of thy walls shall he bring down, lay
low, *and* bring to the ground, *even* to the
dust.

A. M. cir. 3292
B. C. cir. 712
Olymp. XVII. 1
cir. annum
NumæPompilii,
R. Roman., 4

---

[q]Psa. xx. 5——[r]Or, *threshed* [s]Or, *threshed in Madmenah*——[t]Chap. xxvi. 5

---

this [Jesus Christ] is our God: we have waited for him, according to the predictions of the prophets. We have expected him, and we have not been disappointed; therefore will we be glad, and rejoice in his salvation.

Verse 10. *Shall the hand of the Lord rest*—"The hand of JEHOVAH shall give rest"] Heb. תנוח *tenuach, quiescet.* Annon תניח *taniach,* quietem dabit, *shall rest; shall give rest,* ut Græci, *αναπαυσιν δωσει,* et Copt.?—Mr. WOIDE. That is, "shall give peace and quiet to Sion, by destroying the enemy;" as it follows.

As straw is trodden down—"As the straw is threshed"] Hoc juxta ritum loquitur Palæstinæ et multarum Orientis provinciarum, quæ ob pratorum et fœni penuriam paleas preparant esui animantium. Sunt autem carpenta ferrata rotis per medium in serrarum modum se volventibus, quæ stipulam conterunt; et comminuunt in paleas. Quomodo igitur plaustris ferratis paleæ conteruntur, sic conteretur Moab sub eo; sive sub Dei potentia, sive in semetipso, ut nihil in eo integri remaneat. "This is spoken in reference to the mode of threshing in Palestine, and various other Asiatic provinces. Because of the scarcity of meadow land and hay, they make chopped straw for the cattle. They have large wheels studded over with iron teeth or nails, by which, on the out-of-door threshing-floors, they pound and reduce the straw into chaff. As, therefore, the straw is reduced to chaff by bringing the iron-shod wheel over it; so shall Moab be bruised by the power of God, that nothing *whole* shall remain."—*Hieron.* in loc. See the note on chap. xxviii. 27.

For the dunghill—"Under the wheels of the car."] For מדמנה *madmenah,* the *Septuagint, Syriac,* and *Vulgate* read מרכבה *mercabah,* which I have followed. See Joshua xv. 31, compared with xix. 5, where there is a mistake very nearly the same. The keri, במי *bemi,* is confirmed by twenty-eight MSS., seven ancient, and three editions.

Verse 11. *As he that swimmeth spreadeth forth* his hands *to swim*—"As he that sinketh stretcheth out his hands to swim"] There is great obscurity in this place: some understand God as the agent; others, Moab. I have chosen the latter sense, as I cannot conceive that the stretching out of the hands of a swimmer in swimming can be any illustration of the action of God stretching out his hands over Moab to destroy it. I take השחה *hashshocheh,* altering the point on the שׂ *sin,* on the authority of the *Septuagint,* to be the participle of שחה *shachah,* the same with שוח *shuach,* and שחח *shachach, to bow down, to be depressed;* and that the prophet designed a paronomasia here, a figure which he frequently uses between the similar words שחה *shachah,* and שחות *shechoth.* As תחתיו *tachtaiv, in his place,* or *on the spot,* as we say in the preceding verse, gives us an idea of the sudden and complete destruction of Moab; so בקרבו *bekirbo, in the midst of him,* means that this destruction shall be open, and exposed to the view of all: the neighbouring nations shall plainly see him struggling against it, as a man in the midst of the deep waters exerts all his efforts by swimming, to save himself from drowning.—L.

CHAPTER XXVI

This chapter, like the foregoing, is a song of praise, in which thanksgivings for temporal and spiritual mercies are beautifully mingled, though the latter still predominate. Even the sublime and evangelical doctrine of the resurrection seems here to be hinted at, and made to typify the deliverance of the people of God from a state of the lowest misery; the captivity, the general dispersion, or both. This hymn too, like the preceding, is beautifully diversified by the frequent change of speakers. It opens with a chorus of the Church, celebrating the protection vouchsafed by God to his people; and the happiness of the righteous, whom he guards, contrasted with the misery of the wicked, whom he punishes, 1–7. *To this succeeds their own pious resolution of obeying, trusting, and delighting in God,* 8. *Here the prophet breaks in, in his own person, eagerly catching the last words of the chorus, which were perfectly in unison with the feelings of his own soul, and which he beautifully repeats, as one musical instrument reverberates the sound of another on the same key with it. He makes likewise a suitable response to what had been said on the judgments of God, and observes their different effects on the good and the bad; improving the one, and hardening the other,* 9–11. *After this, a chorus of Jews express their gratitude to God for past deliverances, make confession of their sins, and supplicate his power, which they had been long expecting,* 12–18. *To this God makes a gracious reply, promising deliverance that should be as life from the dead,* 19. *And the prophet, (apparently alluding to the command of Moses to the Israelites, when the destroying angel was to go through the land of Egypt,) concludes with exhorting his people to patience and resignation, till God sends the deliverance he has promised,* 20, 21.

A. M. cir. 3292
B. C. cir. 712
Olymp. XVII. 1
cir. annum
NumæPompilii,
R. Roman., 4

IN [a]that day shall this song be sung in the land of Judah; We have a strong city; [b]salvation will *God* appoint *for* walls and bulwarks.

2 [c]Open ye the gates, that the righteous nation which keepeth the [d]truth may enter in.

3 Thou wilt keep *him* [e]in perfect peace, *whose* [f]mind *is* stayed *on thee;* because he trusteth in thee.

4 Trust ye in the LORD for ever: [g]for in the LORD JEHOVAH *is* [h]everlasting strength.

5 For he bringeth down them that dwell on high; [i]the lofty city, he layeth it low; he layeth it low, *even* to the ground; he bringeth it *even* to the dust.

6 The foot shall tread it down, *even* the feet of the poor, *and* the steps of the needy.

7 The way of the just *is* uprightness: [k]thou most upright, dost weigh the path of the just.

8 Yea, [l]in the way of thy judgments, O LORD, have we waited for thee; the desire of *our* soul *is* to thy name, and to the remembrance of thee.

A. M. cir. 3292
B. C. cir. 712
Olymp. XVII. 1
cir. annum
NumæPompilii,
R. Roman., 4

9 [m]With my soul have I desired thee in the night; yea, with my spirit within me will I seek thee early: for when thy judgments *are* in the earth, the inhabitants of the world will learn righteousness.

10 [n]Let favour be showed to the wicked, *yet* will he not learn righteousness: in [o]the land of uprightness will he deal unjustly, and will not behold the majesty of the LORD.

11 LORD, *when* thy hand is lifted up, [p]they will not see: *but* they shall see, and be ashamed for *their* envy [q]at the people; yea, the fire of thine enemies shall devour them.

12 LORD, thou wilt ordain peace for us: for thou also hast wrought all our works [r]in us.

13 O LORD our God, [s]*other* lords beside thee have had dominion over us: *but* by thee

[a]Chap. ii. 11——[b]Chap. lx. 18——[c]Psa. cxviii. 19, 20——[d]Heb. *truths*——[e]Heb. *peace, peace;* chap. lvii. 19——[f]Or, *thought,* or *imagination*——[g]Chap. xlv. 17——[h]Heb. *the rock of ages;* Deut. xxxii. 4——[i]Chap. xxv. 12; xxxii. 19——[k]Psa. xxxvii. 23

[l]Chapter lxiv. 5——[m]Psalm lxiii. 6; Cant. iii. 1——[n]Ecclesiastes viii. 12; Romans ii. 4——[o]Psalm cxliii. 10——[p]Job xxxiv. 27; Psalm xxviii. 5; chapter v. 12——[q]Or, *toward* thy *people*——[r]Or, *for us*——[s]2 Chron. xii. 8

NOTES ON CHAP. XXVI

Verse 1. *We have a strong city*] In opposition to the city of the enemy, which God hath destroyed, chap. xxv. See the note there.

Salvation—for walls and bulwarks] חומת וחל *chomoth vachel, walls and redoubts,* or the *walls and the ditch.* חל *chel* properly signifies the *ditch* or *trench* without the wall; see *Kimchi.* The same rabbin says, This song refers to the time of salvation, *i. e.,* the days of the Messiah.

Verse 2. *The righteous nation*] The converted Gentiles shall have the *gates opened*—a full entrance into all the glories and privileges of the Gospel; being fellow heirs with the converted Jews. The Jewish peculiarity is destroyed, for the middle wall of partition is broken down.

The truth] The Gospel itself—as the fulfilment of all the ancient types, shadows, and ceremonies; and therefore termed *the truth,* in opposition to all those shadowy rites and ceremonies. "The law was given by Moses; *but* grace *and* TRUTH came by Jesus Christ;" John i. 17, and see the note there.

Verse 3. *In perfect peace*] שלום שלום *shalom, shalom,* "peace, peace," *i. e.,* peace upon peace—all kinds of *prosperity*—happiness in this world and in the world to come.

Because he trusteth in thee—"Because they have trusted in thee"] So the *Chaldee,* בטחו *betacho.* The *Syriac* and *Vulgate* read בטחנו *batachnu,* "we have trusted." *Schroeder,* Gram. Heb. p. 360, explains the present reading בטוח *batuach,* impersonally, *confisum est.*

Verse 4. *In the Lord JEHOVAH*—"In JEHOVAH"] In JAH JEHOVAH, Heb.; but see *Houbigant,* and the note on chap. xii. 2.

Everlasting strength] צור עולמים *tsur olamim,* "the rock of ages;" or, according to Rab. *Maimon,*—the *eternal Fountain, Source,* or *Spring.* Does not this refer to the lasting streams from the rock in the desert? And that rock was Christ. **Ye han hoped in the Lord fro the everlastinge worldis.**—Old MS. BIBLE.

Verse 8. *Have we waited for thee*—"We have placed our confidence in thy name"] The *Septuagint, Syriac,* and *Chaldee* read קוינו *kavinu,* without the pronoun annexed.

Verse 9. *Have I desired thee*] *Forty-one* MSS. of Dr. *Kennicott's* and many of *De Rossi's,* (nine ancient,) and *five* editions read אויתיך *ivvithicha.* It is proper to note this; because the second י *yod* being omitted in the text, the *Vulgate* and many others have rendered it in the third person.

When thy judgments, &c.] It would be better to read, When thy judgments were in the earth, the inhabitants of the world have learned (למדו *lamedu*) *righteousness.* Men seldom seek God in *prosperity;* they are apt to rest in an earthly portion; but God in mercy embitters this by ad-

A. M. cir. 3292 B. C. cir. 712 Olymp. XVII. 1 cir. annum NumæPompilii, R. Roman., 4

only will we make mention of thy name.
14 *They are* dead, they shall not live; *they are* deceased, they shall not rise: therefore hast thou visited and destroyed them, and made all their memory to perish.
15 Thou hast increased the nation, O LORD, thou hast increased the nation: thou art glorified: thou hadst removed *it* far *unto* all the ends of the earth.
16 LORD, [t]in trouble have they visited thee, they poured out a [u]prayer *when* thy chastening *was* upon them.
17 Like as a [v]woman with child, *that* draweth near the time of her delivery, is in pain, *and* crieth out in her pangs; so have we been in thy sight, O LORD.
18 We have been with child, we have been in pain, we have as it were brought forth wind; we have not wrought any deliverance in the earth; neither have [w]the inhabitants of the world fallen.
19 [x]Thy dead *men* shall live, *together with* my dead body shall they arise. [y]Awake and sing, ye that dwell in dust: for thy dew *is as* a dew of herbs, and the earth shall cast out the dead.
20 Come, my people, [z]enter thou into thy

[t]Hos. v. 15——[u]Heb. *secret speech*——[v]Chap. xiii. 8; John xvi. 21

[w]Psa. xvii. 14——[x]Ezek. xxxvii. 1, &c.——[y]Dan. xii. 2 [z]Exod. xii. 22, 23

versity; then there is a general cry after himself as our chief, solid, and only permanent good.

Verse 16. *Lord, in trouble have they visited thee*—"O JEHOVAH, in affliction we have sought thee"] So the *Septuagint* and two MSS. have פקדנוך *pekadnucha,* in the first person plural. And so perhaps it should be צקנו *tsaknu,* in the first person; but how the *Septuagint* read this word is not clear; and this last member of the verse is extremely obscure.

For למו *lamo,* "on them," the *Septuagint* read לנו *lanu,* "on us," in the first person likewise; a frequent mistake; see note on chap. x. 29.

Verse 18. *We have—brought forth wind*] The learned Professor *Michaelis* explains this image in the following manner: "Rariorem morbum describi, empneumatosin, aut ventosam molam, dictum; quo quæ laborant diu et sibi et peritis medicis gravidæ videntur, tandemque post omnes veræ graviditatis molestias et labores ventum ex utero emittunt: quem morbum passim describunt medici." Syntagma Comment., vol. ii., p. 165. The *empneumatosis,* or windy inflation of the womb, is a disorder to which females are liable. Some have had this in such wise, for a long time together, that they have appeared to themselves, and even to very skilful medical men, to be pregnant; and after having endured much pain, and even the throes of apparent childbearing, they have been eased and restored to health by the emission of a great quantity of wind from the uterus. This disorder is well known to medical men." The *Syriac* translator seems to have understood it in this manner: Enixi sumus, ut illæ quæ ventos pariunt. "We have brought forth as they who bring forth wind."

In the earth—"In the land"] בארץ *bearets;* so a MS., the *Septuagint, Syriac,* and *Vulgate.*

Verse 19. *My dead body*—"My deceased"] All the ancient Versions render it in the plural; they read נבלותי *niblothai,* my *dead bodies.* The *Syriac* and *Chaldee* read נבלותיהם *niblotheyhem,* their *dead bodies.* No MS. yet found confirms this reading.

The dew of herbs—"The dew of the dawn"] *Lucis,* according to the *Vulgate;* so also the *Syriac* and *Chaldee.*

The deliverance of the people of God from a state of the lowest depression is explained by images plainly taken from the resurrection of the dead. In the same manner the Prophet Ezekiel represents the restoration of the Jewish nation from a state of utter dissolution by the restoring of the dry bones to life, exhibited to him in a vision, chap. xxxvii., which is directly thus applied and explained, ver. 11-13. And this deliverance is expressed with a manifest opposition to what is here said above, ver. 14, of the great lords and tyrants, under whom they had groaned:—

"They are dead, they shall not live;
They are deceased tyrants, they shall not rise:"

that they should be destroyed utterly, and should never be restored to their former power and glory. It appears from hence, that the doctrine of the resurrection of the dead was at that time *a popular and common doctrine;* for an image which is assumed in order to express or represent any thing in the way of allegory or metaphor, whether poetical or prophetical, must be an image *commonly known and understood;* otherwise it will not answer the purpose for which it is assumed.—L.

Kimchi refers these words to the days of the Messiah, and says, "Then many of the saints shall rise from the dead." And quotes Dan. xii. 2. Do not these words speak of the *resurrection* of our blessed Lord; and of that resurrection of the *bodies of men,* which shall be the consequence of *his body* being raised from the dead?

Thy dead men *shall live,*—with *my dead body shall they arise.*] This seems very express.

Verse 20. *Come, my people, enter thou into thy chambers*] An exhortation to patience and resignation under oppression, with a confident expectation of deliverance by the power of God manifestly to be exerted in the destruction of the oppressor. It seems to be an allusion to the command of Moses to the Israelites, when the destroying angel was to go through the land of Egypt, "not to go out at the door of their houses until the morning;" Exod. xii. 22. And before the passage of the Red Sea: "Fear

A. M. cir. 3292 B. C. cir. 712 Olymp. XVII. 1 cir. annum NumæPompilii, R. Roman., 4

chambers, and shut thy doors
about thee: hide thyself as it
were [a]for a little moment, until
the indignation be overpast.
21 For, behold, the LORD [b]cometh out of
his place to punish the inhabitants of the earth for their iniquity: the earth also shall disclose her [c]blood, and shall no more cover her slain.

[a]Psa. xxx. 5; chap. liv. 7, 8; 2 Cor. iv. 17——[b]Mic. i. 3; Jude 14——[c]Heb. *bloods*

ye not, stand still, and see the salvation of JEHOVAH. JEHOVAH shall fight for you, and ye shall hold your peace," Exod. xiv. 13, 14.

Verse 21. *The earth also shall disclose her blood*] Crimes of cruelty and oppression, which have passed away from the eyes of men, God will bring into judgment, and exact punishment for them. O what a reckoning will the kingdoms of the earth have with God, for the torrents of blood which they have shed for the gratification of the lust of power and ambition! Who shall live when he doeth this?

CHAPTER XXVII

Destruction of the enemies of the Church, 1. *God's care of his vineyard,* 2–11. *Prosperity of the descendants of Abraham in the latter days,* 12, 13.

A. M. cir. 3292 B. C. cir. 712 Olymp. XVII. 1 cir. annum NumæPompilii, R. Roman., 4

IN that day the LORD with his
sore and great and strong
sword shall punish leviathan the
[a]piercing serpent, [b]even leviathan
that crooked serpent; and he shall
slay [c]the dragon that *is* in the sea.
2 In that day [d]sing ye unto her,
[e]A vineyard of red wine.

[a]Or, *crossing like a bar*——[b]Psa. lxxiv. 13, 14——[c]Chap. li. 9; Ezek. xxix. 3; xxxii. 2——[d]Chapter v. 1——[e]Psalm lxxx. 8; Jeremiah ii. 21

The subject of this chapter seems to be the nature, the measure, and the design of God's dealings with his people. 1. His judgments inflicted on their great and powerful enemies, ver. 1. 2. His constant care and protection of his favourite vineyard, in the form of a dialogue, ver. 2. 3. The moderation and lenity with which the severity of his judgments have been tempered, ver. 7. 4. The end and design of them, to recover them from idolatry, ver. 9. And, 5. The recalling of them, on their repentance, from their several dispersions, ver. 12. The first verse seems connected with the two last verses of the preceding chapter.—L.

NOTES ON CHAP. XXVII

Verse 1. *Leviathan*] The animals here mentioned seem to be the *crocodile*, rigid by the stiffness of the backbone, so that he cannot readily turn himself when he pursues his prey; hence the easiest way of escaping from him is by making frequent and short turnings: the *serpent* or *dragon*, flexible and winding, which coils himself up in a circular form: and the *sea-monster*, or *whale*. These are used allegorically, without doubt for great potentates, enemies and persecutors of the people of God: but to specify the particular persons or states designed by the prophet under these images, is a matter of great difficulty, and comes not necessarily within the design of these notes. *R. D. Kimchi* says, *leviathan* is a parable concerning the kings of the Gentiles: it is the largest fish in the sea, called also תנין *tannin, the dragon*, or rather the *whale*. By these names the Grecian, Turkish, and Roman empires are intended. The *dragon of the sea* seems to mean some nation having a strong naval force and extensive commerce. See *Kimchi* on the place.

Verse 2. *Sing ye unto her*] ענו לה *anu lah.* Bishop *Lowth* translates this, *Sing ye a responsive song;* and says that ענה *anah, to answer*, signifies occasionally to sing responsively; and that this mode of singing was frequently practised among the ancient Hebrews. See *De Pöes. Sac. Heb. Præl.* xix., at the beginning.

This, indeed, was the ancient method of singing in various nations. The song was divided into distinct portions, and the singers sang *alternately*. There is a fine specimen of this in the song of Deborah and Barak; and also in the Idyls of Theocritus, and the Eclogues of Virgil.

This kind of singing was properly a dialogue in verse, sung to a particular tune, or in the mode which is now termed *recitativo*. I have seen it often practised on funeral occasions among the descendants of the aboriginal Irish. The poems of Ossian are of this kind.

The learned *Bishop* distinguishes the parts of this dialogue thus:—

3. JEHOVAH. It is I, JEHOVAH, that preserve her;
I will water her every moment;
I will take care of her by night;
And by day I will keep guard over her.

4. VINEYARD. I have no wall for my defence:
O that I had a fence of the thorn and brier!

JEHOVAH. Against them should I march in battle,
I should burn them up together.

5. Ah! let her rather take hold of my protection.

VINEYARD. Let him make peace with me!
Peace let him make with me!

A. M. cir. 3292
B. C. cir. 712
Olymp. XVII. 1
cir. annum
NumæPompilii,
R. Roman., 4

3 [f]I the LORD do keep it; I
will water it every moment: lest
any hurt it, I will keep it night
and day.
4 Fury *is* not in me: who would set [g]the
briers *and* thorns against me in battle? I
would [h]go through them, I would burn them
together.
5 Or let him take hold [i]of my strength, *that*
he may [k]make peace with me; *and* he shall
make peace with me.
6 He shall cause them that come
of Jacob [l]to take root: Israel
shall blossom and bud, and fill
the face of the world with fruit.
7 Hath he smitten him, [m]as he smote those
that smote him? *or* is he slain according to
the slaughter of them that are slain by him?
8 [n]In measure, [o]when it shooteth forth, thou
wilt debate with it: [p]he [q]stayeth his rough
wind in the day of the east wind.
9 By this therefore shall the iniquity of

[f]Psa. cxxi. 4, 5——[g]2 Sam. xxiii. 6; ch. ix. 18——[h]Or, *march against*——[i]Ch. xxv. 4——[k]Job xxii. 21——[l]Ch. xxxvii. 31; Hos. xiv. 5, 6——[m]Heb. *according to the stroke of those*

[n]Job xxiii. 6; Psalm vi. 1; Jeremiah x. 24; xxx. 11; xlvi. 28; 1 Corinthians x. 13——[o]Or, *when thou sendest it forth*——[p]Or, *when he removeth it*——[q]Psalm lxxviii. 38

6. JEHOVAH. They that come from the root
of Jacob shall flourish, Israel
shall bud forth;
And they shall fill the face of
the world with fruit.

A vineyard of red wine] The redder the wine, the more it was valued, says *Kimchi*.

Bishop *Lowth* translates, *To the beloved vineyard.* For חמר *chemer, red,* a multitude of MSS. and editions have חמד *chemed, desirable.* This is supported by the *Septuagint* and *Chaldee.*

Verse 3. *Lest* any *hurt it, I will keep it night and day*—"I will take care of her by night; and by day I will keep guard over her"] For פן יפקד *pen yiphkod, lest any visit it,* the *Syriac* read ואפקד *veephkod, and I will visit it.* Twenty MSS. of *Kennicott's*, fourteen of *De Rossi's*, and two of my own, and six editions read אפקד *ephkod, I will visit,* in the first person.

Verse 4. *Fury* is *not in me*—"I have no wall"] For חמה *chemah, anger,* the *Septuagint* and *Syriac* read חומה *chomah, wall.* An ancient MS. has חימה *cheimah.* For בה *bah, in her,* two MSS. read בם *bam, in them,* plural. The vineyard wishes for a wall and a fence of thorns—human strength and protection, (as the Jews were too apt to apply to their powerful neighbours for assistance, and to trust to the shadow of Egypt:) JEHOVAH replies, that this would not avail her, nor defend her against his wrath. He counsels her, therefore, to betake herself to his protection. On which she entreats him to make peace with her.

From the above note it appears that the bishop reads חומה *chomah, wall,* for חמה *chemah, anger* or *fury,* in accordance with the *Syriac* and *Septuagint.* The letter ו *vau* makes the only difference, which letter is frequently absent from many words where its place is supplied by the point **.** *cholem:* it might have been so here formerly; and in process of time both *vau* and *cholem* might have been lost. The *Syriac* supports the learned bishop's criticism, as the word ܫܘܪܐ *shora* is there used; which word in the plural is found, Heb. xi. 30: "By faith the *walls* of Jericho." The bishop thinks the *Septuagint* is on his side: to me, it seems neither *for* nor *against* the criticism. The words in the *Vatican copy* are *εγω πολις οχυρα, I am a fortified city;* which the *Arabic* follows: but instead of οχυρα, the *Codex Alexandrinus* has ισχυρα, *I am a* STRONG *city.*

The word חומה *chomah, wall,* is not found in any MS. in the collections of *Kennicott* and *De Rossi*, nor in any of my own MSS.

However, one of Dr. *Kennicott's* MSS. has חימה *cheimah;* but probably that which now appears to be a י *yod* was formerly a ו *vau,* and now partially obliterated.

This song receives much light from being collated with that in chap. v.; and perhaps the bishop's criticism will find its best support from such a collation. In ver. 5 of that chapter, God threatens to take away the *wall* of his vineyard: this *was* done; and here the vineyard complains, *I have no wall,* and wishes for any kind of defence rather than be thus naked. This is the only *natural* support of the above criticism.

"About Tripoli there are abundance of vineyards and gardens, inclosed, for the most part, with hedges, which chiefly consist of the rhamnus, paliurus, oxyacantha," &c. *Rawolf,* p. 21, 22. A fence of thorns is esteemed equal to a wall for strength, being commonly represented as impenetrable. See Mic. vii. 4; Hos. ii. 6.

Who would set the briers and *thorns against me*—"O that I had a fence of the thorn and brier"] *Seven* MSS., (*two* ancient,) and *one* edition, with the *Syriac, Vulgate,* and Aquila, read ושית *veshayith,* with the conjunction ו *vau* prefixed: *Who would set the briers and thorns.* מי יתנני שמיר שית *mi yitteneni shamir shayith, Who shall give me the brier and thorn,* i. e., for a defence: but hear *Kimchi:* "*Who* (the vineyard) *hath given me* (Jehovah) *the brier and the thorn* instead of good grapes."

Verse 5. *Or*—"Ah"] For או *o* I read אוי *oi,* as it was at first in a MS. The י *yod* was easily lost, being followed by another י *yod.*

Verse 6. *To take root*—"From the root"] For ישרש *yashresh,* I read, with the *Syriac,* משרש *mishshoresh.* And for יציץ ופרח *yatsits uparach,* יציצו פרח *yatsitsu parach,* joining the ו *vau* to the first word, and taking that into construction with the first part of the sentence, *Israel shall bud forth.* I suppose the dialogue to be continued in this verse, which pursues the same image of the allegory, but in the way of metaphor.

Verse 9. *The groves*—"And if the groves"] ולא *velo. Four* MSS., *two* ancient, of *Kennicott's,* and *one* ancient of my own, with the *Septuagint;* this makes a fuller sense.

A. M. cir. 3292 B. C. cir. 712 Olymp. XVII. 1 cir. annum NumæPompilii, R. Roman., 4

Jacob be purged; and this *is* all the fruit to take away his sin; when he maketh all the stones of the altar as chalk-stones that are beaten in sunder, the groves and [r]images shall not stand up.

10 Yet the defenced city *shall be* desolate, *and* the habitation forsaken, and left like a wilderness: [s]there shall the calf feed, and there shall he lie down, and consume the branches thereof.

11 When the boughs thereof are withered, they shall be broken off: the women come, *and* set them on fire: for [t]it *is* a people of no understanding: therefore he that made them will not have mercy on them, and [u]he that formed them will show them no favour.

12 And it shall come to pass in that day, *that* the LORD shall beat off from the channel of the river unto the stream of Egypt, and ye shall be gathered one by one, O ye children of Israel.

13 [v]And it shall come to pass in that day, [w]*that* the great trumpet shall be blown, and they shall come which were ready to perish in the land of Assyria, and the outcasts in the land of Egypt, and shall worship the LORD in the holy mount at Jerusalem.

[r]Or, *sun images*——[s]See chapter xvii. 2; xxxii. 14 [t]Deut. xxxii. 28; chap. i. 3; Jer. viii. 7

[u]Deut. xxxii. 18; chapter xliii. 1, 7; xliv. 2, 21, 24 [v]Chap. ii. 11——[w]Matt. xxiv. 31; Rev. xi. 15

Verse 10. *There shall the calf feed*] That is, the king of Egypt, says *Kimchi.*

Verse 11. *The boughs thereof*—"Her boughs"] קציריה *ketsireyha*, MS. and Vulg.; that is, the boughs of the *vineyard*, referring still to the subject of the dialogue above.

The scarcity of fuel, especially wood, in most parts of the east is so great, that they supply it with every thing capable of burning; cow-dung dried, roots, parings of fruit, withered stalks of herbs and flowers; see Matt. vi. 21-30. Vine-twigs are particularly mentioned as used for fuel in dressing their food, by D'Arvieux; *La Roque*, Palestine, p. 198. Ezekiel says, in his parable of the vine, used figuratively for the people of God, as the vineyard is here: "Shall wood be taken thereof to do any work? or will men take a pin of it to hang any vessel thereon? Behold, it is cast into the fire for fuel;" chap. xv. 3, 4. "If a man abide not in me," saith our Lord, "he is cast forth as a branch of the vine and is withered; and men gather them, and cast them into the fire, and they are burned;" John xv. 6. They employed women and children to gather these things, and they laid them up in store for use. The dressing and pruning their vines afforded a good supply of the last sort of fuel; but the prophet says that the vines themselves of the beloved vineyard shall be blasted, withered, and broken, and the women shall come and gather them up, and carry away the whole of them to make their fires for domestic uses. See *Harmer's* Observations, vol. i., p. 254, &c.

Verse 12. *The channel of the river*] The river *Sabbation*, beyond which the Israelites were carried captive.—*Kimchi.*

Verse 13. *The great trumpet shall be blown*] Does not this refer to the time spoken of by our Lord, Matt. xxiv. 31: *He shall send forth his angels*—the preachers of his Gospel *with a great sound of a trumpet*—the earnest invitation to be saved by Jesus Christ; *and shall gather his elect*—the Jews, his ancient *chosen* people, *from the four winds*—from all parts of the habitable globe in which they have been dispersed.

In this prophet there are several predictions relative to the conversion of Egypt to the true faith, which have not yet been fulfilled, and which *must* be fulfilled, for the truth of God cannot fail. Should Egypt ever succeed in casting off the *Ottoman* yoke, and fully establish its independence, it is most likely that the Gospel of Christ would have a speedy entrance into it; and, according to these prophecies, a wide and permanent diffusion. At present the Mohammedan power is a genuine antichrist. This also the Lord will remove in due time.

CHAPTER XXVIII

This chapter begins with a denunciation of the approaching ruin of the Israelites by Shalmaneser, whose power is compared to a tempest or flood, and his keenness to the avidity with which one plucks and swallows the grape that is soonest ripe, 1–4. *It then turns to the two tribes of Judah and Benjamin, who were to continue a kingdom after the final captivity of their brethren; and gives first a favourable prognostication of their affairs under Hezekiah,* 5, 6; *but soon changes to reproofs and threatenings for their intemperance and their profaneness,* 7, 8. *They are introduced as not only scornfully rejecting, but also mocking and ridiculing, the instructions of the prophet,* 9, 10. *To this God immediately retorts in terms alluding to their own mocking, but differently applied,* 11–13. *The prophet then addresses these scoffers,* 14; *who considered themselves as perfectly secure from every evil,* 15; *and assures them that there was no method under heaven but one, by which they could be saved,* 16; *that every other vain resource should fail in the day of visitation,* 17, 18. *He then farther adds, that the judgments of God were particularly levelled against them; and that all the means to which they trusted for warding them off should be to no purpose,* 19, 20; *as the Almighty, who, on account of his patience and long-*

suffering, is amiably described as unacquainted with punishing, had nevertheless determined to punish them, 21, 22. *The prophet then concludes with a beautiful parable in explanation and defence of God's dealing with his people,* 23–29.

A. M. cir. 3279
B. C. cir. 725
Olymp. XIII. 4
cir. annum
Romuli,
R. Roman., 29

WO to [a]the crown of pride, to
the drunkards of Ephraim,
whose [b]glorious beauty *is* a fading flower, which *are* on the head
of the fat valleys of them that are [c]overcome
with wine!
2 Behold, the Lord hath a mighty and strong
one, [d]*which* as a tempest of hail *and* a destroying storm, as a flood of mighty waters
overflowing, shall cast down to the earth with
the hand.

A. M. cir. 3279
B. C. cir. 725
Olymp. XIII. 4
cir. annum
Romuli,
R. Roman., 29

3 [e]The crown of pride, the
drunkards of Ephraim, shall be
trodden [f]under feet:
4 And [g]the glorious beauty,
which *is* on the head of the fat valley, shall be
a fading flower, *and* as the hasty fruit before
the summer; which *when* he that looketh upon
it seeth, while it is yet in his hand he [h]eateth
it up.
5 In that day shall the LORD of hosts be for
a crown of glory, and for a diadem of beauty,
unto the residue of his people,

[a]Ver. 3——[b]Ver. 4——[c]Heb. *broken*——[d]Chap. xxx. 30; Ezek. xiii. 11

[e]Ver. 1——[f]Heb. *with feet*——[g]Ver. 1——[h]Heb. *swalloweth*

NOTES ON CHAP. XXVIII

Verse 1. *Wo to the crown of pride*] By the crown of pride, &c., *Samaria* is primarily understood. "Sebaste, the ancient Samaria, is situated on a long mount of an oval figure, having first a fruitful valley, and then a ring of hills running round about it;" *Maundrell*, p. 58. "E regione horum ruderum mons est peramœnus, planitie admodum frugifera circumseptus, super quem olim Samaria urbs condita fuit;" Fureri Itinerarium, p. 93. The city, beautifully situated on the top of a round hill, and surrounded immediately with a rich valley and a circle of other hills beyond it, suggested the idea of a chaplet or wreath of flowers worn upon their heads on occasions of festivity, expressed by *the proud crown* and the *fading flower of the drunkards*. That this custom of wearing chaplets in their banquets prevailed among the Jews, as well as among the Greeks and Romans, appears from the following passage of the book of Wisdom:—

"Let us fill ourselves with costly wine and ointments,
And let no flower of the spring pass by us:
Let us crown ourselves with rose-buds before they are withered."

Wisd. ii. 7, 8.

Verse 2. *Behold the Lord hath a mighty and strong one*—"Behold the mighty one, the exceedingly strong one"] אמיץ לאדני *ammits ladonai*, *fortis Domino*, i. e., *fortissimus*, a Hebraism. For לאדני *ladonai, to the Lord, thirty-eight* MSS. of Dr. *Kennicott's* and many of *De Rossi's*, with some of my own, and *two* editions, read ליהוה *laihovah, to* JEHOVAH.

Verse 3. *The crown of pride, the drunkards of Ephraim*—"The proud crown of the drunkards of Ephraim"] I read עטרות *ataroth, crowns*, plural, to agree with the verb תרמסנה *teramasnah*, "shall be trodden down."

Verse 4. *The hasty fruit before the summer*—"The early fruit before the summer"] "No sooner doth the *boccore*, (the early fig,) draw near to perfection in the middle or latter end of June, than the *kermez* or summer fig begins to be formed, though it rarely ripens before August; about which time the same tree frequently throws out a third crop, or the winter fig, as we may call it. This is usually of a much longer shape and darker complexion than the kermez, hanging and ripening upon the tree even after the leaves are shed; and, provided the winter proves mild and temperate, is gathered as a delicious morsel in the spring;" *Shaw*, Travels, p. 370, fol. The image was very obvious to the inhabitants of Judea and the neighbouring countries, and is frequently applied by the prophets to express a desirable object; by none more elegantly than by Hosea, chap. ix. 10:—

"Like grapes in the wilderness I found Israel;
Like the first ripe fig in her prime, I saw your fathers."

Which when *he that looketh upon it seeth*—"Which whoso seeth, he plucketh it immediately"] For יראה *yireh*, which with הראה *haroeh* makes a miserable tautology, read, by a transposition of a letter, יארה *yoreh;* a happy conjecture of Houbigant. The image expresses in the strongest manner the great ease with which the Assyrians shall take the city and the whole kingdom, and the avidity with which they shall seize the rich prey without resistance.

Verse 5. *In that day*] Thus far the prophecy relates to the Israelites, and manifestly denounces their approaching destruction by Shalmaneser. Here it turns to the two tribes of Judah and Benjamin, the remnant of God's people who were to continue a kingdom after the final captivity of the Israelites. It begins with a favourable prognostication of their affairs under Hezekiah; but soon changes to reproofs and threatenings for their intemperance, disobedience, and profaneness.

Jonathan's Targum on this verse is worthy of notice: "In that time Messiah, the Lord of hosts משיחא דיי צבאות *meshicha dayai tsebaoth*, shall be a crown of joy and a diadem of praise to the residue of his people." Kimchi says the rabbins in general are of this opinion. Here then the rabbins, and their most celebrated Targum, give the incommunicable name, יהוה צבאות *Yehovah tsebaoth, the Lord of hosts*, to our ever blessed Redeemer, Jesus Christ.

A. M. cir. 3279
B. C. cir. 725
Olymp. XIII. 4
cir. annum
Romuli,
R. Roman., 29

6 And for a spirit of judgment
to him that sitteth in judgment,
and for strength to them that
turn the battle to the gate.
7 But they also [i]have erred through wine,
and through strong drink are out of the way;
[k]the priest and the prophet have erred through
strong drink, they are swallowed up of wine,
they are out of the way through strong drink;
they err in vision, they stumble *in* judgment.
8 For all tables are full of vomit *and* filthiness, *so that there is* no place
clean.
9 [l]Whom shall he teach knowledge? and whom shall he make
to understand [m]doctrine? *them that are* weaned
from the milk, *and* drawn from the breasts.
10 For precept [n]*must be* upon precept, precept upon precept; line upon line, line upon
line; here a little, *and* there a little:
11 For with [o]stammering [p]lips and another
tongue [q]will he speak to this people.

[i]Prov. xx. 1; Hos. iv. 11——[k]Chap. lvi. 10, 12——[l]Jer. vi. 10——[m]Heb. *the hearing*

[n]Or, hath been——[o]Heb. *stammerings of lips*——[p]1 Cor. xiv. 21——[q]Or, *he hath spoken*

Verse 6. *The battle to the gate*—"The war to the gate *of the enemy*."] That is, who pursue the fleeing enemy even to the very gates of their own city. "But we were upon them even unto the entering of the gate," 2 Sam. xi. 23; that is, we drove the enemy back to their own gates. See also 1 Sam. xvii. 52. The *Targum* says, The Messiah shall give the victory to those who go out to battle, that he may bring them back to their own houses in peace.

Verse 9. *Whom shall he teach knowledge?*—"Whom, say they, would he teach knowledge?"] The scoffers mentioned below, ver. 14, are here introduced as uttering their sententious speeches; they treat God's method of dealing with them, and warning them by his prophets, with contempt and derision. What, say they, doth he treat us as mere infants just weaned? doth he teach us like little children, perpetually inculcating the same elementary lessons, the mere rudiments of knowledge; precept after precept, line after line, here and there, by little and little? imitating at the same time, and ridiculing, in ver. 10, the concise prophetical manner. God, by his prophet, retorts upon them with great severity their own contemptuous mockery, turning it to a sense quite different from what they intended. Yes, saith he, it shall be in fact as you say; ye shall be taught by a strange tongue and a stammering lip; in a strange country; ye shall be carried into captivity by a people whose language shall be unintelligible to you, and which ye shall be forced to learn like children. And my dealing with you shall be according to your own words: it shall be command upon command for your punishment; it shall be line upon line, stretched over you to mark your destruction, (compare 2 Kings xxi. 13;) it shall come upon you at different times, and by different degrees, till the judgments, with which from time to time I have threatened you, shall have their full accomplishment.

Jerome seems to have rightly understood the general design of this passage as expressing the manner in which the scoffers, by their sententious speeches, turned into ridicule the warnings of God by his prophets, though he has not so well explained the meaning of the repetition of their speech in ver. 13. His words are on ver. 9—"Solebant hoc ex persona prophetarum ludentes dicere:" and on ver. 14—"Quod supra diximus, cum irrisione solitos principes Judæorum prophetis dicere, *manda, remanda,* et cætera his similia, per quæ ostenditur, nequaquam eos prophetarum credidisse sermonibus, sed prophetiam habuisse despectui, præsens ostendit capitulum, per quod appellantur viri illusores." *Hieron. in loc.*

And so Jarchi interprets the word משלים *mishelim* in the next verse: Qui dicunt verba irrisionis parabolicè." And the *Chaldee* paraphrases ver. 11 to the same purpose, understanding it as spoken, not of God, but of the people deriding his prophets: "Quoniam in mutatione loquelæ et in lingua subsannationis irridebant contra prophetas, qui prophetabant populo huic."—L.

Verse 10. *For precept* must be *upon precept*] The original is remarkably abrupt and sententious. The hemistichs are these:—

כי צו לצו צו לצו
latsav tsav latsav tsav ki

קו לקו קו לקו
lakav kav lakav kav

זעיר שם זעיר שם
sham zeeir sham zeeir

For,—Command to command, command to command.
Line to line, line to line.
A little there, a little there.

Kimchi says צו *tsav, precept,* is used here for מצוה *mitsvah, command,* and is used in no other place for it but here. צו *tsav* signifies a *little precept,* such as is suited to the capacity of a child; see ver. 9. קו *kav* signifies the *line* that a mason stretches out to build a layer of stones by. After one layer or course is placed, he raises the line and builds another; thus the building is by degrees regularly completed. This is the method of teaching children, giving them such information as their narrow capacities can receive; and thus the prophet dealt with the Israelites. See *Kimchi in loc.*, and see a fine parallel passage, Heb. v. 12-14, by which this may be well illustrated.

My old MS. Bible translates oddly:—

For sende efter sende, sende efter sende:
Abiide efter abiide, abiide efter abiide:
Lityl ther, lytyl ther.

Coverdale is also singular:—

Commande that may be commanded;
Byd that maye be bydden:
Forbyd that maye be forbydden;
Kepe backe that maye be kepte backe:
Here a litle, there a litle.

A. M. cir. 3279 B. C. cir. 725 Olymp. XIII. 4 cir. annum Romuli, R. Roman., 29

12 To whom he said, This *is*
the rest *wherewith* ye may cause
the weary to rest; and this *is* the
refreshing: yet they would not
hear.
13 But the word of the LORD was unto them,
precept upon precept, precept upon precept;
line upon line, line upon line; here a little,
and there a little; that they might go, and fall
backward, and be broken, and snared, and taken.
14 Wherefore hear the word of the LORD,
ye scornful men, that rule this people which
is in Jerusalem.
15 Because ye have said, We have made a
covenant with death, and with hell are we at
agreement; when the overflowing scourge
shall pass through, it shall not come unto us:
[r]for we have made lies our refuge, and under
falsehood have we hid ourselves:
16 Therefore thus saith the Lord GOD,
Behold, I lay in Zion for a foundation [s]a stone, a tried stone, a
precious corner *stone,* a sure
foundation: he that believeth
shall not make haste.
17 Judgment also will I lay to the line, and
righteousness to the plummet: and the hail
shall sweep away [t]the refuge of lies, and the
waters shall overflow the hiding place.
18 And your covenant with death shall be
disannulled, and your agreement with hell
shall not stand; when the overflowing scourge
shall pass through, then ye shall be [u]trodden
down by it.
19 From the time that it goeth forth it shall
take you: for morning by morning shall it
pass over, by day and by night: and it shall
be a vexation only [v]*to* understand the report.
20 For the bed is shorter than that *a man*
can stretch himself *on it:* and the covering

A. M. cir. 3279 B. C. cir. 725 Olymp. XIII. 4 cir. annum Romuli, R. Roman., 29

[r]Amos ii. 4——[s]Gen. xlix. 42; Psa. cxviii. 22; Matt. xxi. 42; Acts iv. 11; Rom. ix. 33; x. 11; Eph. ii. 20; 1 Pet. ii. 6, 7, 8——[t]Ver. 15——[u]Heb. *a treading down to it* [v]Or, when *he shall make* you *to understand doctrine*

Verse 12. *This* is *the rest*—"This is the true rest"] The sense of this verse is: God had warned them by his prophets that their safety and security, their deliverance from their present calamities and from the apprehensions of still greater approaching, depended wholly on their trust in God, their faith and obedience; but they rejected this gracious warning with contempt and mockery.

Verse 15. *A covenant with death*] To be in covenant with, is a kind of proverbial expression to denote *perfect security* from evil and mischief of any sort:—

"For thou shalt be in league with the stones of the field;
And the beasts of the field shall be at peace with thee." Job v. 23.

"And I will make a covenant for them with the beasts of the field,
And with the fowls of heaven, and with the creeping things of the ground." Hos. ii. 18.

That is, none of these shall hurt them. But Lucan, speaking of the Psylli, whose peculiar property it was to be unhurt by the bite of serpents, with which their country abounded, comes still nearer to the expression of Isaiah in this place:—

Gens unica terras
Incolit a sævo serpentum innoxia morsu
Marmaridæ Psylli.——
Pax illis cum morte data est.
Pharsal. ix. 891.

"Of all who scorching Afric's sun endure,
None like the swarthy Psyllians are secure:
With healing gifts and privileges graced,
Well in the land of serpents were they placed:
Truce with the dreadful tyrant death they have,
And border safely on his realm the grave."
ROWE.

We have made a covenant with death, and with hell are we at agreement] עשינו חזה *asinu chozeh*, we have made a *vision*, we have had an *interview*, struck a bargain, and settled all preliminaries. So they had made a *covenant with hell* by *diabolic sacrifice*, כרתנו ברית *carathnu berith*, "We have cut the covenant sacrifice;" they divided it for the contracting parties to *pass between* the separated victim; for the victim was split exactly down the middle, so that even the *spinal marrow was exactly divided* through its whole length; and being set opposite to each other, the contracting parties entered, one at the head part, the other at the feet; and, meeting in the centre, took the covenant oath. Thus, it is intimated, these bad people made an agreement with שאול *sheol*, with *demons*, with whom they had an *interview; i. e.*, meeting them in the covenant sacrifice! To such a pitch had the Israelitish idolatry reached at that time!

Verse 16. *Behold, I lay in Zion*] See the notes on the parallel places in the margin. *Kimchi* understands this of *Hezekiah;* but it most undoubtedly belongs to Jesus Christ alone; and his application of it to himself, even the Jews could not contest. See the margin as above.

Verse 18. *Your covenant with death shall be disannulled*—"Your covenant with death shall be broken"] For כפר *caphar*, which seems not to belong to this place, the *Chaldee* reads תפר *taphar*, which is approved by *Houbigant* and *Secker*. See Jer. xxxiii. 21, where the very same phrase is used. See Prelim. Dissert. p. l.

Verse 20. *For the bed is shorter*] A *mashal* or proverbial saying, the meaning of which is, that

A. M. cir. 3279
B. C. cir. 725
Olymp. XIII. 4
cir. annum Romuli,
R. Roman., 29

narrower than that he can wrap himself *in it.*

21 For the LORD shall rise up as *in* Mount [w]Perazim, he shall be wroth as *in* the valley of [x]Gibeon, that he may do his work, [y]his strange work; and bring to pass his act, his strange act.

22 Now therefore be ye not mockers, lest your bands be made strong: for I have heard from the Lord GOD of hosts [z]a consumption, even determined upon the whole earth.

23 Give ye ear, and hear my voice; hearken, and hear my speech.

24 Doth the ploughman plough all day to sow? doth he open and break the clods of his ground?

25 When he hath made plain the face thereof, doth he not cast abroad the fitches, and scatter the cummin, and cast in [a]the principal wheat and the appointed barley and the [b]rye in their [c]place?

A. M. cir. 3279
B. C. cir. 725
Olymp. XIII. 4
cir. annum Romuli,
R. Roman., 29

26 [d]For [e]his God doth instruct him to discretion, *and* doth teach him.

27 For the fitches are not threshed with a threshing instrument, neither is a cart wheel turned about upon the cummin; but the fitches are beaten out with a staff, and the cummin with a rod.

28 Bread *corn* is bruised; because he will not ever be threshing it, nor break *it with* the wheel of his cart, nor bruise it *with* his horsemen.

29 This also cometh forth from the LORD of hosts, [f]*which* is wonderful in counsel, *and* excellent in working.

---

[w]2 Samuel v. 20; 1 Chronicles xiv. 11——[x]Joshua x. 10, 12; 2 Samuel v. 25; 1 Chronicles xiv. 16——[y]Lamentations iii. 33——[z]Chap. x. 22, 23; Daniel ix. 27——[a]Or, *the wheat in the principal* place, *and barley in the appointed* place——[b]Or, *spelt*——[c]Heb. *border?*——[d]Or, *And he bindeth it in such sort as his God doth teach him*——[e]Ecclesiasticus vii. 15——[f]Psalm xcii. 5; Jeremiah xxxii. 19

---

they will find all means of defence and protection insufficient to secure them, and cover them from the evils coming upon them. מסך *massek*, chap. xxii. 8, the *covering*, is used for the outworks of defence, the barrier of the country; and here, in the allegorical sense, it means much the same thing. Their beds were only mattresses laid on the floor; and the coverlet a sheet, or in the winter a carpet, laid over it, in which the person wrapped himself. For כהתכנס *kehithcannes*, it ought probably to be מהתכנס *mehithcannes*. *Houbigant*, *Secker*.

Verse 21. *As* in *Mount Perazim*] כהר *kehar;* but בהר *bahar*, IN *the mount*, is the reading of two of *Kennicott's*, one of *De Rossi's*, and one of my own MSS.

Verse 22. *The Lord God*] אדני יהוה *Adonai Yehovah*. Adonai is omitted by four of *Kennicott's* MSS., and in the *Septuagint*, *Syriac*, and *Arabic*.

Verse 23. *Give ye ear, and hear my voice*—"Listen ye, and hear my voice"] The foregoing discourse, consisting of severe reproofs, and threatenings of dreadful judgments impending on the Jews for their vices, and their profane contempt of God's warnings by his messengers, the prophet concludes with an explanation and defence of God's method of dealing with his people in an elegant parable or allegory; in which he employs a variety of images, all taken from the science of agriculture. As the *husbandman* uses various methods in preparing his land, and adapting it to the several kinds of seeds to be sown, with a due observation of times and seasons; and when he hath gathered in his harvest, employs methods as various in separating the corn from the straw and the chaff by different instruments, according to the nature of the different sorts of grain; so God, with unerring wisdom, and with strict justice, instructs, admonishes, and corrects his people; chastises and punishes them in various ways, as the exigence of the case requires; now more moderately, now more severely; always tempering justice with mercy; in order to reclaim the wicked, to improve the good, and, finally, to separate the one from the other.

Verse 26. *For his God doth instruct him*] All nations have agreed in attributing agriculture, the most useful and the most necessary of all sciences, to the invention and to the suggestions of their deities. "The Most High hath ordained husbandry," saith the son of Sirach, Ecclus. vii. 15.

Namque Ceres fertur fruges, Liberque liquoris
Vitigeni laticem mortalibus instituisse.
LUCRETIUS, v. 14.

"Ceres has taught mortals how to produce fruits; and Bacchus has taught them how to cultivate the vine."

'Ο δ' ηπιος ανθρωποισι
Δεξια σημαινει, λαους δ' επι εργον εγειρει
Μιμνησκων βιοτοιο· λεγει δ' ὁτε βωλος αριστη
Βουσι τε και μακελησι· λεγει δ' ὁτε δεξιαι ὡραι
Και φυτα γυρωσαι, και σπερματα παντα βαλεσθαι.
ARATUS, *Phænom.* v.

"He, Jupiter, to the human race
Indulgent, prompts to necessary toil
Man provident of life; with kindly signs
The seasons marks, when best to turn the glebe
With spade and plough, to nurse the tender plant,
And cast o'er fostering earth the seeds abroad."

Verses 27, 28. Four methods of threshing are here mentioned, by different instruments; the *flail*, the *drag*, the *wain*, and the *treading of the cattle*. The *staff* or *flail* was used for the *infirmiora semina*, says Jerome, the grain that was *too tender* to be treated in the other methods. The *drag* consisted of a sort of strong planks, made rough at the bottom, with hard stones or iron; it was drawn by horses or oxen over the corn sheaves spread on the floor, the driver sitting upon it. Kempfer has given a print representing the manner of using this instrument, *Amœn. Exot.* p. 682, fig. 3. The *wain* was much like the former; but had *wheels* with *iron teeth,* or *edges* like a *saw:* Ferrata carpenta rotis per medium in serrarum modum se volventibus. Hieron. in loc. From this it would seem that the axle was armed with irŏn teeth or *serrated wheels* throughout. See a description and print of such a machine used at present in Egypt for the same purpose in *Niebuhr's* Voyage en Arabie, Tab. xvii. p. 123; it moves upon three rollers armed with iron teeth or wheels to cut the straw. In Syria they make use of the *drag,* constructed in the very same manner as above described; *Niebuhr,* Description de l'Arabie, p. 140. This not only forced out the grain, but cut the straw in pieces for fodder for the cattle; for in the eastern countries they have no *hay.* See *Harmer's* Observ. I. p. 425. The last method is well known from the law of Moses, which "forbids the ox to be muzzled, when he treadeth out the corn;" Deut. xxv. 4.

Verse 28. *The bread*-corn] I read ולחם *velahem,* on the authority of the *Vulgate* and *Symmachus;* the former expresses the conjunction ו *vau,* omitted in the text, by *autem;* the latter by δε.

Bruise it with *his horsemen*—"Bruise it with the hoofs of his cattle."] For פרשיו *parashaiv, horsemen* or *teeth,* read פרסיו *perasaiv, hoofs.* So the *Syriac, Symmachus, Theodotion,* and the *Vulgate.* The first is read with ש *shin,* the latter with ס *samech,* the pronunciation is nearly the same.

CHAPTER XXIX

Distress of Ariel, or Jerusalem, on Sennacherib's invasion, with manifest allusion, however, to the still greater distress which it suffered from the Romans, 1–4. *Disappointment and fall of Sennacherib described in terms, like the event, the most awful and terrible,* 5–8. *Stupidity and hypocrisy of the Jews,* 9–16. *Rejection of the Jews, and calling of the Gentiles,* 17. *The chapter concludes by a recurrence to the favourite topics of the prophet, viz., the great extension of the Messiah's kingdom in the latter days, and the future restoration of Israel,* 18–24.

A. M. cir. 3292
B. C. cir. 712
Olymp. XVII. 1
cir. annum
NumæPompilii,
R. Roman., 4

WO [a]to[b] Ariel, to Ariel, [c]the city [d]*where* David dwelt! add ye year to year; let them [e]kill sacrifices.

2 Yet I will distress Ariel, and there shall be heaviness and sorrow: and it shall be unto me as Ariel.

A. M. cir. 3292
B. C. cir. 712
Olymp. XVII. 1
cir. annum
NumæPompilii,
R. Roman., 4

[a]Or, *O Ariel,* that is, *the lion of God*——[b]Ezek. xliii. 15, 16——[c]Or, *of the city*——[d]2 Sam. v. 9——[e]Heb. *cut off the heads*

The subject of this and the four following chapters is the invasion of Sennacherib; the great distress of the Jews while it continued; their sudden and unexpected deliverance by God's immediate interposition in their favour; the subsequent prosperous state of the kingdom under Hezekiah; interspersed with severe reproofs, and threats of punishment, for their hypocrisy, stupidity, infidelity, their want of trust in God, and their vain reliance on the assistance of Egypt; and with promises of better times, both immediately to succeed, and to be expected in the future age. The whole making, not one continued discourse, but rather a collection of different discourses upon the same subject; which is treated with great elegance and variety. Though the matter is various, and the transitions sudden, yet the prophet seldom goes far from his subject. It is properly enough divided by the chapters in the common translation.—L.

NOTES ON CHAP. XXIX

Verse 1. *Ariel*] That Jerusalem is here called by this name is very certain: but the reason of this name, and the meaning of it as applied to Jerusalem, is very obscure and doubtful. Some, with the Chaldee, suppose it to be taken from the hearth of the great altar of burnt-offerings, which Ezekiel plainly calls by the same name; and that Jerusalem is here considered as the seat of the fire of God, אור אל *ur el* which should issue from thence to consume his enemies: compare chap. xxxi. 9. Some, according to the common derivation of the word, ארי אל *ari el,* the lion of God, or the strong lion, suppose it to signify the strength of the place, by which it was enabled to resist and overcome all its enemies. Τινες δε φασι την πολιν ούτως ειρησθαι· επει, δια Θεου, λεοντος δικην εσπαραττε τους ανταιροντας. *Procop.* in loc. There are other explanations of this name given: but none that seems to be perfectly satisfactory.—*Lowth.*

From Ezekiel xliii. 15, we learn that Ari-el was the name of the altar of burnt-offerings, put here for the *city* itself in which that altar was. In the second verse it is said, I will distress Ari-el, and it shall be unto me as Ari-el. The first *Ari-el* here seems to mean *Jerusalem,* which should be distressed by the Assyrians: the second *Ari-el* seems to mean the *altar of burnt-offerings.* But why is it said, "Ari-el shall be unto me as Ari-el?" As the altar of burnt-offerings was surrounded daily by the victims which were offered: so the walls of Jerusalem shall be surrounded by the *dead bodies* of those who had rebelled against the Lord, and who should be victims to his justice. The translation of Bishop Lowth appears to embrace both meanings: "I will bring distress upon Ari-el; and it shall be to me as the hearth of the great altar."

Add ye year to year] Ironically. Go on year after year, keep your solemn feasts; yet know, that God will punish you for your hypocritical worship, consisting of mere form destitute of true piety. Probably delivered at the time of some great feast, when they were thus employed.

Verse 2. *There shall be heaviness and sorrow* —"There shall be continual mourning and sor-

A. M. cir. 3292
B. C. cir. 712
Olymp. XVII. 1
cir. annum
NumæPompilii,
R. Roman., 4

3 And I will camp against thee round about, and will lay siege against thee with a mount, and I will raise forts against thee.

4 And thou shalt be brought down, *and* shalt speak out of the ground, and thy speech shall be low out of the dust, and thy voice shall be, as of one that hath a familiar spirit, [f]out of the ground, and thy speech shall [g]whisper out of the dust.

5 Moreover the multitude of thy [h]strangers shall be like small dust, and the multitude of the terrible ones *shall be* [i]as chaff that passeth away: yea, it shall be [k]at an instant suddenly.

6 [l]Thou shalt be visited of the LORD of hosts with thunder, and with earthquake, and great noise, with storm and tempest, and the flame of devouring fire.

7 [m]And the multitude of all the nations that fight against Ariel, even all that fight against her and her munition, and that distress her, shall be [n]as a dream of a night vision.

[f]Ch. viii. 19——[g]Heb. *peep* or *chirp*——[h]Ch. xxv. 5
[i]Job xxi. 18; chap. xvii. 13

[k]Chap. xxx. 13——[l]Chap. xxviii. 2; xxx. 30——[m]Chap. xxxvii. 36——[n]Job xx. 8

row"] Instead of your present joy and festivity.

And it shall be unto me as Ariel—"And it shall be unto me as the hearth of the great altar."] That is, it shall be the seat of the fire of God; which shall issue from thence to consume his enemies. See note on ver. 1. Or, perhaps, all on flame; as it was when taken by the Chaldeans; or covered with carcasses and blood, as when taken by the Romans: an intimation of which more distant events, though not immediate subjects of the prophecy, may perhaps be given in this obscure passage.

Verse 3. *And I will camp against thee round about*—"And I will encamp against thee like David"] For כדור *caddur*, some kind of military engine, כדוד *kedavid, like David*, is the reading of the *Septuagint*, two MSS. of *Kennicott's*, if not two more: but though Bishop Lowth adopts this reading, I think it harsh and unnecessary.

Forts—"Towers"] For מצרת *metsuroth*, read מצדות *metsudoth:* so the *Septuagint* and five MSS. of Dr. *Kennicott's*, one of them ancient, and four of *De Rossi's*.

Verse 4. *And thy speech shall be low out of the dust*—"And from out of the dust thou shalt utter a feeble speech"] That the souls of the dead uttered a feeble stridulous sound, very different from the natural human voice, was a popular notion among the heathens as well as among the Jews. This appears from several passages of their poets; Homer, Virgil, Horace. The pretenders to the art of necromancy, who were chiefly women, had an art of speaking with a feigned voice, so as to deceive those who applied to them, by making them believe that it was the voice of the ghost. They had a way of uttering sounds, as if they were formed, not by the organs of speech, but deep in the chest, or in the belly; and were thence called *εγγαστριμυθοι*, *ventriloqui:* they could make the voice seem to come from beneath the ground, from a distant part, in another direction, and not from themselves; the better to impose upon those who consulted them. Εξεπιτηδες το γενος τουτο τον αμυδρον ηχον επιτηδευονται, ἱνα δια την ασαφειαν της φωνης τον του ψευδους αποδιδρασκωσιν ελεγχον. *Psellus* De Dæmonibus, apud *Bochart*, i. p. 731. "These people studiously acquire, and affect on purpose, this sort of obscure sound; that by the uncertainty of the voice they may the better escape being detected in the cheat." From these arts of the necromancers the popular notion seems to have arisen, that the ghost's voice was a weak, stridulous, almost inarticulate sort of sound, very different from the speech of the living.

Verse 5. *The multitude of thy strangers*—"The multitude of the proud"] For זריך *zarayich, thy strangers*, read זדים *zedim, the proud*, according to the *Septuagint;* parallel to and synonymous with עריצים *aritsim, the terrible*, in the next line: the ר *resh* was at first ד *daleth* in a MS. See note on chap. xxv. 2.

The fifth, sixth, and seventh verses contain an admirable description of the destruction of Sennacherib's army, with a beautiful variety of the most expressive and sublime images: perhaps more adapted to show the greatness, the suddenness, and horror of the event, than the means and manner by which it was effected. Compare chap. xxx. 30-33.

Verse 7. *As a dream*] This is the beginning of the comparison, which is pursued and applied in the next verse. Sennacherib and his mighty army are not compared to a dream because of their sudden disappearance; but the disappointment of their eager hopes is compared to what happens to a hungry and thirsty man, when he awakes from a dream in which fancy had presented to him meat and drink in abundance, and finds it nothing but a vain illusion. The comparison is elegant and beautiful in the highest degree, well wrought up, and perfectly suited to the end proposed. The image is extremely natural, but not obvious: it appeals to our inward feelings, not to our outward senses; and is applied to an event in its concomitant circumstances exactly similar, but in its nature totally different. See *De S. Poës. Hebr.* Prælect. xii. For beauty and ingenuity it may fairly come in competition with one of the most elegant of Virgil, greatly improved from Homer, Iliad xxii. 199, where he has applied to a different purpose, but not so happily, the same image of the ineffectual working of imagination in a dream:—

Ac veluti in somnis, oculos ubi languida pressit
Nocte quies, necquicquam avidos extendere cursus
Velle videmur, et in mediis conatibus ægri
Succidimus; non lingua valet, non corpore notæ
Sufficiunt vires, nec vox, nec verba sequuntur.
Æn., xii. 908.

A. M. cir. 3292 B. C. cir. 712 Olymp. XVII. 1 cir. annum NumæPompilii, R. Roman., 4

8 [o]It shall even be as when a hungry *man* dreameth, and, behold, he eateth; but he awaketh, and his soul is empty: or as when a thirsty man dreameth, and, behold, he drinketh; but he awaketh, and, behold, *he is* faint, and his soul hath appetite: so shall the multitude of all the nations be, that fight against Mount Zion.

9 Stay yourselves, and wonder; [p]cry ye out, and cry: [q]they are drunken, [r]but not with wine; they stagger, but not with strong drink.

10 For [s]the Lord hath poured out upon you the spirit of deep sleep, and hath [t]closed your eyes: the prophets and your [u]rulers, [v]the seers hath he covered.

11 And the vision of all is become unto you as the words of a [w]book [x]that is sealed, which *men* deliver to one that is learned, saying, Read this, I pray thee: [y]and he saith, I cannot; for it *is* sealed.

12 And the book is delivered to him that is not learned, saying, Read this, I pray thee; and he saith, I am not learned.

A. M. cir. 3292 B. C. cir. 712 Olymp. XVII. 1 cir. annum NumæPompilii, R. Roman., 4

13 Wherefore the Lord said, [z]Forasmuch as this people draw near *me* with their mouth, and with their lips do honour me, but have removed their heart far from me, and their fear toward me is taught by [a]the precept of men:

14 [b]Therefore, behold, [c]I will proceed to do a marvellous work among this people, *even* a marvellous work and a wonder: [d]for the wisdom of their wise *men* shall perish, and the understanding of their prudent *men* shall be hid.

15 [e]Wo unto them that seek deep to hide their counsel from the Lord, and their works are in the dark, and [f]they say, [g]Who seeth us? and who knoweth us?

16 Surely your turning of things upside down shall be esteemed as the potter's clay: for shall the [h]work say of him that made it, He made me not? or shall the thing framed say of him that framed it, He had no understanding?

[o]Psa. lxxiii. 20——[p]Or, *take your pleasure and riot* [q]See chap. xxviii. 7, 8——[r]Chap. li. 21——[s]Rom. xi. 8 [t]Psa. lxix. 23; chap. vi. 10——[u]Heb. *heads;* see chap. iii. 2; Jer. xxvi. 8——[v]1 Samuel ix. 9——[w]Or, *letter* [x]Chap. viii. 16

[y]Dan. xii. 4, 9; Rev. v. 1–5, 9; vi. 1——[z]Ezek. xxxiii. 31; Matt. xv. 8, 9; Mark vii. 6, 7——[a]Col. ii. 22 [b]Hab. i. 5——[c]Heb. *I will add*——[d]Jer. xlix. 7; Obad. 8; 1 Cor. i. 19——[e]Chap. xxx. 1——[f]Psalm xciv. 7 [g]Ecclus. xxiii. 18——[h]Chap. xlv. 9; Rom. ix. 20

"And as, when slumber seals the closing sight,
The sick wild fancy labours in the night;
Some dreadful visionary foe we shun
With airy strides, but strive in vain to run;
In vain our baffled limbs their powers essay;
We faint, we struggle, sink, and fall away;
Drain'd of our strength, we neither fight nor fly,
And on the tongue the struggling accents die."

Pitt.

Lucretius expresses the very same image with Isaiah:—

Ut bibere in somnis sitiens quum quærit, et humor
Non datur, ardorem in membris qui stinguere possit;
Sed laticum simulacra petit, frustraque laborat,
In medioque sitit torrenti flumine potans.

iv. 1091.

As a thirsty man desires to drink in his sleep,
And has no fluid to allay the heat within,
But vainly labours to catch the image of rivers,
And is parched up while fancying that he is drinking at a full stream.

Bishop *Stock's* translation of the prophet's text is both elegant and just:—

"As when a hungry man dreameth; and, lo! he is eating:
And he awaketh; and his appetite is unsatisfied.
And as a thirsty man dreameth; and, lo! he is drinking:
And he awaketh; and, lo! he is faint,
And his appetite craveth."

Lucretius almost copies the original.

All that fight against her and her munition—"And all their armies and their towers"] For צביה ומצדתה *tsobeyha umetsodathah*, I read, with the *Chaldee*, צבאם ומצדתם *tsebaam umetsodatham*.

Verse 9. *Stay yourselves, and wonder*] התמהמהו *hithmahmehu, go on what-what-whatting*, in a state of mental indetermination, till the overflowing scourge take you away. See the note on Psa. cxix. 60.

They are drunken, but not with wine] See note on chap. li. 21.

Verse 11. *I cannot; for it* is *sealed*—"I cannot read it; for it is sealed up."] An ancient MS. and the *Septuagint* have preserved a word here, lost out of the text; לקרות *likroth*, (for לקראות,) *αναγνωναι, read it.*

Verse 13. *The Lord*—"Jehovah"] For אדני *Adonai*, sixty-three MSS. of *Kennicott's*, and many of *De Rossi's*, and four editions, read יהוה *Yehovah*, and five MSS. add יהוה.

Kimchi makes some just observations on this verse. *The vision*, meaning the Divine revelation of all the prophets, *is a book or letter that is sealed*—is not easily understood. *This is delivered to one that is learned*—instructed in the law. *Read this; and he saith, I cannot, for it is sealed;* a full proof that he does not wish to know the contents, else he would apply to the prophet to get it explained. See *Kimchi* on the place.

A. M. cir. 3292
B. C. cir. 712
Olymp. XVII. 1
cir. annum
NumæPompilii,
R. Roman., 4

17 *Is* it not yet a very little
while, and [l]Lebanon shall be
turned into a fruitful field, and
the fruitful field shall be esteemed as a forest?
18 And [k]in that day shall the deaf hear
the words of the book, and the eyes of the
blind shall see out of obscurity, and out of
darkness.
19 [l]The meek also [m]shall increase *their*
joy in the LORD, and [n]the poor among men
shall rejoice in the Holy One of Israel.
20 For the terrible one is brought to nought,
and [o]the scorner is consumed, and all that
[p]watch for iniquity are cut off:
21 That make a man an offender for a word,
and [q]lay a snare for him that reproveth in the gate, and turn
aside the just [r]for a thing of
nought.

A. M. cir. 3292
B. C. cir. 712
Olymp. XVII. 1
cir. annum
NumæPompilii,
R. Roman., 4

22 Therefore thus saith the LORD, [s]who
redeemed Abraham, concerning the house of
Jacob, Jacob shall not now be ashamed, neither shall his face now wax pale.
23 But when he seeth his children, [t]the
work of mine hands, in the midst of him,
they shall sanctify my name, and sanctify the
Holy One of Jacob, and shall fear the God
of Israel.
24 They [u]also that erred in spirit [v]shall
come to understanding, and they that mur-
mured shall learn doctrine.

[i]Chap. xxxii. 15——[k]Chap. xxxv. 5——[l]Chap. lxi. 1——[m]Heb. *shall add*——[n]James ii. 5——[o]Chap. xxviii. 14, 22——[p]Mic. ii. 1——[q]Amos v. 10, 12

[r]Prov. xxviii. 21——[s]Josh. xxiv. 3——[t]Chap. xix. 25; xlv. 11; lx. 21; Eph. ii. 10——[u]Chap. xxviii. 7——[v]Heb. *shall know understanding*

And their fear toward me is taught by the precept of men—"And vain is their fear of me, teaching the commandments of men"] I read, for ותהי *vattehi*, ותהו *vethohu*, with the *Septuagint*, Matt. xv. 9; Mark viii. 7; and for מלמדה *melummedah*, מלמדים *melummedim*, with the *Chaldee*.

Verse 17. *And Lebanon shall be turned into a fruitful field*—"Ere Lebanon become like Carmel"] A mashal, or proverbial saying, expressing any great revolution of things; and, when respecting two subjects, an entire reciprocal change: explained here by some interpreters, I think with great probability, as having its principal view beyond the revolutions then near at hand, to the rejection of the Jews, and the calling of the Gentiles. The first were the vineyard of God, כרם אל *kerem El*, (if the prophet, who loves an allusion to words of like sounds, may be supposed to have intended one here,) cultivated and watered by him in vain, to be given up, and to become a wilderness: compare chap. v. 1-7. The last had been hitherto barren; but were, by the grace of God, to be rendered fruitful. See Matt. xxi. 43; Rom. xi. 30, 31. Carmel stands here opposed to Lebanon, and therefore is to be taken as a proper name.

Verse 21. *Him that reproveth in the gate*—"Him that pleaded in the gate"] "They are heard by the treasurer, master of the horse, and other principal officers of the regency of Algiers, who sit constantly in the gate of the palace for that purpose:" that is, the distribution of justice.—*Shaw's* Travels, p. 315, fol. He adds in the note, "That we read of the *elders in the gate*. Deut. xxi. 15; xxv. 7; and, Isa. xxix. 21; Amos v. 10, of *him that reproveth* and *rebuketh in the gate*. The Ottoman court likewise seems to have been called *the Porte*, from the distribution of justice and the despatch of public business that is carried on in the gates of it."

Verse 22. *Who redeemed Abraham*] As God redeemed Abraham from among idolaters and workers of iniquity, so will he redeem those who hear the words of the Book, and are humbled before him, ver. 18, 19.

Concerning the house of Jacob—"The God of the house of Jacob"] I read אל *El* as a noun, not a preposition: the parallel line favours this sense; and there is no address to the house of Jacob to justify the other.

Neither shall his face now wax pale—"His face shall no more be covered with confusion."] "יחורו *yechoro*, Chald. *ut* ὁ μεταβαλει, Theod. εντραπησεται, Syr. נחפרו *necaphro*, *videtur legendum* יחפרו *yechepheru: hic enim solum legitur verbum*, חור *chavar*, *nec in linguis affinibus habet pudoris significationem*."—SECKER. "Here alone is the verb חור *chavar* read; nor has it in the cognate languages the signification of *shame*."

Verse 23. *But when he seeth his children, the work of mine hands*—"For when his children shall see the work of my hands"] For בראותו *birotho* I read בראות *biroth*, with the *Septuagint* and *Syriac*.

CHAPTER XXX

The Jews reproved for their reliance on Egypt, 1–7. *Threatened for their obstinate adherence to this alliance*, 8–17. *Images the most elegant and lofty, by which the intense gloriousness of Messiah's reign at the period when* all Israel *shall be added to the Church is beautifully set forth*, 18–26. *Dreadful fall of Sennacherib's army, an event most manifestly typical of the terrible and sudden overthrow of Antichrist; as, unless this typical reference be admitted, no possible connexion can be imagined between the stupendous events which took place in Hezekiah's reign, and the very remote and inconceivably more glorious displays of Divine vengeance and mercy in the days of the Messiah*, 27–33.

A. M. cir. 3291 B. C. cir. 713 Olymp. XVI. 4 cir. annum NumæPompilii, R. Roman., 3

WO to the rebellious children, saith the LORD, [a]that
take counsel, but not of me; and
that cover with a covering, but
not of my spirit, [b]that they may add sin to
sin:
2 [c]That walk to go down into Egypt, and
[d]have not asked at my mouth; to strengthen
themselves in the strength of Pharaoh, and
to trust in the shadow of Egypt!
3 [e]Therefore shall the strength of Pharaoh
be your shame, and the trust in the shadow
of Egypt *your* confusion.
4 For his princes were at [f]Zoan, and his
ambassadors came to Hanes.
5 [g]They were all ashamed of a people *that*
could not profit them, nor be a help nor profit,
but a shame, and also a reproach.
6 [h]The burden of the beasts of the south:
into the land of trouble and anguish, from
whence *come* the young and old lion, [i]the
viper and fiery flying serpent, they will carry
their riches upon the shoulders of young asses,
and their treasures upon the
bunches of camels, to a people
that shall not profit *them.*
7 [k]For the Egyptians shall
help in vain, and to no purpose: therefore
have I cried [l]concerning this, [m]Their strength
is to sit still.
8 Now go, [n]write it before them in a table,
and note it in a book, that it may be for [o]the
time to come for ever and ever:
9 That [p]this *is* a rebellious people, lying
children, children *that* will not hear the law
of the LORD:
10 [q]Which say to the seers, See not; and to
the prophets, Prophesy not unto us right things,
[r]speak unto us smooth things, prophesy deceits:
11 Get you out of the way, turn aside out
of the path, cause the Holy One of Israel to
cease from before us.
12 Wherefore thus saith the Holy One of
Israel, Because ye despise this word, and
trust in [s]oppression and perverseness, and
stay thereon:

[a]Chap. xxix. 15——[b]Deut. xxix. 19——[c]Chap. xxxi. 1
[d]Num. xxvii. 21; Josh. ix. 14; 1 Kings xxii. 7; Jer. xxi. 2; xlii. 2, 20——[e]Chap. xx. 5; Jer. xxxvii. 5, 7——[f]Chap. xix. 11——[g]Jer. ii. 36——[h]Chap. lvii. 9; Hos. viii. 9; xii. 1——[i]Deut. viii. 15

[k]Jeremiah xxxvii. 7——[l]Or, *to her*——[m]Verse 15; chapter vii. 4——[n]Habakkuk ii. 2——[o]Hebrew, *the latter day*——[p]Deuteronomy xxxii. 20; chapter i. 4; verse 1——[q]Jeremiah xi. 21; Amos ii. 12; vii. 13; Mic. ii. 6——[r]1 Kings xxii. 13; Mic. ii. 11——[s]Or, *fraud*

NOTES ON CHAP. XXX

Verse 1. *And that cover with a covering*—"Who ratify covenants"] Heb. "Who pour out a libation." Sacrifice and libation were ceremonies constantly used, in ancient times by most nations in the ratifying of covenants: a libation therefore is used for a covenant, as in Greek the word σπονδη, for the same reason, stands for both. This seems to be the most easy explication of the Hebrew phrase, and it has the authority of the *Septuagint*, εποιησατε συνθηκας.

Verse 4. *Hanes*] Six MSS. of *Kennicott's*, and perhaps six others, with four of *De Rossi's*, read חנם *chinnam, in vain,* for הנס *Hanes;* and so also the *Septuagint*, who read likewise יגעו *yageu, laboured,* for יגיעו *yaggiu, arrived at.*

Verse 5. *Were—ashamed*] Eight MSS. (one ancient) of *Kennicott's*, and ten of *De Rossi's*, read הביש *hobish*, without א *aleph.* So the *Chaldee* and *Vulgate.*

But a shame—"But proved even a shame"] Four MSS. (three ancient) after כי *ki*, add אם *im, unless*, which seems wanted to complete the phrase in its usual form.

Verse 6. *The burden*] משא *massa* seems here to be taken in its proper sense; the *load*, not the *oracle.* The same subject is continued; and there seems to be no place here for a new title to a distinct prophecy.

Does not *burden of the beasts of the South* in this place relate to the *presents* sent by Hoshea king of Israel to the *South*—to Egypt, which lay *south* of Judea, to engage the Egyptians to succour him against the king of Assyria?

Into the land of trouble and anguish—"Through a land of distress and difficulty"] The same deserts are here spoken of which the Israelites passed through when they came out of Egypt, which Moses describes, Deut. viii. 15, as "that great and terrible wilderness wherein were fiery serpents, and scorpions, and drought; where there was no water." And which was designed to be a kind of barrier between them and Egypt, of which the Lord had said, "Ye shall henceforth return no more that way," Deut. xvii. 16.

Shall not profit them] A MS. adds in the margin the word למו *lamo, them,* which seems to have been lost out of the text: it is authorized by the *Septuagint* and *Vulgate.*

Verse 7. *Their strength* is *to sit still*—"Rahab the Inactive."] The two last words, הם שבת *hem shabeth,* joined into one, make the participle pihel המשבת *hammeshabbeth.* I find the learned Professor Doederlein, in his version of Isaiah, and note on this place, has given the same conjecture; which he speaks of as having been formerly published by him. A concurrence of different persons in the same conjecture adds to it a greater degree of probability.

Verse 8. *For ever and ever*—"For a testimony for ever"] לעד *leed.* So the *Syriac, Chaldee, Vulgate,* and *Septuagint,* in MSS. Pachom. and I. D. II. εις μαρτυριον, which two words have been lost out of the other copies of the *Septuagint.*

Verse 12. *In oppression*—"In obliquity"] בעקש *beakesh,* transposing the two last letters of בעשק *beoshek, in oppression,* which seems not to belong to this place: a very probable conjecture of Houbigant.

A. M. cir. 3291 B. C. cir. 713 Olymp. XVI. 4 cir. annum NumæPompilii, R. Roman., 3

13 Therefore this iniquity shall
be to you [t]as a breach ready to
fall, swelling out in a high wall,
whose breaking [u]cometh suddenly at an instant.
14 And [v]he shall break it as the breaking
of [w]the potters' vessel that is broken in pieces; he shall not spare: so that there shall
not be found in the bursting of it a shred to
take fire from the hearth, or to take water
withal out of the pit.
15 For thus saith the Lord God, the Holy
One of Israel; [x]In returning and rest shall ye
be saved; in quietness and in confidence shall
be your strength: [y]and ye would not.
16 But ye said, No; for we will flee upon
horses; therefore shall ye flee: and, We will
ride upon the swift; therefore shall they that
pursue you be swift.
17 [z]One thousand *shall flee* at the rebuke
of one; at the rebuke of five shall ye flee:
till ye be left as [a]a beacon upon
the top of a mountain, and as an
ensign on a hill.
18 And therefore will the LORD
wait, that he may be gracious unto you, and
therefore will he be exalted, that he may have
mercy upon you: for the LORD *is* a God of
judgment: [b]blessed *are* all they that wait
for him.
19 For the people [c]shall dwell in Zion at
Jerusalem: thou shalt weep no more: he will
be very gracious unto thee at the voice of thy
cry; when he shall hear it, he will answer
thee.
20 And *though* the LORD give you [d]the bread
of adversity, and the water of [e]affliction, yet
shall not thy [f]teachers be removed into a
corner any more, but thine eyes shall see thy
teachers:
21 And thine ears shall hear a word behind
thee, saying, This *is* the way, walk ye in it,

A. M. cir. 3291 B. C. cir. 713 Olymp. XVI. 4 cir. annum NumæPompilii, R. Roman., 3

[t]Psa. lxii. 3——[u]Chap. xxix. 5——[v]Psa. ii. 9; Jer. xix. 11——[w]Heb. *the bottle of potters*——[x]Ver. 7; chap. vii. 4——[y]Matt. xxiii. 37——[z]Rev. xxvi. 8; Deut. xxviii. 25; xxxii. 30; Josh. xxiii. 10

[a]Or, *a tree bereft of branches* or *boughs;* or, *a mast*
[b]Psa. ii. 12; xxxiv. 8; Prov. xvi. 20; Jer. xvii. 7——[c]Ch. lxv. 9——[d]1 Kings xxii. 27; Psa. cxxvii. 2——[e]Or, *oppression*——[f]Psa. lxxiv. 9; Amos viii. 11

Verse 13. *Swelling out in a high wall*—"A swelling in a high wall"] It has been observed before, that the buildings of Asia generally consist of little better than what we call mud walls. "All the houses at Ispahan," says Thevenot, Vol. II., p. 159, "are built of bricks made of clay and straw, and dried in the sun; and covered with a plaster made of a fine white stone. In other places in Persia the houses are built with nothing else but such bricks, made with tempered clay and chopped straw, well mingled together, and dried in the sun, and then used: but the least rain dissolves them." Sir John Chardin's MS. remark on this place of Isaiah is very apposite: Murs en Asie etant faits de terre se fendent ainsi par milieu et de haut en bas. "The walls in Asia being made of earth often cleave from top to bottom." This shows clearly how obvious and expressive the image is. The psalmist has in the same manner made use of it, to express sudden and utter destruction:—

"Ye shall be slain all of you;
Ye shall be like an inclining wall, like a shattered fence." Psa. lxii. 4.

Verse 14. *He shall not spare*—"And spareth it not"] Five MSS. add the conjunction ו *vau* to the negative; ולא *velo.*

Verse 17. *At the rebuke of five shall ye flee*—"At the rebuke of five, ten thousand of you shall flee"] In the second line of this verse a word is manifestly omitted, which should answer to *one thousand* in the first: the *Septuagint* supply πολλοι, רבים *rabbim.* But the true word is רבבה *rebabah,* as I am persuaded any one will be convinced, who will compare the following passages with this place:—

"How should one chase a thousand;
And two put ten thousand (רבבה) to flight?" Deut. xxxii. 30.

"And five of you shall chase a hundred;
And a hundred of you shall chase (רבבה) ten thousand." Lev. xxvi. 8.

Verse 18. *And therefore will he be exalted*—"Even for this shall he expect in silence"] For ירום *yarum, he shall be exalted,* which belongs not to this place, Houbigant reads ידום *yadum, he shall be silent:* and so it seems to be in a MS. Another MS. instead of it reads ישוב *yashub, he shall return.* The mistakes occasioned by the similitude of the letters ד *daleth* and ר *resh* are very frequent, as the reader may have already observed.

Verse 19. *For the people shall dwell in Zion*—"When a holy people shall dwell in Sion"] Λαος ἁγιος, *Septuagint;* עם קדוש *am kadosh.* The word קדוש *kadosh,* lost out of the text, but happily supplied by the *Septuagint,* clears up the sense, otherwise extremely obscure. When the rest of the cities of the land were taken by the king of Assyria, Zion was preserved, and all that were in it.

Thou shalt weep no more—"Thou shalt implore him with weeping"] The negative particle לא *lo* is not acknowledged by the *Septuagint.* It may perhaps have been written by mistake for לו *lo, to him,* of which there are many examples.

Verse 20. Though *the Lord*—"Though JEHOVAH"] For אדני *Adonai,* sixteen MSS. and three editions have יהוה *Yehovah;* many of *De Rossi's* have the same reading; all my own have יהוה *Yehovah.*

Verse 21. *When ye turn to the right hand,*

A. M. cir. 3291
B. C. cir. 713
Olymp. XVI. 4
cir. annum
NumæPompilii,
R. Roman., 3

when ye [g]turn to the right hand,
and when ye turn to the left.
22 [h]Ye shall defile also the
covering of [i]thy graven images
of silver, and the ornament of thy molten
images of gold: thou shalt [k]cast them away
as a menstruous cloth; [l]thou shalt say unto it,
Get thee hence.
23 [m]Then shall he give the rain of thy seed,
that thou shalt sow the ground withal; and
bread of the increase of the earth, and it shall
be fat and plenteous: in that day shall thy
cattle feed in large pastures.
24 The oxen likewise and the young asses
that ear the ground shall eat [n]clean [o]pro-
vender, which hath been winnowed with the
shovel and with the fan.
25 And there shall be [p]upon every high
mountain, and upon every [q]high hill, rivers
and streams of waters in the
day of the great slaughter, when
the towers fall.
26 Moreover [r]the light of the
moon shall be as the light of the sun, and the
light of the sun shall be sevenfold, as the
light of seven days, in the day that the LORD
bindeth up the breach of his people, and
healeth the stroke of their wound.
27 Behold, the name of the LORD cometh
from far, burning *with* his anger, [s]and the
burden *thereof is* [t]heavy: his lips are full of
indignation, and his tongue as a devouring
fire:
28 And [u]his breath, as an overflowing stream,
[v]shall reach to the midst of the neck, to sift
the nations with the sieve of vanity: and *there
shall be* [w]a bridle in the jaws of the people,
causing *them* to err.

[g]Josh. i. 7——[h]2 Chron. xxxi. 1; chap. ii. 20; xxxi. 7——[i]Heb. *the graven images of thy silver*——[k]Heb. *scatter*——[l]Hos. xiv. 8——[m]Matt. vi. 33; 1 Tim. iv. 8——[n]Or, *savoury*——[o]Heb. *leavened*

[p]Chap. ii. 14, 15; xliv. 3——[q]Heb. *lifted up*——[r]Ch. lx. 19, 20——[s]Or, *and the grievousness of flame*——[t]Heb. *heaviness*——[u]Chap. xi. 4; 2 Thess. ii. 8——[v]Chap. viii. 8——[w]Chap. xxxvii. 29

and when ye turn to the left—"Turn not aside, to the right or to the left."] The *Syriac*, *Chaldee*, and *Vulgate*, translate as if, instead of כי—וכי *ki—vechi*, they read לא—ולא *lo—velo*.

Verse 22. *Ye shall defile*—"Ye shall treat as defiled"] The very prohibition of Moses, Deut. vii. 25, only thrown out of the prose into the poetical form: "The graven images of their gods ye shall burn with fire: thou shalt not desire the silver or the gold that is on them; nor take it unto thee, lest thou be snared therein; for it is an abomination to JEHOVAH thy God."

Verse 25. *When the towers fall*—"When the mighty fall."] מגדלים *migdalim*, *μεγαλους*, *Sym.; μεγαλυνομενους*, *Aquila;* רברבין *rabrebin*, *Chald.;* all signifying *mighty ones*.

Verse 26. *Shall be sevenfold*] The text adds כאור שבעת הימים *keor shibath haiyamayim*, "as the light of seven days," a manifest gloss, taken in from the margin; it is not in most of the copies of the *Septuagint*. It interrupts the rhythmical construction, and obscures the sense by a false, or at least an unnecessary, interpretation.

By *moon*, *sun*, *light*, are to be understood the abundance of spiritual and temporal felicity, with which God should bless them in the days of the Messiah, which should be sevenfold, i. e., vastly exceed all that they had ever before possessed.

Verse 27. *And the burden* thereof is *heavy*—"And the flame raged violently"] משאה *massaah;* this word seems to be rightly rendered in our translation, *the flame*, Judg. xx. 38, 40, &c.; a sign of *fire*, Jer. vi. 1; called properly משאת *masseeth*, *an elevation*, from its tending upwards.

Verse 28. *To sift the nations with a sieve of vanity*—"To toss the nations with the van of perdition"] The word להנפה *lahanaphah* is in its form very irregular. *Kimchi* says it is for להניף *lehaniph*. *Houbigant* supposes it to be a mistake, and shows the cause of it; the joining it to the ה *he*, which should begin the following word. The true reading is להניף הגוים *lehaniph haggoyim*, "to sift the nations."

The *Vulgate* seems to be the only one of the ancient interpreters who has explained rightly the sense; but he has dropped the image: ad perdendas gentes in nihilum, "to reduce the nations to nothing." *Kimchi's* explanation is to the following effect: "נפה *naphah* is a van with which they winnow corn; and its use is to cleanse the corn from the chaff and straw: but the van with which God will winnow the nations will be the van of emptiness or perdition; for nothing useful shall remain behind, but all shall come to nothing, and perish. In like manner, a bridle is designed to guide the horse in the right way; but the bridle which God will put in the jaws of the people shall not direct them aright, but shall make them err, and lead them into destruction." This latter image the prophet has applied to the same subject afterwards, ch. xxxvii. 29:—

"I will put my bridle in thy jaws,
And turn thee back by the way in which thou camest."

And as for the former it is to be observed, that the van of the ancients was a large instrument, somewhat like a shovel, with a long handle, with which they tossed the corn mixed with the chaff and chopped straw into the air, that the wind might separate them. See *Hammond* on Matt. iii. 12.

There shall be *a bridle in the jaws*] A metaphor taken from a headstrong, unruly horse: the bridle checks, restrains, and directs him.

A. M. cir. 3291 B. C. cir. 713 Olymp. XVI. 4 cir. annum NumæPompilii, R. Roman., 3
29 Ye shall have a song, as
in the night [x]*when* a holy solemnity is kept; and gladness of
heart, as when one goeth with
a pipe to come into the [y]mountain of the
LORD, to the [z]mighty One of Israel.
30 [a]And the LORD shall cause [b]his glorious
voice to be heard, and shall show the lighting
down of his arm, with the indignation of *his*
anger, and *with* the flame of a devouring fire,
with scattering, and tempest, [c]and hailstones.
31 For [d]through the voice of the LORD shall
the Assyrian be beaten down, A. M. cir. 3291 B. C. cir. 713 Olymp. XVI. 4
[e]*which* smote with a rod.
32 And [f]*in* every place where cir. annum NumæPompilii, R. Roman., 3
the grounded staff shall pass,
which the LORD shall [g]lay upon him, *it* shall
be with tabrets and harps: and in battles of
[h]shaking will he fight [i]with it.
33 [k]For Tophet *is* ordained [l]of old; yea,
for the king it is prepared; he hath made *it*
deep *and* large; the pile thereof *is* fire and
much wood: the breath of the LORD, like a
stream of brimstone, doth kindle it.

---

[x]Psa. xlii. 4——[y]Chap. ii. 3——[z]Heb. *Rock;* Deut. xxxii. 4——[a]Chap. xxix. 6——[b]Heb. *the glory of his voice* [c]Chap. xxviii. 2; xxxii. 19——[d]Chap. xxxvii. 36 [e]Chap. x. 5, 24

[f]Heb. *every passing of the rod founded*——[g]Heb. *cause to rest upon him*——[h]Chap. xi. 15; xix. 16——[i]Or, *against them*——[k]Jeremiah vii. 31; xix. 6, &c.——[l]Heb. *from yesterday*

What the true God does in restraining sinners, has been also attributed to the false gods of the heathen. Thus *Æschylus*, prom. Vinct. 691:—

αλλ' επηναγκαζε νιν
Διος χαλινος προς βιαν πρασσειν ταδε.

"But the bridle of Jupiter violently constrained him to do these things."

Verse 30. *The Lord shall cause his glorious voice to be heard*] *Kimchi* understands this of the great destruction of the Assyrian host by the angel of the Lord. Instead of בזעף אץ *bezaaph ats*, "with swift anger," five of Dr. *Kennicott's* MSS. and one of my own, read בזעם אף *bezaam aph*, "with detestation indignant." For אץ *ats*, "swift," which is the common reading, forty-two of *Kennicott's*, forty-three of *De Rossi's*, and two of my own, have אף *aph*, "wrath or fury." The former reading, אץ *ats*, is not found in any Bible previously to that of *Van der Hooght*, in 1705; and there it seems to be a typographical mistake.

Verse 31. Which *smote with a rod*—"He that was ready to smite with his staff"] "Post אשור *ashshur*, forte excidit אשר *asher*."—SECKER. After אשור *ashshur*, probably אשר *asher*, "which," has been omitted.

Verse 32. *The grounded staff*—"The rod of his correction"] For מוסדה *musadah*, the *grounded* staff, of which no one yet has been able to make any tolerable sense, Le Clerc conjectured מוסרה *musarah, of correction;* (see Prov. xxii. 15;) and so it is in two MSS., (one of them ancient,) and seems to be so in the Bodleian MS. The *Syriac* has רשועבדה *deshuebedah, virgo domans, vel subjectionis,*—"the taming rod, or rod of subjection."

With tabrets and harps] With every demonstration of joy and thanksgiving for the destruction of the enemy in so wonderful a manner: with hymns of praise, accompanied with musical instruments. See ver. 29.

With it—"Against them."] For בה *bah, against her*, fifty-two MSS. and five editions read בם *bam, against them.*

Verse 33. *For Tophet* is *ordained*] Tophet is a valley very near to Jerusalem, to the south-east, called also the valley of Hinnom or Gehenna; where the Canaanites, and afterwards the Israelites, sacrificed their children, by making them pass through the fire, that is, by burning them in the fire, to Molech, as some suppose. It is therefore used for a place of punishment by fire; and by our blessed Saviour in the Gospel for hell-fire, as the Jews themselves had applied it. See Chald. on Isa. xxxiii. 14, where מוקדי עלם *mokedey olam* is rendered "the Gehenna of everlasting fire." Here the place where the Assyrian army was destroyed is called Tophet by a metonymy; for the Assyrian army was destroyed probably at a greater distance from Jerusalem, and quite on the opposite side of it: for Nob is mentioned as the last station, from which the king of Assyria should threaten Jerusalem, chap. x. 32, where the prophet seems to have given a very exact chorographical description of his march in order to attack the city; which however he never reached.—L.

CHAPTER XXXI

The Jews again reproved for their confidence in Egypt, finely contrasted with their neglect of the power and protection of God, 1–3. *Deliverance and protection are, notwithstanding, promised, expressed by two similes; the first remarkably lofty and poetical, the latter singularly beautiful and tender,* 4, 5. *Exhortation to repentance, joined with the prediction of a more reformed period,* 6, 7. *This chapter concludes like the preceding, with a prophecy of the fall of Sennacherib,* 8, 9.

A. M. cir. 3291 B. C. cir. 713 Olymp. XVI. 4 cir. annum NumæPompilii, R. Roman., 3

WO to them [a]that go down to
Egypt for help; and [b]stay
on horses, and trust in chariots,
because *they are* many; and in
horsemen, because they are very strong; but
they look not unto the Holy One of Israel,
[c]neither seek the LORD!
2 Yet he also *is* wise, and will bring evil,
and [d]will not [e]call back his words: but will
arise against the house of the evil-doers, and
against the help of them that work iniquity.
3 Now the Egyptians *are* [f]men, and not
God; and their horses flesh, and not spirit.
When the LORD shall stretch out his hand,
both he that helpeth shall fall,
and he that is holpen shall fall
down, and they all shall fail
together.
4 For thus hath the LORD spoken unto me,
[g]Like as the lion, and the young lion roaring
on his prey, when a multitude of shepherds
is called forth against him, *he* will not be
afraid of their voice, nor abase himself for the
[h]noise of them: [i]so shall the LORD of hosts
come down to fight for Mount Zion, and for
the hill thereof.
5 [k]As birds flying, so will the LORD of hosts
defend Jerusalem; defending [l]also he will

A. M. cir. 3291 B. C. cir. 713 Olymp. XVI. 4 cir. annum NumæPompilii, R. Roman., 3

[a]Chap. xxx. 2; xxxvi. 6; Ezek. xvii. 15——[b]Psa. xx. 7; chap. xxxvi. 9——[c]Dan. ix. 13; Hos. vii. 7——[d]Num. xxiii. 19——[e]Heb. *remove*

[f]Psa. cxlvi. 3, 5——[g]Hos. xi. 10; Amos iii. 8——[h]Or, *multitude*——[i]Chap. xlii. 13——[k]Deut. xxxii. 11; Psa. xci. 4——[l]Psa. xxxvii. 40

NOTES ON CHAP. XXXI

Verse 1. *Wo to them that go down to Egypt*] This is a reproof to the Israelites for forming an alliance with the Egyptians, and not trusting in the Lord.

And stay on horses—"Who trust in horses"] For ועל *veal, and upon*, first twenty MSS. of *Kennicott's*, thirty of *De Rossi's*, one of my own, and the *Septuagint*, *Arabic*, and *Vulgate*, read על *al, upon*, without the conjunction, which disturbs the sense.

Verse 2. *His words*—"His word"] דברו *debaro*, *singular*, without י *yod*, two MSS. of Dr. *Kennicott's*, the *Septuagint*, and *Targ. Hieros.* דרכיו *derachaiv*, *his ways*, is found in one MS.

Verse 3. *He that helpeth* (the Egyptians) *shall fall, and he that is holpen* (the Israelites) *shall fall down—together.*

Verse 4. *Like as the lion*] This comparison is exactly in the spirit and manner, and very nearly approaching to the expression, of *Homer*.

Βη ρ' ιμεν, ὡστε λεων ορεσιτροφος, ὁστ' επιδευης
Δηρον εῃ κρειων, κελεται δε ἑ θυμος αγηνωρ,
Μηλων πειρησοντα, και ες πυκινον δομον ελθειν·
Ειπερ γαρ χ' εὑρῃσι παρ' αυτοφι βωτορας ανδρας
Συν κυσι και δουρεσσι φυλασσοντας περι μηλα,
Ου ρα τ' απειρητος μεμονε σταθμοιο διεσθαι.
Αλλ' ὁγ' αῤ η ἡρπαξε μεταλμενος, ηε και αυτος
Εβλητ' εν πρωτοισι θοης απο χειρος ακοντι.

Iliad xii. 299.

As the bold lion, mountain-bred, now long
Famished, with courage and with hunger stung
Attempts the thronged fold: him nought appals,
Though dogs and armed shepherds stand in guard
Collected; he nathless undaunted springs
O'er the high fence, and rends the trembling prey;
Or, rushing onward, in his breast receives
The well-aimed spear.

Of metaphors, allegories, and comparisons of the Hebrew poets, in which the Divine nature and attributes are represented under images taken from brutes and other low objects; of their effect, their sublimity, and the causes of it; see *De Sac. Poës. Heb.*, Prælect. xvi. sub. fin.

Verse 5. *Passing over*—"Leaping forward"] The generality of interpreters observe in this place an allusion to the deliverance which God vouchsafed to his people when he destroyed the first-born of the Egyptians, and exempted those of the Israelites sojourning among them by a peculiar interposition. The same word is made use of here which is used upon that occasion, and which gave the name to the feast which was instituted in commemoration of that deliverance, פסח *pesach.* But the difficulty is to reconcile the commonly received meaning of that word with the circumstances of the similitude here used to illustrate the deliverance represented as parallel to the deliverance in Egypt.

"As the mother birds hovering over their young,
So shall JEHOVAH God of hosts protect Jerusalem;
Protecting and delivering, *passing over*, and rescuing her."

This difficulty is, I think, well solved by Vitringa, whose remark is the more worthy of observation, as it leads to the true meaning of an important word, which hitherto seems greatly to have been misunderstood, though Vitringa himself, as it appears to me, has not exactly enough defined the precise meaning of it. He says, "פסח *pasach* signifies *to cover, to protect by covering; σκεπασω ὑμας, Septuagint.* JEHOVAH *obteget ostium;* 'The Lord will cover or protect the door:'" whereas it means that particular action or motion by which God at that time placed himself in such a situation as to protect the house of the Israelite against the destroying angel; to spring forward, to throw one's self in the way, in order to cover and protect. *Cocceius* comes nearer to the true meaning than Vitringa, by rendering it *gradum facere*, to march, to step forward; *Lexicon* in voc. The common meaning of the word פסח *pasach* upon other occasions is *to halt, to be lame, to leap*, as in a rude manner of dancing, (as the prophets of Baal did, 1 Kings xviii. 26,) all which agrees very well together; for the motion of a lame person is a perpetual springing forward,

A. M. cir. 3291
B. C. cir. 713
Olymp. XVI. 4
cir. annum
NumæPompilii,
R. Roman., 3

deliver *it; and* passing over he
will preserve *it.*
6 Turn ye unto *him from*
whom the children of Israel have
[m]deeply revolted.
7 For in that day every man shall [n]cast away
his idols of silver, and [o]his idols of gold,
which your own hands have made unto you
for [p]a sin.
8 Then shall the Assyrian [q]fall with the
sword, not of a mighty man;
and the sword, not of a mean
man, shall devour him: but he
shall flee [r]from the sword, and
his young men shall be [s]discomfited.[t]
9 And [u]he [v]shall pass over to [w]his
strong hold for fear, and his princes shall
be afraid of the ensign, saith the LORD,
whose fire *is* in Zion, and his furnace in
Jerusalem.

[m]Hos. ix. 9——[n]Chap. ii. 20; xxx. 22——[o]Heb. *the idols of his gold*——[p]1 Kings xii. 30——[q]See 2 Kings xix. 35, 36; ch. xxxvii. 36——[r]Or, *for fear of the sword*

[s]Or, *tributary*——[t]Heb. *for melting* or *tribute*——[u]Ch. xxxvii. 37; Deut. xxii. 25, in the margin——[v]Heb. *his rock shall pass away for fear*——[w]Or, *his strength*

by throwing himself from the weaker upon the stronger leg. The common notion of God's passage over the houses of the Israelites is, that in going through the land of Egypt to smite the first-born, seeing the blood on the door of the houses of the Israelites, he passed over, or skipped, those houses, and forbore to smite them. But that this is not the true notion of the thing, will be plain from considering the words of the sacred historian, where he describes very explicitly the action: "For JEHOVAH will pass through to smite the Egyptians; and when he seeth the blood on the lintels and on the two side posts, JEHOVAH will spring forward over (or before) the door, ופסח יהוה על הפתח *upasach Yehovah al happethach*, and will not suffer the destroyer to come into your houses to smite *you*," Exod. xii. 23. Here are manifestly two distinct agents, with which the notion of *passing over* is not consistent, for that supposes but one agent. The two agents are the destroying angel passing through to smite every house, and JEHOVAH the Protector keeping pace with him; and who, seeing the door of the Israelite marked with the blood, the token prescribed, *leaps forward, throws himself with a sudden motion in the way*, opposes the destroying angel, and *covers* and *protects* that house against the destroying angel, nor suffers him to smite it. In this way of considering the action, the beautiful similitude of the bird protecting her young answers exactly to the application by the allusion to the deliverance in Egypt. As the mother bird spreads her wings to cover her young, throws herself before them, and opposes the rapacious bird that assaults them, so shall JEHOVAH protect, as with a shield, Jerusalem from the enemy, protecting and delivering, *springing forward* and rescuing her; ὑπερβαινων, as the three other Greek interpreters, *Aquila, Symmachus*, and *Theodotion*, render it. The *Septuagint*, περιποιησεται· instead of which MS. *Pachom.* has περιβησεται, circumeundo proteget, "in going about he shall protect," which I think is the true reading.—*Homer*, Il. viii. 329, expresses the very same image by this word:—

Αιας δ' ουκ αμελησε κασιγνητοιο πεσοντος,
Αλλα θεων περιβη, και οἱ σακος αμφεκαλυψε:

"——But Ajax his broad shield displayed,
And screened his brother with a mighty shade."

——Ὁς Χρυσην αμφιβεβηκας. Il. i. 37.

Which the scholiast explains by περιβεβηκας, ὑπερμαχεις, i. e., "Thou who *strictly guardest* Chryses."—L. On this verse *Kimchi* says, "The angel of the Lord which destroyed the Assyrians is compared to a *lion*, ver. 4, for his *strength;* and here (ver. 5) to *flying birds*, for his *swiftness.*

Verse 6. *Have deeply revolted*—"Have so deeply engaged in revolt."] All the ancient Versions read תעמיקו *taamiku*, in the second person, instead of העמיקו *heemiku, they have deeply revolted*, &c.

Verse 7. *Which your own hands have made unto you for a sin*—"The sin, which their own hands have made."] The construction of the word חטא *chet, sin*, in this place is not easy. The *Septuagint* have omitted it: MSS. *Pachom.* and I. D. II. and *Cod. Marchal.* in margine, supply the omission by the word ἁμαρτιαν, *sin*, or ἁμαρτημα, said to be from Aquila's Version, which I have followed. The learned Professor *Schroeder*, Institut. Ling. Heb. p. 298, makes it to be *in regimine* with ידיכם *yedeychem*, as an epithet, your *sinful hands.* The *Septuagint* render the pronoun in the third person, αἱ χειρες αυτων, *their hands;* and an ancient MS. has, agreeable to that rendering, להם *lahem, to them*, for לכם *lachem, to you;* which word they have likewise omitted, as not necessary to complete the sense.

Verse 8. *Then shall the Assyrian fall, &c.*] Because he was to be discomfited by the angel of the Lord, destroying in his camp, in one night, upwards of *one hundred and eighty thousand* men; and Sennacherib himself fell by the hands of the princes, his own sons. Not *mighty men*, for they were not soldiers; not *mean men*, for they were *princes.*

CHAPTER XXXII

Prophecy of great prosperity under Hezekiah; but, in its highest sense, applicable to Christ, 1–8. *Description of impending calamities,* 9–14. *Rejection of the Jews, and calling of the Gentiles,* 15. *The future prosperity of the Church,* 16–20.

A. M. cir. 3291 B. C. cir. 713 Olymp. XVI. 4 cir. annum NumæPompilii, R. Roman., 3

BEHOLD, a [a]king shall reign
in righteousness, and princes
shall rule in judgment.
2 And a man shall be as a hid-
ing-place from the wind, and [b]a covert from
the tempest; as rivers of water in a dry place,
as the shadow of a [c]great rock in a weary land.
3 And [d]the eyes of them that see shall not be
dim, and the ears of them that hear shall
hearken.
4 The heart also of the [e]rash shall understand knowledge, and the tongue of the stam-
merers shall be ready to speak [f]plainly.

A. M. cir. 3291 B. C. cir. 713 Olymp. XVI. 4 cir. annum NumæPompilii, R. Roman., 3

5 The vile person shall be no
more called liberal, nor the churl
said *to be* bountiful.
6 For the vile person will
speak villany, and his heart will work iniquity,
to practise hypocrisy, and to utter error
against the LORD, to make empty the soul of
the hungry, and he will cause the drink of
the thirsty to fail.
7 The instruments also of the churl *are* evil:
he deviseth wicked devices to destroy the poor
with lying words, even [g]when the needy
speaketh right.

---

[a]Psa. xlv. 1, &c.; Jer. xxiii. 5; Hos. iii. 5; Zech. ix. 9 [b]Chap. iv. 6; xxv. 4——[c]Heb. *heavy*——[d]Chap. xxix. 18; xxxv. 5, 6——[e]Heb. *hasty*——[f]Or, *elegantly* [g]Or, *when he speaketh* against *the poor* in *judgment*

NOTES ON CHAP. XXXII

Verse 1. *Behold, a king shall reign in righteousness*] If King Hezekiah were a type of Christ, then this prophecy may refer to his time; but otherwise it seems to have Hezekiah primarily in view. It is evident, however, that in the fullest sense these words cannot be applied to any man; GOD alone can do all that is promised here.

And princes] ושרים *ve-sarim*, without ל *lamed, to;* so the ancient Versions. An ancient MS. has ושריו *vesaraiv, and* his *princes.*

Verse 2. *As the shadow of a great rock*] The shadow of a great projecting rock is the most refreshing that is possible in a hot country, not only as most perfectly excluding the rays of the sun, but also as having in itself a natural coolness, which it reflects and communicates to every thing about it.

Speluncæque tegant, et saxea procubet umbra.
VIRG. *Georg.* iii. 145.

"Let the cool cave and shady rock protect them."

Επει κεφαλην και γουνατα Σειριος αζει,
Αυαλεος δε τε χρως απο καυματος· αλλα τοτ' ηδη
Ειη πετραιη τε σκιη, και Βιβλινος οινος.
HESIOD. ii. 206.

"When Sirius rages, and thine aching head,
Parched skin, and feeble knees refreshment need;
Then to the rock's projected shade retire,
With Biblin wine recruit thy wasted powers."

Verse 3. *And the eyes of them that see shall not be dim*—"And him the eyes of those that see shall regard"] For ולא *velo, and not, Le Clerc* reads ולו *velo, and to him,* of which mistake the Masoretes acknowledge there are *fifteen* instances; and many more are reckoned by others. The removal of the *negative* restores to the verb its true and usual sense.

Verse 5. *The vile person shall no more be called liberal*] The different epithets here employed require minute explanation.

The vile person—נבל *nabal,* the pampered, fattened, brainless fellow, who eats to live, and lives to eat; who will scarcely part with any thing, and that which he does give he gives with an evil eye and a grudging heart.

Liberal—נדיב *nadib;* the generous, openhearted, princely man, who writes on all his possessions, *For myself and mankind,* and lives only to *get* and to *do* good.

The churl—כילי *kilai,* the avaricious man; he who starves himself amidst his plenty, and will not take the necessaries of life for fear of lessening his stock.

Thus he differs from נבל *nabal,* who feeds himself to the full, and regards no one else; like the rich man in the Gospel. The avaricious man is called כילי *kilai,* from כי *ki, for,* and לי *li, myself;* or contracted from כל *col, all,* and לי *li, to myself:* all is mine; all I have is *my own;* and all I can get is *for myself:* and yet this man enjoys nothing; he withholds

From back and belly too their proper fare:—
O cursed lust of gold, when for thy sake
The wretch throws up his interest in both worlds,
First *starved* in *this,* then *damned* in *that* to come!

Bountiful—שוע *shoa,* he who is abundantly rich; who *rejoices* in his plenty, and deals out to the distressed with a liberal hand.

Verse 6. *The vile person will speak villany*—"The fool will still utter folly"] A sort of proverbial saying, which *Euripides* (Bacchæ, 369) has expressed in the very same manner and words: *Μωρα γαρ μωρος λεγει·* "The fool speaks folly." Of this kind of simple and unadorned proverb or parable, see *De S. Poës,* Hebr. Prælect. xxiv.

Against the Lord—"Against JEHOVAH"] For אל *El,* two MSS. read על *al,* more properly; but both are of nearly the same meaning.

Verse 7. *The instruments also of the churl are evil*—"As for the niggard, his instruments are evil"] His machinations, his designs. The paronomasia, which the prophet frequently deals in, suggested this expression וכלי כליו *vechelai kelaiv.* The first word is expressed with some variety in the MSS. Seven MSS. read וכילי *vekili,* one וכל *vechol,* another וכולי *vecoli.*

To destroy the poor with lying words—"To

A. M. cir. 3291 B. C. cir. 713 Olymp. XVI. 4 cir. annum NumæPompilii, R. Roman., 3

8 But the liberal deviseth liberal things; and by liberal things shall he [h]stand.

9 Rise up, ye women [i]that are at ease; hear my voice, ye careless daughters; give ear unto my speech.

10 [k]Many days and years shall ye be troubled, ye careless women: for the vintage shall fail, the gathering shall not come.

11 Tremble, ye women that are at ease; be troubled, ye careless ones; strip you, and make you bare, and gird *sackcloth* upon *your* loins.

12 They shall lament for the teats, for [l]the pleasant fields, for the fruitful vine.

13 [m]Upon the land of my people shall come up thorns *and* briers; [n]yea, upon all the houses of joy *in* [o]the joyous city:

14 [p]Because the palaces shall be forsaken; the multitude of the city shall be left; the [q]forts and towers shall be for dens for ever, a joy of wild asses, a pasture of flocks;

15 Until [r]the spirit be poured upon us from on high, and [s]the wilderness be a fruitful field, and the fruitful field be counted for a forest.

16 Then judgment shall dwell in the wilderness, and righteousness remain in the fruitful field.

17 [t]And the work of righteousness shall be peace; and the effect of righteousness quietness and assurance for ever.

18 And my people shall dwell in a peaceable habitation, and in sure dwellings, and in quiet resting places;

---

[h]Or, *be established*——[i]Amos vi. 1——[k]Heb. *Days above a year*——[l]Heb. *the fields of desire*——[m]Chap. xxxiv. 13; Hos. ix. 6

[n]Or, *burning upon, &c.*——[o]Chap. xxii. 22——[p]Chap. xxvii. 10——[q]Or, *clifts and watch-towers*——[r]Psa. civ. 30; Joel ii. 28——[s]Ch. xxix. 17; xxxv. 2——[t]James iii. 18

---

defeat the assertions of the poor in judgment"] A word seems to have been lost here, and two others to have suffered a small alteration, which has made the sentence very obscure. The *Septuagint* have happily retained the rendering of the lost word, and restored the sentence in all its parts: Και διασκεδασαι λογους ταπεινων εν κρισει· ולהפר דברי אביון במשפט *ulehapher dibrey ebyon bemishpat*, "And disperse the words of the poor in judgment." They frequently render the verb הפר *haphar* by διασκεδασαι, A MS. reads ולדבר *uledabber*, which gives authority for the preposition ל *lamed, to*, necessary to the sense; and the *Septuagint*, *Syriac*, and *Chaldee* read במשפט *bemishpat*, IN *judgment*.

Verse 8. *Liberal things*—"Generous purposes"] "Of the four sorts of persons mentioned ver. 5, three are described, ver. 6, 7, and 8, but not the fourth."—SECKER. Perhaps for והוא *vehu, and he*, we ought to read וישוע *veshoa, the bountiful*.

Verse 9. *Rise up, ye women*—"ye provinces." *Ye careless daughters*—"ye cities."—*Targum*.

From this verse to the end of the *fourteenth*, the desolation of Judea by the Chaldeans appears to be foretold.

Verse 11. *Gird* sackcloth] שק *sak, sackcloth*, a word necessary to the sense, is here lost, but preserved by the *Septuagint*, MSS. *Alex.* and *Pachom.*, and I. D. II., and edit. *Ald.* and *Comp.*, and the *Arabic* and *Syriac*.

Tremble—be troubled—strip you] פשטה *peshotah*, רגזה *regazah*, &c. These are infinitives, with a paragogic ה *he*, according to *Schultens*, Institut. Ling. Hebr. p. 453, and are to be taken in an imperative sense.

Verse 12. *They shall lament—for the pleasant fields*—"Mourn ye for the pleasant field"] The *Septuagint*, *Syriac*, and *Vulgate* read ספדו *siphdu, mourn ye*, imperative; twelve MSS., (five ancient,) two editions, the *Septuagint*, *Aquila*, *Symmachus*, *Theodotion*, *Syriac*, and *Vulgate*, all read שדה *sadeh, a field;* not שדי *shedey, breasts*.

Verse 13. *Shall come up thorns* and *briers*—"The thorn and the brier shall come up"] All the ancient Versions read ושמיר *veshamir*, with the conjunction. And an ancient MS. has תעלה בו *taaleh bo*, "shall come up in it," which seems to be right; or rather בה *bah:* and there is a rasure in the place of בו *bo* in another ancient MS.

Yea, upon all the houses of joy] For כי *ki*, the ancient Versions, except the *Vulgate*, seem to have read ו *ve*. כי *ki* may perhaps be a mistake for בו *bo*, or בה *bah, in it*, above mentioned. It is not necessary in this place.

The description of impending distress which begins at ver. 13 belongs to other times than that of Sennacherib's invasion, from which they were so soon delivered. It must at least extend to the ruin of the country and city by the Chaldeans. And the promise of blessings which follows was not fulfilled under the Mosaic dispensation; they belong to the KINGDOM of Messiah. Compare ver. 15 with chap. xxix. 17, and see the note there.

Verse 14. *The palaces shall be forsaken*] The house of the sanctuary (the temple) shall be destroyed.—*Targum*.

The forts—"Ophel"] It was a part of Mount Zion, rising higher than the rest, at the eastern extremity, near to the temple, a little to the south of it; called by Micah, chap. iv. 8, "Ophel of the daughter of Zion." It was naturally strong by its situation; and had a wall of its own, by which it was separated from the rest of Zion.

Verse 15. *And the fruitful field*] והכרמל *vehaccarmel*. So *fifteen* MSS., *six* ancient, and *two* editions; which seems to make the noun an appellative.

Verse 17. *The work of righteousness*] Righteousness works and produces peace.

The effect of righteousness] עבדת *abodath, the*

A. M. cir. 3291
B. C. cir. 713
Olymp. XVI. 4
cir. annum
NumæPompilii,
R. Roman., 3

19 [u]When it shall hail, coming down [v]on the forest; [w]and the city shall be low in a low place.

20 Blessed *are* ye that sow beside all waters, that send forth *thither* the feet of [x]the ox and the ass.

A. M. cir. 3291
B. C. cir. 713
Olymp. XVI. 4
cir. annum
NumæPompilii,
R. Roman., 3

[u]Chap. xxx. 30——[v]Zech. xi. 2——[w]Or, *and the city shall be utterly abased*——[x]Ch. xxx. 24

culture. Righteousness, *cultivated* by peace, produces tranquillity of mind and permanent security. Reader, hast thou the principle? If so, dost thou cultivate it? If thou dost, thou hast peace of conscience, joy in the Holy Ghost, and a sure and certain hope of everlasting life.

Verse 19. *The city shall be low in a low place.*—"The city shall be laid level with the plain."] For ובשפלה *ubashephelah*, the *Syriac* reads וכשפלה *ukeshephelah*. *The city*—probably Nineveh or Babylon: but this verse is very obscure. Saltus; Assyriorum regnum: civitas; magnifica Assyriorum castra. Ephrem Syr. *in loc.* For וברד *ubarad*, a MS. has וירד *vaiyered;* and so conjectured Abp. *Secker*, referring to Zech. xi. 2.

Verse 20. *That sow beside all waters*—"Who sow your seed in every well-watered place"] Sir John Chardin's note on this place is:—"This exactly answers the manner of planting rice; for they sow it upon the water, and before sowing, while the earth is covered with water, they cause the ground to be trodden by oxen, horses, and asses, who go mid-leg deep; and this is the way of preparing the ground for sowing. As they sow the rice on the water, they transplant it in the water." *Harmer's* Observ. vol. i. p. 280. "Rice is the food of two-thirds of mankind." Dr. *Arbuthnot.* "It is cultivated in most of the eastern countries." *Miller.* "It is good for all, and at all times." Sir *J. Chardin*, ib. "Le ris, qui est leur principal aliment et leur froment (i. e., des Siamois,) n'est jamais assez arrosé; il croit au milieu de l'eau, et les campagnes ou on le cultive ressemblent plutôt à de marêts que non pas à des terres qu'on laboure avec la charue. Le ris a bien cette force, que quoy qu'il y ait six ou sept pieds d'eau sur lui, il pousse toujours sa tige au dessus; et le tuyau qui le porte s'eleve et croit à proportion de la hauteur de l'eau qui noye son champ. Voyage de l'Evêque de *Beryte*, p. 144. Paris, 1666.—L. "*Rice*, which is the principal grain and aliment of the *Siamese*, can never be too much watered. It grows in the water, and the fields where it is sown resemble *marshes* rather than fields cultivated by ploughing. Rice has that property that although it be covered with water six or seven feet deep, yet it raises its stalk above it; and this grows long in proportion to the depth of the water by which the field is inundated."

CHAPTER XXXIII

This chapter contains the sequel of the prophecy respecting Sennacherib. The prophet addresses himself to the Assyrian monarch, 1–4. *The mercy and power of God acknowledged by the Jews,* 5, 6. *Distress and despair of the Jews at the approach of Sennacherib,* 7–9. *Gracious promise of deliverance,* 10–13. *Dreadful apprehensions of the wicked, and security of the righteous,* 14–17. *The security of the Jews under the reign of Hezekiah, and the wretched condition of Sennacherib and his army,* 18–24.

A. M. cir. 3291
B. C. cir. 713
Olymp. XVI. 4
cir. annum
NumæPompilii,
R. Roman., 3

WO to thee [a]that spoilest, and thou *wast* not spoiled; and dealest treacherously, and they dealt not treacherously with thee! [b]when thou shalt cease to spoil, thou shalt be spoiled; *and* when thou shalt make an end to deal treacherously, they

A. M. cir. 3291
B. C. cir. 713
Olymp. XVI. 4
cir. annum
NumæPompilii,
R. Roman., 3

[a]Chap. xxi. 2; Hab. ii. 8

[b]Rev. xiii. 10

The plan of the prophecy continued in this chapter, and which is manifestly distinct from the foregoing, is peculiarly elegant. To set it in a proper light, it will be necessary to mark the transitions from one part of it to another.

In ver. 1, the prophet addresses himself to Sennacherib, briefly, but strongly and elegantly, expressing the injustice of his ambitious designs, and the sudden disappointments of them.

In ver. 2, the Jews are introduced offering up their earnest supplications to God in their present distressful condition; with expressions of their trust and confidence in his protection.

In verses 3 and 4 the prophet in the name of God, or rather God himself, is introduced addressing himself to Sennacherib, and threatening him that, notwithstanding the terror which he had occasioned in the invaded countries, yet he should fall, and become an easy prey to those whom he had intended to subdue.

In verses 5 and 6, a chorus of Jews is introduced, acknowledging the mercy and power of God, who had undertaken to protect them; extolling it with direct opposition to the boasted power of their enemies, and celebrating the wisdom and piety of their king Hezekiah, who had placed his confidence in the favour of God.

Then follows, in verses 7, 8, and 9, a description of the distress and despair of the Jews, upon the king of Assyria's marching against Jerusalem, and sending his summons to them to surrender, after the treaty he had made with Hezekiah on the conditions of his paying, as he actually did pay to him, three hundred talents of silver and thirty talents of gold. 2 Kings xviii. 14-16.

A. M. cir. 3291
B. C. cir. 713
Olymp. XVI. 4
cir. annum
NumæPompilii,
R. Roman., 3

shall deal treacherously with
thee.
2 O Lord, be gracious unto
us; [c]we have waited for thee:
be thou their arm every morning, our salvation also in the time of trouble.
3 At the noise of the tumult the people fled;
at the lifting up of thyself the nations were
scattered.
4 And your spoil shall be gathered *like* the
gathering of the caterpillar: as the running to
and fro of locusts shall he run upon them.
5 [d]The Lord is exalted; for he dwelleth on
high: he hath filled Zion with
judgment and righteousness.
6 And wisdom and knowledge
shall be the stability of thy times,
and strength of [e]salvation: the fear of the
Lord *is* his treasure.
7 Behold, their [f]valiant ones shall cry without: [g]the ambassadors of peace shall weep
bitterly.
8 [h]The highways lie waste, the wayfaring
man ceaseth: [i]he hath broken the covenant,
he hath despised the cities, he regardeth no
man.

[c]Chap. xxv. 9——[d]Psa. xcvii. 9——[e]Heb. *salvations*
[f]Or, *messengers*

[g]2 Kings xviii. 18, 37——[h]Judg. v. 6——[i]2 Kings xviii. 14, 15, 16, 17

In ver. 10, God himself is again introduced, declaring that he will interpose in this critical situation of affairs, and disappoint the vain designs of the enemies of his people, by discomfiting and utterly consuming them.

Then follows, ver. 11-22, still in the person of God, which however falls at last into that of the prophet, a description of the dreadful apprehensions of the wicked in those times of distress and imminent danger; finely contrasted with the confidence and security of the righteous, and their trust in the promises of God that he will be their never-failing strength and protector.

The whole concludes, in the person of the prophet, with a description of the security of the Jews under the protection of God, and of the wretched state of Sennacherib and his army, wholly discomfited, and exposed to be plundered even by the weakest of the enemy.

Much of the beauty of this passage depends on the explanation above given of ver. 3 and 4, as addressed by the prophet, or by God himself, to Sennacherib; not as it is usually taken, as addressed by the Jews to God, ver. 3, and then ver. 4, as addressed to the Assyrians. To set this in a clear light, it may be of use to compare it with a passage of the Prophet Joel; where, speaking of the destruction caused by the locusts, he sets in the same strong light of opposition as Isaiah does here, the power of the enemy, and the power of Jehovah, who would destroy that enemy. Thus Isaiah to Sennacherib:—

"When thou didst raise thyself up, the nations
were dispersed"— Ver. 3.

"But now will I arise, saith Jehovah;
Now will I be exalted." Ver. 10.

And thus Joel, chap. ii. 20, 21:—

"His stink shall come up, and his ill savour
shall ascend;
Though he hath done great things.
Fear not, O land; be glad and rejoice;
For Jehovah will do great things."—L.

NOTES ON CHAP. XXXIII

Verse 1. *And dealest treacherously*—"Thou plunderer"] See note on chap. xxi. 2.

When thou shalt make an end to deal treacherously—"When thou art weary of plundering"] "כנלתך *cannelothecha, alibi non extat in s. s. nisi f.* Job xv. 29—*simplicius est legere* ככלתך *kechallothecha. Vid.* Capell.; *nec repugnat* Vitringa. *Vid.* Dan. ix. 24. כלה *calah* התים *hatim.*"—Secker.

Verse 2. *Be thou their arm every morning*—"Be thou our strength every morning"] For זרעם *zeroam, their arm*, the *Syriac, Chaldee*, and *Vulgate* read זרענו *zeroenu, our arm*, in the first person of the pronoun, not the third: the edition of Felix Pratensis has זרעתינו *zerootheynu* in the margin.

The prophet is here praying against the enemies of God's people; and yet this part of the prayer seems to be in their behalf: but from the above authorities it appears that our *arm* is the true reading, though I do not find it confirmed by any of *Kennicott's, De Rossi's*, or my own MSS. My old MS. Bible has,—**Be thou oure arm in erly.**

Verse 3. *At the noise of the tumult*—"From thy terrible voice"] For המון *hamon*, "multitude," the *Septuagint* and *Syriac* read אמיך *amica*, "terrible," whom I follow.

Verse 6. *His treasure*—"Thy treasure."] 'O θησαυρος σου, *Sym.* He had in his copy אצרך *otsarcha*, "thy treasure," not אצרו *otsaro*, "his treasure."

Verse 7. *Their valiant ones shall cry without*—"The mighty men raise a grievous cry"] *Three* MSS. read אראלים *erelim*, that is, *lions of God*, or *strong lions*. So they called valiant men heroes; which appellation the Arabians and Persians still use. See *Bochart.* Hieroz. Part I. lib. iii. cap. 1. "Mahomet, ayant reconnu Hamzeh son oncle pour homme de courage et de valeur, lui donne le titre ou surnom d'Assad Allah, qui signifie le lion de Dieu." *D'Herbelot*, p. 427. And for חצה *chatsah*, the *Syriac* and *Chaldee*, read קשה *kashah*, whom I follow. The *Chaldee, Syriac, Aquila, Symmachus*, and *Theodotion* read אראה להם *ereh lahem*, or יראה *yireh*, with what meaning is not clear.

The word אראלם *erellam*, which we translate *valiant ones*, is very difficult; no man knows what it means. *Kimchi* supposes that it is the name of the angel that smote the Assyrian camp! The *Vulgate*, and my old MS., translate

A. M. cir. 3291 B. C. cir. 713 9 [k]The earth mourneth *and*
Olymp. XVI. 4 languisheth: Lebanon is ashamed
cir. annum NumæPompilii, *and* [l]hewn down: Sharon is like
R. Roman., 3 a wilderness; and Bashan and
Carmel shake off *their fruits*.
10 [m]Now will I rise, saith the LORD; now
will I be exalted; now will I lift up myself.
11 [n]Ye shall conceive chaff, ye shall bring
forth stubble: your breath, *as* fire, shall devour you.
12 And the people shall be *as* the burnings
of lime: [o]*as* thorns cut up shall they be
burned in the fire.
13 Hear, [p]ye *that are* far off, what I have
done; and, ye *that are* near, acknowledge my
might.
14 The sinners in Zion are afraid; fearful-
ness hath surprised the hypocrites. Who
among us shall dwell with the devouring fire?
who among us shall dwell with everlasting
burnings?
15 He that [q]walketh [r]righteously, and speaketh [s]uprightly; he that despiseth the gain of
[t]oppressions, that shaketh his hands from
holding of bribes, that stoppeth A. M. cir. 3291 B. C. cir. 713
his ears from hearing of [u]blood, Olymp. XVI. 4
and [v]shutteth his eyes from see- cir. annum NumæPompilii,
ing evil; R. Roman., 3
16 He shall dwell on [w]high: his place
of defence *shall be* the munitions of rocks:
bread shall be given him; his waters *shall
be* sure.
17 Thine eyes shall see the king in his
beauty: they shall behold [x]the land that is
very far off.
18 Thine heart shall meditate terror.
[y]Where *is* the scribe? where *is* the [z]receiver?
where *is* he that counted the towers?
19 [a]Thou shalt not see a fierce people, [b]a
people of deeper speech than thou canst perceive; of a [c]stammering tongue, *that thou
canst* not understand.
20 [d]Look upon Zion, the city of our solemnities: thine eyes shall see [e]Jerusalem a quiet
habitation, a tabernacle *that* shall not be taken
down; [f]not one of [g]the stakes thereof shall
ever be removed, neither shall any of the
cords thereof be broken.

[k]Chap. xxiv. 4——[l]Or, *withered away*——[m]Psa. xii. 5——[n]Psa. vii. 14; chap. lix. 4——[o]Chap. ix. 18——[p]Chap. xlix. 1——[q]Psa. xv. 2; xxiv. 4——[r]Heb. *in righteousnesses*——[s]Heb. *uprightnesses*——[t]Or, *deceits*——[u]Heb. *bloods*——[v]Psa. cxix. 37

[w]Heb. *heights* or *high places*——[x]Heb. *the land of far distances*——[y]1 Cor. i. 20——[z]Heb. *weigher*——[a]2 Kings xix. 32——[b]Deut. xxviii. 49, 50; Jer. v. 15——[c]Or, *ridiculous*——[d]Psa. xlviii. 12——[e]Psa. xlvi. 5; cxxv. 1, 2——[f]Chap. xxxvii. 33——[g]Chap. liv. 2

it *seers;* and most of the Versions understand it in this way. None of the MSS. give us any help, but as we see above in *Lowth*.

Verse 9. *Bashan and Carmel shake off* their fruits—"Bashan and Carmel are stripped of their beauty."] Φανερα εσται, *made manifest. Sept.* They read ונערה *veneerah*.

Verse 11. *Your breath*—"And my spirit"] "For רוחכם *ruchechem, your spirit*, read רוחי כמו *ruchi kemo*." *Secker*. Which reading is confirmed by the *Chaldee*, where מימרי *meymri*, "my word," answers to רוחי *ruchi*, "my spirit."

Verse 14. *The sinners in Zion are afraid*] Zion has been generally considered as a type of the Church of God. Now all the members of God's Church should be holy, and given to good works; sinners in *Zion*, therefore, are portentous beings! but, alas! where are they not? The *Targum* on this verse is worthy of notice: "The sinners in Zion are broken down; fear hath seized the ungodly, who are suffering for their ways. They say, Who among us shall dwell in Zion, where the splendour of the Divine Majesty is like a consuming fire? Who of us shall dwell in Jerusalem, where the ungodly are judged and delivered into hell for an eternal burning?" **Everdurynge brennyngis.** Old MS. Bible.

Verse 15. *That stoppeth his ears from hearing of blood*—"Who stoppeth his ears to the proposal of bloodshed"] A MS. reads בדמים *bedamim*, "in blood."

Verse 18. *Where* is *the scribe?*] The person appointed by the king of Assyria to estimate their number and property in reference to their being heavily taxed.

Where is *the receiver?*] Or he who was to have collected this tribute.

Where is *he that counted the towers?*] That is, the commander of the enemy's forces, who surveyed the fortifications of the city, and took an account of the height, strength, and situation of the walls and towers, that he might know where to make the assault with the greatest advantage; as Capaneus before Thebes is represented in a passage of the Phœnissæ of Euripides, which *Grotius* has applied as an illustration of this place:—

Εκεινος ἑπτα προσβασεις τεκμαιρεται
Πυργων, ανω τε και κατω τειχη μετρων.
Ver. 187.

"To these seven turrets each approach he marks;
The walls from their proud summit to their base
Measuring with eager eye."

He that counted the towers—"Those who were ordered to review the fortified places in Judea, that they might be manned and provisioned for the king of Assyria. So sure was he of gaining Jerusalem and subduing the whole of Judea, that he had already formed all these arrangements."—*Dodd's* notes.

Verse 20. *Look upon Zion*—"Thou shalt see

A. M. cir. 3291 B. C. cir. 713 Olymp. XVI. 4 cir. annum NumæPompilii, R. Roman., 3

21 But there the glorious
LORD *will be* unto us a place
[h]of broad rivers *and* streams;
wherein shall go no galley with
oars, neither shall gallant ship pass thereby.
22 For the LORD *is* our judge, the LORD *is*
our [i]lawgiver,[k] [l]the LORD *is* our king; he
will save us.
23 [m]Thy tacklings are loosed;
they could not well strengthen
their mast, they could not spread
the sail: then is the prey of a
great spoil divided; the lame take the prey.
24 And the inhabitant shall not say, I am
sick: [n]the people that dwell therein *shall be*
forgiven *their* iniquity.

A. M. cir. 3291 B. C. cir. 713 Olymp. XVI. 4 cir. annum NumæPompilii, R. Roman., 3

[h]Heb. *broad of spaces* or *hands*——[i]James iv. 12——[k]Heb. *statute maker*

[l]Psa. lxxxix. 18——[m]Or, *they have forsaken thy tacklings*——[n]Jer. l. 20

Zion"] For חזה *chazeh*, "see," read תחזה *techezeh*, "thou shalt see," with the *Chaldee*.—*Houbigant*. At the end of this verse we find in the Masoretic Bibles this note, חצי הספר *chatsi hassepher*, "the middle of the book;" that is, the middle of the book of Isaiah.

Verse 21. *The glorious Lord*—"The glorious name of JEHOVAH"] I take שם *shem* for a noun, with the *Septuagint* and *Syriac*. See Psa. xx. 1; Prov. xviii. 10.

Verse 23. *Thy tacklings are loosed*] Here the Assyrians are represented under the figure of a *ship* wrecked by a violent storm; and the people on the beach, young, old, feeble, and diseased, gathering the spoil without any to hinder them. *Kimchi*, who understands the whole of this chapter of Hezekiah and the king of Assyria, says, "There are others of our rabbins who apply it all to the days of the Messiah."

Their mast—"Thy mast"] For תרנם *tornam*, "their mast," the *Syriac* reads תרניך *torneycha*, "thy mast;" the *Septuagint* and *Vulgate*, תרנך *tornecha*, ὁ ἱστος σου εκλινεν, "thy mast is fallen aside."—*Septuagint*. They seem to have read נטה *natah* or פנה *panah*, תרנך *tornecha*, or rather, לא כן *lo cun*, "is not firm," the negative having been omitted in the present text by mistake. However, I have followed their sense, which seems very probable, as the present reading is to me extremely obscure.

Verse 24. *And the inhabitant shall not say*] This verse is somewhat obscure. The meaning of it seems to be, that the army of Sennacherib shall by the stroke of God be reduced to so shattered and so weak a condition, that the Jews shall fall upon the remains of them, and plunder them without resistance; that the most infirm and disabled of the people of Jerusalem shall come in for their share of the spoil; the lame shall seize the prey; even the sick and the diseased shall throw aside their infirmities, and recover strength enough to hasten to the general plunder. See above.

The last line of the verse is parallel to the first, and expresses the same sense in other words. Sickness being considered as a visitation from God, a punishment of sin; the forgiveness of sin is equivalent to the removal of a disease. Thus the psalmist:—

"Who forgiveth all thy sin;
And healeth all thine infirmities."
Psa. ciii. 3.

Where the latter line only varies the expression of the former. And our blessed Saviour reasons with the Jews on the same principle: "Whether is it easier to say to the sick of the palsy, Thy sins are forgiven thee; or to say, Arise, and take up thy bed, and walk?" Mark ii. 9. See also Matt. viii. 17; Isa. liii. 4. Qui locus Isaiæ, 1 Pet. ii. 24, refertur ad remissionem peccatorum: hic vero ad sanationem morborum, quia ejusdem potentiæ et bonitatis est utrumque præstare; et, quia peccatis remissis, et morbi, qui fructus sunt peccatorum, pelluntur. "Which passage of Isaiah has reference, in 1 Pet. ii. 24, to *the remission of sins*, and here to *the healing of diseases*, because both are effects of the same power and goodness; and because with the remission of sins was associated the removal of disorders, the fruits of sin."—*Wetstein* on Matt. viii. 17.

That this prophecy was exactly fulfilled, I think we may gather from the history of this great event given by the prophet himself. It is plain that Hezekiah, by his treaty with Sennacherib, by which he agreed to pay him *three hundred* talents of silver and thirty talents of gold, had stripped himself of his whole treasure. He not only gave him all the silver and gold that was in his own treasury and in that of the temple, but was even forced to cut off the gold from the doors of the temple and from the pillars, with which he had himself overlaid them, to satisfy the demands of the king of Assyria: but after the destruction of the Assyrian army, we find that he "had exceeding much riches, and that he made himself treasuries for silver, and for gold, and for precious stones," &c. 2 Chron. xxxii. 27. He was so rich, that out of pride and vanity he displayed his wealth to the ambassadors from Babylon. This cannot be otherwise accounted for, than by the prodigious spoil that was taken on the destruction of the Assyrian army.—L. And thus, in the providence of God, he had the wealth which was exacted from him restored.

CHAPTER XXXIV

The prophet earnestly exhorts all nations to attend to the communication which he has received from Jehovah, as the matter is of the highest importance, and of universal concern, 1. The wrath of God is denounced against all the nations that had provoked to anger the Defender of the cause of Zion, 2, 3. Great crowd of images, by which the final overthrow and utter extermination of every thing that opposes the spread of true religion in the earth are forcibly and majestically set forth; images so very bold and expressive as to render it impossible, without doing great violence to symbolical language, to restrain their import to the calamities which befell the Edomites in the reign of Nebuchadnezzar, or in that of any other potentate, or even to the calamities which the enemies of the Church have yet suffered since the delivery of the prophecy. Edom must therefore be a type of Antichrist, the last grand adversary of the people of God; and consequently this most awful prophecy, in its ultimate signification, remains to be accomplished, 4–15. *The Churches of God, at the period of the consummation, commanded to consult the book of Jehovah, and note the exact fulfilment of these terrible predictions in their minutest details. Not one jot or tittle relative even to the circumstances shadowed forth by the impure animals shall be found to fail; for what the mouth of the Lord has declared necessary to satisfy the Divine justice, his Spirit will accomplish,* 16, 17.

A. M. cir. 3291 B. C. cir. 713 Olymp. XVI. 4 cir. annum NumæPompilii, R. Roman., 3

COME [a]near, ye nations, to
hear; and hearken, ye
people: [b]let the earth hear, and
[c]all that is therein; the world,
and all things that come forth of it.
2 For the indignation of the LORD *is* upon
all nations, and *his* fury upon all their armies:
he hath utterly destroyed them,
he hath delivered them to the
slaughter.
3 Their slain also shall be cast
out, and [d]their stink shall come up out of
their carcasses, and the mountains shall be
melted with their blood.

[a]Psa. xlix. 1——[b]Deut. xxxii. 1 [c]Heb. *the fulness thereof*——[d]Joel ii. 20

This and the following chapter make one distinct prophecy; an entire, regular, and beautiful poem, consisting of two parts: the first containing a denunciation of Divine vengeance against the enemies of the people or Church of God; the second describing the flourishing state of the Church of God consequent upon the execution of those judgments. The event foretold is represented as of the highest importance, and of universal concern: ALL *nations* are called upon to attend to the declaration of it; and the wrath of God is denounced against all the nations, that is, all those that had provoked to anger the Defender of the cause of Zion. Among those, Edom is particularly specified. The principal provocation of Edom was their insulting the Jews in their distress, and joining against them with their enemies, the Chaldeans; see Amos i. 11; Ezek. xxv. 12; xxxv. 15; Psa. cxxxvii. 7. Accordingly the Edomites were, together with the rest of the neighbouring nations, ravaged and laid waste by Nebuchadnezzar; see Jer. xxv. 15-26; Mal. i. 3, 4, and see *Marsham*, Can. Chron. Sæc. xviii., who calls this the age of the destruction of cities. The general devastation spread through all these countries by Nebuchadnezzar may be the event which the prophet has primarily in view in the *thirty-fourth* chapter: but this event, as far as we have any account of it in history, seems by no means to come up to the terms of the prophecy, or to justify so highly wrought and terrible a description; and it is not easy to discover what connexion the extremely flourishing state of the Church or people of God, described in the next chapter, could have with those events, and how the former could be the consequence of the latter, as it is there represented to be. By a figure, very common in the prophetical writings, any city or people, remarkably distinguished as enemies of the people and kingdom of God, is put for those enemies in general. This seems here to be the case with Edom and Botsra. It seems, therefore, reasonable to suppose, with many learned expositors, that this prophecy has a farther view to events still *future;* to some great revolutions to be effected in later times, *antecedent* to that more perfect state of the kingdom of God upon earth, and serving to introduce it, which the Holy Scriptures warrant us to expect.

That the *thirty-fifth* chapter has a view beyond any thing that could be the immediate consequence of those events, is plain from every part, especially from the middle of it, ver. 5, 6; where the miraculous works wrought by our blessed Saviour are so clearly specified, that we cannot avoid making the application: and our Saviour himself has moreover plainly referred to this very passage, as speaking of him and his works, Matt. xi. 4, 5. He bids the disciples of John to go and report to their master the things which they heard and saw; that the blind received their sight, the lame walked, and the deaf heard; and leaves it to him to draw the conclusion in answer to his inquiry, whether he who performed the very works which the prophets foretold should be performed by the Messiah, was not indeed the Messiah himself. And where are these works so distinctly marked by any of the prophets as in this place? and how could they be marked more distinctly? To these the strictly literal interpretation of the prophet's words directs us. According to the allegorical interpretation, they may have a farther view: this part of the prophecy may run parallel with the former, and relate to the future advent of Christ; to the conversion of the Jews, and their restitution to their land; to the extension and purification of the Christian faith; events predicted in the Holy Scriptures as preparatory to it. *Kimchi* says, "This chapter points out the future destruction of Rome, which is here called Bosra; for Bosra was a great city of the Edomites. Now the major part of the *Romans* are Edomites, who profess the law of Jesus. The Emperor Cæsar (qy. Constantine) was an Edomite, and so were all the emperors after him. *The destruction of the Turkish empire is also comprehended in this prophecy.*"—L. As to the last, I say, Amen!

NOTES ON CHAP. XXXIV

Verse 1. *Hearken*—"Attend unto me"] A MS. adds in this line the word אלי *ali, unto me,* after לאמים *leummim;* which seems to be genuine.

A. M. cir. 3291 B. C. cir. 713 Olymp. XVI. 4 cir. annum NumæPompilii, R. Roman., 3

4 And [e]all the hosts of heaven
shall be dissolved, and the heavens shall be [f]rolled together as
a scroll: [g]and all their host shall
fall down as the leaf falleth off from the vine,
and as a [h]falling *fig* from the fig-tree.
5 [i]For my sword shall be bathed in heaven:
behold, [k]it shall come down upon Idumea, and
upon the people of my curse, to judgment.
6 The sword of the Lord is filled with
blood, it is made fat with fatness, *and* with
the blood of lambs and goats, with the fat of
the kidneys of rams: for [l]the Lord hath a
sacrifice in Bozrah, and a great slaughter in
the land of Idumea.
7 And the [m]unicorns shall come down
with them, and the bullocks with the bulls;
and their land shall be [n]soaked with blood,
and their dust made fat with
fatness.
8 For *it is* the day of the Lord's
[o]vengeance, *and* the year of recompenses for the controversy of Zion.
9 [p]And the streams thereof shall be turned
into pitch, and the dust thereof into brimstone, and the land thereof shall become burning pitch.
10 It shall not be quenched night nor day;
[q]the smoke thereof shall go up for ever: [r]from
generation to generation it shall lie waste;
none shall pass through it for ever and ever.
11 [s]But the [t]cormorant and the bittern shall
possess it; the owl also and the raven shall
dwell in it: and [u]he shall stretch out upon
it the line of confusion, and the stones of
emptiness.

A. M. cir. 3291 B. C. cir. 713 Olymp. XVI. 4 cir. annum NumæPompilii, R. Roman., 3

[e]Psa. cii. 36; Ezek. xxxii. 7, 8; Joel ii. 31; iii. 15; Matt. xxiv. 29; 2 Pet. iii. 10——[f]Rev. vi. 14——[g]Chap. xiv. 12——[h]Rev. vi. 13——[i]Jer. xlvi. 10——[k]Jer. xlix. 7, &c.; Mal. i. 4——[l]Ch. lxiii. 1; Jer. xlix. 13; Zeph. i. 7

[m]Or, *rhinoceros*——[n]Or, *drunken*——[o]Ch. lxiii. 4——[p]See Deut. xxix. 23——[q]Rev. xiv. 11; xviii. 18; xix. 3——[r]Mal. i. 4——[s]Ch. xiv. 23; Zeph. ii. 14; Rev. xviii. 2——[t]Or, *pelican*——[u]2 Kings xxi. 13; Lam. ii. 8

Verse 4. *And all the host of heaven*] See note on chap. xxiv. 21, and *De Sacra Poësi Hebrœorum*, Præl. ix.

Verse 5. *For my sword shall be bathed in heaven*—"For my sword is made bare in the heavens"] There seems to be some impropriety in this, according to the present reading: "My sword is made drunken, or is bathed in the heavens;" which forestalls, and expresses not in its proper place, what belongs to the next verse: for the sword of Jehovah was not to be bathed or glutted with blood in the heavens, but in Botsra and the land of Edom. In the heavens it was only prepared for slaughter. To remedy this, Archbishop *Secker* proposes to read, for בשמים *bashshamayim*, בדמם *bedamim;* referring to Jer. xlvi. 10. But even this is premature, and not in its proper place. The *Chaldee*, for רותה *rivvethah*, has תתגלי *tithgalli*, shall be *revealed* or *disclosed:* perhaps he read תראה *teraeh* or נראתה *nirathah*. Whatever reading, different I presume from the present, he might find in his copy, I follow the sense which he has given of it.

Verse 6. *The Lord hath a sacrifice*—"For Jehovah celebrateth a sacrifice"] Ezekiel, chap. xxxix. 16, 17, has manifestly imitated this place of Isaiah. He hath set forth the great leaders and princes of the adverse powers under the same emblems of goats, bulls, rams, fatlings, &c., and has added to the boldness of the imagery, by introducing God as summoning all the fowls of the air, and all the beasts of the field; and bidding them to the feast which he has prepared for them by the slaughter of the enemies of his people:—

"And thou, son of man,
Thus saith the Lord Jehovah,
Say to the bird of every wing,
And to every beast of the field:
Assemble yourselves, and come;
Gather together from every side,
To the sacrifice which I make for you,
A great slaughter on the mountains of Israel.
And ye shall eat flesh and drink blood:
The flesh of the mighty shall ye eat,
And the blood of the lofty of the earth shall ye drink;
Of rams, of lambs, and of goats,
Of bullocks, all of them the fat ones of Bashan;
And ye shall eat fat, till ye are cloyed,
And drink blood, till ye are drunken;
Of my slaughter, which I have slain for you."

The sublime author of the Revelation, chap. xix. 17, 18, has taken this image from Ezekiel, rather than from Isaiah.

Verse 7. *The unicorns shall come down*] ראמים *reemim*, translated *wild goats* by Bishop *Lowth*. The ראם *reem Bochart* thinks to be a species of wild goat in the deserts of Arabia. It seems generally to mean the rhinoceros.

With blood—"With their blood"] מדמם *middamam;* so two ancient MSS. of *Kennicott's*, the *Syriac*, and *Chaldee*.

Verse 8. *The year of recompenses for the controversy of Zion*—"The year of recompense to the defender of the cause of Zion"] As from דון *dun*, דין *din*, *a judge;* so from רוב *rub*, ריב *rib*, *an advocate*, or *defender; Judici* Sionis: *Syriac*.

Verse 11. *The cormorant*] קאת *kaath*, *the pelican*, from the root קיא *ki*, *to vomit*, because it is said she swallows shell-fish, and when the heat of her stomach has killed the fish, she vomits the shells, takes out the dead fish, and eats them.

The bittern] קפד *kippod*, the *hedge-hog*, or *porcupine*.

The owl] ינשוף *yanshoph*, the *bittern*, from נשף *nashaph*, to *blow*, because of the *blowing* noise it makes, almost like the *lowing of an ox*. My old MS. Bible renders the words thus:—**The foule in face like an asse, and the yrchoun, and the snyte** (snipe.)

A. M. cir. 3291
B. C. cir. 713
Olymp. XVI. 4
cir. annum
NumæPompilii,
R. Roman., 3

12 They shall call the nobles
thereof to the kingdom, but none
shall be there, and all her princes
shall be nothing.
13 And [v]thorns shall come up in her palaces,
nettles and brambles in the fortresses thereof:
and [w]it shall be a habitation of dragons, *and*
a court for [x]owls.[y]
14 [z]The wild beasts of the desert shall also
meet with [a]the wild beasts of the island, and
the satyr shall cry to his fellow; the [b]screech
owl also shall rest there, and find for herself
a place of rest.
15 There shall the great owl
make her nest, and lay, and
hatch, and gather under her shadow:
there shall the vultures also
be gathered, every one with her mate.
16 Seek ye out of [c]the book of the LORD and
read; no one of these shall fail, none shall
want her mate, for my mouth it hath commanded,
and his spirit it hath gathered them.
17 And he hath cast the lot for them, and
his hand hath divided it unto them by line:
they shall possess it for ever, from generation
to generation shall they dwell therein.

[v]Chap. xxxii. 13; Hos. ix. 6——[w]Chap. xiii. 21, &c. [x]Or, *ostriches*——[y]Heb. *daughters of the owl*——[z]Heb. *Ziim*——[a]Heb. *Ijim*——[b]Or, *night monster*——[c]Mal. iii. 16

The line of confusion, and the stones of emptiness—"The plummet of emptiness over her scorched plains."] The word חריה *choreyha*, joined to the 12th verse, embarrasses it, and makes it inexplicable. At least I do not know that any one has yet made out the construction, or given any tolerable explication of it. I join it to the 11th verse, and supply a letter or two, which seem to have been lost. *Fifteen* MSS., five ancient, and two editions, read חוריה *choreyha;* the first printed edition of 1486, I think nearer to the truth, חור חריה *chor choreyha*. I read בחרריה *becharereyha*, or על חרריה *al chorereyha;* see Jer. xvii. 6. A MS. has חדיה *chodiah*, and the *Syriac* reads חדוה *chaduah*, *gaudium*, joining it to the two preceding words; which he likewise reads differently, but without improving the sense. However, his authority is clear for dividing the verses as they are here divided. I read שם *shem*, as a noun. They shall boast, יקראו *yikreu;* see Prov. xx. 6.

Verse 13. *And thorns shall come up in her palaces*] ועלו בארמנותיה *vealu bearmenotheyha;* so read all the ancient versions.

A court for owls.] יענה *yaanah*, the *ostrich*, from ענה *anah*, to *cry*, because of the noise it makes. "They *roar*," says Dr. *Shaw*, "sometimes like a *lion*—sometimes like a *bull*. I have often heard them *groan* as if in the utmost distress."

Verse 14. *The wild beasts of the desert*] ציים *tsiyim*, the *mountain cats*.—Bochart.

Wild beasts of the island] איים *aiyim*, the *jackals*.

The satyr] שעיר *seir*, the *hairy one*, probably the *he-goat*.

The screech owl] לילית *lilith*, the *night-bird*, the *night-raven*, *nyctycorax*, from ליל *layil*, or לילה *lailah*, the *night*.

Verse 15. *The great owl*] קפוז *kippoz*, the ακοντιας, or *darter*, a serpent so called because of its suddenly leaping up or *darting* on its prey. Probably the *mongoz* or *ichneumon* may be intended.

The vultures] דיות *daiyoth*, the *black vultures*. My old MS. Bible renders these names curiously: **And ageyn cumen schul debylis: the beste, party of an asse, and party of a man: and the wodwose, the tother schal crien to the tother. There schal byn lampa, that is, thrisse, or a beste habynge the body liic a woman, and hors feet. Ther hadde dichis, the yrchoun, and nurshide out littil chittis. There ben gadred kiitis, the top to the top.** What language!

Every one with her mate.] A MS. adds אל *el* after אשה *ishshah*, which seems necessary to the construction; and so the *Syriac* and *Vulgate*. Another MS. adds in the same place את *eth*, which is equivalent.

Verse 16. *My mouth*—"For the mouth of JEHOVAH"] For הוא *hu*, five MSS., (three ancient,) read יהוה *Yehovah*, and another is so corrected; so likewise the *Septuagint*. Two editions have צום *tsivam;* and so the *Septuagint*, *Vulgate*, and *Arabic*, with the edition of 1486, and a MS. has קבצם *kebatsam*, with the masculine pronoun instead of the feminine: and so in the next verses it is להם *lahem*, instead of להן *lahen*, in fourteen MSS., six of them ancient.—L. To see the importance of these various readings, the Hebrew Bible must be consulted.

CHAPTER XXXV

Flourishing state of the Church of God consequent *to the awful judgments predicted in the preceding chapter. The images employed in the description are so very consolatory and sublime as to oblige us to extend their fulfilment to that period of the Gospel dispensation when Messiah shall take unto himself his great power and reign. The* fifth *and* sixth *verses were* literally *accomplished by our Saviour and his apostles: but that the miracles wrought in the first century were not the only import of the language used by the prophet, is sufficiently plain from the context. They, therefore, have a farther application; and are contemporary with, or rather a consequence of, the judgments of God upon the enemies of the Church in the latter days; and so relate to the greater influence and extension of the Christian faith, the conversion of the Jews, their restoration to their own land, and the second advent of Christ. Much of the imagery of this chapter seems to have been borrowed from the exodus from Egypt: but it is greatly enlivened by the life, sentiments, and passions ascribed to inanimate objects; all nature being represented as rejoicing with the people of God in consequence of their deliverance; and administering in such an unusual manner to their relief and comfort, as to induce some commentators to extend the meaning of the prophecy to the blessedness of the saints in heaven,* 1–10.

A. M. cir. 3291
B. C. cir. 713
Olymp. XVI. 4
cir. annum
NumæPompilii,
R. Roman., 3

THE [a]wilderness and the solitary place shall be glad for
them; and the desert shall rejoice and blossom as the rose.
2 [b]It shall blossom abundantly, and rejoice
even with joy and singing: the glory of Lebanon shall be given unto it, the excellency
of Carmel and Sharon, they shall see the glory
of the LORD, *and* the excellency of our God.
3 [c]Strengthen ye the weak hands, and confirm the feeble knees.
4 Say to them *that are* of a [d]fearful heart,
Be strong, fear not: behold, your God will come *with* vengeance, *even* God *with* a recompense; he will come and save you.
5 Then the [e]eyes of the blind shall be opened,
and [f]the ears of the deaf shall be unstopped.
6 Then shall the [g]lame *man* leap as a hart,
and the [h]tongue of the dumb sing: for in the wilderness shall [i]waters break out, and streams in the desert.
7 And the parched ground shall become a

[a]Chap. lv. 12——[b]Chap. xxxii. 15——[c]Job iv. 3, 4; Heb. xii. 12——[d]Heb. *hasty*——[e]Chap. xxix.1 8; xxxii. 3, 4; xlii. 7; Matt. ix. 27, &c.; xi. 5; xii. 22; xx. 30, &c.; xxi. 14; John ix. 6, 7

[f]Matt. xi. 5; Mark vii. 32, &c.——[g]Matt. xi. 5; xv. 30; xxi. 14; John v. 8, 9; Acts iii. 2, &c.; viii. 7; xiv. 8, &c.——[h]Chap. xxxii. 4; Matt. ix. 32, 33; xii. 22; xv. 30 [i]Chap. xli. 18; xliii. 19; John vii. 38, 39

The various miracles our Lord wrought are the best comment on this chapter, which predicts those wondrous works and the glorious state of the Christian Church. See the parallel texts in the margin.

On this chapter Bishop Lowth has offered some important emendations. I shall introduce his translation, as the best yet given of this singular prophecy:—

1. The desert and the waste shall be glad;
 And the wilderness shall rejoice, and flourish:
2. Like the rose shall it beautifully flourish;
 And the well-watered plain of Jordan shall also rejoice:
 The glory of Lebanon shall be given unto it,
 The beauty of Carmel and of Sharon;
 These shall behold the glory of JEHOVAH,
 The majesty of our God.
3. Strengthen ye the feeble hands,
 And confirm ye the tottering knees.
4. Say ye to the faint-hearted, Be ye strong;
 Fear ye not; behold your God!
 Vengeance will come; the retribution of God:
 He himself will come, and will deliver you.
5. Then shall be unclosed the éyes of the blind;
 And the ears of the deaf shall be opened:
6. Then shall the lame bound like the hart,
 And the tongue of the dumb shall sing;
 For in the wilderness shall burst forth waters,
 And torrents in the desert:
7. And the glowing sand shall become a pool,
 And the thirsty soil bubbling springs:
 And in the haunt of dragons shall spring forth
 The grass with the reed and the bulrush.
8. And a highway shall be there;
 And it shall be called The way of holiness:
 No unclean person shall pass through it:
 But he himself shall be with them, walking in the way,
 And the foolish shall not err therein:
9. No lion shall be there;
 Nor shall the tyrant of the beasts come up thither:
 Neither shall he be found there;
 But the redeemed shall walk in it.
10. Yea, the ransomed of JEHOVAH shall return;
 They shall come to Sion with triumph;
 And perpetual gladness shall crown their heads.
 Joy and gladness shall they obtain;
 And sorrow and sighing shall flee away.

NOTES ON CHAP. XXXV

Verse 1. *Shall be glad*] ישׂשׂום *yesusum;* in one MS. the ם *mem* seems to have been added; and שׂום *sum* is upon a rasure in another. None of the ancient versions acknowledge it; it seems to have been a mistake, arising from the next word beginning with the same letter. *Seventeen* MSS. have ישׂושׂום *yesusum,* both *vaus* expressed; and *five* MSS. ישׂשׂם *yesusum,* without the *vaus.* Probably the true reading is, "The wilderness and the dry place shall be glad." Not *for them.*

Verse 2. *Rejoice even with joy and singing*—"The well-watered plain of Jordan shall also rejoice"] For ורנן *veranen,* the *Septuagint* read ירדן *yarden,* τα ερημα του Ιορδανου, "the deserts of Jordan." *Four* MSS. read גלת *gulath;* see Josh. xv. 19: "Irrigua Jordani;" *Houbigant.* גידת *gidoth,* Ripæ Jordani, "the banks of Jordan;" *Kennicott.* See De S. Poësi Hebr. Prælect. xx. note.

Unto it] For לה *lah, to it, nine* MSS. of *Kennicott's* and *four* of *De Rossi's* read לך *lecha, to thee.* See ibid.

Verse 7. *The parched ground*—"The glowing sand"] שרב *sharab;* this word is Arabic, سراب as well as Hebrew, expressing in both languages the same thing, the *glowing sandy plain,* which in the hot countries at a distance has the appearance of water. It occurs in the Koran, chap. xxiv.: "But as to the unbelievers, their works are like a vapour in a plain, which the

A. M. cir. 3291 B. C. cir. 713 Olymp. XVI. 4 cir. annum NumæPompilii, R. Roman., 3

pool, and the thirsty land
springs of water: in [k]the habitation of dragons, where each
lay, *shall be* [l]grass with reeds
and rushes.
8 And a highway shall be there, and a way,
and it shall be called, The way of holiness;
[m]the unclean shall not pass over it; [n]but it
shall be for those: the way-faring men, though
fools, shall not err *therein.*
9 [o]No lion shall be there, nor
any ravenous beast shall go up
thereon, it shall not be found
there; but the redeemed shall
walk *there:*
10 And the [p]ransomed of the LORD shall
return, and come to Zion with songs and everlasting joy upon their heads: they shall obtain joy and gladness, and [q]sorrow and
sighing shall flee away.

A. M. cir. 3291 B. C. cir. 713 Olymp. XVI. 4 cir. annum NumæPompilii, R. Roman., 3

[k]Ch. xxxiv. 13——[l]Or, *a court for reeds, &c.*——[m]Ch. lii. 1; Joel iii. 17; Rev. xxi. 27——[n]Or, *for he* shall be *with them*——[o]Lev. xxvi. 6; ch. xi. 9; Ezek. xxxiv. 25——[p]Ch. li. 11——[q]Ch. xxv. 8; lxv. 19; Rev. vii. 17; xxi. 4

thirsty traveller thinketh to be water, until, when he cometh thereto, he findeth it to be nothing." Mr. Sale's note on this place is, "The Arabic word *serab* signifies that false appearance which in the eastern countries is often seen on sandy plains about noon, resembling a large lake of water in motion, and is occasioned by the reverberation of the sun beams: 'by the quivering undulating motion of that quick succession of vapours and exhalations which are extracted by the powerful influence of the sun.'—*Shaw*, Trav. p. 378. It sometimes tempts thirsty travellers out of their way; but deceives them when they come near, either going forward, (for it always appears at the same distance,) or quite vanishing." Q. Curtius has mentioned it: "Arenas vapor æstivi solis accendit; camporumque non alia, quam vasti et profundi æquoris species est."—Lib. vii., c. 5. Dr. Hyde gives us the precise meaning and derivation of the word. "Dictum nomen *Barca* הברקה *habberakah, splendorem,* seu *splendentem regionem* notat; cum ea regio radiis solaribus tam copiose collustretur, ut reflexum ab arenis lumen adeo intensè fulgens, a longinquo spectantibus, ad instar corporis solaris, aquarum speciem referat; et hinc arenarum splendor et radiatio, (et linguâ Persicâ petito nomine,) dicitur سراب *serab*, i. e., aquæ superficies seu superficialis aquarum species." Annot. in Peritsol., cap. ii.

"Shall spring forth"] The ה *he* in רבצה *rebitseh* seems to have been at first ם *mem* in MS. Bodl., whence Dr. *Kennicott* concludes it should be רבצים *rebitsim.* But instead of this word the *Syriac, Vulgate,* and *Chaldee* read some word signifying *to grow, spring up,* or *abound.* Perhaps פרצה *paretsah,* or פרצו *paretsu,* or פרץ החציר *parats hachatsir,* as Houbigant reads.—L.

Verse 8. *And a highway*] The word ודרך *vederech* is by mistake added to the first member of the sentence from the beginning of the following member. *Sixteen* MSS. of Dr. *Kennicott's, seven* ancient, and *two* of *De Rossi's,* have it but once; so likewise the *Syriac, Septuagint,* and *Arabic.*

Err therein.] A MS. of Dr. *Kennicott's* adds בו *bo, in it,* which seems necessary to the sense; and so the *Vulgate, per eam,* "by it." One of *De Rossi's* has שם *sham, there.*

But it shall be *for those*—"But he himself shall be with them, walking in the way."] That is, God; see ver. 4. "Who shall dwell among them, and set them an example that they should follow his steps." Our old English Version translated the place to this purpose; our last translators were misled by the authority of the Jews, who have absurdly made a division of the verses in the midst of the sentence, thereby destroying the construction and the sense.

Verse 9. *It shall not be found there*—"Neither shall he be found there"] *Three* MSS. read ולא *velo,* adding the conjunction; and so likewise the *Septuagint* and *Vulgate.* And *four* MSS., *one* ancient, read ימצא *yimmatsa,* the verb, as it certainly ought to be, in the masculine form.

The redeemed shall walk there] גאולים *geulim.* Those whose forfeited inheritances are brought back by the *kinsman,* גואל *goel,* the nearest of kin to the family. This has been considered by all orthodox divines as referring to the incarnation of our Lord, and his sacrificial offering. After גאולים *geulim,* one of *De Rossi's* MSS. adds עד עולם *ad olam, for ever,* "The redeemed shall walk there for ever."

Verse 10. *The ransomed*] פדויי *peduyey,* from פדה *padah,* "to redeem by paying a price." Those for whom a price was paid down to redeem them from bondage and death.

Sighing shall flee away.] אנחה *anachah.* Never was a sorrowful accent better expressed than in this strong guttural word, *an-ach-ah;* nearly the same with the Irish in their funeral wailings, *och-och-on.* The whole nation express all their mournful accents by these *three* monosyllables.

THIS chapter contains the following parts:—

1. We have here blessed promises of the latter-day glory.
2. The prophet may be considered as addressing the teachers of the Gospel, to show them that it was their business to encourage and direct the people in their expectation of redemption.
3. A promise of the manifestation of God among men is given.
4. The miracles which Christ should work are explicitly mentioned.
5. The privileges of Christianity are specified; there shall be, 1. Thorough teaching; 2. Holy walking.
6. Perfect safety.
7. Complete happiness. And—
8. Final glory.

The chapter shows also that no impurity should be tolerated in the Church of God; for as that is the mystical body of Christ, it should be like himself, without spot or wrinkle, or any such thing.

CHAPTER XXXVI

Sennacherib, king of Assyria, comes against Judah, and takes all the fenced cities, 1. *He afterwards sends a great host against Jerusalem; and his general Rabshakeh delivers an insulting and blasphemous message to Hezekiah,* 2–20. *Hezekiah and his people are greatly afflicted at the words of Rabshakeh,* 21, 22.

A. M. cir. 3291
B. C. cir. 713
Olymp. XVI. 4
cir. annum
NumæPompilii,
R. Roman., 3

NOW [a]it came to pass in the fourteenth year of king Hezekiah, *that* Sennacherib king of Assyria came up against all the defenced cities of Judah, and took them.

A. M. cir. 3294
B. C. cir. 710
Olymp. XVII. 3
cir. annum
NumæPompilii,
R. Roman., 6

2 And the king of Assyria sent Rabshakeh from Lachish to Jerusalem unto king Hezekiah with a great army. And he stood by the conduit of the upper pool in the highway of the fuller's field.

3 Then came forth unto him Eliakim, Hilkiah's son, which was over the house, and Shebna the [b]scribe, and Joah, Asaph's son, the recorder.

4 [c]And Rabshakeh said unto them, Say ye now to Hezekiah, Thus saith the great king, the king of Assyria, What confidence *is* this wherein thou trustest?

5 I say, *sayest thou,* (but *they are but* [d]vain words) [e]*I have* counsel and strength for war: now on whom dost thou trust, that thou rebellest against me?

A. M. cir. 3294
B. C. cir. 710
Olymp. XVII. 3
cir. annum
NumæPompilii,
R. Roman., 6

6 Lo, thou trustest in the [f]staff of this broken reed, on Egypt; whereon if a man lean, it will go into his hand, and pierce it: so *is* Pharaoh king of Egypt to all that trust in him.

7 But if thou say to me, We trust in the LORD our God: *is it* not he, whose high places and whose altars Hezekiah hath taken away, and said to Judah and to Jerusalem, Ye shall worship before this altar?

8 Now therefore give [g]pledges, I pray thee, to my master the king of Assyria, and I will give thee two thousand horses, if thou be able on thy part to set riders upon them.

9 How then wilt thou turn away the face of one captain of the least of my master's servants, and put thy trust on Egypt for chariots and for horsemen?

10 And am I now come up without the LORD against this land to destroy it? the LORD said unto me, Go up against this land, and destroy it.

11 Then said Eliakim and Shebna and Joah

---

[a]2 Kings xviii. 13, 17; 2 Chron. xxxii. 1——[b]Or, *secretary*——[c]2 Kings xviii. 19, &c.——[d]Heb. *a word of lips*——[e]Or, but *counsel and strength* are *for the war*——[f]Ezek. xxix. 6, 7——[g]Or, *hostages*

The history of the invasion of Sennacherib, and of the miraculous destruction of his army, which makes the subject of so many of Isaiah's prophecies, is very properly inserted here as affording the best light to many parts of those prophecies, and as almost necessary to introduce the prophecy in the *thirty-seventh* chapter, being the answer of God to Hezekiah's prayer, which could not be properly understood without it. We find the same narrative in the Second Book of Kings, chaps. xviii., xix., xx.; and these chapters of Isaiah, xxxvi., xxxvii., xxxviii., xxxix., for much the greater part, (the account of the sickness of Hezekiah only excepted,) are but a different copy of that narration. The difference of the two copies is little more than what has manifestly arisen from the mistakes of transcribers; they mutually correct each other, and most of the mistakes may be perfectly rectified by a collation of the two copies with the assistance of the ancient versions. Some few sentences, or members of sentences, are omitted in this copy of Isaiah, which are found in the other copy in the Book of Kings. Whether these omissions were made by design or mistake may be doubted.—L.

NOTES ON CHAP. XXXVI

Verse 3. *Then came forth unto him*] Before these words the other copy, 2 Kings xviii. 18, adds, ויקראו אל המלך *vaiyikreu el hammelech,* "And they demanded audience of the king."

Verse 5. *I say*—"Thou hast said"] *Fourteen* MSS. (*three* ancient) of *Kennicott's* and *De Rossi's* have it in the second person, אמרת *amarta;* and so the other copy, 2 Kings xviii. 20.

But they are but *vain words*] דבר שפתים *debar sephathayim, a word of the lips.* Thou dost talk about *counsels,* but thou hast none; about *strength,* but there is none with thee.

Verse 6. *The staff of this broken reed*] A weakened, faithless ally.

On Egypt] The Bodl. MS. adds מלך *melech, the king* of Egypt; and so perhaps the *Chaldee* might read.

It will go into his hand, and pierce it] Will take subsidy after subsidy, and do nothing for it.

Verse 7. *But if thou say*—"But if ye say"] *Two* ancient MSS. have תאמרו *tomeru* in the plural number; so likewise the *Septuagint, Chaldee,* and the other copy, 2 Kings xviii. 22.

Ye shall worship before this altar—"To worship only before this altar"] See 2 Chron. xxxii. 12.

Verse 10. *Am I now come up without the Lord*] Probably some apostate Israelitish priest might have encouraged the king of Assyria by telling him that JEHOVAH had given him a commission against Jerusalem.

A. M. cir. 3294
B. C. cir. 710
Olymp. XVII. 3
cir. innum
NumæPompilii,
R. Roman., 6

unto Rabshakeh, Speak, I pray thee, unto thy servants in the Syrian language; for we understand *it:* and speak not to us in the Jews' language, in the ears of the people that *are* on the wall.

12 But Rabshakeh said, Hath my master sent me to thy master and to thee to speak these words? *hath he* not *sent me* to the men that sit upon the wall, that they may eat their own dung, and drink their own piss with you?

13 Then Rabshakeh stood, and cried with a loud voice in the Jews' language, and said, Hear ye the words of the great king, the king of Assyria.

14 Thus saith the king, Let not Hezekiah deceive you: for he shall not be able to deliver you.

15 Neither let Hezekiah make you trust in the LORD, saying, The LORD will surely deliver us: this city shall not be delivered into the hand of the king of Assyria.

16 Hearken not to Hezekiah: for thus saith the king of Assyria, [h]Make [i]*an agreement* with me *by* a present, and come out to me: [k]and eat ye every one of his vine, and every one of his fig-tree; and drink ye every one the waters of his own cistern;

A. M. cir. 3294
B. C. cir. 710
Olymp. XVII. 3
cir. annum
NumæPompilii,
R. Roman., 6

17 Until I come and take you away to a land like your own land, a land of corn and wine, a land of bread and vineyards.

18 *Beware* lest Hezekiah persuade you, saying, The LORD will deliver us. Hath any of the gods of the nations delivered his land out of the hand of the king of Assyria?

19 Where *are* the gods of Hamath and Arphad? where *are* the gods of Sepharvaim? and have they delivered Samaria out of my hand?

20 Who *are they* among all the gods of these lands, that have delivered their land out of my hand, that the LORD should deliver Jerusalem out of my hand?

21 But they held their peace, and answered him not a word: for the king's commandment was, saying, Answer him not.

22 Then came Eliakim, the son of Hilkiah, that *was* over the household, and Shebna the scribe, and Joah, the son of Asaph, the recorder, to Hezekiah with *their* clothes rent and told him the words of Rabshakeh.

[h]Or, *Seek my favour by a present*

[i]Heb. *Make with me a blessing*——[k]Zech. iii. 10

Verse 12. *That they may eat their own dung*—"Destined to eat their own dung"] לאכל *leechol, that they may eat,* as our translation literally renders it. But the *Syriac* reads מאכל *meechol, that they may not eat,* perhaps rightly, and afterward ומשתות *umishshethoth,* or ושתות *ushethoth,* to the same purpose. *Seventeen* of Dr. *Kennicott's* MSS., *ten* of *De Rossi's* and *two* of my own, read מימי *meymey, the water;* mine have מימי שניהם *meymey sheneyhem,* and write in the margin מימי רגליהם *meymey regaleyhem, the water of their feet,* a modest way of expressing *urine.*

Verse 15. *This city shall not be delivered*] ולא *ve-lo,* AND *this city. Ten* of *Kennicott's* MSS., and *nine* of *De Rossi's,* with *one* (ancient) of my own, add the *conjunction.*

Verse 16. *Make* an agreement] ברכה *berachah, make a blessing with me;* i. e., Give me a ransom for the city, and I will not destroy it; give me the yearly tribute thou hast promised.

Verse 17. *And vineyards*] The other copy, 2 Kings xviii. 32, adds here: "A land of oil-olive, and of honey; that ye may live, and not die: and hearken not unto Hezekiah when he seduceth you."

Verse 19. *Where* are *the gods*] Many MSS. add the conjunction here also: *And,* or *But, where* are *the gods,* &c.

For other matters relative to this chapter, see the notes on 2 Kings xviii. 13, &c.

Of Sepharvaim] The other copy, 2 Kings xviii. 34, adds, of "Henah and Ivah."

Have they delivered] וכי *vechi.* The copulative is not expressed here by the *Septuagint, Syriac, Vulgate,* and *three* MSS.; nor is it in any other copy. Ib. Houbigant reads הכי *hachi,* with the interrogative particle; a probable conjecture, which the ancient Versions above quoted seem to favour.

Verse 21. *But they held their peace*—"But the people held their peace"] The word העם *haam, the people,* is supplied from the other copy, and is authorized by a MS. which inserts it after אתו *otho.*

CHAPTER XXXVII

Hezekiah is greatly distressed, and sends to Isaiah the prophet to pray for him, 1–4. *Isaiah returns a comfortable answer, and predicts the destruction of the king of Assyria and his army,* 5–7. *Sennacherib, hearing that his kingdom was invaded by the Ethiopians, sends a terrible letter to Hezekiah, to induce him to surrender,*

9–13. *Hezekiah goes to the temple, spreads the letter before the Lord, and makes a most affecting prayer,* 14–20. *Isaiah is sent to him to assure him that his prayer is heard; that Jerusalem shall be delivered; and that the Assyrians shall be destroyed,* 21–35. *That very night* a messenger of God *slays one hundred and eighty-five thousand Assyrians,* 36. *Sennacherib returns to Nineveh, and is slain by his own sons,* 37, 38.

A. M. cir. 3294
B. C. cir. 710
Olymp. XVII. 3
cir. annum
NumæPompilii,
R. Roman., 6

AND [a]it came to pass, when king Hezekiah heard *it,* that he rent his clothes, and covered himself with sackcloth, and went into the house of the LORD.

2 And he sent Eliakim, who *was* over the household, and Shebna the scribe, and the elders of the priests covered with sackcloth, unto Isaiah the prophet the son of Amoz.

3 And they said unto him, Thus saith Hezekiah, This day *is* a day of trouble, and of rebuke, and of [b]blasphemy: for the children are come to the birth, and *there is* not strength to bring forth.

4 It may be the LORD thy God will hear the words of Rabshakeh, whom the king of Assyria his master hath sent to reproach the living God, and will reprove the words which the LORD thy God hath heard: wherefore lift up *thy* prayer for the remnant that is [c]left.

5 So the servants of king Hezekiah came to Isaiah.

6 And Isaiah said unto them, Thus shall ye say unto your master, Thus saith the LORD, Be not afraid of the words that thou hast heard, wherewith the servants of the king of Assyria have blasphemed me.

A. M. cir. 3294
B. C. cir. 710
Olymp. XVII. 3
cir. annum
NumæPompilii,
R. Roman., 6

7 Behold, I will [d]send a blast upon him, and he shall hear a rumour, and return to his own land; and I will cause him to fall by the sword in his own land.

8 So Rabshakeh returned, and found the king of Assyria warring against Libnah: for he had heard that he was departed from Lachish.

9 And he heard say concerning Tirhakah king of Ethiopia, He is come forth to make war with thee. And when he heard *it,* he sent messengers to Hezekiah, saying,

10 Thus shall ye speak to Hezekiah king of Judah, saying, Let not thy God, in whom thou trustest, deceive thee, saying, Jerusalem shall not be given into the hand of the king of Assyria.

11 Behold, thou hast heard what the kings of Assyria have done to all lands by destroying them utterly; and shalt thou be delivered?

12 Have the gods of the nations delivered

[a]2 Kings xix. 1, &c.——[b]Or, *provocation*

[c]Heb. *found*——[d]Or, *put a spirit into him*

NOTES ON CHAP. XXXVII

Verse 6. *Thus shall ye say*] כה תאמרון *ko tomerun,* "thus shall ye (*explicitly, earnestly,* and *positively*) say." The paragogic ן *nun* deepens and increases the sense.

Verse 7. *I will send a blast*—"I will infuse a spirit into him"] "נותן בו רוח *nothen bo ruach* never signifies any thing but putting a spirit into a person: this was πνευμα δειλιας, *the spirit of deceit."*—*Secker.* "I will send a blast"—I do not think that Archbishop Secker has hit the true meaning of these words. I believe רוח *ruach* means here a pestilential *wind,* such as the Arabs call *simoom,* that instantly suffocates both man and beast; and is what is termed "the angel of the Lord," God's messenger of death to the Assyrians, ver. 36.

Verse 8. *Rabshakeh returned*] From chap. xxxvi. 2, we learn that the king of Assyria had sent Rabshakeh from Lachish to Jerusalem; now it is likely that Rabshakeh had besieged that place, and that the king of Assyria had taken his station before this city, and despatched Rabshakeh against Jerusalem. But, as in the verse above it is said, "he had departed from Lachish," probably he had been obliged to raise the siege, and sat down before *Libnah,* which promised an easier conquest.

Verse 9. *He heard say concerning Tirhakah king of Ethiopia*] When he heard that Tirhakah king of Ethiopia had come out against him, then he sent that blasphemous *manifesto* which is contained in ver. 10-13, to terrify Hezekiah into submission. How much was this like, in words and spirit, to the manifesto sent to the *Parisians* by the late *Duke of Brunswick,* from the plains of *Champaigne,* in 1792, which was the forerunner of the mighty torrents of human blood which was shed in the French revolution! And what a blast of God fell upon *him* and his *army*—nearly like that which fell on the army of Sennacherib!

He sent messengers—"He sent messengers again"] The word וישמע *vaiyishma,* "and he heard," which occurs the second time in this verse, is repeated by mistake from the beginning of the verse. It is omitted in an ancient MS. It is a mere tautology, and embarrasses the sense. The true reading instead of it is, וישב *veyesheb,* "and he returned," which the *Septuagint* read in this place, απεστρεψε, and which is preserved in the other copy, 2 Kings xix. 9: "He returned and sent," that is, according to the Hebrew idiom, "he sent again."

Verse 12. As *Gozan, and Haran*] חרן *Charan:* but הרן *Haran* is the reading of *four* of *Kennicott's* MSS. and *one* of *De Rossi's.*

A. M. cir. 3294
B. C. cir. 710
Olymp. XVII. 3
cir. annum
NumæPompilii,
R. Roman., 6

them which my fathers have
destroyed, *as* Gozan, and Haran,
and Rezeph, and the children of
Eden which *were* in Telassar?
13 Where *is* the king of [e]Hamath, and the
king of Arphad, and the king of the city of
Sepharvaim, Hena, and Ivah?
14 And Hezekiah received the letter from
the hand of the messengers, and read it: and
Hezekiah went up unto the house of the LORD,
and spread it before the LORD.
15 And Hezekiah prayed unto the LORD,
saying,
16 O LORD of hosts, God of Israel, that
dwellest *between* the cherubims, thou *art* the
God, *even* thou alone, of all the kingdoms of
the earth: thou hast made heaven and earth.
17 [f]Incline thine ear, O LORD, and hear:
open thine eyes, O LORD, and see: and hear
all the words of Sennacherib, which hath sent
to reproach the living God.
18 Of a truth, LORD, the kings of Assyria
have laid waste all the [g]nations, and their
countries,
19 And have [h]cast their gods
into the fire: for they *were* no
gods, but the work of men's
hands, wood and stone: therefore they have destroyed them.

A. M. cir. 3294
B. C. cir. 710
Olymp. XVII. 3
cir. annum
NumæPompilii,
R. Roman., 6

20 Now therefore, O LORD our God, save
us from his hand, that all the kingdoms of the
earth may know that thou *art* the LORD, *even*
thou only.
21 Then Isaiah the son of Amoz sent unto
Hezekiah, saying, Thus saith the LORD God
of Israel, Whereas thou hast prayed to me
against Sennacherib king of Assyria:
22 This *is* the word which the LORD hath
spoken concerning him; The virgin, the
daughter of Zion, hath despised thee, *and*
laughed thee to scorn; the daughter of Jerusalem hath shaken her head at thee.
23 Whom hast thou reproached and blasphemed; and against whom hast thou exalted
thy voice, and lifted up thine eyes on high?
even against the Holy One of Israel.
24 [i]By thy servants hast thou reproached
the Lord, and hast said, By the multitude of

[e]Jer. xlix. 23——[f]Dan. ix. 18——[g]Heb. *lands*

[h]Heb. *given*——[i]Heb. *By the hand of thy servants*

Verse 14. *And read it*—"And read them"] ויקראם *vayikraem*. So MS. Bodl. in this place; and so the other copy; instead of ויקראהו *vaiyikraehu*, "and read IT."

And spread it—"And spread them"] ויפרשהו *vaiyiphresehu*. הו *hu* is upon a rasure in a MS., which probably was at first ם *mem*. The same mistake as in the foregoing note.

Verse 15. *Unto the Lord*—"Before JEHOVAH"] That is, in the sanctuary. For אל *el*, the *Syriac*, *Chaldee*, and the other copy, 2 Kings xix. 15, read לפני *liphney*, "before the face."

Verse 18. *The nations*] הארצות *haratsoth*, "the lands;" instead of this word, which destroys the sense, *ten* of *Kennicott's* and *five* of *De Rossi's* MSS. (*one* ancient) have here גוים *goyim*, "nations;" which is undoubtedly the true reading, being preserved also in the other copy; 2 Kings xix. 17. Another MS. suggests another method of rectifying the sense in this place, by reading מלכם *malcam*, "their king," instead of ארצם *artsam*, "their land;" but it ought to be מלכיהם *malcheyhem*, "all the countries and their kings."

Verse 20. *Save us*—"Save us, we beseech thee"] The supplicating particle, נא *na*, is supplied here from *eighteen* MSS., *three* ancient, of *Dr. Kennicott*, and *ten* of *De Rossi*, and from the other copy; 2 Kings xix. 19.

That thou art *the Lord*, even *thou only*—"That thou JEHOVAH art the only God."] The word אלהים *Elohim*, "God," is lost here in the Hebrew text, but preserved in the other copy; 2 Kings xix. 19. The *Syriac* and *Septuagint* seem here to have had in their copies אלהים *Elohim*, instead of יהוה *Yehovah*.

Verse 21. *Then Isaiah—sent unto Hezekiah*] The *Syriac* and *Septuagint* understand and render the verb passively, *was sent*.

Whereas thou hast prayed to me against Sennacherib—"Thy prayer unto me concerning Sennacherib—*I have heard*"] שמעתי *shamati;* this word, necessary to the sense, is lost in this place out of the Hebrew text. *One* MS. of *Dr. Kennicott's* and *one* of *De Rossi's* have it written above the line in a later hand. The *Septuagint* and *Syriac* found it in their copies; and it is preserved in the other copy; 2 Kings xix. 20.

Verse 23. *Against the Holy One of Israel.*] For אל *el, to*, the other copy has על *al, against*, rather more properly.

Verse 24. *By thy servants*—"By thy messengers"] The text has עבדיך *abdeycha, thy servants;* but the true reading seems to be מלאכיך *malacheycha, thy messengers,* as in the other copy, 2 Kings xix. 23; and as the *Septuagint* and *Syriac* found it in their copies in this place.

Reproached the Lord] אדני *Adonai:* but *one* of my MSS. has יהוה אדני *Yehovah Adonai, Jehovah the Lord.* This reading is not found, I think, in any other MS., but several have יהוה *Yehovah* for אדני *Adonai.*

I will enter into the height of his border—"I will penetrate into his extreme retreats"] The text has מרום *marom, the height* which seems to have been taken by mistake from the line but one above. *Two* MSS. have here מלון *malon*, the *lodge* or *retreat;* which is the word

A. M. cir. 3294
B. C. cir. 710
Olymp. XVII. 3
cir. annum
NumæPompilii,
R. Roman., 6

my chariots am I come up to the height of the mountains, to the sides of Lebanon; and I will cut down [k]the tall cedars thereof, *and* the choice fir trees thereof: and I will enter into the height of his border, *and* [l]the forest of his Carmel.

25 I have digged, and drunk water; and with the sole of my feet have I dried up all the rivers of the [m]besieged places.

26 [n]Hast thou not heard long ago, *how* I have done it; *and* of ancient times, that I have formed it? now have I brought it to pass, that thou shouldest be to lay waste defenced cities *into* ruinous heaps.

27 Therefore their inhabitants *were* [o]of small power, they were dismayed and confounded: they were *as* the grass of the field, and *as* the green herb, *as* the grass on the housetops, and *as corn* blasted before it be grown up.

28 But I know thy [p]abode, and thy going out, and thy coming in, and thy rage against me.

A. M. cir. 3291
B. C. cir. 713
Olymp. XVI. 4
cir. annum
NumæPompilii,
R. Roman., 3

29 Because thy rage against me, and thy tumult, is come up into mine ears, therefore [q]will I put my hook in thy nose, and my bridle in thy lips, and I will turn thee back by the way by which thou camest.

30 And this *shall be* a sign unto thee, Ye shall eat *this* year such as groweth of itself: and the second year that which springeth of the same: and in the third year sow ye, and reap, and plant vineyards, and eat the fruit thereof.

31 And [r]the remnant that is escaped of the house of Judah shall again take root downward, and bear fruit upward:

32 For out of Jerusalem shall go forth a remnant, and [s]they that escape out of Mount Zion: the [t]zeal of the LORD of hosts shall do this.

33 Therefore thus saith the LORD concerning the king of Assyria, He shall not come into this city, nor shoot an arrow there, nor come before it with [u]shields, nor cast a bank against it.

---

[k]Heb. *the tallness of the cedars thereof*, and *the choice of the fir-trees thereof*——[l]Or, *the forest* and *his fruitful field* [m]Or, *fenced and closed*——[n]Or, *Hast thou not heard* how *I have made it long ago*, and *formed it of ancient times? should I now bring it to be laid waste*, and *defenced cities* to be *ruinous heaps?* as 2 Kings xix. 25——[o]Heb. *short of hand*——[p]Or, *sitting*——[q]Ch. xxx. 28; Ezek. xxxviii. 4 [r]Heb. *the escaping of the house of Judah that remaineth* [s]Heb. *the escaping*——[t]2 Kings xix. 31; chap. ix. 7 [u]Heb. *shield*

---

in the other copy, 2 Kings xix. 23, and I think is the true reading.

The forest of his Carmel.] The forest and his fruitful field; that is, I will possess myself of the *whole country.*

Verse 25. *Water*—"Strange waters"] The word זרים *zarim, strange,* lost out of the Hebrew text in this place, is supplied from the other copy. A MS. supplies the word רבים *rabbim, many,* instead of it.

With the sole of my feet] With my *infantry.*

All the rivers of the besieged places—"All the canals of fenced places."] The principal cities of Egypt, the scene of his late exploits, were chiefly defended by deep moats, canals, or large lakes, made by labour and art, with which they were surrounded. See *Harmer's* Observ. ii. p. 304. Claudian introduces Alaric boasting of his conquests in the same extravagant manner:—

"Subsidere nostris
Sub pedibus montes; arescere vidimus amnes.—
Fregi Alpes, galeisque Padum victricibus hausi."

De Bello Getic. 526.

"The mountains have passed away under our feet; we have seen the rivers dried up. I have broken the Alps, and laden out the Po with our victorious helmets."

Verse 26. *Lay waste defenced cities* into *ruinous heaps*—"Lay waste warlike nations. strong fenced cities."] גלים נצים *gallim nitstsim.* It is not easy to give a satisfactory account of these two words, which have greatly embarrassed all the interpreters, ancient and modern. For גלים *gallim* I read גוים *goyim,* as the *Septuagint* do in this place, *εθνη.* The word נצים *netsim* the *Vulgate* renders in this place *compugnantium;* in the parallel place, 2 Kings xix. 25, *pugnantium;* and the *Septuagint μαχιμων, fighting, warlike.* This rendering is as well authorized as any other that I know of; and, with the reading of the *Septuagint*, perfectly clears up the construction. See the *margin* on all the preceding verses.

Verse 27. Corn *blasted*] שדמה *shedemah, parched:* it does not appear that there is any good authority for this word. The true reading seems to be שדפה *shedcphah, blasted,* as it is in six MSS. (two ancient) here, and in the other copy.

Verse 29. *Will I put my hook in thy nose*] Et frænum meum: *Jonathan* vocem מתג *metheg,* interpretatus est זמם *zemam,* i. e., annulum, sive uncum, eumque ferreum, quem infigunt naribus camelæ: eoque trahitur, quoniam illa feris motibus agitur: et hoc est, quod discimus in Talmude; et camela cum annulo narium: scilicet, egreditur die sabbathi. "*And my bridle: Jonathan* interprets the word *metheg* by *zemam,* a ring, or that iron hook which they put in the nostrils of a camel to lead her about, check her in her restiveness, &c. And this is what we mean in the *Talmud,* when we say,

A. M. cir. 3291 B. C. cir. 713 Olymp. XVI. 4 cir. annum NumæPompilii, R. Roman., 3

34 By the way that he came, by the same shall he return, and shall not come into this city, saith the LORD.

35 For I will [v]defend this city to save it for mine own sake, and for my servant David's sake.

36 Then the [w]angel of the LORD went forth, and smote in the camp of the Assyrians a hundred and fourscore and five thousand: and when they arose early in the morning, behold, they *were* all dead corpses.

37 So Sennacherib king of Assyria departed, and went and returned, and dwelt at Nineveh.

38 And it came to pass, as he was worshipping in the house of Nisroch his god, that Adrammelech and Sharezer his sons smote him with the sword; and they escaped into the land of [x]Armenia: and Esar-haddon his son reigned in his stead.

[v]2 Kings xx. 6; chap. xxxviii. 6

[w]2 Kings xix. 35——[x]Heb. *Ararat*

And the camel with the ring of her nostrils shall go out on the Sabbath day."—*Jarchi* in 2 Kings xix. 28. Ponam circulum in naribus tuis. "I will put a ring in thy nostrils."—*Jerome.* Just as at this day they put a ring into the nose of the bear, the buffalo, and other wild beasts, to lead them, and to govern them when they are unruly. Bulls are often ringed thus in several parts of England. The Hindoos compare a person who is the *slave of his wife* to a *cow* led by the *ring* in her nose.

Verse 36. *Then the angel*] Before "the angel," the other copy, 2 Kings xix. 35, adds, "it came to pass the same night, that"——

The Prophet Hosea, chap. i. 7, has given a plain prediction of the miraculous deliverance of the kingdom of Judah:—

"And to the house of Judah I will be tenderly merciful:
And I will save them by JEHOVAH their God.
And I will not save them by the bow;
Nor by sword, nor by battle;
By horses, nor by horsemen."—L.

Verse 38. *His sons smote him*] What an awful punishment of his blasphemy! Who can harden his neck against God, and be successful? God does not lightly pass by blasphemy against himself, his government, his word, his Son, or his people. Let the profligate take care!

CHAPTER XXXVIII

Account of Hezekiah's dangerous sickness and miraculous recovery, 1–9. *Tender and beautiful song of thanksgiving, in which this pious king breathed out the sentiments of a grateful heart, when his life was, as it were, restored. This ode may be adapted to other cases; and will always afford profit and pleasure to those who are not void of feeling and piety,* 10–22.

A. M. cir. 3291 B. C. cir. 713 Olymp. XVI. 4 cir. annum NumæPompilii, R. Roman., 3

IN [a]those days was Hezekiah sick unto death. And Isaiah the prophet the son of Amoz came unto him, and said unto him, Thus saith the LORD, [b]Set[c] thine house in order: for thou shalt die, and not live.

2 Then Hezekiah turned his face toward the wall, and prayed unto the LORD.

[a]2 Kings xx. 1, &c.; 2 Chron. xxxii. 24——[b]2 Sam. xvii. 23; 1 Mac. ix. 55

[c]Heb. *Give charge concerning thy house*

NOTES ON CHAP. XXXVIII

Verse 1. *In those days*] The reader is requested to consult the notes on 2 Kings xx. in reference to the principal parts of this chapter.

Verse 2. *Then Hezekiah turned his face toward the wall*] The furniture of an eastern divan or chamber, either for the reception of company or for private use, consists chiefly of carpets spread on the floor in the middle; and of sofas, or couches ranged on one or more sides of the room, on a part raised somewhat above the floor. On these they repose themselves in the day, and sleep at night. It is to be observed that the corner of the room is the place of honour. Dr. *Pococke*, when he was introduced to the Sheikh of Furshout, found him sitting in the corner of his room. He describes another Arab Sheikh "as sitting in the corner of a large green tent, pitched in the middle of an encampment of Arabs; and the Bey of Girge as placed on a sofa in a corner to the right as one entered the room."—*Harmer's* Observ. ii. p. 60. Lady Mary Montague, giving an account of a visit which she made to the Kahya's lady at Adrianople, says, "She ordered cushions to be given me; and took care to place me in the corner, which is the place of honour." —Letter xxxiii. The reason of this seems to be, that the person so placed is distinguished, and in a manner separated, from the rest of the company, and as it were guarded by the wall on each side. We are to suppose Hezekiah's couch placed in the same situation; in which, turning on either side, he must turn his face to the wall; by which he would withdraw himself from those who were attending upon him in his apartment, in order to address his private prayer to God.

A. M. cir. 3291
B. C. cir. 713
Olymp. XVI. 4
cir. annum
NumæPompilii,
R. Roman., 3

3 And said, [d]Remember now, O LORD, I beseech thee, how I have walked before thee in truth and with a perfect heart, and have done *that which is* good in thy sight. And Hezekiah wept [e]sore.

4 Then came the word of the LORD to Isaiah, saying,

5 Go, and say to Hezekiah, Thus saith the LORD, the God of David thy father, I have heard thy prayer, I have seen thy tears: behold I will add unto thy days fifteen years.

6 And I will deliver thee and this city out of the hand of the king of Assyria: and [f]I will defend this city.

7 And this *shall be* [g]a sign unto thee from the LORD, that the LORD will do this thing that he hath spoken;

A. M. cir. 3291
B. C. cir. 713
Olymp. XVI. 4
cir. annum
NumæPompilii,
R. Roman., 3

8 Behold, I will bring again the shadow of the degrees, which is gone down in the [h]sun dial of Ahaz, ten degrees backward. So the sun returned ten degrees, by which degrees it was gone down.

9 The writing of Hezekiah king of Judah, when he had been sick, and was recovered of his sickness:

10 I said in the cutting off of my days, I shall go to the gates of the grave: I am deprived of the residue of my years.

11 I said, I shall not see the LORD, *even* the LORD, [i]in the land of the living: I shall behold man no more with the inhabitants of the world.

12 [k]Mine age is departed, and is removed from me as a shepherd's tent: I have cut off

[d]Neh. xiii. 14——[e]Heb. *with great weeping*——[f]Chap. xxxvii. 35——[g]2 Kings xx. 8, &c.; chap. vii. 11

[h]Heb. *degrees by* or *with the sun*——[i]Psa. xxvii. 13; cxvi. 9——[k]Job vii. 6

Ver. 3. And he said, I beseech thee, O JEHOVAH, remember now how I have endeavoured to walk before thee in truth, and with a perfect heart; and have done that which is good in thine eyes. And Hezekiah wept, and lamented grievously.—L.

Ver. 4. Now [before Isaiah was gone out into the middle court] the word of JEHOVAH came unto him, saying, Go [back,] and say unto Hezekiah, Thus saith JEHOVAH the God of David thy father, I have heard thy supplication; I have seen thy tears. Behold [I will heal thee; and on the third day thou shalt go up into the house of JEHOVAH.

Ver. 5. And] I will add unto thy days fifteen years. And I will deliver thee, and this city, from the hand of the king of Assyria; and I will protect this city. And [Hezekiah said, By what sign shall I know that I shall go up into the house of JEHOVAH?

Ver. 7. And Isaiah said,] This shall be the sign unto thee from JEHOVAH, that JEHOVAH will bring to effect this word which he hath spoken.

The words in the translation included within crotchets are supplied from the parallel place, 2 Kings xx. 4, 5, to make the narration more perfect. I have also taken the liberty, with *Houbigant*, of bringing forward the two last verses of this chapter, and inserting them in their proper places of the narration with the same mark. *Kimchi's* note on these two verses is as follows: "This and the following verse belong not to the writing of Hezekiah; and I see no reason why they are written here after the writing; for their right place is above, after *And I will protect this city*, ver. 6. And so they stand in the book of Kings," 2 Kings xx. 7, 8. The narration of this chapter seems to be in some parts an abridgment of that of 2 Kings xx. The abridger, having finished his extract here with the eleventh verse, seems to have observed, that the seventh and eighth verses of 2 Kings xx. were wanted to complete the narration: he therefore added them at the end of the chapter, after he had inserted the song of Hezekiah, probably with marks for their insertion in their proper places; which marks were afterwards neglected by transcribers. Or a transcriber might omit them by mistake, and add them at the end of the chapter with such marks. Many transpositions are, with great probability, to be accounted for in the same way.

Verse 6. *I will defend this city.*] The other copy, 2 Kings xx. 6, adds: "for mine own sake, and for the sake of David my servant;" and the sentence seems somewhat abrupt without it.

Verse 8. *Which is gone down*—"By which the sun is gone down"] For בשמש *bashshemesh*, the *Septuagint*, *Syriac*, and *Chaldee* read השמש *hashshemesh.*—*Houbigant.* In the history of this miracle in the book of Kings, (2 Kings xx. 9-11,) there is no mention at all made of the sun, but only of the going backward of the shadow: which might be effected by a supernatural refraction. The first ὁ ἡλιος, *the sun*, in this verse is omitted in the *Septuagint*, MS. Pachom.

Verse 9. *The writing of Hezekiah*] Here the book of Kings deserts us, the song of Hezekiah not being inserted in it. Another copy of this very obscure passage (obscure not only from the concise poetical style, but because it is probably very incorrect) would have been of great service. The MSS. and ancient Versions, especially the latter, will help us to get through some of the many difficulties which we meet with in it.

Verse 11. *The Lord*—"JEHOVAH"] יה *Yah*, יה *Yah*, seems to be יהוה *Yehovah*, in MS. Bodl., and it was so at first written in another. So the *Syriac*. See *Houbigant*. I believe יהוה *Yehovah* was the original reading. See the note on chap. xii. 2.

Verse 12. *Mine age—is removed from me as a shepherd's tent*] רעי *roi* is put for רעה *roeh*, say the rabbins; (*Sal. ben Melec* on the place;) but much more probably is written imperfectly for רעים *roim*, *shepherds*. See note on chap. v. 1.

I shall be removed from this state to another,

A. M. cir. 3291 B. C. cir. 713 Olymp. XVI. 4 cir. annum NumæPompilii, R. Roman., 3

like a weaver my life: he will
cut me off [l]with pining sickness: from day *even* to night
wilt thou make an end of me.

13 I reckoned till morning, *that,* as a lion,
so will he break all my bones: from day *even*
to night wilt thou make an end of me.

14 Like a crane *or* a swallow, so did I
chatter: [m]I did mourn as a dove: mine eyes
fail *with looking* upward: O LORD, I am
oppressed; [n]undertake for me.

15 What shall I say? he hath both spoken
unto me, and himself hath done *it:* I shall
go softly all my years [o]in the bitterness of my
soul.

16 O LORD, by these *things*
men live, and in all these *things*
is the life of my spirit; so wilt
thou recover me, and make
me to live.

17 Behold [p]for peace I had great bitterness: but [q]thou hast in love to my soul *delivered it* from the pit of corruption: for thou
hast cast all my sins behind thy back.

18 For [r]the grave cannot praise thee, death
can *not* celebrate thee: they that go down
into the pit cannot hope for thy truth.

19 The living, the living, he shall praise
thee, as I *do* this day: [s]the father to the
children shall make known thy truth.

[l]Or, *from the* thrum——[m]Chap. lix. 11——[n]Or, *ease me*——[o]Job vii. 11; x. 1——[p]Or, *on my peace* came *great bitterness*

[q]Heb. *thou hast loved my soul from the pit*——[r]Psa. vi. 5; xxx. 9; lxxxviii. 11; cxv. 17; Eccles. ix. 10——[s]Deut. iv. 9; vi. 7; Psa. lxxviii. 3, 4

as a shepherd removes his *tent* from one place to another for the sake of his flock. Is not this a strong intimation of his belief in a future state?

I have cut off like a weaver my life—"My life is cut off as by the weaver"] קפדתי *kippadti.* This verb is rendered passively, and in the third person, by the *Syriac, Chaldee,* and *Vulgate.*

Verse 13. The last line of the foregoing verse מיום עד לילה תשלימני *miyom ad layelah tashlimeni,* "In the course of the day thou wilt finish my web;" or, as the common version has it, "From day *even* to night wilt thou make an end of me," is not repeated at the end of this verse in the Syriac version; and a MS. omits it. It seems to have been inserted a second time in the Hebrew text by mistake.

I reckoned till morning, &c.—"I roared until the morning like the lion"] For שויתי *shivvithi,* the Chaldee has נהמית *nihameith:* he read שאגתי *shaagti,* the proper term for the roaring of a lion; often applied to the deep groaning of men in sickness. See Psa. xxii., xxxii. 3, xxxviii. 9; Job iii. 24. The Masoretes divide the sentence, as I have done; taking כארי *caari, like a lion,* into the first member; and so likewise the *Septuagint.*

Verse 14. *Like—a swallow*—"Like the swallow"] כסים *kesis;* so read two MSS., *Theodot.,* and *Hieron.*

Mine eyes fail] For דלו *dallu* the *Septuagint* read כלו *calu,* εξελιπον. Compare Psa. lxix. 4, cxix. 82, 123; Lam. ii. 11, iv. 17, in the *Hebrew* and in the *Septuagint.*

O LORD—"O Lord"] For יהוה *Yehovah,* thirty MSS. and eight editions read אדני *Adonai.*

Undertake for me—"Contend for me"] עשקה *ashekah,* with ש *shin, Jarchi:* this sense of the word is established by Gen. xxvi. 20: "He called the name of the well עשק *esek,* because they *strove* with him:" התעשקו *hithasseku,* equivalent to יריבו *yaribu,* at the beginning of the verse.

Verse 15. *I shall go softly all my years in the bitterness of my soul*—"Through the rest of my years will I reflect on this bitterness of my soul"] אדדה *eddaddeh; recogitabo,* Vulg., *reputabo,* Hieron. in loc.

Verse 16. *By these* things men *live*—"For this cause shall it be declared"] Περι αυτης γαρ ανηγγελη σοι, και εξηγειρας μου την πνοην, Sept. They read in their copies עליה יחוו לך ותחיי רוחי not very different from the present text, from which all the ancient Versions vary. They entirely omit two words, ולכל בהן *ulecol bahen;* as to which there is some variation in the MSS. One MS. has ובכל *ubechol, and in all;* two others וכל *vechol, and all,* and ten MSS. have בהם *bahem, in them,* in the masculine gender.

Taking this as in the common Version, we may observe, it is not an unfrequent case, that afflictions, and especially such as tend to a speedy death, become the means, not only of saving the *soul,* but also of lengthening the *life.*

Make me to live—"Hast prolonged my life."] A MSS. and the Babylonish Talmud read ותחיני *vetachayeni,* and so the ancient Versions. It must necessarily be in the second person.

Verse 17. *For peace I had great bitterness*—"My anguish is changed into ease"] מר לי מר *mar li mar,* "mutata mihi est amaritudo." Paronomasia; a figure which the prophet frequently admits. I do not always note it, because it cannot ever be preserved in the translation, and the sense seldom depends upon it. But here it perfectly clears up the great obscurity of the passage. See Lowth on the place.

Thou hast rescued] חשכת *chashachta,* with כ *caph,* instead of ק *koph;* so the *Septuagint* and *Vulgate; Houbigant.* See *Chappelow* on Job xxxiii. 18.

From perdition] משחת בלי *mishshachath beli,* ινα μη αποληται, *Sept. ut non periret,* "that it may not perish." *Vulg.* Perhaps inverting the order of the words. See *Houbigant.*

Thou hast in love to my soul] חשקת *chashakta,* "thou hast lovingly embraced" or kissed "my soul out of the pit of corruption."

Verse 19. *Thy truth*] אל אמתך *el amittecha.*

A. M. cir. 3291
B. C. cir. 713
Olymp. XVI. 4
cir. annum
NumæPompilii,
R. Roman., 3

20 The Lord *was ready* to save me: therefore we will sing my songs to the stringed instruments all the days of our life in the house of the Lord.

21 For [t]Isaiah had said, Let them take a lump of figs, and lay *it* for a plaster upon the boil, and he shall recover.

22 [u]Hezekiah also had said, What *is* the sign that I shall go up to the house of the Lord?

---

[t]2 Kings xx. 7

[u]2 Kings xx. 8

A MS. omits אל *el;* and instead of אל *el,* an ancient MS. and one edition read את *eth.* The same mistake as in Psa. ii. 7.

Verse 21. *Let them take a lump of figs, &c.*] God, in effecting this miraculous cure, was pleased to order the use of means not improper for that end. "Folia, et, quæ non maturuere, fici, strumis illinuntur omnibusque quæ emollienda sunt discutiendave."—Plin. *Nat. Hist.* xxiii. 7. "Ad discutienda ea, quæ in corporis parte aliqua coierunt, maxime possunt—ficus arida," &c.—Celsus, v. 11. See the note on 2 Kings xx. 7. *Philemon Holland* translates the passage as a *medical* man:—"The milke or white juice that the figge tree yieldeth is of the same nature that vinegre: and therefore it will cruddle milke as well as rennet, or rendles. The right season of gathering this milkie substance is before that the figs be ripe upon the tree; and then it must be dried in the shadow: thus prepared, *it is good to break impostumes, and keepe ulcer open.*"

CHAPTER XXXIX

The Babylonish monarch sends letters of congratulation and a present to Hezekiah, on account of his recovery from his late dangerous illness, 1. *The king of Judah shows the messengers of Merodach-baladan all the treasures of his house and kingdom,* 2. *The prophet takes occasion from this ostentatious display of the king to predict the captivity of the royal family, and of the people, by the Babylonians,* 3–8.

A. M. cir. 3292
B. C. cir. 712
Olymp. XVII. 1
cir. annum
NumæPompilii,
R. Roman., 4

AT [a]that time Merodach-baladan, the son of Baladan, king of Babylon, sent letters and a present to Hezekiah: for he had heard that he had been sick, and was recovered.

2 [b]And Hezekiah was glad of them, and showed them the house of his [c]precious things, the silver, and the gold, and the spices, and the precious ointment, and all the house of his [d]armour, [e]and all that was found in his treasures: there was nothing in his house, nor in all his dominion, that Hezekiah showed them not.

3 Then came Isaiah the prophet unto king Hezekiah, and said unto him, What said these men? and from whence came they unto thee? And Hezekiah said, They are come from a far country unto me, *even* from Babylon.

4 Then said he, What have they seen in thine house? And Hezekiah answered, All that *is* in mine house have they seen: there is nothing among my treasures that I have not showed them.

5 Then said Isaiah to Hezekiah, Hear the word of the Lord of hosts:

6 Behold, the days come, [f]that all that *is* in thine house, and *that* which thy fathers have laid up in store until this day, shall be carried to Babylon: nothing shall be left, saith the Lord.

7 And of thy sons that shall issue from thee,

---

[a]2 Kings xx. 12, &c.——[b]2 Chron. xxxii. 31
[c]Or, *spicery*

[d]Or, *jewels*——[e]Heb. *vessels* or *instruments*
[f]Jer. xx. 5

NOTES ON CHAP. XXXIX

Hitherto the copy of this history in the second book of Kings has been much the most correct; in this chapter that in Isaiah has the advantage. In the two first verses two mistakes in the other copy are to be corrected from this: for הזקיהו *hizkiyahu,* read ויחזק *vayechezek, and was recovered;* and for וישמע *vaiyishma, he heard,* read וישמח *vaiyismach, he rejoiced.*

Verse 1. *At that time Merodach-baladan*] This name is variously written in the MSS. *Berodach, Medorach, Medarech,* and *Medurach.*

"And ambassadors"] The *Septuagint* add here και πρεσβεις; that is, ומלאכים *umalachim, and ambassadors;* which word seems to be necessary to the sense, though omitted in the Hebrew text both here and in the other copy, 2 Kings xx. 12. For the subsequent narration refers to them all along, "these men, whence came they?" &c.; plainly supposing them to have been personally mentioned before. See *Houbigant.*

Verse 6. *To Babylon*] בבלה *babelah,* so two MSS., (one ancient;) rightly, without doubt, as the other copy (2 Kings xx. 17) has it. This prediction was fulfilled about one hundred and fifty years after it was spoken: see Dan. i. 2, 3-7. What a proof of Divine omniscience!

A. M. cir. 3292
B. C. cir. 712
Olymp. XVII. 1
cir. annum
NumæPompilii,
R. Roman., 4

which thou shalt beget, shall
they take away; and [g]they shall
be eunuchs in the palace of the
king of Babylon.
8 Then said Hezekiah to Isaiah, [h]Good
is the word of the LORD
which thou hast spoken. He
said moreover, For there shall
be peace and truth in my
days.

[g]Fulfilled, Dan. i. 2, 3, 7

[h]1 Sam. iii. 18

Verse 8. *Then said Hezekiah*] The nature of Hezekiah's crime, and his humiliation on the message of God to him by the prophet, is more expressly declared by the author of the book of the Chronicles: "But Hezekiah rendered not again according to the benefit done unto him; for his heart was lifted up; therefore there was wrath upon him, and upon Judah and Jerusalem. Notwithstanding, Hezekiah humbled himself for the pride of his heart, both he and the inhabitants of Jerusalem, so that the wrath of the Lord came not upon them in the days of Hezekiah. And Hezekiah prospered in all his works. Howbeit, in the business of the ambassadors of the princes of Babylon, who sent unto him to inquire of the wonder that was done in the land, God left him, to try him, that he might know all that was in his heart." 2 Chron. xxxii. 25, 26, 30, 31.

There shall be peace and truth in my days.] I rather think these words should be understood as an humble inquiry of the king, addressed to the prophet. "Shall there be prosperity, שלום *shalom*, and truth in MY days?—Shall *I* escape the evil which thou predictest?" Understood otherwise, they manifest a pitiful unconcern both for his own family and for the nation. "So *I* be well, I care not how it may go with others." This is the view I have taken of the passage in 2 Kings xxi. 19. Let the reader judge whether *this*, or the *former*, should be preferred. See the concluding notes on 2 Kings xx.

CHAPTER XL

In this chapter the prophet opens the subject respecting the restoration of the Church with great force and elegance; declaring God's command to his messengers the prophets to comfort his people in their captivity, and to impart to them the glad tidings that the time of favour and deliverance was at hand, 1, 2. *Immediately a harbinger is introduced giving orders, as usual in the march of eastern monarchs, to remove every obstacle, and to prepare the way for their return to their own land,* 3–5. *The same words, however, the New Testament Scriptures authorize us to refer to the opening of the Gospel dispensation. Accordingly, this subject, coming once in view, is principally attended to in the sequel. Of this the prophet gives us sufficient notice by introducing a voice commanding another proclamation, which calls off our attention from all temporary, fading things to the spiritual and eternal things of the Gospel,* 6–11. *And to remove every obstacle in the way of the prophecy in either sense, or perhaps to give a farther display of the character of the Redeemer, he enlarges on the power and wisdom of God, as the Creator and Disposer of all things. It is impossible to read this description of God, the most sublime that ever was penned, without being struck with inexpressible reverence and self-abasement. The contrast between the great Jehovah and every thing reputed great in this world, how admirably imagined, how exquisitely finished! What atoms and inanities are they all before* HIM *who sitteth on the circle of the immense heavens, and views the potentates of the earth in the light of* grasshoppers,—*those poor insects that wander over the barren heath for sustenance, spend the day in continual chirpings, and take up their humble lodging at night on a blade of grass!* 12–26. *The prophet concludes with a most comfortable application of the whole, by showing that all this infinite power and unsearchable wisdom is unweariedly and everlastingly engaged in strengthening, comforting, and saving his people,* 27–31.

A. M. cir. 3292
B. C. cir. 712
Olymp. XVII. 1
cir. annum
NumæPompilii,
R. Roman., 4

COMFORT ye, comfort ye my
people, saith your God.
2 Speak ye [a]comfortably to
Jerusalem, and cry unto her, that
her [b]warfare is accomplished, that
her iniquity is pardoned: [c]for
she hath received of the LORD'S
hand double for all her sins.

[a]Heb. *to the heart*——[b]Or, *appointed time*

[c]See Job xlii. 10; chap. lxi. 7

The course of prophecies which follow, from hence to the end of the book, and which taken together constitute the most elegant part of the sacred writings of the Old Testament, interspersed also with many passages of the highest sublimity, was probably delivered in the latter part of the reign of Hezekiah. The prophet in the foregoing chapter had delivered a very explicit declaration of the impending dissolution of the kingdom, and of the captivity of the royal house of David, and of the people, under the kings of Babylon. As the subject of his subsequent prophecies was to be chiefly of the consolatory kind, he opens them with giving a promise of the restoration of the kingdom, and the return of the people from that captivity, by the merciful interposition of God in their favour. But the views of the prophet are not confined to this event. As the restoration of the royal family, and of the tribe of Judah, which would otherwise have soon become undistinguished, and have been irrecoverably lost, was necessary, in the design and order of Providence, for the fulfilling of God's promises of

A. M. cir. 3292 B. C. cir. 712 Olymp. XVII. 1 cir. annum NumæPompilii, R. Roman., 4

3 [d]The voice of him that crieth in the wilderness, [e]Prepare ye the way of the LORD, [f]make straight in the desert a highway for our God.

4 Every valley shall be exalted, and every mountain and hill shall be made low: [g]and the crooked shall be made [h]straight, and the rough places [i]plain:

[d]Matt. iii. 3; Mark i. 3; Luke iii. 4; John i. 23——[e]Mal. iii. 1

[f]Psa. lxviii. 4; chap. xlix. 11——[g]Ch. xlv. 2——[h]Or, *a straight place*——[i]Or, *a plain place*

establishing a more glorious and an everlasting kingdom, under the Messiah to be born of the tribe of Judah, and of the family of David, the prophet connects these two events together, and hardly ever treats of the former without throwing in some intimations of the latter; and sometimes is so fully possessed with the glories of the future and more remote kingdom, that he seems to leave the more immediate subject of his commission almost out of the question.

Indeed this evangelical sense of the prophecy is so apparent, and stands forth in so strong a light, that some interpreters cannot see that it has any other; and will not allow the prophecy to have any relation at all to the return from the captivity of Babylon. It may therefore be useful to examine more attentively the train of the prophet's ideas, and to consider carefully the images under which he displays his subject. He hears a crier giving orders, by solemn proclamation, to prepare the way of the Lord in the wilderness; to remove all obstructions before JEHOVAH marching through the desert; through the wild, uninhabited, impassable country. The deliverance of God's people from the Babylonish captivity is considered by him as parallel to the former deliverance of them from the Egyptian bondage. God was then represented as their king leading them in person through the vast deserts which lay in their way to the promised land of Canaan. It is not merely for JEHOVAH himself that in both cases the way was to be prepared, and all obstructions to be removed; but for JEHOVAH marching in person at the head of his people. Let us first see how this idea is pursued by the sacred poets who treat of the exodus, which is a favourite subject with them, and affords great choice of examples:—

"When Israel came out of Egypt,
The house of Jacob from the barbarous people;
Judah was his sanctuary,
Israel his dominion." Psa. cxiv. 1, 2.

"JEHOVAH his God is with him;
And the shout of a king is among them:
God brought them out of Egypt"——
Num. xxiii. 21, 22.

"Make a highway for him that rideth through the deserts:
O God, when thou wentest forth before thy people,
When thou marchedst through the wilderness,
The heavens dropped"—— Psa. lxviii. 4, 7.

Let us now see how Isaiah treats the subject of the return of the people from Babylon. They were to march through the wilderness with JEHOVAH at their head, who was to lead them, to smooth the way before them, and to supply them with water in the thirsty desert; with perpetual allusion to the exodus:—

"Come ye forth from Babylon, flee ye from the land of the Chaldeans with the voice of joy:
Publish ye this, and make it heard; utter it forth even to the end of the earth;
Say ye, JEHOVAH hath redeemed his servant Jacob:
They thirsted not in the deserts, through which he made them go;
Waters from the rock he caused to flow for them;
Yea, he clave the rock, and forth gushed the waters."
Chap. xlviii. 20, 21.

"Remember not the former things;
And the things of ancient times regard not:"

(That is, the deliverance from Egypt:)

"Behold, I make a new thing;
Even now shall it spring forth; will ye not regard it?
Yea, I will make in the wilderness a way;
In the desert streams of water."
Chap. xliii. 18, 19.

"But he that trusteth in me shall inherit the land,
And shall possses my holy mountain.
Then will I say: Cast up, cast up the causeway; make clear the way;
Remove every obstruction from the road of my people." Chap. lvii. 13, 14.

"How beautiful appear on the mountains
The feet of the joyful messenger, of him that announceth peace;
Of the joyful messenger of good tidings, of him that announceth salvation;
Of him that saith to Sion, Thy God reigneth!
All thy watchmen lift up their voice, they shout together;
For face to face shall they see, when JEHOVAH returneth to Sion.
Verily not in haste shall ye go forth,
And not by flight shall ye march along:
For JEHOVAH shall march in your front;
And the God of Israel shall bring up your rear." Chap. lii. 7, 8, 12.

Babylon was separated from Judea by an immense tract of country which was one continued desert; that large part of Arabia called very properly Deserta. It is mentioned in history as a remarkable occurrence, that Nebuchadnezzar, having received the news of the death of his father, in order to make the utmost expedition in his journey to Babylon from Egypt and Phœnicia, set out with a few attendants, and passed through this desert. *Berosus apud Joseph.*, Antiq. x. 11. This was the nearest way homewards for the Jews; and whether they actually returned by this way or not, the first thing that would occur on the proposal or thought of their return would be

A. M. cir. 3292
B. C. cir. 712
Olymp. XVII. 1
cir. annum
NumæPompilii,
R. Roman., 4

5 And the [k]glory of the LORD shall be revealed, and all flesh shall see *it* together; for the mouth of the LORD hath spoken *it*.

6 The voice said, Cry. And he said, What shall I cry? [l]All flesh *is* grass, and all the goodliness thereof *is* as the flower of the field.

A. M. cir. 3292
B. C. cir. 712
Olymp. XVII. 1
cir. annum
NumæPompilii,
R. Roman., 4

---

[k]Chap. xxxv. 2; lviii. 8; lx. 1; Exod. xvi. 7; Lev. ix. 23; Num. xiv. 10; xxiv. 16; 1 Kings viii. 11

[l]Job xiv. 2; Psa. xc. 5; cii. 11; ciii. 15; James i. 10; 1 Pet. i. 24

---

the difficulty of this almost impracticable passage. Accordingly the proclamation for the preparation of the way is the most natural idea, and the most obvious circumstance, by which the prophet could have opened his subject.

These things considered, I have not the least doubt that the return of the Jews from the captivity of Babylon is the first, though not the principal, thing in the prophet's view. The redemption from Babylon is clearly foretold, and at the same time is employed as an image to shadow out a redemption of an infinitely higher and more important nature. I should not have thought it necessary to employ so many words in endeavouring to establish what is called the *literal sense* of this prophecy, which I think cannot be rightly understood without it, had I not observed that many interpreters of the first authority, in particular the very learned Vitringa, have excluded it entirely.

Yet obvious and plain as I think this literal sense is, we have nevertheless the irrefragable authority of John the Baptist, and of our blessed Saviour himself, as recorded by all the Evangelists, for explaining this exordium of the prophecy of the opening of the Gospel by the preaching of John, and of the introduction of the kingdom of Messiah; who was to effect a much greater deliverance of the people of God, Gentiles as well as Jews, from the captivity of sin and the dominion of death. And this we shall find to be the case in many subsequent parts also of this prophecy, where passages manifestly relating to the deliverance of the Jewish nation, effected by Cyrus, are, with good reason, and upon undoubted authority, to be understood of the redemption wrought for mankind by Christ.

If the literal sense of this prophecy, as above explained, cannot be questioned, much less surely can the spiritual; which, I think, is allowed on all hands, even by Grotius himself. If both are to be admitted, here is a plain example of the mystical allegory, or double sense, as it is commonly called, of prophecy; which the sacred writers of the New Testament clearly suppose, and according to which they frequently frame their interpretation of passages from the Old Testament. Of the foundation and properties of this sort of allegory, see *De S. Poës. Hebr.* Prælect. xi.

NOTES ON CHAP. XL

Verse 1. *Comfort ye, comfort ye*] "The whole of this prophecy," says *Kimchi*, "belongs to the days of the Messiah."

Verse 2. *Double for all her sins*—"Blessings double to the punishment."] It does not seem reconcilable to our notions of the Divine justice, which always punishes less than our iniquities deserve, to suppose that God had punished the sins of the Jews in double proportion; and it is more agreeable to the tenor of this consolatory message to understand it as a promise of ample recompense for the effects of past displeasure, on the reconciliation of God to his returning people. To express this sense of the passage, which the words of the original will very well bear, it was necessary to add a word or two in the version to supply the elliptical expression of the Hebrew. Compare chap. lxi. 7; Job xlii. 10; Zech. ix. 12. חטאה *chattaah* signifies punishment for sin, Lam. iii. 39; Zech. xiv. 19. But *Kimchi* says, "*Double* here means the *two captivities* and *emigrations* suffered by the Israelites. The *first*, the Babylonish captivity; the *second*, that which they *now* endure." This is not a bad conjecture.

Verse 3. *The voice of him that crieth in the wilderness*—"A voice crieth, In the wilderness"] The idea is taken from the practice of eastern monarchs, who, whenever they entered upon an expedition or took a journey, especially through desert and unpractised countries, sent harbingers before them to prepare all things for their passage, and pioneers to open the passes, to level the ways, and to remove all impediments. The officers appointed to superintend such preparations the Latins call *stratores*. Ipse (Johannes Baptista) se *stratorem* vocat Messiæ, cujus esset alta et elata voce homines in desertis locis habitantes ad itinera et vias Regi mox venturo sternendas et reficiendas hortari.—Mosheim, Instituta, Majora, p. 96. "He (John the Baptist) calls himself the pioneer of the Messiah, whose business it was with a loud voice to call upon the people dwelling in the deserts to level and prepare the roads by which the King was about to march."

Diodorus's account of the marches of Semiramis into Media and Persia will give us a clear notion of the preparation of the way for a royal expedition: "In her march to Ecbatana she came to the Zarcean mountain, which, extending many furlongs, and being full of craggy precipices and deep hollows, could not be passed without taking a great compass about. Being therefore desirous of leaving an everlasting memorial of herself, as well as of shortening the way, she ordered the precipices to be digged down, and the hollows to be filled up; and at a great expense she made a shorter and more expeditious road, which to this day is called from her the road of Semiramis. Afterward she went into Persia, and all the other countries of Asia subject to her dominion; and wherever she went, she ordered the mountains and precipices to be levelled, raised causeways in the plain country, and at a great expense made the ways passable."—*Diod. Sic.* lib. ii.

The writer of the apocryphal book called *Baruch* expresses the same subject by the same images, either taking them from this place of Isaiah, or from the common notions of his countrymen: "For God hath appointed that every high hill, and banks of long continuance, should be cast down, and valleys filled up, to make even the ground, that Israel may go safely in the glory of God." Chap. v. 7.

A. M. cir. 3292
B. C. cir. 712
Olymp. XVII. 1
cir. annum
NumæPompilii,
R. Roman., 4

7 The grass withereth, the
flower fadeth: because the [m]spi-
rit of the LORD bloweth upon it:
surely the people *is* grass.

8 The grass withereth, the
flower fadeth: but the [n]word
of our God shall stand for
ever.

A. M. cir. 3292
B. C. cir. 712
Olymp. XVII. 1
cir. annum
NumæPompilii,
R. Roman., 4

---

[m]Psa. ciii. 16

[n]John xii. 34; 1 Pet. i. 25

The Jewish Church, to which John was sent to announce the coming of Messiah, was at that time in a barren and desert condition, unfit, without reformation, for the reception of her King. It was in this desert country, destitute at that time of all religious cultivation, in true piety and good works unfruitful, that John was sent to prepare the way of the Lord by preaching repentance. I have distinguished the parts of the sentence according to the punctuation of the Masoretes, which agrees best both with the literal and the spiritual sense; which the construction and parallelism of the distich in the Hebrew plainly favours, and of which the Greek of the Septuagint and of the evangelists is equally susceptible.

John was born in the desert of Judea, and passed his whole life in it, till the time of his being manifested to Israel. He preached in the same desert: it was a mountainous country; however not entirely and properly a desert; for though less cultivated than other parts of Judea, yet it was not uninhabited. Joshua (chap. xv. 61, 62) reckons six cities in it. We are so prepossessed with the idea of John's living and preaching in the desert, that we are apt to consider this particular scene of his preaching as a very important and essential part of history: whereas I apprehend this circumstance to be no otherwise important, than as giving us a strong idea of the rough character of the man, which was answerable to the place of his education; and as affording a proper emblem of the rude state of the Jewish Church at that time, which was the true wilderness meant by the prophet, in which John was to prepare the way for the coming of the Messiah.

Verse 4. *Crooked*] The word עקב *akob* is very generally rendered *crooked:* but this sense of the word seems not to be supported by any good authority. *Ludolphus*, Comment. ad Hist. Æthiop. p. 206, says "that in the Ethiopic language it signifies *clivus, locus editus:*" and so the *Syriac* Version renders it in this place, ערמא *arama: Hebrew,* ערמה *aramah, tumulus, acervus.* Thus the parallelism would be more perfect: "the hilly country shall be made level, and the precipices a smooth plain."

Verse 5. "The salvation of our God."] These words are added here by the *Septuagint: το σωτηριον του Θεου,* את ישועת אלהינו *eth yesuath Eloheynu,* as it is in the parallel place, chap. lii. 10. The sentence is abrupt without it, the verb wanting its object; and I think it is genuine. Our English translation has supplied the word *it,* which is equivalent to this addition, from the *Septuagint.*

This omission in the *Hebrew* text is ancient, being prior to the *Chaldee, Syriac,* and *Vulgate* Versions: but the words stand in all the copies of the *Septuagint,* and they are acknowledged by Luke, chap. iii. 6. The whole of this verse is wanting in one of my oldest MSS.

Verse 6. *The voice said, Cry*—"A voice saith, Proclaim"] To understand rightly this passage is a matter of importance; for it seems designed to give us the true key to the remaining part of Isaiah's prophecies, the general subject of which is the restoration of the people and Church of God. The prophet opens the subject with great clearness and elegance: he declares at once God's command to his messengers, (his prophets, as the *Chaldee* rightly explains it,) to comfort his people in captivity, to impart to them the joyful tidings, that their punishment has now satisfied the Divine justice, and the time of reconciliation and favour is at hand. He then introduces a harbinger giving orders to prepare the way for God, leading his people from Babylon, as he did formerly from Egypt, through the wilderness; to remove all obstacles, and to clear the way for their passage. Thus far nothing more appears to be intended than a return from the Babylonish captivity; but the next words seem to intimate something much greater:—

"And the glory of JEHOVAH shall be revealed;
And all flesh shall see together the salvation
of our God."

He then introduces a voice commanding him to make a solemn proclamation. And what is the import of it? that the people—the flesh, is of a vain temporary nature; that all its glory fadeth, and is soon gone; but that the word of God endureth for ever. What is this, but a plain opposition of the flesh to the spirit; of the carnal Israel to the spiritual; of the temporary Mosaic economy to the eternal Christian dispensation? You may be ready to conclude, (the prophet may be disposed to say,) by this introduction to my discourse, that my commission is only to comfort you with a promise of the restoration of your religion and polity, of Jerusalem, of the temple, and its services and worship in all its ancient splendour. These are earthly, temporary, shadowy, fading things, which shall soon pass away, and be destroyed for ever; these are not worthy to engage your attention in comparison of the greater blessings, the spiritual redemption, the eternal inheritance, covered under the veil of the former, which I have it in charge to unfold unto you. The law has only a shadow of good things; the substance is the Gospel. I promise you a restoration of the former, which, however, is only for a time, and shall be done away, according to God's original appointment: but under that image I give you a view of the latter, which shall never be done away, but shall endure for ever. This I take to be agreeable to St. Peter's interpretation of this passage of the prophet, quoted by him, 1 Pet. i. 24, 25: "All flesh is as grass, and all the glory of man as the flower of grass. The grass withereth, and the flower thereof falleth away; but the word of the Lord endureth for ever. And this is the word which by the Gospel is preached unto you." This is the same word of the Lord of which Isaiah speaks, which hath now been preached unto you by the Gospel. The law and the Gospel are frequently opposed to one an-

A. M. cir. 3292
B. C. cir. 712
Olymp. XVII. 4
cir. annum
NumæPompilii,
R. Roman., 4

9 [o]O Zion, that bringest good
tidings, get thee up into the high
mountain; [p]O Jerusalem, that
bringest good tidings, lift up thy
voice with strength; lift *it* up, be not afraid;
say unto the cities of Judah, Behold your God!
10 Behold, the Lord GOD will come [q]with
strong *hand,* and [r]his arm shall rule for him:
behold, [s]his reward *is* with him, and [t]his
work before him.

A. M. cir. 3292
B. C. cir. 712
Olymp. XVII. 1
cir. annum
NumæPompilii,
R. Roman., 4

11 He shall [u]feed his flock like
a shepherd: he shall gather the
lambs with his arm, and carry
them in his bosom, *and* shall
gently lead those [v]that are with young.
12 [w]Who hath measured the waters in the
hollow of his hand, and meted out heaven
with the span, and comprehended the dust of
the earth in [x]a measure, and weighed the
mountains in scales, and the hills in a balance?

---

[o]Or, *O thou that tellest good tidings to Zion;* chap. xli. 27; lii. 7——[p]Or, *O thou that tellest good tidings to Jerusalem*——[q]Or, *against the strong*——[r]Chap. lix. 16 [s]Chap. lxii. 11; Rev. xxii. 12

[t]Or, *recompense for his work;* chap. xlix. 4——[u]Chap. xlix. 10; Ezek. xxxiv. 23; xxxvii. 24; John x. 11; Heb. xiii. 20; 1 Pet. ii. 25; v. 4; Rev. vii. 17——[v]Or, *that give suck*——[w]Prov. xxx. 4——[x]Heb. *a tierce*

---

other by St. Paul, under the images of flesh and spirit: "Having begun in the spirit, are ye now made perfect by the flesh?" Gal. iii. 3.—L.

All the goodliness thereof—"All its glory"] For חסדו *chasdo* read חדו *chadu;* the *Septuagint* and *Vulgate*, and 1 Pet. i. 24.

Verse 7. *The grass withereth*] The whole of this verse is wanting in three of *Kennicott's* and five of *De Rossi's* MSS., and in a very correct and ancient MS. of my own, and also in the *Septuagint* and *Arabic*.

Surely the people—"Verily this people"] So the *Syriac;* who perhaps read העם הזה *haam hazzeh.*

Because the spirit of the Lord—"When the wind of JEHOVAH"] רוח יהוה *ruach Yehovah,* a wind of JEHOVAH, is a Hebraism, meaning no more than a strong wind. It is well known that a hot wind in the east destroys every green thing. Compare Psa. ciii. 16. Two MSS. omit the word יהוה *Yehovah, Jehovah.*

Verse 9. *O Zion, that bringest good tidings*—"O daughter, that bringest glad tidings to Zion"] That the true construction of the sentence is this, which makes Zion the receiver, not the publisher, of the glad tidings, which latter has been the most prevailing interpretation, will, I think, very clearly appear, if we rightly consider the image itself, and the custom and common practice from which it is taken. I have added the word *daughter* to express the feminine gender of the Hebrew participle, which I know not how to do otherwise in our language; and this is absolutely necessary in order to ascertain the image. For the office of announcing and celebrating such glad tidings as are here spoken of, belongs peculiarly to the women. On occasion of any great public success, a signal victory, or any other joyful event, it was usual for the women to gather together, and with music, dances, and songs, to publish and celebrate the happy news. Thus after the passage of the Red Sea, Miriam, and all the women, with timbrels in their hands, formed a chorus, and joined the men in their triumphant song, dancing, and throwing in alternately the refrain or burden of the song:—

"Sing ye to JEHOVAH, for he is greatly exalted;
The horse and his rider hath he cast into the sea."
Exod. xv. 20, 21.

So Jephthah's daughter collected a chorus of virgins, and with dances and songs came out to meet her father, and to celebrate his victory, Judg. xi. 34. After David's conquest of Goliath, "all the women came out of the cities of Israel singing and dancing to meet Saul, with tabrets, with joy, and with instruments of music;" and, forming themselves into two choruses, they sang alternately:—

"Saul has slain his thousands:
And David his ten thousands."
1 Sam. xviii. 6, 7.

And this gives us the true sense of a passage in the sixty-eighth Psalm, which has frequently been misunderstood:—

"JEHOVAH gave the word, (that is, the joyful news,)
The women, who published the glad tidings, were a great company;
The kings of mighty armies did flee, did flee:
And even the matron, who stayed at home, shared the spoil."

The word signifying *the publishers of glad tidings* is the same, and expressed in the same form by the feminine participle, as in this place, and the last distich is the song which they sang. So in this place, JEHOVAH having given the word by his prophet, the joyful tidings of the restoration of Zion, and of God's returning to Jerusalem, (see chap. lii. 8,) the women are exhorted by the prophet to publish the joyful news with a loud voice from eminences, whence they might best be heard all over the country; and the matter and burden of their song was to be, "Behold your God!" See on Psalm lxviii. 11.

Verse 10. *His reward* is *with him, and his work before him.*—"His reward is with him, and the recompense of his work before him."] That is, the reward and the recompense which he bestows, and which he will pay to his faithful servants; this he has ready at hand with him, and holds it out before him, to encourage those who trust in him and wait for him.

Verse 11. *Shall gently lead those that are with young*—"The nursing ewes shall he gently lead."] A beautiful image, expressing, with the utmost propriety as well as elegance, the tender attention of the shepherd to his flock. That the greatest care in driving the cattle in regard to the dams and their young was necessary, appears clearly from Jacob's apology to his brother Esau, Gen. xxxiii. 13: "The flocks and the herds giving suck to their young are

A. M. cir. 3292
B. C. cir. 712
Olymp. XVII. 1
cir. annum
NumæPompilii,
R. Roman., 4

13 [y]Who hath directed the
Spirit of the LORD, or *being*
[z]his counsellor hath taught him.
14 With whom took he coun-
sel, and *who* [a]instructed him, and taught
him in the path of judgment, and taught
him knowledge, and showed to him the way
of [b]understanding?
15 Behold, the nations *are* as a drop of a
bucket, and are counted as the small dust of
the balance: behold, he taketh up the isles as
a very little thing.
16 And Lebanon *is* not sufficient to burn, nor
the beasts thereof sufficient for a burnt-offering.
17 All nations before him *are* as [c]nothing;
and [d]they are counted to him less than nothing, and vanity.
18 To whom then will ye
[e]liken God? or what likeness
will ye compare unto him?
19 [f]The workman melteth a
graven image, and the goldsmith spreadeth it
over with gold, and casteth silver chains.
20 He that [g]*is* so impoverished that he hath
no oblation chooseth a tree *that* will not rot;
he seeketh unto him a cunning workman
[h]to prepare a graven image *that* shall not be
moved.
21 [i]Have ye not known? have ye not
heard? hath it not been told you from the
beginning? have ye not understood from the
foundations of the earth?
22 [k]*It is* he that sitteth upon the circle of
the earth, and the inhabitants thereof *are* as

[y]Job xxi. 22; xxxvi. 22, 23; Wisd. ix. 13; Rom. xi. 34; 1 Cor. ii. 16——[z]Heb. *man of his counsel*——[a]Heb. *made him understand*——[b]Hebrew, *understandings?* [c]Dan. iv. 34——[d]Psa. lxii. 9

[e]Ver. 25; chap. xlvi. 5; Acts xvii. 29——[f]Chap. xli. 6, 7; xliv. 12, &c.; Jer. x. 3, &c.——[g]Heb. *is poor of oblation*——[h]Chap. xli. 7; Jer. x. 4——[i]Psa. xix. 1; Acts xiv. 17; Rom. i. 19, 20——[k]Or, *Him that sitteth*, &c.

with me; and if they should be overdriven, all the flock will die." Which is set in a still stronger light by the following remark of Sir John Chardin: "Their flocks," says he, speaking of those who now live in the east after the patriarchal manner, "feed down the places of their encampments so quick, by the great numbers that they have, that they are obliged to remove them too often, which is very destructive to their flocks, on account of the young ones, who have not strength enough to follow." *Harmer's* Observ. i., p. 126.

Verse 16. *And Lebanon* is *not sufficient*] The image is beautiful and uncommon. It has been imitated by an apocryphal writer, who however comes far short of the original:—

"For all sacrifice is too little for a sweet savour unto thee:
And all the fat is not sufficient for thy burnt-offering." Judith xvi. 16.

Does not the prophet mean here that all the burnt-offerings and sacrifices that could be offered were insufficient to atone for sin? That the nations were as nothing before him, not merely because of his immensity, but because of their insufficiency to make any atonement by their oblations for the iniquities which they had committed? Therefore the Redeemer was to come to Zion, &c.

Verse 19. *And casteth silver chains*—"And forgeth for it chains of silver."] For צורף *tsoreph*, the participle, twenty-seven MSS., five ancient, and three editions, read צרף *tsaraph*, pret. third person.

Verse 20. *Chooseth a tree* that *will not rot*] For what? To make a god out of it! The *rich* we find made theirs of *gold* and *silver;* the *poor man* was obliged to put up with a *wooden god!* From the words "he that hath no oblation chooseth a tree," we may learn that the gold and silver necessary to make the graven image was first *dedicated*, and then formed into a god! How stupid is idolatry! Strange that these people did not perceive that there could be no help in these molten and wooden idols!

Verse 21. *Have ye not known?*] On this verse *Kimchi* has a very interesting comment, an extract of which I subjoin. "The whole world may be considered as a house built up; *heaven* its roof; the *stars* its lamps; and the fruits of the earth its table spread. The *Master* of the house is God, blessed for ever; and *man* is the steward into whose hand all the business of the house is given. If he always consider in his heart that the Master of the house is continually over him, and that he keeps his eye upon his work, and if in consequence he acts wisely, he shall find favour in the eyes of the Master of the house. But if he find wickedness in the house, then will he remove him מן פקידתו *min pekidutho*, 'from his stewardship.' The foolish steward does not think of this; for as his eyes do not see the *Master* of the house, he saith in his heart, 'I will eat and drink what I find in this house, and will take my pleasure in it; nor shall I be careful whether there be a master over this house or not.' When the Lord of the house marks this, he comes and expels him from the house speedily, and with great anger; therefore it is said, ver. 23, *He bringeth the princes to nothing.*" It seems that this parable had been long in use among the Jews, as our blessed Lord alludes to it in his parable of the unjust steward. Or did the rabbin, finding it to his purpose, steal the parable from the Gospel? In both places it has great and peculiar beauties.

Have ye not understood from the foundations of the earth—"Have ye not understood it from the foundations of the earth?"] The true reading seems to be ממוסדות *mimmosedoth*, to answer to מראש *merosh* in the foregoing line. It follows a word ending with מ *mem*, and out of three *mems* concurring, it was an easy mistake to drop the middle one.

Verse 22. *As a curtain*—"As a thin veil"] "It

A. M. cir. 3292 B. C. cir. 712 Olymp. XVII. 1 cir. annum NumæPompilii, R. Roman., 4

grasshoppers; that [l]stretcheth out the heavens as a curtain, and spreadeth them out as a tent to dwell in:

23 That bringeth the [m]princes to nothing; he maketh the judges of the earth as vanity.

24 Yea, they shall not be planted: yea, they shall not be sown: yea, their stock shall not take root in the earth: and he shall also blow upon them, and they shall wither, and the whirlwind shall take them away as stubble.

25 [n]To whom then will ye liken me, or shall I be equal? saith the Holy One.

26 Lift up your eyes on high, and behold who hath created these *things,* that bringeth out their host by number: [o]he calleth them all by names by the greatness of his might, for that *he is* strong in power; not one faileth.

27 Why sayest thou, O Jacob, and speakest, O Israel, My way is hid from the LORD, and my judgment is passed over from my God?

28 Hast thou not known? hast thou not heard, *that* the everlasting God, the LORD, the creator of the ends of the earth, fainteth not, neither is weary? [p]*there is* no searching of his understanding.

29 He giveth power to the faint; and to *them that have* no might he increaseth strength.

30 Even the youths shall faint and be weary, and the young men shall utterly fall;

31 But they that wait upon the LORD [q]shall [r]renew *their* strength; they shall mount up with wings as eagles; they shall run, and not be weary; *and* they shall walk, and not faint.

[l]Job ix. 8; Psa. civ. 2; chap. xlii. 5; xliv. 24; li. 13; Jer. x. 12——[m]Job xii. 21; Psa. cvii. 40——[n]Ver. 18; Deut. iv. 15, &c.——[o]Psa. cxlvii. 4——[p]Psa. cxlvii. 5; Rom. xi. 33——[q]Psa. ciii. 5——[r]Heb. *change*

is usual in the summer season, and upon all occasions when a large company is to be received, to have the court sheltered from heat or inclemency of the weather by a *velum*, umbrella, or veil, as I shall call it; which being expanded on ropes from one side of the parapet wall to the other, may be folded or unfolded at pleasure. The psalmist seems to allude to some covering of this kind in that beautiful expression of spreading out the heavens like a curtain."—*Shaw's* Travels, p. 274.

Verse 24. *And he shall also blow upon them*—"And if he but blow upon them"] The *Septuagint, Syriac, Vulgate*, and MS. *Bodl.*, with another, have גם *gam, only,* without the conjunction ו *vau, and.*

Verse 26. *Lift up your eyes on high*] The rabbins say, He who is capable of meditating on the revolutions of the heavenly bodies, and does not meditate on them, is not worthy to have his name mentioned among men.

Verse 28. There is *no searching of his understanding*—"And that his understanding is unsearchable."] Twenty-four MSS., two editions, the *Septuagint* and *Vulgate*, read ואין *veein,* with the conjunction ו *vau.*

Verse 31. *They shall mount up with wings as eagles*—"They shall put forth fresh feathers like the moulting eagle"] It has been a common and popular opinion that the eagle lives and retains his vigour to a great age; and that, beyond the common lot of other birds, he moults in his old age, and renews his feathers, and with them his youth. "Thou shalt renew thy youth like the eagle," says the psalmist, ciii. 5; on which place St. Ambrose notes, Aquila longam ætatem ducit, dum, vetustis plumis fatiscentibus, nova pennarum successione juvenescit:—"The eagle lives to a very advanced age; and in moulting his youth is renewed with his new feathers."

Phile, De Animalibus, treating of the eagle, and addressing himself to the emperor Michael Palæologus junior, raises his compliment upon the same notion:—

Τουτον συ, βασιλευ, τον πολυν ζωοις βιον,
Αει νεουργων, και κρατυνων την φυσιν.

"Long may'st thou live, O king; still like the eagle
Renew thy youth, and still retain thy vigour."

To this many fabulous and absurd circumstances are added by several ancient writers and commentators on Scripture; see *Bochart*, Hieroz. II. ii. 1. Rabbi Saadias says, Every *tenth* year the eagle flies near the sun; and when not able any longer to bear the burning heat, she falls down into the sea, and soon loses her feathers, and thus renews her vigour. This she does every *tenth* year till the *hundredth*, when, after she has ascended near the sun, and fallen into the sea, she rises no more. How much proof do such stories require! Whether the notion of the eagle's renewing his youth is in any degree well founded or not, I need not inquire; it is enough for a poet, whether profane or sacred, to have the authority of popular opinion to support an image introduced for illustration or ornament.—L.

CHAPTER XLI

The prophet, having intimated the deliverance from Babylon, and the still greater redemption couched under it, resumes the subject. He begins with the Divine vocation of Abraham, the root of the Israelitish family, and his successful exploits against the idolaters, 1–7. *He then recurs to the Babylonish captivity, and encourages the seed of Abraham, the friend of God, not to fear, as all their enemies would be ultimately subdued under them,* 8–16; *and every thing furnished necessary to refresh and comfort them in their passage homewards through the desert,* 17–20. *The prophet then takes occasion to celebrate the prescience of God, from his knowledge of events so very distant, as instanced in the prediction concerning the* messenger of glad tidings *which should be given to Jerusalem to deliver her from all her enemies; and challenges the idols of the heathen to produce the like proof of their pretended divinity,* 21–27. *But they are all vanity, and accursed are they that choose them,* 28, 29.

A. M. cir. 3292
B. C. cir. 712
Olymp. XVII. 1
cir. annum
NumæPompilii,
R. Roman., 4

KEEP [a]silence before me, O
islands; and let the people
renew *their* strength: let them
come near; then let them speak:
let us come near together to judgment.
2 Who raised up [b]the righteous *man* [c]from
the east, called him to his foot, [d]gave the nations before him, and made *him* rule over
kings? he gave *them* as the dust to his sword,
and as driven stubble to his
bow.
3 He pursued them, *and* passed
[e]safely; *even* by the way *that*
he had not gone with his feet.
4 [f]Who hath wrought and done *it,* calling
the generations from the beginning? I
the LORD, the [g]first, and with the last; I
am he.

[a]Zech. ii. 13——[b]Heb. *righteousness*——[c]Ch. xlvi. 11
[d]See Gen. xiv. 14, &c.; ver. 25; chap. xlv. 1

[e]Heb. *in peace*——[f]Ver. 26; ch. xliv. 7; xlvi. 10——[g]Ch. xliii. 10; xliv. 6; xlviii. 12; Rev. i. 17; xxii. 13

NOTES ON CHAP. XLI

Verse 1. *Keep silence before me, O islands*—"Let the distant nations repair to me with new force of mind"] Εγκαινιζεσθε, *Septuagint.* For החרישו *hacharishu, be silent,* they certainly read in their copy החדישו *hachadishu, be renewed;* which is parallel and synonymous with יחלפו כח *yechalephu coach,* "recover their strength;" that is, their strength of mind, their powers of reason; that they may overcome those prejudices by which they have been so long held enslaved to idolatry. A MS. has הר *har,* upon a rasure. The same mistake seems to have been made in this word, Zeph. iii. 17. For יחריש באהבתו *yacharish beahabatho, silebit in directione sua,* as the *Vulgate* renders it; which seems not consistent with what immediately follows, *exultabit super te in laude;* the *Septuagint* and *Syriac* read יחדיש באהבתו *yachadish beahabatho,* "he shall be renewed in his love." אלי *elai, to me,* is wanting in one of *De Rossi's* MSS. and in the *Syriac.*

Verse 2. *The righteous* man] The *Chaldee* and *Vulgate* seem to have read צדיק *tsaddik.* But Jerome, though his translation has *justum,* appears to have read צדק *tsedek;* for in his comment he expresses it by *justum, sive justitiam.* However, I think all interpreters understand it of a person. So the *Septuagint* in MS. *Pachom.* εκαλεσεν αυτον, "he hath called him;" but the other copies have αυτην, *her.* They are divided in ascertaining this person; some explain it of Abraham, others of Cyrus. I rather think that the former is meant; because the character of the righteous man, or righteousness, agrees better with Abraham than with Cyrus. Besides, immediately after the description of the success given by God to Abraham and his posterity, (who, I presume, are to be taken into the account,) the idolaters are introduced as greatly alarmed at this event. Abraham was called out of the east; and his posterity were introduced into the land of Canaan, in order to destroy the idolaters of that country, and they were established there on purpose to stand as a barrier against the idolatry then prevailing, and threatening to overrun the whole face of the earth. Cyrus, though not properly an idolater or worshipper of images, yet had nothing in his character to cause such an alarm among the idolaters, ver. 5-7. Farther, after having just touched upon that circumstance, the prophet with great ease returns to his former subject, and resumes Abraham and the Israelites; and assures them that as God had called them, and chosen them for this purpose, he would uphold and support them to the utmost, and at length give them victory over all the heathen nations, their enemies; ver. 8-16. *Kimchi* is of the same mind and gives the same reasons.

He gave them *as the dust to his sword*—"Hath made them like the dust before his sword"] The image is strong and beautiful; it is often made use of by the sacred poets; see Psa. i. 4; xxxv. 5; Job xxi. 18, and by Isaiah himself in other places, chap. xvii. 13; xxix. 5. But there is great difficulty in making out the construction. The *Septuagint* read קשתם חרבם *kashtam, charbam, their sword, their bow,* understanding it of the sword and bow of the conquered kings: but this is not so agreeable to the analogy of the image, as employed in other places. The *Chaldee* paraphrast and *Kimchi* solve the difficulty by supposing an ellipsis of לפני *liphney* before those words. It must be owned that the ellipsis is hard and unusual: but I choose rather to submit to this, than, by adhering with *Vitringa* to the more obvious construction, to destroy entirely both the image and the sense. But the *Vulgate* by *gladio ejus,* to his sword, and *arcui ejus,* to his bow, seems to express לחרבו *lecharbo, to his sword,* and לקשתו *lekashto, to his bow,* the admission of which reading may perhaps be thought preferable to *Kimchi's* ellipsis.

Verse 3. And *passed safely*—"He passeth in safety"] The preposition seems to have been omitted in the text by mistake; the *Septuagint* and *Vulgate* seem to have had it in their copies; εν ειρηνη, *in pace,* בשלום *beshalom,* "prosperously." It is so in one of *De Rossi's* MSS.

Verse 4. *Who hath wrought and done* it—"Who hath performed and made these things"] A word is here lost out of the text. It is supplied by an ancient MS., אלה *elleh,* "these

A. M. cir. 3292 B. C. cir. 712 Olymp. XVII. 1 cir. annum NumæPompilii, R. Roman., 4

5 The isles saw *it*, and feared;
the ends of the earth were afraid,
drew near, and came.
6 [h]They helped every one his
neighbour; and *every one* said to his brother,
[i]Be of good courage.
7 [k]So the carpenter encouraged the [l]gold-
smith, *and* he that smootheth *with* the hammer
[m]him that smote the anvil, [n]saying, It *is* ready
for the soddering: and he fastened it with
nails, [o]*that* it should not be moved.
8 But thou, Israel, *art* my servant, Jacob
whom I have [p]chosen, the seed of Abraham
my [q]friend.
9 *Thou* whom I have taken from the ends of
the earth, and called thee from the chief men
thereof, and said unto thee, Thou *art* my servant; I have chosen thee, and not cast thee
away.
10 [r]Fear thou not; [s]for I *am* with thee: be
not dismayed; for I *am* thy God: I will
strengthen thee; yea, I will help thee; yea,
I will uphold thee with the right hand of my
righteousness.
11 Behold, all they that were incensed
against thee shall be [t]ashamed and confounded: they shall be as nothing; and [u]they
that strive with thee shall perish.
12 Thou shalt seek them, and shalt not find
them, *even* [v]them that contended with thee:
[w]they that war against thee shall
be as nothing, and as a thing of
nought.
13 For I the LORD thy God
will hold thy right hand, saying unto thee,
[x]Fear not; I will help thee.
14 Fear not, thou worm Jacob, *and* ye [y]men
of Israel; I will help thee, saith the LORD,
and thy Redeemer, the Holy One of Israel.
15 Behold, [z]I will make thee a new sharp
threshing instrument having [a]teeth: thou
shalt thresh the mountains, and beat *them*
small, and shalt make the hills as chaff.
16 Thou shalt [b]fan them, and the wind shall
carry them away, and the whirlwind shall
scatter them: and thou shalt rejoice in the
LORD, *and* [c]shalt glory in the Holy One of
Israel.
17 *When* the poor and needy seek water, and
there is none, *and* their tongue faileth for
thirst, I the LORD will hear them, *I* the God
of Israel will not forsake them.
18 I will open [d]rivers in high places, and
fountains in the midst of the valleys: I will
make the [e]wilderness a pool of water, and the
dry land springs of water.
19 I will plant in the wilderness the cedar,
the shittah tree, and the myrtle, and the oil
tree; I will set in the desert the fir tree, *and*
the pine, and the box tree together:

[h]Chap. xl. 19; xliv. 12——[i]Heb. *Be strong*——[k]Chap. xl. 19——[l]Or, *founder*——[m]Or, *the smiting*——[n]Or, *saying of the sodder, It* is *good*——[o]Chap. xl. 20——[p]Deut. vii. 6; x. 15; xiv. 2; Psa. cxxxv. 4; chap. xliii. 1; xliv. 1——[q]2 Chron. xx. 7; James ii. 23——[r]Ver. 13, 14; chap. xliii. 5——[s]Deut. xxxi. 6, 8

[t]Exod. xxiii. 22; chap. xlv. 24; lx. 12; Zech. xii. 3——[u]Heb. *the men of thy strife*——[v]Heb. *the men of thy contention*——[w]Heb. *the men of thy war*——[x]Ver. 10——[y]Or, *few men*——[z]Mic. iv. 13; 2 Cor. x. 4, 5——[a]Heb. *mouths*——[b]Jer. li. 2——[c]Chap. xlv. 25——[d]Chap. xxxv. 6, 7; xliii. 19; xliv. 3——[e]Psa. cvii. 35

things;" and by the *Septuagint*, ταυτα; and by the *Vulgate*, *hæc;* and by the *Chaldee*, אלן *elin;* all of the same meaning.

Verse 5. *Were afraid*—"And they were terrified"] Three MSS. have ויחרדו *vaiyecheridu*, adding the conjunction ו *vau*, which restores the second member of the sentence to its true poetical form.

Verse 7. That *it should not be moved*—"That it shall not move."] Five MSS., (two ancient,) and the ancient Versions, add the conjunction ו *vau*, "and," reading ולא *velo*, "and not," which seems to be right.

Verse 9. *And called thee from the chief men thereof*—"And called from the extremities thereof"] אציל מאציליה *atsil meatsileyha*, signifies *the arm, axilla, ala;* and is used like כנף *canaph*, "the wing," for any thing extended from the extremity of another, or joined on to it. It is here parallel with and synonymous to מקצות *mikkatsoth*, "from the ends," in the preceding member.

Verse 10. *Be not dismayed*—ואל תשתע *veal tishta*, "AND be not dismayed." The ו *vau* is added by twenty-one of Dr. *Kennicott's* MSS., thirty of *De Rossi's*, and one of my own, and three editions. It makes the sense more complete.

Verse 14. *Fear not, thou worm Jacob*] In the rabbinical commentary on the five books of Moses, *Yelamedenu*, it is asked, Why are the Israelites called a *worm?* To signify, that as the worm does not smite, that is, *gnaw* the cedars, but with its mouth, which is very tender, yet it nevertheless destroys the hard wood; so all the strength of the Israelites is in prayer, by which they smite the wicked of this world, though strong like the cedars, to which they are compared, Ezek. xxxi. 3.

Verse 15. *A new sharp threshing instrument having teeth*—"A threshing wain; a new corn-drag armed with pointed teeth"] See note on chap. xxviii. 27, 28.

Thou shalt thresh the mountains] Mountains and hills are here used metaphorically for the kings and princes of the Gentiles.—*Kimchi.*

Verse 19. *I will plant in the wilderness the cedar*] The two preceding verses express God's

A. M. cir. 3292 B. C. cir. 712 Olymp. XVII. 1 cir. annum NumæPompilii, R. Roman., 4

20 [f]That they may see, and
know, and consider, and understand together, that the hand
of the LORD hath done this, and
the Holy One of Israel hath created it.
21 [g]Produce your cause, saith the LORD;
bring forth your strong *reasons*, saith the
King of Jacob.
22 [h]Let them bring *them* forth, and show us
what shall happen: let them show the former
things, what they *be*, that we may [i]consider
them, and know the latter end of them; or
declare us things for to come.
23 [k]Show the things that are to come hereafter, that we may know that ye *are* gods:
yea, [l]do good, or do evil, that we may be dismayed, and behold *it* together.
24 Behold, [m]ye *are* [n]of nothing, and your
work [o]of naught: an abomination *is he that*
chooseth you.
25 I have raised up *one* from
the north, and he shall come:
from the rising of the sun [p]shall
he call upon my name: [q]and he
shall come upon princes as *upon* mortar, and
as the potter treadeth clay.
26 [r]Who hath declared from the beginning,
that we may know? and beforetime, that we
may say, *He is* righteous? yea, *there is* none
that showeth, yea, *there is* none that declareth,
yea, *there is* none that heareth your words.
27 [s]The first [t]*shall say* to Zion, Behold,
behold them: and I will give to Jerusalem
one that bringeth good tidings.
28 [u]For I beheld, and *there was* no man; even
among them, and *there was* no counsellor, that,
when I asked of them, could [v]answer a word.
29 [w]Behold, they *are* all vanity; their works
are nothing: their molten images *are* wind
and confusion.

[f]Job xii. 9——[g]Heb. *Cause to come near*——[h]Chap. xlv. 21——[i]Heb. *set our heart* upon them——[k]Chap. xlii. 9; xliv. 7, 8; xlv. 3; John xiii. 19——[l]Jer. x. 5——[m]Psa. cxv. 8; chap. xliv. 9, 1 Cor. viii. 4——[n]Or, worse *than nothing*——[o]Or, worse *than of a viper*——[p]Ezra i. 2——[q]Verse 2——[r]Chapter xliii. 9——[s]Verse 4——[t]Chapter xl. 9——[u]Chapter lxix. 5——[v]Heb. *return*——[w]Ver. 24

mercy to them in their passage through the dry deserts, in supplying them with abundant water, when distressed with thirst, in allusion to the exodus. This verse expresses the relief afforded to them, fainting with heat in their journey through that hot country, destitute of shelter, by causing shady trees, and those of the tallest and most beautiful kinds, to spring up for their defence. The apocryphal Baruch, speaking of the return from Babylon, expresses God's protection of his people by the same image: "Even the woods and every sweet-smelling tree shall overshadow Israel by the commandment of God." Chap. v. 8.

The oil tree] This, *Kimchi* says, is not to be understood of the *olive tree*, for the olive is distinguished, Neh. viii. 15; but it means the pine or fir, from which pitch is extracted.

Verse 20. *And consider*] The verb ישימו *yasimu*, without לב *leb* added, cannot signify *to apply the heart*, or *to attend* to a thing, as *Houbigant* has observed; he therefore reads ישמו *yashshemu*, they shall *wonder*. The conjecture is ingenious; but it is much more probable that the word לב *leb* is lost out of the text; for all the ancient versions render the phrase to the same sense, as if it were fully expressed, ישימו לב *yasimu leb;* and the *Chaldee* renders it paraphrastically, yet still retaining the very words in his paraphrase, וישוון דחלתי על לבהון *vishavvun dechalti al lebehon*, "that they may put my fear in their heart." See also ver. 22, where the same phrase is used.

Verse 21. *Bring forth your strong* reasons—"Produce these your mighty powers"] "Let your idols come forward which you consider to be so very strong." *Hieron.* in loc. I prefer this to all other interpretations of this place; and to *Jerome's* own translation of it, which he adds immediately after, Afferte, si quid forte habetis. "Bring it forward, if haply ye have any thing." The false gods are called upon to come forth and appear in person; and to give evident demonstration of their foreknowledge and power by foretelling future events, and exerting their power in doing good or evil.

Verse 23. *That we may be dismayed, and behold* it *together*—"Then shall we be struck at once with admiration and terror."] The word ונרא *venere* is written imperfectly in the *Hebrew* text; the Masoretes supply ה *he* at the end; and so it is read in *twenty-two* MSS. and *four* editions; that is, ונראה *venireh*, and we shall *see*. But the true reading seems to be ונירא *venira*, and we shall *fear*, with י *yod* supplied, from ירא *yara*.

Verse 24. *Your work of naught*—"Your operation is less than naught"] For מאפע *meepha*, read מאפס *meephes;* so the *Chaldee* and *Vulgate*. A manifest error of the text; compare chap. xl. 17. The rabbins acknowledge no such error, but say that the former word signifies the same with the latter, by a change of the two letters ס *samech* and ע *ain.*—*Sal ben Melec* in loc.

Verse 25. *I have raised up* one *from the north*] "That is," says *Kimchi*, "the Messiah. The king of Assyria placed the ten tribes in Chalach and Chabar by the river Gozan, and in the cities of the Medes, 2 Kings xvii. 6, which lands lie northerly and easterly."

He shall come upon princes—"He shall trample on princes"] For יבא *yabo*, *Le Clerc* reads יבס *yebes*, from the *Chaldee*, who seems to read both words. "*Forte legend.* ויבס *vaiyebes* vel וירמס *vaiyirmos: sequitur* ס." "This should perhaps be read ויבס *vaiyebes*, or וירמס *vaiyirmos:* a ס *samech* follows."—*Secker*. See Nah. iii. 14.

Verse 26. *Your words*] אמרתיכם *imrathey-*

chem; but, instead of this, one of my most ancient MSS. has דבריכם *dibreychem.* The meaning is nearly the same: but in this reading this MS. is singular.

Verse 27. *The first* shall say *to Zion, Behold, behold them*—"I first to Zion *gave the word,* Behold they are here"] This verse is somewhat obscure by the transposition of the parts of the sentence, and the peculiar manner in which it is divided into two parallel lines. The verb at the end of the sentence belongs to both parts; and the phrase, *Behold, they are here!* is parallel to *the messenger of glad tidings;* and stands like it, as the accusative case to the verb. The following paraphrase will explain the form and the sense of it. "I first, by my prophets, give notice of these events, saying, Behold, they are at hand! and I give to Jerusalem a messenger of glad tidings."

Verse 28. *Among them*—"Among the idols"] For ומאלה *umeelleh,* I read ומאלים *umeellim,* with the *Septuagint,* και απο των ειδωλων, "*and from* or among the *idols.*" See Exod. xv. 11; Isa. lvii. 5.

R. D. Kimchi has many good observations on this chapter. Bishop *Lowth* follows him in applying it to Abraham, and not to Cyrus; the whole being spoken in the past tense, which is not used, or rarely, in such a case for the future. Almost the whole of the rabbins understand it of Abraham. On *Kimchi's* plan, the following is a paraphrase.

The righteous man—Abram, *from the east*—the land of his nativity, called the land of the children of the east, Gen. xxix. 1.

Brought him to his feet—Whithersoever his feet went, he preached righteousness and truth; as it is written, "There he proclaimed in the name of Jehovah," Gen. xxi. 31. And he called it ויקראהו *vaiyikraehu*—that is, צדק *tsedek,* righteousness, to his feet, enabled him to hold it forth wherever he went.

He called the nations—To leave their idols, and worship him who made the universe. He taught them the way of righteousness, truth, and faith. Was there ever a prodigy like to this? A man who had been an idolater, rising up against all the nations of the earth, reproving their faith, and not fearing before them nor their kings! Who stirred up his heart to do this? Was it not the Lord?

Gave the nations before him—*And made him rule over kings*—Chedorlaomer, and the kings which were with him: whom the Lord *gave as dust to his sword, and stubble to his bow.*

He pursued them—He and his *three hundred and eighteen* servants.

He passed safely—שלום *shalom* for בשלום *beshalom, in safety;* so said, because he lost not one of his men in this expedition. See *Kimchi.*

CHAPTER XLII

The prophet sets forth the meekness of Messiah's character, and the extent and blessings of his kingdom, particularly among the Gentiles, 1–9. *In consequence of this he calls on the whole creation to join him in one song of praise to God,* 10–12. *After which he seems again to glance at the deliverance from the captivity; although the words may full as well apply to the deliverance vouchsafed to the Church; to the overthrow of her most powerful enemies; and to the prevalency of true religion over idolatry and error,* 13–17. *The prophet then reproves the Jews for their blindness and infidelity in rejecting the Messiah, and gives intimations of those judgments which their guilt would draw on them,* 18–25.

A. M. cir. 3292 B. C. cir. 712 Olymp. XVII. 1 cir. annum Numæ Pompilii, R. Roman., 4

BEHOLD [a]my servant, whom
I uphold; mine elect, *in*
whom my soul [b]delighteth; [c]I
have put my spirit upon him: he
shall bring forth judgment to the Gentiles.
2 He shall not cry, nor lift
up, nor cause his voice to be
heard in the street.
3 A bruised reed shall he not
break, and the [d]smoking flax shall he not

[a]Chap. xliii. 10; xlix. 3, 6; lii. 13; liii. 11; Matt. xii. 18, 19, 20; Phil. ii. 7

[b]Matt. iii. 17; xvii. 5; Eph. i. 6——[c]Chap. xi. 2; John iii. 34——[d]Or, *dimly burning*

The prophet, having opened his subject with the preparation for the return from captivity at Babylon, and intimated that a much greater deliverance was covered under the veil of that event, proceeded to vindicate the power of God, as Creator and disposer of all things; and his infinite knowledge, from his prediction of future events, and in particular of that deliverance. He went still farther, and pointed out the instrument by which he should effect the redemption of his people the Jews from slavery; namely, a great conqueror, whom he would call forth from the north and the east to execute his orders. In this chapter he proceeds to the greater deliverance; and at once brings forth into full view, without throwing any veil of allegory over the subject, the Messiah. "Behold my servant, Messiah," says the *Chaldee.* St. Matthew has applied it directly to Christ; nor can it with any justice or propriety be applied to any other person or character whatever.—L.

NOTES ON CHAP. XLII

Verse 1. *Behold my servant, whom I uphold*] אתמך בו *ethmach bo, on whom I lean.* Alluding to the custom of kings leaning on the arm of their most beloved and faithful servant. All, both Jews and Christians, agree, that the seven first verses of this chapter belong to Christ. Now, as they are evidently a continuation of the prophecy in the preceding chapter, that prophecy cannot belong to Cyrus, but to Christ.

He shall bring forth judgment to the Gentiles—"He shall publish judgment to the nations"]

A. M. cir. 3292
B. C. cir. 712
Olymp. XVII. 1
cir. annum
NumæPompilii,
R. Roman., 4

[e]quench: he shall bring forth
judgment unto truth.
4 He shall not fail nor be
[f]discouraged, till he have set
judgment in the earth: [g]and the isles shall
wait for his law.
5 Thus saith God the LORD, [h]he that created
the heavens, and stretched them out; [i]he that
spread forth the earth, and that which cometh
out of it; [k]he that giveth breath unto the
people upon it, and spirit to them that walk
therein:
6 [l]I the LORD have called thee in righteousness, and will hold thine hand, and will keep
thee, [m]and give thee for a covenant of the
people, for [n]a light of the Gentiles;
7 [o]To open the blind eyes, to [p]bring out
the prisoners from the prison, *and* them that
sit in [q]darkness out of the
prison house.
8 I *am* the LORD: that *is* my
name: and my [r]glory will I not
give to another, neither my praise to graven
images.
9 Behold, the former things are come to
pass, and new things do I declare: before
they spring forth I tell you of them.
10 [s]Sing unto the LORD a new song, *and*
his praise from the end of the earth, [t]ye that
go down to the sea, and [u]all that is therein;
the isles, and the inhabitants thereof.
11 Let the wilderness and the cities thereof
lift up *their voice,* the villages *that* Kedar
doth inhabit: let the inhabitants of the rock
sing, let them shout from the top of the mountains.

A. M. cir. 3292
B. C. cir. 712
Olymp. XVII. 1
cir. annum
NumæPompilii,
R. Roman., 4

---

[e]Heb. *quench it*——[f]Heb. *broken*——[g]Gen. xlix. 10——[h]Chap. xliv. 24; Zech. xii. 1——[i]Psa. cxxxvi. 6——[k]Acts xvii. 25——[l]Chap. xliii. 1——[m]Chap. xlix. 8——[n]Chap. xlix. 6; Luke ii. 32; Acts xiii. 47

[o]Chap. xxxv. 5——[p]Chap. lxi. 1; Luke iv. 18; 2 Tim. ii. 26; Heb. ii. 14, 15——[q]Chap. ix. 2——[r]Chap. xlviii. 11——[s]Psa. xxxiii. 3; xl. 3; xcviii. 1——[t]Psa. cvii. 23——[u]Heb. *the fulness thereof*

Four MSS. two ancient, add the conjunction ומשפט *vemishpat.* See Matt. xii. 18.

The word משפט *mishpat, judgment,* like צדקה *tsedakah, righteousness,* is taken in a great latitude of signification. It means *rule, form, order, model, plan; rule of right,* or of *religion;* an *ordinance, institution; judicial process, cause, trial, sentence, condemnation, acquittal, deliverance, mercy,* &c. It certainly means in this place the law to be published by Messiah, the institution of the Gospel.

Verse 4. *He shall not fail nor be discouraged* —"His force shall not be abated nor broken"] Rabbi Meir ita citat locum istum, ut post ירוץ *yaruts,* addat כוחו *cocho, robur ejus,* quod hodie non comparet in textu Hebræo, sed addendum videtur, ut sensus fiat planior. "Rabbi Meir cites this passage so as to add after ירוץ *yaruts* כוחו *cocho, his force,* which word is not found in the present Hebrew text, but seems necessary to be added to make the sense more distinct." *Capell.* Crit. Sac. p. 382. For which reason I had added it in the translation, before I observed this remark of *Capellus.*—L.

Verse 6. *A covenant of the people*—"A covenant to the people"] For עם *am,* two MSS. of *Dr. Kennicott's,* and of my own, read עולם *olam,* the covenant *of the age to come,* or *the everlasting* covenant; which seems to give a clearer and better sense. But I think the word ברית *berith,* here, should not be translated *covenant,* but *covenant sacrifice,* which meaning it often has; and undoubtedly in this place. This gives a still stronger and clearer sense.

Verse 7. *To open the blind eyes*] In this verse the prophet seems to set forth the spiritual redemption, under images borrowed from the temporal deliverance.

Out of the prison house—"*And* from the dungeon."] The *Septuagint, Syriac,* and four MSS., one ancient, add the conjunction ו *vau,* ומבית *umibbeith, and from the house.*

Verse 8. *I* am *the Lord*] אני יהוה *ani Yehovah.* This is the famous tetragrammaton, or name of *four letters,* which we write *Jehovah, Yehovah, Yehveh, Yeveh, Jhuh, Javah,* &c. The letters are Y H U H. The Jews never pronounce it, and the true pronunciation is utterly unknown.

That is *my name*] A name peculiar to myself.

Verse 10. *Ye that go down to the sea*] This seems not to belong to this place; it does not well consist with what follows, "and the fulness thereof." They that go down upon the sea means navigators, sailors, traders, such as do business in great waters; an idea much too confined for the prophet, who means the sea in general, as it is used by the Hebrews, for the distant nations, the islands, the dwellers on the sea-coasts all over the world. I suspect that some transcriber had the 23d verse of Psalm cvii. running in his head, יורדי הים באניות *yoredey haiyam booniyoth,* and wrote in this place יורדי הים *yoredey haiyam* instead of ירעם הים *yiram haiyam,* or יריע *yari,* or ירן *yaran;* "let the sea roar, or shout, or exult." But as this is so different in appearance from the present reading, I do not take the liberty of introducing it into the translation. Conjeceram legendum יגידו *yegidu,* ut ver. 12; sed non favent Versiones. "I would propose to read יגידו *yegidu,* as in ver. 12; but this is not supported by the Versions."—*Secker.*

Verse 11. *Let the wilderness*] The most uncultivated countries, and the most rude and uncivilized people, shall confess and celebrate with thanksgiving the blessing of the knowledge of God graciously imparted to them. By the *desert* is meant Arabia Deserta; by the *rocky country,* Arabia Petræa; by the *mountains,* probably those celebrated ones, Paran, Horeb, Sinai, in the same country; to which also belonged *Kedar,* a clan of Arabians, dwelling for the most part in tents; but there were

A. M. cir. 3292
B. C. cir. 712
Olymp. XVII. 1
cir. annum
NumæPompilii,
R. Roman., 4

12 Let them give glory unto
the LORD, and declare his praise
in the islands.
13 The LORD shall go forth as
a mighty man, he shall stir up jealousy like
a man of war: he shall cry, [v]yea, roar; he
[w]shall prevail against his enemies.
14 I have long time holden my peace; I
have been still, *and* refrained myself: *now*
will I cry like a travailing woman; I will destroy and [x]devour at once.

15 I will make waste mountains
and hills, and dry up all their
herbs; and I will make the rivers
islands, and I will dry up the
pools.
16 And I will bring the blind by a way *that*
they knew not; I will lead them in paths *that*
they have not known: I will make darkness
light before them, and crooked things
[y]straight. These things will I do unto them,
and not forsake them.
17 They shall be [z]turned back, they shall

[v]Chapter xxxi. 4——[w]Or, *behave himself mightily*——[x]Heb. *swallow* or *sup up*

[y]Heb. *into straightness*——[z]Psa. xcvii. 7; chap. i. 29; xliv. 11; xlv. 16

others of them who inhabited or frequented *cities* and *villages*, as may be collected from this place of the prophet. *Pietro della Valle*, speaking of the people of Arabia Deserta, says: "There is a sort of Arabs of that country called Maëdi, who with their herds, of buffaloes for the most part, sometimes live in the *deserts*, and sometimes in *cities;* from whence they have their name, which signifies *wandering*, going from place to place. They have no professed houses; nor are they properly *Bedaui*, or *Beduui*, that is, *Deserticoli*, who are the most noble among them, and never abide within walls, but always go wandering through the open country with their *black tents;* nor are they properly called *Hhadesi*, as they call those who dwell in cities, and lands with fixed houses. These by the latter are esteemed ignoble and base; but both are considered as of low condition." *Viaggi*, Parte III. lett. ii.

The villages that *Kedar doth inhabit*] The *Arabs*, according to the *Targum*.

The inhabitants of the rock] They who dwell in fortified places. The *Vulgate* has *habitatores Petrææ*, "the inhabitants of Arabia Petræa." Those who make the *rock* Jesus Christ, the *inhabitants of the rock*, true believers in him; the *singing*, rejoicing for the salvation they have received; *abuse* and *disgrace* the *passage* and the *pulpit*. I have heard a clergyman, a magistrate, a justice of the quorum, spend an hour in showing from these words, 1. That they meant Jesus Christ, and none other. 2. That he might be fully compared to a *rock*, as the *foundation* on which his Church was built, and on which all true believers rested for their salvation. 3. A *rock*, because of his *strength* and *might* in destroying his enemies, and supporting his friends. 4. A *refreshing rock*, like that in the *wilderness;* and *that rock was Christ*. 5. A *perspective rock*, from which true believers could discover their heavenly inheritance: "When my heart is overwhelmed, lead me to the *rock* that is higher than I," &c. Now all this is true in itself; but false in respect to the words on which it was professedly built, for they have no such meaning.

Verse 14. *I have been still*—"Shall I keep silence for ever"] After מעולם *meolam*, in the copy which the *Septuagint* had before them, followed the word הלעולם *haleolam*, εσιωπησα απ' αιωνος· Μη και αει σιωπησομαι· according to MSS. *Pachom.* and I. D. II. and Edit. *Complut.;* which word, הלעולם *haleolam*, has been omitted in the text by an easy mistake of a transcriber, because of the similitude of the word preceding. *Shall I always keep silence?* like that of *Juvenal:* Semper ego auditor tantum? *Shall I always be a hearer only?*

Verse 15. *I will make the rivers islands*—"I will make the rivers dry deserts"] Instead of איים *iyim, islands*, read ציים *tsiim;* a very probable conjecture of *Houbigant*.

Verse 16. *In paths*] The *Septuagint*, *Syriac*, *Vulgate*, and nine MSS., (two ancient,) read ובנתיבות *ubenotiboth*.

Will I do unto them] עשיתם *asitem*. This word, so written as it is in the text, means "thou wilt do," in the second person. The Masoretes have indeed pointed it for the first person; but the י *yod* in the last syllable is absolutely necessary to distinguish the first person; and so it is written in forty MSS., עשיתים *asithim*.

Jarchi, *Kimchi*, *Sal. ben Melec*, &c., agree that the past time is here put for the future, עשיתי *asithi* for אעשה; and indeed the context necessarily requires that interpretation. Farther it is to be observed that עשיתים *asithim* is put for עשיתי להם *asithi lahem*, "I have done them," for "I have done for them;" as עשיתני *asitheni* is for עשיתי לי *asiti li*, "I have made myself," for "I have made for myself," Ezek. xxix. 2; and in the celebrated passage of Jephthah's vow, Judges xi. 31, והעליתיהו עולה *ve-heelitihu olah* for העליתי לו עולה *heelithi lo olah*, "I will offer him a burnt-offering," for "I will offer unto him (that is, unto JEHOVAH) a burnt-offering;" by an ellipsis of the preposition of which Buxtorf gives many other examples, Thes. Grammat. lib. ii. 17. See also note on chap. lxv. 5. A late happy application of this grammatical remark to that much disputed passage has perfectly cleared up a difficulty which for *two thousand* years had puzzled all the translators and expositors, had given occasion to dissertations without number, and caused endless disputes among the learned on the question, whether Jephthah sacrificed his daughter or not; in which both parties have been equally ignorant of the meaning of the place, of the state of the fact, and of the very terms of the vow; which now at last has been

A. M. cir. 3292, B. C. cir. 712, Olymp. XVII. 1, cir. annum NumæPompilii, R. Roman., 4

be greatly ashamed, that trust in
graven images, that say to the
molten images, Ye *are* our gods.
18 Hear, ye deaf; and look, ye
blind that ye may see.
19 [a]Who *is* blind, but my servant? or
deaf, as my messenger *that* I sent? who *is*
blind as *he that is* perfect, and blind as the
LORD's servant?
20 Seeing many things, [b]but thou observest
not; opening the ears, but he heareth not.
21 The LORD is well pleased for his righteousness' sake; he will magnify the law, and
make [c]*it* honourable.
22 But this *is* a people robbed and spoiled;
[d]*they are* all of them snared in holes, and they
are hid in prison houses: they
are for a prey, and none delivereth; for [e]a spoil, and none saith,
Restore.
23 Who among you will give ear to this? *who*
will hearken and hear [f]for the time to come?
24 Who gave Jacob for a spoil, and Israel
to the robbers? did not the LORD, he against
whom we have sinned? for they would not
walk in his ways, neither were they obedient
unto his law.
25 Therefore he hath poured upon him the
fury of his anger, and the strength of battle:
[g]and it hath set him on fire round about, [h]yet
he knew not; and [i]it burned him, yet he laid
it not to heart.

[a]Ch. xliii. 8; Ezek. xii. 2; see John ix. 39, 41——[b]Rom. ii. 21——[c]Or, him——[d]Or, *in snaring all the young men of them*——[e]Heb. *a treading*——[f]Heb. *for the after time?* [g]2 Kings xxv. 9——[h]Hos. vii. 9——[i]Jer. iv. 4; xxi. 12

cleared up beyond all doubt by my learned friend Dr. Randolph, Margaret Professor of Divinity in the University of Oxford, in his Sermon on Jephthah's Vow, Oxford, 1766.—L.

Verse 19. *As my messenger* that *I sent*—"As he to whom I have sent my messengers"] כמלאכי אשלח *kemalachey eshlach*, ut ad quem nuncios meos misi. The *Vulgate* and *Chaldee* are almost the only interpreters who render it rightly, in consistence with the rest of the sentence, and in perfect agreement with the Hebrew idiom; according to which the ellipsis is to be thus supplied: כלאשר מלאכי אשלח *kelaasher malachey eshlach;* "As he to whom I have sent my messengers."

As he that is *perfect*—"As he who is perfectly instructed"] See note on chap. xliv. 2.

And blind as the Lord's servant—"And deaf, as the servant of JEHOVAH"] For ועור *veivver, and blind*, we must read וחרש *vecheresh, and deaf:* κωφος, *Symmachus*, and so a MS. The mistake is palpable, and the correction self-evident, and admissible though there had been no authority for it.

Verse 20. *Seeing many things*—"Thou hast seen indeed"] The text has ראית רבית *raith rabith*, which the Masoretes in the marginal Keri have corrected to ראות רבות *reoth rabboth;* as indeed *one hundred and seven* MSS., and *five* editions, now have it in the text. This was probably the reading of most of the MSS. of their time; which, though they approved of it, out of some superstition they would not admit into their standard text. But these wretched critics, though they perceived there was some fault, yet did not know where the fault lay, nor consequently how to amend it; and yet it was open enough to a judicious eye: "רבות *rabboth*, sic veteres; et tamen forte legendum, ראות *reoth*, vide cap. vi. 9."—*Secker*. That is, ראית ראות *raith, reoth, seeing, thou shalt see.* I believe no one will doubt of admitting this as the true reading.

But he heareth not—"Yet thou wilt not hear"] For ישמע *yishma*, read תשמע *tishma*, in the second person; so all the ancient Versions and *forty* MSS. of *Kennicott's*, (four of them ancient,) and *seventeen* of *De Rossi's*, and perhaps *five* more. *Two* others have תשמעו *tishmeu*, second person plural.

Verse 21. *He will magnify the law*—"He hath exalted his own praise"] For תורה *torah, the law*, the *Septuagint* read תודה *todah, praise.*

Verse 22. They are *all of them snared in holes*—"All their chosen youths are taken in the toils"] For הפח *hapheach* read הופחו *huphachu*, in the plural number, hophal; as החבאו *hochbau*, which answers to it in the following member of the sentence. *Le Clerc, Houbigant.* הפח *huppach, Secker.*

Verse 24. *We have sinned*—"They have sinned"] For חטאנו *chatanu*, "we have sinned," first person; the *Septuagint* and *Chaldee* read חטאו *chateu*, "they have sinned," in the third person.

Verse 25. *The fury of his anger*—"The heat of his wrath"] For חמה *chammah*, the Bodl. MS. has חמת *chammath*, in *regimine*, more regularly.

It hath set him on fire round about] So thoroughly hardened are the Jewish people, that they are represented as being in a house on fire, and even scorched with the flames, without perceiving their danger, or feeling that they are hurt! What a picture of mental induration! and this is their state to the present day. But by whom shall Jacob arise? for in this sense he is small indeed. Many efforts have been made to Christianize them, but without effect; and is this to be wondered at, while we tell them how great they are, how learned, how wise, how much we owe to them, that they are still the peculiar people of God, &c., &c.? If all this be true, what can they gain by becoming Christians? Whereas a more stupid, proud, hardened, ignorant people can scarcely be found in the civilized world, and they are most grossly ignorant of their own Scriptures.

CHAPTER XLIII

Prediction of that blessed period when God should gather the posterity of Abraham, with tender care, from their several dispersions in every quarter under heaven, and bring them safely to their own land, 1–7. *Struck with astonishment at so clear a display of an event so very remote, the prophet again challenges all the blinded nations and their idols to produce an instance of such foreknowledge,* 8, 9; *and intimates that the Jews should remain,* (*as at this day,*) *a singular monument to witness the truth of the prediction, till it should at length be fulfilled by the irresistible power of God,* 10–13. *He then returns to the nearer deliverance—that from the captivity of Babylon,* 14, 15; *with which, however, he immediately connects another deliverance described by allusions to that from Egypt, but represented as much more wonderful than that; a character which will not at all apply to the deliverance from Babylon, and must therefore be understood of the restoration from the mystical Babylon,* 16–18. *On this occasion the prophet, with peculiar elegance, and by a very strong poetic figure, represents the tender care of God in comforting and refreshing his people on their way through the desert, to be so great as to make even the wild beasts haunting those parched places so sensible of the blessing of those copious streams then provided by him, as to join their hissing and howling notes with one consent to praise God,* 19–21. *This leads to a beautiful contrast of the ingratitude of the Jews, and a vindication of God's dealings with regard to them,* 22–28.

A. M. cir. 3292 B. C. cir. 712 Olymp. XVII. 1 cir. annum NumæPompilii, R. Roman., 4

BUT now thus saith the LORD [a]that created thee, O Jacob, [b]and he that formed thee, O Israel, Fear not: [c]for I have redeemed thee, [d]I have called *thee* by thy name; thou *art* mine.
2 [e]When thou passest through the waters, [f]I *will be* with thee; and through the rivers, they shall not overflow thee: when thou [g]walkest through the fire, thou shalt not be burned; neither shall the flame kindle upon thee.
3 For I *am* the LORD thy God, the Holy One of Israel, thy Saviour: [h]I gave Egypt *for* thy ransom, Ethiopia and Seba for thee.
4 Since thou wast precious in my sight, thou hast been honourable, and I have loved thee: therefore will I give men for thee, and people for thy [i]life.
5 [k]Fear not: for I *am* with thee: I will bring thy seed from the east, and gather thee from the west;
6 I will say to the north, Give up; and to the south, Keep not back: bring my sons from far, and my daughters from the ends of the earth;
7 *Even* every one that is [l]called by my

A. M. cir. 3292 B. C. cir. 712 Olymp. XVII. 1 cir. annum NumæPompilii, R. Roman., 4

[a]Ver. 7.——[b]Ver. 21; chap. xliv. 2, 21, 24——[c]Chap. xliv. 6——[d]Chap. xlii. 6; xlv. 4——[e]Psa. lxvi. 12; xci. 3, &c.——[f]Deut. xxxi. 6, 8——[g]Dan. iii. 25, 27——[h]Prov. xi. 8; xxi. 18——[i]Or, *person*——[k]Chap. xli. 10, 14; xliv. 2; Jer. xxx. 10, 11; xlvi. 27, 28——[l]Chap. lxiii. 19; James ii. 7

NOTES ON CHAP. XLIII

Verse 1. *I have called* thee *by thy name*] "קראתי בשמך *karathi beshimcha.* So all the Versions. But it seems from the seventh verse, and from the thing itself, that we should read קראתיך בשמי *karathicha bishmi,* 'I have called thee by my name;' for this form of speech often occurs—the other never. For chap. xlv. 24, concerning Cyrus, is another matter; but when God calls Jacob Israel, he calls him by the name of God. See Exod. xxxi. 2."—*Secker.*

Verse 3. *I gave Egypt* for *thy ransom*] This is commonly supposed to refer to the time of Sennacherib's invasion; who, when he was just ready to fall upon Jerusalem, soon after his entering Judea, was providentially diverted from that design, and turned his arms against the Egyptians, and their allies the Cushean Arabians, with their neighbours the Sabeans, probably joined with them under Tirhakah. See chap. xx. and chap. xxxvii. 9. Or as there are some reasonable objections to this opinion, perhaps it may mean more generally that God has often saved his people at the expense of other nations, whom he had, as it were in their stead, given up to destruction. Vitringa explains this of Shalmaneser's designs upon the kingdom of Judea after he had destroyed that of Samaria, from which he was diverted by carrying the war against the Egyptians, Cusheans, and Sabeans; but of this I think he has no clear proof in history. It is not to be wondered at that many things of this kind should remain very obscure for the want of the light of history, which in regard to these times is extremely deficient.

"Did not Cyrus overcome these nations? and might they not be given for releasing the Jews? It seems to have been so from chap. xlv. 14."—*Secker.*

Kimchi refers all this to the deliverance of Jerusalem from the invasion of Sennacherib. Tirhakah, king of Ethiopia, had come out to war against the king of Assyria, who was thereupon obliged to raise the siege of Jerusalem. Thus the Ethiopians, Egyptians, and Sabeans were delivered into the hands of the Assyrians as a ransom for Israel.—*Kimchi.* I cannot help thinking this to be a very rational solution of the text.

Verse 7. *Every one that is called by my name*] All who worship the true God, and are obedient to his laws.

I have created him] בראתיו *berathiv.* I have produced him out of nothing.

For my glory] *Ten* MSS., *three* ancient, and the *Syriac* and *Vulgate,* read לכבודי *licabodi,* without the conjunction ו *vau, and.*

A. M. cir. 3292
B. C. cir. 712
Olymp. XVII. 1
cir. annum
NumæPompilii,
R. Roman., 4

name: for [m]I have created him
for my glory, [n]I have formed
him; yea, I have made him.
8 [o]Bring forth the blind people
that have eyes, and the deaf that have ears.
9 Let all the nations be gathered together,
and let the people be assembled: [p]who among
them can declare this, and show us former
things? let them bring forth their witnesses,
that they may be justified: or let them hear,
and say, *It is* truth.
10 [q]Ye *are* my witnesses, saith the LORD,
[r]and my servant whom I have chosen: that
ye may know and believe me, and understand that I *am* he: [s]before me there was [t]no
God formed, neither shall there be after me.
11 I, *even* I, [u]*am* the LORD;
and beside me *there is* no Saviour.
12 I have declared, and have
saved, and I have showed, when *there was*
no [v]strange *god* among you: [w]therefore ye
are my witnesses, saith the LORD, that I
am God.
13 [x]Yea, before the day *was* I *am* he; and
there is none that can deliver out of my hand:
I will work, and who shall [y]let [z]it?
14 Thus saith the LORD, your Redeemer,
the Holy One of Israel; for your sake I
have sent to Babylon, and have brought down
all their [a]nobles, and the Chaldeans, whose
cry *is* in the ships.

---

[m]Psa. c. 3; chap. xxix. 23; John iii. 3, 5; 2 Cor. v. 17; Eph. ii. 10——[n]Ver. 1——[o]Chap. vi. 9; xlii. 19; Ezek. xii. 2——[p]Chap. xli. 21, 22, 26——[q]Chap. xliv. 8——[r]Chap. xlii. 1; lv. 4——[s]Chap. xli. 4; xliv. 6

[t]Or, *nothing formed of God*——[u]Chap. xlv. 21; Hos. xiii. 4——[v]Deut. xxxii. 16; Psa. lxxxi. 9——[w]Chap. xliv. 8; ver. 10——[x]Psa. xc. 2; John viii. 58——[y]Heb. *turn it back?*——[z]Job ix. 12; chap. xiv. 27——[a]Heb. *bars*

I have formed him] יצרתיו *yetsartiv.* I have given him that particular form and shape which are best suited to his station in life.

I have made him] עשיתיו *asithiv.* I have adapted him to the accomplishment of my counsels and designs.

Verse 8. *Bring forth the blind people that have eyes*—"Bring forth the people, blind, although they have eyes"] I understand this of the Gentiles, as the verse following, not of the Jews. Their natural faculties, if they had made a proper use of them, must have led them to the knowledge of the being and attributes of the one true God; "for his eternal power and Godhead," if well attended to, are clearly seen in his works, (Rom. i. 20,) and would have preserved them from running into the folly and absurdity of worshipping idols. They are here challenged to produce the evidence of the power and foreknowledge of their idol gods; and the Jews are just afterwards, ver. 10, appealed to as witnesses for God in this cause, therefore these latter cannot here be meant by the people blind with eyes and deaf with ears.

Verse 9. *Who among them*] *Seven* MSS., *three* ancient, and the first edition, 1486, with the *Syriac* and *Vulgate*, read בכם *bechem*, who among *you;* the present reading is preferable.

Verse 10. *Ye* (the Israelites) are *my witnesses—and my servant* (the prophet) *whom I have chosen*, that whatever has been said before concerning Sennacherib has been literally fulfilled. The *prophet* had predicted it; the *Israelites* saw it accomplished.

Before me there was no God formed, neither shall there be after me.] This is a most difficult place. Was there a time when God was not? No! Yet he says, *before* me. Will there be a time in which God will not exist? No! Yet he says, *after* me. Are not all these words to be referred to his creation? *Before* me, no god created any thing, nor was there any thing pre-existent but myself. And *after* me, *i. e.*, after my creation, such as now exists, there shall be no other class of beings formed. This mode of interpretation frees the passage from all embarrassment, and the context perfectly agrees with it. The words *my servant*, in this verse, the *Targum* understands of *the Messiah.*

Verse 12. *I have declared, and have saved*] My prophets have always predicted your deliverances before they took place; and I have fulfilled their words to the uttermost.

Verse 14. *The Chaldeans, whose cry* is *in the ships*—"The Chaldeans exulting in their ships."] Babylon was very advantageously situated both in respect to commerce, and as a naval power. It was open to the Persian Gulf by the Euphrates, which was navigable by large vessels; and being joined to the Tigris above Babylon by the canal called *Naharmalca* or the Royal River, supplied the city with the produce of the whole country to the north of it, as far as the Euxine and Caspian seas, *Herod.* i. 194. Semiramis was the foundress of this part also of the Babylonian greatness. She improved the navigation of the Euphrates, *Herod.* i. 184; *Strabo*, lib. xvi.; and is said to have had a fleet of three thousand galleys, *Huet*, Hist. du Commerce, chap. xi. We are not to wonder that in later times we hear little of the commerce and naval power of Babylon; for, after the taking of the city by Cyrus, the Euphrates was not only rendered less fit for navigation by being on that occasion diverted from its course and left to spread over the whole country; but the Persian monarchs, residing in their own country, to prevent any invasion by sea on that part of their empire, purposely obstructed the navigation of both the rivers by making cataracts in them, *Strabo*, ib., that is, by raising dams across the channel, and making artificial falls in them, that no vessel of any size or force could possibly come up. Alexander began to restore the navigation of the rivers by demolishing the cataracts upon the Tigris as far up as Seleucia, *Arrian*, lib. vii., but he did not live to finish his great designs; those upon the Euphrates still continued. Ammianus, xxiv. 1, mentions them as subsisting in his time.

The prophet therefore might very justly speak of the Chaldeans as glorying in their naval

A. M. cir. 3292
B. C. cir. 712
Olymp. XVII. 1
cir. annum
NumæPompilii,
R. Roman., 4

15 I *am* the LORD, your Holy One, the Creator of Israel, your King.

16 Thus saith the LORD, which [b]maketh a way in the sea, and [c]a path in the mighty waters;

17 Which [d]bringeth forth the chariot and horse, the army and the power; they shall lie down together, they shall not rise: they are extinct, they are quenched as tow.

18 [e]Remember ye not the former things, neither consider the things of old.

19 Behold, I will do a [f]new thing; now it shall spring forth; shall ye not know it? [g]I will even make a way in the wilderness, *and* rivers in the desert.

20 The beast of the field shall honour me, the dragons and the [h]owls[i]: because [k]I give waters in the wilderness, *and* rivers in the desert, to give drink to my people, my chosen.

21 [l]This people have I formed for myself; they shall show forth my praise.

A. M. cir. 3292
B. C. cir. 712
Olymp. XVII. 1
cir. annum
NumæPompilii,
R. Roman., 4

22 But thou hast not called upon me, O Jacob; but thou [m]hast been weary of me, O Israel.

23 [n]Thou hast not brought me the [o]small cattle of thy burnt-offerings; neither hast thou honoured me with thy sacrifices. I have not caused thee to serve with an offering, nor wearied thee with incense.

24 Thou hast bought me no sweet cane with money, neither hast thou [p]filled me with the fat of thy sacrifices: but thou hast made me to serve with thy sins, thou hast [q]wearied me with thine iniquities.

25 I, *even* I, *am* he that [r]blotteth out thy transgressions [s]for mine own sake, [t]and will not remember thy sins.

26 Put me in remembrance: let us plead

---

[b]Exod. xiv. 16, 22; Psa. lxxvii. 19; chap. li. 10 —— [c]Josh. iii. 13, 16 —— [d]Exod. xiv. 4–9, 25 —— [e]Jer. xvi. 14; xxiii. 7 —— [f]2 Cor. v. 17; Rev. xxi. 5 —— [g]Exod. xvii. 6; Num. xx. 11; Deut. viii. 15; Psa. lxxviii. 16; chap. xxxv. 6; xli. 18 —— [h]Or, *ostriches* —— [i]Heb. *daughters of the owl* —— [k]Chap. xlviii. 21

[l]Psa. cii. 18; ver. 1, 7; Luke i. 74, 75; Eph. i. 5, 6 —— [m]Mal. i. 13 —— [n]Amos v. 25 —— [o]Heb. *lambs* or *kids* —— [p]Heb. *made me drunk*, or *abundantly moistened* —— [q]Ch. i. 14; Mal. ii. 17 —— [r]Chap. xliv. 22; xlviii. 9; Jer. l. 20; Acts iii. 19 —— [s]Ezek. xxxvi. 22, &c. —— [t]Chap. i. 18; Jer. xxxi. 34

---

power in his time; though afterwards they had no foundation for making any such boast.

Verse 15. *The Creator*] For בורא *bore*, "Creator," six MSS. (two ancient) have אלהי *Elohey*, "God."

Verse 19. *Behold, I will do a new thing*] At ver. 16, the prophet had referred to the deliverance from Egypt and the passage through the Red Sea; here he promises that the same power shall be employed in their redemption and return from the Babylonish captivity. This was to be a *new* prodigy.

Verse 20. *The beast of the field shall honour me*—"The wild beast of the field shall glorify me"] The image is elegant and highly poetical. God will give such an abundant miraculous supply of water to his people traversing the dry desert in their return to their country, that even the wild beasts, the serpents, the ostriches, and other animals that haunt those arid regions, shall be sensible of the blessing, and shall break forth into thanksgiving and praises to him for the unusual refreshment which they receive from his so plentifully watering the sandy wastes of Arabia Deserta, for the benefit of his people passing through them.

Verse 22. *But thou hast not called upon me*] The connexion is: But thou, Israel, whom I have chosen, whom I have formed for myself to be my witness against the false gods of the nations; even thou hast revolted from me, hast neglected my worship, and hast been perpetually running after strange gods. The emphasis of this and the following parts of the sentence, on which the sense depends, is laid on the words ME, on MY ACCOUNT, &c. The Jews were diligent in performing the external services of religion; in offering prayers, incense, sacrifices, oblations; but their prayers were not offered with faith; and their oblations were made more frequently to their idols than to the God of their fathers. The Hebrew idiom excludes with a general negative, in a comparative sense, one of two objects opposed to one another: thus, "I will have mercy, and *not* sacrifice," Hos. vi. 6. "For I spoke *not* to your fathers, *nor* commanded them, concerning burnt-offerings or sacrifices; but this thing I commanded them, saying, Obey my voice," Jer. vii. 22, 23. And the meaning of this place of Isaiah seems to be much the same with that of Amos; who however has explained at large both parts of the comparison, and specified the false service opposed to the true:—

"Have ye offered unto me sacrifices and offerings,
In the wilderness forty years, O house of Israel?
Nay, but you have borne the tabernacle of your Moloch,
And Chiun, your images;
The star of your god, which you made to yourselves." Amos v. 25, 26.

But thou hast been weary of me, O Israel—"Neither on my account hast thou laboured, O Israel."] For כי יגעת *ki yagata*, the *Septuagint* and *Vulgate* read ויגעת *veyagata*.—*Houbigant*. The negative is repeated or referred to by the conjunction ו *vau;* as in many other places. See note on chap. xxiii. 4.

Verse 25. *I*, even *I*, am *he*] The original is extremely abrupt: אנכי אנכי הוא *anochi anochi hu*, "I, I, He." Is there any mystery in this form? Does it refer to a plurality of persons in the Godhead?

For mine own sake] In the pardon of sin

A. M. cir. 3292
B. C. cir. 712
Olymp. XVII. 1
cir. annum
NumæPompilii,
R. Roman., 4

together: declare thou, that thou mayest be justified.

27 Thy first father hath sinned, and thy [u]teachers have transgressed against me.

28 Therefore [v]I have profaned the [w]princes of the sanctuary, [x]and have given Jacob to the curse, and Israel to reproaches.

[u]Heb. *interpreters;* Mal. ii. 7, 8——[v]Chap. xlvii. 6; Lam. ii. 2, 6, 7

[w]Or, *holy princes*——[x]Psa. lxxix. 4; Jer. xxiv. 9; Dan. ix. 11; Zech. viii. 13

God can draw no reason but from his own infinite goodness.

Verse 27. *Thy first father hath sinned*] On this *Kimchi* speaks well: "How can ye say that ye have not sinned, seeing your first father, Adam, sinned; and man hath sin impressed on him through natural generation?"

Verse 28. *I have profaned the princes of the sanctuary*—"Thy princes have profaned my sanctuary"] Instead of ואחלל שרי *vaachallel sarey*, read ויחללו שריך *vayechalelu sareycha*. So the *Syriac* and *Septuagint*, και εμιαναν οἱ αρχοντες τα ἁγια μου, "the rulers have defiled my holy things." קדשי *kodshi, Houbigant.* Οἱ αρχοντες σου, "thy rulers," MSS. Pachom. and I. D. II. and Marchal.

To reproaches—"To reproach"] לגדופה *ligeduphah*, in the singular number; so an ancient MS. and the *Septuagint*, *Syriac*, and *Vulgate*. And, alas! what a curse do they still bear, and what reproach do they still suffer! No national crimes have ever equalled those of the Jewish nation, for no nation ever had such privileges to neglect, despise, sin against. When shall this severity of God towards this people have an end? *Answ.* Whenever, with one heart, they turn to him, and receive the doctrine of the Lord Jesus; and not till *then*.

CHAPTER XLIV

This chapter, besides promises of redemption, of the effusion of the Spirit, and success of the Gospel, 1–5, *sets forth, in a very sublime manner, the supreme power and foreknowledge, and absolute eternity, of the one true God; and exposes the folly and absurdity of idolatry with admirable force and elegance,* 6–20. *And to show that the knowledge of future events belongs only to Jehovah, whom all creation is again called to adore for the deliverance and reconciliation granted to his people,* 21–23, *the prophet concludes with setting in a very strong point of view the absolute impotence of every thing considered great and insurmountable in the sight of men, when standing in the way of the Divine counsel; and mentions the future deliverer of the Jewish nation expressly by name, nearly* two hundred years *before his birth,* 24–28.

A. M. cir. 3292
B. C. cir. 712
Olymp. XVII. 1
cir. annum
NumæPompilii,
R. Roman., 4

YET now hear, [a]O Jacob my servant; and Israel, whom I have chosen.

2 Thus saith the LORD that made thee, [b]and formed thee from the womb, *which* will help thee; Fear not, O Jacob, my servant; and thou, [c]Jesurun, whom I have chosen.

3 For I will [d]pour water upon him that is thirsty, and floods upon the dry ground: I will pour my spirit upon thy seed, and my blessing upon thine offspring:

4 And they shall spring up *as* among the grass, as willows by the water courses.

[a]Ver. 21; chap. xli. 8; xliii. 1; Jer. xxx. 10; xlvi. 27, 28
[b]Chap. xliii. 1, 7

[c]Deut. xxxii. 15——[d]Chap. xxxv. 7; Joel ii. 28; John vii. 38; Acts ii. 13

NOTES ON CHAP. XLIV

Verse 2. *Jesurun*] Jeshurun means Israel. This name was given to that people by Moses, Deut. xxxii. 15; xxxiii. 5, 26. The most probable account of it seems to be that in which the Jewish commentators agree; namely, that it is derived from ישר *yashar*, and signifies *upright*. In the same manner, Israel, as a people, is called משלם *meshullam, perfect*, chap. xlii. 19. They were taught of God, and abundantly furnished with the means of rectitude and perfection in his service and worship. *Grotius* thinks that ישרון *yeshurun* is a diminutive of ישראל *yishrael, Israel;* expressing peculiar fondness and affection; Ισραηλιδιον, *O little Israel.*

Verse 4. *They shall spring up* as *among the grass*—"They shall spring up as the grass among the waters"] בבין חציר *bebeyn chatsir.* "They shall spring up *in the midst of*, or rather, *in among, the grass.*" This cannot be right: *eleven* MSS., and *thirteen* editions, have כבין *kebeyn*, or כבן *keben*. Twenty-four MSS. read it without the י *yod*, בבן *beben, in the son of the grass;* and so reads the *Chaldee;* בבן *beben, in the son* of the grass. *Twenty-four* MSS. of Dr. *Kennicott's*, *thirty-three* of *De Rossi's*, and one of my own, with *six* editions, have this reading. The *Syriac*, מבין *mibbeyn*. The true reading is in all probability כבין *kebeyn;* and the word מים *mayim*, which should have followed it, is lost out of the text: but it is happily supplied by the *Septuagint;* ὡς ανα μεσον ὑδατος, *as among the water.* "In every place where there is water, there is always grass; for water makes every thing grow in the east." Sir *John Chardin's* note on 1 Kings xvii. 5. *Harmer's* Observations, i. 54.

A. M. cir. 3292 B. C. cir. 712 Olymp. XVII. 1 cir. annum Numæ Pompilii, R. Roman., 4

5 One shall say, I *am* the
LORD'S; and another shall call
himself by the name of Jacob;
and another shall subscribe *with*
his hand unto the LORD, and surname *himself*
by the name of Israel.
6 Thus saith the LORD, the King of Israel,
[e]and his Redeemer the LORD of hosts; [f]I
am the first, and I *am* the last: and beside
me *there is* no God.
7 And [g]who, as I, shall call, and shall declare it, and set it in order for me, since I
appointed the ancient people? and the things
that are coming, and shall come, let them
show unto them.
8 Fear ye not, neither be
afraid: [h]have not I told thee from
that time, and have declared *it?*
[i]ye *are* even my witnesses. Is
there a God beside me? yea [k]*there is* no
[l]God; I know not *any.*
9 They [m]that make a graven image *are* all
of them vanity; and their [n]delectable things
shall not profit; and they *are* their own witnesses; [o]they see not, nor know; that they
may be ashamed.
10 Who hath formed a god, or molten a
graven image [p]*that* is profitable for nothing?
11 Behold, all his fellows shall be [q]ashamed;
and the workmen, they *are* of men: let them

[e]Ver. 24; chap. xliii. 1, 14——[f]Chap. xli. 4; xlviii. 12; Rev. i. 8, 17; xxii. 13——[g]Chap. xli. 4, 22; xlv. 21 [h]Chap. xli. 22——[i]Chap. xliii. 10, 12——[k]Deut. iv. 35, 39; xxxii. 39; 1 Sam. ii. 2——2 Sam. xxii. 32; chap. xlv. 5——[l]Heb. *rock;* Deut. xxxii. 4——[m]Chap. xli. 24, 29——[n]Heb. *desirable*——[o]Psalm cxv. 4, &c. [p]Jeremiah x. 5; Habakkuk ii. 18——[q]Psalm xcvii. 7; chap. i. 29; xlii. 17; xlv. 16

Verse 5. *Shall call* himself—"Shall be called"] Passive, יקרא *yikkare;* κληθησεται, *Symmachus.*

Another shall subscribe with his hand unto the Lord—"This shall inscribe his hand to JEHOVAH"] Και ἑτερος επιγραψει χειρι (χειρα, *Aq., Sym.*) αυτου, Του Θεου ειμι· "And another shall write upon his hand, I belong to God."—*Sept.* They seem to have read here, as before, ליהוה אני *laihovah ani, I belong to* JEHOVAH. But the repetition of the same phrase without any variation is not elegant. However, they seem to have understood it rightly, as an allusion to the marks, which were made by punctures rendered indelible, by fire or by staining, upon the hand or some other part of the body, signifying the state or character of the person, and to whom he belonged. The slave was marked with the name of his master; the soldier, of his commander; the idolater, with the name or ensign of his god: Στιγματα επιγραφομενα δια των στρατευομενων εν ταις χερσιν· "Punctural inscriptions made by the soldiers on their hands." Aetius apud Turnebum Advers. xxiv. 12. Victuris in cute punctis milites scripti et matriculis inserti jurare solent. "The soldiers having indelible inscriptions on their skin, and inserted in the muster-rolls, are accustomed to make oath." *Vigetius*, ii. 5. And the Christians seem to have imitated this practice, by what *Procopius* says on this place of Isaiah: Το δε ΤΗ ΧΕΙΡΙ, δια το στιζειν ισως πολλους επι καρπων, η βραχιονων, η του σταυρου το σημειον, η την Χριστου προσηγοριαν. "Because many marked their wrists, or their arms, with the sign of the cross, or with the name of Christ." See Rev. xx. 4; *Spencer*, De Leg. Hebr. lib. ii., cap. 20.

Verse 7. *Let them show unto them*—"Let them declare unto us."] For למו *lamo,* unto *them,* the *Chaldee* reads לנו *lanu,* unto *us.* The *Septuagint* read לכם *lachem,* unto *you;* which is preferable to the reading of the text. But למו *lamo,* and לנו *lanu,* are frequently mistaken one for the other, see chap. x. 29; Psa. lxxx. 7; lxiv. 6.

Verse 8. *Fear ye not*] תרהו *tirehu* never occurs. Perhaps it should be תיראו *tireu, fear ye.* Two MSS. read תירהו *tirehu,* and one of mine תהרו *taharu.*

Verses 9, 10. *That they may be ashamed. Who hath formed a god*—"That every one may be ashamed, that he hath formed a god"] The *Bodleian* MS., one of the first extant for its antiquity and authority, instead of מי *mi,* at the beginning of the *tenth* verse, has כי *ki,* which greatly clears up the construction of a very obscure passage. *Doederlein* approves of this reading. The *Septuagint* likewise closely connect in construction the end of ver. 9 with the beginning of ver. 10; and wholly omit the interrogative מי *mi,* which embarrasses the sentence: Αισχυνθησονται οἱ πλὰσσοντες Θεον, και γλυφοντες παντες ανωφελη· "But they shall be confounded that make a god; and they who engrave unprofitable things;" agreeably to the reading of the MS. above mentioned.

Verse 11. *His fellows*] חבריו *chaberaiv:* but עבדיו *abadaiv, his servants* or *worshippers,* is the reading of one of *De Rossi's* MSS., and of the *Chaldee.*

And the workmen, they are *of men*—"Even the workmen themselves shall blush"] I do not know that any one has ever yet interpreted these words to any tolerably good sense: וחרשים המה מאדם *vecharashim hemmah meadam.* The *Vulgate* and our translators, have rendered them very fairly, as they are written and pointed in the text: Fabri enim sunt ex hominibus. "And the workmen they are of men." Out of which the commentators have not been able to extract any thing worthy of the prophet. I have given another explanation of the place; agreeable enough to the context, if it can be deduced from the words themselves. I presume that אדם *adam, rubuit,* may signify *erubuit,* to be red through shame, as well as from any other cause; though I cannot produce any example of it in that particular sense; and the word in the text I would point מאדם *meoddam;* or if any one should object to the irregularity of the number, I would read מאדמים *meoddamim.* But I rather think that the irregularity of the construction has been the cause of the obscurity, and has given occasion to the mistaken punctuation. The singular is sometimes put for the plural. See Psa. lxviii. 31; and the par-

A. M. cir. 3292
B. C. cir. 712
Olymp. XVII. 1
cir. annum
NumæPompilii,
R. Roman., 4

all be gathered together, let them stand up; *yet* they shall fear, *and* they shall be ashamed together.

12 [r]The smith [s]with the tongs both worketh in the coals, and fashioneth it with hammers, and worketh it with the strength of his arms: yea, he is hungry, and his strength faileth: he drinketh no water, and is faint.

13 The carpenter stretcheth out *his* rule; he marketh it out with a line; he fitteth it with planes, and he marketh it out with the compass, and maketh it after the figure of a man, according to the beauty of a man: that it may remain in the house.

14 He heweth him down cedars, and taketh the cypress and the oak, which he [t]strengtheneth for himself among the trees of the forest: he planteth an ash, and the rain doth nourish *it*.

15 Then shall it be for a man to burn: for he will take thereof, and warm himself; yea, he kindleth *it*, and baketh bread; yea, he maketh a god, and worshippeth *it;* he maketh it a graven image, and falleth down thereto.

16 He burneth part thereof in the fire; with part thereof he eateth flesh; he roasteth roast, and is satisfied: yea, he warmeth *himself*, and saith, Aha, I am warm, I have seen the fire:

A. M. cir. 3292
B. C. cir. 712
Olymp. XVII. 1
cir. annum
NumæPompilii,
R. Roman., 4

17 And the residue thereof he maketh a god, *even* his graven image: he falleth down unto it, and worshippeth *it*, and prayeth unto it, and saith, Deliver me; for thou *art* my god.

18 [u]They have not known nor understood: for [v]he hath [w]shut their eyes, that they cannot see; *and* their hearts, that they cannot understand.

19 And none [x]considereth [y]in his heart, neither *is there* knowledge nor understanding to say, I have burned part of it in the fire: yea, also I have baked bread upon the coals thereof; I have roasted flesh and eaten *it:* and shall I make the residue thereof an abomination? shall I fall down to [z]the stock of a tree?

20 He feedeth on ashes: [a]a deceived heart hath turned him aside, that he cannot deliver his soul, nor say, *Is there* not a lie in my right hand?

21 Remember these, O Jacob and Israel; for [b]thou *art* my servant: I have formed

[r]Chap. xl. 19; xli. 6; Jer. x. 3, &c.; Wisd. xiii. 11, &c.——[s]Or, *with an axe*——[t]Or, *taketh courage*——[u]Chap. xlv. 20——[v]2 Thess. ii. 11

[w]Heb. *daubed*——[x]Heb. *setteth to his heart*——[y]Chap. xlvi. 8——[z]Heb. *that which comes of a tree?*——[a]Hos. iv. 11; Rom. i. 21; 2 Thess. ii. 11——[b]Ver. 1. 2

ticiple for the future tense, see Isa. xl. 11.—L.

Verse 12. *The smith with the tongs, &c.*—"The smith cutteth off a portion of iron"] מעצר *meatstsed,* Participium Pihel of עצר *atsad, to cut;* still used in that sense in the *Arabic.* See *Simonis* Lex. Heb. The *Septuagint* and *Syriac* take the word in this form: but they render it *sharpeneth* the iron. See *Castell.* Lex. in voce.

The sacred writers are generally large and eloquent upon the subject of idolatry; they treat it with great severity, and set forth the absurdity of it in the strongest light. But this passage of Isaiah, ver. 12-20, far exceeds any thing that ever was written upon the subject, in force of argument, energy of expression, and elegance of composition. One or two of the apocryphal writers have attempted to imitate the prophet, but with very ill success; Wisd. xiii. 11-19; xv. 7, &c.; Baruch vi., especially the latter, who, injudiciously dilating his matter, and introducing a number of minute circumstances, has very much weakened the force and effect of his invective. On the contrary a heathen author, in the ludicrous way, has, in a line or two, given idolatry one of the severest strokes it ever received:—

Olim truncus eram ficulnus, inutile lignum,
Cum faber incertus, scamnum faceretne Priapum,
Maluit esse Deum. Deus inde ego.
HORAT. *Satyr,* lib. 1. sat. viii.

"Formerly I was the stump of a fig tree, a useless log; when the carpenter, after hesitating whether to make me a *god* or a *stool,* at last determined to make me a *god.* Thus I became a god!"

From the *tenth* to the *seventeenth* verse, a most beautiful strain of irony is carried on against idolatry. And we may naturally think that every idolater, who either read or heard it, must have been for ever ashamed of his own devices.—L.

Verse 14. *He heweth him down*—"He heweth down"] For לכרת *lichroth,* the *Septuagint* and *Vulgate* read כרת *carath* or יכרת *yichroth.*

Verse 16. *With part*—"AND with part"] *Twenty-three* MSS., the *Septuagint,* and *Vulgate* add the conjunction ו *vau,* and ועל *veal.*

Verse 17. *He falleth down unto it*] There were *four* forms of adoration used among the Hebrews: 1. השתחוה HISHTACHAVAH, The prostration of the whole body. 2. קדד KADAD, The bowing of the head. 3. כרע CARA, The bending of the upper part of the body down to the knees. 4. ברך BARACH, Bowing the knee, or kneeling. See on chap. xlix. 23.

Verse 18. *He hath shut their eyes*—"Their eyes are closed up"] The *Septuagint, Chaldee,* and *Vulgate,* for טח *tach,* read טחו *tachu.* See note on chap. vi. 10.

Verse 20. *He feedeth on ashes*] He feedeth

A. M. cir. 3292
B. C. cir. 712
Olymp. XVII. 1
cir. annum
NumæPompilii,
R. Roman., 4

thee; thou *art* my servant: O
Israel, thou shalt not be forgotten of me.
22 [c]I have blotted out, as a
thick cloud, thy transgressions, and, as a
cloud, thy sins: return unto me; for [d]I have
redeemed thee.
23 [e]Sing, O ye heavens; for the LORD hath
done *it:* shout, ye lower parts of the earth:
break forth into singing, ye mountains, O
forest, and every tree therein: for the LORD
hath redeemed Jacob, and glorified himself
in Israel.
24 Thus saith the LORD, [f]thy Redeemer,
and [g]he that formed thee from the womb, I
am the LORD that maketh all *things;* [h]that
stretcheth forth the heavens alone; that
spreadeth abroad the earth by
myself:
25 That [i]frustrateth the tokens
[k]of the liars, and maketh diviners mad; that turneth wise *men* backward,
[l]and maketh their knowledge foolish;
26 [m]That confirmeth the word of his servant,
and performeth the counsel of his messengers;
that saith to Jerusalem, Thou shalt be inhabited; and to the cities of Judah, Ye shall be
built, and I will raise up the [n]decayed places
thereof:
27 [o]That saith to the deep, Be dry, and I
will dry up thy rivers:
28 That saith of Cyrus, *He is* my shepherd,
and shall perform all my pleasure: even saying to Jerusalem, [p]Thou shalt be built; and
to the temple, Thy foundation shall be laid.

[c]Chap. xliii. 25——[d]Chap. xliii. 1; xlviii. 20; 1 Cor. vi. 20; 1 Pet. i. 18, 19——[e]Psa. lxix. 34; xcvi. 11, 12; chap. xlii. 10; xlix. 13; Jer. li. 48; Rev. xviii. 20——[f]Ch. xliii. 14; Ver. 6——[g]Chap. xliii. 1

[h]Job ix. 8; Psa. civ. 2; chap. xl. 22; xlii. 5; xlv. 12; li. 13——[i]Chap. xlvii. 13——[k]Jer. l. 36——[l]1 Cor. i. 20
[m]Zech. i. 6——[n]Heb. *wastes*——[o]See Jer. l. 38; li. 32, 36
[p]2 Chron. xxxvi. 22, 23; Ezra i. 1, &c.; chap. xlv. 13

on that which affordeth no nourishment; a proverbial expression for using ineffectual means, and bestowing labour to no purpose. In the same sense Hosea says, "Ephraim feedeth on wind." Chap. xii. 1.

Verse 22. *I have blotted out, as a thick cloud, thy transgressions, and, as a cloud, thy sins*—"I have made thy transgressions vanish away like a cloud, and thy sins like a vapour"] *Longinus* admired the sublimity of the sentiment, as well as the harmony of the numbers, in the following sentence of *Demosthenes:* Τουτο το ψηφισμα τον τοτε τῃ πολει περισταντα κινδυνον παρελθειν εποιησεν ὡσπερ νεφος. "This decree made the danger then hanging over the city pass away like a cloud." Probably Isaiah alludes here to the smoke rising up from the sin-offering, dispersed speedily by the wind and rendered invisible. He who offered his sacrifice aright was as sure that the sin for which he offered it was blotted out, as that the smoke of the sacrifice was dispersed by the wind, and was no longer discernible.

Verse 24. *By myself*] *Thirteen* MSS., six ancient, confirm the reading of the *Keri,* מאתי *meittai.*

Verse 27. *That saith to the deep, Be dry*—"Who saith to the deep, Be thou wasted"] Cyrus took Babylon by laying the bed of the Euphrates dry, and leading his army into the city by night through the empty channel of the river. This remarkable circumstance, in which the event so exactly corresponded with the prophecy, was also noted by Jeremiah, chap. l. 38, li. 36.

"A drought shall be upon her waters, and they
shall be dried up:—
I will lay her sea dry;
And I will scorch up her springs."

It is proper here to give some account of the means and method by which the stratagem of Cyrus was effected.

The Euphrates, in the middle of the summer, from the melting of the snows on the mountains of Armenia, like the Nile, overflows the country. In order to diminish the inundation, and to carry off the waters, two canals were made by Nebuchadnezzar a hundred miles above the city; the first on the eastern side called Naharmalca, or the Royal River, by which the Euphrates was let into the Tigris; the other on the western side, called Pallacopas, or Naharaga, (נהר אגם *nahar agam,* The river of the pool,) by which the redundant waters were carried into a vast lake, forty miles square, contrived, not only to lessen the inundation, but for a reservoir, with sluices, to water the barren country on the Arabian side. Cyrus, by turning the whole river into the lake by the Pallacopas, laid the channel, where it ran through the city, almost dry; so that his army entered it, both above and below, by the bed of the river, the water not reaching above the middle of the thigh. By the great quantity of water let into the lake, the sluices and dams were destroyed; and being never repaired afterwards, the waters spread over the whole country below, and reduced it to a morass, in which the river is lost. Ingens modo et navigabilis, inde tenuis rivus, despectus emoritur; et nusquam manifesto exitit effluit, ut alii omnes, sed deficit. "And thus a navigable river has been totally lost, it having no exit from this morass. No wonder then that the geographical face of this country is completely changed;" MELA iii. 8; HEROD. i. 185, 190; XENOPHON, *Cyrop.* vii.; ARRIAN vii.

Verse 28. *That saith of Cyrus, He* is *my shepherd*—"Who saith to Cyrus, Thou art my shepherd"] *Pastor meus* es; *Vulg.* The true reading seems to be רעי אתה *roi attah;* the word אתה *attah,* has probably been dropped out of the text. The same word is lost out of the text, Psa. cxix. 57. It is supplied in the *Septuagint* by the word ει, *thou art.*

Saying to Jerusalem] For ולאמר *velemor,* the *Septuagint* and *Vulgate* read האומר *haomer.*

And to the temple] ולהיכל *uleheychal*, as לירושלם *lirushalayim*, before; the preposition is necessary, and the *Vulgate* seems to read so.—*Houbigant.*

That saith of CYRUS, *He is*, or thou art, *my shepherd—Saying to* JERUSALEM, "Thou shalt be built;" *and to the* TEMPLE, "Thy foundation shall be laid."—There is a remarkable beauty and propriety in this verse.

1. Cyrus is called God's shepherd. Shepherd was an epithet which Cyrus took to himself; and what he gave to all good kings.

2. This Cyrus should say to the temple: "Thy foundation shall be laid." Not—thou shalt be *built*. The fact is, only the *foundation* was laid in the days of Cyrus, the *Ammonites* having prevented the building; nor was it resumed till the *second* year of Darius, one of his successors. There is often a precision in the expressions of the prophets which is as honourable to truth, as it is unnoticed by careless readers.

CHAPTER XLV

Prophecy concerning Cyrus, the first king of the Persians. Every obstruction shall be removed out of his way, and the treasures taken from his enemies shall be immense, 1–3. To whom, and on what account, Cyrus was indebted for his wonderful success, 4–6. The prophet refutes the absurd opinion of the Persians, that there were two supreme beings, an evil *and a* good *one, represented by* light *and* darkness, *here declared to be only the operation of the* ONE *true God, 7; and makes a transition to the still greater* work *of God displayed in the dispensation of the Gospel, 8. Great impiety of those who call in question the mysterious providence of God towards his children, 9–12. The remaining part of this chapter, interspersed with strictures on the absurdity of idolatry and some allusions to the dark lying oracles of the heathens, may partly refer to the deliverance begun by Cyrus, but chiefly to the salvation by the Messiah, which, it is declared, shall be of universal extent and everlasting duration, 13–25.*

A. M. cir. 3292
B. C. cir. 712
Olymp. XVII. 1
cir. annum NumæPompilii, R. Roman., 4

THUS saith the LORD to his anointed, to Cyrus, whose [a]right hand I [b]have holden [c]to subdue nations before him; and I will loose the loins of kings, to open before him the two leaved gates; and the gates shall not be shut;

2 I will go before thee, [d]and make the crooked places straight: [e]I will break in pieces the gates of brass, and cut in sunder the bars of iron:

3 And I will give thee the treasures of darkness, and hidden riches of secret places, [f]that

[a]Chap. xli. 13——[b]Or, *strengthened*——[c]Chap. xli. 2; Dan. v. 30

[d]Chapter xl. 4——[e]Psalm cvii. 16——[f]Chapter xli. 23

NOTES ON CHAP. XLV

Verse 1. *Loose the loins of kings*—"ungird the loins of kings"] See the note on chap. v. 27. *Xenophon* gives the following list of the nations conquered by Cyrus: the Syrians, Assyrians, Arabians, Cappadocians, both the Phrygians, Lydians, Carians, Phœnicians, Babylonians. He moreover reigned over the Bactrians, Indians, Cilicians, the Sacæ Paphlagones, and Mariandyni.—*Cyrop.*, lib. i. p. 4, Edit. *Hutchinson*, Quarto. All these kingdoms he acknowledges, in his decree for the restoration of the Jews, to have been given to him by JEHOVAH, the God of heaven. Ezra i. 2.

To open before him the two leaved gates, &c.—"That I may open before him the valves; and the gates shall not be shut"] The gates of Babylon within the city leading from the streets to the river, were providentially left open, when Cyrus's forces entered the city in the night through the channel of the river, in the general disorder occasioned by the great feast which was then celebrated; otherwise, says *Herodotus*, i. 191, the Persians would have been shut up in the bed of the river, and taken as in a net, and all destroyed. And the gates of the palace were opened imprudently by the king's orders, to inquire what was the cause of the tumult without; when the two parties under Gobrias and Gadatas rushed in, got possession of the palace, and slew the king.—XENOPH., *Cyrop.* vii. p. 528.

Verse 2. *The crooked places*—"The mountains"] For הדורים *hadurim, crooked places*, a word not easily accounted for in this place, the *Septuagint* read הררים *hararim*, τα ορη, *the mountains.* Two MSS. have הדרים *hadarim*, without the ו *vau*, which is hardly distinguishable from the reading of the *Septuagint*. The Divine protection that attended Cyrus, and rendered his expedition against Babylon easy and prosperous, is finely expressed by God's going before him, and making the mountains level. The image is highly poetical:—

> At vos, qua veniet, tumidi subsidite montes,
> Et faciles curvis vallibus este viæ.
> OVID, Amor. ii. 16.

"Let the lofty mountains fall down, and make level paths in the crooked valleys."

The gates of brass—"The valves of brass"] Abydenus, *apud, Euseb.* Præp. Evang. ix. 41, says, that the wall of Babylon had brazen gates. And *Herodotus*, i, 179, more particularly: "In the wall all round there are a hundred gates, all of brass; and so in like manner are the sides and the lintels." The gates likewise within the city, opening to the river from the several streets, were of brass; as were those also of the temple of Belus.—*Herod.* i., 180, 181.

Verse 3. *I will give thee the treasures of darkness*] Sardes and Babylon, when taken by Cyrus, were the wealthiest cities in the world. Crœsus, celebrated beyond all the kings of that age for his riches, gave up his treasures to Cyrus, with an exact account in writing of the whole, containing the particulars with

A. M. cir. 3292
B. C. cir. 712
Olymp. XVII. 1
cir. annum
NumæPompilii,
R. Roman., 4

thou mayest know that I, the
LORD, which [g]call *thee* by thy
name, *am* the God of Israel.
4 For [h]Jacob my servant's sake,
and Israel mine elect, I have even called thee
by thy name: I have surnamed thee, though
thou hast [i]not known me.
5 I [k]*am* the LORD, and [l]*there is* none else,
there is no God beside me: [m]I girded thee,
though thou hast not known
me:
6 [n]That they may know from
the rising of the sun, and from
the west, that *there is* none beside me. I *am*
the LORD, and *there is* none else.
7 I form the light, and create darkness: I
make peace, and [o]create evil: I the LORD do
all these *things*.

A. M. cir. 3292
B. C. cir. 712
Olymp. XVII. 1
cir. annum
NumæPompilii,
R. Roman., 4

---

[g]Exod. xxxiii. 12, 17; chap. xliii. 1; xlix. 1——[h]Chap. xliv. 1——[i]1 Thess. iv. 5——[k]Deuteronomy iv. 35, 39; xxxii. 39; chapter xliv. 8; xlvi. 9——[l]Verse 14, 18, 21, 22——[m]Psalm xviii. 32, 39——[n]Psalm cii. 15; chapter xxxvii. 20; Malachi i. 11——[o]Amos iii. 6

---

which each wagon was loaded when they were carried away; and they were delivered to Cyrus at the palace of Babylon.—*Xenoph.* Cyrop. lib. vii. p. 503, 515, 540.

Pliny gives the following account of the wealth taken by Cyrus in Asia. Jam Cyrus, devicta Asia, pondo xxxiv. millia auri invenerat; præter vasa aurea, aurumque factum, et in eo folia, ac platanum, vitemque. Qua victoria argenti quii genta millia talentorum reportavit; et craterem Semiramidis, cujus pondus quindecim talents colligebat. Talentum autem Ægyptium pondo lxxx. patere l. capere Varro tradit.—Nat. Hist. xxxiii. 15. "When Cyrus conquered Asia, he found *thirty-four* thousand pounds weight of gold, besides golden vessels and articles in gold; and leaves, (*folia*, perhaps *solia*, bathing vessels, *Hol.*,) a plane, and vine tree, (of gold.) By which victory he carried away *fifteen thousand* talents of silver; and the cup of Semiramis, the weight of which was *fifteen talents*. The Egyptian talent, according to Varro, was *eighty* pounds." This cup was the *crater*, or large vessel, out of which they filled the drinking cups at great entertainments. Evidently it could not be a *drinking vessel*, which, according to what *Varro* and *Pliny* say, must have weighed 1,200 pounds!

The gold and silver estimated by weight in this account, being converted into pounds sterling, amount to *one hundred and twenty-six millions two hundred and twenty-four thousand* pounds.—*Brerewood*, De Ponderibus, cap. x.

Treasures of darkness may refer to the custom of burying their jewels and money under the ground in their house floors, fearing robbers.

Verse 7. *I form the light, and create darkness*] It was the great principle of the Magian religion, which prevailed in Persia in the time of Cyrus, and in which probably he was educated, that there are two supreme, co-eternal, and independent causes always acting in opposition one to the other; one the author of all good, the other of all evil. The good being they called LIGHT; the evil being, DARKNESS. That when LIGHT had the ascendant, then *good* and *happiness* prevailed among men; when DARKNESS had the superiority, then *evil* and *misery* abounded. An opinion that contradicts the clearest evidence of our reason, which plainly leads us to the acknowledgment of one only Supreme Being, infinitely good as well as powerful. With reference to this absurd opinion, held by the person to whom this prophecy is addressed, God, by his prophet, in the most significant terms, asserts his omnipotence and absolute supremacy:—

"I am JEHOVAH, and none else;
Forming light, and creating darkness,
Making peace, and creating evil:
I JEHOVAH am the author of all these things."

Declaring that those powers whom the Persians held to be the original authors of good and evil to mankind, representing them by *light* and *darkness*, as their proper emblems, are no other than creatures of God, the instruments which he employs in his government of the world, ordained or permitted by him in order to execute his wise and just decrees; and that there is no power, either of good or evil, independent of the one supreme God, infinite in power and in goodness.

There were, however, some among the Persians whose sentiments were more moderate as to this matter; who held the evil principle to be in some measure subordinate to the good; and that the former would at length be wholly subdued by the latter. See *Hyde*, De Relig. Vet. Pers. cap. xxii.

That this opinion prevailed among the Persians as early as the time of Cyrus we may, I think, infer not only from this passage of Isaiah, which has a manifest reference to it, but likewise from a passage in Xenophon's Cyropædia, where the same doctrine is applied to the human mind. Araspes, a noble young Persian, had fallen in love with the fair captive Panthea, committed to his charge by Cyrus. After all his boasting that he was superior to the assaults of that passion, he yielded so far to it as even to threaten violence if she would not comply with his desires. Awed by the reproof of Cyrus, fearing his displeasure, and having by cool reflection recovered his reason; in his discourse with him on this subject he says: "O Cyrus, I have certainly two souls; and this piece of philosophy I have learned from that wicked sophist, Love. For if I had but one soul, it would not be at the same time good and evil; it would not at the same time approve of honourable and base actions; and at once desire to do, and refuse to do, the very same things. But it is plain that I am animated by two souls; and when the good soul prevails, I do what is virtuous; and when the evil one prevails, I attempt what is vicious. But now the good soul prevails, having gotten you for her assistant, and has clearly gained the superiority." Lib. vi. p. 424.

I make peace, and create evil] *Evil* is here evidently put for *war* and its attendant miseries. I will procure *peace* for the Israelites, and destroy Babylon by *war*. *I form light, and create darkness*. Now, as darkness is only the priva-

A. M. cir. 3292
B. C. cir. 712
Olymp. XVII. 1
cir. annum
NumæPompilii,
R. Roman., 4

8 [p]Drop down, ye heavens,
from above, and let the skies
pour down righteousness: let the
earth open, and let them bring
forth salvation, and let righteousness spring
up together; I the LORD have created it.
9 Wo unto him that striveth with [q]his
Maker! *Let* the potsherd *strive* with the
potsherds of the earth. [r]Shall the clay say to
him that fashioneth it, What makest thou?
or thy work, He hath no hands?
10 Wo unto him that saith unto *his* father,
What begettest thou? or to the
woman, What hast thou brought
forth?
11 Thus saith the LORD, the
Holy One of Israel, and his Maker, Ask me
of things to come concerning [s]my sons, and
concerning [t]the work of my hands command
ye me.
12 [u]I have made the earth, and [v]created man
upon it: I, *even* my hands, have stretched out
the heavens, and [w]all their host have I commanded.

A. M. cir. 3292
B. C. cir. 712
Olymp. XVII. 1
cir. annum
NumæPompilii,
R. Roman., 4

[p]Psa. lxxii. 3; xxxv. 11——[q]Chap. lxiv. 8——[r]Chap. xxix. 16; Jer. xviii. 6; Rom. ix. 20——[s]Jer. xxxi. 9——[t]Isa. xxix. 23——[u]Chap. xlii. 5; Jer. xxvii. 5——[v]Gen. i. 26, 27——[w]Gen. ii. 1

tion of light, so the evil of *war* is the privation of *peace*.

Verse 8. *Drop down, ye heavens*] The *eighty-fifth* psalm is a very elegant ode on the same subject with this part of Isaiah's prophecies, the restoration of Judah from captivity; and is, in the most beautiful part of it, a manifest imitation of this passage of the prophet:—

"Verily his salvation is nigh unto them that fear him,
That glory may dwell in our land.
Mercy and truth have met together;
Righteousness and peace have kissed each other.
Truth shall spring from the earth,
And righteousness shall look down from heaven.
Even JEHOVAH will give that which is good,
And our land shall yield her produce.
Righteousness shall go before him,
And shall direct his footsteps in the way."
Psa. lxxxv. 10-14.

See the notes on these verses.

These images of the dew and the rain descending from heaven and making the earth fruitful, employed by the prophet, and some of those nearly of the same kind which are used by the psalmist, may perhaps be primarily understood as designed to set forth in a splendid manner the happy state of God's people restored to their country, and flourishing in peace and plenty, in piety and virtue; but justice and salvation, mercy and truth, righteousness and peace, and glory dwelling in the land, cannot with any sort of propriety, in the one or the other, be interpreted as the consequences of that event; they must mean the blessings of the great redemption by Messiah.

Let the earth open, &c.] Jonathan, in his Targum, refers this to the resurrection of the dead; the earth shall be opened, ויחון מיתיא *veyechon meiteiya*, and the dead shall revive. A plain proof that the ancient Jews believed in a future state, and acknowledged the resurrection of the dead.

Let them bring forth salvation—"Let salvation produce her fruit"] For ויפרו *vaiyiphru*, the *Septuagint*, *Vulgate*, and *Syriac* read ויפרה *vaiyiphrah;* and one MS. has a rasure close after the latter ו *vau*, which probably was ה *he* at first.

Verse 9. *Wo unto him that striveth with his Maker*—"Wo unto him that contendeth with the power that formed him"] The prophet answers or prevents the objections and cavils of the unbelieving Jews, disposed to murmur against God, and to arraign the wisdom and justice of his dispensations in regard to them; in permitting them to be oppressed by their enemies, and in promising them deliverance instead of preventing their captivity. St. Paul has borrowed the image, and has applied it to the like purpose with equal force and elegance: "Nay, but, O man! who art thou that repliest against God? Shall the thing formed say to him that formed it, Why hast thou made me thus? Hath not the potter power over the clay, out of the same lump to make one vessel to honour, and another to dishonour?" Rom. ix. 20, 21. This is spoken, says *Kimchi*, against the king of Babylon, who insulted the Most High, bringing forth the sacred vessels, drinking out of them, and magnifying himself against God.

Or thy work, He hath no hands—"And to the workman, Thou hast no hands"] The *Syriac* renders, as if he had read, ולא היתי פעל ידיך *velo hayithi pheal yadeycha*, "neither am I the work of thy hands;" the *Septuagint*, as if they had read, ולא פעלת ואין ידים לך *velo phaalta veeyn yadim lecha*, "neither hast thou made me; and thou hast no hands." But the fault seems to be in the transposition of the two pronouns; for ופעלך *uphoolcha*, read ופעלו *uphoolo:* and for לו *lo*, read לך *lecha*. So Houbigant corrects it; reading also ופעלו *uphoolo;* which last correction seems not altogether necessary. The *Septuagint*, in MSS. Pachom. and I. D. II. have it thus, *και το εργον ουκ εχεις χειρας*, which favours the reading here proposed.

Verse 11. *Ask me of things to come*—"And he that formeth the things which are to come"] I read ויוצר *veyotser*, without the ו *vau* suffixed; from the *Septuagint*, who join it in construction with the following word, *ὁ ποιησας τα επερχομενα*.

"Do ye question me."—תשאלוני *tishaluni*, *Chald.* recte; præcedit ת *tau;* et sic forte legerunt reliqui Intt.—*Secker*. "The Chaldee has, more properly, תשאלוני *tishaluni*, with a ת *tau* preceding; and thus the other interpreters probably read." The learned bishop therefore reads the passage thus:—

"Thus saith Jehovah, the Holy One of Israel;
And he that formeth the things which are to come;

A. M. cir. 3292
B. C. cir. 712
Olymp. XVII. 1
cir. annum
NumæPompilii,
R. Roman., 4

13 [x]I have raised him up in righteousness, and I will [y]direct all his ways: he shall [z]build my city, and he shall let go my captives, [a]not for price nor reward, saith the LORD of hosts.

14 Thus saith the LORD, [b]The labour of Egypt, and merchandise of Ethiopia and of the Sabeans, men of stature, shall come over unto thee, and they shall be thine: they shall come after thee; [c]in chains they shall come over, and they shall fall down unto thee, they shall make supplication unto thee, *saying,* [d]Surely God *is* in thee; and [e]*there is* none else, *there is* no God.

15 Verily thou *art* a God [f]that hidest thyself, O God of Israel, the Saviour.

16 They shall be ashamed, and also confounded, all of them: they shall go to confusion together *that are* [g]makers of idols.

A. M. cir. 3292
B. C. cir. 712
Olymp. XVII. 1
cir. annum
NumæPompilii,
R. Roman., 4

17 [h]*But* Israel shall be saved in the LORD with an everlasting salvation: ye shall not be ashamed nor confounded world without end.

18 For thus saith the LORD [i]that created the heavens; God himself that formed the earth and made it; he hath established it, he created it not in vain, he formed it to be inhabited: [k]I *am* the LORD; and *there is* none else.

19 I have not spoken in [l]secret, in a dark place of the earth: I said not unto the seed of Jacob, Seek ye me in vain: [m]I the LORD speak righteousness, I declare things that are right.

[x]Ch. xli. 2——[y]Or, *make straight*——[z]2 Chron. xxxvi. 22, 23; Ezra i. 1, &c.; ch. xliv. 28——[a]Ch. lii. 3; see Rom. iii. 24——[b]Psa. lxviii. 31; lxxii. 10, 11; ch. xlix. 23; lx. 9, 10, 14, 16; Zech. viii. 22, 23——[c]Psa. cxlix. 8

[d]1 Cor. xiv. 25——[e]Ver. 5——[f]Psa. xliv. 24; ch. viii. 17; lvii. 17——[g]Ch. xiiv. 11——[h]Ch. xxvi. 4; ver. 25; Rom. xi. 26——[i]Ch. xlii. 5——[k]Ver. 5——[l]Deut. xxx. 11; ch. xlviii. 16——[m]Psa. xix. 8; cxix. 137, 138

Do ye question me concerning my children?
And do ye give me directions concerning the work of my hands?"

Verse 13. *I have raised him up*] This evidently refers to Cyrus, and to what he did for the Jews; and informs us by *whom* he was excited to do it.

Verse 14. *The labour of Egypt*—"The wealth of Egypt"] This seems to relate to the future admission of the Gentiles into the Church of God. Compare Psa. lxviii. 32; lxxii. 10; chap. lx. 6-9. And perhaps these particular nations may be named, by a metonymy common in all poetry, for powerful and wealthy nations in general. See note on chap. lx. 1.

The Sabeans, men of stature—"The Sabeans, tall of stature"] That the Sabeans were of a more majestic appearance than common, is particularly remarked by Agatharchides, an ancient Greek historian quoted by Bochart, Phaleg, ii. 26, *τα σωματα εστι των κατοικουντων αξιολογωτερα.* So also the *Septuagint* understand it, rendering it *ανδρες ὑψηλοι,* "tall men." And the same phrase, אנשי מדה *anshey middah,* is used for persons of extraordinary stature, Num. xiii. 32, and 1 Chron. xx. 6.

They shall make supplication unto thee—"They shall in suppliant guise address thee"] The conjunction ו *vau* is supplied by the ancient Versions, and confirmed by *fifteen* MSS. of *Kennicott's,* (*seven* ancient,) *thirteen* of *De Rossi's,* and *six* editions, ואליך *veelayich. Three* MSS. (*two* ancient) omit the ו *vau* before אליך *elayich* at the beginning of the line.

Verse 15. *Verily thou* art *a God that hidest thyself*] At present, from the nations of the world.

O God of Israel, the Saviour] While thou revealest thyself to the *Israelites* and *savest* them.

Verse 16. *They shall be ashamed*—"They are ashamed"] The reader cannot but observe the sudden transition from the solemn adoration of the secret and mysterious nature of God's counsels in regard to his people, to the spirited denunciation of the confusion of idolaters, and the final destruction of idolatry; contrasted with the salvation of Israel, not from temporal captivity, but the *eternal* salvation by the Messiah, strongly marked by the repetition and augmentation of the phrase, *to the ages of eternity.* But there is not only a sudden change in the sentiment, the change is equally observable in the construction of the sentences; which, from the usual short measure, runs out at once into two distichs of the longer sort of verse. See Prelim. Dissert. p. 66, &c. There is another instance of the same kind, and very like to this, of a sudden transition in regard both to the sentiment and construction in chap. xlii. 17.

"His adversaries"] This line, to the great diminution of the beauty of the distich, is imperfect in the present text: the subject of the proposition is not particularly expressed, as it is in the line following. The version of the *Septuagint* happily supplies the word that is lost: *οἱ αντικειμενοι αυτῳ,* "his adversaries," the original word was צריו *tsaraiv.*—L.

Verse 18. *He formed it to be inhabited*—"For he formed it to be inhabited"] An ancient MS. has כי *ki* before לשבת *lashebeth;* and so the ancient Versions.

Verse 19. *I have not spoken in secret, in a dark place of the earth*] In opposition to the manner in which the heathen oracles gave their answers, which were generally delivered from some deep and obscure cavern. Such was the seat of the Cumean Sybil:—

Excisum Euboicæ latus ingens rupis in antrum.
VIRG. *Æn.* vi. 42.

"A cave cut in the side of a huge rock."

Such was that of the famous oracle at Delphi; of which, says Strabo, lib. ix., *φασι δ' ειναι το μαντειον αντρον κοιλον μετα βαθους, ου μαλα ευρυστομον.* "The oracle is said to be a hollow cavern of considerable depth, with an opening not very

A. M. cir. 3292 B. C. cir. 712 Olymp. XVII. 1 cir. annum Numæ Pompilii, R. Roman., 4
20 Assemble yourselves and come; draw near together, ye *that are* escaped of the nations:
[n]they have no knowledge that set up the wood of their graven image, and pray unto a god *that* cannot save.
21 Tell ye, and bring *them* near; yea, let them take counsel together: [o]who hath declared this from ancient time? *who* hath told it from that time? *have* not I the LORD? [p]and *there is* no God else beside me; a just God and a Saviour: *there is* none beside me.
22 [q]Look unto me, and be ye saved, [r]all the ends of the earth: for I *am* God, and *there is* none else.
23 [s]I have sworn by myself, the word is gone out of my mouth *in* righteousness, and shall not return, That unto me every [t]knee shall bow, [u]every tongue shall swear.
24 [v]Surely, shall *one* say, In the LORD have I [w]righteousness[x] and strength: *even* to him shall *men* come; and [y]all that are incensed against him shall be ashamed.
25 [z]In the LORD shall all the seed of Israel be justified, and [a]shall glory.

[n]Ch. xliv. 17, 18, 19; xlvi. 7; xlviii. 7; Rom. i. 22, 23 —— [o]Ch. xli. 22; xliii. 9; xliv. 7; xlvi. 10; xlviii. 14 —— [p]Ver. 5, 14, 18; ch. xliv. 8; xlvi. 9; xlviii. 3, &c. —— [q]Psa. xxii. 27; lxv. 5 —— [r]Psa. lxv. 3; xcviii. 3 —— [s]Gen. xxii. 16; Jer. xlix. 13; li. 14; Amos vi. 8; Heb. vi. 13

[t]Rom. xiv. 11; Phil. ii. 10 —— [u]Gen. xxxi. 53; Deut. vi. 13; Psa. lxiii. 11; ch. lxv. 16 —— [v]Or, *Surely he shall say of me, In the LORD is all righteousness and strength* —— [w]Jer. xxiii. 5; 1 Cor. i. 30 —— [x]Heb. *righteousnesses* —— [y]Ch. xli. 11 —— [z]Ver. 17 —— [a]1 Cor. i. 31

wide." And Diodorus, giving an account of the origin of this oracle, says "that there was in that place a great chasm or cleft in the earth; in which very place is now situated what is called the Adytum of the temple." Αδυτον· σπηλαιον, η το αποκρυφον μερος του ἱερου. *Hesych.* "Adytum means a cavern, or the hidden part of the temple."

I the Lord speak righteousness, I declare things that are right—"I am JEHOVAH, who speak truth, who give direct answers."] This also is said in opposition to the false and ambiguous answers given by the heathen oracles, of which there are many noted examples; none more so than that of the answer given to Crœsus when he marched against Cyrus, which piece of history has some connexion with this part of Isaiah's prophecies. Let us hear Cicero's account of the Delphic answers in general, and of this in particular: Sed jam ad te venio,

O sancte Apollo, qui umbilicum certum terrarum obsides,
Unde superstitiosa primum sæva evasit vox fera.

Tuis enim oraculis Chrysippus totum volumen implevit, partim falsis, ut ego opinor; partim casu veris, ut fit in omni oratione sæpissime; partim flexiloquis et obscuris, ut interpres egeat interprete, et sors ipsa ad sortes referenda sit; partim ambiguis, et quæ ad dialecticum deferenda sint. Nam cum sors illa edita est opulentissimo regi Asiæ,

Crœsus Halym penetrans magnam pervertet opum vim: hostium vim sese perversurum putavit; pervertit autem suam. Utrum igitur eorum accidisset, verum oraculum fuisset. *De Divinat.* ii. 56. Mountainous countries, and those which abounded in chasms, caves, and grottos, were the places in which oracles were most frequent. The horror and gloom inspired by such places were useful to the lying priests in their system of deception. The terms in which those oracles were conceived, (they were always ambiguous, or equivocal, or false, or illusory,) sometimes the turn of a phrase, or a peculiarity in idiom or construction which might be turned *pro* or *con*, contained the essence of the oracular declaration. Sometimes, in the multitude of guesses, one turned out to be true; at other times, so equivocal was the oracle, that, however the thing fell out, the declaration could be interpreted in that way; as in the above to Crœsus, from the oracle at Delphi, which was: *If Crœsus march against Cyrus, he shall overthrow a great empire:* he, supposing that this promised him success, fought, and lost his own, while he expected to destroy that of his enemy. Here the quack demon took refuge in his designed ambiguity. He predicted the destruction of a great empire, but did not say which it was; and therefore he was safe, howsoever the case fell out. Not one of the predictions of God's prophets is conceived in this way.

Verse 21. *Bring* them *near; yea, let them take counsel together*] For יועצו *yoatsu* or *yivvaatsu*, *let them consult*, the *Septuagint* read ידעו *yedau*, *let them know:* but an ancient MS. has יועדו *yoedu, let them come together by appointment;* which may probably be the true reading.

Verse 22. *Look unto me, and be ye saved, &c.*] This verse and the following contain a plain prediction of the universal spread of the knowledge of God through Christ; and so the *Targum* appears to have understood it; see Rom. xiv. 11; Phil. ii. 10. The reading of the *Targum* is remarkable, viz., אתפנו למימרי *ithpeno lemeymri*, *look to my* WORD, ὁ Λογος, the Lord Jesus.

Verse 23. *I have sworn by myself*] במימרי *bemeymri*, *by my* WORD: and *the word*—פתגם *pithgam*, or *saying*, to distinguish it from the *personal substantial* WORD *meymra*, mentioned before. See the *Targum.*

The word is gone out of my mouth—"Truth is gone forth from my mouth; the word"] So the *Septuagint* distinguish the members of the sentence, preserving the elegance of the construction and the clearness of the sense.

Verse 24. *Surely, shall* one *say, In the Lord have I righteousness and strength*—"Saying, Only to JEHOVAH belongeth salvation and power"] A MS. omits לי *li*, *unto me;* and instead of לי אמר *li amar*, *he said* or *shall say unto me*, the *Septuagint* read, in the copy which they used, לאמר *lemor*, *saying.* For יבא *yabo*, HE *shall come*, in the singular, twelve MSS.

(three ancient) read יבאו *yabeu*, plural; and a letter is erased at the end of the word in two others: and so the Alexandrine copy of the *Septuagint*, *Syriac*, and *Vulgate* read it. For צדקות *tsedakoth*, plural, two MSS. read צדקת *tsidkath*, singular; and so the *Septuagint*, *Syriac*, and *Chaldee*.

Probably these are the words of Cyrus, who acknowledged that all his success came from Jehovah. And this sentiment is in effect contained in his decree or proclamation, Ezra i. 2: "Thus saith Cyrus, king of Persia, The Lord God of heaven hath given me all the kingdoms of the earth," &c.

CHAPTER XLVI

The idols of Babylon represented as so far from being able to bear the burden of their votaries, that they themselves are borne by beasts of burden into captivity, 1, 2. *This beautifully contrasted with the tender care of God, in bearing his people from first to last in his arms, and delivering them from their distress,* 3, 4. *The prophet, then, with his usual force and elegance, goes on to show the folly of idolatry, and the utter inability of idols,* 5–7. *From which he passes with great ease to the contemplation of the attributes and perfections of the true God,* 8–10. *Particularly that prescience which foretold the deliverance of the Jews from the Babylonish captivity, with all its leading circumstances; and also that very remote event of which it is the type in the days of the Messiah,* 11–13.

A. M. cir. 3292 B. C. cir. 712 Olymp. XVII. 1 cir. annum NumæPompilii, R. Roman., 4

BEL [a]boweth down, Nebo stoopeth, their idols were upon the beasts, and upon the cattle: your carriages *were* heavy loaden; [b]*they are* a burden to the weary *beast*.

2 They stoop, they bow down together; they could not deliver the burden, [c]but [d]themselves are gone into captivity.

3 Hearken unto me, O house of Jacob, and all the remnant of the house of Israel, [e]which are borne *by me* from the belly, which are carried from the womb:

4 And *even* to *your* old age [f]I *am* he; and *even* to hoar hairs [g]will I carry *you:* I have made, and I will bear; even I will carry, and will deliver *you*.

5 [h]To whom will ye liken me, and make *me* equal, and compare me, that we may be like?

6 [i]They lavish gold out of the bag, and weigh silver in the balance, *and* hire a goldsmith; and he maketh it a god: they fall down, yea, they worship.

7 [k]They bear him upon the shoulder, they carry him, and set him in his place, and he standeth; from his place shall he not remove; yea, [l]*one* shall cry unto him, yet can he not answer, nor save him out of his trouble.

[a]Chap. xxi. 9; Jer. l. 2; li. 44——[b]Jer. x. 5——[c]Jer. xlviii. 7——[d]Heb. *their soul*——[e]Exod. xix. 4; Deut. i. 31; xxxii. 11; Psa. lxxi. 6; chap. lxiii. 9

[f]Psa. cii. 27; Mal. iii. 6——[g]Psa. xlviii. 14; lxxi. 18——[h]Ch. xl. 18, 25——[i]Ch. xl. 19; xli. 6; xliv. 12, 19; Jer. x. 3——[k]Jer. x. 5——[l]Chap. xlv. 20

NOTES ON CHAP. XLVI

Verse 1. *Their carriages* were *heavy loaden*—"Their burdens are heavy"] For נשאתיכם *nesuotheychem, your burdens*, the *Septuagint* had in their copy נשאתיהם *nesuotheyhem, their burdens.*

Verse 2. *They could not deliver the burden*—"They could not deliver their own charge"] That is, their worshippers, who ought to have been borne by them. See the two next verses. The *Chaldee* and *Syriac* Versions render it in effect to the same purpose, *those that bear them,* meaning their worshippers; but how they can render משא *massa* in an active sense, I do not understand.

For לא *lo, not,* ולא *velo, and they could not,* is the reading of twenty-four of *Kennicott's*, sixteen of *De Rossi's*, and two of my own MSS. The added ו *vau* gives more elegance to the passage.

But themselves—"Even they themselves"] For ונפשם *venaphsham*, an ancient MS. has כי נפשם *ki naphsham*, with more force.

Verse 3. *Which are borne* by me *from the belly*—"Ye that have been borne by me from the birth"] The prophet very ingeniously, and with great force, contrasts the power of God, and his tender goodness effectually exerted towards his people, with the inability of the false gods of the heathen. He like an indulgent father had carried his people in his arms, "as a man carrieth his son," Deut. i. 31. He had protected them, and delivered them from their distresses: whereas the idols of the heathen are forced to be carried about themselves, and removed from place to place, with great labour and fatigue, by their worshippers; nor can they answer, or deliver their votaries, when they cry unto them.

Moses, expostulating with God on the weight of the charge laid upon him as leader of his people, expresses that charge under the same image of a parent's carrying his children, in very strong terms: "Have I conceived all this people? have I begotten them? that thou shouldest say unto me, Carry them in thy bosom, as a nursing father beareth the sucking child, unto the land which thou swarest unto their fathers;" Num. xi. 12.

Verse 7. *They bear him upon the shoulder—and set him in his place*] This is the way in which the Hindoos carry their gods; and indeed so exact a picture is this of the *idolatrous procession* of this people, that the prophet might almost be supposed to have been sitting among the Hindoos when he delivered this prophecy.—WARD'S *Customs*.

A. M. cir. 3292 B. C. cir. 712 Olymp. XVII. 1 cir. annum NumæPompilii, R. Roman., 4

8 Remember this, and show
yourselves men: [m]bring *it* again
to mind, O ye transgressors.
9 [n]Remember the former
things of old: for I *am* God, and [o]*there is* none
else: *I am* God, and *there is* none like me,
10 [p]Declaring the end from the beginning,
and from ancient times *the things* that are not
yet done, saying, [q]My counsel shall stand,
and I will do all my pleasure:
11 Calling a ravenous bird [r]from the east,
[s]the man [t]that executeth my
counsel from a far country: yea,
[u]I have spoken *it,* I will also
bring it to pass; I have purposed *it,* I will also do it.
12 Hearken unto me, ye [v]stout-hearted,
[w]that *are* far from righteousness:
13 [x]I bring near my righteousness; it shall
not be far off, and my salvation [y]shall not
tarry: and I will place [z]salvation in Zion for
Israel my glory.

---

[m]Ch. xliv. 19; xlvii. 7——[n]Deut. xxxii. 7——[o]Ch. xlv. 5, 21——[p]Ch. xlv. 21——[q]Psa. xxxiii. 11; Prov. xix. 21; xxi. 30; Acts v. 39; Heb. vi. 17——[r]Ch. xli. 2, 25

[s]Heb. *the man of my counsel*——[t]Ch. xliv. 28; xlv. 13
[u]Num. xxiii. 19——[v]Psa. lxxvi. 5——[w]Rom. x. 3
[x]Ch. li. 5; Rom. i. 17; iii. 21——[y]Hab. ii. 3——[z]Ch. lxii. 11

Pindar has treated with a just and very elegant ridicule the work of the statuary even in comparison with his own poetry, from this circumstance of its being fixed to a certain station. "The friends of Pytheas," says the Scholiast, "came to the poet, desiring him to write an ode on his victory. Pindar demanded three drachms, (*minæ*, I suppose it should be,) for the ode. No, say they, we can have a brazen statue for that money, which will be better than a poem. However, changing their minds afterwards, they came and offered him what he had demanded." This gave him the hint of the following ingenious exordium of his ode:—

> *Ουκ ανδριαντοποιος ειμ'*
> *'Ωστ' ελινυσσοντα μ' εργαζε-*
> *σθαι αγαλματ' επ' αυτας βαθμιδος*
> *'Εσταοτ'. Αλλ' επι πασας*
> *'Ολκαδος εν τ' ακατῳ γλυκει' αοιδα*
> *Στειχ' απ' Αιγινας διαγγελ-*
> *λοισ' ὁτι Λαμπωνος ὑιος*
> *Πυθεας ευρυσθενης*
> *Νικῃ Νεμειοις παγκρατιου στεφανον.* Nem. v.

Thus elegantly translated by Mr. *Francis* in a note to *Hor. Carm.* iv. 2. 19.

"It is not mine with forming hand
To bid a lifeless image stand
For ever on its base:
But fly, my verses, and proclaim
To distant realms, with deathless fame,
That Pytheas conquered in the rapid race."

Jeremiah, chap. x. 3-5, seems to be indebted to Isaiah for most of the following passage:—

"The practices of the people are altogether vanity:
For they cut down a tree from the forest;
The work of the artificer's hand with the axe;
With silver and with gold it is adorned;
With nails and with hammers it is fastened, that it may not totter.
Like the palm-tree they stand stiff, and cannot speak;
They are carried about, for they cannot go:
Fear them not, for they cannot do harm;
Neither is it in them to do good."

Verse 8. *Show yourselves men*] התאששו *hithoshashu.* This word is rather of doubtful derivation and signification. It occurs only in this place: and some of the ancient interpreters seem to have had something different in their copies. The *Vulgate* read התבוששו *hithbosheshu, take shame to yourselves;* the *Syriac* התבוננו *hithbonenu, consider with yourselves;* the *Septuagint* *στεναξετε· perhaps* התאבלו *hithabbelu, groan* or *mourn, within yourselves.* Several MSS. read התאוששו *hithosheshu,* but without any help to the sense.

Verse 11. *Calling a ravenous bird from the east*—"Calling from the east the eagle"] A very proper emblem for Cyrus, as in other respects, so particularly because the ensign of Cyrus was a golden eagle, ΑΕΤΟΣ *χρυσους,* the very word עיט *ayit,* which the prophet uses here, expressed as near as may be in Greek letters. XENOPH. *Cyrop.* lib. vii. *sub. init. Kimchi* says his father understood this, not of Cyrus, but of the Messiah.

From a far country—"From a land far distant"] Two MSS. add the conjunction ו *vau,* ומארץ *umeerets;* and so the *Septuagint, Syriac,* and *Vulgate.*

Verse 12. *Hearken unto me, ye stout-hearted*—This is an address to the Babylonians, stubbornly bent on the practice of injustice towards the Israelites.

CHAPTER XLVII

The destruction of Babylon is denounced by a beautiful selection of circumstances, in which her prosperous is contrasted with her adverse condition. She is represented as a tender and delicate female reduced to the work and abject condition of a slave, and bereaved of every consolation, 1–4. And that on account of her cruelty, particularly to God's people, her pride, voluptuousness, sorceries, and incantations, 5–11. The folly of these last practices elegantly exposed by the prophet, 12–15. It is worthy of observation that almost all the imagery of this chapter is applied in the book of the Revelation, (in nearly the same words,) to the antitype of the illustrious capital of the Chaldean empire, viz., Babylon the GREAT.

A. M. cir. 3292
B. C. cir. 712
Olymp. XVII. 1
cir. annum
NumæPompilii,
R. Roman., 4

COME [a]down, and [b]sit in the
dust, O virgin daughter of
Babylon; sit on the ground:
there is no throne, O daughter
of the Chaldeans: for thou shalt no more be
called tender and delicate.
2 [c]Take the millstones, and grind meal:
uncover thy locks, make bare the leg, uncover
the thigh, pass over the rivers.
3 [d]Thy nakedness shall be uncovered, yea,
thy shame shall be seen: [e]I will take vengeance, and I will not meet *thee as* a man.
4 *As for* [f]our Redeemer, the LORD of hosts
is his name, the Holy One of Israel.
5 Sit thou [g]silent, and get thee into darkness, O daughter of the Chaldeans: [h]for thou
shalt no more be called, The lady
of kingdoms.

A. M. cir. 3292
B. C. cir. 712
Olymp. XVII. 1
cir. annum
NumæPompilii,
R. Roman., 4

6 [i]I was wroth with my people, [k]I have polluted mine inheritance, and given them into thine hand: thou
didst show them no mercy; [l]upon the ancient
hast thou very heavily laid thy yoke.
7 And thou saidst, I shall be [m]a lady for
ever: *so* that thou didst not [n]lay these *things*
to thy heart, [o]neither didst remember the latter end of it.
8 Therefore hear now this, *thou that art* given
to pleasures, that dwellest carelessly, that
sayest in thine heart, [p]I *am*, and none else
beside me; [q]I shall not sit *as* a widow,
neither shall I know the loss of children:

[a]Jer. xlviii. 18——[b]Ch. iii. 26——[c]Exod. xi. 5; Judg. xvi. 21; Matt. xxiv. 41——[d]Ch. iii. 17; xx. 4; Jer. xiii. 22, 26; Nah. iii. 5——[e]Rom. xii. 19——[f]Chap. xliii. 3, 14; Jer. l. 34——[g]1 Sam. ii. 9——[h]Ver. 7; chap. xiii. 19; Dan. ii. 37——[i]See 2 Sam. xxiv. 14; 2 Chron. xxviii. 9; Zech. i. 15——[k]Ch. xliii. 28——[l]Deut. xxviii. 50——[m]Ver. 5; Rev. xviii. 7——[n]Ch. xlvi. 8——[o]Deut. xxxii. 29——[p]Ver. 10; Zeph. ii. 15——[q]Rev. xviii. 7

NOTES ON CHAP. XLVII

Verse 1. *Come down, and sit in the dust*—"Descend, and sit on the dust"] See note on chap. iii. 26, and on chap. lii. 2.

Verse 2. *Take the mill-stones, and grind meal*—"Take the mill, and grind corn"] It was the work of slaves to grind the corn. They used hand-mills: water-mills were not invented till a little before the time of Augustus, (see the Greek epigram of Antipater, which seems to celebrate it as a new invention, *Anthol. Cephalæ*, 653;) wind-mills, not until long after. It was not only the work of slaves, but the hardest work; and often inflicted upon them as a severe punishment:—

> Molendum in pistrino; vapulandum; habendæ compedes.
>
> TERENT. *Phorm.* ii. 1. 19.
>
> Hominem pistrino dignum.
>
> *Id. Heaut.* iii. 2. 19.

To grind in the mill, to be scourged, to be put in the stocks, were punishments for slaves. Hence a delinquent was said to be *a man worthy of the mill.* The *tread-mill*, now in use in England, is a revival of this ancient usage. But in the east grinding was the work of the female slaves. See Exod. xi. 5; xii. 29, (in the version of the *Septuagint;*) Matt. xxiv. 41; *Homer*, Odyss. xx. 105-108. And it is the same to this day. "Women alone are employed to grind their corn;" *Shaw's* Algiers and Tunis, p. 287. "They are the female slaves, that are generally employed in the east at those hand-mills for grinding corn; it is extremely laborious, and esteemed the lowest employment in the house;" Sir J. *Chardin, Harmer's* Observ. i., p. 153. The words denote that state of captivity to which the Babylonians should be reduced.

Make bare the leg, uncover the thigh] This is repeatedly seen in Bengal, where there are few bridges, and both sexes, having neither shoes nor stockings, truss up their loose garments, and walk across, where the waters are not deep. In the *deeper* water they are obliged to truss *very high*, to which there seems a reference in the *third verse: Thy nakedness shall be uncovered.*

Verse 3. *I will not meet* thee as *a man*—"Neither will I suffer man to intercede with me."] The verb should be pointed, or written, אפגיע *aphgia*, in Hiphil.

Verse 4. *Our Redeemer*—"Our Avenger"] Here a chorus breaks in upon the midst of the subject, with a change of construction, as well as sentiment, from the longer to the shorter kind of verse, for one distich only; after which the former subject and style are resumed. See note on chap. xlv. 16.

Verse 6. *I was wroth with my people*] God, in the course of his providence, makes use of great conquerors and tyrants as his instruments to execute his judgments in the earth; he employs one wicked nation to scourge another. The inflicter of the punishment may perhaps be as culpable as the sufferer; and may add to his guilt by indulging his cruelty in executing God's justice. When he has fulfilled the work to which the Divine vengeance has ordained him, he will become himself the object of it; see chap. x. 5-12. God charges the Babylonians, though employed by himself to chastise his people, with cruelty in regard to them. They exceeded the bounds of justice and humanity in oppressing and destroying them; and though they were really executing the righteous decree of God, yet, as far as it regarded themselves, they were only indulging their own ambition and violence. The Prophet Zechariah sets this matter in the same light: "I was but a little angry, and they helped forward the affliction;" chap. i. 15.—L.

Verse 7. So *that thou didst not*—"Because thou didst not"] For עד *ad*, read על *al;* so two MSS., and one edition. And for אחריתה *acharithah*, "the latter end *of it*," read אחריתך *acharithecha*, "*thy* latter end;" so thirteen MSS., and two editions, and the *Vulgate.* Both the *sixth* and *seventh* verses are wanting in one of my oldest MSS.

A. M. cir. 3292
B. C. cir. 712
Olymp. XVII. 1
cir. annum
NumæPompilii,
R. Roman., 4

9 Beside [r]these two *things* shall come to thee [s]in a moment in one day, the loss of children and widowhood: they shall come upon thee in their perfection [t]for the multitude of thy sorceries, *and* for the great abundance of thine enchantments.

10 For thou [u]hast trusted in thy wickedness: [v]thou hast said, None seeth me. Thy wisdom and thy knowledge, it hath [w]perverted thee; [x]and thou hast said in thine heart, I *am*, and none else beside me.

11 Therefore shall evil come upon thee; thou shalt not know [y]from whence it riseth: and mischief shall fall upon thee; thou shalt not be able to [z]put it off: and [a]desolation shall come upon thee suddenly, *which* thou shalt not know.

12 Stand now with thine enchantments, and with the multitude of thy sorceries, wherein thou hast laboured from thy youth: if so be thou shalt be able to profit, if so be thou mayest prevail.

13 [b]Thou art wearied in the multitude of thy counsels. Let now [c]the [d]astrologers, the stargazers, [e]the monthly prognosticators, stand up, and save thee from *these things* that shall come upon thee.

14 Behold, they shall be [f]as stubble; the fire shall burn them; they shall not deliver [g]themselves from the power of the flame: *there shall* not *be* a coal to warm at, *nor* fire to sit before it.

15 Thus shall they be unto thee with whom thou hast laboured, *even* [h]thy merchants, from thy youth: they shall wander every one to his quarter; none shall save thee.

[r]Chap. li. 19——[s]1 Thess. v. 3——[t]Nah. iii. 4——[u]Psa. lii. 7——[v]Chap. xxix. 15; Ezek. viii. 12; ix. 9——[w]Or, *caused thee to turn away*——[x]Ver. 8——[y]Heb. *the morning thereof*——[z]Heb. *expiate*——[a]1 Thess. v. 3

[b]Chapter lvii. 10——[c]Chapter xliv. 25; Dan. ii. 2——[d]Heb. *viewers of the heavens*——[e]Heb. *that give knowledge concerning the months*——[f]Nah. i. 10; Mal. iv. 1——[g]Heb. *their souls*——[h]Rev. xviii. 11

Verse 9. *These two* things *shall come to thee in a moment*] That is, suddenly. Belshazzar was slain; thus the city became metaphorically a *widow*, the *husband*—the governor of it, being slain. In the time in which the king was slain, the Medes and Persians took the city, and slew many of its inhabitants, see Dan. v. 30, 31. When Darius took the city, he is said to have crucified *three thousand* of its principal inhabitants.

In their perfection—"On a sudden"] Instead of בתמם *bethummam*, "in their perfection," as our translation renders it, the *Septuagint* and *Syriac* read, in the copies from which they translated, פתאם *pithom*, *suddenly;* parallel to רגע *rega*, *in a moment*, in the preceding alternate member of the sentence. The concurrent testimony of the *Septuagint* and *Syriac*, favoured by the context, may be safely opposed to the authority of the present text.

For the multitude—"Notwithstanding the multitude"] ברב *berob*. For this sense of the particle ב *beth*, see Num. xiv. 11.

Verse 11. *Thou shalt not know from whence it riseth*—"Thou shalt not know how to deprecate"] שחרה *shachrah;* so the *Chaldee* renders it, which is approved by *Jarchi* on the place; and *Michaelis* Epim. in Prælect. xix.; see Psa. lxxviii. 34.

Videtur in fine hujus commatis deese verbum, ut hoc membrum prioribus respondeat. "A word appears to be wanting at the end of this clause to connect it properly with the two preceding."—SECKER.

In order to set in a proper light this judicious remark, it is necessary to give the reader an exact verbal translation of the whole verse:—

"And evil shall come upon thee, thou shalt not know how to deprecate it;
And mischief shall fall upon thee, thou shalt not be able to expiate it;
And destruction shall come suddenly upon thee, thou shalt not know"—

What? how to escape, to avoid it, to be delivered from it? perhaps צאת ממנה *tseth mimmennah*, "they could not *go out from it*," Jer. xi. 11. I am persuaded that a phrase is here lost out of the text. But as the ancient versions retain no traces of it, and a wide field lies open to uncertain conjecture, I have not attempted to fill up the chasm, but have in the translation, as others have done before me, palliated and disguised the defect, which I cannot with any assurance pretend to supply.—L.

Verse 13. *From* these things—"What are the events"] For מאשר *measher*, read מה אשר *mah asher*, so the *Septuagint*, "what is to happen to thee."

Verse 15. *To his quarter*—"To his own business"] לעברו *leebro*. Expositors give no very good account of this word in this place. In a MS. it was at first לעבדו *leabdo*, *to his servant* or *work*, which is probably the true reading. The sense however is pretty much the same with the common interpretation: "Every one shall turn aside to his own business; none shall deliver thee."

CHAPTER XLVIII

The Jews reproved for their obstinate attachment to idols, notwithstanding their experience of the Divine providence over them; and of the Divine prescience that revealed by the prophets the most remarkable events which concerned them, that they should not have the least pretext for ascribing any portion of their success to their idols, 1–8. *The Almighty, after bringing them to the furnace for their perverseness, asserts his glorious sovereignty, and repeats his gracious promises of deliverance and consolation,* 9–11. *Prophecy concerning that individual (Cyrus) who shall be an instrument in the hand of God of executing his will on Babylon, and his power on the Chaldeans; and the idols of the people are again challenged to give a like proof of their foreknowledge,* 12–16. *Tender and passionate exclamation of Jehovah respecting the hardened condition of the Jewish nation, to which the very pathetic exclamation of the Divine Saviour when he wept over Jerusalem may be considered a striking parallel,* 17–19. *Notwithstanding the repeated provocations of the house of Israel, Jehovah will again be merciful to them. They are commanded to escape from Babylon; and God's gracious favour towards them is beautifully represented by images borrowed from the exodus from Egypt,* 20, 21. *Certain perdition of the finally impenitent,* 22. *It will be proper here to remark that many passages in this chapter, and indeed the general strain of these prophecies, have a plain aspect to a restoration of the Church in the latter days upon a scale much greater than the world has yet witnessed, when the very violent fall of Babylon the Great, mentioned in the Revelation, of which the Chaldean capital was an expressive type, shall introduce by a most tremendous political convulsion,* (Rev. xvi. 17–21,) *that glorious epoch of the Gospel, which forms so conspicuous a part of the prophecies of the Old Testament, and has been a subject of the prayers of all saints in all ages.*

A. M. cir. 3292
B. C. cir. 712
Olymp. XVII. 1
cir. annum
NumæPompilii,
R. Roman., 4

HEAR ye this, O house of Jacob, which are called by the name of Israel, and [a]are come forth out of the waters of Judah, [b]which swear by the name of the LORD, and make mention of the God of Israel, [c]*but* not in truth, nor in righteousness.

2 For they call themselves [d]of the holy city, and [e]stay themselves upon the God of Israel; The LORD of hosts *is* his name.

3 [f]I have declared the former things from the beginning; and they went forth out of my mouth, and I showed them; I did *them* suddenly, [g]and they came to pass.

4 Because I knew that thou *art* [h]obstinate, and [i]thy neck *is* an iron sinew, and thy brow brass;

5 [k]I have even from the beginning declared *it* to thee; before it came to pass I showed *it* thee: lest thou shouldest say, Mine idol hath done them; and my graven image, and my molten image, hath commanded them.

A. M. cir. 3292
B. C. cir. 712
Olymp. XVII. 1
cir. annum
NumæPompilii,
R. Roman., 4

6 Thou hast heard, see all this; and will not ye declare *it?* I have showed thee new things from this time, even hidden things, and thou didst not know them.

7 They are created now, and not from the beginning; even before the day when thou heardest them not; lest thou shouldest say, Behold, I knew them.

8 Yea, thou heardest not; yea, thou knewest not: yea, from that time *that* thine ear was not opened: for I knew that thou wouldest [l]deal very treacherously, and wast called [m]a transgressor from the womb.

9 [n]For my name's sake [o]will I defer mine anger, and for my praise will I refrain

[a]Psa. lxviii. 26——[b]Deut. vi. 13; chap. lxv. 16; Zeph. i. 5——[c]Jer. iv. 2; v. 2——[d]Ch. lii. 1——[e]Mic. iii. 11; Rom. ii. 17——[f]Ch. xli. 22; xlii. 9; xliii. 9; xliv. 7, 8; xlv. 21: xlvi. 9, 10——[g]Josh. xxi. 45——[h]Heb. *hard*

[i]Exod. lii. 9; Deut. xxxi. 27——[k]Ver. 3——[l]Chap. xxxiii. 1; Jer. iii. 20; v. 11; Hos. v. 7; vi. 7; Mal. ii. 10, 14, 15, 16——[m]Psa. lviii. 3——[n]Psa. lxxix. 9; cvi. 8; chap. xliii. 25; ver. 1; Ezek. xx. 9, 14, 22, 44——[o]Psa. lxxviii. 38

NOTES ON CHAP. XLVIII

Verse 1. *Are come forth out of the waters of Judah*—"Ye that flow from the fountain of Judah"] ממי *mimmey*, "from the *waters.*" Perhaps ממעי *mimmeey*, "from the bowels," so many others have conjectured, or מני יהודה *meni yehudah*, or מיהודה *meyhudah*, "from Judah."—*Secker*. But see *Michaelis* in Prælect, not. 22. And we have עין יעקב *eyn yaakob*, "the fountain of Jacob," Deut. xxxiii. 28, and ממקור ישראל *mimmekor yishrael*, "from the fountain of Israel," Psa. lxviii. 27. Twenty-seven MSS. of *Kennicott's*, six of *De Rossi's* and two of my own, with six editions, have מימי *meymey*, "from the *days;*" which makes no good sense.

Verse 6. *Thou hast heard, see all this*—"Thou didst hear it beforehand; behold, the whole is accomplished"] For חזה *chazeh, see*, a MS. has הזה *hazzeh, this;* thou hast heard the whole of *this:* the *Syriac* has וחזית *vechazith*, "thou hast heard, *and thou hast seen*, the whole." Perhaps it should be הנה *hinneh, behold.* In order to express the full sense, I have rendered it somewhat paraphrastically.

Verse 9. *And for my praise*—"And for the sake of my praise"] I read ולמען תהלתי *ulemaan tehillathi.* The word למען *lemaan*, though not absolutely necessary here, for it may be understood as supplied from the preceding member, yet seems to have been removed from hence to ver. 11; where it is redundant, and where it is not repeated in the *Septuagint.*

A. M. cir. 3292
B. C. cir. 712
Olymp. XVII. 1
cir. annum
NumæPompilii,
R. Roman., 4

for thee, that I cut thee
not off.
10 Behold, [p]I have refined thee,
but not [q]with silver; I have
chosen thee [r]in the furnace of affliction.
11 [s]For mine own sake, *even* for mine own
sake, will I do *it:* for how [t]should *my name*
be polluted: and [u]I will not give my glory
unto another.
12 Hearken unto me, O Jacob and Israel,
my called; [v]I *am* he; I *am* the [w]first, I also
am the last.
13 [x]Mine hand also hath laid the foundation
of the earth, and [y]my right hand
hath spanned the heavens: *when*
[z]I call unto them, they stand up
together.

A. M. cir. 3292
B. C. cir. 712
Olymp. XVII. 1
cir. annum
NumæPompilii,
R. Roman., 4

14 [a]All ye, assemble yourselves, and hear;
which among them hath declared these *things?*
[b]The LORD hath loved him: [c]he will do his
pleasure on Babylon, and his arm *shall be on*
the Chaldeans.
15 I, *even* I, have spoken; yea, [d]I have
called him: I have brought him, and he shall
make his way prosperous.
16 Come ye near unto me, hear ye this; [e]I

[p]Psa. lxvi. 10——[q]Or, *for silver;* see Ezek. xxii. 20, 21, 22——[r]Ecclus. ii. 5——[s]Ver. 9——[t]See Deut. xxxii. 26, 27; Ezek. xx. 9——[u]Chap. xlii. 8——[v]Deut. xxxii. 39——[w]Chap. xli. 4; xliv. 6; Rev. i. 17; xxii. 13

[x]Psa. cii. 25——[y]Or, *the palm of my right hand hath spread out*——[z]Chap. xl. 26——[a]Chap. xli. 22; xliv. 7; xlv. 20, 21——[b]Chap. xlv. 1——[c]Chap. xliv. 28
[d]Chap. xlv. 1, 2, &c.——[e]Chap. xlv. 19

Syriac, and a MS. I have therefore omitted it in the latter place, and added it here.

Verse 10. *I have chosen thee*—"I have tried thee"] For בחרתיך *becharticha*, "I have *chosen* thee," a MS. has בחנתיך *bechanticha*, "I have *tried* thee." And so perhaps read the *Syriac* and *Chaldee* interpreters; they retain the same word בחרתך *bechartach;* but in those languages it signifies, I have *tried* thee. ככסף *kecheseph*, *quasi* argentum, "as silver." *Vulgate.*

I cannot think בכסף *becheseph*, WITH *silver*, is the true reading. ככסף *kecheseph*, LIKE *silver*, as the *Vulgate* evidently read it, I suppose to have been the original reading, though no MS. yet found supports this word; the similarity of the two letters, ב *beth* and כ *caph*, might have easily led to the mistake in the first instance; and it has been but too faithfully copied ever since. כור *cur*, which we translate *furnace*, should be rendered *crucible*, the vessel in which the silver is melted. The meaning of the verse seems to be this: I have purified you, but not as silver is purified; for when it is purified, no dross of any kind is left behind. Had I done this with you, I should have consumed you altogether; but I have put you in the crucible of affliction, in *captivity*, that you may acknowledge your sins, and turn unto me.

Verse 11. *For how should* my name *be polluted*—"For how would my name be blasphemed"] The word שמי *shemi*, *my name*, is dropped out of the text; it is supplied by a MS. which has שמי *shemi;* and by the *Septuagint*, ὁτι το εμον ονομα βεβηλουται. The *Syriac* and *Vulgate* get over the difficulty, by making the verb in the first person; that *I may not be blasphemed.*

Verse 12. *O Jacob*—"O Jacob, my servant"] After יעקב *yaakob*, a MS. of *Kennicott's*, two of *De Rossi's*, and the two old editions of 1486 and 1488, add the word עבדי *abdi*, "my servant," which is lost out of the present text; and there is a rasure in its place in another ancient MS. The Jerusalem Talmud has the same word.

I also am *the last*—"I am the last"] For אף אני *aph ani*, "even I," two ancient MSS. and the ancient Versions, read ואני *veani*, "and I;" more properly.

Verse 14. *Which among them hath declared these* things—"Who among you hath predicted these things"] For בהם *bahem*, "among *them*," twenty-one MSS., nine ancient, and two editions, one of them that of the year 1488, fourteen of *De Rossi's*, and one ancient of my own, have בכם *bachem*, "among *you;*" and so the *Syriac.*

The Lord hath loved him: he will do his pleasure on Babylon—"He, whom JEHOVAH hath loved, will execute his will on Babylon"] That is, Cyrus; so *Symmachus* has well rendered it: Ὁν ὁ Κυριος ηγαπησε ποιησει το θελημα αυτου, "He whom the Lord hath loved will perform his *will.*"

On *the Chaldeans.*] The preposition is lost; it is supplied in the edition of 1486, which has בכשדים *bechasdim*, and so the *Chaldee* and *Vulgate.*

Verse 16. *Come ye near unto me*] After the word קרבו *kirbu*, "draw near," a MS. adds גוים *goyim*, "O ye nations;" which, as this and the two preceding verses are plainly addressed to the idolatrous nations, reproaching their gods as unable to predict future events, is probably genuine.

Hear ye this—"And hear ye this"] A MS. adds the conjunction, ושמעו *vashimu;* and so the *Septuagint*, *Syriac*, and *Vulgate.*

I have not spoken in secret] The Alexandrine copy of the *Septuagint* adds here, ουδε εν τοπῳ γης σκοτεινω, "nor in a dark place of the earth," as in chap. xlv. 19. That it stands rightly, or at least stood very early, in this place of the Version of the *Septuagint*, is highly probable, because it is acknowledged by the *Arabic* Version, and by the *Coptic* MS. *St. Germain de Prez*, Paris, translated likewise from the *Septuagint.* But whether it should be inserted, as of right belonging to the *Hebrew* text, may be doubted; for a transcriber of the *Greek* Version might easily add it by memory from the parallel place; and it is not necessary to the sense.

From the time that it was—"Before the time when *it* began to exist"] An ancient MS. has היותם *heyotham*, "*they* began to exist;" and so another had it at first. From the time that the expedition of Cyrus was planned, there was God managing the whole by the economy of his providence.

A. M. cir. 3292 B. C. cir. 712 Olymp. XVII. 1 cir. annum NumæPompilii, R. Roman., 4

have not spoken in secret from the beginning; from the time that it was, there *am* I: and now [f]the Lord GOD, and his Spirit, hath sent me.

17 Thus saith [g]the LORD, thy Redeemer, the Holy One of Israel; I *am* the LORD thy God which teacheth thee to profit, which [h]leadeth thee by the way *that* thou shouldest go.

18 [i]O that thou hadst hearkened to my commandments! [k]then had thy peace been as a river, and thy righteousness as the waves of the sea:

19 [l]Thy seed also had been as the sand, and the offspring of thy bowels like the gravel thereof; his name should not have been cut off nor destroyed from before me.

A. M. cir. 3292 B. C. cir. 712 Olymp. XVII. 1 cir. annum NumæPompilii, R. Roman., 4

20 [m]Go ye forth of Babylon, flee ye from the Chaldeans, with a voice of singing declare ye, tell this, utter it *even* to the end of the earth; say ye, The LORD hath [n]redeemed his servant Jacob.

21 And they [o]thirsted not *when* he led them through the deserts: he [p]caused the waters to flow out of the rock for them: he clave the rock also, and the waters gushed out.

22 [q]*There is* no peace, saith the LORD, unto the wicked.

---

[f]Ch. lxi. 1; Zech. ii. 8, 9, 11——[g]Ch. xliii. 14; xliv. 6, 24; ver. 20——[h]Psa. xxxii. 8——[i]Deut. xxxii. 29; Psa. lxxxi. 13——[k]Psa. cxix. 165——[l]Gen. xxii. 17; Hos. i. 10

[m]Ch. lii. 11; Jer. l. 8; li. 6, 45; Zech. ii. 6, 7; Rev. xviii. 4
[n]Exod. xix. 4, 5, 6; ch. xliv. 22, 23——[o]See ch. xli. 17, 18
[p]Exod. xvii. 6; Num. xx. 11; Psa. cv. 41——[q]Ch. lvii. 21

Verse 16. *There* am *I*—"I had decreed it"] I take שם *sham* for a verb, not an adverb.

And now the Lord God, and his Spirit, hath sent me—"And now the Lord JEHOVAH hath sent me, and his Spirit"] *Τις εστιν ὁ εν τῳ Ησαιῳ λεγων, Και νυν Κυριος απεστειλε με και το Πνευμα αυτου; εν ᾡ, αμφιβολου οντος του ῥητου, ποτερον ὁ Πατηρ και το Ἁγιον Πνευμα απεστειλαν του Ιησουν, η ὁ Πατηρ απεστειλε τον τε Χριστον και το Ἁγιον Πνευμα· το δευτερον εστιν αληθες.* "Who is it that saith in Isaiah, And now the Lord hath sent me and his Spirit? in which, as the expression is ambiguous, is it the Father and the Holy Spirit who have sent Jesus; or the Father, who hath sent both Christ and the Holy Spirit. The latter is the true interpretation."—*Origen* cont. Cels. lib. i. I have kept to the order of the words of the original, on purpose that the ambiguity, which *Origen* remarks in the Version of the *Septuagint*, and which is the same in the *Hebrew*, might still remain; and the sense which he gives to it, be offered to the reader's judgment, which is wholly excluded in our translation.

Verse 18. *As a river*—"Like the river"] That is, the Euphrates.

Verse 19. *Like the gravel thereof*—"Like that of the bowels thereof"] בצאצאי מעי הים והם הדגים *betseetsaey meey haiyam vehem haddagim;* "As the issue of the bowels of the sea; that is, fishes."—*Salom. ben Melec.* And so likewise *Aben Ezra, Jarchi, Kimchi,* &c.

His name—"Thy name"] For שמו *shemo,* "*his* name," the *Septuagint* had in the copy from which they translated שמך *shimcha, "thy* name."

Verse 20. *Tell this*—"Make it heard"] *Twenty-seven* MSS. of *Kennicott's,* (*ten* ancient,) many of *De Rossi's*, and *two* ancient, of my own, with the *Septuagint, Syriac, Chaldee,* and *Arabic*, and one edition, prefix to the verb the conjunction ו *vau,* והשמיעו *vehashmiu.*

Verse 21. *They thirsted not—through the deserts*] *Kimchi* has a surprising observation upon this place: "If the prophecy," says he, "relates to the return from the Babylonish captivity, as it seems to do, it is to be wondered how it comes to pass, that in the Book of Ezra, in which he gives an account of their return, no mention is made that such miracles were wrought for them; as, for instance, that God clave the rock for them in the desert." It is really much to be wondered, that one of the most learned and judicious of the Jewish expositors of the Old Testament, having advanced so far in a large Comment on Isaiah, should appear to be totally ignorant of the prophet's manner of writing; of the parabolic style, which prevails in the writings of all the prophets, and more particularly in the prophecy of Isaiah, which abounds throughout in parabolical images from the beginning to the end; from "Hear, O heavens, and give ear, O earth," to "the worm and the fire" in the last verse. And how came he to keep his wonderment to himself so long? Why did he not expect that the historian should have related how, as they passed through the desert, cedars, pines, and olive-trees shot up at once on the side of the way to shade them; and that instead of briers and brambles the acacia and the myrtle sprung up under their feet, according to God's promises, chap. xli. 19 and lv. 13? These and a multitude of the like parabolical or poetical images, were never intended to be understood literally. All that the prophet designed in this place, and which he has executed in the most elegant manner, was an amplification and illustration of the gracious care and protection of God vouchsafed to his people in their return from Babylon, by an allusion to the miraculous exodus from Egypt. See *De S. Poësi*, Hebr. Præl. ix.

Verse 22. There is *no peace, saith the Lord, unto the wicked.*] See below, note on chap. lvii. 21. As the destruction of Babylon was determined, God commands his people to hasten out of it; for, saith the Lord, *there is no peace* (prosperity) *to the wicked; ουκ εστι χαιρειν τοις ασεβεσιν, λεγει Κυριος.*—*Sept.* "There is no rejoicing or prosperity to the wicked saith the Lord." **Their is not pese to unrytous men seith the Lord.**—Old MS. Bible.

CHAPTER XLIX

In this chapter the Messiah is introduced, declaring the full extent of his commission, which is not only to be Saviour to the Jews, but also to the Gentiles. The power and efficacy of his word is represented by apt images; the ill success of his ministry among the Jews is intimated, and the great success of the Gospel among the Gentiles, 1–12. *But the prophet, then casting his eye on the happy, though distant, period of Israel's restoration, makes a beautiful apostrophe to the whole creation to shout forth the praises of God on the prospect of this remarkable favour,* 13. *The tender mercies of God to his people, with the prosperity of the Church in general, and the final overthrow of all its enemies, make the subject of the remaining verses,* 14–26.

A. M. cir. 3292
B. C. cir. 712
Olymp. XVII. 1
cir. annum
NumæPompilii,
R. Roman., 4

LISTEN, [a]O isles, unto me;
and hearken, ye people, from
far; [b]The LORD hath called me
from the womb; from the bowels
of my mother hath he made mention of my
name.
2 And he hath made [c]my mouth like a sharp
sword; [d]in the shadow of his hand hath he
hid me, and made me [e]a polished
shaft; in his quiver hath he
hid me;
3 And said unto me, [f]Thou
art my servant, O Israel, [g]in whom I will be
glorified.
4 [h]Then I said, I have labored in vain, I
have spent my strength for nought, and in vain:

[a]Chap. xli. 1——[b]Ver. 5; Jer. i. 5; Matt. i. 20, 21; Luke i. 15, 31; John x. 36; Gal. i. 15——[c]Chap. xi. 4; li. 16; Hos. vi. 5; Heb. iv. 12; Rev. i. 16——[d]Chap. li. 16——[e]Psa. xlv. 5——[f]Chap. xlii. 1; Zech. iii. 8——[g]Chap. xliv. 23; John xiii. 31; xv. 8; Eph. i. 6——[h]Ezek. iii. 19

NOTES ON CHAP. XLIX

Verse 1. *Listen, O isles, unto me*—"Hearken unto me, O ye distant lands"] Hitherto the subject of the prophecy has been chiefly confined to the redemption from the captivity of Babylon; with strong intimations of a more important deliverance sometimes thrown in, to the refutation of idolatry, and the demonstration of the infinite power, wisdom, and foreknowledge of God. The character and office of the Messiah was exhibited in general terms at the beginning of chap. xlii.; but here he is introduced in person, declaring the full extent of his commission, which is not only to restore the Israelites, and reconcile them to their Lord and Father, from whom they had so often revolted, but to be a light to lighten the Gentiles, to call them to the knowledge and obedience of the true God, and to bring them to be one Church together with the Israelites, and to partake with them of the same common salvation procured for all by the great Redeemer and Reconciler of man to God.

Verse 2. *And he hath made my mouth like a sharp sword*—"And he hath made my mouth a sharp sword"] The servant of God, who speaks in the former part of this chapter, must be the Messiah. If any part of this character can in any sense belong to the prophet, yet in some parts it must belong exclusively to Christ; and in all parts to him in a much fuller and more proper sense. Isaiah's mission was to the Jews, not to the distant nations, to whom the speaker in this place addresses himself. "He hath made my mouth a sharp sword;" "to reprove the wicked, and to denounce unto them punishment," says Jarchi, understanding it of Isaiah. But how much better does it suit him who is represented as having "a sharp two-edged sword going out of his mouth," Rev. i. 16; who is himself the Word of God; which word is "quick and powerful, and sharper than any two-edged sword, piercing even to the dividing asunder of soul and spirit, and of the joints and marrow, and is a discerner of the thoughts and intents of the heart;" Heb. iv. 12. This mighty Agent and Instrument of God, "long laid up in store with him, and sealed up among his treasures," is at last revealed and produced by his power, and under his protection, to execute his great and holy purposes. He is compared to a polished shaft stored in his quiver for use in his due time. The polished shaft denotes the same efficacious word which is before represented by the sharp sword. The doctrine of the Gospel pierced the hearts of its hearers, "bringing into captivity every thought to the obedience of Christ." The metaphor of the sword and the arrow, applied to powerful speech, is bold, yet just. It has been employed by the most ingenious heathen writers, if with equal elegance, not with equal force. It is said of Pericles by Aristophanes, (see *Cicero*, Epist. ad Atticum, xii. 6:)—

Οὑτως εκηλει, και μονος των ῥητορων
Το κεντρον εγκατελειπε τοις ακροωμενοις.
Apud. Diod. lib. xii.

His powerful speech
Pierced the hearer's soul, and left behind
Deep in his bosom its keen point infixed.

Pindar is particularly fond of this metaphor, and frequently applies it to his own poetry:—

Επεχε νυν σκοπῳ τοξον,
Αγε, θυμε. τινα βαλλομεν
Εκ μαλθακας αυτε φρε-
νος ευκλεας οϊστους
'Ιεντες—; *Olymp.* ii. 160.

"Come on! thy brightest shafts prepare,
And bend, O Muse, thy sounding bow;
Say, through what paths of liquid air
Our arrows shall we throw?" WEST.

See also ver. 149 of the same ode, and *Olymp.* ix. 17, on the former of which places the *Scholiast* says, τροπικος ὁ λογος· βελη δε τους λογους ειρηκε, δια το οξυ και καιριον των εγκωμιων. "He calls his verses

A. M. cir. 3292
B. C. cir. 712
Olymp. XVII. 1
cir. annum
NumæPompilii,
R. Roman., 4

yet surely my judgment *is* with the LORD, and [i]my work with my God.

5 And now, saith the LORD [k]that formed me from the womb *to be* his servant, to bring Jacob again to him, [l]Though Israel [m]be not gathered, yet shall I be glorious in the eyes of the LORD, and my God shall be my strength.

6 And he said, [n]It is a light thing that thou shouldest be my servant to raise up the tribes of Jacob, and to restore the [o]preserved of Israel: I will also give thee for a [p]light to the Gentiles, that thou mayest be my salvation unto the end of the earth.

7 Thus saith the LORD, the Redeemer of Israel, *and* his Holy One, [q]to [r]him whom man despiseth, to him whom the nation abhorreth, to a servant of rulers, [s]kings shall see and arise, princes also shall worship, because of the LORD that is faithful, *and* the Holy One of Israel, and he shall choose thee.

A. M. cir. 3292
B. C. cir. 712
Olymp. XVII. 1
cir annum
NumæPompilii,
R. Roman., 4

8 Thus saith the LORD, [t]In an acceptable time have I heard thee, and in a day of salvation have I helped thee: and I will preserve thee, [u]and give thee for a covenant of the people, to [v]establish the earth to cause to inherit the desolate heritages;

9 That thou mayest say [w]to the prisoners, Go forth; to them that *are* in darkness, Show yourselves. They shall feed in the ways, and their pastures *shall be* in all high places.

10 They shall not [x]hunger nor thirst; [y]neither shall the heat nor sun smite them: for he that hath mercy on them [z]shall lead them, even by the springs of water shall he guide them.

11 [a]And I will make all my mountains a way, and my highways shall be exalted.

12 Behold, [b]these shall come from far: and, lo, these from the north and from the west; and these from the land of Sinim.

---

[i]Or, *my reward;* ch. xl. 10; lxii. 11——[k]Ver. 1——[l]Or, *That Israel may be gathered to him, and I may,* &c. [m]Matt. xxiii. 37——[n]Or, Art thou *lighter than that thou shouldest,* &c.——[o]Or, *desolations*——[p]Ch. xlii. 6; lx. 3; Luke ii. 32; Acts xiii. 47; xxvi. 18——[q]Chap. liii. 3; Matt. xxvi. 67

[r]Or, *to him that is despised in soul*——[s]Psa. lxxii. 10, 11; verse 23——[t]See Psalm lxix. 13; 2 Corinthians vi. 2——[u]Chapter xlii. 6——[v]Or, *raise up*——[w]Chap. xlii. 7; Zechariah ix. 12——[x]Revelation vii. 16——[y]Psa. cxxi. 6——[z]Psalm xxiii. 2——[a]Chapter xl. 4——[b]Chap. xliii. 5, 6

---

shafts, by a metaphor, signifying the acuteness and the apposite application of his panegyric."

This person, who is (ver. 3) called *Israel,* cannot in any sense be Isaiah. That name, in its original design and full import, can only belong to him who *contended powerfully with God* in behalf of mankind, and prevailed, Gen. xxxii. 28. After all that *Vitringa,* Bp. *Lowth,* and others have said in proof of this chapter speaking of the Messiah, and of him alone, I have my doubts whether sometimes Isaiah, sometimes Cyrus, and sometimes the Messiah, be not intended; the former shadowing out the latter, of whom, in certain respects, they may be considered the *types.* The literal sense should be sought out *first;* this is of the utmost importance both in reading and interpreting the oracles of God.

Verse 5. *And now, saith the Lord*—"And now, thus saith JEHOVAH"] The word כה *coh,* before אמר *amar,* is dropped out of the text: it is supplied by eight MSS. (two ancient) of Dr. *Kennicott's,* two of *De Rossi's,* and the *Septuagint, Syriac,* and *Vulgate.*

Though Israel be not gathered—"And that Israel unto him might be gathered"] Five MSS. (two ancient) confirm the *Keri,* or marginal correction of the Masoretes, לו *lo, unto him,* instead of לא *lo, not,* in the text; and so read *Aquila;* and the *Chaldee, Septuagint,* and *Arabic* omit the negative. But the *Septuagint,* MSS. *Pachom,* and I. D. II. express also the *Keri* לו *lo* by *προς αυτον, to him.*

Verse 6. *And to restore the preserved of Israel*—"And to restore the branches of Israel"] נצירי *netsirey,* or נצורי *netsurey,* as the Masoretes correct it in the marginal reading. This word has been matter of great doubt with interpreters: the *Syriac* renders it *the branch,* taking it for the same with נצר *netser,* chap. xi. 1. See *Michaelis* Epim. in Prælect. xix.

Verse 7. *The Redeemer of Israel,* and *his Holy One*—"The Redeemer of Israel, his Holy One"] "Perhaps we should read לקדושו *likdosho,"* SECKER: that is, *to his Holy One.* The preceding word ends with a ל *lamed,* which might occasion that letter's being lost here. The *Talmud* of Babylon has וקדושו *ukedosho, and his Holy One.*

To him whom man despiseth—"To him whose person is despised"] "Perhaps we should read נבזה *nibzeh,"* SECKER; or בזוי *bazui, Le Clerc;* that is, instead of the active, the passive form, which seems here to be required.

Verse 9. *To them that* are *in darkness*—"And to those that are in darkness"] Fifteen MSS. (five ancient) of Dr. *Kennicott's,* eleven of *De Rossi's,* and one ancient of my own, and the two old editions of 1486 and 1488, and three others, add the conjunction ו *vau* at the beginning of this member. Another MS. had it so at first, and two others have a rasure at the place: and it is expressed by the *Septuagint, Syriac, Chaldee,* and *Vulgate.*

Verse 12. *Behold, these shall come from far*] "Babylon was far and east, ממזרח *mimmizrach,* (*non sic Vett.,*) Sinim, Pelusians, to the south." —SECKER.

The land of Sinim.] Prof. *Doederlein* thought of Syene, the southern limit of Egypt, but does

A. M. cir. 3292
B. C. cir. 712
Olymp. XVII. 1
cir. annum
NumæPompilii,
R. Roman., 4

13 [c]Sing, O heavens; and be joyful, O earth; and break forth into singing, O mountains: for the LORD hath comforted his people, and will have mercy upon his afflicted.

14 [d]But Zion said, The LORD hath forsaken me, and my Lord hath forgotten me.

15 [e]Can a woman forget her sucking child, [f]that she should not have compassion on the son of her womb? yea, they may forget, [g]yet will I not forget thee.

16 Behold, [h]I have graven thee upon the palms of *my* hands; thy walls *are* continually before me.

17 Thy children shall make haste; [i]thy destroyers and they that made thee waste shall go forth of thee.

18 [k]Lift up thine eyes round about, and behold: all these gather themselves together, *and* come to thee. *As* I live, saith the LORD, thou shalt surely clothe thee with them all, [l]as with an ornament, and bind them *on thee,* as a bride *doeth.*

[c]Ch. xliv. 23——[d]See ch. xl. 27——[e]See Psa. ciii. 13; Mal. iii. 17; Matt. vii. 11——[f]Heb. *from having compassion*——[g]Rom. xi. 29——[h]See Exod. xiii. 9; Cant. viii. 6——[i]Ver. 19——[k]Ch. lx. 4——[l]Prov. xvii. 6

not abide by it. *Michaelis* thinks it is right, and promises to give his reasons for so thinking in the second part of his Spicilegium Geographiæ Hebræorum Exteræ. See *Biblioth. Oriental.* Part xi. p. 176.

סין *sin* signifies a *bush*, and סינים *sinim*, *bushes*, *woods*, &c. Probably this means that the land where several of the lost Jews dwell is a woodland. The ten tribes are gone, no one knows whither. On the slave coast in Africa, some Jewish rites appear among the people, and all the males are circumcised. The whole of this land, as it appears from the coast, may be emphatically called ארץ סינים *erets sinim, the land of bushes*, as it is all covered with *woods* as far as the eye can reach. Many of the Indians in North America, which is also a woodland, have a great profusion of rites, apparently in their basis *Jewish*. Is it not possible that the descendants of the *ten* lost tribes are among those in America, or among those in Africa, whom European nations *think they have a right to enslave?* It is of those lost tribes that the twenty-first verse speaks: "And these, where had they been?"

Verse 13. *Break forth into singing, O mountains*—"Ye mountains, burst forth into song"] Three ancient MSS. are without the י *yod* or the conjunction ו *vau* before the verb: and so the *Septuagint*, *Syriac*, and *Vulgate.*

Verse 14. *The Lord* (יהוה *Yehovah*) *hath forsaken me, and my Lord* (אדני *Adonai*) *hath forgotten me.*] But a multitude of MSS. and several ancient editions read יהוה *Yehovah* in both places.

Verse 16. *Behold, I have graven thee upon the palms of* my *hands*—"Behold, on the palms of my hands have I delineated thee"] This is certainly an allusion to some practice, common among the Jews at that time, of making marks on their hands or arms by punctures on the skin, with some sort of sign or representation of the city or temple, to show their affection and zeal for it. They had a method of making such punctures indelible by fire, or by staining. See note on chap. xliv. 5. It is well known, that the pilgrims at the holy sepulchre get themselves marked in this manner with what are called the ensigns of Jerusalem. See *Maundrell*, p. 75, where he tells us how it is performed: and this art is practised by travelling Jews all over the world at this day.

Verse 17. *Thy children shall make haste*—"They that destroyed thee shall soon become thy builders"] Auctor Vulgatæ pro בניך *banayich*, videtur legisse בוניך *bonayich*, unde vertit, *structores tui;* cui et Septuaginta fere consentiunt, qui verterunt ῳκοδομηθης, *ædificata es*, prout in Plantiniana editione habetur; in Vaticana sive Romana legitur, οικοδομηθησῃ, *ædificaberis*. Hisce etiam Targum Jonathanis aliquatenus consentit, ubi, *et ædificabunt*. Confer infra Esai. liv. 13, ad quem locum rabbini quoque notarunt ex tractatu Talmudico Berachot, c. ix., quod non legendum sit בניך *banayich*, id est, *filii tui;* sed בניך *bonayich*, *ædificatores tui*. Confer not. ad librum Prec. Jud. part ii., p. 226, ut et D Wagenseil Sot. p. 253, n. 9. "The author of the *Vulgate* appears to have read בוניך *bonayich* for בניך *banayich*, as he translates it by *structores tui*, 'thy builders.' The *Septuagint* is almost the same with the *Vulgate*, having ῳκοδομηθης, *art built*, as in the *Plantin* edition: but the *Vatican* or *Roman* copy reads οικοδομηθησῃ, *thou shalt be built*. To these readings the *Targum* of *Jonathan* has some sort of correspondence, translating *et ædificabunt*, 'and they shall build.' See chap. liv. 13; on which place the rabbins also remark, in the Talmudic tract *Berachoth*, c. 9, that we should not read בניך *banayich, thy sons*, but בניך *bonayich, thy builders*. See the note in *Prec. Jud.* part ii., p. 226, and also *D. Wagenseil, Sot.* p. 253, n. 9." See also *Breithaupt.* not. ad *Jarchi* in loc.; and the note on this place in De Sac. Poës. Hebr. Prælect. xxxi. Instead of בוניך or בניך *bonayich, thy builders*, several MSS. read בניך *baneycha, thy sons*. So also the *Syriac:* see the above note.

Shall go forth of thee—"Shall become thine offspring."] ממך יצאו *mimmech yetseu*, shall *proceed, spring, issue, from thee*, as thy children. The phrase is frequently used in this sense: see chap. xi. 1; Mic. v. 2; Nah. i. 11. The accession of the Gentiles to the Church of God is considered as an addition made to the number of the family and children of Sion: see ver. 21, 22, and chap. lx. 4. The common rendering, "shall go forth of thee, or depart from thee," is very flat, after their zeal had been expressed by "shall become thy builders:" and as the opposition is kept up in one part of the sentence, one has reason to expect it in the other, which should be parallel to it.

Verse 18. *Bind them* on thee, *as a bride* doeth—"Bind them about thee, as a bride *her jewels.*"] The end of the sentence is manifestly

A. M. cir. 3292
B. C. cir. 712
Olymp. XVII. 1
cir. annum
NumæPompilii,
R. Roman., 4

19 For thy waste and thy desolate places, and the land of thy
destruction, [m]shall even now be
too narrow by reason of the inhabitants, and they that swallowed thee up
shall be far away.
20 [n]The children which thou shalt have,
[o]after thou hast lost the other, shall say again
in thine ears, The place *is* too strait for me:
give place to me that I may dwell.
21 Then shalt thou say in thine heart, Who
hath begotten me these, seeing I have lost my
children, and am desolate, a captive, and removing to and fro? and who hath brought up
these? Behold, I was left alone; these, where
had they *been?*
22 [p]Thus saith the Lord GOD, Behold, I
will lift up mine hand to the Gentiles, and set
up my standard to the people: and they shall
bring thy sons in *their* [q]arms, and thy daughters shall be carried upon *their* shoulders.
23 [r]And kings shall be thy
[s]nursing fathers, and their
[t]queens thy nursing mothers:
they shall bow down to thee with
their face toward the earth, and [u]lick up the
dust of thy feet; and thou shalt know that I
am the LORD: for [v]they shall not be ashamed
that wait for me.
24 [w]Shall the prey be taken from the mighty,
or [x]the lawful captive delivered?
25 But thus saith the LORD, Even the [y]cap-
tives of the mighty shall be taken away, and
the prey of the terrible shall be delivered: for
I will contend with him that contendeth with
thee, and I will save thy children.
26 And I will [z]feed them that oppress thee
with their own flesh; and they shall be drunken with their own [a]blood, as with [b]sweet
wine: and all flesh [c]shall know that I the LORD
am thy Saviour and thy Redeemer, the
Mighty One of Jacob.

[m]See ch. liv. 1, 2; Zech. ii. 4; x. 10——[n]Ch. lx. 4——[o]Matt. iii. 9; Rom. xi. 11, 12, &c.——[p]Ch. lx. 4; lxvi. 20——[q]Heb. *bosom*——[r]Psa. lxxii. 11; ver. 7; ch. lii. 15; lx. 16——[s]Heb. *nourishers*——[t]Heb. *princesses*——[u]Psa. lxxii. 9; Mic. vii. 17——[v]Psa. xxxiv. 22; Rom. v. 5; ix. 33; x. 11——[w]Matt. xii. 29; Luke xi. 21, 22——[x]Heb. *the captivity of the just*——[y]Heb. *captivity*——[z]Ch. ix. 20——[a]Rev. xiv. 20; xvi. 6——[b]Or, *new wine*——[c]Psa. ix. 16; ch. lx. 16

imperfect. Does a bride bind her children, or her new subjects, about her? Sion clothes herself with her children, as a bride clothes herself,—with what? some other thing certainly. The *Septuagint* help us out in this difficulty, and supply the lost word: ὡς κοσμον νυμφη· *as a bride her ornaments.* ככליה כלה *kichleyha callah*, or ככלה כליה *kecallah keleyha.* The great similitude of the two words has occasioned the omission of one of them. See chap. lxi. 10.

Verse 21. *These, where* had *they* been—"These then, where were they?"] The conjunction is added before אלה *elleh*, that is, ואלה *veelleh*, in thirty-two MSS. (nine ancient) of *Kennicott's*, and fifty-four of *De Rossi's;* and so the *Septuagint*, *Chaldee*, and *Vulgate*. See on ver. 12.

Verse 22. *Thus saith the Lord God*—ארני יהוה *Adonai Yehovah.* Adonai is wanting in one MS., in the Alexandrine copy of the *Septuagint*, and in the *Arabic*.

Verse 23. *With* their *face toward the earth*—"With their faces to the earth"] It is well known that expressions of submission, homage, and reverence always have been and are still carried to a great degree of extravagance in the eastern countries. When Joseph's brethren were introduced to him, "they bowed down themselves before him with their faces to the earth," Gen. xlii. 6. The kings of Persia never admitted any one to their presence without exacting this act of adoration; for that was the proper term for it. Necesse est, says the Persian courtier to Conon, si in conspectum veneris, venerari te regem; quod προσκυνειν illi vocant. "It is necessary, if thou shouldest come in sight, to venerate thee as king; which they call *worshipping*."—NEPOS in Conone. Alexander, intoxicated with success, affected this piece of oriental pride: Itaque more Persarum Macedonas venerabundos ipsum salutare, prosternentes humi corpora. "The Macedonians, after the manner of the Persians, saluted their monarch with the ceremony of prostration."—CURTIUS, lib. viii. The insolence of eastern monarchs to conquered princes, and the submission of the latter, is astonishing. Mr. *Harmer*, Observ. ii. 43, gives the following instance of it from D'Herbelot: "This prince threw himself one day on the ground, and kissed the prints that his victorious enemy's horse had made there; reciting some verses in Persian, which he had composed, to this effect:—

"'The mark that the foot of your horse has left upon the dust, serves me now for a crown.

"'The ring which I wear as the badge of my slavery, is become my richest ornament.

"'While I shall have the happiness to kiss the dust of your feet, I shall think that fortune favours me with its tenderest caresses, and its sweetest kisses.'"

These expressions therefore of the prophet are only general poetical images, taken from the manners of the country, to denote great respect and reverence: and such splendid poetical images, which frequently occur in the prophetical writings, were intended only as general amplifications of the subject, not as predictions to be understood and fulfilled precisely according to the letter. For the different kinds of adoration in the east, see the note on chap. xliv. 17.

Verse 24. *Shall the prey be taken from the mighty*—"Shall the prey seized by the terrible be rescued"] For צדיק *tsaddik*, read עריץ

arits. A palpable mistake, like that in chap. xlii. 19. The correction is self-evident from the very terms of the sentence; from the necessity of the strict correspondence in the expressions between the question and the answer made to it, —and it is apparent to the blindest and most prejudiced eye. However, if authority is also necessary, there is that of the *Syriac* and *Vulgate* for it; who plainly read עריץ *arits,* in ver. 24 as well as in ver. 25, rendering it in the former place by the same word as in the latter.—L.

These two last verses contain a glorious promise of deliverance to the persecuted Church of Christ from the *terrible one*—Satan, and all his representatives and vicegerents, persecuting antichristian rulers. They shall at last cease from destroying the Church of God, and destroy one another.

CHAPTER L

In this chapter God vindicates his dealings with his people, whose alienation is owing to themselves, 1. *And, by allusion to the temporal deliverances connected with the drying up of the Red Sea and the Euphrates, asserts his power to save,* 2, 3; *namely, by the obedience and sufferings of the Messiah,* 4–6; *who was at length to prove victorious over all his enemies,* 7–9. *The two last verses exhort to faith and trust in God in the most disconsolate circumstances; with a denunciation of vengeance on those who should trust to their own devices,* 10, 11.

A. M. cir. 3292
B. C. cir. 712
Olymp. XVII. 1
cir. annum
NumæPompilii,
R. Roman., 4

THUS saith the LORD, Where *is* [a]the bill of your mother's divorcement, whom I have put away? or which of my [b]creditors *is it* to whom I have sold you? Behold, for your iniquities [c]have ye sold yourselves, and for your transgressions is your mother put away.
2 Wherefore, when I came, *was there* no man? [d]when I called, *was there* none to answer? [e]Is my hand shortened at all, that it cannot redeem? or have I no power to deliver? behold, [f]at my rebuke I [g]dry up the sea, I make the [h]rivers a wilderness: [i]their fish stinketh, because *there is* no water, and dieth for thirst.
3 [k]I clothe the heavens with blackness, [l]and I make sackcloth their covering.
4 [m]The Lord GOD hath given me the tongue of the learned, that I should know how to speak a word in season to *him that is* [n]weary: he wakeneth morning by morning, he wakeneth mine ear to hear as the learned.
5 The Lord GOD [o]hath opened mine ear, and I was not [p]rebellious, neither turned away back.
6 [q]I gave my back to the smiters, and [r]my

[a]Deut. xxiv. 1; Jer. iii. 8; Hos. ii. 2——[b]See 2 Kings iv. 1; Matt. xviii. 25——[c]Chap. lii. 3——[d]Prov. i. 24; chap. lxv. 12; lxvi. 4; Jer. vii. 13; xxxv. 15——[e]Num. xi. 23; chap. lix. 1——[f]Psa. cvi. 9; Nah. i. 4——[g]Exod. xiv. 21——[h]Josh. iii. 16

[i]Exod. vii. 18, 21——[k]Exod. x. 21——[l]Rev. vi. 12——[m]Exod. iv. 11——[n]Matt. xi. 28——[o]Psa. xl. 6, 7, 8——[p]Matt. xxvi. 39; John xiv. 31; Phil. ii. 8; Heb. x. 5, &c.——[q]Matt. xxvi. 67; xxvii. 26; John xviii. 22——[r]Lam. iii. 30

NOTES ON CHAP. L

Verse 1. *Thus saith the Lord*] This chapter has been understood of the prophet himself; but it certainly speaks more clearly about Jesus of Nazareth than of Isaiah, the son of Amos.

Where is *the bill*—"Where is this bill"] Husbands, through moroseness or levity of temper, often sent bills of divorcement to their wives on slight occasions, as they were permitted to do by the law of Moses, Deut. xxiv. 1. And fathers, being oppressed with debt, often sold their children, which they might do for a time, till the year of release, Exod. xxi. 7. That this was frequently practised, appears from many passages of Scripture, and that the persons and the liberty of the children were answerable for the debts of the father. The widow, 2 Kings iv. 1, complains "that the creditor is come to take unto him her two sons to be bondmen." And in the parable, Matt xviii. 25: "The lord, forasmuch as his servant had not to pay, commands him to be sold, and his wife and children, and all that he had, and payment to be made." Sir John Chardin's MS. note on this place of Isaiah is as follows: En Orient on paye ses dettes avec ses esclaves, car ils sont des principaux meubles; et en plusieurs lieux on les paye aussi de ses enfans. "In the east they pay their debts by giving up their slaves, for these are their chief property of a disposable kind; and in many places they give their children to their creditors." But this, saith God, cannot be my case; I am not governed by any such motives, neither am I urged by any such necessity. Your captivity therefore and your afflictions are to be imputed to yourselves, and to your own folly and wickedness.

Verse 2. *Their fish stinketh*—"Their fish is dried up"] For תבאש *tibaosh, stinketh,* read תיבש *tibash, is dried up;* so it stands in the Bodl. MS., and it is confirmed by the *Septuagint,* ξηρανθησονται, *they shall be dried up.*

Verse 5. *Neither turned away back*—"Neither did I withdraw myself backward"] Eleven MSS. and the oldest edition prefix the conjunction ו *vau;* and so also the *Septuagint* and *Syriac.*

Verse 6. *And my cheeks to them that plucked off the hair*] The greatest indignity that could possibly be offered. See the note on chap. vii. 20.

I hid not my face from shame and spitting.]

A. M. cir. 3292 B. C. cir. 712 Olymp. XVII. 1 cir. annum NumæPompilii, R. Roman., 4

cheeks to them that plucked off
the hair: I hid not my face from
shame and spitting.
7 For the Lord GOD will help
me; therefore shall I not be confounded:
therefore have [s]I set my face like a flint, and
I know that I shall not be ashamed.
8 [t]*He is* near that justifieth me; who will
contend with me? let us stand together: who
is [u]mine adversary? let him come near to me.
9 Behold, the Lord GOD will help me; who
is he *that* shall condemn me? [v]lo, they all
shall wax old as a garment; [w]the moth shall eat them up.
10 Who *is* among you that feareth the LORD, that obeyeth the
voice of his servant, that [x]walketh *in* darkness, and hath no light? [y]let him trust in the
name of the LORD, and stay upon his God.
11 Behold, all ye that kindle a fire, that compass *yourselves* about with sparks: walk in
the light of your fire, and in the sparks *that*
ye have kindled. [z]This shall ye have of mine
hand; ye shall lie down [a]in sorrow.

[s]Ezek. iii. 8, 9——[t]Rom. viii. 32, 33, 34——[u]Heb. *the master of my cause*——[v]Job xiii. 28; Psa. cii. 26; ch. li. 6——[w]Chap. li. 8——[x]Psa. xxiii. 4——[y]2 Chron. xx. 20; Psa. xx. 7——[z]John ix. 19——[a]Psa. xvi. 4

Another instance of the utmost contempt and detestation. It was ordered by the law of Moses as a severe punishment, carrying with it a lasting disgrace; Deut. xxv. 9. Among the Medes it was highly offensive to spit in any one's presence, *Herod.* i. 99; and so likewise among the Persians, *Xenophon*, Cyrop. Lib. i., p. 18.

"They abhor me; they flee far from me;
They forbear not to spit in my face."
Job xxx. 10.

"And JEHOVAH said unto Moses, If her father had but spit in her face, should she not be ashamed seven days?" Num. xxii. 14. On which place Sir John Chardin remarks, that "spitting before any one, or spitting upon the ground in speaking of any one's actions, is through the east an expression of extreme detestation."—*Harmer's* Observ. ii. 509. See also, of the same notions of the Arabs in this respect, *Niebuhr*, Description de l'Arabie, p. 26. It so evidently appears that in those countries spitting has ever been an expression of the utmost detestation, that the learned doubt whether in the passages of Scripture above quoted any thing more is meant than spitting,—not in the face, which perhaps the words do not necessarily imply,—but only in the presence of the person affronted. But in this place it certainly means spitting *in the face;* so it is understood in St. Luke, where our Lord plainly refers to this prophecy: "All things that are written by the prophets concerning the Son of man shall be accomplished; for he shall be delivered to the Gentiles, and shall be mocked and spitefully entreated, and spitted on, *εμπτυσθησεται*," xviii. 31, 32, which was in fact fulfilled; *και ηρξαντο τινες εμπτυειν αυτῳ*, "and some began to spit on him," Mark xiv. 65, xv. 19. If spitting in a person's presence was such an indignity, how much more spitting in his face?

Verse 7. *Therefore have I set my face like a flint*] The Prophet Ezekiel, chap. ii. 8, 9, has expressed this with great force in his bold and vehement manner:

"Behold, I have made thy face strong against their faces,
And thy forehead strong against their foreheads:
As an adamant, harder than a rock, have I made thy forehead;
Fear them not, neither be dismayed at their looks,
Though they be a rebellious house."

Verse 8. *Who will contend with me*] The Bodleian MS. and another add the word הוא *hu;* מי הוא יריב *mi hu yarib*, as in the like phrase in the next verse; and in the very same phrase Job xiii. 19, and so likewise in many other places, Job xvii. 3, xli. 1. Sometimes on the like occasions it is מי זה *mi zeh*, and מי הוא זה *mi hu zeh*, "Who is this one?" The word has probably been lost out of the present text; and the reading of the MSS. above mentioned seems to be genuine.

Verse 10. *Who* is *among you that feareth the Lord*] I believe this passage has been generally, if not *dangerously*, misunderstood. It has been *quoted*, and *preached upon*, to prove that "a man might conscientiously fear God, and be obedient to the words of the law and the prophets; *obey the voice of his servant*—of Jesus Christ himself, that is, be sincerely and regularly obedient to the moral law and the commands of our blessed Lord, and yet *walk in darkness* and *have no light*, no sense of God's approbation, and no evidence of the safety of his state." This is utterly impossible; for Jesus hath said, "He that followeth me shall not walk in darkness, but shall have the light of life." If there be some religious persons who, under the influence of morbid melancholy, are continually writing bitter things against themselves, the word of God should not be bent down to their state. There are other modes of spiritual and Scriptural comfort. But does not the text speak of such a case? And are not the words precise in reference to it? I think not: and Bishop Lowth's translation has set the whole in the clearest light, though he does not appear to have been apprehensive that the *bad use* I mention had been made of the text as it stands in our common Version. The text contains *two questions*, to each of which a particular answer is given:—

Q. 1. "Who is there among you that feareth JEHOVAH?
Ans. *Let him hearken unto the voice of his servant.*
Q. 2. *Who* that walketh in darkness and hath no light?
Ans. *Let him trust in the name of Jehovah;*
And lean himself (prop himself) *upon his God.*"

Now, a man awakened to a sense of his sin and misery, may have a *dread of* JEHOVAH, and *tremble at his word;* and what should such a person do? Why he should hear what God's servant saith: "Come unto me, all ye who labour and are heavy laden; and I will give you rest." There may be a sincere *penitent*, walking in darkness, having no light of salvation; for this is the case of all when they first begin to turn to God. What should such do? They should *trust, believe on, the Lord Jesus*, who died for them, and *lean upon* his all-sufficient merits for the light of salvation which God has promised. Thus acting, they will soon have a sure trust and confidence that God for Christ's sake has forgiven them their sin, and thus they shall have the light of life.

Verse 10. *That obeyeth the voice of his servant*—"Let him hearken unto the voice of his servant"] For שמע *shomea*, pointed as the participle, the *Septuagint* and *Syriac* read ישמע *yishma*, future or imperative. This gives a much more elegant turn and distribution to the sentence.

Verse 11. *Ye that kindle a fire*] The fire of their own kindling, by the light of which they walk with security and satisfaction, is an image designed to express, in general, human devices and mere worldly policy, exclusive of faith, and trust in God; which, though they flatter themselves for a while with pleasing expectations and some appearance of success, shall in the end turn to the confusion of the authors. Or more particularly, as Vitringa explains it, it may mean the designs of the turbulent and factious Jews in the times succeeding those of Christ, who, in pursuit of their own desperate schemes, stirred up the war against the Romans, and kindled a fire which consumed their city and nation.

That compass yourselves *about with sparks*—"Who heap the fuel round about"] "מגוזלי *megozeley, accendentes, Syr.; forte legerunt pro* מאזרי *meazzerey* מאירי *meirey; nam sequitur* אור *ur*."—*Secker*. Lud. Capellus, in his criticism on this place, thinks it should be מאזרי *meazzerey*, from the *Septuagint*, κατισχυοντες.

There are others who are widely different from those already described. Without faith, repentance, or a holy life, they are bold in their professed confidence in God—presumptuous in their trust in the mercy of God; and, while destitute of all preparation for and right to the kingdom of heaven, would think it criminal to doubt their final salvation! Living in this way, what can they have at the hand of God but an endless bed of sorrow! *Ye shall lie down in sorrow.*

But there is a general sense, and accordant to the design of the prophecy, in which these words may be understood and paraphrased: *Behold, all ye that kindle a fire*—provoke war and contention; *compass yourselves about with sparks*—stirring up seditions and rebellions: *walk in the light of your fire*—go on in your lust of power and restless ambition. *Ye shall lie down in sorrow*—it will turn to your own perdition. See the *Targum*. This seems to refer to the restless spirit of the Jews, always stirring up confusion and strife; rebelling against and provoking the Romans, till at last their city was taken, their temple burnt to the ground, and upwards of a million of themselves destroyed, and the rest led into captivity!

CHAPTER LI

The prophet exhorts the children of Abraham to trust in the Lord; and briefly, but beautifully, describes the great blessedness which should be the consequence, 1–3. *Then, turning to the Gentiles, encourages them to look for a portion in the same salvation,* 4, 5; *the everlasting duration of which is majestically described,* 6. *And as it is everlasting, so is it sure to the righteous, notwithstanding all the machinations of their enemies,* 7, 8. *The faithful, then, with exultation and joy, lift their voices, reminding God of his wondrous works of old, which encourage them to look now for the like glorious accomplishment of these promises,* 9–11. *In answer to this the Divinity is introduced comforting them under their trials, and telling them that the deliverer was already on his way to save and to establish them,* 12–16. *On this the prophet turns to Jerusalem to comfort and congratulate her on so joyful a prospect. She is represented, by a bold image, as a person lying in the streets, under the intoxicating effects of the cup of the Divine wrath, without a single person from among her own people appointed to give her consolation, and trodden under the feet of her enemies; but, in the time allotted by theDivine providence,* the cup of trembling *shall be taken out of her hand, and put into that of her oppressors; and she shall drink it no more again for ever,* 17–22.

A. M. cir. 3292
B. C. cir. 712
Olymp. XVII. 1
cir. annum
NumæPompilii,
R. Roman., 4

HEARKEN [a]to me, [b]ye that follow after righteousness, ye that seek the LORD: look unto the rock *whence* ye are hewn, and to the hole of the pit *whence* ye are digged.

2 [c]Look unto Abraham your father, and unto Sarah *that* bare you: [d]for I called him alone, and [e]blessed him, and increased him.

3 For the LORD [f]shall comfort Zion: he

[a]Ver. 7——[b]Rom. ix. 30, 31, 32——[c]Rom. iv. 1, 16; Heb. xi. 11, 12——[d]Gen. xii. 1, 2

[e]Gen. xxiv. 1, 35——[f]Psa. cii. 13; chap. xl. 1; lii. 9; lxi. 2; lxvi. 13; Zech. i. 17; ver. 12

NOTES ON CHAP. LI

Verse 1. *Ye that follow after righteousness*] The people who, feeling the want of salvation, seek the Lord in order to be justified.

The rock] Abraham.

The hole of the pit] Sarah; as explained in ver. 2.

Verse 2. *I called him alone*] As I have made out of one a great nation; so, although ye are

A. M. cir. 3292 B. C. cir. 712 Olymp. XVII. 1 cir. annum NumæPompilii, R. Roman., 4

will comfort all her waste places; and he will make her wilderness like Eden, and her desert [g]like the garden of the LORD: joy and gladness shall be found therein, thanksgiving and the voice of melody.

4 Hearken unto me, my people; and give ear unto me, O my nation: [h]for a law shall proceed from me, and I will make my judgment to rest [i]for a light of the people.

5 [k]My righteousness *is* near; my salvation is gone forth, [l]and mine arms shall judge the people: [m]the isles shall wait upon me, and [n]on mine arm shall they trust.

6 [o]Lift up your eyes to the heavens, and look upon the earth beneath: for [p]the heavens shall vanish away like smoke, [q]and the earth shall wax old like a garment, and they that dwell therein shall die in like manner: but my salvation shall be for ever, and my righteousness shall not be abolished.

7 [r]Hearken unto me, ye that know righteousness, the people [s]in whose heart *is* my law; [t]fear ye not the reproach of men, neither be ye afraid of their revilings.

8 For [u]the moth shall eat them up like a garment, and the worm shall eat them like wool: but my righteousness shall be for ever, and my salvation from generation to generation.

A. M. cir. 3292 B. C. cir. 712 Olymp. XVII. 1 cir. annum NumæPompilii, R. Roman., 4

9 [v]Awake, awake, [w]put on strength, O arm of the LORD; awake, [x]as in the ancient days, in the generations of old. [y]*Art* thou not it that hath cut [z]Rahab, *and* wounded the [a]dragon?

10 *Art* thou not it which hath [b]dried the sea, the waters of the great deep; that hath made the depths of the sea a way for the ransomed to pass over?

11 Therefore [c]the redeemed of the LORD shall return, and come with singing unto Zion; and everlasting joy *shall be* upon their head: they shall obtain gladness and joy: *and* sorrow and mourning shall flee away.

12 I, *even* I, *am* he [d]that comforteth you: who *art* thou, that thou shouldest be afraid [e]of a man *that* shall die, and of the son of man *which* shall be made [f]*as* grass;

13 And forgettest the LORD thy Maker, [g]that hath stretched forth the heavens, and laid the

[g]Gen. xiii. 10; Joel ii. 3——[h]Ch. ii. 3; xlii. 4——[i]Ch. xlii. 6——[k]Ch. xlvi. 13; lvi. 1; Rom. i. 16, 17——[l]Psa. lxvii. 4; xcviii. 9——[m]Ch. lx. 9——[n]Rom. i. 16——[o]Ch. xl. 26——[p]Psa. cii. 26; Matt. xxiv. 35; 2 Pet. iii. 10, 12 [q]Ch. l. 9——[r]Ver. 1——[s]Psa. xxxvii. 31——[t]Matt. x. 28; Acts v. 41——[u]Ch. l. 9——[v]Psa. xliv. 23; ch. lii. 1

[w]Psa. xciii. 1; Rev. xi. 17——[x]Psa. xliv. 1——[y]Job xxvi. 12——[z]Psa. lxxxvii. 4; lxxxix. 10——[a]Psa. lxxiv. 13, 14; ch. xxvii. 1; Ezek. xxix. 3——[b]Exod. xiv. 21; ch. xliii. 16——[c]Ch. xxxv. 10——[d]Ver. 3; 2 Cor. i. 3 [e]Psa. cxviii. 6——[f]Ch. xl. 6; 1 Pet. i. 24——[g]Job ix. 8; Psa. civ. 2; ch. xl. 22; xlii. 5; xliv. 24

brought low and minished, yet I can restore you to happiness, and greatly multiply your number.

Verse 4. *My people—O my nation—*"O ye peoples—O ye nations"] For עמי *ammi, my people*, the Bodleian MS. and another read עמים *ammim, ye peoples;* and for לאומי *leumi, my nation*, the Bodleian MS. and *eight* others, (*two* of them ancient,) and *four* of *De Rossi's*, read לאמים *leummim, ye nations;* and so the *Syriac* in both words. The difference is very material; for in this case the address is made, not to the Jews, but to the Gentiles, as in all reason it ought to be; for this and the two following verses express the call of the Gentiles, the islands, or the distant lands on the coasts of the Mediterranean and other seas. It is also to be observed that God in no other place calls his people לאמי *leummi, my nation.* It has been before remarked that transcribers frequently omitted the final ם *mem* of nouns plural, and supplied it, for brevity's sake, and sometimes for want of room at the end of a line, by a small stroke thus עמי׳; which mark, being effaced or overlooked, has been the occasion of many mistakes of this kind.

A law shall proceed from me] The new law, the Gospel of our Lord Jesus. *Kimchi* says, "After the war with Gog and Magog the King Messiah will teach the people to walk in the ways of the Lord."

Verse 5. *My righteousness* is *near*] The word צדק *tsedek, righteousness*, is used in such a great latitude of signification, for justice, truth, faithfulness, goodness, mercy, deliverance, salvation, &c., that it is not easy sometimes to give the precise meaning of it without much circumlocution; it means here the faithful completion of God's promises to deliver his people.

Verse 6. *My salvation shall be for ever*] Aben Ezra says, From this verse divines have learnt the immortality of the soul. Men shall perish as the earth does, because they are formed from it; but they who are filled with the salvation of God shall remain for ever. See *Kimchi.*

Verse 11. *They shall obtain gladness and joy;* and *sorrow and mourning shall flee away.*] *Nineteen* MSS. and the *two* oldest editions have ישגו *yasigu;* and *forty-six* MSS. of *Kennicott's* and *ten* of *De Rossi's*, and the same *two* editions, and agreeably to them the *Chaldee* and *Syriac*, have ונסו *venasu;* and so both words are expressed, chap. xxxv. 10, of which place this is a repetition. And from comparing both together it appears that the ו *vau* in this place is become by mistake in the present text final ן *nun* of the preceding word.

Verse 13. *Of the oppressor, as if he, &c.*]

A. M. cir. 3292 B. C. cir. 712 Olymp. XVII. 1 cir. annum NumæPompilii, R. Roman., 4

foundations of the earth; and hast
feared continually every day because
of the fury of the oppressor,
as if he [h]were ready to destroy?
[i]and where *is* the fury of the oppressor?

14 The captive exile hasteneth that he may
be loosed, [k]and that he should not die in the
pit, nor that his bread should fail.

15 But I *am* the LORD thy God, that [l]divided
the sea, whose waves roared: The
LORD of hosts *is* his name.

16 And [m]I have put my words in thy mouth,
and [n]I have covered thee in the shadow of
mine hand, [o]that I may plant the heavens,
and lay the foundations of the earth, and say
unto Zion, Thou *art* my people.

17 [p]Awake, awake, stand up, O Jerusalem,
which [q]hast drunk at the hand of the LORD
the cup of his fury; [r]thou hast
drunken the dregs of the cup of
trembling, *and* wrung *them* out.

A. M. cir. 3292 B. C. cir. 712 Olymp. XVII. 1 cir. annum NumæPompilii, R. Roman., 4

18 *There is* none to guide her
among all the sons *whom* she hath brought
forth; neither *is there any* that taketh her
by the hand of all the sons *that* she hath
brought up.

19 [s]These two *things* [t]are come unto thee;
who shall be sorry for thee? desolation, and
[u]destruction, and the famine, and the sword:
[v]by whom shall I comfort thee?

20 [w]Thy sons have fainted, they lie at the
head of all the streets, as a wild bull in a
net: they are full of the fury of the LORD,
the rebuke of thy God.

21 Therefore hear now this, thou afflicted,
and drunken, [x]but not with wine.

---

[h]Or, *made* himself *ready*——[i]Job xx. 7——[k]Zech. ix. 11——[l]Psa. lxxiv. 13; Job xxvi. 12; Jer. xxxi. 35 [m]Deut. xviii. 18; chap. lix. 21; John iii. 34——[n]Chap. xlix. 2——[o]Chap. lxv. 17; lxvi. 22——[p]Chap. lii. 1 [q]Job xxi. 20; Jer. xxi. 15, 16

[r]See Deut. xxviii. 28, 34; Psa. lx. 3; lxxv. 8; Ezek. xxiii. 32, 33, 34; Zech. xii. 2; Rev. xiv. 10——[s]Chap. xlvii. 9——[t]Hebrew, *happened*——[u]Hebrew, *breaking*——[v]Amos vii. 2——[w]Lam. ii. 11, 12——[x]See ver. 17; Lam. iii. 15

"The כ *caph* in כאשר *keasher* seems clearly to have changed its situation from the end of the preceding word to the beginning of this; or rather, to have been omitted by mistake there, because it was here. That it was there the *Septuagint* show by rendering המציקך *hammetsikech* θλιβοντος σε, *of him that oppressed* thee. And so they render this word in both its places in this verse. The *Vulgate* also has the pronoun in the first instance; *furoris ejus qui* te *tribulabat.*" Dr. *Jubb.* The correction seems well founded; I have not conformed the translation to it, because it makes little difference in the sense.

Verse 14. *The captive exile hasteneth that he may be loosed*—"He marcheth on with speed, who cometh to set free the captive"] Cyrus, if understood of the temporal redemption from the captivity of Babylon; in the spiritual sense, the Messiah, who comes to open the prison to them that are bound.

Verse 16. *That I may plant the heavens*—"To stretch out the heavens"] In the present text it is לנטע *lintoa, "to plant* the heavens:" the phrase is certainly very obscure, and in all probability is a mistake for לנטות *lintoth.* This latter is the word used in ver. 13 just before, in the very same sentence; and this phrase occurs very frequently in Isaiah, chap. xl. 22, xlii. 5, xliv. 24, xlv. 12; the former in no other place. It is also very remarkable, that in the Samaritan text, Num. xxiv. 6, these two words are twice changed by mistake, one for the other, in the same verse.

Verse 17. *The cup of trembling*] כום התרעלה *cos hattarelah,* "the cup of mortal poison," veneni mortiferi.—MONTAN. This may also allude to the ancient custom of taking off criminals by a cup of poison. Socrates is well known to have been sentenced by the Areopagus to drink a cup of the juice of hemlock, which occasioned his death. See the note on Heb. ii. 9, and see also Bishop Lowth's note on ver. 21.

Verse 19. *These two* things—*desolation, and destruction, and the famine, and the sword*] That is, desolation by famine, and destruction by the sword, taking the terms alternately: of which form of construction see other examples. *De S. Poësi,* Heb. Præl. xix., and Prelim. Dissert. p. xxx. The *Chaldee* paraphrast, not rightly understanding this, has had recourse to the following expedient: "Two afflictions are come upon thee, and when *four* shall come upon thee, *depredation,* and *destruction,* and the *famine,* and the *sword*—" Five MSS. have הרעב *haraab,* without the conjunction ו *vau;* and so the *Septuagint* and *Syriac.*

By whom shall I comfort thee—"Who shall comfort thee"] A MS., the *Septuagint, Syriac, Chaldee,* and *Vulgate* have it in the third person, ינחמך *yenachamech,* which is evidently right.

Verse 20. *As a wild bull in a net: they are full, &c.*—"Like the oryx taken in the toils; drenched to the full"] "Perhaps מכמרה מלאים *michmerah meleim.*" SECKER. The demonstrative ה *he,* prefixed to מלאים *meleim, full,* seems improper in this place.

Verse 21. *Drunken, but not with wine*] *Æschylus* has the same expression:—

Αοινοις εμμανεις θυμωμασι· *Eumen.* 863.

Intoxicated with passion, not with wine.

Schultens thinks that this circumlocution, as he calls it, gradum adfert incomparabiliter majorem; and that it means, not simply *without wine,* but *much more than with wine. Gram. Heb.* p. 182. See his note on Job xxx. 38.

The bold image of the cup of God's wrath, often employed by the sacred writers, (see note

A. M. cir. 3292
B. C. cir. 712
Olymp. XVII. 1
cir. annum
NumæPompilii,
R. Roman., 4

22 Thus saith thy Lord the LORD, and thy God [y]*that* pleadeth the cause of his people, Behold I have taken out of thine hand the cup of trembling, *even* the dregs of the cup of my fury; thou shalt no more drink it again:

23 But [z]I will put it into the hand of them that afflict thee; which have [a]said to thy soul, Bow down, that we may go over: and thou hast laid thy body as the ground, and as the street, to them that went over.

[y]Jer. l. 34——[z]Jer. xxv. 17, 26, 28; Zech. xii. 2

[a]Psa. lxvi. 11, 12

on chap. i. 22,) is nowhere handled with greater force and sublimity than in this passage of Isaiah, ver. 17-23. Jerusalem is represented in person as staggering under the effects of it, destitute of that assistance which she might expect from her children; not one of them being able to support or to lead her. They, abject and amazed, lie at the head of every street, overwhelmed with the greatness of their distress; like the oryx entangled in a net, in vain struggling to rend it, and extricate himself. This is poetry of the first order, sublimity of the highest character.

Plato had an idea something like this: "Suppose," says he, "God had given to men a medicating potion inducing fear, so that the more any one should drink of it, so much the more miserable he should find himself at every draught, and become fearful of every thing both present and future; and at last, though the most courageous of men, should be totally possessed by fear: and afterwards, having slept off the effects of it, should become himself again." *De Leg.* i., near the end. He pursues at large this hypothesis, applying it to his own purpose, which has no relation to the present subject. *Homer* places two vessels at the disposal of Jupiter, one of good, the other of evil. He gives to some a potion mixed of both; to others from the evil vessel only: these are completely miserable. Iliad xxiv. 527-533.

Δοιοι γαρ τε πιθοι κατακειαται εν Διος ουδει
Δωρων, οἱα διδωσι, κακων, ἑτερος δε εαων.
Ὡ μεν καμμιξας δῳη Ζευς τερπικεραυνος,
Αλλοτε μεν τε κακῳ ὁγε κυρεται, αλλοτε δ' εσθλῳ·
Ὡ δε κε των λυγρων δῳη, λωβητον εθηκε.
Και ἑ κακη βουβρωστις επι χθονα διαν ελαυνει·
Φοιτᾳ δ' ουτε θεοισι τετιμενος, ουτι βροτοισιν.

"*Two urns* by Jove's high throne have ever stood,
The source of *evil* one, and one of *good;*
From thence the cup of mortal man he fills,
Blessings to *these*, to *those* distributes *ills;*
To most he *mingles both:* the wretch decreed
To taste the *bad unmixed*, is cursed indeed:
Pursued by wrongs, by meagre famine driven,
He wanders outcast both of earth and heaven."
POPE.

Verse 23. *Them that afflict thee*—"Them who oppress thee"] The *Septuagint*, *Chaldee*, *Syriac*, and *Vulgate* appear to have read מוניך *monayich*, as in chap. xl. 26."—SECKER.

Which have said to thy soul, Bow down—"Who say to thee, Bow down thy body"] A very strong and most expressive description of the insolent pride of eastern conquerors; which, though it may seem greatly exaggerated, yet hardly exceeds the strict truth. An example has already been given of it in the note to chap. xlix. 23. I will here add one or two more. "Joshua called for all the men of Israel; and said unto the captains of the men of war that went with him, Come near, put your feet upon the necks of these kings," Josh. x. 24. "Adonibezek said, Threescore and ten kings, having their thumbs and their great toes cut off, gathered their meat under my table: As I have done, so hath God requited me," Judg. i. 7. The Emperor Valerianus, being through treachery taken prisoner by Sapor king of Persia, was treated by him as the basest and most abject slave: for the Persian monarch commanded the unhappy Roman to bow himself down, and offer him his back, on which he set his foot, in order to mount his chariot or horse, whenever he had occasion.—LACTANTIUS, *De Mort. Persec.* cap. v. AUREL. VICTOR. *Epitome*, cap. xxxii.—L.

CHAPTER LII

Jerusalem, in manifest allusion to the strong figure employed in the close of the preceding chapter, is represented as fallen asleep in the dust, and in that helpless state bound by her enemies. The prophet, with all the ardour natural to one who had such joyful news to communicate, bids her awake, arise, put on her best attire, (holiness to the Lord,) and ascend her lofty seat; and then he delivers the message he had in charge, a very consolatory part of which was, that "no more *should enter into her the uncircumcised and the polluted,*" 1–6. *Awaking from her stupefaction, Jerusalem sees the* messenger *of such joyful tidings on the eminence from which he spied the coming deliverance. She expresses, in beautiful terms, her joy at the news, repeating with peculiar elegance the words of the crier,* 7. *The rapturous intelligence, that Jehovah was returning to resume his residence on his holy mountain, immediately spreads to others on the watch, who all join in the glad acclamation,* 8; *and, in the ardour of their joy, they call to the very ruins of Jerusalem to sing along with them, because Jehovah maketh bare his holy arm in the sight of all the nations, and all the ends of the earth are about to see the salvation of Israel's God,* 9, 10. *To complete the deliverance, they are commanded to march in triumph out of Babylon, earnestly exhorted to have nothing to do with any of her abominations, and assured that Jehovah will guide them in all their way,* 11, 12. *The prophet then passes to the procuring cause of this great blessedness to the house of Israel in particular, and to the world in general, viz., the humiliation, sufferings, death, burial, resurrection, and ascension of Jesus Christ; a very celebrated and clear prophecy, which takes up the remainder of this and the whole of the following chapter.*

A. M. cir. 3292
B. C. cir. 712
Olymp. XVII. 1
cir. annum
NumæPompilii,
R. Roman., 4

AWAKE, [a]awake; put on thy
strength, O Zion; put on thy
beautiful garments, O Jerusalem, [b]the holy city: for [c]hence-
forth there shall no more come into thee the
uncircumcised [d]and the unclean.

2 [e]Shake thyself from the dust; arise, *and*
sit down, O Jerusalem: [f]loose thyself from the
bands of thy neck, O captive daughter of Zion.

3 For thus saith the LORD, [g]ye have sold
yourselves for nought; and ye shall be redeemed without money.

4 For thus saith the Lord GOD,
My people went down aforetime
into [h]Egypt to sojourn there;
and the Assyrian oppressed them
without cause.

A. M. cir. 3292
B. C. cir. 712
Olymp. XVII. 1
cir. annum
NumæPompilii,
R. Roman., 4

5 Now therefore, what have I here, saith the
LORD, that my people is taken away for
nought? they that rule over them make them
to howl, saith the LORD; and my name continually every day *is* [i]blasphemed.

6 Therefore my people shall know my name:
therefore *they shall know* in that day that I

[a]Chap. li. 9, 17——[b]Neh. xi. 1; chap. xlviii. 2; Matt. iv. 5; Rev. xxi. 2——[c]Chap. xxxv. 8; lx. 21; Nah. i. 15——[d]Rev. xxi. 27——[e]See chap. iii. 26; li. 23

[f]Zech. ii. 7——[g]Psa. xliv. 12; chap. xlv. 13; Jer. xv. 13——[h]Gen. xlvi. 6; Acts vii. 14——[i]Ezek. xx. 27; Rom. ii. 24

NOTES ON CHAP. LII

Verse 1. *There shall no more come into thee*—For יבא *yabo*, "shall come," לבא *lebo*, "to come," is the reading of *five* of *Kennicott's* and *two* of *De Rossi's* MSS. This is the better reading, כי לא יוסיף לבא *ki lo yosiph lebo*, "There shall not add to come."

The uncircumcised and the unclean.] Christians have turned many passages of the prophets against the Jews; and it is not to be wondered at, that in support of their obstinate and hopeless cause, they should press a prophecy into their service, and make it speak against the Christians. This *Kimchi* does in this place; for he says, by the uncircumcised, the *Christians* are meant; and by the unclean, the *Turks*. The *Christians* are *uncircumcised;* and the *Turks*, though circumcised, and using many ablutions, are *unclean* in their works.

Verse 2. *Sit down, O Jerusalem*—"Ascend thy lofty seat, O Jerusalem"] The literal rendering here is, according to our English translation, "arise, sit;" on which a very learned person remarks: "So the old versions. But sitting is an expression of mourning in Scripture and the ancients; and doth not well agree with the rising just before." It does not indeed agree, according to our ideas; but, considered in an oriental light, it is perfectly consistent. The common manner of sitting in the eastern countries is upon the ground or the floor with the legs crossed. The people of better condition have the floors of their chambers or divans covered with carpets for this purpose; and round the chamber broad couches, raised a little above the floor, spread with mattresses handsomely covered, which are called sofas. When sitting is spoken of as a posture of more than ordinary state, it is quite of a different kind; and means sitting on high, on a chair of state or throne called the *musnud;* for which a footstool was necessary, both in order that the person might raise himself up to it, and for supporting the legs when he was placed in it. "Chairs," says Sir *John Chardin*, "are never used in Persia, but at the coronation of their kings. The king is seated in a chair of gold set with jewels, three feet high. The chairs which are used by the people in the east are always so high as to make a footstool necessary. And this proves the propriety of the style of Scripture, which always joins the footstool to the throne." (Isa. lxvi. 1; Psa. cx. 1.) *Voyages*, tom. ix. p. 85, 12mo. Besides the six steps to Solomon's throne, there was a footstool of gold fastened to the seat, 2 Chron. ix. 18, which would otherwise have been too high for the king to reach, or to sit on conveniently.

When Thetis comes to wait on Vulcan to request armour for her son, she is received with great respect, and seated on a silver-studded throne, a chair of ceremony, with a footstool:—

> Την μεν επειτα καθεισεν επι θρονου αργυροηλου,
> Καλου, δαιδαλεου· ὑπο δε θρηνυς ποσιν ηεν.
> *Iliad* xviii. 389.

> "High on a throne, with stars of silver graced,
> And various artifice, the queen she placed;
> A footstool at her feet." POPE.

Ὁ γαρ θρονος αυτος μονον ελευθεριος εστι καθεδρα συν ὑποποδιῳ. *Athenæus*, v. 4. "A throne is nothing more than a handsome sort of chair with a footstool."—L.

Verse 4. *Thus saith the Lord God*] אדני יהוה *Adonai Yehovah;* but *Adonai* is wanting in *twelve* of *Kennicott's*, *five* of *De Rossi's*, and two of my own MSS.; and by the *Septuagint* and *Arabic*. Some MSS. have יהוה צבאות *Yehovah tsebaoth*, "Lord of hosts;" and others have יהוה אלהים *Yehovah Elohim*, "Lord God."

Verse 5. *They that rule over them*—"They that are lords over them"] For משלו *moshelo*, singular, in the text, more than a hundred and twenty MSS. (*De Rossi* says, codices innumeri, "numberless copies") have משליו *moshelaiv*, plural, according to the Masoretical correction in the margin; which shows that the Masoretes often superstitiously retained apparent mistakes in the text, even when they had sufficient evidence to authorize the introduction of the true reading.

Make them to howl—"Make their boast of it"] For יהילילו *yeheililu*, "make them to howl," five MSS., (two ancient,) have יהללו *yehalelu*, "make their boast;" which is confirmed by the *Chaldee* paraphrast, *who renders it* משתבחין *mishtabbechin*. *Ulaloo* is not only the cry itself, but also the name of the funeral song of the *Irish*. The *Arabs* have a cry very much resembling this.

Verse 6. *Therefore my people shall know*]

A. M. cir. 3292 B. C. cir. 712 Olymp. XVII. 1 cir. annum NumæPompilii, R. Roman., 4

am he that doth speak: behold,
it is I.
7 [k]How beautiful upon the
mountains are the feet of him
that bringeth good tidings, that publisheth
peace; that bringeth good tidings of good,
that publisheth salvation; that saith unto
Zion, [l]Thy God reigneth!

8 Thy watchmen shall lift up
the voice; with the voice together
shall they sing: for they shall
see eye to eye, when the LORD
shall bring again Zion.
9 Break forth into joy, sing together, ye waste
places of Jerusalem: [m]for the LORD hath comforted
his people, [n]he hath redeemed Jerusalem.

A. M. cir. 3292 B. C. cir. 712 Olymp. XVII. 1 cir. annum NumæPympilli, R. Roman., 4

[k]Nah. i. 15; Rom. x. 15——[l]Psa. xciii. 1; xcvi. 10; xcvii. 1——[m]Chap. li. 3——[n]Chap. xlviii. 20

The word לכן *lachen*, occurring the second time in this verse, seems to be repeated by mistake. It has no force nor emphasis as a repetition; it only embarrasses the construction and the sense. It was not in the copies from which the *Septuagint*, *Syriac*, and *Vulgate* were translated; it was not in the copy of the *Septuagint* from which the *Arabic* was translated; but in the *Aldine* and *Complutensian* editions δια τουτο is repeated; probably so corrected, in order to make it conformable with the Hebrew text.

I am he that doth speak—"I am he, JEHOVAH, that promised"] For הוא *hu*, the Bodleian MS. and another have יהוה *Yehovah;* "For I am JEHOVAH that promised;" and another ancient MS. adds יהוה *Yehovah* after הוא *hu*. The addition of JEHOVAH seems to be right in consequence of what was said in the preceding line, "My people shall know my *name*."

Verse 7. *How beautiful*] The watchmen discover afar off, on the mountains, the messenger bringing the expected and much-wished-for news of the deliverance from the Babylonish captivity. They immediately spread the joyful tidings, ver. 8, and with a loud voice proclaim that JEHOVAH is returning to Zion, to resume his residence on his holy mountain, which for some time he seemed to have deserted. This is the *literal* sense of the place.

"How beautiful on the mountains are the feet of the joyful messenger," is an expression highly poetical: for, how welcome is his arrival! how agreeable are the tidings which he brings!

Nahum, chap. i. 15, who is generally supposed to have lived after Isaiah, has manifestly taken from him this very pleasing image; but the imitation does not equal the beauty of the original:—

"Behold upon the mountain the feet of the joyful messenger,
Of him that announceth peace!
Celebrate, O Judah, thy festivals; perform thy vows:
For no more shall pass through thee the wicked one;
He is utterly cut off."

But it must at the same time be observed that Isaiah's subject is infinitely more interesting and more sublime than that of Nahum; the latter denounces the destruction of the capital of the Assyrian empire, the most formidable enemy of Judah; the ideas of the former are in their full extent evangelical; and accordingly St. Paul has, with the utmost propriety, applied this passage to the preaching of the Gospel, Rom. x. 15. The joyful tidings here to be proclaimed, "Thy God, O Zion, reigneth," are the same that John the Baptist, the messenger of Christ, and Christ himself, published: "The kingdom of heaven is at hand."

From the use made of this by our Lord and the apostles, we may rest assured that the preachers of the Gospel are particularly intended. *Mountains* are put for the whole land of Judea, where the Gospel was first preached. There seems to be an allusion to a battle fought, and the messengers coming to announce the victory, which was so decisive that a *peace* was the consequence, and the king's throne established in the land.

There appear to have been two sorts of *messengers* among the Jews: one sort always employed to bring evil tidings; the other to bring good. The names also and persons of these different messengers appear to have been well known; so that at a distance they could tell, from seeing the messenger, what sort of tidings he was bringing. See a case in point, 2 Sam. xviii. 19-27. Ahimaaz and Cushi running to bring tidings of the defeat of Absalom and his rebel army. *Ahimaaz is a* GOOD *man, and bringeth* GOOD *tidings.*

Verse 8. *Thy watchmen lift up the voice*—"All thy watchmen lift up their voice"] There is a difficulty in the construction of this place which, I think, none of the ancient versions or modern interpreters have cleared up satisfactorily. Rendered word for word it stands thus: "The voice of thy watchmen: they lift up their voice." The sense of the first member, considered as elliptical, is variously supplied by various expositors; by none, as it seems to me, in any way that is easy and natural. I am persuaded there is a mistake in the present text, and that the true reading is כל צפיך *col tsophayich, all thy watchmen*, instead of קול צפיך *kol tsophayich, the voice of thy watchmen*. The mistake was easy from the similitude in sound of the two letters כ *caph* and ק *koph*. And in one MS. the ק *koph* is upon a rasure. This correction perfectly rectifies the sense and the construction.—L.

They shall see eye to eye] May not this be applied to the prophets and apostles; the one predicting, and the other discovering in the prediction the truth of the prophecy. The meaning of both Testaments is best understood by bringing them *face to face.*

When the Lord shall bring again Zion—"When JEHOVAH returneth to Zion"] So the *Chaldee:* כד יתיב שכנתיה לציון *cad yethib shechinteih letsiyon*, "when he shall place the shechinah in Zion." God is considered as having deserted his people during the captivity; and at the restoration, as returning himself with them to Zion, his former habitation. See Psa. lx. 1; Isa. xl. 9, and note.

Verse 9. *He hath redeemed Jerusalem*—"He

A. M. cir. 3292 B. C. cir. 712 Olymp. XVII. 1 cir. annum NumæPompilii, R. Roman., 4

10 [o]The LORD hath made bare
his holy arm in the eyes of all
the nations; and [p]all the ends
of the earth shall see the salvation of our God.
11 [q]Depart ye, depart ye, go ye out from
thence, touch no unclean *thing;* go ye out
of the midst of her; [r]be ye clean,
that bear the vessels of the LORD.
12 For [s]ye shall not go out
with haste, nor go by flight: [t]for
the LORD will go before you; and [u]the God
of Israel *will* [v]*be* your rereward.
13 Behold, [w]my servant shall [x]deal pru-

[o]Psa. xcviii. 2, 3——[p]Luke iii. 6——[q]Chap. xlviii. 20; Jer. l. 8; li. 6, 45; Zech. ii. 6, 7; 2 Cor. vi. 17; Rev. xviii. 4——[r]Lev. xxii. 2, &c.——[s]See Exod. xii. 33, 39——[t]Mic. ii. 13——[u]Num. x. 25; chap. lviii. 8; see Exod. xiv. 19——[v]Heb. *gather you up*——[w]Chap. xlii. 1——[x]Or, *prosper;* chap. liii. 10; Jer. xxiii. 5

hath redeemed Israel."] For the word ירושלם *yerushalaim*, which occurs the second time in this verse, MS. Bodleian and another read ישראל *yisrael.* It is upon a rasure in a third; and left unpointed at first, as suspected, in a fourth. It was an easy mistake, by the transcriber casting his eye on the line above: and the propriety of the correction, both in regard to sense and elegance, is evident.

Verse 11. *Depart ye, depart ye, go ye out from thence*] The Prophet Jeremiah seems to have had his eye on this passage of Isaiah, and to have applied it to a subject directly opposite. It is here addressed by the prophet in a way of encouragement and exhortation to the Jews coming out of Babylon. Jeremiah has given it a different turn, and has thrown it out, as a reproach of the heathen upon the Jews when they were driven from Jerusalem into captivity:—

"Depart; ye are polluted, depart; depart ye,
forbear to touch.
Yea, they are fled, they are removed: they
shall dwell here no more." Lam. iv. 15.

Of the metrical distribution of these lines, see the Prelim. Dissert., p. lviii. note.

Verse 13. *My servant shall deal prudently*] ישכיל *yaskil, shall prosper*, or *act prosperously.* The subject of Isaiah's prophecy, from the fortieth chapter inclusive, has hitherto been, in general, the deliverance of the people of God. This includes in it *three distinct parts;* which, however, have a close connexion with one another; that is, 1. The deliverance of the Jews from the captivity of Babylon; 2. The deliverance of the Gentiles from their miserable state of ignorance and idolatry; and, 3. The deliverance of mankind from the captivity of sin and death. These *three subjects* are subordinate to one another; and the *two* latter are shadowed out under the image of the former. They are covered by it as by a veil; which however is transparent, and suffers them to appear through it. *Cyrus* is expressly named as the immediate agent of God in effecting the first deliverance. A *greater person* is spoken of as the Agent who is to effect the two latter deliverances, called the *servant*, the *elect, of God*, in whom his soul delighteth; *Israel*, in whom God will be glorified. Now these three subjects have a very near relation to one another; for as the *Agent* who was to effect the *two latter* deliverances,—that is, the Messiah,—was to be born a Jew, with particular limitations of *time, family*, and *other circumstances;* the *first deliverance* was necessary in the order of providence, and according to the determinate counsel of God, to the accomplishment of the *two latter deliverances;* and the *second deliverance* was necessary to the *third*, or rather was involved in it, and made an essential part of it. This being the case, Isaiah has not treated the *three subjects* as quite *distinct* and *separate* in a methodical and orderly manner, like a philosopher or a logician, but has taken them in their connective veiw. He has handled them as a prophet and a *poet;* he has *allegorized the former*, and under the image of it has *shadowed out the two latter:* he has thrown them all together, has mixed one with another, has passed from this to that with rapid transitions, and has painted the whole with the strongest and boldest imagery. The *restoration of the Jews* from captivity, the *call of the Gentiles*, the *redemption by Messiah*, have hitherto been handled interchangeably and alternately. *Babylon* has hitherto been kept pretty much in sight; at the same time, that strong intimations of something *much greater* have frequently been thrown in. But here *Babylon* is at once dropped, and I think hardly ever comes in sight again; unless perhaps in chap. lv. 12, and lvii. 14. The prophet's views are almost wholly engrossed by the *superior part* of his subject. He introduces the *Messiah* as appearing at first in the *lowest state of humiliation*, which he had just touched upon before, (chap. l. 5, 6,) and obviates the offence which would be occasioned by it, by declaring the *important* and *necessary cause* of it, and foreshowing the glory which should follow it.

This seems to me to be the nature and the true design of this part of Isaiah's prophecies; and this view of them seems to afford the best method of resolving difficulties, in which expositors are frequently engaged, being much divided between what is called the *literal* and the *mystical sense*, not very properly; for the *mystical* or *spiritual* sense is very often the *most literal* sense of all.

Abarbanel seems to have had an idea of this kind, as he is quoted by Vitringa on chap. xlix. 1, who thus represents his sentiments: Censet Abarbanel prophetam hic *transitum* facere a *liberatione ex exilio Babylonico* ad *liberationem ex exilio Romano;* et, quod hic animadversu dignum est, observat liberationem ex exilio Babylonico esse אות וראיה *oth veraayah*, signum et argumentum liberationis futuræ; atque adeo orationem prophetæ de duabus hisce liberationibus in superioribus concionibus sæpe inter se permisceri. Verba ejus: "Et propterea verba, sive res, in prophetia superiore inter se permixtæ occurrunt; modo *de liberatione Babylonica*, modo *de liberatione extrema* accipiendæ, ut orationis necessitas exigit." Nullum hic vitium, nisi quod redemptionem veram et spiritualem a Messia vero Jesu adductam, non agnoscat. "Abarbanel supposes that the prophet here makes a transition from the de-

A. M. cir. 3292
B. C. cir. 712
Olymp. XVII. 1
cir. annum
NumæPompilii,
R. Roman., 4

dently, [y]he shall be exalted and extolled, and be very high.

14 As many were astonished at thee; his [z]visage was so marred more than any man, and his form more than the sons of men.

15 [a]So shall he sprinkle many nations; [b]the kings shall shut their mouths at him: for *that* [c]which had not been told them shall they see; and *that* which they had not heard shall they consider.

A. M. cir. 3292
B. C. cir. 712
Olymp. XVII. 1
cir. annum
NumæPompilii,
R. Roman., 4

[y]Phil. ii. 9——[z]Psa. xxii. 6, 7; ch. liii. 2, 3——[a]Ezek. xxxvi. 25; Acts ii. 33; Heb. ix. 13, 14——[b]Chap. xlix. 7, 23——[c]Chap. lv. 5; Rom. xv. 21; xvi. 25, 26; Eph. iii. 5, 9

liverance from the *Babylonish* captivity to the deliverance from the *Roman* captivity; and (which is worthy of particular note) he observes that the deliverance from the Babylonish captivity is a *sign* and *pledge* of the future redemption; and that on this account it is we find in the preceding prophecies the circumstances of the two captivities intimately blended together. His words are the following: 'And, therefore, the words or subjects in the foregoing prophecy are very much intermixed; in one passage the redemption from the Babylonish captivity being treated of, in another the redemption from the general dispersion, as may be collected from the obvious import of the words.' No fault can be found with the above remark, except that the true and spiritual redemption procured by Jesus the Messiah is not acknowledged."—L.

Verse 14. *As many were astonished at thee*—"As many were astonished at him"] For עליך *aleicha* read עליו *alaiv.* So the *Syriac, Chaldee,* and *Vulgate* in a MS.; and so likewise two ancient MSS.

His visage was so marred more than any man] Most interpreters understand this of the indignities offered to our blessed Lord: but *Kimchi* gives it another turn, and says, "It means the Jewish people, who are considered by most nations as having an appearance different from all the people of the earth." Poor Jews! they have in general a very disagreeable look, partly affected, and partly through neglect of neatness and cleanliness. Most Christians think they carry the impress of their reprobation on every feature of their face. However this may be, it should never be forgotten that the greatest men that ever flourished as kings, judges, magistrates, lawgivers, heroes, and poets, were of Jewish extraction. *Isaiah* was a Jew; so was *Paul;* and so was Jesus of *Nazareth.*

Verse 15. *So shall he sprinkle many nations*] I retain the common rendering, though I am by no means satisfied with it. "יזה *yazzeh,* frequent in the law, means only to sprinkle: but the water sprinkled is the accusative case; the thing on which has על *al* or אל *el.* Θαυμασονται, *ὁ*, makes the best apodosis. ינהג *yenahag* would do. ינהרו *yinharu* is used chap. ii. 2, Jer. xxxi. 12, chap. li. 14, but is unlike. 'Kings shall shut,' &c., is good, but seems to want a first part."—Secker. Munster translates it, *faciet loqui,* (*de se;*) and in his note thus explains it: יזה *yazzeh proprie significat* spargere *et* stillas disseminare; *hic vero capitur pro* loqui, *et verbum disseminare.* "יזה *yazzeh* properly signifies *to sprinkle,* and *to scatter about drops;* but it here means *to speak,* and *to disseminate the word.*" This is pretty much as the *Rabbins Kimchi* and *Sal. ben Melec* explain it, referring to the expression of "dropping the word." But the same objection lies to this as to the common rendering; it ought to be יזה (דבר) על גוים *yazzeh* (*debar*) *al goyim.* Bishop *Chandler,* Defence, p. 148, says, "that to sprinkle is used for to surprise and astonish, as people are that have much water thrown upon them. And this sense is followed by the *Septuagint.*" This is ingenious, but rather too refined. Dr. *Durell* conjectures that the true reading may be יחזו *yechezu, they shall regard,* which comes near to the θαυμασονται of the *Septuagint,* who seem to give the best sense of any to this place.

"I find in my papers the same conjecture which Dr. *Durell* made from θαυμασονται in the *Septuagint.* And it may be added that חזה *chazah* is used to express 'looking on any thing with admiration,' Psa. xi. 7; xvii. 15; xxvii. 4; lxiii. 2; Cant. vi. 13. It is particularly applied to 'looking on God,' Exod. xxiv. 11, and Job xix. 26. *Gisbert Cuper,* in Observ. lib. ii. 1, though treating on another subject, has some observations which show how nearly ὁραω and θαυμαζω are allied, which, with the peculiar sense of the verb חזה *chazah* above noted, add to the probability of θαυμασονται being the version of יחזו *yechezu* in the text: οἱ δε νυ λαοι Παντες ες αυτον ὁρωσι. *Hesiod., id est, cum veneratione quadam admirantur. Hinc* ὁραω *et* θαυμαζω *junxit Themistius* Or. i. Ειτα παυσονται οἱ ανθρωποι προς σε μονον ὁρωντες, και σε μονον θαυμαζοντες. *Theophrastus in Charact.* c. 3. Ενθυμη ὡς αποβλεπουσιν εις σε οἱ ανθρωποι. Hence the rendering of this verse seems to be—

"So many nations shall look on him with admiration;
Kings shall stop their mouths—" Dr. Jubb.

Does not sprinkling the nations refer to the conversion and baptism of the Gentiles? Many nations shall become proselytes to his religion.

Kings shall shut their mouths at him] His Gospel shall so prevail that all opposition shall be finally overcome; and kings and potentates shall be overwhelmed with confusion, and become speechless before the doctrines of his truth. When they hear these *declared* they shall attentively *consider* them, and their conviction of their truth shall be the consequence.

For that which had not been told them] The mystery of the Gospel so long concealed. See Rom. xv. 21; xvi. 25.

Shall they see] With the eyes of their faith; God enlightening both *organ* and *object.*

And that which they had not heard] The redemption of the world by Jesus Christ; the conversion of the Gentiles, and making them one flock with the converted Jews.—Trapp.

CHAPTER LIII

This chapter foretells the sufferings of the Messiah, the end for which he was to die, and the advantages resulting to mankind from that illustrious event. It begins with a complaint of the infidelity of the Jews, 1; *the offence they took at his mean and humble appearance,* 2; *and the contempt with which they treated him,* 3. *The prophet then shows that the Messiah was to suffer for sins not his own; but that our iniquities were laid on him, and the punishment of them exacted of him, which is the meritorious cause of our obtaining pardon and salvation,* 4–6. *He shows the meekness and placid submission with which he suffered a violent and unjust death, with the circumstances of his dying with the wicked, and being buried with the great,* 7–9; *and that, in consequence of his atonement, death, resurrection, and intercession, he should procure pardon and salvation to the multitudes, insure increasing prosperity to his Church, and ultimately triumph over all his foes,* 10, 11. *This chapter contains a beautiful summary of the most peculiar and distinguishing doctrines of Christianity.*

A. M. cir. 3292 B. C. cir. 712 Olymp. XVII. 1 cir. annum NumæPompilii, R. Roman., 4

WHO [a]hath believed our [b]report?[c] and to whom is [d]the
arm of the LORD revealed?
2 For [e]he shall grow up before
him as a tender plant, and as a root out of a
dry ground: [f]he hath no form
nor comeliness; and when we
shall see him, *there is* no beauty
that we should desire him.
3 [g]He is despised and rejected of men; a

[a]John xii. 38; Rom. x. 16——[b]Or, *doctrine*——[c]Heb. *hearing*——[d]Chap. li. 9; Rom. i. 16; 1 Cor. i. 18

[e]Chap. xi. 1——[f]Chap. lii. 14; Mark ix. 12——[g]Psa. xxii. 6; chap. xlix. 7

NOTES ON CHAP. LIII

That this chapter speaks of none but JESUS must be evident to every unprejudiced reader who has ever heard the history of his sufferings and death. The Jews have endeavoured to apply it to their sufferings in captivity; but, alas for their cause! they can make nothing out in this way. Allowing that it belongs to our blessed Lord, (and the best men and the best scholars agree in this,) then who can read verses 4, 5, 6, 8, 10, without being convinced that his death was a vicarious sacrifice for the sins of mankind? On the *first* and *second* verses of this chapter I have received the following remarks from an unknown hand.

"Verse 1. *Who hath believed our report?*] The report of the *prophets*, of *John the Baptist*, and *Christ's own report of himself*. The Jews did not *receive the report*, and for this reason he was not manifested to them as the promised Messiah. 'He came unto his own, but his own received him not.' Before the FATHER *he grew up as a tender plant:* but to the JEWS he was as *a root out of a dry ground*. 'He hath no form nor comeliness; and when we shall see him, there is no beauty that we should desire him.'

"Verse 2. *For he shall grow up*] Supposes something to have preceded; as it might be asked, what or who shall 'grow up before him,' &c. As the translation now stands, no correct answer can be given to this question. The translation then is wrong, the connexion broken, and the sense obscured. זרוע *zeroa*, translated *the arm*, from the root *zara*. 1. *To sow*, or *plant;* also *seed*, &c. 2. The *limb* which reaches from the shoulder to the hand, called the *arm;* or more properly beginning at the shoulder and ending at the elbow. The translator has given the wrong sense of the word. It would be very improper to say, *the arm of the Lord should grow up before him;* but by taking the word in its former sense, the connexion and metaphor would be restored, and the true sense given to the text. זרע *zera* signifies, not only the *seed of herbs*, but *children, offspring*, or *posterity*. The same word we find Gen. iii. 15, where CHRIST is the Seed promised. See also Gen. xxii. 17, 18; xxvi. 4; xxviii. 14. Hence the SEED of the *woman*, the SEED promised to the patriarchs is, according to Isaiah, the *Seed of the Lord*, the Child born, and the Son given; and according to St. John, 'the Son of God, the only-begotten of the Father, full of grace and truth.' זרע then, in this place, should be understood to mean JESUS CHRIST, and him alone. To speak here of the *manifestation of the arm* or *power* of God would be irregular; but to suppose the text to speak of the *manifestation of Jesus Christ* would be very proper, as the whole of the chapter is written concerning him; particularly his humiliation and sufferings, and the reception he should meet with from the Jewish nation.

"The first verse of this chapter is quoted John xii. 38, and the former part of the same verse Rom. x. 16. But no objection of importance can be brought forward from either of these quotations against the above explanation, as they are quoted to show the unbelief of the Jews in not receiving Christ as the promised Messiah."

He hath no form nor comeliness—"He hath no form nor any beauty"] *Ουκ ειδος αυτῳ, ουδε αξιωμα, ἱνα ειδωμεν αυτον· ουδε θεωρια, ἱνα επιθυμωμεν αυτον.* "He hath no form, nor any beauty, that we should regard him; nor is his countenance such that we should desire him." *Symmachus;* the only one of the ancients that has translated it rightly.

Verse 3. *Acquainted with grief*] For וידוע *vidua, familiar with grief*, eight MSS. and one edition have וידע *veyada, and knowing grief;* the *Septuagint, Syriac*, and *Vulgate* read it ויודע *veyodea*.

We hid as it were our faces from him—"As one that hideth his face from us"] For וכמסתר *uchemaster, four* MSS. (*two* ancient) have וכמסתיר *uchemastir, one* MS. ומסתיר *umastir*. For פנים *panim, two* MSS. have פניו *panaiv;* so likewise the *Septuagint* and *Vulgate*. Mourners covered up the lower part of their faces, and their heads, 2 Sam. xv. 30; Ezek. xxix. 17; and lepers were commanded by the law, Lev. xii. 45, to cover their upper lip. From which circumstance it seems that the *Vulgate, Aquila, Symmachus*, and the Jewish commenta-

A. M. cir. 3292
B. C. cir. 712
Olymp. XVII. 1
cir. annum
NumæPompilii,
R. Roman., 4

man of sorrows, and [h]acquainted
with grief: and [i]we [k]hid as it
were *our* faces from him; he
was despised, and [l]we esteemed
him not.
4 Surely [m]he hath borne our griefs, and
carried our sorrows: yet we did esteem him
stricken, smitten of God, and afflicted.
5 But he *was* [n]wounded [o]for our transgressions, *he was* bruised for our iniquities: the
chastisement of our peace *was* upon him; and
with his [p]stripes [q]we are healed.
6 [r]All we like sheep have gone
astray; we have turned every one
to his own way; and the LORD [s]hath
laid on him the iniquity of us all.

A. M. cir. 3292
B. C. cir. 712
Olymp. XVII. 1
cir. annum
NumæPompilii,
R. Roman., 4

7 He was oppressed, and he was afflicted,
yet [t]he opened not his mouth: [u]he is
brought as a lamb to the slaughter, and as a
sheep before her shearers is dumb, so he
openeth not his mouth.
8 [v]He was taken from prison and from judgment: and who shall declare his generation?
for [w]he was cut off out of the land of the

[h]Heb. iv. 15——[i]Or, *he hid as it were* his *face from us* [k]Heb. *as a hiding of faces from him*, or *from us*——[l]John i. 10, 11——[m]Matt. viii. 17; Heb. ix. 28; 1 Pet. ii. 24 [n]Or, *tormented*——[o]Rom. iv. 25; 1 Cor. xv. 3; 1 Pet. iii. 18——[p]1 Pet. ii. 24

[q]Heb. *bruise*——[r]Psa. cxix. 176; 1 Pet. ii. 25——[s]Heb. *hath made the iniquities of us all to meet on him*——[t]Matt. xxvi. 63; xxvii. 12, 14; Mark xiv. 61; xv. 5; 1 Pet. ii. 23 [u]Acts viii. 32——[v]Or, *He was taken away by distress and judgment; but*, &c.——[w]Dan. ix. 26

tors have taken the word נגוע *nagua*, *stricken*, in the next verse, as meaning stricken with the *leprosy:* εν αφη οντα, *Sym.;* αφημενον, *Aq.; leprosum*, *Vulg.* So my old MS. Bible. I will insert the whole passage as curious:—

There is not schap to him, ne fairnesse,
And we seegen him, and he was not of sigte,
And we desiriden him dispisid; and the last of men:
Man of souaris and witing infirmitie;
And as hid his cheer and despisid;
Wherfor ne we settiden bi him:
Verili our seeknesse he toke and our sorewis he bair,
And we helden him as leprous and smyten of God, and meekid;
He forsoth wounded is for our wickednesse,
Defoulid is for our hidous giltis
The discipline of our pese upon him,
And with his wanne wound we ben helid.

Verse 4. *Surely he hath borne our griefs*—"Surely our infirmities he hath borne"] *Seven* MSS. (*two* ancient) and *three* editions have חליינו *cholayeynu* in the plural number.

And carried our sorrows—"And our sorrows, he hath carried them"] *Seventeen* MSS. (*two* ancient) of Dr. *Kennicott's*, *two* of *De Rossi's*, and *two* editions have the word הוא *hu*, *he*, before סבלם *sebalam*, "carrieth them," in the text; *four* other MSS. have it in the margin. This adds force to the sense, and elegance to the construction.

Verse 5. *The chastisement of our peace*—"The chastisement by which our peace is effected"] *Twenty-one* MSS. and *six* editions have the word fully and regularly expressed, שלמינו *shelomeynu;* pacificationum nostrarum, "our pacification;" that by which we are brought into a state of peace and favour with God. *Ar. Montan.*

Verse 6. *The iniquity of us all.*] For עון *avon*, "iniquity," the ancient interpreters read עונות *avonoth*, "iniquities," plural; and so the *Vulgate* in MS. Blanchini. And the Lord hath הפגיע בו *hiphgia bo*, caused to meet in him the iniquities of us all. He was the subject on which all the rays collected on the focal point fell. These fiery rays, which should have fallen on all mankind, diverged from Divine justice to the east, west, north, and south, were deflected from them, and *converged* in him. So the Lord hath caused to meet in him the punishment due to the iniquities of ALL.

Verse 8. *And who shall declare his generation*—"And his manner of life who would declare"] A learned friend has communicated to me the following passages from the Mishna, and the Gemara of Babylon, as leading to a satisfactory explication of this difficult place. It is said in the former, that before any one was punished for a capital crime, proclamation was made before the prisoner by the public crier, in these words: כל מי שיודע לו זכות יבא וילמד עליו *col mi shioda lo zachoth yabo vayilmad alaiv*, "whosoever knows any thing of this man's innocence, let him come and declare it." Tract. Sandhedrim. Surenhus. Part iv. p. 233. On which passage the Gemara of Babylon adds, that "before the death of Jesus this proclamation was made for forty days; but no defence could be found." On which words Lardner observes: "It is truly surprising to see such falsities, contrary to well-known facts." Testimonies, Vol. I. p. 198. The report is certainly false; but this false report is founded on the supposition that there was such a custom, and so far confirms the account given from the Mishna. The Mishna was composed in the middle of the second century according to Prideaux; Lardner ascribes it to the year of Christ 180.

Casaubon has a quotation from Maimonides which farther confirms this account:—Exercitat. in Baronii Annales, Art. lxxvi. Ann. 34. Num. 119. Auctor est Maimonides in Perek xiii. ejus libri ex opere Jad, solitum fieri, ut cum reus, sententiam mortis passus, a loco judicii exibat ducendus ad supplicium, præcedoret ipsum הכרוז κηρυξ, præco; et hæc verba diceret: *Ille* exit occidendus morte *illa*, quia transgressus est transgressione *illa*, in loco *illo*, tempore *illo*, et sunt ejus rei testes *ille* et *ille*. Qui noverit aliquid ad ejus innocentiam probandam, veniat, et loquatur pro eo. "It was customary when sentence of death was passed upon a criminal, and he was led out from the seat of judgment to the place of punishment, a crier went before, and spoke as follows:—'This man is going out to suffer death by —— because he has transgressed by —— such a transgression, in such a place, in such a time; and

A. M. cir. 3292
B. C. cir. 712
Olymp. XVII. 1
cir. annum
NumæPompilii,
R. Roman., 4

living: for the transgression of my people [x]was he stricken.

9 [y]And he made his grave with the wicked, and with the rich in his [z]death; because he had done no violence, neither *was any* [a]deceit in his mouth.

[x]Heb. was *the stroke upon him*——[y]Matt. xxvii. 57, 58, 60——[z]Heb. *deaths*——[a]1 Pet. ii. 22; 1 John iii. 5

the witnesses against him are ——. He who may know any thing relative to his innocence, let him come and speak in his behalf.' "

Now it is plain from the history of the four Evangelists, that in the trial and condemnation of Jesus no such rule was observed; though, according to the account of the Mishna, it must have been in practice at that time, no proclamation was made for any person to bear witness to the innocence and character of Jesus; nor did any one voluntarily step forth to give his attestation to it. And our Saviour seems to refer to such a custom, and to claim the benefit of it, by his answer to the high priest, when he asked him of his disciples and of his doctrine: "I spoke openly to the world; I ever taught in the synagogue and in the temple, whither the Jews always resort; and in secret have I said nothing. Why askest thou me? ask them who heard me, what I have said unto them: behold, they know what I said;" John xviii. 20, 21. This, therefore, was one remarkable instance of hardship and injustice, among others predicted by the prophet, which our Saviour underwent in his trial and sufferings.

St. Paul likewise, in similar circumstances, standing before the judgment seat of Festus, seems to complain of the same unjust treatment; that no one was called, or would appear, to vindicate his character. "My manner of life (την βιωσιν μου, דורי *dori*, 'my generation') from my youth, which was at the first among my own nation at Jerusalem, know all the Jews, who knew me from the beginning, *if they would testify;* that after the straitest sect of our religion I lived a Pharisee;" Acts xxvi. 4, 5.

דור *dor* signifies age, duration, the time which one man or many together pass in this world, in this place; the course, tenor, or manner of life. The verb דור *dor* signifies, according to Castell, ordinatam vitam sive ætatem egit, ordinavit, ordine constituit. "He passed a certain course of life, he ordained," &c. In Arabic, *curavit, administravit,* "he took care of, administered to."

Was he stricken—"He was smitten to death"] The *Septuagint* read למות *lemaveth*, εις θανατον, "to death." And so the *Coptic* and *Saidic* Versions, from the *Septuagint;* MSS. St. Germain de Prez.

"Origen," (*Contra* Celsum, lib. i. p. 370, edit. 1733,) after having quoted at large this prophecy concerning the Messiah, "tells us, that having once made use of this passage in a dispute against some that were accounted wise among the Jews, one of them replied, that the words did not mean one man, but *one people*, the *Jews*, who were smitten of God and dispersed among the Gentiles for their conversion; that he then urged many parts of this prophecy to show the absurdity of this interpretation, and that he seemed to press them the hardest by this sentence, απο των ανομιων του λαου μου ηχθη εις θανατον, 'for the iniquity of my people was he smitten to death.' " Now as Origen, the author of the Hexapla, must have understood Hebrew, we cannot suppose that he would have urged this last quotation as so decisive if the Greek Version had not agreed here with the Hebrew text; nor that these wise Jews would have been at all distressed by this quotation, unless their Hebrew text had read agreeably to εις θανατον, "to death," on which the argument principally depended; for, by quoting it immediately, they would have triumphed over him, and reprobated his Greek version. This, whenever they could do it, was their constant practice in their disputes with the Christians. Jerome, in his Preface to the Psalms, says, Nuper cum Hebræo disputans, quædam pro Domino Salvatore de Psalmis testimonia protulisti: volensque ille te illudere, per sermones fere singulos asserebat, non ita haberi in Hebræo, ut tu de LXX. opponebas. "Lately disputing with a Hebrew,—thou advancedst certain passages out of the Psalms which bear testimony to the Lord the Saviour; but he, to elude thy reasoning, asserted that almost all thy quotations have an import in the Hebrew text different from what they had in the Greek." And Origen himself, who laboriously compared the Hebrew text with the *Septuagint*, has recorded the necessity of arguing with the Jews from such passages only as were in the *Septuagint* agreeable to the Hebrew: ἱνα προς Ιουδαιοις διαλεγομενοι μη προφερωμεν αυτοι τα μη κειμενα εν τοις αντιγραφοις αυτων, και ἱνα συγχρησωμεθα τοις φερομενοις παρ' εκεινοις. See *Epist. ad African.* p. 15, 17. Wherefore as Origen had carefully compared the Greek version of the *Septuagint* with the Hebrew text, and speaks of the contempt with which the Jews treated all appeals to the Greek version where it differed from their Hebrew text; and as he puzzled and confounded the learned Jews by urging upon them the reading εις θανατον, "unto death," in this place; it seems almost impossible not to conclude, both from Origen's argument and the silence of his Jewish adversaries, that the Hebrew text at that time actually had למות *lemaveth*, "to death," agreeably to the version of the *Septuagint*.—Dr. *Kennicott.*

Verse 9. *With the rich in his death*—"With the rich man was his tomb"] It may be necessary to introduce Bishop *Lowth's* translation of this verse before we come to his very satisfactory criticisms:—

And his grave was appointed with the wicked;
But with the rich man was his tomb:
Although he had done no wrong,
Neither was there any guile in his mouth.

Among the various opinions which have been given on this passage, I have no doubt in giving my assent to that which makes the ב *beth* in במותיו *bemothaiv* radical, and renders it *excelsa sua*. This is mentioned by Aben Ezra as received by some in his time; and has been long since approved by Schindler, Drusius, and many other learned Christian interpreters.

The most simple tombs or monuments of old

A. M. cir. 3292
B. C. cir. 712
Olymp. XVII. 1
cir. annum
NumæPompilii,
R. Roman., 4

10 Yet it pleased the LORD to
bruise him; he hath put *him* to
grief: [b]when thou shalt make
his soul [c]an offering for sin, he
shall see *his* seed, [d]he shall prolong *his* days, and [e]the pleasure
of the LORD shall prosper in his
hand.

[b]Or, *when his soul shall make an offering*——[c]2 Cor. v. 21; 1 Pet. ii. 24

[d]Romans vi. 9——[e]Ephesians i. 5, 9; 2 Thess. i. 11

consisted of hillocks of earth heaped up over the grave; of which we have numerous examples in our own country, generally allowed to be of very high antiquity. The Romans called a monument of this sort very properly *tumulus;* and the Hebrews as properly במות *bamoth,* "high place," for that is the form of the noun in the singular number; and *sixteen* MSS. and the *two* oldest editions express the word fully in this place, במותיו *bamothaiv.* Tumulus et collem et sepulchrum fuisse significat. Potest enim tumulus sine sepulchro interpretatione collis interdum accipi. Nam et terræ congestio super ossa tumulus dicitur. "*Tumulus* signifies a sepulchre with a hillock of earth raised over it. The word is sometimes restrained to the bank of earth; for the heaping up of the earth over the bones is named the *tumulus.*"—Servius, Æn. iii. 22. And to make the tumulus still more elevated and conspicuous, a pillar or some other ornament was often erected upon it:—

Τυμβον χευαντες, και επι στηλην ερυσαντες, .
Πηξαμεν ακροτατῳ τυμβῳ ευηρες ερετμον.
Odyss. xii. 14.

"A rising tomb, the silent dead to grace,
Fast by the roarings of the main we place;
The rising tomb a *lofty column* bore,
And *high above it* rose the *tapering oar.*"
POPE.

The tomb therefore might with great propriety be called the *high place.* The Hebrews might also call such a tomb במות *bamoth,* from the situation, for they generally chose to erect them on *eminences.* The sepulchre of Joseph of Arimathea, in which the body of Christ was laid, was upon a hill, Mount Calvary. See chap. xxii. 16, and the note there.

"It should be observed that the word במותיו *bamothaiv* is not formed from במות *bamoth,* the plural of במה *bamah,* the feminine noun, but from במותים *bamothim,* the plural of a masculine noun, במות *bamoth.* This is noted because these two nouns have been negligently confounded with one another, and absurdly reduced to one by very learned men. So *Buxtorf,* lex. in voc. במה *bamah,* represents במותי *bamotey,* though plainly without any pronoun suffixed, as it governs the word ארץ *arets* following it, as only another form of במות *bamoth;* whereas the truth is, that במות *bamoth* and במותים *bamothim* are different words, and have through the whole Bible very different significations; במה *bamah,* whether occurring in the singular or plural number, always signifying a *place* or *places* of *worship;* and במותים *bamothim* always signifying *heights.* Thus in Deut. xxxii. 13; Isa. lviii. 14; Amos iv. 13; and Micah i. 3, במותי ארץ *bamothey arets* signifies 'the heights of the earth;' Isa. xiv. 14, במותי עב *bamothey ab,* 'the heights of the clouds;' and in Job ix. 8, במותי ים *bamothey yam,* 'the heights of the sea,' i. e., the high waves of the sea, as Virgil calls a wave *præruptus aquæ mons,* 'a broken mountain of water.' These being all the places where this word occurs without a suffix, the sense of it seems nearly determined by them. It occurs in other instances with a pronoun suffixed, which confirm this signification. Unluckily, our English Bible has not distinguished the feminine noun במה *bamah* from the masculine singular noun במות *bamoth;* and has consequently always given the signification of the latter to the former, always rendering it a *high place;* whereas the true sense of the word appears plainly to be, in the very numerous passages in which it occurs, 'a place of worship,' or 'a sacred court,' or 'a sacred inclosure;' whether appropriated to the worship of idols or to that of the true God, for it is used of both, *passim.* Now as the Jewish graves are shown, from 2 Chron. xxxii. 33, and Isa. xxii. 16, to have been in high situations, to which may be added the custom of another eastern nation from *Osbeck's* Travels, who says, vol. i. p. 339, 'the Chinese graves are made on the side of hills;' 'his heights' becomes a very easy metaphor to express 'his sepulchre.'"—JUBB.

The exact completion of this prophecy will be fully shown by adding here the several circumstances of the burial of Jesus, collected from the accounts of the evangelists:—

"There was a rich man of Arimathea, named Joseph, a member of the sanhedrin, and of a respectable character, who had not consented to their counsel and act; he went to Pilate and begged the body of Jesus: and he laid it in his own new tomb, which had been hewn out of the rock, near to the place where Jesus was crucified; having first wound it in fine linen with spices, as the manner of the Jews was to bury the rich and great."

It has been supposed that קברו *kibro, his grave,* and במתיו *bemothaiv, in his death,* may have been transposed, as also the prefix ב *be* originally placed before רשעים *reshaim, the wicked.* Thus:—

ויתן ברשעים את מתיו
mothaiv eth bireshayim vaiyitten

ואת עשיר קברו
kibro ashir veeth

Yea, his death was appointed among the wicked,
And with a rich man, his tomb.

By these alterations it is supposed the text would be freed from all embarrassment. But see the preceding notes of Bishop *Lowth,* and the various readings of *De Rossi,* in loc.

Verse 10. *To grief*—"With affliction"] For החלי *hecheli,* the verb, the construction of which seems to be hard and inelegant in this place, the *Vulgate* reads בחלי *bocholi,* in infirmitate, "with infirmity."

When thou shalt make his soul—"If his soul

A. M. cir. 3292
B. C. cir. 712
Olymp. XVII. 1
cir. annum
NumæPompilii,
R. Roman., 4

11 He shall see of the travail
of his soul, *and* shall be satisfied: [f]by his knowledge
shall [g]my righteous [h]servant[i]
justify many; [k]for he shall bear their
iniquities.
12 [l]Therefore will I divide him *a portion*
with the great, [m]and he shall
divide the spoil with the strong;
because he hath poured out his
soul unto death: and he was
[n]numbered with the transgressors; and he
bare the sin of many, and [o]made intercession
for the transgressors.

[f]John xvii. 3; 2 Pet. i. 3——[g]1 John ii. 1——[h]Chap. xlii. 1; xlix. 3——[i]Rom. v. 18, 19——[k]Ver. 4, 5——[l]Psa. ii. 8; Phil. ii. 9——[m]Col. ii. 15——[n]Mark xv. 28; Luke xxii. 37——[o]Luke xxiii. 34; Rom. viii. 34; Heb. vii. 25; ix. 24; 1 John ii. 1

shall make"] For תשים *tasim*, a MS. has תשם *tasem*, which may be taken passively, "If his soul shall be made—" agreeably to some copies of the *Septuagint*, which have δωται. See likewise the *Syriac*.

When thou shalt make his soul an offering] The word נפש *nephesh, soul*, is frequently used in *Hebrew* to signify *life*. Throughout the New Testament the salvation of men is uniformly attributed to the *death* of Christ.

He shall see his *seed*] True converts, genuine Christians.

He shall prolong his *days*] Or this spiritual progeny shall prolong their days, i. e., Christianity shall endure to the end of time.

And the pleasure of the Lord] To have all men saved and brought to the knowledge of the truth.

Shall prosper in his hand.] Shall go on in a state of progressive prosperity; and so completely has this been thus far accomplished, that every succeeding century has witnessed more Christianity in the world than the preceding, or any former one.

Verse 11. *Shall be satisfied*—"And be satisfied"] The *Septuagint, Vulgate, Syriac*, and a MS. add the conjunction to the verb, וישבע *vaiyisba*.

Shall my righteous servant justify—"Shall my servant justify"] Three MSS., (two of them ancient,) omit the word צדיק *tsaddik;* it seems to be only an imperfect repetition, by mistake, of the preceding word. It makes a solecism in this place; for according to the constant usage of the Hebrew language, the adjective, in a phrase of this kind, ought to follow the substantive; and צדיק עבדי *tsaddik abdi*, in Hebrew, would be as absurd as "shall my *servant righteous* justify," in English. Add to this, that it makes the hemistich too long.

Verse 12. *He bare the sin of many*] רבים *rabbim*, the *multitudes*, the *many that* were *made sinners* by *the offences of one;* i. e., the whole human race; for *all have sinned —all have fallen;* and for all that have sinned, and for all that have fallen, Jesus Christ died. The רבים *rabbim* of the *prophet* answers to the οἱ πολλοι, of the apostle, Rom. v. 15, 19. As the πολλοι of the apostle means all that have sinned; so the רבים *rabbim* of the prophet means those for whom Christ died; i. e., all that have sinned.

And made intercession for the transgressors.] For יפגיע *yaphgia*, in the future, a MS. has הפגיע *hiphgia*, preterite, rather better, as agreeable with the other verbs immediately preceding in the sentence.

He made intercession for the transgressors.— This was literally fulfilled at his death, "Father, forgive them; they know not what they do!" Luke xxiii. 34. And to make intercession for transgressors is one part of his *mediatorial* office. Heb. vii. 25, and ix. 24.

In this chapter the *incarnation, preaching, humiliation, rejection, sufferings, death, atonement, resurrection*, and *mediation* of Jesus Christ are all predicted, together with the prevalence of his Gospel, and the *extension* of his *kingdom* through all ages.

CHAPTER LIV

Some suppose this chapter to have been addressed to the Gentiles; some, to the Jewish Church; and some, to the Christian, in its first stage. On comparing the different parts of it, particularly the seventh *and* eighth *verses, with the remainder, the most obvious import of the prophecy will be that which refers it to the future conversion of the Jews, and to the increase and prosperity of that nation, when reconciled to God after their long rejection, when their glory and security will far surpass what they were formerly in their most favoured state,* 1–17.

A. M. cir. 3292
B. C. cir. 712
Olymp. XVII. 1
cir annum
NumæPompilii,
R. Roman., 4

[a]SING, O barren, thou *that*
didst not bear; break forth
into singing, and cry aloud, thou
that didst not travail with child:
for [b]more *are* the children of
the desolate than the children
of the married wife, saith the
LORD.

[a]Zeph. iii. 14; Gal. iv. 27——[b]1 Sam. ii. 5

NOTES ON CHAP. LIV

Verse 1. *Sing, O barren, thou* that *didst not bear*—"Shout for joy, O thou barren, that didst not bear"] The Church of God under the Old Testament, confined within the narrow bounds of the Jewish nation, and still more so in respect of the very small number of true be-

A. M. cir. 3292
B. C. cir. 712
Olymp. XVII. 1
cir. annum
NumæPompilii,
R. Roman., 4

2 [c]Enlarge the place of thy tent, and let them stretch forth the curtains of thine habitations; spare not, lengthen thy cords, and strengthen thy stakes;

3 For thou shalt break forth on the right hand and on the left: [d]and thy seed shall inherit the Gentiles, and make the desolate cities to be inhabited.

4 Fear not; for thou shalt not be ashamed: neither be thou confounded; for thou shalt not be put to shame: for thou shalt forget the shame of thy youth, and shalt not remember the reproach of thy widowhood any more.

5 [e]For thy Maker *is* thine Husband; the [f]LORD of hosts *is* his name; and thy Redeemer the Holy One of Israel; [g]The God of the whole earth shall he be called.

6 For the LORD [h]hath called thee as a woman forsaken and grieved in spirit, and a wife of youth, when thou wast refused, saith thy God.

7 [i]For a small moment have I forsaken thee; but with great mercies will I gather thee.

8 In a little wrath I hid my face from thee for a moment; [k]but with everlasting kindness will I have mercy on thee, saith the LORD thy Redeemer.

A. M. cir. 3292
B. C. cir. 712
Olymp. XVII. 1
cir. annum
NumæPompilii,
R. Roman., 4

9 For this *is as* the waters of [l]Noah unto me: for *as* I have sworn that the waters of Noah should no more go over the earth; so have I sworn that I would not be wroth with thee, nor rebuke thee.

10 For [m]the mountains shall depart, and the hills be removed: [n]but my kindness shall not depart from thee, neither shall the covenant of my peace be removed, saith the LORD that hath mercy on thee.

11 O thou afflicted, tossed with tempest, *and* not comforted, behold, I will lay thy stones with [o]fair colours, and lay thy foundations with sapphires.

12 And I will make thy windows of agates, and thy gates of carbuncles, and all thy borders of pleasant stones.

13 And all thy children *shall be* [p]taught of the LORD; and [q]great *shall be* the peace of thy children.

14 In righteousness shalt thou be established:

[c]Ch. xlix. 19, 20——[d]Ch. lv. 5; lxi. 9——[e]Jer. iii. 14——[f]Luke i. 32——[g]Zech. xiv. 9; Rom. iii. 29——[h]Ch. lxii. 4——[i]Psa. xxx. 5; ch. xxvi. 20; lx. 10; 2 Cor. iv. 17——[k]Ch. lv. 3; Jer. xxxi. 3——[l]Gen. viii. 21; ix. 11; ch. lv. 11; see Jer. xxxi. 35, 36——[m]Psa. xlvi. 2; ch. li. 6; Matt. v. 18——[n]Psa. lxxxix. 33, 34——[o]1 Chron. xxix. 2; Rev. xxi. 18, &c.——[p]Ch. xi. 9; Jer. xxxi. 54; John vi. 45; 1 Cor. ii. 10; 1 Thess. iv. 9; 1 John ii. 20——[q]Psa. cxix. 165

lievers, and which sometimes seemed to be deserted of God her husband, is *the barren woman, that did not bear*, and was *desolate.* She is exhorted to rejoice, and to express her joy in the strongest manner, on the reconciliation of her husband, (see ver. 6,) and on the accession of the Gentiles to her family. The converted Gentiles are all along considered by the prophet as a new accession of adopted children, admitted into the original Church of God, and united with it. See chap. xlix. 20, 21.

Verse 4. *For thou shalt forget the shame of thy youth*] That is, "The bondage of Egypt: *widowhood*, the captivity of Babylon."—*Secker.*

Verse 7. *For a small moment*—"In a little anger"] So the *Chaldee* and *Syriac*, either reading רגז *regaz*, for רגע *rega;* or understanding the latter word as meaning the same with the former, which they both make use of. See Psa. xxx. 5, xxxv. 20, in the *Septuagint*, where they render רגע *rega* by οργη, *anger.*

Verse 8. *I hid my face from thee for a moment*] The word רגע *rega* is omitted by the *Septuagint*, *Syriac*, and two MSS. of *Kennicott's*, and two of *De Rossi's*. It seems to embarrass rather than to help the sentence. Forte reponi debet pro שצף *shetseph*, quod potest a קצף *ketseph* errore scribæ originem duxisse. "Perhaps it ought to be substituted for שצף *shetseph*, an error probably made by some scribe from its similarity to קצף *ketseph.*"—*Secker.*

Thy Redeemer—גאלך *goalech:* but for this word three of *De Rossi's* MSS. have מרחמך *merachamech, thy commiserator.*

Verse 9. *For this* is as *the waters of Noah unto me*—"The same will I do now, as in the days of Noah"] כימי *kimey*, in one word, in a MS., and some editions; and so the *Syriac*, *Chaldee*, *Vulgate*, *Symmachus*, *Theodotion*, *Abarbanel*, *Sal. ben Melec*, and *Kimchi* acknowledge that their copies vary in this place. It is certain that these two words כי מי *ki mey*, were written formerly as *one.* Taken as two כי מי *ki mey*, they signify *for* as *the waters* —when as one, כימי *kimey*, they signify *as the days.* This latter reading is found in about four of *Kennicott's* and *De Rossi's* MSS. In one of my own it appears to have been intended as *one word:* but he who added the *points*, which are by a much *later hand* than the MS. itself, has pointed the letters so as to make the *two words* which are commonly found in the text. For *the waters*, *Symmachus*, *Theodotion*, the *Syriac*, *Vulgate*, and *Arabic* have *days.* The former seems to make the best sense; and the ancient *Versions*, except the *Septuagint*, support it.

Verse 11. *Behold, I will lay thy stones*—"Behold, I lay thy stones"] These seem to be general images to express beauty, magnificence, purity, strength, and solidity, agreeably to the ideas of the eastern nations; and to have never been intended to be strictly scrutinized, or minutely and particularly explained, as if they

A. M. cir. 3292
B. C. cir. 712
Olymp. XVII. 1
cir. annum
NumæPompilii,
R. Roman., 4

thou shalt be far from oppression; for thou shalt not fear: and from terror; for it shall not come near thee.

15 Behold, they shall surely gather together, *but* not by me: whosoever shall gather together against thee shall fall for thy sake.

16 Behold, I have created the smith that bloweth the coals in the fire, and that bringeth forth an instrument for his work; and I have created the waster to destroy.

17 No weapon that is formed against thee shall prosper; and every tongue *that* shall rise against thee in judgment thou shalt condemn. This *is* the heritage of the servants of the LORD, [r]and their righteousness *is* of me, saith the LORD.

[r]Chap. xlv. 24, 25; Psa. iv. 1; xxxv. 28; li. 14; lxix. 27; lxxxix. 16; cxxxii. 9

had each of them some precise, moral, or spiritual meaning. Tobit, in his prophecy of the final restoration of Israel, describes the New Jerusalem in the same oriental manner: "For Jerusalem shall be built up with sapphires, and emeralds, and precious stones; thy walls, and towers, and battlements, with pure gold. And the streets of Jerusalem shall be paved with beryl, and carbuncle, and stones of ophir." Tob. xiii. 16, 17. Compare also Rev. xxi. 18-21.

Verse 15. *Shall fall for thy sake*—"Shall come over to thy side."] For יפול *yippol*, twenty-eight MSS. (eight ancient) have יפל *yipal*, in its more common form. For the meaning of the word in this place, see Jer. xxxvii. 13.

CHAPTER LV

This chapter first displays the fulness, freeness, excellence, and everlasting nature of the blessings of the Gospel, and foretells again the enlargement of Messiah's kingdom, 1–5. *This view leads the prophet to exhort all to seize the precious opportunity of sharing in such blessings, which were not, however, to be expected without repentance and reformation,* 6, 7. *And as the things now and formerly predicted were so great as to appear incredible, the prophet points to the omnipotence of God, who would infallibly accomplish his word, and bring about those glorious deliverances which he had promised; the happy effects of which are again set forth by images beautiful and poetical in the highest degree,* 8–13.

A. M. cir. 3292
B. C. cir. 712
Olymp. XVII. 1
cir. annum
NumæPompilii,
R. Roman., 4

HO, [a]every one that thirsteth, come ye to the waters, and he that hath no money; [b]come ye, buy, and eat; yea, come, buy wine and milk without money and without price.

2 Wherefore do ye [c]spend money for *that which is* not bread? and your labour for *that which* satisfieth not? hearken diligently unto me, and eat ye *that which is* good, and let your soul delight itself in fatness.

3 Incline your ear, and [d]come unto me: hear, and your soul shall live: [e]and I will make an everlasting covenant with you, *even* the [f]sure mercies of David.

[a]John iv. 14; vii. 37; Rev. xxi. 6; xxii. 17——[b]Ecclus. li. 25; Matt. xiii. 44, 46; Rev. iii. 18——[c]Heb. *weigh*
[d]Matt. xi. 28

[e]Gen. ix. 16; xvii. 13, 19; Lev. xxiv. 8; 2 Sam. xxiii. 5; chap. liv. 8; lxi. 8; Jer. xxxii. 40——[f]2 Sam. vii. 8, &c.; Psa. lxxxix. 28; Acts xiii. 34

NOTES ON CHAP. LV

Verse 1. *Ho, every one that thirsteth*] "Water," says *Kimchi*, "is a metaphor for the *law* and *wisdom:* as the world cannot subsist without water, so it is impossible that it can subsist without *wisdom.* The *law* is also compared to *wine* and *milk:* to *wine* because *wine* rejoiceth the heart, as it is written: 'The statutes of the Lord are right, rejoicing the heart,' Psa. xix. 8. It is compared also to *milk*, because *milk* is the subsistence of the child; so are the *words of the law* the *nourishment* of his soul who walks in the Divine teaching, and grows up under it."

Come, buy wine and milk] In ancient times our forefathers used what is now called the *old third person singular*, ending in *eth*, for the *imperative mood.* We have a fine example of this in the first verses of this chapter. I shall present them as they stand in my old MS. Bible:—**Alle gee thirstinge cummeth to wateris: and gee that han not sylver, goth forth and bieth, and etith. Cummeth, bieth without silver, and without eny chaungyng, wyn and mylc. Heerith gee, heering me and etith gode thinge, and deliten schal in fattnesse your soule. Bowith in your eie and cummeth to mee, heerith and liven schal your soule. And I schal smyten with gou, everlastynge covenant, the faithful mercies of David.**

Verse 2. *Wherefore do ye spend*] Why should ye be so zealously attached to a doctrine from which your souls derive neither comfort nor nourishment?

Verse 3. *I will make an everlasting covenant*] Heb. אכרתה לכם ברית עולם *echrethah lachem berith olam*, "I will cut the old or everlasting covenant sacrifice with you." That covenant sacrifice which was pointed out of old from the very beginning; and which is to last to the con-

A. M. cir. 3292
B. C. cir. 712
Olymp. XVII. 1
cir. annum
NumæPompilii,
R. Roman., 4

4 Behold, I have given him [g]*for* a witness to the people, [h]a leader and commander to the people.

5 [i]Behold, thou shalt call a nation *that* thou knowest not, [k]and nations *that* knew not thee shall run unto thee because of the LORD thy God, and for the Holy One of Israel; [l]for he hath glorified thee.

6 [m]Seek ye the LORD while he may be found, call ye upon him while he is near:

7 [n]Let the wicked forsake his way, and [o]the unrighteous man [p]his thoughts: and let him return unto the LORD, [q]and he will have mercy upon him; and to our God, for [r]he will abundantly pardon.

8 [s]For my thoughts *are* not your thoughts, neither *are* your ways my ways, saith the LORD.

9 [t]For *as* the heavens are higher than the earth, so are my ways higher than your ways, and my thoughts than your thoughts.

10 For [u]as the rain cometh down, and the snow from heaven, and returneth not thither, but watereth the earth, and maketh it bring forth and bud, that it may give seed to the sower, and bread to the eater:

A. M. cir. 3292
B. C. cir. 712
Olymp. XVII. 1
cir. annum
NumæPompilii,
R. Roman., 4

11 [v]So shall my word be that goeth forth out of my mouth: it shall not return unto me void, but it shall accomplish that which I please, and it shall prosper *in the thing* whereto I sent it.

12 [w]For ye shall go out with joy, and be led forth with peace: the mountains and the hills shall [x]break forth before you into singing, and [y]all the trees of the field shall clap *their* hands.

13 [z]Instead of [a]the thorn shall come up the fir tree, and instead of the brier shall come up the myrtle tree: and it shall be to the LORD [b]for a name, for an everlasting sign *that* shall not be cut off.

[g]John xviii. 37; Rev. i. 5——[h]Jer. xxx. 9; Ezek. xxxiv. 23; Hos. iii. 5; Dan. ix. 25——[i]Chap. lii. 15; Eph. ii. 11, 12——[k]Chap. lx. 5——[l]Chap. lx. 9; Acts iii. 13——[m]Psa. xxxii. 6; Matt. v. 25; xxv. 11; John vii. 34; viii. 21; 2 Cor. vi. 1, 2; Heb. iii. 13——[n]Chap. i. 16——[o]Heb. *the man of iniquity*

[p]Zech. viii. 17——[q]Psa. cxxx. 7; Jer. iii. 12——[r]Heb. *he will multiply to pardon*——[s]2 Sam. vii. 19——[t]Psa. ciii. 11——[u]Deut. xxxii. 2——[v]Chap. liv. 9——[w]Chap. xxxv. 10; lxv. 13, 14——[x]Psa. xcvi. 12; xcviii. 8; chap. xiv. 8; xxxv. 1, 2; xlii. 11——[y]1 Chron. xvi. 33——[z]Chap. xli. 19——[a]Mic. vii. 4——[b]Jer. xiii. 11

summation of ages; viz., the Lamb of God that was slain from the foundation of the world.

The sure mercies of David] That is, says *Kimchi*, "The MESSIAH," called here *David;* as it is written, "David my servant shall be a prince over you."

Verse 6. *Seek ye the Lord while he may be found*] Rab. *David Kimchi* gives the true sense of this passage: "Seek ye the Lord, *because* he may be found: call upon him, *because* he is near. Repent before ye die, for after death there is no conversion of the soul."

Verse 9. *For* as *the heavens are higher*] I am persuaded that כ *caph*, the particle of comparison, is lost in this place, from the likeness of the particle כי *ki*, immediately preceding it. So *Houbigant* and *Secker*. And their remark is confirmed by all the ancient Versions, which express it; and by the following passage of Psa. ciii. 11, which is almost the same:—

כי כגבה שמים על הארץ

haarets al shamayim chigboah ki

גבר חסדו על יראיו

yereaiv al chasdo gabar

"For as the heavens are high above the earth,
So high is his goodness over them that fear him."

Where, by the nature of the sentence, the verb in the second line ought to be the same with that in the first; גבה *gabah*, not גבר *gabar:* so Archbishop *Secker* conjectured; referring however to Psa. cxvii. 2.

Verse 12. *The mountains and the hills*] These are highly poetical images to express a happy state attended with joy and exultation.

Ipsi lætitia voces ad sidera jactant
Intonsi montes: ipsæ jam carmina rupes,
Ipsa sonant arbusta. VIRG. Ecl. v. 61.

"The mountain tops unshorn, the *rocks* rejoice;
The lowly *shrubs* partake of human voice."
DRYDEN.

Verse 13. *Instead of the thorn*—"Instead of the thorny bushes"] These likewise (see note on the preceding verse, and on chap. liv. 11) are general poetical images, expressing a great and happy change for the better. The wilderness turned into a paradise, Lebanon into Carmel: the desert of the Gentiles watered with the heavenly snow and rain, which fail not to have their due effect, and becoming fruitful in piety and righteousness: or, as the *Chaldee* gives the moral sense of the emblem, "instead of the wicked shall arise the just; and instead of sinners, such as fear to sin." Compare chap. xxxv. 1, 2; xli. 19.

And instead of] The conjunction ו *vau* is added, ותחת *vetachath*, in forty-five MSS. of *Kennicott's* several of *De Rossi's*, and five editions; and it is acknowledged by all the ancient Versions. The Masoretes therefore might have safely received it into the text, and not have referred us for it to the margin. But this is no uncommon case with them. Even in our own *Version* the best reading is very often found in the *margin*.

CHAPTER LVI

Whoever would partake of the blessings of the Gospel is required to be holy in all manner of life and conversation. And he that will be so is declared to be accepted according to this gracious dispensation, the blessings of which are large as the human race, without any respect to persons or to nations, 1–8. *At the ninth verse begins a different subject, or new section of prophecy. It opens with calling on the enemies of the Jews,* (*the Chaldeans, or perhaps the Romans,*) *as beasts of prey against them, for the sins of their rulers, teachers, and other profane people among them, whose guilt drew down judgments on the nation,* 9–12.

A. M. cir. 3292 B. C. cir. 712 Olymp. XVII. 1 cir. annum NumæPompilii, R. Roman., 4

THUS saith the LORD, Keep ye [a]judgment, and do justice: [b]for my salvation *is* near to come, and my righteousness to be revealed.

2 Blessed *is* the man *that* doeth this, and the son of man *that* layeth hold on it; [c]that keepeth the sabbath from polluting it, and keepeth his hand from doing any evil.

3 Neither let [d]the son of the stranger, that hath joined himself to the LORD, speak, saying, The LORD hath utterly separated me from his people: neither let the eunuch say, Behold, I *am* a dry tree.

4 For thus saith the LORD unto the eunuchs that keep my sabbaths, and choose *the things* that please me, and take hold of my covenant;

5 Even unto them will I give in [e]mine house and within my walls a place [f]and a name better than of sons and of daughters: I will give them an everlasting name, that shall not be cut off.

A. M. cir. 3292 B. C. cir. 712 Olymp. XVII. 1 cir. annum NumæPompilii, R. Roman., 4

6 Also the sons of the stranger, that join themselves to the LORD, to serve him, and to love the name of the LORD, to be his servants, every one that keepeth the sabbath from polluting it, and taketh hold of my covenant;

7 Even them will I [g]bring to my holy mountain, and make them joyful in my house of prayer: [h]their burnt-offerings and their sacrifices *shall be* accepted upon mine altar; for [i]mine house shall be called a house of prayer [k]for all people.

8 The LORD God [l]which gathereth the outcasts of Israel saith, [m]Yet will I gather *others* to him, [n]beside those that are gathered unto him.

9 [o]All ye beasts of the field, come to devour, *yea,* all ye beasts in the forest.

[a]Or, *equity*——[b]Chap. xlvi. 13; Matt. iii. 2; iv. 17; Rom. xiii. 11, 12——[c]Chap. lviii. 13——[d]See Deut. xxiii. 1, 2, 3; Acts viii. 27; x. 1, 2, 34; xvii. 4; xviii. 7; 1 Pet. i. 1——[e]1 Tim. iii. 15——[f]John i. 12; 1 John iii. 1 [g]Chap. ii. 2; 1 Pet. i. 1, 2

[h]Rom. xii. 1; Heb. xiii. 15; 1 Pet. ii. 5——[i]Matt. xxi. 13; Mark xi. 17; Luke xix. 46——[k]Mal. i. 11 [l]Psa. cxlvii. 2; chap. xi. 12——[m]John x. 16; Eph. i. 10; ii. 14, 15, 16——[n]Hebrew, *to his gathered* [o]Jer. xii. 9

NOTES ON CHAP. LVI

Verse 2. *That keepeth the Sabbath from polluting it*] *Kimchi* has an excellent note here. "The Sabbath is sanctified when it is *distinguished in dignity;* and *separated* from *other days.* 1. As to the *body,* in meat, drink, and clean clothing. 2. As to the *soul,* that it be empty of worldly occupations, and be busily employed in the words of the law and wisdom, and in meditation on the works of the Lord." The *rabbins* say, "Jerusalem had never been destroyed, had not the Sabbaths been profaned in it."

Verse 5. *I will give them an everlasting name*] For לו *lo, him,* in the singular, it is evident that we ought to read למו *lamo, them,* in the plural: so read the *Septuagint, Syriac, Chaldee,* and *Vulgate.*

Verse 6. *The sons of the stranger*] The Gentiles.

That join themselves to the Lord] Who shall enter into the Christian covenant by baptism and faith in Christ, as the Jews and proselytes did by *circumcision.*

To serve him] To live according to the Gospel, and ever do that which is right in the sight of the Lord.

To love the name of the Lord] The name of JESUS, the Christ, the *Saviour* of sinners, the *Anointed* of God, and the Giver of the Holy Spirit to his followers.

To be his servants] To worship no other God but JEHOVAH, and to trust in none for salvation but his CHRIST.

That keepeth the Sabbath] That observes it as a type of the *rest* that remains for the people of God.

And taketh hold of my covenant] בבריתי *biberithi,* "of my covenant sacrifice;" as without this he can do nothing good; and without it nothing can be acceptable to the infinite majesty of the Most High.

Verse 7. Shall be *accepted*] A word is here lost out of the text: it is supplied from the *Septuagint,* יהיו *yihyu,* εσονται, "they shall be." —*Houbigant.*

Verse 9. *All ye beasts of the field*] Here manifestly begins a new section. The prophet in the foregoing chapters, having comforted the faithful Jews with many great promises of God's favour to be extended to them, in the restoration of their ruined state, and in the

A. M. cir. 3292
B. C. cir. 712
Olymp. XVII. 1
cir. annum
NumæPompilii,
R. Roman., 4

10 His watchmen *are* [p]blind:
they are all ignorant, [q]they *are*
all dumb dogs, they cannot bark;
[r]sleeping, lying down, loving to
slumber.
11 Yea, *they are* [s]greedy [t]dogs *which* [u]can
[v]never have enough, and they *are* shepherds
that cannot understand: they all
look to their own way, every one
for his gain, from his quarter.
12 Come ye, *say they,* I will
fetch wine; and we will fill ourselves with
strong drink; [w]and to-morrow shall be as this
day, *and* much more abundant.

[p]Matt. xv. 14; xxiii. 17; Luke vi. 39; xxiii. 16 — [q]Phil. iii. 2 — [r]Or, *dreaming,* or *talking in their sleep* — [s]Heb. *strong of appetite* — [t]Mic. iii. 11 — [u]Heb. *know not to be satisfied* — [v]Ezek. xxxiv. 2, 3 — [w]Psa. x. 6; Prov. xxiii. 35; chap. xxii. 13; Luke xii. 19; 1 Cor. xv. 32

enlargement of his Church by the admission of the Gentiles; here on a sudden makes a transition to the more disagreeable part of the prospect, and to a sharp reproof of the wicked and unbelievers; and especially of the negligent and faithless governors and teachers, of the idolaters and hypocrites, who would still draw down his judgments upon the nation. Probably having in view the destruction of their city and polity by the Chaldeans, and perhaps by the Romans. The same subject is continued in the next chapter; in which the charge of corruption and apostasy becomes more general against the whole Jewish Church. Some expositors have made great difficulties in the 9th verse of this chapter, where there seems to be none. It is perfectly well explained by Jeremiah, chap. xii. 7, 9, where, having introduced God declaring his purpose of punishing his people, by giving them up as a prey to their enemies the Chaldeans, a charge to these his agents is given in words very nearly the same with those of Isaiah in this place:—

"I have forsaken my house; I have deserted my heritage;
I have given up the beloved of my soul into the hands of her enemies.—
Come away, be gathered together, all ye beasts of the field;
Come away to devour."

All ye beasts in the forest—"All ye beasts of the forest."] Instead of ביער *baiyaar*, three MSS. have יער *yaar*, without the preposition; which seems to be right, and is confirmed by all the ancient Versions.

Verse 10. *His watchmen* are *blind*] *Kimchi* observes, "The flock is intrusted to the care of these watchmen. The wild beasts come; these dogs bark not; and the wild beasts devour the flock. Thus they do not *profit* the flock. Yea, they *injure* it; for the owner trusts in them, that they will watch and be faithful; but they are not. These are the false teachers and careless shepherds."

Dumb dogs, they cannot bark] See note on chap. lxii. 6.

Sleeping—"Dreamers"] הזים *hozim*, ενυπνιαζομενοι, *Septuagint.* This seems to be the best authority for the meaning of this word, which occurs only in this place: but it is to be observed, that eleven MSS. of *Kennicott's* and *De Rossi's*, and four editions, have חזים *chazim*, *seers*, or *those who see;* and so the *Vulgate* seems to have read, videntes vana, "seeing vain things."

Loving to slumber.] לנום *lanum:* but six of *Kennicott's* and seven of *De Rossi's* MSS. read לנוס *lanus, to fly,* "to change their residence:" but what connexion such reading can have with the *sense* of the passage, I cannot discern. What is taken for ס *samech* here is, I have no doubt, a *narrow* formed final ם *mem*, which has been mistaken for the above. Many instances occur in my own MSS., where the final ם *mem* is similar to the *samech;* and yet no such change was intended by the scribe.

Verse 11. *Greedy dogs*] Insatiably feeding themselves with the fat, and clothing themselves with the wool, while the flock is scattered, ravaged, and starved! O what an abundance of these dumb and greedy dogs are there found hanging on and prowling about the flock of Christ! How can any careless, avaricious, hireling minister read this without agitation and dismay?

Verse 12. *I will fetch wine*—"Let us provide wine"] For אקחה *ekchah*, first person singular, an ancient MS. has נקחה *nikchah*, first person plural; and another ancient MS. has אך *ak* upon a rasure. So the *Syriac, Chaldee,* and *Vulgate* render it. The spirit of this epicurean sentiment is this: Let us indulge ourselves in the present time to the utmost, and instead of any gloomy forebodings of the future, let us expect nothing but increasing hilarity for every day we shall live. Thus they,

"Counting on long years of pleasure here,
Are quite unfurnished for the world to come."

CHAPTER LVII

After mentioning the removal of righteous persons as an awful symptom of the approach of Divine judgments, 1, 2, *the prophet goes on to charge the nation in general with idolatry, and with courting the unprofitable alliance of idolatrous kings,* 3–12. *In opposition to such vain confidence, the prophet enjoins trust in God, with whom the penitent and humble are sure to find acceptance, and from whom they should obtain temporal and spiritual deliverances,* 13–19. *Awful condition of the wicked and finally impenitent,* 20, 21.

A. M. cir. 3292
B. C. cir. 712
Olymp. XVII. 1
cir. annum
NumæPompilii,
R. Roman., 4

THE righteous perisheth, and
no man layeth *it* to heart:
and [a]merciful [b]men *are* taken
away, [c]none considering that the
righteous is taken away [d]from the evil *to*
come.
2 He shall [e]enter into peace: they shall
rest [f]in their beds, *each one* walking [g]*in* his
uprightness.
3 But draw near hither, [h]ye sons of the
sorceress, the seed of the adulterer and the whore.
4 Against whom do ye sport
yourselves? against whom make
ye a wide mouth, *and* draw out the tongue?
are ye not children of transgression, a [i]seed
of falsehood,
5 Enflaming yourselves [k]with idols [l]under
every green tree, [m]slaying the children in the
valleys under the clifts of the rocks?

[a]Heb. *men of kindness*, or *godliness*——[b]Psa. xii. 1; Mic. vii. 2——[c]1 Kings xiv. 13; see 2 Kings xxii. 20; Wisd. iv. 20, &c.——[d]Or, *from that which is evil*——[e]Or, *go in peace;* Luke ii. 29——[f]2 Chron. xvi. 14

[g]Or, *before him*——[h]Matthew xvi. 4——[i]Chapter i. 4——[k]Or, *among the oaks;* chap. i. 29——[l]2 Kings xvi. 4; xvii. 10; Jer. ii. 20——[m]Lev. xviii. 21; xx. 2; 2 Kings xvi. 3, xxiii. 10; Jer. vii. 31; Ezek. xvi. 20; xx. 26

NOTES ON CHAP. LVII

I shall give Bishop *Lowth's* translation of the two first verses, and give the substance of his criticisms with additional evidence.

Ver. 1. The righteous man perisheth, and no one considereth;
And pious men are taken away, and no one understandeth,
That the righteous man is taken away because of the evil.
2. He shall go in peace: he shall rest in his bed;
Even the perfect man: he that walketh in the straight path.

Verse 1. *The righteous perisheth*—הצדק אבד *hatstsadik abad.* There is an emphasis here which seems intended to point out a particular person. See below. *Perisheth*—As the root עבד *abad* signifies the straying of cattle, their passing away from one pasture to another, I feel inclined to follow the grammatical meaning of the word "perish," *pereo.* So the *Vulgate*, *justus periit*, from *per*, BY or THROUGH, and *eo*, to GO. In his death the righteous man may be said to have passed *through* life, and to have passed by men, i. e., gone or passed before them into the eternal world. A similar mode of speech is used by our Saxon ancestors to express death: **ᵹeꝼoꞃon ꞅıꞇe.** he went out of sight; and **ᵹeꝼoꞃ,** he went away; and **ꝼoꞃðꝼoꞃen,** to fare forth, to die.

There are very few places in Isaiah where Jesus Christ is not intended; and I am inclined to think that *He* is intended here, THAT Just One; and perhaps Stephen had this place in view, when he thus charged the Jews, "Ye denied *τον ἁγιον και δικαιον*, that HOLY and JUST One," Acts iii. 14. That his death was not laid to heart by the wicked Jewish people, needs no proof.

Merciful men] If the *first* refers to *Christ*, this may well refer to the *apostles*, and to others of the primitive Christians, who were *taken away*, some by death and martyrdom, and others by a providential escape from the city that they knew was devoted to destruction.

The evil to come.] That destruction which was to come upon this disobedient people by the Romans.

Verse 2. *He shall enter into peace*—"He shall go in peace"] יבוא שלום *yabo shalom;* the expression is elliptical, such as the prophet frequently uses. The same sense is expressed at large and in full terms, Gen. xv. 15: ואתה תבא אל אבותיך בשלום *veattah tibbo al abotheycha beshalom*, "and thou shalt go to thy fathers in peace."

They shall rest in their beds, each one *walking* in *his uprightness*—"He shall rest in his bed; even the perfect man."] This obscure sentence is reduced to a perfectly good sense, and easy construction by an ingenious remark of Dr. Durell. He reads ינוח על משכבו תם *yanuach al mishcabo tam*, "the perfect man shall rest in his bed." Two MSS. (one of them ancient) have ינוח *yanuach*, singular; and so the *Vulgate* renders it, *requiescat*, "he shall rest." The verb was probably altered to make it plural, and so consistent with what follows, after the mistake had been made in the following words, by uniting משכבו *mishcabo* and תם *tam* into one word. See *Merrick's* Annotations on the Psalms, Addenda; where the reader will find that J. S. Moerlius, by the same sort of correction, and by rescuing the adjective תם *tam*, which had been swallowed up in another word in the same manner, has restored to a clear sense a passage before absolutely unintelligible:—

כי אין חרצבות למו
lemo chartsubboth ein ki
תם ובריא אולם:
ulam ubari tham

"For no distresses happen to them;
Perfect and firm is their strength."
Psa. lxxiii. 4.

To follow on my application of this to our Lord:—HE, the JUST ONE, *shall enter into peace*—the peaceable, prosperous possession of the glorious mediatorial kingdom. *They shall rest upon their beds*—the hand of wrong and oppression can reach these persecuted followers of Christ no more. (But see below.) *The perfect man walking in his uprightness.* This may be considered as a general declaration. The separated spirit, though disunited from its body, walking in conscious existence in the paradise of God, reaping the fruit of *righteousness.* The word which we render *their beds*, משכבותם *mishkebotham*, the learned bishop supposes to be two words; and to be compounded of משכבו *mishkabo*, *his bed*, and תם *tam*, *the upright* or *perfect man.* This is the reading both of the *Syriac* and *Vulgate*, and it is favoured by the *Chaldee;* and one of *De Rossi's* MS. has משכבו

A. M. cir. 3292
B. C. cir. 712
Olymp. XVII. 1
cir. annum
NumæPompilii,
R. Roman., 4

6 Among the smooth *stones* of
the stream *is* thy portion; they,
they *are* thy lot: even to them
hast thou poured a drink-offering, thou hast offered a meat-offering.
Should I receive comfort in these?
7 [n]Upon a lofty and high mountain hast thou
set [o]thy bed: even thither wentest thou up to
offer sacrifice.
8 Behind the doors also and the posts hast
thou set up thy remembrance:
for thou hast discovered *thyself*
to another than me, and art gone
up; thou hast enlarged thy bed,
and [p]made thee *a covenant* with them; [q]thou
lovedst their bed [r]where thou sawest *it*.
9 And [s]thou [t]wentest to the king with ointment, and didst increase thy perfumes, and
didst send thy messengers far off, and didst
debase *thyself even* unto hell.

[n]Ezek. xvi. 16, 25——[o]Ezek. xxiii. 41——[p]Or, *hewed it for thyself* larger *than theirs*——[q]Ezek. xvi. 26, 28; xxiii. 2-20

[r]Or, *thou providest room*——[s]Or, *thou respectedst the king*——[t]Chap. xxx. 6; Ezek. xvi. 33; xxiii. 16; Hosea vii. 11; xii. 1

mishkabo, his bed, without the word תם *tam,* which has been added by a later hand. Bishop *Lowth,* as we have seen, adopts this separation of the word; and for ינוחו *yanuchu, they shall rest,* reads ינוח *yanuach, he shall rest,* which is supported by two of Dr. *Kennicott's* MSS., and by the *Vulgate, Septuagint,* and *Arabic.* The word תם *tam,* taken from משכבותם *mishkebotham,* should begin the latter clause of the verse; and then the interpolated words, *each one,* which our translators supplied, may be very well spared. The verse may be then read and paraphrased thus:—

He shall enter into peace: he shall rest upon
his bed;
The perfect man walking in his uprightness.

The *bed* must signify the *grave;* the walking in uprightness after death, the conscious existence of the happy spirit, and its eternal progression in happiness and perfection: נכחו *nechocho, straight before him;* proceeding into the unlimited extent of eternal glory, increasing in happiness, and increasing in perfection.

My old MS. Bible translates very nervously:—

The rightwise man perishith,
And there is not that bethinke in his herte.
And men of mercy ben gedrid,
For there is not that understonde:
From the face forsoth of malice,
Gedrid is the rigtwise.
Cumm pese: reste it in his bed
That geede in his rigt rewlinge.

It has been often remarked that, previously to the execution of God's judgments upon a wicked place, he has removed good men from it, that they might not suffer with the wicked. When great and good men are removed by death, or otherwise, from any place, the remaining inhabitants have much cause to tremble.

Verse 6. *Among the smooth* stones *of the stream*—"Among the smooth stones of the valley"] The Jews were extremely addicted to the practice of many superstitious and idolatrous rites, which the prophet here inveighs against with great vehemence. Of the worship of rude stones consecrated, there are many testimonials of the ancients. They were called Βαιτυλοι and Βαιτυλια· probably from the stone which Jacob erected at Beth-el, pouring oil upon the top of it. This practice was very common in different ages and places. *Arnobius,* lib. i., gives an account of his own practice in this respect before he became a Christian: Si quando conspexeram lubricatum lapidem, et ex olivi unguine sordidatum; tanquam inesset vis præsens, adulabar, affabar, et beneficia poscebam nihil sentiente de trunco.—"When I have met with a smooth stone, smeared with oil, supposing a spiritual power to be connected with it, I worshipped it, paid my addresses to it, and requested blessings," &c. *Clemens* Alex., Strom. lib. vii., speaks of a worshipper of every smooth stone in a proverbial way, to denote one given up to superstition. And accordingly Theophrastus has marked this as one strong feature in the character of the superstitious man: Και των λιπαρων λιθων των εν ταις τριοδοις παριων, εκ της ληκυθου ελαιου καταχειν, και επι γονατα πεσων και προσκυνησας απαλλαττεσθαι. "Passing by the anointed stones in the streets, he takes out his phial of oil, and pours it on them; and having fallen on his knees, and made his adorations, he departs." *Kimchi* says: "When they found a beautiful polished stone in a brook or river, they paid Divine adoration to it." This idolatry is still prevalent among the Hindoos. The stone which is the object of their adoration is called *salgram.* They are found about eighty miles from the source of the river Sown, in the viceroyalty of Bahar, on the coast of Bengal. *Ayeen Akbery* vol. ii. p. 29.

Verse 8. *Behind the doors also and the posts hast thou set up thy remembrance*—"Behind the door, and the door-posts, hast thou set up thy memorial"] That is, the image of their tutelary gods, or something dedicated to them; in direct opposition to the law of God, which commanded them to write upon the door-posts of their house, and upon their gates, the words of God's law; Deut. vi. 9; xi. 20. If they chose for them such a situation as more private, it was in defiance of a particular curse denounced in the law against the man who should make a graven or a molten image, and put it in a secret place; Deut. xxvii. 15. An ancient MS., with another, has אחר *achar,* without the conjunction ו *vau, and.*

Verse 9. *And thou wentest to the king with ointment*—"And thou hast visited the king with a present of oil"] That is, the king of Assyria, or Egypt. Hosea, chap. xii. 1, reproaches the Israelites for the same practice:—

"They make a covenant with Assyria,
And oil is carried to Egypt."

It is well known, that in all parts of the east, whoever visits a great person must carry him a present. "It is counted uncivil," says *Maundrell,* p. 26, "to visit in this country without

A. M. cir. 3292
B. C. cir. 712
Olymp. XVII. 1
cir. annum
NumæPompilii,
R. Roman., 4

10 Thou art wearied in the greatness of thy way; [u]*yet* saidst thou not, There is no hope: thou hast found the [v]life of thine hand; therefore thou wast not grieved.

11 And [w]of whom hast thou been afraid or feared, that thou hast lied, and hast not remembered me, nor laid *it* to thy heart? [x]have not I held my peace even of old, and thou fearest me not?

12 I will declare thy righteousness, and thy works; for they shall not profit thee.

13 When thou criest, let thy companies deliver thee; but the wind shall carry them all away; vanity shall take *them:* but he that putteth his trust in me shall possess the land, and shall inherit my holy mountain;

14 And shall say, [y]Cast ye up, cast ye up, prepare the way, take up the stumbling block out of the way of my people.

15 For thus saith the high and lofty One that inhabiteth eternity, [z]whose name *is* Holy; [a]I dwell in the high and holy *place,* [b]with him also *that is* of a contrite and humble spirit, [c]to revive the spirit of the humble, and to revive the heart of the contrite ones.

16 [d]For I will not contend for ever, neither will I be always wroth: for the spirit should

[u]Jeremiah ii. 25——[v]Or, *living*——[w]Chap. li. 12, 13——[x]Psalm l. 21——[y]Chap. xl. 3; lxii. 10——[z]Job vi. 10; Luke i. 49——[a]Psalm lxviii. 4; Zechariah ii. 13——[b]Psa. xxxiv. 18; li. 17; cxxxviii. 6; chap. lxvi. 2——[c]Psalm cxlvii. 3; chap. lxi. 1——[d]Psalm lxxxv. 5; ciii. 9; Mic. vii. 18

an offering in hand. All great men expect it as a tribute due to their character and authority; and look upon themselves as affronted, and indeed defrauded, when the compliment is omitted." Hence שור *shur, to visit* a person, is equivalent to making him a present; and תשורה *teshurah* signifies a *present* made on such occasions; as our translators have rightly rendered it, 1 Sam. ix. 7; on which Jarchi says, Menachem exponit תשורה *teshurah,* quod significat oblationem sive manus, ut aliquis aspiciat faciem regis, aut alicujus magnatis. "Menachem expounds תשורה *teshurah* of an offering or gift which is presented in order to be admitted into the presence of the king or some great man."

Verse 10. Yet *saidst thou not, There is no hope*—"Thou hast said, There is hope"] In one of the MSS. at Koningsberg, collated by Lilienthal, the words לא אמרת *lo amarta,* are left in the text unpointed, as suspected; and in the margin the corrector has written ותאמרי *vattomari.* Now if we compare Jer. ii. 25 and xviii. 12, we shall find that the subject is in both places quite the same with this of Isaiah; and the sentiment expressed, that of a desperate resolution to continue at all hazards in their idolatrous practices; the very thing that in all reason we might expect here. Probably, therefore, the latter is the true reading in this place.—L.

Verse 11. *Nor laid* it *to thy heart*—"Nor revolved it in thy hand"] *Eight* MSS., (*four* ancient,) and the *two* oldest editions, with another, add the conjunction ו *vau,* ולא *velo:* which is confirmed by all the ancient Versions.

Even of old—"And winked"] For ומעולם *umeolam,* which makes no good sense or construction in this place, *twenty-three* MSS. (*seven* ancient) and *three* editions have מעלם, (to be thus pointed מעלם *malim;*) Παρορω, *Septuagint; quasi non videns,* "as if not seeing," *Vulgate.* See Psa. x. 1. The truth of this reading, so confirmed, admits of no doubt. In one of my own MSS. the ו *vau* has been written, but afterwards struck out. *Is it not because I was silent, and winked?*

Verse 12. *Thy righteousness*—"My righteousness"] For צדקתך *tsidkathech,* THY *righteousness,* the *Syriac, Septuagint,* MSS. *Alex.* and *Pachom.,* and I. D. II., and *Marchal.* and *οἱ* Γ, and the *Arabic,* read צדקי *tsidki,* MY *righteousness.*

Verse 13. *Let thy companies deliver thee*—"Let thine associates deliver thee"] *Thirty-nine* MSS. (*ten* ancient) of Dr. *Kennicott's,* and *two* of my own, and the two oldest editions have יצילך *yatstsiluchu,* plural.

Verse 14. *And shall say*—"Then will I say"] ואמר *vaomer,* to be pointed as the first person future. They are the words of God, as it is plain from the conclusion of the verse; *my* people, עמי *ammi.*

Verse 15. *For thus saith the high and lofty One*—"For thus saith JEHOVAH, the high and the lofty"] A MS. adds יהוה *Yehovah,* after אמר *amar,* and edition Prag. 1518. So the *Septuagint, Alex.,* and *Arabic.* An ancient MS. adds יה *Yah.*

With him also that is *of a contrite and humble spirit*] *Twelve* MSS. have את *eth,* without the conjunction ו *vau.* Pro ואת *veeth,* forte legendum ואראה *veerah:* confer Psa. cxiii. 5, *et* cxxxviii. 6.—SECKER. "We should perhaps read ואראה *veerah,* instead of ואת *veeth.* See Psa. cxiii. 5, and cxxxviii. 6."

Verse 16. *For I will not contend for ever*] The learned have taken a great deal of pains to little purpose on the latter part of this verse, which they suppose to be very obscure. After all their labours upon it, I think the best and easiest explication of it is given in the two following elegant passages of the Psalms, which I presume are exactly parallel to it, and very clearly express the same sentiment.

"But he in his tender mercy will forgive their sin,
And will not destroy them;
Yea, oftentimes will he turn away his wrath,
And will not rouse up his indignation:
For he remembereth that they are but flesh,
A breath that passeth, and returneth not."
Psa. lxxviii. 38, 39.

A. M. cir. 3292 B. C. cir. 712 Olymp. XVII. 1 cir. annum NumæPompilii, R. Roman., 4

fail before me, and the souls [e]*which* I have made.
17 For the iniquity of [f]his covetousness was I wroth, and smote him: [g]I hid me, and was wroth, [h]and he went on [i]frowardly in the way of his heart.
18 I have seen his ways, and [k]will heal him: I will lead him also, and restore comforts unto him and to [l]his mourners.
19 I create [m]the fruit of the lips; Peace, peace [n]to *him that is* far off, and to *him that is* near, saith the LORD; and I will heal him.
20 [o]But the wicked *are* like the troubled sea, when it cannot rest, whose waters cast up mire and dirt.
21 [p]*There is* no peace, saith my God, to the wicked.

[e]Num. xvi. 22; Job xxxiv. 14; Heb. xii. 9——[f]Jer. vi. 13——[g]Chap. viii. 17; xlv. 15——[h]Chap. ix. 13 [i]Heb. *turning away*

[k]Jer. iii. 22——[l]Chap. lxi. 2——[m]Heb. xiii. 15 [n]Acts ii. 39; Eph. ii. 17——[o]Job xv. 20, &c.; Prov. iv. 16——[p]Chap. xlviii. 22

"He will not always contend,
Neither will he for ever hold his wrath:
As a father yearneth towards his children,
So is JEHOVAH tenderly compassionate towards them that fear him:
For he knoweth our frame;
He remembereth that we are but dust."
Psa. ciii. 9, 13, 14.

In the former of these two passages the second line seems to be defective both in measure and sense. I suppose the word אותם *otham, them,* is lost at the end; which seems to be acknowledged by the *Chaldee* and *Vulgate,* who render as if they had read ולא ישחית אותם *velo yaschith otham.*—L.

For the spirit] רוח *ruach, the animal life.*

And the souls] נשמות *neshamoth, the immortal spirits.* The *Targum* understands this of the resurrection. *I will restore the souls of the dead,* i. e., to their bodies.

Verse 17. *For the iniquity of his covetousness was I wroth*—"Because of his iniquity for a short time was I wroth"] For בצעו *bitso,* I read בצע *betsa, a little while,* from בצע *batsa, he cut off;* as the *Septuagint* read and render it, βραχυ τι, "a certain short space." *Propter iniquitatem* avaritiæ ejus, "because of the iniquity of his avarice," the rendering of the *Vulgate,* which our translators and I believe all others follow, is surely quite beside the purpose.

Verse 18. *I have seen his ways*] Probably these verses refer to the restoration of the Jews from captivity.

Verse 19. *I create the fruit of the lips*] "The sacrifice of praise," saith St. Paul, Heb. xiii. 15, "is the fruit of the lips." God creates this fruit of the lips, by giving new subject and cause of thanksgiving by his mercies conferred on those among his people, who acknowledge and bewail their transgressions, and return to him. The great subject of thanksgiving is peace—reconciliation and pardon, offered to them that are nigh, and to them that are afar off; not only to the Jew, but also to the Gentile, as St. Paul more than once applies those terms, Eph. ii. 13, 17. See also Acts ii. 39.

Peace to him that is *far off*—"That is, to the penitent; *and to* him that is *near,* i. e., the righteous."—*Kimchi.*

Verse 21. There is *no peace, saith my God*] For אלהי *Elohai, twenty-two* MSS. (*five* ancient) of *Kennicott's, thirty* of *De Rossi's,* and *one* ancient of my own, read יהוה *Yehovah;* the *Vulgate, Septuagint, Alex.,* and *Arabic,* and three MSS. have both. This verse has reference to the *nineteenth.* The perseveringly wicked and impenitent are excluded from all share in that peace above mentioned, that reconcilement and pardon which is promised to the *penitent* only. The forty-eighth chapter ends with the same declaration, to express the exclusion of the unbelievers and impenitent from the benefit of the foregoing promises.—L.

CHAPTER LVIII

This elegant chapter contains a severe reproof of the Jews on account of their vices, particularly their hypocrisy in practising and relying on outward ceremonies, such as fasting and bodily humiliation, without true repentance, 1–5. *It then lays down a clear and comprehensive summary of the duties they owed to their fellow creatures,* 6, 7. *Large promises of happiness and prosperity are likewise annexed to the performance of these duties in a variety of the most beautiful and striking images,* 8–12. *Great temporal and spiritual blessedness of those who keep holy the Sabbath day,* 13, 14.

A. M. cir. 3292 B. C. cir. 712 Olymp. XVII. 1 cir. annum NumæPompilii, R. Roman., 4

CRY [a]aloud, spare not, lift up thy voice like a trumpet, and show my people their transgression, and the house of Jacob their sins.
2 Yet they seek me daily, and

[a]Heb. *with the throat*

NOTES ON CHAP. LVIII

Verse 1. *Cry aloud, spare not*] Never was a louder cry against the hypocrisy, nor a more cutting reproof of the wickedness, of a people professing a national established religion, having all the forms of godliness without a particle of its power. This chapter has been often appointed to be read on political fast days for the success of wars carried on for—God *knows*

A. M. cir. 3292 B. C. cir. 712 Olymp. XVII. 1 cir. annum NumæPompilii, R. Roman., 4

delight to know my ways, as a
nation that did righteousness,
and forsook not the ordinance of
their God: they ask of me the
ordinances of justice; they take delight in approaching to God.
3 [b]Wherefore have we fasted, *say they,* and
thou seest not? *wherefore* have we [c]afflicted
our soul, and thou takest no knowledge? Behold, in the day of your fast ye find pleasure,
and exact all your [d]labours[e].
4 [f]Behold, ye fast for strife and debate, and
to smite with the fist of wickedness: [g]ye shall
not fast as *ye do this* day, to make your voice
to be heard on high.
5 Is it [h]such a fast that I have chosen?
[i]a[k] day for a man to afflict his soul? *is it* to
bow down his head as a bulrush, and [l]to
spread sackcloth and ashes *under him?* wilt
thou call this a fast, and an acceptable day to the LORD?

A. M. cir. 3292 B. C. cir. 712 Olymp. XVII. 1 cir. annum NumæPompilii, R. Roman., 4

6 *Is* not this the fast that I
have chosen? to loose the bands
of wickedness, [m]to undo [n]the heavy burdens,
and [o]to let the [p]oppressed go free, and that
ye break every yoke?
7 *Is it* not [q]to deal thy bread to the hungry,
and that thou bring the poor that are [r]cast
out to thy house? [s]when thou seest the naked,
that thou cover him; and that thou hide not
thyself from [t]thine own flesh?
8 [u]Then shall thy light break forth as the
morning, and thine health shall spring forth
speedily: and thy righteousness shall go before thee; [v]the glory of the LORD [w]shall be
thy rereward.
9 Then shalt thou call, and the LORD shall
answer; thou shalt cry, and he shall say,

[b]Mal. iii. 14——[c]Lev. xvi. 29, 31; xxiii. 27——[d]Or, *things wherewith ye grieve others*——[e]Heb. *griefs* [f]1 Kings xxi. 9, 12, 13——[g]Or, *ye fast not as this day* [h]Zech. vii. 5——[i]Lev. xvi. 29——[k]Or, *to afflict his soul for a day*——[l]Esth. iv. 3; Job ii. 8; Dan. ix. 3; Jonah iii. 6

[m]Neh. v. 10, 11, 12——[n]Heb. *the bundles of the yoke* [o]Jer. xxxiv. 9——[p]Heb. *broken*——[q]Ezek. xviii. 7, 16; Matt. xxv. 35——[r]Or, *afflicted*——[s]Job xxxi. 19 [t]Gen. xxix. 14; Neh. v. 5——[u]Job xi. 17——[v]Exod. xiv. 19; chap. lii. 12——[w]Heb. *shall gather thee up*

what purposes, and originating in—God *knows* what motives. Politically speaking, was ever any thing more injudicious?

Verse 3. *Have we afflicted our soul*—"Have we afflicted our souls"] *Twenty-seven* MSS. (*six* ancient) of Dr. *Kennicott's*, *thirty-six* of *De Rossi's*, and *two* of my own, and the old edition of 1488 have the noun in the plural number, נפשינו *naphsheynu, our souls;* and so the *Septuagint*, *Chaldee*, and *Vulgate*. This reading is undoubtedly genuine.

In the day of your fast ye find pleasure] Fast days are generally called *holidays*, and holidays are days of idleness and pleasure. In numberless cases the *fast* is turned into a *feast*.

And exact all your labours.] Some disregard the most sacred fast, and will oblige their servant to *work* all day long; others use fast days for the purpose of settling their accounts, posting up their books, and drawing out their bills to be ready to collect their debts. These are sneaking hypocrites; the others are daringly irreligious.

Verse 4. *Ye fast for strife and debate*] How often is this the case! A whole nation are called to fast to implore God's blessing on wars carried on for the purposes of wrath and ambition.

To smite with the fist of wickedness: ye shall not fast as ye do this *day*—"To smite with the fist the poor. Wherefore fast ye unto me in this manner"] I follow the version of the *Septuagint*, which gives a much better sense than the present reading of the Hebrew. Instead of רשע לא *resha lo*, they seem to have read in their copy רש על מה לי *rash al mah lli.* The four first letters are the same, but otherwise divided in regard to the words; the four last are lost, and א *aleph* added in their place, in order to make some sort of sense with רשע ל. The version of the *Septuagint* is, και τυπτετε πυγμαις ταπεινον· ἱνα τι μοι νηστευετε—— as above.

Verse 6. *Let the oppressed go free*] How can any nation pretend to fast or worship God at all, or dare to profess that they believe in the existence of such a Being, while they carry on the *slave trade*, and traffic in the souls, blood, and bodies, of men! O ye most flagitious of knaves, and worst of hypocrites, cast off at once the mask of religion; and deepen not your endless perdition by professing the *faith* of our *Lord Jesus Christ*, while ye continue in this traffic!

Verse 7. *Deal thy bread to the hungry*] But this thou canst not do, if thou eat it *thyself.* When a man fasts, suppose he do it through a religious motive, he should give the food of that day, from which he abstains, to the poor and hungry, who, in the course of providence, are called to sustain many involuntary fasts, besides suffering general privations. Wo to him who saves a day's victuals by his religious fast! He should either give them or their value in money to the poor. See ver. 6.

That thou bring the poor that are cast out to thy house—"To bring the wandering poor into thy house"] πτωχους αστεγους, *Septuagint; egenos* vagosque, *Vulgate;* and מטלטלין *metaltelin, Chaldee.* They read, instead of מרודים *merudim,* הנודים *hanudim.* מר *mer* is upon a rasure in the Bodleian MS. The same MS. reads ביתה *bayethah,* in *domum,* "into the house."—L.

Verse 8. *And thine health shall spring forth speedily*—"And thy wounds shall speedily be healed over"] Et cicatrix vulneris tui cito obducetur; "And the scar of thy wounds shall be speedily removed." *Aquila's* Version, as reported by Jerome, with which agrees that of the *Chaldee.*

The glory—"And the glory"] Sixteen MSS.

A. M. cir. 3292
B. C. cir. 712
Olymp. XVII. 1
cir. annum
NumæPompilii,
R. Roman., 4

Here I *am.* If thou take away from the midst of thee the yoke, the putting forth of the finger, and [x]speaking vanity;

10 And *if* thou draw out thy soul to the hungry, and satisfy the afflicted soul; then shall thy light rise in obscurity, and thy darkness *be* as the noon day:

11 And the LORD shall guide thee continually, and satisfy thy soul in [y]drought, and make fat thy bones: and thou shalt be like a watered garden, and like a spring of water, whose waters [z]fail not.

12 And *they that shall be* of thee [a]shall build the old waste places: thou shalt raise up the foundations of many generations; and thou shalt be called, The repairer of the breach, The restorer of paths to dwell in.

A. M. cir. 3292
B. C. cir. 712
Olymp. XVII. 1
cir. annum
NumæPompilii,
R. Roman., 4

13 If [b]thou turn away thy foot from the sabbath, *from* doing thy pleasure on my holy day; and call the sabbath a delight, the holy of the LORD, honourable; and shalt honour him, not doing thine own ways, nor finding thine own pleasure, nor speaking *thine own* words;

14 [c]Then shalt thou delight thyself in the LORD; and I will cause thee to [d]ride upon the high places of the earth, and feed thee with the heritage of Jacob thy father: [e]for the mouth of the LORD hath spoken *it.*

[x]Psa. xii. 2——[y]Heb. *droughts*——[z]Heb. *lie* or *deceive*——[a]Chap. lxi. 4——[b]Chap. lvi. 2

[c]Job xxii. 26——[d]Deut. xxxii. 13; xxxiii. 29——[e]Chap. i. 20; xl. 5; Mic. iv. 4

(five ancient) of Dr. *Kennicott's*, and the *Septuagint*, *Syriac*, and *Vulgate* add the conjunction ו *vau*, וכבוד *vechabod.*

Verse 10. *And* if *thou draw out thy soul to the hungry*—"If thou bring forth thy bread to the hungry"] "To draw out thy soul to the hungry," as our translators rightly enough express the present Hebrew text, is an obscure phrase, and without example in any other place. But instead of נפשך *naphshecha, thy soul,* eight MSS. (three ancient) of *Kennicott's* and three of *De Rossi's* read לחמך *lachmecha, thy bread;* and so the *Syriac* renders it. The *Septuagint* express both words, *τον αρτον εκ της ψυχης σου*, "thy bread from thy soul." I cannot help thinking, however, that this reading is a gloss, and should not be adopted. To *draw out the soul* in relieving the poor, is to do it, not of constraint or necessity, but cheerfully, and is both nervous and elegant. His *soul pities* and his *hand gives.*

Verse 11. *And make fat thy bones*—"And he shall renew thy strength"] Chaldæus forte legit יחליף עצמתך *yachaliph otsmathecha; confer cap.* xl. 29, 31, *et* xli. 1.—SECKER. "The *Chaldee* perhaps read יחליף עצמתך *yachaliph otsmathecha.*" The *Chaldee* has וגופך יחיי בחיי עלמא *veguphach yechaiyey bechaiyey alma,* "and he will vivify thy body in life eternal." The rest of the ancients seem not to know what to make of יחליץ *yachalits;* and the rendering of the *Vulgate,* which seems to be the only proper one, *ossa tua liberabit,* "he will deliver thy bones," makes no sense. I follow this excellent emendation; to favour which it is still farther to be observed that three MSS., instead of עצמתיך *atsmotheycha,* have עצמתך *otsmathecha,* singular.—L.

Verse 12. *The restorer of paths to dwell in*—"The restorer of paths to be frequented by inhabitants."] To this purpose it is rendered by the *Syriac, Symmachus,* and *Theodotion.*

Verse 13. *If thou turn away thy foot from the Sabbath*] The meaning of this seems to be, that they should be careful not to take their pleasure on the Sabbath day, by paying visits, and taking country jaunts; not going, as *Kimchi* interprets it, more than a Sabbath day's journey, which was only *two thousand* cubits beyond the city's suburbs. How vilely is this rule transgressed by the inhabitants of this land! They seem to think that the Sabbath was made only for their recreation!

From *doing thy pleasure*] The *Septuagint, Syriac,* and *Chaldee,* for עשות *asoth,* manifestly express מעשות *measoth.* So likewise a MS. has it, but with the omission of the words שבת רגלך *shabbath raglecha.*—L.

The holy of the Lord—"And the holy feast of JEHOVAH"] Twenty-eight MSS. (seven ancient) add the conjunction ו *vau,* ולקדוש *velikedosh;* and so the *Syriac, Chaldee,* and *Vulgate.* One of my own has the same reading.

Nor speaking thine own *words*—"From speaking vain words."] It is necessary to add some epithet to make out the sense; the *Septuagint* say, *angry* words; the *Chaldee,* words of violence. If any such epithet is lost here, the safest way is to supply it by the prophet's own expression, ver. 9, ודבר און *vedabar aven, vain words;* that is, profane, impious, injurious, &c.

"The additional epithet seems unnecessary; the *Vulgate* and *Syriac* have it not; and the sense is good without it; two ways, first by taking ודבר *vedabar* for a noun, and דבר *dabur* for the participle pahul, and rendering,—

'From pursuing thy pleasure, and the thing resolved on.'

Or, secondly, by supposing the force of the preposition מ *mem* to have been continued from the verb ממצוא *mimmetso* to the verb ודבר *vedabber* immediately following; and rendering,—

'From executing thy pleasure, and from speaking words concerning it.'

But the first seems the easier rendering."—Dr. JUBB.

Verse 14. *Then shalt thou delight thyself*] If all *fasts* and religious observances be carried on in the spirit and manner recommended above, God's blessing will attend every ordinance. But in public fasts, prescribed not in the Book of God, but by the rulers of nations in general (very unfit persons) care should be taken that the *cause is good*, and that God's blessing may be *safely* implored in it.

France has lately fasted and prayed that they might be able to subjugate Spain, restore and establish the horrible inquisition, and utterly destroy all the liberties of the people! Is this such a fast as God hath chosen?—A. D. 1823.

CHAPTER LIX

This chapter contains a more general reproof of the wickedness of the Jews, 1–8. *After this they are represented confessing their sins, and deploring the unhappy consequences of them,* 9–15. *On this act of humiliation God, ever ready to pardon the penitent, promises that he will have mercy on them; that the Redeemer will come, mighty to save; and that he will deliver his people, subdue his enemies, and establish a new and everlasting covenant,* 16–21.

A. M. cir. 3292
B. C. cir. 712
Olymp. XVII. 1
cir. annum
NumæPompilii,
R. Roman., 4

BEHOLD, the LORD's hand is not [a]shortened, that it cannot save; neither his ear heavy, that it cannot hear:

2 But your iniquities have separated between you and your God, and your sins [b]have hid *his* face from you, that he will not hear.

3 For [c]your hands are defiled with blood, and your fingers with iniquity; your lips have spoken lies, your tongue hath muttered perverseness.

4 None calleth for justice, nor *any* pleadeth for truth: they trust in vanity, and speak lies; [d]they conceive mischief, and bring forth iniquity.

5 They hatch [e]cockatrice' eggs, and weave the spider's web: he that eateth of their eggs dieth, and [f]that which is crushed breaketh out into a viper.

A. M. cir. 3292
B. C. cir. 712
Olymp. XVII. 1
cir. annum
NumæPompilii,
R. Roman., 4

6 [g]Their webs shall not become garments, neither shall they cover themselves with their works: their works *are* works of iniquity, and the act of violence *is* in their hands.

7 [h]Their feet run to evil, and they make haste to shed innocent blood: their thoughts *are* thoughts of iniquity; wasting and [i]destruction *are* in their paths.

[a]Numbers xi. 23; chap. l. 2——[b]Or, *have made him hide*——[c]Chap. i. 15——[d]Job xv. 35; Psalm vii. 14——[e]Or, *adders'*——[f]Or, *that which is sprinkled is as if there brake out a viper*——[g]Job viii. 14, 15——[h]Proverbs i. 16; Romans iii. 15——[i]Hebrew, *breaking*

The foregoing elegant chapter contained a severe reproof of the Jews, in particular for their hypocrisy in pretending to make themselves accepted with God by fasting and outward humiliation without true repentance; while they still continued to oppress the poor, and indulge their own passions and vices; with great promises however of God's favour on condition of their reformation. This chapter contains a more general reproof of their wickedness, bloodshed, violence, falsehood, injustice. At ver. 9 they are introduced as making, themselves, an ample confession of their sins, and deploring their wretched state in consequence of them. On this act of humiliation a promise is given that God, in his mercy and zeal for his people, will rescue them from this miserable condition; that the Redeemer will come like a mighty hero to deliver them; he will destroy his enemies, convert both Jews and Gentiles to himself, and give them a new covenant, and a law which shall never be abolished.

As this chapter is remarkable for the beauty, strength, and variety of the images with which it abounds; so is it peculiarly distinguished by the elegance of the composition, and the exact construction of the sentences. From the first verse to the two last it falls regularly into stanzas of four lines, (see Prelim. Dissert. p. xxi.,) which I have endeavoured to express as nearly as possible in the form of the original.—L.

NOTES ON CHAP. LIX

Verse 2. *His face*] For פנים *panim, faces,* I read *panaiv, his face.* So the *Syriac, Septuagint, Alexandrian, Arabic,* and *Vulgate.* פני *panai,* MS. Forte legendum פני *panai,* nam מ *mem,* sequitur, et loquitur Deus; confer cap. lviii. 14. "We should perhaps read פני *panai;* for מ *mem* follows, and God is the speaker."—SECKER. I rather think that the speech of God was closed with the last chapter, and that this chapter is delivered in the person of the prophet.—L.

Verse 3. *Your tongue*—"And your tongue"] An ancient MS., and the *Septuagint* and *Vulgate,* add the conjunction.

Verse 4. *They conceive mischief, and bring forth iniquity.*] There is a curious propriety in this mode of expression; a thought or purpose is compared to *conception;* a word or act, which is the consequence of it, to the *birth of a child.* From the *third* to the *fifteenth* verse inclusive may be considered a true statement of the then moral state of the Jewish people; and that they were, in the most proper sense of the word, guilty of the iniquities with which they are charged.

A. M. cir. 3292
B. C. cir. 712
Olymp. XVII. 1
cir. annum
NumæPompilii,
R. Roman., 4

8 The way of peace they know not; and *there is* no [k]judgment in their goings: [l]they have made them crooked paths: whosoever goeth therein shall not know peace.

9 Therefore is judgment far from us, neither doth justice overtake us: [m]we wait for light, but behold obscurity; for brightness, *but* we walk in darkness.

10 [n]We grope for the wall like the blind, and we grope as if *we had* no eyes: we stumble at noon day as in the night; *we are* in desolate places as dead *men.*

11 We roar all like bears, and [o]mourn sore like doves: we look for judgment, but *there is* none; for salvation, *but* it is far off from us.

12 For our transgressions are multiplied before thee, and our sins testify against us: for our transgressions *are* with us; and *as for* our iniquities, we know them:

13 In transgressing and lying against the LORD, and departing away from our God, speaking oppression and revolt, conceiving and uttering [p]from the heart words of falsehood.

A. M. cir. 3292
B. C. cir. 712
Olymp. XVII. 1
cir. annum
NumæPompilii,
R. Roman., 4

14 And judgment is turned away backward, and justice standeth afar off: for truth is fallen in the street, and equity cannot enter.

15 Yea, truth faileth; and he *that* departeth from evil [q]maketh himself a prey: and the LORD saw *it* and [r]it displeased him that *there was* no judgment.

16 [s]And he saw that *there was* no man, and [t]wondered that *there was* no intercessor: [u]therefore his arm brought salvation unto him; and his righteousness, it sustained him.

17 [v]For he put on righteousness as a breastplate, and a helmet of salvation upon his head; and he put on the garments of ven-

---

[k]Or, *right*——[l]Psa. cxxv. 5; Prov. ii. 15——[m]Jer. viii. 15——[n]Deut. xxviii. 29; Job v. 14; Amos viii. 9——[o]Chap. xxxviii. 14; Ezek. vii. 16——[p]Matt. xii. 34——[q]Or, *is accounted mad*

[r]Hebrew, *it was evil in his eyes*——[s]Ezek. xxii. 30——[t]Mark vi. 6——[u]Psalm xcviii. 1; chapter lxiii. 5——[v]Wisd. v. 18, 19; Ephesians vi. 14, 17; 1 Thessalonians v. 8

Verse 8. *Whosoever goeth therein shall not know peace*—"Whoever goeth in them knoweth not peace"] For בה *bah,* singular, read בם *bam,* plural, with the *Septuagint, Syriac, Vulgate,* and *Chaldee.* The ה *he* is upon a rasure in one MS. Or, for נתיבותיהם *nethibotheyhem,* plural, we must read נתיבתם *nethibatham,* singular, as it is in an ancient MS., to preserve the grammatical concord.—L.

Verse 10. *We stumble at noon day as in the night*—"We stumble at mid-day, as in the twilight"] I adopt here an emendation of Houbigant, נשגגה *nishgegah,* instead of the second, נגששה *negasheshah,* the repetition of which has a poverty and inelegance extremely unworthy of the prophet, and unlike his manner. The mistake is of long standing, being prior to all the ancient versions. It was a very easy and obvious mistake, and I have little doubt of our having recovered the true reading in this ingenious correction.

Verse 11. But *it is far off from us*—"And it is far distant from us."] The conjunction ו *vau* must necessarily be prefixed to the verb, as the *Syriac, Chaldee,* and *Vulgate* found it in their copies; ורחקה *verachakah,* "and far off."

Verse 14. *Justice standeth afar off*] צדקה *tsedakah, righteousness,* put here, says Kimchi, for *alms to the poor.* This casts some light on Matt. vi. 1: "Take heed that you do not your alms," ελεημοσυνην. But the best copies have δικαιοσυνην, *righteousness;* the former having been inserted in the text at first merely as the explanation of the genuine and original word.

Verse 15. *And the Lord saw* it—"And JEHOVAH saw it ——"] This third line of the stanza appears manifestly to me to be imperfect by the loss of a phrase. The reader will perhaps more perfectly conceive my idea of the matter if I endeavour to supply the supposed defect. I imagine it might have stood originally in this manner:—

לו	ויחר	יהוה	וירא
lo	*veyachar*	*Yehovah*	*vaiyar*

משפט	אין	כי	בעיניו	וירע
mishpat	*ein*	*ki*	*beeyinaiv*	*veyera*

"And JEHOVAH saw it, and he was wroth;
And it displeased him, that there was no judgment."

We have had already many examples of mistakes of omission; this, if it be such, is very ancient, being prior to all the versions.—L.

Verse 16. *And wondered that* there was *no intercessor*] This and the following verses some of the most eminent rabbins understand as spoken of the Messiah. Kimchi says that Rabbi Joshua ben Levi proposes this objection: "It is written, 'Behold, he will come in the clouds of heaven as the son of man,' Dan. vii. 13; and elsewhere it is written, 'He cometh lowly, and riding upon an ass,' Zech. ix. 9. How can these texts be reconciled? Thus: If the Jews have merit, he will come unto them in the clouds of heaven; but if they be destitute of merit, he will come unto them riding upon an ass." Now out of their own mouth they may be condemned. They were truly destitute of all merit when Jesus Christ came into Jerusalem riding upon an ass, according to the letter of the above prophecy; and they neither acknowledged nor received him. And that they were destitute of merit their destruction by the Romans, which shortly followed their rejection of him, sufficiently proves.

Verse 17. For *clothing*—"For his clothing"] תלבשת *tilbosheth.* "I cannot but think that

A. M. cir. 3292 B. C. cir. 712 Olymp. XVII. 1 cir. annum NumæPompilii, R. Roman., 4

geance *for* clothing, and was
clad with zeal as a cloak.
18 [w]According to *their* [x]deeds,
accordingly we will repay, fury to
his adversaries, recompense to his enemies;
to the islands he will repay recompense.
19 [y]So shall they fear the name of the
LORD from the west, and his
glory from the rising of the sun.
When the enemy shall come in
[z]like a flood, the Spirit of the
LORD shall [a]lift up a standard against
him.
20 And [b]the Redeemer shall come to

[w]Chap. lxiii. 6; Psa. xxviii. 4; Jer. l. 29; Matt. xvi. 27; Rev. xx. 12; xxii. 12——[x]Heb. *recompenses*

[y]Psa. cxiii. 3; Mal. i. 11——[z]Rev. xii. 15——[a]Or, *put him to flight*——[b]Rom. xi. 26

this word, תלבשת *tilbosheth*, is an interpolation. 1. It is in no one ancient version. 2. It is redundant in the sense, as it is before expressed in בגדי *bigdey*. 3. It makes the hemistich just so much longer than it ought to be, if it is compared with the others adjoining. 4. It makes a form of construction in this clause less elegant than that in the others. 5. It might probably be in some margin a various reading for בגדי *bigdey*, and thence taken into the text. This is more probable, as its form is such as it would be if it were *in regimine*, as it must be before נקם *nakam*."—Dr. JUBB. Two sorts of armour are mentioned: a *breast-plate* and a *helmet*, to bring *righteousness* and *salvation* to those who fear him; and the *garments of vengeance* and the *cloak of zeal* for the destruction of all those who finally oppose him, and reject his Gospel.

Verse 18. *According to* their *deeds, accordingly he will repay*—"He is mighty to recompense; he that is mighty to recompense will requite"] The former part of this verse, as it stands at present in the Hebrew text, seems to me to be very imperfect, and absolutely unintelligible. The learned Vitringa has taken a great deal of pains upon it after Cocceius, who he says is the only one of all the interpreters, ancient or modern, who has at all understood it, and has opened the way for him. He thinks that both of them together have clearly made out the sense; I do not expect that any third person will ever be of that opinion. He says, Videtur sententia ad verbum sonare: quasi propter facta [adversariorum] quasi propter rependet; excandescentiam, &c., et sic reddidit Pagnimus. "According to the height of their demerits, he will repay them to the height: fury to his adversaries, recompense to his enemies," &c.—*Waterland.* This he converts, by a process which will not much edify my reader, into Secundum summe merita, secundum summe (*merita*) rependet; which is his translation. They that hold the present Hebrew text to be absolutely infallible must make their way through it as they can; but they ought surely to give us somewhat that has at least the appearance of sense. However, I hope the case here is not quite desperate; the *Chaldee* leads us very fairly to the correction of the text, which is both corrupted and defective. The paraphrase runs thus: מרי גמליא הוא גמלא ישלם *marey gumlaiya hu gimla yeshallem*, "The Lord of retribution, he will render recompense." He manifestly read בעל *baal* instead of כעל *keal*. מרי גמליא *marey gumlaiya* is בעל גמלות *baal gemuloth;* as מרי מרירותא *marey merirutha* is בעל אף *baal aph*. Prov. xxii. 24. And so in the *Chaldee* paraphrase on Isa. xxxv. 4: מרי גמליא יי הוא יתגלי *marey gamlaiya yeya hu yithgeley*, "The Lord of retribution, Jehovah himself, shall be revealed;" words very near to those of the prophet in this place. The second כעל *keal*, which the *Chaldee* has omitted, must be read בעל *baal* likewise. With this only addition to the *Chaldee*, which the Hebrew text justifies, we are supplied with the following clear reading of the passage:—

בעל גמלות הוא
hu gemuloth baal
בעל גמלות ישלם
yeshallem gemuloth baal

The Lord of retributions, he
The Lord of retributions, shall repay.

The כ *caph* in כעל *keal* twice seems to have been at first ב *beth*, in MS. This verse in the *Septuagint* is very imperfect. In the first part of it they give us no assistance: the latter part is wholly omitted in the printed copies; but it is thus supplied by MSS. Pachom. and I. D. II: Τοις ὑπεναντιοις αυτου· αμυναν τοις εχθροις αυτου· ταις νησοις αποδομα αποτισει.—L.

Verse 19. *When the enemy shall come in like a flood*] This all the rabbins refer to the coming of the Messiah. If ye see a generation which endures much tribulation, then (say they) expect him, according to what is written: "When the enemy shall come in like a flood, the Spirit of the Lord shall lift up a standard against him."

Kimchi says, he that was the standard-bearer always began the battle by first smiting at the enemy. Here then the Spirit of the Lord is the standard-bearer, and strikes the first blow. They who go against sin and Satan with the Holy Spirit at their head, are sure to win the day.

The Spirit of the Lord shall lift up a standard against him—"Which a strong wind driveth along."] Quam spiritus Domini cogit, "Which the Spirit of the Lord drives on."—*Vulg.* נוססה *nosesah*, pihel à נוס *nus* fugit. *Kimchi* says his father thus explained this word: נוססה *nosesah* interpretatur in significatione fugæ, et ait, spiritus Domini *fugabit* hostem;— nam secundum eum נוססה *nosesah* est ex conjugatione quadrata, ejusque radix est נוס *nus:* "nosesah he interpreted in the signification of *flight,*—*The Spirit of the Lord shall put the enemy to flight;* for according to him the root of the word is נוס *nus, he put to flight.*" The object of this action I explain otherwise. The conjunction ו *vau*, prefixed to רוח *ruach*, seems necessary to the sense; it is added by the corrector in one of the Koningsberg MSS., collated by Lilienthal. It is added also in one of my own.

Verse 20. *Unto them that turn from trans-*

A. M. cir. 3292 B. C. cir. 712 Zion, and unto them that turn
Olymp. XVII. 1 from transgression in Jacob,
cir. annum NumæPompilii, saith the LORD.
R. Roman., 4 21 [c]As for me, this *is* my covenant with them, saith the LORD; My Spirit
that *is* upon thee, and my words which I have
put in thy mouth, shall not de- A. M. cir. 3292 B. C. cir. 712
part out of thy mouth, nor out Olymp. XVII. 1
of the mouth of thy seed, nor cir. annum NumæPompilii,
out of the mouth of thy seed's R. Roman., 4
seed, saith the LORD, from henceforth and for
ever.

[c]Heb. viii. 10; x. 16

gression in Jacob—"And shall turn away iniquity from Jacob"] So the *Septuagint* and St. Paul, Rom. xi. 26, reading instead of לשבי *leshabey* and ביעקב *beyaacob*, והשיב *veheshib* and מיעקב *meyaacob*. The *Syriac* likewise reads והשיב *veheshib;* and the *Chaldee*, to the same sense, ולהשיב *ulehashib*. Our translators have expressed the sense of the present reading of the Hebrew text: "And unto them that turn from transgression in Jacob."

Verse 21. *This* is *my covenant with them*—"This is the covenant which I make with them"] For אותם *otham, them*, twenty-four MSS., (four ancient,) and nine editions have אתם *ittam, with them.*

My Spirit that is *upon thee*] This seems to be an address to the *Messiah; Kimchi* says it is to the *prophet*, informing him that the spirit of prophecy should be given to all Israelites in the days of the Messiah, as it was then given to *him*, i. e., to the prophet.

And my words which I have put in thy mouth] Whatsoever Jesus spoke was the *word* and *mind* of God himself; and must, as such, be implicitly received.

Nor out of the mouth of thy seed] The *same doctrines* which Jesus preached, all his faithful ministers preach; and his *seed*—genuine Christians, who are all *born of God*, believe; and *they* shall continue, and the doctrines remain in the *seed's seed* through all generations—for ever and ever. This is God's *covenant*, ordered in all things and sure.

CHAPTER LX

The glorious prospect displayed in this chapter seems to have elevated the prophet even above his usual majesty. The subject is the very flourishing condition of the Church of Jesus Christ at that period of the Gospel dispensation when both Jews and Gentiles shall become one fold under one Shepherd. The imagery employed is of the most consolatory and magnificent description. This blessed state of the world shall follow a time of gross darkness, 1, 2. *The universal diffusion of vital godliness beautifully set forth by a great variety of images,* 3–14. *The everlasting duration and spotless purity of this kingdom of Christ,* 15–21. *A time appointed in the counsels of Jehovah for the commencement of this happy period; and when this time arrives, the particulars of the prophecy shall have a speedy accomplishment,* 22.

A. M. cir. 3292 B. C. cir. 712 ARISE, [a]shine; [b]for thy light
Olymp. XVII. 1 is come, and [c]the glory of
cir. annum NumæPompilii, the LORD is risen upon thee.
R. Roman., 4 2 For, behold, the darkness
shall cover the earth, and gross A. M. cir. 3292 B. C. cir. 712
darkness the people: but the Olymp. XVII. 1
LORD shall arise upon thee, and cir. annum NumæPompilii,
his glory shall be seen upon thee. R. Roman., 4

[a]Eph. v. 14——[b]Or, *be enlightened; for thy light cometh*——[c]Mal. iv. 2

The subject of this chapter is the great increase and flourishing state of the Church of God by the conversion and accession of the heathen nations to it, which is set forth in such ample and exalted terms, as plainly show that the full completion of this prophecy is reserved for future times. This subject is displayed in the most splendid colours under a great variety of images highly poetical, designed to give a general idea of the glories of that perfect state of the Church of God which we are taught to expect in the latter times; when the fulness of the Gentiles shall come in, and the Jews shall be converted and gathered from their dispersions, and the kingdoms of this world shall become the kingdoms of our Lord and of his Christ.

Of the use in prophecy of general or common poetical images, in setting forth the greatness and importance of a future event universally, without descending to particulars, or too minutely explaining circumstances, I have already pretty largely treated in the twentieth prelection on the Hebrew poetry; and have more than once observed in these notes that such images are not always to be applied particularly to persons and things, and were never intended to be minutely explained. I shall add here the opinion of a very learned and judicious person upon this subject: "It is, I think, a mark of right understanding in the language of prophecy, and in the design of prophecy too, to keep to what appears the design and meaning of the prophecy in general, and what the whole of it laid together points out to us; and not to suffer a warm imagination to mislead us from the real intention of the spirit of prophecy, by following uncertain applications of the parts of it." *Lowman* on the Revelation, note on chap. xix. 21.—L. To this testimony I must add my own. This is one of the most glorious chapters in the whole of the Old Testament. The splendour, glory, and excellence of the Church of Christ are here pointed out in language which the Spirit of God alone is capable of using. But *when* shall this state of blessedness take place? Lord, *thou* only knowest.

NOTES ON CHAP. LX

Verse 1. *Arise*] Call upon God through Christ, for his salvation; and,

Shine] אורי *ori, be illuminated;* for till thou

A. M. cir. 3292
B. C. cir. 712
Olymp. XVII. 1
cir. annum
NumæPompilii,
R. Roman., 4

3 And the [d]Gentiles shall come
to thy light, and kings to the
brightness of thy rising.
4 [e]Lift up thine eyes round
about, and see: all they gather themselves
together, [f]they come to thee: thy sons shall
come from far, and thy daughters shall be
nursed at *thy* side.
5 Then thou shalt see, and flow together,
and thine heart shall fear, and be enlarged;
because [g]the [h]abundance of the sea
shall be converted unto thee, the [i]forces
of the Gentiles shall come unto
thee.
6 The multitude of camels shall
cover thee, the dromedaries of Midian
and [k]Ephah; all they from [l]Sheba shall
come: they shall bring [m]gold and incense; and
they shall show forth the praises of the LORD.
7 All the flocks of [n]Kedar shall be gathered
together unto thee, the rams of Nebaioth shall
minister unto thee: they shall come up with
acceptance on mine altar, and [o]I will glorify
the house of my glory.

[d]Chap. xlix. 6, 23; Rev. xxi. 24——[e]Chap. xlix. 18
[f]Chap. xlix. 20, 21, 22; lxvi. 12——[g]Rom. xi. 25
[h]Or, *noise of the sea shall be turned toward thee*

[i]Or, *wealth;* ver. 11; chap. lxi. 6——[k]Gen. xxv. 4
[l]Psa. lxxii. 10——[m]Chap. lxi. 6; Matt. ii. 11——[n]Gen. xxv. 13——[o]Hag. ii. 7, 9

arise and call upon God, thou wilt never receive true light.

For thy light is come] כי בא אורך *ki ba orech, for thy light cometh.* The Messiah is at the door; who, while he is a light to lighten the Gentiles, will be the glory—the effulgence, of his people Israel.

Verse 2. *Darkness shall cover the earth*] This is the state of the Gentile people.

Verse 3. *And the Gentiles shall come*] This has been in some sort already fulfilled. The Gentiles have received the light of the Gospel from the land of Judea, and the Gentile *kings* have embraced that Gospel; so that many nations of the earth are full of the doctrine of Christ.

Verse 4. *Shall be nursed at* thy *side*—"Shall be carried at the side."] For תאמנה *teamanah, shall be nursed,* the *Septuagint* and *Chaldee* read תנשאנה *tinnasenah, shall be carried.* A MS. has על כתף תנשאנה *al catheph tinnasenah,* "shall be carried on the shoulder;" instead of על צד תאמנה *al tsad teamanah,* "shall be nursed on the side." Another MS. has both כתף *catheph* and צד *tsad.* Another MS. has it thus: תנשאנה: תאמנה *tinnasenah : teamanah,* with a line drawn over the first word. Sir John Chardin says that it is the general custom in the east to carry their children astride upon the hip with the arm round their body. His MS. note on this place is as follows:—Coutume en Orient de porter les enfans sur le coste à califourchon sur la hanche: cette facon est generale aux Indes; les enfans se tiennent comme cela, et la personne qui les porte les embrasse et serre par le corps; parceque sont (ni) emmaillottès, ni en robes qui les embrassent. "In the east it is the custom to carry the children on the haunch, with the legs astride. This is the general custom in India. The children support themselves in this way, and the arm of the nurse goes round the body and presses the child close to the side; and this they can easily do, as the children are not swathed, nor encumbered with clothes." Non brachiis occidentalium more, sed humeris, divaricatis tibiis, impositos circumferunt. "They carry them about, not in their arms after the manner of the western nations, but on their shoulders; the children being placed astride." *Cotovic.* Iter. Syr. cap. xiv. This last quotation seems to favour the reading על כתף *al catheph, on the shoulder,* as the *Septuagint* likewise do: but upon the whole I think that על צד תנשאנה *al tsad tinnasenah* is the true reading, which the *Chaldee* favours; and I have accordingly followed it. See chap. lxvi. 12.—L. This mode of carrying children is as common in *India* as carrying them in the arms is in *Europe.*

Verse 5. *Then thou shalt see*—"Then shalt thou fear"] For תראי *tirai, thou shalt see,* as ours and much the greater number of the translators, ancient and modern, render it, forty MSS. (ten ancient) of *Kennicott's,* and twenty-eight of *De Rossi's,* with one ancient of my own, and the old edition of 1488, have תיראי *tirai, thou shalt fear:* the true reading, confirmed by the perfect parallelism of the sentences: the heart *ruffled* and *dilated* in the second line answering to the *fear* and *joy* expressed in the first. The Prophet Jeremiah, chap. xxxiii. 9, has the same natural and elegant sentiment:—

"And this city shall become to me a name of joy;
A praise and an honour for all the nations of the earth;
Which shall hear all the good that I do unto them:
And they shall fear, and they shall tremble, at all the goodness
And at all the prosperity that I procure unto her."

And David:—

"I will praise thee, for I am fearfully and wonderfully made." PSA. cxxxix. 14.

His tibi me rebus quædam divina voluptas
Percipit atque horror. LUCRET. iii. 28.

Recenti mens trepidat metu,
Plenoque Bacchi pectore turbidum
Lætatur. HOR. *Carm.* ii. 19. l. 5.—L.

Verse 6. *The praises of the Lord*—"And the praise of JEHOVAH."] Thirty-three MSS. and three editions have ותהלת *uthehillath,* in the singular number; and so read the ancient versions, and one of my own MSS.

Verse 7. *The rams of Nebaioth shall minister unto thee*] Vitringa on the place understands their ministering, and ascending or going up on the altar, as offering themselves voluntarily: ipsi se, non expectato sacerdote alio, gloriæ et

A. M. cir. 3292
B. C. cir. 712
Olymp. XVII. 1
cir. annum
NumæPompilii,
R. Roman., 4

8 Who *are* these *that* fly as a cloud, and as the doves to their windows?

9 [p]Surely the isles shall wait for me, and the ships of Tarshish first, [q]to bring thy sons from far, [r]their silver and their gold with them, [s]unto the name of the LORD thy God, and to the Holy One of Israel, [t]because he hath glorified thee.

10 And [u]the sons of strangers shall build up thy walls, [v]and their kings shall minister unto thee: for [w]in my wrath I smote thee, [x]but in my favour have I had mercy on thee.

11 Therefore thy gates [y]shall be open continually; they shall not be shut day nor night; that *men* may bring unto thee the [z]forces of the Gentiles, and *that* their kings *may be* brought.

12 [a]For the nation and kingdom that will not serve thee shall perish; yea, *those* nations shall be utterly wasted.

13 [b]The glory of Lebanon shall come unto thee, the fir tree, the pine tree, and the box together, to beautify the place of my sanctuary; and I will make [c]the place of my feet glorious.

14 The sons also of them that afflicted thee shall come bending unto thee; and all they that despised thee shall [d]bow themselves down at the soles of thy feet; and they shall call thee, The city of the LORD, [e]the Zion of the Holy One of Israel.

A. M. cir. 3292
B. C. cir. 712
Olymp. XVII. 1
cir. annum
NumæPompilii,
R. Roman., 4

15 Whereas thou hast been forsaken and hated, so that no man went through *thee,* I will make thee an eternal excellency, a joy of many generations.

16 Thou shalt also suck the milk of the Gentiles, [f]and shalt suck the breast of kings: and thou shalt know that [g]I the LORD *am* thy Saviour and thy Redeemer, the Mighty One of Jacob.

17 For brass I will bring gold, and for iron I will bring silver, and for wood brass, and for stones iron: I will also make thy officers peace, and thine exactors righteousness.

18 Violence shall no more be heard in thy land, wasting nor destruction within thy borders; but thou shalt call [h]thy walls Salvation, and thy gates Praise.

19 The [i]sun shall be no more thy light by day; neither for brightness shall the moon give light unto thee: but the LORD shall be unto thee an everlasting light, and [k]thy God thy glory.

20 [l]Thy sun shall no more go down; neither

[p]Psa. lxxii. 10; chap. xlii. 4; li. 5——[q]Gal. iv. 26——[r]Psa. lxviii. 30; Zech. xiv. 14——[s]Jer. iii. 17——[t]Chap. lv. 5——[u]Zech. vi. 15——[v]Chap. xlix. 23; Rev. xxi. 24——[w]Chap. lvii. 17——[x]Chap. liv. 7, 8——[y]Rev. xxi. 25——[z]Or, *wealth;* ver. 5——[a]Zech. xiv. 17, 19; Matt. xxi. 44

[b]Chap. xxxv. 2; xli. 19——[c]See 1 Chron. xxviii. 2; Psa. cxxxii. 7——[d]Chap. xlix. 23; Rev. iii. 9——[e]Heb. xii. 22; Rev. xiv. 1——[f]Chap. xlix. 23; lxi. 6; lxvi. 11, 12——[g]Chap. xliii. 3——[h]Chap. xxvi. 1——[i]Rev. xxi. 23; xxii. 5——[k]Zech. ii. 5——[l]See Amos viii. 9

sanctificationi divini nominis ultro ac libenter oblaturi. "They, waiting for no priest, go and freely offer themselves to the glory and sanctification of the sacred name." This gives a very elegant and poetical turn to the image. It was a general notion that prevailed with sacrificers among the heathen, that the victim's being brought without reluctance to the altar was a good omen; and the contrary a bad one. Sabinus petit aliquanto tristior; quod sacrificanti hostia aufugerat. *Sueton.* Titus, cap. x. Accessit dirum omen, profugus altaribus tauris. "It was an omen of dreadful portent when the victim fled away from the altar." *Tacit.* Hist. iii. 56.—L.

Verse 8. *And as the doves to their windows*—"And like doves upon the wing?"] Instead of אל *el, to,* forty-two MSS. of *Kennicott's,* and one of mine, have על *al, upon.* For ארבתיהם *arubboteyhem, their windows,* read אברתיהם *ebrotheyhem, their wings,* transposing a letter.—*Houbigant.* The *Septuagint* render it *συν νεοσσοις,* "with their young;" they read אפרחיהם *ephrocheyhem,* nearer to the latter than to the present reading.—L.

Verse 9. *The ships of Tarshish first*—"The ships of Tarshish among the first"] For בראשנה *barishonah* twenty-five MSS. and the *Syriac* read כבראשנה *kebarishonah,* "as at the first." The ships of Tarshish AS at the first; that is, *as* they brought gold and silver in the days of Solomon.

Verse 13. *And I will make the place of my feet glorious*—"And that I may glorify the place whereon I rest my feet"] The temple of Jerusalem was called the house of God, and the place of his rest or residence. The visible symbolical appearance of God, called by the Jews the schechinah, was in the most holy place, between the wings of the cherubim, above the ark. This is considered as the throne of God, presiding as King over the Jewish state; and as a footstool is a necessary appendage to a throne, (see note on chap. lii. 2,) the ark is considered as the footstool of God, and is so called, Psa. xcix. 5, 1 Chron. xxviii. 2.

The glory of Lebanon] That is, the cedar.

Verse 19. *Neither for brightness shall the moon give light unto thee*—"Nor by night shall the brightness of the moon enlighten thee"] This line, as it stands in the present text, seems to be defective. The *Septuagint* and *Chaldee* both express *the night,* which is almost necessary to answer to *day* in the preceding line, as well as to perfect the sense here. I therefore

A. M. cir. 3292 B. C. cir. 712 Olymp. XVII. 1 cir. annum NumæPompilii, R. Roman., 4

shall thy moon withdraw itself:
for the LORD shall be thine everlasting light, and the days of
thy mourning shall be ended.
21 [m]Thy people also *shall be* all righteous:
[n]they shall inherit the land for ever, [o]the
branch of my planting, [p]the work
of my hands, that I may be
glorified.
22 [q]A little one shall become
a thousand, and a small one a strong nation:
I the LORD will hasten it in his time.

[m]Chap. lii. 1; Rev. xxi. 27——[n]Psa. xxxvii. 11, 22; Matt. v. 5

[o]Chap. lxi. 3; Matt. xv. 13; John xv. 2——[p]Chap. xxix. 23; xlv. 11; Eph. ii. 10——[q]Matt. xiii. 31, 32

think that we ought, upon the authority of the *Septuagint and Chaldee,* to read either ולילה *velailah, and by night,* instead of ולנגה *ulenogah, and for brightness;* or ולנגה בלילה *ulenogah ballailah,* adding the word בלילה *ballailah, by night.*—L.

Verse 21. *Of my planting*] מטעי *mattai;* so, with the *Keri,* read forty-four MSS. (seven ancient) and six editions; with which agree the *Syriac, Chaldee,* and *Vulgate.*

Verse 22. *I the Lord will hasten it in his time*] There is a time set for the fulfilment of this prophecy: that time must come before it begins to take place; but when it does begin, the whole will be performed in a short space. It is not, therefore, the time determined for the event that shall be hastened, but all the circumstances of the event; all the parts of the prediction shall be speedily completed. **I the Lorde in hys tyme sodeynly schal doun thys.**—Old MS. Bible. And because it is the LORD, therefore it will be done: for although it be difficult, he is almighty.

CHAPTER LXI

The subject of the preceding chapter is continued in this; and to give it the greater solemnity, the Messiah is introduced describing his character and office, and confirming the large promises made before, 1–9. *In consequence of this the Jewish Church is introduced, praising God for the honour done her by her restoration to favour, and by the accession of the Gentiles, which is beautifully described by allusions to the rich pontifical dress of the high priest; a happy similitude to express the ornaments of a restored nation and of a renewed mind,* 10. *Certainty of the prophecy illustrated by a figure drawn from the vegetable kingdom,* 11.

A. M. cir. 3292 B. C. cir. 712 Olymp. XVII. 1 cir. annum NumæPompilii, R. Roman., 4

THE [a]Spirit of the Lord GOD
is upon me; because the
LORD [b]hath anointed me to
preach good tidings unto the
meek; he hath sent me [c]to bind up the
broken-hearted, to proclaim [d]liberty to the
captives, and the opening of
the prison to *them that are*
bound;
2 [e]To proclaim the acceptable
year of the LORD, and [f]the day of vengeance
of our God; [g]to comfort all that mourn;

[a]Chap. xi. 2; Luke iv. 18; John i. 32; iii. 34——[b]Psa. xlv. 7——[c]Psa. cxlvii. 3; chap. lvii. 15——[d]Chap. xlii. 7; see Jer. xxxiv. 8

[e]See Lev. xxv. 9——[f]Chap. xxxiv. 8; lxiii. 4; lxvi. 14; Mal. iv. 1, 3; 2 Thess. i. 7, 8, 9——[g]Chap. lvii. 18; Matt. v. 4

NOTES ON CHAP. LXI

Verse 1. *The Spirit of the Lord God is upon me*—"The Spirit of JEHOVAH is upon me"] The *Septuagint, Vulgate,* and St. Luke, (chap. iv. 18,) and a MS., and two old editions omit the word אדני *Adonai, the Lord;* which was probably added to the text through the superstition of the Jews, to prevent the pronunciation of the word יהוה *Yehovah* following. See *Kennicott* on the state of the printed Hebrew text, vol. i., p. 510.

In most of Isaiah's prophecies there is a primary and secondary sense, or a remote subject illustrated by one that is near. The deliverance of the Jews from their captivity in Babylon is constantly used to shadow forth the salvation of men by Jesus Christ. Even the prophet himself is a typical person, and is sometimes intended to represent the great Saviour. It is evident from Luke iv. 18 that this is a prophecy of our blessed Lord and his preaching; and yet it is as evident that it primarily refers to Isaiah preaching the glad tidings of deliverance to the Jews.

The opening of the prison—"Perfect liberty"] פקח קוח *pekach koach.* Ten MSS. of *Kennicott's,* several of *De Rossi's,* and one of my own, with the *Complutensian,* have פקחקוח *pekachkoach* in one word; and so the *Septuagint* and *Vulgate* appear to have taken it: not merely opening of prisons, but every kind of liberty—complete redemption.

The proclaiming of perfect liberty to the bound, and the year of acceptance with JEHOVAH, is a manifest allusion to the proclaiming of the year of jubilee by sound of trumpet. See Lev. xxv. 9, &c. This was a year of general release of debts and obligations, of bondmen and bondwomen, of lands and possessions which had been sold from the families and tribes to which they belonged. Our Saviour, by applying this text to himself, (Luke iv. 18, 19,) a text so manifestly relating to the institution

A. M. cir. 3292 B. C. cir. 712 Olymp. XVII. 1 cir. annum NumæPompilii, R. Roman., 4

3 To appoint unto them that
mourn in Zion, [h]to give unto
them beauty for ashes, the oil
of joy for mourning, the gar-
ment of praise for the spirit of heaviness;
that they might be called trees of righteousness, [i]the planting of the LORD, [k]that he might
be glorified.

4 And they shall [l]build the old wastes, they
shall raise up the former desolations, and they
shall repair the waste cities, the desolations
of many generations.

5 And [m]strangers shall stand
and feed your flocks, and the sons
of the alien *shall be* your ploughmen and your vinedressers.

6 [n]But ye shall be named the Priests of the
LORD: *men* shall call you the Ministers of
our God: [o]ye shall eat the riches of the Gentiles, and in their glory shall ye boast yourselves.

7 [p]For your shame *ye shall have* double;
and *for* confusion they shall rejoice in their
portion: therefore in their land they shall

[h]Psa. xxx. 11——[i]Chap. lx. 21——[k]John xv. 8——[l]Ch. xlix. 8; lviii. 12; Ezek. xxxvi. 33, 36——[m]Eph. ii. 12

[n]Exod. xix. 6; ch. lx. 17; lxvi. 21; 1 Pet. ii. 5, 9; Rev. i. 6; v. 10——[o]Ch. lx. 5, 11, 16——[p]Ch. xl. 2; Zech. ix. 12

above mentioned, plainly declares the typical design of that institution.

Verse 3. *To appoint unto them that mourn in Zion*—"To impart *gladness* to the mourners of Zion"] A word necessary to the sense is certainly lost in this place, of which the ancient Versions have preserved no traces. Houbigant, by conjecture, inserts the word ששון *sason, gladness*, taken from the line next but one below, where it stands opposed to אבל *ebel, sorrow* or *mourning*, as the word lost here was to אבלי *abeley, mourners:* I follow him.—L.

Beauty for ashes—"A beautiful crown instead of ashes"] In times of mourning the Jews put on sackcloth, or coarse and sordid raiment, and spread dust and ashes on their heads; on the contrary, splendid clothing and ointment poured on the head were the signs of joy. "Feign thyself to be a mourner," says Joab to the woman of Tekoah, "and put on now mourning apparel, and anoint not thyself with oil," 2 Sam. xiv. 2. These customs are at large expressed in the Book of Judith: "She pulled off the sackcloth which she had on, and put off the garments of her widowhood, and washed her body all over with water and anointed herself with precious ointment, and braided the hair of her head, and put on a tire [mitre, marg.] upon it; and put on her garments of gladness;" chap. x. 3.—L.

פאר תחת אפר *peer tachath ephar, glory for ashes;* a paronomasia which the prophet often uses: a *chaplet, crown*, or other ornament of the head (for so the *Vulgate* renders the word here and in the 10th verse; in which last place the *Septuagint* agree in the same rendering,) *instead of dust and ashes*, which before covered it; and the costly ointments used on occasions of festivity, instead of the ensigns of sorrow.—L.

Trees of righteousness—"Trees approved"] Heb. *oaks of righteousness* or *truth;* that is, such as by their flourishing condition should show that they were indeed "the scion of God's planting, and the work of his hands;" under which images, in the preceding chapter, ver. 21, the true servants of God, in a highly improved state of the Church, were represented; that is, says Vitringa on that place, "commendable for the strength of their faith, their durability, and firmness."

Verse 4. *"And they that spring from thee"*] A word is lost here likewise. After ובנו *ubanu*, "they shall build," add ממך *mimmecha*, they that spring *from thee*. Four MSS. have it so, (two of them ancient,) and one of mine has it in the margin, and it is confirmed by chap. lviii. 12, where the sentence is the very same, this word being here added. *Kimchi* makes the same remark: "the word ממך *mimmecha* is omitted here; but is found in chap. lviii. 12."

The desolations of many generations] It seems that these words cannot refer to the Jews in the Babylonish captivity, for they were not there many generations; but it may refer to their dispersions and state of ruin since the advent of our Lord; and consequently this may be a promise of the restoration of the Jewish people.

Verse 5. *Strangers shall—feed your flocks*] Gentiles shall first preach to you the salvation of Christ, and feed with Divine knowledge the Jewish congregations.

Verse 7. *For your shame*—"Instead of your shame"] The translation of this verse, which is very confused, and probably corrupted in the Hebrew, is taken from the *Syriac* Version; except that the latter has not expressed the word משנה *mishneh, double*, in the first place. Five MSS. add the conjunction ו *vau* to שמחת *simchath*. The *Syriac* reads תרנו *taronnu*, and תירשו *tirashu*, in the second person, "*ye* shall rejoice, *ye* shall inherit." And for להם *lahem, to them*, two MSS., (one of them ancient,) three of *De Rossi's*, and the *Syriac*, read לכם *lahem, to you*, in the second person likewise.

The Version of the *Septuagint* is imperfect in this place; the first half of the verse is entirely omitted in all the printed copies. It is supplied by MSS. *Pachom.* and I. D. II. in the following manner:—

Αντι της αισχυνης ὑμων της διπλης,
Και αντι της εντροπης αγαλλιασεται ἡ μερις αυτων·
Δια τουτο την γην αυτων εκ δευτερου—

"Instead of your shame *ye shall have* double,
And instead of your confusion their portion shall rejoice;
Therefore, they shall possess their land a second time."

In which the two MSS. agree, except that I. D. II. has by mistake ἡμερας, *day*, for ἡ μερις, *the part.* And *Cod. Marchal.*, in the margin, has pretty nearly the same supplement as from *Theodotion.*—L.

A. M. cir. 3292
B. C. cir. 712
Olymp. XVII. 1
cir. annum
NumæPompilii,
R. Roman., 4

possess the double: everlasting
joy shall be unto them.
8 For [q]I the LORD love judgment, [r]I hate robbery for burnt-offering; and I will direct their work in truth,
[s]and I will make an everlasting covenant with them.
9 And their seed shall be known among the Gentiles, and their offspring among the people: all that see them shall acknowledge them, [t]that they *are* the seed *which* the LORD hath blessed.
10 [u]I will greatly rejoice in the LORD, my soul shall be joyful in my God; for [v]he hath clothed me with the garments of salvation, he hath covered me with the robe of righteousness, [w]as a bridegroom [x]decketh *himself* with ornaments, and as a bride adorneth *herself* with her jewels.
11 For as the earth bringeth forth her bud, and as the garden causeth the things that are sown in it to spring forth; so the Lord GOD will cause [y]righteousness and [z]praise to spring forth before all the nations.

[q]Psa. xi. 7——[r]Chap. i. 11, 13——[s]Chap. lv. 3——[t]Gen. xli. 7; xiii. 15; xv. 18; xvii. 8; xxiv. 7; xxvi. 3; xxviii. 4, 13; chap. lxv. 23——[u]Hab. iii. 18——[v]Psa. cxxxii. 9, 16——[w]Chap. xlix. 18; Rev. xxi. 2——[x]Heb. *decketh as priest*——[y]Psa. lxxii. 3; lxxxv. 11——[z]Chap. lx. 18; lxii. 7

Verse 8. *I hate robbery for burnt-offering*—"Who hate rapine and iniquity"] The *Syriac*, and *Chaldee* prefix the conjunction ו *vau*, instead of the preposition ב *beth*, to עולה *olah*, which they render *iniquity* or *oppression;* and so the *Septuagint*, αδικιας. The difference lies in the *punctuation;* בעולה *beolah*, in a *burnt-offering* בעולה *beavelah*, in *iniquity*. The *letters* are the same in both words. Five of *De Rossi's* MSS. confirm this reading.

Verse 9. *Their seed shall be known among the Gentiles*] Both Jews and Gentiles are to make but *one fold* under one shepherd, Christ Jesus. But still, notwithstanding this, they may retain their peculiarity and national distinction; so that though they are known to be Christians, yet they shall appear to be converted Jews. After their conversion to Christianity this will necessarily be the case for a long time. Strange nations are not so speedily amalgamated, as to lose their peculiar cast of features, and other national distinctions.

Verse 10. *I will greatly rejoice in the Lord*] These may be the words of the Jews now converted, and brought into the Church of Christ, and with the Gentiles made fellow heirs of the blessings of the new covenant.

As a bridegroom decketh himself *with ornaments*—"As the bridegroom decketh himself with a priestly crown"] An allusion to the magnificent dress of the high priest, when performing his functions; and particularly to the mitre, and crown or plate of gold on the front of it, Exod. xxix. 6. The bonnet or mitre of the priests also was made, as Moses expresses it, "for glory and for beauty," Exod. xxviii. 40. It is difficult to give its full force to the prophet's metaphor in another language. The version of *Aquila* and *Symmachus* comes nearest to it: ως νυμφιον ιερατευομενον στεφανῳ· "as a bridegroom decked with a priestly crown."—L.

Verse 11. *The Lord God*—"The Lord JEHOVAH"] "אדני *Adonai, the Lord*, makes the line longer than the preceding and following; and the *Septuagint, Alexandrian*, (and MSS. *Pachom.* and I. D. II.,) and *Arabic*, do not so render it. Hence it seems to be interpolated."—Dr. JUBB. Three MSS. have it not. See on ver. 1 of this chapter. Both words אדני יהוה *Adonai Yehovah*, are wanting in one of my MSS.; but are supplied in the margin by a later hand.

CHAPTER LXII

The prophet opens this chapter with ardent prayers that the happy period of reconciliation just now promised, and here again foretold, may be hastened, 1–5. *He then calls upon the faithful, particularly the priests and Levites, to join him, urging the promises, and even the oath, of Jehovah, as the foundation of their request,* 6–9. *And, relying on this oath, he goes on to speak of the general restoration promised, as already performing; and calls to the people to march forth, and to the various nations among whom they are dispersed to prepare the way for them, as God had caused the order for their return to be universally proclaimed,* 10–12.

A. M. cir. 3292
B. C. cir. 712
Olymp. XVII. 1
cir. annum
NumæPompilii,
R. Roman., 4

FOR Zion's sake will I not hold my peace, and for Jerusalem's sake [a]I will not rest, until the righteousness thereof go forth as brightness, and the salvation thereof as a lamp *that* burneth.
2 [b]And the Gentiles shall see thy righteousness, and all kings

[a]Ver. 7——[b]Chap. lx. 3

NOTES ON CHAP. LXII

Verse 1. *For Zion's sake will I not hold my peace*] These are the words of JEHOVAH declaring his purpose relative to the events predicted in the preceding chapter.

Thou shalt be called by a new name] Viz., CHRISTIAN—or, as in the fourth verse, חפצי בה

A. M. cir. 3292
B. C. cir. 712
Olymp. XVII. 1
cir. annum
NumæPompilii,
R. Roman., 4

thy glory: [c]and thou shalt be
called by a new name, which
the mouth of the LORD shall
name.

3 Thou shalt also be [d]a crown of glory in
the hand of the LORD, and a royal diadem in
the hand of thy God.

4 [e]Thou shalt no more be termed [f]Forsaken;
neither shall thy land any more be termed
[g]Desolate: but thou shalt be called [h]Hephzi-
bah, and thy land [i]Beulah: for the LORD delighteth in thee, and thy land shall be married.

5 For *as* a young man marrieth
a virgin, *so* shall thy sons marry
thee: and [k]*as* the bridegroom rejoiceth over the bride, *so* [l]shall
thy God rejoice over thee.

A. M. cir. 3292
B. C. cir. 712
Olymp. XVII. 1
cir. annum
NumæPompilii,
R. Roman., 4

6 [m]I have set watchmen upon thy walls, O
Jerusalem, *which* shall never hold their peace
day nor night: [n]ye that make mention of the
LORD, keep not silence,

7 And give him no [o]rest, till he establish,
and till he make Jerusalem [p]a praise in the
earth.

---

[c]See verse 4, 12; chapter lxv. 15——[d]Zech. ix. 16——[e]Hos. i. 10; 1 Pet. ii. 10——[f]Chap. xlix. 14; liv. 6, 7——[g]Chap. liv. 1——[h]That is, *My delight is in her*——[i]That is, *Married*

[k]Heb. *with the joy of the bridegroom*——[l]Chap. lxv. 19——[m]Ezek. iii. 17; xxxiii. 7——[n]Or, *ye that are the LORD'S remembrancers*——[o]Heb. *silence*——[p]Chap. lxi. 11; Zeph. iii. 20

---

chephtsi bah, "my delight is in her"—because she has now received that command, "This is my beloved Son, in whom I am well pleased; HEAR HIM."

Verse 4. *Thy land Beulah*] בעולה *beulah, married.* In the prophets, a *desolate land* is represented under the notion of *a widow;* an *inhabited land*, under that of a *married woman*, who has both *a husband* and *children.*

Verse 5. *For* as *a young man*—so] The particles of comparison are not at present in the *Hebrew* Text: but the *Septuagint*, *Syriac*, and *Chaldee* seem to have read in their copies כ *caph* prefixed to the verb, כי כיבעל *ki keyibal*, which seems to have been omitted by mistake of a transcriber, occasioned by the repetition of the same two letters. And before the verb in the second line a MS. adds כן *ken, so;* which the *Septuagint*, *Syriac*, and *Chaldee* seem also to have had in their copies. In the third line of this verse the same MS. has in like manner וכמשוש *vechimsos*, and two MSS. and the *Babylonish Talmud* כמשוש *kimsos*, adding the כ *caph;* and in the fourth line, the *Babylonish Talmud* likewise adds כן *ken, so*, before the verb.

Sir *John Chardin*, in his note on this place, tells us, "that it is the custom in the east for youths, that were never married, always to marry virgins; and widowers, however young, to marry widows."—HARMER, *Observ.* ii. p. 482.

So *shall thy sons marry thee.*] For בניך *banayich, thy sons*, Bishop *Lowth* reads, *restorer* or *builder*, as he does not consider the word as the plural of בן *ben, a son*, but the participle *benoni* of the verb בנה *banah, he built.* I do not see that we gain much by this translation. *Thy sons shall dwell in thee, Vulgate;* and so the *Septuagint* and *Chaldee.*

Verse 6. *Ye that make mention of the Lord, keep not silence*] The faithful, and in particular the priests and Levites, are exhorted by the prophet to beseech God with unremitted importunity (compare Luke xviii. 1, &c.) to hasten the redemption of Sion. The image in this place is taken from the temple service; in which there was appointed a constant watch, day and night, by the Levites: and among them this seems to have belonged particularly to the singers, see 1 Chron. ix. 33. Now the watches in the east, even to this day, are performed by a loud cry from time to time of the watchmen, to mark the time, and that very frequently, and in order to show that they themselves are constantly attentive to their duty. Hence the watchmen are said by the prophet, chap. lii. 8, *to lift up their voice;* and here they are commanded, *not to keep silence;* and the greatest reproach to them is, *that they are dumb dogs; they cannot bark; dreamers; sluggards, loving to slumber*, chap. lvi. 10. "The watchmen in the camp of the caravans go their rounds crying one after another, 'God is one, he is merciful:' and often add, 'Take heed to yourselves.'" TAVERNIER, *Voyage de Perse*, Liv. i. chap. x. The hundred and thirty-fourth Psalm gives us an example of the temple watch. The whole Psalm is nothing more than the alternate cry of two different divisions of the watch. The first watch addresses the second, reminding them of their duty; the second answers by a solemn blessing. The address and the answer seem both to be a set form, which each division proclaimed, or sung aloud, at stated intervals, to notify the time of the night:—

FIRST CHORUS

"Come on now, bless ye JEHOVAH, all ye servants of JEHOVAH;
Ye that stand in the house of JEHOVAH in the nights;
Lift up your hands towards the sanctuary,
And bless ye JEHOVAH."

SECOND CHORUS

"JEHOVAH bless thee out of Sion;
He that made heaven and earth."

"Ye who stand in the *place of the watch*, in the house of the sanctuary of the Lord; and ye praise through the nights;"—says the *Chaldee* paraphrase on the second line. And this explains what is here particularly meant by proclaiming, or making remembrance of, the name of JEHOVAH: the form, which the watch made use of on these occasions, was always a short sentence, expressing some pious sentiment, of which JEHOVAH was the subject; and it is remarkable, that the custom in the east in this respect also still continues the very same; as appears by the example above given from *Tavernier.*

A. M. cir. 3292
B. C. cir. 712
Olymp. XVII. 1
cir. annum
NumæPompilii,
R. Roman., 4

8 The LORD hath sworn by his
right hand, and by the arm of his
strength, [q]Surely I will no more
[r]give thy corn *to be* meat for
thine enemies; and the sons of the stranger
shall not drink thy wine, for the which thou
hast laboured:
9 But they that have gathered it shall eat it,
and praise the LORD; and they that have
brought it together shall drink it [s]in the courts
of my holiness.
10 Go through, go through the gates; [t]prepare ye the way of the people;
cast up, cast up the highway;
gather out the stones; [u]lift up a
standard for the people.

A. M. cir. 3292
B. C. cir. 712
Olymp. XVII. 1
cir. annum
NumæPompilii,
R. Roman., 4

11 Behold, the LORD hath proclaimed unto
the end of the world, [v]Say ye to the daughter
of Zion, Behold, thy salvation cometh; behold,
his [w]reward *is* with him, and his [x]work before him.
12 And they shall call them, The holy people, The redeemed of the LORD: and thou shalt
be called, Sought out, A city [y]not forsaken.

---

[q]Heb. *If I give, &c.*——[r]Deut. xxix. 31, &c.; Jer. v. 17——[s]See Deut. xii. 12; xiv. 23, 26; xvi. 11, 14——[t]Chap. xl. 3; lvii. 14

[u]Chap. xi. 12——[v]Zech. ix. 9; Matt. xxi. 5; John xii. 15——[w]Chap. xl. 10; Rev. xxii. 12——[x]Or, *recompense*——[y]Ver. 4

And this observation leads to the explanation of an obscure passage in the Prophet Malachi, chap. ii. 12.

"JEHOVAH will cut off the man that doeth this;
The watchman and the answerer, from the tabernacles of Jacob;
And him that presenteth an offering to JEHOVAH God of hosts."

ער וענה *er veoneh, the master and the scholar,* says our translation, after the *Vulgate: the son and the grandson,* says the *Syriac* and *Chaldee,* as little to the purpose: *Arias Montanus* has given it *vigilantem et respondentem,* "the watchman and the answerer;" that is, the Levite and "him that presenteth an offering to JEHOVAH," that is, the priest.—L. *Ye that make mention of the Lord, keep not silence.* Is not this clause an address to the ministers of Christ, to continue in supplication for the conversion of the Jewish people? *Kimchi* seems to think that the watchmen are the *interceding angels!*

Verse 9. *But they that have gathered it shall eat it, and praise the Lord*] This and the following line have reference to the law of Moses: "Thou mayest not eat within thy gates the tithe of thy corn, or of thy wine, or of thy oil; but thou must eat them before the Lord thy God, in the place which the Lord thy God shall choose," Deut. xii. 17, 18. "And when ye shall come into the land, and shall have planted all manner of trees for food, then ye shall count the fruit thereof as uncircumcised: three years it shall be as uncircumcised unto you; it shall not be eaten of. But in the fourth year all the fruit thereof shall be holy to praise the Lord withal. And in the fifth year ye shall eat the fruit thereof," Lev. xix. 23-25. This clearly explains the force of the expressions, "shall praise JEHOVAH," and "shall drink it in my sacred courts."

Five MSS., one ancient, have יאכלוהו *yocheluhu, they shall eat it,* fully expressed: and so likewise ישתוהו *yishtuhu, they shall drink it,* is found in nineteen MSS., three of them ancient.—L.

Verse 10. *Of the people*—"For the people"] Before the word העם *haam, the people,* two MSS. insert יהוה *Yehovah;* one MS. adds the same word after; and eight MSS., three ancient, instead of העם *haam,* have יהוה *Yehovah,* and so likewise one edition. But though it makes a good sense either way, I believe it to be an interpolation, as the ancient Versions do not favour it. The *Septuagint* indeed read עמי *ammi, my people.*—L.

Verse 11. *Unto the end of the world*—אל קצה הארץ *el ketseh haarets*—Instead of אל *el, to,* עד *ad,* UNTO, is the reading of two of *Kennicott's* MSS.; and one of mine has מקצה *mikketseh,* "FROM the end of the earth."

Behold, thy salvation cometh—"Lo, thy Saviour cometh"] So all the ancient Versions render the word ישעך *yishech.*

Behold, his reward] See note on chap. xl. 10, 11. This *reward* he carries as it were in his hand. *His work is before him*—he perfectly knows what is to be done; and is perfectly able to do it. He will do what God should do, and what man cannot do; and men should be *workers with him.* Let no man fear that the promise shall not be fulfilled on account of its difficulty, its greatness, the hinderances in the way, or the unworthiness of the person to whom it is made. It is God's work; he is *able* to do it, and as *willing* as he is able.

Verse 12. *They shall call them*—These characteristics seem to be put in their inverted order.—1. God will not *forsake* them. 2. They shall be *sought out.* 3. They shall be *redeemed.* And, 4. Be in consequence a *holy people.* 1. When God *calls,* it is a proof that he has not *forsaken.* 2. When he *seeks,* it is a proof he is *waiting* to be *gracious.* 3. When the *atonement* is exhibited, *all things are then ready.* 4. And when that is received, *holiness* of *heart* and *life* is then to be kept continually in view, as this is the genuine work of God's Spirit; and without *holiness* none shall see the Lord.

CHAPTER LXIII

The prophet, (or rather the Church he represents,) sees the great Deliverer, long promised and expected, making his appearance, after having crushed his enemies, like grapes in the wine-vat. The comparison suggests a lively idea of the wrath of Omnipotence, which its unhappy objects can no more resist than the grapes can resist the treader. Indeed, there is so much pathos, energy, and sublimity in this remarkable passage, as hardly any thing can be conceived to exceed. The period to which it refers must be the same with that predicted in the nineteenth *chapter of the Revelation, some parts of which are expressed in the same terms with this, and plainly enough refer to the very sudden and total overthrow of Antichrist, and of all his adherents and auxiliaries, of which the destruction of Babylon, the capital of Chaldea, and of Bozra, the chief city of the Edomites, was the prototype,* 1–6. *At the* seventh *verse commences a penitential confession and supplication of the Jews, as uttered in their present dispersion,* 7–19.

A. M. cir. 3292
B. C. cir. 712
Olymp. XVII. 1
cir. annum
NumæPompilii,
R. Roman., 4

WHO *is* this that cometh from
Edom, with dyed garments
from Bozrah? this *that is* [a]glo-
rious in his apparel, travelling in
the greatness of his strength? I
that speak in righteousness,
mighty to save.
2 Wherefore [b]*art thou* red in

A. M. cir. 3292
B. C. cir. 712
Olymp. XVII. 1
cir. annum
NumæPompilii,
R. Roman., 4

[a]Heb. *decked*

[b]Rev. xix. 13

The very remarkable passage with which this chapter begins seems to me to be, in a manner, detached from the rest, and to stand singly by itself; having no immediate connexion with what goes before, or with what follows, otherwise than as it may pursue the general design, and stand in its proper place in the order of prophecy. It is by many learned interpreters supposed that Judas Maccabeus and his victories make the subject of it. What claim Judas can have to so great an honour will, I think, be very difficult to make out; or how the attributes of the great person introduced can possibly suit him. Could Judas call himself the *announcer of righteousness*, mighty to save? Could he talk of the *day of vengeance being in his heart*, and the *year of his redeemed being come?* or that *his own arm wrought salvation for him?* Besides, what were the great exploits of Judas in regard to the Idumeans? He overcame them in battle, and slew twenty thousand of them. And John Hyrcanus, his brother Simon's son and successor, who is called in to help out the accomplishment of the prophecy, gave them another defeat some time afterward, and compelled them by force to become proselytes to the Jewish religion, and to submit to circumcision: after which they were incorporated with the Jews, and became one people with them. Are these events adequate to the prophet's lofty prediction? Was it so great an action to win a battle with considerable slaughter of the enemy, or to force a whole nation by dint of the sword into Judaism? or was the conversion of the Idumeans, however effected, and their admission into the Church of God, equivalent to a most grievous judgment and destruction, threatened in the severest terms? But here is another very material circumstance to be considered, which, I presume, entirely excludes Judas Maccabeus, and even the Idumeans, properly so called. For the Idumea of the prophet's time was quite a different country from that which Judas conquered. For during the Babylonish captivity the Nabatheans had driven the Edomites out of their country; who upon that took possession of the southern parts of Judea, and settled themselves there; that is, in the country of the whole tribe of Simeon and in half of that of Judah. See Prideaux, ad. an. 740 and 165. And the metropolis of the Edomites, and of the country thence called Idumea, which Judas took, was *Hebron*, 1 Macc. v. 65, not Bozrah.

I conclude, therefore, that this prophecy has not the least relation to Judas Maccabeus. It may be asked, to whom, and to what event does it relate? I can only answer, that I know of no event in history to which, from its importance and circumstances, it can be applied: unless, perhaps, to the destruction of Jerusalem and the Jewish polity; which in the Gospel is called the *coming of Christ* and *the days of vengeance*, Matt. xvi. 28; Luke xxi. 22. But though this prophecy must have its accomplishment, there is no necessity for supposing that it has been already accomplished. There are prophecies, which intimate a great slaughter of the enemies of God and his people, which remain to be fulfilled; these in Ezekiel, chap. xxxviii., and in the Revelation of St. John, chap. xx., are called *Gog* and *Magog*. This prophecy of Isaiah may possibly refer to the same or the like event. We need not be at a loss to determine the person who is here introduced, as *stained with treading the wine-press*, if we consider how St. John in the Revelation has applied this image of the prophet, Rev. xix. 13, 15, 16. Compare chap. xxxiv.—L.

NOTES ON CHAP. LXIII

Verse 1. *Who* is *this that cometh from Edom*] Probably both Edom and Bozrah are only figurative expressions, to point out the place in which God should discomfit his enemies. *Edom* signifies *red*, and *Bozrah*, *a vintage*. *Kimchi* interprets the whole of the destruction of Rome.

I that speak in righteousness—"I who publish righteousness"] A MS. has המדבר *hammedabber*, with the demonstrative article added with greater force and emphasis: *The announcer* of righteousness. A MS. has צדקה *tsedakah*, without ב *be* prefixed; and so the *Septuagint* and *Vulgate*. And *thirty-eight* MSS. (*seven* ancient) of Dr. *Kennicott's*, and many of *De Rossi's*, and *one* of my own, add the conjunction ו *vau* to רב *rab*, *and mighty;* which the *Septuagint*, *Syriac*, and *Vulgate* confirm.—L.

Verse 2. *Wherefore* art thou *red in thine apparel*] For ללבושך *lilebushecha*, *twenty-nine* MSS. (*nine* ancient) of *Kennicott's*, and *thirty* of *De Rossi's*, and *one* edition, have ללבושיך

A. M. cir. 3292
B. C. cir. 712
Olymp. XVII. 1
cir. annum
NumæPompilii,
R. Roman., 4

thine apparel, and thy garments
like him that treadeth in the
winefat?
3 I have [c]trodden the wine-
press alone; and of the people *there was* none
with me: for I will tread them in mine anger,
and trample them in my fury; and their blood
shall be sprinkled upon my garments, and I
will stain all my raiment.
4 For the [d]day of vengeance *is* in mine
heart, and the year of my redeemed is
come.
5 [e]And I looked, and [f]*there was* none to
help; and I wondered that *there was* none to
uphold: therefore mine own
[g]arm brought salvation unto me;
and my fury, it upheld me.
6 And I will tread down the
people in mine anger, and [h]make them drunk
in my fury, and I will bring down their
strength to the earth.
7 I will mention the [i]loving-kindnesses of
the LORD, *and* the praises of the LORD,
according to all that the LORD hath bestowed
on us, and the great goodness toward the house
of Israel, which he hath bestowed on them
according to his mercies, and according to the
multitude of his loving-kindnesses.

[c]Lam. i. 15; Rev. xiv. 19, 20; xix. 15——[d]Chap. xxxiv. 8; lxi. 2——[e]Chap. xli. 28; lix. 16——[f]John xvi. 32——[g]Psa. xcviii. 1; chap. lix. 16——[h]Rev. xvi. 6——[i]Psa. xxv. 6; lxxxix. 49

lilebusheycha in the plural; so the *Septuagint* and *Syriac*. And all the ancient Versions read it with מ *mem*, instead of the first ל *lamed*. But the true reading is probably מלבושך *malbushecha* in the singular, as in ver. 3.—L.

Verse 3. *And of the people* there was *none with me*] I was wholly abandoned by them: but a good meaning is, No man has had any part in making the atonement; it is entirely the work of the Messiah alone. No created being could have any part in a sacrifice that was to be of infinite merit.

And I will stain—"And I have stained"] For אגאלתי *egalti*, a verb of very irregular formation, compounded, as they say, of the two forms of the preterite and future, a MS. has אגאלהו *egalehu*, the regular future with a pleonastic pronoun added to it, according to the Hebrew idiom: "And all my raiment, I have stained it." The necessity of the verb's being in the past tense seems to have given occasion to the alteration made in the end of the word. The conversive ו *vau* at the beginning of the sentence affects the verb, though not joined to it; of which there are many examples:—

anithani remim umikkarney

ומקרני רמים עניתני

"And thou wilt hear me (or hear thou me) from among the horns of the unicorns," Psa. xxii. 22.—L.

Instead of על בגדי *al begadai, upon my garments*, one of my ancient MSS. has לארץ בגדי *laarets begadai, to the earth:* but this word is partly effaced, and על *al* written in the margin by a later hand.

Verse 5. *And my fury*—"And mine indignation"] For וחמתי *vachamathi, nineteen* MSS. (*three* ancient) of *Kennicott's, nine* of *De Rossi's*, and *one* of mine, and *four* editions, have וצדקתי *vetsidkathi, and my righteousness;* from chap. lix. 16, which I suppose the transcriber retained in his memory. It is true that the Versions are in favour of the common reading; but that noticed above seems to stand on good authority, and is a reading both pleasing and impressive. Opposite, in the margin, my MS. has the common reading by a later hand.

Verse 6. *And make them drunk in my fury*—"And I crushed them in mine indignation"] For ואשכרם *vaashkerem, and I made them drunken, twenty-seven* MSS., (*three* ancient,) *twelve* of *De Rossi's*, and the old edition of 1488, have ואשברם *vaashabberem, and I crushed them:* and so the *Syriac* and *Chaldee*. The *Septuagint* have omitted this whole line.

Verse 7. *I will mention the loving-kindnesses of the Lord*] The prophet connects the preceding mercies of God to the Jews with the present prospect he has of their redemption by the Messiah; thus making a *circle* in which eternal goodness revolves. The remaining part of this chapter, with the whole chapter following, contains a penitential confession and supplication of the Israelites in their present state of dispersion, in which they have so long marvellously subsisted, and still continue to subsist, as a people; cast out of their country; without any proper form of civil polity or religious worship; their temple destroyed, their city desolated and lost to them, and their whole nation scattered over the face of the earth, apparently deserted and cast off by the God of their fathers, as no longer his peculiar people.

They begin with acknowledging God's great mercies and favours to their nation, and the ungrateful returns made to them on their part, that by their disobedience they had forfeited the protection of God, and had caused him to become their adversary. And now the prophet represents them, induced by the memory of the great things that God had done for them, as addressing their humble supplication for the renewal of his mercies. They beseech him to regard them in consideration of his former loving-kindness, they acknowledge him for their Father and Creator, they confess their wickedness and hardness of heart, they entreat his forgiveness, and deplore their present miserable condition under which they have so long suffered. It seems designed as a formulary of humiliation for the Israelites, in order to their conversion.

The whole passage is in the elegiac form, pathetic and elegant; but it has suffered much in our present copy by the mistakes of transcribers.

The praises of the Lord—"The praise of JEHOVAH"] For תהלות *tehilloth*, plural, *twenty-*

A. M. cir. 3292 B. C. cir. 712 Olymp. XVII. 1 cir. annum NumæPompilii, R. Roman., 4

8 For he said, Surely they *are*
my people, children *that* will not
lie: so he was their Saviour.
9 [k]In all their affliction he was
afflicted, [l]and the angel of his presence saved
them [m]in his love and in his pity he redeemed them; and [n]he bare them, and carried them all the days of old.
10 But they [o]rebelled, and [p]vexed his holy
Spirit: [q]therefore he was turned to be their
enemy, *and* he fought against them.
11 Then he remembered the days of old,
Moses, *and* his people, *saying,* Where *is* he
that [r]brought them up out of the sea with the
[s]shepherd of his flock? [t]where
is he that put his holy Spirit
within him?
12 That led *them* by the right
hand of Moses, [u]with his glorious arm, [v]divid-
ing the water before them, to make himself
an everlasting name?
13 [w]That led them through the deep as a
horse in the wilderness, *that* they should not
stumble?
14 As a beast goeth down into the valley,
the Spirit of the LORD caused him to rest:
so didst thou lead thy people, [x]to make thyself a glorious name.

[k]Judg. x. 16; Zech. ii. 8; Acts ix. 4——[l]Exod. xiv. 19; xxiii. 20, 21; xxxiii. 14; Malachi iii. 1; Acts xii. 11——[m]Deut. vii. 7, 8——[n]Exod. xix. 4; Deut. i. 31; xxxii. 11, 12; chap. xlvi. 3, 4——[o]Exod. xv. 24; Num. xiv. 11; Psa. lxxviii. 56; xcv. 9——[p]Psa. lxxviii. 40; Acts vii. 51; Eph. iv. 30

[q]Exod. xxiii. 21——[r]Exod. xiv. 30; xxxii. 11, 12; Num. xiv. 13, 14, &c.; Jer. ii. 6——[s]Or, *shepherds*, as Psa. lxxvii. 20——[t]Num. xi. 17, 25; Neh. ix. 20; Dan. iv. 8; Hag. ii. 5——[u]Exod. xv. 6——[v]Exod. xiv. 21; Joshua iii. 16——[w]Psalm cvi. 9——[x]2 Samuel vii. 23

nine MSS. (*three* ancient) and *two* editions, have תהלת *tehillath*, in the singular number; and so the *Vulgate* renders it; and one of the Greek versions, in the margin of Cod. Marchal. and in the text of MSS. Pachom. and I. D. II. *την αινεσιν* Κυριου, "the praise of the Lord."—L.

Verses 8, 9. *So he was their Saviour. In all their affliction*—"And he became their Saviour in all their distress"] I have followed the translation of the *Septuagint* in the latter part of the *eighth*, and the former part of the *ninth* verse; which agrees with the present text, a little differently divided as to the members of the sentence. They read מכל *miccol, out of all*, instead of בכל *bechol, in all*, which makes no difference in the sense; and צר *tsar* they understand as ציר *tsir*. Και *εγενετο αυτοις εις σωτηριαν εκ πασης θλιψεως αυτων· ου πρεσβυς, ουδε αγγελος·* "And he was salvation to them in all their tribulation; neither an ambassador nor an angel, but himself saved them." An angel of his presence means an angel of superior order, in immediate attendance upon God. So the angel of the Lord says to Zacharias, "I am Gabriel, that stand in the presence of God," Luke i. 19. The presence of JEHOVAH, Exod. xxxiii. 14, 15, and the angel, Exod. xxxiii. 20, 21, is JEHOVAH himself; here an angel of his presence is opposed to JEHOVAH himself, as an angel is in the following passages of the same book of Exodus. After their idolatrous worshipping of the golden calf, "when God had said to Moses, I will send an angel before thee—I will not go up in the midst of thee—the people mourned," Exod. xxxiii. 2-4. God afterwards comforts Moses, by saying, "My presence (that is, I myself in person, and not by an angel) will go with thee," ver. 14. *Αυτος προπορευσομαι σου*, "I myself will go before thee," as the *Septuagint* render it.

The MSS. and editions are much divided between the two readings of the text and margin in the common copies, לא *lo, not*, and לו *lo, to him.* All the ancient Versions express the chetib reading, לא *lo, not.*

And he bare them and carried them all the days of old—"And he took them up, and he bore them, all the days of old."] See the note on chap. xlvi. 3.—L.

Verse 10. And *he fought against them*] *Twenty-six* MSS. (*ten* ancient) and the *first* edition, with another, add the conjunction ו *vau,* והוא *vehu, and he.*

Verse 11. *Moses* and *his people*—"Moses his servant"] For עמו *ammo, his people,* two MSS. (*one* of them ancient) and *one* of my own, (ancient,) and *one* of *De Rossi's*, and the old edition of 1488, and the *Syriac*, read עבדו *abdo, his servant.* These two words have been mistaken one for the other in other places; Psa. lxxviii. 71, and lxxx. 5, for עמו *ammo, his people,* and עמך *ammecha, thy people,* the *Septuagint* read עבדו *abdo, his servant,* and עבדך *abdecha, thy servant.*

Where is he that brought them up out of the sea with the shepherd of his flock? where &c.—"How he brought them up from the sea, with the shepherd of his flock; how," &c.] For איה *aiyeh, how,* interrogative, twice, the *Syriac* Version reads איך *eich, how,* without interrogation, as that particle is used in the *Syriac* language, and sometimes in the *Hebrew.* See Ruth iii. 18; Eccles. ii. 16.

The shepherd of his flock] That is, Moses. The MSS. and editions vary in this word; some have it רעה *roeh,* in the singular number; so the *Septuagint, Syriac,* and *Chaldee.* Others רעי *roey,* plural, *the shepherds.*—L.

Verses 13, 14. *That led them through the deep—As a beast goeth down into the valley*] In both these verses there is an allusion to the Israelites going through the Red Sea, in the bottom of which they found no more inconvenience than a horse would in running in the desert, where there was neither *stone* nor *mud;* nor a beast in the valley, where all was *plain* and *smooth.*

Verse 14. *The Spirit of the Lord caused him to rest*—"The Spirit of JEHOVAH conducted them"] For תניחנו *tenichennu, caused him to rest,* the *Septuagint* have *ὡδηγησεν αυτους, conducted them;* they read תנחם *tanchem.* The *Syriac, Chaldee,* and *Vulgate* read תנחנו *tan-*

A. M. cir. 3292
B. C. cir. 712
Olymp. XVII. 1
cir. annum
NumæPompilii,
R. Roman., 4

15 [y]Look down from heaven, and behold [z]from the habitation of thy holiness and of thy glory: where *is* thy zeal and thy strength, [a]the sounding [b]of thy bowels and of thy mercies toward me? are they restrained?
16 [c]Doubtless thou *art* our father, though Abraham [d]be ignorant of us, and Israel acknowledge us not: thou, O LORD *art* our Father, [e]our Redeemer; thy name *is* from everlasting.
17 O LORD, why hast thou [f]made us to err from thy ways *and* [g]hardened our heart from thy fear? [h]Return, for thy servants' sake, the tribes of thine inheritance.
18 [i]The people of thy holiness have possessed *it* but a little while: [k]our adversaries have trodden down thy sanctuary.
19 We are *thine:* thou never barest rule over them: [l]they were not called by thy name.

[y]Deut. xxvi. 15; Psa. lxxx. 14——[z]Psa. xxxiii. 14——[a]Or, *the multitude*——[b]Jer. xxxi. 20; Hos. xi. 8——[c]Deut. xxxii. 6; 1 Chron. xxix. 10; chap. lxiv. 8——[d]Job xiv. 21; Eccles. ix. 5——[e]Or, *our Redeemer from everlasting* is *thy name*

[f]Psa. cxix. 10——[g]See chap. vi. 10, with John xii. 40; Rom. ix. 18——[h]Num. x. 36; Psa. xc. 13——[i]Deut. vii. 6; xxvi. 19; chap. lxii. 12; Dan. viii. 24——[k]Psa. lxxiv. 7——[l]Or, *thy name was not called upon them;* chap. lxv. 1

chennu, conducted him. Two MSS. have the word without the י *yod* in the middle.

Verse 15. *And thy strength*—"And thy mighty power"] For גבורתיך *geburotheycha,* plural, *thirty-two* MSS. (*seven* ancient) and *twenty-one* of *De Rossi's,* and *seven* editions, have גבורתך *geburathecha,* singular.

Are they restrained?] For אלי *elai, from* (or in regard to) *me,* the *Septuagint* and *Syriac* read אלינו *eleynu, from us.*—L.

Verse 16. *Our Redeemer; thy name* is *from everlasting*—"O deliver us for the sake of thy name."] The present text reads, as our translation has rendered it, "Our Redeemer, thy name is from everlasting." But instead of מעולם *meolam, from everlasting,* an ancient MS. has למען *lemaan, for the sake of,* which gives a much better sense. To show the impropriety of the present reading, it is sufficient to observe, that the *Septuagint* and *Syriac* translators thought it necessary to add עלינו *aleynu, upon us,* to make out the sense; That is, "Thy name is *upon us,* or we are called by thy name, from of old." And the *Septuagint* have rendered גאלנו *goalenu,* in the *imperative* mood, ῥυσαι ἡμας, *deliver us.*—L.

Verse 17. *Why hast thou made us to err*] A mere *Hebraism,* for why hast thou *permitted* us to err. So, *Lead us not into temptation;* do not *suffer* us to fall into that to which we are tempted.

Verse 18. *The people of thy holiness have possessed* it *but a little while*—"It is little that they have taken possession of thy holy mountain"] The difficulty of the construction in this place is acknowledged on all hands. *Vitringa* prefers that sense as the least exceptionable which our translation has expressed; in which however there seems to be a great defect; that is, the want of what in the speaker's view must have been the principal part of the proposition, the object of the verb, *the land,* or *it,* as our translators supply it, which surely ought to have been expressed, and not to have been left to be supplied by the reader. In a word, I believe there is some mistake in the text; and here the *Septuagint* help us out; they had in their copy הר *har, mountain,* instead of עם *am, people,* του ορους του ἁγιου σου, *the mountain of thy Holy One.* "Not only have our enemies taken possession of Mount Sion, and trodden down thy sanctuary; even far worse than this has befallen us; thou hast long since utterly cast us off, and dost not consider us as thy peculiar people."—L.

CHAPTER LXIV

The whole of this chapter, which is very pathetic and tender, may be considered as a formulary of prayer and humiliation intended for the Jews in order to their conversion, 1–12.

A. M. cir. 3292
B. C. cir. 712
Olymp. XVII. 1
cir. annum
NumæPompilii,
R. Roman., 4

O THAT thou wouldest [a]rend the heavens, that thou wouldest come down, that the [b]mountains might flow down at thy presence,
2 As *when* [c]the melting fire burneth, the fire causeth the waters to boil, to make thy name known to thine adversaries, *that* the nations may tremble at thy presence!

[a]Psa. cxliv. 5——[b]Judg. v. 5; Mic. i. 4

[c]Heb. *the fire of meltings*

NOTES ON CHAP. LXIV

Verse 1. *O that thou wouldest rend the heavens*—This seems to allude to the wonderful manifestation of God upon Mount Sinai.

Verse 2. *As* when *the melting fire burneth*—"As the fire kindleth the dry fuel"] המסים *hamasim.* "It means *dry stubble,* and the root is המס *hamas,*" says *Rabbi Jonah,* apud *Sal. ben Melec* in loc. Which is approved by *Schultens,* Orig. Heb. p. 30.

"The fire kindling the stubble does not seem like enough to the melting of the mountains to be brought as a simile to it. What if thus?—

A. M. cir. 3292
B. C. cir. 712
Olymp. XVII. 1
cir. annum
NumæPompilii,
R. Roman., 4

3 When [d]thou didst terrible
things *which* we look not for,
thou camest down, the mountains flowed down at thy presence.
4 For since the beginning of the world [e]*men*
have not heard, nor perceived by the ear,
neither hath the eye [f]seen, O
God, beside thee, *what* he hath
prepared for him that waiteth
for him.
5 Thou meetest him that rejoiceth [g]and
worketh righteousness, [h]*those that* remember

[d]Exod. xxxiv. 10; Judg. v. 4, 5; Psa. lxviii. 8; Hab. iii. 3, 6——[e]Psa. xxxi. 19; 1 Cor. ii. 9

[f]Or, *seen a God besides thee,* which *doeth so for him,* &c. [g]Acts x. 35——[h]Chap. xxvi. 8

'That the mountains might flow down at thy presence!
As the fire of things smelted burneth,
As the fire causeth the waters to boil—'

There is no doubt of the Hebrew words of the second line bearing that version."—Dr. Jubb.

I submit these different interpretations to the reader's judgment. For my own part I am inclined to think that the text is much corrupted in this place. The ancient Versions have not the least traces of either of the above interpretations. The *Septuagint* and *Syriac* agree exactly together in rendering this line by, "As the wax melted before the fire," which can by no means be reconciled with the present text. The *Vulgate*, for המסים *hamasim*, read ימסו *yemasu*.

That *the nations*] For גוים *goyim*, *the nations*, four MSS. (one of them ancient) have הרים *harim*, *the mountains*.—L.

Verse 4. *For since the beginning of the world men have not heard*—"For never have men heard"] St. Paul is generally supposed to have quoted this passage of Isaiah, 1 Cor. ii. 9; and Clemens Romanus in his first epistle has made the same quotation, very nearly in the same words with the apostle. But the citation is so very different both from the *Hebrew* text and the version of the *Septuagint*, that it seems very difficult, if not impossible, to reconcile them by any literal emendation, without going beyond the bounds of temperate criticism. One clause, "neither hath it entered into the heart of man," (which, by the way, is a phrase purely Hebrew, עלה על לב *alah al leb*, and should seem to belong to the prophet,) is wholly left out; and another is repeated without force or propriety; viz., "nor perceived by the ear," after, "never have heard:" and the sense and expression of the apostle is far preferable to that of the Hebrew text. Under these difficulties I am at a loss what to do better, than to offer to the reader this, perhaps disagreeable, alternative: either to consider the *Hebrew* text and *Septuagint* in this place as wilfully disguised and corrupted by the Jews; of which practice in regard to other quotations in the New Testament from the Old, they lie under strong suspicions, (see Dr. *Owen* on the version of the *Septuagint*, sect. vi.-ix.;) or to look upon St. Paul's quotation as not made from Isaiah, but from one or other of the two apocryphal books, entitled, The Ascension of Esaiah, and the Apocalypse of Elias, in both of which this passage was found; and the apostle is by some supposed in other places to have quoted such apocryphal writings. As the first of these conclusions will perhaps not easily be admitted by many, so I must fairly warn my readers that the second is treated by Jerome as little better than heresy. See his comment on this place of Isaiah.—L. I would read the whole verse thus; "Yea, from the time of old they have not heard, they have not hearkened to, an eye hath not seen a God besides thee. He shall work for that one that waiteth for him." This I really think on the whole to be the best translation of the original.

The variations on this place are as follows: for שמעו *shameu, they* have heard, a MS. and the *Septuagint* read שמענו *shamanu, we* have heard: for the second לא *lo, not, sixty-nine* MSS. and four editions have ולא *velo, and not,* and the *Syriac, Chaldee,* and *Vulgate.* And so ועין *veayin, and eye, Septuagint* and *Syriac.* את *eth, the,* (emphatic,) is added before אלהים *Elohim, God,* in MS. *Bodleian.* למחכי *limechakkey,* to them *that wait,* plural, two MSS. and all the ancient Versions.—L.

Verse 5. *Thou meetest him that rejoiceth and worketh righteousness*—"Thou meetest with joy those who work righteousness"] The *Syriac* reads פוגע אתה שש בעשי *poga attah shesh baashi*, as above.

In those is continuance, and we shall be saved—"Because of our deeds, for we have been rebellious"] בהם עולם ונושע *bahem olam venivvashea.* I am fully persuaded that these words as they stand in the present Hebrew text are utterly unintelligible; there is no doubt of the meaning of each word separately; but put together they make no sense at all. I conclude, therefore, that the copy has suffered by mistakes of transcribers in this place. The corruption is of long standing; for the ancient interpreters were as much at a loss for the meaning as the moderns, and give nothing satisfactory. The *Septuagint* render these words by δια τουτο επλανηθημεν, *therefore we have erred:* they seem to have read עליהם נפשע *aleyhem niphsha,* without helping the sense. In this difficulty what remains but to have recourse to conjecture? Archbishop *Secker* was dissatisfied with the present reading: he proposed הבט עלינו ונושע *hebet aleynu venivvashea;* "look upon us, and we shall, or that we may, be saved:" which gives a very good sense, but seems to have no sufficient foundation. Besides, the word ונושע *venivvashea,* which is attended with great difficulties, seems to be corrupted as well as the two preceding; and the true reading of it is, I think, given by the *Septuagint,* ונפשע *veniphsha,* επλανηθημεν, *we have erred,* (so they render the verb פשע *pasha,* chap. xlvi. 8, and Ezek. xxiii. 12,) parallel to ונחטא *vannecheta,* ἡμαρτομεν, *we have sinned.* For בהם עולם *bahem olam,* which means nothing, I would propose המעללינו *hammaaleleynu,* "because of our deeds; which I presume was first altered to במעלליהם *bemaaleleyhem,* an

A. M. cir. 3292
B. C. cir. 712
Olymp. XVII. 1
cir annum
NumæPompilii,
R. Roman., 4

thee in thy ways: behold, thou
art wroth; for we have sinned:
[i]in those is continuance, and we
shall be saved.
6 But we are all as an unclean *thing,* and
all [k]our righteousnesses *are* as filthy rags;
and we all do [l]fade as a leaf: and our iniquities, like the wind, have taken us away.
7 And [m]*there is* none that calleth upon thy
name, that stirreth up himself to take hold of
thee: for thou hast hid thy face from us, and
hast [n]consumed us, [o]because of our iniquities.
8 [p]But now, O LORD, thou *art* our Father;
we *are* the clay, [q]and thou our potter; and
we all *are* [r]the work of thy
hand.
9 Be not [s]wroth very sore, O
LORD, neither remember iniquity
for ever: behold, see, we beseech thee, [t]we
are all thy people.
10 Thy holy cities are a wilderness, Zion
is a wilderness, [u]Jerusalem a desolation.
11 [v]Our holy and our beautiful house, where
our fathers praised thee, is burned up with fire:
and all [w]our pleasant things are laid waste.
12 [x]Wilt thou refrain thyself for these
things, O LORD? [y]wilt thou hold thy peace
and afflict us very sore?

A. M. cir. 3292
B. C. cir. 712
Olymp. XVII. 1
cir. annum
NumæPompilii,
R. Roman., 4

---

[i]Mal. iii. 6——[k]Phil. iii. 9——[l]Psa. xc. 5, 6——[m]Hos. vii. 7——[n]Heb. *melted*——[o]Heb. *by the hand,* as Job ix. 4——[p]Chap. lxiii. 16——[q]Chap. xxix. 16; xlv. 9; Jer. xviii. 6; Rom. ix. 20, 21——[r]Eph. ii. 10

[s]Psa. lxxiv. 1, 2; lxxix. 8——[t]Psa. lxxix. 13——[u]Psa. lxxix. 1; chap. iii. 8; Jer. vi. 1; ix. 11——[v]2 Kings xxv. 9; Psa. lxxiv. 7; 2 Chron. xxxvi. 12——[w]Ezek. xxiv. 21, 25——[x]Chap. xlii. 24——[y]Psa. lxxxiii. 1

---

easy and common mistake of the third person plural of the pronoun for the first, (see note on chap. xxxiii. 2,) and then with some farther alteration to בהם עולם *behem olam.* The עליהם *aleyhem,* which the *Septuagint* probably found in their copy, seems to be a remnant of במעלליהם *bemaaleleyhem.*

This, it may be said, is imposing your sense upon the prophet. It may be so; for perhaps these may not be the very words of the prophet: but however it is better than to impose upon him what makes no sense at all; as they generally do, who pretend to render such corrupted passages. For instance, our own translators: "in *those* is continuance, and we shall be saved:" in those—in whom, or what? There is no antecedent to the relative. "In the ways of God," say some: "with our fathers," says *Vitringa,* joining it in construction with the verb, קצפת *katsaphta,* "thou hast been angry with them, our fathers;" and putting ונחטא *vannecheta,* "for we have sinned," in a parenthesis. But there has not been any mention of *our fathers:* and the whole sentence, thus disposed, is utterly discordant from the *Hebrew* idiom and construction. In those is *continuance;* עולם *olam* means a *destined* but hidden and *unknown* portion of time; but cannot mean continuation of time, or *continuance,* as it is here rendered. Such forced interpretations are equally conjectural with the boldest critical emendation; and generally have this farther disadvantage, that they are altogether unworthy of the sacred writers.—L.

Coverdale renders the passage thus:—**But lo, thou art angrie, for we offende, and have been ever in synne; and there is not one whole.** This is, I am afraid, *making a sense.*

After all that this very learned prelate has done to reduce these words to sense and meaning, I am afraid we are still far from the prophet's mind. Probably בהם *bahem, in them,* refers to דרכיך *deracheycha, thy ways,* above. עולם *olam* may be rendered *of old,* or during the whole of the Jewish economy; and ונושע *venivvashea,* "and shall we be saved?" Thus: —Thou art wroth, for we have sinned in them (thy ways) of old; and can we be saved? For we are all as an unclean thing, &c.

Verse 6. *As filthy rags*] עדים *iddim.* Rab. Mosheh ben Maimon interpretatur עדים *iddim,* vestes quibus mulier se abstergit post congressum cum marito suo. *Alii* pannus menstruatus. *Alii* panni mulieris parientis.—**And we ben made as unclene alle we: and as the cloth of the woman rooten blode flowing, all our rigtwisnesses.** —Old MS. Bible. If preachers knew properly the meaning of this word, would they make such a liberal use of it in their public ministry? And why should any use a word, the meaning of which he does not understand? How many in the congregation blush for the incautious man and his "filthy rags!"

Verse 7. There is *none*] Twelve MSS. have אין *ein,* without the conjunction ו *vau* prefixed; and so read the *Chaldee* and *Vulgate.*

And hast consumed us because of our iniquities—"And hast delivered us up into the hands of our iniquities."] For ותמוגנו *vattemugenu,* "hast dissolved us," the *Septuagint, Syriac,* and *Chaldee* had in their copies תמגננו *temaggenenu,* "hast delivered us up." *Houbigant. Secker.*

Verse 8. *But, now, O Lord, thou* art *our Father*—"But thou, O JEHOVAH, thou art our Father"] For ועתה *veattah, and now,* five MSS., one of them ancient, and the two oldest editions, 1486 and 1488, have ואתה *veattah, and thou;* and so the *Chaldee* seems to have read. The repetition has great force. The other word may be well spared. "But now, O Lord, thou art our Father." How very affectionate is the complaint in this and the following verses! But how does the distress increase, when they recollect the desolations of the temple, and ruin of public worship, ver. 11: "Our holy and beautiful house, where our fathers praised thee, is burnt up with fire," &c.

We all are *the work of thy hand*] Three MSS. (two of them ancient) and the *Septuagint* read מעשה *maaseh, the work,* without the conjunction ו *vau* prefixed. And for ידך *yadecha, thy hand,* the *Bodleian,* and two others MSS., the *Septuagint, Syriac,* and *Vulgate* read ידיך *yadeycha, thy hands,* in the plural number.—L.

Verse 9. *Neither remember iniquity*] For

לעד תזכר *laad tizcor*, one of my MSS. has לעד תקצף *laad tiktsoph*, "be not *angry*," as in the preceding clause. This has been partially obliterated, and תזכר *tizcor*, written in the margin by a later hand: but this MS. abounds with words of this kind, all altered by later hands.

CHAPTER LXV

We have here a vindication of God's dealings with the Jews, 1, 2. *To this end the prophet points out their great hypocrisy, and gives a particular enumeration of their dreadful abominations, many of which were committed under the specious guise of sanctity*, 3–5. *For their horrid impieties, (recorded in writing before Jehovah,) the wrath of God shall certainly come upon them to the uttermost; a prediction which was exactly fulfilled in the first and second centuries in the reigns of the Roman emperors Vespasian, Titus, and Hadrian, when the whole Jewish polity was dissolved, and the people dispersed all over the world*, 6, 7. *Though God had rejected the Jews, and called the Gentiles, who sought him not*, (Rom. ix. 24–26,) *yet a remnant from among the former shall be preserved, to whom he will in due time make good all his promises*, 8–10. *Denunciation of Divine vengeance against those idolaters who set in order a table for Gad, and fill out a libation to Meni, ancient idolatries, which, from the context, and from the chronological order of the events predicted, have a plain reference to the idolatries practised by Antichrist under the guise of Christianity*, 11, 12. *Dreadful fate which awaits these gross idolaters beautifully contrasted with the great blessedness reserved for the righteous*, 13–16. *Future restoration of the posterity of Jacob, and the happy state of the world in general from that most glorious epoch, represented by the strong figure of the creation of* NEW heavens and a NEW earth, *wherein dwelleth righteousness, and into which no distress shall be permitted to enter*, 17–19. *In this new state of things the term of human life shall be greatly protracted, and shall possess none of that uncertainty which attaches to it in "the heavens and the earth which are now." This is elegantly illustrated by the longevity of a tree; manifestly alluding to the* oak *or* cedar of Lebanon, *some individuals of which are known to have lived from seven to ten centuries*, 20–23. *Beautiful figures shadowing forth the profound peace and harmony of the Church of Jesus Christ, which shall immediately follow the total overthrow of Antichrist; with a most gracious promise that the great chain of Omnipotence shall be put upon every adversary, so that none will be able any longer to hurt and destroy in all God's holy mountain*, 24, 25.

A. M. cir. 3292
B. C. cir. 712
Olymp. XVII. 1
cir. annum
NumæPompilii,
R. Roman., 4

I [a]AM sought of *them that* asked not *for me;* I am found of *them that* sought me not: I said, Behold me, behold me, unto a nation *that* [b]was not called by my name.

2 [c]I have spread out my hands all the day unto a rebellious people, which walketh in a way *that was* not good, after their own thoughts;

3 A people [d]that provoketh me to anger

[a]Rom. ix. 24, 25, 26, 30; x. 20; Eph. ii. 12, 13 — [b]Chap. lxiii. 19 — [c]Rom. x. 21 — [d]Deut. xxxii. 21

This chapter contains a defence of God's proceedings in regard to the Jews, with reference to their complaint in the chapter preceding. God is introduced declaring that he had called the Gentiles, though they had not sought him; and had rejected his own people for their refusal to attend to his repeated call; for their obstinate disobedience, their idolatrous practices, and detestable hypocrisy. That nevertheless he would not destroy them all; but would preserve a remnant, to whom he would make good his ancient promises. Severe punishments are threatened to the apostates; and great rewards are promised to the obedient in a future flourishing state of the Church.—L.

NOTES ON CHAP. LXV

Verse 1. *I am sought of* them that *asked not* for me—"I am made known to those that asked not for me"] נדרשתי *nidrashti*, εμφανης εγενομην, the *Septuagint*, *Alexandrian*, and *St. Paul*, Rom. x. 20; who has however inverted the order of the phrases, εμφανης εγενομην, "I was made manifest," and ευρεθην, "I was found," from that which they have in the *Septuagint*. נדרשתי *nidrashti* means, "I am sought so as to be found." *Vitringa.* If this be the true meaning of the word, then שאלו *shaalu*, "that asked," which follows, should seem defective, the verb wanting its object: but two MSS., one of them ancient, have שאלוני *shealuni*, "asked me;" and another MS. שאלו לי *shealu li*, "asked for me;" one or other of which seems to be right. But *Cocceius* in Lex., and *Vitringa* in his translation, render נדרשתי *nidrashti*, by "I have answered;" and so the verb is rendered by all the ancient Versions in Ezek. xx. 3, 31. If this be right, the translation will be, 'I have answered those that asked not." I leave this to the reader's judgment; but have followed in my translation the *Septuagint* and *St. Paul*, and the MSS. above mentioned. בקשני *bikeshuni* is written regularly and fully in above a hundred MSS. and in the oldest edition, בקשוני *bikeshuni*.—L.

Verse 3. *That sacrificeth in gardens, and burneth incense upon altars of brick*—"Sacrificing in the gardens, and burning incense on the tiles"] These are instances of heathenish superstition, and idolatrous practices, to which the Jews were immoderately addicted before the

A. M. cir. 3292
B. C. cir. 712
Olymp. XVII. 1
cir. annum
NumæPompilii,
R. Roman., 4

continually to my face; [e]that sacrificeth in gardens, and burneth incense [f]upon altars of brick;

4 [g]Which remain among the graves, and lodge in the monuments; [h]which eat swine's flesh, and [i]broth of abominable *things is in* their vessels;

[e]Chap. i. 29; lxvi. 17; see Lev. xvii. 5——[f]Heb. *upon bricks*

[g]Deut. xviii. 11——[h]Chap. lxvi. 17; see Lev. xi. 7
[i]Or, *pieces*

Babylonish captivity. The heathen worshipped their idols in groves; whereas God, in opposition to this species of idolatry, commanded his people, when they should come into the promised land, to destroy all the places wherein the Canaanites had served their gods, and in particular to burn their groves with fire, Deut. xii. 2, 3. These apostate Jews sacrificed upon altars built of bricks; in opposition to the command of God in regard to his altar, which was to be of unhewn stone, Exod. xx. 25. Et pro uno altari, quod impolitis lapidibus Dei erat lege constructum, coctos lateres et agrorum cespites hostiarum sanguine cruentabant. "And instead of one altar which, according to the law of God, was to be constructed of unhewn stones, they stained the bricks and turfs of the fields with the blood of their victims." *Hieron.* in loc. Or it means, perhaps, that they sacrificed upon the roofs of their houses, which were always flat, and paved with brick, or tile, or plaster of terrace. An instance of this idolatrous practice we find in 2 Kings xxiii. 12, where it is said that Josiah "beat down the altars that were on the top of the upper chamber of Ahaz, which the kings of Judah had made." See also Zeph. i. 5. Sir *John Chardin's* MS. note on this place of Isaiah is as follows: "Ainsi font tous les Gentiles, sur les lieux elevés, et sur les terrasses, appellez *latcres*, parceque sont faits de briq." "Who dwell in the sepulchres, and lodge in the caverns," for the purposes of necromancy and divination; to obtain dreams and revelations. Another instance of heathenish superstition: so Virgil:—

Huc dona sacerdos
Cum tulit, et cæsarum ovium sub nocte silenti
Pellibus incubuit stratis, somnosque petivit:
Multa modis simulacra videt volitantia miris,
Et varias audit voces, fruiturque deorum
Colloquio, atque imis Acheronta affatur Avernis.
Æn. vii. 86.—L.

"Here in distress the Italian nations come,
Anxious, to clear their doubts, and learn their doom.
First, on the fleeces of the slaughtered sheep,
By night the sacred priest dissolves in sleep:
When in a train, before his slumbering eye,
Thin airy forms and wondrous visions fly.
He calls the powers who guard the infernal floods,
And talks inspired, familiar with the gods."
PITT.

There was a practice exactly like this which prevailed among the Highlanders of Scotland; an authentic account of this is given by Sir Walter Scott, in a note on his poem called *The Lady of the Lake.* It is as follows:—

"The Highlanders, like all rude people, had various superstitious modes of inquiring into futurity. One of the most noted was the *Taghairm,* mentioned in the text. A person was wrapped up in the skin of a newly-slain bullock, and deposited beside a waterfall, or at the bottom of a precipice, or in some other strange, wild, and unusual situation, where the scenery around him suggested nothing but objects of horror. In this situation he revolved in his mind the question proposed; and whatever was impressed upon him by his exalted imagination passed for the inspiration of the disembodied spirits who haunt these desolate recesses. In some of the Hebrides, they attributed the same oracular power to a large black stone by the sea-shore, which they approached with certain solemnities; and considered the first fancy which came into their own minds after they did so, to be the undoubted dictate of the tutelar deity of the stone; and as such to be, if possible, punctually complied with. Martin has recorded the following curious modes of Highland augury, in which the Taghairm, and its effects upon the person who was subjected to it, may serve to illustrate the text.

"It was an ordinary thing among the over-curious to consult an invisible oracle concerning the fate of families and battles, &c. This was performed three different ways; the first was by a company of men, one of whom, being detached by lot, was afterwards carried to a river, which was the boundary between two villages. Four of the company laid hold on him; and, having shut his eyes, they took him by the legs and arms, and then, tossing him to and again, struck his hips with force against the bank. One of them cried out, What is it you have got here? Another answers, A log of birch-wood. The other cries again, Let his invisible friends appear from all quarters, and let them relieve him by giving an answer to our present demands; and in a few minutes after, a number of little creatures came from the sea, who answered the question, and disappeared suddenly. The man was then set at liberty; and they all returned home, to take their measures according to the prediction of their false prophets; but the poor deluded fools were abused; for the answer was still ambiguous. This was always practised in the night, and may literally be called the works of darkness.

"I had an account from the most intelligent and judicious men in the Isle of Skie, that, about sixty-two years ago, the oracle was thus consulted only once, and that was in the parish of Kilmartin, on the east side, by a wicked and mischievous race of people, who are now extinguished, both root and branch.

"The second way of consulting the oracle was by a party of men, who first retired to solitary places, remote from any house; and there they singled out one of their number, and wrapt him in a big cow's hide, which they folded about him. His whole body was covered with it, except his head, and so left in this posture all night, until his invisible friends relieved him, by giving a proper answer to the question in hand; which he received, as he fancied, from several persons that he found about him all that time. His consorts returned to him at the break

A. M. cir. 3292 B. C. cir. 712 Olymp. XVII. 1 cir. annum Numæ Pompilii, R. Roman., 4

5 [k]Which say, Stand by thyself, come not near to me; for I am holier than thou. These *are* a smoke in my [l]nose, a fire that burneth all the day.

6 Behold, [m]*it is* written before me: [n]I will not keep silence, [o]but will recompense, even recompense into their bosom,

7 Your iniquities, and [p]the iniquities of your fathers together, saith the LORD, [q]which have burned incense upon the mountains, [r]and blasphemed me upon the hills: therefore will I measure their former work into their bosom.

8 Thus saith the LORD, As the new wine is found in the cluster, and *one* saith, Destroy it not; for [s]a blessing *is* in it: so will I do for my servants' sakes, that I may not destroy them all.

[k]See Matt. ix. 11; Luke v. 30; xviii. 11; Jude 19——[l]Or, *anger*——[m]Deut. xxxii. 34; Mal. iii. 16——[n]Psa. l. 3——[o]Psa. lxxix. 12; Jer. xvi. 18; Ezek. xi. 21——[p]Exod. xx. 5——[q]Ezek. xviii. 6——[r]Ezek. xx. 27, 28——[s]Joel ii. 14

of day, and then he communicated his news to them; which often proved fatal to those concerned in such unwarrantable inquiries.

"There was a third way of consulting, which was a confirmation of the second above mentioned. The same company who put the man into the hide took a live cat, and put him on a spit. One of the number was employed to turn the spit; and one of his consorts inquired of him, What are you doing? He answered, I roast this cat until his friends answer the question; which must be the same that was proposed by the man shut up in the hide. And afterwards, a very big cat (in allusion to the story of 'the King of the Cats,' in Lord Lyttleton's Letters, and well known in the Highlands as a nursery tale) comes, attended by a number of lesser cats, desiring to relieve the cat turned upon the spit, and then answers the question. If this answer proved the same that was given to the man in the hide, then it was taken as a confirmation of the other, which, in this case, was believed infallible.

"Mr. Alexander Cooper, present minister of North-Vist, told me that one John Erach, in the Isle of Lewis, assured him it was his fate to have been led by his curiosity with some who consulted this oracle, and that he was a night within the hide, as above-mentioned; during which time he felt and heard such terrible things, that he could not express them. The impression it made on him was such as could never go off; and he said for a thousand worlds he would never again be concerned in the like performance, for this had disordered him to a high degree. He confessed it ingenuously, and with an air of great remorse; and seemed to be very penitent under a just sense of so great a crime. He declared this about five years since, and is still living in the Lewis for any thing I know."—*Description of the Western Isles*, p. 110. See also PENNANT'S *Scottish Tour*, vol. ii. p. 361.

Verse 4. *Which remain among the graves*] "For the purpose of evoking the dead. They lodged in desert places that demons might appear to them; for demons do appear in such places, to those who do believe in them."—*Kimchi.*

In the monuments—"In the caverns"] בנצורים *bannetsurim*, a word of doubtful signification. An ancient MS. has בצורים *batstsurim*, another בצרים *batstsurim*, "in the rocks;" and *Le Clerc* thinks the *Septuagint* had it so in their copy. They render it by εν τοις σπηλαιοις, "in the caves."

Which eat swine's flesh] This was expressly forbidden by the law, Lev. xi. 7, but among the heathen was in principal request in their sacrifices and feasts. Antiochus Epiphanes compelled the Jews to eat swine's flesh, as a full proof of their renouncing their religion, 2 Mac. vi. 18 and vii. 1. "And the broth of abominable meats," for lustrations, magical arts, and other superstitious and abominable practices.

In *their vessels*] For כליהם *keleyhem*, a MS. had at first בכליהם *bichleyhem.* So the *Vulgate* and *Chaldee*, (and the preposition seems necessary to the sense,) "in their vessels."

Verse 5. *For I am holier than thou*] So the *Chaldee* renders it. קדשתיך *kedashticha* is the same with קדשתי ממך *kadashti mimmecha.* In the same manner חזקתני *chazaktani*, Jer. xx. 7, is used for חזקת ממני *chazacta mimmenni*, "thou art stronger than I."—L.

Verse 6. *Behold*, it is *written before me*] Their sin is registered in heaven, calling aloud for the punishment due to it.

I will—recompense into their bosom] The bosom is the place where the Asiatics have their pockets, and not in their skirts like the inhabitants of the west. Their loose flowing garments have scarcely any thing analogous to *skirts.*

Into their bosom] For על *al*, *ten* MSS. and *five* editions have אל *el.* So again at the end of this verse, *seventeen* MSS. and *four* editions have אל *al.*—L.

Verse 7. *Your iniquities, and the iniquities of your fathers*—"Their iniquities, and the iniquities of their fathers"] For the pronoun affixed of the second person כם *chem, your*, twice, read הם *hem, their*, in the third person; with the *Septuagint* and *Houbigant.*—L.

Verse 8. *A blessing* is *in it*] The Hebrews call all things which serve for food ברכה *berachah*, "a blessing." On this verse *Kimchi* remarks: "As the cluster of grapes contains, besides the juice, the bark, and the kernels, so the Israelites have, besides the just, sinners among them. Now as the cluster must not be destroyed because there is a *blessing*, a nutritive part in it; so Israel shall not be destroyed, because there are righteous persons in it. But as the bark and kernels are thrown away, when the wine is pressed out, so shall the sinners be purged away from among the just, and on their return from exile, shall not be permitted to enter into the land of Israel;" Ezek. xx. 38.

For my servant's sakes—"For the sake of my servant"] It is to be observed that one of the Koningsburg MSS. collated by Lilienthal points

A. M. cir. 3292
B. C. cir. 712
Olymp. XVII. 1
cir. annum
NumæPompilii,
R. Roman., 4

9 And I will bring forth a seed
out of Jacob, and out of Judah
an inheritor of my mountains:
and mine [t]elect shall inherit it,
and my servants shall dwell there.
10 And [u]Sharon shall be a fold of flocks,
and [v]the valley of Achor a place for the
herds to lie down in, for my people that have
sought me.
11 But ye *are* they that forsake the LORD,
that forget [w]my holy mountain, that prepare
[x]a table for that [y]troop, and that
furnish the drink-offering unto
that [z]number.
12 Therefore will I number
you to the sword, and ye shall all bow down
to the slaughter: [a]because when I called, ye
did not answer; when I spake, ye did not hear;
but did evil before mine eyes, and did choose
that wherein I delighted not.
13 Therefore thus saith the Lord GOD, Behold, my servants shall eat, but ye shall be

A. M. cir. 3292
B. C. cir. 712
Olymp. XVII. 1
cir. annum
NumæPompilii,
R. Roman., 4

[t]Ver. 15, 22; Matt. xxiv. 22; Rom. xi. 5, 7——[u]Chap. xxxiii. 9; xxxv. 2——[v]Josh. vii. 24, 26; Hos. ii. 15 [w]Chap. lvi. 7; lvii. 13; ver. 25

[x]Ezek. xxiii. 41; 1 Cor. x. 21——[y]Or, *Gad*——[z]Or, *Meni*——[a]2 Chron. xxxvi. 15, 16; Prov. i. 24, &c.; chap. lxvi. 4; Jer. vii. 13; Zech. vii. 7; Matt. xxi. 34–43

the word עבדי *abdi*, singular; that is, "my servant," meaning the Messiah; and so read the *Septuagint*, which gives a very good sense. In two of my old MSS. it is pointed עבדי *abadai*, and עבדי *abdi*, "my servant," this confirms the above reading.

Verse 9. *An inheritor of my mountains*—"An inheritor of my mountain"] הרי *hari*, in the singular number; so the *Septuagint* and *Syriac;* that is, of Mount Sion. See ver. 11 and chap. lvi. 7, to which Sion, the pronoun feminine singular, added to the verb in the next line, refers; ירשוה *yereshuah*, "shall inherit her."—L.

Verse 10. *Sharon—and the valley of Achor*] Two of the most fertile parts of Judea; famous for their rich pastures; the former to the west, not far from Joppa; the latter north of Jericho, near Gilgal.

Verse 11. *That prepare a table for that troop*—"Who set in order a table for Gad"] The disquisitions and conjectures of the learned concerning Gad and Meni are infinite and uncertain: perhaps the most probable may be, that Gad means good fortune, and Meni the moon. "But why should we be solicitous about it?" says Schmidius. "It appears sufficiently, from the circumstances, that they were false gods; either stars, or some natural objects; or a mere fiction. The Holy Scriptures did not deign to explain more clearly what these objects of idolatrous worship were; but chose rather, that the memory of the knowledge of them should be utterly abolished. And God be praised, that they are so totally abolished, that we are now quite at a loss to know what and what sort of things they were." Schmidius on the place, and on Jud. ii. 13, Bibl. Hallensia.

Jerome, on the place, gives an account of this idolatrous practice of the apostate Jews, of making a feast, or a lectisternium, as the Romans called it, for these pretended deities. Est in cunctis urbibus, et maxime in Ægypto, et in Alexandria, idololatriæ vetus consuetudo, ut ultimo die anni, et mensis ejus qui extremus est, ponant mensam refertam varii generis epulis, et poculum mulso mixtum; vel præteriti anni vel futuri fertilitatem auspicantes. Hoc autem faciebant et Israelitæ, omnium simulachrorum portenta venerantes; et nequaquam altari victimas, sed hujusmodi mensæ liba fundebant. "In all cities, and especially in Egypt and Alexandria, it was an ancient idolatrous custom on the last day of the year, to spread a table covered with various kinds of viands, and a goblet mixed with new wine, referring to the fertility either of the past or coming year. The Israelites did the same, worshipping all kinds of images, and pouring out libations on such tables," &c. See also *Le Clerc* on the place; and on lxvi. 17, and Dav. Millii Dissert. v.

The allusion to Meni, which signifies *number*, is obvious. If there had been the like allusion to Gad, which might have been expected, it might perhaps have helped to let us into the meaning of that word. It appears from Jerome's version of this place, that the words τῳ δαιμονιω, *to a demon*, (or δαιμονι, as some copies have it,) and τῃ τυχῃ, *to fortune*, stood in his time in the Greek version in an inverted order from that which they have in the present copies; the latter then answering to גד *gad*, the former to מני *meni:* by which some difficulty would be avoided; for it is commonly supposed that גד *gad* signifies τυχη, *fortune*. See Gen. xxx. 11, apud *Sept*. This matter is so far well cleared up by MSS. Pachom. and I. D. II., which agree in placing these two words in that order, which Jerome's version supposes.—L.

My Old MS. Bible translates: **That putten the borde of fortune; and offreden licours upon it;** and so the *Vulgate*.

Ἑτοιμαζοντες τῳ δαιμονιῳ τραπεζαν, και πληρουντες τῃ τυχῃ κερασμα. "Preparing a table for the demon, and filling up, or pouring out, a libation to fortune."—*Septuagint*.

Ye have set up an aulter unto fortune
And geven rich drink offeringes unto treasure.
COVERDALE.

Verse 12. *Therefore will I number you*] Referring to *Meni*, which signifies *number*. "Rabbi Eliezar said to his disciples, Turn to God one day before you die. His disciples said, How can a man know the day of his death? He answered, Therefore it is necessary that you should turn to God to-day, for possibly ye may die to-morrow."

Verse 13. *My servants shall eat, but ye shall be hungry*] Rabbi Joachan ben Zachai said in a parable: There was a king who invited his servants, but set them no time to come to the feast. The prudent and wary who were among them adorned themselves; and, standing at the gate of the king's house, said, Is there any thing lacking in the king's house? i. e., Is there any work to be done in it? But the foolish

A. M. cir. 3292
B. C. cir. 712
Olymp. XVII. 1
cir. annum
Numæ Pompilii,
R. Roman., 4

hungry: behold, my servants
shall drink, but ye shall be thirsty:
behold, my servants shall rejoice,
but ye shall be ashamed:
14 Behold, my servants shall sing for joy
of heart, but ye shall cry for sorrow of heart,
and [b]shall howl for [c]vexation of spirit.
15 And ye shall leave your name [d]for a
curse unto [e]my chosen: for the Lord GOD
shall slay thee, and [f]call his servants by another name:
16 [g]That he who blesseth himself in the
earth shall bless himself in the God of truth;
and [h]he that sweareth in the earth shall swear
by the God of truth; because the former
troubles are forgotten, and because they are
hid from mine eyes.
17 For, behold, I create [i]new heavens and
a new earth: and the former shall not be remembered, nor [k]come into
mind.
18 But be ye glad and rejoice
for ever *in that* which I create:
for, behold, I create Jerusalem a rejoicing,
and her people a joy.
19 And [l]I will rejoice in Jerusalem, and
joy in my people; and the [m]voice of weeping
shall be no more heard in her, nor the voice
of crying.
20 There shall be no more thence an infant
of days, nor an old man that hath not filled
his days: for the child shall die a hundred
years old; [n]but the sinner *being* a hundred
years old shall be accursed.
21 And [o]they shall build houses, and inhabit *them;* and they shall plant vineyards,
and eat the fruit of them.
22 They shall not build, and another in-

A. M. cir. 3292
B. C. cir. 712
Olymp. XVII. 1
cir. annum
Numæ Pompilii,
R. Roman., 4

[b]Matt. viii. 12; Luke xiii. 28——[c]Heb. *breaking*——[d]See Jer. xxix. 22; Zech. viii. 13——[e]Ver. 9. 22——[f]Ch. lxii. 2; Acts xi. 26——[g]Psalm lxxii. 17; Jer. iv. 2——[h]Deut. vi. 13; Psa. lxiii. 11; chap. xix. 18; xlv. 23; Zeph. i. 5

[i]Chap. li. 16; lxvi. 22; 2 Pet. iii. 13; Rev. xxi. 1——[k]Heb. *come upon the heart*——[l]Chap. lxii. 5——[m]Chap. xxxv. 10; li. 11; Rev. vii. 17; xxi. 4——[n]Eccles. viii. 12——[o]See Lev. xxvi. 16; Deut. xxviii. 30; chap. lxii. 8; Amos ix. 14

which were among them went, and mocking said, When shall the feast be, in which there is no labour? Suddenly, the king sought out his servants: they who were adorned entered in, and they who were still polluted entered in also. The king was glad when he met the *prudent;* but he was angry when he met the *foolish.* Therefore he said, Let *those* sit down, and let them eat; but let *these* stand and look on.

This parable is very like that of the wise and foolish virgins, Matt. xxv., and that of the marriage of the king's son, Matt. xxii.

Verse 15. *Shall slay thee*—"Shall slay you"] For והמיתך *vehemithecha, shall slay thee,* the *Septuagint* and *Chaldee* read והמיתכם *vehemithechem, shall slay you,* plural.

Verse 17. *I create new heavens and a new earth*] This has been variously understood. Some Jews and some Christians understand it *literally.* God shall change the state of the atmosphere, and render the earth more fruitful. Some refer it to what they call the Millennium; others, to a glorious state of religion; others, to the re-creation of the earth after it shall have been destroyed by fire. I think it refers to the full conversion of the Jews *ultimately;* and primarily to the deliverance from the Babylonish captivity.

Verse 18. *Rejoice for ever* in that *which I create*—"Exult in the age to come which I create"] So in chap. ix. 5 אבי עד *abi ad,* πατηρ του μελλοντος αιωνος, "the father of the age to come," *Sept.* See Bishop Chandler, Defence of Christianity, p. 136.

Verse 19. *The voice of weeping,* &c.] "Because of untimely deaths shall no more be heard in thee; for natural death shall not happen till men be full of days; as it is written, ver. 20: *There shall be no more thence an infant of days,* i. e., the people shall live to *three* or *five hundred* years of age, as in the days of the patriarchs; and if one die at *one hundred* years, it is because of his sin; and even at that age he shall be reputed an *infant;* and they shall say of him, An infant is dead. These things shall happen to Israel in the days of the Messiah."—*Kimchi.*

Verse 20. *Thence*—"There"] For משם *mishsham, thence,* the *Septuagint, Syriac,* and *Vulgate,* read שם *sham, there.*

Verse 22. *They shall not build, and another inhabit*] The reverse of the curse denounced on the disobedient, Deut. xxviii. 30: "Thou shalt build a house, and thou shalt not dwell therein; thou shalt plant a vineyard, and shalt not gather the grapes thereof."

For as the days of a tree] It is commonly supposed that the oak, one of the most long-lived of the trees, lasts about a thousand years; being five hundred years growing to full perfection, and as many decaying: which seems to be a moderate and probable computation. See *Evelyn,* Sylva, B. III. chap. iii. The present emperor of China, in his very ingenious and sensible poem entitled *Eloge de Moukden,* a translation of which in French was published at Paris, 1770, speaks of a tree in his country which lives more than a hundred ages: and another, which after fourscore ages is only in its prime, pp. 37, 38. But his imperial majesty's commentators, in their note on the place, carry the matter much farther; and quote authority, which affirms, that the tree last mentioned by the emperor, the immortal tree, after having lived ten thousand years, is still only in its prime. I suspect that the Chinese enlarge somewhat in their national chronology, as well as in that of their trees. See *Chou King,* Preface, by Mons. de Guignes. The prophet's idea seems

A. M. cir. 3292
B. C. cir. 712
Olymp. XVII. 1
cir. annum
NumæPompilii,
R. Roman., 4

habit; they shall not plant, and
another eat: for [p]as the days of
a tree *are* the days of my people,
and [q]mine elect [r]shall long enjoy the work of their hands.
23 They shall not labour in vain, [s]nor bring
forth for trouble; for [t]they *are* the seed of
the blessed of the LORD, and their offspring
with them.

[p]Psa. xcii. 12——[q]Ver. 9, 15——[r]Heb. *shall make them continue long*, or *shall wear out*

24 And it shall come to pass,
that [u]before they call, I will
answer; and while they are yet
speaking, I will hear.

A. M. cir. 3292
B. C. cir. 714
Olymp. XVII. 1
cir. annum
NumæPompilii,
R. Roman., 4

25 The [v]wolf and the lamb shall feed together, and the lion shall eat straw like the
bullock: [w]and dust *shall be* the serpent's meat.
They shall not hurt nor destroy in all my holy
mountain, saith the LORD.

[s]Deut. xxviii. 41; Hos. ix. 12——[t]Ch. lxi. 9——[u]Psa. xxxii. 5; Dan. ix. 21——[v]Ch. xi. 6, 7, 9——[w]Gen. iii. 14

to be, that they shall live to the age of the antediluvians; which seems to be very justly expressed by the days of a tree, according to our notions. The rabbins have said that this refers to the tree of life, which endures five hundred years.—L.

Verse 23. *They shall not labour in vain*—"My chosen shall not labour in vain"] I remove בחירי *bechirai, my elect*, from the end of the twenty-second to the beginning of the twenty-third verse, on the authority of the *Septuagint*, *Syriac*, and *Vulgate*, and a MS.; contrary to the division in the Masoretic text.—L. The *Septuagint* is beautiful: My chosen shall not labour in vain, neither shall they beget children for the curse; for the seed is blessed of the Lord, and their posterity with them."

Nor bring forth for trouble—"Neither shall they generate a short-lived race"] לבהלה *labbehalah, in festinationem*, "what shall soon hasten away." Εις καταραν, *for a curse*, *Sept.* They seem to have read לאלה *lealah*.—Grotius. But Psa. lxxviii. 33 both justifies and explains the word here:—

ויכל בהבל ימיהם

yemeyhem bahebel vayechal

ושנותם בבהלה

babbehalah ushenotham

"And he consumed their days in vanity;
And their years in haste."

μετα σπουδης, say the *Septuagint*. Jerome on this place of Isaiah explains it to the same purpose: "*εις ανυπαρξιαν, hoc est*, ut esse desistant."

Verse 24. *Before they call, I will answer*] I will give them all they crave for, and more than they can desire.

Verse 25. *The wolf and the lamb, &c.*] The glorious salvation which Jesus Christ procures is for men, and for men only: fallen spirits must still abide under the curse: "He took not on him the nature of angels, but the seed of Abraham."

Shall feed together] For כאחד *keechad, as one*, an ancient MS. has יחדו *yachdav, together;* the usual word, to the same sense, but very different in the letters. The *Septuagint*, *Syriac*, and *Vulgate* seem to agree with the MSS.—L.

CHAPTER LXVI

This chapter treats of the same subject with the foregoing. God, by his prophet, tells the Jews, who valued themselves much on their temple and pompous worship, that the Most High dwelleth not in temples made with hands; and that no outward rites of worship, while the worshippers are idolatrous and impure, can please him who looketh at the heart, 1–3. *This leads to a threatening of vengeance for their guilt, alluding to their making void the law of God by their abominable traditions, their rejection of Christ, persecution of his followers, and consequent destruction by the Romans. But as the Jewish ritual and people shadow forth the system of Christianity and its professors; so, in the prophetical writings, the idolatries of the Jews are frequently put for the idolatries afterwards practised by those bearing the Christian name. Consequently, if we would have the plenitude of meaning in this section of prophecy, which the very context requires, we must look through the type into the antitype, viz., the very gross idolatries practised by the members of Antichrist, the pompous heap of human inventions and traditions with which they have encumbered the Christian system, their most dreadful persecution of Christ's spiritual and true worshippers, and the awful judgments which shall overtake them in the great and terrible day of the Lord,* 4–6. *The mighty and sudden increase of the Church of Jesus Christ at the period of Antichrist's fall represented by the very strong figure of Sion being delivered of a man-child before the time of her travail, the meaning of which symbol the prophet immediately subjoins in a series of interrogations for the sake of greater force and emphasis,* 7–9. *Wonderful prosperity and unspeakable blessedness of the world when the posterity of Jacob, with the fulness of the Gentiles, shall be assembled to Messiah's standard,* 10–14. *All the wicked of the earth shall be gathered together to the battle of that great day of God Almighty, and the slain of Jehovah shall be many,* 15–18. *Manner of the future restoration of the Israelites from their several dispersions throughout the habitable globe,* 19–21. *Perpetuity of this new economy of grace to the house of Israel,* 22. *Righteousness shall be universally diffused in the earth; and the memory of those who have transgressed against the Lord shall be had in continual abhorrence,* 23, 24. *Thus this great prophet, after tracing the principal events of* time, *seems at length to have terminated his views in* eternity, *where all revolutions cease, where the blessedness of the righteous shall be unchangeable as the new heavens, and the misery of the wicked as the fire that shall not be quenched.*

A. M. cir. 3292
B. C. cir. 712
Olymp. XVII. 1
cir. annum
NumæPompilii,
R. Roman., 4

THUS saith the LORD, [a]The
heaven *is* my throne, and
the earth *is* my footstool: where
is the house that ye build unto
me? and where *is* the place of my rest?
2 For all those *things* hath mine hand made,
and all those *things* have been, saith the
LORD: [b]but to this *man* will I look, [c]*even* to
him that is poor and of a contrite spirit, and
[d]trembleth at my word.
3 [e]He that killeth an ox *is as if* he slew a
man; he that sacrificeth a [f]lamb, *as if* he
[g]cut off a dog's neck; he that
offereth an oblation, *as if he offer-*
ed swine's blood; he that [h]burneth
incense, *as if* he blessed an idol.
Yea, they have chosen their own ways, and
their soul delighteth in their abominations.
4 I also will choose their [i]delusions, and
will bring their fears upon them; [k]because
when I called, none did answer; when I
spake, they did not hear: but they did evil
before mine eyes, and chose *that* in which I
delighted not.

A. M. cir. 3292
B. C. cir. 712
Olymp. XVII. 1
cir. annum
NumæPompilii,
R. Roman., 4

---

[a]1 Kings viii. 27; 2 Chron. vi. 18; Matt. v. 34, 35; Acts vii. 48, 49; xvii. 24——[b]Chap. lvii. 15; lxi. 1 [c]Psa. xxxiv. 18; li. 17——[d]Ezra ix. 4; x. 3; Prov. xxviii. 14; ver. 5

[e]Chapter i. 11——[f]Or, *kid*——[g]Deuteronomy xxiii. 18——[h]Hebrew, *maketh a memorial of*, Lev. ii. 2 [i]Or, *devices*——[k]Proverbs i. 24; chapter lxv. 12; Jer. vii. 13

NOTES ON CHAP. LXVI

This chapter is a continuation of the subject of the foregoing. The Jews valued themselves much upon their temple, and the pompous system of services performed in it, which they supposed were to be of perpetual duration; and they assumed great confidence and merit to themselves for their strict observance of all the externals of their religion. And at the very time when the judgments denounced in verses 6 and 12 of the preceding chapter were hanging over their heads, they were rebuilding, by Herod's munificence, the temple in a most magnificent manner. God admonishes them, that "the Most High dwelleth not in temples made with hands;" and that a mere external worship, how diligently soever attended, when accompanied with wicked and idolatrous practices in the worshippers, would never be accepted by him. This their hypocrisy is set forth in strong colours, which brings the prophet again to the subject of the former chapter; and he pursues it in a different manner, with more express declaration of the new economy, and of the flourishing state of the Church under it. The increase of the Church is to be sudden and astonishing. They that escape of the Jews, that is, that become converts to the Christian faith, are to be employed in the Divine mission to the Gentiles, and are to act as priests in presenting the Gentiles as an offering to God; see Rom. xv. 16. And both, now collected into one body, shall be witnesses of the final perdition of the obstinate and irreclaimable.

These two chapters manifestly relate to the calling of the Gentiles, the establishment of the Christian dispensation, and the reprobation of the apostate Jews, and their destruction executed by the Romans.—L.

Verse 2. *And all those* things *have been*—"And all these things are mine"] A word absolutely necessary to the sense is here lost out of the text: לי *li, mine.* It is preserved by the *Septuagint* and *Syriac.*

Verse 3. *He that killeth an ox* is as if *he slew a man*—"He that slayeth an ox killeth a man"] These are instances of wickedness joined with hypocrisy; of the most flagitious crimes committed by those who at the same time affected great strictness in the performance of all the external services of religion. God, by the Prophet Ezekiel, upbraids the Jews with the same practices: "When they had slain their children to their idols, then they came the same day into my sanctuary to profane it," chap. xxiii. 39. Of the same kind was the hypocrisy of the Pharisees in our Saviour's time: "who devoured widows' houses, and for a pretence made long prayers," Matt. xxiii. 14.

The generality of interpreters, by departing from the literal rendering of the text, have totally lost the true sense of it, and have substituted in its place what makes no good sense at all; for it is not easy to show how, in any circumstances, sacrifice and murder, the presenting of legal offerings and idolatrous worship, can possibly be of the same account in the sight of God.

He that offereth an oblation, as if he offered *swine's blood*—"That maketh an oblation *offereth* swine's blood"] A word here likewise, necessary to complete the sense, is perhaps irrecoverably lost out of the text. The *Vulgate* and *Chaldee* add the word *offereth,* to make out the sense; not, as I imagine, from any different reading, (for the word wanted seems to have been lost before the time of the oldest of them, as the *Septuagint* had it not in their copy,) but from mere necessity.

Le Clerc thinks that מעלה *maaleh* is to be repeated from the beginning of this member; but that is not the case in the parallel members, which have another and a different verb in the second place. "דם *dam,* sic Versiones; putarem tamen legendum participium aliquod, et quidem זבח *zabach,* cum sequatur ח *cheth,* nisi jam præcesserat."—SECKER. *Houbigant* supplies אכל *achal, eateth.* After all, I think the most probable word is that which the *Chaldee* and *Vulgate* seem to have designed to represent; that is, מקריב *makrib, offereth.*

In their abominations.] ובשקוציהם *ubeshikkutseyhem,* "and in their abominations;" two

A. M. cir. 3292 B. C. cir. 712 Olymp. XVII. 1 cir. annum NumæPompilii, R. Roman., 4

5 Hear the word of the LORD, [l]ye that tremble at his word; Your brethren that hated you, that cast you out for my name's sake, said, [m]Let the LORD be glorified: but [n]he shall appear to your joy, and they shall be ashamed.

6 A voice of noise from the city, a voice from the temple, a voice of the LORD that rendereth recompense to his enemies.

7 Before she travailed, she brought forth; before her pain came, she was delivered of a man child.

8 Who hath heard such a thing? who hath seen such things? Shall the earth be made to bring forth in one day: *or* shall a nation be born at once? for as soon as Zion travailed, she brought forth her children.

9 Shall I bring to the birth, and not [o]cause to bring forth? saith the LORD: shall I cause to bring forth, and shut *the womb?* saith thy God.

10 Rejoice ye with Jerusalem, and be glad with her, all ye that love her: rejoice for joy with her, all ye that mourn for her:

A. M. cir. 3292 B. C. cir. 712 Olymp. XVII. 1 cir. annum NumæPompilii, R. Roman., 4

11 That ye may suck, and be satisfied with the breasts of her consolations; that ye may milk out, and be delighted with the [p]abundance of her glory.

12 For thus saith the LORD, Behold, [q]I will extend peace to her like a river, and the glory of the Gentiles like a flowing stream; then shall ye [r]suck, ye shall be [s]borne upon *her* sides, and be dandled upon *her* knees.

13 As one whom his mother comforteth, so will I comfort you; and ye shall be comforted in Jerusalem.

14 And when ye see *this,* your heart shall rejoice, and [t]your bones shall flourish like an herb: and the hand of the LORD shall be known toward his servants, and *his* indignation toward his enemies.

[l]Ver. 1——[m]Chap. v. 19——[n]2 Thess. i. 10; Tit. ii. 13——[o]Or, *beget*——[p]Or, *brightness*

[q]Chap. xlviii. 18; lx. 5——[r]Chap. lx. 16——[s]Chap. xlix. 22; lx. 4——[t]See Ezek. xxxvii. 1, &c.

copies of the *Machazor,* and one of *Kennicott's* MSS. have ובגלוליהם *ubegilluleyhem,* "and in their idols." So the *Vulgate* and *Syriac.*

Verse 5. *Your brethren that hated you—said*—"Say ye to your brethren that hate you"] The *Syriac* reads אמרו לאחיכם *imru laacheychem;* and so the *Septuagint,* Edit. Comp. ειπατε αδελφοις ὑμων· and MS. Marchal. has αδελφοις· and so Cyril and Procopius read and explain it. It is not easy to make sense of the reading of the *Septuagint* in the other editions; ειπατε αδελφοι ἡμων τοις μισουσιν ὑμας· but for ἡμων, *our,* MS. I. D. II. also has ὑμων, *your.*

Verse 6. *A voice of noise from the city, a voice from the temple, a voice of the Lord*] It is very remarkable that similar words were spoken by Jesus, son of Ananias, previously to the destruction of Jerusalem. See his very affecting history related by *Josephus,* WAR, B. vi., chap. v.

Verse 8. *Who hath seen*—"And who hath seen"] Twenty MSS., (four ancient,) of *Kennicott's,* and twenty-nine of *De Rossi's,* and two ancient of my own, and the two oldest editions, with two others, have ומי *umi,* adding the conjunction ו *vau;* and so read all the ancient versions. AND *who hath seen?*

Verse 9. *Shall I bring to the birth*] האני אשביר *haani ashbir,* num ego matricem frangam; MONTANUS. The word means that which immediately precedes the appearance of the fetus—*the breaking forth* of the *liquor amnii.* This also is an expression that should be studiously avoided in prayers and sermons.

Verse 11. *With the abundance of her glory*—"From her abundant stores."] For מזין *mizziz, from the splendour,* two MSS. and the old edition of 1488, have מזין *mizziv;* and the latter ז *zain* is upon a rasure in three other MSS. It is remarkable that *Kimchi* and *Sal. ben Melec,* not being able to make any thing of the word as it stands in the text, say it means the same with מזין *mizziv;* that is, in effect, they admit of a various reading, or an error in the text. But as *Vitringa* observes, what sense is there in sucking nourishment from the *splendour* of her glory? He therefore endeavours to deduce another sense of the word זיז *ziz;* but, as far as it appears to me, without any authority. I am more inclined to accede to the opinion of those learned rabbins, and to think that there is some mistake in the word; for that in truth is their opinion, though they disguise it by saying that the corrupted word means the very same with that which they believe to be genuine. So in chap. xli. 24 they say that אפע *apha, a viper,* means the same with אפס *ephes, nothing;* instead of acknowledging that one is written by mistake instead of the other. I would propose to read in this place מזין *mizzin* or מזן *mizzen,* which is the reading of one of *De Rossi's* MS., (instead of מזין *meziz,*) *from the stores,* from זון *zun, to nourish, to feed;* see Gen. xlv. 23; 2 Chron. xi. 23; Psa. cxliv. 13. And this perhaps may be meant by Aquila, who renders the word by απο παντοδαπιας· with which that of the *Vulgate, ab* omnimoda *gloria,* and of Symmachus and Theodotion, nearly agree. The Chaldee follows a different reading, without improving the sense; מיין *meyin, from the wine.*—L.

Verse 12. *Like a river, and—like a flowing stream*—"Like the great river, and like the overflowing stream"] That is, the Euphrates, (it ought to have been pointed כנהר *cannahar,* ut fluvius ille, *as the river,*) and the Nile.

Then shall ye suck—"And ye shall suck at the breast"] These two words על שד *al shad, at the*

A. M. cir. 3292
B. C. cir. 712
Olymp. XVII. 1
cir. annum
NumæPompilii,
R. Roman., 4

15 [u]For, behold, the LORD
will come with fire, and with his
chariots like a whirlwind, to
render his anger with fury, and
his rebuke with flames of fire.
16 For by fire and by [v]his sword will the
LORD plead with all flesh: and the slain of
the LORD shall be many.
17 [w]They that sanctify themselves, and purify themselves in the gardens [x]behind one
tree in the midst, eating swine's flesh, and the
abomination, and the mouse,
shall be consumed together, saith
the LORD.
18 For I *know* their works and
their thoughts; it shall come that I will gather
all nations and tongues; and they shall come,
and see my glory.
19 [y]And I will set a sign among them, and
I will send those that escape of them unto the
nations, *to* Tarshish, Pul, and Lud, that draw
the bow, *to* Tubal, and Javan, *to* the isles afar

A. M. cir. 3292
B. C. cir. 712
Olymp. XVII. 1
cir. annum
NumæPompilii,
R. Roman., 4

[u]Chap. ix. 5; 2 Thess. i. 8——[v]Chap. xxvii. 1

[w]Ch. lxv. 3, 4——[x]Or, *one after another*——[y]Luke ii. 34

breast, seem to have been omitted in the present text, from their likeness to the two words following; על צד *al tsad, at the side*. A very probable conjecture of *Houbigant*. The *Chaldee* and *Vulgate* have omitted the two latter words instead of the two former. See note on chap. lx. 4.

Verse 15. *The Lord will come with fire*—"JEHOVAH shall come as a fire"] For באש *baesh, in fire*, the *Septuagint* had in their copy כאש *kaesh, as a fire; ὡς πυρ*.

To render his anger with fury—"To breathe forth his anger in a burning heat"] Instead of להשיב *lehashib*, as pointed by the Masoretes, *to render*, I understand it as להשב *lehashshib, to breathe*, from נשב *nashab*.

Verse 17. *Behind one* tree—"After the rites of Achad"] The Syrians worshipped a god called Adad, *Plin.* Nat. Hist. xxxvii. 11; Macrob. Sat. i. 23. They held him to be the highest and greatest of the gods, and to be the same with Jupiter and the sun; and the name Adad, says *Macrobius*, signifies *one;* as likewise does the word Achad in Isaiah. Many learned men therefore have supposed, and with some probability, that the prophet means the same pretended deity. אחד *achad*, in the *Syrian* and *Chaldean* dialects, is חד *chad;* and perhaps by reduplication of the last letter to express perfect unity, it may have become חדד *chadad*, not improperly expressed by Macrobius *Adad*, without the aspirate. It was also pronounced by the Syrians themselves, with a weaker aspirate, הדד *hadad;* as in Benhadad, Hadadezer, names of their kings, which were certainly taken from their chief object of worship. This seems to me to be a probable account of this name.

But the Masoretes correct the text in this place. Their marginal reading is אחת *achath*, which is the same word, only in the feminine form; and so read thirty MSS. (six ancient) and the two oldest editions. This *Le Clerc* approves, and supposes it to mean Hecate, or the moon; and he supports his hypothesis by arguments not at all improbable. See his note on the place.

Whatever the particular mode of idolatry which the prophet refers to might be, the general sense of the place is perfectly clear. But the *Chaldee* and *Syriac*, and after them *Symmachus* and *Theodotion*, cut off at once all these difficulties, by taking the word אחד *achad* in its common meaning, not as a proper name; the two latter rendering the sentence thus: Οπισω αλληλων εν μεσῳ εσθιοντων το κρεας το χοιρειον; "One after another, in the midst of those that eat swine's flesh." I suppose they all read in their copies אחד אחד *achad achad, one by one*, or perhaps אחד אחר אחד *achad achar achad, one after another*. See a large dissertation on this subject in *Davidis Millii* Dissertationes Selectæ, Dissert. vi.—L.

I know not what to make of this place; it is certain that our translation makes no sense, and that of the learned prelate seems to me too refined. *Kimchi* interprets this of the Turks, who are remarkable for ablutions. "Behind one in the midst" he understands of a large fish-pond placed in the middle of their gardens. Others make אחד *achad a deity*, as above; and a deity of various names it is supposed to be, for it is *Achad*, and *Chad*, and *Hadad*, and *Achath*, and *Hecat*, an Assyrian idol. **Behynd the fyrst tree or the gate withine forth.**—Old MS. Bible.

Verse 18. *For I* know *their works*] A word is here lost out of the present text, leaving the text quite imperfect. The word is יודע *yodea, knowing*, supplied from the *Syriac*. The *Chaldee* had the same word in the copy before him, which he paraphrases by קדמי גלן *kedemi gelon*, their deeds *are manifest before me;* and the Aldine and Complutensian editions of the *Septuagint* acknowledge the same word επισταμαι, which is verified by MS. *Pachom.* and the *Arabic* version. I think there can be little doubt of its being genuine. The concluding verses of this chapter refer to the complete restoration of the Jews, and to the destruction of all the enemies of the Gospel of Christ, so that the earth shall be filled with the knowledge and glory of the Lord. Talia sæcla currite! Lord, hasten the time!

It shall come—"And I come"] For באה *baah*, which will not accord with any thing in the sentence, I read בא *ba*, with a MS.; the participle answering to יודע *yodea*, with which agree the *Septuagint*, *Syriac*, and *Vulgate*. Perhaps it ought to be ובא *veba, when* I shall come, Syr.; and so the *Septuagint*, according to Edit. Ald. and Complut., and Cod. Marchal.

Verse 19. *That draw the bow*] I much suspect that the words משכי קשת *moshechey kesheth, who draw the bow*, are a corruption of the word משך *meshek, Moschi*, the name of a nation situated between the Euxine and Caspian seas; and properly joined with תבל *tubal*, the Tibareni. See *Bochart*, Phaleg. iii. 12. The *Septuagint* have μοσοχ, without any thing of the *drawers of the bow:* the word being once taken for a participle, *the bow* was added to make

A. M. cir. 3292
B. C. cir. 712
Olymp. XVII. 1
cir. annum
NumæPompilii,
R. Roman., 4

off, that have not heard my fame, neither have seen my glory; [z]and they shall declare my glory among the Gentiles.

20 And they shall bring all your brethren [a]*for* an offering unto the LORD out of all nations upon horses, and in chariots, and in [b]litters, and upon mules, and upon swift beasts, to my holy mountain Jerusalem, saith the LORD, as the children of Israel bring an offering in a clean vessel into the house of the LORD.

21 And I will also take of them for [c]priests *and* for Levites, saith the LORD.

22 For as [d]the new heavens and the new earth, which I will make, shall remain before me, saith the LORD, so shall your seed and your name remain.

23 And [e]it shall come to pass *that* [f]from one new moon to another, and from one sabbath to another, [g]shall all flesh come to worship before me, saith the LORD.

24 And they shall go forth, and look upon [h]the carcasses of the men that have transgressed against me: for their [i]worm shall not die, neither shall their fire be quenched; and they shall be an abhorring unto all flesh.

[z]Mal. i. 11——[a]Rom. xv. 16——[b]Or, *couches*——[c]Exod. xix. 6; ch. lxi. 6; 1 Pet. ii. 9; Rev. i. 6——[d]Chap. lxv. 17; 2 Pet. iii. 13; Rev. xxi. 1——[e]Zech. xiv. 16——[f]Heb. *from new moon to his new moon, and from sabbath to his sabbath*——[g]Psa. lxv. 2; chap. xlix. 26——[h]Ver. 16——[i]Mark ix. 44, 46, 48

sense of it קשת *kesheth, the bow,* is omitted in a MS. and by the *Septuagint.*

That have not heard my fame—"Who never heard my name"] For שמעי *shimi, my fame,* I read, with the *Septuagint* and *Syriac,* שמי *shemi, my name.*

Verse 20. *And in chariots*—"And in counes"] There is a sort of vehicle much used in the east, consisting of a pair of hampers or cradles, thrown across a camel's back, one on each side; in each of which a person is carried. They have a covering to defend them from the rain and the sun. *Thevenot* calls them *counes,* i. p. 356. *Maillet* describes them as covered cages hanging on both sides of a camel. "At Aleppo," says Dr. *Russell,* "women of inferior condition in longer journeys are commonly stowed, one on each side of a mule, in a sort of covered cradles." Nat. Hist. of Aleppo, p. 89. These seem to be what the prophet means by the word צבים *tsabbim.* *Harmer's* Observations, i. p. 445.

Verse 21. And *for Levites*] For ללוים *laleviyim,* fifty-nine MSS., (eight ancient,) have וללוים *velaleviyim,* adding the conjunction ו *vau,* which the sense seems necessarily to require: and so read all the ancient versions. See Josh. iii. 3, and the various readings on that place in *Kennicott's* Bible.

Verse 24. *For their worm shall not die*] These words of the prophet are applied by our blessed Saviour, Mark ix. 44, to express the everlasting punishment of the wicked in Gehenna, or in hell. Gehenna, or the valley of Hinnom, was very near to Jerusalem to the south-east: it was the place where the idolatrous Jews celebrated that horrible rite of making their children pass through the fire, that is, of burning them in sacrifice to Moloch. To put a stop to this abominable practice, Josiah defiled, or desecrated, the place, by filling it with human bones, 2 Kings xxiii. 10, 14; and probably it was the custom afterwards to throw out the carcasses of animals there, when it also became the common burying place for the poorer people of Jerusalem. Our Saviour expressed the state of the blessed by sensible images; such as paradise, Abraham's bosom, or, which is the same thing, a place to recline next to Abraham at table in the kingdom of heaven. See Matt. viii. 11. Cœnabat Nerva cum paucis. Veiento *proximus,* atque etiam *in sinu* recumbebat. "The Emperor Nerva supped with few. *Veiento* was the first in his estimation, and even reclined in his bosom." *Plin. Epist.* iv. 22. Compare John xiii. 23; for we could not possibly have any conception of it, but by analogy from worldly objects. In like manner he expressed the place of torment under the image of Gehenna; and the punishment of the wicked by the worm which there preyed on the carcasses, and the fire that consumed the wretched victims. Marking however, in the strongest manner, the difference between Gehenna and the invisible place of torment; namely, that in the former the suffering is transient:—the worm itself which preys upon the body, dies; and the fire which totally consumes it, is soon extinguished:—whereas in the figurative Gehenna the instruments of punishment shall be everlasting, and the suffering without end; "for there the worm dieth not, and the fire is not quenched."

These emblematical images, expressing heaven and hell, were in use among the Jews before our Saviour's time; and in using them he complied with their notions. "Blessed is he that shall eat bread in the kingdom of God," says the Jew to our Saviour, Luke xiv. 15. And in regard to Gehenna, the Chaldee paraphrast, as I observed before on chap. xxx. 33, renders everlasting or continual burnings by "the Gehenna of everlasting fire." And before his time the son of Sirach, chap. vii. 17, had said, "The vengeance of the ungodly is fire and worms." So likewise the author of the book of Judith, chap. xvi. 17: "Wo to the nations rising up against my kindred: the Lord Almighty will take vengeance of them in the day of judgment, in putting fire and worms in their flesh;" manifestly referring to the same emblem.—L.

Kimchi's conclusion of his notes on this book is remarkable:—

"Blessed be God who hath created the mountains and the hills,
And hath endued me with strength to finish the book of salvation:
He shall rejoice us with good tidings and reports;

He shall show us a token for good;—
And the end of his miracles he shall cause to approach us."

Several of the Versions have a peculiarity in their terminations:—

And they shall be to a satiety of sight to all flesh.
VULGATE.

And thei schul ben into fyllyng of sigt to all fleshe.
Old MS. BIBLE.

And they shall be as a vision to all flesh.
SEPTUAGINT.

And the wicked shall be punished in hell till the righteous shall say,—It is enough.
CHALDEE.

They shall be an astonishment to all flesh;
So that they shall be a spectacle to all beings.
SYRIAC.

The end of the prophecy of Isaiah the prophet.
Praise to God who is truly praiseworthy.
ARABIC.

One of my old Hebrew MSS. after the twenty-first verse repeats the twenty-third: "And it shall come to pass that from one new moon to another, and from one Sabbath to another, shall all flesh come to worship before me, saith the Lord."

MASORETIC NOTES

Number of verses in this book, 1295.

Middle verse,—Chap. xxxiii. 21.

Masoretic sections, 26.

חזק *chazak*, Be strong.

In the course of these notes the reader will have often observed two MSS. of the *Septuagint* referred to by Bp. Lowth, and marked I. B. II., I. D. II. They are both in the British Museum. The *former* contains the prophets, and was written about the tenth or eleventh century; and because it once belonged to Pachomius, patriarch of Constantinople, in the beginning of the sixteenth century, the bishop often quotes it by the title MS. Pachom. The *other* contains many of the historical books, beginning with *Ruth*, and ending with *Ezra;* and has also the Prophet Isaiah. This MS. consists of two parts,—one apparently written in the eleventh or twelfth century; the other, in the beginning of the fourteenth. Dr. *Grabe* and Dr. *Woide*, as well as Bp. *Lowth*, considered these MSS. of great value and authority.

It may be necessary to say something of the Hebrew MSS. which I have also frequently quoted. The collations of *Kennicott* and *De Rossi* have been long before the public; and to describe them would be useless. The collections of the *latter* Bp. Lowth had never seen, else he could have strengthened his authorities: these, for the first time, I have in the preceding notes incorporated with Bishop Lowth's references, and thus added double strength to the learned prelate's authorities. But of my own I should say something, as they form no part of the above collections; and yet are among the oldest MSS. known to exist. Independently of rolls, which contain only the Megillah, Esther, and the Pentateuch, they are *ten* in number, and formerly belonged to the Rev. Cornelius Schulting, a Protestant minister of Amsterdam. After his death in 1726, they were sold by public auction, and came into the possession of the Rev. John Van der Hagen, a reformed minister of the same place.

In 1733, Jo. Christ. Wolf described these MSS. in the fourth volume of his Bibliotheca Hebræa, p. 79. A few years ago I had the singular good fortune to purchase the whole of these at Utrecht; a collection of MSS., which Dr. *Kennicott* complains that he could not by any entreaties obtain the privilege of collating. These are his own words,—"Wolfius, (Bib. Heb. iv. 79-82,) memorat codices 10. olim penes Schultingium; quorum plurimi postea erant penes Rev. Joh. Van der Hagen. Usum Codd. Hagenianorum obtinere nulla potuit à me precatio." Dissert. Gener. p. 78. sub Cod. 84. Dr. *Kennicott* supposed that three of those MSS. had been collated for him: but in this I believe he was mistaken; as he was also in supposing that only the greater part of the ten MSS. of Schulting had fallen into the hands of Mr. Van der Hagen; for the fact is, the whole ten were purchased by Van der Hagen, and the same ten are now in my library, being precisely those described by Wolfius, as above. I have collated the Prophet Isaiah throughout, in two of the most ancient of these MSS.; and have added their testimony in many places to the various readings collected by *Kennicott* and *De Rossi.* The very bad state of my health, and particularly of my eyes, prevented a more extensive collation of these very ancient and invaluable MSS. Some of the oldest are without any date. They are marked with the ten first letters of the alphabet. Cod. C. was written A. D. 1076,—D. in 1286,—G. in 1215,—H. in 1309,—I. in 1136. In most of these there is an ample harvest of important various readings.

Bishop Lowth, in giving an account of his labours on this prophet, takes a general view of the difficulties and helps he met with in his work. This being of considerable importance, I shall lay an abstract of it before the reader, as a proper supplement to the preceding sheets. He observes:—

"The Masoretic punctuation,—by which the pronunciation of the language is given, and the forms of the several parts of speech, the construction of the words, the distribution and limits of the sentences, and the connexion of the several members, are fixed,—is in effect an interpretation of the Hebrew text made by the Jews of late ages, probably not earlier than the eight century; and may be considered as *their* translation of the Old Testament. Where the words unpointed are capable of various meanings, according as they may be variously pronounced and constructed, the Jews by their pointing have determined them to one meaning and construction; and the sense which they thus give is *their* sense of the passage, just as the rendering of a translator into another language is *his* sense. The points have been considered as part of the Hebrew text, and as giving the meaning of it on no less than Divine authority. Accordingly our public translations in the modern tongues, for the use of the Church among Protestants, and so likewise the modern Latin translations, are for the most part close copies of the Hebrew pointed text, and are in reality only versions at second hand, translations of the Jews' interpretation of the Old Testament.

"To what a length an opinion lightly taken up, and embraced with a full assent without due examination, may be carried, we may see in another example of much the same kind. The learned of the Church of Rome, who have taken the liberty of giving translations of

Scripture in the modern languages, have for the most part subjected and devoted themselves to a prejudice equally groundless and absurd. The Council of Trent declared the Latin translation of the Scriptures, called the Vulgate, which had been for many ages in use in their Church, to be authentic; a very ambiguous term, which ought to have been more precisely defined than the fathers of this council chose to define it. Upon this ground many contended that the Vulgate Version was dictated by the Holy Spirit; at least was providentially guarded against all error; was consequently of Divine authority, and more to be regarded than even the original Hebrew and Greek texts.

"But a very fruitful source of error proceeded from the Jewish coypists consulting more the fair appearance of their copy than the correctness of it, by wilfully leaving mistakes uncorrected, lest by erasing they should diminish the beauty and the value of the transcript, (for instance, when they had written a word or part of a word wrong, and immediately saw their mistake, they left the mistake uncorrected, and wrote the word anew after it;) their scrupulous regard to the evenness and fulness of their lines, which induced them to cut off from the ends of lines a letter or letters for which there was not sufficient room, (for they never divided a word, so that the parts of it should belong to two lines,) and to add to the ends of lines letters wholly insignificant, by way of expletives to fill up a vacant space: their custom of writing part of a word at the end of a line, where there was not room for the whole, and then giving the whole word at the beginning of the next line.

"These circumstances considered, it would be the most astonishing of all miracles, if the Hebrew writings of the Old Testament had come down to us through their hands absolutely pure, and free from all mistakes whatsoever.

"The ancient VERSIONS, as the principal sources of emendation, and highly useful in rectifying as well as in explaining the Hebrew text, are contained in the London Polyglot.

"The *Greek* Version, commonly called the Septuagint, or of the seventy interpreters, probably made by different hands, (the number of them uncertain,) and at different times, as the exigence of the Jewish Church at Alexandria and in other parts of Egypt required, is of the first authority, and of the greatest use in correcting the Hebrew text, as being the most ancient of all; and as the copy from which it was translated appears to have been free from many errors which afterwards by degrees got into the text. But the Greek Version of Isaiah is not so old as that of the Pentateuch by a hundred years and more, having been made in all probability after the time of Antiochus Epiphanes, when the reading of the prophets in the Jewish synagogues began to be practised; and even after the building of Onias' temple, to favour which there seems to have been some artifice employed in a certain passage of Isaiah (chap. xix. 18) in this Version. And it unfortunately happens that Isaiah has had the hard fate to meet with a Greek translator very unworthy of him, there being hardly any book of the Old Testament so ill rendered in that Version as this of Isaiah.

"The *Arabic* Version is sometimes referred to as verifying the reading of the Septuagint, being, for the most part at least, taken from that Version.

"The *Chaldee* paraphrase of Jonathan ben Uzziel, made about or before the time of our Saviour, though it often wanders from the text in a wordy allegorical explanation, yet very frequently adheres to it closely, and gives a verbal rendering of it; and accordingly is sometimes of great use in ascertaining the true reading of the Hebrew text.

"The *Syriac* Version stands next in order of time, but is superior to the Chaldee in usefulness and authority, as well in ascertaining as in explaining the Hebrew text. It is a close translation of the Hebrew language into one of near affinity to it. It is supposed to have been made as early as the first century.

"The fragments of the three Greek Versions of *Aquila*, *Symmachus*, and *Theodotion*, all made in the second century, which are collected in the Hexapla of Montfauçon, are of considerable use for the same purpose.

"The *Vulgate*, being for the most part the translation of Jerome, made in the fourth century, is of service in the same way, in proportion to its antiquity.

"In referring to Dr. Kennicott's Collections, I have given the whole number of manuscripts or editions which concur in any particular reading; what proportion that number bears to the whole number of collated copies which contain the Book of Isaiah, may be seen by comparing it with the catalogue of copies collated, which is given at the end of that book in the doctor's edition of the Hebrew Bible.

"Among the manuscripts which have been collated, I consider those of the tenth, eleventh, and twelfth centuries as ancient, comparatively and in respect of the rest. Therefore in quoting a number of manuscripts, where the variation is of some importance, I have added, that so many of that number are *ancient*, that is, are of the centuries above mentioned.

"The design of the notes is to give the reasons and authorities on which the translation is founded; to rectify or to explain the words of the text; to illustrate the ideas, the images, and the allusions of the prophet, by referring to objects, notions, and customs which peculiarly belong to his age and his country; and to point out the beauties of particular passages. If the reader would go deeper into the mystical sense, into theological, historical, and chronological disquisitions, there are many learned expositors to whom he may have recourse, who have written full commentaries on this prophet, to which title the present work has no pretensions. The sublime and spiritual uses to be made of this peculiarly evangelical prophet, must be all founded on a faithful representation of the literal sense which his words contain. This is what I have endeavoured closely and exactly to express."

IN conclusion, it may be necessary to give some account of what I have ventured to superadd to the labours of this very learned prelate. After consulting the various commentators, who have spent much time and labour in their endeavours to illustrate this prophet, I found their interpretations of many of the most important prophecies strangely different, and often at variance. Former commentators have taken especial care to bring forth in the most prominent point of view all those passages which have been generally understood to refer to our blessed Lord, and the Christian dispensation. Later critics, especially those on the continent, have adopted the Jewish plan of interpretation, referring the parts belonging to the Messiah in his sufferings, &c., to the prophet himself, or to the children of the captivity in their state of *suffering;* and those passages which speak of the *redemption of the world*, and the *glorious state of the Christian Church*, they apply to the *deliverance of the Israelites from the Babylonish captivity.* It is really painful to see what labour and learning these critics spend to rob the prophet of his title of *evangelical;* and to show that even the sacred writers of the New Testament, in their application of select passages to our Lord, only followed the popular custom of *accommodating* passages of the Sacred Writings to occurrences and events, to which their leading circumstances bore some kind of resemblance, the application being only intended to convey the idea of *similitude*, and not of *identity*.

While I have cautiously handled those passages, the application of which was *dubious*, I have taken care to give my opinion with firmness on those which seem to have no other meaning than what they derive from their application to the great work of redemption by Jesus Christ, and the glory that should follow the outpouring of his Spirit. Many readers will no doubt suppose that I should have dwelt more on the *spiritual* parts of this inimitable book; but to this there would be scarcely any end. Who could exhaust the stores of this prophet! and if any thing were left unsaid, some would still be unsatisfied, to say nothing of the volume being thereby swollen beyond all reasonable bounds. I have marked enough for the reader's meditation; and have thrown out a sufficient number of hints to be improved by ministers of the word of God. To another class it may appear too *critical;* but this chiefly applies to the learned bishop, whose plan, as by far the best in my judgment, I have followed; and whose collection of various readings I felt it my duty to complete, a thing that none of his editors have attempted before. I have therefore added the various readings collected by De Rossi to those of Dr. Kennicott, which the bishop had cited as authorities, on which he built his alterations and critical conjectures.

INTRODUCTION TO THE BOOK

OF THE

PROPHET JEREMIAH

THE Prophet Jeremiah, son of Hilkiah, was of the sacerdotal race, and a native of *Anathoth,* a village in the tribe of *Benjamin,* within a few miles of Jerusalem, which had been appointed for the use of the priests, the descendants of Aaron, Josh. xxi. 18. He was called to the prophetic office when very young; probably when he was fourteen years of age, and in the thirteenth of the reign of Josiah, A. M. 3375, B. C. 629. He continued to prophesy till after the destruction of Jerusalem by the Chaldeans, which took place A. M. 3416; and it is supposed that about two years after he died in Egypt. Thus it appears that he discharged the arduous duties of the prophetic office for upwards of *forty* years.

Being very young when called to the prophetic office, he endeavoured to excuse himself on account of his youth and incapacity for the work; but, being overruled by the Divine authority, ne undertook the task, and performed it with matchless zeal and fidelity in the midst of a most crooked and perverse people, by whom he was continually persecuted, and whom he boldly reproved, often at the hazard of his life.

His attachment to his country was strong and fervent; he foresaw by the light of prophecy the ruin that was coming upon it. He might have made terms with the enemy, and not only saved his life, but have gained ease and plenty; but he chose rather to continue with his people, and take his part in all the disasters that befell them.

After the destruction of Jerusalem, Nebuchadnezzar having made *Gedaliah* governor of Judea, the fractious Jews rose up against him, and put him to death; they then escaped to *Tahpanhes* in Egypt, carrying Jeremiah with them; who, continuing to testify against their wickedness and idolatry, at length fell a victim to his faithfulness: they filled up the measure of their iniquity, as tradition reports, by stoning the prophet to death. God marked this murderous outrage by his peculiar displeasure; for in a few years after they were almost all miserably destroyed by the Chaldean armies which had invaded Egypt; and even this destruction had been foretold by the prophet himself, chap. xliv: "They were consumed by the sword and by the famine until there was an end of them, a small remnant only escaping," ver. 14, 27, 28.

The pitch of desperate wickedness to which the Jews had arrived previously to their captivity was truly astonishing. They had exhausted all the means that infinite *mercy,* associated with infinite *justice,* could employ for the salvation of sinners; and they became in consequence *desperately wicked;* no wonder, therefore, that wrath fell upon them to the *uttermost.* It seems that their hardness and darkness had proceeded to such lengths that they abandoned themselves to all the abominations of idolatry to avenge themselves on God, because he would not bear with their continual profligacy. Were ever people more highly favoured, more desperately ungrateful, or more signally punished! What a lesson is their history to the nations of the earth, and especially to those who have been favoured with the light of revelation!

I should have entered into a particular discussion relative to the history of those times mentioned by this prophet, had they not passed already in review in the Books of *Kings* and *Chronicles;* in which much of the historical parts of this prophet has been anticipated; and to which, in order to avoid repetition, I must refer my readers. What is farther necessary to be added will be found in the following notes.

As a writer, the character of Jeremiah has been well drawn by Bishop *Lowth.* On comparing him with *Isaiah,* the learned prelate says: "Jeremiah is by no means wanting either in elegance or sublimity; although, generally speaking, inferior to Isaiah in both. St. Jerome has objected to him a certain *rusticity* in his diction; of which, I must confess, I do not discover the smallest trace. His thoughts, indeed, are somewhat less elevated, and he is commonly more large and diffuse in his sentences; but the reason of this may be, that he is mostly taken up with the gentler passions of *grief* and *pity,* for the expressing of which he has a peculiar talent. This is most evident in the *Lamentations,* where those passions altogether predominate; but it is often visible also in his *Prophecies;* in the former part of the book more especially, which is principally *poetical.* The middle parts are for the most part *historical;* but the last part, consisting of *six* chapters, is entirely *poetical;* and contains several oracles distinctly marked, in which this prophet falls very little short of the loftiest style of Isaiah."

It has often been remarked, that although several of the prophecies in this book have their *dates* distinctly noted, and most of the rest may be ascertained from collateral evidence; yet there is a strange *disorder* in the *arrangement.* "There is," says Dr. *Blayney,* "a preposterous jumbling together of the prophecies of the reigns of Jehoiakim and Zedekiah in the seventeen chapters which follow the twentieth, according to the Hebrew copies; so that, without any apparent reason, many of the *latter* reigns *precede* those of the *former;* and in the *same reign,* the *last* delivered are put *first,* and the *first, last.*" In order to prevent the confusion arising from this, Dr. *Blayney* has transposed the chapters where he thought it needful, without altering the numerals as they stand in our common Bibles.

This defect has been noticed, and attempts made to remedy it, by others. Dr. *John George Dahler,* Professor of Theology in the Protestant seminary of Strasburg, has just now published the *first volume* of a work, entitled, Jeremie, *traduit sur le Texte original, accompagnê de Notes Explicatives, Historiques, et Critiques, 8vo.,* (antedated) *Strasbourg,* 1824. After a *preface,* and very judicious *historical introduction,* consisting, the first of *twenty-two,* the second of *thirty-six* pages, the *text* and *notes* follow. The poetical parts of the text are translated in the *hemistich* manner, as the original appears in the best copies; and the whole is divided into *sections;* each of which is introduced with judicious observations relative to time, place, circumstances, and the matter contained in that section. The discourses or prophecies delivered under a particular reign, are all produced under that reign in their chronological order. A table of this arrangement I shall here introduce, and refer to the use of it afterwards:—

TABLE I

Prophecies under Josiah

Chap. i. 1–19.
iv. v.–vi. 30.
ii. 1.–iii. 5.
iii. 6.–iv. 4.
xvii. 19–27.
xlvii. 1–7.

Under Jehoiakim

vii. 1.–ix. 25.
xxvi. 1–24.
xlvi. 2–12.
x. 1–16.
Chap. xiv. 1.–xv. 21.
xvi. 1.–xvii. 18.
xviii. 1–23.
xix. 1.–xx. 13.
xx. 14–18.
xxiii. 9–40.
xxxv. 1–19.
xxv. 1–38.
xxxvi. 1–32.
xlv. 1–5.
xii. 14–17.
x. 17–25.

Under Jeconiah

xiii. 1–27.

Under Zedekiah

Chap. xxiii. 1.–xxii. 8.
xi. 1–17.
xi. 18.–xii. 13.
xxiv. 1–10.
xxix. 1–32.
xxvii. 1.–xxviii. 17.
xlix. 34–39.
li. 59–64.
xxi. 1–14.
xxxiv. 1–7.
xxxvii. 1–10.
xxxiv. 8–22.
xxxvii. 11–21.
xxxviii. 1–28.

Chap. xxxix. 15–18.
xxxii. 1–44.
xxxiii. 1–26.
xxxix. 1–10.

After the destruction of Jerusalem

xxxix. 11–14.
xl. 1.–xli. 18.
xlii. 1.–xliii. 7.
xxx. 1.–xxxi. 40.

Prophecies delivered in Egypt

Chap. xliii. 8–13.
xliv. 1–30.
xlvi. 13–28.

Prophecies relative to strange nations

xlvi. 1, and xlix. 1–6.

Chap. xlviii. 1–47.
xlix. 7-22.
xlix. 23–27.
xlix. 28–33.
l. 1.–li. 58–64.

Historical Appendix

lii. 1–34.

The kings under whom Jeremiah prophesied succeeded each other in the following order: 1. Josiah; 2. Jehoahaz; 3. Jehoiachin, or Jeconiah; 4. Jehoiakim; 5. Zedekiah.

To render the *transpositions* evident which have taken place in these prophetical discourses, we have only to look at those which bear the date of their delivery.

TABLE II

Chap.		
i.	1.	Delivered the thirteenth year of Josiah.
iii.	6.	Under Josiah.
xxi.	1.	Under Zedekiah.
xxiv.	1.	After the carrying away of Jeconiah, son of Jehoiakim.
xxv.	1.	The fourth year of Jehoiakim.
xxvi.	1.	The beginning of the reign of Jehoiakim.
xxviii.	1.	The beginning of the reign of Zedekiah.
xxix.	1.	After the carrying away of Jeconiah.
xxxii.	1.	The tenth year of Zedekiah.
xxxiv.	1.	(Under Zedekiah) during the siege of Jerusalem.
xxxiv.	8.	(Under Zedekiah) when he had obliged his subjects to give liberty to the Israelites whom they had reduced to slavery.
xxxv.	1.	Under Jehoiakim.
xxxvi.	1.	Under Jehoiakim.
xxxvii.	1.	Under Zedekiah during the siege of Jerusalem.
xxxvii.	11.	Under Zedekiah.
xxxviii.	1.	Under Zedekiah.
xxxix.	15.	Under Zedekiah while Jeremiah was in prison.
xlv.	1.	The fourth year of Jehoiakim.
xlvi.	2.	The fourth year of Jehoiakim.
xlix.	34.	In the beginning of the reign of Zedekiah.
li.	59.	The fourth year of Zedekiah.

Taking into consideration the order of the reigns, a child may perceive that the above prophecies are not in the order of the times of their delivery; and that the *sheets* or *skins* on which the text of that MS. was written, from which the present copies have derived their origin, have been pitifully interchanged, huddled and tacked together, without connexion or arrangement.

To remedy this defect, Dr. *Blayney* has arranged the chapters in the following order which he terms a new arrangement of the chapters in Jeremiah, from chap. xx. to chap. xlvi., inclusive: xx., xxii., xxiii., xxv., xxvi., xxxv., xxxvi., xlv., xxiv., xxix., xxx., xxxi., xxvii., xxviii., xxi., xxxiv., xxxvii., xxxii., xxxiii., xxxviii., xxxix. 15–18, xxxix. 1–14, xl., xli., xlii., xliii., xliv., xlvi., &c.

The preceding and subsequent chapters Dr. *Blayney* thought sufficiently correct for all the general purposes of chronology; and it is according to this order that he prints the text in his edition and translation of this prophet.

Dr. *Dahler*, as we have seen, is more circumstantial. Where he has *dates*, as are shown in the preceding table, he produces the text in that order; where there are not *positive* dates, he ascertains several by circumstantial intimations, which bear great evidence of accuracy; but there is a numerous class of discourses which he is obliged to insert in this work by *critical conjecture*. In such a case as this, when the *arrangement* of the common text is so evidently *defective*, and in many respects *absurd*, this procedure is quite allowable; for although the present text as to its arrangement has the sanction of *antiquity*, yet when a remedy is found, it would be absurd, if not sinful, to follow an order which we may rest satisfied never did proceed from the inspired writer.

I hope none will suppose that these observations detract any thing from the Divine inspiration of the book. The prophet delivered his discourses at particular times in *select portions*, during *forty* or *forty-three* years; these were afterwards gathered together and stitched up without any attention to chronological arrangement. Though the Spirit of the Lord directed the prophet, yet it would be absurd to suppose that it guided the hand of every *collector* or *scribe* into whose custody these several parcels might come. Suppose a man buy a copy of the Bible *in sheets*, and not knowing how to collate them, stitches the whole confusedly together, so that in many places the sense cannot be made out from a preceding to a following sheet, would it not be singularly foolish for any person to say, "As God is the Fountain of wisdom and Author of reason, such incongruities cannot proceed from him, therefore this book was not given by Divine revelation." A child in a printer's office might reply, "Cut the stitching asunder, that is man's work; collate the sheets and put them in their proper order, and you will soon see that every paragraph is in harmony with the rest, and contains the words of Divine wisdom."

Many an ancient MS., which appeared mutilated and imperfect, I have restored to order and perfection by cutting the binding asunder, and restoring the sheets and leaves to those places from which the ignorance and unskilfulness of the binder had detached them. May we not be allowed to treat the dislocations in the writings of a prophet in the same way, when it is evident that in the lapse of time his work has suffered by the hand of the careless and ignorant.

But it may be asked, "After all the evidence I have, and the concessions I have made, why I have not transposed those disjointed chapters, and produced them in the order in which I think they should be read?" I answer, Were I to give a new translation with notes of this prophet separately, as Drs. *Blayney* and *Dahler* have done, I should feel it my duty to do what the objection states; but as my province as a general commentator requires me to take up all the *books* of the sacred volume in the *order* in which I find them in the present authorized version, though convinced that this arrangement is neither correct nor convenient; so I take up the *parts* of each, however transposed, in the same manner, directing the reader by *tables* and *notes* to regulate his use of the work so as to produce general edification with as little embarrassment as possible.

For general purposes, Dr. *Blayney's* chronological arrangement may be sufficient; but for greater accuracy Table I. may be preferred. These may at least be considered in the light of *helps* to a better understanding of these several prophecies; but no man is bound to follow either, farther than he is convinced that it follows what is specifically set down by the prophet himself, or fairly deducible from strong circumstantial evidence.

In my notes on this prophet I have availed myself, as far as my plan would permit, of the best helps within my reach. The *various readings* of *Kennicott* and *De Rossi* I have carefully consulted, and occasionally strengthened the evidence in behalf of those readings, more particularly recommended by collations from my own MSS. I regret that I have not been able, for the reasons mentioned at the conclusion of the notes on Isaiah, to produce all the various readings of importance found in these ancient MSS., and especially in the Book of *Lamentations*, which is contained in *five* of them; but like the woman in the Gospels, *I have done what I could*, and must leave the rest to those who, with better abilities, may possess the greater advantages of youth and strength, with unimpaired sight.

Reader! God designs thee a blessing by every portion of his word: in thy reading seek for *this;* and if these notes be helpful to thee, give Him the glory.

A. C.

Eastcott, Nov. 1, 1824.

THE BOOK

OF THE

PROPHET JEREMIAH

Chronological notes relative to the commencement of Jeremiah's prophesying

Year from the Creation, according to Archbishop Usher, 3375.—Year from the Deluge, according to the generally received Hebrew text, conferred with Acts vii. 4, 1719.—Fourth year of the *thirty-seventh* Olympiad.—Year from the building of Rome according to the Varronian account, 125.—Year before the vulgar era of Christ's nativity, 629.—Twelfth year of Ancus Martius, the fourth king of the Romans: this was the *one hundred and twentieth* year before the expulsion of the Tarquins.—Nineteenth year of Phraortes, the second king of Media.—Twenty-third year of Archidamus, king of Lacedæmon, of the family of the Proclidæ.—Sixteenth year of Eurycrates II., king of Lacedæmon, of the family of the Eurysthenidæ.—Third year of Sadyattes, king of Lydia, which was the *eighty-second* year before the conquest of this kingdom by Cyrus.—Twelfth year of Philip, the sixth king of Macedon, or the *two hundred and ninety-third* before the commencement of the reign of Alexander the Great.—Thirteenth year of Josiah, king of Judah.—Epoch of the building of Cyrene by Battus, according to some chronologers.

CHAPTER I

General title to the whole Book, 1–3. *Jeremiah receives a commission to prophesy concerning nations and kingdoms, a work to which in the Divine purpose he had been appointed before his birth,* 4–10. *The vision of* the rod of an almond tree *and of the* seething pot, *with their signification,* 11–16. *Promises of Divine protection to Jeremiah in the discharge of the arduous duties of his prophetical office,* 17–19.

A. M. 3375 B. C. 629 Ol. XXXVII. 4 Anci Martii, R. Roman., 12

THE words of Jeremiah the
son of Hilkiah, of the priests
that *were* [a]in Anathoth in the
land of Benjamin:
2 To whom the word of the LORD came in
the days of Josiah the son of Amon king of
Judah, [b]in the thirteenth year of his reign.

A. M. cir. 3394—3416 B. C. cir. 610—588 Ol. XLII. 3—XLVIII. 1

3 It came also in the days of
Jehoiakim the son of Josiah king
of Judah, [c]unto the end of the
eleventh year of Zedekiah the
son of Josiah king of Judah,
[d]unto the carrying away of Jerusalem
captive [e]in the fifth
month.

A. M. 3375 B. C. 629 Ol. XXXVII. 4 Anci Martii, R. Roman., 12

4 Then the word of the LORD
came unto me, saying,
5 Before I [f]formed thee in the
belly [g]I knew thee; and before
thou camest forth out of the womb I [h]sanctified
thee, *and* I [i]ordained thee a prophet unto
the nations.

[a]Joshua xxi. 18; 1 Chronicles vi. 60; chapter xxxii. 7, 8, 9——[b]Chap. xxv. 3——[c]Chap. xxxix. 2——[d]Chap. lii. 12, 15——[e]2 Kings xxv. 8——[f]Isaiah xlix. 1, 5; Ecclesiasticus xlix. 7——[g]Exodus xxxiii. 12, 17——[h]Luke i. 15, 41; Galatians i. 15, 16——[i]Hebrew, *gave*

NOTES ON CHAP. I

Verse 1-3. *The words of Jeremiah*] These three verses are the *title* of the Book; and were probably added by Ezra when he collected and arranged the sacred books, and put them in that order in which they are found in Hebrew Bibles in general. For particulars relative to this prophet, the times of his prophesying, and the arrangement of his discourses, see the *introduction.*

Eleventh year of Zedekiah] That is, the last year of his reign; for he was made prisoner by the Chaldeans in the fourth month of that year, and the *carrying away of the inhabitants of Jerusalem* was in the fifth month of the same year.

Verse 4. *The word of the Lord came unto me*] Then I first felt the inspiring influence of the Divine Spirit, not only revealing to me the subjects which he would have me to declare to the people, but also the *words* which I should use in these declarations.

Verse 5. *Before I formed thee*] I had destined thee to the prophetic office before thou wert born: I had formed my plan, and appointed thee to be my envoy to his people. St. Paul speaks of his own call to preach the Gospel to the Gentiles in similar terms, Gal. i. 15, 16.

A. M. 3375
B. C. 629
Ol. XXXVII. 4
Anci Martii,
R. Roman.,
12

6 Then said I, [k]Ah, Lord GOD! behold, I cannot speak: for I *am* a child.

7 But the LORD said unto me, Say not, I *am* a child; for thou shalt go to all that I shall send thee, and [l]whatsoever I command thee thou shalt speak.

8 [m]Be not afraid of their faces; for [n]I *am* with thee to deliver thee, saith the LORD.

9 Then the LORD put forth his hand, and [o]touched my mouth. And the LORD said unto me, Behold, I have [p]put my words in thy mouth.

10 [q]See, I have this day set thee over the nations and over the kingdoms, to [r]root out, and to pull down, and to destroy, and to throw down, to build, and to plant.

A. M. 3375
B. C. 629
Ol. XXXVII. 4
Anci Martii,
R. Roman.,
12

11 Moreover the word of the LORD came unto me, saying, Jeremiah, what seest thou? And I said, I see a rod of an almond tree.

12 Then said the LORD unto me, Thou hast well seen: for I will hasten my word to perform it.

13 And the word of the LORD came unto me the second time, saying, What seest thou? And I said, I see [s]a seething pot; and the face thereof *is* [t]toward the north.

14 Then the LORD said unto me, Out of the [u]north an evil [v]shall break forth upon all the inhabitants of the land.

---

[k]Exod. iv. 10; vi. 12, 30; Isa. vi. 5——[l]Num. xxii. 20, 38; Matt. xxviii. 20——[m]Ezek. ii. 6; iii. 9; ver. 17 [n]Exod. iii. 12; Deut. xxxi. 6, 8; Josh. i. 5; chap. xv. 20; Acts xxvi. 17; Heb. xiii. 6

[o]Isa. vi. 7——[p]Isa. li. 16; chap. v. 14——[q]1 Kings xix. 17——[r]Ch. xviii. 7, 8, 9, 10; 2 Cor. x. 4, 5——[s]Ezek. xi. 3, 7; xxiv. 3——[t]Heb. *from the face of the north* [u]Chap. iv. 6; vi. 1——[v]Heb. *shall be opened*

Verse 6. *I cannot speak*] Being very young, and wholly inexperienced, I am utterly incapable of conceiving aright, or of clothing these Divine subjects in suitable language. Those who are really *called of God* to the sacred ministry are such as have been brought to a deep acquaintance with themselves, feel their own ignorance, and know their own weakness. They know also the awful responsibility that attaches to the work; and nothing but the authority of God can induce such to undertake it. They whom God never called *run*, because of worldly honour and emolument: the others hear the call with *fear* and *trembling*, and can go only in the strength of Jehovah.

"How *ready* is the man to *go*,
Whom God hath never sent!
How *timorous, diffident*, and *slow*,
God's chosen instrument!"

Verse 7. *Whatsoever I command thee*] It is my words and message, not thine own, that thou shalt deliver. I shall teach thee; therefore thy youth and inexperience can be no hinderance.

Verse 8. *Be not afraid of their faces*] That is, the *Jews*, whom he knew would persecute him because of the message which he brought. To be *fore*-warned is to be half armed. He knew what he was to expect from the disobedient and the rebellious, and must now be prepared to meet it.

Verse 10. *I have—set thee over the nations*] God represents his messengers the prophets as *doing* what he commanded them to declare *should be done*. In this sense they *rooted up, pulled down*, and *destroyed*—declared God's judgments; they *builded up* and *planted*—declared the promises of his *mercy*. Thus God says to Isaiah, chap. vi. 10: "Make the heart of this people fat—and shut their eyes." Show them that they are *stupid* and *blind;* and that, because they have shut their eyes and hardened their hearts, God will in his judgments leave them to their hardness and darkness.

Verse 11. *A rod of an almond tree.*] שקד *shaked*, from שקד *shakad*, "to be ready," "to hasten," "to *watch* for an opportunity to do a thing," to *awake;* because the almond tree is the *first* to flower and bring forth fruit. *Pliny* says, Floret prima omnium amygdala mense Januario; Martio vero pomum maturat. It blossoms in *January*, when other trees are locked up in their winter's repose; and it bears fruit in *March*, just at the commencement of spring, when other trees only begin to *bud*. It was here the symbol of that *promptitude* with which God was about to fulfil his promises and threatenings. As a *rod*, says *Dahler*, is an instrument of punishment, the rod of the almond may be intended here as the symbol of that punishment which the prophet was about to announce.

Verse 12. *I will hasten my word*] Here is a paronomasia. *What dost thou see?* I see שקד *shaked*, "an almond," the *hastening* tree: that which first *awakes*. *Thou hast well seen, for* (שקד *shoked*) *I will hasten my word*. I will awake, or watch over my word for the first opportunity to inflict the judgments which I threaten. The judgment shall come speedily; it shall soon *flourish*, and come to *maturity*.

Verse 13. *A seething pot—toward the north.*] We find, from Ezekiel xxiv. 3, &c., that a *boiling pot* was an emblem of *war*, and the desolations it produces. Some have thought that by the seething pot *Judea* is intended, *agitated* by the invasion of the Chaldeans, whose land lay *north* of Judea. But Dr. *Blayney* contends that מפני צפונה *mippeney tsaphonah* should be translated, *From the face of the north*, as it is in the margin; for, from the next verse, it appears that the evil was to come *from the north;* and therefore the *steam*, which was designed as an emblem of that evil, must have arisen from that quarter also. The pot denotes the empire of the Babylonians and Chaldeans lying to the north of Judea, and pouring forth its multitudes like a *thick vapour*, to overspread the land. Either of these interpretations will suit the text.

Verse 14. *Shall break forth*] תפתח *tippath-*

A. M. 3375
B. C. 629
Ol. XXXVII. 4
Anci Martii,
R. Roman.,
12

15 For, lo, I will [w]call all the families of the kingdoms of the north, saith the LORD; and they shall come, and they shall [x]set every one his throne at the entering of the gates of Jerusalem, and against all the walls thereof round about, and against all the cities of Judah.

16 And I will utter my judgments against them touching all their wickedness, [y]who have forsaken me, and have burned incense unto other gods, and worshipped the works of their own hands.

17 Thou therefore [z]gird up thy loins, and arise, and speak unto them all that I command thee: [a]be not dismayed at their faces, lest I [b]confound thee before them.

18 For, behold, I have made thee this day [c]a defenced city, and an iron pillar, and brazen walls against the whole land, against the kings of Judah, against the princes thereof, against the priests thereof, and against the people of the land.

19 And they shall fight against thee; but they shall not prevail against thee; [d]for I *am* with thee, saith the LORD, to deliver thee.

---

[w]Chap. v. 15; vi. 22; x. 22; xxv. 9——[x]Chap. xxxix. 3; xliii. 10——[y]Deut. xxviii. 20; chap. xvii. 13——[z]1 Kings xviii. 46; 2 Kings iv. 29; ix. 1; Job xxxviii. 3; Luke xii. 35; 1 Pet. i. 18——[a]Exod. iii. 12; ver. 8; Ezek. ii. 6——[b]Or, *break to pieces*——[c]Isa. l. 7; chap. vi. 27; xv. 20——[d]Ver. 8

---

ach, shall be opened. The door shall be thrown abroad, that these calamities may pass out freely.

Verse 15. *Shall set every one his throne at the entering of the gates*] As the gates of the cities were the ordinary places where justice was administered, so the enemies of Jerusalem are here represented as conquering the whole land, assuming the reins of government, and laying the whole country under their own laws; so that the Jews should no longer possess any *political power:* they should be wholly subjugated by their enemies.

Verse 16. *I will utter my judgments*] God denounced his judgments: the conquest of their cities, and the destruction of the realm, were the facts to which these judgments referred; and these facts prove that the threatening was fulfilled.

Worshipped the works of their own hands.] *Idolatry* was the source of all their wickedness, and was the cause of their desolations. For למעשי *lemaasey, the works*, more than a hundred MSS. of *Kennicott's* and *De Rossi's*, with many editions, have למעשה *lemaaseh, the work.* Idolatry was their ONE great WORK, the *business* of their *life*, their *trade.*

Verse 17. *Gird up thy loins*] Take courage and be ready, lest I confound thee; take courage and be resolute, פן *pen*, lest by their opposition thou be terrified and confounded. God is often represented as *doing* or *causing to be done*, what he only *permits* or *suffers* to be done. Or, do not fear them, I will not suffer thee to be confounded. So *Dahler*, Ne crains pas que je te confonde a leurs yeux, "Do not fear that I shall confound thee before them." It is well known that the phrase, *gird up thy reins*, is a metaphor taken from the *long robes* of the Asiatics; which, on going a journey, or performing their ordinary work, they were obliged to truss up under their girdles, that the motions of the body might not be impeded.

Verse 18. *I have made thee this day a defenced city, and an iron pillar, and brazen walls*] Though thou shalt be exposed to persecutions and various indignities, they shall not prevail against thee. To their attacks thou shalt be as an *impregnable city;* as *unshaken* as an *iron pillar;* and as *imperishable* as a *wall of brass.* None, therefore, can have less cause to apprehend danger than thou hast. The issue proved the truth of this promise: he outlived all their insults; and saw Jerusalem destroyed, and his enemies, and the enemies of his Lord, carried into captivity. Instead of חומות *chomoth, walls*, many MSS. and editions read חמת *chomath, a wall*, which corresponds with the singular nouns preceding.

Verse 19. *They shall not prevail against thee*] Because I am determined to defend and support thee against all thy enemies. One of the ancients has said, *Θεου θελοντος, και επι ῥιπος πλεῃ Σωζῃ·* Thestius, apud Theophil. ad Autolyc. lib. ii. "God protecting thee, though thou wert at sea upon a twig, thou shouldst be safe."

CHAPTER II

God expresses his continued regard for his people, long since chosen, 1–3. *He then expostulates with them on their ungrateful and worse than heathen return to his regard,* 4–11; *at which even the inanimate creation must be astonished,* 12, 13. *After this their guilt is declared to be the sole cause of the calamities which their enemies had power to inflict on them,* 14–17. *They are upbraided for their alliances with idolatrous countries,* 18, 19; *and for their strong propensity to idolatry, notwithstanding all the care and tender mercy of God,* 20–29. *Even the chastenings of the Almighty have produced in this people no repentance,* 30. *The chapter concludes with compassionately remonstrating against their folly and ingratitude in revolting so deeply from God, and with warning them of the fearful consequences,* 31, 37.

A. M. 3375
B. C. 629
Ol. XXXVII. 4
Anci Martii,
R. Roman.,
12

MOREOVER the word of the
LORD came to me, saying,
2 Go and cry in the ears of
Jerusalem, saying, Thus saith
the LORD; I remember [a]thee, the kindness of
thy [b]youth, the love of thine espousals, [c]when
thou wentest after me in the wilderness, in a
land *that was* not sown.
3 [d]Israel *was* holiness unto the LORD, *and*
[e]the first-fruits of his increase: [f]all that devour him shall offend; evil shall come upon
them, saith the LORD.
4 Hear ye the word of the LORD, O house
of Jacob, and all the families of the house of
Israel:
5 Thus saith the LORD, [g]What iniquity
have your fathers found in me, that they are
gone far from me, [h]and have walked after
vanity, and are become vain?
6 Neither said they, Where *is* the LORD
that [i]brought us up out of the
land of Egypt, that led us through
the [k]wilderness, through a land
of deserts and of pits, through a
land of drought, and of the shadow of death,
through a land that no man passed through,
and where no man dwelt?
7 And I brought you into [l]a [m]plentiful country, to eat the fruit thereof and the goodness
thereof; but when ye entered, ye [n]defiled my
land, and made mine heritage an abomination.
8 The priests said not, Where *is* the LORD?
and they that handle the [o]law knew me not:
the pastors also transgressed against me, [p]and
the prophets prophesied by Baal, and walked
after *things that* [q]do not profit.
9 Wherefore [r]I will yet plead with you, saith
the LORD, and [s]with your children's children
will I plead.
10 For pass [t]over the isles of Chittim, and

A. M. 3375
B. C. 629
Ol. XXXVII. 4
Anci Martii,
R. Roman.,
12

[a]Or, *for thy sake*——[b]Ezek. xvi. 8, 22, 60; xxiii. 3, 8, 19; Hos. ii. 15——[c]Deut. ii. 7——[d]Exod. xix. 5, 6 [e]James i. 18; Rev. xiv. 4——[f]Chap. xii. 14; see chap. l. 7 [g]Isa. v. 4; Mic. vi. 3——[h]2 Kings xvii. 15; Jonah ii. 8 [i]Isa. lxiii. 9, 11, 13; Hos. xiii. 4——[k]Deut. viii. 15; xxxii. 10——[l]Or, *the land of Carmel*

[m]Num. xiii. 27; xiv. 7, 8; Deut. viii. 7, 8, 9——[n]Lev. xviii. 25, 27, 28; Num. xxxv. 33, 34; Psa. lxxviii. 58, 59; cvi. 38; chap. iii. 1; xvi. 18——[o]Mal. ii. 6, 7; Rom. ii. 20——[p]Chap. xxiii. 13——[q]Ver. 11; Hab. ii. 18 [r]Ezek. xx. 35, 36; Mic. vi. 2——[s]Exod. xx. 5; Lev. xx. 5——[t]Or, *over to*

NOTES ON CHAP. II

Verse 2. *I remember thee*] The *youth* here refers to their *infant political state* when they came out of Egypt; they just then began to be a *people.* Their *espousals* refer to their receiving the law at Mount Sinai, which they solemnly accepted, Exod. xxiv. 6-8, and which acceptance was compared to a *betrothing* or *espousal.* Previously to this they were no *people,* for they had no *constitution* nor *form of government.* When they received the *law,* and an *establishment in the Promised Land,* then they became a *people* and a *nation.*

Wentest after me] Receivedst my law, and wert obedient to it; confiding thyself wholly to my guidance, and being conscientiously attached to my worship. The *kindness* was that which God showed them by taking *them* to be his people, not *their kindness* to *him.*

Verse 3. *Israel* was *holiness unto the Lord*] Fully *consecrated* to his service.

The first fruits of his increase] They were as wholly the Lord's, as the first fruits were the property of the priests according to the law, Num. xviii. 13. These the priests alone had a right to devote to their own use.

All that devour him shall offend] As they were *betrothed* to the Lord, they were considered his *especial property;* they therefore who injured them were considered as laying violent hands on the property of God. They who persecute God's children have a grevious burden to bear, an awful account to give.

Verse 5. *What iniquity have your fathers found in me*] Have they ever discovered any thing *cruel, unjust, oppressive* in my *laws?* Any thing *unkind* or *tyrannical* in my *government?* Why then have they become *idolaters?*

Verse 6. *Through the wilderness*] Egypt was the *house of their bondage:* the *desert* through which they passed after they came out of Egypt, was a place where the *means of life* were not to be found; where no one family could subsist, much less a company of 600,000 men. God mentions these things to show that it was by the bounty of an *especial providence* that they were fed and preserved alive. Previously to this, it was a *land through which no man passed, and in which no man dwelt.* And why? because it did not produce the means of life; it was the *shadow of death* in its appearance, and the *grave* to those who committed themselves to it.

Verse 7. *And I brought you into a plentiful country*] The land of *Canaan.*

My land] The *particular property of God,* which he gave to them as an inheritance, they being his peculiar people.

Verse 8. *They that handle the law*] ותפשי *vethophe shey, they that draw out the law;* they whose office it is to *explain* it, *draw out* its spiritual meanings, and show to what its testimonies refer.

The pastors also] Kings, political and civil rulers.

Prophesied by Baal] Became his prophets, and were inspired with the words of *lying spirits.*

Verse 9. *I will yet plead with you*] אריב *arib,* I will maintain my *process,* vindicate my own conduct, and prove the wickedness of yours.

Verse 10. *The isles of Chittim*] This is the island of *Cyprus,* according to Josephus. In 1 Maccabees, chap. viii. 5, it is taken for *Macedonia. Besides this, how they* (the Romans) *had discomfited in battle Philip* and *Perseus,*

A. M. 3375 B. C. 629 Ol. XXXVII. 4 Anci Martii, R. Roman., 12

see; and send unto Kedar, and
consider diligently, and see if
there be such a thing:
11 [u]Hath a nation changed
their gods, which *are* [v]yet no gods? [w]but my
people have changed their glory for [x]*that
which* doth not profit.
12 [y]Be astonished, O ye heavens, at this, and
be horribly afraid, be ye very desolate, saith
the LORD.
13 For my people have committed two evils;
they have forsaken me the [z]Fountain of living
waters, *and* hewed them out cisterns, broken
cisterns that can hold no water.
14 *Is* Israel [a]a servant? *is* he a home-born
slave? why is he [b]spoiled?
15 [c]The young lions roared upon him, *and*
[d]yelled, and they made his land waste: his
cities are burned without inhabitant.
16 Also the children of Noph
and [e]Tahapanes, [f]have broken
the crown of thy head.
17 [g]Hast thou not procured this
unto thyself, in that thou hast forsaken the
LORD thy God, when [h]he led thee by the
way?
18 And now what hast thou to do [i]in the
way of Egypt, to drink the waters of [k]Sihor?
or what hast thou to do in the way of Assyria,
to drink the waters of the river?
19 Thine own [l]wickedness shall correct
thee, and thy backslidings shall reprove thee:
know therefore and see that *it is* an evil *thing*
and bitter, that thou hast forsaken the LORD
thy God, and that my fear *is* not in thee,
saith the Lord GOD of hosts.
20 For of old time I have broken thy yoke,
and burst thy bands; and [m]thou saidst, I will

[u]Mic. iv. 5——[v]Psa. cxv. 4; Isa. xxxvii. 19; chap. xvi. 20——[w]Psa. cvi. 20; Rom. i. 23——[x]Ver. 8——[y]Isa. i. 2; chap. vi. 19——[z]Psa. xxxvi. 9; chap. xvii. 13; xviii. 14; John iv. 14——[a]See Exod. iv. 22——[b]Heb. *become a spoil?*——[c]Isa. i. 7; chap. iv. 7

[d]Heb. *gave out their voice*——[e]Chap. xliii. 7, 8, 9
[f]Or, *feed on thy crown;* Deut. xxxiii. 20; Isa. viii. 8
[g]Chap. iv. 18——[h]Deut. xxxii. 10——[i]Isa. xxx. 1, 2
[k]Josh. xiii. 3——[l]Isa. iii. 9; Hos. v. 5——[m]Exod. xix. 8; Josh. xxiv. 18; Judg. x. 16; 1 Sam. xii. 10

king of the Chittims. Chittim was the grandson of Japhet; and *Bochart* has made it appear that the countries inhabited by the *Chittim* were *Italy* and the adjacent provinces of *Europe*, lying along the coast of the Mediterranean Sea; and probably this is the prophet's meaning.

Send unto Kedar] The name of an *Arabian tribe.* See if nations either near or remote, cultivated or stupid, have acted with such fickleness and ingratitude as you have done! *They* have *retained* their gods to whom they had no obligation; ye have *abandoned* your God, to whom ye owe your life, breath, and all things!

Verse 12. *Be astonished, O ye heavens*] Or, *the heavens are astonished.* The original will admit either sense. The conduct of this people was so altogether bad, that among all the iniquities of mankind, neither heaven nor earth had witnessed any thing so excessively sinful and profligate.

Verse 13. *Two evils*] *First,* they *forsook God,* the Fountain of life, light, prosperity, and happiness. *Secondly,* they hewed out broken cisterns; they *joined themselves to idols,* from whom they could receive neither temporal nor spiritual good! Their conduct was the excess of folly and blindness. What we call here *broken cisterns,* means more properly such vessels as were *ill made, not staunch, ill put together,* so that the water *leaked through them.*

Verse 14. Is *Israel a servant?*] Is he a *slave* purchased with money, or a *servant born in the family?* He is a *son* himself. If so, then, *why is he spoiled?* Not because God has not shown him love and kindness; but because he forsook God, turned to and is joined with idols.

Verse 15. *The young lions roared upon him*] The Assyrians, who have sacked and destroyed the kingdom of Israel, with a fierceness like that of pouncing upon their prey.

Verse 16. *The children of Noph and Tahapanes*] Noph and Tahapanes were two cities of Egypt, otherwise called *Memphis* and *Daphni.* It is well known that the good king was defeated by the Egyptians, and slain in battle. Thus was the *crown of Judah's head broken.*

Verse 18. *What hast thou to do in the way of Egypt*] Why dost thou *make alliances* with Egypt?

To drink the waters of Sihor?] This means the *Nile.* See on Isa. xxiii. 3.

The way of Assyria] Why *make alliances* with the Assyrians? All such connexions will only expedite thy ruin.

To drink the waters of the river?] The *Euphrates,* as נהר *nahar* or הנהר *hannahar* always means *Euphrates,* the country between the *Tigris* and *Euphrates,* is termed to this day *Maher alnahar,* "the country beyond the river," i. e., *Mesopotamia.*

Instead of cleaving to the Lord, they joined affinity and made alliances with those two nations, who were ever jealous of them, and sought their ruin. *Egypt* was to them a *broken reed* instead of a *staff; Assyria* was a *leaky cistern,* from which they could derive no *help.*

Verse 20. *Of old time I have broken thy yoke*] It is thought by able critics that the verbs should be read in the *second person singular,* THOU *hast broken thy yoke,* THOU *hast burst thy bonds;* and thus the *Septuagint,* *συνετριψας τον ζυγον σου,* "thou hast broken thy yoke." And the *Vulgate,* Confregisti jugum meum, rupisti, vincula mea; "Thou hast broken my yoke; thou hast burst my bonds;" and so the *Arabic.* But the *Chaldee* gives it a meaning which removes the difficulty: "I have broken the yoke of the people from thy neck; I have cut your bonds asunder." And when this was done, they did promise fair; for "thou saidst, I will not trans-

A. M. 3375 B. C. 629 Ol. XXXVII. 4 Anci Martii, R. Roman., 12

not [n]transgress; when [o]upon
every high hill and under every
green tree thou wanderest,
[p]playing the harlot.
21 Yet I had [q]planted thee a noble vine,
wholly a right seed: how then art thou turned
into [r]the degenerate plant of a strange vine
unto me?
22 For though thou [s]wash thee with nitre,
and take thee much soap, *yet* [t]thine iniquity
is marked before me, saith the Lord GOD.
23 [u]How canst thou say, I am not polluted,
I have not gone after Baalim? see thy way
[v]in the valley, know what thou hast done:
[w]*thou art* a swift dromedary traversing her
ways;
24 [x]A[y] wild ass [z]used to the
wilderness, *that* snuffeth up the
wind at [a]her pleasure; in her
occasion who can [b]turn her
away? all they that seek her will not weary
themselves; in her mouth they shall
find her.
25 Withhold thy foot from being unshod, and thy throat from thirst: but
[c]thou saidst, [d]There is no hope; no; for
I have loved [e]strangers, and after them
will I go.
26 As the thief is ashamed when he is found,
so is the house of Israel ashamed; they, their
kings, their princes, and their priests, and
their prophets,

A. M. 3375 B. C. 629 Ol. XXXVII. 4 Anci Martii, R. Roman., 12

---

[n]Or, *serve*——[o]Deut. xii. 2; Isa. lvii. 5, 7; chap. iii. 6——[p]Exod. xxxiv. 15, 16——[q]Exod. xv. 17; Psa. xliv. 2; lxxx. 8; Isa. v. 1, &c.; lx. 21; Matt. xxi. 33; Mark xii. 1; Luke xx. 9——[r]Deut. xxxii. 32; Isa. i. 21; v. 4——[s]Job ix. 30——[t]Deut. xxxii. 34; Job xiv. 17; Hos. xiii. 12

[u]Prov. xxx. 12——[v]Chap. vii. 31——[w]Or, *O swift dromedary*——[x]Job xxxix. 5, &c.; chap. xiv. 6——[y]Or, *O wild ass, &c.*——[z]Heb. *taught*——[a]Heb. *the desire of her heart*——[b]Or, *reverse it*——[c]Chap. xviii. 12——[d]Or, *is the case desperate?*——[e]Deut. xxxii. 16; chap. iii. 13

---

gress;" but still *they played the harlot*—committed idolatrous acts in the high places, where the heathen had built their altars, pretending that *elevation* of this kind assisted their devotion.

Verse 21. *I had planted thee a noble vine*] I gave thee the fullest instruction, the purest ordinances, the highest privileges; and reason would that I should expect thee to *live suitably to such advantages;* but instead of this thou *art become degenerate;* the *tree* is deteriorated, and the *fruit* is *bad.* Instead of being true worshippers, and of a holy life and conversation, ye are become idolaters of the most corrupt and profligate kind. See Isa. v. 1, &c., where the same image is used.

Verse 22. *For though thou wash thee with nitre*] It should be rendered *natar* or *natron,* a substance totally different from our *nitre.* It comes from the root נתר *nathar,* to dissolve, loosen, because a solution of it in water is abstersive, taking *out spots,* &c., from clothes. It is still used in the *east* for the purpose of *washing.* If *vinegar* be poured on it, Dr. *Shaw* says, a strong effervescence is the immediate consequence, which illustrates Prov. xxv. 20: "The singing of songs to a heavy heart is like vinegar upon natron;" that is, there is no affinity between them; opposition and strife are occasioned by any attempt to unite them.

Thine iniquity is marked before me] No washing will take out *thy spots;* the *marks* of thy idolatry and corruption are too deeply rooted to be extracted by any human means.

Verse 23. *See thy way in the valley*] The *valley of Hinnom,* where they offered their own children to Moloch, an idol of the Ammonites.

A swift dromedary traversing her ways] Dr. *Blayney* translates, "A fleet dromedary that hath taken to company with her."

Dr. *Dahler* rather paraphrases, thus:—

Semblable a une dromedaire en chaleur,
Qui court d'une cote a l'autre.

"Like to a dromedary in her desire for the male,
Which runs hither and thither."

This is an energetic comparison; and shows the unbridled attachment of those bad people to idolatry, and the abominable practices by which it was usually accompanied.

Verse 24. *A wild ass used to the wilderness*] Another comparison to express the same thing.

Snuffeth up the wind] In a high fever from the inward heat felt at such times, these animals open their mouths and nostrils as wide as possible, to take in large draughts of fresh air, in order to cool them.

In her mouth they shall find her.] The meaning is, that although such animals are exceedingly fierce and dangerous when they are in this state; yet, as soon as they have found the male, the desire is satisfied, and they become quiet and governable as before. But it was not so with this idolatrous people: their desires were ever fierce and furious; they were never satiated, one indulgence always leading to another. The brute beasts had only a short season in which this appetite prevailed; but *they* acted without restraint or limit.

Verse 25. *Withhold thy foot from being unshod*] When it was said to them, "Cease from discovering thy feet; prostitute thyself no more to thy idols."

And thy throat from thirst] Drink no more of their libations, nor use those potions which tend only to increase thy appetite for pollution. Thou didst say, There is no hope: it is useless to advise me thus; I am determined; I have loved *these strange gods,* and to them will I cleave.

Verse 26. *As the thief is ashamed*] As the pilferer is confounded when he is caught in the fact; so shalt thou, thy kings, princes, priests, and prophets, be confounded, when God shall arrest thee in thy idolatries, and deliver thee into the hands of thine enemies.

A. M. 3375
B. C. 629
Ol. XXXVII. 4
Anci Martii,
R. Roman.,
12

27 Saying to a stock, Thou *art* my father; and to a stone, Thou hast [f]brought me forth: for they have turned [g]*their* back unto me, and not *their* face: but in the time of their [h]trouble they will say, Arise, and save us.

28 But [i]where *are* thy gods that thou hast made thee? let them arise, if they [k]can save thee in the time of thy [l]trouble: for [m]*according to* the number of thy cities are thy gods, O Judah.

29 [n]Wherefore will ye plead with me? ye all have transgressed against me, saith the LORD.

30 In vain have I [o]smitten your children; they received no correction: your own sword hath [p]devoured your prophets, like a destroying lion.

31 O generation, see ye the word of the LORD. [q]Have I been a wilderness unto Israel? a land of darkness? wherefore say my people, [r]We [s]are lords; [t]we will come no more unto thee?

32 Can a maid forget her ornaments, *or* a bride her attire? yet my people [u]have forgotten me days without number.

33 Why trimmest thou thy way to seek love? therefore hast thou also taught the wicked ones thy ways.

34 Also in thy skirts is found [v]the blood of the souls of the poor innocents: I have not found it by [w]secret search, but upon all these.

35 [x]Yet thou sayest, Because I am innocent, surely his anger shall turn from me. Behold, [y]I will plead with thee, [z]because thou sayest, I have not sinned.

36 [a]Why gaddest thou about so much to change thy way? [b]thou also shalt be ashamed of Egypt, [c]as thou wast ashamed of Assyria.

37 Yea, thou shalt go forth from him, and [d]thine hands upon thine head: for the LORD hath rejected thy confidences, and thou shalt not prosper in them.

[f]Or, *begotten me*——[g]Heb. *the hinder part of the neck*——[h]Judg. x. 10; Psa. lxxviii. 34; Isa. xxvi. 16——[i]Deut. xxxii. 37; Judg. x. 14——[k]Isa. xlv. 20——[l]Heb. *evil*——[m]Chap. xi. 13——[n]Ver. 23, 35——[o]Isa. i. 5 ix. 13; chap. v. 3——[p]2 Chron. xxxvi. 16; Neh. ix. 26; Matt. xxiii. 29, &c.; Acts vii. 52; 1 Thess. ii. 15——[q]Ver. 5

[r]Heb. *We have dominion*——[s]Psa. xii. 4——[t]Deut. xxxii. 15——[u]Psa. cvi. 21; chap. xiii. 25; Hos. viii. 14——[v]Psa. cvi. 38; chap. xix. 4——[w]Heb. *digging*——[x]Ver. 23, 29——[y]Ver. 9——[z]Prov. xxviii. 13; 1 John i. 8, 10——[a]Ver. 18; chap. xxxi. 22; Hos. v. 13; xii. 1——[b]Isa. xxx. 3; chap. xxxvii. 7——[c]2 Chron. xxviii. 16, 20, 21——[d]2 Sam. xiii. 19

Verse 27. *Thou* art *my father*] By thee we have been produced, and by thee we are sustained. This was the property of the true God; for he is the *Author* and *Supporter* of *being*. How deeply fallen and brutishly ignorant must they be when they could attribute this to the stock of a tree!

Verse 28. According *to the number of thy cities are thy gods*] Among heathen nations every city had its *tutelary deity*. Judah, far sunk in idolatry, had adopted this custom. The Church of Rome has refined it a little: every city has its *tutelary saint*, and this saint has a procession and worship peculiar to himself. So here; not much of the old idolatry is lost.

Verse 31. *Have I been a wilderness unto Israel?*] Have I ever withheld from you any of the blessings necessary for your support?

A land of darkness] Have you, since you passed through the wilderness, and came out of the darkness of Egypt, ever been brought into similar circumstances? You have had food and all the necessaries of life for your bodies; and my ordinances and word to enlighten and cheer your souls. I have neither *been a wilderness* nor *a land of darkness to you.*

We are lords] We wish to be our own masters; we will neither brook religious nor civil restraint; we will regard no laws, human or Divine. It was this disposition that caused them to fall in so fully with the whole system of idolatry.

Verse 32. *Can a maid forget her ornaments*] This people has not so much attachment to me as young females have to their dress and ornaments. They never forget them; and even when arrived at old age, look with pleasure on the dress and ornaments which they have worn in their youth.

Days without number.] That is, for many years; during the whole reign of Manasses, which was *fifty-five* years, the land was deluged with idolatry, from which the *reform* by good King Josiah his grandson had not yet purified it.

Verse 33. *Why trimmest thou thy way*] Ye have used a multitude of artifices to gain alliances with the neighbouring idolatrous nations.

Hast thou also taught the wicked ones thy ways.] Ye have made even these idolaters worse than they were before. Dr. *Blayney* translates, "Therefore have I taught calamity thy ways." A prosopopœia: "I have instructed calamity where to find thee." Thou shalt not escape punishment.

Verse 34. *The blood of the souls of the poor innocents*] We find from the sacred history that Manasseh had filled Jerusalem with innocent blood; see 2 Kings xxi. 16, and Ezek. xxxiv. 10.

I have not found it by secret search, but upon all these.] Such deeds of darkness and profligacy are found only in Israel. Dr. *Blayney* translates, "I have not found it in a digged hole, but upon every oak." Others cover the blood that it may not appear; but ye have shed it openly, and sprinkled it upon your consecrated oaks, and gloried in it.

Verse 35. *Because I am innocent*] They continued to assert their innocence, and therefore expected that God's judgments would be speedily removed!

I will plead with thee] I will maintain my *process*, follow it up to conviction, and inflict the deserved punishment.

Verse 36. *Why gaddest thou about*] When they had departed from the Lord, they sought foreign alliances for support. 1. The *Assyrians*, 2 Chron. xxviii. 13-21; but they injured instead of helping them. 2. The *Egyptians:* but in this they were utterly disappointed, and were ashamed of their confidence. See chap. xxxvii. 7, 8, for the fulfilment of this prediction.

Verse 37. *Thou shalt go forth from him, and thine hands upon thine head*] Thou shalt find all thy confidence in vain,—thy hope disappointed,—and thy state reduced to desperation. *The hand being placed on the head* was the evidence of deep sorrow, occasioned by utter desolation. See the case of Tamar, when ruined and abandoned by her brother Amnon, 2 Sam. xiii. 19.

Thou shalt not prosper in them.] They shall all turn to thy disadvantage; and this, as we shall see in the history of this people, was literally fulfilled. O what a grievous and bitter thing it is to sin against the Lord, and have him for an enemy!

CHAPTER III

The first five verses of this chapter allude to the subject of the last; and contain earnest exhortations to repentance, with gracious promises of pardon, notwithstanding every aggravation of guilt, 1–5. *At the* sixth *verse a new section of prophecy commences, opening with a complaint against Judah for having exceeded in guilt her sister Israel, already cast off for her idolatry,* 6–11. *She is cast off, but not forever; for to this same Israel, whose place of captivity (Assyria) lay to the north of Judea, pardon is promised on her repentance, together with a restoration to the Church of God, along with her sister Judah, in the latter days,* 12–20. *The prophet foretells the sorrow and repentance of the children of Israel under the Gospel dispensation,* 21. *God renews his gracious promises,* 22; *and they again confess their sins. In this confession their not deigning to name the idol Baal, the source of their calamities, but calling him in the abstract* shame, *or* a thing of shame, *is a nice touch of the pencil, extremely beautiful and natural,* 22–25.

A. M. 3375
B. C. 629
Ol. XXXVII. 4
Anci Martii,
R. Roman.,
12

THEY [a]say, If a man put
away his wife, and she go
from him, and become another
man's, [b]shall he return unto her
again? shall not that [c]land be greatly polluted? but thou hast [d]played the harlot with
many lovers; [e]yet return again to me, saith
the LORD.
2 Lift up thine eyes unto [f]the high places,
and see where thou hast not been lien with.
[g]In the ways hast thou sat for
them, as the Arabian in the
wilderness; [h]and thou hast
polluted the land with thy
whoredoms and with thy wickedness.
3 Therefore the [i]showers have been withholden, and there hath been no latter rain;
and thou hast a [k]whore's forehead, thou re-
fusedst to be ashamed.
4 Wilt thou not from this time cry unto me,

[a]Heb. *saying*——[b]Deut. xxiv. 4——[c]Ch. ii. 7——[d]Ch. ii. 20; Ezek. xvi. 26, 28, 29——[e]Ch. iv. 1; Zech. i. 3——[f]See Deut. xii. 2; ch. ii. 20——[g]Gen. xxxviii. 14; Prov. xxiii. 28; Ezek. xvi. 24, 25——[h]Ch. ii. 7; ver. 9——[i]Lev. xxvi. 19; Deut. xxviii. 23, 24; chap. ix. 12; xiv. 4——[k]Chap. v. 3; vi. 15; viii. 12; Ezek. iii. 7; Zeph. iii. 5

NOTES ON CHAP. III

Verse 1. *If a man put away his wife*] It was ever understood, by the law and practice of the country, that if a woman were divorced by her husband, and became the wife of another man, the first husband could never take her again. Now Israel had been married unto the Lord; joined in solemn covenant to him to worship and serve him only. Israel turned from following him, and became idolatrous. On this ground, considering idolatry as a *spiritual whoredom*, and the precept and practice of the law to illustrate this case, Israel could never more be restored to the Divine favour: but God, this first husband, in the plenitude of his mercy, is willing to receive this adulterous spouse, if she will abandon her idolatries and return unto him. And this and the following chapters are spent in affectionate remonstrances and loving exhortations addressed to these sinful people, to make them sensible of their own sin, and God's tender mercy in offering to receive them again into favour.

Verse 2. *As the Arabian in the wilderness*] They were as fully intent on the practice of their idolatry as the *Arab* in the desert is in lying in wait to plunder the caravans. Where they have not cover to lie in ambush, they scatter themselves about, and run hither and thither, raising themselves up on their saddles to see if they can discover, by *smoke, dust*, or other *token*, the approach of any travellers.

Verse 3. *There hath been no latter rain*] The *former rain*, which prepared the earth for tillage, fell in the beginning of *November*, or a little sooner; and the *latter rain* fell in the middle of *April*, after which there was scarcely any rain during the summer.

Verse 4. *Wilt thou not—cry unto me, My father*] Wilt thou not allow me to be thy Creator and Preserver, and cease thus to acknowledge idols? See on chap. ii. 27.

A. M. 3375
B. C. 629
Ol. XXXVII. 4
Anci Martii,
R. Roman.,
12

My father, thou *art* [l]the guide of
[m]my youth?
5 [n]Will he reserve *his anger*
for ever? will he keep *it* to the
end? Behold, thou hast spoken and done evil
things as thou couldest.

A. M. cir. 3392
B. C. cir. 612
Ol. cir. XLII. 1
TarquiniiPrisci,
R. Roman.,
cir. annum 5

6 The LORD said also unto me
in the days of Josiah the king,
Hast thou seen *that* which
[o]backsliding Israel hath done?
she is [p]gone up upon every high mountain
and under every green tree, and there hath
played the harlot.
7 [q]And I said, after she had done all these
things, Turn thou unto me. But she returned
not. And her treacherous [r]sister Judah saw *it.*
8 And I saw, when [s]for all the causes
whereby backsliding Israel committed adultery I had [t]put her away, and given her a bill
of divorce; [u]yet her treacherous sister Judah
feared not, but went and played the harlot
also.
9 And it came to pass through the [v]lightness
of her whoredom, that she [w]defiled the land,
and committed adultery with
[x]stones and with stocks.

A. M. cir. 3392
B. C. cir. 612
Ol. cir. XLII. 1
TarquiniiPrisci,
R. Roman.,
cir. annum 5

10 And yet for all this her
treacherous sister Judah hath
not turned unto me [y]with her whole heart,
but [z]feignedly, saith the LORD.
11 And the LORD said unto me, [a]The backsliding Israel hath justified herself more than
treacherous Judah.
12 Go and proclaim these words toward [b]the
north, and say, Return, thou backsliding Israel, saith the LORD; *and* I will not cause mine
anger to fall upon you: for I *am* [c]merciful,
saith the LORD, *and* I will not keep *anger*
for ever.
13 [d]Only acknowledge thine iniquity, that
thou hast transgressed against the LORD thy
God, and hast [e]scattered thy ways to the
[f]strangers [g]under every green tree, and ye
have not obeyed my voice, saith the LORD.
14 Turn, O backsliding children, saith the
LORD; [h]for I am married unto you: and I
will take you [i]one of a city, and two of a
family, and I will bring you to Zion:

[l]Prov. ii. 17——[m]Chap. ii. 2; Hos. ii. 15——[n]Psa. lxxvii. 7, &c.; ciii. 9; Isa. lvii. 16; ver. 12——[o]Ver. 11, 14; chap. vii. 24——[p]Chap. ii. 23——[q]2 Kings xvii. 13 [r]Ezek. xvi. 46; xxiii. 2, 4——[s]Ezek. xxiii. 9——[t]2 Kings xvii. 6, 18——[u]Ezek. xxiii. 11, &c.——[v]Or, *fame* [w]Chap. ii. 7; ver. 2——[x]Chap. ii. 27

[y]2 Chron. xxxiv. 33; Hos. vii. 14——[z]Heb. *in falsehood*——[a]Ezek. xvi. 51; xxiii. 11——[b]2 Kings xvii. 6 [c]Psa. lxxxvi. 15; ciii. 8, 9; ver. 5——[d]Lev. xxvi. 40, &c.; Deut. xxx. 1, 2, &c.; Prov. xxviii. 13——[e]Ver. 2; Ezek. xvi. 15, 24, 25——[f]Chap. ii. 25——[g]Deut. xii. 2 [h]Chap. xxxi. 38; Hos. ii. 19, 20——[i]Rom. xi. 5

Verse 5. *Will he reserve* his anger *for ever?*] Why should not wrath be continued against thee, as thou continuest transgression against the Lord?

Verse 6. *The Lord said also unto me in the days of Josiah the king*] This is a new discourse, and is supposed to have been delivered after the *eighteenth* year of the reign of Josiah. Here the prophet shows the people of Judah the transgressions, idolatry, obstinacy, and punishment of their brethren, the ten tribes, whom he calls to return to the Lord, with the most gracious promises of restoration to their own country, their reunion with their brethren of Judah, and every degree of prosperity in consequence. He takes occasion also to show the Jews how much more culpable they were than the Israelites, because they practised the same iniquities while they had the punishment and ruin of the others before their eyes. He there fore exhorts them to return to God with all their hearts, that they might not fall into the same condemnation. See the following verses.

Verse 7. *And I said*] By the prophets *Elijah, Elisha, Hosea, Amos, &c.*; for all these prophesied to that rebellious people, and exhorted them to return to the Lord.

Verse 8. *I had put her away*] Given them up into the hands of the Assyrians.

Verse 9. *The lightness of her whoredom*] The *grossness* of her idolatry: worshipping objects the most degrading, with rites the most impure.

Verse 11. *Backsliding Israel hath justified herself more*] She was less offensive in my eyes, and more excusable, than treacherous Judah. So it is said, Luke xviii. 14, the humbled *publican* went down to his house *justified rather than* the boasting *Pharisee.* The one was more to be pitied than the other, and more likely to receive the mercy of God.

Verse 12. *Proclaim these words toward the north*] The countries where the ten tribes were then in captivity, Mesopotamia, Assyria, Media, &c., see 2 Kings xvii. 6; these lay *north* of Judea. How tender and compassionate are the exhortations in this and the following verses! Could these people believe that God had sent the prophet and yet prefer the land of their bondage to the blessings of freedom in their own country, and the approbation of their God?

Verse 14. *I will take you one of a city, and two of a family*] If there should be but *one of a city* left, or one willing to return, and *two only of a whole tribe,* yet will I receive these, and bring them back from captivity into their own land. I have heard these words most sinfully applied to show the nature of a fancied eternal decree of election, that has appointed in several cases one only out of a whole city, and *two out of a whole family,* to be eternally saved, leaving the rest, according to the decree of reprobation, to perish everlastingly! And yet these persons, who spoke thus of the Fountain of eternal goodness and mercy, professed to be-

A. M. cir. 3392
B. C. cir. 612
Ol. cir. XLII. 1
TarquiniiPrisci,
R. Roman.,
cir. annum 5

15 And I will give you [k]pastors according to mine heart, which shall [l]feed you with knowledge and understanding.

16 And it shall come to pass, when ye be multiplied and increased in the land, in those days, saith the LORD, they shall say no more, The ark of the covenant of the LORD: [m]neither shall it [n]come to mind: neither shall they remember it; neither shall they visit *it;* neither shall [o]*that* be done any more.

17 At that time they shall call Jerusalem the throne of the LORD; and all the nations shall be gathered unto it, [p]to the name of the LORD, to Jerusalem: neither shall they [q]walk any more after the [r]imagination of their evil heart.

18 In those days [s]the house of Judah shall walk [t]with the house of Israel, and they shall come together out of the land of [u]the north to [v]the land that I have [w]given for an inheritance unto your fathers.

A. M. cir. 3392
B. C. cir. 612
Ol. cir. XLII.1
TarquiniiPrisci,
R. Roman.,
cir. annum 5

19 But I said, How shall I put thee among the children, and give thee [x]a [y]pleasant land, [z]a goodly heritage of the hosts of nations? and I said, Thou shalt call me, [a]My father; and shalt not turn away [b]from me.

20 Surely *as* a wife treacherously departeth from her [c]husband, so [d]have ye dealt treacherously with me, O house of Israel, saith the LORD.

21 A voice was heard upon [e]the high places, weeping *and* supplications of the children of Israel: for they have perverted their way, *and* they have forgotten the LORD their God.

22 [f]Return, ye backsliding children, *and* [g]I will heal your backslidings. Behold, we

[k]Chap. xxiii. 4; Ezek. xxxiv. 23; Eph. iv. 11——[l]Acts xx. 28——[m]Isa. lxv. 17——[n]Heb. *come upon the heart*——[o]Or, it *be magnified*——[p]Isa. lx. 9——[q]Chap. xi. 8——[r]Or, *stubbornness*——[s]See Isa. xi. 13; Ezek. xxxvii. 16-22; Hos. i. 11——[t]Or, *to*——[u]Ver. 12; chap. xxxi. 8——[v]Amos ix. 15

[w]Or, *caused your fathers to possess*——[x]Psa. cvi. 24; Ezek. xx. 6; Dan. viii. 9; xi. 16, 41, 45——[y]Heb. *land of desire*——[z]Heb. *a heritage of glory* or *beauty*——[a]Isa. lxiii. 16——[b]Heb. *from after me*——[c]Heb. *friend*——[d]Isa. xlviii. 8; chap. v. 11——[e]Isa. xv. 2——[f]Ver. 14; Hos. xiv. 1——[g]Hos. vi. 1; xiv. 4

lieve in Him who by the grace of God tasted death for every man.

Verse 15. *I will give you pastors according to mine heart*] The pastor means either the *king* or the *prophet;* and the pastors here promised may be either kings or prophets, or both. These shall be according to God's own heart; they shall be of his own choosing and shall be qualified by himself: and in consequence they shall feed the people with knowledge, דעה *deah,* that Divine truth concerning the true God and the best interests of man, which was essentially necessary to their salvation; and *understanding*—השכיל *haskeil,* the full interpretation of every point, that in receiving the truth they might become wise, holy, and happy.

Verse 16. *The ark of the covenant of the Lord*] This symbol of the Divine presence, given to the Jews as a token and pledge of God's dwelling among them, shall be no longer necessary, and shall no longer exist; for in the days of the Messiah, to which this promise seems to relate, God's worship shall not be confined either to *one place* or to *one people.* The temple of God shall be among men, and every where God be adored through Christ Jesus.

Neither shall that *be done any more.*] The ark shall be no more established, nor carried from place to place; nor shall men go to visit it. All its ceremonies and importance shall cease; and, if lost, shall never be *rebuilt.*

Verse 17. *They shall call Jerusalem the throne of the Lord*] The new Jerusalem, the universal Church of Christ, shall be God's throne: and wherever he is acknowledged as *the Lamb of God who takes away the sin of the world,* there God sits on his throne, and holds his court.

Verse 18. *The house of Judah shall walk with the house of Israel*] That is, in those days in which the Jews shall be brought in with the fulness of the Gentiles.

Out of the land of the north] From Chaldea. This prophecy has two aspects: one refers to the return from the Babylonish captivity; the other, to the glorious days of Christianity. But the words may refer to that gathering together of the Jews, not only from Chaldea, but from the countries of their dispersion over the face of the whole earth, and uniting them in the Christian Church.

Verse 19. *How shall I put thee among the children*] As if he had said, How can ye be accounted a holy seed, who are polluted? How can ye be united to the people of God, who walk in the path of sinners? How can ye be taken to heaven, who are unholy within, and unrighteous without?

And I said, Thou shalt call me, My father] This is the answer to the above question. They could *not be put among the children* unless they became legal *members* of the heavenly family: and they could not become members of this family unless they abandoned *idolatry,* and took the Lord for their portion. Nor could they be continued in the privileges of the heavenly family, unless they *no more turned away from their heavenly Father.*

Verse 21. *A voice was heard upon the high places*] Here the Israelites are represented as assembled together to bewail their idolatry and to implore mercy. While thus engaged, they hear the gracious call of Jehovah—

Verse 22. *Return, ye backsliding children*] This they gladly receive, and with one voice make their confession to him: "Behold, we come unto thee, for thou art Jehovah our God;" and thence to the end of the chapter, show the reasons why they return unto God. 1. Because he

A. M. cir. 3392
B. C. cir. 612
Ol. cir. XLII. 1
TarquiniiPrisci,
R. Roman.,
cir. annum 5

come unto thee; for thou *art* the LORD our God.
23 [h]Truly in vain *is salvation hoped for* from the hills, *and from* the multitude of mountains: [i]truly in the LORD our God *is* the salvation of Israel.
24 [k]For shame hath devoured the labour of our fathers from our youth; their flocks and their herds, their sons and their daughters.
25 We lie down in our shame, and our confusion covereth us: [l]for we have sinned against the LORD our God, we and our fathers, from our youth even unto this day, and [m]have not obeyed the voice of the LORD our God.

[h]Psa. cxxi. 1, 2——[i]Psa. iii. 8——[k]Chap. xi. 13; Hos. ix. 10——[l]Ezra ix. 7——[m]Chap. xxii. 21

is the true God. 2. Because the idols did not profit them: they could give no help in time of trouble. 3. Because it is the prerogative of God alone to give salvation. 4. Because they had no kind of prosperity since they had abandoned the worship of their Maker. And this was not only their case, but it was the case of their *forefathers*, who all suffered in consequence of their idolatry and disobedience. 5. These reasons are concluded with a hearty confession of sin, at the thought of which they are *confounded;* for the remembrance of their sin was grievous to them, and the burden was intolerable. This confession ended, God appears in the next chapter with gracious promises, and proper directions how they are to return, and how to conduct themselves in future.

Verse 24. *For shame hath devoured*] The word *shame*, here and in chap. xi. 13; Hos. ix. 10, is supposed to signify Baal, the idol which they worshipped. That thing or shame which has brought you into contempt, confusion, and ruin. Sooner or later every sinner must be *ashamed* of his conduct; next, *confounded;* and, lastly, *ruined* by it, unless by true faith and hearty repentance he returns to the Lord.

CHAPTER IV

Sequel of the exhortations and promises addressed to Israel in the preceding chapter, 1, 2. *The prophet then addresses the people of Judah and Jerusalem, exhorting to repentance and reformation, that the dreadful visitation with which they were threatened might be averted,* 3, 4. *He then sounds the alarm of war,* 5, 6. *Nebuchadnezzar, like a fierce lion, is, from the certainty of the prophecy, represented to be on his march; and the disastrous event to have been already declared,* 7–9. *And as the lying prophets had flattered the people with the hopes of peace and safety, they are now introduced, (when their predictions are falsified by the event,) excusing themselves; and, with matchless effrontery, laying the blame of the deception upon God,* ("*And* they *said,*" *&c., so the text is corrected by Kennicott,)* 10. *The prophet immediately resumes his subject; and, in the person of God, denounces again those judgments which were shortly to be inflicted by Nebuchadnezzar,* 11–18. *The approaching desolation of Jerusalem lamented in language amazingly energetic and exquisitely tender,* 19–21. *The incorrigible wickedness of the people the sole cause of these calamities,* 22. *In the remaining verses the prophet describes the sad catastrophe of Jerusalem by such a beautiful assemblage of the most striking and afflictive circumstances as form a picture of a land "swept with the besom of destruction." The earth seems ready to return to its original chaos; every ray of light is extinguished, and succeeded by a frightful gloom; the mountains tremble, and the hills shake, under the dreadful apprehension of the wrath of Jehovah; all is one awful solitude, where not a vestige of the human race is to be seen. Even the fowls of heaven, finding no longer whereon to subsist, are compelled to migrate; the most fruitful places are become a dark and dreary desert, and every city is a ruinous heap. To complete the whole, the dolorous shrieks of Jerusalem, as of a woman in peculiar agony, break through the frightful gloom; and the appalled prophet pauses, leaving the reader to reflect on the dreadful effects of apostasy and idolatry,* 23–31.

A. M. cir. 3392
B. C. cir. 612
Ol. cir. XLII. 1
TarquiniiPrisci,
R. Roman.,
cir. annum 5

IF thou wilt return, O Israel, saith the LORD, [a]return unto me: and if thou wilt put away thine abominations out of my sight, then shalt thou not remove.
2 [b]And thou shalt swear, The LORD liveth, [c]in truth, in judg-

[a]Chap. iii. 1, 22; Joel ii. 12——[b]Deut. x. 29; Isa. xlv. 23; lxv. 16; see chap. v. 2; Zech. viii. 8——[c]Isa. xlviii. 1

NOTES ON CHAP. IV

Verse 1. *Shalt thou not remove.*] This was spoken *before* the Babylonish captivity; and here is a promise that if they will return from their idolatry, they *shall not be led into captivity.* So, even that positively threatened judgment would have been averted had they returned to the Lord.

Verse 2. *Thou shalt swear, The Lord liveth*] Thou shalt not *bind* thyself by any false god; thou shalt acknowledge ME as the Supreme. Bind thyself BY me, and TO me; and do this *in truth*, in *judgment*, and in *righteousness*.

A. M. cir. 3392
B. C. cir. 612
Ol. cir. XLII. 1
TarquiniiPrisci,
R. Roman.,
cir. annum 5

ment, and in righteousness; [d]and the nations shall bless themselves in him, and in him shall they [e]glory.

3 For thus saith the LORD to the men of Judah and Jerusalem, [f]Break up your fallow ground, and [g]sow not among thorns.

4 [h]Circumcise yourselves to the LORD, and take away the foreskins of your heart, ye men of Judah and inhabitants of Jerusalem: lest my fury come forth like fire, and burn that none can quench *it,* because of the evil of your doings.

5 Declare ye in Judah, and publish in Jerusalem; and say, Blow ye the trumpet in the land: cry, gather together, and say, [i]Assemble yourselves, and let us go into the defenced cities.

6 Set up the standard toward Zion: [k]retire, stay not: for I will bring evil from the [l]north, and a great [m]destruction.

7 [n]The lion is come up from his thicket, and [o]the destroyer of the Gentiles is on his way; he is gone forth from his place [p]to make thy land desolate; *and* thy cities shall be laid waste, without an inhabitant.

A. M. cir. 3392
B. C. cir. 612
Ol. cir. XLII. 1
TarquiniiPrisci,
R. Roman.,
cir. annum 5

8 For this [q]gird you with sackcloth, lament and howl: for the fierce anger of the LORD is not turned back from us.

9 And it shall come to pass at that day saith the LORD, *that* the heart of the king shall perish, and the heart of the princes; and the priests shall be astonished, and the prophets shall wonder.

10 Then said I, Ah, Lord GOD! [r]surely thou hast greatly deceived this people and Jerusalem, [s]saying, Ye shall have peace; whereas the sword reacheth unto the soul.

11 At that time shall it be said to this people and to Jerusalem, [t]A dry wind of the high places in the wilderness toward the daughter of my people, not to fan nor to cleanse,

12 *Even* [u]a full wind from those *places* shall come unto me: now also [v]will I [w]give sentence against them.

---

[d]Gen. xxii. 18; Psa. lxxii. 17; Gal. iii. 8——[e]Isa. xlv. 25; 1 Cor. i. 31——[f]Hos. x. 12——[g]Matt. xiii. 7, 22 [h]Deut. x. 16; xxx. 6; chap. ix. 26; Col. ii. 11; Rom. ii. 28, 29——[i]Chap. viii. 14——[k]Or, *strengthen*——[l]Chap. i. 13, 14, 15; vi. 1, 22——[m]Heb. *breaking*

[n]2 Kings xxiv. 1; ch. v. 6; Dan. vii. 4——[o]Ch. xxv. 9 [p]Isa. i. 7; chap. ii. 15——[q]Isa. xxii. 12; chap. vi. 26 [r]Ezek. xiv. 9; 2 Thess. ii. 11——[s]Ch. v. 12; xiv. 13 [t]Ch. li. 1; Ezek. xvii. 10; Hos. xiii. 15——[u]Or, *a fuller wind than those*——[v]Ch. i. 16——[w]Heb. *utter judgments*

The nations shall bless themselves in him] They shall be so fully convinced of the power and goodness of Jehovah in seeing the change wrought on thee, and the mercies heaped upon thee, that their usual mode of benediction shall be, *May the God of Israel bless thee!*

Verse 3. *Break up your fallow ground*] *Fallow* ground is either that which, having been *once tilled,* has *lain long uncultivated;* or, *ground slightly ploughed,* in order to be ploughed again previously to its being sown. Ye have been long *uncultivated* in righteousness; let true repentance *break up* your fruitless and hardened hearts; and when the *seed* of the *word of life* is sown in them, take heed that worldly cares and concerns do not arise, and, like *thorns,* choke the good seed.

Verse 4. *Circumcise yourselves*] Put away every thing that has a tendency to grieve the Spirit of God, or to render your present holy resolutions unfruitful.

Verse 5. *Blow ye the trumpet*] Give full information to all parts of the land, that the people may assemble together and defend themselves against their invaders.

Verse 6. *I will bring evil from the north*] From the land of Chaldea.

Verse 7. *The lion is come up*] Nebuchadnezzar, king of Babylon. "The king (Nebuchadnezzar) is come up from his tower."—*Targum.*

The destroyer of the Gentiles] Of the *nations:* of all the people who resisted his authority. He destroyed them all.

Verse 8. *Lament and howl*] הילילו *heililu.* The aboriginal Irish had a funeral song called the *Caoinian,* still continued among their descendants, one part of which is termed the *ulaloo:* this is sung responsively or alternately, and is accompanied with a *full chorus of sighs and groans.* It has been thought that Ireland was originally peopled by the Phœnicians: if so, this will account for the similarity of many words and customs among both these people.

Verse 9. *The heart of the king shall perish*] Shall lose all courage.

Verse 10. *Ah, Lord God! surely thou hast greatly deceived this people*] The *Targum* paraphrases this verse thus: "And I said, Receive my supplication, O Lord God; for, behold, the false prophets deceive this people and the inhabitants of Jerusalem, saying, Ye shall have peace." The prophet could not reconcile this *devastation* of the country with the *promises* already made; and he appears to ask the question, Hast thou not then deceived this people in saying there shall be peace, i. e., prosperity?

Whereas the sword reacheth unto the soul.] That is, the life; the people being generally *destroyed.*

Verses 11-13. *A dry wind—a full wind—as clouds—as a whirlwind*] All these expressions appear to refer to the *pestilential winds, suffocating vapours,* and *clouds and pillars of sand* collected by *whirlwinds,* which are so common and destructive in the east, (see on Isa. xxi. 1;) and these images are employed here to

A. M. cir. 3392
B. C. cir. 612
Ol. cir. XLII. 1
TarquiniiPrisci,
R. Roman.,
cir. annum 5

13 Behold, he shall come up
as clouds, and [x]his chariots *shall*
be as a whirlwind: [y]his horses
are swifter than eagles. Wo
unto us! for we are spoiled.
14 O Jerusalem, [z]wash thine heart from
wickedness, that thou mayest be saved. How
long shall thy vain thoughts lodge within thee?
15 For a voice declareth [a]from Dan, and
publisheth affliction from Mount Ephraim.
16 Make ye mention to the nations; behold,
publish against Jerusalem, *that* watchers come
[b]from a far country, and give out their voice
against the cities of Judah.
17 [c]As keepers of a field, are they against
her round about; because she hath been rebellious against me, saith the LORD.
18 [d]Thy way and thy doings have procured
these *things* unto thee; this *is* thy wickedness, because it is bitter, because it reacheth
unto thine heart.
19 My [e]bowels, my bowels! I am pained at
[f]my very heart; my heart maketh a noise in
me; I cannot hold my peace, because thou
hast heard, O my soul, the sound of the
trumpet, the alarm of war.
20 [g]Destruction upon destruction is cried; for the whole land
is spoiled: suddenly are [h]my
tents spoiled, *and* my curtains in
a moment.

A. M. cir. 3392
B. C. cir. 612
Ol. cir. XLII. 1
TarquiniiPrisci,
R. Roman.,
cir. annum 5

21 How long shall I see the standard, *and*
hear the sound of the trumpet?
22 For my people *is* foolish, they have not
known me: they *are* sottish children, and
they have none understanding; [i]they *are*
wise to do evil, but to do good they have no
knowledge.
23 [k]I beheld the earth, and, lo, *it was* [l]with-
out form and void; and the heavens, and
they *had* no light.
24 [m]I beheld the mountains, and, lo, they
trembled, and all the hills moved lightly.
25 I beheld, and, lo, *there was* no man, and
[n]all the birds of the heavens were fled.
26 I beheld, and, lo, the fruitful place *was*
a wilderness, and all the cities thereof were
broken down at the presence of the LORD,
and by his fierce anger.
27 For thus hath the LORD said, The whole
land shall be desolate; [o]yet will I not make a
full end.

---

[x]Isa. v. 28——[y]Deut. xxviii. 49; Lam. iv. 19; Hos. viii. 1; Hab. i. 8——[z]Isa. i. 16; James iv. 8——[a]Chap. viii. 16——[b]Chap. v. 15——[c]2 Kings xxv. 1, 4——[d]Psa. cvii. 17; Isa. l. 1; chap. ii. 17, 19——[e]Isa. xv. 5; xvi. 11; xxi. 3; xxii. 4; chap. ix. 1, 10; see Luke xix. 42

[f]Hebrew, *the walls of my heart*——[g]Psalm xlii. 7; Ezekiel vii. 26——[h]Chap. x. 20——[i]Romans xvi. 19——[k]Isa. xxiv. 19——[l]Gen. i. 2——[m]Isa. v. 25; Ezek. xxxviii. 20——[n]Zeph. i. 3——[o]Chap. v. 10, 18; xxx. 11; xlvi. 28

---

show the overwhelming effect of the invasion of the land by the Chaldeans.

Verse 13. *Wo unto us!*] The people, deeply affected with these threatened judgments, interrupt the prophet with the lamentation—*Wo unto us, for we are spoiled!* The prophet then resumes:—

Verse 14. *O Jerusalem, wash thine heart*] Why do ye not put away *your wickedness, that ye may be saved* from these tremendous judgments? *How long shall thy vain thoughts* of safety and prosperity *lodge within thee?* Whilst thou continuest a rebel against God, and provokest him daily by thy abominations!

Verse 15. *For a voice declareth from Dan*] *Dan* was a city in the tribe of Dan, north of Jerusalem; the first city in Palestine, which occurs in the way from Babylon to Jerusalem.

Affliction from Mount Ephraim.] Between Dan and Jerusalem are the *mountains of Ephraim.* These would be the first places attacked by the Chaldeans; and the rumour from thence would show that the land was invaded.

Verse 16. *Watchers come from a far country*] Persons to besiege fortified places.

Verse 17. *As keepers of a field*] In the eastern countries grain is often sown in the *open country;* and, when nearly ripe, guards are placed at different distances round about it to preserve it from being plundered. Jerusalem was watched, like one of these fields, by guards all round about it; so that none could enter to give assistance, and none who wished to escape were permitted to go out.

Verse 19. *My bowels*] From this to the *twenty-ninth* verse the prophet describes the ruin of Jerusalem and the desolation of Judea by the Chaldeans in language and imagery scarcely paralleled in the whole Bible. At the sight of misery the *bowels* are first affected; pain is next felt by a sort of stricture in the *pericardium;* and then, the heart becoming strongly affected by irregular palpitations, a gush of tears, accompanied with wailings, is the issue.—"My bowels, my bowels! I am pained at my very heart, (the walls of my heart;) my heart maketh a noise in me; I cannot hold my peace." Here is nature, and fact also.

Verse 20. *Destruction upon destruction*] Cities burnt, and their inhabitants destroyed.

My tents spoiled] Even the solitary dwellings in the fields and open country do not escape.

Verse 23. *I beheld the earth,* (the land,) *and lo* it was *without form and void*] תהו ובהו *tohu vabohu;* the very words used in Genesis to denote the formless state of the chaotic mass before God had brought it into order.

Verse 24. *The mountains—hills*] Princes, rulers, &c., were astonished and fled.

Verse 25. *The birds of the heavens were fled.*]

A. M. cir. 3392 B. C. cir. 612 Ol. cir. XLII. 1 TarquiniiPrisci, R. Roman., cir. annum 5

28 For this [p]shall the earth mourn, and [q]the heavens above be black: because I have spoken *it,* I have purposed *it,* and [r]will not repent, neither will I turn back from it.

29 The whole city shall flee for the noise of the horsemen and bowmen; they shall go into thickets, and climb up upon the rocks: every city *shall be* forsaken, and not a man dwell therein.

30 And *when* thou *art* spoiled, what wilt thou do? Though thou clothest thyself with crimson, though thou deckest thee with ornaments of gold, [s]though thou rentest thy [t]face with painting, in vain shalt thou make thyself fair; [u]*thy* lovers will despise thee, they will seek thy life.

31 For I have heard a voice as of a woman in travail, *and* the anguish as of her that bringeth forth her first child, the voice of the daughter of Zion, *that* bewaileth herself, *that* [v]spreadeth her hands, *saying,* Wo *is* me now! for my soul is wearied because of murderers.

[p]Hos. iv. 3——[q]Isa. v. 30; l. 3——[r]Num. xxiii. 19; chap. vii. 16——[s]2 Kings ix. 30; Ezek. xxiii. 40——[t]Heb. *eyes*——[u]Chap. xxii. 20, 22; Lam. i. 2, 19——[v]Isa. i. 15; Lam. i. 17

The land was so desolated that even the fowls of heaven could not find meat, and therefore fled away to another region. How powerfully energetic is this description! See Zeph. i. 3.

Verse 30. *Though thou rentest thy face with painting*] This probably refers to the custom of introducing *stibium*, a preparation of antimony, between the eye and the lids, in order to produce a fine lustre, which occasions a distension of the eye-lid in the time of the operation. In order to heighten the effect from this, some may have introduced a *more than ordinary quantity*, so as nearly to *rend* the eye-lid itself. Though thou make use of every means of address, of cunning, and of solicitation, to get assistance from the neighbouring states, it will be all in vain. Reference is here particularly made to the practice of *harlots* to allure men.

Verse 31. *Bringeth forth her first child*] In such a case the fear, danger, and pain were naturally the greatest.

Spreadeth her hands] The gesture indicated by nature to signify distress, and implore help. We have met with this figure in other parts, and among the classic writers it is frequent.

CHAPTER V

The prophet, having described the judgments impending over his countrymen, enlarges on the corruptions which prevailed among them. Their profession of religion was all false and hypocritical, 1, 2. *Though corrected, they were not amended, but persisted in their guilt,* 3. *This was not the case with the low and ignorant only,* 4; *but more egregiously so with those of the higher order, from whose knowledge and opportunities better things might have been expected,* 5. *God therefore threatens them with the most cruel enemies,* 6; *and appeals to themselves if they should be permitted to practise such sins unpunished,* 7–9. *He then commands their enemies to raze the walls of Jerusalem,* 10; *that devoted city, whose inhabitants added to all their other sins the highest contempt of God's word and prophets,* 11–13. *Wherefore his word, in the mouth of his prophet, shall be as fire to consume them,* 14; *the Chaldean forces shall cruelly afflict them,* 15–17; *and farther judgments await them as the consequence of their apostasy and idolatry,* 18, 19. *The chapter closes with a most melancholy picture of the moral condition of the Jewish people at that period which immediately preceded the Babylonish captivity,* 20–31.

A. M. cir. 3392 B. C. cir. 612 Ol. cir. XLII. 1 TarquiniiPrisci, R. Roman., cir. annum 5

RUN ye to and fro through the streets of Jerusalem, and see now, and know, and seek in the broad places thereof, [a]if ye can find a man, [b]if there be *any* that executeth judgment, that seeketh the truth; [c]and I will pardon it.

2 And [d]though they say, [e]The LORD liveth; surely they [f]swear falsely.

[a]Ezek. xxii. 30——[b]Gen. xviii. 23, &c.; Psa. xii. 1——[c]Gen. xviii. 26——[d]Tit. i. 16——[e]Chap. iv. 2——[f]Chap. vii. 9

NOTES ON CHAP. V

Verse 1. *Broad places*] Market-places, and those where there was most public resort.

If ye can find a man] A certain philosopher went through the streets of Athens with a lighted lamp in his hand; and being asked what he sought, answered, "I am seeking to find a MAN." So in Jerusalem none was found, on the most diligent search, who acted worthy the character of a rational being.

I will pardon it.] I will spare the city for the sake of *one righteous person.* So at the intercession of Abraham, God would have spared Sodom if there had been *ten* righteous persons found in it; Gen. xviii. 26.

Verse 2. *The Lord liveth*] Though they profess to *bind themselves* by Jehovah, as if they acknowledged him their God and only Lord, yet they *swore falsely;* for not believing in him, they took *a false oath;* one by which they did not believe themselves bound, not acknowledging him as their Lord. See on chap. iv. 2.

A. M. cir. 3392
B. C. cir. 612
Ol. cir. XLII. 1
TarquiniiPrisci,
R. Roman.,
cir. annum 5

3 O LORD, *are* not [g]thine eyes upon the truth? thou hast [h]stricken them, but they have not grieved; thou hast consumed them, *but* [i]they have refused to receive correction: they have made their faces harder than a rock; they have refused to return.

4 Therefore I said, Surely these *are* poor; they are foolish: for [k]they know not the way of the LORD, *nor* the judgment of their God.

5 I will get me unto the great men, and will speak unto them; for [l]they have known the way of the LORD, *and* the judgment of their God: but these have altogether [m]broken the yoke, *and* burst the bonds.

6 Wherefore [n]a lion out of the forest shall slay them, [o]*and* a wolf of the [p]evenings shall spoil them, [q]a leopard shall watch over their cities: every one that goeth out thence shall be torn in pieces: because their transgressions are many, *and* their backslidings [r]are increased.

7 How shall I pardon thee for this? thy children have forsaken me, and [s]sworn by *them* [t]*that are* no gods: [u]when I had fed them to the full, they then committed adultery, and assembled themselves by troops in the harlots' houses.

A. M. cir. 3392
B. C. cir. 612
Ol. cir. XLII. 1
TarquiniiPrisci,
R. Roman.,
cir. annum 5

8 [v]They were *as* fed horses in the morning: every one [w]neighed after his neighbour's wife.

9 [x]Shall I not visit for these *things?* saith the LORD: [y]and shall not my soul be avenged on such a nation as this?

10 [z]Go ye up upon her walls, and destroy; [a]but make not a full end: take away her battlements; for they *are* not the LORD's.

11 For [b]the house of Israel and the house of Judah have dealt very treacherously against me, saith the LORD.

12 [c]They have belied the LORD, and said, [d]*It is* not he; neither shall evil come upon us; [e]neither shall we see sword nor famine:

13 And the prophets shall become wind, and the word *is* not in them: thus shall it be done unto them.

14 Wherefore thus saith the LORD God of

[g]2 Chron. xvi. 9——[h]Isa. i. 5; ix. 13; chap. ii. 30——[i]Chap. vii. 28; Zeph. iii. 2——[k]Chap. vii. 8——[l]Mic. iii. 1——[m]Psa. ii. 3——[n]Chap. iv. 7——[o]Psa. civ. 20; Hab. i. 8; Zeph. iii. 3——[p]Or, *deserts*——[q]Hos. xiii. 7——[r]Heb. *are strong*——[s]Josh. xxiii. 7; Zeph. i. 5

[t]Deut. xxxii. 21; Gal. iv. 8——[u]Deut. xxxii. 15——[v]Ezek. xxii. 11——[w]Chap. xiii. 27——[x]Ver. 29; chap. ix. 9——[y]Chap. xliv. 22——[z]Chap. xxxix. 8——[a]Chap. iv. 27; ver. 18——[b]Chap. iii. 20——[c]2 Chron. xxxvi. 16; chap. iv. 10——[d]Isa. xxviii. 15——[e]Chap. xiv. 13

Verse 4. *These* are *poor*] They are ignorant; they have no education; they know no better.

Verse 5. *I will get me unto the great men*] Those whose circumstances and rank in life gave them opportunities of information which the others could not have, for the reasons already given.

These have altogether broken the yoke] These have cast aside all restraint, have acted above law, and have trampled all moral obligations under their feet; and into their vortex the lower classes of the people have been swept away. *Solon* said, "The laws are like cobwebs; they entangle the small fry, but the great ones go through them, and carry all away with them."

Verse 6. *Wherefore a lion*] Nebuchadnezzar, according to the general opinion; who is called here a *lion* for his courage and violence, a *bear* for his rapaciousness, and a *leopard* for his activity. *Dahler* supposes the *Scythians* to be intended, both here and in chap. iv. 7.

Verse 7. *In the harlots' houses.*] In places consecrated to idolatry. In the language of the prophets, adultery generally signifies *idolatry.* This we have often seen.

Verse 8. *After his neighbour's wife.*] This may have been *literally* true, as the abominations of idolatry, in which they were so deeply practised, would necessarily produce such a state of things as that here mentioned.

Verse 10. *Go ye up upon her walls*] This is the permission and authority given to the Chaldeans to pillage Jerusalem.

Take away her battlements] Some translate נטישות *netishoth, branches;* others, *vines.* Destroy the *branches,* cut down the *stem;* but do not damage the *root.* Leave so many of the people that the state may be regenerated. The *Septuagint, Syriac,* and *Arabic* read, "Leave her foundations, for they are the Lord's;" and this agrees with "Destroy, but make not a full end."

Verse 12. *They have belied the Lord*] כחשו *kichashu.* They have *denied* or disavowed the Lord.

It is *not he*] לוא הוא *lo hu, he is not;* there is no such being; therefore this evil shall not come upon us. On their premises, this conclusion was just. There is no judge; therefore there shall be no judgment. Thus they denied the Lord. They were atheists at heart.

Verse 13. *And the prophets shall become wind*] What are the prophets? Empty persons. Their words are wind; we hear the *sound* of their threatenings, but of the matter of the threatenings we shall hear no more.

And the word is *not in them*] There is no inspirer, but may their own predictions fall on their own heads! This seems the natural sense of this passage.

Verse 14. *Because ye speak this word*] Because ye thus treat my message, "I will make my words in thy mouth fire." They have said *they are but air;* but I will make them *fire,*

A. M. cir. 3392
B. C. cir. 612
Ol. cir. XLII. 1
TarquiniiPrisci,
R. Roman.,
cir. annum 5

hosts, Because ye speak this
word, [f]behold, I will make my
words in thy mouth fire, and this
people wood, and it shall devour them.
15 Lo, I will bring a [g]nation upon you
[h]from far, O house of Israel, saith the LORD:
it *is* a mighty nation, it *is* an ancient nation,
a nation whose language thou knowest not,
neither understandest what they say.
16 Their quiver *is* as an open sepulchre,
they *are* all mighty men.
17 And they shall eat up thine [i]harvest, and
thy bread, *which* thy sons and thy daughters
should eat: they shall eat up thy flocks and
thine herds: they shall eat up thy vines and
thy fig trees: they shall impoverish thy
fenced cities, wherein thou trustedst, with the
sword.
18 Nevertheless in those days, saith the
LORD, I [k]will not make a full end with you.
19 And it shall come to pass, when ye shall
say, [l]Wherefore doeth the LORD our God all
these *things* unto us? then shalt thou answer
them, Like as ye have [m]forsaken me, and
served strange gods in your land, so [n]shall ye
serve strangers in a land *that is*
not yours.
20 Declare this in the house of
Jacob, and publish it in Judah,
saying,
21 Hear now this, O [o]foolish people, and
without [p]understanding; which have eyes, and
see not; which have ears, and hear not:
22 [q]Fear ye not me? saith the LORD: will
ye not tremble at my presence, which have
placed the sand *for* the [r]bound of the sea by
a perpetual decree, that it cannot pass it: and
though the waves thereof toss themselves, yet
can they not prevail; though they roar, yet
can they not pass over it?
23 But this people hath a revolting and a
rebellious heart; they are revolted and gone.
24 Neither say they in their heart, Let us
now fear the LORD our God, [s]that giveth rain,
both the [t]former and the latter, in his
season: [u]he reserveth unto us the appointed
weeks of the harvest.
25 [v]Your iniquities have turned away these
things, and your sins have withholden good
things from you.
26 For among my people are found wicked

[f]Ch. i. 9——[g]Deut. xxviii. 49; Isa. v. 26; ch. i. 15; vi. 22——[h]Isa. xxxix. 3; ch. iv. 16——[i]Lev. xxvi. 16; Deut. xxviii. 31, 33——[k]Ch. iv. 27——[l]Deut. xxix. 24, &c.; 1 Kings ix. 8, 9; ch. xiii. 22; xvi. 10——[m]Ch. ii. 13——[n]Deut. xxviii. 48——[o]Isa. vi. 9; Ezek. xii. 2; Matt. xiii. 14; John xii. 40; Acts xxviii. 26; Rom. xi. 8——[p]Heb. *heart*; Hos. vii. 11——[q]Rev. xv. 4——[r]Job xxvi. 10; xxxviii. 10, 11; Psa. civ. 9; Prov. viii. 29——[s]Psa. cxlvii. 8; ch. xiv. 22; Matt. v. 45; Acts xiv. 17——[t]Deut. xi. 14; Joel ii. 23——[u]Gen. viii. 22——[v]Chap. iii. 3

and a *fire* too that shall *devour them.* And how this was to be done, and by whom, is mentioned in the next verse.

Verse 15. *I will bring a nation*] The *Scythians*, says *Dahler;* the *Babylonians*, whose antiquity was great, that empire being founded by Nimrod.

Whose language thou knowest not] The Chaldee, which, though a dialect of the Hebrew, is so very different in its words and construction, that in hearing it spoken they could not possibly collect the meaning of what was said.

Verse 16. *Their quiver* is *an open sepulchre*] They are such exact archers as never to miss their mark; every arrow is sure to slay one man.

Verse 18. *I will not make a full end*] There are more evils in store for you. You shall not only be spoiled, and all your property destroyed, but ye shall be carried into *captivity; and ye shall serve strangers in a land that is not yours*, ver. 19.

Verse 22. *Which have placed the sand* for *the bound of the sea*] What can I not do, who confine the sea, that enormous mass of waters, and prevent it from overflowing the earth; not by immense *mountains* and *rocks*, but by the *sand*, no particle of which is in cohesion with another? The most tremendous waves cannot displace nor pass over this simple barrier.

Verse 23. *They are revolted and gone.*] They have abandoned me, and are gone farther and farther into transgression. They are gone *entirely* away from truth and righteousness.

Verse 24. *Giveth rain, both the former and the latter*] See the note on chap. iii. 3.

The appointed weeks of the harvest.] As the early rains fell in the northern parts of Judea about the end of *September*, in the *civil year* of the Hebrews, so the *latter rains* fell before harvest, in the months of *March* and *April.* The appointed weeks of the harvest were those which fell between the *passover* and *pentecost.* In the southern parts the harvest was earlier than in the northern. Dr. *Blayney* translates, "A sufficiency of the appointed things of harvest he secureth to us."

If the word שבעת *weeks*, be read with a שׂ *sin* instead of a שׁ *shin*, it will signify *fulness* or *sufficiency;* and thus the *Septuagint* and *Vulgate* have read it. I think the present reading is much to be preferred. God *appoints a harvest time*, and in his good providence he generally gives *harvest weather.*

Verse 25. *Your iniquities have turned away these* things] When these appointed weeks of harvest do not come, should we not examine and see whether this be not in God's judgments? Have not our iniquities turned away these good things from *us?*

Verse 26. *They lay wait, as he that setteth*

A. M. cir. 3392
B. C. cir. 612
Ol. cir. XLII. 1
TarquiniiPrisci,
R. Roman.,
cir. annum 5

men: [w]they [x]lay wait, as he that
setteth snares; they set a trap,
they catch men.
27 As a [y]cage is full of birds,
so *are* their houses full of deceit: therefore
they are become great, and waxen rich:
28 They are waxen [z]fat, they shine: yea,
they overpass the deeds of the wicked: they
judge not [a]the cause, the cause of the fatherless, [b]yet they prosper; and the right of the
needy do they not judge.

29 [c]Shall I not visit for
these *things?* saith the LORD:
shall not my soul be avenged on such a nation as
this?
30 [d]A wonderful and [e]horrible thing is committed in the land;
31 The prophets prophesy [f]falsely, and the
priests [g]bear rule by their means; and my
people [h]love *to have it* so: and what will ye
do in the end thereof?

A. M. cir. 3392
B. C. cir. 612
Ol. cir. XLII. 1
TarquiniiPrisci,
R. Roman.,
cir. annum 5

---

[w]Or, *they pry as fowlers lie in wait*——[x]Prov. i. 11, 17, 18; Hab. i. 15——[y]Or, *coop*——[z]Deut. xxxii. 15——[a]Isa. i. 23; Zech. vii. 10——[b]Job xii. 6; Psa. lxxiii. 12; chap. xii. 1

[c]Ver. 9; Mal. iii. 5——[d]Or, *Astonishment and filthiness*——[e]Chap. xxiii. 14; Hos. vi. 10——[f]Chap. xiv. 14; xxiii. 25, 26; Ezek. xiii. 6——[g]Or, *take into their hands*——[h]Mic. ii. 11

---

snares] A metaphor taken from *fowlers*, who, having fixed their nets, lie down and keep out of sight, that when birds come, they may be ready to draw and entangle them.

Verse 27. *As a cage is full of birds*] There is no doubt that the reference here is to a *decoy* or *trap-cage*, as Dr. *Blayney* has rendered it; in these the fowlers put several tame birds, which when the wild ones see, they come and light on the cage, and fall into the snare.

Verse 28. *They judge not the cause, yet they prosper*] Perhaps we might be justified in translating, "And shall they prosper?"

Verse 30. *A wonderful and horrible thing is committed in the land*] *Dahler* translates: "Strange crimes and horrible trespasses have been committed in the land." These have been already detailed; but this may refer to what follows.

Verse 31. *The prophets prophesy falsely*] The false prophets predict favourable things, that they may please both the princes and the people.

The priests bear rule by their means] The false prophets affording them all that their influence and power can procure, to enable them to keep their places, and feed on the riches of the Lord's house.

And my people love to have it so] Are perfectly satisfied with this state of things, because they are permitted to continue in their sins without reproof or restraint. The prophets and the priests united to deceive and ruin the people. The prophets gave out false predictions; by their means the priests got the government of the people into their own hands; and so infatuated were the people that they willingly abandoned themselves to those blind guides, and would not hearken to the voice of any reformer. In my Old Bible the words stand thus:—**Stonyng and mervailis ben made in the erthe, prophets propheciden lesing; and prestis flappiden with joye with ther hondes, and my peple lovid siche thingis.** False prophets and worldly priests have been in all ages the bane of religion, and the ruin of many souls. When profligate people stand up on behalf of profligate priests, corruption must then be at its height.

CHAPTER VI

Jeremiah, in the spirit of prophecy, seeing the Chaldeans on their march, bids his people set up the usual signals of distress, and spread the general alarm to betake themselves to flight, 1. *Then, by a beautiful allusion to the custom of shepherds moving their flocks to the richest pastures, Jerusalem is singled out as a place devoted to be eaten up or trodden down by the armies of the Chaldeans, who are called up against her, and whose ardour and impatience are so great that the soldiers, when they arrive in the evening, regret they have no more day, and desire to begin the attack without waiting for the light of the morning,* 2–5. *God is then represented as animating and directing the besiegers against this guilty city, which sinned as incessantly as a fountain flows,* 6, 7, *although warned of the fatal consequence,* 8. *He intimates also, by the gleaning of the grapes, that one invasion should carry away the remains of another, till their disobedience, hypocrisy, and other sins should end in their total overthrow,* 9–15. *And to show that God is clear when he judgeth, he mentions his having in vain admonished and warned them, and calls upon the whole world to witness the equity of his proceedings,* 16–18, *in punishing this perverse and hypocritical people,* 19, 20, *by the ministry of the cruel Chaldeans,* 21–23. *Upon this a chorus of Jews is introduced expressing their fears and alarm,* 24, 25; *to which the prophet echoes a response full of sympathy and tenderness,* 26. *The concluding verses, by metaphors taken from the process of refining gold and silver, represent all the methods hitherto used to amend them as wholly ineffectual,* 27–30.

A. M. cir. 3392
B. C. cir. 612
Ol. cir. XLII. 1
TarquiniiPrisci,
R. Roman.,
cir. annum 5

O YE children of Benjamin, gather yourselves to flee out of the midst of Jerusalem, and blow the trumpet in Tekoa, and set up a sign of fire in [a]Beth-haccerem: [b]for evil appeareth out of the north, and great destruction.

2 I have likened the daughter of Zion to a [c]comely and delicate *woman*.

3 The shepherds with their flocks shall come unto her; [d]they shall pitch *their* tents against her round about; they shall feed every one in his place.

4 [e]Prepare ye war against her; arise, and let us go up [f]at noon. Wo unto us! for the day goeth away, for the shadows of the evening are stretched out.

5 Arise, and let us go by night, and let us destroy her palaces.

6 For thus hath the LORD of hosts said, Hew ye down trees, and [g]cast a mount against Jerusalem: this *is* the city to be visited; she *is* wholly oppression in the midst of her.

7 [h]As a fountain casteth out her waters, so she casteth out her wickedness: [i]violence and spoil is heard in her; before me continually *is* grief and wounds.

A. M. cir. 3392
B. C. cir. 612
Ol. cir. XLII. 1
TarquiniiPrisci,
R. Roman.,
cir. annum 5

8 Be thou instructed, O Jerusalem, lest [k]my soul [l]depart from thee; lest I make thee desolate, [m]a land not inhabited.

9 Thus saith the LORD of hosts, They shall thoroughly glean the remnant of Israel as a vine: turn back thine hand as a grape-gatherer into the baskets.

10 To whom shall I speak, and give warning, that they may hear? behold, their [n]ear *is* uncircumcised, and they cannot hearken: behold, [o]the word of the LORD is unto them a reproach; they have no delight in it.

11 Therefore I am full of the fury of the LORD; [p]I am weary with holding in: I will pour it out [q]upon the children abroad, and upon the assembly of young men together: for even the husband with the wife shall be taken, the aged with *him that is* full of days.

12 And [r]their houses shall be turned unto others, *with their* fields and wives together: for I will stretch out my hand upon the inhabitants of the land, saith the LORD.

[a]Neh. iii. 14——[b]Chap. i. 14; iv. 6——[c]Or, *dwelling at home*——[d]1 Kings xxv. 1, 4; chap. iv. 17——[e]Ch. li. 27; Joel iii. 9——[f]Chap. xv. 8——[g]Or, *pour out the engine of shot*——[h]Isa. lvii. 20——[i]Psa. lv. 9, 10, 11; chap. xx. 8; Ezek. vii. 11, 23——[k]Ezek. xxiii. 18; Hos. ix. 12——[l]Heb. *be loosed* or *disjointed* [m]Lev. xvi. 22; 2 Sam. xxiv. 6, in the margin——[n]Chap. vii. 26; Acts vii. 61; see Exod. vi. 12——[o]Chap. xx. 8——[p]Chap. xx. 9——[q]Chap. ix. 21——[r]Deut. xxviii. 30; chap. viii. 10

NOTES ON CHAP. VI

Verse 1. *O ye children of Benjamin, gather yourselves to flee*] As the invading armies are fast approaching, the prophet calls on the inhabitants of Jerusalem to sound an alarm, and collect all the people to arm themselves and go against the invaders. They are called the children of Benjamin, because Jerusalem was in the tribe of Benjamin.

Tekoa] Was a city about *twelve* miles to the south of Jerusalem.

Beth-haccerem] Was the name of a small village situated on an eminence between Jerusalem and Tekoa. On this they were ordered to set up a *beacon*, or *kindle a large fire*, which might be seen at a distance, and give the people to understand that an enemy was entering the land.

Out of the north] From *Babylon*. The *Scythians.—Dahler.*

Verse 3. *The shepherds with their flocks*] The chiefs and their battalions. The invading army is about to spoil and waste all the fertile fields round about the city, while engaged in the siege.

Verse 4. *Prepare ye war against her*] The words of the invaders exciting each other to the assault, and impatient lest any time should be lost; lest the besieged should have time to strengthen themselves, or get in supplies.

Verse 5. *Arise, and let us go by night*] Since we have lost the day, let us not lose the night; but, taking advantage of the darkness, let us make a powerful assault while they are under the impression of terror.

Verse 6. *Hew ye down trees*] To form machines.

And cast a mount] That may overlook the city, on which to place our engines.

This is *the city to be visited*] We are sure of success, for their God will deliver it into our hands; for it is full of oppression, and he has consigned it to destruction.

Verse 7. *As a fountain casteth out her waters*] The inhabitants are incessant in their acts of iniquity; they do nothing but sin.

Verse 8. *Be thou instructed*] Still there is respite: if they would even now return unto the Lord with all their heart, the advancing Chaldeans would be arrested on their march and turned back.

Verse 9. *They shall thoroughly glean the remnant of Israel as a vine: turn back thine hand*] The Chaldeans are here exhorted to *turn back* and glean up the remnant of the inhabitants that were left after the capture of Jerusalem; for even that remnant did not profit by the Divine judgments that fell on the inhabitants at large.

Verse 10. *The word of the Lord is unto them a reproach*] It is an object of *derision; they despise it.*

Verse 11. *I am full of the fury of the Lord*] God has given me a dreadful revelation of the judgments he intends to inflict: my soul is

A. M. cir. 3392
B. C. cir. 612
Ol. cir. XLII. 1
TarquiniiPrisci,
R. Roman.,
cir. annum 5

13 For from the least of them
even unto the greatest of them
every one *is* given to [s]covetous-
ness; and from the prophet even
unto the priest every one dealeth falsely.
14 They have [t]healed also the [u]hurt *of the
daughter* of my people slightly, [v]saying, Peace,
peace; when *there is* no peace.
15 Were they [w]ashamed when they had committed abomination? nay, they were not at
all ashamed, neither could they blush: therefore they shall fall among them that fall: at
the time *that* I visit them they shall be cast
down, saith the LORD.
16 Thus saith the LORD, Stand ye in the
ways, and see, and ask for the [x]old paths,
where *is* the good way, and walk therein, and
ye shall find [y]rest for your souls. But they
said, We will not walk *therein.*
17 Also I set [z]watchmen over you, *saying,*
Hearken to the sound of the trumpet. But
they said, We will not hearken.
18 Therefore hear, ye nations, and know, O
congregation, what *is* among them.
19 [a]Hear, O earth: behold, I will bring evil
upon this people, *even* [b]the fruit of their
thoughts, because they have not
hearkened unto my words, nor to
my law, but rejected it.
20 [c]To what purpose cometh
there to me incense [d]from Sheba, and the
sweet cane from a far country? [e]your burnt-
offerings *are* not acceptable, nor your sacrifices sweet unto me.
21 Therefore thus saith the LORD, Behold,
I will lay stumbling blocks before this people,
and the fathers and the sons together shall
fall upon them; the neighbour and his friends
shall perish.
22 Thus saith the LORD, Behold, a people
cometh from the [f]north country, and a great
nation shall be raised from the sides of the
earth.
23 They shall lay hold on bow and spear;
they *are* cruel, and have no mercy; their voice
[g]roareth like the sea; and they ride upon
horses, set in array as men for war against
thee, O daughter of Zion.
24 We have heard the fame thereof: our
hands wax feeble: [h]anguish hath taken hold
of us, *and* pain, as of a woman in travail.
25 Go not forth into the field, nor walk by

[s]Isa. lvi. 11; chap. viii. 10; xiv. 18; xxiii. 11; Mic. iii. 5, 11——[t]Chap. viii. 11; Ezek. xiii. 10——[u]Heb. *bruise*, or *breach*——[v]Chap. iv. 10; xiv. 13; xxiii. 17 [w]Chap. iii. 3; viii. 12——[x]Isa. viii. 20; chap. xviii. 15; Mal. iv. 4; Luke xvi. 29——[y]Matt. xi. 29

[z]Isa. xxi. 11; lviii. 1; chap. xxv. 4; Ezek. iii. 17; Hab. ii. 1——[a]Isa. i. 2——[b]Prov. i. 31——[c]Psa. xl. 6; l. 7, 8, 9; Isa. i. 11; lvi. 3; Amos v. 21; Mic. vi. 6, &c.——[d]Isa. lx. 6——[e]Ch. vii. 21——[f]Ch. i. 15; v. 15; x. 22; l. 41, 42, 43——[g]Isa. v. 30——[h]Ch. iv. 31; xiii. 21; xlix. 24; l. 43

burdened with this prophecy. I have endeavoured to suppress it; but I must pour it forth upon the *children*, on the *young people*, on *husbands* and *wives*, on the *old* and the *superannuated*. All must partake in these judgments.

Verse 14. *They have healed also the hurt* of the daughter *of my people slightly*] *Of the daughter* is not in the text, and is here improperly added: it is, however, in some MSS.

Peace, peace] Ye shall have *prosperity*—when there was none; and when God had determined that there should be none. Here the *prophets prophesied falsely;* and the people continued in sin, being deceived by the priests and the prophets.

Verse 16. *Thus saith the Lord, Stand ye in the ways, and see*] Let us observe the metaphor. A *traveller* is going to a particular city; he comes to a place where the road divides into several paths, he is afraid of going astray; he stops short,—endeavours to find out the right path: he cannot fix his choice. At last he sees another traveller; he inquires of him, gets proper directions—proceeds on his journey—arrives at the desired place—and *reposes* after his fatigue. There is an excellent sermon on these words in the works of our first poet, *Geoffrey Chaucer;* it is among the Canterbury Tales, and is called *Chaucer's Tale.* The text, I find, was read by him as it appears in my old MS. Bible:—**Standith upon weies and seeth, and asketh of the olde pathes; What is the good weie? and goth in it, and gee schul fynden refresching to your soulis.** The soul needs *rest;* it can only find this by *walking in the good way.* The *good way* is that which has been *trodden* by the *saints from the beginning:* it is the *old way*, the way of *faith* and *holiness.* BELIEVE, LOVE, OBEY; be *holy*, and be *happy.* This is the *way;* let us *inquire* for it, and *walk* in it. But these bad people said, *We will not walk* in it. Then they took another way, walked over the precipice, and fell into the bottomless pit; where, instead of *rest*, they find—

————————a fiery deluge, fed
With ever-burning sulphur, unconsumed.

Verse 17. *I set watchmen*] I have sent prophets to warn you.

Verse 20. *Incense from Sheba*] Sheba was in Arabia, famous for the best incense. It was situated towards the southern extremity of the peninsula of Arabia; and was, in respect of Judea, *a far country.*

And the sweet cane from a far country] The *calamus aromaticus*, which, when dried and pulverized, yields a very fine aromatic smell; see on Isa. xliii. 24. This was employed in making the *holy anointing oil.* See Exod. xxx. 23.

Verse 23. *They shall lay hold on bow and spear*] Still pointing out the Chaldeans; or

A. M. cir. 3392
B. C. cir. 612
Ol. cir. XLII. 1
TarquiniiPrisci,
R. Roman.,
cir. annum 5

the way; for the sword of the
enemy *and* fear *is* on every side.
26 O daughter of my people,
[i]gird *thee* with sackcloth, [k]and
wallow thyself in ashes: [l]make thee mourning,
as for an only son, most bitter lamentation:
for the spoiler shall suddenly come upon us.
27 I have set thee *for* a tower *and* [m]a fortress
among my people, that thou mayest know and
try their way.
28 [n]They *are* all grievous revolters, [o]walking with slanders:
they are [p]brass and iron; they
are all corrupters.
29 The bellows are burned, the lead is
consumed of the fire; the founder melteth
in vain: for the wicked are not plucked
away.
30 [q]Reprobate [r]silver shall *men* call them,
because the LORD hath rejected them.

[i]Chap. iv. 8——[k]Chap. xxv. 34; Mic. i. 10——[l]Zech. xii. 10——[m]Chap. i. 18; xv. 20——[n]Chap. v. 23——[o]Chap. ix. 4——[p]Ezek. xxii. 18——[q]Isa. i. 22——[r]Or, *refuse silver*

according to *Dahler*, the *Scythians*, who had before their invasion of Palestine overrun many parts of Asia, and had spread consternation wherever their name was heard.

Verse 27. *I have set thee for a tower* and *a fortress*] Dr. *Blayney* translates, *I have appointed thee to make an assay among my people.* The words refer to the *office of an assayer of silver and gold;* and the *manner* of *assaying* here intended is by the *cupel*, a flat broad iron ring filled with the ashes of burnt bones. To separate the alloy from the silver they add a portion of *lead;* and when all is fused together, and brought into a state of ebullition, the cupel absorbs the lead, and with it the dross or alloy, and the silver is left pure and motionless on the top of the cupel. The people are here represented under the notion of *alloyed silver.* They are full of *impurities;* and they are put into the hands of the prophet, the *assayer*, to be purified. The *bellows* are placed, the *fire* is lighted up, but all to no purpose: so intensely commixed is the alloy with the silver, that it cannot be separated. The nozzle of the *bellows* is even *melted* with the intensity of the fire used to effect the refinement; and the *lead is carried off* by the action of the heat; and the *assayer melteth in vain*, for the alloy still continues in union with the metal. The assayer gives up the process,—will not institute one more expensive or tedious—pronounces the mass unfit to be coined, and denominates it *reprobate silver*, ver. 30. Thus, the evil habits and dispositions of the Israelites were so ingrained that they would not yield to either the *ordinary* or *extraordinary* means of salvation. God pronounces them *reprobate silver*,—not sterling,—full of alloy;—having neither the image nor the superscription of the Great King either on their hearts or on their conduct. Thus he gave them up as incorrigible, and their adversaries prevailed against them. This should be a warning to other nations, and indeed to the Christian Church; for if God did not spare the natural branches, neither will he spare these.

CHAPTER VII

Here begins another section of prophecy, ending with the ninth *chapter. It opens with exhorting to amendment of life, without which the confidence of the Jews in their temple is declared vain,* 1–11. *God bids them take warning from the fate of their brethren the Israelites, who had been carried away captive on account of their sins without any regard to that sacred place,* (Shiloh,) *where the ark of God once resided,* 12–15. *The iniquities of Judah are so great in the sight of God that the prophet is commanded not to intercede for the people,* 16; *the more especially as they persisted in provoking God by their idolatrous practices,* 17–20. *The Jewish sacrifices, if not accompanied with obedience to the moral law, are of no avail,* 21–24. *Notwithstanding the numerous messages of mercy from the time of the exodus, the people revolted more and more; and have added to their other sins this horrible evil,* the setting up of their abominations in the temple of Jehovah; *or, in other words, they have encumbered the Mosaic economy, which shadowed forth the glorious truths of Christianity, with a heterogeneous admixture of the idolatrous, impure, and cruel rites of heathenism; consequently, the whole land shall be utterly desolated,* 25–34.

A. M. cir. 3394
B. C. cir. 610
Ol. cir. XLII. 3
TarquiniiPrisci,
R. Roman.,
cir. annum 7

THE word that came to Jeremiah from the LORD, saying,
2 [a]Stand in the gate of the
LORD's house, and proclaim there
this word, and say, Hear the
word of the LORD, all *ye of* Judah, that enter in at these gates
to worship the LORD.

[a]Jeremiah, chap. xxvi. 2

NOTES ON CHAP. VII

Verse 1. *The word that came to Jeremiah*] This prophecy is supposed to have been delivered in the *first year of the reign of Jehoiakim*, son of Josiah, who, far from following the example of his pious father, restored idolatry, maintained bad priests and worse prophets, and filled Jerusalem with abominations of all kinds.

A. M. cir. 3394
B. C. cir. 610
Ol. cir. XLII. 3
TarquiniiPrisci,
R. Roman.,
cir. annum 7

3 Thus saith the LORD of hosts, the God of Israel, [b]Amend your ways and your doings, and I will cause you to dwell in this place.

4 [c]Trust ye not in lying words, saying, The temple of the LORD, The temple of the LORD, The temple of the LORD, *are* these.

5 For if ye throughly amend your ways and your doings; if ye throughly [d]execute judgment between a man and his neighbour;

6 *If* ye oppress not the stranger, the fatherless, and the widow, and shed not innocent blood in this place, [e]neither walk after other gods to your hurt:

7 [f]Then will I cause you to dwell in this place, in [g]the land that I gave to your fathers, for ever and ever.

8 Behold, [h]ye trust in [i]lying words, that cannot profit.

9 [k]Will ye steal, murder, and commit adultery, and swear falsely, and burn incense unto Baal, and [l]walk after other gods whom ye know not;

10 [m]And come and stand before me in this house, [n]which [o]is called by my name, and say, We are delivered to do all these abominations?

11 Is [p]this house, which is called by my name, become a [q]den of robbers in your eyes? Behold, even I have seen *it*, saith the LORD.

A. M. cir. 3394
B. C. cir. 610
Ol. cir. XLII. 3
TarquiniiPrisci,
R. Roman.,
cir. annum 7

12 But go ye now unto [r]my place which *was* in Shiloh, [s]where I set my name at the first, and see [t]what I did to it for the wickedness of my people Israel.

13 And now, because ye have done all these works, saith the LORD, and I spake unto you, [u]rising up early and speaking, but ye heard not; and I [v]called you, but ye answered not;

14 Therefore will I do unto *this* house, which is called by my name, wherein ye trust, and unto the place which I gave to you and to your fathers, as I have done to [w]Shiloh.

15 And I will cast you out of my sight, [x]as I have cast out all your brethren, [y]*even* the whole seed of Ephraim.

16 Therefore [z]pray not thou for this people, neither lift up cry nor prayer for them, neither make intercession to me: [a]for I will not hear thee.

17 Seest thou not what they do in the cities of Judah and in the streets of Jerusalem?

[b]Chap. xviii. 11; xxvi. 13——[c]Mic. iii. 11——[d]Chap. xxii. 3——[e]Deut. vi. 14, 15; viii. 19; xi. 28; chap. xiii. 10 [f]Deut. iv. 40——[g]Chap. iii. 18——[h]Ver. 4——[i]Chap. v. 31; xiv. 13, 14——[k]1 Kings xviii. 21; Hos. iv. 1, 2; Zeph. i. 5——[l]Exod. xx. 3; ver. 6——[m]Ezek. xxiii. 39 [n]Heb. *whereupon my name is called*——[o]Ver. 11, 14, 30; chap. xxxii. 34; xxxiv. 15——[p]Isa. lvi. 7

[q]Matt. xxi. 13; Mark xi. 17; Luke xix. 46——[r]Josh. xviii. 1; Judg. xviii. 31——[s]Deut. xii. 11——[t]1 Sam. iv. 10, 11; Psa. lxxviii. 60; chap. xxvi. 6——[u]2 Chron. xxxvi. 15; ver. 25; chap. xi. 7——[v]Prov. i. 24; Isa. lxv. 12; lxvi. 4——[w]1 Sam. iv. 10, 11; Psa. lxxviii. 60; chap. xxvi. 6——[x]2 Kings xvii. 23——[y]Psa. lxxviii. 67, 68 [z]Exod. xxxii. 10; chap. xi. 14; xiv. 11——[a]Chap. xv. 1

Verse 2. *Stand in the gate of the Lord's house*] There was a show of public worship kept up. The temple was considered God's residence; the usual ceremonies of religion restored by Josiah were still observed; and the people were led to consider the temple and its services as *sacred things*, which would be preservatives to them in case of the threatened invasion.

Verse 4. *The temple of the Lord*] In the *Chaldee* the passage stands thus:—"Do not trust in the words of lying prophets, which say, Before the temple of the Lord ye shall worship; Before the temple of the Lord ye shall sacrifice; Before the temple of the Lord ye shall adore; thrice in the year ye shall appear before it." This the *Targumist* supposes to have been the reason why the words are here *thrice* repeated. They rather seem to express the conviction which the people had, that they should be safe while their temple service continued; for they supposed that God would not give it up into profane hands. But *sacred places* and *sacred symbols* are nothing in the sight of God when the heart is not right with him.

Verse 5. *If ye throughly amend your ways*] Literally, *If in making good ye fully make good your ways.* God will no longer admit of *half-hearted* work. *Semblances* of piety cannot deceive him; he will not accept *partial* reformation; there must be a *thorough amendment.*

Verse 9. *Will ye steal, murder*] Will you continue to commit such abominations, and pretend to worship *me;* and thus defile the place that is called by my name; and so make my house a *den of robbers? I have seen this,*—and can you expect to escape condign punishment? Ye shall not escape.

Verse 12. *But go ye now unto my place which was in Shiloh*] See what I did to my tabernacle and ark formerly: after a long residence at Shiloh, for the iniquity of the priests and the people, I suffered it to fall into the hands of the Philistines, and to be carried captive into their land, and to be set up in the house of their idols. And because of *your* iniquities, I will deal with you and this temple in the same way; for as I spared not Shiloh, though my ark was there, but made it a victim of my wrath, so will I do to Jerusalem and her temple.

Verse 15. *The whole seed of Ephraim.*] Taken here for all the *ten* tribes, that of Ephraim being the principal.

Verse 16. *Therefore pray not thou for this people*] They have filled up the measure of their iniquity, and they must become examples of my justice. How terrible must the state of

A. M. cir. 3394
B. C. cir. 610
Ol. cir. XLII. 3
TarquiniiPrisci,
R. Roman.,
cir. annum 7

18 [b]The children gather wood,
and the fathers kindle the fire,
and the women knead *their*
dough, to make cakes to the
[c]queen of heaven, and to [d]pour out drink-
offerings unto other gods, that they may provoke me to anger.
19 [e]Do they provoke me to anger? saith
the LORD: *do they* not *provoke* themselves to
the confusion of their own faces?
20 Therefore thus saith the Lord GOD; Behold, mine anger and my fury shall be poured
out upon this place, upon man, and upon
beast, and upon the trees of the field, and
upon the fruit of the ground; and it shall
burn, and shall not be quenched.
21 Thus saith the LORD of hosts, the God
of Israel; [f]Put your burnt-offerings unto your
sacrifices, and eat flesh.
22 [g]For I spake not unto your fathers, nor
commanded them in the day that I brought
them out of the land of Egypt, [h]concerning
burnt-offerings or sacrifices.
23 But this thing commanded I them, saying, [i]Obey my voice, and [k]I will be your
God, and ye shall be my people: and walk
ye in all the ways that I have
commanded you, that it may be
well unto you.
24 [l]But they hearkened not,
nor inclined their ear, but [m]walked in the
counsels *and* in the [n]imagination of their evil
heart, and [o]went[p] backward, and not forward.
25 Since the day that your fathers came forth
out of the land of Egypt unto this day I have
even [q]sent unto you all my servants the prophets; [r]daily rising up early and sending *them:*
26 [s]Yet they hearkened not unto me, nor
inclined their ear, but [t]hardened their neck:
[u]they did worse than their fathers.
27 Therefore [v]thou shalt speak all these
words unto them; but they will not hearken
to thee: thou shalt also call unto them; but
they will not answer thee.
28 But thou shalt say unto them, This *is* a
nation that obeyeth not the voice of the LORD
their God, [w]nor receiveth [x]correction: [y]truth
is perished, and is cut off from their mouth.
29 [z]Cut off thine hair, *O Jerusalem,* and
cast *it* away, and take up a lamentation on
high places; for the LORD hath rejected and
forsaken the generation of his wrath.

A. M. cir. 3394
B. C. cir. 610
Ol. cir. XLII. 3
TarquiniiPrisci,
R. Roman.,
cir. annum 7

[b]Chap. xliv. 17, 19——[c]Or, *frame,* or *workmanship of heaven*——[d]Ch. xix. 13——[e]Deut. xxxii. 16, 21——[f]Isa. i. 11; ch. vi. 20; Amos v. 21; see Hos. viii. 13——[g]1 Sam. xv. 22; Psa. li. 16, 17; Hos. vi. 6——[h]Heb. *concerning the matter of*——[i]Exod. xv. 26; Deut. vi. 3; ch. xi. 4, 7 [k]Exod. xix. 5; Lev. xxvi. 12——[l]Psa. lxxxi. 11; chap. xi. 8——[m]Deut. xxix. 19; Psa. lxxxi. 12

[n]Or, *stubbornness*——[o]Heb. *were*——[p]Chap. ii. 27; xxxii. 33; Hos. iv. 16——[q]2 Chron. xxxvi. 15; chap. xxv. 4; xxix. 19——[r]Ver. 13——[s]Ver. 24; chap. xi. 8; xvii. 23; xxv. 3, 4——[t]Neh. ix. 17, 29; chap. xix. 15——[u]Ch. xvi. 12——[v]Ezek. ii. 7——[w]Chap. v. 3; xxxii. 33 [x]Or, *instruction*——[y]Chap. ix. 3——[z]Job i. 20; Isa. xv. 2; chap. xvi. 6; xlviii. 37; Mic. i. 16

that place be, where God refuses to pour out the spirit of supplication on his ministers and people in its behalf!

Verse 18. *The children gather wood*] Here is a description of a *whole family* gathered together, and acting unitedly in idolatrous worship. 1. The *children* go and collect wood, and bring it to the place of sacrifice. 2. The *fathers* lay it in order, and kindle a fire. 3. The *mother* and her *maids* knead dough, make their batch, and out of it form *cakes*, and bake them for the honour of the queen of heaven; most probably the *moon*, though perhaps not exclusive of the *sun* and *planets*, generally called the *host of heaven.* Family worship is a most amiable and becoming thing when performed according to truth. What a pity that so few families show such zeal for the worship of God as those apostate Israelites did for that of their idols!

Verse 21. *Put your burnt-offerings unto your sacrifices, and eat flesh.*] I will receive neither sacrifice nor oblation from you; therefore you may take the beasts intended for sacrifice, and slay and eat them for your *common nourishment.* See on ver. 29.

Verse 23. *This thing commanded I them—Obey my voice*] It was not *sacrifices* and *oblations* which I required of your fathers in the wilderness, but *obedience;* it was to *walk in that way* of righteousness which I have commanded; then I should have acknowledged them for *my people*, and I should have been *their God;* and then it would have *been well with them.* But to my commands, 1. *They hearkened not*—paid no regard to my word. 2. They *inclined not the ear*—showed no disposition to attend to my counsels. 3. They *walked in the imaginations of their evil heart*—followed its irregular and impure motions, rather than the holy dictates of my Spirit. 4. They *went backward and not forward.* Instead of becoming more wise, obedient, and holy, they grew more corrupt; so that they became more profligate than their fathers.

Verse 28. *Nor receiveth correction*] They have profited neither by *mercies* nor by *judgments:* blessings and corrections have been equally lost upon them.

Verse 29. *Cut off thine hair*] גזי נזרך *gozzi nizrech, shear thy nazarite.* The Nazarite was one who took upon him a particular vow, and *separated* himself from all worldly connexions for a certain time, that he might devote himself without interruption to the service of God; and during all this time no razor was to pass on his

A. M. cir. 3394
B. C. cir. 610
Ol. cir. XLII. 3
TarquiniiPrisci,
R. Roman.,
cir. annum 7

30 For the children of Judah
have done evil in my sight, saith
the LORD: [a]they have set their
abominations in the house which
is called by my name, to pollute it.
31 And they have built the high [b]places
of Tophet, which *is* in the valley of the son of
Hinnom, to [c]burn their sons and their daughters in the fire; [d]which I commanded *them*
not, neither [e]came it into my heart.
32 Therefore, behold, [f]the days come, saith
the LORD, that it shall no more be called
Tophet, nor the valley of the son of Hinnom,
but the valley of slaughter: [g]for
they shall bury in Tophet, till
their be no place.

A. M. cir. 3394
B. C. cir. 610
Ol. cir. XLII. 3
TarquiniiPrisci,
R. Roman.,
cir. annum 7

33 And the [h]carcasses of this
people shall be meat for the fowls of the heaven, and for the beasts of the earth; and none
shall fray *them* away.
34 Then will I cause to [i]cease from the
cities of Judah, and from the streets of Jerusalem, the voice of mirth, and the voice of
gladness, the voice of the bridegroom, and the
voice of the bride: for [k]the land shall be
desolate.

---

[a]2 Kings xxi. 4, 7; 2 Chron. xxxiii. 4, 5, 7; chap. xxiii. 11; xxxii. 34; Ezek. vii. 20; viii. 5, 6, &c.; Dan. ix. 27 —— [b]2 Kings xxiii. 10; chap. xix. 5; xxxii. 35 —— [c]Psa. cvi. 38 —— [d]See Deut. xvii. 3 —— [e]Heb. *came it upon my heart* —— [f]Chap. xix. 6

[g]2 Kings xxiii. 10; chapter xix. 11; Ezekiel vi. 5 —— [h]Deut. xxviii. 26; Psa. lxxix. 2; chap. xii. 9; xvi. 4; xxxiv. 20 —— [i]Isa. xxiv. 7, 8; chap. xvi. 9; xxv. 10; xxxv. 11; Ezek. xxvi. 13; Hos. ii. 11; Rev. xviii. 23 —— [k]Lev. xxvi. 33; Isa. i. 7; iii. 26

---

head, for none of his hair was to be taken off. After the vow was over, he shaved his head and beard, and returned to society. See Num. vi. 2, &c., and the notes there. Jerusalem is here considered under the notion of a Nazarite, by profession devoted to the service of God: but that profession was empty; it was not accompanied with any suitable practice. God tells them here to cut off their hair; to make no vain pretensions to holiness or religion; to throw off the mask, and attempt no longer to impose upon themselves and others by their hypocritical pretensions. On the same ground he orders them, ver. 21, to devote to common use the animals destined for sacrifice; and to make no more vain shows of religion while their hearts were not right with him. Dr. *Blayney* thinks the address is to the *prophet*, who was a Nazarite by virtue of his office, and who was called to cut off his hair as a token of *mourning* for the desolations which were coming upon his people. That *cutting off the hair* was a sign of *distress* and *mourning* may be seen, Ezra ix. 3; Isa. xv. 2; Jer. xli. 5, &c. But I think the other the more natural construction.

On high places] That the lamentation may be heard to the greater distance.

The generation of his wrath.] Persons exposed to punishment: used here as *children of wrath*, Eph. ii. 3.

Verse 31. *Tophet—in the valley of the son of Hinnom*] Tophet was the place in that valley where the continual fires were kept up, in and through which they consecrated their children to Moloch.

Verse 32. *The valley of slaughter*] The place where the slaughtered thousands of this rebellious people shall be cast, in order to their being burnt, or becoming food for the beasts of the field and the fowls of the air, ver. 33. These words are repeated, and their meaning more particularly explained, chap. xix. 6-15.

Verse 34. *Then will I cause to cease—the voice of mirth*] There shall no longer be in Jerusalem any *cause of joy;* they shall neither marry nor be given in marriage, for the land shall be totally desolated. Such horrible sins required such a horrible punishment. And they must be *horrible*, when they move God to destroy the work of his own hands.

CHAPTER VIII

The judgments threatened in the last chapter are here declared to extend to the very dead, whose tombs should be opened, and the carcasses treated with every mark of indignity, 1–3. *From this the prophet returns to reprove them for their perseverance in transgression,* 4–6; *and for their thoughtless stupidity, which even the instinct of the brute creation, by a beautiful contrast, is made to upbraid,* 7–9. *This leads to farther threatenings, expressed in a variety of striking terms,* 10–13. *Upon which a chorus of Jews is introduced, expressing their terror on the news of the invasion,* 14, 15; *which is greatly heightened in the next verse by the prophet's hearing the snorting of Nebuchadnezzar's horses even from Dan, and then seeing the devastation made by his army,* 16, *whose cruelties God himself declares no entreaties will soften,* 17. *On this declaration the prophet laments most bitterly the fate of the daughter of his people, changing the scene unawares to the place of her captivity, where she is introduced answering in mournful responses to the prophet's dirge,* 18–22. *The variety of images and figures used to diversify the same subject is equally pleasing and astonishing. The dress is generally new, always elegant.*

A. M. cir. 3394
B. C. cir. 610
Ol. cir. XLII. 3
TarquiniiPrisci,
R. Roman.,
cir. annum 7

AT that time, saith the LORD, they shall bring out the bones of the kings of Judah, and the bones of his princes, and the bones of the priests, and the bones of the prophets, and the bones of the inhabitants of Jerusalem, out of their graves:

2 And they shall spread them before the sun, and the moon, and all the host of heaven, whom they have loved, and whom they have served, and after whom they have walked, and whom they have sought, and [a]whom they have worshipped: they shall not be gathered, [b]nor be buried; they shall be for [c]dung upon the face of the earth.

3 And [d]death shall be chosen rather than life by all the residue of them that remain of this evil family, which remain in all the places whither I have driven them, saith the LORD of hosts.

4 Moreover thou shalt say unto them, Thus saith the LORD; Shall they fall, and not arise? shall he turn away, and not return?

5 Why *then* is this people of Jerusalem [e]slidden back by a perpetual backsliding? [f]they hold fast deceit, [g]they refuse to return.

6 [h]I hearkened and heard, *but* they spake not aright: no man repented him of his wickedness, saying, What have I done? every one turned to his course, as the horse rusheth into the battle.

7 Yea, [i]the stork in the heaven knoweth her appointed times; and [k]the turtle and the crane and the swallow observe the time of their coming; but [l]my people know not the judgment of the LORD.

8 How do ye say, We *are* wise, [m]and the

[a]2 Kings xxiii. 5; Ezek. iii. 16——[b]Chap. xxii. 19
[c]2 Kings ix. 36; Psa. lxxxiii. 10; chap. ix. 22; xvi. 4
[d]Job iii. 21, 22; vii. 15, 16; Rev. ix. 6

[e]Chap. vii. 24——[f]Chap. ix. 6——[g]Chap. v. 3
[h]2 Pet. iii. 9——[i]Isa. i. 3——[k]Cant. ii. 12——[l]Chap. v. 4, 5——[m]Rom. ii. 17

NOTES ON CHAP. VIII

Verse 1. *They shall bring out the bones*] This and the two following verses are a continuation of the preceding prophecy, and should not have been separated from the foregoing chapter.

In order to pour the utmost contempt upon the land, the victorious enemies dragged out of their graves, caves, and sepulchres, the bones of kings, princes, prophets, priests, and the principal inhabitants, and exposed them in the open air; so that they became, in the order of God's judgments, a reproach to them in the vain confidence they had in the *sun, moon,* and *the host of heaven*—all the planets and stars, whose worship they had set up in opposition to that of Jehovah. This custom of raising the bodies of the dead, and scattering their bones about, seems to have been general. It was the highest expression of hatred and contempt. *Horace* refers to it:—

Barbarus, heu, cineres insistet victor, et urbem
 Eques sonante verberabit ungula:
Quæque carent ventis et solibus ossa Quirini
 (Nefas videre) dissipabit insolens.
Epod. xvi. 11.

"Barbarians fell shall wanton with success,
 Scatter the city's flaming ruins wide;
 Or through her streets in vengeful triumph ride,
 And her great founder's hallowed ashes spurn,
 That slept uninjured in the sacred urn."
FRANCIS.

See this judgment referred to, Baruch ii. 24, 25.

Verse 4. *Moreover thou shalt say*] Dr. *Blayney* very properly observes, "In that part of the prophecy which follows next, the difference of speakers requires to be attended to; the transition being quick and sudden, but full of life and energy. The prophet at first, in the name of God, reproves the people's incorrigibility; he charges their wise ones with folly, and threatens them with grievous calamities, ver. 4-13. In the three next verses he seems to apostrophize his countrymen in his own person, and as one of the people that dwelt in the open towns, advising those that were in the like situation to retire with him into some of the fortified cities, and there wait the event with patience, since there was nothing but terror abroad, and the noise of the enemy, who had already begun to ravage the country, ver. 14-16. God speaks, ver. 17, and threatens to bring foes against them that should be irresistible. The prophet appears again in his own person, commiserating the daughter of his people, who is heard bewailing her forlorn case in a distant land; while the voice of God, like that of conscience, breaks in upon her complaints, and shows her that all this ruin is brought upon her by her own infidelities, ver. 18-20. The prophet once more resumes his discourse; he regrets that no remedy can be found to close up the wounds of his country, and pathetically weeps over the number of her slain, ver. 21, chap. ix. 1."

Shall they fall, and not arise? shall he turn away, and not return?] That is, It is as possible for sinners to return from their sin to God, for his grace is ever at hand to assist, as it is for God, who is pouring out his judgments, to return to them on their return to him. But these *held fast deceit, and refused to return;* they would not be undeceived.

Verse 6. *As the horse rusheth into the battle.*] This strongly marks the unthinking, careless desperation of their conduct.

Verse 7. *The stork in the heaven*] The *birds of passage* know the times of their going and return, and punctually observe them; they obey the dictates of nature, but my people do not obey my law.

Verse 8. *The pen of the scribes* is *in vain.*]

A. M. cir. 3394
B. C. cir. 610
Ol. cir. XLII. 3
TarquiniiPrisci,
R. Roman.,
cir. annum 7

law of the LORD *is* with us? Lo, certainly [n]in vain made he *it;* the pen of the scribes *is* in vain.

9 [o]The [p]wise *men* are ashamed, they are dismayed and taken: lo, they have rejected the word of the LORD; and [q]what wisdom *is* in them?

10 Therefore [r]will I give their wives unto others, *and* their fields to them that shall inherit *them:* for every one from the least even unto the greatest is given to [s]covetousness, from the prophet even unto the priest every one dealeth falsely.

11 For they have [t]healed the hurt of the daughter of my people slightly, saying, [u]Peace, peace; when *there is* no peace.

12 Were they [v]ashamed when they had committed abomination; nay, they were not at all ashamed, neither could they blush: therefore shall they fall among them that fall: in the time of their visitation they shall be cast down, saith the LORD.

13 [w]I will surely consume them, saith the LORD: *there shall be* no grapes [x]on the vine, nor figs on the [y]fig tree, and the leaf shall fade; and *the things that* I have given them shall pass away from them.

14 Why do we sit still? [z]assemble yourselves, and let us enter into the defenced cities, and let us be silent there: for the LORD our God hath put us to silence, and given us [a]water of [b]gall to drink, because we have sinned against the LORD.

A. M. cir. 3394
B. C. cir. 610
Ol. cir. XLII. 3
TarquiniiPrisci,
R. Roman.,
cir. annum 7

15 We [c]looked for peace, but no good *came; and* for a time of health, and behold trouble!

16 The snorting of his horses was heard from [d]Dan: the whole land trembled at the sound of the neighing of his [e]strong ones; for they are come, and have devoured the land, and [f]all that is in it; the city, and those that dwell therein.

17 For, behold, I will send serpents, cockatrices, among you, which *will* not *be* [g]charmed, and they shall bite you, saith the LORD.

18 *When* I would comfort myself against sorrow, my heart *is* faint [h]in me.

19 Behold the voice of the cry of the daughter of my people [i]because of them that dwell in [k]a far country: *Is* not the LORD in Zion? *is* not her king in her? Why have they [l]provoked me to anger with their graven images, *and* with strange vanities?

20 The harvest is past, the summer is ended, and we are not saved.

21 [m]For the hurt of the daughter of my people am I hurt; I am [n]black; astonishment hath taken hold on me.

22 *Is there* no [o]balm in Gilead; *is there* no physician there? why then is not the health of the daughter of my people [p]recovered?

[n]Or, *the false pen of the scribes worketh for falsehood;* Isa. x. 1——[o]Chap. vi. 15——[p]Or, *have they been ashamed,* &c.——[q]Heb. *the wisdom of what thing*
[r]Deut. xxviii. 30; chap. vi. 12; Amos v. 11; Zeph. i. 13
[s]Isa. lvi. 11; chap. vi. 13——[t]Chap. vi. 14——[u]Ezek. xiii. 10——[v]Chap. iii. 3; vi. 15——[w]Or, *in gathering I will consume*——[x]Isa. v. 1, &c.; Joel i. 7——[y]Matt. xxi. 19; Luke xiii. 6, &c.——[z]Chap. iv. 5

[a]Chap. ix. 15; xxiii. 15——[b]Or, *poison*——[c]Chap. xiv. 19——[d]Chap. iv. 15——[e]Judg. v. 22; chap. xlvii. 3
[f]Heb. *the fulness thereof*——[g]Psa. lviii. 4, 5; Eccles. x. 11——[h]Heb. *upon*——[i]Heb. *because of the country of them that are far off*——[k]Isa. xxxix. 3——[l]Deut. xxxii. 21; Isa. i. 4——[m]Chap. iv. 19; ix. 1; xiv. 17
[n]Joel ii. 6; Nah. ii. 10——[o]Gen. xxxvii. 25; xliii. 11; chap. xlvi. 11; li. 8——[p]Heb. *gone up*

The *deceitful pen* of the scribes. They have written falsely, though they had the truth before them. It is too bold an assertion to say that "the Jews have never falsified the sacred oracles;" they have done it again and again. They have written falsities when they knew they were such.

Verse 10. *Therefore will I give their wives*] From this to the end of ver. 15 is repeated from chap. vi. 13-15.

Verse 16. *The snorting of his horses was* From this to the end of ver. 15 is repeated from Babylon to Jerusalem; and it was by this city, after the battle of Carchemish, that Nebuchadnezzar, in pursuing the Egyptians, entered Palestine.

The whole land trembled at the sound of the neighing of his strong ones] Of his *war horses.* This is a fine image; so terrible was the united neighing of the cavalry of the Babylonians that the reverberation of the air caused the ground to tremble. This is better, and more majestic, than the celebrated line of *Virgil:*—

Quadrupe-dante pu-trem soni-tu quatit ungula campum. It would be much easier to *shake the ground* with the *prancings* of many horses, than to cause an *earthquake* by the sound of the *neighing* of the troops of cavalry.

Verse 17. *I will send serpents*] These were symbols of the enemies that were coming against them; a foe that would rather slay them and destroy the land than get booty and ransom.

Verse 20. *The harvest is past*] The siege of Jerusalem lasted *two years;* for Nebuchadnezzar came against it in the *ninth* year of Zedekiah, and the city was taken in the *eleventh;* see 2 Kings xxv. 1-3. This seems to have been a proverb: "We expected deliverance the *first year*—none came. We hoped for it the *second year*—we are disappointed; we are not saved—no deliverance is come."

Verse 22. Is there *no balm in Gilead?*] Yes, the most excellent in the world. "Is there no physician there?" Yes, persons well skilled to apply it. "Why then is not the health of the daughter of my people recovered?" Because ye have not applied to the physician, nor used the balm. Ye die because ye will not use the remedy. But to apply this metaphor:—The *Israelites* are represented as a *man dying* through disease; and a disease for the cure of which the *balm of Gilead* was well known to be a *specific*, when judiciously applied by a physician. But though there be *balm* and a *physician*, the people are not cured; neither their spiritual nor political evils are removed. But what may all this *spiritually* mean? The people are morally diseased; they have sinned against God, and provoked him to destroy them. They are warned by the prophet to repent and turn to God: they refuse, and sin on. Destruction is come upon them. Might they not have avoided it? Yes. Was it the fault of God? No. Did he not send his prophets with the richest offers of mercy? Did he not give them time, the best instructions, and the most effectual means of returning to him? Has not *mercy*, the heavenly *balm*, been ever at hand? And has not GOD, the great *Physician*, been ever ready to apply it? Yes. Why then are they not converted and healed? Because they would not apply to the Divine Physician, nor receive the only remedy by which they could be spiritually healed. They, then, that sin against the only remedy must perish, because they might have had it, but would not. It is not because there is a deficiency of grace, nor of the means of grace, that men are not saved; but because they either make no use, or a bad use, of them. Jesus Christ, by the grace of God, has tasted death for every man; but few are saved, because *they* WILL NOT *come unto him that they may have life.*

In my old MS. Bible the text is rendered thus:—

Whether gumm is not in Galaad? Or a leche is not there? Why than the hid wounde of the daughter of my peple is not alle helid?

How shall they escape who neglect so great a salvation? Reader, lay this to heart; and, while there is time, apply heartily to the great Physician for thy cure.

CHAPTER IX

The prophet bitterly laments the terrible judgments about to be inflicted upon his countrymen, and points ou some of the evils which have provoked the Divine Majesty, 1–9. *Judea shall be utterly desolated, and the inhabitants transplanted into heathen countries,* 10–17. *In allusion to an ancient custom, a band of mourning women is called to lament over the ruins of Jerusalem,* 17, 18; *and even the funeral dirge is given in terms full of beauty, elegance, and pathos,* 19–22. *God is the fountain of all good; man, merely an instrument by which a portion of this good is distributed in the earth; therefore none should glory in his wisdom, might, or riches,* 23, 24. *The judgments of God shall fall, not upon the land of Judea only, but also upon many heathen nations,* 25, 26.

A. M. cir. 3394 B. C. cir. 610 Ol. cir. XLII. 3 TarquiniiPrisci, R. Roman., cir. annum 7

O [a]THAT[b] my head were waters, and mine eyes a
fountain of tears, that I might
weep day and night for the slain
of the daughter of my people!
2 O that I had in the wilderness a lodging
place of way-faring men; that I might leave
my people, and go from them!
for [c]they *be* all adulterers, an
assembly of treacherous men.
3 And [d]they bend their tongues
like their bow *for* lies: but they are
not valiant for the truth upon the earth;
for they proceed from evil to evil, and

A. M. cir. 3394 B. C. cir. 610 Ol. cir. XLII. 3 TarquiniiPrisci, R. Roman., cir. annum 7

[a]Heb. *Who will give my head, &c.*——[b]Isa. xxii. 4; chap. iv. 19; xiii. 17; xiv. 17; Lam. ii. 11; iii. 48

[c]Chapter v. 7, 8——[d]Psalm lxiv. 3; Isaiah lix. 4 13, 15

NOTES ON CHAP. IX

Verse 1. *O that my head were waters*] מי יתן ראשי מים *mi yitten roshi mayim*, "who will give to my head waters?" My mourning for the sins and desolations of my people has already exhausted the source of tears: I wish to have a fountain opened there, that I may weep day and night for the slain of my people. This has been the sorrowful language of many a pastor who has preached long to a hardened, rebellious people, to little or no effect. This verse belongs to the preceding chapter.

Verse 2. *O that I had in the wilderness*] In the eastern countries there are no such *inns* or *houses of entertainment* as those in Europe. There are in different places public buildings called *caravanserais*, where travellers may *lodge:* but they are without *furniture* of any kind, and without food. Indeed they are often without a *roof*, being mere *walls* for a protection against the wild beasts of the desert. I wish to hide myself any where, in the most uncomfortable circumstances, that I may not be obliged any longer to witness the abominations of this people who are shortly to be visited with the most grievous punishments. Several interpreters suppose this to be the speech of GOD. I cannot receive this. I believe this verse to be spoken by the prophet, and that God proceeds with the next verse, and so on to the *ninth* inclusive.

Verse 3. *They bend their tongues* like *their bow* for *lies*] And their lies are such that they as fully *take away life* as the *keenest arrow* shot from the best strung bow. The false prophets told the people that there was no desolation at hand: the people believed them; made no preparation for their defence; did not return to the Lord; and the sword came and destroyed them.

They are not valiant for the truth] They are *bold* in sin, and *courageous* to support their

A. M. cir. 3394
B. C. cir. 610
Ol. cir. XLII. 3
TarquiniiPrisci,
R. Roman.,
cir. annum 7

they [e]know not me, saith the
LORD.
4 [f]Take ye heed every one of
his [g]neighbour, and trust ye not
in any brother: for every brother will utterly
supplant, and every neighbour will [h]walk with
slanders.
5 And they will [i]deceive every one his
neighbour, and will not speak the truth: they
have taught their tongues to speak lies, *and*
weary themselves to commit iniquity.
6 Thine habitation *is* in the midst of deceit;
through deceit they refuse to know me, saith
the LORD.
7 Therefore thus saith the LORD of hosts,
Behold, [k]I will melt them, and try them;
[l]for how shall I do for the daughter of my
people?
8 Their tongue *is as* an arrow shot out; it
speaketh [m]deceit: *one* speaketh [n]peaceably
to his neighbour with his mouth, but [o]in heart
he layeth [p]his wait.
9 [q]Shall I not visit them for these *things?*
saith the LORD: shall not my soul be avenged
on such a nation as this?
10 For the mountains will I take up a weeping and wailing, and [r]for the [s]habitations of
the wilderness a lamentation, because they are
[t]burned up, so that none can pass through
them; neither can *men* hear the
voice of the cattle; [u]both [v]the
fowl of the heavens and the beast
are fled; they are gone.

A. M. cir. 3394
B. C. cir. 610
Ol. cir. XLII. 3
TarquiniiPrisci,
R. Roman.,
cir. annum 7

11 And I will make Jerusalem [w]heaps, *and*
[x]a den of dragons; and I will make the cities
of Judah [y]desolate, without an inhabitant.
12 [z]Who *is* the wise man that may understand this? and *who is he* to whom the mouth
of the LORD hath spoken, that he may declare
it, for what the land perisheth *and* is burned up
like a wilderness, that none passeth through?
13 And the LORD saith, Because they have
forsaken my law which I set before them, and
have not obeyed my voice, neither walked
therein;
14 But have [a]walked after the [b]imagination
of their own heart, and after Baalim, [c]which
their fathers taught them:
15 Therefore thus saith the LORD of hosts,
the God of Israel; Behold, I will [d]feed them,
even this people, [e]with wormwood, and give
them water of gall to drink.
16 I will [f]scatter them also among the heathen, whom neither they nor their fathers have
known: [g]and I will send a sword after them
till I have consumed them.
17 Thus saith the LORD of hosts, Consider
ye, and call for [h]the mourning women, that

[e]1 Sam. ii. 12; Hos. iv. 1——[f]Chap. xii. 6; Mic. vii. 5, 6——[g]Or, *friend*——[h]Chap. vi. 28——[i]Or, *mock* [k]Isa. i. 25; Mal. iii. 3——[l]Hos. xi. 8——[m]Psa. xii. 2; cxx. 3, ver. 3——[n]Psa. xxviii. 3; lv. 21——[o]Heb. *in the midst of him*——[p]Or, *wait for him*——[q]Ch. v. 9. 29 [r]Ch. xii. 4; xxiii. 10; Hos. iv. 3——[s]Or, *pastures* [t]Or, *desolate*——[u]Heb. *from the fowl even to*, &c.——[v]Ch. iv. 25

[w]Isa. xxv. 2——[x]Isa. xiii. 22; xxxiv. 13; chap. x. 22 [y]Heb. *desolation*——[z]Psa. cvii. 43; Hos. xiv. 9 [a]Chap. iii. 17; vii. 43——[b]Or, *stubbornness*——[c]Gal. i. 14——[d]Psa. lxxx. 5——[e]Chap. viii. 14; xxii. 15; Lam. iii. 15, 19——[f]Lev. xxvi. 33; Deut. xxviii. 64 [g]Lev. xxvi. 33; chap. xliv. 27; Ezek. v. 2, 12——[h]2 Chron. xxxv. 25; Job iii. 8; Eccles. xii. 5; Amos v. 16; Matt. ix. 23

lies; but the *truth* they neither patronize nor support.

Verse 5. And *weary themselves to commit iniquity.*] O, what a drudgery is sin! and how much labour must a man take in order to get to hell! The tenth part of it, in *working together with God,* would bring him to the gate of glory.

Verse 7. *Behold, I will melt them*] I will put them in the *furnace of affliction,* and see if this will be a means of purging away their dross. See on chap. vi. 27.

Verse 10. *Both the fowl of the heavens and the beast are fled*] The land shall be so utterly devastated, that neither beast nor bird shall be able to live in it.

Verse 11. *A den of dragons*] תנים *tannim* is supposed to mean here *jackals;* the *chakal* is a beast frequent in the east, an attendant on the lion, the refuse of whose prey he devours. It is an animal that seems to have been bred originally between the *wolf* and the *dog.* The original is sometimes interpreted, *dragons, whales,* &c.

Verse 12. *Who is the wise man*] To whom has God revealed these things? He is the truly wise man. But it is to his prophet alone that God has revealed these things, and the speedy fulfilment of the predictions will show that the prophet has not spoken of himself.

Verse 15. *I will feed them—with wormwood*] They shall have the deepest sorrow and heaviest affliction. They shall have *poison* instead of *meat* and *drink.*

Verse 17. *Call for the mourning women*] Those whose office it was to make lamentations at funerals, and to bewail the dead, for which they received *pay.* This custom continues to the present in Asiatic countries. In *Ireland* this custom also prevails, which no doubt their ancestors brought from the east. I have often witnessed it, and have given a specimen of this elsewhere. See the note on Matt. ix. 23. The first lamentations for the dead consisted only in the sudden bursts of inexpressible grief, like that of David over his son Absalom, 2 Sam. xix. 4. But as men grew refined, it was not deemed

A. M. cir. 3394
B. C. cir. 610
Ol. cir. XLII. 3
TarquiniiPrisci, R. Roman., cir. annum 7

they may come; and send for
cunning *women*, that they may
come:
18 And let them make haste,
and take up a wailing for us, that [i]our eyes
may run down with tears, and our eyelids gush
out with waters.
19 For a voice of wailing is heard out of
Zion, How are we spoiled! we are greatly
confounded, because we have forsaken the
land, because [k]our dwellings have cast *us* out.
20 Yet hear the word of the LORD, O ye
women, and let your ear receive the word of
his mouth, and teach your daughters wailing,
and every one her neighbour lamentation.
21 For death is come up into our windows,
and is entered into our palaces,
to cut off [l]the children from
without, *and* the young men
from the streets.
22 Speak, Thus saith the LORD, Even the
carcasses of men shall fall [m]as dung upon the
open field, and as the handful after the harvestman, and none shall gather *them*.
23 Thus saith the LORD, [n]Let not the wise
man glory in his wisdom, neither let the
mighty *man* glory in his might, let not the
rich *man* glory in his riches:
24 But [o]let him that glorieth glory in this,
that he understandeth and knoweth me, that I
am the LORD which exercise loving-kindness,
judgment, and righteousness, in the earth:

A. M. cir. 3394
B. C. cir. 610
Ol. cir. XLII. 3
TarquiniiPrisci, R. Roman., cir. annum 7

[i]Chap. xiv. 17——[k]Lev. xviii. 28; xx. 22——[l]Chap. vi. 11

[m]Chap. viii. 2; xvi. 4——[n]Eccles. ix. 11——[o]1 Cor. i. 31; 2 Cor. x. 17

sufficient for the surviving relatives to vent their sorrows in these natural, artless expressions of wo, but they endeavoured to join others as partners in their sorrows. This gave rise to the custom of *hiring persons to weep at funerals*, which the *Phrygians* and *Greeks* borrowed from the *Hebrews*. *Women* were generally employed on these occasions, because the tender passions being predominant in this sex, they succeeded better in their parts; and there were never wanting persons who would let out their services to hire on such occasions. Their lamentations were sung to the pipe as we learn from Matt. ix. 23. See the funeral ceremonies practised at the burial of Hector, as described by Homer:—

Οἱ δ' επει εισαγαγον κλυτα δωματα, τον μεν επειτα
Τρητοις εν λεχεεσσι θεσαν, παρα δ' εἱσαν αοιδους,
Θρηνων εξαρχους, οἱ τε στονοεσσαν αοιδην
Οἱ μεν αρ' εθρηνεον, επι δε στεναχοντο γυναικες.
IL. lib. xxiv., ver. 719.

"Arrived within the royal house, they stretched
The breathless Hector on a sumptuous bed,
And *singers* placed beside him, who should chant
The *strain funereal;* they with many a *groan*
The *dirge began;* and still at every close
The *female train* with *many a groan replied.*"
COWPER.

St. Jerome tells us that even to his time this custom continued in Judea; that women at funerals, with dishevelled hair and naked breasts, endeavoured in a modulated voice to invite others to lament with them. The poem before us, from the *seventeenth* to the *twenty-second* verse, is both an illustration and confirmation of what has been delivered on this subject, and worthy of the reader's frequent perusal, on account of its affecting pathos, moral sentiments, and fine images, particularly in the *twenty-first* verse, where *death* is decribed in as animated a prosopopœia as can be conceived. See *Lowth's twenty-second* Prelection, and *Dodd*. The *nineteenth* verse is supposed to be the funeral song of the women.

"How are we spoiled!
We are greatly confounded!
For we have forsaken the land;
Because they have destroyed our dwellings."

Verse 20. *Teach your daughters*] This is not a common dirge that shall last only till the body is consigned to the earth; it must last longer; teach it to your children, that it may be continued through every generation, till God turn again your captivity.

Verse 21. *For death is come up into our windows*] Here DEATH is personified, and represented as scaling their wall; and after having slain the *playful children* without, and the *vigorous youth* employed in the labours of the field, he is now come into the private houses, to destroy the aged and infirm; and into the palaces, to destroy the king and the princes.

Verse 22. *And as the handful after the harvestman*] The reapers, after having cut enough to fill their hand, threw it down; and the binders, following after, collected those handfuls, and bound them in sheaves. *Death* is represented as having *cut down* the inhabitants of the land, as the *reapers do the corn;* but so general was the *slaughter*, that there was none to *bury the dead*, to gather up these handfuls; so that they lay in a state of putrescence, *as dung upon the open field.*

Verse 23. *Let not the wise* man *glory in his wisdom*] Because God is the Fountain of all good, neither *wisdom*, nor *might*, nor *riches*, nor *prosperity* can come but *from* or *through* him. Nothing can be more rational than that the Source of all our blessings should be acknowledged. *Riches* cannot deliver in the day of death; *strength* cannot avail against him; and as a shield against him, our *wisdom* is foolishness.

Verse 24. *But let him that glorieth*] To *glory* in a thing is to depend on it as the means or cause of procuring *happiness*. But there can be no happiness but in being *experimentally acquainted* with that God *who exercises loving-kindness, judgment*, and *righteousness in the earth.* He who has God's mercy for his portion may well exult; for he need not fear the power of any adversary.

A. M. cir. 3394
B. C. cir. 610
Ol. cir. XLII. 3
TarquiniiPrisci,
R. Roman.,
cir. annum 7

[p]for in these *things* I delight,
saith the LORD.
25 Behold, the days come,
saith the LORD, that [q]I will
[r]punish all *them which are* circumcised with
the uncircumcised;
26 Egypt, and Judah, and Edom, [s]and the
children of Ammon, and Moab,
and all *that are* [t]in the [u]utmost corners, that dwell in the
wilderness: for all *these* nations *are* uncircumcised, and all the house
of Israel *are* [v]uncircumcised, in the
heart.

[p]Mic. vi. 8; vii. 18——[q]Rom. ii. 8, 9——[r]Heb. *visit upon*——[s]Judith xiv. 10——[t]Heb. *cut off into corners*, or *having the corners* of their hair *polled*——[u]Ch. xxv. 23; xlix. 32——[v]Lev. xxvi. 41; Ezek. xliv. 7; Rom. ii. 28, 29

Sometimes the ancient heathen poets uttered sentiments of morality far beyond their dispensation. Witness PHOCYLIDES on this subject:—

Μη γαυρου σοφιῃ, μητ' αλκῃ, μητ' ενι πλουτῳ·
Εἱς Θεος εστι σοφος, δυνατος θ' ἁμα, και τολυολβος.

"If *wisdom*, *strength*, or *riches* be thy lot,
Boast not; but rather think thou hast them not.
ONE GOD alone from whom those gifts proceed
Is *wise*, is *mighty*, and is *rich indeed*."

Verse 25. *I will punish all* them which are *circumcised with the uncircumcised*] Do not imagine that *you*, because of your crimes, are the only objects of my displeasure; the *circumcised* and the *uncircumcised*, the *Jew* and the *Gentile*, shall equally feel the stroke of my justice, their transgressions being alike, after their advantages and disadvantages are duly compared. In like manner, *other nations* also were delivered into the hands of Nebuchadnezzar; these he immediately enumerates: *Egypt* and *Edom*, and the *Moabites* and the *Ammonites*, and the *Arabians of the desert*. All these nations were *uncircumcised* in that way which God required that rite to be practised as a sign of his *covenant;* and the Israelites, that did practise it as a sign of that covenant, did not attend to its spiritual meaning, for they were all *uncircumcised in heart*. And it may be remarked, that these people were in general confederated against the Chaldeans.

Verse 26. *All* that are *in the utmost corners*] כל קצוצי פאה *col ketsutsey pheah*. These words have been variously understood. The *Vulgate* translates: Omnes qui attonsi sunt in comam; "All who have their hair cut short." The *Targum*, *Septuagint*, *Syriac*, and *Arabic* have understood it nearly in the same way; and so our margin. Others think that the *insular* or *peninsular* situation of the people is referred to. Dr. *Blayney* thinks the *Arabians* are meant, who dwelt in the great desert, between Mesopotamia and Palestine. I really think our marginal reading should be preferred, as expressing the sense of all the ancient Versions.

CHAPTER X

The Jews, about to be carried into captivity, are here warned against the superstition and idolatry of that country to which they were going. Chaldea was greatly addicted to astrology, and therefore the prophet begins with warning them against it, 1, 2. *He then exposes the absurdity of idolatry in short but elegant satire; in the midst of which he turns, in a beautiful apostrophe, to the one true God, whose adorable attributes repeatedly strike in view, as he goes along, and lead him to contrast his infinite perfections with those despicable inanities which the blinded nations fear,* 3–16. *The prophet again denounces the Divine judgments,* 17, 18; *upon which Jerusalem laments her fate, and supplicates the Divine compassion in her favour,* 19–25.

A. M. cir. 3397
B. C. cir. 607
Ol. XLIII. 2
TarquiniiPrisci,
R. Roman.,
cir. annum 10

HEAR ye the word which the
LORD speaketh unto you, O
house of Israel:
2 Thus saith the LORD, [a]Learn
not the way of the heathen, and be not dismayed at the signs of heaven;
for the heathen are dismayed at
them.
3 For the [b]customs of the people *are* vain: for [c]*one* cutteth a tree out of

[a]Lev. xviii. 3; xx. 23——[b]Heb. *statutes*, or *ordinances*, *are vanity*——[c]Isa. xl. 19, 20; xliv. 9, 10, &c.; xlv. 20

NOTES ON CHAP. X

Verse 1. *Hear ye the word which the Lord speaketh unto you*] Dr. *Dahler* supposes this discourse to have been delivered in the *fourth* year of the reign of *Jehoiakim*. It contains an invective against idolatry; showing its absurdity, and that the Creator alone should be worshipped by all mankind.

Verse 2. *Learn not the way of the heathen*] These words are more particularly addressed to the ten tribes scattered among the heathen by the Assyrians, who carried them away captive; they may also regard those in the land of Israel, who still had the customs of the former heathen settlers before their eyes.

Be not dismayed at the signs of heaven; for the heathen are dismayed] The Chaldeans and Egyptians were notoriously addicated to astrology; and the Israelites here are cautioned against it. The *signs* of the heavens may mean either the *sun*, *moon*, *planets*, and particular *stars* or *constellations;* or the *figures* or *characters* by which they represented these heavenly bodies.

Verse 3. *The customs of the people* are *vain*]

A. M. cir. 3397
B. C. cir. 607
Ol. XLIII. 2
TarquiniiPrisci, R. Roman.,
cir. annum 10

the forest, the work of the hands
of the workman, with the axe.
4 They deck it with silver and
with gold; they [d]fasten it with
nails and with hammers, that it move not.
5 They *are* upright as the palm tree, [e]but
speak not: they must needs be [f]borne, because they cannot go. Be not afraid of them;
for [g]they cannot do evil, neither also *is it* in
them to do good.
6 Forasmuch as *there is* none [h]like unto
thee, O LORD; thou *art* great, and thy name
is great in might.
7 [i]Who would not fear thee, O King of
nations? for [k]to thee doth it appertain: forasmuch as [l]among all the wise *men* of the nations, and in all their kingdoms, *there is* none
like unto thee.

A. M. cir. 3397
B. C. cir. 607
Ol. XLIII. 2
TarquiniiPrisci, R. Roman.,
cir. annum 10

8 But they are [m]altogether
[n]brutish and foolish: the stock
is a doctrine of vanities.
9 Silver spread into plates is
brought from Tarshish, and [o]gold from Uphaz,
the work of the workman, and of the hands of
the founder: [p]blue and purple *is* their clothing: they *are* all [q]the work of cunning *men*.
10 But the LORD *is* the [r]true God, he *is*
[s]the living God, and an [t]everlasting [u]King:
at his wrath the earth shall tremble, and the nations shall not be able to abide his indignation.
11 [v]Thus shall ye say unto them, [w]The
gods that have not made the heavens and the
earth, *even* [x]they shall perish from the earth,
and from under these heavens.
12 He [y]hath made the earth by his power,
he hath [z]established the world by his wisdom,

---

[d]Isa. xli. 7; xlvi. 7——[e]Psa. cxv. 5; cxxxv. 16; Hab. ii. 19; 1 Cor. xii. 2——[f]Psa. cxv. 7; Isa. xlvi. 1, 7 [g]Isa. xli. 23——[h]Exod. xv. 11; Psa. lxxxvi. 8, 10 [i]Rev. xv. 4——[k]Or, *it liketh thee*——[l]Psa. lxxxix. 6 [m]Heb. *in one*, or *at once*——[n]Psa. cxv. 8; Isa. xli. 29; Hab. ii. 18; Zech. x. 2; Rom. i. 21, 22

[o]Dan. x. 5——[p]Bar. vi. 12, 72——[q]Psa. cxv. 4 [r]Heb. *God of truth;* Psa. xxxi. 5——[s]1 Tim. vi. 17 [t]Heb. *king of eternity*——[u]Psa. x. 16——[v]In the Chaldean language——[w]See Psa. xcvi. 5——[x]Ver. 15; Isa. ii. 18; Zech. xiii. 2——[y]Gen. i. 1, 6, 9; Psa. cxxxvi. 5, 6; chap. li. 15, &c.——[z]Psa. xciii. 1

חקות *chukkoth;* the statutes and principles of the science are vain, empty, and illusory. They are founded in nonsense, ignorance, idolatry, and folly.

One *cutteth a tree out of the forest*] See the notes on Isa. xl. 19, and xliv. 9, &c., which are all parallel places and where this conduct is strongly ridiculed.

Verse 5. *They* are *upright as the palm tree*] As straight and as stiff as the trees out of which they are hewn.

Verse 7. *Who would not fear thee*] Who would not *worship* thee as the Author and Giver of all good? The *fear of God* is often taken for the whole of true *religion*.

Among all the wise men *of the nation*] Not even the wisest and most cultivated of the nations have ever found out any one equal to thee; but so exalted and holy art thou, that in all their wisdom and research they have never been able to find out the *true God*.

Verse 8. *The stock* is *a doctrine of vanities.*] Dr. *Blayney* translates,—"The wood itself is a rebuker of vanities." The very tree out of which the god is hewn demonstrates the vanity and folly of the idolaters; for, can all the art of man make out of a log of wood an animate and intelligent being?

Verse 9. *Brought from Tarshish*] Some suppose this to be *Tartessus* in *Spain*, from which the Phœnicians brought much silver. *Uphaz*, *Calmet* thinks to be the river *Pison;* some think *Ophir* is intended.

Blue and purple is *their clothing*] These were the most precious dyes; very rare, and of high price.

Verse 10. *But the Lord*] The original word should be preserved, however we agree to pronounce it: יהוה *Yehovah is the true God.* He is without beginning, and without end. This is *true* of no being else.

He is the living God] His being is underived; and he gives *life* to all. He is the very *Fountain* whence all *life* is derived.

And an everlasting king] As he has *made*, so he *governs*, all things. His *sway* is felt both in the heavens and in the earth.

At his wrath the earth shall tremble] All storms, tempests, tornadoes, and earthquakes are the effects of his power; and when the *nations* are destroyed, or turned upside down, it is the effect of his displeasure.

Verse 11. *Thus shall ye say unto them*] This is the message you shall deliver to the Chaldean idolaters.

The gods that have not made the heavens and the earth, even *they shall perish*] Both they and their worshippers shall be destroyed; and idolatry shall *finally* be destroyed from the earth; and the heavens shall look no more on so great an abomination. It is suffered for a *while:* but in the *end* shall be destroyed. This verse is written in a sort of *Hebræo-Syriaco-Chaldee;* such a dialect as I suppose was spoken at that time in Babylon, or during the captivity. As it is a message to the Babylonians, therefore, it is given in their own language. The *Chaldee* makes it the beginning of the copy of the epistle which the Prophet Jeremiah sent to the rest of the elders of the captivity who were in Babylon. All the ancient Versions acknowledge this verse; and it is found in all MSS. hitherto collated, except one of Dr. *Kennicott's* numbered 526; and he has included it between lines, as doubting its authenticity. Dr. *Blayney* supposes that some public teacher during the captivity, deducing it by direct inference from the prophet's words, had it inserted in the margin, and perhaps usually read together with this section, in the assemblies of the people, in order that they might have their answer always ready, whenever they were mo-

A. M. cir. 3397
B. C. cir. 607
Ol. XLIII. 2
TarquiniiPrisci,
R. Roman.,
cir. annum 10

and [a]hath stretched out the heavens by his discretion.
13 [b]When he uttereth his
voice, *there is* a [c]multitude of
waters in the heavens, and [d]he causeth the
vapours to ascend from the ends of the earth;
he maketh lightnings [e]with rain, and bringeth
forth the wind out of his treasures.
14 [f]Every man [g]is [h]brutish in *his* knowledge: [i]every founder is confounded by the
graven image: [k]for his molten image *is* falsehood, and *there is* no breath in them.
15 They *are* vanity, *and* the
work of errors: in the time of
their visitation [l]they shall perish.
16 [m]The Portion of Jacob *is*
not like them: for he *is* the former of all
things; and [n]Israel *is* the rod of his inheritance: [o]The LORD of hosts *is* his name.

A. M. cir. 3404
B. C. cir. 600
Ol. cir. XLV. 1
TarquiniiPrisci,
R. Roman.,
cir. annum 17

17 [p]Gather up thy wares out
of the land, O [q]inhabitant of the
fortress.
18 For thus saith the LORD,
Behold, I will [r]sling out the inhabitants of

---

[a]Job ix. 8; Psa. civ. 2; Isa. xl. 22——[b]Job xxxviii. 34——[c]Or, *noise*——[d]Psa. cxxxv. 7——[e]Or, *for rain* [f]Chap. li. 17, 18——[g]Or, *is more brutish than to know* [h]Prov. xxx. 2——[i]Isa. xlii. 17; xliv. 11; xlv. 16 [k]Hab. ii. 18——[l]Verse 11——[m]Psalm xvi. 5; lxxiii. 26; cxix. 57; chap. li. 19; Lamentations iii. 24——[n]Deuteronomy xxxii. 9; Psalm lxxiv. 2——[o]Isaiah xlvii. 4; li. 15; liv. 5——chap. xxxi. 35; xxxii. 18; l. 34——[p]See chap. vi. 1; Ezek. xii. 3, &c.——[q]Heb. *inhabitress* [r]1 Sam. xxv. 29; chap. xvi. 18

---

lested on the point of religion, or importuned to join the idolatrous worship of the Chaldeans.

Dahler has left it entirely out of the text, and introduces it in a note thus:—"After ver. 10 the Hebrew text is interrupted by a verse written in the Chaldean or Babylonish tongue. It is thus expressed:—

Ye shall say unto them, Let the gods perish!
Who have not made the heavens and the earth.
Let them be banished from above the earth,
and from under the heavens.

This verse can be considered only as a foreign insertion, not only on account of the difference of the language, but also because it interrupts the natural course of the ideas, and of the connexion of the *tenth* and *twelfth* verses."

As a curiosity I shall insert it in *Hebrew*, which the reader may compare with the *Chaldee* text, which I also subjoin.

כזאת תאמרו להם האלהים אשר לא עשו השמים והארץ יאבדו מן הארץ ומן תחת השמים אלה *cazoth tomeru lahem; haelohim asher lo asu hashshamayim vehaarets, yobedu min haarets, umin tachath hashshamayim elleh.* כדנא תאמרון להון אלהיא די שמיא וארקא לא עבדו יאבדו מארעא ומן תחות שמיא אלה: *kidna temerun lehon; elahaiya di shemaiya vearka la abadu, yebadu meara umin techoth shemaiya elleh.*

The *Hebrew* is the translation of *Leusden;* the *Chaldee* is that of the common text. Had not *all the ancient Versions* acknowledged it, I also, principally on account of the *strangeness* of the language, as being neither *Chaldee* nor *Syriac*, should have doubted its authenticity.

Verse 13. *When he uttereth his voice, there is a multitude of waters*] This is a plain allusion to a storm of thunder and lightning, and the abundance of rain which is the consequence. Water is composed of two *gases, hydrogen* and *oxygen:* the electric or galvanic spark decomposes them, and they become *air;* when recomposed, they form *water.* The lightning acts upon the *hydrogen* and *oxygen*, which are found in the atmospheric air: they are decomposed, and water or rain is the consequence; which, being heavier than the air falls down in the form of rain.

This verse and the *three* following are the same in substance, and nearly in words, as chap. li. 16, and following.

Verse 14. *Every man is brutish*] נבער *nibar*, is a boor, acts as a brute, who may suppose that a *stock* of a *tree*, formed *like a man*, may be an intellectual being; and therefore shuns the *form* as though it had *life.* See Isa. xliv. 10, 11. Of which verses, by the way, Dr. *Blayney* gives the following version to correct that of Bishop *Lowth:*—

Verse 10. Who hath formed a god?
Or set up a graven image that profiteth not?
11. Behold, all that are connected with it shall be ashamed,
And the artificers, they above all men!
They shall assemble all of them; they shall stand forth;
They shall fear; they shall be ashamed at the same time.

"That is, while they stand before the image they have set up, and worship it with a *religious dread*, the glaring absurdity of their conduct shall lead to their *shame* and *disgrace.*" With due deference to this learned man, I think this interpretation too refined.

Verse 16. *The Portion of Jacob* is *not like them*] Every nation had its tutelary god; this was its *portion;* in reference to this God says Deut. iv. 19, "He has divided the sun, moon, and stars, to all the nations under the heaven." And the Lord had taken the Israelites to be his *portion;* for "the Lord's portion is his people," Deut. xxxii. 9, and David says, "The Lord is the portion of mine inheritance," Psa. xvi. 5; cxix. 57. And hence Isaiah terms the *smooth stones of the brook*, to which Divine honours were paid, the *portion* of those idolaters, chap. lvii. 6. But in the text he says, "The PORTION, i. e., the God of Jacob is not like them; for he is the former of all things," and they are formed by their foolish worshippers.

Verse 17. *Gather up thy wares*] Pack up your goods, or what necessaries of life your enemies will permit you to carry away; for,

Verse 18. *I will sling out the inhabitants of the land*] I will *project* you with *violence* from your country. I will send you all into captivity. This discourse, from ver. 17, is supposed to have

A. M. cir. 3404 B. C. cir. 600 Ol. cir. XLV. 1 TarquiniiPrisci, R. Roman., cir. annum 17

the land at this once, and will distress them, [s]that they may find *it so.*

19 [t]Wo is me for my hurt! my wound is grievous: but I said, [u]Truly this *is* a grief, and [v]I must bear it.

20 [w]My tabernacle is spoiled, and all my cords are broken: my children are gone forth of me, and they *are* not: *there is* none to stretch forth my tent any more, and to set up my curtains.

21 For the pastors are become brutish, and have not sought the LORD: therefore they shall not prosper, and all their flocks shall be scattered.

22 Behold, the noise of the bruit is come, and a great commotion out of the [x]north country, to make the cities of Judah desolate, *and* a [y]den of dragons.

23 O LORD, I know that the [z]way of man *is* not in himself: *it is* not in man that walketh to direct his steps.

24 O LORD, [a]correct me, but with judgment; not in thine anger, lest thou [b]bring me to nothing.

25 [c]Pour out thy fury upon the heathen [d]that know thee not, and upon the families that call not on thy name: for they have eaten up Jacob, and [e]devoured him, and consumed him, and have made his habitation desolate.

---

[s]Ezek. vi. 10——[t]Chap. iv. 19; viii. 21; ix. 1——[u]Psa. lxxvii. 10——[v]Mic. vii. 9——[w]Chap. iv. 20——[x]Chap. i. 15; iv. 6; v. 15; vi. 22——[y]Chap. ix. 11——[z]Prov. xvi. 1; xx. 24——[a]Psa. vi. 1; xxxviii. 1; chap. xxx. 11——[b]Heb. *diminish me*——[c]Psa. lxxix. 6——[d]Job xviii. 21; 1 Thess. iv. 5; 2 Thess. i. 8——[e]Chap. viii. 16

---

been delivered in the *eleventh year* of Jehoiakim.

Verse 19. *This* is *a grief, and I must bear it.*] Oppressive as it is, I have deserved it, and worse; but even in this *judgment* God remembers *mercy.*

Verse 20. *My tabernacle is spoiled*] The city is taken, and all our villages ruined and desolated.

Verse 21. *The pastors are become brutish*] The king and his counsellors, who, by refusing to pay the promised tribute to Nebuchadnezzar, had kindled a new war.

Verse 22. *The noise of the bruit is come*] How this silly French word *bruit,* which signifies *noise,* got in here, I cannot imagine. The simple translation is this: "The voice of the report! behold, it is come; yea, great commotion from the land of the north; (Chaldea;) to make the cities of Judea a desolation, a habitation of wild beasts." That is, the *report* we had heard of the projected invasion of Judea by Nebuchadnezzar is confirmed. He has entered the land; the Chaldeans are at the doors, and the total desolation of Judea is their sole object.

Verse 23. *O Lord, I know that the way of man* is *not in himself*] I will not pretend to dispute with thee; thou dost every thing wisely and justly; we have sinned, and thou hast a right to punish; and to choose that sort of punishment thou thinkest will best answer the ends of justice. We cannot choose; thou hast appointed us to captivity; we must not repine: yet,

Verse 24. *Correct me, but with judgment*] Let not the punishment be to the uttermost of the demerit of the offence; else *we shall be brought to nothing*—totally and irrecoverably ruined.

Verse 25. *Pour out thy fury upon the heathen*] Even those who are now the executors of thy justice upon us will, in their turn, feel its scourge; for if judgment begins at us, who have been called *thy house* and *thy people,* shall they who have *not acknowledged thee* escape? It is impossible. The families and tribes which invoke thee not shall have thy fury poured out upon them, and especially they who "have eaten up Jacob and consumed him, and have made his habitation desolate." This was fulfilled in the *Chaldeans.* Nebuchadnezzar was punished with madness, his son was slain in his revels, and the city was taken and sacked by Cyrus; and the Babylonish empire was finally destroyed! This verse has been often quoted against those ungodly families who set not up the worship of God in their houses. These are spiritual *Chaldeans,* worse indeed than the Chaldeans ever were: they acknowledge God and his Christ; and yet neither worship nor serve him. How can that family expect the blessing of God, where the worship of God is not daily performed? No wonder their servants are wicked, their children profligate, and their goods cursed! What an awful reckoning shall such heads of families have with the Judge in the great day, who have refused to petition for that mercy which they might have had for the asking.

CHAPTER XI

The prophet proclaims the tenor of God's covenant with the Jews of old, 1–5; *and then reproves them for their hereditary disobedience,* 6–19. *In consequence of this the Almighty is introduced, declaring he will show them no pity,* 11–13; *forbidding Jeremiah to intercede,* 14; *rejecting their sacrifices,* 15; *and in a word, condemning this fair but unfruitful tree to the fire,* 16, 17. *In what remains of the chapter the prophet predicts evil to his neighbours of Anathoth, who had conspired against him,* 18–23. *"Let us," said they, "destroy this tree, with the fruit thereof," &c., alluding to what Jeremiah had said in the sixteenth verse.*

A. M. cir. 3406
B. C. cir. 598
Ol. cir. XLV. 3
TarquiniiPrisci,
R. Roman.,
cir. annum 19

THE word that came to Jeremiah from the LORD, saying,
2 Hear ye the words of this
covenant, and speak unto the
men of Judah, and to the inhabitants of Jerusalem;
3 And say thou unto them, Thus saith the
LORD God of Israel; [a]Cursed *be* the man
that obeyeth not the words of this covenant,
4 Which I commanded your fathers in the
day *that* I brought them forth out of the land
of Egypt, [b]from the iron furnace, saying,
[c]Obey my voice, and do them, according to
all which I command you: so shall ye be my
people, and I will be your God:
5 That I may perform the [d]oath which I
have sworn unto your fathers, to give them a
land flowing with milk and honey, as *it is*
this day. Then answered I, and said, [e]So be
it, O LORD.
6 Then the LORD said unto me, Proclaim
all these words in the cities of Judah, and in
the streets of Jerusalem, saying, Hear ye the
words of this covenant, [f]and do them.
7 For I earnestly protested unto your fathers
in the day *that* I brought them up out of the
land of Egypt, *even* unto this day, [g]rising
early and protesting, saying, Obey my voice.
8 [h]Yet they obeyed not, nor inclined their
ear, but [i]walked every one in the [k]imagina-
tion of their evil heart: therefore
I will bring upon them all the
words of this covenant, which I
commanded *them* to do; but they
did *them* not.

A. M. cir. 3406
B. C. cir. 598
Ol. cir. XLV. 3
TarquiniiPrisci,
R. Roman.,
cir. annum 19

9 And the LORD said unto me, [l]A conspiracy
is found among the men of Judah, and among
the inhabitants of Jerusalem.
10 They are turned back to [m]the iniquities
of their forefathers, which refused to hear my
words; and they went after other gods to
serve them: the house of Israel and the house
of Judah have broken my covenant which I
made with their fathers.
11 Therefore thus saith the LORD, Behold,
I will bring evil upon them, which they shall
not be able [n]to escape; and [o]though they shall
cry unto me, I will not hearken unto them.
12 Then shall the cities of Judah and inhabitants of Jerusalem go, and [p]cry unto the
gods unto whom they offer incense: but they
shall not save them at all in the time of their
[q]trouble.
13 For *according to* the number of thy
[r]cities were thy gods, O Judah; and *according to* the number of the streets of Jerusalem
have ye set up altars to *that* [s]shameful thing,
even altars to burn incense unto Baal.
14 Therefore [t]pray not thou for this people,
neither lift up a cry or prayer for them: for

[a]Deut. xxvii. 26; Gal. iii. 10——[b]Deut. iv. 20; 1 Kings viii. 51——[c]Lev. xxvi. 3, 12; chap. vii. 23——[d]Deut. vii. 12, 13; Psa. cv. 9, 10——[e]Heb. *Amen;* Deut. xxvii. 15-26——[f]Rom. ii. 13; James i. 22——[g]Chap. vii. 13, 25; xxxv. 15——[h]Chap. vii. 26——[i]Chap. iii. 17; vii. 24; ix. 14——[k]Or, *stubbornness*

[l]Ezek. xxii. 25; Hos. vi. 9——[m]Ezek. xx. 18——[n]Heb. *to go forth of*——[o]Psa. xviii. 41; Prov. i. 28; Isa. i. 15; chap. xiv. 12; Ezek. viii. 18; Mic. iii. 4; Zech. vii. 13——[p]Deut. xxxii. 37, 38——[q]Heb. *evil*——[r]Chap. ii. 28——[s]Heb. *shame;* chap. iii. 24; Hos. ix. 10——[t]Exod. xxxii. 10; chap. vii. 16; xiv. 11; 1 John v. 16

NOTES ON CHAP. XI

Verse 1. *The word that came to Jeremiah*] This discourse is supposed to have been delivered in the first year of the reign of Zedekiah. See *Dahler.*

Verse 2. *Hear ye the words of this covenant*] It is possible that the prophet caused the words of the covenant made with their fathers in the desert (Exod. xxiv. 4-8) to be read to them on this occasion; or, at least, the *blessings and the cursings* which Moses caused to be pronounced to the people as soon as they had set foot in Canaan, Deut. xxvii., xxviii.

Verse 3. *Cursed* be *the man that obeyeth not*] After the reading, the prophet appears to *sum up* the things contained in what was read to them; as if he had said, "Ye hear what the Lord saith unto you: remember, the sum of it is this: The man is cursed who obeyeth not; and he is blessed who obeys. From these declarations God will not depart."

Verse 5. *So be it, O Lord*] Let thy promises be fulfilled; and let the incorrigible beware of thy threatenings!

Verse 6. *Proclaim all these words*] Let the same covenant, with the blessings and cursings, be read in every city of Judah, and in all the streets of Jerusalem, that all the people may know their duty, their privileges, and their danger.

Verse 9. *A conspiracy is found*] They were all *fratres conjurati,* sworn brothers, determined to cast off the Divine yoke, and no longer to have God to reign over them.

Verse 10. *They are turned back to the iniquities of their forefathers*] A great reformation had taken place under the reign of Josiah, and the public worship of idols had been abolished, and most of the high places destroyed; but under the reign of his son and his successors, they had *turned back again* to idolatry, and were become worse than ever. It required a *captivity* to cure them of this propensity; and God sent one: after that, there was no idolatry among the Jews.

Verse 12. *Go, and cry unto the gods*] See chap. ii. 28.

Verse 14. *Therefore pray not thou for this people*] I am determined to give them up into

A. M. cir. 3406 B. C. cir. 598 Ol. cir. XLV. 3 TarquiniiPrisci, R. Roman., cir. annum 19

I will not hear *them* in the time
that they cry unto me for their
[u]trouble.
15 [v]What [w]hath my beloved
to do in mine house, *seeing* she hath [x]wrought
lewdness with many, and [y]the holy flesh is
passed from thee? [z]when thou doest evil,
then thou [a]rejoicest.
16 The LORD called thy name, [b]A green
olive tree, fair, *and* of goodly fruit: with the
noise of a great tumult he hath kindled fire
upon it, and the branches of it are broken.
17 For the LORD of hosts, [c]that planted
thee, hath pronounced evil against thee, for
the evil of the house of Israel and of the house
of Judah, which they have done against themselves
to provoke me to anger in offering
incense unto Baal.
18 And the LORD hath given me knowledge
of it, and I know *it:* then thou showedst me
their doings.
19 But I *was* like a lamb *or* an ox *that* is
brought to the slaughter; and
I knew not that [d]they had devised
devices against me, *saying,*
Let us destroy [e]the tree with the
fruit thereof, [f]and let us cut him off from
[g]the land of the living, that his name may be
no more remembered.
20 But, O LORD of hosts, that judgest righteously,
that [h]triest the reins and the heart, let
me see thy vengeance on them: for unto thee
have I revealed my cause.
21 Therefore thus saith the LORD of the
men of Anathoth, [i]that seek thy life, saying,
[k]Prophesy not in the name of the LORD, that
thou die not by our hand:
22 Therefore thus saith the LORD of hosts,
Behold, I will [l]punish them: the young men
shall die by the sword; their sons and their
daughters shall die by famine:
23 And there shall be no remnant of them:
for I will bring evil upon the men of Anathoth,
even [m]the year of their visitation.

---

[u]Heb. *evil*——[v]Psa. l. 16; Isa. i. 11, &c.——[w]Heb. *What is to my beloved in my house?*——[x]Ezek. xvi. 25, &c.——[y]Hag. ii. 12, 13, 14; Titus i. 15——[z]Or, *when thy evil is*——[a]Prov. ii. 14——[b]Psa. lii. 8; Rom. xi. 17 [c]Isa. v. 2; chap. ii. 21——[d]Chap. xviii. 18——[e]Heb. *the stalk with his bread*

[f]Psa. lxxxiii. 4——[g]Psa. xxvii. 13; cxvi. 9; cxlii. 5 [h]1 Sam. xvi. 7; 1 Chron. xxviii. 9; Psa. vii. 9; chap. xvii. 10; xx. 12; Rev. ii. 23——[i]Chap. xii. 5, 6——[k]Isa. xxx. 10; Amos ii. 12; vii. 13, 16; Mic. ii. 6——[l]Heb. *visit upon*——[m]Chap. xxiii. 12; xlvi. 21; xlviii. 44; l. 27; Luke xix. 44

---

the hands of their enemies; I will neither hear thy intercession, nor regard their prayers. Their measure is *full.*

Verse 15. *What hath my beloved to do in mine house*] This has been supposed to refer to *Abraham, Moses,* or such eminent servants of God, whose intercession was very powerful. Were even *they* to appear as intercessors, their prayer should not be regarded. Others think that this is an *endearing expression,* which properly belonged to the Israelites. When God took them into covenant with himself, they were *espoused* to him, and therefore his *beloved;* but now that they have forsaken him, and *joined themselves to another,* what have they to do with his house or its ordinances, which they wish now to frequent with *vows* and *sacrifices,* when they see the evil fast coming upon them? This is probably the sense of this very obscure passage. Dr. *Blayney* translates, "What hath my beloved to do in my house whilst she practiseth wickedness? Shall vows and holy flesh (sacrifices) be allowed to come from thee? When thou art malignant, shalt thou rejoice?"

Verse 16. *The Lord called thy name, A green olive tree*] That is, he made thee like a green olive—fair, flourishing, and fruitful; but thou art degenerated, and God hath given the Chaldeans permission to burn thee up.

Verse 18. *The Lord hath given me knowledge of it*] The men of Anathoth had conspired against his life, because he reproved them for their sins, and denounced the judgments of God against them. Of this God had given him a secret warning, that he might be on his guard.

Verse 19. *I* was *like a lamb* or *an ox*] *Dahler* translates, "I was like a fattened lamb that is led to the slaughter." *Blayney,* "I was like a tame lamb that is led to slaughter." The word אלוף *alluph,* which we translate *ox,* is taken by both as an *adjective,* qualifying the noun כבש *kebes, a lamb.* It may probably signify a lamb brought up in the house—fed at home, (אלוף *alluph,*) instructed or nourished at home; perfectly innocent and unsuspecting, while leading to the slaughter. This meaning the word will bear in Arabic, for الف *alaf* signifies *accustomed, familiar,* (to or with any person or thing;) a *companion,* a *comrade,* an *intimate friend.* I therefore think that ככבש אלוף *kechebes alluph* signifies, *like the familiar lamb*—the lamb *bred up in the house,* in a state of *friendship* with the family. The people of Anathoth were Jeremiah's *townsmen;* he was *born* and *bred* among them; they were his *familiar friends;* and now they lay wait for his life! All the *Versions* understood אלוף *alluph* as an epithet of כבש *kebes,* a *chosen, simple, innocent* lamb.

Let us destroy the tree with the fruit] Let us slay the prophet, and his prophecies will come to an end. The *Targum* has, *Let us put mortal poison in his food;* and all the Versions understand it something in the same way.

Verse 20. *Let me see thy vengeance on them*] Rather, *I shall see* (אראה *ereh*) *thy punishment inflicted on them.*

Verse 22. *Behold, I will punish them*] And the punishment is, *Their young men shall die by the sword* of the Chaldeans; and *their sons and daughters shall die by the famine* that shall come on the land through the desolations occasioned by the Chaldean army.

Verse 23. *The year of their visitation.*] This punishment shall come in that year in which I shall visit their iniquities upon them.

CHAPTER XII

This chapter is connected with the foregoing. The prophet expostulates with God concerning the ways of Providence in permitting the wicked to prosper, 1–4. *It is intimated to him that he must endure still greater trials,* 5, *from his false and deceitful brethren,* 6; *but that still heavier judgments awaited the nation for their crimes,* 7–13. *That God, however, would at length have compassion on them; restore them to their land; and turn his judgments against those that oppressed them, if not prevented by their becoming converts to the true religion,* 14–17.

A. M. cir. 3406
B. C. cir. 598
Ol. cir. XLV. 3
TarquiniiPrisci, R. Roman., cir. annum 19

RIGHTEOUS [a]*art* thou, O
LORD, when I plead with
thee: yet [b]let me talk with thee
of *thy* judgments: [c]Wherefore
doth the way of the wicked prosper? *where-*
fore are all they happy that deal very treacherously?
2 Thou hast planted them, yea, they have
taken root: [d]they grow, yea, they bring forth
fruit: [e]thou *art* near in their mouth, and far
from their reins.
3 But thou, O LORD, [f]knowest me: thou
hast seen me, and [g]tried mine heart [h]toward
thee: pull them out like sheep for the slaughter, and prepare them for [i]the day of slaughter.

A. M. cir. 3406
B. C. cir. 598
Ol. cir. XLV. 3
TarquiniiPrisci, R. Roman., cir. annum 19

4 How long shall [k]the land
mourn, and the herbs of every
field wither, [l]for the wickedness of them that dwell therein?
[m]the beasts are consumed, and the birds; because they said, He shall not see our last end.
5 If thou hast run with the footmen, and
they have wearied thee, then how canst thou
contend with horses? and *if* in the land of
peace, *wherein* thou trustedst, *they wearied*
thee, then how wilt thou do in [n]the swelling
of Jordan?
6 For even [o]thy brethren, and the house
of thy father, even they have dealt treacherously with thee; yea, [p]they have called a

---

[a]Psa. li. 4——[b]Or, *let me reason the case with thee*——[c]Job xii. 6; xxi. 7; Psa. xxxvii. 1, 35; lxxiii. 3, &c.; chap. v. 28; Hab. i. 4; Mal. iii. 15——[d]Heb. *they go on*——[e]Isa. xxix. 13; Matt. xv. 8; Mark vii. 6——[f]Psa. xvii. 3; cxxxix. 1——[g]Chap. xi. 20

[h]Heb. *with thee*——[i]James v. 5——[k]Chap. xxiii. 10; Hos. iv. 3——[l]Psa. cvii. 34——[m]Chap. iv. 25; vii. 20; ix. 10; Hos. iv. 3——[n]Josh. iii. 15; 1 Chron. xii. 15; chap. xlix. 19; l. 44——[o]Chap. ix. 4; xi. 19, 21——[p]Or, *they cried after thee fully*

NOTES ON CHAP. XII

Verse 1. *Righteous* art *thou, O Lord, when I plead with thee*] The prophet was grieved at the prosperity of the wicked; and he wonders how, consistently with God's righteousness, vice should often be in affluence, and piety in suffering and poverty. He knows that God is righteous, that every thing is done well; but he wishes to inquire how these apparently unequal and undeserved lots take place. On this subject he wishes to reason with God, that he may receive instruction.

Verse 2. *Thou* art *near in their mouth*] They have no sincerity: they have something of the *form* of religion, but nothing of its *power.*

Verse 3. *But thou, O Lord, knowest me*] I know that the very secrets of my heart are known to thee; and I am glad of it, for *thou knowest that my heart is towards thee*—is upright and sincere.

Verse 4. *How long shall the land mourn*] These hypocrites and open sinners are a curse to the country; *pull them out, Lord,* that the land may be delivered of that which is the cause of its desolation.

Verse 5. *If thou hast run with the footmen*] If the smallest evils to which thou art exposed cause thee to make so many bitter complaints, how wilt thou feel when, in the course of thy prophetic ministry, thou shalt be exposed to much greater, from enemies much more powerful? *Footmen* may here be the symbol of *common evil events; horsemen,* of evils much more terrible. If thou have sunk under small difficulties, what wilt thou do when great ones come?

And if *in the land of peace,* wherein *thou trustedst*] I believe the meaning is this, "If in a country now enjoying peace thou scarcely thinkest thyself in safety, what wilt thou do in the swellings of Jordan? in the time when the enemy, like an overflowing torrent, shall deluge every part of the land?"

The overflowing of Jordan, which generally happened in harvest, drove the lions and other beasts of prey from their coverts among the bushes that lined its banks; who, spreading themselves through the country, made terrible havoc, slaying men, and carrying off the cattle.

Perhaps by *footmen* may be meant the *Philistines, Edomites,* &c., whose armies were composed principally of *infantry;* and by the *horses,* the *Chaldeans,* who had abundance of *cavalry* and chariots in their army. But still the words are *proverbial,* and the above is their meaning.

Verse 6. *For even thy brethren, and the house of thy father*] Thou hast none to depend on but God: even thy brethren will betray thee when they have it in their power.

A. M. cir. 3406
B. C. cir. 598
Ol. cir. XLV. 3
TarquiniiPrisci,
R. Roman.,
cir. annum 19

multitude after thee: [q]believe
them not, though they speak
[r]fair words unto thee.
7 I have forsaken mine house,
I have left mine heritage; I have given [s]the
dearly beloved of my soul into the hand of her
enemies.
8 Mine heritage is unto me as a lion in the
forest; it [t]crieth [u]out against me: therefore
have I hated it.
9 Mine heritage *is* unto me *as* a [v]speckled
bird, the birds round about *are* against her;
come ye, assemble all the beasts of the field,
[w]come [x]to devour.
10 Many [y]pastors have destroyed [z]my
vineyard, they have [a]trodden my portion
under foot, they have made my [b]pleasant portion a desolate wilderness.
11 They have made it desolate, *and being*
desolate [c]it mourneth unto me; the whole
land is made desolate, because
[d]no man layeth *it* to heart.
12 The spoilers are come upon
all high places through the wilderness: for the sword of the LORD shall devour
from the *one* end of the land even to the *other*
end of the land: no flesh shall have peace.
13 [e]They have sown wheat, but shall reap
thorns: they have put themselves to pain,
but shall not profit: and [f]they shall be
ashamed of your revenues because of the
fierce anger of the LORD.

A. M. cir. 3401
B. C. cir. 603
Ol. XLIV. 2
TarquiniiPrisci,
R. Roman.,
cir. annum 14

14 Thus saith the LORD against
all mine evil neighbours, that
[g]touch the inheritance which I
have caused my people Israel to
inherit; Behold, I will [h]pluck them out of
their land, and pluck out the house of Judah
from among them.
15 [i]And it shall come to pass, after that I

[q]Prov. xxvi. 25——[r]Heb. *good things*——[s]Heb. *the love*——[t]Or, *yelleth*——[u]Heb. *giveth out his voice*——[v]Or, *having talons*——[w]Or, *cause them to come*——[x]Isa. lvi. 9; chap. vii. 33——[y]Chap. vi. 3——[z]Isa. v. 1, 5

[a]Isa. lxiii. 18——[b]Heb. *portion of desire*——[c]Ver. 4——[d]Isa. xlii. 25——[e]Lev. xxvi. 16; Deut. xxviii. 38; Mic. vi. 15; Hag. i. 6——[f]Or, *ye*——[g]Zech. ii. 8——[h]Deut. xxx. 3; chap. xxxii. 37——[i]Ezek. xxviii. 25

Believe them not] Do not trust to them; do not commit thyself to them; they are in heart thy enemies, and will betray thee.

Verse 7. *I have forsaken mine house*] I have abandoned my temple.

I have given the dearly beloved of my soul] The people once in covenant with me, and inexpressibly dear to me while faithful.

Into the hand of her enemies.] This was a condition in the covenant I made with them; if they forsook me, they were to be abandoned to their enemies, and cast out of the good land I gave to their fathers.

Verse 8. *Mine heritage is unto me as a lion*] The people are *enraged* against me; they *roar like a furious lion* against their God. They have proceeded to the most open acts of the most flagrant iniquity.

Verse 9. Is *unto me* as *a speckled bird*] A bird of *divers colours.* This is a people who have corrupted the worship of the true God with heathenish rites and ceremonies; therefore, the different nations, (see ver. 10,) whose gods and forms of worship they have adopted, shall come and spoil them. As far as you have followed the surrounding nations in their worship, so far shall they prevail over your state. Every one shall take that which is his own; and wherever he finds his own gods, he will consider the land consecrated to them, and take it as his property, because those very gods are the objects of his worship. The fable of the *daw* and *borrowed plumes* is no mean illustration of this passage.

Dahler translates the whole verse thus:—

Birds of prey! inundate *with blood my heritage.*
Birds of prey! come against her from all sides.
Run together in crowds, ye savage beasts!
Come to the carnage!

Verse 10. *Many pastors have destroyed my vineyard*] My people have had many kinds of enemies which have fed upon their richest pastures; the Philistines, the Moabites, Ammonites, Assyrians, Egyptians, and now the *Chaldeans.*

Verse 11. *No man layeth* it *to heart.*] Notwithstanding all these desolations, from which the land every where mourns, and which are so plainly the consequences of the people's crimes, no man layeth it to heart, or considereth that these are God's judgments; and that the only way to have them removed is to repent of their sins, and turn to God with all their hearts.

Verse 12. *The sword of the Lord shall devour*] It is the sword of the Lord that has devoured, and will devour: this is what no man layeth to heart. They think these things come in the course of events.

Verse 13. *They have sown wheat, but shall reap thorns*] All their projects shall fail: none of their enterprises shall succeed. They are enemies to God, and therefore cannot have his blessing.

Verse 14. *Against all mine evil neighbours*] All the neighbouring nations who have united in desolating Judea shall be desolated in their turn: they also are *wicked,* and they shall be punished. If I make them executors of my justice, it is to them no proof of my approbation. God often uses one wicked nation to scourge another; and afterwards scourges the scourger by some other scourge. In some places a felon who was condemned to be hanged is made the common hangman for the county; he himself being still under the sentence of death,—

Till soon some trusty brother of the trade
Shall do for *him* what *he* has done for *others.*

Verse 15. *I will return, and have compassion*

A. M. cir. 3401
B. C. cir. 603
Ol. XLIV. 2
TarquiniiPrisci,
R. Roman.,
cir. annum 14

have plucked them out I will return, and have compassion on
them, [k]and will bring them
again, every man to his heritage,
and every man to his land.
16 And it shall come to pass, if they will
diligently learn the ways of my people, [l]to
swear by my name, The LORD
liveth; (as they taught my people
to swear by Baal;) then shall they
be [m]built in the midst of my
people.

A. M. cir. 3401
B. C. cir. 603
Ol. cir. XLV. 2
TarquiniiPrisci,
R. Roman.,
cir. annum 14

17 But if they will not [n]obey, I will utterly
pluck up and destroy that nation, saith the LORD.

[k]Amos ix. 14——[l]Chap. iv. 2

[m]Eph. ii. 20, 21; 1 Pet. ii. 5——[n]Isa. lx. 12

on them] This is a promise of restoration from the captivity, and an intimation also that some of their enemies would turn to the true God with them; *learn the ways of his people;* that is, would abjure idols, and take Jehovah for their God; *and be built in the midst of his people*, that is, Jew and Gentile forming *one Church* of the Most High.

Verse 17. *I will—destroy that nation*] Several of them did not obey, and are destroyed. Of the Moabites, Ammonites, and Chaldeans, not one vestige remains. The *sixteenth* verse is supposed to be a promise of the conversion of the Gentiles. See Eph. ii. 13-22.

From the *thirteenth* verse to the end is a different discourse, and *Dahler* supposes it to have been delivered in the *seventh* or *eighth* year of the reign of *Jehoiakim.*

CHAPTER XIII

This chapter contains an entire prophecy. The symbol of the linen girdle, left to rot for a considerable time, was a type of the manner in which the glory of the Jews should be marred during the course of their long captivity, 1–11. *The scene of hiding the girdle being laid near the Euphrates, intimated that the scene of the nation's distress should be Chaldea, which that river waters. The next three verses, by another emblem frequently used to represent the judgments of God, are designed to show that the calamities threatened should be extended to every rank and denomination,* 12–14. *This leads the prophet to a most affectionate exhortation to repentance,* 15–17. *But God, knowing that this happy consequence would not ensue, sends him with an awful message to the royal family particularly, and to the inhabitants of Jerusalem in general, declaring the approaching judgments in plain terms,* 18–27. *The ardent desire for the reformation of Jerusalem, with which the chapter concludes, beautifully displays the compassion and tender mercy of God.*

A. M. cir. 3405
B. C. cir. 599
Ol. cir. XLV. 2
TarquiniiPrisci,
R. Roman.,
cir. annum 18

THUS saith the LORD unto
me, Go and get thee [a]a linen
girdle, and put it upon thy loins,
and put it not in water.
2 So I got a girdle according to the word
of the LORD, and put *it* on my [b]loins.
3 And the word of the LORD came unto
me the second time, saying,
4 Take the girdle that thou
hast got, which *is* upon thy loins,
and arise, go to Euphrates, and
hide it there in a hole of the rock.

A. M. cir. 3405
B. C. cir. 599
Ol. cir. XLV. 2
TarquiniiPrisci,
R. Roman.,
cir. annum 18

5 So I went and hid it by Euphrates, as the
LORD commanded me.
6 And it came to pass after many days, that
the LORD said unto me, Arise, go to Euphrates,

[a]Lev. vi. 10

[b]Isa. xi. 5

NOTES ON CHAP. XIII

Verse 1. *Thus saith the Lord unto me*] This discourse is supposed to have been delivered under the reign of *Jeconiah*, the son and successor of Jehoiakim, who came to the throne in the *eighteenth* year of his age; when the Chaldean generals had encamped near to Jerusalem, but did not besiege it in form till Nebuchadnezzar came up with the great body of the army. In these circumstances the prophet predicts the captivity; and, by a symbolical representation of a rotten girdle, shows the people their totally corrupt state; and by another *of bottles filled with wine*, shows the destruction and madness of their counsels, and the confusion that must ensue.

Go and get thee a linen girdle] This was either a vision, or God simply describes the thing in order that the prophet might use it in the way of illustration.

Put it not in water.] After having worn it let it not be washed, that it may more properly represent the uncleanness of the Israelites; for *they* were represented by the *girdle;* for "as the girdle cleaveth to the loins of a man, so have I caused to cleave unto me the whole house of Israel, and the whole house of Judah." And as a girdle is as well for *ornament* as *use;* God took them *for a name*, and *for a praise*, and *for a glory*, ver. 11.

Verse 4. *Go to Euphrates, and hide it there*] Intending to point out, by this distant place, the *country* into which they were to be carried away captive.

A. M. cir. 3405
B. C. cir. 599
Ol. cir. XLV. 2
TarquiniiPrisci,
R. Roman.,
cir. annum 18

and take the girdle from thence,
which I commanded thee to hide
there.
7 Then I went to Euphrates,
and digged, and took the girdle from the place
where I had hid it; and, behold, the girdle
was marred, it was profitable for nothing.
8 Then the word of the LORD came unto
me, saying,
9 Thus saith the LORD, After this manner
[c]will I mar the pride of Judah, and the great
pride of Jerusalem.
10 This evil people, which refuse to hear my
words, which [d]walk in the [e]imagination of
their heart, and walk after other gods, to serve
them, and to worship them, shall even be as
this girdle, which is good for nothing.
11 For as the girdle cleaveth to the loins of
a man, so have I caused to cleave unto me
the whole house of Israel and the whole house
of Judah, saith the LORD; that [f]they might
be unto me for a people, and [g]for a name, and
for a praise, and for a glory: but they would
not hear.
12 Therefore thou shalt speak unto them
this word; Thus saith the LORD God of Israel, Every bottle shall be filled with wine:
and they shall say unto thee, Do we not certainly know that every bottle
shall be filled with wine?

A. M. cir. 3405
B. C. cir. 599
Ol. cir. XLV. 2
TarquiniiPrisci,
R. Roman.,
cir. annum 18

13 Then shalt thou say unto
them, Thus saith the LORD, Behold, I will fill all the inhabitants of this land,
even the kings that sit upon David's throne, and
the priests, and the prophets, and all the inhabitants of Jerusalem, [h]with drunkenness.
14 And [i]I will dash them [k]one against another, even the fathers and the sons together,
saith the LORD: I will not pity, nor spare,
nor have mercy, [l]but destroy them.
15 Hear ye, and give ear; be not proud: for
the LORD hath spoken.
16 [m]Give glory to the LORD your God, before he cause [n]darkness, and before your feet
stumble upon the dark mountains, and, while
ye [o]look for light, he turn it into [p]the shadow
of death, *and* make *it* gross darkness.
17 But if ye will not hear it, my soul shall
weep in secret places for *your* pride; and
[q]mine eye shall weep sore, and run down
with tears, because the LORD'S flock is carried
away captive.
18 Say unto [r]the king and to the queen,
Humble yourselves, sit down: for your [s]principalities shall come down, *even* the crown of
your glory.

---

[c]Lev. xxvi. 19——[d]Chap. ix. 14; xi. 8; xvi. 12——[e]Or, *stubbornness*——[f]Exod. xix. 5——[g]Chap. xxxiii. 9——[h]Isa. li. 17, 21; lxviii. 6; chap. xxv. 27; li. 7——[i]Psa. ii. 9——[k]Heb. *a man against his brother*

[l]Heb. *from destroying them*——[m]Josh. vii. 19——[n]Isa. v. 30, viii. 22; Amos viii. 9——[o]Isa. lix. 9——[p]Psa. xliv. 19——[q]Chap. ix. 1; xiv. 17; Lam. i. 2, 16; ii. 18——[r]See 2 Kings xxiv. 12; chap. xxii. 26——[s]Or, *head-tires*

Verse 7. *And, behold, the girdle was marred; it was profitable for nothing.*] This symbolically represented the state of the Jews: they were corrupt and abominable; and God, by sending them into captivity, "marred the pride of Judah, and the great pride of Jerusalem," ver. 9.

Verse 12. *Every bottle shall be filled with wine?*] The bottles were made for the purpose of being filled with wine; and it is likely, from the promising appearance of the *season* and the *grapes*, that there was a great likelihood of a *copious vintage;* and this made them say, "Do we not certainly know that every bottle shall be filled with wine? Have we not every prospect that it will be so? Do we need a revelation to inform us of this?"

Verse 13. *Behold, I will fill all the inhabitants of this land—with drunkenness.*] You pretend to take this *literally*, but it is a *symbol. You*, and your *kings*, and *priests*, and *prophets*, are represented by these bottles. The *wine* is God's *wrath* against you, which shall first be shown by *confounding* your deliberations, filling you with foolish plans of defence, causing you from your divided counsels to fall out among yourselves, so that like so many drunken men you shall reel about and jostle each other; defend yourselves without plan, and fight without order, till ye all fall an easy prey into the hands of your enemies. The ancient adage is here fulfilled:—

Quos Deus vult perdere, prius dementat.

"Those whom God determines to destroy, he first renders foolish."

Verse 16. *Give glory to—God*] Confess your sins and turn to him, that these sore evils may be averted.

While ye look for light] While ye expect *prosperity*, he turned it into the *shadow of death*—sent you adversity of the most *distressing* and *ruinous kind.*

Stumble upon the dark mountains] Before you meet with those great *obstacles*, which, having no *light*—no proper understanding in the matter, ye shall be utterly unable to surmount.

Verse 17. *My soul shall weep in secret places*] If you will not hearken to the Lord, there is no remedy: destruction must come; and there is nothing left for me, but to go in secret, and mourn and bewail your wretched lot.

Verse 18. *Say unto the king and to the queen*] Probably Jeconiah and his mother, under whose tutelage, being young when he began to reign, he was left, as is very likely.

A. M. cir. 3405
B. C. cir. 599
Ol. cir. XLV. 2
TarquiniiPrisci,
R. Roman.,
cir. annum 18

19 The cities of the south shall be shut up, and none shall open *them;* Judah shall be carried away captive all of it, it shall be wholly carried away captive.

20 Lift up your eyes, and behold them [t]that come from the north: where *is* the flock *that* was given thee, thy beautiful flock?

21 What wilt thou say when he shall [u]punish thee? for thou hast taught them *to be* captains, *and* as chief over thee: shall not [v]sorrows take thee, as a woman in travail?

22 And if thou say in thine heart, [w]Wherefore come these things upon me? For the greatness of thine iniquity are [x]thy skirts discovered, *and* thy heels [y]made bare.

23 Can the Ethiopian change his skin, or the leopard his spots? *then* may ye also do good, that are [z]accustomed to do evil.

A. M. cir. 3405
B. C. cir. 599
Ol. XLIII. 4
TarquiniiPrisci,
R. Roman.,
cir. annum 18

24 Therefore will I scatter them [a]as the stubble that passeth away by the wind of the wilderness.

25 [b]This *is* thy lot, the portion of thy measures from me, saith the LORD; because thou hast [c]forgotten me, and trusted in [d]falsehood.

26 Therefore [e]will I discover thy skirts upon thy face, that thy shame may appear.

27 I have seen thine adulteries, and thy [f]neighings, the lewdness of thy whoredom, *and* thine abominations [g]on the hills in the fields. Wo unto thee, O Jerusalem! wilt thou not be made clean? [h]when *shall it* once *be?*

[t]Ch. vi. 22——[u]Heb. *visit upon*——[v]Ch. vi. 24——[w]Ch. v. 19; xvi. 10——[x]Isa. iii. 17; xlvii. 2, 3; ver. 26; Ezek. xvi. 37, 38, 39; Nah. iii. 5——[y]Or, *shall be violently taken away*——[z]Heb. *taught*——[a]Psa. i. 4; Hos. xiii. 3

[b]Job xx. 29; Psa. xi. 6——[c]Psa. l. 22; Isa. lxv. 11; chap. xxiii. 27——[d]Chap. x. 14——[e]Ver. 22; Lam. i. 8; Ezek. xvi. 37; xxiii. 29; Hos. ii. 10——[f]Chap. v. 8——[g]Isa. lxv. 7; chap. ii. 20; iii. 2, 6; Ezek. vi. 13——[h]Heb. *after when yet?*

Sit down] Show that ye have *humbled* yourselves; for your state will be destroyed, and your glorious crown taken from your heads.

Verse 19. *The cities of the south shall be shut up*] Not only the cities of the *north*, the quarter at which the Chaldeans entered, but the cities of the *south* also; for he shall proceed from one extremity of the land to the other, spreading devastation every where, and carrying off the inhabitants.

Verse 20. *Where* is *the flock—thy beautiful flock?*] Jerusalem is addressed. Where are the prosperous multitudes of men, women, and children? Alas! are they not driven before the Babylonians, who have taken them captive?

Verse 21. *Thou hast taught them* to be *captains*, and *as chief over thee*] This is said of their enemies, whether Assyrians or Chaldeans: for ever since Ahaz submitted himself to the king of Assyria, the kings of Judah never regained their *independence*. Their enemies were thus taught to be their lords and masters.

Verse 22. *Are thy skirts discovered*] Thy defenceless state is every where known; thou art not only *weak*, but ignominiously so. It is thy *scandal* to be in so depressed a condition; thou art lower than the basest of thy adversaries, and thou art so because of thy sin.

Verse 23. *Can the Ethiopian change his skin*] Can a *black*, at his own pleasure, change the *colour* of his *skin?* Can the *leopard* at will change the *variety* of his *spots?* These things are natural to them, and they cannot be altered; so sin, and especially your attachment to idolatry, is become a *second nature;* and we may as well expect the Ethiopian to change his skin, and the leopard his spots, *as you to do good, who have been accustomed to do evil.* It is a matter of the utmost difficulty to get a sinner, deeply rooted in vicious habits, brought to the knowledge of himself and God. But the expression does not imply that the thing is as impossible in a *moral* as it is in a *natural* sense: it only shows that it is *extremely difficult*, and not to be often expected; and a thousand matters of fact prove the truth of this. But still, what is impossible to man is possible to God. See on ver. 27.

Verse 24. *The wind of the wilderness.*] Some strong tempestuous wind, proverbially severe, coming from the desert to the south of Judea.

Verse 25. *Trusted in falsehood.*] In *idols*, and in *lying prophets.*

Verse 26. *Therefore will I discover thy skirts upon thy face*] It was the custom to punish lewd women by stripping them naked, and exposing them to public view; or by throwing their clothes over their heads, as here intimated. Was this the way to correct the evil?

Verse 27. *I have seen thine adulteries*] Thy *idolatries* of different kinds, practised in various ways; no doubt often accompanied with gross debauchery.

Wo unto thee, O Jerusalem! wilt thou not be made clean?] We see from this, that though the thing was difficult, yet it was not *impossible*, for these *Ethiopians* to change their *skin*, for these *leopards* to change their *spots.* It was only their obstinate refusal of the grace of God that rendered it impossible. Man cannot change himself; but he may pray to God to do it, and come to him through Christ, that he *may* do it. To enable him to pray and believe, the power is still at hand. If he will not use it, he must perish.

CHAPTER XIV

This chapter begins with foretelling a drought that should greatly distress the land of Judea, the effects of which are described in a most pathetic manner, 1–6. *The prophet then, in the people's name, makes a confession of sins, and supplication for pardon,* 7–9. *But God declares his purpose to punish, forbidding Jeremiah to pray for the people,* 10–12. *False prophets are then complained of, and threatened with destruction, as are also those who attend to them,* 13–16. *The prophet, therefore, bewails their misery,* 17, 18; *and though he had just now been forbidden to intercede for them, yet, like a tender pastor, who could not cease to be concerned for their welfare, he falls on the happy expedient of introducing themselves as supplicating in their own name that mercy which he was not allowed to ask in his,* 19–22.

A. M. cir. 3399
B. C. cir. 605
Ol. XLIII. 4
TarquiniiPrisci,
R. Roman.,
cir. annum 12

THE word of the LORD that came to Jeremiah concerning [a]the dearth.

2 Judah mourneth, and [b]the gates thereof languish; they are [c]black unto the ground; and [d]the cry of Jerusalem is gone up.

3 And their nobles have sent their little ones to the waters: they came to the pits, *and* found no water; they returned with their vessels empty; they were [e]ashamed and confounded, [f]and covered their heads.

4 Because the ground is chapt, for there was no rain in the earth, the ploughmen were ashamed, they covered their heads.

A. M. cir. 3399
B. C. cir. 605
Ol. XVIII. 4
TarquiniiPrisci,
R. Roman.,
cir. annum 12

5 Yea, the hind also calved in the field, and forsook *it,* because there was no grass.

6 And [g]the wild asses did stand in the high places, they snuffed up the wind like dragons; their eyes did fail, because *there was* no grass.

7 O LORD, though our iniquities testify against us, do thou *it* [h]for thy name's sake: for our backslidings are many; we have sinned against thee.

8 [i]O the hope of Israel, the Saviour thereof in time of trouble, why shouldest thou be as a stranger in the land, and as a way-faring man *that* turneth aside to tarry for a night?

[a]Heb. *the words of the dearths,* or *restraints*——[b]Isa. iii. 26——[c]Chap. viii. 21——[d]See 1 Sam. v. 12

[e]Psa. xl. 14——[f]2 Sam. xv. 30——[g]Chap. ii. 24
[h]Psa. xxv. 11——[i]Chap. xvii. 13

NOTES ON CHAP. XIV

Verse 1. *The word—that came—concerning the dearth.*] This discourse is supposed to have been delivered, after the *fourth* year of Jehoiakim. *Concerning the dearth.* We have no historic record of any dearth that may fall in with the time of this prophecy, and perhaps it does not refer to any particular dearth: but this was a calamity to which Judea was very liable. They had ordinarily very dry summers, for scarcely any rain fell from *April* to the middle of *October;* and during much of this time, the rivers were generally either very low or entirely dry. They kept the rain of the winter in tanks and reservoirs; and if little fell in winter, a dearth was unavoidable. See an account of a dearth in the time of Elijah, 1 Kings xviii. 5, through which almost all the cattle were lost.

Verse 2. *The gates thereof languish*] The *gates* being the places of public resort, they are put here for the *people.*

They are black unto the ground] Covered from head to foot with a black garment, the emblem of sorrow and calamity.

Verse 3. *Their nobles have sent their little ones*] So general was this calamity, that the servants no longer attended to their lords, but every one was interested alone for himself; and the *nobles* of the land were obliged to employ their *own children* to scour the land, to see if any water could be found in the tanks or the pits. In the dearth in the time of Elijah, Ahab the king, and Obadiah his counsellor, were obliged to traverse the land *themselves,* in order to find out water to keep their cattle alive. This and the three following verses give a lively but distressing picture of this dearth and its effects.

Verse 4. *The ground is chapt*] The cracks in the earth before the descent of the rains are in some places a cubit wide, and deep enough to receive the greater part of a human body.

Verse 6. *Snuffed up the wind like dragons*] תנים *tannim* here probably means the *hippopotamus,* who, after feeding under the water, is obliged to come to the surface in order to take in fresh draughts of air; or it may mean the *wild asses.*

Verse 7. *O Lord, though our iniquities testify against us*] We deeply acknowledge that we have sinned, and deserve nothing but death. Yet *act for thy name's sake*—work in our behalf, that we perish not.

Verse 8. *O the hope of Israel*] O thou who art the only object of the *hope* of this people.

The Saviour thereof in time of trouble] Who hast never yet abandoned them that seek thee.

Why shouldest thou be as a stranger in the land] As one who has no interest in the prosperity and safety of the country.

And as a way-faring man] A traveller on his journey.

That *turneth aside to tarry for a night?*] Who stays the shortest time he can; and takes up his lodging in a *tent* or *caravanserai,* for the dead of the night, that he may pursue his journey by break of day. Instead of *dwelling among us,* thou hast scarcely paid the most transient visit to thy land. O come once more, and dwell among us.

A. M. cir. 3399
B. C. cir. 605
Ol. XLIII. 4
TarquiniiPrisci,
R. Roman.,
cir. annum 12

9 Why shouldest thou be as a man astonied, as a mighty man [k]*that* cannot save? yet thou, O LORD, [l]*art* in the midst of us, and [m]we are called by thy name; leave us not.

10 Thus saith the LORD unto this people, [n]Thus have they loved to wander, they have not refrained their feet, therefore the LORD doth not accept them; [o]he will now remember their iniquity, and visit their sins.

11 Then said the LORD unto me, [p]Pray not for this people for *their* good.

12 [q]When they fast, I will not hear their cry; and [r]when they offer burnt-offering and an oblation, I will not accept them: but [s]I will consume them by the sword, and by the famine, and by the pestilence.

13 [t]Then said I, Ah, Lord GOD! behold, the prophets say unto them, Ye shall not see the sword, neither shall ye have famine; but I will give you [u]assured peace in this place.

14 Then the LORD said unto me, [v]The prophets prophesy lies in my name: [w]I sent them not, neither have I commanded them, neither spake unto them: they prophesy unto you a false vision and divination, and a thing of nought, and the deceit of their heart.

15 Therefore thus saith the LORD concerning the prophets that prophesy in my name, and I sent them not, [x]yet they say, Sword and famine shall not be in this land; By sword and famine shall those prophets be consumed.

16 And the people to whom they prophesy shall be cast out in the streets of Jerusalem because of the famine and the sword; [y]and they shall have none to bury them, them, their wives, nor their sons, nor their daughters: for I will pour their wickedness upon them.

17 Therefore thou shalt say this word unto them; [z]Let mine eyes run down with tears night and day, and let them not cease: [a]for the virgin daughter of my people is broken with a great breach, with a very grievous blow.

18 If I go forth into [b]the field, then behold the slain with the sword! and if I enter into

[k]Isa. lix. 1——[l]Exod. xxix. 45, 46; Lev. xxvi. 11, 12——[m]Heb. *thy name is called upon us;* Dan. ix. 18, 19——[n]See ch. ii. 23, 24, 25——[o]Hos. viii. 13; ix. 9——[p]Exod. xxxii. 10; chap. vii. 16; xi. 14——[q]Prov. i. 28; Isa. i. 15; lviii. 3; ch. xi. 11; Ezek. viii. 18; Mic. iii. 4; Zech. vii. 13——[r]Chap. vi. 20; vii. 21, 22——[s]Chap. ix. 16——[t]Chap. iv. 10——[u]Heb. *peace of truth*——[v]Chap. xxvii. 10——[w]Chap. xxiii. 21; xxvii. 15; xxix, 8. 9——[x]Chap. v. 12, 13——[y]Psa. lxxix. 3——[z]Chap. ix. 1; xiii. 17; Lam. i. 16; ii. 18——[a]Chap. viii. 21——[b]Ezek. vii. 15

Verse 9. *Yet thou, O Lord,* art *in the midst of us*] Thy ark, temple, and sacred rites, are all here; and thou thyself, who art every where present, art here also: but alas! thou dost not *reveal* thyself as the Father of mercies, who forgivest iniquity, transgression, and sin.

We are called by thy name; leave us not.] Let us call thee our Father, and say thou to us, "Ye are my sons and daughters!" O leave us not!

Verse 10. *Thus have they loved to wander*] And the measure of your iniquity being now full, ye must be punished.

Verse 11. *Pray not for this people*] They are ripe for destruction, intercede not for them. O, how dreadful is the state of that people in reference to whom the Lord says to his ministers, *Pray not for them;* or, what amounts nearly to a prohibition, withholds from his ministers the spirit of prayer and intercession in behalf of the people!

Verse 13. *Ah, Lord God! behold, the prophets say unto them*] True, Lord, they are exceedingly wicked; but the false prophets have deceived them; this is some mitigation of their offence. This plea God does not admit; and why? the people believed them, without having any proof of their Divine mission.

Verse 14. *The prophets prophesy lies*] They say they have *visions*, but they have them by *divination*, and they are false. The people should know their character, and avoid them; but they love to have it so, and will not be undeceived.

Verse 15. *By sword and famine shall those prophets be consumed.*] Jeremiah had told Jehoiakim that, if he rebelled against Nebuchadnezzar, he should be overthrown, and the land wasted by *sword* and *famine:* the false prophets said there shall be neither *sword* nor *famine*, but *peace* and *prosperity*. The king believed *them*, and withheld the *tribute*. Nebuchadnezzar, being incensed, invaded and destroyed the land; and the false prophets fell in these calamities. See 2 Kings xxv. 3; Lam. ii. 11-19.

Verse 16. *And the people—shall be cast out*] They shall be destroyed, because they preferred *their lying words* to *my truth*, proclaimed by thee.

Verse 17. *For the virgin daughter of my people is broken*] *First*, the land was sadly distressed by *Pharaoh-necho*, king of Egypt. *Secondly*, it was laid under a heavy tribute by *Nebuchadnezzar*. And, *thirdly*, it was nearly desolated by a *famine* afterwards. In a few years all these calamities fell upon them; these might be well called *a great breach, a very grievous blow*.

Verse 18. *If I go forth into the field, then behold the slain with the sword*] Every place presents frightful spectacles; the wounded, the dying, the starving, and the slain; none to bury the dead, none to commiserate the dying, none to bring either relief or consolation. Even the *prophets* and the *priests* are obliged to leave the cities, and wander about in unfrequented and unknown places, seeking for the neces-

A. M. cir. 3399
B. C. cir. 605
Ol. XLIII. 4
TarquiniiPrisci,
R. Roman.,
cir. annum 12

the city, then behold them that are sick with famine! yea, both the prophet and the priest [c]go about into a land that they know not.

19 [d]Hast thou utterly rejected Judah? hath thy soul loathed Zion? why hast thou smitten us, and [e]*there is* no healing for us? [f]we looked for peace, and *there is* no good; and for the time of healing, and behold trouble!

20 We acknowledge, O LORD, our wickedness, *and* the iniquity of our fathers: for [g]we have sinned against thee.

21 Do not abhor *us,* for thy name's sake, do not disgrace the throne of thy glory: [h]remember, break not thy covenant with us.

22 [i]Are there *any* among the [k]vanities of the Gentiles that can cause rain? or can the heavens give showers? [l]*art* not thou he, O LORD our God? therefore we will wait upon thee: for thou hast made all these *things.*

[c]Or, *make merchandise against a land, and* men *acknowledge* it *not;* chap. v. 13——[d]Lam. v. 22——[e]Ch. xv. 18——[f]Ch. viii. 15——[g]Psa. cvi. 6; Dan. ix. 8

[h]Psa. lxxiv. 2, 20; cvi. 45——[i]Zech. x. 1, 2——[k]Deut. xxxii. 21——[l]Psa. cxxxv. 7; cxlvii. 8; Isa. xxx. 23; chap. v. 24; x. 13

saries of life. Dr. *Blayney* thinks that the *going about of the prophets and priests of the land,* is to be understood thus:—"They went trafficking about with their false doctrines and lying predictions, as pedlars do with their wares, seeking their own gain." I think the other sense preferable.

Verse 19. *We looked for peace*] We expected prosperity when Josiah purged the land of idolatry.

And there is *no good*] For we have relapsed into our former ways.

Verse 20. *We acknowledge, O Lord, our wickedness*] This the prophet did in behalf of the people; but, alas! they did not join him.

Verse 21. *Do not disgrace the throne of thy glory*] The temple. Let not this sacred place be profaned by impious and sacrilegious hands.

Break not thy covenant] See Exod. xxiv. 7, 8; xix. 5. *They* had already broken the covenant, and they wish God to fulfil his part. They ceased to *be his people,* for they abandoned themselves to idolatry; and yet they wished Jehovah *to be their Lord;* to defend, support, and fill them with all good things! But when the conditions of a covenant are broken by one of the contracting parties, the other party is not bound; and the covenant is necessarily annulled.

Verse 22. *Are there* any *among the vanities of the Gentiles*] Probably the dearth was now coming, as there had been a long want of rain. It was the prerogative of the true God to give rain and send showers at the prayers of his people.

Therefore we will wait upon thee] If thou do not undertake for us, we must be utterly ruined.

CHAPTER XV

God declares to Jeremiah that not even Moses and Samuel, whose prayers had been so prevalent, could divert him from his purpose of punishing so wicked a people, 1. *Accordingly their captivity is again announced in a variety of images so full of terror,* 2–9, *that the prophet complains of his own hard fate in being obliged to deliver such unwelcome messages,* 10; *for which too he is reproved,* 11–14. *Immediately he appeals to God for his sincerity, and supplicates pardon,* 15–18; *and God tempers his reproof with promising again to protect him in the faithful discharge of his duty,* 19–21.

A. M. cir. 3399
B. C. cir. 605
Ol. XLIII. 4
TarquiniiPrisci,
R. Roman.,
cir. annum 12

THEN said the LORD unto me, [a]Though [b]Moses and [c]Samuel stood before me, *yet* my mind *could* not *be* toward this people: cast *them* out of my sight, and let them go forth.

2 And it shall come to pass, if they say unto thee, Whither shall

[a]Ezek. xiv. 14, &c.

[b]Exod. xxxii. 11, 12; Psa. xcix. 6——[c]1 Sam. vii. 9

NOTES ON CHAP. XV

Verse 1. *Though Moses and Samuel*] *Moses* had often supplicated for the people; and in consequence they were spared. See Exod. xxxii. 11 and following verses, Num. xiv. 13. *Samuel* also had prayed for the people, and God heard him, 1 Sam. vii. 9; but if these or the most holy men were now to supplicate for this people, he would not spare them.

Cast them *out of my sight, and let them go forth.*] Do not bring them into my *presence* by your prayers; *let them go forth* into captivity.

Verse 2. *Whither shall we go forth?—Such as* are *for death, to death*] Some shall be destroyed by the *pestilence,* here termed *death.* See chap. xviii. 21. Others shall be slain by the *sword* in battle, and in the sackage of cities. Others shall perish by *famine,* shall be starved to death through the mere want of the necessaries of life; and the rest shall go into *captivity.* There shall be *different* sorts of punishments inflicted on them according to the nature of their transgressions. Some shall be punished in one way, and some in another.

A. M. cir. 3399
B. C. cir. 605
Ol. XLIII. 4
TarquiniiPrisci,
R. Roman.,
cir. annum 12

we go forth? then thou shalt tell
them, Thus saith the LORD;
[d]Such as *are* for death, to death;
and such as *are* for the sword,
to the sword; and such as *are* for the famine,
to the famine; and such as *are* for the captivity, to the captivity.

3 And I will [e]appoint over them four [f]kinds,
saith the LORD: the sword to slay, and the
dogs to tear, and [g]the fowls of the heaven,
and the beasts of the earth, to devour and
destroy.

4 And [h]I will cause them to be [i]removed
into all kingdoms of the earth, because of
[k]Manasseh the son of Hezekiah king of Judah,
for *that* which he did in Jerusalem.

5 For [l]who shall have pity upon thee, O
Jerusalem? or who shall bemoan thee? or
who shall go aside [m]to ask how thou doest?

6 [n]Thou hast forsaken me, saith the LORD,
thou art [o]gone backward: therefore will I
stretch out my hand against thee, and destroy
thee; [p]I am weary with repenting.

7 And I will fan them with a fan in the
gates of the land; I will bereave *them* of
[q]children, I will destroy my people, *since* [r]they return not from
their ways.

A. M. cir. 3399
B. C. cir. 605
Ol. XLIII. 4
TarquiniiPrisci,
R. Roman.,
cir. annum 12

8 Their widows are increased to
me above the sand of the seas: I have brought
upon them [s]against the mother of the young
men, a spoiler at noonday: I have caused *him* to
fall upon it suddenly, and terrors upon the city.

9 [t]She that hath borne seven languisheth:
she hath given up the ghost; [u]her sun is gone
down while *it was* yet day: she hath been
ashamed and confounded: and the residue of
them will I deliver to the sword before their
enemies, saith the LORD.

10 [v]Wo is me, my mother, that thou hast
borne me a man of strife and a man of contention to the whole earth! I have neither
lent on usury, nor men have lent to me on
usury; *yet* every one of them doth curse me.

11 The LORD said, Verily it shall be well
with thy remnant, verily [w]I will cause [x]the
enemy to entreat thee *well* in the time of evil
and in the time of affliction.

12 Shall iron break the northern iron and the
steel?

---

[d]Ch. xliii. 11; Ezek. v. 2, 12; Zech. xi. 9——[e]Lev. xxvi. 16, &c.——[f]Heb. *families*——[g]Ch. vii. 33; Deut. xxviii. 26——[a]Heb. *I will give them for a removing* [i]Deut. xxviii. 25; ch. xxiv. 9; Ezek. xxiii. 46——[k]2 Kings xxi. 11, &c.; xxiii. 26; xxiv. 3, 4——[l]Isa. li. 19 [m]Heb. *to ask of thy peace*——[n]Ch. ii. 13——[o]Ch. vii. 24

[p]Hos. xiii. 14——[q]Or, *whatsoever is dear*——[r]Isa. ix. 13; ch. v. 3; Amos iv. 10, 11——[s]Or, *against the mother city a young man spoiling*, &c.; or *against the mother* and *the young men*——[t]1 Sam. ii. 5——[u]Amos viii. 9 [v]Job iii. 1, &c.; ch. xx. 14——[w]Or, *I will entreat the enemy for thee*——[x]Ch. xxxix. 11, 12; xl. 3, 4, 5

Verse 3. *I will appoint over them four kinds*] There shall appear *four* instruments of my justice. 1. The *sword* to slay. 2. The *dogs* to tear what is slain. 3. The *fowls* of the heaven to feed on the dead carcasses. And, 4. The wild *beasts* to destroy all that the fowls have left.

Verse 4. *I will cause them to be removed into all kingdoms of the earth*] This seems to have respect to the *succeeding* state of the Jews in their *different generations;* and never was there a prophecy more literally fulfilled; and it is still a standing monument of Divine truth. Let *infidelity* cast its eyes on the scattered Jews whom it may meet with in every civilized nation of the world; and then let it deny the truth of this prophecy, if it can. The Jews are scattered through every nation, and yet *are not a nation;* nor do they form even *a colony* on any part of the face of the earth. Behold the truth and the justice of God!

Verse 5. *Who shall go aside to ask how thou doest?*] Perhaps there is not a more despised nor a more degraded people under the sun. Scarcely any one thinks himself called upon to do a kind office for a Jew. Their character is bad in society, and they are not at all solicitous to redeem it.

Verse 6. *I am weary with repenting.*] With repeatedly *changing my purpose.* I have often, after purposing to punish, showed them mercy. I will do it no longer; it is useless. I took them often at their promise, and in every instance they have failed.

Verse 7. *I will fan them with a fan*] There is no pure grain; all is chaff.

In the gates of the land] The places of public justice: and there it shall be seen that the judgments that have fallen upon them have been highly merited. And from these places of fanning they shall go out into their captivity.

Verse 8. *The mother of the young men*] The *metropolis* or mother city, *Jerusalem.*

Verse 9. *She that hath borne seven*] She that hath had a numerous offspring; Jerusalem, the parent of so many cities, villages, and families in the land. *Seven* signifies a *complete* or *full* number.

Verse 10. *A man of contention to the whole earth!*] To the whole LAND, to all his countrymen; though he had done nothing to merit their displeasure.

Verse 11. *I will cause the enemy to entreat thee* well *in the time of evil*] This was literally fulfilled; see chap. xxxix. 11, &c. Nebuchadnezzar had given strict charge to Nebuzar-adan, commander in chief, to look well to Jeremiah, to do him no harm, and to grant him all the privileges he was pleased to ask.

Verse 12. *Shall iron break the northern iron and the steel?*] Shall our weak forces be able to oppose and overcome the powers of the Chal-

A. M. cir. 3399 B. C. cir. 605 Ol. XLIII. 4 TarquiniiPrisci, R. Roman., cir. annum 12

13 Thy substance and thy treasures will I give to the [y]spoil without price, and *that* for all thy sins, even in all thy borders.

14 And I will make *thee* to pass with thine enemies [z]into a land *which* thou knowest not: for a [a]fire is kindled in mine anger, *which* shall burn upon you.

15 O LORD, [b]thou knowest: remember me, and visit me, and [c]revenge me of my persecutors, take me not away in thy long-suffering: know that [d]for thy sake I have suffered rebuke.

16 Thy words were found, and I did [e]eat them; and [f]thy word was unto me the joy and rejoicing of mine heart: for [g]I am called by thy name, O LORD God of hosts.

17 [h]I sat not in the assembly of the mockers, nor rejoiced; I sat alone because of thy hand: for thou hast filled me with indignation.

A. M. cir. 3399 B. C. cir 605 Ol. XLIV. 4 TarquiniiPrisci, R. Roman., cir. annum 12

18 Why is my [i]pain perpetual, and my wound incurable, *which* refuseth to be healed? wilt thou be altogether unto me [k]as a liar, *and as* waters *that* [m]fail?

19 Therefore thus saith the LORD, [n]If thou return, then will I bring thee again, *and* thou shalt [o]stand before me: and if thou [p]take forth the precious from the vile, thou shalt be as my mouth: let them return unto thee; but return not thou unto them.

20 And I will make thee unto this people a fenced brazen [q]wall: and they shall fight against thee, [r]but they shall not prevail against thee: for I *am* with thee to save thee and to deliver thee, saith the LORD.

21 And I will deliver thee out of the hand of the wicked, and I will redeem thee out of the hand of the terrible.

---

[y]Psa. xliv. 12; chap. xvii. 3——[z]Chap. xvi. 13; xvii. 4 [a]Deut. xxxii. 22——[b]Chap. xii. 3——[c]Chap. xi. 20; xx. 12——[d]Psa. lxix. 7——[e]Ezek. iii. 1, 3; Rev. x. 9, 10 [f]Job xxiii. 12; Psa. cxix. 72, 111

[g]Heb. *thy name is called upon me*——[h]Psa. i. 1; xxvi. 4, 5——[i]Ch. xxx. 15——[k]See ch. i. 18, 19——[l]Job vi. 15, &c. [m]Heb. *be not sure*——[n]Zech. iii. 7——[o]Ver. 1——[p]Ezek. xxii. 26; xliv. 23——[q]Ch. i. 18; vi. 27——[r]Ch. xx. 11, 12

---

deans? נחשת *nechasheth,* which we here translate *steel,* properly signifies brass or copper united with tin, which gives it much hardness, and enables it to bear a good edge.

Verse 13. *Thy substance—will I give to the spoil without price*] *Invaluable property* shall be given up to thy adversaries. Or, *without price*—thou shalt have nothing for it in return.

Verse 15. *O Lord—remember me, and visit me*] Let me not be carried away into captivity; and it does not appear that he had ever been taken to Babylon. After the capture of the city he went into Egypt; and either died there, or was put to death by his countrymen.

Verse 16. *Thy word was—the joy and rejoicing of mine heart*] When I did receive the prophetic message, I did rejoice in the honour thou hadst done me; and I faithfully testified thy will to them. They have become mine enemies; not because there was any evil in me, but because I was faithful to thee.

Verse 18. *Wilt thou be altogether unto me as—waters* that *fail?*] Meaning either springs, which in the height of summer grow dry; or, like that phenomenon in the sandy desert, where, by a peculiar action of the air on the rising vapours, the resemblance of water is produced, so that the traveller, deceived, rejoices that he is come, in the sandy desert, to the verge of a beautiful lake; but the farther he travels, it is still at the same distance, and at last vanishes; and he finds the whole was an illusion, for the waters have *failed.* Nothing can exceed the disappointment of the farmer whose subsistence absolutely depends on the periodical rains, when these *fail,* or fall short of their usual *quantity.* Some times the *rice* is sown and springs up in the most promising manner; but the latter rains *fail,* and whole fields of young rice wither and perish.

Verse 19. *If thou return*] By repentance unto me,—

Then will I bring thee again] Restore thee to thy own country. But some think the words are spoken to the prophet in reference to his ministry. He had greatly repined because of the persecutions which he endured. The Lord reprehends him, and is about to take from him the prophetic gift; but exhorts him first to take the *precious* from the *vile*—not to attend to the deceitful words of the people, but boldly declare the message he had given him; not to return unto the people, but let the people return unto him. And then he should be as *God's mouth*—his words should appear to be what they were, the genuine words of God; and the people should be obliged to acknowledge them as such.

Verse 20. *I will make thee—a fenced brazen wall*] While thou art faithful to me, none of them shall be able to prevail against thee.

Verse 21. *I will deliver thee out of the hand of the wicked*] From the power of this evil people.

And I will redeem thee out of the hand of the terrible.] Out of the power of the Chaldean armies. Every thing took place as God had promised, for no word of his can ever fall to the ground.

CHAPTER XVI

On account of the evils which threatened his country, the prophet is forbidden to encumber himself with a wife and family, or to bear any share in the little joys and sorrows of his neighbours, which were to be forgotten and absorbed in those public calamities, 1–9, *which their sins should draw on them,* 10–13. *A future restoration however is intimated,* 14, 15, *after those calamities should be endured,* 16–18; *and the conversion of the Gentiles is foretold,* 19–21.

A. M. cir. 3400
B. C. cir. 604
Ol. XLIV. 1
TarquiniiPrisci, R. Roman., cir. annum 13

THE word of the LORD came
also unto me, saying,
2 Thou shalt [a]not take thee a
wife, neither shalt thou have
sons or daughters in this place.
3 For thus saith the LORD concerning the
sons and concerning the daughters that are
born in this place, and concerning their mothers that bare them, and concerning their
fathers that begat them in this land;
4 They shall die of [b]grievous deaths; they
shall not be [c]lamented; neither shall they be
buried; *but* they shall be [d]as dung upon the
face of the earth: and they shall be consumed
by the sword, and by famine; and their [e]car-
casses shall be meat for the fowls of heaven,
and for the beasts of the earth.
5 For thus saith the LORD, [f]Enter not into
the house of [g]mourning, neither go to lament
nor bemoan them: for I have taken away my
peace from this people, saith the LORD, *even*
loving-kindness and mercies.
6 Both the great and the small shall die in
this land: they shall not be buried, [h]neither
shall *men* lament for them, nor [i]cut themselves, nor [k]make themselves
bald for them:

A. M. cir. 3400
B. C. cir. 604
Ol. XLIV. 1
TarquiniiPrisci, R. Roman., cir. annum 13

7 Neither shall *men* [l]tear *themselves* for them in mourning, to
comfort them for the dead; neither shall *men*
give them the cup of consolation to [m]drink for
their father or for their mother.
8 Thou shalt not also go into the house of
feasting, to sit with them to eat and to drink.
9 For thus saith the LORD of hosts, the
God of Israel; Behold, [n]I will cause to cease
out of this place in your eyes, and in your
days, the voice of mirth, and the voice of
gladness, the voice of the bridegroom, and
the voice of the bride.
10 And it shall come to pass, when thou
shalt show this people all these words, and
they shall say unto thee, [o]Wherefore hath
the LORD pronounced all this great evil against
us? or what *is* our iniquity? or what *is* our
sin that we have committed against the LORD
our God?
11 Then shalt thou say unto them, [p]Be-
cause your fathers have forsaken me, saith the
LORD, and have walked after other gods, and

[a]1 Cor. vii. 26——[b]Chap. xv. 2——[c]Chap. xxii. 18, 19; xxv. 33——[d]Psa. lxxxiii. 10; chap. viii. 2; ix. 22——[e]Psa. lxxix. 2; chap. vii. 33; xxxiv. 20——[f]Ezek. xxiv. 17, 22, 23——[g]Or, *mourning feast*——[h]Chap. xxii. 18——[i]Lev. xix. 28; Deut. xiv. 1; chap. xli. 5; xlvii. 5——[k]Isa. xxii. 12; chap. vii. 29

[l]Or, *break bread for them,* as Ezek. xxiv. 17; Hos. ix. 4; see Deut. xxvi. 14; Job xlii. 11——[m]Prov. xxxi. 6, 7——[n]Isa. xxiv. 7, 8; chap. vii. 34; xxv. 10; Ezek. xxvi. 13; Hos. ii. 11; Rev. xviii. 23——[o]Deut. xxix. 24; chap. v. 19; xiii. 22; xxii. 8——[p]Deuteronomy xxix. 25; chap. xxii. 9

NOTES ON CHAP. XVI

Verse 1. *The word of the Lord came also unto me*] This discourse *Dahler* supposes to have been delivered some time in the *reign of Jehoiakim.*

Verse 2. *Thou shalt not take thee a wife*] As it would be very inconvenient to have a family when the threatened desolations should come on the place. The reason is given in the following verses.

Verse 4. *They shall die of grievous deaths*] All *prematurely;* see chap. xiv. 16.

As dung upon the face of the earth] See chap. viii. 2.

Be meat for the fowls] See chap. vii. 33.

Verse 5. *Enter not into the house of mourning*] The public calamities are too great to permit individual losses to come into consideration.

Verse 6. *Nor cut themselves*] A custom of the heathen forbidden to the Jews, Lev. xix. 28, Deut. xiv. 1, and which appears now to have prevailed among them; because, having become idolaters, they conformed to all the customs of the heathen. They *tore their hair, rent their garments, cut their hands, arms,* and *faces.* These were not only *signs of sorrow,* but were even supposed to give ease to the dead, and appease the angry deities. The *Hindoos,* on the death of a relation, express their grief by loud lamentations, and not unfrequently *bruise* themselves in an agony of grief with whatever they can lay hold on.

Verse 8. *Thou shalt not also go into the house of feasting*] *Funeral banquets* were made to commemorate the dead, and comfort the surviving relatives; and *the cup of consolation,* strong mingled wine, was given to those who were deepest in distress, to divert their minds and to soothe their sorrows. These kinds of ceremonies were common among almost all the nations of the world on funeral occasions. The *Canaanites,* the *Jews,* the *Persians, Arabians, New Zealanders, Huns,* &c., &c.

A. M. cir. 3400 B. C. cir. 604 Ol. XLIV. 1 TarquiniiPrisci, R. Roman., cir. annum 13

have served them, and have
worshipped them, and have forsaken me, and have not kept
my law;
12 And ye have done [q]worse than your
fathers; for, behold, [r]ye walk every one after
the [s]imagination of his evil heart, that they
may not hearken unto me:
13 [t]Therefore will I cast you out of this
land [u]into a land that ye know not, *neither* ye
nor your fathers; and there shall ye serve
other gods day and night; where I will not
show you favour.
14 Therefore, behold, the [v]days come, saith
the LORD, that it shall no more be said, The
LORD liveth, that brought up the children of
Israel out of the land of Egypt;
15 But, The LORD liveth, that brought up
the children of Israel from the land of the
north, and from all the lands whither he
had driven them: and [w]I will bring them
again into their land that I gave unto their
fathers.
16 Behold, I will send for many [x]fishers,
saith the LORD, and they shall fish them;
and after will I send for many
hunters, and they shall hunt them
from every mountain, and from
every hill, and out of the holes
of the rocks.
17 For mine [y]eyes *are* upon all their ways:
they are not hid from my face, neither is their
iniquity hid from mine eyes.
18 And first I will recompense their iniquity
and their sin [z]double; because [a]they have defiled my land, they have filled mine inheritance with the carcasses of their detestable and
abominable things.
19 O LORD, [b]my strength, and my fortress,
and [c]my refuge in the day of affliction, the
Gentiles shall come unto thee from the ends
of the earth, and shall say, Surely our fathers
have inherited lies, vanity, and *things* [d]where-
in *there is* no profit.
20 Shall a man make gods unto himself, and
[e]they *are* no gods?
21 Therefore, behold, I will this once cause
them to know, I will cause them to know mine
hand and my might; and they shall know
that [f]my name *is* [g]The LORD.

[q]Ch. vii. 26——[r]Ch. xiii. 10——[s]Or, *stubbornness* ——[t]Deut. iv. 26, 27, 28; xxviii. 36, 63, 64, 65——[u]Ch. xv. 14 ——[v]Isa. xliii. 18; ch. xxiii. 7, 8——[w]Ch. xxiv. 6; xxx. 3; xxxii. 37——[x]Amos iv. 2; Hab. i. 15——[y]Job xxxiv. 21; Prov. v. 21; xv. 3; chap. xxxii. 19

[z]Isa. xl. 2; ch. xvii. 18——[a]Ezek. xliii. 7, 9——[b]Psa. xviii. 2——[c]Ch. xvii. 17——[d]Isa. xliv. 10; ch. ii. 11; x. 5 ——[e]Isa. xxxvii. 19; ch. ii. 11; Gal. iv. 8——[f]Exod. xv. 3; chap. xxxiii. 2; Amos v. 8——[g]Or, *JEHOVAH;* Psa. lxxxiii. 18

Verse 12. *And ye have done worse than your fathers*] The sins of the fathers would not have been visited on the children, had they not followed their example, and become even worse than they.

Verse 13. *Will I cast you out of this land*] See chap. vii. 15, and ix. 15.

Verse 14. *The Lord liveth, that brought up*] See Isa. xliii. 18.

Verse 15. *The land of the north*] Chaldea: and their deliverance thence will be as remarkable as the deliverance of their fathers from the land of Egypt.

Verse 16. *I will send for many fishers—for many hunters*] I shall raise up enemies against them some of whom shall destroy them by *wiles*, and others shall ruin them by *violence*. This seems to be the meaning of these symbolical *fishers* and *hunters.*

Verse 18. *The carcasses of their detestable—things.*] Either meaning the *idols* themselves, which were only *carcasses* without life; or the *sacrifices* which were made to them.

Verse 19. *The Gentiles shall come*] Even the days shall come when the Gentiles themselves, ashamed of their confidence, shall renounce their idols, and acknowledge that their fathers had believed lies, and worshipped vanities. This may be a prediction of the *calling of the Gentiles* by the Gospel of Christ; if so, it is a *light* amidst much *darkness.* In such dismal accounts there is need of some gracious promise relative to an amended state of the world.

Verse 20. *Shall a man make gods unto himself?*] Can any be so silly, and so preposterously absurd? Yes, fallen man is capable of any thing that is base, mean, vile, and wicked, till influenced and converted by the grace of Christ.

Verse 21. *Therefore, behold, I will this once*] I will not now change my purpose. They shall be visited and carried into captivity; nothing shall prevent this: and they shall know that my name is JEHOVAH. Since they would not receive the abundance of my *mercies*, they shall know what the true God can do in the way of *judgment.*

CHAPTER XVII

This chapter begins with setting forth the very strong bias which the people of Judah had to idolatry, with the fatal consequences, 1–4. The happiness of the man that trusteth in Jehovah is then beautifully contrasted with the opposite character, 5–8. God alone knows the deceitfulness and wretchedness of the heart of man, 9, 10. The comparison of a bird's hatching the eggs of another of a different species, which will soon forsake her, is highly expressive of the vanity of ill-acquired riches, which often disappoint the owner, 11. *The prophet continues the same subject in his own person, appeals to God for his sincerity, and prays that the evil intended him by his enemies may revert on their own heads,* 12–18. *The remaining part of the chapter is a distinct prophecy relating to the due observance of the Sabbath, enforced both by promises and threatenings,* 19–27.

A. M. cir. 3400
B. C. cir. 604
Ol. XLIV. 1
TarquiniiPrisci, R. Roman., cir. annum 13

THE sin of Judah *is* written
with a [a]pen of iron, *and*
with the [b]point of a diamond:
it is [c]graven upon the table of
their heart, and upon the horns of your altars;
2 Whilst their children remember their altars
and their [d]groves by the green trees upon the
high hills.
3 O my mountain in the field, [e]I will give
thy substance *and* all thy treasures to the spoil,
and thy high places for sin, throughout all
thy borders.
4 And thou, even [f]thyself, shalt discontinue
from thine heritage that I gave thee; and I
will cause thee to serve thine enemies in [g]the
land which thou knowest not: for [h]ye have
kindled a fire in mine anger, *which* shall burn
for ever.
5 Thus saith the LORD; [i]Curs-
ed *be* the man that trusteth in
man, and maketh [k]flesh his arm,
and whose heart departeth from
the LORD.
6 For he shall be [l]like the heath in the
desert, and [m]shall not see when good cometh;
but shall inhabit the parched places in the
wilderness, [n]*in* a salt land and not inhabited.
7 [o]Blessed *is* the man that trusteth in the
LORD, and whose hope the LORD is.
8 For he shall be [p]as a tree planted by the
waters, and *that* spreadeth out her roots by
the river, and shall not see when heat cometh,
but her leaf shall be green; and shall not be
careful in the year of [q]drought, neither shall
cease from yielding fruit.
9 The heart *is* deceitful above all *things,*

[a]Job xix. 24——[b]Heb. *nail*——[c]Prov. iii. 3; 2 Cor. iii. 3——[d]Judg. iii. 7; 2 Chron. xxiv. 18; xxxiii. 3, 19; Isa. i. 29; xvii. 8; ch. ii. 20——[e]Ch. xv. 13——[f]Heb. *in thyself* [g]Ch. xvi. 13——[h]Ch. xv. 14——[i]Isa. xxx. 1, 2; xxxi. 1

[k]See Isa. xxxi. 3——[l]Chap. xlviii. 6——[m]Job xx. 17 [n]Deut. xxix. 23——[o]Psa. ii. 12; xxxiv. 8; cxxv. 1; cxlvi. 5; Prov. xvi. 20; Isa. xxx. 18——[p]Job viii. 16; Psa. i. 3——[q]Or, *restraint*

NOTES ON CHAP. XVII

Verse 1. *The sin of Judah*] Idolatry.

Is *written with a pen of iron*] It is deeply and indelibly written in their *heart*, and shall be as indelibly written in their *punishment*. Writing with the *point of a diamond* must refer to *glass*, or some *vitrified* substance, as it is distinguished here from engraving with a *steel burine*, or *graver*. Their altars show what the deities are which they worship. There may be reference here to the different methods of recording events in those days:—1. A pen or stile of iron, for engraving on lead or wood. 2. A point of a diamond, for writing on vitreous substances. 3. Writing on tables of brass or copper. 4. Writing on the horns of the altars the names of the deities worshipped there. This is probable.

In several parts of India, and all through Ceylon, an *iron* or *steel pen* is used universally; with these the natives form the letters by incisions on the outer rind of the palm leaf. Books written in this way are very durable. This pen is *broad* at the *top*, has a very *fine sharp point*, and is *sharp* at *one side* as a knife, to shave and prepare the palm leaf. A pen of this description now lies before me.

Verse 2. *Whilst their children remember*] Even the rising generation have their *imagination* stocked with *idol images*, and their *memories* with the frantic rites and ceremonies which they saw their parents observe in this abominable worship.

Verse 3. *O my mountain in the field*] The prophet here addresses the *land of Judea*, which was a *mountainous* country, Deut. iii. 25; but *Jerusalem* itself may be meant, which is partly built upon *hills* which, like itself, are elevated above the rest of the country.

Verse 5. *Cursed* be *the man that trusteth in man*] This reprehends their vain confidence in trusting in *Egypt*, which was *too feeble* itself to help, and, had it been otherwise, too ill disposed towards them to help them *heartily*. An *arm of flesh* is put here for a *weak* and *ineffectual support*. And he who, in reference to the salvation of his soul, trusts in an *arm of flesh*—in *himself* or *others*, or in any thing he has *done* or *suffered*, will inherit a curse instead of a blessing.

Verse 6. *He shall be like the heath in the desert*] כערער *kearar;* or, like a blasted *tree*, without moisture, parched and withered.

Shall not see when good cometh] Shall not be sensible of it: the previous drought having rendered it incapable of absorbing any more vegetable juices.

A salt land] Barren; and therefore unfit to be *inhabited*.

Verse 8. *As a tree planted by the waters*] Which is sufficiently supplied with *moisture*, though the heat be intense, and there be no rain; for the roots being spread out by the river, they absorb from it all the moisture requisite for the flourishing vegetation of the tree.

Shall not see when heat cometh] Shall not feel any damage by *drought*, for the reason already assigned. It shall be strong and vigorous, its *leaf* always *green;* and shall produce plenty of fruit in its season.

Verse 9. *The heart* is *deceitful*] עקב הלב *akob halleb*, "the heart is supplanting—tortuous—full of windings—insidious;" lying ever at the catch; striving to avail itself of every

A. M. cir. 3400
B. C. cir. 604
Ol. XLIV. 1
TarquiniiPrisci,
R. Roman.,
cir. annum 13

and desperately wicked: who can know it?

10 I the LORD [r]search the heart, *I* try the reins, [s]even to give every man according to his ways, *and* according to the fruit of his doings.

11 *As* the partridge [t]sitteth *on eggs,* and hatcheth *them* not; *so* he that getteth riches, and not by right, [u]shall leave them in the midst of his days, and at his end shall be [v]a fool.

12 A glorious high throne from the beginning *is* the place of our sanctuary.

13 O LORD, [w]the hope of Israel, [x]all that forsake thee shall be ashamed, *and* they that depart from me shall be [y]written in the earth, because they have forsaken the LORD, the [z]Fountain of living waters.

A. M. cir. 3400
B. C. cir. 604
Ol. XLIV. 1
TarquiniiPrisci,
R. Roman.,
cir. annum 13

14 Heal me, O LORD, and I shall be healed; save me, and I shall be saved: for [a]thou *art* my praise.

15 Behold, they say unto me, [b]Where *is* the word of the LORD? let it come now.

16 As for me, [c]I have not hastened from *being* a pastor [d]to follow thee: neither have I desired the woful day; thou knowest: that which came out of my lips was *right* before thee.

17 Be not a terror unto me: [e]thou *art*

[r]1 Sam. xvi. 7; 1 Chron. xxviii. 9; Psa. vii. 9; cxxxix. 23, 24; Prov. xvii. 3; chap. xi. 20; xx. 12; Rom. viii. 27; Rev. ii. 23——[s]Psa. lxii. 12; chap. xxxii. 19; Rom. ii. 6——[t]Or, *gathereth* young *which she hath not brought forth*——[u]Psa. lv. 23——[v]Luke xii. 20

[w]Chap. xiv. 8——[x]Psa. lxxiii. 27; Isa. i. 21——[y]See Luke x. 20——[z]Chap. ii. 13——[a]Deut. x. 28; Psa. cix. 1; cxlviii. 14——[b]Isa. v. 19; Ezek. xii. 22; Amos v. 18; 2 Pet. iii. 4——[c]Chap. i. 4, &c.——[d]Heb. *after thee*——[e]Chap. xvi. 19

favourable circumstance to gratify its propensities to pride, ambition, evil desire, and corruption of all kinds.

And desperately wicked] ואנש הוא *veanush hu*, and is *wretched*, or *feeble; distressed beyond all things*, in consequence of the wickedness that is in it. I am quite of Mr. *Parkhurst's* opinion, that this word is here badly translated, as אנש *anash* is never used in Scripture to denote *wickedness* of any kind. My old MS. Bible translates thus:—**Schrewid is the herte of a man; and unserchable: who schal knowen it?**

Who can know it?] It even hides itself from itself; so that its owner does not know it. A corrupt heart is the worst enemy the fallen creature can have; it is full of evil devices,—of deceit, of folly, and abomination; and its owner knows not what is in him till it boils over, and is often past remedy before the evil is perceived. Therefore, trust not in man, whose purposes are continually changing, and who is actuated only by motives of *self-interest*.

Verse 10. *I the Lord search the heart*] The Lord is called by his apostles, Acts i. 24, Καρδιογνωστης, *the Knower of the heart.* To him alone can this epithet be applied; and it is from him alone that we can derive that *instruction* by which we can in any measure *know ourselves*.

Verse 11. As *the partridge*] קרא *kore*. It is very likely that this was a bird different from our partridge. The text Dr. *Blayney* translates thus:—

(As) the koré that hatcheth what it doth not lay,
(So is) he who getteth riches, and not according to right.

"The covetous man," says *Dahler*, "who heaps up riches by unjust ways, is compared to a bird which hatches the eggs of other fowls. And as the young, when hatched, and able at all to shift for themselves, abandon her who is not their mother, and leave her nothing to compensate her trouble, so the covetous man loses those unjustly-gotten treasures, and the fruit of his labour."

And at his end shall be a fool.] Shall be reputed as such. He was a fool all the way through; he lost his soul to get wealth, and this wealth he never enjoyed. To him also are applicable those strong words of the poet:—

"O cursed lust of gold! when for *thy* sake
The wretch throws up his interest in *both worlds*.
First *starved* in *this*, then *damned* in *that to come*." BLAIR.

Verse 12. *A glorious high throne*] As he is *cursed* who trusts in *man*, so he is *blessed* who trusts in GOD. He is here represented as on a *throne* in his temple; to him in the *means of grace* all should resort. He is the support, and a *glorious support*, of all them that trust in him.

Verse 13. *Written in the earth*] They shall never come to true honour. Their names shall be written in the dust; and the first wind that blows over it shall mar every letter, and render it illegible.

Verse 14. *Heal me—and I shall be healed*] That is, I shall be *thoroughly* healed, and *effectually* saved, if thou undertake for me.

Thou art *my praise.*] The whole glory of the work of salvation belongs to thee alone.

Verse 15. *Where* is *the word of the Lord?*] Where is the accomplishment of his *threatenings?* Thou hast said that the city and the temple should both be destroyed. No such events have yet taken place. But they did take place, and every tittle of the menace was strictly fulfilled.

Verse 16. *I have not hastened from* being *a pastor*] Dr. *Blayney* translates thus: "But I have not been in haste to outrun thy guidance." I was obliged to utter thy prediction; but I have not hastened the evil day. For the credit of my prophecy I have not desired the calamity to come speedily; I have rather pleaded for *respite*. I have followed thy steps, and proclaimed thy truth. I did not desire to be a prophet; but thou hast commanded, and I obeyed.

Verse 17. *Be not a terror unto me*] Do not

A. M. cir. 3400
B. C. cir. 604
Ol. cir. XLII. 2
TarquiniiPrisci,
R. Roman.,
cir. annum 13

my hope in the day of
evil.
18 [f]Let them be confounded
that persecute me, but [g]let not
me be confounded: let them be dismayed,
but let not me be dismayed: bring upon them
the day of evil, and [h]destroy[i] them with
double destruction.

A. M. cir. 3393
B. C. cir. 611
Ol. cir. XLII. 2
TarquiniiPrisci,
R. Roman.,
cir. annum 6

19 Thus saith the LORD unto
me; Go and stand in the gate
of the children of the people,
whereby the kings of Judah
come in, and by the which they go out, and
in all the gates of Jerusalem;
20 And say unto them, [k]Hear ye the word
of the LORD, ye kings of Judah, and all
Judah, and all the inhabitants of Jerusalem,
that enter in by these gates:
21 Thus saith the LORD; [l]Take heed to
yourselves, and bear no burden on the sabbath
day, nor bring *it* in by the gates of Jerusalem;
22 Neither carry forth a burden out of your
houses on the sabbath day, neither do ye any
work, but hallow ye the sabbath day, as I
[m]commanded your fathers.
23 [n]But they obeyed not, neither inclined
their ear, but made their neck stiff, that they
might nor hear, nor receive
instruction.

A. M. cir. 3393
B. C. cir. 611
Ol. cir. XLII. 2
TarquiniiPrisci,
R. Roman.,
cir. annum 6

24 And it shall come to pass, if
ye diligently hearken unto me,
saith the LORD, to bring in no burden through
the gates of this city on the sabbath day, but
hallow the sabbath day, to do no work therein;
25 [o]Then shall there enter into the gates of
this city kings and princes sitting upon the
throne of David, riding in chariots and on
horses, they, and their princes, the men of
Judah, and the inhabitants of Jerusalem: and
this city shall remain for ever.
26 And they shall come from the cities of
Judah, and from [p]the places about Jerusalem,
and from the land of Benjamin, and from [q]the
plain, and from the mountains, and from [r]the
south, bringing burnt-offerings, and sacrifices,
and meat-offerings, and incense, and bringing
[s]sacrifices of praise, unto the house of the LORD.
27 But if ye will not hearken unto me to
hallow the sabbath day, and not to bear a
burden, even entering in at the gates of Jerusalem on the sabbath day; then [t]will I kindle
a fire in the gates thereof, [u]and it shall devour
the palaces of Jerusalem, and it shall not be
quenched.

---

[f]Psa. xxxv. 4; xl. 14; lxx. 2——[g]Psa. xxv. 2——[h]Heb. *break them with a double breach*——[i]Ch. xi. 20——[k]Ch. xix. 8; xxii. 2——[l]Num. xv. 32, &c.; Neh. xiii. 19——[m]Exod. xx. 8; xxiii. 12; xxxi. 13; Ezek. xx. 12

[n]Ch. vii. 24, 26; xi. 10——[o]Ch. xxii. 4——[p]Ch. xxxii. 44; xxxiii. 13——[q]Zech. vii. 7——[r]Zech. vii. 7——[s]Psa. cvii. 22; cxvi. 17——[t]Ch. xxi. 14; xlix. 27; Lam. iv. 11; Amos i. 4, 7, 10, 12; ii. 2, 5——[u]2 Kings xxv. 9; ch. lii. 13

---

command me to predict miseries, and abandon me to them and to my enemies.

Verse 18. *Let them be confounded*] They shall be confounded. These words are to be understood as simple *predictions*, rather than *prayers*.

Verse 19. *The gate of the children of the people*] I suppose the most *public gate* is meant; that through which there was the greatest thoroughfare.

Verse 20. *Ye kings of Judah, and all Judah*] This last clause is wanting in eight of *Kennicott's* and *De Rossi's* MSS., in the *Arabic*, and some copies of the *Septuagint*.

Verse 21. *Take heed to yourselves and bear no burden*] From this and the following verses we find the ruin of the Jews attributed to the breach of the Sabbath; as this led to a neglect of sacrifice, the ordinances of religion, and all public worship, so it necessarily brought with it all immorality. This *breach* of the *Sabbath* was that which let in upon them all the *waters of God's wrath*.

Verse 24. *If ye diligently hearken unto me*] So we find that though their destruction was *positively* threatened, yet still there was an unexpressed proviso that, *if they did return to the Lord*, the calamities should be averted, and a succession of princes would have been continued on the throne of David, ver. 25, 26.

Verse 27. *But if ye will not hearken*] Then their sin lay at their own door. How fully were they warned; and how basely did they reject the counsel of God against themselves!

CHAPTER XVIII

The type of the potter's vessel, and its signification, 1–10. *The inhabitants of Judah and Jerusalem exhorted to repentance,* 11; *but on their refusal, (which is represented to be as unnatural as if a man should prefer the snowy Lebanon or barren rock to a fruitful plain, or other waters to the cool stream of the fountain,) their destruction is predicted,* 12–17. *In consequence of these plain reproofs and warnings of Jeremiah, a conspiracy is formed against him,* 18. *This leads him to appeal to God for his integrity,* 19, 20; *who puts a most dreadful curse in the mouth of his prophet, strongly indicative of the terrible fate of his enemies,* 21–23.

A. M. cir. 3396
B. C. cir. 608
Ol. XLIII. 1
TarquiniiPrisci,
R. Roman.,
cir. annum 9

THE word which came to Jeremiah from the LORD, saying,
2 Arise, and go down to the potter's house, and there I will cause thee to hear my words.
3 Then I went down to the potter's house, and, behold, he wrought a work on the [a]wheels.
4 And the vessel [b]that he made of clay was marred in the hand of the potter: so he [c]made it again another vessel, as seemed good to the potter to make *it*.
5 Then the word of the LORD came to me, saying,
6 O house of Israel, [d]cannot I do with you as this potter? saith the LORD. Behold, [e]as the clay *is* in the potter's hand, so *are* ye in mine hand, O house of Israel.
7 *At what* instant I shall speak concerning a nation, and concerning a kingdom, to [f]pluck up, and to pull down, and to destroy *it;*
8 [g]If that nation, against whom I have pronounced, turn from their evil, [h]I will repent of the evil that I thought to do unto them.

[a]Or, *frames* or *seats*——[b]Or, *that he made was marred, as clay in the hand of the potter*——[c]Heb. *returned and made*

[d]Isa. xlv. 9; Wisd. xv. 7; Rom. ix. 20, 21——[e]Isa. lxi. 8——[f]Chap. i. 10——[g]Ezek. xviii. 21; xxxiii. 11 [h]Chap. xxvi. 3; Jonah iii. 10

NOTES ON CHAP. XVIII

Verse 1. *The word which came to Jeremiah*] This discourse is supposed to have been delivered some time in the reign of Jehoiakim, probably within the first three years.

Verse 2. *Go down to the pottter's house*] By this similitude God shows the absolute state of dependence on himself in which he has placed mankind. They are as clay in the hands of the potter; and in reference to every thing *here below*, he can shape their destinies as he pleases. Again; though while under the providential care of God they may go *morally astray*, and *pervert themselves*, yet they can be reclaimed by the almighty and all-wise Operator, and become such vessels as *seemeth good for him to make*. In considering this parable we must take heed that in running parallels we do not *destroy* the *free agency* of man, nor *disgrace* the *goodness* and *supremacy* of God.

Verse 3. *He wrought a work on the wheels.*] אל האבנים *al haabnayim, upon the stones*, the potter's wheel being usually made of such; the spindle of the moving stone being placed on a stone below, on which it turned, and supported the stone above, on which the vessel was manufactured, and which alone had a rotatory motion. The potter's wheel in the present day seems to differ very little from that which was in use between *two* and *three thousand* years ago.

Verse 4. *The vessel—was marred in the hands of the potter*] It did not stand in the working; it got out of shape; or some *gravel* or *small stone* having been incorporated with the mass of clay, made a breach in that part where it was found, so that the potter was obliged to knead up the clay afresh, place it on the wheel, and form it anew; and then it was *such a vessel as seemed good to the potter* to make it.

Verse 6. *Cannot I do with you as this potter?*] Have I not a right to do with a people whom I have created as reason and justice may require? If they do not answer my intentions, may I not reject and destroy them; and act as this potter, make a new vessel out of that which at first did not succeed in his hands?

It is generally supposed that St. Paul has made a very different use of this similitude from that mentioned above. See Rom. ix. 20, &c. His words are, "Hath not the potter power over the clay, of the same lump to make one vessel unto honour, and another unto dishonour?" To this every sensible and pious man will answer, *Undoubtedly he has.* But would any potter make an exceedingly fair and good vessel on purpose to dash it to pieces when he had done? Surely no! And would, or could, the God of infinite perfection and love make millions of immortal souls on purpose for eternal perdition, as the horrible decree of reprobation states? No! This is a lie against all the attributes of God. But does not the text state that he can, out of the same lump, the same mass of human nature, make one vessel to honour, and another to dishonour? Yes. But the text does not say, what the horrible decree says, that he makes one part, and indeed the greater, for eternal perdition. But what then is the meaning of the text? Why evidently this: As out of the *same* mass of clay a potter may make a *flagon* for the table and a certain utensil for the chamber, the one for a more honourable, the other for a less honourable use, though both equally necessary to the owner; so God, out of the same *flesh and blood*, may make the *tiller of the field* and the *prophet of the Most High;* the one in a more honourable, the other in a less honourable employ; yet both equally necessary in the world, and equally capable of bringing glory to God in their respective places. But if the vessel be marred in his hand, under his providential and gracious dealings, he may reject it as he did the *Jews*, and make another vessel, such as he is pleased with, of the *Gentiles;* yet even these *marred vessels*, the *reprobate Jews*, are not finally rejected; for all Israel shall be saved in (through) the Lord, *i. e.*, Jesus Christ. And should the *Gentiles* act as the *Jews* have done, then *they* also shall be cut off, and God will call his Church by another name. See on Rom. ix. 22, and below.

Verses 7-10. At what *instant I shall speak concerning a nation*, &c.—*If that nation, against whom*, &c.—*And* at what *instant*, &c.—*If it do evil*, &c.] These verses contain what may be called *God's decree* by which the whole of his conduct towards man is regulated. If he purpose destruction against an offending person, if that person repent and turn to God, he shall *live* and not *die*.

A. M. cir. 3396
B. C. cir. 608
Ol. XLIII. 1
TarquiniiPrisci,
R. Roman.,
cir. annum 9

9 And *at what* instant I shall speak concerning a nation, and concerning a kingdom, to build and to plant *it;*

10 If it do evil in my sight, that it obey not my voice, then I will repent of the good, wherewith I said I would benefit them.

11 Now therefore go to, speak to the men of Judah, and to the inhabitants of Jerusalem, saying, Thus saith the LORD; Behold, I frame evil against you, and devise a device against you: [i]return ye now, every one from his evil way, and make your ways and your doings good.

12 And they said, [k]There is no hope: but we will walk after our own devices, and we will every one do the imagination of his evil heart.

13 Therefore thus saith the LORD; [l]Ask ye now among the heathen, who hath heard such things: the virgin of Israel hath done [m]a very horrible thing.

14 Will *a man* leave [n]the snow of Lebanon *which cometh* from the rock of the field? *or* shall the cold flowing waters that come from another place be forsaken?

15 Because my people hath forgotten [o]me, they have burned incense to [p]vanity, and they have caused them to stumble in their ways *from* the [q]ancient paths, to walk in paths, *in* a way not cast up;

16 To make their land [r]desolate, *and* a perpetual [s]hissing; every one that passeth thereby shall be astonished, and wag his head.

17 [t]I will scatter them [u]as with an east wind before the enemy; [v]I will show them the back, and not the face, in the day of their calamity.

A. M. cir. 3396
B. C. cir. 608
Ol. XLIII. 1
TarquiniiPrisci,
R. Roman.,
cir. annum 9

18 Then said they, [w]Come, and let us devise devices against Jeremiah; [x]for the law shall not perish from the priest, nor counsel from the wise, nor the word from the prophet. Come, and let us smite him [y]with the tongue, and let us not give heed to any of his words.

19 Give heed to me, O LORD, and hearken to the voice of them that contend with me.

20 [z]Shall evil be recompensed for good? for [a]they have digged a pit for my soul. Remember that I stood before thee to speak good for them, *and* to turn away thy wrath from them.

21 Therefore [b]deliver up their children to the famine, and [c]pour out their *blood* by the force of the sword; and let their wives be bereaved of their children, and *be* widows; and let their men be put to death; *let* their young men *be* slain by the sword in battle.

22 Let a cry be heard from their houses, when thou shalt bring a troop suddenly upon them: for [d]they have digged a pit to take me, and hid snares for my feet.

23 Yet, LORD, thou knowest all their counsel against me [e]to slay *me:* [f]forgive not their iniquity, neither blot out their sin from thy sight, but let them be overthrown before thee; deal *thus* with them in the time of thine anger.

[i]2 Kings xxvii. 13; ch. vii. 3; xxv. 5; xxvi. 13; xxxv. 15 —— [k]Ch. ii. 25 —— [l]Ch. ii. 10; 1 Cor. v. 1 —— [m]Ch. v. 30 —— [n]Or, *my fields for a rock,* or for *the snow of Lebanon? shall the running waters be forsaken for the strange cold* waters? —— [o]Ch. ii. 13, 32; iii. 21; xiii. 25; xvii. 13 —— [p]Ch. x. 15; xvi. 19 —— [q]Ch. vi. 16 —— [r]Ch. xix. 8; xlix. 13; l. 13

[s]1 Kings ix. 8; Lam. ii. 15; Mic. vi. 16 —— [t]Ch. xiii. 24 —— [u]Psa. xlviii. 7 —— [v]See ch. ii. 27 —— [w]Ch. xi. 19 —— [x]Lev. x. 11; Mal. ii. 7; John vii. 48, 49 —— [y]Or, *for the tongue* —— [z]Psa. cix. 4, 5 —— [a]Psa. xxxv. 7; lvii. 6; ver. 22 —— [b]Psa. cix. 9, 10 —— [c]Heb. *pour them out* —— [d]Ver. 20 —— [e]Heb. *for death* —— [f]Psa. xxxv. 4; cix. 14; ch. xi. 20; xv. 15

If he purpose peace and salvation to him that walketh uprightly, if he turn from God to the world and sin, he shall *die* and not *live.*

Verse 12. *There is no hope*] See chap. ii. 25.

Verse 13. *The virgin of Israel*] Instead of ישראל *Yisrael, three* of *Kennicott's* and *De Rossi's* MSS., with the Alexandrian copy of the *Septuagint,* have ירושלם *Yerushalem, Jerusalem.*

Verse 14. *Will* a man *leave the snow of Lebanon*] Lebanon was the highest mountain in Judea. Would any man in his senses abandon a *farm* that was always watered by the melted snows of Lebanon, and take a *barren rock* in its place? How stupid therefore and absurd are my people, who abandon the everlasting God for the worship of idols!

Verse 16. *A perpetual hissing*] שריקות *sherikoth,* a *shrieking, hissing;* an expression of contempt.

Verse 17. *I will scatter them as with an east wind*] It is the property of this wind, almost every where, to parch up, blast, and destroy grain and trees, and even cattle and men suffer from it. Hence the old metrical proverb:—

"When the wind blows from the east,
'Tis good for neither man nor beast."

Verse 18. *Come, and let us devise devices*] Let us form a conspiracy against him, accuse him of being a *false prophet,* and a contradicter of the words of God, for God has promised us protection, and *he* says we shall be destroyed, and that God will forsake his people.

Let us smite him with the tongue] ON *the tongue;* so it should be rendered. Lying and false testimony are punished in the eastern countries, to the present day, by smiting the person on the mouth with a strong piece of leather like the sole of a shoe. Sometimes a bodkin is run through the tongue. Blasphemy, calumny, and cursing of parents, are usually punished in that way among the Chinese.

Verse 20. *They have digged a pit for my soul.*] For my *life;* this they wish to take away.

Stood before thee to speak good for them] I was their continual intercessor.

Verse 21. *Therefore deliver up their children*] The execrations in these verses should be considered as simply *prophetic declarations* of the judgments which God was about to pour out on them.

If we consider them in their *grammatical* meaning, then they are not directions to us, to whom our Lawgiver has said, "Love your *enemies.*"

CHAPTER XIX

By the significant type of breaking a potter's vessel, Jeremiah is directed to predict the utter desolation of Judah and Jerusalem, 1–15. *The prophets taught frequently by* symbolic actions *as well as by* words.

A. M. cir. 3397
B. C. cir. 607
Ol. XLIII. 2
TarquiniiPrisci,
R. Roman.,
cir. annum 10

THUS saith the LORD, Go and get a potter's earthen bottle, and *take* of the ancients of the people, and of the ancients of the priests;

2 And go forth unto [a]the valley of the son of Hinnom, which *is* by the entry of [b]the east gate, and proclaim there the words that I shall tell thee,

3 [c]And say, Hear ye the word of the LORD, O kings of Judah, and inhabitants of Jerusalem; Thus saith the LORD of hosts, the God of Israel; Behold, I will bring evil upon this place, the which whosoever heareth, his ears shall [d]tingle.

4 Because they [e]have forsaken me, and have estranged this place, and have burned incense in it unto other gods, whom neither they nor their fathers have known, nor the kings of Judah, and have filled this place with [f]the blood of innocents;

5 [g]They have built also the high places of Baal, to burn their sons with fire *for* burnt-offerings unto Baal, [h]which I commanded not, nor spake *it,* neither came *it* into my mind:

A. M. cir. 3397
B. C. cir. 607
Ol. XLIII. 2
TarquiniiPrisci,
R. Roman.,
cir. annum 10

6 Therefore, behold, the days come, saith the LORD, that this place shall no more be called Tophet, nor [i]The valley of the son of Hinnom, but The valley of slaughter.

7 And I will make void the counsel of Judah and Jerusalem in this place; [k]and I will cause them to fall by the sword before their enemies, and by the hands of them that seek their lives: and their [l]carcasses will I give to be meat for the fowls of the heaven, and for the beasts of the earth.

8 And I will make this city [m]desolate, and a hissing: every one that passeth thereby shall be astonished and hiss because of all the plagues thereof.

9 And I will cause them to eat the [n]flesh of their sons and the flesh of their daughters, and they shall eat every one the flesh of his friend in the siege and straitness, wherewith their enemies, and they that seek their lives, shall straiten them.

10 [o]Then shalt thou break the bottle in the sight of the men that go with thee,

---

[a]Josh. xv. 8; 2 Kings xxiii. 10; chap. vii. 31——[b]Heb. *the sun gate*——[c]Chap. xvii. 20——[d]1 Sam. iii. 11; 2 Kings xxi. 12——[e]Deut. xxviii. 20; Isa. lxv. 11; chap. ii. 13, 17, 19; xv. 6; xvii. 13——[f]2 Kings xxi. 16; chap. ii. 34——[g]Chap. vii. 31, 32; xxxii. 35

[h]Lev. xviii. 21——[i]Josh. xv. 8——[k]Lev. xxvi. 17; Deut. xxviii. 25——[l]Psa. lxxix. 2; chap. vii. 33; xvi. 4; xxxiv. 20——[m]Chap. xviii. 16; xlix. 13; l. 13——[n]Lev. xxvi. 29; Deut. xxviii. 53; Isa. ix. 20; Lam. iv. 10——[o]So chap. li. 63, 64

NOTES ON CHAP. XIX

Verse 1. *Go and get a potter's earthen bottle*] This discourse was also delivered some time in the reign of *Jehoiakim.* Under the type of breaking a potter's earthen bottle or jug, Jeremiah shows his enemies that the word of the Lord should stand, that Jerusalem should be taken and sacked, and they all carried into captivity.

Ancients of the priests] The chiefs of the *twenty-four* classes which David had established. See 1 Chron. xxiv. 4.

Verse 4. *Estranged this place*] Ye have devoted my temple to a widely different purpose from that for which it was erected.

Verse 5. *Offerings unto Baal*] A general name for all the popular idols; Baal, Moloch, Ashtaroth, &c.

Verse 7. *I will make void the counsel of Judah*] Probably this refers to some determination made to proclaim themselves *independent,* and pay no more tribute to the Chaldeans.

To be meat for the fowls] See on chap. vii. 33.

Verse 9. *I will cause them to eat the flesh of their sons*] This was literally fulfilled when Jerusalem was besieged by the Romans. This also the prophet might have had in view.

A. M. cir. 3397
B. C. cir. 607
Ol. XLIII. 2
TarquiniiPrisci,
R. Roman.,
cir. annum 10

11 And shalt say unto them, Thus saith the LORD of hosts; [p]Even so will I break this people and this city, as *one* breaketh a potter's vessel, that cannot [q]be made whole again: and they shall [r]bury *them* in Tophet, till *there be* no place to bury.

12 Thus will I do unto this place, saith the LORD, and to the inhabitants thereof, and *even* make this city as Tophet:

13 And the houses of Jerusalem, and the houses of the kings of Judah, shall be defiled [s]as the place of Tophet, because of all the houses upon whose [t]roofs they have burned incense unto all the host of heaven, and [u]have poured out drink-offerings unto other gods.

14 Then came Jeremiah from Tophet, whither the LORD had sent him to prophesy; and he stood in [v]the court of the LORD'S house, and said to all the people,

15 Thus saith the LORD of hosts, the God of Israel; Behold, I will bring upon this city and upon all her towns all the evil that I have pronounced against it, because [w]they have hardened their necks, that they might not hear my words.

[p]Psa. ii. 9; Isa. xxx. 14; Lam. iv. 2——[q]Heb. *be healed*——[r]Chap. vii. 32——[s]2 Kings xxiii. 10——[t]2 Kings xxiii. 12; ch. xxxii. 29; Zeph. i. 5——[u]Ch. vii. 18——[v]See 2 Chron. xx. 5——[w]Ch. vii. 26; xvii. 23

Verse 11. *Even so will I break this people and this city*] The breaking of the bottle was the symbolical representation of the destruction of the city and of the state.

That cannot be made whole again] This seems to refer rather to the final destruction of Jerusalem by the Romans, than to what was done by the Chaldeans. Jerusalem was *healed* after 70 years: but nearly 1800 years have elapsed since Jerusalem was taken and destroyed by the Romans; and it was then so broken, *that it could not be made whole again.*

Verse 12. *And* even *make this city as Tophet*] A place of slaughter and destruction.

Verse 14. *Then came Jeremiah from Tophet*] He had probably gone to the *valley of Hinnom,* and there repeated the discourse which he had a little before delivered to the chief priests and elders.

Verse 15. *Because they have hardened their necks*] A metaphor taken from unruly and unbroken oxen, who resist the yoke, break and run away with their gears. So this people had broken and destroyed the yoke of the law.

CHAPTER XX

Jeremiah, on account of his prophesying evil concerning Judah and Jerusalem, is beaten and imprisoned by Pashur, chief governor of the temple, 1, 2. *On the following day the prophet is released, who denounces the awful judgments of God which should fall upon the governor and all his house, as well as upon the whole land of Judah, in the approaching Babylonish captivity,* 3–6. *Jeremiah then bitterly complains of the reproaches continually heaped upon him by his enemies; and, in his haste, resolves to speak no more in the name of Jehovah; but the word of the Lord is in his heart as a burning flame, so that he is not able to forbear,* 7–10. *The prophet professes his trust in God, whom he praises for his late deliverance,* 11–13. *The remaining verses, which appear to be out of their place, contain Jeremiah's regret that he was ever born to a life of so much sorrow and trouble,* 14–18. *This complaint resembles that of Job; only it is milder and more dolorous. This excites our pity, that our horror. Both are highly poetical, and embellished with every circumstance that can heighten the colouring. But such circumstances are not always to be too literally understood or explained. We must often make allowances for the strong figures of eastern poetry.*

A. M. cir. 3397
B. C. cir. 607
Ol. XLIII. 2
TarquiniiPrisci,
R. Roman.,
cir. annum 10

NOW Pashur the son of [a]Immur the priest, who *was* also chief governor in the house of the LORD, heard that Jeremiah prophesied these things.

2 Then Pashur smote Jeremiah the prophet, and put him in the stocks that *were* in the high gate of Benjamin, which *was* by the house of the LORD.

3 And it came to pass on the morrow, that Pashur brought forth Jeremiah out of the

[a]1 Chronicles, chap. xxiv. 14

NOTES ON CHAP. XX

Verse 1. *Pashur—chief governor*] Pashur was probably one of the chief priests of the *twenty-four* classes.

Verse 2. *Put him in the stocks*] Probably such a place near the gate as we term the *lock-up,* the *coal-hole;* or it may mean a sort of *dungeon.*

Verse 3. *The Lord hath not called thy name Pashur*]—Security on all sides. This name thou hast had, but not by Divine appointment.

A. M. cir. 3397
B. C. cir. 607
Ol. XLIII. 2
TarquiniiPrisci,
R. Roman.,
cir. annum 10

stocks. Then said Jeremiah unto him, The LORD hath not called thy name Pashur, but [b]Magor-missabib.

4 For thus saith the LORD, Behold, I will make thee a terror to thyself, and to all thy friends: and they shall fall by the sword of their enemies, and thine eyes shall behold *it:* and I will give all Judah into the hand of the king of Babylon, and he shall carry them captive into Babylon, and shall slay them with the sword.

5 Moreover I [c]will deliver all the strength of this city, and all the labours thereof, and all the precious things thereof, and all the treasures of the kings of Judah will I give into the hand of their enemies, which shall spoil them, and take them, and carry them to Babylon.

6 And thou, Pashur, and all that dwell in thine house, shall go into captivity: and thou shalt come to Babylon, and there thou shalt die, and shalt be buried there, thou, and all thy friends, to whom thou hast [d]prophesied lies.

7 O LORD, thou hast deceived me, and I was [e]deceived: [f]thou art stronger than I, and hast prevailed: [g]I am in derision daily, every one mocketh me.

8 For since I spake, I cried out, [h]I cried violence and spoil; because the word of the LORD was made a reproach unto me, and a derision, daily.

A. M. cir. 3397
B. C. cir. 607
Ol. XLIII. 2
TarquiniiPrisci,
R. Roman.,
cir. annum 10

9 Then I said, I will not make mention of him, nor speak any more in his name. But *his word* was in mine heart as a [i]burning fire shut up in my bones, and I was weary with forbearing, and [k]I could not *stay.*

10 [l]For I heard the defaming of many, fear on every side. Report, *say they,* and we will report it. [m]All [n]my familiars watched for my halting, *saying,* Peradventure he will be enticed, and we shall prevail against him, and we shall take our revenge on him.

11 But [o]the LORD *is* with me as a mighty terrible one: therefore my persecutors shall stumble, and they shall not [p]prevail: they shall be greatly ashamed; for they shall not prosper: *their* [q]everlasting confusion shall never be forgotten.

12 But, O LORD of hosts, that [r]triest the righteous, *and* seest the reins and the heart, [s]let me see thy vengeance on them: for unto thee have I opened my cause.

13 Sing unto the LORD, praise ye the LORD:

---

[b]That is, *fear round about;* Psa. xxxi. 13; ver. 10; ch. vi. 25; xlvi. 5; xlix. 29——[c]2 Kings xx. 17; xxiv. 12-16; xxv. 13, &c.; ch. iii. 24——[d]Ch. xiv. 13, 14; xxviii. 15; xxix. 21——[e]Or, *enticed*——[f]Ch. i. 6, 7——[g]Lam. iii. 14
[h]Ch. vi. 7——[i]Job xxxii. 18, 19; Psa. xxxix. 3

[k]Job xxxii. 18; Acts xviii. 5——[l]Psa. xxxi. 13
[m]Heb. *every man of my peace*——[n]Job xix. 19; Psa. xli. 9; lv. 13, 14; Luke xi. 53, 54——[o]Ch. i. 8, 19——[p]Ch. xv. 20; xvii. 18——[q]Chap. xxiii. 40——[r]Chap. xi. 20; xvii. 10——[s]Psa. liv. 7; lix. 10

But Magor-missabib—Fear on every side. This name hath God given thee; because, in the course of his providence, thou shalt be placed in the circumstances signified by it: *thou shalt be a terror to thyself.*

Verse 6. *And thou, Pashur—shall go into captivity*] Thou shalt suffer for the false prophecies which thou hast delivered, and for thy insults to my prophet.

Verse 7. *O Lord, thou hast deceived me*] Thou hast promised me protection; and, lo! I am now delivered into the hands of my enemies. These words were probably spoken when Pashur smote him, and put him in prison.

I think our translation of this passage is very exceptionable. My old Bible reads, **Thou laddist me aside Lord; and I was lad aside.** The original word is פתיתני *pittithani,* thou hast *persuaded me,* i. e., to go and prophesy to this people. I went, faithfully declared thy message, and now I am likely to perish by their cruelty. As the root פתה *pathah* signifies to *persuade* and *allure,* as well as to *deceive,* the above must be its meaning in this place. Taken as in our Version, it is highly irreverent. It is used in the same sense here as in Gen. ix. 27: *God shall enlarge* (*persuade,* margin) *Japheth; and he shall dwell in the tents of Shem.*

Verse 8. *I cried violence and spoil*] This was the burden of the message thou didst give me.

Verse 9. *I will not make mention of him*] I will renounce the prophetic office, and return to my house.

As a burning fire shut up in my bones] He felt stings of conscience for the hasty and disobedient resolution he had formed; he felt ashamed of his own weakness, that did not confide in the promise and strength of God; and God's word was in him as a strongly raging fire, and he was obliged to deliver it, in order to get rid of the tortures which he felt from suppressing the solemn message which God had given. It is as dangerous to refuse to go when called, as it is to run without a call. On this subject, see on chap. i. 6.

Verse 10. *Report—and we will report it.*] Let us spread calumnies against him every where; or let us spread reports of dangers coming upon him, that we may intimidate him, and cause him to desist.

Verse 11. *But the Lord* is *with me as a mighty terrible one*] Thus was he, by his strong confidence in the strong God, delivered from all his fears, and enabled to go on comfortably with his work.

A. M. cir. 3398
B. C. cir. 606
Ol. XLIII. 3
TarquiniiPrisci,
R. Roman.,
cir. annum 11

for [t]he hath delivered the soul
of the poor from the hand of evil
doers.
14 [u]Cursed *be* the day wherein
I was born: let not the day wherein my
mother bare me be blessed.
15 Cursed *be* the man who brought tidings
to my father, saying, A man child is born
unto thee; making him very glad.
16 And let that man be as the cities which
the LORD [v]overthrew, and repented not: and let him [w]hear the
cry in the morning, and the
shouting at noontide;
17 [x]Because he slew me not from the womb
or that my mother might have been my grave
and her womb *to be* always great *with me.*
18 [y]Wherefore came I forth out of the
womb to [z]see labour and sorrow, that my
days should be consumed with shame?

[t]Psa. xxxv. 9, 10; cix. 30, 31——[u]Job iii. 3; chap. xv. 10——[v]Gen. xix. 25——[w]Chap. xviii. 22——[x]Job iii. 10, 11——[y]Job iii. 20——[z]Lam. iii. 1

Verse 13. *Sing unto the Lord*] He was so completely delivered from all fear, that although he remained in the same circumstances, yet he exults in the Divine protection, and does not fear the face of any adversary.

Verse 14. *Cursed* be *the day wherein I was born*] If we take these words *literally*, and suppose them to be in their proper place, they are utterly inconsistent with that state of confidence in which he exulted a few minutes before. If they are the language of Jeremiah, they must have been spoken on a prior occasion, when probably he had given way to a passionate hastiness. They might well comport with the state he was in ver. 9. I really believe these verses have got out of their proper place, which I conjecture to be between the *eighth* and *ninth* verses. There they will come in very properly; and might have been a part of his complaint in those moments when he had purposed to flee from God as did Jonah, and prophesy no more in his name. Transpositions in this prophet are frequent; therefore place these *five* verses after the *eighth*, and let the chapter end with the *thirteenth*, and the whole will form a piece of exquisite poetry; where the state of *despair*, and the *hasty resolutions* he had formed while under its influence, and the state of *confidence* to which he was raised by the succouring influence of God, will appear to be both illustrative of each other, and are touched with a delicacy and fervour which even a cold heart must admire. See Job iii. 3, and the notes there. The two passages are very similar.

Verse 15. *A man child is born*] **Borun is to thee a knave child.**—Old MS. Bible. This is the old English word for *man* or *servant;* and is so used by *Wiclif*, Rev. xii. 5.

Verse 16. *And let him hear the cry*] Let him be in continual alarms.

Verse 18. *Wherefore came I forth*] It would have been well had I never been born, as I have neither comfort in my life, nor comfort in my work.

CHAPTER XXI

Nebuchadnezzar being come up against Jerusalem, Zedekiah sends Pashur and Zephaniah to the prophet to request him to intercede with God in behalf of his people, 1, 2. *But he is declared to be against Jerusalem, and the whole land of Judah; and the only mitigation of their punishment must proceed from their surrendering to the king of Babylon,* 3–10. *Prophecy concerning the house of the king of Judah,* 11, 12. *Notwithstanding the amazing fortifications round about Jerusalem, in which the people vainly trust, the Lord will most assuredly visit them for their iniquities; the city shall be taken by the Chaldeans,* 13, 14.

A. M. cir. 3415
B. C. cir. 589
Ol. XLVII. 4
TarquiniiPrisci,
R. Roman.,
cir. annum 28

THE word which came unto
Jeremiah from the LORD,
when king Zedekiah sent unto
him [a]Pashur the son of Melchiah, and [b]Zephaniah the son
of Maaseiah the priest, saying,
2 [c]Inquire, I pray thee, of
the LORD for us; (for Nebuchad-

[a]Chap. xxxviii. 1——[b]2 Kings xxv. 18; chap. xxix. 25; xxxvii. 3——[c]Chap. xxxvii. 3, 7

NOTES ON CHAP. XXI

Verse 1. *The word which came unto Jeremiah*] The chapters in the remaining parts of this prophecy seem strangely *interchanged.* This subject has been mentioned in the *introduction*, and some *tables* given; and to these the critical reader is requested to refer. The discourse here was delivered about the *ninth* year of the reign of Zedekiah. This chapter, observes Dr. *Blayney*, contains the first of those prophecies which were delivered by Jeremiah, *subsequent* to the revolt of Zedekiah, and the breaking out of the war thereupon; and which are continued on to the *taking of Jerusalem*, related in chap. xxix., in the following order:—ch. xxi., xxxiv., xxxvii., xxxii., xxxiii., xxxviii., xxxix.

Pashur the son of Melchiah] There can be little doubt that this Pashur was a different person from him who was called the son of *Immur* in the preceding chapter.

Verse 2. *Inquire, I pray thee*] See whether

A. M. cir. 3415
B. C. cir. 589
Ol. XLVII. 4
TarquiniiPrisci,
R. Roman.,
cir. annum 28

rezzar king of Babylon maketh war against us; if so be that the LORD will deal with us according to all his wondrous works, that he may go up from us.

3 Then said Jeremiah unto them, Thus shall ye say to Zedekiah:

4 Thus saith the LORD God of Israel; Behold, I will turn back the weapons of war that *are* in your hands, wherewith ye fight against the king of Babylon, and *against* the Chaldeans, which besiege you without the walls, and [d]I will assemble them into the midst of this city.

5 And I myself will fight against you with an [e]outstretched hand and with a strong arm, even in anger, and in fury, and in great wrath.

6 And I will smite the inhabitants of this city, both man and beast: they shall die of a great pestilence.

7 And afterward, saith the LORD, [f]I will deliver Zedekiah king of Judah, and his servants, and the people, and such as are left in this city from the pestilence, from the sword, and from the famine, into the hand of Nebuchadrezzar king of Babylon, and into the hand of their enemies, and into the hand of those that seek their life: and he shall smite them with the edge of the sword; [g]he shall not spare them, neither have pity, nor have mercy.

8 And unto this people thou shalt say, Thus saith the LORD; Behold, [h]I set before you the way of life, and the way of death.

A. M. cir. 3415
B. C. cir. 589
Ol. XLVII. 4
TarquiniiPrisci,
R. Roman.,
cir. annum 28

9 He that [i]abideth in this city shall die by the sword, and by the famine, and by the pestilence: but he that goeth out, and falleth to the Chaldeans that besiege you, he shall live, and [k]his life shall be unto him for a prey.

10 For I have [l]set my face against this city for evil, and not for good, saith the LORD; [m]it shall be given into the hand of the king of Babylon, and he shall [n]burn it with fire.

11 And touching the house of the king of Judah, *say,* Hear ye the word of the LORD;

12 O house of David, thus saith the LORD; [o]Execute [p]judgment [q]in the morning, and deliver *him that is* spoiled out of the hand of the oppressor, lest my fury go out like fire, and burn that none can quench *it,* because of the evil of your doings.

13 Behold, [r]I *am* against thee, O [s]inhabitant of the valley, *and* rock of the plain, saith the LORD; which say, [t]Who shall come down against us? or who shall enter into our habitations?

14 But I will [u]punish you according to the [v]fruit of your doings, saith the LORD: and I will kindle a fire in the forest thereof, and [w]it shall devour all things round about it.

---

[d]Isa. xiii. 4——[e]Exod. vi. 6——[f]Chap. xxxvii. 17; xxxix. 5; lii. 9——[g]Deut. xxiii. 50; 2 Chron. xxxvi. 17
[h]Deut. xxx. 19——[i]Chap. xxxviii. 2, 17, 18——[k]Chap. xxxix. 18; xlv. 5——[l]Lev. xvii. 10; chap. xliv. 11; Amos ix. 4——[m]Chap. xxxviii. 3

[n]Chap. xxxiv. 2, 22; xxxvii. 10; xxxviii. 18, 23; lii. 13
[o]Chap. xxii. 3; Zech. vii. 9——[p]Heb. *Judge*——[q]Psa. ci. 8——[r]Ezek. xiii. 8——[s]Heb. *inhabitress*——[t]Chap. xlix. 4——[u]Heb. *visit upon*——[v]Prov. i. 31; Isa. iii. 10, 11——[w]2 Chron. xxxvi. 19; chap. lii. 13

God intends to deliver us *into* or *out of* the hand of the Chaldeans.

Verse 4. *I will turn back the weapons*] Every attempt you make to repel the Chaldeans shall be unsuccessful.

I will assemble them into the midst of this city.] I will deliver the city into their hands.

Verse 6. *They shall die of a great pestilence.*] The *sword* may appear to be that of *man,* though I have given the Chaldeans their commission; but the *pestilence* shall appear to be the immediate act of GOD.

Verse 7. *Nebuchadrezzar*] This name is spelt as above in *twenty-six* places of this book; and in *ten* places it is spelt *Nebuchadnezzar,* which is the common orthography. The difference is only a ר *resh* for a נ *nun;* but the MSS. are various on this point. It is the same person who is intended by both names; and here all the *Versions,* except the *Arabic,* which omits the name, have it in the usual form.

Verse 8. *Behold, I set before you the way of life, and the way of death.*] Meaning *escape* or *destruction* in the *present* instance. This is explained in the next verse.

Verse 10. *He shall burn it with fire.*] What a heavy message to all; and especially to them who had any fear of God, or reverence for the temple and its sacred services!

Verse 12. *Execute judgment in the morning*] Probably the time for dispensing judgment was *the morning,* when the people were going to their work; but the words may mean, Do justice *promptly,* do not *delay.* Let justice be administered *as soon* as required.

Verse 13. *O inhabitant of the valley,* and *rock of the plain*] Dr. *Blayney* translates: "O thou inhabitant of the levelled hollow of a rock." With all his explanation I cannot see the good sense of this translation. Jerusalem itself, though partly on *two hills,* was also extended in the valley; and *Zion,* the *city of David,* was properly *a rock,* strongly fortified both by nature and art; and by its ancient possessors, the *Jebusites,* was deemed impregnable.

Who shall come down against us?] Probably

the words of those *courtiers* who had persuaded Zedekiah to rebel against the king of Babylon.

Verse 14. *I will kindle a fire in the forest thereof*] I will send destruction into its *centre*, that shall spread to every part of the *circumference*, and so consume the whole.

The beginning of the *thirty-fourth* chapter should follow here. See the arrangement on ver. 1.

CHAPTER XXII

This section of prophecy, extending to the end of the eighth verse of the next chapter, is addressed to the king of Judah and his people. It enjoins on them the practice of justice and equity, as they would hope to prosper, 1–4; *but threatens them, in case of disobedience, with utter destruction,* 5–9. *The captivity of Shallum, the son of Josiah, is declared to be irreversible,* 10–12; *and the miserable and unlamented end of Jeconiah, contemptuously called Coniah, is foretold,* 13–19. *His family is threatened with the like captivity, and his seed declared to be for ever excluded from the throne,* 20–30.

A. M. cir. 3406
B. C. cir. 598
Ol. cir. XLV. 3
TarquiniiPrisci, R. Roman., cir. annum 19

THUS saith the LORD; Go down to the house of the king of Judah, and speak there this word,

2 And say, Hear the word of the LORD, O king of Judah, that sittest upon the throne of David, thou, and thy servants, and thy people that enter in by these gates:

3 Thus saith the LORD; [b]Execute ye judgment and righteousness, and deliver the spoiled out of the hand of the oppressor: and [c]do no wrong, do no violence to the stranger, the fatherless, nor the widow, neither shed innocent blood in this place.

4 For if ye do this thing indeed, [d]then shall there enter in by the gates of this house kings sitting [e]upon the throne of David, riding in chariots and on horses, he, and his servants, and his people.

5 But if ye will not hear these words, [f]I swear by myself, saith the LORD, that this house shall become a desolation.

A. M. cir. 3406
B. C. cir. 598
Ol. cir. XLV. 3
TarquiniiPrisci, R. Roman., cir. annum 19

6 For thus saith the LORD unto the king's house of Judah; Thou *art* Gilead unto me, *and* the head of Lebanon: *yet* surely I will make thee a wilderness, *and* cities *which* are not inhabited.

7 And I will prepare destroyers against thee, every one with his weapons: and they shall cut down [g]thy choice cedars, [h]and cast *them* into the fire.

8 And many nations shall pass by this city, and they shall say every man to his neighbour, [i]Wherefore hath the LORD done thus unto this great city?

9 Then they shall answer, [k]Because they have forsaken the covenant of the LORD their God, and worshipped other gods, and served them.

10 Weep ye not for [l]the dead, neither bemoan him: *but* weep sore for him [m]that goeth away: for he shall return no more, nor see his native country.

---

[a]Chap. xvii. 20——[b]Chap. xxi. 12——[c]See ver. 17——[d]Chap. xvii. 25——[e]Heb. *for David upon his throne*——[f]Heb. vi. 13, 17——[g]Isa. xxxvii. 24——[h]Chap. xxi. 14——[i]Deut. xxix. 24, 25; 1 Kings ix. 8, 9——[k]2 Kings xxii. 17; 2 Chron. xxxiv. 25——[l]2 Kings xxii. 20——[m]Ver. 11

NOTES ON CHAP. XXII

Verse 1. *Go down to the house of the king of Judah, and speak there this word*] This is supposed by *Dahler* to have been published in the *first* year of the reign of Zedekiah.

Verse 2. *O king of Judah—thou, and thy servants*] His *ministers* are here addressed, as chiefly governing the nation; and who had counselled Zedekiah to rebel.

Verse 6. *Thou* art *Gilead unto me,* and *the head of Lebanon*] Perhaps in allusion, says *Dahler*, to the *oaks* of *Gilead*, and the *cedars* of Mount *Lebanon*, of which the palace was constructed. *Lebanon* was the highest mountain in Israel, and *Gilead* the richest and most fertile part of the country; and were, therefore, proper emblems of the reigning *family*. Though thou art the richest and most powerful, I, who raised thee up, can bring thee down and make thee a wilderness.

Verse 7. *They shall cut down thy choice cedars*] The destruction of the country is expressed under the symbol of the destruction of a *fine forest;* a multitude of fellers come against it, each with his axe; and, there being no resistance, every tree is soon *felled* to the earth. "These destroyers," God says, "I have prepared, קדשתי *kiddashti, I have sanctified*—consecrated, to this work. They have their commission from me."

Verse 8. *Many nations shall pass*] These words seem borrowed from Deut. xxix. 22, &c.

Verse 10. *Weep ye not for the dead*] Josiah, dead in consequence of the wound he had received at Megiddo, in a battle with Pharaoh-necho, king of Egypt; but he died in peace with God.

But *weep sore for him that goeth away*] Namely, Jehoahaz, the son of Josiah, called below *Shallum*, whom Pharaoh-necho had carried captive into Egypt from which it was proph-

A. M. cir. 3406 B. C. cir. 598 Ol. cir. XLV. 3 TarquiniiPrisci, R. Roman., cir. annum 19

11 For thus saith the LORD touching [n]Shallum the son of Josiah king of Judah, which reigned instead of Josiah his father, [o]which went forth out of this place; He shall not return thither any more:

12 But he shall die in the place whither they have led him captive, and shall see this land no more.

13 [p]Wo unto him that buildeth his house by unrighteousness, and his chambers by wrong; [q]*that* useth his neighbour's service without wages, and giveth him not for his work;

14 That saith, I will build me a wide house and [r]large chambers, and cutteth him out [s]windows; and *it is* ceiled with cedar, and painted with vermilion.

15 Shalt thou reign, because thou closest *thyself* in cedar? [t]did not thy father eat and drink, and do judgment and justice, *and* then [u]*it was* well with him?

16 He judged the cause of the poor and needy; then *it was* well *with him: was* not this to know me? saith the LORD.

17 [v]But thine eyes and thine heart *are* not but for thy covetousness, and for to shed innocent blood, and for oppression, and for [w]violence, to do *it*.

18 Therefore thus saith the LORD concerning Jehoiakim the son of Josiah king of Judah; [x]They shall not lament for him, *saying,* [y]Ah my brother! or, Ah sister! they shall not lament for him, *saying,* Ah lord! or, Ah his glory!

[n]See 1 Chron. iii. 15, with 2 Kings xxiii. 30——[o]2 Kings xxiii. 34——[p]2 Kings xxiii. 35; ver. 18——[q]Lev. xix. 13; Deut. xxiv. 14, 15; Mic. iii. 10; Hab. ii. 9; James v. 4

[r]Heb. *thorough-aired*——[s]Or, *my windows*——[t]2 Kings xxiii. 25——[u]Psa. cxxviii. 2; Isa. iii. 10——[v]Ezek. xix. 6——[w]Or, *incursion*——[x]Chap. xvi. 4, 6——[y]See 1 Kings xiii. 30

esied he should never return, 2 Kings xxiii. 30-34. He was called *Shallum* before he ascended the throne, and *Jehoahaz* afterwards; so his brother *Eliakim* changed his name to *Jehoiakim*, and *Mattaniah* to *Zedekiah*.

Verse 13. *Wo unto him that buildeth his house*] These evils, charged against Jehoiakim, are nowhere else *circumstantially* related. We learn from 2 Kings xxiii. 35-37, that he taxed his subjects heavily, to give to Pharaoh-necho, king of Egypt: "He exacted the silver and gold of the people of the land, and did that which was evil in the sight of the Lord." The *mode* of taxation is here intimated; he took the *wages of the hirelings*, and caused the *people to work without wages* in his *own buildings*, &c.

Verse 15. *Shalt thou reign, &c.*] Dost thou think thou art a great king, because thou dwellest in a splendid palace?

Verse 18. *They shall not lament for him*, saying, *Ah my brother!*] These words were no doubt the burden of some *funeral dirge. Alas!* a *brother*, who was our *lord* or *governor*, is gone. *Alas, our sister!* his QUEEN, who has lost her *glory* in losing her husband. הדה *hodah* is feminine, and must refer to the *glory* of the queen.

The mournings in the east, and lamentations for the dead, are loud, vehement, and distressing. For a *child* or a *parent* grief is expressed in a variety of impassioned sentences, each ending with a *burden* like that in the text, "Ah my child!" "Ah my mother!" as the prophet in this place: הוי אחי *hoi achi*, "Ah my brother!" הוי אחות *hoi achoth*, "Ah sister!" הוי אדון *hoi adon*, "Ah lord!" הוי הדה *hoi hodah*, "Ah the glory."

Mr. *Ward*, in his Manners and Customs of the Hindoos, gives two examples of lamentation; one of a *mother* for the death of her *son*, one of a *daughter* for her departed *mother*. "When a woman," says he, "is overwhelmed with grief for the death of her child, she utters her grief in some such language as the following:—

Ah, my Hureedas, where is he gone?—'Ah my child, my child!'
My golden image, Hureedas, who has taken?—'Ah my child, my child!'
I nourished and reared him, where is he gone?—'Ah my child, my child!'
Take me with thee.—'Ah my child my child!'
He played round me, like a golden top.—'Ah my child, my child!'
Like his face I never saw one.—'Ah my child, my child!'
The infant continually cried, *Ma Ma!*—'Ah my child, my child!'
Ah my child, crying, *Ma!* come into my lap.—'Ah my child, my child!'
Who shall now drink milk?—'Ah my child, my child!'
Who shall now stay in my lap?—'Ah my child, my child!'
Our support is gone!—'Ah my child, my child!'

"The lamentations for a mother are in some such strains as these:—

Mother! where is she gone?—'Ah my mother, my mother!'
You are gone, but what have you left for me?—'Ah my mother, my mother!'
Whom shall I now call mother, mother?—'Ah my mother, my mother!'
Where shall I find such a mother?—'Ah my mother, my mother!' "

From the above we may conclude that the funeral lamentations, to which the prophet refers, generally ended in this way, in each of the verses or interrogatories.

There is another intimation of this ancient and universal custom in 1 Kings xiii. 30, where the *old prophet*, who had deceived the *man of God*, and who was afterwards slain by a lion, is represented as mourning over him, and saying, הוי אחי *hoi achi*, "Alas, my brother!" this being the *burden* of the lamentation which he

A. M. cir. 3406 B. C. cir. 598 Ol. cir. XLV. 3 TarquiniiPrisci, R. Roman., cir. annum 19

19 [z]He shall be buried with the burial of an ass, drawn and cast forth beyond the gates of Jerusalem.

20 Go up to Lebanon, and cry; and lift up thy voice in Bashan, and cry from the passages: for all thy lovers are destroyed.

21 I spake unto thee in thy [a]prosperity; *but* thou saidst, I will not hear. [b]This *hath been* thy manner from thy youth, that thou obeyedst not my voice.

22 The wind shall eat up all [c]thy pastors, and [d]thy lovers shall go into captivity; surely then shalt thou be ashamed and confounded for all thy wickedness.

23 O [e]inhabitant of Lebanon, that makest thy nest in the cedars, how gracious shalt thou be when pangs come upon thee, [f]the pain as of a woman in travail!

24 *As* I live, saith the LORD, [g]though Coniah the son of Jehoiakim king of Judah [h]were the signet upon my right hand, yet would I pluck thee thence;

25 And I will give thee into the hand of them that seek thy life, and into the hand *of them* whose face thou fearest, even into the hand of Nebuchadrezzar king of Babylon, and into the hand of the Chaldeans.

A. M. cir. 3406 B. C. cir. 598 Ol. cir. XLV. 3 TarquiniiPrisci, R. Roman., cir. annum 19

26 [i]And I will cast thee out, and thy mother that bare thee, into another country, where ye were not born; and there shall ye die.

27 But to the land whereunto they [k]desire to return, thither shall they not return.

28 *Is* this man Coniah a despised broken idol? *is he* [l]a vessel wherein *is* no pleasure? wherefore are they cast out, he and his seed, and are cast into a land which they know not?

29 [m]O earth, earth, earth, hear the word of the LORD.

30 Thus saith the LORD, Write ye this man [n]childless, a man *that* shall not prosper in his days: for no man of his seed shall prosper, [o]sitting upon the throne of David, and ruling any more in Judah.

[z]2 Chron. xxxvi. 6; chap. xxxvi. 30——[a]Heb. *prosperities*——[b]Chap. iii. 25; vii. 23, &c.——[c]Chap. xxiii. 1 [d]Ver. 20——[e]Heb. *inhabitress*——[f]Chap. vi. 24 [g]See 2 Kings xxiv. 6, 8; 1 Chron. iii. 16; chap. xxxvii. 1 [h]Cant. viii. 6

[i]2 Kings xxiv. 15; 2 Chron. xxxvi. 10——[k]Heb. *lift up their mind;* chap. xliv. 14——[l]Psa. xxxi. 12; chap. xlviii. 38; Hos. viii. 8——[m]Deut. xxxii. 1; Isa. i. 2; xxxiv. 1; Mic. i. 2——[n]See 1 Chron. iii. 16, 17; Matt. i. 12——[o]Chap. xxxvi. 30

had used on this occasion. Similar instances may be seen in other places, Jer. xxx. 7; Ezek. vi. 11; Joel i. 15; and particularly Amos v. 16, 17, and Rev. xviii. 10-19.

Verse 19. *With the burial of an ass*] Cast out, and left unburied, or buried without any *funeral solemnities*, and without such lamentations as the above.

Verse 20. *Go up to Lebanon*] Probably *Anti-Libanus*, which, together with *Bashan* and *Abarim*, which we here translate *passages*, were on the way by which the captives should be led out of their own country.

Verse 21. *I spake unto thee in thy prosperity*] In all states and circumstances I warned thee by my prophets; and thou wilt only be *ashamed* of thy conduct when thou shalt be stripped of all thy excellencies, and reduced to poverty and disgrace, ver. 22.

Verse 22. *The wind shall eat up all thy pastors*] A *blast* from God's mouth shall carry off thy kings, princes, prophets, and priests.

Verse 23. *How gracious shalt thou be*] A strong irony.

Verse 24. *Though Coniah*] Called *Jeconiah*, probably on ascending the throne. See on ver. 10.

The signet upon my right hand] The most precious seal, ring, or armlet. Though dearer to me than the most splendid gem to its possessor.

Verse 26. *I will cast thee out, and thy mother*] See all this fulfilled, 2 Kings xxiv. 12, 13. All were carried by Nebuchadnezzar into captivity together.

Verse 28. Is *this man Coniah a despised broken idol?*] These are probably the exclamations of the *people*, when they heard those solemn denunciations against their *king* and their *country*.

Verse 29. *O earth*] These are the words of the *prophet* in reply: O land! unhappy land! desolated land! *Hear the judgment of the Lord!*

Verse 30. *Write ye this man childless*] Though he had *seven* sons, 1 Chron. iii. 17, yet, having no *successor*, he is to be entered on the *genealogical tables* as one *without children*, for none of his posterity ever sat on the throne of David.

CHAPTER XXIII

Sequel of the discourse which commenced in the preceding chapter. The prophet denounces vengeance against the pastors of Israel who have scattered and destroyed the flock of the Lord, 1, 2. *He concludes with gracious promises of deliverance from the Babylonish captivity, and of better times under the Messiah, when the converts to Christianity, who are the true Israel of God, shadowed forth by the old dispensation, shall be delivered, by the glorious light of the Gospel, from worse than Chaldean bondage, from the captivity of sin and death. But this prophecy will not have its fullest accomplishment till that period arrives which is fixed in the Divine counsel for the restoration of Israel and Judah from their various dispersions, of which their deliverance from the Chaldean domination was a type; when Jesus the Christ, the righteous Branch, the Root and Offspring of David, and the only legitimate Heir to the throne, shall take unto himself his great power, and reign gloriously over the whole house of Jacob,* 3–8. *At the* ninth *verse a new discourse commences. Jeremiah expresses his horror at the great wickedness of the priests and prophets of Judah, and declares that the Divine vengeance is hanging over them. He exhorts the people not to listen to their false promises,* 9–22; *and predicts the utter ruin that shall fall upon all pretenders to inspiration,* 23–32, *as well as upon all scoffers at true prophecy,* 33–40.

A. M. cir 3406
B. C. cir. 598
Ol. cir. XLV. 3
TarquiniiPrisci,
R. Roman.,
cir. annum 19

WO [a]be unto the pastors that
destroy and scatter the
sheep of my pasture! saith the
LORD.
2 Therefore thus saith the LORD God of
Israel against the pastors that feed my people;
Ye have scattered my flock, and driven them
away, and have not visited them: [b]behold, I
will visit upon you the evil of your doings,
saith the LORD.
3 And [c]I will gather the remnant of my
flock out of all countries whither I have driven
them, and will bring them again
to their folds; and they shall be
fruitful and increase.
4 And I will set up [d]shepherds
over them which shall feed them: and they
shall fear no more, nor be dismayed, neither
shall they be lacking, saith the LORD.
5 Behold, [e]the days come, saith the LORD,
that I will raise unto David a righteous Branch,
and a King shall reign and prosper, [f]and shall
execute judgment and justice in the earth.
6 [g]In his days Judah shall be saved, and

A. M. cir. 3406
B. C. cir. 598
Ol. cir. XLV. 3
TarquiniiPrisci,
R. Roman,
cir. annum 19

[a]Chap. x. 21; xxii. 22; Ezek. xxxiv. 2——[b]Exod. xxxii. 34——[c]Chap. xxxii. 37; Ezek. xxxiv. 13, &c. [d]Chap. iii. 15; Ezek. xxxiv. 23, &c.

[e]Isa. iv. 2; xi. 1; xl. 10, 11; ch. xxxiii. 14, 15, 16; Dan. ix. 24; Zech. iii. 8; vi. 12; John i. 45——[f]Psa. lxxii. 2; Isa. xxxii. 1, 18; ix. 7——[g]Deut. xxxiii. 28; Zech. xiv. 11

NOTES ON CHAP. XXIII

Verse 1. *Wo be unto the pastors*] There shall a curse fall on the kings, princes, priests, and prophets; who, by their vicious conduct and example, have brought desolation upon the people.

Verse 2. *Ye have scattered my flock*] The bad government both in Church and State was a principal cause of the people's profligacy.

Verse 5. *I will raise unto David a righteous Branch*] As there has been no *age*, from the Babylonish captivity to the destruction of Jerusalem by the Romans, in which such a state of prosperity existed, and no *king* or *governor* who could answer at all to the character here given, the passage has been understood to refer to our blessed Lord, Jesus Christ, who was a *branch* out of the *stem of Jesse;* a *righteous king;* by the power of his Spirit and influence of his religion *reigning, prospering,* and *executing judgment* and *justice in the earth.*

Verse 6. *In his days Judah shall be saved*] The real *Jew* is not one who has his circumcision in the flesh, but in the spirit. The real *Israel* are true believers in Christ Jesus; and the genuine *Jerusalem* is the Church of the first-born, and made free, with all her children, from the bondage of sin, Satan, death, and hell. All these exist only in the *days of the Messiah.* All that went before were the *types* or *significators* of these glorious Gospel excellencies.

And this is *his name whereby he shall be called, THE LORD OUR RIGHTEOUSNESS.*] I shall give the *Hebrew* text of this important passage: וזה שמו אשר יקראו יהוה צדקנו *vezeh shemo asher yikreo Yehovah tsidkenu,* which the *Septuagint* translate as follows, Και τουτο το ονομα αυτου ὁ καλεσει αυτον Κυριος, Ιωσεδεκ, "And this is his name which the Lord shall call him, Josedek."

Dahler translates the text thus:—

> Et voici le nom dont on l'appellera:
> L'Eternel, *Auteur de* notre felicité.

"And this is the name by which he shall be called; The Lord, *the Author of* our happiness."

Dr. *Blayney* seems to follow the *Septuagint;* he translates thus, "And this is the name by which Jehovah shall call him, OUR RIGHTEOUSNESS."

In my old MS. Bible, the first English translation ever made, it is thus:—**And this is the name that thei schul clepen him: oure rigtwise Lord.**

Coverdale's, the first complete English translation of the Scriptures ever *printed*, (1535,) has given it thus:—**And this is the name that they shall call him: even the Lorde oure rightuous Maker.**

Matthews (1549) and *Becke* (1549) follow *Coverdale* literally; but our present translation of the clause is borrowed from *Cardmarden*, (Rouen, 1566,) "Even the Lord our righteousness."

A. M. cir. 3406
B. C. cir. 598
Ol. cir. XLV. 3
TarquiniiPrisci,
R. Roman.,
cir. annum 19

Israel [h]shall dwell safely: and [i]this *is* his name whereby he shall be called, [k]THE LORD OUR RIGHTEOUSNESS.

7 Therefore, behold, [l]the days come, saith the LORD, that they shall no more say, The LORD liveth, which brought up the children of Israel out of the land of Egypt;

8 But, The LORD liveth, which brought up and which led the seed of the house of Israel out of the north country, [m]and from all countries whither I have driven them; and they shall dwell in their own land.

A. M cir 3406
B. C. cir. 598
Ol. cir. XLV. 3
TarquiniiPrisci,
R. Roman.,
cir. annum 19

9 Mine heart within me is broken because of the prophets; [n]all my bones shake; I am like a drunken man, and like a man whom wine hath overcome, because of the LORD, and because of the words of his holiness.

A. M. cir. 3399
B. C. cir. 605
Ol. cir. XLV. 4
TarquiniiPrisci,
R. Roman.,
cir. annum 12

10 For [o]the land is full of adulterers; for [p]because of [q]swearing the land mourneth; [r]the pleasant places of the wilderness are dried up, and their [s]course is evil, and their force *is* not right.

11 For [t]both prophet and priest are profane; yea, [u]in my house have I found their wickedness, saith the LORD.

12 [v]Wherefore their way shall be unto them as slippery *ways* in the darkness: they shall be driven on, and fall therein: for I [w]will bring evil upon them, *even* the year of their visitation, saith the LORD.

13 And I have seen [x]folly [y]in the prophets of Samaria; [z]they prophesied in Baal, and [a]caused my people Israel to err.

14 I have seen also in the prophets of Jerusalem [b]a horrible thing: [c]they commit

[h]Chap. xxxii. 37——[i]Chap. xxxiii. 16; 1 Cor. i. 30——[k]Heb. *Jehovah-tsidkenu*——[l]Chap. xvi. 14, 15——[m]Isa. xliii. 5, 6; ver. 3——[n]See Hab. iii. 16——[o]Chap. v. 7, 8; ix. 2——[p]Hos. iv. 2, 3——[q]Or, *cursing*——[r]Chap. ix. 10; xii. 4——[s]Or, *violence*

[t]Chap. vi. 13; viii. 10; Zeph. iii. 4——[u]Chap. vii. 30; xi. 15; xxxii. 34; Ezek. viii. 11; xxiii. 39——[v]Psa. xxxv. 6; Prov. iv. 19; chap. xiii. 16——[w]Chap. xi. 23——[x]Or *an absurd thing*——[y]Heb. *unsavoury*——[z]Chap. ii. 8——[a]Isa. ix. 16——[b]Or, *filthiness*——[c]Chap. xxix. 23

Dr. *Blayney* thus accounts for his translation:—"Literally, according to the Hebrew idiom,—'And this is his name by which Jehovah shall call, Our Righteousness;' a phrase exactly the same as, 'And Jehovah shall call him so;' which implies that God would make him such as he called him, that is, *our Righteousness*, or the author and means of our salvation and acceptance. So that by the same metonymy Christ is said to 'have been made of God unto us wisdom, and righteousness, and sanctification, and redemption,' 1 Cor. i. 30.

"I doubt not that some persons will be offended with me for depriving them, by this translation, of a favourite argument for proving the Divinity of our Saviour from the Old Testament. But I cannot help it; I have done it with no ill design, but purely because I think, and am morally sure, that the text, as it stands, will not properly admit of any other construction. The *Septuagint* have so translated before me, in an age when there could not possibly be any bias or prejudice either *for* or *against* the fore-mentioned doctrine, a doctrine which draws its *decisive* proofs from the New Testament only."

Dahler paraphrases,—"This Prince shall be surnamed by his people, 'The Lord, the author of our happiness.' The people shall feel themselves happy under him; and shall express their gratitude to him."

I am satisfied that both the *translation* from *Cardmarden* downwards, and the *meaning* put on these words, are incorrect. I prefer the translation of *Blayney* to all others; and that it speaks any thing about the *imputed* righteousness of Christ, cannot possibly be proved by any man who understands the original text. As to those who put the *sense* of their *creed* upon the words, they must be content to stand out of the list of Hebrew critics. I believe *Jesus* to be *Jehovah;* but I doubt much whether this text calls him so. No doctrine so vitally important should be rested on an interpretation so dubious and unsupported by the text. That all our righteousness, holiness, and goodness, as well as the whole of our salvation, come *by* HIM, *from* HIM, and *through* HIM, is fully evident from the Scriptures; but this is not one of the passages that support this most important truth. See on chap. xxxiii.

Verse 7. *The Lord liveth which brought up*] See on chap. xvi. 14, 15.

Verse 9. *Mine heart within me is broken because of the prophets*] The first word of this clause is לנבאים *lannebiim*, which we incorporate with the whole clause, and translate, "Because of the prophets." But as a new prophecy begins here, it is evident that the word is the *title* to this prophecy; and is thus distinguished both by *Blayney* and *Dahler*, CONCERNING THE PROPHETS. This discourse was delivered probably in the reign of *Jehoiakim*.

All my bones shake] He was terrified even by his own message, and shocked at the profanity of the false prophets.

Verse 10. *The land is full of adulterers*] Of idolaters. Of persons who *break their faith* to ME, as an *impure wife* does to her *husband*.

The pleasant places of the wilderness are dried up] He speaks here, most probably, in reference to *dearth*. Profane oaths, false swearing, evil courses, violence, &c., had provoked God to send this among other judgments; see ver. 19.

Verse 11. *In my house*] They had even introduced idolatry into the Temple of God!

Verse 13. *I have seen folly in the prophets of Samaria*] This was not to be wondered at, for their religion was a system of corruption.

Verse 14. *I have seen also in the prophets of Jerusalem*] That is, the prophets of Jerusalem,

A. M. cir. 3399 B. C. cir 605 Ol. XLIII. 4 TarquiniiPrisci, R. Roman., cir. annum 12

adultery, and [d]walk in lies: they [e]strengthen also the hands of evil doers, that none doth return from his wickedness: they are all of them unto me as [f]Sodom, and the inhabitants thereof as Gomorrah.

15 Therefore thus saith the LORD of hosts concerning the prophets; Behold, I will feed them with [g]wormwood, and make them drink the water of gall: for from the prophets of Jerusalem is [h]profaneness gone forth into all the land.

16 Thus saith the LORD of hosts, Hearken not unto the words of the prophets that prophesy unto you: they make you vain: [i]they speak a vision of their own heart, *and* not out of the mouth of the LORD.

17 They say still unto them that despise me, The LORD hath said, [k]Ye shall have peace; and they say unto every one that walketh after the [l]imagination of his own heart, [m]No evil shall come upon you.

18 For [n]who hath stood in the [o]counsel of the LORD, and hath perceived and heard his word? who hath marked his word, and heard *it?*

19 Behold, a [p]whirlwind of the LORD is gone forth in fury, even a grievous whirlwind: it shall fall grievously upon the head of the wicked.

A. M. cir. 3399 B. C. cir. 605 Ol. XLIII. 4 TarquiniiPrisci, R. Roman., cir. annum 12

20 The [q]anger of the LORD shall not return until he have executed, and till he have performed the thoughts of his heart: [r]in the latter days ye shall consider it perfectly.

21 [s]I have not sent these prophets, yet they ran: I have not spoken to them, yet they prophesied.

22 But if they had [t]stood in my counsel, and had caused my people to hear my words, then they should have [u]turned them from their evil way, and from the evil of their doings.

23 *Am* I a God at hand, saith the LORD, and not a God afar off?

24 Can any [v]hide himself in secret places that I shall not see him? saith the LORD. [w]Do not I fill heaven and earth? saith the LORD.

25 I have heard what the prophets said, that prophesy lies in my name, saying, I have dreamed, I have dreamed.

26 How long shall *this* be in the heart of the prophets that prophesy lies? yea, *they are* prophets of the deceit of their own heart;

27 Which think to cause my people to forget my name by their dreams which they tell

[d]Ver. 26——[e]Ezek. xiii. 23——[f]Deut. xxxii. 32; Isa. i. 9, 10——[g]Chap. viii. 14; ix. 15——[h]Or, *hypocrisy* [i]Chap. xiv. 14; ver. 21——[k]Chap. vi. 14; viii. 11; Ezek. xiii. 10; Zech. x. 2——[l]Or, *stubbornness;* chap. xiii. 10 [m]Mic. iii. 11

[n]Job xv. 8; 1 Cor. ii. 16——[o]Or, *secret*——[p]Chap. xxv. 32; xxx. 23——[q]Chap. xxx. 24——[r]Gen. xlix. 1 [s]Chap. xiv. 14; xxvii. 15; xxix. 9——[t]Ver. 18——[u]Jer. xxv. 5——[v]Psa. cxxxix. 7, &c.; Amos ix. 2, 3——[w]1 Kings viii. 27; Psa. cxxxix. 7

while professing a pure *faith,* have followed the ways, and become as corrupt as the prophets of *Samaria.*

They are all of them unto me as Sodom] Incorrigible, brutish sinners, who will as surely be destroyed as *Sodom* and *Gomorrah* were.

Verse 16. *Hearken not unto the words of the prophets*] That is, of those who promise you *safety,* without requiring you to forsake your sins and turn unto the Lord; see ver. 17.

Verse 18. *Who hath stood in the counsel of the Lord*] Who of *them* has ever received a word of prophecy from me? *My word* is not *in them.*

Verse 19. *Behold, a whirlwind*] The *simoom:* the hot pestilential wind blowing from the south, frequently mentioned or referred to in the sacred writings; see ver. 10.

Verse 20. *In the latter days ye shall consider it*] I give you warning: and this punishment which I now threaten shall surely take place; a short time will determine it; ye shall not escape.

Verse 21. *I have not sent these prophets, yet they ran*] Not to save souls, but to profit themselves.

I have not spoken to them, yet they prophesied.] They never received the word at my mouth; yet they went, publishing their own deceits, and pretending them to be revelations from God. The churches which have *legal emoluments* are ever in danger of being overrun and ruined by worldly and self-interested priests.

Verse 23. Am *I a God at hand,—and not a God afar off?*] You act as if you thought I could not see you! Am I not omnipresent? *Do not I fill the heavens and the earth?* ver. 24.

Verse 27. *By their dreams*] Dreams were anciently reputed as a species of inspiration; see Num. xii. 6; 1 Sam. xxviii. 6; Joel iii. 1; Dan. vii. 1. In the Book of *Genesis* we find many examples; and although many mistook the workings of their own vain *imaginations* in sleep for *revelations* from God, yet he has often revealed himself in this way: but such dreams were easily distinguished from the others. They were always such as had no connexion with the *gratification of the flesh;* they were such as contained *warnings against sin,* and *excitements* to *holiness;* they were always *consecutive—well connected,* with a proper *beginning* and *ending;* such as possessed the *intellect* more than the *imagination.* Of such dreams the Lord says, (ver. 28:) *The prophet that hath a dream, let him tell a dream*—permit him to show what he has thus received from the Lord: but let him tell it as a *dream,* and speak

A. M. cir. 3399 B. C. cir. 605 Ol. XLIII. 4 TarquiniiPrisci, R. Roman., cir. annum 12

every man to his neighbour, [x]as
their fathers have forgotten my
name for Baal.
28 The prophet [y]that hath a
dream, let him tell a dream; and he that hath
my word, let him speak my word faithfully.
What *is* the chaff to the wheat? saith the
LORD.
29 *Is* not my word like as a fire? saith the
LORD; and like a hammer *that* breaketh the
rock in pieces?
30 Therefore, behold, [z]I *am* against the
prophets, saith the LORD, that steal my words
every one from his neighbour.
31 Behold, I *am* against the prophets, saith
the LORD, [a]that use their tongues, and say,
He saith.
32 Behold, I *am* against them
that prophesy false dreams, saith
the LORD, and do tell them, and
cause my people to err by their
lies, and by [b]their lightness; yet I sent
them not, nor commanded them: therefore
they shall not profit this people at all, saith
the LORD.
33 And when this people, or the prophet, or
a priest, shall ask thee, saying, What *is* [c]the
burden of the LORD? thou shalt then say unto
them, what burden? [d]I will even forsake you,
saith the LORD.
34 And *as for* the prophet, and the priest,
and the people, that shall say, The burden of
the LORD, I will even [e]punish that man and
his house.

[x]Judg. iii. 7; viii. 33, 34——[y]Heb. *with whom is*——[z]Deut. xviii. 20; chap. xiv. 14, 15

[a]Or, *that smooth their tongues*——[b]Zeph. iii. 4——[c]Mal. i. 1——[d]Ver. 39——[e]Heb. *visit upon*

my word faithfully, lest he may have been deceived.

Verse 28. *What* is *the chaff to the wheat? saith the Lord.*] Do not mingle these *equivocal matters* with *positive revelations.* Do not consider a *dream,* even from a prophet, as that *positive inspiration* which my prophets receive when their *reason, judgment,* and *spiritual feelings* are all in full and in regular exercise. Mix none of your *own devices* with my *doctrines.*

Verse 29. Is *not my word like as a fire?*] It enlightens, warms, and penetrates every part. When it is communicated to the true prophet, it is *like a fire* shut up in his bones; he cannot retain it, he must publish it: and when published, it is like a *hammer* that breaks the rock in pieces; it is ever accompanied by a *Divine power,* that causes both sinner and saint to *feel* its *weight* and *importance.*

In the original words there is something singular: הלוא כה דברי כאש *halo coh debari kaesh,* "Is not thus my word like fire?" I suspect, with Dr. *Blayney,* that כה *coh, thus,* was formerly written כח *coach, strength* or *power;* and so it was understood by the *Targumist:* "Are not all my words strong, like fire?" and probably the author of the Epistle to the Hebrews read it thus, and had it in view when he wrote: "For the word of God is quick and powerful, and sharper than any two-edged sword," Heb. iv. 12. This admitted, the text would read, "Is not my word powerful, like fire?" or, "Is not the power of my word like fire?" But however we understand the words, let us take heed lest we think, as some have thought and affirmed, that the sacred writings are quite sufficient of themselves to enlighten, convince, and convert the soul, and that there is no need of the Holy Spirit. *Fire itself* must be *applied* by an *agent* in order to produce its effects; and surely the *hammer* cannot *break the rock in pieces,* unless *wielded* by an *able workman.* And it is God's *Spirit* alone that can thus *apply* it; for we find it frequently *read* and frequently *spoken,* without producing any salutary effects. And by this very thing the true preachers of the word of God may be distinguished from the *false, non-commissioned ones;* those who run, though they are not sent, ver. 21. The word of him who has his commission from heaven shall be as a *fire* and as a *hammer;* sinners shall be convinced and converted to God by it. But the others, though they steal the word from their neighbour—borrow or pilfer a good sermon, yet they do not profit the people at all, because God did not send them, ver. 32; for the *power* of God does not in their ministry accompany the word.

There may be an allusion to the practice in some mining countries, of *roasting stones* containing ore, before they are subjected to the *hammer,* in order to *pulverize* them. In Cornwall I have seen them *roast the tin stones* in the fire, before they placed them under the action of the *hammers* in the *stamp mill.* The fire separated the *arsenic* from the ore, and then they were easily reduced to powder by the hammers of the mill; afterwards, *washing* the mass with water, the grains of *tin* sank to the bottom, while the lighter parts went off with the water, and thus the metal was procured clean and pure. If this be the allusion, it is very appropriate.

Verse 30. *I* am *against the prophets*] Three cases are mentioned here which excited God's disapprobation: 1. The prophets who *stole the word* from their neighbour; who associated with the true prophets, got some intelligence from them, and then went and published it as a revelation which themselves had received, ver. 30. 2. The prophets who used their *tongues;* הלקחים לשונם *hallokechim leshonam, who lick* or *smooth with their tongues*—gave their own counsels as Divine revelations, flattering them in their sins, and promising peace, when God had not spoken; and prefaced them, "Thus saith the Lord," ver. 31. 3. The prophets who made up false stories, which they termed prophecies, revealed to them in *dreams;* and thus *caused the people to err,* ver. 32.

Verse 33. *What* is *the burden of the Lord?*] The word משא *massa,* here used, signifies *burden, oracle, prophetic discourse;* and is used by almost every prophet. But the persons in the

A. M. cir. 3399 B. C. cir. 605 Ol. XLIII. 4 TarquiniiPrisci, R. Roman., cir. annum 12

35 Thus shall ye say every
one to his neighbour, and every
one to his brother, What hath
the LORD answered? and, What
hath the LORD spoken?
36 And the burden of the LORD shall ye
mention no more: for every man's word shall
be his burden; for ye have perverted the words
of the living God, of the LORD of hosts our God.
37 Thus shalt thou say to the prophet, What
hath the LORD answered thee? and, What hath
the LORD spoken?
38 But since ye say, The burden of the
LORD; therefore thus saith the
LORD; Because ye say this
word, The burden of the LORD,
and I have sent unto you, saying,
Ye shall not say, The burden of the
LORD;
39 Therefore, behold, I, even I, [f]will utterly
forget you, and [g]I will forsake you, and the
city that I gave you and your fathers, *and cast
you* out of my presence:
40 And I will bring [h]an everlasting reproach
upon you, and a perpetual shame, which shall
not be forgotten.

[f]Hos. iv. 6——[g]Ver. 33 [h]Chap. xx. 11

text appear to have been *mockers*. "Where is this *burden* of the Lord?"—"What is the *burden* now?" To this insolent question the prophet answers in the following verses.

I will even forsake you] I will punish the prophet, the priest, and the people, that speak thus, ver. 34. Here are *burdens*.

Verse 36. *Every man's word shall be his burden*] Ye say that all God's messages are *burdens*, and to *you* they shall be such: whereas, had you used them as you ought, they would have been *blessings* to you.

For ye have perverted the words of the living God] And thus have sinned against your own souls.

Verse 39. *I will utterly forget you, and I will forsake you and the city*] Dr. *Blayney* translates:—*I will both take you up altogether, and will cast you off together with the city.* Ye are a *burden* to me: but I will take you up, and then cast you off. I will do with you as a man weary with his burden will do; cast it off his shoulders, and bear it no more.

Verse 40. *I will bring an everlasting reproach upon you*] And this reproach of having rebelled against so good a God, and rejected so powerful a Saviour, follows them to this day through all their dispersions, in every part of the habitable earth. The word of the Lord cannot fail.

CHAPTER XXIV

Under the emblem of the good and bad figs is represented the fate of the Jews already gone into captivity with Jeconiah, and of those that remained still in their own country with Zedekiah. It is likewise intimated that God would deal kindly with the former, but that his wrath would still pursue the latter, 1–10.

A. M. cir. 3406 B. C. 598 Ol. XLV. 3 Anno TarquiniiPrisci, R. Roman., 19

THE [a]LORD showed me, and,
behold, two baskets of figs
were set before the temple of the
LORD, after that Nebuchadrezzar
[b]king of Babylon had carried away captive
[c]Jeconiah the son of Jehoiakim king of Judah,
and the princes of Judah, with
the carpenters and smiths from
Jerusalem, and had brought
them to Babylon.
2 One basket *had* very good figs, *even* like
the figs *that are* first ripe; and the other basket

[a]Amos vii. 1, 4; viii. 1——[b]2 Kings xxiv. 12, &c.; 2 Chron. xxxvi. 10——[c]See chap. xxii. 24, &c.; xxix. 2

NOTES ON CHAP. XXIV

Verse 1. *The Lord showed me, and, behold, two baskets of figs*] Besides the *transposition* of *whole chapters* in this book, there is not unfrequently a transposition of *verses*, and *parts of verses*. Of this we have an instance in the verse before us; the first clause of which should be the last. Thus:—

"After that Nebuchadrezzar king of Babylon had carried away captive Jeconiah, the son of Jehoiakim king of Judah, with the carpenters and smiths from Jerusalem, and had brought them to Babylon, the Lord showed me, and, behold, two baskets of figs *were* set before the temple of the Lord."

Verse 2. "One basket *had* very good figs, *even* like the figs *that are* first ripe; and the other basket *had* very naughty figs, which could not be eaten, they were so bad."

This arrangement restores these verses to a better sense, by restoring the *natural connexion*.

This prophecy was undoubtedly delivered in the first year of the reign of Zedekiah.

Under the type of *good* and *bad figs*, God represents the state of the persons who had already been carried captives into Babylon, with their king Jeconiah, compared with the state of those who should be carried away with Zedekiah. Those already carried away, being the *choice* of the people, are represented by the *good figs:* those now remaining, and soon to be carried into captivity, are represented by the *bad figs, that were good for nothing.* The *state*

A. M. 3406
B. C. 598
Ol. XLV. 3
Anno
TarquiniiPrisci,
R. Roman., 19

had very naughty figs, which could not be eaten, [d]they were so bad.

3 Then said the LORD unto me, What seest thou, Jeremiah? And I said, Figs; the good figs, very good; and the evil, very evil, that cannot be eaten, they are so evil.

4 Again the word of the Lord came unto me, saying,

5 Thus saith the LORD, the God of Israel; Like these good figs, so will I acknowledge [e]them that are carried away captive of Judah, whom I have sent out of this place into the land of the Chaldeans for *their* good.

6 For I will set mine eyes upon them for good, and [f]I will bring them again to this land: and [g]I will build them, and not pull *them* down; and I will plant them, and not pluck *them* up.

7 And I will give them [h]a heart to know me, that I *am* the LORD: and they shall be [i]my people, and I will be their God: for they shall return unto me [k]with their whole heart.

A. M. 3406
B. C. 598
Ol. XLV. 3
Anno
TarquiniiPrisci,
R. Roman., 19

8 And as the evil [l]figs, which cannot be eaten, they are so evil; surely thus saith the LORD, So will I give Zedekiah the king of Judah, and his princes, and the residue of Jerusalem, that remain in this land, and [m]them that dwell in the land of Egypt:

9 And I will deliver them [n]to [o]be removed into all the kingdoms of the earth for *their* hurt, [p]*to be* a reproach and a proverb, a taunt [q]and a curse, in all places whither I shall drive them.

10 And I will send the sword, the famine, and the pestilence, among them, till they be consumed from off the land that I gave unto them and to their fathers.

[d]Heb. *for badness*——[e]Heb. *the captivity*——[f]Ch. xii. 15; xxix. 10——[g]Chap. xxxii. 41; xxxiii. 7; xlii. 10——[h]Deut. xxx. 6; ch. xxxii. 39; Ezek. xi. 19; xxxvi. 26, 27——[i]Chap. xxx. 22; xxxi. 33; xxxii. 38——[k]Chap. xxix. 13

[l]Ch. xxix. 17——[m]See chap. xliii. xliv——[n]Heb. *for removing, or vexation*——[o]Deut. xxviii. 25, 37; 1 Kings ix. 7; 2 Chron. vii. 20; chap. xv. 4; xxix. 18; xxxiv. 17——[p]Psa. xliv. 13, 14——[q]Chap. xxix. 18, 22

also of the *former* in their captivity was vastly preferable to the *state* of *those* who were now about to be delivered into the hand of the king of Babylon. The *latter* would be treated as *double rebels;* the *former*, being the most respectable of the inhabitants, were treated well; and even in captivity, a marked distinction would be made between them, God ordering it so. But the prophet sufficiently explains his own meaning.

Set before the temple]—As an offering of the first-fruits of that kind.

Verse 2. *Very good figs*] Or, figs of the *early sort.* The fig-trees in Palestine, says Dr. *Shaw*, produce fruit thrice each year. The first sort, called *boccore*, those here mentioned, come to perfection about the middle or end of June. The *second* sort, called *kermez*, or summer fig, is seldom ripe before August. And the *third*, which is called the *winter* fig, which is larger, and of a darker complexion than the preceding, hangs all the winter on the tree, ripening even when the leaves are shed, and is fit for gathering in the beginning of *spring.*

Could not be eaten] The *winter fig*,—then in its *crude* or unripe state; the spring not being yet come.

Verse 5. *Like these good figs, so will I acknowledge*] Those already carried away into captivity, I esteem as far more excellent than those who still remain in the land. They have not sinned so deeply, and they are now penitent; and, therefore, *I will set mine eyes upon them for good*, ver. 6. I will watch over them by an especial providence, and they shall be restored to their own land.

Verse 7. *They shall be my people*] I will renew my *covenant* with them, for *they will return to me with thei· whole heart.*

Verse 8. *So will I give Zedekiah*] I will treat these as they deserve. They shall be carried into captivity, and scattered through all nations. Multitudes of those never returned to Judea; the others returned at the end of *seventy years.*

Verse 10. *I will send the sword*] Many of them fell by sword and famine in the war with the Chaldeans, and many more by such means afterwards. The first received their captivity as a correction, and turned to God; the latter still hardened their hearts more and more, and probably very many of them never returned: perhaps they are now amalgamated with heathen nations. Lord, how long?

CHAPTER XXV

This chapter contains a summary of the judgments denounced by Jeremiah against Judah, Babylon, and many other nations. It begins with reproving the Jews for disobeying the calls of God to repentance, 1–7; *on which account their captivity, with that of other neighbouring nations, during* seventy *years, is foretold,* 8–11. *At the expiration of that period, (computing from the invasion of Nebuchadnezzar in the fourth year of Jehoiakim, to the famous edict of the first year of Cyrus,) an end was to be put to the Babylonian empire,* 12–14. *All this is again declared by the emblem of that cup of wrath which the prophet, as it should seem in a vision, tendered to all the nations which he enumerates,* 15–29. *And for farther confirmation, it is a third time repeated in a very beautiful and elevated strain of poetry,* 30–38. *The talent of diversifying the ideas, images, and language, even when the subject is the same, or nearly so, appears no where in such perfection as among the sacred poets.*

A. M. 3397
B. C. 607
Ol. XLV. 2
Anno TarquiniiPrisci,
R. Roman., 10

THE word that came to Jeremiah concerning all the people of Judah [a]in the fourth year of Jehoiakim the son of Josiah king of Judah, that *was* the first year of Nebuchadrezzar king of Babylon.

2 The which Jeremiah the prophet spake unto all the people of Judah, and to all the inhabitants of Jerusalem, saying,

3 [b]From the thirteenth year of Josiah the son of Amon king of Judah, even unto this day, that *is* the three and twentieth year, the word of the LORD hath come unto me, and I have spoken unto you, rising early and speaking; [c]but ye have not hearkened.

4 And the LORD hath sent unto you all his servants the prophets, [d]rising early and sending *them*; but ye have not hearkened, nor inclined your ear to hear.

5 They said, [e]Turn ye again now every one from his evil way, and from the evil of your doings, and dwell in the land that the LORD hath given unto you and to your fathers for ever and ever:

6 And go not after other gods to serve them, and to worship them, and provoke me not to anger with the works of your hands; and I will do you no hurt.

A. M. 3397
B. C. 607
Ol. XLV. 2
Anno TarquiniiPrisci,
R. Roman., 10

7 Yet ye have not hearkened unto me, saith the LORD; that ye might [f]provoke me to anger with the works of your hands to your own hurt.

8 Therefore thus saith the LORD of hosts; Because ye have not heard my words,

9 Behold, I will send and take [g]all the families of the north, saith the LORD, and Nebuchadrezzar the king of Babylon, [h]my servant, and will bring them against this land, and against the inhabitants thereof, and against all these nations round about, and will utterly destroy them, and [i]make them an astonishment, and a hissing, and perpetual desolations.

10 Moreover [k]I will take from them the [l]voice of mirth, and the voice of gladness, the voice of the bridegroom, and the voice of the bride, [m]the sound of the millstones, and the light of the candle.

11 And this whole land shall be a desolation, *and* an astonishment; and these nations shall serve the king of Babylon seventy years.

[a]Chap. xxxvi. 1——[b]Chap. i. 2——[c]Chap. vii. 13; xi. 7, 8, 10; xiii. 10, 11; xvi. 12; xvii. 23; xviii. 12; xix. 15; xxii. 21——[d]Ch. vii. 13, 25; xxvi. 5; xxix. 19——[e]2 Kings xvii. 13; ch. xviii. 11; xxxv. 15; Jonah iii. 8 [f]Deut. xxxii. 21; chap. vii. 19; xxxii. 30

[g]Chap. i. 15——[h]Chap. xxvii. 6; xliii. 10; see Isa. xliv. 28; xlv. 1; chap. xl. 2——[i]Chap. xviii. 16——[k]Heb. *I will cause to perish from them*——[l]Isa. xxiv. 7; chap. vii. 34; xvi. 9; Ezek. xxvi. 13; Hos. ii. 11; Rev. xviii. 23 [m]Eccles. xii. 4

NOTES ON CHAP. XXV

Verse 1. *The word that came to Jeremiah—in the fourth year*] This prophecy, we see, was delivered in the *fourth* year of Jehoiakim, and the chapter that contains it is utterly out of its place. It should be between chapters xxxv. and xxxvi.

The defeat of the Egyptians by Nebuchadnezzar at Carchemish, and the subsequent taking of Jerusalem, occurred in this year, *viz.*, the fourth year of *Jehoiakim.*

The first year of Nebuchadrezzar] This king was associated with his father *two years* before the death of the latter. The Jews reckon his reign from this time, and this was the *first* of those two years; but the Chaldeans date the commencement of his reign two years later, *viz.*, at the death of his father.

Verse 7. *That ye might provoke*] Ye would not hearken; but chose to provoke me with anger.

Verse 9. *Behold, I will send*] At this time Nebuchadrezzar had not invaded the land, according to this Version; but the Hebrew may be translated, "Behold I am sending, and have taken all the families;" that is, all the *allies* of the king of Babylon.

Instead of ואל *veel, "and* TO Nebuchadrezzar," as in the common Hebrew Bible, *seven* MSS. of *Kennicott's* and *De Rossi's*, and *one* of my own, have ואת *veeth*, "AND Nebuchadrezzar," which is undoubtedly the true reading.

Verse 10. *I will take from them*] See chap. vii. 34, and xvi. 9.

The sound of the mill-stones, and the light of the candle.] These two are conjoined, because they generally ground the corn *before day*, by the light of the candle. Sir J. *Chardin* has remarked, that every where in the morning may be heard the *noise of the mills;* for they generally grind *every day* just as much as is necessary for the day's consumption. Where then the *noise of the mill* is not *heard*, nor the *light of the candle seen*, there must be desolation; because these things are heard and seen in every inhabited country.

Verse 11. *Shall serve the king of Babylon seventy years.*] As this prophecy was delivered in the *fourth* year of Jehoiakim, and in the *first* of Nebuchadnezzar, and began to be accomplished in the same year, (for then Nebuchadnezzar invaded Judea, and took Jerusalem,)

A. M. 3397 B. C. 607 Ol. XLIII. 2 Anno TarquiniiPrisci, R. Roman., 10

12 And it shall come to pass, [n]when seventy years are accomplished, *that* I will [o]punish the king of Babylon, and that nation, saith the LORD, for their iniquity, and the land of the Chaldeans, [p]and will make it perpetual desolations.

13 And I will bring upon that land all my words which I have pronounced against it, *even* all that is written in this book, which Jeremiah hath prophesied against all the nations.

14 [q]For many nations [r]and great kings shall [s]serve themselves of them also: [t]and I will recompense them according to their deeds, and according to the works of their own hands.

15 For thus saith the LORD God of Israel unto me; Take the [u]wine cup of this fury at my hand, and cause all the nations, to whom I send thee, to drink it.

16 And [v]they shall drink, and be moved, and be mad, because of the sword that I will send among them.

17 Then took I the cup at the LORD's hand, and made all the nations to drink, unto whom the LORD had sent me:

18 *To wit,* Jerusalem, and the cities of Judah, and the kings thereof, and the princes thereof, to make them [w]a desolation, an astonishment, a hissing, and [x]a curse; as *it is* this day;

19 [y]Pharaoh king of Egypt, and his servants, and his princes, and all his people;

20 And all [z]the mingled people, and all the kings of [a]the land of Uz, [b]and all the kings of the land of the Philistines, and Ashkelon, and Azzah, and Ekron, and [c]the remnant of Ashdod,

21 [d]Edom, and [e]Moab, and the children of [f]Ammon,

22 And all the kings of [g]Tyrus, and all the kings of Zidon, and the kings of the [h]isles which *are* beyond the [i]sea,

23 [k]Dedan, and Tema, and Buz, and all [l]*that are* in the utmost corners,

24 And [m]all the kings of Arabia, and all the kings of the [n]mingled people that dwell in the desert,

[n]2 Chron. xxxvi. 21, 22; Ezra i. 1; ch. xxix. 10; Dan. ix. 2; 2 Kings xxiv. 1——[o]Heb. *visit upon*——[p]Isa. xiii. 19; xiv. 23; xxi. 1, &c.; xlvii. 1; ch. l. 3, 13, 23, 39, 40, 45; li. 25, 26——[q]Ch. l. 9; li. 27, 28——[r]Ch. l. 41; li. 27 [s]Ch. xxvii. 7——[t]Ch. l. 29; li. 6, 24——[u]Job xxi. 20; Psa. lxxv. 8; Isa. li. 17; Rev. xiv. 10——[v]Ch. li. 7; Ezek. xxiii. 34; Nah. iii. 11——[w]Ver. 9, 11——[x]Ch. xxiv. 9

[y]Ch. xlvi. 2, 25——[z]Ver. 24——[a]Job i. 1——[b]Ch. xlvii. 1, 5, 7——[c]See Isa. xx. 1——[d]Ch. xlix. 7, &c. [e]Ch. xlviii. 1——[f]Ch. xlix. 1——[g]Ch. xlvii. 4——[h]Or, *region by the sea side*——[i]Ch. xlix. 23——[k]Ch. xlix. 8 [l]Heb. *cut off into corners*, or *having the corners* of the hair *polled;* ch. ix. 26; xlix. 32——[m]2 Chron. ix. 14——[n]See ver. 20; ch. xlix. 31; l. 3; Ezek. xxx. 5

seventy years from this time will reach down to the first year of Cyrus, when he made his proclamation for the restoration of the Jews, and the rebuilding of Jerusalem. See the note on Isa. xiii. 19, where the subject is farther considered in relation to the reign of Nebuchadnezzar, and the city of Babylon.

Verse 12. *And that nation*] הגוי ההוא *haggoi hahu.* Dr. *Blayney* contends that this should be translated *his nation*, and that ההוא *hahu* is the substantive pronoun used in the genitive case. It is certainly more clear and definite to read, "I will punish the king of Babylon, and HIS nation."

Will make it perpetual desolations] See the note on Isa. xiii. 19, where the fulfilment of this prophecy is distinctly marked.

Verse 14. *Many nations and great kings*] The *Medes* and the *Persians*, under Cyrus; and several princes, his vassals or allies.

Verse 15. *Take the wine cup of this fury*] For an ample illustration of this passage and simile, see the note on Isa. li. 21.

Verse 17. *Then took I the cup—and made all the nations to drink*] This *cup of God's wrath* is merely symbolical, and simply means that the prophet should declare to all these people that they shall fall under the Chaldean yoke, and that this is a punishment inflicted on them by God for their iniquities. "Then I took the cup;" I declared publicly the tribulation that God was about to bring on Jerusalem, the cities of Judah, and all the nations.

Verse 19. *Pharaoh king of Egypt*] This was *Pharaoh-necho*, who was the principal cause of instigating the neighbouring nations to form a league against the Chaldeans.

Verse 20. *All the mingled people*] The strangers and foreigners; Abyssinians and others who had settled in Egypt.

Land of Uz] A part of Arabia near to Idumea. See on Job. i. 1.

Verse 22. *Tyrus and—Zidon*] The most ancient of all the cities of the Phœnicians.

Kings of the isles which are *beyond the sea.*] As the *Mediterranean* Sea is most probably meant, and the Phœnicians had numerous colonies on its *coasts*, I prefer the *marginal* reading, *the kings of the region by the sea side.*

Verse 23. *Dedan*] Was son of Abraham, by Keturah, Gen. xxv. 3.

Tema] Was one of the sons of Ishmael, in the north of Arabia, Gen. xxxvi. 15.

Buz] Brother of *Uz*, descendants of Nahor, brother of Abraham, settled in Arabia Deserta, Gen. xxii. 21.

Verse 24. *The mingled people*] Probably the *Scenite Arabians.*

A. M. 3397
B. C. 607
Ol. XLIII. 2
Anno
TarquiniiPrisci,
R. Roman., 10

25 And all the kings of Zimri, and all the kings of [o]Elam, and all the kings of the Medes,

26 [p]And all the kings of the north, far and near, one with another, and all the kingdoms of the world, which *are* upon the face of the earth: [q]and the king of Sheshach shall drink after them.

27 Therefore thou shalt say unto them, Thus saith the LORD of hosts, the God of Israel; [r]Drink ye, and [s]be drunken, and spue, and fall, and rise no more, because of the sword which I will send among you.

28 And it shall be, if they refuse to take the cup at thine hand to drink, then shalt thou say unto them, Thus saith the LORD of hosts; Ye shall certainly drink.

29 For, lo, [t]I begin to bring evil on the city [u]which [v]is called by my name, and should ye be utterly unpunished? Ye shall not be unpunished: for [w]I will call for a sword upon all the inhabitants of the earth, saith the LORD of hosts.

30 Therefore prophesy thou against them all these words, and say unto them, The LORD shall [x]roar from on high, and utter his voice from [y]his holy habitation; he shall mightily roar upon [z]his habitation; he shall give [a]a shout, as they that tread *the grapes,* against all the inhabitants of the earth.

31 A noise shall come *even* to the ends of the earth; for the LORD hath [b]a controversy with the nations, [c]he will plead with all flesh; he will give them *that are* wicked to the sword, saith the LORD.

A. M. 3397
B. C. 607
Ol. XLIII. 2
Anno
TarquiniiPrisci,
R. Roman., 10

32 Thus saith the LORD of hosts, Behold, evil shall go forth from nation to nation, and [d]a great whirlwind shall be raised up from the coasts of the earth.

33 [e]And the slain of the LORD shall be at that day from *one* end of the earth even unto the *other* end of the earth: they shall not be [f]lamented, [g]neither gathered, nor buried; they shall be dung upon the ground.

34 [h]Howl, ye shepherds, and cry; and wallow yourselves *in the ashes,* ye principal of the flock: for [i]the days of your slaughter and of your dispersions are accomplished; and ye shall fall like [k] a pleasant vessel.

35 And [l]the shepherds shall have no way to flee, nor the principal of the flock to escape.

36 A voice of the cry of the shepherds, and a howling of the principal of the flock, *shall be heard:* for the LORD hath spoiled their pasture.

37 And the peaceable habitations are cut down because of the fierce anger of the LORD.

38 He hath forsaken [m]his covert, as the lion: for their land is [n]desolate because of the fierceness of the oppressor, and because of his fierce anger.

---

[o]Ch. xlix. 34——[p]Ch. l. 9——[q]Ch. li. 41——[r]Hab. ii. 16——[s]Isa. li. 21; lxiii. 6——[t]Prov. xi. 31; ch. xlix. 12; Ezek. ix. 6; Obad. 16; Luke xxiii. 31; 1 Pet. iv. 17——[u]Heb. *upon which my name is called*——[v]Dan. ix. 18, 19——[w]Ezek. xxxviii. 21——[x]Isa. xlii. 13; Joel iii. 16; Amos i. 2——[y]Psa. xi. 4; ch. xvii. 12——[z]1 Kings ix. 3; Psa. cxxxii. 14——[a]Isa. xvi. 9; chap. xlviii. 33

[b]Hos. iv. 1; Mic. vi. 2——[c]Isa. lxvi. 16; Joel iii. 2——[d]Ch. xxiii. 19; xxx. 23——[e]Isa. lxvi. 16——[f]Ch. xvi. 4, 6——[g]Psa. lxxix. 3; ch. viii. 2; Rev. xi. 9——[h]Ch. iv. 8; vi. 26——[i]Heb. *your days for slaughter*——[k]Heb. *a vessel of desire*——[l]Heb. *flight shall perish from the shepherds, and escaping from, &c.*; Amos ii. 14——[m]Psa. lxxvi. 2——[n]Heb. *a desolation*

Verse 25. *Zimri*] Descendants of Abraham, by Keturah, Gen. xxv. 2, 6.

Elam] Called Elymais by the Greeks, was on the south frontier of Media, to the north of Susiana, not far from Babylon.

Verse 26. *The kings of the north, far and near*] The *first* may mean Syria; the *latter*, the *Hyrcanians* and *Bactrians.*

And the king of Sheshach shall drink after them.] *Sheshach* was an ancient king of Babylon, who was deified after his death. Here it means either *Babylon*, or *Nebuchadnezzar* the king of it. After it has been the occasion of ruin to so many other nations, Babylon itself shall be destroyed by the *Medo-Persians.*

Verse 27. *Be drunken, and spue*] Why did we not use the word *vomit,* less offensive than the other, and yet of the same signification?

Verse 29. *The city which is called by my name*] Jerusalem, which should be *first* given up to the destruction.

Verse 32. *Evil shall go forth from nation to nation*] One nation after another shall fall before the Chaldeans.

Verse 33. *From* one *end of the earth*] From one end of the *land* to the other. All *Palestine* shall be desolated by it.

Verse 34. *Howl, ye shepherds*] Ye kings and chiefs of the people.

Ye shall fall like a pleasant vessel.] As a fall will break and utterly ruin a precious vessel of crystal, agate, &c., so your overthrow will be to you irreparable ruin.

Verse 38. *As the lion*] Leaving the banks of Jordan when overflowed, and coming with ravening fierceness to the champaign country.

CHAPTER XXVI

Jeremiah, by the command of God, goes into the court of the Lord's house; and foretells the destruction of the temple and city, if not prevented by the speedy repentance of the people, 1–7. *By this unwelcome prophecy his life was in great danger; although saved by the influence of Ahikam, the son of Shaphan, who makes a masterly defence for the prophet,* 8–18. *Urijah is condemned, but escapes to Egypt; whence he is brought back by Jehoiakim, and slain,* 20–23. *Ahikam befriends Jeremiah,* 24.

A. M. 3394
B. C. 610
Ol. XLII. 3
Anno
TarquiniiPrisci,
R. Roman., 7

IN the beginning of the reign of Jehoiakim the son of Josiah king of Judah came this word from the LORD, saying,

2 Thus saith the LORD; Stand in [a]the court of the LORD's house, and speak unto all the cities of Judah, which come to worship in the LORD's house, [b]all the words that I command thee to speak unto them; [c]diminish not a word:

3 [d]If so be they will hearken, and turn every man from his evil way, that I may [e]repent me of the evil, which I purpose to do unto them, because of the evil of their doings.

4 And thou shalt say unto them, Thus saith the LORD; [f]If ye will not hearken to me to walk in my law, which I have set before you,

5 To hearken to the words of my servants the prophets, [g]whom I sent unto you, both rising up early, and sending *them,* but ye have not hearkened;

6 Then will I make this house like [h]Shiloh, and will make this city [i]a curse to all the nations of the earth.

7 So the priests and the prophets and all the people heard Jeremiah speaking these words in the house of the LORD.

8 Now it came to pass, when Jeremiah had made an end of speaking all that the LORD had commanded *him* to speak unto all the people, that the priests and the prophets and all the people took him, saying, Thou shalt surely die.

A. M. 3394
B. C. 610
Ol. XLII. 3
Anno
TarquiniiPrisci,
R. Roman., 7

9 Why hast thou prophesied in the name of the LORD, saying, This house shall be like Shiloh, and this city shall be desolate without an inhabitant? And all the people were gathered against Jeremiah in the house of the LORD.

10 When the princes of Judah heard these things, then they came up from the king's house unto the house of the LORD, and sat down [k]in the entry of the new gate of the LORD's *house.*

11 Then spake the priests and the prophets unto the princes and to all the people, saying, [l]This man *is* worthy to die; [m]for he hath prophesied against this city, as ye have heard with your ears.

12 Then spake Jeremiah unto all the princes and to all the people, saying, The LORD sent me to prophesy against this house and against this city all the words that ye have heard.

13 Therefore now [n]amend your ways and your doings, and obey the voice of the LORD your God; and the LORD will [o]repent him of the evil that he hath pronounced against you.

14 As for me, behold, [p]I *am* in your hand: do with me [q]as seemeth good and meet unto you.

[a]Chap. xix. 14——[b]Ezek. iii. 10; Matt. xxviii. 20——[c]Acts xx. 27——[d]Chap. xxxvi. 3——[e]Chap. xviii. 8; Jonah iii. 8, 9——[f]Lev. xxvi. 14, &c.; Deut. xxviii. 15——[g]Chap. vii. 13, 25; xi. 7; xxv. 3, 4——[h]1 Sam. iv. 10, 11; Psa. lxxviii. 60; chap. vii. 12, 14——[i]Isa. lxv. 15; chap. xxiv. 9——[k]Or, *at the door*——[l]Heb. *The judgment of death is for this man*——[m]Chap. xxxviii. 4——[n]Chap. vii. 3——[o]Ver. 3, 19——[p]Chap. xxxviii. 5——[q]Hebrew, *as it is good and right in your eyes*

NOTES ON CHAP. XXVI

Verse 1. *In the beginning of the reign of Jehoiakim*] As this prophecy must have been delivered in the *first* or *second* year of the reign of Jehoiakim, it is totally out of its place here. Dr. *Blayney* puts it before chap. xxxvi.; and Dr. *Dahler* immediately after chap. ix., and before chap. xlvi.

Verse 4. *If ye will not hearken*] This and several of the following verses are nearly the same with those in chap. vii. 13, &c., where see the notes.

Verse 8. *And all the people*] That were in company with the priests and the prophets.

Verse 10. *The princes of Judah*] The king's court; his cabinet counsellors.

Verse 12. *The Lord sent me to prophesy*] My commission is from him, and my words are his own. I sought not this painful office. I did not run before I was sent.

Verse 13. *Therefore now amend your ways*] If ye wish to escape the judgment which I have predicted, turn to God, and iniquity shall not be your ruin.

Verse 14. *As for me, behold, I* am *in your hand*] I am the messenger of God; you may do with me what you please; but if you slay me, you will bring innocent blood upon yourselves.

A. M. 3394 B. C. 610 Ol. XLII. 3 Anno TarquiniiPrisci, R. Roman., 7

15 But know ye for certain, that if ye put me to death, ye shall surely bring innocent blood upon yourselves, and upon this city, and upon the inhabitants thereof: for of a truth the LORD hath sent me unto you to speak all these words in your ears.

16 Then said the princes and all the people unto the priests and to the prophets; This man *is* not worthy to die: for he hath spoken to us in the name of the LORD our God.

17 [r]Then rose up certain of the elders of the land, and spake to all the assembly of the people, saying,

18 [s]Micah the Morasthite prophesied in the days of Hezekiah king of Judah, and spake to all the people of Judah, saying, Thus saith the LORD of hosts; [t]Zion shall be ploughed *like* a field, and Jerusalem shall become heaps, and the mountain of the house as the high places of a forest.

19 Did Hezekiah king of Judah and all Judah put him at all to death? [u]did he not fear the LORD, and besought [v]the LORD, and the LORD [w]repented him of the evil which he had pronounced against them? [x]Thus might we procure great evil against our souls.

A. M. 3394 B. C. 610 Ol. XLII. 3 Anno TarquiniiPrisci, R. Roman., 7

20 And there was also a man that prophesied in the name of the LORD, Urijah the son of Shemaiah of Kirjath-jearim, who prophesied against this city and against this land according to all the words of Jeremiah:

21 And when Jehoiakim the king, with all his mighty men, and all the princes, heard his words, the king sought to put him to death: but when Urijah heard it, he was afraid, and fled, and went into Egypt;

22 And Jehoiakim the king sent men into Egypt, *namely*, Elnathan the son of Achbor, and *certain* men with him into Egypt.

23 And they fetched forth Urijah out of Egypt, and brought him unto Jehoiakim the king; who slew him with the sword, and cast his dead body into the graves of the [y]common people.

24 Nevertheless [z]the hand of Ahikam the son of Shaphan was with Jeremiah, that they should not give him into the hand of the people to put him to death.

---

[r]See Acts v. 34, &c.——[s]Mic. i. 1——[t]Mic. iii. 12 [u]2 Chronicles xxxii. 26——[v]Hebrew, *the face of the LORD*

[w]Exod. xxxii. 14; 2 Sam. xxiv. 16——[x]Acts v. 39 [y]Heb. *sons of the people*——[z]2 Kings xxii. 12, 14; chap. xxxix. 14

Verse 16. *This man* is *not worthy to die*] The whole court acquitted him.

Verse 17. *Certain of the elders*] This is really a fine defence, and the argument was perfectly conclusive. Some think that it was Ahikam who undertook the prophet's defence.

Verse 18. *Micah the Morasthite*] The same as stands among the prophets. Now all these prophesied as hard things against the land as Jeremiah has done; yet they were not put to death, for the people saw that they were sent of God.

Verse 20. *Urijah—who prophesied*] The process against Jeremiah is finished at the *nineteenth* verse; and the case of Urijah is next brought on, for he was also to be tried for his life; but hearing of it he fled to Egypt. He was however condemned in his absence; and the king sent to Egypt, and brought him thence and slew him, and caused him to have an ignominious burial, ver. 21-23.

Verse 24. *The hand of Ahikam—was with Jeremiah*] And it was probably by his influence that Jeremiah did not share the same fate with Urijah. The Ahikam mentioned here was probably the father of Gedaliah, who, after the capture of Jerusalem, was appointed governor of the country by Nebuchadnezzar, chap. xl. 5. Of the Prophet *Urijah*, whether he was true or false, we know nothing but what we learn from this place.

That they should not give him into the hand of the people] Though acquitted in the supreme court, he was not out of danger; there was a popular prejudice against him, and it is likely that Ahikam was obliged to conceal him, that they might not put him to death. The genuine ministers of God have no favour to expect from those who are HIS enemies.

CHAPTER XXVII

Ambassadors being come from several neighbouring nations to solicit the king of Judah to join in a confederacy against the king of Babylon, Jeremiah is commanded to put bands and yokes upon his neck, (the emblems of subjection and slavery,) and to send them afterwards by those ambassadors to their respective princes; intimating by this significant type that God had decreed their subjection to the Babylonian empire, and that it was their wisdom to submit. It is farther declared that all the conquered nations shall remain in subjection to the Chaldeans during the reign of Nebuchadnezzar, and those of his son and grandson, even till the arrival of that period in which the Babylonians shall have filled up the measure of their iniquities; and that then the mighty Chaldean monarchy itself, for a certain period the paramount power of the habitable globe, shall be visited with a dreadful storm of Divine wrath, through the violence of which it shall be dashed to pieces like a potter's vessel, the fragments falling into the hands of many nations and great kings, 1–11. *Zedekiah, particularly, is admonished not to join in the revolt against Nebuchadnezzar, and warned against trusting to the suggestions of false prophets,* 11–18. *The chapter concludes with foretelling that what still remained of the sacred vessels of the temple should be carried to Babylon, and not restored till after the destruction of the Chaldean empire,* 19–22.

A. M. 3409
B. C. 595
Ol. XLVI. 2
Anno
TarquiniiPrisci,
R. Roman., 22

IN the beginning of the reign of Jehoiakim the son of Josiah [a]king of Judah came this word unto Jeremiah from the LORD, saying,

2 Thus [b]saith the LORD to me; Make thee bonds and yokes, [c]and put them upon thy neck,

3 And send them to the king of Edom, and to the king of Moab, and to the king of the Ammonites, and to the king of Tyrus, and to the king of Zidon, by the hand of the messengers which come to Jerusalem unto Zedekiah king of Judah;

4 And command them [d]to say unto their masters, Thus saith the LORD of hosts, the God of Israel; Thus shall ye say unto your masters;

5 [e]I have made the earth, the man and the beast that *are* upon the ground, by my great power and by my outstretched arm, and [f]have given it unto whom it seemed meet unto me.

A. M. 3409
B. C. 595
Ol. XLVI. 2
Anno
TarquiniiPrisci,
R. Roman., 22

6 [g]And now have I given all these lands into the hand of Nebuchadnezzar, the king of Babylon, [h]my servant; and [i]the beasts of the field have I given him also to serve him.

7 [k]And all nations shall serve him, and his son, and his son's son, [l]until the very time of his land come: [m]and then many nations and great kings shall serve themselves of him.

8 And it shall come to pass, *that* the nation and kingdom which will not serve the same Nebuchadnezzar the king of Babylon, and that will not put their neck under the yoke of the king of Babylon, that nation will I punish, saith the LORD, with the sword, and with the famine, and with the pestilence, until I have consumed them by his hand.

9 Therefore hearken not ye to your prophets, nor to your diviners, nor to your [n]dreamers, nor to your enchanters, nor to your sorcerers, which speak unto you, saying, Ye shall not serve the king of Babylon:

---

[a]See ver. 3, 12, 19, 20; chap. xxviii. 1——[b]Or, *hath the LORD said*——[c]Chap. xxviii. 10, 12; so Ezek. iv. 1; xii. 3; xxiv. 3, &c.——[d]Or, *concerning their masters, saying*——[e]Psa. cxv. 15; cxlvi. 6; Isa. xlv. 12

[f]Psa. cxv. 16; Dan. iv. 17, 25, 32——[g]Ch. xxviii. 14——[h]Ch. xxv. 9; xliii. 10; Ezek. xxix. 18, 20——[i]Ch. xxviii. 14; Dan. ii. 38——[k]2 Chron. xxxvi. 20——[l]Ch. xxv. 12; l. 27; Dan. v. 26——[m]Ch. xxv. 14——[n]Heb. *dreams*

NOTES ON CHAP. XXVII

Verse 1. *In the beginning of the reign of Jehoiakim*] It is most evident that his prophecy was delivered about the *fourth* year of ZEDEKIAH, and not *Jehoiakim*, as in the text. See chap. xxviii. 1. *Three* of *Kennicott's* MSS. (*one* in the text, a *second* in the margin, and the *third* upon a rasure) have *Zedekiah;* so likewise have the *Syriac* and the *Arabic*. *Houbigant*, *Lowth*, *Blayney*, *Dahler*, and others declare for this reading against that in the present text. And it is clear from the *third* and *twelfth* verses, where *Zedekiah* is expressly mentioned, that this is the true reading.

Verse 2. *Make thee bonds and yokes*] Probably *yokes* with *straps*, by which they were attached to the neck. This was a symbolical action, to show that the several kings mentioned below should be brought under the dominion of the Chaldeans.

Verse 5. *I have made the earth*] I am the Creator and Governor of all things, and I dispose of the several kingdoms of the world as seemeth best to me.

Verse 6. *And now have I given*] These kingdoms are at my sovereign disposal; and at present, for the punishment of their rulers and people, I shall give them into the hands of Nebuchadnezzar, king of Babylon.

Verse 7. *And all nations shall serve him*, (Nebuchadnezzar,) *and his son*, (Evil-merodach, chap. lii. 31,) *and his son's son*, (Belshazzar, Dan. v. 11.) All which was literally fulfilled.

Verse 9. *Therefore hearken not ye to your prophets*] Who pretend to have a revelation from heaven.

Nor to your diviners] קסמיכם *kosemeychem, from* קסם *kasam*, to *presage* or *prognosticate*. Persons who *guessed* at futurity by certain signs in the animate or inanimate creation.

Nor to your dreamers] חלמתיכם *chalomotheychem*, from חלם *chalam*, to *break in pieces;* hence חלום *chalom, a dream*, because it consists of *broken fragments*. Dream-interpreters, who, from these *broken shreds* patch up a meaning by their own interpolations.

Nor to your enchanters] ענניכם *oneneychem*, from ענן *anan, a cloud*—cloud-mongers. Diviners by the flight, colour, density, rarity, and shape of clouds.

Nor to your sorcerers] כשפיכם *cashshapheychem*, from כשף *kashaph*, to *discover;* the discoverers, the finders out of hidden things, stolen

A. M. 3409
B. C. 595
Ol. XLVI. 2
Anno
TarquiniiPrisci,
R. Roman., 22

10 [o]For they prophesy a lie unto you, to [p]remove you far from your land; and that I should drive you out, and ye should perish.

11 But the nations that bring their neck under the yoke of the king of Babylon, and serve him, those will I let remain still in their own land, saith the LORD; and they shall till it, and dwell therein.

12 I spake also to [q]Zedekiah king of Judah according to all these words, saying, Bring your necks under the yoke of the king of Babylon, and serve him and his people, and live.

13 [r]Why will ye die, thou and thy people, by the sword, by the famine, and by the pestilence, as the LORD hath spoken against the nation that will not serve the king of Babylon?

14 Therefore hearken not unto the words of the prophets that speak unto you, saying, Ye shall not serve the king of Babylon: for they prophesy [s]a lie unto you.

15 For I have not sent them, saith the LORD, yet they prophesy [t]a lie in my name; that I may drive you out, and that ye might perish, ye, and the prophets that prophesy unto you.

16 Also I spake to the priests and to all this people, saying, Thus saith the LORD; Hearken not to the words of your prophets that prophesy unto you, saying, Behold, [u]the vessels of the LORD's house shall now shortly be brought again from Babylon: for they prophesy a lie unto you.

A. M. 3409
B. C. 595
Ol. XLVI. 2
Anno
TarquiniiPrisci,
R. Roman., 22

17 Hearken not unto them; serve the king of Babylon, and live: wherefore should this city be laid waste?

18 But if they *be* prophets, and if the word of the LORD be with them, let them now make intercession to the LORD of hosts, that the vessels which are left in the house of the LORD, and *in* the house of the king of Judah, and at Jerusalem, go not to Babylon.

19 For thus saith the LORD of hosts [v]concerning the pillars, and concerning the sea, and concerning the bases, and concerning the residue of the vessels that remain in this city,

20 Which Nebuchadnezzar king of Babylon took not, when he carried away [w]captive Jeconiah the son of Jehoiakim king of Judah from Jerusalem to Babylon, and all the nobles of Judah and Jerusalem;

21 Yea, thus saith the LORD of hosts, the God of Israel, concerning the vessels that remain *in* the house of the LORD, and *in* the house of the king of Judah and of Jerusalem;

22 They shall be [x]carried to Babylon, and there shall they be until the day that I [y]visit them, saith the LORD; then [z]will I bring them up, and restore them to this place.

---

[o]Ver. 14——[p]Ch. xxxii. 31; Deut. xxviii. 25; Ezek. xii. 3——[q]Ch. xxviii. 1; xxxviii. 17——[r]Ezek. xviii. 31——[s]Ch. xiv. 14; xxiii. 21; xxix. 8, 9——[t]Heb. *in a lie*, or *lyingly*——[u]2 Chron. xxxvi. 7, 10; ch. xxviii. 3; Dan. i. 2

[v]2 Kings xxv. 13, &c.; ch. lii. 17, 20, 21——[w]2 Kings xxiv. 14, 15; chap. xxiv. 1——[x]2 Kings xxv. 13; 2 Chron. xxxvi. 18——[y]2 Chron. xxxvi. 21; chap. xxix. 10; xxxii. 5——[z]Ezra i. 7; vii. 19

---

goods, &c. Persons also who use *incantations*, and either by *spells* or *drugs* pretend to find out mysteries, or produce supernatural effects. Every nation in the world had persons who pretended to find out hidden things, or foretell future events; and such were gladly encouraged by the ignorant multitude; and many of them were mere apes of the prophets of God. Man knows that he is *short-sighted*, feels pain at the uncertainty of futurity, and wishes to have his doubts resolved by such persons as the above, to put an end to his uncertainty.

Verse 13. *Why will ye die*] If ye resist the king of Babylon, to whom I have given a commission against you, ye shall be destroyed by the sword and by famine; but if ye submit, ye shall escape all these evils.

Verse 16. *The vessels of the Lord's house*] Which had been carried away by Nebuchadnezzar under the reigns of Jehoiakim and Jeconiah, 2 Chron. xxxvi. 7-10.

Shall now shortly be brought again] This is a lie. They shall not be restored till I bring them up, ver. 22, which was after the captivity, when they were sent back by Cyrus, the Lord inclining his heart to do it, Ezra i. 7, and vii. 19.

Verse 19. *Concerning the pillars*] Two brazen columns placed by Solomon in the pronaos or portico of the temple, *eighteen* cubits high, and *twelve* in circumference, 1 Kings vii. 15-22; Jer. lii. 11.

The sea] The brazen sea, *ten* cubits in diameter, and *thirty* in circumference. It contained water for different washings in the Divine worship, and was supported on *twelve* brazen oxen. Perhaps these are what are called the *bases* here. See the parallel places in the margin, and the notes on them.

Verse 22. *They shall be carried to Babylon*] Far from those already taken being brought back, those which now remain shall be carried thither, unless ye submit to the Chaldeans. They did not submit, and the prophecy was literally fulfilled; see chap. lii. 17-23; 2 Kings xxv. 13, and the other places in the *margin*.

CHAPTER XXVIII

One of those pretended prophets spoken of in the preceding chapter, having contradicted and opposed Jeremiah, receives an awful declaration that, as a proof to the people of his having spoken without commission, he should die in the then current year; which accordingly came to pass in the seventh month, 1–17.

A. M. 3409
B. C. 595
Ol. XLVI. 2
Anno
TarquiniiPrisci,
R. Roman., 22

AND [a]it came to pass the
same year, in the beginning
of the reign of Zedekiah king of
Judah, in the fourth year, *and* in
the fifth month, *that* Hananiah the son of Azur
the prophet, which *was* of Gibeon, spake unto
me in the house of the LORD, in the presence
of the priests and of all the people, saying,
2 Thus speaketh the LORD of hosts, the
God of Israel, saying, I have broken [b]the
yoke of the king of Babylon.
3 [c]Within [d]two full years will I bring again
into this place all the vessels of the LORD's
house, that Nebuchadnezzar king of Babylon
took away from this place, and carried them
to Babylon:
4 And I will bring again to this place Jeconiah the son of Jehoiakim king of Judah, with
all the [e]captives of Judah, that went into
Babylon, saith the LORD: for I will break the
yoke of the king of Babylon.
5 Then the prophet Jeremiah said unto the
prophet Hananiah in the presence of the
priests, and in the presence of all the people
that stood in the house of the LORD,
6 Even the prophet Jeremiah said, [f]Amen:
the LORD do so: the LORD per-
form thy words which thou hast
prophesied, to bring again the
vessels of the LORD's house,
and all that is carried away captive, from
Babylon into this place.

A. M. 3409
B. C. 595
Ol. XLVI. 2
Anno
TarquiniiPrisci,
R. Roman., 22

7 Nevertheless hear thou now this word that
I speak in thine ears, and in the ears of all
the people;
8 The prophets that have been before me and
before thee of old prophesied both against
many countries, and against great kingdoms,
of war, and of evil, and of pestilence.
9 [g]The prophet which prophesieth of peace,
when the word of the prophet shall come to
pass, *then* shall the prophet be known, that
the LORD hath truly sent him.
10 Then Hananiah the prophet took the
[h]yoke from off the prophet Jeremiah's neck,
and brake it.
11 And Hananiah spake in the presence of
all the people, saying, Thus saith the LORD;
Even so will I break the yoke of Nebuchadnezzar king of Babylon [i]from the neck of all
nations within the space of two full years.
And the prophet Jeremiah went his way.

[a]Chap. xxvii. 1——[b]Chap. xxvii. 12——[c]Chap. xxvii. 16——[d]Heb. *two years of days*

[e]Heb. *captivity*——[f]1 Kings i. 36——[g]Deut. xviii. 22 [h]Chap. xxvii. 2——[i]Chap. xxvii. 7

NOTES ON CHAP. XXVIII

Verse 1. *And it came to pass the same year—the fifth month*] Which commenced with the first new moon of *August*, according to our calendar. This verse gives the *precise date* of the prophecy in the preceding chapter; and proves that *Zedekiah*, not *Jehoiakim*, is the name that should be read in the *first* verse of that chapter.

Hananiah the son of Azur the prophet] One who called himself a prophet; who pretended to be in commerce with the Lord, and to receive revelations from him. He was probably a *priest;* for he was of Gibeon, a sacerdotal city in the tribe of Benjamin.

Verse 2. *Thus speaketh the Lord*] What awful impudence! when he knew in his conscience that God had given him no such commission.

Verse 3. *Within two full years*] Time sufficient for the Chaldeans to destroy the city, and carry away the rest of the sacred vessels; but he did not live to see the end of this short period.

Verse 6. *Amen; the Lord do so*] O that it might be according to thy word! May the people find this to be true!

Verse 8. *The prophets that have been before me*] Namely, Joel, Amos, Hosea, Micah, Zephaniah, Nahum, Habakkuk, and others; all of whom denounced similar evils against a corrupt people.

Verse 9. *When the word of the prophet shall come to pass*] Here is the criterion. . He is a true prophet who specifies things that he says shall happen, and also fixes the *time* of the event; and the things do happen, and in that time.

You say that Nebuchadnezzar shall not overthrow this city; and that in *two years* from this time, not only the sacred vessels *already taken away* shall be restored, but also that *Jeconiah* and *all the Jewish captives* shall be restored, and the *Babylonish yoke* broken, see verses 2, 3, 4. Now *I* say that Nebuchadnezzar will come *this year*, and destroy this city, and lead away the rest of the people into captivity, and the rest of the sacred vessels; and that there will be no restoration of any kind till *seventy* years from this time.

Verse 10. *Then Hananiah—took the yoke—and brake it.*] He endeavoured by this symbolical act to persuade them of the truth of his prediction.

A. M. 3409
B. C. 595
Ol. XLVI. 2
Anno
TarquiniiPrisci,
R. Roman., 22

12 Then the word of the LORD came unto Jeremiah *the prophet,* (after that Hananiah the prophet had broken the yoke from off the neck of the prophet Jeremiah,) saying,
13 Go and tell Hananiah, saying, Thus saith the LORD; Thou hast broken the yokes of wood; but thou shalt make for them yokes of iron.
14 For thus saith the LORD of hosts, the God of Israel; [k]I have put a yoke of iron upon the neck of all these nations, that they may serve Nebuchadnezzar king of Babylon; and they shall serve him: and [l]I have given him the beasts of the field also.
15 Then said the prophet Jeremiah unto Hananiah the prophet, Hear now, Hananiah; The LORD hath not sent thee; but [m]thou makest this people to trust in a lie.
16 Therefore thus saith the LORD; Behold, I will cast thee from off the face of the earth: this year thou shalt die, because thou hast taught [n]rebellion [o]against the LORD.
17 So Hananiah the prophet died the same year in the seventh month.

[k]Deut. xxviii. 48; chap. xxvii. 4, 7——[l]Chap. xxvii. 6——[m]Chap. xxix. 31; Ezek. xiii. 22——[n]Deuteronomy xiii. 5; chapter xxix. 32——[o]Hebrew, *revolt*

Verse 13. *Yokes of iron.*] Instead of Nebuchadnezzar's yoke *being broken,* this captivity shall be more *severe* than the *preceding.* All these nations shall have a *yoke of iron* on their neck. He shall *subdue them,* and take all *their property,* even the *beasts of the field.*

Verse 15. *Hear now, Hananiah; the Lord hath not sent thee*] This was a bold speech in the presence of those priests and people who were prejudiced in favour of this false prophet, who prophesied to them smooth things. In such cases men wish to be *deceived.*

Verse 16. *This year thou shalt die*] By this shall the people know *who* is the *true prophet.* Thou hast taught *rebellion against the Lord,* and God will cut thee off; and this shall take place, not within *seventy years,* or *two years,* but in *this very year,* and within *two months* from this time.

Verse 17. *So Hananiah—died the same year in the seventh month.*] The prophecy was delivered in the *fifth month,* (ver. 1,) and Hananiah died in the *seventh month.* And thus God, in mercy, gave him about *two months,* in which he might prepare to meet his Judge. Here, then, the *true prophet* was *demonstrated,* and the *false prophet detected.* The death of Hananiah, thus predicted, was God's *seal* to the words of his prophet; and must have gained his other predictions great credit among the people.

CHAPTER XXIX

This chapter contains the substance of two letters sent by the prophet to the captives in Babylon. In the first he recommends to them patience and composure under their present circumstances, which were to endure for seventy *years,* 1–14; *in which, however, they should fare better than their brethren who remained behind,* 15–19. *But, finding little credit given to this message, on account of the suggestions of the false prophets, Ahab the son of Kolaiah, and Zedekiah, the son of Maaseiah, who flattered them with the hopes of a speedy end to their captivity, he sends a second, in which he denounces heavy judgments against those false prophets that deceived them,* 20–23; *as he did afterwards against Shemaiah the Nehelamite, who had sent a letter of complaint against Jeremiah, in consequence of his message,* 24–32.

A. M. cir. 3407
B. C. cir. 597
Ol. cir. XLV. 4
TarquiniiPrisci,
R. Roman.,
cir. annum 20

NOW these *are* the words of the letter that Jeremiah the prophet sent from Jerusalem unto the residue of the [a]elders which were carried away captives, and to the priests, and to the prophets, and to all the people whom Nebuchadnezzar had [b]carried away captive from Jerusalem to Babylon;
2 (After that [c]Jeconiah the king and the queen, and the [d]eunuchs, the princes of Judah and Jerusalem, and the car-

[a]Ezra x. 14——[b]2 Kings xxv. 21——[c]2 Kings xxiv. 12, &c.; chap. xxii. 26; xxviii. 4——[d]Or, *chamberlains*

NOTES ON CHAP. XXIX

Verse 1. *Now these* are *the words of the letter*] This transaction took place in the *first* or *second* year of Zedekiah. It appears that the prophet had been informed that the Jews who had already been carried into captivity had, through the instigations of false prophets, been led to believe that they were to be brought out of their captivity speedily. Jeremiah, fearing that this delusion might induce them to take some hasty steps, ill comporting with their present state, wrote a letter to them, which he entrusted to an embassy which Zedekiah had sent on some political concerns to Nebuchadnezzar. The letter was directed to the elders, priests, prophets, and people who had been carried away captives to Babylon.

A. M. cir. 3407
B. C. cir. 597
Ol. cir. XLV. 4
TarquiniiPrisci, R. Roman., cir. annum 20

penters, and the smiths, were departed from Jerusalem;)

3 By the hand of Elasah the son of Shaphan, and Gemariah the son of Hilkiah, (whom Zedekiah king of Judah sent unto Babylon to Nebuchadnezzar king of Babylon) saying,

4 Thus saith the LORD of hosts, the God of Israel, unto all that are carried away captives, whom I have caused to be carried away from Jerusalem unto Babylon;

5 [e]Build ye houses, and dwell *in them,* and plant gardens, and eat the fruit of them;

6 Take ye wives, and beget sons and daughters; and take wives for your sons, and give your daughters to husbands, that they may bear sons and daughters; that ye may be increased there, and not diminished.

7 And seek the peace of the city whither I have caused you to be carried away captives, [f]and pray unto the LORD for it: for in the peace thereof shall ye have peace.

8 For thus saith the LORD of hosts, the God of Israel; Let not your prophets and your diviners, that *be* in the midst of you, [g]deceive you, neither hearken to your dreams which ye cause to be dreamed.

A. M. cir. 3407
B. C. cir. 597
Ol. cir. XLV. 4
TarquiniiPrisci, R. Roman., cir. annum 20

9 [h]For they prophesy [i]falsely unto you in my name: I have not sent them, saith the LORD.

10 For thus saith the LORD, That after [k]seventy years be accomplished at Babylon I will visit you, and perform my good word toward you, in causing you to return to this place.

11 For I know the thoughts that I think toward you, saith the LORD, thoughts of peace, and not of evil, to give you an [l]expected end.

12 Then shall ye [m]call upon me, and ye shall go and pray unto me, and I will hearken unto you.

13 And [n]ye shall seek me, and find *me,* when ye shall search for me [o]with all your heart.

14 And [p]I will be found of you, saith the LORD: and I will turn away your captivity, and [q]I will gather you from all the nations, and from all the places whither I have driven you, saith the LORD; and I will bring you again into the place whence I caused you to be carried away captive.

---

[e]Ver. 28——[f]Ezra vi. 10; 1 Mac. xii. 11; 1 Tim. ii. 2——[g]Ch. xiv. 14; xxiii. 21; xxvii. 14, 15; Eph. v. 6——[h]Ver. 31——[i]Heb. *in a lie*——[k]2 Chron. xxxvi. 21, 22; Ezra i. 1; chap. xxv. 12; xxvii. 22; Dan. ix. 2

[l]Heb. *end and expectation*——[m]Dan. ix. 3, &c.——[n]Lev. xxvi. 39, 40, &c.; Deut. xxx. 1, &c.——[o]Chap. xxiv. 7——[p]Deut. iv. 7; Psa. xxxii. 6; xlvi. 1; Isa. lv. 6——[q]Chap. xxiii. 3, 8; xxx. 3; xxxii. 37

Verse 4. *Thus saith the Lord of hosts*] This was the commencement of the letter.

Verse 5. *Build ye houses*] Prepare for a long continuance in your present captivity. Provide yourselves with the *necessaries* of life, and multiply in the land, that ye may become a powerful people.

Verse 7. *Seek the peace of the city*] Endeavour to promote, as far as you can, the *prosperity* of the places in which ye sojourn. Let no disaffection appear in word or act. Nothing can be more reasonable than this. Wherever a man lives and has his nourishment and support, that is his country as long as he resides in it. If things go well with that country, his interest is promoted by the general prosperity, he lives at comparative ease, and has the necessaries of life cheaper; and unless he is in a state of cruel servitude, which does not appear to have been the case with those Israelites to whom the prophet writes, (those of the first captivity,) they must be nearly, if not altogether, in as good a state as if they had been in the country that gave them birth. And in this case they were much better off than their brethren now in Judea, who had to contend with *famine* and *war*, and scarcely any thing before them but God's curse and extermination.

Verse 8. *Neither hearken to your dreams*] Rather, *dreamers;* for it appears there was a class of such persons, who not only had acquired a facility of dreaming themselves, but who undertook to interpret the dreams of others.

Verse 10. *For thus saith the Lord*] It has been supposed that a very serious *transposition* of verses has taken place here; and it has been proposed to read after ver. 9 the *sixteenth* to the *nineteenth* inclusive; then the *tenth*, and on to the *fourteenth* inclusive; then the *twentieth*, the *fifteenth*, the *twenty-first*, and the rest regularly to the end.

That after seventy years be accomplished] לפי מלאת *lephi meloth*, "at the mouth of the accomplishment," or "fill to the mouth." Seventy years is the *measure* which must be *filled;* —*fill this to the brim;*—complete this measure, and then you shall be visited and released. The whole *seventy* must be completed; expect no enlargement before that time.

Verse 11. *Thoughts of peace*] Here God gives them to understand, 1. That his love was moved towards them. 2. That he would perform his good word, his promises often repeated, to them. 3. That for the fulfilment of these they must *pray, seek*, and *search*. 4. That he would *hearken*, and they should *find* him; provided, 5. They *sought* him with their *whole heart*, ver. 10-13.

Verse 14. *I will gather you from all the na-*

A. M. cir. 3407
B. C. cir. 597
Ol. cir. XLV. 4
TarquiniiPrisci,
R. Roman.,
cir. annum 20

15 Because ye have said, The
LORD hath raised us up prophets
in Babylon;
16 *Know* that thus saith the
LORD of the king that sitteth upon the throne
of David, and of all the people that dwelleth
in this city, *and* of your brethren that are not
gone forth with you into captivity;
17 Thus saith the LORD of hosts; Behold,
I will send upon them the [r]sword, the famine,
and the pestilence, and will make them like
[s]vile figs, that cannot be eaten, they are so evil.
18 And I will persecute them with the sword,
with the famine, and with the pestilence, and
[t]will deliver them to be removed to all the
kingdoms of the earth, [u]to be [v]a curse, and an
astonishment, and a hissing, and a reproach,
among all the nations whither I have driven
them:
19 Because they have not hearkened to my
words, saith the LORD, which [w]I sent unto
them by my servants the prophets, rising up
early and sending *them;* but ye would not
hear, saith the LORD.
20 Hear ye therefore the word of the
LORD, all ye of the captivity, whom I have
sent from Jerusalem to Babylon:

A. M. cir. 3407
B. C. cir. 597
Ol. cir. XLV. 4
TarquiniiPrisci,
R. Roman.,
cir. annum 20

21 Thus saith the LORD of
hosts, the God of Israel, of Ahab
the son of Kolaiah, and of Zedekiah the son
of Maaseiah, which prophesy a lie unto you
in my name; Behold, I will deliver them into
the hand of Nebuchadnezzar king of Babylon;
and he shall slay them before your eyes;
22 [x]And of them shall be taken up a curse
by all the captivity of Judah which *are* in
Babylon, saying, The LORD make thee like
Zedekiah, and like Ahab, [y]whom the king of
Babylon roasted in the fire;
23 Because [z]they have committed villany in
Israel, and have committed adultery with their
neighbours' wives, and have spoken lying
words in my name, which I have not commanded
them; even I know, and *am* a Witness,
saith the LORD.
24 *Thus* shalt thou also speak to Shemaiah
the [a]Nehelamite, saying,
25 Thus speaketh the LORD of hosts, the
God of Israel, saying, Because thou hast sent
letters in thy name unto all the people that
are at Jerusalem, [b]and to Zephaniah the son

---

[r]Chap. xxiv. 10——[s]Chap. xxiv. 8——[t]Deut. xxviii. 25; 2 Chron. xxix. 8; chap. xv. 4; xxiv. 9; xxxiv. 17 [u]Heb. *for a curse*——[v]Chap. xxvi. 6; chap. xlii. 18

[w]Chap. xxv. 4; xxxii. 33——[x]See Gen. xlviii. 20; Isa. lxv. 15——[y]Dan. iii. 6——[z]Chap. xxiii. 14——[a]Or, *dreamer*——[b]2 Kings xxv. 18; chap. xxi. 1

---

tions] A quotation from Deut. xxx. 3, and see also Deut. iv. 7.

Verse 15. *Because ye have said*] The *Septuagint* very properly insert this verse between the *twentieth* and the *twenty-first*, and thus the *connexion* here is not disturbed, and the connexion below completed.

Verse 17. *Behold, I will send upon them the sword*] Do not envy the state of *Zedekiah* who sits on the throne of David, nor that of the *people* who are now in the land whence ye have been carried captive, (ver. 16,) for "I will send the sword, the pestilence, and the famine upon them;" and afterwards shall cause them to be carried into a miserable captivity *in all nations*, (ver. 18;) but *ye* see the worst of *your own* case, and you have God's promise of enlargement when the proper time is come. The reader will not forget that the prophet is addressing the captives in Babylon.

Verse 20. *Hear ye therefore the word*] Dr. *Blayney* thinks there were *two letters* written by the prophet to the captives in Babylon, and that the *first* ends with this verse. That having heard, on the return of the embassy (Elasah and Gemariah, whom Zedekiah had sent to Babylon, and to whom the prophet entrusted the above letter, ver. 3,) that the captives had not received his advices favourably, because they were deceived by false prophets among them, who promised them a *speedier* deliverance, he therefore wrote a *second letter*, beginning with the *fifteenth* verse, and going on with the *twenty-first*, &c., in which he denounces God's judgments on three of the chief of those, Ahab, Zedekiah, and Shemaiah.

Verse 21. *He shall slay them before your eyes.*] Nebuchadnezzar would be led by political reasons to punish these pretended prophets, as their predictions tended to make his Israelitish subjects uneasy and disaffected, and might excite them to rebellion. He therefore slew them; two of them, it appears, he *burnt alive*, viz., *Ahab* and *Zedekiah*, who are supposed by the rabbins to be the *two elders* who endeavoured to seduce *Susanna*, see ver. 23. Burning *alive* was a Chaldean punishment, Dan. iii. 6, and Amos. ii. 1. From them other nations borrowed it.

Verse 23. *Have committed adultery with their neighbours' wives*] This is supposed to refer to the case of *Susanna*. See above.

Verse 24. *Speak to Shemaiah*] Zephaniah was the *second priest*, *sagan*, or chief priest's deputy, and Seraiah, high priest, when Jerusalem was taken. See chap. lii. 24. Shemaiah directs his letter to the former, and tells him that God had appointed him to supply the place of the high priest, who was probably then absent. His name was either *Azariah* or *Seraiah* his son, but called *Jehoiada* from the remarkable zeal and courage of that pontiff. See the passages in the margin.—*Dodd.* After the taking of Jerusalem, Zephaniah was put to death by

A. M. cir. 3407
B. C. cir. 597
Ol. cir. XLV. 4
TarquiniiPrisci,
R. Roman.,
cir. annum 20

of Maaseiah the priest, and to all the priests, saying,

26 The LORD hath made thee priest in the stead of Jehoiada the priest, that ye should be [c]officers in the house of the LORD, for every man *that is* [d]mad, and maketh himself a prophet, that thou shouldest [e]put him in prison, and in the stocks.

27 Now therefore why hast thou not reproved Jeremiah of Anathoth, which maketh himself a prophet to you?

28 For therefore he sent unto us *in* Babylon, saying, This *captivity is* long: [f]build ye houses, and dwell *in them;* and plant gardens, and eat the fruit of them.

29 And Zephaniah the priest read this letter in the ears of Jeremiah the prophet.

30 Then came the word of the LORD unto Jeremiah, saying,

31 Send to all them of the captivity, saying, Thus saith the LORD concerning Shemaiah the Nehelamite; Because that Shemaiah hath prophesied unto you, [g]and I sent him not, and he caused you to trust in a lie:

32 Therefore thus saith the LORD; Behold I will punish Shemaiah the Nehelamite, and his seed: he shall not have a man to dwell among this people: neither shall he behold the good that I will do for my people, saith the LORD; [h]because he hath taught [i]rebellion against the LORD.

[c]Chap. xx. 1——[d]2 Kings ix. 11; Acts xxvi. 24——[e]Chap. xx. 2——[f]Ver. 5——[g]Chap. xxviii. 15——[h]Chap. xxviii. 16——[i]Heb. *revolt*

Nebuchadnezzar at Riblah; see chap. xxxvii. 3. The history of Jehoiada may be seen 2 Kings xi. 3, &c.

Verse 26. *For every man* that is *mad, and maketh himself a prophet*] *Mad,* משגע *meshugga, in ecstatic rapture;* such as appeared in the prophets, whether *true* or *false,* when under the influence, the one of God, the other of a demon. See 2 Kings ix. 11; Hos. ix. 7.

Verse 32. *I will punish Shemaiah*] 1. He shall have no posterity to succeed him. 2. His family, *i. e., relations,* &c., shall not be found among those whom I shall bring back from captivity. 3. Nor shall *he* himself see the good that I shall do for my people. And all this shall come upon him and his because he hath taught rebellion against the Lord. He excited the people to reject Jeremiah, and to receive the lying words of the *false prophets;* and these led them to rebel.

CHAPTER XXX

This and the following chapter must relate to a still future restoration of the posterity of Jacob from their several dispersions, as no deliverance hitherto afforded them comes up to the terms of it; for, after the return from Babylon, they were again enslaved by the Greeks and Romans, contrary to the prediction in the eighth *verse; in every papistical country they have laboured under great civil disabilities, and in some of them have been horribly persecuted; upon the ancient people has this mystic Babylon very heavily laid her yoke; and in no place in the world are they at present their own masters; so that this prophecy remains to be fulfilled in the reign of David,* i. e., *the Messiah; the* type, *according to the general structure of the prophetical writings, being put for the* antitype. *The prophecy opens by an easy transition from the temporal deliverance spoken of before, and describes the mighty revolutions that shall precede the restoration of the descendants of Israel,* 1–9, *who are encouraged to trust in the promises of God,* 10, 11. *They are, however, to expect corrections; which shall have a happy issue in a future period,* 12–17. *The great blessings of Messiah's reign are enumerated,* 18–22; *and the wicked and impenitent declared to have no share in them,* 23, 24.

A. M. cir. 3417
B. C. cir. 587
Ol. XLVIII. 2
TarquiniiPrisci,
R. Roman.,
cir. annum 30

THE word that came to Jeremiah from the LORD, saying,

2 Thus speaketh the LORD God of Israel, saying, Write thee all the words that I have spoken unto thee in a book.

3 For, lo, the days come, saith the LORD, that [a]I will bring again

[a]Ver. 18; chap. xxxii. 44; Ezek. xxxix. 25; Amos ix. 14, 15

NOTES ON CHAP. XXX

Verse 1. *The word that came to Jeremiah from the Lord*] This prophecy was delivered about *a year after the taking of Jerusalem;* so *Dahler.* Dr. *Blayney* supposes it and the following chapter to refer to the *future restoration* of both *Jews* and *Israelites* in the times of the Gospel; though also touching at the restoration from the *Babylonish captivity,* at the end of

A. M. cir. 3417 B. C. cir. 587 Ol. XLVIII. 2 TarquiniiPrisci, R. Roman., cir. annum 30

the captivity of my people Israel and Judah, saith the LORD: [b]and I will cause them to return to the land that I gave to their fathers, and they shall possess it.

4 And these *are* the words that the LORD spake concerning Israel and concerning Judah.

5 For thus saith the LORD; We have heard a voice of trembling, [c]of fear, and not of peace.

6 Ask ye now, and see whether [d]a man doth travail with child? wherefore do I see every man with his hands on his loins, [e]as a woman in travail, and all faces are turned into paleness?

7 [f]Alas! for that day *is* great, [g]so that none *is* like it: it *is* even the time of Jacob's trouble; but he shall be saved out of it.

8 For it shall come to pass in that day, saith the LORD of hosts, *that* I will break his yoke from off thy neck, and will burst thy bonds, and strangers shall no more serve themselves of him.

9 But they shall serve the LORD their God, and [h]David their King, whom I will [i]raise up unto them.

10 Therefore [k]fear thou not, O my servant Jacob, saith the LORD; neither be dismayed, O Israel: for, lo, I will save thee from afar, and thy seed [l]from the land of their captivity; and Jacob shall return, and shall be in rest, and be quiet, and none shall make *him* afraid.

11 For I *am* with thee, saith the LORD, to save thee: [m]though I make a full end of all nations whither I have scattered thee, [n]yet will I not make a full end of thee: but I will correct thee [o]in measure, and will not leave thee altogether unpunished.

12 For thus saith the LORD, [p]Thy bruise *is* incurable, *and* thy wound *is* grievous.

---

[b]Chap. xvi. 15——[c]Or, there is *fear, and not peace*——[d]Heb. *a male*——[e]Chap. iv. 31; vi. 24——[f]Joel ii. 11, 31; Amos v. 18; Zeph. i. 14, &c.——[g]Dan. xii. 1——[h]Isa. lv. 3, 4; Ezek. xxxiv. 23; xxxvii. 24; Hos. iii. 5

[i]Luke i. 69; Acts ii. 30; xiii. 23——[k]Isa. xli. 13; xliii. 5; xliv. 2; chap. xlvi. 27, 28——[l]Chap. iii. 18——[m]Amos ix. 8——[n]Ch. iv. 27——[o]Psa. vi. 1; Isa. xxvii. 8; ch. x. 24; xlvi. 28——[p]2 Chron. xxxvi. 16; chap. xv. 18

---

seventy years. Supposing these two chapters to be penned after the taking of Jerusalem, which appears the most natural, they will refer to the same events, *one captivity* shadowing forth *another*, and *one restoration* being the *type* or *pledge* of the *second*.

Verse 2. *Write thee all the words that I have spoken unto thee in a book.*] The *book* here recommended I believe to be the *thirtieth* and *thirty-first* chapters; for among the Hebrews any portion of writing, in which the subject was *finished*, however small, was termed ספר *sepher*, a BOOK, a *treatise* or *discourse*.

Verse 3. *The days come*] *First*, After the conclusion of the *seventy* years. *Secondly*, Under the *Messiah*.

That I will bring again the captivity of Israel] The *ten tribes*, led captive by the king of *Assyria*, and dispersed among the *nations*.

And Judah] The people carried into *Babylon* at *two different times;* first, under *Jeconiah*, and, secondly, under *Zedekiah*, by Nebuchadnezzar.

Verse 5. *We have heard a voice of trembling*] This may refer to the state and feelings of the people during the war which Cyrus carried on against the Babylonians. *Trembling* and *terror* would no doubt affect them, and put an end to *peace* and all prosperity; as they could not tell what would be the issue of the struggle, and whether their state would be better or worse should their present masters fall in the conflict. This is well described in the next verse, where *men* are represented as being, through pain and anguish, like *women in travail*. See the same comparison Isa. xiii. 6-8.

Verse 7. *Alas! for that day* is *great*] When the Medes and Persians, with all their forces shall come on the Chaldeans, it will be *the day of Jacob's trouble*—trial, dismay, and uncertainty; but *he shall be delivered out of it*—the Chaldean empire shall fall, but the Jews shall be delivered by Cyrus. Jerusalem shall be destroyed by the Romans, but the *Israel of God* shall be delivered from its ruin. Not one that had embraced Christianity perished in the sackage of that city.

Verse 8. *I will break his yoke*] That is, the yoke of *Nebuchadnezzar*.

Of him.] Of *Jacob*, (ver. 7,) viz., the then captive Jews.

Verse 9. *But they shall serve the Lord their God, and David their King*] This must refer to the *times of the Messiah;* and hence the *Chaldee* has, "They shall obey the Lord their God, וישת מאון למשיחה בר דוד *veyishta meun limschicha bar David*, and they shall obey the Messiah, the Son of David." This is a very remarkable version; and shows that it was a version, not according to the *letter*, but according to their *doctrine* and their *expectation*. David was long since dead; and none of his descendants ever reigned over them after the Babylonish captivity, nor have they since been a *regal nation*. *Zerubbabel*, under the Persians, and the *Asmoneans*, can be no exception to this. They have been *no nation* since; they are no nation now; and it is only in the *latter days* that they can expect to be a *nation*, and that must be a *Christian nation*.

Christ is promised under the name of his progenitor, *David*, Isa. lv. 3, 4; Ezek. xxxiv. 23, 24, xxxvii. 24, 25; Hos. iii. 5.

Verse 11. *Though I make a full end of all nations*] Though the Persians destroy the nations whom they vanquish, yet they shall not destroy *thee*.

Verse 12. *Thy bruise* is *incurable*] אנוש *anush, desperate*, not *incurable;* for the *cure* is promised in ver. 17, *I will restore health unto thee, and I will heal thee of thy wounds.*

A. M. cir. 3417
B. C. cir. 587
Ol. XLVIII. 2
TarquiniiPrisci,
R. Roman.,
cir. annum 30

13 *There is* none to plead thy cause, [q]that thou mayest be bound up: [r]thou hast no healing medicines.

14 [s]All thy lovers have forgotten thee; they seek thee not; for I have wounded thee with the wound [t]of an enemy, with the chastisement [u]of a cruel one, for the multitude of thine iniquity; [v]*because* thy sins were increased.

15 Why [w]criest thou for thine affliction? thy sorrow *is* incurable for the multitude of thine iniquity: *because* thy sins were increased, I have done these things unto thee.

16 Therefore all they that devour thee [x]shall be devoured; and all thine adversaries, every one of them shall go into captivity; and they that spoil thee shall be a spoil, and all that prey upon thee will I give for a prey.

17 [y]For I will restore health unto thee, and I will heal thee of thy wounds, saith the LORD; because they called thee an Outcast, *saying,* This *is* Zion, whom no man seeketh after.

18 Thus saith the LORD; Behold, [z]I will bring again the captivity of Jacob's tents, and [a]have mercy on his dwelling-places; and the city shall be builded upon her own [b]heap, and the palace shall remain after the manner thereof.

A. M. cir. 3417
B. C. cir. 587
Ol. XLVIII. 2
TarquiniiPrisci,
R. Roman.,
cir. annum 30

19 And [c]out of them shall proceed thanksgiving and the voice of them that make merry: [d]and I will multiply them, and they shall not be few; I will also glorify them, and they shall not be small.

20 Their children also shall be [e]as aforetime, and their congregation shall be established before me, and I will punish all that oppress them.

21 And their nobles shall be of themselves, [f]and their governor shall proceed from the midst of them: and I will [g]cause him to draw near, and he shall approach unto me: for who *is* this that engaged his heart to approach unto me? saith the LORD.

22 And ye shall be [h]my people, and I will be your God.

23 Behold, the [i]whirlwind of the LORD goeth forth with fury, a [k]continuing whirlwind: it shall [l]fall with pain upon the head of the wicked.

24 The fierce anger of the LORD shall not return, until he have done *it,* and until he have performed the intents of his heart: [m]in the latter days ye shall consider it.

[q]Heb. *for binding up,* or *pressing*——[r]Chap. viii. 22——[s]Lam. i. 2——[t]Job xiii. 24; xvi. 9; xix. 11——[u]Job xxx. 21——[v]Ch. v. 6——[w]Ch. xv. 18——[x]Exod. xxiii. 22; Isa. xxxiii. 1; xli. 11; ch. x. 25——[y]Ch. xxxiii. 6——[z]Ver. 3; chap. xxxiii. 7, 11——[a]Psa. cii. 13——[b]Or, *little hill*

[c]Isa. xxxv. 10; li. 11; ch. xxxi. 4, 12, 13; xxxiii. 10, 11——[d]Zech. x. 8——[e]Isa. i. 26——[f]Gen. xlix. 10——[g]Num. xvi. 5——[h]Ch. xxiv. 7; xxxi. 1, 33; xxxii. 38; Ezek. xi. 20; xxxvi. 28; xxxvii. 27——[i]Ch. xxiii. 19, 20; xxv. 32——[k]Heb. *cutting*——[l]Or, *remain*——[m]Gen. xlix. 1

Verse 13. There is *none to plead thy cause*] All thy friends and allies have forsaken thee.

Verse 15. *Thy sorrow* is *incurable*] אנוש *anush, desperate.* See ver. 12.

Verse 16. *They that devour thee*] The Chaldeans,

Shall be devoured] By the *Medes* and *Persians.*

All that prey upon thee will I give for a prey.] The *Assyrians* were destroyed by the *Babylonians;* the *Babylonians,* by the *Medes* and *Persians;* the *Egyptians* and *Persians* were destroyed by the *Greeks,* under Alexander. All these nations are now *extinct;* but the *Jews,* as a distinct people, still exist.

Verse 18. *The city shall be builded upon her own heap*] Be re-edified from its own *ruins.* See the book of *Nehemiah, passim.*

And the palace shall remain] Meaning, the *king's house* shall be restored; or, more probably, the *temple shall be rebuilt;* which was true, for after the Babylonish captivity it was rebuilt by Nehemiah, &c. By the *tents,* distinguished from the *dwelling-places of Jacob,* we may understand all *the minor dispersions of the Jews,* as well as those *numerous synagogues* found in large cities.

Verse 19. *I will multiply them*] They shall be *very numerous;* even where at present they have but *tents.*

I will also glorify them] I will put *honour* upon them every where, so that they shall be no longer *contemptible.* This will be a very great *change,* for they are now *despised* all over the earth.

Verse 20. *Their children also*] They shall have the education of their own children as formerly.

And their congregation] Their religious *assemblies.*

Shall be established] Being, in the latter days, incorporated with those "who serve the Lord their God, and worship the Messiah, the son of David."

Verse 21. *Their nobles shall be of themselves*] *Strangers* shall not rule over them; and—

Their governor shall proceed from the midst of them] Both *Nehemiah* and *Zerubbabel,* their nobles and governors after the return from Babylon, were *Jews.*

Verse 22. *Ye shall be my people*] The *old covenant* shall be renewed.

Verse 23. *The whirlwind of the Lord*] A grievous tempest of desolation,—

Shall fall with pain upon the head of the wicked.] On Nebuchadnezzar and the Chaldeans.

Verse 24. *In the latter days ye shall consider it.*] By the *latter days* the Gospel dispensation is generally meant; and that restoration which is the principal topic in this and the succeeding chapter refers to this time. Had the Jews properly *considered* this subject, they would long ere this have been brought into the liberty of the Gospel, and saved from the maledictions under which they now groan. Why do not the Jews read their own prophets more conscientiously?

CHAPTER XXXI

This chapter continues the subject of the preceding in a beautiful vision represented at a distant period. God is introduced expressing his continual regard for Israel, and promising to restore them to their land and liberty, 1–5. *Immediately heralds appear, proclaiming on Mount Ephraim the arrival of the great year of jubilee, and summoning the people to gather unto Zion,* 6. *Upon which God resumes the speech; and makes such gracious promises both of leading them tenderly by the way, and making them happy in their own land, that all the nations of the world are called upon to consider with deep attention this great salvation,* 7–14. *The scene is then diversified by a very happy invention. Rachel, the mother of Joseph and Benjamin, is represented as risen from her tomb, in a city of Benjamin near Jerusalem, looking about for her children, and bitterly lamenting their fate, as none of them are to be seen in the land of their fathers,* 15. *But she is consoled with the assurance that they are not lost, and that they shall in due time be restored,* 16, 17. *To this another tender and beautiful scene immediately succeeds. Ephraim, (often put for the* TEN tribes,) *comes in view. He laments his past errors, and expresses the most earnest desires of reconciliation; upon which God, as a tender parent, immediately forgives him,* 18–20. *The virgin of Israel is then directed to prepare for returning home,* 21, 22; *and the vision closes with a promise of abundant peace and security to Israel and Judah in the latter days,* 23–26. *The blessed condition of Israel under the Messiah's reign is then beautifully contrasted with their afflicted state during the general dispersion,* 27, 28. *In the remaining part of the chapter the promises to the posterity of Jacob of the impartial administration of justice, increasing peace and prosperity, the universal diffusion of righteousness, and stability in their own land after a general restoration in Gospel times, are repeated, enlarged on, and illustrated by a variety of beautiful figures,* 29–40.

A. M. cir. 3417
B. C. cir. 587
Ol. XLVIII. 2
TarquiniiPrisci,
R. Roman.,
cir. annum 30

AT [a]the same time, saith the
LORD, [b]will I be the God of
all the families of Israel, and
they shall be my people.

2 Thus saith the LORD, The
people *which were* left of
the sword found grace in
the wilderness; *even* Israel,

[a]Chap. xxx. 24

[b]Chap. xxx. 22

NOTES ON CHAP. XXXI

Dr. *Blayney* has introduced this and the preceding chapter with the following excellent observations:—

"There are many prophecies," says he, "in various parts of the Old Testament, which announce the future restoration of Israel to their own land, and the complete re-establishment of both their civil and religious constitution in the latter days, meaning the times of the Gospel dispensation. These two chapters contain a prophecy of this kind; which must necessarily be referred to these times, because it points out circumstances which certainly were not fulfilled at the return of the Jews from the Babylonish captivity, nor have hitherto had their completion. For the people who returned from Babylon were the people of Judah only, who had been carried away captive by Nebuchadnezzar; but here it is foretold, that not only should the captivity of Judah be restored, but the captivity of Israel also, meaning those ten tribes which were carried away before, by Shalmaneser king of Assyria; and who still remain in their several dispersions, having never returned, in a national capacity at least, to their own land, whatever some few individuals have done. But the terms of the prophecy entitle us to expect, not an obscure and partial, but a complete and universal, restoration; when God will manifest himself, as formerly, the God and Patron of all the families of Israel, and not of a few only. Again it is promised that, after this restoration, they should no more fall under the dominion of foreigners, but be governed by princes and magistrates of their own nation, independently of any but God, and David their king. But this was not the case with the Jews who returned from Babylon. They then indeed had a leader, Zerubbabel, one of their own nation, and also of the family of David; but both the nation and their leader continued still in a state of vassalage, and the most servile dependence upon the Persian monarchy. And when the Grecian monarchy succeeded, they changed their masters only, but not their condition; till at length under the Asmonean princes they had for a while an independent government of their own, but without any title to the name of David. At last they fell under the Roman yoke; since which time their situation has been such as not to afford the least ground to pretend that the promised restoration has yet taken place. It remains therefore to be brought about in future under the reign of the Messiah, emphatically distinguished by the name of David; when every particular circumstance predicted concerning it will no doubt be verified by a distinct and unequivocal accomplishment. There is no particular date annexed to this prophecy, whereby to ascertain the precise time of its delivery.

A. M. cir. 3417
B. C. cir. 587
Ol. XLVIII. 2
TarquiniiPrisci, R. Roman., cir. annum. 30

when [c]I went to cause him to
rest.
3 The LORD hath appeared [d]of old unto me, *saying,* Yea,
[e]I have loved thee with [f]an everlasting love: therefore [g]with loving-kindness have I [h]drawn thee.

[c]Num. x. 33; Deut. i. 33; Psa. xcv. 11; Isa. lxiii. 14——[d]Heb. *from afar*——[e]Mal. i. 2

[f]Rom. xi. 28, 29——[g]Or, *have I extended loving-kindness unto thee*——[h]Hos. xi. 4

But it may not unreasonably be presumed to have followed immediately after the preceding one, in which the restoration of the people from their Babylonish captivity is in direct terms foretold. From hence the transition is natural and easy to the more glorious and general restoration which was to take place in a more distant period, and was designed for the ultimate object of the national hopes and expectations. Both events are frequently thus connected together in the prophetic writings; and perhaps with this design, that when that which was nearest at hand should be accomplished, it might afford the clearest, and strongest, and most satisfactory kind of evidence that the latter, how remote soever its period, would in like manner be brought about by the interposition of Providence in its due season. But though this prophecy relates wholly to one single subject, it seems naturally to divide itself into three distinct parts. The first part, after a short preface, in which the prophet is required to commit to writing the matters revealed to him, commences with representing, in a style of awe and energy, the consternation and distress which, in some future day of visitation, should fall upon all nations, preparatory to the scene of Jacob's deliverance, ver. 5-9. Israel is encouraged to confide in the Divine assurance of restoration and protection, ver. 10, 11. He is prepared previously to expect a severe chastisement for the multitude of his sins; but consoled with the prospect of a happy termination, ver. 12-17. This is followed by an enumeration at large of the blessings and privileges to which the Jews should be restored upon their re-admission into God's favour, ver. 18-22. Again, however, it is declared that the anger of JEHOVAH would not subside till his purposed vengeance against the wicked should have been fully executed; and then, but not till then, an entire reconciliation would take place between him and all the families of Israel, ver. 23, chap. xxxi. 1. The second part of this prophecy begins chap. xxxi. 2, and is marked by a sudden transition to a distant period of time, represented in a vision, and embellished with a variety of beautiful scenes and images. God announces the renewal of his ancient love for Israel; and promises, in consequence thereof, a speedy restoration of their former privileges and happiness, ver. 2-5. Already the heralds have proclaimed on Mount Ephraim the arrival of the joyful day; they summon the people to re-assemble once more in Zion; and promulge by special command the glad tidings of salvation which God had accomplished for them. God himself declares his readiness to conduct home the remnant of Israel from all parts of their dispersion, to compassionate and relieve their infirmities, and to provide them with all necessary accommodations by the way, ver. 6-9. The news is carried into distant lands; and the nations are summoned to attend to the display of God's power and goodness in rescuing his people from their stronger enemies, and in supplying them after their return with all manner of good things to the full extent of their wants and desires, ver. 10-14. Here the scene changes; and two new personages are successively introduced, in order to diversify the same subject, and to impress it more strongly. Rachel first; who is represented as just risen from the grave, and bitterly bewailing the loss of her children; for whom she anxiously looks about, but none are to be seen. Her tears are dried up; and she is consoled with the assurance that they are not lost for ever, but shall in time be brought back to their ancient borders, ver. 15-17. Ephraim comes next. He laments his past undutifulness with great contrition and penitence, and professes an earnest desire of amendment. These symptoms of returning duty are no sooner discerned in him, than God acknowledges him once more as a darling child and resolves with mercy to receive him, ver. 18-20. The virgin of Israel is then earnestly exhorted to hasten the preparations for their return; and encouraged with having the prospect of a signal miracle wrought in her favour, ver. 21, 22. And the vision closes at last with a promise that the Divine blessing should again rest upon the land of Judah; and that the men of Judah should once more dwell there, cultivating it according to the simplicity of ancient institutions, and fully discharged from every want, ver. 23-26. In the third part, by way of appendix to the vision, the following gracious promises are specifically annexed: That God would in time to come supply all the deficiencies of Israel and Judah; and would be as diligent to restore as he had ever been to destroy them; and would not any more visit the offences of the fathers upon the children, ver. 27-30. That he would make with them a better covenant than he had made with their forefathers, ver. 31-34. That they should continue his people by an ordinance as firm and as lasting as that of the heavens, ver. 35-37. And that Jerusalem should again be built, enlarged in its extent, and secure from future desolation, ver. 38-40."

Verse 1. *At the same time*] This discourse was delivered at the same time with the former; and, with that, constitutes the *Book* which God ordered the prophet to write.

Will I be the God of all the families of Israel] I shall bring back the *ten tribes*, as well as their brethren the *Jews*. The restoration of the *Israelites* is the principal subject of this chapter.

Verse 2. *The people* which were *left of the sword*] Those of the *ten tribes* that had escaped death by the sword of the Assyrians.

Found grace in the wilderness] The place of their exile; a *wilderness*, compared to their own land.—*Dahler*. See Isa. xl. 3.

Verse 3. *I have loved thee with an everlasting love*] ואהבת עולם אהבתיך *veahabath olam ahabtich*, "and with the old love I have loved thee." "Also, with a love of long standing have

A. M. cir. 3417 B. C. cir. 587 Ol. XLVIII. 2 TarquiniiPrisci, R. Roman., cir. annum 30

4 Again, [i]I will build thee, and thou shalt be built, O virgin of Israel: thou shalt again be adorned with thy [k]tabrets, [l]and shalt go forth in the dances of them that make merry.

5 [m]Thou shalt yet plant vines upon the mountains of Samaria: the planters shall plant, and shall [n]eat *them* as common things.

6 For there shall be a day, *that* the watchmen upon the mount Ephraim shall cry, [o]Arise ye, and let us go up to Zion unto the LORD our God.

7 For thus saith the LORD; [p]Sing with gladness for Jacob, and shout among the chief of the nations: publish ye, praise ye, and say, O LORD, save thy people, the remnant of Israel.

8 Behold, I will bring them [q]from the north country, and [r]gather them from the coasts of the earth, *and* with them the blind and the lame, the woman with child and her that travaileth with child together: a great company shall return thither.

9 [s]They shall come with weeping, and with [t]supplications will I lead them: I will cause them to walk [u]by the rivers of waters in a straight way, wherein they shall not stumble: for I am a father to Israel, and Ephraim *is* my [v]first-born.

10 Hear the word of the LORD, O ye nations, and declare *it* in the isles afar off, and

[i]Chap. xxxiii. 7——[k]Exod. xv. 20; Judg. xi. 34; Psa. cxlix. 3——[l]Or, *timbrels*——[m]Isa. lxv. 21; Amos ix. 14 ——[n]Heb. *profane* them; Deut. xx. 6; xxviii. 30——[o]Isa. ii. 3; Mic. iv. 2——[p]Isa. xii. 5, 6

[q]Chap. iii. 12, 18; xxiii. 8——[r]Ezek. xx. 34, 41; xxxiv. 13——[s]Psa. cxxvi. 5, 6; chap. l. 4——[t]Or, *favours;* Zech. xii. 10——[u]Isa. xxxv. 8; xliii. 19; xlix. 10, 11——[v]Exod. iv. 22

I loved thee."—*Blayney.* "But I love thee always."—*Dahler.* I still bear to the Jewish people that love which I showed to their fathers in Egypt, in the wilderness, and in the promised land. Can it be supposed, by any person seriously considering the context, that these words are spoken of *God's decree of election* in behalf of the Jews? Those who make it such, act most injudiciously on their own principle; for, how few of the Jews have ever given evidence that they were the *children of God,* from their restoration from Babylon to the present day! The words refer simply to their state as a people, most wondrously preserved by the providence and mercy of God, as a *standing* proof of the Divine authority of the Scriptures, and as an evidence of God's displeasure against sin.

Therefore with loving-kindness have I drawn thee.] "Therefore have I lengthened out mercy to thee."—*Blayney.*

> C'est pourquoi je t'ai conservé ma grace.—*Dahler.*

> "Therefore I have preserved my grace to thee."

The exiles, who had not for a long time received any proofs of the Divine protection, are represented as deploring their state; but God answers, that though this may seem to be the case, he has *always* loved them; and this *continued* love he will show by bringing them out of their captivity. However *creeds* may fare, this is the sense of the passage; all the context proves this.

Verse 4. *O virgin of Israel*] Israelites in general; now called *virgin,* because restored to their ancient *purity.*

With thy tabrets] Women in general played on these; they were used in times of *rejoicing,* and accompanied with *dancing.* To these customs, still preserved, the prophet alludes.

Verse 5. *Thou shalt yet plant vines upon the mountains of Samaria*] This was the regal city of the Israelites, as *Jerusalem* was of the Jews.

Shall eat them *as common things.*] By the law of Moses no man was permitted to eat of the fruit of his vineyard till the fifth year after planting. For the first *three* years it was considered uncircumcised, unclean, not fit to be eaten; in the *fourth* year it was *holy to the Lord,* the fruit belonged to Him; in the *fifth* year he might use it for himself, Lev. xix. 23-25. But in the time here mentioned the fruit should be considered *common*—lawful at all times to be eaten.

Verse 6. *For there shall be a day*] Literally, *for this is the day,* or *the day is come.* The *watchmen*—the prophets.

Arise ye, and let us go up to Zion] Let both *Israelites* and *Jews* join together in the worship of the Lord.

Verse 7. *The chief of the nations*] The same as Jacob or Israel; for most certainly this people was once the *most honourable* on the face of the earth.

O Lord, save thy people] Let the Jews earnestly intercede in behalf of their Israelitish brethren; or let them rejoice and praise the Lord, who *hath saved* the remnant of Israel. So Dr. *Blayney* thinks the clause should be understood.

Verse 8. *I will bring them from the north country*] From Babylon.

From the coasts of the earth] The ten tribes were carried away partly into Assyria by Tiglath-pileser, and partly into Mesopotamia and Media by Shalmaneser, 2 Kings xv. 29; xvii. 6. Assyria and Media, being very distant from Palestine, might have been called, in prophetic language, *the coasts of the earth.*

The blind and the lame] I will so effectually remove all difficulties out of the way, so provide for them on the journey, so supernaturally support their bodies and minds, that the veriest invalids shall safely proceed to, and happily arrive at, the end of their journey.

Verse 9. *They shall come with weeping*] Duly penetrated with a sense of their sins, they shall deeply deplore them; and, while weeping for them, earnestly *supplicate* God to have mercy upon them.

By the rivers of waters] I will so guide and provide for them in the arid deserts, that they

A. M. cir. 3417
B. C. cir. 587
Ol. XLVIII. 2
TarquiniiPrisci,
R. Roman.,
cir. annum 30

say, He that scattered Israel
[w]will gather him, and keep him,
as a shepherd *doth* his flock.
11 For [x]the LORD hath redeem-
ed Jacob, and ransomed him [y]from the hand
of *him that was* stronger than he.
12 Therefore they shall come and sing in
[z]the height of Zion, and shall flow together to
[a]the goodness of the LORD, for wheat, and for
wine, and for oil, and for the young of the flock
and of the herd: and their soul shall be as a
[b]watered garden; [c]and they shall not sorrow
any more at all.
13 Then shall the virgin rejoice in the dance,
both young men and old together: for I will
turn their mourning into joy, and will comfort
them, and make them rejoice from their sorrow.
14 And I will satiate the soul of the priests
with fatness, and my people shall be satisfied
with my goodness, saith the LORD.
15 Thus saith the LORD; [d]A voice was
heard in [e]Ramah, lamentation, *and* bitter
weeping; Rachel weeping for her
children refused to be comforted
for her children, because [f]they
were not.
16 Thus saith the LORD; Refrain thy voice
from weeping, and thine eyes from tears: for
thy work shall be rewarded, saith the LORD;
and [g]they shall come again from the land of
the enemy.
17 And there is hope in thine end, saith the
LORD, that thy children shall come again to
their own border.
18 I have surely heard Ephraim bemoaning
himself *thus;* Thou hast chastised me, and I
was chastised, as a bullock unaccustomed *to
the yoke:* [h]turn thou me, and I shall be
turned; for thou *art* the LORD my God.
19 Surely [i]after that I was turned, I repented; and after that I was instructed, I smote
upon *my* thigh: I was ashamed, yea, even
confounded, because I did bear the reproach
of my youth.

[w]Isa. xl. 11; Ezek. xxxiv. 12, 13, 14——[x]Isa. xliv. 23 xlviii. 20——[y]Isa. xlii. 24, 25——[z]Ezek. xvii. 23; xx. 40 [a]Hos. iii. 5——[b]Isa. lviii. 11

[c]Isa. xxxv. 10; lxv. 19; Rev. xxi. 4——[d]Matt. ii. 17, 18——[e]Josh. xviii. 25——[f]Gen. xlii. 13——[g]Ver. 4, 5; Ezra i. 5; Hos. i. 11——[h]Lam. v. 21——[i]Deut. xxx. 2

shall find streams of water whenever necessary. Every one knows of how much consequence water is to travellers in the eastern deserts.

Ephraim is *my first-born.*] Ephraim, being the most considerable, is often put for the whole of the *ten tribes.*

Verse 12. *And shall flow together*] Perhaps this may refer to their assembling at the *three* great national feasts, the passover, pentecost, and tabernacles.

Their soul shall be as a watered garden] Full of the light, life, and power of God; so that they shall rejoice evermore, pray without ceasing, and give thanks in every thing.

Verse 14. *And I will satiate the soul of the priests*] The worship of God being restored, they shall have their proper share of the victims brought to the temple.

Verse 15. *A voice was heard in Ramah*] The Ramah mentioned here, (for there were several towns of this name,) was situated in the tribe of Benjamin, about *six* or *seven* miles from Jerusalem. Near this place *Rachel* was buried; who is here, in a beautiful figure of poetry, represented as coming out of her grave, and lamenting bitterly for the loss of her children, none of whom presented themselves to her view, all being slain or gone into exile. St. Matthew, who is ever fond of accommodation, applies these words, chap. ii. 17, 18, to the massacre of the children at Bethlehem. That is, they were suitable to that occasion, and therefore he so applied them; but they are not a prediction of that event.

Verse 16. *They shall come again from the land of the enemy.*] This could not be said of the *murdered innocents* at Bethlehem; they never came again; but the Jews, who had gone into captivity, did come again from the *land of their enemy* to *their own border.*

Verse 18. *I have surely heard Ephraim bemoaning himself*] The exiled Israelites are in a state of deep repentance.

Thou hast chastised me, and I was chastised] I was at first like an unbroken and untoward steer, the more I was chastised the more I rebelled; but now I have benefited by thy correction.

Turn thou me] I am now *willing* to take thy yoke upon me, but I have no *power.* I can only *will* and *pray.* Take the matter into thy own hand, and fully convert my soul.

Verse 19. *After that I was turned*] Converted from my sin, folly, and idolatry.

I repented] To *conviction of sin,* I now added *contrition for sin.* Conviction, in this sense of the word, must precede contrition or repentance. As soon as a man sees himself lost and undone, he is *convicted* of sin; when *convicted,* he begins to *mourn.* Thus *contrition* follows *conviction.*

I smote upon my *thigh*] My sorrow grew deeper and deeper; I smote upon my thigh through the extremity of my distress. This was a usual sign of deep affliction. See Ezek. xxi. 12. It was the same among the ancient Greeks. So Homer:—

Ως εφατ'· αυταρ Αρης θαλερω πεπληγετο μηρω
Χερσι καταπρηνεσσ', ολοφυρομενος δε προσηυδα.
IL. lib. xv. 113.

"She spake; and with expanded arms, his *thighs*
Smiting, thus *sorrowful,* the god exclaimed."
COWPER.

A. M. cir. 3417 B. C. cir. 587 Ol. XLVIII. 2 TarquiniiPrisci, R. Roman., cir. annum 30

20 *Is* Ephraim my dear son? *is he* a pleasant child? for since I spake against him, I do earnestly remember him still: [k]therefore my bowels [l]are troubled for him; [m]I will surely have mercy upon him, saith the LORD.

21 Set thee up waymarks, make thee high heaps: [n]set thine heart toward the highway, *even* the way *which* thou wentest: turn again, O virgin of Israel, turn again to these thy cities.

22 How long wilt thou [o]go about, O thou [p]backsliding daughter? for the LORD hath created a new thing in the earth, A woman shall compass a man.

23 Thus saith the LORD of hosts, the God of Israel; As yet they shall use this speech in the line of Judah and in the cities thereof, when I shall bring again their captivity; [q]The LORD bless thee, O habitation of justice, *and* [r]mountain of holiness.

[k]Deut. xxxii. 36; Isa. lxiii. 15; Hos. xi. 8——[l]Heb. *sound*——[m]Isa. lvii. 18; Hos. xiv. 4——[n]Chap. l. 5

[o]Chap. ii. 18, 23, 36——[p]Chap. iii. 6, 8, 11, 12, 14, 22——[q]Psa. cxxii. 5, 6, 7, 8; Isa. i. 26——[r]Zech. viii. 3

———————— αυταρ Αχιλλευς
Μηρω πληξαμενος Πατροκληα προσεειπεν.
IL. lib. xvi. 124.

"Achilles saw it, *smote his thigh*, and said——."
COWPER.

I have often seen persons in deep grief act thus.

Verse 20. Is *Ephraim my dear son?*] It is impossible to conceive any thing more *tenderly affectionate* than this. Let us consider the whole account. The *ten tribes*, called here *Ephraim*, for the reason before alleged, are represented as acknowledging their sins. I have heard Ephraim bemoaning himself; and in his lamentation he says, 1. *Thou hast chastised me.* 2. Though he at first rebelled against the chastisement, yet at last he submitted and acknowledged his offences. 3. He turned from all his offences; he was *converted.* 4. After his conversion, (שובי *shubi,*) he *repented;* after conviction came *contrition*, as before stated. 5. Being in a state of godly sorrow, he was instructed, הודעי *hivvadei*, he got a thorough *knowledge* of the desperate wickedness of his heart and life. 6. Having received this *instruction*, he was filled with *excessive grief;* which is signified here by *smiting on his thigh.* See above. 7. He finds that from his *youth up* he had been sinning against God; and although his youthful sins had long passed from his memory, yet the light of God brought them back, and he was ashamed and confounded at the sight of them. 8. In this state of confusion and distress God sees him; and, commiserating his state, thus speaks:—

1. *Is Ephraim my dear son?* Bad as he is in his own sight, and in the sight of my justice, he is now a *penitent*, and to me is *precious.* 2. However loathsome and disfigured he may be with sin and sorrow, he is to me a *pleasant child* --a *child of delights;* one in whose conversion I delight, and my angels rejoice. 3. I did speak against him: כי מדי דברי בו *ki middey dabberi bo*, for "from the abundance of my speaking in him;" accusing, threatening, promising, exhorting, encouraging; "I do still earnestly remember him." God has taken much pains with him, and is unwilling to give him up; but now that he repents, he has not received the grace of God utterly in vain. 4. God feels a *yearning* desire towards him; המו מעי לו *hamu meai lo*, "my bowels are agitated for him." I feel nothing towards him but *pity* and *love.* When a sinner turns to God, God ceases to be angry with him. 5. God expresses his determination to save him; רחם ארחמנו *rachem arachamennu*, "I will be affectionately merciful to him, with tender mercy, saith the Lord." He shall find that I treat him as a *father* does a returning prodigal son. So every penitent is sure to find mercy at the hand of God.

Verse 21. *Set thee up waymarks*] Alluding to stones, or *heaps of stones*, which travellers in the desert set up to ascertain the way, that they may know how to return. Mark the way to Babylon: thither *ye shall certainly go;* but *from it* ye shall as certainly *return.*

Verse 22. *A woman shall compass a man*] נקבה תסובב גבר *nekebah tesobeb gaber*, "A weak woman shall compass or circumvent a strong man." This place has given much trouble to Biblical critics. By many Christian writers it is considered a prophecy of the *miraculous conception of the holy virgin;* but as I am sure no such meaning is in the *words*, nor in the *context*, so I am satisfied no such meaning can be fairly brought out of them. *Houbigant* thinks there is a small error in the text, i. e., תשובב *teshobeb*, shall *return*, and not תסובב *tesobeb*, shall *compass.* This reading is found in *two* of *Kennicott's* MSS., and *he* contends that the passage should be read, "The wife shall return to her husband;" alluding to the conversion of the Jewish people, called above a *backsliding daughter.* This makes a good sense; but I do not see why this should be called *a new thing in the earth.* After all, I think it likely that the Jews in their present distressed circumstances are represented under the similitude of a *weak defenceless female* נקבה *nekebah;* and the *Chaldeans* under that of a *fierce strong man*, גבר *gaber*, who had prevailed over and oppressed this *weak woman.* But, notwithstanding the disparity between them, God would cause the *woman*—the *weak defenceless Jews*, to *compass*—to overcome, the *strong man*—the *powerful Babylonians.* And this the prophet says would be *a new thing in the land;* for in such a case the lame would take the prey. The context favours both these meanings. Dr. *Blayney* gives a sense very near to this: "A weak woman shall repulse a strong or mighty man." It is most likely a proverbial expression.

Verse 23. *The Lord bless thee, O habitation of justice*] After their return they shall be remarkably prosperous. *Piety* and *industry* shall go hand in hand; they shall have their *husbandmen*, their *shepherds*, and *neatherds*,

A. M. cir. 3417
B. C. cir. 587
Ol. XLVIII. 2
TarquiniiPrisci, R. Roman., cir. annum 30

24 And there shall dwell in Judah itself, and [s]in all the cities thereof together, husbandmen, and they *that* go forth with flocks.

25 For I have satiated the weary soul, and I have replenished every sorrowful soul.

26 Upon this I awaked, and beheld; and my sleep was sweet unto me.

27 Behold, the days come, saith the LORD, that [t]I will sow the house of Israel and the house of Judah, with the seed of man, and with the seed of beast.

28 And it shall come to pass, *that* like as I have [u]watched over them, [v]to pluck up, and to break down, and to throw down, and to destroy, and to afflict; so will I watch over them, [w]to build, and to plant, saith the LORD.

29 [x]In those days they shall say no more, The fathers have eaten a sour grape, and the children's teeth are set on edge.

30 [y]But every one shall die for his own iniquity: every man that eateth the sour grape, his teeth shall be set on edge.

31 Behold, the [z]days come, saith the LORD, that I will make a new covenant with the house of Israel, and with the house of Judah:

A. M. cir. 3417
B. C. cir. 587
Ol. XLVIII. 2
TarquiniiPrisci, R. Roman., cir. annum 30

32 Not according to the covenant that I made with their fathers, in the day *that* [a]I took them by the hand, to bring them out of the land of Egypt; which my covenant they brake, [b]although I was a husband unto them, saith the LORD.

33 [c]But this shall *be* the covenant that I will make with the house of Israel; After those days, saith the LORD, [d]I will put my law in their inward parts, and write it in their hearts; [e]and will be their God, and they shall be my people.

34 And they shall teach no more every man his neighbour, and every man his brother, saying, Know the LORD: for [f]they shall all know me, from the least of them unto the greatest of them, saith the LORD: for [g]I will forgive their iniquity, and I will remember their sin no more.

35 Thus saith the LORD; [h]which giveth the sun for a light by day, *and* the ordinances of the moon and of the stars for a light by night, which divideth [i]the sea when the waves thereof roar; [k]The LORD of hosts *is* his name:

---

[s]Ch. xxxiii. 12, 13——[t]Ezek. xxxvi. 9, 10, 11; Hos. ii. 23; Zech. x. 9——[u]Ch. xliv. 27——[v]Ch. i. 10; xviii. 7——[w]Ch. xxiv. 6——[x]Ezek. xviii. 2, 3——[y]Gal. vi. 5, 7——[z]Ch. xxxii. 40; xxxiii. 14; Ezek. xxxvii. 26; Heb. viii. 8-12; x. 16, 17——[a]Deut. i. 31——[b]Or, *should I have continued a husband unto them?*——[c]Chap. xxxii. 40

[d]Psa. xl. 8; Ezek. xi. 19, 20; xxxvi. 26, 27; 2 Cor. iii. 3——[e]Chap. xxiv. 7; xxx. 22; xxxii. 38——[f]Isa. liv. 13; John vi. 45; 1 Cor. ii. 10; 1 John ii. 20——[g]Chap. xxxiii. 8; l. 20; Mic. vii. 18; Acts x. 43; xiii. 39; Rom. xi. 27——[h]Gen. i. 16; Psa. lxxii. 5, 17; lxxxix. 2, 36, 37; cxix. 89——[i]Isa. li. 15——[k]Chap. x. 16

---

ver. 24. And Jerusalem shall become a *righteous city*, and the *temple* shall be a *place of holiness;* so the weary there shall have *rest*, and the *sorrowful* shall be abundantly *comforted*, ver. 24, 25.

Verse 26. *Upon this I awaked*] It appears that the prophecy, commencing with chap. xxx. 2 and ending with ver. 25 of this chapter, was delivered to the prophet in a dream. *Dahler* supposes it to be a *wish;* that the prophet, though he could not hope to live to that time, might be permitted to awake up from his tomb; and, having seen this prosperity, would be content to return to his grave.

Verse 27. *I will sow—with the seed of man and with the seed of beast.*] I will multiply both men and cattle.

Verse 29. *The fathers have eaten a sour grape*] A proverbial expression for, "The children suffer for the offences of their parents." This is explained in the next verse: "Every one shall die for his own iniquity." No child shall suffer Divine punition for the sin of his father; only so far as he acts in the same way can he be said to bear the sins of his parents.

Verse 31. *A new covenant*] The Christian dispensation.

Verse 33. *After those days*] When vision and prophecy shall be sealed up, and Jesus have assumed that *body which was prepared for him*, and have laid down his life for the redemption of a lost world, and, having ascended on high, shall have obtained the gift of the Holy Spirit to purify the heart; then God's law shall, by it, be *put in their inward parts, and written on their hearts;* so that all *within* and all *without* shall be holiness to the Lord. Then God will be truly *their God*, received and acknowledged as their *portion*, and the sole object of their devotion; and they shall be *his people*, filled with holiness, and made partakers of the Divine nature, so that they shall perfectly love him and worthily magnify his name.

Verse 34. *And they shall teach no more*] It shall be a time of universal *light* and *knowledge;* all shall *know God in Christ, from the least to the greatest;* the *children* shall be taught to *read the New Covenant*, and to *understand* the *terms* of their salvation.

I will forgive their iniquity] It shall be a time of GENERAL PARDON; multitudes shall be daily in the Christian Church receiving the witness of God's Spirit, and in their life and conversation witnessing a good confession. How wonderfully is this prophecy fulfilled in the age of *Bibles*, *Sunday schools*, and *village preaching*.

A. M. cir. 3417
B. C. cir. 587
Ol. XLVIII. 2
TarquiniiPrisci,
R. Roman.,
cir. annum 30

36 [l]If those ordinances depart from before me, saith the LORD, *then* the seed of Israel also shall cease from being a nation before me for ever.

37 Thus saith the LORD; [m]If heaven above can be measured, and the foundations of the earth searched out beneath, I will also cast off all the seed of Israel for all that they have done, saith the LORD.

38 Behold, the days come, saith the LORD, that the city shall be built to the LORD, [n]from the tower of Hananeel unto the gate of the corner.

39 And [o]the measuring line shall yet go forth over against it upon the hill Gareb, and shall compass about to Goath.

40 And the whole valley of the dead bodies, and of the ashes, and all the fields unto the brook of Kidron, [p]unto the corner of the horse-gate toward the east, [q]*shall be* holy unto the LORD; it shall not be plucked up, nor thrown down any more for ever.

[l]Psa. cxlviii. 6; Isa. liv. 9, 10; ch. xxxiii. 20——[m]Ch. xxxiii. 22——[n]Neh. iii. 1; Zech. xiv. 10

[o]Ezek. xl. 8; Zech. ii. 1——[p]2 Chron. xxiii. 15; Neh. iii. 28——[q]Joel iii. 17

Verse 36. *If those ordinances*] As sure as the *sun* shall give light to the *day*, and the *moon* to the *night*, so surely shall the Jews continue to be a distinct people. The same thing is expressed in other words in the next verse. Hitherto this prophecy has been literally fulfilled; the Jews are still a distinct people from all the dwellers upon earth. Every attempt that has been made in any country to *naturalize* and unite them with the people of that country, has proved abortive. The well-circumstanced attempt made this year (1830) in England, when the strongest interest was excited in their behalf, has also utterly failed. And why? Because of God's *purpose* expressed in chap. xxxi. 35-37 of the BOOK *of the Prophet* JEREMIAH.

Verse 38. *The city shall be built to the Lord*] This cannot mean the city built after the return from Babylon, for two reasons: 1. This is to be much *greater* in *extent;* 2. It is to be *permanent,* never to be *thrown down*, ver. 40. It must therefore mean, if taken literally at all, the city that is to be built by them when they are brought in with the fulness of the Gentiles.

The tower of Hananeel] This stood in the *northeast* part of the city; from thence the wall proceeded to the *corner gate*, (probably the same as the *old gate*,) thus named from its running out into an *angle* in that part.

Verse 39. *Upon the hill Gareb*] *Gareb* and *Goath* are out of the limits of this city. The latter is supposed to be *Golgotha;* that is, the *heap of Gotha*, which, being the place where our Lord was crucified, was *without the city*. These hills were a little to the north-west of the old city walls: but are destined to be *within* the new city. See Dr. *Blayney* on all these verses.

Verse 40. *The whole valley of the dead bodies*] The valley of the son of *Hinnom*.

And all the fields unto the brook of Kidron, unto the corner of the horse-gate toward the east] All these places, the *fuller's field*, &c., shall be consecrated to the Lord, and become a part of this new city; so that this will appear to be a city much more extensive than the city of Jerusalem ever was; and to be suited to that time, when the people shall have the law written in their hearts, and God shall have filled the land with the seed of man, and with the seed of beast. Talia sæcla currite! "Make speed, ye happy times!"

CHAPTER XXXII

Jeremiah, now confined for his faithful admonitions, foretells the fate of the king and city, 1–5. *According to the direction of God, he buys of his cousin Hanameel a field in Anathoth; the contract, or deed of sale, being subscribed, sealed, and witnessed, and delivered to Baruch, together with a duplicate not sealed, who is commanded to put them into an earthern vessel that they may remain there for many days,* 6–14. *This transaction of the prophet, which is entered and subscribed in the public register, God constitutes a sign or pledge of the Jews' return from the Babylonish captivity, and of their again possessing houses, fields, and vineyards, in their own land, and by their own right, according to their tribes and families,* 15. *Jeremiah's prayer, in which he recounts God's marvellous acts towards the children of Israel, and deeply deplores the lamentable state of the country, and the numerous provocations which have led to it,* 16–25. *After which God is introduced declaring his purpose of giving up his people into the hands of their enemies,* 26–35; *promising, however, to restore them in due time to their ancient possessions, and to make with them an everlasting covenant,* 36–44.

A. M. 3415
B. C. 589
Ol. XLVII. 4
Anno
TarquiniiPrisci,
R. Roman., 28

THE word that came to Jeremiah from the LORD [a]in the
tenth year of Zedekiah king of
Judah, which *was* the eighteenth
year of Nebuchadrezzar.
2 For then the king of Babylon's army besieged Jerusalem: and Jeremiah the prophet
was shut up [b]in the court of the prison, which
was in the king of Judah's house.
3 For Zedekiah king of Judah had shut him
up, saying, Wherefore dost thou prophesy,
and say, Thus saith the LORD, [c]Behold, I will
give this city into the hand of the king of
Babylon, and he shall take it;
4 And Zedekiah king of Judah [d]shall not
escape out of the hand of the Chaldeans, but
shall surely be delivered into the hand of the
king of Babylon, and shall speak with him
mouth to mouth, and his eyes shall behold
his eyes;
5 And he shall lead Zedekiah to Babylon,
and there shall he be [e]until I visit him, saith
the LORD: [f]though ye fight with
the Chaldeans, ye shall not
prosper.
6 And Jeremiah said, The
word of the LORD came unto me, saying,
7 Behold, Hanameel the son of Shallum
thine uncle shall come unto thee, saying, Buy
thee my field that *is* in Anathoth: for the
[g]right of redemption *is* thine to buy *it.*
8 So Hanameel mine uncle's son came to
me in the court of the prison according to the
word of the LORD, and said unto me, Buy my
field, I pray thee, that *is* in Anathoth, which
is in the country of Benjamin: for the right
of inheritance *is* thine, and the redemption *is*
thine; buy *it* for thyself. Then I knew that
this *was* the word of the LORD.
9 And I bought the field of Hanameel
my uncle's son, that *was* in Anathoth, and
[h]weighed him the money, *even* [i]seventeen
shekels of silver.
10 And I [k]subscribed the evidence, and

[a]2 Kings xxv. 1, 2; Jer. xxxix. 1——[b]Neh. iii. 25; chap. xxxiii. 1; xxxvii. 21; xxxviii. 6; xxxix. 14——[c]Ch. xxxiv. 2——[d]Ch. xxxiv. 3; xxxviii. 18, 23; xxxix. 5; lii. 9——[e]Ch. xxvii. 22——[f]Ch. xxi. 4; xxxiii. 5——[g]Leviticus xxv. 24, 25, 32; Ruth iv. 4——[h]Gen. xxiii. 16; Zech. xi. 12——[i]Or, *seven shekels and ten* pieces *of silver*——[k]Heb. *wrote in the book*

NOTES ON CHAP. XXXII

Verse 1. *The word that came*] This prophecy bears its own *date:* it was delivered in the *tenth* year of *Zedekiah,* which answered to the *eighteenth* of Nebuchadnezzar. It appears from 2 Kings xxv. 8, that the *eleventh* year of Zedekiah was the *nineteenth* of Nebuchadnezzar; and consequently, that the *eighteenth* of that monarch must have been the *tenth* of the Jewish king.

Verse 2. *Then the king of Babylon's army besieged Jerusalem*] The siege had commenced the *year before,* and continued a *year after,* ending in the *fifth* month of the following year; consequently, the siege must have lasted about *eighteen* months and *twenty-seven* days. See 2 Kings xxv. 18.

Verse 4. *And shall speak with him mouth to mouth*] He shall be reduced to a state of the most abject servitude. The *slave* was obliged to fix his eyes on every motion of the master whilst giving his orders, who often condescended to give them only by *dumb signs.*

Verse 7. *The right of redemption* is *thine*] The law had established that the estates of a family should never be alienated. If, therefore, a man through poverty was obliged to sell his patrimony, the *nearest relative* had a right to purchase it before all others, and even to redeem it, if it had been sold to another. This is what is called the *right of goel,* or *kinsman,* Lev. xxv. 25. And in the year of jubilee the whole reverted to its ancient master, Lev. xxv. 13.

Verse 8. *This* was *the word of the Lord.*] It was by his appointment that I was to make this purchase. The whole was designed as a symbolical act, to show the people that there would be a *return* from Babylon, that each family should re-enter on its former possessions, and that a man might safely purchase on the certainty of this event.

Verse 9. *Weighed him the money*] It does not appear that there was any *coined* or *stamped* money among the Jews before the captivity; the Scripture, therefore, never speaks of *counting* money, but of *weighing* it.

Seventeen shekels of silver.] The shekel at this time must have been a *nominal* coin; it was a thing of a certain *weight,* or a certain *worth. Seventeen* shekels was the *weight* of the silver paid: but it might have been in *one ingot,* or piece. The shekel has been valued at from *two shillings and threepence* to *two shillings and sixpence,* and even at *three shillings;* taking the purchase-money at a *medium* of the value of the shekel, it would amount only to about *two pounds two shillings and sixpence.* But as estates bore value only in proportion to the *number of years before the jubilee,* and the field in question was then in the hands of the *Chaldeans,* and this cousin of Jeremiah was not likely to come back to enjoy it after *seventy* years, (nor could he then have it, as a jubilee would intervene and restore it to the original family,) and money must now be very scarce and high in its value, the *seventeen* shekels might have been a sufficient sum for a field in those circumstances, and one probably not large in its dimensions.

Verse 10. *I subscribed the evidence*] We have here all the circumstances of this legal act: 1. An offer is made of the reversion of the ground, till the jubilee, to him who would then of right come into possession. 2. The price is agreed on, and the silver *weighed* in the balances. 3. A *contract* or *deed* of sale is drawn

A. M. 3415
B. C. 589
Ol. XLVII. 4
Anno
TarquiniiPrisci,
R. Roman., 28

sealed *it,* and took witnesses, and
weighed *him* the money in the
balances.
11 So I took the evidence of
the purchase, *both* that which was sealed *according* to the law and custom, and that which was open:
12 And I gave the evidence of the purchase unto [l]Baruch the son of Neriah, the son of Maaseiah, in the sight of Hanameel mine uncle's *son,* and in the presence of the [m]witnesses that subscribed the book of the purchase, before all the Jews that sat in the court of the prison.
13 And I charged Baruch before them, saying,
14 Thus saith the LORD of hosts, the God of Israel; Take these evidences, this evidence of the purchase, both which is sealed, and this evidence which is open; and put them in an earthen vessel, that they may continue many days.
15 For thus saith the LORD of hosts, the God of Israel; Houses and fields and vineyards [n]shall be possessed again in this land.
16 Now when I had delivered the evidence of the purchase unto Baruch the son of Neriah, I prayed unto the LORD, saying,
17 Ah Lord GOD! behold, [o]thou hast made the heaven and the earth by thy great power and stretched-out arm, *and* [p]there is nothing [q]too hard for thee:
18 Thou showest [r]loving-kindness unto thousands, and recompensest the iniquity of the fathers into the bosom of their children after them: the Great, [s]the Mighty God, [t]the LORD of hosts, *is* his name,
19 [u]Great in counsel, and mighty in [v]work: for thine [w]eyes *are* open upon all the ways of the sons of men: [x]to give every one according to his ways, and according to the fruit of his doings:
20 Which hast set signs and wonders in the land of Egypt, *even* unto this day, and in Israel, and among *other* men; and hast made thee [y]a name, as at this day;
21 And [z]hast brought forth thy people Israel out of the land of Egypt with signs, and with wonders, and with a strong hand, and with a stretched-out arm, and with great terror;
22 And hast given them this land, which thou didst swear to their fathers to give them, [a]a land flowing with milk and honey;
23 And they came in, and possessed it; but [b]they obeyed not thy voice, neither walked in thy law; they have done nothing of all that thou commandedst them to do: therefore thou hast caused all this evil to come upon them:
24 Behold the [c]mounts, they are come unto the city to take it; and the city [d]is given into the hand of the Chaldeans, that fight against

[l]Ch. xxxvi. 4——[m]See Isa. viii. 2——[n]Ver. 37, 43——[o]2 Kings xix. 15——[p]Gen. xviii. 14; ver. 27; Luke i. 37 [q]Or, *hid from thee*——[r]Exod. xx. 6; xxxiv. 7; Deut. v. 9, 10 [s]Isa. ix. 6——[t]Ch. x. 16——[u]Isa. xxviii. 29——[v]Heb. *doing* [w]Job xxxiv. 21; Psa. xxxiii. 13; Prov. v. 21; chap. xvi. 17

[x]Ch. xvii. 10——[y]Exod. ix. 16; 1 Chron. xvii. 21; Isa. lxiii. 12; Dan. ix. 15——[z]Exod. vi. 6; 2 Sam. vii. 23; 1 Chron. xvii. 21; Psa. cxxxvi. 11, 12——[a]Exod. iii. 8, 17; chap. xi. 5——[b]Neh. ix. 26; ch. xi. 8; Dan. ix. 10–14 [c]Or, *engines of shot;* chap. xxxiii. 4——[d]Ver. 25, 36

up; to which both parties agreeing, 4. *Witnesses* are brought forward to see it *signed* and *sealed;* for the contract was both *subscribed* and *sealed.* 5. A *duplicate* of the deed was drawn, which was not to be *sealed,* but to lie *open* for the inspection of those concerned, in some public place where it might be safe, and always to be seen. 6. The original, which was *sealed up,* was put in an *earthen pitcher,* in order to be preserved from accidents. 7. This was delivered by the purchaser into the hands of a third party, to be preserved for the use of the purchaser, and *witnesses* were called to attest this *delivery.* 8. They subscribed the *book of the purchase,* perhaps a *town book,* or *register,* where such purchases were entered. *Baruch* was a *scribe* by profession; and the deeds were delivered into his hands, before witnesses, to be preserved as above. Perhaps the *law,* in this case, required that the *instrument* should be thus lodged. But, in the present case, *both the deeds,* the *orignal* and the *duplicate,* were put into the earthen pitcher, because the city was about to be burnt; and, if lodged as *usual,* they would be destroyed in the general conflagration. See ver. 14.

Verse 15. *Houses and fields—shall be possessed again*] That is, this is an evidence that the captivity shall not last long: houses, &c., shall here be possessed again, either by their present owners or immediate descendants. The *young* might return; at least, all *under ten years* of age: there was no natural impossibility that *they* should not live till they should be *fourscore.*

Verse 16. *I prayed unto the Lord*] And what a prayer! What weight of matter, sublimity of expression, profound veneration, just conception, Divine unction, powerful pleading, and strength of faith! Historical, without flatness; condensed, without obscurity; confessing the greatest of crimes against the most righteous of Beings, without despairing of his mercy, or presuming on his goodness: a confession that, in fact, acknowledges that God's *justice should* smite and destroy, had not his infinite goodness said, I will pardon and spare.

Verse 19. *Thine eyes* are *open upon all the*

A. M. 3415
B. C. 589
Ol. XLVII. 4
Anno
TarquiniiPrisci,
R. Roman., 28

it, because of [e]the sword, and of the famine, and of the pestilence: and what thou hast spoken is come to pass; and, behold, thou seest *it.*

25 And thou hast said unto me, O Lord GOD, Buy thee the field for money, and take witnesses; [f]for [g]the city is given into the hand of the Chaldeans.

26 Then came the word of the LORD unto Jeremiah, saying,

27 Behold, I *am* the LORD, the [h]God of all flesh: [i]is there any thing too hard for me?

28 Therefore thus saith the LORD; Behold, [k]I will give this city into the hand of the Chaldeans, and into the hand of Nebuchadrezzar king of Babylon, and he shall take it:

29 And the Chaldeans, that fight against this city, shall come, and [l]set fire on this city, and burn it with the houses, [m]upon whose roofs they have offered incense unto Baal, and poured out drink-offerings unto other gods, to provoke me to anger.

30 For the children of Israel and the children of Judah [n]have only done evil before me from their youth: for the children of Israel have only provoked me to anger with the work of their hands, saith the LORD.

31 For this city hath been to me *as* [o]a provocation of mine anger and of my fury from the day that they built it even unto this day; [p]that I should remove it from before my face.

32 Because of all the evil of the children of Israel, and of the children of Judah, which they have done to provoke me to anger, [q]they, their kings, their princes, their priests, and their prophets, and the men of Judah, and the inhabitants of Jerusalem.

A. M. 3415
B. C. 589
Ol. XLVII. 4
Anno
TarquiniiPrisci,
R. Roman., 28

33 And they have turned unto me the [r]back,[s] and not the face: though I taught them, [t]rising up early and teaching *them,* yet they have not hearkened to receive instruction.

34 But they [u]set their abominations in the house, which is called by my name, to defile it.

35 And they built the high places of Baal, which *are* in the valley of the son of Hinnom, to [v]cause their sons and their daughters to pass through *the fire* unto [w]Molech; [x]which I commanded them not, neither came it into my mind, that they should do this abomination, to cause Judah to sin.

36 And now therefore thus saith the LORD, the God of Israel, concerning this city, whereof ye say, [y]It shall be delivered into the hand of the king of Babylon by the sword, and by the famine, and by the pestilence;

37 Behold, I will [z]gather them out of all countries, whither I have driven them in mine anger, and in my fury, and in great wrath; and I will bring them again unto this place, and I will cause them [a]to dwell safely:

38 And they shall [b]be my people, and I will be their God:

39 And I will [c]give them one heart, and one way, that they may fear me [d]for ever, for the good of them, and of their children after them:

[e]Ch. xiv. 12——[f]Or, *though*——[g]Ver. 24——[h]Num. xvi. 22——[i]Ver. 17——[k]Ver. 3——[l]Ch. xxi. 10; xxxvii. 8, 10; lii. 13——[m]Ch. xix. 13——[n]Ch. ii. 7; iii. 25; vii. 22–26; xxii. 21; Ezek. xx. 28——[o]Heb. *for my anger*——[p]2 Kings xxiii. 27; xxiv. 3——[q]Isa. i. 4, 6; Dan. ix. 8——[r]Heb. *neck*——[s]Ch. ii. 27; vii. 24——[t]Ch. vii. 13

[u]Ch. vii. 30, 31; xxiii. 11; Ezek. viii. 5, 6——[v]Ch. vii. 31; xix. 5——[w]Lev. xviii. 21; 1 Kings xi. 33——[x]Chap. vii. 31——[y]Ver. 24——[z]Deut. xxx. 3; ch. xxiii. 3; xxix. 14; xxxi. 10; Ezek. xxxvii. 21——[a]Ch. xxiii. 6; xxxiii. 16——[b]Ch. xxiv. 7; xxx. 22; xxxi. 33——[c]Chap. xxiv. 7; Ezek. xi. 19, 20——[d]Heb. *all days*

ways of—men] Thou art omniscient, and knowest all things; thou art omnipresent, and seest all things.

Verse 24. *Behold the mounts*] The huge terraces raised up to plant their engines on, that they might throw darts, stones, &c., into the city.

Because of the sword, and of the famine, and of the pestilence] The city was now reduced to extreme necessity; and from the siege continuing nearly a year longer, we may conclude that the besieged made a noble defence.

Verse 29. *With the houses, upon whose roofs*] As it is most probable that *Baal* was the *sun,* they might have chosen the *tops* of the houses, which were always flat, with battlements around, to offer incense and sacrifice to him at his *rising,* and while he was *in sight* above the horizon.

Verse 30. *For the children of Israel and the children of Judah have only done evil*] They have all been transgressors from their earliest history.

For the children of Israel] The ten tribes.

Have only provoked me to anger with the work of their hands] They have been sinners beyond all others, being *excessive idolaters.* Their *hands* have formed the *objects* of their *worship.*

Verse 33. *Though I taught them, rising up early and teaching* them] From the frequent reference to this, we may naturally conclude that *morning preaching* prevailed much in Judea.

Verse 37. *Behold, I will gather them out of all countries*] A promise often repeated. See chap. xxix. 14, and the notes on chap. xxxi. 8, &c.

Verse 39. *I will give them one heart*] And that a *clean one.*

A. M. 3415
B. C. 589
Ol. XLVII. 4
Anno
TarquiniiPrisci,
R. Roman., 28

40 And [e]I will make an everlasting covenant with them, that I will not turn away [f]from them, to do them good; but [g]I will put my fear in their hearts, that they shall not depart from me.

41 Yea, [h]I will rejoice over them to do them good, and [i]I will plant them in this land [k]assuredly with my whole heart and with my whole soul.

42 For thus saith the LORD; [l]Like as I have brought all this great evil upon this people, so will I bring upon them all the good that I have promised them.

43 And [m]fields shall be bought in this land, [n]whereof ye say, *It is* desolate without man or beast; it is given into the hand of the Chaldeans.

44 Men shall buy fields for money, and subscribe evidences, and seal *them,* and take witnesses in [o]the land of Benjamin, and in the places about Jerusalem, and in the cities of Judah, and in the cities of the mountains, and in the cities of the valley, and in the cities of the south: for [p]I will cause their captivity to return, saith the LORD.

[e]Isa. lv. 3; chap. xxxi. 31——[f]Heb, *from after them* [g]Chap. xxxi. 33——[h]Deut. xxx. 9; Zeph. iii. 17——[i]Ch. xxiv. 6; xxxi. 28; Amos ix. 15

[k]Heb. *in truth,* or *stability*——[l]Chap. xxxi. 28 [m]Ver. 15——[n]Chap. xxxiii. 10——[o]Chap. xvii. 26 [p]Chap. xxxiii. 7, 11, 26

And one way] And that a *holy and safe one:* and to have this *clean heart,* and to *walk in this good way, will be for the good of them and their children after them.* God's blessing is a profitable inheritance. They shall have but *one object* of *worship,* and *one way* of salvation; and being saved from sin, idolatry, and destruction, they must necessarily be happy within and happy without.

Verse 41. *Yea, I will rejoice over them to do them good*] Nothing can please God better than our coming to him to receive the good which, *with his whole heart* and *his whole soul,* he is ready to impart. How exceedingly condescending are these words of God!

Verse 42. *Will I bring upon them all the good that I have promised*] God's word cannot fail. The Jews have never yet received the good that God has promised. Nothing like the fulfilment of these promises took place after their return from Babylon; therefore there remaineth yet a *rest* for these ancient people of God; and it is under the *Christian* dispensation that they are to have it.

Verse 44. *Men shall buy fields for money*] This is a reference to the symbolical purchase mentioned at the beginning of the chapter; *that* may be considered by them as a sure sign of their restoration, not only to the *same land,* but to their respective inheritances in that land. This the power of God could alone perform.

CHAPTER XXXIII

In this chapter the prophet predicts a restoration of Israel and Judah to the favour of God, attended with such glorious circumstances as shall astonish all the world, 1–9. *Their prosperity from that period is then described by a beautiful enumeration of circumstances,* 10–13. *This leads to the promise of the Messiah, the grand subject of the prophetical writings, and the happiness and stability which the children of Israel shall enjoy under his government; promises which, in so far as they respect the great body of the Jews, remain still to be fulfilled,* 14–26.

A. M. 3416
B. C. 588
Ol. XLVIII. 1
Anno
TarquiniiPrisci,
R. Roman., 29

MOREOVER the word of the LORD came unto Jeremiah the second time, (while he was yet [a]shut up in the court of the prison,) saying,

2 Thus saith the LORD the [b]Maker thereof, the LORD that formed it, to establish it; [c]the[d] LORD *is* his name;

3 [e]Call unto me, and I will answer thee, and

[a]Ch. xxxii. 2, 3——[b]Isa. xxxvii. 26——[c]Or, *JEHOVAH*

[d]Exod. xv. 3; Amos v. 8; ix. 6——[e]Psa. xci. 15; ch. xxix

NOTES ON CHAP. XXXIII

Verse 1. *Moreover the word of the Lord*] This was in the *eleventh* year of the reign of Zedekiah, Jeremiah being still *shut up in prison:* but he was now in the *court of the prison,* where the elders and the king's officers, &c., might consult him with the greater ease; for they continued to inquire, foolishly thinking, that if he would but prophesy good things, that these must come; or that he had sufficient power with God to induce him to alter his mind,—destroy the Chaldeans, and deliver the city.

Verse 2. *Thus saith the Lord the Maker thereof*] עשה *osah, the doer of it.* That is, he who is to perform *that* which he is now about to promise. Thus translated by *Dahler:*—Voici ce que dit l'Eternel, qui *fait* ce qu'il a *dit.*— "Thus saith the Lord, who doth that which he hath said." The word *Jehovah,* not *Lord,* should be used in all such places as this.

Verse 3. *Call unto me, and I will answer thee*] To me alone it belongs to reveal what is future; and the stupendous things which are now coming are known only to myself. These idolaters go to their gods to get information

A. M. 3416 B. C. 588 Ol. XLVIII. 1 Anno TarquiniiPrisci, R. Roman., 29

show thee great and [f]mighty
things which thou knowest not.
4 For thus saith the LORD, the
God of Israel, concerning the
houses of this city, and concerning the houses
of the kings of Judah, which are thrown down
by [g]the mounts, and by the sword;
5 [h]They come to fight with the Chaldeans,
but *it is* to fill them with the dead bodies of
men, whom I have slain in mine anger and in
my fury, and for all whose wickedness I have
hid my face from this city.
6 Behold, [i]I will bring it health and cure,
and I will cure them, and will reveal unto
them the abundance of peace and truth.
7 And [k]I will cause the captivity of Judah
and the captivity of Israel to return, and will
build them, [l]as at the first.
8 And I will [m]cleanse them from all their
iniquity, whereby they have sinned against
me; and I will [n]pardon all their iniquities,
whereby they have sinned, and whereby they
have transgressed against me.
9 [o]And it shall be to me a name of joy, a
praise and an honour before all the nations
of the earth, which shall hear all the good
that I do unto them: and they shall [p]fear
and tremble for all the goodness and for all
the prosperity that I procure unto it.
10 Thus saith the LORD; Again
there shall be heard in this place,
[q]which ye say *shall be* desolate
without man and without beast,
even in the cities of Judah, and in the streets
of Jerusalem, that are desolate, without man,
and without inhabitant, and without beast,
11 The [r]voice of joy, and the voice of gladness, the voice of the bridegroom, and the
voice of the bride, the voice of them that shall
say, [s]Praise the LORD of hosts: for the LORD *is*
good; for his mercy *endureth* for ever: *and* of
them that shall bring [t]the sacrifice of praise
into the house of the LORD. For [u]I will cause
to return the captivity of the land, as at the
first, saith the LORD.
12 Thus saith the LORD of hosts; [v]Again in
this place, which is desolate without man and
without beast, and in all the cities thereof,
shall be a habitation of shepherds causing
their flocks to lie down.
13 [w]In the cities of the mountains, in the
cities of the vale, and in the cities of the south,
and in the land of Benjamin, and in the places
about Jerusalem, and in the cities of Judah,
shall the flocks [x]pass again under the hands
of him that telleth *them,* saith the LORD.
14 [y]Behold, the days come, saith the LORD,
that [z]I will perform that good thing which

A. M. 3416 B. C. 588 Ol. XLVIII. 1 Anno TarquiniiPrisci, R. Roman., 29

[f]Or, *hidden;* Isa. xlviii. 6——[g]Ch. xxxii. 24——[h]Ch. xxxii. 5——[i]Ch. xxx. 17——[k]Ch. xxx. 3; xxxii. 44; ver. 11——[l]Isa. i. 26; chap. xxiv. 6; xxx. 20; xxxi. 4, 28; xlii. 10——[m]Ezek. xxxvi. 25; Zech. xiii. 1; Heb. ix. 13, 14——[n]Chap. xxxi. 34; Mic. vii. 18——[o]Isa. lxii. 7; chap. xiii. 11——[p]Isa. lx. 5

[q]Ch. xxxii. 43——[r]Ch. vii. 34; xvi. 9; xxv. 10; Rev. xviii. 23——[s]1 Chron. xvi. 8, 34; 2 Chron. v. 13; vii. 3; Ezra iii. 11; Psa. cxxxvi. 1; Isa. xii. 4——[t]Lev. vii. 12; Psa. cvii. 22; cxvi. 17——[u]Ver. 7——[v]Isa. lxv. 10; ch. xxxi. 24; l. 19——[w]Ch. xvii. 26; xxxii. 44——[x]Lev. xxvii 32——[y]Ch. xxiii. 5; xxxi. 27, 31——[z]Ch. xxix. 10

relative to the issue of the present commotions; but there is no light in them. Ask *thou,* O Jeremiah, and I will tell *thee* the great and mighty things which *even thou* knowest not.

Verse 4. *Thus saith the Lord*] This is a new confirmation of what has already been said, viz., The city shall fall, a number of the inhabitants shall perish, the rest shall be carried into captivity; but the *nation* shall be preserved, and the people return from their captivity.

Verse 6. *Behold I will bring it health and cure*] ארכה *aruchah,* an *extensive plaister;* or, as we phrase it, *a plaister as large as the sore.* I will repair the losses of families by numerous births, and bless the land with fertility.

Verse 7. *The captivity of Judah and the captivity of Israel*] This must respect the latter times, for the *ten tribes* did not return with the Jews at the termination of the *seventy* years.

Verse 8. *I will cleanse them*] These promises of pardon and holiness must be referred to their state under the Gospel, when they shall have received Jesus as the promised Messiah.

Verse 9. *They shall fear and tremble*] The surrounding nations shall be persuaded that it is the hand of the Almighty that has wrought this change in your behalf; and shall *fear* to molest you, and *tremble* lest they should incur the displeasure of your God by doing you any kind of evil.

Verse 11. *The voice of them that shall say, Praise the Lord of hosts*] That is, the voice of the *Levites* in the sacred service: intimating that the temple should be rebuilt, and the public service restored.

Verse 12. *A habitation of shepherds*] See on chap. xxxi. 12.

Verse 14. *Behold, the days come*] See chap. xxiii. 5, and xxxi. 31.

That good thing which I have promised] By my prophets: for those who have predicted the captivity have also foretold its conclusion, though not in such express terms as Jeremiah did. See Hos. i. 10, &c.; ii. 15, &c.; vi. 11, &c.; Amos ix. 14, &c., and Jer. iii. 12, &c. The *end* of the captivity has been foretold by Micah, chap. vii. 9, &c.; Zephaniah, iii. 10, &c.; and by Jeremiah, chap. xvi. 15; xxiii. 3; xxix. 10;

A. M. 3416 B. C. 588 Ol. XLVIII. 1 Anno Tarquinii Prisci, R. Roman., 29

I have promised unto the house
of Israel and to the house of
Judah.
15 In those days, and at that
time, will I cause the [a]Branch of righteousness to grow up unto David; and he shall execute judgment and righteousness in the land.
16 [b]In those days shall Judah be saved, and
Jerusalem shall dwell safely: and this *is the
name* wherewith she shall be called, [c]The LORD
our Righteousness.
17 For thus saith the LORD; [d]David shall
never [e]want a man to sit upon the throne of
the house of Israel;
18 Neither shall the priests the Levites
want a man before me to [f]offer burnt-offerings,
and to kindle meat-offerings, and to do sacrifice continually.
19 And the word of the LORD came unto
Jeremiah, saying,
20 Thus saith the LORD; [g]If ye can break
my covenant of the day, and my covenant of
the night, and that there should not be day
and night in their season;
21 *Then* may also [h]my covenant be broken
with David my servant, that he
should not have a son to reign
upon his throne; and with the
Levites, the priests, my ministers.

A. M. 3416 B. C. 588 Ol. XLVIII. 1 Anno Tarquinii Prisci, R. Roman., 29

22 As [i]the host of heaven cannot be numbered, neither the sand of the sea measured:
so will I multiply the seed of David my servant, and the Levites that minister unto me.
23 Moreover the word of the LORD came to
Jeremiah, saying,
24 Considerest thou not what this people
have spoken, saying, [k]The two families which
the LORD hath chosen, he hath even cast them
off? thus they have despised my people, that
they should be no more a nation before them.
25 Thus saith the LORD; If [l]my covenant
be not with day and night, *and if* I have not
[m]appointed the ordinances of heaven and
earth;
26 [n]Then will I cast away the seed of Jacob,
and David my servant, *so* that I will not take
any of his seed *to be* rulers over the seed of
Abraham, Isaac, and Jacob: for [o]I will cause
their captivity to return, and have mercy on
them.

[a]Isa. iv. 2; xi. 1; chap. xxiii. 5——[b]Chap. xxiii. 6——[c]Heb. *Jehovah-tsidkenu*——[d]Heb. *there shall not be cut off from David*——[e]2 Sam. vii. 16; 1 Kings ii. 4; Psa. lxxxix. 29, 36; Luke i. 32, 33——[f]Rom. xii. 1; xv. 16; 1 Pet. ii. 5, 9; Rev. i. 6

[g]Psa. lxxxix. 37; Isa. liv. 9; chap. xxxi. 36; ver. 25——[h]Psa. lxxxix. 34——[i]Gen. xiii. 16; xv. 5; xxii. 17; chap. xxxi. 37——[k]Ver. 21, 22——[l]Ver. 20; Gen. viii. 22——[m]Psa. lxxiv. 16, 17; civ. 19; chap. xxxi. 35, 36——[n]Ch. xxxi. 37——[o]Ver. 7, 11; Ezra ii. 1

xxxii. 37. The *Targum* explains verses 14, 15, and 16 of the Messiah.

Verse 16. *And this* is the name *wherewith she shall be called, The Lord our Righteousness.*] See what has been said on chap. xxiii. 6, which is generally supposed to be a strictly parallel passage: but they are very different, and I doubt whether they mean exactly the same thing. As to our translation here, it is ignorant, and almost impious; it says that *Jerusalem*, for that is the antecedent, shall be called *The Lord our Righteousness.* The pronoun לה *lah*, which is translated *her*, is the *masculine* affix, in the *Chaldaic* form, which frequently occurs; and Dr. *Blayney* translates, "And this is He whom Jehovah shall call our righteousness," or Justification. Perhaps there is a sense which these words will bear far more congenial to the scope of the place. I will give the original, as before: וזה אשר יקרא לה יהוה צדקנו *vezeh asher yikra lah, Yehovah tsidkenu*, "And this one who shall call to her *is* the Lord our Justification;" that is, the salvation of the Jews shall take place when Jesus Christ is proclaimed to them as their Justifier, and they receive him as such.

Instead of לה *lah, her* or *him*, Chaldaice, the *Vulgate*, *Chaldee*, and *Syriac* have read לו *lo, him*, less ambiguously; and this reading is supported by one or two MSS. This emendation renders the passage here more conformable to that in chap. xxiii. 6; but if the translation above be admitted, all embarrassment is gone. One of my own MSS. has לה *loh*, with the masculine points, and no mappik on the ה *he;* and for *tsidkenu* has צדקינו *tsidkeynu*, the contracted plural form, *our righteousness:* but this may be a mistake. The passages in this and the *twenty-third* chapter were not, I am satisfied, intended to express the same thing. I suppose that above refers to the preaching or proclaiming Christ crucified to the Jews, when the time shall arrive in which they shall be incorporated with the Gentile Church. *Dahler* translates this as he did that in chap. xxiii., which is a perfect oversight: but paraphrastic renderings are too often introduced by this learned foreigner.

Verse 18. *Neither shall the priests the Levites want a man*] This is a repetition of the promise made to Phinehas, Num. xxv. 13.

Verse 20. *If ye can break my covenant of the day*] See the note on chap. xxxi. 36.

Verse 22. *So will I multiply the seed of David*] This must be understood of the spiritual David, Jesus Christ, and his progeny, genuine Christians. The two families which God chose for the priesthood, that of Aaron and Phinehas, or, on its being taken away from him, that of Ithamar, 1 Sam. ii. 35, are both extinct. Nor has the office of high priest, or priest of

any kind offering sacrifice, been exercised among the Jews for nearly *eighteen hundred* years; therefore what is said here of the priesthood must refer to the spiritual priesthood, at the head of which is Jesus Christ.

Verse 24. *The two families which the Lord hath chosen*] Some think these refer to the two kingdoms of Israel and Judah; but they never can be considered as two distinct families, being of one and the same race. Others think that the families of Jacob and David are intended; but neither were these distinct. If the two families which had the priesthood be not meant, then the regal family of David, and the sacerdotal family of Jacob through Levi, may be designed. See ver. 26. Following the spiritual interpretation, neither the regal nor sacerdotal family has failed; for Jesus is a King and a Priest, and all true believers in him are kings and priests unto God and the Lamb. And the highest King that ever reigned is He who is the seed of David, King of kings and Lord of lords, who has all power in heaven and in earth.

CHAPTER XXXIV

This chapter contains two prophecies: the first, delivered during the siege of Jerusalem, predicts to Zedekiah the taking and burning of the city, with his own peaceful death and honourable burial, 1–7. *The second was delivered when the Chaldeans had for some time broken up the siege. It reproves the Jews for their conduct towards their brethren of the poorer sort, whom they released, by a solemn covenant, from bondage, in the extremity of their danger; but compelled to return to it when they thought that danger over,* 8–11. *For this God threatens them with the sword, pestilence, and famine; and with the return of the Chaldeans, who should take the city, destroy it and the other cities by fire, and make an utter desolation of the whole land of Judea,* 12–22.

A. M. 3415 B. C. 589 Ol. XLVII. 4 Anno TarquiniiPrisci, R. Roman., 28

THE word which came unto Jeremiah from the LORD, ([a]when Nebuchadnezzar king of Babylon, and all his army, and [b]all the kingdoms of the earth [c]of his dominion, and all the people, fought against Jerusalem, and against all the cities thereof,) saying,

2 Thus saith the LORD, the God of Israel; Go and speak to Zedekiah king of Judah, and tell him, Thus saith the LORD; Behold [d]I will give this city into the hand of the king of Babylon, and [e]he shall burn it with fire:

3 And [f]thou shalt not escape out of his hand, but shalt surely be taken, and delivered into his hand; and thine eyes shall behold the eyes of the king of Babylon, and [g]he shall speak with thee mouth to mouth, and thou shalt go to Babylon.

4 Yet hear the word of the LORD, O Zedekiah king of Judah; Thus saith the LORD of thee, Thou shalt not die by the sword:

5 *But* thou shalt die in peace: and with [h]the burnings of thy fathers, the former kings which were before thee, [i]so shall they burn *odours* for thee; and [k]they will lament thee, *saying,* Ah lord! for I have pronounced the word, saith the LORD.

[a]2 Kings xxv. 1, &c.; chap. xxxix. 1; lii. 4——[b]Chap. i. 15——[c]Heb. *the dominion of his hand*——[d]Chap. xxi. 10; xxxii. 3, 28——[e]Chap. xxxii. 29; ver. 22

[f]Chap. xxxii. 4——[g]Heb. *his mouth shall speak to thy mouth*——[h]See 2 Chron. xvi. 14; xxi. 19——[i]Dan ii. 46 [k]See chap. xxii. 18

NOTES ON CHAP. XXXIV

Verse 1. *The word which came unto Jeremiah*] This discourse was delivered in the *tenth* year of the reign of Zedekiah. The chapter contains two discourses; one, ver. 1-7, which concerns the taking of the city, and Zedekiah's captivity and death; the other, ver. 8-22, which is an invective against the inhabitants of Jerusalem for having Hebrew male and female slaves. These, having been manumitted at the instance of the prophet, were afterwards brought back by their old masters, and put in the same thraldom; for which God threatens them with severe judgments.

Nebuchadnezzar—and all his army, and all the kingdoms of the earth of his dominion] That is, his army was composed of soldiers gathered out of Babylon, and out of all his tributary dominions: one hundred and twenty provinces.

Verse 2. *He shall burn it with fire*] This was a newly-added circumstance. Among many ancient nations they burned the bodies of the more illustrious dead. Odours were used in the burning: they then gathered the ashes, and put them into an urn or pitcher, sometimes into a strong vessel, and buried them. Many of these have been digged up in different parts of England, where the Romans had stations.

Verse 3. *Thou shalt not escape*] This, however, he had attempted, but was taken in his flight. See chap. xxxix. 4, and lii. 7, &c.

Verse 5. *Thou shalt die in peace*] Thou shalt not die a *violent* death; and at thy death thou shalt have all those funereal solemnities which were usual at the demise of kings. See 2 Chron. xvi. 14.

So shall they burn odours *for thee*] Scented wood and other odoriferous substances are placed on the funeral pile of the rich Hindoos, and burned with the body.

And they will lament thee, saying, *Ah lord!*] They will recite the funeral dirge that begins with those words. See the note on chap. xxii. 18.

A. M. 3415 B. C. 589 Ol. XLVII. 4 Anno TarquiniiPrisci, R. Roman., 28

6 Then Jeremiah the prophet
spake all these words unto Zedekiah king of Judah in Jerusalem,

7 When the king of Babylon's army fought
against Jerusalem, and against all the cities of
Judah that were left, against Lachish, and
against Azekah: for [l]these defenced cities remained of the cities of Judah.

A. M. cir. 3415 B. C. cir. 589 Ol. XLVII. 4 TarquiniiPrisci, R. Roman., cir. annum 28

8 *This is* the word that came
unto Jeremiah from the LORD,
after that the king Zedekiah had
made a covenant with all the
people which *were* at Jerusalem, to proclaim
[m]liberty unto them;

9 [n]That every man shauld let his man-servant, and every man his maid-servant, *being*
a Hebrew or a Hebrewess, go free; [o]that
none should serve himself of them, *to wit,* of
a Jew his brother.

10 Now when all the princes, and all the
people, which had entered into the covenant,
heard that every one should let his man-
servant, and every one his maid-servant, go
free, that none should serve themselves of them
any more, then they obeyed, and let *them* go.

11 But [p]afterward they turned, and caused
the servants and the handmaids, whom they
had let go free, to return, and brought them
into subjection for servants and for handmaids.

A. M. cir. 3415 B. C. cir. 589 Ol. XLVII. 4 TarquiniiPrisci, R. Roman., cir. annum 28

12 Therefore the word of the
LORD came to Jeremiah from the
LORD, saying,

13 Thus saith the LORD, the
God of Israel; I made a covenant with your
fathers in the day that I brought them forth
out of the land of Egypt, out of the house
of bondmen, saying,

14 At the end of [q]seven years let ye go
every man his brother a Hebrew, which
[r]hath been sold unto thee; and when he hath
served thee six years, thou shalt let him go
free from thee: but your fathers hearkened not
unto me, neither inclined their ear.

15 And ye were [s]now turned, and had done
right in my sight, in proclaiming liberty every
man to his neighbour; and ye had [t]made a
covenant before me [u]in the house [v]which is
called by my name:

16 But ye turned and [w]polluted my name,
and caused every man his servant, and every
man his handmaid, whom he had set at liberty
at their pleasure, to return, and brought them
into subjection, to be unto you for servants
and for handmaids.

17 Therefore thus saith the LORD; Ye have
not hearkened unto me, in proclaiming liberty,
every one to his brother, and every man to his
neighbour: [x]behold, I proclaim a liberty for
you, saith the LORD, [y]to the sword, to the pes-

---

[l]2 Kings xviii. 13; xix. 8; 2 Chron. xi. 5, 9——[m]Exod. xxi. 2; Lev. xxv. 10; ver. 14——[n]Neh. v. 11——[o]Lev. xxv. 39-46——[p]See ver. 21; chap. xxxvii. 5——[q]Exod. xxi. 2; xxiii. 10; Deut. xv. 12——[r]Or, *hath sold himself*

[s]Heb. *to-day*——[t]So 2 Kings xxiii. 3; Neh. x. 29——[u]Chap. vii. 10——[v]Heb. *whereupon my name is called*——[w]Exod. xx. 7; Lev. xix. 42——[x]Matt. vii. 2; Gal. vi. 7; James ii. 13——[y]Chap. xxxii. 24, 36

Verse 6. ***Spake all these words unto Zedekiah*]** **He delivered this message at the hazard of his life. Jeremiah feared God, and had no other fear.**

Verse 7. ***Against Lachish, and against Azekah*]** **These were two cities of Judah of considerable importance: they had been strongly fortified by Rehoboam, 2 Chron. xi. 9-11; 2 Chron. xxxii. 9.**

Verse 8. ***The word that came unto Jeremiah*]** **Here the *second* discourse begins, which was delivered probably a short time, even a few days, after the former.**

***Zedekiah had made a covenant*]** **We find no account elsewhere of this covenant: "Every man should let his man-servant and his maid-servant go free;" i. e., as we learn from ver. 14, on the *sabbatical year;* for the *seventh* year was the *year of release.* See Deut. xv. 12.**

Verse 11. ***But afterward they turned*]** **They had agreed to manumit them at the end of the *seventh* year; but when the *seventh* year was ended, they recalled their engagement, and detained their servants. This, I believe, is what is here meant.**

Verse 16. ***Ye—polluted my name*]** **Had made the covenant in my name, calling me to witness it; now ye have dishonoured my name, by breaking that covenant, and acting contrary to my law.**

Verse 17. ***I proclaim a liberty for you*]** **Ye proclaimed *liberty* to your slaves, and afterward resumed your *authority* over them; and I had in consequence *restrained* the sword from cutting you off: but now I give *liberty* to the *sword,* to the *pestilence,* and to the *famine,* and to the *captivity,* to destroy and consume you, and *enslave* you: for ye shall be removed to all the kingdoms of the earth. The prophet loves to express the *conformity* between the *crime* and its *punishment.* You promised to give *liberty* to your *enslaved* brethren; I was pleased, and *bound* the sword in its sheath. You broke your promise, and brought them again into *bondage;* I gave *liberty* to the sword, pestilence, and famine, to destroy multitudes of you, and *captivity* to take the rest. Thus you are punished *according* to your crimes, and in the *punishment* you may see the *crime.* Sword, pestilence, and famine are frequently joined together, as**

A. M. cir. 3415 B. C. cir. 589 Ol. XLVII. 4 TarquiniiPrisci, R. Roman., cir. annum 28

tilence, and to the famine; and I will make you [z]to be [a]removed into all the kingdoms of the earth.

18 And I will give the men that have transgressed my covenant, which have not performed the words of the covenant which they had made before me, when [b]they cut the calf in twain, and passed between the parts thereof,

19 The princes of Judah, and the princes of Jerusalem, the eunuchs, and the priests, and all the people of the land, which passed between the parts of the calf;

20 I will even give them into the hand of their enemies, and into the hand of them that seek their life: and their [c]dead bodies shall be for meat unto the fowls of the heaven, and to the beasts of the earth.

21 And Zedekiah king of Judah, and his princes, will I give into the hand of their enemies, and into the hand of them that seek their life, and into the hand of the king of Babylon's army, [d]which are gone up from you.

22 [e]Behold, I will command, saith the LORD, and cause them to return to this city; and they shall fight against it, [f]and take it, and burn it with fire: and [g]I will make the cities of Judah a desolation without an inhabitant.

[z]Heb. *for a removing*——[a]Deut. xxviii. 25, 64; chap. xxix. 18——[b]See Gen. xv. 10, 17——[c]Chap. vii. 33; xvi. 4; xix. 7

[d]See chap. xxxvii. 5, 11——[e]Chap. xxxvii. 8, 10——[f]Chap. xxxviii. 3; xxxix. 1, 2, 8; lii. 7, 13——[g]Chap. ix. 11; xliv. 2, 6

being often the effects of each other. The *sword* or *war* produces *famine; famine*, the *pestilence*.

Verse 18. *When they cut the calf in twain, and passed between the parts thereof*] This was the ancient and most solemn way of making a covenant. 1. A calf as sacrifice was offered to God to secure his approbation and support. 2. The *victim* was then *exactly divided* from the nose to the rump; the *spinal marrow* being divided longitudinally, in the most careful manner, that the *half* of it might remain on *each side*. 3. These divided parts were laid opposite to each other, a passage being left between them. 4. The contracting parties entered this passage at each end, met in the middle, and there took the covenant oath; adjudging themselves to death should they break this covenant. 5. Then they both feasted on the victim. In reference to this last circumstance, God says he *will give their bodies* for *meat to the fowls of heaven* and *to the beasts*. This is a farther conformity between the crime and the punishment. See my notes on Gen. xv. 9-17.

Verse 21. *The king of Babylon's army, which are gone up from you.*] Nebuchadnezzar, hearing that there was an Egyptian army coming to the relief of Jerusalem, raised the siege, went out, and met and defeated the Egyptians. It was in the interim this prophecy was delivered.

Verse 22. *I will—cause them to return*] They did return; re-invested the city; and, after an obstinate defence, took it, plundered it, and burned it to the ground, taking *Zedekiah* and his *princes* captive.

CHAPTER XXXV

Jeremiah is commanded to go to the Rechabites, who, on the approach of the Chaldean army, took refuge in Jerusalem; and to try their obedience to the command of Jonadab, (*or Jehonadab*, 2 Kings x. 15, 16,) *their great progenitor, who lived in the reign of Jehu, king of Israel, upwards of* two hundred and fifty *years before this time, offers them wine to drink, which they refuse,* 1–11. *Hence occasion is taken to upbraid the Jews with their disobedience to God, their heavenly Father,* 12–17; *and a blessing is pronounced on the Rechabites,* 18, 19.

A. M. cir. 3397 B. C. cir. 607 Ol. XLIII. 2 TarquiniiPrisci, R. Roman., cir. annum 10

THE word which came unto Jeremiah from the LORD in the days of Jehoiakim the son of Josiah king of Judah, saying,

2 Go unto the house of the [a]Rechabites, and speak unto them, and bring them into the house of the LORD, into one of

[a]2 Kings x. 15; 1 Chron. ii. 55

NOTES ON CHAP. XXXV

Verse 1. *The word which came—in the days of Jehoiakim*] What strange confusion in the placing of these chapters! Who could have expected to hear of *Jehoiakim* again, whom we have long ago buried; and we have now arrived in the history at the very last year of the last Jewish king.

This discourse was probably delivered in the *fourth* or *fifth* year of Jehoiakim's reign.

Verse 2. *The house of the Rechabites*] The *Rechabites* were not descendants of *Jacob;* they were *Kenites*, 1 Chron. ii. 55, a people originally settled in that part of *Arabia Petræa*, called the *land of Midian;* and most probably the descendants of *Jethro*, the father-in-law of Moses. Compare Num. x. 29-32, with Judg. i. 16; iv. 11.

A. M. cir. 3397 B. C. cir. 607 Ol. XLIII. 2 TarquiniiPrisci, R. Roman., cir. annum 10

[b]the chambers, and give them wine to drink.

3 Then I took Jaazaniah the son of Jeremiah, the son of Habaziniah, and his brethren, and all his sons, and the whole house of the Rechabites;

4 And I brought them into the house of the LORD, into the chamber of the sons of Hanan, the son of Igdaliah, a man of God which *was* by the chamber of the princes, which *was* above the chamber of Maaseiah the son of Shallum, [c]the keeper of the [d]door:

5 And I set before the sons of the house of the Rechabites pots full of wine, and cups, and I said unto them, Drink ye wine.

6 But they said, We will drink no wine: for [e]Jonadab the son of Rechab our father commanded us, saying, Ye shall drink no wine, *neither* ye, nor your sons for ever:

A. M. cir. 3397 B. C. cir. 607 Ol. XLIII. 2 TarquiniiPrisci, R. Roman., cir. annum. 10

7 Neither shall ye build house, nor sow seed, nor plant vineyard, nor have *any*: but all your days ye shall dwell in tents; [f]that ye may live many days in the land where ye *be* strangers.

8 Thus have we obeyed the voice of Jonadab the son of Rechab our father in all that he hath charged us, to drink no wine all our days, we, our wives, our sons, nor our daughters;

9 Nor to build houses for us to dwell in: neither have we vineyard, nor field, nor seed:

10 But we have dwelt in tents, and have obeyed, and done according to all that Jonadab our father commanded us.

---

[b]1 Kings vi. 5——[c]2 Kings xii. 9; xxv. 18; 1 Chron. ix. 18, 19——[d]Heb. *threshold*, or *vessel*——[e]2 Kings x. 15——[f]Exod. xx. 12; Eph. vi. 2, 3

Those mentioned here seem to have been a tribe of Nomades or Scenite Arabs, who fed their flocks in the deserts of Judea; they preserved the simple manners of their ancestors, considering the life of the *inhabitants of cities* and *large towns* as the death of *liberty;* believing that they would dishonour themselves by using that *sort of food* that would oblige them to live a *sedentary* life. Jonadab, one of their ancestors, had required his children and descendants to abide faithful to the customs of their forefathers; to continue to live in *tents*, and to nourish themselves on the produce of their *flocks;* to abstain from the *cultivation* of the *ground*, and from that particularly of the *vine* and its produce. His descendants religiously observed this rule, till the time when the armies of the Chaldeans had entered Judea; when, to preserve their lives, they retired within the walls of Jerusalem. But even there we find, from the account in this chapter, they did not quit their frugal manner of life: but most scrupulously observed the law of Jonadab their ancestor, and probably of this family.

When the children of *Hobab*, or *Jethro*, the father-in-law of Moses, were invited by him to accompany them in their journeying to the Promised Land, it is very likely that they continued their ancient usages, and lived a *patriarchal life*. Their property, consisting in nothing but their *cattle* and *tents*, was easily removable from place to place; and their manner of living was not likely to excite the *envy* or *jealousy* of those who had learnt to relish the luxuries of life; and therefore we may naturally conclude that as they were enemies to none, so they had no enemies themselves. Nature has few wants. Most of those which we feel are *factitious;* and howsoever what we call civilization may furnish us with the *conveniences* and *comforts* of *life*, let us not deceive ourselves by supposing that these very things do not create the very wants which they are called in to supply; and most certainly do not contribute to the comfort of life, when the term of life is considerably abridged by their use.

But it is time to return to the case of the Rechabites before us.

Verse 3. *The whole house of the Rechabites*] That is, the *family*—the chiefs of which are here specified.

Verse 4. *Igdaliah, a man of God*] A prophet or holy man, having some office in the temple.

Verse 5. *Pots full of wine, and cups*] The *cups* were to draw the wine out of the *pots*, in order to drink it.

Verse 6. *We will drink no wine*] The reason is given above. Their whole religious and political institution consisted in obedience to *three* simple precepts, each of which has an appropriate spiritual meaning:—

1. *Ye shall drink no wine*] Ye shall preserve your bodies in temperance, shall use nothing that would deprive you of the exercise of your sober reason at any time; lest in such a time ye should do what might be prejudicial to yourselves, injurious to your neighbour, or dishonourable to your God.

2. *Neither shall ye build house*] Ye shall not become residents in any place; ye shall not court earthly possessions; ye shall live free from ambition and from envy, that ye may be free from contention and strife.

3. *But—ye shall dwell in tents*] Ye shall imitate your forefathers, Abraham, Isaac, and Jacob, and the rest of the patriarchs, *who dwelt in tents*, being *strangers and pilgrims* upon earth, looking for a heavenly country, and being determined to have nothing here that would indispose their minds towards that place of endless rest, or prevent them from passing through *temporal* things so as not to lose those that are *eternal*.

There must necessarily be more in these injunctions than meets the eye in the *letter* of this account.

Verse 8. *Thus have we obeyed the voice*] We have considered these precepts so very *reasonable*, so very *useful*, so *conducive* to the *health of both body and mind*, and sanctioned by such a respectable *antiquity* that we scrupulously and religiously observe them.

A. M. cir. 3397
B. C. cir. 607
Ol. XLIII. 2
TarquiniiPrisci,
R. Roman.,
cir. annum 10

11 But it came to pass, when Nebuchadrezzar king of Babylon came up into the land, that we said, Come, and let us go to Jerusalem for fear of the army of the Chaldeans, and for fear of the army of the Syrians: so we dwell at Jerusalem.

12 Then came the word of the LORD unto Jeremiah, saying,

13 Thus saith the LORD of hosts, the God of Israel; Go and tell the men of Judah and the inhabitants of Jerusalem, Will ye not [g]receive instruction to hearken to my words? saith the LORD.

14 The words of Jonadab the son of Rechab, that he commanded his sons not to drink wine, are performed; for unto this day they drink none, but obey their father's commandment: [h]notwithstanding I have spoken unto you, [i]rising early and speaking; but ye hearkened not unto me:

15 [k]I have sent also unto you all my servants the prophets, rising up early and sending *them*, saying, [l]Return ye now every man from his evil way, and amend your doings, and go not after other gods to serve them, and ye shall dwell in the land which I have given to you and to your fathers: but ye have not inclined your ear, nor hearkened unto me.

A. M. cir. 3397
B. C. cir. 607
Ol. XLIII. 2
TarquiniiPrisci,
R. Roman.,
cir. annum 10

16 Because the sons of Jonadab the son of Rechab have performed the commandment of their father, which he commanded them; but this people hath not hearkened unto me:

17 Therefore thus saith the LORD God of hosts, the God of Israel; Behold, I will bring upon Judah and upon all the inhabitants of Jerusalem all the evil that I have pronounced against them: [m]because I have spoken unto them, but they have not heard; and I have called unto them, but they have not answered.

18 And Jeremiah said unto the house of the Rechabites, Thus saith the LORD of hosts, the God of Israel; Because ye have obeyed the commandment of Jonadab your father, and kept all his precepts, and done according unto all that he hath commanded you:

19 Therefore thus saith the LORD of hosts, the God of Israel; [n]Jonadab the son of Rechab shall not want a man to [o]stand before me for ever.

[g]Chap. xxxii. 33——[h]2 Chron. xxxvi. 15——[i]Chap. vii. 13; xxv. 3——[k]Chap. vii. 25; xxv. 4——[l]Chap. xviii. 11; xxv. 5, 6

[m]Prov. i. 24; Isa. lxv. 12; lxvi. 4; chap. vii. 13——[n]Heb. *There shall not a man be cut off from Jonadab the son of Rechab to stand*, &c.——[o]Chap. xv. 19

Verse 11. *But—when Nebuchadnezzar—came up*] If at present we appear to be acting contrary in any respect to our institutions, in being found in the city, *necessity* alone has induced us to take this temporary step. We have sought the *shelter of the city* for the *preservation of our lives; so now we dwell at Jerusalem.*

Verse 14. *The words of Jonadab—are performed—but ye hearkened not unto me.*] The Lord, knowing the fidelity of this people, chose to try them in this way, that he might, by their conscientious obedience to the precepts of their forefathers, show the Jews, to their confusion, their ingratitude to him, and their neglect of his precepts, which if a man do, he shall live by them.

Verse 17. *I will bring upon Judah and upon all the inhabitants of Jerusalem all the evil*] Having, by the conduct of the Rechabites, clearly and fully convicted them of *ingratitude* and *rebellion*, he now proceeds to pronounce sentence against them.

Verse 19. *Thus saith the Lord—Jonadab—shall not want a man to stand before me for ever.*] His name shall ever be honourable, and his posterity shall enjoy my continual protection; and there shall never be found a time in which men of his spirit shall be wanting as patterns of genuine simplicity, filial obedience, purity of manners, and deadness to the world. True Christians may be considered as the genuine *successors* of these ancient *Rechabites;* and some suppose that the *Essenes*, in our Lord's time, were literally their *descendants*, and that these were they who followed our Lord particularly, and became the *first converts* to the Gospel. If so, the prophecy is *literally* fulfilled: *they shall never want a man to stand before God*, to proclaim his salvation, and minister to the edification and salvation of others, as long as the earth shall endure.

CHAPTER XXXVI

God commands Jeremiah to write down in one roll or volume all the predictions he had uttered against Israel and Judah, and all the surrounding nations, from the day of his vocation to the prophetic office, that the house of Judah might have abundant warning of the dreadful calamities with which their country was about to be visited, if not prevented by a timely repentance, 1–3. The prophet employs Baruch the scribe, the son of Neriah, to write from his mouth all the words of the Lord, and then to read them publicly upon a fast day in the Lord's house, 4–8. *A general fast is proclaimed in the following year, viz., the* fifth *year of the reign of Jehoiakim; upon which occasion Baruch, in obedience to the prophet's command, reads the words of Jeremiah to all the people at the entry of the new gate of the temple*, 9, 10. *The princes, hearing of this, send for Baruch, who reads the roll to them; at the contents of which they are greatly alarmed, and solemnly resolve to give information to the king, at the same time advising both the prophet and his scribe to hide themselves*, 11–19. *Jehoiakim likewise having sent for the roll, Jehudi reads to him a part; and then the king, though advised to the contrary by some of his princes, having cut the leaves, throws the whole into the fire*, 20–25, *and orders Jeremiah and Baruch to be seized; but they could not be found, because a special providence of God had concealed them*, 26. *Jeremiah is commanded to re-write his prophecies, and to denounce the judgments of God against the king who had destroyed the first roll*, 27–31. *Baruch accordingly writes from the mouth of Jeremiah a new copy, with numerous additions*, 32.

A. M. 3397
B. C. 607
Ol. XLIII. 2
Anno
TarquiniiPrisci,
R. Roman., 10

AND it came to pass in the fourth year of Jehoiakim, the son of Josiah king of Judah, *that* this word came unto Jeremiah from the LORD, saying,

2 Take thee a [a]roll of a book, and [b]write therein all the words that I have spoken unto thee against Israel, and against Judah, and against [c]all the nations, from the day I spake unto thee, from the days of [d]Josiah, even unto this day.

3 [e]It may be that the house of Judah will hear all the evil which I purpose to do unto them; that they may [f]return every man from his evil way; that I may forgive their iniquity and their sin.

4 Then Jeremiah [g]called Baruch the son of Neriah: and [h]Baruch wrote from the mouth of Jeremiah all the words of the LORD, which he had spoken unto him, upon a roll of a book.

5 And Jeremiah commanded Baruch, saying, I *am* shut up; I cannot go into the house of the LORD:

A. M. 3397
B. C. 607
Ol. XLIII. 2
Anno
TarquiniiPrisci,
R. Roman., 10

6 Therefore go thou, and read in the roll, which thou hast written from my mouth, the words of the LORD in the ears of the people in the LORD's house upon [i]the fasting day: and also thou shalt read them in the ears of all Judah that come out of their cities.

7 [k]It may be [l]they will present their supplication before the LORD, and will return every one from his evil way: for great *is* the anger and the fury that the LORD hath pronounced against this people.

8 And Baruch the son of Neriah did according to all that Jeremiah the prophet commanded him, reading in the book the words of the LORD in the LORD's house.

9 And it came to pass in the fifth year of Jehoiakim the son of Josiah king of Judah, in the ninth month, *that* they proclaimed

[a]Isa. viii. 1; Ezek. ii. 9; Zech. v. 1——[b]Chap. xxx. 2——[c]Chap. xxv. 15, &c.——[d]Chap. xxv. 3——[e]Ver. 7; chap. xxvi. 3——[f]Chap. xviii. 8; Jonah iii. 8

[g]Chap. xxxii. 12——[h]See chap. xlv. 1——[i]Lev. xvi. 29; xxii. 27, 32; Acts xxvii. 9——[k]Ver. 3——[l]Heb. *their supplication shall fall*

NOTES ON CHAP. XXXVI

Verse 1. *And it came to pass in the fourth year*] About the end of this year, see ver. 9. This discourse also bears its own *date*, and was probably delivered at a time when the people enjoyed peace, and were about to celebrate one of their annual fasts.

Verse 2. *Take thee a roll of a book*] Take a sufficient quantity of parchment; cut and stitch it together, that it may make a roll on which to write the words that I have already spoken, that they may serve for a testimony to future generations. The *Jewish rolls*, several of which now lie before me, were made of vellum, or of *sheep-skins* dressed in the *half-tanned* or Basil manner. These were cut into certain lengths, and those parts were all stitched together, and rolled upon a roller. The *matter* was written on these skins in *columns* or *pages*. Sometimes *two rollers* are used, that as the matter is read from the roll in the left hand, the reader may coil it on the roller in his right. In this form the *Pentateuch* is written which is read in the synagogues.

Verse 3. *It may be that the house of Judah will hear*] It was yet possible to avert the judgments which had been so often denounced against them. But in order to this they must—1. *Hear* what God has spoken. 2. Every man *turn* from his evil way. 3. If they do so, God graciously promises to *forgive their iniquity and their sin.*

Verse 4. *Then Jeremiah called Baruch*] This man, so useful to the prophet, and so faithfully attached to him, was by office a *scribe;* which signifies, not only a writer, but also a man in office; a chancellor, secretary, &c., a learned man; one acquainted with laws and customs.

Verse 6. *Upon the fasting day*] A day when multitudes of people would be gathered together from all parts to implore the mercy of God. This was a favourable time to read these tremendous prophecies.

Verse 7. *Present their supplication*] "Let their supplication fall," that they may fall down before God, and deplore their sins.

Verse 9. *In the ninth month*] Answering to a part of our *December*.

A. M. 3398 B. C. 606 Ol. XLIII. 3 Anno TarquiniiPrisci, R. Roman., 11

a fast before the LORD to all the people in Jerusalem, and to all the people that came from the cities of Judah unto Jerusalem.

10 Then read Baruch in the book the words of Jeremiah in the house of the LORD, in the chamber of Gemariah the son of Shaphan the scribe, in the higher court, at the [m]entry [n]of the new gate of the LORD's house, in the ears of all the people.

11 When Michaiah the son of Gemariah, the son of Shaphan, had heard out of the book all the words of the LORD,

12 Then he went down into the king's house, into the scribe's chamber: and, lo, all the princes sat there, *even* Elishama the scribe, and Delaiah the son of Shemaiah, and Elnathan the son of Achbor, and Gemariah the son of Shaphan, and Zedekiah the son of Hananiah, and all the princes.

13 Then Michaiah declared unto them all the words that he had heard, when Baruch read the book in the ears of the people.

14 Therefore all the princes sent Jehudi the son of Nethaniah, the son of Shelemiah, the son of Cushi, unto Baruch, saying, Take in thine hand the roll wherein thou hast read in the ears of the people, and come. So Baruch the son of Neriah took the roll in his hand, and came unto them.

15 And they said unto him, Sit down now, and read it in our ears. So Baruch read *it* in their ears.

16 Now it came to pass, when they had heard all the words, they were afraid both one and other, and said unto Baruch, We will surely tell the king of all these words.

A. M. 3398 B. C. 606 Ol. XLIII. 3 Anno TarquiniiPrisci, R. Roman., 11

17 And they asked Baruch, saying, Tell us now, How didst thou write all these words at his mouth?

18 Then Baruch answered them, He pronounced all these words unto me with his mouth, and I wrote *them* with ink in the book.

19 Then said the princes unto Baruch, Go, hide thee, thou and Jeremiah; and let no man know where ye be.

20 And they went in to the king into the court, but they laid up the roll in the chamber of Elishama the scribe, and told all the words in the ears of the king.

21 So the king sent Jehudi to fetch the roll: and he took it out of Elishama the scribe's chamber. And Jehudi read it in the ears of the king, and in the ears of all the princes which stood beside the king.

22 Now the king sat in [o]the winterhouse in the ninth month: and *there was a fire* on the hearth burning before him.

23 And it came to pass, *that* when Jehudi had read three or four leaves, he cut it with the penknife, and cast *it* into the fire that *was* on the hearth, until all the roll was consumed in the fire that *was* on the hearth.

24 Yet they were not afraid, nor [p]rent their garments, *neither* the king, nor any of his servants that heard all these words.

25 Nevertheless Elnathan and Delaiah and Gemariah had made intercession to the king

[m]Or, *door*——[n]Chap. xxvi. 10——[o]See Amos iii. 15

[p]2 Kings xxii. 11; Isa. xxxvi. 22; xxxvii. 1

Verse 10. *In the chamber of Gemariah*] He was one of the princes of Judah. See ver. 12.

Verse 17. *How didst thou write all these words?—At his mouth?*] So the text should be pointed. They wished to know whether he had not copied them, or whether he wrote as Jeremiah prophesied.

Verse 19. *Go, hide thee, thou and Jeremiah*] They saw that the king would be displeased, and most probably seek their lives; and as they believed the prophecy was from God, they wished to save both the prophet and his scribe; but they were obliged to inform the king of what they had heard.

Verse 22. *Winterhouse*] A warm apartment suited to the season of the year, (*December,*) when in Palestine there is often snow upon the ground, though it does not last long. *A fire on the hearth*—a *pan* or *brazier* of burning coals. This is the case to the present day. In cold weather the rich burn wood in brass or earthen pans, placed in any part of the room; the indigent burn sticks on the floor.

Verse 23. *When Jehudi had read three or four leaves*] Rather columns; for the law, and the sacred Hebrew Books, are written in *columns* of a certain breadth. דלתות *delathoth*, signifies *gates* or *openings* between column and column, or between section and section.

He cut it with the penknife] בתער הספר *bethaar hassopher*, "the knife of the scribe," properly enough *penknife*.

And cast it *into the fire*] To show his contempt for God's words.

Verse 25. *Elnathan and Delaiah and Gemariah*] Three of the princes wished to *save the roll*, and entreated the king that it might not be burnt. They would have saved it *out of the fire*, but the king would not permit it to be done.

A. M. 3398 B. C. 606 that he would not burn the roll:
Ol. XLIII. 3 but he would not hear them.
Anno TarquiniiPrisci, 26 But the king commanded
R. Roman., 11 Jerahmeel the son [q]of Hamme-
lech, and Seraiah the son of Azriel, and She-
lemiah the son of Abdeel, to take Baruch the
scribe and Jeremiah the prophet: but the
LORD hid them.

A. M. cir. 3399 B. C. cir. 605 27 Then the word of the LORD
Ol. XLIII 4 came to Jeremiah, after that the
TarquiniiPrisci, R. Roman., king had burned the roll, and the
cir. annum 12 words which Baruch wrote at
the mouth of Jeremiah, saying,

28 Take thee again another roll, and write
in it all the former words that were in the
first roll, which Jehoiakim the king of Judah
hath burned.

29 And thou shalt say to Jehoiakim king of
Judah, Thus saith the LORD; Thou hast
burned this roll, saying, Why hast thou written therein, saying, The king of Babylon shall
certainly come and destroy this A. M. cir. 3399 B. C. cir. 605
land, and shall cause to cease Ol. XLIII. 4
from thence man and beast? TarquiniiPrisci, R. Roman.,

30 Therefore thus saith the cir. annum 12
LORD of Jehoiakim king of Judah; [r]He shall
have none to sit upon the throne of David: and
his dead body shall be [s]cast out in the day to
the heat, and in the night to the frost.

31 And I will [t]punish him and his seed and
his servants for their iniquity; and I will
bring upon them, and upon the inhabitants of
Jerusalem, and upon the men of Judah, all
the evil that I have pronounced against them;
but they hearkened not.

32 Then took Jeremiah another roll, and
gave it to Baruch the scribe, the son of
Neriah; who wrote therein from the mouth of
Jeremiah all the words of the book which
Jehoiakim king of Judah had burned in the
fire: and there were added besides unto them
many [u]like words.

---

[q]Or, *of the king*——[r]Chap. xxii. 30——[s]Chap. xxii. 19

[t]Heb. *visit upon;* chap. xxiii. 34——[u]Heb. *as they*

Verse 26. *But the Lord hid them.*] They had, at the counsel of some of the princes, hidden themselves, ver. 19. And now, though a diligent search was made, the Lord did not permit them to be found.

Verse 28. *Take thee again another roll*] There was no duplicate of the former preserved; and now God inspired the prophet with the same matter that he had given him before; and there is to be added the heavy judgment that is to fall on Jehoiakim and his courtiers.

Verse 30. *He shall have none to sit upon the throne of David*] He shall have no *successor*, and himself shall have an untimely end, and shall not even be buried, but his body be exposed to the open air, both night and day. He who wishes to hide his crimes, or take away the evidence which is against him, adds thereby to his iniquities, and is sure in consequence to double his punishment. See the threatening against Jehoiakim, chap. xxii. 19, and the note there.

Verse 32. *There were added—many like words.*] All the first roll, with many other threatenings, and perhaps more minute declarations which were merely of a temporary importance and local application; and the Holy Spirit did not think proper to record them here.

CHAPTER XXXVII

Zedekiah succeeds Coniah, the son of Jehoiakim, in the Jewish throne, and does that which is evil in the sight of the Lord, 1, 2. *The king sends a message to Jeremiah,* 3–5. *God suggests an answer; and foretells the return of the Chaldean army, who should most assuredly take and burn the city,* 6–10. *Jeremiah, in attempting to leave this devoted city, and retire to his possession in the country, is seized as a deserter, and cast into a dungeon,* 11–15. *The king, after a conference with him, abates the rigour of his confinement,* 16–21.

A. M. 3406—3416 B. C. 598—588 Ol. XLV. 3—XLVIII. 1
AND king [a]Zedekiah the son
of Josiah reigned instead
of Coniah the son of Jehoiakim, whom Nebuchadrezzar
king of Babylon made king in the land of
Judah.

2 [b]But neither he, nor his ser- A. M. 3406—3416
vants, nor the people of the land, B. C. 598—588
did hearken unto the words of Ol. XLV. 3—
the LORD, which he spake [c]by XLVIII. 1
the prophet Jeremiah.

3 And Zedekiah the king sent Jehucal the

---

[a]2 Kings xxiv. 17; 2 Chron. xxxvi. 10; chap. xxii. 24

[b]2 Chron. xxxvi. 12, 14——[c]Heb. *by the hand of the prophet*

NOTES ON CHAP. XXXVII

Verse 1. *And king Zedekiah the son of Josiah*] Of the siege and taking of Jerusalem referred to here, and the making of Zedekiah king instead of Jeconiah, see 2 Kings xxiv. 1, &c., and the notes there.

Verse 3. *Zedekiah—to the prophet Jeremiah*]

A. M. cir. 3414 B. C. cir. 590 Ol. XLVII. 3 TarquiniiPrisci, R. Roman., cir. annum 27

son of Shelemiah and [d]Zephaniah the son of Maaseiah the priest to the prophet Jeremiah, saying, Pray now unto the LORD our God for us.

4 Now Jeremiah came in and went out among the people: for they had not put him into prison.

5 Then [e]Pharaoh's army was come forth out of Egypt: [f]and when the Chaldeans that besieged Jerusalem heard tidings of them, they departed from Jerusalem.

6 Then came the word of the LORD unto the prophet Jeremiah, saying,

7 Thus saith the LORD, the God of Israel; Thus shall ye say to the king of Judah, [g]that sent you unto me to inquire of me; Behold, Pharaoh's army, which is come forth to help you, shall return to Egypt into their own land.

8 [h]And the Chaldeans shall come again, and fight against this city, and take it, and burn it with fire.

9 Thus saith the LORD; Deceive not [i]yourselves, saying, The Chaldeans shall surely depart from us: for they shall not depart.

10 [k]For though ye had smitten the whole army of the Chaldeans that fight against you, and there remained *but* [l]wounded men among them, *yet* should they rise up every man in his tent, and burn this city with fire.

A. M. cir. 3414 B. C. cir. 590 Ol. XLVII. 3 TarquiniiPrisci, R. Roman. cir. annum 27

11 [m]And it came to pass, that when the army of the Chaldeans was [n]broken up from Jerusalem for fear of Pharaoh's army,

12 Then Jeremiah went forth out of Jerusalem to go into the land of Benjamin, [o]to separate himself thence in the midst of the people.

13 And when he was in the gate of Benjamin, a captain of the ward *was* there, whose name *was* Irijah, the son of Shelemiah, the son of Hananiah; and he took Jeremiah the prophet, saying, Thou fallest away to the Chaldeans.

14 Then said Jeremiah, *It is* [p]false; I fall not away to the Chaldeans. But he hearkened not to him: so Irijah took Jeremiah, and brought him to the princes.

15 Wherefore the princes were wroth with Jeremiah, and smote him, [q]and put him in prison in the house of Jonathan the scribe: for they had made that the prison.

---

[d]Ch. xxi. 1, 2; xxix. 25; lii. 24——[e]See 2 Kings xxiv.; Ezek. xvii. 15——[f]Ver. 11; ch. xxxiv. 21——[g]Ch. xxi. 2——[h]Chap. xxxiv. 22——[i]Heb. *souls*——[k]Chap. xxi. 4, 5

[l]Heb. *thrust through*——[m]Ver. 5——[n]Heb. *made to ascend*——[o]Or, *to slip away from thence in the midst of the people*——[p]Heb. *falsehood*, or *a lie*——[q]Chap. xxxviii. 26

He was willing to hear a message from the Lord, provided it were according to his own mind. He did not fully trust in his own prophets.

Verse 4. *Now Jeremiah came in and went out*] After the siege was raised, he had a measure of liberty; he was not *closely confined*, as he afterwards was. See ver. 16.

Verse 5. *Then Pharaoh's army*] This was *Pharaoh-hophra* or *Apries*, who then reigned in Egypt in place of his father *Necho*. See Ezek. xxix. 6, &c. Nebuchadnezzar, hearing that the Egyptian army, on which the Jews so much depended, was on their march to relieve the city, suddenly raised the siege, and went to meet them. In the interim Zedekiah sent to Jeremiah to inquire of the Lord to know whether they might consider themselves in safety.

Verse 7. *Pharaoh's army—shall return to Egypt*] They were defeated by the Chaldeans; and, not being hearty in the cause, returned immediately to Egypt, leaving Nebuchadnezzar unmolested to recommence the siege.

Verse 10. *For though ye had smitten the whole army*] Strong words; but they show how fully God was determined to give up this city to fire and sword, and how fully he had instructed his prophet on this point.

Verse 12. *Jeremiah went forth*] At the time that Nebuchadnezzar had raised the siege, and gone to meet the Egyptian army.

Go into the land of Benjamin] To *Anathoth*, his native city.

To separate himself thence] "To receive a portion thereof among the people;"—*Blayney:* who supposes that Jeremiah went to receive a portion of the proceeds of his patrimony at *Anathoth*, which had, previously to the siege, been in the hands of the Chaldeans. The siege being now raised, he thought of looking thus after his own affairs. The *Chaldee* is to the same sense. "He went that he might divide the inheritance which he had there among the people."

Dahler translates, "He went to withdraw himself from *the siege*, as many others *of the inhabitants*." I believe he went to withdraw himself from a city devoted to destruction, and in which he could no longer do any good.

Verse 13. *Thou fallest away to the Chaldeans.*] Thou art a deserter, and a traitor to thy country. As he had always declared that the Chaldeans should take the city, &c., his enemies took occasion from this to say he was in the interest of the Chaldeans, and that he wished now to go to them, and betray the place.

Verse 15. *And smote him*] Without any *proof* of the alleged treachery, without any form of *justice*.

In prison in the house of Jonathan] In Asiatic countries there is an apartment in the houses of the officers of the law, to confine all

A. M. cir. 3415
B. C. cir. 589
Ol. XLVII. 4
TarquiniiPrisci,
R. Roman.,
cir. annum 28

16 When Jeremiah was entered into [r]the dungeon, and into the [s]cabins, and Jeremiah had remained there many days;

17 Then Zedekiah the king sent, and took him out: and the king asked him secretly in his house, and said, Is there *any* word from the LORD? And Jeremiah said, There is: for, said he, thou shalt be delivered into the hand of the king of Babylon.

18 Moreover Jeremiah said unto king Zedekiah, What have I offended against thee, or against thy servants, or against this people, that ye have put me in prison?

19 Where *are* now your prophets which prophesied unto you, saying, The king of Babylon shall not come against you, nor against this land?

20 Therefore hear now, I pray thee, O my lord the king: [t]let my supplication, I pray thee, be accepted before thee; that thou cause me not to return to the house of Jonathan the scribe, lest I die there.

21 Then Zedekiah the king commanded that they should commit Jeremiah [u]into the court of the prison, and that they should give him daily a piece of bread out of the bakers' street, [v]until all the bread in the city were spent. Thus Jeremiah remained in the court of the prison.

[r]Gen. xl. 15; xli. 14; Exod. xii. 29; chap. xxxviii. 6 —— [s]Or, *cells*

[t]Heb. *let my supplication fall* —— [u]Chap. xxxii. 2; xxxviii. 13, 28 —— [v]Chap. xxxviii. 9; lii. 6

the accused that are brought before them. Jonathan was a *scribe* or *secretary*, and had a prison of this kind in his house.

Verse 16. *Entered into the dungeon, and into the cabins*] The dungeon was probably a deep pit; and the cabins or *cells*, niches in the sides, where different malefactors were confined. See *Blayney*.

Verse 17. *Is there* any *word from the Lord?*] Is there any farther revelation?

There is:—thou shalt be delivered] What bold faithfulness! And to a king, in whose hands his life now lay.

Verse 19. *Where* are *now your prophets*] *They* told you that the Chaldeans should *not* come; I told you they *would*. According to my word the Chaldeans *are come*, and are departed only for a short time.

Verse 20. *Cause me not to return to the house of Jonathan*] He had been ill used in this man's custody, so as to endanger his life, the place being cold, and probably unhealthy.

Verse 21. *Then Zedekiah—the court of the prison*] Was contiguous to the king's house, where the prisoners could readily see their friends.

Give him daily a piece of bread out of the bakers' street] From the public stores; which he received till all the provisions were spent.

CHAPTER XXXVIII

The princes of Judah, taking offence at Jeremiah on account of his predicting the destruction of Jerusalem and the temple by the Chaldeans, cause him to be cast into a deep and miry dungeon, 1–6. *Ebed-melech, an Ethiopian, gets the king's permission to take him out,* 7–13. *Jeremiah advises the king, who consulted him privately, to surrender to the Chaldeans,* 14–23. *The king promises the prophet that he will not put him to death, and requires him not to reveal what had passed to the princes; to whom he accordingly gives an evasive answer, telling them only so much of the conference as related to his request for his life,* 24–28.

A. M. cir. 3415
B. C. cir. 589
Ol. XLVII. 4
TarquiniiPrisci,
R. Roman.,
cir. annum 28

THEN Shephatiah the son of Mattan, and Gedaliah the son of Pashur, and [a]Jucal the son of Shelemiah, and [b]Pashur the son of Malchiah, [c]heard the words that Jeremiah had spoken unto all the people, saying,

2 Thus saith the LORD, [d]He that remaineth in this city shall die by the sword, by the famine, and by the pestilence: but he that goeth forth to the Chaldeans shall live; for he shall have his life for a prey, and shall live.

3 Thus saith the LORD, [e]This city shall

[a]Chap. xxxvii. 3 —— [b]Chap. xxi. 1 —— [c]Chap. xxi. 8 —— [d]Chap. xxi. 9 —— [e]Chap. xxi. 10; xxxii. 3

NOTES ON CHAP. XXXVIII

Verse 1. *Then Shephatiah*] This was the *faction*—what *Dahler* terms the *Antitheocratic faction*—who were enemies to Jeremiah, and sought his life.

Verse 3. *This city shall surely be given*] This was a testimony that he constantly bore: he

A. M. cir. 3415 B. C. cir. 589 Ol. XLVII. 4 TarquiniiPrisci, R. Roman., cir. annum 28

surely be given into the hand of the king of Babylon's army, which shall take it.

4 Therefore the princes said unto the king, We beseech thee, [f]let this man be put to death: for thus he weakeneth the hands of the men of war that remain in this city, and the hands of all the people, in speaking such words unto them: for this man seeketh not the [g]welfare of this people, but the hurt.

5 Then Zedekiah the king said, Behold, he *is* in your hand: for the king *is* not *he that* can do *any* thing against you.

6 [h]Then took they Jeremiah, and cast him into the dungeon of Malchiah the son [i]of Hammelech, that *was* in the court of the prison: and they let down Jeremiah with cords. And in the dungeon *there was* no water, but mire: so Jeremiah sunk in the mire.

7 [k]Now when Ebed-melech the Ethiopian, one of the eunuchs which was in the king's house, heard that they had put Jeremiah in the dungeon (the king then sitting in the gate of Benjamin;)

8 Ebed-melech went forth out of the king's house, and spake to the king, saying,

9 My lord the king, these men have done evil in all that they have done to Jeremiah the prophet, whom they have cast into the dungeon; and [l]he is like to die for hunger in the place where he is: for *there is* no more bread in the city.

10 Then the king commanded Ebed-melech the Ethiopian, saying, Take from hence thirty men [m]with thee, and take up Jeremiah the prophet out of the dungeon, before he die.

11 So Ebed-melech took the men with him, and went into the house of the king under the treasury, and took thence old cast clouts and old rotten rags, and let them down by cords into the dungeon to Jeremiah.

12 And Ebed-melech the Ethiopian said unto Jeremiah, Put now *these* old cast clouts and rotten rags under thine armholes under the cords. And Jeremiah did so.

13 [n]So they drew up Jeremiah with cords, and took him up out of the dungeon: and Jeremiah remained [o]in the court of the prison.

14 Then Zedekiah the king sent, and took Jeremiah the prophet unto him into the [p]third entry that *is* in the house of the LORD: and the king said unto Jeremiah, I will ask thee a thing; hide nothing from me.

15 Then Jeremiah said unto Zedekiah, If I declare *it* unto thee, wilt thou not surely put me to death? and if I give thee counsel, wilt thou not hearken unto me?

[f]See chap. xxvi. 11——[g]Heb. *peace*——[h]Chap. xxxvii. 21——[i]Or, *of the king*

[k]Chap. xxxix. 16——[l]Heb. *he will die*——[m]Heb. *in thine hand*——[n]Ver. 6——[o]Ch. xxxvii. 21——[p]Or, *principal*

had the authority of God for it. He knew it was true, and he never wavered nor equivocated.

Verse 4. *Let this man be put to death*] And they gave their reasons plain enough: but the *proof* was wanting.

Verse 5. *He* is *in your hand*] Ye have power to do as you please; I must act by your counsel. Poor weak prince! you respect the prophet, you fear the cabal, and you sacrifice an innocent man to your own weakness and their malice!

Verse 6. *So Jeremiah sunk in the mire.*] Their obvious design was, that he might be stifled in that place.

Verse 7. *Ebed-melech*] *The servant of the king*, one of the eunuchs who belonged to the palace. Perhaps it should be read, "Now, a servant of the king, a Cushite, one of the eunuchs," &c.

The king then sitting in the gate of Benjamin] To give audience, and to administer justice. We have often seen that the *gates* of cities were the places of public judicature.

Verse 9. *My lord the king, these men have done evil*] He must have been much in the king's confidence, and a humane and noble spirited man, thus to have raised his voice against the powerful cabal already mentioned.

There is *no more bread in the city.*] They had defended it to the last extremity; and it appears that bread had been afforded to the prophet according to the king's commandment, as long as there was any remaining. See chap. xxxvi. 21.

Verse 10. *Take from hence thirty men*] The king was determined that he should be rescued by force, if the princes opposed.

Verse 11. *Went into the house of the king—and took thence*] The eastern kings had their wardrobes always well furnished; as garments were a usual present to ambassadors, &c. I cannot think that, in the proper acceptation of the words, these were in any part of the king's house.

Old cast clouts, and old rotten rags] The fact seems to be this: there were several garments that had been *used*, and would not be used again; and there were others which, through continuing long there, had by *insects*, &c., been rendered *useless*. These he took, tied to the cord, let down to the prophet, that he might roll them round the ropes, and place them under his arm-pits, so that in being hauled up he might not suffer injury from the ropes, which in this case must sustain the whole weight of his body.

Verse 14. *Into the third entry*] A place

A. M. cir. 3415
B. C. cir. 589
Ol. XLVII. 4
TarquiniiPrisci,
R. Roman.,
cir. annum 28

16 So Zedekiah the king sware secretly unto Jeremiah, saying, *As* the LORD liveth, [q]that made us this soul, I will not put thee to death, neither will I give thee into the hand of these men that seek thy life.

17 Then said Jeremiah unto Zedekiah, Thus saith the LORD, the God of hosts, the God of Israel; If thou wilt assuredly [r]go forth [s]unto the king of Babylon's princes, then thy soul shall live, and this city shall not be burned with fire; and thou shalt live, and thine house:

18 But if thou wilt not go forth to the king of Babylon's princes, then shall this city be given into the hand of the Chaldeans, and they shall burn it with fire, and [t]thou shalt not escape out of their hand.

19 And Zedekiah the king said unto Jeremiah, I am afraid of the Jews that are fallen to the Chaldeans, lest they deliver me into their hand, and they [u]mock me.

20 But Jeremiah said, They shall not deliver *thee.* Obey, I beseech thee, the voice of the LORD, which I speak unto thee: so it shall be well unto thee, and thy soul shall live.

21 But if thou refuse to go forth, this *is* the word that the LORD hath showed me:

22 And, behold, all the women that are left in the king of Judah's house *shall be* brought forth to the king of Babylon's princes, and those *women* shall say, [v]Thy friends have set thee on, and have prevailed against thee: thy feet are sunk in the mire, *and* they are turned away back.

A. M. cir. 3415
B. C. cir. 589
Ol. XLVII. 4
TarquiniiPrisci,
R. Roman.,
cir. annum 28

23 So they shall bring out all thy wives and [w]thy children to the Chaldeans: and [x]thou shalt not escape out of their hand, but shalt be taken by the hand of the king of Babylon: and [y]thou shalt cause this city to be burned with fire.

24 Then said Zedekiah unto Jeremiah, Let no man know of these words, and thou shalt not die.

25 But if the princes hear that I have talked with thee, and they come unto thee, and say unto thee, Declare unto us now what thou hast said unto the king, hide it not from us, and we will not put thee to death; and also what the king said unto thee:

26 Then thou shalt say unto them, [z]I presented my supplication before the king, that he would not cause me to return [a]to Jonathan's house, to die there.

27 Then came all the princes unto Jeremiah, and asked him: and he told them according to all these words that the king had commanded. So [b]they left off speaking with him; for the matter was not perceived.

A. M. 3415
—3416
B. C. 589
—588
Ol. XLVII. 4
—XLVIII,. 1

28 So [c]Jeremiah abode in the court of the prison until the day that Jerusalem was taken: and he was *there* when Jerusalem was taken.

---

[q]Isa. lvii. 16——[r]2 Kings xxiv. 12——[s]Chap. xxxix. 3——[t]Chap. xxxii. 4; xxxiv. 3; ver. 23——[u]1 Sam. xxxi. 4——[v]Heb. *Men of thy peace*——[w]Chap. xxxix. 6; xli. 10——[x]Ver. 18——[y]Heb. *thou shalt burn,* &c. [z]Chap. xxxvii. 28——[a]Chap. xxxvii. 15——[b]Heb. *they were silent from him*——[c]Ch. xxxvii. 21; xxxix. 14

---

to enter which *two* others must be passed through.

Verse 16. *As the Lord liveth, that made us this soul*] He is the *living* God, and he is the Author of that *life* which each of us possesses; and as sure as he *lives,* and we *live* by him, I will not put thee to *death,* nor give thee into the hands of those men who seek thy *life.* A very solemn oath; and the first instance on record of the profane custom of swearing *by the soul.*

Verse 17. *Wilt assuredly go*] On the king's obedience to the advice of the prophet the safety of the city depended.

Unto the king of Babylon's princes] The generals of the army then returning to the siege from the defeat of the Egyptians; for Nebuchadnezzar himself was then at Riblah, in Syria, chap. xxxix. 5, 6.

Verse 19. *They mock me.*] Insult me, and exhibit me in triumph.

Verse 22. *All the women—brought forth*] I think this place speaks of a kind of defection among the women of the harem; many of whom had already *gone forth* privately to the principal officers of the Chaldean army, and made the report mentioned in the end of this verse. These were the *concubines* or women of the second rank.

Verse 23. *They shall bring out all thy wives and thy children*] These were the women of the *first rank,* by whom the king had children. These had no temptation to go out to the Chaldeans, nor would they have been made welcome; but the others being young, and without children, would be well received by the Chaldean princes.

Verse 26. *I presented my supplication*] This was telling the *truth,* and *nothing* but the truth, but not the *whole* truth. The king did not wish him to defile his conscience, nor did he propose any thing that was not consistent with the truth.

Verse 27. *The matter was not perceived.*]

They did not question him farther; and the king's commandment to remove him from the house of Jonathan being well known, they took for granted that they had all the information that they sought. And he was most certainly not obliged to relate any thing that might embroil this weak king with his factious but powerful princes, or affect his own life. He related simply what was necessary, and no more.

CHAPTER XXXIX

This chapter gives an account of the siege and taking of Jerusalem; the flight, capture, and punishment of Zedekiah; the burning of the city; and the carrying away of the people, (a few of the meanest excepted,) to Babylon, 1–10; *also of the release of Jeremiah, and the special orders of Nebuchadnezzar concerning him,* 11–14. *The remaining verses relate to the subject of the preceding chapter; and contain promises of personal safety to Ebed-melech the Ethiopian amidst the public calamities, on account of his piety, and his humanity to the prophet,* 15–18.

A. M. 3414 B. C. 590 Ol. XLVII. 3 Anno TarquiniiPrisci, R. Roman., 27

IN the [a]ninth year of Zedekiah king of Judah, in the tenth month, came Nebuchadrezzar king of Babylon and all his army against Jerusalem, and they besieged it.

A. M. 3416 B. C. 588 Ol. XLVIII. 1 Anno TarquiniiPrisci, R. Roman., 29

2 *And* in the eleventh year of Zedekiah, in the fourth month, the ninth *day* of the month, the city was broken up.

3 [b]And all the princes of the king of Babylon came in, and sat in the middle gate, *even* Nergal-sharezer, Samgar-nebo, Sarsechim, Rab-saris, Nergal-sharezer, Rab-mag, with all the residue of the princes of the king of Babylon.

A. M. 3416 B. C. 588 Ol. XLVIII. 1 Anno TarquiniiPrisci, R. Roman., 29

4 [c]And it came to pass, *that* when Zedekiah the king of Judah saw them, and all the men of war, then they fled, and went forth out of the city by night, by the way of the king's garden, by the gate betwixt the two walls: and he went out the way of the plain.

5 But the Chaldeans' army pursued after them, and [d]overtook Zedekiah in the plains of Jericho: and when they had taken him, they brought him up to Nebuchadnezzar king of Babylon to [e]Riblah in the land of Hamath, where he [f]gave judgment upon him.

6 Then the king of Babylon slew the sons of Zedekiah in Riblah before his eyes: also the

[a]2 Kings xv. 1–4; chap. lii. 4–7——[b]Chap. xxxviii. 17 [c]2 Kings xxv. 4, &c.; chap. lii. 7, &c.

[d]Chap. xxxii. 4; xxxviii. 18, 23——[e]2 Kings xxiii. 33 [f]Heb. *spake with him judgments;* chap. iv. 12

NOTES ON CHAP. XXXIX

Verse 1 *In the ninth year of Zedekiah—in the tenth month*] This month is called *Tebeth* in Esther ii. 16. It began with the first new moon of our *January*, and it was on the tenth day of this month that Nebuchadnezzar invested the city.

Verse 2. *The eleventh year—in the fourth month*] This month in the Hebrew calendar is called *Thammuz*, and commences with the first new moon of our *July*. The siege had lasted just *eighteen* months.

The city was broken up.] A breach was made in the wall by which the Chaldeans entered.

Verse 3. *Sat in the middle gate*] The city of Jerusalem stood upon *two* hills, *Sion* to the south, and *Acra* to the north, with a deep valley between them. The *gate of the centre*, as the term seems plainly to import, was a gate of communication in the middle of the valley, between the *two* parts of the city, sometimes called the *higher* and the *lower* city. The Chaldeans entered the city on the *north* side by a breach in the walls, and rushing forward and posting themselves in this gate, in the very heart or centre of the city, became thereby masters at will of the whole. Zedekiah with his troop, perceiving this, fled out of the opposite gate on the *south* side. See *Blayney*. This is likely; but we know nothing positively on this subject.

Nergal-sharezer] These were the principal commanders; but Dr. *Blayney* thinks that instead of *six* persons, we have in reality but *three*, as the name that follows each is a *title* of office. Thus, *Nergal-sharezer*, who was *Samgar; Nebu-sarsechim*, who was *Rab-saris;* and *Nergal-sharezer*, who was *Rab-mag*. As *Nergal-sharezer* occurs *twice* here, and we know that *Nebuzar-adan* was general-in-chief, the first Nergal-sharezer is probably a mistake for Nebuzar-adan, or some other of the commanders. But these things are as uncertain as they are unimportant.

Verse 4. *Went forth out of the city by night*] Probably there was a *private passage under ground*, leading without the walls, by which Zedekiah and his followers might escape unperceived, till they had got some way from the city.

The way of the plain.] There were two roads from Jerusalem to Jericho. One passed over the mount of Olives; but, as this might have retarded his flight, he chose *the way of the plain*, and was overtaken near Jericho, perhaps about sixteen or eighteen miles from Jerusalem. He had probably intended to have passed the Jordan, in order to escape to Egypt, as the Egyptians were then his professed allies.

Verse 5. *To Riblah*] This city was situated on the northern frontier of Palestine, and Hamath was a large city belonging also to Syria. See Gen. x. 18.

A. M. 3416
B. C. 588
Ol. XLVIII. 1
Anno
TarquiniiPrisci,
R. Roman., 29

king of Babylon slew all the nobles of Judah.

7 Moreover [g]he put out Zedekiah's eyes, and bound him [h]with chains, to carry him to Babylon.

8 [i]And the Chaldeans burnt the king's house, and the houses of the people, with fire, and brake down the walls of Jerusalem.

9 [k]Then Nebuzar-adan the [l]captain [m]of the guard carried away captive into Babylon the remnant of the people that remained in the city, and those that fell away, that fell to him, with the rest of the people that remained.

10 But Nebuzar-adan the captain of the guard left of the poor of the people, which had nothing, in the land of Judah, and gave them vineyards and fields [n]at the same time.

11 Now Nebuchadrezzar king of Babylon gave charge concerning Jeremiah [o]to Nebuzaradan the captain of the guard, saying,

12 Take him, and [p]look well to him, and do him no harm; but do unto him even as he shall say unto thee.

13 So Nebuzar-adan the captain of the guard sent, and Nebushasban, Rab-saris, and Nergal-sharezer Rab-mag, and all the king of Babylon's princes;

A. M. 3416
B. C. 588
Ol. XLVIII. 1
Anno
TarquiniiPrisci,
R. Roman., 29

14 Even they sent, [q]and took Jeremiah out of the court of the prison, and committed him [r]unto Gedaliah the son of [s]Ahikam the son of Shaphan, that he should carry him home: so he dwelt among the people.

15 Now the word of the LORD came unto Jeremiah, while he was shut up in the court of the prison, saying,

16 Go and speak to [t]Ebed-melech the Ethiopian, saying, Thus saith the LORD of hosts, the God of Israel; Behold [u]I will bring my words upon this city for evil, and not for good; and they shall be *accomplished* in that day before thee.

17 But I will deliver thee in that day, saith the LORD: and thou shalt not be given into the hand of the men of whom thou *art* afraid.

18 For I will surely deliver thee, and thou shalt not fall by the sword, but [v]thy life shall be for a prey unto thee: [w]because thou hast put thy trust in me, saith the LORD.

---

[g]Ezek. xii. 13, compared with chap. xxxii. 4——[h]Heb. *with two brazen chains* or *fetters*——[i]2 Kings xxv. 9; chap. xxxviii. 18; lii. 13——[k]2 Kings xxv. 11, &c.; chap. lii. 15, &c.——[l]Or, *chief marshal*——[m]Heb. *chief of the executioners*, or *slaughtermen;* and so ver. 10, 11, &c.; see Gen. xxxvii. 26

[n]Hebrew, *in that day*——[o]Hebrew, *by the hand of*——[p]Hebrew, *set thine eyes upon him*——[q]Chapter xxxviii. 28——[r]Chapter xl. 5——[s]Chapter xxvi. 24——[t]Chapter xxxviii. 7, 12——[u]Daniel ix. 12 [v]Chapter xxi. 9; xlv. 5——[w]1 Chron. v. 20; Psalm xxxvii. 40

Verse 7. *Bound him with chains*] **Margin: "Two brazen chains;" one for his hands, and the other for his feet.**

Verse 9. *Those that fell away*] **That deserted to the Chaldeans during the siege.**

Verse 10. *Left of the poor of the people*] **The very refuse of the inhabitants, who were not worthy of being carried away; and among them he divided the fields and vineyards of those whom he took away.**

Verse 12. *Take him—look well to him*] **Nebuchadnezzar had heard that this prophet had foretold his capture of the city, and had frequently used all his influence to induce Zedekiah to pay the tribute, and not rebel against him; and on this account would be inclined to show the prophet especial favour.**

Verse 16. *Go and speak to Ebed-melech*] **The king's servant, the Cushite.**

Verse 18. *I will surely deliver thee*] **Thou hast feared the Lord, and not the king, nor his princes, and thou hast taken the part of the prophet, and become his intercessor. Thou shalt not be slain. Thou hast put thy trust in me; thou shalt therefore be safe whithersoever thou goest. They that fear God need fear nothing besides.**

CHAPTER XL

This and the four following chapters contain a distinct account of what passed in the land of Judah from the taking of Jerusalem to the retreat of the remnant of the people to Egypt; together with the prophecies of Jeremiah concerning that place, whither he himself accompanied them. In this chapter we have an account of the enlargement of Jeremiah by Nebuzar-adan, the captain of the guard, who advises him to put himself under the jurisdiction of Gedaliah, the son of Ahikam, whom the king of Babylon had made governor over the land of Judea, 1–5. *The prophet and many of the dispersed Jews repair to Gedaliah,* 6–12. *Johanan acquaints the governor of a conspiracy against him, but is not believed,* 13–16.

A. M. 3416
B. C. 588
Ol. XLVIII. 1
Anno TarquiniiPrisci, R. Roman., 29

THE word that came to Jeremiah from the LORD, [a]after that Nebuzar-adan the captain of the guard had let him go from Ramah, when he had taken him being bound in [b]chains among all that were carried away captive of Jerusalem and Judah, which were carried away captive unto Babylon.

2 And the captain of the guard took Jeremiah, and [c]said unto him, The LORD thy God hath pronounced this evil upon this place.

3 Now the LORD hath brought *it,* and done according as he hath said: [d]because ye have sinned against the LORD, and have not obeyed his voice, therefore this thing is come upon you.

4 And now, behold, I loose thee this day from the chains which [e]*were* upon thine hand. [f]If it seem good unto thee to come with me into Babylon, come; and [g]I will look well unto thee: but if it seem ill unto thee to come with me into Babylon, forbear: behold, [h]all the land *is* before thee: whither it seemeth good and convenient for thee to go, thither go.

5 Now while he was not yet gone back, *he said,* Go back also to Gedaliah the son of Ahikam the son of Shaphan, [i]whom the king of Babylon hath made governor over the cities of Judah, and dwell with him among the people: or go wheresoever it seemeth convenient unto thee to go. So the captain of the guard gave him victuals and a reward, and let him go.

6 [k]Then went Jeremiah unto Gedaliah the son of Ahikam to [l]Mizpah, and dwelt with him among the people that were left in the land.

A. M. 3416
B. C. 588
Ol. XLVIII. 1
Anno TarquiniiPrisci, R. Roman., 29

7 [m]Now when all the captains of the forces which *were* in the fields, *even* they and their men, heard that the king of Babylon had made Gedaliah the son of Ahikam governor in the land, and had committed unto him men, and women, and children, and of [n]the poor of the land, of them that were not carried away captive to Babylon;

8 Then they came to Gedaliah to Mizpah, [o]even Ishmael the son of Nethaniah, and Johanan and Jonathan the sons of Kareah, and Seraiah the son of Tanhumeth, and the sons of Ephai the Netophathite, and Jezaniah the son of a Maachathite, they and their men.

9 And Gedaliah the son of Ahikam the son of Shaphan sware unto them and to their men, saying, Fear not to serve the Chaldeans: dwell in the land, and serve the king of Babylon, and it shall be well with you.

10 As for me, behold, I will dwell at Mizpah, [p]to serve the Chaldeans, which will come unto us: but ye, gather ye wine, and summer fruits, and oil, and put *them* in your vessels, and dwell in your cities that ye have taken.

11 Likewise when all the Jews that *were* in Moab, and among the Ammonites, and in Edom, and that *were* in all the countries, heard that the king of Babylon had left a

[a]Chap. xxxix. 14——[b]Or, *manacles*——[c]Chap. l. 7——[d]Deut. xxix. 24, 25; Dan. ix. 11——[e]Or, are *upon thine hand*——[f]Chap. xxxix. 12——[g]Heb. *I will set mine eye upon thee*

[h]Gen. xx. 15——[i]2 Kings xxv. 22, &c.——[k]Chap. xxxix. 14——[l]Judg. xx. 1——[m]2 Kings xxv. 23, &c.——[n]Chap. xxxix. 10——[o]Chap. xli. 1——[p]Heb. *to stand before;* Deut. i. 38

NOTES ON CHAP. XL.

Verse 1. *The word that came to Jeremiah*] This and the four following chapters contain a particular account of what passed in the land of Judea from the taking of the city to the retreat of the people into Egypt, and the prophecies of Jeremiah concerning them there.

Had let him go from Ramah] This has embarrassed most of the commentators. Dr. *Blayney* has thrown much light upon it by his translation and note:—

"The word that came to Jeremiah from Jehovah, after that Nebu-Zaradan captain of the guards had taken him, and let him go from Ramah: for he had been bound with chains among all the captives of Jerusalem and Judah, who were carried away captive to Babylon."

"HAD TAKEN HIM, AND LET HIM GO.—Most interpreters have understood בקחתו אתו *bekachto otho* of Nebuchadnezzar's having first taken Jeremiah as a captive unto Ramah. But if the order of the sentence be well observed, as well as the more common use of the verb לקח *lakach*, it will, I think, rather appear that those words relate to his *taking* or having him brought to him, in order to give him his discharge."

Verse 2. *The Lord thy God hath pronounced*] I know that thou art a true prophet, for what thou hast predicted from thy God is come to pass.

Verse 4. *Come; and I will look well unto thee*] Thou art now at full liberty to do as thou pleasest; either to come to Babylon or to stay in thy own land.

Verse 5. *Go back also to Gedaliah*] If thou wilt stay in thy own land, thou hadst best put thyself under the protection of thy countryman Gedaliah, whom the King of Babylon has made governor of the land.

Verse 8. *Ishmael the son of Nethaniah*] This is he who afterwards murdered Gedaliah. He had

A. M. 3416 B. C. 588 Ol. XLVIII. 1 Anno TarquiniiPrisci, R. Roman., 29

remnant of Judah, and that he had set over them Gedaliah the son of Ahikam the son of Shaphan;

12 Even all the Jews returned out of all places whither they were driven, and came to the land of Judah, to Gedaliah, unto Mizpah, and gathered wine and summer fruits very much.

13 Moreover Johanan the son of Kareah, and all the captains of the forces that *were* in the fields, came to Gedaliah to Mizpah,

14 And said unto him, Dost thou certainly know that [q]Baalis the king of the Ammonites hath sent Ishmael the son of Nethaniah [r]to slay thee? But Gedaliah the son of Ahikam believed them not.

A. M. 3416 B. C. 588 Ol. XLVIII. 1 Anno TarquiniiPrisci, R. Roman., 29

15 Then Johanan the son of Kareah spake to Gedaliah in Mizpah secretly, saying, Let me go, I pray thee, and I will slay Ishmael the son of Nethaniah, and no man shall know *it:* wherefore should he slay thee, that all the Jews which are gathered unto thee should be scattered, and the remnant in Judah perish?

16 But Gedaliah the son of Ahikam said unto Johanan the son of Kareah, Thou shalt not do this thing: for thou speakest falsely of Ishmael.

[q]See chap. xli. 10

[r]Heb. *to strike thee in soul?*

been employed to do this by Baalis, king of the Ammonites, with whom he appears to have taken refuge during the siege. See ver. 14.

Verse 14. *But Gedaliah the son of Ahikam believed them not.*] The account given of this man proves him to have been a person of uncommon greatness of soul. Conscious of his own integrity and benevolence, he took the portrait of others from his own mind; and therefore believed evil of no man, because he felt none towards any in his own breast. He may be reproached for being too credulous and confident: but any thing of this kind that may be justly charged against him serves only to show the greatness of his mind. A *little soul* is ever suspicious, and ready to believe the worst of every person and thing. A great mind acts always on the contrary.

Verse 16. *Thou shalt not do this thing*] He cannot be so base.

***Thou speakest falsely of Ishmael.*] He thought it quite possible that the man who was capable of becoming an *assassin* was capable of telling a *lie;* and therefore he would not credit what he said. Had he been a little more distrustful, he would have saved his own life. The next chapter shows that Johanan's information was too true. So noble Gedaliah lost his life by not believing that evil of others of which he himself was incapable.**

CHAPTER XLI

Ishmael executes his conspiracy against Gedaliah the governor and his companions, and attempts to carry away the Jews who were with him captives to the Ammonites, 1–10; *but Johanan recovers them, and purposes to flee into Egypt,* 11–18.

A. M. 3416 B. C. 588 Ol. XLVIII. 1 Anno TarquiniiPrisci, R. Roman., 29

NOW it came to pass in the seventh month, [a]*that* Ishmael the son of Nethaniah the son of Elishama, of the seed royal, and the princes of the king, even ten men with him, came unto Gedaliah the son of Ahikam to Mizpah; and there they did eat bread together in Mizpah.

2 Then arose Ishmael the son of Nethaniah, and the ten men that were with him, and [b]smote Gedaliah the son of Ahikam the son of Shaphan with the sword, and slew him, whom the king of Babylon had made governor over the land.

A. M. 3416 B. C. 588 Ol. XLVIII. 1 Anno TarquiniiPrisci, R. Roman., 29

3 Ishmael also slew all the Jews that were with him, *even* with Gedaliah, at Mizpah, and the Chaldeans that were found there, *and* the men of war.

4 And it came to pass the second day after he had slain Gedaliah, and no man knew *it,*

5 That there came certain from Shechem, from Shiloh, and from Samaria, *even* fourscore men, [c]having their beards shaven, and their clothes rent, and having cut themselves,

[a]2 Kings xxv. 25; chap. xl. 6, 8——[b]2 Kings xxv. 25

[c]Lev. xix. 27, 28; Deut. xiv. 1; Isa. xv. 2

NOTES ON CHAP XLI

Verse 1. *Now—in the seventh month*] Answering to the first new moon in our month of *October*.

***There they did eat bread together*] This was the same as making a solemn covenant; for he who *ate bread* with another was ever reputed a *friend*.**

Verse 2. *Smote Gedaliah*] See the preceding chapter, ver. 14.

Verse 5. *Having their beards shaven*] All these were signs of deep mourning, probably on account of the destruction of the city.

A. M. 3416
B. C. 588
Ol. XLVIII. 1
Anno
TarquiniiPrisci,
R. Roman., 29

with offerings and incense in their hand, to bring *them* to [d]the house of the LORD.

6 And Ishmael the son of Nethaniah went forth from Mizpah to meet them, [e]weeping all along as he went: and it came to pass, as he met them, he said unto them, Come to Gedaliah the son of Ahikam.

7 And it was *so,* when they came into the midst of the city, that Ishmael the son of Nethaniah slew them, *and* [f]*cast them* into the midst of the pit, he, and the men that *were* with him.

8 But ten men were found among them that said unto Ishmael, Slay us not: for we have treasures in the field, of wheat, and of barley, and of oil, and of honey. So he forbare, and slew them not among their brethren.

9 Now the pit wherein Ishmael had cast all the dead bodies of the men, whom he had slain [g]because [h]of Gedaliah, *was* it [i]which Asa the king had made for fear of Baasha king of Israel: *and* Ishmael the son of Nethaniah filled it with *them that were* slain.

10 Then Ishmael carried away captive all the residue of the people that *were* in Mizpah, [k]*even* the king's daughters, and all the people that remained in Mizpah, [l]whom Nebuzaradan the captain of the guard had committed to Gedaliah the son of Ahikam: and Ishmael the son of Nethaniah carried them away captive, and departed to go over to [m]the Ammonites.

11 But when Johanan the son of Kareah, and all [n]the captains of the forces that *were* with him, heard of all the evil that Ishmael the son of Nethaniah had done,

A. M. 3416
B. C. 588
Ol. XLVIII. 1
Anno
TarquiniiPrisci,
R. Roman., 29

12 Then they took all the men, and went to fight with Ishmael the son of Nethaniah, and found him by [o]the great waters that *are* in Gibeon.

13 Now it came to pass *that* when all the people which *were* with Ishmael saw Johanan the son of Kareah, and all the captains of the forces that *were* with him, then they were glad.

14 So all the people that Ishmael had carried away captive from Mizpah cast about and returned, and went unto Johanan the son of Kareah.

15 But Ishmael the son of Nethaniah escaped from Johanan with eight men, and went to the Ammonites.

16 Then took Johanan the son of Kareah, and all the captains of the forces that *were* with him, all the remnant of the people whom he had recovered from Ishmael the son of Nethaniah, from Mizpah, after *that* he had slain Gedaliah the son of Ahikam, *even* mighty men of war, and the women, and the children, and the eunuchs, whom he had brought again from Gibeon:

17 And they departed, and dwelt in the habitation of [p]Chimham, which is by Beth-lehem, to go to enter into Egypt,

18 Because of the Chaldeans: for they were afraid of them, because Ishmael the son of Nethaniah had slain Gedaliah the son of Ahikam, [q]whom the king of Babylon made governor in the land.

---

[d]See 2 Kings xxv. 9; 1 Sam. i. 7——[e]Heb. *in going and weeping*——[f]So 1 Mac. vii. 19——[g]Or, *near Gedaliah* [h]Heb. *by the hand,* or *by the side of Gedaliah*

[i]1 Kings xv. 22; 2 Chron. xvi. 6——[k]Chap. xliii. 6 [l]Chap. xl. 7——[m]Chap. xl. 14——[n]Chap. xl. 7, 8, 13 [o]2 Sam. ii. 13——[p]2 Sam. xix. 37, 38——[q]Chap. xl. 5

Verse 6. *Weeping all along as he went*] This felonious hypocrite pretended that he also was deeply afflicted, and wished to bear them company in their sorrow.

Come to Gedaliah] He will appoint you vineyards and fields.

Verse 7. *Slew them*] He kept the murder of Gedaliah secret, and no doubt had a band of his assassins lodged in Mizpah; and he decoyed these fourscore men thither that he might have strength to slay them. He kept *ten* alive because they told him they had treasures hidden in a field, which they would show him. Whether he kept his word with them is not recorded. He could do nothing good or great; and it is likely that, when he had possessed himself of those treasures, he served them as he had served their companions. *Grain* is preserved to the present day in subterranean pits, called *mattamores,* in different parts of the east.

Verse 9. *Now the pit—was it which Asa the king had made for fear of Baasha*] See 1 Kings xv. 22. Asa made this cistern as a reservoir for water for the supply of the place; for he built and fortified *Mizpah* at the time that he was at war with Baasha, king of Israel.

Verse 10. *Carried away captive*] He took all these that he might sell them for slaves among the Ammonites.

Verse 14. *Went unto Johanan*] They were weary of the tyranny of Ishmael, and were glad of an opportunity to abandon him.

Verse 16. *The women,—children, and the eunuchs*] These were all, most probably, persons who belonged to the palace and harem of Zedekiah: some of them his own concubines and their children.

Verse 17. *Dwelt in the habitation of Chimham*] The estate that David gave Chimham, the son of Barzillai. See 2 Sam. xix. 37, &c. He took this merely as a resting-place; as he designed to carry all into Egypt, fearing the *Chaldeans*, who would endeavour to revenge the death of Gedaliah.

CHAPTER XLII

Johanan and the remnant of the people desire Jeremiah to ask counsel of God what they should do, 1–3. *The prophet assures them of safety in Judea, but destruction in Egypt,* 4–18; *and reproves their hypocrisy in asking counsel with which they had no intention to comply,* 19–22.

A. M. 3416
B. C. 588
Ol. XLVIII. 1
Anno Tarquinii Prisci, R. Roman., 29

THEN all the captains of the forces, [a]and Johanan the son of Kareah, and Jezaniah the son of Hoshaiah, and all the people, from the least even unto the greatest, came near,

2 And said unto Jeremiah the prophet, [b]Let, we beseech thee, our supplication be accepted before thee, and [c]pray for us unto the LORD thy God, *even* for all this remnant; (for we are left *but* [d]a few of many, as thine eyes do behold us:)

3 That the LORD thy God may show us [e]the way wherein we may walk, and the thing that we may do.

4 Then Jeremiah the prophet said unto them, I have heard *you;* behold, I will pray unto the LORD your God according to your words; and it shall come to pass, *that* [f]whatsoever thing the LORD shall answer you, I will declare it unto you; I will [g]keep nothing back from you.

5 Then they said to Jeremiah, [h]The LORD be a true and faithful Witness between us, if we do not even according to all things for the which the LORD thy God shall send thee to us.

6 Whether *it be* good, or whether *it be* evil, we will obey the voice of the LORD our God, to whom we send thee; [i]that it may be well with us, when we obey the voice of the LORD our God.

A. M. 3416
B. C. 588
Ol. XLVIII. 1
Anno Tarquinii Prisci, R. Roman., 29

7 And it came to pass after ten days, that the word of the LORD came unto Jeremiah.

8 Then called he Johanan the son of Kareah, and all the captains of the forces which *were* with him, and all the people from the least even to the greatest,

9 And said unto them, Thus saith the LORD, the God of Israel, unto whom ye sent me to present your supplication before him;

10 If ye will still abide in this land, then [k]will I build you, and not pull *you* down; and I will plant you, and not pluck *you* up: for [l]I repent me of the evil that I have done unto you.

11 Be not afraid of the king of Babylon, of whom ye are afraid; be not afraid of him, saith the LORD: [m]for I *am* with you to save you, and to deliver you from his hand.

12 And [n]I will show mercies unto you, that he may have mercy upon you, and cause you to return to your own land.

[a]Chap. xl. 8, 13; xli. 11——[b]Or, *Let our supplication fall before thee*——[c]1 Sam. vii. 8; xii. 19; Isa. xxxvii. 4; James v. 16——[d]Lev. xxvi. 22——[e]Ezra viii. 21 [f]1 Kings xxii. 14

[g]1 Sam. iii. 18; Acts xx. 20——[h]Gen. xxxi. 50 [i]Deut. vi. 3; chap. vii. 23——[k]Chap. xxiv. 6; xxxi. 28; xxxiii. 7;——[l]Deut. xxxii. 36; chap. xviii. 8——[m]Isa. xliii. 5; Rom. viii. 31——[n]Psa. cvi. 45, 46

NOTES ON CHAP. XLII

Verse 1. *The captains of the forces*] The different leaders of the small bands or companies, collected from different parts of the land. The principal are those here named.

Verse 3. *That the Lord thy God may show us*] They all thought there was no safety in Jerusalem or in Judea, and therefore determined to leave the land: but they did not know which might be the safest direction to take; for though they inclined to Egypt, yet they wished to know the mind of God on that point.

Verse 5. *The Lord be a true and faithful Witness*] The Lord is such; and as ye have bound yourselves to obey his voice, he will register the covenant, and bless or curse according as ye shall conduct yourselves in this matter.

Verse 7. *After ten days*] All this time he was waiting upon God; for it is evident the prophets could not prophesy when they pleased, any more than the disciples of our Lord could work miracles when they wished. The gift of prophecy and the gift of miracles were both dependent on the will of the Most High, and each of them was given only for the moment; and when the necessity was over, the influence ceased.

Verse 10. *For I repent me of the evil*] The meaning is, As I have punished you only because you continued to be rebellious, I will arrest this punishment as soon as you become

A. M. 3416
B. C. 588
Ol. XLVIII. 1
Anno TarquiniiPrisci,
R. Roman., 29

13 But if [o]ye say, We will not
dwell in this land, neither obey
the voice of the LORD your
God,
14 Saying, No; but we will go into the
land of Egypt, where we shall see no war,
nor hear the sound of the trumpet, nor have
hunger of bread; and there will we dwell:
15 And now therefore hear the word of the
LORD, ye remnant of Judah, Thus saith the
LORD of hosts, the God of Israel; If ye [p]wholly
set [q]your faces to enter into Egypt, and go to
sojourn there;
16 Then it shall come to pass, *that* the sword,
[r]which ye feared, shall overtake you there in
the land of Egypt, and the famine, whereof ye
were afraid, [s]shall follow close after you there
in Egypt; and there ye shall die.
17 [t]So shall it be with all the men that set
their faces to go into Egypt to sojourn there;
they shall die [u]by the sword, by the famine,
and by the pestilence: and [v]none of them
shall remain or escape from the evil that I
will bring upon them.
18 For thus saith the LORD of hosts, the
God of Israel; As mine anger
and my fury hath been [w]poured
forth upon the inhabitants of
Jerusalem; so shall my fury be
poured forth upon you, when ye shall enter
into Egypt: and [x]ye shall be an execration,
and an astonishment, and a curse, and a reproach; and ye shall see this place no more.
19 The LORD hath said concerning you, O
ye remnant of Judah; [y]Go ye not into Egypt:
know certainly that I have [z]admonished you
this day.
20 For [a]ye dissembled in your hearts, when
ye sent me unto the LORD your God, saying,
[b]Pray for us unto the LORD our God: and
according unto all that the LORD our God shall
say, so declare unto us, and we will do *it*.
21 And *now* I have this day declared *it* to
you; but ye have not obeyed the voice of the
LORD your God, nor any *thing* for the which
he hath sent me unto you.
22 Now therefore know certainly that [c]ye
shall die by the sword, by the famine, and by
the pestilence, in the place whither ye desire
[d]to go *and* to sojourn.

[o]Ch. xliv. 16——[p]Deut. xvii. 16; ch. xliv. 12, 13, 14——[q]Luke ix. 51——[r]Ezek. xi. 8——[s]Heb. *shall cleave after you*——[t]Heb. *So shall all the men be*——[u]Chap. xxiv. 10; ver. 22——[v]See ch. xliv. 14, 28——[w]Ch. vii. 20

[x]Ch. xviii. 16; xxiv. 9; xxvi. 6; xxix. 18, 22; xliv. 12; Zech. viii. 13——[y]Deut. xvii. 16——[z]Heb. *testified against you*——[a]Or, *ye have used deceit against your souls*——[b]Ver. 2——[c]Ver. 17; Ezek. vi. 11——[d]Or, *to go to sojourn*

obedient to my word. You need not fear the king of Babylon if you have me for your helper; and I will so show mercy to you that he shall see it, and cease from afflicting you, as he shall see that I am on your side.

Verse 15. *If ye—set your faces to enter into Egypt, &c.*] Every evil that ye dreaded by staying in your own land shall come upon you in Egypt.

Verse 16. *The sword—and the famine—shall follow close after you*] Shall be at your heels; shall overtake and destroy you; *for there ye shall die.*

Verse 19. *Go ye not into Egypt*] Why? Because God knew, such was their miserable propensity to idolatry, that they would there adopt the worship of the country, and serve idols.

Verse 20. *For ye dissembled in your hearts*] What a most miserable and incorrigible people! Ingratitude, hypocrisy, rebellion, and cruelty seem to have been enthroned in their hearts! And what are they still? Just what their fathers were, except in the mere article of *idolatry;* and that they do not practise because they are indifferent to their own religion and to that of all others. Examine their devotions and their lives, and see whether Charity herself can say they believe in the God of Abraham!

Verse 21. *Ye have not obeyed the voice*] Though ye have requested to have this particular revelation of the Divine will, and promised obedience, yet have ye not done one thing for which ye sent me to inquire of the Lord.

Verse 22. *Now therefore know certainly*] As ye have determined to disobey, God has determined to punish. Ye may now follow the full bent of your wicked devices, and I will follow the requisitions of my justice. Ye shall die by the sword, by the pestilence, and by the famine, in the place whither ye desire to go to sojourn. Thus was their doom *sealed.*

With such dispositions and with such rebellion of heart, it is strange that they should put themselves to any trouble to inquire of the Lord relative to their future operations. They did not intend to obey; but as a matter of curiosity they would inquire to hear what the prophet might say; and if according to their own inclination, they would obey.

CHAPTER XLIII

The leading men, discrediting Jeremiah's prophecy, carry the people into Egypt, 1–7. Jeremiah, by a type, foretells the conquest of Egypt by Nebuchadnezzar, 8–13. This mode of conveying instruction by actions was very expressive, and frequently practised by the prophets. The image of Nebuchadnezzar arraying himself with Egypt, as a shepherd puts on his garment, is very noble. Egypt at this time contended with Babylon for the empire of the east; yet this mighty kingdom, when God appoints the revolution, shifts its owner with as much ease as a shepherd removes his tent or garment, which the new proprietor has only to spread over him. See ver. 12.

A. M. 3416
B. C. 588
Ol. XLVIII. 1
Anno
TarquiniiPrisci,
R. Roman., 29

AND it came to pass, *that* when Jeremiah had made an end of speaking unto all the people all the words of the LORD their God, for which the LORD their God had sent him to them, *even* all these words,

2 [a]Then spake Azariah the son of Hoshaiah, and Johanan the son of Kareah, and all the proud men, saying unto Jeremiah, Thou speakest falsely: the LORD our God hath not sent thee to say, Go not into Egypt to sojourn there:

3 But Baruch the son of Neriah setteth thee on against us, for to deliver us into the hand of the Chaldeans, that they might put us to death, and carry us away captives into Babylon.

4 So Johanan the son of Kareah, and all the captains of the forces, and all the people, obeyed not the voice of the LORD, to dwell in the land of Judah.

5 But Johanan the son of Kareah, and all the captains of the forces, took [b]all the remnant of Judah, that were returned from all nations, whither they had been driven to dwell in the land of Judah;

6 *Even* men, and women, and children, [c]and the king's daughters, [d]and every person that Nebuzar-adan the captain of the guard had left with Gedaliah the son of Ahikam the son of Shaphan, and Jeremiah the prophet, and Baruch the son of Neriah.

A. M. 3416
B. C. 588
Ol. XLVIII. 1
Anno
TarquiniiPrisci,
R. Roman., 29

7 So they came into the land of Egypt: for they obeyed not the voice of the LORD: thus came they *even* to [e]Tahpanhes.

A. M. 3417
B. C. 587
Ol. XLVIII. 2
TarquiniiPrisci,
R. Roman.,
cir. annum 30

8 Then came the word of the LORD unto Jeremiah in Tahpanhes, saying,

9 Take great stones in thine hand, and hide them in the clay in the brick-kiln, which *is* at the entry of Pharaoh's house in Tahpanhes, in the sight of the men of Judah;

10 And say unto them, Thus saith the LORD of hosts, the God of Israel; Behold, I will send and take Nebuchadrezzar the king of Babylon, [f]my servant, and will set his throne upon these stones that I have hid; and he shall spread his royal pavilion over them.

11 [g]And when he cometh, he shall smite the land of Egypt, *and deliver* [h]such *as are* for death to death; and such *as are* for captivity to captivity; and such *as are* for the sword to the sword.

12 And I will kindle a fire in the houses of [i]the gods of Egypt; and he shall burn them

[a]Chap. xlii. 1——[b]Chap. xl. 11, 12——[c]Chap. xli. 10——[d]Chap. xxxix. 10; xl. 7——[e]Chap. ii. 16; xliv. 1, called *Hanes;* Isa. xxx. 4

[f]Chap. xxv. 9; xxvii. 6; see Ezek. xxix. 18, 20——[g]Ch. xliv. 13; xlvi. 13——[h]Chap. xv. 2; Zech. xi. 9——[i]Chap. xlvi. 25

NOTES ON CHAP. XLIII

Verse 2. *Thou speakest falsely*] They had no other colour for their rebellion than *flatly to deny* that God had spoken what the prophet related.

Verse 6. *Men, and women, and children, and the king's daughters*] See the note on chap. xli. 10. It is truly surprising that the Chaldeans should have left behind any of the royal family of Judah! But, 1. Perhaps they knew not there were any. 2. If they did know, they might think, being children of *concubines*, they could not inherit. Or, 3. That being females, they were not eligible. And they had taken care to seize all Zedekiah's sons, and slay them before his eyes.

Verse 7. *Came they* even *to Tahpanhes*] This city was called *Daphne* by the Greeks, and was situated at the extremity of Lower Egypt, near to Heliopolis. It was called *Daphne Pelusiaca.* They halted at this place, most probably for the purpose of obtaining the king's permission to penetrate farther into Egypt. It was at this place that, according to St. Jerome, tradition says the faithful Jeremiah was stoned to death by these rebellious wretches; for whose welfare he had watched, prayed, gone through many indignities, and suffered every kind of hardship. And now he sealed the truth of his Divine mission with his blood.

Verse 9. *Take great stones*] This discourse seems to have been delivered about a year after the destruction of Jerusalem. They pretended that they dared not stay in *Judea* for fear of the *Chaldeans.* The prophet here assures them that *Nebuchadnezzar* shall come to Egypt, extend his conquests in that kingdom, and place his tent over the very place where these stones were laid up, and destroy them. How these prophecies were fulfilled, see at the end of chap. xliv.

Verse 11. *Such* as are *for death to death*] See the note on chap. xv. 2.

Verse 12. *He shall burn them, and carry them away captives*] Some of these gods, such as were of *wood*, he will burn; those of *metal* he will carry away. Some of them were of *gold.* See below.

Shall array himself with the land of Egypt]

A. M. cir. 3417 B. C. cir. 587 Ol. XLVIII. 2 Anno TarquiniiPrisci, R. Roman., 30

and carry them away captives:
and he shall array himself with
the land of Egypt, as a shepherd
putteth on his garment; and he
shall go forth from thence in peace.

13 He shall break also the
[k]images of [l]Bethshemesh, that *is*
in the land of Egypt; and the
houses of the gods of the Egyptians shall he burn with fire.

[k]Heb. *statues*, or *standing images* — [l]Or, *the house of the sun*

Shall take all its wealth, and all its grandeur; shall take all its spoils.

As a shepherd putteth on his garment] With as much ease, and with as little opposition; and with as full a confidence that it is now his own.

He shall go forth from thence in peace.] He shall suffer no interruption, nor endure any disaster in his return from his Egyptian expedition. See the proof of all this in the notes at the end of chap. xliv.

Verse 13. *He shall break also the images of Beth-shemesh*] בית שמש *beith shemesh* is, literally, *the house* or *temple of the sun;* which was worshipped here, and whose images are said to have been of *solid gold.* These Nebuchadnezzar was to break and carry away; and the *houses of the gods*—all the temples of Egypt, he was to burn with fire. Beth-shemesh is the same as Heliopolis.

CHAPTER XLIV

Jeremiah reproves the Jews in Egypt for continuing in idolatry after the exemplary judgments inflicted by God on their nation for that sin, 1–14; *and, upon their refusing to reform, denounces destruction to them, and to that kingdom wherein they sought protection,* 15–30.

A. M. cir. 3433 B. C. cir. 571 Ol. cir. LII. 2 Servii Tullii, R. Roman., cir. annum 8

THE word that came to Jeremiah concerning all the
Jews which dwell in the land of
Egypt, which dwell at [a]Migdol,
and at [b]Tahpanhes, and at [c]Noph, and in the
country of Pathros, saying,
2 Thus saith the LORD of hosts, the God of
Israel; Ye have seen all the evil that I have
brought upon Jerusalem, and upon all the
cities of Judah; and, behold, this day they *are*
[d]a desolation, and no man dwelleth therein,
3 Because of their wickedness which they
have committed to provoke me to anger, in
that they went [e]to burn incense, *and* to [f]serve
other gods, whom they knew not,
neither they, ye, nor your fathers.
4 Howbeit [g]I sent unto you all
my servants the prophets, rising early and
sending *them*, saying, O, do not this abominable thing that I hate.
5 But they hearkened not, nor inclined their
ear to turn from their wickedness, to burn no
incense unto other gods.
6 Wherefore [h]my fury and mine anger was
poured forth, and was kindled in the cities of
Judah and in the streets of Jerusalem; and
they are wasted *and* desolate, as at this day.

[a]Exod. xiv. 2; ch. xlvi. 14——[b]Ch. xliii. 7——[c]Isa. xix. 13——[d]Chap. ix. 11; xxxiv. 22——[e]Chap. xix. 4

[f]Deut. xiii. 6; xxxii. 17——[g]2 Chron. xxxvi. 15; chap. vii. 25; xxv. 4; xxvi. 5; xxix. 19——[h]Chap. xlii. 18

NOTES ON CHAP. XLIV

Verse 1. *The word that came to Jeremiah concerning all the Jews*] *Dahler* supposes this discourse to have been delivered in the *seventeenth* or *eighteenth* year after the taking of Jerusalem.

Which dwell at Migdol] A city of Lower Egypt, not far from Pelusium.

Tahpanhes] *Daphne Pelusiaca,* the place to which the emigrant Jews first went.

Noph] מפס *Maphes,* Targum. *Memphis,* a celebrated city of Middle Egypt, and the capital of its district.

The country of Pathros] A district of Upper Egypt, known by the name of the *Thebais.* See *Bochart,* Lib. Phaleg, lib. iv., c. 22. Thus we find that the Jews were scattered over the principal parts of Egypt.

Verse 2. *No man dwelleth therein*] The desolation of the land of Judea must have been exceedingly great when this, in almost any sense, could be spoken of it.

Verse 4. *O, do not this abominable thing*] A strong specimen of affectionate entreaty. One of the finest figures of poetry, when judiciously managed, the *anthropopathia,* the ascribing *human passions* to God, is often used by this prophet: so God is said to *grieve,* to *mourn,* to have his *bowels moved* with compassion, to *repent,* to be *angry,* &c. Here he is represented as *tenderly expostulating: O, do not;* or, *I entreat you, do not that abominable thing which I hate.* 1. *Do it not:* your *God* commands. 2. *O, do it not:* your *Father entreats.* 3. It is *an abominable* thing, and should *not be done.* 4. *I hate it,* and on that account ye should abstain from it.

Verse 5. *But they hearkened not*] 1. They disregarded the *authority* of their God. 2. They were not *moved* by the *entreaties* of their most affectionate Father. 3. In abominations they

A. M. cir. 3433
B. C. cir. 571
Ol. cir. LII. 2
Servii Tullii,
R. Roman.,
cir. annum 8

7 Therefore now thus saith the
LORD, the God of hosts, the God
of Israel; Wherefore commit ye
this great evil [i]against your
souls, to cut off from you man and woman,
child and suckling, [k]out of Judah, to leave
you none to remain;
8 In that ye [l]provoke me unto wrath with
the works of your hands, burning incense unto
other gods in the land of Egypt, whither ye
be gone to dwell, that ye might cut yourselves
off, and that ye might be [m]a curse and a reproach among all the nations of the earth?
9 Have ye forgotten the [n]wickedness of your
fathers, and the wickedness of the kings of
Judah, and the wickedness of their wives, and
your own wickedness, and the wickedness of
your wives, which they have committed in the
land of Judah, and in the streets of Jerusalem?
10 They are not [o]humbled *even* unto this
day, neither have they [p]feared, nor walked in
my law, nor in my statutes, that I set before
you and before your fathers.
11 Therefore thus saith the LORD of hosts,
the God of Israel; Behold [q]I will set my face
against you for evil, and to cut off all Judah.
12 And I will take the remnant of Judah,
that have set their faces to go into the land of
Egypt to sojourn there, and [r]they shall all be
consumed, *and* fall in the land of Egypt;
they shall *even* be consumed by the sword *and*
by the famine: they shall die, from the least
even unto the greatest, by the sword and by
the famine: and [s]they shall be an execration,
and an astonishment, and a curse, and a reproach.
13 [t]For I will punish them that
dwell in the land of Egypt, as I
have punished Jerusalem, by the
sword, by the famine, and by the
pestilence:
14 So that none of the remnant of Judah,
which are gone into the land of Egypt to sojourn there, shall escape or remain, that they
should return into the land of Judah, to the
which they [u]have a desire to return to dwell
there: for [v]none shall return but such as shall
escape.
15 Then all the men which knew that their
wives had burned incense unto other gods, and
all the women that stood by, a great multitude,
even all the people that dwelt in the land of
Egypt, in Pathros, answered Jeremiah, saying,
16 *As for* the word that thou hast spoken
unto us in the name of the LORD, [w]we will
not hearken unto thee.
17 But we will certainly do [x]whatsoever
thing goeth forth out of our own mouth, to
burn incense unto the [y]queen [z]of heaven, and
to pour out drink-offerings unto her, as we
have done, we, and our fathers, our kings, and
our princes, in the cities of Judah, and in the
streets of Jerusalem: for *then* had we plenty
of [a]victuals, and were well, and saw no evil.
18 But since we left off to burn incense to
the queen of heaven, and to pour out drink-
offerings unto her, we have wanted all *things,*
and have been consumed by the sword and by
the famine.
19 [b]And when we burned incense to the
queen of heaven, and poured out drink-offerings
unto her, did we make her cakes to worship

[i]Num. xvi. 38; chap. vii. 19——[k]Heb. *out of the midst of Judah*——[l]Chap. xxv. 6, 7——[m]Chap. xlii. 18; ver. 12——[n]Heb. *wickedness*, or *punishments*, &c.——[o]Heb. *contrite;* Psa. li. 17——[p]Prov. xxviii. 14——[q]Lev. xvii. 10; xx. 5, 6; chap. xxi. 10; Amos ix. 4

[r]Chap. xlii. 15, 16, 17, 22——[s]Chap. xlii. 18——[t]Ch. xliii. 11——[u]Heb. *lift up their soul*——[v]Ver. 28——[w]So chap. vi. 16——[x]Num. xxx. 12; Deut. xxiii. 23; Judg. xi. 36; see ver. 25——[y]Or, *frame of heaven*——[z]Chap. vii. 18——[a]Heb. *bread*——[b]Chap. vii. 18

delighted. And, 4. They *loved that* which *God hated;* and, apparently, *because* he hated it.

Verse 7. This *great evil against your souls*] Will not *self-interest* weigh with you? See what ruin your conduct has brought upon your country. Your fathers sinned as you are doing; and where are they now? Either destroyed, or in captivity. And you are now taking the same way to your own destruction.

Verse 9. *Have ye forgotten the wickedness of your fathers*] It seems that the *women* were principal agents in idolatrous practices; for the *queens*—the *wives,* of rulers and of common people, burnt incense to the *queen of heaven,* (the moon,) ver. 17, and poured out drink-offerings to her.

Verse 15. *Then all the men—and all the women*] We have not seen the women in determined rebellion before. Here they make a common cause with their idolatrous husbands.

Verse 19. *And when we burned incense to the queen of heaven*] The MOON seems to have been called מלכת *melecheth,* as the SUN was called מלך *molech.* The Hindoos pour out water to the sun thrice a day; and to the moon whenever they worship her.

The idolatrous worship of these people was a sort of imitation of the worship of the true God; only sacrifice was not common in it. The factious women here tell us in what it consisted. 1. They burnt incense to the moon, and perhaps

A. M. cir. 3433
B. C. cir. 571
Ol. cir. LII. 2
Servii Tullii,
R. Roman.,
cir. annum. 8

her, and pour out drink-offerings unto her, without our [c]men?
20 Then Jeremiah said unto
all the people, to the men, and to
the women, and to all the people which had
given him *that* answer, saying,
21 The incense that ye burned in the cities
of Judah, and in the streets of Jerusalem, ye,
and your fathers, your kings, and your princes,
and the people of the land, did not the LORD
remember them, and came it *not* into his mind?
22 So that the LORD could no longer bear,
because of the evil of your doings *and* because
of the abominations which ye have committed;
therefore is your land [d]a desolation, and an
astonishment, and a curse, without an inhabitant, [e]as at this day.
23 Because ye have burned incense, and because ye have sinned against the LORD, and
have not obeyed the voice of the LORD, nor
walked in his law, nor in his statutes, nor in
his testimonies; [f]therefore this evil is happened unto you, as at this day.
24 Moreover Jeremiah said unto all the people, and to all the women, Hear the word of the
LORD, all Judah [g]that *are* in the land of Egypt:
25 Thus saith the LORD of hosts, the God
of Israel, saying; [h]Ye and your wives have
both spoken with your mouths, and fulfilled
with your hand, saying, We will surely perform
our vows that we have vowed, to burn incense
to the queen of heaven, and to pour out drink-
offerings unto her: ye will surely
accomplish your vows, and surely
perform your vows.

A. M. cir. 3433
B. C. cir. 571
Ol. cir. LII. 2
Servii Tullii,
R. Roman.,
cir. annum 8

26 Therefore hear ye the word
of the LORD, all Judah that dwell in the land
of Egypt; Behold, [i]I have sworn by my great
name, saith the LORD, that [k]my name shall no
more be named in the mouth of any man of
Judah in all the land of Egypt, saying, The
Lord GOD liveth.
27 [l]Behold, I will watch over them for evil,
and not for good; and all the men of Judah
that *are* in the land of Egypt [m]shall be consumed by the sword and by the famine, until
there be an end of them.
28 Yet [n]a small number that escape the
sword shall return out of the land of Egypt
into the land of Judah, and all the remnant
of Judah, that are gone into the land of Egypt
to sojourn there, shall know whose [o]words
shall stand, [p]mine or theirs.
29 And this *shall be* a sign unto you, saith
the LORD, that I will punish you in this place,
that ye may know that my words shall [q]surely
stand against you for evil:
30 Thus saith the LORD; Behold, [r]I will
give Pharaoh-hophra king of Egypt into the
hand of his enemies, and into the hand of
them that seek his life; as I gave [s]Zedekiah
king of Judah into the hand of Nebuchadrezzar king of Babylon, his enemy, and that
sought his life.

[c]Or, *husbands*——[d]Chap. xxv. 11, 18, 38——[e]Ver. 6——[f]Dan. ix. 11, 12——[g]Chap. xliii. 7; ver. 15——[h]Ver. 15 &c.——[i]Gen. xxii. 16——[k]Ezek. xx. 39——[l]Chap. i. 10; xxxi. 28; Ezek. vii. 6

[m]Ver. 12——[n]Ver. 14; Isa. xxvii. 13——[o]Ver. 17, 25, 26——[p]Heb. *from me*, or *them*——[q]Psa. xxxiii. 11——[r]Chap. xlvi. 25, 26; Ezek. xxix. 3, &c.; xxx. 21, &c.——[s]Chap. xxxix. 5

to the sun and the planets. 2. They poured out libations to her. 3. They made and consecrated cakes to her. All these were prescribed in the worship of the true GOD. See, among others, Exod. xxix. 23, &c.; Lev. ii. 4; xxiii. 16; and Num. vi. 15. And the women vindicate their conduct by asserting that they did all this by the consent of their husbands: "Did we worship her without our men?"

Verse 22. *Therefore is your land a desolation*] I grant that ye and your husbands have joined together in these abominations; and what is the consequence? "The Lord could no longer bear because of your evil doings; and therefore is your land a desolation, and an astonishment, and a curse, without an inhabitant, this day."

Verse 30. *Behold I will give Pharaoh-hophra*] That is, *Pharaoh Apries.* How this and the prophecies in the preceding chapter were fulfilled, we learn from ancient historians. The sum of such information is this: the subjects of *Pharaoh Apries* rebelling, he sent *Amasis*, one of his generals, to reduce them to their duty. But no sooner had *Amasis* begun to make his speech, than they fixed a helmet on his head, and proclaimed him king. *Amasis* accepted the title, and confirmed the Egyptians in their revolt; and the greater part of the nation declaring for him, *Apries* was obliged to retire into Upper Egypt; and the country being thus weakened by intestine war, was attacked and easily overcome by Nebuchadnezzar, who on quitting it left *Amasis* his viceroy. After Nebuchadnezzar's departure, *Apries* marched against *Amasis;* but, being defeated at *Memphis*, was taken prisoner, carried to *Sais*, and was strangled in his own palace, thus verifying this prophecy. See *Herodotus* in Euterpe.

Thus Nebuchadnezzar made an easy conquest of the land. He conquered it as easily as "a shepherd puts on his cloak: he went thence in peace," having clothed himself with its spoils; and left all quiet under a viceroy of his own choosing. The rebellion of Pharaoh's subjects was the "fire that God kindled in Egypt," chap. xliii. 12. And thus was he "delivered into the hands of his enemies," his revolted people; and "into the hand of him who sought his life," i. e., *Amasis* his general. And thus the whole prophecy was literally fulfilled.

CHAPTER XLV

This chapter is evidently connected with the subject treated of in the thirty-sixth. *Baruch, who had written the prophecies of Jeremiah, and read them publicly in the temple, and afterwards to many of the princes, is in great affliction because of the awful judgments with which the land of Judah was about to be visited; and also on account of the imminent danger to which his own life was exposed, in publishing such unwelcome tidings,* 1–3. *To remove Baruch's fear with respect to this latter circumstance, the prophet assures him that though the total destruction of Judea was determined because of the great wickedness of the inhabitants, yet his life should be preserved amidst the general desolation,* 4, 5.

A. M. cir. 3397 B. C. cir. 607 Ol. XLIII. 2 Anno TarquiniiPrisci, R. Roman., 10

THE [a]word that Jeremiah the prophet spake unto Baruch the son of Neriah, when he had written these words in a book at the mouth of Jeremiah, in the fourth year of Jehoiakim [b]the son of Josiah king of Judah, saying,

2 Thus saith the LORD, the God of Israel, unto thee, O Baruch,

3 Thou didst say, Wo is me now! for the LORD hath added grief to my sorrow; I fainted in my sighing, and I find no rest.

4 Thus shalt thou say unto him, The LORD saith thus; Behold, [c]*that* which I have built will I break down, and that which I have planted I will pluck up, even this whole land.

5 And seekest thou great things for thyself? seek *them* not: for, behold, [d]I will bring evil upon all flesh, saith the LORD: but thy life will I give unto thee [e]for a prey in all places whither thou goest.

[a]Ch. xxxvi. 1, 4, 32——[b]2 Kings xxiii. 34——[c]Isa. v. 5

[d]Chap. xxv. 26——[e]Chap. xxi. 9; xxxviii. 2; xxxix. 18

NOTES ON CHAP. XLV

Verse 1. *The word that Jeremiah—spake unto Baruch*] This is another instance of shameless transposition. This discourse was delivered in the *fourth* year of Jehoiakim, several years before Jerusalem was taken by the Chaldeans. It is a simple appendage to chap. xxxvi., and there it should have been inserted.

Verse 3. *Thou didst say, Wo is me now!*] All that were the enemies of Jeremiah became his enemies too; and he needed these promises of support.

The Lord hath added grief to my sorrow] He had mourned for the desolations that were coming on his country, and now he mourns for the dangers to which he feels his own life exposed; for we find, from chap. xxxvi. 26, that the king had given commandment to take both Baruch and Jeremiah, in order that they might be put to death at the instance of his nobles.

Verse 4. *Behold*, that *which I have built*] I most certainly will fulfil all those threatenings contained in the roll thou hast written; for I will destroy this whole land.

Verse 5. *And seekest thou great things for thyself?*] Nothing better can be expected of this people: thy hopes in reference to *them* are vain. Expect no national amendment, till national judgments have taken place. And as for any *benefit* to *thyself*, think it sufficient that God has determined to preserve thy life amidst all these dangers.

But thy life will I give unto thee for a prey] This is a proverbial expression. We have met with it before, chap. xxi. 9, xxxviii. 2, xxxix. 18; and it appears to have this meaning. As a *prey* or *spoil* is that which is gained from a vanquished enemy, so it is preserved with pleasure as the proof and reward of a man's own valour. So Baruch's life should be doubly precious unto him, not only on account of the dangers through which God had caused him to pass safely, but also on account of those services he had been enabled to render, the consolations he had received, and the continual and very evident interposition of God in his behalf. All these would be dearer to him than the *spoils* of a vanquished foe to the hero who had overcome in battle.

Spoil may signify *unlooked-for gain.* The preservation of his life, in such circumstances, must be more than he could reasonably expect; but his life should be safe, and he should have it as a *spoil*, whithersoever he should go. This assurance must have quieted all his fears.

CHAPTER XLVI

The difference between the preceding and the subsequent prophecies in point of composition is very remarkable; the last excelling much in majesty and elegance. This chapter (of which the first *verse forms a general title to this and the five chapters following) contains two distinct prophecies relating to Egypt. The first was delivered previous to an engagement between Pharaoh-necho, king of Egypt, and Nebuchadnezzar, king of Babylon; in which the Egyptians were routed in Carchemish with great slaughter, as here predicted. The prophet sees the mighty preparations; but they are all declared to be of no avail, as God had decreed their fall,* 1–6. *The king of Egypt, however, is represented as marching with all the confidence of victory, like a river overflowing its banks, and threatening all around with its inundation,* 7, 8. *But this immense armament of Pharaoh-necho, consisting of various nations, shall, by a righteous judgment of God, receive such a signal overthrow near the river Euphrates, that the political consequence of Egypt shall be thereby irretrievably ruined, and its remaining power become contemptible in the sight of the nations,* 9–12. *The other prophecy, beginning at the* thirteenth *verse, relates to the memorable overthrow of the Egyptians by Nebuchadnezzar, subsequent to his siege of Tyre, in the* sixteenth *year after the destruction of Jerusalem,* 13–26. *The promise, in the conclusion of the chapter, of preservation to the Jews, (who have for many ages continued a distinct people, when the various nations of antiquity who oppressed them, or with whom they had any intercourse, have long ago ceased to have any separate and visible existence,) has been most remarkably fulfilled; and is a very signal act of providence, and a pledge of the restoration of Israel to the Divine favour, when the time of the Gentiles shall be fulfilled,* 27, 28.

A. M. cir. 3397
B. C. cir. 607
Ol. XLIII. 2
TarquiniiPrisci,
R. Roman.,
cir. annum 10

THE word of the LORD which came to Jeremiah the prophet against [a]the Gentiles;
2 Against Egypt, [b]against the army of Pharaoh-necho king of Egypt, which was by the river Euphrates in Carchemish, which Nebuchadrezzar king of Babylon smote in the fourth year of Jehoiakim the son of Josiah king of Judah.
3 [c]Order ye the buckler and shield, and draw near to battle.
4 Harness the horses; and get up, ye horsemen, and stand forth with *your* helmets; furbish the spears, *and* put on the brigandines.
5 Wherefore have I seen them dismayed *and* turned away back? and their mighty ones are [d]beaten down, and are [e]fled apace, and look not back: *for* [f]fear *was* round about, saith the LORD.
6 Let not the swift flee away, nor the mighty man escape; they shall [g]stumble, and fall toward the north by the river Euphrates.
7 Who *is* this *that* cometh up [h]as a flood, whose waters are moved as the rivers?
8 Egypt riseth up like a flood, and *his* waters are moved like the rivers; and he saith, I will go up, *and* will cover the earth; I will destroy the city and the inhabitants thereof.
9 Come up, ye horses; and rage, ye chariots;

[a]Chap. xxv. 15, &c.——[b]2 Kings xxxiii. 29; 2 Chron. xxxv. 20——[c]So chap. li. 11, 12; Nah. ii. 1; iii. 14
[d]Heb. *broken in pieces*

[e]Heb. *fled a flight*——[f]Chap. vi. 25; xlix. 29——[g]Dan. xi. 19——[h]See Isaiah viii. 7, 8; chap. xlvi. 2; Daniel xi. 22

NOTES ON CHAP. XLVI

Verse 1. *The word of the Lord—against the Gentiles*] This is a general title to the following collection of prophecies, written concerning different nations, which had less or more connexion with the Jews, either as *enemies, neighbours*, or *allies*.

They were not written at the same time; and though some of them bear dates, yet it would be difficult to give them any chronological arrangement. *Dahler's* mode of ascertaining the times of their delivery may be seen in the table in the *introduction*.

Verse 2. *Pharaoh-necho*] This was the person who defeated the army of Josiah, in which engagement Josiah received a mortal wound, of which he died, greatly regretted, soon after at *Megiddo*. After this victory, he defeated the Babylonians, and took Carchemish; and, having fortified it, returned to his own country. *Nabopolassar* sent his son *Nebuchadnezzar* with an army against him, defeated him with immense slaughter near the river Euphrates, retook *Carchemish*, and subdued all the revolted provinces, according to the following prophecies.

Verse 3. *Order ye the buckler*] This is the call to the general armament of the people against the Chaldeans.

Verse 4. *Furbish the spears*] Cleanse, brighten, and sharpen them; from the Franco-Gallic *fourbir*, to polish, brighten.

Brigandines.] A coat of mail, especially that which was made *scale fashion;* one plate overlapping the other, like the scales of fish.

Verse 5. *Wherefore have I seen them dismayed*] What! such a numerous, formidable, and well-appointed army panic-struck? So that they have *turned back—fled apace*, and *looked not round;* while their *mighty ones*—their generals and commanders, striving to rally them, are *beaten down*.

Verse 6. *Let not the swift flee away*] Even the swiftest shall not be able to escape.

They shall—fall toward the north] By the *Euphrates*, which was northward of Judea. Here the Egyptian army was routed with great slaughter.

Verse 7. *Who* is *this* that *cometh up as a flood*] The vast concourse of people is here represented as a *river:* for instance, the Jordan, suddenly swollen with the rains in harvest, rolling its waters along, and overflowing the whole country. A fine image to represent the incursions of vast armies carrying all before them. Such was the army of Pharaoh-necho in its march to Carchemish.

Verse 9. *The Ethiopians*] Heb. *Cush, Phut,* and the *Ludim*. This army was composed of many nations. *Cush*, which we translate *Ethiopians*, almost invariably means the *Arabians;* and here, those *Arabs* that bordered on Egypt near the Red Sea. *Phut* probably means the *Libyans;* for *Phut* settled in *Libya*, according

A. M. cir. 3397
B. C. cir. 607
Ol. XLIII. 2
TarquiniiPrisci, R. Roman., cir. annum 10

and let the mighty men come forth; [i]the Ethiopians and [k]the Libyans, that handle the shield; and the Lydians, [l]that handle *and* bend the bow.

10 For this *is* [m]the day of the Lord GOD of hosts, a day of vengeance, that he may avenge him of his adversaries: and [n]the sword shall devour, and it shall be satiate and made drunk with their blood: for the Lord GOD of hosts [o]hath a sacrifice in the north country by the river Euphrates.

11 [p]Go up into Gilead, and take balm, [q]O virgin, the daughter of Egypt: in vain shalt thou use many medicines; *for* [r]thou [s]shalt not be cured.

12 The nations have heard of thy shame, and thy cry hath filled the land: for the mighty man hath stumbled against the mighty, *and* they are fallen both together.

13 The word that the LORD spake to Jeremiah the prophet, how Nebuchadrezzar king of Babylon should come *and* [t]smite the land of Egypt.

A. M. cir. 3397
B. C. cir. 607
Ol. XLIII. 2
TarquiniiPrisci, R. Roman., cir. annum 10

14 Declare ye in Egypt, and publish in Migdol, and publish in Noph and in Tahpanhes: say ye, [u]Stand fast, and prepare thee; for [v]the sword shall devour round about thee.

15 Why are thy valiant *men* swept away? they stood not, because the LORD did drive them.

16 He [w]made many to fall, yea, [x]one fell upon another: and they said, Arise, and let us go again to our own people, and to the land of our nativity, from the oppressing sword.

17 They did cry there, Pharaoh king of Egypt *is but* a noise; he hath passed the time appointed.

18 *As* I live, saith the King, [y]whose name *is* the LORD of hosts, Surely as Tabor *is* among the mountains, and as Carmel by the sea, *so* shall he come.

19 O [z]thou daughter dwelling in Egypt, [a]furnish thyself [b]to go into captivity: for

[i]Heb. *Cush*——[k]Heb. *Put*——[l]Isa. lxvi. 19——[m]Isa. xiii. 6; Joel i. 15; ii. 1——[n]Deut. xxxii. 42; Isa. xxxiv. 6 [o]Isa. xxxiv. 6; Zeph. i. 7; see Ezek. xxxix. 17——[p]Chap. viii. 22; li. 8——[q]Isa. xlvii. 1——[r]Heb. *no cure* shall be *unto thee*——[s]Ezek. xxx. 21

[t]Isa. xix. 1; chap. xliii. 10, 11; Ezek. xxix., xxx., xxxii. [u]Ver. 3, 4——[v]Ver. 10——[w]Heb. *multiplied the faller* [x]Lev. xxvi. 37——[y]Isa. xlvii. 4; xlviii. 2; chap. xlviii. 15 [z]See chap. xlviii. 18——[a]Heb. *make thee instruments of captivity*——[b]Isa. xx. 4

to Josephus. *Phut* and *Cush* were two of the sons of *Ham*, and brothers to *Mitsraim*, the father of the Egyptians, Gen. x. 6; and the *Ludim* were descended from *Mitsraim;* see Gen. x. 13. *Bochart* contends that the *Ludim* were *Ethiopians*, and that they were famous for the *use of the bow*. *Phaleg*, lib. iv. 26.

Verse 10. *For this* is *the day of the Lord God of hosts*] The prophet represents this as a *mighty sacrifice*, where innumerable victims were slain.

Verse 11. *Go up into Gilead, and take balm*] An irony. Egypt is so completely enfeebled by this overthrow, that her political wound is utterly incurable. This figure is used with the more propriety here, as the Egyptians have been celebrated from the remotest antiquity for their *knowledge of medicine*.

Verse 12. *The nations have heard of thy shame*] Of thy disgrace, by this prodigious slaughter of thy troops.

Verse 13. *How Nebuchadrezzar—should come* and *smite the land of Egypt*.] See on chap. xliv. This was after Amasis had driven Pharaoh-necho into Upper Egypt. See chap. xliv. 30.

Verse 14. *Migdol*] Magdolum, a city of Lower Egypt. *Noph*, Memphis. *Tahpanhes*, Daphne. See before, chap. xliv. 1.

Round about thee.] The Phœnicians, Philistines, Ammonites, Moabites, and Edomites, all prostrated by the arms of the Chaldeans.

Verse 15. *They stood not, because the Lord did drive them.*] The Lord panic-struck them, and *drove* them back.

Verse 16. *One fell upon another*] In their terror and confusion ranks fell on ranks, and overturned each other.

Let us go again to our own people] Let us flee to our own country with all possible speed. These were the auxiliaries.

Verse 17. *They did cry there*] Dr. *Blayney* translates this cry thus:—

——— "O Pharaoh, king of Egypt,
A tumult hath frustrated the appointed meeting."

These allies sent their excuse to Pharaoh, that the disasters they had met with had prevented them from joining him as they had intended.

Verse 18. *As Tabor is among the mountains*] This mountain is situated in the plain of Esdraelon in Galilee, on the confines of the tribes of Zebulun and Issachar, Josh. xix. 22. It stood by itself, separated from all the other mountains by deep valleys, and is the highest of the whole.

And as Carmel by the sea] Carmel is a mountain on the coast of the Mediterranean Sea, on the southern frontier of the tribe of Asher. Were the Egyptians as distinguished for valour and strength as the mountains Tabor and Carmel are for height among the other mountains in their vicinity, they should not be able to stand the shock of the Chaldean army.

Verse 19. *Furnish thyself to go into captivity*] The thing is unavoidable; prepare for this calamity.

A. M. cir. 3398
B. C. cir. 606
Ol. XLIII. 3
TarquiniiPrisci,
R. Roman.,
cir. annum 11

Noph shall be waste and desolate
without an inhabitant.
20 Egypt *is like* a very fair
[c]heifer, *but* destruction cometh;
it cometh [d]out of the north.
21 Also her hired men *are* in the midst of
her like [e]fatted bullocks; for they also are
turned back, *and* are fled away together: they
did not stand, because [f]the day of their calamity
was come upon them, *and* the time of
their visitation.
22 [g]The voice thereof shall go like a serpent;
for they shall march with an army, and
come against her with axes, as hewers of wood.
23 They shall [h]cut down her forest, saith
the LORD, though it cannot be searched; because
they are more than [i]the grasshoppers,
and *are* innumerable.
24 The daughter of Egypt shall be confounded:
she shall be delivered into the hand
of [k]the people of the north.
25 The LORD of hosts, the God of Israel,
saith; Behold, I will punish the [l]multitude[m]
of [n]No, and Pharaoh, and Egypt,
[o]with their gods, and their kings;
even Pharaoh, and *all* them that
trust in him:

A. M. cir. 3398
B. C. cir. 606
Ol. XLIII. 3
TarquiniiPrisci,
R. Roman.,
cir. annum 11

26 [p]And I will deliver them into the hand
of those that seek their lives, and into the hand
of Nebuchadrezzar king of Babylon, and into
the hand of his servants: and [q]afterward it
shall be inhabited, as in the days of old, saith
the LORD.
27 [r]But fear not thou, O my servant Jacob,
and be not dismayed, O Israel; for, behold, I
will save thee from afar off, and thy seed from
the land of their captivity; and Jacob shall
return, and be in rest and at ease, and none
shall make *him* afraid.
28 Fear thou not, O Jacob my servant, saith
the LORD: for I *am* with thee; for I will
make a full end of all the nations whither
I have driven thee: but I will not make
[s]a full end of thee, but correct thee in measure,
yet will I [t]not leave thee wholly unpunished.

---

[c]So Hos. x. 11——[d]Ch. i. 14; xlvii. 2; ver. 6, 10 [e]Heb. *bullocks of the stall*——[f]Psa. xxxvii. 13; ch. l. 27 [g]See Isa. xxix. 4——[h]Isa. x. 34——[i]Judg. vi. 5——[k]Ch. i. 15——[l]Or, *nourisher*——[m]Heb. *Amon*——[n]Ezek. xxx. 14, 15, 16; Nah. iii. 8——[o]Ch. xliii. 12, 13; Ezek. xxx. 13 [p]Ch. xliv. 30; Ezek. xxxii. 11——[q]Ezek. xxix. 11, 13, 14 [r]Isa. xli. 13, 14; xliii. 5; xliv. 2; ch. xxx. 10, 11——[s]Ch. x. 24; xxx. 11——[t]Or, *not utterly cut thee off*

Verse 20. *Egypt* is like *a very fair heifer*] Fruitful and useful; but destruction cometh out of the north, from Chaldea. It may be that there is an allusion here to *Isis*, worshipped in Egypt under the form of a beautiful cow.

Verse 21. *Are fled away together*] Perhaps there is a reference here to the case of a cow stung with gnats. She runs hither and thither, not knowing where to go; so shall it be with this scattered people.

Verse 22. *The voice—shall go like a serpent*] See Isa. xxix. 4, and the note there.

Verse 23. *They shall cut down her forest*] Supposed to mean her cities, of which Egypt had no fewer than *one thousand* and *twenty*.

Verse 24. *The hand of the people of the north*] The Chaldeans.

Verse 25. *The multitude of No*] אמון מנא *Amon minno*, the Amon of No, called by the Greeks Διοσπολις, or *Jupiter's city*. It was the famous *Thebes*, celebrated anciently for its hundred gates. *Amon* was the name by which the Egyptians called Jupiter, who had a famous temple at Thebes.

The word Pharaoh is twice repeated here; and Dr. *Dahler* thinks that one may design *Pharaoh Hophrah*, and the other *Amasis*, the new king.

Verse 26. *Afterward it shall be inhabited*] That is, within *forty years*, as Ezekiel had predicted, chap. xxix. 13.

Verse 27. *Fear not—my servant Jacob*] In the midst of wrath God remembers mercy. Though Judah shall be destroyed, Jerusalem taken, the temple burnt to the ground, and the people carried into captivity, yet the *nation* shall not be destroyed. A seed shall be preserved, out of which the nation shall revive.

Verse 28. *I will make a full end of all the nations whither I have driven thee; but I will not make a full end of thee*] The Jews still remain as a *distinct people*, while the *Assyrians*, *Chaldeans*, *Egyptians*, &c., are no more!

ON this subject, I cannot withhold from my readers the following very judicious remarks of Bp. *Newton*, in his Dissertations on the Prophecies.

"The preservation of the Jews through so many ages, and the total destruction of their enemies, are wonderful events; and are made still more wonderful by being signified beforehand by the spirit of prophecy, as particularly in the passage before us. Their preservation is really one of the most illustrious acts of Divine Providence. They are dispersed among all nations, yet not confounded with any. The drops of rain which fall, nay the great rivers which flow into the ocean, are soon mingled with and lost in that immense body of waters. And the same, in all human probability, would have been the fate of the Jews; they would have been mingled and lost in the common mass of mankind: but, on the contrary, they flow into all parts of the world, mix with all nations, and yet keep separate from all. They still live as a distinct people; and yet they nowhere live according to their own laws, nowhere elect their own magistrates, nowhere enjoy the full exercise of their religion. Their solemn feasts and sacrifices are limited to one certain place; and that hath been now for many ages in the hands of strangers and aliens, who will not suffer them to come thither. No people have continued unmixed so long as they have done; not only of those who have sent colonies into foreign countries, but even of those who have remained in their own country. The northern nations have come in swarms into the more southern parts of Europe: but where are they now to be discerned and distinguished? The Gauls went forth in great bodies to seek their fortune in foreign parts; but what traces or footsteps of them are now remaining any where? In France, who can separate the race of the ancient Gauls from the various other people who from time to time have settled there? In Spain, who can distinguish between the first possessors, the Spaniards, and the Goths and Moors, who conquered and kept possession of the country for some ages? In England, who can pretend to say certainly which families are derived from the ancient Britons, and which from the Romans, Saxons, Danes, and Normans? The most ancient and honourable pedigrees can be traced up only to a certain period; and beyond that there is nothing but conjecture and uncertainty, obscurity and ignorance. But the Jews can go up higher than any nation; they can even deduce their pedigree from the beginning of the world. They may not know from what particular tribe or family they are descended; but they know certainly that they all sprang from the stock of Abraham. And yet the contempt with which they have been treated, and the hardships they have undergone in almost all countries, should, one would think, have made them desirous to forget or renounce their original: but they profess it; they glory in it; and after so many wars, massacres, and persecutions, they still subsist; they are still very numerous. And what but a supernatural power could have preserved them in such a manner as no other nation upon earth has been preserved? Nor is the providence of God less remarkable in the destruction of their enemies, than in their own preservation. For, from the beginning, who have been the great enemies and oppressors of the Jewish nation, removed them from their own land, and compelled them into captivity and slavery? The Egyptians afflicted them much, and detained them in bondage several years. The Assyrians carried away captive the ten tribes of Israel; and the Babylonians, afterwards, the two remaining tribes of Judah and Benjamin. The Syro-Macedonians, especially Antiochus Epiphanes, cruelly persecuted them; and the Romans utterly dissolved the Jewish state, and dispersed the people so as that they have never been able to recover their city and country again. And where are now those great and famous monarchies, which in their turn subdued and oppressed the people of God? Are they not vanished as a dream; and not only their power, but their very names, lost in the earth? The Egyptians, Assyrians, and Babylonians were overthrown and entirely subjugated by the Persians; and the Persians, it is remarkable, were the restorers of the Jews as well as the destroyers of their enemies. The Syro-Macedonians were swallowed up by the Romans; and the Roman empire, great and powerful as it was, was broken into pieces by the incursions of the northern nations; while the Jews are subsisting as a distinct people at this day. And what a wonder of providence is it, that the vanquished should so many ages survive the victors; and the former be spread all over the world, while the latter are no more! Nay, not only nations have been punished for their cruelties to the Jews, but Divine vengeance has pursued even single persons who have been their persecutors and oppressors. The first-born of Pharaoh was destroyed; and he himself, with his host, drowned in the sea. Nebuchadnezzar was stricken with madness, and the crown was transferred from his family to strangers. Antiochus Epiphanes and Herod died in great agonies, with ulcers and vermin issuing from them. Flaccus, governor of Egypt, who barbarously plundered and oppressed the Jews of Alexandria, was afterwards banished and slain; and Caligula, who persecuted the Jews for refusing to do Divine honours to his statue, was murdered in the flower of his age, after a short and wicked reign. But where are now,—since they have absolutely rejected the Gospel, and been no longer the peculiar people of God,—where are now such visible manifestations of a Divine interposition in their favour? The Jews would do well to consider this point; for, rightly considered, it may be an effectual means of opening their eyes, and of turning them to Christ our Saviour." See Bp. *Newton* on the prophecies, dissert. viii. sect. 2. And see the notes on Ezekiel, where the calamities of these miserable people are largely detailed.

CHAPTER XLVII

Among the nations doomed to suffer from the hostilities of Nebuchadnezzar are the Philistines, (see chap. xxv. 20.) *And the calamities predicted in this chapter befell them probably during the long siege of Tyre, when their country was desolated to prevent their giving Tyre or Sidon any assistance,* 1–5. *The whole of this chapter is remarkably elegant. The address to the sword of Jehovah, at the close of it, is particularly a very beautiful and bold personification,* 6, 7.

A. M. cir. 3387
B. C. cir. 617
Ol. cir. XL. 4
Anci Martii,
R. Roman.,
cir. annum 24

THE word of the LORD that
came to Jeremiah the pro-
phet [a]against the Philistines, [b]be-
fore that Pharaoh smote [c]Gaza.
2 Thus saith the LORD; Behold, [d]waters rise
up [e]out of the north, and shall be an overflowing flood, and shall overflow the land, and [f]all
that is therein; the city and them that dwell
therein: then the men shall cry, and all the
inhabitants of the land shall howl.
3 At the [g]noise of the stamping of the hoofs
of his strong *horses, at* the rushing of his
chariots, *and at* the rumbling of his wheels,
the fathers shall not look back to *their* children for feebleness of hands;

[a]Chap. xxv. 20; Ezek. xxv. 15, 16; Zeph. ii. 4, 5 —— [b]Amos i. 6, 7, 8 —— [c]Heb. *Azzah* —— [d]Isa. viii. 7; chap. xlvi. 7, 8 —— [e]Ch. i. 14; xlvi. 20 —— [f]Heb. *the fulness thereof* —— [g]Ch. viii. 16; Nah. iii. 2 —— [h]Ch. xxv. 2 —— [i]Ezek. xxv. 16; Amos i. 8; ix. 7

A. M. cir. 3387
B. C. cir. 617
Ol. cir. XL. 4
Anci Martii,
R. Roman.,
cir. annum 24

4 Because of the day that cometh to spoil all the Philistines,
and to cut off from [h]Tyrus and
Zidon every helper that remain-
eth: for the LORD will spoil the Philistines,
[i]the remnant of [k]the country of [l]Caphtor.
5 [m]Baldness is come upon Gaza; [n]Ashkelon
is cut off *with* the remnant of their valley:
how long wilt thou [o]cut thyself?
6 O thou [p]sword of the LORD, how long *will
it be* ere thou be quiet? [q]put up thyself into
thy scabbard, rest, and be still.
7 [r]How can it be quiet, seeing the LORD hath
[s]given it a charge against Ashkelon, and against
the sea shore? there hath he [t]appointed it.

[k]Heb. *the isle* —— [l]Gen. x. 14 —— [m]Amos i. 7; Mic. i. 16; Zeph. ii. 4, 7; Zech. ix. 5 —— [n]Ch. xxv. 20 —— [o]Ch. xvi. 6; xli. 5; xlviii. 37 —— [p]Deut. xxxii. 41; Ezek. xxi. 3, 4, 5 —— [q]Heb. *gather thyself* —— [r]Heb. *how canst thou?* —— [s]Ezek. xiv. 17 —— [t]Mic. vi. 9

NOTES ON CHAP. XLVII

Verse 1. *The word of the Lord—against the Philistines*] The *date* of this prophecy cannot be easily ascertained. Dr. *Blayney* thinks it was delivered about the *fourth year* of *Zedekiah*, while *Dahler* assigns it some time in the reign of *Josiah.*

Before that Pharaoh smote Gaza.] We have no historical relation of any Egyptian king smiting Gaza. It was no doubt smitten by some of them; but *when*, and by *whom*, does not appear either from sacred or profane history.

Verse 2. *Waters rise up out of the north*] *Waters* is a common prophetic image for a *multitude of people.* The *north* here, as in other places of this prophecy, means *Chaldea.*

Verse 3. *The stamping of the hoofs*] At the *galloping sound,*—

Quadrupedante putrem sonitu quatit ungula campum,

is a line of *Virgil*, (*Æn.* viii. 596,) much celebrated; and quoted here by *Blayney*, where the galloping sound of the horses' hoofs is *heard.* In the *stamping* of the *horses*, the *rushing* of the *chariots*, and the *rumbling* of the *wheels*, our translators intended to convey the *sense* by the *sound* of the words; and they have not been unsuccessful. Their translation of the original is at the same time sufficiently literal.

The fathers shall not look back] Though their children are left behind, they have neither *strength* nor *courage* to go back to bring them off.

Verse 4. *To spoil all the Philistines*] These people, of whom there were *five seignories*, occupied the coast of the Mediterranean Sea, to the south of the Phœnicians.

Tyrus and Zidon] Places sufficiently remarkable both in the Old and New Testament, and in profane history. They belonged to the Phœnicians; and at this time were depending on the succour of their allies, the Philistines. But their expectation was cut off.

The remnant of the country of Caphtor.] *Crete*, or *Cyprus.* Some think it was a district along the coast of the Mediterranean, belonging to the Philistines; others, that the *Cappadocians* are meant.

Verse 5. *Baldness is come upon Gaza*] They have *cut off their hair* in token of deep sorrow and distress.

Ashkelon is cut off] Or *put to silence;* another mark of the deepest sorrow. Ashkelon was one of the *five seignories* of the Philistines, *Gaza* was another.

The remnant of their valley] Or *plain;* for the whole land of the Philistines was a *vast plain*, which extended along the coast of the Mediterranean Sea from Phœnicia to the frontiers of Egypt. The whole of this plain, the territory of the Philistines, shall be desolated.

Verse 6. *O thou sword of the Lord*] This is a most grand prosopopœia—a dialogue between the sword of the Lord and the prophet. Nothing can be imagined more sublime.

Put up thyself into thy scabbard, rest, and be still.] Shed no more blood, destroy no more lives, erase no more cities, desolate no more countries. *Rest:*—hast thou not been long enough at this work of judgment? *O be still:* —let wars and desolations cease for ever.

Verse 7. *How can it be quiet*] This is the *answer* of the *Sword.* I am the officer of God's judgments, and he has given me a commission against Ashkelon, and against the sea shore; all the coast where the Philistines have their territories. The measure of their iniquities is full; and these God hath appointed this sword to ravage. The Philistines were ever the implacable enemies of the Jews, and the basest and worst of all idolaters. On these accounts the sword of the Lord had its commission against them; and it did its office most fearfully and effectually by the hand of the Chaldeans.

CHAPTER XLVIII

The following prophecy concerning the Moabites is supposed to have had its accomplishment during the long siege of Tyre in the reign of Nebuchadnezzar. The whole of this chapter is poetry of the first order. The distress of the cities of Moab, with which it opens, is finely described. The cries of one ruined city resound to those of another, 1–3. *The doleful helpless cry of the children is heard,* 4; *the highways, on either hand, resound with the voice of weeping,* 5; *and the few that remain resemble a blasted tree in the wide howling waste,* 6. *Chemosh, the chief god of the Moabites, and the capital figure in the triumph, is represented as carried off in chains, with all his trumpery of priests and officers,* 7. *The desolation of the country shall be so general and sudden that, by a strong figure, it is intimated that there shall be no possibility of escape, except it be in the speediest flight,* 8, 9. *And some idea may be formed of the dreadful wickedness of this people from the consideration that the prophet, under the immediate inspiration of the Almighty, pronounces a curse on those who do the work of the Lord negligently, in not proceeding to their utter extermination,* 10. *The subject is then diversified by an elegant and well-supported comparison, importing that the Moabites increased in insolence and pride in proportion to the duration of their prosperity,* 11; *but this prosperity is declared to be nearly at an end; the destroyer is already commissioned against Moab, and his neighbours called to sing the usual lamentation at his funeral,* 13–18. *The prophet then represents some of the women of Aroer and Ammon, (the extreme borders of Moab,) standing in the highways, and asking the fugitives of Moab, What intelligence? They inform him of the complete discomfiture of Moab,* 19–24, *and of the total annihilation of its political existence,* 25. *The Divine judgments about to fall upon Moab are farther represented under the expressive metaphor of a cup of intoxicating liquor, by which he should become an object of derision because of his intolerable pride, his magnifying himself against Jehovah, and his great contempt for the children of Israel in the day of their calamity,* 26, 27. *The prophet then points out the great distress of Moab by a variety of striking figures, viz., by the failure of the customary rejoicings at the end of harvest, by the mournful sort of music used at funerals, by the signs which were expressive among the ancients of deep mourning, as shaving the head, clipping the beard, cutting the flesh, and wearing sackcloth; and by the methods of catching wild beasts in toils, and by the terror and pitfall,* 28–46. *In the close of the chapter it is intimated that a remnant shall be preserved from this general calamity whose descendants shall be prosperous in the latter days,* 47.

A. M. cir. 3420
B. C. cir. 584
Ol. XLIX. 1
TarquiniiPrisci,
R. Roman.,
cir. annum 33

AGAINST [a]Moab thus saith the LORD of hosts, the God of Israel; Wo unto [b]Nebo! for it is spoiled: [c]Kiriathaim is confounded *and* taken: [d]Misgab is confounded and dismayed.

2 [e]*There shall be* no more praise of Moab: in [f]Heshbon they have devised evil against it; come, and let us cut it off from *being* a nation. Also thou shalt [g]be cut down, O Madmen; the sword shall [h]pursue thee.

3 [i]A voice of crying *shall be* from Horonaim, spoiling and great destruction.

A. M. cir. 3420
B. C. cir. 584
Ol. XLIX. 1
TarquiniiPrisci,
R. Roman.,
cir. annum 33

4 Moab is destroyed; her little ones have caused a cry to be heard.

5 [k]For in the going up of Luhith [l]continual weeping shall go up; for in the going down of Horonaim the enemies have heard a cry of destruction.

6 [m]Flee, save your lives, and be like [n]the [o]heath in the wilderness.

[a]Isa. xv., xvi.; chap. xxv. 21; xxvii. 3; Ezek. xxv. 9; Amos ii. 1, 2——[b]Num. xxxii. 38; xxxiii. 47; Isa. xv. 2——[c]Num. xxxii. 37——[d]Or, *The high place*——[e]Isa. xvi. 14——[f]Isa. xv. 4——[g]Or, *be brought to silence;* Isa. xv. 1——[h]Heb. *go after thee*——[i]Ver. 5——[k]Isa. xv. 5——[l]Heb. *weeping with weeping*——[m]Chap. li. 6——[n]Or, *a naked tree*——[o]Ch. xvii. 6

NOTES ON CHAP. XLVIII

Verse 1. *Against Moab*] This was delivered some time after the destruction of Jerusalem. The Moabites were in the neighbourhood of the Ammonites, and whatever evils fell on the one would naturally involve the other. See Isa. xv. and xvi. on this same subject.

Wo unto Nebo! for it is spoiled] This was a city in the tribe of Reuben, afterwards possessed by the Moabites. It probably had its name from *Nebo*, one of the principal idols of the Moabites.

Kiriathaim] Another city of the Moabites.

Misgab is confounded] There is no place of this name known; and therefore several learned men translate המשגב *hammisgab*, literally, *The high tower*, or *fortress*, which may apply to *Kiriathaim*, or any other high and well-fortified place.

Verse 2. *No more praise of Moab*] "The glory of Moab, that it had never been conquered," (*Dahler*,) is now at an end. Dr. *Blayney* translates:—

"Moab shall have no more glorying in Heshbon;
They have devised evil against her (saying.)"

And this most certainly is the best translation of the original. He has marked also a double *paronomasia* in this and the next verse, a figure in which the prophets delight; בחשבון חשבו *becheshbon chashebu*, "in Cheshbon they have devised," and מדמן תדמי *madmen tiddommi*, "Madmena, thou shalt be dumb."

Verse 3. *Horonaim*] Another city of Moab, near to Luhith. At this latter place the *hill country* of Moab commenced. "It is a place," says *Dahler*, "situated upon a height between *Areopolis* and *Zoar*."

A. M. cir. 3420 B. C. cir. 584 Ol. XLIX. 1 TarquiniiPrisci, R. Roman., cir. annum 33

7 For because thou hast trusted in thy works and in thy treasures, thou shalt also be taken: and [p]Chemosh shall go forth into captivity *with* his [q]priests and his princes together.

8 And [r]the spoiler shall come upon every city, and no city shall escape: the valley also shall perish, and the plain shall be destroyed, as the LORD hath spoken.

9 [s]Give wings unto Moab, that it may flee and get away: for the cities thereof shall be desolate, without any to dwell therein.

10 [t]Cursed *be* he that doeth the work of the LORD [u]deceitfully, and cursed *be* he that keepeth back his sword from blood.

11 Moab hath been at ease from his youth, and he [v]hath settled on his lees, and hath not been emptied from vessel to vessel, neither hath he gone into captivity: therefore his taste [w]remained in him, and his scent is not changed.

12 Therefore, behold, the days come, saith the LORD, that I will send unto him wanderers, that shall cause him to wander, and shall empty his vessels, and break their bottles.

A. M. cir. 3420 B. C. cir. 584 Ol. XLIX. 1 TarquiniiPrisci, R. Roman., cir. annum 33

13 And Moab shall be ashamed of [x]Chemosh, as the house of Israel [y]was ashamed of [z]Beth-el their confidence.

14 How say ye, [a]We *are* mighty and strong men for the war?

15 [b]Moab is spoiled, and gone up *out of* her cities, and [c]his chosen young men are [d]gone down to the slaughter, saith [e]the King, whose name *is* the LORD of hosts.

16 The calamity of Moab *is* near to come, and his affliction hasteth fast.

17 All ye that are about him, bemoan him; and all ye that know his name, say, [f]How is the strong staff broken, *and* the beautiful rod!

18 [g]Thou daughter that dost inhabit [h]Dibon, come down from *thy* glory, and sit in thirst; for [i]the spoiler of Moab shall come upon thee, *and* he shall destroy thy strong holds.

[p]Num. xxi. 29; Judg. xi. 24; see Isa. xlvi. 1, 2; chap. xliii. 12——[q]Chap. xlix. 3——[r]Chap. vi. 26; ver. 18——[s]Psa. lv. 6; ver. 28——[t]See Judg. v. 23; 1 Sam. xv. 3, 9; 1 Kings xx. 42——[u]Or, *negligently*——[v]Zeph. i. 12——[w]Heb. *stood*

[x]Judg. xi. 24; 1 Kings xi. 7——[y]Hos. x. 6——[z]1 Kings xii. 29——[a]Isa. xvi. 6——[b]Ver. 8, 9, 18——[c]Heb. *the choice of*——[d]Chap. l. 27——[e]Chap. xlvi. 18; li. 57——[f]See Isa. ix. 4; xiv. 4, 5——[g]Isa. xlvii. 1; chap. xlvi. 19——[h]Num. xxi. 30; Isa. xv. 2——[i]Ver. 8

Verse 6. *Flee, save your lives*] The enemy is in full pursuit of you.

Be like the heath] כערוער *caaroer*, "like Aroer;" which some take for a *city*, others for a *blasted* or *withered tree*. It is supposed that a place of this name lay towards the north, in the land of the Ammonites, on a branch of the river Jabbok; surrounded by *deserts*. Save yourselves by getting into the wilderness, where the pursuing foe will scarcely think it worth his while to follow you, as the wilderness itself must soon destroy you.

Verse 7. *Chemosh shall go forth into captivity*] The grand national idol of the Moabites, Num. xxi. 29; Judg. xi. 24. Ancient idolaters used to take their gods with them to the field of battle. This was probably in imitation of the Israelites, who took the *ark* with them in such cases.

Verse 9. *Give wings unto Moab*] There is no hope in resistance, and to escape requires the *speediest* flight. I cannot conceive how *Dahler* came to translate thus: Tirez Moab par les chevaux, "Drag Moab away by the hair of the head."

Verse 10. *Cursed* be *he that doeth the work of the Lord deceitfully*] Moab is doomed to destruction, and the Lord pronounces a curse on their enemies if they do not proceed to utter extirpation. God is the Author of life, and has a sovereign right to dispose of it as he pleases; and these had forfeited theirs long ago by their idolatry and other crimes.

Verse 11. *Moab hath been at ease*] The metaphor here is taken from the mode of preserving wines. They let them rest upon their lees for a considerable time, as this improves them both in strength and flavour; and when this is sufficiently done, they rack, or pour them off into other vessels. Moab had been very little molested by war since he was a nation; he had never gone out of his own land. Though some had been carried away by Shalmaneser forty years before this, he has had neither wars nor captivity.

Therefore his taste remained in him] Still carrying on the allusion to the curing of wines; by resting long upon the *lees*, the *taste* and *smell* are both improved. See the note on Isa. xxv. 6.

Verse 12. *I will send unto him wanderers, that shall cause him to wander*] Dr. *Blayney* renders צעים *tsaim, tilters;* those who elevate one end of the wine cask when nearly run out, that the remains of the liquor may be the more effectually drawn off at the cock. And this seems to be well supported by the following words,—

And shall empty his vessels] I will send such as will carry the whole nation into captivity.

Verse 13. *Beth-el their confidence.*] Alluding to the golden calves which Jeroboam had there set up, and commanded all the Israelites to worship.

Verse 17. *How is the strong staff broken*] The *sceptre*. The sovereignty of Moab is destroyed.

Verse 18. *That dost inhabit Dibon*] This was anciently a city of the Reubenites, afterwards inhabited by the Moabites, about two leagues north of the river Arnon, and about six to the east of the Dead Sea.—*Dahler*.

A. M. cir. 3420
B. C. cir. 584
Ol. XLIX. 1
TarquiniiPrisci,
R. Roman.,
cir. annum 33

19 O [k]inhabitant of [l]Aroer,
[m]stand by the way, and espy;
ask him that fleeth, and her that
escapeth, *and* say, What is done?
20 Moab is confounded; for it is broken
down: [n]howl and cry; tell ye it in [o]Arnon,
that Moab is spoiled,
21 And judgment is come upon [p]the plain
country; upon Holon, and upon Jahazah, and
upon Mephaath,
22 And upon Dibon, and upon Nebo, and
upon Beth-diblathaim,
23 And upon Kiriathaim, and upon Beth-ga-
mul, and upon Beth-meon,
24 And upon [q]Kerioth, and upon Bozrah,
and upon all the cities of the land of Moab,
far or near.
25 [r]The horn of Moab is cut off, and his
[s]arm is broken, saith the LORD.
26 [t]Make ye him drunken: for he magnified
himself against the LORD: Moab also shall wallow in his vomit, and he also shall be in derision.
27 For [u]was not Israel a derision unto thee?
[v]was he found among thieves? for since thou
spakest of him, thou [w]skippedst for joy.
28 O ye that dwell in Moab, leave the
cities, and [x]dwell in the rock, and be like
[y]the dove *that* maketh her nest in the sides
of the hole's mouth.
29 We have heard the [z]pride of Moab, (he
is exceeding proud,) his loftiness, and his
arrogancy, and his pride, and the haughtiness of his heart.
30 I know his wrath, saith
the LORD; but *it shall* not *be* so;
[a]his [b]lies shall not so effect *it*.
31 Therefore [c]will I howl for
Moab, and I will cry out for all Moab; *mine
heart* shall mourn for the men of Kir-heres.
32 [d]O vine of Sibmah, I will weep for thee
with the weeping of Jazer: thy plants are
gone over the sea, they reach *even* to the sea
of Jazer: the spoiler is fallen upon thy summer fruits and upon thy vintage.
33 And [e]joy and gladness is taken from the
plentiful field, and from the land of Moab;
and I have caused wine to fail from the wine-
presses: none shall tread with shouting; *their*
shouting *shall be* no shouting.
34 [f]From the cry of Heshbon *even* unto
Elealeh, *and even* unto Jahaz, have they
uttered their voice, [g]from Zoar *even* unto Horonaim, *as* a heifer of three years old: for the
waters also of Nimrim shall be [h]desolate.
35 Moreover I will cause to cease in Moab,
saith the LORD, [i]him that offereth in the high
places, and him that burneth incense to his gods.
36 Therefore [k]mine heart shall sound for
Moab like pipes, and mine heart shall sound
like pipes for the men of Kir-heres: because
[l]the riches *that* he hath gotten are perished.
37 For [m]every head *shall be* bald, and every
beard [n]clipped: upon all the hands *shall be*
cuttings, and [o]upon the loins sackcloth.
38 *There shall be* lamentation generally
upon all the housetops of Moab, and in the

A. M. cir. 3420
B. C. cir. 584
Ol. XLIX. 1
TarquiniiPrisci
R. Roman.,
cir. annum 33

[k]Heb. *inhabitress*——[l]Deut. ii. 36——[m]1 Sam. iv. 13, 16——[n]Isa. xiv. 7——[o]See Num. xxi. 13——[p]Ver. 8——[q]Ver. 41; Amos ii. 2——[r]Psa. lxxv. 10——[s]See Ezek. xxx. 21——[t]Chap. xxv. 15, 27——[u]Zeph. ii. 8——[v]See chap. ii. 26——[w]Or, *movedst thyself*——[x]Psa. lv. 6, 7; ver. 9——[y]Cant. ii. 14——[z]Isa. xvi. 6, &c.——[a]Isa. xvi. 6; chap. l. 36

[b]Or, *those on whom he stayeth* (Heb. *his bars) do not right*——[c]Isa. xv. 2; xvi. 7, 11——[d]Isa. xvi. 8, 9——[e]Isa. xvi. 10; Joel i. 12——[f]Isa. xv. 4, 5, 6——[g]Isa. xv. 5, 6; ver. 5——[h]Heb. *desolations*——[i]Isa. xv. 2; xvi. 12——[k]Isa. xv. 5; xvi. 11——[l]Isa. xv. 7——[m]Isa. xv. 2, 3; chapter xlvii. 5——[n]Hebrew, *diminished*——[o]Genesis xxxvii. 34

Verse 19. *O inhabitant of Aroer*] See the note on ver. 6. This place, being at a greater distance, is counselled to watch for its own safety, and inquire of every passenger, *What is done?* that it may know when to pack up and be gone.

Verse 20. *Tell ye it in Arnon*] Apprize the inhabitants there that the territories of Moab are invaded, and the country about to be destroyed, that they may provide for their own safety.

Verse 21. *Upon Holon, &c.*] All these were cities of the Moabites, but several of them are mentioned in no other place.

Verse 25. *The horn of Moab is cut off, and his arm is broken*] His political and physical powers are no more.

Verse 27. *Was not Israel a derision unto thee?*] Didst thou not mock my people, and say their God was no better than the gods of other nations? See Ezek. xxv. 8.

Was he found among thieves?] Did the Israelites come to *rob* and *plunder* you? Why then mock them, and rejoice at their desolation, when their enemies prevailed over them? This the Lord particularly resents.

Verse 28. *Dwell in the rock*] Go to the most inaccessible places in the mountains.

The hole's mouth.] And into the most secret caves and holes of the earth.

Verse 29. *The pride of Moab*] See on Isa. xvi. 1.

Verse 32. *O vine of Sibmah*] See on Isa. xvi. 8.

Verse 34. As *a heifer of three years old*] Which runs lowing from place to place in search of her calf, which is lost or taken from her.

Verse 37. *For every head* shall be *bald*]

A. M. cir. 3420
B. C. cir. 584
Ol. XLIX. 1
TarquiniiPrisci,
R. Roman.,
cir. annum 33

streets thereof: for I have broken
Moab like [p]a vessel wherein *is*
no pleasure, saith the LORD.
39 They shall howl, *saying,*
How is it broken down! how hath Moab
turned the [q]back with shame! so shall Moab
be a derision and a dismaying to all them
about him.
40 For thus saith the LORD; Behold, [r]he shall
fly as an eagle, and shall [s]spread his wings
over Moab.
41 [t]Kerioth [u]is taken, and the strong holds
are surprised, and [v]the mighty men's hearts in
Moab at that day shall be as the heart of a
woman in her pangs.
42 And Moab shall be destroyed [w]from
being a people, because he hath magnified
himself against the LORD.
43 [x]Fear, and the pit, and the snare, *shall be*
upon thee, O inhabitant of Moab,
saith the LORD.
44 He that fleeth from the fear
shall fall into the pit; and he that
getteth up out of the pit shall be taken in the
snare: for [y]I will bring upon it, *even* upon
Moab, the year of their visitation, saith the
LORD.
45 They that fled stood under the shadow of
Heshbon because of the force: but [z]a fire shall
come forth out of Heshbon, and a flame from
the midst of Sihon, and [a]shall devour the corner of Moab, and the crown of the head of the
[b]tumultuous ones.
46 [c]Wo be unto thee, O Moab! the people
of Chemosh perisheth: for thy sons are taken
[d]captives, and thy daughters captives.
47 Yet will I bring again the captivity of
Moab [e]in the latter days, saith the LORD.
Thus far *is* the judgment of Moab.

[p]Chap. xxii. 28——[q]Heb. *neck*——[r]Deut. xxviii. 49; chap. xlix. 22; Dan. vii. 4; Hos. viii. 1; Hab. i. 8——[s]Isa. viii. 8——[t]Ver. 24——[u]Or, *The cities*——[v]Isa. xiii. 8; xxi. 3; chap. xxx. 6; xlix. 22, 24; l. 43; li. 30; Mic. iv. 9

[w]Psa. lxxxiii. 4; Isa. vii. 8——[x]Isa. xxiv. 17, 18——[y]See chap. xi. 23——[z]Num. xxi. 28——[a]Num. xxiv. 17——[b]Heb. *children of noise*——[c]Num. xxi. 29——[d]Heb. *in captivity*——[e]Chap. xlix. 6, 39

These, as we have seen before, were signs of the deepest distress and desolation.

Verse 40. *He shall fly as an eagle*] The enemy will pounce upon him, carry him off, and tear him to pieces.

Verse 42. *Moab shall be destroyed from* being *a people*] They shall not have a king or *civil governor:* and I doubt whether there be any evidence that they were ever reinstated in their *national character.* They were captivated by the Chaldeans; and probably many returned with the Jews on the edict of Cyrus: but as to their being an *independent nation* after this, where is the positive proof?

Verse 43. *Fear, and the pit, and the snare*] See the note on Isa. xxiv. 17, 18.

Verse 45. *They that fled stood under the shadow of Heshbon*] Heshbon being a fortified place, they who were worsted in the fight fled to it, and rallied under its walls; but, instead of safety, they found themselves disappointed, betrayed, and ruined. See ver. 2, and the note there.

But a fire shall come forth out of Heshbon] Jeremiah has borrowed this part of his discourse from an ancient poet quoted by Moses, Num. xxi. 28; where see the notes.

The crown of the head] The choicest persons of the whole nation.

Verse 46. *The people of Chemosh*] The Moabites, who worshipped *Chemosh* as their supreme god.

Verse 47. *Will I bring again the captivity of Moab in the latter days*] I have already expressed doubts (see ver. 42) whether the Moabites were ever restored to their national distinction. The expressions in this chapter, relative to their total destruction as a people, are so strong and so frequent, that they leave little room for a limited interpretation. That many of them returned on the edict of Cyrus, by virtue of which the Jews were restored, I doubt not; but neither the *Ammonites, Moabites, Philistines,* nor even the *Jews* themselves, were ever restored to their national consequence. Perhaps the restoration spoken of here, which was to take place in the *latter days,* may mean the conversion of these people, in their existing remnants, to the faith of the Gospel. Several judicious interpreters are of this opinion. The Moabites were partially restored; but never, as far as I have been able to learn, to their national consequence. Their conversion to the Christian faith must be the main end designed by this prophecy.

CHAPTER XLIX

This chapter is a collection of prophecies relating to several nations in the neighbourhood of Judea; and, like those preceding, are supposed to have been fulfilled by the ministry of Nebuchadnezzar during the thirteen years' siege of Tyre. The chapter opens with a prophecy concerning the Ammonites, whose chief city, Rabbah, shall be destroyed; and Malcom, the supreme divinity of the people, with all his retinue of priests and officers, carried into captivity, 1–5. *Promise that the Ammonites shall be restored to their liberty,* 6. *Prophecy against the Edomites, (very like that most dreadful one in the thirty-fourth chapter of Isaiah against the same people,) who shall be utterly exterminated, after the similitude of Sodom and Gomorrah,* 7–22. *Prophecy against Damas-*

cus, 23–27; and against Kedar, 28, 29. Utter desolation of the kingdoms of Hazor foretold, 30–33. The polity of the Elamites shall be completely dissolved, and the people dispersed throughout the nations, 34–38. The Elamites shall be delivered from their captivity in the latter days, 39. It will be proper here to observe that these predictions should not be so explained as if they admitted of merely a private interpretation; for, as Bishop Lowth remarks upon Isaiah's prophecy concerning the Idumeans, "by a figure very common in the prophetical writings, any city or people, remarkably distinguished as enemies of the people and kingdom of God, is put for those enemies in general;" therefore, it is under the Gospel dispensation that these prophecies shall be accomplished to their fullest extent upon all the antichristian nations that have sinned after the similitude *of the ancient enemies of the people of God under the Mosaic economy.*

A. M. cir. 3421 B. C. cir. 583 Ol. XLIX. 2 TarquiniiPrisci, R. Roman., cir. annum 34

[a]CONCERNING [b]the Ammonites, thus saith the LORD; Hath Israel no sons? hath he no heir? why *then* doth [c]their king inherit [d]Gad, and his people dwell in his cities?

2 Therefore, behold, the days come, saith the LORD, that I will cause an alarm of war to be heard in [e]Rabbah of the Ammonites; and it shall be a desolate heap, and her daughters shall be burned with fire: then shall Israel be heir unto them that were his heirs, saith the LORD.

3 Howl, O Heshbon, for Ai is spoiled: cry, ye daughters of Rabbah, [f]gird you with sackcloth; lament, and run to and fro by the hedges; for [g]their king shall go into captivity, *and* his [h]priests and his princes together.

4 Wherefore gloriest thou in the valleys, [i]thy flowing valley, [j]O [k]backsliding daughter? that trusted in her treasures, [l]*saying,* Who shall come unto me?

5 Behold, I will bring a fear upon thee, saith the Lord GOD of hosts, from all those that be about thee; and ye shall be driven out every man right forth; and none shall gather up him that wandereth.

6 And [m]afterward I will bring again the captivity of the children of Ammon, saith the LORD.

A. M. cir. 3417 B. C. cir. 587 Ol. XLVIII. 2 TarquiniiPrisci, R. Roman., cir. annum 30

7 [n]Concerning Edom, thus saith the LORD of hosts; [o]*Is* wisdom no more in Teman? [p]is counsel perished from the prudent? is their wisdom vanished?

8 [q]Flee ye, [r]turn back, dwell deep, O inhabitants of [s]Dedan; for I will bring the cala-

[a]Or, *Against*——[b]Ezek. xxi. 28; xxv. 2; Amos i. 13; Zeph. ii. 8, 9——[c]Or, *Melcom*——[d]Amos i. 13 [e]Ezek. xxv. 5; Amos i. 14——[f]Isa. xxxii. 11; chap. iv. 8; vi. 26——[g]Or, *Melcom;* 1 Kings xi. 5, 33——[h]Chap. xlviii. 7; Amos i. 15

[i]Or, *thy valley floweth away*——[k]Chap. iii. 14; vii. 24 [l]Chap. xxi. 13——[m]So ver. 39; chap. xlviii. 47 [n]Ezek. xxv. 12; Amos i. 11——[o]Obad. 8——[p]See Isa. xix. 11——[q]Ver. 30——[r]Or, *they are turned back* [s]Chap. xxv. 23

NOTES ON CHAP. XLIX

Verse 1. CONCERNING THE AMMONITES] This prophetic discourse was also delivered *after* the capture of Jerusalem.

Hath Israel no sons?—no heir?] The Ammonites, it appears, took advantage of the depressed state of Israel, and invaded their territories in the tribe of Gad, hoping to make them their own for ever. But the prophet intimates that God will preserve the descendants of Israel, and will bring them back to their forfeited inheritances.

Why then *doth their king*] מלכם *Malcom* or *Milcom*, the chief idol of the Ammonites. That the idol *Milcom* is here meant is sufficiently evident from ver. 3, where it is said: "Milcom (not *their king*) shall go into captivity; his PRIESTS and his princes together." *Milcom* is also called *Molech. Malcom* is put here for the *Ammonites*, as the *people of Chemosh* in the preceding chapter are put for the *Moabites* in general.

Verse 3. *Run to and fro by the hedges*] It is supposed that this may refer to the women making lamentations for the dead, that were in general buried by the walls of their *gardens;* but others think that it refers to the *smaller cities* or *villages*, called here the *daughters of Rabbah*, the metropolis; the inhabitants of which are exhorted to seek safety somewhere else, as none can be expected from them, now that the enemy is at hand.

Verse 4. *Wherefore gloriest thou*] Though thy valleys be fruitful, yet glory not in them. Though thou have much political and military power, do not trust in them, nor in the multitude of thy cities; a stronger than thou is coming against thee.

Verse 6. *Afterward I will bring again*] The *Ammonites* are supposed to have returned with the Moabites and Israelites, on permission given by the edict of Cyrus.

Verse 7. CONCERNING EDOM] This is a new and separate discourse.

Teman] A part of Idumea, put here for the whole country.

Verse 8. *Dwell deep*] An allusion to the custom of the Arabs, who, when about to be attacked by a powerful foe, strike their tents, pack up their utensils, lade their camels, which they can do in *a couple of hours*, and set off to the great desert, and so *bury themselves in it* that no enemy either will or can pursue, as it is the Arabs alone that know the deserts, and can find *water* and *provender* for their support.

Dedan] Was a city of Idumea, not far from Teman.

A. M. cir. 3417 B. C. cir. 587 Ol. XLVIII. 2 TarquiniiPrisci, R. Roman., cir. annum 30

mity of Esau upon him, the time *that* I will visit him.

9 If [t]grape-gatherers come to thee, would they not leave *some* gleaning grapes? if thieves by night, they will destroy [u]till they have enough.

10 [v]But I have made Esau bare, I have uncovered his secret places, and he shall not be able to hide himself: his seed is spoiled, and his brethren, and his neighbours, and [w]he *is* not.

11 Leave thy fatherless children, I will preserve *them* alive; and let thy widows trust in me.

12 For thus saith the LORD; Behold, [x]they whose judgment *was* not to drink of the cup have assuredly drunken; and *art* thou he *that* shall altogether go unpunished? thou shalt not go unpunished, but thou shalt surely drink *of it*.

13 For [y]I have sworn by myself, saith the LORD, that [z]Bozrah shall become a desolation, a reproach, a waste, and a curse; and all the cities thereof shall be perpetual wastes.

14 I have heard a [a]rumour from the LORD, and an ambassador is sent unto the heathen, *saying,* Gather ye together, and come against her, and rise up to the battle.

A. M. cir. 3417 B. C. cir. 587 Ol. XLVIII. 2 TarquiniiPrisci, R. Roman., cir. annum 30

15 For, lo, I will make thee small among the heathen, *and* despised among men.

16 Thy terribleness hath deceived thee, *and* the pride of thine heart, O thou that dwellest in the clefts of the rock, that holdest the height of the hill: [b]though thou shouldest make thy [c]nest as high as the eagle, [d]I will bring thee down from thence, saith the LORD.

17 Also Edom shall be a desolation: [e]every one that goeth by it shall be astonished, and shall hiss at all the plagues thereof.

18 [f]As in the overthrow of Sodom and Gomorrah and the neighbour *cities* thereof, saith the LORD, no man shall abide there, neither shall a son of man dwell in it.

19 [g]Behold, he shall come up like a lion from [h]the swelling of Jordan against the habitation of the strong: but I will suddenly make him run away from her: and who *is* a chosen *man, that* I may appoint over her? for [i]who *is* like me? and who will [k]appoint me the time? and [l]who *is* that shepherd that will stand before me?

---

[t]Obad. 5——[u]Heb. *their sufficiency*——[v]Mal. i. 3 [w]Isa. xvii. 14——[x]Chap. xxv. 29; Obad. 16——[y]Gen. xxii. 16; Isa. xlv. 23; Amos vi. 8——[z]Isa. xxxiv. 6; lxiii. 1——[a]Obad. 1, 2, 3——[b]Obad. 4

[c]Job xxxix. 27——[d]Amos ix. 2——[e]Ch. xviii. 16; l. 13 [f]Gen. xix. 25; Deut. xxix. 23; chap. l. 40; Amos iv. 11 [g]Chap. l. 44, &c.——[h]Chap. xii. 5——[i]Exod. xv. 11 [k]Or, *convent me in judgment*——[l]Job xli. 10

Verse 9. *If grape-gatherers*] Both in vintage and harvest every grape and every stalk are not gathered; hence the gleaners get something for their pains: but your enemies shall not leave one of you behind; all shall be carried into captivity.

Verse 10. *I have made Esau bare*] I have stripped him of all defence, and have discovered his hiding-places to his enemies.

Verse 11. *Leave thy fatherless children*] The connexion of this with the context is not easy to be discerned; but, as a general maxim, it is of great importance. *Widows* and *orphans* are the peculiar care of God. He is as the best of fathers to the one, and the most loving of husbands to the other. Even the widows and orphans of Esau, who escape the general destruction, shall be taken care of by the Lord.

Verse 12. Art *thou he* that *shall altogether go unpunished?*] A similar form of speech appears, chap. xxv. 29. Others, less wicked than thou, have been punished; and canst *thou* expect to escape? Thou shalt not escape.

Verse 13. *Bozrah shall become a desolation*] *Bozrah,* a city of Idumea, is here put for the whole country.

Verse 14. *I have heard a rumour*] The Lord has revealed to me what he is about to do to the Edomites.

An ambassador is sent] I believe this means only that God has given *permission,* and has *stirred up* the hearts of these nations to go against those whom he has doomed to destruction.

Verse 16. *O thou that dwellest*] All *Idumea* is full of *mountains* and *rocks,* and these rocks and mountains full of caves, where, in time of great heats, and in time of war, the people take shelter.

Verse 18. *As in the overthrow of Sodom*] The destruction of Sodom and Gomorrah and the neighbouring cities was so terrible, that, when God denounces judgments against incorrigible sinners, he tells them they shall be like Sodom and Gomorrah.

No man shall abide there] It shall be so desolate as not to be habitable. Travellers may lodge on the ground for a night; but it cannot become a permanent dwelling.

Verse 19. *Behold, he shall come up like a lion*] See the note on chap. xii. 5. The similitude used here is well illustrated by Dr. *Blayney:* "When I shall occasion a like commotion in her (Idumea) as a fierce and strong lion may be supposed to do in the sheep-folds, then I will cause him (the man of whom it is said in the preceding verse that he should not dwell in it) to run away from her as the affrighted shepherds and their flocks run from the lion."

A chosen man] Nebuchadnezzar. That is, God has *chosen* this man, and given him a commission against Idumea.

A. M. cir. 3417
B. C. cir. 587
Ol. XLVIII. 2
TarquiniiPrisci,
R. Roman.,
cir. annum 30

20 [m]Therefore hear the counsel of the LORD, that he hath taken against Edom; and his purposes, that he hath purposed against the inhabitants of Teman: Surely the least of the flock shall draw them out: surely he shall make their habitations desolate with them.

21 [n]The earth is moved at the noise of their fall, at the cry the noise thereof was heard in the [o]Red Sea.

22 Behold, [p]he shall come up and fly as the eagle, and spread his wings over Bozrah: and at that day shall the heart of the mighty men of Edom be as the heart of a woman in her pangs.

A. M. cir. 3404
B. C. cir. 600
Ol. cir. XLV. 1
TarquiniiPrisci,
R. Roman.,
cir. annum 17

23 [q]Concerning Damascus. Hamath is confounded, and Arpad: for they have heard evil tidings: they [r]are faint-hearted; [s]*there is* sorrow [t]on the sea; it cannot be quiet.

24 Damascus is waxed feeble, *and* turneth herself to flee, and fear hath seized on *her:* [u]anguish and sorrows have taken her, as a woman in travail.

A. M. cir. 3404
B. C. cir. 600
Ol. cir. XLV. 1
TarquiniiPrisci,
R. Roman.,
cir. annum 17

25 How is [v]the city of praise not left, the city of my joy!

26 [w]Therefore her young men shall fall in her streets, and all the men of war shall be cut off in that day, saith the LORD of hosts.

27 And I will kindle a [x]fire in the wall of Damascus, and it shall consume the palaces of Ben-hadad.

A. M. cir. 3403
B. C. cir. 601
Ol. XLIV. 4
TarquiniiPrisci,
R. Roman.,
cir. annum 16

28 [y]Concerning Kedar, and concerning the kingdoms of Hazor, which Nebuchadrezzar king of Babylon shall smite, thus saith the LORD; Arise ye, go up to Kedar, and spoil [z]the men of the east.

29 Their [a]tents and their flocks shall they take away: they shall take to themselves their curtains, and all their vessels, and their camels, and they shall cry unto them, [b]Fear *is* on every side.

30 [c]Flee, [d]get you far off, dwell deep, O ye inhabitants of Hazor, saith the LORD; for Nebuchadrezzar king of Babylon hath taken coun-

---

[m]Chap. l. 45——[n]Chap. l. 46——[o]Heb. *weedy sea*——[p]Chap. iv. 13; xlviii. 40, 41——[q]Isa. xvii. 1; xxxvii. 13; Amos i. 3; Zeph. ix. 1, 2——[r]Heb. *melted*——[s]Isa. lvii. 20——[t]Or, *as on the sea*

[u]Isa. xiii. 8; ch. 31; vi. 24; xxx. 6; xlviii. 41; ver. 22——[v]Ch. xxxiii. 9; li. 41——[w]Ch. l. 30; li. 4——[x]Amos i. 4——[y]Isa. xxi. 13——[z]Judg. vi. 5; Job i. 3——[a]Psa. cxx. 5——[b]Ch. vi. 25; xlvi. 5——[c]Ver. 8——[d]Heb. *flit greatly*

Verse 20. *The inhabitants of Teman*] Taken here for the whole of Idumea. These are a kind of synonyms which prevent monotony, and give variety to the poet's versification.

Surely the least of the flock shall draw them out] They shall be like timid sheep; the weakest foe shall overcome them.

Verse 21. *The earth is moved*] The whole state is represented here as a *vast building* suddenly thrown down, so as to cause the earth to tremble, and the noise to be heard at a great distance.

Verse 22. *He shall come up and fly as the eagle*] Nebuchadnezzar. See chap. xlviii. 40.

Verse 23. CONCERNING DAMASCUS.] This is the *head* or *title* of another prophecy. *Damascus* was one of the principal cities of Syria. It was taken by David, 2 Sam. viii. 6, was retaken in the reign of Solomon, 1 Kings xi. 24, &c., and regained its independence. Its kings were often at war with the ten tribes, and once it joined with them for the destruction of Judah. To defend himself against these powerful enemies Ahaz made a league with the king of Assyria, who besieged Damascus, took, and demolished it. From that time we hear nothing of Damascus till we meet with it in this prophecy. It appears to have been rebuilt and restored to some consequence. It made an obstinate resistance to Nebuchadnezzar; but was at last taken and sacked by him. At present it is both a large and populous city, with considerable commerce.

Hamath is confounded] This is a city of Syria, on the *Orontes.* The Greeks called it *Epiphania.*

Arpad] Not far from Damascus.

Sorrow on the sea] They are like the troubled sea, that cannot rest.

Verse 25. *How is the city of praise not left*] Damascus is so ruined that she can no more be called a *praiseworthy* or *happy city.*

Verse 27. *The palaces of Ben-hadad.*] Damascus was a seat of the Syrian kings, and *Ben-hadad* was a name common to several of its kings.

Verse 28. CONCERNING KEDAR, AND CONCERNING THE KINGDOMS OF HAZOR] This is the *title* of another new prophecy.

Kedar was the name of one of the sons of Ishmael (Gen. xxv. 13) who settled in Arabia, and who gave name to a powerful tribe of Arabs who used to traffic with the Tyrians in cattle. It appears from this prophecy that Nebuchadnezzar got a commission to go against and reduce them to great misery.

Verse 29. *Their tents and their flocks*] This description of *property* shows that they were *Scenite* or *Nomad Arabs;* persons who dwell in *tents,* and whose principal property was *cattle,* especially *camels,* of the whole of which they were plundered by the Chaldeans.

Verse 30. *Dwell deep*] Retire into the depths of the *desert.* See on ver. 8.

Inhabitants of Hazor] I cannot find this place. It was no doubt in Arabia, and a place of considerable importance; but it is now no more

A. M. cir. 3403 B. C. cir. 601 Ol. XLIV. 4 TarquiniiPrisci, R. Roman., cir. annum 16

sel against you, and hath conceived a purpose against you.
31 Arise, get you up unto [e]the [f]wealthy nation, that dwelleth without care, saith the LORD, which have neither gates nor bars, *which* [g]dwell alone.
32 And their camels shall be a booty, and the multitude of their cattle a spoil; and I will [h]scatter into all winds [i]them *that are* [k]in the utmost corners, and I will bring their calamity from all sides thereof, saith the LORD.
33 And Hazor [l]shall be a dwelling for dragons, *and* a desolation for ever: [m]there shall no man abide there, nor *any* son of man dwell in it.

A. M. cir. 3406 B. C. cir. 598 Ol. cir. XLV. 3 TarquiniiPrisci, R. Roman., cir. annum 19

34 The word of the LORD that *came* to Jeremiah the prophet against [n]Elam in the beginning of the reign of Zedekiah king of Judah, saying,
35 Thus saith the LORD of hosts; Behold, I will break [o]the bow of Elam, the chief of their might.
36 And upon Elam will I bring the four winds from the four quarters of heaven, and [p]will scatter them toward all those winds; and there shall be no nation whither the outcasts of Elam shall not come.
37 For I will cause Elam to be dismayed before their enemies, and before them that seek their life: and I will bring evil upon them, *even* my fierce anger, saith the LORD; [q]and I will send the sword after them, till I have consumed them:
38 And I will [r]set my throne in Elam, and will destroy from thence the king and the princes, saith the LORD.
39 But it shall come to pass [s]in the latter days, *that* I will bring again the captivity of Elam, saith the LORD.

[e]Ezek. xxxviii. 11——[f]Or, *that is at ease*——[g]Num. xxiii. 9; Deut. xxxiii. 28; Mic. vii. 14——[h]Ezek. v. 10; ver. 36——[i]Chap. ix. 26; xxv. 23——[k]Heb. *cut off into corners*, or *that have the corners* of their hair *polled*

[l]Chap. ix. 11; x. 22; Mal. i. 3——[m]Ver. 18——[n]Chap. xxv. 25——[o]See Isa. xxii. 6——[p]Ver. 32——[q]Chap. ix. 16; xlviii. 2——[r]See chap. xliii. 10——[s]Chap. xlviii. 47; ver. 6

Verse 31. *The wealthy nation*] גוי שליו *goi sheleiv*, "the peaceable nation"—

Have neither gates nor bars] The Arabs, who had nothing but their tents; no cities, nor even *permanent villages*.

Verse 32. *The utmost corners*] Even in these utmost inaccessible recesses the sword and pillage shall reach them. "'The utmost corners;' insulated coasts; the peninsula of Arabia."—*Blayney*.

Verse 33. *Hazor shall be a dwelling for dragons*] Shall be turned into a *wilderness*.

A desolation for ever] Never to be repeopled.

There shall no man abide there] It may occasionally be *visited*, but never made a permanent abode.

Verse 34. THE WORD—AGAINST ELAM] Another new head of prophecy. As this was delivered in the beginning of the reign of Zedekiah, it can have no natural nor historical connexion with the other prophecies in this various chapter. Some think that by *Elam* Persia is always meant; but this is not at all likely. It was a part of the Babylonian empire in the time of Daniel, (chap. viii. 2,) and is most probably what is called *Elymais* by the Greeks. This, with Susiana, Nebuchadnezzar subdued, and took from Astyages, king of Media.

Verse 35. I *will break the bow of Elam*] They were eminent archers; and had acquired their power and eminence by their dexterity in the use of the bow. See Isa. xxii. 6. *Strabo*, *Livy*, and others speak of their eminence in archery.

Verse 36. *Will I bring the four winds*] Nebuchadnezzar and his armies, gathered out of different provinces, and attacking this people at all points in the same time.

There shall be no nation, &c.] They shall be scattered through the *one hundred* and *twenty-seven* provinces of which the Babylonish empire is composed.

Verse 38. *I will set my throne in Elam*] This is spoken either of *Nebuchadnezzar* or *Cyrus*. It is certain that Cyrus did render himself master of *Elymais* and *Media*, which are in the land of Elam.

Verse 39. *I will bring again the captivity of Elam*] As this is to be in *the latter days*, probably it may mean the *spiritual freedom* which these people would receive under the Gospel dispensation. Under Cyrus, the *Elamites*, collected out of all quarters, were united with the *Persians*, their neighbours, and became, with them, masters of the east. See *Calmet* and *Dahler*. There are still, however, difficulties on this subject. Who the *Elamites* were is still a question. That which appears to be nearest the truth is, that the *Elamites* and *Persians* were two *distinct people*, and continued so till blended together under Cyrus. It is in this light that I have considered the subject in the preceding notes. Neighbouring people are frequently confounded in history, and sometimes the name of a people is given to those who have the same *character*.

CHAPTER L

This and the following chapter contain a prophecy relating to the fall of Babylon, interspersed with several predictions relative to the restoration of Israel and Judah, who were to survive their oppressors, and, on their repentance, to be pardoned and brought to their own land. This chapter opens with a prediction of the complete destruction of all the Babylonish idols, and the utter desolation of Chaldea, through the instrumentality of a great northern nation, 1–3. *Israel and Judah shall be reinstated in the land of their forefathers after the total overthrow of the great Babylonish empire,* 4, 5. *Very oppressive and cruel bondage of the Jewish people during the captivity,* 6, 7. *The people of God are commanded to remove speedily from Babylon, because an assembly of great nations are coming out of the north to desolate the whole land,* 8–10. *Babylon, the hammer of the whole earth, the great desolator of nations, shall itself become a desolation on account of its intolerable pride, and because of the iron yoke it has rejoiced to put upon a people whom a mysterious Providence had placed under its domination,* 11–34. *The judgments which shall fall upon Chaldea, a country addicted to the grossest idolatry, and to every species of superstition, shall be most awful and general, as when God overthrew Sodom and Gomorrah,* 35–40. *Character of the people appointed to execute the Divine judgments upon the oppressors of Israel,* 41–45. *Great sensation among the nations at the very terrible and sudden fall of Babylon,* 46.

A. M. 3409 B. C. 595 Ol. XLVI. 2 Anno TarquiniiPrisci, R. Roman., 22

THE word that the LORD spake [a]against Babylon *and* against the land of the Chaldeans [b]by Jeremiah the prophet.

2 Declare ye among the nations, and publish, and [c]set up a standard; publish, *and* conceal not: say, Babylon is taken, [d]Bel is confounded, Merodach is broken in pieces; [e]her idols are confounded, her images are broken in pieces.

3 [f]For out of the north there cometh up [g]a nation against her, which shall make her land desolate, and none shall dwell therein: they shall remove, they shall depart, both man and beast.

4 In those days, and in that time, saith the LORD, the children of Israel shall come, [h]they and the children of Judah together, [i]going and weeping: they shall go, [k]and seek the LORD their God.

5 They shall ask the way to Zion with their faces thitherward, *saying,* Come, and let us join ourselves to the LORD in [l]a perpetual covenant *that* shall not be forgotten.

[a]Isa. xiii. 1; xxi. 1; xlvii. 1——[b]Heb. *by the hand of Jeremiah*——[c]Heb. *lift up*——[d]Isa. xlvi. 1; chap. li. 44 [e]See chap. xliii. 12, 13——[f]Chap. li. 48

[g]Isa. xiii. 17, 18, 20; ver. 39, 40——[h]Hos. i. 11 [i]Ezra iii. 12, 13; Psa. cxxvi. 5, 6; chap. xxxi. 9; Zech. xii. 10——[k]Hos. iii. 5——[l]Chap. xxxi. 31, &c.; xxxii. 40

NOTES ON CHAP. L

Verse 1. THE WORD THAT THE LORD SPAKE AGAINST BABYLON] This is also a new head of discourse.

The prophecy contained in this and the following chapter was sent to the captives in Babylon in the *fourth* year of the reign of Zedekiah. They are very important; they predict the total destruction of the Babylonish empire, and the return of the Jews from their captivity. These chapters were probably composed, with several additions, out of the book that was then sent by Jeremiah to the captives by the hand of Seraiah. See chap. li. 59-64.

Verse 2. *Declare ye among the nations*] God's determination relative to this empire.

Set up a standard] Show the people where they are to assemble.

Say, Babylon is taken] It is a thing so firmly determined, that it is as good as already done.

Bel] The tutelar deity of Babylon *is confounded,* because it cannot save its own city.

Merodach] Another of their idols, *is broken to pieces;* it was not able to save *itself,* much less the whole empire.

Her idols are confounded] It is a reproach to have acknowledged them.

Her images] Great and small, golden and wooden, *are broken to pieces;* even the *form* of them no longer appears.

Verse 3. *Out of the north there cometh up a nation*] The *Medes,* who formed the chief part of the army of Cyrus, lay to the *north* or *north-east* of Babylon.

Shall make her land desolate] This war, and the consequent taking of the city, *began* those disasters that brought Babylon in process of time to *complete desolation;* so that now it is not known where it stood, the whole country being a total solitude.

Verse 4. *In those days, and in that time*] In the times in which Babylon shall be opposed by the Medes and Persians, both Israel and Judah, seeing the commencement of the fulfilling of the prophecies, shall begin to seek the Lord with much prayer, and broken and contrite hearts. When the decree of Cyrus comes, they shall be ready to set off for their own country, deploring their offences, yet rejoicing in the mercy of God which has given them this reviving in their bondage.

Verse 5. *Let us join ourselves to the Lord in a perpetual covenant*] All our *former covenants* have been *broken;* let us now make one that shall *last for ever.* He shall be the LORD OUR GOD, and WE will no more worship *idols.* This covenant they have kept to the present day; whatever their present moral and spiritual state may be, they are no idolaters, in the gross sense of the term.

The description that is here given of the

A. M. 3409
B. C. 595
Ol. XLVI. 2
Anno
TarquiniiPrisci,
R. Roman., 22

6 My people hath been [m]lost
sheep: their shepherds have
caused them to go astray, they
have turned them away *on* [n]the
mountains: they have gone from mountain to
hill, they have forgotten their [o]resting place.
7 All that found them have [p]devoured them:
and [q]their adversaries said, [r]We offend not,
because they have sinned against the LORD,
[s]the habitation of justice, even the LORD, [t]the
Hope of their fathers.
8 [u]Remove out of the midst of Babylon, and
go forth out of the land of the
Chaldeans, and be as the he-goats
before the flocks.
9 [v]For, lo, I will raise and
cause to come up against Babylon an assembly
of great nations from the north country: and
they shall [w]set themselves in array against
her; from thence she shall be taken: their
arrows *shall be* as of a mighty [x]expert man;
[y]none shall return in vain.
10 And Chaldea shall be a spoil: [z]all that
spoil her shall be satisfied, saith the LORD.

A. M. 3409
B. C. 595
Ol. XLVI. 2
Anno
TarquiniiPrisci,
R. Roman., 22

[m]Isa. liii. 6; ver. 17; 1 Pet. ii. 25——[n]Chap. ii. 20; iii. 6, 23——[o]Heb. *place to lie down in*——[p]Psa. lxxix. 7 [q]Chap. xl. 2, 3; Zech. xi. 5——[r]See chap. ii. 3; Dan. ix. 16——[s]Psa. xc. 1; xci. 1

[t]Psa. xxii. 4——[u]Isa. xlviii. 20; chap. li. 6, 45; Zech. ii. 6, 7; Rev. xviii. 4——[v]Chap. xv. 14; li. 27; Ver. 3, 41——[w]Ver. 14, 29——[x]Or, *destroyer*——[y]2 Sam. i. 22——[z]Rev. xvii. 16

state of this people, their feelings and their conduct, finely exhibit the state of *real penitents*, who are fervently seeking the salvation of their souls.

1. *In those days*, when Jesus Christ is manifested in the flesh; *and in that time*, when through him is preached the remission of sins, and the people who hear are pricked in their conscience.

2. *The children of Israel and the children of Judah together.*—No distinctions being then felt or attended to; for all feel themselves *sinners*, who have come short of the glory of God. Even national distinctions and religious differences, which bind men fastest, and hold them longest, are absorbed in the deep and overpowering concern they feel for their eternal interests.

3. *Going and weeping shall they go.*—Religious *sorrow* does not preclude *activity* and *diligence*. While they are *weeping* for their sins, they are *going on* in the path of duty, seeking the Lord while he may be found, and calling upon him while he is near.

4. *They shall ask the way to Zion.—Real penitents* are the most *inquisitive* of all mortals; but their inquiries are limited to one object, *they ask the way to Zion*. What shall we do to be saved? How shall we shun the perdition of ungodly men, &c.

5. *With their faces thitherward.*—They have *turned* FROM *sin*, and *turned* TO *God*. They have left the paths of the destroyer, and their hearts are towards God, and the remembrance of his name. Thus they are profiting by that light which has convinced them of sin, righteousness, and judgment.

6. *Come, and let us join ourselves to the Lord.*—Religion is a *social principle*, and begets a *social feeling* in the soul. No man who feels his own sore, and the plague of his heart, wishes to venture *alone* in the way to heaven. He feels he wants counsel, support, comfort, and the company of those who will watch over him in love. Like David, the true penitent is a companion of all those who fear the Lord. These heavenly feelings come from one and the same Spirit, and lead to the same end; hence they say,—

7. *Let us join ourselves to the Lord in a perpetual covenant.* It is said, that *to be undecided, is to be decided.* They who are not *determined* to go to heaven, will never reach it. If the heart be not *laid under obligation*, it will do nothing. "I hope I am in earnest; I trust I shall be in earnest about the salvation of my soul; it is very proper I should be so;" and such like, show an *irresolute* soul. Such persons are ever learning, and never able to come to the knowledge of the truth.

Let us therefore bind ourselves. We have trifled too long; been *indecisive* too long; have *halted* too long between two opinions. We know now that *Jehovah* is God; let us, therefore, enter into a *covenant* with him. Let this covenant be a *perpetual* one: let us not make it for a *day*, for any *particular time*, but *for ever;* and let it never be *broken*. Let *our part* be kept inviolable: *we* ARE *and* WILL BE *thy people;* and God's part will never fail, I AM *and* WILL BE *your God.*

The covenant requires a *sacrifice.*—Hence ברית *berith* signifies *both*. Christ crucified is the great covenant sacrifice. By him God becomes united to us, and through him we become united to God.

Verse 6. *My people hath been lost sheep*] He pities them; for their pastors, kings, and prophets have caused them to err.

They have gone from mountain to hill] In all *high places* they have practised idolatry.

Verse 7. *Their adversaries said, We offend not*] God has abandoned them; we are only fulfilling his designs in plaguing them.

Verse 8. *Remove out of the midst of Babylon*] The sentence of destruction is gone out against it; prepare for your flight, that ye be not overwhelmed in its ruin.

Be as the he-goats before the flocks.] Who always run to the head of the flock, giving the example for others to follow. This may be addressed to the elders and persons of authority among the people.

Verse 9. *An assembly of great nations*] The army of Cyrus was composed of Medes, Persians, Armenians, Caducians, Sacæ, &c. Though all these did not come from the *north;* yet they were arranged under the *Medes*, who did come from the north, in reference to Babylon.

Their arrows] They are such expert archers, that they shall never miss their mark.

Verse 10. *Chaldea shall be a spoil*] She has been a spoiler, and she shall be spoiled. They had destroyed Judea, God's *heritage;* and now God shall cause her to be destroyed.

A. M. 3409
B. C. 595
Ol. XLVI. 2
Anno
TarquiniiPrisci,
R. Roman., 22

11 [a]Because ye were glad, because ye rejoiced, O ye destroyers of mine heritage, because ye are grown [b]fat [c]as the heifer at grass, and [d]bellow as bulls;

12 Your mother shall be sore confounded; she that bare you shall be ashamed: *behold,* the hindermost of the nations *shall be* a wilderness, a dry land, and a desert.

13 Because of the wrath of the LORD it shall not be inhabited, [e]but it shall be wholly desolate: [f]every one that goeth by Babylon shall be astonished, and hiss at all her plagues.

14 [g]Put yourselves in array against Babylon round about: all ye [h]that bend the bow, shoot at her, spare no arrows: for she hath sinned against the LORD.

15 Shout against her round about: she hath [i]given her hand: her foundations are fallen, [k]her walls are thrown down: for [l]it *is* the vengeance of the LORD: take vengeance upon her; [m]as she hath done, do unto her.

16 Cut off the sower from Babylon, and him that handleth the [n]sickle in the time of harvest: for fear of the oppressing sword [o]they shall turn every one to his people, and they shall flee every one to his own land.

A. M. 3409
B. C. 595
Ol. XLVI. 2
Anno
TarquiniiPrisci,
R. Roman., 22

17 Israel *is* [p]a scattered sheep; [q]the lions have driven *him* away: first [r]the king of Assyria hath devoured him; and last this [s]Nebuchadrezzar king of Babylon hath broken his bones.

18 Therefore thus saith the LORD of hosts, the God of Israel; Behold, I will punish the king of Babylon and his land, as I have punished the king of Assyria.

19 [t]And I will bring Israel again to his habitation, and he shall feed on Carmel and Bashan, and his soul shall be satisfied upon Mount Ephraim and Gilead.

20 In those days, and in that time, saith the LORD, [u]the iniquity of Israel shall be sought for, and *there shall be* none; and the sins of Judah, and they shall not be found: for I will pardon them [v]whom I reserve.

21 Go up against the land [w]of Merathaim, *even* against it, and against the inhabitants of [x]Pekod:[y] waste and utterly destroy after them, saith the LORD, and do [z]according to all that I have commanded thee.

[a]Isa. xlvii. 6——[b]Heb. *big,* or *corpulent*——[c]Hos. x. 11——[d]Or, *neigh as steeds*——[e]Chap. xxv. 12——[f]Ch. xlix. 17——[g]Ver. 9; chap. li. 2——[h]Chap. xlix. 35; ver. 29——[i]1 Chron. xxix. 24; 2 Chron. xxx. 8; Lam. v. 6; Ezek. xvii. 18——[k]Chap. li. 58——[l]Chap. li. 6, 11——[m]Psa. cxxxvii. 8; ver. 29; Rev. xviii. 6——[n]Or, *scythe*

[o]Isa. xiii. 14; chap. li. 9——[p]Ver. 6——[q]Chap. ii. 15——[r]2 Kings xvii. 6——[s]2 Kings xxiv. 10, 14——[t]Isa. lxv. 10; chap. xxxiii. 12; Ezek. xxxiv. 13, 14——[u]Chap. xxxi. 34——[v]Isa. i. 9——[w]Or, *of the rebels*——[x]Ezek. xxiii. 23——[y]Or, *visitation*——[z]See 2 Sam. xvi. 11; 2 Kings xviii. 25; 2 Chron. xxxvi. 23; Isa. x. 6; xliv. 28; xlviii. 14; chap. xxxiv. 22

Verse 11. *As the heifer at grass*] Ye were wanton in the desolations ye brought upon Judea.

Verse 12. *Your mother*] Speaking to the Chaldeans: BABYLON, the *metropolis,* or mother city, shall be a wilderness, a dry land, a desert, neither fit for man nor beast.

Verse 15. *Shout against her round about*] Encompass her with lines and with troops; let none *go in* with relief, none *come out* to escape from her ruin.

Verse 16. *Cut off the sower*] Destroy the gardens and the fields, that there may be neither fruits nor tillage.

Verse 17. *Israel*] All the descendants of Jacob have been harassed and spoiled, first by the Assyrians, and afterwards by the Chaldeans. They acted towards them as a lion to a sheep which he has caught; first he devours all the flesh, next he breaks all the bones to extract the marrow.

Verse 18. *As I have punished the king of Assyria.*] The Assyrians were overthrown by the *Medes* and the *Chaldeans.* The *king* is here taken for all their kings, generals, &c., Tiglath-pileser, Shalmaneser, Sennacherib, Esar-haddon, &c. To them succeeded the Chaldean or Babylonish kings. Nebuchadnezzar came against Judea several times; and at last took the city and burnt it, profaned and demolished the temple, wasted the land, and carried the princes and people into captivity.

Verse 19. *I will bring Israel again*] This seems to refer wholly to the ten tribes; for Carmel, Bashan, Mount Ephraim, and Gilead, were in their territories.

Verse 20. *In those days and in that time*] This phrase appears to take in the whole of an epoch, from its commencement to its end. See ver. 4.

I will pardon them] So as to deliver them from their captivity, and exact no more *punishment* from *them whom I reserve;* namely, the *remnant* left in the Babylonish captivity.

Verse 21. *Go up against the land of Merathaim—and against the inhabitants of Pekod*] No such *places* as these are to be found any where else; and it is not likely that *places* are at all meant. The ancient *Versions* agree in rendering the first as an *appellative,* and the last as a *verb,* except the Chaldee, which has *Pekod* as a proper name. Dr. *Blayney* translates:—

"Against the land of bitternesses, go up:
Upon it, and upon its inhabitants, visit, O sword!"

Dr. *Dahler* renders thus:—

A. M. 3409 B. C. 595 Ol. XLVI. 2 Anno TarquiniiPrisci, R. Roman., 22
22 [a]A sound of battle *is* in the
land, and of great destruction.
23 How is [b]the hammer of the
whole earth cut asunder and
broken! how is Babylon become a desolation
among the nations!
24 I have laid a snare for thee, and thou
art also taken, O Babylon, [c]and thou wast
not aware: thou art found, and also caught,
because thou hast striven against the LORD.
25 The LORD hath opened his armoury, and
hath brought forth [d]the weapons of his indignation: for this *is* the work of the Lord GOD
of hosts in the land of the Chaldeans.
26 Come against her [e]from the utmost border, open her storehouses: [f]cast her up as
heaps, and destroy her utterly: let nothing of
her be left.
27 Slay all her [g]bullocks; let them go down
to the slaughter: wo unto them! for their day
is come, the time of [h]their visitation.
28 The voice of them that flee and escape
out of the land of Babylon, [i]to declare in
Zion the vengeance of the LORD our God,
the vengeance of his temple.
29 Call together the archers against Babylon: [k]all ye that bend the bow, camp against
it round about; let none thereof escape:
[l]recompense her according to her
work; according to all that she
hath done, do unto her: [m]for she
hath been proud against the
LORD, against the Holy One of Israel.
30 [n]Therefore shall her young men fall in
the streets, and all her men of war shall be
cut off in that day, saith the LORD.
31 Behold, I *am* against thee, *O thou* [o]most
proud, saith the Lord GOD of hosts: for [p]thy
day is come, the time *that* I will visit thee.
32 And [q]the most proud shall stumble and
fall, and none shall raise him up: and [r]I will
kindle a fire in his cities, and it shall devour
all round about him.
33 Thus saith the LORD of hosts; The
children of Israel and the children of Judah
were oppressed together: and all that took
them captives held them fast; they refused to
let them go.
34 [s]Their Redeemer *is* strong; [t]the LORD of
hosts *is* his name: he shall thoroughly plead
their cause, that he may give rest to the land,
and disquiet the inhabitants of Babylon.
35 A sword *is* upon the Chaldeans, saith
the LORD, and upon the inhabitants of Babylon, and [u]upon her princes, and upon [v]her
wise *men*.

[a]Ch. li. 54——[b]Isa. xiv. 6; ch. li. 20——[c]Ch. li. 8, 31, 39, 57; Dan. v. 30, 31——[d]Isa. xiii. 5——[e]Heb. *from the end*——[f]Or, *tread her*——[g]Psa. xxii. 12; Isa. xxxiv. 7; ch. xlvi. 21——[h]Ch. xlviii. 44; ver. 31——[i]Ch. li. 10, 11

[k]Ver. 14——[l]Ver. 15; ch. li. 56; Rev. xviii. 6——[m]Isa. xlvii. 10——[n]Ch. xlix. 26; li. 4——[o]Heb. *pride*——[p]Ver. 27——[q]Heb. *pride*——[r]Ch. xxi. 14——[s]Rev. xviii. 8 [t]Isa. xlvii. 4——[u]Dan. v. 30——[v]Isa. xlvii. 13

"March against the country doubly rebellious,
And against its inhabitants *worthy* of punishment."

The latter of these two versions I take to be the most literal. The words are addressed to the *Medes* and *Persians;* and the country is *Chaldea*, doubly rebellious by its *idolatry* and its insufferable *pride*. In these *two*, it was exceeded by no other land.

Verse 23. *The hammer of the whole earth*] Nebuchadnezzar dashed to pieces the nations against whom he warred. He was the scourge of the Lord.

Verse 24. *I have laid a snare for thee*] It was not by *storm* that Cyrus took the city. The *Euphrates* ran through it; he dug a channel for the river in another direction, to divert its stream; he waited for that time in which the inhabitants had delivered themselves up to debauchery: in the dead of the night he turned off the stream, and he and his army entered by the *old channel*, now void of its waters. This was the *snare* of which the prophet here speaks. See *Herodotus*, lib. i., c. 191.

Verse 26. *Open her store-houses*] At the time that Cyrus took the city, it was full of provisions and treasures of all kinds; the walls had suffered no injury; and when the inhabitants heard that the enemy was *within*, they thought they must have *arisen out of the earth* in the centre of the city!

Verse 27. *Slay all her bullocks*] Princes, magistrates, &c., &c.

Verse 28. *Declare in Zion the vengeance of the Lord*] Zion was desolated by Babylon; tell Zion that God hath desolated the desolator.

The vengeance of his temple.] Which Nebuchadnezzar had pillaged, profaned, and demolished, transporting its sacred vessels to Babylon, and putting them in the temple of his god Bel.

Verse 29. *Call together the archers*] The preceding verses are the prediction: here, God calls the *Medes* and *Persians* to fulfil it.

Verse 31. O thou *most proud*] זדון *zadon*. PRIDE in the abstract; proudest of all people.

Verse 32. *And the most proud*] זדון *zadon*, as before. Here *pride* is personified and addressed, as if possessing a being and rational powers.

Verse 34. *Their Redeemer* is *strong*] And it was not that he *wanted power*, and that Nebuchadnezzar had *much*, that Jerusalem was taken; but because the people had *sinned*, and would *not return;* and therefore *national sins* called for *national punishments*. These have

A. M. 3409 B. C. 595 Ol. XLVI. 2 Anno TarquiniiPrisci, R. Roman., 22

36 A sword *is* [w]upon the [x]liars;[y] and they shall dote: a sword *is* upon her mighty men; and they shall be dismayed.

37 A sword *is* upon their horses, and upon their chariots, and upon all [z]the mingled people that *are* in the midst of her; and [a]they shall become as women: a sword *is* upon her treasures; and they shall be robbed.

38 [b]A drought *is* upon her waters; and they shall be dried up: for it *is* the land of [c]graven images, and they are mad upon *their* idols.

39 [d]Therefore the wild beasts of the desert with the wild beasts of the islands shall dwell *there*, and the owls shall dwell therein: [e]and it shall be no more inhabited for ever; neither shall it be dwelt in from generation to generation.

40 [f]As God overthrew Sodom and Gomorrah and the neighbour *cities* thereof, saith the LORD; *so* shall no man abide there, neither shall any son of man dwell therein.

41 [g]Behold, a people shall come from the north, and a great nation, and many kings shall be raised up from the coasts of the earth.

42 [h]They shall hold the bow and the lance: [i]they *are* cruel, and will not show mercy: [k]their voice shall roar like the sea, and they shall ride upon horses, *every one* put in array, like a man to the battle, against thee, O daughter of Babylon.

A. M. 3409 B. C. 595 Ol. XLVI. 2 Anno TarquiniiPrisci, R. Roman., 22

43 The king of Babylon hath heard the report of them, and his hands waxed feeble: [l]anguish took hold of him, *and* pangs as of a woman in travail.

44 [m]Behold, he shall come up like a lion from the swelling of Jordan unto the habitation of the strong: but I will make them suddenly run away from her: and who *is* a chosen *man, that* I may appoint over her? for who *is* like me? and who will [n]appoint me the time? and [o]who *is* that shepherd that will stand before me?

45 Therefore hear ye [p]the counsel of the LORD, that he hath taken against Babylon; and his purposes, that he hath purposed against the land of the Chaldeans: Surely the least of the flock shall draw them out: surely he shall make *their* habitation desolate with them.

46 [q]At the noise of the taking of Babylon the earth is moved, and the cry is heard among the nations.

---

[w]Isa. xliv. 25; chap. xlviii. 30——[x]Or, *chief stays* [y]Heb. *bars*——[z]Chap. xxv. 20, 24; Ezek. xxx. 5——[a]Ch. li. 30; Nah. iii. 13——[b]Isa. xliv. 27; chap. li. 32, 36; Rev. xvi. 12——[c]Ver. 2; chap. li. 44, 47, 52——[d]Isa. xiii. 21, 22; xxxiv. 14; chap. li. 37; Rev. xviii. 2——[e]Isa. xiii. 20; chap. xxv. 12——[f]Gen. xiii. 10; xix. 24, 25, 28; Deut. xxix. 23; Isa. i. 9; xiii. 19; ch. xlix. 18; Lam. iv. 6; Amos iv. 11; Zeph. ii. 9; 2 Pet. ii. 6; Jude 7——[g]Ver. 9; ch. vi. 22; xxv. 14; li. 27; Rev. xvii. 16——[h]Ch. vi. 22——[i]Isa. xiii. 18——[k]Isa. v. 30——[l]Ch. xlix. 24——[m]Ch. xlix. 19, &c.——[n]Or, *convent me to plead*——[o]Job xli. 10; ch. xlix. 19——[p]Isa. xiv. 24, &c.; ch. li. 11——[q]Rev. xviii. 9

---

taken place; and now the Lord of hosts shows them that the *power of the Chaldeans* is mere *weakness* against his *might*.

Verse 35. *A sword*] War and its calamities, or any grievous plague; and so in the following verses.

Verse 38. *A drought* is *upon her waters*] May not this refer to the *draining of the channel of the Euphrates*, by which the army of Cyrus entered the city. See on ver. 24. The original is, however, חרב *chereb*, a sword, as in the preceding verses, which signifies war, or any calamity by which the thing on which it falls is ruined.

Verse 39. *The wild beasts of the desert*] *Dahler* translates these various terms, "The wild cats, the jackals, and the ostriches." And *Blayney* the same. *Wicklif*, "Dragons, woodewoses, and ostriches." *Coverdale*, "Wild beestes, apes, and estriches."

Verse 40. *As God overthrew Sodom*] As the very *ground* on which these cities stood, with all the *plain*, now lies under the *Dead Sea;* so *Babylon* and the *adjacent country* shall be rendered totally barren and unfruitful, and utterly incapable of being inhabited. And this is the *fact* concerning both countries. See chap. xlix. 18.

Verse 41. *Behold, a people shall come from the north*] This and the two following verses are nearly the same with chap. vi. 22-24. But *here*, destroyers against *Babylon* are intended; *there*, destroyers against *Jerusalem*.

Verse 44. *Behold, he shall came up like a lion*] The same words as in chap. xlix. 19, &c., where see the note.

Verse 46. *At the noise of the taking of Babylon*] See the note on the parallel place, chap. xlix. 21. In the *forty-ninth* chapter, these words are spoken of *Nebuchadnezzar; here*, of *Cyrus*. The taking of Babylon was a wonder to all the surrounding nations. It was thought to be impregnable.

CHAPTER LI

Sequel of the prophecies of Jeremiah against Babylon. The dreadful, sudden, and final ruin that shall fall upon the Chaldeans, who have compelled the nations to receive their idolatrous rites, (see an instance in the third *chapter of Daniel,) set forth by a variety of beautiful figures; with a command to the people of God, (who have made continual intercession for the conversion of their heathen rulers,) to flee from the impending vengeance,* 1–14. *Jehovah, Israel's God, whose infinite power, wisdom, and understanding are every where visible in the works of creation, elegantly contrasted with the utterly contemptible objects of the Chaldean worship,* 15–19. *Because of their great oppression of God's people, the Babylonians shall be visited with cruel enemies from the north, whose innumerable hosts shall fill the land, and utterly extirpate the original inhabitants,* 20–44. *One of the figures by which this formidable invasion is represented is awfully sublime. "The* SEA *is come up upon Babylon; she is covered with the multitude of the waves thereof." And the account of the sudden desolation produced by this great armament of a multitude of nations, (which the prophet, dropping the figure, immediately subjoins,) is deeply afflictive. "Her cities are a desolation, a dry land, and a wilderness; a land wherein no man dwelleth, neither doth any son of man pass thereby." The people of God a third time admonished to escape from Babylon, lest they be overtaken with her plagues,* 45, 46. *Other figures setting forth in a variety of lights the awful judgments with which the Chaldeans shall be visited on account of their very gross idolatries,* 47–58. *The significant emblem with which the chapter concludes, of Seraiah, after having read the book of the Prophet Jeremiah against Babylon, binding a stone to it, and casting it into the river Euphrates, thereby prefiguring the very sudden downfall of the Chaldean city and empire,* 59–64, *is beautifully improved by the writer of the Apocalypse,* chap. xviii. 21, *in speaking of* Babylon the GREAT, *of which the other was a most expressive type; and to which many of the passages interspersed throughout the Old Testament Scriptures relative to Babylon must be ultimately referred, if we would give an interpretation in every respect equal to the terrible import of the language in which these prophecies are conceived.*

A. M. 3409
B. C. 595
Ol. XLVI. 2
Anno
TarquiniiPrisci,
R. Roman., 22

THUS saith the LORD; Behold, I will raise up against Babylon, and against them that dwell in the [a]midst of them that rise up against me, [b]a destroying wind;

2 And will send unto Babylon [c]fanners that shall fan her, and shall empty her land; [d]for in the day of trouble they shall be against her round about.

3 Against *him that* bendeth [e]let the archer bend his bow, and against *him that* lifteth himself up in his brigandine: and spare ye not her young men; [f]destroy ye utterly all her host.

4 Thus the slain shall fall in the land of the Chaldeans, [g]and *they that are* thrust through in her streets.

5 For Israel *hath* not *been* forsaken, nor Judah of his God, of the LORD of hosts; though their land was filled with sin against the Holy One of Israel.

6 [h]Flee out of the midst of Babylon, and deliver every man his soul; be not cut off in her iniquity; for [i]this *is* the time of the LORD's vengeance; [k]he will render unto her a recompense.

7 [l]Babylon *hath been* a golden cup in the LORD's hand, that made all the earth drunken: [m]the nations have drunken of her wine; therefore the nations [n]are mad.

8 Babylon is suddenly [o]fallen and destroyed: [p]howl for her; [q]take balm for her pain, if so be she may be healed.

9 We would have healed Babylon, but she is not healed: forsake her, and [r]let us go every one into his own country: [s]for her

[a]Heb. *heart*——[b]2 Kings xix. 7; chap. iv. 11——[c]Ch. xv. 7——[d]Chap. l. 14——[e]Chap. l. 14——[f]Chap. l. 21——[g]Chap. xlix. 26; l. 30, 37——[h]Chap. l. 8; Rev. xviii. 4——[i]Chap. l. 15, 28——[k]Chap. xxv. 14

[l]Rev. xvii. 4——[m]Rev. xiv. 8——[n]Chap. xxv. 16——[o]Isa. xxi. 9; Rev. xiv. 8; xviii. 2——[p]Chap. xlviii. 20; Rev. xviii. 9, 11, 19——[q]Chap. xlvi. 11——[r]Isa. xiii. 4; chap. l. 16——[s]Rev. xviii. 5

NOTES ON CHAP. LI

Verse 1. *Thus saith the Lord*] This chapter is a continuation of the preceding prophecy.

A destroying wind.] Such as the *pestilential winds* in the east; and here the emblem of a *destroying army*, carrying all before them, and wasting with fire and sword.

Verse 2. *And will send—fanners*] When the corn is trodden out with the feet of cattle, or crushed out with a heavy wheel armed with iron, with a shovel they throw it up against the wind, that the chaff and broken straw may be separated from it. This is the image used by the prophet; these people shall be trodden, crushed, and fanned by their enemies.

Verse 5. *For Israel* hath *not* been *forsaken*] God still continued his prophets among them; he had never cast them wholly off. Even in the midst of *wrath*—highly deserved and inflicted *punishment*, he has remembered *mercy;* and is now about to crown what he has done by restoring them to their own land. I conceive אשם *asham*, which we translate *sin*, as rather signifying *punishment*, which meaning it often has.

Verse 7. *Made all the earth drunken*] The cup of God's wrath is the *plenitude of punishment*, that he inflicts on transgressors. It is represented as *intoxicating* and making them *mad.*

Verse 8. *Babylon is suddenly fallen and destroyed*] These appear to be the words of some of the spectators of Babylon's misery.

Verse 9. *We would have healed Babylon*] Had it been in our power, we would have saved her; but we could not turn away the judgment of God.

A. M. 3409 B. C. 595 judgment reacheth unto heaven,
Ol. XLVI. 2 and is lifted up *even* to the skies.
Anno TarquiniiPrisci, 10 The LORD hath [t]brought
R. Roman., 22 forth our righteousness: come,
and let us [u]declare in Zion the work of the
LORD our God.
11 [v]Make [w]bright the arrows; gather the
shields: [x]the LORD hath raised up the spirit
of the kings of the Medes: [y]for his device *is*
against Babylon, to destroy it; because it *is*
[z]the vengeance of the LORD, the vengeance
of his temple.
12 [a]Set up the standard upon the walls of
Babylon, make the watch strong, set up the
watchmen, prepare the [b]ambushes: for the
LORD hath both devised and done that
which he spake against the inhabitants of
Babylon.
13 [c]O thou that dwellest upon many waters,
abundant in treasures, thine end is come, *and*
the measure of thy covetousness.
14 [d]The LORD of hosts hath sworn [e]by
himself, *saying,* Surely I will fill thee with
men, [f]as with caterpillars; and A. M. 3409 B. C. 595
they shall [g]lift [h]up a shout Ol. XLVI. 2
against thee. Anno TarquiniiPrisci
15 [i]He hath made the earth by R. Roman., 22
his power, he hath established the world by
his wisdom, and [k]hath stretched out the heaven by his understanding.
16 [l]When he uttereth *his* voice, *there is* a
[m]multitude of waters in the heavens; and [n]he
causeth the vapours to ascend from the ends
of the earth: he maketh lightnings with rain,
and bringeth forth the wind out of his treasures.
17 [o]Every man [p]is brutish by *his* knowledge; every founder is confounded by the
graven image: [q]for his molten image *is* falsehood, and *there is* no breath in them.
18 [r]They *are* vanity, the work of errors: in
the time of their visitation they shall perish.
19 [s]The Portion of Jacob *is* not like them;
for he *is* the former of all things: and *Israel*
is the rod of his inheritance: the LORD of
hosts *is* his name.

[t]Psa. xxxvii. 6——[u]Chap. l. 28——[v]Chap. xlvi. 4——[w]Heb. *pure*——[x]Isa. xiii. 17; ver. 28——[y]Chap. l. 45——[z]Chap. l. 28——[a]Nah. ii. 1; iii. 14——[b]Heb. *liers in wait*——[c]Rev. xvii. 1, 15——[d]Chap. xlix. 13; Amos vi. 8——[e]Heb. *by his soul*——[f]Nah. iii. 15

[g]Heb. *utter*——[h]Chap. l. 15——[i]Gen. i. 1, 6; chap. x. 12, &c.——[k]Job ix. 8; Psa. civ. 2; Isa. xl. 22——[l]Chap. x. 13——[m]Or, *noise*——[n]Psa. cxxxv. 7——[o]Chap. x. 14——[p]Or, *is more brutish than to know*——[q]Chap. l. 2——[r]Chap. x. 15——[s]Chap. x. 16

Verse 10. *The Lord hath brought forth our righteousness.*] This is the answer of the Jews. God has vindicated our cause.

Verse 11. *Make bright the arrows*] This is the prophet's address to Babylon.

The Lord hath raised up the spirit of the kings of the Medes] Of Cyaxares king of Media, called *Darius the Mede* in Scripture; and of Cyrus king of Persia, presumptive heir of the throne of Cyaxares, his uncle. Cambyses, his father, sent him, Cyrus, with 30,000 men to assist his uncle Cyaxares, against Neriglissar king of Babylon, and by these was Babylon overthrown.

Verse 12. *Set up the standard*] A call to the enemies of Babylon to invest the city and press the siege.

Verse 13. *O thou that dwellest upon many waters*] Thou who hast an abundant supply of waters. It was built on the confluence of the Tigris and Euphrates; the latter running through the city. But the *many waters* may mean the many nations which belonged to the Babylonish empire; nations and people are frequently so called in Scripture.

Verse 14. *I will fill thee with men*] By means of these very waters through the channel of thy boasted river, thou shalt be filled with men, suddenly appearing as an army of *locusts;* and, without being expected, shall lift up a terrific cry, as soon as they have risen from the channel of the river.

Verse 15. *He hath made the earth by his power*] The *omnipotence* of God is particularly manifested in the works of *creation.*

He hath established the world by his wisdom] The *omniscience* of God is particularly seen in the *government* of תבל *tebel,* the inhabited surface of the globe. What a profusion of wisdom and skill is apparent in that wondrous *system of providence* by which he governs and provides for every living thing.

And hath stretched out the heaven by his understanding.] Deep thought, comprehensive design, and consummate skill are especially seen in the formation, magnitudes, distances, revolutions, and various affections of the heavenly bodies.

Verse 16. *When he uttereth* his *voice*] Sends *thunder.*

There is *a multitude of waters*] For the *electric spark,* by decomposing atmospheric air, converts the *hydrogen* and *oxygen* gases, of which it is composed, into *water;* which falls down in the form of *rain.*

Causeth the vapours to ascend] He is the Author of that power of *evaporation* by which the water is *rarified,* and, being lighter than the air, ascends in form of *vapour,* forms clouds, and is ready to be sent down again to water the earth by the action of his *lightnings,* as before. And by those same lightnings, and the agency of heat in general, *currents of air* are formed, moving in various directions, which we call *winds.*

Verse 17. *Every man is brutish by* his *knowledge*] He is brutish for want of real knowledge; and he is brutish when he acknowledges that an idol is any thing in the world. These verses, from *fifteen* to *nineteen,* are transcribed from chap. x. 12-16.

A. M. 3409
B. C. 595
Ol. XLVI. 2
Anno
TarquiniiPrisci,
R. Roman., 22

20 [t]Thou *art* my battle axe *and* weapons of war: for [u]with thee will I break in pieces the nations, and with thee will I destroy kingdoms;

21 And with thee will I break in pieces the horse and his rider; and with thee will I break in pieces the chariot and his rider;

22 With thee also will I break in pieces man and woman; and with thee will I break in pieces [v]old and young; and with thee will I break in pieces the young man and the maid;

23 I will also break in pieces with thee the shepherd and his flock; and with thee will I break in pieces the husbandman and his yoke of oxen; and with thee will I break in pieces captains and rulers.

24 [w]And I will render unto Babylon and to all the inhabitants of Chaldea all their evil that they have done in Zion in your sight, saith the LORD.

25 Behold, I *am* against thee, [x]O destroying mountain, saith the LORD, which destroyest all the earth: and I will stretch out mine hand upon thee, and roll thee down from the rocks, [y]and will make thee a burnt mountain.

26 And they shall not take of thee a stone for a corner, nor a stone for foundations; but [z]thou shalt be [a]desolate for ever, saith the LORD.

A. M. 3409
B. C. 595
Ol. XLVI. 2
Anno
TarquiniiPrisci,
R. Roman., 22

27 [b]Set ye up a standard in the land, blow the trumpet among the nations, [c]prepare the nations against her, call together against her [d]the kingdoms of Ararat, Minni, and Ashchenaz; appoint a captain against her; cause the horses to come up as the rough caterpillars.

28 Prepare against her the nations with [e]the kings of the Medes, the captains thereof, and all the rulers thereof, and all the land of his dominion.

29 And the land shall tremble and sorrow, for every purpose of the LORD shall be performed against Babylon, [f]to make the land of Babylon a desolation without an inhabitant.

30 The mighty men of Babylon have forborne to fight, they have remained in *their* holds: their might hath failed; [g]they became as women: they have burned her dwellingplaces; [h]her bars are broken.

31 [i]One post shall run to meet another, and one messenger to meet another, to show the king of Babylon that his city is taken at *one* end,

[t]Isa. x. 5, 15; chap. l. 23——[u]Or, *in thee*, or *by thee* [v]So 2 Chron. xxxvi. 17——[w]Chap. l. 15, 29——[x]Isa. xiii. 2; Zech. iv. 7——[y]Rev. viii. 8——[z]Chap. l. 40 [a]Heb. *everlasting desolations*

[b]Isa. xiii. 2——[c]Chap. xxv. 14——[d]Chap. l. 41 [e]Ver. 11——[f]Chap. l. 13, 39, 40; ver. 43——[g]Isa. xix. 16; chap. xlviii. 41; l. 37——[h]Lam. ii. 9; Amos i. 5; Nah. iii. 13——[i]Chap. l. 24

Verse 20. *Thou* art *my battle axe*] I believe *Nebuchadnezzar* is meant, who is called, chap. l. 23, the *hammer* of the whole earth. Others think the words are spoken of *Cyrus*. All the verbs are in the past tense: "With thee have I broken in pieces," &c., &c.

Verse 24. *And I will render*] The ו *vau* should be translated *but*, of which it has here the full power: "*But* I will render unto Babylon."

Verse 25. *O destroying mountain*] An epithet which he applies to the Babylonish government; it is like a *burning mountain*, which, by vomiting continual streams of *burning lava*, inundates and destroys all towns, villages, fields, &c., in its vicinity.

And roll thee down from the rocks] I will tumble thee from the rocky base on which thou restest. The combustible matter in thy bowels being exhausted, thou shalt appear as an *extinguished* crater; and the *stony matter* which thou castest out shall not be of sufficient substance to make a *foundation stone* for solidity, or a *corner stone* for beauty, ver. 26. Under this beautiful and most expressive metaphor, the prophet shows the nature of the Babylonish government; setting the nations on fire, deluging and destroying them by its troops, till at last, exhausted, it tumbles down, is extinguished, and leaves nothing as a basis to erect a new form of government on; but is altogether *useless*, like the cooled lava, which is, properly speaking, fit for no human purpose.

Verse 27. *Set ye up a standard*] Another summons to the *Medes* and *Persians* to attack Babylon.

Ararat, Minni] The Greater and Lesser Armenia.

And Ashchenaz] A part of Phrygia, near the Hellespont. So *Bochart*, Phaleg, lib. i. c. 3, lib. iii. c. 9. Concerning *Ashchenaz Homer* seems to speak, Il. ii. 370, 371:—

> Φορκυς αυ Φρυγας ηγε, και Ασκανιος θεοειδης,
> Τηλ' εξ Ασκανιης.

"Ascanius, godlike youth, and Phorcys led
The Phrygians from Ascania's distant land."

Calmet thinks that the *Ascantes*, who dwelt in the vicinity of the Tanais, are meant.

Verse 29. *And the land shall tremble*] It is represented here as trembling under the numerous armies that are passing over it, and the prancing of their horses.

Verse 30. *The mighty men—have forborne to fight*] They were panic-struck when they found the Medes and Persians within their walls, and at once saw that resistance was useless.

Verse 31. *One post shall run to meet another*] As the city was taken by *surprise*, in the manner already related, so now messengers, one

A. M. 3409
B. C. 595
Ol. XLVI. 2
Anno
TarquiniiPrisci,
R. Roman., 22

32 And that [k]the passages are
stopped, and the reeds they have
burned with fire, and the men
of war are affrighted.
33 For thus saith the LORD of hosts, the
God of Israel; The daughter of Babylon *is*
[l]like a threshing-floor, [m]*it* [n]*is* time to thresh
her: yet a little while, [o]and the time of her
harvest shall come.
34 Nebuchadrezzar the king of Babylon
hath [p]devoured me, he hath crushed me, he
hath made me an empty vessel, he hath
swallowed me up like a dragon, he hath filled
his belly with my delicates, he hath cast me out.
35 [q]The violence done to me and to my
[r]flesh *be* upon Babylon, shall the [s]inhabitant
of Zion say: and my blood upon the inhabitants of Chaldea, shall Jerusalem say.
36 Therefore thus saith the LORD; Behold,
[t]I will plead thy cause, and take
vengeance for thee; [u]and I will
dry up her sea, and make her
springs dry.

A. M. 3409
B. C. 595
Ol. XLVI. 2
Anno
TarquiniiPrisci,
R. Roman., 22

37 [v]And Babylon shall become heaps, a
dwelling-place for dragons, [w]an astonishment,
and a hissing, without an inhabitant.
38 They shall roar together like lions: they
shall [x]yell as lions' whelps.
39 In their heat I will make their feasts, and
[y]I will make them drunken, that they may
rejoice, and sleep a perpetual sleep, and not
wake, saith the LORD.
40 I will bring them down like lambs to the
slaughter, like rams with he-goats.
41 How is [z]Sheshach taken! and how is
[a]the praise of the whole earth surprised! how
is Babylon become an astonishment among
the nations!

[k]Ch. l. 38——[l]Isa. xxi. 10; Mic. iv. 13; Amos i. 3——[m]Isa. xli. 15; Hab. iii. 12——[n]Or, *in the time that he thresheth her*——[o]Isa. xvii. 5, &c.; Hos. vi. 11; Joel iii. 13; Rev. xiv. 15, 18——[p]Ch. l. 17——[q]Heb. *My violence*

[r]Or, *remainder*——[s]Heb. *inhabitress*——[t]Ch. l. 34——[u]Ch. l. 38——[v]Isa. xiii. 22; ch. l. 39; Rev. xviii. 2——[w]Ch. xxv. 9, 18——[x]Or, *shake themselves*——[y]Ver. 57——[z]Ch. xxv. 26——[a]Isa. xiii. 19; ch. xlix. 25; Dan. iv. 30

after another, were despatched to give the king information of what was done; viz., that the city was taken at *one end. Herodotus* tells us that the *extreme parts* of the city were taken, before those of the *centre* knew any thing of the invasion. *Herodot.* lib. i. c. 191.

Verse 32. *That the passages are stopped*] Either the *bridges* or *slips* for boats, by which the inhabitants passed from one side to the other, and may mean the principal gates or passes in the city, which the victorious army would immediately seize, that they might prevent all communication between the inhabitants.

The reeds they have burned with fire] What this means I cannot tell, unless it refer to something done *after* the taking of the city. *Setting fire to the reeds* in the marshy ground, in order the better to clear the places, and give a freer passage to the water, that it may neither stagnate nor turn the solid ground into a marsh. Dr. *Blayney* thinks it refers to the *firing of the houses*, in order to throw the inhabitants into the greater confusion; but no historian makes any mention of *burning the city*, except what is said ver. 30, "They have burned her dwelling places;" and this may be a poetical expression. That they burnt nothing before they took the city must be evident from the circumstance of their taking the city by *surprise*, in the night time, with the greatest *secrecy*. Still there might have been some gates, barricadoes, or wooden works, serving for barracks or such like, which obstructed some of the great passages, which, when they had entered, they were obliged to *burn*, in order to get themselves a ready passage through the city. This is the more likely because this *burning of reeds* is connected with the *stopping of the passages*, *burning the dwelling places*, and *breaking the bars*.

Verse 33. *The daughter of Babylon* is *like a threshing floor*] The threshing wheel is gone over her; she is trodden under foot.

Verse 34. *Nebuchadrezzar—hath devoured me*] These are the words of Judea; he has taken away all my riches.

He hath cast me out.] He shall vomit all up; i. e., they shall be regained.

Verse 35. *The violence done to me*—be *upon Babylon,—and my blood upon the inhabitants of Chaldea*] Zion begins to speak, ver. 34, and ends with this verse. The answer of Jehovah begins with the next verse. Though the Chaldeans have been the instrument of God to punish the Jews, yet in return they, being themselves exceedingly wicked, shall suffer for all the carnage they have made, and for all the blood they have shed.

Verse 36. *I will dry up her sea*] Exhaust all her treasures.

Verse 37. *Without an inhabitant.*] See chap. l. 39.

Verse 39. *In their heat I will make their feasts*] It was on the night of a feast day, while their hearts were *heated* with wine and revelry, that Babylon was taken; see Dan. v. 1-3. This feast was held in honour of the goddess *Sheshach*, (or perhaps of *Bel*,) who is mentioned, ver. 41, as being taken with her worshippers. As it was in the *night* the city was taken, many had retired to rest, and *never awoke;* slain in their beds, *they slept a perpetual sleep.*

Verse 41. *How is Sheshach taken!*] Perhaps the city is here called by the name of its idol.

The praise of the whole earth] One of the *seven wonders* of the world; superexcellent for the height, breadth, and compass of its *walls*, its *hanging gardens*, the *temple of Belus*, &c., &c.

Verse 42. *The sea is come up*] A multitude of foes have inundated the city.

A. M. 3409
B. C. 595
Ol. XLVI. 2
Anno TarquiniiPrisci,
R. Roman., 22

42 [b]The sea is come up upon
Babylon: she is covered with
the multitude of the waves
thereof.
43 [c]Her cities are a desolation, a dry land,
and a wilderness, a land wherein no man
dwelleth, neither doth *any* son of man pass
thereby.
44 [d]And I will punish Bel in Babylon, and I
will bring forth out of his mouth that which
he hath swallowed up: and the nations shall
not flow together any more unto him: yea,
[e]the wall of Babylon shall fall.
45 [f]My people, go ye out of the midst of
her, and deliver ye every man his soul from
the fierce anger of the LORD.
46 And [g]lest your heart faint, and ye fear
[h]for the rumour that shall be heard in the
land; a rumour shall both come *one* year, and
after that in *another* year *shall come* a rumour,
and violence in the land, ruler against ruler.
47 Therefore, behold, the days come, that
[i]I will [k]do judgment upon the graven images
of Babylon: and her whole land shall be confounded,
and all her slain shall fall in the
midst of her.
48 Then [l]the heaven and the earth, and all
that *is* therein, shall sing for Babylon: [m]for
the spoilers shall come unto her from the
north, saith the LORD.
49 [n]As Babylon *hath caused* the slain of
Israel to fall, so at Babylon shall fall the slain
of all [o]the earth.

A. M. 3409
B. C. 595
Ol. XLVI. 2
Anno TarquiniiPrisci,
R. Roman., 22

50 [p]Ye that have escaped the
sword, go away, stand not still:
remember the LORD afar off, and
let Jerusalem come into your
mind.
51 [q]We are confounded, because we have
heard reproach; shame hath covered our faces:
for strangers are come into the sanctuaries of
the LORD's house.
52 Wherefore, behold, the days come, saith
the LORD, [r]that I will do judgment upon her
graven images: and through all her land the
wounded shall groan.
53 [s]Though Babylon should mount up to
heaven, and though she should fortify the
height of her strength, *yet* from me shall
spoilers come unto her, saith the LORD.
54 [t]A sound of a cry *cometh* from Babylon,
and great destruction from the land of the
Chaldeans:
55 Because the LORD hath spoiled Babylon,
and destroyed out of her the great voice;
when her waves do roar like great waters, a
noise of their voice is uttered:
56 Because the spoiler is come upon her,
even upon Babylon, and her mighty men are
taken, every one of their bows is broken: [u]for
the LORD God of recompenses shall surely
requite.
57 [v]And I will make drunk her princes, and
her wise *men*, her captains, and her rulers,
and her mighty men: and they shall sleep a
perpetual sleep, and not wake, saith [w]the King,

[b]See Isa. viii. 7, 8——[c]Chap. l. 39, 40; ver. 29——[d]Isa. xlvi. 1; chap. l. 2——[e]Ver. 58——[f]Ver. 6; chap. l. 8; Rev. xviii. 4——[g]Or, *let not*——[h]2 Kings xix. 7——[i]Chap. l. 2; ver. 52——[k]Heb. *visit upon*——[l]Isa. xliv. 23; xlix. 43; Rev. xviii. 20——[m]Chap. l. 3, 41

[n]Or, *Both Babylon* is *to fall, O ye slain of Israel, and with Babylon*, &c.——[o]Or, *the country*——[p]Ch. xliv. 28——[q]Psa. xliv. 15, 16; lxxix. 4——[r]Ver. 47——[s]Ch. xlix. 16; Amos ix. 2; Obad. 4——[t]Ch. l. 22——[u]Psa. xciv. 1; ch. lvi. 29; ver. 24——[v]Ver. 39——[w]Ch. xlvi. 18; xlviii. 15

Verse 44. *I will punish Bel in Babylon*] Bel or Belus was their supreme deity.

That which he hath swallowed up] The sacred vessels of the temple of Jerusalem, which were taken thence by Nebuchadnezzar, and dedicated to him in his temple at Babylon.

The wall of Babylon shall fall.] It shall cease to be a defence; and shall moulder away until, in process of time, it shall not be discernible.

Verse 45. *My people, go ye out*] A warning to all the Jews in Babylon to leave the city, and escape for their lives.

Verse 46. *A rumour shall—come* one *year*] A year before the capture of the city there shall be a rumour of war,—and in that year Belshazzar was defeated by Cyrus. In the *following year* the city was taken.

Verse 48. *The heaven and the earth—shall sing for Babylon*] Its fall shall be a subject of universal rejoicing.

Verse 50. *Ye that have escaped the sword*] The Jews.

Let Jerusalem come into your mind.] Pray for its restoration; and embrace the first opportunity offered of returning thither.

Verse 51. *Strangers are come into the sanctuaries*] The lamentation of the pious Jews for the profanation of the temple by the Chaldeans.

Verse 53. *Though Babylon should mount up to heaven*] Though it were fortified even to the skies, it shall fall by the enemies that I will send against it.

Verse 55. *The great voice*] Its *pride* and insufferable boasting.

Verse 56. *The Lord God of recompenses*] The fall of Babylon is an act of Divine justice; whatever it suffers, it is in consequence of its crimes.

Verse 57. *I will make drunk her princes*] See on ver. 39.

A. M. 3409
B. C. 595
Ol. XLVI. 2
Anno TarquiniiPrisci, R. Roman., 22

whose name *is* the LORD of
hosts.
58 Thus saith the LORD of
hosts; [x]The [y]broad walls of
Babylon shall be utterly [z]broken, and her high
gates shall be burned with fire; and [a]the people shall labour in vain, and the folk in the
fire, and they shall be weary.
59 The word which Jeremiah the prophet
commanded Seraiah the son of Neriah, the
son of Maaseiah, when he went [b]with Zedekiah the king of Judah into Babylon in the
fourth year of his reign. And *this* Seraiah
was a [c]quiet prince.
60 So Jeremiah wrote in a book all the evil
that should come upon Babylon, *even* all these
words that are written against Babylon.
61 And Jeremiah said to
Seraiah, When thou comest to
Babylon, and shalt see, and shalt
read all these words;
62 Then shalt thou say, O LORD, thou hast
spoken against this place, to cut it off, that
[d]none shall remain in it, neither man nor
beast, but that it shall be [e]desolate for ever.
63 And it shall be, when thou hast made an
end of reading this book, [f]*that* thou shalt bind
a stone to it, and cast it into the midst of
Euphrates:
64 And thou shalt say, Thus shall Babylon sink, and shall not rise from the evil
that I will bring upon her: [g]and they shall
be weary. Thus far *are* the words of Jeremiah.

[x]Or, *The walls of broad Babylon*——[y]Verse 44 [z]Or, *made naked*——[a]Habakkuk ii. 13——[b]Or, *on the behalf of*

[c]Or, *prince of Menucha*, or *chief chamberlain*——[d]Ch. l. 3, 39; verse 29——[e]Heb. *desolations*——[f]See Rev. xviii. 21——[g]Ver. 58

Verse 58. *The broad walls of Babylon*] Herodotus, who saw these walls, says, "The city was a regular square, each side of which was *one hundred and twenty* stadia, the circumference *four hundred and eighty* stadia. It was surrounded by a wall *fifty* cubits broad, and *two hundred* cubits high; and each side had *twenty-five* brazen gates."—*Herod.*, lib. i. c. 178. Had not Cyrus resorted to *stratagem*, humanly speaking, he could not have taken this city. For the destruction of this wall and its very vestiges, see on Isa. xiii. 19.

Verse 59. *The word which Jeremiah*] On account of the message sent by Jeremiah to the Jewish captives in Babylon.

Verse 60. *Wrote in a book*] Whether this book contained any more than is recorded in this place we do not know; probably it contained no more than what is found in verses 62-64. A *book*, ספר *sepher*, signifies, in Hebrew, any writing, *great* or *small*.

Verse 64. *Thus shall Babylon sink, &c.*] This is the emblem of its overthrow and irretrievable ruin. See Rev. xviii. 21, where we find that this is an emblem of the total ruin of *mystical Babylon*.

Herodotus relates a similar action of the *Phocæans*, who, having resolved to leave their country, and never return to it again, *μυδρον σιδηρεον κατεποντωσαν, και ωμοσαν μη πριν ες Φωκαιην ἡξειν, πριν η τον μυδρον τουτον αναφηναι·* "threw a mass of iron into the sea, and swore that they would never return to Phocæa till that iron mass should rise and swim on the top." The story is this: The Phocæans, being besieged by Harpagus, general of the Persians, demanded one day's truce to deliberate on the propositions he had made to them relative to their surrendering their city; and begged that in the mean while he would take off his army from the walls. Harpagus having consented, they carried their wives, children, and their most valuable effects, aboard their ships; then, throwing a mass of iron into the sea, bound themselves by an oath never to return till that iron should rise to the top and swim. See *Herodotus*, lib. i. c. 165.

Horace refers to this in his epode *Ad Populum Romanum*, Epode xvi. ver. 25:—

Sed juremus in hæc: simul imis saxa renarint
Vadis levata, ne redire sit nefas.

"As the Phocæans oft for freedom bled,
At length with imprecated curses fled."
FRANCIS.

Thus far are *the words of Jeremiah.*] It appears that the following chapter is not the work of this prophet: it is not his style. The author of it writes *Jehoiachin;* Jeremiah writes him always *Jeconiah*, or *Coniah*. It is merely historical, and is very similar to 2 Kings xxiv. 18-xxv. 30. The author, whoever he was, relates the capture of Jerusalem, the fate of Zedekiah, the pillage and burning of the city and the temple. He mentions also certain persons of distinction who were slain by the Chaldeans. He mentions the number of the captives that were carried to Babylon at three different times; and concludes with the deliverance of King Jehoiachin from prison in Babylon, in which he had been for thirty-seven years. It is very likely that the whole chapter has been compiled from some chronicle of that time; or it was designed as a *preface* to the Book of the *Lamentations;* and would stand with great propriety before it, as it contains the *facts* on which that inimitable poem is built. Were it allowable, I would remove it to that place.

CHAPTER LII

This chapter was added after Jeremiah's time probably by Ezra, after the return from the captivity, of which it gives a short account, nearly the same as in 2 Kings xxiv. 18–20, *and* xxv. *It is very properly subjoined to the preceding prophecies, in order to show how exactly they were fulfilled. It likewise forms a proper introduction to the following Lamentations, as it gives an account of the mournful events which gave rise to them. Zedekiah's evil reign and rebellion against Nebuchadnezzar,* 1–3. *Jerusalem is taken by the Chaldeans after a siege of* eighteen *months,* 4–7. *Zedekiah pursued and taken in the plains of Jericho, and his whole army dispersed,* 8, 9. *The king's sons and all the princes of Judah slain in Riblah,* 10. *Zedekiah has his eyes put out by order of the Chaldean monarch; and is afterward bound in chains, carried to Babylon, and imprisoned for life,* 11. *Nebuzar-adan, the captain of the guard, burns and spoils the city and temple,* 12–19. *The two pillars of the temple, with their dimensions and ornaments,* 20–23. *The officers of the temple, and several others, carried away captives into Babylon, and then slain by order of Nebuchadnezzar,* 24–27. *The number of Jews that Nebuchadnezzar carried away captive in the* seventh *year of his reign,* 28; *in his* eighteenth *year,* 29; *and in his* twenty-third *year* 30. *Evil-merodach, the son of Nebuchadnezzar, in the year of his accession to the throne of Babylon,* (*which was in the* thirty-seventh *year of the captivity, and the* one hundred and ninety-first *from the building of Rome, according to the computation of Varro,*) *orders Jehoiachin to be taken out of prison, and treats him kindly for the remainder of his life,* 31–34.

A. M. 3406–3416 B. C. 598–588 Ol. XLV. 3–XLVIII. 1

ZEDEKIAH *was* [a]one and twenty years old when he [b]began to reign, and he reigned eleven years in Jerusalem. And his mother's name *was* Hamutal the daughter of Jeremiah of Libnah.

2 And he did *that which was* evil in the eyes of the LORD, according to all that Jehoiakim had done.

A. M. cir. 3411 B. C. cir. 593 Ol. XLVI. 4 TarquiniiPrisci, R. Roman., cir. annum 24

3 For through the anger of the LORD it came to pass in Jerusalem and Judah, till he had cast them out from his presence, that Zedekiah rebelled against the king of Babylon.

A. M. 3414 B. C. 590 Ol. XLVII. 3 Anno TarquiniiPrisci, R. Roman., 27

4 And it came to pass in the [c]ninth year of his reign, in the tenth month, in the tenth *day* of the month, *that* Nebuchadrezzar king of Babylon came, he and all his army, against Jerusalem, and pitched against it, and built forts against it round about.

A. M. 3414–3416 B. C. 590–588 Ol. XLVII. 3–XLVIII. 1

5 So the city was besieged unto the eleventh year of king Zedekiah.

A. M. 3416 B. C. 588 Ol. XLVIII. 1 Anno TarquiniiPrisci, R. Roman., 29

6 And in the fourth month, in the ninth *day* of the month, the famine was sore in the city, so that there was no bread for the people of the land.

7 Then the city was broken up, and all the men of war fled, and went forth out of the city by night by the way of the gate between the two walls, which *was* by the king's garden; (now the Chaldeans *were* by the city round about:) and they went by the way of the plain.

8 But the army of the Chaldeans pursued after the king, and overtook Zedekiah in the plains of Jericho; and all his army was scattered from him.

9 [d]Then they took the king, and carried him up unto the king of Babylon to Riblah in the land of Hamath; where he gave judgment upon him.

10 [e]And the king of Babylon slew the sons of Zedekiah before his eyes: he slew also all the princes of Judah in Riblah.

11 Then he [f]put out the eyes of Zedekiah; and the king of Babylon bound him in [g]chains,

[a]2 Kings xxiv. 18——[b]Heb. *reigned*——[c]2 Kings xxv. 1–27; chap. xxxix. 1; Zech. viii. 19

[d]Chap. xxxii. 4——[e]Ezek. xii. 13——[f]Heb. *blinded* [g]Or, *fetters*

NOTES ON CHAP. LII

Verse 1. *Zedekiah* was *one and twenty years old*] See 2 Kings xxiv. 18.

Verse 2. *And he did—evil*] This and the following verse are the same as 2 Kings xxiv. 19.

Verse 3. *Through the anger of the Lord*] Here is a king given to a people in God's anger, and taken away in his displeasure.

Verse 4. *Ninth year—tenth month*] Answering nearly to our January.

Verse 5. *So the city was besieged*] It held out *one year and six months.*

Verse 6. *And in the fourth month*] See the notes on chap. xxxix. 1, &c. The *fourth* month answers nearly to our July.

Verse 8. *The army of the Chaldeans pursued*] See on 2 Kings xxv. 5.

Verse 9. *King of Babylon to Riblah*] See the note on chap. xxxix. 5.

Verse 11. *He put out the eyes of Zedekiah*] See on chap. xxxix. 7.

A. M. 3416 B. C. 588 Ol. XLVIII. 1 Anno TarquiniiPrisci, R. Roman., 29

and carried him to Babylon, and put him in [h]prison till the day of his death.

12 [i]Now in the fifth month, in the tenth *day* of the month, [k]which *was* the nineteenth year of Nebuchadrezzar king of Babylon, [l]came Nebuzar-adan, [m]captain[n] of the guard, *which* [o]served the king of Babylon, into Jerusalem,

13 And burned the house of the LORD, and the king's house; and all the houses of Jerusalem, and all the houses of the great *men,* burned he with fire:

14 And all the army of the Chaldeans, that *were* with the captain of the guard, brake down all the walls of Jerusalem round about.

15 [p]Then Nebuzar-adan the captain of the guard carried away captive *certain* of the poor of the people, and the residue of the people that remained in the city, and those that fell away, that fell to the king of Babylon, and the rest of the multitude.

16 But Nebuzar-adan the captain of the guard left *certain* of the poor of the land for vinedressers and for husbandmen.

17 [q]Also the [r]pillars of brass that *were* in the house of the LORD, and the bases, and the brazen sea that *was* in the house of the LORD the Chaldeans brake, and carried all the brass of them to Babylon.

18 [s]The caldrons also, and the [t]shovels, and the snuffers, and the [u]bowls, and the spoons, and all the vessels of brass wherewith they ministered, took they away.

19 And the basins, and the [v]firepans, and the bowls, and the caldrons, and the candlesticks, and the spoons, and the cups; *that* which *was* of gold *in* gold, and *that* which *was* of silver *in* silver, took the captain of the guard away.

A. M. 3416 B. C. 588 Ol. XLVIII. 1 Anno TarquiniiPrisci, R. Roman., 29

20 The two pillars, one sea, and twelve brazen bulls that were under the bases, which king Solomon had made in the house of the LORD: [w]the [x]brass of all these vessels was without weight.

21 And *concerning* the [y]pillars, the height of one pillar *was* eighteen cubits; and a [z]fillet of twelve cubits did compass it; and the thickness thereof *was* four fingers: *it was* hollow.

22 And a chapiter of brass *was* upon it; and the height of one chapiter *was* five cubits, with network and pomegranates upon the chapiters round about, all *of* brass. The second pillar also and the pomegranates *were* like unto these.

23 And there were ninety and six pomegranates on a side; *and* [a]all the pomegranates upon the network *were* a hundred round about.

24 And [b]the captain of the guard took Seraiah the chief priest, [c]and Zephaniah the second priest, and the three keepers of the [d]door:

25 He took also out of the city an eunuch, which had the charge of the men of war; and seven men of them that [e]were near the king's person, which were found in the city; and the [f]principal scribe of the host, who mustered the people of the land; and threescore men of the people of the land, that were found in the midst of the city.

26 So Nebuzar-adan the captain of the guard took them, and brought them to the king of Babylon to Riblah.

27 And the king of Babylon smote them, and put them to death in Riblah in the land of Hamath. Thus [g]Judah was carried away captive out of his own land.

---

[h]Heb. *house of the wards*——[i]Zech. vii. 5; viii. 19——[k]See ver. 29——[l]Chap. xxxix. 9——[m]Or, *chief marshal*——[n]Heb. *chief of the executioners,* or *slaughtermen;* and so ver. 14, &c.——[o]Heb. *stood before*——[p]Chap. xxxix. 8, 9——[q]Chap. xxvii. 19——[r]See 1 Kings vii. 15, 23, 27, 50——[s]Exod. xxvii. 3; 2 Kings xxv. 14, 15, 16——[t]Or, *instruments to remove the ashes*

[u]Or, *basins*——[v]Or, *censers*——[w]1 Kings vii. 47——[x]Heb. *their brass*——[y]1 Kings vii. 15; 2 Kings xxv. 17; 2 Chronicles iii. 15——[z]Hebrews, *thread*——[a]See 1 Kings vii. 20——[b]2 Kings xxv. 18——[c]Chap. xxi. 1; xxix. 25——[d]Hebrew, *threshold*——[e]Hebrew, *saw the face of the king*——[f]Or, *scribe of the captain of the host*——[g]Lam. i. 3

Verse 12. *Now in the fifth month*] Answering nearly to our August.

Verse 13. *And burned the house of the Lord*] Thus perished this magnificent structure, after it had stood *four hundred and twenty-four* years *three* months and *eight* days. It was built A. M. 2992, and destroyed A. M. 3416.

Verse 15. *Those that fell away*] The deserters to the Chaldeans during the siege.

Verse 16. *The poor of the land*] See on chap. xxxix. 1.

Verse 17. *Also the pillars*] See on chap. xxvii. 19.

Verses 18-23. In reference to these verses see the parallel texts in the margin, the various readings there, and the notes.

Verse 24. *The second priest*] See the note on 2 Kings xxv. 18.

The three keepers] The priests who stood at the door to receive the offerings of the people, see 2 Kings xx. 9, and xxiii. 4.

Verse 25. *Seven men—that were near the*

A. M. 3404 B. C. 600 Ol. XLV. 1 Anno TarquiniiPrisci, R. Roman., 17

28 [h]This *is* the people whom
Nebuchadrezzar carried away
captive: in the [i]seventh year
[k]three thousand Jews and three
and twenty:

A. M. 3415 B. C. 589 Ol. XLVII. 4 Anno TarquiniiPrisci, R. Roman., 28

29 [l]In the eighteenth year of
Nebuchadrezzar he carried away
captive from Jerusalem eight
hundred thirty and two [m]persons:

A. M. 3420 B. C. 584 Ol. XLIX. 1 Anno TarquiniiPrisci, R. Roman., 33

30 In the three and twentieth
year of Nebuchadrezzar Nebuzar-adan the captain of the guard
carried away captive of the Jews
seven hundred forty and five persons: all the
persons *were* four thousand and
six hundred.

A. M. 3442 B. C. 562 Ol. LIV. 3 Anno Servii Tullii, R. Roman., 17

31 [n]And it came to pass in the
seven and thirtieth year of the
captivity of Jehoiachin king of Judah, in the
twelfth month, in the five and twentieth *day*
of the month, *that* Evil-merodach king of
Babylon in the *first* year of his reign [o]lifted
up the head of Jehoiachin king of Judah, and
brought him forth out of prison,
32 And spake [p]kindly unto him, and set his
throne above the throne of the kings that *were*
with him in Babylon,
33 And changed his prison garments: [q]and

[h]2 Kings xxiv. 2——[i]See 2 Kings xxiv. 12——[k]See 2 Kings xxiv. 14——[l]See ver. 12; ch. xxxix. 9——[m]Heb. *souls*——[n]2 Kings xxv. 27, 28, 29, 30——[o]Gen. xiv. 13, 20——[p]Heb. *good things with him*——[q]2 Sam. ix. 13

king's person] These were privy counsellors.

Verses 28-30. On these verses Dr. *Blayney* has some sensible remarks; I will extract the substance. These verses are not inserted in 2 Kings xxv. Are we to conclude from these verses that the whole number of the Jews which Nebuchadnezzar, in all his expeditions, carried away, was no more than *four thousand six hundred?* This cannot be true; for he carried away more than twice that number at one time; and this is expressly said to have been in the *eighth* year of his reign, 2 Kings xxiv. 12-16. Before that time he had carried off a number of captives from Jerusalem, in the *first* year of his reign, among whom were *Daniel* and his companions, Dan. i. 3-6. These are confessedly not noticed here. And as the taking and burning of Jerusalem is in this very chapter said to have been in the *fourth* and *fifth* months of the *nineteenth* year of the reign of Nebuchadnezzar, those who were carried into captivity at the date of those events cannot possibly be the same with those that are said to be carried away either in the *eighteenth* or *twenty-third* year of that prince. Nor, indeed, is it credible that the number carried away at the time that the city was taken, and the whole country reduced, could be so few as *eight hundred and thirty-two*, (see ver. 29;) supposing a mistake in the date of the year, which some are willing to do without sufficient grounds.

Here then we have *three* deportations, and those the most considerable ones, in the *first*, in the *eighth*, and *nineteenth* years of Nebuchadnezzar, sufficiently distinguished from those in the *seventh*, *eighteenth*, and *twenty-third* years. So that it seems most reasonable to conclude with Abp. *Usher*, in *Chronologia Sacra*, that by the latter *three* the historian meant to point out deportations of a minor kind, not elsewhere noticed in direct terms in Scripture.

The *first* of these, said to have been in the *seventh* year of Nebuchadnezzar, was one of those that had been picked up in several parts of Judah by the band of Chaldeans, Syrians, and others, whom the king of Babylon sent against the land previously to his own coming, 2 Kings xxiv. 2.

That in the *eighteenth* year corresponds with the time when the Chaldean army broke off the siege before Jerusalem, and marched to meet the Egyptian army, at which time they might think it proper to send off the prisoners that were in camp, under a guard to Babylon.

And the *last*, in the *twenty-third* year of Nebuchadnezzar, was when that monarch, being engaged in the siege of Tyre, sent off Nebuzar-adan against the Moabites, Ammonites, and other neighbouring nations, who at the same time carried away the gleanings of Jews that remained in their own land, amounting in all to no more than *seven hundred* and *forty-five*.

Josephus speaks of this expedition against the Moabites and Ammonites, which he places in the *twenty-third* year of Nebuchadnezzar; but mentions nothing done in the land of Israel at that time. Only he says that after the conquest of those nations, Nebuchadnezzar carried his victorious arms against Egypt, which he in some measure reduced, and carried the Jews whom he found there captives to Babylon. But the Egyptian expedition was not till the *twenty-seventh* year of Jehoiachin's captivity, i. e., the *thirty-fifth* of Nebuchadnezzar, as may be collected from Ezek. xxix. 17; so that those who were carried away in the *twenty-third* year were not from Egypt, but were, as before observed, the few Jews that remained in the land of Judah.

Verse 31. *In the twelfth month*] Answering nearly to our *twenty-fifth* of *April*, A. M. 3442.

Lifted up the head of Jehoiachin] This phrase is taken from Gen. xl. 13. It is founded on the observation that those who are in sorrow *hold down* their heads, and when they are comforted, or the cause of their sorrow removed, *they lift up their heads.* The Hebrew phrase, *lift up the head*, signifies to *comfort*, *cheer*, *make happy.*

Verse 32. *Spake kindly*] Conversed freely with him.

Set his throne] Gave him a more respectable *seat* than any of the captive princes, or better than even his own princes had, probably near his person.

Verse 33. *And changed his prison garments*] That is, Jehoiachin changed his own garments, that he might be suited in that respect to the state of his elevation. Kings also, in token of

A. M. 3442 B. C. 562 Ol. LIV. 3 Anno Servii Tullii, R. Roman., 17

he did continually eat bread before him all the days of his life.

34 And *for* his diet, there was a continual diet given him of the king of Babylon, [r]every day a portion until the day of his death, all the days of his life.

[r]Heb. *the matter of the day in his day*

favour, gave caftans or robes to those whom they wish to honour.

And he did continually eat bread before him] Was a constant guest at the king's table.

Verse 34. *And—there was a continual diet given him*] This was probably a ration allowed by the king for the support of Jehoiachin's household. For other particulars, see the note on 2 Kings xxv. 30.

All the days of his life.] I believe these words have been by mistake added from the preceding verse. *There*, they are proper; *here*, they are tautological. They are wanting in the *Septuagint* and in the *Arabic*.

The preceding words, עד יום מותו *ad yom motho*, "to the day of his death," are wanting in two of *De Rossi's* and one of *Kennicott's* MSS.

Coverdale ends thus: **All the days of his life untill he died.** This is better than the common Version.

Immediately after this verse my old MS. Bible adds the following words: **And done is aftir that into caitifte is brougt Israel, and Jerusalem is destroide, satte Jerempe the prophet weepund, and weiled with this lamentation Jerusalem; and with bitter inwit sighand and criand weilawai, seide.** Then follows in red letters: **Here beginneth the Lamentation of Jerempe, that is intitle Cenoth; with the sortynge out of Ebrue letters.** Aleph: **How sittith aloon the city**, &c. See something of a similar kind from other authorities, at the beginning of Lamentations.

Masoretic Notes.

Number of verses in this Book, 1365.

Middle verse, chap. xxviii. 11.

Masoretic sections, 31.

INTRODUCTION

TO THE

LAMENTATIONS

OF

JEREMIAH

THIS book, like the several books of the Pentateuch, is denominated in Hebrew איכה *eicah, how,* from its first word; and sometimes קינות *kinnoth, lamentations,* from its subject. In the *Septuagint* it is termed ΘΡΗΝΟΙ ΤΟΥ ΙΕΡΕΜΙΟΥ, for the same reason. The *Syriac* and *Arabic* copy or follow the *Septuagint;* and so does the *Vulgate,* from the *Lamentationes* of which, the book has that name which it bears in our language. In the *Chaldee* it has no name; and in it, and perhaps anciently in the *Hebrew,* it was written consecutively with the last chapter of Jeremiah.

It is one of the books of the מגילות *Megilloth,* or Roll, among the Jews; and because it relates to the ruin of their affairs, and contains promises of restoration, it is peculiarly prized, and frequently read. The five Megilloth are: *Ecclesiastes, Canticles, Lamentations, Ruth,* and *Esther.*

There has been little difference among learned men concerning the *author* of this book. The whole current of antiquity and modern times has pointed out Jeremiah as the writer: of this the style is a sufficient evidence. Mr. *John Henry Pareau,* in a Dissertation prefixed to his Translation and Notes on this book, (8vo. Lugd. Bat. 1790,) has proved this point amply from a general collation of the prophecy of Jeremiah with select passages in this book. I have heard of but one learned man who has entertained serious doubts on the subject, Mr. *Herman Van der Hardt,* who has supposed the five chapters were written by *Daniel, Shadrach, Meshach, Abednego,* and *Jeconiah.* To this opinion I suppose none has ever been converted.

There has been more difference of opinion relative to the *subject* and *occasion.* Some have thought the book was composed on the *death of Josiah;* others that it was composed on occasion of the *destruction of Jerusalem,* and the *various desolations* connected with it. To *this* all its parts and its general phraseology seem best to apply; and this is the sentiment most generally embraced at present. This will receive much proof from a minute consideration of the book itself.

The *composition* of this poem is what may be called very technical. Every chapter, except the last, is an *acrostic.* Of the *two first,* each verse begins with a several letter of the Hebrew alphabet, in the order of the letters, with this exception, that in the *second, third,* and *fourth* chapters, the פ *phe* is put before the ע *ain;* whereas in all the acrostic Psalms the latter preceded the former, as it does in all *grammars* of the Hebrew language. In the *first* and *second* chapters each verse is composed of *three hemistichs* or half verses, except the *seventh* verse of the *first,* and the *nineteenth* of the *second* chapter, which have each *four* hemistichs.

The *third* chapter contains *sixty-four* verses, each, as before, formed of *three hemistichs,* but with this difference, that each hemistich begins with the same letter, so that the whole alphabet is *thrice* repeated in this chapter.

The *fourth* chapter is made up of *twenty-two* verses, according to the number of the Hebrew letters; but the composition is different from all the rest, for each verse consists of only *two* hemistichs, and those much shorter than any in the preceding chapters.

I have called this an inimitable poem; better judges are of the same opinion. "Never," says Bishop *Lowth,* "was there a more rich and elegant variety of beautiful images and adjuncts arranged together within so small a compass, nor more happily chosen and applied."

"One would think," says Dr. *South,* "that every letter was written with a tear; every word, the sound of a breaking heart: that the author was compacted of sorrows; disciplined to grief from his infancy; one who never breathed but in sighs, nor spoke but in a groan."

"Nor can we too much admire," says Dr. *Blayney,* "the full and graceful flow of that pathetic eloquence in which the author pours forth the effusions of a patriotic heart, and piously weeps over the ruins of his venerable country. But it was observed before that the prophet's peculiar talent lay in working up and expressing the passions of grief and *pity;* and, unhappily for him as a man and a citizen, he met with a subject but too well calculated to give his genius its full display."

David in several places has forcibly depicted the sorrows of a heart oppressed with penitential sorrow; but where, in a composition of such length, have bodily misery and mental agony been more successfully painted? All the expressions and images of sorrow are here exhibited in various combinations, and in various points of view. *Misery* has no expression that the author of the *Lamentations* has not employed. Patriots! you who tell us you burn for your country's welfare, look at the prophecies and history of this extraordinary man; look at his *Lamentations;* take him through his life to his death, and learn from him what true patriotism means! The man who watched, prayed, and lived for the welfare of his country; who choose to share her adversities, her sorrows, her wants, her afflictions, and disgrace, where he might have been a companion of princes, and have sat at the table of kings; who only ceased to live for his country when he ceased to breathe;—that was a patriot, in comparison with whom almost all others are obscured, minished, and brought low, or are totally annihilated!

THE
LAMENTATIONS
OF
JEREMIAH

Chronological notes relative to the Book of the Lamentations

Year from the Creation, according to Archbishop Usher, 3416.—Year of the Jewish era of the world, 3173. —Year from the Deluge, 1760.—First year of the *forty-eighth* Olympiad.—Year from the building of Rome, according to the Varronian account, 166.—Year before the birth of Christ, 584.—Year before the vulgar era of Christ's nativity, 588.—Year of the Julian Period, 4126.—Year of the era of Nabonassar, 160.—Cycle of the Sun, 10.—Cycle of the Moon, 3.—Second year after the fourth Sabbatic year after the *seventeenth* Jewish jubilee, according to Helvicus.—Twenty-ninth year of Tarquinius Priscus, the fifth king of the Romans: this was the *seventy-ninth* year before the commencement of the consular government. —Thirty-eighth year of Cyaxares or Cyaraxes, the fourth king of Media.—Eighteenth year of Agasicles, king of Lacedæmon, of the family of the Proclidæ.—Twentieth year of Leon, king of Lacedæmon, of the family of the Eurysthenidæ. Thirty-second year of Alyattes II., king of Lydia. This was the father of the celebrated Crœsus.—Fifteenth year of Æropas, the seventh king of Macedon.—Nineteenth year of Nebuchadnezzar, king of Babylon.—Eleventh year of Zedekiah, the last king of Judah.

CHAPTER I

The prophet begins with lamenting the dismal reverse of fortune that befell his country, confessing at the same time that her calamities were the just consequence of her sins, 1–6. Jerusalem herself is then personified and brought forward to continue the sad complaint, and to solicit the mercy of God, 7–22.

A. M. cir. 3416
B. C. cir. 588
Ol. XLVIII. 1
TarquiniiPrisci, R. Roman., cir. annum 29

HOW doth the city sit solitary,
that was full of people:
[a]*how* is she become as a widow!
she *that was* great among the
nations, *and* [b]princess among the
provinces, *how* is she become
tributary!
2 She [c]weepeth sore in the

A. M. cir. 3416
B. C. cir. 588
Ol. XLVIII. 1
TarquiniiPrisci, R. Roman., cir. annum 29

[a]Isa. xlvii. 7, 8——[b]Ezra iv. 20

[c]Jer. xiii. 17

In all copies of the *Septuagint*, whether of the Roman or Alexandrian editions, the following words are found as a part of the text: Και εγενετο μετα το αιχμαλωτισθηναι τον Ισραηλ, και Ιερουσαλημ ερημωθηναι, εκαθισεν Ιερεμιας κλαιων, και εθρηνησεν τον θρηνον τουτον επι Ιερουσαλημ, και ειπεν·—"And it came to pass after Israel had been carried away captive, and Jerusalem was become desolate, that Jeremiah sat weeping: and he lamented with this lamentation over Jerusalem; and he said."

The *Vulgate* has the same, with some variations:—"Et factum est, postquam in captivitatem redactus est Israel, et Jerusalem deserta est, sedit Jeremias propheta flens, et planxit lamentatione hac in Jerusalem, et amaro animo suspirans et ejulans, dixit." The translation of this, as given in the *first translation* of the Bible into English, may be found at the end of Jeremiah, taken from an ancient MS. in my own possession.

I subjoin another taken from the *first* PRINTED *edition* of the English Bible, that by *Coverdale*, 1535. "And it came to passe, (after Israel was brought into captyvitie, and Jerusalem destroyed;) that Jeremy the prophet sat weeping, mournynge, and makinge his mone in Jerusalem; so that with an hevy herte he sighed and sobbed, sayenge."

Matthew's Bible, printed in 1549, refines upon this: "It happened after Israell was brought into captyvite, and Jerusalem destroyed, that Jeremy the prophet sate wepyng, and sorrowfully bewayled Jerusalem; and syghynge and hewlynge with an hevy and wooful hert, sayde."

Becke's Bible of the same date, and *Cardmarden's* of 1566, have the same, with a trifling change in the *orthography*.

On this *Becke* and others have the following note:—"These words are read in the LXX. interpreters: but not in the Hebrue."

All these show that it was the ancient opinion

A. M. cir. 3416 B. C. cir. 588 Ol. XLVIII 1. TarquiniiPrisci, R. Roman., cir. annum 29

[d]night, and her tears are on her
cheeks: [e]among all her lovers
[f]she hath none to comfort *her:*
all her friends have dealt treacherously with her, they are become her enemies.
3 [g]Judah is gone into captivity because of
affliction, and [h]because of great servitude:
[i]she dwelleth among the heathen, she findeth
no rest: all her persecutors overtook her between the straits.
4 The ways of Zion do mourn, because none
come to the solemn feasts: all her gates are
desolate: her priests sigh, her
virgins are afflicted, and she *is*
in bitterness.
5 Her adversaries [k]are the
chief, her enemies prosper; for the LORD hath
afflicted her [l]for the multitude of her transgressions: her [m]children are gone into captivity before the enemy.
6 And from the daughter of Zion all her
beauty is departed: her princes are become
like harts *that* find no pasture, and they are
gone without strength before the pursuer.

[d]Job vii. 3; Psalm vi. 6——[e]Jeremiah iv. 30; xxx. 14; ver. 19——[f]Verses 9, 16, 17, 21——[g]Jeremiah lii. 27——[h]Hebrew, *for the greatness of servitude*

[i]Deuteronomy xxviii. 64, 65; chapter ii. 9——[k]Deuteronomy xxviii. 43, 44——[l]Jeremiah xxx. 14, 15; Daniel ix. 7, 16——[m]Jer. lii. 28

that the Book of Lamentations was composed, not over the death of *Josiah*, but on account of the *desolations of Israel and Jerusalem.*

The *Arabic* copies the *Septuagint.* The *Syriac* does not acknowledge it; and the *Chaldee* has these words only: "Jeremiah the great priest and prophet said."

NOTES ON CHAP. I

Verse 1. *How doth the city sit solitary*]. Sitting down, with the elbow on the knee, and the head supported by the hand, without any company, unless an oppressor near,—all these were signs of mourning and distress. The coin struck by Vespasian on the capture of Jerusalem, on the obverse of which there is a *palm-tree*, the emblem of Judea, and under it a woman, the emblem of Jerusalem, sitting, leaning as before described, with the legend *Judea capta*, illustrates this expression as well as that in Isa. xlvii. 1. See the note on Isa. iii. 26, where the subject is farther explained.

Become as a widow] Having lost her *king. Cities* are commonly described as the *mothers* of their *inhabitants*, the *kings* as *husbands*, and the *princes* as *children.* When therefore they are bereaved of these, they are represented as *widows*, and *childless.*

The *Hindoo* widow, as well as the *Jewish*, is considered the most destitute and wretched of all human beings. She has her hair cut short, throws off all ornaments, eats the coarsest food, fasts often, and is all but an outcast in the family of her late husband.

Is she become tributary!] Having no longer the political form of a nation; and the remnant that is left paying tribute to a foreign and heathen conqueror.

Verse 2. *Among all her lovers*] Her allies; her *friends*, instead of helping her, have helped her enemies. Several who sought her friendship when she was in prosperity, in the time of David and Solomon, are now among her enemies.

Verse 3. *Between the straits.*] She has been brought into such difficulties, that it was impossible for her to escape. Has this any reference to the circumstances in which Zedekiah and the princes of Judah endeavoured to escape from Jerusalem, *by the way of the gates between the two walls?* Jer. lii. 7.

Verse 4. *The ways of Zion do mourn*] A fine prosopopœia. The ways in which the people trod coming to the sacred solemnities, being now no longer frequented, are represented as *shedding tears;* and the *gates* themselves partake of the general distress. All poets of eminence among the Greeks and Romans have recourse to this image. So *Moschus*, in his Epitaph on *Bion*, ver. 1-3:—

Αιλινα μοι στροναχειτε ναπαι, και Δωριον ὑδωρ
Και ποταμοι κλαιοιτε τον ἱμεροεντα Βιωνα.
Νυν φυτα μοι μυρεσθε, και αλσεα νυν γοαοισθε, κ. τ. λ.

"Ye winds, with grief your waving summits bow,
Ye Dorian fountains, murmur as ye flow;
From weeping urns your copious sorrows shed,
And bid the rivers mourn for Bion dead.
Ye shady groves, in robes of sable hue,
Bewail, ye plants, in pearly drops of dew;
Ye drooping flowers, diffuse a languid breath,
And die with sorrow, at sweet Bion's death."
FAWKES.

So *Virgil*, Æn. vii., ver. 759:—

Te nemus Anguitiæ, vitrea te Fucinus unda
Te liquidi flevere lacus.

"For thee, wide echoing, sighed th' Anguitian woods;
For thee, in murmurs, wept thy native floods."

And more particularly on the *death of Daphnis*, Eclog. v. ver. 24:—

Non ulli pastos illis egere diebus
Frigida, Daphni, boves ad flumina: nulla neque amnem
Libavit quadrupes, nec graminis attigit herbam.
Daphni, tuum Pœnos etiam ingemuisse leones
Interitum, montesque feri, sylvæque loquuntur.

"The swains forgot their sheep, nor near the brink
Of running waters brought their herds to drink:
The thirsty cattle of themselves abstained
From water, and their grassy fare disdained.
The death of Daphnis woods and hills deplore;
The Libyan lions hear, and hearing roar."
DRYDEN.

Verse 5. *Her adversaries are the chief*] They have now *supreme dominion* over the whole land.

A. M. cir. 3416
B. C. cir. 588
Ol. XLVIII. 1
TarquiniiPrisci,
R. Roman.,
cir. annum 29

7 Jerusalem remembered in the days of her affliction and of her miseries all [n]her pleasant things that she had in the days of old, when her people fell into the hand of the enemy, and none did help her: the adversaries saw her, *and* did mock at her sabbaths.

8 [o]Jerusalem hath grievously sinned; therefore she [p]is removed: all that honoured her despise her, because [q]they have seen her nakedness: yea, she sigheth, and turneth backward.

9 Her filthiness *is* in her skirts; she [r]remembereth not her last end; therefore she came down wonderfully: [s]she had no comforter. O LORD, behold my affliction: for the enemy hath magnified *himself*.

10 The adversary hath spread out his hand upon [t]all her [u]pleasant things: for she hath seen *that* [v]the heathen entered into her sanctuary, whom thou didst command *that* [w]they should not enter into thy congregation.

11 All her people sigh, [x]they seek bread; they have given their pleasant things for meat [y]to relieve the soul: see, O LORD, and consider; for I am become vile.

12 [z]*Is it* nothing to you, all ye that [a]pass by? behold, and see [b]if there be any sorrow like unto my sorrow, which is done unto me, wherewith the LORD hath afflicted *me* in the day of his fierce anger.

A. M. cir. 3416
B. C. cir. 588
Ol. XLVIII. 1
TarquiniiPrisci,
R. Roman.,
cir. annum 29

13 From above hath he sent fire into my bones, and it prevaileth against them: he hath [c]spread a net for my feet, he hath turned me back: he hath made me desolate *and* faint all the day.

14 [d]The yoke of my transgressions is bound by his hand: they are wreathed, *and* come up upon my neck: he hath made my strength to fall, the LORD hath delivered me into *their* hands, *from whom* I am not able to rise up.

15 The LORD hath trodden under foot all my mighty *men* in the midst of me: he hath called an assembly against me to crush my young men: [e]the LORD hath trodden [f]the virgin, the daughter of Judah, *as* in a wine-press.

16 For these *things* I weep; [g]mine eye, mine eye runneth down with water, because [h]the comforter that should [i]relieve my soul is far from me: my children are desolate, because the enemy prevailed.

[n]Or, *desirable;* ver. 10——[o]1 Kings viii. 46——[p]Heb. *is become a removing,* or *wandering*——[q]Jer. xiii. 22, 26; Ezek. xvi. 37; xxiii. 29; Hos. ii. 10——[r]Deut. xxxii. 29; Isa. xlvii. 7——[s]Ver. 2, 17, 21——[t]Ver. 7——[u]Or, *desirable*——[v]Jer. li. 51——[w]Deut. xxiii. 3; Neh. xiii. 1 [x]Jer. xxxviii. 9; lii. 6; chap. ii. 12; iv. 4

[y]Or, *to make the soul to come again*——[z]Or, It is *nothing*——[a]Heb. *pass by the way*——[b]Dan. ix. 12 [c]Ezek. xii. 13; xvii. 20——[d]Deut. xxviii. 48——[e]Isa. lxiii. 3; Rev. xiv. 19, 20; xix. 15——[f]Or, *the winepress of the virgin,* &c.——[g]Jer. xiii. 17; xiv. 17; chap. ii. 18 [h]Ver. 2. 9——[i]Heb. *bring back*

Verse 7. *Did mock at her Sabbaths.*] משבתה *mishbatteha.* Some contend that *Sabbaths* are not intended here. The *Septuagint* has κατοικεσια αυτης, "her habitation;" the *Chaldee,* על טובהא *al tubaha,* "her good things;" the *Syriac,* [Syriac] *al toboroh,* "her breach." The *Vulgate* and *Arabic* agree with the Hebrew. Some of my oldest MSS. have the word in the plural number, משבתיה *mishbatteyha,* "her Sabbaths." A multitude of *Kennicott's* MSS. have the same reading. The Jews were despised by the heathen for *keeping the Sabbath. Juvenal* mocks them on that account:—

—— cui septima quæque fuit lux
Ignava et partem vitæ non attigit ullam.
Sat. v.

"To whom every seventh day was a blank, and formed not any part of their life."

St. Augustine represents *Seneca* as doing the same:—Inutiliter id eos facere affirmans, quod septimani ferme partem ætatis suæ perdent vacando, et multa in tempore urgentia non agendo lædantur. "That they lost the seventh part of their life in keeping their Sabbaths; and injured themselves by abstaining from the performance of many necessary things in such times." He did not consider that the Roman calendar and customs gave them many more idle days than God had prescribed in Sabbaths to the Jews. The Sabbath is a most wise and beneficent ordinance.

Verse 9. *She remembereth not her last end*] Although evident marks of her pollution appeared about her, and the land was defiled by her sinfulness even to its utmost borders, she had no thought or consideration of what must be the consequence of all this at the last.—*Blayney.*

Verse 11. *They have given their pleasant things*] Jerusalem is compared to a woman brought into great straits, who parts with her jewels and trinkets in order to purchase by them the necessaries of life.

Verse 12. Is it *nothing to you, all ye that pass by?*] The desolations and distress brought upon this city and its inhabitants had scarcely any parallel. Excessive abuse of God's accumulated mercies calls for singular and exemplary punishment.

Verse 14. *The yoke of my transgressions*] I am now tied and bound by the chain of my sins; and it is so *wreathed,* so *doubled* and *twisted* round me, that I cannot free myself. A fine representation of the miseries of a penitent soul, which feels that nothing but the pitifulness of God's mercy can loose it.

Verse 15. *Called an assembly*] The Chaldean

A. M. cir. 3416
B. C. cir. 588
Ol. XLVIII. 1
TarquiniiPrisci,
R. Roman.,
cir. annum 29

17 [k]Zion spreadeth forth her hands, *and* [l]*there is* none to comfort her: the LORD hath commanded concerning Jacob, *that* his adversaries *should be* round about him: Jerusalem is as a menstruous woman among them.

18 The LORD is [m]righteous; for I have [n]rebelled against his [o]commandment: hear, I pray you, all people, and behold my sorrow: my virgins and my young men are gone into captivity.

19 I called for my lovers, *but* [p]they deceived me: my priests and mine elders gave up the ghost in the city, [q]while they sought their meat to relieve their souls.

A. M. cir. 3416
B. C. cir. 588
Ol. XLVIII. 1
TarquiniiPrisci,
R. Roman.,
cir. annum 29

20 Behold, O LORD; for I *am* in distress: my [r]bowels are troubled: mine heart is turned within me; for I have grievously rebelled: [s]abroad the sword bereaveth, at home *there is* as death.

21 They have heard that I sigh: [t]*there is* none to comfort me: all mine enemies have heard of my trouble; they are glad that thou hast done *it:* thou wilt bring [u]the day *that* thou hast [v]called, and they shall be like unto me.

22 [w]Let all their wickedness come before thee; and do unto them, as thou hast done unto me for all my transgressions: for my sighs *are* many, and [x]my heart *is* faint.

---

[k]Jer. iv. 31——[l]Ver. 2, 9——[m]Neh. ix. 33; Dan. ix. 7, 14——[n]1 Sam. xii. 14, 15——[o]Heb. *mouth*——[p]Ver. 2; Jer. xxx. 14——[q]Ver. 11——[r]Job xxx. 27; Isa. xvi. 11; Jer. iv. 19; xlviii. 36; ch. ii. 11; Hos. xi. 8——[s]Deut. xxxii. 25; Ezek. vii. 15——[t]Ver. 2——[u]Isa. xiii. &c.; Jer. xlvi. &c.——[v]Or, *proclaimed*——[w]Psa. cix. 15——[x]Chap. v. 17

---

army, composed of various nations, which God commissioned to destroy Jerusalem.

Verse 17. *Zion spreadeth forth her hands*] Extending the hands is the form in supplication.

Jerusalem is as a menstruous woman] To whom none dared to approach, either to help or comfort, because of the law, Lev. xv. 19-27.

Verse 19. *I called for my lovers*] My allies; the *Egyptians* and others.

Verse 20. *Abroad the sword bereaveth*] WAR is through the *country; and at home death;* the pestilence and famine rage in the city; calamity in every shape is fallen upon me.

Virgil represents the calamities of Troy under the same image:—

——— Nec soli pœnas dant sanguine Teucri:
Quondam etiam victis redit in præcordia virtus;
Victoresque cadunt Danai. Crudelis ubique
Luctus, ubique *Pavor*, et *plurima mortis imago.*
Æneid. lib. ii. 366.

"Not only Trojans fall; but, in their turn,
The vanquished triumph, and the victors mourn.
Ours take new courage from despair and night;
Confused the fortune is, confused the fight.
All parts resound with *tumults*, *plaints*, and *fears;*
And grisly death in *sundry shapes* appears."
DRYDEN.

So Milton—

"——————————Despair
Tended the sick, busiest from couch to couch;
And over them triumphant Death his dart
Shook." *Par. Lost*, B. xi. 489.

Jeremiah, chap. ix. 21, uses the same image:—

Death is come up into our windows:
He hath entered our palaces,
To cut off the infants without,
And the young men in our streets.

So *Silius Italicus*, II. 548:—

Mors graditur, vasto pandens cava guttura rictu,
Casuroque inhians populo.

"Death stalks along, and opens his hideous throat to gulp down the people."

Verse 21. *They have heard that I sigh*] My affliction is public enough; but no one comes to comfort me.

They are glad that thou hast done it] On the contrary, they exult in my misery; and they see that THOU hast done what *they* were incapable of performing.

Thou wilt bring the day that *thou hast called, and they shall be like unto me.*] Babylon shall be visited in her turn; and thy judgments poured out upon her shall equal her state with my own. See the last six chapters of the preceding prophecy for the accomplishment of this prediction.

Verse 22. *Let all their wickedness come before thee*] That is, Thou wilt call their crimes also into remembrance; and thou wilt do unto them by siege, sword, famine, and captivity, what thou hast done to me. Though thy judgments, because of thy long-suffering, are slow; yet, because of thy righteousness, they are sure.

For my sighs are *many*] My desolations continue; and *my heart* is *faint*—my political and physical strength almost totally destroyed.

Imprecations in the sacred writings are generally to be understood as *declarative* of the evils they indicate; or, that such evils will take place. No prophet of God ever wished desolation on those against whom he was directed to prophesy.

CHAPTER II

The prophet shows the dire effects of the Divine anger in the miseries brought on his country; the unparalleled calamities of which he charges, in a great measure, on the false prophets, 1–14. *In this desperate condition, the astonishment and by-word of all who see her, Jerusalem is directed to sue earnestly for mercy and pardon,* 15–22.

A. M. cir. 3416
B. C. cir. 588
Ol. XLVIII. 1
TarquiniiPrisci,
R. Roman.,
cir. annum 29

HOW hath the LORD covered the daughter of Zion with a cloud in his anger, [a]*and* cast down from heaven unto the earth [b]the beauty of Israel, and remembered not [c]his footstool in the day of his anger!

2 The LORD hath swallowed up all the habitations of Jacob, [d]and hath not pitied: he hath thrown down in his wrath the strong holds of the daughter of Judah; he hath [e]brought *them* down to the ground: [f]he hath polluted the kingdom and the princes thereof.

3 He hath cut off in *his* fierce anger all the horn of Israel: [g]he hath drawn back his right hand from before the enemy, [h]and he burned against Jacob like a flaming fire, *which* devoureth round about.

4 [i]He hath bent his bow like an enemy: he stood with his right hand as an adversary, and slew [k]all [l]*that were* pleasant to the eye in the tabernacle of the daughter of Zion: he poured out his fury like fire.

5 [m]The LORD was as an enemy: he hath swallowed up Israel, [n]he hath swallowed up all her palaces: he hath destroyed his strong holds, and hath increased in the daughter of Judah mourning and lamentation.

A. M. cir. 3416
B. C. cir. 588
Ol. XLVIII. 1
TarquiniiPrisci,
R. Roman.,
cir. annum 29

6 And he hath violently [o]taken away his [p]tabernacle, [q]as *if it were of* a garden: he hath destroyed his places of the assembly: [r]the LORD hath caused the solemn feasts and sabbaths to be forgotten in Zion, and hath despised in the indignation of his anger the king and the priest.

7 The LORD hath cast off his altar, he hath abhorred his sanctuary, he hath [s]given up into the hand of the enemy the walls of her palaces; [t]they have made a noise in the house of the LORD, as in the day of a solemn feast.

8 The LORD hath purposed to destroy the wall of the daughter of Zion: [u]he hath stretched out a line, he hath not withdrawn his hand from [v]destroying: therefore he made the rampart and the wall to lament; they languished together.

[a]Matt. xi. 23——[b]2 Sam. i. 19——[c]1 Chron. xxviii. 2; Psa. xcix. 5; cxxxii. 7——[d]Ver. 17, 21; chap. iii. 43——[e]Heb. *made to touch*——[f]Psa. lxxxix. 39——[g]Psa. lxxiv. 11——[h]Psa. xxxix. 46——[i]Isa. lxiii. 10; ver. 5——[k]Heb. *all the desirable of the eye*

[l]Ezek. xxiv. 25——[m]Ver. 4; Jer. xxx. 14——[n]2 Kings xxv. 9; Jer. lii. 13——[o]Psa. lxxx. 12; lxxxix. 40; Isa. v. 5——[p]Or, *hedge*——[q]Isa. i. 8——[r]Chap. i. 4; Zeph. iii. 18——[s]Heb. *shut up*——[t]Psa. lxxiv. 4——[u]2 Kings xxi. 13; Isa. xxxiv. 11——[v]Heb. *swallowing up*

NOTES ON CHAP. II

Verse 1. *How hath the Lord covered the daughter of Zion with a cloud*] The women in the eastern countries wear *veils*, and often very costly ones. Here, Zion is represented as being *veiled* by the hand of God's judgment. And what is the veil? A *dark cloud*, by which she is entirely obscured.

Instead of אדני *Adonai, lord, twenty-four* of Dr. *Kennicott's* MSS., and some of the most ancient of my own, read יהוה *Yehovah*, LORD, as in ver. 2.

The beauty of Israel] His *Temple*.

His footstool] The ark of the covenant, often so called. The rendering of my old MS. Bible is curious:—**And record not of his litil steging-stole of his feet, in the dai of his woodnesse.** To be *wood* signifies, in our ancient language, to be *mad*.

Verse 2. *The Lord hath swallowed up*] It is a strange figure when thus applied: but Jehovah is here represented as having swallowed down Jerusalem and all the cities and fortifications in the land: that is, he has permitted them to be destroyed. See ver. 5.

Verse 3. *The horn of Israel*] His *power* and *strength*. It is a metaphor taken from cattle, whose principal strength lies in their *horns*.

Hath drawn back his right hand] He did not support us when our enemies came against us.

Verse 4. *He hath bent his bow—he stood with his right hand*] This is the attitude of the archer. He first bends his bow; then sets his arrow upon the string; and, lastly, placing his right hand on the lower end of the arrow, in connexion with the string, takes his aim, and prepares to let fly.

Verse 6. *As* if it were of *a garden*] "As it were the garden of his own hedging."—*Blayney*.

The Lord hath caused the solemn feasts] By delivering us up into the hands of the enemy our religious worship is not only suspended, but all Divine ordinances are destroyed.

Verse 7. *They have made a noise in the house of the Lord*] Instead of the silver trumpets of the sanctuary, nothing but the sounds of warlike instruments are to be heard.

Verse 8. *He hath stretched out a line*] The *line of devastation;* marking what was to be pulled down and demolished.

A. M. cir. 3416
B. C. cir. 588
Ol. XLVIII. 1
TarquiniiPrisci, R. Roman., cir. annum 29

9 Her gates are sunk into the ground; he hath destroyed and [w]broken her bars: [x]her king and her princes *are* among the Gentiles: [y]the law *is* no *more;* her [z]prophets also find no vision from the LORD.

10 The elders of the daughter of Zion [a]sit upon the ground, *and* keep silence: they have [b]cast up dust upon their heads; they have [c]girded themselves with sackcloth: the virgins of Jerusalem hang down their heads to the ground.

11 [d]Mine eyes do fail with tears, [e]my bowels are troubled, [f]my liver is poured upon the earth, for the destruction of the daughter of my people; because [g]the children and the sucklings [h]swoon in the streets of the city.

12 They say to their mothers, Where *is* corn and wine? when they swooned as the wounded in the streets of the city, when their soul was poured out into their mothers' bosom.

13 What thing shall I take to witness for thee? [i]what thing shall I liken to thee, O daughter of Jerusalem? what shall I equal to thee, that I may comfort thee, O virgin daughter of Zion? for thy breach *is* great like the sea: who can heal thee?

14 Thy [k]prophets have seen vain and foolish things for thee: and they have not [l]discovered thine iniquity, to turn away thy captivity; but have seen for thee false burdens and causes of banishment.

15 [m]All that pass [n]by [o]clap *their* hands at thee; they hiss [p]and wag their head at the daughter of Jerusalem, *saying, Is* this the city that *men* call [q]The perfection of beauty, The joy of the whole earth?

16 [r]All thine enemies have opened their mouth against thee: they hiss and gnash the teeth: they say, [s]We have swallowed *her* up: certainly this *is* the day that we looked for; we have found, [t]we have seen *it*.

17 The LORD hath done *that* which he had [u]devised; he hath fulfilled his word that he had commanded in the days of old: [v]he hath thrown down, and hath not pitied: and he hath caused *thine* enemy to [w]rejoice over thee, he hath set up the horn of thine adversaries.

18 Their heart cried unto the LORD, O

[w]Jer. li. 30——[x]Deut. xxviii. 36; 2 Kings xxiv. 15; xxv. 7; chap. i. 3; iv. 20——[y]2 Chron. xv. 3——[z]Psa. lxxiv. 9; Ezek. vii. 26——[a]Job ii. 13; Isa. iii. 26; chap. iii. 28——[b]Job ii. 12——[c]Isa. xv. 3; Ezek vii. 18; xxvii. 31——[d]Psa. vi. 7; chap. iii. 48, &c. [e]Chap. i. 20——[f]Job xvi. 13; Psa. xxii. 14——[g]Ver. 19; chapter iv. 4——[h]Or, *faint*——[i]Chapter i. 12; Dan. ix. 12

[k]Jer. ii. 8; v. 31; xiv. 14; xxiii. 16; xxvii. 14; xxix. 8, 9; Ezek. xiii. 2——[l]Isa. lviii. 1——[m]1 Kings ix. 8; Jer. xviii. 16; Nah. iii. 19; Ecclus. xii. 18——[n]Heb. *by the way*——[o]Ezek. xxv. 6——[p]2 Kings xix. 21; Psa. xliv. 14 [q]Psa. xlviii. 2; l. 2——[r]Job xvi. 9, 10; Psa. xxii. 13; chap. iii. 46——[s]Psa. lvi. 2——[t]Psa. xxxv. 21——[u]Lev. xxvi. 16, &c.; Deut. xxviii. 15, &c.——[v]Ver. 2——[w]Psa. xxxviii. 16; lxxxix. 42

Verse 9. *Her gates are sunk into the ground*] The consequence of their being long thrown down and neglected. From this it appears that the captivity had already lasted a considerable time.

Her king and her princes are *among the Gentiles*] Zedekiah and many of the princes were then prisoners in Babylon, another proof that the captivity had endured some time; unless all this be spoken *prophetically*, of what *should be done.*

Verse 10. *Sit upon the ground*] See the note on chap. i. 1.

Keep silence] No words can express their sorrows: small griefs are eloquent, great ones dumb.

Verse 11. *Swoon in the streets of the city.*] Through the excess of the famine.

Verse 12. *When their soul was poured out into their mothers' bosom.*] When, in endeavouring to draw nourishment from the breasts of their exhausted mothers, they breathed their last in their bosoms! How dreadfully afflicting was this!

Verse 13. *What thing shall I take*] Or, rather, as Dr. *Blayney*, "What shall I urge to thee?" How shall I comfort thee?

Thy breach is *great like the sea*] Thou hast a *flood* of *afflictions*, a *sea* of *troubles*, an *ocean* of *miseries*.

Verse 14. *They have not discovered thine iniquity*] They did not reprove for sin; they flattered them in their transgressions; and instead of turning away thy captivity, by turning thee from thy sins, they have pretended visions of good in thy favour, and false burdens for thy enemies.

Verse 15. *The perfection of beauty*] This probably only applied to the *temple*. Jerusalem never was a fine or splendid city; but the temple was most assuredly the most splendid building in the world.

Verse 16. *This* is *the day that we looked for*] Jerusalem was the envy of the surrounding nations: they longed for its destruction, and rejoiced when it took place.

Verse 17. *The Lord hath done* that] This and the *sixteenth* verse should be interchanged, to follow the order of the letters in the Hebrew alphabet; as the *sixteenth* has פ *phe* for its acrostic letter, and the *seventeenth* has ע *ain*, which should precede the other in the order of the alphabet.

Verse 18. *O wall of the daughter of Zion*] חומת בת ציון *chomath bath tsiyon, wall of the daughter of Zion.* These words are probably those of the passengers, who appear to be affected by the desolations of the land; and they address the people, and urge them to plead with God day and night for their restoration.

A. M. cir. 3416
B. C. cir. 588
Ol. XLVIII. 1
TarquiniiPrisci,
R. Roman.,
cir. annum 29

[x]wall of the daughter of Zion, [y]let tears run down like a river day and night: give thyself no rest; let not the apple of thine eye cease.

19 Arise, [z]cry out in the night: in the beginning of the watches [a]pour out thine heart like water before the face of the LORD: lift up thy hands toward him for the life of thy young children, [b]that faint for hunger [c]in the top of every street.

20 Behold, O LORD, and consider to whom thou hast done this. [d]Shall the women eat their fruit, *and* children [e]of a span long? [f]shall the priest and the prophet be slain in the sanctuary of the LORD?

21 [g]The young and the old lie on the ground in the streets: my virgins and my young men are fallen by the sword; thou hast slain *them* in the day of thine anger; [h]thou hast killed, *and* not pitied.

22 Thou hast called as in a solemn day [i]my terrors round about, so that in the day of the LORD's anger none escaped nor remained: [k]those that I have swaddled and brought up hath mine enemy consumed.

[x]Ver. 8——[y]Jer. xiv. 17; ch. i. 16——[z]Psa. cxix. 147——[a]Psa. lxii. 8——[b]Ver. 11——[c]Isa. li. 20; ch. iv. 1; Nah. iii. 10——[d]Lev. xxvi. 29; Deut. xxviii. 53; Jer. xix. 9; ch. iv. 10; Ezek. v. 10——[e]Or, *swaddled with their hands*——[f]Ch. iv. 13, 16——[g]2 Chron. xxxvi. 17——[h]Ch. iii. 43——[i]Psa. xxxi. 13; Jer. vi. 25; xliv. 5——[k]Hos. ix. 12, 13

But what is the meaning of *wall of the daughter of Zion?* I answer, I do not know. It is certainly harsh to say, "O wall of the daughter of Zion, let tears run down like a river day and night." Zion's *ways* may *lament*, and her *streets mourn;* but how the *walls* can be said to *weep* is not so easy to be understood, because there is no parallel for it. One of my most ancient MSS. *omits* the three words; and in it the text stands thus: "Their heart cried unto the Lord, Let tears run down like a river day and night; give thyself no rest," &c.

Let not the apple of thine eye cease.] בת עין *bath ayin* means either the *pupil* of the *eye*, or the *tears*. Tears are the produce of the eye, and are here elegantly termed *the daughter of the eye*. Let not thy tears cease. But with what propriety can we say to the *apple* or *pupil* of the eye, *Do not cease?* *Tears* are most certainly meant.

Verse 19. *Arise, cry out in the night*] This seems to refer to Jerusalem besieged. Ye who keep the night watches, pour out your hearts before the Lord, instead of calling the time of night, &c.; or, when you call it, send up a fervent prayer to God for the safety and relief of the place.

Verse 20. *Consider to whom thou hast done this*] Perhaps the best sense of this difficult verse is this: "Thou art our *Father*, we are thy *children;* wilt thou *destroy thy own offspring?* Was it ever heard that a mother devoured her own child, a helpless infant of a span long?" That it was foretold that there should be such distress in the siege,—that mothers should be obliged to eat their own children, is evident enough from Lev. xxvi. 29; Deut. xxviii. 53, 56, 57; but the former view of the subject seems the most natural, and is best supported by the *context*. The *priest* and the *prophet* are slain; the *young* and *old* lie on the ground in the streets; the *virgins* and *young men* are fallen by the sword. "THOU hast slain them in the day of thine anger; THOU hast killed, and not pitied." See chap. iv. 10.

Verse 22. *Thou hast called as in a solemn day*] It is by thy influence alone that so many enemies are called together at one time; and they have so hemmed us in that none could escape, and none remained unslain or uncaptivated. Perhaps the figure is the collecting of the people in Jerusalem on one of the solemn annual festivals. God has called terrors together to feast on Jerusalem, similar to the convocation of the people from all parts of the land to one of those annual festivals. The indiscriminate slaughter of young and old, priest and prophet, all ranks and conditions, may be illustrated by the following verses from *Lucan*, which appear as if a translation of the *nineteenth*, *twentieth*, and *twenty-first* verses of this chapter:—

Nobilitas cum plebe perit; lateque vagatur
Ensis, et a nullo revocatum est pectore ferrum.
Stat cruor in Templis; multaque rubentia cæde
Lubrica saxa madent. Nulli sua profuit ætas.
Non senes extremum piguit vergentibus annis
Præcipitasse diem; nec primo in limine vitæ,
Infanti miseri nascentia rumpere fata.

Pharsal. lib. ii., 101.

"With what a slide devouring slaughter passed,
And swept promiscuous orders in her haste;
O'er noble and plebeian ranged the sword,
Nor pity nor remorse one pause afford!
The sliding streets with blood were clotted o'er,
And sacred temples stood in pools of gore.
The ruthless steel, impatient of delay,
Forbade the sire to linger out his day:
It struck the bending father to the earth,
And cropped the wailing infant at its birth."

ROWE.

CHAPTER III

The prophet, by enumerating his own severe trials, 1–20, *and showing his trust in God,* 21, *encourages his people to the like resignation and trust in the Divine and never-failing mercy,* 22–27. *He vindicates the goodness of God in all his dispensations, and the unreasonableness of murmuring under them,* 28–39. *He recommends self-examination and repentance; and then, from their experience of former deliverances from God, encourages them to look for pardon for their sins, and retribution to their enemies,* 40–66.

A. M. cir. 3416
B. C. cir. 588
Ol. XLVIII. 1
TarquiniiPrisci,
R. Roman.,
cir. annum 29

I *AM* the man *that* hath seen
affliction by the rod of his
wrath.
2 He hath led me, and brought
me into darkness, but not *into* light.
3 Surely against me is he turned; he turneth
his hand *against me* all the day.
4 [a]My flesh and my skin hath he made old;
he hath [b]broken my bones.
5 He hath builded against me, and compassed *me* with gall and travail.
6 [c]He hath set me in dark places, as *they
that be* dead of old.
7 [d]He hath hedged me about, that I cannot
get out: he hath made my chain heavy.
8 Also [e]when I cry and shout, he shutteth
out my prayer.
9 He hath inclosed my ways
with hewn stone, he hath made
my paths crooked.
10 [f]He *was* unto me *as* a bear
lying in wait, *and as* a lion in secret places.
11 He hath turned aside my ways, and
[g]pulled me in pieces: he hath made me desolate.
12 He hath bent his bow, and [h]set me as a
mark for the arrow.
13 He hath caused [i]the [k]arrows of his
quiver to enter into my reins.
14 I was a [l]derision to all my people; *and*
[m]their song all the day.
15 [n]He hath filled me with [o]bitterness, he
hath made me drunken with wormwood.
16 He hath also broken my teeth [p]with

A. M. cir. 3416
B. C. cir. 588
Ol. XLVIII. 1
TarquiniiPrisci,
R. Roman.,
cir. annum 29

[a]Job xvi. 3——[b]Psa. li. 8; Isa. xxxviii. 13; Jer. l. 17——[c]Psa. lxxxviii. 5, 6; cxliii. 3——[d]Job iii. 23; xix. 8; Hos. ii. 6——[e]Job xxx. 20; Psa. xxii. 2——[f]Job x. 16; Isa. xxxviii. 13; Hos. v. 14; xiii. 7, 8

[g]Hos. vi. 1——[h]Job vii. 20; xvi. 12; Psa. xxxviii. 2——[i]Job vi. 4——[k]Heb. *sons*——[l]Jer. xx. 7——[m]Job xxx. 9; Psa. lxix. 12; ver. 63——[n]Jer. ix. 15——[o]Heb. *bitternesses*——[p]Prov. xx. 17

NOTES ON CHAP. III

Verse 1. *I* am *the man* that *hath seen affliction*] Either the prophet speaks here of himself, or he is personating his miserable countrymen. This and other passages in this poem have been applied to Jesus Christ's passion; but, in my opinion, without any foundation.

Verse 2. *He hath—brought* me into *darkness*] In the sacred writings, *darkness* is often taken for *calamity; light,* for *prosperity.*

Verse 5. *He hath builded against me*] Perhaps there is a reference here to the *mounds* and *ramparts* raised by the Chaldeans in order to take the city.

Verse 7. *He hath hedged me about*] This also may refer to the lines drawn round the city during the siege. But these and similar expressions in the following verses may be merely metaphorical, to point out their *straitened, oppressed,* and *distressed* state.

Verse 9. *He hath inclosed my ways with hewn stone*] He has put insuperable obstacles in my way; and confounded all my projects of deliverance, and all my expectations of prosperity.

Verse 12. *He hath bent his bow, and set me as a mark for the arrow.*] One might conjecture that the following thought in the *Toozek i Teemour* was borrowed from this:—

"One addressed the caliph Aaly, and said, 'If the *heavens* were a *bow,* and the *earth* the *cord* thereof; if *calamities* were *arrows, man* the *butt* for those arrows; and the holy blessed *God* the unerring *marksman;* where could the sons of Adam flee for succour?' The caliph replied, 'The children of Adam must flee unto the Lord.'" This was the state of poor Jerusalem. It seemed as a *butt* for all God's *arrows;* and each *arrow* of *calamity* entered into the soul, for God was the *unerring marksman.*

Verse 13. *The arrows of his quiver*] בני אשפתו *beney ashpatho,* "The sons of his quiver." The *issue* or *effect;* the subject, adjunct, or accident, or produce of a thing, is frequently denominated its *son* or *child.* So *arrows* that *issue* from a *quiver* are here termed *the sons of the quiver.*

Verse 15. *He hath filled me with bitterness*] במרורים *bimrorim,* with bitternesses, bitter upon bitter.

He hath made me drunken with wormwood.] I have drunk the cup of misery till I am intoxicated with it. Almost in all countries, and in all languages, *bitterness* is a metaphor to express *trouble* and *affliction.* The reason is, there is nothing more disagreeable to the *taste* than the one; and nothing more distressing to the *mind* than the other. An Arabic poet, *Amralkeis,* one of the writers of the *Moallakat,* terms a man grievously afflicted ناقع حنظل *a pounder of wormwood.*

Verse 16. *He hath also broken my teeth with gravel stones*] What a figure to express *disgust, pain,* and the consequent incapacity of *taking food* for the support of life; a man, instead of bread, being obliged to eat *small pebbles,* till all his teeth are *broken to pieces* by endeavouring to grind them. One can scarcely read this description without feeling the *toothache.* The next figure is not less expressive.

A. M. cir. 3416 B. C. cir. 588 Ol. XLVIII. 1 TarquiniiPrisci, R. Roman., cir. annum 29

gravel stones, he hath [q]covered
me with ashes.
17 And thou hast removed my
soul far off from peace: I forgat
[r]prosperity.
18 [s]And I said, My strength and my hope
is perished from the LORD:
19 [t]Remembering mine affliction and my
misery, [u]the wormwood and the gall.
20 My soul hath *them* still in remembrance,
and is [v]humbled in me.
21 This I [w]recall to my mind, therefore have
I hope.
22 [x]*It is of* the LORD's mercies that we are
not consumed, because his compassions fail
not.
23 *They are* new [y]every morning: great *is*
thy faithfulness.
24 The LORD *is* my [z]portion,
saith my soul: therefore will I
hope in him.
25 The LORD *is* good unto
them that [a]wait for him, to the soul *that*
seeketh him.
26 *It is* good that *a man* should both hope
[b]and quietly wait for the salvation of the
LORD.
27 [c]*It is* good for a man that he bear the
yoke in his youth.
28 [d]He sitteth alone and keepeth silence,
because he hath borne *it* upon him.
29 [e]He putteth his mouth in the dust; if
so be there may be hope.
30 [f]He giveth *his* cheek to him that smiteth
him: he is filled full with reproach.
31 [g]For the LORD will not cast off for ever:

[q]Or, *rolled me in the ashes*——[r]Heb. *good*——[s]Psa. xxxi. 22——[t]Or, *Remember*——[u]Jer. ix. 15——[v]Heb. *bowed* [w]Heb. *make to return to my heart*——[x]Mal. iii. 6——[y]Isa. xxxiii. 2——[z]Psa. xvi. 5; lxxiii. 26; cxix. 57; Jer. x. 16

[a]Psalm cxxx. 6; Isaiah xxx. 18; Micah vii. 7——[b]Psa. xxxvii. 7——[c]Psalm xc. 12; cxix. 71——[d]Jeremiah xv. 17; chapter ii. 10——[e]Job xlii. 6——[f]Isaiah l. 6; Matthew v. 39——[g]Psalm xciv. 14

He hath covered me with ashes.] הכפישני באפר *hichphishani beepher*, "he hath plunged me into the dust." To be thrown into a mass or bed of perfect *dust*, where the eyes are blinded by it, the ears stopped, and the mouth and lungs filled at the very first attempt to respire after having been thrown into it—what a horrible idea of *suffocation* and *drowning!* One can scarcely read this without feeling a suppression of breath, or a stricture upon the lungs! Did ever man paint sorrow like this man?

Verse 17. *Thou hast removed my soul*] Prosperity is at such an utter distance from me, that it is impossible I should ever reach it; and as to *happiness*, I have forgotten whether I have ever tasted of it.

Verse 18. *And my hope*] That first, that last support of the miserable—it is gone! it is perished! The sovereign God alone can revive it.

Verse 20. *My soul—is humbled in me.*] It is evident that in the preceding verses there is a *bitterness* of *complaint* against the *bitterness* of *adversity*, that is not becoming to *man* when under the chastising hand of God; and, while indulging this feeling, all *hope* fled. Here we find a different feeling; he *humbles* himself under the mighty hand of God, and then his *hope* revives, ver. 21.

Verse 22. It is of *the Lord's mercies that we are not consumed*] Being thus *humbled*, and seeing *himself* and his *sinfulness* in a proper point of view, he finds that God, instead of dealing with him in *judgment*, has dealt with him in *mercy;* and that though the affliction was excessive, yet it was less than his iniquity deserved. If, indeed, any sinner be kept out of hell, it is because God's *compassion* faileth not.

Verse 23. They are *new every morning*] Day and night proclaim the mercy and compassion of God. Who could exist throughout the *day*, if there were not a continual superintending Providence? Who could be preserved in the *night*, if the Watchman of Israel ever slumbered or slept?

Verse 24. *The Lord* is *my portion*] See on Psa. cxix. 57.

Verse 26. It is *good that* a man *should both hope*] *Hope* is essentially necessary to *faith;* he that *hopes not*, *cannot believe;* if there be no *expectation*, there can be no *confidence.* When a man *hopes* for salvation, he should not only *wait* for it, but use every means that may lead to it; for *hope* cannot live, if there be no *exercise.* If *hope* become *impatient*, *faith* will be impossible: for who can believe for his salvation when his mind is *agitated?* He must therefore *quietly wait.* He must *expect*, and yet be *dumb*, as the words imply; ever feeling his *utter unworthiness;* and, without *murmuring*, struggle into life.

Verse 27. *That he bear the yoke in his youth.*] Early *habits*, when good, are invaluable. Early *discipline* is equally so. He who has not got under wholesome restraint in youth will never make a useful man, a good man, nor a happy man.

Verse 28. *He sitteth alone*] He has learned that necessary lesson of *independence*, that shows him how *he is to serve himself;* to *give no trouble to others;* and *keep his troubles*, as far as possible, *in his own bosom.*

Verse 29. *He putteth his mouth in the dust*] Lives in a state of deep humility.

If so be there may be hope.] Because there is room for hope.

Verse 30. *He giveth* his *cheek to him that smiteth*] He has that love that is not provoked. He is not quarrelsome, nor apt to resent injuries; he suffers long and is kind. Or, it may be rendered, "let him give his cheek."

He is filled full with reproach.] Though all this take place, yet let his "trust be in God, who will not cast off for ever." God will take his part, and bring him safely through all hardships.

Verse 31. *The Lord*] אדני *Adonai;* but one

A. M. cir. 3416
B. C. cir. 588
Ol. XLVIII. 1
TarquiniiPrisci,
R. Roman.,
cir. annum 29

32 But though he cause grief,
yet will he have compassion according to the multitude of his
mercies.
33 For [h]he doth not afflict [i]willingly, nor
grieve the children of men.
34 To crush under his feet all the prisoners
of the earth,
35 To turn aside the right of a man before
the face of [k]the Most High,
36 To subvert a man in his cause, [l]the LORD
[m]approveth not.
37 Who *is* he [n]*that* saith, and it cometh to
pass, *when* the LORD commanded *it* not?
38 Out of the mouth of the Most High proceedeth not [o]evil and good?
39 [p]Wherefore doth a living man [q]complain,
a man for the punishment of his sins?
40 Let us search and try our
ways, and turn again to the
LORD.
41 [s]Let us lift up our heart
with *our* hands unto God in the heavens.
42 [t]We have transgressed and have rebelled:
thou hast not pardoned.
43 Thou hast covered with anger, and persecuted us: [u]thou hast slain, thou hast not
pitied.
44 Thou hast covered thyself with a cloud,
[v]that *our* prayer should not pass through.
45 Thou hast made us *as* the [w]offscouring
and refuse in the midst of the people.
46 [x]All our enemies have opened their
mouths against us.
47 [y]Fear and a snare is come upon us,
[z]desolation and destruction.

A. M. cir. 3416
B. C. cir. 588
Ol. XLVIII. 1
TarquiniiPrisci,
R. Roman.,
cir. annum 29

---

[h]Ezek. xxxiii. 11; Heb. xii. 10——[i]Heb. *from his heart*——[k]Or, *a superior*——[l]Hab. i. 13——[m]Or, *seeth not*——[n]Psa. xxxiii. 9——[o]Job ii. 10; Isa. xlv. 7; Amos iii. 6——[p]Prov. xix. 3

[q]Or, *murmur*——[r]Mic. vii. 9——[s]Psa. lxxxvi. 4 [t]Dan. ix. 5——[u]Chap. ii. 17, 21——[v]Ver. 8——[w]1 Cor. iv. 13——[x]Chap. ii. 16——[y]Isa. xxiv. 17; Jer. xlviii. 43 [z]Isa. li. 19

---

of my ancient MSS. has יהוה *Yehovah.* The above verse is quoted in reference to our Lord's passion, by Matt. xxvi. 62.

Verse 33. *For he doth not afflict willingly*] It is no pleasure to God to afflict men. He takes no delight in our pain and misery: yet, like a tender and intelligent parent, he uses the rod; not to gratify himself, but to profit and save us.

Verse 34. *To crush under his feet*] He can neither gain credit nor pleasure in trampling upon those who are already *bound*, and in suffering; such he knows to be the state of man here below. From which it most assuredly follows, that God never afflicts us but for our good, nor chastises but that we may be partakers of his holiness.

All the prisoners of the earth] By the *prisoners of the earth*, or *land*, Dr. *Blayney* understands those insolvent debtors who were put in prison, and there obliged to work out the debt. Yet this is mercy in comparison with those who put them in prison, and keep them there, when they know that it is impossible, from the state of the laws, to lessen the debt by their confinement.

In verses 34, 35, and 36, certain acts of tyranny, malice, and injustice are specified, which men often indulge themselves in the practice of towards one another, but which the Divine goodness is far from countenancing or approving by any similar conduct.—*Blayney.*

Verse 35. *To turn aside the right of a man*] To make a man lose his right, because one of the higher orders opposes him. Dr. *Blayney* thinks that עליון *elyon,* instead of being referred to *God,* should be considered as pointing out one of the *chief* of the people. I do not see that we gain any thing by this. The evil fact is, *turning aside the right of a man;* and the aggravation of it is, doing it *before the face of the Most High;* that is, in a court of justice, where God is ever considered to be present.

Verse 36. *To subvert a man in his cause*] To prevent his having justice done him in a lawsuit, &c., by undue interference, as by suborning false witnesses, or exerting any kind of influence in opposition to truth and right.—*Blayney.*

The Lord approveth not.] Instead of אדני *Adonai,* seventeen MSS., of *Kennicott's*, and one ancient of my own, have יהוה *Yehovah. Approveth not,* לא ראה *lo raah,* doth not see, turns away his face from it, abhors it.

Verse 39. *Wherefore doth a living man complain*] He who has his life still lent to him has small cause of complaint. How great soever his affliction may be, he is still *alive;* therefore, he may seek and find mercy unto eternal life. Of this, *death* would deprive him; therefore let not a *living* man complain.

Verse 40. *Let us search*] How are we to get the pardon of our sins? The prophet tells us: 1. Let us examine ourselves. 2. "Let us turn again to the Lord." 3. "Let us lift up our heart;" let us make fervent prayer and supplication for mercy. 4. "Let us lift up our hand;" let us solemnly promise to be his, and bind ourselves in a covenant to be the Lord's only: so much *lifting up the hand to God* implies. Or, let us put our heart on our hand, and offer it to God; so some have translated this clause. 5. "We have transgressed;" let our confession of sin be fervent and sincere. 6. And to us who profess *Christianity* it may be added, *Believe on the Lord Jesus Christ* as having *died for thee;* and thou shalt not perish, but have everlasting life. Verses 46, 47, 48, beginning with פ *phe,* should, as to the order of the alphabet, follow 49, 50, 51, which begin with ע *ain,* which in its grammatical position precedes the former.

Verse 47. *Fear and a snare*] See on Jer. xlviii. 13.

A. M. cir. 3416
B. C. cir. 588
Ol. XLVIII. 1
TarquiniiPrisci,
R. Roman.,
cir. annum 29

48 [a]Mine eye runneth down with rivers of water for the destruction of the daughter of my people.

49 [b]Mine eye trickleth down, and ceaseth not, without any intermission.

50 Till the LORD [c]look down, and behold from heaven.

51 Mine eye affecteth [d]mine heart [e]because of all the daughters of my city.

52 Mine enemies chased me sore, like a bird, [f]without cause.

53 They have cut off my life [g]in the dungeon, and [h]cast a stone upon me.

54 [i]Waters flowed over mine head; *then* [k]I said, I am cut off.

55 [l]I called upon thy name, O LORD, out of the low dungeon.

56 [m]Thou hast heard my voice: hide not thine ear at my breathing, at my cry.

57 Thou [n]drewest near in the day *that* I called upon thee: thou saidst, Fear not.

A. M. cir. 3416
B. C. cir. 588
Ol. XLVIII. 1
TarquiniiPrisci,
R. Roman.,
cir. annum 29

58 O LORD, thou hast [o]pleaded the causes of my soul; [p]thou hast redeemed my life.

59 O LORD, thou hast seen my wrong: [q]judge thou my cause.

60 Thou hast seen all their vengeance *and* all their [r]imaginations against me.

61 Thou hast heard their reproach, O LORD, *and* all their imaginations against me;

62 The lips of those that rose up against me, and their device against me all the day.

63 Behold their [s]sitting down, and their rising up; [t]I *am* their music.

64 [u]Render unto them a recompense, O LORD, according to the work of their hands.

65 Give them [v]sorrow of heart, thy curse unto them.

66 Persecute and destroy them in anger [w]from under the [x]heavens of the LORD.

---

[a]Jer. iv. 19; ix. 1; xiv. 17; ch. ii. 11——[b]Psa. lxxvii. 2; ch. i. 16——[c]Isa. lxiii. 15——[d]Heb. *my soul*——[e]Or, *more than all*——[f]Psa. xxxv. 7, 19; lxix. 4; cix. 3; cxix. 161——[g]Jer. xxxvii. 16; xxxviii. 6, 9, 10——[h]Dan. vi. 17 [i]Psa. lxix. 2; cxxiv. 4, 5——[k]Psa. xxxi. 22; Isa. xxxviii. 10, 11; ver. 18——[l]Psa. cxxx. 1; Jonah ii. 2

[m]Psa. iii. 4; vi. 8; xviii. 6; lxvi. 19; cxvi. 1——[n]James iv. 8——[o]Psa. xxxv. 1; Jer. li. 36——[p]Psa. lxxi. 23 [q]Psa. ix. 4; xxxv. 23——[r]Jer. xi. 19——[s]Psa. cxxxix. 2 [t]Ver. 14——[u]Psa. xxviii. 4; see Jer. xi. 20; 2 Tim. iv. 14 [v]Or, *obstinacy of heart*——[w]Deut. xxv. 19; Jer. x. 11 [x]Psa. viii. 3

Verse 48. *Mine eye runneth down*] I weep incessantly.

Verse 51. *Mine eye affecteth mine heart*] What I *see* I *feel*. I *see* nothing but *misery;* and I *feel*, in consequence, nothing but *pain*. There have been various translations of the original: but they all amount to this.

The daughters of my city.] The villages about Jerusalem.

Verse 52. *Mine enemies chased me*] From this to the end of the chapter the prophet speaks of his own personal sufferings, and especially of those which he endured in the *dungeon*. See Jer. xxxviii. 6, &c.

Verse 56. *Hide not thine ear at my breathing*] He dared not even to *complain*, nor to *cry*, nor to *pray aloud:* he was obliged to *whisper* his prayer to God. It was only a *breathing*.

Verse 57. *Fear not.*] How powerful is this word when spoken by the Spirit of the Lord to a disconsolate heart. To *every mourner* we may say, on the authority of God, *Fear not!* God will plead thy cause, and redeem thy soul.

Verse 60. *Thou hast seen—all their imaginations*] Every thing is open to the eye of God. Distressed soul! though *thou* knowest not *what* thy enemies *meditate* against thee; yet he who *loves thee* does, and will infallibly defeat all *their* plots, and save *thee*.

Verse 65. *Give them sorrow of heart*] They shall have a *callous* heart, *covered* with *obstinacy*, and thy *execration*. The former is their *state*, the latter their *fate*. This is the consequence of their hardening their hearts from thy fear. *Blayney* translates, "Thou wilt give with a hearty concordance thy curse unto them." That is, Thou wilt give it to them freely, and without reserve; intimating that God felt no longer any bowels of compassion for them. Formerly he inflicted punishments with reluctance, while there was any hope of amendment: but, in the instance before us, the case was so hopeless, that God acts according to the simple principle of vindictive justice. The prophet therefore considers them on the utmost verge of final reprobation: another plunge, and they are lost for ever.

Verse 66. *Persecute and destroy them*] Thou wilt pursue them with destruction. These are all *declaratory*, not *imprecatory*.

From under the heavens of the Lord.] This verse seems to allude to the Chaldaic prediction, in Jer. x. 11. By their conduct they will bring on themselves the curse denounced against their enemies.

The *Septuagint* and *Vulgate* seem to have read "From under heaven, O Jehovah:" and the *Syriac* reads, "Thy heavens, O Jehovah!" None of these makes any material change in the meaning of the words.

It has already been noticed in the *introduction*, that this chapter contains a *triple acrostic*, *three* lines always beginning with the same letter; so that the Hebrew alphabet is thrice repeated in this chapter, *twenty-two* multiplied by *three* being equal to *sixty-six*.

CHAPTER IV

The present deplorable state of the nation is now contrasted with its ancient prosperity, 1–12; *and the unhappy change ascribed, in a great degree, to the profligacy of the priests and prophets,* 13–16. *The national calamities are tenderly lamented,* 17–20. *The ruin of the Edomites also, who had insulted the Jews in their distress, is ironically predicted,* 21. See Psa. cxxxvii. 7, and Obadiah 10–12. *The chapter closes with a gracious promise of deliverance from the Babylonish captivity,* 22.

A. M. cir. 3416
B. C. cir. 588
Ol. XLVIII. 1
TarquiniiPrisci, R. Roman., cir. annum 29

HOW is the gold become dim!
how is the most fine gold
changed! the stones of the sanctuary are poured out [a]in the
top of every street.
2 The precious sons of Zion, comparable to
fine gold, how are they esteemed [b]as earthen
pitchers, the work of the hands of the potter!
3 Even the [c]sea monsters draw out the
breast, they give suck to their young ones:
the daughter of my people *is become* cruel,
[d]like the ostriches in the wilderness.
4 [e]The tongue of the suckling child cleaveth
to the roof of his mouth for
thirst: [f]the young children ask
bread, *and* no man breaketh *it*
unto them.
5 They that did feed delicately are desolate
in the streets: they that were brought up in
scarlet [g]embrace dunghills.
6 For the [h]punishment of the iniquity of
the daughter of my people is greater than the
punishment of the sin of Sodom, that was
[i]overthrown as in a moment, and no hands
stayed on her.
7 Her Nazarites were purer than snow, they

A. M. cir. 3416
B. C. cir. 588
Ol. XLVIII. 1
TarquiniiPrisci, R. Roman., cir. annum 29

[a]Chap. ii. 19——[b]Isa. xxx. 14; Jer. xix. 11; 2 Cor. iv. 7
[c]Or, *sea calves*——[d]Job xxxix. 14, 16

[e]Psa. xxii. 15——[f]See chap. ii. 11, 12——[g]Job xxiv. 8
[h]Or, *iniquity*——[i]Gen. xix. 25

NOTES ON CHAP. IV

Verse 1. *How is the gold become dim*] The prophet contrasts, in various affecting instances, the wretched circumstances of the Jewish nation, with the flourishing state of their affairs in former times. Here they are compared to gold, זהב *zahab*, native gold from the mine, which, contrary to its nature, is become *dim*, is tarnished; and even the *fine*, the *sterling gold*, כתם *kethem*, that which was stamped to make it *current*, is *changed* or *adulterated*, so as to be no longer passable. This might be applied to the *temple*, but particularly to the fallen *priests* and apostate *prophets*.

The stones of the sanctuary] אבני קדש *abney kodesh*, the *holy stones;* the Jewish godly men, who were even then the *living stones* of which God *built his Church*.

Verse 2. *The precious sons of Zion*] The Jewish priests and Jewish believers.

Comparable to fine gold] Who were of the *pure standard* of holiness; holy, because God who called them is holy; but now esteemed no better than *earthen pitchers*—vessels of dishonour in comparison of what they once were.

Verse 3. *Even the sea monsters draw out the breast*] The *whales* give suck to their young ones. The word תנין *tannin*, signifies all *large* and *cruel* creatures, whether *aquatic* or *terrestrial;* and need not here be restrained to the *former* sort. My Old MS. Bible translates curiously: **Bot and the cruel bestis that ben clepid Lamya, and thei nakeden ther tetis, geve ther whelpis souken.**

Like the ostriches in the wilderness.] For her carelessness about her *eggs*, and her inattention to her *young*, the ostrich is proverbial.

Verse 4. *The tongue of the sucking child*] See the note on chap. ii. 12.

Verse 5. *Embrace dunghills.*] Lie on *straw* or *rubbish*, instead of the costly carpets and sofas on which they formerly stretched themselves.

Verse 6. *For the punishment*] He thinks the punishment of *Jerusalem* far greater than that of *Sodom*. That was destroyed *in a moment*, while all her inhabitants were in *health* and *strength;* Jerusalem fell by the most *lingering* calamities; her men *partly destroyed by the sword*, and *partly by the famine*.

Instead of *no hands stayed on her*, *Blayney* translates, "Nor were hands weakened in her." Perhaps the meaning is, "Sodom was destroyed in a moment without any human labour." It was a judgment from *God himself:* so the sacred text: "The LORD rained down fire and brimstone from the Lord out of heaven." See Gen. xix. 24.

Verse 7. *Her Nazarites were purer than snow*] נזיר *nazir* does not always signify a *person separated* under a *religious vow;* it sometimes denotes what is *chief* or *eminent*. It is applied to *Joseph*, Gen. xlix. 26. *Blayney* therefore translates here, HER NOBLES.

"Her nobles were purer than snow, they were
whiter than milk;
They were ruddier on the bone than rubies;
their veining was the sapphires."

On which he remarks:—"In the first line the *whiteness* of their skin is described; and in the second, their flesh;" and as נזר *gazar* signifies to *divide* and *intersect*, as the *blue veins* do on the surface of the body, these are without doubt intended.

Milk will most certainly well apply to the *whiteness* of the *skin;* the beautiful *ruby* to the *ruddiness* of the *flesh;* and the *sapphire*, in its clear transcendent *purple*, to the *veins* in a fine complexion. The reverse of this state, as described in the following verse, needs no explanation. The *face* was a dismal *dark brown*, the

A. M. cir. 3416
B. C. cir. 588
Ol. XLVIII. 1
TarquiniiPrisci,
R. Roman.,
cir. annum 29

were whiter than milk, they were more ruddy in body than rubies, their polishing *was* of sapphire:

8 Their visage is [k]blacker [l]than a coal; they are not known in the streets: [m]their skin cleaveth to their bones; it is withered, it is become like a stick.

9 *They that be* slain with the sword are better than *they that be* slain with hunger: for these [n]pine away, stricken through for *want of* the fruits of the field.

10 [o]The hands of the [p]pitiful women have sodden their own children: they were their [q]meat in the destruction of the daughter of my people.

11 The LORD hath accomplished his fury; [r]he hath poured out his fierce anger, and [s]hath kindled a fire in Zion, and it hath devoured the foundations thereof.

12 The kings of the earth, and all the inhabitants of the world, would not have believed that the adversary and the enemy should have entered into the gates of Jerusalem.

13 [t]For the sins of her prophets, *and* the iniquities of her priests, [u]that have shed the blood of the just in the midst of her,

A. M. cir. 3416
B. C. cir. 588
Ol. XLVIII. 1
TarquiniiPrisci,
R. Roman.,
cir. annum 29

14 They have wandered *as* blind *men* in the streets, [v]they have polluted themselves with blood, [w]so [x]that men could not touch their garments.

15 They cried unto them, Depart ye; [y]*it is* [z]unclean; depart, depart, touch not: when they fled away and wandered, they said among the heathen, They shall no more sojourn *there*.

16 The [a]anger of the LORD hath divided them; he will no more regard them: [b]they respected not the persons of the priests, they favoured not the elders.

17 As for us, [c]our eyes as yet failed for our vain help: in our watching we have watched for a nation *that* could not save *us*.

18 [d]They hunt our steps, that we cannot go in our streets: our end is near, our days are fulfilled; for [e]our end is come.

---

[k]Heb. *darker than blackness*——[l]Chap. v. 10; Joel ii. 6; Nah. ii. 10——[m]Psa. cii. 5——[n]Heb. *flow out* [o]Chap. ii. 20——[p]Isa. xlix. 15——[q]Deut. xxviii. 57; 2 Kings vi. 29——[r]Jer. vii. 20——[s]Deut. xxxii. 22; Jer. xxi. 14——[t]Jer. v. 31; vi. 13; xiv. 14; xxiii. 11, 21; Ezek. xxii. 26, 28; Zeph. iii. 4

[u]Matt. xxiii. 31, 37——[v]Jer. ii. 34——[w]Or, *in that they could not but touch*——[x]Num. xix. 16——[y]Or, *ye polluted*——[z]Lev. xiii. 45——[a]Or, *face*——[b]Chap. v. 12 [c]2 Kings xxiv. 7; Isa. xx. 5; xxx. 6, 7; Jer. xxxvii. 7; Ezek. xxix. 16——[d]2 Kings xxv. 4, 5——[e]Ezek. vii. 2, 3, 6; Amos viii. 2

---

flesh gone, the *skin* shrivelled, and apparently wrapped round the *bones*.

Verse 10. *The hands of the pitiful women have sodden their own children*] See on chap. ii. 20. But here there is a reference to mothers eating their own children; and this was done, not by mothers cruel and brutal, but by נשים רחמניות *nashim rachmaniyoth*, the *compassionate*, the *tender-hearted mothers*. From these horrible scenes it is well to pass with as hasty a step as possible.

Verse 12. *The kings of the earth*] Jerusalem was so well fortified, both by nature and art, that it appeared as a miracle that it should be taken at all.

Verse 13. *For the sins of her prophets*, and *the iniquities of her priests*] These most wretched beings, under the pretence of *zeal for the true religion*, persecuted the *genuine prophets*, *priests*, and *people of God*, and caused their blood to be shed in the midst of the city, in the most open and public manner; exactly as the murderous priests, and blood-thirsty preachers, under the reign of bloody Queen Mary, did in England. However, the profligate priests and idolatrous prophets in Jerusalem, only *shed* the blood of the saints of God there: but the sanguinary papists, in the above reign, *burnt* the blood here, for they *burnt the people alive;* and at the same time, in their worse than Molochean cruelty, consigned, with all the fervour peculiar to their then ruthless Church, the *souls* of those whom they thus massacred, to the bitter pains of eternal death! O earth, cover not thou their blood!

Verse 14. *They have wandered* as *blind* men *in the streets*] Rather, "They ran frantic through the streets, they were stained with blood." This was in their pretended zeal for their cause. Bishop *Bonner*, who was at the head of those sanguinary executions in England, was accustomed to *buffet* the poor Protestants, when on their examinations they were too powerful for him in argument:—

"He proved his doctrine orthodox,
By apostolic blows and knocks."

Just as his *elder brethren*, the false priests and prophets of Jerusalem.

Verse 15. *When they fled away*] These priests and prophets were so *bad*, that the very *heathen* did not like to permit them to sojourn among them. The prophet now resumes the history of the siege.

Verse 17. *We have watched for a nation*] Viz., the Egyptians, who were their pretended allies, but were neither *able* nor *willing* to help them against the Chaldeans.

Verse 18. *We cannot go in our streets*] Supposed to refer to the *darts* and other *missiles* cast from the mounds which they had raised on the outside of the walls, by which those who walked in the streets were grievously annoyed, and could not shield themselves.

A. M. cir. 3416
B. C. cir. 588
Ol. XLVIII. 1
TarquiniiPrisci,
R. Roman.,
cir. annum 29

19 Our persecutors are [f]swifter
than the eagles of the heaven:
they pursued us upon the mountains, they laid wait for us in the
wilderness.
20 The [g]breath of our nostrils, the anointed
of the LORD, [h]was taken in their pits, of whom
we said, Under his shadow we shall live among
the heathen.
21 [i]Rejoice and be glad, O daughter of
Edom, that dwellest in the land
of Uz; [k]the cup also shall pass
through unto thee: thou shalt be
drunken, and shalt make thyself
naked.
22 [l]The [m]punishment of thine iniquity is
accomplished, O daughter of Zion; he will
no more carry thee away into captivity: [n]he
will visit thine iniquity, O daughter of Edom;
he will [o]discover thy sins.

[f]Deut. xxviii. 49; Jer. iv. 13——[g]Gen. ii. 7; chap. ii. 9——[h]Jer. lii. 9; Ezek. xii. 13; xix. 4, 8——[i]Like Eccles. xi. 9

[k]Jer. xxv. 15, 16, 21; Obad. 10——[l]Isa. xl. 2——[m]Or, *Thine iniquity*——[n]Psa. cxxxvii. 7——[o]Or, *carry thee captive for thy sins*

Verse 19. *They pursued us upon the mountains*] They hunted down the poor Jews like wild beasts in every part of the country by their marauding parties, whilst the great army besieged Jerusalem. But this may apply to the pursuit of Zedekiah. See what follows.

Verse 20. *The breath of our nostrils, the anointed of the Lord*] That is, Zedekiah the king, who was as *the life of the city*, was taken in his flight by the Chaldeans, and his eyes were put out; so that he was wholly unfit to perform any function of government; though they had fondly hoped that if they surrendered and should be led captives, yet they should be permitted to live under their own laws and king in the land of their bondage.

Verse 21. *Rejoice and be glad, O daughter of Edom*] A strong irony.

The cup also shall pass through unto thee] Thou who hast triumphed in our disasters shalt shortly have enough of thy own. They had joined themselves to the Chaldeans, (see Psa. cxxxvii. 7,) and therefore they should share in the desolations of Babylon.

Verse 22. *The punishment of thine iniquity is accomplished, O daughter of Zion*] On the contrary: Rejoice, O Jerusalem, for thy captivity will soon end; thy sufferings are nearly completed; thou shalt soon return to thy own land: but he will *visit thy iniquity, O Edom; he will discover thy sins.* When sin is *pardoned*, it is said to be *covered:* here, God says he will *not cover the sins of Edom*—he will not *pardon them;* they shall drink the cup of wrath.

The promise in this last verse may refer to Jerusalem under the Gospel. When they receive Christ crucified, they shall be gathered from all nations, become one with the Church among the Gentiles, be one flock under one and the same Shepherd, and shall be *carried no more into captivity.*

CHAPTER V

This chapter is, as it were, an epiphonema, *or conclusion to the four preceding, representing the nation as groaning under their calamities, and humbly supplicating the Divine favour,* 1–22.

A. M. cir. 3416
B. C. cir. 588
Ol. XLVIII. 1
TarquiniiPrisci,
R. Roman.,
cir. annum 29

[a]REMEMBER, O LORD, what
is come upon us: consider,
and behold [b]our reproach.
2 [c]Our inheritance is turned to
strangers, our houses to aliens.
3 We are orphans and fatherless, our mothers *are* as widows.
4 We have drunken our water
for money; our wood [d]is sold
unto us.

[a]Psa. lxxxix. 50, 51——[b]Chap. ii. 15; Psa. lxxix. 4

[c]Psa. lxxix. 1——[d]Heb. *cometh for price*

NOTES ON CHAP. V

Verse 1. *Remember, O Lord*] In the *Vulgate, Syriac,* and *Arabic,* this is headed, "The prayer of Jeremiah." In my old MS. Bible: **Here bigynneth the orison of Jeremye the prophete.**

Though this chapter consists of exactly *twenty-two* verses, the *number of letters* in the *Hebrew alphabet,* yet the *acrostic* form is no longer observed. Perhaps any thing so technical was not thought proper when in agony and distress (under a sense of God's displeasure on account of sin) they prostrated themselves before him to ask for mercy. Be this as it may, no attempt appears to have been made to throw these verses into the form of the preceding chapters. It is properly a *solemn prayer of all the people,* stating their past and present sufferings, and praying for God's mercy.

Behold our reproach.] הביט *hebita.* But many MSS. of *Kennicott's,* and the oldest of my own, add the ה *he paragogic,* הביטה *hebitah,* "Look down earnestly with commiseration;" for *paragogic letters* always *increase* the sense.

Verse 2. *Our inheritance is turned to strangers*] The greater part of the Jews were either slain or carried away captive; and even those who were left under *Gedaliah* were not *free,* for they were vassals to the *Chaldeans.*

Verse 4. *We have drunken our water for money*] I suppose the meaning of this is, that every thing was taxed by the Chaldeans, and that they kept the management in their own

A. M. cir. 3416 B. C. cir. 588 Ol. XLVIII. 1 TarquiniiPrisci, R. Roman., cir. annum 29

5 [e]Our [f]necks *are* under persecution: we labour, *and* have
no rest.
6 [g]We have given the hand
[h]*to* the Egyptians, *and to* the Assyrians, to be
satisfied with bread.
7 [i]Our fathers have sinned, *and* [k]*are* not;
and we have borne their iniquities.
8 [l]Servants have ruled over us: *there is*
none that doth deliver *us* out of their hand.
9 We gat our bread with *the peril of* our
lives because of the sword of the wilderness.
10 Our [m]skin was black like an oven because of the[n] terrible famine.
11 [o]They ravished the women in Zion, *and*
the maids in the cities of Judah.
12 Princes are hanged up by
their hand: [p]the faces of elders
were not honoured.
13 They took the young men
[q]to grind, and the children fell under the
wood.
14 The elders have ceased from the gate,
the young men from their music.
15 The joy of our heart is ceased; our
dance is turned into mourning.
16 [r]The [s]crown is fallen *from* our head:
wo unto us, that we have sinned!
17 For this [t]our heart is faint; [u]for these
things our eyes are dim.
18 Because of the mountain of Zion, which
is desolate, the foxes walk upon it.

[e]Deut. xxviii. 48; Jer. xxviii. 14——[f]Heb. *On our necks are we persecuted*——[g]Gen. xxiv. 2; Jer. l. 15——[h]Hos. xii. 1——[i]Jer. xxxi. 29; Ezek. xviii. 2——[k]Gen. xlii. 13; Zech. i. 5——[l]Neh. v. 15——[m]Job xxx. 30; Psa. cxix. 83; chap. iv. 8

[n]Or, *terrors* or *storms*——[o]Isa. xiii. 16; Zech. xiv. 2——[p]Isa. xlvii. 6; chap. iv. 16——[q]Judg. xvi. 21——[r]Job xix. 9; Psa. lxxxix. 39——[s]Heb. *The crown of our head is fallen*——[t]Chap. i. 22——[u]Psalm vi. 7; chapter ii. 11

hands, so that *wood* and *water* were both sold, the people not being permitted to help themselves. They were now so lowly reduced by servitude, that they were obliged to pay dearly for those things which formerly were *common* and of *no price*. A poor *Hindoo* in the country never buys *fire-wood*, but when he comes to the city he is obliged to purchase his fuel, and considers it as a matter of great hardship.

Verse 5. *Our necks* are *under persecution*] We feel the yoke of our bondage; we are driven to our work like the *bullock*, which has a yoke upon his neck.

Verse 6. *We have given the hand* to *the Egyptians*] We have sought alliances both with the Egyptians and Assyrians, and made covenants with them in order to get the necessaries of life. Or, wherever we are now driven, we are obliged to submit to the people of the countries in order to the preservation of our lives.

Verse 7. *Our fathers have sinned*, and are *not*] *Nations*, as such, cannot be punished in the *other world;* therefore national judgments are to be looked for only in this life. The punishment which the Jewish nation had been meriting for a series of years came now upon them, because they copied and increased the sins of their fathers, and the cup of their iniquity was full. Thus the *children* might be said to *bear the sins of the fathers*, that is, in *temporal punishment*, for in no other way does God visit these upon the children. See Ezek. xviii. 1, &c.

Verse 8. *Servants have ruled over us*] To be subject to such is the most painful and dishonourable bondage:—

> Quio domini faciant, audent cum talia fures?
> *Virg.* Ecl. iii. 16.

> "Since slaves so insolent are grown,
> What may not masters do?"

Perhaps he here alludes to the Chaldean *soldiers*, whose will the wretched Jews were obliged to obey.

Verse 9. *We gat our bread with* the peril of *our lives*] They could not go into the wilderness to feed their cattle, or to get the necessaries of life, without being harassed and plundered by marauding parties, and by these were often exposed to the peril of their lives. This was predicted by Moses, Deut. xxviii. 31.

Verse 10. *Our skin was black—because of the terrible famine.*] Because of the *searching winds* that burnt up every green thing, destroying vegetation, and in consequence producing a famine.

Verse 11. *They ravished the women in Zion*, and *the maids in the cities of Judah.*] The evil mentioned here was predicted by Moses, Deut. xxviii. 30, 32, and by Jeremiah, chap. vi. 12.

Verse 12. *Princes are hanged up by their hand*] It is very probable that this was a species of punishment. They were suspended from hooks in the wall by their hands till they died through torture and exhaustion. The body of Saul was fastened to the wall of Bethshan, probably in the same way; but his head had already been taken off. They were hung in this way that they might be devoured by the fowls of the air. It was a custom with the Persians after they had slain, strangled, or beheaded their enemies, to hang their bodies upon poles, or empale them. In this way they treated *Histiæus* of Miletum, and *Leonidas* of Lacedæmon. See *Herodot.* lib. vi. c. 30, lib. vii. c. 238.

Verse 13. *They took the young men to grind*] This was the work of female slaves. See the note on Isa. xlvii. 2.

Verse 14. *The elders have ceased from the gate*] There is now no more justice administered to the people; they are under military law, or disposed of in every sense according to the caprice of their masters.

Verse 16. *The crown is fallen* from *our head*] At feasts, marriages, &c., they used to crown themselves with garlands of flowers; all festivity of this kind was now at an end. Or it may refer to their having lost all *sovereignty*, being made *slaves*.

Verse 18. *The foxes walk upon it.*] *Foxes*

A. M. cir. 3416
B. C. cir. 588
Ol. XLVIII. 1
TarquiniiPrisci,
R. Roman.,
cir. annum 29

19 Thou, O Lord, [v]remain-
est for ever; [w]thy throne from
generation to generation.
20 [x]Wherefore dost thou forget
us for ever, *and* forsake us [y]so long time?
21 [z]Turn thou us unto thee,
O Lord, and we shall be turned;
renew our days as of old.
22 [a]But thou hast utterly rejected us; thou art very wroth against us.

[v]Psa. ix. 7; x. 16; xxix. 10; xc. 2; cii. 12, 26, 27; cxlv. 13; Hab. i. 12——[w]Psa. xlv. 6——[x]Psa. xiii. 1

[y]Heb. *for length of days?*——[z]Psa. lxxx. 3, 7, 19; Jer. xxxi. 18——[a]Or, *For wilt thou utterly reject us?*

are very numerous in Palestine, see on Judges xv. 4. It was usual among the Hebrews to consider all desolated land to be the resort of wild beasts; which is, in fact, the case every where when the inhabitants are removed from a country.

Verse 19. *Thou, O Lord, remainest for ever*] Thou sufferest no *change.* Thou didst once *love* us; O let that love be renewed towards us!

Verse 21. *Renew our days as of old.*] Restore us to our former state. Let us regain our country, our temple, and all the Divine offices of our religion; but, more especially, thy favour.

Verse 22. *But thou hast utterly rejected us*] It appears as if thou hadst sealed our final reprobation, because thou showest against us *exceeding great wrath.* But *convert us, O Lord, unto thee, and we shall be converted.* We are now greatly humbled, *feel* our *sin,* and *see* our *folly:* once more restore us, and we shall never again forsake thee! He heard the prayer; and at the end of *seventy* years they were restored to their own land.

This last verse is well rendered in the first printed edition of our Bible, 1535:—**Renue our daies as in olde tyme, for thou hast now banished us longe ynough, and bene sore displeased at us.**

My old MS. Bible is not less nervous:—**Newe thou our dais as fro the begynnynge: bot castand aweie thou hast put us out: thou wrathedist ugein us hugely.**

Dr. *Blayney* translates, "For surely thou hast cast us off altogether:" and adds, "כי *ki* ought certainly to be rendered as *causal;* God's having rejected his people, and expressed great indignation against them, being the *cause* and *ground* of the preceding application, in which they pray to be restored to his favour, and the enjoyment of their ancient privileges."

Pareau thinks no good sense can be made of this place unless we translate interrogatively, as in Jer. xiv. 19,—

"Hast thou utterly rejected Judah?
Hath thy soul loathed Sion?"

On this ground he translates here,

An enim prorsus nos rejecisses?
Nobis iratus esses usque adeo?

"Hast thou indeed utterly cast us off?
Wilt thou be angry with us for ever?"

Wilt thou extend thy wrath against us so as to show us no more mercy? This agrees well with the *state* and *feelings* of the complainants.

Masoretic Notes

Number of verses in this Book, 154.

Middle verse, chap. iii. 34.

In one of my oldest MSS., the *twenty-first* verse is repeated at the conclusion of the *twenty-second* verse. In another, yet older, there is only the first word of it, השיבנו *hashibenu, Convert us!*

Having given in the preceding *preface* and *notes* what I judge necessary to explain the principal difficulties in this very fine and affecting poem, very fitly termed The Lamentations, as it justly stands at the *head* of every composition of the kind, I shall add but a few words, and these shall be by way of recapitulation chiefly.

The Hebrews were accustomed to make *lamentations* or *mourning songs* upon the death of great men, princes, and heroes, who had distinguished themselves in arms; and upon any *occasion of public miseries and calamities. Calmet* thinks they had *collections* of these sorts of Lamentations: and refers in proof to 2 Chron. xxxv. 25: "And Jeremiah lamented for Josiah; and all the singing men and the singing women spake of Josiah in their lamentations, to this day; and made them an ordinance in Israel: and, behold, they are written in the Lamentations."

From this verse it is evident, that Jeremiah had composed a funeral elegy on *Josiah:* but, from the complexion of *this Book,* it is most evident that *it* was not composed on the death of *Josiah,* but upon the *desolations of Jerusalem,* &c., as has already been noted. His *lamentation for Josiah* is therefore lost. It appears also, that on particular occasions, perhaps *anniversaries,* these *lamentations* were sung by men and women singers, who performed their *several parts;* for these were all *alternate* or *responsive songs.* And it is very likely, that this book was sung in the same way; the *men* commencing with א *aleph,* the *women* responding with ב *beth,* and so on. Several of this sort of songs are still extant. We have those which *David* composed on the death of his son *Absalom,* and on the death of his friend *Jonathan.* And we have those made by *Isaiah, Jeremiah,* and *Ezekiel,* on the desolation of *Egypt, Tyre, Sidon,* and *Babylon.* See Isa. xiv. 4, 5; xv.; xvi.; Jer. vii. 29; ix. 10; xlviii. 32; Ezek. xix. 1; xxviii. 11; xxxii. 2; Jer. ix. 17. Besides these, we have *fragments* of others in different places; and references to some, which are now finally lost.

In the *two* first *chapters* of this book, the prophet describes, principally, the calamities of the siege of Jerusalem.

In the *third,* he deplores the persecutions which he himself had suffered; though he may in this be *personifying* the city and state; many of his own sufferings being illustrative of the calamities that fell generally upon the city and people at large.

The *fourth* chapter is employed chiefly on the ruin and desolation of the city and temple; and upon the misfortunes of *Zedekiah,* of whom he speaks in a most respectful, tender, and affecting manner:—

"The anointed of Jehovah, the breadth of our nostrils, was taken in their toils,
Under whose shadow we said, We shall live among the nations."

At the end he speaks of the cruelty of the Edomites, who had insulted Jerusalem in her miseries, and contributed to its demolition. These he threatens with the wrath of God.

The *fifth* chapter is a kind of *form of prayer* for the Jews, in their dispersions and captivity. In the conclusion of it, he speaks of their fallen royalty; attributes all their calamities to their rebellion and wickedness; and acknowledges that there can be no end to their misery, but in their restoration to the Divine favour.

This last chapter was probably written some considerable time *after* the rest: for it supposes the temple to be so deserted, that the *foxes walked undisturbed among its ruins*, and that the people were already in captivity.

The poem is a monument of the *people's* iniquity and rebellion; of the displeasure and judgment of GOD against them; and of the piety, eloquence, and incomparable ability of the *poet.*

INTRODUCTION TO THE BOOK

OF THE

PROPHET EZEKIEL

EZEKIEL the prophet was the son of *Buzi;* and was of the sacerdotal race, as himself informs us, chap. i. 3, and was born at a place called *Saresa,* as the *pseudo-Epiphanius* tells us in his Lives of the Prophets. He was carried captive by Nebuchadnezzar into Babylon, with Jeconiah king of Judah, and *three thousand* other captives of the principal inhabitants, and was sent into Mesopotamia, where he received the prophetic gift; which is supposed, from an obscure expression in his prophecies, chap. i. 1, to have taken place in the *thirtieth* year of his age. He had then been in captivity *five* years; and continued to prophesy about *twenty-two* years, from A. M. 3409 to A. M. 3430, which answers to the *fourteenth* year after the destruction of Jerusalem.

About *three* months and *ten* days after this conquest of Jerusalem, Nebuchadnezzar made another descent, and again besieged the city; and Jehoiachin, who succeeded his father Jehoiakim, was obliged to surrender. The victorious Chaldeans carried off all the inhabitants of note into Babylon, leaving none behind but the very poorest of the people. See 2 Kings xxiv. 8–16. These captives were fixed at *Tel-abib,* and other places on the river Chebar, which flows into the east side of the Euphrates at Carchemish, nearly *two hundred* miles northward of Babylon. There, as Archbishop *Newcome* observes, he was present in body, though, in visionary representation, he was sometimes taken to Jerusalem.

With this same learned writer I am of opinion that, the better to understand the propriety and force of these Divine revelations, the circumstances and dispositions of the Jews in their own country, and in their state of banishment, and the chief historical events of that period, should be stated and considered. Most writers on this Prophet have adopted this plan; and Archbishop *Newcome's* abstract of this history is sufficient for every purpose.

"Zedekiah, uncle to the captive king Jehoiachin, was advanced by Nebuchadnezzar to the kingdom of Judah; and the tributary king bound himself to subjection by a solemn oath in the name of Jehovah, Ezek. xvii. 18. But notwithstanding the Divine judgments which had overwhelmed Judah during the reigns of his two immediate predecessors, he did evil in the sight of God, 2 Chron. xxxvi. 12. Jerusalem became so idolatrous, impure, oppressive, and blood-thirsty, that God is represented as smiting his hands together through astonishment at such a scene of iniquity, chap. xxii. 13. The Prophet Jeremiah was insulted, rejected, and persecuted; false prophets abounded, whose language was, 'Ye shall not serve the king of Babylon,' Jer. xxvii. 9. 'I have broken the yoke of the king of Babylon,' Jer. xxviii. 2. They even limited the restoration of the sacred vessels, and the return of Jehoiachin and his fellow captives, to so short an interval as *two years,* Jer. xxviii. 3, 4. Zedekiah, blinded by his vices and these delusions, flattered by the embassies which he had received from Edom, Moab, Ammon, Tyre, and Sidon, Jer. xxvii. 3, and probably submitting with his accustomed timidity to the advice of evil counsellors, Jer. xxviii. 25, rebelled against his powerful conquerors, and sent ambassadors into Egypt for assistance, Ezek. xvii. 15. Hence arose a third invasion of the Chaldeans. Pharaoh-hophra, king of Egypt, did not advance to the assistance of Zedekiah till Jerusalem was besieged, Jer. xxxvii. 5. The Babylonians raised the siege with the design of distressing the Egyptians in their march, and of giving battle when advantage offered: but Pharaoh, with perfidy and pusillanimity, returned to his own country; and left the rebellious and perjured king of Judah to the rage of his enemies, Jer. xxxvii. 7. Before the siege was thus interrupted, Zedekiah endeavoured to conciliate the favour of God by complying so far with the Mosaic law as to proclaim the sabbatical year a year of liberty to Hebrew servants, Exod. xxi. 2. But such was his impiety and so irresolute and fluctuating were his counsels, that, on the departure of the Chaldeans, he revoked his edict, Jer. xxxiv. 11; upon which God, by the Prophet Jeremiah, proclaimed liberty to the sword, to the pestilence, and to the famine; and commissioned these messengers of his wrath to avenge himself on his people, Jer. xxxiv. 17. When the siege was resumed, we have a farther instance of Zedekiah's extreme infatuation; his rejection of Jeremiah's counsel, given him by the authority of God, to preserve himself, his family, and his city, by a surrender to the Chaldeans. Thus, after a siege of *eighteen* months, Jerusalem was stormed and burnt, Jer. xxxix. 1, 2; Zedekiah was taken in his flight; his sons were slain before his eyes; his eyes were afterwards put out, agreeably to the savage custom of eastern conquerors; and he was carried in chains to Babylon, Jer. xxxix. 5–7.

"The exiles on the river Chebar were far from being awakened to a devout acknowledgment of God's justice by the punishment inflicted on them: they continued rebellious and idolatrous, Ezek. ii. 3; xx. 39, they hearkened to false prophets and prophetesses, Ezek. xiii. 2, 17; and they were so alienated that he refused to be inquired of by them. In vain did Ezekiel endeavour to attract and win them by the charms of his flowing and insinuating eloquence; in vain did he assume a more vehement tone to awe and alarm them by heightened scenes of calamity and terror.

"We know few particulars concerning the Jews at Babylon. They enjoyed the instruction and example of the Prophet Daniel, who was carried away captive to that city in the *third* year of Jehoiakim, *eight* years before the captivity of Ezekiel, Dan. i. 1. Jeremiah cautioned them not to be deceived by their false prophets and diviners, Jer. xxix. 8, 9, 15, 21; against some of whom he denounced fearful judgments. He exhorted them to seek the peace of the city where they dwelt; to take wives, build houses, and plant gardens, till their restoration after *seventy* years, Jer. xxix. 5, 6, 7, 10. He also comforted them by a prediction of all the evil which God designed to inflict on Babylon: he assured them that *none should remain* in that proud city, but that it should be *desolate for ever*. The messenger, when he had read the book containing these denunciations, was commanded 'to bind a stone to it, and cast it into the Euphrates, and say, Thus shall Babylon sink, and shall not rise from the evil which I will bring on her,' Jer. li. 59–64. It farther appears, by Divine hymns now extant, see Psa. lxxix., cii., cvi., and cxxxvii., that God vouchsafed to inspire some of these Babylonian captives with his Holy Spirit. Nebuchadnezzar appointed Gedaliah ruler of the people that remained in Judea, 2 Kings xxv. 23; Jer. xl. 5; and the scattered military commanders and their men, together with other Jews who had taken refuge in the neighbouring countries, Jer. xl. 7, 11, submitted to his government on the departure of the Chaldeans. The Jews employed themselves in gathering the fruits of the earth, Jer. xl. 12, and a calm succeeded the tempest of war: but it was soon interrupted by the turbulence of this devoted people. Ishmael slew Gedaliah; and compelled the wretched remains of the Jews in Mizpah, the seat of Gedaliah's government, to retire with him towards the country of the Ammonites, Jer. xli. 10; a people hostile to the Chaldeans, Jer. xxvii. 3. Johanan raised a force to revenge this mad and cruel act, Jer. xli. 11–15; pursued Ishmael, overtook him, and recovered from him the people whom he had forced to follow him: but the assassin himself escaped with *eight* men to his place of refuge. The succeeding event furnishes another signal instance of human infatuation. Johanan, through fear of the Chaldeans, many of whom Ishmael had massacred, together with Gedaliah, Jer. xli. 3, conceived a design of retreating to Egypt, Jer. xli. 17; but before he executed this resolution, he formally consulted the Prophet Jeremiah. The prophet answered him in the name of Jehovah,

Jer. xlii., that if Johanan and the people abode in Judea, God would 'build them, and not pull them down: would plant them, and not pluck them up;' but if they went to sojourn in Egypt, they should 'die by the sword, by famine, and by pestilence;' and should become an 'execration, and an astonishment, and a curse, and a reproach.' Notwithstanding this awful assurance, and the many prophecies of Jeremiah, which the most calamitous events had lately verified, Johanan defied the living God and his prophet, and madly adhered to his determination. Not long after the destruction of Jerusalem, the siege of Tyre was undertaken by Nebuchadnezzar. It continued for the space of *thirteen* years; and many think that the conquest of the Sidonians, Philistines, Ammonites, Moabites, and Idumeans, coincided with this period, the Chaldean being able to make powerful detachments from his vast forces. See the prophecies, Jer. xxvii. 2, 3; xlviii., xlix., and Ezek. xxv. After the reduction of that famous city, Nebuchadnezzar made his descent on Egypt, which he subdued and ravaged throughout; and at this time Johanan and his Jewish colonists experienced the vengeance of the conqueror, together with the Egyptians. So widely did Nebuchadnezzar spread his victories and devastations, that, according to the learned chronologer *Marsham*, Lond. edit. 1672, fol. p. 556, s. 18, this might justly be called the era of the subversion of cities.

——————— Omnis eo terrore Ægyptus, et Indi,
Omnis Arabs, omnes vertebant terga Sabæi. Virg. *Æn.* viii. 705.

'The trembling Indians and Egyptians yield:
Arabs and soft Sabæans quit the field.' "

I may add that the stroke fell upon no people so heavily as upon the Jews, for no other nation possessed privileges like them, and no other nation had sinned so deeply against God. Their crimes were seen in their punishment.

The principal design of this prophet was to comfort his companions in tribulation during their captivity, and to render it light by the most positive promises of their restoration to their own land, the re-building of the temple, and the re-establishment of the Divine worship, all their enemies being finally destroyed.

That Ezekiel is a very *obscure* writer, all have allowed who have attempted to explain his prophecies. The Jews considered him inexplicable. There is a tradition that the rabbins held a consultation whether they should admit Ezekiel into the sacred canon. And it was likely to be carried in the negative, when Rabbi *Ananias* rose up and said he would undertake to remove every difficulty from the account of *Jehovah's chariot*, chap. i., which is confessedly the most difficult part in the whole book. His proposal was received; and to assist him in his work, and that he might complete it to his credit, they furnished him with *three hundred barrels of oil* to light his lamp during the time he might be employed in the study of this part of his subject! This extravagant grant proved at once the conviction the rabbins had of the difficulty of the work; and it is not even intimated that Rabbi *Ananias* succeeded in any tolerable degree, if indeed he undertook the task; and they believe that to this hour the *chariot* mentioned in chap. i., and the account of the *temple* described at the conclusion of the book, have not been explained.

I believe it may be affirmed with truth that these parts of the prophecy have had as many *different explanations* as there have been *expositors!* Yet each has been sanguine in the hope that he had removed all difficulties; while every successor felt that the whole work was yet to be done, and that the *Gordian knot* was not likely to be untied unless by himself. And it is to be lamented that in these circumstances the work still remains as to its principal difficulties; and I certainly do not attempt to add another to Ezekiel's commentators with the most distant hope of being able to solve those particular difficulties.

After all, with the exception of the *chariot*, *Gog and Magog*, the peculiarities in the description of the *temple*, and some matters of this kind, the major part of the prophecy is very intelligible, and highly edifying; and does not present more difficulties than have been found in the preceding prophets, and may be found in those which follow. I have in the following notes done what I could, as a help to a better understanding of this part of the sacred writings.

The ancient *Versions* give some help; but it is astonishing how difficult it is to settle the text by a collation of MSS. This has not yet been properly done; and we cannot know the *true meaning* till we can ascertain the *true reading*. But after having laboured in this way, I must express myself as the learned professor of the oriental tongues at Parma, *J. B. De Rossi:* Tanta hic in suffixis præsertim pronominibus codicum inconstantia ac varietas, ut tæduerit me laboris mei, ac verius ego quod olim de uno Zachariæ versu (xi. 5) dolens inquiebat *Norzius,* de toto Ezechielis libro usurpare possim, angustiatam fuisse animam meam ob varietates multas, et avertisse faciem meam ab eis. "That there is so much inconstancy and variation among the MSS., especially in the *suffixed pronouns*, that I was weary of my labour; and I could more truly say of the whole book of Ezekiel, than *Norzius* did relative to one passage in Zechariah, who, bitterly complaining of the many variations he met with, said, 'My soul was perplexed with them, and I turned away my face from them.' " As most of our printed editions have been taken from a very inadequate collation of MSS., especially of this prophet, much remains to be done to restore the text to a proper state of purity. When this is done it is presumed that several of the difficulties in this book will be removed. In many instances Abp. *Newcome* has been very successful.

On the famous controversy relative to Gog and Magog, I must refer the reader to the notes on chap. xxxviii. and xxxix., where the best accounts I have met with are detailed. There are only *two schemes* that appear at all probable; that which makes Gog *Antiochus Epiphanes*, king of Assyria, and that which makes him *Cambyses*, king of Persia. The former, as being the most probable, and the best supported in all its parts by the marks given in the prophecy, I have in a certain measure adopted, for want of one more satisfactory to my own mind.

The character of Ezekiel as a poet has been drawn at large by some of the most eminent critics of these and other countries. *Lowth, Michaelis,* and *Eichhorn,* are the chief. Abp. *Newcome* has quoted largely from the latter; and from his work, which is now very scarce and extremely dear, I shall present my readers with the following extracts:—

"The two first visions are so accurately polished, chap. i.–vii., viii.–xi., and demanded so much art to give them their last perfection and proportion, that they cannot possibly be an unpremeditated work. And if, according to the commonly received opinion, they were publicly read by Ezekiel as we read them now, he must have seriously designed them as a picture, and finished them in form. The intention of his visions might make this necessary. He designed no doubt to make deep impressions upon the people whom he was to guide; and by highly labouring the Divine appearances, to open their ears for his future oracles and representations. The more complete, divine, and majestic the Divine appearances were which he represented, the deeper veneration was impressed upon the mind towards the prophet to whom such high visions were communicated. Most of the parts which compose Ezekiel, as they are generally works of art, are full of artificial and elaborate plans.

"The peculiarities of language in the first chapter are to be found in the middle and end of the book. The same enthusiasm which in the beginning of his prophecies produced the magnificent Divine appearances, must also have built the temple of God at the conclusion. As in the beginning every thing is first proposed in high allegorical images, and afterwards the same ideas are repeated in plain words, thus also in the middle and at the end in every piece, allegorical representation is succeeded by literal. Throughout the style is rather prose than verse; and rough, hard, and mixed with the Chaldee.

"The division of Ezekiel into two parts has been adopted by several writers. They continue the former part to the *thirty-ninth* chapter, and consider the last *nine* chapters from the *fortieth* as a separate book. This division is possible. From the *eleventh* chapter a new elevated scene commences. Before there was nothing but oracles, full of misfortunes, punishments, death, and ruin; visions concerning the destruction of the government, and concerning the flight and state of the last king; and pictures of the universal corruption, idolatry, and superstition of Israel. From the *fortieth* chapter a new temple rises before the eyes of the holy seer; he walks round about it in Palestine; he measures the city and country for their new inhabitants; he orders sacrifices, feasts, and customs. In short, a Magna Charta is planned for priests, kings, and people, in future and better times. Lastly, from hence prosaic expressions predominate; at least the prophet elevates himself by poetical colouring much more rarely than before.

"A generally acknowledged character of Ezekiel is, that he minutely distinguishes every thing in its smallest parts. What the more ancient prophets brought together in one single picture, and to which they only alluded, and what they explained with the utmost brevity, and showed only from one side, *that* he explains and unfolds formally, and represents from all possible sides.

"Another character, and a principal one, which distinguishes his oracle is, that no other prophet has given so free a course to his imagination. Almost every thing is dressed in symbolical actions, in fables, narrations, allegories, or in the still higher poetry of visions. And as they are very complicate, there resound from all sides complaints of darkness. Whoever can look on these things with the eye of an eagle, and is not disturbed from the principal object by what is not essential; he alone is able to comprehend the sense of the whole composition, and he scarcely conceives how any one can complain of obscurity. Meanwhile, how different soever the species of composition are which he hazards, they are all worked out in the same general form. What he represents in one image, picture, or vision, in allegory, parable, or narration, is explained in a short speech, which God, who is at his right hand, enables him to pronounce.

"It is evident that he has shown an inexhaustible imagination and power of invention throughout all the pages of his book. He uses all sorts of prophetical poetry to appear always great and magnificent; and it cannot be denied that he has given all kinds, excellent pieces, both in design and execution. Particularly, he is so used to ecstasies and visions that he adopts the language proper to these, where he has no visions to describe.

"If the dress of vision fitted any prophet, it was certainly Ezekiel: he was even naturally led to it by his situation, and by the subjects which he was to represent. He was to describe and foretell to his fellow captives several facts which happened in Palestine, in Jerusalem, and in the king's palace. A narration and description in simple prose could not possibly suit a prophet; he must give his object the requisite prophetic dignity, by a particular dress.

"He therefore brought the scene of events nearer. For this purpose he chose high ecstasies, such as the Greek and Roman poets pretended to in their flights of enthusiasm; the hand of Jehovah came upon him, and carried him to that place where what he intended to propose to his countrymen in their exile might be seen and considered. All ecstasies in my opinion are nothing but dresses, nothing but poetical fictions; and a poet of another age, and of another tone, of an inferior imagination and poetical endowments, would have given the same ideas quite another dress.

"Accustomed to this kind of poetry, he represented the restitution of the Jewish state in a sublime vision. His imagination placed him upon graves, where he stood on the dried bones of the dead. He saw how the graves opened, the bones were clothed with flesh, and the dead came forth by a new creation. Could there be a more lively fiction for this case? Another poet would have represented the restoration of the Jews in simple words; and would only have compared it to a resurrection, or give it some other ornamental delineation. To view this intuitively in an example, compare Ezek. xxxvii. 1–14 and Isa. xxvi. 19.

'Thy dead shall live, their dead bodies shall rise:
Awake and sing, ye that dwell in dust:
For thy dew is as the dew of herbs,
And the earth shall cast forth the mighty dead.'

"And, however numerous the fictions of Ezekiel are, they all appear in magnificent dress, and each in its peculiar splendid one. Lustre shines in him on every side; and if the poet has here and there overloaded his subject with ornaments, we shall be unable to refuse our admiration to his genius, notwithstanding these defects.

"The first part of his book may be an instance. The barren genius of Moses was gone when God appeared only in a fiery bush in the wilderness; and as the world improved in cultivation, a more luxuriant one succeeded in his place, which in process of time demanded wonderful figures and giant forms, that the representation of the Divine appearance might please. Isaiah had already appeared in a higher style than Moses. To him God manifested himself in the pomp of an oriental king; and this piece makes a strong impression by its unity and gains on us by its elevated simplicity, majesty, and dignity, Isa. vi. But Ezekiel differs widely. Before him stands the chariot-throne of God, with wonderful forms; he summons all the pomp which nature and art can furnish; he abundantly employs fiction and composition to give his Divine appearance dignity, elevation, and majesty; and thus to make a suitable expression. The whole creation must lend him its most noble forms. Men, oxen, lions, and eagles support the throne: the Hebrew history must furnish all its most wonderful scenes, to surround the chariot-throne with the greatest pomp imaginable. I admire the master-hand of the artist, who knew how to compose in such a manner. I am astonished at the richness of *his* imagination, that could give dignity to all the exalted scenes of the Hebrew history, and could combine them in one body. But, notwithstanding this, the scene in Ezekiel is far from making the same deep and heart-striking impression with that of Isaiah. A short view of the whole in Isaiah does wonders; in Ezekiel the prospect is dispersed; and as it is not rounded, it astonishes rather than impresses. In Isaiah there is a majestic silence, which is only interrupted by the heavenly cry of the seraphs, Isa. vi. 3; in Ezekiel, the noise of the restless wheels and moving wings confounds us. In Isaiah, the eye is delighted with artless majesty; in Ezekiel, it is consumed by the brightness of the fire which shines round about the chariot-throne.

"The author of the Revelation, whose poetry is in the same style with that of Ezekiel, and full of imagination, has for the most part avoided the rocks upon which his predecessor struck; and, happily for the most part, has cut off the wild shoots of a heated imagination. He also has fictions of wonders and giant forms; but he has produced them only so far as to give the reader a full image before his eyes. He does not pursue them minutely, and he does not distract or pain his reader.

"On the contrary, it was a happy invention that his lofty poems are sometimes interrupted by short speeches; they are not only useful for the illustration of his symbols, but also for the repose of the mind. By this change, his readers are agreeably entertained; and their imagination finds resting places, so as to soar more easily after the imagination of the poet.

"Ezekiel is a great poet, full of originality; and, in my opinion, whoever censures him as if he were only an imitator of the old prophets, can never have felt his power. He must not in general be compared with Isaiah and the rest of the old prophets. Those are great, Ezekiel is also great; those in *their* manner of poetry, Ezekiel in *his;* which he had invented for himself, if we may form our judgment from the Hebrew monuments still extant." Thus far a judicious critic, who but indirectly admits the prophet's *inspiration.*

Bp. *Lowth,* who has done so much to elucidate the Hebrew *poetry,* has also given fine critical judgments on the comparative merits of the *prophets. Isaiah* is his favorite and him he places always at the *head,* and with *him* all others are compared. Of *Ezekiel,* his character is very high and accurately drawn; and my readers will naturally expect that I should produce what he says on this subject, rather than attempt any thing of my own; for this would resemble the attempt *to write an Iliad after Homer*.

"*Ezekiel*," says this learned prelate, "is inferior to *Jeremiah* in *elegance*, but is equal to *Isaiah* in SUBLIMITY, though in a different species of the *sublime*. He is *bold*, *vehement*, *tragical*, and deals very much in *amplification*. His SENTIMENTS are *lofty*, *animated*, *poignant*, and full of *indignation*. His IMAGES are *fertile*, *magnificent*, and sometimes rather bordering on *indelicacy*. His DICTION is *grand*, *weighty*, *austere*, *rough*, and sometimes *uncultivated*. He abounds in *repetitions*, not for the sake of *beauty* or *grace*, but from *vehemence* and *indignation*. Whatever his *subject* be, he keeps it always in his eye, without the least deviation, and is so much taken up with it that he has scarcely any regard to *order* or *connection*. In other things he may be perhaps *exceeded* by the other prophets, but in that species for which he was particularly turned, that is, *force*, *impetuosity*, *weight*, and *grandeur*, no writer ever equalled him. His *diction* is *clear* enough; almost all his *obscurity* arises from his *subjects*. His VISIONS are particularly *obscure;* which, however, as in *Hosea*, *Amos*, and *Zechariah*, are delivered in a *plain historical narration*.

"The greater part of the book, particularly the middle of it, is *poetical;* whether we regard the *matter* or the *language*. But some passages are so *rough* and *unpolished*, that we are frequently at a loss to what species of writing we ought to refer them. As to STYLE, *Isaiah*, *Jeremiah*, and *Ezekiel* may be placed with propriety enough in the same rank among the *Hebrews*, as *Homer*, *Simonides*, and *Æschylus* among the *Greeks*."

Nothing need be added, and indeed nothing can be added, to this character; it is as fairly as it is fully drawn; and every paragraph in the book will show its propriety. But could we satisfactorily fathom the prophet's meaning in those places where he is *peculiarly obscure*, we should feel the force and propriety of the bishop's character still more, as in those very places the prophet is *peculiarly sublime*. The prophecy was delivered that it might be understood and be profitable; and no doubt it was fully apprehended by those to whom it was originally given, and for whose sake it was sent from heaven. As to the portions which respect a very *remote futurity*, they will be understood when the events take place; which will, in such times, be an additional argument in favour of Divine revelation, when it is seen with what precision and accuracy prophets have foreseen and described such very remote and apparently contingent events.

To the general reader the following table, taken from *Calmet*, may be useful:—

A Chronological Table of the Prophecies of Ezekiel

A. M.

3405. Ezekiel is led captive to Babylon with King Jeconiah. From this year the epoch of these prophecies must be taken.

3409. The first *vision* by the river Chebar, chap. i. The circumstances which followed Ezekiel's vocation to the prophetic office, chap. i., ii.

He draws upon a tile or bed of clay the plan of Jerusalem, and the siege that it was about to endure; and he remains lying on this plan, on his left side, *three hundred* and *ninety* days, chap. iv. See under A. M. 3420.

3410. He turns on his right side, and lies *forty* days, which point out the *forty* years of the sins of Judah, To this time chap. v., vi., vii. refer.

About the month of *September*, this being the *sixth* year of the captivity of Jeconiah, he had the visions related, chap. viii., ix., x., xi.

3411. Prophecies and figurative actions by which he points out the flight, capture, and blinding of Zedekiah, chap. xii. and the *seven* following.

Zedekiah rebels against Nebuchadnezzar, chap. xvii. 15, 17.

The prophet charges the elders of Judah with hypocrisy, who came to consult him, chap. xx., xxi.. xxii., xxiii.

3414. The siege of *Jerusalem* by Nebuchadnezzar. This was a sabbatic year, Jer. xxiv. 8, &c. The siege did not begin till about the middle of the winter, 2 Kings xxv. 1. The prophet's wife dies on the same day of the siege, and he is forbidden to mourn for her, chap. xxiv. 1, 2.

3415. Predictions against Egypt, chap. xxix. 16. Nebuchadnezzar puts to flight Pharaoh-hophra, and returns to the siege of Jerusalem *three hundred* and *ninety* days before it was taken.

3416. Predictions against *Tyre*, chap. xxvi.–xxviii., the *first* day of the *first* month.

In the *seventh* day of the same month, God shows the prophet the miseries to be brought on Egypt by Nebuchadnezzar, chap. xxx.

In the *third* month of the same year, the prophet had another vision against *Egypt*, chap. xxxi.

Jerusalem is taken the *ninth* of the *fourth* month. Zedekiah was taken prisoner near Jericho. He is brought to Riblah, where, after seeing his children slain, his eyes are put out, he is laden with chains and led to Babylon. Thus were fulfilled and reconciled the seemingly contradictory prophecies concerning him.

3417. Ezekiel being informed of the taking of Jerusalem the *fifth* day of the *tenth* month, he predicts the ruin of the remnant that was left there under Gedaliah, chap. xxxiv. 21–29.

He afterwards foretells the ruin of *Egypt*, chap. xxxii. 1, 16, 32; and that of the *Idumeans*, chap. xxv. 12.

3419. The commencement of the siege of *Tyre*, which lasted *thirteen* years.

To the same time we must refer the miseries of the Sidonians, the Amalekites, the Moabites, and the Idumeans, pointed out by Jeremiah, chap. xxvii., xlviii., xlix.; Ezek. xxv.

3420. End of the *forty* years mentioned chap. iv. 5, 6, and of the *three hundred* and *ninety* years from the separation of Israel and Judah. The *forty* years commence with the renewal of the covenant under Josiah.

3430. The vision in which God showed the prophet the rebuilding of the city and the temple, and the restoration of the kingdom of Israel, chap. xl. 1 to the end of the book.

This vision took place on the *tenth* of the *first* month, *fourteen* years after the taking of Jerusalem.

3432. Taking of the city of *Tyre*, by Nebuchadnezzar, to whom God promises the spoils of Egypt, as a compensation for the trouble and loss he sustained before Tyre, chap. xxix. 17–20.

Nebuchadnezzar enters *Egypt*. Amasis had been made king by the Cyrenians, who had rebelled against Pharaoh-hophra. *Herodotus*, lib. iv. c. 159, and lib. ii. cc. 161, 162.

3433. The king of Babylon overruns and subdues the whole of Egypt; commits the greatest outrages; and carries off captives the inhabitants, the Jews, and others whom he found there. See Jer. xliii., xliv., xlvi.; Ezek. xxix., xxx., xxxi.

Nebuchadnezzar leaves *Amasis* king of Lower Egypt; *Hophra*, or *Apries*, having escaped to the Thebais.

3442. Death of Nebuchadnezzar.

Evil-merodach succeeds him; and sets Jeconiah at liberty, and makes him his companion, 2 Kings xv. 27 and Jer. lii. 31.

THE BOOK

OF THE

PROPHET EZEKIEL

Chronological Notes relative to the commencement of Ezekiel's prophesying

Year from the Creation, according to Archbishop Usher, 3409.—Year of the Jewish era of the world, 3166.—Year from the Deluge, 1753.—Second year of the *forty-sixth* Olympiad.—Year from the building of Rome, according to the Varronian or generally received account, 159.—Year from the building of Rome, according to Cato and the Fasti Consulares, 158.—Year from the building of Rome, according to Polybius the historian, 157.—Year from the building of Rome, according to Fabius Pictor, 153.—Year of the Julian Period, 4119.—Year of the era of Nabonassar, 153.—Year from the foundation of Solomon's temple, 409.—Year since the destruction of the kingdom of Israel by Shalmaneser, king of Assyria, 126.—Second year after the third Sabbatic year after the *seventeenth* Jewish jubilee, according to Helvicus. Year before the birth of Christ, 591.—Year before the vulgar era of Christ's nativity, 595.—Cycle of the Sun, 3.—Cycle of the Moon, 15.—Twenty-second year of Tarquinius Priscus, the fifth king of the Romans: this was the *eighty-sixth* year before the consulship of Lucius Junius Brutus, and Publius Valerius Poplicola.—Thirty-first year of Cyaxares, or Cyaraxes, the fourth king of Media.—Eleventh year of Agasicles, king of Lacedæmon, of the family of the Proclidæ.—Thirteenth year of Leon, king of Lucedæmon, of the family of the Eurysthenidæ.—Twenty-fifth year of Alyattes II., king of Lydia, and father of the celebrated Crœsus.—Eighth year of Æropas, the seventh king of Macedon.—Sixth and last year of Psammis, king of Egypt, according to Helvicus, an accurate chronologer. This Egyptian king was the immediate predecessor of the celebrated Apries, called Vaphres by Eusebius, and Pharaoh-hophra by Jeremiah, chap. xliv. 30.—First year of Baal, king of the Tyrians. Twelfth year of Nebuchadnezzar, king of Babylon.—Fourth year of Zedekiah, the last king of Judah.

CHAPTER I

This chapter contains that extraordinary vision of the Divine glory with which the prophet was favoured when he received the commission and instructions respecting the discharge of his office, which are contained in the two following chapters. The time of this Divine manifestation to the prophet, 1–3. *The vision of the four living creatures, and of the four wheels,* 4–25. *Description of the firmament that was spread over them, and of the throne upon which one sat in appearance as a man,* 26–28. *This vision, proceeding in a whirlwind from the* NORTH, *seems to indicate the dreadful judgments that were coming upon the whole land of Judah through the instrumentality of the cruel Chaldeans, who lay to the north of it.* See Jer. i. 14; iv. 6; and vi. 1.

A. M. 3409 B. C. 595 Ol. XLVI. 2 Anno TarquiniiPrisci, R. Roman., 22

NOW it came to pass in the thirtieth year, in the fourth *month,* in the fifth *day* of the month, as I *was* among the [a]captives [b]by the river of Chebar, *that* [c]the heavens were opened, and I saw [d]visions of God.

A. M. 3409 B. C. 595 Ol. XLVI. 2 Anno TarquiniiPrisci, R. Roman., 22

---

[a]Heb. *captivity*——[b]Ver. 3; chap. iii. 15, 23; x. 15, 20, 22; xliii. 3

[c]So Matt. iii. 16; Acts vii. 56; x. 11; Rev. xix. 11——[d]Chap. viii. 3

NOTES ON CHAP. I

Verse 1. *In the thirtieth year*] We know not what this date refers to. Some think it was the *age of the prophet;* others think the date is taken from the *time* that Josiah *renewed the covenant* with the people, 2 Kings xxii. 3, from which *Usher, Prideaux,* and *Calmet* compute the *forty* years of *Judah's transgression,* mentioned chap. iv. 6.

Abp. *Newcome* thinks there is an error in the text, and that instead of בשלשים *bisheloshim,* in the *thirtieth,* we should read בחמישית *bachamishith,* in the *fifth,* as in the *second* verse. "Now it came to pass in the fifth year, in the fourth month, in the fifth day of the month," &c. But this is supported by none of the ancient *Versions,* nor by any MS. The *Chaldee* paraphrases the verse, "And it came to pass *thirty* years after the high priest Hilkiah had found the book of the law, in the house of the sanctuary," &c. This was in the *twelfth* year of

A. M. 3409
B. C. 595
Ol. XLVI. 2
Anno
TarquiniiPrisci,
R. Roman., 22

2 In the fifth *day* of the month,
which *was* the fifth year of [e]king
Jehoiachin's captivity.
3 The word of the LORD came
expressly unto [f]Ezekiel the priest, the son
of Buzi, in the land of the Chaldeans by the
river Chebar; and [g]the hand of the LORD was
there upon him.
4 And I looked, and, behold, [h]a whirlwind
came [i]out of the north, a great cloud, and a
fire [k]infolding itself, and a brightness *was*
about it, and out of the midst thereof as the
colour of amber, out of the midst of the fire.

A. M. 3409
B. C. 595
Ol. XLVI. 2
Anno
TarquiniiPrisci,
R. Roman., 22

5 [l]Also out of the midst thereof *came* the likeness of four
living creatures. And [m]this *was*
their appearance; they had [n]the
likeness of a man.
6 And every one had four faces, and every
one had four wings.
7 And their feet *were* [o]straight feet; the
sole of their feet *was* like the sole of a calf's
foot: and they sparkled [p]like the colour of
burnished brass.
8 [q]And *they had* the hands of a man under
their wings on their four sides; and they

[e]2 Kings xxiv. 12, 15——[f]Heb. *Jehezkel*——[g]1 Kings xviii. 46; 2 Kings iii. 15; ch. iii. 14, 22; viii. 1; xl. 1——[h]Jer. xxiii. 19; xxv. 32——[i]Jer. i. 14; iv. 6; vi. 1

[k]Heb. *catching itself*——[l]Rev. iv. 6, &c.——[m]Ch. x. 8, &c.——[n]Ver. 10; ch. x. 14, 21——[o]Heb. *a straight foot*——[p]Dan. x. 6; Rev. i. 15——[q]Chap. x. 18, 21

Josiah's reign. The *thirtieth* year, computed as above, comes to A. M. 3409, the *fourth* year from the captivity of Jeconiah, and the *fifth* of the reign of Zedekiah. Ezekiel was then among the captives who had been carried way with Jeconiah, and had his dwelling near the river *Chebar*, *Chaborus*, or *Aboras*, a river of Mesopotamia, which falls into the *Euphrates* a little above *Thapsacus*, after having run through Mesopotamia from east to west.—*Calmet.*

Fourth month] *Thammuz*, answering nearly to our *July*.

I saw visions of God.] Emblems and symbols of the Divine Majesty. He particularly refers to those in this chapter.

Verse 2. *Jehoiachin's captivity*] Called also Jeconiah and Coniah; see 2 Kings xxiv. 12. He was carried away by Nebuchadnezzar; see 2 Kings xxiv. 14.

Verse 3. *The hand of the Lord*] I was filled with his power, and with the influence of the prophetic spirit.

Verse 4. *A whirlwind came out of the north*] Nebuchadnezzar, whose land, Babylonia, lay north of Judea. *Chaldea* is thus frequently denominated by Jeremiah.

A great cloud, and a fire infolding itself] A mass of fire concentrated in a *vast cloud*, that the flames might be more distinctly observable, the fire never escaping from the cloud, but issuing, and then returning in upon itself. It was in a state of powerful agitation; but always involving itself, or returning back to the centre whence it appeared to issue.

A brightness was *about it*] A fine tinge of light surrounded the cloud, in order to make its limits the more discernible; beyond which verge the turmoiling fire did not proceed.

The colour of amber] This was in the centre of the cloud; and this amber-coloured substance was the centre of the labouring flame. The word ηλεκτρον, which we translate *amber*, was used to signify a compound metal, very bright, made of gold and brass.

Verse 5. *Also out of the midst thereof* came—*four living creatures.*] As the amber-coloured body was the *centre* of the *fire*, and this *fire* was in the *centre* of the *cloud;* so out of this amber-coloured igneous centre came the *living creatures* just mentioned.

Verse 6. *Every one had four faces*] There were *four* several figures of these living creatures, and each of these figures had *four* distinct faces: but as the face of the *man* was that which was presented to the prophet's view, so that he saw it more plainly than any of the others; hence it is said, ver. 5, that each of these figures had *the likeness of a man;* and the whole of this compound image bore a general resemblance to the human figure.

Verse 7. *Their feet* were *straight feet*] There did not seem to be any flexure at the knee, nor were the legs separated in that way as to indicate progression by walking. I have before me several ancient *Egyptian* images of *Isis*, *Osiris*, *Anubis*, &c., where the legs are *not separated*, nor is there any bend at the knees; so that if there was any motion at all, it must have been by *gliding*, not progressive walking. It is a remark of *Ælian*, that the gods are never represented as *walking*, but always *gliding;* and he gives this as a criterion to discern common angelic appearances from those of the *gods:* all other spiritual beings *walked progressively*, rising on one foot, while they stretched out the other; but the deities always *glided* without *gradual* progressive motions. And *Heliodorus* in his Romance of *Theogines* and *Charicha*, gives the same reason for the *united feet of the gods*, &c., and describes the same appearances.

Like the sole of a calf's foot] Before it is stated to be a *straight foot;* one that did not lay down a *flat horizontal sole*, like that of the human foot.

And they sparkled like the colour of burnished brass.] I suppose this refers rather to the *hoof* of the calf's foot, than to the whole appearance of the *leg*. There is scarcely any thing that gives a higher lustre than highly *polished* or *burnished brass*. Our blessed Lord is represented with legs like *burnished brass*, Rev. i. 15.

Verse 8. They had *the hands of a man under their wings*] I doubt much whether the arms be not here represented as all covered with feathers, so that they had the appearance of wings, only the hand was bare; and I rather think that this is the meaning of their having "the hands of a man under their wings."

A. M. 3409
B. C. 595
Ol. XLVI. 2
Anno
TarquiniiPrisci,
R. Roman., 22

four had their faces and their wings.

9 [r]Their wings *were* joined one to another; [s]they turned not when they went; they went every one straight forward.

10 As for [t]the likeness of their faces, they four [u]had the face of a man, [v]and the face of a lion, on the right side: [w]and they four had the face of an ox on the left side; [x]they four also had the face of an eagle.

11 Thus *were* their faces: and their wings *were* [y]stretched upward; two *wings* of every one *were* joined one to another, and [z]two covered their bodies.

12 And [a]they went every one straight forward: [b]whither the spirit was to go, they went; *and* [c]they turned not when they went.

13 As for the likeness of the living creatures, their appearance *was* like burning coals of fire, [d]*and* like the appearance of lamps: it went up and down among the living creatures; and the fire was bright, and out of the fire went forth lightning.

A. M. 3409
B. C. 595
Ol. XLVI. 2
Anno
TarquiniiPrisci,
R. Roman., 22

14 And the living creatures [e]ran and returned [f]as the appearance of a flash of lightning.

15 Now as I beheld the living creatures, behold [g]one wheel upon the earth by the living creatures, with his four faces.

16 [h]The appearance of the wheels and their work *was* [i]like unto the colour of a beryl: and they four had one likeness: and their appearance and their work *was* as it were a wheel in the middle of a wheel.

17 When they went, they went upon their four sides: [k]*and* they turned not when they went.

[r]Ver. 11——[s]Ver. 12; chap. x. 11——[t]See Rev. iv. 7——[u]Num. ii. 10——[v]Num. ii. 3——[w]Num. ii. 18——[x]Num. ii. 25——[y]Or, *divided above*——[z]Isa. vi. 2

[a]Ver. 9; chap. x. 22——[b]Ver. 20——[c]Ver. 9, 17——[d]Rev. iv. 5——[e]Zech. iv. 10——[f]Matt. xxiv. 27——[g]Ch. x. 9——[h]Chap. x. 9, 10——[i]Dan. x. 6——[k]Ver. 12

Verse 9. *Their wings* were *joined one to another*] When their wings were extended, they formed a sort of canopy level with their own heads or shoulders; and on this canopy was the throne, and the "likeness of the man" upon it, ver. 26.

They turned not when they went] The wings did not flap in flying, or move in the manner of oars, or of the hands of a man in swimming, in order to their passing through the air; as they *glided* in reference to their *feet*, so they *soared* in reference to their *wings*.

Verse 10. *As for the likeness of their faces*] There was but one body to each of those compound animals: but each body had four faces; the face of a *man* and of a *lion* on the right side; the face of an *ox* and an *eagle* on the left side. Many of these compound images appear in the Asiatic idols. Many are now before me: some with the head and feet of a *monkey*, with the body, arms, and *legs* of a *man*. Others with the head of the *dog;* body, arms, and legs human. Some with the head of an *ape;* all the rest human. Some with one head and eight arms; others with six heads or faces, with twelve arms. The head of a lion and the head of a cock often appear; and some with the head of a cock, the whole body human, and the legs terminating in *snakes*. All these were symbolical, and each had its own appropriate meaning. Those in the text had theirs also, could we but find it out.

Verse 12. *They went every one straight forward*] Not by *progressive stepping*, but by *gliding*.

Whither the spirit was to go] Whither that *whirlwind* blew, they went, being borne on by the wind, see ver. 4.

Verse 13. *Like burning coals of fire*] The whole substance appeared to be of flame; and among them frequent coruscations of fire, like vibrating lamps, often emitting lightning, or rather sparks of fire, as we have seen struck out of strongly ignited iron in a forge. The flames might be something like what is called *warring wheels* in pyrotechny. They seemed to conflict together.

Verse 14. *The living creatures ran and returned*] They had a circular movement; they were in rapid motion, but did not increase their distance from the spectator. So I think this should be understood.

Verse 15. *One wheel upon the earth*] It seems at first view there were *four wheels*, one for each of the living creatures; that is, the creatures were compound, so were the wheels, for there was "a wheel in the middle of a wheel." And it is generally supposed that these wheels cut each other at right angles up and down: and this is the manner in which they are generally represented; but most probably the *wheel within* means merely the *nave* in which the spokes are inserted, in reference to the *ring, rim*, or *periphery*, where these *spokes* terminate from the centre or nave. I do think this is what is meant by the wheel within a wheel; and I am the more inclined to this opinion, by some fine Chinese drawings now before me, where their *deities* are represented as *walking upon wheels*, the wheels themselves *encompassed with fire*. The wheel is simply by itself, having a projecting axis; so of *these* it is said, "their appearance and their work was, as it were, a wheel within a wheel." There were either two peripheries or rims with their spokes, or the *nave* answered for the wheel within. I have examined models of what are called Ezekiel's wheels, which are designed to move equally in all directions: but I plainly saw that this was impossible; nor can any kind of complex wheel move in this way.

Verse 18. *As for their rings*] The *strakes* which form the *rim* or *periphery*.

A. M. 3409
B. C. 595
Ol. XLVI. 2
Anno
TarquiniiPrisci,
R. Roman., 22

18 As for their rings, they were so high that they were dreadful; and their [l]rings *were* [m]full of eyes round about them four.

19 And [n]when the living creatures went, the wheels went by them: and when the living creatures were lifted up from the earth, the wheels were lifted up.

20 [o]Whithersoever the spirit was to go, they went, thither *was their* spirit to go; and the wheels were lifted up over against them: [p]for the spirit [q]of the living creature *was* in the wheels.

21 [r]When those went, *these* went; and when those stood, *these* stood; and when those were lifted up from the earth, the wheels were lifted up over against them: for the spirit [s]of the living creature *was* in the wheels.

22 [t]And the likeness of the firmament upon the heads of the living creature *was* as the colour of the terrible crystal, stretched forth over their heads above.

23 And under the firmament *were* their wings straight, the one toward the other: every one had two, which covered on this side, and every one had two, which covered on that side, their bodies.

24 [u]And when they went, I heard the noise of their wings, [v]like the noise of great waters, as [w]the voice of the Almighty, the voice of speech, as the noise of a host: when they stood, they let down their wings.

25 And there was a voice from the firmament that *was* over their heads, when they stood, *and* had let down their wings.

26 [x]And above the firmament that *was* over their heads *was* the likeness of a throne, [y]as the appearance of a sapphire stone: and upon the likeness of the throne *was* the likeness as the appearance of a man above upon it.

27 [z]And I saw as the colour of amber, as the appearance of fire round about within it, from the appearance of his loins even upward, and from the appearance of his loins even downward, I saw as it were the appearance of fire, and it had brightness round about.

28 [a]As the appearance of the bow that is in the cloud in the day of rain, so *was* the appearance of the brightness round about. [b]This *was* the appearance of the likeness of the glory of the LORD. And when I saw *it*, [c]I fell upon my face, and I heard a voice of one that spake.

[l]Or, *strakes*——[m]Ch. x. 12; Zech. iv. 10——[n]Ch. x. 16, 17——[o]Ver. 12——[p]Ch. x. 17——[q]Or, *of life* [r]Ver. 19, 20; chap. x. 17——[s]Or, *of life*——[t]Chap. x. 1 [u]Chap. x. 5——[v]Chap. xliii. 2; Dan. x. 6; Rev. i. 15

[w]Job xxxvii. 4, 5; Psa. xxix. 3, 4; lxviii. 33——[x]Chap. x. 1——[y]Exod. xxiv. 10——[z]Chap. viii. 2——[a]Rev. iv. 3; x. 1——[b]Chap. iii. 23; viii. 4——[c]Chap. iii. 23; Dan. viii. 17; Acts ix. 4; Rev. i. 17

They were dreadful] They were exceedingly great in their diameter, so that it was tremendous to look from the part that touched the ground to that which was opposite above.

Were *full of eyes*] Does not this refer to the appearance of *nails* keeping on the spokes, or strakes or bands upon the rim?

Verse 19. *When the living creatures went, the wheels went*] The *wheels* were attached to the living creatures, so that, in progress, they had the same motion.

Verse 20. *The spirit of the living creature* was *in the wheels.*] That is, the wheels were *instinct with a vital spirit;* the wheels were *alive*, they also were *animals*, or endued with *animal life*, as the creatures were that stood upon them. Here then is the *chariot of Jehovah.* There are *four wheels*, on each of which one of the *compound animals* stands; the four compound animals form the *body* of the *chariot*, their wings spread horizontally above, forming the canopy or covering of this chariot; on the top of which, or upon the extended wings of the four living creatures, was the throne, on which was the appearance of a man, ver. 26.

Verse 22. *The colour of the terrible crystal*] Like a *crystal*, well cut and well polished, with various *faces*, by which rays of light were refracted, assuming either a variety of prismatic colours, or an insufferably brilliant splendour. This seems to be the meaning of the *terrible crystal. Newcome* translates, *fearful ice.* The common translation is preferable.

Verse 23. *Every one had two, which covered on this side*] While they employed two of their wings to form a foundation for the *firmament* to rest on, two other wings were let down to cover the lower part of their bodies: but this they did only when they *stood*, ver. 24.

Verse 24. *The noise of their wings*] When the whirlwind drove the wheels, the wind rustling among the wings was like the noise of *many waters;* like a *waterfall*, or *waters dashing continually against the rocks*, or *rushing down precipices.*

As the voice of the Almighty] Like distant thunder; for this is termed the *voice of God*, Psa. xviii. 13; Exod. ix. 23, 28, 29; xx. 18.

Verse 26. *A sapphire*] The pure oriental sapphire, a large well cut specimen of which is now before me, is one of the most beautiful and resplendent blues that can be conceived. I have sometimes seen the heavens assume this illustrious hue. The human form above this canopy is supposed to represent Him who, in the fulness of time, was manifested in the flesh.

Verse 27. *The colour of amber*] There are

specimens of amber which are very pure and beautifully transparent. One which I now hold up to the light gives a most beautiful *bright yellow* colour. Such a splendid appearance had the august Being who sat upon this throne from the reins upward; but from thence downward he had the appearance of *fire*, burning with a clear and brilliant flame. For farther particulars see the notes on chap. x.

Verse 28. *As the appearance of the bow*] Over the canopy on which this glorious personage sat there was a fine *rainbow*, which, from the description here, had all its colours vivid, distinct, and in perfection—red, orange, yellow, green, blue, indigo, and violet. In all this description we must understand every *metal*, every *colour*, and every *natural appearance*, to be in their utmost perfection of *shape*, *colour*, and *splendour*. "And this," as above described, "was the appearance of the likeness of the glory of the Lord." Splendid and glorious as it was, it was only the "appearance of the likeness," a faint representation of the real thing.

I have endeavoured to explain these appearances as correctly as possible; to show their forms, positions, colours, &c. But who can explain their meaning? We have conjectures in abundance; and can it be of any use to mankind to increase the number of those conjectures? I think not. I doubt whether the whole does not point out the state of the Jews, who were about to be subdued by Nebuchadnezzar, and carried into captivity. And I am inclined to think that the "living creatures, wheels, fires, whirlwinds," &c., which are introduced here, point out, emblematically, the various means, sword, fire, pestilence, famine, &c., which were employed in their destruction; and that *God appears* in all this to show that Nebuchadnezzar is only his *instrument* to inflict all these calamities. What is in the following chapter appears to me to confirm this supposition. But we have the *rainbow*, the token of God's covenant, to show that though there should be a destruction of the city, temple, &c., and sore tribulation among the people, yet there should not be a total ruin; after a long captivity they should be restored. The rainbow is an illustrious token of mercy and love.

CHAPTER II

The prophet, having been overwhelmed with the glorious vision in the preceding chapter, is here strengthened and comforted, 1, 2; *and then commissioned to declare to the rebellious house of Israel the terrible judgments that would very shortly come upon the whole land, if they repented not; with a gracious assurance to Ezekiel that God would be constantly with him while executing the duties of his office,* 3–5. *The prophet is also commanded to be fearless, resolute, and faithful in the discharge of it,* 6–8, *as he must be the messenger of very unpleasing tidings, which will expose him to great persecution,* 9, 10.

A. M. 3409 B. C. 595 Ol. XLVI. 2 Anno TarquiniiPrisci, R. Roman., 22

AND he said unto me, Son of
man, [a]stand upon thy feet,
and I will speak unto thee.
2 And [b]the spirit entered into
me when he spake unto me, and set me upon
my feet, that I heard him that spake unto me.
3 And he said unto me, Son of
man, I send thee to the children
of Israel, to a rebellious [c]nation
that hath rebelled against me:
[d]they and their fathers have transgressed
against me, *even* unto this very day.

A. M. 3409 B. C. 595 Ol. XLVI. 2 Anno TarquiniiPrisci, R. Roman., 22

[a]Dan. x. 11——[b]Chap. iii. 24——[c]Heb. *nations*

[d]Jer. iii. 25; chap. xx. 18, 21, 30

NOTES ON CHAP. II

Verse 1. *And he said unto me*] In the last verse of the preceding chapter we find that the prophet was so penetrated with awe at the sight of the glory of God in the mystical chariot, that "he fell upon his face;" and, while he was in this posture of adoration, he heard the voice mentioned here. It is evident, therefore, that the present division of these chapters is wrong. Either the *first* should end with the words, "This was the appearance of the likeness of the glory of the Lord," ver. 28; or the *first verse* of this chapter should be added to the preceding, and this begin with the *second* verse.

Verse 2. *And the spirit entered into me*] This *spirit* was different to that mentioned above, by which the wheels, &c., were moved. The *spirit of prophecy* is here intended; whose office was not merely to enable him to *foresee* and *foretell* future events, but to purify and refine his heart, and qualify him to be a successful preacher of the word of life.

He who is sent by the God of all grace to convert sinners must be influenced by the Holy Ghost; otherwise he can neither be saved himself, nor become the instrument of salvation to others.

And set me upon my feet] That he might *stand* as a servant before his master, to receive his orders.

Verse 3. *Son of man*] This appellative, so often mentioned in this book, seems to have been given first to this *prophet;* afterwards to *Daniel;* and after that to the MAN *Christ Jesus.* Perhaps it was given to the two former to remind them of their frailty, and that they should not be exalted in their own minds by the extraordinary revelations granted to them; and that they should feel themselves of the same nature with those to whom they were sent; and, from the common principle of *humanity*, deeply interest themselves in the welfare of their unhappy countrymen. To the *latter* it might have been appropriated merely to show that though all his actions demonstrated him to be GOD, yet that he was also really MAN; and that in the *man* Christ Jesus dwelt all the fulness of the

A. M. 3409
B. C. 595
Ol. XLVI. 2
Anno
TarquiniiPrisci,
R. Roman., 22

4 [e]For *they are* [f]impudent children and stiff-hearted. I do send thee unto them; and thou shalt say unto them, Thus saith the Lord GOD.

5 [g]And they, whether they will hear, or whether they will forbear, (for they *are* a rebellious house,) yet [h]shall know that there hath been a prophet among them.

6 And thou, son of man, [i]be not afraid of them, neither be afraid of their words, though [k]briers [l]and thorns *be* with thee, and thou dost dwell among scorpions: [m]be not afraid of their words, nor be dismayed at their looks, [n]though they *be* a rebellious house.

7 [o]And thou shalt speak my words unto them, [p]whether they will hear, or whether they will forbear: for they *are* [q]most rebellious.

8 But thou, son of man, hear what I say unto thee; Be not thou rebellious like that rebellious house: open thy mouth, and [r]eat that I give thee.

9 And when I looked, behold, [s]a hand *was* sent unto me; and, lo, [t]a roll of a book *was* therein:

10 And he spread it before me; and it *was* written within and without: and *there was* written therein lamentations, and mourning, and wo.

---

[e]Chap. iii. 7——[f]Heb. *hard of face*——[g]Chap. iii. 11, 26, 27——[h]Ch. xxxiii. 33——[i]Jer. i. 8, 17; Luke xii. 4 [k]Or, *rebels*——[l]Isa. ix. 18; Jer. vi. 28; Mic. vii. 4

[m]Chap. iii. 9; 1 Pet. iii. 14——[n]Chap. iii. 9, 26, 27 [o]Jer. i. 7, 17——[p]Ver. 5——[q]Heb. *rebellion*——[r]Rev. x. 9——[s]Chap. viii. 3; Jer. i. 9——[t]Chap. iii. 1

Godhead bodily. When the *acts* of Christ are considered, it is more easy to believe his *eternal Godhead*, than to be convinced that the person we hear speaking, and see working, is also a *man* like unto ourselves.

I send thee to the children of Israel] To those who were now in captivity, in Chaldea particularly; and to the Jews in general, both far and near.

Verse 4. *Thou shalt say unto them, Thus saith the Lord*] Let them know that what thou hast to declare is the message of the LORD, that they may receive it with reverence.

Every preacher of God's word should take heed that it is God's message he delivers to the people. Let him not suppose, because it is according to his own *creed* or *confession of faith*, that therefore it is God's word. False doctrines and fallacies without end are foisted on the world in this way. Bring the *creed* first to the *Word of God*, and scrupulously try whether it be right; and when this is done, leave it where you please; take the Bible, and warn them from God's word recorded there.

Verse 5. *Yet shall know that there hath been a prophet among them.*] By this they shall be assured of *two* things: 1. That God in his mercy had given them due warning. 2. That themselves were inexcusable, for not taking it.

Verse 6. *Be not afraid of them*] They will maltreat thee for thy message; but let not the apprehension of this induce thee to suppress it. Though they be *rebels*, fear them not; I will sustain and preserve thee.

Verse 7. *Whether they will hear*] Whether they receive the message, or persecute thee for it, declare it to them, that they may be without excuse.

Verse 8. *Open thy mouth and eat that I give thee.*] Take *my word* as thou wouldst take thy *proper food;* receive it into thy heart; ponder it there, that it may be the means of *strengthening* and *preserving thy soul*, as proper nourishment will strengthen the body, and preserve from death. And the people to whom such messages of God may come should so hear it, read, mark, learn, and *inwardly digest* it, that it may become efficient nourishment to their souls.

Verse 9. *A hand* was *sent*] Here the *hand* signifies not only the instrument of conveyance, but an *emblem* of the Divine *power*, which the *hand of God* always signifies.

A roll of a book] מגלת ספר *megillath sepher.* All ancient books were written so as to be *rolled up;* hence *volumen*, a *volume*, from *volvo*, *I roll.*

Verse 10. *It* was *written within and without*] Contrary to the state of rolls in general, which are written on the *inside* only. The *Hebrew rolls* are generally written in this way. There are several of such Hebrew rolls before me, all written on the *inside* only, consisting of skins of vellum, or parchment, or basil, a sort of half-tanned sheep or goat skin, sewed together, extending to several yards in length. Other Asiatic books were written in the same way. A Sanscrit roll of *sixty* feet in length, also before me, is written all on the *inside;* and a *Koran*, written in exceedingly small characters, about two inches broad and twelve feet long, and weighing but about half an ounce. But the *roll* presented to the prophet was written on *both sides*, because the prophecy was long, and to the same effect; that they might see the mind of God wherever they looked.

There was *written therein lamentations, and mourning, and wo.*] What an awful assemblage! קינים והגה והי *kinim, vahegeh, vehi, lamentations*, and a *groan*, and *alas! Lamentations* on all hands; *a groan* from the dying; and *alas*, or *Wo is me!* from the survivors. It was the *letter* that killeth, and is the ministration of death. What a mercy to have that which is emphatically called Το Ευαγγελιον, The *glad tidings*, the *good news! Christ Jesus is come into the world to save sinners;* and he wills that *all men should be saved and come to the knowledge of the truth.* Here are *rejoicings, thanksgivings*, and *exultation.*

CHAPTER III

This chapter contains more particular instructions to the prophet. It begins with repeating his appointment to his office, 1–3. *Ezekiel is then informed that his commission is, at this time, to the house of Israel exclusively,* 4–6; *that his countrymen would pay little regard to him,* 7; *that he must persevere in his duty notwithstanding such great discouragement; and he is endued with extraordinary courage and intrepidity to enable him fearlessly to declare to a disobedient and gainsaying people the whole counsel of God,* 8–11. *The prophet is afterwards carried by the spirit that animated the cherubim and wheels, and by which he received the gift of prophecy, to a colony of his brethren in the neighbourhood, where he remained seven days overwhelmed with astonishment,* 12–15. *He is then warned of the awful importance of being faithful in his office,* 16–21; *commanded to go forth into the plain that he may have a visible manifestation of the Divine Presence,* 22; *and is again favoured with a vision of that most magnificent set of symbols described in the first chapter, by which the glorious majesty of the God of Israel was in some measure represented,* 23. *See also* Isa. vi. 1–18; Dan. x. 5–19; *and* Rev. i. 10–16; iv. 1–11, *for other manifestations of the Divine glory, in all of which some of the imagery is very similar. The prophet receives directions relative to his future conduct,* 24–27.

A. M. 3409 B. C. 595 Ol. XLVI. 2 Anno TarquiniiPrisci, R. Roman., 22

MOREOVER he said unto me, Son of man, eat that thou findest; [a]eat this roll, and go speak unto the house of Israel.

2 So I opened my mouth, and he caused me to eat that roll.

3 And he said unto me, Son of man, cause thy belly to eat, and fill thy bowels with this roll that I give thee. Then did I [b]eat *it;* and it was in my mouth [c]as honey for sweetness.

4 And he said unto me, Son of man, go, get thee unto the house of Israel, and speak with my words unto them.

5 For thou *art* not sent to a people [d]of a strange speech and of a hard language, *but* to the house of Israel;

6 Not to many people [e]of a strange speech and of a hard language, whose words thou canst not understand. [f]Surely, [g]had I sent thee to them, they would have hearkened unto thee.

A. M. 3409 B. C. 595 Ol. XLVI. 2 Anno TarquiniiPrisci, R. Roman., 22

7 But the house of Israel will not hearken unto thee; [h]for they will not hearken unto me: [i]for all the house of Israel *are* [k]impudent and hard-hearted.

8 Behold, I have made thy face strong against their faces, and thy forehead strong against their foreheads.

9 [l]As an adamant harder than flint have I made thy forehead: [m]fear them not, neither be dismayed at their looks, though they *be* a rebellious house.

10 Moreover he said unto me, Son of man, all my words that I shall speak unto thee, receive in thine heart, and hear with thine ears.

11 And go, get thee to them of the captivity, unto the children of thy people, and speak unto them, and tell them, [n]Thus saith the Lord GOD; whether they will hear, or whether they will forbear.

12 Then [o]the spirit took me up, and I

[a]Chap. ii. 8, 9——[b]Rev. x. 9; see Jer. xv. 16——[c]Psa. xix. 10; cxix. 103——[d]Heb. *deep of lip, and heavy of tongue;* and so ver. 6——[e]Heb. *deep of lip and heavy of language*——[f]Or, *If I had sent thee, &c., would they not have hearkened unto thee?*

[g]Matt. xi. 21, 23——[h]John xv. 20——[i]Ch. ii. 4 [k]Heb. *stiff of forehead, and hard of heart*——[l]Isa. l. 7; Jer. i. 18; xv. 20; Mic. iii. 8——[m]Jer. i. 8, 17; ch. ii. 6 [n]Chap. ii. 5, 7; ver. 27——[o]Ver. 14; chap. viii. 3; see 1 Kings xviii. 12; 2 Kings ii. 16; Acts viii. 39

NOTES ON CHAP. III

Verse 1. *Eat this roll, and go speak*] This must have passed in vision; but the meaning is plain. Receive my word—let it enter into thy soul; *digest* it—let it be thy *nourishment;* and let it be thy meat and drink to do the will of thy Father who is in heaven.

Verse 3. *It was in my mouth as honey*] It was joyous to me to receive the Divine message, to be thus let into the secrets of the Divine counsel, and I promised myself much comfort in that intimate acquaintance with which I was favoured by the Supreme Being. In Rev. x. 10 we find St. John receiving a little book, which he ate, and found it sweet as *honey* in his *mouth,* but after he had eaten it, it made his *belly bitter,* signifying that a deep consideration of the awful matter contained in God's word against sinners, which multitudes of them will turn to their endless confusion, must deeply afflict those who know any thing of the worth of an immortal spirit.

Verse 5. *Thou* art *not sent to a people of a strange speech*] I neither send thee to thy adversaries, the *Chaldeans,* nor to the *Medes* and *Persians,* their enemies. Even these would more likely have hearkened unto thee than thy own countrymen.

Verse 7. *Impudent and hard-hearted.*] "Stiff of forehead, and hard of heart."—*Margin.* The marginal readings on several verses here are very nervous and very correct.

Verse 12. *Then the Spirit took me up*] This, as *Calmet* remarks, has been variously understood. 1. An impetuous *wind* carried him to the place where his brethren sojourned. 2. The *Holy Spirit,* which filled his heart, transported

A. M. 3409
B. C. 595
Ol. XLVI. 2
Anno
TarquiniiPrisci,
R. Roman., 22

heard behind me a voice of a
great rushing, *saying,* Blessed
be the glory of the LORD from
his place.
13 *I heard* also the noise of the wings of
the living creatures that [p]touched one another, and the noise of the wheels over against
them, and a noise of a great rushing.
14 So [q]the spirit lifted me up and took me
away, and I went [r]in bitterness, in the [s]heat
of my spirit; but the [t]hand of the LORD was
strong upon me.
15 Then I came to them of the captivity at
Tel-abib, that dwelt by the river of Chebar,
and [u]I sat where they sat, and remained
there astonished among them seven days.
16 And it came to pass at the end of seven
days, that the word of the LORD
came unto me, saying,
17 [v]Son of man, I have made
thee a [w]watchman unto the
house of Israel: therefore hear the word at
my mouth, and give them warning from me.
18 When I say unto the wicked, Thou
shalt surely die; and thou givest him not
warning, nor speakest to warn the wicked
from his wicked way, to save his life; the
same wicked *man* [x]shall die in his iniquity;
but his blood will I require at thine
hand.
19 Yet if thou warn the wicked, and he
turn not from his wickedness, nor from his
wicked way, he shall die in his iniquity; [y]but
thou hast delivered thy soul.

[p]Heb. *kissed*——[q]Ver. 12; chap. viii. 3——[r]Heb. *bitter*——[s]Heb. *hot anger*——[t]2 Kings iii. 15; ch. i. 3; viii. 1; xxxvii. 1——[u]Job ii. 13; Psa. cxxxvii. 1

[v]Chap. xxxiii. 7, 8, 9——[w]Isa. lii. 8; lvi. 10; lxii. 6; Jer. vi. 17——[x]Chap. xxxiii. 6; John viii. 21, 24 [y]Isa. xlix. 4, 5; Acts xx. 26

him in a moment to the place where the captives were. 3. Or, he was so *transported* with heavenly ardour in his mind, that he ran immediately off, and seemed to fly to the place where God commanded him to go. The promptitude and impetuosity of his spirit seemed to furnish him with *wings* on the occasion. However this may be understood, the going to the captives was *real.*

A voice of a great rushing] This was the noise made by the wings of the living creatures that formed the chariot of Jehovah. See the notes on chap. i. and x.

Blessed be *the glory of the Lord*] Probably the acclamation of the living creatures: "Let God be blessed from the throne of his glory! He deserves the praises of his creatures in all the dispensations of his mercy and justice, of his providence and grace."

Verse 13. *A great rushing.*] All the living *creatures* and the *wheels* being then in motion.

Verse 14. *I went in bitterness*] Being filled with indignation at the wickedness and obstinacy of my people, I went, determining to speak the word of God without disguise, and to reprove them *sharply* for their rebellion; and yet I was greatly distressed because of the heavy message which I was commanded to deliver.

Verse 15. *I came to them of the captivity*] Because the hand of the Lord was strong upon him and supported him, he soon reached the place.

Tel-abib] תל אביב "a heap of corn." So the *Vulgate: acervum novarum frugum,* "a heap of new fruits." ܠܬܠܐ ܟܒܘ *letola chib,* "to the hill Chib," or *the hill of grief.—Syriac.*

Seven days.] Perhaps God kept him all this time without an immediate revelation, that the *bitterness* and *heat of spirit* of which he speaks above might be *subdued,* and that he might speak God's words in God's own Spirit. Had he gone in a better spirit he had probably been employed in his work as soon as he had gained the place of labour.

Verse 17. *I have made thee a watchman*] The care and welfare of all this people I have laid on thee. Thou must *watch* for their *safety, preach* for their *edification,* and *pray* for their *eternal welfare.* And that thou mayest be successful, *receive the word at my mouth, and warn them from me.*

God is particularly jealous lest *any words* but *his own* be taught for *Divinc doctrines.* He will not have human *creeds,* no more than TRADITIONS, taught instead of his own word. No word can be successful in the salvation of sinners but that which comes from God. Every minister of the Gospel should be familiar with his Maker by *faith* and *prayer;* God will then hold communion with his spirit; otherwise, what he preaches will be destitute of spirit and life, and his *hackneyed texts* and *sermons,* instead of being the bread from heaven, will be like the dry mouldy Gibeonitish crusts.

Verse 18. *Thou shalt surely die*] That is, If he turn not from his wickedness, *and thou givest him not warning,* as above, *he shall die in his iniquity,* which he should not have committed; *but his blood will I require at thy hand*—I will visit *thy soul* for the loss of *his.* O how awful is this! Hear it, ye *priests,* ye *preachers,* ye *ministers* of the Gospel; ye, especially, who have entered into the ministry *for a living;* ye who *gather a congregation* to yourselves that ye may feed upon their fat, and clothe yourselves with their wool; in whose parishes and in whose congregations souls are dying unconverted from day to day, who have never been solemnly warned by you, and to whom you have never shown the way of salvation, probably because ye know nothing of it yourselves! O what a perdition awaits *you!* To have the blood of every soul that has died in your parishes or in your congregations unconverted laid at your door! To suffer a common damnation for *every* soul that perishes through your neglect! How *many loads* of endless wo must such have to bear! Ye take your *tithes,* your *stipends,* or your *rents,* to the last

A. M. 3409
B. C. 595
Ol. XLVI. 2
Anno
TarquiniiPrisci,
R. Roman., 22

20 Again, When a [z]righteous *man* doth turn from his [a]righteousness, and commit iniquity, and I lay a stumbling-block before him, he shall die: because thou hast not given him warning, he shall die in his sin, and his righteousness which he hath done shall not be remembered; but his blood will I require at thine hand.

21 Nevertheless if thou warn the righteous *man,* that the righteous sin not, and he doth not sin, he shall surely live, because he is warned; also thou hast delivered thy soul.

22 [b]And the hand of the LORD was there upon me; and he said unto me, Arise, go forth [c]into the plain, and I will there talk with thee.

23 Then I arose, and went forth into the plain: and, behold, [d]the glory of the LORD stood there, as the glory which I [e]saw by the river of Chebar: [f]and I fell on my face.

A. M. 3409
B. C. 595
Ol. XLVI. 2
Anno
TarquiniiPrisci.
R. Roman., 22

24 Then [g]the spirit entered into me, and set me upon my feet, and spake with me, and said unto me, Go, shut thyself within thine house.

25 But thou, O son of man, behold, [h]they shall put bands upon thee, and shall bind thee with them, and thou shalt not go out among them:

26 And [i]I will make thy tongue cleave to the roof of thy mouth, that thou shalt be dumb, and shalt not be to them [k]a reprover: [l]for they *are* a rebellious house.

27 [m]But when I speak with thee, I will open thy mouth, and thou shalt say unto them, [n]Thus saith the Lord GOD; he that heareth, let him hear; and he that forbeareth, let him forbear: [o]for they *are* a rebellious house.

---

[z]Ch. xviii. 24; xxxiii. 12, 13——[a]Heb. *righteousnesses*——[b]Ver. 14; chap. i. 3——[c]Chap. viii. 4——[d]Chap. i. 28——[e]Chap. i. 1——[f]Chap. i. 28——[g]Chap. ii. 2

[h]Ch. iv. 8——[i]Ch. xxiv. 27; Luke i. 20, 22——[k]Heb. *a man reproving*——[l]Ch. ii. 5, 6, 7——[m]Ch. xxiv. 27; xxxiii. 22——[n]Ver. 11——[o]Ver. 9, 26; chap. xii. 2, 3

---

grain, and the last *penny;* while the souls over whom you made yourselves watchmen have perished, and are perishing, through *your* neglect. O worthless and hapless men! better for you had ye never been born! Vain is your boast of *apostolical authority,* while ye do not the *work of apostles!* Vain your boast of *orthodoxy,* while ye neither *show* nor *know* the *way of salvation!* Vain your pretensions to a *Divine call,* when ye do not the work of *evangelists!* The state of the most wretched of the human race is enviable to that of such ministers, pastors, teachers, and preachers.

But let not this discourage the *faithful minister* who *teaches every man,* and *warns every man, in all wisdom, that he may present every man perfect in Christ Jesus.* If after such teaching and warning they will sin on, and die in their sins, their blood will be upon themselves; but *thou,* O man of God, *hast delivered thine own soul.*

Verse 20. *When a righteous* man *doth turn from his righteousness*] Which these words plainly state he may do, *and commit iniquity,* and die in his sin; and consequently die eternally, which is also here granted; if he have not been warned, though he die in his sin, the *blood*—the life and salvation, of this person also will God require at the watchman's hand. Pastor hunc occidit, quia eum tacendo morti tradidit. "This man the pastor kills; for in being silent, he delivers him over to death."—GREGORY. From these passages we see that a *righteous man* may *fall from grace,* and *perish everlastingly.* Should it be said that it means the *self-righteous,* I reply, this is absurd; for self-righteousness is a *fall* itself, and the sooner a man falls from it the better for himself. Real, genuine righteousness of heart and life is that which is meant. Let him that standeth take heed lest he fall.

And I lay a stumbling-block before him] That is, I permit him to be tried, and he fall in the trial. God is repeatedly represented as doing things which he only *permits* to be done. He lays a stumbling-block, *i. e.,* he permits one to be laid.

Verse 22. *Arise, go forth into the plain*] Into a place remote from observation and noise; a place where the glory of God might have sufficient room to manifest itself, that the prophet might see all its movements distinctly.

Verse 24. *The spirit—said unto me, Go, shut thyself within thine house.*] Hide thyself for the present. The reason is immediately subjoined.

Verse 25. *They shall put bands upon thee*] Thy countrymen will rise up against thee; and, to prevent thy prophesying, will confine thee.

Verse 26. *I will make thy tongue cleave to the roof of thy mouth*] I will not give thee any message to deliver to them. They are so rebellious, it is useless to give them farther warning.

Verse 27. *I will open thy mouth*] When it is necessary to address them again, thou shalt sum up what thou hast said in this one speech: *Thus saith the Lord,* "He that heareth, let him hear; and he that forbeareth, let him forbear." Let him who feels obedience to the voice of God his interest, be steadfast. Let him who disregards the Divine monition go in his own way, and abide the consequences.

CHAPTER IV

Ezekiel delineates Jerusalem, and lays siege to it, as a type of the manner in which the Chaldean army should surround that city, 1–3. *The prophet commanded to lie on his left side* three hundred and ninety *days, and on his right side* forty *days, with the signification,* 4–8. *The scanty and coarse provision allowed the prophet during his symbolical siege, consisting chiefly of the worst kinds of grain, and likewise ill-prepared, as he had only cow's dung for fuel, tended all to denote the scarcity of provision, fuel, and every necessary of life, which the Jews should experience during the siege of Jerusalem,* 9–17.

A. M. 3409
B. C. 595
Ol. XLVI. 2
Anno Tarquinii Prisci, R. Roman., 22

THOU also, son of man, take thee a tile, and lay it before thee, and pourtray upon it the city, *even* Jerusalem:

2 And lay siege against it, and build a fort against it, and cast a mount against it; set the camp also against it, and set [a]*battering* rams against it round about.

3 Moreover take thou unto thee [b]an iron pan, and set it *for* a wall of iron between thee and the city: and set thy face against it, and it shall be besieged, and thou shalt lay siege against it. [c]This *shall be* a sign to the house of Israel.

A. M. 3409
B. C. 595
Ol. XLVI. 2
Anno Tarquinii Prisci, R. Roman., 22

4 Lie thou also upon thy left side, and lay

[a]Or, *chief leaders;* chap. xxi. 22——[b]Or, *a flat plate, or slice*——[c]Chap. xii. 6, 11; xiv. 24, 27

NOTES ON CHAP. IV

Verse 1. *Take thee a tile*] A *tile,* such as we use in covering houses, will give us but a very inadequate notion of those used anciently; and also appear very insufficient for the figures which the prophet was commanded to pourtray on it. A *brick* is most undoubtedly meant; yet, even the larger dimensions here, as to *thickness,* will not help us through the difficulty, unless we have recourse to the ancients, who have spoken of the dimensions of the bricks commonly used in building. *Palladius,* De Re Rustica, lib. vi. c. 12, is very particular on this subject:—Sint vero lateres longitudine pedum duorum, latitudine unius, altitudine quatuor unciarum. "Let the bricks be two feet long, one foot broad, and four inches thick." Edit. *Gesner,* vol. iii. p. 144. On such a surface as this the whole siege might be easily pourtrayed. There are some *brick-bats* before me which were brought from the ruins of ancient *Babylon,* which have been made of clay and straw kneaded together and *baked in the sun;* one has been more than *four inches* thick, and on one side it is *deeply impressed* with characters; others are smaller, well made, and finely impressed on one side with Persepolitan characters. These have been for *inside* or *ornamental* work; to such bricks the prophet most probably alludes.

But the tempered clay out of which the bricks were made might be meant here; of this substance he might *spread out* a sufficient quantity to receive all his figures. The figures were, 1. Jerusalem. 2. A fort. 3. A mount. 4. The camp of the enemy. 5. Battering rams, and such like engines, round about. 6. A wall round about the city, between it and the besieging army.

Verse 2. Battering *rams*] כרים *carim.* This is the earliest account we have of this military engine. It was a long beam with a head of brass, like the head and horns of a *ram,* whence its name. It was hung by chains or ropes, between two beams, or *three legs,* so that it could admit of being drawn backward and forward some yards. Several stout men, by means of ropes, pulled it as far back as it could go; and then, suddenly letting it loose, it struck with great force against the wall which it was intended to batter and bring down. This machine was not known in the time of *Homer,* as in the siege of Troy there is not the slightest mention of such. And the first notice we have of it is *here,* where we see that it was employed by Nebuchadnezzar in the siege of Jerusalem, A. M. 3416. It was afterwards used by the *Carthaginians* at the siege of *Gades,* as *Vitruvius* notes, lib. x. c. 19, in which he gives a circumstantial account of the invention, fabrication, use, and improvement of this machine. It was for the want of a machine of this kind, that the ancient sieges lasted so long; they had nothing with which to beat down or undermine the walls.

Verse 3. *Take thou unto thee an iron pan*] מחבת *machabath,* a *flat plate* or *slice,* as the margin properly renders it: such as are used in some countries to bake bread on, called a *griddle* or *girdle,* being suspended above the fire, and kept in a proper degree of heat for the purpose. A *plate* like this, stuck perpendicularly in the earth, would show the nature of a *wall* much better than any *pan* could do. The Chaldeans threw such a wall round Jerusalem, to prevent the besieged from receiving any succours, and from escaping from the city.

This shall be *a sign to the house of Israel.*] This shall be an emblematical representation of what shall actually take place.

Verse 4. *Lie thou also upon thy left side*] It appears that all that is mentioned here and in the following verses was done, not in *idea,* but in *fact.* The prophet lay down on *his left side* upon a couch to which he was *chained,* ver. 5, for *three hundred and ninety days;* and afterwards he lay in the same manner, upon his *right side,* for *forty days.* And thus was signified the state of the Jews, and the punishment that was coming upon them. 1. The *prophet* himself represents the Jews. 2. His *lying,* their state of depression. 3. His being *bound,* their helplessness and captivity. 4. The *days* signify *years,* a *day for a year;* during which they were to bear their iniquity, or the temporal punishment due to their sins. 5. The *three hundred and ninety days,* during which he was to lie on his left side, and bear the iniquity of the house of Israel, point out *two*

A. M. 3409 B. C. 595 Ol. XLVI. 2 Anno TarquiniiPrisci, R. Roman., 22

the iniquity of the house of Israel upon it: *according* to the number of the days that thou shalt lie upon it thou shalt bear their iniquity.

5 For I have laid upon thee the years of their iniquity, according to the number of the days, three hundred and ninety days: [d]so shalt thou bear the iniquity of the house of Israel.

6 And when thou hast accomplished them, lie again on thy right side, and thou shalt bear the iniquity of the house of Judah forty days: I have appointed thee [e]each day for a year.

7 Therefore thou shalt set thy face toward the siege of Jerusalem, and thine arm *shall be* uncovered, and thou shalt prophesy against it.

8 [f]And, behold, I will lay bands upon thee, and thou shalt not turn thee [g]from one side to another, till thou hast ended the days of thy siege.

9 Take thou also unto thee wheat, and barley, and beans, and lentiles, and millet, and [h]fitches, and put them in one vessel, and make thee bread thereof, *according* to the number of the days that thou shalt lie upon thy side, three hundred and ninety days shalt thou eat thereof.

10 And thy meat which thou shalt eat *shall be* by weight, twenty shekels a day: from time to time shalt thou eat it.

11 Thou shalt drink also water by measure, the sixth part of a hin: from time to time shalt thou drink.

12 And thou shalt eat it *as* barley cakes, and thou shalt bake it with dung that cometh out of man, in their sight.

[d]Num. xiv. 34——[e]Heb. *a day for a year, a day for a year*

[f]Chap. iii. 25——[g]Heb. *from thy side to thy side* [h]Or, *spelt*

things: the *first*, The *duration* of the *siege* of Jerusalem. *Secondly*, The *duration* of the *captivity* of the *ten* tribes, and that of Judah. 6. The prophet lay *three hundred and ninety days* upon his left side, and *forty* days upon his right side, in all *four hundred and thirty* days. Now Jerusalem was besieged the *ninth* year of the reign of Zedekiah, 2 Kings xxv. 1, 2, and was not taken till the *eleventh* year of the same prince, 2 Kings xxv. 2. But properly speaking, the siege did not continue the *whole* of that time; it was interrupted; for Nebuchadnezzar was obliged to *raise* it, and go and meet the Egyptians, who were coming to its succour. This consumed a considerable portion of time. After he had defeated the Egyptians, he returned and recommenced the siege, and did not leave it till the city was taken. We may, therefore, conclude that the *four hundred and thirty days* only comprise the time in which the city was *actually besieged*, when the city was encompassed with walls of circumvallation, so that the besieged were reduced to a state of the utmost distress. The siege commenced the *tenth* day of the *tenth* month of the *ninth* year of Zedekiah; and it was taken on the *ninth* day of the *fourth* month of the *eleventh* year of the same king. Thus the siege had lasted, in the whole, *eighteen months*, or *five hundred and ten days*. Subtract for the time that Nebuchadnezzar was obliged to interrupt the siege, in order to go against the Egyptians, *four months and twenty days*, or *one hundred and forty days*, and there will remain *four hundred and thirty days*, composed of 390+40=430. See *Calmet* on this place. See also at the end of this chapter.

Verse 6. *Forty days*] Reckon, says Archbishop Newcome, near *fifteen* years and *six* months in the reign of Manasseh, *two* years in that of Amon, *three* months in that of Jehoahaz, *eleven* years in that of Jehoiakim, *three* months and *ten* days in that of Jehoiachin, and *eleven* years in that of Zedekiah; and there arises a period of *forty* years, during which gross idolatry was practised in the kingdom of Judah. *Forty days* may have been employed in spoiling and desolating the city and the temple.

Verse 9. *Take thou also unto thee wheat*] In times of *scarcity*, it is customary in all countries to mix several kinds of coarser grain with the finer, to make it last the longer. This *mashlin*, which the prophet is commanded to take, of wheat, barley, beans, lentiles, millet, and fitches, was intended to show how scarce the necessaries of life should be during the siege.

Verse 10. *Twenty shekels a day*] The whole of the above grain, being ground, was to be formed into one *mass*, out of which he was to make *three hundred and ninety loaves; one loaf* for *each day;* and this loaf was to be of *twenty shekels* in weight. Now a *shekel*, being in weight about half an ounce, this would be *ten* ounces of bread for each day; and with this *water* to the amount of one *sixth* part of a *hin*, which is about a pint and a half of our measure. All this shows that so reduced should provisions be during the siege, that they should be obliged to eat the *meanest* sort of aliment, and that by *weight*, and their *water* by *measure;* each man's allowance being scarcely a *pint and a half*, and *ten ounces*, a little more than *half a pound* of *bread*, for each day's support.

Verse 12. *Thou shalt bake it with dung*] Dried ox and cow dung is a common fuel in the east; and with this, for want of wood and coals, they are obliged to prepare their food. Indeed, dried excrement of every kind is gathered. Here, the prophet is to prepare his bread with *dry human excrement*. And when we know that this did not come in contact with the bread, and was only used to warm the plate, (see ver. 3,) on which the bread was laid over the fire, it removes all the horror and much of the disgust. This was required to show the extreme

A. M. 3409 B. C. 595 Ol. XLVI. 2 Anno TarquiniiPrisci, R. Roman., 22

13 And the LORD said, Even
thus [i]shall the children of Israel
eat their defiled bread among
the Gentiles, whither I will
drive them.
14 Then said I, [k]Ah Lord GOD! behold,
my soul hath not been polluted: for from my
youth up even till now have I not eaten of
[l]that which dieth of itself, or is torn in
pieces; neither came there [m]abominable flesh
into my mouth.
15 Then he said unto me, Lo, I have given
thee cow's dung for man's dung,
and thou shalt prepare thy
bread therewith.
16 Moreover he said unto me,
Son of man, behold, I will break the [n]staff of
bread in Jerusalem: and they shall [o]eat bread
by weight, and with care; and they shall
[p]drink water by measure, and with astonishment:
17 That they may want bread and water,
and be astonied one with another, and [q]consume away for their iniquity.

[i]Hos. ix. 3——[k]Acts x. 14——[l]Exod. xxii. 31; Lev. xi. 40; xvii. 15——[m]Deut. xiv. 3; Isa. lxv. 4——[n]Lev. xxvi. 26; Psa. cv. 16; Isa. iii. 1; ch. v. 16; xiv. 13——[o]Ver. 10; ch. xii. 19——[p]Ver. 11——[q]Lev. xxvi. 39; ch. xxiv. 23

degree of wretchedness to which they should be exposed; for, not being able to *leave the city* to collect the dried excrements of beasts, the inhabitants during the siege would be obliged, literally, to use dried human ordure for fuel. The very circumstances show that this was the plain fact of the case. However, we find that the prophet was relieved from using this kind of fuel, for *cows' dung* was substituted at his request. See ver. 15.

Verse 14. *My soul hath not been polluted*] There is a remarkable similarity between this expostulation of the prophet and that of St. Peter, Acts x. 14.

Verse 16. *I will break the staff of bread*] They shall be besieged till all the bread is consumed, till the famine becomes *absolute;* see 2 Kings xxv. 3: "And on the ninth of the *fourth* month, the famine prevailed in the city; and THERE WAS NO BREAD for the people of the land." All this was accurately foretold, and as accurately fulfilled.

Abp. *Newcome* on ver. 6 observes: "This number of years will take us back, with sufficient exactness, from the year in which Jerusalem was sacked by Nebuchadnezzar to the first year of Jeroboam's reign, when national idolatry began in Israel. The period of days seems to predict the duration of the siege by the Babylonians, ver. 9, deducting from the year *five months and twenty-nine days,* mentioned 2 Kings xxv. 1-4, the time during which the Chaldeans were on their expedition against the Egyptians; see Jer. xxxvii. 5." This amounts nearly to the same as that mentioned above.

CHAPTER V

In this chapter the prophet shows, under the type of hair, *the judgments which God was about to execute on the inhabitants of Jerusalem by famine, sword, and dispersion,* 1–4. *The type or allegory is then dropped, and God is introduced declaring in plain terms the vengeance that was coming on the whole nation which had proved so unworthy of those mercies with which they had hitherto been distinguished,* 5–17.

A. M. cir. 3410 B. C. cir. 594 Ol. XLVI. 3 TarquiniiPrisci, R. Roman., cir. annum 23

AND thou, son of man, take
thee a sharp knife, take thee
a barber's razor, [a]and cause *it*
to pass upon thine head and
upon thy beard: then take thee balances to
weigh, and divide the *hair.*
2 [b]Thou shalt burn with fire a third part in
the midst of [c]the city, when [d]the days of the siege
are fulfilled: and thou shalt take
a third part, *and* smite about it
with a knife: and a third part
thou shalt scatter in the wind;
and I will draw out a sword after them.
3 [e]Thou shalt also take thereof a few in
number, and bind them in thy [f]skirts.
4 Then take of them again, and [g]cast them

[a]See Lev. xxi. 5; Isa. vii. 20; chap. xliv. 20——[b]Ver. 12——[c]Chap. iv. 1——[d]Chap. iv. 8, 9——[e]Jer. xl. 6; lii. 16——[f]Heb. *wings*——[g]Jer. xli. 1, 2, &c.; xliv. 14

NOTES ON CHAP. V

Verses 1-4. *Take thee a sharp knife*] Among the Israelites, and indeed among most ancient nations, there were very few *edge-tools.* The *sword* was the chief; and this was used as a *knife,* a *razor,* &c., according to its different *length* and *sharpness.* It is likely that only *one* kind of instrument is here intended; a *knife* or short *sword,* to be employed as a *razor.*

Here is a new emblem produced, in order to mark out the coming evils. 1. The *prophet* represents the Jewish *nation.* 2. His *hair,* the *people.* 3. The *razor,* the *Chaldeans.* 4. The *cutting* the *beard* and *hair,* the *calamities, sorrows,* and *disgrace* coming upon the people. *Cutting off the hair* was a sign of *mourning;* see on Jer. xlv. 5; xlviii. 37; and also a sign of great *disgrace;* see 2 Sam. x. 4. 5. He is ordered to divide the hair, ver. 2, into *three equal* parts, to intimate the *different degrees* and *kinds of punishment* which should fall upon the people. 6. The *balances,* ver. 1, were to represent the Divine justice, and the exactness with which

A. M. cir. 3410
B. C. cir. 594
Ol. XLVI. 3
TarquiniiPrisci,
R. Roman.,
cir. annum 23

into the midst of the fire, and burn them in the fire; *for* thereof shall a fire come forth into all the house of Israel.

5 Thus saith the Lord GOD; This *is* Jerusalem: I have set it in the midst of the nations and countries *that are* round about her.

6 And she hath changed my judgments into wickedness more than the nations, and my statutes more than the countries that *are* round about her: for they have refused my judgments and my statutes, they have not walked in them.

7 Therefore thus saith the Lord GOD; Because ye multiplied more than the nations that *are* round about you, *and* have not walked in my statutes, neither have kept my judgments, [h]neither have done according to the judgments of the nations that *are* round about you;

8 Therefore thus saith the Lord GOD; Behold, I, even I, *am* against thee, and will execute judgments in the midst of thee in the sight of the nations.

A. M. cir. 3410
B. C. cir. 594
Ol. XLVI. 3
TarquiniiPrisci,
R. Roman.,
cir. annum 23

9 [i]And I will do in thee that which I have not done, and whereunto I will not do any more the like, because of all thine abominations.

10 Therefore the fathers [k]shall eat the sons in the midst of thee, and the sons shall eat their fathers; and I will execute judgments in thee, and the whole remnant of thee will I [l]scatter into all the winds.

11 Wherefore, *as* I live, saith the Lord GOD; Surely, because thou hast [m]defiled my sanctuary with all thy [n]detestable things, and with all thine abominations, therefore will I also diminish *thee;* [o]neither shall mine eye spare, neither will I have any pity.

12 [p]A third part of thee shall die with the pestilence, and with famine shall they be con-

[h]Jer. ii. 10, 11; chap. xvi. 47——[i]Lam. iv. 6; Dan. ix. 12; Amos iii. 2——[k]Lev. xxvi. 29; Deut. xxviii. 53 2 Kings vi. 29; Jer. xix. 9; Lam. ii. 20; iv. 10; Bar. ii. 3 [l]Ver. 12; Lev. xxvi. 33; Deut. xxviii. 64; chap. xii. 14; Zech. ii. 6——[m]2 Chronicles xxxvi. 14; chap. vii. 20; viii. 5, &c.; xxiii. 38——[n]Chap. xi. 21——[o]Chap. vii. 4, 9; viii. 18; ix. 10——[p]See ver. 2; Jer. xv. 2; xxi. 9; chap. vi. 12

God's judgments should be distributed among the offenders. 7. This *hair*, divided into *three parts*, is to be disposed of thus: 1. A *third* part is to be *burnt* in the midst of the city, to show that so many should perish by famine and pestilence during the siege. 2. Another third part he was to *cut in small portions* about the city, (that figure which he had pourtrayed upon the brick,) to signify those who should perish in different *sorties*, and in *defending* the *walls*. 3. And the remaining third part he was to *scatter* in the *wind*, to point out those who should be driven into *captivity*. And, 4. The *sword following* them was intended to show that their lives should be at the will of their captors, and that many of them should perish by the *sword* in their dispersions. 5. The *few hairs* which he was to take in his skirts, ver. 3, was intended to represent those few Jews that should be left in the land under *Gedaliah*, after the taking of the city. 6. The throwing a part of these last into the fire, ver. 4, was intended to show the miseries that these suffered in *Judea*, in *Egypt*, and finally in their being also carried away into *Babylon* on the conquest of Egypt by Nebuchadnezzar. See these transactions particularly pointed out in the notes on Jeremiah, chapters xl., xli., xlii. Some think that this prophecy may refer to the persecution of the Jews by *Antiochus Epiphanes*.

Verse 5. *This* is *Jerusalem: I have set it in the midst of the nations*] I have made this city the most eminent and the most illustrious in the world. Some think that these words refer to its *geographical situation*, as being equally in *the centre of the habitable world.* But any point on a globe is its centre, no matter where laid down; and it would not be difficult to show that even this *literal sense* is tolerably correct. But the point which is the *centre* of the greatest portion of land that can be exhibited on one hemisphere is the capital of the *British empire.* See my *Sermon on the universal spread of the Gospel.*

Verse 6. *She hath changed my judgments*] God shows the reason why he deals with Jerusalem in greater severity than with the surrounding nations; because she was more wicked than they. Bad and idolatrous as they were, they had a greater degree of *morality* among them than the Jews had. Having fallen from the true God, they became *more abominable* than others in proportion to the height, eminence, and glory from which they had fallen. This is the common case of *backsliders;* they frequently, in their fall, become tenfold more the children of wrath than they were before.

Verse 9. *I will do in thee that which I have not done*] The destruction of Jerusalem by *Nebuchadnezzar* was one of the greatest calamities that ever fell on any nation or place *before;* and that by the *Romans* under Titus exceeded all that has taken place *since.* These two sackages of that city have no parallel in the history of mankind.

Verse 10. *The fathers shall eat the sons*] Though we have not this fact so particularly stated in *history*, yet we cannot doubt of it, considering the extremities to which they were reduced during the siege. The same is referred to by Jeremiah, Lam. iv. 10. Even the *women*, who were remarkable for *kindness* and *humanity, boiled* their own children, and ate them during the siege.

Will I scatter into all the winds.] Disperse you, by captivity, among all the nations of the earth.

Verse 12. *A third part of thee*] See the note on ver. 1-4.

A. M. cir. 3410 B. C. cir. 594 Ol. XLVI. 3 TarquiniiPrisci, R. Roman., cir. annum 23

sumed in the midst of thee: and a third part shall fall by the sword round about thee; and [q]I will scatter a third part into all the winds, and [r]I will draw out a sword after them.

13 Thus shall mine anger [s]be accomplished, and I will [t]cause my fury to rest upon them, [u]and I will be comforted: [v]and they shall know that I the LORD have spoken *it* in my zeal, when I have accomplished my fury in them.

14 Moreover [w]I will make thee waste, and a reproach among the nations that *are* round about thee, in the sight of all that pass by.

15 So it shall be a [x]reproach and a taunt, an instruction and an astonishment unto the nations that *are* round about thee, when I shall execute judgments in thee in anger and in fury and in [y]furious rebukes. I the LORD have spoken *it*.

16 When I shall [z]send upon them the evil arrows of famine, which shall be for *their* destruction, *and* which I will send to destroy you: and I will increase the famine upon you, and will break your [a]staff of bread.

17 So will I send upon you famine and [b]evil beasts, and they shall bereave thee; and [c]pestilence and blood shall pass through thee; and I will bring the sword upon thee. I the LORD have spoken *it*.

[q]Jeremiah ix. 16; verse 2, 10; chapter vi. 8——[r]Leviticus xxvi. 33; verse 2; chapter xii. 14——[s]Lamentations iv. 11; chapter vi. 12; vii. 8——[t]Chap. xxi. 17 [u]Deuteronomy xxxii. 36; Isaiah i. 24——[v]Chapter xxxvi. 6; xxxviii. 19——[w]Leviticus xxvi. 31, 32; Nehemiah ii. 17——[x]Deut. xxviii. 37; 1 Kings ix. 7; Psa. lxxix. 4; Jer. xxiv. 9; Lam. ii. 15——[y]Chap. xxv. 17——[z]Deut. xxxii. 23, 24——[a]Lev. xxvi. 26; ch. iv. 16; xiv. 13 [b]Lev. xxvi. 22; Deut. xxxii. 24; chap. xiv. 21; xxxiii. 27; xxxiv. 25——[c]Chap. xxxviii. 22

Verse 13. *I will cause my fury to rest*] My displeasure, and the evidences of it, shall not be *transient;* they shall be *permanent* upon you, and among you. And is not this dreadfully true to the present day?

Verse 16. *The evil arrows of famine*] Famine and pestilence are represented as *poisoned arrows*, inflicting death wherever they *wound*. The ancients represented them in the same way.

Verse 17. *So will I send upon you famine and evil beasts, and they shall bereave thee*] Wild beasts always multiply in depopulated countries. In England, *wolves* abounded when the country was thinly peopled, it is now full of inhabitants, and there is not one wolf in the land. Nebuchadnezzar and his Chaldeans may be called here *evil beasts*. He is often compared to a *lion*, Jer. iv. 7; Dan. vii. 14; on account of the ravages made by him and his Chaldean armies.

CHAPTER VI

In this chapter, which forms a distinct section, the prophet denounces the judgments of God against the Jews for their idolatry, 1–7; *but tells them that a remnant shall be saved, and brought to a sense of their sins by their severe afflictions,* 8–14.

A. M. cir. 3410 B. C. cir. 594 Ol. XLVI. 3 TarquiniiPrisci, R. Roman., cir. annum 23

AND the word of the LORD came unto me, saying,

2 Son of man, [a]set thy face toward the [b]mountains of Israel, and prophesy against them,

3 And say, Ye mountains of Israel, hear the word of the Lord GOD; Thus saith the Lord GOD to the mountains, and to the hills, to the rivers, and to the valleys; Behold, I, *even* I, will bring a sword upon you, and [c]I will destroy your high places.

4 And your altars shall be desolate, and your [d]images shall be broken: and [e]I will cast down your slain *men* before your idols.

5 And I will [f]lay the dead carcasses of the

[a]Chap. xx. 46; xxi. 2; xxv. 2——[b]Chap. xxxvi. 1 [c]Lev. xxvi. 30

[d]Or, *sun images;* and so ver. 6——[e]Lev. xxvi. 30 [f]Heb. *give*

NOTES ON CHAP. VI

Verse 2. *Set thy face toward the mountains of Israel*] This is a new prophecy, and was most probably given after the *four hundred and thirty* days of his lying on his left and right side were accomplished. By *Israel* here, Judea is simply meant; not the *ten tribes*, who had long before been carried into captivity. Ezekiel uses this term in reference to the Jews only.

The *mountains* may be addressed here particularly, because it was on them the chief scenes of idolatry were exhibited.

Verse 4. *Your images shall be broken*] Literally, your *sun images;* representations of the sun, which they worshipped. See the margin.

Verse 5. *Will scatter your bones round about*

A. M. cir. 3410 B. C. cir. 594 Ol. XLVI. 3 TarquiniiPrisci, R. Roman., cir. annum 23

children of Israel before their idols; and I will scatter your bones round about your altars.

6 In all your dwelling-places the cities shall be laid waste, and the high places shall be desolate; that your altars may be laid waste and made desolate, and your idols may be broken and cease, and your images may be cut down, and your works may be abolished.

7 And the slain shall fall in the midst of you, and [g]ye shall know that I *am* the LORD.

8 [h]Yet will I leave a remnant, that ye may have *some* that shall escape the sword among the nations, when ye shall be scattered through the countries.

9 And they that escape of you shall remember me among the nations whither they shall be carried captives, because [i]I am broken with their whorish heart, which hath departed from me, and [k]with their eyes, which go a whoring after their idols: and [l]they shall loathe themselves for the evils which they have committed in all their abominations.

10 And they shall know that I *am* the LORD, *and that* I have not said in vain that I would do this evil unto them.

11 Thus saith the Lord GOD; Smite [m]with thine hand, and stamp with thy foot, and say, Alas for all the evil abominations of the house of Israel! [n]for they shall fall by the sword, by the famine, and by the pestilence.

12 He that is far off shall die of the pestilence; and he that is near shall fall by the sword; and he that remaineth and is besieged shall die by the famine: [o]thus will I accomplish my fury upon them.

13 Then [p]shall ye know that I *am* the LORD, when their slain *men* shall be among their idols round about their altars, [q]upon every high hill, [r]in all the tops of the mountains, and [s]under every green tree, and under every thick oak, the place where they did offer sweet savour to all their idols.

14 So will I [t]stretch out my hand upon them, and make the land desolate, yea, [u]more desolate than the wilderness toward [v]Diblath, in all their habitations: and they shall know that I *am* the LORD.

[g]Ver. 13; ch. vii. 4, 9; xi. 10, 12; xii. 15——[h]Jer. xliv. 28; ch. v. 2, 12; xii. 16; xiv. 22——[i]Psa. lxxviii. 40; Isa. vii. 13; xliii. 24; lxiii. 10——[k]Num. xv. 39; ch. xx. 7, 24 [l]Lev. xxvi. 39; Job xlii. 6; ch. xx. 43; xxxvi. 31

[m]Chap. xxi. 14——[n]Chap. v. 12——[o]Chap. v. 13 [p]Ver. 7——[q]Jer. ii. 20——[r]Hos. iv. 13——[s]Isa. lvii. 5 [t]Isa. v. 25——[u]Or, *desolate from the wilderness* [v]Num. xxxiii. 46; Jer. xlviii. 22

your altars.] This was literally fulfilled by the Chaldeans. According to *Baruch*, chap. ii. 24, 25, they opened the sepulchres of the principal people, and threw the bones about on every side.

Verse 9. *They that escape of you shall remember me*] Those that escape the sword, the pestilence, and the famine, and shall be led into captivity, shall plainly see that it is God who has done this; and shall humble themselves on account of their abominations, leave their idolatry, and worship me alone. And this they have done from the Babylonish captivity to the present day.

Verse 11. *Smite with thine hand, and stamp with thy foot*] Show the utmost marks of thy astonishment and indignation, and dread of the evils that are coming upon them. Some have contended for the propriety of *clapping* and *stamping* in public worship from these words! It is scarcely a breach of charity to think that such persons are themselves incapable either of attending on or conducting the worship of God. To be consistent, they should copy the prophet in his other typical actions as well as these; and then we shall hear of their *lying on their left side* for *three hundred and ninety* days, and on *their right side* for *forty* days; *shaving their heads, burning their hair, baking their bread with dung,* &c. Now all these things, because they were typical and commanded, were proper in the prophet: in such persons as the above they would be evidences of insanity. Such extravagant acts are no part of God's worship.

Verse 14. *And make the land—more desolate than the wilderness toward Diblath*] *Diblath* or *Diblathayim* is situated in the land of Moab. It is mentioned Num. xxxiii. 46, *Almon-Diblathaim;* and in Jer. xlviii. 22, *Beth-Diblathaim.* It was a part of that horrible wilderness mentioned by Moses, Deut. viii. 15, "wherein were fiery serpents, and scorpions, and drought." The precise reason why it is mentioned here is not very evident. Some think it is the same as *Riblah*, where Nebuchadnezzar slew the princes of Israel, and put out Zedekiah's eyes; the principal difference lying between the ד *daleth* and the ר *resh*, which in MSS. is often scarcely discernible; and hence vast multitudes of *various readings. Five*, probably *six*, of *Kennicott's* MSS. have רבלתה *riblathah*, as likewise *two* of my oldest MSS.; though in the margin of one a later hand directs the word to be read בדלת *bedaleth, with daleth.* But all the *Versions* read the word with a D. This may appear a matter of little importance, but we should take pains to recover even one lost *letter* of the *word* of God.

CHAPTER VII

This chapter, which also forms a distinct prophecy, foretells the dreadful destruction of the land of Israel, or Judah, (for after the captivity of the ten tribes these terms are often used indiscriminately for the Jews in general,) on account of the heinous sins of its inhabitants, 1–15; *and the great distress of the small remnant that should escape,* 16–19. *The temple itself, which they had polluted with idolatry, is devoted to destruction,* 20–22; *and the prophet is directed to make a chain, as a type of that captivity, in which both king and people should be led in bonds to Babylon,* 23–27. *The whole chapter abounds in bold and beautiful figures, flowing in an easy and forcible language.*

A. M. cir. 3410
B. C. cir. 594
Ol. XLVI. 3
TarquiniiPrisci, R. Roman., cir. annum 23

MOREOVER the word of the
LORD came unto me, saying,
2 Also, thou son of man, thus
saith the Lord GOD unto the
land of Israel; [a]An end, the end is come
upon the four corners of the land.
3 Now *is* the end *come* upon thee, and I
will send mine anger upon thee, and [b]will
judge thee according to thy ways, and will
[c]recompense upon thee all thine abominations.
4 And [d]mine eye shall not spare thee, neither will I have pity: but I will recompense
thy ways upon thee, and thine abominations
shall be in the midst of thee: [e]and ye shall
know that I *am* the LORD.
5 Thus saith the Lord GOD; An
evil, an only evil, behold, is come.
6 An end is come, the end is
come: it [f]watcheth for thee;
behold, it is come.
7 [g]The morning is come unto thee, O thou
that dwellest in the land: [h]the time is come,
the day of trouble *is* near, and not the
[i]sounding again of the mountains.
8 Now will I shortly [k]pour out my fury
upon thee, and accomplish mine anger upon
thee: [l]and I will judge thee according to thy
ways, and will recompense thee for all thine
abominations.
9 And [m]mine eye shall not spare, neither will

[a]Ver. 3, 6; Amos viii. 2; Matt. xxiv. 6, 13, 14——[b]Ver. 8, 9——[c]Heb. *give*——[d]Ver. 9; chap. v. 11; viii. 18; ix. 10——[e]Ver. 27; chap. vi. 7; xii. 20

[f]Heb. *awaketh against thee*——[g]Ver. 10——[h]Ver. 12; Zeph. i. 14, 15——[i]Or, *echo*——[k]Chap. xx. 8, 21 [l]Ver. 3——[m]Ver. 4

NOTES ON CHAP. VII

Verse 2. *An end, the end is come*] Instead of קץ בא הקץ *kets ba hakkets, one* MS. of *Kennicott's one* of *De Rossi's*, and *one* of *my own*, read קץ בא בא הקץ *kets ba, ba hakkets*, "The end cometh, come is the end." This reading is supported by all the ancient Versions, and is undoubtedly genuine. *The end* COMETH: the termination of the Jewish state *is coming*, and while I am speaking, it *is come*. The destruction is at the door. The *later* hand, who put the *vowel points* to the ancient MS. that has the above reading, did not put the points to the first בא *ba*, but struck his pen gently across it, and by a mark in the margin intimated that it should be blotted out. All my ancient MSS. were without the points originally; but they have been added by modern hands, with a different ink; and they have in multitudes of instances corrected, or rather changed, important readings, to make them quadrate with the *masora*. But the original reading, in almost every case, is discernible.

The end is come upon the four corners of the land.] This is not a *partial* calamity; it shall cover and sweep the whole land. The cup of your iniquity is full, and my forbearing is at an end. This whole chapter is *poetical*.

Verse 4. *Thine abominations shall be in the midst of thee*] They shall ever stare thee in the face, upbraid thee with thy ingratitude and disobedience, and be witnesses against thee.

Verse 5. *An evil, an only evil*] The great, the sovereign, the last exterminating evil, is come: the sword, the pestilence, the famine, and the captivity. Many MSS. read אחר *achar, after*. So evil cometh after evil; one instantly succeeds another.

Verse 6. *An end is come, the end is come: it watcheth for thee*] This is similar to the *second* verse; but there is a *paronomasia*, or play upon letters and words, which is worthy of note. קץ בא בא הקץ הקיץ אליך *kets ba, ba hakkets, hekits elayich.* קצר *katsah* signifies to make an *end* or *extremity*, by cutting off something, and יקץ *yakats* signifies to *awake from sleep:* hence קיץ *kits*, the *summer*, as the earth and its productions seem then to awake from the sleep of winter. The *end* or final destruction is here *personified;* and represented as an *executioner* who has *arisen early* from his sleep, and is *waiting* for his orders to execute judgment upon these offenders. Hence it is said—

Verse 7. *The morning is come unto thee*] Every note of *time* is used in order to show the *certainty* of the thing. The *morning* that the executioner has *watched* for is come; the *time* of that *morning*, in which it should take place, and the *day* to which that *time, precise hour* of that *morning*, belongs, in which judgment shall be executed. All, all is come.

And not the sounding again of the mountains.] The hostile troops are advancing! Ye hear a *sound*, a *tumultuous noise;* do not suppose that this proceeds from festivals upon *the mountains;* from the joy of *harvestmen*, or the treaders *of the wine-press*. It is the *noise* of those by whom ye and your country are to fall. ולא הד הרים *velo hed harim*, and not the reverberation of sound, or reflected sound, or *re-*

A. M. cir. 3410 B. C. cir. 594 Ol. XLVI. 3 TarquiniiPrisci, R. Roman., cir. annum 23

I have pity: I will recompense
[n]thee according to thy ways and
thine abominations *that* are in
the midst of thee; [o]and ye shall
know that I *am* the LORD that smiteth.
10 Behold the day, behold, it is come: [p]the
morning is gone forth; the rod hath blossomed, pride hath budded.
11 [q]Violence is risen up into a rod of wickedness: none of them *shall remain,* nor of
their [r]multitude, nor of any of [s]theirs; [t]nei-
ther *shall there be* wailing for them.
12 [u]The time is come, the day draweth near:
let not the buyer rejoice, nor the seller mourn:
for wrath *is* upon all the multitude thereof.
13 For the seller shall not return to that
which is sold, [v]although they were yet alive:
for the vision *is* touching the
whole multitude thereof, *which*
shall not return; neither shall
any strengthen himself [w]in [x]the
iniquity of his life.
14 They have blown the trumpet, even to
make all ready: but none goeth to the battle:
for my wrath *is* upon all the multitude thereof.
15 [y]The sword *is* without, and the pestilence and the famine within: he that *is* in the
field shall die with the sword; and he that *is* in
the city, famine and pestilence shall devour him.
16 But [z]they that escape of them shall
escape, and shall be on the mountains like
doves of the valleys, all of them mourning,
every one for his iniquity.
17 All [a]hands shall be feeble, and all

[n]Heb. *upon thee*——[o]Ver. 4——[p]Ver. 7——[q]Jer. vi. 7——[r]Or, *tumult*——[s]Or, *their tumultuous persons* [t]Jer. xvi. 5, 6; ch. xxiv. 16, 22——[u]Ver. 7——[v]Heb. *though their life* were *yet among the living*——[w]Or, *whose life* is *in his iniquity*——[x]Hebrew, *his iniquity*——[y]Deut. xxxii. 25; Lam. i. 20; chap. v. 12——[z]Chap. vi. 8——[a]Isa. xiii. 7; Jer. vi. 24; chap. xxi. 7

echoing from the mountains. "Now will I shortly pour out," ver. 8. Here they come!

Verse 10. *Behold the day*] The same words are repeated, sometimes varied, and pressed on the attention with *new figures* and *new circumstances*, in order to alarm this infatuated people. Look at the *day!* It is come!

The morning is gone forth] It will wait no longer. The *rod* that is to chastise you hath *blossomed;* it is quite ready.

Pride hath budded.] Your insolence, obstinacy, and daring opposition to God have brought forth their proper fruits.

Verse 11. *Violence is risen up into a rod of wickedness*] The prophet continues his metaphor: "Pride has budded."—And what has it brought forth? *Violence* and *iniquity.* To meet these, the *rod of God* cometh. There is such a vast rapidity of succession in the ideas of the prophet that he cannot wait to find language to clothe each. Hence we have broken sentences; and, consequently, *obscurity.* Something must be *supplied* to get the sense, and most critics alter words in the text. *Houbigant,* who rarely acknowledges himself to be puzzled, appears here completely nonplussed. He has given a meaning; it is this: "Violence hath burst forth from the rod; salvation shall not proceed from them, nor from their riches, nor from their turbulence: there shall be no respite for them." *Calmet* has given no less than *five* interpretations to this verse. The simple meaning seems to be, that such and so great is their wickedness that it must be punished; and from this punishment, neither their multitude nor struggles shall set them free. They may strive to evade the threatened stroke; but they shall not succeed, nor shall they have any respite. Our *Version* is to be understood as saying,—None of the people shall be left; all shall be slain, or carried into captivity: nor shall any of theirs, their princes, priests, wives, or children, escape. And so deserved shall their desolation appear, that none shall *lament* them. This may be as good a sense as any, and it is nearest to the letter.

Verse 12. *Let not the buyer rejoice, nor the seller mourn*] Such is now the state of public affairs, that he who through want has been obliged to *sell his inheritance,* need not *mourn* on the account; as of this the enemy would soon have deprived him. And he who *has bought it* need not *rejoice* in his bargain, as he shall soon be stripped of his purchase, and either fall by the sword, or be glad to flee for his life.

Verse 13. *For the seller shall not return*] In the sale of all heritages among the Jews, it was always understood that the heritage must return to the family on the *year of jubilee,* which was every *fiftieth* year; but in this case the *seller* should not return to possess it, as it was not likely that he should be *alive* when the next jubilee should come; and if he were even to live till that time, he could not possess it, as he would then be in captivity. And the reason is particularly given; *for the vision*—the prophetic declaration of a *seventy* years' captivity, regards the whole multitude of the people; and *it shall not return,* i. e., it will be found to be strictly true, without any abatement.

Verse 14. *They have blown the trumpet*] Vain are all the efforts you make to collect and arm the people, and stand on your own defence; for all shall be dispirited, and none *go to the battle.*

Verse 15. *The sword* is *without*] *War* through all the *country,* and *pestilence* and *famine* within the city, shall destroy the whole, except a small remnant. He who endeavours to flee from the one shall fall by the other.

Verse 16. *They—shall be on the mountains like doves of the valleys*] Rather, *like mourning doves* הגאיות *haggeayoth,* chased from their dove-cotes, and separated from their mates.

Verse 17. *All knees shall be weak* as *water.*] *Calmet* understands this curiously: La frayeur dont on sera saisi, fera qu'on ne pourra retenir

A. M. cir. 3410
B. C. cir. 594
Ol. XLVI. 3
TarquiniiPrisci,
R. Roman.,
cir. annum 23

knees shall [b]be weak *as* water.

18 They shall also [c]gird *themselves* with sackcloth, and [d]horror shall cover them; and shame *shall be* upon all faces, and baldness upon all their heads.

19 They shall cast their silver in the streets, and their gold shall be [e]removed: their [f]silver and their gold shall not be able to deliver them in the day of the wrath of the LORD: they shall not satisfy their souls, neither fill their bowels: [g]because it is [h]the stumbling-block of their iniquity.

20 As for the beauty of his ornament, he set it in majesty: [i]but they made the images of their abominations *and* of their detestable things therein: therefore have I [k]set it far from them.

21 And I will give it into the hands of the strangers for a prey, and to the wicked of the earth for a spoil; and they shall pollute it.

22 My face will I turn also from them, and they shall pollute my secret *place:* for the [l]robbers shall enter into it, and defile it.

A. M. cir. 3410
B. C. cir. 594
Ol. XLVI. 3
Tarquinii Prisci,
R. Roman.,
cir. annum 23

23 Make a chain: for [m]the land is full of bloody crimes, and the city is full of violence.

24 Wherefore I will bring the worst of the heathen, and they shall possess their houses: I will also make the pomp of the strong to cease; and [n]their holy places shall be defiled.

25 [o]Destruction cometh; and they shall seek peace, and *there shall be* none.

26 [p]Mischief shall come upon mischief, and rumour shall be upon rumour; [q]then shall they seek a vision of the prophet; but the law shall perish from the priest, and counsel from the ancients.

27 The king shall mourn, and the prince shall be clothed with desolation, and the hands of the people of the land shall be troubled: I will do unto them after their way, and [r]according to their deserts will I judge them; [s]and they shall know that I *am* the LORD.

---

[b]Heb. *go into water*——[c]Isa. iii. 24; xv. 2, 3; Jer. xlviii. 37; Amos viii. 10——[d]Psa. lv. 5——[e]Heb. *for a separation*, or *uncleanness*——[f]Prov. xi. 4; Zeph. i. 18; Ecclus. v. 8——[g]Or, *because their iniquity* is their *stumbling block*——[h]Chap. xiv. 3, 4; xliv. 12

[i]Jer. vii. 30——[k]Or, *made it unto them an unclean thing*——[l]Or, *burglars*——[m]2 Kings xxi. 16; ch. ix. 9; xi. 6——[n]Or, *they shall inherit their holy places*——[o]Heb. *Cutting off*——[p]Deut. xxxii. 23; Jer. iv. 20——[q]Psa. lxxiv. 9; Lam. ii. 9; chap. xx. 1, 3——[r]Heb. *with their judgments*——[s]Ver. 4

---

son urine. D'autres l'expliquent d'une autre soüillure plus honteuse. I believe him to be nearly about right. *St. Jerome* is exactly the same: Pavoris magnitudine, urina polluet genua, nec valebit profluentes aquas vesica prohibere. This and other malretentions are often the natural effect of extreme fear or terror.

Verse 19. *They shall cast their silver in the streets*] Their riches can be of no use; as in a time of *famine* there is no necessary of life to be *purchased*, and *gold* and *silver cannot fill their bowels.*

It is the stumbling-block of their iniquity.] They loved riches, and placed in the possession of them their supreme happiness. Now they find a *pound* of *gold* not worth an *ounce* of *bread.*

Verse 20. *As for the beauty of his ornament*] Their *beautiful temple* was their highest *ornament*, and God made it *majestic* by his presence. But they have even taken its riches to make their *idols*, which they have brought into the very courts of the Lord's house; and therefore God hath *set it*—the temple, *from him*—given it up to pillage. Some say it means, "They took their ornaments, which were their pride, and made them into images to worship."

Verse 22. *The robbers shall enter into it*] The Chaldeans shall not only destroy the city; but they shall enter the temple, deface it, plunder it, and burn it to the ground.

Verse 23. *Make a chain*] Point out the *captivity;* show them that it shall come, and show them the reason: "Because the land is full of bloody crimes," &c.

Verse 24. *The worst of the heathen*] The Chaldeans; the most cruel and idolatrous of all nations.

Verse 25. *They shall seek peace*] They see now that their ceasing to pay the tribute to the king of Babylon has brought the Chaldeans against them; and now *they sue for peace* in vain. He will not hear: he is resolved on their destruction.

Verse 26. *Then shall they seek a vision*] Vision shall perish from the prophet, the law from the priest, and counsel from the ancients. Previously to great national judgments, God restrains the influences of his Spirit. His word is not accompanied with the usual unction; and the *wise men* of the land, the *senators* and celebrated *statesmen*, devise foolish schemes; and thus, in endeavouring to avert it, they hasten on the national ruin. How true is the saying, Quem Deus vult perdere, prius dementat. "Those whom God designs to destroy, he first infatuates."

CHAPTER VIII

Here begins a section of prophecy extending to the twelfth *chapter. In this chapter the prophet is carried in vision to Jerusalem,* 1–4; *and there shown the idolatries committed by the rulers of the Jews, even within the temple. In the beginning of this vision, by the noblest stretch of an inspired imagination,* idolatry *itself is personified, and made an* idol; *and the image sublimely called, from the provocation it gave God, the* IMAGE OF JEALOUSY, 5. *The prophet then proceeds to describe the three principal superstitions of this unhappy people: the* Egyptian, 6–12, *the* Phœnician, 13, 14, *and the* Persian, 15, 16; *giving the striking features of each, and concluding with a declaration of the heinousness of their sins in the sight of God, and the consequent greatness of their punishment,* 17, 18.

A. M. 3410
B. C. 594
Ol. XLVI. 3
Anno Tarquinii Prisci, R. Roman., 23

AND it came to pass in
the sixth year, in the
sixth *month,* in the fifth *day*
of the month, *as* I sat in mine
house, and [a]the elders of Judah sat before
me, that [b]the hand of the Lord GOD fell
there upon me.
2 [c]Then I beheld, and lo a likeness as the
appearance of fire: from the
appearance of his loins even
downward, fire; and from his
loins even upward, as the appearance of brightness, [d]as the colour of
amber.
3 And he [e]put forth the form of a hand,
and took me by a lock of mine head; and

A. M. 3410
B. C. 594
Ol. XLVI. 3
Anno Tarquinii Prisci, R. Roman., 23

[a]Chap. xiv. 1; xx. 1; xxxiii. 31——[b]Chap. i. 3; iii. 22

[c]Chap. i. 26, 27——[d]Chap. i. 4——[e]Dan. v. 5

NOTES ON CHAP. VIII

Verse 1. *In the sixth year, in the sixth* month, *in the fifth* day *of the month*] This, according to Abp. *Usher*, was the *sixth* year of Ezekiel's captivity. The *sixth* day of the *fifth* month of the *ecclesiastical year*, which answers to August, A. M. 3410.

This chapter and the *three* following contain but *one vision*, of which I judge it necessary, with *Calmet*, to give a general idea, that the attention of the reader may not be too much divided.

The prophet, in the visions of God, is carried to Jerusalem, to the northern gate of the temple, which leads by the north side to the court of the priests. There he sees the glory of the Lord in the same manner as he did by the river Chebar. At one side he sees the *image of jealousy*. Going thence to the court of the people, he sees through an opening in the wall *seventy* elders of the people, who were worshipping all sorts of beasts and reptiles, which were painted on the wall. Being brought thence to the gate of the door of the house, he saw women weeping for *Tammuz* or *Adonis*. As he returned to the court of the priests, between the porch and the altar, he saw *twenty-five* men with their backs to the sanctuary and their faces towards the east, worshipping the *rising sun*. This is the substance of the vision contained in the *eighth* chapter.

About the same time he saw *six men* come from the higher gate with *swords* in their hands; and among them, one with an *ink-horn*. Then the Divine Presence left the cherubim, and took post at the entrance of the temple, and gave orders to the man with the *ink-horn* to put a *mark* on the foreheads of those who sighed and prayed because of the abominations of the land; and then commanded the men with the *swords* to go forward, and slay every person who had not this mark. The prophet, being left alone among the dead, fell on his face, and made intercession for the people. The Lord gives him the reason of his conduct; and the man with the ink-horn returns, and reports to the Lord what was done. These are the general contents of the *ninth* chapter.

The Lord commands the same person to go in between the *wheels* of the cherubim, and take his hand full of live coals, and scatter them over the city. He went as commanded, and one of the cherubim gave him the coals; at the same time the glory of the Lord, that had removed to the threshold of the house, now returned, and stood over the cherubim. The cherubim, wheels, wings, &c., are here described as in the *first* chapter. This is the substance of the *tenth* chapter.

The prophet then finds himself transported to the east gate of the temple, where he saw *twenty-five* men, and among them *Jaazaniah* the son of Azur, and *Pelatiah* the son of Benaiah, princes of the people, against whom the Lord commands him to prophesy, and to threaten them with the utmost calamities, because of their crimes. Afterwards God himself speaks, and shows that the Jews who should be left in the land should be driven out because of their iniquities, and that those who had been led captive, and who acknowledged their sins and repented of them, should be restored to their own land. Then the glory of the Lord arose out of the city, and rested for a time on one of the mountains on the east of Jerusalem, and the prophet being carried in vision by the Spirit to Chaldea, lost sight of the chariot of the Divine glory, and began to show to the captivity what the Lord had shown to him. This is the substance of the *eleventh* chapter.

We may see from all this what induced the Lord to abandon his people, his city, and his temple; the abominations of the people in public and in private. But because those carried away captives with Jeconiah acknowledged their sins, and their hearts turned to the Lord, God informs them that they shall be brought back and restored to a happy state both in temporal and spiritual matters, while the others, who had filled up the measure of their iniquities, should be speedily brought into a state of desolation and ruin. This is the sum and intent of the vision in these *four* chapters.

Verse 2. *The appearance of fire*] See the note on chap. i. 27.

Verse 3. *The image of jealousy*] סמל הקנאה

A. M. 3410
B. C. 594
Ol. XLVI. 3
Anno
Tarquinii Prisci,
R. Roman., 23

[f]the spirit lifted me up between the earth and the heaven, and [g]brought me in the visions of God to Jerusalem, to the door of the inner gate that looketh toward the north; [h]where *was* the seat of the image of jealousy, which [i]provoketh to jealousy.

4 And, behold, the glory of the God of Israel *was* there, according to the vision that I [k]saw in the plain.

5 Then said he unto me, Son of man, lift up thine eyes now the way toward the north. So I lifted up mine eyes the way toward the north, and behold northward at the gate of the altar this image of jealousy in the entry.

6 He said furthermore unto me, Son of man, seest thou what they do? *even* the great abominations that the house of Israel committeth here, that I should go far off from my sanctuary? but turn thee yet again, *and* thou shalt see greater abominations.

7 And he brought me to the door of the court; and when I looked, behold a hole in the wall.

8 Then said he unto me, Son of man, dig now in the wall: and when I had digged in the wall, behold a door.

9 And he said unto me, Go in, and behold the wicked abominations that they do here.

10 So I went in and saw; and behold every form of creeping things, and abominable beasts, and all the idols of the house of Israel, pourtrayed upon the wall round about.

11 And there stood before them seventy men of the ancients of the house of Israel, and in the midst of them stood Jaazaniah the son of Shaphan, with every man his censer in his hand; and a thick cloud of incense went up.

12 Then said he unto me, Son of man, hast thou seen what the ancients of the house of Israel do in the dark, every man in the chambers of his imagery? for they say, [l]The LORD seeth us not; the LORD hath forsaken the earth.

13 He said also unto me, Turn thee yet again, *and* [m]thou shalt see greater abominations that they do.

14 Then he brought me to the door of the gate of the LORD's house which *was* toward

[f]Chap. iii. 14——[g]Gen. xlvi. 2; 2 Chron. xxvi. 5; ch. xi. 1, 24; xl. 2——[h]Jer. vii. 30; xxxii. 34; chap. v. 11

[i]Deut. xxxii. 16, 21——[k]Chap. i. 28; iii. 22, 23——[l]Ch. ix. 9——[m]Ver. 6, 15

semel hakkinah. We do not know certainly of what *form* this image was, nor what *god* it represented. Some say it was the image of Baal, which was placed in the temple by Manasses; others, that it was the image of *Mars;* and others, that it was the image of *Tammuz* or *Adonis. Calmet* supports this opinion by the following reasons:—1. The *name* agrees perfectly with him. He was represented as a beautiful youth, beloved by Venus; at which Mars, her paramour, being incensed and filled with *jealousy,* sent a large boar against Adonis, which killed him with his tusks. Hence it was the image of him who fell a victim to *jealousy.* 2. The prophet being returned towards the northern gate, where he had seen the *image of jealousy,* ver. 14, there saw the *women lamenting for Tammuz.* Now *Tammuz,* all agree, signifies *Adonis;* it was that therefore which was called the *image of jealousy.* 3. The Scripture often gives to the heathen idols names of degradation; as Baal-zebub, *god of flies;* Baalzebul, *god of dung.* It is likely that it was *Adonis* who is called *The dead,* Lev. xix. 27, 28; Deut. xiv. 9, because he was worshipped as one *dead.* And the women represented as worshipping him were probably *adulteresses,* and had suffered through the *jealousy* of their husbands. And this worship of the *image of jealousy provoked God to jealousy,* to destroy this bad people.

Verse 4. *The vision that I saw in the plain.*] See the note on chap. iii. 23; see also chap. i. 3.

Verse 7. *A hole in the wall.*] This we find was not large enough to see what was doing within; and the prophet is directed to dig, and make it larger, ver. 8; and when he had done so and entered, he says,—

Verse 10. *And saw—every form of creeping things*] It is very likely that these images pourtrayed on the wall were the objects of *Egyptian* adoration: the *ox,* the *ape,* the *dog,* the *crocodile,* the *ibis,* the *scarabœus* or *beetle,* and various other things. It appears that these were privately worshipped by the sanhedrin or great Jewish council, consisting of *seventy* or *seventy-two* persons, *six* chosen out of every tribe, as representatives of the people. The images were pourtrayed upon the wall, as we find those ancient idols are on the walls of the *tombs of the kings and nobles of Egypt.* See the plates to *Belzoni's* Travels, the *Isaic Tomb* in the Bodleian Library, and the *Egyptian hieroglyphics* in general. *Virgil* speaks of these, *Æn.* lib. viii.:—

Omnigenumque Deum monstra, et latrator Anubis.

"All kinds of gods, monsters, and barking dogs."

Verse 11. *Jaazaniah the son of Shaphan*] Shaphan was a scribe, or what some call comptroller of the temple, in the days of Josiah; and *Jaazaniah* his son probably succeeded him in this office. He was at the head of this band of idolaters.

Verse 14. *There sat women weeping for Tammuz.*] This was *Adonis,* as we have already

A. M. 3410
B. C. 594
Ol. XVLI. 3
Anno
Tarquinii Prisci,
R. Roman., 23

the north; and, behold, there sat women weeping for Tammuz.

15 Then said he unto me, Hast thou seen *this,* O son of man? turn thee yet again, *and* thou shalt see greater abominations than these.

16 And he brought me into the inner court of the LORD'S house, and, behold, at the door of the temple of the LORD, [n]between the porch and the altar, [o]*were* about five and twenty men, [p]with their backs toward the temple of the LORD, and their faces toward the east; and they worshipped [q]the sun toward the east.

17 Then he said unto me, Hast thou seen *this,* O son of man? [r]Is it a light thing to the house of Judah that they commit the abominations which they commit here? for they have [s]filled the land with violence, and have returned to provoke me to anger: and, lo, they put the branch to their nose.

A. M. 3410
B. C. 594
Ol. XLVI. 3
Anno
Tarquinii Prisci,
R. Roman., 23

18 [t]Therefore will I also deal in fury: mine [u]eye shall not spare, neither will I have pity; and though they [v]cry in mine ears with a loud voice, *yet* will I not hear them.

---

[n]Joel ii. 17——[o]Ch. xi. 1——[p]Jer. ii. 27; xxxii. 33 [q]Deut. iv. 19; 2 Kings xxiii. 5, 11; Job xxxi. 26; Jer. xliv. 17——[r]Or, *Is there* any *thing lighter than to commit*

[s]Chap. ix. 9——[t]Chap. v. 13; xvi. 42; xxiv. 13 [u]Chap. v. 11; vii. 4, 9; ix. 5, 10——[v]Prov. i. 28; Isa. i. 15; Jer. xi. 11; xiv. 12; Mic. iii. 4; Zech. vii. 13

---

seen; and so the *Vulgate* here translates. My old MS. Bible reads, **There saten women, mornynge a mawmete of lecherye that is cleped Adonydes.** He is fabled to have been a beautiful youth beloved by Venus, and killed by a wild boar in Mount Lebanon, whence springs the river *Adonis,* which was fabled to *run blood* at his festival in August. The women of Phœnicia, Assyria, and Judea worshipped him as *dead,* with deep lamentation, wearing *priapi* and other obscene images all the while, and they prostituted themselves in honour of this idol. Having for some time mourned him as *dead,* they then supposed him revivified, and broke out into the most extravagant rejoicings. Of the appearance of the river at this season, Mr. *Maundrell* thus speaks: "We had the good fortune to see what is the foundation of the opinion which *Lucian* relates, viz., that this stream at certain seasons of the year, especially about the feast of Adonis, is of a *bloody colour,* proceeding from a kind of sympathy, as the heathens imagined, for the death of Adonis, who was killed by a wild boar in the mountain out of which this stream issues. Something like this we saw actually come to pass, for the water was stained to a surprising redness; and, as we observed in travelling, had stained the sea a great way into a reddish hue." This was no doubt occasioned by a red ochre, over which the river ran with violence at this time of its increase. *Milton* works all this up in these fine lines:—

"Thammuz came next behind,
Whose annual *wound* in Lebanon allured
The Syrian damsels to lament his fate,
In amorous ditties all a summer's day;
While smooth Adonis, from his native rock,
Ran *purple* to the sea, *suffused with blood*
Of Thammuz, yearly wounded. The love tale
Infected *Sion's daughters* with like heat:
Whose wanton passions in the sacred porch
Ezekiel saw, when by the vision led,
His eye surveyed the dark idolatries
Of alienated Judah." *Par. Lost,* b. i. 446.

Tammuz signifies *hidden* or *obscure,* and hence the worship of his image was in some *secret place.*

Verse 16. *Five and twenty men*] These most probably represented the *twenty-four courses* of the *priests,* with the *high priest* for the *twenty-fifth.* This was the *Persian* worship, as their turning their faces to the east plainly shows they were worshipping the *rising sun.*

Verse 17. *They put the branch to their nose.*] This is supposed to mean some branch or branches, which they carried in succession in honour of the idol, and with which they covered their faces, or from which they inhaled a pleasant smell, the branches being odoriferous. That the heathens carried branches of trees in their sacred ceremonies is well known to all persons acquainted with classic antiquity; and it is probable that the heathen borrowed those from the use of such branches in the Jewish feast of tabernacles. There are many strange, and some filthy, interpretations given of this clause; but the former are not worth repeating, and I abominate the latter too much to submit to defile my paper with them. Probably the Brahminic *Linga* is here intended.

It really seems that at this time the Jews had incorporated every species of idolatry in their impure worship,—*Phœnician, Egyptian,* and *Persian.* I might add that some imagine the *image of jealousy* to be a personification of *idolatry* itself.

CHAPTER IX

The vision in this chapter seems intended to denote the general destruction of the inhabitants of Jerusalem, excepting a few pious individuals that were distressed at the abominations that were committed in the land; who in order to be delivered from the general calamity, were MARKED, *in allusion, perhaps, to the custom of eastern princes, who marked their servants in the forehead, or rather to the custom very frequent among the Pagan*

worshippers, of indelibly imprinting on different parts of their body the marks of their idols. To indicate, likewise, that God was soon to forsake the temple, the shechinah, or glorious symbol of his presence, is seen to remove from the inner sanctuary to the threshold or door of the temple, 1–7. ***The prophet intercedes for his people; but God, on account of the greatness of their sins, will not be entreated,*** 8–11.

A. M. 3410
B. C. 594
Ol. XLVI. 3
Anno
Tarquinii Prisci,
R. Roman., 23

HE cried also in mine ears
with a loud voice, saying,
Cause them that have charge
over the city to draw near,
even every man *with* his [a]destroying weapon
in his hand.
2 And, behold, six men came from the
way of the higher gate, [b]which lieth toward
the north, and every man [c]a slaughter weapon
in his hand; [d]and one man among them *was*
clothed with linen, with a writer's inkhorn
[e]by his side: and they went in, and stood beside the brazen altar.
3 And [f]the glory of the God of Israel was gone
up from the cherub, whereupon he was, to the
threshold of the house. And
he called to the man clothed
with linen, which *had* the
writer's inkhorn by his side;

A. M. 3410
B. C. 594
Ol. XLVI. 3
Anno
Tarquinii Prisci,
R. Roman., 23

4 And the LORD said unto him, Go through
the midst of the city, through the midst of
Jerusalem, and [g]set [h]a mark upon the foreheads of the men [i]that sigh and that cry for all
the abominations that be done in the midst
thereof.
5 And to the others he said in [k]mine hearing, Go ye after him through the city, and
smite: [l]let not your eye spare, neither have
ye pity:
6 [m]Slay [n]utterly old *and* young, both maids,

[a]Jer. xxii. 7——[b]Heb. *which is turned*——[c]Heb. *a weapon of his breaking in pieces*——[d]Lev. xvi. 4; ch. x. 6, 7; Rev. xv. 6——[e]Heb. *upon his loins*——[f]See ch. iii. 23; viii. 4; x. 4, 18; xi. 22, 23——[g]Heb. *mark a mark*

[h]Exod. xii. 7; Rev. vii. 3; ix. 4; xiii. 16, 17; xx. 4——[i]Psa. cxix. 53, 136; Jer. xiii. 17; 2 Cor. xii. 21; 2 Pet. ii 8——[k]Heb. *mine ears*——[l]Ver. 10; chap. v. 11——[m]2 Chron. xxxvi. 17——[n]Heb. *to destruction*

NOTES ON CHAP. IX

Verse 1. *Cause them that have charge over the city*] By those *six* men with destroying weapons the *Chaldeans* are represented, who had received commission to destroy the city; and when the *north* is mentioned in such cases, *Chaldea* and the *Chaldean armies* are generally intended. There appears to have been *six men* with a sort of *slaughter-bills*, and *one man* with an *inkhorn*. These may represent the *seven* counsellors of the eastern monarchs, who always saw the king's face, and knew all the secrets of the government. One of them was that *minister* who had the office of *reporting* concerning *criminals*, who carried *the book of death* and the *book of life* into the presence of the king, where the names were entered of criminals who were *destined* to *suffer*, and of those who were either considered as *innocent* or *recommended to mercy;* those of the *former* in the *book of death*, those of the *latter* in the *book of life*. This person with the inkhorn might be termed, in our phrase, the *recorder*.

Verse 2. *Stood beside the brazen altar.*] To signify that the people against whom they had their commission were, for their crimes, to be sacrificed to the demands of Divine justice.

Verse 3. *And he called to the man*] The person here who called was that who sat on the chariot of the Divine glory. See chap. i. 26.

Verse 4. *Set a mark upon the foreheads of the men that sigh*] This is in allusion to the ancient every-where-used custom of setting marks on servants and slaves, to distinguish them from others. It was also common for the worshippers of particular idols to have their idol's *mark* upon their *foreheads*, *arms*, &c. These are called *sectarian marks* to the present day among the *Hindoos* and others in India. Hence by this mark we can easily know who is a follower of *Vishnoo*, who of *Siva*, who of *Bramah*, &c. The original words, והתוית תו *vehithvitha tau*, have been translated by the Vulgate, *et signa thau*, "and mark thou tau on the foreheads," &c. St. Jerome and many others have thought that the letter *tau* was that which was ordered to be placed on the foreheads of those mourners; and Jerome says, that this Hebrew letter ת *tau* was formerly written like a *cross*. So then the people were to be *signed with the sign of the cross!* It is certain that on the ancient Samaritan coins, which are yet extant, the letter ת *tau* is in the form +, which is what we term St. *Andrew's cross*. The sense derived from this by many commentators is, that God, having ordered those penitents to be marked with this figure, which is the sign of the cross, intimated that there is no redemption nor saving of life but by the cross of Christ, and that this will avail none but the real penitent. All this is true in itself, but it is not true in respect to this place. The Hebrew words signify literally, *thou shalt make a mark*, or *sign a sign*, but give no intimation what that *mark* or *sign* was. It was intended here to be what the sprinkling of the blood of the paschal lamb on the lintels and door-posts of the Israelites was, namely, a notice to the destroying angel what house he should spare. As the whole of this matter only passed in *vision* we are bound to neither *letter*, nor any other kind of *figure*. The symbolical action teaches us that God, in general judgments, will make a distinction between the *innocent* and the *guilty*, between the *penitent* and the *hardened sinner*.

Verse 6. *Begin at my sanctuary.*] Let those who have sinned against most mercy, and most privileges, be the first victims of justice. Those who know their Lord's will, and do it not, shall be beaten with many stripes. The unfaithful

A. M. 3410
B. C. 594
Ol. XLVI. 3
Anno
Tarquinii Prisci,
R. Roman., 23

and little children, and women: but [o]come not near any man upon whom *is* the mark; and [p]begin at my sanctuary. [q]Then they began at the ancient men which *were* before the house.

7 And he said unto them, Defile the house, and fill the courts with the slain: go ye forth. And they went forth, and slew in the city.

8 And it came to pass, while they were slaying them, and I was left, that I [r]fell upon my face, and cried, and said, [s]Ah Lord GOD! wilt thou destroy all the residue of Israel in thy pouring out of thy fury upon Jerusalem?

9 Then said he unto me, The iniquity of the house of Israel and Judah *is* exceeding great, and [t]the land is [u]full of blood, and the city full of [v]perverseness: for they say, [w]The LORD hath forsaken the earth, and [x]the LORD seeth not.

10 And as for me also, mine [y]eye shall not spare, neither will I have pity, *but* [z]I will recompense their way upon their head.

11 And, behold, the man clothed with linen, which *had* the inkhorn by his side, [a]reported the matter, saying, I have done as thou hast commanded me.

[o]Rev. ix. 4——[p]Jer. xxv. 29; 1 Pet. iv. 17——[q]Chap. viii. 11, 12, 16——[r]Num. xiv. 5; xvi. 4, 22, 45; Josh. vii. 6——[s]Ch. xi. 13——[t]2 Kings xxi. 16; chap. viii. 17

[u]Heb. *filled with*——[v]Or, *wresting* of judgment [w]Ch. viii. 12——[x]Psa. x. 11; Isa. xxix. 15——[y]Ch. v. 11. vii. 4; viii. 18——[z]Ch. xi. 21——[a]Heb. *returned the word*

members of Christ's church will be first visited and most punished. But let not those who belong to the *synagogue of Satan* exult in this; for if judgment begin at the house of God, what will the end be of them who obey not the Gospel! However, the truly *penitent* of all descriptions in such cases shall be safe. The command of God is, "Set a mark on all them that sigh and cry;" and his command to the destroyers is, "Come not near any man on whom is the mark."

Verse 7. *Defile the house*] A dreadful sentence, Let it be polluted, I will no more dwell in it; I now utterly forsake it.

Verse 8. *Wilt thou destroy all the residue of Israel, in thy pouring out of thy fury upon Jerusalem?*] These destroyers had slain the *seventy* elders, the *twenty-five* adorers of the sun, and the women that mourned for Tammuz; and on seeing this slaughter the prophet fell on his face, and began to make intercession.

Verse 9. *For they say, The Lord hath forsaken the earth*] את הארץ *eth haarets,* "this land." He has no more place in Israel; he has quite abandoned it; he neither sees nor cares, and he can be no longer the object of worship to any man in Israel. This seems to be the meaning; and God highly resents it, because it was bringing him on a level with idols and provincial deities, who had, according to supposition, regency only in some one place.

Verse 10. *Mine eye shall not spare*] They say, *the Lord seeth not:* this is false; I have seen all their iniquities, and do see all their abominations; and I will bring deserved judgment upon them, and then that eye which now sees will neither pity nor spare.

Verse 11. *I have done as thou hast commanded me.*] Angels and men must all give account of their conduct to God; for although he is every where, and his eye sees all things, yet they must personally account for all that they have done. *I have done as thou hast commanded me.* The penitents are all signed; the penitents are all safe. This is good news for them that mourn.

CHAPTER X

The same august vision which appeared to the prophet at first, is repeated here; and coals of fire are scattered over the city to intimate that it was to be burned. The symbol of the Divine presence is likewise represented as removing farther and farther from the temple, to signify that God's protection was about to be withdrawn from it, 1–22. It may not be improper to remark, that whatever is particularly intended by the cherubim, wheels, firmament, throne, &c., described in this and the first chapter, the prophet several times informs us (chap. i. 28; iii. 25; viii. 4; x. 4, 18,) *that his vision was a manifestation or similitude of the* GLORY *of Jehovah; or, in other words, consisted of a set of hieroglyphics by which this glory was in some measure represented. It is also worthy of observation, that the faces of the living creatures, of which we have an account in the* fourth *chapter of the Apocalypse, are precisely the same with those of Ezekiel's cherubim; and we may readily collect, as Mr. Mede remarks, the quarter of the heavens in which each cherub was situated in reference to the other three, from the consideration that as Ezekiel saw the vision proceeding from the* NORTH, (see chap. i. 4, 10,) *the human face of the cherubim was towards him, or the* south; *on his right hand, or the* east, *was the face of a lion; on his left hand, or the* west, *the face of an ox; and towards the* north, *the face of an eagle.*

A. M. 3410
B. C. 594
Ol. XLVI. 3
Anno
Tarquinii Prisci,
R. Roman., 23

THEN I looked, and, behold, in the [a]firmament that was above the head of the cherubims there appeared over them as it were a sapphire stone, as the appearance of the likeness of a throne.

2 [b]And he spake unto the man clothed with linen, and said, Go in between the wheels, even under the cherub, and fill [c]thine hand with [d]coals of fire from between the cherubims, and [e]scatter *them* over the city. And he went in my sight.

3 Now the cherubims stood on the right side of the house, when the man went in; and the cloud filled the inner court.

4 [f]Then the glory of the LORD [g]went up from the cherub, *and stood* over the threshold of the house; and [h]the house was filled with the cloud, and the court was full of the brightness of the LORD's glory.

5 And the [i]sound of the cherubims' wings was heard *even* to the outer court, as [k]the voice of the Almighty God when he speaketh.

6 And it came to pass, *that* when he had commanded the man clothed with linen, saying, Take fire from between the wheels, from between the cherubims; then he went in, and stood beside the wheels.

7 And *one* cherub [l]stretched forth his hand from between the cherubims unto the fire that *was* between the cherubims, and took *thereof*, and put *it* into the hands of *him that was* clothed with linen: who took *it*, and went out.

8 [m]And there appeared in the cherubims, the form of a man's hand under their wings.

9 [n]And when I looked, behold the four wheels by the cherubims, one wheel by one cherub, and another wheel by another cherub: and the appearance of the wheels *was* as the colour of a [o]beryl stone.

10 And *as for* their appearances, they four had one likeness, as if a wheel had been in the midst of a wheel.

[a]Ch. i. 22, 26——[b]Ch. ix. 2, 3——[c]Heb. *the hollow of thine hand*——[d]Ch. i. 13——[e]See Rev. viii. 5——[f]See ver. 18; chap. i. 28; ix. 3——[g]Heb. *was lifted up*

[h]1 Kings viii. 10, 11; chap. xliii. 5——[i]Chap. i. 24 [k]Psa. xxix. 3, &c.——[l]Heb. *sent forth*——[m]Chap. i. 8; ver. 21——[n]Chap. i. 15——[o]Chap. i. 16

NOTES ON CHAP. X

Verse 1. *As it were a sapphire stone*] See the note on chap. i. 22, 26. The *chariot*, here mentioned by the prophet, was precisely the same as that which he saw at the river *Chebar*, as himself tells us, ver. 15, of which see the description in chap. i.

Verse 2. *Coals of fire*] These were to signify the burning of the city by the Chaldeans. It seems that the space between the *four* wheels, which was all on fire, was that from which those coals were taken.

Verse 3. *On the right side of the house*] The right hand always marked the *south* among the Hebrews.

Verse 4. *The glory of the Lord went up*] This is repeated from chap. ix. 3.

The house was filled with the cloud] This is a fact similar to what occurred frequently at the *tabernacle* in the wilderness, and in the *dedication of the temple* by Solomon. What is mentioned here was the *Divine shechinah*, the symbolical representation of the majesty of God.

Verse 5. *As the voice of the Almighty God*] That is, as *thunder;* for this was called the *voice of God.*

Verse 8. *The form of a man's hand under their wings.*] I am still of opinion that the *hands* and *wings* were not distinct. The *arms* were *feathered like wings*, and the *hand* terminated the arm; but as the long front feathers of the wings would extend much beyond the fingers, hence the *hands* would appear to *be under the wings*. See on chap. i. 8. The *human hand* might be intended to show that God helps and punishes *man* by *man;* and that, in the general operations of his providence, he makes use of *human agency.*

Verse 9. *The colour of a beryl stone.*] אבן תרשיש *eben Tarshish*, "the stone of Tarshish." The *Vulgate* translates it *chrysolith; Symmachus*, the *jacinct;* the *Septuagint*, the *carbuncle*. In the parallel place, chap. i. 16, it is כעין תרשיש *keeyn Tarshish*, "like the eye of Tarshish;" i. e., the *colour* of tarshish, or the stone so called, which the *Vulgate* translates *visio maris*, "like the sea," i. e., *azure*. The *beryl* is a gem of a *green* colour, passing from one side into *blue*, on the other side into *yellow*. The *chrysolith* is also *green*, what is called *pistachio green;* but the *chrysolith* of the ancients was our *topaz*, which is of a fine *wine yellow*. The *beryl*, or *chrysolith*, is most likely what is here meant by *tarshish*. One name among the ancients served for several kinds of gems that were nearly of the *same colour*. The moderns go more by *chemical characters* than by *colour*.

Verse 10. *A wheel had been in the midst of a wheel.*] It is difficult to comprehend this description. It is generally supposed to mean one wheel within another, cutting each other at right angles. This, in my opinion, will not account for the *motions* attributed to these wheels; nor can I see how, on this supposition, they could have any motion; for if one was moved on its axis, the other must be dragged contrary to its axis. I have conjectured it rather to mean a wheel within a wheel, or a wheel with two rims, working on the same axis. See on chap. i. 16-18. It is however no matter of *faith;* and the reader may judge as he thinks proper. For other matters relative to this *chariot, wheels, cherubim, wings*, &c., I

A. M. 3410
B. C. 594
Ol. XLVI. 3
Anno
Tarquinii Prisci,
R. Roman., 23

11 [p]When they went, they
went upon their four sides;
they turned not as they went,
but to the place whither the
head looked they followed it; they turned not
as they went.
12 And their whole [q]body, and their backs,
and their hands, and their wings, and [r]the
wheels, *were* full of eyes round about, *even*
the wheels that they four had.
13 As for the wheels, [s]it was cried unto them
in my hearing, O wheel.
14 [t]And every one had four faces: the first
face *was* the face of a cherub, and the second
face *was* the face of a man, and the third the
face of a lion, and the fourth the face of an
eagle.
15 And the cherubims were lifted up. This
is [u]the living creature that I saw by the river
of Chebar.
16 [v]And when the cherubims went, the
wheels went by them: and when the cherubims
lifted up their wings to mount up from the
earth, the same wheels also turned not from
beside them.
17 [w]When they stood, *these*
stood; and when they were
lifted up, *these* lifted up
themselves *also:* for the spirit
[x]of the living creature *was* in them.
18 Then [y]the glory of the LORD [z]departed
from off the threshold of the house, and stood
over the cherubims.
19 And [a]the cherubims lifted up their
wings, and mounted up from the earth in
my sight: when they went out, the wheels
also *were* beside them, and *every one* stood
at the door of the east gate of the LORD'S
house; and the glory of the God of Israel
was over them above.
20 [b]This *is* the living creature that I saw
under the God of Israel [c]by the river of Chebar;
and I knew that they *were* the cherubims.
21 [d]Every one had four faces apiece, and
every one four wings; [e]and the likeness of
the hands of a man *was* under their wings.
22 And [f]the likeness of their faces *was* the
same faces which I saw by the river of Chebar,
their appearances and themselves: [g]they went
every one straight forward.

[p]Ch. i. 17——[q]Heb. *flesh*——[r]Ch. i. 18——[s]Or, *they were called in my hearing, wheel,* or, *galgal*——[t]Ch. i. 6, 10——[u]Ch. i. 5——[v]Ch. i. 19——[w]Ch. i. 12, 20, 21

[x]Or, *of life*——[y]Ver. 4——[z]Hos. ix. 12——[a]Ch. xi. 22——[b]Ch. i. 22; ver. 15——[c]Ch. i. 1——[d]Ch. i. 6; ver. 14——[e]Chap. i. 8; ver. 8——[f]Chap. i. 10——[g]Chap. i. 12

must refer to the notes on the *first* chapter. And perhaps from the whole of this vision and its difficulties, he will see the propriety of the council of rabbins ordering Rabbi Ananias *three hundred* barrels of oil to light his lamp during the time it would be necessary for him to employ in explaining this one vision.

Verse 13. *As for the wheels, it was cried unto them—O wheel.*] Never was there a more unfortunate and unmeaning translation. The word הגלגל *haggalgal*, may signify, simply, *the roller*, or *a chariot*, or *roll on*, or *the swift roller.* **And he clepide ilke wheelis volible, or turninge about.** Old MS. Bible. Any of these will do: "and as to the wheels," לאופנים *laophannim*, "they were called in my hearing" הגלגל *haggalgal*, "the chariot." The gentleman who took for his text "O wheel!" and made God's decree of eternal predestination out of it, must have borrowed some of Rabbi Ananias's *three hundred* barrels of oil! But such working of God's word cannot be too severely reprehended.

As these wheels are supposed to represent Divine *Providence*, bringing about the *designs* of the Most High, how like is the above הגלגל *haggalgal*, taken as a verb, "roll on," to those words of Virgil in his Pollio:—

Talia sæcla, suis dixerunt, *currite*, fusis,
Concordes stabili fatorum numine Parcæ.

"The Fates, when they this happy web have spun,
Shall bless the sacred clue, and bid it *swiftly run.*"

Verse 14. *The first*—was *the face of a cherub*] In chap. i. 10, this is called the "face of an ox;" here, the "face of a cherub:" hence, a *cherub* was in the likeness of an *ox*, at least, as to its *head.* כרוב *kerub* never occurs as a verb; and its meaning cannot be precisely ascertained. *Parkhurst* thinks the כ *caph* to be here the note of *similitude;* and then translates כ *ke*, "like," רב *rab* or רוב *rob*, "the mighty one;" and, in consequence, makes the *cherubim* an emblem of the *Holy Trinity.* See his *lengthy* Dissertation under כרב in his Hebrew and English Lexicon.

Verse 20. *And I knew that they* were *the cherubims.*] This formation of the plural is quite improper. In general, Hebrew nouns of the masculine gender end in ים *im*, in the plural; the *s*, therefore, should never be added to such. *Cherub* is singular; *cherubim* is plural. The *s* should be uniformly expunged.

I have already referred to the *end of this chapter* for farther information relative to this glorious chariot of Jehovah; but I must say that I have met with nothing on the subject that entirely satisfies myself. In the preceding notes I have endeavoured to make the literal meaning as plain as possible; and have occasionally given some intimations relative to the *general design* of this sublime vision. My readers are already apprised that I do not like *conjectures* on *Divine things;* many points, that had originally no other origin, are now incorporated with *creeds* of which it is deemed sinful to doubt. Because some learned and pious men have written to prove that this symbolical compound figure is a representation of the *Holy Trinity;* therefore, the sentiment now passes current. Now this is not *proved;* and I suppose never can be proved. The continuator of the *Historical Discourses of Saurin* has made some sensible remarks on the subject of this vision; and these I shall lay here before the intelligent reader. They deserve attention.

This intelligent writer observes: "For the right interpretation of this vision, the following rules should be laid down:—

"The *first* rule is this:—An explanation, which accounts for all the parts contained in the vision, is much more probable than those which explain only one part.

"The *second* is this:—An explanation which is conformable to the present circumstances of the prophet, and of the people to whom he is sent, as well as to the nature of the things which he is called upon to say to them, is incomparably more probable than those explanations which go in quest of past or future events, which have no connexion with the immediate circumstances of the prophet, nor with the end of his mission. These rules, which appear incontestable, being laid down, we observe, that their opinion who think that God here draws out a plan of the government of his providence, applied to the present state of the Jews, accounts for all that Ezekiel saw; and that in a manner which refers to the end of the prophet's mission, and all that he had to say to this rebellious people. Why wish God to represent to his prophet the future state of the Christian Church, which was not to be founded till after a series of time, rather than the state of the Jewish Church, and the chastisements which hung over the heads of that hardened people? The people having revolted from God, and persevering obstinately in that revolt, notwithstanding the menaces of the prophet, it was proper to show to Ezekiel, in order that he might declare it to the rebellious, that Providence had its eyes open to all that had been done, all that had hitherto happened, and that it had seized upon the rod to smite. The people imagined, but too much according to the errors of infidelity, that God saw every thing with indifference and had given the world up to chance. It was necessary, therefore, to divest them of these fatal prejudices; and to teach them that the Supreme Being did not behold with the same eye order and disorder, contempt of his laws and submission to his will; and that all the revolutions of states are directed by a superior intelligence, which cannot be imposed upon. The Jewish people imagined but too much that the prophets exaggerated when they threatened them with the severest chastisements. They repeated with emphasis and complacency the promises of God made to the patriarchs; that their posterity should not only be more numerous than the stars of heaven, and the sand which covers the sea-shore; but that it should subsist for ever and ever. God had declared to Abraham, 'I will establish my covenant between me and thee, and thy seed after thee, in their generations, for an everlasting covenant, to be a God unto thee and thy seed after thee,' Gen. xvii. 7. It was proper, therefore, to show this stiff-necked people that the threatenings of God and his promises were not contradictory. That the people, conformable to the promises given by God to the patriarchs, should not be destroyed; but that, notwithstanding, they should be severely chastised, to correct them for their propensity to idolatry, and their scandalous irregularities.

"These suppositions, which are reasonable, being granted, we shall have no difficulty to perceive the sense of this celebrated vision. We shall not follow the order observed by Ezekiel, in the description of what he saw; he raises himself from the nearest to the most distant objects, going back from effects to their general cause. We will begin with the First Cause which gives motion to all that happens, traces out the plan, and procures the execution, according to the rules of his ineffable wisdom, and agreeably to the nature of those creatures which are the object of his agency. Next, we will proceed to consider the effects of this universal Providence, and the intelligent secondary causes which he frequently employs in the administration of the government of the universe.

" 'Ezekiel saw a firmament which was above the heads of the animals; there was the resemblance of a throne like a sapphire stone; and over the resemblance of the throne, there was, as it were, the resemblance of a man.' This vast transparent *firmament* represents to us the heaven, the peculiar residence of the Lord of the earth; and where he hath established the throne of his empire. This 'appearance of a man' was the emblem of Providence or God; considered as taking care of all the creatures whom he hath made. Man is the symbol of intelligence. The mind of man, with respect to his knowledge and wisdom, is a weak sketch of that mind which knows all things, and whose wisdom is unbounded. And yet, of all sublunary beings, there is none that approaches so near to the Divine nature as man. Under this emblem also it is that God, considered as seeing all things, and directing all, would be represented. This resemblance of man was *seated* upon a *throne*, to show that God governs all things as Lord, and that without agitation and without labour.

"The *shining metal*, and the *fire* which surrounded him who sat on the throne, were the symbol of his glory and his judgments, which are poured upon the wicked as a fire which nothing can withstand; agreeably to Isaiah, chap. xxxiii. 14.

"The Jews acknowledged that there was a Providence which governs the whole universe with infinite wisdom. The psalmist gives us a description of it, equally just and pathetic, in Psa. civ. 27, &c. Christians, no less than Jews, admit this important truth; and the Gospel establishes it no less strongly than the law. See Matt. vi. 26; x. 29, 30. To raise the mind of the prophet up to the first Mover of those events which strike and admonish us in all the revolutions which happen to individuals, families, and states, God shows him *four wheels* above the firmament, over which the emblem of Providence was placed on a throne. These wheels are a symbol of those perpetual revolutions, which are observed in the earth; and which, by turns, lift up and abase individuals and nations. They are of a prodigious *height*, to show that man cannot fathom or know all that is great, wonderful, and astonishing, in the ways of Providence. See Job xi. 7, 8; Rom. xi.

33, 34; Isa. lv. 8, 9. These wheels move themselves every way, and are full of eyes in the vast circle of their felloes. This shows, that all which God does he effects without pain; and that the eye of his wisdom ordereth all events. The wheels did not move of themselves; but they followed the impulse of the four living creatures; 'when the living creatures went, they went.' This shows that, in the government of the world, all the living creatures are subject to Providence; and that God subordinates the creatures one to another. He directs what those holy intelligences ought to do, who serve him as ministers, and are here represented by the four animals. And these intelligences, enlightened and supported by the Supreme Wisdom, contribute, as far as is suitable, to all that happens to mankind. The angels whom Ezekiel saw were in number *four*, in reference to the *four* cardinal points of the world; to show that their ministry extends every where, and that there is no part of the universe which the Providence of God does not govern in an immediate manner, or by the means of his ministers. The extraordinary shape of these angels, which appeared to the prophet in vision, is symbolical; for it is not to be supposed that those heavenly ministers are really thus formed. The 'four faces, wings, and arms of a man,' denote the sublime qualities of these immediate ministers of the Deity; qualities entirely essential to fill up the extent of their duty. The face of a *man* denotes their intelligence; of a *lion*, their intrepid courage; of an *ox*, their patience and perseverance in labour; and of an *eagle*, their great penetration, their sublime sight into heavenly things, and their readiness to rise up into all that is great and Divine. The 'wings being stretched out,' signifies that they are always ready to set forward, and run with rapidity wherever the commands of their great Master call them. The 'wings bent down,' are a symbol of that profound respect in which these heavenly ministers stand before the Lord of the universe. Under the wings there were men's arms, to show that zeal produces application and labour. Labour, without zeal, can never be supported; and zeal, without application, is only a hypocritical ardour, which amounts to nothing with that supreme Master who requires sincere homage from those who serve him. If God chose to make known to Ezekiel that his providence extends to all things, and that even in this life it often takes up the rod to chastise nations and individuals, he would also show beforehand that he wished not the destruction of the Jewish people, whom he was about to visit in his anger, but only its correction and amendment. This is signified by the 'precious metal,' which the prophet found unmelted in the midst of the fiery cloud. This cloud of fire, urged on by a whirlwind, and involving on all sides the metal, represented the judgments of God which were about to fall upon this rebellious nation, not to destroy, but to humble and purify it. Nothing is more proper than afflictions to bring men back to their duty. As fire purifies metals, so the paternal chastisements of God have a tendency to purify the soul and heart, if the man be not entirely incorrigible. The people upon whom God was about to pour the vials of his anger, were not worthy of his lenity. But that great God, who is firm in his promises, remembers the covenant of peace he had made with the patriarchs. This covenant is made sensible to the prophet under the image of a *rainbow*, which was round about him who appeared upon the throne. Every one knows, that this splendid phenomenon, which seems to join heaven and earth together, was given to Noah and his posterity as a symbol of the covenant which God then made with mankind, and by which he declared to them that the earth should undergo a deluge no more. Thus, the Pagans considered the *Iris* as the messenger of the gods. See *Virgil, Æn.* lib. iv. ver. 694. But whereas the rainbow to the Jews was a symbol of peace, the *Iris* of the Pagans was a messenger of trouble. On the sight of this bow, the symbol of grace, Ezekiel was to be encouraged; and persuaded that his people were not threatened with an utter destruction. The event fully justified all that the prophet had contemplated, with surprise, in this enigmatical picture. The Chaldeans, the rod of the Lord's just severity, ravaged Judea; the people were carried away captive; they groaned for *seventy* years in a foreign land; but they were protected in a miraculous manner against the bloody designs of the cruel Haman; and at length, favoured with various decrees of the kings of Persia, they had permission, not only to return to their own country, but also to rebuild Jerusalem and the temple." See Dr. *Dodd's* notes on this place.

CHAPTER XI

This chapter denounces the judgments of God against those wicked persons who remained in Jerusalem, and made a mock of the types and predictions of the prophets, 1–13; *compare* ver. 3 *with* Jer. i. 13. *God promises to favour those who were gone into captivity, and intimates their restoration from the Babylonish yoke,* 14–21. *Then the shechinah, or symbol of the Divine Presence, is represented forsaking the city, as in the foregoing chapter it did the temple,* 22, 23; *and the prophet returns in vision to the place from which he set out,* (chap. viii. 1, &c.,) *in order to communicate his instructions to his brethren of the captivity,* 24, 25.

A. M. 3410
B. C. 594
Ol. XLVI. 3
Anno
Tarquinii Prisci,
R. Roman., 23

MOREOVER [a]the spirit lifted me up, and brought me unto [b]the east gate of the LORD's house, which looketh eastward: and behold [c]at the door of the gate five and

[a]Chap. iii. 12, 14; viii. 3; ver. 24 — [b]Chap. x. 19 — [c]See chap. viii. 16

NOTES ON CHAP. XI

Verse 1. *At the door of the gate five and twenty men*] The same persons, no doubt, who appear, chap. viii. 16, worshipping the sun.

Jaazaniah the son of Azur] In chap. viii. 16, we find a *Jaazaniah* the son of *Shaphan*. If *Shaphan* was also called *Azur*, they may be the same person. But it is most likely that

A. M. 3410
B. C. 594
Ol. XLVI. 3
Anno
Tarquinii Prisci,
R. Roman., 23

twenty men; among whom I
saw Jaazaniah the son of
Azur, and Pelatiah the son of
Benaiah, princes of the people.
2 Then said he unto me, Son of man, these
are the men that devise mischief, and give
wicked counsel in this city:
3 Which say, [d]*It is* not [e]near; let us build
houses: [f]this *city is* the caldron, and we *be*
the flesh.
4 Therefore prophesy against them, prophesy, O son of man.
5 And [g]the Spirit of the LORD fell upon me,
and said unto me, Speak; Thus saith the
LORD; Thus have ye said, O house of Israel:
for I know the things that come into your
mind, *every one of* them.
6 [h]Ye have multiplied your slain in this
city, and ye have filled the streets thereof
with the slain.
7 Therefore thus saith the Lord GOD; [i]Your
slain whom ye have laid in the midst of it,
they *are* the flesh, and this *city is* the caldron:
[k]but I will bring you forth out of the midst
of it.
8 Ye have feared the sword, and I will bring
a sword upon you, saith the Lord GOD.
9 And I will bring you out of the midst
thereof, and deliver you into the hands of
strangers, and [l]will execute judgments among
you.
10 [m]Ye shall fall by the sword; I will judge
you in [n]the border of Israel;
[o]and ye shall know that I *am*
the LORD.
11 [p]This *city* shall not be
your caldron, neither shall ye be the flesh in
the midst thereof; *but* I will judge you in the
border of Israel:
12 And [q]ye shall know that I *am* the LORD:
[r]for ye have not walked in my statutes, neither executed my judgments, but [s]have done
after the manners of the heathen that *are*
round about you.
13 And it came to pass, when I prophesied,
that [t]Pelatiah the son of Benaiah died. Then
[u]fell I down upon my face, and cried with a
loud voice, and said, Ah, Lord GOD! wilt thou
make a full end of the remnant of Israel?
14 Again the word of the LORD came unto
me, saying,
15 Son of man, thy brethren, *even* thy
brethren, the men of thy kindred, and all the
house of Israel wholly, *are* they unto whom
the inhabitants of Jerusalem have said, Get
you far from the LORD: unto us is this land
given in possession.
16 Therefore say, Thus saith the Lord GOD;
Although I have cast them far off among the
heathen, and although I have scattered them
among the countries, [v]yet will I be to them
as a little sanctuary in the countries where
they shall come.
17 Therefore say, Thus saith the Lord

A. M. 3410
B. C. 594
Ol. XLVI. 3
Anno
Tarquinii Prisci,
R. Roman., 23

[d]Or, It is *not* for us *to build houses near*——[e]Ch. xii. 22, 27; 2 Pet. iii. 4——[f]See Jer. i. 13; ch. xxiv. 3, &c. [g]Ch. ii. 2; iii. 24——[h]Ch. vii. 23; xxii. 3, 4——[i]Ch. xxiv. 3, 6, 10, 11; Mic. iii. 3——[k]Ver. 9——[l]Ch. v. 8——[m]2 Kings xxv. 19, 20, 21; Jer. xxxix. 6; lii. 10

[n]1 Kings viii. 65; 2 Kings xiv. 25——[o]Psa. ix. 16; ch. vi. 7; xiii. 9, 14, 21, 23——[p]See ver. 3——[q]Ver. 10 [r]Or, *which have not walked*——[s]Lev. xviii. 3, 24, &c.; Deut. xii. 30, 31; ch. viii. 10, 14, 16——[t]Ver. 1; Acts v. 5 [u]Chap. ix. 8——[v]Psa. xc. 1; xci. 9; Isa. viii. 14

there were two of this name, and both chiefs among the people.

Verse 3. It is *not near*] That is, the threatened invasion.

This city is *the caldron, and we* be *the flesh.*] See the vision of the *seething pot*, Jer. i. 13. These infidels seem to say: "We will run all risks, we will abide in the city. Though it be the *caldron*, and we the *flesh*, yet we will share its fate: if it perish, we will perish with it." Or they may allude to the above prediction of Jeremiah, in order to ridicule it: "We were to have been *boiled* long ago: but the fulfilment of that prediction is not near yet."

Verse 7. *Your slain—they* are *the flesh*] Jerusalem is the *caldron*, and those who have been slain in it, they are the flesh; and though ye purpose to stay and share its fate, ye shall not be permitted to do so; ye shall be carried into captivity.

Verse 9. *And deliver you into the hands of strangers*] This seems to refer chiefly to Zedekiah and his family.

Verse 11. *I will judge you in the border of Israel.*] Though *Riblah* was in Syria, yet it was on the very *frontiers* of Israel; and it was here that Zedekiah's sons were slain, and his own eyes put out.

Verse 13. *Pelatiah the son of Benaiah died.*] Most probably he was struck dead the very hour in which Ezekiel prophesied against him. His death appears to have resembled that of Ananias and Sapphira, Acts v. 1, &c.

Verse 15. *Get you far from the Lord*] These are the words of the inhabitants of Jerusalem, against those of Israel who had been carried away to Babylon with Jeconiah. *Go ye far from the Lord:* but as for us, the land of Israel is given to us for a possession; *we* shall never be removed from it, and *they* shall never return to it.

Verse 16. *Yet will I be to them as a little*

A. M. 3410
B. C. 594
Ol. XLVI. 3
Anno
Tarquinii Prisci,
R. Roman., 23

GOD; I will even gather you
from the people, and assemble
you out of the countries where
ye have been scattered, and I
will give you the land of Israel.
18 And they shall come thither, and [x]they
shall take away all the detestable things
thereof and all the abominations thereof from
thence.
19 And [y]I will give them one heart, and I
will put [z]a new spirit within you; and I will
take [a]the stony heart out of their flesh, and
will give them a heart of flesh:
20 [b]That they may walk in my statutes,
and keep mine ordinances, and do them:
[c]and they shall be my people, and I will be
their God.
21 But *as for them* whose heart walketh
after the heart of their detestable things and their abominations, [d]I will recompense their
way upon their own heads,
saith the Lord GOD.
22 Then did the cherubims [e]lift up their
wings, and the wheels beside them; and the
glory of the God of Israel *was* over them above.
23 And [f]the glory of the LORD went up
from the midst of the city, and stood [g]upon
the mountain [h]which *is* on the east side of
the city.
24 Afterwards [i]the spirit took me up, and
brought me in a vision by the Spirit of God
into Chaldea, to them of the captivity. So
the vision that I had seen went up from me.
25 Then I spake unto them of the captivity
all the things that the LORD had showed me.

[w]Jer. xxiv. 5; chap. xxviii. 25; xxxiv. 13; xxxvi. 24 —— [x]Chap. xxxvii. 23 —— [y]Jer. xxxii. 39; chap. xxxvi. 26, 27; see Zeph. iii. 9 —— [z]Psa. li. 10; Jer. xxxi. 33; xxxii. 39; chap. xviii. 31 —— [a]Zech. vii. 12

[b]Psa. cv. 45 —— [c]Jer. xxiv. 7; ch. xiv. 11; xxxvi. 28; xxxvii. 27 —— [d]Chap. ix. 10; xxii. 31 —— [e]Chap. i. 19; x. 19 —— [f]Chap. viii. 4; ix. 3; x. 4, 18; xliii. 4 —— [g]See Zech. xiv. 4 —— [h]Chap. xliii. 2 —— [i]Chap. viii. 3

sanctuary] Though thus exiled from their own land, yet not forgotten by their God. While in their captivity, I will dispense many blessings to them; and I will restore them to their own land, ver. 17, from which they shall put away all idolatry, ver. 18.

Verse 19. *And I will give them one heart*] A whole system of *renewed affections.*

And I will put a new spirit within you] To direct and influence these new affections.

And I will take the stony heart out of their flesh] That which would not receive the impressions of my Spirit.

And will give them a heart of flesh] One that is capable of receiving and retaining these impressions.

Verse 20. *That they may walk in my statutes*] The holiness of their lives shall prove the work of God upon their hearts. Then it shall appear that *I am their God,* because I have done such things *in* them and *for* them; and their *holy conduct* shall show that they are *my people.* See on chap. xxxvi. 25, &c.

Verse 21. *But* as for them *whose heart walketh*] Them whose affections are attached to idolatry, they shall have such reward as their idols can give them, and such a recompense as Divine justice shall award them.

Verse 23. *The glory of the Lord went up from the midst of the city*] This vision is no mean proof of the *long-suffering of God.* He did not abandon this people *all at once;* he departed by *little and little.* FIRST, he left the *temple.* SECONDLY, he stopped a little at the gate of the city. THIRDLY, he departed entirely from the city and went to the *Mount of Olives,* which lay on the *east* side of the city. Having tarried there for some time to see if they would repent and turn to him,—FOURTHLY, he departed to *heaven.* The vision being now concluded, the prophet is taken away by the Spirit of God into Chaldea, and there announces to the captive Israelites what God had showed him in the preceding visions, and the good that he had spoken concerning them; who at first did not seem to profit much by them, which the prophet severely reproves.

CHAPTER XII

The prophet proceeds, by a variety of types and parables, to convince those of the captivity that their brethren who were left behind to sustain the miseries of a siege and the insults of a conqueror, would be in a much worse condition than they who were already settled in a foreign land. In the beginning of this chapter he foretells the approaching captivity of Judah by action instead of words, 1–7. He predicts particularly the flight, capture, captivity, and sufferings of Zedekiah and his followers, 8–16, compared with Jer. lii. 11. *He is to eat his food with trembling and signs of terror, as an emblem of the consternation of the Jews when surrounded by their enemies, 17–20; and then he answers the objections and bywords of scoffers and infidels, who either disbelieved his threatenings, or supposed the accomplishment of them very distant, 21–28. Josephus* (Antiq. xi. 10) *tells us that Zedekiah thought the prophecy of Ezekiel in the* thirteenth *verse inconsistent with that of Jeremiah,* (chap. xxxiv. 3,) *and resolved to believe neither. Both, however, were literally fulfilled; and the event convinced him that they were not irreconcilable. Thus, blinded by infidelity, sinners rush on to that destruction against which they are sufficiently warned.*

A. M. 3410
B. C. 594
Ol. XLVI. 3
Anno
Tarquinii Prisci,
R. Roman., 23

THE word of the LORD also came unto me, saying,

2 Son of man, thou dwellest in the midst of [a]a rebellious house, which [b]have eyes to see, and see not; they have ears to hear, and hear not: [c]for they *are* a rebellious house.

3 Therefore, thou son of man, prepare thee [d]stuff for removing, and remove by day in their sight; and thou shalt remove from thy place to another place in their sight: it may be they will consider, though they *be* a rebellious house.

4 Then shalt thou bring forth thy stuff by day in their sight, as stuff for removing: and thou shalt go forth at even in their sight, [e]as they that go forth into captivity.

5 [f]Dig thou through the wall in their sight, and carry out thereby.

6 In their sight shalt thou bear *it* upon *thy* shoulders, *and* carry *it* forth in the twilight: thou shalt cover thy face, that thou see not the ground: [g]for I have set thee *for* a sign unto the house of Israel.

7 And I did so as I was commanded: I brought forth my stuff by day, as stuff for captivity, and in the even I [h]digged through the wall with mine hand; I brought *it* forth in the twilight, *and* I bare *it* upon *my* shoulder in their sight.

8 And in the morning came the word of the LORD unto me, saying,

A. M. 3410
B. C. 594
Ol. XLVI. 3
Anno
Tarquinii Prisci,
R. Roman., 23

9 Son of man, hath not the house of Israel, [i]the rebellious house, said unto thee, [k]What doest thou?

10 Say thou unto them, Thus saith the Lord GOD; This [l]burden *concerneth* the prince in Jerusalem, and all the house of Israel that *are* among them.

11 Say, [m]I *am* your sign: like as I have done, so shall it be done unto them: [n]they[o] shall remove *and* go into captivity.

12 And [p]the prince that *is* among them shall bear upon *his* shoulder in the twilight, and shall go forth; they shall dig through the wall to carry out thereby: he shall cover his face, that he see not the ground with *his* eyes.

13 My [q]net also will I spread upon him, and he shall be taken in my snare: and [r]I will bring him to Babylon *to* the land of the Chaldeans; yet shall he not see it, though he shall die there.

14 And [s]I will scatter toward every wind all that *are* about him to help him, and all his bands; and [t]I will draw out the sword after them.

15 [u]And they shall know that I *am* the LORD, when I shall scatter them among the nations, and disperse them in the countries.

[a]Chap. ii. 3, 6, 7, 8; iii. 26, 27——[b]Isa. vi. 9; xlii. 20; Jer. v. 21; Matt. xiii. 13, 14——[c]Chap. ii. 5——[d]Or, *instruments*——[e]Heb. *as the goings forth of captivity* [f]Heb. *Dig for thee*——[g]Isa. viii. 18; chap. iv. 3; xxiv. 24; ver. 11——[h]Heb. *digged for me*——[i]Chap. ii. 5——[k]Ch. xvii. 12; xxiv. 19——[l]Mal. i. 1

[m]Ver. 6——[n]Heb. *by removing go into captivity*——[o]2 Kings xxv. 4, 5, 7——[p]Jer. xxxix. 4——[q]Job xix. 6; Lam. i. 13; Jer. lii. 9; chap. xvii. 20——[r]2 Kings xxv. 7; Jer. lii. 11; chap. xvii. 16——[s]2 Kings xxv. 4, 5; chap. v. 10——[t]Chap. v. 2, 12——[u]Psa. ix. 16; chap. vi. 7, 14; xi. 10; ver. 16, 20

NOTES ON CHAP. XII

Verse 2. *Which have eyes to see, and see not*] It is not want of *grace* that brings them to destruction. *They have eyes to see*, but they will not *use* them. No man is lost because he had not *sufficient grace to save him*, but because he abused that grace.

Verse 3. *Prepare thee stuff for removing*] Get carriages to transport thy goods to another place; signifying by this the *captivity* that was at hand.

Verse 5. *Dig thou through the wall*] This refers to the manner in which Zedekiah and his family would escape from the city. They escaped by night through a *breach in the wall*. See Jer. xxxix. 2-4; and 2 Kings xxv. 4.

Verse 6. *Thou shalt cover thy face, that thou see not the ground*] Referring to the blinding of Zedekiah: even the *covering of the face* might be intended to signify that in this way Zedekiah should be carried to Babylon *on men's shoulders* in some sort of *palanquin*, with a *cloth tied over his eyes*, because of the recent wounds made by extracting them. All the prophecies from this to the *twentieth* chapter are supposed to have been delivered in the *sixth* year of Zedekiah, *five* years before the taking of Jerusalem. How accurate the prediction! and how exactly fulfilled!

Verse 10. *This burden*] This prediction concerning the *prince*. By this I point out the capture, misery, and ruin of *Zedekiah*.

Verse 13. *I will bring him to Babylon—yet shall he not see it*] Because Nebuchadnezzar caused him to have his eyes put out at *Riblah*. To Babylon he was carried in his blind state, and there he died. In saying, *My net also will I spread upon him*, there is probably a reference to an ancient manner of fighting. One, who was called the *retiarius*, had a small casting net, which if he could throw over his antagonist's head, he then despatched him with his sword; if he missed his throw, he was obliged to run in order to get his net once more adjusted for another throw. In the mean time the other pursued him with all his speed to prevent this, and to despatch *him;* hence he

A. M. 3410 B. C. 594 Ol. XLVI. 3 Anno Tarquinii Prisci, R. Roman., 23

16 [v]But I will leave [w]a few
men of them from the sword,
from the famine, and from the
pestilence; that they may declare all their abominations among the
heathen whither they come; and they shall
know that I *am* the LORD.

17 Moreover the word of the LORD came to
me, saying,

18 Son of man, [x]eat thy bread with quaking, and drink thy water with trembling and
with carefulness;

19 And say unto the people of the land,
Thus saith the Lord GOD of the inhabitants
of Jerusalem, *and* of the land of Israel; They
shall eat their bread with carefulness, and
drink their water with astonishment, that her
land may [y]be desolate from [z]all that is therein,
[a]because of the violence of all them that dwell
therein.

20 And the cities that are inhabited shall be
laid waste, and the land shall be desolate;
and ye shall know that I *am* the LORD.

21 And the word of the LORD came unto me,
saying,

22 Son of man, what *is* that proverb *that*
ye have in the land of Israel, saying, [b]The
days are prolonged, and every
vision faileth?

23 Tell them, therefore,
Thus saith the Lord GOD; I
will make this proverb to cease, and they shall
no more use it as a proverb in Israel; but say
unto them, [c]The days are at hand, and the
effect of every vision.

24 For [d]there shall be no more any [e]vain
vision nor flattering divination within the
house of Israel.

25 For I *am* the LORD: I will speak, and
[f]the word that I shall speak shall come to
pass; it shall be no more prolonged: for in
your days, O rebellious house, will I say the
word, and will perform it, saith the Lord GOD.

26 Again the word of the LORD came to
me, saying,

27 [g]Son of man, behold, *they of* the house
of Israel say, The vision that he seeth *is* [h]for
many days *to come,* and he prophesieth of the
times *that are* far off.

28 [i]Therefore say unto them, Thus saith
the Lord GOD; There shall none of my words
be prolonged any more, but the word which
I have spoken shall be done, saith the Lord
GOD.

A. M. 3410 B. C. 594 Ol. XLVI. 3 Anno Tarquinii Prisci, R. Roman., 23

[v]Ch. vi. 8, 9, 10——[w]Heb. *men of number*——[x]Ch. iv. 16——[y]Zech. vii. 14——[z]Heb. *the fulness thereof* [a]Psa. cvii. 34——[b]Ver. 27; chap. xi. 3; Amos vi. 3; 2 Pet. iii. 4

[c]Joel ii. 1——Zeph. i. 14——[d]Chapter xiii. 23 [e]Lam. ii. 14——[f]Isaiah lv. 11; ver. 28; Daniel ix. 12; Luke xxi. 33——[g]Ver. 22——[h]2 Peter iii. 4——[i]Ver. 23, 25

was called *secutor:* the *first* the *netman,* the *second* the *pursuer.*

Verse 18. *Eat thy bread with quaking*] Assume the manner of a person who is every moment afraid of his life, who has nothing but a morsel of bread to eat, and a little water to drink. Thus signifying the *siege,* and the *straits* to which they should be reduced. See this explained, ver. 19.

Verse 22. *The days are prolonged, and every vision faileth?*] These are the words of the infidels and scoffers, who, because vengeance was not speedily executed on an evil work, set their heart to do iniquity. "These predictions either will not come in our days, or will wholly fail; why then should *we* disquiet ourselves about them?" Strange, that the very means used by the most gracious God to bring sinners to repentance, should be made by them the very instruments of their own destruction! See 2 Pet. iii. 4.

Verse 23. *The days are at hand*] Far from *failing* or being *prolonged,* time is posting on, and the destruction threatened is at the door.

Verse 25. *In your days—will I say the word, and will perform it*] Even these mockers shall *live* to see and *feel* this desolation. This is more particularly intimated in the following verses.

Verse 28. *There shall none of my words be prolonged any more*] He had waited to be gracious; they abused his mercy; and at last the protracted wrath rushed upon them with irresistible force.

CHAPTER XIII

This chapter denounces heavy judgments against the lying prophets who flattered the people, in the midst of their sin and danger, with false hopes of peace and security, 19. *The work of these deceivers is beautifully compared to a frail and insufficient piece of building, which can never stand against the battering elements of heaven, (the Chaldean forces,) which God will commission against it,* 10–16. *In the remaining part of the chapter woes are denounced against false prophetesses who practised vain rites and divinations, with the view of promoting their own gain by deceiving the people,* 17–23.

A. M. 3410
B. C. 594
Ol. XLVI. 3
Anno
Tarquinii Prisci,
R. Roman., 23

AND the word of the LORD
came unto me, saying,
2 Son of man, prophesy
against the prophets of Israel
that prophesy, and say thou unto [a]them [b]that
prophesy out of their own [c]hearts, Hear ye
the word of the LORD;
3 Thus saith the Lord GOD; Wo unto the
foolish prophets, that [d]follow their own spirit,
[e]and have seen nothing!
4 O Israel, thy prophets are [f]like the foxes
in the deserts.
5 Ye [g]have not gone up into the [h]gaps,
neither [i]made up the hedge for the house of
Israel to stand in the battle in the day of the
LORD.
6 [k]They have seen vanity and lying divination, saying, The LORD saith: and the LORD
hath not sent them: and they have made
others to hope that they would confirm the
word.
7 Have ye not seen a vain vision, and have
ye not spoken a lying divination, whereas ye
say, The LORD saith *it;* albeit I have not
spoken?

8 Therefore thus saith the
Lord GOD; Because ye have
spoken vanity, and seen lies,
therefore, behold, I *am* against
you, saith the Lord GOD.
9 And mine hand shall be upon the prophets
that see vanity, and that divine lies: they
shall not be in the [l]assembly of my people,
[m]neither shall they be written in the writing
of the house of Israel, [n]neither shall they enter
into the land of Israel; [o]and ye shall know that
I *am* the Lord GOD.
10 Because, even because they have seduced
my people, saying, [p]Peace; and *there was*
no peace; and one built up [q]a wall, and, lo,
others [r]daubed it with untempered *mortar:*
11 Say unto them which daub *it* with untempered *mortar,* that it shall fall: [s]there
shall be an overflowing shower; and ye, O
great hailstones, shall fall; and a stormy wind
shall rend *it.*
12 Lo, when the wall is fallen, shall it not
be said unto you, Where *is* the daubing wherewith ye have daubed *it?*
13 Therefore thus saith the Lord GOD; I

A. M. 3410
B. C. 594
Ol. XLVI. 3
Anno
Tarquinii Prisci,
R. Roman., 23

[a]Ver. 17——[b]Heb. *them that are prophets out of their own hearts*——[c]Jer. xiv. 14; xxiii. 16, 26——[d]Heb. *walk after*——[e]Or, *and* things which *they have not seen* [f]Cant. ii. 15——[g]Psa. cvi. 23, 30; ch. xxii. 30——[h]Or, *breaches*——[i]Heb. *hedged the hedge*

[k]Ver. 23; chap. xii. 24; xxii. 28——[l]Or, *secret,* or *council*——[m]Ezra ii. 59, 62; Neh. vii. 5; Psa. lxix. 28 [n]Chap. xx. 38——[o]Chap. xi. 10, 12——[p]Jer. vi. 14; viii. 11——[q]Or, *a slight wall*——[r]Chap. xxii. 28 [s]Chap. xxxviii. 22; Ecclus. xlix. 9

NOTES ON CHAP. XIII

Verse 2. *That prophesy out of their own hearts*] Who are *neither inspired* nor *sent* by ME. *They are prophets out of their own hearts.* They have their mission from their own *assumption*, and proceed in it from their own *presumption.* Such either go of *themselves*, or are sent by *man.* Such prophets, ministers, preachers, and clergy have been a curse to the Church and to the world for some thousands of years.

Verse 4. *Thy prophets are like the foxes in the deserts.*] The cunning of the *fox* in obtaining his prey has been long proverbial. These false prophets are represented as the foxes who, having got their prey by great subtlety, run to the desert to hide both themselves and it. So the false prophets, when the event did not answer to their prediction, *got out of the way*, that they might not be overwhelmed with the reproaches and indignation of the people.

Verse 5. *Ye have not gone up into the gaps*] Far from opposing sinners, who are bringing down the wrath of God upon the place, you prevent their repentance by your flattering promises and false predictions. Ye have neither by prayers, example, nor advice, contributed any thing for the preservation of the place, or the salvation of the people's souls.

Verse 9. *They shall not be in the assembly of my people*] They shall not be reputed members of my Church. They shall not be reckoned in the genealogy of true Israelites that return from captivity; and they shall never have a possession in the land; they shall be exhereditated and expatriated. They shall all perish in the siege, by the sword, the famine, and the pestilence.

Verse 10. *One built up a wall*] A true prophet is as *a wall of defence* to the people. These false prophets pretend to *be a wall of defence;* but their *wall* is bad, and their *mortar* is worse. One gives a *lying vision*, another pledges himself that it is *true;* and the people believe what *they* say, and trust not in God, nor turn from their sins. The city is about to be besieged; it needs stronger fortifications than what it possesses. The prophet should be as a *brazen wall* for its defence; and such my prophets would have been had the people received the word from my mouth. But ye have prevented this by your *lying vanities;* and when you have perverted the people, you pretend to raise up a *rampart* of specious prophecy, full of fine promises, for their *defence.* What one false prophet says, another confirms; and this is like daubing over a *bad wall* with *bad mortar*, which prevents its blemishes and weaknesses being discovered, though it has no tendency to strengthen the building.

Verse 11. *There shall be an overflowing shower*] That shall wash off this bad mortar; sweep away the ground on which the wall

A. M. 3410
B. C. 594
Ol. XLVI. 3
Anno
Tarquinii Prisci,
R. Roman., 23

will even rend *it* with a stormy wind in my fury; and there shall be an overflowing shower in mine anger, and great hailstones in *my* fury to consume *it*.

14 So will I break down the wall that ye have daubed with untempered *mortar*, and bring it down to the ground, so that the foundation thereof shall be discovered, and it shall fall, and ye shall be consumed in the midst thereof: [t]and ye shall know that I *am* the LORD.

15 Thus will I accomplish my wrath upon the wall, and upon them that have daubed it with untempered *mortar*, and will say unto you, The wall *is* no *more*, neither they that daubed it;

16 *To wit*, the prophets of Israel which prophesy concerning Jerusalem, and which [u]see visions of peace for her, and *there is* no peace, saith the Lord GOD.

17 Likewise, thou son of man, [v]set thy face against the daughters of thy people, [w]which prophesy out of their own heart; and prophesy thou against them,

A. M. 3410
B. C. 594
Ol. XLVI. 3
Anno
Tarquinii Prisci,
R. Roman., 23

18 And say, Thus saith the Lord GOD; Wo to the *women* that sew pillows to all [x]arm holes, and make kerchiefs upon the head of every stature to hunt souls! Will ye [y]hunt the souls of my people, and will ye save the souls alive *that come* unto you?

19 And will ye pollute me among my people [z]for handfuls of barley and for pieces of bread, to slay the souls that should not die, and to save the souls alive that should not live, by your lying to my people that hear *your* lies?

20 Wherefore thus saith the Lord GOD; Behold, I *am* against your pillows, wherewith ye there hunt the souls [a]to make *them* fly, and I will tear them from your arms, and will let the souls go, *even* the souls that ye hunt to make *them* fly.

21 Your kerchiefs also will I tear, and deliver my people out of your hand, and they shall be no more in your hand to be hunted;

[t]Ver. 9, 21, 23; ch. xiv. 8——[u]Jer. vi. 14; xxviii. 9——[v]Chap. xx. 46; xxi. 2——[w]Ver. 2——[x]Or, *elbows*——[y]2 Pet. ii. 14——[z]See Prov. xxviii. 21; Micah iii. 5——[a]Or, *into gardens*

stands, and level it with the earth. In the eastern countries, where the walls are built with *unbaked bricks*, desolations of this kind are often occasioned by tempestuous rains. Of this sort of materials were the walls of ancient cities made, and hence the reason why no vestige of them remains. Witness Babylon, which was thus built. See the note on chap. iv. 1.

Verse 17. *Set thy face against the daughters of thy people, which prophesy*] From this it appears that there were *prophetesses* in the land of Israel, that were really *inspired* by the Lord: for as a *false religion* necessarily implies a *true one*, of which it is the *ape;* so *false prophetesses* necessarily imply *true ones*, whom they endeavoured to imitate.

That there were *true prophetesses* among the Jews is evident enough from such being mentioned in the sacred writings. *Miriam*, the sister of Moses, Exod. xv. 20; Num. xii. 2; *Deborah*, Judg. iv. 4; *Huldah*, 2 Kings xxii. 14; *Anna*, the daughter of Phanuel, Luke ii. 36; the *four daughters* of Philip the deacon, Acts xxi. 9.

Calmet observes that there was scarcely a heresy in the primitive Church that was not supported and fomented by seducing women.

Verse 18. *That sew pillows to all arm holes*] I believe this refers to those *cushions* which are so copiously provided in the eastern countries for the apartments of women; on which they sit, lean, rest their heads, and prop up their arms. I have several drawings of eastern ladies, who are represented on *sofas;* and often with their *arm thrown over a pillow*, which is thereby pressed close to their side, and against which they thus recline. The prophet's discourse seems to point out that state of softness and effeminacy to which the predictions of those false prophetesses allured the inhabitants of Jerusalem. A careless voluptuous life is that which is here particularly reprehended.

And make kerchiefs] The word *kerchief* is French, *couvre chef*, that which *covers the head;* hence *handkerchief* and *neck handkerchief*, and *pocket handkerchief*, are pitifully improper; because none of them is used to *cover the head*, from which *alone*, that article of dress has its name. But what are we to understand by *kerchiefs* here? Probably some kind of *ornamental dress* which rendered women more enticing, so that they could the more successfully hunt or inveigle souls (men) into the worship of their false gods. These they put on heads of every *stature—women of all ages*, קומה *komah*, of every *woman* that *rose up* to inveigle men to idolatry.

The word מספחות *mispachoth*, translated here *kerchiefs*, and by the *Vulgate cervicalia, bolsters*, *Calmet* contends, means a sort of *nets* used in hunting, and in every place where it occurs it will bear this meaning; and hence the *use* to which it is here said to be applied, to *hunt souls*.

Verse 20. *The souls that ye hunt to make them fly.*] לפרחות *lephorechoth*, into the *flower gardens*, says *Parkhurst*. These false prophetesses decoyed men into these gardens, where probably some impure rites of worship were performed, as in that of אשרה *Asherah* or *Venus*. See *Parkhurst* under פרח.

Verse 21. *Your kerchiefs*] *Nets*, or *amulets*, as some think.

A. M. 3410
B. C. 594
Ol. XLVI. 3
Anno
Tarquinii Prisci,
R. Roman., 23

[b]and ye shall know that I *am* the LORD.

22 Because with lies ye have made the heart of the righteous sad, whom I have not made sad: and [c]strengthened the hands of the wicked, that he should not return from his wicked way, [d]by [e]promising him life:

23 Therefore [f]ye shall see no more vanity, nor divine divinations: for I will deliver my people out of your hand: [g]and ye shall know that I *am* the LORD.

[b]Ver. 9——[c]Jer. xxiii. 14——[d]Or, *that I should save his life*——[e]Heb. *by quickening him*

[f]Ver. 6, &c.; chap. xii. 24; Mic. iii. 6——[g]Ver. 9; chap. xiv. 8; xv. 7

Verse 22. *With lies ye have made the heart of the righteous sad*] Here is the *ministry* of these false prophetesses, and its effects. *They told lies:* they would *speak*, and they had no *truth* to tell; and therefore spoke *falsities*. They "saddened the souls of the righteous, and strengthened the hands of the wicked." They promised them life, and prevented them from repenting and turning from their sins.

Verse 23. *Ye shall see no more vanity*] They pretended *visions;* but they were *empty* of *reality*.

Nor divine divinations] As God would not speak to them, they employed *demons*. Where God is not, because of the iniquity of the people, the *devil* is, to strengthen and support that iniquity. And if he cannot have his *priests*, he will have his *priestesses;* and these will have a Church like themselves, full of lying doctrines, and bad works.

CHAPTER XIV

Here God threatens those hypocrites who pretended to worship him, while they loved and practised idolatry, 1–11. *He declares his irreversible purpose of punishing so guilty a nation, in behalf of which no intercession of the people of God shall be of any avail. The gross idolaters of Jerusalem and Judah shall be visited with God's four sore judgments,* famine, 12–14; wild beasts, 15, 16; *the* sword, 17, 18; *and* pestilence, 19–21. *A remnant shall be delivered from the wrath coming upon the whole land,* 22, 23.

A. M. 3410
B. C. 594
Ol. XLVI. 3
Anno
Tarquinii Prisci,
R. Roman., 23

THEN [a]came certain of the elders of Israel unto me, and sat before me.

2 And the word of the LORD came unto me, saying,

3 Son of man, these men have set up their idols in their heart, and put [b]the stumbling-block of their iniquity before their face: [c]should I be inquired of at all by them?

4 Therefore speak unto them, and say unto them, Thus saith the Lord GOD; Every man of the house of Israel that setteth up his idols in his heart, and putteth the stumbling-block of his iniquity before his face, and cometh to the prophet; I the LORD will answer him that cometh according to the multitude of his idols:

5 That I may take the house of Israel in their own heart, because they are all estranged from me through their idols.

6 Therefore say unto the house of Israel, Thus saith the Lord GOD; Repent, and turn [d]*yourselves* from your idols; and turn away your faces from all your abominations.

7 For every one of the house of Israel, or of the stranger that sojourneth in Israel, which separateth himself from me, and setteth up his

[a]Ch. viii. 1; xx. 1; xxxiii. 31——[b]Ch. vii. 19; ver. 4, 7——[c]2 Kings iii. 13——[d]Or, others

NOTES ON CHAP. XIV

Verse 1. *Then came certain of the elders of Israel unto me*] These probably came to tempt him, or get him to say something that would embroil him with the government. They were bad men, as we shall see in the third verse.

Verse 3. *These men have set up their idols in their heart*] Not only in their houses; in the *streets;* but they had them in their *hearts*. These were *stumbling-blocks* of iniquity; they *fell over them*, and broke the neck of their souls. And should God be inquired of by such miscreants as these?

Verse 4. *According to the multitude of his idols*] I will treat him as an idolater, as a flagrant idolater.

Verse 7. *And cometh to a prophet*] Generally supposed to mean a *false prophet*.

I the Lord will answer him by myself] I shall discover to him, by my own true prophet, what shall be the fruit of his ways. So, while their false prophets were assuring them of peace and prosperity, God's prophets were predicting the calamities that afterwards fell upon them. Yet they believed the *false prophets* in preference to the *true*. Ahab, about to engage with the Syrians, who had possession of Ramoth-Gilead, asked Micaiah, the prophet of the Lord, concerning the event; who told him he

A. M. 3410
B. C. 594
Ol. XLVI. 3
Anno
Tarquinii Prisci,
R. Roman., 23

idols in his heart, and putteth
the stumbling block of his iniquity before his face, and cometh to a prophet to inquire of
him concerning me; I the LORD will answer
him by myself:
8 And [e]I will set my face against that man,
and will make him a [f]sign and a proverb,
and I will cut him off from the midst of my
people; [g]and ye shall know that I *am* the
LORD.
9 And if the prophet be deceived when he
hath spoken a thing, I the LORD [h]have deceived that prophet, and I will stretch out my
hand upon him, and will destroy him from
the midst of my people Israel.
10 And they shall bear the punishment of
their iniquity: the punishment of the prophet
shall be even as the punishment of him that
seeketh *unto him;*
11 That the house of Israel may [i]go no
more astray from me, neither be polluted any
more with all their transgressions; [k]but that
they may be my people, and I may be their
God, saith the Lord GOD.
12 The word of the LORD came again to
me, saying,
13 Son of man, when the land sinneth
against me by trespassing grievously, then
will I stretch out mine hand upon it, and will
break the [l]staff of the bread
thereof, and will send famine
upon it, and will cut off man
and beast from it:

A. M. 3410
B. C. 594
Ol. XLVI. 3
Anno
Tarquinii Prisci,
R. Roman., 23

14 [m]Though these three men, Noah, Daniel,
and Job, were in it, they should deliver *but*
their own souls [n]by their righteousness, saith
the Lord GOD.
15 If I cause [o]noisome beasts to pass through
the land, and they [p]spoil it, so that it be desolate, that no man may pass through because
of the beasts:
16 [q]*Though* these three men *were* [r]in it, *as*
I live, saith the Lord GOD, they shall deliver
neither sons nor daughters; they only shall
be delivered, but the land shall be desolate.
17 Or *if* [s]I bring a sword upon that land,
and say, Sword, go through the land; so that
I [t]cut off man and beast from it:
18 [u]Though these three men *were* in it, *as*
I live, saith the Lord GOD, they shall deliver
neither sons nor daughters, but they only
shall be delivered themselves.
19 Or *if* I send [v]a pestilence into that land,
and [w]pour out my fury upon it in blood, to
cut off from it man and beast:
20 [x]Though Noah, Daniel, and Job, *were* in
it, *as* I live, saith the Lord GOD, they shall deliver neither son nor daughter; they shall *but*
deliver their own souls by their righteousness.

---

[e]Lev. xvii. 10; xx. 3, 5, 6; Jer. xliv. 11; chap. xv. 7 —[f]Num. xxvi. 10; Deut. xxviii. 37; chap. v. 15——[g]Chap. vi. 7——[h]1 Kings xxii. 23; Job xii. 16; Jer. iv. 10; 2 Thess. ii. 11——[i]2 Pet. ii. 15——[k]Chap. xi. 20; xxxvii. 27——[l]Lev. xxvi. 26; Isa. iii. 1; chap. iv. 16; v. 16 —[m]Jer. xv. 1; ver. 16, 18, 20; see Jer. vii. 16; xi. 14; xiv. 11——[n]Prov. xi. 4——[o]Lev. xxvi. 22; chap. v. 17——[p]Or, *bereave*——[q]Ver. 14, 18, 20——[r]Heb. *in the midst of it*——[s]Lev. xxvi. 25; chap. v. 12; xxi. 3, 4; xxix. 8; xxxviii. 21——[t]Chap. xxv. 13; Zeph. i. 3——[u]Ver. 14——[v]2 Sam. xxiv. 15; chap. xxxviii. 22 —[w]Chap. vii. 8——[x]Ver. 14

---

should lose the battle. He then inquired of Zedekiah, a false prophet, who promised him a glorious victory. Ahab believed the latter, marched against the enemy, was routed, and slain in the battle, 1 Kings xxii. 10, &c.

Verse 9. *I the Lord have deceived that prophet*] That is, he ran before he was sent; he willingly became the servant of Satan's illusions; and I *suffered* this to take place, because he and his followers refused to consult and serve me. I have often had occasion to remark that it is common in the Hebrew language to state a thing as done by the Lord which he only *suffers* or *permits* to be done; for so absolute and universal is the government of God, that the smallest occurrence cannot take place without his *will* or *permission.*

Verse 10. *The punishment of the prophet*] They are both equally guilty: both have left the Lord, and both shall be equally punished.

Verse 13. *By trespassing grievously*] Having been frequently warned, and having refused to leave their sin, and so filled up the measure of their iniquity.

Verse 14. *Though—Noah, Daniel, and Job*] The intercession even of the holiest of men shall not avert my judgments. *Noah,* though a righteous man, could not by his intercession preserve the old world from being drowned. *Job,* though a righteous man, could not preserve his children from being killed by the fall of their house. Daniel, though a righteous man, could not prevent the captivity of his country. *Daniel* must have been *contemporary* with *Ezekiel.* He was taken captive in the *third* year of Jehoiakim, Dan. i. 1. After this Jehoiakim reigned *eight* years, 2 Kings xxiii. 36. And this prophecy, as appears from chap. viii. 1, was uttered in the *sixth* year of Jehoiachin's captivity, who succeeded Jehoiakim, and reigned only *three* months, 2 Kings xxiv. 6, 8. Therefore at this time Daniel had been *fourteen* years in captivity. See *Newcome.* Even at this time he had gained much public celebrity. From this account we may infer that *Job* was as *real* a *person* as *Noah* or *Daniel;* and of their identity no man has pretended to doubt. When God, as above, has determined to punish a nation,

A. M. 3410
B. C. 594
Ol. XLVI. 3
Anno
Tarquinii Prisci,
R. Roman., 23

21 For thus saith the Lord
God; [y]How much more when
[z]I send my four sore judgments upon Jerusalem, the
sword, and the famine, and the noisome beast,
and the pestilence, to cut off from it man and
beast?
22 [a]Yet, behold, therein shall be left a
remnant that shall be brought forth, *both* sons
and daughters: behold, they shall come forth
unto you, and [b]ye shall see
their way and their doings:
and ye shall be comforted concerning the evil that I have
brought upon Jerusalem, *even* concerning all
that I have brought upon it.
23 And they shall comfort you, when ye see
their ways and their doings: and ye shall
know that I have not done [c]without cause all
that I have done in it, saith the Lord God.

A. M. 3410
B. C. 594
Ol. XLVI. 3
Anno
Tarquinii Prisci,
R. Roman., 23

[y]Or, *Also when*——[z]Chap. v. 17; xxxiii. 27

[a]Chap. vi. 8——[b]Chap. xx. 43——[c]Jer. xxii. 8, 9

no intercession shall avail. *Personal holiness* alone can prevent these evils; but the holiness of any man can only avail for himself.

Verse 21. *My four sore judgments*] Sword, *war.* Famine, occasioned by *drought.* Pestilence, epidemic diseases which sweep off a great part of the inhabitants of a land. The noisome beast, the multiplication of *wild beasts* in consequence of the general destruction of the inhabitants.

Verse 22. *Behold, they shall come forth unto you*] Though there shall be great desolations in the land of Judea, yet a *remnant shall be left that shall come here also as captives;* and their account of the abominations of the people shall prove to you with what propriety I have acted in abandoning them to such general destruction. This speech is addressed to those who were already in captivity; i. e., those who had been led to Babylon with their king Jeconiah.

Verse 23. *Ye shall know that I have not done without cause*] There is no part of the conduct of God towards man that is not dictated by the purest principles of *justice, equity,* and *truth.* He does nothing but what is *right;* and whatever is right to be done, that *ought* to be done. In God's *justice* there is no *severity;* in God's *mercy* there is no *caprice.* He alone doth all things *well;* for he is the Fountain of justice and mercy.

CHAPTER XV

The Jewish nation, about to be destroyed by the Chaldeans, compared to a barren vine which is fit for nothing but to be cast into the fire, 1–8.

A. M. 3410
B. C. 594
Ol. XLVI. 3
Anno
Tarquinii Prisci,
R. Roman., 23

AND the word of the Lord
came unto me, saying,
2 Son of man, What is the
vine tree more than any tree,
or than a branch which is among the trees
of the forest?
3 Shall wood be taken thereof to do any
work? or will men take a pin of it to hang
any vessel thereon?
4 Behold, [a]it is cast into the fire for fuel;
the fire devoureth both the
ends of it, and the midst of it
is burned. [b]Is it meet for *any*
work?
5 Behold, when it was whole, it was [c]meet
for no work: how much less shall it be meet
yet for *any* work, when the fire hath devoured
it, and it is burned?
6 Therefore thus saith the Lord God; As
the vine tree among the trees of the forest,

A. M. 3410
B. C. 594
Ol. XLVI. 3
Anno
Tarquinii Prisci,
R. Roman., 23

[a]John xv. 6——[b]Heb. *Will it prosper?*

[c]Heb. *made* fit

NOTES ON CHAP. XV

Verse 2. *What is the vine tree more than any tree*] It is certain that the *vine* is esteemed only on account of its *fruit.* In some countries, it is true, it grows to a considerable size and thickness: but, even then, it is not of a sufficient density to work into furniture. But whatever may be said of the *stock* of the vine, it is the *branch* that the prophet speaks of here; and I scarcely know the branch of any tree in the forest more useless than is the branch of the vine. Out of it who can even make a *pin* to drive into a mud wall, or *hang any vessel on?* A vine would never be cultivated for the sake of its *wood;* it is really *worthless* but as it bears *fruit.* What is *Israel?* Good for nothing, but as God influenced them to bring forth fruit to his glory. But now that they have ceased to be *fruitful,* they are *good* for nothing, but, like a withered branch of the vine, to be burnt.

Verse 4. *The fire devoureth both the ends of it, and the midst of it is burned.*] Judea is like a vine branch thrown into the fire, which seizes on *both the ends,* and *scorches* the *middle:* so both the extremities of the land is wasted; and the middle, Jerusalem, is now threatened with a siege, and by and by will be totally destroyed.

Verse 6. *Therefore thus saith the Lord*] As surely as I have allotted such a *vine branch,* or *vine branches,* for *fuel;* so surely have I appointed the *inhabitants of Jerusalem* to be consumed.

A. M. 3410
B. C. 594
Ol. XLVI. 3
Anno
Tarquinii Prisci,
R. Roman., 23

which I have given to the fire
for fuel, so will I give the
inhabitants of Jerusalem.
7 And [d]I will set my face
against them: [e]they shall go out from *one*
fire, and *another* fire shall devour them; [f]and
ye shall know that I *am* the
LORD, when I set my face
against them.
8 And I will make the land
desolate, because they have [g]committed a
trespass, saith the Lord GOD.

[d]Leviticus xvii. 10; chapter xiv. 8——[e]Isaiah xxiv. 18——[f]Chapter vi. 7; vii. 4; xi. 10; xx. 38, 42, 44——[g]Hebrew, *trespassed a trespass*

The design of this parable is to abate the pride of the Jews; to show them that, in their best estate, they had nothing but what they had received, and therefore deserved nothing; and now, having fallen from all righteousness, they can have no expectation of any thing but judgment unmixed with mercy.

Verse 7. *They shall go out from* one *fire, and* another *fire shall devour them*] If they escape the *sword*, they shall perish by the *famine;* if they escape the *famine*, they shall be led away *captives*. To escape will be *impossible*. It will be to them according to the proverb:—

Incidit in Scyllam, cupiens vitare Charybdim.

"Out of the scald, into the flame."

Verse 8. *They have committed a trespass*] They have *prevaricated;* they are the worst of sinners, and shall have the heaviest of punishments. Can men suppose that it is possible to hide even their dark hearts from God?

CHAPTER XVI

In this chapter the mercy of God to Jerusalem, (or the Jewish Church and nation,) is set forth by the emblem of a person that should take up an exposed infant, bring her up with great tenderness, and afterwards marry her, 1-14. *She is then upbraided with her monstrous ingratitude in departing from the worship of God, and polluting herself with the idolatries of the nations around her, under the figure of a woman that proves false to a tender and indulgent husband,* 15–52. *But, notwithstanding these her heinous provocations, God promises, after she should suffer due correction, to restore her again to his favour,* 53–63. *The mode of describing apostasy from the true religion to the worship of idols under the emblem of* adultery, (*a figure very frequent in the sacred canon,*) *is pursued with great force, and at considerable length, both in this and the* twenty-third *chapter; and is excellently calculated to excite in the Church of God the highest detestation of all false worship.*

A. M. 3410
B. C. 594
Ol. XLVI. 3
Anno
Tarquinii Prisci,
R. Roman., 23

AGAIN the word of the
LORD came unto me, saying,
2 Son of man, [a]cause Jerusalem to know her abominations,
3 And say, Thus saith the
Lord GOD unto Jerusalem; Thy
[b]birth [c]and thy nativity *is* of
the land of Canaan; [d]thy father *was* an Amorite, and thy mother a Hittite.

[a]Chap. xx. 4; xxii. 2; xxxiii. 7, 8, 9——[b]Heb. *cutting out*, or *habitation*——[c]Ch. xxi. 30——[d]Ver. 45

NOTES ON CHAP. XVI

Verse 2. *Cause Jerusalem to know her abominations*] And such a revelation of impurity never was seen before or since. Surely the state of the Jews, before the Babylonish captivity, was the most profligate and corrupt of all the nations of the earth. This chapter contains God's *manifesto* against this most abominable people; and although there are many *metaphors* here, yet all is not metaphorical. Where there was so much *idolatry*, there must have been adulteries, fornications, prostitutions, and lewdness of every description. The description of the prophet is sufficiently clear, except where there is a reference to ancient and obsolete *customs*. What a description of crimes! The *sixth satire of Juvenal* is its counterpart. General remarks are all that a commentator is justified in bestowing on this very long, very circumstantial, and caustic invective. For its *key*, see on the *thirteenth* and *sixty-third* verses.

Verse 3. *Thy birth and thy nativity* is *of the land of Canaan*] It would dishonour Abraham to say that you sprung from *him:* ye are rather *Canaanites* than *Israelites*. The Canaanites were accursed; so are ye.

Thy father was *an Amorite, and thy mother a Hittite.*] These tribes were the most famous, and probably the most corrupt, of all the Canaanites. So Isaiah calls the princes of Judah *rulers of Sodom*, chap. i. 10; and John the Baptist calls the Pharisees *a generation* or *brood of vipers*, Matt. iii. 7. There is a fine specimen of this kind of *catachresis* in Dido's invective against Æneas:—

Nec tibi Diva parens, generis nec Dardanus auctor,
Perfide; sed duris genuit te cautibus horrens
Caucasus, Hyrcanæque admorunt ubera tigres.
Æn. lib. iv. 365.

"False as thou art, and more than false, *forsworn;*
Not sprung from noble blood, nor goddess born:
But hewn from hardened entrails of a rock,—
And rough Hyrcanian tigers gave thee suck."
DRYDEN.

This is strong: but the invective of the prophet exceeds it far. It is the essence of

A. M. 3410
B. C. 594
Ol. XLVI. 3
Anno
Tarquinii Prisci,
R. Roman., 23

4 And *as for* thy nativity,[e]in
the day thou wast born, thy
navel was not cut, neither wast
thou washed in water [f]to
supple *thee;* thou wast not salted at all, nor
swaddled at all.
5 None eye pitied thee, to do any of these
unto thee, to have compassion upon thee;
but thou wast cast out in the open field, to
the loathing of thy person, in the day that
thou wast born.
6 And when I passed by thee, and saw thee
[g]polluted in thine own blood, I said unto
thee *when thou wast* in thy blood, Live; yea,
I said unto thee *when thou wast* in thy blood,
Live.
7 [h]I have [i]caused thee to multiply as the bud
of the field, and thou hast increased and
waxen great, and thou art come to [k]excellent
ornaments: *thy* breasts are fashioned, and
thine hair is grown, where thou *wast* naked
and bare.

A. M. 3410
B. C. 594
Ol. XLVI. 3
Anno
Tarquinii Prisci,
R. Roman., 23

8 Now when I passed by thee,
and looked upon thee, behold,
thy time *was* the time of love;
[l]and I spread my skirt over
thee, and covered thy nakedness: yea, I sware
unto thee, and entered into a covenant with
thee, saith the Lord GOD, and [m]thou becamest
mine.
9 Then washed I thee with water; yea, I
throughly washed away thy [n]blood from thee,
and I anointed thee with oil.
10 I clothed thee also with broidered work,
and shod thee with badgers' skin, and I
girded thee about with fine linen, and I covered thee with silk.
11 I decked thee also with ornaments, and
I [o]put bracelets upon thy hands, [p]and a chain
on thy neck.
12 And I put a jewel on thy [q]forehead, and
ear-rings in thine ears, and a beautiful crown
upon thine head.
13 Thus wast thou decked with gold and

[e]Hos. ii. 3——[f]Or, *when I looked* upon thee——[g]Or, *trodden under foot*——[h]Exod. i. 7——[i]Heb. *made thee a million*——[k]Heb. *ornament of ornaments*

[l]Ruth iii. 9——[m]Exod. xix. 5; Jer. ii. 2——[n]Heb. *bloods*——[o]Gen. xxiv. 22, 47——[p]Prov. i. 9——[q]Heb. *nose;* see Isa. iii. 21

degradation to its subject; and shows the Jews to be as base and contemptible as they were abominable and disgusting.

Verse 4. As for *thy nativity, &c.*] This verse refers to what is ordinarily done for every infant on its birth. The *umbilical cord*, by which it received all its nourishment while in the womb, being no longer necessary, is cut at a certain distance from the abdomen: on this part a knot is tied, which firmly uniting the sides of the tubes, they coalesce, and incarnate together. The extra part of the cord on the outside of the ligature, being cut off from the circulation by which it was originally fed, soon drops off, and the part where the ligature was is called the navel. In many places, when this was done, the infant was plunged into *cold water;* in all cases *washed*, and sometimes with a *mixture of salt and water*, in order to give a greater firmness to the skin, and constringe the pores. The last process was *swathing* the body, to support mechanically the tender muscles till they should acquire sufficient strength to support the body. But among savages this latter process is either wholly neglected, or done very slightly: and the less it is done, the better for the infant; as this kind of unnatural *compression* greatly impedes the *circulation* of the blood, the *pulsation* of the heart, and the due inflation of the lungs; respiration, in many cases, being rendered oppressive by the tightness of these bandages.

Verse 5. *Thou wast cast out in the open field*] This is an allusion to the custom of some heathen and barbarous nations, who exposed those children in the open fields to be devoured by wild beasts who had any kind of deformity, or whom they could not support.

Verse 6. *I said—Live*] I received the exposed child from the death that awaited it, while in such a state as rendered it at once an object of horror, and also of compassion.

——————Modo primos
Edere vagitus, et adhuc a matre rubentem.

Verse 8. Was *the time of love*] Thou wast marriageable.

I spread my skirt over thee] I *espoused* thee. This was one of their initiatory marriage ceremonies. See Ruth iii. 9.

I—entered into a covenant with thee] Married thee. *Espousing* preceded *marriage.*

Verse 10. *I clothed thee also with broidered work*] Cloth on which various *figures*, in various *colours*, were wrought by the needle.

With badgers' skin] See Exod. xxv. 5. The same kind of skin with which the tabernacle was covered.

Fine linen] בשש *beshesh, with cotton.* I have seen cloth of this kind enveloping the finest mummies.

I covered thee with silk.] משי *meshi.* Very probably the produce of the silk-worm.

Verse 12. *I put a jewel on thy forehead*] על אפך *al appech*, upon thy *nose.* This is one of the most common ornaments among ladies in the east. European translators, not knowing what to make of *a ring in the nose*, have rendered it, *a jewel on thy forehead* or *mouth*, (though they have sometimes a piece of *gold* or *jewel* fastened to the centre of their *forehead.*) I have already spoken of this Asiatic custom, so often referred to in the sacred writings: see Gen. xxiv. 22, 42; Exod. xxxii. 2; Job. xlii. 11; Prov. xi. 22; Isa. iii. 21; Hos. ii. 13.

Verse 13. *Thus wast thou decked, &c.*] The *Targum* understands all this of the *tabernacle*

A. M. 3410
B. C. 594
Ol. XLVI. 3
Anno
Tarquinii Prisci,
R. Roman., 23

silver; and thy raiment *was of* fine linen, and silk, and broidered work; [r]thou didst eat fine flour, and honey, and oil: and thou wast exceeding [s]beautiful, and thou didst prosper into a kingdom.

14 And [t]thy renown went forth among the heathen for thy beauty: for it *was* perfect through my comeliness, which I had put upon thee, saith the Lord GOD.

15 [u]But thou didst trust in thine own beauty, [v]and playedst the harlot because of thy renown, and pouredst out thy fornications on every one that passed by; his it was.

16 [w]And of thy garments thou didst take, and deckedst thy high places with divers colours, and playedst the harlot thereupon: *the like things* shall not come, neither shall it be *so*.

17 Thou hast also taken thy fair jewels of my gold and of my silver, which I had given thee, and madest to thyself images [x]of men, and didst commit whoredom with them,

18 And tookest thy broidered garments, and coveredst them: and thou hast set mine oil and mine incense before them.

19 [y]My meat also which I gave thee, fine flour, and oil, and honey, *wherewith* I fed thee, thou hast even set it before them for [z]a sweet savour: and *thus* it was, saith the Lord GOD.

20 [a]Moreover thou hast taken thy sons and thy daughters, whom thou hast borne unto me, and these hast thou sacrificed unto them [b]to be devoured. *Is this* of thy whoredoms a small matter,

21 That thou hast slain my children, and delivered them to cause them to pass through *the fire* for them?

22 And in all thine abominations and thy

[r]Deut. xxxii. 13, 14——[s]Psa. xlviii. 2——[t]Lam. ii. 15——[u]See Deut. xxxii. 15; Jer. vii. 4; Mic. iii. 11——[v]Isa. i. 21; lvii. 8; Jer. ii. 20; iii. 2, 6, 20; chap. xxiii. 3, 8, 11, 12; Hos. i. 2

[w]2 Kings xxiii. 7; chap. vii. 20; Hos. ii. 8——[x]Heb. *of a male*——[y]Hos. ii. 8——[z]Heb. *a savour of rest*——[a]2 Kings xvi. 3; Psa. cvi. 37, 38; Isa. lvii. 5; Jer. vii. 31; xxxii. 35; chap. xx. 26; xxiii. 37——[b]Heb. *to devour*

service, the *book of the law*, the *sacerdotal vestments*, &c.

Thou didst prosper into a kingdom.] Here the figure explains itself: by this *wretched infant*, the low estate of the Jewish nation in its *origin* is pointed out; by the *growing up of this child into woman's estate*, the increase and multiplication of the people; by her being *decked out and ornamented*, her tabernacle service, and religious ordinances; by her *betrothing* and consequent *marriage*, the *covenant* which God made with the Jews; by her *fornication* and *adulteries*, their *apostasy* from God, and the establishment of *idolatrous worship*, with all its abominable rites; by her *fornication* and *whoredoms* with the *Egyptians* and *Assyrians*, the sinful alliances which the Jews made with those nations, and the incorporation of *their* idolatrous worship with that of Jehovah; by her *lovers being brought against her*, and *stripping her naked*, the delivery of the Jews into the hands of the Egyptians, Assyrians, and Chaldeans, who stripped them of all their excellencies, and at last carried them into captivity.

This is the *key* to the whole of this long chapter of metaphors; and the reader will do well to forget the *figures*, and look at the *facts*. The *language* and *figures* may in many places appear to us exceptionable: but these are quite in conformity to those *times* and *places*, and to every reader and hearer would appear perfectly appropriate, nor would engender either a thought or passion of an irregular or improper kind. *Custom* sanctions the *mode*, and prevents the *abuse*. Among *naked savages* irregular passions and propensities are not known to predominate above those in civilized life. And why? Because such sights are *customary*, and therefore in themselves innocent. And the same may be said of the *language* by which such states and circumstances of life are described. Had Ezekiel spoken in such language as would have been called *chaste* and *unexceptionable* among *us*, it would have appeared to his auditors as a *strange dialect*, and would have lost at least one half of its *power* and *effect*. Let this be the prophet's apology for the apparent indelicacy of his metaphors; and mine, for not entering into any particular discussion concerning them. See also on ver. 63.

Verse 15. *Thou didst trust in thine own beauty*] Riches, strength, alliances, &c.; never considering that all they possessed came from God; therefore *it was his comeliness which he had put upon them*. Witness their *original abject state*, and the degree of *eminence* to which they had arrived afterwards through the protecting power of God.

Verse 17. *And madest to thyself images of men*] צלמי זכר *tsalmey zachar, male images*. *Priapi* are here meant, which were carried about in the ceremonies of Osiris, Bacchus, and Adonis; and were something like the *lingam* among the Hindoos. *Herodotus*, lib. ii, c. 48, 49, gives us an account of these *male images:* Πηχυαια αγαλματα νευροσπαστα, τα περιφορεουσι κατα κωμας ται γυναικες, νευον το αιδοιον, ου πολλῳ τεῳ ελασσον εον του αλλου σωματος. This was done at the worship of Bacchus in Egypt: and they who wish to see more may consult *Herodotus* as above. In this *phallic* worship the women were principally concerned.

Verse 18. *Hast set mine oil and mine incense before them.*] It appears that they had made use of the holy vestments, and the different kinds of offerings which belonged to the Lord, to honour their idols.

Verse 21. *To cause them to pass through* the fire] Bp. *Newcome* quotes a very apposite passage from *Dionysius Halicarnass.* Ant. Rom. lib.

A. M. 3410
B. C. 594
Ol. XLVI. 3
Anno
Tarquinii Prisci,
R. Roman., 23

whoredoms thou hast not remembered the days of thy [c]youth, [d]when thou wast naked and bare, *and* wast polluted in thy blood.

23 And it came to pass after all thy wickedness, (wo, wo unto thee! saith the Lord GOD;)

24 *That* [e]thou hast also built unto thee an [f]eminent place, and [g]hast made thee a high place in every street.

25 Thou hast built thy high place [h]at every head of the way, and hast made thy beauty to be abhorred, and hast opened thy feet to every one that passed by, and multiplied thy whoredoms.

26 Thou hast also committed fornication with [i]the Egyptians thy neighbours, great of flesh; and hast increased thy whoredoms, to provoke me to anger.

27 Behold, therefore, I have stretched out my hand over thee, and have diminished thine ordinary *food,* and delivered thee unto the will of them that hate thee, [k]the [l]daughters of the Philistines, which are ashamed of thy lewd way.

28 [m]Thou hast played the whore also with the Assyrians, because thou wast unsatiable; yea, thou hast played the harlot with them, and yet couldest not be satisfied.

29 Thou hast moreover multiplied thy fornication in the land of Canaan [n]unto Chaldea; and yet thou wast not satisfied herewith.

30 How weak is thine heart, saith the Lord GOD, seeing thou doest all these *things,* the work of an imperious whorish woman;

31 [o]In that [p]thou buildest thine eminent place in the head of every way, and makest thine high place in every street; and hast not been as a harlot, in that thou scornest hire;

32 *But as* a wife that committeth adultery, *which* taketh strangers instead of her husband!

33 They give gifts to all whores: but [q]thou givest thy gifts to all thy lovers, and [r]hirest them, that they may come unto thee on every side for thy whoredom.

34 And the contrary is in thee from *other* women in thy whoredoms, whereas none followeth thee to commit whoredoms: and in that thou givest a reward, and no reward is given unto thee, therefore thou art contrary.

35 Wherefore, O harlot, hear the word of the LORD:

36 Thus saith the Lord GOD; Because thy filthiness was poured out, and thy nakedness discovered through thy whoredoms with thy lovers, and with all the idols of thy abominations, and by [s]the blood of thy children, which thou didst give unto them;

37 Behold, therefore [t]I will gather all thy lovers, with whom thou hast taken pleasure, and all *them* that thou hast loved, with all *them* that thou hast hated; I will even gather them round about against thee, and will discover thy nakedness unto them, that they may see all thy nakedness.

A. M. 3410
B. C. 594
Ol. XLVI. 3
Anno
Tarquinii Prisci,
R. Roman., 23

[c]Jer. ii. 2; ver. 43, 60; Hos. xi. 1——[d]Ver. 4, 5, 6——[e]Ver. 31——[f]Or, *brothel house*——[g]Isa. lvii. 5, 7; Jer. ii. 20; iii. 2——[h]Prov. ix. 14——[i]Chap. viii. 10, 14; xx. 7, 8; xxiii. 19, 20, 21——[k]2 Chron. xxviii. 18, 19; ver. 57——[l]Or, *cities*——[m]2 Kings xvi. 7, 10; 2 Chron. xxviii. 23; Jer. ii. 18, 36——[n]Ch. xxiii. 14, &c.——[o]Or, *in thy daughters* is *thine*, &c.——[p]Ver. 24, 39——[q]Isa. xxx. 3; Hos. viii. 9——[r]Heb. *bribest*——[s]Ver. 20; Jer. ii. 34——[t]Jer. xiii. 22, 26; Lam. i. 8; chap. xxiii. 9, 10, 22, 29; Hos. ii. 10; viii. 10; Nah. iii. 5

i., s. 88, p. 72, and marg. p. 75, Edit. Hudson: *Μετα δε τουτο, πυρκαϊας προ των σκηνων γενεσθαι κελευσας, εξαγει τον λεων τας φλογας ὑπερθρωσκοντα, της ὁσιωσεως των μιασματων ἑνεκα.* "And after this, having ordered that fires should be made before the tents, he brings out the people to leap over the flames, for the purifying of their pollutions." This example shows that we are not always to take passing through the fire for being entirely consumed by it. Among the Israelites this appears to have been used as a rite of consecration.

Verse 24. *Thou hast also built unto thee an eminent place*] גב *gab*, a *stew* or *brothel;* Vulg. *lupanar;* Septuag. οικημα πορνικον. So my old MS. Bible, **a bordel house.** "Thou hast builded thy stewes and bordell houses in every place."—*Coverdale's* Bible, 1535. *Bordel* is an *Italian* word: how it got so early into our language I know not. Our modern word *brothel* is a corruption of it. *Diodati* translates, Tu hai edificato un bordello, "Thou hast built a brothel." Houses of this kind were of a very ancient date.

Verse 26. *Great of flesh*] The most extensive idolaters. Bene vasatis—longa mensura incognita nervi.—Juv. *Sat.* ix. 34. This is the allusion.

Verse 27. *Have diminished thine ordinary*] חקך *chukkech* means here the household provision made for a wife—food, clothing, and money.

Verse 36. *Thy filthiness was poured out*] נחשתך *nechushtech.* As this word signifies a sort of *metal,* (brass,) it is generally supposed to mean *money.* They had given *money* literally to these heathen nations to procure their friendship and assistance; but the word also

A. M. 3410
B. C. 594
Ol. XLVI. 3
Anno
Tarquinii Prisci,
R. Roman., 23

38 And I will judge thee, [u]as [v]women that break wedlock and [w]shed blood are judged; and I will give thee blood in fury and jealousy.

39 And I will also give thee into their hand, and they shall throw down [x]thine eminent place, and shall break down thy high places: [y]they shall strip thee also of thy clothes, and shall take [z]thy fair jewels, and leave thee naked and bare.

40 [a]They shall also bring up a company against thee, [b]and they shall stone thee with stones, and thrust thee through with their swords.

41 And they shall [c]burn thine houses with fire, and [d]execute judgments upon thee in the sight of many women: and I will cause thee to [e]cease from playing the harlot, and thou also shalt give no hire any more.

42 So [f]will I make my fury toward thee to rest, and my jealousy shall depart from thee, and I will be quiet, and will be no more angry.

43 Because [g]thou hast not remembered the days of thy youth, but hast fretted me in all these *things;* behold, therefore, [h]I also will recompense thy way upon *thine* head, saith the Lord God: and thou shalt not commit this lewdness above all thine abominations.

44 Behold, every one that useth proverbs shall use *this* proverb against thee, saying, As *is* the mother, *so is* her daughter.

A. M. 3410
B. C. 594
Ol. XLVI. 3
Anno
Tarquinii Prisci,
R. Roman., 23

45 Thou *art* thy mother's daughter, that loathed her husband and her children; and thou *art* the sister of thy sisters, which loathed their husbands and their children: [i]your mother *was* a Hittite, and your father an Amorite.

46 And thine elder sister *is* Samaria, she and her daughters that dwell at thy left hand: and [k]thy [l]younger sister, that dwelleth at thy right hand, *is* Sodom and her daughters.

47 Yet hast thou not walked after their ways, nor done after their abominations: but [m]as *if that were* a very little *thing,* [n]thou wast corrupted more than they in all thy ways.

48 *As* I live, saith the Lord God, [o]Sodom thy sister hath not done, she nor her daughters, as thou hast done, thou and thy daughters.

49 Behold, this was the iniquity of thy sister Sodom, pride, [p]fulness of bread, and abundance of idleness, was in her and in her daughters, neither did she strengthen the hand of the poor and needy.

50 And they were haughty, and [q]committed abomination before me: therefore [r]I took them away, as I saw *good.*

51 Neither hath Samaria committed half of thy sins; but thou hast multiplied thine abo-

[u]Heb. *with judgments of*——[v]Lev. xx. 10; Deut. xxii. 22; ch. xxiii. 45——[w]Gen. ix. 6; Exod. xxi. 12; see ver. 20, 36——[x]Ver. 24, 31——[y]Ch. xxiii. 26; Hos. ii. 3 [z]Heb. *instruments of thine ornament*——[a]Ch. xxiii. 10, 47 [b]John viii. 5, 7——[c]Deut. xiii. 16; 2 Kings xxv. 9; Jer. xxxix. 8; lii. 13——[d]Ch. v. 8; xxiii. 10, 48——[e]Ch. xxiii. 27

[f]Chap. v. 13——[g]Ver. 22; Psalm lxxviii. 42——[h]Ch. ix. 10, 11, 21; xxii. 31——[i]Ver. 3——[k]Deuteronomy xxxii. 32; Isaiah i. 10——[l]Hebrew, *lesser than thou* [m]Or, *that was loathed as a small* thing——[n]2 Kings xxi. 9; chap. v. 6, 7; ver. 48, 51——[o]Matt. x. 15; xi. 24 [p]Gen. xiii. 10——[q]Gen. xiii. 13; xviii. 30; xix. 5 [r]Gen. xix. 24

means *verdigris*, the *poisonous rust of copper* or *brass.* It is properly translated in our version *filthiness, poisonous filth.* Does it not refer to that *venereal virus* which is engendered by promiscuous connexions?

Verse 39. *They shall strip thee also of thy clothes—thy fair jewels*] Alluding to a lot common enough to prostitutes, their maintainers in the end stripping them of all they had given them.

Verse 42. *I will be quiet, and will be no more angry.*] I will completely abandon thee; have nothing more to do with thee; think no more of thee. When God in judgment ceases to reprehend, this is the severest judgment.

Verse 43. *Thou hast not remembered the days of thy youth*] Thy former low beginning, when God made thee a people, who wast no people. He who maintains not a proper recollection of past mercies is not likely to abide steadfast in the faith. Ingratitude to God is the commencement, if not the parent, of many crimes.

Verse 44. *As* is *the mother,* so is *her daughter.*] כאמה בתה *keimmah bittah*, "As the mother, her daughter." As is the *cause*, so is the *effect.* As is the *breeding*, so is the *practice.* A *silken purse* cannot be made out of a *swine's ear.* What is bred in the *bone* seldom comes out of the *flesh.* All such proverbs show the necessity of early holy *precepts*, supported by suitable *example.*

Verse 46. *Thine elder sister* is *Samaria, she and her daughters that dwell at thy left*] It is supposed that the prophet by *Sodom* in this place means the Israelites that dwelt beyond Jordan, in the land of the *Moabites* and *Ammonites;* or rather of the *Moabites* and *Ammonites* themselves. Literally, Sodom could not be called the *younger sister* of Jerusalem, as it existed before Jerusalem had a name. In looking *east* from Jerusalem, Samaria was on the *left*, and Sodom on the *right hand;* that is, the *first* was on the *north*, the *second* on the *south* of Jerusalem.

Verse 49. *This was the iniquity of thy sister Sodom*] If we are to take this place literally,

A. M. 3410
B. C. 594
Ol. XLVI. 3
Anno
Tarquinii Prisci,
R. Roman., 23

minations more than they,
and [s]hast justified thy sisters
in all thine abominations
which thou hast done.
52 Thou also, which hast judged thy sisters,
bear thine own shame for thy sins that thou
hast committed more abominable than they:
they are more righteous than thou: yea, be
thou confounded also, and bear thy shame, in
that thou hast justified thy sisters.
53 [t]When I shall bring again their captivity,
[u]the captivity of Sodom and her daughters,
and the captivity of Samaria and her daughters, then *will I bring again* the captivity of
thy captives in the midst of them.
54 That thou mayest bear thine own shame,
and mayest be confounded in all that thou
hast done, in that thou art [v]a comfort unto
them.
55 When thy sisters, Sodom and her daughters, shall return to their former estate, and
Samaria and her daughters shall return
to their former estate, then thou and thy
daughters shall return to your former
estate.
56 For thy sister Sodom was not [w]mentioned
by thy mouth in the day of thy [x]pride,
57 Before thy wickedness was discovered, as
at the time of *thy* [y]reproach of
the daughters of [z]Syria, and
all *that are* round about her,
[a]the daughters of the Philistines, which [b]despise thee round about.
58 [c]Thou hast [d]borne thy lewdness and
thine abominations, saith the LORD.
59 For thus saith the Lord GOD; I will
even deal with thee as thou hast done, which
hast [e]despised [f]the oath in breaking the
covenant.
60 Nevertheless I will [g]remember my covenant with thee in the days of thy youth, and
I will establish unto thee [h]an everlasting
covenant.
61 Then [i]thou shalt remember thy ways,
and be ashamed, when thou shalt receive thy
sisters, thine elder and thy younger: and I
will give them unto thee for [k]daughters, [l]but
not by thy covenant.
62 [m]And I will establish my covenant with
thee; and thou shalt know that I *am* the
LORD:
63 That thou mayest [n]remember, and be
confounded, [o]and never open thy mouth any
more because of thy shame, when I am pacified toward thee for all that thou hast done,
saith the Lord GOD.

[s]Jer. iii. 11; Matt. xii. 41, 42——[t]See Isa. i. 9; ver. 60, 61——[u]Jer. xx. 16——[v]Ch. xiv. 22, 23——[w]Heb. *for a report*, or *hearing*——[x]Heb. *prides*, or *excellencies* [y]2 Kings xvi. 5; 2 Chron. xxviii. 18; Isa. vii. 1; xiv. 28 [z]Heb. *Aram.*——[a]Ver. 27——[b]Or, *spoil*

[c]Chap. xxiii. 49——[d]Heb. *borne them*——[e]Chap. xvii. 13, 16——[f]Deut. xxix. 12, 14——[g]Psa. cvi. 45——[h]Jer. xxxii. 40; l. 5——[i]Ch. xx. 43; xxxvi. 31——[k]Isa. liv. 1; lx. 4; Gal. iv. 26, &c.——[l]Jer. xxxi. 31, &c.——[m]Hos. ii. 19. 20——[n]Ver. 61——[o]Rom. iii. 19

Sodom was guilty of other crimes besides that for which she appears to have been especially punished; in addition to her unnatural crime, she is charged with *pride*, *luxury*, *idleness*, and *uncharitableness;* and these were sufficient to sink any city to the bottomless pit.

Verse 52. *They are more righteous than thou*] תצדקנה ממך *tetsuddaknah mimmech*, "They shall be justified more than thou." They are less guilty in the sight of God, for their crimes were not accompanied with so many *aggravations*. This phrase casts light on Luke xviii. 14: "This man went down to his house justified rather than the other." Less blame in the sight of God was attached to him. He always had fewer advantages, and now he was a true *penitent;* while the other was boasting of what he *had done*, and what he had *not done*.

Verse 60. *I will remember my covenant*] That is, the covenant I made with Abraham *in the day of thy youth*, when in *him* thou didst *begin* to be a nation.

Verse 61. *Thy sisters, thine elder and thy younger*] The *Gentiles*, who were *before* the Jews were called, and *after* the Jews were cast off, are here termed the *elder* and *younger sister*. These were to be given to Jerusalem for *daughters;* the latter should be converted to God by the ministry of men who should spring out of the Jewish Church. The *former*, who were *patriarchs*, &c., profited by the *Lamb who was slain from the foundation of the world*. Among the latter the Gospel was preached, first by *Christ* and his *apostles*, and since by persons raised up from among themselves.

But not by thy covenant.] This was the *ancient covenant*, the conditions of which they *broke*, and the blessings of which they *forfeited;* but by that *new covenant*, or the *renewal* to the Gentiles of that *covenant* that was made *originally* with Abraham while he was a *Gentile*, promising that in *his seed all the nations of the earth should be blessed;* that *covenant* which respected the incarnation of Christ, and was ratified by the blood of his cross.

Verse 63. *When I am pacified toward thee*] This intimates that the Jews shall certainly share in the blessings of the Gospel covenant, and that they shall be restored to the favour and image of God. And *when* shall this be? Whenever *they* please. They might have enjoyed them *eighteen hundred* years ago; but they would not come, though *all things were then ready*. They may enjoy them *now;* but they still *choose* to shut their eyes against the light, and contradict and blaspheme. As they do *not turn to the Lord*, the *veil* still continues on their hearts. Let their *elder brethren* pray for them.

For a *key* to the principal metaphors in this chapter, the reader is referred to the note on the *thirteenth* verse, which, if he regard not, he will neither do justice to himself nor to the prophet. The whole chapter is a tissue of invective; sharp, cutting, and confounding; every where well sustained, in every respect richly merited; and in no case leaving any room to the delinquent for justification or response.

CHAPTER XVII

This chapter begins with a new allegory or parable, 1–10; *to which an explanation is immediately subjoined,* 11–21. *In the remaining verses the prophet, by a beautiful metaphor, makes an easy and natural transition to the Messiah, and predicts the security, increasing prosperity, and ultimate universality of his kingdom,* 22–24. *From the beauty of its images, the elegance of its composition, the perspicuity of its language, the rich variety of its matter, and the easy transition from one part of the subject to another, this chapter forms one of the most beautiful and perfect pieces of its kind that can possibly be conceived in so small a compass; and then the unexpected change from objects that presented nothing to the view but gloom and horror, to a prospect of ineffable glory and beauty, has a most happy effect. Every lowering cloud is dispelled, and the fields again smile in the beams of midday. The traveller, who this moment trembled as he looked around for shelter, now proceeds on his way rejoicing.*

A. M. 3410 B. C. 594 Ol. XLVI. 3 Anno Tarquinii Prisci, R. Roman., 23
AND the word of the LORD
came unto me, saying,
2 Son of man, put forth a
riddle, and speak a parable
unto the house of Israel;
3 And say, Thus saith the Lord GOD; [a]A
great eagle with great wings, long-winged,
full of feathers, which had [b]divers colours,
came unto Lebanon, and [c]took the highest
branch of the cedar;
4 He cropped off the top of his young
twigs, and carried it into a land of traffic:
he set it in a city of merchants.
5 He took also of the seed
of the land, and [d]planted it
in [e]a fruitful field; he placed *it* by great
waters, *and* set it [f]*as* a willow tree.
6 And it grew, and became a spreading
vine [g]of low stature, whose branches turned
toward him, and the roots thereof were under
him: so it became a vine, and brought forth
branches, and shot forth sprigs.
7 There was also another great eagle with

A. M. 3410 B. C. 594 Ol. XLVI. 3 Anno Tarquinii Prisci, R. Roman., 23

[a]See ver. 12, &c.——[b]Heb. *embroidering*——[c]2 Kings xxiv. 12

[d]Heb. *put it in a field of seed*——[e]Deut. viii. 7, 8, 9 [f]Isa. xliv. 4——[g]Ver. 14

NOTES ON CHAP. XVII

Verse 2. *Son of man, put forth a riddle*] Riddle, rædels or rædelse, Anglo-Saxon, from arædan, to *divine;* a thing that must be curiously *investigated* and *sifted*, to find out the meaning; and hence, *riddle*, a sort of coarse sieve to clean corn, to separate coarse chaff and straws from the pure grain. An instrument formerly used for *divination.* This is not far removed from the Hebrew חידה *chidah*, from חד *chad*, to *penetrate;* not that which *penetrates the mind*, but which *we* must *penetrate* to find out the sense.

Verse 3. *A great eagle*] Nebuchadnezzar. See Jer. xlviii. 40; xlix. 22; Dan. vii. 4. And see here, ver. 12, where it is so applied.

Great wings] Extensive empire.

Long-winged] Rapid in his conquests.

Full of feathers] Having multitudes of subjects.

Divers colours] People of various nations.

Came unto Lebanon] Came against Judea.

The highest branch] King Jehoiachin he took captive to Babylon.

The cedar] The Jewish state and king.

Verse 4. *The top of his young twigs*] The princes of Judah.

A land of traffic] Chaldea.

A city of merchants] Babylon; for which this city was the most celebrated of all the cities of the east. Its situation procured it innumerable advantages; its two rivers, the *Tigris* and *Euphrates*, and the *Persian Gulf*, gave it communication with the richest and the most distant nations.

Verse 5. *The seed of the land*] Zedekiah, brother of Jehoiachin.

Planted it in a fruitful field] Made him king of Judea in place of his brother.

Placed it by great waters] Put him under the protection of Babylon, situated on the confluence of the *Tigris* and *Euphrates*.

And *set it* as *a willow tree*] Made him *dependent* on this city of great waters, as the *willow* is on humidity.

Verse 6. *A spreading vine of low stature*] The Jewish state having then no height of dominion, it must abide under the wings or branches of the Chaldean king.

Whose branches turned toward him, and the roots—under him] Zedekiah was wholly dependent on Nebuchadnezzar, both for his elevation to the throne, and his support on it.

Verse 7. *Another great eagle*] Pharaoh-hophra, or Apries, king of Egypt.

With great wings] Extensive dominion.

And many feathers] Numerous subjects.

Did bend her roots] Looked to him for support in her intended rebellion against Nebuchadnezzar.

A. M. 3410
B. C. 594
Ol. XLVI. 3
Anno
Tarquinii Prisci,
R. Roman., 23

great wings and many feathers: and, behold, [h]this vine did bend her roots toward him, and shot forth her branches toward him, that he might water it by the furrows of her plantation.

8 It was planted in a good [i]soil by great waters, that it might bring forth branches, and that it might bear fruit, that it might be a goodly vine.

9 Say thou, Thus saith the Lord GOD; Shall it prosper? [k]shall he not pull up the roots thereof, and cut off the fruit thereof, that it wither? it shall wither in all the leaves of her spring, even without great power, or many people to pluck it up by the roots thereof.

10 Yea, behold, *being* planted, shall it prosper? [l]shall it not utterly wither, when the east wind toucheth it? it shall wither in the furrows where it grew.

11 Moreover the word of the LORD came unto me, saying,

12 Say now to [m]the rebellious house, Know ye not what these *things mean?* tell *them,* Behold, [n]the king of Babylon is come to Jerusalem, and hath taken the king thereof, and the princes thereof, and led them with him to Babylon:

13 [o]And hath taken of the king's seed, and made a covenant with him, [p]and hath [q]taken an oath of him: he hath also taken the mighty of the land:

14 That the kingdom might be [r]base, that it might not lift itself up, [s]*but* that by keeping of his covenant it might stand.

A. M. 3410
B. C. 594
Ol. XLVI. 3
Anno
Tarquinii Prisci,
R. Roman., 23

15 But [t]he rebelled against him in sending his ambassadors into Egypt, [u]that they might give him horses and much people. [v]Shall he prosper? shall he escape that doeth such *things?* or shall he break the covenant, and be delivered?

16 *As* I live, saith the Lord GOD, surely [w]in the place *where* the king *dwelleth* that made him king, whose oath he despised, and whose covenant he brake, *even* with him in the midst of Babylon he shall die.

17 [x]Neither shall Pharaoh with *his* mighty army and great company make for him in the war, [y]by casting up mounts, and building forts, to cut off many persons:

18 Seeing he despised the oath by breaking the covenant, when, lo, he had [z]given his hand, and hath done all these *things,* he shall not escape.

19 Therefore thus saith the Lord GOD; *As* I live, surely mine oath that he hath despised, and my covenant that he hath broken, even it will I recompense upon his own head.

20 And I will [a]spread my net upon him, and he shall be taken in my snare, and I will bring him to Babylon, and [b]will plead with him there for his trespass that he hath trespassed against me.

---

[h]Ver. 15——[i]Heb. *field*——[k]2 Kings xxv. 7——[l]Ch. xix. 12; Hos. xiii. 15——[m]Ch. ii. 5; xii. 9——[n]Ver. 3; 2 Kings xxiv. 11–16——[o]2 Kings xxiv. 17——[p]2 Chron. xxxvi. 13——[q]Heb. *brought him to an oath*——[r]Ver. 6; ch. xxix. 14——[s]Heb. *to keep his covenant, to stand to it*

[t]2 Kings xxiv. 20; 2 Chron. xxxvi. 13——[u]Deut. xvii. 16; Isa. xxxi. 1, 3; xxxvi. 6, 9——[v]Ver. 9——[w]Jer. xxxii. 5; xxxiv. 3; lii. 11; ch. xii. 13——[x]Jer. xxxvii. 7 [y]Jer. lii. 4; ch. iv. 2——[z]1 Chron. xxix. 24; Lam. v. 6 [a]Chap. xii. 13; xxxii. 3——[b]Chap. xx. 36

Verse 8. *It was planted in a good soil*] Though he depended on Babylon, he lived and reigned as Nebuchadnezzar's vicegerent in the land of Judea.

Verse 9. *Shall it prosper?*] Shall Zedekiah succeed in casting off the yoke of the king of Babylon, to whom he had *sworn* fealty?

Shall he not pull up the roots] Nebuchadnezzar will come and dethrone him.

And cut off the fruit] The children of Zedekiah.

The leaves] All the nobles; all shall perish with Zedekiah.

Verse 10. *Shall—utterly wither*] The *regal* government shall be no more restored. Zedekiah shall be the *last king,* and the monarchy shall finally terminate with him.

Verse 12. *Know ye not what these* things mean?] They are explained in this and the following verses.

Verse 14. *That the kingdom might be base*] Have no political *consequence;* and at last sink into a *miserable government* under Gedaliah.

Verse 15. *Sending his ambassadors into Egypt*] Zedekiah must have sent his ambassadors into Egypt, between the *sixth* month of his *sixth* year, and the *fifth* month of his *seventh* year. Compare chap. viii. 1, with chap. xx. 1.—See *Newcome.*

Verse 16. *In the midst of Babylon he shall die.*] His eyes were put out; he was carried to Babylon, and never returned.

Verse 18. *Seeing he despised the oath*] This God particularly resents. He had bound himself by oath, in the presence of Jehovah, to be faithful to the covenant that he made with Nebuchadnezzar, and he took the first opportunity to break it; therefore he shall not escape.

Verse 20. *I will spread my net upon him*] See the note on chap. xii. 13.

A. M. 3410
B. C. 594
Ol. XLVI. 3
Anno
Tarquinii Prisci,
R. Roman., 23

21 And [c]all his fugitives with all his bands shall fall by the sword, and they that remain shall be scattered toward all winds: and ye shall know that I the LORD have spoken *it*.

22 Thus saith the Lord GOD; I will also take of the highest [d]branch of the high cedar, and will set *it;* I will crop off from the top of his young twigs [e]a tender one, and will [f]plant *it* upon a high mountain and eminent:

23 [g]In the mountain of the height of Israel will I plant it: and it shall bring forth boughs, and bear fruit, and be a goodly cedar: and [h]under it shall dwell all fowl of every wing; in the shadow of the branches thereof shall they dwell.

24 And all the trees of the field shall know that I the LORD [i]have brought down the high tree, have exalted the low tree, have dried up the green tree, and have made the dry tree to flourish: [k]I the LORD have spoken and have done *it*.

[c]Chap. xii. 14——[d]Isa. xi. 1; Jer. xxiii. 5; Zech. iii. 8 [e]Isa. liii. 2——[f]Psa. ii. 6

[g]Isa. ii. 2, 3; ch. xx. 40; Mic. iv. 1——[h]See ch. xxxi. 6; Dan. iv. 12——[i]Luke i. 52——[k]Ch. xxii. 14; xxiv. 14

Verse 21. *All his fugitives*] All who attempted to escape with him, and all that ran to Egypt, &c., shall fall by the sword.

Verse 22. *I will also take of the highest branch of the high cedar*] I will raise up *another monarchy*, which shall come in the *line of David*, namely, the *Messiah;* who shall appear as a *tender plant*, as to his incarnation; but he shall be *high and eminent;* his Church, the royal city, the highest and purest ever seen on the face of the earth.

Verse 23. *In the mountain of the height of Israel*] He shall make his appearance at the *temple*, and found his Church at *Jerusalem*.

Shall bring forth boughs] Apostles, evangelists, and their successors in the Gospel ministry.

And bear fruit] Multitudes of souls shall be converted by their preaching.

And under it shall dwell all fowl of every wing] All the nations of the earth shall receive his Gospel.

In the shadow of the branches thereof shall they dwell.] Trust in him alone for salvation, and be saved in their trusting.

Verse 24. *All the trees of the field shall know*] All the people of Israel and of Chaldea.

I the Lord have brought down the high tree] Have dethroned Jehoiachin.

Have exalted the low tree] Put Zedekiah, brother of Jehoiachin, in his place.

Have dried up the green tree] Zedekiah, who had numerous children, but who were all slain before his eyes at Riblah.

And have made the dry tree to flourish] Have raised up a rod out of the stem of Jesse, the family of David being then apparently dried up and extinct. This was the promised Messiah, of the increase and government of whose kingdom and peace there shall be no end; upon the throne of David, and upon his kingdom, to order and establish it with judgment and with justice, from henceforth, even for ever. THE ZEAL OF THE LORD OF HOSTS WILL PERFORM THIS.

The *high* and *green tree*, says *Newcome*, refers to Nebuchadnezzar; the *low* and the *dry tree*, to the Jews.

CHAPTER XVIII

The Jews, in Ezekiel's time, complained of God's dealing hardly with them in punishing them for the sins of their forefathers, 1, 2; *their* temporal *calamities having been long threatened as the consequence of the national guilt,* (Jer. xv. 4, &c.;) *and, from the general complexion of this chapter, it appears that the Jews so interpreted the second commandment of the Decalogue and other passages of like import, as if the sins of the forefathers were visited upon the children, independently of the moral conduct of the latter, not only in this world, but in that which is to come. To remove every foundation for such an unworthy idea of the Divine government, God assures them, with an oath, that he had no respect of persons,* 3, 4; *strongly intimating that the great mysteries in Providence, (mysterious only on account of the limited capacity of man,) are results of the most impartial administration of justice; and that this would be particularly manifested in the rewards and punishments of another life; when every ligament that at present connects societies and nations together shall be dissolved, and each person receive according to his work, and bear his own burden. This is illustrated by a variety of examples: such as that of a just or righteous man,* 5–9; *his wicked son,* 10–13; *and again the just son of this wicked person,* 14–20. *Then a wicked man repenting, and finding mercy, whose former wickedness shall be no impediment to his salvation,* 21–23; *and a righteous man revolting, and dying in his sins, whose former righteousness shall be of no avail,* 24. *The conduct of the Divine Providence is then vindicated,* 25–29; *and all persons, without any exception, most earnestly exhorted to repentance,* 30, 31; *because the Lord hath no pleasure in the death of the sinner,* 32. *As the whole of this chapter is taken up with the illustration of a doctrine nearly connected with the comfort of man, and the honour of the Divine government, the prophet, with great propriety, lays aside his usual mode of figure and allegory, and treats his subject with the utmost plainness and perspicuity.*

A. M. 3410
B. C. 594
Ol. XLVI. 3
Anno
Tarquinii Prisci,
R. Roman., 23

THE word of the LORD came unto me again, saying,
2 What mean ye, that ye use this proverb concerning the land of Israel, saying, The [a]fathers have eaten sour grapes, and the children's teeth are set on edge?
3 *As* I live, saith the Lord GOD, ye shall not have *occasion* any more to use this proverb in Israel.
4 Behold, all souls are mine; as the soul of the father, so also the soul of the son is mine: [b]the soul that sinneth, it shall die.
5 But if a man be just, and do [c]that which is lawful and right,
6 [d]*And* hath not eaten upon the mountains, neither hath lifted up his eyes to the idols of the house of Israel, neither hath [e]defiled his neighbour's wife, neither hath come near to a [f]menstruous woman,
7 And hath not [g]oppressed any, *but* hath restored to the debtor his [h]pledge, hath spoiled none by violence, hath [i]given his bread to the hungry, and hath covered the naked with a garment;
8 He *that* hath not given forth upon [k]usury, neither hath taken any increase, *that* hath withdrawn his hand from iniquity, [l]hath executed true judgment between man and man,

[a]Jer. xxxi. 29; Lam. v. 7——[b]Ver. 20; Rom. vi. 23——[c]Heb. *judgment and justice*——[d]Ch. xxii. 9——[e]Lev. xviii. 20; xx. 10——[f]Lev. xviii. 19; xx. 18——[g]Exod. xxii. 21; Lev. xix. 15; xxv. 14——[h]Exod. xxii. 26; Deut. xxiv. 12, 13——[i]Deut. xv. 7, 8; Isa. lviii. 7; Matt. xxv. 35, 36——[k]Exod. xxii. 25; Lev. xxv. 36, 37; Deut. xxiii. 19; Neh. xv. 7; Psa. v. 5——[l]Deut. i. 16; Zech. viii. 16

NOTES ON CHAP. XVIII

Verse 2. *The fathers have eaten sour grapes, and the children's teeth are set on edge?*] We have seen this proverb already, Jer. xxxi. 29, &c., and have considered its general meaning. But the subject is here proposed in greater detail, with a variety of circumstances, to adapt it to all those cases to which it should apply. It refers simply to these questions: How far can the moral evil of the parent be extended to his offspring? And, Are the faults and evil propensities of the parents, not only transferred to the children, but punished in them? Do parents transfer their evil nature, and are their children punished for their offences?

Verse 3. As *I live, saith the Lord God, ye shall not have* occasion *any more to use this proverb in Israel.*] I will now, by this present declaration, settle this question for ever. And hence God has *sworn* to what follows. After this, who will dare to doubt the judgment pronounced?

Verse 4. *All souls are mine*] Equally so; I am the Father of the spirits of all flesh, and shall deal *impartially* with the whole.

The soul that sinneth, it shall die.] None shall *die* for *another's crimes;* none shall be saved by *another's righteousness.* Here is the *general* judgment relative to the *righteousness* and *unrighteousness* of men, and the *influence* of one *man's state* on *that of another;* particularly in respect to their moral *conduct.*

Verse 5. *If a man be just, and do that which is lawful and right*] If he be *just* or *holy* within, and do what is according to *law* and *equity.* What is meant by this, is immediately specified.

Verse 6. 1. *Hath not eaten upon the mountains*] Idolatrous worship was generally performed on *mountains* and *hills;* and those who offered sacrifices *feasted* on the sacrifice, and thus held *communion* with the idol.

2. *Neither hath lifted up his eyes to the idols*] Has paid them no religious adoration; has trusted in them for nothing, and has not made prayer nor supplication before them.

3. *Neither hath defiled his neighbour's wife*] Has had no adulterous connexion with any woman; to which idolatrous feasts and worship particularly led.

4. *Neither hath come nigh to a menstruous woman*] Has abstained from the use of the marriage-bed during the periodical indisposition of his wife. This was absolutely forbidden by the law; and both the man and the woman who disobeyed the command were to be put to death, Lev. xx. 18. For which *Calmet* gives this reason: "It has been believed, and experience confirms it, that the children conceived at such times are either leprous, or monsters, or deformed by their diminutiveness, or by the disproportion of their members." There are other reasons for this law, should those of the learned commentator be found invalid.

Verse 7. 5. *Hath not oppressed any*] Has not used his power or influence to oppress, pain, or injure another.

6. *Hath restored to the debtor his pledge*] Has carefully surrendered the pawn or pledge when its owner came to *redeem* it. As the *pledge* is generally of *more worth* than that for which it is pledged, an unprincipled man will make some pretence to keep it; which is highly abominable in the sight of God.

7. *Hath spoiled none by violence*] Either by robbery or personal insult. For a man may be spoiled both ways.

8. *Hath given his bread to the hungry*] Has been kind-hearted and charitable; especially to them that are in the deepest want.

9. *Hath covered the naked with a garment*] Has divided both his *bread* and his *clothing* with the necessitous. These are two branches of the same root.

Verse 8. 10. *Hath not given forth upon usury*] בנשך לא יתן *beneshech lo yitten.* נשך *nasach* signifies to *bite; usury* is properly so termed, because it *bites* into and *devours* the *principal.* Usury signifies, with us, exacting *unlawful interest* for money; and taking the *advantage* of a man's necessities to advance him cash on *exorbitant profit.* This *bites* the *receiver* in his *property,* and the *lender* in his *salvation.*

A. M. 3410
B. C. 594
Ol. XLVI. 3
Anno
Tarquinii Prisci,
R. Roman., 23

9 Hath walked in my statutes, and hath kept my judgments, to deal truly; he *is* just, he shall surely [m]live, saith the Lord GOD.

10 If he beget a son *that is* a [n]robber, [o]a shedder of blood, and [p]*that* doeth the like to *any* one of these *things,*

11 And that doeth not any of those *duties,* but even hath eaten upon the mountains, and defiled his neighbour's wife,

12 Hath oppressed the poor and needy, hath spoiled by violence, hath not restored the pledge, and hath lifted up his eyes to the idols, hath [q]committed abomination,

13 Hath given forth upon usury, and hath taken increase: shall he then live? he shall not live: he hath done all these abominations; he shall surely die; [r]his [s]blood shall be upon him.

14 Now, lo, *if* he beget a son, that seeth all his father's sins which he hath done, and considereth, and doeth not such like,

15 [t]*That* hath not eaten upon the mountains, neither hath lifted up his eyes to the idols of the house of Israel, hath not defiled his neighbour's wife,

16 Neither hath oppressed any, [u]hath not withholden the pledge, neither hath spoiled by violence, *but* hath given his bread to the hungry, and hath covered the naked with a garment,

17 *That* hath taken off his hand from the poor, *that* hath not received usury nor increase, hath executed my judgments, hath walked in my statutes; he shall not die for the iniquity of his father, he shall surely live.

18 *As for* his father, because he cruelly oppressed, spoiled his brother by violence, and did *that* which *is* not good among his people, lo, even [v]he shall die in his iniquity.

19 Yet say ye, Why? [w]doth not the son bear the iniquity of the father? When the son hath done that which is lawful and right, *and* hath kept all my statutes, and hath done them, he shall surely live.

20 [x]The soul that sinneth, it shall die. [y]The son shall not bear the iniquity of the father, neither shall the father bear the ini-

[m]Chap. xx. 11; Amos v. 4——[n]Or, *breaker up of a house*——[o]Gen. ix. 6; Exod. xxi. 12; Num. xxxv. 31 [p]Or, *that doeth to his brother besides any of these*——[q]Ch. viii. 6, 17——[r]Lev. xx. 9, 11, 12, 13, 16, 27; chap. iii. 18; xxxiii. 4; Acts xviii. 6——[s]Heb. *bloods*

[t]Ver. 6, &c.——[u]Heb. *hath not pledged the pledge,* or *taken to pledge*——[v]Chap. iii. 18——[w]Exod. xx. 5; Deut. v. 9; 2 Kings xxiii. 26; xxiv. 3, 4——[x]Ver. 4——[y]Deut. xxiv. 16; 2 Kings xiv. 6; 2 Chronicles xxv. 4; Jeremiah xxxi. 29, 30

11. *Neither hath taken any increase*] In lending has not required more than was *lent;* and has not taken that product of the cash *lent,* which was more than the *value* for its *use.* This may be a part of the *tenth* article.

12. *That hath withdrawn his hand from iniquity*] Never *associates* with those who act contrary to *justice* and *equity;* his hand or influence being never found among *evil workers.*

13. *Hath executed true judgment between man and man*] Being neither swayed by *prejudice, fear,* nor *favour.*

These *thirteen points* concern his *social* and *civil* relations.

Verse 9. *Hath walked in my statutes*] Not only acknowledging them to be right, but acting according to them. Especially in every thing that relates to my worship, changing nothing, neglecting nothing.

And hath kept my judgments, to deal truly] Has attended to my Divine direction, both with respect to things *forbidden,* and things *commanded.* These concern men in their *religious* conduct.

He is *just*] צדיק הוא *tsaddik hu.* He is a *righteous* man; he has given to all *their due;* he has *abstained* from every appearance of evil, and done that which was *lawful* and *right* in the sight of God.

He shall surely live] He has *lived to* me, and he shall *live with* me.

Verse 10. *If he beget a son*] Who is the reverse of the above righteous character, according to the *thirteen articles* already specified and explained.

Verse 13. *Shall he then live?*] Because his father was a righteous man, shall the father's holiness be imputed to him? No!

He shall surely die; his blood shall be upon him.] He shall suffer for his own crimes.

Verse 14. *Now, lo,* if *he beget a son that seeth all his father's sins—and considereth*] Lays to heart the evil of his father's life, and the dreadful consequences of a life of rebellion against God.

And doeth not such like] Is quite a different man in moral *feeling* and *character;* and acts up to the *thirteen points* already laid down.

Verse 17. *He shall not die for the iniquity of his father*] He shall no more be affected by his father's *crimes,* than his father was *benefited* by his *grandfather's righteousness.*

Verse 20. *The soul that sinneth, it shall die.*] Hitherto we have had to do with the *simple cases* of the *righteous* and the *wicked;* of him who *lived and died a holy man,* and of him who *lived and died a wicked man.* But there are *two cases* behind: 1. That of the *wicked man,* who *repents* and *turns to God.* 2. That of the *righteous man,* who *backslides,* and *does not return to God* by repentance. On both these cases God decides thus:—

A. M. 3410
B. C. 594
Ol. XLVI. 3
Anno
Tarquinii Prisci,
R. Roman., 23

quity of the son: [z]the righteousness of the righteous shall
be upon him, [a]and the wickedness of the wicked shall be
upon him.
21 But [b]if the wicked will turn from all his
sins that he hath committed, and keep all
my statutes, and do that which is lawful
and right, he shall surely live, he shall not
die.
22 [c]All his transgressions that he hath committed, they shall not be mentioned unto
him: in his righteousness that he hath done
he shall live.
23 [d]Have I any pleasure at all that the
wicked should die? saith the Lord God: *and*
not that he should return from his ways, and
live?
24 But [e]when the righteous turneth away
from his righteousness, and committeth iniquity, *and* doeth according to all the abominations that the wicked *man* doeth, shall he
live? [f]All his righteousness that he hath
done shall not be mentioned: in his trespass
that he hath trespassed, and
in his sin that he hath sinned,
in them shall he die.
25 Yet ye say, [g]The way of
the Lord is not equal. Hear now, O house of
Israel; Is not my way equal? are not your
ways unequal?
26 [h]When a righteous *man* turneth away
from his righteousness, and committeth iniquity, and dieth in them; for his iniquity
that he hath done shall he die.
27 Again, [i]when the wicked *man* turneth
away from his wickedness that he hath committed, and doeth that which is lawful and
right, he shall save his soul alive.
28 Because he [k]considereth, and turneth
away from all his transgressions that he hath
committed, he shall surely live, he shall not
die.
29 [l]Yet saith the house of Israel, The way
of the Lord is not equal. O house of Israel,
are not my ways equal? are not your ways
unequal?
30 [m]Therefore I will judge you, O house of

A. M. 3410
B. C. 594
Ol. XLVI. 3
Anno
Tarquinii Prisci,
R. Roman., 23

[z]Isa. iii. 10, 11——[a]Rom. ii. 9——[b]Ver. 27; chap. xxxiii. 12, 19——[c]Chap. xxxiii. 16——[d]Ver. 32; chap. xxxiii. 11; 1 Tim. ii. 4; 2 Pet. iii. 9

[e]Chap. iii. 20; xxxiii. 12, 13, 18——[f]2 Pet. ii. 20
[g]Ver. 29; chap. xxxiii. 17, 20——[h]Ver. 24——[i]Ver. 21
[k]Ver. 14——[l]Ver. 25——[m]Chap. vii. 3; xxxiii. 20

Verse 21. *But if the wicked will turn from all his sins*] And afterwards walk according to the character of the righteous already specified; shall he find mercy, and be for ever saved? Yes.

Verse 22. *All his transgressions*] Shall be so completely forgiven by God's mercy, that they *shall not be even mentioned to him;* and if he live and die in this recovered state, he shall live with God to all eternity. And why? Hear the reason:—

Verse 23. *Have I any pleasure at all that the wicked should die?*] No! That is foreign to him whose name is love, and whose nature is mercy. On the contrary he "wills that he should return from his evil ways and live."

And if God can have *no pleasure* in the *death of the wicked,* he cannot have made a *decree* to abandon him to the evil of his nature, and then damn him for what he could not avoid: for as God can *do* nothing with which he is *not pleased,* so he can *decree* nothing with which he is *not pleased.* But he is "not pleased with the death of a sinner;" therefore he cannot have *made a decree* to bring him to this *death.*

Verse 24. *When the righteous turneth away from his righteousness*] Here is the *second* case. Can a man who was once holy and pure, fall away so as to perish everlastingly? Yes. For God says, "If he turn away from his righteousness;" not his *self-righteousness,* the gloss of theologians: for God never speaks of turning away from *that,* for, in his eyes, that is a *nonentity.* There is no righteousness or holiness but what himself infuses into the soul of man, and as to *self-righteousness,* i. e., a man's *supposing* himself to be *righteous* when he has not the *life of God* in his soul, it is the delusion of a dark and hardened heart; therefore it is the *real righteous principle* and *righteous practice* that God speaks of here. And he tells us, that a man may so "turn away from this," and so "commit iniquity," and "act as the wicked man," that *his righteousness shall be no more mentioned* to his account, than the *sins* of the *penitent backslider* should be *mentioned* to his condemnation; and "in the sin that he," this once righteous man, "hath sinned, and in the trespass that he hath trespassed, in them shall he die." O, how awful a termination of a life once distinguished for righteousness and true holiness! So then, God himself informs us that a *righteous man* may not only *fall foully,* but *fall finally.* But to such righteous persons the devil will ever preach, "Ye shall not surely die; ye shall be as God." Touch, taste, and handle; ye cannot ultimately fall. Thus we find, by the manner of treating these *two cases,* that *God's way is equal,* ver. 25; just, merciful, and impartial. And to prove this, he sums up his conduct in the above cases, in the following verses, 26, 27, 28, 29. And then, that the "wicked may not die in his sins," and that the "backslider may return and find mercy," he thus exhorts:—

Verse 30. *Repent, and turn* yourselves *from all your transgressions*] There is still life; still a God that has *no pleasure* in the death of a sinner, one who is ever ready to give his

A. M. 3410
B. C. 594
Ol. XLVI. 3
Anno
Tarquinii Prisci,
R. Roman., 23

Israel, every one according to
his ways, saith the Lord God.
[n]Repent, and turn [o]*yourselves*
from all your transgressions;
so iniquity shall not be your ruin.
31 [p]Cast away from you all your transgressions, whereby ye have transgressed; and
make you a [q]new heart and a
new spirit: for why will ye
die, O house of Israel?
32 For [r]I have no pleasure
in the death of him that dieth, saith the
Lord God: wherefore turn [s]*yourselves*, and
live ye.

[n]Matt. iii. 2; Rev. ii. 5——[o]Or, others——[p]Eph. iv. 22, 23——[q]Jer. xxxii. 39; chap. xi. 19; xxxvi. 26

[r]Lam. iii. 33; ver. 23; chap. xxxiii. 11; 2 Pet. iii. 9——[s]Or, others

Holy Spirit to all them that ask him; therefore "repent and turn, so iniquity shall not be your ruin."

Verse 31. *Cast away*] With a holy violence, dash away every transgression and incentive to it.

Make you a new heart] Call upon God for it, and he will give it: for as sure as you *earnestly call on God through Christ* to save you, so surely you shall be saved; and the *effect* will so speedily follow, that God is pleased to attribute that in some sort to *yourselves*, which is done by *his grace alone;* because ye earnestly *call* upon him for it, *come* in the right way to receive it, and are *determined* never to *rest* till you have it.

For why will ye die] Why should you go to *hell* while the kingdom of God is open to receive you? Why should you be the *devil's slaves*, when ye may be *Christ's freemen?* WHY WILL YE DIE? Every word is emphatic. *Why*—show God or man one *reason. Will*—obstinacy alone, —a determination not to be saved, or a *voluntary* listlessness about salvation,—can prevent you. *Ye*—children of so many mercies, fed and supported by a kind God all your life; *ye*, who are redeemed by the blood of Jesus Christ; *ye*, who have made many promises to give up yourselves to God; *ye*, who have been dedicated to the ever-blessed Trinity, and promised to renounce the devil and all his works, the pomps and vanities of this wicked world, and all the sinful lusts of the flesh; *why will* YE *die? Die!*—what is this? A separation from God and the glory of his power **for** ever! *Die!*—forfeiting all the purposes for which your immortal souls were made! *Die*—to know what the *worm* is that *never dieth*, and what that *fire* is which is *never quenched!* Why will ye die?

Verse 32. *For I have no pleasure*] God repeats what he had so solemnly declared before. Can ye doubt his sincerity? his ability? his willingness? the efficacy of the blood of his covenant?

Wherefore turn yourselves, *and live ye.*] Reader, now give God thy heart.

Though every man comes into the world with a *fallen nature—a soul infected with sin*, yet no man is damned on that account. He who *refuses* that grace which *pardons sin* and *heals infected nature*, who permits the *evil principle* to break out into *transgression*, and *continues* and dies in his iniquity and sin, and will not come unto Christ that he may have life; he, and he only, goes to perdition. Nor will the righteousness of a parent or relation help his sinful soul: no man can have more grace than is necessary to *save himself;* and none can have that, who does not receive it *through Christ Jesus.* It is the mercy of God in Christ which renders the *salvation of a sinner possible;* and it is that mercy alone which can *heal* the *backslider.* The atoning blood *blots out all that is past;* the same blood *cleanses from all unrighteousness.* Who believes so as to *apply* for this redemption? Who properly thanks God for having provided such a Saviour?

CHAPTER XIX

This chapter contains two beautiful examples of the parabolic kind of writing; the one lamenting the sad catastrophe of Jehoahaz and Jehoiakim, 1–9, and the other describing the desolation and captivity of the whole people, 10–14. In the first parable, the lioness is Jerusalem. The first of the young lions is Jehoahaz, deposed by the king of Egypt; and the second lion is Jehoiakim, whose rebellion drew on himself the vengeance of the king of Babylon. In the second parable the vine is the Jewish nation, which long prospered, its land being fertile, its princes powerful, and its people flourishing; but the judgments of God, in consequence of their guilt, had now destroyed a great part of the people, and doomed the rest to captivity.

A. M. 3410
B. C. 594
Ol. XLVI. 3
Anno
Tarquinii Prisci,
R. Roman., 23

MOREOVER [a]take thou up
a lamentation for the
princes of Israel,
2 And say, What *is* thy
mother? A lioness: she lay
down among lions, she nourished her whelps among young
lions.

[a]Chap. xxvi. 17; xxvii. 2

NOTES ON CHAP. XIX

Verse 1. *Moreover take thou up a lamentation*] Declare what is the great subject of sorrow in Israel. Compose a funeral dirge. Show the melancholy fate of the kings who proceeded from Josiah. The prophet deplores the misfortune of *Jehoahaz* and *Jehoiakim*, under the figure of *two lion whelps*, which were *taken by hunters*, and *confined in cages.* Next he shows the *desolation of Jerusalem* under *Zedekiah*, which he compares to a *beautiful vine* pulled up by the roots, withered, and at last burned. *Calmet* justly observes, that the style of this

A. M. 3410
B. C. 594
Ol. XLVI. 3
Anno
Tarquinii Prisci,
R. Roman., 23

3 And she brought up one
of her whelps: [b]it became a
young lion, and it learned to
catch the prey; it devoured
men.
4 The nations also heard of him; he was
taken in their pit, and they brought him with
chains unto the land of [c]Egypt.
5 Now when she saw that she had waited,
and her hope was lost, then she [d]took another
of her whelps, *and* made him a young lion.
6 [e]And he went up and down among the
lions, [f]he became a young lion, and learned
to catch the prey, *and* devoured men.
7 And he knew [g]their desolate palaces, and
he laid waste their cities; and the land was
desolate, and the fulness thereof, by the noise
of his roaring.

[b]Ver. 6; 2 Kings xxiii. 31, 32——[c]2 Kings xxiii. 33; 2 Chron. xxxvi. 4; Jer. xxii. 11, 12——[d]2 Kings xxiii. 34 [e]Jer. xxiii. 13-17——[f]Ver. 3——[g]Or, *their widows* [h]2 Kings xxiv. 2——[i]Ver. 4

8 [h]Then the nations set
against him on every side
from the provinces, and
spread their net over him:
[i]he was taken in their pit.
9 [k]And they put him in ward [l]in chains,
and brought him to the king of Babylon:
they brought him into holds, that his voice
should no more be heard upon [m]the mountains of Israel.
10 Thy mother *is* [n]like a vine [o]in thy blood,
planted by the waters: she was [p]fruitful
and full of branches by reason of many
waters.
11 And she had strong rods for the sceptres
of them that bare rule, and her [q]stature was
exalted among the thick branches, and she

A. M. 3410
B. C. 594
Ol. XLVI. 3
Anno
Tarquinii Prisci,
R. Roman., 23

[k]2 Chron. xxxvi. 6; Jer. xxii. 18——[l]Or, *in hooks* [m]Ezek. vi. 2——[n]Chap. xvii. 6——[o]Or, *in thy quietness*, or *in thy likeness*——[p]Deut. viii. 7, 8, 9——[q]So chap. xxxi. 3; Dan. iv. 11

song is beautiful, and the allegory well supported throughout.

Verse 2. *What* is *thy mother? A lioness*] *Judea* may here be the *mother;* the *lioness*, Jerusalem. *Her lying down among lions*, her having confederacy with the neighbouring *kings;* for *lion* here means *king*.

Verse 3. *She brought up one of her whelps*] *Jehoahaz*, son of Josiah, whose father was conquered and slain by Pharaoh-necho, king of Egypt.

It learned to catch the prey] His reign was a reign of oppression and cruelty. He made his *subjects* his *prey*, and devoured their *substance*.

Verse 4. *The nations also heard of him*] The king of Egypt, whose subjects were of divers nations, marched against Jerusalem, took *Jehoahaz* prisoner, and brought him to Egypt. Thus—

He was taken in their pit] Here is an allusion to those *trap-pits* digged in forests, into which the wild beasts fall, when the huntsmen, surrounding a given portion of the forest, drive the beasts in; by degrees narrowing the inclosure, till the animals come to the place where the pits are, which, being lightly covered over with *branches* and *turf*, are not perceived, and the beasts tread on them and fall in. Jehoahaz reigned only *three* months before he was dethroned by the king of Egypt, against whom it is apparent some craft was used, here signified by the *pit*, into which he fell.

Verse 5. *When she saw that she had waited*] Being very weak, the Jews found that they could not resist with any *hope* of success; so the king of Egypt was permitted to do as he pleased.

She took another of her whelps] Jehoiakim.

And made him a young lion.] King of Judea.

Verse 6. *And he went up and down among the lions*] He became a perfect heathen, and made Judea as idolatrous as any of the surrounding nations. He reigned *eleven* years, a monster of iniquity, 2 Kings xxiii. 30, &c.

Verse 8. *The nations set against him*] The Chaldeans, Syrians, Moabites, and Ammonites, and the king of Babylon—king of many nations.

He was taken] The city was taken by Nebuchadnezzar; and Jehoiakim was taken prisoner, and sent in *chains* to *Babylon*.

Verse 9. *That his voice should no more be heard*] He continued in prison many years, till the reign of Evil-merodach, who set him at liberty, but never suffered him to return to the *mountains of Israel*. "The unhappy fate of these princes, mentioned ver. 4, 8, 9, is a just subject of lamentation."—*Newcome*.

Verse 10. *Thy mother* (Jerusalem) is *like a vine in thy blood*] Of this expression I know not what to make. Some think the meaning is, "A vine planted by the waters to produce the *blood of the grape*." See Deut. xxxii. 14. Others, for בדמך *bedamecha, in thy blood*, would read ברמון *berimmon, in* or *at a pomegranate;* like a vine planted by or beside a pomegranate-tree, by which it was to be supported. And so the *Septuagint* and *Arabic* appear to have read. *Calmet* reads כרמך *carmecha, thy vineyard*, instead of בדמך *bedamecha, in thy blood*. Here is no change but a ר *resh* for a ד *daleth*. This reading is supported by one of *Kennicott's* and one of *De Rossi's* MSS.: "Thy mother is like a vine in thy vineyard, planted by the waters." Though this is rather an unusual construction, yet it seems the best *emendation*. Of the textual reading no sense can be made. There is a corruption somewhere.

Full of branches] Many *princes*. See next verse.

Verse 11. *She had strong rods*] *Zedekiah*, and his many *sons*.

Her stature was exalted] Zedekiah grew *proud* of his numerous offspring and prosperity; and although he copied the example of *Jehoiakim*, yet he thought he might safely rebel against the king of Babylon.

A. M. 3410
B. C. 594
Ol. XLVI. 3
Anno
Tarquinii Prisci,
R. Roman., 23

appeared in her height with
the multitude of her branches.
12 But she was plucked up
in fury, she was cast down to
the ground, and the [r]east wind dried up her
fruit: her strong rods were broken and withered; the fire consumed them.
13 And now she *is* planted in the wilderness, in a dry and thirsty
ground.
14 [s]And fire is gone out of
a rod of her branches, *which*
hath devoured her fruit, so that she hath no
strong rod *to be* a sceptre to rule. [t]This
is a lamentation, and shall be for a lamentation.

A. M. 3410
B. C. 594
Ol. XLVI. 3
Anno
Tarquinii Prisci,
R. Roman., 23

[r]Chap. xvii. 10; Hos. xiii. 15——[s]Judg. ix. 15; 2 Kings xxiv. 20; chap. xvii. 18——[t]Lam. iv. 20

Verse 12. *But she was plucked up in fury*] Jerusalem; taken after a violent and most destructive siege; Nebuchadnezzar being violently *enraged* against Zedekiah for breaking his oath to him.

She was cast down to the ground] Jerusalem was totally ruined, by being burned to the ground.

Her strong rods were broken] The *children* of Zedekiah were slain before his eyes, and after that his *own eyes pulled out;* and he was laden with chains, and carried into Babylon.

Verse 13. *And now she* is *planted in the wilderness*] In the land of *Chaldea,* whither the people have been carried captives; and which, compared with their own land, was to them a *dreary wilderness.*

Verse 14. *Fire is gone out*] A vindictive and murderous disposition has taken hold—

Of a rod of her branches] Ishmael, son of Nethaniah, who was of the blood-royal of Judah,—

Hath devoured her fruit] Hath assassinated *Gedaliah,* slain many people, and carried off others into the country of the Ammonites. But he was pursued by Jonathan, the son of Kareah, who slew many of his adherents, and delivered much of the people.

She hath no strong rod] None of the blood-royal of Judah left. And from that time not one of her own royal race ever sat upon the throne of Israel.

This is *a lamentation*] This is a most lamentable business.

And shall be for a lamentation.] These predictions shall be so punctually fulfilled, and the catastrophe shall be so complete, that it shall ever remain as a lamentation; as this state of Jerusalem shall never be restored. Even to the present day this, to a Jew, is a subject of mourning.

CHAPTER XX

A deputation of the elders of Israel, as usual, in their distress, came to request Ezekiel to ask counsel of God, 1. *In reply to this, God commands the prophet to put them in mind of their rebellion and idolatry: In Egypt,* 2–9, *in the wilderness,* 10–27, *and in Canaan,* 28–32. *Notwithstanding which the Lord most graciously promises to restore them to their own land, after they should be purged from their dross,* 33–44. *The five last verses of this chapter ought to begin the next, as they are connected with the subject of that chapter, being a prophecy against Jerusalem, which lay to the south of Chaldea, where the prophet then was, and which here and elsewhere is represented under the emblem of a forest doomed to be destroyed by fire,* 45–49.

A. M. 3411
B. C. 594
Ol. XLVI. 4
Anno
Tarquinii Prisci,
R. Roman., 24

AND it came to pass in the
seventh year, in the fifth
month, the tenth *day* of the
month, *that* [a]certain of the
elders of Israel came to inquire of the LORD,
and sat before me.
2 Then came the word of the LORD unto
me, saying,
3 Son of man, speak unto
the elders of Israel, and say
unto them, Thus saith the
Lord GOD; Are ye come to
inquire of me? *As* I live, saith the Lord GOD,
[b]I will not be inquired of by you.
4 Wilt thou [c]judge [d]them, son of man, wilt
thou judge *them?* [e]cause them to know

A. M. 3411
B. C. 593
Ol. XLVI. 4
Anno
Tarquinii Prisci,
R. Roman., 24

[a]Chap. viii. 1; xiv. 1——[b]Ver. 31; chap. xiv. 3——[c]Or, *plead for them*——[d]Ch. xxii. 2; xxiii. 36——[e]Ch. xvi. 2

NOTES ON CHAP. XX

Verse 1. *In the seventh year*] Of the captivity of Jeconiah, (see chap. viii. 1,) and *the seventh of the reign* of Zedekiah.

The fifth month, *the tenth* day] That is, according to Abp. *Usher, Monday,* August 27, A.M. 3411.

Certain of the elders of Israel] What these came to inquire about is not known. They were doubtless hypocrites and deceivers, from the manner in which God commands the prophet to treat them. It seems to have been such a deputation of elders as those mentioned chap. viii. 1 and xiv. 1.

Verse 3. *I will not be inquired of by you.*] I will not hear you. I will have nothing to do with you.

Verse 4. *Wilt thou judge them*] If thou wilt *enter into any discussion with them,* show them *the abomination of their fathers.* The whole chapter is a consecutive history of the *unfaithfulness, ingratitude, rebellion,* and *idolatry* of the Jews, from the earliest times to that day; and vindicates the sentence which God had pronounced against them, and which he was about to execute more fully in delivering them and the city into the hands of the Chaldeans.

A. M. 3411 B. C. 593 Ol. XLVI. 4 Anno Tarquinii Prisci, R. Roman., 24

the abominations of their
fathers:
5 And say unto them, Thus
saith the Lord God; In the
day when [f]I chose Israel, and [g]lifted up mine
hand unto the seed of the house of Jacob,
and made myself [h]known unto them in the
land of Egypt, when I lifted up mine hand
unto them, saying, [i]I *am* the LORD your
God;
6 In the day *that* I lifted up mine hand
unto them, [k]to bring them forth of the land
of Egypt into a land that I had espied for
them, flowing with milk and honey, [l]which
is the glory of all lands:
7 Then said I unto them, [m]Cast ye away
every man [n]the abominations of his eyes, and
defile not yourselves with [o]the idols of Egypt:
I *am* the LORD your God.
8 But they rebelled against me, and would
not hearken unto me: they
did not every man cast away
the abominations of their
eyes, neither did they forsake
the idols of Egypt: then I said, I will [p]pour
out my fury upon them, to accomplish my
anger against them in the midst of the land
of Egypt.
9 [q]But I wrought for my name's sake, that
it should not be polluted before the heathen,
among whom they *were*, in whose sight I
made myself known unto them, in bringing
them forth out of the land of Egypt.
10 Wherefore I [r]caused them to go forth
out of the land of Egypt, and brought them
into the wilderness.
11 [s]And I gave them my statutes, and
[t]showed them my judgments, [u]which *if* a
man do, he shall even live in them.
12 Moreover also I gave them my [v]sabbaths,

[f]Exod. vi. 7; Deut. vii. 6——[g]Or, *sware;* and so ver. 6, &c.; Exod. vi. 8——[h]Exod. iii. 8; iv. 31; Deut. iv. 34——[i]Exod. xx. 2——[k]Exod. iii. 8, 17; Deut. viii. 7, 8, 9; Jer. xxxii. 22——[l]Psa. xlviii. 2; ver. 15; Dan. viii. 9; xi. 16, 41; Zech. vii. 14——[m]Chap. xviii. 31——[n]2 Chron. xv. 8——[o]Lev. xvii. 7; xviii. 3; Deut. xxix. 16, 17, 18; Josh. xxiv. 14——[p]Chap. vii. 8; ver. 13, 21——[q]See Exod. xxxii. 12; Num. xiv. 13, &c.; Deut. ix. 28; ver. 14, 22; chap. xxxvi. 21, 22——[r]Exod. xiii. 18——[s]Deut. iv.8; Neh. ix. 13, 14; Psa. cxlvii. 19, 20——[t]Heb. *made them to know*——[u]Lev. xviii. 5; ver. 13, 21; Rom. x. 5; Gal. iii. 12——[v]Exod. xx. 8; xxxi. 13, &c.; xxxv. 2; Deut. v. 12; Neh. ix. 14

Verse 5. *I chose Israel*] They did not choose *me* for *their God*, till I had chosen *them* to be *my people*.

I lifted up mine hand] I bound myself in a covenant to them to continue to be their God, if they should be faithful, and continue to be my people. Among the Jews the *juror* lifted up his right hand to heaven; which explains Psa. cxliv. 8: "Their right hand is a right hand of falsehood." This is a form used in England, Scotland, and Ireland.

Verse 6. *To bring them forth of the land of Egypt*] When they had been long in a very disgraceful and oppressive bondage.

A land that I had espied for them] God represents himself as having *gone over different countries* in order to *find* a comfortable residence for these people, whom he considered as his children.

Flowing with milk and honey] These were the characteristics of a *happy and fruitful country*, producing without intense labour all the *necessaries* and *comforts* of life. Of the happiest state and happiest place, a fine poet gives the following description:—

Ver erat æternum, placidique tepentibus auris
Mulcebant Zephyri natos sine semine flores.
Mox etiam fruges tellus inarata ferebat:
Nec renovatus ager gravidis canebat aristis.
Flumina jam *lactis*, jam *flumina nectaris* ibant:
Flavaque de viridi *stillabant* ilice *mella*.

OVID'S *Metam.* lib. i., 107.

On flowers unsown soft Zephyr spreads his wing,
And time itself was one eternal spring;
Ensuing years the yellow harvest crowned,
The bearded blade sprang from the untilled ground,
And laden, unrenewed, the fields were found.
Floods were with *milk*, and *floods* with *nectar filled*,
And *honey* from the sweating *oaks* distilled.

In the flourishing state of Judea every mountain was cultivated as well as the valleys. Among the very rocks the vines grew luxuriantly.

Verse 7. *Cast ye away—the abominations*] Put away all your idols; those incentives to idolatry that ye have looked on with delight.

Verse 8. *They did not—cast away*] They continued attached to the *idolatry* of Egypt; so that, had I consulted my *justice* only, I should have consumed them *even in Egypt* itself. This is a circumstance that Moses has not mentioned, namely, their provoking God by their idolatry, *after* he had sent Moses and Aaron to them in *Egypt*.

Verse 9. *But I wrought for my name's sake*] I bare with them and did not punish them, lest the heathen, who had known my promises made to them, might suppose that I had either broken them through some caprice, or was not able to fulfil them.

Verse 10. *I caused them to go forth*] Though greatly oppressed and degraded, they were not *willing* to leave their *house of bondage*. I was obliged to *force them away*.

Verse 11. *I gave them my statutes*] I showed them what they should do in order to be safe, comfortable, wise, and happy; and what they should avoid in order to be uninjured in body, mind, and possessions. Had they attended to these things, they should have *lived by them*. They would have been holy, healthy, and happy.

Verse 12. *I gave them my Sabbaths*] The religious observance of the Sabbath was the *first statute* or *command* of God to men. This

A. M. 3411
B. C. 593
Ol. XLVI. 4
Anno
Tarquinii Prisci,
R. Roman., 24

to be a sign between me and them, that they might know that I *am* the LORD that sanctify them.

13 But the house of Israel [w]rebelled against me in the wilderness: they walked not in my statutes, and they [x]despised my judgments, which *if* a man do, he shall even live in them; and my sabbaths they greatly [y]polluted: then I said, I would pour out my fury upon them in the [z]wilderness, to consume them.

14 [a]But I wrought for my name's sake, that it should not be polluted before the heathen, in whose sight I brought them out.

15 Yet also [b]I lifted up my hand unto them in the wilderness, that I would not bring them into the land which I had given *them,* flowing with milk and honey, [c]which *is* the glory of all lands;

16 [d]Because they despised my judgments, and walked not in my statutes, but polluted my sabbaths: for [e]their heart went after their idols.

17 [f]Nevertheless mine eye spared them from destroying them, neither did I make an end of them in the wilderness.

18 But I said unto their children in the wilderness, Walk ye not in the statutes of your fathers, neither observe their judgments, nor defile yourselves with their idols:

[w]Num. xiv. 22; Psa. lxxviii. 40; xcv. 8, 9, 10——[x]Ver. 16, 24; Prov. i. 25——[y]Exod. xvi. 27——[z]Num. xiv. 29; xxvi. 65; Psa. cvi. 23——[a]Ver. 9, 22——[b]Num. xiv. 28; Psa. xcv. 11; cvi. 26——[c]Ver. 6——[d]Ver. 13, 24 [e]Num. xv. 39; Psa. lxxviii. 37; Amos v. 25, 26; Acts vii. 42, 43——[f]Psa. lxxviii. 38——[g]Deut. v. 32, 33; vi., vii., viii., x., xi., xii

19 I *am* the LORD your God; [g]walk in my statutes, and keep my judgments, and do them;

A. M. 3411
B. C. 593
Ol. XLVI. 4
Anno
Tarquinii Prisci,
R. Roman., 24

20 [h]And hallow my sabbaths; and they shall be a sign between me and you, that ye may know that I *am* the LORD your God.

21 Notwithstanding [i]the children rebelled against me: they walked not in my statutes, neither kept my judgments to do them, [k]which *if* a man do, he shall even live in them; they polluted my sabbaths: then I said, [l]I would pour out my fury upon them, to accomplish my anger against them in the wilderness.

22 [m]Nevertheless I withdrew mine hand, and [n]wrought for my name's sake, that it should not be polluted in the sight of the heathen, in whose sight I brought them forth.

23 I lifted up mine hand unto them also in the wilderness, that [o]I would scatter them among the heathen, and disperse them through the countries;

24 [p]Because they had not executed my judgments, but had despised my statutes, and had polluted my sabbaths, and [q]their eyes were after their fathers' idols.

25 Wherefore [r]I gave them also statutes *that were* not good, and judgments whereby they should not live;

[h]Ver. 12; Jer. xvii. 22——[i]Num. xxv. 1, 2; Deut. ix. 23, 24; xxxi. 27——[k]Ver. 11, 13——[l]Ver. 8, 13 [m]Psalm lxxviii. 38; ver. 17——[n]Ver. 9, 14——[o]Leviticus xxvi. 33; Deuteronomy xxviii. 64; Psalm cvi. 27; Jeremiah xv. 4——[p]Ver. 13, 16——[q]See chap. vi. 9 [r]See Psalm lxxxi. 12; ver. 39; Romans i. 24; 2 Thess. ii. 11

institution was *a sign between God and them,* to keep them in remembrance of the creation of the world, of the *rest* that he designed them in Canaan, and of the eternal inheritance among the saints in light. Of these things the Sabbath was a *type* and *pledge.*

Verse 13. *But the house of Israel rebelled*] They acted in the *wilderness* just as they had done in *Egypt;* and he spared them there for the same reason. See ver. 9.

Verse 15. *I lifted up my hand*] Their provocations in the wilderness were so great, that I vowed never to bring them into the promised land. I did not *consume* them, but I *disinherited* them. See the note on ver. 5.

Verse 18. *But I said unto their children*] These I chose in their fathers' stead; and to them I purposed to give the inheritance which their fathers by disobedience lost.

Verse 22. *I withdrew mine hand*] I had just lifted it up to crush them as in a moment; for they also were idolatrous, and walked in the steps of their fathers.

Verse 25. *I gave them also statutes* that were *not good*] What a foolish noise has been made about this verse by *critics,* believers and infidels! How is it that God can be said "to give a people statutes that were not good, and judgments whereby they could not live?" I answer, in *their sense* of the words, God never gave any such, at any time, to any people. Let any man produce *an example* of this kind if he can; or show even the *fragment* of such a law, sanctioned by the Most High! The simple meaning of this place and all such places is, that when they had rebelled against the Lord, despised his statutes, and polluted his Sabbaths—in effect cast him off, and given themselves wholly to their idols, then he *abandoned* them, and they abandoned themselves to the customs and ordinances of the heathen. That this is the meaning of the words, requires no proof to them who are the least acquainted with the *genius* and *idioms* of the Hebrew language, in which God is a thousand times said *to do,* what in the course of his *providence* or *justice* he only *permits* to be done.

A. M. 3411
B. C. 593
Ol. XLVI. 4
Anno
Tarquinii Prisci,
R. Roman., 24

26 And I polluted them in their own gifts, in that they caused to pass [s]through *the fire* all that openeth the womb, that I might make them desolate, to the end that they [t]might know that I *am* the LORD.

27 Therefore, son of man, speak unto the house of Israel, and say unto them, Thus saith the Lord GOD; Yet in this your fathers have [u]blasphemed me, in that they have [v]committed a trespass against me.

28 *For* when I had brought them into the land, *for* the which I lifted up mine hand to give it to them, then [w]they saw every high hill, and all the thick trees, and they offered there their sacrifices, and there they presented the provocation of their offering: there also they made their [x]sweet savour, and poured out there their drink-offerings.

29 Then [y]I said unto them, What *is* the high place whereunto ye go? And the name thereof is called Bamah unto this day.

30 Wherefore say unto the house of Israel, Thus saith the Lord GOD; Are ye polluted after the manner of your fathers? and commit ye whoredom after their abominations?

31 For when ye offer [z]your gifts, when ye make your sons to [a]pass through the fire, ye pollute yourselves with all your idols, even unto this day: and [b]shall I be inquired of by you, O house of Israel? *As* I live, saith the Lord GOD, I will not be inquired of by you.

32 And that [c]which cometh into your mind shall not be at all, that ye say, We will be as the heathen, as the families of the countries, to serve wood and stone.

33 *As* I live, saith the Lord GOD, surely with a mighty hand, and [d]with a stretched-out arm, and with fury poured out, will I rule over you:

34 And I will bring you out from the people, and will gather you out of the countries wherein ye are scattered, with a mighty hand, and with a stretched-out arm, and with fury poured out.

35 And I will bring you into the wilderness of the people, and there [e]will I plead with you face to face.

36 [f]Like as I pleaded with your fathers in the wilderness of the land of Egypt, so will I plead with you, saith the Lord GOD.

37 And I will cause you to [g]pass under the rod, and I will bring you into [h]the bond of the covenant:

[s]2 Kings xvii. 17; xxi. 6; 2 Chron. xxviii. 3; xxxiii. 6; Jer. xxxii. 35; chap. xvi. 20, 21——[t]Chap. vi. 7——[u]Rom. ii. 24——[v]Heb. *trespassed a trespass*——[w]Isa. lvii. 5, &c.; chap. vi. 13——[x]Chap. xvi. 19——[y]Or, *I told them what the high place* was, or *Bamah*——[z]Ver. 26——[a]2 Kings xvi. 3; xxi. 6; xxiii. 10——[b]Ver. 3——[c]Chap. xi. 5——[d]Jer. xxi. 5——[e]Jer. ii. 9, 35; chap. xvii. 20——[f]See Numbers xiv. 21, 22, 23, 28, 29——[g]Leviticus xxvii. 32; Jeremiah xxxiii. 13——[h]Or, *a delivering*

Verse 26. *I polluted them in their own gifts*] I *permitted* them to pollute themselves by the offerings which they made to their idols. Causing their children to pass through the fire was one of those *pollutions;* but, did God ever *give them a statute* or *judgment* of *this kind?* No. He ever inveighs against such things, and they incur his heaviest displeasure and curse. See on ver. 31.

Verse 29. *What* is *the high place*] מה הבמה *mah habbamah,* "what is the high place?" What is it good for? Its being a *high place* shows it to be a *place of idolatry.* I called it במה *bamah,* to mark it with *infamy;* but ye continue to frequent it, even while it is called במה *bamah,* to the present day!

Verse 31. *Ye pollute yourselves*] This shows the sense in which God says, ver. 26, "I polluted them in their own gifts." They *chose* to pollute themselves, and I *permitted* them to do so. See on verses 25, 26.

Verse 32. *And that which cometh into your mind*] Ye wish to be naturalized among *idolaters,* and make a part of such nations. But this *shall not be at all;* you shall be preserved as a *distinct people.* Ye shall not be permitted to mingle yourselves with the people of those countries: even *they,* idolaters as they are, will *despise* and *reject you.* Besides, I will change your place, restore your captivity; yet not in *mercy,* but *in fury poured out;* and reserve you for sorer evils, ver. 34.

Verse 35. *I will bring you into the wilderness of the people*] I will bring you out of your captivity, and bring you into *your own land,* which you will find to be a *wilderness,* the consequence of your crimes.

There will I plead with you] There I will be your king, and rule you with a sovereign rule; and the dispensations of my justice and mercy shall either *end you* or *mend you.*

Verse 37. *I will cause you to pass under the rod*] This alludes to the custom of *tithing* the *sheep.* I take it from the rabbins. The sheep were all penned; and the shepherd stood at the door of the fold, where only one sheep could come out *at once.* He had in his hand a *rod* dipped in *vermillion;* and as they came out, he counted one, two, three, four, five, six, seven, eight, nine; and as the *tenth* came out, he marked it with the rod, and said, "This is the *tenth;*" and that was set apart for the Lord.

I will bring you into the bond of the covenant] You shall be placed under the same *obligations* as before, and acknowledge your-

A. M. 3411
B. C. 593
Ol. XLVI. 4
Anno
Tarquinii Prisci,
R. Roman., 24

38 And [i]I will purge out
from among you the rebels,
and them that transgress
against me: I will bring them
forth out of the country where they sojourn,
and [k]they shall not enter into the land of
Israel: [l]and ye shall know that I *am* the LORD.
39 As for you, O house of Israel, thus saith
the Lord GOD; [m]Go ye, serve ye every one
his idols, and hereafter *also,* if ye will not
hearken unto me: [n]but pollute ye my holy
name no more with your gifts, and with your
idols.
40 For [o]in mine holy mountain, in the
mountain of the height of Israel, saith the
Lord GOD, there shall all the house of Israel,
all of them in the land, serve me: there [p]will
I accept them, and there will I require your
offerings, and the [q]first-fruits of your oblations,
with all your holy things.
41 I will accept you with your [r]sweet[s]
savour, when I bring you out from the people,
and gather you out of the countries wherein
ye have been scattered; and I will be sanctified
in you before the heathen.
42 [t]And ye shall know that I *am* the LORD,
[u]when I shall bring you into the land of
Israel, into the country *for* the which I lifted
up mine hand to give it to
your fathers.
43 And [v]there shall ye remember
your ways, and all
your doings, wherein ye have been defiled; and
[w]ye shall loathe yourselves in your own sight
for all your evils that ye have committed.
44 [x]And ye shall know that I *am* the LORD,
when I have wrought with you [y]for my
name's sake, not according to your wicked
ways, nor according to your corrupt doings,
O ye house of Israel, saith the Lord GOD.
45 Moreover, the word of the LORD came
unto me, saying,
46 [z]Son of man, set thy face toward the
south, and drop *thy word* toward the south, and
prophesy against the forest of the south field;
47 And say to the forest of the south, Hear
the word of the LORD; Thus saith the Lord
GOD; Behold, [a]I will kindle a fire in thee,
and it shall devour [b]every green tree in thee,
and every dry tree: the flaming flame shall
not be quenched, and all faces [c]from the
south to the north shall be burned therein.
48 And all flesh shall see that I the LORD
have kindled it: it shall not be quenched.
49 Then said I, Ah Lord GOD! they say of
me, Doth he not speak parables?

A. M. 3411
B. C. 593
Ol. XLVI. 4
Anno
Tarquinii Prisci,
R. Roman., 24

[i]Chap. xxxiv. 17, 20; Matt. xxv. 32, 33——[k]Jer. xliv. 14——[l]Chap. vi. 7; xv. 7; xxiii. 49——[m]Judg. x. 14; Psa. lxxxi. 12; Amos iv. 4——[n]Isa. i. 13; chap. xxiii. 38, 39——[o]Isa. ii. 2, 3; chap. xvii. 23; Mic. iv. 1——[p]Isa. lvi. 7; lx. 7; Zech. viii. 20, &c.; Mal. iii. 4; Rom. xii. 1 [q]Or, *chief*——[r]Heb. *savour of rest*

[s]Eph. v. 2; Phil. iv. 18——[t]Ver. 38, 44; chap. xxxvi. 23; xxxviii. 23——[u]Chap. xi. 17; xxxiv. 13; xxxvi. 24 [v]Chap. xvi. 61——[w]Lev. xxvi. 39; chap. vi. 9; Hos. v. 15——[x]Ver. 38; chap. xxiv. 24——[y]Chap. xxxvi. 22 [z]Chap. vi. 2; xxi. 2——[a]Jer. xxi. 14——[b]Deut. xii. 2; Luke xxiii. 31——[c]Chap. xxi. 4

selves bound; ye shall feel your obligation, and live according to its nature.

Verse 38. *I will purge out from among you the rebels*] The incorrigibly wicked I will destroy; those who *will not* receive him whom I have appointed for this purpose as the Saviour of Israel. And I will gather you *who believe* out of all the countries where you sojourn, and bring you into your own land; but those of you who *will not believe*—will not receive the Son of David to reign over you, shall never enter into the land of Israel, but die in your dispersions. This is what the contradicting and blaspheming Jews of the present day have to expect. And thus, both of you *shall know that he is Jehovah,* fulfilling his *threatenings* against the one, and his *promises* to the other.

Verse 39. *Go ye, serve ye every one his idols*] Thus, God *gave* them *statutes that were not good,* and *judgments whereby they could not live,* by thus *permitting* them to take their own way, serve their gods, and follow the *maxims* and *rites* of that abominable worship.

Verse 40. *For in mine holy mountain*] The days shall come in which all *true* ISRAELITES shall receive HIM whom I have *sent* to be the *true sacrifice* for the life of the world; and shall bring to Jerusalem—the *pure Christian Church,* their offerings, which I will there accept, for they will give me thanks for my unspeakable gift.

Verse 42. *And ye shall know*] Shall acknowledge *that I am Jehovah.*

Verse 43. *And there shall ye remember your ways*] Ye shall be ashamed of your past conduct, and of your long opposition to the Gospel of your salvation.

These promises may, in a certain limited sense, be applied to the restoration from the Babylonish captivity; but they must have their proper fulfilment when the Jews shall accept Jesus as their Saviour, and in consequence be brought back from all their dispersions to their own land.

Verse 46. *Set thy face toward the south*] Towards *Judea,* which lay south from Babylon, or Mesopotamia, where the prophet then dwelt.

The forest of the south field] The *city of Jerusalem,* as full of inhabitants as the forest is of trees.

Verse 47. *I will kindle a fire*] I will send war, "and it shall devour every green tree," the most eminent and substantial of the inhabitants; and *every dry tree,* the lowest and meanest also.

The flaming flame shall not be quenched] The

fierce ravages of Nebuchadnezzar and the Chaldeans shall not be stopped till the whole land is ruined.

All faces from the south to the north shall be burned] From the one end of the land to the other there shall be nothing but fear, dismay, terror, and confusion, occasioned by the wide-wasting violence of the Chaldeans. Judea lay in length from north to south.

Verse 48. *All flesh*] All the people shall see that this war is a judgment of the Lord.

It shall not be quenched.] Till the whole land shall be utterly ruined.

Verse 49. *Ah Lord God!*] O my God, consider my situation; who will believe what I shall say? They put the evil day far from them.

Doth he not speak parables?] הלא ממשל משלים הוא *halo memashshel meshalim hu*, "Is not he a maker of parables?" Is it not his custom to deal in *enigmas?* His figures are not to be understood; we should not trouble ourselves with them. We are not obliged to fathom his meaning; and perhaps after all it does not refer to *us*, or will not be accomplished in *our time*, if it even respect the land. Thus they turned aside what might have done them good, and rejected the counsel of God against themselves.

By dividing the word with our neighbour we often lose the benefit both of threatenings and promises. They voluntarily shut their own eyes; and then God, in judgment, sealed them up in darkness.

CHAPTER XXI

The prophet goes on to denounce the fate of Jerusalem and Judea; using signs of vehement grief, to denote the greatness of the calamity, 2–7. *He then changes the emblem to that of a sharp and bright sword, still denoting the same sad event,* 8–17; *and, becoming yet more explicit, he represents the king of Babylon, who was to be employed by God in this work, as setting out to take vengeance on both the Jews and the Ammonites, for joining with Egypt in a confederacy against him. He is described as standing at the parting of the roads leading to the respective capitals of the Jews and Ammonites; and doubting which to attack first, he commits the decision of the matter to his arts of divination, performed by mingling arrows inscribed with the names of the different nations or cities, and then marching against that whose name was written on the arrow first drawn from the quiver. In this case the name* Jerusalem *comes forward; and therefore he proceeds against it,* 18–24. *History itself could scarcely be more explicit than this prophecy. The profane prince Zedekiah is then declared to be given up by God, and his kingdom devoted to utter destruction, for that breach of oath of which the prophet foretells he should be guilty,* 25–27. *The remaining verses form a distinct prophecy relating to the destruction of the Ammonites, which was fulfilled about five years after the destruction of Jerusalem,* 28–32.

A. M. 3411
B. C. 593
Ol. XLVI. 4
Anno Tarquinii Prisci, R. Roman., 24

AND the word of the LORD came unto me, saying,
2 [a]Son of man, set thy face toward Jerusalem, and [b]drop *thy word* toward the holy places, and prophesy against the land of Israel,

3 And say to the land of Israel, Thus saith the LORD; Behold, I *am* against thee, and will draw forth my sword out of his sheath, and will cut off from thee [c]the righteous and the wicked.

[a]Chap. xx. 46——[b]Deut. xxxii. 2; Amos vii. 16; Mic. ii. 6, 11——[c]Job ix. 22

NOTES ON CHAP. XXI

Verse 2. *Set thy face toward Jerusalem*] This is a continuation of the preceding prophecy; and in this chapter the prophet sets before them, in the *plainest language*, what the foregoing metaphors meant, so that they could not complain of his *parables*.

Verse 3. *Behold, I* am *against thee*] Dismal news! When God is *against us*, who can be *for us?*

And will draw forth my sword] War.

And will cut off from thee] The land of Judea.

The righteous and the wicked.] All shall be *removed from thee*. Some shall be *cut off*—removed by the *sword;* shall be slain in *battle*, or by the *pestilence;* and some shall be *cut off*—die by the *famine;* and some shall be *cut off*—removed from the land by *captivity*. Now, among the two latter classes there might be *many righteous* as well as *wicked*. And when all the provisions were consumed, so that there was no more bread in the city, during the siege by Nebuchadnezzar, the righteous must have suffered as well as the wicked; for they could not be preserved alive, but by miracle, when there was no bread; nor was their perishing for want any loss to them, because the Lord would take them straight to his glory. And however men in general are unwilling to die, yet there is no instance, nor can there be, of any man's complaint that he got to heaven *too soon*. Again, if God had permitted *none* to be carried off captive but the *wicked*, the case of these would be utterly hopeless, as there would be none to set a good example, to preach repentance, to reprove sin, or to show God's willingness to forgive sinners. But God, in his mercy, permitted many of the *righteous* to be carried off also, that the wicked might not be totally abandoned, or put beyond the reach of being saved. Hence, both *Ezekiel* and *Daniel*, and indeed several *others, prophets* and *righteous men*, were *thus cut off from the land*, and carried into captivity. And how much was God's glory and the good of men promoted by this! What a seed of salvation was sown, even in the heathen countries, by thus *cutting off the righteous with the wicked!* To this we owe, under God, many of the *Psalms*, the *whole of the Book of Ezekiel*, all the prophecies of *Daniel*, the

A. M. 3411
B. C. 593
Ol. XLVI. 4
Anno
Tarquinii Prisci,
R. Roman., 24

4 Seeing then that I will cut
off from thee the righteous and
the wicked, therefore shall my
sword go forth out of his
sheath against all flesh, [d]from the south to the
north:
5 That all flesh may know that I the LORD
have drawn forth my sword out of his sheath:
it [e]shall not return any more.
6 [f]Sigh therefore, thou son of man, with the
breaking of *thy* loins: and with bitterness
sigh before their eyes.
7 And it shall be, when they say unto thee,
Wherefore sighest thou? that thou shalt
answer, For the tidings; because it cometh:
and every heart shall melt, and [g]all hands
shall be feeble, and every spirit shall faint,
and all knees [h]shall be weak *as* water: behold,
it cometh, and shall be brought to pass, saith
the Lord GOD.
8 Again the word of the LORD came unto
me, saying,
9 Son of man, prophesy and say, Thus saith
the LORD; Say, [i]A sword, a
sword is sharpened, and also
furbished:
10 It is sharpened to make a
sore slaughter; it is furbished that it may
glitter: should we then make mirth? [k]it
contemneth the rod of my son, *as* every
tree.
11 And he hath given it to be furbished
that it may be handled: this sword is sharpened, and it is furbished, to give it into the
hand of [l]the slayer.
12 Cry and howl, son of man: for it shall
be upon my people, it *shall be* upon all the
princes of Israel: [m]terrors by reason of the
sword shall be upon my people: [n]smite therefore upon *thy* thigh.
13 [o]Because *it is* [p]a trial, and what if *the
sword* contemn even the rod? [q]it shall be no
more, saith the Lord GOD.
14 Thou, therefore, son of man, prophesy,
and [r]smite *thine* [s]hands together, and let the
sword be doubled the third time, the sword

A. M. 3411
B. C. 593
Ol. XLVI. 4
Anno
Tarquinii Prisci,
R. Roman., 24

---

[d]Chap. xx. 47——[e]So Isa. xlv. 23; lv. 11——[f]Isa. xxii. 4——[g]Chap. vii. 17——[h]Heb. *shall go into water* [i]Deut. xxxii. 41; ver. 15, 28——[k]Or, it is *the rod of my son, it despiseth every tree*——[l]Ver. 19——[m]Or, *they are thrust down to the sword with my people*

[n]Jer. xxxi. 19——[o]Or, *When the trial* hath been, *what then? shall they not also belong to the despising rod*——[p]Job ix. 23; 2 Cor. viii. 2——[q]Ver. 27 [r]Num. xxiv. 10; ver. 17; chap. vi. 11——[s]Heb. *hand to hand*

---

bright example of *Shadrach, Meshach,* and *Abed-nego,* the *decrees* passed *in favour of the religion of the true God* by *Nebuchadnezzar, Cyrus, Darius,* &c. And to this dispensation of God's merciful providence we owe the *Books* and *example* of *Ezra* and *Nehemiah.* Where then is the *injustice,* so loudly declaimed against, of God's thus cutting off *from the land of Judea* the *righteous* with the *wicked?* The *righteous* were not cut off for the *crimes of the wicked,* (see chap. xviii.,) nor were these crimes visited upon them; yet several of them shared in the common calamity, but none *perished.* Those that were removed by a violent death, (and I believe we shall find few such,) got a speedier entrance into eternal glory.

Verse 4. *From the south to the north*] The whole land shall be ravaged from one end to the other.

Verse 5. *It shall not return any more.*] That is, till all the work that I have designed for it is done. Nor did it; for Nebuchadnezzar never rested till he had subdued all the lands from the south to the north, from the *Euphrates* to the *Nile.*

Verse 6. *Sigh—with the breaking of* thy *loins*] Let thy mourning for this sore calamity be like that of a woman in the pains of travail.

Verse 7. *Wherefore sighest thou?*] The prophet was a *sign* unto them. His sighing and mourning showed them how *they* should act.

All knees shall be weak as *water*] See the note on chap. vii. 17.

Verse 10. *It contemneth the rod of my son*] "It," the sword of Nebuchadnezzar, "contemneth the rod," despises the power and influence *of my son*—Israel, the Jewish people: "Out of Egypt have I called MY SON."

As every tree.] As all the *stocks,* kindreds, and nations, over which I have already given him commission. Can the *rod of Israel* be spared, when the *trees* of *Assyria, Egypt,* &c., have been cut down?

Verse 11. *This sword is sharpened*] It is prepared for the slaughter, it is *furbished;* from the French, *fourbir,* to polish, brighten. He shall have *splendid* victories every where. Some complain of corruption in the original in this place; but I think without sufficient reason.

Verse 12. *Smite—upon* thy *thigh.*] See on Jer. xxxi. 19. So HOMER, Il. xv. ver. 113:—

Ὡς εφατ'· αυταρ Αρης θαλερω πεπληγετο μηρω
Χερσι καταπρηνεσσ', ολοφυρομενος δε προσηυδα.

"She spake; and, with expanded arms his thighs
Smiting, thus sorrowful the god exclaimed."
COWPER.

Verse 13. *Because* it is *a trial*] This will be a trial of strength and skill between the Chaldeans and the Jews; and a *trial* of faith and patience to the righteous.

And what if the sword, (Nebuchadnezzar,) *contemn even the rod?*] Overthrow Zedekiah? It will do so; for the regal government of Judea *shall be no more.* Or, *it is tried;* that is, the *sword.* Nebuchadnezzar has already shown himself strong and skilful.

Verse 14. *Let the sword be doubled the third*

A. M. 3411
B. C. 593
Ol. XLVI. 4
Anno
Tarquinii Prisci,
R. Roman., 24

of the slain: it *is* the sword of
the great *men that are* slain,
which entereth into their
[t]privy chambers.
15 I have set the [u]point of the sword against
all their gates, that *their* heart may faint, and
their ruins be multiplied: ah! [v]*it is* made
bright, *it is* [w]wrapped up for the slaughter.
16 [x]Go thee one way or other, *either* on
the right hand, [y]*or* on the left, whithersoever
thy face *is* set.
17 I will also [z]smite mine hands together,
and [a]I will cause my fury to rest: I the LORD
have said *it*.
18 The word of the LORD came unto me
again, saying,
19 Also, thou son of man, appoint thee two
ways, that the sword of the king of Babylon
may come: both twain shall come forth out
of one land: and choose thou a
place, choose *it* at the head of
the way to the city.
20 Appoint a way, that the
sword may come to [b]Rabbath of the Ammonites, and to Judah in Jerusalem the defenced.
21 For the king of Babylon stood at the
[c]parting of the way, at the head of the two
ways, to use divination: he made *his* [d]arrows
bright, he consulted with [e]images, he looked
in the liver.
22 At his right hand was the divination for
Jerusalem, to appoint [f]captains, [g]to open the
mouth in the slaughter, to [h]lift up the voice
with shouting, [i]to appoint *battering* rams
against the gates, to cast a mount, *and* to
build a fort.
23 And it shall be unto them as a false
divination in their sight, [k]to them that [l]have

[t]1 Kings xx. 30; xxii. 25——[u]Or, *glittering*, or *fear*——[v]Ver. 10, 28——[w]Or, *sharpened*——[x]Ch. xiv. 17——[y]Heb. *set thyself, take the left hand*——[z]Ver. 14; ch. xxii. 13——[a]Ch. v. 13——[b]Jer. xlix. 2; ch. xxv. 5; Amos. i. 14

[c]Heb. *mother of the way*——[d]Or, *knives*——[e]Heb. *teraphim*——[f]Or, battering *rams;* chap. iv. 2——[g]Heb. *rams*——[h]Jer. li. 14——[i]Chap. iv. 2——[k]Or, *for the oaths made unto them*——[l]Chap. xvii. 13, 15, 16, 18

time] The sword has been *doubled*, and it shall come the *third time*. Nebuchadnezzar came against Judea THRICE. 1. Against *Jehoiakim*. 2. Against *Jeconiah*. 3. Against *Zedekiah*. The sword had already been *doubled;* it is to come now *the third time, i. e.*, against Zedekiah.

The sword of the slain] חרב חללים *chereb chalalim*, "the sword of the *soldiers*," of the *Chaldeans*. So in the next clause, היא חרב חלל הגדול *hi chereb chalal haggadol*, "it is the sword of that *great soldier*," that eminent *king* and *conqueror*. This is the meaning of the word חלל *chalal*, that is so ill rendered in almost every place of its occurrence, in our Version. See Dr. *Kennicott*.

Verse 15. *Wrapped up*] It is not a blunt sword, it is carefully sharpened and preserved for the slaughter.

Verse 16. *Go thee one way or other*] Thou shalt prosper, O sword, whithersoever thou turnest; against Ammon, or Judea, or Egypt.

Verse 19. *Appoint thee two ways*] Set off from Babylon, and lay down two ways, either of which thou mayest take; that to the *right*, which leads to *Jerusalem;* or that to the *left*, which leads to *Rabbath* of the Ammonites, ver. 20. But why against the *Ammonites?* Because both they and the Moabites were united with Zedekiah against the Chaldeans, (see Jer. xxvii. 3,) though they afterwards fought against Judea, chap. xii. 6.

Verse 21. *For the king of Babylon stood at the parting of the way*] He was in doubt which way he should first take; whether to humble the Ammonites by taking their metropolis, *Riblath*, or go at once against Jerusalem. In this case of uncertainty, he made use of *divination*. And this was of *three* kinds: 1. By *arrows*. 2. By *images* or *talismans*. 3. By inspecting the *entrails* of a sacrifice offered on the occasion.

1. *He made bright his arrows*. This might be after the manner in which the divination is still practised among the Arabs. These arrows were without head or wing. They took three. On one they wrote, *Command me, Lord*. On the second, *Forbid me, Lord*. The third was *blank*. These were put in a bag, and the querist put in his hand and took one out. If it was *Command me*, he set about the business immediately; if it was *Forbid me*, he rested for a *whole year;* if it was the *blank* one, he drew again. On all occasions the Arabs consulted futurity by such *arrows*. See *D'Herbelot*, under the word ACDAH.

2. As to the *images*, the Hebrew calls them תרפים *teraphim*. See the note on Gen. xxxi. 19.

3. And as to the *liver*, I believe it was only inspected to see whether the animal offered in sacrifice were *sound* and *healthy*, of which the state of the *liver* is the most especial indication. When the liver is sound, the animal is healthy; and it would have been a bad omen to any who offered sacrifice, to find that the animal they had offered to their gods was *diseased;* as, in that case, they would have taken for granted that the sacrifice was not accepted.

Verse 22. *At his right hand was the divination for Jerusalem*] He had probably written on *two* arrows; *one, Jerusalem;* the *other, Riblath;* the *third*, left *blank*. He drew, and that on which *Jerusalem* was written came to his hand; in consequence of which he marched immediately against that city. It was ripe for destruction; and had he marched *before* or *after*, it would have fallen; but he never considered himself as sure of the conquest till now.

Verse 23. *To them that have sworn oaths*] To Zedekiah and his *ministers*, who had bound themselves by the oath of the Lord to be faithful to the Chaldeans, and to pay them the

A. M. 3411
B. C. 593
Ol. XLVI. 4
Anno
Tarquinii Prisci,
R. Roman., 24

sworn oaths: but he will call to remembrance the iniquity, that they may be taken.

24 Therefore thus saith the Lord GOD; Because ye have made your iniquity to be remembered, in that your transgressions are discovered, so that in all your doings your sins do appear; because, *I say*, that ye are come to remembrance, ye shall be taken with the hand.

25 And thou [m]profane wicked prince of Israel, [n]whose day is come, when iniquity *shall have* an end,

26 Thus saith the Lord GOD; Remove the diadem, and take off the crown: this *shall* not *be* the same: [o]exalt *him that is* low, and abase *him that is* high.

27 [p]I will overturn, overturn, overturn it: [q]and it shall be no *more*, until he come whose right it is; and I will give it *him*.

28 And thou, son of man, prophesy and say, Thus saith the Lord GOD [r]concerning the Ammonites, and concerning their reproach; even say thou, [s]The sword, the sword *is* drawn: for the slaughter *it is* furbished, to consume because of the glittering:

A. M. 3411
B. C. 593
Ol. XLVI. 4
Anno
Tarquinii Prisci,
R. Roman.. 24

29 Whiles they [t]see vanity unto thee, whiles they divine a lie unto thee, to bring thee upon the necks of *them that are* slain, of the wicked, [u]whose day is come, when their iniquity *shall have* an end.

30 [v]Shall [w]I cause *it* to return into his sheath? [x]I will judge thee in the place where thou wast created, [y]in the land of thy nativity.

31 And I will [z]pour out mine indignation upon thee, I will [a]blow against thee in the fire of my wrath, and deliver thee into the hand of [b]brutish men, *and* skilful to destroy.

32 Thou shalt be for fuel to the fire; thy blood shall be in the midst of the land; [c]thou shalt be no *more* remembered: for I the LORD have spoken *it*.

---

[m]2 Chron. xxxvi. 13; Jer. lii. 2; chap. xvii. 19 —— [n]Ver. 29; chap. xxxv. 5 —— [o]Ch. xvii. 24; Luke i. 52 —— [p]Heb. *perverted, perverted, perverted will I make it* —— [q]Gen. xlix. 10; ver. 13; Luke i. 32, 33; John i. 49 —— [r]Jer. xlix. 1; chap. xxv. 2, 3, 6; Zeph. ii. 8, 9, 10

[s]Ver. 9, 10 —— [t]Chap. xii. 24; xxii. 28 —— [u]Ver. 25; Job xviii. 20; Psa. xxxvii. 13 —— [v]Or, *Cause it to return* —— [w]Jer. xlvii. 6, 7 —— [x]Gen. xv. 14; ch. xvi. 38 —— [y]Chap. xvi. 3 —— [z]Chap. vii. 8; xiv. 19; xxii. 22 —— [a]Chap. xxii. 20, 21 —— [b]Or, *burning* —— [c]Chap. xxv. 10

---

promised tribute. The *oaths* may refer, farther, to the *alliances* formed with the Egyptians, Ammonites, and others. They will not believe that Nebuchadnezzar shall succeed against them, while they expect the powerful assistance of the Egyptians.

Verse 25. *And thou profane wicked prince of Israel*] Zedekiah, called here *profane*, because he had broken his oath; and *wicked*, because of his opposition to God and his prophet.

Whose day is come] Who in a short time shalt be delivered into the hands of thy enemies.

Verse 26. *Exalt* him that is *low*] Give Gedaliah the government of Judea.

Abase him that is *high*.] Depose Zedekiah—remove his diadem, and take off his crown.

Verse 27. *I will overturn*] I will utterly destroy the Jewish government. Perverted will I make it. See the margin.

Until he come whose—is] משפט *mishpat*, the judgment; *i. e.*, till the coming of the son of David, the Lord Jesus; who, in a mystic and spiritual sense, shall have the throne of Israel, and whose *right it is*. See the famous prophecy, Gen. xlix. 10, and Luke i. 32. The עוה *avah*, which we translate *overturn*, is *thrice* repeated here; to point out, say the rabbins, the *three* conquests of Jerusalem, in which *Jehoiakim*, *Jeconiah*, and *Zedekiah* were *overthrown*.

Verse 28. *Concerning the Ammonites*] They had reproached and insulted Judea in its low estate, see chap. xxv. This prophecy against them was fulfilled about *five* years after the taking of Jerusalem. See Joseph. Ant. lib. x. c. 11; and Jer. xxvii., xlviii., xlix.; Ezek. xxv.

Verse 30. *I will judge thee*] This seems to refer to Nebuchadnezzar, who, after his return from Jerusalem, became insane, and lived like a beast for *seven* years; but was afterwards restored, and acknowledged the Lord.

Verse 32. *Thou shalt be no* more *remembered*] The empire of the *Chaldeans* was destroyed, and the power transferred to the *Persians;* the Persian empire was destroyed, and given to the *Greeks;* the Grecian empire was destroyed, and given to the *Mohammedans;* and the destruction of the Mohammedans is at no great distance.

CHAPTER XXII

This chapter contains a recital of the sins of Jerusalem, 1–12; *for which God threatens it with severe judgments,* 13–16, *in order to purify it from the dross,* 17–22. *And as the corruption is general, pervading prophets, priests, princes, and people; so, it is declared, shall be the punishment,* 23–31.

A. M. cir. 3411
B. C. cir. 593
Ol. XLVI. 4
Tarquinii Prisci,
R. Roman.,
cir. annum 24

MOREOVER the word of the LORD came unto me, saying,

2 Now, thou son of man, [a]wilt thou [b]judge, wilt thou judge [c]the [d]bloody city? yea, thou shalt [e]show her all her abominations.

3 Then say thou, Thus saith the Lord GOD; The city sheddeth blood in the midst of it, that her time may come, and maketh idols against herself to defile herself.

4 Thou art become guilty in thy blood that thou hast [f]shed, and hast defiled thyself in thine idols which thou hast made; and thou hast caused thy days to draw near, and art come *even* unto thy years: [g]therefore have I made thee a reproach unto the heathen, and a mocking to all countries.

5 *Those that be* near, and *those that be* far from thee, shall mock thee, *which art* [h]infamous *and* much vexed.

6 Behold, [i]the princes of Israel, every one were in thee to their [k]power to shed blood.

7 In thee have they [l]set light by father and mother: in the midst of thee have they [m]dealt by [n]oppression with the stranger: in thee have they vexed the fatherless and the widow.

8 Thou hast [o]despised mine holy things, and hast [p]profaned my sabbaths.

9 In thee are [q]men [r]that carry tales to shed blood: [s]and in thee they eat upon the mountains: in the midst of thee they commit lewdness.

A. M. cir. 3411
B. C. cir. 593
Ol. XLVI. 4
Tarquinii Prisci,
R. Roman.,
cir. annum 24

10 In thee have they [t]discovered their father's nakedness: in thee have they humbled her that was [u]set apart for pollution.

11 And [v]one hath committed abomination [w]with his neighbour's wife; and [x]another [y]hath [z]lewdly defiled his daughter-in-law: and another in thee hath humbled his [a]sister, his father's daughter.

12 In thee [b]have they taken gifts to shed blood; [c]thou hast taken usury and increase, and thou hast greedily gained of thy neighbours by extortion, and [d]hast forgotten me, saith the Lord GOD.

13 Behold, therefore, I have [e]smitten mine hand at thy dishonest gain which thou hast made, and at thy blood which hath been in the midst of thee.

14 [f]Can thine heart endure, or can thine hands be strong, in the days that I shall deal with thee? [g]I the LORD have spoken *it,* and will do *it.*

15 And [h]I will scatter thee among the heathen, and disperse thee in the countries, and [i]will consume thy filthiness out of thee.

16 And thou [k]shalt take thine inheritance

[a]Chap. xx. 4; xxiii. 36——[b]Or, *plead for*——[c]Chap. xxiv. 6, 9; Nah. iii. 1——[d]Heb. *city of bloods*——[e]Heb. *make her know;* chap. xvi. 2——[f]2 Kings xxi. 16 [g]Deut. xxviii. 37; 1 Kings ix. 7; chap. v. 14; Dan. ix. 16 [h]Heb. *polluted of name, much in vexation*——[i]Isa. i. 23; Mic. iii. 1, 2, 3; Zeph. iii. 3——[k]Heb. *arm*——[l]Deut. xxvii. 16——[m]Exod. xxii. 21, 22——[n]Or, *deceit*——[o]Ver 26——[p]Lev. xix. 30; chap. xxiii. 38——[q]Heb. *men of slanders*——[r]Exod. xxiii. 1; Lev. xix. 16——[s]Chap. xviii. 6, 11——[t]Lev. xviii. 7, 8; xx. 11; 1 Cor. v. 1

[u]Lev. xviii. 19; xx. 18; chap. xviii. 6——[v]Or, *every one* [w]Lev. xviii. 20; xx. 10; Deut. xxii. 22; Jer. v. 8; chap. xviii. 11——[x]Or, *every one*——[y]Lev. xviii. 15; xx. 12 [z]Or, *by lewdness*——[a]Lev. xviii. 9; xx. 17——[b]Exod. xxiii. 8; Deut. xvi. 19; xxvii. 25——[c]Exod. xxii. 25; Lev. xxv. 36; Deut. xxiii. 19; chap. xviii. 13——[d]Deut. xxxii. 18; Jer. iii. 21; chap. xxiii. 35——[e]Chap. xxi. 17 [f]See chap. xxi. 7——[g]Chap. xvii. 24——[h]Deut. iv. 27; xxviii. 25, 64; chap. xii. 14, 15——[i]Chap. xxiii. 27, 48 [k]Or, *shalt be profaned*

NOTES ON CHAP. XXII

Verse 2. *Wilt thou judge the bloody city*] Pronounce the sentence of death against the murderers.

Show her all her abominations.] And a most revolting and dreadful catalogue of these is in consequence exhibited.

Verse 3. *Her time may come*] Till now, it was my long-suffering; she has fulfilled her days—completed the time of her probation; has not mended, but is daily worse; therefore her judgment can linger no longer.

Verse 4. *Thou art become guilty in thy blood*] Thou art guilty of blood.

Verse 5. Those that be *near*] Both *distant* as well as *neighbouring* provinces consider thee the most abandoned of characters; and through thee many have been involved in distress and ruin.

Verse 6. *Behold, the princes*] Ye are a vile and murderous people, and your princes have been of the same character. *Like people, like prince.*

Verse 7. *In thee have they set light*] The children do not reverence their parents. Parental affection and filial respect do not exist among you. The *stranger* is not only not succoured, but he is *oppressed.* The *widows* and *fatherless* are *vexed* by wrongs and exactions.

Verse 8. *Thou hast despised*] All my ordinances are not only neglected, but treated with contempt; and my Sabbaths profaned. There is not only no *power* of godliness among you, but there is no *form.*

Verse 9. *In thee are men that carry tales*] Witnesses that will swear any thing, even where life is concerned.

They eat upon the mountains] Sacrifice to *idols,* and celebrate their *festivals.*

Verse 10. *In thee have they discovered*] They are guilty of the most abominable *incest* and unnatural lust.

In thee have they humbled] In their unholy

A. M. cir. 3411
B. C. cir. 593
Ol. XLVI. 4
Tarquinii Prisci,
R. Roman.,
cir. annum 24

in thyself in the sight of the
heathen, and [l]thou shalt know
that I *am* the LORD.
17 And the word of the LORD
came unto me, saying,
18 Son of man, [m]the house of Israel is to
me become dross: all they *are* brass, and
tin, and iron, and lead, in the midst of the
furnace; they are *even* the [n]dross of silver.
19 Therefore thus saith the Lord GOD;
Because ye are all become dross, behold,
therefore I will gather you into the midst of
Jerusalem.
20 [o]*As* they gather silver, and brass, and
iron, and lead, and tin, into the midst of the
furnace, to blow the fire upon it, to melt *it;*
so will I gather *you* in mine anger and in
my fury, and I will leave *you there,* and
melt you.
21 Yea, I will gather you, and [p]blow upon
you in the fire of my wrath, and ye shall be
melted in the midst thereof.
22 As silver is melted in the midst of the
furnace, so shall ye be melted in the midst
thereof: and ye shall know that I the LORD
have [q]poured out my fury upon you.
23 And the word of the LORD came unto me,
saying,
24 Son of man, say unto her, Thou *art* the
land that is not cleansed, nor rained upon in
the day of indignation.
25 [r]*There is* a conspiracy of her prophets in
the midst thereof, like a roaring lion ravening
the prey: they [s]have devoured
souls: [t]they have taken the
treasure and precious things:
they have made her many
widows in the midst thereof.

A. M. cir. 3411
B. C. cir. 593
Ol. XLVI. 4
Tarquinii Prisci,
R. Roman.,
cir. annum 24

26 [u]Her priests have [v]violated my law, and
have [w]profaned mine holy things; they have
put no [x]difference between the holy and profane, neither have they showed *difference*
between the unclean and the clean, and have
hid their eyes from my sabbaths, and I am
profaned among them.
27 [y]Her princes in the midst thereof *are* like
wolves ravening the prey, to shed blood, *and*
to destroy souls, to get dishonest gain.
28 And [z]her prophets have daubed them
with untempered *mortar,* [a]seeing vanity, and
divining lies unto them, saying, Thus saith
the Lord GOD, when the LORD hath not
spoken.
29 [b]The people of the land have used [c]op-
pression, and exercised robbery, and have
vexed the poor and needy: yea, they have
[d]oppressed the stranger [e]wrongfully.
30 [f]And I sought for a man among them,
that should [g]make up the hedge, and [h]stand in
the gap before me for the land, that I should
not destroy it: but I found none.
31 Therefore have I [i]poured out mine indignation upon them; I have consumed them
with the fire of my wrath: [k]their own way have
I recompensed upon their heads, saith the
Lord GOD.

---

[l]Psa. ix. 16; ch. vi. 7.——[m]Isa. i. 22; Jer. vi. 28, &c.; see Psa. cxix. 119——[n]Heb. *drosses*——[o]Heb. according *to the gathering*——[p]Ch. xxii. 20, 21, 22——[q]Ch. xx. 8, 33; ver. 31——[r]Hos. vi. 9——[s]Matt. xxiii. 14——[t]Mic. iii. 11; Zeph. iii. 3, 4——[u]Mal. ii. 8——[v]Heb. *offered violence to*——[w]Lev. xxii. 2, &c.; 1 Sam. ii. 29——[x]Lev. x. 10; Jer. xv. 19; chap. xlv. 23

[y]Isa. i. 23; chap. xxii. 6; Mic. iii. 2, 3, 9, 10, 11; Zeph. iii. 3——[z]Chap. xiii. 10——[a]Chap. xiii. 6, 7; xxi. 29 [b]Jer. v. 26, 27, 28; chap. xviii. 12——[c]Or, *deceit* [d]Exod. xxii. 21; xxiii. 9; Lev. xix. 33; chap. xxii. 7 [e]Heb. *without right*——[f]Jer. v. 1——[g]Chap. xiii. 5 [h]Psa. cvi. 23——[i]Ver. 22——[k]Chap. ix. 10; xi. 21; xvi. 43

---

and unnatural connexions, they have not abstained from those set apart because of their infirmities. The catalogue of crimes that follow is too plain to require comment.

Verse 16. *Thou shalt know that I* am *the Lord.*] I shall so deal with and punish thee, that thou shalt be obliged to own the vindictive hand of a sin-avenging God.

Verse 18. *The house of Israel is to me become dross*] They are all like *base metal—brass, tin, iron,* and *lead* alloyed together with *silver.* Ye must be put in the furnace, and subjected to the most intense fire, till your impurities are consumed away. No *ordinary* means will avail any thing; the most *violent* must be resorted to.

Verse 19. *I will gather you*] Jerusalem is represented here as the *fining pot;* all the people are to be gathered together in *it,* and the *Chaldean fire* is to *melt* the whole. And God will increase thy sufferings: as the refiner *blows the fire* with his bellows, so God will *blow upon you* with the *fire of his wrath,* ver. 21.

Verse 24. *Thou* art *the land that is not cleansed*] Thou art like a country where there is no *rain,* either *to cleanse* the *garments,* or *fertilize* the *ground.*

Verse 25. There is *a conspiracy*] The false prophets have united together to say and support the same things; and have been the cause of the destruction of souls, and the death of many, so that *widows,* through their means, are multiplied in thee.

Verse 26. *Her priests*] Even they whose lips should preserve knowledge, have not instructed the people: they *have violated my law,* not only in their private conduct, but in their careless and corrupt manner of serving in my temple.

Verse 27. *Her princes*] Are as bad as her *priests;* they are rapacious, and grievously oppress the people by unjust impositions in order to increase their revenues.

Verse 28. *Her prophets*] Even those who profess themselves to be my prophets, have been unfaithful in the discharge of their office; have *soothed* the people in their sins, and pretended to have oracles of *peace* and *safety* when I had not spoken to them.

Verse 29. *The people*] All that have power or authority have abused it; *vexed* and *oppressed* the *poor*, the *needy*, and the *stranger*.

Verse 30. *I sought for a man*] I saw that there was a grievous breach made in the *moral state* and *feeling* of the people, and I sought for a man that would stand in the gap; that would faithfully exhort, reprove, and counsel, with all long-suffering and doctrine. But none was to be found!

Verse 31. *Therefore*] Because of the *profligacies* already mentioned; because of the *false worship* so generally practised; because of the *false prophets* tolerated; because of the unholy and profane *priesthood;* because of the oppressive *princes;* because of the *unfaithful* and deceiving *prophets;* because of the oppressions of *petty officers;* and because of the *total corruption of manners* in all *ranks, places, offices,* &c.;—

Have I poured out mine indignation—consumed them with the fire of my wrath] Considering the above, has there not been sufficient reason why I should abandon such a people, and pour out upon them such a destructive storm of calamities?

CHAPTER XXIII

The idolatries of Samaria and Jerusalem are represented in this chapter by the bad practices of two common harlots, for which God denounces severe judgments against them, 1–49. *See the* sixteenth *chapter, where the same metaphor is enlarged upon as here, it being the prophet's view to excite the utmost detestation of the crime against which he inveighs.*

A. M. cir. 3411
B. C. cir. 593
Ol. XLVI. 4
Tarquinii Prisci,
R. Roman.,
cir. annum 24

THE word of the LORD came
again unto me, saying,
2 Son of man, there were
[a]two women, the daughters of
one mother:
3 And [b]they committed whoredoms in
Egypt; they committed whoredoms in [c]their
youth: there were their breasts pressed, and
there they bruised the teats of their virginity.
4 And the names of them *were* Aholah the
elder, and Aholibah her sister: and [d]they
were mine, and they bare sons and daughters.
Thus *were* their names; Samaria *is* [e]Aholah, and Jerusalem [f]Aholibah.
5 And Aholah played the
harlot when she was mine; and she doted on
her lovers, on [g]the Assyrians *her* neighbours,
6 *Which were* clothed with blue, captains
and rulers, all of them desirable young men,
horsemen riding upon horses.
7 Thus she [h]committed her whoredoms with
them, with all them *that were* [i]the chosen men
of Assyria, and with all on whom she doted:

A. M. cir. 3411
B. C. cir. 593
Ol. XLVI. 4
Tarquinii Prisci,
R. Roman.,
cir. annum 24

[a]Jer. iii. 7, 8, 10; ch. xvi. 46——[b]Lev. xvii. 7; Josh. xxiv. 14; ch. xx. 8——[c]Ch. xvi. 22——[d]Ch. xvi. 8, 20
[e]That is, *His tent*, or *tabernacle*——[f]That is, *My tabernacle in her;* 1 Kings viii. 29——[g]2 Kings xv. 19; xvi. 7; xvii. 3; Hos. viii. 9——[h]Heb. *bestowed her whoredoms upon them*——[i]Heb. *the choice of the children of Ashur*

NOTES ON CHAP. XXIII

Verse 2. *Son of man, there were two women*] All the Hebrews were derived from *one source*, Abraham and Sarah; and, till the schism under Rehoboam, formed but one people: but as these ten tribes and a half separated from Judah and Benjamin, they became two distinct people under different kings; called the kingdom of Judah, and the kingdom of Israel. They are called here, because of their consanguinity, *two sisters*. The elder, Samaria, (for there was the *seat of government* for the kingdom of Israel,) was called אהלה *aholah*, "a tent." The younger, Judah, was called אהליבה *aholibah*, "my tent is in her," because the temple of God was in Jerusalem, the seat of the government of the kingdom of Judah.

Verse 5. *And Aholah played the harlot*] Without entering into detail here, or following the *figures*, they both became idolatrous, and received the impure rites of the Egyptians, Assyrians, and Chaldeans; of which connexion the prophet speaks here as he did in chap. xvi., which see.

In this chapter there are many of what we would call indelicate expressions, because a parallel is run between *idolatry* and *prostitution*, and the circumstances of the latter illustrate the peculiarities of the former. In such cases, perhaps, the *matter* alone was given to the prophet, and he was left to use his own language, and amplify as he saw good. *Ezekiel* was among the *Jews* what *Juvenal* was among the Romans,—a rough reprover of the most abominable vices. They both spoke of things as they found them; stripped vice naked, and scourged it publicly. The original is still more rough than the translation; and surely there is no need of a *comment* to explain imagery that is but too generally understood. I have said enough on chap. xvi., and to that I must refer the reader. It is true that there are a few things here in the shade that might be illustrated by *anatomy;* and it would not be difficult to do it: but they are not necessary to salvation, and I shall not take off the covering. They were sufficiently understood by those for whose use they were originally designed.

Verse 6. *Clothed with blue*] The *purple* dye was highly valued among the ancients, and at

A. M. cir. 3411
B. C. cir. 593
Ol. XLVI. 4
Tarquinii Prisci,
R. Roman.,
cir. annum 24

with all their idols she defiled
herself.
8 Neither left she her whoredoms *brought* [k]from Egypt:
for in her youth they lay with her, and they
bruised the breasts of her virginity, and
poured their whoredom upon her.
9 Wherefore I have delivered her into the
hand of her lovers, into the hand of the [l]As-
syrians, upon whom she doted.
10 These [m]discovered her nakedness: they
took her sons and her daughters, and slew her
with the sword: and she became [n]famous
among women: for they had executed judgment upon her.
11 And [o]when her sister Aholibah saw *this,*
[p]she [q]was more corrupt in her inordinate love
than she, and in her whoredoms [r]more than
her sister in *her* whoredoms.
12 She doted upon the [s]Assyrians *her* neighbours, [t]captains and rulers clothed most gorgeously, horsemen riding upon horses, all of
them desirable young men.
13 Then I saw that she was defiled, *that*
they *took* both one way,
14 And *that* she increased her whoredoms:
for when she saw men pourtrayed upon the
wall, the images of the Chaldeans pourtrayed
with vermilion,
15 Girded with girdles upon their loins, exceeding in dyed attire upon their heads, all of
them princes to look to, after the manner of
the Babylonians of Chaldea, the land of their
nativity:
16 [u]And [v]as soon as she saw them with her
eyes, she doted upon them, and sent messengers unto them into Chaldea.
17 And the [w]Babylonians
came to her into the bed of
love, and they defiled her with
their whoredom, and she was
polluted with them, and [x]her mind was [y]alien-
ated from them.

A. M. cir. 3411
B. C. cir. 593
Ol. XLVI. 4
Tarquinii Prisci,
R. Roman.,
cir. annum 24

18 So she discovered her whoredoms, and
discovered her nakedness: then [z]my mind
was alienated from her, like as my mind was
alienated from her sister.
19 Yet she multiplied her whoredoms in
calling to remembrance the days of her youth,
[a]wherein she had played the harlot in the land
of Egypt.
20 For she doted upon their paramours,
[b]whose flesh *is as* the flesh of asses, and
whose issue *is like* the issue of horses.
21 Thus thou calledst to remembrance the
lewdness of thy youth, in bruising thy teats
by the Egyptians for the paps of thy youth.
22 Therefore, O Aholibah, thus saith the
Lord GOD; [c]Behold, I will raise up thy lovers
against thee, from whom thy mind is alienated; and I will bring them against thee on
every side;
23 The Babylonians, and all the Chaldeans,
[d]Pekod, and Shoa, and Koa, *and* all the Assyrians with them: [e]all of them desirable
young men, captains, and rulers, great lords
and renowned, all of them riding upon horses.
24 And they shall come against thee with
chariots, wagons, and wheels, and with an
assembly of people, *which* shall set against
thee buckler and shield and helmet round
about: and I will set judgment before them,
and they shall judge thee according to their
judgments.
25 And I will set my jealousy against thee,

[k]Ver. 3——[l]2 Kings xvii. 3, 4, 5, 6, 23; xviii. 9, 10, 11——[m]Ch. xvi. 37, 41——[n]Heb. *a name*——[o]Jer. iii. 8——[p]Jer. iii. 11; ch. xvi. 47, 51——[q]Heb. *she corrupted her inordinate love more than,* &c.——[r]Heb. *more than the whoredoms of her sister*——[s]2 Kings xvi. 7, 10; 2 Chron. xxviii. 16–23; chap. xvi. 28

[t]Ver. 6, 23——[u]2 Kings xxiv. 1; chap. xvi. 29——[v]Hebrew, *at the sight of her eyes*——[w]Hebrew, *children of Babel*——[x]Ver. 22, 28——[y]Hebrew, *loosed,* or *disjointed*——[z]Jeremiah vi. 8——[a]Ver. 3——[b]Chap. xvi. 26——[c]Chap. xvi. 37; verse 28——[d]Jeremiah l. 21——[e]Ver. 12

first was only used by kings; at last it was used among the military, particularly by officers of high rank in the country.

Verse 14. *Men pourtrayed upon the wall*] See on chap. viii. 10.

Verse 20. *She doted upon their paramours*] פלגשיהם *pillagsheyhem,* their *harlots* or *concubines.* Anciently *harlot* meant in our language either the *male* or *female* prostitute.

Whose flesh is as *the flesh of asses*] See on chap. xvi. 25.

Verse 23. *Pekod, and Shoa, and Koa*] פקוד ושוע וקוע. These names have been thought to designate certain people bordering on the Chaldeans; but no geographer has ever been able to find them out.

In our old translations these names were considered *appellatives—rulers, mighty men,* and *tyrants.* Others, following the literal import of the words, have translated, *visiting, shouting,* and *retreating.* Others have applied them to the *habits* of the Chaldean soldiers. *Pekod* signifying the *muster* or *review* of armies; *Shoa,* the *magnificence* of their *uniform* and

A. M. cir. 3411
B. C. cir. 593
Ol. XLVI. 4
Tarquinii Prisci,
R. Roman.,
cir. annum 24

and they shall deal furiously
with thee: they shall take
away thy nose and thine ears;
and thy remnant shall fall by
the sword: they shall take thy sons and thy
daughters; and thy residue shall be devoured
by the fire.
26 [f]They shall also strip thee out of thy
clothes, and take away thy [g]fair jewels.
27 Thus [h]will I make thy lewdness to cease
from thee, and [i]thy whoredom *brought* from
the land of Egypt: so that thou shalt not lift
up thine eyes unto them, nor remember
Egypt any more.
28 For thus saith the Lord God; Behold,
I will deliver thee into the hand *of them*
[k]whom thou hatest, into the hand *of them*
[l]from whom thy mind is alienated:
29 And they shall deal with thee hatefully,
and shall take away all thy labour, and [m]shall
leave thee naked and bare: and the nakedness
of thy whoredoms shall be discovered, both
thy lewdness and thy whoredoms.
30 I will do these *things* unto thee, because
thou hast [n]gone a whoring after the heathen,
and because thou art polluted with their idols.
31 Thou hast walked in the way of thy
sister; therefore will I give her [o]cup into
thine hand.
32 Thus saith the Lord God; Thou shalt
drink of thy sister's cup deep and large: [p]thou
shalt be laughed to scorn and had in derision;
it containeth much.
33 Thou shalt be filled with drunkenness and
sorrow, with the cup of astonishment and desolation, with the cup of thy
sister Samaria.

A. M. cir. 3411
B. C. cir. 593
Ol. XLVI. 4
Tarquinii Prisci,
R. Roman.,
cir. annum 24

34 Thou shalt [q]even drink it
and suck *it* out, and thou shalt
break the sherds thereof, and pluck off thine
own breasts: for I have spoken *it,* saith the
Lord God.
35 Therefore thus saith the Lord God; Because thou [r]hast forgotten me, and [s]cast me
behind thy back, therefore bear thou also thy
lewdness and thy whoredoms.
36 The Lord said moreover unto me; Son
of man, wilt thou [t]judge [u]Aholah and Aholibah? yea, [v]declare unto them their abominations;
37 That they have committed adultery, and
[w]blood *is* in their hands, and with their idols
have they committed adultery, and have also
caused their sons, [x]whom they bare unto me,
to pass for them through *the fire,* to devour
them.
38 Moreover this they have done unto me:
they have defiled my sanctuary in the same
day, and [y]have profaned my sabbaths.
39 For when they had slain their children
to their idols, then they came the same day
into my sanctuary to profane it; and, lo, [z]thus
have they done in the midst of mine house.
40 And furthermore, that ye have sent for
men [a]to come from far, [b]unto whom a messenger *was* sent; and, lo, they came; for whom
thou didst [c]wash thyself, [d]paintedst thy eyes,
and deckedst thyself with ornaments.

[f]Ch. xvi. 39——[g]Heb. *instruments of thy decking* [h]Ch. xvi. 41; xxii. 15——[i]Ver. 3, 19——[k]Ch. xvi. 37 [l]Ver. 17——[m]Ch. xvi. 39; ver. 26——[n]Ch. vi. 9——[o]Jer xxv. 15, &c.——[p]Ch. xxii. 4, 5——[q]Psa. lxxv. 8; Isa. li. 17——[r]Jer. ii. 32; iii. 21; xiii. 25; ch. xxii. 12——[s]1 Kings xiv. 9; Neh. ix. 26——[t]Ch. xx. 4; xxii. 2

[u]Or, *plead for*——[v]Isa. lviii. 1——[w]Ch. xvi. 38; ver. 45——[x]Ch. xvi. 20, 21, 36, 45; xx. 26, 31——[y]Ch. xxii. 8 [z]2 Kings xxi. 4——[a]Heb. *coming*——[b]Isa. lvii. 9 [c]Ruth iii. 3——[d]2 Kings ix. 30; Jer. iv. 30——[e]Heb. *honourable*——[f]Esth. i. 6; Isa. lvii. 7; Amos ii. 8; vi. 4 [g]Prov. vii. 17; chap. xvi. 18, 19; Hos. ii. 8

arms; and *Koa,* the marks or *embroidery* of the clothes of the captains and generals. *Grotius* thought that they might be names of contiguous nations: *Pekod,* the *Bactrians; Shoa,* a people of *Armenia;* and *Koa,* the *Medes.* I have nothing to add that would satisfy myself, or be edifying to my readers.

Verse 25. *Shall take away thy nose*] A punishment frequent among the Persians and Chaldeans, as ancient authors tell. Adulteries were punished in this way; and to this *Martial* refers:—

Quis tibi persuasit nares abscindere mœcho?

"Who has counselled thee to cut off the adulterer's nose?"

Women were thus treated in Egypt. See *Calmet.*

Verse 26. *They shall also strip thee*] See on chap. xvi. 39.

Verse 32. *Thou shalt drink of thy sister's cup*] Thou shalt be ruined and desolated as Samaria was.

Verse 34. *Thou shalt—pluck off thine own breasts*] Thou shalt *tear them;* a frequent action in extreme sorrow and desolation. *Weeping, tearing the bosom, and beating the breasts.*

Tunc vero rupique sinus, et pectora planxi.
Ovid's Ep. 5.

Verse 38. *They have defiled my sanctuary*] By placing idols there.

Verse 40. *Thou didst wash thyself, paintedst thy eyes, and deckedst thyself with ornaments.*] This is exactly the way in which a loose female in Bengal adorns herself to receive guests. She first bathes, then rubs black paint around her

A. M. cir. 3411
B. C. cir. 593
Ol. XLVI. 4
Tarquinii Prisci,
R. Roman.,
cir. annum 24

41 And satest upon a [e]stately [f]bed, and a table prepared before it, [g]whereupon thou hast set mine incense and mine oil.

42 And a voice of a multitude being at ease *was* with her: and with the men [h]of the common sort *were* brought [i]Sabeans from the wilderness, which put bracelets upon their hands, and beautiful crowns upon their heads.

43 Then said I unto *her that was* old in adulteries, Will they now commit [k]whoredoms with her, and she *with them?*

44 Yet they went in unto her, as they go in unto a woman that playeth the harlot: so went they in unto Aholah and unto Aholibah, the lewd women.

45 And the righteous men, they shall [l]judge them after the manner of adulteresses, and after the manner of women that shed blood; because they *are* adulteresses, and [m]blood *is* in their hands.

A. M. cir. 3411
B. C. cir. 593
Ol. XLVI. 4
Tarquinii Prisci,
R. Roman.,
cir. annum 24

46 For thus saith the Lord GOD, [n]I will bring up a company upon them, and will give them [o]to be removed and spoiled.

47 [p]And the company shall stone them with stones, and [q]despatch them with their swords; they [r]shall slay their sons and their daughters, and burn up their houses with fire.

48 Thus [s]will I cause lewdness to cease out of the land, [t]that all women may be taught not to do after your lewdness.

49 And they shall recompense your lewdness upon you, and ye shall [u]bear the sins of your idols: [v]and ye shall know that I *am* the Lord GOD.

[h]Heb. *of the multitude of men*——[i]Or, *drunkards*——[k]Heb. *her whoredoms*——[l]Chap. xvi. 38——[m]Ver. 37——[n]Chap. xvi. 40——[o]Heb. *for a removing and spoil*——[p]Chap. xvi. 41——[q]Or, *single them out*——[r]2 Chron. xxxvi. 17, 19; chap. xxiv. 21——[s]Chap. xxii. 15; ver. 27——[t]Deut. xiii. 11; 2 Pet. ii. 6——[u]Ver. 35——[v]Chap. xx. 38, 42, 44; xxv. 5

eyes, and then covers her body with ornaments. —WARD'S *Customs*.

Verse 41. *And satest upon a stately bed*] Hast raised a stately altar to thy idols; probably alluding to that which Ahaz ordered to be made, after the similitude of that which he saw at Damascus. The *bed* here is in allusion to the *sofas* on which the ancients were accustomed to recline at their meals; or to the couches on which they place Asiatic brides, with incense pots and sweetmeats on a table before them.

Verse 42. *And a voice of a multitude*] This seems to be an account of an idolatrous festival, where a riotous multitude was assembled, and fellows of the baser sort, with *bracelets* on their arms and *chaplets* on their heads, performed the religious rites.

Verse 45. *And the righteous men*] אנשים צדיקים *anashim tsaddikim*. The Chaldeans, thus called because they are appointed by God to *execute judgment* on these criminals.

Verse 47. *Shall stone them with stones*] As they did adulteresses under the law. See Lev. xx. 10, Deut. xxii. 22, compared with John viii. 3.

Verse 48. *Thus will I cause lewdness to cease*] *Idolatry;* and from that time to the present day the Jews never relapsed into idolatry.

Verse 49. *Ye shall bear the sins of your idols*] The punishment due to your adultery; your apostasy from God, and setting up idolatry in the land.

CHAPTER XXIV

The prophet now informs those of the captivity of the very day on which Nebuchadnezzar was to lay siege to Jerusalem, (*compare* Jer. lii. 4,) *and describes the fate of that city and its inhabitants by a very apt similitude,* 1–14. *As another sign of the greatness of those calamities, the prophet is forbidden to mourn for his wife, of whom he is to be deprived; intimating thereby that the sufferings of the Jews should be so astonishing as to surpass all expressions of grief; and that private sorrow, however affectionate and tender the object, ought to be absorbed in the public calamities,* 15–18. *The prophet, having farther expressed his prediction in plain terms, intimates that he was to speak to* them *no more till they should have the news of these prophecies having been fulfilled,* 19–27.

A. M. 3414
B. C. 590
Ol. XLVII. 3
Anno
Tarquinii Prisci,
R. Roman., 27

AGAIN in the ninth year, in the tenth month, in the tenth *day* of the month, the [a]word of the LORD came unto me, saying,

2 Son of man, write thee the name of the day, *even* of this same day: the king of Babylon set himself against Jerusalem [b]this same day.

A. M. 3414
B. C. 590
Ol. XLVII. 3
Anno
Tarquinii Prisci,
R. Roman., 27

3 [c]And utter a parable unto the rebellious

[a]Chap. xxiii. 1——[b]2 Kings xxv. 1; Jer. xxxixl; lii. 4.——[c]Chap. xvii. 12

NOTES ON CHAP. XXIV

Verse 1. *The ninth year*] This prophecy was given in the *ninth* year of Zedekiah, about *Thursday*, the *thirtieth* of *January*, A. M. 3414; the very day in which the king of Babylon commenced the siege of Jerusalem.

Verse 3. *Set on a pot*] The *pot* was Jeru-

A. M. 3414
B. C. 590
Ol. XLVII. 3
Anno
Tarquinii Prisci,
R. Roman., 27

house, and say unto them, Thus saith the Lord GOD; [d]Set on a pot, set *it* on, and also pour water into it:

4 Gather the pieces thereof into it, *even* every good piece, the thigh, and the shoulder; fill *it* with the choice bones.

5 Take the choice of the flock, and [e]burn also the bones under it, *and* make it boil well, and let them seethe the bones of it therein.

6 Wherefore thus saith the Lord GOD; Wo to [f]the bloody city, to the pot whose scum *is* therein, and whose scum is not gone out of it! bring it out piece by piece; let no [g]lot fall upon it.

7 For her blood is in the midst of her; she set it upon the top of a rock; [h]she poured it not upon the ground, to cover it with dust;

8 That it might cause fury to come up to take vengeance; [i]I have set her blood upon the top of a rock, that it should not be covered.

9 Therefore thus saith the Lord GOD; [k]Wo to the bloody city! I will even make the pile for fire great.

10 Heap on wood, kindle the fire, consume the flesh, and spice it well, and let the bones be burned.

A. M. 3414
B. C. 590
Ol. XLVII. 3
Anno
Tarquinii Prisci,
R. Roman., 27

11 Then set it empty upon the coals thereof, that the brass of it may be hot, and may burn, and *that* [l]the filthiness of it may be molten in it, *that* the scum of it may be consumed.

12 She hath wearied *herself* with lies, and her great scum went not forth out of her: her scum *shall be* in the fire.

13 In thy filthiness *is* lewdness; because I have purged thee, and thou wast not purged, thou shalt not be purged from thy filthiness any more, [m]till I have caused my fury to rest upon thee.

14 [n]I the LORD have spoken *it:* it shall come to pass, and I will do *it;* I will not go back; [o]neither will I spare, neither will I repent; according to thy ways, and according to thy doings, shall they judge thee, saith the Lord GOD.

15 Also the word of the LORD came unto me, saying,

16 Son of man, behold, I take away from thee the desire of thine eyes with a stroke:

---

[d]See Jer. i. 13; chap. xi. 3——[e]Or, *heap*——[f]Chap. xxii. 3; xxiii. 37; ver. 9——[g]See 2 Sam. viii. 2; Joel iii. 3; Obad. 11; Nah. iii. 10——[h]Lev. xvii. 13; Deut. xii. 16, 24——[i]Matt. vii. 2——[k]Ver. 6; Nah. iii. 1; Hab. ii. 12 [l]Chap. xxii. 15——[m]Chap. v. 13; viii. 18; xvi. 42 [n]1 Sam. xv. 29——[o]Chap. v. 11

---

salem; the *flesh*, the inhabitants in general; *every good piece*, *the thigh* and *the shoulder*, King Zedekiah and his family; the *bones*, the soldiers; and *the setting on* the *pot*, the commencement of the siege. The prophet was then in *Mesopotamia;* and he was told particularly to mark the day, &c., that it might be seen how precisely the spirit of prophecy had shown the very day in which the siege took place. Under the same image of a *boiling pot*, Jeremiah had represented the siege of Jerusalem, chap. i. 13. Ezekiel was a priest; the action of boiling pots was familiar to him, as these things were much in use in the temple service.

Verse 5. *Make it boil well*] Let it boil over, that its own scum may augment the fire, that the *bones*—the soldiers, may be *seethed therein.* Let its contentions, divided counsels, and disunion be the means of increasing its miseries, רתח רתחיה *rattach rethacheyha*, let it bubble its bubbling; something like that of the poet:—

"Bubble, bubble, toil and trouble:
Fire burn, and cauldron bubble."

Very like the noise made by ebullition, when a *pot of thick broth*, "sleek and slab," is set over a fierce fire. Such was that here represented, in which all the *flesh*, the *fat*, and the *bones* were to be boiled, and generally dissolved together.

Verse 6. *Let no lot fall upon it.*] Pull out the flesh indiscriminately; let no piece be *chosen* for *king* or *priest;* thus showing that all should be involved in one indiscriminate ruin.

Verse 7. *For her blood is in the midst of her*] She gloried in her idol sacrifices; she offered them upon a *rock*, where the blood should *remain evident;* and she poured none upon the *ground* to cover it with dust, in horror of that moral evil that required the blood of an innocent creature to be shed, in order to the atonement of the offender's guilt. To "cover the blood of the victim," was a command of the law, Lev. xvii. 13; Deut. xii. 24.

Verse 8. *That it might cause fury*] This very blood shall be against them, as the blood of *Abel* was against *Cain.*

Verse 10. *Heap on wood*] Let the siege be *severe*, the carnage great, and the ruin and catastrophe complete.

Verse 13. *In thy filthiness* is *lewdness*] זמה *zimmah*, a word that denominates the *worst kinds of impurity; adultery, incest*, &c., and the *purpose, wish, design*, and *ardent desire* to do these things. Hers were not *accidental* sins, they were *abominations by design;* and they were the worse in her, because God had *cleansed her*, had separated the Israelites from idolatry and idolatrous nations, and by his institutions removed from them all idolatrous incentives. But they formed *alliances* with the *heathen*, and adopted all their abominations; therefore God would not spare them. See ver. 14.

Verse 16. *Behold, I take away from thee the desire of thine eyes*] Here is an intimation that the stroke he was to suffer was to be above

A. M. 3414
B. C. 590
Ol. XLVII. 3
Anno
Tarquinii Prisci,
R. Roman., 27

yet neither shalt thou mourn
nor weep, neither shall thy
tears [p]run down.
17 [q]Forbear to cry, [r]make no
mourning for the dead, [s]bind the tire of thine
head upon thee, and [t]put on thy shoes upon
thy feet, and [u]cover not *thy* [v]lips, and eat not
the bread of men.
18 So I spake unto the people in the morning:
and at even my wife died; and I did in
the morning as I was commanded.
19 And the people said unto me, [w]Wilt thou
not tell us what these *things are* to us, that
thou doest *so?*
20 Then I answered them, The word of the
LORD came unto me, saying,
21 Speak unto the house of Israel, Thus saith
the Lord GOD; Behold, [x]I will profane my
sanctuary, the excellency of your strength,
[y]the desire of your eyes, and [z]that which your
soul pitieth; [a]and your sons and your daughters
whom ye have left, shall fall by the
sword.
22 And ye shall do as I have done: [b]ye
shall not cover *your* lips, nor
eat the bread of men.
23 And your tires *shall be*
upon your heads, and your
shoes upon your feet: [c]ye shall not mourn nor
weep; but [d]ye shall pine away for your iniquities,
and mourn one toward another.
24 Thus [e]Ezekiel is unto you a sign: according
to all that he hath done shall ye do:
[f]and when this cometh, [g]ye shall know that
I *am* the Lord GOD.
25 Also, thou son of man, *shall it* not *be* in
the day when I take from them [h]their
strength, the joy of their glory, the desire of
their eyes, and [i]that whereupon they set their
minds, their sons and their daughters,
26 *That* [k]he that escapeth in that day shall
come unto thee, to cause *thee* to hear *it* with
thine ears?
27 [l]In that day shall thy mouth be opened
to him which is escaped, and thou shalt speak,
and be no more dumb: and [m]thou shalt be a
sign unto them; and they shall know that I
am the LORD.

A. M. 3414
B. C. 590
Ol. XLVII. 3
Anno
Tarquinii Prisci,
R. Roman., 27

[p]Heb. *go*——[q]Heb. *Be silent*——[r]Jer. xvi. 5, 6, 7——[s]See Lev. x. 6; xxi. 10——[t]2 Sam. xv. 30——[u]Mic. iii. 7——[v]Heb. *upper lip;* and so ver. 22; Lev. xiii. 45——[w]Chap. xii. 9; xxxvii. 18——[x]Jer. vii. 14; chap. vii. 20, 21, 22——[y]Psa. xxvii. 4——[z]Heb. *the pity of your soul*——[a]Chap. xxiii. 47

[b]Jer. xvi. 6, 7; ver. 17——[c]Job xxvii. 15; Psa. lxxviii. 64——[d]Lev. xxvi. 39; ch. xxxiii. 10——[e]Isa. xx. 3; ch. iv. 3; xii. 6, 11——[f]Jer. xvii. 15; John xiii. 19; xiv. 29——[g]Chap. vi. 7; xxv. 5——[h]Ver. 21——[i]Heb. *the lifting up of their soul*——[k]Chap. iii. 21, 22——[l]Chap. iii. 26, 27; xxix. 21; xxxiii. 22——[m]Ver. 24

all grief; that it would be so great as to prevent the relief of tears.

Curæ leves loquuntur, graviores silent,

is a well-accredited maxim in such cases. Superficial griefs affect the more easily moved passions; great ones affect the soul itself, in its powers of reasoning, reflecting, comparing, recollecting, &c., when the sufferer feels all the weight of wo.

Neither shall thy tears run down.] Τουτο γαρ ιδιον των οφθαλμων εν τοις μεγαλοις κακοις· εν μεν γαρ ταις μετριαις συμφοραις αφθονως τα δακρυα καταῤῥει, ————εν δε τοις ὑπερβαλλουσι δεινοις φευγει και τα δακρυα και προδιδωσι και τους αφθαλμους· Achill. Tat. lib. 3. c. 11. For this is the case with the eyes in great calamities: in light misfortunes tears flow freely, but in heavy afflictions tears fly away, and betray the eyes.

Verse 17. *Make no mourning*] As a *priest*, he could make no public mourning, Lev. xxi. 1, &c.

Bind the tire of thine head] This seems to refer to the high priest's bonnet; or perhaps, one worn by the ordinary priests: it might have been a black veil to cover the head.

Put on thy shoes upon thy feet] Walking barefoot was a sign of grief.

Cover not thy *lips*] Mourners covered the under part of the face, from the nose to the bottom of the chin.

Eat not the bread of men.] לחם אנשים *lechem anashim*, "the bread of miserable men," i. e., *mourners;* probably, the funeral banquet.

Verse 18. *At even my wife died*] The prophet's wife was a type of the city, which was to him exceedingly dear. The *death of his wife* represented the *destruction of the city* by the Chaldeans; see ver. 21, where the *temple* is represented to be the *desire of his eyes*, as his *wife* was, ver. 16.

Verse 19. *Wilt thou not tell us*] In the following verses he explains and applies the whole of what he had *done* and *said*.

Verse 27. *In that day shall thy mouth be opened*] That is, When some one who shall have escaped from Jerusalem, having arrived among the captives, shall inform them of the destruction of the city, the temple, the royal family, and the people at large; till then he might suppress his tears and lamentations. And we find from chap. xxxiii. 21, that one did actually escape from the city, and informed the prophet and his brethren in captivity that the *city was smitten*.

Thus he was not only a prophet to foretell such things, but he was also a *sign* or *portent*, shadowing them out by circumstances in his own person and family; and thus the prediction, agreeing so perfectly with the event, proved that the previous information was from the Lord.

CHAPTER XXV

This chapter contains threatenings of the heavy judgments of God against the Ammonites, 1–7; *Moabites,* 8–11; *Edomites,* 12–14; *and Philistines,* 15–17; *on account of their hatred to his people, and their insulting them in the time of their distress. These prophecies were fulfilled by the instrumentality of Nebuchadnezzar, about* five *years after the destruction of Jerusalem. The same events were predicted by several of the other prophets, as may be seen from the citation of parallel texts in the margin.*

A. M. 3414
B. C. 590
Ol. XLVII. 3
Anno
Tarquinii Prisci,
R. Roman., 27

THE word of the LORD came again unto me, saying,

2 Son of man, [a]set thy face [b]against the Ammonites, and prophesy against them;

3 And say unto the Ammonites, Hear the word of the Lord GOD; Thus saith the Lord GOD; [c]Because thou saidst, Aha, against my sanctuary, when it was profaned; and against the land of Israel, when it was desolate; and against the house of Judah, when they went into captivity;

4 Behold, therefore I will deliver thee to the [d]men of the east for a possession, and they shall set their palaces in thee, and make their dwellings in thee: they shall eat thy fruit, and they shall drink thy milk.

5 And I will make [e]Rabbah [f]a stable for camels, and the Ammonites a couching-place for flocks: [g]and ye shall know that I *am* the LORD.

6 For thus saith the Lord GOD; Because thou [h]hast clapped *thine* [i]hands, and stamped with the [k]feet, and [l]rejoiced in [m]heart with all thy despite against the land of Israel;

A. M. 3414
B. C. 590
Ol. XLVII. 3
Anno
Tarquinii Prisci,
R. Roman., 27

7 Behold, therefore I will [n]stretch out mine hand upon thee, and will deliver thee for [o]a spoil to the heathen; and I will cut thee off from the people, and I will cause thee to perish out of the countries: I will destroy thee; and [p]thou shalt know that I *am* the LORD.

8 Thus saith the Lord GOD; Because that [q]Moab and [r]Seir do say, Behold, the house of Judah *is* like unto all the heathen;

9 Therefore, behold, I will open the [s]side of Moab from the cities, from his cities *which are* on his frontiers, the glory of the country, Beth-jeshimoth, Baal-meon, and Kiriathaim,

10 [t]Unto the men of the east [u]with the Ammonites, and will give them in possession, that the Ammonites [v]may not be remembered among the nations.

[a]Chap. vi. 2; xxxv. 2——[b]Jer. xlix. 1, &c.; chap. xxi. 28; Amos i. 13; Zeph. ii. 9——[c]Prov. xvii. 5; chap. xxvi. 2——[d]Heb. *children*——[e]Chap. xxi. 20——[f]Isa. xvii. 2; xxxii. 14; Zeph. ii. 14, 15——[g]Chap. xxiv. 24; xxvi. 6; xxxv. 9——[h]Job xxvii. 23; Lam. ii. 15; Zeph. ii. 15
[i]Heb. *hand*

[k]Heb. *foot*——[l]Chap. xxxvi. 5; Zeph. ii. 8, 10
[m]Heb. *soul*——[n]Chap. xxxv. 3——[o]Or, *meat*——[p]Ch. xxii. 16; xxiv. 24——[q]Isa. xv., xvi.; Jer. xlviii. 1, &c.; Amos ii. 1——[r]Chap. xxxv. 2, 5, 12——[s]Heb. *shoulder of Moab*——[t]Ver. 4——[u]Or, *against the children of Ammon*——[v]Chap. xxi. 32

NOTES ON CHAP. XXV

Verse 1. *The word of the Lord*] The chronological order of this chapter is after chap. xxxiii. 21, &c. See Abp. *Newcome.*

Verse 2. *Set thy face against the Ammonites*] We have already seen, chap. xxi. 19, &c., that when Nebuchadnezzar left Babylon, he was in doubt whether he should besiege Riblath, the capital of the Ammonites, or Jerusalem, the capital of the Jews, first: and having used his divination, he was determined, by the result, to attack Jerusalem the first. He did so; and the Ammonites, seeing the success of his arms, made friends with him, and exulted in the ruin of the Jews. God resents this, and predicts their downfall with that of Edom, Moab, and the Philistines. The fulfilment of this prediction is not noted in Scripture: but *Josephus* tells us, that about *five* years after the taking of Jerusalem, Nebuchadnezzar turned his arms against the *Ammonites* and *Moabites*, and afterwards against *Egypt;* and having subdued those nations, he returned to Babylon. *Joseph.* Antiq., l. x., c. ii. *Berosus* states, as quoted by Josephus, contra App., that Nebuchadnezzar subdued Syria, Arabia, Phœnicia, and Egypt: and consequently, that he had brought under his dominion the Ammonites, Moabites, and Idumeans, who were included among the *Philistines.* See *Calmet.*

Verse 4. *Will deliver thee to the men of the east*] Probably the *Scenite Arabs, Ishmaelites,* and people of Kedar, who seized upon the provinces of the vanquished *Ammonites,* &c. The following description suits this people only, living on fruits, the milk of their flocks, using camels, &c. Some think the *people of the east* mean the *Chaldeans.*

Verse 7. *I will cause thee to perish*] Except in history, the name of the Ammonites does not now exist.

Verse 8. *Moab and Seir do say*] *Seir* means the *Idumeans.* It appears that both these, with the Ammonites, had made a league with Zedekiah, Jer. xxvii. 3, which they did not keep; and it is supposed that they even joined with the Chaldeans.

Verse 9. *I will open the side*] כתף *ketheph,* the shoulder, the strongest frontier place. *Beth-jeshimoth, Baal-meon,* and *Kiriathaim* were strong frontier towns of Moab.

Verse 10. *That the Ammonites*] The Syriac

A. M. 3414
B. C. 590
Ol. XLVII. 3
Anno
Tarquinii Prisci,
R. Roman., 27

11 And I will execute judgments upon Moab; and they shall know that I *am* the LORD.

12 Thus saith the Lord GOD; [w]Because that Edom hath dealt against the house of Judah [x]by taking vengeance, and hath greatly offended, and revenged himself upon them;

13 Therefore thus saith the Lord GOD; I will also stretch out mine hand upon Edom, and will cut off man and beast from it; and I will make it desolate from Teman; and [y]they of Dedan shall fall by the sword.

14 And [z]I will lay my vengeance upon Edom by the hand of my people Israel: and they shall do in Edom according to mine anger and according to my fury; and they shall know my vengeance, saith the Lord GOD.

15 Thus saith the Lord GOD; [a]Because [b]the Philistines have dealt by revenge, and have taken vengeance with a despiteful heart, to destroy *it* [c]for the old hatred;

16 Therefore thus saith the Lord GOD; Behold, [d]I will stretch out mine hand upon the Philistines, and I will cut off the [e]Cherethims, [f]and destroy the remnant of the [g]sea coasts.

17 And I will [h]execute great [i]vengeance upon them with furious [k]rebukes; [l]and they shall know that I *am* the LORD, when I shall lay my vengeance upon them.

[w]2 Chron. xxviii. 17; Psa. cxxxvii. 7; Jer. xlix. 7, 8, &c.; chap. xxxv. 2, &c.; Amos i. 11; Obad. 10, &c.; &c.; 1 Esd. iv. 45——[x]Heb. *by revenging revengement* [y]Or, *they shall fall by the sword unto Dedan*——[z]See Isa. xi. 14; Jer. xlix. 2; 1 Mac. v. 3; 2 Mac. x. 16, 17 [a]Jer. xxv. 20; xlvii. 1, &c.; Joel iii. 4, &c.; Amos i. 6

[b]2 Chron. xxviii. 18——[c]Or, *with perpetual hatred* [d]Zeph. ii. 4, &c.——[e]1 Sam. xxx. 14——[f]Jer. xlvii. 4 [g]Or, *haven of the sea*——[h]Chap. v. 15——[i]Hebrew, *vengeances*——[k]1 Chron. xii. 17; Psa. lxviii. 30; Isa. ii. 4; xvii. 13; Micah iv. 3; Malachi iii. 11——[l]Psalm ix. 16

has, "That Rabbah of the sons of Ammon be not remembered."

Verse 12. *Because that Edom hath dealt*] The Edomites were the most inveterate enemies of the Jews from the very earliest times, and ever did all that they could to annoy them.

Verse 13. *I will make it desolate from Teman*] *Teman* and *Dedan* were both cities of the Moabites, and apparently at each extremity of the land.

Verse 14. *I will lay my vengeance upon Edom*] God will not allow men to insult those whom he has cast down. His judgment is sufficient; to add more is an insult to God.

By the hand of my people Israel] This was fulfilled by the Maccabees, who not only defeated them and brought them under complete subjection, but obliged them to receive circumcision, *Joseph.* Antiq. l. xiii., c. 17; 1 Macc. v. 65; 2 Macc. x. 16.

Verse 15. *Because the Philistines*] They were as inimical to the Jews as the Ammonites, &c., were. Nebuchadnezzar punished them because they had assisted the Tyrians during the time he was besieging their city.

I will cut off the Cherethims] See the note on 2 Sam. viii. 18.

The remnant of the sea coasts.] The different seignories of the Philistines inhabited the coast of the Mediterranean Sea, from Judea to Egypt. For other matters relative to these prophecies, see the passages in the margin.

CHAPTER XXVI

This prophecy, beginning here and ending in the twentieth verse of the twenty-eighth *chapter, is a declaration of the judgments of God against Tyre, a very famous commercial city of antiquity, which was taken by Nebuchadnezzar after an arduous siege of thirteen years. The prophet begins with introducing Tyre insulting Jerusalem, and congratulating herself on the prospect of accession to her commerce now that this city was no more,* 1, 2. *Upon which God denounces utter destruction to Tyre, and the cities depending on her,* 3–6. *We have then a particular account of the person raised up in the course of the Divine providence to accomplish this work. We see, as it were, his mighty hosts, (which are likened to the* waves *of the sea for their multitude,) raising the mounds, setting the engines, and shaking the walls; we hear the noise of the horsemen, and the sound of their cars; we see the clouds of smoke and dust; we see the sword bathed in blood, and hear the groans of the dying. Tyre, (whose buildings were very splendid and magnificent, and whose walls were* one hundred and fifty *feet in height, with a proportionable breadth,) immediately disappears; her strong (and as she thought impregnable) towers are thrown down; and her very dust is buried in the sea. Nothing remains but the bare rock,* 7–14. *The scene is then varied. The isles and adjacent regions, by a very strong and beautiful figure, are represented to be shaken, as with a mighty earthquake by violent concussion occasioned by the fall of Tyre. The groans of the dying reach the ears of the people inhabiting these regions. Their princes, alarmed for themselves and grieved for Tyre, descend from their thrones, lay aside their robes, and clothe themselves with—sackcloth?—no, but with* trembling! *Arrayed in this astonishing attire, the prophet introduces them as a chorus of mourners, lamenting Tyre in a funeral song or dirge, as customary on the death of renowned personages. And pursuing the same image still farther, in the person of God, he performs the last sad office for her. She is brought forth from her place in solemn pomp; the pit is dug for her; and she is buried, to rise no more,* 15–21. *Such is the prophecy concerning Tyre, comprehending both the city on the continent and that on the island, and most punctually fulfilled in regard to both. That on the continent was razed to the ground by Nebuchadnezzar, B. C.* 572, *and that on the island by Alexander the Great, B. C.* 332. *And at present, and for ages past, this ancient and renowned city, once the emporium of the world, and by her great naval superiority the centre of a powerful monarchy, is literally what the prophet has repeatedly foretold it should be, and what in his time was, humanly speaking, so highly improbable*—a BARE rock, a place to spread nets on!

A. M. 3416
B. C. 588
Ol. XLVIII. 1
Anno Tarquinii Prisci, R. Roman., 29

AND it came to pass in the eleventh year, in the first *day* of the month, *that* the word of the LORD came unto me, saying,

2 Son of man, [a]because that Tyrus hath said against Jerusalem, [b]Aha, she is broken *that was* the gates of the people: she is turned unto me: I shall be replenished, *now* she is laid waste:

3 Therefore, thus saith the Lord GOD: Behold, I *am* against thee, O Tyrus, and will cause many nations to come up against thee, as the sea causeth his waves to come up.

4 And they shall destroy the walls of Tyrus, and break down her towers: I will also scrape her dust from her, and [c]make her like the top of a rock.

5 It shall be *a place for* the spreading of nets, [d]in the midst of the sea: for I have spoken *it,* saith the Lord GOD: and it shall become a spoil to the nations.

A. M. 3416
B. C. 588
Ol. XLVIII. I
Anno Tarquinii Prisci, R. Roman, 29

6 And her daughters which *are* in the field shall be slain by the sword; [e]and they shall know that I *am* the LORD.

7 For thus saith the Lord GOD; Behold, I will bring upon Tyrus Nebuchadrezzar king of Babylon, [f]a king of kings, from the north, with horses, and with chariots, and with horsemen, and companies, and much people.

8 He shall slay with the sword thy daughters in the field: and he shall [g]make a fort against thee, and [h]cast a mount against thee, and lift up the buckler against thee.

9 And he shall set engines of war against thy walls, and with his axes he shall break down thy towers.

10 By reason of the abundance of his horses their dust shall cover thee: thy walls shall shake at the noise of the horsemen, and of the wheels, and of the chariots, when he shall enter into thy gates, [i]as men enter into a city wherein is made a breach.

[a]Isa. xxiii.; Jer. xxv. 22; xlvii. 4; Amos i. 9; Zech. ix. 2 —— [b]Chap. xxv. 3; xxxvi. 2 —— [c]Ver. 14 —— [d]Chap. xxvii. 32 —— [e]Chap. xxv. 5

[f]Ezra vii. 12; Dan. ii. 37 —— [g]Chap. xxi. 22 —— [h]Or, *pour out the engine of shot* —— [i]Heb. *according to the enterings of a city broken up*

Verse 1. *The eleventh year*] This was the year in which Jerusalem was taken; the *eleventh* of the captivity of Jeconiah, and the *eleventh* of the reign of Zedekiah. What *month* we are not told, though the *day* is mentioned. There have been many conjectures about this, which are not of sufficient consequence to be detailed.

Verse 2. *Tyrus hath said*] From this it would appear that Jerusalem *had been* taken, which was on the *fourth* month of this year; but it is possible that the prophet speaks of the event beforehand.

She is broken that was *the gates of the people*] Jerusalem, a general emporium.

I shall be replenished] The merchandise that went to Jerusalem will come to me, (to Tyre.)

Verse 3. *Will cause many nations to come up against thee*] We have already seen that the empire of the Chaldeans was composed of many different provinces, and that Nebuchadnezzar's army was composed of soldiers from different nations: these may be the people meant; but I doubt whether this may not refer to the different nations which in successive ages fought against Tyre. It was at last finally destroyed in the *sixteenth* century of the Christian era.

Verse 4. *I will also scrape her dust from her*] I will totally destroy her fortifications, and leave her nothing but a barren rock, as she was before. This cannot refer to the capture of Tyre by Nebuchadnezzar. It flourished long after his time.

Verse 5. A place for *the spreading of nets*] A place for the habitation of some poor fishermen, who spent the fishing season there, and were accustomed to dry their nets upon the rocks. See on ver. 11.

Verse 6. *And her daughters*] The places dependent on Tyre. As there were *two* places called *Tyre,* one on the *main land,* and the other on a *rock* in the sea, opposite to that on the main land, sometimes the one seems to be spoken of, and sometimes the other. That on the *land, Palætyre,* was soon taken; but that in the sea cost Nebuchadnezzar *thirteen years* of siege and blockade. The two formed only *one city,* and one state.

Verse 7. *Nebuchadrezzar—king of kings*] An ancient title among those proud Asiatic despots بدشاه شاهنشاه *shahinshah* and *padshah,* titles still in use.

Verse 8. *Thy daughters in the field*] This seems to be spoken of *Palætyre,* or Tyre on the main land; for *forts, mounts, engines of war, horses,* and *chariots* could not be brought to act against the other.

A. M. 3416
B. C. 588
Ol. XLVIII. 1
Anno
Tarquinii Prisci,
R. Roman., 29

11 With the hoofs of his
horses shall he tread down all
thy streets: he shall slay thy
people by the sword, and thy
strong garrisons shall go down to the
ground.
12 And they shall make a spoil of thy
riches, and make a prey of thy merchandise:
and they shall break down thy walls, and destroy [k]thy pleasant houses: and they shall lay
thy stones and thy timber and thy dust in the
midst of the water.
13 [l]And I will cause the noise of [m]thy songs
to cease; and the sound of thy harps shall be
no more heard.
14 And [n]I will make thee like the top of
a rock: thou shalt be *a place* to spread
nets upon; thou shalt be built no more: for
I the LORD have spoken *it,* saith the Lord
GOD.
15 Thus saith the Lord GOD to Tyrus;
Shall not the isles [o]shake at the sound of thy
fall, when the wounded cry, when the slaughter is made in the midst of thee?
16 Then all the [p]princes of the sea shall
[q]come down from their thrones, and lay away
their robes, and put off their broidered garments: they shall clothe themselves with
[r]trembling; [s]they shall sit upon the ground,
and [t]shall tremble at *every*
moment, and [u]be astonished
at thee.
17 And they shall take up a
[v]lamentation for thee, and say to thee, How
art thou destroyed, *that wast* inhabited
[w]of seafaring men, the renowned city,
which wast [x]strong in the sea, she and her
inhabitants, which cause their terror *to be*
on all that haunt it!
18 Now shall [y]the isles tremble in the day
of thy fall; yea, the isles that *are* in the sea
shall be troubled at thy departure.
19 For thus saith the Lord GOD; When I
shall make thee a desolate city, like the cities
that are not inhabited; when I shall bring up
the deep upon thee, and great waters shall
cover thee;
20 When I shall bring thee down [z]with
them that descend into the pit, with the people of old time, and shall set thee in the low
parts of the earth, in [a]places desolate of old,
with them that go down to the pit, that thou
be not inhabited; and I shall set glory [b]in
the land of the living;
21 [c]I will make thee [d]a terror, and thou *shalt
be* no *more:* [e]though thou be sought for, yet
shalt thou never be found again, saith the
Lord GOD.

[k]Heb. *houses of thy desire*——[l]Isa. xiv. 11; xxiv. 8; Jer. vii. 34; xvi. 9; xxv. 10——[m]Isa. xxiii. 16; ch. xxviii. 13; Rev. xviii. 22——[n]Ver. 4, 5——[o]Jer. xlix. 21; ver. 18; ch. xxvii. 28; xxxi. 16——[p]Isa. xxiii. 8——[q]Jonah iii. 6——[r]Heb. *tremblings*——[s]Job ii. 13——[t]Chap. xxxii. 10——[u]Chap. xxvii. 35

[v]Jer. vii. 29; chap. xix. 1; xxvii. 2, 32; xxviii. 12; xxxii. 2; Rev. xviii. 9——[w]Heb. *of the seas*——[x]Isa. xxiii. 4 [y]Ver. 15——[z]Chap. xxxii. 18, 24——[a]Job iii. 14; Psa. cix. 10; Isa. xlix. 19; lix. 10; Amos vii. 9——[b]Chap. xxxii. 23, 26, 27, 32——[c]Chap. xxvii. 36; xxviii. 19 [d]Heb. *terrors*——[e]Psa. xxxvii. 36

Verse 12. *And they shall lay thy stones and thy timber and thy dust in the midst of the water.*] This answers to the taking of Tyre by Alexander; he actually took the timbers, stones, rubbish, &c. of *old Tyre*, and filled up the space between it and new Tyre, and thus connected the latter with the main land; and this he was obliged to do before he could take it.

Verse 14. *Thou shalt be built no more*] If this refer to Nebuchadnezzar's capture of the city, *old Tyre* must be intended: that was destroyed by him, and never rebuilt. But I doubt whether the whole of this prophecy do not refer to the taking of Tyre by Alexander, *three hundred* years after its capture by Nebuchadnezzar. Indeed it may include more recent conquests of this important city. It went through a variety of vicissitudes till 1289, when it and the neighbouring towns were sacked and ravaged by the Mamelukes. Mr. *Maundrell*, who visited this place, says, "it is a Babel of broken walls, pillars, vaults, &c., there being not so much as *one entire house left!* Its present inhabitants are only a few *poor wretches*, harbouring themselves in the *vaults*, and subsisting chiefly on *fishing;* who seem to be preserved in this place by Divine Providence as a visible argument how God has fulfilled his word concerning Tyre, that it should be *the top of a rock, a place for fishers to dry their nets on.*"

Verse 15. *The isles shake at the sound of thy fall*] All those which had traded with this city, which was the grand mart, and on which they all depended. Her ruin involved them all, and caused general wailing.

Verse 16. *The princes of the sea*] The chief maritime states, such as *Leptis, Utica, Carthage, Gades*, &c. See *Calmet.*

Verse 17. *Wast strong in the sea*] The strength of Tyre was so great, that Alexander despaired of being able to reduce it unless he could *fill up that arm of the sea that ran between it and the main land.* And this work cost his army *seven months* of labour.

Verse 20. *And I shall set glory in the land of the living.*] Judea so called, the land of the living God.

Verse 21. *Yet shalt thou never be found again*] This is literally true; there is not the smallest vestige of the *ancient Tyre*, that which was erected on the main land. Even the ground seems to have been washed away; and the new Tyre is in nearly a similar state. I think this prophecy must be extended to the whole duration of Tyre. If it now be found to be in the state here described, it is sufficient to show the truth of the prophecy. And now it is found precisely in the state which the above prophetic declarations, taken according to the letter, point out! No word of God can ever fall to the ground.

Notwithstanding the former destructions, Tyre was a place of some consequence in the time of St. Paul. There was a Church there, (see Acts xxi. 3, 4, &c.,) which afterwards became famous. *Calmet* observes, it afforded a great number of martyrs for the Christian Church.

CHAPTER XXVII

This chapter may be considered as the second part of the prophecy concerning Tyre. The prophet pursues his subject in the manner of those ancient lamentations or funeral songs, in which the præficiæ *or mourning women first recounted whatever was great or praiseworthy in the deceased, and then mourned his fall. Here the riches, glory, and extensive commerce of Tyre are enlarged upon,* 1–25. *Her downfall is then described in a beautiful allegory, executed in a few words, with astonishing brevity, propriety, and perspicuity,* 26; *upon which all the maritime and commercial world are represented as grieved and astonished at her fate, and greatly alarmed for their own,* 27–36. *Besides the view which this chapter gives of the conduct of Providence, and the example with which it furnishes the critic and man of taste of a very elegant and highly finished piece of composition, it likewise affords the antiquary a very curious and interesting account of the wealth and commerce of ancient times. And to the mind that looks for "a city that hath foundations," what a picture does the whole present of the mutability and inanity of all earthly things! Many of the places mentioned in ancient history have, like Tyre, long ago lost their political consequence; the geographical situation of others cannot be traced; they have sunk in the* deep waters *of oblivion; the* east wind *hath carried them away.*

A. M. 3416
B. C. 588
Ol. XLVIII. 1
Anno Tarquinii Prisci, R. Roman., 29

THE word of the LORD came
again unto me, saying,
2 Now, thou son of man,[a] take
up a lamentation for Tyrus;
3 And say unto Tyrus, [b]O thou that art
situate at the entry of the sea, *which art* [c]a
merchant of the people for
many isles, Thus saith the
Lord GOD; O Tyrus, thou hast
said, [d]I *am* [e]of perfect beauty.
4 Thy borders *are* in the [f]midst of the seas,
thy builders have perfected thy beauty.

[a]Chap. xix. 1; xxvi. 17; xxviii. 12; xxxii. 2——[b]Chap. xxviii. 2——[c]Isa. xxiii. 3

[d]Chap. xxviii. 12——[e]Heb. *perfect of beauty*——[f]Heb. *heart*

NOTES ON CHAP. XXVII

Verse 2. *Take up a lamentation for Tyrus*] This is a singular and curious chapter. It gives a very circumstantial account of the trade of Tyre with different parts of the world, and the *different sorts of merchandise* in which she trafficked. The *places* and the *imports* are as regularly entered here as they could have been in a European custom-house.

Verse 3. *The entry of the sea*] Tyre was a small island, or rather rock, in the sea, at a short distance from the main land. We have already seen that there was another Tyre on the main land; but they are both considered as one city.

Verse 4. *Thy builders have perfected thy beauty.*] Under the allegory of a *beautiful ship*, the prophet, here and in the following verses, paints the glory of this ancient city. *Horace* describes the *commonwealth of Rome* by the same allegory, and is as minute in his description, *Carm.* lib. i. Od. xiv:—

O *navis*, referent in *mare* te novi
Fluctus? O quid agis? Fortiter occupa
Portum. Nonne vides, ut
Nudum *remigio latus*,
Et *malus* celeri saucius *Africo*,
Antennæque gemant? ac sine *funibus*
Vix durare *carinæ*
Possint imperiosius
Æquor? non tibi sunt *integra lintea;*
Non Di, quos iterum pressa voces malo:
Quamvis Pontica *pinus*,
Sylvæ filia nobilis,
Jactes et genus, et nomen inutile
Nil *pictis* timidus *navita puppibus*
Fidit. Tu, nisi, *ventis*
Debes ludibrium, cave.

Unhappy *vessel*, shall the *waves* again
Tumultuous bear thee to the faithless *main?*
What, would thy madness thus with *storms* to sport?
Cast firm your anchor in the friendly *port*.
Behold thy *naked decks*, the *wounded mast*,
And *sail-yards* groan beneath the *southern blast*.
Nor, without *ropes*, thy *keel* can longer brave
The rushing fury of the imperious *wave:*
Torn are thy *sails;* thy *guardian gods* are lost,
Whom you might call, in future *tempests* tost.
What, though majestic in your pride you stood,
A noble daughter of the *Pontic wood*,
You now may vainly boast an empty name,
Of birth conspicuous in the rolls of fame.
The *mariner*, when *storms* around him rise,
No longer on a *painted stern* relies.
Ah! yet take heed, lest these *new tempests* sweep,
In sportive rage, thy glories to the *deep*.

FRANCIS.

A. M. 3416
B. C. 588
Ol. XLVIII. 1
Anno
Tarquinii Prisci,
R. Roman., 29

5 They have [g]made all thy *ship* boards of fir trees of [h]Senir: they have taken [i]cedars from Lebanon to make masts for thee.

6 *Of* the oaks of Bashan have they made thine oars: [k]the [l]company of the Ashurites have made thy benches *of* ivory, *brought* out of [m]the isles of Chittim.

7 Fine linen with broidered work from Egypt was that which thou spreadest forth to be thy sail; [n]blue and purple from the isles of Elishah was that which covered thee.

8 The inhabitants of Zidon and Arvad were thy mariners: thy wise *men,* O Tyrus, *that* were in thee, were thy pilots.

9 The ancients of [o]Gebal and the wise *men* thereof were in thee thy [p]calkers[q]; all the ships of the sea with their mariners were in thee to occupy thy merchandise.

10 They of Persia and of Lud and of [r]Phut were in thine army, thy men of war: they hanged the shield and helmet in thee; they set forth thy comeliness.

A. M. 3416
B. C. 588
Ol. XLVIII. 1
Anno
Tarquinii Prisci,
R. Roman., 29

11 The men of Arvad with thine army *were* upon thy walls round about, and the Gammadims were in thy towers: they hanged their shields upon thy walls round about; they have made [s]thy beauty perfect.

12 [t]Tarshish *was* thy merchant by reason of the multitude of all *kind of* riches; with silver, iron, tin, and lead, they traded in thy fairs.

13 [u]Javan, Tubal, and Meshech, they *were* thy merchants: they traded [v]the persons of men and vessels of brass in thy [w]market.

14 They of the house of [x]Togarmah traded in thy fairs with horses and horsemen and mules.

[g]Heb. *built*——[h]Deut. iii. 9——[i]Judg. ix. 15——[k]Or, *they have made thy hatches of ivory well trodden*——[l]Heb. *the daughter*——[m]Jer. ii. 10——[n]Or, *purple and scarlet* [o]1 Kings v. 18; Psa. lxxxiii. 7

[p]Or, *stoppers of chinks*——[q]Heb. *strengtheners* [r]Jer. xlvi. 9; chap. xxx. 5; xxxviii. 5——[s]Ver. 3——[t]Gen. x. 4; 2 Chron. xx. 36——[u]Gen. x. 2——[v]Rev. xviii. 13 [w]Or, *merchandise*——[x]Gen. x. 3; chap. xxxviii. 6

I give this as a striking parallel to many passages in this chapter.

Verse 5. *Fir trees of Senir*] *Senir* is a mountain which the Sidonians called Sirion, and the Hebrews *Hermon*, Deut. iii. 9. It was beyond Jordan, and extended from Libanus to the mountains of Gilead.

Verse 6. Of *the oaks of Bashan*] Some translate *alder*, others the *pine*.

The company of the Ashurites] The word אשרים *asherim* is by several translated *boxwood*. The *seats* or *benches* being made of this wood inlaid with *ivory*.

Isles of Chittim] The Italian islands; the islands of Greece; Cyprus. *Calmet* says *Macedonia* is meant.

Verse 7. *Fine linen*] שש *shesh*, *cotton cloth*. In this sense the word is generally to be understood.

To be thy sail] Probably the flag—*ensign* or *pennant*, is meant.

Blue and purple from the isles of Elishah] *Elis*, a part of the *Peloponnesus*.

Verse 8. *Zidon* and *Arvad*] Or *Arad*. Two powerful cities on the Phœnician coast, in the neighbourhood of Tyre, from which Tyre had her sailors; and the best instructed of her own inhabitants were her pilots or steersmen.

Verse 9. *The ancients of Gebal*] This was a city of Phœnicia, near Mount Libanus, Josh. xiii. 5. It was called *Biblos* by the Greeks.

Thy calkers] Those who repaired their vessels; *paying*, as it is termed, pitched hemp into the seams, to prevent the water from oozing through.

To occupy thy merchandise.] That is, to be thy *agents* or *factors*.

Verse 10. *They of Persia*] Lud, the Lydians; *Phut*, a people of Africa, see Gen. x. 6. From these places they had auxiliary troops; for as they traded with the then known world, were rich, and could afford to give good pay, they no doubt had soldiers and sailors from every part. Skilful and desperate men will go any where after their *price*.

Verse 11. *The Gammadims were in thy towers*] Some think these were a people of Phœnicia; others, that *tutelar images* are meant; others, that the word expresses *strong men*, who acted as *guards*. The *Vulgate* reads *Pygmæi*, the pygmies, who were fabled to be a little people of a *cubit* in height, from גמד *gomed*, a *cubit;* and we are told that this little people were celebrated for their wars with the *cranes;* but nothing of this kind can enter into this description. Probably a people inhabiting the promontories of Phœnicia are here intended; and their hanging their *shields upon the walls* is a proof that *soldiers* are meant, and persons of skill and prowess too.

Verse 12. *Tarshish* was *thy merchant*] After having given an account of the *naval* and *military* equipment of this city, he now speaks of the various *places* and *peoples* with whom the Tyrians traded, and the different kinds of merchandise imported from those places.

By *Tarshish* some understand the *Carthaginians;* some think *Tartessus*, near the straits of Gibraltar, is meant; others, *Tharsis* in Cilicia. The place was famous for all the useful metals, *silver, iron, tin,* and *lead.* All these they might have had from *Britain.*

Verse 13. *Javan, Tubal, and Meshech*] The Ionians, the Tybarenians, and the Cappadocians, or Muscovites.

They traded the persons of men] That is, they trafficked in *slaves.* The bodies and souls of men were bought and sold in those days, as in our degenerate age. With these also they traded in brazen vessels.

Verse 14. *Togarmah*] The *Sarmatians.* Some think *Cappadocia.* With these they dealt

A. M. 3416
B. C. 588
Ol. XLVIII. 1
Anno
Tarquinii Prisci,
R. Roman., 29

15 The men of [y]Dedan *were* thy merchants; many isles *were* the merchandise of thine hand: they brought thee *for* a present horns of ivory and ebony.

16 Syria *was* thy merchant by reason of the multitude of [z]the wares of thy making: they occupied in thy fairs with emeralds, purple, and broidered work, and fine linen, and coral, and [a]agate.

17 Judah, and the land of Israel, they *were* thy merchants: they traded in thy market [b]wheat of [c]Minnith, and Pannag, and honey, and oil, and [d]balm.[e]

18 Damascus *was* thy merchant in the multitude of the wares of thy making, for the multitude of all riches; in the wine of Helbon, and white wool.

19 Dan also and Javan [f]going to and fro occupied in thy fairs: bright iron, cassia, and calamus, were in thy market.

20 [g]Dedan *was* thy merchant in [h]precious clothes for chariots.

A. M. 3416
B. C. 588
Ol. XLVIII. 1
Anno
Tarquinii Prisci,
R. Roman., 29

21 Arabia, and all the princes of [i]Kedar, [k]they occupied with thee in lambs, and rams, and goats: in these *were they* thy merchants.

22 The merchants of [l]Sheba and Raamah, they *were* thy merchants: they occupied in thy fairs with chief of all spices, and with all precious stones, and gold.

23 [m]Haran, and Canneh, and Eden, the merchants of [n]Sheba, Asshur, *and* Chilmad, *were* thy merchants.

24 These *were* thy merchants in [o]all sorts *of things,* in blue [p]clothes, and broidered work, and in chests of rich apparel, bound with cords, and made of cedar, among thy merchandise.

25 [q]The ships of Tarshish did sing of thee in thy market: and thou wast replenished, and made very glorious [r]in the midst of the seas.

26 Thy rowers have brought thee into great

[y]Gen. x. 7——[z]Heb. *thy works*——[a]Heb. *chrysoprase*——[b]1 Kings v. 9, 11; Ezra iii. 7; Acts xii. 20——[c]Judg. xi. 33——[d]Jer. viii. 22——[e]Or, *rosin*——[f]Or, *Meuzal*——[g]Gen. xxv. 3——[h]Heb. *clothes of freedom*——[i]Gen. xxv. 13; Isa. lx. 7

[k]Heb. *they* were *the merchants of thy hand*——[l]Gen. x. 7; 1 Kings x. 1, 2; Psa. lxxii. 10, 15; Isa. lx. 6——[m]Gen. xi. 31; 2 Kings xix. 12——[n]Gen. xxv. 3——[o]Or, *excellent things*——[p]Heb. *foldings*——[q]Psa. xlviii. 7; Isa. ii. 16; xxiii. 14——[r]Ver. 4

in *horses, mules,* and *horsemen;* or probably *draught horses* and *war horses* are intended.

Verse 15. *The men of Dedan*] Dedan was one of the descendants of Abraham by Keturah, and dwelt in Arabia, Gen. xxv. 3. *Ivory* and *ebony* might come from that quarter. By way of distinction ivory is called both in Hebrew שן *shen,* and in Arabic سن *shen,* the TOOTH, as that beautiful substance is the *tooth* of the *elephant.*

Verse 16. *Syria*] These were always a mercantile people. For the precious stones mentioned here see the notes on Exod. xxviii. 17.

Verse 17. *Judah, and the land of Israel—traded in thy market wheat*] The words have been understood as articles of merchandise, not names of *places.* So the Jews traded with the Tyrians in *wheat, stacte, balsam, honey, oil,* and *resin.*

Verse 18. *Damascus—wine of Helbon*] Now called by the Turks Haleb, and by us Aleppo.

White wool.] Very fine wool: wool of a fine quality. Some think *Milesian wool* is meant.

Verse 19. *Dan also and Javan*] It is probable that both these words mean some of the Grecian islands.

Going to and fro] They both *took* and *brought—imported* and *exported:* but מאוזל *meuzal,* from *uzal,* may be a proper name. What place is signified I cannot tell, unless it be *Azal,* a name, according to *Kamoos,* of the capital of Arabia Felix.

Verse 20. *Dedan*] Possibly the descendants of *Dedan,* son of *Raamah,* see Gen. x. 7.

In precious clothes for chariots.] Either fine carpets, or rich housings for horses, camels, &c., used for riding.

Verse 21. *Arabia, and all the princes of Kedar*] Arabia Deserta, on the confines of the Dead Sea. The *Kedarenes* inhabited the same country. These brought *lambs, rams,* and *goats* for the consumption of the city.

Verse 22. *Sheba and Raamah*] Inhabitants of Arabia Felix, at the entrance of the Persian Gulf, who were famous for their riches and spices.

Verse 23. *Haran*] In Mesopotamia; well known in Scripture.

Canneh] Or *Chalane;* see Gen. x. 10. It is supposed to be a cape or port of Arabia Felix, on the Indian Sea.

Eden] Equally famous: supposed to have been situated near the confluence of the *Tigris* and *Euphrates.*

Sheba] Different from that in ver. 22. This was probably near the country of the Edomites.

Asshur] Perhaps the Assyrians.

Chilmad] Possibly *Cholmadora,* on the Euphrates. *Ptol.* lib. v., cap. 15. For several of these places, and the persons from whom they derived their names, see Gen. x., and the notes there; and see *Calmet.*

Verse 24. *These* were *thy merchants in all sorts* of things] The above people traded with the Tyrians in a great variety of the most valuable merchandise: *blue* or *purple cloth, boxes of cedar, covered with skins, and bound with silken cords,* and *sealed with an engraved seal, finely cut, &c.* See the *Chaldee.*

Verse 25. *The ships of Tarshish*] The ships of *Tharsis,* in Cilicia, were the chief of those which traded with thee.

Verse 26. *Thy rowers have brought thee into great waters*] Tyre is still considered under

A. M. 3416
B. C. 588
Ol. XLVIII. 1
Anno
Tarquinii Prisci,
R. Roman., 29

waters: [s]the east wind hath broken thee in the [t]midst of the seas.

27 Thy [u]riches, and thy fairs, thy merchandise, thy mariners, and thy pilots, thy calkers, and the occupiers of thy merchandise, and all thy men of war, that *are* in thee, [v]and in all thy company which *is* in the midst of thee, shall fall into the [w]midst of the seas in the day of thy ruin.

28 The [x]suburbs [y]shall shake at the sound of the cry of thy pilots.

29 And [z]all that handle the oar, the mariners, *and* all the pilots of the sea, shall come down from their ships, they shall stand upon the land;

30 And shall cause their voice to be heard against thee, and shall cry bitterly, and shall [a]cast up dust upon their heads, they [b]shall wallow themselves in the ashes:

31 And they shall [c]make themselves utterly bald for thee, and gird them with sackcloth, and they shall weep for thee with bitterness of heart *and* bitter wailing.

A. M. 3416
B. C. 588
Ol. XLVIII. 1
Anno
Tarquinii Prisci,
R. Roman., 29

32 And in their wailing they shall [d]take up a lamentation for thee, and lament over thee, *saying,* [e]What *city is* like Tyrus, like the destroyed in the midst of the sea.

33 [f]When thy wares went forth out of the seas, thou filledst many people; thou didst enrich the kings of the earth with the multitude of thy riches and of thy merchandise.

34 In the time *when* [g]thou shalt be broken by the seas in the depths of the waters, [h]thy merchandise and all thy company in the midst of thee shall fall.

35 [i]All the inhabitants of the isles shall be astonished at thee, and their kings shall be sore afraid, they shall be troubled in *their* countenance.

36 The merchants among the people [k]shall hiss at thee; [l]thou shalt be [m]a terror, and [n]never *shalt be* any more.

[s]Psa. xlviii. 7——[t]Heb. *heart*——[u]Prov. xi. 4; ver. 34; Rev. xviii. 9, &c.——[v]Or, *even with all*——[w]Heb. *heart* [x]Or, *waves*——[y]Ch. xxvi. 15, 18——[z]Rev. xviii. 17, &c. [a]Job ii. 12; Rev. xviii. 19——[b]Esth. iv. 1, 3; Jer. vi. 26

[c]Jer. xvi. 6; xlvii. 5; Mic. i. 16——[d]Ch. xxvi. 17; ver. 2 [e]Rev. xviii. 18——[f]Rev. xviii. 19——[g]Ch. xxvi. 19 [h]Ver. 27——[i]Ch. xxvi. 15, 16——[k]Jer. xviii. 16——[l]Ch. xxvi. 21——[m]Heb. *terrors*——[n]Heb. shalt *not* be *for ever*

the allegory of a *ship;* and all the vessels of different nations trading with her are represented as towing her into deep waters—bringing her into great affluence. But while in this state, a stormy *east wind*, or a destructive wind, meaning the Chaldeans, arises, and dashes her to pieces! See the ode from *Horace*, already quoted on ver. 4.

Verse 27. *Thy riches*] This vast ship, laden with all kinds of valuable wares, and manned in the best manner, being wrecked, all her *valuables, sailors, officers*, &c., went to the bottom.

Verse 28. *The cry of thy pilots.*] When the ship was dashed against the rocks by the violence of the winds and the waves, and all hope of life was taken away, then a universal cry was set up by all on board. I have heard this cry, and nothing more dismal can be imagined, when the ship by a violent tempest is driving among *rocks* on a lee shore. Then "All lost! cut away the boat!" is more dreadful than the cry of *fire* at midnight.

Verse 30. *Shall cry bitterly*] All that were on the land, seeing this dreadful sight, a gallant ship perishing with all her men and goods, are represented as setting up a dismal cry at this heart-rending sight. But what must they have felt who were on board? Reader, wert thou ever *shipwrecked?* Wert thou ever in a *hurricane* on a *lee rocky shore*, where the helm had lost its power, and the sails were rendered useless? Dost thou remember that apparently last moment, when the ship drove up to the tremendous rocks, riding on the back of a mountainous surge? Then what was the universal cry? Hast thou ever heard any thing so terrific? so appalling? so death and judgment-like? No. It is impossible. These are the circumstances, this is the cry, that the prophet describes; disorder, confusion, dismay, and ruin. And this is a scene which the present writer has witnessed, himself a part of the wretched, when all hope of life was taken away, the yawning gulf opened, and nothing presented itself to support body or soul but that God who gave to both their being, and ultimately rescued him and his forlorn companions from one of the worst of deaths, by heaving the ship from the rocks by the agency of a tremendous receding wave. My soul hath these things still in remembrance, and therefore is humbled within me.

Verse 32. *What* city is *like Tyrus*] This, to the end of the chapter, is the lamentation.

Verse 36. *Shall hiss at thee*] שרקו *shareku*, shall *shriek* for thee. This powerfully expresses the sensation made on the feelings of the spectators on the shore when they saw the vessel swallowed up.

CHAPTER XXVIII

The first part of this chapter relates to a king of Tyre, probably the same who is called in the Phœnician annals Ithobalus. He seems to have been a vain man, who affected Divine honours. The prophet treats his foolish pretensions with severe irony, and predicts his doom, 1–10. *He then takes up a funeral dirge and lamentation over him, in which his former pomp and splendour are finely contrasted with his fall, in terms that seem frequently to allude to the fall of Lucifer from heaven,* (Isa. xiv.,) 11–19. *The overthrow of Sidon, the mother city of Tyre, is next announced,* 20–23; *and the chapter concludes with a promise to the Jews of deliverance from all their enemies, and particularly of their restoration from the Babylonish captivity,* 24–26.

A. M. 3416
B. C. 588
Ol. XLVIII. 1
Anno
Tarquinii Prisci,
R. Roman., 29

THE word of the LORD came again unto me, saying,

2 Son of man, say unto the prince of Tyrus, Thus saith the Lord GOD; Because thine heart *is* lifted up, and [a]thou hast said, I *am* a god, I sit *in* the seat of God, [b]in the [c]midst of the seas; [d]yet thou *art* a man, and not God, though thou set thine heart as the heart of God:

3 Behold, [e]thou *art* wiser than Daniel; there is no secret that they can hide from thee:

4 With thy wisdom and with thine understanding thou hast gotten thee riches, and hast gotten gold and silver into thy treasures:

5 [f]By [g]thy great wisdom *and* by thy traffic hast thou increased thy riches, and thine heart is lifted up because of thy riches:

6 Therefore thus saith the Lord GOD; Because thou hast set thine heart as the heart of God;

7 Behold, therefore I will bring strangers upon thee, [h]the terrible of the nations: and they shall draw their swords against the beauty of thy wisdom, and they shall defile thy brightness.

A. M. 3416
B. C. 588
Ol. XLVIII. 1
Anno
Tarquinii Prisci,
R. Roman., 29

8 They shall bring thee down to the pit, and thou shalt die the deaths of *them that are* slain in the midst of the seas.

9 Wilt thou yet [i]say before him that slayeth thee, I *am* God; but thou *shalt be* a man, and no God, in the hand of him that [k]slayeth thee.

10 Thou shalt die the deaths of [l]the uncircumcised by the hand of strangers: for I have spoken *it*, saith the Lord GOD.

11 Moreover the word of the LORD came unto me, saying,

12 Son of man, [m]take up a lamentation upon the king of Tyrus, and say unto him, Thus saith the Lord GOD; [n]Thou sealest up the sum, full of wisdom, and perfect in beauty.

13 Thou hast been in [o]Eden the garden of God; every precious stone *was* thy covering, the [p]sardius, topaz, and the diamond, the [q]beryl, the onyx, and the jasper, the sapphire, the [r]emerald, and the carbuncle, and gold:

[a]Ver. 9——[b]Chap. xxvii. 3, 4——[c]Hebrew, *heart*——[d]Isaiah xxxi. 3——[e]Zechariah ix. 2——[f]Hebrew, *By the greatness of thy wisdom*——[g]Psalm lxii. 10; Zechariah ix. 3——[h]Chap. xxx. 11; xxxi. 12; xxxii. 12

[i]Ver. 2——[k]Or, *woundeth*——[l]Chap. xxxi. 18; xxxii. 19, 21, 25, 27——[m]Chap. xxvii. 2——[n]Chap. xxvii. 3; ver. 3——[o]Chap. xxxi. 8, 9——[p]Or, *ruby*——[q]Or, *chrysolite*——[r]Or, *chrysoprase*

NOTES ON CHAP. XXVIII

Verse 2. *Say unto the prince of Tyrus*] But who was this prince of Tyrus? Some think *Hiram;* some, *Sin;* some, the *devil;* others, *Ithobaal*, with whom the chronology and circumstances best agree. *Origen* thought the guardian angel of the city was intended.

I am a god] That is, I am absolute, independent, and accountable to none. He was a man of great pride and arrogance.

Verse 3. *Thou* art *wiser than Daniel*] Daniel was at this time living, and was reputable for his great wisdom. This is said *ironically.* See chap. xiv. 14; xxvi. 1.

Verse 5. *By thy great wisdom*] He attributed every thing to himself; he did not acknowledge a Divine providence. As he got all by himself, so he believed he could keep all by himself, and had no need of any foreign help.

Verse 7. *I will bring strangers upon thee*] The Chaldeans.

Verse 9. *Wilt thou yet say before him that slayeth thee*] Wilt thou continue thy pride and arrogance when the sword is sheathed in thee, and still imagine that thou art self-sufficient and independent?

Verse 10. *The deaths of the uncircumcised*] *Two* deaths, *temporal* and *eternal.* Ithobaal was taken and killed by Nebuchadnezzar.

Verse 12. *Thou sealest up*] This has been translated, "Thou drawest thy own likeness." "Thou formest a portrait of thyself; and hast represented thyself the perfection of wisdom and beauty." I believe this to be the meaning of the place.

Verse 13. *Thou hast been in Eden*] This also is a strong irony. Thou art like *Adam*, when in his innocence and excellence he was in the garden of Eden!

Every precious stone was *thy covering*] For a description of these stones see the note on Exod. xxviii. 17.

Verse 14. *Thou* art *the anointed cherub that covereth*] The irony is continued; and here he is likened to the CHERUB that guarded the gates of Paradise, and kept the way of the tree

A. M. 3416
B. C. 588
Ol. XLVIII. 1
Anno
Tarquinii Prisci,
R. Roman., 29

the workmanship of [s]thy tabrets and of thy pipes was
prepared in thee in the day
that thou wast created.
14 Thou *art* the anointed [t]cherub that
covereth: and I have set thee *so:* thou wast
upon [u]the holy mountain of God; thou hast
walked up and down in the midst of the
stones of fire.
15 Thou *wast* perfect in thy ways from the
day that thou wast created, till iniquity was
found in thee.
16 By the multitude of thy merchandise
they have filled the midst of thee with violence, and thou hast sinned: therefore I will
cast thee as profane out of the mountain of
God: and I will destroy thee, [v]O covering
cherub, from the midst of the stones of
fire.
17 [w]Thine heart was lifted up because of
thy beauty, thou hast corrupted thy wisdom
by reason of thy brightness: I will cast thee
to the ground, I will lay thee before kings,
that they may behold thee.

A. M. 3416
B. C. 588
Ol. XLVIII. 1
Anno
Tarquinii Prisci,
R. Roman., 29

18 Thou hast defiled thy
sanctuaries by the multitude
of thine iniquities, by the iniquity of thy traffic; therefore
will I bring forth a fire from the midst of
thee, it shall devour thee, and I will bring
thee to ashes upon the earth in the sight of
all them that behold thee.
19 All they that know thee among the people shall be astonished at thee: [x]thou shalt be
[y]a terror, and never *shalt* thou *be* any more.
20 Again the word of the LORD came unto
me, saying,
21 Son of man, [z]set thy face [a]against Zidon,
and prophesy against it,
22 And say, Thus saith the Lord GOD;
[b]Behold, I *am* against thee, O Zidon; and I
will be glorified in the midst of thee: and
[c]they shall know that I *am* the LORD, when
I shall have executed judgments in her, and
shall be [d]sanctified in her.
23 [e]For I will send into her pestilence, and
blood into her streets; and the wounded shall
be judged in the midst of her by the sword

[s]Ch. xxvi. 13——[t]See Exod. xxv. 20; ver. 16——[u]Ch. xx. 40——[v]Ver. 14——[w]Ver. 2, 5——[x]Ch. xxvi. 21; xxvii. 36——[y]Heb. *terrors*——[z]Ch. vi. 2; xxv. 2; xxix. 2

[a]Isa. xxiii. 4, 12; Jer. xxv. 22; xxvii. 3; ch. xxxii. 30
[b]Exod. xiv. 4, 17; ch. xxxix. 13——[c]Psa. ix. 16——[d]Ch. xx. 41; xxxvi. 23; ver. 25——[e]Ch. xxxviii. 22

of life; or to one of the cherubs whose wings, spread out, covered the mercy-seat.

Thou wast upon the holy mountain of God] The irony is still continued; and now he is compared to *Moses*, and afterwards to one of the *chief angels*, who has walked up and down among the stones of fire; that is, thy floors have been paved with precious stones, that shone and sparkled like fire.

Lucan, describing the splendour of the apartments of *Cleopatra*, queen of Egypt, speaks in nearly a similar language:—

Nec summis crustata domus, sectisque nitebat
Marmoribus, stabatque sibi non segnis *achates*,
Purpureusque lapis, totusque effusus in aula
Calcabatur onyx— *Pharsal.* lib. x.

Rich as some fane by slavish zealots reared,
For the proud banquet stood the hall prepared:
Thick *golden plates* the latent beams infold,
And the high roof was fretted o'er with *gold.*
Of solid *marble* all the walls were made,
And *onyx* e'en the *meaner floor* inlaid;
While *porphyry* and *agate* round the court
In massy columns rose, a proud support.
Of solid *ebony* each post was wrought,
From swarthy Meroë profusely brought.
With *ivory* was the entrance crusted o'er,
And polished *tortoise* hid each shining door;
While on the cloudy spots enchased was seen
The trusty *emerald's* never-fading green.
Within the royal beds and couches shone,
Beamy and bright with many a costly *stone*,
The glowing *purple* rich. ROWE.

Verse 15. *Thou* wast *perfect in thy ways*] The irony seems still to be kept up. Thou hast been like the angels, like Moses, like the cherubs, like Adam, like God, till thy iniquity was found out.

Verse 16. *I will cast thee as profane*] Thou shalt be cast down from thine eminence.

From the midst of the stones of fire.] Some, supposing that *stones of fire* means the *stars*, have thought that the whole refers to the *fall of Satan.*

Verse 18. *Thou hast defiled thy sanctuaries*] Irony continued. As God, as the angels, as the cherubim, thou must have had thy sanctuaries; but thou hast defiled them: and as Adam, thou hast polluted thy Eden, and hast been expelled from Paradise.

Verse 19. *Thou shalt be a terror*] Instead of being an object of *adoration* thou shalt be a subject of horror, and at last be destroyed with thy city, so that nothing but thy name shall remain. It was entirely burnt by Alexander the Great, as it had been before by Nebuchadnezzar.

Verse 22. *I* am *against thee, O Zidon*] Sidon for a long time had possessed the empire of the sea and of all Phœnicia, and Tyre was one of its colonies; but in process of time, the daughter became greater than the mother. It seems to have been an independent place at the time in which Tyre was taken; but it is likely that it was taken by the Chaldeans soon after the former.

Verse 23. *And the wounded*] חלל *chalal*, the *soldiery*. All its supports shall be taken away, and its defenders destroyed.

A. M. 3416
B. C. 588
Ol. XLVIII. 1
Anno
Tarquinii Prisci,
R. Roman., 29

upon her on every side; and they shall know that I *am* the LORD.

24 And there shall be no more [f]a pricking brier unto the house of Israel, nor *any* grieving thorn of all *that are* round about them, that despised them; and they shall know that I *am* the Lord GOD.

25 Thus saith the Lord GOD; When I shall have [g]gathered the house of Israel from the people among whom they are scattered, and shall be [h]sanctified in them in the sight of the heathen, then shall they dwell in their land that I have given to my servant Jacob.

26 And they shall [i]dwell [k]safely therein, and shall [l]build houses, and [m]plant vineyards; yea, they shall dwell with confidence, when I have executed judgments upon all those that[n]despise them round about them; and they shall know that I *am* the LORD their God.

[f]Num. xxxiii. 55; Josh. xxiii. 13——[g]Isa. xi. 12; xi. 17; xx. 41; xxxiv. 13; xxxvii. 21——[h]Ver. 22

[i]Jer. xxiii. 6; ch. xxxvi. 28——[k]Or, *with confidence* [l]Isa. lxv. 21; Amos ix. 14——[m]Jer. xxxi. 5——[n]Or, *spoil*

Verse 24. *There shall be no more a pricking brier*] Nothing to excite Israel to idolatry when restored from their captivity. Perhaps there is an allusion to *Jezebel*, daughter of *Ethbaal*, king of Sidon, and wife to Ahab, king of Israel, who was the greatest curse to Israel, and the universal restorer of idolatry in the land, see 1 Kings xvi. 31. Sidon being destroyed, there would come no encourager of idolatry from that quarter.

Verse 25. *When I shall have gathered the house of Israel*] In their long captivity, God had been preparing the land for them so as to make it a *safe dwelling;* and hence he executed judgments on all the heathen nations round about by means of the Chaldeans. Thus Tyre and Sidon were destroyed, as were the Ammonites and others who had been the inveterate enemies of the Jews. Judgment first began at his own house, then proceeded to the heathen nations; and when they were brought down, then he visited and redeemed his people. Thus God's ways are proved to be all equal; partialities and caprices belong not to him.

CHAPTER XXIX

This and the three following chapters foretell the conquest of Egypt by Nebuchadnezzar, which he accomplished in the twenty-seventh *year of Jehoiachin's captivity. The same event is foretold by Jeremiah,* chap. xlvi. 13, &c. *The prophecy opens with God's charging the king of Egypt (Pharaoh-hophra) with the same extravagant pride and profanity which were in the preceding chapter laid to the charge of the prince of Tyre. He appears, like him, to have affected Divine honours; and boasted so much of the strength of his kingdom, that, as an ancient historian* (Herodotus) *tells us, he impiously declared that God himself could not dispossess him. Wherefore the prophet, with great majesty, addresses him under the image of one of those crocodiles or monsters which inhabited that river, of whose riches and revenue he vaunted; and assures him that, with as much ease as a fisherman drags the fish he has hooked, God would drag him and his people into captivity, and that their carcasses should fall a prey to the beasts of the field and to the fowls of heaven,* 1–7. *The figure is then dropped; and God is introduced denouncing, in plain terms, the most awful judgments against him and his nation, and declaring that the Egyptians should be subjected to the Babylonians till the fall of the Chaldean empire,* 8–12. *The prophet then foretells that Egypt, which was about to be devastated by the Babylonians, and many of the people carried into captivity, should again become a kingdom; but that it should never regain its ancient political importance; for, in the lapse of time, it should be even* the BASEST of the kingdoms, *a circumstance in the prophecy most literally fulfilled, especially under the Christian dispensation, in its government by the Mameluke slaves,* 13–16. *The prophecy, beginning at the* seventeenth *verse, is connected with the foregoing, as it relates to the same subject, though delivered about* seventeen *years later. Nebuchadnezzar and his army, after the long siege of Tyre, which made every head bald by constantly wearing their helmets, and wore the skin off every shoulder by carrying burdens to raise the fortifications, were disappointed of the spoil which they expected, by the retiring of the inhabitants to Carthage. God, therefore, promises him Egypt for his reward,* 17–20. *The chapter concludes with a prediction of the return of the Jews from the Babylonish captivity,* 21.

A. M. 3415
B. C. 589
Ol. XLVII. 4
Anno
Tarquinii Prisci,
R. Roman., 28

IN the tenth year, in the tenth *month,* in the twelfth *day* of the month, the word of the LORD came unto me, saying,

2 Son of man, [a]set thy face against Pharaoh king of Egypt, and prophesy against him, and [b]against all Egypt:

3 Speak, and say, Thus saith the Lord GOD; [c]Behold, I *am* against thee, Pharaoh king of Egypt, the great [d]dragon that lieth in the midst of his rivers, [e]which hath said, My river *is* mine own, and I have made *it* for myself.

4 But [f]I will put hooks in thy jaws, and I will cause the fish of thy rivers to stick unto thy scales, and I will bring thee up out of the midst of thy rivers, and all the fish of thy rivers shall stick unto thy scales.

5 And I will leave thee *thrown* into the wilderness, thee and all the fish of thy rivers: thou shalt fall upon the [g]open fields; [h]thou shalt not be brought together, nor gathered: [i]I have given thee for meat to the beasts of the field and to the fowls of the heaven.

6 And all the inhabitants of Egypt shall know that I *am* the LORD, because they have been a [k]staff of reed to the house of Israel.

A. M. 3415
B. C. 589
Ol. XLVII. 4
Anno
Tarquinii Prisci,
R. Roman., 28

7 [l]When they took hold of thee by thy hand, thou didst break, and rend all their shoulder: and when they leaned upon thee, thou brakest, and madest all their loins to be at a stand.

8 Therefore thus saith the Lord GOD; Behold, I will bring [m]a sword upon thee, and cut off man and beast out of thee.

9 And the land of Egypt shall be desolate and waste; and they shall know that I *am* the LORD: because he hath said, The river *is* mine, and I have made *it.*

10 Behold, therefore I *am* against thee, and against thy rivers, [n]and I will make the land of Egypt [o]utterly waste *and* desolate, [p]from[q] the tower of [r]Syene even unto the border of Ethiopia.

11 [s]No foot of man shall pass through it, nor foot of beast shall pass through it, neither shall it be inhabited forty years.

12 [t]And I will make the land of Egypt desolate in the midst of the countries *that are* desolate, and her cities among the cities

[a]Chap. xxviii. 21——[b]Isa. xix. 1; Jer. xxv. 19; xlvi. 2, 25——[c]Jer. xliv. 30; ch. xxviii. 22; ver. 10——[d]Psa. lxxiv. 13, 14; Isa. xxvii. 1; li. 9; ch. xxxii. 2——[e]See ch. xxviii. 2——[f]Isa. xxxvii. 29; ch. xxxviii. 4——[g]Heb. *face of the field*——[h]Jer. viii. 2; xvi. 4; xxv. 33——[i]Jer. vii. 33; xxxiv. 20

[k]2 Kings xviii. 21; Isa. xxxvi. 6——[l]Jer. xxxvii. 5, 7, 11; ch. xvii. 17——[m]Ch. xiv. 17; xxxii. 11, 12, 13——[n]Ch. xxx. 12——[o]Heb. *wastes of wastes*——[p]Or, *from Migdol to Syene;* Exod. xiv. 2; Jer. xliv. 1——[q]Chap. xxx. 6——[r]Heb. *Seveneh*——[s]Chap. xxxii. 13——[t]Chap. xxx. 7, 26

NOTES ON CHAP. XXIX

Verse 1. *In the tenth year*] Of Zedekiah; and *tenth* of the captivity of Jeconiah.

The ten month, *in the twelfth* day *of the month*] Answering to *Monday,* the first of *February,* A. M. 3415.

Verse 2. *Set thy face against Pharaoh king of Egypt*] This was Pharaoh-hophra or Pharaoh-apries, whom we have so frequently met with in the prophecies of Jeremiah, and much of whose history has been given in the notes.

Verse 3. *The great dragon*] התנים *hattannim* should here be translated *crocodile,* as that is a *real* animal, and numerous in the *Nile;* whereas the *dragon* is wholly *fabulous.* The original signifies any large animal.

The midst of his rivers] This refers to the several *branches* of the Nile, by which this river empties itself into the Mediterranean. The ancients termed them septem ostia Nili, "the seven mouths of the Nile." The *crocodile* was the *emblem* of *Egypt.*

Verse 4. *I will put hooks in thy jaws*] Amasis, one of this king's generals, being proclaimed king by an insurrection of the people, dethroned *Apries,* and seized upon the kingdom; and Apries was obliged to flee to Upper Egypt for safety.

I will cause the fish—to stick unto thy scales] Most fish are sorely troubled with a species of *insect* which bury their heads in their flesh, under their *scales,* and suck out the vital juices. The allusion seems to be to this. *Pharaoh* was the *crocodile;* the *fish,* the *common people;* and the *sticking to his scales,* the *insurrection* by which he was *wasted* and despoiled of his kingdom.

Verse 5. *I will leave thee* thrown *into the wilderness*] Referring to his being obliged to take refuge in Upper Egypt. But he was afterwards taken prisoner, and strangled by Amasis. *Herod.* lib. ii. s. 169.

Verse 6. *They have been a staff of reed*] An inefficient and faithless ally. The Israelites expected assistance from them when Nebuchadnezzar came against Jerusalem; and they made a feint to help them, but retired when Nebuchadnezzar went against them. Thus were the Jews deceived and ultimately ruined, see ver. 7.

Verse 10. *From the tower of Syene*] ממגדל סונה *mimmigdol seveneh,* "from Migdol to Syene." Syene, now called *Essuan,* was the last city in Egypt, going towards Ethiopia. It was famous for a well into which the rays of the sun fell *perpendicularly* at *midday.*

Verse 12. *Shall be desolate forty years*] The country from Migdol or Magdolan, which was on the isthmus between the Mediterranean and the Red Sea, was so completely ruined, that it might well be called *desert;* and it is

A. M. 3415
B. C. 589
Ol. XLVII. 4
Anno
Tarquinii Prisci,
R. Roman., 28

that are laid waste shall be desolate forty years: and I will scatter the Egyptians among the nations, and will disperse them through the countries.
13 Yet thus saith the Lord GOD; At the [u]end of forty years will I gather the Egyptians from the people whither they were scattered:
14 And I will bring again the captivity of Egypt, and will cause them to return *into* the land of Pathros, into the land of their [v]habitation; and they shall be there a [w]base [x]kingdom.
15 It shall be the basest of the kingdoms; neither shall it exalt itself any more above the nations: for I will diminish them, that they shall no more rule over the nations.
16 And it shall be no more [y]the confidence of the house of Israel, which bringeth *their* iniquity to remembrance, when they shall look after them: but they shall know that I *am* the Lord GOD.
17 And it came to pass in the seven and twentieth year, in the first *month,* in the first *day* of the month, the word of the LORD came unto me, saying,

A. M. 3432
B. C. 572
Ol. LII. 1
Anno
Servii Tullii,
R. Roman., 7

18 Son of man, [z]Nebuchadrezzar king of Babylon caused his army to serve a great service against Tyrus: every head *was* made bald, and every shoulder *was* peeled; yet had he no wages, nor his army, for Tyrus, for the service that he had served against it:
19 Therefore thus saith the Lord GOD; Behold, I will give the land of Egypt unto Nebuchadrezzar king of Babylon; and he shall take her multitude, and [a]take her spoil, and take her prey; and it shall be the wages for his army.
20 I have given him the land of Egypt [b]*for* his labour wherewith he [c]served against it because they wrought for me, saith the Lord GOD.
21 In that day [d]will I cause the horn of the house of Israel to bud forth, and I will give thee [e]the opening of the mouth in the midst of them; and they shall know that I *am* the LORD.

[u]Isa. xix. 23; Jer. xlvi. 26——[v]Or, *birth*——[w]Heb. *low*——[x]Chapter xvii. 6, 14——[y]Isaiah xxx. 2, 3; xxxvi. 4, 6

[z]Jer. xxvii. 6; chap. xxvi. 7, 8——[a]Heb. *spoil her spoil, and prey her prey*——[b]Or, for *his hire*——[c]Jer. xxv. 9——[d]Psa. cxxxii. 17——[e]Chap. xxiv. 27

probable that this desolation continued during the whole of the *reign of Amasis*, which was just *forty years.* See *Herod.* lib. iii. c. 10; and see *Calmet.*

Verse 13. *Will I gather the Egyptians*] It is probable that Cyrus gave permission to the Egyptians brought to Babylon by Nebuchadnezzar, to return to their own country. And if we reckon from the commencement of the war against Pharaoh-hophra by Nebuchadnezzar, to the *third* or *fourth* year of Cyrus, the term will be about *forty* years.

Verse 14. Into *the land of Pathros*] Supposed to mean the *Delta*, a country included between the branches of the Nile; called Δ *delta*, from its being in the form of the Greek letter of that name. It may mean the *Pathrusim*, in Upper Egypt, near to the Thebaid. This is most likely.

Shall be there a base kingdom.] That is, it shall continue to be *tributary.* It is upwards of *two thousand* years since this prophecy was delivered, and it has been uninterruptedly fulfilling to the *present hour.* 1. Egypt became tributary to the *Babylonians*, under Amasis. 2. After the ruin of the Babylonish empire, it became subject to the *Persians.* 3. After the Persians, it came into the hands of the *Macedonians.* 4. After the Macedonians it fell into the hands of the *Romans.* 5. After the division of the Roman empire it was subdued by the *Saracens.* 6. About A. D. 1250, it came into the hands of the *Mameluke* slaves. 7. Selim, the *ninth* emperor of the Turks, conquered the Mamelukes, A. D. 1517, and annexed Egypt to the *Ottoman empire*, of which it still continues to be a province, governed by a *pacha* and *twenty-four beys*, who are always advanced from *servitude* to the administration of public affairs. So true is it that Egypt, once so glorious, is the *basest of kingdoms.* See *Newton* on the prophecies.

Verse 17. *The seven and twentieth year*] That is, of the *captivity of Jeconiah, fifteen* years after the taking of *Jerusalem;* about *April* 20, 3432. The *preceding* prophecy was delivered one year before the taking of Jerusalem; *this*, sixteen years after; and it is supposed to be the last which this prophet wrote.

Verse 18. *Caused his army to serve a great service against Tyrus*] He was *thirteen* years employed in the siege. See *Joseph.* Antiq. lib. x. c. 11. In this siege his soldiers endured great hardships. Being continually on duty, their *heads became bald* by wearing their helmets; and their *shoulders bruised and peeled* by carrying baskets of earth to the fortifications, and wood, &c., to build towers, &c.

Yet had he no wages, nor his army] The Tyrians, finding it at last impossible to defend their city, put all their wealth aboard their vessels, sailed out of the port, and escaped for Carthage; and thus Nebuchadnezzar lost all the spoil of one of the richest cities in the world.

Verse 20. *I have given him the land of Egypt* for *his labour*] Because he fulfilled the designs of God against Tyre, God promises to *reward* him with the spoil of Egypt.

Verse 21. *Will I cause the horn of the house of Israel to bud*] This may refer generally to the *restoration;* but particularly to *Zerubbabel,* who became one of the leaders of the people from Babylon. Or it may respect *Daniel,* or *Mordecai,* or *Jeconiah,* who, about this time, was brought out of prison by Evil-merodach, and afterwards kindly treated.

CHAPTER XXX

This chapter describes, with great force and elegance, the ruin of Egypt and all her allies by the Chaldeans under Nebuchadnezzar, 1–11; *with an amplification of the distress of the principal cities of Egypt on that occasion,* 12–19. *The remaining verses are a short prophecy relating to the same event, and therefore annexed to the longer one preceding, although this was predicted sooner,* 20–26.

A. M. 3432
B. C. 572
Olymp. LII. 1
Anno Servii Tullii, R. Roman., 7

THE word of the LORD
came again unto me,
saying,
2 Son of man, prophesy and
say, Thus saith the Lord GOD; [a]Howl ye, Wo
worth the day!
3 For [b]the day *is* near, even the day of the
LORD *is* near, a cloudy day; it shall be the
time of the heathen.
4 And the sword shall come upon Egypt,
and great [c]pain shall be in Ethiopia, when
the slain shall fall in Egypt, and they [d]shall
take away her multitude, and [e]her foundations shall be broken down.
5 Ethiopia, and [f]Libya, and Lydia, and [g]all
the mingled people, and Chub, and the [h]men
of the land that is in league, shall fall with
them by the sword.
6 Thus saith the LORD; They also that uphold Egypt shall fall; and the pride of her
power shall come down: [i]from [k]the tower of
Syene shall they fall in it by the sword, saith
the Lord GOD.
7 [l]And they shall be desolate in the midst
of the countries *that are* desolate, and her
cities shall be in the midst of the cities *that
are* wasted.
8 And they shall know that
I *am* the LORD, when I have
set a fire in Egypt, and *when*
all her helpers shall be [m]de-
stroyed.
9 In that day [n]shall messengers go forth
from me in ships to make the careless Ethiopians afraid, and great pain shall come upon
them, as in the day of Egypt: for, lo, it cometh.
10 Thus saith the Lord GOD: [o]I will also
make the multitude of Egypt to cease by the
hand of Nebuchadrezzar king of Babylon.
11 He and his people with him, [p]the terrible of the nations, shall be brought to destroy the land: and they shall draw their
swords against Egypt, and fill the land with
the slain.
12 And [q]I will make the rivers [r]dry, and
[s]sell the land into the hand of the wicked:
and I will make the land waste, and [t]all that
is therein, by the hand of strangers: I the
LORD have spoken *it.*
13 Thus saith the Lord GOD; I will also
[u]destroy the idols, and I will cause *their*
images to cease out of Noph; [v]and there shall
be no more a prince of the land of Egypt:
[w]and I will put a fear in the land of Egypt.

A. M. 3432
B. C. 572
Olymp. LII. 1
Anno Servii Tullii, R. Roman., 7

[a]Isa. xiii. 6——[b]Chap. vii. 7, 12; Joel ii. 1; Zeph. i. 7——[c]Or, *fear*——[d]Chap. xxix. 19——[e]Jer. l. 15——[f]Heb. *Phut;* chap. xxvii. 10——[g]Jer. xxv. 20, 24——[h]Heb. *children*——[i]Or, *from Migdol to Syene*——[k]Chap. xxix. 10——[l]Chap. xxix. 12

[m]Heb. *broken*——[n]Isa. xviii. 1, 2——[o]Chap. xxix. 19——[p]Chap. xxviii. 7——[q]Isa. xix. 5, 6——[r]Heb. *drought*——[s]Isa. xix. 4——[t]Heb. *the fulness thereof*——[u]Isa. xix. 1; Jer. xliii. 12; xlvi. 25; Zech. xiii. 2——[v]Zech. x. 11——[w]Isa. xix. 16

NOTES ON CHAP. XXX

Verse 2. *Howl ye, Wo worth the day!*] My Old MS. Bible,—**Goule gee, woo woo to the day!** הילילו הה ליום *heylilu, hah laiyom!* "Howl ye, Alas for the day!" The reading in our present text is taken from *Coverdale's* Bible, 1535. The expressions signify that a most dreadful calamity was about to fall on Egypt and the neighbouring countries, called here the "time of the heathen," or of the *nations;* the day of calamity to them. They are afterwards specified, Ethiopia, Libya, Lydia, and *Chub,* and the *mingled people,* probably persons from different nations, who had followed the ill fortune of Pharaoh-hophra or Pharaoh-apries, when he fled from Amasis, and settled in Upper Egypt.

Verse 5. *Lydia*] This place is not well known. The *Ludim* were contiguous to Egypt, Gen. xi. 13.

Chub] The Cubians, placed by Ptolemy in the *Mareotis.* But probably instead of וכוב *vechub,* "and Chub," we should read וכל *vechol,* "and ALL the men of the land," &c. The *Septuagint* adds "the Persians and the Cretans."

Verse 7. *Shall be desolate*] All these countries shall be desolated, and the places named shall be *chief* in these desolations.

Verse 9. *Messengers go forth from me in ships*] Ships can ascend the Nile up to Syene or Essuan, by the *cataracts;* and when Nebuchadnezzar's vessels went up, they struck terror into the Ethiopians. They are represented here as the "messengers of God."

Verse 12. *I will make the rivers dry*] **As the**

A. M. 3432
B. C. 572
Ol. LII. 1
Anno
Servii Tullii,
R. Roman., 7

14 And I will make [x]Pathros desolate, and will set fire
in [y]Zoan,[z] [a]and will execute
judgments in No.
15 And I will pour my fury upon [b]Sin, the
strength of Egypt; [c]and I will cut off the
multitude of No.
16 And I will [d]set fire in Egypt: Sin shall
have great pain, and No shall be rent asunder,
and Noph *shall have* distresses daily.
17 The young men of [e]Aven and of [f]Pibeseth
shall fall by the sword: and these
cities shall go into captivity.
18 [g]At Tehaphnehes also the day shall be
[h]darkened, when I shall break there the yokes
of Egypt: and the pomp of her strength shall
cease in her: as for her, a cloud shall cover
her, and her daughters shall go into captivity.
19 Thus will I execute judgments in Egypt:
and they shall know that I *am* the LORD.

A. M. 3416
B. C. 588
Ol. XLVIII. 1
Anno
Tarquinii Prisci,
R. Roman., 29

20 And it came to pass in
the eleventh year, in the first
month, in the seventh *day* of
the month, *that* the word of
the LORD came unto me, saying,
21 Son of man, I have [i]broken the arm of
Pharaoh king of Egypt; and lo, [k]it shall not
be bound up to be healed, to
put a roller to bind it, to
make it strong to hold the
sword.
22 Therefore thus saith the Lord GOD; Behold,
I *am* against Pharaoh king of Egypt,
and will [l]break his arms, the strong, and that
which was broken; and I will cause the
sword to fall out of his hand.
23 [m]And I will scatter the Egyptians
among the nations, and will disperse them
through the countries.
24 And I will strengthen the arms of the
king of Babylon, and put my sword in his
hand: but I will break Pharaoh's arms, and
he shall groan before him with the groanings
of a deadly wounded *man.*
25 But I will strengthen the arms of the
king of Babylon, and the arms of Pharaoh
shall fall down; and [n]they shall know that
I *am* the LORD, when I shall put my sword
into the hand of the king of Babylon, and he
shall stretch it out upon the land of Egypt.
26 [o]And I will scatter the Egyptians among
the nations, and disperse them among the
countries; and they shall know that I *am*
the LORD.

[x]Ch. xxix. 14——[y]Psa. lxxviii. 12, 43——[z]Or, *Tanis* [a]Nah. iii. 8, 9, 10——[b]Or, *Pelusium*——[c]Jer. xlvi. 25 [d]Ver. 8——[e]Or, *Heliopolis*——[f]Or, *Pubastum*

[g]Jer. ii. 16——[h]Or, *restrained*——[i]Jer. xlviii. 25 [k]Jer. xlvi. 11——[l]Psa. xxxvii. 17——[m]Ver. 26; ch. xxix. 12——[n]Psa. ix. 16——[o]Ver. 23; ch. xxix. 12

overflowing of the Nile was the grand cause of fertility to Egypt, the *drying* it up, or preventing that *annual inundation,* must be the cause of dearth, famine, &c. By *rivers,* we may understand the *various canals* cut from the Nile to carry water into the different parts of the land. When the Nile did not rise to its usual height, these canals were quite dry.

Verse 13. Their *images to cease out of Noph*] Afterwards *Memphis,* and now *Cairo* or *Kahira.* This was the seat of Egyptian idolatry; the place where *Apis* was particularly worshipped.

No more a prince of the land of Egypt] Not one, from that time to the present day. See the note on chap. xxix. 14.

Verse 14. *I will make Pathros desolate*] See the preceding chapter, ver. 14.

Zoan] *Tanis,* the ancient capital of Egypt.

No.] *Diospolis,* or *Thebes,* the city of Jupiter.

Verse 15. *My fury upon Sin*] *Pelusium,* a strong city of Egypt, on the coast of the Mediterranean Sea.

Verse 16. *Noph*] *Cairo* or *Kahira;* see ver. 13.

Verse 17. *Aven*] Or *On, the famous Heliopolis,* or city of the sun.

Pibeseth] *Bubastum* or *Bubaste,* by a slight alteration of the letters. It is situated on the eastern branch of the Nile, towards Arabia.

Verse 18. *Tehaphnehes*] Called also *Tahapanes,* Jer. ii. 16. This is the *Pelusian Daphne.*

Break there the yokes] The sceptres. Nubuchadnezzar broke the sceptre of Egypt when he confirmed the kingdom to *Amasis,* who had rebelled again t *Apries.*

Verse 20. *In the eleventh year, in the first* month, *in the seventh* day] This was the *eleventh* year of the captivity of Jeconiah, and the date here answers to April 26, A. M. 3416; a prophecy anterior by several years to that already delivered. In collecting the writings of Ezekiel, more care was taken to put all that related to *one subject* together, than to attend to *chronological arrangement.*

Verse 21. *I have broken the arm of Pharaoh*] Perhaps this may refer to his defeat by Nebuchadnezzar, when he was coming with the Egyptian army to succour Jerusalem.

Verse 22. *I will cause the sword to fall out of his hand.*] When the arm is broken, the sword will naturally fall. But these expressions show that the Egyptians would be rendered wholly useless to Zedekiah, and should never more recover their political strength. This was the case from the time of the rebellion of Amasis.

Verse 26. *I will scatter the Egyptians*] Several fled with *Apries* to Upper Egypt; and when Nebuchadnezzar wasted the country, he carried many of them to Babylon. See on chap. xxix. 12.

CHAPTER XXXI

This very beautiful chapter relates also to Egypt. The prophet describes to Pharaoh the fall of the king of Nineveh, (see the books of Nahum, Jonah, and Zephaniah,) under the image of a fair cedar of Lebanon, once exceedingly tall, flourishing, and majestic, but now cut down and withered, with its broken branches strewed around, 1–17. *He then concludes with bringing the matter home to the king of Egypt, by telling him that this was a picture of his approaching fate,* 18. *The beautiful cedar of Lebanon, remarkable for its loftiness, and in the most flourishing condition, but afterwards cut down and deserted, gives a very lively painting of the great glory and dreadful catastrophe of both the Assyrian and Egyptian monarchies. The manner in which the prophet has embellished his subject is deeply interesting; the colouring is of that kind which the mind will always contemplate with pleasure.*

A. M. 3416
B. C. 588
Ol. XLVIII. 1
Anno
Tarquinii Prisci,
R. Roman., 29

AND it came to pass in the eleventh year, in the third *month,* in the first *day* of the month, *that* the word of the LORD came unto me, saying,

2 Son of man, speak unto Pharaoh king of Egypt, and to his multitude; [a]Whom art thou like in thy greatness?

3 [b]Behold, the Assyrian *was* a cedar in Lebanon [c]with fair branches, and with a shadowing shroud, and of a high stature; and his top was among the thick boughs.

4 [d]The waters [e]made him great, the deep [f]set him up on high with her rivers running round about his plants, and sent out her [g]little rivers unto all the trees of the field.

5 Therefore [h]his height was exalted above all the trees of the field, and his boughs were multiplied, and his branches became long because of the multitude of waters, [i]when he shot forth.

6 All the [k]fowls of heaven made their nests in his boughs, and under his branches did all the beasts of the field bring forth their young, and under his shadow dwelt all great nations.

7 Thus was he fair in his greatness, in the length of his branches: for his root was by great waters.

A. M. 3416
B. C. 588
Ol. XLVIII. 1
Anno
Tarquinii Prisci,
R. Roman., 29

8 The cedars in the [l]garden of God could not hide him: the fir trees were not like his boughs, and the chesnut trees were not like his branches; nor any tree in the garden of God was like unto him in his beauty.

9 I have made him fair by the multitude of his branches; so that all the trees of Eden, that *were* in the garden of God, envied him.

10 Therefore thus saith the Lord GOD; Because thou hast lifted up thyself in height, and he hath shot up his top among the thick boughs, and [m]his heart is lifted up in his height;

11 I have therefore delivered him into the hand of the mighty one of the heathen; [n]he shall surely deal with him: I have driven him out for his wickedness.

12 And strangers, [o]the terrible of the nations, have cut him off, and have left him: [p]upon the mountains and in all the valleys his branches are fallen, and his boughs are broken by all the rivers of the land; and all the people of the earth are gone down from his shadow, and have left him.

[a]Ver. 18——[b]Dan. iv. 10——[c]Heb. *fair of branches* [d]Jer. li. 36——[e]Or, *nourished*——[f]Or, *brought him up* [g]Or, *conduits*——[h]Dan. iv. 11——[i]Or, *when it sent them forth*

[k]Chap. xvii. 23; Dan. iv. 12——[l]Gen. ii. 8; xiii. 10; chap. xxviii. 13——[m]Dan. v. 20——[n]Heb. *in doing he shall do unto him*——[o]Chap. xxviii. 7——[p]Chap. xxxii. 5; xxxv. 8

NOTES ON CHAP. XXXI

Verse 1. *In the eleventh year*] On *Sunday,* June 19, A. M. 3416, according to Abp. Usher; a *month* before Jerusalem was taken by the Chaldeans.

Verse 3. *Behold, the Assyrian* was *a cedar*] Why is the *Assyrian* introduced here, when the whole chapter concerns *Egypt?* Bp. *Lowth* has shown that אשור ארז *ashshur erez* should be translated *the tall cedar, the very stately cedar;* hence there is reference to his *lofty top;* and all the following description belongs to *Egypt,* not to *Assyria.* But see on ver. 11.

Verse 4. *The waters made him great*] Alluding to the fertility of Egypt by the *overflowing of the Nile.* But *waters* often mean *peoples.* By means of the different nations under the Egyptians, that government became very opulent. These nations are represented as *fowls* and *beasts,* taking shelter under the protection of this great political Egyptian tree, ver. 6.

Verse 8. *The cedars in the garden of God*] Egypt was one of the most eminent and affluent of all the neighbouring nations.

Verse 11. *The mighty one of the heathen*] Nebuchadnezzar. It is worthy of notice, that Nebuchadnezzar, in the *first* year of his reign, rendered himself master of *Nineveh,* the capital of the *Assyrian* empire. See *Sedar Olam.* This happened about *twenty* years before Ezekiel delivered this prophecy; on this account,

A. M. 3416
B. C. 588
Ol. XLVIII. 1
Anno
Tarquinii Prisci,
R. Roman., 29

13 [q]Upon his ruin shall all the fowls of the heaven remain, and all the beasts of the field shall be upon his branches:

14 To the end that none of all the trees by the waters exalt themselves for their height, neither shoot up their top among the thick boughs, neither their trees [r]stand up in their height, all that drink water: for [s]they are all delivered unto death, [t]to the nether parts of the earth, in the midst of the children of men, with them that go down to the pit.

15 Thus saith the Lord GOD; In the day when he went down to the grave I caused a mourning: I covered the deep for him, and I restrained the floods thereof, and the great waters were stayed: and I caused Lebanon [u]to mourn for him, and all the trees of the field fainted for him.

16 I made the nations to [v]shake at the sound of his fall, when I [w]cast him down to hell with them that descend into the pit: and [x]all the trees of Eden, the choice and best of Lebanon, all that drink water, [y]shall be comforted in the nether parts of the earth.

17 They also went down into hell with him unto *them that be* slain with the sword; and *they that were* his arm, *that* [z]dwelt under his shadow in the midst of the heathen.

18 [a]To whom art thou thus like in glory and in greatness among the trees of Eden? yet shalt thou be brought down with the trees of Eden unto the nether parts of the earth: [b]thou shalt lie in the midst of the uncircumcised with *them that be* slain by the sword. This *is* Pharaoh and all his multitude, saith the Lord GOD.

[q]Isa. xviii. 6; ch. xxxii. 4——[r]Or, *stand upon themselves for their height*——[s]Psa. lxxxii. 7——[t]Ch. xxxii. 18 [u]Heb. *to be black*——[v]Chap. xxvi. 15

[w]Isa. xiv. 15——[x]Isa. xiv. 8——[y]Chap. xxxii. 31 [z]Lam. iv. 20——[a]Ver. 2; chap. xxxii. 19——[b]Chap. xxviii. 10; xxxii. 19, 21, 24, &c.

Ashshur, ver. 3, may relate to the *Assyrians*, to whom it is possible the prophet here compares the Egyptians. But see on ver. 3.

Verse 13. *Upon his ruin shall all the fowls*] The fall of Egypt is likened to the fall of a great tree; and as the fowls and beasts sheltered under its branches before, ver. 6, so they now feed upon its ruins.

Verse 14. *To the end that none of all the trees*] Let this ruin, fallen upon Egypt, teach all the nations that shall hear of it to be *humble*, because, however *elevated*, God can soon bring them down; and *pride* and *arrogance*, either in *states* or *individuals*, have the peculiar abhorrence of God. Pride does not suit the sons of men; it made devils of *angels*, and makes fiends of *men*.

Verse 15. *I caused Lebanon to mourn for him*] All the confederates of Pharaoh are represented as deploring his fall, ver. 16, 17.

Verse 17. *They also went down into hell with him*] Into *remediless destruction*.

Verse 18. *This* is *Pharaoh*] All that I have spoken in this allegory of the *lofty cedar* refers to *Pharaoh*, king of Egypt, his princes, confederates, and people. *Calmet* understands the whole chapter of the *king of Assyria*, under which he allows that *Egypt* is adumbrated; and hence on this verse he quotes,—

Mutato nomine, de te fabula narratur.

What is said of Assyria belongs to thee, O Egypt.

CHAPTER XXXII

The prophet goes on to predict the fall of the king of Egypt, under the figure of an animal of prey, such as a lion or crocodile, caught, slain, and his carcass left a prey to the fowls and wild beasts, 1–6. *The figure is then changed; and the greatness of his fall (described by the darkening of the sun, moon, and stars) strikes terror into all the surrounding nations,* 7–10. *The prophet adds, that the overthrow of the then reigning Egyptian dynasty was to be effected by the instrumentality of the king of Babylon, who should leave Egypt so desolate, that its waters, (alluding to the metaphor used in the* second *verse,) should run as pure and smooth as oil, without the foot of man or the hoof of a beast to disturb them,* 11–16. *A beautiful, nervous, and concise description of a land ruined and left utterly desolate. In the remaining part of the chapter the same event is pourtrayed by one of the boldest figures ever attempted in any composition, and which at the same time is executed with astonishing perspicuity and force. God is introduced ordering a place in the lower regions for the king of Egypt and his host,* 17, 18. *The prophet delivers his messsage, pronounces their fate, and commands those who buried the slain to drag him and his multitudes to the subterraneous mansions,* 19, 20. *At the tumult and commotion which this mighty work occasions, the infernal shades are represented as roused from their couches to learn the cause. They see and congratulate the king of Egypt, on his arrival among them,* 21. *Pharaoh being now introduced into this immense subterraneous cavern, (see the* fourteenth *chapter of Isaiah, where a similar imagery is employed,) the prophet leads him all around the sides of the pit; shows him the gloomy mansions of former tyrants, tells their names as he goes along; beautifully contrasts their former pomp and destructive ambition, when they were a terror to the surrounding states, with their present most abject and help-*

less condition; declares that all these oppressors of mankind have not only been cut off out of the land of the living, but have gone down into the grave uncircumcised, *that is, they have died in their sins, and therefore shall have no resurrection to eternal life; and concludes with showing Pharaoh the place destined for him in the midst of the uncircumcised, and of them that have been slain by the sword,* 22–32. *This prophetic ode may be considered as a finished model in that species of writing which is appropriated to the exciting of terror. The imagery throughout is sublime and terrible; and no reader of sensibility and taste can accompany the prophet in this funeral procession, and visit the mansions of Hades, without being impressed with a degree of awe nearly approaching to horror.*

A. M. 3417
B. C. 587
Ol. XLVIII. 2
Anno
Tarquinii Prisci,
R. Roman., 30

AND it came to pass in the
twelfth year, in the
twelfth month, in the first *day*
of the month, *that* the word of
the LORD came unto me, saying,
2 Son of man, [a]take up a lamentation for
Pharaoh king of Egypt, and say unto him,
[b]Thou art like a young lion of the nations,
[c]and thou *art* as a [d]whale in the seas: and
thou camest forth with thy rivers, and troub-
ledst the waters with thy feet, and [e]fouledst
their rivers:
3 Thus saith the Lord GOD; I will therefore
[f]spread out my net over thee with a company
of many people; and they shall bring thee up
in my net.
4 Then [g]will I leave thee upon the land, I
will cast thee forth upon the open field, and
[h]will cause all the fowls of the heaven to remain upon thee, and I will fill the beasts of
the whole earth with thee.
5 And I will lay thy flesh [i]upon the mountains, and fill the valleys with thy height.
6 I will also water with thy blood [k]the land
wherein thou swimmest, *even*
to the mountains; and the
rivers shall be full of thee.
7 And when I shall [l]put thee

A. M. 3417
B. C. 587
Ol. XLVIII. 2
Anno
Tarquinii Prisci,
R. Roman., 30

out, [m]I will cover the heaven, and make the
stars thereof dark; I will cover the sun with
a cloud, and the moon shall not give her light.
8 All the [n]bright lights of heaven will I make
[o]dark over thee, and set darkness upon thy
land, saith the Lord GOD.
9 I will also [p]vex the hearts of many people,
when I shall bring thy destruction among the
nations, into the countries which thou hast
not known.
10 Yea, I will make many people [q]amazed
at thee, and their kings shall be horribly
afraid for thee, when I shall brandish my
sword before them; and [r]they shall tremble at
every moment, every man for his own life, in
the day of thy fall.
11 [s]For thus saith the Lord GOD; The
sword of the king of Babylon shall come upon
thee.
12 By the swords of the mighty will I cause

[a]Chap. xxvii. 2; ver. 16——[b]Chap. xix. 3, 6; xxxviii. 13——[c]Chap. xxix. 3——[d]Or, *dragon*——[e]Chap. xxxiv. 18——[f]Chap. xii. 13; xvii. 20; Hos. vii. 12——[g]Chap. xxix. 5——[h]Chap. xxxi. 13——[i]Chap. xxxi. 12——[k]Or, *the land of thy swimming*——[l]Or, *extinguish*

[m]Isa. xiii. 10; Joel ii. 31; iii. 15; Amos viii. 9; Rev. vi. 12, 13; Matt. xxiv. 29——[n]Heb. *light of the light in heaven*——[o]Heb. *them dark*——[p]Heb. *provoke to anger*, or *grief*——[q]Chap. xxvii. 35——[r]Chap. xxvi. 16
[s]Jer. xlvi. 26; chap. xxx. 4

NOTES ON CHAP. XXXII

Verse 1. *In the twelfth year, in the twelfth month, in the first* day *of the month*] On *Wednesday*, March 22, the *twelfth* year of the captivity of Jeconiah, A. M. 3417.

Instead of the *twelfth* year, *five* of *Kennicott's* MSS., and *eight* of *De Rossi's*, *read* בעשתי עשרה *in the eleventh* year. This reading is supported by the *Syriac;* and is confirmed by an excellent MS. of my own, about *four hundred* years old.

Verse 2. *Thou art like a young lion—and thou* art *as a whale in the seas*] Thou mayest be likened to *two* of the fiercest animals in the creation; to a lion, the fiercest on the *land;* to a *crocodile*, תנים *tannim*, (see chap. xxix. 3,) the fiercest in the *waters*. It may, however, point out the *hippopotamus*, as there seems to be a reference to his mode of *feeding*. He walks deliberately into the water over head, and pursues his way in the same manner; still keeping on his feet, and feeding on the plants, &c., that grow at the bottom. Thus he *fouls the water* with his feet.

Verse 5. *And fill the valleys with thy height.*] Some translate, with *the worms*, which should proceed from the putrefaction of his flesh.

Verse 6. *The land wherein thou swimmest*] Egypt; so called, because intersected with *canals*, and *overflowed* annually by the *Nile*.

Verse 7. *I will cover the heaven*] Destroy the *empire*.

Make the stars thereof dark] Overwhelm all the *dependent states*.

I will cover the sun] The *king* himself.

And the moon shall not give her light.] The *queen* may be meant, or some *state* less than the kingdom.

Verse 8. *And set darkness upon thy land*] As I did when a former king refused to let my people go to the wilderness to worship me. I will involve *thee*, and thy *house*, and thy *people*, and the whole *land*, in desolation and wo.

Verse 9. *I will also vex the hearts*] Even the remote nations, who had no connexion with thee, shall be amazed at the judgments which have fallen upon thee.

Verse 14. *Cause their rivers to run like oil*] Bring the whole state into quietness, there being no longer a political *hippopotamus* to *foul*

A. M. 3417
B. C. 587
Ol. XLVIII. 2
Anno
Tarquinii Prisci,
R. Roman., 30

thy multitude to fall, [t]the terrible of the nations, all of them: and [u]they shall spoil the pomp of Egypt, and all the multitude thereof shall be destroyed.

13 I will destroy also all the beasts thereof from beside the great waters; [v]neither shall the foot of man trouble them any more, nor the hoofs of beasts trouble them.

14 Then will I make their waters deep, and cause their rivers to run like oil, saith the Lord GOD.

15 When I shall make the land of Egypt desolate, and the country shall be [w]destitute of that whereof it was full, when I shall smite all them that dwell therein, [x]then shall they know that I *am* the LORD.

16 This *is* the [y]lamentation wherewith they shall lament her: the daughters of the nations shall lament her: they shall lament for her, *even* for Egypt, and for all her multitude, saith the Lord GOD.

17 It came to pass also in the twelfth year, in the fifteenth *day* of the month, that the word of the LORD came unto me, saying,

18 Son of man, wail for the multitude of Egypt, and [z]cast them down, *even* her, and the daughters of the famous nations, unto the nether parts of the earth, with them that go down into the pit.

19 [a]Whom dost thou pass in beauty? [b]go down, and be thou laid with the uncircumcised.

20 They shall fall in the midst of *them that are* slain by the sword: [c]she is delivered to the sword: draw her and all her multitudes.

21 [d]The strong among the mighty shall speak to him out of the midst of hell with them that help him: they are [e]gone down, they lie uncircumcised, slain by the sword.

22 [f]Asshur *is* there and all her company: his graves *are* about him: all of them slain, fallen by the sword:

23 [g]Whose graves are set in the sides of the pit, and her company is round about her grave; all of them slain, fallen by the sword, which [h]caused [i]terror in the land of the living.

24 There *is* [k]Elam and all her multitude round about her grave, all of them slain, fallen by the sword, which are [l]gone down uncircumcised into the nether parts of the earth, [m]which caused their terror in the land of the living; yet have they borne their shame with them that go down to the pit.

25 They have set her a bed in the midst of the slain with all her multitude: her graves *are* round about him: all of them uncircumcised, slain by the sword: though their terror was caused in the land of the living, yet have they borne their shame with them that go down to the pit: he is put in the midst of *them that be* slain.

26 There *is* [n]Meshech, Tubal, and all her

[t]Ch. xxviii. 7——[u]Ch. xxix. 19——[v]Ch. xxix. 11——[w]Heb. *desolate from the fulness thereof*——[x]Exod. vii. 5; xiv. 4, 18; Psa. ix. 16; ch. vi. 7——[y]Ver. 2; 2 Sam. i. 17; 2 Chron. xxxv. 25; ch. xxvi. 17——[z]Ch. xxvi. 20; xxxi. 14——[a]Ch. xxxi. 2, 18——[b]Ver. 21, 24, &c.; ch. xxviii. 10

[c]Or, *the sword is laid*——[d]Isa. i. 31; xiv. 9, 10; ver. 27——[e]Ver. 19, 25, &c.——[f]Ver. 24, 26, 29, 30——[g]Isa. xiv. 15——[h]Ch. xxvi. 17, 20; ver. 24, 25, 26, 27, 32——[i]Or, *dismaying*——[k]Jer. xlix. 34, &c.——[l]Ver. 21——[m]Ver. 23——[n]Gen. x. 2; chap. xxvii. 13; xxxviii. 2

the waters—to disturb the peace of the country.

Verse 15. *Shall be destitute of that whereof it was full*] Of *corn*, and all other necessaries of life.

Verse 17. *In the twelfth year*] Two of *Kennicott's* MSS., *one* of *De Rossi's*, and *one* of my own, (that mentioned ver. 1,) have, *in the* ELEVENTH *year;* and so has the *Syriac*, as before. This prophecy concerns the *people of Egypt*.

Verse 18. *Cast them down*] Show them that they shall be cast down. Proclaim to them a *casting down* prophecy.

Verse 19. *Whom dost thou pass in beauty?*] How little does it signify, whether a mummy be well embalmed, wrapped round with rich stuff, and beautifully painted on the outside, or not. Go down into the *tombs*, examine the *niches*, and see whether one dead carcass be preferable to another.

Verse 21. *Out of the midst of hell*] שאול *sheol*, the *catacombs*, the *place of burial*. There is something here similar to Isa. xiv. 9, where the descent of the king of Babylon to the state of the dead is described.

Verse 22. *Asshur* is *there*] The mightiest conquerors of the earth have gone down to the grave before thee; there they and their soldiers lie together, all slain by the sword.

Verse 23. *Whose graves are set in the sides of the pit*] Alluding to the *niches* in the sides of the subterranean caves or burying-places, where the bodies are laid. These are numerous in Egypt.

Verse 24. *There* is *Elam*] The Elamites, not far from the Assyrians; others think that *Persia* is meant. It was invaded by the joint forces of Cyaxares and Nebuchadnezzar.

Verse 26. *There* is *Meshech, Tubal*] See on chap. xxvii. 13.

A. M. 3417
B. C. 587
Ol. XLVIII. 2
Anno
Tarquinii Prisci,
R. Roman., 30

multitude: her graves *are*
round about him: all of them
[o]uncircumcised, slain by the
sword, though they caused
their terror in the land of the living.
27 [p]And they shall not lie with the mighty
that are fallen of the uncircumcised, which
are gone down to hell [q]with their weapons
of war: and they have laid their swords
under their heads, but their iniquities shall
be upon their bones, though *they were*
the terror of the mighty in the land of the
living.
28 Yea, thou shalt be broken in the midst
of the uncircumcised, and shalt lie with *them*
that are slain with the sword.
29 There *is* [r]Edom, her kings, and all her
princes, which with their might are [s]laid by
them that were slain by the sword: they shall
lie with the uncircumcised,
and with them that go down
to the pit.
30 [t]There *be* the princes of
the north, all of them, and all the [u]Zidonians
which are gone down with the slain; with
their terror they are ashamed of their might;
and they lie uncircumcised with *them that be*
slain by the sword, and bear their shame with
them that go down to the pit.
31 Pharaoh shall see them, and shall be
[v]comforted over all his multitude, *even* Pharaoh and all his army slain by the sword, saith
the Lord GOD.
32 For I have caused my terror in the land
of the living: and he shall be laid in the midst
of the uncircumcised with *them that are* slain
with the sword, *even* Pharaoh and all his multitude, saith the Lord GOD.

A. M. 3417
B. C. 587
Ol. XLVIII. 2
Anno
Tarquinii Prisci,
R. Roman., 30

[o]Ver. 19, 20, &c.——[p]Ver. 21; Isa. xiv. 18, 19——[q]Heb. *with weapons of their war*——[r]Chap. xxv. 12, &c.

[s]Heb. *given*, or *put*——[t]Chap. xxxviii. 6, 15; xxxix. 2
[u]Chap. xxviii. 21——[v]Chap. xxxi. 16

Verse 27. *Gone down to hell with their weapons of war*] Are buried in their armour, and with their weapons lying by their sides. It was a very ancient practice, in different nations, to bury a warrior's weapons in the same grave with himself.

Verse 29. *There* is *Edom*] All the glory and pomp of the *Idumean* kings, who also helped to oppress the Israelites, are gone down into the grave. Their kings, princes, and all their mighty men lie mingled with the *uncircumcised*, not distinguished from the *common dead:*

"Where they an equal honour share,
Who buried or unburied are.
Where Agamemnon knows no more
Than Irus, he condemned before.
Where fair Achilles and Thersites lie,
Equally naked, poor, and dry."

Verse 30. *There be the princes of the north*] The kings of Media and Assyria, and all the *Zidonians*—the kings of *Tyre, Sidon*, and *Damascus*. See *Calmet*.

Verse 31. *Pharaoh shall see them*] Pharaoh also, who said he was *a god*, shall be found among the vulgar dead.

And shall be comforted] Shall console himself, on finding that all other proud boasters are in the same circumstances with himself. Here is a reference to a *consciousness* after death.

Verse 32. *I have caused my terror in the land of the living*] I have spread dismay through Judea, the land of the *living God*, where the *living oracles* were delivered, and where the upright *live* by faith. When Pharaoh-necho came against Josiah, defeated, and slew him at Megiddo, fear and terror were spread through all the land of Judea; and the allusion here is probably to that circumstance. But even he is now laid with the *uncircumcised*, and is no more to be distinguished from the common dead.

Much of the phraseology of this chapter may be illustrated by comparing it with Isa. xiv., where see the notes, which the intelligent reader will do well to consult.

CHAPTER XXXIII

The prophet, after having addressed several other nations, returns now to his own; previously to which he is told, as on a former occasion, the duty of a watchman, the salvation or ruin of whose soul depends on the manner in which he discharges it. An awful passage indeed; full of important instruction both to such as speak, and to such as hear, the word of God, 1–9. *The prophet is then directed what answer to make to the cavils of infidelity and impiety; and to vindicate the equity of the Divine government by declaring the general terms of acceptance with God to be* (as told before, chap. xviii.) *without respect of persons; so that the ruin of the finally impenitent must be entirely owing to themselves,* 10–20. *The prophet receives the news of the destruction of Jerusalem by the Chaldeans, about a year and four months after it happened, according to the opinion of some, who have been led to this conjecture by the date given to this prophecy in the* twenty-first *verse, as it stands in our common Version: but some of the manuscripts of this prophet consulted by Dr. Kennicott have in this place* the ELEVENTH year, *which is probably the genuine reading. To check the vain confidence of those who expected to hold out by possessing themselves of its other fastnesses, the utter desolation of all Judea is foretold,* 21–29. *Ezekiel is informed that among those that attended his instructions were a great number of hypocrites, against whom he delivers a most awful message. When the Lord is* destroying *these hypocrites, then shall they know that there hath been a prophet among them,* 30–33.

A. M. cir. 3416
B. C. cir. 588
Ol. XLVIII. 1
Tarquinii Prisci, R. Roman., cir. annum 29

AGAIN the word of the LORD came unto me, saying,

2 Son of man, speak [a]to the children of thy people, and say unto them, [b]When [c]I bring the sword upon a land, if the people of the land take a man of their coasts, and set him for their [d]watchman:

3 If when he seeth the sword come upon the land, he blow the trumpet, and warn the people;

4 Then [e]whosoever heareth the sound of the trumpet and taketh not warning; if the sword come, and take him away, [f]his blood shall be upon his own head.

5 He heard the sound of the trumpet, and took not warning; his blood shall be upon him. But he that taketh warning shall deliver his soul.

6 But if the watchman see the sword come, and blow not the trumpet, and the people be not warned; if the sword come, and take *any* person from among them, [g]he is taken away in his iniquity; but his blood will I require at the watchman's hand.

7 [h]So thou, O son of man, I have set thee a watchman unto the house of Israel; therefore thou shalt hear the word at my mouth, and warn them from me.

8 When I say unto the wicked, O wicked *man,* thou shalt surely die; if thou dost not speak to warn the wicked from his way, that wicked *man* shall die in his iniquity; but his blood will I require at thine hand.

9 Nevertheless, if thou warn the wicked of his way to turn from it; if he do not turn from his way, he shall die in his iniquity; but thou hast delivered thy soul.

A. M. cir. 3416
B. C. cir. 588
Ol. XLVIII. 1
Tarquinii Prisci, R. Roman., cir. annum 29

10 Therefore, O thou son of man, speak unto the house of Israel; Thus ye speak, saying, If our transgressions and our sins *be* upon us, and we [i]pine away in them, [k]how should we then live?

11 Say unto them, *As* I live, saith the Lord GOD, [l]I have no pleasure in the death of the wicked; but that the wicked turn from his way and live: turn ye, turn ye from your evil ways; for [m]why will ye die, O house of Israel?

12 Therefore, thou son of man, say unto the children of thy people, [n]The righteousness of the righteous shall not deliver him in the day of his transgression: as for the wickedness of the wicked, [o]he shall not fall thereby in the day that he turneth from his wickedness; neither shall the righteous be able to live for his *righteousness* in the day that he sinneth.

13 When I shall say to the righteous, *that* he shall surely live; [p]if he trust to his own righteousness, and commit iniquity, all his righteousness shall not be remembered; but for his iniquity that he hath committed he shall die for it.

14 Again, [q]when I say unto the wicked, Thou shalt surely die; if he turn from his sin, and do [r]that which is lawful and right;

15 *If* the wicked [s]restore the pledge, [t]give again that he had robbed, walked in [u]the sta-

[a]Chap. iii. 11——[b]Chap. xiv. 17——[c]Heb. *A land when I bring a sword upon her*——[d]2 Sam. xviii. 24, 25; 2 Kings ix. 17; ver. 7; Hos. ix. 8——[e]Heb. *he that hearing heareth*——[f]Chap. xviii. 13——[g]Ver. 8 [h]Chap. iii. 17, &c.——[i]Chap. xxiv. 23——[k]So Isa. xlix. 14; chap. xxxvii. 11——[l]2 Sam. xiv. 14; chap. xviii. 23, 32; 2 Pet. iii. 9——[m]Chap. xviii. 31——[n]Chap. iii. 20; xviii. 24, 26, 27——[o]2 Chron. vii. 14——[p]Chap. iii. 20; xviii. 24——[q]Chap. iii. 18, 19; xviii. 27——[r]Heb. *judgment and justice*——[s]Chap. xviii. 7——[t]Exod. xxii. 1, 4; Lev. vi. 2, 4, 5; Num. v. 6, 7; Luke xix. 8——[u]Lev. xviii. 5; chap. xx. 11, 13, 21

NOTES ON CHAP. XXXIII

Verse 2. *Son of man—if the people of the land take a man*] The first *ten* verses of this chapter are the same with chap. iii. 17-22; and to what is said there on this most important and awful subject I must refer the reader. *Here* the PEOPLE *choose* the *watchman; there,* the Lord appoints him. When God chooses, the people should approve.

Verse 10. *If our transgressions and our sins* be *upon us*] They *are* upon us, as a grievous burden, too weighty for us to bear: how then can we *live* under such a load?

We pine away in them] In such circumstances how consoling is that word: "Come unto me, all ye who are heavy laden, and I will give you rest!"

Verse 11. As *I live, saith the Lord God, I have no pleasure in the death of the wicked*] From this to the twentieth verse inclusive is nearly the same with chap. xviii., on which I wish the reader to consult the notes.

Verse 13. *If he trust to his own righteousness, and commit iniquity*] If he trust in his *acting according to the statutes and ordinances of religion,* and according to the *laws relative to rights and wrongs among men,* and in

A. M. cir. 3416
B. C. cir. 588
Ol. XLVIII. 1
Tarquinii Prisci,
R. Roman.,
cir. annum 29

tutes of life, without commit-
ting iniquity; he shall surely
live, he shall not die.
16 [v]None of his sins that he
hath committed shall be mentioned unto him:
he hath done that which is lawful and right;
he shall surely live.
17 [w]Yet the children of thy people say, The
way of the Lord is not equal: but as for them,
their way is not equal.
18 [x]When the righteous turneth from his
righteousness, and committeth iniquity, he
shall even die thereby.
19 But if the wicked turn from his wickedness, and do that which is lawful and right, he
shall live thereby.
20 Yet ye say, [y]The way of the Lord is not
equal. O ye house of Israel, I will judge you
every one after his ways.
21 And it came to pass in the twelfth year
[z]of our captivity, in the tenth *month,* in the
fifth *day* of the month, [a]*that* one that had
escaped out of Jerusalem came unto me, saying, [b]The city is smitten.
22 Now [c]the hand of the LORD was upon
me in the evening, afore he that was escaped
came; and had opened my mouth, until
he came to me in the morning; [d]and my
mouth was opened, and I was no more
dumb.

A. M. 3416
B. C. 588
Ol. XLVIII. 1
Anno
Tarquinii Prisci,
R. Roman., 29

23 Then the word of the
LORD came unto me, saying,
24 Son of man, [e]they that inhabit those [f]wastes of the land
of Israel speak, saying, [g]Abraham was one,
and he inherited the land: [h]but we *are* many;
the land is given us for inheritance.
25 Wherefore say unto them, Thus saith the
Lord GOD; [i]Ye eat with the blood, and [k]lift
up your eyes towards your idols, and [l]shed
blood: and shall ye possess the land?
26 [m]Ye stand upon your sword, ye work
abomination, and ye [n]defile every one his
neighbour's wife: and shall ye possess the
land?
27 Say thou thus unto them, Thus saith the
Lord GOD; *As* I live, surely [o]they that *are* in
the wastes shall fall by the sword, and him
that *is* in the open field [p]will I give to the
beasts [q]to be devoured, and they that *be* in the
forts and [r]in the caves shall die of the pestilence.
28 [s]For I will lay the land [t]most desolate,
and the [u]pomp of her strength shall cease;
and the [v]mountains of Israel shall be desolate,
that none shall pass through.
29 Then shall they know that I *am* the
LORD, when I have laid the land most desolate because of all their abominations which
they have committed.

---

[v]Chap. xviii. 22——[w]Ver. 20; chap. xviii. 25, 29——[x]Chap. xviii. 26, 27——[y]Ver. 17; chap. xviii. 25, 29——[z]Chap. i. 2——[a]Chap. xxiv. 26——[b]2 Kings xxv. 4——[c]Chap. i. 3——[d]Chap. xxiv. 27——[e]Chap. xxxiv. 2——[f]Ver. 27; chap. xxxvi. 4——[g]Isaiah li. 2; Acts vii. 5——[h]See Micah iii. 11; Matthew iii. 9; John viii. 39

[i]Gen. ix. 4; Lev. iii. 17; vii. 26; xvii. 10; xix. 26; Deut. xii. 16——[k]Ch. xviii. 6——[l]Ch. xxii. 6, 9——[m]Wisd. ii. 11——[n]Chap. xviii. 6; xxii. 11——[o]Ver. 24——[p]Ch. xxxix. 4——[q]Heb. *to devour him*——[r]Judg. vi. 2; 1 Sam. xiii. 6——[s]Jer. xliv. 2, 6, 22; chap. xxxvi. 34, 35——[t]Heb. *desolation and desolation*——[u]Chap. vii. 24; xxiv. 21; xxx. 6, 7——[v]Chap. vi. 2, 3, 6

---

other respects commit iniquity, *he shall die for it.*

Verse 19. *He shall live thereby*] "The *wages* of sin is death;" the "gift of God is eternal life." It is a miserable trade by which a man *cannot live;* such a trade is *sin.*

Verse 21. *In the twelfth year of our captivity, in the tenth* month, *in the fifth* day *of the month*] Instead of the *twelfth year,* the *eleventh* is the reading of *seven* of *Kennicott's* MSS., *one* of *De Rossi's,* and the *Syriac.* My own, mentioned in the preceding chapter, reads with the present text. This was on *Wednesday, Jan.* 25, A. M. 3416 or 3417.

One that had escaped out of Jerusalem] After it had been taken by the Chaldeans.

Came unto me, saying, THE CITY IS SMITTEN.] This very message God had promised to the prophet, chap. xxiv. 26.

Verse 22. *My mouth was opened*] They had now the fullest evidence that I had spoken from the Lord. I therefore spoke freely and fully what God delivered to me, chap. xxiv. 27.

Verse 24. *Abraham was one*] If he was called to inherit the land when he was alone, and had the whole to himself, why may we not expect to be established here, who are his posterity, and are *many?* They wished to remain in the land and be happy after the Chaldeans had carried the rest away captives.

Verse 25. *Ye eat with the blood*] Abraham was *righteous,* ye are *unrighteous.* Eating of *blood,* in any way dressed, or of *flesh* from which the blood had not been *extracted,* was and is in the sight of God abominable. All such practices he has absolutely and for ever forbidden. Let the vile blood-eaters hear and tremble. See the note on Acts xv. 20, and the passages in the margin.

Verse 26. *Ye stand upon your sword*] Ye live by plunder, rapine, and murder. Ye are every way impure; and shall ye possess the land? No.

Verse 27. *They that* are *in the wastes*] He seems to speak of those Jews who had fled to *rocks, caves,* and *fortresses,* in the *mountains;*

A. M. 3416
B. C. 588
Ol. XLVIII. 1
Anno
Tarquinii Prisci,
R. Roman., 29

30 Also, thou son of man,
the children of thy people
still are talking [w]against thee
by the walls and in the doors
of the houses, and [x]speak one to another,
every one to his brother, saying, Come, I pray
you, and hear what is the word that cometh
forth from the LORD.
31 And [y]they come unto thee [z]as the people
cometh, and [a]they [b]sit before thee *as* my people, and they hear thy words, but they will
not do them: for [c]with their
mouth [d]they show much love,
but [e]their heart goeth after
their covetousness.
32 And, lo, thou *art* unto them as [f]a very
lovely song of one that hath a pleasant voice,
and can play well on an instrument: for they
hear thy words, but they do them not.
33 [g]And when this cometh to pass, (lo, it
will come,) then [h]shall they know that a
prophet hath been among them.

[w]Or, *of thee*——[x]Isa. xxix. 13——[y]Chap. xiv. 1; xx. 1, &c.——[z]Heb. *according to the coming of the people* [a]Or, *my people set before thee*

[b]Ch. viii. 1——[c]Psa. lxxviii. 36, 37; Isa. xxix. 13 [d]Heb. *they make loves*, or *jests*——[e]Matt. xiii. 22 [f]Heb. *a song of loves*——[g]1 Sam. iii. 20——[h]Chap. ii. 5

whose death he predicts, partly by the *sword*, partly by *wild beasts*, and partly by *famine.*

Verse 30. *The people still are talking against thee*] בך *bach* should be rather translated, "concerning thee," than "against thee;" for the following verses show that the prophet was much respected. The *Vulgate* translates, *de te;* the *Septuagint*, περι σου, "concerning thee;" both right.

Talking by the walls and in the doors of the houses is not a custom peculiar to the *Copts*, mentioned by Bp. *Pococke;* it is a practice among *idle people*, and among those who are *resting from their work*, in *every country*, when the *weather permits.* Gossiping *in the inside of the house* is not less frequent, and much more blamable.

Verse 31. *As the people cometh*] As they are accustomed to come on public days, Sabbaths, &c.

With their mouth they show much love] They respected the prophet, but would not bend themselves to follow his precepts. They loved *earthly things*, and did not relish those of *heaven.*

Verse 32. *As a very lovely song*] They admired the *fine voice* and *correct delivery* of the prophet; this was *their religion*, and this is the *whole* of the religion of thousands to the present day; for never were *itching ears* so multiplied as now.

Verse 33. *When this cometh to pass—then shall they know that a prophet hath been among them.*] What I have predicted, (and it is even now at the doors,) then they will be convinced that there was a prophet among them, by whose ministry they did not profit as they ought.

CHAPTER XXXIV

The prophet is commanded to declare the dreadful judgments of God against the covetous shepherds of Israel, who feed themselves, and not their flocks; by which emblem the priests and Levites are intended, who in Ezekiel's time were very corrupt, and the chief cause of Israel's apostasy and ruin, 1–10. *From this gloomy subject the prophet passes to the blessedness of the true Israel of God under the reign of* DAVID, *the Great Shepherd of the sheep, our Lord Jesus Christ being named after this prince by a figure exceedingly frequent in the sacred oracles, of putting the type for the antitype,* 11–31.

A. M. cir. 3417
B. C. cir. 587
Ol. XLVIII. 2
Tarquinii Prisci,
R. Roman.,
cir. annum 30

AND the word of the LORD
came unto me, saying,
2 Son of man, prophesy
against the [a]shepherds of Isra-
el, prophesy, and say unto them, Thus saith
the Lord GOD unto the shepherds, [b]Wo *be* to
the shepherds of Israel that do
feed themselves! should not
the shepherds feed the flocks?
3 [c]Ye eat the fat, and ye
clothe you with the wool, [d]ye kill them that
are fed: *but* ye feed not the flock.

[a]Chap. xxxiii. 24——[b]Jer. xxiii. 1; Zech. xi. 17——[c]Isa. lvi. 11; Zech. xi. 16

[d]Chapter xxxiii. 25, 26; Micah iii. 1, 2, 3; Zechariah xi. 5

NOTES ON CHAP. XXXIV

Verse 2. *Prophesy against the shepherds of Israel*] The *shepherds* include, first, the *priests* and *Levites;* secondly, the *kings, princes*, and *magistrates.* The *flock* means the whole of the *people.* The *fat* and the *wool*, the *tithes* and *offerings*, the *taxes* and *imposts.* The reprehensible *feeding* and *clothing* with these, as to the priests and Levites, the using these *tithes* and *offerings*, not to enable them the better to fulfil the work of the *ministry*, but to pamper their own bodies, and support them in an idle voluptuous life; and in reference to the *state*, the employing the *taxes* and *imposts*, not for the support and administration of *justice* and good *government*, but to subsidize heathen powers, and maintain their own luxury and idolatrous prodigality.

Verse 3. *Ye eat the fat*] I think החלב *hacheleb* should be translated *the milk;* and so most of the Versions understand it. Or they lived on the *fat sheep*, and took the *wool* of all.

"The *priests*," says *Calmet*, "ate the tithes,

A. M. cir. 3417
B. C. cir. 587
Ol. XLVIII. 2
Tarquinii Prisci,
R. Roman.,
cir. annum 30

4 [e]The diseased have ye not
strengthened, neither have ye
healed that which was sick,
neither have ye bound up *that*
which was broken, neither have ye brought
again that which was driven away, neither
have ye [f]sought that which was lost; but with
[g]force and with cruelty have ye ruled them.

5 [h]And they were [i]scattered,
[k]because *there is* no shepherd:
[l]and they became meat to all
the beasts of the field, when
they were scattered.
6 My sheep wandered through all the mountains, and upon every high hill: yea, my flock
was scattered upon all the face of the earth,

A. M. cir. 3417
B. C. cir. 587
Ol. XLVIII. 2
Tarquinii Prisci,
R. Roman.,
cir. annum 30

[e]Ver. 16; Zech. xi. 16——[f]Luke xv. 4——[g]1 Pet. v. 3
[h]Chap. xxxiii. 21, 28

[i]1 Kings xxii. 17; Matt. ix. 36——[k]Or, *without a shepherd;* and so ver. 8——[l]Isa. lvi. 9; Jer. xii. 9; ver. 8

the first-fruits, and the offerings of the people; the *princes* received the tributes and imposts; and instead of instructing and protecting them, the latter took away their *lives* by the cruelties they practised against them: the former destroyed their *souls* by the poison of their doctrine, and by their bad example. The *fat sheep* point out the *rich*, to whom these pastors often disguised the truth, by a cruel condescension and complaisance."

Verse 4. *The diseased have ye not strengthened*] No person is fit for the office of a shepherd, who does not *well understand* the *diseases* to which sheep are incident, and the *mode of cure*. And is any man fit for the *pastoral office*, or to be a shepherd of souls, who is not well acquainted with the *disease of sin* in all its *varieties*, and the *remedy* for this disease, and the proper mode of administering it, in those various cases? He who does not know Jesus Christ as his *own Saviour*, never can recommend him to others. He who is not saved, will not save.

Neither have ye healed that which was sick] The prophet first speaks of the *general disease;* next, of the different kinds of spiritual infirmity.

Neither have ye bound up that which was *broken*] If a sheep have broken a leg, a proper shepherd knows how to *set the bones*, and splint and bind it till the bones knit and become strong. And the *skilful* spiritual pastor knows, if one of the flock be overtaken in a fault, how to restore such. Those *sudden falls*, where there was not a strong propensity to sin, are, to the soul, as a *broken bone* to the body.

Neither have ye brought again] A proper shepherd *loves* his sheep: he feels *interested* for their welfare; he acquaints himself with them all, so that he knows and can distinguish each. He knows also their *number*, and frequently counts to see that none is missing; if one be *lost* or *strayed*, he goes immediately and *seeks* it; and as he is constantly on the *watch*, it cannot have strayed *far* before he is apprised of its absence from the flock; and the *less* it has strayed, the *sooner* it is found and brought back to the fold.

The shepherds of Israel knew nothing about their flock; they might have been *diseased*, *infirm*, *bruised*, *maimed*, their *limbs broken*, *strayed*, and *lost;* for they *watched not* over them. When they got *fat sheep* and *wool* for their *table* and their *clothing*, they regarded nothing else; as they considered the flock *given them* for their *own use*, and scarcely ever supposed that they were to give any thing in return for the milk and the wool.

But with force and with cruelty] *Exacting tithes* and dues by the strong arm of the law, with the most *ungodly feeling;* and with a *cruelty* of *disposition* that proved it was the *fat* and the *wool* they sought, and not the safety or comfort of the flock.

Verse 5. *And they were scattered*] There was no discipline kept up; and the flock, the Church, became disorganized, and separated from each other, both in affection and fellowship. And the consequence was, the grievous wolves, false and worldly interested teachers, seized on and made a prey of them. Of the *communion of saints* such shepherds know nothing, farther than that it makes a part of the common *creed*.

Verse 6. *My sheep wandered through all the mountains*] They all became idolaters, and lost the knowledge of the true God. And could it be otherwise while they had such pastors?

"Himself a wanderer from the narrow way;
His silly sheep, no wonder that they stray!"

Reader, if thou be a *minister*, a *preacher*, or a person in *holy orders*, or *pretended holy orders*, or art one *pretending to holy orders*, look at the qualifications of a good shepherd as laid down by the prophet.

1. He professes to be a *shepherd*, and to be *qualified* for the office.

2. In consequence he *undertakes the care of a flock*. This supposes that he believes the great Bishop of souls has *called him* to the pastoral office; and that office implies that he is to give all diligence to *save the souls of them that hear him*.

HIS QUALIFICATIONS

1. He is *skilful;* he knows the *disease of sin* and its consequences; for the Eternal Spirit, by whom he is called, has convinced him of sin, of righteousness, and of judgment.

2. He knows well the *great remedy* for this disease, the passion and sacrificial death of the Lord Jesus Christ.

3. He is skilful, and knows *how to apply* this remedy.

4. The flock over which he watches is, in its *individuals*, either,—1. *Healthy* and *sound*. 2. Or, in a *state* of *convalescence*, returning to health. 3. Or, still under the *whole power* of the *general disease*. 4. Or, some are *dying* in a state of *spiritual weakness*. 5. Or, some are *fallen into sin*, and sorely bruised and broken in their souls by that fall. 6. Or, some have been *driven away* by some sore *temptation* or *cruel usage*. 7. Or, some have *wandered* from the flock, are got into strange pastures, and are perverted by erroneous doctrines. Or, 8. Some

A. M. cir. 3417
B. C. cir. 587
Ol. XLVIII. 2
Tarquinii Prisci, R. Roman., cir. annum 30

and none did search or seek
after them.
7 Therefore, ye shepherds,
hear the word of the LORD;
8 *As* I live, saith the Lord GOD, surely because my flock became a prey, and my flock [m]became meat to every beast of the field, because *there was* no shepherd, neither did my shepherds search for my flock, [n]but the shepherds fed themselves, and fed not my flock;
9 Therefore, O ye shepherds, hear the word of the LORD;
10 Thus saith the Lord GOD; Behold, I *am* against the shepherds; and [o]I will require my flock at their hand, and cause them to cease from feeding the flock; neither shall the shepherds [p]feed themselves any more: for I will deliver my flock from their mouth, that they may not be meat for them.
11 For thus saith the Lord GOD; Behold,
I, *even* I, will both search my sheep, and seek them out.
12 [q]As a shepherd seeketh out his flock in the day that he is among his sheep *that are* scattered; so will I seek out my sheep, and will deliver them out of all places where they have been scattered in [r]the cloudy and dark day.
13 And [s]I will bring them out from the people, and gather them from the countries, and will bring them to their own land, and feed them upon the mountains of Israel by the rivers, and in all the inhabited places of the country.
14 [t]I will feed them in a good pasture, and upon the high mountains of Israel shall their fold be: [u]there shall they lie in a good fold, and *in* a fat pasture shall they feed upon the mountains of Israel.
15 I will feed my flock, and I will cause

[m]Ver. 5, 6——[n]Ver. 2, 10——[o]Chap. iii. 18; Hebrews xiii. 17——[p]Ver. 2. 8——[q]Hebrew, *According to the seeking*——[r]Chap. xxx. 3; Joel ii. 2——[s]Isaiah lxv. 9, 10; Jeremiah xxiii. 3; chap. xxviii. 25; xxxvi. 24; xxxvii. 21, 22——[t]Psalm xxiii. 2——[u]Jeremiah xxxiii. 12

wolf has got among them, and scattered the whole flock. Now, the true shepherd, the pastor of God's choosing, knows—

1. How to keep the *healthy* in health; and cause them to grow in grace, and in the knowledge of Jesus Christ.

2. How to *nourish, feed,* and *care for* the *convalescent,* that they may be brought into a state of spiritual *soundness.*

3. How to *reprove,* instruct, and awaken those who are still under the *full power* of the *disease of sin.*

4. How to *find out* and *remove* the cause of all that *spiritual weakness* of which he sees some slowly *dying.*

5. How to deal with those who have *fallen into some scandalous sin,* and restore them from their *fall.*

6. How to *find out* and *turn aside* the *sore temptation* or *cruel usage* by which some have been *driven away.*

7. How to *seek* and *bring back* to the fold those who have *strayed* into strange pastures, and have had their souls perverted by *erroneous doctrines;* and knows also how, by a godly *discipline,* to preserve him in the flock, and keep the flock honourably together.

8. How to *oppose, confound,* and *expel* the *grievous wolf,* who has got among the flock, and is *scattering* them from each other, and from God. He knows how to *preach, explain,* and *defend* the truth. He is well acquainted with the *weapons* he is to use, and the *spirit* in which he is to employ them.

In a word, the true shepherd gives up his life *to* the sheep; spends and is spent for the glory of God; and gives up his life *for* the sheep, in defence of them, and in labouring for their welfare. And while he is thus employed, it is the duty of the flock to feed and clothe him; and see that neither he nor his family lack the *necessaries* and *conveniencies* of life. The *labourer* is worthy of his meat. He who does not *labour,* or, because of his *ignorance* of God and salvation, *cannot labour,* in the word and doctrine, deserves neither meat nor drink; and if he exact that by law, which he has not honestly earned by a proper discharge of the *pastoral function,* let him read this chapter, and learn from it what a fearful *account* he shall have to give to the chief Shepherd at the great day; and what a dreadful *punishment* shall be inflicted on him, when the blood of the souls lost through his neglect or inefficiency is visited upon him! See the notes on chap. iii. 17, &c.

Verse 7. *Therefore, ye shepherds,* (ye *bad* and *wicked shepherds,*) *hear the word of the Lord*] In the preceding character of the *good shepherd* the reader will find, by reversing the particulars, the character of a *bad shepherd;* and therefore I may be excused from entering into farther detail.

Verse 10. *I will—cause them to cease from feeding the flock*] God, in this country, *unpriested* a whole hierarchy who fed not the flock, but *ruled them with force and cruelty;* and he raised up a new set of shepherds better qualified, both by sound doctrine and learning, to feed the flock. Let these be faithful, lest God cause *them to cease,* and raise up other feeders.

Verse 12. *Cloudy and dark day.*] Times of general distress and persecution; in such times the shepherd should be especially watchful.

Verse 13. *I will—feed them upon the mountains*] When I bring back the people from their captivity, I will raise up to them a holy and diligent priesthood, who shall in all places give them sound instruction. But this, and some of the following promises, belong to the *Christian Church,* as we shall find below.

A. M. cir. 3417
B. C. cir. 587
Ol. XLVIII. 2
Tarquinii Prisci,
R. Roman.,
cir. annum 30

them to lie down, saith the
Lord GOD.
16 [v]I will seek that which
was lost, and bring again that
which was driven away, and will bind up *that
which was* broken, and will strengthen that
which was sick: but I will destroy [w]the fat and
the strong; I will feed them [x]with judgment.
17 And *as for* you, O my flock, thus saith
the Lord GOD: [y]Behold, I judge between
[z]cattle and cattle, between the rams and the
[a]he-goats.
18 *Seemeth it* a small thing unto you to
have eaten up the good pasture, but ye must
tread down with your feet the residue of
your pastures? and to have drunk of the deep
waters, but ye must foul the residue with
your feet?
19 And *as for* my flock, they eat that which
ye have trodden with your feet; and they
drink that which ye have
fouled with your feet.
20 Therefore thus saith the
Lord GOD unto them; [b]Be-
hold, I, even I, will judge between the fat
cattle and between the lean cattle.
21 Because ye have thrust with side and
with shoulder, and pushed all the diseased
with your horns, till ye have scattered them
abroad;
22 Therefore will I save my flock, and they
shall no more be a prey; and [c]I will judge
between cattle and cattle.
23 And I will set up one [d]Shepherd over
them, and he shall feed them, [e]*even* my servant David; he shall feed them, and he shall
be their Shepherd.
24 And [f]I the LORD will be their God, and
my Servant David [g]a Prince among them; I
the LORD have spoken *it*.

[v]See ver. 4; Isa. xl. 11; Mic. iv. 6; Matt. xviii. 11; Mark ii. 17; Luke v. 32——[w]Isa. x. 16; Amos iv. 1——[x]Jer. x. 24——[y]Chap. xx. 37, 38; ver. 20, 22; Zech. x. 3; Matt. xxv. 32, 33——[z]Heb. *small cattle of lambs and kids*——[a]Heb. *great he-goats*

[b]Ver. 17——[c]Ver. 17——[d]Isa. xl. 11; Jer. xxiii. 4, 5; John x. 11; Heb. xiii. 20; 1 Pet. ii. 25; v. 4——[e]Jer. xxx. 9; chap. xxxvii. 24, 25; Hos. iii. 5——[f]Ver. 30; Exod. xxix. 45; chap. xxxvii. 27——[g]Chap. xxxvii. 22; Luke i. 32, 33

Verse 16. *I will destroy the fat and the strong*] I will destroy those cruel and imperious shepherds who abuse their authority, and tyrannize over the flock.

Verse 17. *And* as for *you, O my flock*] After having spoken to the *shepherds*, he now addresses the *flock*.

I judge between cattle and cattle] Between *false* and *true* professors; between them that have only the *form* and them that have the *power* of godliness; between the *backslider in heart* and the *upright man*.

Verse 18. *Have eaten up the good pasture*] Arrogate to yourselves all the promises of God, and will hardly permit the simple believer to claim or possess any token of God's favour.

Ye must foul the residue with your feet?] Ye abuse God's mercies; you *consume much* upon yourselves, and ye *spoil more*, on which the *poor* would have been glad to *feed*. There are some who would rather give food to their *sporting dogs* than to the *poor* around them, who are ready to starve, and who would be glad of the crumbs that fall from the table of those *masters!*

Verse 20. *I will judge between the fat cattle and between the lean cattle.*] Between the *rich* and the *poor;* those who *fare sumptuously* every day and those who have not the *necessaries of life*.

Verse 23. *I will set up one Shepherd—my servant David*] DAVID, king of Israel, had been dead upwards of *four hundred years;* and from that time till now there never was a ruler of any kind, either in the Jewish *Church* or *state*, of the name of *David*. This, then, must be some *typical person;* and from the texts marked in the margin we understand that *Jesus Christ* alone is meant, as both *Old* and *New* TESTAMENTS agree in this. And from this one *Shepherd* all Christian *ministers* must derive their authority to teach, and their grace to teach effectually.

By the kind providence of God it appears that he has not permitted any *apostolic succession* to be preserved, lest the members of his Church should seek that in an *uninterrupted succession* which must be found in the HEAD *alone*. The *papists* or *Roman Catholics*, who boast of an *uninterrupted succession*, which is a mere fable that never was and never can be proved, have raised up *another head*, the POPE. And I appeal to themselves, in the fear of God, whether they do not in *heart* and in *speech* trace up all their *authority* to *him*, and only compliment Christ as having appointed *Peter* to be the first bishop of Rome, (which is an *utter falsity*, for he was never appointed to such an office there, nor ever held such an office in that city, nor, in their sense, *any where else;*) and they hold also that the popes of Rome are not so much *Peter's successors* as *God's vicars;* and thus both God and Peter are nearly *lost sight of* in their *papal enumerations*. With them the *authority of the Church* is all in all; the *authority of Christ* is seldom mentioned.

Verse 24. *I the Lord will be their God, and my Servant David a Prince*] Here we find God and his Christ are *all in all* in his Church, and Jesus is still PRINCE *among them;* and to him the *call* and *qualifications* of all genuine pastors belong, and *from* him they must be derived. And he has blotted out what is called *uninterrupted succession*, that every Christian minister may seek and receive credentials from himself. Here is the grand reason why the *uninterrupted succession cannot be made out*. And here is the proof also that the Church that *pretends to*

A. M. cir. 3417
B. C. cir. 587
Ol. XLVIII. 2
Tarquinii Prisci, R. Roman., cir. annum 30

25 And [h]I will make with them a covenant of peace, and [i]will cause the evil beasts to cease out of the land: and they [k]shall dwell safely in the wilderness, and sleep in the woods.

26 And I will make them and the places round about [l]my hill [m]a blessing: and I will [n]cause the shower to come down in his season; there shall be [o]showers of blessing.

27 And [p]the tree of the field shall yield her fruit, and the earth shall yield her increase, and they shall be safe in their land, and shall know that I *am* the LORD, when I have [q]broken the bands of their yoke, and delivered them out of the hand of those that [r]served themselves of them.

28 And they shall no more [s]be a prey to the heathen, neither shall the beast of the land devour them; but [t]they shall dwell safely, and none shall make *them* afraid.

29 And I will raise up for them a [u]plant [v]of renown, and they shall be no more [w]consumed with hunger in the land, [x]neither bear the shame of the heathen any more.

30 Thus shall they know that [y]I the LORD their God *am* with them, and *that* they, *even* the house of Israel, *are* my people, saith the Lord GOD.

31 And ye my [z]flock, the flock of my pasture, *are* men, *and* I *am* your God, saith the Lord GOD.

---

[h]Ch. xxxvii. 26——[i]Lev. xxvi. 6; Isa. xi. 6–9; xxxv. 9; Hos. ii. 18——[k]Ver. 28; Jer. xxiii. 6——[l]Isa. lvi. 7; chap. xx. 40——[m]Gen. xii. 2; Isa. xix. 24; Zech. viii. 13——[n]Lev. xxvi. 4——[o]Psa. lxviii. 9; Mal. iii. 10——[p]Lev. xxvi. 4; Psa. lxxxv. 12; Isa. iv. 2

[q]Lev. xxvi. 13; Jer. ii. 20——[r]Jer. xxv. 14——[s]See ver. 8——chap. xxxvi. 4——[t]Ver. 25; Jer. xxx. 10; xlvi. 27——[u]Isa. xi. 1; Jer. xxiii. 5——[v]Or, *for renown*; [w]Heb. *taken away*——[x]Ch. xxxvi. 3, 6, 15——[y]Ver. 24; chap. xxxvii. 27——[z]Psa. c. 3; John x. 11

---

it, and builds upon it, must be a *false Church;* for it is founded on a falsity; an *uninterrupted succession* which does not exist either in *history* or in *fact*.

Verse 25. *I will make with them a covenant of peace*] The original is emphatic: וכרתי להם ברית שלום *vecharatti lahem berith shalom*, "And I will cut with them the peace covenant;" that is, a *covenant sacrifice*, procuring and establishing peace between God and man, and between man and his fellows. I need not tell the reader that the *cutting* refers to the ancient mode of *making covenants*. The blood was poured out; the animal was divided from mouth to tail, exactly in *two;* the divisions placed *opposite to each other;* the contracting parties entered into the space, going in at each end, and met in the *middle*, and *there* took the *covenant oath*. He is the *Prince of peace*, and through him come glory to God in the highest, and *peace* and good will to men upon earth.

And will cause the evil beasts to cease] These *false* and *ravenous pastors*. Christ purges them out of his Church, and destroys that *power* by which they lorded it over God's heritage.

Verse 26. *The shower to come down*] The Holy Spirit's influence.

There shall be showers of blessing.] Light, life, joy, peace, and power shall be manifest in all the *assemblies of Christ's people*.

Verse 29. *I will raise up—a plant of renown*] מטע לשם *matta leshem*, "a plantation to the name;" to the name of CHRIST. A *Christian Church* composed of men who are *Christians*, who have the spirit of *Christ* in them, and do not bear his *name* in vain. I believe the words might be applied to the *Christian Church;* but that Christ may be called a *plant* or *plantation* here,—as he is elsewhere called a *branch* and a *rod*, Isa. iv. 2; xi. 1; so Jer. xxiii. 5; xxxv. 15,—is most probable. He is the Person of *name*, לשם *leshem*, JESUS; the *Saviour*, CHRIST; the *Anointer*, long *spoken* of before he was manifested in the flesh, and since the *daily theme* in the Church militant. It is he who hath loved us, and washed us from our sins in his own blood, no other *name* being given under heaven among men by which we can be saved; he who has a *name* above every *name*, and at whose *name* every knee shall bow; through whose *name*, by faith in his *name*, the diseased are healed; and in whose *name* all our prayers and supplications must be presented to God to make them acceptable. This is the Person of NAME!

They shall be no more consumed with hunger] For this glorious *plant of name* is the *Bread of life;* and this is broken in all the assemblies of his people where his *name* is properly proclaimed.

Verse 31. *And ye my flock*] That is, under the allegory of a *flock* of *sheep*, I point out *men;* under that of a *pasture*, my *Church;* and under that of a *shepherd*, the *Messiah*, through whom I am become *your God*. And he who is your God is אדני יהוה *Adonai Yehovah*, the self-existent Being; the *Governor* and *Director*, as well as the *Saviour* and *Judge* of men.

CHAPTER XXXV

The prophet having formerly predicted the ruin of Edom, the same with Seir, (chap. xxv. 12,) *now resumes and pursues the subject at greater length, intimating, as did also Isaiah,* (chap. xxi. 11, 12,) *that though other nations should recover their liberty after the fall of the Babylonian monarchy, the Edomites should continue in bondage for their very despiteful behaviour towards the children of Israel in the day of their calamity,* 1–15.

A. M. cir. 3417
B. C. cir. 587
Ol. XLVIII. 2
Tarquinii Prisci,
R. Roman.,
cir. annum 30

MOREOVER the word of the LORD came unto me, saying,

2 Son of man, [a]set thy face against [b]Mount Seir, and [c]prophesy against it.

3 And say unto it, Thus saith the Lord GOD; Behold, O Mount Seir, I *am* against thee, and [d]I will stretch out mine hand against thee, and I will make thee [e]most desolate.

4 [f]I will lay thy cities waste, and thou shalt be desolate, and thou shalt know that I *am* the LORD.

5 [g]Because thou hast had a [h]perpetual hatred, and hast [i]shed *the blood of* the children of Israel, by the [k]force of the sword in the time of their calamity, [l]in the time *that their* iniquity *had* an end:

6 Therefore, *as* I live, saith the Lord GOD, I will prepare thee unto blood, and blood shall pursue thee: [m]sith thou hast not hated blood, even blood shall pursue thee.

7 Thus will I make Mount Seir [n]most desolate, and cut off from it [o]him that passeth out and him that returneth.

8 [p]And I will fill his mountains with his slain *men:* in thy hills, and in thy valleys, and in all thy rivers, shall they fall that are slain with the sword.

A. M. cir. 3417
B. C. cir. 587
Ol. XLVIII. 2
Tarquinii Prisci,
R. Roman.,
cir. annum 30

9 [q]I will make thee perpetual desolations, and thy cities shall not return: [r]and ye shall know that I *am* the LORD.

10 Because thou hast said, These two nations and these two countries shall be mine, and we will [s]possess it; [t]whereas [u]the LORD was there:

11 Therefore, *as* I live, saith the Lord GOD, I will even do, [v]according to thine anger, and according to thine envy which thou hast used out of thy hatred against them; and I will make myself known among them, when I have judged thee.

12 [w]And thou shalt know that I *am* the LORD, *and that* I have heard all thy blasphemies which thou hast spoken against the mountains of Israel, saying, They are laid desolate, they are given us [x]to consume.

[a]Chap. vi. 2——[b]Deut. ii. 5——[c]Jer. xlix. 7, 8; chap. xxv. 12; Amos i. 11; Obad. 10, &c.——[d]Chap. vi. 14——[e]Heb. *desolation and desolation;* so ver. 7——[f]Ver. 9——[g]Chap. xxv. 12; Obad. 10——[h]Or, *hatred of old;* chap. xxv. 15——[i]Heb. *poured out the children*——[k]Heb. *hands*——[l]Psa. cxxxvii. 7; chap. xxi. 25, 29; Dan. ix. 24; Obad. 11——[m]Psa. cix. 17——[n]Heb. *desolation and desolation;* ver. 3

[o]Judg. v. 6; chap. xxix. 11——[p]Chap. xxxi. 12; xxxii. 5——[q]Jer. xlix. 17, 18; ver. 4; chap. xxv. 13; Mal. i. 3, 4——[r]Chap. vi. 7; vii. 4, 9; xxxvi. 11——[s]Psa. lxxxiii. 4, 12; chap. xxxvi. 5; Obad. 13——[t]Or, *though the LORD was there*——[u]Psa. xlviii. 1, 3; cxxxii. 13, 14; chap. xlviii. 35——[v]Matt. vii. 2; James ii. 13——[w]Chap. vi. 7; Psa. ix. 16——[x]Heb. *to devour*——[y]1 Sam. ii. 3; Rev. xiii. 6——[z]Heb. *magnified*

NOTES ON CHAP. XXXV

Verse 2. *Set thy face against Mount Seir*] That is, against the *Edomites*. This prophecy was probably delivered about the time of the preceding, and before the destruction of Idumea by Nebuchadnezzar, which took place about *five years after*.

Calmet supposes that *two destructions of Idumea* are here foretold; one by Nebuchadnezzar, and the other by the *Jews* after their return from their captivity.

Verse 3. *Most desolate.*] Literally, "A desolation and a wilderness."

Verse 5. *A perpetual hatred*] The Edomites were the descendants of *Esau;* the Israelites, the descendants of *Jacob*. Both these were brothers; and between them there was contention even in the womb, and they lived generally in a state of enmity. Their descendants kept up the ancient feud: but the Edomites were implacable; they had not only a *rooted* but *perpetual enmity* to the Israelites, harassing and distressing them by all possible means; and they seized the opportunity, when the Israelites were most harassed by other enemies, to make inroads upon them, and cut them off wherever they found them.

To afflict the afflicted is cruel. This is scarcely of man, bad as he is. He must be possessed by the *malignant spirit* of the *devil*, when he wounds the wounded, insults over the miseries of the afflicted, and seeks opportunities to add affliction to those who are already under the rod of God.

Verse 6. *Blood shall pursue thee*] Thou lovest blood, and thou shalt have blood. It is said that Cyrus and *two hundred thousand* men were slain in an ambush by Thomyris, queen of the Scythians, and that she cut off his head, and threw it into a vessel filled with blood, with this severe sarcasm:—

Satia te sanguine quem sititsti, Cyre.
"O Cyrus, now satisfy thyself with blood."

Hence, the *figure:*—

"*Sarcasmus*, with this biting taunt doth kill:
Cyrus, thy thirst was blood, now drink thy fill."

Verse 9. *Perpetual desolations*] Thou shalt have perpetual desolation for thy perpetual hatred.

Verse 10. *These two nations*] Israel and Judah. The Idumeans thought of conquering and possessing both; and they would have succeeded, but only *the Lord was there;* and this spoiled their projects, and blasted their hopes.

Verse 12. *They are laid desolate, they are given us to consume.*] They exulted in seeing Judea overrun; and they rejoiced in the prospect of completing the ruin, when the Chaldeans had withdrawn from the land.

Verse 13. *Thus with your mouth ye have*

A. M. cir. 3417
B. C. cir. 587
Ol. XLVIII. 2
Tarquinii Prisci,
R. Roman.,
cir. annum 30

13 Thus [y]with your mouth ye
have [z]boasted against me, and
have multiplied your words
against me: I have heard *them*.
14 Thus saith the Lord GOD; [a]When the
whole earth rejoiceth, I will make thee
desolate.
15 [b]As thou didst rejoice at
the inheritance of the house
of Israel, because it was desolate, so will I do unto thee:
[c]thou shalt be desolate, O Mount Seir, and
all Idumea, *even* all of it: and they shall
know that I *am* the LORD.

A. M. cir. 3417
B. C. cir. 587
Ol. XLVIII. 2
Tarquinii Prisci,
R. Roman.,
cir annum 30

[a]Isa. lxv. 13, 14

[b]Obad. xii. 15——[c]Ver. 3, 4

boasted against me] Ye have said you would enter into those lands, and take them for your inheritance; though ye knew that God had promised them to the Israelites, and that you should never have them for your portion.

Verse 14. *When the whole earth rejoiceth*] When the whole *land* shall rejoice in the restoration of the Jews, I will make thee desolate. Probably this refers to the time of the *Maccabees*.

Verse 15. *So will I do unto thee*] Others shall rejoice in thy downfall as thou hast rejoiced at their downfall.

This whole chapter strongly inculcates this maxim: Do as thou wouldst be done by; and what thou wouldst not have done to thee, do not to others. And from it we learn that every man may, in some sort, be said to make his own temporal good or evil; for as he does to others, God will take care to do to him, whether it be evil or good, weal or wo. Would you not be slandered or backbitten? Then do not slander nor backbite. Wouldst thou wish to live in peace? Then do not disturb the peace of others. Be merciful, and thou shalt obtain mercy.

CHAPTER XXXVI

The Edomites or Idumeans, during the Babylonish captivity, took possession of the mountainous parts of Judea, and the fortresses which commanded the country, intending to exclude the Jews if ever they should return from their captivity. The prophet therefore, by a beautiful personification, addresses the mountains of Israel; and, ascribing to them passions and emotions similar to those of his own breast, consoles them with the prospect of being soon rid of those usurping foes; of being freed from the dishonour of idols under which they groaned; and of flourishing again in their ancient glory under their rightful owners, 1–15. *The idolatry and other sins of the Jews are then declared to be the cause of their captivity and dispersion,* 16–20; *from which however they are promised a deliverance in terms of great force and beauty,* 21–38. *This chapter contains also, under the type of the happy condition of the Israelites after their restoration from the Babylonish captivity, a glorious prophecy of the rich blessings of the Gospel dispensation.*

A. M. cir. 3417
B. C. cir. 587
Ol. XLVIII. 2
Tarquinii Prisci,
R. Roman.,
cir. annum 30

ALSO, thou son of man,
prophesy unto the [a]moun-
tains of Israel, and say, Ye
mountains of Israel, hear the
word of the LORD:
2 Thus saith the Lord GOD; Because [b]the
enemy hath said against you, Aha, [c]even the
ancient high places [d]are ours in possession:
3 Therefore prophesy and say, Thus saith
the Lord GOD; [e]Because they have made *you*
desolate, and swallowed you up on every side,
that ye might be a possession unto the residue
of the heathen, [f]and [g]ye are taken up in the lips of talkers, and
are an infamy of the people:
4 Therefore, ye mountains of
Israel, hear the word of the Lord GOD; Thus
saith the Lord GOD to the mountains, and to
the hills, to the [h]rivers, and to the valleys, to the
desolate wastes, and to the cities that are forsaken, which [i]became a prey and [k]derision to the
residue of the heathen that *are* round about;
5 Therefore thus saith the Lord GOD;
[l]Surely in the fire of my jealousy have I

A. M. cir. 3417
B. C. cir. 587
Ol. XLVIII. 2
Tarquinii Prisci,
R. Roman.,
cir. annum 30

[a]Ch. vi. 2, 3——[b]Ch. xxv. 3; xxvi. 2——[c]Deut. xxxii. 13——[d]Ch. xxxv. 10——[e]Heb. *Because for because* [f]Deut. xxviii. 37; 1 Kings ix. 7; Lam. ii. 15; Dan. ix. 16

[g]Or, *ye are made to come upon the lip of the tongue* [h]Or, *bottoms*, or *dales*——[i]Ch. xxxiv. 28——[k]Psa. lxxix. 4——[l]Deut. iv. 24; chap. xxxviii. 19

NOTES ON CHAP. XXXVI

Verse 1. *Prophesy unto the mountains of Israel*] This is a part of the preceding prophecy, though it chiefly concerns the Jews. In it they are encouraged to expect a glorious restoration; and that none of the evil wishes of their adversaries should take place against them.

Verse 2. *Because the enemy hath said*] The Idumeans thought they would shortly be put in possession of all the strong places of Israel; *the ancient high places shall be ours.*

Verse 4. *Therefore—thus saith the Lord God to the mountains, &c.*] They shall neither possess *mountain* nor *valley, hill* nor *dale, fountain* nor *river;* for though in my justice I made you desolate, yet they shall not profit by your disasters. See ver. 5, 6, and 7.

A. M. cir. 3417
B. C. cir. 587
Ol. XLVIII. 2
Tarquinii Prisci, R. Roman., cir. annum 30

spoken against the residue of the heathen, and against all Idumea, [m]which have appointed my land into their possession with the joy of all *their* heart, with despiteful minds, to cast it out for a prey.

6 Prophesy therefore concerning the land of Israel, and say unto the mountains, and to the hills, to the rivers, and to the valleys, Thus saith the Lord GOD; Behold, I have spoken in my jealousy and in my fury, because ye have [n]borne the shame of the heathen:

7 Therefore thus saith the Lord GOD; I have [o]lifted up mine hand, Surely the heathen that *are* about you, they shall bear their shame.

8 But ye, O mountains of Israel, ye shall shoot forth your branches, and yield your fruit to my people of Israel; for they are at hand to come.

9 For, behold, I *am* for you, and I will turn unto you, and ye shall be tilled and sown:

10 And I will multiply men upon you, all the house of Israel, *even* all of it: and the cities shall be inhabited, and [p]the wastes shall be builded:

11 And [q]I will multiply upon you man and beast: and they shall increase and bring fruit: and I will settle you after your old estates, and will do better *unto you* than at your beginnings: [r]and ye shall know that I *am* the LORD.

12 Yea, I will cause men to walk upon you, *even* my people Israel; [s]and they shall possess thee, and thou shalt be their inheritance, and thou shalt no more henceforth [t]bereave them *of men*.

13 Thus saith the Lord GOD; Because they say unto you, [u]Thou *land* devourest up men, and hast bereaved thy nations;

A. M. cir. 3417
B. C. cir. 587
Ol. XLVIII. 2
Tarquinii Prisci, R. Roman., cir. annum 30

14 Therefore thou shalt devour men no more, neither [v]bereave thy nations any more, saith the Lord GOD.

15 [w]Neither will I cause *men* to hear in thee the shame of the heathen any more, neither shalt thou bear the reproach of the people any more, neither shalt thou cause thy nations to fall any more, saith the Lord GOD.

16 Moreover the word of the LORD came unto me, saying,

17 Son of man, when the house of Israel dwelt in their own land, [x]they defiled it by their own way and by their doings: their way was before me as [y]the uncleanness of a removed woman.

18 Wherefore I poured my fury upon them [z]for the blood that they had shed upon the land, and for their idols *wherewith* they had polluted it:

19 And I [a]scattered them among the heathen and they were dispersed through the countries: [b]according to their way and according to their doings I judged them.

20 And when they entered unto the heathen, whither they went, they [c]profaned my holy name, when they said to them, These *are* the people of the LORD, and are gone forth out of his land.

21 But I had pity [d]for mine holy name, which the house of Israel had profaned among the heathen, whither they went.

22 Therefore say unto the house of Israel,

[m]Chap. xxxv. 10, 12——[n]Psa. cxxiii. 3, 4; chap. xxxiv. 29; ver. 15——[o]Ch. xx. 5——[p]Ver. 33; Isa. lviii. 12; lxi. 4; Amos ix 14——[q]Jer. xxxi. 27; xxxiii. 12 [r]Chap. xxxv. 9; xxxvii. 6, 13——[s]Obad. 17, &c.——[t]See Jer. xv. 7

[u]Num. xiii. 32——[v]Or, *cause to fall*——[w]Chap. xxxiv. 29——[x]Lev. xviii. 25, 27, 28; Jer. ii. 7——[y]Lev. xv. 19, &c.——[z]Chap. xvi. 36, 38; xxiii. 37——[a]Chap. xxii. 15——[b]Chap. vii. 3; xviii. 30; xxxix. 24——[c]Isa. lii. 5; Rom. ii. 24——[d]Chap. xx. 9, 14

Verse 8. *For they are at hand to come.*] The restoration of the Jews is so absolutely determined that you may rest assured it will take place; and be as confident relative to it, as if you saw the different families entering into the Israelitish borders. It was near at hand in God's determination, though there were about *fifty-eight* of the *seventy* years unelapsed.

Verse 9. *Ye shall be tilled and sown*] The land shall be *cultivated* as it formerly was, when *best peopled* and at *peace*.

Verse 11. *I will multiply upon you man and beast*] The *agriculturalist* and the *beast of burden*.

And will do better unto you *than at your beginnings*] I agree with *Calmet*, that it would be difficult to show the literal fulfilment of this prophecy from the days of Zerubbabel to the birth of Christ. The colouring is too high for that period; and the whole falls in better with Gospel than with Jewish times.

Verse 17. *When the house of Israel dwelt in their own land*] Had they continued faithful to me, they had never been removed from it: but they polluted it with their crimes; and I abhorred the land on that account, and gave both them and it up to the destroyers.

Verse 20. *And when they entered unto the heathen*] So bad were they, and so deeply fallen, that they *profaned the Lord's name among the heathen;* and, on their account, the true God was blasphemed. *These*, say they, *are the people*

A. M. cir. 3417
B. C. cir. 587
Ol. XLVIII. 2
Tarquinii Prisci, R. Roman., cir. annum 30

Thus saith the Lord GOD; I do not *this* for your sakes, O house of Israel, [e]but for mine holy name's sake, which ye have profaned among the heathen, whither ye went.
23 And I will sanctify my great name, which was profaned among the heathen, which ye have profaned in the midst of them; and the heathen shall know that I *am* the LORD, saith the Lord GOD, when I shall be [f]sanctified in you before [g]their eyes.
24 For [h]I will take you from among the heathen, and gather you out of all countries, and will bring you into your own land.
25 [i]Then will I sprinkle clean water upon you, and ye shall be clean: [k]from all your filthiness, and from all your idols, will I cleanse you.
26 A [l]new heart also will I give you, and a new spirit will I put within you: and I will take away the stony heart out of your flesh: and I will give you a heart of flesh.
27 And I will put my [m]Spirit within you, and cause you to walk in my statutes, and ye shall keep my judgments, and do *them*.

[e]Psa. cvi. 8——[f]Chap. xx. 41; xxviii. 22——[g]Or, *your*——[h]Chap. xxxiv. 13; xxxvii. 21

[i]Isa. lii. 15; Heb. x. 22——[k]Jer. xxxiii. 8——[l]Jer. xxxii. 39; chap. xi. 19——[m]Chap. xi. 19; xxxvii. 14

of Jehovah! O what an abominable people are these! and what a being must that God be who can have and own such for his people!

Verse 23. *I will sanctify my great name*] By changing your hearts and your conduct, I shall show my hatred to vice, and my love to holiness: but it is not *for your sakes*, but for *my holy name's sake*, that I shall do you good in your latter days.

Verse 24. *I will take you from among the heathen*] This does not relate to the restoration from Babylon merely. The Jews are at this day scattered in all *Heathen, Mohammedan*, and *Christian countries*. From these they are to be gathered, and brought to repossess their own land.

Verse 25. *Then*—at the time of this great restoration—*will I sprinkle clean water upon you*—the *truly cleansing water;* the influences of the HOLY SPIRIT typified by *water*, whose property it is to *cleanse, whiten, purify, refresh*, render *healthy* and *fruitful*.

From all your filthiness] From every sort of external and internal abomination and pollution.

And from all your idols] False gods, false worship, false opinions, and false hopes.

Will I cleanse you.] Entirely separate you.

Verse 26. *A new heart also will I give you*] I will change the whole of your infected nature; and give you new appetites, new passions; or, at least, the old ones *purified* and *refined*. The *heart* is generally understood to mean all the *affections* and *passions*.

And a new spirit will I put within you] I will renew your *minds*, also *enlighten* your *understanding, correct* your *judgment*, and *refine* your *will;* so that you shall have a *new spirit* to actuate your new *heart*.

I will take away the stony heart] That heart that is *hard, impenetrable*, and *cold;* the affections and passions that are unyielding, frozen to good, unaffected by heavenly things; that are slow to credit the words of God. I will entirely remove this heart: it is the opposite to that which I have promised you; and you cannot have the *new heart* and the *old heart* at the same time.

And I will give you a heart of flesh.] One that can *feel*, and that can *enjoy;* that can feel *love to God* and to *all men*, and be a proper habitation for the living God.

Verse 27. *And I will put my Spirit within you*] To keep the *heart of flesh alive*, the *feeling heart* still *sensible*, the *loving heart* still *happy*. I will *put my Spirit*, the *great principle* of light, life, and love, within you, to actuate the *new spirit*, and to influence the *new affections* and *passions;* that the *animal* spirit may not become *brutish*, that the *mental* powers become not *foolish*. I will put my Spirit within you, so that as the *new spirit* may influence the *new heart*, so will MY SPIRIT influence YOUR *new spirit*, that each may have a proper *mover;* and then all will be pure, regular, and harmonious, when *passion* is influenced by *reason*, and *reason* by the *Holy Ghost*.

And the *cause* shall be evidenced by the *effects;* for I will *cause you to walk in my statutes*—not only to *believe* and *reverence* my appointments relative to what I command you to *perform;* but ye shall *walk in them*, your *conduct* shall be regulated by them. "And ye shall keep my judgments;" whatsoever I enjoin you to avoid. And ye shall *do them*—ye shall not only *avoid* every appearance of *evil*, but keep all my ordinances and commandments unblamably.

Here is the salvation that God promises to give to restored Israel; and here is the salvation that is the birthright of every *Christian believer: the complete destruction of all sin in the soul, and the complete renewal of the heart;* no *sin* having any place *within*, and no *unrighteousness* having any place *without*.

"But where are they that are thus saved?" *Ans.* Wherever *true Christians* are to be found. "But I know many *true Christians* that have not this salvation, but daily mourn over their evil hearts?" *Ans.* They may be *sincere*, but they are not *true Christians;* i. e., such as are saved from their sins; the true Christians are those who are *filled* with the *nature* and *Spirit of Christ*. But I will ask a question in my turn: "Do those you mention think it a *virtue* to be always *mourning* over their *impurities?*" Most certainly. Then it is a pity they were not *better instructed*. It is right they should *mourn* while they feel an *impure heart;* but why do they not apply to that *blood which cleanses from all unrighteousness*, and to that *Spirit* which *cleanses the very thoughts of the heart by his inspiration?* Many employ that time in *brooding* and

A. M. cir. 3417
B. C. cir. 587
Ol. XLVIII. 2
Tarquinii Prisci,
R. Roman.,
cir. annum 30

28 [n]And ye shall dwell in
the land that I gave to your
fathers; [o]and ye shall be my
people, and I will be your God.
29 I will also [p]save you from all your uncleannesses: and [q]I will call for the corn, and
will increase it, and [r]lay no famine upon you.
30 [s]And I will multiply the fruit of the
tree, and the increase of the field, that ye
shall receive no more reproach of famine
among the heathen.
31 Then [t]shall ye remember your own evil
ways, and your doings that *were* not good,
and [u]shall loathe yourselves in your own sight
for your iniquities and for your abominations.
32 [v]Not for your sakes do I *this,* saith the
Lord GOD, be it known unto you: be ashamed
and confounded for your own ways, O house
of Israel.
33 Thus saith the Lord GOD; In the day
that I shall have cleansed you from all your
iniquities I will also cause *you* to dwell in
the cities, [w]and the wastes
shall be builded.
34 And the desolate land
shall be tilled, whereas it lay
desolate in the sight of all that passed by.
35 And they shall say, This land that was
desolate is become like the garden of [x]Eden;
and the waste and desolate and ruined cities
are become fenced, *and* are inhabited.
36 Then the heathen that are left round
about you shall know that I the LORD build
the ruined *places, and* plant that that was
desolate: [y]I the LORD have spoken *it,* and I
will do *it.*
37 Thus saith the Lord GOD; [z]I will yet
for this be inquired of by the house of Israel,
to do *it* for them; I will [a]increase them with
men like a flock.
38 As the [b]holy flock, as the flock of Jerusalem in her solemn feasts; so shall the waste
cities be filled with flocks of men: and they
shall know that I *am* the LORD.

[n]Chap. xxviii. 25; xxxvii. 25——[o]Jer. xxx. 22; chap. xi. 20; xxxvii. 27——[p]Matt. i. 21; Rom. xi. 26——[q]See Psa. cv. 16——[r]Chap. xxxiv. 29——[s]Chap. xxxiv. 27
[t]Ch. xvi. 61, 63——[u]Lev. xxvi. 39; ch. vi. 9; xx. 43

[v]Deut. ix. 5; ver. 22——[w]Ver. 10——[x]Isa. li. 3; chap. xxviii. 13; Joel ii. 3——[y]Chap. xvii. 24; xxii. 14; xxxvii. 14——[z]See chap. xiv. 3; xx. 3, 31——[a]Ver. 10
[b]Heb. *flock of holy things*

mourning over their impure hearts, which should be spent in prayer and faith before God, that their impurities might be washed away. In what a state of nonage are many members of the Christian Church!

Verse 28. *Ye shall be my people*] Wholly given up to me in body, soul, and spirit.

And I will be your God.] To fill you with love, joy, peace, meekness, gentleness, long-suffering, fidelity, and goodness, to *occupy* your *whole soul,* and *gratify* your *every desire.*

Verse 29. *I will also save you from all your uncleannesses*] I repeat it; "I WILL save you from all your sins."

Verse 30. *Ye shall receive no more reproach of famine*] Ye shall be daily and hourly fed with the *bread that endures unto eternal life.* "But will not those get *proud,* who are *thus saved,* if there be any such? and will they not *undervalue* the *blood of the covenant,* for then they shall *not need it?*" *Ans.* Hear what the Lord saith,—

Verse 31. *Then shall ye remember your own evil ways*] Ye shall never forget that ye were once *slaves of sin,* and *sold under sin; children of the wicked one; heirs to all God's curses,* with no *hope* beyond *hell.* Such cleansed people never forget *the horrible pit* and the *miry clay* out of which they have been brought. And can they then be *proud?* No; *they loathe themselves in their own sight.* They never *forgive themselves* for having sinned against so *good a God,* and so *loving a Saviour.* And can they *undervalue* HIM by whose blood they were bought, and by whose blood they were cleansed? No! That is impossible: they *now see Jesus* as they *ought to see him;* they see him *in his splendour,* because they *feel him* in his *victory* and *triumph* over sin. To them *that thus believe he is precious,* and he was never *so precious* as *now.* As to their not *needing him* when thus saved from their sins, we may as well say, as soon may the *creation* not need the *sustaining hand of God,* because the *works are finished!* Learn this, that *as* it requires the *same power* to *sustain* creation as to *produce* it, so it requires the *same Jesus* who *cleansed* to *keep clean.* They feel that it is only through his *continued indwelling,* that they are kept *holy,* and *happy,* and *useful.* Were he to leave them the original darkness and kingdom of death would soon be restored.

Verse 35. *This land that was desolate* by sin, *is become like the garden of Eden* by righteousness.—Satan's blast is removed; God's blessing has taken place.

Verse 36. *Then the heathen*] They shall see how powerful Jehovah is, and how *fully he saves* those who come unto and worship him.

Verse 37. *Thus saith the Lord God*] In answer to the question, "Who shall have such blessings?" we say, they that *pray,* that *seek* earnestly, that *strive* to enter in at the strait gate. "Thus saith the Lord, I will yet for this be inquired of by the house of Israel." Neither *Jew* nor *Gentile* shall be thus saved who do not *earnestly pray* to God; and for *this thing;* for this *complete salvation;* this setting up of the kingdom of Christ upon earth, and particularly in their *own souls.*

Verse 38. *As the holy flock*] The *Church of Christ,* without spot, or wrinkle, or any such thing.

The flock of Jerusalem] The Jerusalem that is *from above, the city of the living God,* the *place* where *his Majesty dwells.* As they came in ancient times to the solemn national feasts, so shall they come when they have fully returned unto the Lord, and received his salvation by Christ Jesus.

I do not ask my reader's pardon for having considered this most beautiful chapter as relating, not to the restoration from the Babylonish captivity, but to the redemption under the new covenant by Jesus Christ. There is no period of the Jewish history from that time until now, to which it can be applied. It must belong to the *Gospel dispensation;* and if the *Jews* will still refuse, contradict, and blaspheme, let no *Christian* have any fellowship with them in their opposition to this *Almighty Saviour.* Let none be *indifferent* to his *salvation;* let all *plead* his *promises;* and let the *messengers of the Churches* proclaim to the Christian world a FREE, a FULL, and a PRESENT SALVATION! And may great grace rest upon themselves, and upon all their flocks!

CHAPTER XXXVII

This chapter treats of the same subject with the preceding, in a beautiful and significant vision. Under the emblem of the open valley being thickly strewed with very dry bones is represented the hopeless state of the Jews when dispersed throughout the provinces of the Chaldean empire. But God, contrary to every human probability, restores these bones to life, thereby prefiguring the restoration of that people from the Babylonish captivity, and their resettlement in the land of their forefathers, 1–14. *The prophet then makes an easy and elegant transition to the blessedness of the people of God under the Gospel dispensation, in the plenitude of its manifestation; when the genuine converts to Christianity, the* spiritual *Israel, shall be no longer under the domination of heathen and anti-christian rulers, but shall be collected together into one visible kingdom, and constitute but one flock under one Shepherd,* 15–28. *The vision of the dry bones reviving is considered by some as having a remote view to the general resurrection.*

A. M. cir. 3417
B. C. cir. 587
Ol. XLVIII. 2
Tarquinii Prisci, R. Roman., cir. annum 30

THE [a]hand of the LORD was upon me, and carried me out [b]in the spirit of the LORD, and set me down in the midst of the valley which *was* full of bones,
2 And caused me to pass by them round about: and, behold, *there were* very many in the open [c]valley; and, lo, *they were* very dry.
3 And he said unto me, Son of man, can these bones live? And I answered, O Lord GOD, [d]thou knowest.
4 Again he said unto me, Prophesy upon these bones, and say unto them, O ye dry bones, hear the word of the LORD.
5 Thus saith the Lord GOD unto these bones; Behold, I will [e]cause breath to enter into you, and ye shall live:

A. M. cir. 3417
B. C. cir. 587
Ol. XLVIII. 2
Tarquinii Prisci, R. Roman., cir. annum 30

6 And I will lay sinews upon you, and will bring up flesh upon you, and cover you with skin, and put breath in you, and ye shall live; [f]and ye shall know that I *am* the LORD.
7 So I prophesied as I was commanded; and as I prophesied, there was a noise, and behold a shaking, and the bones came together, bone to his bone.
8 And when I beheld, lo, the sinews and the flesh came up upon them, and the skin covered them above: but *there was* no breath in them.

---

[a]Ch. i. 3——[b]Ch. iii. 14; viii. 3; xi. 24; Luke iv. 1 v. 21; Rom. iv. 17; 2 Cor. i. 9——[e]Psa. civ. 30; ver. 9
[c]Or, *champaign*——[d]Deut. xxxii. 36; 1 Sam. ii. 6; John
[f]Chap. vi. 7; xxxv. 12; Joel ii. 27; iii. 17

NOTES ON CHAP. XXXVII

Verse 1. *The hand of the Lord was upon me*] The prophetic influence was communicated.

And carried me out in the spirit] Or, And the Lord brought me out in the spirit; that is, a spiritual vision, in which all these things were doubtless transacted.

The valley which was *full of bones*] This vision of the *dry bones* was designed, *first,* as an emblem of the then *wretched* state of the Jews; *secondly,* of the general resurrection of the body.

Verse 3. *Can these bones live?*] Is it possible that the persons whose bones these are can return to life?

Verse 4. *Prophesy upon these bones*] Declare to your miserable countrymen the gracious designs of the Lord; show them that their state, however deplorable, is not hopeless.

Verse 5. *Behold, I will cause breath*] רוח *ruach* signifies both *soul, breath,* and *wind;* and sometimes the *Spirit of God. Soul* is its proper meaning in this vision, where it refers to the bones: "I will cause the SOUL to enter into you."

Verse 6. *I will lay sinews upon you*] Observe the progress: 1. Here are the *bones.* 2. The *ligaments,* called here *sinews,* are to be added in order to *unite* the bones, that the *skeleton* might be complete. 3. The *flesh* (the whole *muscular system,* the *subjacent* and *superjacent muscles,* including the *arterial* and *venous system*) clothes this skeleton. 4. The *skin* (the *dermis* and *epidermis,* or *cutis* and *cuticle*) envelopes the whole of these muscles or flesh; and now these bodies are in the state that the body of Adam was before it received the animal and intellectual principle from God. 5. *There was no breath in them*—they had not yet received their *souls.* 6. The *wind,* רוח *ruach,* the *soul,* came into them. They were endued with animal and intellectual life; and they *arose* and evidenced a complete restoration to life, and began to perform its functions, ver. 10.

A. M. cir. 3417
B. C. cir. 587
Ol. XLVIII. 2
Tarquinii Prisci,
R. Roman.,
cir. annum 30

9 Then said he unto me,
Prophesy unto the [g]wind, prophesy, son of man, and say to
the wind, Thus saith the Lord
God; [h]Come from the four winds, O breath, and breathe upon these slain, that they may live.
10 So I prophesied as he commanded me, [i]and the breath came into them, and they lived, and stood up upon their feet, an exceeding great army.
11 Then he said unto me, Son of man, these bones are the whole house of Israel: behold, they say, [k]Our bones are dried, and our hope is lost: we are cut off for our parts.
12 Therefore prophesy and say unto them, Thus saith the Lord God; Behold, [l]O my people, I will open your graves, and cause you to come up out of your graves, and [m]bring you into the land of Israel.

A. M. cir. 3417
B. C. cir. 587
Ol. XLVIII. 3
Tarquinii Prisci,
R. Roman.,
cir. annum 30

13 And ye shall know that I *am* the Lord, when I have opened your graves, O my people, and brought you up out of your graves,
14 And [n]shall put my Spirit in you, and ye shall live, and I shall place you in your own land: then shall ye know that I the Lord have spoken *it*, and performed *it*, saith the Lord.
15 The word of the Lord came again unto me, saying,
16 Moreover, thou son of man, [o]take thee one stick, and write upon it, For Judah, and for [p]the children of Israel his companions: then take another stick, and write

[g]Or, *breath*——[h]Psa. civ. 30; ver. 5——[i]Rev. xi. 11 [k]Psalm cxli. 7; Isa. xlix. 14——[l]Isa. xxvi. 19; Hos. xiii. 14

[m]Chap. xxxvi. 24; ver. 25——[n]Chap. xxxvi. 27 [o]See Num. xvii. 2——[p]2 Chron. xi. 12, 13, 16; xv. 9; xxx. 11, 18

Verse 9. *Prophesy unto the wind*] רוח *ruach*. Address thyself to the *soul*, and command it to enter into these well-organized bodies, that they may live.

Come from the four winds] Souls, *come from all parts* where ye are scattered; and reanimate these bodies from which ye have been so long separated. The *four winds* signify *all parts*—in *every direction.* Literally it is, "Souls, come from the four souls;" "Breath, come from the four breaths;" or, "Wind, come from the four winds." But here רוח *ruach* has both of its most general meanings, *wind* or *breath*, and *soul.*

Verse 11. *These bones are the whole house of Israel*] That is, their state is represented by *these bones;* and their restoration to their own land is represented by the *revivification* of these bones.

Verse 12. *I will open your graves*] Here is a pointed allusion to the *general resurrection;* a doctrine properly credited and understood by the Jews, and to which our Lord refers, John v. 25, 28, 29: "The hour is coming when they that are in their graves shall hear his voice, and come forth."

And cause you to come up out of your graves] I am determined that ye shall be restored; so that were ye even *in your graves*, as mankind at the general resurrection, yet my all-powerful *voice* shall *call you forth.*

Verse 13. *When I have opened your graves*] When I shall have done for you what was *beyond* your *hope*, and deemed *impossible*, then shall ye know that I am *Jehovah.*

Verse 14. *And shall put my Spirit*] רוחי *ruchi.* Here רוח *ruach* is taken for the *Holy Ghost.* They were *living souls, animal* and *intellectual beings*, when they had received their souls, as mentioned above: but they could only become *spiritual, holy*, and *obedient* creatures by the *Spirit of God* actuating *their spirits.* See the notes on chap. xxxvi. 25, 26, 27.

Three *degrees* or *processes* have been remarked in this mystic vision. When the prophet was commanded to *prophesy*—to foretell, on the authority of God, that there should be a restoration to their own land,—

1. There was a *noise*, which was followed by a general *shaking*, during which the *bones* became arranged and united.

2. The *flesh* and *skin* came upon them, so that the *dry bones* were no longer seen.

3. The *spirit* or *soul* came into them, and they *stood up* perfectly vivified.

Perhaps these might be illustrated by *three* periods of time, which marked the *regeneration* of the *Jewish polity.*

1. The *publication* of the *edict of Cyrus* in behalf of the Jews, which caused a *general shaking* or *stir* among the people, so that the *several families* began to *approach each other.* and prepare for their return to Judea, Ezra i. 2, 3. But though partially restored, they were obliged to discontinue the rebuilding of their temple.

2. The *edict* published by *Darius* in the *second* year of his reign, Ezra iv. 23, 24, which removed the impediments thrown in the way of the Jews. Ezra vi. 6, 7, &c.

3. The *mission of Nehemiah*, with orders from Artaxerxes to complete the building of the temple and the city, Neh. ii. 7, &c. Then the Jews *became a great army*, and found themselves in sufficient force to defend themselves and city against all their enemies.

As to the *spiritual uses* of this curious vision, I must leave them to preachers. I have given the *literal* meaning, and what the different parts refer to; and if they found their observations on these, they may profit their hearers.

Verse 16. *Son of man, take thee one stick*] The *two sticks* mentioned in this symbolical transaction represented, as the text declares, the two kingdoms of Israel and Judah, which were formed in the days of Rehoboam, and continued distinct till the time of the captivity. The kingdom of *Judah* was composed of the tribes of *Judah* and *Benjamin*, with the *Levites;* all the rest went off in the schism with Jero-

A. M. cir. 3417
B. C. cir. 587
Ol. XLVIII. 2
Tarquinii Prisci,
R. Roman.,
cir. annum 30

upon it, For Joseph, the stick
of Ephraim, and *for* all the
house of Israel his companions:
17 And [q]join the one to another into one
stick, and they shall become one in thine
hand.
18 And when the children of thy people
shall speak unto thee, saying, [r]Wilt thou not
show us what thou *meanest* by these?
19 [s]Say unto them, Thus saith the Lord
GOD; Behold, I will take [t]the stick of Joseph,
which *is* in the hand of Ephraim, and the
tribes of Israel his fellows, and will put them
with him, *even* with the stick of Judah, and
make them one stick, and they shall be one
in mine hand.
20 And the sticks whereon thou writest
shall be in thine hand [u]before their eyes.
21 And say unto them, Thus saith the Lord
GOD; Behold, [v]I will take the children of
Israel from among the heathen, whither they
be gone, and will gather them on every side,
and bring them into their own land:
22 And I[w]will make them one nation in the
land upon the mountains of Israel; and [x]one
king shall be king to them all: and they shall
be no more two nations, neither shall they be
divided into two kingdoms any more at all:
23 [y]Neither shall they defile themselves any
more with their idols, nor
with their detestable things,
nor with any of their transgressions: but [z]I will save them
out of all their dwelling-places, wherein they
have sinned, and will cleanse them: so shall
they be my people, and I will be their God.
24 And [a]David my servant *shall be* king
over them; and [b]they all shall have one shepherd: [c]they shall also walk in my judgments,
and observe my statutes, and do them.
25 [d]And they shall dwell in the land that I
have given unto Jacob my servant, wherein
your fathers have dwelt; and they shall
dwell therein, *even* they, and their children,
and their children's children [e]for ever: and
[f]my servant David *shall be* their prince for
ever.
26 Moreover I will make a [g]covenant of
peace with them; it shall be an everlasting
covenant with them: and I will place them,
and [h]multiply them, and will set my [i]sanctu-
ary in the midst of them for evermore.
27 [k]My tabernacle also shall be with them:
yea, I will be [l]their God, and they shall be
my people.
28 [m]And the heathen shall know that I the
LORD do [n]sanctify Israel, when my sanctuary shall be in the midst of them for evermore.

[q]See ver. 22, 24——[r]Ch. xii. 9; xxiv. 19——[s]Zech. x. 6 [t]Ver. 16, 17——[u]Ch. xii. 3——[v]Ch. xxxvi. 24——[w]Isa. xi. 13; Jer. iii. 18; l. 4; Hos. i. 11——[x]Ch. xxxiv. 23, 24; John x. 16——[y]Ch. xxxvi. 25——[z]Ch. xxxvi. 28, 29 [a]Isa. xl. 11; Jer. xxiii. 5; xxx. 9; ch. xxxiv. 23, 24; Hosea iii. 5; Luke i. 32——[b]Ver. 22; John x. 16

[c]Ch. xxxvi. 27——[d]Ch. xxxvi. 28——[e]Isa. lx. 21; Joel iii. 20; Amos ix. 15——[f]Ver. 24; John xii. 34——[g]Psa. lxxxix. 3; Isa. lv. 3; Jer. xxxii. 40; ch. xxxiv. 25——[h]Ch. xxxvi. 10, 37——[i]2 Cor. vi. 16——[k]Lev. xxvi. 11, 12; chap. xliii. 7; John i. 14——[l]Chap. xi. 20; xiv. 11; xxxvi. 28——[m]Chap. xxxvi. 23——[n]Chap. xx. 12

boam, and formed the kingdom of Israel. Though some out of those tribes did rejoin themselves to Judah, yet no *whole tribe* ever returned to that kingdom. Common sufferings in their captivity became the means of reviving a kinder feeling; and to encourage this, God promises that he will reunite them, and restore them to their own land; and that there shall no more be any divisions or feuds among them. To represent this in such a way as would make it a subject of *thought*, *reflection*, and *inquiry*, the prophet is ordered to take the *two sticks* mentioned above, to *write on them* the distinguishing names of the divided kingdoms, and then by a *notch*, *dovetail*, *glue*, or some such method, to unite them both before the people. He did so; and on their inquiry, showed them the full meaning of this symbolical action.

Verse 19. *The stick of Joseph, which* is *in the hand of Ephraim*] Jeroboam, the first king of the ten tribes, was an *Ephraimite*. *Joseph* represents the ten tribes in general; they were in the hand of *Ephraim*, that is, *under the government of Jeroboam*.

Verse 22. *I will make them one nation*] There was no distinction after the return from Babylon.

And one king shall be king to them all] Politically speaking, they never had a *king* from that day to this; and the grand junction and government spoken of here must refer to another time—to that in which they shall be brought into the Christian Church with the fulness of the Gentiles; when JESUS, the *King of kings* and *Lord of lords*, shall rule over all.

Verse 24. *And David my servant* shall be *King*] That this refers to *Jesus Christ*, see proved, chap. xxxiv. 23.

Verse 25. *The land that I have given unto Jacob my servant*] Jacob means here the *twelve tribes;* and the *land given to them* was the whole land of *Palestine;* consequently, the promise states that, when they return, they are to possess the whole of the *Promised Land*.

Verse 26. *Covenant of peace*] See this explained chap. xxxiv. 25.

Verse 27. *My tabernacle*] Jesus Christ, the true tabernacle, in whom dwelt all the fulness of the Godhead bodily.

CHAPTER XXXVIII

The sublime prophecy contained in this and the following chapter relates to Israel's victory over Gog, and is very obscure. It begins with representing a prodigious armament of many nations combined together under the conduct of Gog, with the intention of overwhelming the Jews, after having been for some time resettled in their land subsequent to their return from the Babylonish captivity, 1–9. *These enemies are farther represented as making themselves sure of the spoil,* 10–13. *But in this critical conjuncture when Israel, to all human appearance, was about to be swallowed up by her enemies, God most graciously appears, to execute by terrible judgments the vengeance threatened against these formidable adversaries of his people,* 14–16. *The prophet, in terms borrowed from human passions, describes, with awful emphasis, the fury of Jehovah as coming up to his face; and the effects of it so dreadful, as to make all the animate and inanimate creation tremble, and even to convulse with terror the whole frame of nature,* 17–23.

A. M. cir. 3417
B. C. cir. 587
Ol. XLVIII. 2
Tarquinii Prisci,
R. Roman.,
cir. annum 30

AND the word of the LORD
came unto me, saying,
2 [a]Son of man, [b]set thy face
against [c]Gog, the land of Ma-
gog, [d]the chief prince of [e]Meshech and Tubal,
and prophesy against him,
3 And say, Thus saith the Lord GOD; Behold, I *am* against thee, O Gog, the chief
prince of Meshech and Tubal:
4 And [f]I will turn thee back, and put hooks
into thy jaws, and I will bring thee forth,
and all thine army, horses and horsemen, [g]all
of them clothed with all sorts *of armour, even*
a great company *with* bucklers
and shields, all of them
handling swords:
5 Persia, Ethiopia, and [h]Libya
with them; all of them with shield and helmet.
6 [i]Gomer, and all his bands; the house of
[k]Togarmah of the north quarters, and all his
bands: *and* many people with thee.
7 [l]Be thou prepared, and prepare for thyself,
thou, and all thy company that are assembled
unto thee, and be thou a guard unto them.
8 [m]After many [n]days thou shalt be visited:
in the latter years thou shalt come into the

A. M. cir. 3417
B. C. cir. 587
Ol. XLVIII. 2
Tarquinii Prisci,
R. Roman.,
cir. annum 30

[a]Chap. xxxix. 1——[b]Chap. xxxv. 2, 3——[c]Rev. xx. 8——[d]Or, *prince of the chief*——[e]Chap. xxxii. 26——[f]2 Kings xix. 28; chap. xxix. 4; xxxix. 2——[g]Ch. xxiii. 12

[h]Or, *Phut;* chap. xxvii. 10; xxx. 5——[i]Gen. x. 2 [k]Chap. xxvii. 14——[l]Like Isa. viii. 9, 10; Jer. xlvi. 3, 4, 14; li. 12——[m]Gen. xlix. 1; Deut. iv. 30; ver. 16 [n]Isa. xxix. 6

NOTES ON CHAP. XXXVIII

Verse 2. *Son of man, set thy face against Gog, the land of Magog*] This is allowed to be the most difficult prophecy in the Old Testament. It is difficult to us, because we know not the *king* nor *people* intended by it: but I am satisfied they were well known by these names in the time that the prophet wrote.

I have already remarked in the *introduction* to this book that there are but *two* opinions on this subject that appear to be at all probable: 1. That which makes GOG *Cambyses*, king of *Persia;* and, 2. That which makes him ANTIOCHUS EPIPHANES, king of *Syria*. And between these *two* (for one or other is supposed to be the person intended) men are much divided.

Calmet, one of the most judicious commentators that ever wrote on the Bible, declares for *Cambyses;* and supports his opinion, in opposition to all others, by many arguments.

Mr. *Mede* supposes the *Americans* are meant, who were originally colonies of the Scythians, who were descendants of *Magog*, son of *Japheth. Houbigant* declares for the *Scythians*, whose neighbours were the people of *Rosh, Meshech*, and *Tubal*, that is the *Russians, Muscovites*, and *Tybareni* or *Cappadocians*. Several eminent critics espouse this opinion. *Rabbi David Kimchi* says the *Christians* and *Turks* are meant: and of later opinions there are several, founded in the ocean of conjecture. *Calmet* says expressly, that GOG is *Cambyses*, king of Persia, who on his return from the land of Egypt, died in *Judea*. The Rev. *David Martin*, pastor of the Waloòn church at Utrecht, concludes, after examining all previous opinions, that *Antiochus Epiphanes*, the great enemy of the Israelites, is alone intended here; and that *Gog*, which signifies *covered*, is an allusion to the well-known *character* of Antiochus, whom historians describe as an *artful, cunning*, and *dissembling* man. See Dan. viii. 23, 25; xi. 23, 27, 32. *Magog* he supposes to mean the country of *Syria*. Of this opinion the following quotation from *Pliny*, Hist. Nat., lib. v., c. 23, seems a proof; who, speaking of Cœle-Syria, says: Cœle habet Apamiam Marsyia amne divisam a Nazarinorum Tetrarchia. Bambycem quam alio nomine Hierapolis vocatur, Syris vero Magog. "Cœle-Syria has Apamia separated from the tetrarchy of the Nazarenes by the river Marsyia; and Bambyce, otherwise called Hierapolis; but by the Syrians, MAGOG."

I shall at present examine the text by this latter opinion.

Chief prince of Meshech and Tubal] These probably mean the auxiliary forces, over whom Antiochus was supreme; they were the *Muscovites* and *Cappadocians*.

Verse 4. *I will turn thee back*] Thy enterprise shall fail.

Verse 5. *Persia*] That a part of this country was tributary to *Antiochus*, see 1 Macc. iii. 31.

Ethiopia, and Libya] That these were auxiliaries of Antiochus is evident from Dan. xi. 43: "The Libyans and Ethiopians shall be at his steps."

Verse 6. *Gomer, and all his bands; the house of Togarmah*] The *Cimmerians* and *Turcomanians*, and other northern nations.— *Calmet.*

Verse 8. *In the latter years thou shalt come*] This was fulfilled about *four hundred* years after.—*Martin*. The expedition of *Cambyses* against Egypt was about *twelve* years after the return of the Jews from Babylon.—*Calmet.*

A. M. cir. 3417
B. C. cir. 587
Ol. XLVIII. 2
Tarquinii Prisci,
R. Roman.,
cir. annum 30

land *that is* brought back from the sword, [n]*and is* gathered out of many people, against [o]the mountains of Israel, which have been always waste: but it is brought forth out of the nations, and they shall [p]dwell safely all of them.

9 Thou shalt ascend and come [q]like a storm, thou shalt be [r]like a cloud to cover the land, thou, and all thy bands, and many people with thee.

10 Thus saith the Lord GOD; It shall also come to pass *that* at the same time shall things come into thy mind, and thou shalt [s]think an evil thought:

11 And thou shalt say, I will go up to the land of unwalled villages; I will [t]go to them that are at rest, [u]that dwell [v]safely, all of them dwelling without walls, and having neither bars nor gates,

12 [w]To take a spoil, and to take a prey, to turn thine hand upon [x]the desolate places *that are now* inhabited, [y]and upon the people *that are* gathered out of the nations, which have gotten cattle and goods, that dwell in the [z]midst of the land.

13 [a]Sheba, and [b]Dedan, and the merchants [c]of Tarshish, with all [d]the young lions thereof, shall say unto thee, Art thou come to take a spoil? hast thou gathered thy company to take a prey? to carry away silver and gold, to take away cattle and goods, to take a great spoil?

14 Therefore, son of man, prophesy and say unto Gog, Thus saith the Lord GOD; [e]In that day when my people of Israel [f]dwelleth safely, shalt thou not know *it?*

A. M. cir. 3417
B. C. cir 587
Ol. XLVIII. 2
Tarquinii Prisci,
R. Roman.,
cir. annum 30

15 [g]And thou shalt come from thy place out of the north parts, thou, [h]and many people with thee, all of them riding upon horses, a great company, and a mighty army:

16 [i]And thou shalt come up against my people of Israel, as a cloud to cover the land; [k]it shall be in the latter days, and I will bring thee against my land, [l]that the heathen may know me, when I shall be sanctified in thee, O Gog, before their eyes.

17 Thus saith the Lord GOD; *Art* thou he of whom I have spoken in old time, [m]by my servants the prophets of Israel, which prophesied in those days *many* years that I would bring thee against them?

18 And it shall come to pass at the same time when Gog shall come against the land of Israel, saith the Lord GOD, *that* my fury shall come up in my face.

19 For [n]in my jealousy [o]*and* in the fire of my wrath have I spoken, [p]Surely in that day there shall be a great shaking in the land of Israel;

20 So that [q]the fishes of the sea, and the fowls of the heaven, and the beasts of the field, and all creeping things that creep upon the earth, and all the men that *are* upon the face of the earth, shall shake at my presence, [r]and the mountains shall be thrown down, and

[n]Ver. 12; chap. xxxiv. 13——[o]Chap. xxxvi. 1, 4, 8——[p]Jer. xxiii. 6; chap. xxviii. 26; xxxiv. 25, 28; ver. 11——[q]Isa. xxviii. 2——[r]Jer. iv. 13; ver. 16——[s]Or, *conceive a mischievous purpose*——[t]Jer. xlix. 31——[u]Ver. 8——[v]Or, *confidently*——[w]Heb. *To spoil the spoil, and to prey the prey;* chap. xxix. 19——[x]Chap. xxxvi. 34, 35——[y]Ver. 8——[z]Heb. *navel;* Judg. ix. 37

[a]Chap. xxvii. 22, 23——[b]Chap. xxvii. 15, 20——[c]Ch. xxvii. 12——[d]See chap. x. 3, 5——[e]Isa. iv. 1——[f]Ver. 8——[g]Chap. xxxix. 2——[h]Ver. 6——[i]Ver. 9——[k]Ver. 8——[l]Exod. xiv. 4; chap. xxxvi. 23; xxxix. 21——[m]Heb. *by the hands*——[n]Chap. xxxvi. 5, 6; xxxix. 25——[o]Psa. lxxxix. 46——[p]Hag. ii. 6, 7; Rev. xvi. 18——[q]Hos. iv. 3——[r]Jer. iv. 24; Nah. i. 5, 6

Verse 9. *Thou shalt ascend and come like a storm*] It is observable that Antiochus is thus spoken of by Daniel, chap. xi. 40: *The king of the north*—Antiochus, *shall come against him* (the king of the south is the king of Egypt) *like a whirlwind.*

Verse 10. *Shall things come into thy mind, and thou shalt think an evil thought*] Antiochus purposed to invade and destroy *Egypt,* as well as *Judea;* see Dan. xi. 31, 32, 36. This *Calmet* interprets of Cambyses, his cruelties in Egypt, and his evil design to destroy the Israelites.

Verse 12. *To take a spoil—and a prey*] When Antiochus took Jerusalem he gave the pillage of it to his soldiers, and spoiled the temple of its riches, which were immense. See *Joseph.* WAR, B. i. c. 1.

Verse 13. *Sheba, and Dedan*] The Arabians, anciently great plunderers; and *Tarshish,* the inhabitants of the famous isle of Tartessus, the most noted merchants of the time. They are here represented as coming to Antiochus before he undertook the expedition, and *bargaining for the spoils of the Jews. Art thou come to take a spoil, to carry away silver and gold, cattle and goods?*

Verse 16. *When I shall be sanctified in thee, O Gog*] By the defeat of his troops under *Lysias,* his general. 1 Mac. iii. 32, 33, &c., and chap. vi. 6.

Verse 17. Art *thou he of whom I have spoken in old time*] This prophecy concerning Antiochus and the Jews was delievered about *four hundred* years before the events took place.—*Martin. Calmet* maintains that Cambyses is spoken of, and refers to ancient prophecies, especially Isa. xiv., xv., xvi. 20, 21.

A. M. cir. 3417
B. C. cir. 587
Ol. XLVIII. 2
Tarquinii Prisci,
R. Roman.,
cir. annum 30

the [s]steep places shall fall,
and every wall shall fall to
the ground.
21 And I will [t]call for [u]a
sword against him throughout all my mountains, saith the Lord God: [v]every man's sword
shall be against his brother.
22 And I will [w]plead against him with [x]pes-
tilence and with blood; and [y]I will rain upon
him, and upon his bands, and
upon the many people that
are with him, an overflowing
rain, and [z]great hailstones,
fire, and brimstone.
23 Thus will I magnify myself, and [a]sanc-
tify myself; [b]and I will be known in the eyes
of many nations, and they shall know that I
am the LORD.

A. M. cir. 3417
B. C. cir. 587
Ol. XLVIII. 2
Tarquinii Prisci,
R. Roman.,
cir. annum 30

[s]Or, *towers*, or *stairs*——[t]Psa. cv. 16——[u]Chap. xiv. 17——[v]Judg. vii. 22; 1 Sam. xiv. 20; 2 Chron. xx. 23——[w]Isa. lxvi. 16; Jer. xxv. 31——[x]Ch. v. 17——[y]Psa. xi. 6; Isa. xxix. 6; xxx. 30——[z]Chap. xiii. 11; Rev. xvi. 21——[a]Chap. xxxvi. 23——[b]Psa. ix. 16; chap. xxxvii. 28; xxxix. 7; ver. 16

Verse 21. *I will call for a sword against him*] Meaning *Judas Maccabeus*, who defeated his army under Lysias, making a horrible carnage. —*Martin*. Cambyses had no wars in the mountains of Israel.

Verse 22. *Great hailstones, fire, and brimstone.*] These are probably figurative expressions, to signify that the whole tide of the war should be against him, and that his defeat and slaughter should be great. Abp. *Newcome* supposes all the above prophecy remains yet to be fulfilled. Where such eminent scribes are divided, who shall decide!

CHAPTER XXXIX

The prophet goes on to denounce the Divine judgments against Gog and his army, 1–7; *and describes their dreadful slaughter,* 8–10, *and burial,* 11–16, *in terms so very lofty and comprehensive, as must certainly denote some very extraordinary interposition of Providence in behalf of the Jews. And to amplify the matter still more, the prophet, with peculiar art and propriety, delays the summoning of all the birds and beasts of prey in nature to feast on the slain, (in allusion to the custom of feasting on the remainder of sacrifices,) till after the greater multitudes are buried; to intimate that even the remainder, and as it were the stragglers of such mighty hosts, would be more than sufficient to satisfy their utmost rapacity,* 17–20. *The remaining verses contain a prediction of the great blessedness of the people of God in Gospel times, and of the stability of the kingdom of Christ,* 21–29. *It will be proper to remark that the great northern expedition against the natural Israel, described in this and the preceding chapter, is, from its striking resemblance in the main particulars, put by the writer of the Apocalypse,* (chap. xx. 7–10,) *for a much more formidable armament of a multitude of nations in the four quarters of the earth against the pure Christian Church,* the MYSTICAL Israel; *an event still extremely remote, and which it is thought shall immediately precede the destruction of the world by fire, and the general judgment.*

A. M. cir. 3417
B. C. cir. 587
Ol. XLVIII. 2
Tarquinii Prisci,
R. Roman.,
cir. annum 30

THEREFORE, [a]thou son
of man, prophesy against
Gog, and say, Thus saith
the Lord GOD; Behold, I *am*
against thee, O Gog, the chief prince of
Meshech and Tubal;
2 And I will turn thee back, and [b]leave but
the sixth part of thee, [c]and will cause thee
to come up from [d]the north parts, and
will bring thee upon the mountains of
Israel:
3 And I will smite thy bow out of thy left
hand, and will cause thine
arrows to fall out of thy right
hand.
4 [e]Thou shalt fall upon the
mountains of Israel, thou, and
all thy bands, and the people that *is* with
thee: [f]I will give thee unto the ravenous
birds of every [g]sort, and *to* the beasts of the
field [h]to be devoured.
5 Thou shalt fall upon [i]the open field: for
I have spoken *it*, saith the Lord GOD.
6 [k]And I will send a fire on Magog, and

A. M. cir. 3417
B. C. cir. 587
Ol. XLVIII. 2
Tarquinii Prisci,
R. Roman.,
cir. annum 30

[a]Ch. xxxviii. 2, 3——[b]Or, *strike thee with six plagues;* or, *draw thee back with a hook of six teeth,* as chap. xxxviii. 4——[c]Chap. xxxviii. 15——[d]Heb. *the sides of the north*——[e]Chap. xxxviii. 21; ver. 17——[f]Chap. xxxiii. 27——[g]Heb. *wing*——[h]Heb. *to devour*——[i]Heb. *the face of the field*——[k]Chap. xxxviii. 22; Amos i. 4

NOTES ON CHAP. XXXIX

Verse 2. *And leave but the sixth part of thee*] The margin has, *strike thee with six plagues;* or, *draw thee back with a hook of six teeth.*

Verse 3. *I will smite thy bow out of thy left hand*] The *Persians* whom Antiochus had in his army, chap. xxxviii. 5, were famous as *archers*, and they may be intended here. The *bow* is held by the *left hand;* the *arrow* is pulled and discharged by the *right.*

Verse 6. *I will send a fire on Magog*] On Syria. I will destroy the Syrian troops.

And among them that dwell carelessly in the isles] The auxiliary troops that came to Antiochus from the borders of the Euxine Sea.—*Martin.*

A. M. cir. 3417
B. C. cir. 587
Ol. XLVIII. 2
Tarquinii Prisci,
R. Roman.,
cir. annum 30

among them that dwell [l]care-
lessly in [m]the isles: and they
shall know that I *am* the
LORD.
7 [n]So will I make my holy name known in
the midst of my people Israel; and I will not
let them [o]pollute my holy name any more:
[p]and the heathen shall know that I *am* the
LORD, the Holy One in Israel.
8 [q]Behold, it is come, and it is done, saith
the Lord GOD; this *is* the day [r]whereof I
have spoken.
9 And they that dwell in the cities of Israel
shall go forth, and shall set on fire and burn
the weapons, both the shields and the bucklers, the bows and the arrows, and the [s]hand-
staves, and the spears, and they shall [t]burn
them with fire seven years:
10 So that they shall take
no wood out of the field,
neither cut down *any* out of
the forests; for they shall
burn the weapons with fire: [u]and they shall
spoil those that spoiled them, and rob those
that robbed them, saith the Lord GOD.
11 And it shall come to pass in that day,
that I will give unto Gog a place there of
graves in Israel, the valley of the passengers
on the east of the sea; and it shall stop the
[v]*noses* of the passengers: and there shall they
bury Gog and all his multitude: and they
shall call *it* The valley of [w]Hamon-gog.
12 And seven months shall the house of
Israel be burying of them, [x]that they may
cleanse the land.
13 Yea, all the people of the land shall

A. M. cir. 3417
B. C. cir. 587
Ol. XLVIII. 2
Tarquinii Prisci,
R. Roman.,
cir. annum 30

[l]Or, *confidently*——[m]Psa. lxxii. 10——[n]Ver. 22——[o]Lev. xviii. 21; chap. xx. 39——[p]Chap. xxxviii. 16, 23——[q]Rev. xvi. 17; xxi. 6——[r]Chap. xxxviii. 17

[s]Or, *javelins*——[t]Or, *make a fire of them*——[u]Isa. xiv. 2——[v]Or, *mouths*——[w]That is, *The multitude of Gog*——[x]Deut. xxi. 23; ver. 14, 16

Verse 7. *In the midst of my people Israel*] This defeat of Gog is to be in Israel: and it was *there* according to this prophecy, that the immense army of Antiochus was so completely defeated.

And I will not let them *pollute my holy name any more*] See on 1 Macc. i. 11, &c., how Antiochus had *profaned the temple, insulted Jehovah and his worship*, &c. God permitted that as a scourge to his disobedient people; but now the scourger shall be scourged, and he shall *pollute the sanctuary no more.*

Verse 9. *And shall set on fire—the weapons*] The Israelites shall make bonfires and fuel of the weapons, tents, &c., which the defeated Syrians shall leave behind them, as expressive of the joy which they shall feel for the destruction of their enemies; and to keep up, in their *culinary consumption*, the memory of this great event.

They shall burn them with fire seven years] These may be *figurative* expressions, after the manner of the Asiatics, whose language abounds with such descriptions. They occur every where in the prophets. As to the number *seven*, it is only a certain for an indeterminate number. But as the slaughter was great, and the *bows, arrows, quivers, shields, bucklers, handstaves*, and *spears* were in vast multitudes, it must have taken a long time to gather them up in the different parts of the *fields* of battle, and the *roads* in which the Syrians had *retreated*, throwing away their *arms* as they proceeded; so there might have been a long time employed in collecting and burning them. And as all seem to have been doomed to the fire, there might have been some found at different intervals and burned, during the *seven years* here mentioned. *Mariana*, in his History of Spain, lib. xi., c. 24, says, that after the Spaniards had given that signal overthrow to the Saracens, A. D. 1212, they found such a vast quantity of lances, javelins, and such like, that they served them for *four years* for fuel. And probably these instruments obtained by the Israelites were used in general for *culinary firewood*, and might *literally* have served them for *seven years;* so that during that time *they should take no wood out of the fields, nor out of the forests* for the purpose of *fuel*, ver. 10.

Verse 11. *The valley of the passengers on the east of the sea*] That is, of *Gennesareth*, according to the *Targum*. The valley near this lake or sea is called *the Valley of the Passengers*, because it was a great road by which the merchants and traders from Syria and other eastern countries went into Egypt; see Gen. xxxvii. 17, 25. See *Calmet* here.

There shall they bury Gog and all his multitude] Some read, "There shall they bury Gog, that is, all his multitude." Not Gog, or Antiochus himself, for he was not in this battle; but his *generals, captains*, and *soldiers*, by whom he was represented. As to *Hamon-gog*, we know no valley of this name but here. But we may understand the words thus: the place where this great slaughter was, and where the multitudes of the slain were buried, might be better called *Hamon-gog*, the *valley of the multitude of Gog*, than the *valley of passengers;* for so great was the carnage there, that the way of the passengers shall be stopped by it. See the text.

Verse 12. *And seven months*] It shall require a long time to bury the dead. This is another figurative expression; which, however, may admit of a good deal of *literal* meaning. Many of the Syrian soldiers had secreted themselves in different places during the pursuit after the battle, where they died of their wounds, of hunger, and of fatigue; so that they were not all found and buried till *seven months* after the defeat of the Syrian army. This slow process of burying is distinctly related in the three following verses, and extended even to a *bone*, ver. 15; which, when it was found by a passenger, the place was marked, that the buriers might see and *inter* it. *Seven months* was little time enough for all this work; and in that country putrescency does not easily take place; the

A. M. cir. 3417
B. C. cir. 587
Ol. XLVIII. 2
Tarquinii Prisci,
R. Roman.,
cir. annum 30

bury *them;* and it shall be to
them a renown, the day that
[y]I shall be glorified, saith the
Lord GOD.
14 And they shall sever out [z]men of continual employment, passing through the land
to bury with the passengers those that remain
upon the face of the earth,[a]to cleanse it: after
the end of seven months shall they search.
15 And the passengers *that* pass through
the land, when *any* seeth a man's bone, then
shall he [b]set up a sign by it, till the buriers
have buried it in the valley of Hamon-gog.
16 And also the name of the city *shall be*
[c]Hamonah. Thus shall they [d]cleanse the
land.
17 And, thou son of man, thus saith the
Lord GOD; [e]Speak [f]unto every feathered fowl,
and to every beast of the field, [g]Assemble
yourselves, and come; gather yourselves on
every side to my [h]sacrifice that I do sacrifice
for you, *even* a great sacrifice [i]upon the
mountains of Israel, that ye may eat flesh,
and drink blood.
18 [k]Ye shall eat the flesh of the mighty,
and drink the blood of the princes of the
earth, of rams, of lambs, and of [l]goats, of
bullocks, all of them [m]fatlings of Bashan.
19 And ye shall eat fat till ye be full, and
drink blood till ye be drunken, of my sacrifice which I have sacrificed for you.
20 [n]Thus ye shall be filled
at my table with horses and
chariots, [o]with mighty men,
and with all men of war,
saith the Lord GOD.

A. M. cir. 3417
B. C. cir. 587
Ol. XLVIII. 2
Tarquinii Prisci,
R. Roman.,
cir. annum 30

21 [p]And I will set my glory among the
heathen, and all the heathen shall see my
judgment that I have executed, and [q]my
hand that I have laid upon them.
22 [r]So the house of Israel shall know that
I *am* the LORD their God from that day and
forward.
23 [s]And the heathen shall know that the
house of Israel went into captivity for their
iniquity: because they trespassed against me,
therefore [t]hid I my face from them, and
[u]gave them into the hand of their enemies:
so fell they all by the sword.
24 [v]According to their uncleanness and according to their transgressions have I done
unto them, and hid my face from them.
25 Therefore thus saith the Lord GOD; [w]Now
will I bring again the captivity of Jacob,
and have mercy upon the [x]whole house of
Israel, and will be jealous for my holy name;
26 [y]After that they have borne their shame,
and all their trespasses whereby they have trespassed against me, when they [z]dwelt safely
in their land, and none made *them* afraid.
27 [a]When I have brought them again from
the people, and gathered them out of their

[y]Ch. xxviii. 22——[z]Heb. *men of continuance*——[a]Ver. 12——[b]Heb. *build*——[c]That is, *the multitude*——[d]Ver. 12——[e]Rev. xix. 17; [f]Heb. *to the fowl of every wing* [g]Isa. xviii. 6; xxxiv. 6; Jer. xii. 9; Zeph. i. 7——[h]Or, *slaughter*——[i]Ver. 4——[k]Rev. xix. 18——[l]Heb. *great goats*——[m]Deut. xxxii. 14; Psa. xxii. 12——[n]Psa. lxxvi. 6; chap. xxxviii. 4

[o]Rev. xix. 18——[p]Chap. xxxviii. 16, 23——[q]Exod. vii. 4——[r]Ver. 7, 28——[s]Chap. xxxvi. 18, 19, 20, 23——[t]Deut. xxxi. 17; Isa. lix. 2——[u]Lev. xxvi. 25——[v]Chap. xxxvi. 19——[w]Jer. xxx. 3, 18; chap. xxxiv. 13; xxxvi. 21——[x]Chap. xx. 40; Hos. i. 11 [y]Dan. ix. 16——[z]Lev. xxvi. 5, 6——[a]Chap. xxviii. 25, 26

scorching winds serving to desiccate the flesh, and preserve it from decomposition.

Verse 17. *Gather yourselves—to my sacrifice*] This is an allusion to a custom common in the east: when a sacrifice is made, the friends and neighbours of the party sacrificing are invited to come and feast on the sacrifice.

Verse 18. *Ye shall—drink the blood of the princes of the earth*] I need not mention the custom of the Scandinavians: they were accustomed to drink the blood of their enemies out of the skulls of the dead. But this is spoken of *fowls* and *beasts* here—*rams, lambs*, and *goats*. The feast shall be as grateful and as plenteous to the *fowls* and *beasts*, as one made of the above animals, the fattest and best of their kind, (because fed in the fertile fields of Bashan,) would be to the guests of him who makes a sacrifice.

Verse 19. *And ye shall eat fat—and drink blood*] *Who* shall eat and drink, &c.? Not the *Jews;* though *Voltaire* says they ate *human flesh*, and are invited here by the prophet to *eat the flesh and drink the blood of their enemies;* which is a most unprincipled falsehood. It is the *fowls* and the *beasts* that God invites, ver. 17: "Speak to every feathered fowl, and to every beast of the field, assemble yourselves—that ye may eat flesh and drink blood;" nor are the persons altered in all these verses, 17, 18, 19, 20: so the assertion of *Voltaire* is either through *brutish ignorance* or *Satanic malice.*

Verse 25. *Now will I bring again the captivity of Jacob*] Both *they* and the *heathen* shall know that it was for their iniquity that I gave them into the hands of their enemies: and now I will redeem them from those hands in such a way as to prove that I am a *merciful God*, as well as a *just God.*

Verse 26. *After that they have borne their shame*] After they shall have borne the *punishment* due to a line of conduct which is their *shame* and reproach, viz. *idolatry.*

Verse 27. *When I have—gathered them*]

A. M. cir. 3417
B. C. cir. 587
Ol. XLVIII. 2
Tarquinii Prisci,
R. Roman.,
cir. annum 30

enemies' lands, and [b]am sanctified in them in the sight of many nations;

28 [c]Then shall they know that I *am* the Lord their God, [d]which caused them to be led into captivity among the heathen: but I have gathered them unto their own land, and have left none of them any more there.

A. M. cir. 3417
B. C. cir. 587
Ol. XLVIII. 2
Tarquinii Prisci,
R. Roman.,
cir annum 30

29 [e]Neither will I hide my face any more from them, for I have [f]poured out my Spirit upon the house of Israel, saith the Lord God.

[b]Chap. xxxvi. 23, 24; xxxviii. 16——[c]Chap. xxxiv. 30; ver. 22——[d]Heb. *by my causing of them,* &c.——[e]Isa. liv. 8——[f]Joel ii. 28; Zech. xii. 10; Acts ii. 17

Antiochus had before captured many of the Jews, and sold them for *slaves;* see Dan. xi. 33.

Verse 28. *And have left none of them any more there.*] All that *chose* had liberty to return; but many remained behind. This promise may therefore refer to a *greater restoration,* when not a Jew shall be left behind. This, the next verse intimates, will be in the *Gospel dispensation.*

Verse 29. *For I have poured out my Spirit*] That is, I will pour out my Spirit; see the notes on chap. xxxvi. 25-29, where this subject is largely considered. This *Spirit* is to enlighten, quicken, purify, and cleanse their hearts; so that, being completely changed, they shall become God's people, and be a praise in the earth. Now, they are a proverb of reproach; then, they shall be eminently distinguished.

A NEW PLAN OF THE TEMPLE AT JERUSALEM

[*For an explanation of this plan, and of the accompanying map of the division of the Land of Canaan, see at the end of chap.* xlviii.]

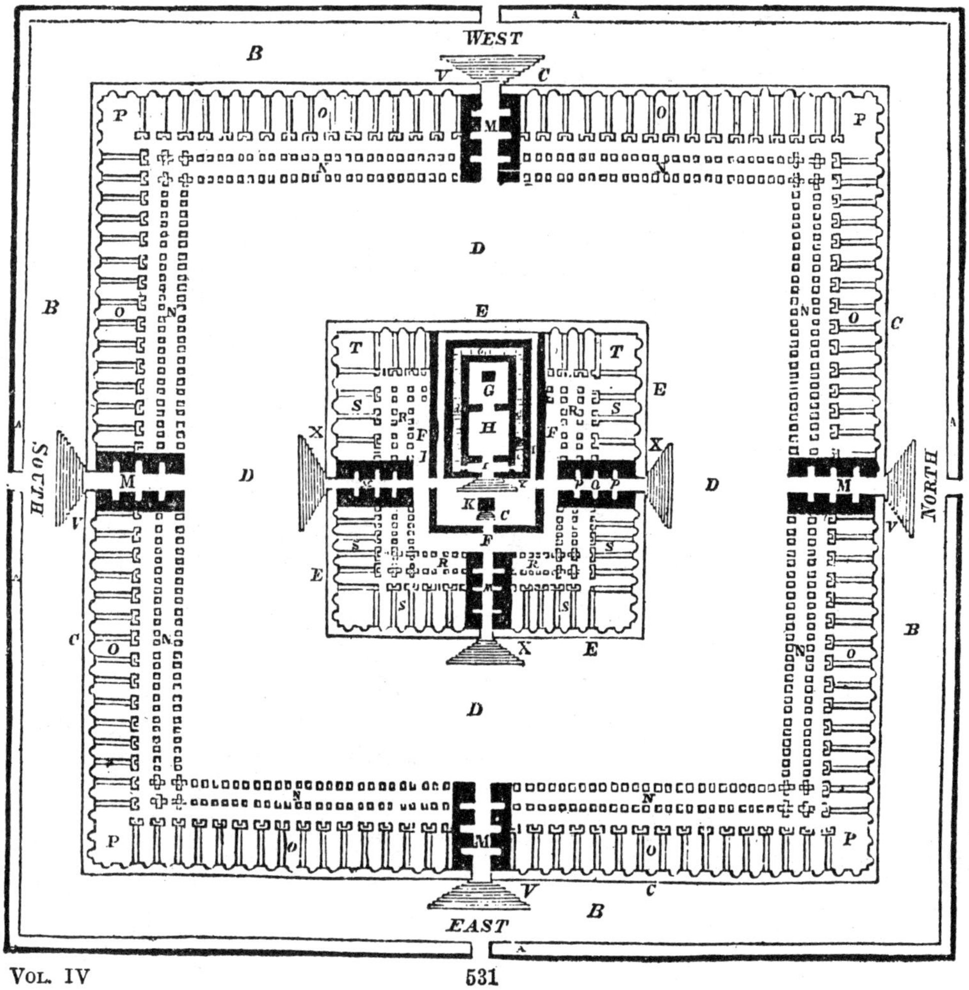

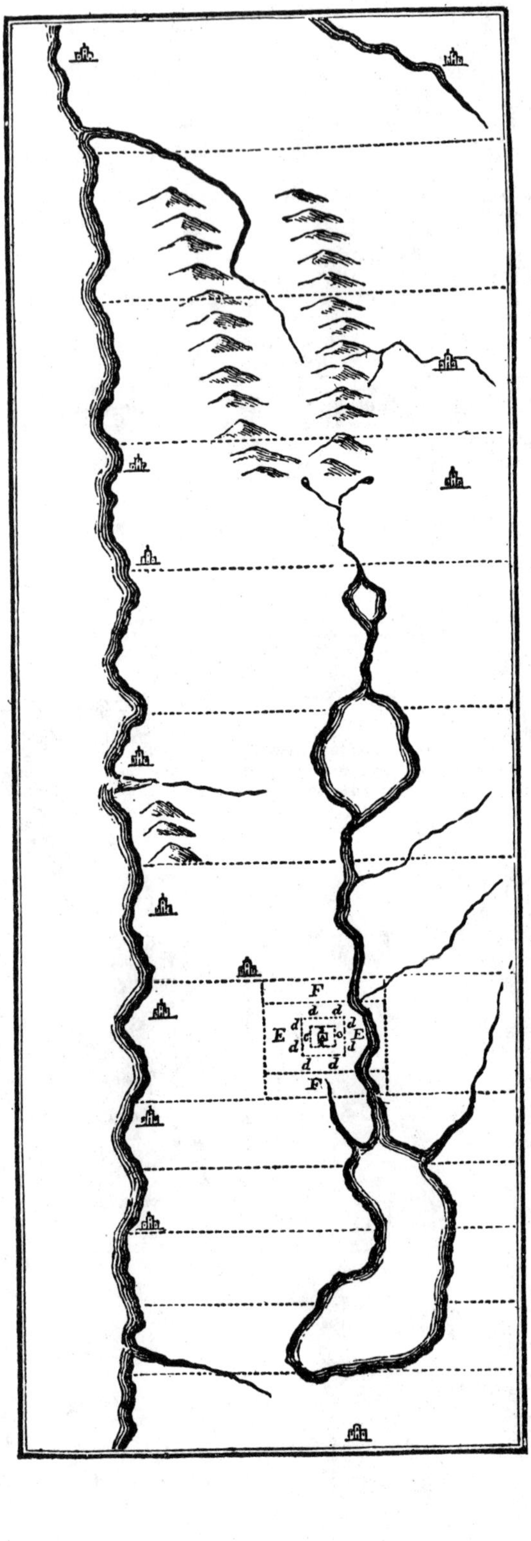

DIVISION OF THE LAND OF CANAAN

CHAPTER XL

The prophecy or vision, which begins here, continues to the end of the Book. The Temple of Jerusalem lying in ruins when Ezekiel had this vision, (for its date is the fourteenth *year after the destruction of Jerusalem by Nebuchadnezzar,) the Jews needed consolation. If they were not promised a restoration of the temple, they would not feel so great an interest in returning home. It is thought by some that no model of Solomon's Temple had remained. To direct them, therefore, in the dimensions, parts, order, and rules of their new temple might be one reason why Ezekiel is so particular in the description of the old; to which the new was conformable in figure and parts, though inferior in magnificence, on account of the poverty of the nation at the time. Whatever was august or illustrious in the prophetic figures, and not literally fulfilled in or near their own times, the ancient Jews properly considered as belonging to the time of the Messiah. Accordingly, upon finding that the latter temple fell short of the model of the temple here described by Ezekiel, they supposed the prophecy to refer, at least in part, to the period now mentioned. And we, who live under the Gospel dispensation, have apostolical authority for the assertion that the temple and temple worship were emblematic of Christ's Church, frequently represented in the New Testament under the metaphor of a temple, in allusion to the symmetry, beauty, and firmness of that of Solomon; to its orderly worship; and to the manifestations it had of the Divine Presence. This chapter commences with the time, manner, and end of the vision,* 1–5. *We have next a description of the east gate,* 6–19, *the north gate,* 20–22, *and the south gate,* 24–31. *A farther description of the east gate,* 32–34, *and of the north gate,* 35–38. *Account of the eight tables,* 39–43; *of the chambers,* 44–47; *and of the porch of the temple,* 48, 49.

A. M. 3430 B. C. 574 Olymp. LI. 3 Anno Servii Tullii, R. Roman., 5

IN the five and twentieth year of our captivity, in the beginning of the year, in the tenth *day* of the month, in the fourteenth year after that [a]the city was smitten, in the selfsame day [b]the hand of the LORD was upon me, and brought me thither.

A. M. 3430 B. C. 574 Olymp. LI. 3 Anno Servii Tullii, R. Roman., 5

[a]Chap. xxxiii. 21

[b]Chap. i. 3

NOTES ON CHAP. XL

Verse 1. *In the five and twentieth year of our captivity*] According to the date here given, this prophecy was delivered on Tuesday, April 20, A. M. 3430, in the *twenty-fifth* year of the captivity of *Jeconiah*, and *fourteen* years after the taking of Jerusalem.

The temple here described by Ezekiel is, in all probability, the same which he saw before his captivity, and which had been burned by the Chaldeans *fourteen* years before this vision. On comparing the Books of Kings and Chronicles with this prophet, we shall find the same dimensions in the parts described by both; for instance, the temple, or place which comprehended the sanctuary, the holy place, and the vestibule or porch before the temple, is found to measure equally the same both in Ezekiel and the Kings. Compare 1 Kings vi. 3-16, with chap. xli. 2, &c. The inside ornaments of the temple are entirely the same; in both we see two courts; an inner one for the priests, and an outer one for the people. Compare 1 Kings vi. 29-36; 2 Chron. iv. 9; and Ezek. xli. 16, 17, and xlviii. 7-10. So that there is room to suppose that, in all the rest, the temple of Ezekiel resembled the old one; and that God's design in retracing these ideas in the prophet's memory was to preserve the remembrance of the plan, the dimensions, the ornaments, and whole structure of this Divine edifice; and that at the return from captivity the people might more easily repair it, agreeably to this model. The prophet's applying himself to describe this edifice was a motive of hope to the Jews of seeing themselves one day delivered from captivity, the temple rebuilt, and their nation restored to its ancient inheritance. Ezekiel touches very slightly upon the description of the temple or house of the Lord, which comprehended the holy place or sanctuary, and which are so exactly described in the Books of Kings. He dwells more largely upon the gates, the galleries, and apartments, of the temple, concerning which the history of the kings had not spoken, or only just taken notice of by the way.

This is the judgment of *Calmet;* and although every Biblical critic is of the same opinion, yet more labour is spent on *rebuilding* this temple of *Ezekiel* than was spent on that built by Solomon! The Jesuits, *Prada* and *Villalpand*, have given *three* folio volumes on this temple, with abundance of cuts, where the different parts are exhibited after the finest models of *Grecian* and *Roman* architecture! But still the building is incomplete. Now, of what consequence is all this to the Christian, or to any other reader? I confess I see not. While, then, we have the exact dimensions and accurate description in 1 Kings and 2 Chronicles, of that built by Solomon, in imitation of which this *plan by Ezekiel* was drawn, we need not be very solicitous about the *manner of measuring* and *describing* used by the prophet: as, when we have laboured through the whole, we have only the measurements and description of that built by Solomon, and delineated by a hand not less faithful in the First Book of Kings, chap. vi., and 2 Chron. ii., iii., iv., v. and vi.

As the prophet knew that the Chaldeans had utterly destroyed the temple, he thought it necessary to preserve an *exact description* of it, that on their restoration the people might build one on the same model. As to *allegorical meanings* relative to this temple, I can say nothing: God has given no *data* by which any thing of this kind can be known or applied; and as to those who have laboured in this way, perhaps "Solomon's Temple Spiritualized, by *John Bunyan*," is equally good with their well-intended inventions. Those who wish to enter much into the particulars of this temple must have recourse to the more voluminous expositors, who

A. M. 3430
B. C. 574
Olymp. LI. 3
Anno
Servii Tullii,
R. Roman., 5

2 [c]In the visions of God
brought he me into the land
of Israel, [d]and set me upon
a very high mountain, [e]by
which *was* as the frame of a city on the
south.
3 And he brought me thither, and, behold,
there was a man, whose appearance *was* [f]like
the appearance of brass, [g]with a line of flax
in his hand, [h]and a measuring reed; and he
stood in the gate.
4 And the man said unto me, [i]Son of man,
behold with thine eyes, and hear with thine
ears, and set thine heart upon all that I shall
show thee; for to the intent that I might
show *them* unto thee *art* thou brought
hither: [k]declare all that thou seest to the
house of Israel.
5 And behold [l]a wall on the outside of the
house round about, and in the man's hand a
measuring reed of six cubits *long* by the
cubit and a hand breadth: so he measured
the breadth of the building, one reed; and
the height, one reed.
6 Then came he unto the gate [m]which looketh toward the east, and went up the stairs
thereof, and measured the threshold of the
gate, *which was* one reed broad; and the
other threshold *of the gate, which was* one
reed broad.
7 And *every* little chamber *was* one reed
long, and one reed broad; and between the
little chambers *were* five cubits;
and the threshold of the gate by
the porch of the gate within
was one reed.
8 He measured also the porch of the gate
within, one reed.
9 Then measured he the porch of the gate,
eight cubits: and the posts thereof, two
cubits; and the porch of the gate *was* inward.
10 And the little chambers of the gate eastward *were* three on this side, and three on
that side; they three *were* of one measure:
and the posts had one measure on this side
and on that side.
11 And he measured the breadth of the
entry of the gate, ten cubits; *and* the length
of the gate, thirteen cubits.
12 The [n]space also before the little chambers *was* one cubit *on this side,* and the space
was one cubit on that side: and the little
chambers *were* six cubits on this side, and six
cubits on that side.
13 He measured then the gate from the
roof of *one* little chamber to the roof of another: the breadth *was* five and twenty
cubits, door against door,
14 He made also posts of threescore cubits,
even unto the posts of the court round about
the gate.
15 And from the face of the gate of the
entrance unto the face of the porch of the
inner gate *were* fifty cubits.

A. M. 3430
B. C. 574
Olymp. LI. 3
Anno
Servii Tullii,
R. Roman., 5

[c]Chap. viii.——[d]Rev. xxi. 10——[e]Or, *upon which* [f]Chap. i. 7; Dan. x. 6——[g]Chap. xlvii. 3——[h]Rev. xi. 1; xxi. 15

[i]Chap. xliv. 5——[k]Chap. xliii. 10——[l]Chap. xlii. 20 [m]Heb. *whose face* was *the way toward the east*——[n]Heb. *limit,* or *bound*

on this subject seem to have thought that they could never say enough. See also the accompanying *map*.

Verse 2. *Set me upon a very high mountain*] Mount *Moriah*, the mount on which Solomon's temple was built, 2 Chron. iii. 1.

Verse 3. *A man, whose appearance* was *like—brass*] Like *bright polished brass*, which strongly reflected the rays of light. Probably he had what we would term a *nimbus* or *glory* round his head. This was either an *angel;* or, as some think, a personal appearance of our blessed Lord.

Verse 4. *Declare all that thou seest to the house of Israel*] That they may know how to build the second temple, when they shall be restored from their captivity.

Verse 5. *A measuring reed of six cubits* long] The Hebrew cubit is supposed to be about *twenty and a half* inches; and a palm, about *three* inches more; the length of the rod about *ten* feet *six* inches.

The breadth—one reed; and the height, one reed.] As this *wall* was as *broad* as it was *high*, it must have been a kind of *parapet*, which was carried, of the same dimensions, all round the temple. See AAAA in the plan.

Verse 6. *Went up the stairs thereof*] As the temple was built upon an eminence, there must have been steps on the outside, opposite to each door, to ascend by. And it appears there were *steps* to go up from *one court* to *another*, see ver. 22, 26, 34, 37; and also from the *court of the priests* to the *sanctuary*, ver. 49. See MMMMM in the plan.

Verse 7. *And* every *little chamber* was *one reed*] These were the chambers of the buildings which were within the inclosure of the temple round the court, and these chambers appear to have been numerous. See the map, which has been carefully copied from that of *Calmet*.

Verse 9. *The porch of the gate*] See account of the *gates* in the plan.

Verse 15. *Fifty cubits.*] The length of the building. See MMMMM in the plan.

A. M. 3430
B. C. 574
Olymp. LI. 3
Anno
Servii Tullii,
R. Roman., 5

16 And *there were* [o]narrow[p] windows to the little chambers, and to their posts within the gate round about, and likewise to the [q]arches: and windows *were* round about [r]inward: and upon *each* post *were* palm trees.

17 Then brought he me into [s]the outward court, and, lo, *there were* [t]chambers, and a pavement made for the court round about: [u]thirty chambers *were* upon the pavement.

18 And the pavement by the side of the gates over against the length of the gates *was* the lower pavement.

19 Then he measured the breadth from the forefront of the lower gate unto the forefront of the inner court [v]without, a hundred cubits eastward and northward.

20 And the gate of the outward court [w]that looked toward the north, he measured the length thereof, and the breadth thereof.

21 And the little chambers thereof *were* three on this side, and three on that side; and the posts thereof and the [x]arches thereof were after the measure of the first gate: the length thereof *was* fifty cubits, and the breadth five and twenty cubits.

22 And their windows, and their arches, and their palm trees, *were* after the measure of the gate that looketh toward the east: and they went up unto it by seven steps; and the arches thereof *were* before them.

23 And the gate of the inner court *was* over against the gate toward the north, and toward the east; and he measured from gate to gate a hundred cubits.

24 After that he brought me toward the south, and behold a gate toward the south: and he measured the posts thereof and the arches thereof according to these measures.

25 And *there were* windows in it and in the arches thereof round about, like those windows: the length *was* fifty cubits, and the breadth five and twenty cubits.

A. M. 3430
B. C. 574
Olymp. LI. 3
Anno
Servii Tullii,
R. Roman., 5

26 And *there were* seven steps to go up to it, and the arches thereof *were* before them: and it had palm trees, one on this side, and another on that side, upon the posts thereof.

27 And *there was* a gate in the inner court toward the south: and he measured from gate to gate toward the south a hundred cubits.

28 And he brought me to the inner court by the south gate: and he measured the south gate according to these measures;

29 And the little chambers thereof, and the posts thereof, and the arches thereof, according to these measures: and *there were* windows in it, and in the arches thereof round about: *it was* fifty cubits long, and five and twenty cubits broad.

30 And the arches round about *were* [y]five and twenty cubits long, and five cubits [z]broad.

31 And the arches thereof *were* toward the utter court; and palm trees *were* upon the posts thereof: and the going up to it *had* eight steps.

32 And he brought me into the inner court toward the east: and he measured the gate according to these measures.

33 And the little chambers thereof, and the posts thereof, and the arches thereof, *were* according to these measures: and *there were* windows therein and in the arches thereof round about: *it was* fifty cubits long, and five and twenty cubits broad.

34 And the arches thereof *were* toward the outward court; and palm trees *were* upon the posts thereof, on this side, and on that side: and the going up to it *had* eight steps.

35 And he brought me to the north gate, and measured *it* according to these measures;

---

[o]1 Kings vi. 4——[p]Heb. *closed*——[q]Or, *galleries*, or *porches*——[r]Or, *within*——[s]Rev. xi. 2——[t]1 Kings vi. 5 [u]Chap. xlv. 5

[v]Or, *from without*——[w]Heb. *whose face* was——[x]Or, *galleries*, or *porches*——[y]See verses 21, 25, 33, 36 [z]Hebrew, *breadth*

Verse 17. *The outward court*] This was the court of the people.

Verse 21. *And the little chambers thereof* were *three, &c.*] See the plan.

Arches] Porch. The arch was not known at this period.

Verse 24. *According to these measures.*] The same measures that had been used at the eastern court.

Verse 30. *And the arches round about* were *five and twenty cubits long*] That the *five cubits broad* should be *read twenty-five* is evident from verses 21, 25, 29, 33, and 36. The word ועשרים *veesrim*, *twenty*, has probably been lost out of the text. Indeed the whole verse is wanting in *two* of *Kennicott's* MSS., *one* of *De Rossi's*, and *one* of mine, (Cod. B.) It has been added in the margin of mine by a later hand. It is reported to have been anciently wanting in many MSS.

A. M. 3430
B. C. 574
Olymp. LI. 3
Anno
Servii Tullii,
R. Roman., 5

36 The little chambers thereof,
the posts thereof, and the arches
thereof, and the windows to it
round about: the length *was* fifty
cubits, and the breadth five and twenty cubits.
37 And the posts thereof *were* toward the
utter court; and palm trees *were* upon the
posts thereof, on this side, and on that side:
and the going up to it *had* eight steps.
38 And the chambers and the entries thereof *were* by the posts of the gates, where they
washed the burnt-offering.
39 And in the porch of the gate *were* two
tables on this side, and two tables on that
side, to slay thereon the burnt-offering and
[a]the sin-offering and [b]the trespass-offering.
40 And at the side without, [c]as one goeth
up to the entry of the north gate, *were* two
tables; and on the other side, which *was* at
the porch of the gate, *were* two tables.
41 Four tables *were* on this side, and four
tables on that side, by the side of the gate;
eight tables, whereupon they slew *their sacrifices.*
42 And the four tables *were* of hewn stone
for the burnt-offering, of a cubit and a half
long, and a cubit and a half broad, and one
cubit high: whereupon also they laid the instruments wherewith they slew the burnt-
offering and the sacrifice.
43 And within *were* [d]hooks, a hand
broad, fastened round about: and upon the
tables *was* the flesh of the
offering.
44 And without the inner gate
were the chambers of [e]the sing-
ers in the inner court, which *was* at the side
of the north gate; and their prospect *was*
toward the south: one at the side of the east
gate *having* the prospect toward the north.
45 And he said unto me, This chamber,
whose prospect *is* toward the south, *is* for the
priests, [f]the keepers of the [g]charge of the
house.
46 And the chamber whose prospect *is*
toward the north *is* for the priests, [h]the keepers of the charge of the altar: these *are* the
sons of [i]Zadok among the sons of Levi,
which come near to the LORD to minister
unto him.
47 So he measured the court, a hundred
cubits long, and a hundred cubits broad, four-
square; and the altar *that was* before the
house.
48 And he brought me to the porch of the
house, and measured *each* post of the porch,
five cubits on this side, and five cubits on
that side: and the breadth of the gate *was*
three cubits on this side, and three cubits on
that side.
49 [k]The length of the porch *was* twenty
cubits, and the breadth eleven cubits; and *he
brought me* by the steps whereby they went
up to it: and *there were* [l]pillars by the posts,
one on this side, and another on that side.

A. M. 3430
B. C. 574
Olymp. LI. 3
Anno
Servii Tullii,
R. Roman., 5

[a]Lev. iv. 2, 3——[b]Lev. v. 6; vi. 6; vii. 1——[c]Or, *at the step*——[d]Or, *endirons*, or *the two hearthstones* [e]1 Chron. vi. 31——[f]Lev. viii. 35; Num. iii. 27, 28, 32, 38; xviii. 5; 1 Chron. ix. 23; 2 Chron. xiii. 11; Psa. cxxxiv. 1——[g]Or, *ward*, or *ordinance;* and so ver. 46——[h]Num. xviii. 5; chap. xliv. 15——[i]1 Kings ii. 35; chap. xliii. 19; xliv. 15, 16——[k]1 Kings vi. 3 [l]1 Kings vii. 21

Verse 39. *The porch of the gate*] The north gate of the court of the priests. See Q in the plan.

Two tables] Some say of *marble*. See *dddd* in the plan.

Verse 41. *Four tables*] These were in the porch of the north gate, in the court of the priests: on them they slew, flayed, and cut up the victims. See *dddd* in the plan.

Verse 47. *He measured the court*] This was the court of the priests. See FFF in the plan.

Verse 48. *Breadth of the gate*] It is evident that the gate was a bivalve, or had folding doors. The length of the porch was *twenty* cubits. *Josephus* says the vestibule was *twenty* cubits long and *ten* broad. Antiq. lib. viii. 3, 2.

Verse 49. *By the steps*] This was a flight of steps that led to the temple; there were *eight* steps in each flight. See YY in the plan.

CHAPTER XLI

In this chapter the prophet gives us a circumstantial account of the measures, parts, chambers, and ornaments of the temple, 1–26.

A. M. 3430
B. C. 574
Olymp. LI. 3
Anno
Servii Tullii,
R. Roman., 5

AFTERWARD he brought me to the temple, and measured the posts, six cubits broad on the one side, and six cubits broad on the other side, *which was* the breadth of the tabernacle.

2 And the breadth of the [a]door *was* ten cubits; and the sides of the door *were* five cubits on the one side, and five cubits on the other side: and he measured the length thereof, forty cubits: and the breadth, [b]twenty cubits.

3 Then went he inward, and measured the post of the door, two cubits; and the door six cubits; and the breadth of the door, seven cubits.

4 So [c]he measured the length thereof, twenty cubits; and the breadth, twenty cubits, before the temple: and he said unto me, This *is* the most holy *place*.

5 After he measured the wall of the house, six cubits; and the breadth of *every* side chamber, four cubits, round about the house on every side.

6 [d]And the side chambers *were* three, [e]one over another, and [f]thirty in order; and they entered into the wall which *was* of the house for the side chambers round about, that they might [g]have hold, but they had not hold in the wall of the house.

7 And [h]*there* [i]*was* an enlarging, and a winding about still upward to the side chambers: for the winding about of the house went still upward round about the house: therefore the breadth of the house *was still* upward, and so increased *from* the lowest *chamber* to the highest by the midst.

A. M. 3430
B. C. 574
Olymp. LI. 3
Anno
Servii Tullii,
R. Roman., 5

8. I saw also the height of the house round about: the foundations of the side chambers *were* [k]a full reed of six great cubits.

9 The thickness of the wall, which *was* for the side chamber without, *was* five cubits: and *that* which *was* left *was* the place of the side chambers that *were* within.

10 And between the chambers *was* the wideness of twenty cubits round about the house on every side.

11 And the doors of the side chambers *were* toward *the place that was* left, one door toward the north, and another door toward the south: and the breadth of the place that was left *was* five cubits round about.

12 Now the building that *was* before the separate place at the end toward the west *was* seventy cubits broad; and the wall of the building *was* five cubits thick round about, and the length thereof ninety cubits.

13 So he measured the house, a hundred cubits long: and the separate place, and the

[a]Or, *entrance*——[b]1 Kings vi. 2——[c]1 Kings vi. 20; 2 Chron. iii. 8——[d]1 Kings vi. 5, 6——[e]Heb. *side chamber over side chamber*

[f]Or, *three and thirty times*, or *foot*——[g]Heb. *be holden*——[h]Heb. it was *made broader, and went round* [i]1 Kings vi. 8——[k]Chap. xl. 5

NOTES ON CHAP. XLI

Verse 1. *To the temple*] He had first described the courts and the porch. See chap. xl.

Verse 2. *The breadth of the door*] This was the door, or gate, of the sanctuary, (see *gates*, 3, in the plan,) and this *doorway* was filled up with folding gates. The measurements are exactly the same as those of Solomon's temple. See 1 Kings vi. 2, 17.

Verse 4. *The length thereof, twenty cubits*] This is the measurement of the sanctuary, or holy of holies. See G in the plan. This also was the exact measurement of Solomon's temple, see 1 Kings vi. 20. This, and the other resemblances here, sufficiently prove that Ezekiel's temple and that of Solomon were on the same plan; and that the latter temple was intended to be an exact resemblance of the former.

Verse 6. *The side chambers* were *three*] We find by *Joseph*. Antiq. viii. 3, 2, that round Solomon's temple were chambers *three* stories high, each story consisting of *thirty* chambers. It is supposed that *twelve* were placed to the *north* of the temple, *twelve* to the *south*, and ***six*** to the *east*.

Entered into the wall] The beams were admitted into the outer wall, but they rested on projections of the inner wall.

Verse 7. *An enlarging, and a winding about*] Perhaps a winding staircase that widened upward as the inner wall decreased in thickness; this wall being six cubits thick as high as the first story, five from the floor of the second story to that of the third, and four from the floor to the ceiling of the third story: and thus there was a rest of one cubit in breadth to support the stories.—*Newcome.*

Verse 9. *The thickness of the wall*] See LLL in the plan.

The place of the side chambers] A walk, or gallery of communication along the chambers, *five* cubits broad, ver. 11.

Verse 11. *And the doors*] See the plan, *aa. bb.*

Verse 12. *The length thereof ninety cubits.*] The temple, with the buildings which surrounded it, was *eighty-one* cubits long; add *ten* cubits for the vestibule, or *five* for the breadth of the separate place, and five for its wall; in all, *ninety* cubits. See the plan, LHIL. By the *separate place* I suppose the temple itself is meant.

Verse 13. *So he measured the house*] The

A. M. 3430
B. C. 574
Olymp. LI. 3
Anno
Servii Tullii,
R. Roman., 5

building, with the walls thereof, a hundred cubits long;

14 Also the breadth of the face of the house, and of the separate place toward the east, a hundred cubits.

15 And he measured the length of the building over against the separate place which *was* behind it, and the [l]galleries thereof on the one side and on the other side, a hundred cubits, with the inner temple, and the porches of the court;

16 The door posts, and [m]the narrow window, and the galleries round about on their three stories, over against the door, [n]ceiled with wood round about, [o]and from the ground up to the windows, and the windows *were* covered;

17 To that above the door, even unto the inner house, and without, and by all the wall round about within and without, by [p]measure.

18 And *it was* made [q]with cherubims and palm trees, so that a palm tree *was* between a cherub and a cherub; and *every* cherub had two faces;

19 [r]So that the face of a man *was* toward the palm tree on the one side, and the face of a young lion toward the palm tree on the other side: *it was* made through all the house round about.

20 From the ground unto above the door *were* cherubims and palm trees made, and *on* the wall of the temple.

A. M. 3430
B. C. 574
Olymp. LI. 3
Anno
Servii Tullii,
R. Roman., 5

21 The [s]posts of the temple *were* squared *and* the face of the sanctuary; the appearance *of the one* as the appearance *of the other.*

22 [t]The altar of wood *was* three cubits high, and the length thereof two cubits; and the corners thereof, and the length thereof, and the walls thereof, *were* of wood: and he said unto me, This *is* [u]the table that *is* [v]before the LORD.

23 [w]And the temple and the sanctuary had two doors.

24 And the doors had two leaves *apiece,* two turning leaves; two *leaves* for the one door, and two leaves for the other *door.*

25 And *there were* made on them, on the doors of the temple, cherubims and palm trees, like as *were* made upon the walls; and *there were* thick planks upon the face of the porch without.

26 And *there were* [x]narrow windows and palm trees on the one side and on the other side, on the sides of the porch, and *upon* the side chambers of the house, and thick planks.

---

[l]Or, *several walks,* or, *walks with pillars*——[m]Chap. xl. 16; ver. 26——[n]Heb. *ceiling of wood*——[o]Or, *and the ground unto the windows*——[p]Heb. *measures*

[q]1 Kings vi. 29——[r]See chap. i. 10——[s]Heb. *post* ——[t]Exod. xxx. 1——[u]Ch. xliv. 16; Mal. i. 7, 12——[v]Exod. xxx. 8——[w]1 Kings vi. 31-35——[x]Ch. xl. 16; ver. 16

---

temple, taken from the wall which encompassed it from the western side to the vestibule, was *one hundred and one* cubits; *five* for the separate place, *nine* for the wall and the chambers attached to the temple, *sixty* for the sanctuary and the holy place, *ten* for the vestibule, and *twelve* for the two great walls on the west and east of the temple; in all, *one hundred and one cubits.* See the plan, GHI.

Verse 14. *The breadth of the face of the house*] That is, the front. See the plan, FRR.

Verse 18. *A palm tree* was *between a cherub and a cherub*] That is, the palm trees and the cherubs were alternated; and each cherub had two faces, one of a *lion,* and the other of a *man;* one of which was turned to the palm tree on the right, the other to the palm tree on the left.

Verse 20. *From the ground unto above the door*] The temple was *thirty* cubits high, 1 Kings vi. 2, the gate was *fourteen* cubits, chap. xl. 48. The *palm trees* and the *cherubim* were the same height as the *gate* or *door.* The windows were above the door.

Verse 22. *The altar of wood*] This was the altar of incense, and was covered with plates of gold.

Verse 25. There were *thick planks*] The wood, or planks, were thick and strong; for the cherubim and palm trees were carved in *relief,* out of their substance, and unless they had been of considerable thickness, this could not have been done.

CHAPTER XLII

This chapter gives us a description of the priests' chambers and their use, with the dimensions of the holy mount on which the temple stood, 1-20.

A. M. 3430
B. C. 574
Olymp. LI. 3
Anno
Servii Tullii,
R. Roman., 5

THEN he brought me forth into the utter court, the way toward the north: and he brought me into [a]the chamber that *was* over against the [b]separate place, and which *was* before the building toward the north.

2 Before the length of a hundred cubits *was* the north door, and the breadth *was* fifty cubits.

3 Over against the twenty *cubits* which *were* for the inner court, and over against the pavement which *was* for the utter court, *was* [c]gallery against gallery in three *stories.*

4 And before the chambers *was* a walk of ten cubits' breadth inward, a way of one cubit; and their doors toward the north.

5 Now the upper chambers *were* shorter: for the galleries [d]were higher than these, [e]than the lower, and than the middlemost of the building.

6 For they *were* in three *stories,* but had not pillars as the pillars of the courts: therefore *the building* was straitened more than the lowest and the middlemost from the ground.

7 And the wall that *was* without over against the chambers, toward the utter court on the forepart of the chambers, the length thereof *was* fifty cubits.

8 For the length of the chambers that *were* in the utter court *was* fifty cubits: and, lo, before the temple *were* a hundred cubits.

9 And [f]from under these chambers *was* [g]the entry on the east side, [h]as one goeth into them from the utter court.

10 The chambers *were* in the thickness of the wall of the court toward the east, over against the separate place, and over against the building.

11 And [i]the way before them *was* like the appearance of the chambers which *were* toward the north, as long as they, *and* as broad as they: and all their goings out *were* both according to their fashions, and according to their doors.

A. M. 3430
B. C. 574
Olymp. LI. 3
Anno
Servii Tullii,
R. Roman., 5

12 And according to the doors of the chambers that *were* toward the south *was* a door in the head of the way *even* the way directly before the wall toward the east, as one entereth into them.

13 Then said he unto me, The north chambers *and* the south chambers, which *are* before the separate place, they *be* holy chambers, where the priests that approach unto the LORD [k]shall eat the most holy things: there shall they lay the most holy things, and [l]the meat-offering, and the sin-offering, and the trespass-offering; for the place *is* holy.

14 [m]When the priests enter therein, then shall they not go out of the holy *place* into the utter court, but there they shall lay their garments wherein they minister; for they *are* holy; and shall put on other garments, and shall approach to *those things* which *are* for the people.

15 Now when he had made an end of measuring the inner house, he brought me forth toward the gate whose prospect *is* toward the east, and measured it round about.

16 He measured the east [n]side with the measuring reed, five hundred reeds, with the measuring reed round about.

17 He measured the north side, five hundred reeds, with the measuring reed round about.

18 He measured the south side five hundred reeds, with the measuring reed.

19 He turned about to the west side, *and* measured five hundred reeds, with the measuring reed.

20 He measured it by the four sides: [o]it had a wall round about, [p]five hundred *reeds* long, and five hundred broad, to make a separation between the sanctuary and the profane place.

[a]Chap. xli. 12, 15——[b]Chap. xli. 12, 13, 14; xlii. 10, 13——[c]Chap. xli. 16——[d]Or, *did eat of these*——[e]Or, and *the building* consisted *of the lower and the middlemost*——[f]Or, *from the place*——[g]Or, *he that brought me*

[h]Or, *as he came*——[i]Ver. 4——[k]Lev. vi. 16, 26; xxiv. 9——[l]Lev. ii. 3, 10; vi. 14, 17, 25, 29; vii. 1; x. 13, 14; Num. xviii. 9, 10——[m]Chap. xliv. 19——[n]Heb. *wind*——[o]Chap. xl. 5——[p]Chap. xlv. 2

NOTES ON CHAP. XLII

Verse 1. *He brought me forth into the utter court*] He brought him out from the temple into the *court of the priests.* This, in reference to the temple, was called the *outer court;* but the *court of the people* was beyond this.

Verse 4. *A walk of ten cubits' breadth inward*] This seems to have been a sort of *parapet.*

Verse 14. *They shall lay their garments wherein they minister*] The priests were not permitted to wear their *robes* in the *outer court.* These vestments were to be used *only when they ministered;* and when they had done, they were to deposit them in one of the chambers mentioned in the *thirteenth* verse.

Verses 16-19. *He measured the east—north—south—west side*] Each of which was *five hundred* reeds: and, as the building was square, the *area* must have been nearly *thirteen thousand* paces. No wonder this was called a city. See chap. xl. 2.

Verse 20. *It had a wall round about—to make a separation between the sanctuary and the profane place.*] The *holy place* was that which was consecrated to the Lord; into which no heathen, nor stranger, nor any in a state of impurity, might enter. The *profane place* was that in which men, women, Gentiles, pure or impure, might be admitted. *Josephus* says *War*, lib. vi., c. 14, that in his time there was a wall built before the entrance *three* cubits high, on which there were posts fixed at certain distances, with inscriptions on them in *Latin* and *Greek*, containing the laws which enjoined *purity* on those that entered; and forbidding all strangers to enter, on pain of death. See *Calmet*.

CHAPTER XLIII

The glory of the Lord is represented as returning to the temple, 1–6; *where God promises to fix his residence, if the people repent and forsake those sins which caused him to depart from them,* 7–12. *Then the measures of the altar, and the ordinances relating to it, are set down,* 13–27.

A. M. 3430
B. C. 574
Olymp. LI. 3
Anno Servii Tullii, R. Roman., 5

AFTERWARD he brought me
to the gate, *even* the gate
[a]that looketh toward the east:
2 [b]And behold, the glory of the
God of Israel came from the way of the east:
and [c]his voice *was* like a noise of many
waters: [d]and the earth shined with his glory.
3 And *it was* [e]according to the appearance
of the vision which I saw, *even* according to
the vision that I saw [f]when I came [g]to destroy the city: and the visions *were* like the
vision that I saw [h]by the river Chebar; and
I fell upon my face.
4 [i]And the glory of the LORD came into the
house by the way of the gate
whose prospect *is* toward the east.
5 [k]So the spirit took me up,
and brought me into the inner
court; and, behold, [l]the glory of the LORD
filled the house.
6 And I heard *him* speaking unto me out
of the house; and [m]the man stood by me.
7 And he said unto me, Son of man, [n]the
place of my throne, and [o]the place of the soles
of my feet, [p]where I will dwell in the midst
of the children of Israel for ever, and my
holy name shall the house of Israel [q]no more
defile, *neither* they, nor their kings, by their

A. M. 3430
B. C. 574
Olymp. LI. 3
Anno Servii Tullii, R. Roman., 5

[a]Chap. x. 19; xliv. 1; xlvi. 1——[b]Chap. xi. 23——[c]Chap. i. 24; Rev. i. 15; xiv. 2; xix. 1, 6——[d]Chap. x. 4; Rev. xviii. 1——[e]Chap. i. 4, 28; viii. 4——[f]Or, *when I came to* prophesy *that the city should be destroyed;* see ch. ix. 1 5——[g]So Jer. i. 10——[h]Chap. i. 3; iii. 23

[i]See chap. x. 19; xliv. 2——[k]Chap. iii. 12, 14; viii. 3——[l]1 Kings viii. 10, 11; chap. xliv. 4——[m]Chap. xl. 3——[n]Psa. xcix. 1——[o]1 Chron. xxviii. 2; Psa. xcix. 5——[p]Exod. xxix. 45; Psa. lxviii. 16; cxxxii. 14; Joel iii. 17; John i. 14; 2 Cor. vi. 16——[q]Chap. xxxix. 7

NOTES ON CHAP. XLIII

Verse 2. *The glory of the God of Israel came from the way of the east*] This was the *chariot of cherubim, wheels*, &c., which he saw at the river Chebar. And this glory, coming from the east, is going to enter into the *eastern gate* of the temple, and thence to shine out upon the whole earth. Is there not a *mystery* here? All knowledge, all religion, and all arts and sciences, have travelled, according to the *course of the sun*, FROM EAST TO WEST! From that quarter the Divine glory at first came; and thence the rays of Divine light continue to diffuse themselves over the face of the earth. From thence came the *Bible*, and through that the *new covenant*. From thence came the *prophets*, the *apostles*, and the *first missionaries*, that brought the knowledge of God to *Europe*, to the *isles of the sea*, and to the *west first*, and afterwards to these *northern regions*.

Verse 5. *The spirit took me up*] And, to follow this thought for a moment, how many men has this heavenly *Spirit taken up;* filled them with his own *influence*, and sent them to every country, and nation, and tongue, and people, to testify the Gospel of the grace of God, and to preach among the Gentiles the unsearchable riches of Christ! What spiritual *temples* have been raised, beautified, and filled with the *glory of God!* And this light is shining and burning more and more unto the perfect day, when the whole earth shall be filled with the glory of God!

Verse 7. *Son of man, the place of my throne*] The *throne* refers to his *majesty;* the *soles of his feet*, to his *condescension* in *dwelling among men*.

Where I will dwell in the midst of the children of Israel] The *tabernacle* and *temple* were types of the *incarnation* of *Jesus Christ:* "Destroy THIS TEMPLE, and after three days I will raise it up;—but this he spake of the temple of his body;" John ii. 19, 21. And in THAT TEMPLE "dwelt all the fulness of the Godhead bodily." Into this *immaculate humanity* did the *glory* of the Supreme God enter; and thus, "God was in Christ reconciling the world unto himself." And this Jesus is *Immanuel*, GOD *with* US. In him we find united the *ineffable majesty* of God, with the *abjectness of man*. He humbled himself in human nature, not only to bear the *form of a servant*, but to *suffer death upon the cross* as a malefactor *slave!* But by these means he has purchased *eternal redemption* for us; and the *spiritual Israel*, who find redemption in his blood, shall be raised up wherever his *holy name* shall be proclaimed; and shall not, like the old apostate Israel, *defile* that *great name* by idolatry or a life of wickedness, but

A. M. 3430
B. C. 574
Olymp. LI. 3
Anno
Servii Tullii,
R. Roman., 5

whoredom, nor by the [r]carcasses
of their kings in their high
places.
8 [s]In their setting of their
threshold by my thresholds, and their posts
by my posts, [t]and the wall between me and
them, they have even defiled my holy name
by their abominations that they have committed: wherefore I have consumed them in
mine anger.
9 Now let them put away their whoredom,
and [u]the carcasses of their kings, far from
me, [v]and I will dwell in the midst of them
for ever.
10 Thou son of man, [w]show the house to
the house of Israel, that they may be ashamed
of their iniquities: and let them measure the
[x]pattern.
11 And if they be ashamed of all that they
have done, show them the form of the house,
and the fashion thereof, and the goings out
thereof, and the comings in thereof, and all
the forms thereof, and all the ordinances
thereof, and all the forms thereof, and all
the laws thereof: and write *it* in their
sight, that they may keep the whole form
thereof, and all the ordinances
thereof, and do them.
12 This *is* the law of the
house; Upon [y]the top of the
mountain the whole limit thereof round
about *shall be* most holy. Behold, this *is*
the law of the house.
13 And these *are* the measures of the altar
after the cubits: [z]The cubit *is* a cubit and a
hand breadth; even the [a]bottom *shall be* a
cubit, and the breadth a cubit, and the border
thereof by the [b]edge thereof round about
shall be a span: and this *shall be* the higher
place of the altar.
14 And from the bottom *upon* the ground
even to the lower settle *shall be* two cubits,
and the breadth one cubit; and from the
lesser settle *even* to the greater settle *shall be*
four cubits, and the breadth *one* cubit.
15 So [c]the altar *shall be* four cubits; and
from [d]the altar and upward *shall be* four
horns.
16 And the altar *shall be* twelve *cubits*
long, twelve broad, square in the four squares
thereof.
17 And the settle *shall be* fourteen *cubits*

[r]Lev. xxvi. 30; Jer. xvi. 18——[s]See 2 Kings xvi. 14; xxi. 4, 5, 7; chap. viii. 3; xxiii. 39; xliv. 7——[t]Or, *for there was but a wall between me and them*——[u]Ver. 7 [v]Ver. 7——[w]Chap. xl. 4

[x]Or, *sum*, or *number*——[y]Chap. xl. 2——[z]Chap. xl. 5; xli. 8——[a]Heb. *bosom*——[b]Heb. *lip*——[c]Heb. *Harel*, that is, *the mountain of God*——[d]Heb. *Ariel*, that is, *the lion of God;* Isa. xxix. 1

they shall show forth the virtues of Him who has called them from darkness into his marvellous light.

Verse 8. *In their setting of their threshold*] They had even gone so far as to set up their idol altars by those of Jehovah; so that their abominable idols were found in the very house of God! therefore, "he consumed them in his anger."

Verse 9. *Now let them put away their whoredom*] Their *idolatry.*

And the carcasses of their kings] It appears that God was displeased with their *bringing their kings so near his temple.* David was buried in the *city of David*, which was on *Mount Zion*, near to the temple; and so were almost all the kings of Judah; but God requires that the place of his temple and its vicinity shall be kept unpolluted; and when they *put away* all kinds of defilement, then will he *dwell among them.*

Verse 10. *Show the house to the house of Israel*] Show them this holy house where the holy God dwells, that they may be *ashamed of their iniquities.* Their name, their profession, their temple, their religious services, all bound them to a holy life; all within them, all without them, should have been *holiness unto the Lord.* But alas! they have been bound by no ties, and they have sinned against all their obligations; nevertheless, *let them measure the pattern*, let them see the rule by which they should have walked, and let them measure themselves by this standard, and walk accordingly.

Verse 11. *And if they be ashamed*] If, in a spirit of true repentance, they acknowledge their past transgressions, and purpose in his help never more to offend their God, then teach them every thing that concerns my worship, and their profiting by it.

Verse 12. *This* is *the law of the house*] From the top of the mountain on which it stands, to the bottom, *all round about*, all shall be holy; no buildings shall be erected in any part, nor place nor spot be appropriated to a common use; all shall be considered as being *most holy.*

Verse 13. *The cubit* is *a cubit and a hand breadth*] It is the same cubit by which all the previous admeasurements were made, and was a hand breadth or *four* inches longer than the Babylonian cubit.

Verse 15. *So the altar*] ההראל *haharel*, "the mount of God."

And from the altar] ומהאריאל *umihaariel*, "and from the lion of God." Perhaps the first was a name given to the *altar* when *elevated* to the honour of God, and on which the victims were offered to him; and the second, the *lion of God*, may mean the *hearth*, which might have been thus called, because it *devoured* and consumed the burnt-offerings, as a lion does his prey. See on Isa. xxix. 1.

Verse 17. *And the settle*] The *ledge* on

A. M. 3430 B. C. 574 Olymp. LI. 3 Anno Servii Tullii, R. Roman., 5

long and fourteen broad in the four squares thereof; and the border about it *shall be* half a cubit; and the bottom thereof *shall be* a cubit about; and [e]his stairs shall look toward the east.

18 And he said unto me, Son of man, thus saith the Lord GOD; These *are* the ordinances of the altar in the day when they shall make it, to offer burnt-offerings thereon, and to [f]sprinkle blood thereon.

19 And thou shalt give to [g]the priests the Levites that be of the seed of Zadok, which approach unto me, to minister unto me, saith the Lord GOD, [h]a young bullock for a sin-offering.

20 And thou shalt take of the blood thereof, and put *it* on the four horns of it, and on the four corners of the settle, and upon the border round about: thus shalt thou cleanse and purge it.

21 Thou shalt take the bullock also of the sin-offering, and he [i]shall burn it in the appointed place of the house, [k]without the sanctuary.

22 And on the second day thou shalt offer a kid of the goats without blemish for a sin-offering; and they shall cleanse the altar, as they did cleanse *it* with the bullock.

A. M. 3430 B. C. 574 Olymp. LI. 3 Anno Servii Tullii, R. Roman., 5

23 When thou hast made an end of cleansing *it*, thou shalt offer a young bullock without blemish, and a ram out of the flock without blemish.

24 And thou shalt offer them before the LORD, [l]and the priests shall cast salt upon them, and they shall offer them up *for* a burnt-offering unto the LORD.

25 [m]Seven days shalt thou prepare every day a goat *for* a sin-offering: they shall also prepare a young bullock, and a ram out of the flock, without blemish.

26 Seven days shall they purge the altar and purify it; and they shall [n]consecrate themselves.

27 And when these days are expired, it shall be, *that* upon the [o]eighth day, and *so* forward, the priests shall make your burnt-offerings upon the altar, and your [p]peace-offerings; and I will [q]accept you, saith the Lord GOD.

[e]See Exodus xx. 26——[f]Leviticus i. 5——[g]Chap. xliv. 15——[h]Exodus xxix. 10, 12; Leviticus viii. 14, 15; chap. xlv. 18, 19——[i]Exodus xxix. 14——[k]Hebrew xiii. 11——[l]Leviticus ii. 13——[m]Exodus xxix. 35, 36; Leviticus viii. 33——[n]Hebrew, *fill their hands;* Exodus xxix. 24——[o]Leviticus ix. 1——[p]Or, *thank-offerings*——[q]Job xlii. 8; chapter xx. 40, 41; xliii. 27; Romans xii. 1; 1 Peter ii. 5, 20

which the priests walked round the altar, see ver. 14. By these settles or ledges the altar was narrowed towards the top. "The ascent shall look toward the east;" this ascent was an inclined plane. But these *settles*, or more properly *ledges*, as Bp. *Newcome* translates, may be thus computed. The altar itself was *ten* feet high and *twenty* broad; the same as that of Solomon, 2 Chron. iv. 1.

	Cubits
For the base, ver. 13, is in height - - -	1
From the surface of the base to the first ledge, ver. 14, is - - - - - - - -	1
From the lower ledge to the upper, ver. 14, are - - - - - - - - - - - - - -	4
From the upper ledge to the ariel or hearth, ver. 15, are - - - - - - - - - -	4
In all - - -	10

	Cubits
And as to the breadth, the upper ledge, ver. 17, was - - - - - - - - - - - - -	14
Add a cubit on each side for the higher ledge, ver. 14, latter part - - - - - - - -	2
Add a cubit on each side for the lower ledge, ver. 14, former part - - - - - - - -	2
Add a cubit on each side for the base, ver. 13,	2
In all - - -	20

The altar of burnt-offerings, described Exod. xxvii. 1, xxxviii. 1, was smaller than this, because it was to be removed from place to place with the tabernacle. This was designed for a permanent temple. See Bp. *Newcome* on this chapter.

Verse 19. *The priests—that be of the seed of Zadok*] It was this Zadok that was put in the place of Abiathar, by Solomon, 1 Kings ii. 35, in whose family the priesthood had continued ever since.

Verse 25. *Seven days shalt thou prepare*] These are, in general, ordinances of the LAW; and may be seen by consulting the parallel passages. All these directions are given that they might follow them, when they should be put in possession of their own land. For in several cases the prophet enters into particulars, as if he had supposed that the book of the law had perished.

CHAPTER XLIV

This chapter gives an account of the glory of God having returned to the temple, 1–4. *The Jews reproved for suffering idolatrous priests to pollute it with their ministrations,* 5–8. *Ordinances respecting the conduct of the priests, and the maintenance due to them,* 9–31.

A. M. 3430
B. C. 574
Olymp. LI. 3
Anno
Servii Tullii,
R. Roman., 5

THEN he brought me back the way of the gate of the outward sanctuary [a]which looketh toward the east; and it *was* shut.

2 Then said the LORD unto me; This gate shall be shut, it shall not be opened, and no man shall enter in by it; [b]because the LORD, the GOD of Israel, hath entered in by it, therefore it shall be shut.

3 *It is* for the prince; the prince, he shall sit in it to [c]eat bread before the LORD; [d]he shall enter by the way of the porch of *that* gate, and shall go out by the way of the same.

4 Then brought he me the way of the north gate before the house: and I looked, and, [e]behold, the glory of the LORD filled the house of the LORD: [f]and I fell upon my face.

5 And the LORD said unto me, [g]Son of man, [h]mark well, and behold with thine eyes, and hear with thine ears all that I say unto thee concerning all the ordinances of the house of the LORD, and all the laws thereof; and mark well the entering in of the house, with every going forth of the sanctuary.

6 And thou shalt say to the [i]rebellious, *even* to the house of Israel, Thus saith the Lord GOD; O ye house of Israel, [k]let it suffice you of all your abominations.

A. M. 3430
B. C. 574
Olymp. LI. 3
Anno
Servii Tullii,
R. Roman., 5

7 [l]In that ye have brought *into my sanctuary* [m]strangers,[n] [o]uncircumcised in heart, and uncircumcised in flesh, to be in my sanctuary, to pollute it, *even* my house, when ye offer [p]my bread, [q]the fat and the blood, and they have broken my covenant because of all your abominations.

8 And ye have not [r]kept the charge of mine holy things; but ye have set keepers of my [s]charge in my sanctuary for yourselves.

9 Thus saith the Lord GOD; [t]No stranger, uncircumcised in heart, nor uncircumcised in flesh, shall enter into my sanctuary, of any stranger that *is* among the children of Israel.

10 [u]And the Levites that are gone away far from me, when Israel went astray, which went astray away from me after their idols; they shall even bear their iniquity.

11 Yet they shall be ministers in my sanctuary, [v]*having* charge at the gates of the house, and ministering to the house: [w]they shall slay the burnt-offering and the sacrifice for the people, and [x]they shall stand before them to minister unto them.

12 Because they ministered unto them before

[a]Chap. xliii. 1——[b]Chap. xliii. 4——[c]Gen. xxxi. 54; 1 Cor. x. 18——[d]Chap. xlvi. 2, 8——[e]Chap. iii. 23; xliii. 5——[f]Chap. i. 28——[g]Chap. xl. 4——[h]Heb. *set thine heart*——[i]Chap. ii. 5——[k]Chap. xlv. 9; 1 Pet. iv. 3 [l]Chap. xliii. 8; ver. 9; Acts xxi. 28——[m]Heb. *children of a stranger*——[n]Lev. xxii. 25

[o]Lev. xxvi. 41; Deut. x. 16; Acts vii.5 1——[p]Lev. xxi. 6, 8, 17, 21——[q]Lev. iii. 16; xvii. 11——[r]Lev. xxii. 2, &c.——[s]Or, *ward*, or *ordinance;* and so ver. 14, 16; chap. xl. 45——[t]Ver. 7——[u]See 2 Kings xxiii. 8, &c.; 2 Chron. xxix. 4, ´; chap. xlviii. 11——[v]1 Chron. xxvi. 1 [w]2 Chron. xxix. 34; [x]Num. xvi. 9

NOTES ON CHAP. XLIV

Verse 1. *The outward sanctuary*] In opposition to the temple itself, which was the inner sanctuary.

Verse 2. *This gate shall be shut*] It was not to be opened on *ordinary occasions*, nor at all on the *week days:* but only on the *Sabbaths* and the *new moons*. See the account of the *gates* (4) in the explanation of the plan.

This verse has been adduced by the Roman Catholics to prove the *perpetual virginity* of the mother of our Lord; and it may be allowed to be as much to the purpose as any other that has been brought to prove this very precarious point, on which no stress should ever be laid by any man. Mary was a virgin when she brought forth Jesus.

Verse 5. *Mark well, and behold*] Take notice of every thing; register all so fully that thou shalt be able to give the most minute information to the children of Israel.

Verse 7. *The fat and the blood*] These never went into common use; they were wholly offered to God. The *blood* was poured out; the *fat* consumed.

Because of all your abominations.] Several MSS. of *Kennicott's* and *De Rossi's* read *their abominations*, referring to the *strangers* mentioned before.

Verse 10. *And the Levites that are gone away far from me*] This refers to the schism of Jeroboam, who, when he set up a new worship, got as many of the priests and Levites to join him in his idolatry as he could. These, on the return from the captivity, should not be permitted to perform the functions of *priests* in the new temple; but they might be continued as *keepers of all the charge of the house*—be treasurers, guards of the temple, porters, &c.; see

A. M. 3430
B. C. 574
Olymp. LI. 3
Anno
Servii Tullii,
R. Roman., 5

their idols, and [y]caused [z]the house of Israel to fall into iniquity; therefore have I [a]lifted up mine hand against them, saith the Lord GOD, and they shall bear their iniquity.

13 [b]And they shall not come near unto me, to do the office of a priest unto me, nor to come near to any of my holy things, in the most holy *place:* but they shall [c]bear their shame, and their abominations which they have committed.

14 But I will make them [d]keepers of the charge of the house, for all the service thereof, and for all that shall be done therein.

15 [e]But the priests the Levites, [f]the sons of Zadok, that kept the charge of my sanctuary [g]when the children of Israel went astray from me, they shall come near to me to minister unto me, and they [h]shall stand before me to offer unto me [i]the fat and the blood, saith the Lord GOD:

16 They shall enter into my sanctuary, and they shall come near to [k]my table, to minister unto me, and they shall keep my charge.

17 And it shall come to pass, *that* when they enter in at the gates of the inner court, [l]they shall be clothed with linen garments; and no wool shall come upon them, whiles they minister in the gates of the inner court, and within.

18 [m]They shall have linen bonnets upon their heads, and shall have linen breeches upon their loins; they shall not gird *themselves* [n]with [o]any thing that causeth sweat.

19 And when they go forth into the utter court, *even* into the utter court of the people, [p]they shall put off their garments wherein they ministered, and lay them in the holy chambers, and they shall put on other garments; and they shall [q]not sanctify the people with their garments.

20 [r]Neither shall they shave their heads, nor suffer their locks to grow long; they shall only poll their heads.

21 [s]Neither shall any priest drink wine, when they enter into the inner court.

22 Neither shall they take for their wives a [t]widow, nor her that is [u]put away: but they shall take maidens of the seed of the house of Israel, or a widow [v]that had a priest before.

23 And [w]they shall teach my people *the difference* between the holy and profane, and cause them to discern between the unclean and the clean.

24 And [x]in controversy they shall stand in judgment; *and* they shall judge it according to my judgments; and they shall keep my laws and my statutes in all mine assemblies; [y]and they shall hallow my sabbaths.

25 And they shall come at no [z]dead person to defile themselves: but for father, or for mother, or for son, or for daughter, for brother, or for sister that hath had no husband, they may defile themselves.

26 And [a]after he is cleansed, they shall reckon unto him seven days.

27 And in the day that he goeth into the

[y]Isa. ix. 16; Mal. ii. 8——[z]Heb. *were for a stumbling block of iniquity unto*, &c.; ch xiv 3, 4——[a]Psa. cvi. 26——[b]2 Kings xxiii. 9; Num. xviii. 3——[c]Ch. xxxii. 30; xxxvi. 7——[d]Num. xviii. 4; 1 Chron. xxiii. 28, 32——[e]Ch. xl. 46; xliii. 19——[f]1 Sam. ii. 35——[g]Ver. 10——[h]Deut. x. 8——[i]Ver. 7——[k]Ch. xli. 22——[l]Exod. xxviii. 39, 40, 43; xxxix. 27, 28——[m]Exod. xxviii. 40, 42; xxxix. 28

[n]Or, *in sweating* places——[o]Heb. *in*, or *with sweat.*——[p]Ch. xlii. 14——[q]Ch. xlvi. 20; see Exod. xxix. 37; xxx 29; Lev. vi. 27; Matt. xxiii. 17, 19——[r]Lev. xxi. 5——[s]Lev. x. 9——[t]Lev. xxi. 7, 13, 14——[u]Heb. *thrust forth*——[v]Heb. *from a priest*——[w]Lev. x. 10, 11; ch. xxii. 26; Mal. ii. 7——[x]Deut. xvii. 8, &c.; 2 Chron. xix. 8, 10——[y]See ch. xxii. 26——[z]Lev. xxi. 1, &c.——[a]Num. vi. 10; xix. 11, &c.

ver. 11-15. The whole of these passages refer to the period of time when the second temple was built.

Verse 16. *Come near to my table*] To place the *shew-bread* there, and to burn incense on the golden altar in the holy of holies.

Verse 17. *No wool shall come upon them*] The reason is plain; wool is more apt than *linen* to contract *dirt* and breed *insects;* linen breeds none; besides, this is a *vegetable*, and the other an *animal* substance. It was an ancient maxim, that whatever was taken from a *dead body* was impure in matters of religion, and should not be permitted to enter into the temple. The Egyptian priests always wore *linen* on their bodies, and shoes of *matting* or *rushes* on their feet. The Mohammedans never write the Koran upon *vellum* or *skin* of any kind, as they would consider that as a defilement.

Verse 20. *Neither shall they shave their heads*] The priests of *Isis* shaved their heads close to the skin; the priests of *Budhoo* do so still; their ordinances oblige them to shave their heads every *tenth day.* To let the hair grow *long* would have been improper; therefore the Lord commands them to *poll*—cut the hair *short*, but not to shave.

Verse 22. *Neither shall they take for their wives a widow*] This was prohibited to the *high priest* only, by Moses, Lev. xxi. 13, 14.

Verse 25. *And they shall come at no dead person to defile themselves*] Touching the dead defiles a *Hindoo* now, as it formerly did a *Jew;* and they must bathe to become clean again.

A. M. 3430 B. C. 574 Olymp. LI. 3 Anno Servii Tullii, R. Roman., 5

sanctuary, [b]unto the inner court, to minister in the sanctuary, [c]he shall offer his sin-offering, saith the Lord GOD.

28 And it shall be unto them for an inheritance: I [d]*am* their inheritance: and ye shall give them no possession in Israel: I *am* their possession.

29 [e]They shall eat the meat-offering, and the sin-offering, and the trespass-offering; and [f]every [g]dedicated thing in Israel shall be theirs.

30 And the [h]first[i] of all the first-fruits of all *things*, and every oblation of all, of every *sort* of your oblations, shall be the priest's: [k]ye shall also give unto the priest the first of your dough, [l]that he may cause the blessing to rest in thine house.

31 The priest shall not eat of any thing that is [m]dead of itself, or torn, whether it be fowl or beast.

[b]Ver. 17——[c]Lev. iv. 3——[d]Num. xviii. 20; Deut. x. 9; xviii. 1, 2; Josh. xiii. 14, 33——[e]Lev. vi. 18, 29; vii. 6——[f]Lev. xxvii. 21, 28, compared with Num. xviii. 14——[g]Or, *devoted*

[h]Or, *chief*——[i]Exod. xiii. 2; xxii. 29, 30; xxiii. 19; Num. iii. 13; xviii. 12, 13——[k]Num. xv. 20; Neh. x. 37 [l]Prov. iii. 9, 10; Mal. iii. 10——[m]Exod. xxii. 31; Lev. xxii. 8

Verse 28. *I* am *their inheritance*] Those who affect to form their ecclesiastical matters on the model of the Jewish Church have with one consent left this out of the question. They will not live on the *free-will offerings of the people;* but must have vast revenues, and these secured to them by *law.* That every minister of God should be supported by the altar I grant; but I think, instead of that method of paying the parochial clergy which I see is so much objected to, and breeds so much dissension between the pastors and their flocks, it would be better, *on these accounts*, to assign them a portion of land adequate to their supply, or let the state maintain them as it does its other officers. In Israel God was their *inheritance* and their *possession;* but *they* had the *breast* and *shoulder* of all sin-offerings and trespass-offerings, and all *dedicated things* were theirs; and they had a portion of all the *dough* that was prepared for bread. These were considered as the *Lord's property*, and these he gave to *them;* and this is always implied in the *Lord's being their inheritance* and their *possession.* They had a plentiful support.

Hitherto *tithes* have been thought the best mode of paying the *clergy*, and providing for the *poor* of each parish; but these matters have undergone such *alterations* since the time of their institution, that some emendation of the system is at present absolutely necessary.

There should be a public acknowledgment of God in every nation, and this should be provided for by the *state* in a way the least burdensome to the *people*, that all may rejoice in the benefit. Happy the nations that have a Bible so correct, and a *Liturgy* so pure, as those in the British empire! In such cases, a religion established by the state is an unutterable blessing to the nation; only keep it to the Bible, and to the Liturgy, and all, under God, will be well; but when the sermon is against these, all is bad.

CHAPTER XLV

The several portions of land appointed for the sanctuary, 1–5, *the city,* 6, *and the prince,* 7, 8. *Regulations concerning the weights and measures,* 9–12; *with ordinances respecting the provisions for the ordinary and extraordinary sacrifices,* 13–25.

A. M. 3430 B. C. 574 Olymp. LI. 3 Anno Servii Tullii, R. Roman., 5

MOREOVER, [a]when ye shall [b]divide by lot the land for inheritance, ye shall [c]offer an oblation unto the LORD, [d]a holy portion of the land: the length *shall be* the length of five and twenty thousand *reeds*, and the breadth *shall be* ten thousand. This *shall be* holy in all the borders thereof round about.

2 Of this there shall be for the sanctuary [e]five hundred *in length*, with five hundred *in breadth*, square round about; and fifty cubits round about for the [f]suburbs thereof.

[a]Heb. *when ye cause the land to fall*——[b]Chap. xlvii. 22 [c]Chap. xlviii. 8

[d]Hebrew, *holiness*——[e]Chapter xlii. 20——[f]Or, *void places*

NOTES ON CHAP. XLV

Verse 1. *When ye shall divide by lot*] That is, when on your repossessing your land, every family settles according to the allotment which they *formerly* had; for it is certain that the *land* was not divided afresh by lot after the Babylonish captivity. The allotment mentioned and described here was merely for the *service* of the *temple*, the use of the *priests*, and the *prince* or governor of the people. A division of the *whole land* is not intended.

Verse 2. *Of this there shall be for the sanctuary*] See the plan, A.

A. M. 3430
B. C. 574
Olymp. LI. 3
Anno
Servii Tullii,
R. Roman., 5

3 And of this measure shalt thou measure the length of five and twenty thousand, and the breadth of ten thousand: [g]and in it shall be the sanctuary *and* the most holy *place*.

4 [h]The holy *portion* of the land shall be for the priests the ministers of the sanctuary, which shall come near to minister unto the LORD: and it shall be a place for their houses, and a holy place for the sanctuary.

5 [i]And the five and twenty thousand of length, and the ten thousand of breadth, shall also the Levites, the ministers of the house, have for themselves, for a possession for [k]twenty chambers.

6 And [l]ye shall appoint the possession of the city five thousand broad, and five and twenty thousand long, over against the oblation of the holy *portion:* it shall be for the whole house of Israel.

7 [m]And *a portion shall be* for the prince on the one side and on the other side of the oblation of the holy portion, and of the possession of the city, before the oblation of the holy *portion,* and before the possession of the city, from the west side westward, and from the east side eastward: and the length *shall be* over against one of the portions, from the west border unto the east border.

8 In the land shall be his possession in Israel: and [n]my princes shall no more oppress my people; and *the rest of* the land shall they give to the house of Israel according to their tribes.

9 Thus saith the Lord GOD; [o]Let it suffice you, O princes of Israel: [p]remove violence and spoil, and execute judgment and justice, take away your [q]exactions from my people, saith the Lord GOD.

A. M. 3430
B. C. 574
Olymp. LI. 3
Anno
Servii Tullii,
R. Roman., 5

10 Ye shall have just [r]balances, and a just ephah, and a just bath.

11 The ephah and the bath shall be of one measure, that the bath may contain the tenth part of an homer, and the ephah the tenth part of an homer: the measure thereof shall be after the homer.

12 And the [s]shekel *shall be* twenty gerahs: twenty shekels, five and twenty shekels, fifteen shekels shall be your maneh.

13 This *is* the oblation that ye shall offer: the sixth part of an ephah of an homer of wheat, and ye shall give the sixth part of an ephah of an homer of barley:

14 Concerning the ordinance of oil, the bath of oil, *ye shall offer* the tenth part of a bath out of the cor, *which is* an homer of ten baths; for ten baths *are* an homer:

15 And one [t]lamb out of the flock, out of two hundred, out of the fat pastures of Israel; for a meat-offering, and for a burnt-offering, and for [u]peace-offerings, [v]to make reconciliation for them, saith the Lord GOD.

16 All the people of the land [w]shall give this oblation [x]for the prince in Israel.

17 And it shall be the prince's part *to give* burnt-offerings, and meat-offerings, and drink-offerings, in the feasts, and in the new moons, and in the sabbaths, in all solemnities of the house of Israel: he shall prepare the sin-offering, and the meat-offering, and the burnt-offering, and the [y]peace-offerings, to make reconciliation for the house of Israel.

---

[g]Chap. xlviii. 10——[h]Ver. 1; chap. xlviii. 10, &c. [i]Ch. xlviii. 13——[k]See ch. xl. 17——[l]Ch. xlviii. 15 [m]Chap. xlviii. 21——[n]Chap. xlvi. 18; see Jer. xxii. 17; chap. xxii. 27——[o]Chap. xliv. 6——[p]Jer. xxii. 3

[q]Heb. *expulsions*——[r]Lev. xix. 35, 36; Prov. xi. 1 [s]Exod. xxx. 13; Lev. xxvii. 25; Num. iii. 47——[t]Or, *kid* [u]Or, *thank-offerings*——[v]Lev. i. 4——[w]Heb. *shall be for* [x]Or, *with*——[y]Or, *thank-offerings*

Verse 3. *And of this measure*] See the plan, A, B, C, D, E.

Verse 4. *The holy* portion] See the plan, A.

Verse 5. *And the five and twenty thousand*] See the plan, B.

Verse 6. *Ye shall appoint*] See the plan, FF.

Verse 7. A portion shall be *for the prince*] נשיא *nasi,* he who had the authority of *chief magistrate;* for there was neither *king* nor *prince* among the Jews after the Babylonish captivity. For these allotments and divisions, see the plan, EE, FF, GG.

Verse 8. *My princes shall no more oppress my people*] By exorbitant taxes to maintain profligate courts, or subsidize other powers to help to keep up a system of tyranny in the earth. The former princes even robbed the temple of God to give subsidies to other states.

Verse 9. *Take away your exactions from my people*] This is the voice of God to all the rulers of the earth.

Take away your exactions; do not oppress the people; they are *mine.* Abolish all oppressive taxes.

Verse 10. *Ye shall have just balances*] This appreciation of *weights, measures,* and *money* was intended to show them that they must not

A. M. 3430
B. C. 574
Olymp. LI. 3
Anno
Servii Tullii,
R. Roman., 5

18 Thus saith the Lord GOD: In the first *month,* in the first *day* of the month, thou shalt take a young bullock without blemish, and [z]cleanse the sanctuary.

19 [a]And the priest shall take of the blood of the sin-offering, and put *it* upon the posts of the house, and upon the four corners of the settle of the altar, and upon the posts of the gate of the inner court.

20 And so thou shalt do the seventh *day* of the month [b]for every one that erreth, and for *him that is* simple: so shall ye reconcile the house.

21 [c]In the first *month,* in the fourteenth day of the month, ye shall have the passover, a feast of seven days; unleavened bread shall be eaten.

22 And upon that day shall the prince prepare for himself and for all the people of the land [d]a bullock *for* a sin-offering.

23 And [e]seven days of the feast he shall prepare a burnt-offering to the LORD, seven bullocks and seven rams without blemish daily the seven days; [f]and a kid of the goats daily *for* a sin-offering.

24 [g]And he shall prepare a meat-offering of an ephah for a bullock, and an ephah for a ram, and a hin of oil for an ephah.

25 In the seventh *month,* in the fifteen day of the month, shall he do the like in the [h]feast of the seven days, according to the sin-offering, according to the burnt-offering, and according to the meat-offering, and according to the oil.

[z]Lev. xvi. 16——[a]Chap. xliii. 20——[b]Lev. iv. 27
[c]Exod. xii. 18; Lev. xxiii. 5, 6; Num. ix. 2, 3; xxviii. 16, 17; Deut. xvi. 1, &c.

[d]Lev. iv. 14——[e]Lev. xxiii. 8——[f]See Num. xxviii. 15, 22, 30; xxix. 5, 11, 16, 19, &c.——[g]Ch. xlvi. 5, 7
[h]Lev. xxiii. 34; Num. xxix. 12; Deut. xvi. 13

introduce those to which they had been accustomed in the captivity, but those which God had prescribed to their forefathers. See the notes on the parallel places.

Verse 16. *All—this oblation for the prince*] A present or offering to the prince.

Verse 18. *Thou shalt take a young bullock —and cleanse the sanctuary.*] There is nothing of this in the Mosaic law; it seems to have been a new ceremony. An *annual* purification of the sanctuary may be intended.

Verse 20. *For* him that is *simple*] That wants understanding to conduct himself properly.

Verse 25. *In the seventh* month] He shall do at the feast of tabernacles the same things that he was desired to do on the *passover.* The prince should offer the same number of victims, of the same quality, and with the same ceremonies, as during the above *seven* days. The offerings were, sin-offerings, burnt-offerings, and peace-offerings.

CHAPTER XLVI

Ordinances of worship prescribed for the prince and for the people, 1–15; *and the gifts he may bestow on his sons and servants,* 16–18. *A description of the courts appointed for boiling or baking any part of the holy oblations,* 19–24.

A. M. 3430
B. C. 574
Olymp. LI. 3
Anno
Servii Tullii,
R. Roman., 5

THUS saith the Lord GOD; The gate of the inner court that looketh toward the east shall be shut the six working days; but on the sabbath it shall be opened, and in the day of the new moon it shall be opened.

2 [a]And the prince shall enter by the way of the porch of *that* gate without, and shall stand by the post of the gate, and the priest shall prepare his burnt-offering and his peace-offerings, and he shall worship at the threshold of the gate: then he shall go forth: but the gate shall not be shut until the evening.

3 Likewise the people of the land shall worship at the door of this gate before the LORD in the sabbaths and in the new moons.

4 And the burnt-offering that [b]the prince shall offer unto the LORD in the sabbath day *shall be* six lambs without blemish, and a ram without blemish.

[a]Chap. xliv. 3; ver. 8

[b]Chap. xlv. 17

NOTES ON CHAP. XLVI

Verse 4. *The burnt-offerings that the prince shall offer*] The *chief magistrate* was always obliged to *attend the public worship of God,* as well as the *priest,* to show that the *civil* and *ecclesiastical* states were both under the same government of the Lord; and that no one was capable of being *prince* or *priest,* who did not acknowledge God in all his ways. It is no wonder that those lands mourn, where neither the *established priest* nor the *civil magistrate*

A. M. 3430
B. C. 574
Olymp. LI. 3
Anno
Servii Tullii,
R. Roman., 5

5 [c]And the meat-offering *shall*
be an ephah for a ram, and the
meat-offering for the lambs [d]as
he shall be able to give, and a
hin of oil to an ephah.
6 And in the day of the new moon *it shall*
be a young bullock without blemish, and six
lambs, and a ram: they shall be without
blemish.
7 And he shall prepare a meat-offering, an
ephah for a bullock, and an ephah for a ram,
and for the lambs according as his hand shall
attain unto, and a hin of oil to an ephah.
8 [e]And when the prince shall enter, he
shall go in by the way of the porch of *that*
gate, and he shall go forth by the way thereof.
9 But when the people of the land [f]shall
come before the LORD in the solemn feasts,
he that entereth in by the way of the north
gate to worship shall go out by the way of
the south gate; and he that entereth by the
way of the south gate shall go forth by the
way of the north gate: he shall not return
by the way of the gate whereby he came in,
but shall go forth over against it.
10 And the prince in the midst of them,
when they go in, shall go in; and when they
go forth, shall go forth.
11 And in the feasts and in the solemnities
[g]the meat-offering shall be an ephah to a bullock, and an ephah to a ram, and to the
lambs as he is able to give, and a hin of oil
to an ephah.
12 Now when the prince shall prepare a
voluntary burnt-offering or peace-offerings
voluntarily unto the LORD, [h]*one*
shall then open him the gate
that looketh toward the east,
and he shall prepare his burnt
offering and his peace-offerings, as he did on
the sabbath day: then he shall go forth; and
after his going forth *one* shall shut the gate.
13 [i]Thou shalt daily prepare a burnt-offering unto the LORD *of* a lamb [k]of the first year
without blemish: thou shalt prepare it [l]every
morning.
14 And thou shalt prepare a meat-offering
for it every morning, the sixth part of an
ephah, and the third part of a hin of oil, to
temper with the fine flour; a meat-offering
continually by a perpetual ordinance unto
the LORD.
15 Thus shall they prepare the lamb, and
the meat-offering, and the oil, every morning
for a continual burnt-offering.
16 Thus saith the Lord GOD; If the prince
give a gift unto any of his sons, the inheritance thereof shall be his sons'; it *shall be*
their possession by inheritance.
17 But if he give a gift of his inheritance
to one of his servants, then it shall be his to
[m]the year of liberty; after it shall return to
the prince; but his inheritance shall be his
sons' for them.
18 Moreover [n]the prince shall not take of
the people's inheritance by oppression, to
thrust them out of their possession; *but* he
shall give his sons' inheritance out of his own
possession: that my people be not scattered
every man from his possession.

A. M. 3430
B. C. 574
Olymp. LI. 3
Anno
Servii Tullii,
R. Roman., 5

[c]Chap. xlv. 29; ver. 7, 11——[d]Heb. *the gift of his hand;* Deut. xvi. 17——[e]Ver. 2——[f]Exod. xxiii. 14-17; Deut. xvi. 16——[g]Ver. 5

[h]Chap. xliv. 3; ver. 2——[i]Exod. xxix. 38; Num. xxviii. 3——[k]Heb. *a son of his year*——[l]Heb. *morning by morning*——[m]Lev. xxv. 10——[n]Chap. xlv. 8

either fear or love God. Ungodly priests and profligate magistrates are a curse to any land. In no country have I found *both* so exemplary for uprightness, as in Britain.

Verse 7. *According as his hand shall attain unto*] According to his ability, to what the providence of God has put in his hand, i. e., his power. This proportion of offerings is different from that prescribed by the Mosaic law, Num. xv. 4-12.

Verse 9. *He that entereth in by the way of the north, &c.*] As the *north* and the *south* gates were opposite to each other, he that came in at the north must go out at the south; he that came in at the south must go out at the north. No person was to come in at the *east* gate, because there was no gate at the *west;* and the people were not permitted to *turn round* and go out at the same place by which they came in; for this was like turning their backs on God, and the decorum and reverence with which public worship was to be conducted would not admit of this. Besides, returning by the same way must have occasioned a great deal of confusion, where so many people must have jostled each other, in their meetings in different parts of this space.

Verse 10. *And the prince in the midst of them*] Even *he* shall act in the same way: he must also go straight forward, and never turn his back to go out at the same gate by which he entered. The prince and the people were to begin and end their worship at the same time.

Verse 13. *Thou shalt prepare it every morning.*] The *evening* offering is entirely omitted, which makes an important difference between this and the old laws. See Exod. xxix. 31-46.

Verse 17. *To the year of liberty*] That is,

A. M. 3430
B. C. 574
Olymp. LI. 3
Anno
Servii Tullii,
R. Roman., 5

19 After he brought me
through the entry, which *was* at
the side of the gate, into the
holy chambers of the priests,
which looked toward the north: and, behold,
there *was* a place on the two sides westward.
20 Then said he unto me, This *is* the place
where the priests shall [o]boil the trespass-
offering and the sin-offering, where they shall
[p]bake the meat-offering; that they bear *them*
not out into the utter court, [q]to sanctify the
people.
21 Then he brought me forth into the utter
court, and caused me to pass by the four corners of the court; and, behold,
[r]in every corner of the court
there was a court.
22 In the four corners of the
court *there were* courts [s]joined of forty
cubits long and thirty broad: these four
[t]corners *were* of one measure.
23 And *there was* a row *of building* round
about in them, round about them four, and
it was made with boiling places under the
rows round about.
24 Then said he unto me, These *are* the
places of them that boil, where the ministers of
the house shall [u]boil the sacrifice of the people.

[o]2 Chron. xxxv. 13——[p]Lev. ii. 4, 5, 7——[q]Chap. xliv. 19——[r]Heb. *a court in a corner of a court, and a court in a corner of a court*

[s]Or, *made with chimneys*——[t]Hebrew, *cornered*
[u]See verse 20; Leviticus viii. 31; 1 Kings xix. 21; 2 Kings vi. 29

to the year of *jubilee*, called the *year of liberty*, because there was then a general release. All servants had their liberty, and all alienated estates returned to their former owners.

Verse 19. *He brought me through the entry*] The prophet had entered by the north gate of the court of the priests, where he had seen, a little before, the glory of the Lord, and where he had received all those directions from chap. xliv. 4, 5, to this chapter. From that gate, (see plan Q,) he entered the vestibule by a gate which was by the side of the apartments of the priests, which were along this aisle, (see S,) to the right of the vestibule towards the west. At the extremity of a row of chambers, he remarked, at the west, the place where they *boiled the flesh* of the sin-offerings, (see T.) They did not boil there the flesh of *all sorts* of victims, there were other kitchens appointed for that, (see PP:) but that only which could not be eaten but in the *outer court*, and by the *priests* which were sanctified; such were the parts of the offerings for sins of commission and ignorance, and the offerings of *flour* with which they were accompanied.

Verse 20. *The trespass-offering*] Part of this, and of the sin-offering, and the flour-offering, was the portion of the priests. See Num. xviii. 9, 10.

Verse 23. It was *made with boiling places*] These were uncovered apartments, where they kept fires for dressing those parts of the peace-offerings, which were made in the temple by individuals through a principle of devotion. On these their families and their friends feasted; and portions were sent to the poor, the widows, and the orphans. And thus the spirit of devotion was the means of preserving the spirit of mercy, charity, and benevolence in the land. How true is that word, "Godliness is profitable for all things."

CHAPTER XLVII

The vision of the holy waters issuing out of the temple, and their virtue; an emblem of the power of God's grace under the Gospel, capable of healing all but the incorrigibly impenitent, represented by the marshy ground that cannot be healed, 1–12. *Also a description of the several divisions of the Holy Land indiscriminately shared betwixt Jews and proselytes; to denote that in after times the privileges now enjoyed by the Jews should be also extended to the Gentiles,* 13–23.

A. M. 3430
B. C. 574
Olymp. LI. 3
Anno
Servii Tullii,
R. Roman., 5

AFTERWARD he brought me
again unto the door of the
house; and, behold, [a]waters issued out from under the [b]thresh-
old of the house eastward: for the fore front
of the house *stood toward* the
east, and the waters came down
from under from the right side
of the house, at the south *side*
of the altar.

[a]Joel iii. 18; Zech. xiii. 1; xiv. 8; Rev. xxii. 1

[b]Psa. lxxxiv. 10, in the margin

NOTES ON CHAP. XLVII

Verse 1. *Behold, waters issued out from under the threshold*] Ezekiel, after having made the whole compass of the *court of the people*, is brought back by the *north gate* into the *courts of the priests;* and, having reached the gate of the temple, he saw waters which had their spring under the threshold of that gate, that looked towards the east; and which, passing to the south of the altar of burnt-offerings on the right of the temple, ran from the west to the east, that they might fall into the brook Kidron, and thence be carried into the Dead Sea. Literally, no such waters were ever in the temple; and because there were none, Solomon had what is called the *brazen sea* made, which held water for the use of the

A. M. 3430 B. C. 574 Olymp. LI. 3 Anno Servii Tullii, R. Roman., 5

2 Then brought he me out of
the way of the gate northward,
and led me about the way without unto the utter gate by the
way that looketh eastward; and, behold,
there ran out waters on the right side.

3 And when [e]the man that had the line in
his hand went forth eastward, he measured a
thousand cubits, and he brought me through
the waters; the [d]waters *were* to the ankles.

4 Again he measured a thousand, and
brought me through the waters; the waters
were to the knees. Again he measured a
thousand, and brought me through; the
waters *were* to the loins.

5 Afterward he measured a thousand; *and
it was a* river that I could not pass over: for
the waters were risen, [e]waters
to swim in, a river that could
not be passed over.

6 And he said unto me, Son
of man, hast thou seen *this?* Then he
brought me, and caused me to return to the
brink of the river.

7 Now when I had returned, behold, at the
[f]bank of the river *were* very many [g]trees on
the one side and on the other.

8 Then said he unto me, These waters issue
out toward the east country, and go down
into the [h]desert, and go into the sea: *which
being* brought forth into the sea, the waters
shall be healed.

9 And it shall come to pass, *that* every
thing that liveth, which moveth, whither-

[c]Chap. xl. 3——[d]Heb. *waters of the ankles*——[e]Heb. *waters of swimming*——[f]Heb. *lip*

[g]Ver. 12; Rev. xxii. 2——[h]Or, *plain;* see Deut. iii. 17; iv. 49; Josh. iii. 16

temple. It is true that the water which supplied this *sea* might have been brought by pipes to the place: but a fountain producing *abundance of water* was not there, and could not be there, on the top of such a hill; and consequently these waters, as well as those spoken of in Joel iii. 18, and in Zech. xiv. 8, are to be understood *spiritually* or *typically;* and indeed the whole complexion of the place here shows, that they are thus to be understood. Taken in this view, I shall proceed to apply the whole of this vision to the effusion of light and salvation by the outpouring of the Spirit of God under the Gospel dispensation, by which the knowledge of the true God was multiplied in the earth; and have only one previous remark to make, that the farther the waters flowed from the temple, the deeper they grew.

With respect to the *phraseology* of this chapter, it may be said that *St. John* had it particularly in view while he wrote his celebrated description of the paradise of God, Rev. xxii. The *prophet* may therefore be referring to the same thing which the *apostle* describes, viz., the *grace* of the *Gospel*, and its *effects* in the world.

Verse 2. *There ran out waters*] מים מפכים *mayim mephaccim*, the waters seem to have been at first *in small quantity;* for the words imply that they *oozed* or *dropped out.* They were at first so small that they came *guttatim, drop by drop;* but they increased so, that they became a river in which one could swim.

Verses 3-5. *He measured a thousand cubits,—the waters were to the* ANKLES; *a thousand more,—the waters were to the* KNEES; *a thousand more,—they became a* RIVER that could *not be forded.* The *waters were risen*, and they *were waters to* SWIM *in.*

I. This may be applied to the *gradual* discoveries of the *plan* of *salvation,*—1. In the *patriarchal* ages. 2. In the giving of the *law.* 3. In the *ministry* of *John the Baptist.* And, 4. In the *full manifestation* of *Christ* by the communication of the *Holy Ghost.*

II. This vision may be applied also to the *growth* of a *believer* in the grace and knowledge of God. There is—1. The *seed* of the kingdom. 2. The *blade* from that seed. 3. The *ear* out of that blade. And, 4. The *full corn* in that *ear.*

III. It may be applied to the discoveries a penitent believer receives of the *mercy* of God in his salvation. He is—1. *A little child,* born of God, born from above, and begins to *taste the bread of life,* and live on the *heavenly food.* 2. He grows up and increases in stature and strength, and becomes a *young man.* 3. He becomes *matured* in the *Divine life,* and has his spiritual senses exercised so as to become a *father* in Christ. In other words, the grace of God appears to come *drop by drop;* it is given as it can be used; it is a *seed of light,* and multiplies itself. The penitent at first can scarcely believe the infinite goodness of his Maker; he however ventures to follow on with the conducting angel, the minister of the Gospel, in his descriptions of the plenitude of that salvation, provided in that *living Temple* in which alone the *well-spring* of life is to be found. 4. In thus following on to know the Lord he finds a continual increase of light and life, till at last he is carried by the *streams* of *grace* to the *ocean* of *eternal mercy;* then

"Plunged in the Godhead's deepest sea,
And lost in his immensity."

IV. These waters may be considered as a type of the progress which Christianity shall make in the world. 1. There were only a few poor fishermen. 2. Afterwards many Jews. 3. Then the Gentiles of Asia Minor and Greece. 4. The continent and isles of Europe. And, 5. Now spreading through Africa, Asia, and America, at present these waters are no longer a river, but an immense sea; and the Gospel fishers are daily bringing multitudes of souls to Christ.

Verse 9. *Every thing—whithersoever the rivers shall come, shall live*] *Life* and *salvation* shall continually accompany the *preaching* of the Gospel; the *death of sin* being removed, the life of righteousness shall be brought in.

There shall be a very great multitude of fish] On the above plan this must refer to *genuine converts* to the Christian faith; true believers, who have got life and salvation by the streams

A. M. 3430
B. C. 574
Olymp. LI. 3
Anno
Servii Tullii,
R. Roman., 5

soever the [i]rivers shall come, shall live: and there shall be a very great multitude of fish, because these waters shall come thither: for they shall be healed; and every thing shall live whither the river cometh.

10 And it shall come to pass, *that* the fishers shall stand upon it from En-gedi even unto En-eglaim; they shall be a *place* to spread forth nets; their fish shall be according to their kinds, as the fish [k]of the great sea, exceeding many.

11 But the miry places thereof and the marshes thereof [l]shall not be healed; they shall be given to salt.

12 And [m]by the river upon the bank thereof, on this side and on that side, [n]shall grow all trees for meat, [o]whose leaf shall not fade, neither shall the fruit thereof be consumed: it shall bring forth [p]new fruit according to his months, because their waters they issued out of the sanctuary; and the fruit thereof shall be for meat, and the leaf thereof [q]for [r]medicine.

A. M. 3430
B. C. 574
Olymp. LI. 3
Anno
Servii Tullii,
R. Roman., 5

13 Thus saith the Lord God; This *shall be* the border, whereby ye shall inherit the land according to the twelve tribes of Israel: [s]Joseph *shall have* two portions.

14 And ye shall inherit it, one as well as another: *concerning* the which I [t]lifted [u]up mine hand to give it unto your fathers: and this land shall [v]fall unto you for inheritance.

15 And this *shall be* the border of the land toward the north side, from the great sea, [w]the way of Hethlon, as men go to [x]Zedad;

16 [y]Hamath, [z]Berothah, Sibraim, which *is* between the border of Damascus and the border of Hamath; [a]Hazar-hatticon, which *is* by the coast of Hauran.

17 And the border from the sea shall be

[i]Heb. *two rivers*——[k]Num. xxxiv. 6; Josh. xxiii. 4; chap. xlviii. 28——[l]Or, *and* that which *shall not be healed*——[m]Ver. 7——[n]Heb. *shall come up*——[o]Job viii. 16; Psa. i. 3; Jer. xvii. 8——[p]Or, *principal*——[q]Or, *for bruises and sores*——[r]Rev. xxii. 2

[s]Gen. xlviii. 5; 1 Chron. v. 1; chap. xlviii. 4, 5——[t]Or, *swore*——[u]Gen. xii. 7; xiii. 15; xv. 7; xvii. 8; xxvi. 3; xxviii. 13; chap. xx. 5, 6, 28, 42——[v]Chap. xlviii. 29——[w]Chap. xlviii. 1——[x]Num. xxxiv. 8——[y]Num. xxxiv. 8——[z]2 Sam. viii. 8——[a]Or, *the middle village*

of God's grace. The *apostles* were *fishers of men; converts* were *the fish* caught. See below. As the waters flow into the Dead *Sea*, where no fish, it is said, can live, *its* waters must be healed, that is, made capable of preserving life; and so its nature be thus far most surprisingly altered.

Verse 10. *The fishers shall stand upon it*] On the above plan of interpretation these must mean—1. The *apostles* of our Lord Jesus. 2. The *preachers* of the everlasting Gospel. See Matt. iv. 19.

From En-gedi] At the southern extremity of the Dead Sea.

Unto En-eglaim] At the northern extremity of the same.

Their fish shall be according to their kinds] Every kind of fish, and the fish all excellent of their kinds. All *nations*, and *kindreds*, and *people* shall be called by the Gospel; it shall not be an excluding system like that of Judaism, for its Author tasted death for every man.

Verse 11. *The miry places*] "Point out," says *Calmet*, "the schismatics and heretics who do not live by the Spirit of Jesus Christ, but separate from his Church; and the evil Christians who dishonour that Church, of which they are corrupt members." A description applicable to the Roman Catholic Church, that is both schismatic and heretic from the Church of Jesus Christ, which is built on the *foundation of the prophets and apostles, Jesus himself being the chief corner stone;* for the Church of Rome, leaving this foundation, is now built on the foundation of councils and traditions, and lying miracles; the popes in their succession being its only corner stones.

Verse 12. *Shall grow all trees for meat, whose leaf shall not fade*] A description that suits the righteous, who are still producing—1. The *fruits* of *faith*. 2. The *fruits* of the *Spirit*. 3. The *fruits* of *love* to God, obedience to his holy will, and love to all men. Benevolence, mercy, charity, kindness, &c.

The leaf thereof for medicine.] See Rev. xxii. 1-5. Even the *leaves*, the holy *profession* of the righteous, is a spiritual medicine. Righteousness is thus encouraged in the world. The *profession* points out the salvation, as it shows the nature and sufficiency of that salvation; for a just creed contains all the articles of the Christian faith.

Verse 13. *Joseph* shall have two *portions.*] That is, In *Ephraim* and *Manasseh*, his two sons, who each had a separate inheritance.

Verse 15. *The way of Hethlon, as men go to Zedad.*] Probably Hethlon is the same as Cuthlon, a city of Syria, between Antioch and Laodicea, according to Antoninus. Some of these places are not known; but see the same kind of division, Num. xxxiv. 7-12.

Verse 16. *Hamath*] Emesa or Amesa, in Syria.—*Calmet*.

Berothah] Berytus, now Baruth or Beeroth, which David took from Hadarezer, king of Syria, 2 Sam. viii. 8; but these things are very uncertain.

Sibraim] Sabarim or Sepharvaim, according to the Syriac, between Hamath and Damascus.

Hazar-hatticon] The middle Hazar; or *middle village*, as the *margin*.

Hauran.] The city Aurana, and the district Auranitis, are in the north-east limit of the Holy Land.

Verse 17. *The border from the sea*] The north border *eastward* is ascertained ver. 15, 16;

A. M. 3430
B. C. 574
Olymp. LI. 3
Anno
Servii Tullii,
R. Roman., 5

[b]Hazar-enan, the border of Damascus, and the north northward, and the border of Hamath. And *this is* the north side.

18 And the east side ye shall measure [c]from Hauran, and from Damascus, and from Gilead, and from the land of Israel *by* Jordan, from the border unto the east sea. And *this is* the east side.

19 And the south side southward, from Tamar *even* to [d]the waters of [e]strife *in* Kadesh, the [f]river to the great sea. And *this is* the south side [g]southward.

20 The west side also *shall be* the great sea from the border, till a man come over against [h]Hamath. This *is* the west side.

21 So shall ye divide this land unto you according to the tribes of Israel.

22 And it shall come to pass, *that* ye shall divide it by lot for an inheritance unto you, [i]and to the strangers that sojourn among you, which shall beget children among you: [k]and they shall be unto you as born in the country among the children of Israel; they shall have inheritance with you among the tribes of Israel.

23 And it shall come to pass, *that* in what tribe the stranger sojourneth, there shall ye give *him* his inheritance, saith the Lord GOD.

[b]Num. xxxiv. 9; chap. xlviii. 1——[c]Heb. *from between*——[d]Num. xx. 13; Deut. xxxii. 51; Psa. lxxxi. 7; chap. xlviii. 28——[e]Or, *Meribah*

[f]Or, *valley*——[g]Or, *toward Teman*——[h]Num. xiii. 21; xxxiv. 8; Josh. xiii. 5——[i]See Eph. iii. 6; Rev. vii. 9, 10 [k]Rom. x. 12; Gal. iii. 28; Col. iii. 11

here it is shown how far it extends itself *northward.*

Hazar-enan] The village of Enan, Num. xxxiv. 9, placed to the north of Cæsarea Philippi. *Ziphron*, see Num. xxxiv. 9, called *Zaphion* by the Syriac.

Verse 18. *The east sea*] The same as the *Dead Sea.*

Verse 19. *Tamar*] Called *Hazazon Tamar*, or *Engedi*, 2 Chron. xx. 2.

The river] Besor, which runs into the sea near Gaza.

Verse 20. *The great sea*] The Mediterranean.

From the border] The southern border, mentioned ver. 19.

Verse 22. *And to the strangers that sojourn*] In former divisions of the land, no place was given to *strangers;* but in this division, (which seems to have no other reference than to the Gospel, for literally such a division never took place,) the *strangers* are to have an *inheritance;* intimating the calling of the Gentiles into the Church of Christ, to an inheritance that is incorruptible, undefiled, and that fadeth not away. Glory be to God for his unspeakable gift! Amen. Amen.

CHAPTER XLVIII

This chapter contains a description of the several portions of the land belonging to each tribe, together with the portion allotted to the sanctuary, city, suburb, and prince, 1–29; *as also the measure and gates of the new city,* 30–35.

A. M. 3430
B. C. 574
Olymp. LI. 3
Anno
Servii Tullii,
R. Roman., 5

NOW these *are* the names of the tribes. [a]From the north end to the coast of the way of Hethlon, as one goeth to Hamath, Hazar-enan, the border of Damascus northward, to the coast of Hamath; for these are his sides east *and* west; [b]a *portion for* Dan.

2 And by the border of Dan, from the east side unto the west side, a *portion for* Asher.

3 And by the border of Asher, from the east side even unto the west side, a *portion for* Naphtali.

4 And by the border of Naphtali, from the east side unto the west side, a *portion for* Manasseh.

5 And by the border of Manasseh, from the east side unto the west side, a *portion for* Ephraim.

6 And by the border of Ephraim, from the east side even unto the west side, a *portion for* Reuben.

7 And by the border of Reuben, from the east side unto the west side, a *portion for* Judah.

8 And by the border of Judah, from the east side unto the west side, shall be [c]the

[a]Chap. xlvii. 15, &c.——[b]Heb. *one* portion

[c]Chap. xlv. 1–6

NOTES ON CHAP. XLVIII

Verse 1. *Now these* are *the names of the tribes.*] See the division mentioned Num. xxxiv. 7-12, which casts much light upon this.

Verse 9. *The oblation*] This was a portion of land *twenty-five thousand* cubits in length, by *ten thousand* broad; in the centre of which was the temple, which must be destined for the use of the priests, the Levites, and the prince.

A. M. 3430 B. C. 574 Olymp. LI. 3 Anno Servii Tullii, R. Roman., 5

offering which ye shall offer of
five and twenty thousand *reeds*
in breadth, and *in* length as one
of the *other* parts, from the
east side unto the west side: and the sanctuary shall be in the midst of it.
9 The oblation that ye shall offer unto the
LORD *shall be* of five and twenty thousand in
length, and of ten thousand in breadth.
10 And for them, *even* for the priests, shall
be *this* holy oblation; toward the north five
and twenty thousand *in length,* and toward
the west ten thousand in breadth, and toward
the east ten thousand in breadth, and toward
the south five and twenty thousand in length:
and the sanctuary of the LORD shall be in the
midst thereof.
11 [d]*It* [e]*shall be* for the priests that are
sanctified of the sons of Zadok; which have
kept my [f]charge, which went not astray when
the children of Israel went astray, [g]as the
Levites went astray.
12 And *this* oblation of the land that is
offered shall be unto them a thing most holy
by the border of the Levites.
13 And over against the border of the priests
the Levites *shall have* five and twenty thousand in length, and ten thousand in breadth:
all the length *shall be* five and twenty thousand, and the breadth ten thousand.
14 [h]And they shall not sell of it, neither exchange nor alienate the first-fruits of the
land: for *it is* holy unto the LORD.
15 [i]And the five thousand that are left in
the breadth over against the five and twenty
thousand, shall be [k]a profane *place* for the
city, for dwelling, and for suburbs: and the
city shall be in the midst thereof.
16 And these *shall be* the measures thereof;
the north side four thousand
and five hundred, and the south
side four thousand and five hundred, and on the east side four
thousand and five hundred, and the west side
four thousand and five hundred.
17 And the suburbs of the city shall be
toward the north two hundred and fifty, and
toward the south two hundred and fifty, and
toward the east two hundred and fifty, and
toward the west two hundred and fifty.
18 And the residue in length over against
the oblation of the holy *portion shall be* ten
thousand eastward, and ten thousand westward: and it shall be over against the oblation
of the holy *portion;* and the increase thereof
shall be for food unto them that serve the city.
19 [l]And they that serve the city shall serve
it out of all the tribes of Israel.
20 All the oblation *shall be* five and twenty
thousand by five and twenty thousand: ye
shall offer the holy oblation foursquare, with
the possession of the city.
21 [m]And the residue *shall be* for the prince,
on the one side and on the other of the holy
oblation, and of the possession of the city,
over against the five and twenty thousand of
the oblation toward the east border, and westward over against the five and twenty thousand toward the west border, over against the
portions for the prince: and it shall be the
holy oblation; [n]and the sanctuary of the
house *shall be* in the midst thereof.
22 Moreover from the possession of the
Levites, and from the possession of the city
being in the midst *of that* which is the
prince's between the border of Judah and the
border of Benjamin, shall be for the prince.
23 As for the rest of the tribes from the

A. M. 3430 B. C. 574 Olymp. LI. 3 Anno Servii Tullii, R. Roman., 5

[d]Chap. xliv. 15——[e]Or, *The sanctified* portion shall be *for the priests*——[f]Or, *ward,* or *ordinance*——[g]Chap. xliv. 10

[h]Exod. xxii. 29; Lev. xxvii. 10, 28, 33——[i]Chap. xlv. 6——[k]Chap. xlii. 20——[l]Chap. xlv. 6——[m]Chap. xlv. 7——[n]Ver 8, 10

Verse 15. *And the five thousand that are left*] The territory of the Levites was *twenty-five thousand* square cubits, ver. 20. But their city was only *four thousand five hundred* square cubits, see ver. 13 and 16; there remained, therefore, *ten thousand* cubits square to be divided, of which *five thousand* cubits in breadth, by *twenty-five thousand* in length, on the east and west sides, were reserved for a sort of *second city;* or for suburbs where laymen might dwell who were employed by those priests and Levites who lodged in the temple and in the city, ver. 18. And another space of *one thousand* cubits in breadth, by *twenty-five thousand* in length, which extended only from north to south, was for fields and gardens appointed for the support of those lay servants. On which we may remark, there was no cultivated land between the portion of the Levites and that of the prince, but only on the east and west sides. See chap. xlv. 6, and the map FF.

Verse 21. *And the residue—for the prince*] His portion was alongside that of the Levites, from west to east; these were on each side *twenty-five thousand* cubits in length, from the east to the west, by *twelve thousand five hun-*

A. M. 3430
B. C. 574
Olymp. LI. 3
Anno
Servii Tullii
R. Roman., 5

east side unto the west side,
Benjamin *shall have* [o]a *portion.*
24 And by the border of Benjamin, from the east side unto
the west side, Simeon *shall have* a *portion.*
25 And by the border of Simeon, from the east side unto the west side, Issachar a *portion.*
26 And by the border of Issachar, from the east side unto the west side, Zebulun a *portion.*
27 And by the border of Zebulun, from the east side unto the west side, Gad a *portion.*
28 And by the border of Gad, at the south side southward, the border shall be even from Tamar *unto* [p]the waters of [q]strife *in* Kadesh, *and* to the river toward the great sea.
29 [r]This *is* the land which ye shall divide by lots unto the tribes of Israel for inheritance, and these *are* their portions, saith the Lord GOD.
30 And these *are* the goings out of the city on the north side, four thousand and five hundred measures.
31 [s]And the gates of the city *shall be* after the names of the tribes of Israel: three gates northward; one gate of Reuben, one gate of Judah, one gate of Levi.
32 And at the east side four thousand and five hundred: and three gates; and one gate of Joseph, one gate of Benjamin, one gate of Dan.
33 And at the south side four thousand and five hundred measures: and three gates; one gate of Simeon, one gate of Issachar, one gate of Zebulun.
34 At the west side four thousand and five hundred, *with* their three gates; one gate of Gad, one gate of Asher, one gate of Naphtali.
35 *It was* round about eighteen thousand *measures:* [t]and the name of the city from *that* day *shall be,* [u]The [v]LORD *is* there.

---

[o]Heb. *one* portion——[p]Chap. xlvii. 19——[q]Heb. *Meribah-kadesh*——[r]Chap. xlvii. 14, 21, 22——[s]Rev. xxi. 12, &c.——[t]Jer. xxxiii. 16

[u]Heb. *Jehovah-shammah;* see Exod. xvii. 15; Judg. vi. 24——[v]Psa. ii. 6; ix. 11; lxxvi. 2; xcix. 2; Jer. iii. 17; Joel iii. 21; Zech. ii. 10; Rev. xxi. 3; xxii. 3

---

dred cubits in breadth from north to south. The space both above and below was equal, between the tribe of Judah and that of Benjamin to north and south; and the portion of the Levites, which had Judah and Benjamin to the north and south, and the portion of the *prince* to the east and to the west. See the *map.*

Verse 28. *From Tamar—in Kadesh*] The former was on the *south* of the Dead Sea; and the latter, or Kadesh-Barnea, was still farther south, and at the extremity of the portion of *Gad,* which was the most *southern* tribe, as *Dan* was the most *northern.*

Verse 30. *These* are *the goings out*] Each of the four sides of the city was *four thousand five hundred* cubits long. There were three gates on each side, as mentioned below; and the whole circumference of the city was *eighteen thousand* cubits. See the map, plan B, *dddd.*

The rector of New Haven College, in New England, supposes the preceding representations to refer to the happy state of the Church in what is called the Millennium. Leaving this period out of the question, the following observations are worthy of notice:—

"The Jews, for whom this vision was intended, would conceive their country to be divided to the *twelve tribes,* in lots of a regular and mathematical form; and not confused or intermixed, as in Joshua's time. Their city laid out larger than before; and exactly *four-square,* with regular suburbs; the temple and appendages much more commodious for their sacrifices, and the habitations of the priests and Levites regularly formed round about the temple. So that this whole plan of the division of the country, laying out of the city, temple, and all the appendages, appears to be perfectly regular and uniform, as if it were drawn all at one time, and by one hand, who had power to effect it; and therefore conveyed to the Jews the most complete idea they were capable of conceiving of the most perfect church, commonwealth, city, temple, and conveniences, for Divine worship. I. The Holy Land, as described chap. xlvii. and xlviii., according to the original grant, being about *two hundred and fifty* miles long, north and south, and about *one hundred and fifty* miles wide, is divided, by parallel lines east and west, to the twelve tribes, each of them having a portion *twenty* miles wide. Only between Judah and Benjamin there is a *holy portion* near *ten* miles wide; in the middle of which is the *holy oblation, twenty-five thousand* cubits; that is, about *ten* miles square for the priests, Levites, city, and temple, chap. xlv. 1; xlviii. 8; the two ends are for the prince, chap. xlv. 7, &c. II. The *holy oblation,* lying in the middle of the *holy portion,* is *twenty-five thousand* cubits square, which is near *ten* miles; of which *ten thousand* cubits, or *four* miles, are taken off from the north side for a habitation for the priests, and as much for the Levites on the south side, chap. xlv. 4, 5, and xlviii. 20; and *five thousand* cubits in the middle for the city portion, chap. xlv. 6; in the middle of which is the city, *four thousand five hundred* cubits square, which is nearly *two* miles, chap. xlviii. 15, 16. Round about this is left *two hundred and fifty* cubits, near *thirty* rods, for suburbs, ver. 17. The remaining *ten thousand* cubits on the east side, and the *ten thousand* cubits on the west side, are for the profit of those who serve the city, out of all the tribes, ver. 18, 19. The sanctuary is in the midst of the city, chap.

xlviii. 8. III. The *sanctuary* or temple, and its appendages, were entirely surrounded with a wall *six* cubits high and *six* cubits thick, chap. xl. 5; and *five hundred* cubits long on each side, chap. xlii. 15, &c., and xlv. 2. In the middle square stands the temple, which was surrounded by a wall *one hundred* cubits long on each side, chap. xli. 13, and *six* cubits thick, chap. xli. 6. The side-chambers on the outside *four* cubits, ver. 6. The Holy of Holies, at the west end, was *twenty* cubits square on the inside, ver. 4. The holy place, or outer court at the east end, was *forty* cubits, ver. 12. The length of the porch on the north side was *twenty* cubits; the breadth was *eleven* cubits, chap. xl. 49; and the width of the separate place on the south side *twenty* cubits. On each side of the temple, towards the *four* gates in the outer wall, stood *two* courts, *eight* in the whole, each *one hundred* cubits square, chap. xl. 19, 23, 27. In each of these were *thirty-six* little chambers or buildings, about *six* cubits square, viz., *six* at the entrance of the gate, chap. xl. 7, 17, 20, &c., and *thirty* on the pavement, ver. 17, &c., which were for lodgings for the priests, for hanging up their garments, and their part of the sacrifices, chap. xlii. 13."

Calmet has constructed a map to show the position of the tribes, and the *quantum* of space each was to possess. As this will give a better view of the subject than any written description can, I have inserted one constructed for this work, which, consulting the places said to be connected with the possessions of the different tribes, shows that the tribes did not all possess the same *quantum* of space, *five* of the southern tribes possessing only one half as much as those of the north.

Verse 35. *The name of the city from that day* shall be, *The Lord* is *there.*] It would have been better to have retained the original words:—

יהוה שמה YEHOVAH SHAMMAH.

This is an allusion to the *shechinah*, or symbol of the Divine Presence, which was in the *first*, but most certainly was *not* in the *second* temple; but Ezekiel tells us that the Divine Presence should be in the *city* of which he speaks; and should be there so fully and so powerfully, that it should give name to the city itself; and that the very name, *Jehovah shammah*, should remind all men of the supereminently glorious Being who had condescended to make this city his habitation.

Two points must be considered here:—1. That the prophet intended that, when they should be restored, they should build the temple, and divide the land as he here directs, if the thing could be found to be practicable. 2. That he had *another temple*, another *holy city*, another *Promised Land*, in view. The land of Immanuel, the city of the New Jerusalem; and his temple, the Christian Church, which is the house of the living God, 1 Tim. iii. 15, in which the presence of Christ shall ever be found; and all its inhabitants, all that believe on his name, shall be temples of the Holy Ghost. Nor can there be any reasonable doubt that the prophet here, by the Spirit of God, not only points out the return of the Israelites from the Babylonish captivity, and what was to befall them previously to the advent of Jesus Christ; but also the glorious spread of the Gospel in the earth, and the final conversion of the tribes of Israel by the preaching of that Gospel.

In conclusion, I think it necessary to state, that there are but few of the prophets of the Old Testament who have left a more valuable treasure to the Church of God than Ezekiel. It is true, he is in several places obscure; but there is a great proportion of the work that is in the highest degree edifying; and several portions that for the depth of the salvation predicted, and the accuracy and minuteness of the description, have nothing equal to them in the Old Testament Scriptures. On such portions, I have felt it my duty to be very particular, that I might be able to point out spiritual beauties and excellencies in this book which are beyond all praise; while I passed slightly over prophecies and symbols which I did not fully understand; but have left to time, by the fulfilment of the events, to prove to successive generations with what heavenly wisdom this *much neglected* prophet has spoken. And I take this opportunity to recommend this book to the serious perusal of every pious man; and while he wonders at the extent of the wisdom by which Ezekiel has fathomed the depth of so many Divine mysteries, let him give God the glory for this additional testimony to the unsearchable riches of Christ, and that plenary salvation which he has purchased for, and freely offers to, the vilest of the vile, and to the whole of the descendants of Adam.

MASORETIC NOTES.—Number of verses, 1,273. Middle verse, chap. xxvi. 1. Masoretic sections, 29.

DESCRIPTION OF THE PLAN OF EZEKIEL'S TEMPLE

As I utterly despair of making the prophet's description of this temple intelligible without a plan, I have introduced one drawn up with great labour and skill by *Dom. August. Calmet*, where the measurements, distances, gates, chambers, courts, inclosures, &c., are all carefully entered as far as they could possibly be ascertained from Ezekiel's description; which, it must be allowed, though wondrously circumstantial, is in several respects obscure. But by referring to the places, both in Kings and Chronicles, as well as in this prophet, where the same things are mentioned, this obscurity will be considerably diminished, if not entirely removed. At the same time, for a description of the temple in general, I beg leave to refer the reader to 1 Kings vi., at the end, where this subject is considered at large.

THE PLAN

[Let it be observed that the Hebrew cubit is about twenty inches and a half.]

AAAA The first inclosure, or wall of *six hundred* cubits, i. e., *one thousand and twenty-five* royal feet in length on each side, chap. xlv. 2; and *six* cubits or *ten* feet *three* inches high, and as many in breadth, chap. xl. 5.

BBBB The court of the Gentiles, or first court, *fifty* cubits in breadth, or *eighty-five* feet *five* inches, chap. xl. 2.

CCCC The outward wall of the court of Israel, or inclosure, *five hundred* cubits square, i. e., *eight hundred and fifty-four* feet *two* inches. This wall might be *thirty* cubits high, taken from the level of the threshold of the gate.

DDDD The court of Israel, *one hundred* cubits, or *one hundred and seventy* feet *ten* inches broad, chap. xl. 19.

EEEE The outer wall, or inclosure of the court of the priests, *two hundred* cubits, or *three hundred and forty-one* feet *eight* inches square, is supposed to be *thirty* cubits, or *fifty-one* feet *three* inches in height.

FFF The court of the priests, *one hundred* cubits, or *one hundred and seventy* feet *ten* inches square, chap. xl. 7; xli. 14, 15.

G The Sanctuary, or Holy of Holies, *twenty* cubits, or *thirty-four* feet *two* inches square, chap. xli. 4; 1 Kings vi. 2.

H The holy place, *forty* cubits long by *twenty* broad, or *sixty-eight* feet *two* inches long by *thirty-four* feet *two* inches broad, chap. xli. 2, and 1 Kings vi. 2.

I The vestibule or porch, *twenty* cubits in breadth, by *ten* (or according to Ezekiel, *eleven*) cubits in length, i. e., *thirty-four* feet *two* inches long by *seventeen* feet *one* inch broad, chap. xl. 48; 1 Kings vi. 3.

K The altar of burnt-offerings, *twelve* cubits, or *twenty* feet *six* inches square, according to Ezekiel, chap. xliii. 12, 13, &c., or *ten* cubits high by *twenty* broad, i. e., *seventeen* feet *one* inch high, and *thirty-four* feet *two* inches broad, according to 2 Chron. iv. 1.

LLL The wall of separation which encompassed the Temple, and the altar of burnt-offerings, of which the Scriptures do not give the dimensions. It was *twenty* cubits from the buildings in the court of the priests, and *five* from the Temple, chap. xli. 9, 10. *Josephus* makes it *three* cubits high, *Antiq.* lib. viii. c. 2.

MMMMMM Gates of the court of Israel, and of the court of the priests, all of the same dimensions, chap. xl. 1, 22, 36. Each of the porches was *fifty* cubits long, i. e., *eighty-five* feet *five* inches (as much as the depth of the aisles, chap. xl. 15) and *twenty-five* cubits, or *forty-two* feet *eight* inches and a *half* in breadth in the opening, and *sixty* cubits high, i. e., *one hundred and two* feet *six* inches, chap. xl. 14. On each side of the porches there were *three* chambers, each *six* cubits square, chap. xl. 6. And the separations between the *three* chambers were *five* cubits in thickness, chap. xl. 6.

NNNNNNNN Galleries around the court of Israel, chap. xl. I place there *thirty* pillars on a line of *two hundred* cubits in length, which is the same proportion as those given for *one hundred* cubits long, 1 Kings vii. 2, 3, 4, for the court of the palace of Solomon.

OOOOOOO Chambers or apartments round the court of Israel; there were *thirty* on both sides of the gate, or *fifteen* on each side, chap. xl. 17.

PPPP The kitchens of the Temple, *forty* cubits, or *sixty-eight* feet *four* inches long by *thirty* cubits, or *fifty-one* feet *three* inches broad, chap. xlv. 21, 22, 23, 24.

Q The north gate of the court of the priests, where the victims were prepared, and where they slew the animals designed for sacrifice, chap. xl. 38, 39.

RRRR Galleries around the court of the priests, chap. xlii. 3.

SSSSSS Apartments continued round the court of the priests. The aisle, which was to the south of the eastern gate, was for the priests employed as *guards* of the Temple, chap. xl. 45. The aisle on the north side of the said gate was appointed for the *singers*, chap. xl. 44; the aisle that was on the eastern side of the south gate was for the *priests* employed about the *altar*, chap. xl. 46; the aisles which were to the west of the north gate and of the south gate, contained the halls where the priests ate, chap. xlii. 13.

TT The kitchens of the court of the priests were those where they dressed the trespass-offering, sin-offering, and the meat-offerings, *forty* cubits, or *sixty-eight* feet *four* inches long, and *thirty* cubits, or *fifty-one* feet *five* inches broad, chap. xlvi. 20. He speaks only of that on the *north*.

VVVV Flights of steps which led to the court of the people. In each flight there were *seven steps*, chap. xl. 22-26.

XXX Flights of steps which led to the court of the priests; in each there were *eighty steps*, chap. xl. 31, 34, 37.

YY A flight of steps which led to the porch of the Temple, *eight steps* in each, chap. xl. 49.

aaa Chambers about the Temple, *thirty-three* in number, Ezekiel makes them *four* cubits in breadth, chap. xli. 5; but in 1 Kings vi. 5, 6, they are stated to be *five* cubits in the *lower* stage, *six* in the *second*, and *seven* in the *third*.

bb Flights of steps opposite to the chambers, which were continued round the temple, chap. xli. 7, and 1 Kings vi. 8.

c The steps of the altar of burnt-offerings turned toward the east, chap. xliii. 15, 16.

dddd Tables of hewn stone, which were in the portico of the north gate of the priests' court, where they slew, flayed, and cut up the victims. Each table was *one and a half* cubits square, chap. xl. 38, 39-41.

The great walls of the temple were all *six* cubits, or *ten* feet *three* inches thick. These walls were: 1. That which formed the first inclosure; 2. The wall of the court of Israel: 3. The wall of the court of the priests; and, 4. The walls of the Temple. But the outward wall of the *thirty-three* chambers, which were round the holy place and the sanctuary, was only *five* cubits broad, and *fifteen* high; i. e., *eight* feet *six* inches *and a half* in thickness, and *twenty-five* feet *seven* inches *and a half* in height, chap. xli. 9, 12.

All the gates of the two courts, that of Israel and that of the priests, are of the same dimensions. The wall where was the opening was *six* cubits, or *ten* feet *three* inches in thickness. The gate was *eight* cubits, or *thirteen* feet *eight* inches wide; and the opening of the gate was one cubit, and the gate was *thirteen* cubits, or *twenty-two* feet *two* inches *and a half* high, chap. xl. 9, 11.

The *western* gate of the Temple is not mentioned by Ezekiel, because, according to his plan, the king's palace was not to be near the temple; and consequently this gate, which was the gate of the king, did not exist. But this was not followed, as we find that, after the return from Babylon, there were gates on the *western* side of the Temple, according to *Josephus;* and *before* the captivity the *western* gate did most certainly exist, see chap. xliii. 8; 2 Kings xi. 6; xvi. 18; 1 Chron. ix. 24; xxvi. 16, 18.

1. The gate of the porch of the holy place was *fourteen* cubits wide, i. e., *twenty-three* feet *eleven* inches, chap. xl. 48; 1 Kings vi. 3.

2. The gate of the holy place was *ten* cubits, or *seventeen* feet *one* inch wide, chap. xli. 1, 2.

3. The gate of the *sanctuary* was *six* cubits, or *ten* feet *three* inches wide. The wall of the separation was only *two* cubits, chap. xli. 1, 3.

4. The *east* gate of the court of the priests was shut all the week, and was not opened but

on the Sabbath and new moons, according to Ezekiel. It was there that the king had his *seat*, a sort of tribunal, chap. xliv. 2-4; xlvi. 1, 2, &c.

Calmet observes, with respect to his plan, that he assigns only *two* galleries to the apartments which were around the court of Israel; but those which were around the court of the priests had *three*, chap. xlii. 3, 5, 6. There is another difference between the palace (atrium) of the court of the priests, and that of the court of Israel. The walls of the first were built with *three* rows of hewn stones and one of cedar alternately, 1 Kings vi. 36; but this is not said to be the same in the structure of the outward court, or that of the people.

In the Old Testament we find no mention of the *court of the Gentiles*. Only *two* courts are mentioned there, one of the *priests*, the other of the *people;* one the *inner*, the other the *outer* court; but it is certain that such a court did exist, and is here marked BBBB.

The height of the aisles, or apartments that were around the *two* courts, is not mentioned any where in the Scriptures; but they are here fixed at *thirty* cubits; for the temple was not higher, neither was Solomon's palace. See 1 Kings vii. 2.

Explanation of the plan for the division of the land of Canaan, according to Ezekiel's vision, chap. xlviii.

A The Temple of the Lord, *five hundred* cubits square, chap. xlv. 2.

BB The city of the Levites, *four thousand five hundred* cubits square, and *eighteen thousand* in compass, chap. xlviii. 16.

cccc Suburbs of the city of the Levites, *two hundred and fifty* cubits in breadth, chap. xlviii. 17.

dddd The *twelve* gates of the Levitical city, *four* on each side, chap. xlviii. 31-34.

EE City of the lay persons or workmen employed in the service of the priests and of the Levites, *five thousand* broad by *twenty-five thousand* cubits long, chap. xlv. 6.

FF Cultivated ground for the maintenance of the lay artisans, chap. xlviii. 15.

GG Portion of the prince of Israel, *tweny-five thousand* cubits long by *twelve thousand five hundred* broad, chap. xlviii. 21.

The whole extent of the land from Kadesh-barnea south to Hethlon or Hamath north, was about *two hundred and twenty* miles, its mean breadth about *one* hundred.

INTRODUCTION TO THE BOOK

OF THE

PROPHET DANIEL

DANIEL is said to have descended from the royal family of David; and he appears to have been carried into Babylon when very young, in the *fourth* year of Jehoiakim king of Judah, A. M. 3398, B. C. 602, or 606 before the vulgar era. He and his three fellow-captives, *Hananiah, Mishael*, and *Azariah*, being likely youths, were chosen to be about the king's court, and were appointed to have an education suitable to the employments for which they were destined. As they had been carefully bred up in the Mosaic institutions, they regulated their conduct by them, even in the court of a heathen king, where they were in the capacity of *slaves;* hence, though ordered to be fed from the royal table, they would not touch that food, because the Chaldeans ate of meat forbidden by the Mosaic law, and probably even that which might be dominated *clean* became defiled by having been *sacrificed to idols* before it was prepared for common use. At their earnest request, the officer under whose care they were placed permitted them to use *vegetables* only; and finding that they grew healthy and strong by this aliment, did not oblige them to use the portion sent from the king's table.

Daniel appears to have been instructed in all the wisdom of the Chaldeans, which was at that time greatly superior to the learning of the ancient Egyptians; and he was soon distinguished in the Babylonish court, as well for his wisdom and strong understanding as for his deep and steady piety.

His interpretation of Nebuchadnezzar's dream of the *variously compounded metallic image* raised his credit so high at the court that he was established governor of the province of Babylon, and made chief of all the *Magians*, or wise men in that country. The chief facts and incidents of his history are so particularly woven throughout the book bearing his name, and undoubtedly written by himself, that they need not be detailed here.

The reputation of Daniel was so great, even in his *lifetime*, that it became a proverb. "*Thou art wiser than Daniel*," said Ezekiel ironically to the king of Tyre, chap. xxviii. 3; and by the same prophet God ranks him among the most holy and exemplary of men, when he declares, speaking relative to Jerusalem, which had been condemned to destruction, "Though these three men, Noah, Daniel, and Job, were in it, they should deliver but their own lives by their righteousness," chap. xiv. 14, 20.

Josephus, Ant. lib. x., c. 12, says that God bestowed many favours on him: that he was advanced to the rank of the most considerable prophets; that he enjoyed the favour of princes, and the affection of the people during his life; and that after his death his memory became immortal. He observes also that, in the complexion of his predictions, he differs widely from all other prophets; they foretold scarcely any thing but *disastrous* events; on the contrary, he predicts the most *joyous* events, and *fixes the times of accomplishment* with more circumstantial precision than they did. And this is so true, that we cannot help thinking that God had given this eminent man a greater degree of light to fix the times when his predictions should issue, than he had given in general to all his predecessors, who simply declared the mind of God in relation to things *future*, without attempting to indicate the *distance of time* in which they should be fulfilled. There are but very few exceptions to this either in *Isaiah* or *Jeremiah*. And in this respect the prophecy of the *seventy weeks* of Daniel exceeds all that have gone before, as the incidents and transactions relative to its fulfilment were so various, and yet so fixed and declared *six hundred* years before the time, that when the time came in which they were predicted to take place, they were *expected*, and occurred exactly according to the *prediction*, and the *expectations* founded upon it. This prophet therefore, far from occupying a lower place among divinely inspired men, deserves to be placed in the front rank with all those who have been most distinguished among the men who have partaken most largely of the prophetic gift.

The rabbins have endeavoured to degrade Daniel, and have placed his prophecies among the *hagiographa*, books which they consider to possess a *minor degree of inspiration;* and it is probable that he meets with this treatment from them because his prophecies are proofs too evident that *Jesus Christ* is the true *Messiah*, and that he came at the very time that Daniel said the *Prince Messiah* should come. But the testimony and sayings of such men are infinitely overpowered by the testimony of *Ezekiel*, which has been produced above; and the testimony of our Lord, who gives him the title of *prophet*, Matt. xxiv. 15, without the slightest intimation that he was to wear this title with abatement.

It is very probable that Daniel did not return at the general restoration from the Babylonish captivity. At that time, if alive, he must have been an old man; and it is most likely that he finished his days in Babylon, though some Asiatic authors hold that he returned to Judea with Ezra, came back afterward to Persia, and died in the city of *Susa*.

Josephus speaks of his skill in *architecture*, Antiq. lib. x., c. 12, and that he built a famous tower at *Ecbatane* or *Susa*, which remained to his time, and was so exquisitely finished that it always appeared as if newly built. In this tower or palace the kings of Persia were interred; and in consideration of its *founder*, the guard of it was always chosen from the *Jews*.

Daniel is famous among the orientalists. The author of the *Tareekh Muntekheb* says that Daniel flourished in the time of *Lohorasp*, king of Persia; and consequently in that of *Ceresh*, or Cyrus, who gave him the government of Syria; that he taught these two princes the knowledge of the true God; that he preached the true faith through the whole of the Babylonian Irak; and was, on the death of Nebuchadnezzar, sent by Bahman, (Artaxerxes Longimanus,) son of Asfendiar, who then reigned in Persia, into Judea; and that, having returned, he died at *Shouster*, or *Susa*, the capital of Persia, where he lies interred.

Some have supposed that the Zoroaster or Zeradusht of the Persians is a confused picture of the Prophet Daniel. The account given by Abul Pharaje, in his *fifth* dynasty, may be considered favourable to this opinion. He says, "Zeradusht, author of the Magiouseiah *Magism*, or sect of the worshippers of fire, flourished in the reign of *Cambasous*, (Cambyses;) that he was a native of the province of Adherbigian, or Media, or, according to others, of Assyria; that he foretold to his disciples the coming of the Messiah, who should be pointed out by a *star* which should appear in the day time at his birth; that they should have the first information of his advent; that he should be born of a virgin; and that they should present him with gifts; because he is the Word that made the heavens." See *Pococke's* Abul Pharajius, p. 83 of the *Arabic*, and 54 of the *Latin*.

D'Herbelot, on this account, makes the following remark: "We may see by these words of the historian, that the prophecy of Balaam was pretty generally known throughout the east, and that the *Magi*, who came to worship our Lord, were the true *Magians* of Persia, and not Arab kings."

The account given by Abul Pharaje makes Daniel and Zeradusht contemporary, and thus far is favourable to the opinion that the history of the former may be disguised under that of the latter. There have been several Zoroasters, of whom many fables are told; and no wonder, when the persons themselves are generally fabulous.

The Asiatics make him the *inventor* of رمل *remel*, or *geomancy;* and among them he passes for the author of a work entitled *Assoul ol Tabeer*, "The Principles of the Interpretation of Dreams." I have in my own library a very ancient work which pretends to be drawn from this, and is entitled *Somnia Daniel;* it was printed in the infancy of printing, but without date; small 4to. There is an Arabic work in the French king's library, No. 410, entitled *Odhmet al Mancoul, an Danial an Nabi*, "The Traditionary Predictions of Daniel the Prophet;" which is said to contain many falsities, built on the foundation of Daniel's prophecies; but it has never been given to the public, and I have no other notice of it than the above from *D'Herbelot.* But although all these are curious from their *antiquity*, yet they are doubtless impostures.

Abul Pharaje, in his history of the dynasties, says, that the *seventy weeks* of Daniel are to be dated from the *twentieth* year of اردشير درازدست *Ardsheer Dirazdest*, the *Artaxerxes Longimanus* of the Greeks, (called *Bahman* above,) and the same to whom Nehemiah was ساقي *sakee*, or cup-bearer. Other orientalists are of the same opinion. This shall be considered more at large when we come to the prophecy itself. Artaxerxes had the name of *Longimanus*, or Long-handed, from the great extent of his dominions.

Daniel cannot be ranked among the Hebrew *poets:* his book is all in *prose;* and it is written partly in *Hebrew*, and partly in *Chaldee*. The Chaldee, or Syro-Chaldaic part, begins with מלכא לעלמין חיי *malka lealmin chei*, "O king, live for ever!" and continues to the end of the *seventh* chapter.

In the interpretation of his prophecies I have endeavoured to follow the best critics and chronologists; and, without an extended comment, to give in as short a space as possible the meaning of every place. On the *metallic images* and *seventy weeks* I have been obliged to be more prolix, as these are of too much importance to be slightly handled. It is not my province to enter into the controversy about the date when the seventy weeks commence; even they who disagree so much from each other on this point come so near to the general issue that the difference is immaterial.

The chronology of the several events mentioned in this book *Calmet* endeavours to fix as follows:—

A. M.

3398. Daniel led captive to Babylon, chap. i. 1–7.
3399. Death of Nabopolassar, father of Nebuchadnezzar.
3401. Jehoiakim revolts against Nebuchadnezzar, 2 Kings xxiv. 1.
3402. Dream of the compound statue, Dan. ii. 1, &c.
Daniel and his companions promoted to honour at court.
Birth of Cyrus, son of Cambyses and Mandane.
3405. Jehoiakim is taken and put to death by the Chaldeans.
Jeconiah is raised to his throne, but reigns only *three* months and *ten* days.
Zedekiah, last king of Judah, succeeds; and reigns *eleven* years.
3416. Taking of Jerusalem, and destruction of the temple, 1 Chron. xxxvi.
3434. Return of Nebuchadnezzar to Babylon after his great conquests in Phœnicia, Judea, Egypt, &c.
His dream of the great tree, chap. iv. 7, &c.
3435. He becomes insane, which lasts for *seven* years, chap. iv. 32, 33.
3442. He becomes sane, and re-ascends the throne.
The golden image set up. The *three* Hebrews cast into the fiery furnace, chap. iii.
Death of Nebuchadnezzar after a reign of *forty-three* years, according to *Berosus*.
Evil-Merodach succeeds him, and reigns *two* years.—*Berosus*.
He sets Jeconiah at liberty, Jer. lii. 31.
3444. Belshazzar his son succeeds, Dan. vii. 1.
Daniel's vision of the *four* beasts, representing the *four* great empires, chap. vii.
3447. Vision of the ram and he-goat, chap. viii.
The death of Belshazzar, chap. v.
3449. Darius the Mede, called *Cyaxares* by Xenophon, and *Astyages* in the Apocrypha, son of Astyages, king of the Medes, and maternal great uncle to Belshazzar, succeeds him in the government of Chaldea, chap. v. 30, 31. See Isa. xiii. 1, &c.
The visions of Daniel related, chap. ix., x., xi., xii.
Cyrus attacks the Medes in the *first* or *second* year of Darius the Mede, chap. x. 1.

A. M.

3455. Daniel is cast into the den of lions, chap. vi.

3456. Death of Darius. Cyrus succeeds him.

3457. End of the Babylonish captivity *declared* by *Cyrus*, in the *first* year of his reign, 2 Chron. xxxvi. 22, and Ezra i. 1; but afterward interrupted. See below.

3485. Termination of Jeremiah's *seventy* years under *Darius Hystaspes*, who gives orders to *continue* the rebuilding of the temple.

3550. Commencement of the *seventy* weeks, chap. ix. 24.
Nehemiah returns to Jerusalem, Neh. ii. 1-6.

In this chronology *Calmet* differs from *Usher.*

As a writer, this prophet is simple, yet pure and correct: and he is so conscientious that he relates the very words of those persons whom he introduces as speaking. He writes *Hebrew* where what he delivers is a bare narrative; but he relates in *Chaldee* the conversations which he had with the wise men and the kings; and in the same language he relates Nebuchadnezzar's edict, which he made after Daniel had interpreted his dream concerning the great metalline image. This is a proof of his great and conscientious accuracy; and exhibits this prophet in a most advantageous point of view. Daniel writes both *Hebrew* and *Chaldee* with great purity.

This book divides itself into two parts. Part I is *historical*, and is contained in the six former chapters. Part II. is *prophetical*, and occupies the other six.

THE BOOK

OF THE

PROPHET DANIEL

Chronological Notes relative to the commencement of Daniel's prophesying

Year from the Creation, according to Archbishop Usher, 3397.—Year of the Jewish era of the world, 3154. —Year from the Deluge, 1741.—Second year of the *forty-third* Olympiad.—Year from the building of Rome, according to the Varronian or generally received account, 147.—Year from the building of Rome, according to Cato and the Fasti Consulares, 146.—Year from the building of Rome, according to Polybius the historian, 145.—Year from the building of Rome, according to Fabius Pictor, 411.—Year of the Julian Period, 4107.—Year of the era of Nabonassar, 141.—Year from the foundation of Solomon's temple, 397.—Year since the destruction of the kingdom of Israel by Shalmaneser, king of Assyria, 114. —Fourth year after the first Sabbatic year after the *seventeenth* Jewish jubilee, according to Helvicus.—Year before the birth of Christ, 603.—Year before the vulgar era of Christ's nativity, 607.—Cycle of the Sun, 19.—Cycle of the Moon, 3.—Tenth year of Tarquinius Priscus, the fifth king of the Romans.—Nineteenth year of Cyaxares or Cyaraxes, the fourth king of Media.—Forty-fourth year of Archidamus, king of Lacedæmon, of the family of the Proclidæ.—First year of Leon, king of Lacedæmon, of the family of Eurysthenidæ.—Thirteenth year of Alyattes II., king of Lydia, and father of the celebrated Crœsus. —Thirty-fourth year of Philip, the sixth king of Macedon.—Eleventh year of Pharaoh-necho, called Necus by Herodotus. This king was the immediate predecessor of Psammis; and Psammis was succeeded by the celebrated Pharaoh-hophra, called also Apries.—Eighth year of Ithobalus, king of the Tyrains, according to Helvicus.—Third year (ending) of Jehoiakim, king of Judah; for the principal part of A. M. 3397 corresponded to the *fourth* year of this prince.

CHAPTER I

This chapter begins with giving a short account of Nebuchadnezzar's conquest of Judea, when Jehoiakim became tributary to him; and consequently the seventy years' captivity and vassalage began, 1, 2. *On this expedition (taking Egypt in his way) the king of Babylon set out towards the end of the third year of Jehoiakim, but did not take Jerusalem before the* ninth *month of the year following. Hence the seeming discrepancy between Daniel and Jeremiah,* (chap. xxv. 1,) *the one computing from the time of his setting out on the expedition, and the other from the time in which the purpose of it was accomplished. We have next an account of the manner in which Daniel and his companions were brought up at the king's court,* 3–7. *They reject the daily provision of meat granted by the king, lest they should be defiled, and are allowed to live on pulse,* 8–16. *Their great proficiency in the wisdom of that time,* 17–20. *Daniel flourishes till the reign of Cyrus the Persian,* 21.

A. M. 3397 B. C. 607 Ol. XLIII. 2 Anno TarquiniiPrisci, R. Roman., 10

IN the third year of the reign of Jehoiakim king of Judah [a]came Nebuchadnezzar king of Babylon unto Jerusalem, and besieged it.

A. M. cir. 3398 B. C. cir. 606 Ol. XLIII. 3 TarquiniiPrisci. R. Roman., cir. annum 11

2 And the LORD gave Jehoiakim king of Judah into his hand, with [b]part of the vessels of the house of God: which he carried [c]into the land of Shinar to the house

[a]2 Kings xxiv. 1; 2 Chron. xxxvi. 6——[b]Jer. xxvii. 19, 20——[c]Gen. x. 10; xi. 2; Isa. xi. 11; Zech. v. 11

NOTES ON CHAP. I

Verse 1. *In the third year of the reign of Jehoiakim*] This king was raised to the throne of Judea in the place of his brother *Jehoahaz*, by *Pharaoh-necho*, king of Egypt, 2 Kings xxiii. 34-36, and continued tributary to him during the first *three* years of his reign; but in the *fourth*, which was the *first* of Nebuchadnezzar, Jer. xxv. 1, Nebuchadnezzar completely defeated the Egyptian army near the Euphrates, Jer. xlvi. 2; and this victory put the neighbouring countries of Syria, among which *Judea* was the chief, under the Chaldean government. Thus Jehoiakim, who had *first* been tributary to Egypt, became now the vassal of the king of Babylon, 2 Kings xxiv. 1.

At the end of three years Jehoiakim rebelled

A. M. cir. 3398 B. C. cir. 606 Ol. XLIII. 3 TarquiniiPrisci, R. Roman., cir. annum 11

of his god; [d]and he brought the vessels into the treasure house of his god.

3 And the king spake unto Ashpenaz the master of his eunuchs, that he should bring *certain* of the children of Israel, and of the king's seed, and of the princes;

4 Children [e]in whom *was* no blemish, but well favoured, and skilful in all wisdom, and cunning in knowledge, and understanding science, and such as *had* ability in them to stand in the king's palace, and [f]whom they might teach the learning and the tongue of the Chaldeans.

5 And the king appointed them a daily provision of the king's meat, and of [g]the wine which he drank: so nourishing them three years, that at the end thereof they might [h]stand before the king.

6 Now among these were of the children of Judah, Daniel Hananiah, Mishael, and Azariah:

7 [i]Unto whom the prince of the eunuchs gave names: [k]for he gave unto Daniel *the name* of Belteshazzar; and to Hananiah, of

[d]2 Chron. xxxvi. 7——[e]See Lev. xxiv. 19, 20——[f]Acts vii. 22——[g]Heb. *the wine of his drink*

[h]Ver. 19; Gen. xli. 46; 1 Kings x. 8——[i]Gen. xli. 45; 2 Kings xxiv. 17——[k]Chap. iv. 8; v. 12

against Nebuchadnezzar, who, then occupied with other wars, did not proceed against Jerusalem till *three years after*, which was the *eleventh* and last of Jehoiakim, 2 Kings xxiii. 36.

There are some difficulties in the chronology of this place. *Calmet* takes rather a different view of these transactions. He connects the history thus: Nabopolassar, king of Babylon, finding that one of his lords whom he had made governor of Cœlesyria and Phœnicia had revolted from him, and formed an alliance with the king of Egypt, sent Neubuchadnezzar his son, whom he invested with the authority of *king*, to reduce those provinces, as was customary among the easterns when the heir presumptive was sent on any important expedition or embassy. This young prince, having quelled the insurrection in those parts, marched against Jerusalem about the *end* of the *third* or *beginning* of the *fourth* year of the reign of Jehoiakim, king of Judah. He soon took the city, and put Jehoiakim in chains with the design of carrying him to Babylon; but, changing his mind, he permitted him to resume the reins of government under certain oppressive conditions. At this year, which was A. M. 3398, the *seventy years* of the Babylonish captivity commence. Nabopolassar dying in the interim, Nebuchadnezzar was obliged to return speedily to Babylon, leaving his generals to conduct the Jewish captives to Babylon, among whom were Daniel and his companions.

Verse 2. *Part of the vessels of the house of God*] He took the richest and finest of them for the service of his god *Bel*, and left what were necessary for carrying on the public worship of *Jehovah*, (for he did not attempt to alter the civil or religious constitution of Judea;) for leaving Jehoiakim on the throne, he only laid the land under tribute. The Chaldeans carried these sacred vessels away at *three* different times. 1. In the war spoken of in this place. 2. In the taking of Jerusalem and Jeconiah a few months after, 2 Kings xxiv. 13. 3. *Eleven years* after, under the reign of Zedekiah, when the city and temple were totally destroyed, and the land ruined, 2 Kings xxv. 8-15.

The land of Shinar] This was the ancient name of Babylon. See Gen. xi. 2.

The treasure house of his god.] This was *Bel*, who had a splendid temple in Babylon, and was the tutelar god of the city and empire.

Verse 3. *Master of his eunuchs*] This word *eunuchs* signifies officers about or in the palace, whether literally eunuchs or not.

Verse 4. *Children*] ילדים *yeladim, youths, young men;* and so the word should be rendered throughout this book.

Skilful in all wisdom] Rather, persons capable of every kind of literary accomplishment, that they might be put under proper instruction. And as *children of the blood* and of the *nobles* were most likely, from the care usually taken of their initiatory education, to profit most by the elaborate instruction here designed, the master of the eunuchs, the king's chamberlain, was commanded to choose the youths in question out of such.

Verse 5. *A daily provision*] *Athenæus*, lib. iv., c. 10, says: The kings of Persia, (who succeeded the kings of Babylon, on whose empire they had seized,) were accustomed to order the food left at their own tables to be delivered to their courtiers.

So nourishing them three years] This was deemed a sufficient time to acquire the *Chaldee language*, and the *sciences* peculiar to that people. I suppose they had good *introductory books, able teachers*, and a *proper method;* else they would have been obliged, like us, to send their children *seven years* to *school*, and *as many* to the *university*, to teach them any tolerable measure of useful and ornamental literature! O how reproachful to the nations of Europe, and particularly to our own, is this *backward* mode of instruction. And what is generally learned after this vast expense of *time* and *money?* A little *Latin, Greek*, and *mathematics;* perhaps a little *moral philosophy;* and by this they are *entitled*, not *qualified*, to teach others, and especially to teach the people the important *science of salvation!* To such shepherds, (and there are many such,) the hungry sheep look up, and are not fed; and if all are not such, no thanks to our plan of national education.

Verse 6. *Now among these*] There were no doubt several noble youths from other provinces: but the four mentioned here were Jews, and are supposed to have all been of royal extraction.

Verse 7. *Unto whom the prince of the eunuchs gave names*] This change of names, *Calmet* properly remarks, was a mark of dominion and authority. It was customary for

A. M. cir. 3398 B. C. cir. 606 Ol. XLIII. 3 TarquiniiPrisci, R. Roman., cir. annum 11

Shadrach; and to Mishael, of Meshach; and to Azariah, of Abed-nego.

8 But Daniel purposed in his heart that he would not defile himself [l]with the portion of the king's meat, nor with the wine which he drank: therefore he requested of the prince of the eunuchs that he might not defile himself.

9 Now [m]God had brought Daniel into favour and tender love with the prince of the eunuchs.

10 And the prince of the eunuchs said unto Daniel, I fear my lord the king who hath appointed your meat and your drink: for why should he see your faces [n]worse liking than the children which *are* of your [o]sort? then shall ye make *me* endanger my head to the king.

11 Then said Daniel to [p]Melzar, whom the prince of the [q]eunuchs had set over Daniel, Hananiah, Mishael, and Azariah,

12 Prove thy servants, I beseech thee, ten days; and let them give us [r]pulse [s]to eat, and water to drink.

A. M. cir. 3398 B. C. cir. 606 Ol. XLIII. 3 TarquiniiPrisci, R. Roman., cir. annum 11

13 Then let our countenances be looked upon before thee, and the countenance of the children that eat of the portion of the king's meat: and as thou seest, deal with thy servants.

14 So he consented to them in this matter, and proved them ten days.

15 And at the end of ten days their countenances appeared fairer and fatter in flesh than all the children which did eat the portion of the king's meat.

16 Thus Melzar took away the portion of their meat, and the wine that they should drink; and gave them pulse.

17 As for these four children, [t]God gave them [u]knowledge and skill in all learning and wisdom; and [v]Daniel had [w]understanding in all visions and dreams.

[l]Deut. xxxii. 38; Ezek. iv. 13; Hos. ix. 3——[m]See Gen. xxxix. 21; Psa. cvi. 46; Prov. xvi 7——[n]Heb. *sadder*——[o]Or, *term*, or *continuance*——[p]Or, *the steward* [q]2 Kings ix. 32; xx. 18; Isa. xxxix. 7; Acts viii. 27

[r]Heb. *of pulse*——[s]Heb. *that we may eat*, &c.——[t]1 Kings iii. 12; James i. 5, 17——[u]Acts vii. 22——[v]Or, *he made Daniel understand*——[w]Num. xii. 6; 2 Chron. xxvi. 5; chap. v. 11, 12, 14; x. 1

masters to impose new names upon their slaves; and rulers often, on their ascending the throne, assumed a name different from that which they had before.

דניאל Daniel signifies "God is my Judge." This name they changed into בלטשאצר Belteshatstsar; in Chaldee, "The treasure of Bel," or "The despository of the secrets (or *treasure*) of Bel."

חנניה Hananiah signifies, "The Lord has been gracious to me;" or "He to whom the Lord is gracious." This name was changed into שדרך Shadrach, Chaldee, which has been variously translated: "The inspiration of the sun;" "God, the author of evil, be propitious to us;" "Let God preserve us from evil."

מישאל Mishael signifies, "He who comes from God." Him they called מישך Meshach, which in Chaldee signifies, "He who belongs to the goddess Sheshach," a celebrated deity of the Babylonians, mentioned by Jeremiah, chap. xxv. 26.

עזריה Azariah, which signifies "The Lord is my Helper," they changed into אבד נגו Abed-nego, which in Chaldee is "the servant of Nego," who was one of their divinities; by which they meant either the *sun*, or the *morning star;* whether *Jupiter* or *Venus*.

The vicious pronunciation of this name should be carefully avoided; I mean that which lays the accent on the first syllable, and hurries to the end, without attending to the natural division of the word *Abed-Nego*.

Verse 8. *But Daniel—would not defile himself*] I have spoken of this resolution in the introduction. The chief reasons why Daniel would not eat meat from the royal table were probably these three:—1. Because they ate unclean beasts, which were forbidden by the Jewish law. 2. Because they ate, as did the heathens in general, beasts which had been strangled, or not properly blooded. 3. Because the animals that were eaten were first offered as victims to their gods. It is on this account that Athenæus calls the beasts which were served up at the tables of the Persian kings, *ἱερια, victims*, lib. iv. c. 10, p. 145.

Verse 11. *Then said Daniel to Melzar*] Melzar was an officer under Ashpenaz, whose office it was to attend to the food, clothing, &c., of these royal captives. Others think מלצר *meltsar*, master of the inn or hotel, the name of an *office*.

Verse 12. *Give us pulse to eat*] הזרעים *hazzeraim*, seeds or grain, such as barley, wheat, rye, and peas, &c. Though a vegetable diet might have produced that healthiness of the system in general, and of the countenance particularly, as mentioned here; yet we are to understand that there was an especial blessing of God in this, because this spare diet was taken on a religious account.

Verse 17. *As for these four children*] *Young men* or *youths*. Our translation gives a false idea.

In all visions and dreams.] That is, such as are *Divine;* for as to dreams in general, they have as much signification as they have connexion, being the effects of the state of the *body*, of the *mind*, or of the *circumstances* of the dreamer. A dream may be considered *supernatural*, if it have nothing preposterous,

A. M. cir. 3401
B. C. cir. 603
Ol. XLIV. 2
TarquiniiPrisci,
R. Roman.,
cir. annum 14

18 Now at the end of the days that the king had said he should bring them in, then the prince of the eunuchs brought them in before Nebuchadnezzar.

19 And the king communed with them; and among them all was found none like Daniel, Hananiah, Mishael, and Azariah: therefore [x]stood they before the king.

20 [y]And in all matters of [z]wisdom *and* understanding, that the king inquired of them, he found them ten times better than all the magicians *and* astrologers that *were* in all his realm.

21 [a]And Daniel continued *even* unto the first year of king Cyrus.

[x]Genesis xli. 46; ver. 5——[y]1 Kings x. 1——[z]Hebrew, *wisdom of understanding*——[a]Chap. vi. 28; x. 1 He lived to see that glorious time of the return of his people from the Babylonian captivity, though he did not die then; so *till* is used, Psalm cx. 1; cxii. 8

nothing monstrous, and nothing irregular. If the whole order and consequences of the things be preserved in them, from beginning to end, then we may presume they are supernatural. In such dreams Daniel had understanding.

Verse 18. *Now at the end of the days*] That is, at the end of *three years*, ver. 5.

Verse 19. *And among them all*] All the young noble captives from different nations.

Therefore stood they before the king.] It appears that only *four* were wanting.

Verse 20. *Magicians* and *astrologers*] Probably the same as *philosophers* and *astronomers* among us.

Verse 21. *The first year of king Cyrus.*] That is, to the *end of the Chaldean empire.* And we find Daniel alive in the *third* year of Cyrus, see chap. x. 1.

CHAPTER II

Nebuchadnezzar, in the second year of his reign, (or in the fourth, according to the Jewish account, which takes in the first two years in which he reigned conjointly with his father,) had a dream which greatly troubled him; but of which nothing remained in the morning but the uneasy impression. Hence the diviners, when brought in before the king, could give no interpretation, as they were not in possession of the dream, 1–13. *Daniel then, having obtained favour from God, is made acquainted with the dream, and its interpretation,* 14–19; *for which he blesses God in a lofty and beautiful ode,* 20–23; *and reveals both unto the king, telling him first the particulars of the dream,* 24–35, *and then interpreting it of the four great monarchies. The then existing* Chaldean *empire, represented by the head of gold, is the first; the next is the* Medo-Persian; *the third, the* Macedonian *or* Grecian; *the fourth, the* Roman, *which should break every other kingdom in pieces, but which in its last stage, should be divided into ten kingdoms, represented by the ten toes of the image, as they are in another vision* (chap. vii.) *by the ten horns of the fourth beast. He likewise informs the king that in the time of this last monarchy,* viz., *the Roman, God would set up the kingdom of the Messiah; which, though small in its commencement, should ultimately be extended over the whole earth,* 36–45. *Daniel and his three friends, Hananiah, Mishael, and Azariah, (named by the prince of the eunuchs, Shadrach, Meshach, and Abed-nego,) are then promoted by the king to great honour,* 46–49.

A. M. 3401
B. C. 603
Ol. XLIV. 2
Anno
TarquiniiPrisci,
R. Roman., 14

AND in the second year of the reign of Nebuchadnezzar, Nebuchadnezzar dreamed dreams, [a]wherewith his spirit was troubled, and [b]his sleep brake from him.

2 [c]Then the king commanded to call the magicians, and the

[a]Gen. xli. 8; chap. iv. 5——[b]Esth. vi. 1; chap. vi. 18——[c]Gen. xli. 8; Exod. vii. 11; chap. v. 7

NOTES ON CHAP. II

Verse 1. *The second year of the reign of Nebuchadnezzar*] That is, the *second* year of his reigning *alone*, for he was king *two* years before his father's death. See the notes on chap. i. 1. This was therefore the *fifth* year of his reign, and the *fourth* of the captivity of Daniel.

Nebuchadnezzar dreamed dreams wherewith his spirit was troubled] The dream had made a deep and solemn impression upon his mind; and, having forgotten all but general circumstances, his mind was distressed.

Verse 2. *The magicians*] חרטמים *chartummim.* See the note on Gen. xli. 8.

The astrologers] אשפים *ashshaphim.* Perhaps from נשף *nashaph,* to *breathe,* because they laid claim to Divine *inspiration;* but probably the persons in question were the *philosophers* and *astronomers* among the Babylonians.

The sorcerers] מכשפים *mechashshephim.* See the note on Deut. xviii. 10, and on Exod. xxii. 18, and Lev. xix. 31, where several of these *arts* are explained.

The Chaldeans] Who these were is difficult to be ascertained. They might be a college of learned men, where all arts and sciences were professed and taught. The Chaldeans were the most ancient philosophers of the world; they might have been originally inhabitants of the

A. M. 3401 B. C. 603 Ol. XLIV. 2 Anno TarquiniiPrisci, R. Roman., 14

astrologers, and the sorcerers, and the Chaldeans, for to show the king his dreams. So they came and stood before the king.

3 And the king said unto them, I have dreamed a dream, and my spirit was troubled to know the dream.

4 Then spake the Chaldeans to the king in Syriac, [d]O king, live for ever: tell thy servants the dream, and we will show the interpretation.

5 The king answered and said to the Chaldeans, The thing is gone from me: if ye will not make known unto me the dream, with the interpretation thereof, ye shall be [e]cut [f]in pieces, and your houses shall be made a dunghill.

6 [g]But if ye show the dream, and the interpretation thereof, ye shall receive of me gifts and [h]rewards and great honour: therefore show me the dream, and the interpretation thereof.

7 They answered again and said, Let the king tell his servants the dream, and we will show the interpretation of it.

8 The king answered and said, I know of certainty that ye would [i]gain the time, because ye see the thing is gone from me.

9 But if ye will not make known unto me the dream, [k]*there is but* one decree for you: for ye have prepared [l]lying and corrupt words to speak before me, till the time be changed: therefore tell me the dream, and I shall know that ye can show me the interpretation thereof.

A. M. 3401 B. C. 603 Ol. XLIV. 2 Anno TarquiniiPrisci, R. Roman., 14

10 The Chaldeans answered before the king, and said, There is not a man upon the earth that can show the king's matter: therefore *there is* no king, lord, nor ruler, *that* asked such things at any magician, or astrologer, or Chaldean.

11 And *it is* a rare thing that the king requireth, and there is none other that can show it before the king, [m]except the gods, whose dwelling is not with flesh.

12 For this cause the king was angry and very furious, and commanded to destroy all the wise *men* of Babylon.

13 And the decree went forth that the wise *men* should be slain; and they sought Daniel and his fellows to be slain.

14 Then Daniel [n]answered with counsel and wisdom to Arioch the [o]captain [p]of the king's guard, which was gone forth to slay the wise *men* of Babylon:

[d]1 Kings i. 31; chap. iii. 9; v. 10; vi. 6, 21——[e]Ezra vi. 11; 2 Kings x. 27; chap. iii. 29——[f]Chald. *made pieces*——[g]Chap. v. 16——[h]Or, *fee;* chap. v. 17; ver. 48 [i]Chald. *buy;* Eph. v. 16

[k]Esth. iii. 15; iv. 11; ix. 14——[l]Prov. vi. 17; xii. 19; xxi. 6; xxvi. 28——[m]Ver. 28; chap. v. 11——[n]Chald. *returned*——[o]Or, *chief marshal*——[p]Chald. *chief of the executioners,* or *slaughtermen;* Gen. xxxvii. 36

Babylonian Irak; and still have preserved to themselves exclusively the name of *Chaldeans*, to distinguish themselves from other nations and peoples who inhabited the *one hundred and twenty* provinces of which the Babylonish government was composed.

Verse 4. *Then spake the Chaldeans to the king in Syriac*] ארמית *aramith*, the language of *Aram* or *Syria*. What has been generally called the Chaldee.

O king, live for ever] מלכא לעלמין חיי *Malca leolmin cheyi.* With these words the *Chaldee* part of Daniel commences; and continues to the end of the *seventh* chapter. These kinds of compliments are still in use in the East Indies. A superior gives a blessing to an inferior by saying to him, when the latter is in the act of doing him reverence, "*Long life to thee.*" A poor man, going into the presence of a king to solicit a favour, uses the same kind of address: *O father*, thou art the support of the destitute; *mayest thou live to old age!*—WARD'S *Customs.*

Verse 5. *Ye shall be cut in pieces*] This was arbitrary and tyrannical in the extreme; but, in the order of God's providence, it was overruled to serve the most important purpose.

Verse 8. *That ye would gain the time*] The king means either that they wished to prolong the time that he might recollect it, or get indifferent about it; or that they might invent something in the place of it; or make their escape to save their lives, after having packed up their valuables. See ver. 9.

Verse 10. *There is not a man upon the earth*] The thing is utterly impossible to man. This was their decision: and when Daniel gave the dream, with its interpretation, they knew that the *spirit of the holy gods was in him.* So, even according to their own theology, he was immeasurably greater than the wisest in Babylon or in the world.

Verse 13. *They sought Daniel and his fellows*] As the decree stated that all the wise men of Babylon should be slain, the *four* young Hebrews, being reputed among the *wisest*, were considered as sentenced to death also.

Verse 14. *Captain of the king's guard*] Chief of the *king's executioners* or *slaughter men.* Margin, רב טבחיא *rab tabachaiya*, chief of the butchers, he that took off the heads of those whom the king ordered to be slain, because they had in any case displeased him. "Go and bring me the head of Giaffer." The honourable butcher went and brought the head in a bag on a dish. It was Herod's chief butcher that brought the head of John the Baptist in a dish

A. M. 3401 B. C. 603 Ol. XLIV. 2 Anno TarquiniiPrisci, R. Roman., 14

15 He answered and said to Arioch the king's captain, Why *is* the decree *so* hasty from the king? Then Arioch made the thing known to Daniel.

16 Then Daniel went in, and desired of the king that he would give him time, and that he would show the king the interpretation.

17 Then Daniel went to his house, and made the thing known to Hananiah, Mishael, and Azariah, his companions:

18 [q]That they would desire mercies [r]of the God of heaven concerning this secret; [s]that Daniel and his fellows should not perish with the rest of the wise *men* of Babylon.

19 Then was the secret revealed unto Daniel [t]in a night vision. Then Daniel blessed the God of heaven.

20 Daniel answered and said, [u]Blessed be the name of God for ever and ever: [v]for wisdom and might are his:

21 And he changeth [w]the times and the seasons: [x]he removeth kings, and setteth up kings: [y]he giveth wisdom unto the wise, and knowledge to them that know understanding:

22 [z]He revealeth the deep and secret things: [a]he knoweth what *is* in the darkness, and [b]the light dwelleth with him.

A. M. 3401 B. C. 603 Ol. XLIV. 2 Anno TarquiniiPrisci, R. Roman., 14

23 I thank thee, and praise thee, O thou God of my fathers, who hast given me wisdom and might, and hast made known unto me now what we [c]desired of thee: for thou hast *now* made known unto us the king's matter.

24 Therefore Daniel went in unto Arioch, whom the king had ordained to destroy the wise *men* of Babylon: he went and said thus unto him: Destroy not the wise *men* of Babylon: bring me in before the king, and I will show unto the king the interpretation.

25 Then Arioch brought in Daniel before the king in haste, and said thus unto him, [d]I have found a man of the [e]captives of Judah, that will make known unto the king the interpretation.

26 The king answered and said to Daniel, whose name *was* Belteshazzar, Art thou able to make known unto me the dream which I have seen, and the interpretation thereof?

27 Daniel answered in the presence of the king, and said, The secret which the king hath demanded cannot the wise *men*, the astrologers, the magicians, the soothsayers, show unto the king;

[q]Matt. xviii. 12——[r]Chald. *from before God*——[s]Or, *that they should not destroy Daniel, &c.*——[t]Num. xii. 6 Job xxxiii. 15, 16——[u]Psa. cxiii. 2; cxv. 18——[v]Jer. xxxii. 19——[w]Esth. i. 13; 1 Chron. xxix. 30; chap. vii. 25; xi. 6

[x]Job xii. 18; Psa. lxxv. 6, 7; Jer. xxvii. 5; chap. iv. 17 [y]James i. 5——[z]Job xii. 22; Psa. xxv. 14; ver. 28, 29 [a]Psa. cxxxix. 11, 12; Heb. iv. 13——[b]Chap. v. 11, 14; James i. 17——[c]Ver. 18——[d]Chald. *That I have found* [e]Chald. *children of the captivity of Judah*

to the delicate daughter of Herodias. This was the custom of the country. No law, no judge, no jury. The will or caprice of the king governed all things. Happy England! know and value thy excellent privileges!

Verse 16. *That he would give him time*] That is, that he might seek unto God for a revelation of the thing. The Chaldeans dared not even to promise *this;* they would only pledge themselves for the *interpretation*, provided the king would furnish the *dream*. Daniel engages both to find the *lost dream*, and to give the proper *interpretation.*

Verse 18. *That they would desire mercies*] For this Daniel had requested a little time; and doubtless both he and his *three* companions prayed incessantly till God gave the wished for revelation; but whether it was given that *same night*, we do not know.

Verse 19. *Then was the secret revealed—in a night vision.*] Daniel either dreamed it, or it was represented to his mind by an immediate inspiration.

Verse 20. *Wisdom and might are his*] He knows all things, and can do all things.

Verse 21. *He changeth the times*] Time, duration, succession are his, and under his dominion. It is in the course of his providence that one king is put down, and another raised up; and therefore he can distinctly tell what he has purposed to do in the great empires of the earth.

Verse 23. *I thank thee and praise thee*] No wonder he should feel gratitude, when God by this merciful interference had saved both the life of him and his fellows; and was about to reflect the highest credit on the God of the Jews, and on the people themselves.

Verse 24. *Destroy not the wise* men] The decree was suspended till it should be seen whether Daniel could tell the dream, and give its interpretation.

Verse 27. *Cannot the wise* men] Cannot your own able men, aided by your gods, tell you the secret? This question was necessary in order that the king might see the foolishness of depending on the one, or worshipping the other.

The soothsayers] One of our old words: "The tellers of truth:" but גזרין *gazerin* is the name of *another class* of those curious artists, unless we suppose it to mean the same as the CHALDEANS, ver. 2. They are supposed to be persons who divined by *numbers*, *amulets*, &c. There are many conjectures about them, which, whatever learning they show, cast little light upon this place.

A. M. 3401 B. C. 603 Ol XLIV. 2 Anno TarquiniiPrisci, R. Roman., 14

28 [f]But there is a God in heaven that revealeth secrets, and [g]maketh known to the king Nebuchadnezzar [h]what shall be in the latter days. Thy dream, and the visions of thy head upon thy bed, are these;

29 As for thee, O king, thy thoughts [i]came *into thy mind* upon thy bed, what should come to pass hereafter: [k]and he that revealeth secrets maketh known unto thee what shall come to pass.

30 [l]But as for me, this secret is not revealed to me for *any* wisdom that I have more than any living, [m]but for *their* sakes that shall make known the interpretation to the king, [n]and that thou mightest know the thoughts of thy heart.

31 Thou, O king, [o]sawest, and behold a great image. This great image, whose brightness *was* excellent, stood before thee; and the form thereof *was* terrible.

32 [p]This image's head *was* of fine gold, his breast and his arms of silver, his belly and his [q]thighs of brass,

33 His legs of iron, his feet part of iron and part of clay.

34 Thou sawest till that a stone was cut out [r]without [s]hands, which smote the image upon his feet *that were* of iron and clay, and brake them to pieces.

A. M. 3401 B. C. 603 Ol. XLIV. 2 Anno TarquiniiPrisci, R. Roman., 14

35 Then was the iron, the clay, the brass, the silver, and the gold, broken to pieces together, and became [t]like the chaff of the summer threshing-floors; and the wind carried them away, that [u]no place was found for them: and the stone that smote the image [v]became a great mountain, [w]and filled the whole earth.

36 This *is* the dream; and we will tell the interpretation thereof before the king.

37 [x]Thou, O king, *art* a king of kings: [y]for the God of heaven hath given thee a kingdom, power, and strength, and glory.

38 [z]And wheresoever the children of men dwell, the beasts of the field and the fowls of the heaven hath he given into thine hand, and hath made thee ruler over them all. [a]Thou *art* this head of gold.

39 And after thee shall arise [b]another kingdom [c]inferior to thee, and another third kingdom of brass, [d]which shall bear rule over all the earth.

40 And [e]the fourth kingdom shall be strong as iron: forasmuch as iron breaketh in pieces and subdueth all *things:* and as iron that breaketh all these, shall it break in pieces and bruise.

41 And whereas thou sawest [f]the feet and toes, part of potters' clay, and part of iron,

[f]Gen. xl. 8; xli. 16; ver. 18, 47; Amos iv. 13——[g]Chald. *hath made known*——[h]Gen. xlix. 1——[i]Chald. *came up*——[k]Ver. 22, 28——[l]So Gen. xli. 16; Acts iii. 12 [m]Or, *but for the intent that the interpretation may be made known to the king*——[n]Ver. 47——[o]Chald. *wast seeing* [p]See ver. 38, &c.——[q]Or, *sides*——[r]Or, *which* was *not in hands;* as ver. 45

[s]Chap. viii. 25; Zech. iv. 6; 2 Cor. v. 1; Heb. ix. 24 [t]Psa. i. 4; Hos. xiii. 3——[u]Psa. xxxvii. 10, 36——[v]Isa. ii. 2, 3——[w]Psa. lxxx. 9——[x]Ezra vii. 12; Isa. xlvii. 5; Jer. xxvii. 6, 7; Ezek. xxvi. 7; Hos. viii. 10——[y]Ezra i. 2 [z]Chap. iv. 21, 22; Jer. xxvii. 6——[a]Ver. 32——[b]Chap. v. 28, 31——[c]Ver. 32——[d]1 Mac. i. 3——[e]Chap. vii. 7, 23——[f]Ver. 33

Verse 28. *There is a God in heaven*] To distinguish him from those idols, the works of men's hands; and from the false gods in which the Chaldeans trusted.

In the latter days.] A phrase which, in the prophets, generally means the *times of the Messiah*. God is about to show what shall take place from this time to the latest ages of the world. And the vision most certainly contains a very extensive and consecutive prophecy; which I shall treat more largely at the close of the chapter, giving in the mean time a short exposition.

Verse 31. *A great image*] Representing the *four great monarchies.*

Verse 32. *Head* was *of fine gold*] The *Babylonish empire,* the first and greatest.

Breast and his arms of silver] The *Medo-Persian empire,* under Cyrus, &c.

His belly and his thighs of brass] The *Macedonian empire,* under Alexander the Great, and his successors.

Verse 33. *His legs of iron*] The *Roman government.*

His feet part of iron and part of clay.] The same, mixed with the barbaric nations, and divided into *ten* kingdoms. See at the end of the chapter.

Verse 34. *A stone was cut out*] The *fifth* monarchy; the spiritual kingdom of the Lord Jesus, which is to last for ever, and diffuse itself over the whole earth.

Verse 35. *The stone—became a great mountain*] There is the kingdom אבן *eben,* of the *stone,* and the kingdom of the *mountain.* See at the end of the chapter.

Verse 37. *The God of heaven*] Not given by thy own gods, nor acquired by thy own skill and prowess; it is a Divine gift.

Power] To rule this kingdom.

And strength] To defend it against all foes.

And glory.] Great honour and dignity.

Verse 38. *Thou* art *this head of gold*] See on ver. 31-34, and at the end.

A. M. 3401
B. C. 603
Ol. XLIV. 2
Anno
TarquiniiPrisci,
R. Roman., 14

the kingdom shall be divided; but there shall be in it of the strength of the iron, forasmuch as thou sawest the iron mixed with miry clay.

42 And *as* the toes of the feet *were* part of iron, and part of clay, *so* the kingdom shall be partly strong, and partly [g]broken.

43 And whereas thou sawest iron mixed with miry clay, they shall mingle themselves with the seed of men: but they shall not cleave [h]one to another, even as iron is not mixed with clay.

44 And in [i]the days of these kings [k]shall the God of heaven set up a kingdom, [l]which shall never be destroyed: and the [m]kingdom shall not be left to other people, [n]*but* it shall break in pieces and consume all these kingdoms, and it shall stand for ever.

45 [o]Forasmuch as thou sawest that the stone was cut out of the mountain [p]without hands, and that it brake in pieces the iron, the brass, the clay, the silver, and the gold; the great God hath made known to the king what shall come to pass [q]hereafter: and the dream *is* certain, and the interpretation thereof sure.

A. M. 3401
B. C. 603
Ol. XLIV. 2
Anno
TarquiniiPrisci,
R. Roman., 14

46 [r]Then the king Nebuchadnezzar fell upon his face, and worshipped Daniel, and commanded that they should offer an oblation [s]and sweet odours unto him.

47 The king answered unto Daniel, and said, Of a truth *it is,* that your God *is* a God of gods, and a Lord of kings, [t]and a revealer of secrets, seeing thou couldest reveal this secret.

48 Then the king made Daniel a great man, [u]and gave him many great gifts, and made him ruler over the whole province of Babylon, and [v]chief of the governors over all the wise *men* of Babylon.

49 Then Daniel requested of the king, [w]and he set Shadrach, Meshach, and Abed-nego over the affairs of the province of Babylon: but Daniel [x]*sat* in the gate of the king.

[g]Or, *brittle*——[h]Chald. *this with this*——[i]Chald. *their days*——[k]Ver. 28——[l]Chap. iv. 3, 34; vi. 26; vii. 14, 27; Mic. iv. 7; Luke i. 32, 33——[m]Chald. *kingdom thereof* [n]Psa. ii. 9; Isa. lx. 12; 1 Cor. xv. 24——[o]Ver. 35; Isa. xxviii. 16——[p]Or, *which* was *not in hand*——[q]Chald. *after this*——[r]See Acts x. 25; xiv. 13; xxviii. 6 [s]Ezra vi. 10——[t]Ver. 28——[u]Ver. 6——[v]Chap. iv. 9; v. 11——[w]Chap. iii. 12——[x]Esth. ii. 19, 21; iii. 2

Verse 44. *A kingdom which shall never be destroyed*] The extensive and extending empire of Christ.

Shall not be left to other people] All the preceding empires have swallowed up each other successively; but this shall remain to the end of the world.

Verse 45. *The dream* is *certain*] It contains a *just representation* of things as they shall be.

And the interpretation thereof sure.] The parts of the dream being truly explained.

Verse 46. *The king—fell upon his face*] Prostrated himself: this was the fullest act of adoration among the ancients.

Worshipped Daniel] Supposing him to be a god, or Divine being. No doubt Daniel forbade him; for to receive this would have been gross idolatry.

Verse 47. *Your God* is *a God of gods*] He is greater than all others.

And a Lord of kings] He governs both in heaven and earth.

Verse 48. *Made Daniel a great man*] By, 1. Giving him many rich gifts. 2. By making him *governor* over the whole province of Babylon. And, 3. By making him the *chief* or *president* over all the *wise men.*

Verse 49. *Daniel requested of the king, and he set Shadrach, Meshach, and Abed-nego over the affairs of the province of Babylon*] He wished his *three* companions promoted, who had shared his anxieties, and helped him by their prayers. They all had places of trust, in which they could do much good, and prevent much evil.

Daniel sat *in the gate of the king.*] That is, was the chief officer in the palace; and the greatest confidant and counsellor of the king. But whatever his influence and that of his friends was, it extended only over the province of Babylon; not through the empire.

A DISCOURSE ON NEBUCHADNEZZAR'S DREAM,
chap. ii. 41-45.

I shall now consider this most important vision more at large, and connect it with a portion of the previous history of the Jewish people.

The kingdoms of Israel and Judah after a series of the most unparalleled ingratitude and rebellion, against displays of mercy and benevolence, only equalled by their rebellions, were at last, according to repeated threatenings, given over into the hands of their enemies. The inhabitants of the former country were subdued and carried away captives by the Assyrians; and those of the latter, by the Chaldeans.

The people of Israel never recovered their ancient territories; and were so disposed of by their conquerors, that they either became amalgamated with the heathen nations, so as to be utterly undistinguishable; or they were transported to some foreign and recluse place of settlement, that the land of their residence, though repeatedly sought for and guessed at, has for more than *two thousand* years been totally unknown.

Judah, after having been harassed by the Chaldeans, Egyptians, and others, was at last invaded by Nebuchadnezzar, king of Babylon; Jerusalem besieged and taken; and Jehoiachin the king, who had before become tributary to the Babylonians, with his mother, wives, officers of state, and chief military commanders, princes, and mighty men of valour, to the amount of *ten thousand;* and all the *artificers, smiths,* &c., to the number of *one thousand,* with all that were *fit for war,* he carried captives to Babylon; leaving only the poorest of the people behind, under the government of *Mattaniah,* son of the late king Josiah, and uncle to Jehoiachin; and, having changed his name to *Zedekiah,* gave him a nominal authority as king over the wretched remains of the people. Zedekiah, after having reigned *nine* years, rebelled against Nebuchadnezzar, who, coming against Jerusalem with all his forces, besieged it; and having reduced it to the last extremity by famine, and made a breach in the walls, took the city, pillaged and destroyed the temple by fire, slew the sons of Zedekiah before his face, then put out his eyes, and carried him *bound in brazen fetters* to Babylon, 2 Kings, chap. xxiv. and xxv. Thus, the *temple* of God, the most glorious building ever laid on the face of the earth, was profaned, pillaged, and burnt, with the king's palace, and all the houses of the Jewish nobility, in the *eleventh* year of *Zedekiah,*—the *nineteenth* of *Nebuchadnezzar,*—the *first* of the *forty-eight Olympiad,*—the *one hundred and sixtieth* current year of the era of *Nabonassar,*—*four hundred and twenty-four* years, *three* months, and *eight* days from the time in which *Solomon* laid its *foundation stone!*

In the same month in which the city was taken, and the temple burnt, *Nebuzar-adan,* commander in chief of the Babylonish forces, carried off the spoils of the temple, with the Jewish treasures, and the principal part of the residue of the people; and brought them also to Babylon. And thus *Judah* was carried away out of her own land, *four hundred and sixty-eight* years after *David* began to reign over it; from the *division* under *Rehoboam, three hundred and eighty-eight* years; from the *destruction* of the *kingdom* of *Israel, one hundred and thirty-four* years; in the year of the world, *three thousand four hundred and sixteen;* and before the *nativity* of our Lord, *five hundred and eighty-eight.*

In the *fourth* year of Jehoiakim, king of Judah, A. M. 3397, B. C. 607, Nebuchadnezzar, having besieged Jerusalem, and made its king tributary, carried away a number of captives; and among them was the Prophet *Daniel,* then in his youth, who became, for his wisdom, and knowledge of future events, very eminent at Babylon; and, with some other Jewish captives, great favourites of Nebuchadnezzar the king; who made *Daniel* president of all the wise men of his city. It was in the *second* year of the reign of this king, that a circumstance occurred which, though at first it threatened the destruction of the prophet, finally issued in the increase of his reputation and celebrity.

As prophecy is one of the strongest proofs of the authenticity of what professes to be a *Divine revelation,* God endued this man with a large portion of his Spirit, so that he clearly predicted some of the most astonishing political occurrences and changes which have ever taken place on the earth; no less than the rise, distinguishing characteristics, and termination of the FOUR *great monarchies* or *empires,* which have been so celebrated in all the histories of the world. And as the Babylonian, under which he then lived, was one of these monarchies, and was shortly to be absorbed by the *Medo-Persian,* which was to succeed it, he made Nebuchadnezzar, the then reigning monarch, by means of a most singular *dream,* the particulars of which he had forgotten, the instrument that appeared to give birth to a prediction, in which the ruin of his own empire was foretold; as well as other mighty changes which should take place in the political state of the world, for at least the term of *one thousand* years next ensuing. Nor did the prophetic Spirit in this eminent man limit his predictions to these; but showed at the same time the origin and nature of that FIFTH *monarchy,* which, under the great King of kings, should be administered and prevail to the end of time.

The dream itself, with its interpretation, and the exact and impressive manner in which the predictions relative to the *four* great monarchies have been fulfilled, and those which regard the *fifth* monarchy are in the course of being accomplished, are the subjects to which I wish to call the reader's most serious and deliberate attention.

This image, so circumstantially described from the *thirty-eighth* to the *forty-fourth* verse, was, as we learn from the prophet's general solution, intended to point out the rise and fall of *four* different *empires* and *states;* and the final prevalence and establishment of a *fifth* empire, that shall never have an end, and which shall commence *in the last days,* ver. 28; a phrase commonly used in the *prophets* to signify the *times of the Messiah,* and in the New Testament, his *advent* to judge the world.

Before we proceed to particular parts, we may remark in general, that the whole account strongly indicates:—

1. The especial *providence* of God in behalf of the Jews at that time. For, although suffering grievously because of their sins, being deprived of both their political and personal liberty, God shows them that he has not *abandoned* them; and the existence of a *prophet* among them is a proof of his fatherly care and unremitted attention to their eternal welfare.

2. The particular *interference* of God to manifest the superiority of his truth, to wean an idolatrous nation from their vanity and superstition, and lead them to that God who is the fountain of truth, the revealer of secrets, and the governor of all things.

And, 3. The direct *inspiration* of God immediately teaching his servant things which could be known only to God himself, and thus showing the Babylonians that his prophets had spoken by an unerring Spirit; that the *Jews* were the depositaries of the true religion; that HE was the only true God; and as he was *omniscient,* so he was *omnipotent;* and the things which his *wisdom* had *predicted,* his *power* could and *would* accomplish.

The sum of the account given in this chapter is the following:—

1. Nebuchadnezzar, king of Babylon, in the *second* year of his reign, about A. M. 3401, and B. C. 603, had a remarkable dream, which, although it made a deep impression on his mind, yet, on his awakening, he found it impossible to recollect; the general impression only remaining.

2. He summoned his wise men, astrologers, &c., told them that he had a dream or vision, which he had forgotten; and commanded them

to tell him the dream, and give its interpretation.

3. They request the king to tell them the dream; and promise, then, to make known the meaning. This he could not do, having forgotten it; yet he insists on their compliance on pain of death.

4. To tell the king his dream they find impossible; and a decree for the destruction of the wise men of Babylon is issued, in which Daniel and his fellows are included.

5. Daniel, hearing of it, speaks to *Arioch*, captain of the king's guard or the royal executioner; desires to be brought before the king; and promises to tell the dream, &c.

6. He is introduced; and immediately tells the king what he had dreamed, and shows him its interpretation.

THE DREAM

A vast image, exceedingly luminous, of terrible form, and composed of different substances, appears in a night vision to the king, of which the following is the description:—

I. Its *head* was of fine *gold*.

II. Its *breast* and *arms* of *silver*.

III. Its *belly* and *thighs* of *brass*.

IV. Its *legs* of *iron*, and its *feet* and *toes* of *iron* and *clay*. While gazing on this image he sees,—

V. A *stone* cut out of a mountain without hands, which smites the image on its feet, and dashes it all to pieces; and the gold, and silver, brass, iron, and clay become as small and as light as chaff.

VI. A *wind* carries the whole away, so that no place is found for them.

VII. The *stone* becomes a *great mountain*, and fills the earth.

In order to explain this, certain DATA must be laid down.

1. This image is considered a political representation of as many different governments, as it was composed of materials; and as all these materials are successively inferior to each other, so are the governments in a descending ratio.

2. The *human figure* has been used, both by *historians* and *geographers*, to represent the rise, progress, establishment, and decay of empires, as well as the *relative situation* and importance of the different parts of the government. Thus *Florus*, in the *proœmium* to his Roman history, represents the Romans under the form of a *human being*, in its different stages, from infancy to old age, *viz*.

Si quis ergo populum Romanum quasi *hominem* consideret, totamque ejus *ætatem* percenseat, ut CŒPERIT, utque ADOLEVERIT, ut quasi ad quemdam JUVENTÆ florem pervenerit; ut postea velut CONSENUERIT, quatuor gradus progressusque ejus inveniet.

1. *Prima ætas* sub *Regibus* fuit, prope ducentos quinquaginta per annos, quibus circum ipsam matrem suam cum finitimis luctatus est. Hæc erit ejus INFANTIA.

2. Sequens a Bruto, Collatinoque *consulibus*, in Appium Claudium, Quinctiumque Fulvium consules, ducentos quinquaginta annos habet, quibus Italiam subegit. Hoc fuit tempus viris armisque exercitatissi mum! ideo quis ADOLESCENTIAM dixerit.

3. Dehinc ad Cæsarem Augustum, ducenti quinquaginta anni, quibus totum orbem pacavit. Hic jam ipsa JUVENTA Imperii, et quasi quædam robusta MATURITAS.

4. A Cæsare Augusto in sæculum, nostrum, sunt non multo minus anni ducenti, quibus inertia Cæsarum quasi CONSENUIT atque DECOXIT. *L. An. Flori* PROŒM.

1. INFANCY; *first stage*—under KINGS, from Romulus to Tarquinius Superbus; about *two hundred and fifty* years.

2. YOUTH; *second stage*—under CONSULS, from Brutus and Collatinus to Appius Claudius and M. Fulvius; about *two hundred and fifty* years.

3. MANHOOD; *third stage*—the empire from the conquest of Italy to Cæsar Augustus; about *two hundred and fifty* years.

4. OLD AGE; *fourth stage*—from Augustus, through the *twelve* Cæsars, down to A. D. 200; about *two hundred* years.

Geographers have made similar representations. The *Germanic* empire, in the totality of its dependent states, has been represented by a *map* in the *form of a man;* different parts being pointed out by *head*, *breast*, *arm*, *belly*, *thighs*, *legs*, *feet*, &c., according to their geographical and political relation to the empire in general.

3. Different *metals* are used to express different *degrees of political strength*, excellence, durability, &c.

4. *Clay*, *earth*, *dust*, are emblems of *weakness*, *instability*, &c.

5. *Mountains* express, in Scripture, *mighty empires*, *kingdoms*, and *states*.

6. *Stone* signifies Jesus Christ, Gen. xlix. 24; "From thence" (of the posterity of Jacob) "is the Shepherd, the Stone of Israel." That our blessed Lord, "the good shepherd," John x. 11-17, is here intended, will appear most plainly from the following passages; Isa. viii. 14: "And he shall be for a sanctuary; but for a STONE of stumbling and for a ROCK of offence to both the houses of Israel." Isa. xxviii. 16: "Thus saith the Lord God, Behold, I lay in Zion for a foundation a STONE, a tried STONE, a precious corner STONE, a sure foundation; he that believeth shall not make haste." 1 Peter ii. 4, 6, 8. Collate these with Psa. cxviii. 22: "The STONE which the builders refused is become the head STONE of the corner." Matt. xxi. 42; Mark xii. 10; Luke xx. 17; Acts iv. 11; in which latter quotations the whole is positively applied to Christ; as also 1 Peter ii. 4-8: "To whom coming as unto a living STONE," &c.; who seems to have all the preceding passages in view. See also Isa. ii. 2: "The mountain of the Lord's house shall be established in the top of the mountains," &c.

7. This stone is said to be cut out without hands, ver. 34. *Without hands* signifies that which is *spiritual*. So 2 Cor. v. 1, *a house not made with hands* means a *spiritual* building.

EXPLANATION

The *Chaldean* empire, called the *Assyrian* in its commencement, the *Chaldean* from the country, the *Babylonish* from its chief city.

I. HEAD OF GOLD. This was the first monarchy, begun by *Nimrod*, A. M. 1771, B. C. 2233, and ending with the death of Belshazzar, A. M. 3466, B. C. 538, after having lasted nearly *seventeen hundred* years. In the time of Nebuchadnezzar it extended over *Chaldea*, *Assyria*, *Arabia*, *Syria*, and *Palestine*. HE, Nebuchadnezzar, was *the head of gold*.

II. BREASTS AND ARMS OF SILVER. The *Medo-Persian* empire; which properly began under *Darius* the *Mede*, allowing him to be the same with *Cyaxares*, son of *Astyages*, and uncle to Cyrus the great, son of *Cambyses*. He first fought under his uncle Cyaxares; defeated *Neriglissar*, king of the Assyrians, and *Crœsus*, king of the Lydians; and, by the capture of Babylon, B. C. 538, terminated the Chaldean empire. On the death of his father Cambyses, and his uncle Cyaxares, B. C. 536, he became sole governor of the Medes and Persians, and thus established a potent empire on the ruins of that of the *Chaldeans*.

III. Belly and thighs of brass. The *Macedonian* or *Greek* empire, founded by *Alexander the Great*. He subdued *Greece*, penetrated into *Asia*, took *Tyre*, reduced *Egypt*, overthrew *Darius Codomanus* at *Arbela*, Oct. 2, A. M. 3673, B. C. 331, and thus terminated the *Persian* monarchy. He crossed the *Caucasus*, subdued *Hyrcania*, and penetrated *India* as far as the *Ganges;* and having conquered all the countries that lay between the *Adriatic sea* and this *river*, the Ganges, he died A. M. 3681, B. C. 323; and after his death his empire became divided among his generals, *Cassander*, *Lysimachus*, *Ptolemy*, and *Seleucus*. Cassander had *Macedon* and *Greece;* Lysimachus had *Thrace*, and those parts of *Asia* which lay on the *Hellespont* and *Bosphorus;* Ptolemy had *Egypt*, *Lybia*, *Arabia*, *Palestine*, and *Cœlesyria;* Seleucus had *Babylon*, *Media*, *Susiana*, *Persia*, *Assyria*, *Bactria*, *Hyrcania*, and all other provinces, even to the *Ganges*. Thus this empire, founded on the ruin of that of the Persians, "had rule over all the earth."

IV. Legs of iron, and feet and toes of iron and clay. I think this means, in the first place, the *kingdom* of the Lagidæ, in *Egypt;* and the *kingdom* of the Seleucidæ, in *Syria*. And, *secondly*, the Roman *empire*, which was properly composed of them.

1. Ptolemy Lagus, one of Alexander's generals, began the new kingdom of *Egypt*, A. M. 3692, B. C. 312, which was continued through a long race of sovereigns, till A. M. 3974, B. C. 30; when *Octavius Cæsar* took Alexandria, having in the preceding year defeated *Anthony* and *Cleopatra* at the battle of *Actium*, and so Egypt became a *Roman province*. Thus ended the kingdom of the *Lagidæ*, after it had lasted *two hundred and eighty-two* years.

2. Seleucus Nicator, another of Alexander's generals, began the new kingdom of *Syria*, A. M. 3692, B. C. 312, which continued through a long race of sovereigns, till A. M. 3939, B. C. 65, when *Pompey* dethroned *Antiochus Asiaticus*, and Syria became a Roman province after it had lasted *two hundred and forty-seven* years.

That the *two legs of iron* meant the kingdom of the *Lagidæ* and that of the *Seleucidæ*, seems strongly intimated by the characters given in the text. "And the fourth kingdom shall be strong as iron. Forasmuch as iron breaketh in pieces and subdueth all things; and as iron that breaketh all these, shall it break in pieces and bruise," ver. 40. 1. The *iron* here not only marks the *strength* of these kingdoms, but also their *violence* and *cruelty* towards the people of God. History is full of the miseries which the kings of *Egypt* and *Syria* inflicted on the Jews. 2. It is said that these *legs* should *break in pieces and bruise*. How many generals and princes were destroyed by *Seleucus Nicator*, and by *Ptolemy*, son of *Lagus! Seleucus*, particularly, could not consider himself secure on his throne till he had destroyed Antigonus, Nicanor, and Demetrius; and *Ptolemy* endeavoured to secure himself by the ruin of *Perdiccas*, and the rest of his enemies. 3. The *dividing of the kingdom*, the *iron and clayey mixture* of the *feet*, point out the continual divisions which prevailed in those empires; and the *mixture of the good and evil qualities* which appeared in the successors of *Seleucus* and *Ptolemy;* none of them possessing the good qualities of the founders of those monarchies; neither their valour, wisdom, nor prudence. 4. The efforts which these princes made to *strengthen* their respective governments by *alliances*, which all proved not only *useless* but *injurious*, are here pointed out by their *mingling themselves with the seed of men.* "But they shall not cleave one to another," ver. 43. *Antiochus Theos*, king of Syria, married both *Laodice* and *Berenice*, daughters of *Ptolemy Philadelphus*, king of Egypt. *Antiochus Magnus*, king of Syria, gave his daughter *Cleopatra* to *Ptolemy Epiphanes*, king of Egypt; but these marriages, instead of being the means of consolidating the *union* between those kingdoms, contributed more than any thing else to *divide* them, and excite the most bloody and destructive wars.

In chap. vii. 7, the prophet, having the same subject in view, says, "I saw in the night visions, and behold a fourth beast, dreadful and terrible, and strong exceedingly; and it had great iron teeth: it devoured and brake in pieces, and stamped the residue with the feet of it;" and in chap. viii. 22: "Now that being broken," the horn of the *rough goat*, the *Grecian monarchy*, "whereas four stood up for it, four kingdoms shall stand up out of the nation, but not in his power." These and other declarations point out those peculiar circumstances that distinctly mark the kingdom of the *Seleucidæ*, and that of the *Lagidæ;* both of which rose out of the Macedonian or Grecian empire, and both terminated in that of the *Romans*.

2. These two legs of iron became absorbed in the Roman government, which also partook of the *iron* nature; strong, military, and extensive in its victories; and by its various conquests united to and amalgamated with itself various nations, some *strong*, and some *weak*, so as to be fitly represented in the *symbolical image* by *feet* and *toes*, partly of *iron* and partly of *clay*. Thus, as the *Lagidæ* and *Seleucidæ* arose out of the wreck of the *Grecian empire;* so the *Roman empire* arose out of their ruin. But the empire became *weakened* by its *conquests;* and although, by mingling themselves *with the seed* of men, that is, by strong leagues, and *matrimonial alliances*, as mentioned above, they endeavoured to secure a perpetual sovereignty, yet they did not *cleave to each other*, and they also were swallowed up by the *barbarous northern nations;* and thus terminated those *four* most powerful monarchies.

V. "A stone cut out of the mountain without hands."

1. That Jesus Christ has been represented by a *stone*, we have already seen; but *this stone* refers chiefly to his *Church*, which is represented as a *spiritual building*, which he supports as a *foundation stone*, *connects* and strengthens as a *corner stone*, and finishes and *adorns* as a *top stone*. He is called a *stone* also in reference to the prejudice conceived against him by his countrymen. Because he did not come in *worldly pomp* they therefore refused to receive him; and to them he is

represented as a *stone of stumbling, and rock of offence.*

2. But *here* he is represented under another notion, viz., that of a *stone projected from a catapult, or some military engine,* which smote the image on its feet; that is, it smote the then *existing government* at its *foundation,* or principles of support; and by destroying these, brought the whole into ruin.

3. By this *stroke* the *clay,* the *iron,* the *brass,* the *silver,* and the *gold* were *broken to pieces, and became like chaff which the wind carried away.* Now we have already seen that the *Roman empire,* which had absorbed the kingdoms of the *Lagidæ* and *Seleucidæ,* was represented by the *legs of iron, and feet and toes of iron and clay;* but as we find that not only the *iron and clay,* but also the *brass, silver,* and *gold* were confounded and destroyed by that stroke, it follows that there was then remaining in and compacted with the Roman government, something of the distinguishing marks and principles of all the *preceding empires;* not only as to their *territorial possessions,* but also as to their distinctive *characteristics.* There were at the time here referred to in the Roman empire, the *splendour* of the CHALDEANS, the *riches* of the PERSIANS, the *discipline* of the GREEKS, and the *strength* of the EGYPTIAN and SYRIAN governments, mingled with the *incoherence* and imbecility of those empires, kingdoms, and states which the Romans had subdued. In short, with every political excellence, it contains the principles of its own destruction, and its persecution of the Church of Christ accelerated its ruin.

4. As the *stone* represents *Christ* and his *governing influence,* it is here said to be a *kingdom,* that is, a state of *prevailing rule* and *government;* and was to arise *in the days of those kings* or kingdoms, ver. 44. And this is *literally* true; for its rise was when the Roman government, partaking of all the characteristics of the preceding empires, was at its *zenith of imperial splendour,* military glory, legislative authority, and literary eminence. It took place a few years after the battle of Actium, and when Rome was at peace with the whole world, *September* 2, B. C. 31.

5. This *stone* or government was *cut out of the mountain,* arose *in* and *under* the *Roman government,* Judea being, at the time of the birth of Christ, a *Roman province.*

6. It was *cut out without hands;* probably alluding to the miraculous birth of our Lord, but particularly to the *spiritual* nature of his kingdom and government, in which no *worldly policy, human maxims,* or *military force* were employed; for it was not *by might nor power, but by the Spirit of the Lord of hosts.*

Two things may be here distinguished: 1. The government or *kingdom* of the STONE. 2. The government or kingdom of the MOUNTAIN.

1. The *kingdom* of the STONE *smites, breaks to pieces,* and *destroys* all the other kingdoms, till no vestige of them remains, and till the whole earth is subdued by it.

2. The *kingdom* of the MOUNTAIN fills, and continues to govern, all that has been thus subdued, maintaining endless peace and righteousness in the earth.

First, The stone began to *strike the image,* when the *apostles* went out into every part of the Roman empire, pulling down idolatry, and founding Christian Churches.

Secondly, But the great blow was given to the heathen Roman empire by the *conversion of Constantine,* just at the time when it was an epitome of the *four great monarchies,* being under the government of FOUR EMPERORS *at once,* A. D. 308: CONSTANTIUS, who governed *Gaul, Spain,* and *Britain;* GALERIUS, who had *Illyricum, Thrace,* and *Asia;* SEVERUS, who had *Italy* and *Africa;* and MAXIMIN, who had the *East* and *Egypt.*

1. The conversion of Constantine took place while he was in Gaul, A. D. 312, by the appearance of a *luminous cross* in the sky above the sun, a little after *noon-day,* with this inscription, Εν τουτῳ νικα, "By this conquer;" *Euseb.* De Vit. Const. lib. i. cap. 28. In A. D. 324 he totally defeated *Licinius,* who had shared the empire with him, and became sole emperor. He terminated the reign of idolatry in A. D. 331, by an edict ordering the destruction of all the heathen temples. This made CHRISTIANITY the religion of the *empire.*

2. The *stroke* which thus destroyed idolatry in the Roman empire is continual in its *effects;* and must be so till idolatry be destroyed over the face of the earth, and the universe filled with the knowledge of Christ.

3. This *smiting* has been continued by all the means which God in his providence and mercy has used for the dissemination of Christianity, from the time of *Constantine* to the present: and particularly *now,* by means of the *British and Foreign Bible Society,* and its countless ramifications, and by the numerous *missionaries* sent by Christian societies to almost every part of the globe. Thus far the kingdom of the *stone.*

In ver. 44, the *kingdom of the stone,* grown into a *great mountain* and filling the whole earth, is particularly described by various characters.

1. It is a *kingdom* which the *God of heaven sets up.* That this means the *whole dispensation of the Gospel,* and the *moral effects* produced by it in the *souls of men* and in the *world,* needs little proof; for our Lord, referring to *this* and other prophecies in this book, calls its influence and his Gospel *the kingdom of God,* and *the kingdom of heaven;* showing thereby that it is a kingdom *not of this world*—not raised by human *ambition,* the *lust of rule,* or *military conquest;* but a *spiritual kingdom,* raised and maintained by the *grace of God* himself, in which he *himself lives and rules,* governing by his own laws, influencing and directing by his own Spirit; producing, not *wars and contentions,* but *glory to God in the highest,* and *on earth peace and good will among men.*

2. This is called the *kingdom of heaven,* because it is to be a counterpart of the *kingdom of glory. The kingdom of God,* says the apostle, is *righteousness, peace,* and *joy in the Holy Ghost,* (Rom. xiv. 17;) *righteousness,* without any *sin; peace,* without inward *disturbance; joy,* without any mental *unhappiness.* An *eternity* of righteousness, peace, and spiritual joy constitutes HEAVEN; nor can we conceive in that state any thing higher or more excellent than these.

3. This kingdom *shall never be destroyed:* it is the *everlasting Gospel,* and the work of the *everlasting* GOD. As it neither originates in nor is dependent on the *passions* of men, it cannot be *destroyed.* All other governments, from the imperfection of their nature, contain in them the seeds of their own destruction. *Kings* die, *ministers* change, *subjects* are not permanent;

new relations arise, and with them *new measures*, *new passions*, and *new projects;* and these produce *political changes*, and often *political ruin.* But *this* government, being the government of GOD, cannot be affected by the changes and chances to which mortal things are exposed.

4. *This kingdom shall not be left to other people.* Every dispensation of God, prior to Christianity, supposed another by which it was to be succeeded. 1. Holy *patriarchs* and their *families* were the *first* people among whom the kingdom of God was found. 2. *Hebrews*, in *Egypt* and in the *wilderness*, were the *next.* 3. *Jews*, in the *promised land*, were a *third* denomination. 4. And after the division of the kingdoms, captivity, and dispersion of the Jews, the *Israel of God* became a *fourth* denomination. 5. Under the Gospel, CHRISTIAN is the name of the *people of this kingdom.* Every thing in the construction of the Gospel system, as well as its own declarations, shows that it is not to be *succeeded* by any other dispensation: its *name* can never be changed; and CHRISTIAN will be the only denomination of the *people of God* while sun and moon endure. All former *empires* have changed, and the very *names* of the people have changed with them. The *Assyrians* were lost in the *Chaldeans* and *Babylonians;* the *Babylonians* were lost in the *Medes;* the *Medes* in the *Persians;* the *Persians* in the *Greeks;* and the *Greeks* in the *Syrians* and *Egyptians;* these in the *Romans;* and the *Romans* in the *Goths*, and a variety of other nations. Nor does the *name* of those ancient governments, nor the people who lived under them, remain on the face of the earth in the present day! They are only found in the *page of history.* This spiritual kingdom shall never be *transferred*, and the name of its *subjects* shall never be changed.

5. *It shall break in pieces and consume all these kingdoms;* that is, the preaching and influence of Christianity shall destroy *idolatry* universally. They did so in the Roman empire, which was the epitome of all the rest. But this was not done by the *sword*, nor by any *secular influence.* Christians wage no wars for the propagation of Christianity; for the religion of Christ breathes nothing but *love to God, and peace and good will to all mankind.* The sum of the Gospel is contained in these words of Christ: "God so loved the world that he gave his only-begotten Son, that whosoever believeth on him should not perish, but have everlasting life;—for the Son of man is not come to destroy men's lives, but to save."

For his own cause, God fights in the course of his providence. He depresses one, and exalts another; but permits not his own people to join with him in the *infliction of judgments.* It is by his own Spirit and energy that his kingdom is propagated and maintained in the world; and by the same his enemies are confounded. All *false religions*, as well as falsified and corrupted systems of Christianity, have had recourse to the *sword*, because they were conscious they had NO GOD, no influence but what was merely *human.*

6. The kingdom of Christ *breaks in pieces and consumes all other kingdoms;* that is, it destroys every thing in every earthly government where it is received, that is opposed to the glory of God and the peace and happiness of men, and yet in such a way as to leave all political governments unchanged. No law or principle in Christianity is directed against the *political code* of any country. *Britain* is Christian without the alteration of her *Magna Charta* or her constitution. All the other empires, kingdoms, and states on the face of the earth, may become Christian *and preserve their characteristic forms of political government.* If there be in them any thing hostile to Christianity, and the peace and happiness of the subject, the WIND of *God*—the *Divine Spirit*, will *fan* or *winnow* it away, so that *no more place shall be found* for it. But this he will do in the way of his ordinary *providence;* and by his influence on their hearts, dispose truly Christianized rulers to alter or abrogate whatever their laws contain inimical to the mild sway of the sceptre of Christ.

7. *And it shall stand for ever.* This is its final characteristic. It shall prevail over the whole world; it shall pervade every government; it shall be the basis of every code of laws; it shall be professed by every people of the earth: "The *Gentiles* shall come to its light, and *kings* to the brightness of its rising." The whole earth shall be subdued by its influence, and the whole earth filled with its glory.

8. The actual constitution, establishment, and maintenance of this kingdom belong to the LORD; yet he will use *human means* in the whole administration of his government. His WORD must be *distributed*, and that word must be PREACHED. Hence, under God, BIBLES and MISSIONARIES are the grand means to be employed in things *concerning* his kingdom. BIBLES must be printed, sent out, and dispersed; MISSIONARIES, called of God to the work, and filled with the Divine Spirit, must be *equipped*, *sent out*, and *maintained;* therefore *expenses* must necessarily be incurred. Here the people *now* of the kingdom must be helpers. It is the duty, therefore, of every soul professing Christianity to lend a helping hand to send forth the *Bible;* and wherever the Bible is sent, to send a missionary, full of faith and of the Holy Ghost, to enforce its truths.

9. The *duration* of the *kingdom of the mountain* upon *earth.* The world has now lasted nearly *six thousand* years, and a very ancient tradition has predicted its termination at the close of that period. Its duration has been divided into *three* grand periods, each comprising *two thousand years*, which should be closed by a period *without terminating* limits; and these have been supposed to have their *types* in the *six days' work of the creation*, and the *seventh* day, called *Sabbath* or *rest.*

1. There have been *two thousand* years from the creation *without any written revelation* from God; this was called the *patriarchal dispensation.*

2. There have been *two thousand* years *under the law*, where there has been a *written revelation*, a *succession of prophets*, and a Divine *ecclesiastical establishment.* This has been termed the *Mosaic dispensation.*

3. *One thousand eight hundred and twenty-nine* years have passed since the true epoch of the nativity of our blessed Lord; and this is called the *Gospel* or *Christian dispensation*, which is now within *one hundred and seventy-one years* of closing its *two thousand!*

According to the ancient tradition there were, 1. *Two thousand* years *void;* that is, without the law. 2. *Two thousand* years under the law. And, 3. *Two thousand* years under the Messiah. And at the termination of the *third* the endless

Sabbath should commence. The comments on this ancient tradition go on to state, that at the termination of each day's work of the creation it was said, *The evening and the morning were the first, second, third, fourth, fifth,* and *sixth day;* but when the *Sabbath* is introduced, and God is said to *rest from his work,* and to have *hallowed this day,* there is no mention of *the evening and the morning* being the *seventh* day. That is left without termination; and therefore a proper type of the *eternal Sabbath,* that *rest which remains for the people of God.*

And are we indeed so near that time when the elements of all things shall be dissolved by fervent heat; when the heavens shall be shrivelled up like a scroll, and the earth and all it contains be burned up? Is the *fifth empire,* the *kingdom of the stone* and *the kingdom of the mountain,* so near its termination? Are all vision and prophecy about to be sealed up, and the whole earth to be illuminated with the bright beams of the Sun of righteousness? Are the finally incorrigible and impenitent about to be swept off the face of the earth by the besom of destruction, while the righteous shall be able to lift up their heads with ineffable joy, knowing their final redemption is at hand? Are we so near the eve of that period when "they who turn many to righteousness shall shine as the stars for ever and ever?" What sort of persons should we then be in all holy conversation and godliness? Where is our zeal for God? Where the sounding of our bowels over the perishing nations who have not yet come under the yoke of the Gospel? Multitudes of whom are not under the yoke, because they have never heard of it; and they have not heard of it, because those who enjoy the blessings of the Gospel of Jesus have not felt (or have not obeyed the feeling) the imperious duty of dividing their *heavenly bread* with those who are famishing with *hunger,* and giving the *water of life* to those who are dying of *thirst.* How shall they appear in that great day when the conquests of the Lion of the tribe of Judah are ended; when the mediatorial kingdom is delivered up unto the Father, and the Judge of quick and dead sits on the great white throne, and to those on his left hand says, "I was hungry, and ye gave me no meat; I was thirsty, and ye gave me no drink." I say, How shall they appear who have made no exertions to tell the lost nations of the earth the necessity for *preparing to meet their God;* and showing them the *means* of doing it, by affording them the blessings of the Gospel of the grace of God? Let us beware lest the *stone* that struck the motley image, and dashed it to pieces, *fall* on US, and *grind us to powder.*

Bibles are sent out by millions into heathen countries; but *how shall they hear without a preacher;* and *how shall they understand the things which they read, unless* those who know the things of God teach them? Let us haste, then, and send *missionaries* after the *Bibles.* God is mightily at work in the earth: let us be *workers together with him, that we receive not the grace of God in vain.* He that giveth to those *poor* (emphatically POOR, for they are without God in the world, and consequently without the *true riches*) lendeth unto the Lord; and let him look what he layeth out, and it shall be paid unto him again. For "he that *converteth a sinner* from the error of his ways shall *save a soul from death,* and hide a multitude of sins." God does not call on *us* to shake hands with all secular, social, and family comfort, and bid farewell to the whole; and go to the heathen with the glad tidings of great joy: but he loudly calls on us to assist in sending *those* who, in the true spirit of sacrifice, the love of Christ constraining them, say, "Here are we! O Lord, send US." Let these servants of God run to and fro; that by their ministry knowledge may be increased. Amen.

CHAPTER III

Nebuchadnezzar, having erected an image, whose height (including probably a very high pedestal) was sixty cubits, and the breadth six, ordered a numerous assembly, which he had convened, to fall down and worship it; threatening, at the same time, that whosoever refused should be cast into a fiery furnace, 1–7; *a punishment not uncommon in that country,* (see Jer. xxix. 22.) *Daniel's three companions, Shadrach, Meshach, and Abed-nego, who were present, being observed to refrain from this idolatrous worship, were accused before the king; who, in great wrath, commanded them to comply with his orders on pain of death,* 8–15. *But these holy men, with the greatest composure and serenity, expressed their firm resolution not to worship his gods or his images, whatever might be the consequence,* 16–18. *Upon which the king, unaccustomed to have his will opposed, in the height of his wrath, ordered the furnace to be made seven times hotter than usual, and these men to be cast into it, bound by the most mighty of his army, who were killed by the flame in the execution of this service,* 19–23. *On this occasion God* literally *performed his promise by Isaiah,* (chap. xliii. 2:) *"When thou walkest through the fire, thou shalt not be burnt; neither shall the flame kindle upon thee;" for an angel of God, ap-*

pearing in the furnace, protected these young men, and counteracted the natural violence of the fire; which, only consuming the cords with which they were bound, left them to walk at liberty, and in perfect safety, in the midst of the furnace. The king, astonished at this prodigy, called to them to come out of the furnace, and blessed God for sending an angel to deliver his servants; and commanded all his subjects, upon pain of death, not to speak irreverently of the God of Shadrach, Meshach, and Abed-nego, who were promoted to great power and honour, 24–30. *A striking example of the interposition of Providence in favour of true and inflexible piety.*

A. M. cir. 3424
B. C. cir. 580
Ol. cir. L. 1
TarquiniiPrisci, R. Roman., cir. annum 37

NEBUCHADNEZZAR the king made [a]an image of gold, whose height *was* threescore cubits, *and* the breadth thereof six cubits: he set it up in the plain of Dura, in the [b]province of Babylon.

2 Then Nebuchadnezzar the king sent to gather together the princes, the governors, and the captains, the judges, the treasurers, the counsellors, the sheriffs, and all the rulers of the provinces, to come to the dedication of the image which Nebuchadnezzar the king had set up.

[a]Ver. 5, 7, 10, 12, 14

[b]Chap. ii. 48

NOTES ON CHAP. III

Verse 1. *Nebuchadnezzar the king made an image of gold*] It is supposed that the history given here did not occur till the close, or near the end, of Nebuchadnezzar's reign. For it was after his insanity, as we see chap. iv. 33-36, and this happened near the close of his reign. The authorized version, which is followed in the margin, fixes the date of this event *seventeen* years earlier, and *ten* years before the king's insanity. A few observations on this image may be necessary:—

1. It is not likely that this image was in *human* form—the dimensions show the improbability of this; for what proportion is there between *sixty* cubits (*ninety* feet) in length, and *six* cubits (*nine* feet) in breadth?

2. It is not likely that this image was *all of gold;* for this would have required more of this precious metal than the whole *province* of Babylon could produce; for as I suppose the *sixty* cubits apply to the perpendicular *altitude,* so I take it for granted that the *six* cubits intend the *diameter.* Now a column of gold of this height in diameter, upon the supposition that the pillar was circular, contains *five thousand seven hundred and twenty-five and a half* cubic feet; and as there are *nineteen thousand* avoirdupois ounces in a cubic foot, the weight of the whole pillar would be *eight million two hundred and sixty-two thousand eight hundred and six* pounds *ten ounces* of gold.

3. It might have been a *pillar* on which an *image* of the god *Bel* was erected. The image itself might be of *gold,* or more probably *gilt,* that is, covered with *thin plates* of gold, and on this account it might be called the *golden image;* and most probably the height of the image may be confounded with the height of the pillar. Or perhaps it was no more than a pillar, on the sides of which their gods and sacred emblems were engraven, surmounted with *Bel* on the top.

The plain of Dura] The situation of this place is not exactly known; there was a town or city called *Dura,* or *Doura,* in Mesopotamia, near the Tigris.

Verse 2. *Sent to gather together the princes*] It is not easy to show what these different offices were, as it is difficult to ascertain the meaning of the *Chaldee* words. *Parkhurst* analyzes them thus:—

The PRINCES] אחשדרפניא *achashdarpenaiya,* from אחש *achash, great* or *eminent,* and דר *dar,* "to go about freely," and פנים *panim,* "the presence." Satraps or privy counsellors who had free access to the presence of the king.

The GOVERNORS] סגניא *signaiya, lieutenants* or *viceroys,* for סגן *sagan,* among the Hebrews, was the name of the high priest's *deputy.*

The CAPTAINS] פחותא *pachavatha,* from פח *pach, to extend,* because set over those provinces that had been *annexed* to the kingdom by conquest. *Pashas*—This word and office are still in use in Asiatic countries. By corruption we pronounce *bashaw.*

The JUDGES] אדרגזריא *adargazeraiya,* from אדר *adar, noble* or *magnificent,* and גזר *gazar, to decree.* The nobles, the assistants to the king in making laws, statutes, &c. The same probably in Babylon, as the *House of Lords* in England.

The TREASURERS] גדבריא *gedaberaiya,* from גנז *ganaz,* (the ז *zain* being changed into ד *daleth,* according to the custom of the *Chaldee,*) to *treasure up,* and בר *bar, pure.* Those who kept the current coin, or were over the *mint;* the treasurers of the exchequer in Babylon.

The COUNSELLORS] דתבריא *dethaberaiya,* from דת *dath,* a *statute,* and בר *bar,* "to declare the meaning of the law;" for in all ages and countries there has been what is termed *the glorious uncertainty of the law;* and therefore there must be a class of men whose business it is to explain it. What a pity that law cannot be tendered to the people as other sciences are, in plain, unsophisticated, and intelligible terms, and by persons whose business it is to show what is *just* and *right,* and not pervert *truth, righteousness,* and *judgment.*

The SHERIFFS] תפתיא *tiphtaye,* from תפת *taphath,* in Hebrew, שפת *shaphath,* "to set in order." Probably civil magistrates.

And all the rulers of the provinces] All other state or civil officers, not only to grace the solemnity, but to maintain order. My old Bible renders them: **Satrapis, or wiise men. Magistratis. Jugis. Duykis, Tyrauntis, or stronge men. Prefectis, and alle the Princes of Cuntreese.**

A. M. cir. 3424
B. C. cir. 580
Ol. cir. L. 1
TarquiniiPrisci, R. Roman., cir. annum 37

3 Then the princes, the governors and captains, the judges, the treasurers, the counsellors, the sheriffs, and all the rulers of the provinces, were gathered together unto the dedication of the image that Nebuchadnezzar the king had set up; and they stood before the image that Nebuchadnezzar had set up.

4 Then a herald cried [c]aloud, To you [d]it is commanded, [e]O people, nations, and languages,

5 *That* at what time ye hear the sound of the cornet, flute, harp, sackbut, psaltery, [f]dulcimer, [g]and all kinds of music, ye fall down and worship the golden image that Nebuchadnezzar the king hath set up:

6 And whoso falleth not down and worshippeth shall the same hour [h]be cast into the midst of a burning fiery furnace.

7 Therefore at that time, when all the people heard the sound of the cornet, flute, harp, sackbut, psaltery, and all kinds of music, all the people, the nations, and the languages, fell down *and* worshipped the golden image that Nebuchadnezzar the king had set up.

8 Wherefore at that time certain Chaldeans [i]came near, and accused the Jews.

A. M. cir. 3424
B. C. cir. 580
Ol. cir. L. 1
TarquiniiPrisci, R. Roman., cir. annum 37

9 They spake and said to the king Nebuchadnezzar, [k]O king, live for ever.

10 Thou, O king, hast made a decree, that every man that shall hear the sound of the cornet, flute, harp, sackbut, psaltery, and dulcimer, and all kinds of music, shall fall down and worship the golden image:

11 And whoso falleth not down and worshippeth, *that* he should be cast into the midst of a burning fiery furnace.

12 [l]There are certain Jews whom thou hast set over the affairs of the province of Babylon, Shadrach, Meshach, and Abed-nego; these men, O king, [m]have not regarded thee: they serve not thy gods, nor worship the golden image which thou hast set up.

13 Then Nebuchadnezzar in *his* rage and fury commanded to bring Shadrach, Meshach, and Abed-nego. Then they brought these men before the king.

14 Nebuchadnezzar spake and said unto

[c]Chald. *with might*——[d]Chald. *they command* [e]Chap. iv. 1; vi. 25——[f]Or, *singing*——[g]Chald. *symphony*——[h]Jer. xxix. 22; Rev. xiii. 15

[i]Chapter vi. 12——[k]Chapter ii. 4; v. 10; vi. 6, 21 [l]Chapter ii. 49——[m]Chald. *have set no regard upon thee*

Verse 4. *Then a herald cried aloud*] כרוזא קרא בחיל *caroza kara bechayil*, "a crier called with might." **A bedel cried mightili.**—Old MS. Bible.

Verse 5. *The sound of the* CORNET] There is not less difficulty in ascertaining the precise meaning of these *musical instruments* than there is in the *offices* in ver. 2. קרנא *karna*, here translated *cornet*, is the common *blowing horn*, which makes a deep and hollow sound, as well as one shrill and piercing.

FLUTE] משרוקיתא *mashrokitha*, from שרק *sharak, to whistle, shriek*. A wind instrument which made a strong and shrill noise, such as the *hautbois* or *clarionet*.

HARP] קיתרס *kithros, cytharus;* κιθαρα. Some kind of stringed instrument. It seems to be formed from the Greek word.

SACKBUT] סבכא *sabbecha*. The Greek has it σαμβυκη, from which our word *sackbut*, from סבך *sabach*, to *interweave;* probably on account of the number of chords, for it seems to have been a species of harp.

PSALTERY] פסנתרין *pesanterin;* Greek, ψαλτηριον. A stringed instrument, struck with a plectrum; that called *santeer* in Egypt is probably the same. Dr. *Russel* says: "It is a large triangle, and has two bottoms two inches from each other, with about twenty catguts of different sizes." It was the ancient *psalterium*, and most probably the same as *David's harp*.

DULCIMER] סומפניה *sumponeyah;* Greek, συμφωνεια. Probably a kind of *tamboor, tambourine*, or *tomtom drum*. It does not mean the same as the Greek *symphonia*, which signifies a *concert* or *harmony of many instruments*, for here one kind of instrument only is intended.

All kinds of music] כל זני זמרא *col zeney zemara, the whole stock*, or *band, of music;* the preceding being the chief, the most common, and the most sonorous. My old MS. Bible has, **Trumpe, and Pipe, and Harpe: Sambuke, Santrie, and Synfonye, and al kynde of musykes.**

Verse 6. *Shall the same hour*] This is the first place in the Old Testament where we find the division of time into *hours*. The Greeks say that *Anaximander* was the inventor. He had it probably from the Chaldeans, among whom this division was in use long before Anaximander was born.

Be cast into the midst of a burning fiery furnace.] This was an ancient mode of punishment among the Chaldeans, if we may credit the tradition that Abram was cast into such a fire by this idolatrous people because he would not worship their idols.

Verse 8. *Accused the Jews.*] That is, Shadrach, Meshach, and Abed-nego. The other Jews were left unnoticed; and probably at this time Daniel was too high to be touched; but we may rest assured that he was not found among these idolaters, see ver. 12.

A. M. cir. 3424
B. C. cir. 580
Ol. cir. L. 1
TarquiniiPrisci,
R. Roman.,
cir. annum 37

them, *Is it* [n]true, O Shadrach, Meshach, and Abed-nego, do not ye serve my gods, nor worship the golden image which I have set up?

15 Now if ye be ready that at what time ye hear the sound of the cornet, flute, harp, sackbut, psaltery, and dulcimer, and all kinds of music, ye fall down and worship the image which I have made; [o]*well:* but if ye worship not, ye shall be cast the same hour into the midst of a burning fiery furnace: [p]and who *is* that God that shall deliver you out of my hands?

16 Shadrach, Meshach, and Abed-nego, answered and said to the king, O Nebuchadnezzar, [q]we *are* not careful to answer thee in this matter.

17 If it be *so,* our God whom we serve is able to deliver us from the burning fiery furnace, and he will deliver *us* out of thine hand, O king.

18 [r]But if not, be it known unto thee, O king, that we will not serve thy gods, nor worship the golden image which thou hast set up.

A. M. cir. 3424
B. C. cir. 580
Ol. cir. L. 1.
TarquiniiPrisci
R. Roman.,
cir. annum 37

19 Then was Nebuchadnezzar [s]full of fury, and the form of his visage was changed against Shadrach, Meshach, and Abed-nego: *therefore* he spake, and commanded that they should heat the furnace one seven times more than it was wont to be heated.

20 And he commanded the [t]most mighty men that *were* in his army to bind Shadrach, Meshach, and Abed-nego, *and* to cast *them* into the burning fiery furnace.

21 Then these men were bound in their [u]coats, their hosen, and their [v]hats, and their *other* garments, and were cast into the midst of the burning fiery furnace.

22 Therefore because the king's [w]commandment was urgent, and the furnace exceeding hot, the [x]flame of the fire slew those men that took up Shadrach, Meshach, and Abed-nego.

23 And these three men, Shadrach, Meshach, and Abed-nego, fell down bound into the midst of the burning fiery furnace.

[n]Or, *of purpose,* as Exod. xxi. 13——[o]As Exod. xxxii. 32; Luke xiii. 9——[p]Exod. v. 2; 2 Kings xviii. 35 [q]Matt. x. 19

[r]2 Mac. vii. 2——[s]Chald. *filled*——[t]Chald. *mighty of strength*——[u]Or, *mantles*——[v]Or, *turbans*——[w]Chald. *word*——[x]Or, *sparks*

Verse 16. *We* are *not careful*] We have no need to put thee to any farther trouble; we have made up our minds on this subject, and have our answer ready: *Be it known unto thee,* WE WILL NOT SERVE THY GODS. This was as honest as it was decisive.

Verse 17. *If it be so*] Thou mayest cast us into the furnace; the terror of it has no effect on our minds to induce us to alter the resolution we have taken, nor shall the fire change our purpose. We serve a God who is able to deliver us. Should he not, we are equally determined; but we are satisfied that in some way or other he will deliver us out of thy hand. Thy power cannot affect us in the kingdom of our God to which we shall ascend from thy furnace, should he permit the fire to kindle upon us. "Render to Cæsar the things which are Cæsar's," is a maxim of Jesus Christ; but when Cæsar arrogates to himself the things that are the Lord's, then, and in such cases, his authority is to be resisted. God does not desire Cæsar's things; Cæsar's must not have the things of God.

Verse 19. *Then was Nebuchadnezzar full of fury*] How strange is this, after having had so many proofs of the supremacy of Jehovah! He had seen how God poured contempt upon his authority in the case of the *three* Hebrews, and yet he will try his strength once more! How infatuated is man!

Seven times more] As hot as it could be made. *Seven* expresses the great intensity of the heat.

Verse 20. *The most mighty men*] The generals, or chief officers of his army; not *strong* men; there was no need of such.

Verse 21. *Their hats*] This word, *hat,* is found only in this place in the Old Testament. The word סרבל *sarbal* properly means an outer garment. *Herodotus,* who lived about *one hundred* years after Daniel, says, "the dress of the Babylonians consisted of a tunic of linen reaching down to the feet; over this a tunic of woollen; and over all a white short cloak or mantle, χλανιδιον; and on their heads they wore *turbans,* μιτρησι." Following this, Mr. *Parkhurst* translates the verse thus: "Then these three men were bound [בסרבליהון *besarbaleyhon*] in their CLOAKS, [פטישיהון *patesheyhon*] their TURBANS, [וכרבלתהון *vecharbelathehon*] and in their UPPER (woollen) TUNICS, [ולבושיהון *ulebushehon*] and their UNDER (linen) TUNICS." And as, according to this interpretation, their סרבלי *sarbaley* were their *outermost garments,* we see the propriety with which it is observed at ver. 27 that these *were not changed* by the fire.

Verse 23. *And these three men—fell down bound*] There is a most evident want of connexion between this and the following verse; and it is between these verses that the apocryphal Song of the Three Children, as it is called, has been inserted by St. Jerome and others; but with this note: Quæ sequuntur in Hebræis voluminibus non reperi; "What follows I have not found in the Hebrew books." And then begins, "They walked in the midst of the flame, praising God, and blessing the Lord." The

A. M. cir. 3424
B. C. cir. 580
Ol. cir. L. 1
TarquiniiPrisci, R. Roman., cir. annum 37

24 Then Nebuchadnezzar the king was astonied, and rose up in haste, *and* spake, and said unto his [y]counsellors, Did not we cast three men bound into the midst of the fire? They answered and said unto the king, True, O king.

25 He answered and said, Lo, I see four men loose, [z]walking in the midst of the fire, and [a]they have no hurt; and the form of the fourth is like [b]the Son of God.

26 Then Nebuchadnezzar came near to the [c]mouth of the burning fiery furnace, *and* spake, and said, Shadrach, Meshach, and Abed-nego, ye servants of the most high God, come forth, and come *hither*. Then Shadrach, Meshach, and Abed-nego, came forth of the midst of the fire.

27 And the princes, governors, and captains, and the king's counsellors, being gathered together, saw these men, [d]upon whose bodies the fire had no power, nor was a hair of their head singed, neither were their coats changed, nor the smell of fire had passed on them.

A. M. cir. 3424
B. C. cir. 580
Ol. cir. L. 1
TarquiniiPrisci, R. Roman., cir. annum 37

28 *Then* Nebuchadnezzar spake, and said, Blessed *be* the God of Shadrach, Meshach, and Abed-nego, who hath sent his angel, and delivered his servants that [e]trusted in him, and have changed the king's word, and yielded their bodies, that they might not serve nor worship any god, except their own God.

29 [f]Therefore [g]I make a decree, That every people, nation, and language, which speak [h]any thing amiss against the God of Shadrach, Meshach, and Abed-nego, shall be [i]cut [k]in pieces, and their houses shall be made a dunghill: [l]because there is no other god that can deliver after this sort.

30 Then the king [m]promoted Shadrach, Meshach, and Abed-nego, in the province of Babylon.

[y]Or, *governors*——[z]Isa. xliii. 2——[a]Chald. *there is no hurt in them*——[b]Job i. 6; xxxviii. 7; Psa. xxxiv. 7; ver. 28——[c]Chald. *door*——[d]Heb. xi. 34——[e]Psa. xxxiv. 7, 8; Jer. xvii. 7; ch. vi. 22, 23——[f]Ch. vi. 26——[g]Chald. *a decree is made by me*——[h]Chald. *error*——[i]Chap. ii. 5——[k]Chald. *made pieces*——[l]Chap. vi. 27——[m]Chald. *made to prosper*

Septuagint and *Arabic* read the *twenty-fourth* verse thus: "Then Nebuchadnezzar heard them singing praise, and was astonished." To connect the two verses *Houbigant* adds two verses found in the *Vulgate*, which are the *forty-ninth* and the *twenty-third:* "But an angel of the Lord went down with Azariah and his companions into the furnace, and drove out the flame of fire from the furnace; and they walked in the midst of the furnace." This verse (the *forty-ninth*) has been added to show the *reason* of Nebuchadnezzar's *astonishment*, and also to account for the appearance of a *fourth* person in the furnace, as in ver. 25.

Verse 25. *Is like the Son of God.*] A most improper translation. What notion could this idolatrous king have of the *Lord Jesus Christ?* for so the place is understood by thousands. בר אלהין *bar elahin* signifies *a son of the gods*, that is, a Divine person or *angel;* and so the king calls him in ver. 28: "God hath sent his ANGEL, and delivered his servants." And though even from this some still contend that it was the *Angel of the covenant*, yet the Babylonish king knew just as much of the one as he did of the other. No other ministration was necessary; a single angel from heaven was quite sufficient to answer this purpose, as that which stopped the mouths of the lions when Daniel was cast into their den.

Verse 27. *Upon whose bodies the fire had no power*] The heathens boasted that their priests could walk on burning coals unhurt; and *Virgil* mentions this of the priests of Apollo of Soracte:—

Summe Deum, sancti custos Soractis Apollo!
Quem primi colimus, cui pineus ardor acervo
Pascitur; et medium, freti pietate, per ignem
Cultores multa premimus vestigia pruna.
VIRG. *Æn.* xi. 785.

O Phœbus, guardian of Soracte's woods
And shady hills; a god above the gods;
To whom our natives pay the rites divine,
And burn whole crackling groves of hallowed pine;
Walk through the fire in honour of thy name,
Unhurt, unsinged, and *sacred from the flame.*
PITTS.

But *Varro* tells us that they anointed the soles of their feet with a species of unguent that preserved them from being burnt. Very lately a female showed many feats of this kind, putting red hot iron upon her arms, breasts, &c., and passing it over her hair without the slightest inconvenience; but in the case of the three Hebrews all was supernatural, and the king and his officers well knew it.

Verse 28. *Blessed* be *the God of Shadrach, &c.*] Here is a noble testimony from a heathen. And what produced it? The intrepidly pious conduct of these three noble Jews. Had they been time-servers, the name of the true God had not been known in Babylon. What honour does the Lord put on them that are steadfast in the faith!

Verse 29. *Speak any thing amiss*] Though by the decree the king does not oblige the people to worship the true God, yet he obliges them to treat him with reverence.

Verse 30. *Then the king promoted, &c.*] He restored them to the offices which they held before the charge of disobedience and treason was brought against them.

At the end of this verse the *Septuagint* add, "And he advanced them to be governors over all the Jews that were in his kingdom." This may be the meaning of the latter verse. They were more likely to be set over the *Jews* than over the *Chaldeans*.

CHAPTER IV

Nebuchadnezzar, after having subdued all the neighbouring countries, and greatly enriched and adorned his own, became so intoxicated with his prosperity, as to draw down upon himself a very remarkable judgment, of which this chapter gives a particular account, in the very words of the edict or proclamation which the Babylonish monarch issued on his restoration to the throne. This state document begins with Nebuchadnezzar's acknowledging the hand of God in his late malady, 1–3. *It then gives an account of the dream of Nebuchadnezzar, which portended the loss of his kingdom and reason for seven years, on account of his pride and arrogance,* 4–18. *So it was explained by Daniel,* 19–27, *and so it was verified by the event,* 28–33. *It then recites how, at the end of the period fixed by the God of heaven for the duration of his malady, the Chaldean monarch became sensible of his dependence on the Supreme Being, and lifted up his eyes to heaven in devout acknowledgment of the sovereign majesty of the King of kings, the Ruler of the earth, whose dominion alone is universal, unchangeable, and everlasting,* 34–37.

A. M. cir. 3434
B. C. cir. 570
Ol. cir. LII. 3
Servii Tullii, R. Roman., cir. annum 9

NEBUCHADNEZZAR the king, [a]unto all people, nations, and languages, that dwell in all the earth; Peace be multiplied unto you.

2 [b]I thought it good to show the signs and wonders [c]that the high God hath wrought toward me.

3 [d]How great *are* his signs! and how mighty *are* his wonders! his kingdom *is* [e]an everlasting kingdom, and his dominion *is* from generation to generation.

4 I Nebuchadnezzar was at rest in mine house, and flourishing in my palace:

5 I saw a dream which made me afraid, [f]and the thoughts upon my bed and the visions of my head [g]troubled me.

6 Therefore made I a decree to bring in all the wise *men* of Babylon before me, that they might make known unto me the interpretation of the dream.

7 [h]Then came in the magicians, the astrologers, the Chaldeans, and the soothsayers: and I told the dream before them; but they did not make known unto me the interpretation thereof.

A. M. cir. 3434
B. C. cir. 570
Ol. cir. LII. 3
Servii Tullii, R. Roman., cir. annum 9

8 But at the last Daniel came in before me, [i]whose name *was* Belteshazzar, according to the name of my god, [k]and in whom *is* the spirit of the holy gods: and before him I told the dream, *saying,*

9 O Belteshazzar, [l]master of the magicians, because I know that the spirit of the holy gods *is* in thee, and no secret troubleth thee, tell me the visions of my dream that I have seen, and the interpretation thereof.

10 Thus *were* the visions of mine head in my bed; [m]I saw, and behold [n]a tree in the midst of the earth, and the height thereof *was* great.

11 The tree grew, and was strong, and the height thereof reached unto heaven, and the sight thereof to the end of all the earth:

[a]Chap. iii. 4; vi. 25——[b]Chald. *It was seemly before me*——[c]Chap. iii. 26——[d]Chap. vi. 27——[e]Ver. 34; chap. ii. 44; vi. 26——[f]Chap. ii. 28, 29——[g]Chap. ii. 1

[h]Chap. ii. 2——[i]Chap. i. 7——[k]Isa. lxiii. 11; ver. 18; chap. ii. 11; v. 11, 14——[l]Chap. ii. 48; v. 11——[m]Chald. *I was seeing*——[n]Ezek. xxxi. 3, &c.; ver. 20

NOTES ON CHAP. IV

Verse 1. *Nebuchadnezzar the king, unto all people*] This is a regular *decree*, and is one of the most ancient on record; and no doubt was copied from the *state papers* of Babylon. Daniel has preserved it in the *original language*.

Verse 2. *I thought it good to show*] A part of the decree was a recital of the wonders wrought by the hand of the true God in his kingdom and on his person.

Verse 3. *How great* are *his signs!*] There are no preternatural signs like his! His *wonders*—miraculous interferences, are mighty—they surpass all human power. He is the *Sovereign of all kings*, and his *dominion is everlasting;* and *every generation* is a proof of his all-governing influence. These are very fine sentiments, and show how deeply his mind was impressed with the majesty of God.

Verse 4. *I—was at rest*] I had returned to my palace in Babylon after having subdued Syria, Phœnicia, Judea, Egypt, and Arabia. It was probably these great conquests that puffed him up with pride, and brought that chastisement upon him which he afterwards describes. See the dream of the *emblematical tree* explained.

Verse 5. *I saw a dream*] See this dream circumstantially explained in the following verses.

Verse 10. *I saw—a tree*] This vision Nebuchadnezzar says *made him afraid.* What a mercy it is that God has hidden futurity from us! Were he to show every man the lot that is before him, the misery of the human race would be complete.

Great men and princes are often represented, in the language of the prophets, under the similitude of *trees;* see Ezek. xvii. 5, 6; xxxi. 3, &c.; Jer. xxii. 15; Psa. i. 3; xxxvii. 35.

A. M. cir. 3434
B. C. cir. 570
Ol. cir. LII. 3
Servii Tullii,
R. Roman.,
cir. annum 9

12 The leaves thereof *were* fair, and the fruit thereof much, and in it *was* meat for all: [o]the beasts of the field had shadow under it, and the fowls of the heaven dwelt in the boughs thereof, and all flesh was fed of it.

13 I saw in the visions of my head upon my bed, and, behold, [p]a watcher and [q]a holy one came down from heaven;

14 He cried [r]aloud, and said thus, [s]Hew down the tree, and cut off his branches, shake off his leaves, and scatter his fruit: [t]let the beasts get away from under it, and the fowls from his branches.

15 Nevertheless leave the stump of his roots in the earth, even with a band of iron and brass, in the tender grass of the field; and let it be wet with the dew of heaven, and *let* his portion *be* with the beasts in the grass of the earth:

16 Let his heart be changed from man's, and let a beast's heart be given unto him; and let seven [u]times pass over him.

17 This matter *is* by the decree of the watchers, and the demand by the word of the holy ones: to the intent [v]that the living may know [w]that the Most High ruleth in the kingdom of men, and giveth it to whomsoever he will, and setteth up over it the basest of men.

A. M. cir. 3434
B. C. cir. 570
Ol. cir. LII. 3
Servii Tullii
R. Roman.,
cir. annum 9

18 This dream I king Nebuchadnezzar have seen. Now thou, O Belteshazzar, declare the interpretation thereof, [x]forasmuch as all the wise *men* of my kingdom are not able to make known unto me the interpretation: but thou *art* able; [y]for the spirit of the holy gods *is* in thee.

19 Then Daniel, [z]whose name *was* Belteshazzar, was astonied for one hour, and his thoughts troubled him. The king spake, and said, Belteshazzar, let not the dream, or the interpretation thereof, trouble thee. Belteshazzar answered and said, My lord, [a]the dream *be* to them that hate thee, and the interpretation thereof to thine enemies.

20 [b]The tree that thou sawest, which grew, and was strong, whose height reached unto the heaven, and the sight thereof to all the earth;

21 Whose leaves *were* fair, and the fruit thereof much, and in it *was* meat for all; under which the beasts of the field dwelt,

---

[o]Ezek. xvii. 23; xxxi. 6; see Lam. iv. 20——[p]Psa. ciii. 20; ver. 17, 23——[q]Deut. xxxiii. 2; chap. viii. 13; Zech. xiv. 5; Jude 14——[r]Chald. *with might*——[s]Matt. iii. 10——[t]Ezek. xxxi. 12

[u]Chap. xi. 13; xii. 7——[v]Psa. ix. 16——[w]Chap. ii. 21; v. 21; ver. 25, 32——[x]Gen. xli. 8, 15; chap. v. 8, 15 [y]Ver. 8——[z]Ver. 8——[a]See 2 Sam. xviii. 32; Jer. xxix. 7 [b]Ver. 10, 11, 12

Verse 13. *A watcher and a holy one*] These are both *angels;* but, according to the Chaldean oracles, of *different orders.* They appear, according to their opinions, to be a kind of *judges* of *human actions* who had the power of *determining the lot* of men; see ver. 17.

Verse 14. *Hew down the tree*] As the tree was to be cut down, the beasts are commanded to *flee away from under his branches.* His courtiers, officers, &c., all abandoned him as soon as his insanity appeared; but he soon fled from the society of men.

Verse 15. *Leave the stump*] Let him not be destroyed, nor his kingdom alienated.

Verse 16. *Let his heart be changed*] Let him conceive himself to be a *beast,* and act as such, herding among the beasts of the field.

Let seven times pass over him.] Let him continue in this state for *seven years.* I knew a man who was thus changed in his heart—in his imagination. He believed himself to be a *bear,* and would imitate the ursal growl, &c.; and the case did not appear to be hypochondriacal. Whether he ever came to sound mind, I know not.

Verse 17. *This matter* is *by the decree of the watchers*] See on ver. 13.

The Most High ruleth] He never leaves the government of the world to man, to second causes, or to fortuitous occurrences. What are thus called are his *agents;* they are no *moving causes.*

And setteth up—the basest of men.]

"Tyrants and kings from Jove proceed
Those are permitted, these decreed."

The *throne* ennobles no man: to be properly filled, the *man* must be *noble.* Some of the *greatest* and some of the *meanest* of men have sat on the throne. Kings differ in *education,* seldom in *intellect,* from the common mass of men; the *power* and *authority* are from God. The king himself may be given either in *mercy* or in *wrath.* When *James* II. ruled this kingdom, it might well be said, God hath *set up over it the basest of men.* His *successor* was one of the best. The *former* nearly ruined it both in a civil and religious point of view; the *latter* was the means of restoring it in both these respects.

Verse 19. *Daniel—was astonied for one hour*] He saw the design of the dream, and he felt the great delicacy of interpreting it. He was not puzzled by the difficulties of it. He felt for the king, and for the nation; and with what force and delicacy does he express the general portent; "The dream to them that hate thee, and the interpretation thereof to thine enemies!"

Verse 20. *The tree that thou sawest*] The

A. M. cir. 3434
B. C. cir. 570
Ol. cir. LII. 3
Servii Tullii,
R. Roman.,
cir. annum 9

and upon whose branches the
fowls of the heaven had their
habitation:
22 [c]It *is* thou, O king, that art
grown and become strong: for thy greatness
is grown, and reacheth unto heaven, [d]and thy
dominion to the end of the earth.
23 [e]And whereas the king saw a watcher
and a holy one coming down from heaven,
and saying, Hew the tree down, and destroy
it; yet leave the stump of the roots thereof
in the earth, even with a band of iron and
brass, in the tender grass of the field; and
let it be wet with the dew of heaven, [f]and
let his portion *be* with the beasts of the field,
till seven times pass over him;
24 This *is* the interpretation, O king, and
this *is* the decree of the Most High, which is
come upon my lord the king:
25 That they shall [g]drive thee from men,
and thy dwelling shall be with the beasts of
the field, and they shall make thee [h]to eat
grass as oxen, and they shall wet thee with
the dew of heaven, and seven times shall pass
over thee, [i]till thou know that the Most High
ruleth in the kingdom of men, and [k]giveth it
to whomsoever he will.
26 And whereas they commanded to leave
the stump of the tree roots; thy kingdom
shall be sure unto thee, after that thou
shalt have known that the [l]heavens do
rule.
27 Wherefore, O king, let my counsel be
acceptable unto thee, and [m]break off thy sins
by righteousness, and thine iniquities by
showing mercy to the poor; [n]if it may be [o]a[p]
lengthening of thy tranquillity.

A. M. cir. 3434
B. C. cir. 570
Ol. cir. LII. 3
Servii Tullii,
R. Roman.,
cir. annum 9

28 All this came upon the king
Nebuchadnezzar.
29 At the end of twelve months
he walked [q]in the palace of the
kingdom of Babylon.
30 The king [r]spake, and said, Is not this
great Babylon, that I have built for the house
of the kingdom by the might of my power,
and for the honour of my majesty?
31 [s]While the word *was* in the king's mouth,
there fell [t]a voice from heaven, *saying,* O
king Nebuchadnezzar, to thee it is spoken;
The kingdom is departed from thee.
32 And [u]they shall drive thee from men,
and thy dwelling *shall be* with the beasts of
the field: they shall make thee to eat grass as
oxen, and seven times shall pass over thee,
until thou know that the Most High ruleth in
the kingdom of men, and giveth it to whomsoever
he will.
33 The same hour was the thing fulfilled
upon Nebuchadnezzar: and he was driven
from men, and did eat grass as oxen, and his
body was wet with the dew of heaven, till his
hairs were grown like eagles' *feathers,* and
his nails like birds' *claws.*

A. M. cir. 3441
B. C. cir. 563
Ol. LIV. 2
Servii Tullii,
R. Roman.,
cir. annum 16

34 And [v]at the end of the days
I Nebuchadnezzar lifted up
mine eyes unto heaven, and mine
understanding returned unto
me, and I blessed the Most High, and I
praised and honoured him [w]that liveth for
ever, whose dominion *is* [x]an everlasting dominion,
and his kingdom *is* from generation
to generation:
35 And [y]all the inhabitants of the earth *are*
reputed as nothing: and [z]he doeth according

[c]Chap. ii. 38——[d]Jer. xxvii. 6, 7, 8——[e]Ver. 13
[f]Chap. v. 21——[g]Ver. 32; chap. v. 21, &c.——[h]Psa. cvi.
20——[i]Ver. 17, 32; Psa. lxxxiii. 18——[k]Jer. xxvii. 5
[l]Matt. xxi. 25; Luke xv. 18, 21——[m]1 Pet. iv. 8
[n]Psa. xli. 1, &c.——[o]Or, *a healing of thine error*

[p]1 Kings xxi. 29——[q]Or, *upon*——[r]Prov. xvi. 18;
chap. v. 20——[s]Chap. v. 5; Luke xii. 20——[t]Ver. 24
[u]Ver. 25——[v]Ver. 26——[w]Chap. xii. 7; Rev. iv. 10
[x]Psa. x. 16; chap. ii. 44; vii. 14; Mic. iv. 7; Luke i. 33
[y]Isa. xl. 15, 17——[z]Psa. cxv. 3; cxxxv. 6

dream is so fully interpreted in the following verses that it needs no comment.

Verse 26. *Thy kingdom shall be sure unto thee*] No new king was set up; Evil-merodach his son was regent during his father's insanity.

Verse 27. *Break off thy sins by righteousness*] Do *justice.* Thou hast been an *oppressive* man; *show mercy to the poor,* many of whom have been made such by thyself: witness the whole nation of the Jews. He was to cease from his *sins—repent, and bring forth fruits meet for repentance,* in order that he might find mercy at the hand of God.

Verse 30. *Is not this great Babylon*] Here his heart was inflated with pride; he attributed every thing to himself, and acknowledged God in nothing. The *walls, hanging gardens, temple of Bel,* and the *royal palace,* all built by Nebuchadnezzar, made it the greatest city in the world.

Verse 31. *While the word* was *in the king's mouth*] How awful to a victorious and proud king: "Thy kingdom is departed from thee!" All thy goods and gods are gone in a moment!

Verse 32. *They shall make thee, &c.*] Thou shalt be made *to eat grass as oxen.* The madness that fell upon him induced him to forsake society, and to run to the woods and deserts,

A. M. cir. 3441
B. C. cir. 563
Ol. LIV. 2
Servii Tullii,
R. Roman.,
cir. annum 16

to his will in the army of
heaven, and *among* the inhabitants of the earth: and [a]none
can stay his hand, or say unto
him, [b]What doest thou?
36 At the same time my reason returned
unto me; [c]and for the glory of my kingdom,
mine honour and brightness returned unto
me; and my counsellors and my lords sought
unto me; and I was established
in my kingdom, and excel-
lent majesty was [d]added unto
me.
37 Now I Nebuchadnezzar praise and extol
and honour the king of heaven, [e]all whose
works *are* truth, and his ways judgment:
[f]and those that walk in pride he is able to
abase.

[a]Job xxxiv. 29——[b]Job ix. 12; Isa. xlv. 9; Rom. ii. 20——[c]Ver. 26——[d]Job xlii. 12; Prov. xxii. 4; Matt. vi. 33——[e]Psa. xxxiii. 4; Rev. xv. 3; xvi. 7——[f]Exod. xviii. 11; chap. v. 20

where he lived like a wild beast, his *hairs* growing long and thick, so as to be a substitute for clothing; and his *nails* strong and hooked, that he might the better climb trees and grub up the ground, in order to get *roots* and *earth-nuts*. It was the *mercy* of God that thus *clothed* and *accoutred* him. His case seems much like that of the maniac in the Gospel, whose dwelling was among the tombs and in the mountains, and who shunned the society of men.

Verse 36. *My reason returned*] Every thing was fulfilled that was exhibited by the *dream* and its *interpretation*. It is very likely that this unfortunate king had so concealed himself that the place of his retreat was not found out; and the providence of God had so watched over every thing, that, on his return to his palace, he found his *counsellors* and his *lords*, who received him gladly, and cleaved to and served him as they had formerly done.

Verse 37. *Now I—praise and extol*] It is very probable that Nebuchadnezzar was a true convert; that he relapsed no more into idolatry, and died in the faith of the God of Israel. It is supposed that he lived *seventeen* years after his restoration. But the authorized Version, which is followed in the margin, states the date of this decree to be B. C. 563, the year preceding Nebuchadnezzar's death.

CHAPTER V

In the commencement of this chapter we are informed how Belshazzar, the grandson of Nebuchadnezzar, when rioting in his palace, and profaning the sacred vessels of the temple, 1–4, *was suddenly terrified with the appearance of the fingers of a man's hand, which wrote a few words on the wall before him,* 5, 6. *The wise men and astrologers were immediately called in to show the king the interpretation; but they could not so much as read the writing, because (as Houbigant and others have conjectured) though the words are in the Chaldee tongue, yet they were written in the Samaritan or ancient Hebrew characters, with which the wise men of Babylon were very probably unacquainted, as the Jews were at that time a despised people, and the knowledge of their language not a fashionable attainment,* 7–9. *Daniel, who had been so highly esteemed by Nebuchadnezzar for his superior wisdom, appears to have been altogether unknown to* Belshazzar, *till the queen (the same who had been the wife of Nebuchadnezzar according to the general opinion, or the queen consort according to others) had informed him,* 10–12. *Upon the queen's recommendation, Daniel is called in,* 13–16; *who boldly tells this despotic king, that as he had not benefited by the judgments inflicted on his grandfather, but gave himself up to pride and profanity, and had added to his other sins an utter contempt for the God of the Jews by drinking wine out of the sacred vessels of Jehovah in honour of his idols,* 17–23; *the Supreme Being, the Ruler of heaven and earth, had written his condemnation in three words,* Mene, Tekel, Peres, 24, 25; *the first of which is repeated in the copies containing the Chaldean original; but all the ancient Versions, except the Syriac, are without this repetition. Daniel then gives the king and his lords the fearful import of the writing,* viz., *that the period allotted for the duration of the Chaldean empire was now completed,* (see Jer. xxv. 12–14,) *and that the kingdom was about to be transferred to the Medes and Persians,* 26–28. *However unwelcome such an interpretation must have been to Belshazzar, yet the monarch, overwhelmed with its clearness and certainty, commanded the prophet to be honoured,* 29. *And that very night the prediction was fulfilled, for the king was slain,* 30, *and the city taken by the Medes and Persians,* 31. *This great event was also predicted by Isaiah and Jeremiah; and the manner in which it was accomplished is recorded by Herodotus and Xenophon.*

A. M. cir. 3466
B. C. cir. 538
Ol. cir. LX. 3
Servii Tullii,
R. Roman.,
cir. annum 41

BELSHAZZAR the king
[a]made a great feast to a
thousand of his lords, and
drank wine before the thousand.
2 Belshazzar, whiles he tasted

[a]Esther, chap. i. 3

NOTES ON CHAP. V.

Verse 1. *Belshazzar the king made a great feast*] This chapter is out of its place, and should come in after the *seventh* and *eighth*. There are difficulties in the *chronology*. After the death of *Nebuchadnezzar*, *Evil-merodach* his son ascended the throne of Babylon. Having reigned about *two* years, he was slain by his brother-in-law, *Neriglissar*. He reigned *four*

A. M. cir. 3466 B. C. cir. 538 Ol. cir. LX. 3 Servii Tullii, R. Roman., cir. annum 41

the wine, commanded to bring
the [b]golden and silver vessels
[c]which his [d]father Nebuchadnezzar had [e]taken out of the
temple which *was* in Jerusalem; that the
king, and his princes, his wives, and his concubines, might drink therein.

3 Then they brought the golden vessels that
were taken out of the temple of the house of
God which *was* at Jerusalem; and the king,
and his princes, his wives, and his concubines,
drank in them.

4 They drank wine, [f]and praised the gods
of gold, and of silver, of brass, of iron, of
wood, and of stone.

5 [g]In the same hour came
forth fingers of a man's hand,
and wrote over against the
candlestick upon the plaster of
the wall of the king's palace: and the king
saw the part of the hand that wrote.

6 Then the king's [h]countenance [i]was changed, and his thoughts troubled him, so that
the [k]joints[l] of his loins were loosed, and his
[m]knees smote one against another.

7 [n]The king cried [o]aloud to bring in [p]the
astrologers, the Chaldeans, and the soothsayers. *And* the king spake, and said to the
wise *men* of Babylon, Whosoever shall read
this writing, and show me the interpretation

[b]1 Chron. xxviii. 17; Ezra vi. 5; ver. 3, 23——[c]Chap. i. 2; Jer. lii. 19——[d]Or, *grandfather;* as Jer. xxvii. 7; 2 Sam. ix. 7; 2 Chron. xv. 16; ver. 11, 13——[e]Chald. *brought forth*——[f]Rev. ix. 20——[g]Chap. iv. 31

[h]Chald. *brightnesses;* ver. 9——[i]Chald. *changed it*
[k]Or, *girdles;* Isa. v. 27——[l]Chald. *bindings,* or *knots*
[m]Nah. ii. 10——[n]Chap. ii. 2; iv. 6——[o]Chald. *with might*——[p]Isa. xlvii. 13

years, and was succeeded by his son *Laborosoarchod,* who reigned only *nine months.* At his death *Belshazzar,* the son of *Evil-merodach,* was raised to the throne, and reigned *seventeen years,* and was slain, as we read here, by Cyrus, who surprised and took the city on the night of this festivity. This is the chronology on which Archbishop *Usher,* and other learned chronologists, agree; but the Scripture mentions only *Nebuchadnezzar, Evil-merodach,* and *Belshazzar,* by name; and Jeremiah, chap. xxvii. 7, expressly says, "All nations shall serve him (Nebuchadnezzar,) and his son (Evil-merodach,) and his son's son (Belshazzar,) until the very time of his land come;" i. e., till the time in which the empire should be seized by Cyrus. Here there is no mention of *Neriglissar* nor *Laborosoarchod;* but as they were *usurpers,* they might have been purposely passed by. But there remains one difficulty still: *Belshazzar* is expressly called the *son of Nebuchadnezzar* by the queen mother, ver. 11: "There is a man in thy kingdom, in whom is the spirit of the holy gods: and in the days of THY FATHER light and understanding and wisdom, like the wisdom of the gods, was found in him: whom the king NEBUCHADNEZZAR THY FATHER, the king, I say, thy father, made master of the magicians." The solution of this difficulty is, that in Scripture the name of *son* is indifferently given to *sons* and *grandsons,* and even to *great grandsons.* And perhaps the *repetition* in the above verse may imply this: "The king, Nebuchadnezzar thy father, the king thy father." The king thy father's father, and consequently thy grandfather. If it have not some such meaning as this, it must be considered an *idle repetition.* As to the *two other kings, Neriglissar* and *Laborosoarchod,* mentioned by *Josephus* and *Berosus,* and by whom the chronology is so much puzzled, they might have been some *petty kings,* or *viceroys,* or *satraps,* who affected the kingdom, and produced disturbances, one for *four years,* and the other for *nine months;* and would in consequence not be acknowledged in the Babylonish chronology, nor by the sacred writers, any more than finally unsuccessful rebels are numbered among the kings of those nations which they have disturbed. I believe the only sovereigns we can acknowledge here are the following: 1. *Nabopolassar;* 2. *Nebuchadnezzar;* 3. *Evil-merodach;* 4. *Belshazzar;* and with this last the Chaldean empire ended.

To a thousand of his lords] Perhaps this means *lords* or *satraps,* that were each over *one thousand men.* But we learn from antiquity that the *Persian* kings were very profuse in their entertainments; but it does not follow that the *Chaldeans* were so too. Besides, *one thousand lords* and their appropriate attendants would have been very inconvenient in a *nocturnal assembly.* The text, however, supports the common translation. Literally, "Belshazzar the king made bread for his lords a thousand; and against the thousand he drank wine." That is, say some, he was a very great drinker.

Verse 2. *Whiles he tasted the wine*] He relished it, got heated by it, and when WINE got *fully in,* WIT went *wholly out;* and in consequence he acted the profane part of which we immediately read.

Verse 4. *And praised the gods of gold*] They had gods of *all sorts,* and of *all metals;* with *wooden* gods, and *stone* gods, beside!

Verse 5. *Fingers of a man's hand*] The fingers were collected about the *style* or *pen* as in the act of writing.

Verse 6. *The king's countenance was changed*] Here is a very natural description of fear and terror. 1. The face grows pale; 2. The mind becomes greatly agitated; 3. Pains seize on the lower part of the back and kidneys; 4. A universal tremor takes place, so that the knees smite against each other; 5. And lastly, either a *syncope* takes place, or the *cry of distress* is uttered, ver. 7: "The king cried."

Verse 7. *Whosoever shall read this writing*] He knew it must be some awful portent, and wished to know what.

Verse 8. *They could not read the writing*] Because it was in the *pure Hebrew,* not the *Chaldean, character.* See below.

Verse 10. *The queen—came*] This is generally allowed to have been the *widow* of Nebu-

A. M. cir. 3466 B. C. cir. 538 Ol. cir. LX. 3 Servii Tullii, R. Roman., cir. annum 41

thereof, shall be clothed with [q]scarlet, and *have* a chain of gold about his neck, [r]and shall be the third ruler in the kingdom.

8 Then came in all the king's wise *men:* [s]but they could not read the writing, nor make known to the king the interpretation thereof.

9 Then was king Belshazzar greatly [t]troubled, and his [u]countenance was changed in him, and his lords were astonied.

10 *Now* the queen by reason of the words of the king and his lords came into the banquet house: *and* the queen spake and said, [v]O king, live for ever: let not thy thoughts trouble thee, nor let thy countenance be changed:

11 [w]There is a man in thy kingdom, in whom *is* the spirit of the holy gods; and in the days of thy [x]father light and understanding wisdom, like the wisdom of the gods, was found in him; whom the king Nebuchadnezzar thy [y]father, the king, *I say,* thy father, made [z]master of the magicians, astrologers, Chaldeans, *and* soothsayers;

12 [a]Forasmuch as an excellent spirit, and knowledge, and understanding, [b]interpreting of dreams, and showing of hard sentences, and [c]dissolving of [d]doubts, were found in the same Daniel, [e]whom the king named Belteshazzar: now let Daniel be called, and he will show the interpretation.

13 Then was Daniel brought in before the king. *And* the king spake and said unto Daniel, *Art* thou that Daniel, which *art* of the children of the captivity of Judah, whom the king my [f]father brought out of Jewry?

14 I have even heard of thee, that [g]the spirit of the gods *is* in thee, and *that* light and understanding and excellent wisdom is found in thee.

15 And now [h]the wise *men,* the astrologers, have been brought in before me, that they should read this writing, and make known unto me the interpretation thereof: but they could not show the interpretation of the thing:

16 And I have heard of thee, that thou canst [i]make interpretations, and dissolve doubts: [k]now if thou canst read the writing, and make known to me the interpretation thereof, thou shalt be clothed with scarlet, and *have* a chain of gold about thy neck, and shalt be the third ruler in the kingdom.

17 Then Daniel answered and said before the king, Let thy gifts be to thyself, and give thy [l]rewards to another; yet I will read the writing unto the king, and make known to him the interpretation.

18 O thou king, [m]the most high God gave Nebuchadnezzar thy father a kingdom, and majesty, and glory, and honour:

19 And for the majesty that he gave him, [n]all people, nations, and languages, trembled and feared before him: whom he would he slew; and whom he would he kept alive; and whom he would he set up; and whom he would he put down.

20 [o]But when his heart was lifted up, and his mind hardened [p]in pride, he was [q]deposed

[q]Or, *purple*——[r]Chap. vi. 2——[s]Chap. ii. 27; iv. 7——[t]Chap. ii. 1——[u]Chald. *brightnesses;* ver. 6——[v]Chap. ii. 4; iii. 9——[w]Chap. ii. 48; iv. 8, 9, 18——[x]Or, *grandfather;* ver. 2——[y]Or, *grandfather;* ver. 2——[z]Chap. iv. 9——[a]Chap. vi. 3——[b]Or, *of an interpreter,* &c.——[c]Or, *of a dissolver*

[d]Chald. *knots*——[e]Chap. i. 7——[f]Or, *grandfather*——[g]Ver. 11, 12——[h]Ver. 7, 8——[i]Chald. *interpret*——[k]Ver. 7——[l]Or, *fee,* as chap. ii. 6——[m]Chap. ii. 37, 38; iv. 17, 22, 25——[n]Jer. xxvii. 7; chap. iii. 4——[o]Chap. iv. 30, 37——[p]Or, *to deal proudly;* Exod. xviii. 11——[q]Chald. *made to come down*

chadnezzar; if so, she was the queen *Amiyt*, daughter of *Astyages*, sister of *Darius* the Mede, and aunt of *Cyrus*, according to *Polyhistor*, cited by *Cedrenus*. See *Calmet*. Others think that *Nitocris* was the person who is said to be queen when Cyrus took the city; and is stated to have been a lady of eminent wisdom and discretion, and to have had the chief direction of the public affairs. She was the mother of *Labynithus;* and, if this be the same as *Belshazzar*, she must be the person here introduced.

Verse 11. *Nebuchadnezzar thy father*] See the note on ver. 1.

Verse 16. *Dissolve doubts*] *Untie knots—unbind what is bound.* An expression used in the east to signify a *judge* of eminent wisdom and skill.

Verse 17. *Let thy gifts be to thyself*] They could be of little use to any, as the city was *in a few hours* to be taken and pillaged.

Verse 18. *Nebuchadnezzar thy father*] Or *grandfather*, as the *margin* reads, ver. 2. See the notes on ver. 1.

Verse 19. *Whom he would he slew*] The genuine character of a *despot*, whose *will* is the only *rule* of his conduct.

Verse 20. *He was deposed from his kingly throne*] Became insane; and the reins of government were taken out of his hands.

A. M. cir. 3466
B. C. cir. 538
Ol. cir. LX. 3
Servii Tullii,
R. Roman.,
cir. annum 41

from his kingly throne, and they took his glory from him:
21 And he was [r]driven from the sons of men; and [s]his heart was made like the beasts, and his dwelling *was* with the wild asses: they fed him with grass like oxen, and his body was wet with the dew of heaven; [t]till he knew that the most high God ruled in the kingdom of men, and *that* he appointeth over it whomsoever he will.
22 And thou his son, O Belshazzar, [u]hast not humbled thine heart, though thou knewest all this;
23 [v]But hast lifted up thyself against the Lord of heaven; and they have brought the vessels of his house before thee, and thou, and thy lords, thy wives, and thy concubines, have drunk wine in them; and thou hast praised the gods of silver, and gold, of brass, iron, wood, and stone, [w]which see not, nor hear, nor know: and the God in whose hand thy breath *is,* [x]and whose *are* all thy ways, hast thou not glorified:
24 Then was the part of the hand sent from him; and this writing was written.

A. M. cir. 3466
B. C. cir. 538
Ol. cir. LX. 3
Servii Tullii,
R. Roman.,
cir. annum 41

25 And this *is* the writing that was written, MENE, MENE, TEKEL, UPHARSIN.
26 This *is* the interpretation of the thing: MENE; God hath numbered thy kingdom, and finished it.
27 TEKEL; [y]Thou art weighed in the balances, and art found wanting.
28 PERES; Thy kingdom is divided, and given to the [z]Medes and [a]Persians.
29 Then commanded Belshazzar, and they clothed Daniel with scarlet, and *put* a chain of gold about his neck, and made a proclamation concerning him, [b]that he should be the third ruler in the kingdom.
30 [c]In that night was Belshazzar the king of the Chaldeans slain.
31 [d]And Darius the Median took the kingdom, [e]*being* [f]about threescore and two years old.

[r]Chap. iv. 32, &c.——[s]Or, *he made his heart equal,* &c.——[t]Chap. iv. 17, 25——[u]2 Chronicles xxxiii. 23; xxxvi. 12——[v]Ver. 3, 4——[w]Psalm cxv. 5, 6——[x]Jeremiah x. 23——[y]Job xxxi. 6; Psalm lxii. 9; Jeremiah vi. 30——[z]Foretold, Isa. xxi. 2; ver. 31; chap. ix. 1 [a]Chap. vi. 28——[b]Ver. 7——[c]Jeremiah li. 31, 39, 57——[d]Chap. vi. 1, 6, 9, 25, 28; ix. 1, 2; xi. 1——[e]Chald. he as *the son of*, &c.——[f]Or, *now*

Verse 22. *Hast not humbled thine heart*] These *judgments* and **mercies** have had no good effect upon thee.

Verse 23. *But hast lifted up thyself against the Lord*] And the highest evidence of this rebellion was, the profaning the sacred vessels of the Lord's house.

Verse 24. *Then was the part of the hand sent*] This was the filling up of the cup of thy iniquity; **this** last act made thee ripe for destruction.

Verse 25. *And this* is *the writing*] Had the words been written in the *Chaldean* character, every wise man there, every one that could read the *alphabet of his own language*, could have read and interpreted them. Let it be observed, —1. That the *character* which we now call *Hebrew* is the *Chaldean* character. 2. That the true *Hebrew* character is that which we call the *Samaritan.* 3. Daniel could easily read this, for it was the character used by the Jews previously to the *Babylonish* captivity. 4. It appears that it was simply on account of the strangeness of the *character* that the Chaldeans could not read it.

I shall set down the words in both characters, by which the least learned reader may see that it was quite possible that one might be well known, while the other might be unintelligible.

Hebrew

מנא מנא תקל ופרסין

Samaritan

ࠌࠍࠀ ࠌࠍࠀ ࠕࠒࠋ ࠅࠐࠓࠎࠉࠍ

In ancient times, no doubt, these letters differed more from each other than they appear to do now; for we know that the Samaritan on *ancient coins*, though radically the same, differs very much from that now used in printing.

It should be observed, that *each word* stands for a *short sentence;* מנא *mene* signifies NUMERATION; תקל *tekel*, WEIGHING; and פרס *peres*, DIVISION. And so the *Arabic* translates them. مقيسن *mokeeson*, measured; موزون *mewzonon*, weighed; مقسوم *mokesoomon*, divided. All the ancient Versions, except the *Syriac*, read the words simply *Mene*, *Tekel*, *Phares*, as they are explained in the following verses; without the repetition of *Mene*, and without the *conjunction* ו *vau*, and *plural termination*, ין *in*, in *Peres*.

Verse 29. *Clothed Daniel with scarlet*] ארגונא *argevana*, more probably with *purple*. The *gold chain* about the neck was an emblem of magisterial authority. It is often thus mentioned in Scripture.

Verse 30. *In that night was Belshazzar—slain.*] Xenophon says, he was despatched by two lords, *Gadatas* and *Gobrias*, who went over to Cyrus, to avenge themselves of certain wrongs which Belshazzar had done them. We have already seen that Cyrus entered the city by the bed of the Euphrates, which he had emptied, by cutting a channel for the waters, and directing them into the marshy country.

Verse 31. *Darius the Median took the kingdom*] This is supposed to be the same as *Cyaxares*, son of *Astyages* and maternal uncle of *Cyrus*, to whom he gave the throne of Babylon, after himself had had the honour of taking the city.

Daniel speaks nothing of the war that raged between the *Babylonians* and the *Medes;* but Isaiah speaks particularly of it, chap. xiii., xiv., xlv., xlvi., xlvii.; and so does Jeremiah, chap. l., li. I need not add, that it is largely spoken of by profane authors. The Medes and Persians were confederates in the war; the former under *Darius,* the latter under *Cyrus.* Both princes are supposed to have been present at the taking of this city. *Mandane,* daughter of Astyages, was mother of Cyrus, and sister to Cyaxares.

CHAPTER VI

Darius the Median, who succeeded Belshazzar in the kingdom of Babylon, having heard of Daniel's extraordinary wisdom and understanding, constitutes him the chief of the three presidents who were over the whole empire, and purposed also to make him prime minister or viceroy, 1–3. *This great partiality of the king towards a stranger of Jewish extraction, and who had been carried captive into Chaldea, raised up a great many enemies to Daniel; and a scheme was even contrived by the presidents and princes to ruin him,* 4–15; *which succeeded so far that he was cast into a den of lions, but was miraculously delivered,* 16–23. *Darius, who was greatly displeased with himself for having been entrapped by the governors of the provinces to the prejudice of his faithful minister, is pleased and astonished at this deliverance; punished Daniel's enemies with the same kind of death which they had designed for the prophet; and made a decree that, throughout his dominions, the God of Daniel should be had in the greatest veneration,* 24–38.

A. M. cir. 3466
B. C. cir. 538
Ol. cir. LX. 3
Servii Tullii, R. Roman., cir. annum 41

IT pleased Darius to set [a]over the kingdom a hundred and twenty princes, which should be over the whole kingdom;

2 And over these three presidents; of whom Daniel *was* first: that the princes might give accounts unto them, and the king should have no damage.

3 Then this Daniel was preferred above the presidents and princes, [b]because an excellent spirit *was* in him; and the king thought to set him over the whole realm.

A. M. cir. 3467
B. C. cir. 537
Ol. cir. LX. 4
Servii Tullii, R. Roman., cir. annum 42

4 [c]Then the presidents and princes sought to find occasion against Daniel concerning the kingdom; but they could find none occasion nor fault; forasmuch as he *was* faithful, neither was there any error or fault found in him.

A. M. cir. 3467
B. C. cir. 537
Ol. cir. LX. 4
Servii Tullii, R. Roman., cir. annum 42

5 Then said these men, We shall not find any occasion against this Daniel, except we find *it* against him concerning the law of his God.

6 Then these presidents and princes [d]assembled together to the king, and said thus unto him, [e]King Darius, live for ever.

7 All the presidents of the kingdom, the governors, and the princes, the counsellors, and the captains, have consulted together to establish a royal statute, and to make a firm [f]decree, that whosoever shall ask a petition of any god or man for thirty days, save of thee, O king, he shall be cast into the den of lions.

8 Now, O king, establish the decree, and

[a]Esther i. 1——[b]Chap. v. 12——[c]Eccles. iv. 4——[d]Or, *came tumultuously*

[e]Nehemiah ii. 3; verse 21; chapter ii. 4——[f]Or, *interdict*

NOTES ON CHAP. VI

Verse 1. *A hundred and twenty princes*] A chief or *satrap* over every province which belonged to the Medo-Persian empire. Afterwards we find it enlarged to *one hundred and twenty-seven* provinces, by the victories of *Cambyses* and *Darius Hystaspes.* See Esth. i. 1. *Josephus* reckons *three hundred and sixty* satrapies or lordships; but this is most probably an exaggeration or mistake.

Verse 2. *Three presidents*] Each having *forty* of these presidents accountable to him for their administration.

Daniel was *first*] As being established over that part where was the seat of government. He was confirmed in his offices by Darius.

Verse 3. *The king thought to set him over the whole realm*] Intended to make him *grand vizier* or *emir ul amrim.* This partiality of the king made Daniel the object of the other presidents, and the grandees of the kingdom.

Verse 4. *Sought to find occasion against Daniel*] But they found no blemish in his administration, for he was *faithful to his king:* this was a *virtue.* But he was also *faithful to his God:* this they hoped to construe into a *crime,* and make it the cause of his ruin.

Verse 7. *Whosoever shall ask a petition*] What pretence could they urge for so silly an ordinance? Probably to *flatter* the ambition of the king, they pretend to make him *a god* for *thirty* days; so that the whole empire should make prayer and supplication to him, and pay him Divine honours! This was the bait; but their real object was to destroy Daniel.

Verse 8. *According to the law of the Medes and Persians*] I do not think that this is to be understood so as to imply that whatever laws or ordinances the Medes or Persians once enacted, they never changed them. This would argue extreme folly in legislators in any country. Nothing more appears to be meant than that the decree should be enacted, written, and

A. M. cir. 3467
B. C. cir. 537
Ol. cir. LX. 4
Servii Tullii,
R. Roman.,
cir. annum 42

sign the writing, that it be not changed, according to the [g]law of the Medes and Persians, which [h]altereth not.

9 Wherefore king Darius signed the writing and the decree.

10 Now when Daniel knew that the writing was signed, he went into his house; and his windows being open in his chamber [i]toward Jerusalem, he kneeled upon his knees [k]three times a day, and prayed, and gave thanks before his God, as he did aforetime.

11 Then these men assembled, and found Daniel praying and making supplication before his God.

12 [l]Then they came near, and spake before the king concerning the king's decree; Hast thou not signed a decree, that every man that shall ask *a petition* of any god or man within thirty days, save of thee, O king, shall be cast into the den of lions? The king answered and said, The thing *is* true, [m]according to the law of the Medes and Persians, which altereth not.

13 Then answered they and said before the king, That Daniel, [n]which *is* of the children of the captivity of Judah, [o]regardeth not thee, O king, nor the decree that thou hast signed, but maketh his petition three times a day.

14 Then the king, when he heard *these* words, [p]was sore displeased with himself, and set *his* heart on Daniel to deliver him: and he laboured till the going down of the sun to deliver him.

15 Then these men assembled unto the king, and said unto the king, Know, O king, that [q]the law of the Medes and Persians *is*, That no decree nor statute which the king establisheth may be changed.

16 Then the king commanded, and they brought Daniel, and cast *him* into the den of lions. *Now* the king spake and said unto Daniel, Thy God, whom thou servest continually, he will deliver thee.

17 [r]And a stone was brought, and laid upon the mouth of the den; [s]and the king sealed it with his own signet, and with the signet of his

[g]Esth. i. 19; viii. 8; ver. 12, 15——[h]Chald. *passeth not* [i]1 Kings viii. 44, 48; Psa. v. 7; Jonah ii. 4——[k]Psa. lv. 17; Acts ii. 1, 2, 15; iii. 1; x. 9

[l]Chap. iii. 8——[m]Ver. 8——[n]Chap. i. 6; v. 13 [o]Chap. iii. 12——[p]So Mark vi. 26——[q]Ver. 8——[r]Lam. iii. 53——[s]So Matt. xxvii. 66

registered, according to the legal forms among the Medes and Persians; and this one to be made absolute for *thirty* days. The laws were such among this people, that, when once passed with the usual formalities, the *king* could not change them at his own will. This is the utmost that can be meant by the law of the Medes and Persians that could not be changed.

Verse 10. *Now when Daniel knew that the writing was signed*] He saw *what* was *designed*, and he knew *whom* he *served*.

His windows being open] He would not shut them to conceal himself, but "kneeled down with his face turned toward Jerusalem, and prayed thrice each day, giving thanks to God as usual." When the Jews were in distant countries, in prayer they turned their faces towards *Jerusalem;* and when in Jerusalem, they turned their faces towards the *temple.* Solomon, in his prayer at the dedication of the temple, 1 Kings viii. 48, had entreated God to hear the prayers of those who might be in strange lands, or in captivity, when they should *turn their faces towards their own land*, which *God gave unto their fathers;* and towards *the city which he had chosen*, and *the house which was dedicated to his name.* It was in reference to this that Daniel turned his face towards Jerusalem when he prayed.

Verse 12. *Shall be cast into the den of lions*] Either this was the royal *menagerie*, like that place in the *Tower* of London, where wild beasts are kept for the king's pleasure, and the public amusement; or they were kept for the purpose of devouring certain criminals, which the laws might consign to that kind of death. This is most likely, from the case before us.

Verse 14. *The king—was sore displeased with himself*] And well he might, when through his excessive folly he passed a law that, for its ostensible object, would have been a disgrace almost to an idiot.

And set his *heart on Daniel*] He strove by every means to get the law annulled. He had no doubt spoken to several of his lords in private, and had gone from *one* to *another* till the going down of the sun.

Verse 15. *Then these men assembled*] Having got favourable answers, as we may presume, from many individuals, he called a *parliament;* but they now collectively joined to urge the *execution* of the law, not its *repeal.*

Verse 16. *Then the king commanded*] With a heavy heart he was obliged to warrant this murderous conspiracy. But when passing sentence his last words were affecting: "Thy God, whom thou servest continually, he will deliver thee." He is *thy* God: *thou servest him*, not occasionally, but *continually;* therefore "he will deliver thee." Daniel had now the same kind of opportunity of showing his fidelity to God, as his *three* Hebrew companions before. The *lions* were not less terrible than the *fiery furnace.*

Verse 17. *A stone was brought*] All this *precaution* served the purposes of the Divine Providence. There could be no trick nor collusion here; if Daniel be preserved, it must be by the power of the Supreme God. The same precaution was taken by the Jews, in the case

A. M. cir. 3467
B. C. cir. 537
Ol. cir. LX. 4
Servii Tullii,
R. Roman.,
cir. annum 42

lords; that the purpose might not be changed concerning Daniel.

18 Then the king went to his palace and passed the night fasting: neither were [t]instruments of music brought before him: [u]and his sleep went from him.

19 Then the king arose very early in the morning, and went in haste unto the den of lions.

20 And when he came to the den, he cried with a lamentable voice unto Daniel: *and* the king spake and said to Daniel, O Daniel, servant of the living God, [v]is thy God, whom thou servest continually, able to deliver thee from the lions

21 Then said Daniel unto the king, [w]O king, live for ever.

22 [x]My God hath sent his angel, and hath [y]shut the lions' mouths, that they have not hurt me: forasmuch as before him innocency was found in me; and also before thee, O king, have I done no hurt.

23 Then was the king exceeding glad for him, and commanded that they should take Daniel up out of the den. So Daniel was taken up out of the den, and no manner of hurt was found upon him, [z]because he believed in his God.

A. M. cir. 3467
B. C. cir. 537
Ol. cir. LX. 4
Servii Tullii,
R. Roman.,
cir. annum 42

24 And the king commanded, [a]and they brought those men which had accused Daniel, and they cast *them* into the den of lions, them, [b]their children, and their wives; and the lions had the mastery of them, and brake all their bones in pieces or ever they came at the bottom of the den.

25 [c]Then king Darius wrote unto all people, nations, and languages, that dwell in all the earth; Peace be multiplied unto you.

26 [d]I make a decree, That in every dominion of my kingdom men [e]tremble and fear before the God of Daniel: [f]for he *is* the living God, and steadfast for ever, and his kingdom *that* which shall not be [g]destroyed, and his dominion *shall be even* unto the end.

27 He delivereth and rescueth, [h]and he worketh signs and wonders in heaven and in earth, who hath delivered Daniel from the [i]power of the lions.

28 So this Daniel prospered in the reign of Darius, [k]and in the reign of [l]Cyrus the Persian.

[t]Or, *table*——[u]Chap. ii. 1——[v]Chap. iii. 15——[w]Ch. ii. 4——[x]Chap. iii. 28——[y]Heb. xi. 33——[z]Heb. xi. 33——[a]Deut. xix. 19——[b]Esth. ix. 10; see Deut. xxiv. 16; 2 Kings xiv. 6

[c]Chap. iv. 1——[d]Chap. iii. 29——[e]Psa. xcix. 1——[f]Chap. iv. 34——[g]Chap. ii. 44; iv. 3, 34; vii. 14, 27; Luke i. 33——[h]Chap. iv. 3——[i]Heb. *hand*——[k]Chap. i. 21——[l]Ezra i. 1, 2

of the *burial of our blessed Lord;* and this very thing has served as one of the strongest proofs of the certainty of his resurrection and their unmixed wickedness.

Verse 18. *Passed the night fasting*] He neither ate nor drank, had no music to solace, nor sweet odours burnt or brought before him, and he passed the night without sleep. All this points out his great sincerity; and when it is considered that Darius could not be less than *sixty-two* or *sixty-three* years of age at this time, it shows more fully the depth of his concern.

Verse 19. *The king arose very early*] By the break of day.

Verse 20. *He cried with a lamentable voice*] His heart, full of grief, affected his speech.

Servant of the living God] The king was convinced that, unless his God saved him, his destruction was inevitable.

Verse 22. *My God hath sent his angel*] Such a one as that who attended Shadrach, Meshach, and Abed-nego, in the fiery furnace, and blew aside the flames, so that they could not hurt them.

Before him innocency was found in me] Because I was innocent God has preserved me; and now that I am preserved, my innocence is fully proved.

Verse 23. *No manner of hurt was found upon him*] And why? *Because he believed in his God.* How mighty is *faith?* It interests that power in the behalf of the believer by which the sea is dried up, the mountains removed, the dead raised to life, sin forgiven, the heart purified, Satan vanquished, death conquered, and God himself delighted and glorified! See Heb. xi.

Verse 24. *They brought those men*] It was perfectly just that they should suffer that death to which they had endeavoured to subject the innocent; but it was savage cruelty to destroy the *women* and *children* who had no part in the transgression.

Verse 25. *Then king Darius wrote*] And the substance of this *decree*, which was made by a heathen king, was to point out the *perfections* of the *true God*, and the *fidelity* of his devoted servant.

Verse 26. *I make a decree that—men tremble and fear before the God of Daniel*] As in the case of the *three* Hebrews, chap. iii. 29. The true God was known by his servants, and by the deliverances he wrought for them. See his characters in this decree. 1. He is the *living God*, the Author and Giver of life; all others are *dead* gods. 2. He is *steadfast for ever.* All things *change;* but he is unchangeable. 3. He has a *kingdom;* for as he made all things, so he *governs* all things. 4. His *kingdom shall not be destroyed.* No human power can prevail against it, because it is upheld by his omnipotence. 5. His *dominion* is without *end.* It is an everlasting dominion, under an everlasting rule, by an everlasting God. 6. He *delivereth* them that are in danger and bondage. 7. He *rescueth* those who have fallen into the hands of their enemies, and implore his succour. 8. He *worketh signs* in the *heavens.* 9. And *wonders* upon *earth;* showing that both are under his sway, and are parts of his dominion. 10. And to complete all, *He hath delivered Daniel.* Before our own eyes he has given the fullest proof of his *power* and *goodness,* in rescuing his faithful servant from the teeth of the lions. What a fine eulogium on the great God and his faithful servant!

Verse 28. *So this Daniel prospered*] He had served *five* kings: *Nebuchadnezzar, Evil-merodach, Belshazzar, Darius,* and *Cyrus.* Few courtiers have had so long a reign, served so many masters without flattering any, been more successful in their management of public affairs, been so useful to the states where they were in office, or have been more owned of God, or have left such an example to posterity.

Where shall we find ministers like *Samuel* and *Daniel?* None so wise, so holy, so disinterested, so useful, have ever since appeared in the nations of the earth.

CHAPTER VII

The prophet having, in the preceding chapters of this book, related some remarkable events concerning himself and his brethren in the captivity, and given proof of his being enabled, by Divine assistance, to interpret the dreams of others, enters now into a detail of his own visions, returning to a period prior to the transactions recorded in the last chapter. The first in order of the prophet's visions is that of the four beasts, which arose out of a very tempestuous ocean, 1–9; *and of one like the Son of man who annihilated the dominion of the fourth beast, because of the proud and blasphemous words of one of its horns,* 9–14. *An angel deciphers the hieroglyphics contained in this chapter, declaring that the* FOUR beasts, *diverse one from another, represent the* FOUR PARAMOUNT empires *of the habitable globe, which should succeed each other; and are evidently the same which were shadowed forth to Nebuchadnezzar by another set of hieroglyphics,* (*see the* second *chapter,*) 15–26. *But for the consolation of the people of God, it is added that, at the time appointed in the counsel of Jehovah, "the kingdom and dominion, and the greatness of the kingdom under the whole heaven, shall be given to the saints of the Most High;" and that this kingdom shall never be destroyed or transferred to another people, as all the preceding dominations have been, but shall itself stand for ever,* 27, 28. *It will be proper to remark that the period of* a time, times, and a half, *mentioned in the twenty-fifth verse as the duration of the dominion of the little horn that made war with the saints, (generally supposed to be a symbolical representation of the papal power,) had most probably its commencement in A. D.* 755 *or* 756, *when Pepin, king of France, invested the pope with temporal power. This hypothesis will bring the conclusion of the period to about the year of Christ* 2000, *a time fixed by Jews and Christians for some remarkable revolution; when the world, as they suppose, will be renewed, the wicked cease from troubling the Church, and the saints of the Most High have dominion over the whole habitable globe. But this is all hypothesis.*

A. M. cir. 3449
B. C. cir. 555
Ol. cir. LVI. 2
Servii Tullii,
R. Roman.,
cir. annum 24

IN the first year of Belshazzar
king of Babylon [a]Daniel [b]had
a dream and [c]visions of his head
upon his bed: then he wrote the
dream, *and* told the sum of the [d]matters.
2 Daniel spake and said, I saw
in my vision by night, and, behold,
the four winds of the
heaven strove upon the great sea.
3 And four great beasts [e]came up from

[a]Num. xii. 6; Amos iii. 7——[b]Chald. *saw*

[c]Chald. ii. 28——[d]Or, *words*——[e]Rev. xiii. 1

NOTES ON CHAP. VII

Verse 1. *In the first year of Belshazzar*] This is the same Belshazzar who was slain at the taking of Babylon, as we have seen at the conclusion of chap. v. That chapter should have followed both this and the succeeding. The reason why the *fifth* chapter was put in an improper place was, that all the *historic parts* might be together, and the *prophetic* be by themselves; and, accordingly, the former end with the preceding chapter, and the latter with this. The division therefore is not *chronological* but merely *artificial.*

Told the sum of the matters.] That he might not forget this extraordinary dream, he wrote down the leading particulars when he arose.

Verse 2. *The four winds of the heaven strove upon the great sea*] The idea of *strife* is taken here from the effects that must be produced, were the east, the west, the north, and the south winds to rise tempestuously, and *meet* on the surface of the sea. By the *great sea,* the Mediterranean is meant; and is so called to distinguish it from those *lakes* called *seas* by the Hebrews; such as the *Sea* of *Galilee, Dead Sea, Sea* of *Tiberias,* &c.; but even that may refer to *Asia,* the scene of all these contentions. This dream is the same in meaning, under *different emblems,* as that of Nebuchadnezzar's metallic image; but in Daniel's dream several circumstances are added. It is supposed that Daniel had this dream about *forty-eight* years after Nebuchadnezzar had the vision of the great image.

Verse 3. *Four great beasts came up from the*

A. M. cir. 3449
B. C. cir. 555
Ol. cir. LVI. 2
Servii Tullii, R. Roman., cir. annum 24

the sea, diverse one from another.
4 The first *was* [f]like a lion, and had eagle's wings: I beheld till the wings thereof were plucked, [g]and it was lifted up from the earth, and made stand upon the feet as a man, and a man's heart was given to it.
5 [h]And behold another beast, a second, like to a bear, and [i]it raised up itself on one side, and *it had* three ribs in the mouth of it between the teeth of it:

[f]Deut. xxviii. 49; 2 Sam. i. 23; Jer. iv. 7, 13; xlviii. 40; Ezek. xvii. 3; Hab. i. 8——[g]Or, *wherewith*——[h]Chap. ii. 39——[i]Or, *it raised up one dominion*

sea] The term *sea*, in Hebrew ים *yam*, from המה *hamah, to be tumultuous, agitated*, &c., seems to be used here to point out the then known *terraqueous globe*, because of its generally agitated state; and the *four winds striving*, point out those predatory wars that prevailed almost universally among men, from the days of Nimrod, the founder of the Assyrian or Babylonish monarchy, down to that time, and in the end gave birth to the *four great monarchies* which are the subject of this vision.

Diverse one from another.] The *people* were *different;* the *laws* and *customs* different; and the *administration* of each differently executed.

Verse 4. *The first* was *like a lion, and had eagle's wings*] Bp. *Newton* well remarks, that these *great beasts*, as explained by the angel, ver. 17, are *kingdoms.* They arise out of a stormy and tempestuous sea; that is, out of the *wars* and commotions of the world; and they are called *great* in comparison of other states and kingdoms, and are denominated *beasts* for their tyrannical and cruel oppression.

These *four beasts* are indeed monstrous productions; a *lion with eagle's wings;* a *bear with three ribs* in its mouth; a *leopard with four wings, and four heads;* and a *beast with ten horns.* But such emblems and hieroglyphics were usual among the eastern nations, as may be seen in the monuments of antiquity. A *winged lion*, and such-like fictitious animals, may be seen in many parts of the ruins of *Persepolis. Horns* are attributed to beasts which naturally have none, being used in hieroglyphic writings for symbols of *strength* and *power.* And such figures are supposed to be the symbols of different nations; and are not more strange than many that are still used in *heraldry.* I believe the science of heraldry arose out of the knowledge gained from the symbols used in the Sacred Writings; and the little acquaintance anciently obtained of the meaning of some of the Egyptian hieroglyphics. Hence our wiverons, griffins, unicorns, with a congeries of natural and unnatural things, split eagles, *two*-headed swans, &c., &c., &c.

The *beast like a lion* is the kingdom of the *Babylonians;* and the king of Babylon is compared to a *lion*, Jer. iv. 7; Isa. v. 29; and is said to fly as an *eagle*, Jer. xlviii. 40; Ezek. xvii. 3, 7. The *lion* is considered the *king of the beasts*, and the *eagle* the *king of the birds;* and therefore the kingdom of Babylon, which was signified by the *golden head* of the great image, was the first and noblest of all the kingdoms; and was the greatest then in being. The *wings* of the *eagle* denote the *rapidity* with which the *lion*—Nebuchadnezzar, made his conquests; for in a few years, by his own arms, he brought his empire to such an extent, and raised it to such a degree of eminence, as was truly surprising; and all tended to show with what propriety this *eagle-winged lion* is here made his emblem.

The wings thereof were plucked] Lydia, Media, and Persia, which had been provinces of the Babylonish empire, cast off the yoke, and put themselves under kings of their own. Besides, the rapidity of its conquests was stopped by its wars with the *Medes* and *Persians;* by whom it was at last conquered, and *divided* between Darius the Mede and Cyrus the Persian.

And it was lifted up from the earth] That is, the *wings were plucked*, rendered unfit for farther flight, *by which it had* before *been lifted up from the earth;* making its conquests almost with the rapidity of an eagle's flight. In what a short time did Nebuchadnezzar, who is here chiefly intended, conquer Syria, Phœnicia, Judea, Egypt, Arabia, &c.! But on his death the *wings were plucked;* and no farther extension of the empire took place under *Evil-merodach* or *Belshazzar*, till it was lost by the latter, and became divided as we have seen above.

And made stand upon the feet as a man] This I think refers to the taming of Nebuchadnezzar's pride. He had acted like a fierce and ravening *lion.* God struck him with insanity; he then lived the life of a beast, and had a *beast's heart*—disposition, and habits. At last God restored him.

And a man's heart was given to it.] He became *humane, humble*, and *pious;* and in this state he appears to have died.

Verse 5. *Another beast—like to a bear*] This was the *Medo-Persian* empire, represented here under the symbol of the *bear*, as the largest species of these animals was found in *Media*, a mountainous, cold, and rough country, covered with *woods.* The Medes and Persians are compared to a *bear* on account of their *cruelty* and *thirst after blood*, a bear being a most voracious and cruel animal; the *bear* is termed by Aristotle *an all-devouring animal;* and the Medo-Persians are known to have been great *robbers* and *spoilers.* See Jer. li. 48-56. The Persians were notorious for the cruelty of their punishments. See *Calmet.*

Raised up itself on one side] Cyrus arose on the borders of Chaldea, and thus the *bear* appeared to put itself in the position to attack the *lion.*

It had *three ribs in the mouth of it*] As if it had just finished its repast on some animal that it had seized. Some think *three tusks, curved* like ribs, are meant; others *three throats*, עלעין *illin*, by which it (Cyrus) had absorbed the *three* empires of the Babylonians, Medes, and Persians; for these symbolic animals do not so much denote *four empires*, as *four kings.* See ver. 17. Others think *three rows of teeth* are meant, to denote the *triple* power of the Medes, Persians, and Babylonians,

A. M. cir. 3449
B. C. cir. 555
Ol. cir. LVI. 2
Servii Tullii,
R. Roman.,
cir. annum 24

and they said thus unto it, Arise, devour much flesh.
6 After this I beheld, and lo another, like a leopard, which had upon the back of it four wings of a fowl; the beast had also [k]four heads; and dominion was given to it.
7 After this I saw in the night visions, and behold [l]a fourth beast, dreadful and terrible, and strong exceedingly; and it had great iron teeth: it devoured and brake in pieces, and stamped the residue with the feet of it: and it *was* diverse from all the beasts that *were* before it; [m]and it had ten horns.
8 I considered the horns, and, behold, [n]there came up among them another little horn, before whom there were three of the first horns

[k]Chapter viii. 8, 22——[l]Chapter ii. 40; verse 19, 23——[m]Chap. ii. 41; Rev. xiii. 1——[n]Ver. 20, 21, 24; chap. viii. 9

conjoined. Or the *east, north,* and *south,* which were subdued by the Persians. But the *ribs* being between the teeth of the *bear* may show how Babylon, Lydia, and Egypt were ground and oppressed by the *bear*—the Persians; though, as ribs strengthen the body, they were a powerful support to their conquerors.

Verse 6. *Another, like a leopard—four wings—four heads*] This was the *Macedonian* or *Greek empire;* and Alexander the Great its king. Alexander and his subjects are fitly compared to a *leopard.* 1. The leopard is remarkable for its swiftness. Alexander and the Macedonians were very rapid in their conquests. 2. The leopard is a *spotted* animal; a proper emblem of the *various nations,* with their various customs and languages, which constituted the Macedonian empire. It may refer to the *character* of Alexander himself, sometimes *mild,* at others *cruel; sober* and *drunken; continent* and *lecherous;* having a great power of self-government, and at other times being a slave to his passions. 3. The leopard, though small, is not afraid to attack the lion.

Four wings of a fowl] The *Babylonian* empire was represented with *two wings;* and they sufficiently marked the *rapidity* of Nebuchadnezzar's conquests; but the *Macedonian* has here *four wings;* for nothing, in the history of the world, was equal to the conquests of Alexander, who ran through all the countries from Illyricum and the Adriatic Sea to the Indian Ocean and the River Ganges; and in *twelve* years subdued part of Europe, and all Asia.

The beast had also four heads] Signifying the empire after the death of Alexander, divided between his *four* generals. *Cassander* reigning over *Macedon* and *Greece; Lysimachus,* over *Thrace* and *Bithynia; Ptolemy,* over *Egypt;* and *Seleucus,* over *Syria.*

Dominion was given to it.] It was not owing to the skill, courage, or valour of Alexander and his troops, that he made those wondrous conquests; the nations were *given* to him. For, as Bishop *Newton* says, had he not been assisted by the mighty power of God, how could he, with only *thirty thousand* men, have overcome Darius with *six hundred thousand;* and in so short a time have brought the countries from Greece as far as India into subjection?

Verse 7. *I saw—a fourth beast—it had great iron teeth*] This is allowed, on all hands, to be the Roman empire. It was *dreadful, terrible,* and *exceeding strong: it devoured, and brake* in pieces, and stamped the residue, that is, the remains of the former kingdoms, *with its feet.* It reduced *Macedon* into a Roman province about *one hundred and sixty-eight* years before Christ; the kingdom of *Pergamos* about *one hundred and thirty-three* years; *Syria* about *sixty-five;* and *Egypt* about *thirty* years before Christ. And, besides the remains of the Macedonian empire, it subdued many other provinces and kingdoms; so that it might, by a very usual figure, be said to *devour the whole earth, to tread it down, and break it to pieces;* and became in effect, what the Roman writers delight to call it, *the empire of the whole world.*

It (the fourth beast) was *diverse from all the beasts that* were *before it*] Not only in its *republican* form of government, but also in *power* and *greatness, extent of dominion,* and *length of duration.*

It had ten horns] The *ten* kingdoms into which the Roman empire was afterwards divided. *Calmet* says, *ten* Syrian kings: and he finds them thus:—1. Seleucus Nicator. 2. Antiochus Soter. 3. Antiochus Theos. 4. Antiochus Callinicus. 5. Seleucus Ceraunus. 6. Antiochus the Great. 7. Seleucus, surnamed Philopater, brother of Antiochus Epiphanes. 8. Laomedon of Mitylene, to whom Syria and Phœnicia had been intrusted. 9. Antigone. And, 10. His son Demetrius, who possessed those provinces, with the title of *kings.* This is too much like forced work. There are different opinions concerning these *ten* kings; or rather which they were that constituted this division of the Roman empire. They are reckoned thus:—1. The Roman senate. 2. The *Greeks,* in *Ravenna.* 3. The *Lombards* in *Lombardy.* 4. The *Huns* in *Hungary.* 5. The *Alemans,* in *Germany.* 6. The *Franks* in France. 7. The *Burgundians* in *Burgundy.* 8. The *Saracens* in Africa, and a part of Spain. 9. The *Goths,* in other parts of Spain. 10. And the *Saxons, in Britain.*

Verse 8. *Another little horn*] Among Protestant writers this is considered to be the popedom.

Before whom there were three of the first horns plucked up] These were probably, 1. The exarchate of *Ravenna.* 2. The kingdom of the *Lombards.* And, 3. The *state of Rome.* The *first* was given to the Pope, Stephen II., by Pepin, king of France, A. D. 755; and this constituted the pope's temporal princes. The *second* was given to St. Peter by Charlemagne, in 774. The *third,* the *state of Rome,* was vested in the pope, both in spirituals and temporals, and confirmed to him by *Lewis the pious.* These are the *three* horns which were *plucked up from the roots* before the *little horn.*

Were *eyes like the eyes of a man*] Intimating *cunning* and *superintendence;* for the pope calls himself *Episcopus episcoporum,* the *Overseer of overseers.*

A. M. cir. 3449
B. C. cir. 555
Ol. cir. LVI. 2
Servii Tullii,
R. Roman.,
cir. annum 24

plucked up by the roots: and, behold, in this horn *were* eyes like the eyes [o]of man, [p]and a mouth speaking great things.

9 [q]I beheld till the thrones were cast down, and [r]the Ancient of days did sit, [s]whose garment *was* white as snow, and the hair of his head like the pure wool: his throne *was like* the fiery flame, [t]*and* his wheels *as* burning fire.

10 [u]A fiery stream issued and came forth from before him: [v]thousand thousands ministered unto him, and ten thousand times ten thousand stood before him: [w]the judgment was set, and the books were opened.

11 I beheld then because of the voice of the great words which the horn spake: [x]I beheld *even* till the beast was slain, and his body destroyed, and given to the burning flame.

12 As concerning the rest of the beasts, they had their dominion taken away: yet [y]their lives were prolonged for a season and time.

13 I saw in the night visions, and, behold, [z]*one* like the Son of man came with the clouds of heaven, and came to [a]the Ancient of days, and they brought him near before him.

A. M. cir. 3449
B. C. cir. 555
Ol. cir. LVI. 2
Servii Tullii,
R. Roman.,
cir. annum 24

14 [b]And there was given him dominion, and glory, and a kingdom, that all [c]people, nations, and languages, should serve him: his dominion *is* [d]an everlasting dominion, which shall not pass away, and his kingdom *that* which shall not be destroyed.

15 I Daniel [e]was grieved in my spirit in the midst of *my* [f]body, and the visions of my head troubled me.

16 I came near unto one of them that stood by, and asked him the truth of all this. So he told me, and made me know the interpretation of the things.

17 [g]These great beasts, which are four, *are* four kings, *which* shall arise out of the earth.

[o]Rev. ix. 7——[p]Psa. xii. 3; ver. 25; Rev. xiii. 5——[q]Rev. xx. 4——[r]Psa. xc. 2; ver. 13, 22——[s]Psa. civ. 2; Rev. i. 14——[t]Ezek. i. 15, 16——[u]Psa. l. 3; xcvii. 3; Isa. xxx. 33; lxvi. 15——[v]1 Kings xxii. 19; Psa. lxviii. 17; Heb. xii. 22; Rev. v. 11——[w]Rev. xx. 4, 12——[x]Rev xix. 20——[y]Chald. *a prolonging in life was given them*

[z]Ezek. iv. 26; Matt. xxiv. 30; xxvi. 64; Rev. i. 7, 13; xiv. 14——[a]Ver. 9——[b]Psa. ii. 6, 7, 8; viii. 6; cx. 1, 2; Matt. xi. 27; xxviii. 18; John iii. 35; 1 Cor. xv. 27; Eph. i. 22——[c]Chap. iii. 4——[d]Psa. cxlv. 13; ch. ii. 44; ver. 27; Mic. iv. 7; Luke i. 33; John xii. 34; Heb. xii. 28——[e]Ver. 28——[f]Chald. *sheath*——[g]Ver. 3

And a mouth speaking great things.] Full of boasting; pretending to unlimited jurisdiction; binding and loosing at pleasure; promising to absolve from all sins, present, past, and future; and threatening to send to everlasting destruction all kings, kingdoms, and individuals, who would dare to dispute his power and authority.

Verse 9. *The thrones were cast down*] דמיו might be translated *erected;* so the Vulgate, *positi sunt*, and so all the versions; but that ours is a proper translation, is sufficiently evident from chap. iii. 6, 15, 20; vi. 17, &c.; where the original word can be used in no other sense than that of *throwing* or *casting down*. There is a reference here to preparations made for a general assize, or to the convocation of the sanhedrin, where the father of the consistory sat with his assessors on each side in the form of a semicircle, and the people stood before them.

The Ancient of days] God Almighty; and this is the only place in the sacred writings where God the Father is represented in a *human form*.

Verse 10. *A fiery stream issued*] This is not spoken of the *final judgment;* but of that which he was to execute upon this *fourth beast*, the Roman empire; and the *little* boasting *horn*, which is a part of the fourth beast, and must fall when the other falls.

Verse 11. *I beheld then because of the voice* (or, *the beast will be destroyed because*) *of the great words which the horn spake—his body destroyed*] When the dominion was taken from the rest of the *beasts*, their *bodies* were not destroyed, but suffered to continue still in being; but when the dominion shall be taken away from *this beast*, his *body* shall be totally destroyed; because *other kingdoms* succeeded to those, but no other earthly kingdom shall succeed to this.—Bishop *Newton*.

Verse 13. One *like the Son of man came with the clouds of heaven*] This most certainly points out the Lord Jesus, בר אנש *bar enosh*, the Son of miserable man; who took our nature upon him that he might redeem us unto himself. To prove himself to be the Messiah he applies, before the high priests, these words of the Prophet Daniel to himself, Matt. xxiv. 30.

Near before him.] The Ancient of days.

Verse 14. *And there was given him dominion*] This also is applied to our Lord Jesus by himself, after his resurrection, Matt. xxviii. 18.

His dominion is *an everlasting dominion*] Christianity shall increase, and prevail to the end of the world. See the parallel passages in the margin.

Verse 15. *I Daniel was grieved, &c.*] The words in the original are uncommonly emphatic. *My spirit was grieved*, or *sickened*, בגו נדנה *bego nidneh, within its sheath* or *scabbard*. Which I think proves, 1. That the human *spirit* is different from the *body*. 2. That it has a proper subsistence independently of the body, which is only its *sheath* for a certain time. 3. That the spirit may exist independently of its body, as the *sword* does independently of its *sheath*.

Verse 17. *These great beasts*—are *four kings*]

A. M. cir. 3449
B. C. cir. 555
Ol. cir. LVI. 2
Servii Tullii,
R. Roman.,
cir. annum 24

18 But [h]the saints of the
[i]Most High shall take the kingdom, and possess the kingdom
for ever, even for ever and ever.
19 Then I would know the truth of [k]the
fourth beast, which was diverse [l]from all the
others, exceeding dreadful, whose teeth *were*
of iron, and his nails *of* brass; *which* devoured, brake in pieces, and stamped the
residue with his feet;
20 And of the ten horns that *were* in his
head, and *of* the other which came up, and
before whom three fell; even *of* that horn
that had eyes, and a mouth that spake very
great things, whose look *was* more stout than
his fellows.
21 I beheld, [m]and the same horn made
war with the saints and prevailed against
them;
22 [n]Until the Ancient of days came, [o]and
judgment was given to the
saints of the Most High; and
the time came that the saints
possessed the kingdom.

A. M. cir. 3449
B. C. cir. 555
Ol. cir. LVI. 2
Servii Tullii,
R. Roman.,
cir. annum 24

23 Thus he said, The fourth beast shall be
[p]the fourth kingdom upon earth, which shall
be diverse from all kingdoms, and shall devour the whole earth, and shall tread it down,
and break it in pieces.
24 [q]And the ten horns out of this kingdom
are ten kings *that* shall arise: and another
shall rise after them; and he shall be diverse
from the first, and he shall subdue three
kings.
25 [r]And he shall speak *great* words against
the Most High, and shall [s]wear out the saints
of the Most High, and [t]think to change times
and laws: and [u]they shall be given into his
hand [v]until a time and times and the dividing
of time.

---

[h]Isa. lx. 12, 13, 14; ver. 22, 27; 2 Tim. ii. 11, 12; Rev. ii. 26, 27; iii. 21; xx. 4——[i]Chald. *high ones*, that is, *things* or *places*——[k]Ver. 7——[l]Chald. *from all those* [m]Chap. viii. 12, 24; xi. 31; Rev. xi. 7; xiii. 7; xvii. 14; xix. 19——[n]Ver. 9

[o]Ver. 18; 1 Cor. vi. 2; Rev. i. 6; v. 10; xx. 4——[p]Ch. ii. 40——[q]Ver. 7, 8, 20; Rev. xvii. 12——[r]Isa. xxxvii. 23; ch. viii. 24, 25; xi. 28, 30, 31, 36; 1 Mac. i. 46; Rev. xiii. 5, 6——[s]Rev. xvii. 6; xviii. 24——[t]Ch. ii. 21 [u]Rev. xiii. 7——[v]Chap. xii. 7; Rev. xii. 14

See the preceding verses, where the following explanations are inserted and illustrated.

Verse 18. *But the saints of the Most High shall take the kingdom*] I doubt whether this be the true sense of the original *Chaldee*, ויקבלון מלכותא קדישי עליונין *vikabbelun malcutha kaddishey elyonin*, "But the supreme holy ones shall receive the kingdom;" or, "they shall receive the kingdom of the supreme saints." Properly translated by *Montanus*, Et suscipient regnum sanctorum altissimorum. Whatever we may think of the *patriarchs* and the *Jews* in their best times, there has never been so *much holiness of heart possessed*, and so much *righteousness practised*, as by the genuine disciples of Christ. Christianity alone has provided a full redemption for man. They are the *chief saints*, and to them God gives the kingdom: and this Gospel dispensation, called often *the kingdom of God, and the kingdom of heaven*, shall last for ever, during the whole lapse of time; *and for ever and ever*—throughout eternity, shall they and its blessings endure.

Verse 19. *His nails* of *brass*] This is not mentioned in the *seventh* verse, where the description of the beast is given. It might be *added*, for the first time, by the person who is now explaining the fourth beast. *Houbigant* thinks it has been lost out of the text: but such loss is not intimated by any MS.; nor does any of the *ancient Versions* acknowledge this addition in the *seventh* verse.

Verse 21. *The same horn made war with the saints, and prevailed against them.*] Those who make *Antiochus* the *little horn*, make the *saints* the *Jewish people*. Those who understand the *popedom* by it, see this as referring to the cruel persecutions of the popes of Rome against the *Waldenses* and *Albigenses*, and the *Protestant* Church in general.

Verse 22. *Saints of the Most High*] *To the supereminent saints;* see the note on ver. 18.

Verse 25. *He shall speak* great *words against the Most High*] Sermones quasi Deus loquetur; "He shall speak as if he were God." So St. *Jerome* quotes from *Symmachus*. To none can this apply so well or so fully as to the popes of Rome. They have assumed *infallibility*, which belongs only to God. They profess to forgive sins, which belongs only to God. They profess to open and shut heaven, which belongs only to God. They profess to be higher than all the kings of the earth, which belongs only to God. And they go *beyond* God in pretending to loose whole nations from their oath of allegiance to their kings, when such kings do not please them! And they go *against* God when they give *indulgences for sin*. This is the *worst* of all blasphemies!

And shall wear out the saints] By wars, crusades, massacres, inquisitions, and persecutions of all kinds. What in this way have they not done against all those who have protested against their *innovations*, and refused to submit to their *idolatrous worship?* Witness the exterminating crusades published against the *Waldenses* and *Albigenses*. Witness *John Huss*, and *Jerome* of *Prague*. Witness the *Smithfield fires* in England! Witness *God* and man against this bloody, persecuting, ruthless, and impure Church!

And think to change times and laws] Appointing fasts and feasts; canonizing persons whom he chooses to call *saints;* granting pardons and indulgences for sins; instituting new modes of worship utterly unknown to the Christian Church; new articles of faith; new rules

A. M. cir. 3449
B. C. cir. 555
Ol. cir. LVI. 2
Servii Tullii,
R. Roman.,
cir. annum 24

26 [w]But the judgment shall sit, and they shall take away his dominion, to consume and to destroy *it* unto the end.

27 And the [x]kingdom and dominion, and the greatness of the kingdom under the whole heaven, shall be given to the people of the saints of the Most High, [y]whose kingdom *is* an everlasting kingdom, [z]and all [a]dominions shall serve and obey him.

28 Hitherto *is* the end of the matter. As for me Daniel, [b]my cogitations much troubled me, and my countenance changed in me: but I [c]kept the matter in my heart.

[w]Ver. 10, 22——[x]Ver. 14, 18, 22; chapter ii. 42; Obadiah 21; Matthew xxv. 34; Mark xi. 10; Luke xii. 32——[y]Chapter ii. 44; Luke i. 33; John xii. 34; Revelation xi. 15——[z]Isaiah lx. 12——[a]Or, *rulers* [b]Ver. 15; chapter viii. 27; x. 8, 16——[c]Luke ii. 19, 51

of practice; and reversing, with pleasure, the laws both of God and man.—*Dodd.*

Until a time and times and the dividing of time.] In prophetic language a *time* signifies a *year;* and a *prophetic year* has a *year* for *each day. Three years and a half* (a *day* standing for a *year,* as in chap. ix. 24) will amount to *one thousand two hundred and sixty years,* if we reckon *thirty* days to each month, as the Jews do.

If we knew precisely when the papal power began to exert itself in the *antichristian* way, then we could at once fix the time of its destruction. The *end* is probably not very distant; it has already been grievously shaken by the French. In 1798 the French republican army under General *Berthier* took possession of the city of Rome, and entirely superseded the whole papal power. This was a deadly wound, though at present it appears to be healed; but it is but *skinned over,* and a dreadful cicatrice remains. The *Jesuits,* not JESUS, are now the Church's doctors.

If the papal power, as a *horn* or *temporal power,* be intended here, which is most likely, (and we know that that power was given in 755 to Pope Stephen II. by *Pepin,* king of France,) counting *one thousand two hundred and sixty* years from that, we are brought to A. D. 2015, about *one hundred and ninety* years from the present [A. D. 1825.] But I neither lay stress upon nor draw conclusions from these dates. If the Church of Rome will *reform itself,* it will then be the *true Christian* Church, and will never be destroyed. Let it throw aside all that is ritually *Jewish;* all that is *heathen;* all that which pretends to be of God, and which is only of *man;* all doctrines that are not in the Bible; and all *rites* and *ceremonies* which are not of the appointment of *Christ* and his *apostles;* and then, all hail the once Roman, but now, after such a change, the HOLY, *Catholic Church!* Every true Protestant would wish rather the *reform* than the extinction of this Church.

Verse 27. *The kingdom and dominion*] The people of the saints of the Most High, or the people who are the supereminent saints, shall have the kingdom. Whatever name they may be distinguished by among men, these are the people, and theirs is the Church, that no lapse of time shall injure, and no power be able to destroy; but shall last as long as time shall endure.

Verse 28. *The end of the matter.*] So said the expounding angel; and he said so because the purpose of God had determined it. In considering these things, and looking at the evils that shall come upon the world before those auspicious times can take place, I may say, with Daniel, *My cogitations much troubled me, and my countenance changed in me: but I keep the matter* of my conjectures and consequent feelings *in my own heart.*

CHAPTER VIII

This chapter contains Daniel's vision of the ram *and* he-goat, 1–14; *referring, as explained by the angel, to the Persian and Grecian monarchies,* 15–26. *The* little horn *mentioned in the* ninth *verse,* (*or* fierce king, *as interpreted in the* twenty-third,) *is supposed by some to denote Antiochus Epiphanes; but seems more properly to apply to the Roman power in general, by which the polity and temple of the Jews were destroyed, on account of the great transgressions of these ancient people of God; and particularly because of their very obstinate and unaccountable rejection of the glorious doctrines of Christianity, which had been preached among them by Jesus Christ and his apostles, and the truth of which God had attested "by signs and wonders, and by divers miracles and gifts of the Holy Ghost." Daniel is then informed of the* two thousand and three hundred *prophetic days* (*that is, years*) *which must elapse before the sanctuary be cleansed; or, in other words, before righteousness shall prevail over the whole earth. This period is supposed, with considerable probability, to have had its commencement when Alexander the Great invaded Asia, in the year before Christ* 334. *This will bring the close of it to about the end of the* SIXTH chiliad *of the world; when, as already observed, some astonishing changes are expected to take place in the moral condition of the human race; when the power of Antichrist, both Papal and Mohammedan, shall be totally annihilated, and universal dominion given to the saints of the Most High. The chapter concludes with the distress of Daniel on account of the fearful judgments with which his country should be visited in after ages,* 27.

A. M. cir. 3451
B. C. cir. 553
Ol. cir. LVI. 4
Servii Tullii,
R. Roman.,
cir. annum 26

IN the third year of the reign
of King Belshazzar a vision
appeared unto me, *even unto* me
Daniel, after that which appeared unto me [a]at the first.
2 And I saw in a vision; and it came to
pass, when I saw, that I *was* at [b]Shushan *in*
the palace, which *is* in the province of Elam;
and I saw in a vision, and I was by the river
of Ulai.
3 Then I lifted up mine eyes, and saw, and
behold, there stood before the river a ram
which had *two* horns: and the *two* horns
were high; but one *was* higher
than [c]the other, and the higher
came up last.
4 I saw the ram pushing west-
ward, and northward, and southward; so that
no beasts might stand before him, neither *was*
there any that could deliver out of his hand;
[d]but he did according to his will, and became
great.
5 And as I was considering, behold, a he-goat
came from the west on the face of the whole
earth, and [e]touched not the ground: and the
goat *had* [f]a [g]notable horn between his eyes.

A. M. cir. 3451
B. C. cir. 553
Ol. cir. LVI. 4
Servii Tullii,
R. Roman.,
cir. annum 26

[a]Chap. vii. 1——[b]Esth. i. 2——[c]Heb. *the second*——[d]Chap. v. 19; xi. 3, 16

[e]Or, *none touched* him *in the earth*——[f]Heb. *a horn of sight*——[g]Ver. 21

NOTES ON CHAP. VIII

Verse 1. *In the third year of the reign of —Belshazzar*] We now come once more to the *Hebrew*, the *Chaldee* part of the book being finished. As the Chaldeans had a particular interest both in the *history* and *prophecies* from chap. ii. 4 to the end of chap. vii., the whole is written in *Chaldee;* but as the prophecies which remain concern times posterior to the Chaldean monarchy, and principally relate to the *Church and people of God generally*, they are written in the Hebrew language, this being the tongue in which God chose to reveal all his counsels given under the *Old Testament* relative to the *New*.

Verse 2. *I saw in a vision*] Daniel was at this time in Shushan, which appears to have been a strong place, where the kings of Persia had their summer residence. It was the capital of the province of Elam or the Elymais; which province was most probably added to the Chaldean territories by Nebuchadnezzar; see Jer. xlix. 34, 35. Here was Daniel's ordinary residence; and though here at this time, he, in *vision*, saw himself on the *banks of the river Ulai*. This is the same as the river *Euleus*, which divided Shushan or Susiana from Elymais.

Verse 3. *A ram which had* two *horns*] In the former vision there were *four beasts*, pointing out *four empires;* in this we have but *two*, as only *two empires* are concerned here, *viz.*, the *Grecian* and the *Persian*. The Babylonish empire is not mentioned; its fate was before decided, and it was now at its close.

By the *ram*, the empire of the Medes and Persians was pointed out, as explained by the angel Gabriel, ver. 20; and particularly Cyrus, who was the founder of that empire. Cyrus was the son of Cambyses, king of Persia; and grandson of Astyages, king of Media, by his daughter Mandane, who had been given in marriage to Cambyses. Cyrus, marrying Roxana, the daughter and only child of his uncle Cyaxares, called in Scripture *Ahasuerus*, succeeded to both crowns, and thus united Media and Persia. A *ram* was the symbol of the Persians; and a ram's head with two horns, one higher than the other, appears as such in different parts of the ruins of *Persepolis*. See the plates of these ruins in the supplement to the seventh volume of the ancient part of the *Universal History*.

This ram had *two horns;* that is, *two kingdoms, viz., Media* and *Persia;* but one was *higher than the other;* and the higher *came up last. Media*, signified by the *shorter horn*, was the more *ancient* of the two kingdoms. *Persia*, the *higher horn*, had come up but lately, and was of little historic or political consequence till the time of Cyrus; but in the reigns of this prince and his immediate successors, Persia attained a political consequence greatly superior to that possessed at any time by the kingdom of Media; therefore, it is said to have been the *higher*, and to have come up *last*.

Verse 4. *I saw the ram pushing westward*] The Persians, who are signified by the *ram*, as well as their *founder Cyrus*, pushed their conquests *west, north* and *south*. The principal theatre of their wars, says *Calmet*, was against the SCYTHIANS, *northward;* against the GREEKS, *westward;* and against the EGYPTIANS, *southward*.

He did according to his will] There was no other nation at that time that could stay the progress of the Persian arms.

Verse 5. *Behold, a he-goat*] This was *Alexander the Great;* and a *goat* was a very proper symbol of the Grecian or Macedonian people. Bp. *Newton* very properly observes that, *two hundred* years before the time of Daniel, they were called *Ægeadæ*, the *goats' people;* the origin of which name is said to be as follows: Caranus, their first king, going with a multitude of Greeks to seek a new habitation in Macedonia, was advised by an oracle to take the *goats* for his guides; and afterwards, seeing a herd of goats flying from a violent storm, he followed them to *Edessa*, and there fixed the seat of his empire, and made the *goats* his ensigns or standards; and called the place *Æge* or *Ægea*, the *goats' town;* and the people *Ægeadæ*, the *goats' people;* names which are derived from αιξ, αιγος, a *goat*. The city *Æge* or *Ægea*, was the usual burying-place of the Macedonian kings; and, in reference to this origin, Alexander called his son by Roxana, *Alexander Ægus*, Alexander the *goat*. All this shows the very great propriety of the symbol here used.

Came from the west] Europe lies westward of Asia.

On the face of the whole earth] Carrying every thing before him.

A. M. cir. 3451 B. C. cir. 553 Ol. cir. LVI. 4 Servii Tullii, R. Roman., cir. annum 26

6 And he came to the ram
that had *two* horns, which I had
seen standing before the river,
and ran unto him in the fury of
his power.
7 And I saw him come close unto the ram,
and he was moved with choler against him,
and smote the ram, and brake his two horns:
and there was no power in the ram to stand before him, but he cast him down to the ground,
and stamped upon him: and there was none
that could deliver the ram out of his hand.
8 Therefore the he-goat waxed
very great: and when he was
strong, the great horn was broken; and for it came up [h]four
notable ones toward the four winds of
heaven.
9 [i]And out of one of them came forth a
little horn, which vexed exceeding great,
[k]toward the south, and toward the east, and
toward the [l]pleasant *land*.
10 [m]And it waxed great, *even* [n]to [o]the host
of heaven; and [p]it cast down *some* of the

[h]Ch. vii. 6; xi. 4; ver. 22——[i]Ch. vii. 8; xi. 21 [k]Ch. xi. 25; 1 Mac. i. 16-19——[l]Psa. xlviii. 2; Ezek. xx. 6, 15; ch. xi. 16, 41, 45——[m]Ch. xi. 28——[n]Or, *against the host*——[o]So Isa. xiv. 13——[p]Rev. xii. 4

Touched not the ground] Seemed to fly from conquest to conquest. By the time Alexander was *thirty* years of age he had conquered all Asia: and, because of the rapidity of his conquests, he is represented as a *leopard* with four wings, in the preceding vision.

A notable horn between his eyes.] This, says the angel, is the *first king*, ver. 21, that is, the first kingdom of the Greeks in Asia, which was erected by Alexander; and continued some years in his brother *Philip Aridæus*, and in his two young sons, *Alexander Ægus* and *Hercules*. See *Newton*.

Verse 6. *And he came to the ram.*] This and the following verse give an account of the overthrow of the Persian empire by Alexander.

And ran unto him in the fury of his power] The conflicts between the Greeks and the Persians were excessively severe. Alexander first vanquished the generals of Darius, at the river *Granicus*, in Phrygia; he next attacked and totally routed Darius, at the straits of *Issus*, in Cilicia; and afterwards at the plains of *Arbela*, in Assyria. One can hardly read these words, says Bp. *Newton*, "the ram—which I had seen standing by the river, ran unto him in the fury of his power," without having the image of Darius' army standing and guarding the *river Granicus;* and of Alexander on the *other side*, with his forces plunging in swimming across the stream, and rushing on the enemy, with all the fire and fury that can be conceived.

Verse 7. *And brake his two horns*] Subdued Persia and Media; sacked and burnt the royal city of *Persepolis*, the capital of the Persian empire, and, even in its *ruins*, one of the wonders of the world to the present day. This he did because "he was moved with choler" against Darius, who had endeavoured to draw off his captains with bribes, and had laboured to induce some of his friends to assassinate him. Alexander, finding this, would listen to no proposals of peace; and was determined never to rest till he had destroyed Darius and his whole empire. In Media, Darius was seized and made prisoner by some of his own treacherous subjects, and afterwards basely murdered.

There was no power in the ram to stand before him] Alexander's victories over the Persians were as *easy* as they were *rapid* and *decisive*.

He cast him down to the ground, and stamped upon him] Totally destroyed the *family*, and overturned the whole *monarchy*.

Verse 8. *The he-goat waxed very strong*] He had subdued nearly the whole of the then known world.

The great horn was broken] Alexander died in the height of his conquests, when he was but about *thirty-three* years of age. His natural brother, Philip Aridæus, and his two sons, Alexander Ægus and Hercules, kept up the show and name of the Macedonian kingdom for a time; but they were all murdered within *fifteen* years; and thus *the great horn*, the Macedonian kingdom, *was broken*, Alexander's family being now cut off.

And for it came up four notable ones] The regal family being all dead, the governors of provinces usurped the title of kings; and Antigonus, one of them, being slain at the battle of *Ipsus*, they were reduced to *four*, as we have already seen. 1. SELEUCUS, who had Syria and Babylon, from whom came the *Seleucidæ*, famous in history. 2. LYSIMACHUS, who had Asia Minor. 3. PTOLEMY, son of *Lagus*, who had Egypt, from whom sprang the *Lagidæ*. And, 4. CASSANDER, who had Greece and the neighbouring countries. These held dominion *towards the four winds of heaven. Cassander* had the *western* parts, *Lysimachus* had the *northern* regions, *Ptolemy* possessed the *southern* countries, and *Seleucus* had the *eastern* provinces.

Verse 9. *Out of one of them came forth a little horn*] Some think that *Antiochus Epiphanes* is meant; but Bp. *Newton* contends that it is the *Roman* government that is intended; and although very *great* at its *zenith*, yet very *little* in its *rising*.

Waxed—great toward the south] The Romans made *Egypt* a province of their empire, and it continued such for some centuries.

Toward the east] They conquered *Syria*, and made it a province.

Toward the pleasant land.] *Judea*, so called Psa. cvi. 24; Jer. iii. 19; Dan. xi. 16, 41. It is well known that they took Judea, and made it a province; and afterwards burnt the city and the temple, and scattered the Jews over the face of the earth.

Verse 10. *The host of heaven*] The *Jewish hierarchy*. The *stars*, the *priests* and *Levites*. The *powers* or *host of heaven* are probably intended by our Lord, Matt. xxiv. 29, to signify the whole Jewish hierarchy.

A. M. cir. 3451
B. C. cir. 553
Ol. cir. LVI. 4
Servii Tullii,
R. Roman.,
cir. annum 26

host and of the stars to the ground, and stamped upon them.

11 Yea, [q]he magnified *himself* even [r]to [s]the prince of the host, [t]and [u]by him [v]the daily *sacrifice* was taken away, and the place of his sanctuary was cast down.

12 And [w]a [x]host was given *him* against the daily *sacrifice* [y]by reason of transgression, and it cast down [z]the truth to the ground; and [a]it practised, and prospered.

13 Then I heard [b]one saint speaking, and another saint said unto [c]that[d] certain *saint* which spake, How long *shall be* the vision *concerning* the daily *sacrifice,* and the transgression of [e]desolation, to give both the sanctuary and the host to be trodden under foot?

14 And he said unto me, Unto two thousand and three hundred [f]days; [g]then shall the sanctuary be [h]cleansed.

15 And it came to pass, when I, *even* I Daniel, had seen the vision, and [i]sought for the meaning, then, behold, there stood before me [k]as the appearance of a man.

16 And I heard a man's voice [l]between *the banks of* Ulai, which called, and said, [m]Gabriel, make this *man* to understand the vision.

A. M. cir. 3451
B. C. cir. 553
Ol. cir. LVI. 4
Servii Tullii,
R. Roman.,
cir. annum 26

17 So he came near where I stood: and when he came, I was afraid, and [n]fell upon my face: but he said unto me, Understand, O son of man, for at the time of the end *shall be* the vision.

18 [o]Now as he was speaking with me, I was in a deep sleep on my face toward the ground: [p]but he touched me, and [q]set me upright.

19 And he said, Behold, I will make thee know what shall be in the last end of the indignation; [r]for at the time appointed the end *shall be.*

20 [s]The ram which thou sawest having *two* horns *are* the kings of Media and Persia.

21 [t]And the rough goat *is* the king of Grecia: and the great horn that *is* between his eyes [u]*is* the first king.

22 [v]Now that being broken, whereas four stood up for it, four kingdoms shall stand up out of the nation, but not in his power.

23 And in the latter time of their kingdom, [w]when the transgressors [x]are come to the full, a king [y]of fierce countenance, and understanding dark sentences, [z]shall stand up.

---

[q]Jer. xlviii. 26, 42; chap. xi. 36; ver. 25——[r]Or, *against*——[s]Josh. v. 14——[t]Chap. xi. 31; xii. 11; 1 Mac. i. 44–64——[u]Or, *from him*——[v]Exod. xxix. 38; Num. xxviii. 3; Ezek. xlvi. 13——[w]Chap. xi. 31——[x]Or, *the host was given over for the transgression against the daily* sacrifice——[y]1 Mac. i. 11, &c.; 2 Mac. iv. 13, 17 [z]Psa. cxix. 43, 142; Isa. lix. 14——[a]Ver. 4; chap. xi. 28, 36——[b]Chap. iv. 13; xii. 6; 1 Pet. i. 12——[c]Or, *the numberer of secrets*, or *the wonderful numberer*——[d]Hebrew, *Palmoni*

[e]Or, *making desolate;* ch. xi. 31; xii. 11; 1 Mac. i. 54 [f]Heb. *evening morning*——[g]1 Mac. iv. 36, &c.——[h]Heb. *justified*——[i]See ch. xii. 8; 1 Pet. i. 10, 11——[k]Ezek. i. 26——[l]Ch. xii. 6, 7——[m]Ch. ix. 21; Luke i. 19, 26 [n]Ezek. i. 28; Rev. i. 17——[o]Ch. x. 9, 10; Luke ix. 32 [p]Ezek. ii. 2——[q]Heb. *made me stand upon my standing* [r]Ch. ix. 27; xi. 27, 35, 36; xii. 7; Hab. ii. 3——[s]Ver. 3 [t]Ver. 5——[u]Ch. xi. 3——[v]Ver. 8; ch. xi. 4——[w]1 Mac. i. 11, &c.; ii. 15——[x]Heb. *are accomplished*——[y]Deut. xxviii. 50——[z]Ver. 6

Verse 11. *Even to the prince of the host*] They seemed, in this case, to fight against God himself.

The daily sacrifice *was taken away*] By the destruction of the city and temple; and has never been restored from that day until now.

Verse 12. *And a host was given* him] That is, *power;* or perhaps *the host of heaven*—the *priesthood*—the whole sacrificial system, by reason of *transgression.* They had filled up the measure of their iniquities, in rejecting the Lord that bought them; and the *daily sacrifice,* being no longer of use, was given up with the rest to destruction.

Cast down the truth] Probably the whole Jewish ritual and religion.

Practised, and prospered.] Prosperity or success followed all their acts.

Verse 13. *One saint speaking, and another saint said*] One *angel* asked another how long the sanctuary was to be trodden down?

Verse 14. *Unto two thousand and three hundred days*] Though literally it be *two thousand three hundred evenings and mornings*, yet I think the *prophetic day* should be understood here, as in other parts of this prophet, and must signify so many *years.* If we date these years from the vision of the he-goat, (Alexander's invading Asia,) this was A. M. 3670, B. C. 334; and *two thousand three hundred* years from that time will reach to A. D. 1966, or *one hundred and forty-one* years from the present A. D. 1825. This will bring it near to the time mentioned chap. vii. 25, where see the note.

Verse 15. *As the appearance of a man.*] Supposed to be the *Messiah.*

Verse 17. *At the time of the end* shall be *the vision.*] Or, as *Houbigant*, "The vision shall have an end at the proper time."

Verse 20. *The ram which thou sawest*] See this explained under the vision itself, ver. 3, &c.

Verse 22. *But not in his power.*] The *four kingdoms* which shall arise out of the Macedonian empire shall not be of Alexander's power or *family*, nor have his strength and dignity.

Verse 23. *When the transgressors are come to the full*] When the utmost degradation has taken place, by the *buying* and *selling* of the *high priesthood;* for *Onias* was ejected for a

A. M. cir. 3451
B. C. cir. 553
Ol. cir. LVI. 4
Servii Tullii,
R. Roman.,
cir. annum 26

24 And his power shall be
mighty, [a]but not by his own
power: and he shall destroy
wonderfully, [b]and shall prosper,
and practise, [c]and shall destroy the mighty
and the [d]holy people.
25 And [e]through his policy also he shall
cause craft to prosper in his hand; [f]and he
shall magnify *himself* in his heart, [g]and by
[h]peace shall destroy many: [i]he shall also
stand up against the Prince of princes; but
he shall be [k]broken without
hand.
26 [l]And the vision of the
evening and the morning which
was told *is* true: [m]wherefore shut thou
up the vision; for it *shall be* for many
days.
27 [n]And I Daniel fainted, and was sick
certain days; afterward I rose up, [o]and did
the king's busines and I was astonished at
the vision, [p]but none understood *it*.

A. M. cir. 3451
B. C. cir. 553
Ol. cir. LVI. 4
Servii Tullii,
R. Roman.,
cir. annum 26

[a]Rev. xvii. 13, 17——[b]Ver. 12; chap. xi. 36——[c]Ver. 10; chap. vii. 25——[d]Heb. *people of the holy ones* [e]Chap. xi. 21, 23, 24——[f]Ver. 11; chap. xi. 36; 2 Mac. ix. 4, 7, 8, 11——[g]1 Mac. i. 30, &c.——[h]Or, *prosperity*

[i]Ver. 11; ch. xi. 36——[k]Job xxxiv. 20; Lam. iv. 6; ch. ii. 34, 45; 1 Mac. vi. 8–13; 2 Mac. ix. 9, &c.——[l]Ch. x. 1——[m]Ezek. xii. 27; ch. x. 14; xii. 4, 9; Rev. xxii. 10 [n]Ch. vii. 28; x. 8, 16——[o]Ch. vi. 2, 3——[p]See ver. 16

sum of money, to make room for wicked *Jason;* and Jason again was supplanted for a greater sum by a worse man, if possible, than himself, *Menelaus;* and the golden vessels of the temple were sold to pay for this sacrilegious purchase. Thus transgressions were come to the full, before the Romans had commission to destroy Jerusalem and its temple, &c.

A king of fierce countenance] The *Roman government*, as before; for *king* is often taken for *kingdom* or *empire.*

Understanding dark sentences] Very learned and skilful in all things relating to government and its intrigues. The *learning* of Rome is proverbial to the present time.

Verse 24. *But not by his own power*] The strength of the other kingdoms consisted in themselves; but the Roman empire, as a *horn* or *kingdom* of the *goat*, was *not mighty by its own power*—was not strong by virtue of the *goat*, but drew its nourishment and strength from Rome and Italy. There grew the trunk and body of the tree; though the branches extended over Greece, Asia, Syria, and Egypt.—Bp. *Newton.*

Shall destroy wonderfully] In the taking of Jerusalem by the Romans *ninety-seven thousand* Jews were made captives, and *eleven hundred thousand* were slain. So they destroyed this once mighty and holy people!

Verse 25. *He shall cause craft to prosper*] They subdued as many by their *diplomatic skill* and *political intrigues* as they did by the *sword.*

He shall also stand up against the Prince of princes] Against *Christ;* for it was by the *Roman* authority that he was condemned to death and crucified; and their persecutions had nearly destroyed the Christian religion; but the house was founded on a *rock.*

But he shall be broken without hand.] The tide was turned by the invisible hand of God; and thus heathen Rome was overcome, and converted to Christianity.

Verse 26. *The vision of the evening and the morning which was told* is *true*] That mentioned in ver. 14.

For it shall be *for many days.*] Not less than *two thousand three hundred* years!

Verse 27. *Daniel fainted*] To foresee the desolations that were coming on the land, the city, the temple, and the people.

Did the king's business] Transacted the affairs of state that belonged to my department, after having been sick for certain days through the effects of this vision. He had a pious and feeling heart; and he was distressed for the desolations that were coming upon his people.

CHAPTER IX

Daniel, understanding from the prophecies of Jeremiah that the seventy *years' captivity was now terminating, pours out his soul in fervent prayer to God, and earnestly supplicates pardon and restoration for his captive people,* 1–12. *When thus supplicating God in behalf of Israel, the angel Gabriel is sent to inform him of the* seventy *prophetic weeks, or* four hundred and ninety *natural years, which should elapse from the date of the edict to rebuild Jerusalem and the temple to the death of the Messiah,* 20–27; *a prophecy most exactly fulfilled by the event, according to the computation of the best chronologers. Dean Prideaux states the commencement of these* seventy *prophetic weeks to have been in the month Nisan, in the year of the Julian period* 4256, *which corresponds with* A. M. 3546, B. C. 458, *according to the Usherian account. How awfully are the Jews blinded, who, in contradiction to so clear a prophecy, still expect the Messiah who was* cut off, *and, after suffering, is entered into his glory!*

A. M. cir. 3466
B. C. cir. 538
Ol. cir. LX. 3
Servii Tullii,
R. Roman.,
cir. annum 41

IN the first year [a]of Darius
the son of Ahasuerus, of the
seed of the Medes, [b]which was
made king over the realm of the
Chaldeans;
2 In the first year of his reign I Daniel
understood by books the number of the years,
whereof the word of the LORD came to [c]Jere-
miah the prophet, that he would accomplish
seventy years in the desolations of Jerusalem.
3 [d]And I set my face unto the Lord GOD, to
seek by prayer and supplications, with fasting, and sackcloth, and ashes:
4 And I prayed unto the LORD my God, and
made my confession, and said, O [e]Lord, the
great and dreadful God, keeping the covenant
and mercy to them that love him, and to them
that keep his commandments;
5 [f]We have sinned, and have committed
iniquity, and have done wickedly, and have
rebelled, even by departing from thy precepts
and from thy judgments:
6 [g]Neither have we hearkened unto thy servants the prophets, which spake in thy name
to our kings, our princes, and our fathers,
and to all the people of the land.
7 O Lord, [h]righteousness [i]*belongeth* unto
thee, but unto us confusion of faces, as at this
day; to the men of Judah, and to the inhabitants of Jerusalem, and unto all Israel, *that*
are near, and *that are* far off,
through all the countries
whither thou hast driven them,
because of their trespass that
they have trespassed against thee.

A. M. cir. 3466
B. C. cir. 538
Ol. cir. LX. 3
Servii Tullii,
R. Roman.,
cir. annum 41

8 O Lord, to us *belongeth* [k]confusion of face
to our kings, to our princes, and to our
fathers, because we have sinned against thee.
9 [l]To the Lord our God *belong* mercies and
forgivenesses, though we have rebelled
against him;
10 [m]Neither have we obeyed the voice of the
LORD our God, to walk in his laws, which he
set before us by his servants the prophets.
11 Yea, [n]all Israel have transgressed thy
law, even by departing, that they might not
obey thy voice; therefore the curse is poured
upon us, and the oath that *is* written in the
[o]law of Moses the servant of God, because
we have sinned against him.
12 And he hath [p]confirmed his words, which
he spake against us, and against our judges
that judged us, by bringing upon us a great
evil: [q]for under the whole heaven hath not
been done as hath been done upon Jerusalem.
13 [r]As *it is* written in the law of Moses, all
this evil is come upon us: [s]yet [t]made we not
our prayer before the LORD our God, that we
might turn from our iniquities, and understand thy truth.

---

[a]Chap. i. 21; v. 31; vi. 28——[b]Or, *in which he*, &c. [c]2 Chron. xxxvi. 21; Jer. xxv. 11, 12; xxix. 10——[d]Neh. i. 4; chap. vi. 10; Jer. xxix. 12, 13; James iv. 8, 9, 10 [e]Exod. xx. 6; Deut. vii. 9; Neh. i. 5; ix. 32——[f]1 Kings viii. 47, 48; Neh. i. 6, 7; ix. 33, 34; Psa. cvi. 6; Isa. lxiv. 5, 6, 7; Jer. xiv. 7; ver. 15; Bar. i. 17, 18——[g]2 Chron. xxxvi. 15, 16; ver. 10——[h]Neh. ix. 33; Bar. i. 15 [i]Or, *thou* hast, &c.

[k]Ver. 7; Bar. i. 15——[l]Neh. ix. 17; Psa. cxxx. 4, 7 [m]Ver. 6——[n]Isa. i. 4, 5, 6; Jer. viii. 5, 10——[o]Lev. xxvi. 14, &c.;Deut. xxvii. 15, &c.; xxviii. 15, &c.; xxix. 20, &c.; xxx. 17, 18; xxxi. 17, &c.; xxxii. 19, &c.; Lam. ii. 17 [p]Zech. i. 6——[q]Lam. i. 12; ii. 13; Ezek. v. 9; Amos iii. 2 [r]Lev. xxvi. 14, &c.; Deut. xxviii. 15; Lam. ii. 17 [s]Isa. ix. 13; Jer. ii. 30; v. 3; Hos. vii. 7, 10——[t]Heb. *intreated we not the face of the*, &c.

NOTES ON CHAP. IX

Verse 1. *In the first year of Darius*] This is the same Darius the *Mede*, spoken of before, who succeeded Belshazzar, king of the Chaldeans. See chap. v. 31.

Verse 2. *I Daniel understood by books*] The prophecy referred to here is found Jer. xxv. 12; xxix. 10. The people must have been satisfied of the Divine inspiration of Jeremiah, or his prophecies would not have been so speedily collected nor so carefully preserved. It appears that there was a copy of them then in Daniel's hands.

Verse 3. *I set my face—to seek by prayer*] He found that the time of the promised deliverance could not be at any great distance; and as he saw nothing that indicated a speedy termination of their oppressive captivity, he was very much afflicted, and earnestly besought God to put a speedy end to it; and how earnestly he seeks, his own words show. He *prayed*, he *supplicated*, he *fasted*, he put *sackcloth* upon his body, and he put *ashes* upon his head. He uses that kind of prayer prescribed by Solomon in his prayer at the dedication of the temple. See 1 Kings viii. 47, 48.

Verse 4. *Keeping the covenant*] Fidelity and truth are characteristics of God. He had never yet broken his engagements to his followers, and was ever showing *mercy* to men.

Verse 7. *All Israel*, that are *near, and* that are *far off*] He prays both for *Judah* and *Israel*. The latter were more dispersed, and had been much longer in captivity.

Verse 9. *Mercies and forgivenesses*] From God's *goodness* flow God's *mercies;* from his *mercies, forgivenesses.*

Verse 11. *Therefore the curse is poured upon us*] It is probable that he alludes here to the punishment of certain criminals by pouring *melted metal* upon them; therefore he uses the word תתך *tittach, it is poured out*, like melted

A. M. cir. 3466
B. C. cir. 538
Ol. cir. LX. 3
Servii Tullii,
R. Roman.,
cir. annum 41

14 Therefore hath the LORD [u]watched upon the evil, and brought it upon us: for [v]the LORD our God *is* righteous in all his works which he doeth: [w]for we obeyed not his voice.

15 And now, O Lord our God, [x]that hast brought thy people forth out of the land of Egypt with a mighty hand, and hast [y]gotten thee [z]renown, as at this day; [a]we have sinned, we have done wickedly.

16 O Lord, [b]according to all thy righteousness, I beseech thee, let thine anger and thy fury be turned away from thy city Jerusalem, [c]thy holy mountain: because for our sins, [d]and for the iniquities of our fathers, [e]Jerusalem and thy people [f]*are become* a reproach to all *that are* about us.

17 Now therefore, O our God, hear the prayer of thy servant, and his supplications, [g]and cause thy face to shine upon thy sanctuary [h]that is desolate, [i]for the Lord's sake.

18 [k]O my God, incline thine ear, and hear; open thine eyes, [l]and behold our desolations, and the city [m]which [n]is called by thy name: for we do not [o]present our supplications before thee for our righteousnesses, but for thy great mercies.

19 O Lord, hear; O Lord, forgive; O Lord, hearken and do; defer not, [p]for thine own sake, O my God: for thy city and thy people are called by thy name.

A. M. cir. 3466
B. C. cir. 538
Ol. cir. LX. 3
Servii Tullii,
R. Roman.,
cir. annum 41

20 [q]And whiles I was speaking, and praying, and confessing my sin and the sin of my people Israel, and presenting my supplication before the LORD my God for the holy mountain of my God;

21 Yea, whiles I *was* speaking in prayer, even the man [r]Gabriel, whom I had seen in the vision at the beginning, being caused to fly [s]swiftly, [t]touched me [u]about the time of the evening oblation.

22 And he informed *me,* and talked with me, and said, O Daniel, I am now come forth [v]to give thee skill and understanding.

23 At the begining of thy supplications the [w]commandment came forth, and [x]I am come to show *thee;* [y]for thou *art* [z]greatly beloved: therefore [a]understand the matter, and consider the vision.

24 Seventy weeks are determined upon thy people and upon thy holy city, [b]to finish the transgression, and [c]to make an end of sins, [d]and to make reconciliation for iniquity, and to bring in everlasting righteousness, and to seal up the vision [e]and [f]prophecy, [g]and to anoint the Most Holy.

---

[u]Jer. xxxi. 28; xliv. 27——[v]Neh. ix. 33; ver. 7——[w]Ver. 10——[x]Exod. vi. 1, 6; xxxii. 11; 1 Kings viii. 51; Neh. i. 10——Jer. xxxii. 21——[y]Heb. *made thee a name*——[z]Exod. xiv. 18; Neh. ix. 10; Jer. xxxii. 20——[a]Ver. 5——[b]1 Sam. xii. 7; Psa. xxxi. 1; lxxi. 2; Mic. vi. 4, 5——[c]Ver. 20; Zech. viii. 3——[d]Exod. xx. 5——[e]Lam. ii. 15, 16——[f]Psa. xliv. 13, 14; lxxix. 4——[g]Num. vi. 25; Psa. lxvii. 1; lxxx. 3, 7, 19——[h]Lam. v. 18——[i]Ver. 19; John xvi. 24——[k]Isa. xxxvii. 17——[l]Exod. iii. 7; Psa. lxxx. 14, &c.——[m]Jer. xxv. 29——[n]Heb. *whereupon thy name is called*

[o]Heb. *cause to fall;* Jer. xxxvi. 7——[p]Psa. lxxix. 9, 10; cii. 15, 16——[q]Psa. xxxii. 5; Isa. lxv. 24——[r]Chap. viii. 16——[s]Heb. *with weariness*, or *flight*——[t]Chap. viii. 18; x. 10, 16——[u]1 Kings xviii. 36——[v]Heb. *to make thee skilful of understanding*——[w]Heb. *word*——[x]Chap. x. 12——[y]Chap. x. 11, 19——[z]Heb. a man *of desires*——[a]Matt. xxiv. 15——[b]Or, *to restrain*——[c]Or, *to seal up;* Lam. iv. 22——[d]Isa. liii. 10——[e]Isa. liii. 11; Jer. xxiii. 5, 6; Heb. ix. 12; Rev. xiv. 6——[f]Heb. *prophet*——[g]Psalm xlv. 7; Luke i. 35; John i. 41; Hebrews ix. 11

---

metal, for this is the proper meaning of the root נתך *nathach.*

Verse 14. *The Lord watched upon the evil*] In consequence of our manifold rebellions he hath now watched for an opportunity to bring these calamities upon us.

Verse 17. *And cause thy face to shine*] Give us proof that thou art reconciled to us.

Verse 19. *Thy city and thy people are called by thy name.*] The *holy city,* the *city of the great King.* I think it scarcely possible for any serious man to read these impressive and pleading words without feeling a measure of the prophet's earnestness.

Verse 21. *The man Gabriel*] Or the angel Gabriel, who had appeared to me as a *man.* איש *ish* is the same here as *person*—the person *Gabriel.*

Being caused to fly swiftly] God hears with delight such earnest, humble, urgent prayers; and sends the *speediest* answer. Gabriel himself was ordered on this occasion to make *more than usual speed.*

Verse 24. *Seventy weeks are determined*] This is a most important prophecy, and has given rise to a variety of opinions relative to the proper mode of explanation; but the chief difficulty, if not the only one, is to find out the *time* from which these *seventy weeks* should be *dated.* What is here said by the angel is not a direct answer to Daniel's prayer. He prays to know when the *seventy weeks of the captivity* are to *end.* Gabriel shows him that there are *seventy weeks determined* relative to a *redemption* from *another sort of captivity,* which shall commence with the *going forth of the edict to restore and rebuild Jerusalem,* and shall terminate with the *death of Messiah the Prince,* and the total *abolition of the Jewish sacrifices.* In the four following verses he enters into the particulars of this most important *determination,* and leaves them with Dan-

A. M. cir. 3466
B. C. cir. 538
Ol. cir. LX. 3
Servii Tullii,
R. Roman.,
cir. annum 41

25 [h]Know therefore and understand, *that* [i]from the going forth of the commandment [k]to restore and to build Jerusalem unto [l]the Messiah [m]the Prince *shall be* seven weeks, and threescore and two weeks: the street [n]shall be built again, and the [o]wall, [p]even [q]in troublous times.

[h]Ver. 23; Matt. xxiv. 15——[i]Ezra iv. 24; vi. 1, 15; vii. 1; Neh. ii. 1, 3, 5, 6, 8——[k]Or, *to build again Jerusalem;* as 2 Sam. xv. 25; Psa. lxxi. 20——[l]John i. 41; iv. 25——[m]Isa. lv. 4——[n]Heb. *shall return and be builded*——[o]Or, *breach,* or *ditch*——[p]Neh. iv. 8, 16, 17, 18——[q]Heb. *in strait of times;* Neh. vi. 15

iel for his comfort, who has left them to the Church of God for the *confirmation* of its faith, and a *testimony* to the truth of Divine revelation. They contain the fullest confirmation of Christianity, and a complete refutation of the Jewish cavils and blasphemies on this subject.

Of all the writers I have consulted on this most noble prophecy, Dean *Prideaux* appears to me the most clear and satisfactory. I shall therefore follow his method in my explanation, and often borrow his words.

Seventy weeks are determined—The Jews had *Sabbatic years,* Lev. xxv. 8, by which their years were divided into weeks of years, as in this important prophecy, each week containing *seven* years. The *seventy weeks* therefore here spoken of amount to *four hundred and ninety* years.

In ver. 24 there are *six events* mentioned which should be the consequences of the incarnation of our Lord:—

I. *To finish* (לכלא *lechalle, to restrain,*) *the transgression*, which was effected by the preaching of the Gospel, and pouring out of the Holy Ghost among men.

II. *To make an end of sins;* rather ולהתם חטאות *ulehathem chataoth*, "to make an end of *sin-offerings;*" which our Lord did when he offered his spotless soul and body on the cross *once* for all.

III. *To make reconciliation* (ולכפר *ulechapper,* "to make atonement or expiation") *for iniquity;* which he did by the once offering up of himself.

IV. *To bring in everlasting righteousness,* צדק עלמים *tsedek olamim,* that is, "the righteousness, or righteous ONE, of ages;" that person who had been the object of the faith of mankind, and the subject of the predictions of the prophets through all the ages of the world.

V. *To seal up* (ולחתם *velachtom,* "to finish or complete") *the vision and prophecy;* that is, to put an end to the necessity of any farther revelations, by completing the canon of Scripture, and fulfilling the prophecies which related to his person, sacrifice, and the glory that should follow.

VI. *And to anoint the Most Holy,* קדש קדשים *kodesh kodashim,* "the Holy of holies." משח *mashach, to anoint,* (from which comes משיח *mashiach, the Messiah,* the anointed one,) signifies in general, to consecrate or appoint to some special office. Here it means the consecration or appointment of our blessed Lord, the Holy One of Israel, to be the Prophet, Priest, and King of mankind.

Verse 25. *From the going forth of the commandment to restore and to build Jerusalem*] The foregoing events being all accomplished by Jesus Christ, they of course determine the prophecy to him. And if we reckon back *four hundred and ninety* years, we shall find the time of the going forth of this command.

Most learned men agree that the death of Christ happened at the passover in the month *Nisan,* in the *four thousand seven hundred and forty-sixth* year of the Julian period. *Four hundred and ninety* years, reckoned back from the above year, leads us directly to the month *Nisan* in the *four thousand two hundred and fifty-sixth* year of the same period; the very month and year in which *Ezra* had his commission from *Artaxerxes Longimanus,* king of Persia, (see Ezra vii. 9,) to restore and rebuild Jerusalem. See the commission in *Ezra,* chap. vii. 11-26, and *Prideaux's* Connexions, vol. ii. p. 380.

The above *seventy* weeks, or *four hundred and ninety* years, are divided, in ver. 25, into *three distinct periods,* to each of which particular events are assigned. The three periods are,—

I. *Seven* weeks, that is, *forty-nine* years.

II. *Sixty-two* weeks, that is, *four hundred and thirty-four* years.

III. *One* week, that is, *seven* years.

To the *first* period of seven *weeks* the restoration and repairing of Jerusalem are referred; and so long were *Ezra* and *Nehemiah* employed in restoring the sacred constitutions and civil establishments of the Jews, for this work lasted *forty-nine* years after the commission was given by Artaxerxes.

From the above *seven* weeks the *second* period of *sixty-two* weeks, or *four hundred and thirty-four* years more, commences, at the end of which the prophecy says, *Messiah the Prince should come,* that is, *seven* weeks, or *forty-nine* years, should be allowed for the restoration of the Jewish state; from which time till the public entrance of the Messiah on the work of the ministry should be *sixty-two weeks,* or *four hundred and thirty-four years,* in all *four hundred and eighty-three* years.

From the coming of our Lord, the *third period* is to be dated, viz., "He shall confirm the covenant with many for one week," that is, *seven* years, ver. 27.

This confirmation of the covenant must take in the ministry of *John the Baptist* with that of our Lord, comprehending the term of *seven* years, during the whole of which he might be well said to confirm or ratify the new covenant with mankind. Our Lord says, "The law was until John;" but from his first public preaching *the kingdom of God,* or Gospel dispensation, commenced.

These *seven* years, added to the *four hundred and eighty-three,* complete the *four hundred and ninety* years, or *seventy* prophetic weeks; so that the whole of this prophecy, from the times and corresponding events, has been fulfilled to the very letter.

Some imagine that the *half* of the last *seven years* is to be referred to the total destruction of the Jews by *Titus,* when the daily sacrifice for ever ceased to be offered; and that the

A. M. cir. 3466
B. C. cir. 538
Ol. cir. LX. 3
Servii Tullii,
R. Roman.,
cir. annum 41

26 And after threescore and two weeks [r]shall Messiah be cut off, [s]but[t] not for himself: [u]and [v]the people of the prince that shall come [w]shall destroy the city [x]and the sanctuary; [y]and the end thereof *shall be* [z]with a flood, and unto the end of the war [a]desolations are determined.

[r]Isa. liii. 8; Mark ix. 12; Luke xxiv. 26, 46——[s]1 Pet. ii. 21; iii. 18——[t]Or, *and shall have nothing;* John xiv. 30 [u]Or, *and [the Jews] they shall be no more his people;* chap. xi. 17, or, and the *Prince's* [*Messiah's*, ver. 25] *future people*——[v]Matt. xxii. 7——[w]Luke xix. 44——[x]Matt. xxiv. 2——[y]Matt. xxiv. 6, 14——[z]Isa. viii. 7, 8; chap. xi. 10, 22; Nah. i. 8

27 And he shall confirm [b]the [c]covenant with [d]many for one week: and in the midst of the week he shall cause the sacrifice and the oblation to cease, [e]and for the overspreading of [f]abominations he shall make *it* desolate, [g]even until the consummation, and that determined shall be poured [h]upon the desolate.

A. M. cir. 3466
B. C. cir. 538
Ol. cir. LX. 3
Servii Tullii,
R. Roman.,
cir. annum 41

[a]Or, *it shall be cut off by desolations*——[b]Or, *a* [c]Isa. xlii. 6; lv. 3; Jer. xxxi. 31; Ezek. xvi. 60, 61, 62 [d]Isa. liii. 11; Matt. xxvi. 28; Rom. v. 15, 19; Heb. ix. 28 [e]Or, *and upon the battlements shall be the idols of the desolator*——[f]Matt. xxiv. 15; Mark xiii. 14; Luke xxi. 20 [g]See Isa. x. 22, 23; xxviii. 22; chap. xi. 36; Luke xxi. 24; Rom. xi. 26——[h]Or, *upon the desolator*

intermediate space of *thirty-seven* years, from our Lord's death till the destruction of the city, is passed over as being of no account in relation to the prophecy, and that it was on this account that the last seven years are *divided.* But Dean *Prideaux* thinks that the whole refers to our Lord's preaching connected with that of the Baptist. וחצי *vachatsi,* says he, signifies in the *half part* of the week; that is, in the latter three years and a half in which he exercised himself in the public ministry, he caused, by the sacrifice of himself, all other sacrifices and oblations to cease, which were instituted to signify his.

In the latter parts of ver. 26 and 27 we find the THIRD PART of this great prophecy, which refers to what should be done *after* the completion of these *seventy* weeks.

Verse 26. *And the people of the prince that shall come shall destroy the city and the sanctuary*] By the "prince" *Titus*, the son of *Vespasian*, is plainly intended; and "the people of that prince" are no other than the *Romans*, who, according to the prophecy, *destroyed the sanctuary*, הקדש *hakkodesh*, the *holy place* or temple, and, as a *flood*, swept away all, till the total destruction of that obstinate people finished the war.

Verse 27. *And for the overspreading of abominations he shall make* it *desolate*] This clause is remarkably obscure. כנף שקוצים משמם *kenaph shikkutsim meshomem*, "And upon the wing of abominations causing amazement." This is a literal translation of the place; but still there is no determinate sense. A *Hebrew* MS., written in the *thirteenth* century, has preserved a very remarkable reading here, which frees the place from all embarrassment. Instead of the above reading, this valuable MS. has ובהיכל יהיה שיקוץ *ubeheychal yihyey shikkuts;* that is, "And in the temple (of the Lord) there shall be abomination." This makes the passage plain, and is strictly conformable to the facts themselves, for the temple was profaned; and it agrees with the prediction of our Lord, who said that *the abomination that maketh desolate should stand in the holy place*, Matt. xxiv. 15, and quotes the words as *spoken* δια Δανιηλ του φροφητου, *by Daniel the prophet.* That the above reading gives the true sense, there can be little doubt, because it is countenanced by the most eminent ancient *versions.*

The *Vulgate* reads, Et erit in templo abominatio, "And in the temple there shall be abomination."

The *Septuagint*, Και επι το ἱερον βδελυγμα των ερημωσεων, "And upon the temple there shall be the abomination of desolation."

The *Arabic*, "And upon the sanctuary there shall be the abomination of ruin."

The above reading is celebrated by *J. D. Michaelis*, Epist. De Ebdom. Dan., p. 120: Vix insignius exemplum reperiri posse autumem, ostensuro in codicibus Hebræis latere lectiones dignissimas quæ eruantur, &c. "A more illustrious example can, I think, hardly be found, to show that various readings lie hid in Hebrew MSS., which are most worthy of being exhibited." Vid. *Bib. Heb.* KENNICOTT, *Dis. Gen.*

I have only to add that this mode of reckoning years and periods by *weeks* is not solely Jewish. *Macrobius*, in his book on Scipio's dream, has these remarkable words: Sed a sexta usque ad *septimam septimanam* fit quidem diminutio, sed occulta, et quæ detrimentum suum aperta defectione non prodat: ideo nonnullarum rerumpublicarum hic mos est, ut post *sextam* ad militiam nemo cogatur; Somn. Scip., lib. i. c. vi., *in fine.* "From the *sixth* to the *seventh week*, there is a diminution of strength; but it is hidden, and does not manifest itself by any outward defect. Hence it was the custom in some republics not to oblige a man to go to the wars after the *sixth week*, i. e., after *forty-two* years of age."

Having now gone through the whole of this important prophecy, and given that interpretation which the original seemed best to warrant, I shall next proceed to notice the principal various readings found in the Collections of *Kennicott* and *De Rossi*, with those from my own MSS., which the reader may collate with the words of the common printed text.

Verse 24. שבעים שבעים נחתך על עמך ועל עיר קדשך
לכלא הפשע ולחתם חטאות
ולכפר עון ולהביא צדק עלמים
ולחתם חזון ונביא ולמשח קדש קדשים:

Verse 25. ותדע ותשכל
מן מצא דבר להשיב ולבנות ירושלם
עד משיח נגיד שבעים שבעה
ושבעים ששים ושנים תשוב
ונבנתה רחוב וחרוץ ובצוק העתים:

Verse 26. ואחרי השבעים ששים ושנים
יכרת משיח ואין לו.
והעיר והקדש ישחית עם נגיד הבא
וקצו בשטף.
ועד קץ מלחמה נחרצת שממות:
Verse 27. והגביר ברית לרבים שבוע אחד.
והצי השבוע ישבית זבח ומנחה.
ועל כנף שקוצים משמם.
ועד כלה ונחרצה תתך על שומם:

Of the whole passage *Houbigant* gives the following translation:—

Verse 24. Seventy weeks are determined upon thy people, and the city of thy sanctuary:
That sin may be restrained, and transgressions have an end;
That iniquity may be expiated, and an everlasting righteousness brought in;
That visions and prophecies may be sealed up, and the Holy of holies anointed.
Verse 25. Know therefore and understand:—
From the edict which shall be promulgated, to return and rebuild Jerusalem, there shall be seven weeks.
Then it shall be fully rebuilt, with anxiety, in difficult times.
Thence, to the Prince Messiah, there shall be sixty-two weeks.
Verse 26. And after sixty-two weeks the Messiah shall be slain, and have no justice.
Afterwards he shall waste the city and the sanctuary, by the prince that is to come.
And his end shall be in straits; and to the end of the war desolation is appointed.
Verse 27. And for one week he shall confirm a covenant with many;
And in the middle of the week he shall abrogate sacrifice and offering;
And in the temple there shall be the abomination of desolation,
Until the ruin which is decreed rush on after the desolation.

In this translation there are some peculiarities.

Instead of "the street shall be built again, and the wall," ver. 25, he translates רחוב וחרוץ (with the prefix ב *beth* instead of ו *vau* in the latter word,) "it shall be fully (the city and all its walls) rebuilt with anxiety."

Instead of ואין לו "but not for himself," he translates, "Nor shall justice be done him;" supposing that דין "justice" was originally in the verse.

Instead of "the people of the prince," ver. 26, he translates "by the prince," using עם *im* as a preposition, instead of עם *am*, "the people."

Instead of "and for the overspreading," he translates ועל כנף "in the temple;" following the Septuagint, *και επι το ἱερον*. This rendering is at least as good as ours: but see the *marginal* readings here, and the preceding notes.

Houbigant contends also that the arrangement of the several members in these passages is confused. He proposes one alteration, which is important, *viz.*, From the promulgation of the decree to rebuild Jerusalem shall be seven weeks; and unto Messiah the prince, sixty-two weeks. All these alterations he vindicates in his notes at the end of this chapter. In the text I have inserted Houbigant's dots, or marks of distinction between the different members of the verses.

Various Readings

Verse 24. שבעים, שבועים *weeks* written *full*, so to prevent mistakes, in *thirteen* of *Kennicott's*, *four* of *De Rossi's*, and *one* ancient of my own.

שבעים *Seventy-one* of *Kennicott's*, and *one* of *De Rossi's*, have שבועים "weeks, weeks, weeks;" that is, "many weeks:" but this is a mere mistake.

לכלא "to restrain." לכלה "to consume," is the reading of *twenty-nine* of *Kennicott's*, *thirteen* of *De Rossi's*, and *one* ancient of my own.

ולחתם "and to seal up." *Forty-three* of *Kennicott's twelve* of *De Rossi's*, and *one* of my own, have ולחתם "to make an end." One reads ולחתום, more *full.*

חטאות "sins." חטאת "sin," in the singular, is the reading of *twenty-six* of *De Rossi's;* and so, in the second instance where this word occurs, *two* of my MSS.

עלמים "everlasting." *Two* of my oldest MSS. read שלמים, and so in the next instance.

ונביא "and the prophet." The conjunction is omitted by *two* of *Kennicott's.*

ותשכל "and understand." *One* of my MSS. has ותשכיל.

Verse 25. מן מוצא "from the publication." One MS. of *De Rossi's* omits the מן "from," and instead of either, *one* of my oldest MSS. has למוצא "to the publication."

משיח "Messiah." *Nine* MSS. read the word with the point *sheva*, which makes it read, in regimine, "the anointed of the prince." But this is evidently the effect of carelessness, or rather design.

שבעה "seven." *Two* MSS. add the conjunction ו *vau*, "and."

ולבנות "and to build." One of mine omits the conjunction.

שבעים שבעה "seven weeks." *One* of *Kennicott's* has שבעים שנה "seventy years."

ושבעים "and weeks." *One* of *Kennicott's* has ושבוע "and a week."

ששים "sixty." A few add the conjunction ו *vau*, "*and* sixty;" and another has ששה "six;" and another שבעים "seventy." Wherever this word signifies *weeks*, *two* of my oldest MSS. write it *full* שבועים. In *one* of my MSS. השבועים ששים are omitted in the text, but added by a later hand in the margin.

וחרוץ "and the ditch." One MS. has העיר "the city." And for רחב "street," one of mine has רחוב of the same meaning, but more *full*.

ובצוק "and in straits," or *anxiety*. One MS. without *and*, as the *Vulgate* and *Septuagint*.

Verse 26. והקדש "and the holy place or sanctuary." But *two* of my most ancient MSS., and *four* of *Kennicott's*, leave out the ו *vau*, and read והעיר הקדש "and the holy city," or "city of holiness," instead of "the city and sanctuary." In one MS. ו is omitted in והעיר.

וקצו "and its end." *One* MS. omits the conjunction ו *and;* one omits the following קץ "the end;" reading thus: "and unto the war." But a more singular reading is that of one of my own MSS. written about A. D. 1136, which has וקיצו "and its summer."

ששים "sixty." But one of *Kennicott's* MSS.

has ששים שבעים "sixty weeks;" and another adds the conjunction, AND *sixty*.

ישחית "shall destroy." But one of *De Rossi's* has ישחת "shall be destroyed."

עם "the people." עם *im*, "with," is the reading of one of *Kennicott's*, with the *Septuagint*, *Theodotion*, *Syriac*, *Hexapla*, *Vulgate*, and *Arabic*.

בשטף "with a flood." *One* MS. has השטף "the flood."

ועל בנף "and upon the wing." Nearly *twenty* MSS. have ועד "and unto," &c.

Verse 27. ועד קץ "and unto the end." עד־ "to the end;" and one has ועל "and upon."

קץ "the end." One has עת "the time;" and another both, עת קץ "the time of the end."

ועל כנף שקוצים "and upon the wing (or battlement) abomination." Instead of this, one of the Parisian MSS. numbered *three hundred and thirteen* in *Kennicott's*, has ובהיכל יהיה שיקוץ "and in the temple there shall be abomination." See the preceding notes. This is a similar reading to *Theodotion*, the *Vulgate*, *Septuagint*, *Syriac Hexapla*, and the *Arabic;* and is countenanced by our Lord, Matt. xxiv. 15. After all that has been said on this reading, (which may be genuine, but is less liable to suspicion, as the MS. appears to be the work of some *Christian;* it is written from the *left to the right hand*, and is accompanied by the *Vulgate Latin*,) if this be an attempt to accommodate the *Hebrew* to the *Vulgate*, it should be stated that they who have examined this MS. closely, have asserted that there is no evidence that the writer has endeavoured to conform the Hebrew to the Latin text, unless this be accounted such. The ancient versions give this reading great credit.

שקוצים "abominations." One of mine has less fully שקצים

משמם "desolation." *One* of mine has more fully משומם.

ועד "and unto," is wanting in one of mine; ועל "and upon" is the reading in *one* other.

על שומם "until the desolation." שומם "the desolation." *One* of mine has שמם without the ו *vau*. על is wanting; but is added in the margin, by a later hand, in another of these ancient MSS.

I have thus set down almost all the variations mentioned by *Kennicott* and *De Rossi*, and those furnished by *three* ancient MSS. of my own, that the learned reader may avail himself of every help to examine thoroughly this important prophecy. Upwards of *thirty* various readings in the compass of *four* verses, and several of them of great moment.

CHAPTER X

This and the two following chapters give an account of Daniel's last vision, wherein the succession of the Persian and Grecian monarchies is described, together with the wars that should take place between Syria and Egypt under the latter monarchy. The last part of the vision (*from* chap. xi. 36) *seems to relate chiefly to the persecutions of the Church in the times of Antichrist, till it be purified from all its pollutions; after which will follow that glorious kingdom of the saints spoken of in the* seventh *and* eighth *chapters. This chapter begins with an account of Daniel's fasting and humiliation,* 1–3. *Then we have a description of the Divine person who appeared to the prophet, not unlike him who appeared to the apostle in the isle of Patmos,* 4–21. *See* Rev. i. 10–16.

A. M. 3470 IN the third year of Cyrus king
B. C. 534 of Persia a thing was re-
Ol. LXI. 3 vealed unto Daniel, [a]whose name
Anno Tarquinii Superbi, was called Belteshazzar; [b]and
R. Roman., 1 the thing *was* true, [c]but the time appointed
was [d]long; and [e]he understood the thing, and
had understanding of the vision.
2 In those days I Daniel was mourning
three [f]full weeks.
3 I ate no [g]pleasant bread, A. M. 3470
neither came flesh nor wine in B. C. 534
my mouth, [h]neither did I anoint Ol. LXI. 3
myself at all, till three whole Anno Tarquinii Superbi,
weeks were fulfilled. R. Roman., 1
4 And in the four and twentieth day of the
first month, as I was by the side of the great
river, which *is* [i]Hiddekel;
5 Then [k]I lifted up mine eyes, and looked,

[a]Chap. i. 7——[b]Chap. viii. 26; Rev. xix. 9——[c]Ver. 14——[d]Heb. *great*——[e]Chap. i. 17; viii. 16

[f]Heb. *weeks of days*——[g]Heb. *bread of desires*——[h]Matt. vi. 17——[i]Gen. ii. 14——[k]Josh. v. 13

NOTES ON CHAP. X

Verse 1. *In the third year of Cyrus*] Which answers to the *first* year of Darius the Mede.

The time appointed was *long*] וצבא גדול *vetsaba gadol*, but the *warfare long;* there will be many contentions and wars before these things can be accomplished.

Verse 2. *I—was mourning three full weeks.*] The weeks are most probably dated from the time of the termination of the last vision. *Calmet* proves this by several reasons.

Verse 3. *I ate no pleasant bread*] This fast was rather a general *abstinence;* living all the while on *coarse* and *unsavoury food;* drinking nothing but *water;* not using the *bath*, and most probably wearing *haircloth* next the skin, during the whole of the time.

Verse 4. *By the side of—Hiddekel*] The same as the *Tigris*, the great river of Assyria;

A. M. 3470
B. C. 534
Ol. LXI. 3
Anno Tarquinii Superbi, R. Roman., 1

and [l]behold [m]a certain man clothed in linen, whose loins *were* [n]girded with [o]fine gold of Uphaz:

6 His body also *was* [p]like the beryl, and his face [q]as the appearance of lightning, [r]and his eyes as lamps of fire, and his arms [s]and his feet like in colour to polished brass, [t]and the voice of his words like the voice of a multitude.

7 And I Daniel [u]alone saw the vision: for the men that were with me saw not the vision; but a great quaking fell upon them, so that they fled to hide themselves.

8 Therefore I was left alone, and saw this great vision, [v]and there remained no strength in me: for my [w]comeliness [x]was turned in me into corruption, and I retained no strength.

9 Yet heard I the voice of his words: [y]and when I heard the voice of his words, then was I in a deep sleep on my face, and my face toward the ground.

10 [z]And, behold, a hand touched me, which [a]set me upon my knees and *upon* the palms of my hands.

11 And he said unto me, O Daniel, [b]a [c]man greatly beloved, understand the words that I speak unto thee, and [d]stand upright: for unto thee am I now sent. And when he had spoken this word unto me, I stood trembling.

12 Then said he unto me, [e]Fear not, Daniel: for from the first day that thou didst set thine heart to understand, and to chasten thyself before thy God, [f]thy words were heard, and I am come for thy words.

13 [g]But the prince of the kingdom of Persia withstood me one and twenty days: but, lo, [h]Michael, [i]one of the chief princes, came to help me; and I remained there with the kings of Persia.

14 Now I am come to make thee understand what shall befall thy people [k]in the latter days: [l]for yet the vision *is* for *many* days.

15 And when he had spoken such words unto me, [m]I set my face toward the ground, and I became dumb.

16 And, behold, [n]*one* like the similitude of the sons of men [o]touched my lips: then I

[l]Ch. xii. 6, 7——[m]Heb. *one man*——[n]Rev. i. 13, 14, 15; xv. 6——[o]Jer. x 9——[p]Ezek. i. 16——[q]Ezek. i. 14——[r]Rev. i. 14; xix. 12——[s]Ezek. i. 7; Rev. i. 15——[t]Ezek. i. 24; Rev. i. 15——[u]2 Kings vi. 17; Acts ix. 7——[v]Ch. viii. 27——[w]Or, *vigour*——[x]Ch. vii. 28——[y]Ch. viii. 18——[z]Jer. i. 9; ch. ix. 21; Rev. i. 17——[a]Heb. *moved*

[b]Ch. ix. 23——[c]Heb. *a man of desires*——[d]Heb. *stand upon thy standing*——[e]Rev. i. 17——[f]Ch. ix. 3, 4, 22, 23; Acts x. 4——[g]Ver. 20——[h]Ver. 21; ch. xii. 1; Jude 9; Rev. xii. 7——[i]Or, *the first*——[k]Gen. xlix. 1; ch. ii. 28——[l]Ch. viii. 26; ver. 1; Hab. ii. 3——[m]Ver. 9; ch. viii. 18——[n]Ch. viii. 15——[o]Ver. 10; Jer. i. 9

as the *Euphrates* of Syria, and the *Nile* of Egypt.

Verse 5. *Clothed in linen*] The description is intended to point out the *splendour* of the garments.

Gold of Uphaz] The same as *Ophir*.

Verse 6. *His body also* was *like the beryl*] The description of this person is very similar to that of our Lord in Rev. i. 13-15.

Verse 7. *The men that were with me saw not the vision*] An exactly parallel case with what occurred at the conversion of Saul of Tarsus, Acts ix. 7. There was a Divine influence which they all felt, but only Daniel saw the corporeal appearance.

Verse 9. *Was I in a deep sleep*] I fell into a swoon.

Verse 10. *A hand touched me*] Nothing was *apparent* or *palpable* but a *hand*. A hand had written Belshazzar's fate upon the wall; and the *hand* is frequently mentioned when the *power* or *majesty* of *God* is intended. Perhaps by *hand* God himself may be meant. It is remarkable that in a very ancient MS. of the Septuagint, more than a *thousand* years old, now in the imperial library of Vienna, adorned with paintings which have been engraved for the catalogue of Lambechius, and transferred to that of Nesselius, all the appearances of God are represented by a *hand in the clouds*.

Verse 12. *I am come for thy words*] On account of thy prayers I am sent to comfort and instruct thee.

Verse 13. *But the prince of the kingdom of Persia withstood me*] I think it would go far to make a *legend* or a precarious *tale* of this important place to endeavour to maintain that either a *good* or *evil* ANGEL is intended here. *Cyrus* alone was the *prince of Persia*, and God had destined him to be the deliverer of his people; but there were some matters, of which we are not informed, that caused him to hesitate for some time. Fearing, probably, the greatness of the work, and not being fully satisfied of his ability to execute it, he therefore for a time *resisted the secret inspirations* which God had sent him. The opposition might be in reference to the building of the temple.

But lo, Michael] Gabriel, who speaks, did not leave Cyrus till Michael came to take his place. Michael, *he who is like God*, sometimes appears to signify the *Messiah*, at other times the *highest* or *chief archangel*. Indeed there is no archangel mentioned in the whole Scripture but this *one*. See Jude 9; Rev. xii. 7.

Verse 14. *For yet the vision* is *for* many *days*.] There are many things which remain yet to be revealed, and the time of their accomplishment is very distant.

Verse 15. *I set my face toward the ground*] He was standing upright, ver. 11, and he now

A. M. 3470
B. C. 534
Olymp. LXI. 3
Anno Tarquinii Superbi,
R. Roman., 1

opened my mouth, and spake, and said unto him that stood before me, O my lord, by the vision [p]my sorrows are turned upon me, and I have retained no strength.

17 For how can [q]the servant of this my lord talk with this my lord? for as for me, straightway there remained no strength in me, neither is there breath left in me.

18 Then there came again and touched me *one* like the appearance of a man, and he strengthened me,

19 [r]And said, O man greatly beloved, [s]fear not: peace *be* unto thee, be strong, yea, be strong. And when he had spoken unto me, I was strengthened, and said, Let my lord speak, for thou hast strengthened me.

A. M. 3470
B. C. 534
Olymp. LXI. 3
Anno Tarquinii Superbi,
R. Roman., 1

20 Then said he, Knowest thou wherefore I come unto thee? and now will I return to fight [t]with the king of Persia: and when I am gone forth, lo, the prince of Grecia shall come.

21 But I will show thee that which is noted in the scripture of truth: and *there is* none that [u]holdeth with me in these things, [v]but Michael your prince.

[p]Ver. 8——[q]Or, *this servant of my lord*——[r]Ver. 11——[s]Judg. vi. 23

[t]Ver. 13——[u]Heb. *strengtheneth himself*——[v]Ver. 13; Jude 9; Rev. xii. 7

bent his body in reverence, and looked down upon the ground.

And became dumb.] Found himself unable to speak.

Verse 16. *Like the similitude of the sons of men*] I think Gabriel is here meant, who appeared to Daniel in a *human form;* and so in ver. 18, and see also chap. ix. 21.

Touched my lips] Before this he was unable to speak.

By the vision] The vision that I have already had, and of which I have not a proper knowledge has greatly afflicted me, because I see it intimates grievous calamities to my people. See chap. ix. 26.

Verse 17. *Neither is there breath*] He could not breathe freely; he was almost suffocated with sorrow.

Verse 19. *O man, greatly beloved*] איש חמדות *ish chamudoth,* man of delights; the most amiable of men.

Let my lord speak] I am now so strengthened and encouraged, that I shall be able to bear any revelation that thou mayest make.

Verse 20. *Knowest thou wherefore I come*] So high art thou in the favour of God, that he hath sent me unto thee to give thee farther satisfaction; though I was elsewhere employed upon a most important mission, and I must speedily return to accomplish it, *viz.:*—

To fight with the king of Persia] To remove all the scruples of Cyrus, and to excite him to do all that God designs him to do for the restoration of my people, and the rebuilding of the city and temple of Jerusalem. Nothing less than a supernatural agency in the mind of Cyrus can account for his decree in favour of the Jews. He had no natural, no political inclination to it; and his reluctance to obey the heavenly motions is here represented as a *fight between him and the angel.*

The prince of Grecia shall come.] I believe this refers to Alexander the Great, who was to destroy the *Persian* empire. See the *second* and *third* verses of the following chapter.

Verse 21. *Noted in the scripture of truth*] Perhaps this refers to what he had already *written* down. See the preceding visions, which Daniel did not fully understand, though a general impression from them had filled his heart with sorrow.

Michael your prince.] The archangel mentioned before, ver. 13, and who has been always supposed to be appointed by God as the guardian of the Jewish nation. It appears that God chose to make use of the ministry of angels in this work; that angels, as they could be only in *one place* at *one time,* could not produce influence where *they were* not; and that, to carry on the operation on the mind of the Persian king, it was necessary that either *Gabriel* or *Michael* should be *present* with him, and when one went on another commission another took his place; see ver. 13. But we know so little of the invisible world that we cannot safely *affirm* any thing *positively.*

CHAPTER XI

This chapter gives a more particular explanation of those events which were predicted in the eighth *chapter. The prophet had foretold the partition of Alexander's kingdom into four parts. Two of these, in which were included Egypt and Syria, the one to the* north, *the other to the* south, *in respect of Judea, appear to take up the chief attention of the prophet, as his people were particularly concerned in their fate; these being the countries in which by far the greatest number of the Jews were, and still are, dispersed. Of these countries he treats (according to the views of the most enlightened expositors) down to the conquest of Macedon, A. M.* 3836, *B. C.* 168, *when he begins to speak of the Romans,* 1–30; *and then of the Church under that power,* 31–35. *This leads him to speak of Antichrist, who was to spring up in that quarter,* 36–39; *and of those powers which* at the TIME of the end, *or the latter days of the Roman monarchy, (as this term is generally understood,) were to* push at *it, and overthrow many countries,* 40–43. *By the* king of the SOUTH, *in the fortieth verse, the dominion of the Saracens, or Arabs, is supposed to be intended, which was an exceeding great plague to the Roman empire in the east, and also to several papistical countries, for the space of* one hundred and fifty *years,* i. e.

from A. D. 612, *when Mohammed and his followers first began their depredations, to A. D.* 762, *when Bagdad was built, and made the capital of the caliphs of the house of Abbas; from which epoch the Saracens became a more settled people. By the* king of the NORTH *in the same verse the prophet is supposed by some to design that great scourge of eastern Christendom, the Ottoman or Othman empire, by which, after about a* hundred and fifty *years of almost uninterrupted hostilities, the Roman empire in the east was completely overturned, A. D.* 1453. *The chapter concludes with a prediction of the final overthrow of this northern power, and of the manner in which this great event shall be accomplished,* 44, 45. *But it should be observed that, notwithstanding the very learned observations of Bishop Newton and others upon this chapter, their scheme of interpretation presents very great and insurmountable difficulties; among which the very lengthy detail of events in the Syrian and Egyptian histories, comprising a period of less than* two hundred *years, and the rather uncouth transition to the incomparably greater transactions in Antichristian times, and of much longer duration, which are passed over with unaccountable brevity, are not the least. On all these subjects, however, the reader must judge for himself. See the notes.*

A. M. 3470 B. C. 534 Olymp. LXI. 3 Anno Tarquinii Superbi, R. Roman., 1

ALSO I, [a]in the first year of [b]Darius the Mede, *even* I, stood to confirm and to strengthen him.

2 And now will I show thee the truth. Behold, there shall stand up yet three kings in Persia; and the fourth shall be far richer than *they* all: and by his strength through his riches he shall stir up all against the realm of Grecia.

3 And [c]a mighty king shall stand up, that shall rule with great dominion, and [d]do according to his will.

4 And when he shall stand up, [e]his kingdom shall be broken, and shall be divided toward the four winds of heaven, and not to his posterity, [f]nor according to his dominion which he ruled: for his kingdom shall be plucked up, even for others beside those.

[a]Chap. ix. 1——[b]Chap. v. 31——[c]Chap. vii. 6; viii. 5 [d]Ch. viii. 4; ver. 16, 36——[e]Ch. viii. 8——[f]Ch. viii. 22

NOTES ON CHAP. XI

Verse 1. *In the first year of Darius the Mede*] This is a continuation of the preceding discourse. Bp. *Newton*, who is ever judicious and instructing, remarks: It is the usual method of the Holy Spirit to make the latter prophecies explanatory of the former; and thus revelation "is a shining light, that shineth more and more unto the perfect day." The four great empires shown to Nebuchadnezzar, under the symbol of a *great image*, were again more particularly represented to Daniel under the forms of *four great wild beasts*. In like manner, the memorable events that were revealed to Daniel in the vision of the *ram* and *he-goat*, are here more clearly revealed in this last vision by an angel; so that this latter prophecy may not improperly be said to be a comment on the former. It comprehends many signal events. The types, figures, and symbols of the things are not exhibited in this, as in most other visions, and then expounded by the angel; but the angel *relates* the whole: and, not by way of *vision*, but by *narration*, informs Daniel of that which is *noted in the Scripture of truth*, chap. x. 21.

Verse 2. *There shall stand up yet three kings*] Gabriel had already spoken of *Cyrus*, who was now reigning; and after him *three* others should arise. These were, 1. *Cambyses*, the son of Cyrus. 2. *Smerdis*, the Magian, who was an impostor, who pretended to be another son of Cyrus. And, 3. *Darius*, the son of *Hystaspes*, who married *Mandane*, the daughter of Cyrus.

Cambyses reigned *seven* years and *five* months; *Smerdis* reigned only *seven* months; and *Darius Hystaspes* reigned *thirty-six* years.

The fourth shall be far richer than they *all*] This was *Xerxes*, the son of Darius, of whom *Justin* says: "He had so great an abundance of riches in his kingdom, that although rivers were dried up by his numerous armies, yet his wealth remained unexhausted."

He shall stir up all against the realm of Grecia.] His military strength was such, that *Herodotus*, who lived in that time, informs us that his army amounted to *five* millions, *two hundred and eighty-three* thousand, *two hundred and twenty* men. Besides these, the Carthaginians furnished him with an army of *three hundred thousand* men, and a fleet of *two hundred* ships. He led an army against the Greeks of *eight hundred thousand* men, and *twelve hundred and seven* ships, with *three banks of rowers* each. As he marched along, he obliged all the people of the countries through which he passed to join him.

Verse 3. *A mighty king shall stand up*] This was *Alexander the Great*. It is not said that this mighty king shall stand up against *Xerxes*, for he was not born till *one hundred* years after that monarch; but simply that he should *stand up*, i. e., that he should reign in Greece.

Verse 4. *His kingdom shall be broken*] Shall, after his death, be *divided* among his *four* chief generals, as we have seen before. See chap. viii. 22.

And not to his posterity] The *family of Alexander* had a most tragical end: 1. His wife *Statira* was murdered soon after his death by his other wife *Roxana*. 2. His brother *Aridæus*, who succeeded him, was killed, together with his wife *Euridice*, by command of *Olympias*, Alexander's mother, after he had been king about six years and some months. 3. *Olympias* herself was killed by the soldiers in revenge. 4. *Alexander Ægus*, his son, together with *his* mother *Roxana*, was slain by order of Cassander. 5. Two years after, his other son *Hercules*, with his mother *Barsine*, was privately murdered by Polysperchon; so that in

A. M. 3470
B. C. 534
Olymp. LXI. 3
Anno Tarquinii
Superbi,
R. Roman., 1

5 And the king of the south
shall be strong, and *one* of his
princes; and he shall be strong
above him, and have dominion;
his dominion *shall be* a great dominion.
6 And in the end of years they [g]shall join
themselves together: for the king's daughter
of the south shall come to the king of the
north to make [h]an agremeent: but she shall
not retain the power of the arm; neither shall
he stand, nor his arm: but she shall be given
up, and they that brought her, and [i]he that
begat her, and he that strengthened her in
these times.
7 But out of a branch of her roots shall *one*
stand up [k]in his estate, which
shall come with an army, and
shall enter into the fortress of
the king of the north, and shall
deal against them, and shall prevail:

A. M. 3470
B. C. 534
Olymp. LXI. 3
Anno Tarquinii
Superbi,
R. Roman., 1

8 And shall also carry captives into Egypt
their gods, with their princes, *and* with [l]their
precious vessels of silver and of gold; and
he shall continue *more* years than the king of
the north.
9 So the king of the south shall come into
his kingdom, and shall return into his own
land.
10 But his sons [m]shall be stirred up, and
shall assemble a multitude of great forces:

[g]Heb. *shall associate themselves*——[h]Heb. *rights*——[i]Or, *whom she brought forth*

[k]Or, *in his place*, or *office;* ver. 20——[l]Heb. *vessels of their desire*——[m]Or, *shall war*

fifteen years after his death not one of his family or posterity remained alive!

"Blood calls for blood." He (Alexander) was the great butcher of men. He was either poisoned, or killed himself by immoderate drinking, when he was only *thirty-two* years and *eight* months old: and a retributive Providence destroyed all his posterity, so that neither *root* nor *branch* of them was left on the face of the earth. Thus ended Alexander, the great butcher; and thus ended his family and posterity.

Verse 5. *The king of the south*] This was *Ptolemy Lagus*, one of his generals, who had the government of Egypt, Libra, &c., which are on the south of Judea. He was strong, for he had added Cyprus, Phœnicia, Caria, &c., to his kingdom of Egypt.

And one *of his princes—shall be strong above him*] This was *Seleucus Nicator*, who possessed Syria, Babylon, Media, and the neighbouring countries. This was *the king of the north*, for his dominions lay *north* of Judea.

Verse 6. *In the end of years*] Several historical circumstances are here passed by.

The king's daughter of the south] *Berenice*, daughter of Ptolemy Philadelphus, king of Egypt, was married to *Antiochus Theos*, king of Syria. These two sovereigns had a bloody war for some years; and they agreed to terminate it by the above marriage, on condition that Antiochus would put away his wife *Laodice* and her children, which he did; and *Berenice* having brought an immense fortune to her husband, all things appeared to go on well for a time.

But she shall not retain the power of the arm] זרע *zaro, her posterity*, shall not reign in that kingdom.

But she shall be given up] Antiochus recalled his former wife Laodice and her children; and she, fearing that he might recall Berenice, caused him to be poisoned and her to be murdered, and set her son Callinicus upon the throne.

And they that brought her] Her Egyptian women, striving to defend their mistress, were many of them killed.

And he that begat her] Or, as the margin, "he whom she brought forth;" the son being murdered, as well as the mother, by order of Laodice.

And he that strengthened her] Probably her *father* Ptolemy, who was excessively fond of her, and who had died a few years before.

Verse 7. *But out of a branch of her roots*] A branch from the same root from which she sprang. This was *Ptolemy Euergetes*, her brother, who, to avenge his sister's death, marched with a great army against *Seleucus Callinicus*, took some of his best places, indeed all Asia, from Mount Taurus to India, and returned to Egypt with an immense booty, *forty thousand* talents of silver, precious vessels, and images of their gods *two thousand five hundred*, without Callinicus daring to offer him battle. I can but touch on these historic facts, for fear of extending these notes to an immoderate length.

Verse 8. *He shall continue* more *years*] *Seleucus Callinicus* died (an exile) by a fall from his horse; and *Ptolemy Euergetes* survived him four or five years.—Bp. *Newton.*

Verse 9. *So the king of the south*] Ptolemy Euergetes—

Shall come into his *kingdom*] That of Seleucus Callinicus.

And shall return] Having heard that a sedition had taken place in Egypt, Ptolemy Euergetes was obliged to return speedily in order to repress it; else he had wholly destroyed the kingdom of Callinicus.

Verse 10. *But his sons shall be stirred up*] That is, the sons of *Callinicus*, who were *Seleucus Ceraunus* and *Antiochus*, afterwards called *the Great.*

Shall assemble a multitude] Seleucus Ceraunus did assemble a multitude of forces in order to recover his father's dominions; but, not having money to pay them, they became mutinous, and he was poisoned by two of his own generals. His brother Antiochus was then proclaimed king; so that *one only* of the sons did *certainly come, and overflow, and pass through;* he retook Seleucia, and regained Syria. He *then returned*, and overcame Nicolaus the Egyptian general; and seemed disposed to invade Egypt, as he came even to *his fortress*, to the frontiers of Egypt.

A. M. 3470 B. C. 534 Olymp. LXI. 3 Anno Tarquinii Superbi, R. Roman., 1

and *one* shall certainly come, [n]and overflow, and pass through: [o]then shall he return, and be stirred up, [p]*even* to his fortress.

11 And the king of the south shall be moved with choler, and shall come forth and fight with him, *even* with the king of the north: and he shall set forth a great multitude; but the multitude shall be given into his hand.

12 *And* when he hath taken away the multitude, his heart shall be lifted up; and he shall cast down *many* ten thousands: but he shall not be strengthened *by it.*

13 For the king of the north shall return, and shall set forth a multitude greater than the former, and shall certainly come [q]after certain years with a great army and with much riches.

14 And in those times there shall many stand up against the king of the south: also [r]the robbers of thy people shall exalt themselves to establish the vision; but they shall fall.

A. M. 3470 B. C. 534 Olymp. LXI. 3 Anno Tarquinii Superbi, R. Roman., 1

15 So the king of the north shall come, and cast up a mount, and take [s]the most fenced cities: and the arms of the south shall not withstand, neither [t]his chosen people, neither *shall there be any* strength to withstand.

16 But he that cometh against him [u]shall do according to his own will, and [v]none shall stand before him: and he shall stand in the [w]glorious [x]land, which by his hand shall be consumed.

17 He shall also [y]set his face to enter with the strength of his whole kingdom, and [z]up-

[n]Isa. viii. 8; chap. ix. 26——[o]Or, *then shall he be stirred up again*——[p]Ver. 7——[q]Heb. *at the end of times, even years;* chap. iv. 16; xii. 7——[r]Heb. *the children of robbers*——[s]Heb. *the city of munitions*

[t]Heb. *the people of his choices*——[u]Ch. viii. 4, 7: ver. 3, 36——[v]Josh. i. 5——[w]Or, *goodly land;* ch. viii .9; ver. 41, 45——[x]Heb. *the land of ornament*——[y]2 Chron. xx. 3 [z]Or, *much uprightness,* or *equal conditions*

Verse 11. *The king of the south*] Ptolemy Philopater, who succeeded his father *Euergetes*.

Shall come forth and fight with him] He did come forth to Raphia, where he was met by Antiochus, when a terrible battle was fought between these two kings.

And he (Antiochus, the king of the north) *shall set forth a great multitude*] Amounting to *sixty-two thousand* foot, *six thousand* horse, and *one hundred and two* elephants; but yet the multitude was *given into his hand*, the hand of the *king of the south;* for Ptolemy gained a complete victory. Raphia, and other neighbouring towns, declared for the victor; and Antiochus was obliged to retreat with his scattered army to Antioch, from which he sent to solicit a peace. See 3 Macc. i. 1-6, and *Polybius*, lib. v.

Verse 12. *His heart shall be lifted up*] Had Ptolemy improved his victory, he might have dispossessed Antiochus of his whole empire; but giving way to *pride*, and a criminally *sensual life*, he made peace on dishonourable terms; and though he had gained a great victory, yet his kingdom *was not strengthened by it*, for his subjects were displeased, and rebelled against him, or at least became considerably disaffected.

Verse 13. *The king of the north shall return —after certain years*] In about *fourteen* years Antiochus did return, Philopater being dead, and his son Ptolemy Epiphanes being then a minor. He brought a much larger army and more riches; these he had collected in a late eastern expedition.

Verse 14. *Many stand up against the king of the south*] Antiochus, and Philip king of Macedon, united together to overrun Egypt.

Also the robbers of thy people] The *Jews*, who revolted from their religion, and joined Ptolemy, under *Scopas*,—

Shall exalt themselves to establish the vision] That is, to build a temple like that of Jerusalem, in Egypt, hoping thereby to fulfil a prediction of Isaiah, chap. xxx. 18-25, which seemed to intimate that the Jews and the Egyptians should be one people. They now revolted from Ptolemy, and joined Antiochus; and this was the means of contributing greatly to the accomplishment of prophecies that foretold the calamities that should fall upon the Jews.

But they shall fall.] For Scopas came with a great army from Ptolemy; and, while Antiochus was engaged in other parts, reduced *Cœlesyria* and *Palestine*, subdued the Jews, placed guards on the coasts of Jerusalem, and returned with great spoils to Egypt.

Verse 15. *So the king of the north*] Antiochus came to recover Judea. Scopas was sent by Ptolemy to oppose him; but he was defeated near the fountains of Jordan, and was obliged to take refuge in *Sidon* with *ten thousand* men. Antiochus pursued and besieged him; and he was obliged by famine to surrender at discretion, and their lives only were spared. Antiochus afterwards besieged *several of the fenced cities*, and took them; in short, carried all before him; so that the king of the south, Ptolemy, and *his chosen people*, his ablest generals, were not able to oppose him.

Verse 16. *He shall stand in the glorious land*] Judea. For he reduced *Palestine;* and the Jews supplied him with provisions, and assisted him to reduce the garrison that Scopas had left in the citadel of Jerusalem.

Which by his hand shall be consumed] Or, *which shall be perfected in his hand.* For Antiochus showed the Jews great favour: he brought back those that were dispersed, and reestablished them in the land; freed the priests and Levites from all tribute, &c.

Verse 17. *He shall also set his face to enter*]

A. M. 3470
B. C. 534
Olymp. LXI. 3
Anno Tarquinii
Superbi,
R. Roman., 1

right ones with him; thus shall
he do: and he shall give him
the daughter of women, [a]cor-
rupting her: but she shall not
stand *on his side,* [b]neither be for him.
18 After this shall he turn his face unto the
isles, and shall take many: but a prince [c]for
his own behalf shall cause [d]the reproach offered by him to cease; without his own reproach he shall cause *it* to turn upon him.
19 Then he shall turn his face toward the
fort of his own land: but he
shall stumble and fall, [e]and not
be found.
20 Then shall stand up [f]in his
estate [g]a raiser of taxes *in* the glory of the
kingdom: but within few days he shall be
destroyed, neither in [h]anger, nor in battle.
21 And [i]in his estate [k]shall stand up a vile
person, to whom they shall not give the honour
of the kingdom: but he shall come in peaceably, and obtain the kingdom by flatteries.

[a]Heb. *to corrupt*——[b]Chap. ix. 26——[c]Heb. *for him*
[d]Heb. *his reproach*——[e]Job xx. 8; Psa. xxxvii. 36; Ezek. xxvi. 21——[f]Or, *in his place;* ver. 7

[g]Heb. *one that causeth an exactor to pass over*——[h]Heb. *angers*——[i]Or, *in his place*——[k]Chap. vii. 8; viii. 9 23, 25

Antiochus purposed to have marched his army into Egypt; but he thought it best to proceed by *fraudulence;* and therefore proposed a treaty of marriage between him and his daughter Cleopatra, called here *the daughter of women,* because of her great beauty and accomplishments. And this he appeared to do, having "upright ones with him." Or, as the *Septuagint* have it και ευθεια παντα μετ' αυτου ποιησει, "and he will make all things straight with him;" that is, he acted as if he were influenced by nothing but the most *upright views.* But he intended his daughter to be a snare to Ptolemy, and therefore purposed to *corrupt her* that she might betray her husband.

But she shall not stand on his side] On the contrary, her husband's interests became more dear to her than her father's; and by her means Ptolemy was put upon his guard against the intentions of Antiochus.

Verse 18. *Shall he turn his face unto the isles*] Antiochus had fitted out a great fleet of *one hundred* large ships and *two hundred* smaller, and with this fleet subdued most of the *maritime places* on the *coast* of the Mediterranean, and took many of the isles, *Rhodes, Samos, Eubœa, Colophon,* and others.

But a prince for his own behalf] Or, *a captain.* The consul *Acilius Glabrio caused the reproach to cease;* beat and routed his army at the straits of Thermopylæ, and expelled him from Greece. So he obliged him to pay the tribute which he hoped to impose on others; for he would grant him peace only on condition of paying the expense of the war, *fifteen thousand* talents; *five hundred* on the spot,—*two thousand five hundred* when the peace should be ratified by the senate,—and the remaining *twelve thousand* in *twelve* years, each year *one thousand.* See *Polybius* in his Legations, and *Appian* in the Wars of Syria. And thus,—

Without his own reproach] Without losing a battle, or taking a false step, *Acilius* caused *the reproach* which he was bringing upon the Romans *to turn upon himself.*

Verse 19. *He shall turn his face toward the fort of his own land*] After this shameful defeat, Antiochus fled to Sardis, thence to Apamea, and the next day got into Syria, and to *Antioch,* his *own fort,* whence he sent ambassadors to treat for peace; and was obliged to engage to pay the immense sum of money mentioned above.

But he shall stumble and fall] Being under the greatest difficulties how to raise the stipulated sums, he marched into his eastern provinces to exact the arrears of taxes; and, attempting to plunder the temple of *Jupiter Belus* at Elymais, he was opposed by the populace, and he and his attendants slain. This is the account that *Diodorus Siculus, Strabo,* and *Justin* give of his death. But it is variously related by others; some saying that he was assassinated by some of his own people whom he had punished for being drunk at a feast.—So *Aurelius Victor.* St. *Jerome* says he lost his life in a battle against the inhabitants of Elymais. In short, the manner of his death is uncertain; and perhaps even this circumstance is referred to by the prophet, when he says, "He shall stumble and fall, and NOT BE FOUND."

Verse 20. *Then shall stand up in his estate a raiser of taxes*] *Seleucus Philopater* succeeded his father *Antiochus.* He sent his treasurer *Heliodorus* to seize the money deposited in the temple of Jerusalem, which is here called *the glory of the kingdom,* see 2 Macc. ix. 23. He was so cramped to pay the annual tax to the Romans, that he was obliged to burden his subjects with continual taxes.

He shall be destroyed, neither in anger—fighting against an enemy, *nor in battle*—at the head of his troops; but basely and treacherously, by the hand of *Heliodorus* his treasurer, who hoped to reign in his stead.

Verse 21. *In his estate shall stand up a vile person*] This was Antiochus, surnamed *Epiphanes—the Illustrious.* They *did not give him the honour of the kingdom:* he was at Athens, on his way from Rome, when his father died; and Heliodorus had declared himself king, as had several others. But *Antiochus came in peaceably,* for he obtained *the kingdom by flatteries.* He *flattered Eumenes,* king of Pergamus, and *Attalus* his brother, and got their assistance. He *flattered* the Romans, and sent ambassadors to court their favour, and pay them the arrears of the tribute. He *flattered* the Syrians, and gained their concurrence; and as he *flattered* the Syrians, so they flattered him, giving him the epithet of *Epiphanes*—the *Illustrious.* But that he was what the prophet here calls him, a *vile person,* is fully evident from what *Polybius* says of him, from *Athenæus,* lib. v.: "He was every man's companion: he resorted to the common shops, and prattled with the workmen: he frequented the common taverns, and ate and drank with the meanest fellows, singing debauched songs,"

A. M. 3470
B. C. 534
Ol. LXI. 3
Anno Tarquinii Superbi,
R. Roman., 1

22 [l]And with the arms of a flood shall they be overflown from before him, and shall be broken; [m]yea, also the prince of the covenant.
23 And after the league *made* with him [n]he shall work deceitfully: for he shall come up, and shall become strong with a small people.
24 He shall enter [o]peaceably even upon the fattest places of the province; and he shall do *that* which his fathers have not done, nor his fathers' fathers; [p]he shall scatter among them the prey, and spoil, and riches: *yea,* and he shall [q]forecast his devices against the strong holds, even for a time.
25 And he shall stir up his power and his courage against the king of the south with a great army; and the king of the south shall be stirred up to battle with a very great and mighty army; but he shall not stand: for they shall forecast devices against him.
26 Yea, they that feed of the portion of his meat shall destroy him, and his army shall [r]overflow: and many shall fall down slain.
27 And both these kings' [s]hearts *shall be* to

[l]Ver. 10——[m]Chap. viii. 10, 11, 25——[n]Chap. viii. 25——[o]Or, *into the peaceable and fat,* &c.——[p]1 Mac. iii. 28, &c.——[q]Heb. *think his thoughts*——[r]Ver. 10, 22——[s]Heb. *their hearts*

&c., &c. On this account a contemporary writer, and others after him, instead of *Epiphanes,* called him *Epimanes*—the *Madman.*

Verse 22. *And with the arms of a flood*] The arms which were *overflown* before him were his competitors for the crown. They were vanquished by the forces of Eumenes and Attalus; and were dissipated by the arrival of Antiochus from Athens, whose presence disconcerted all their measures.

The prince of the covenant] This was *Onias,* the high priest, whom he removed, and put *Jason* in his place, who had given him a great sum of money; and then put wicked *Menelaus* in his room, who had offered him a larger sum. Thus he acted *deceitfully* in the *league* made with *Jason.*

Verse 23. *He shall come up*] From Rome, where he had been a hostage for the payment of the tax laid on his father.

Shall become strong with a small people.] At first he had but *few* to espouse his cause when he arrived at *Antioch,* the people having been greatly divided by the many claimants of the crown; but being supported by Eumenes and Attalus, his *few people* increased, and he became *strong.*

Verse 24. *He shall enter peaceably even upon the fattest places*] The very richest provinces—Cœlesyria and Palestine.

He shall do that *which his fathers have not done, nor his fathers' fathers*] He became profuse in his liberalities, and *scattered among them the prey* of his enemies, *the spoil* of temples, and *the riches* of his friends, as well as his own revenues. He spent much in public shows, and bestowed largesses among the people. We are told in 1 Macc. iii. 30, that "in the liberal giving of gifts he abounded above all the kings that went before him." These are nearly the words of the prophet; and perhaps without any design to copy them on the part of the apocryphal writer. He would sometimes go into the streets, and throw about a handful of money, crying out, "Let him take it, to whom Fortune sends it."

He shall forecast his devices] As Eulæus and Lenæus, who were the guardians of the young Egyptian king Ptolemy Philometer, demanded from Antiochus the restitution of Cœlesyria and Palestine, which he refused, he foresaw that he might have a war with that kingdom; and therefore *he forecast devices*—fixed a variety of plans to prevent this; visited the *strong holds* and frontier places to see that they were in a state of defence. And this he did *for a time*—he employed some years in hostile preparations against Egypt.

Verse 25. *He shall stir up his power*] Antiochus marched against Ptolemy, *the king of the south,* (Egypt,) with a great army; and the Egyptian generals had raised a *mighty force.*

Stirred up to battle] The two armies met between Pelusium and Mount Casius; *but he* (the king of the south) *could not stand*—the Egyptian army was defeated. The next campaign he had greater success; he routed the Egyptian army, took Memphis, and made himself master of all Egypt, except *Alexandria,* see 1 Macc. i. 16-19. And all these advantages he gained by *forecasting devices;* probably by *corrupting* his ministers and captains. Ptolemy Macron gave up Cyprus to Antiochus; and the Alexandrians were led to renounce their allegiance to Potlemy Philometer, and took *Euergetes,* or Physcon his younger brother, and made him king in his stead. All this was doubtless by the *corruptions* of Antiochus. See below.

Verse 26. *Yea, they that feed of the portion of his meat*] This is the proof of what has been last noted, that the intrigues of Antiochus, *corrupting* the *ministers* and *officers* of Ptolemy, were the cause of all the disasters that fell on the Egyptian king. They *that fed of the portion of his meat*—who were in his confidence and pay, and possessed the secrets of the state, betrayed him; and these were the means of destroying *him and his army,* so that he was defeated, as was before observed.

Verse 27. *And both these kings' hearts* shall be *to do mischief*] That is, *Antiochus,* and *Ptolemy Philometer,* who was nephew to the former, and whose interest he now pretended to have much at heart, since the Alexandrians had renounced their allegiance to him, and set his younger brother *Euergetes* upon the throne. When Antiochus came to Memphis, he and Philometer had frequent conferences at the *same table;* and at these times they *spoke lies* to each other, Antiochus professing great friendship to his nephew and concern for his interests, yet in his heart designing to ruin the

A. M. 3470
B. C. 534
Olymp. LXI. 3
Anno Tarquinii Superbi,
R. Roman., 1

do mischief, and they shall speak
lies at one table; but it shall
not prosper: for [t]yet the end
shall be at the time appointed.
28 Then shall he return into his land [u]with
great riches; and [v]his heart *shall be* against
the holy covenant; and he shall do *exploits,*
and return to his own land.

A. M. 3470
B. C. 534
Olymp. LXI. 3
Anno Tarquinii Superbi,
R. Roman., 1

29 At the time appointed he
shall return, and come toward
the south; [w]but it shall not be
as the former, [x]or as the latter.
30 [y]For the ships of Chittim shall come
against him: therefore he shall be grieved,
and return, and have indignation [z]against the
holy covenant: so shall he do; he shall even

[t]Ver. 29, 35, 40; chap. viii. 19——[u]1 Mac. i. 19
[v]Ver. 22; 1 Mac. i. 20, &c.; 2 Mac. v. 11, 14, &c.

[w]Ver. 23——[x]Ver. 25——[y]Num. xxiv. 24; Jer. ii. 10
[z]Ver. 28; 1 Mac. i. 30, 44, &c.; 2 Mac. v. 24, &c.

kingdom by fomenting the discords which already subsisted between the two brothers. On the other hand, Philometer professed much *gratitude* to his uncle for the interest he took in his affairs, and laid the blame of the war upon his minister Eulæus; while at the same time he *spoke lies*, determining as soon as possible to accommodate matters with his brother, and join all their strength against their deceitful uncle.

But it shall not prosper] Neither succeeded in his object; for *the end* of the *appointed time* was not yet come.

Verse 28. *Then shall he return into his land with great riches*] Antiochus did return, laden with riches, from the spoils that he took in Egypt; see 1 Macc. i. 19, 20. And hearing that there had been a report of his death, at which the citizens of Jerusalem had made great rejoicings,—

His heart shall be *against the holy covenant*] He was determined to take a severe revenge, and he had an ostensible pretext for it; for Jason, who had been deprived of the high priesthood, hearing the report of the death of Antiochus, raised forces, marched against Jerusalem, took it, and obliged Menelaus, the high priest, to shut himself up in the castle. Antiochus brought a great army against Jerusalem; took it by storm; slew *forty thousand* of the inhabitants; sold as many more for *slaves;* boiled swine's flesh, and sprinkled the temple and the altar with the broth; broke into the holy of holies; took away the golden vessels and other sacred treasures, to the value of *one thousand eight hundred* talents; restored Menelaus to his office; and made one *Philip*, a Phrygian, governor of Judea. 1 Macc. i. 24; 2 Macc. v. 21. *Prideaux* and *Newton*. These are what we term *exploits;* which having finished, *he returned to his own land.*

Verse 29. *At the time appointed he shall return*] Finding that his treachery was detected, and that the two brothers had united their counsel and strength for their mutual support, he threw off the mask; and having collected a great army early in the spring, he passed through *Cœlesyria;* entered Egypt; and the inhabitants of Memphis having submitted to him, he came by easy marches to Alexandria. But, says the prophet, "it shall not be as the former or as the latter:" he had not the *same success* as the *former*, when he overthrew the Egyptian army at *Pelusium;* nor as the *latter*, when he took *Memphis*, and subdued all Egypt, except *Alexandria*. See the reason.

Verse 30. *For the ships of Chittim shall come against him*] *Chittim* is well known to mean the *Roman empire*. Antiochus, being now in full march to besiege Alexandria, and within *seven miles* of that city, heard that ships were arrived there from Rome, with *legates* from the senate. He went to salute them. They delivered to him the letters of the senate, in which he was commanded, on pain of the displeasure of the Roman people, to put an end to the war against his nephews. Antiochus said he would go and consult his friends; on which *Popilius*, one of the legates, took his staff, and instantly drew a circle round Antiochus on the sand where he stood, and commanded him not to pass that circle till he had given a definitive answer. Antiochus, intimidated, said, *he would do whatever the senate enjoined;* and in a few days after began his march, and returned to Syria. This is confirmed by *Polybius*, *Livy*, *Velleius*, *Paterculus*, *Valerius Maximus*, and *Justin*.

Therefore he shall be grieved] "Grieving and groaning," says Polybius; both mortified, humbled, and disappointed.

Have indignation against the holy covenant] For he vented his rage against the Jews; and he sent his general, *Apollonius*, with *twenty-two thousand* men against Jerusalem, plundered and set fire to the city, pulled down the houses round about it, slew much of the people, and built a castle on an eminence that commanded the temple, and slew multitudes of the poor people who had come up to worship, polluted every place, so that the temple service was totally abandoned, and all the people fled from the city. And when he returned to Antioch he published a decree that all should conform to the *Grecian worship;* and the Jewish worship was totally abrogated, and the temple itself consecrated to *Jupiter Olympius*. How great must the wickedness of the people have been when God could tolerate this!

In the transacting of these matters *he had intelligence with them that forsake the holy covenant;* with wicked *Menelaus* the high priest; and the *apostate Jews* united with him, who gave from time to time such information to Antiochus as excited him against Jerusalem, the temple, and the people. See 1 Macc. i. 41, 62; 2 Macc. vi. 1-9; confirmed by *Josephus*, War, book i. chap. 1, s. 1. The concluding reflection of Bp. *Newton* here is excellent:—

"It may be proper to stand a little here, and reflect how particular and circumstantial this prophecy is, concerning Egypt and Syria, from the death of *Alexander* to the time of *Antiochus Epiphanes*. There is not so concise, comprehensive, and regular an account of their kings and affairs to be found in any authors of those times. The prophecy is really more perfect

A. M. 3470
B. C. 534
Olymp. LXI. 3
Anno Tarquinii Superbi,
R. Roman., 1

return, [a]and have intelligence
with them that forsake the holy
covenant.
31 And arms shall stand on his
part, [b]and they shall pollute the sanctuary of
strength, and shall take away the daily *sacrifice,* [c]and they shall place the abomination
that [d]maketh desolate.
32 [e]And such as do wickedly against the
covenant shall he [f]corrupt by flatteries: [g]but
the people that do know their God
shall be strong, and do *exploits.*
33 [h]And they that understand
among the people shall instruct
many: [i]yet they shall fall by the sword, and by
flame, by captivity, and by spoil, *many* days.
34 Now when they shall fall, they [k]shall be
holpen with a little help: [l]but many shall
cleave to them with flatteries.
35 And *some* of them of understanding shall

[a]1 Mac. i. 43, 52; 2 Mac. v. 15, 23——[b]Chap. viii. 11; xii. 11; 1 Mac. i. 37, 39, 41, 45, 46——[c]1 Mac. i. 54, 59; iv. 38——[d]Or, *astonisheth*——[e]1 Mac. i. 43, 52; 2 Mac. iv. 13, 14; v. 15

[f]Or, *cause to dissemble*——[g]1 Mac. i. 62; ii. 41, 42, 43; 2 Mac. v. 27; vi. 19, 20; vii. 1, &c.——[h]Mal. ii. 7 [i]Heb. xi. 35, &c.——[k]1 Mac. iii. 2; 2 Mac. viii. 1 [l]2 Mac. xii. 40; xiii. 21

than any *history*, and is so wonderfully exact, not only *to the time* of Antiochus Epiphanes, but likewise equally so *beyond that time*, that we may conclude in the words of the inspired writer, 'No one could thus declare *the times and seasons*, but he who *hath them in his own power*.'"

Verse 31. *And arms shall stand on his part*] After Antiochus, *arms*, that is, the Romans, *shall stand up:* for *arms* in this prophecy every where denote *military power;* and *standing up*, the power in *activity* and *conquering*. Both Sir *Isaac Newton* and Bp. *Newton* agree, that what follows is spoken of the *Romans*. Hitherto Daniel has described the actions of the kings of the *north* and of the *south*, that of the kings of *Syria* and *Egypt;* but, upon the conquest of Macedon by the Romans, he has left off describing the actions of the Greeks, and begun to describe those of the *Romans in Greece*, who conquered Macedon, Illyricum, and Epirus, in the year of the era of *Nabonassar*, 580. *Thirty-five* years after, by the *will* of *Attalus*, they inherited all Asia westward of Mount Taurus; *sixty-five* years after they conquered the kingdom of Syria, and reduced it into a province; and *thirty-four* years after they did the same to Egypt. By all these steps the Roman *arms stood up* over the Greeks; and after *ninety-five years* more, by making war upon the Jews, *they polluted the sanctuary of strength*,—the temple, (so called by reason of its *fortifications*,) *and took away the daily* sacrifice *and placed the abomination that maketh desolate*, or of the *desolator;* for that this *abomination* was thus placed *after* the time of Christ, appears from Matt. xxiv. 15.

In the *sixteenth* year of the Emperor Adrian, A. D. 132, they placed this *abomination* by building a temple to *Jupiter Capitolinus*, where the temple of God in Jerusalem stood; upon which the Jews, under *Barchocab*, rose up against the Romans. But in this war they had *fifty* cities demolished, *nine hundred and fifty* of their best towns destroyed, and *eighty thousand* men were slain by the sword; and in the end of the war, A. D. 136, were banished Judea on pain of death; and thenceforth the land *became desolate*. See Observations on Daniel, and Bp. Newton on the Prophecies.

Verse 32. *Such as do wickedly against the covenant*] This is understood of the *Christian Jews;* for the NEW had now succeeded to the OLD, the whole of the Jewish ritual having been abolished, and Jerusalem filled with heathen *temples*. *And he*—the Roman power, did all he could by *flatteries*, as well as threats, to *corrupt* the Christians, and cause them to sacrifice to the statues of the emperors.

But the people that do know their God] The genuine Christians.

Shall be strong] Shall be strengthened by his grace and Spirit.

And do exploits.] Continue steadfast in all temptations, hold fast their faith, and enjoy a good conscience.

Verse 33. *And they that understand*] The *apostles* and *primitive Christians* in general, who *understood* from the *prophets*, and his own *actions*, that JESUS was the true MESSIAH.

Instruct many] Preach the Gospel every where, and convert multitudes to the faith.

Yet they shall fall by the sword, and by flame, by captivity, and by spoil, many *days*.] They were exposed to the malice and fury of their enemies, during TEN STATE PERSECUTIONS, and suffered all kinds of tortures, with but little intermission, for *three hundred* years.—*Newton*.

Verse 34. *Now when they shall fall*] When the storm of the *tenth* persecution under *Diocletian*, which lasted *ten* years, *fell upon them*, they were sorely oppressed.

They shall be holpen with a little help] By Constantine; who, while he removed all persecution, and promoted the temporal prosperity of the Christian Church, yet added little to its spiritual perfection and strength. For many, now seeing the Christians in prosperity,—

Cleave to them with flatteries.] Became *Christians* BECAUSE the EMPEROR was *such*.

Verse 35. *And some of them of understanding*] Disputes on certain points of religion soon agitated the Christian Church; and now, having no outward persecution, they began to persecute each other. And many excellent men, *men of understanding*, *fell* victims because they would not embrace erroneous doctrines, when professed by the *state*. But this was permitted,—

To try them, and to purge, and to make them *white*] To bring all to the pure profession, possession, and practice of Christianity.

To the time of the end] To the time that God shall cause pure and undefiled religion every where to prevail. But when is the time appointed for this?

A. M. 3470
B. C. 534
Olymp. LXI. 3
Anno Tarquinii Superbi,
R. Roman., 1

fall, [m]to try [n]them, and to purge, and to make *them* white, [o]*even* to the time of the end: [p]because *it is* yet for a time appointed.

36 And the king [q]shall do according to his will; and he shall [r]exalt himself, and magnify himself above every god, and shall speak marvellous things [s]against the God of gods, and shall prosper [t]till the indignation be accomplished: for that that is determined shall be done.

[m]Chap. xii. 10; 1 Pet. i. 7——[n]Or, *by them*——[o]Chap. viii. 17, 19; ver. 40——[p]Ver. 29——[q]Ver. 16——[r]Chap. vii. 8, 25; viii. 25; 2 Thess. ii. 4; Rev. xiii. 5, 6——[s]Chap. viii. 11, 24, 25——[t]Chap. ix. 27——[u]1 Tim. iv. 3 [v]Isa. xiv. 13; 2 Thess. ii. 4

A. M. 3470
B. C. 534
Olymp. XLI. 3
Anno Tarquinii Superbi,
R. Roman., 1

37 Neither shall he regard the God of his fathers, [u]nor the desire of women, [v]nor regard any god: for he shall magnify himself above all.

38 [w]But [x]in his estate shall he honour the god of [y]forces: [z]and a god whom his fathers knew not shall he honor with gold, and silver, and with precious stones, and [a]pleasant things.

39 Thus shall he do in the [b]most strong holds with a strange god, whom he shall ac-

[w]Or, *But in his stead*——[x]Heb. *as for the Almighty God, in his seat he shall honour, yea, he shall honour a god, whom,* &c.——[y]Or, *munitions*——[z]Hebrew, *Mauzzim*, or *gods protectors*——[a]Heb. *things desired;* Isa. xliv. 9 [b]Hebrew, *fortresses of munitions*

Verse 36. *And the king shall do according to his will*] This may apply to *Antiochus*, who exalted himself above every god, called himself a god, sported with all religion, profaned the temple, &c., &c. But others think an *antichristian power* in the Church is intended; for in the language of this prophecy *king* is taken for *power*, a *kingdom*, &c. That such a power did spring up in the Church that acted in an arbitrary manner against all laws, human and Divine, is well known. This power showed itself in the *Greek emperors* in the *east*, and in the *bishops of Rome* in the *west*. And this is to continue.

Till the indignation be accomplished: for that that is determined shall be done.] This is the same as what was called in chap. viii. 19, *the last end of the indignation;* and chap. ix. 27, *the consummation;* and means the *end* or *consummation* of God's indignation against the Jews. And this seems more clearly expressed, chap. xii. 7: "When he shall have accomplished to scatter the power of the holy people." We see this still subsisting in the Church of Rome; and it was a saying of *Rabbi David Kimchi*, "When Rome shall be laid waste, then shall be redemption for Israel." For the destruction of Rome and the restoration of the Jews shall fall out about the same time.—Bp. *Newton.*

Verse 37. *Neither shall he regard the God of his fathers*] That God who sent the *evangelists* and *apostles* to preach the *pure doctrine.* These *true fathers of the Christian Church*, and their God, this Church has not regarded, but put *councils*, and *traditions*, and *apocryphal writings* in their place.

Nor the desire of women] Both the Greek and Latin Church, in their antichristian enactments, have discouraged, and in several cases *proscribed, marriage*, under the pretence of *greater chastity*, to the discredit of God's ordinance, and Christianity itself.

Nor regard any god] For the mandates and decrees of that Church have been often in defiance of God and his word; for it has magnified itself above all power and authority in heaven and on earth. It professes to hold the keys, and to open and shut heaven at pleasure, both to states and individuals.

Verse 38. *Shall he honour the god of forces*] מעזים *mauzzim*, or *gods protectors*, as in the *margin;* worshipping *saints* and *angels* as *guardians*, and *protectors*, and *mediators;* leaving out, in general, the *true God*, and the *only Mediator*, Jesus Christ.

And a god whom his fathers knew not] For these *gods guardians*, the *Virgin Mary, saints*, and *angels*, were utterly unknown as *mediators* and *invocable guardians* in the primitive apostolic Church.

Shall he honour with gold, and silver, and with precious stones] How literally does this apply to the *Church of Rome!* See the house of our lady at *Loretto;* the *shrines of saints;* the *decorated images, costly apparel, gold, jewels*, &c., profusely used about *images of saints, angels*, and the *blessed virgin*, in different popish churches. This superstition began to prevail in the *fourth* century, and was established in 787, by the *seventh* general council; for in that the *worship of images* was enacted.

Verse 39. *In the most strong holds with a strange god*] Bishop *Newton* proposed the following translation, after justly finding fault with our common Version: "Thus shall he do to the defenders of Mauzzim, together with the strange god whom he shall acknowledge: he shall multiply honour, and he shall cause him to rule over many; and the earth he shall divide for a reward." The *defenders* of *Mauzzim*, these saint and angel *gods protectors*, were the monks, priests, and bishops; of whom it may be truly said, "They were increased with honour, ruled over many, and divided the land for gain." They have been honoured and reverenced almost to adoration; their jurisdiction was extended over the *purses* and *consciences* of men; they have been enriched with the noblest buildings and largest endowments, and the *choicest lands* have been appropriated for Church *lands.* These are points of such public notoriety, that they require no proof.—*Newton.*

Verse 40. *At the time of the end shall the king of the south push at him*] These kings are to be understood in reference to the times of which the prophet speaks. While the kingdoms of *Egypt* and *Syria* were subsisting, the *king of the south and the north* applied to them exclusively: but they did not exist at the time of which the prophet speaks; therefore *other southern* and *northern* powers must be sought. These we may find in the *Saracens*, who were of the *Arabians*, who came from the *south*, headed by the false prophet *Mohammed*, who

A. M. 3470
B. C. 534
Olymp. LXI. 3
Anno Tarquinii Superbi, R. Roman., 1

knowledge *and* increase with glory: and he shall cause them to rule over many, and shall divide the land for [c]gain.

40 [d]And at the time of the end shall the king of the south push at him: and the king of the north shall come against him [e]like a whirlwind, with chariots, [f]and with horsemen, and with many ships; and he shall enter into the countries, [g]and shall overflow and pass over.

41 He shall enter also into the [h]glorious[i] land, and many *countries* shall be overthrown: but these shall escape out of his hands, [k]*even* Edom, and Moab, and the chief of the children of Ammon.

42 He shall [l]stretch forth his hand also upon the countries: and the land of Egypt shall not escape.

43 But he shall have power over the treasures of gold and of silver, and over all the precious things of Egypt: and the Libyans and the Ethiopians *shall be* [m]at his steps.

44 But tidings out of the east and out of the north shall trouble him: therefore he shall go forth with great fury to destroy, and utterly to make away many.

45 And he shall plant the tabernacles of his palaces between the seas in [n]the [o]glorious[p] holy mountain; [q]yet he shall come to his end and none shall help him.

[c]Heb. *a price*——[d]Ver. 35——[e]Psa. lviii. 9; Prov. i. 27; x. 25; Isa. xxi. 1; xl. 24; xli. 16; lxvi. 15; Zech. ix. 14 [f]Ezek. xxxviii. 4, 15; Rev. ix. 16——[g]Ver. 10, 22 [h]Or, *goodly land;* ver. 16——[i]Heb. *land of delight,* or *ornament*

[k]Isa. xi. 14——[l]Heb. *send forth*——[m]Exod. xi. 8; Judg. iv. 10——[n]Psa. xlviii. 2; ver. 16, 41; 2 Thess. ii. 4 [o]Or, *goodly*——[p]Hebrew, *mountain of delight of holiness*——[q]1 Mac. vi. 8–16; 2 Thess. ii. 8; Revelation xix. 20

pushed at him—made war on the *Greek emperor Heraclius*, and with amazing rapidity deprived him of Egypt, Syria, and many of his finest provinces.

And the king of the north] The *Turks*, who were originally *Scythians*, seized on the remains of the Greek empire; and in process of time rendered themselves masters of the whole. They are represented as coming like a *whirlwind, with chariots, and with horsemen;* their armies being chiefly composed of *cavalry.*

And with many ships] With these they got possession of many *islands* and *maritime countries;* and were so powerful in their fleets, that they entirely defeated the Venetians; and at last their fleets became of the utmost consequence to them in besieging, and afterwards taking, *Constantinople*, A. D. 1453, which they hold to the present day. So *they entered into the countries, and overflowed*, rendering themselves masters of all Asia Minor and Greece.

Verse 41. *He shall enter also into the glorious land*] Entirely subdue Judea.

And many countries *shall be overthrown*] Aleppo, Damascus, Gaza, and many other cities were forced to submit to them; and they hold them still.

But these shall escape—Edom and Moab, and the chief of the children of Ammon.] These and other Arabians they have never been able to subdue. They still occupy the deserts; and receive a yearly pension of *forty thousand* crowns of gold from the Ottoman emperors, to permit the caravans, with the pilgrims for Mecca, to have a free passage.

Verse 42. *He shall stretch forth his hand*] *He*—the *Ottoman emperors*, have *stretched forth the hand*, not only on *European*, but also upon *Asiatic* and *African* countries. *Egypt* has not escaped; it is a province of the Turkish government, as are also Fez, Morocco, Algiers, and many other African countries. And as the prophecy says they "got power over the silver and gold, and the precious things of Egypt," so it was; for when *Selim* conquered Egypt, A. D. 1517, he took all its spoils; and the immense sums drawn from it to the present day, and the wretchedness of the land in consequence, are almost incredible.

The Libyans and the Ethiopians] The *Cushim*—unconquered *Arabs*, all sought their friendship; and many of them are tributary to the present time.

Verse 44. *But tidings out of the east and out of the north shall trouble him*] This part of the prophecy is allowed to be yet *unfulfilled;* and what is portented, the course of prophetic events will show. Were we to understand it as applying to *Antiochus*, then the *news* might be of the *preparations* which he heard, that the provinces of the *east*, and *Artaxerxes*, king of *Armenia*, on the *north*, were intending to rise up against him. But if the *Turkish* power be understood, as in the preceding verses, it may mean that the *Persians* on the *east*, and the *Russians* on the *north*, will at some time greatly embarrass the Ottoman government. And how completely has this been fulfilled; first, by the total destruction of the Egyptian fleet, by the combined fleets of England, France, and Russia, in the Bay of Navarino; and, secondly, by the total overthrow of the Turkish army by the Russians, in the years 1828 and 1829, when the sultan was obliged to accept any conditions that the emperor of Russia was pleased to give! [N.B.—The former part of this note was written for the first edition of this work, printed in 1825.]

Verse 45. *He shall plant the tabernacles*] He shall make a last stand in *Judea*, and there shall his power be smitten.

He shall come to his end, and none shall help him.] All his confederate and tributary kingdoms, states, and provinces shall desert him, and leave that government to come to a shameful end.

In the interpretation of this chapter I have generally followed Bp. *Newton*, in his most excellent *Dissertations on the Prophecies*, consulting other eminent authors occasionally.

From the beginning of the chapter to the end of ver. 30 all is very clear and plain, relative to the Grecian, Syrian, and Egyptian histories; from the *thirty-first* verse to the end, the mode of interpretation is not so satisfactory, in its application to the times since Christ. Yet possibly these alone may be intended; though the whole might be, with considerable ease, applied to the remaining part of the *Syrian* and *Egyptian* history. It is a wonderful piece of prophecy, and of great utility to the cause of Divine revelation.

CHAPTER XII

The proper conclusion to the great revolutions predicted in this and the following chapters is the general resurrection, *of which the beginning of this chapter (if to be literally understood) gives some intimation*, 1–3. *Daniel is then commanded to shut up the words and to seal the book to the time of the end*, 4; *and is informed of the three grand symbolical periods of a* time, times, and a half, twelve hundred and ninety *days, and* thirteen hundred and thirty-five *days*, 4–12; *at the end of the last of which Daniel shall rest and stand in his lot*, 13. *It is generally thought by commentators that the termination of the last period is the epoch of the* FIRST resurrection. See Rev. xx. 4, 5.

A. M. 3470 B. C. 534 Olymp. LXI. 3 Anno Tarquinii Superbi, R. Roman., 1

AND at that time shall [a]Michael stand up, the great
prince which standeth for the
children of thy people: [b]and
there shall be a time of trouble, such as never
was since there was a nation *even* to that
same time: and at that time thy people [c]shall
be delivered, every one that shall be found
[d]written in the book.
2 And many of them that sleep in the dust
of the earth shall awake, [e]some to everlasting
life, and some to shame [f]*and*
everlasting contempt.
3 And [g]they that be [h]wise
shall shine [i]as the brightness of
the firmament; [k]and they that turn many
to righteousness [l]as the stars for ever and
ever.
4 [m]But thou, O Daniel, [n]shut up the words,
and seal the book, *even* to [o]the time of the
end: many shall run to and fro, and knowledge shall be increased.

A. M. 3470 B. C. 534 Olymp. LXI. 3 Anno Tarquinii Superbi, R. Roman., 1

[a]Ch. x. 13, 21——[b]Isa. xxvi. 20, 21; Jer. xxx. 7; Matt. xxiv. 21; Rev. xvi. 18——[c]Rom. xi. 26——[d]Exod. xxxii. 32; Psa. lvi. 8; lxix. 28; Ezek. xiii. 9; Luke x. 20; Phil. iv. 3; Rev. iii. 5; xiii. 8——[e]Matt. xxv. 46; John v. 28, 29; Acts xxiv. 15

[f]Isa. lxvi. 24; Rom. ix. 21——[g]Ch. xi. 33, 35——[h]Or, *teachers*——[i]Prov. iv. 18; Wisd. iii. 7; Matt. xiii. 43——[k]James v. 20——[l]1 Cor. xv. 41, 42——[m]Chap. viii. 26; ver. 9——[n]Rev. x. 4; xxii. 10——[o]Chap. x. 1; ver. 9

NOTES ON CHAP. XII

Verse 1. *And at that time Michael shall stand up*] Michael the archangel, as has already been observed, was ever reputed the guardian of the Jewish people.

Every one that shall be found written in the book] All that truly fear, love, and obey the Lord. On the phrase, "written in the book, the book of life," &c., see the passages in the margin, and the notes on those passages.

Verse 2. *Many of them that sleep in the dust of the earth*] This prophecy has been referred to the future *restoration of the Jews*. It will be also true of the state of mankind at the general judgment.

Verse 3. *And they that be wise*] Those who are thoroughly instructed in Christ's word and doctrine, *shall shine*—shall be eminently distinguished in the Christian Church by the holiness of their lives, and the purity of their creed.

And they that turn many to righteousness] They who, by preaching Christ crucified among their brethren, shall be the means of converting them to the Christian faith; shall be *as the stars*—bright luminaries in the Gospel kingdom of Jesus Christ. This also may be applied to the case of holy and useful men, particularly the faithful ministers of the Gospel, in the day of judgment. See the parallel texts in the margin, and the notes on them.

Verse 4. *Shut up the words, and seal the book*] When a prophet received a prediction concerning what was at a considerable distance of time, he shut his book, did not communicate his revelation for some time after. This Daniel was commanded to do, chap. viii. 26. See also Isa. xxix. 10, 11; Rev. xxii. 10. Among the ancients, those were said to *seal*, who in the course of their reading stamped the places of which they were *yet doubtful*, in order to keep them in memory, that they might refer to them again, as not yet fully understood. This custom *Salmasius*, in his book *De modo Usurarum*, p. 446, proves from *Hesychius*.

Many shall run to and fro] Many shall endeavour to *search out* the sense; *and knowledge shall be increased* by these means; though the meaning shall not be *fully* known till the events take place: THEN the seal shall be broken, and the sense become plain. This seems to be the meaning of this verse, though another has been put on it, viz., "Many shall run to and fro preaching the Gospel of Christ, and therefore religious knowledge and true wisdom shall be increased." This is true in itself; but it is not the meaning of the prophet's words.

A. M. 3470
B. C. 534
Olymp. LXI. 3
Anno Tarquinii Superbi,
R. Roman., 1

5 Then I Daniel looked, and,
behold, there stood other two,
the one on this side of the [p]bank
of the river, and the other on
that side of the bank [q]of the river.
6 And *one* said to [r]the man clothed in linen,
which *was* [s]upon the waters of the river, [t]How
long *shall it be to* the end of these wonders?
7 And I heard the man clothed in linen,
which *was* upon the waters of the river, when
he [u]held up his right hand and his left hand
unto heaven, and sware by him [v]that liveth
for ever [w]that *it shall be* for a time, times, and
[x]a half; [y]and when he shall have accomplished to scatter the power of [z]the holy people, all
these *things* shall be finished.
8 And I heard, but I understood not: then
said I, O my Lord, what *shall be* the end of
these *things?*
9 And he said, Go thy way,
Daniel: for the words *are* closed
up and sealed [a]till the time of
the end.
10 [b]Many shall be purified, and made white,
and tried; [c]but the wicked shall do wickedly:
and none of the wicked shall understand; but
[d]the wise shall understand.
11 And from the time [e]*that* the daily *sacri-*
fice shall be taken away, and [f]the abomination that [g]maketh desolate set up, *there*
shall be a thousand two hundred and ninety
days.
12 Blessed *is* he that waiteth, and cometh
to the thousand three hundred and five and
thirty days.
13 But [h]go thou thy way till the end *be:*
[i]for [k]thou shalt rest, [l]and stand in thy lot at
the end of the days.

[p]Heb. *lip*——[q]Ch. x. 4——[r]Ch. x. 5——[s]Or, *from above*——[t]Ch. viii. 13——[u]Deut. xxxii. 40; Rev. x. 5, 6 [v]Ch. iv. 34——[w]Ch. vii. 25; xi. 13; Rev. xii. 14——[x]Or, *part*——[y]Luke xxi. 24; Rev. x. 7——[z]Ch. viii. 24 [a]Ver. 4——[b]Ch. xi. 35; Zech. xiii. 9——[c]Hos. xiv. 9; Rev. ix. 20; xxii. 11——[d]Chap. xi. 33, 35; John vii. 17; viii. 47; xviii. 37——[e]Chap. viii. 11; xi. 31——[f]Hebrew, *to set up the abomination*, &c.——[g]Or, *astonisheth*——[h]Verse 9——[i]Or, *and thou*, &c.——[k]Isa. lvii. 2; Rev. xiv. 13——[l]Psa. i. 5

Verse 5. *Behold, there stood other two*] Probably two angels. We know no more of them, unless they be the same as those called *saints*, chap. viii. 13, which see. The *river* was most likely the *Tigris*.

Verse 6. *The man clothed in linen*] Gabriel, in a human form. Thus he is represented, chap. x. 5.

Verse 7. *Which* was *upon the waters*] By this description, he was standing on the water. This is very similar to the description of the angel, Rev. x. 5, 6, and in the seventh verse there seems to be a reference to this prophecy, "a time, times, and a half." See the note on chap. vii. 25.

Verse 8. *I heard, but I understand not*] Could not comprehend what the *time, times,* and *half time* should refer to. These make *three* years and *a half* of prophetic time, answering to *one thousand two hundred and sixty* years.

Verse 9. *The words* are *closed up*] The prophecy shall not be understood, but in its accomplishment; and then the depth of the wisdom and providence of God will be clearly seen in these matters. See on ver. 4. We must wait "till the time of the end;" and this, it appears from the following calculations, will not arrive before the TWENTIETH CENTURY. We here see the reason why these prophecies are at present so imperfectly understood. *God has sealed them.*

Verse 10. *Many shall be purified*] During the interim, the great work of God's providence and grace shall be carried on in the salvation of men; who, in the midst of trials, temptations, and difficulties, shall be *purified* and *made white*—be fully saved from their sins.

None of the wicked shall understand] Because they are wicked, and *will* continue in their sins, the eyes of their *understanding* shall be closed, and their hearts hardened; so that they shall not see the light of the glorious Gospel.

But the wise] Those who open their hearts to God, that he may pour in his light, shall *understand* the things that make for their peace.

Verse 11. *From the time* that *the daily* sacrifice *shall be taken away*] See the notes on chap. xi. 25-27.

The abomination that maketh desolate set up] I believe, with Bp. *Newton*, that this is a *proverbial* phrase; and may be applied to any thing substituted in the *place* of, or set up in opposition to, the ordinances of God, his worship, his truth, &c. Adrian's temple, built in the place of God's temple at Jerusalem, the church of St. Sophia turned into a Mohammedan mosque, &c., &c., may be termed *abominations that make desolate.* Perhaps Mohammedanism may be the abomination; which sprang up A. D. 612. If we reckon *one thousand two hundred and ninety* years, ver. 11, from that time, it will bring us down to A. D. 1902, when we might presume from this calculation, that the religion of the FALSE PROPHET will cease to prevail in the world; which from the present year, 1825, is distant only *seventy-seven* years.

Verse 12. *Blessed* is *he that waiteth*] He who implicitly depends on God, expecting, as his truth cannot fail, that these predictions shall be accomplished in due time.

And cometh to the thousand three hundred and five and thirty days.] This is *seventy-five* days more than what is included in the *three* years and a *half*, or the *time, times, and a half* in the *seventh* verse; and as we have met with so many instances of *prophetical days* and *years,* this undoubtedly is another instance; and as a *day* stands for a *year,* this must mean a period of *one thousand three hundred and thirty-five* years, which period is to bring *all these wonders to an end,* ver. 6. But we are left totally in the dark relative to the *time from which these one thousand three hundred and thirty-five years* are to be reckoned. If, however, we reckon them from the above epoch, A. D. 612, when *Mohammedanism* arose, they lead us to A. D. 1947, when the *fulness of the Gentiles* shall be brought in; and thus a final closure of vision and prophecy be made, as then all the great events relative to the salvation of men shall have taken place. Wars and contentions will probably then cease over the whole world; Jews and Gentiles become one fold, under one Shepherd and Bishop of souls; and the triune God be properly worshipped and glorified, from generation to generation, over the face of the whole earth. But all these conjectures may be founded in darkness. We have not chronological data; and "the times and seasons God has reserved in his own power."

Verse 13. *But go thou thy way till the end be*] Here is proper advice for every man. 1. Thou hast a *way*—a *walk in life,* which God has assigned thee; *walk in that way,* it is *thy way.* 2. There will be an *end* to thee of all earthly things. Death is at the door, and eternity is at hand; *go on to the end*—be faithful unto death. 3. There is a *rest* provided for the people of God. Thou shalt *rest;* thy *body,* in the *grave;* thy *soul,* in the *Divine favour* here, and finally in *paradise.* 4. As in the promised land there was a *lot* for *each* of *God's people,* so in heaven there is a *lot* for *thee.* Do not *lose* it, do not *sell* it, do not let thy enemy *rob thee* of it. Be determined to *stand in thy own lot at the end of the days.* See that thou keep the faith; die in the Lord Jesus, that thou mayest rise and reign with him to all eternity. Amen.

MASORETIC NOTES

Number of verses in this book, 357

Middle verse, chap. v. 30

Masoretic sections, 7

Finished correcting for the press, March 1st, 1831.—A. C.

INTRODUCTION TO THE BOOK

OF THE

PROPHET HOSEA

HOSEA, the son of *Beeri*, is the first of the minor prophets. *Epiphanius* says that he was of the town of *Belemoth*, in the tribe of *Issachar;* which is no other, in all probability, than *Beelmeon*, towards Esdraelon, in this tribe. The rabbins say that *Bura* was his father, who is mentioned in the *Chronicles*, and was prince of the tribe of *Reuben* at the time when *Tiglath-pileser* carried some of the tribes of *Israel* into captivity. But if it be so, *Hosea* must be said to be of the tribe of *Reuben;* and a native of *Beelmeon*, beyond *Jordan*. This prophet lived in the kingdom of *Samaria;* and his prophecies for the most part have a view to this state, though there are likewise some particular things which concern the kingdom of *Judah*.

We read, in the introduction to his prophecy, that he prophesied under the kings of *Judah*, *Uzziah*, *Jotham*, *Ahaz*, and *Hezekiah*, and under *Jeroboam* II., king of *Israel*. If he prophesied in the reign of all these princes, he must have lived a very long time; for there are a *hundred and twelve* years from the beginning of *Uzziah's* reign to the end of *Hezekiah's* reign. *Uzziah* began to reign A. M. 3194, and *Hezekiah's* reign ended in 3306. Add, if you please, *twenty* or *five and twenty* years, which might be the age of *Hosea* when he began to prophesy; and this will make *one hundred and thirty-two*, or *one hundred and thirty-seven* years. And if we were to take *ten* years from *Uzziah*, and as many from *Hezekiah*, during which *Hosea* might not have prophesied, there will still remain *one hundred and twelve*, or *one hundred and fifteen* years.

In the whole collection of *Hosea's* prophecies, we find nothing which proves that he prophesied so long. And, besides, why should his prophecies be dated in the title by the reigns of the kings of *Judah*, when he did not live under their dominion? It is therefore very probable that this title is not *Hosea's*, but some ancient transcriber's; and that the true beginning of this prophet's work is at these words: "The beginning of the word of the Lord by Hosea." It is our opinion that he began about the end of *Jeroboam's* reign, who was the second king of *Israel* of this name. See *Calmet*.

St. *Jerome* and many others believe *Hosea* to be the oldest prophet, whose writings are in our possession; and that he was witness to the *first* captivity of the *four* tribes carried away by *Tiglath-pileser*, and the extinction of the kingdom of *Samaria* by *Shalmaneser*. St. *Jerome* will have it that he prophesied even afterwards. The *first* verses of chap. i. have a view to the death of *Zechariah*, king of *Israel*, and son of *Jeroboam* II. From the *sixth* verse of the *first* chapter to the *third* chapter, is a prediction of the captivity of *Israel:* but after he has foretold this captivity, he declares the return and end of it. He inveighs strongly against the disorders which prevailed in the kingdom of the *ten* tribes. It appears that in his time there were idols; not only at *Dan*, *Beth-el*, and *Samaria*, but likewise at *Gilgal*, upon *Tabor*, at *Sichem*, *Beer-sheba*, and upon the mountains of *Gilead*. He speaks of the *Israelites* as of a people entirely corrupted, and the measure of whose sins was filled up; he foretells that their golden calves should be pulled down, cast upon the ground, and carried into *Assyria*.

He reflects, with the same severity, upon the irregularities which reigned in *Judah*. He stands up against those who went to worship false gods at *Gilgal*. He speaks of *Sennacherib's* invading the territories of *Judah*. He foretells that the people of *Judah* should still continue some time in their country after the captivity of the *ten* tribes; but that after this they themselves should likewise be carried captives beyond the *Euphrates*, from whence the Lord would bring them back after a certain number of years. The style of *Hosea* is obscure, and his expressions often dubious and perplexed. The things whereof he speaks contribute farther to his obscurity, by reason of their distance, and our ignorance of the history of those times.

In the beginning of *Hosea's* prophecy, we read that the Lord directed him "to take unto him a wife of whoredoms, and children of whoredoms;" that is, to marry a woman who, before her marriage, had lived a debauched life, but who, after her marriage, should retire from all bad conversation, and whose children should be legitimate, notwithstanding that, by reason of the blemish which their mother had contracted by her former life, they were called *the children of whoredoms*. This prostitute woman, and the children who were to be born of her, were a figure and a kind of real prophecy which described the idolatry and infidelity of *Samaria* and the *ten* tribes, formerly the Lord's spouse, but who afterwards became idolatrous and corrupt.

The children of this faithless woman are children of prostitution, since they imitate the idolatry of their mother. God gives these children the names of *Jezreel*, *God will disperse; Lo-rechamah*, or *Without mercy;* and *Lo-ammi*, *Thou art no longer my people;* to show,—1. That God was going to revenge upon the house of *Jehu*, king of *Israel*, the sins which he had committed at *Jezreel*, when he usurped the kingdom of the *ten* tribes. 2. That the Lord would treat his idolatrous and sinful people without mercy. 3. That he would reject them, and no more look upon them as his people.

Hosea is concise, sententious, and abrupt. It is his manner to omit the connexive and adversative particles; an observation which we should recollect when we observe them occasionally supplied by versions or manuscripts. These are among the causes of that obscurity for which he is remarkable: but the greatest difficulties arise from the corrupt readings which deform the printed text. He chiefly addresses Israel; but introduces frequent mention of Judah. He not only inveighs against the vices of the people, but sharply arraigns the conduct of their kings, princes, and priests.

Like many of the Hebrew prophets, he tempers denunciations of God's vengeance against an idolatrous and vicious people, with promises of abundant mercies in store for them; and his transitions from one of these subjects to the other are rapid and unexpected. He abounds with short and lively comparisons; and, like the best Greek and Roman writers, often omits the particle of similitude. These comparisons he sometimes accumulates in the spirit of that poetry which is most admired. See chap. vi. 3, 4, ix. 10, xi. 11, xiii. 3, xiv. 5, 6, 7. He has often a GREAT FORCE OF EXPRESSION. See chap. i. 7, ii. 3, 18, 21, 22, iv. 2, vi. 5, xi. 4, *l.* 1, xii. 1, *l.* 1. He is sometimes HIGHLY ANIMATED. See chap. iv. 14, v. 8, viii, 1, ix. 5, 14, xiii. 10, 14. Many BEAUTIFUL PASSAGES occur in this prophet, as in the SIMILES throughout; in the ALLEGORIES, chap. ii. 2, 20, vii. 11, 12, viii. 7, *l.* 2, 3, 4, x. 11, 12, 13, xiii. 15; in the PATHOS, chap. xi. 3, *l.* 1, 2, and ver. 8, 9; in the FIGURES, chap. xiii. 12, xiv. 2, *l.* 5. There are also some parts which are truly SUBLIME, as chap. v. 14. 15, viii. 7, *l.* 1, x. 8, *l.* 2, 3, xiii. 7, 8.

I have already, at the beginning of Isaiah, given a table of the chronological succession of all the prophets: that of Archbishop *Newcome* on the *twelve* minor prophets I subjoin here, because it contains some differences from the preceding.

ORDER AND TIME IN WHICH THE TWELVE MINOR PROPHETS FLOURISHED

1. JONAH prophesied between 823 B. C. and 783 B. C. in the reign of Jeroboam II., king of Israel. See 2 Kings xiv. 25.

2. Amos prophesied from about 823 B. C. to about 785 B. C. in the reign of Uzziah, king of Judah, and in that of Jeroboam II., king of Israel. See Amos i. 1.

3. Hosea flourished from about 809 B. C. to about 698 B. C., in the reigns of Uzziah, Jotham, Ahaz, and Hezekiah, kings of Judah, and in that of Jeroboam II., king of Israel. See Hos. i. 1. [But see the observations in the preceding page.]

4. Micah flourished between 757 B. C. and 698 B. C., in the reigns of Jotham, Ahaz, and Hezekiah, kings of Judah. See Mic. i. 1.

5. Nahum is supposed to have prophesied between 720 B. C. and 698 B. C., in the reign of Hezekiah.

6. Joel is supposed to have prophesied between 697 B. C. and 660 B. C., in the reign of Manasseh.

7. Zephaniah prophesied between 640 B. C. and 609 B. C., in the reign of Josiah. See Zeph. i. 1.

8. Habakkuk is thought to have prophesied between 606 B. C. and 598 B. C., in the reign of Jehoiakim.

9. Obadiah prophesied soon after 587 B. C., between the taking of Jerusalem by Nebuchadnezzar, and the destruction of the Edomites by the same prince.

10. Haggai prophesied about 520 B. C. after the return from Babylon. See Haggai i. 1.

11. Zechariah prophesied from 520 B. C. to about 518 B. C.; and was contemporary with Haggai. See Zech. i. 1.

12. Malachi is generally believed to have prophesied about 436 B. C.

THE BOOK

OF THE

PROPHET HOSEA

Chronological Notes relative to the commencement of Hosea's prophesying, upon the supposition that this event took place in the last year of the reign of Jeroboam II., king of Israel

Year of the world, according to the Usherian account, 3219.—Year of the Julian period, 3929.—Year since the Flood, 1563.—Year from the vocation of Abram, 1136.—Year from the foundation of Solomon's temple, 227.—Year before the First Olympiad, 9.—Year before the building of Rome, 32.—Year before the vulgar era of Christ's nativity, 785.—Cycle of the Sun, 9.—Cycle of the Moon, 15.—Second year of Cœnus, the second king of Macedon; which was the thirtieth from the foundation of the monarchy.—Thirteenth year of Agamestor, perpetual archon of the Athenians.—Thirteenth year of Ardysus, king of Lydia.—Twelfth year of Amulius Sylvius, king of the Albans.—Twenty-fifth year of Charilaus, king of the Lacedæmonians.—Forty-first year of Jeroboam II., king of Israel.—Twenty-sixth year of Uzziah, king of Judah.

CHAPTER I

Under the figure of a wife proving false to her marriage vows, and bearing children that would follow her example, the prophet represents the shameful idolatry of the ten tribes, which provoked God to cast them off. The whole passage is information by action instead of words. The names of the children are all emblematical. The first is intended to put Israel in mind of their unrepented guilt, and the acts of cruelty committed in their palace of Jezreel, (1 Kings xxi. 1.) *The second and third, signifying* not finding mercy, *and* not my peope, *denote that, in consequence of their guilt, they were to be rejected of God,* 1–9. *God promises, however, to repair the loss to his Church by calling in the Gentiles,* 10; *and by uniting all the children of God under one head, the Messiah, in the latter days,* 11.

A. M. cir. 3219
B. C. cir. 785
Ante U. C. 32
Amulii Sylvii, R. Alban., cir. annum 12

THE word of the LORD that
came unto Hosea, the son
of Beeri, in the days of [a]Uz-
ziah, Jotham, Ahaz, *and* Heze-
kiah, kings of Judah, and in the days of [b]Je-
roboam the son of Joash, king
of Israel.

2 The beginning of the word
of the LORD by Hosea. And the
LORD said to Hosea, [c]Go, take unto thee a

[a]Isa. i. 1——[b]2 Kings xiv. 23

[c]So chap. iii. 1

NOTES ON CHAP. I

Verse 1. *Hosea, the son of Beeri*] See the preceding account of this prophet.

In the days of Uzziah, &c.] If we suppose, says Bp. *Newcome*, that Hosea prophesied during the course of *sixty-six* years, and place him from the year 790 before Christ to the year 724, he will have exercised his office *eight* years in the reign of *Jeroboam* the second, *thirty-three* years in the reign of *Uzziah*, the whole reigns of *Jotham* and *Ahaz*, and *three* years in the reign of *Hezekiah;* but will not have survived the taking of Samaria. But see the preceding account of this prophet.

I think the *first* verse to be a *title* to this book added by the compiler of his prophecies, and that it relates more to facts which took place *in those reigns*, and had been *predicted* by Hosea, who would only be said to have prophesied under all those kings, *by his predictions*, which were consecutively fulfilled under them. By those, though dead, he continued to speak. The prophet's work properly begins at ver. 2; hence called, "The beginning of the word of the Lord by Hosea."

Verse 2. *A wife of whoredoms*] That is, says *Newcome*, a wife from among the *Israelites*, who were remarkable for spiritual fornication, or idolatry. God calls himself the *husband* of Israel; and this chosen nation owed him the fidelity of a wife. See Exod. xxxiv. 15; Deut. xxxi. 16; Judge. ii. 17; Isa. liv. 5; Jer. iii. 14; xxxi. 32; Ezek. xvi. 17; xxiii. 5, 27; Hos. 2, 5; Rev. xvii. 1, 2. He therefore says, with indignation, Go join thyself in marriage to one of those who have committed fornication against me, and raise up children who, by the power of example, will themselves swerve to idolatry. See chap. v. 7. And thus show them that they are *radically* depraved.

A. M. cir. 3219
B. C. cir. 785
Ante U. C. 32
Amulii Sylvii,
R. Alban.,
cir. annum 12

wife of whoredoms, and children
of whoredoms: for [d]the land
hath committed great whoredom, *departing* from the LORD.
3 So he went and took Gomer the daughter
of Diblaim; which conceived, and bare him
a son.
4 And the LORD said unto him, Call his
name Jezreel; for yet a little *while*, [e]and I
will [f]avenge the blood of Jezreel upon the
house of Jehu, [g]and will cause to cease the
kingdom of the house of Israel.
5 [h]And it shall come to pass at that day,
that I will break the bow of Israel in the
valley of Jezreel.
6 And she conceived again, and bare a
daughter. And *God* said unto
him, Call her name [i]Lo-ru-
hamah: [k]for [l]I will no more have
mercy upon the house of Israel;
[m]but I will utterly take them away.
7 [n]But I will have mercy upon the house of
Judah, and will save them by the LORD their
God, and [o]will not save them by bow, nor by
sword, nor by battle, by horses, nor by horsemen.
8 Now when she had weaned Lo-ruhamah,
she conceived, and bare a son.
9 Then said *God*, call his name [p]Lo-ammi:
for ye *are* not my people, and I will not be
your *God*.
10 Yet [q]the number of the children of Israel

[d]Deut. xxxi. 16; Psa. lxxiii. 27; Jer. ii. 13; Ezek. xxiii. 3, &c.——[e]2 Kings x. 11——[f]Heb. *visit*——[g]2 Kings xv. 10, 12——[h]2 Kings xv. 29——[i]That is, *Not having obtained mercy*——[k]2 Kings xvii. 6, 23

[l]Heb. *I will not add any more to*——[m]Or, *that I should altogether pardon them*——[n]2 Kings xix. 35——[o]Zech. iv. 6; ix. 10——[p]That is, *Not my people*——[q]Gen. xxxii. 12; Romans ix. 27, 28

Verse 3. *He went and took Gomer*] All this appears to be a real transaction, though having a typical meaning. If he took an *Israelite*, he must necessarily have taken an *idolatress;* one who had worshipped the calves of Jeroboam at Dan or at Bethel.

Verse 4. *Call his name Jezreel*] יזרעאל that is, *God will disperse*. This seems to intimate that a dispersion or sowing of Israel shall take place; which happened under Shalmaneser, king of Assyria, 2 Kings xvii. 5, 6. But the word refers also to the name of *a city*, where Jehu slew Jezebel and all the children of Ahab. 2 Kings ix. 10, 36, and x. 6.

This was one of those *prophetic* names which we so often meet with in the Scriptures; *e. g.*, Japheth, Abraham, Israel, Judah, Joshua, Zerubbabel, Solomon, Sheer-jashub, &c.

The blood of Jezreel] Not Jehu's vengeance on Ahab's family, but his acts of cruelty while he resided at Jezreel, a city in the tribe of Issachar, Josh. xix. 18, where the kings of Israel had a palace, 1 Kings xxi. 1.

Will cause to cease the kingdom] Either relating to the cutting off of the kingdom of Israel by the Assyrians, see ver. 6, or to the ceasing of the kingdom of Israel from the house of *Jehu*, 2 Kings x. 30, and which was fulfilled, 2 Kings xv. 10.—*Newcome.*

Verse 5. *In the valley of Jezreel*] This also is supposed to relate either to some signal defeat of the Israelites by the Assyrians, which took place in the valley of Jezreel; or to the death of Zechariah, the fourth lineal descendant of Jehu, which may have happened here. See 2 Kings xv. 10.—*Newcome.*

Verse 6. *Call her Lo-ruhamah*] לא רחמה, "Not having obtained mercy." This also was a *prophetic* or *typical* name; and the reason of its imposition is immediately given:

For I will no more have mercy] כי לא אוסיף עיד ארחם *ki lo osiph od arachem*, "For I will no more add to have mercy upon the house of Israel." This refers to the total destruction of that kingdom.

Verse 7. *But I will have mercy upon the house of Judah*] I will spare them as a kingdom after Israel has been carried away into captivity by the Assyrians.

And will save them by the Lord their God] Remarkably fulfilled in the supernatural defeat of the army of the Assyrians, see 2 Kings xix. 35; and so they were saved not by *bow*, nor by *sword*, nor by *battle*, nor by *horses*, nor by *horsemen*. The former expression may mean, not in *war by horses*, *i. e.*, yoked to war *chariots*, nor *by horsemen*—nor by cavalry, however efficient such troops might have then been deemed.

Verse 9. *Call his name Lo-ammi*] לא עמי *Lo-ammi*, "Not my people;" for which the reason is immediately given:

Ye are not my people, and I will not be your God.] The word GOD is not added here by any of the ancient versions or MSS.; and yet the construction absolutely requires it, as *Houbigant* properly observes, who thinks the present reading לא אהיה לכם *lo eheyeh lachem*, "I will not be to you," a corruption of the word אלהיכם *eloheychem*, "your God." It is strange that no various reading occurs on this verse in any MS. yet discovered. In *two* of the oldest of mine there is a *blank* of *half a line* left after the last word; and so it is in the Masoretic Bibles, though the sense is not complete; for it is evidently continued in the following verse. Probably God refers to the words, Exod. iii. 14: אהיה אשר אהיה *I am that I am. I am*, אהיה *eheyeh,—I shall be*, hath sent me unto you. I will not be your *eheyeh*, *i. e.*, I will not be your God.

Verse 10. *Yet the number of the children of Israel*] God had promised that the children of Israel should be as the sand of the sea. See Gen. xxxii. 12; Rom. ix. 25, 26. And though for their iniquities he had thinned and scattered them, yet the spirit and design of his promise and covenant shall be fulfilled. An Israel there shall be. In the place of the reprobated people,

A. M. cir. 3219 B. C. cir. 785 Ante U. C. 32 Amulii Sylvii, R. Alban., cir. annum 12

shall be as the sand of the sea, which cannot be measured nor numbered; [r]and it shall come to pass, *that* [s]in the place where it was said unto them, [t]Ye *are* not my people, *there* it shall be said unto them, *Ye are* [u]the sons of the living God.

11 [v]Then shall the children of Judah and the children of Israel be gathered together, and appoint themselves one head, and they shall come up out of the land: for great *shall be* the day of Jezreel.

[r]Rom. ix. 25, 26; 1 Pet. ii. 10——[s]Or, *instead of that*——[t]Chap. ii. 23——[u]John i. 12; 1 John iii. 1——[v]Isa. xi. 12, 13; Jer. iii. 18; Ezek. xxxiv. 23; xxxvii. 16–24

who were now no longer his people, there shall be found an Israel that shall be the *children of the living God.* See the above scriptures, and 1 Pet. ii. 10. This must mean either the Israelites after their conversion to Christianity, or even the Gentiles themselves converted to God, and now become the *true Israel.*

Verse 11. *The children of Judah and the children of Israel*] After the return from Babylon, the distinction between Israel and Judah was entirely destroyed; and those of them that did return were all included under one denomination, *Jews;* and the *one head* may refer to Zerubbabel their leader, and afterwards under Ezra and Nehemiah. In the more extensive view of the prophet the *one Head* may mean *Jesus Christ,* under whom the true Israel, Jews and Gentiles, shall be finally gathered together; so that there shall be one flock, and one Shepherd over that flock.

They shall come up out of the land] Assyria and Chaldea in particular; but also from the various places of their dispersions in general.

Great shall be *the day of Jezreel.*] He alludes to the meaning of the word, the *seed of God.* God who has dispersed—*sown,* them in different lands, shall gather them together; and that day of God's power shall be great and glorious. It was a wonderful *seed time* in the Divine justice; it shall then be a wonderful *harvest* in the Divine mercy. He sowed them among the nations in his wrath; he shall reap them and gather them in his bounty.

CHAPTER II

The prophet exhorts his people to speak and to act as became those who obtained mercy of God; and to remonstrate strongly against the conduct of their mother, (Samaria,) whose captivity is threatened on account of her forsaking God, and ascribing her prosperity to idols, 1–5. *As an amplification of this threatening, the prophet enumerates a series of afflictions which were to befall her to bring her to a sense of her duty to God; and of her folly in seeking after idols, and falsely ascribing to them the blessings of Providence,* 6–13. *After these corrections, however, God promises to conduct Israel safely to their own land; perhaps alluding to their restoration from the Babylonish captivity, for this prophecy is supposed to have been delivered about* two hundred and fifty *years prior to this event,* 14, 15. *He farther engages to deal with them as a tender husband, and not as a severe master, as were the idols which they served,* 16, 17. *The rest of the chapter promises the people of God, the true Israel, security from every evil, with the possession of every blessing, under a new covenant; and that in terms full of beauty, energy, and consolation. Heaven and earth, and whatever they contain; all nature, and the God of nature, are represented as uniting to make the people of God happy; so that if they only breathe a wish, one part of nature, animate or inanimate, echoes it to another, and all join in sweet harmony to transmit it to the ear of the Almighty. "I will hear, saith the* LORD, *I will hear the heavens, and they shall hear the earth; and the earth shall hear the corn, and the wine, and the oil; and they shall hear Jezreel."*

A. M. cir. 3219 B. C. cir. 785 Ante U. C. 32 Amulii Sylvii, R. Alban., cir. annum 12

SAY ye unto your brethren, [a]Ammi; and to your sisters, [b]Ruhamah.

2 Plead with your mother, plead: for [c]she *is* not my wife, neither *am* I her husband: let her therefore put away her [d]whoredoms out of her sight, and her adulteries from between her breasts;

[a]That is, *My people*——[b]That is, *Having obtained mercy*——[c]Isa. l. 1——[d]Ezek. xvi. 25

NOTES ON CHAP. II

Verse 1. *Say ye unto your brethren, Ammi*] I prefer the interpretation of these proper names. *Say ye unto your brethren,* MY PEOPLE; *and to your sisters, who have* OBTAINED MERCY.

Verse 2. *Plead with your mother*] People of Judah, accuse your mother, (Jerusalem,) who has abandoned my worship, and is become idolatrous; convince her of her folly and wickedness, and let her return to him from whom she has so deeply revolted.

A. M. cir. 3219
B. C. cir. 785
Ante U. C. 32
Amulii Sylvii,
R. Alban.,
cir. annum 12

3 Lest [e]I strip her naked, and
set her as in the day that she
was [f]born, and make her [g]as
a wilderness, and set her like a
dry land, and slay her with [h]thirst.
4 And I will not have mercy upon her children;
for they *be* the [i]children of whoredoms.
5 [k]For their mother hath played the harlot:
she that conceived them hath done shamefully:
for she said, I will go after my lovers,
[l]that give *me* my bread and my water, my
wool and my flax, mine oil and my [m]drink.
6 Therefore, behold, [n]I will hedge up thy
way with thorns, and [o]make a wall, that she
shall not find her paths.
7 And she shall follow after her lovers, but
she shall not overtake them; and she shall
seek them, but shall not find *them:* then shall
she say, [p]I will go and return to my [q]first husband;
for then *was it* better with me than
now.
8 For she did not [r]know that [s]I gave her
corn, and [t]wine, and oil, and
multiplied her silver and gold,
[u]*which* they prepared for Baal.
9 Therefore will I return, and
[v]take away my corn in the time thereof, and
my wine in the season thereof, and will [w]recover
my wool and my flax *given* to cover
her nakedness.
10 And now [x]will I discover her [y]lewdness
in the sight of her lovers, and none shall deliver
her out of mine hand.
11 [z]I will also cause all her mirth to cease,
her [a]feast days, her new moons, and her Sabbaths,
and all her solemn feasts.
12 And I will [b]destroy her vines and her
fig-trees, [c]whereof she hath said, These *are*
my rewards that my lovers have given me:
and [d]I will make them a forest, and the beasts
of the field shall eat them.
13 And I will visit upon her the days of
Baalim, wherein she burned incense to them,

[e]Jer. xiii. 22, 26; Ezekiel xvi. 37, 39——[f]Ezekiel xvi. 4——[g]Ezek. xix. 13——[h]Amos viii. 11, 13——[i]John viii. 41——[k]Isa. i. 21; Jer. iii. 1, 6, 8, 9; Ezek. xvi. 15, 16, &c.——[l]Ver. 8, 12; Jer. xliv. 17——[m]Heb. *drinks*——[n]Job iii 23; xix. 8; Lam. iii. 7, 9——[o]Heb. *wall a wall*——[p]Chapter v. 15; Luke xv. 18——[q]Ezek. xvi. 8——[r]Isa. i. 3——[s]Ezek. xvi. 17, 18, 19——[t]Heb. *new wine*——[u]Or, *wherewith they made Baal;* chap. viii. 4——[v]Ver. 3——[w]Or, *take away*——[x]Ezek. xvi. 37; xxiii. 29——[y]Heb. *folly* or *villany*——[z]Amos viii. 10——[a]1 Kings xii. 32; Amos viii. 5——[b]Heb. *make desolate*——[c]Ver. 5——[d]Psa. lxxx. 12, 13; Isa. v. 5

Verse 3. *Lest I strip her naked*] Lest I expose her to infamy, want, and punishment. The punishment of an adulteress among the ancient Germans was this: "They shaved off her hair, stripped her naked in the presence of her relatives, and in this state drove her from the house of her husband." See on Isa. iii. 17; and see also Ezek. xvi. 39; xxiii. 26. However reproachful this might be to such delinquents, it had no tendency to promote their moral reformation.

And set her like a dry land] The Israelites, if obedient, were promised a land flowing with milk and honey; but, should they be disobedient, the reverse. And this is what God here threatens against disobedient Israel.

Verse 4. *They* be *the children of whoreaoms.*] They are all idolaters; and have been consecrated to idols, whose marks they bear.

Verse 5. *That give* me *my bread*] See the note on Jer. xliv. 17, 18, where nearly the same words are found and illustrated.

Verse 6. *I will hedge up thy way with thorns*] I will put it out of your power to escape the judgments I have threatened; and, in spite of all your attachment to your idols, you shall find that they can give you neither *bread*, nor *water*, nor *wool*, nor *flax*, nor *oil*, nor *drink*. And ye shall be brought into such circumstances, that the pursuit of your expensive idolatry shall be impossible. And she shall be led so deep into captivity, as never to find the road back to her own land. And this is the fact; for those who were carried away into Assyria have been lost among the nations, few of them having ever returned to Judea. And, if in being, where they are now is utterly unknown.

Verse 8. *For she did not know that I gave her corn*] How often are the gifts of God's *immediate bounty* attributed to fortuitous causes—to any cause but the right one!

Which *they prepared for Baal.*] And how often are the gifts of God's bounty perverted into means of dishonouring him! God gives us *wisdom*, *strength*, and *property;* and we use them to sin against him with the greater *skill*, *power*, and *effect!* Were the goods those of the *enemy*, in whose service they are employed, the crime would be the less. But the crime is deeply engrained, when God's property is made the instrument to dishonour himself.

Verse 9. *Therefore will I return, and take away*] In the course of my providence, I will withhold those benefits which she has prostituted to her idolatrous services. And I will neither give the land rain, nor fruitful seasons.

Verse 10. *In the sight of her lovers*] Her idols, and her faithful or faithless allies.

Verse 11. *Her feast days*] Jerusalem shall be pillaged and destroyed; and therefore all her joyous assemblies, and religious feasts, &c., shall cease.

Verse 12. *These* are *my rewards*] They attributed all the blessings of Providence as rewards received from the idols which they worshipped.

Verse 13. *Days of Baalim*] To *visit* signifies to *inflict punishment; the days* are taken for the *acts* of idolatrous worship committed on them; and *Baalim* means the *multitude* of false

A. M. cir. 3219
B. C. cir. 785
Ante U. C. 32
Amulii Sylvii,
R. Alban.,
cir. annum 12

and she [e]decked herself with her earrings and her jewels, and she went after her lovers, and forgat me, saith the LORD.

14 Therefore, behold, I will allure her, and
[f]bring her into the wilderness, and speak
[g]comfortably [h]unto her.

15 And I will give her vineyards from
thence, and [i]the valley of Achor for a door of
hope: and she shall sing there, as in [k]the days
of her youth, and [l]as in the day when she
came up out of the land of Egypt.

16 And it shall be at that day, saith the
LORD, that thou shalt call me [m]Ishi; and shalt
call me no more [n]Baali.

17 For [o]I will take away the names of
Baalim out of her mouth, and they shall no
more be remembered by their
name.

18 And in that day will I
make a [p]covenant for them with
the beasts of the field, and with the fowls of
heaven, and *with* the creeping things of the
ground: and [q]I will break the bow and the
sword, and the battle out of the earth, and
will make them to [r]lie down safely.

19 And I will betroth thee unto me for ever;
yea, I will betroth thee unto me in righteousness, and in judgment, and in lovingkindness,
and in mercies.

20 I will even betroth thee unto me in faithfulness; and [s]thou shalt know the LORD.

21 And it shall come to pass in that day, [t]I
will hear, saith the LORD, I will hear the hea-

[e]Ezekiel xxiii. 40, 42——[f]Ezekiel xx. 35——[g]Or, *friendly*——[h]Hebrew, *to her heart*——[i]Joshua vii. 26; Isaiah lxv. 10——[k]Jeremiah ii. 2; Ezekiel xvi. 8, 22, 60——[l]Exodus xv. 1——[m]That is, *My husband* [n]That is, *My lord*

[o]Exod. xxiii. 13; Josh. xxiii. 7; Psa. xvi. 4; Zech. xiii. 2——[p]Job v. 23; Isa. xi. 6–9; Ezek. xxxiv. 25 [q]Psa. xlvi. 9; Isa. ii. 4; Ezek. xxxix. 9, 10; Zech. ix. 10 [r]Lev. xxvi. 5; Jer. xxiii. 6——[s]Jer. xxxi. 33, 34; John xvii. 3——[t]Zech. viii. 12

gods worshipped by them. *Baal* was a general name for a *male* idol, as *Astarte* was for a *female*. *Baalim* includes all the *male idols*, as *Ashtaroth* all those that were *female*. But the species of idol was often designated by some adjunct; as *Baal*-Zebub, *Baal*-Peor, *Baal*-Zephon, *Baal*-Berith, &c.

Her earrings] נזמה *nizmah*, signifies rather a *nose jewel*. These are worn by females in the East to the present day, in great abundance.

And her jewels] וחליתה *vechelyatah*, rings, armlets, bracelets, ankle-rings, and ornaments of this kind.

Verse 14. *I will allure her, and bring her into the wilderness, and speak comfortably unto her.*] After inflicting many judgments upon her, I will restore her again. I will deal with her as a very affectionate husband would do to an unfaithful wife. Instead of making her a *public example*, he takes her in private, talks to and reasons with her; puts her on her good behaviour; promises to pass by all, and forgive all, if she will now amend her ways. In the meantime he provides what is necessary for her wants and comfortable support; and thus, opening a *door of hope* for her, she may be fully reconciled; *rejoice* as at the beginning, when he first took her by the hand, and she became his bride. This is most probably the simple meaning of the above *metaphorical* expressions. The *valley of Achor* was very fruitful; it lay to the north of Jericho, not far from Gilgal. See Isa. lxv. 10.

Verse 15. *She shall sing there*] There she shall sing the *responsive song*, as on high festival occasions, and in marriage ceremonies. The Book of *Canticles* is of this sort.

Verse 16. *Thou shalt call me Ishi*] That is, *my man*, or *my husband;* a title of *love* and *affection; and not* BAALI, *my master*, a title exciting *fear* and *apprehension;* which, howsoever good in itself, was now rendered improper to be applied to Jehovah, having been prostituted to false gods. This intimated that they should scrupulously avoid idolatry; and they had such a full proof of the inefficacy of their idolatrous worship that, after their captivity, they never more served idols.

Verse 18. *Will I make a covenant for them*] I will make an *agreement* between them and the birds, beasts, and reptiles, so that they shall not be injured by those; their *flocks* shall not be destroyed, nor their *crops* spoiled. I will also prevent every species of *war*, that they may no more have the calamities that arise from that source. They shall also be safe from robbers and nightly alarms; for *I will make them to lie down in safety.*

Verse 19. *I will betroth thee unto me*] The people are always considered under the emblem of a *wife* unfaithful to her husband.

In righteousness] According to law, reason, and equity.

In judgment] According to what is fit and becoming.

In lovingkindness] Having the utmost affection and love for thee.

In mercies.] Forgiving and blotting out all past miscarriages. Or there may be an allusion here to the dowry given by the husband to his wife: "I will give righteousness," &c., as a dowry.

Verse 20. *In faithfulness*] Thou shalt no more prostitute thyself to idols, but be *faithful* to him who calls himself *thy husband.*

Thou shalt know the Lord.] There shall be no more *infidelity* on *thy part* nor *divorce* on *mine;* and thou shalt experience me to be the sole, present, and eternal good of thy immortal spirit: and when this conviction is fully rooted, then there can be no more idolatry, for it shall be seen that an idol is nothing in the world.

Verse 21. *I will hear, saith the Lord*] The sentence is repeated, to show how fully the thing was determined by the Almighty, and

A. M. cir. 3219
B. C. cir. 785
Ante U. C. 32
Amulii Sylvii,
R. Alban.,
cir. annum 12

vens, and they shall hear the
earth;
22 And the earth shall hear the
corn, and the wine, and the oil;
[u]and they shall hear Jezreel.
23 And [v]I will sow her unto me in the earth,
[w]and I will have mercy upon her
that had not obtained mercy;
and I [x]will say to *them which*
were not my people, Thou *art*
my people; and they shall say, *Thou art* my
God.

[u]Ch. i. 4——[v]Jer. xxxi. 27; Zech. x. 9——[w]Ch. i. 6——[x]Chap. i. 10; Zech. xiii. 9; Rom. ix. 26; 1 Pet. ii. 10

how implicitly they might depend on the Divine promise.

I will hear the heavens] The visible heavens, the atmosphere, where vapours are collected. The *clouds*, when they wish to deposit their fertilizing showers upon the earth.

They shall hear the earth] When it seems to supplicate for rain.

Verse 22. *Shall hear the corn, and the wine*] When they seem to express a desire to supply the wants of man.

And they shall hear Jezreel.] The destitute people who are in want of the necessaries of life.

This most elegant gradation in the exertion of the influences of nature, for the supply of the wants of man, may be considered thus:—

1. There is a concord, harmony, and mutual influence, which God has established in the parts of created nature, in reference to the support and preservation of the human race.

2. God alone is the author of all this; and unless he give his command, communicate his *energetic influence* to the different parts of nature, these effects will not, cannot be produced.

3. *Jezreel*, the people who have been *dispersed* for their iniquities, and now about to be *sown* or *planted* in their own land, will require the most *fostering care*. See on ver. 23.

4. They are heard in desiring *oil*, *wine*, and *corn*. These are necessary to the support and comfort of life; and to those the desire of animal life naturally aspires.

5. These products are looked for from the EARTH. *On* it, and *by* it, grass grows for the cattle, and corn for the service of man.

6. The seeds or germs, whence proceed corn, wine, and oil, live and grow in the earth; but cannot come to perfection, unless the earth be impregnated with the dews and rains from the clouds. They are therefore represented as imploring the heavens to collect their clouds, to pour down their fructifying moisture upon it.

7. The clouds, or materials of which they are composed, not being able to arrange themselves, nor aggregate themselves so as to meet those demands, prevent drought, and maintain an effective vegetation, are represented as calling upon the heavens to form, arrange, and supply them with the requisite quantity of moisture.

8. God, who is the author of all being and all bounty, dependent on nothing, comes forward and says, *I will hear the heavens*, the clouds which are gathered in the atmosphere; he will arrange the particles, saturate those that are *light*, till they become sufficiently *impregnated* with the necessary fluid; and then direct them in his providence *where* to deposit their contents. And,

9. When brought to the proper place, he will *shake* them with his *winds*, or *strike* them with his *thunder*, so as to cause them to fall down in drops to fertilize the earth with their showers.

Thus then—

1. God works upon the *heavens*.

2. In them the *clouds* are collected.

3. The *clouds* drop their moisture upon the earth.

4. The *earth* exerts its vegetative influence upon the *germs* which it contains.

5. *They* expand, increase, and become matured, under the genial influences of the *heavens*, *sun*, *air*, *water*, from the clouds, &c.

6. *Man* receives and applies those bounties of Providence, and *variously prepares* them for the support and comfort of life.

Take all this in still fewer words:—

As *Jezreel* or the *Israelites* are here considered as perishing for want of food, all inanimate nature is represented as invoking God in their behalf.

1. The *heavens* have prayed that they be stored with *clouds*, that they may drop down fatness upon the *earth*.

2. The Lord answers the heavens, and *clouds* are formed.

3. The *earth* invokes the *clouds*, that they may drop down their fatness into its bosom.

4. The *bottles of heaven* are, consequently, unstopped for this purpose.

5. Then the *corn*, *vine*, and *olive*, implore the *earth* to put forth its vegetative energy.

6. The *earth* answers; and *corn*, *wine*, and *oil* are produced.

7. *Jezreel* cries for the necessaries of life, and the abundance of the above supplies all his wants.

All these are dependent on each other, as the links are which constitute a chain; and God has the government of the whole; and he manages all for the benefit of man. How wondrous is this *providence!* How gracious is this GOD!

Here is a series of *prosopopœias* together. Corn, wine, oil, the earth, the clouds and their contents, the *heavens*, sun, moon, &c., are all represented as intelligent beings, speaking to and influencing each other. GOD is at *one end* of the *chain*, and MAN at the *other;* and by means of the *intermediate links* the *latter* is kept in a state of continued dependence upon the *former* for life, breath, and all things.

Verse 23. *I will sow her*] Alluding to the import of the name *Jezreel*, the seed of God. Then shall it appear that God *has shown mercy to them that had not obtained mercy.* Then the *covenant* of God will be renewed; for he will call them *his people* who were *not his people;* and they shall call Jehovah *their God*, who before had *him* not for the object of their worship. It does not appear that these promises have had their fulfilment among the Jews. They must either be understood of the blessings experienced by the *Gentiles* on their conversion to God by the preaching of the Gospel, or are yet to be fulfilled to the Jews on their embracing the Gospel, and being brought back to their own land.

The sentences in the latter part of this verse are very abrupt, but exceedingly expressive; leaving out those words *supplied* by the translators, and which unnerve the passage, it stands thus: *I will say to* NOT MY PEOPLE, THOU MY PEOPLE; and they shall say, MY GOD.

CHAPTER III

By the prophet's taking back his wife, for whom he (her friend or husband) still retained his affection, though she had proved unfaithful; by his entering into a new contract with her; and by his giving her hopes of reconciliation, after she should for some time prove, as in a state of widowhood, the sincerity of her repentance; is represented the gracious manner in which God will restore the Jews from the Babylonish captivity, 1–4. *It is also very strongly intimated that the whole house of Israel will be added to the Church of Christ in the latter days,* 5.

A. M. cir. 3219
B. C. cir. 785
Ante U. C. 32
Amulii Sylvii,
R. Alban.,
cir. annum 12

THEN said the LORD unto
me, [a]Go yet, love a woman
beloved of *her* [b]friend, yet an
adulteress, according to the love
of the LORD toward the children of Israel,
who look to other gods, and love flagons [c]of
wine.
2 So I bought her to me for fifteen *pieces*
of silver, and *for* a homer of
barley, and a [d]half homer of
barley:
3 And I said unto her, Thou
shalt [e]abide for me many days; thou shalt
not play the harlot, and thou shalt not be for
another man: so *will* I also *be* for thee.
4 For the children of Israel shall abide many

A. M. cir. 3219
B. C. cir. 785
Ante U. C. 32
Amulii Sylvii,
R. Alban.,
cir. annum 12

---

[a]Chap. i. 2——[b]Jer. iii. 20——[c]Heb. *of grapes*

[d]Heb. *lethech*——[e]Deut. xxi. 13

NOTES ON CHAP. III

Verse 1. *Go yet, love a woman*] This is a different command from that mentioned in the *first* chapter. *That* denoted the infidelity of the kingdom of Israel, and God's divorce of *them.* He gave them up to their *enemies,* and caused them to be *carried into captivity.* The *woman* mentioned *here* represents one who was a *lawful wife* joining herself to a *paramour;* then divorced by her *husband;* afterwards repenting, and desirous to be joined to her spouse; ceasing from her adulterous commerce, but not yet *reconciled* to him. This was the state and disposition of the Jews under the Babylonish captivity. Though separated from their own *idols,* they continued *separated from their God.* He is still represented as having affectionate feelings towards them; awaiting their *full repentance* and *contrition,* in order to renew the marriage covenant. These things are pointed out by the symbolical actions of the prophet.

Beloved of her *friend*] Or, *a lover of evil;* or, *loving another:* for the Hebrew words אהבת רע mean one who *loves evil* or a *friend:* because רע signifies a *friend,* or *evil,* according as it is *pointed.* The former seems to be its best sense here; רֵעַ *rea* is a *friend;* רַע *ra* is *evil.*

According to the love of the Lord] This woman, who had proved false to her husband, was still beloved by him, though he could not acknowledge her; as the Israelites were beloved by the Lord, while they were *looking after other gods.* The *flagons of wine* were probably such as were used for *libations,* or drunk in idol feasts. Others think that the words should be translated *cakes of dried grapes, sweet cakes, consecrated wafers.*

Verse 2. *Fifteen* pieces *of silver*] If they were *shekels,* the price of this woman was about *two* pounds *five* shillings.

A homer of barley] As the homer was about *eight bushels,* or something more, the *homer and half* was about *twelve* or *thirteen* bushels.

Verse 3. *Thou shalt abide for me many days*] He did not take her home, but made a contract with her that, if she would abstain from her evil ways, he would take her to himself after a sufficient trial. In the meantime he gave her the *money* and the *barley* to subsist upon, that she might not be under the temptation of becoming again unfaithful.

So will *I also* be *for thee.*] That is, if *thou,* Israel, wilt keep thyself separate from thy idolatry, and give me proof, by thy total abstinence from idols, that thou wilt be my faithful worshipper, I will receive thee again, and in the meantime support thee with the *necessaries of life* while thou art in the land of thy captivity. This is farther illustrated in the following verses.

Verse 4. *Many days without a king*] Hitherto this prophecy has been literally fulfilled. Since the destruction of the temple by the Romans they have neither had *king* nor *prince,* nor any *civil government* of their own, but have lived in different nations of the earth as *mere exiles.* They have neither *priests* nor *sacrifices,* nor *urim* nor *thummim;* no *prophet,* no *oracle,* no *communication* of any kind from *God.*

Without an image—ephod—teraphim] The *Septuagint* read, *Ουδε ουσης θυσιας, ουδε οντος θυσιαστηριου, ουδε ἱερατειας, ουδε δηλων*: "Without a sacrifice, without an altar, without a priesthood, and without oracles;" that is, the *urim* and *thummim.* The *Vulgate, Arabic,* and *Syriac* read nearly the same. Instead of מצבה *matstsebah,* an *image,* they have evidently read מזבח

A. M. cir. 3219
B. C. cir. 785
Ante U. C. 32
Amulii Sylvii,
R. Alban.,
cir. annum 12

days [f]without a king, and
without a prince, and without
sacrifice, and without [g]an image,
and without an [h]ephod, and
without [i]teraphim:

5 Afterward shall the children
of Israel return, and [k]seek the
LORD their God, and [l]David
their king; and shall fear the
LORD and his goodness in the [m]latter days.

[f]Chap. x. 3; Song of the three children, ver. 15 —— [g]Heb. *a standing,* or *statue,* or *pillar;* Isa. xix. 19 —— [h]Exod. xxviii. 6 —— [i]Judg. xviii. 5

[k]Jer. l. 4, 5; Chap. v. 6 —— [l]Jer. xxx. 9; Ezek. xxxiv. 23, 24; xxxvii. 22, 24 —— [m]Isa. ii. 2; Jer. xxx. 24; Ezek. xxxviii. 8, 16; Dan. ii. 28; Mic. iv. 1

mizbeach, an *altar;* the letters of these words being very similar, and easily mistaken for each other. But instead of either, one, if not two, of *Kennicott's* MSS. has מנחה *minchah,* an *oblation.*

What is called *image* may signify any kind of *pillar,* such as God forbade them to erect, Lev. xxvi. 1, lest it should be an incitement to idolatry.

The *ephod* was the high priest's garment of ceremony; the *teraphim* were some kind of *amulets, telesms,* or *idolatrous images;* the *urim* and *thummim* belonged to the *breastplate,* which was attached to the *ephod.*

Instead of *teraphim* some would read *seraphim,* changing the ת *tau* into ש *sin;* these are an order of the celestial hierarchy. In short, all the time that the Israelites were in captivity in Babylon, they seem to have been as wholly without *forms* of *idolatrous worship* as they were without the *worship of God;* and this may be what the prophet designs: they were totally without any kind of public worship, whether *true* or *false.* As well without *images* and *teraphim,* as they were without *sacrifice* and *ephod,* though still idolaters in their hearts. They were in a state of the most miserable darkness, which was to *continue many days;* and it has continued now nearly *eighteen hundred* years, and must continue yet longer, till they acknowledge him as their *Saviour* whom they crucified as a *blasphemer.*

Verse 5. *Afterward shall the children of Israel return*] Shall *repent* of their iniquities, *and seek the Lord;* lay aside their *mock worship,* and serve the true God *in spirit and in truth.*

And David their king] Or as the *Targum,* "They shall obey the Messiah, the Son of David, their King;" and thus look believingly upon him whom they have pierced, and mourn. And then shall their long *spiritual darkness* and *dismal captivity* have an end; but not before. The *Messiah,* as *David,* is promised in Jer. xxx. 9; Ezek. xxxiv. 23; xxxvii. 22, 24, 25, (where see the notes,) and in this place of *Hosea.* Some think that the *family* of David is intended; but if we go to the rigour of the letter, the *house of Israel* was scarcely ever perfectly submissive to David. And we know that after the death of Solomon they never acknowledged the house of David till they were all carried away captive; and certainly never *since.* And to say that *Zerubbabel* is here meant, is not supportable, as the very *short* and *imperfect obedience* of the Jews to Zerubbabel can never comport with the *high terms* of this and similar prophecies. We are obliged, therefore, from the evidence of these *prophecies,* from the evidence of the above *facts,* from the evidence of the *rabbins* themselves, and from the evidence of the *New Testament,* to consider these texts as applying solely to JESUS CHRST, the promised MESSIAH, who has been a *light to lighten the Gentiles,* and will yet be the *glory of his people Israel.* There is a strange propensity in some men to deny these evidences of Christianity, while they profess to believe its doctrines.

CHAPTER IV

The prophet charges his people with their enormous sins, 1, 2; *in consequence of which they are threatened with heavy judgments,* 3–5. *God himself is then introduced complaining of the ignorance and obstinacy of Israel; and as their priests had a large share in the common guilt, it is declared that they shall be visited with a proportionable share of the common ruin,* 6–11. *The sins of idolatry and divination are then particularly reproved,* 12–14; *and Judah admonished to beware of these sins, which would leave her rebellious sister Israel helpless and desolate as a lamb in a desert,* 15, 16. *In the remaining verses the style is varied, but the subject is the same. Ephraim is given up to idolatry, and the necessary consequence declared to be a bitter draught! Immediately we see him bound in the wings of a mighty tempest, and driven as chaff before the wind, either to destruction or captivity,* 17–19.

A. M. cir. 3224
B. C. cir. 780
Ante U. C. 27
Amulii Sylvii,
R. Alban.,
cir. annum 17

HEAR the word of the LORD,
ye children of Israel: for
the LORD hath a [a]controversy
with the inhabitants of the land,
Because *there is* no truth, nor
mercy, nor [b]knowledge of God
in the land.
2 By swearing, and lying, and

[a]Isa. i. 18; iii. 13, 14; Jer. xxv. 31; Chap. xii. 2; Mic. vi. 2 —— [b]Jer. iv. 22; v. 4

NOTES ON CHAP. IV

Verse 1. *The Lord hath a controversy*] ריב *rib,* what we should call a *lawsuit,* in which God is *plaintiff,* and the Israelites *defendants.* It is Jehovah *versus* Israel and Judah.

But *when* has God a controversy with any land?—*Answer.* When there is *no truth, nor*

A. M. cir. 3224 B. C. cir. 780 Ante U. C. 27 Amulii Sylvii, R. Alban., cir. annum 17

killing, and stealing, and com-
mitting adultery, they break out,
and [c]blood toucheth blood.
3 Therefore [d]shall the land
mourn, and [e]every one that dwelleth therein
shall languish, with the beasts of the field,
and with the fowls of heaven; yea, the fishes
of the sea also shall be taken away.
4 Yet let no man strive, nor reprove another: for thy people *are* as they [f]that strive
with the priest.
5 Therefore shalt thou fall
[g]in the day, and the prophet
also shall fall with thee in the
night, and I will [h]destroy thy
mother.
6 [i]My people are [k]destroyed for lack of
knowledge: because thou hast rejected knowledge, I will also reject thee, that thou shalt
be no priest to me: seeing thou hast forgotten
the law of thy God, I will also forget thy children.

A. M. cir. 3224 B. C. cir. 780 Ante U. C. 27 Amulii Sylvii, R. Alban., cir. annum 17

[c]Heb. *bloods*——[d]Jer. iv. 28; xii. 4; Amos v. 16; viii. 8 [e]Zeph. i. 3

[f]Deut. xvii. 12——[g]See Jer. vi. 4, 5; xx. 8——[h]Heb. *cut off*——[i]Isa. v. 13——[k]Heb. *cut off*

mercy, nor knowledge of God in the land. These refer to the *minds* of the people. But wherever these righteous *principles* are wanting, there will soon be a vicious *practice;* hence it is added,

Verse 2. *By swearing, and lying*] Where there is no *truth* there will be *lies and perjury;* for false swearing is brought in to confirm lying statements. And when there is no *mercy*, *killing, slaying,* and *murders*, will be frequent. And where there is *no knowledge of God*, no conviction of his *omnipresence* and *omniscience*, private offences, such as stealing, adulteries, &c., will prevail. These, sooner or later, *break out*, become a *flood*, and carry all before them. *Private stealing* will assume the form of a *public robbery*, and *adulteries* become *fashionable*, especially among the higher orders; and suits of *crim. con.* render them more public, scandalous, and corrupting. By the examination of *witnesses*, and reading of *infamous letters* in a court of justice, people are taught the *wiles* and *stratagems* to be used to accomplish these ends, and prevent detection; and also how to *avoid* those circumstances which have led to the detection of others. Every *report* of such matters is an *experimental lecture* on *successful debauchery*.

Blood toucheth blood.] Murders are not only frequent, but assassinations are mutual. Men go out to *kill each other;* as in our duels, the frenzy of cowards; and as there is no law regarded, and no justice in the land, the nearest akin slays the murderer. Even in our land, where *duels* are so frequent, if a man kill his antagonist, it is *murder;* and so generally brought in by an honest *coroner* and his jury. It is then brought into court; but who is *hanged* for it? The very murder is considered as an *affair of honour*, though it began in a dispute about a *prostitute;* and it is directed to be brought in manslaughter; and the murderer is slightly fined for having hurried his neighbour, perhaps once his *friend*, into the eternal world, *with all his imperfections on his head!* No wonder that a land *mourns* where these prevail; and that God should have a *controversy* with it. Such crimes as these are sufficient to bring God's curse upon any land. And how does God show his displeasure? See the following verse.

Verse 3. *Therefore shall the land mourn*] Fruitful seasons shall be denied.

That dwelleth therein shall languish] *Endemic* and *epidemic disorders* shall prevail, and multitudes shall die; so that *mourning* shall be found in all quarters.

The beasts of the field, and with the fowls] There is a death of cattle and domestic animals, in consequence of the badness of the season.

The fishes of the sea also shall be taken away.] Those immense shoals which at certain seasons frequent the coasts, which are caught in millions, and become a very useful home supply, and a branch of most profitable traffic, they shall be directed by the unseen influence of God to avoid our coasts, as has frequently been the case with herrings, mackerel, pilchards, &c.; and so this source of supply and wealth has been shut up, because of the iniquities of the land.

Verse 4. *Yet let no man strive*] Or, *no man contendeth.* All these evils stalk abroad unreproved, for all are guilty. None can say, "Let me pluck the *mote* out of thy eye," because he knows that "there is a *beam* in his own."

For thy people are] The *people* and the *priest* are alike *rebels* against the Lord; the priests having become idolaters, as well as the people. Bp. *Newcome* renders this clause, "And as *is* the provocation of the priest, *so is that of my people.*" The whole clause in the original is ועמך כמריבי כהן *veammecha kimeribey cohen*, "and thy people as the rebellions of the priest." But one of my oldest MSS. omits כהן *cohen*, "priest;" and then the text may be read, *And thy people are as rebels.* In this MS. כהן *cohen* is added in the margin by a much later hand.

Verse 5. *Therefore shalt thou fall in the day*] In the most open and public manner, without *snare* or *ambush*.

And the prophet also shall fall—in the night] The false prophet, when employed in taking prognostications from stars, meteors, &c.

And I will destroy thy mother.] The *metropolis* or *mother city. Jerusalem* or *Samaria* is meant.

Verse 6. *My people are destroyed for lack of knowledge*] They have not the knowledge of God, nor of sacred things, nor of their own interest, nor of the danger to which they are exposed. They walk on blindly, and perish.

Because thou hast rejected knowledge] So they might have become wise, had they not rejected the means of improvement.

Thou shalt be no priest to me] If this be the true reading, there must be reference to some *particular priest*, well known, to whom these words are personally addressed; unless by

A. M. cir. 3224
B. C. cir. 780
Ante U. C. 27
Amulii Sylvii,
R. Alban.,
cir. annum 17

7 [l]As they were increased, so they sinned against me: [m]*therefore* will I change their glory into shame.

8 They eat up the sin of my people, and they [n]set their heart on their iniquity.

9 And there shall be, [o]like people, like priest: and I will [p]punish them for their ways, and [q]reward them their doings.

10 For [r]they shall eat, and not have enough: they shall commit whoredom, and shall not increase: because they have left off to take heed to the Lord.

11 Whoredom and wine and new wine [s]take away the heart.

12 My people ask counsel at their [t]stocks, and their staff declareth unto them: for [u]the spirit of whoredoms hath caused *them* to err, and they have gone a whoring from under their God.

13 [v]They sacrifice upon the tops of the mountains, and burn incense upon the hills, under oaks and poplars and elms, because the shadow thereof *is* good: [w]therefore your daughters shall commit whoredom, and your spouses shall commit adultery.

14 [x]I will not punish your daughters when they commit whoredom, nor your spouses when they commit adultery: for themselves are separated with whores, and they sacrifice with harlots: therefore the people *that* [y]doth not understand shall [z]fall.

15 Though thou, Israel, play the harlot, *yet* let not Judah offend; [a]and come not ye unto Gilgal, neither go ye up to [b]Beth-aven, [c]nor swear, The Lord liveth.

16 For Israel [d]slideth back as a backsliding

[l]Chap. xiii. 6——[m]1 Samuel ii. 30; Malachi ii. 9; Philippians iii. 19——[n]Hebrew, *lift up their soul to their iniquity*——[o]Isa. xxiv. 2; Jer. v. 31——[p]Heb. *visit upon*——[q]Heb. *cause to return*——[r]Lev. xxvi. 26; Mic. vi. 14; Hag. i. 6——[s]Isa. xxviii. 7; See Eccles. vii. 7——[t]Jer. ii. 27; Hab. ii. 19

[u]Isa. xliv. 20; Chap. v. 4——[v]Isa. i. 29; lvii. 5, 7; Ezek. vi. 13; xx. 28——[w]Amos vii. 17; Rom. i. 28——[x]Or, *Shall I not*, &c.——[y]Ver. 1, 6——[z]Or, *be punished*——[a]Chap. ix. 15; xii. 11; Amos iv. 4; v. 5——[b]1 Kings xii. 29; Chap. x. 5——[c]Amos viii. 14; Zeph. i. 5——[d]Jer. iii. 6; vii. 24; viii. 5; Zech. vii. 11

priest the whole *priesthood* is meant, and then it may apply to the *priests of Jeroboam's calves.*

Verse 7. *Will I change their glory into shame.*] As the idolaters at Dan and Bethel have changed my glory into the similitude of an ox that eateth grass, (Rom. i. 23,) so will I change their *glory* into *shame* or ignominy. In the day of my wrath, their calf-gods shall not deliver them.

Verse 8. *They eat up the sin of my people*] חטאת *chattath*, the *sin-offering*, though it be offered contrary to the law; for their *hearts are set on iniquity*, they *wish* to do whatever is contrary to God.

Verse 9. *Like people, like priest*]

"The priest a wanderer from the narrow way;
The silly sheep, no wonder that they stray."

I will punish them] Both priest and people; both equally bad.

Verse 10. *They shall eat, and not have enough*] Whatever means they may use to *satisfy* or *gratify* themselves shall be ineffectual.

Verse 11. *Whoredom and wine*] These debaucheries go generally *together*.

Take away the heart.] Darken the understanding, deprave the judgment, pervert the will, debase all the passions, &c.

Verse 12. *At their stocks*] They consult their *wooden gods.*

And their staff declareth] They use divination by *rods;* see the note on Ezek. xxi., where this sort of divination (*rabdomancy*) is explained.

Verse 13. *Under oaks*] אלון *allon*, from אלל *alal*, he was *strong.* Hence, the *oak*, in Latin, is called *robur;* which word means also, *strength*, the oak being the *strongest* of all the trees of the forest.

The shadow thereof is *good*] Their "daughters committed whoredom, and their spouses committed adultery." 1. Their deities were worshipped by prostitution. 2. They *drank* much in their idol worship, ver. 11, and thus their passions became inflamed. 3. The *thick groves* were favourable to the whoredoms and adulteries mentioned here. In imitation of these, some nations have their public gardens.

Verse 14. *I will not punish*] Why should you be stricken any more; ye will revolt more and more. When God, in judgment, removes his judgments, the case of that people is desperate. While there is *hope*, there is *correction.*

Themselves are separated] There is a reference here to certain debaucheries which should not be described. The state of the people at this time must have been abominable beyond all precedent; animal, sensual, bestial, diabolical: women consecrating themselves to serve their idols by public prostitution; boys dismembered like the *Galli* or priests of Cybele; men and women acting unnaturally; and all conjoining to act diabolically.

Verse 15. *Let not Judah offend*] Israel was *totally* dissolute; Judah was not so. Here she is exhorted to maintain her integrity. If the former will go to what was once *Beth-el*, the *house of God*, now *Beth-aven*, the *house of iniquity*, because Jeroboam has set up his calves there, let not Judah imitate them. *Gilgal* was the place where the covenant of circumcision was renewed when the people passed over Jordan; but was rendered infamous by the worship of idols, after Jeroboam had set up his idolatry.

Verse 16. *Israel slideth back*] They are un-

A. M. cir. 3224
B. C. cir. 780
Ante U. C. 27
Amulii Sylvii,
R. Alban.,
cir. annum 17

heifer: now the LORD will feed
them as a lamb in a large place.
17 Ephraim *is* joined to idols:
[e]let him alone.
18 Their drink [f]is sour: they have
committed whoredom continually: [g]her
[h]rulers *with* shame do love,
Give ye.
19 [i]The wind hath bound
her up in her wings, and [k]they
shall be ashamed because of their sacrifices.

[e]Matt. xv. 14——[f]Heb. *is gone*——[g]Mic. iii. 11; vii. 3
[h]Heb. *shields;* Psa. lxxiv. 9

[i]Psa. i. 4; lxxxiii. 13; Isa. xi. 15; xli. 16; lvii. 13; Jer. iv. 11, 12; li. 1——[k]Isa. i. 29; Jer. ii. 26

tractable, like an unbroken heifer or steer, that *pulls back*, rather than *draw in the yoke*.

Will feed them as a lamb in a large place.] A species of irony. Ye shall go to Assyria, and be scattered among the nations; ye may *sport yourselves* in the extensive empire, wither ye shall be carried captives.

Verse 17. *Ephraim*] The ten tribes.

Is *joined to idols*] Is become incorporated with false gods.

Let him alone.] They are irreclaimable, leave them to the consequences of their vicious conduct.

Verse 18. *Their drink is sour*] Or rather, *he is gone after their wine*. The enticements of idolatry have carried them away.

Her rulers with *shame do love*] Rather, *have loved shame;* they glory in their abominations.

Give ye.] Perhaps it would be better to read, *Her rulers have committed, &c. They have loved gifts. What a shame!* These were *their rulers*, literally, *their shields*. Justice and judgment were perverted.

Verse 19. *The wind hath bound her*] A parching wind has blasted them in their *wings*—coasts, borders; or they are carried away into captivity, as with the most rapid blight. These two last verses are very obscure.

CHAPTER V

This chapter begins with threatening the Israelites for ensnaring the people to idolatry by their sacrifices and other rites on Mizpah and Tabor, 1–5. *Their sacrifices, however costly, are declared to be unacceptable,* 6; *and their substance is devoted to the locust,* 7. *Nor is judgment to stop here. The cities of Judah are called upon, in a very animated manner, to prepare for the approach of enemies. Benjamin is to be pursued; Ephraim is to be desolate; and all this is intimated to Israel, that they may by repentance avert the judgment,* 8, 9. *The following verses contain farther denunciations,* 10–13, *expressed in terms equally terrible and sublime,* 14. *The Lord afflicts not willingly the children of men; he visits them with temporal calamities that he may heal their spiritual malady,* 15.

A. M. cir. 3224
B. C. cir. 780
Ante U. C. 27
Amulii Sylvii,
R. Alban.,
cir. annum 17

HEAR ye this, O priests; and
hearken, ye house of Israel;
and give ye ear, O house of the
king; for judgment *is* toward
you, because [a]ye have been a snare on Mizpah, and a net spread upon Tabor.
2 And the revolters are [b]profound to make
slaughter, [c]though I *have been* [d]a Rebuker
of them all.
3 [e]I know Ephraim, and
Israel is not hid from me: for
now, O Ephraim, [f]thou com-
mittest whoredom, *and* Israel is
defiled.
4 [g]They [h]will not frame their doings to
turn unto their God: for [i]the spirit of whoredoms *is* in the midst of them, and they have
not known the LORD.

[a]Chap. vi. 9——[b]Isa. xxix. 15——[c]Or, *and*, &c.
[d]Heb. *a correction*——[e]Amos iii. 2

[f]Ezek. xxiii. 5, &c.; ch. iv. 17——[g]Heb. *They will not give*
[h]Or, *Their doings will not suffer* them——[i]Chap. iv. 12

NOTES ON CHAP. V

Verse 1. *Hear ye this, O priests*] A process is instituted against the *priests*, the *Israelites*, and the *house of the king;* and they are called on to appear and defend themselves. The accusation is, that they have *ensnared* the people, caused them to practise idolatry, both at *Mizpah* and *Tabor*. Mizpah was situated beyond Jordan, in the mountains of Gilead; see Judg. xi. 29. And Tabor was a beautiful mountain in the tribe of Zebulum. Both these places are said to be eminent for *hunting*, &c.; and hence the natural occurrence of the words *snare* and *net*, in speaking of them.

Verse 2. *The revolters are profound to make slaughter*] Here may be a reference to the practice of *hunters*, making *deep pits* in the ground, and lightly covering them over, that the beasts, not discovering them, might fall in, and become a prey.

Though I have been *a Rebuker*] "I will bring *chastisement* on them all." As they have made *victims* of others to their *idolatry*, I will make *victims* of them to my *justice*. Some have thought that as many as wished to depart from the idolatrous worship set up by Jeroboam, were *slaughtered;* and thus *Jeroboam the son of Nebat* MADE *Israel to sin*.

Verse 3. *I know Ephraim*] I know the whole to be idolaters.

Verse 4. *They will not frame their doings*]

A. M. cir. 3224
B. C. cir. 780
Ante U. C. 27
Amulii Sylvii,
R. Alban.,
cir. annum 17

5 And [k]the pride of Israel doth testify to his face: therefore shall Israel and Ephraim fall in their iniquity: Judah also shall fall with them.

6 [l]They shall go with their flocks and with their herds to seek the LORD; but they shall not find *him;* he hath withdrawn himself from them.

7 They have [m]dealt treacherously against the LORD: for they have begotten strange children: now shall [n]a month devour them with their portions.

8 [o]Blow ye the cornet in Gibeah, *and* the trumpet in Ramah: [p]cry aloud *at* [q]Beth-aven, [r]after thee, O Benjamin.

9 Ephraim shall be desolate in the day of rebuke: among the tribes of Israel have I made known that which shall surely be.

10 The princes of Judah were like them that [s]remove the bound: *therefore* I will pour out my wrath upon them like water.

A. M. cir. 3224
B. C. cir. 780
Ante U. C. 27
Amulii Sylvii,
R. Alban.,
cir. annum 17

11 Ephraim *is* [t]oppressed *and* broken in judgment, because he willingly walked after [u]the commandment.

12 Therefore *will* I *be* unto Ephraim as a moth, and to the house of Judah [v]as [w]rottenness.

13 When Ephraim saw his sickness, and Judah *saw* his [x]wound, then went Ephraim [y]to the Assyrian, [z]and sent [a]to King Jareb: yet could he not heal you, nor cure you of your wound.

14 For [b]I *will be* unto Ephraim as a lion, and as a [c]young lion to the house of Judah: I, *even* I, will tear and go away; I will take away, [d]and none shall rescue *him.*

15 I will go *and* return to my place, [e]till [f]they acknowledge their offence, and seek my face: [g]in their affliction they will seek me early.

---

[k]Chap. vii. 10——[l]Prov. i. 28; Isa. i. 15; Jer. xi. 11; Ezek. viii. 18; Mic. iii. 4; John vii. 34——[m]Isa. xlviii. 8; Jer. iii. 20; v. 11; Chap. vi. 7; Mal. ii. 11——[n]Zech. xi. 8——[o]Chap. viii. 1; Joel ii. 1——[p]Isa. x. 30 [q]Josh. vii. 2; chap. iv. 15——[r]Judg. v. 14——[s]Deut. xix. 14; xxvii. 17——[t]Deut. xxviii. 33——[u]1 Kings xii. 28; Mic. vi. 16

[v]Prov. xii. 4——[w]Or, *a worm*——[x]Jer. xxx. 12——[y]2 Kings xv. 19; chap. vii. 11; xii. 1——[z]Chap. x. 6——[a]Or *to the king of Jareb;* or, *to the king* that *should plead* [b]Lam. iii. 10; chap. xiii. 7, 8——[c]Isa. xxx. 6——[d]Psa. l. 22——[e]Heb. *till they be guilty*——[f]Lev. xxvi. 40, 41; Jer. xxix. 12, 13; Ezek. vi. 9; xx. 43; xxxvi. 31——[g]Psa. lxxviii. 34

They never *purpose* to turn to God, they have fully imbibed the spirit of idolatry.

Verse 5. *The pride of Israel doth testify to his face*] The effrontery with which they practise idolatry manifests, not only their insolence, but the deep depravity of their heart; but their pride and arrogance shall be humbled.

Verse 6. *They shall go with their flocks*] They shall *offer many sacrifices,* professing to *seek* and be reconciled to the Lord; but they shall not *find him.* As they still retain the spirit of their idolatry, he has withdrawn himself from them.

Verse 7. *Now shall a month devour them*] In a month's time the king of Assyria shall be upon them, and oblige them to purchase their lives and liberties by a grievous tax of *fifty* shekels per head. This Menahem, king of Israel, gave to *Pul,* king of Assyria, 2 Kings xv. 16-20. Instead of *month,* some translate the original *locust.* "The locusts shall devour them."

Verse 8. *Blow ye the cornet in Gibeah*] Gibeah and Ramah were cities of Judah, in the tribe of Benjamin.

After thee, O Benjamin] An abrupt call of warning. "Benjamin, fly for thy life! The enemy is just behind thee!" This is a prediction of the invasion of the Assyrians, and the captivity of the *ten* tribes.

Verse 9. *Among the tribes of Israel have I made known*] They have got sufficient warning; it is their own fault that they have not taken it.

Verse 10. *Like them that remove the bound*] As execrable as they who remove the *land-mark.* They have leaped over law's inclosure, and scaled all the walls of right; they have despised and broken all laws, human and Divine.

Verse 11. *Walked after the commandment.*] Jeroboam's commandment to worship his calves at Dan and Beth-el. Many of them were not *forced* to do this; they did it *willingly.*

Verse 12. *Unto Ephraim as a moth*] I will consume them by little and little, as a moth frets a garment.

Verse 13. *When Ephraim saw his sickness*] When both Israel and Judah felt their own weakness to resist their enemies, instead of calling upon and trusting in *me,* they sought sinful alliances, and trusted in their idols.

King Jareb] This name occurs nowhere in Scripture but here and in chap. x. 6. The *Vulgate* and *Targum* render ירב *yareb,* an *avenger,* a person whom they thought able to *save them* from their enemies. It is well known that *Menahem,* king of Israel, sought alliance with *Pul* and *Tiglath-pileser,* kings of Assyria, and *Ahaz,* king of Judah. These were the *protectors* that Ephraim sought after. See 2 Kings xv. and xvi. But far from *healing them* by making them tributary, the Assyrians made their *wound* more dangerous.

Verse 14. *I* will be—*as a lion*] כשחל *cashshachel,* as a *panther* or *lioness.*

Verse 15. *I will go* and *return to my place*] I will abandon them till they acknowledge their offences. This had the wished-for effect, as we shall see in the following chapter; for they repented and turned to God, and he had mercy upon them. These two verses are considered as instances of the *true sublime.*

CHAPTER VI

The prophet earnestly exhorts to repentance, 1–3. God is then introduced as very tenderly and pathetically remonstrating against the backslidings of Ephraim and Judah, 4–11.

A. M. cir. 3224
B. C. cir. 780
Ante U. C. 27
Amulii Sylvii,
R. Alban.,
cir. annum 17

COME, and let us return unto
the LORD: for [a]he hath torn,
and [b]he will heal us; he hath
smitten, and he will bind us up.
2 [c]After two days will he revive us: in the
third day he will raise us up, and we shall
live in his sight.
3 [d]Then shall we know, *if* we follow on to
know the LORD: his going forth is prepared
[e]as the morning; and [f]he shall
come unto us [g]as the rain, as
the latter *and* former rain unto
the earth.
4 [h]O Ephraim, what shall I do unto thee?
O Judah, what shall I do unto thee? for your
[i]goodness *is* [k]as a morning cloud, and as the
early dew it goeth away.
5 Therefore have I hewed *them* [l]by the

[a]Deuteronomy xxxii. 39; 1 Samuel ii. 6; Job. v. 18; Chapter v. 14——[b]Jeremiah xxx. 17——[c]1 Corinthians xv. 4——[d]Isaiah liv. 13——[e]2 Samuel xxiii. 4——[f]Psalm lxxii. 6——[g]Job xxix. 23——[h]Chap. xi. 8——[i]Or, *mercy*, or *kindness*——[k]Chap. xiii. 3——[l]Jer. i. 10; v. 14

NOTES ON CHAP. VI

Verse 1. *Come, and let us return unto the Lord*] When God had purposed to abandon them, and they found that he had *returned to his place*—to his temple, where alone he could be successfully sought; they, feeling their weakness, and the fickleness, weakness, and unfaithfulness of their idols and allies, now resolve to "return to the Lord;" and, referring to what he said, chap. v. 14: "I will tear and go away;" they say, he "hath torn, but he will heal us;" their allies had *torn*, but they gave them no healing. While, therefore, they acknowledge the *justice* of God in their punishment, they depend on his well-known mercy and compassion for restoration to life and health.

Verse 2. *After two days will he revive*] Such is his power that in *two* or *three* days he can restore us. He can realize all our hopes, and give us the strongest token for good.

In the third day he will raise us up] In so short a time can he give us complete deliverance. These words are supposed to refer to the *death and resurrection of our Lord;* and it is thought that the apostle refers to them, 1 Cor. xv. 4: "Christ rose again the third day, according to the Scriptures;" and this is the *only place* in the *Scriptures*, i. e., of the Old Testament, where his resurrection on the *third* day seems to be hinted at. The original, יקמנו *yekimenu*, has been translated, *he will raise him up*. Then they who trusted in him could believe that they should be *quickened* together with him.

And we shall live in his sight.] *His resurrection* being a proof of *theirs.*

Verse 3. *Then shall we know*] We shall have the fullest evidence that we have not believed in vain.

If *we follow on to know the Lord*] If we *continue* to be as much in *earnest* as we *now* are.

His going forth] The manifestation of his mercy to our souls is as certain as the *rising of the sun* at the appointed time.

And he shall come unto us as the rain] As surely as the early and the latter rain come. The first, to prepare the earth for the seed; this fell in *autumn:* the second, to prepare the full ear for the harvest; this fell in *spring.* Here is strong confidence; but not misplaced, however worthless the persons were. As surely as the *sun*, who is *now set*, is running his course to *arise* on us in the *morning*, and make a glorious *day* after a dreary *night;* so surely shall the Lord *come again from his place*, and the Sun of righteousness shall arise on our souls with healing in his wings. He is already *on his way* to save us.

Verse 4. *O Ephraim, what shall I do unto thee?*] This is the answer of the Lord to the above pious resolutions; sincere while they lasted, but frequently forgotten, because the people were fickle. Their *goodness* (for goodness it was while it endured) was *like the morning cloud that fadeth away* before the rising sun, or like the *early dew* which is speedily evaporated by heat. Ephraim and Judah had too much *goodness* in them to admit of their total rejection, and too much *evil* to admit of their being placed among the children. Speaking after the manner of men, the *justice* and *mercy* of God seem puzzled how to act toward them. When *justice* was about to *destroy* them for their iniquity, it was prevented by their *repentance* and *contrition:* when *mercy* was about to pour upon them as penitents its choicest blessings, it was prevented by their *fickleness* and *relapse!* These things induce the just and merciful God to exclaim, "O Ephraim, what shall I do unto thee? O Judah, what shall I do unto thee?" The only thing that could be done in such a case was that which God did.

Verse 5. *Therefore have I hewed* them *by the prophets*] I have sent my prophets to testify against their fickleness. They have smitten them with the most solemn and awful threatenings; they have, as it were, slain them by the words of my mouth. But to what purpose?

Thy judgments are as *the light* that *goeth forth*] Instead of ומשפטיך אור יצא *umispateycha or yetse*, "and thy judgments a light that goeth forth," the *versions* in general have read ומשפטי כאור *umishpati keor*, "and my judgment *is* as the light." The final ך *caph* in the common reading has by mistake been taken from אור *aur*, and joined to משפטי *mishpati;* and thus turned it from the *singular* to the *plural* number, with the postfix ך *cha*. The proper reading is, most probably, "And my judgment is as the light going forth." It shall be both *evident* and *swift;* alluding both to the *velocity* and *splendour* of light.

A. M. cir. 3224
B. C. cir. 780
Ante U. C. 27
Amulii Sylvii,
R. Alban.,
cir. annum 17

prophets; I have slain them by
[m]the words of my mouth: [n]and
thy judgments *are as* the light
that goeth forth.
6 For I desired [o]mercy, and [p]not sacrifice;
and the [q]knowledge of God more than burnt
offerings.
7 But they [r]like men [s]have transgressed the
covenant: there [t]have they dealt treacherously against me.
8 [u]Gilead *is* a city of them that work iniquity, *and is* [v]polluted with blood.
9 And as troops of robbers
wait for a man, *so* [w]the company
of priests murder in the way
[x]by consent: for they commit
[y]lewdness.
10 I have seen [z]a horrible thing in the house
of Israel: there *is* [a]the whoredom of Ephraim,
Israel is defiled.
11 Also, O Judah, [b]he hath set a harvest
for thee, [c]when I returned the captivity of
my people.

A. M. cir. 3224
B. C. cir. 780
Ante U. C. 27
Amulii Sylvii,
R. Alban.,
cir. annum 17

[m]Jer. xxiii. 29; Heb. iv. 12——[n]Or, *that thy judgments might be*, &c.——[o]1 Sam. xv. 22; Eccles. v. 1; Mic. vi. 8; Matt. ix. 13; xii. 7——[p]Psa. l. 8, 9; Prov. xxi. 3; Isa. i. 11——[q]Jer. xxii. 16; John. xvii. 3——[r]Or, *like Adam;* Job xxxi. 33——[s]Chap. viii. 1

[t]Chap. v. 7——[u]Chap. xii. 11——[v]Or, *cunning for blood*——[w]Jer. xi. 9; Ezek. xxii. 25; Chap. v. 1, 2 [x]Heb. *with* one *shoulder*, or *to Shechem*——[y]Or, *enormity*——[z]Jer. v. 31——[a]Chap. iv. 12, 13, 17——[b]Jer. li. 33; Joel iii. 13; Rev. xiv. 15——[c]Isa. cxxvi. 1

Verse 6. *I desired mercy, and not sacrifice*] I taught them righteousness by my prophets; for I desired mercy. I was more willing to *save* than to *destroy;* and would rather see them full of *penitent* and *holy resolutions*, than behold them offering the *best* and most *numerous victims* upon my altar. See Matt. ix. 13.

Verse 7. *But they like men* (כאדם *keadam*, "like Adam") *have transgressed the covenant*] They have sinned against light and knowledge as *he* did. This is *sense*, the other is scarcely so. There was a striking similarity in the two cases. *Adam, in Paradise*, transgressed the commandment, and I *cast him out: Israel*, in possession of the *promised land*, transgressed my covenant, and I cast *them* out, and sent them into captivity.

Verse 8. *Gilead* is *a city of them that work iniquity*] In this place Jacob and Laban made their covenant, and set up a *heap of stones*, which was called *Galeed*, the *heap of testimony;* and most probably idolatry was set up here. Perhaps the very *heap* became the object of superstitious adoration.

Verse 9. *As troops of robbers*] What a sad picture is this of the state of the priesthood! The country of Gilead was infamous for its robberies and murders. The idolatrous priests there formed themselves into companies, and kept possession of the roads and passes; and if they found any person going to Jerusalem to worship the true God, they put him to death. The reason is given:—

For they commit lewdness.] They are gross idolaters.

Verse 10. *I have seen a horrible thing*] That is, the idolatry that prevailed in Israel to such a degree that the whole land was defiled.

Verse 11. *O Judah, he hath set a harvest for thee*] Thou also hast transgressed; thy *harvest* will come; thou shalt be *reaped down* and sent into captivity. The *sickle* is already thrust in. That which thou *hast sowed* shalt thou *reap.* They who *sow* unto the *flesh* shall *reap corruption.*

When I returned the captivity of my people.] Bp. *Newcome* translates, "Among those who lead away the captivity of my people." There is thy harvest; they who have led Israel into captivity shall lead thee also into the same. The Assyrians and Babylonians were the same kind of people; equally idolatrous, equally oppressive, equally cruel. From the common reading some suppose this to be a *promise of return from captivity.* It is true that *Judah* was gathered together again and brought back to their own land; but the majority of the *Israelites* did not return, and are not now to be found.

CHAPTER VII

Here God complains that though he had employed every means for reforming Israel, they still persisted in their iniquity, without fearing the consequences, 1, 2; *that those who ought to check their crimes were pleased with them,* 3; *and that they all burned with adultery, as an oven when fully heated, and ready to receive the kneaded dough,* 4. *The* fifth *verse alludes to some recent enormities; the* sixth *charges them with dividing their time between inactivity and iniquity; the* seventh *alludes to their civil broils and conspiracies; (see* 2 Kings xv. 10, 14, 25;) *the* eighth *to their joining themselves with idolatrous nations; and the* ninth *describes the sad consequence. The* tenth *verse reproves their pride and open contempt of God's worship; the* eleventh *reproves their foolish conduct in applying for aid to their enemies; (see* 2 Kings xv. 19, *and* xvii. 4;) *the* twelfth *and* thirteenth *threaten them with punishments; the* fourteenth *charges them with hypocrisy in their acts of humiliation; the* fifteenth *with ingratitude; and the image of the deceitful bow, in the* sixteenth *verse, is highly expressive of their frequent apostasies; and their hard speeches against God shall be visited upon them by their becoming a reproach in the land of their enemies.*

A. M. cir. 3224
B. C. cir. 780
Ante U. C. 27
Amulii Sylvii,
R. Alban.,
cir. annum 17

WHEN I would have healed Israel, then the iniquity of Ephraim was discovered, and the [a]wickedness of Samaria: for [b]they commit falsehood; and the thief cometh in *and* the troop of robbers [c]spoileth without.

2 And they [d]consider not in their hearts *that* I [e]remember all their wickedness: now [f]their own doings have beset them about; they are [g]before my face.

3 They make the king glad with their wickedness, and the princes [h]with their lies.

4 [i]They *are* all adulterers, as an oven heated by the baker, [k]*who* ceaseth [l]from raising after he hath kneaded the dough, until it be leavened.

5 In the day of our king the princes have made *him* sick [m]with bottles of wine; he stretched out his hand with scorners.

A. M. cir. 3224
B. C. cir. 780
Ante U. C. 27
Amulii Sylvii,
R. Alban.,
cir. annum 17

6 For they have [n]made ready their heart like an oven, whiles they lie in wait: their baker sleepeth all the night; in the morning it burneth as a flaming fire.

7 They are all hot as an oven, and have devoured their judges; [o]all their kings [p]are fallen: [q]*there is* none among them that calleth unto me.

8 Ephraim, he [r]hath mixed himself among the people; Ephraim is a cake not turned.

9 [s]Strangers have devoured his strength, and he knoweth *it* not: yea, gray hairs are [t]there

[a]Heb. *evils*——[b]Chap. v. 1; vi. 10——[c]Hebrew, *strippeth*——[d]Heb. *say not to*——[e]Jer. xvii. 1——[f]Psa. ix. 16; Prov. v. 22——[g]Psa. xc. 8——[h]Rom. i. 32 [i]Jer. ix. 2——[k]Or, *the raiser will cease*

[l]Or, *from waking*——[m]Or, *with heat through wine* [n]Or, *applied*——[o]Chapter viii. 4——[p]2 Kings xv. 10, 14, 25, 30——[q]Isa. lxiv. 7——[r]Psa. cvi. 35——[s]Chap. viii. 7——[t]Hebrew, *sprinkled*

NOTES ON CHAP. VII

Verse 1. *When I would have healed Israel*] As soon as one wound was healed, another was discovered. Scarcely was one sin blotted out till another was committed.

The thief cometh in] Their own princes spoil them.

The troop of robbers spoileth without.] The Assyrians, under different leaders, waste and plunder the country.

Verse 2. *They consider not in their hearts*] They do not consider that *my eye is upon all their ways;* they do not think that I *record* all their wickedness; and they know not their *own* evil *doings* are as a *host of enemies encompassing* them about.

Verse 3. *They make the king glad*] They pleased Jeroboam by coming readily into his measures, and heartily joining with him in his idolatry. And they professed to be perfectly happy in their change, and to be greatly advantaged by their new gods; and that the religion of the state now was better than that of Jehovah. Thus, they made all their rulers, "glad with their lies."

Verse 4. *As an oven heated by the baker*] *Calmet's* paraphrase on this and the following verses expresses pretty nearly the sense: Hosea makes a twofold comparison of the Israelites; to an *oven*, and to *dough*. Jeroboam set fire to his own *oven*—his kingdom—and put the leaven in his dough; and afterwards went to rest, that the fire might have time to heat his *oven*, and the *leaven* to raise his *dough*, that the false principles which he introduced might infect the whole population. This prince, purposing to make his subjects relinquish their ancient religion, put, in a certain sense, the fire to his own oven, and mixed his dough with leaven. At first he used no violence; but was satisfied with exhorting them, and proclaiming a feast. This *fire* spread very rapidly, and the *dough* was very soon impregnated by the *leaven*. All Israel was seen running to this feast, and partaking in these innovations. But what shall become of the *oven*—the *kingdom;* and the *bread*—the *people?* The *oven* shall be consumed by these flames; the king, the princes, and the people shall be enveloped in the burning, ver. 7. Israel was *put under the ashes*, as a *loaf* well kneaded and leavened; but not being carefully *turned*, it was burnt on one side before those who prepared it could eat of it; and *enemies* and *strangers* came and carried off the loaf. See ver. 8 and 9. Their lasting captivity was the consequence of their wickedness and their apostasy from the religion of their fathers. On this explication verses 4, 5, 6, 7, 8, and 9, may be easily understood.

Verse 7. *All their kings are fallen*] There was a pitiful slaughter among the idolatrous kings of Israel; *four* of them had fallen in the time of this prophet. Zechariah was slain by Shallum; Shallum, by Menahem; Pekahiah, by Pekah; and Pekah, by Hoshea, 2 Kings xv. All were idolaters, and all came to an untimely death.

Verse 8. *A cake not turned.*] In the East, having heated the *hearth*, they sweep one corner, put the cake upon it, and cover it with embers; in a short time they *turn* it, cover it again, and continue this several times, till they find it sufficiently baked. All travellers into Asiatic countries have noted this.

Verse 9. *Gray hairs are here and there upon him, yet he knoweth not.*] The kingdom is grown old in iniquity; the time of their captivity is at hand, and they are apprehensive of no danger. They are in the state of a *silly old man*, who through age and infirmities is become nearly *bald*, and the few *remaining hairs* on his head are quite *gray*. But he does not consider his latter end; is making no provision for that eternity on the brink of which he is constantly standing; does not apply to the sovereign Physician to heal his spiritual diseases; but calls in the *doctors* to cure him of *old age* and *death!* This miserable state and preposterous conduct we witness every day. O how fast

A. M. cir. 3224
B. C. cir. 780
Ante U. C. 27
Amulii Sylvii,
R. Alban.,
cir. annum 17

and there upon him, yet he
knoweth not.
10 And the [u]pride of Israel
testified to his face: and [v]they
do not return to the LORD their God, nor seek
him for all this.
11 [w]Ephraim also is like a silly dove without heart: [x]they call to Egypt, they go to
Assyria.
12 When they shall go, [y]I will spread my
net upon them; I will bring them down as
the fowls of the heaven; I will chastise them,
[z]as their congregation hath heard.
13 Wo unto them! for they have fled from
me: [a]destruction unto them! because they have
transgressed against me: though
[b]I have redeemed them, yet they
have spoken lies against me.
14 [c]And they have not cried
unto me with their heart, when they howled
upon their beds: they assemble themselves
for corn and wine, *and* they rebel against me.
15 Though I [d]have bound *and* strengthened
their arms, yet do they imagine mischief
against me.
16 [e]They return, *but* not to the Most High:
[f]they are like a deceitful bow: their princes
shall fall by the sword for the [g]rage of their
tongue: this *shall be* their derision [h]in the
land of Egypt.

[u]Chap. v. 5——[v]Isa. ix. 13——[w]Chap. xi. 11
[x]See 2 Kings xv. 19; xvii. 4; chap. v. 13; ix. 3; xii. 1
[y]Ezek. xii. 13——[z]Lev. xxvi. 14, &c.; Deut. xxviii. 15,
&c.; 2 Kings xvii. 13, 18

[a]Heb. *spoil*——[b]Mic. vi. 4——[c]Job xxxv. 9, 10; Psa.
lxxviii. 36; Jer. iii. 10; Zech. vii. 5——[d]Or, *chastened*
[e]Chap. xi. 7——[f]Psalm lxxvii. 57——[g]Psalm lxxiii. 9
[h]Chapter ix. 3, 6

does the human being cling to his native earth! Reader, hear the voice of an old man:—

O my *coevals!* remnants of yourselves,
Shall *our* pale wither'd hands be *still stretch'd out?*
Trembling at once with *eagerness* and *age;*
With *avarice* and *ambition* grasping—fast
Grasping at *air!* For what hath *earth* beside?
We want but *little;* nor THAT LITTLE *long.*

Verse 10. *The pride of Israel*] The same words as at chap. v. 5, where see the note.

Verse 11. *Ephraim also is like a silly dove without heart*] A bird that has *little understanding;* that is *easily snared* and taken; that is careless about its *own young,* and seems to live without *any kind of thought.* It has been made, by those who, like itself, are *without heart,* the *symbol of conjugal affection.* Nothing *worse* could have been chosen, for the dove and its mate are continually quarrelling.

They call to Egypt, they go to Assyria.] They strive to make these their allies and friends; but in this they showed that they were *without heart,* had not a *sound understanding;* for these were rival nations, and Israel could not attach itself to the one without incurring the jealousy and displeasure of the other. Thus, like the *silly dove,* they were constantly falling into *snares;* sometimes of the Egyptians, at others of the Assyrians. By the former they were *betrayed;* by the latter, *ruined.*

Verse 12. *When they shall go*] To those nations for help—

I will spread my net upon them] I will cause them to be taken by those in whom they trusted.

I will bring them down] They shall no sooner set off to seek this foreign help, than *my net* shall *bring them down to the earth.* The allusion to the *dove,* and to the mode of taking the *fowls of heaven,* is still carried on.

As their congregation hath heard.] As in their *solemn assemblies* they before have heard; in the *reading of my law,* and the denunciation of my wrath against *idolaters.*

Bishop *Newcome* translates: "I will chastise them when they hearken to their assembly." That is, when they take the counsel of their elders to go down to Egypt for help, and trust in the arm of the Assyrians for succour.

Verse 13. *Wo unto them!*] They shall have *wo,* because they *have fled from me.* They shall have *destruction,* because they *have transgressed against me.*

Though I have redeemed them] Out of Egypt; and given them the fullest proof of my love and power.

Yet they have spoken lies against me.] They have represented me as rigorous and cruel; and my service as painful and unprofitable.

Verse 14. *They have not cried unto me with their heart*] They say they have sought me, but could not find me; that they have cried unto me, but I did not answer. I know they have *cried,* yea, *howled;* but could I hear them when all was forced and hypocritical, not one sigh coming from their *heart?*

They assemble themselves for corn and wine] In dearth and famine they call and howl: but they assemble themselves, not to seek ME, but to invoke their false gods for corn and wine.

Verse 15. *Though I have bound* and *strengthened their arms*] Whether I dealt with them in *judgment* or *mercy,* it was all one; in all circumstances they rebelled against me.

Verse 16. *They return,* but *not to the Most High*] They go to their idols.

They are like a deceitful bow] Which, when it is *reflexed,* in order to be strung, suddenly *springs back* into its *quiescent curve;* for the *eastern bows* stand in their quiescent state in a curve, something like ; and in order to be strung must be *bended back* in the *opposite direction.* This bending of the bow requires both *strength* and *skill;* and if not properly done, it will fly back, and regain its former position; and in this recoil endanger the archer—may even break an arm. I have been in this danger myself in bending the Asiatic bow. For want of this knowledge not one commentator has hit the meaning of the passage.

Shall fall by the sword] Their *tongue* has been enraged against ME; the *sword* shall be enraged against them. They have *mocked* me, (ver. 5,) and their fall is now a subject of *derision in the land of Egypt*. What they have sown, that do they now reap.

CHAPTER VIII

This chapter begins with threatening some hostile invasion in short and broken sentences, full of rapidity, and expressive of sudden danger and alarm: "The trumpet to thy mouth; he cometh as an eagle," 1. *And why? For their hypocrisy,* 2; *iniquity,* 3; *treason (see* 2 Kings xv. 13, 17) *and idolatry,* 4; *particularly the worshipping of the calves of Dan and Beth-el,* 5, 6. *The folly and unprofitableness of pursuing evil courses is then set forth in brief but very emphatic terms. The labour of the wicked is vain, like sowing of the wind; and the fruit of it destructive as the whirlwind. Like corn blighted in the bud, their toil shall have no recompense; or if it should have a little, their enemies shall devour it,* 7. *They themselves, too, shall suffer the same fate, and shall be treated by the nations of Assyria and Egypt as the vile sherds of a broken vessel,* 8, 9. *Their incorrigible idolatry is again declared to be the cause of their approaching captivity under the king of Assyria. And as they delighted in idolatrous altars, there they shall have these in abundance,* 10–14. *The last words contain a prediction of the destruction of the fenced cities of Judah, because the people trusted in these for deliverance, and not in the Lord their God.*

A. M. cir. 3244
B. C. cir. 760
Ante U. C. 7
Amulii Sylvii, R. Alban., cir. annum 37

SET [a]the trumpet to [b]thy
mouth. *He shall come* [c]as
an eagle against the house of the
LORD, because [d]they have transgressed my covenant, and trespassed against
my law.
2 [e]Israel shall cry unto me, My God, [f]we
know thee.
3 Israel hath cast off *the thing that is* good:
the enemy shall pursue him.
4 [g]They have set up kings, but
not by me: they have made
princes, and I knew *it* not: [h]of
their silver and their gold have
they made them idols, that they may be cut off.
5 Thy calf, O Samaria, hath cast *thee* off;
mine anger is kindled against them: [i]how
long *will it be* ere they attain to innocency?
6 For from Israel *was* it also: the workman made it; therefore it *is* not God; but

A. M. cir. 3244
B. C. cir. 760
Ante U. C. 7
Amulii Sylvii, R. Alban., cir. annum 37

---

[a]Chapter v. 8——[b]Hebrew, *the roof of thy mouth* ——[c]Deuteronomy xxviii. 49; Jeremiah iv. 13; Habakkuk i. 8——[d]Chapter vi. 7——[e]Psalm lxxviii. 34; chapter v. 15——[f]Titus i. 16——[g]2 Kings xv. 13, 17, 25, Shallum, Menahem, Pekahiah——[h]Chapter ii. 8; xiii. 2——[i]Jeremiah xiii. 27

NOTES ON CHAP. VIII

Verse 1. Set *the trumpet to thy mouth*] Sound another alarm. Let them know that an enemy is fast approaching.

As an eagle against the house of the Lord] If this be a prophecy against *Judah*, as some have supposed, then by the *eagle* Nebuchadnezzar is meant, who is often compared to this king of birds. See Ezek. xvii. 3; Jer, xlviii. 40; xlix. 22; Dan. vii. 4.

But if the prophecy be against *Israel*, which is the most likely, then *Shalmaneser*, king of Assyria, is intended, who, for his rapidity, avarice, rapacity, and strength, is fitly compared to this royal bird. He is represented here as *hovering over the house of God*, as the eagle does over the prey which he has just espied, and on which he is immediately to pounce.

Verse 2. *Israel shall cry*] The rapidity of the eagle's flight is well imitated in the rapidity of the sentences in this place.

My God, we know thee.] The same sentiment, from the same sort of persons, under the same feelings, as that in the Gospel of St. Matthew, chap. vii. 22: "Lord, have we not prophesied in thy name? and in thy name have cast out devils? Then will I profess unto them, I never KNEW YOU."

Verse 4. *They have set up kings, but not by me*] Properly speaking, not one of the kings of Israel, from the defection of the ten tribes from the house of David, was the *anointed* of the Lord.

I knew it *not*] It had not my *approbation*. In this sense the word *know* is frequently understood.

That they may be cut off.] That is, They shall be cut off in consequence of their idolatry.

Verse 5. *Thy calf, O Samaria, hath cast* thee *off*] Bishop *Newcome* translates: "Remove far from thee thy calf, O Samaria!" Abandon thy idolatry; for *my anger is kindled against thee.*

How long will it be *ere they attain to innocency?*] How long will ye continue your guilty practices? When shall it be said that ye are from these vices? The *calf* or *ox*, which was the object of the idolatrous worship of the Israelites, was a supreme deity in Egypt; and it was there they learned this idolatry. A white ox was worshipped under the name of *Apis*, at Memphis; and another ox under the name of *Mnevis*, was worshipped at On, or Heliopolis. To Osiris the males of this genus were consecrated, and the females to Isis. It is a most ancient superstition, and still prevails in the East. The cow is a most sacred animal among the Hindoos.

Verse 6. *The workman made it; therefore it is not God*] As God signifies the supreme eternal Good, the Creator and Upholder of all things, therefore the workman cannot make

A. M. cir. 3244
B. C. cir. 760
Ante U. C. 7
Amulii Sylvii,
R. Alban.,
cir. annum 37

the calf of Samaria shall be
broken in pieces.
7 For [k]they have sown the
wind, and they shall reap the
whirlwind: it hath no [l]stalk: the bud shall
yield no meal: if so be it yield, [m]the strangers
shall swallow it up.
8 [n]Israel is swallowed up: now shall they
be among the Gentiles [o]as a vessel wherein
is no pleasure.
9 For [p]they are gone up to Assyria, [q]a wild
ass alone by himself: Ephraim [r]hath hired
[s]lovers.
10 Yea, though they have hired among the
nations, now [t]will I gather them, and they
shall [u]sorrow [v]a little for the burden of [w]the
king of princes.
11 Because Ephraim hath
made [x]many altars to sin,
altars shall be unto him to
sin.
12 I have written to him [y]the great things
of my law, *but* they were counted as a strange
thing.
13 [z]They [a]sacrifice flesh *for* the sacrifices
of mine offerings, and eat *it;* [b]*but* the LORD
accepteth them not; [c]now will he remember
their iniquity, and visit their sins: [d]they shall
return to Egypt.
14 [e]For Israel hath forgotten [f]his Maker,
and [g]buildeth temples: and Judah hath multiplied fenced cities: but [h]I will send a fire
upon his cities, and it shall devour the palaces
thereof.

[k]Prov. xxii. 8; Ch. x. 12, 13——[l]Or, *standing corn*——[m]Ch. vii. 9——[n]2 Kings xvii. 6——[o]Jer. xxii. 28; xlviii. 38——[p]2 Kings xv. 19——[q]Jer. ii. 24——[r]Isa. xxx. 6; Ezek. xvi. 33, 34——[s]Heb. *loves*——[t]Ezek. xvi. 37; Ch. x. 10——[u]Or, *begin*——[v]Or, *in a little while*, as Hag. ii. 6——[w]Isa. x. 8; Ezek. xxvi. 7; Dan. ii. 37——[x]Ch. xii. 11

[y]Deut. iv. 6, 8; Psa. cxix. 18; cxlvii. 19, 20——[z]Jer. vii. 21; Zech. vii. 6——[a]Or, *in the sacrifices of mine offerings they*, &c.——[b]Jer. xiv. 10, 12; Ch. v. 6; ix. 4; Amos v. 22——[c]Ch. ix. 9; Amos viii. 7——[d]Deut. xxviii. 68; ch. ix. 3, 6; xi. 5——[e]Deut. xxxii. 18——[f]Isa. xxix. 23; Eph. ii. 10——[g]1 Kings xii. 31——[h]Jer. xvii. 27; Amos ii. 5

Him who made all things. This is an overwhelming argument against all idols. Nothing need be added. *The workman has made them; therefore they are not God.*

Verse 7. *They have sown the wind, and they shall reap the whirlwind*] As the husbandman reaps the same kind of grain which he has sown, but in far greater abundance, *thirty, sixty*, or *one hundred* fold; so he who sows the wind shall have a whirlwind to reap. The *vental* seed shall be multiplied into a *tempest;* so they who sow the seed of unrighteousness shall reap a harvest of judgment. This is a fine, bold, and energetic metaphor.

It hath no stalk] Nothing that can yield a *blossom.* If it have a *blossom*, that blossom shall not yield *fruit;* if there be *fruit*, the sower shall not enjoy it, for *strangers shall eat it.* The meaning is, the labours of this people shall be utterly unprofitable and vain.

Verse 8. *Now shall they be among the Gentiles*] They shall be carried into captivity, and there be as a vessel wherein there is no pleasure; one soiled, unclean, infectious, to be despised, abhorred, not used. The allusion is to a rotten, corrupted skin-bottle; a bottle made of goat, deer, or calf hide, still commonly used in Asia and Africa. Some of them are splendidly ornamented. This is the case with one now before me made of a goat's skin well dressed, variously painted, and ornamented with leather fringes, tassels, &c. In such a bottle there might be pleasure; but the Israelites are compared to such a bottle, rough, ill-dressed, not ornamented, old, musty, and putrid. This shows the force of the comparison.

Verse 9. *They are gone up to Assyria*] For succour.

A wild ass alone by himself] Like that animal, jealous of its liberty, and suffering no rival. If we may credit *Pliny* and others, one male wild ass will keep a whole flock of females to himself, suffer no other to approach them, and even bite off the genitals of the colts, lest in process of time they should become his rivals. "Mares singuli fæminarum gregibus imperitant; timent libidinis æmulos, et ideo gravidas custodiunt, morsuque natos mares castrant."—*Hist. Nat.*, lib. viii., c. 30. The Israelites, with all this selfishness and love of liberty, took no step that did not necessarily lead to their thraldom and destruction.

Ephraim hath hired lovers.] Hath subsidized the neighbouring heathen states.

Verse 10. *For the burden of the king of princes.*] The exactions of the Assyrian king, and the princes of the provinces.

Verse 11. *Many altars to sin*] Though it does not appear that the Jews in Babylon were obliged to worship the idols of the country, except in the case mentioned by Daniel, yet it was far otherwise with the Israelites in Assyria, and the other countries of their dispersion. Because they had made many altars to sin while they were in their own land, they were obliged to *continue* in the land of their captivity a similar system of idolatry against their will. Thus they felt and saw the evil of their idolatry, without power to help themselves.

Verse 12. *I have written to him the great things of my law*] I have as it were inscribed my laws to them, and they have treated them as matters in which they had no interest.

Verse 13. *They sacrifice flesh*] Bp. *Newcome* translates thus: "They sacrifice gifts appointed unto me, and eat flesh." They offer to their idols the things which belong to Jehovah; or, while pretending to offer unto the Lord, they eat and drink idolatrously; and therefore the Lord will not accept them.

They shall return to Egypt.] Many of them did return to Egypt after the conquest of Palestine by Shalmaneser, and many after the ruin of Jerusalem by Nebuchadnezzar; but they had in effect returned to Egypt by setting up the worship of the golden calves, which were in imitation of the Egyptian *Apis*.

Verse 14. *Israel hath forgotten his Maker*] And therefore built *temples* to other gods. *Judah* had lost all confidence in the Divine protection, and therefore built many fenced cities. But the *fire* of God's anger burnt up both the temples and the fortified cities.

CHAPTER IX

The prophet reproves the Israelites for their sacrifices and rejoicings on their corn-floors, by which they ascribed to idols, as the heathen did, the praise of all their plenty, 1. *For which reason they are threatened with famine and exile,* 2, 3, *in a land where they should be polluted, and want the means of worshipping the God of their fathers, or observing the solemnities of his appointment,* 4, 5. *Nay more; they shall speedily fall before the destroyer, be buried in Egypt, and leave their own pleasant places desolate,* 6–9. *God is then introduced declaring his early favour for his people, and the delight he took in their obedience; but now they had so deeply revolted, all their glory will take wing, God will forsake them, and their offspring be devoted to destruction,* 10–16.

A. M. cir. 3244
B. C. cir. 760
Ante U. C. 7
Amulii Sylvii, R. Alban., cir. annum 37

REJOICE not, O Israel, for
joy, as *other* people: for
thou [a]hast gone a whoring from
thy God, thou hast loved a [b]re-
ward [c]upon every corn-floor.
2 [d]The floor and the [e]wine-press shall not
feed them, and the new wine shall fail in her.
3 They shall not dwell in [f]the LORD's
land; [g]but Ephraim shall return to Egypt,
and [h]they shall eat unclean *things* [i]in Assyria.
4 [k]They shall not offer wine *offerings* to
the LORD, [l]neither shall they be pleasing unto
him: [m]their sacrifices *shall be* unto them as
the bread of mourners; all that
eat thereof shall be polluted: for
their bread [n]for their soul shall
not come into the house of the
LORD.
5 What will ye do in [o]the solemn day, and
in the day of the feast of the LORD?
6 For, lo, they are gone because of [p]de-
struction: [q]Egypt shall gather them up,
Memphis shall bury them: [r]the [s]pleasant
places for their silver, [t]nettles shall possess
them: thorns *shall be* in their tabernacles.
7 The days of visitation are come, the days
of recompense are come; Israel shall know

A. M. cir. 3244
B. C. cir. 760
Ante U. C. 7
Amulii Sylvii, R. Alban., cir. annum 37

---

[a]Chap. iv. 12; v. 4, 7——[b]Jer. xliv. 17; chap. ii. 12——[c]Or, *in*, &c.——[d]Ch. ii. 9, 12——[e]Or, *wine-fat*——[f]Lev. xxv. 23; Jer. ii. 7; xvi. 18——[g]Ch. viii. 13; xi. 5; not into Egypt itself, but into another bondage as bad as that——[h]Ezek. iv. 13; Dan. i. 8——[i]2 Kings xvii. 6; ch. xi. 11

[k]Ch. iii. 4——[l]Jer. vi. 20; ch. viii. 13——[m]Deut. xxvi. 14——[n]Lev. xvii. 11——[o]Ch. ii. 11——[p]Hebrew, *spoil*——[q]Ch. vii. 16; ver. 3——[r]Or, *their silver shall be desired, the nettle*, &c.——[s]Heb. *the desire*——[t]Isa. v. 6; xxxii. 13; xxxiv. 13; chap. x. 8

NOTES ON CHAP. IX

Verse 1. *Rejoice not*] Do not imitate the heathens, nor serve their idols. Do not *prostitute* thy soul and body in practising their impurities. Hitherto thou hast acted as a *common harlot*, who goes even to the common *threshing places;* connects herself with the meanest, in order to get a *hire* even of the *grain* there threshed out.

Verse 3. *But Ephraim shall return to Egypt*] See on chap. viii. 12.

Verse 4. *As the bread of mourners*] By the law, a dead body, and every thing that related to it, the house where it lay, and the persons who touched it, were all polluted and unclean, and whatever they touched was considered as defiled. See Deut. xxvi. 14; Num. xix. 11, 13, 14.

For their bread for their soul] The bread for the common support of *life* shall not be sanctified to them by having the *first-fruits* presented at the temple.

Verse 5. *What will ye do in the solemn day*] When ye shall be despoiled of every thing by the Assyrians; for the Israelites who remained in the land after its subjection to the Assyrians did worship the true God, and offer unto him the sacrifices appointed by the law, though in an imperfect and schismatic manner; and it was a great mortification to them to be deprived of their religious *festivals* in a land of strangers. See *Calmet.*

Verse 6. *For, lo, they are gone*] Many of them fled to Egypt to avoid the *destruction;* but they went there only to *die.*

Memphis] Now *Cairo*, or *Kahira*, found them *graves.*

The pleasant places *for their silver*] The fine estates or *villas* which they had purchased by their money, being now neglected and uninhabited, are covered with *nettles;* and even in their *tabernacles, thorns* and *brambles* of different kinds grow. These are the fullest marks of *utter desolation.*

Verse 7. *The days of visitation*] Of punishment *are come.*

The prophet is *a fool*] Who has pretended to foretell, on Divine authority, peace and plenty; for behold all is desolation.

A. M. cir. 3244
B. C. cir. 760
Ante U. C. 7
Amulii Sylvii,
R. Alban.,
cir. annum 37

it: the prophet *is* a fool, [u]the [v]spiritual man *is* mad, for the multitude of thine iniquity, and the great hatred.

8 The [w]watchman of Ephraim *was* with my God: *but* the prophet *is* a snare of a fowler in all his ways, *and* hatred [x]in the house of his God.

9 [y]They have deeply corrupted *themselves,* as in the days of [z]Gibeah: [a]*therefore* he will remember their iniquity, he will visit their sins.

10 I found Israel likes grapes in the wilderness; I saw your fathers as the [b]first ripe in the fig tree [c]at her first time: *but* they went to [d]Baal-peor, and [e]separated themselves [f]unto *that* shame; [g]and *their* abominations were according as they loved.

A. M. cir. 3244
B. C. cir. 760
Ante U. C. 7
Amulii Sylvii,
R. Alban.,
cir. annum 37

11 *As for* Ephraim, their glory shall fly away like a bird, from the birth, and from the womb, and from the conception.

12 [h]Though they bring up their children, yet [i]will I bereave them, *that there shall* not *be* a man *left:* yea, [k]wo also to them when I [l]depart from them!

13 Ephraim, [m]as I saw Tyrus, *is* planted in a pleasant place; [n]but Ephraim shall bring forth his children to the murderer.

14 Give them, O LORD: what wilt thou give? give them[o] a [p]miscarrying womb and dry breasts.

15 All their wickedness [q]*is* in Gilgal: for

---

[u]Heb. *man of the spirit*——[v]Ezek. xiii. 3, &c.; Mic. ii. 11; Zeph. iii. 4——[w]Jer. vi. 17; xxxi. 6; Ezek. iii. 17; xxxiii. 7——[x]Or, *against*——[y]Isa. xxxi. 6; ch. x. 9 [z]Judg. xix. 22——[a]Ch. viii. 13——[b]Isa. xxviii. 4; Mic. vii. 1——[c]See chap. ii. 15——[d]Num. xxv. 3; Psa. cvi. 28 [e]Chap. iv. 14——[f]Jer. xi. 13; see Judg. vi. 32

[g]Psa. lxxxi. 12; Ezek. xx. 8; Amos iv. 5——[h]Job xxvii. 14——[i]Deut. xxviii. 41, 62——[k]Deut. xxxi. 17; 2 Kings xvii. 18; ch. v. 6——[l]See 1 Sam. xxviii. 15, 16 [m]See Ezek. xxvi., xxvii., xxviii.——[n]Ver. 16; ch. xiii. 16 [o]Luke xxiii. 29——[p]Heb. *that casteth the fruit*——[q]Ch. iv. 15; xii. 11

The spiritual man] איש הרוח *ish haruach, the man of spirit,* who was *ever pretending* to be under a *Divine afflatus.*

Is *mad*] He is now *enraged* to see every thing falling out contrary to his prediction.

Verse 8. *The watchman of Ephraim*] The true prophet, *was with*—faithful to, *God.*

The prophet] The *false prophet* is the *snare of a fowler;* is continually deceiving the people, and leading them into *snares,* and infusing into their hearts deep hatred against God and his worship.

Verse 9. *They have deeply corrupted* themselves, *as in the days of Gibeah*] This relates to that shocking rape and murder of the Levite's wife, mentioned Judg. xix. 16, &c.

Verse 10. *I found Israel like grapes in the wilderness*] While they were faithful, they were as *acceptable* to me as *ripe grapes* would be to a *thirsty traveller* in the desert.

I saw your fathers] Abraham, Isaac, Jacob, Moses, Joshua, Caleb, Samuel, &c.

As the first ripe] Those grapes, whose bud having come first, and being exposed most to the sun, have been the *first ripe* upon the tree; which tree was now in the vigour of youth, and bore fruit for the *first time.* A metaphor of the *rising prosperity* of the Jewish state.

But *they went to Baal-peor*] The same as the Roman *Priapus,* and worshipped with the most impure rites.

And their *abominations were according as they loved.*] Or, "they became as abominable as the *object* of their love." So Bp. *Newcome.* And this was superlatively abominable.

Verse 11. *Their glory shall fly away*] It shall suddenly spring away from them, and return no more.

From the birth] "So that there shall be no birth, no carrying in the womb, no conception."—*Newcome.* They shall cease to glory in their *numbers;* for no *children* shall be *born,* no woman shall be *pregnant,* for none shall *conceive.* Here judgment blasts the very *germs* of population.

Verse 12. *Though they bring up their children*] And were they even to have children, I would *bereave them* of them; for, when I *depart from them,* they shall have all manner of wretchedness and wo.

Verse 13. *Ephraim, as I saw Tyrus*] Tyre was strongly situated on a rock in the sea; Samaria was on a mountain, both strong and pleasant. But the strength and beauty of those cities shall not save them from destruction.

Ephraim shall bring forth his children to the murderer.] The people shall be destroyed, or led into captivity by the Assyrians. Of the grandeur, wealth, power, &c., of Tyre, see the notes on Ezekiel, chap. xxvii. and xxviii.

Verse 14. *Give them, O Lord: what wilt thou give?*] There is an uncommon beauty in these words. The prophet, seeing the evils that were likely to fall upon his countrymen, begins to make intercession for them; but when he had formed the first part of his petition, "Give them, O Lord!" the prophetic light discovered to him that the petition would not be answered, and that God was about to give them something widely different. Then changing his petition, which the Divine Spirit had interrupted, by signifying that he must not proceed in his request, he asks the question, then, "What wilt thou give them?" and the answer is, "Give them a miscarrying womb, and dry breasts." And this he is commanded to announce. It is probable that the Israelites had prided themselves in the *fruitfulness* of their families, and the numerous *population* of their country. God now tells them that this shall be no more; their wives shall be barren, and their land cursed.

Verse 15. *All their wickedness* is *in Gilgal*] though we are not directly informed of the fact,

A. M. cir. 3244
B. C. cir. 760
Ante U. C. 7
Amulii Sylvii,
R. Alban.,
cir. annum 37

there I hated them; [r]for the
wickedness of their doings I will
drive them out of mine house,
I will love them no more: [s]all
their princes *are* revolters.
16 Ephraim is smitten, their root is dried
up, they shall bear no fruit: yea, [t]though
they bring forth, yet will I slay
even [u]the beloved *fruit* of their
womb.
17 My God will cast them
away, because they did not hearken unto him:
and they shall be [v]wanderers among the
nations.

[r]Chap. i. 6——[s]Isa. i. 23——[t]Ver. 13——[u]Heb. *the desires;* Ezek. xxiv. 21——[v]Deut. xxviii. 64, 65

yet we have reason to believe they had been guilty of some scandalous practices of idolatry in *Gilgal.* See chap. iv. 15.

For there I hated them] And therefore he determined, "for the wickedness of their doings, to drive them out of his house," so that they should cease to be a part of the heavenly family, either as *sons* or *servants;* for he would "love them no more," and bear with them no longer.

Verse 16. *Ephraim is smitten*] The thing being determined, it is considered as already done.

Their root is dried up] They shall never more be a kingdom. And they never had any political form from their captivity by the Assyrians to the present day.

Yea, though they bring forth] See the note on ver. 11, 12.

Verse 17. *My God will cast them away*] Here the prophet seems to apologize for the severity of these denunciations; and to vindicate the Divine justice, from which they proceeded. It is—

Because they did not hearken unto him] That "my God," the fountain of mercy and kindness, "will cast them away."

And they shall be wanderers among the nations.] And where they have *wandered* to, who can tell? and in what nations to be found, no man knows. *Wanderers* they are; and perhaps even now unknown to themselves. Some have thought they have found them in one country; some, in another; and a very pious writer, in a book entitled, *The Star in the West,* thinks he has found their descendants in the *American Indians;* among whom he has discovered many *customs,* apparently the same with those of the *ancient Jews,* and commanded in the *Law.* He even thinks that the word *Je-ho-vah* is found in their solemn festal cry, *Ye-ho-wa-he.* If they be this long lost people, they are utterly unknown to themselves; their origin being lost in a very remote antiquity.

CHAPTER X

This chapter treats of the same subject, but elegantly varied. It begins with comparing Israel to a fruitful vine but corrupted by too much prosperity, 1. *It next reproves and threatens them for their idolatry,* 2; *anarchy,* 3; *and breach of covenant,* 4. *Their idolatry is then enlarged on; and its fatal consequences declared in terms full of sublimity and pathos,* 5–8. *God is now introduced complaining of their excessive guilt; and threatening them with captivity in terms that bear a manifest allusion to their favourite idolatry, the worshipping the similitude of a calf or heifer,* 9–11. *Upon which the prophet, in a beautiful allegory suggested by the preceding metaphors, exhorts them to repentance; and warns them of the dreadful consequences of their evil courses, if obstinately persisted in,* 12–15.

A. M. cir. 3264
B. C. cir. 740
A. U. C. cir. 14
Romuli,
R. Roman.,
cir. annum 14

ISRAEL *is* [a]an [b]empty vine,
he bringeth forth fruit unto
himself: according to the multitude of his fruit [c]he hath increased the altars; according
to the goodness of his land
[d]they have made goodly
[e]images.

[a]Nah. ii. 2——[b]Or, *a vine emptying the fruit which it giveth*

[c]Chap. viii. 11; xii. 11——[d]Chap. viii. 4——[e]Heb. *statues,* or *standing images*

NOTES ON CHAP. X

Verse 1. *Israel* is *an empty vine*] Or, *a vine that casteth its grapes.*

He bringeth forth fruit] Or, *he laid up fruit for himself.* He abused the blessings of God to the purposes of idolatry. He was prosperous; but his prosperity corrupted his heart.

According to the multitude of his fruit] He became idolatrous in proportion to his prosperity; and in proportion to their wealth was the costliness of their images, and the expensiveness of their idol worship. True is the homely saying of old *Quarles:*—

"So God's best gifts, usurp'd by wicked ones,
To poison turn, by their con-ta-gi-ons."

Another poet, of a higher order, but worse school, says:—

Effodiuntur opes, irritamenta malorum.—Ovid.

Of which the words of St. Paul are nearly a literal rendering,—

Ῥιζα γαρ παντων των κακων εστιν ἡ φιλαργυρια.

"For the love of money is the root of all these evils" 1 Tim. vi. 10. Pity that this beautiful

A. M. cir. 3264 B. C. cir. 740 A. U. C. cir. 14 Romuli, R. Roman., cir. annum 14

2 [f]Their heart is [g]divided;
now shall they be found faulty:
he shall [h]break down their altars,
he shall spoil their images.
3 [i]For now they shall say, We have no
king, because we feared not the LORD; what
then should a king do to us?
4 They have spoken words, swearing falsely
in making a covenant: thus judgment springeth up [k]as hemlock in the furrows of the
field.
5 The inhabitants of Samaria shall fear because of [l]the calves of [m]Beth-aven: for the
people thereof shall mourn over it, and [n]the
priests thereof *that* rejoiced on
it, [o]for the glory thereof, because
it is departed from it.
6 It shall be also carried unto
Assyria *for* a present to [p]King Jareb:
Ephraim shall receive shame, and Israel shalt
be ashamed [q]of his own counsel.
7 [r]*As for* Samaria, her king is cut off as
the foam upon [s]the water.
8 [t]The high places also of Aven, [u]the sin of
Israel, shall be destroyed: [v]the thorn and the
thistle shall come up on their altars; [w]and
they shall say to the mountains, Cover us;
and to the hills, Fall on us.

[f]Or, *He hath divided their heart*——[g]1 Kings xviii. 21; Matt. vi. 24——[h]Heb. *behead*——[i]Ch. iii. 4; xi. 5; Mic. iv. 9; ver. 7——[k]See Deut. xxix. 18; Amos v. 7; vi. 12; Acts viii. 23; Heb. xii. 15——[l]1 Kings xii. 28, 29; chap. viii. 5, 6——[m]Chap. iv. 15

[n]Or, *Chemarim;* 2 Kings xxiii. 5; Zeph. i. 4——[o]1 Sam. iv. 21, 22; ch. ix. 11——[p]Ch. v. 13——[q]Ch. xi. 6 [r]Ver. 3, 15——[s]Heb. *the face of the water*——[t]Ch. iv. 15 [u]Deut. ix. 21; 1 Kings xii. 30——[v]Chap. ix. 6——[w]Isa. ii. 19; Luke xxiii. 30; Rev. vi. 16; ix. 6

metal, on which God has bestowed such a large portion of mineral perfection, and then hid in the earth, should, on its being *digged up* by man, become the *incentive* to so many *vices*, and draw away his heart from the Creator of all things, and the fountain of ineffable perfection and goodness.

Verse 2. *Their heart is divided*] They wish to serve God and Mammon, Jehovah and Baal: but this is impossible. Now GOD will do in *judgment* what *they* should have done in *contrition*, "break down their altars, and spoil their images."

Verse 3. *We have no king*] We have rejected the King of kings; and had we any king, he would be of no service to us in this state, as he would be a captive like ourselves; nor could we have the approbation of God, as we now justly lie under his displeasure.

Verse 4. *They have spoken words*] Vain, empty, deceitful *words*.

Swearing falsely] This refers to the alliances made with strange powers, to whom they promised fidelity without intending to be faithful; and from whom they promised themselves protection and support, notwithstanding God was against them, and they knew it. All their words were vain, and in the end as *bitter as gall.*

Judgment springeth up as hemlock] As our land lies without cultivation, so that we have nothing but noxious weeds instead of crops; so we have no administration of justice. What is done in this way is a perversion of law, and is as hurtful to society as hemlock would be to animal life. All this may refer to the anarchy that was in the kingdom of Israel before Hoshea's reign, and which lasted, according to Archbishop *Usher, nine* years. They then, literally, "had no king."

Verse 5. *The inhabitants of Samaria shall fear*] According to *Calmet*, shall worship the calves of Beth-aven; those set up by Jeroboam, at Beth-el. *Fear* is often taken for religious reverence.

The people thereof shall mourn] On seeing the object of their worship carried into captivity, as well as themselves.

And the priests thereof] כמרים *kemarim.* The priests of Samaria, says *Calmet*, are here called *kemarim*, that is, *black coats*, or *shouters*, because they made loud cries in their sacrifices. Instead of יגילו *yagilu*, "they shall rejoice;" learned men propose ילילו *yalilu*, "shall howl," which is likely to be the true reading, but it is not supported by any of the MSS. yet discovered. But the *exigentia loci*, the necessity of the place, requires some such word.

Verse 6. *A present to King Jareb*] See on chap. v. 13. If this be a proper name, the person intended is not known in history: but it is most likely that *Pul*, king of Assyria, is intended, to whom Menahem, king of Israel, appears to have given one of the golden calves, to insure his assistance.

Verse 7. *Her king is cut off as the foam*] As lightly as a puff of wind blows off the foam that is formed below by a fall of water, so shall the kings of Israel be cut off. We have already seen that not less than *four* of them died by assassination in a very short time. See on chap. vii. 7.

Verse 8. *The high places*] Idol temples.

Of Aven] Beth-aven.

The thorn and the thistle shall come up on their altars] Owing to the uncultivated and unfrequented state of the land, and of their places of idol worship, the people being all carried away into captivity.

"And they shall say to the mountains, Cover us,
And to the hills, Fall on us."

"This sublime description of fear and distress our Lord had in view, Luke xxiii. 30, which may be a reference, and not a quotation. However, the *Septuagint*, in the *Codex Alexandrinus*, has the same order of words as occurs in the evangelist. The parallelism makes the passages more beautiful than Rev. vi. 16; and Isa. ii. 19 wants the animated dramatic form. That there is a reference to the caverns that abounded in the mountainous countries of Palestine, see the note on Isa. ii. 19."—*Newcome.*

A. M. cir. 3264
B. C. cir. 740
A. U. C. cir. 14
Romuli,
R. Roman.,
cir. annum 14

9 [x]O Israel, thou hast sinned
from the days of Gibeah: there
they stood: [y]the battle in Gibeah
against the children of iniquity
did not overtake them.
10 [z]*It is* in my desire that I should chastise
them; and [a]the people shall be gathered
against them, [b]when they shall bind themselves in their two furrows.
11 And Ephraim *is as* [c]a heifer *that is*
taught *and* loveth to tread out *the corn;* but
I passed over upon [d]her fair neck: I will
make Ephraim to ride; Judah shall plough,
and Jacob shall break his clods.
12 [e]Sow to yourselves in righteousness, reap
in mercy; [f]break up your fallow ground: for
it is time to seek the LORD, till
he come and rain righteousness
upon you.

A. M. cir. 3264
B. C. cir. 740
A. U. C. cir. 14
Romuli,
R. Roman.,
cir. annum 14

13 [g]Ye have ploughed wicked-
ness, ye have reaped iniquity; ye have eaten
the fruit of lies: because thou didst trust
in thy way, in the multitude of thy mighty
men.
14 [h]Therefore shall a tumult arise among
thy people, and all thy fortresses shall be
spoiled, as Shalman spoiled [i]Beth-arbel in the
day of battle: [k]the mother was dashed in
pieces upon *her* children.
15 So shall Beth-el do unto you because of
[l]your great wickedness: in a morning [m]shall
the king of Israel utterly be cut off.

[x]Chap. ix. 9——[y]See Judg. xx——[z]Deut. xxviii. 63——[a]Jer. xvi. 16; Ezek. xxiii. 46, 47; chap. viii. 10——[b]Or, *when I shall bind them for their two transgressions*, or *in their two habitations*——[c]Jer. l. 11; Mic. iv. 13

[d]Heb. *the beauty of her neck*——[e]Prov. xviii. 21——[f]Jer. iv. 3——[g]Job iv. 8; Prov. xxii. 8; ch. viii. 7; Gal. vi. 7, 8——[h]Ch. xiii. 16——[i]2 Kings xviii. 34; xix. 13——[k]Ch. xiii. 16——[l]Heb. *the evil of your evil*——[m]Ver. 7

Verse 9. *Thou hast sinned from the days of Gibeah*] This is another reference to the horrible rape and murder of the Levite's wife, Judg. xix. 13, 14.

There they stood] Only one tribe was nearly destroyed, viz., that of *Benjamin.* They were *the criminals, the children of iniquity;* the others were faultless, and *stood* only for the rights of justice and mercy.

Verse 10. *When they shall bind themselves in their two furrows.*] "When they are chastised for their two iniquities," i. e., the calves in Dan and Beth-el.—*Newcome.* But this double iniquity may refer to what Jeremiah says, chap. xi. 13: "My people have committed *two* evils." —1. They have forsaken me. 2. They have joined themselves to idols.

Verse 11. *Ephraim* is as *a heifer* that is *taught*] One thoroughly broken in to the yoke.

And *loveth to tread out*] Goes peaceably in the yoke; and is pleased because, *not being muzzled,* she eats of the corn.

I passed over upon her fair neck] I brought the yoke upon it, that she should not tread out the corn merely, but draw the plough and drag the harrow. These operations of husbandry are all referred to here, with some others. *Ephraim* shall *tread out the corn,* that there may be *seed* for the fields.

Judah shall plough] That the *furrows* may receive it.

Jacob shall break his clods.] Harrow—that the seed may be covered with the mould.

Israel very frequently made great depredations on Judah; and as this heifer *loved to tread out the corn,* and not *plough,* it is therefore added that he should be made to *plough,* be *put under the yoke,* namely, that of the Assyrians. What is added, "Judah and Jacob shall plough for themselves," means, that Judah should not now plough for Israel, but for *himself;* as Israel shall no more make depredations upon him.—*Dodd.*

Verse 12. *Sow to yourselves in righteousness*] Let the seed you sow be of the best kind, and in just measure.

Reap in mercy] By the blessing of God on this ploughing, sowing, and harrowing, you may expect a good crop in harvest.

Break up your fallow ground] Do not be satisfied with a *slight furrow;* let the land that was *fallowed* (slightly ploughed) be broken up again with a *deep furrow.*

For it is *time to seek the Lord*] This should be immediately done: the season is passing; and if you do not get the seed in the ground, the early rain will be past, and your fields will be unfruitful.

Rain righteousness upon you.] God will give you the early rain in due time, and in proper measure. Here are the metaphors, and the application cannot be difficult. Here are *ploughing, fallowing, sowing, harrowing, watering, reaping, threshing,* and *feeding* on the produce of well-directed labour. All may be applied to the human heart, and the work of God upon it. Correction, contrition, conversion, receiving the grace of Christ, bringing forth fruit, &c.

Verse 13. *Ye have ploughed wickedness*] Ye have laboured sinfully.

Ye have reaped iniquity] The *punishment* due to your iniquity.

Ye have eaten the fruit of lies] Your *false worship* and your *false gods* have brought you into *captivity* and *misery.*

Because thou didst trust in thy way] Didst confide in thy own counsels, and in *thy mighty men,* and not in the God who made you.

Verse 14. *Shall a tumult arise*] The enemy shall soon fall upon thy people, and take all thy *fortified* places.

As Shalman spoiled Beth-arbel] Some think that this refers to *Jerubbaal,* or *Gideon's* victory over *Zalmunna,* general of the Midianites; see Judg. vii., viii. Others think that an allusion is made here to the destruction of *Arbela,* a city *of Armenia,* by *Shalmaneser,* here called *Shalman;* and this while he was only general of the Assyrian forces, and not yet *king.* I think the history to which this refers is unknown. It seems that it was distinguished by some remarkable ferocities.

The mother was dashed in pieces upon her children.] But *when*, *where*, *how*, and by *whom*, still remain unknown. Conjecture in such a case must be useless.

Verse 15. *So shall Beth-el do unto you*] This shall be the consequence of your *idolatry*.

In a morning shall the king of Israel utterly be cut off.] Suddenly, unexpectedly. *Hoshea*, the king of Israel, shall be cut off by the Assyrians. There are some allusions to facts in this chapter, which cannot be easily verified, as we have not sufficient acquaintance with the history of those times.

CHAPTER XI

This chapter gives a very pathetic representation of God's tender and affectionate regard for Israel, by metaphors chiefly borrowed from the conduct of mothers toward their tender offspring. From this, occasion is taken to reflect on their ungrateful return to the Divine goodness, and to denounce against them the judgments of the Almighty, 1–7. *But suddenly and unexpectedly the prospect changes. Beams of mercy break from the clouds just now fraught with vengeance. God, to speak in the language of men, feels the relentings of a tender parent; his bowels yearn; his mercy triumphs; his rebellious child shall yet be pardoned. As the lion of the tribe of Judah, he will employ his power to save his people, he will call his children from the land of their captivity; and, as doves, they will fly to him, a faithful and a holy people,* 8–12.

A. M. cir. 3264
B. C. cir. 740
A. U. C. cir. 14
Romuli,
R. Roman.,
cir. annum 14

WHEN [a]Israel *was* a child,
then I loved him, and
[b]called my [c]son out of Egypt.
2 *As* they called them, so they
went from them: [d]they sacrificed unto Baalim, and burned incense to graven images.
3 [e]I taught Ephraim also to go, taking them by their arms; but they knew not that [f]I healed them.
4 I drew them with cords of a man, with bands of love: and [g]I was to
them as they that [h]take off the
yoke on their jaws, and [i]I laid
meat unto them.
5 [k]He shall not return into the land of Egypt, but the Assyrian shall be his king, [l]because they refused to return.
6 And the sword shall abide on his cities, and shall consume his branches, and devour *them* [m]because of their own counsels.

[a]Chapter ii. 15——[b]Matthew ii. 15——[c]Exodus iv. 22, 23——[d]2 Kings xvii. 16; chapter ii. 13; xiii. 2
[e]Deuteronomy i. 31; xxxii. 10, 11, 12; Isaiah xlvi. 3
[f]Exod. xv. 26

[g]Lev. xxvi. 13——[h]Heb. *lift up*——[i]Psa. lxxviii. 25; chap. ii. 8——[k]See chap. viii. 13; ix. 3——[l]2 Kings xvii. 13, 14; Cir. 728, they became tributaries to Salmanasser——[m]Chap. x. 6

NOTES ON CHAP. XI

Verse 1. *When Israel* was *a child*] In the infancy of *his political existence*.

I loved him, and called my son out of Egypt.] Where he was greatly oppressed; and in this I gave the proof of my *love*. I *preserved* my people in their affliction there, and *brought* them safely out of it.

Verse 3. *I taught Ephraim also to go*] An allusion to a mother or nurse *teaching a child to walk*, directing it how to *lift and lay its feet*, and supporting it in the meantime *by the arms*, that it may use its feet with the greater ease. This is a passage truly pathetic.

Verse 4. *I drew them with cords of a man*] This is a reference to *leading strings*, one end of which is held by the child, the other by the nurse, by which the little one, feeling some support, and gaining confidence, endeavours to walk. God, their heavenly Father, made use of every means and method to teach them to walk in the right and only safe path; for, as the *Targum* says, "As beloved children are drawn, I drew them by the strength of love."

That take off the yoke on their jaws] I did every thing that mercy could suggest, and justice permit, to make their *duty* their *delight* and *profit*. There appears to be here an illusion to the *moving and pulling forward* the *collar* or *yoke of beasts* which have been hard at work, to let in the cool air between it and their neck, so as to refresh them, and prevent that *heat*, which with the *sweat* would scald their necks, and take off not only the *hair*, but the *skin*. I have often done this at the land ends, in ploughing, when at the *turnings* the cattle were permitted a few moments to draw their breath after the hard pull that terminated the furrow at either end of the field:—

And I laid meat unto them] Giving them at the same time a bite of *grass* or *hay*, to encourage them to go on afresh. The metaphor is strong and expressive; and he who ever had or saw the management of cattle in the *plough* or *cart* must admire it. Thus God acted with the people on *whose necks* was the *yoke of his law*. How many privileges, advantages, and comforts did he mingle with his precepts, to make them at once a righteous and happy people!

Verse 5. *He shall not return into—Egypt*] I have brought them thence already, with the design that the *nation* should never return thither again; but as they have sinned, and forfeited my favour and protection, they shall go *to Assyria;* and this *because they refused to return* to me. This view of the verse removes every difficulty.

Verse 6. *The sword shall abide on his cities*] Israel was agitated with external and intestine wars from the time of *Jeroboam the Second.*

A. M. cir. 3264
B. C. cir. 740
A. U. C. cir. 14
Romuli,
R. Roman.,
cir. annum 14

7 And my people are bent to [n]backsliding from me: [o]though they called them to the Most High, [p]none at all would exalt *him.*

8 [q]How shall I give thee up, Ephraim? *how* shall I deliver thee, Israel? how shall I make thee as [r]Admah? *how* shall I set thee as Zeboim? [s]mine heart is turned within me, my repentings are kindled together.

9 I will not execute the fierceness of mine anger, I will not return to destroy Ephraim: [t]for I *am* God, and not man; the Holy One in the midst of thee: and I will not enter into the city.

10 They shall walk after the LORD: [u]he shall roar like a lion: when he shall roar, then the children shall tremble [v]from the west.

11 They shall tremble as a bird out of Egypt, [w]and as a dove out of the land of Assyria: [x]and I will place them in their houses, saith the LORD.

12 [y]Ephraim compasseth me about with lies, and the house of Israel with deceit: but Judah yet ruleth with God, and is faithful [z]with the saints.

[n]Jer. iii. 6, &c.; viii. 5; chap. iv. 16——[o]Chap. vii. 16
[p]Heb. *together they exalted not*——[q]Jer. ix. 7; ch. vi. 4
[r]Gen. xiv. 8; xix. 24, 25; Deut. xxix. 23; Amos iv. 11
[s]Deut. xxxii. 36; Isa. lxii. 15; Jer. xxxi. 20

[t]Num. xxiii. 19; Isa. lv. 8, 9; Mal. iii. 6——[u]Isa. xxxi. 4; Joel iii. 16; Amos i. 2——[v]Zech. viii. 7——[w]Isa. lx. 8; chap. vii. 11——[x]Ezek. xxviii. 25, 26; xxxvii. 21, 25
[y]Chap. xii. 1——[z]Or, *with the most holy*

Although *Zechariah* his son reigned *twelve* years, yet it was in *continual troubles;* and he was at last slain by the rebel *Shallum,* who, having reigned one month, was slain by *Menahem. Pekahiah* succeeded his father Menahem, and reigned two years, and was killed by *Pekah,* son of Remaliah. He joined Rezin, king of Syria, and made an irruption into the land of Judah; but Ahaz having obtained succour from *Tiglath-Pileser,* king of Assyria, Pekah was defeated, and the tribes of Reuben, Gad, Naphtali, and the half-tribe of Manasseh, were carried away captives by the Assyrian king; and in a short time after, *Hosea,* son of Elah, slew Pekah, and usurped the kingdom, which he could not possess without the assistance of *Shalmaneser,* who for his services imposed a tribute on the Israelitish king. Wishing to rid himself of this yoke, he applied to the king of Egypt; but this being known to Shalmaneser, he came against Samaria, and after a three years' siege took and destroyed it. Thus the sword rested on their cities; it continued in the land till all was ruined. See *Calmet.*

Verse 7. *Though they called them to the Most High*] *Newcome* is better: "*And* though *they call on him together because of the yoke, he will not raise it.* He shall receive no *refreshment.*" See the metaphor, ver. 4.

Verse 8. *How shall I give thee up*] See the notes on chap. vi. 4, where we have similar words from similar feeling.

Mine heart is turned within me] *Justice* demands thy *punishment; Mercy* pleads for thy *life.* As thou *changest,* Justice resolves to *destroy,* or Mercy to *save.* My heart is oppressed, and I am weary with *repenting*—with so frequently changing my purpose. All this, though spoken after the manner of men, shows how merciful, compassionate, and loath to punish, the God of heaven is. What *sinner* or *saint* upon earth has not been a subject of these *gracious* operations?

Verse 9. *I will not execute*] Here is the *issue* of this conflict in the Divine mind. Mercy triumphs over Judgment; Ephraim shall be spared. *He is God, and not man.* He cannot be affected by human caprices. They are now *penitent,* and implore mercy; he will not, as *man* would do, punish them for former offences, when they have fallen into his hand. The *holy place* is in Ephraim, and *God is in this holy place;* and he will not *go into the cities,* as he did into Sodom and Gomorrah, to destroy them. Judgment is his strange work. How exceedingly affecting are these two verses!

Verse 10. *They shall walk after the Lord*] They shall discern the operations of his providence, when,

He shall roar like a lion] When he shall utter his majestic voice, Cyrus shall make his decree. The *people shall tremble*—be in a state of commotion; every one hurrying to avail himself of the opportunity to return to his own land.

Verse 11. *They shall tremble as a bird*] Those of them that are in *Egypt* shall also be called thence, and shall *speed* hither *as a bird.* Those in *Assyria* shall also be called to return, and they shall *flee as doves* to their windows. All shall, in the fulness of time, return to their own land. And,

I will place them in their houses, saith the Lord.] They shall have their *temple* once more, and all their holy ordinances.

Verse 12. *Ephraim compasseth me about with lies*] I think this verse does not well *unite* with the *above;* it belongs to *another subject,* and should begin the following chapter, as in the Hebrew.

Judah yet ruleth with God] There is an allusion here to Gen. xxxii. 24, where *Jacob,* having "wrestled with the Angel," had his name changed to *Israel,* one that *rules with God.* That glory the *Israelites* had lost by their idolatry; but *Judah* still retained the true worship, and alone deserved the name of Israel.

Bp. *Newcome* translates this clause thus:—"But hereafter they shall come down a people of God, even a faithful people of saints."

Even allowing this to be the most correct view of the original, I do not see what we gain by this change.

CHAPTER XII

The prophet, in very pointed terms, describes the unprofitableness and destruction attending vicious courses; particularly such as Ephraim pursued, who forsook God, and courted the alliance of idolatrous princes, 1. *Judah is also reproved,* 2. *He is reminded of the extraordinary favour of God to his father Jacob, in giving him the birthright; and exhorted, after his example, to wrestle with God (the Angel of the covenant, the same unchangeable Jehovah) for a blessing; and to love mercy and execute justice,* 3–6. *Ephraim is accused of pursuing practices that are deceitful, although pretending to integrity,* 7, 8. *God then threatens to deprive this people of their possessions,* 9, *as they had rejected every means of reformation,* 10, *and given themselves up to gross impieties,* 11. *And, as an aggravation of their guilt, they are reminded from what humble beginnings they had been raised,* 12, 13. *The Divine judgments about to fall upon Israel are declared to be the result of great provocation,* 14.

A. M. cir. 3279
B. C. cir. 725
A. U. C. cir. 29
Romuli,
R. Roman.,
cir. annum 29

EPHRAIM [a]feedeth on wind,
and followeth after the east
wind: he daily increaseth lies
and desolation; [b]and they do
make a covenant with the Assyrians, and [c]oil
is carried into Egypt.
2 [d]The LORD hath also a controversy with
Judah, and will [e]punish Jacob according to
his ways; according to his doings will he recompense him.
3 He took his brother [f]by the heel in the
womb, and by his strength he [g]had [h]power
with God:

[a]Chap. viii. 7——[b]2 Kings xvii. 4; chap. v. 13; chap. vii. 11——[c]Isa. xxx. 6; lvii. 9——[d]Chap. iv. 1; Mic. vi. 2——[e]Heb. *visit upon*——[f]Gen. xxv. 26——[g]Heb. *was a prince* or *behaved himself princely*——[h]Gen. xxxii. 24, &c.

A. M. cir. 3279
B. C. cir. 725
A. U. C. cir. 29
Romuli,
R. Roman.,
cir. annum 29

4 Yea, he had power over the
Angel, and prevailed: he wept,
and made supplication unto
him: he found him *in* [i]Beth-el,
and there he spake with us;
5 Even the LORD God of hosts; the LORD
is his [k]memorial.
6 [l]Therefore turn thou to thy God: keep
mercy and judgment, and [m]wait on thy God
continually.
7 *He is* [n]a merchant, [o]the balances of deceit *are* in his hand: he loveth to [p]oppress.
8 And Ephraim said, [q]Yet I am become

[i]Gen. xxviii. 12, 19; xxxv. 9, 10, 15——[k]Exod. iii. 15——[l]Ch. xiv. 1; Mic. vi. 8——[m]Psa. xxxvii. 7——[n]Or, *Canaan:* see; Ezek. xvi. 3——[o]Prov. xi. 1; Amos viii. 5——[p]Or, *deceive*——[q]Zech. xi. 5; Rev. iii. 17

NOTES ON CHAP. XII

Verse 1. *Ephraim feedeth on wind*] He forms and follows empty and unstable counsels.

Followeth after the east wind] They are not only empty, but *dangerous* and *destructive*. The *east wind* was, and still is, in all countries, a *parching, wasting, injurious* wind.

He daily increaseth lies] He promises himself safety from foreign alliances. He "made a covenant with the Assyrians," and *sent* a subsidy of "oil to Egypt." The latter *abandoned* him; the *former oppressed* him.

Verse 2. *The Lord hath also a controversy with Judah*] The rest of the prophecy belongs both to Judah and Israel. He reproaches both with their ingratitude, and threatens them with God's anger. In order to make their infidelity the more hateful, and their malice the more sensible, he opposes to them the righteousness, obedience, and piety of their father Jacob. He recalls to their minds the benefits they had received since they returned from Egypt. He speaks afterwards of their kings; and how, in their ingratitude, they refused to have him for their monarch. Having mentioned this fact, he subjoins reflections, exhortations, invectives, and threatenings; and continues this subject in *this* and the *two* following *chapters.—Calmet.*

Verse 3. *He took his brother by the heel*] See on Gen. xxv. 26, and xxxii. 24, &c.

Verse 4. *He had power over the Angel*] Who represented the invisible Jehovah.

He wept, and made supplication] He entreated with tears that God would bless him; and he *prevailed.* The circumstance of his *weeping* is not mentioned in *Genesis.*

He found him in *Beth-el*] It was there that God made those glorious promises to Jacob relative to his posterity. See Gen. xxviii. 13-15.

Verse 5. *The Lord* is *his memorial.*] He is the same God as when Jacob so successfully wrestled with him.

Verse 6. *Therefore turn thou to thy God*] Because he is the same, and cannot change. Seek him as faithfully and as fervently as Jacob did, and you will find him the same merciful and compassionate Being.

Verse 7. He is *a merchant*] Or a *Canaanite;* referring to the *Phœnicians,* famous for their traffic. Ephraim is as corrupt as those heathenish traffickers were. He kept, as many in all ages have done, a *weight* and a *weight;* a *heavy* one to *buy* with and a *light* one to *sell* by.

Verse 8. *I am become rich*] They boasted in their riches, notwithstanding the *unjust manner* in which they were acquired.

In *all my labours they shall find none iniquity in me*] This is frequently the language of merchants, tradesmen, &c. None are so full of professions of equity and justice, while all the time they are endeavouring to overreach, both in buying and selling. "Sir, I cannot afford it at that price." "It is not *mine* for that money." "I assure you that it cost me more than you offer." "I am sorry I cannot take your money; but if I did, I should lose by the article," &c., &c., &c. I have heard such lan-

A. M. cir. 3279 B. C. cir. 725 A. U. C. cir. 29 Romuli, R. Roman., cir. annum 29

rich, I have found me out substance: [r]*in* all my labours they shall find none iniquity in me [s]that *were* sin.

9 And [t]I *that am* the LORD thy God from the land of Egypt [u]will yet make thee to dwell in tabernacles, as in the days of the solemn feasts.

10 [v]I have also spoken by the prophets, and I have multiplied visions, and used similitudes, [w]by the ministry of the prophets.

11 [x]*Is there* iniquity *in* Gilead? surely they are vanity: they sacrifice bullocks in [y]Gilgal; yea, their [z]altars *are* as heaps in the furrows of the fields.

12 And Jacob [a]fled into the country of Syria, and Israel [b]served for a wife, and for a wife he kept *sheep*.

13 [c]And by a prophet the LORD brought Israel out of Egypt, and by a prophet was he preserved.

14 [d]Ephraim provoked *him* to anger [e]most bitterly: therefore shall he leave his [f]blood upon him, [g]and his [h]reproach shall his Lord return unto him.

[r]Or, *all my labours suffice me not:* he shall have *punishment of iniquity in whom* is *sin*——[s]Heb. *which*——[t]Ch. xiii. 4——[u]Lev. xxiii. 42, 43; Neh. viii. 17; Zech. xiv. 16——[v]2 Kings xvii. 13——[w]Heb. *by the hand*——[x]Chap. v. 1; vi. 8——[y]Chap. iv. 15; ix. 15; Amos iv. 4; v. 5——[z]Ch. viii. 11; x. 1

[a]Gen. xxviii. 5; Deut. xxvi. 5——[b]Gen. xxix. 20, 28——[c]Exod. xii. 50, 51; xiii. 3; Psa. lxxvii. 20; Isa. lxiii. 11; Mic. vi. 4——[d]2 Kings xvii. 11–18——[e]Heb. *with bitterness*——[f]Heb. *bloods;* see Ezek. xviii. 13; xix. 10; xxiv. 7, 8——[g]Dan. xi. 18——[h]Deut. xxviii. 37; Lam. iii. 61–66

guage over and over, when I knew every word was false. *Truth* is a sacred thing in the sight of God; but who regards it as he should? There are, however, many noble exceptions among merchants and tradesmen. Bp. *Newcome* gives another turn to the subject, by translating:—

"All his labours shall not be found *profitable* unto him,
For the iniquity wherewith he hath sinned."

Verse 9. *And I—the Lord thy God*] I who brought thee out of the land of Egypt, will again make thee to dwell in tabernacles. This appears to be a *threatening.* I will reduce you to as miserable a state in the land of your captivity, as you often were through your transgressions in the wilderness. This was the opinion of some of the ancients on this verse; and the *context* requires it to be understood in this way. I do not think that the *feast of tabernacles* is referred to.

Verse 10. *I have also spoken*] I have used every means, and employed every method, to instruct and save you. I have sent *prophets,* who spake *plainly,* exhorting, warning, and beseeching you to return to me. They have had *Divine visions,* which they have declared and *interpreted.* They have used *similitudes, symbols, metaphors, allegories,* &c., in order to fix your attention, and bring you back to your duty and interest. And, alas! all is in vain; you have not profited by my condescension. This text *St. Paul* seems to have had full in view, when he wrote, Heb. i. 1: "God who, at SUNDRY TIMES and in DIVERS MANNERS, spake in *time past* unto the FATHERS by the PHOPHETS." See the note on the above.

Dr. *Dodd* supposes that there are *three* distinct kinds of prophecy mentioned here: 1. Immediate inspiration, when God declares the very words. 2. Vision; a representation of *external objects* to the *mind,* in as lively a manner as if there were conveyed by the *senses.* 3. Parables and apt resemblances.

Verse 11. *Iniquity* in *Gilead*] Gilgal and Gilead are equally iniquitous, and equally idolatrous. Gilead, which was beyond Jordan, had already been brought under subjection by Tiglath-Pileser. Gilgal, which was on this side Jordan, shall share the same fate; because it is now as idolatrous as the other.

Their altars are *as heaps*] They occur everywhere. The whole land is given to idolatry.

Verse 12. *Served for a wife*] Seven years for *Rachel.*

For a wife he kept sheep.] Seven years for *Leah;* having been cheated by Laban, who gave him first *Leah,* instead of *Rachel;* and afterwards made him serve seven years more before he would confirm his first engagement. Critics complain of want of connection here. Why is this isolated fact predicted? Thus, in a detached sentence, the prophet speaks of the low estate of their ancestors, and how amply the providence of God had preserved and provided for them. This is all the connection the place requires.

Verse 13. *By a prophet* (Moses) *the Lord brought Israel out of Egypt, and by a prophet* (Joshua) *was he preserved.*] Joshua succeeded Moses, and brought the Israelites into the promised land; and when they passed the Jordan at Gilgal, he received the covenant of circumcision; and yet this same place was now made by them the seat of idolatry! How blind and how ungrateful!

Verse 14. *Therefore shall he leave his blood upon him*] He will not remove his guilt. These are similar to our Lord's words, John iii. 36, ix. 41: "He that believeth not on the Son of God, shall not see life, for the wrath of God ABIDETH ON HIM"—shall not be removed by any remission, as he rejects the only way in which he can be saved. *Because ye say, We see; therefore,* YOUR SIN REMAINETH, i. e., it still stands charged against you. Your miseries and destruction are of your own procuring; your perdition is of yourselves. God is as *merciful* as he is *just.*

CHAPTER XIII

This chapter begins with observing that the fear of God leads to prosperity, but sin to ruin; a truth most visibly exemplified in the sin and punishment of Ephraim, 1–3. *As an aggravation of their guilt, God reminds them of his former favours,* 4, 5; *which they had shamefully abused,* 6; *and which now expose them to dreadful punishments,* 7, 8. *He, however, tempers these awful threatenings with gracious promises; and, on their repentance, engages to save them, when no other could protect them,* 9–11. *But, alas! instead of repenting, Ephraim is filling up the measure of his iniquity,* 12, 13. *Notwithstanding this, God promises to put forth his almighty power in behalf of his people, and, as it were, raise them from the dead,* 14; *although, in the mean-time, they must be visited with great national calamities, compared first to the noxious and parching east wind,* 15, *and described immediately after in the plainest terms,* 16.

A. M. cir. 3279
B. C. cir. 725
A. U. C. cir. 29
Romuli,
R. Roman.,
cir. annum 29

WHEN Ephraim spake trem-
bling, he exalted himself
in Israel: but [a]when he offended
in Baal, he died.
2 And now [b]they sin more and more, and
[c]have made them molten images of their silver, *and* idols according to their own understanding, all of it the work of the craftsmen:
they say of them, Let [d]the men that sacrifice
[e]kiss the calves.
3 Therefore they shall be [f]as the morning
cloud, and as the early dew that passeth away,
[g]as the chaff *that* is driven with the whirlwind
out of the floor, and as the
smoke out of the chimney.
4 Yet [h]I *am* the LORD thy God
from the land of Egypt, and
thou shalt know no god but me: for [i]*there is*
no saviour beside me.
5 [k]I did know thee in the wilderness, [l]in
the land of [m]great drought.
6 [n]According to their pasture, so were they
filled; they were filled, and their heart was
exalted; therefore [o]have they forgotten me.
7 Therefore [p]I will be unto them as a lion:
as [q]a leopard by the way will I observe *them:*

A. M. cir. 3279
B. C. cir. 725
A. U. C. cir. 29
Romuli,
R. Roman.,
cir. annum 29

[a]2 Kings xvii. 16, 18; chap. xi. 2——[b]Heb. *they add to sin*——[c]Chap. ii. 8; viii. 4——[d]Or, *the sacrifices of men*——[e]1 Kings xix. 18——[f]Chap. vi. 4——[g]Dan. ii. 35——[h]Isa. xliii. 11; chap. xii. 9

[i]Isa. xliii. 11; xlv. 21——[k]Deut. ii. 7; xxxii. 10——[l]Deut. viii. 15; xxxii. 10——[m]Heb. *droughts*——[n]Deut. viii. 12, 14; xxxii. 15——[o]Chap. viii. 14——[p]Lam. iii. 10; chap. v. 14——[q]Jer. v. 6

NOTES ON CHAP. XIII

Verse 1. *When Ephraim spake trembling*] When he was meek and humble, of a broken heart and contrite spirit.

He exalted himself in Israel] He became great in God's sight; he rose in the Divine esteem in proportion as he sank in his own. But this did not continue.

He offended in Baal] He became an idolater.

He died.] The sentence of death from the Divine justice went out against him.

This has been differently understood: "As soon as Ephraim spake (To your tents, O Israel!) There was a trembling or commotion: then the kingdom was exalted in Israel." Thus taken, it refers to the division of the *ten* tribes from Rehoboam, son of Solomon, 1 Kings xii. 16, &c., and the establishment of the kingdom of Israel under Jeroboam in opposition to that of Judah; which breach was never healed.

Verse 2. *And now they sin more and more*] They increase in every kind of vice, having abandoned the great Inspirer of virtue.

Let the men that sacrifice kiss the calves.] This was the *test.* If there be a Jew that pretends to sacrifice, and whose conversion is dubious, let him come openly and *kiss the calves.* This will show what he is; no *real* Jew will do this. If he be an *idolater,* he will not scruple. This was the ancient method of *adoration.* 1. They *kissed* the idol. 2. When the statue was too high or too far off, they presented the hand, in token of alliance. 3. They brought that hand respectfully to their mouths, and kissed it. This was the genuine act of *adoration; from ad, to,* and *os, oris,* the *mouth.* So PLINY, *Hist. Nat.,* lib. xxviii., c. 1. Adorando, dexteram ad oscula referimus.

And APULEIUS, *Asin.,* lib. iv.: Admoventes oribus suis dexteram, ut ipsam prorsus deam religiosis adorationibus venerabantur. See *Calmet,* and see the note on Job xxxi. 17.

Verse 3. *Therefore they shall be as the morning* CLOUD—*as the early* DEW—*as the* CHAFF—*as the* SMOKE] *Four* things, most easy to be driven about and dissipated, are employed here to show how they should be *scattered* among the nations, and dissipated by captivity.

Verse 4. *I* am *the Lord thy God*] This was the first discovery I made of myself to you, and the *first commandment* I gave; and I showed you that besides me there was no Saviour. There is a remarkable addition in the Septuagint here: "But I am Jehovah thy God, who stretched out the heavens and created the earth. And I showed them not to thee, that thou shouldest walk after them. And I brought thee up out of the land of Egypt," &c. This might have been once in the Hebrew text.

Verse 5. *I did know thee*] I *approved* of thee; I *loved* thee; and by miraculously providing for thee in that land of *drought,* I demonstrated my love.

Verse 6. *According to their pasture*] They had a rich pasture, and were amply supplied with every good. They became *exalted in their heart, forgat their God,* and became a prey to their enemies. "He that exalteth himself shall be abased."

Verse 7. *I will be unto them as a lion*] שחל *shachal* is supposed to mean here the *black lion,* frequent in Ethiopia.

A. M. cir. 3279
B. C. cir. 725
A. U. C. cir. 29
Romuli,
R. Roman.,
cir. annum 29

8 I will meet them [r]as a bear
that is bereaved *of her whelps,*
and will rend the caul of their
heart, and there will I devour
them like a lion: [s]the wild beast shall tear
them.
9 O Israel, [t]thou hast destroyed thyself;
[u]but in me [v]*is* thine help.
10 [w]I will be thy king: [x]where *is any*
other that may save thee in all thy cities? and
thy judges of whom [y]thou saidst, Give me a
king and princes?
11 [z]I gave thee a king in
mine anger, and took *him* away
in my wrath.
12 [a]The iniquity of Ephraim
is bound up; his sin *is* hid.
13 [b]The sorrows of a travailing woman
shall come upon him: he *is* [c]an unwise son;
for he should not [d]stay [e]long in *the place of*
the breaking forth of children.
14 [f]I will ransom them from [g]the power
of the grave; I will redeem them from death;

A. M. cir. 3279
B. C. cir. 725
A. U. C. cir. 29
Romuli,
R. Roman.,
cir. annum 29

[r]2 Sam. xvii. 8; Prov. xvii. 12——[s]Heb. *the beast of the field*——[t]Prov. vi. 32; chap. xiv. 1; Mal. i. 9——[u]Ver. 4 [v]Heb. *in thy help*——[w]Rather, *Where is thy king?* King Hoshea being then in prison; 2 Kings xvii. 4——[x]Deut. xxxii. 38; chap. x. 3; ver. 4

[y]1 Sam. viii. 5, 19——[z]1 Sam. viii. 7; x. 19; xv. 22, 23; xvi. 1; chap. x. 3——[a]Deut. xxxii. 34; Job xiv. 17 [b]Isa. xiii. 8; Jer. xxx. 6——[c]Prov. xxii. 3——[d]2 Kings xix. 3——[e]Heb. *a time*——[f]Isa. xxv. 8; Ezek. xxxvii. 12 [g]Hebrew, *the hand*

As a leopard] נמר *namar*, so termed from its *spotted skin*, for *to be spotted* is the signification of the root.

Will I observe them] The leopard, tiger, and panther will hide themselves in thick bushwood, near where they expect any prey to pass; and as soon as it comes near, spring suddenly upon it. To this is the allusion in the text: "By the way will I observe them;" watch for them as the leopard does. They shall be greatly harassed even on their way to Assyria, when going into captivity.

Verse 8. *As a bear—bereaved*] This is a figure to denote excessive ferocity. See the note on 2 Sam. xvii. 8, where a remarkable instance is given.

And will rend the caul of their heart] Every savage beast goes first to the *seat of the blood* when it has seized its prey; as in this fluid they delight more than in the most delicate parts of the flesh.

There will I devour them like a lion] לביא *labi*, the *old strong lion;* drinking the blood, tearing the flesh, and breaking the bones to extract the marrow.

The wild beast shall tear them] Probably this refers to the *chakal* or *jackal*, who frequently hunts down the prey, which the lion takes the liberty to devour, while the *jackal* stands by, and afterwards picks the bones. Hence he has been called the *lion's* PROVIDER, and *the lion's waiting-man.*

Verse 9. *O Israel, thou hast destroyed thyself*] These evils come not by my *immediate infliction;* they are the consequences of *thy own crimes.* In the above terrifying figures of the ferocious beasts, the prophet only shows what they would meet with from the hand of the *Assyrians* in the war, the famine, and the captivity; God being represented as *doing* what he only *permits* to be done.

But in me is *thine help.*] "Though thou hast destroyed thyself, yet in me alone can thy help be found"—*Newcome.* And others read, *And who* will *help thee?* reading מי *mi, who*, for בי *bi, in me.* Though this is countenanced by the *Syriac*, yet there is no evidence of it in any of the MSS. yet collated, nor do I think it to be the true reading.

Verse 10. *Give me a king and princes?*] Referring to the time in which they cast off the Divine theocracy and chose *Saul* in the place of *Jehovah.*

Verse 11. *I gave thee a king in mine anger*] Such was *Saul;* for they highly offended God when they clamoured to have a king like the heathen nations that were around them.

Took him *away in my wrath.*] Permitted *him* and the *Israelites* to fall before the Philistines. Others think that *Shalmaneser* was the *king thus given*, and *Hoshea* the king thus *taken away.*

Verse 12. *The iniquity of Ephraim* is *bound up*] It is *registered* in my court of justice; the *death warrant* is in store, and will be produced in due time. Though there be not at present the judgment inflicted which such glaring transgressions demand, yet it will surely come. Such crimes cannot go unpunished.

Verse 13. *The sorrows of a travailing woman*] These judgments shall come suddenly and *unavoidably.*

The place of *the breaking forth of children.*] As there is a critical time in parturition in which the mother in hard labour may by skilful assistants be eased of her burden, which, if neglected, may endanger the life both of parent and child; so there was a time in which Ephraim might have returned to God, but they would not; therefore they are now in danger of being finally destroyed. And, speaking after the manner of men, he must be deemed an *unwise son*, who if he had power and consideration, would prolong his stay in the porch of life, where he must necessarily be suffocated; so is Ephraim, who, though warned of his danger, having yet power to escape, continued in his sin, and is now come to destruction. I could illustrate the allusion in the text farther, and show the accurate propriety of the original; but the subject forbids it.

Verse 14. *I will ransom them from the power of the grave*] In their captivity they are represented as *dead* and *buried*, which is a similar view to that taken of the Jews in the Babylonish captivity by Ezekiel in his *vision of the valley of dry bones.* They are now lost as to the purpose for which they were made, for which God had wrought so many miracles for them and for their ancestors; but the gracious purpose of God shall not be utterly defeated. He will bring them out of that grave, and ran-

A. M. cir. 3279
B. C. cir. 725
A. U. C. cir. 29
Romuli,
R. Roman.,
cir. annum 29

[h]O death, I will be thy plagues;
O grave, I will be thy destruction;
[i]repentance shall be hid
from mine eyes.
15 Though [k]he be fruitful among *his*
brethren, [l]an east wind shall come, the wind
of the LORD shall come up from the wilderness,
and his spring shall become dry, and his
fountain shall be dried up: he
shall spoil the treasure of all
[m]pleasant vessels.
16 [n]Samaria shall become desolate;
[o]for she hath rebelled against her
God: [p]they shall fall by the sword: their
infants shall be dashed in pieces, and their
women with child shall be ripped up.

[h]1 Cor. xv. 54, 55——[i]Jer. xv. 6; Rom. xi. 29——[k]See Gen. xli. 52; xlviii. 19——[l]Jer. iv. 11; Ezek. xvii. 10; xix. 12; ch. iv. 19——[m]Heb. *vessels of desire;* Nah. ii. 9

[n]Fulfilled, cir. 721; 2 Kings xvii. 6——[o]2 Kings xviii. 12——[p]2 Kings viii. 12; xv. 16; Isa. xiii. 16; chap. x. 14, 15; Amos i. 13; Nah. iii. 10

som them from that death; for as they have *deserved* that death and disgraceful burial, they must be *redeemed* and *ransomed* from it, or still lie under it. And who can do this but God himself? And he will do it. In the prospect of this the prophet exclaims, in the person of the universal Redeemer, "O death, I will be thy plagues;" I will bring into thy reign the principle of its destruction. The *Prince of life* shall lie for a time under thy power, that he may destroy that power.

O grave, I will be thy destruction] I will put an end to thy dreary domination by rising from the dead, and bringing life and immortality to life by my Gospel, and by finally raising from the death the whole human race in the day of the general resurrection.

שאול *sheol,* which we translate *grave,* is the *state of the dead.* מות *maveth,* which we translate *death,* is the *principle* of *corruption* that renders the body unfit to be longer the tenement of the soul, and finally decomposes it. *Sheol* shall be destroyed, for it must deliver up all its dead. *Maveth* shall be annihilated, for the *body shall be raised incorruptible.* See the use which the apostle makes of this passage, 1 Cor. xv. 54, 55; but he does not quote from the Hebrew, nor from any of the ancient versions. He had to apply the subject anew; and the Spirit, which had originally given the words, chose to adapt them to the subject then in hand, which was the *resurrection of the dead in the last day.* Instead of דבריך *debareycha, thy plagues, one* of my oldest MSS., *ninety-six* of *Kennicott's* and *thirty-two* of *De Rossi's,* have דברך *debarcha, thy plague,* that which shall *carry thee off,* as the *plague* does them who are affected by it. To *carry off, carry away,* is one of the regular meanings of the verb דבר *dabar.*

Repentance shall be hid from mine eyes.] On these points I will not *change my purpose;* this is the signification of *repentance* when attributed to God.

Verse 15. *Though he be fruitful*] יפריא *yaphri;* a paronomasia on the word אפרים *ephrayim,* which comes from the same root פרה *parah,* to be fruitful, to *sprout,* to *bud.*

An east wind shall come] As the east wind parches and blasts all vegetation, so shall *Shalmaneser* blast and destroy the Israelitish state.

Verse 16. *Samaria shall become desolate*] This was the capital of the Israelitish kingdom. What follows is a simple prophetic declaration of the cruelties which should be exercised upon this hapless people by the Assyrians in the sackage of the city.

CHAPTER XIV

By the terrible denunciation of vengeance which concludes the preceding chapter, the prophet is led to exhort Israel to repentance, furnishing them with a beautiful form of prayer, very suitable to the occasion, 1–3. *Upon which God, ever ready to pardon the penitent, is introduced making large promises of blessings, in allusion to those copious dews which refresh the green herbs, and which frequently denote, not only temporal salvation, but also the rich and refreshing comforts of the Gospel,* 4–7. *Their reformation from idolatry is foretold, and their consequent prosperity, under the emblem of a green flourishing fir tree,* 8; *but these promises are confined to those who may bring forth the fruits of righteousness, and the wicked are declared to have no share in them,* 9.

A. M. cir. 3279
B. C. cir. 725
A. U. C. cir. 29
Romuli,
R. Roman.,
cir. annum 29

O ISRAEL, [a]return unto the
LORD thy God; [b]for thou
hast fallen by thine iniquity.
2 Take with you words, and
turn to the LORD: say unto him,
Take away all iniquity, and [c]receive
us graciously: so will we
render [d]the calves of our lips.

[a]Chap. xii. 6; Joel ii. 13——[b]Chap. xiii. 9

[c]Or, *give good*——[d]Heb. xiii. 15

NOTES ON CHAP. XIV

Verse 1. *O Israel, return unto the Lord*] These words may be considered as addressed to the people now in captivity; suffering much, but having still much more to suffer if they did not repent. But it seems all these evils might yet be prevented, though so positively predicted, if the people would repent and return; and the very exhortation to this repent-

A. M. cir. 3279
B. C. cir. 725
A. U. C. cir. 29
Romuli,
R. Roman.,
cir. annum 29

3 [e]Asshur shall not save us;
[f]we will not ride upon horses:
[g]neither will we say any more
to the work of our hands, *Ye
are* our gods: [h]for in thee the fatherless
findeth mercy.
4 I will heal [i]their backsliding, I will love
them [k]freely: for mine anger is
turned away from him.
5 I will be as [l]the dew
unto Israel: he shall [m]grow as
the lily, and [n]cast forth his roots as Lebanon.
6 His branches [o]shall spread, and [p]his

[e]Jer. xxxi. 18, &c.; chap. v. 13; xii. 1——[f]Deut. xvii. 16; Psa. xxxiii. 17; Isa. xxx. 2, 16; xxxi. 1——[g]Chap. ii. 17; ver. 8——[h]Psa. x. 14; lxviii. 5

[i]Jer. v. 6; xiv. 7; ch. xi. 7——[k]Eph. i. 6——[l]Job xxix. 19; Prov. xix. 12——[m]Or, *blossom*——[n]Heb. *strike*
[o]Heb. *shall go*——[p]Psa. lii. 8; cxxviii. 3; Ecclus. l. 10

ance shows that they still had power to repent, and that God was ready to save them and avert all these evils. All this is easily accounted for on the doctrine of the *contingency of events*, i. e., the poising a multitude of events on the possibility of being and not being, and leaving the will of man to turn the scale; and that God will not foreknow a thing *as absolutely certain*, which his will has determined to make *contingent*. A doctrine against which some solemn men have blasphemed, and philosophic infidels declaimed; but without which fate and dire necessity must be the universal governors, *prayer* be a useless meddling, and Providence nothing but the ineluctable adamantine chain of unchangeable events; all virtue is vice, and vice virtue; or there is no distinction between them, each being eternally determined and unalterably fixed by a sovereign and uncontrollable will and unvarying necessity, from the operation of which no soul of man can escape, and no occurrence in the universe be otherwise than it is. From such blasphemy, and from the *monthly* publications which avouch it, good Lord, deliver us!

Verse 2. *Take with you words*] And you may be assured that you pray aright, when you use the words which God himself has put in your mouths. On this very ground there is a potency in the Lord's Prayer, when offered up believingly, beyond what can be found in any human composition. And it may be presumed that it was this consideration that induced our *reformers* to introduce it so *frequently* in the public liturgy.

See the order of God's directions here:—

1. Hearing these merciful invitations, believe them to be *true*.

2. Cast aside your idols; and return to God as your Maker, King, and Saviour.

3. *Take with you* the *words* by which you have been encouraged, and plead them before God.

4. Remember your iniquity, deeply deplore it, and beg of God to *take it all away*.

5. Let faith be in exercise to receive what God waits to impart. "Receive us graciously;" וקח טוב *vekach tob, receive*, or *let us receive good;* when thou has emptied us of evil, fill us with goodness.

6. Be then determined, through grace, to live to his glory, "so shall we render thee the calves" (פרים *parim*, for which the *versions* in general read פרי *peri, fruits*, omitting the מ *mem*) "of our lips;" the sacrifices of *praise, thanksgiving, gratitude*, and the hearty *obedience* which our *lips* have often promised.

7. Having thus determined, specify your *resolutions* to depend on God alone for all that can make you wise, useful, holy, and happy. The *resolutions* are,—

1. *Asshur shall not save us*—We will neither trust in, nor fear, this rich and powerful king. We will not look either to riches or power for true rest and peace of mind.

2. *We will not ride upon horses*—We shall no more fix our hopes on the proud Egyptian cavalry, to deliver us out of the hands of enemies to whom thy Divine justice has delivered us. We will expect no rest nor happiness in the elegances of life, and gratification of our senses.

3. *Neither will we say any more to the work of our hands*, Ye are *our gods*—We will not trust in any thing *without* us; nor even in any good thing we are able to do through thy grace; knowing we have nothing but what we have received. We will trust in thy infinite mercy for our final salvation.

4. And we will do all this from the conviction, that *in thee the fatherless findeth mercy;* for we are all alike helpless, desolate, perishing *orphans*, till translated into thy family.

Verse 4. *I will heal their backsliding*] Here is the *answer* of God to these prayers and resolutions. See its parts:—

1. Ye have backslidden and fallen, and are grievously and mortally wounded by that fall; but I, who am the Author of life, and who redeem from death, will *heal* all these wounds and spiritual diseases.

2. *I will love them freely*—נדבה *nedabah*, after a *liberal, princely* manner. I will love them so as to do them incessant good. It shall not be a love of *affection* merely, but shall be a *beneficial love*. A love that not only *feels delight in itself*, but fills them with *delight* who are its objects, by making them unutterably and supremely happy.

3. *For mine anger is turned away from him*—Because he has turned back to me. Thus God and man become *friends*.

Verse 5. *I will be as the dew unto Israel*] On these metaphors I gladly avail myself of the elegant and just observations of Bp. *Lowth*. "These verses (5, 6, 7) contain gracious promises of God's favour and blessings upon Israel's conversion. In the *fifth* verse, it is described by that refreshment which copious *dews* give to the grass in summer. If we consider the nature of the climate, and the necessity of *dews* in so hot a country, not only to refresh, but likewise to preserve life; if we consider also the beauty of the oriental *lilies*, the fragrance of the *cedars* which grow upon Lebanon, the beauteous appearance which the spreading *olive trees* afforded, the exhilarating coolness caused by the shade of such trees, and the *aromatic*

A. M. cir. 3279
B. C. cir. 725
A. U. C. cir. 29
Romuli,
R. Roman.,
cir. annum 29

beauty shall be as the olive tree,
and [q]his smell as Lebanon.
7 [r]They that dwell under his
shadow shall return; they shall
revive *as* the corn, and [s]grow as the vine:
the [t]scent thereof *shall be* as the wine of
Lebanon.
8 Ephraim *shall say,* [u]What have I to do
any more with idols? [v]I have heard *him,* and
observed him: I *am* like a green
fir tree. [w]From me is thy fruit
found.
9 [x]Who *is* wise, and he shall
understand these *things?* prudent, and he
shall know them? for [y]the ways of the
LORD *are* right, and the just shall walk
in them: but the transgressors shall fall
therein.

[q]Gen. xxvii. 27; Cant. iv. 11——[r]Psa. xci. 1——[s]Or, *blossom*——[t]Or, *memorial*——[u]Ver. 3——[v]Jer. xxxi. 18 [w]James i. 17——[x]Psa. cvii. 43; Jer. ix. 12; Dan. xii. 10; Ecclus. xxxix. 24, 27; John viii. 47; xviii. 37——[y]Psa. cxix. 14, 27, 33; cxlv. 17; Prov. x. 29; Luke ii. 34; 2 Cor. ii. 16; 1 Pet. ii. 7, 8

smell exhaled by the *cedars;* we shall then partly understand the force of the metaphors here employed by the prophet; but their full energy no one can conceive, till he feels both the *want,* and enjoys the *advantage,* of the particulars referred to in that climate where the prophet wrote."—*Lowth's twelfth* and *nineteenth* prelection; and *Dodd* on the place.

What a glorious prophecy! What a wonderful prophet! How sublime, how emergetic, how just! The great master prophet, Isaiah, alone could have done this better. And these promises are not for *Israel* merely after the flesh; they are for all the people of God. *We* have a lot and portion in the matter; God also places his love upon *us.* Here the reader must feel some such sentiment as the shepherd in *Virgil,* when enraptured with the elegy which his associate had composed on their departed friend. The phraseology and metaphors are strikingly similar; and therefore I shall produce it.

Tale tuum carmen nobis, divine poeta,
Quale *sopor fessis in gramine,* quale *per æstum*
Dulcis aquæ saliente sitim restinguere rivo.
Nec calamis solum æquiparas, sed voce magistrum.
Fortunate puer! tu nunc eris *alter* ab illo.
Nos tamen hæc quocunque modo tibi nostra vicissim
Dicemus, Daphninque tuum tollemus ad astra:
Daphnin ad astra feremus: *amavit nos quoque Daphnis.*

VIRGIL. *Ecl.* v., ver. 45.

"O heavenly poet, such thy verse appears,
So sweet, so charming to my ravish'd ears,
As to the *weary swain* with cares oppress'd,
Beneath the *sylvan shade, refreshing rest;*
As to the *feverish traveller,* when first
He finds a *crystal stream* to quench his *thirst.*
In singing, as in piping, you excel;
And scarce your master could perform so well.
O fortunate young man! at least your lays
Are *next* to *his,* and claim the second praise.
Such as they are, my rural songs I join
To raise your Daphnis to the powers divine;
For Daphnis was *my friend,* as well as *thine.*"

Verse 7. *They that dwell under his shadow shall return*] The *Targum* is curious: "They shall be gathered together from the midst of their captivity; they shall dwell under the shadow of *his* CHRIST, and the dead shall revive."

They shall revive as the corn] The justness and beauty of this metaphor is not generally perceived. After the corn has been a short time above the earth, in a single spike, the blades begin to separate, and the stalk to spring out of the centre. The side leaves turn back to make way for the protruding stalk; and fall bending down to the earth, assuming a *withered* appearance, though still attached to the plant. To look at the corn in this state, no one, unacquainted with the circumstance, could entertain any sanguine hope of a copious *harvest.* In a short time other leaves spring out; the former freshen, and begin to stand erect; and the whole seems *to revive from a vegetative death.* This is the circumstance to which the prophet refers; "they shall revive as the corn." Of this a prudent and profitable use may be made.

1. When a soul is first "drawn by the cords of love," chap. xi. 4, every thing seems to it promising, comfortable, and delightful, like the corn in its *first state.*

2. But when the Spirit of judgment brings to the light of conscience the hidden things of iniquity, and repentance is deepened into *contrition,* the broken and the contrite heart groans, and thinks that *all is lost;* deep distress takes place, and discouragement succeeds discouragement. This answers to the corn in its *second state.*

3. By and by the pardon comes, and God's love is shed abroad in the heart by the Holy Ghost; every hope is *revived* and realized, the *full corn* in the ear becomes manifest; and this answers to the corn in its *third state.* "They shall revive as the corn." Glory be to God for his unspeakable gift!

Verse 8. *What have I to do any more with idols?*] The conversion of Ephraim is now as complete as if was sincere. God hears and observes this.

I am like a green fir tree.] Perhaps these words should be joined to the preceding, as *Newcome* has done, and be a part of God's speech to Ephraim. "I have heard him; and I have seen him as a flourishing fir tree." He is become strong and vigorous; and from his present appearance of healthiness, his future increase and prosperity may be safely anticipated.

From me is thy fruit found.] All thy goodness springs from the principle of grace which I have planted in thy soul; for as the earth cannot bring forth fruit without the blessing of God, sending the *dews* and *rains,* with the *genial rays* of the sun; so neither can the soul of man, even of the most pious, bear fruit, without a continual influence from the Most High.

Without the *former*, neither *grass* could grow for *cattle*, nor *corn* for the service of *man;* without the *latter*, no seeds of righteousness could take root, no stalk of promise could grow, no fruit of grace could be produced. And the unclean spirit, which was cast out, would soon return; and, finding his former house empty, swept, and garnished, would re-enter with seven demons of greater power and worse influence; and the latter end of that man would be worse than the first. Reader, ever consider that all *thy good* must be derived from God; and all that good must be preserved in thee by his continued influence of *light, love,* and *power* upon thy soul.

Verse 9. *Who is wise, and he shall understand these* things?] What things? Those which relate to the *backslidings, iniquity,* and *punishment* of Israel; and to the *mercy* and *kindness* of God in their promised restoration. *The things* which belong to the work of *sin* in the heart; *the things* which belong to the work of *grace* in the soul; and particularly *the things* mentioned in this wonderful chapter.

Prudent, and he shall know them?] He who endeavours to *understand* them, who lays his heart to them, such a person shall understand them.

For the ways of the Lord are *right*] This is the *conclusion* which the prophet makes from the whole. All God's conduct, both in the *dispensation of justice* and *mercy,* is right: all as it should be, all as it must be; because he is too wise to err, too good to be unkind.

The just shall walk in them] This is a truth which he will always acknowledge; and illustrate it by a righteous and godly life.

But the transgressors shall fall therein.] Howsoever good they might have been before, if they do not consider the necessity of depending upon God; of receiving all their light, life, power, and love from him; ever evidencing that *faith* which *worketh* by *love;* maintaining an obedient conduct, and having respect to all God's precepts; they shall fall, even in the "way of righteousness." When still using the *Divine ordinances,* and *associating with God's people,* they shall perish from the way; and be like Ephraim, who once "spoke trembling," and "was exalted in Israel," who was "God's beloved son," and "called out of Egypt;" yet, by "offending in Baal," giving way to "the idols of his heart," fell from God, fell into the hands of his enemies, and became a wretched thrall in a heathen land.

"Whoso is wise, let him understand these things!
Whoso is prudent, let him know them!"——

He who is well instructed will make a proper application of what he has here read; will tremble at the *threatenings,* and embrace the *promises,* of his God.

The *Targum* is worthy the most serious attention.

"The ways of the Lord are right, and the just who walk in them shall live for ever; but the ungodly, because they have not walked in them, shall be delivered into hell."

How instructive, how convincing, how awakening, and yet how consolatory, are the words of this prophecy! Reader, lay them to heart. A godly mind cannot consider them in vain; such shall know them, and know that the ways of the Lord are right.

INTRODUCTION TO THE BOOK

OF THE

PROPHET JOEL

JOEL, the son of *Pethuel,* the second of the twelve minor prophets, was, as is said, of the tribe of *Reuben,* and city of *Bethoran;* or rather *Betharan,* for *Bethoran* was on this side *Jordan,* in the tribe of *Ephraim,* and *Betharan* was on the other side of the river, in the tribe of *Reuben.* Joel prophesied in the kingdom of Judah; and it is the opinion of some critics that he did not appear there till after the removal of the ten tribes and the destruction of the kingdom of *Israel.* We do not know distinctly the year wherein he began to prophesy, nor that in which he died. He speaks of a great famine, and an inundation of locusts, which ravaged *Judea;* but as these are evils not uncommon in that country, and all sorts of events have not been registered in history, we can infer nothing from thence towards fixing the particular period of *Joel's* prophecy.

St. Jerome, followed by many others, both ancients and moderns, believed *Joel* to have been contemporary with *Hosea,* according to this rule laid down by him, that when there is no certain proof of the time wherein any prophet lived, we are to be directed in our conjectures by the time of the preceding prophet, whose epoch is better known. But this rule is not always certain, and should not hinder us from following another system, if we have good reason for doing so. The *Hebrews* maintain that *Joel* prophesied under *Manasseh;* and as collateral circumstances seem to preponderate in favour of this hypothesis, it has been accordingly followed in the margin. Under the idea of an enemy's army, the prophet represents a cloud of locusts, which in his time fell upon *Judea,* and caused great desolation. This, together with the caterpillars, and the drought, brought a terrible famine upon the land. God, being moved with the calamities and prayers of his people, scattered the locusts, and the wind blew them into the sea. These misfortunes were succeeded by plenty and fertility. After this, the prophet foretold the day of the Lord, and the vengeance he was to exercise in the valley of *Jezreel.* He speaks of the *teacher of righteousness,* whom God was to send; and of the Holy Spirit, which was to descend upon all flesh. He says that *Jerusalem* will be inhabited for ever; that salvation will come out from thence; and that whosoever shall call upon the name of the Lord shall be saved. All this relates to the new covenant, and the time of the Messiah. See *Calmet.*

Bishop *Lowth* observes that "the style of Joel differs much from that of Hosea; but, though of a different kind, is equally poetical. It is elegant, perspicuous, clear, diffusive, and flowing; and, at the same time, very sublime, nervous, and animated. He displays the whole power of poetic description in the first and second chapters; and, at the same time, his fondness for metaphors, comparisons, and allegories; nor is the connection of his subjects less remarkable than the graces of his diction. It is not to be denied that in some places he is very obscure; which every attentive reader will perceive, especially in the end of this prophecy." Præl. xxi.; and see *Dodd.* The two first chapters are inimitably beautiful; and the language, in force, and often in *sound,* well adapted to the subject. See the note on ver. 1.

THE BOOK

OF THE

PROPHET JOEL

Chronological Notes relative to the commencement of Joel's prophesying, upon the supposition that this event took place about six hundred and ninety *years before the commencement of the Christian era.*

Year from the Creation, according to Archbishop Usher, 3314.—Year of the Julian Period, 4024.—Year since the Flood, 1658.—Year from the foundation of Solomon's temple, 322.—Year since the division of Solomon's monarchy into the kingdoms of Israel and Judah, 285.—Year since the extinction of the kingdom of Israel by Shalmaneser, king of Assyria, 31.—Third year of the *twenty-second* Olympiad.—Year from the building of Rome, according to the Varronian computation, 64.—Year before the vulgar era of Christ's nativity, 690.—Cycle of the Sun, 20.—Cycle of the Moon, 15.—Third year of Eryxias, the last decennial archon of the Athenians.—First year of Anaxidamus, king of Lacedæmon, of the family of the Proclidæ.—Thirty-fifth year of Eurycrates I., king of Lacedæmon, of the family of the Eurysthenidæ.—Eleventh year of Deioces, the first king of the Medes.—Fortieth year of Perdiccas I., king of Macedon.—Twenty-ninth year of Gyges, king of Lydia.—Ninth year of Manasseh, king of Judah.

CHAPTER I

This and the beginning of the next chapter contain a double prophecy, applicable in its primary sense to a plague of locusts which was to devour the land, and to be accompanied with a severe drought and famine; and in its secondary sense it denotes the Chaldean invasion. Both senses must be admitted: for some of the expressions will apply only to the dearth by insects; others to the desolation by war. The contexture of both is beautiful and well conducted. In this chapter the distress of every order of people is strongly painted; and not only does the face of nature languish when the God of nature is displeased, 1–19; *but the very beasts of the field, by a bold figure, are represented as supplicating God in their distress, and reproaching the stupidity of man,* 20.

A. M. cir. 3314
B. C. cir. 690
Ol. cir. XXII. 3
NumæPompilii, R. Roman., cir. annum 26

THE word of the LORD that
came to Joel the son of Pethuel.
2 Hear this, ye old men, and
give ear, all ye inhabitants of
the land. [a]Hath this been in
your days, or even in the days of
your fathers?

A. M. cir. 3314
B. C. cir. 690
Ol. cir. XXII. 3
NumæPompilii, R. Roman., cir. annum 26

---

[a]Joel, chap. ii. 2

NOTES ON CHAP. I

Verse 1. *The word of the Lord that came to Joel*] See the *introduction* for some account of this prophet, whose history is very obscure. Bishop *Newcome* thinks that he prophesied while the kingdom of Judah subsisted, and refers to chap. ii. 1, 15, (see also chap. i. 14, and the note there,) but not long before its subversion as his words, chap. iii. 1, seem to imply that its captivity was approaching. See 2 Kings xxi. 10-15. He therefore favours the conjecture of *Drusius*, that this prophet lived under *Manasseh*, and before his conversion, 2 Chron. xxxiii. 13; that is, some time from before Christ 697 to (suppose) 660.

Verse 2. *Ye old men*] Instead of הזקנים *hazzekenim old men*, a few MSS. have הכהנים *haccohanim*, *ye priests*, but improperly.

Hath this been in your days] He begins very abruptly; and before he proposes his *subject*, excites attention and alarm by intimating that he is about to announce disastrous events, such as the *oldest man* among them has never seen, nor any of them learnt from the histories of ancient times.

A. M. cir. 3314
B. C. cir. 690
Ol. cir. XXII. 3
NumæPompilii,
R. Roman.,
cir. annum 26

3 [b]Tell ye your children of it,
and *let* your children *tell* their
children, and their children another generation.

4 [c]That[d] which the palmerworm hath left
hath the locust eaten: and that which the
locust hath left hath the cankerworm eaten;
and that which the cankerworm hath left
hath the caterpillar eaten.

5 Awake, ye drunkards, and weep; and
howl, all ye drinkers of wine, because of the
new wine; [e]for it is cut off from your mouth.

6 For [f]a nation is come up upon my land,
strong, and without number, [g]whose teeth *are*
the teeth of a lion, and he hath the cheek-
teeth of a great lion.

7 He hath [h]laid my vine waste, and [i]barked
my fig tree: he hath made it
clean bare, and cast *it* away;
the branches thereof are made
white.

A. M. cir. 3314
B. C. cir. 690
Ol. cir. XXII. 3
NumæPompilii,
R. Roman.,
cir. annum 26

8 [k]Lament like a virgin girded with sackcloth for [l]the husband of her youth.

9 [m]The meat-offering and the drink-
offering is cut off from the house of the
LORD; the priests, the LORD's ministers,
mourn.

10 The field is wasted, [n]the land mourneth;
for the corn is wasted: [o]the new wine is
[p]dried up, the oil languisheth.

11 [q]Be ye ashamed, O ye husbandmen;
howl, O ye vine-dressers, for the wheat
and for the barley; because the harvest of the
field is perished.

---

[b]Psa. lxxviii. 4——[c]Deut. xxviii. 38; chap. ii. 25——[d]Heb. *The residue of the palmerworm*——[e]Isa. xxxii. 10——[f]So Prov. xxx. 25, 26, 27; chap. ii. 2, 11, 25——[g]Rev. ix. 8——[h]Isa. v. 6

[i]Heb. *laid my fig tree for a barking*——[k]Isa. xxii. 12——[l]Prov. ii. 17; Jer. iii. 4——[m]Ver. 13; chap. ii. 14——[n]Jer. xii. 11; xiv. 2——[o]Isa. xxiv. 7; ver. 12——[p]Or, *ashamed*——[q]Jer. xiv. 3, 4

Verse 3. *Tell ye your children of it*] To heighten the effect, he still conceals the subject, and informs them that it is such as should be handed down from father to son through all generations.

Verse 4. *That which the palmerworm hath left*] Here he begins to open his message, and the words he chooses show that he is going to announce a devastation of the land by *locusts*, and a *famine* consequent on their depredations. What the different *insects* may be which he specifies is not easy to determine. I shall give the words of the original, with their etymology.

The *palmerworm*, גזם *gazam*, from the same root, *to cut short;* probably the *caterpillar*, or some such *blight*, from its *cutting the leaves of the trees into pieces* for its nourishment.

The *locust*, ארבה *arbeh*, from רבה *rabah*, to *multiply*, from the immense increase and multitude of this insect.

Cankerworm, ילק *yelek*, from לק *lak*, to *lick* or *lap* with the tongue; the *reference* is uncertain.

Caterpillar, חסיל *chasil*, from חסל *chasal*, to *consume*, to *eat up;* the *consumer*. Bishop *Newcome* translates the *first grasshopper;* the *second, locust;* the *third, devouring locust;* and the *fourth, consuming locust.* After all that has been said by interpreters concerning these *four* animals, I am fully of opinion that the *arbeh*, or *locust* himself, is the *gazam*, the *yelek*, and the *chasil;* and that these different names are used here by the prophet to point out the locust in its different states, or progress from *embryo* to *full growth.* See the note on chap. ii. 2.

Verse 5. *Awake, ye drunkards*] The general destruction of vegetation by these devouring creatures has totally prevented both *harvest* and *vintage;* so that there shall not be *wine* even for *necessary* uses, much less for the purposes of *debauchery.* It is well known that the ruin among the vines by locusts prevents the vintage for several years after.

Verse 6. *A nation is come up upon my land*] That real *locusts* are intended there can be little doubt; but it is thought that this may be a *double prophecy*, and that the destruction by the *Chaldeans* may also be intended, and that the *four* kinds of *locusts* mentioned above may mean the *four* several attacks made on Judea by them. The *first* in the last year of Nabonassar, (father of Nebuchadnezzar,) which was the *third* of Jehoiakim; the *second* when Jehoiakim was taken prisoner in the *eleventh* year of his reign; the *third* in the *ninth* year of Zedekiah; and the *fourth three* years after, when Jerusalem was destroyed by Nebuchadnezzar. Others say that they mean *four powers* which have been enemies of the Jews: 1. The *palmerworm*, the Assyrians and Chaldeans. 2. The *locust*, the Persians and Medes. 3. The *cankerworm*, the Greeks, and particularly Antiochus Epiphanes. 4. The *caterpillar*, the Romans. Others make them *four* kings; Tiglath-pileser, Shalmaneser, Sennacherib, and Nebuchadnezzar. But of such similitudes there is no end; and the best of them is arbitrary and precarious.

Verse 7. *He hath laid my vine waste*] The locusts have eaten off both *leaves* and *bark.* חשף חשפה *chasoph chasaphah*, he hath *made it clean bare;* שדד שדה *suddad sadeh, the field is laid waste*, ver. 10; and כשד משדי *kesod mishshaddai*, a *destruction from the Almighty*, ver. 15; are all *paronomasias* in which this prophet seems to delight.

Verse 8. *Lament like a virgin—for the husband of her youth.*] *Virgin* is a very improper *version* here. The original is בתולה *bethulah*, which signifies a *young woman* or *bride* not a *virgin*, the proper Hebrew for which is עלמה *almah.* See the notes on Isa. vii. 14, and Matt. i. 23.

Verse 9. *The meat-offering and the drink-offering is cut off*] The crops and the vines being destroyed by the locusts, the total devasta-

A. M. cir. 3314
B. C. cir. 690
Ol. cir. XXII. 3
NumæPompilii,
R. Roman.,
cir. annum 26

12 [r]The vine is dried up, and the fig tree languisheth, the pomegranate tree, the palm tree also, and the apple tree, *even* all the trees of the field, are withered: because [s]joy is withered away from the sons of men.

13 [t]Gird yourselves, and lament, ye priests: howl, ye ministers of the altar; come, lie all night in sackcloth, ye ministers of my God: for [u]the meat-offering and the drink-offering is withholden from the house of your God.

14 [v]Sanctify ye a fast, call [w]a [x]solemn assembly, gather the elders *and* [y]all the inhabitants of the land *into* the house of the LORD your God, and cry unto the LORD.

15 [z]Alas for the day! for [a]the day of the LORD *is* at hand, and as a destruction from the Almighty shall it come.

16 Is not the meat cut off before our eyes, *yea,* [b]joy and gladness from the house of our God?

17 The [c]seed is rotten under their clods, the garners are laid desolate, the barns are broken down; for the corn is withered.

18 How do [d]the beasts groan! the herds of cattle are perplexed, because they have no pasture; yea, the flocks of sheep are made desolate.

19 O LORD, [e]to thee will I cry: for [f]the fire hath devoured the [g]pastures of the wilderness, and the flame hath burned all the trees of the field.

20 The beasts of the field [h]cry also unto thee: for [i]the rivers of waters are dried up, and the fire hath devoured the pastures of the wilderness.

---

[r]Ver. 10——[s]Isa. xxiv. 11; Jer. xlviii. 33; see Psa. iv. 7; Ias. ix. 3——[t]Ver. 8; Jer. iv. 8——[u]Ver. 9——[v]2 Chron. xx. 3, 4; chap. ii. 15, 16——[w]Lev. xxiii. 36 [x]Or, day of *restraint*——[y]2 Chron. xx. 13——[z]Jer. xxx. 7

[a]Isa. xiii. 6, 9; chap. ii. 1——[b]See Deut. xii. 6, 7; xvi. 11, 14, 15——[c]Heb. *grains*——[d]Hos. iv. 3——[e]Psa. l. 15——[f]Jer. ix. 10; chap. ii. 3——[g]Or, *habitations* [h]Job xxxviii. 41; Psa. civ. 21; cxlv. 15——[i]1 Kings xvii. 7; xviii. 5

---

tion in plants, trees, corn, &c., is referred to and described with a striking variety of expression in this and the following verses.

Verse 12. *The vine is dried up*] Dr. *Shaw* observes that in Barbary, in the month of June, the locusts collect themselves into compact bodies a furlong or more square, and march on, eating up every thing that is green or juicy, and letting nothing escape them, whether vegetables or *trees*.

They destroy the *pomegranate*, the *palm*, the *apple*, (תפוח *tappuach*, the *citron tree*,) the *vine*, the *fig*, and every *tree of the field*. See the note on chap. ii. 2.

Verse 14. *Call a solemn assembly*] עצרה *atsarah* signifies a time of *restraint*, as the *margin* has it. The clause should be translated—*consecrate a fast, proclaim a time of restraint;* that is, of total abstinence from *food*, and from all *secular employment*. All the elders of the land and the representatives of the people were to be collected at the *temple* to cry unto the Lord, to confess their sins, and pray for mercy. The *temple* was not yet destroyed. This prophecy was delivered before the captivity of Judah.

Verse 15. *Alas for the day!*] The *Syriac repeats* this; the *Vulgate*, *Septuagint*, and *Arabic*, thrice: "Alas, alas, alas, for the day!"

As a destruction from the Almighty] The destruction that is now coming is no ordinary calamity; it is as a signal judgment immediately inflicted by the Almighty.

Verse 17. *The seed is rotten under their clods*] When the sprout was cut off as low as possible by the locusts, there was no farther germination. The seed rotted away.

Verse 18. *How do the beasts groan!*] I really think that the *neighing* of horses, or *braying* of asses, is wonderfully expressed by the sound of the original: מה נאנחה בהמה *mah* NEENCHAH *behemah*, how do the horses *neigh!* how do the asses *bray!* בהמה *behemah* is a collective name for all *domestic cattle*, and those used in *husbandry*.

Cattle are perplexed] They are looking everywhere, and wandering about to find some grass, and know not which way to run.

Verse 19. *O Lord, to thee will I cry*] Let this calamity come as it may, *we have sinned*, and should humble ourselves before God; and it is such a calamity as God alone can remove, therefore unto him must we cry.

The fire hath devoured the pastures] This may either refer to a *drought*, or to the effects of the locusts; as the ground, after they have passed over it, everywhere appears as if a *sheet of flame* had not only *scorched*, but *consumed* every thing.

Verse 20. *The beasts of the field cry also unto thee*] Even the cattle, wild and tame, are represented as supplicating God to have mercy upon them, and send them provender! There is a similar affecting description of the effects of a drought in Jeremiah, chap. xiv. 6.

The rivers of waters are dried up] There must have been a *drought* as well as a *host of locusts;* as some of these expressions seem to apply to the effects of *intense heat*.

For המדבר *hammidbar*, "the wilderness," one of my oldest MSS. reads מדבר *midbar*, "wilderness" simply, as in ver. 19. *Eight* or *ten* of Dr. *Kennicott's* have the same reading.

CHAPTER II

The prophet sounds the alarm of a dreadful calamity, the description of which is most terribly worked up, 1–11. *Exhortation to repentance, fasting, and prayer, that the Divine judgments may be averted,* 12–17. *God will in due time take vengeance on all the enemies of pure and undefiled religion,* 18–20. *Great prosperity of the Jews subsequent to their return from the Babylonish captivity,* 21–27. *Joel then makes an elegant transition to the outpouring of the Holy Ghost on the day of pentecost,* 28–30; *for so these verses are explained by one of the twelve apostles of the Lamb. See* Acts ii. 16–21. *Prophecy concerning the destruction of Jerusalem, which was shortly to follow the opening of the Gospel dispensation,* 31. *Promises of safety to the faithful and penitent; promises afterwards remarkably fulfilled to the Christians in their escape to Pella from the desolating sword of the Roman army,* 32.

A. M. cir. 3314 B. C. cir. 690 Ol. cir. XXII. 3 NumæPompilii, R. Roman., cir. annum 26

BLOW [a]ye the [b]trumpet in
Zion, and [c]sound an alarm
in my holy mountain: let all the
inhabitants of the land tremble:
for [d]the day of the LORD cometh, for *it is*
nigh at hand;

A. M. cir. 3314 B. C. cir. 690 Ol. cir. XXII. 3 NumæPompilii, R. Roman., cir. annum 26

2 [e]A day of darkness and of
gloominess, a day of clouds and
of thick darkness, as the morning spread upon the mountains:
[f]a great people and a strong; [g]there hath
not been ever the like, neither shall be any

[a]Jer. iv. 5; Ver. 15——[b]Or, *cornet*——[c]Numbers x. 5, 9 [d]Chap. i. 15; Obad. 15; Zeph. i. 14, 15

[e]Amos v. 18, 20——[f]Ver. 5, 11, 25; Chap. i. 6 [g]Exod. x. 14

NOTES ON CHAP. II

Verse 1. *Blow ye the trumpet in Zion*] This verse also shows that the temple was still standing. All assemblies of the people were collected by the sound of the *trumpet.*

The day of the Lord cometh] This phrase generally means a day of judgment or punishment.

Verse 2. *A day of darkness, &c.*] The depredations of the locusts are described from the *second* to the *eleventh* verse, and their destruction in the *twentieth.* Dr. *Shaw,* who saw locusts in Barbary in 1724 and 1725, thus describes them:—

"I never observed the *mantes,* bald *locusts,* to be gregarious. But the *locusts,* properly so called, which are so frequently mentioned by *sacred* as well as *profane* writers, are sometimes so beyond expression. Those which I saw in 1724 and 1725 were much bigger than our common grasshopper; and had brown spotted wings, with legs and bodies of a bright yellow. Their first appearance was toward the latter end of *March,* the wind having been for some time south. In the middle of *April* their numbers were so vastly increased that, in the heat of the day, they formed themselves into large and numerous swarms; flew in the air like a succession of clouds; and, as the prophet Joel expresses it, (ii. 10,) they darkened the sun. When the wind blew briskly, so that these swarms were crowded by others, or thrown one upon another, we had a lively idea of that comparison of the psalmist, (Psa. cix. 23,) of being 'tossed up and down as the locust.' In the month of *May,* when the ovaries of those insects were ripe and turgid, each of these *swarms* began gradually to disappear; and retired into the *Mettijiah,* and other adjacent plains, where they deposited their eggs. These were no sooner hatched in June, than each of these broods collected itself into a compact body of a furlong or more in square; and, marching immediately forward in the direction of the sea, they let nothing escape them; eating up every thing that was green and juicy, not only the lesser kinds of vegetables, but the *vine* likewise; the *fig tree,* the *pomegranate,* the *palm,* and the *apple tree, even all the trees of the field,* Joel i. 12; in doing which *they kept their ranks like men of war;* climbing over, as they advanced, every tree or wall that was in their way. Nay, they entered into our very houses and bedchambers, like *so many thieves.* The inhabitants, to stop their progress, made a variety of pits and trenches all over their fields and gardens, which they filled with water; or else they heaped up in them heath, stubble, and such like combustible matter, which were severally set on fire upon the approach of the *locusts.* But this was all to no purpose, for the trenches were quickly filled up, and the fires extinguished, by infinite swarms succeeding one another; while the front was regardless of danger, and the rear pressed on so close, that a retreat was altogether impossible. A day or two after one of these broods was in motion, others were already hatched to march and glean after them; gnawing off the very bark, and the young branches, of such trees as had before escaped with the loss only of their fruit and foliage. So justly have they been compared by the prophet *Joel* (chap. ii. 3) to *a great army;* who further observes, that 'the land is as the garden of Eden before them, and behind them a desolate wilderness.'

"Having lived near a month in this manner (like a *μυριοστομον ξιφος,* or *sword with ten thousand edges,* to which they have been compared,) upon the ruin and destruction of every vegetable substance which came in their way, they arrived at their full growth, and threw off their *nympha state* by casting their outward skin. To prepare themselves for this change, they clung by their hinder feet to some bush, twig, or corner of a stone; and immediately, by using an undulating motion, their heads would first break out, and then the rest of their bodies. The whole transformation was performed in seven or eight minutes, after which they lay for a short time in a torpid and seemingly languishing condition; but as soon as the sun and air had hardened their wings, by drying up the moisture which remained upon them, after casting their sloughs, they reassumed their former voracity, with an addition both of strength and

A. M. cir. 3314
B. C. cir. 690
Ol. cir. XXII. 3
NumæPompilii,
R. Roman.,
cir. annum 26

more after it, *even* to the years [h]of many generations.

3 [i]A fire devoureth before them; and behind them a flame burneth: the land *is* as [k]the garden of Eden before them, [l]and behind them a desolate wilderness; yea, and nothing shall escape them.

4 [m]The appearance of them *is* as the appearance of horses; and as horsemen, so shall they run.

5 [n]Like the noise of chariots on the tops of mountains shall they leap, like the noise of a flame of fire that devoureth the stubble, [o]as a strong people set in battle array.

6 Before their face the people shall be much pained: [p]all faces shall gather [q]blackness.

7 They shall run like mighty men; they shall climb the wall like men of war; and they shall march every one on his ways, and they shall not one break their ranks.

A. M. cir. 3314
B. C. cir. 690
Ol. cir. XXII. 3
NumæPompilii,
R. Roman.,
cir. annum 26

8 Neither shall one thrust another; they shall walk every one in his path: and *when* they fall upon the [r]sword, they shall not be wounded.

9 They shall run to and fro in the city; they shall run upon the wall, they shall climb up upon the houses: they shall [s]enter in at the windows [t]like a thief.

10 [u]The earth shall quake before them; the heavens shall tremble: [v]the sun and the moon shall be dark, and the stars shall withdraw their shining:

[h]Heb. *of generation and generation*——[i]Ch. i. 19, 20——[k]Gen. ii. 8; xiii. 10; Isa. li. 3——[l]Zech. vii. 14——[m]Rev. ix. 7——[n]Rev. ix. 9——[o]Ver. 2——[p]Jer. viii. 21; Lam. iv. 8; Nah. ii. 10——[q]Heb. *pot*——[r]Or, *dart*——[s]Jer. ix. 21——[t]John x. 1——[u]Psa. xviii. 7——[v]Isa. xiii. 10; Ezek. xxxii. 7; Ver. 31; chap. iii. 15; Matt. xxiv. 29

agility. Yet they did not continue long in this state before they were entirely dispersed, as their parents were before, after they had laid their eggs; and as the direction of the marches and flights of them both was always to the northward, and not having strength, as they have sometimes had, to reach the opposite shores of *Italy*, *France*, or *Spain*, it is probable they perished in the sea, a grave which, according to these people, they have in common with other winged creatures."—*Travels*, 4to. edition, pp. 187, 188.

A day of darkness] They sometimes obscure the sun. And *Thuanus* observes of an immense crowd, that "they darkened the sun at mid-day."

As the morning spread upon the mountains] They appeared suddenly: as the sun, in rising behind the mountains, *shoots his rays* over them. *Adanson*, in his voyage to *Senegal*, says: "Suddenly there came over our heads a thick cloud which *darkened the air, and deprived us of the rays of the sun*. We soon found that it was owing to a cloud of *locusts*." Some clouds of them are said to have darkened the sun for a mile, and others for the space of *twelve miles!* See on ver. 10.

Verse 3. *A fire devoureth before them*] They consume like a general conflagration. "They destroy the ground, not only for the time, but burn trees for two years after." Sir *Hans Sloane*, Nat. Hist. of Jamaica, vol. i., p. 29.

Behind them a flame burneth] "Wherever they feed," says *Ludolf*, in his History of Ethiopia, "their leavings seem as if *parched with fire*."

Nothing shall escape them.] "After devouring the herbage," says *Adanson*, "with the fruits and leaves of trees, they attacked even the *buds* and the very *bark;* they did not so much as spare the *reeds with which the huts were thatched*."

Verse 4. *The appearance of horses*] The *head* of the locust is remarkably like that of the *horse;* and so *Ray* on Insects describes them: *Caput oblongum, equi instar, prona spectans*—"They have an oblong head, like to that of a horse, bending downward." On this account, the *Italians* call them *cavaletta*, cavalry. *Bochart* remarks, from an *Arabic writer*, that the *locusts* resemble *ten* different kinds of *animals:* 1. The HORSE in its *head*. 2. The ELEPHANT in its *eyes*. 3. The BULL in its *neck*. 4. The STAG in its *horns*. 5. The LION in its *breast*. 6. The SCORPION in its *belly*. 7. The EAGLE in its *wings*. 8. The CAMEL in its *thighs*. 9. The OSTRICH in its *feet*. And 10. The SERPENT in its *tail*. *Vid. Hieroz.*, vol. ii., p. 475, edit. 1692. But its most prominent resemblance is to the *horse*, which the prophet mentions; and which the *Arabic writer* puts in the *first place*, as being the *chief*.

Verse 5. *Like the noise of chariots*] *Bochart* also remarks:—"The locusts fly with a *great noise*, so as to be heard *six miles off*, and while they are eating the fruits of the earth, the *sound* of them is like that of a *flame driven by the wind*."—*Ibid.*, p. 478.

Verse 6. *All faces shall gather blackness.*] Universal mourning shall take place, because they know that such a plague is irresistible.

Verse 7. *Like mighty men—like men of war* (*and as horsemen*, ver. 4)] The prophet does not say *they are such*, but they *resemble*. They are *locusts;* but in their operations they are LIKE the above.

They shall not break their ranks] See the account on ver. 2, from Dr. *Shaw*.

Verse 8. *They shall not be wounded.*] They have hard scales like a coat of mail; but the expression refers to the *utter uselessness* of all means to prevent their depredations. See *Shaw's* account above.

Verse 10. *The earth shall quake—the heavens shall tremble*] Poetical expressions, to point out *universal consternation* and *distress*. The *earth quaked* to see itself deprived of its *verdure;* the *heavens trembled* to find themselves deprived of their *light*.

The sun and the moon shall be dark] *Bochart* relates that "their multitude is sometimes

A. M. cir. 3314
B. C. cir. 690
Ol. cir. XXII. 3
NumæPompilii,
R. Roman.,
cir. annum 26

11 [w]And the LORD shall utter
his voice before [x]his army: for
his camp *is* very great: [y]for *he*
is strong that executeth his
word: for the [z]day of the LORD *is* great and
very terrible; and [a]who can abide it?
12 Therefore also now, saith the LORD, [b]turn
ye *even* unto me with all your heart, and with
fasting, and with weeping, and with mourning:
13 And [c]rend your heart, and not [d]your
garments, and turn unto the LORD your God:
for he *is* [e]gracious and merciful, slow to anger, and of great kindness, and repenteth him
of the evil.
14 [f]Who knoweth *if* he will return and repent, and leave [g]a blessing behind him; *even*
[h]a meat-offering and a drink-offering unto
the LORD your God?
15 [i]Blow the trumpet in Zion, [k]sanctify a
fast, call a solemn assembly:

16 Gather the people, [l]sanctify
the congregation, [m]assemble the
elders, [n]gather the children, and
those that suck the breasts: [o]let
the bridegroom go forth of his chamber, and
the bride out of her closet.

A. M. cir. 3314
B. C. cir. 690
Ol. cir. XXII. 3
NumæPompilii,
R. Roman.,
cir. annum 26

17 Let the priests, the ministers of the
LORD, weep [p]between the porch and the
altar, and let them say, [q]Spare thy people, O
LORD, and give not thine heritage to reproach,
that the heathen should [r]rule over them:
[s]wherefore should they say among the people,
Where *is* their God?
18 Then will the LORD [t]be jealous for his
land, [u]and pity his people.
19 Yea, the LORD will answer and say unto
his people, Behold, I will send you [v]corn, and
wine, and oil, and ye shall be satisfied therewith: and I will no more make you a reproach among the heathen:

[w]Jer. xxv. 30; chap. iii. 16; Amos i. 2——[x]Ver. 25——[y]Jer. l. 34; Rev. xviii. 8——[z]Jer. xxx. 7; Amos v. 18; Zeph. i. 15——[a]Num. xxiv. 23; Mal. iii. 2——[b]Jer. iv. 1; Hos. xii. 6; xiv. 1——[c]Psa. xxxiv. 18; li. 17——[d]Gen. xxxvii. 34; 2 Sam. i. 11; Job i. 20——[e]Exod. xxxiv. 6; Psa. lxxxvi. 5, 15; Jonah iv. 2——[f]Josh. xiv. 12; 2 Sam. xii. 22; 2 Kings xix. 4; Amos v. 15; Jonah iii. 9; Zeph. ii. 3

[g]Isa. lxv. 8; Hag. ii. 19——[h]Chap. i. 9, 13——[i]Num. x. 3; ver. 1——[k]Chap. i. 14——[l]Exod. xix. 10, 22——[m]Chap. i. 14——[n]2 Chron. xx. 13——[o]1 Cor. vii. 5——[p]Ezek. viii. 16; Matt. xxiii. 35——[q]Exod. xxxii. 11, 12; Deut. ix. 26–29——[r]Or, *use a by-word against them*——[s]Psa. xlii. 10; lxxix. 10; cxv. 2; Mic. vii. 10——[t]Zech. i. 14; viii. 2——[u]Deut. xxxii. 36; Isa. lx. 10——[v]See chap. i. 10; Mal. iii. 10, 11, 12

so immense as to obscure the heavens for the space of *twelve miles!*"—*Ibid.* p. 479.

Verse 11. *The Lord shall utter his voice*] Such a *mighty force* seems as if summoned by the Almighty, and the noise they make in coming announces their approach, while yet afar off.

Verse 12. *Turn ye* even *to me*] *Three means* of turning are recommended: *Fasting, weeping, mourning,* i. e., *continued sorrow.*

Verse 13. *Rend your heart*] Let it not be merely a rending of your *garments*, but let your *hearts* be truly contrite. Merely *external* worship and *hypocritical pretensions* will only increase the evil, and cause God to meet you with heavier judgments.

For he is *gracious*] Good and benevolent in his own nature.

Merciful] Pitying and forgiving, as the effect of *goodness* and *benevolence.*

Slow to anger] He is not easily provoked to punish, because he is *gracious* and *merciful.*

Of great kindness] Exuberant goodness to all them that return to him.

And repenteth him of the evil.] Is ever ready to *change* his *purpose* to *destroy*, when he finds the culprit willing to be *saved.* See the notes on Exod. xxxiv. 6, 7.

Verse 14. *Who knoweth* if *he will return*] He may yet interpose and turn aside the calamity threatened, and so far preserve the land from these ravagers, that there will be food for *men* and *cattle*, and a sufficiency of *offerings* for the temple service. Therefore—

Verse 15. *Blow the trumpet*] Let no time be lost, let the alarm be sounded.

Verse 16. *Gather the children*] Let all share in the humiliation, for all must feel the judgment, should it come. Let no *state* nor *condition* among the people be exempted. The *elders*, the *young persons*, the *infants*, the *bridegroom*, and the *bride;* let all leave their houses, and go to the temple of God.

Verse 17. *Let the priests—weep between the porch and the altar*] The altar of burnt-offerings stood before the porch of the temple, 2 Chron. viii. 12, and between them there was an open space of *fifteen* or *twenty* cubits. It was there that the priests prostrated themselves on such occasions. It was into this place that the priests brought the *sacrifice* or *victim of atonement;* and where the high priest laid his hands on the head of the victim confessing his sins.

Let them say] The following was the form to be used on this occasion, "Spare thy people," &c. And if this be done with a rent heart, &c., "then will the Lord be jealous for his land, and pity his people," ver. 18. He will surely save, if ye seriously return to and penitently seek him.

Verse 19. *Yea, the Lord will answer*] It is not a *peradventure;* it will *surely* be done; if ye seek God as *commanded*, ye will find him as *promised.*

I will send you corn and wine] He will either prevent the *total* ravaging of the land, or so bless it with extraordinary *vegetable strength*, that ye shall have plentiful crops.

Verse 20. *I will remove far off from you the northern* army] "That is, the *locusts;* which might enter Judea by the *north*, as Circassia and Mingrelia abound with them. Or the locusts may be thus called, because they spread terror like the *Assyrian* armies, which entered

A. M. cir. 3314
B. C. cir. 690
Ol. cir. XXII. 3
NumæPompilii,
R. Roman.,
cir. annum 26

20 But [w]I will remove far off
from you [x]the northern *army,*
and will drive him into a land
barren and desolate, with his
face [y]toward the east sea, and his hinder part
[z]toward the utmost sea, and his stink shall
come up, and his ill savour shall come up, because [a]he hath done great things.
21 Fear not, O land; be glad and rejoice:
for the LORD will do great things.
22 Be not afraid, [b]ye beasts of the field:
for [c]the pastures of the wilderness do spring,
for the tree beareth her fruit, the fig tree and
the vine do yield their strength.
23 Be glad then, ye children of Zion, and
[d]rejoice in the LORD your God: for he hath
given you [e]the former rain [f]moderately, and
he [g]will cause to come down for you [h]the
rain, the former rain, and the
latter rain in the first *month.*
24 And the floors shall be full
of wheat, and the fats shall overflow with wine and oil.
25 And I will restore to you the years [i]that
the locust hath eaten, the cankerworm, and
the caterpillar, and the palmerworm, [k]my
great army which I sent among you.
26 And ye shall [l]eat in plenty, and be satisfied, and praise the name of the LORD your
God, that hath dealt wondrously with you:
and my people shall never be ashamed.
27 [m]And ye shall know that I *am* [n]in the
midst of Israel, and *that* [o]I *am* the LORD
your God, and none else: and my people shall
never be ashamed.
28 [p]And it shall come to pass afterward,

A. M. cir. 3314
B. C. cir. 690
Ol. cir. XXII. 3
NumæPompilii,
R. Roman.,
cir. annum 26

[w]See Exod. x. 19——[x]Jer. i. 14——[y]Ezek. xlvii. 18; Zech. xiv. 8——[z]Deut. xi. 24——[a]Heb. *he hath magnified to do*——[b]Chap. i. 18, 20——[c]Zech. viii. 12; See chap. i. 19——[d]Isa. xli. 16; lxi. 10; Hab. iii. 18; Zech. x. 7——[e]Or, *a teacher of righteousness* [f]Heb. *according to righteousness*——[g]Lev. xxvi. 4; Deut. xi. 14; xxviii. 12——[h]James v. 7——[i]Ch. i. 4 [k]Ver. 11——[l]Lev. xxvi. 5; Psa. xxii. 26; see Lev. xxvi. 26; Mic. vi. 14——[m]Ch. iii. 17——[n]Lev. xxvi. 11, 12; Ezek. xxxvii. 26, 27, 28——[o]Isa. xlv. 5, 21, 22; Ezek. xxxix. 22, 28——[p]Isa. xliv. 3; Ezek. xxxix. 29; Acts ii. 17

Judea by the *north.* See Zeph. ii. 13."—*Newcome.* Syria, which was *northward* of Judea, was infested with them; and it must have been a *northern* wind that brought them into Judea, in the time of *Joel;* as God promises to *change* this wind, and carry them into a *barren and desolate land,* Arabia Deserta. "And his face toward the east sea," i. e., the *Dead Sea,* which lay *eastward* of Jerusalem. "His hinder part toward the utmost sea," the *western sea,* i. e., the *Mediterranean.*

And his stink shall come up] After having been drowned by millions in the Mediterranean, the reflux of the tide has often brought them back, and thrown them in heaps upon the shore, where they putrefied in such a manner as to infect the air and produce pestilence, by which both *men* and *cattle* have died in great multitudes. See *Bochart,* Hieroz., vol. ii., p. 481.

Livy, and St. *Augustine* after him, relate that there was such an immense crowd of locusts in Africa that, having eaten up every green thing, a wind arose that carried them into the sea, where they perished; but being cast upon the shore, they putrefied, and bred such a *pestilence,* that *eighty thousand* men died of it in the kingdom of *Massinissa,* and *thirty thousand* in the garrison of *Utica,* in which only *ten* remained alive. See *Calmet* and *Livy,* lib. xc., and *August. De Civitate Dei,* lib. iv., c. 31. We have many testimonies of a similar kind.

Because he hath done great things] Or, כי *ki, although* he have done great things, or, *after* he has done them, i. e., in almost destroying the whole country.

Verse 21. *Fear not—for the Lord will do great things.*] The words are *repeated* from the preceding verse; Jehovah will do great things in *driving them away,* and supernaturally restoring the land to fertility.

Verse 23. *The former rain moderately*] המורה לצדקה *hammorch litsedakah,* "the former rain in righteousness," that is, in *due time* and in *just proportion.* This rain fell after *autumn,* the other in *spring.* See Hosea vi. 3.

In the first month.] בראשון *barishon,* "as aforetime." So Bp. *Newcome.* In the month *Nisan.*—Syriac.

Verse 25. *I will restore—the years*] It has already been remarked that the *locusts* not only destroyed the produce of *that year,* but so completely ate up all *buds,* and *barked the trees,* that they did not recover for *some years.* Here God promises that he would either *prevent* or *remedy* that evil; for he would *restore the years* that the *locusts, cankerworm, caterpillar,* and *palmerworm* had eaten.

Verse 26. *Praise the name of the Lord your God, that hath dealt wondrously with you*] In so destroying this formidable enemy; and so *miraculously* restoring the land to *fertility,* after so great a devastation.

Verse 28. *Shall come to pass afterward*] אחרי כן *acharey ken,* "after this;" the same, says *Kimchi,* as *in the latter days,* which always refers to the *days of the Messiah;* and thus this prophecy is to be interpreted: and we have the testimony of St. Peter, Acts ii. 17, that this prophecy relates to *that mighty effusion of the Holy Spirit* which took place after the day of pentecost. Nor is there any evidence that such an *effusion* took place, nor such effects were produced, from the days of this prophet till the day of *pentecost.* And the *Spirit* was poured out then *upon all flesh,* that is, on people of different countries, speaking the languages of almost all the people of the earth; which intimated that these were the *first-fruits* of the conversion of all the nations of the world. For there was scarcely a tongue in the universe that

A. M. cir. 3314 B. C. cir. 690 Ol. cir. XXII. 3 NumæPompilii, R. Roman., cir. annum 26

that I [q]will pour out my Spirit
upon all flesh; [r]and your sons
and [s]your daughters shall prophesy, your old men shall dream
dreams, your young men shall see visions:
29 And also upon [t]the servants and upon
the handmaids in those days will I pour out
my Spirit.
30 And [u]I will show wonders in the heavens
and in the earth, blood, and fire, and pillars
of smoke.
31 [v]The sun shall be turned
into darkness, and the moon into
blood, [w]before the great and
the terrible day of the LORD
come.
32 And it shall come to pass, *that* [x]whoso-
ever shall call on the name of the LORD shall
be delivered: for [y]in Mount Zion and in Jerusalem shall be deliverance, as the LORD hath
said, and in [z]the remnant whom the LORD
shall call.

[q]Zech. xii. 10; John vii. 39——[r]Isa. liv. 13——[s]Acts xxi. 9——[t]1 Cor. xii. 13; Gal. iii. 28; Col. iii. 11 [u]Matt. xxiv. 29; Mark xiii. 24; Luke xxi. 11, 25 [v]Verse 10; Isaiah xiii. 9, 10; chap. iii. 1, 15; Matthew xxiv. 29; Mark xiii. 24; Luke xxi. 25; Rev. vi. 12 [w]Malachi iv. 5——[x]Romans x. 13——[y]Isa. xlvi. 13; lix. 20; Obad. 17; Romans xi. 26——[z]Isa. xi. 11, 16; Jer. xxxi. 7; Mic. iv. 7; v. 3, 7, 8; Rom. ix. 27; xi. 5, 7

was not to be found among the *Parthians, Medes, Elamites, Mesopotamians, Jews, Cappadocians*, people of *Pontus*, of *Asia, Phrygia, Pamphylia, Egypt, Libya, Cyrene, Rome, Crete*, and *Arabia*, who were residents at Jerusalem at that time; and on whom this mighty gift was poured out, each hearing and apprehending the truths of the Gospel, in his own language wherein he was born. Thus we have Divine authority for saying, *that* was the fulfilment of *this* prophecy by *Joel*. And the mighty and rapid spread of the Gospel of Christ in the *present day*, by means of the translation of the Scriptures into almost all the regular languages of the world, and the sending *missionaries* to all nations, who preach the Gospel in those tongues, are farther proofs that the great promise is in the *fullest progress* to be speedily fulfilled, even in the utmost sense of the words.

Your sons and your daughters shall prophesy] Shall *preach*—exhort, pray, and instruct, so as to benefit the Church.

Your old men shall dream dreams] Have my will represented to them in this way, as the others by *direct inspiration*.

Your young men shall see visions] Have true representations of Divine things made upon their *imaginations* by the power of God; that they shall have as full an evidence of them as they could have of any thing that came to the *mind* through the medium of the *senses*.

Verse 29. *And also upon the servants and upon the handmaids*] The gifts of teaching and instructing men shall not be *restricted* to any one *class* or *order* of people. He shall call and qualify the men of his own choice; and shall take such out of all *ranks, orders, degrees*, and offices in society. And he will pour out his Spirit upon them; and they shall be endowed with all the gifts and graces necessary to convert sinners, and build up the Church of Christ on its most holy faith.

And this God *has done*, and is *still doing*. He left the *line of Aaron*, and took his *apostles* indiscriminately from *any tribe*. He passed by the *regular order* of the *priesthood*, and the *public schools* of the most celebrated doctors, and took his *evangelists* from among *fishermen, tent-makers*, and even the *Roman tax-gatherers*. And he, lastly, passed by the *Jewish tribes*, and took the *Gentile converts*, and made *them* preachers of righteousness to the inhabitants of the whole earth. The same practice he continues to the present day; yet he did not then pass by a man *brought up at the feet of Gamaliel*, no more than he would *now* a man *brought up in a celebrated seminary of learning*. He is ever free to use his *own gifts*, in his *own way;* and when *learning* is sanctified, by being *devoted to the service of God*, and the *possessor* is humble and pious, and has those *natural gifts* necessary for a *public teacher*, perhaps we might safely say, God would in many cases *prefer such:* but he will have *others*, as intimated in the prophecy, that we may see the conversion of men is not by *human might*, nor *power*, but *by the Spirit of the Lord of hosts*. The learned man can do nothing without his *Spirit;* the *unlearned* must have his *gifts* and *graces*, without which both their labours would be unprofitable; and thus the *excellency of the power is of God*, and no *flesh can glory in his presence*. See my sermon on this passage.

Verse 30. *Wonders in the heavens and in the earth*] This refers to those dreadful sights, dreadful portents, and destructive commotion, by which the Jewish polity was finally overthrown, and the Christian religion established in the Roman empire. See how our Lord applies this prophecy, Matt. xxiv. 29, and the parallel texts.

Verse 31. *The sun shall be turned into darkness*] The Jewish polity civil and ecclesiastical, shall be entirely destroyed.

Before the great and the terrible day of the Lord come.] In the taking and sacking of Jerusalem, and burning of the temple, by the Romans, under *Titus*, the son of Vespasian. This was, perhaps, the *greatest* and most *terrible day* of God's vengeance ever shown to the world, or that ever will be shown, till the great day of the general judgment. For a full view of this subject, I wish to refer the reader to the notes on Matt. xxiv.

Verse 32. *Whosoever shall call on the name of the Lord*] כל אשר יקרא בשם יהוה *col asher yikra beshem Yehovah*, "All who shall *invoke* in the name of Jehovah." That CHRIST is the *Jehovah* here mentioned appears plain from Rom. x. 15, where the reader had better consult the notes. "This refers," says Bp. *Newcome*, "to the safety of the Christians during the Jewish and the Roman war." It may: but it has a much more extensive meaning, as the use of it by St. Paul, as above, evidently shows. *Every man who invokes Jehovah* for mercy and salvation *by* or *in the name*, JESUS—that very name given under heaven among men for this purpose—*shall be saved.* Nor is there salvation in any other; and those who reject *him* had better lay these things to heart before it be too late.

For in Mount Zion and in Jerusalem] Our blessed Lord first began to preach the Gospel in *Mount Zion*, in the *temple*, and throughout *Jerusalem. There* he formed his Church, and *thence* he sent his apostles and evangelists to every part of the globe: "Go ye into all the world, and preach the Gospel to every creature." Of the Jews there was but a *remnant*, a very small number, that received the doctrine of the Gospel, here termed the remnant that the Lord should call; קרא *kore, whom he calleth.* Many were called who would not obey: but those who obeyed the call were saved; and still he *delivers* those who *call upon him;* and he is still calling on men to come to him that they may be saved.

CHAPTER III

The prophecy in this chapter is thought by some to relate to the latter times of the world, when God shall finally deliver his people from all their adversaries; and it must be confessed that the figures employed are so lofty as to render it impossible to restrain the whole of their import to any events prior to the commencement of the Christian era. The whole prophecy is delivered in a very beautiful strain of poetry; but what particular events are referred to is at present very uncertain, 1–21.

A. M. cir. 3314
B. C. cir. 690
Ol. cir. XXII. 3
NumæPompilii,
R. Roman.,
cir. annum 26

FOR, behold, [a]in those days,
and in that time, when I
shall bring again the captivity
of Judah and Jerusalem,
2 [b]I will also gather all nations, and
will bring them down into [c]the valley of
Jehoshaphat, and [d]will plead
with them there for my people and *for* my heritage Israel, whom they have scattered among the nations, and parted my land.

A. M. cir. 3314
B. C. cir. 690
Ol. cir. XXII. 3
NumæPompilii,
R. Roman.,
cir. annum 26

[a]Jer. xxx. 3; Ezek. xxxviii. 14——[b]Zech. xiv. 2, 3, 4

[c]2 Chron. xx. 26; ver. 42——[d]Isa. lxvi. 16; Ezek. xxxviii. 22

NOTES ON CHAP. III

Verse 1. *For, behold, in those days*] According to the preceding prophecy, *these days* should refer to *Gospel times*, or to such as should *immediately precede* them. But this is a part of the prophecy which is difficult to be understood. All interpreters are at *variance* upon it; some applying its principal parts to *Cambyses;* his unfortunate expedition to Egypt; the destruction of *fifty thousand* of his troops (by the moving pillars of sand) whom he had sent across the desert to plunder the rich temple of Jupiter Ammon; his return to Judea, and dying of a wound which he received from his own sword, in mounting his horse, which happened at *Ecbatane*, at the foot of Mount *Carmel.* On which his army, composed of different nations, seeing themselves without a head, fell out, and fought against each other, till the whole were destroyed. And this is supposed to be what *Ezekiel* means by *Gog* and *Magog*, and the destruction of the former. See Ezek. xxxviii. and xxxix.

Others apply this to the *victories* gained by the *Maccabees*, and to the destruction brought upon the enemies of their country; while several consider the whole as a figurative prediction of the *success of the Gospel* among the nations of the earth. It may refer to those times in which the Jews shall be brought in with the fulness of the Gentiles, and be re-established in their own land. Or there may be portions in this prophecy that refer to *all the events;* and to *others* that have not fallen yet within the range of human conjecture, and will be only known when the time of fulfilment shall take place. In this painful uncertainty, rendered still more so by the discordant opinions of many wise and learned men, it appears to be my province, as I have nothing in the form of a new conjecture to offer, to confine myself to an explanation of the *phraseology* of the chapter; and then leave the reader to apply it as may seem best to his own judgment.

I shall bring again the captivity of Judah and Jerusalem.] This may refer to the return from the Babylonish captivity; extending also to the restoration of *Israel*, or the *ten tribes.*

Verse 2. *The valley of Jehoshaphat*] There is no such valley in the land of Judea; and hence the word must be *symbolical.* It signifies the *judgment of God*, or *Jehovah judgeth;* and may mean some place (as Bp. *Newcome* imagines) where Nebuchadnezzar should gain a great battle, which would utterly discomfit the ancient enemies of the Jews, and resemble the victory which Jehoshaphat gained over the Ammonites, Moabites, and Edomites, 2 Chron. xx. 22-26.

And parted my land.] The above nations had frequently entered into the territories of Israel; and divided among themselves the lands they had thus overrun.

While the Jews were in captivity, much of the land of Israel was seized on, and occupied by the *Philistines*, and other nations that bordered on Judea.

A. M. cir. 3314
B. C. cir. 690
Ol. cir. XXII. 3
NumæPompilii,
R. Roman.,
cir. annum 26

3 And they have [e]cast lots for
my people; and have given a
boy for a harlot, and sold a girl
for wine, that they might drink.
4 Yea, and what have ye to do with me, [f]O
Tyre, and Zidon, and all the coasts of Palestine? [g]will ye render me a recompense? and
if ye recompense me, swiftly *and* speedily will
I return your recompense upon your own
head;
5 Because ye have taken my silver and my
gold, and have carried into your temples my
goodly [h]pleasant things:
6 The children also of Judah and the children of Jerusalem have ye sold unto [i]the
Grecians, that ye might remove them far
from their border.
7 Behold, [k]I will raise them out of the place
whither ye have sold them, and will return
your recompense upon your own head:
8 And I will sell your sons and your daughters into the hand of the chil-
dren of Judah, and they shall
sell them to the [l]Sabeans, to
a people [m]far off; for the LORD
hath spoken *it*.

A. M. cir. 3314
B. C. cir. 690
Ol. cir. XXII. 3
NumæPompilii,
R. Roman.,
cir. annum 26

9 [n]Proclaim ye this among the Gentiles;
[o]Prepare war, wake up the mighty men, let all
the men of war draw near; let them come up.
10 [p]Beat your ploughshares into swords, and
your [q]pruning hooks into spears: [r]let the
weak say, I *am* strong.
11 [s]Assemble yourselves, and come, all ye
heathen, and gather yourselves together round
about: thither [t]cause [u]thy mighty ones to
come down, O Lord.
12 Let the heathen be wakened, [v]and
come up to the valley of Jehoshaphat: for
there will I sit to [w]judge all the heathen
round about.
13 [x]Put ye in the sickle, for [y]the harvest is
ripe: come, get you down; for the [z]press

[e]Obad. 11; Nah. iii. 10——[f]Amos i. 6, 9——[g]Ezek. xxv. 15, 16, 17——[h]Heb. *desirable;* Dan. xi. 38——[i]Heb. *the sons of the Grecians*——[k]Isa. xliii. 5, 6; xlix. 12; Jer. xxiii. 8——[l]Ezek. xxiii. 42——[m]Jer. vi. 20——[n]See Isa. viii. 9, 10; Jer. xlvi. 3, 4; Ezek. xxxviii. 7——[o]Heb. *sanctify*

[p]See Isa. ii. 4; Mic. iv. 3——[q]Or, *scythes*——[r]Zech. xii. 8——[s]Ver. 2——[t]Or, *the LORD shall bring down* [u]Psa. ciii. 20; Isa. xiii. 3——[v]Ver. 2——[w]Psa. xcvi. 13; xcviii. 9; cx. 6; Isa. ii. 4; iii. 13; Mic. iv. 3——[x]Matt. xiii. 39; Rev. xiv. 15, 18——[y]Jeremiah li. 33; Hosea vi. 11——[z]Isa. lxiii. 3; Lam. i. 15; Rev. xiv. 19, 20

Verse 3. *Have given a boy for a harlot*] To such wretched circumstances were the poor Jews reduced in their captivity, that their children were sold by their oppressors; and both *males* and *females* used for the *basest purposes.* And they were often bartered for the necessaries or luxuries of life. Or this may refer to the issue of the Chaldean war in Judea, where the captives were divided among the victors. And being set in companies, *they cast lots for them:* and those to whom they fell sold them for various purposes; the boys to be slaves and catamites, the girls to be prostitutes; and in return for them they got *wine* and *such things.* I think this is the meaning of the text.

Verse 4. *What have ye to do with me*] Why have the *Tyrians* and *Sidonians* joined their other enemies to oppress my people? for they who touch my people touch *me.*

Will ye render me a recompense?] Do you think by this to avenge yourselves upon the Almighty? to retaliate upon God! Proceed, and speedily will I return your recompense; I will retaliate.

Verse 5. *Ye have taken my silver and my gold*] The Chaldeans had spoiled the temple, and carried away the *sacred vessels,* and put them in the temple of their own god in Babylon.

Verse 6. *Sold unto the Grecians*] These were the descendants of *Javan,* Gen. x. 2-5. And with them the *Tyrians* trafficked, Ezek. xxvii. 19.

That ye might remove them far from their border.] Intending to send them *as far off* as possible, that it might be impossible for them to get back to reclaim the land of which you had dispossessed them.

Verse 7. *I will raise them*] I shall find means to bring them back from *the place whither ye have sold them,* and they shall retaliate upon you the injuries they have sustained. It is said that Alexander and his successors set at liberty many Jews that had been sold into Greece. And it is likely that many returned from different lands, on the publication of the edict of Cyrus.—*Newcome.*

Verse 8. *I will sell your sons*] When *Alexander* took Tyre, he reduced into slavery all the lower people, and the women. *Arrian,* lib. ii., says that *thirty thousand* of them were *sold. Artaxerxes Ochus* destroyed *Sidon,* and subdued the other cities of *Phœnicia.* In all these wars, says *Calmet,* the Jews, who obeyed the Persians, did not neglect to purchase Phœnician slaves, whom they sold again to the *Sabeans,* or *Arabs.*

Verse 9. *Prepare war*] Let all the enemies of God and of his people join together; let them even call all the tillers of the ground to their assistance, instead of labouring in the field; let every *peasant* become a *soldier.* Let them turn their *agricultural implements* into *offensive weapons,* so that *the weak,* being well armed, may confidently say, *I am strong:* yet, when thus collected and armed, *Jehovah will bring down thy mighty ones;* for so the clause in ver. 11 should be rendered.

Verse 12. *Let the heathen be wakened*] The heathen *shall be wakened.*

The valley of Jehoshaphat] Any place where God may choose to display his judgments against his enemies.

Verse 13. *Put ye in the sickle*] The destruc-

A. M. cir. 3314
B. C. cir. 690
Ol. cir. XXII. 3
NumæPompilii,
R. Roman.,
cir. annum 26

is full, and the fats overflow;
for their wickedness *is* great.
14 Multitudes, multitudes in
[a]the valley of [b]decision: for [c]the
day of the LORD *is* near in the valley of
decision.
15 The [d]sun and the moon shall be darkened,
and the stars shall withdraw their shining.
16 The LORD also shall [e]roar out of Zion,
and utter his voice from Jerusalem; and [f]the
heavens and the earth shall shake: [g]but the
LORD *will be* the [h]hope of his people, and the
strength of the children of Israel.
17 So [i]shall ye know that I
am the LORD your God dwelling
in Zion, [k]my holy mountain:
then shall Jerusalem be [l]holy,
and there shall [m]no strangers pass through
her any more.
18 And it shall come to pass in that day
that the mountains shall [n]drop down new
wine, and the hills shall flow with milk, [o]and
all the rivers of Judah shall [p]flow with
waters, and [q]a fountain shall come forth of
the house of the LORD, and shall water [r]the
valley of Shittim.

[a]Verse 2——[b]Or, *concision*, or *threshing*——[c]Chapter ii. 1——[d]Chapter ii. 10, 31——[e]Jeremiah xxv. 30; chapter ii. 11; Amos i. 2——[f]Haggai ii. 6——[g]Isaiah li. 5, 6——[h]Hebrew *place of repair*, or *harbour* [i]Chapter ii. 27

[k]Dan. xi. 45; Obad. 16; Zech. viii. 3——[l]Heb. *holiness*——[m]Isa. xxxv. 8; lii. 1; Nah. i. 15; Zech. xiv. 21; Rev. xxi. 27——[n]Amos ix. 13——[o]Psa. xxx. 25 [p]Heb. *go*——[q]Psa. xlvi. 4; Ezek. xlvii. 1; Zech. xiv. 8; Rev. xxii. 1——[r]Num. xxv. 1

tion of his enemies is represented here under the metaphor of reaping down the harvest; and of gathering the grapes, and treading them in the wine-presses.

Verse 14. *Multitudes, multitudes*] המנים המנים *hamonim, hamonim, crowds upon crowds*, in *the valley of decision*, or *excision:* the same as the valley of Jehoshaphat, the place where God is to execute judgment on his enemies.

Verse 15. *The sun and the moon shall be darkened*] High and mighty states shall be eclipsed, and brought to ruin, and the *stars*—petty states, princes, and governors—*shall withdraw their shining;* withhold their *influence* and *tribute* from the kingdoms to which they have belonged, and set up themselves as *independent governors*.

Verse 16. *The Lord also shall roar out of Zion*] His temple and worship shall be re-established there, and he will thence denounce his judgments against the nations. "The heavens and the earth shall shake." There shall be great commotions in powerful empires and their dependencies; but in all these things his own people shall be unmoved, for God shall be their *hope* and *strength*.

Verse 17. *So shall ye know*] By the judgments I execute on your enemies, and the support I give to yourselves, that I am the all-conquering Jehovah; and that I have again taken up my residence in Jerusalem. All this may refer, ultimately, to the restoration of the Jews to their own land; when *holiness to the Lord* shall be their motto; and no *strange* god, nor *impure people*, shall be permitted to enter the city, or even *pass through it;* they shall have neither civil nor religious connections with any who do not worship the true God in *spirit* and in *truth*. This, I think, must refer to Gospel times. It is a promise not ye fulfilled.

Verse 18. *In that day*] After their return from their captivities.

The mountains shall drop down new wine] A poetic expression for great fertility. Happy times: peace and plenty. The vines shall grow luxuriantly on the sides of the mountains; and the hills shall produce such rich pastures that the flocks shall yield abundance of milk.

And all the rivers of Judah] Far from being generally dry in the summer, shall have their *channels* always full of water.

And a fountain shall come forth of the house of the Lord] See the account of the *typical waters* in Ezekiel, chap. xlvii., to which this seems to have a reference; at least the subject is the same, and seems to point out the *grace of the Gospel*, the *waters of salvation*, that shall flow from Jerusalem, and water the valley of *Shittim*. *Shittim* was in the *plains of Moab* beyond Jordan; Num. xxxiii. 49; Josh. iii. 1; but as no stream of water could flow from the temple, pass across Jordan, or reach this plain, the *valley of Shittim* must be considered *symbolical*, as *the valley of Jehoshaphat*. But as *Shittim* may signify *thorns*, it may figuratively represent the most *uncultivated and ferocious inhabitants of the earth* receiving the Gospel of Christ, and being civilized and saved by it. We know that *briers and thorns* are emblems of *bad men;* see Ezek. ii. 6. Thus all the figures in this verse will point out the happy times of the Gospel: *the mountains shall drop down new wine; the hills flow with milk;* the *thorny valleys* become fertile, &c. Similar to those almost parallel words of the prince of poets:—

Mistaque ridenti colocasia fundet acantho.—
Ipsæ lacte domum referent destenta capellæ
Ubera: nec magnos metuent armenta leones.—
Molli paullatim flavescet campus arista,
Incultisque rubens pendebit sentibus uva:
Et duræ quercus sudabunt roscida mella.
VIRG. *Ecl.* iv. 20.

Unbidden earth shall wreathing ivy bring,
And fragrant herbs the promises of spring.
The goats with streaming dugs shall homeward speed;
And lowing herds, secure from lions, feed.
Unlabour'd harvests shall the fields adorn,
And cluster'd grapes shall grow on every thorn:
The *knotted oaks* shall *showers of honey weep.*
DRYDEN.

A. M. cir. 3314
B. C. cir. 690
Ol. cir. XXII. 3
NumæPompilii,
R. Roman.,
cir. annum 26

19 [s]Egypt shall be a desolation, and [t]Edom shall be a desolate wilderness, for the violence *against* the children of Judah, because they have shed innocent blood in their land.

20 But Judah shall [u]dwell [v]for ever, and Jerusalem from generation to generation.

21 For I will [w]cleanse their blood *that* I have not cleansed: [x]for [y]the LORD dwelleth in Zion.

[s]Isa. xix. 1, &c.——[t]Jer. xlix. 17; Ezek. xxv. 12, 13; Amos i. 11; Obad. 10——[u]Or, *abide*——[v]Amos ix. 15

[w]Isa. iv. 4——[x]Ezek. xlviii. 35; ver. 17; Rev. xxi. 3
[y]Or, *even I the LORD that dwelleth in Zion*

Verse 19. *Egypt shall be a desolation*] While peace, plenty, and prosperity of every kind, shall crown my people, all their *enemies* shall be as a *wilderness;* and those who have *used violence* against the saints of God, and *shed the blood of innocents* (of the holy MARTYRS) *in their land,* when they had *political power;* these and all such shall fall under the just judgments of God.

Verse 20. *But Judah shall dwell for ever*] The true Church of Christ shall be supported, while all false and persecuting Churches shall be annihilated. The promise may also belong to the full and final restoration of the Jews, when they shall dwell at Jerusalem as a distinct people professing the faith of our Lord Jesus Christ.

Verse 21. *For I will cleanse their blood*] נקיתי *nikkeythi, I will avenge* the slaughter and martyrdom of my people, which I have not *yet avenged.* Persecuting *nations* and persecuting *Churches* shall all come, sooner or later, under the stroke of vindictive justice.

For the Lord dwelleth in Zion.] He shall be the life, soul, spirit, and defence of his Church for ever.

THIS prophet, who has many things similar to Ezekiel, ends his prophecy nearly in the same way:

Ezekiel says of the glory of the Church, יהוה שמה *Yehovah shammah,* THE LORD IS THERE.

Joel says, יהוה שכן בציון *Yehovah shochen betsiyon,* THE LORD DWELLETH IN ZION.

Both point out the continued indwelling of Christ among his people.

INTRODUCTION TO THE BOOK

OF THE

PROPHET AMOS

AMOS, the third of the minor prophets, was, it is said, of the little town of Tekoa, in the tribe of Judah, about *four* leagues southward of Jerusalem. There is no good proof, however, that he was a native of this place; but only that he retired thither when he was driven from Beth-el, which was in the kingdom of the *ten* tribes. It is very probable that he was born within the territories of Israel, and that his mission was directed principally to this kingdom.

As he was prophesying in Beth-el, where the golden calves were, in the reign of Jeroboam the second, about the year of the world 3217; before the birth of Jesus Christ, 783; before the vulgar era, 787; Amaziah, the high priest of Beth-el, accused him before King Jeroboam, saying, "Amos hath conspired against thee in the midst of the house of Israel: the land is not able to bear all his words. For thus Amos saith, Jeroboam shall die by the sword, and Israel shall surely be led away captive out of their own land." Amaziah said therefore unto Amos, "O thou seer, go, flee thee away into the land of Judah, and there eat bread, and prophesy there: but prophesy not again any more at Beth-el; for it is the king's chapel, and it is the king's court."

Amos answered Amaziah, "I was no prophet, neither was I a prophet's son; but I was a herdman, and a gatherer of sycamore fruit. And the Lord took me as I followed the flock; and the Lord said unto me, Go, prophesy unto my people Israel. Now, therefore, hear thou the word of the Lord; Thou sayest, Prophesy not against Israel, and drop not thy word against the house of Isaac. Therefore thus saith the Lord, Thy wife shall be a harlot in the city, and thy sons and thy daughters shall fall by the sword, and thy land shall be divided by line; and thou shalt die in a polluted land, and Israel shall surely go into captivity forth of his land."

After this the prophet retired into the kingdom of Judah, and dwelt in the town of Tekoa, where he continued to prophesy. He complains in many places of the violence offered him by endeavouring to oblige him to silence, and bitterly exclaims against the disorders of Israel.

He began to prophesy the second year before the earthquake, which happened in the reign of King Uzziah; and which Josephus, with most of the ancient and modern commentators, refers to this prince's usurpation of the priest's office, when he attempted to offer incense to the Lord.

The first of his prophecies, in order of time, are those of the *seventh* chapter. The others he pronounced in the town of Tekoa, whither he retired. His two first chapters are against Damascus, the Philistines, Tyrians, Edomites, Ammonites, Moabites, the kingdom of Judah, and that of the ten tribes. The evils with which he threatens them refer to the times of Shalmaneser, Tiglath-pileser, Sennacherib, and Nebuchadnezzar, who did so much mischief to these provinces, and at last led the Israelites into captivity.

He foretold the misfortunes into which the kingdom of Israel should fall after the death of Jeroboam the Second, who was then living. He foretold the death of King Zechariah; the invasion of the lands belonging to Israel by Pul and Tiglath-pileser, kings of Assyria; and speaks of the captivity of the ten tribes, and of their return into their own country.

He makes sharp invectives against the sins of Israel; against their effeminacy and avarice, their harshness to the poor, the splendour of their buildings, and the delicacy of their tables. He reproves the people of Israel for going to Beth-el, Dan, Gilgal, and Beer-sheba, which were the most famous pilgrimages of the country; and for swearing by the gods of these places.

The time and manner of his death are not known. Some old authors relate that Amaziah, priest of Beth-el, whom we have spoken of, provoked by the discourses of the prophet, had his teeth broken in order to silence him. Others say that Hosea, or Uzziah, the son of Amaziah, struck him with a stake upon the temples, and knocked him down, and almost killed him; that in this condition he was carried to Tekoa, where he died, and was buried with his fathers. This is the account these authors give us. On the contrary, it is the opinion of others, that he prophesied a long time at Tekoa after the adventure he had with Amaziah: and the prophet taking no notice of the ill treatment which he is said to have received from Uzziah, his silence is no argument that he suffered nothing from him.

St. Jerome observes, that there is nothing great and sublime in the style of Amos. He applies these words of St. Paul to him, *rude in speech, though not in knowledge.* He says farther, that as every one chooses to speak of his own art, Amos generally makes use of comparisons taken from the country life wherein he had been brought up. St. Austin shows that there was a certain kind of eloquence in the sacred writers, directed by the spirit of wisdom, and so proportioned to the nature of the things they treated of, that even they who accuse them of rusticity and unpoliteness in their way of writing, could not choose a style more suitable, were they to have spoken on the same subject, to the same persons, and in the same circumstances.

Bishop Lowth is not satisfied with the judgment of St. Jerome. His authority, says the learned prelate, has occasioned many commentators to represent this prophet as entirely rude, void of eloquence, and wanting in all the embellishments of style; whereas any one who reads him with due attention will find him, though a herdsman, not a whit behind the very chiefest prophets; almost equal to the greatest in the loftiness of his sentiments; and not inferior to any in the splendour of his diction, and the elegance of his composition. And it is well observed, that the same heavenly Spirit which inspired Isaiah and Daniel in the palace, inspired David and Amos in their shepherds' tents; always choosing proper interpreters of his will, and sometimes perfecting praise even out of the mouths of babes: at one time using the eloquence of some; at another, making others eloquent to subserve his great purposes. See *Calmet* and *Dodd.*

Archbishop *Newcome* speaks also justly of this prophet: "Amos borrows many images from the scenes in which he was engaged; but he introduces them with skill, and gives them tone and dignity by the eloquence and grandeur of his manner. We shall find in him many affecting and pathetic, many elegant and sublime, passages. No prophet has more magnificently described the Deity; or more gravely rebuked the luxurious: or reproved injustice and oppression with greater warmth, and a more generous indignation. He is a prophet on whose model a preacher may safely form his style and manner in luxurious and profligate times."

THE BOOK

OF THE

PROPHET AMOS

Chronological Notes relative to this Book

Year from the Creation, according to Archbishop Usher, 3217.—Year of the Julian Period, 3927.—Year since the Flood, 1561.—Year from the foundation of Solomon's temple, 225.—Year since the division of Solomon's monarchy into the kingdoms of Israel and Judah, 188.—Year since the first Olympic games were celebrated in Elis by the Idæi Dactyli, 667.—Year since the restoration of the Olympic games at Elis by Lycurgus, Iphitus, and Cleosthenes, 97.—Year before the conquest of Corœbus at Olympia, vulgarly called the first Olympiad, 11.—Year before the building of Rome, according to the Varronian computation, 34.—Year before the birth of Christ, 783.—Year before the vulgar era of Christ's nativity, 787.—Cycle of the Sun, 7.—Cycle of the Moon, 13.—Twenty-eighth and last year of Caranus, the founder of the kingdom of Macedon.—Twenty-third year of Nicander, king of Lacedæmon, of the family of the Proclidæ.—Twenty-seventh year of Alcamenes, king of Lacedæmon, of the family of the Eurysthenidæ.—Eleventh year of Ardysus, king of Lydia.—Eleventh year of Agamestor, perpetual archon of the Athenians.—Tenth year of Amulius Sylvius, king of the Albans.—Fifth year of Telestus, monarch of Corinth.—Sixth year of Sosarmus, king of the Medes, according to some chronologers.—Thirty-ninth year of Jeroboam II., king of Israel.—Twenty-fourth year of Uzziah, king of Judah.

CHAPTER I

This chapter denounces judgments against the nations bordering on Palestine, enemies to the Jews, viz., the Syrians, 1–5; *Philistines,* 6–8; *Tyrians,* 9, 10; *Edomites,* 11, 12; *and Ammonites,* 13–15. *The same judgments were predicted by other prophets, and fulfilled, partly by the kings of Assyria, and partly by those of Babylon; though, like many other prophecies, they had their accomplishment by degrees, and at different periods. The prophecy against the Syrians, whose capital was Damascus, was fulfilled by Tiglath-pileser, king of Assyria; see* 2 Kings xvi. 9. *The prophecy against Gaza of the Philistines was accomplished by Hezekiah,* 2 Kings xviii. 8; *by Pharaoh,* Jer. xlvii. 1; *and by Alexander the Great; see* Quintius Curtius, lib. iv. c. 6. *The prophecy against Ashdod was fulfilled by Uzziah,* 2 Chron. xxvi. 6; *and that against Ashkelon by Pharaoh,* Jer. xlvii. 5. *All Syria was also subdued by Pharaoh-necho; and again by Nebuchadnezzar, who also took Tyre, as did afterwards Alexander. Nebuchadnezzar also subdued the Edomites,* Jer. xxv. 9, 21, *and* xxvii. 3, 6. *Judas Maccabeus routed the remains of them,* 1 Macc. v. 3; *and Hyrcanus brought them under entire subjection. The Ammonites were likewise conquered by Nebuchadnezzar. The earthquake, which the prophet takes for his era, is perhaps referred to in* Zech. xiv. 5, *and also in* Isa. v. 25. Josephus *ascribes it to Uzziah's invasion of the priestly office; see* 2 Chron. xxvi. 16.

A. M. cir. 3217
B. C. cir. 787
Ante U. C. 34
Amulii Sylvii,
R. Alban.,
cir. annum 10

THE words of Amos, [a]who was among the herdmen of [b]Tekoa, which he saw concerning Israel [c]in the days of Uzziah king of Judah, and in the days of [d]Jeroboam the son of Joash king of Israel, two years before the [e]earthquake.

---

[a]Chap. vii. 14——[b]2 Sam. xiv. 2; 2 Chron. xx. 20——[c]Hos. i. 1——[d]Chap. vii. 10——[e]Zech. xiv. 5

NOTES ON CHAP. I

Verse 1. *The words of Amos*] This person and the father of Isaiah, though named alike in our translation, were as different in their names as in their persons. The father of Isaiah, אמוץ *Amots;* the prophet before us, עמוס *Amos.* The first, *aleph, mem, vau, tsaddi;* the second, *ain, mem, vau, samech.* For some account of this prophet see the *introduction.*

Among the herdmen] He seems to have been among the very lowest orders of life, a herds-

A. M. cir. 3217
B. C. cir. 787
Ante U. C. 34
Amulii Sylvii,
R. Alban.,
cir. annum 10

2 And he said, The Lord will
[f]roar from Zion, and utter his
voice from Jerusalem; and the
habitations of the shepherds shall
mourn, and the top of [g]Carmel shall wither.
3 Thus saith the Lord; For three transgressions of [h]Damascus, [i]and for four, I will not
[k]turn away *the punishment* thereof; [l]because
they have threshed Gilead with threshing instruments of iron:
4 [m]But I will send a fire into
the house of Hazael, which shall
devour the palaces of Ben-
hadad.
5 I will break also the [n]bar of Damascus,
and cut off the inhabitants from [o]the plain of
Aven, and him that holdeth the sceptre from
[p]the house of Eden: and [q]the people of Syria
shall go into captivity [r]unto Kir, saith the
Lord.

[f]Jer. xxv. 30; Joel iii. 16——[g]1 Sam. xxv. 2; Isa. xxxiii. 9——[h]Isa. viii. 4; xvii. 1; Jer. xlix. 23; Zech. ix. 1 [i]Or, *yea, for four*——[k]Or, *convert it*, or *let it be quiet:* and so verse 6, &c.

[l]2 Kings x. 33; xiii. 7——[m]Jer. xvii. 27; xlix. 27; verse 7, 10, 12; chap. ii. 2, 5——[n]Jer. li. 30; Lam. ii. 9 [o]Or, *Bikath-aven*——[p]Or, *Beth-eden*——[q]Fulfilled, 2 Kings xvi. 9——[r]Chap. ix. 7

man, one who tended the flocks of *others* in the open fields, and *a gatherer of sycamore fruit.* Of whatever species this was, whether a kind of *fig*, it is evident that it was *wild fruit;* and he probably collected it for his own subsistence, or to dispose of either for the service of his employer, or to increase his scanty wages.

Before the earthquake.] Probably the same as that referred to Zech. xiv. 5, if הרעש *haraash* do not mean some *popular tumult.*

Verse 2. *The Lord will roar from Zion*] It is a pity that our translators had not followed the hemistich form of the Hebrew:—

Jehovah from Zion shall roar,
And from Jerusalem shall give forth his voice;
And the pleasant dwellings of the shepherds shall mourn,
And the top of mount Carmel shall wither.

Carmel was a very fruitful mountain in the tribe of Judah, Josh. xv. 55; Isa. xxxv. 2.

This introduction was natural in the mouth of a *herdsman* who was familiar with the roaring of lions, the bellowing of bulls, and the lowing of kine. The roaring of the lion in the forest is one of the most terrific sounds in nature; when near, it strikes terror into the heart of both man and beast.

Verse 3. *For three transgressions of Damascus, and for four*] These expressions of *three* and *four*, so often *repeated* in this chapter, mean *repetition, abundance*, and any thing that goes towards *excess. Very, very exceedingly;* and so it was used among the ancient Greek and Latin poets. See the passionate exclamation of Ulysses, in the storm, *Odyss.*, lib. v., ver. 306:—

Τρις μακαρες Δαναοι και τετρακις, οἱ τοτ' ολοντο
Τροιῃ εν ευρειῃ, χαριν Ατρειδῃσι φεροντες.

"*Thrice happy* Greeks! and *four times* who were slain
In Atreus' cause, upon the Trojan plain."

Which words *Virgil* translates, and puts in the mouth of his hero in similar circumstances, *Æn.* i. 93.

Extemplo Æneæ solvuntur frigore membra:
Ingemit; et, duplicis tendens ad sidera palmas,
Talia voce refert: *O terque quaterque beati!*
Queis ante ora patrum Trojæ sub mœnibus altis
Contigit oppetere.

"Struck with unusual fright, the Trojan chief
With lifted hands and eyes invokes relief.
And *thrice*, and *four times happy* those, he cried,
That under Ilion's walls before their parents died."

Dryden.

On the words, *O terque quaterque*, Servius makes this remark, "Hoc est *sæpius;* finitus numerous pro infinito." *"O thrice and four times*, that is, *very often*, a finite number for an infinite." Other poets use the same form of expression. So Seneca in *Hippolyt.*, Act. ii. 694.

O ter quaterque prospero fato dati,
Quos hausit, et peremit, et leto dedit
Odium dolusque!

"O *thrice* and *four times* happy were the men
Whom hate devoured, and fraud, hard pressing on,
Gave as a prey to death."

And so the ancient oracle quoted by *Pausanias*, Achaic., lib. vii., c. 6: *Τρις μακαρες κεινοι και τετρακις ανδρες εσονται;* "Those men shall be *thrice* and *four times* happy."

These quotations are sufficient to show that this form of speech is neither unfrequent nor *inelegant*, being employed by the most correct writers of antiquity.

Damascus was the capital of Syria.

Verse 4. *Ben-hadad.*] He was son and successor of Hazael. See the cruelties which they exercised upon the Israelites, 2 Kings x. 32; xiii. 7, &c.; and see especially 2 Kings viii. 12, where these cruelties are predicted.

The *fire* threatened here is the *war* so successfully carried on against the Syrians by Jeroboam II., in which he took Damascus and Hamath, and reconquered all the ancient possessions of Israel. See 2 Kings xiv. 25, 26, 28.

Verse 5. *The bar of Damascus*] The *gates*, whose long traverse bars, running from wall to wall, were their strength. I will throw it open; and the *gates* were forced, and the city taken, as above.

The plain of Aven—the house of Eden] These are names, says *Bochart*, of the *valley of Damascus.* The *plain of Aven*, or *Birkath-Aven*, *Calmet* says, is a city of Syria, at present called *Baal-Bek*, and by the Greeks *Heliopolis;* and is situated at the end of that long valley

A. M. cir. 3217
B. C. cir. 787
Ante U. C. 34
Amulii Sylvii,
R. Alban.,
cir. annum 10

6 Thus saith the LORD; For
three transgressions of [s]Gaza,
and for four, I will not turn
away *the punishment* thereof;
because they [t]carried away captive the whole
captivity, [u]to deliver *them* up to Edom:
7 [v]But I will send a fire on the wall of Gaza,
which shall devour the palaces thereof:
8 And I will cut off the inhabitant [w]from
Ashdod, and him that holdeth the sceptre
from Ashkelon, and I will [x]turn mine hand
against Ekron: and [y]the remnant of the
Philistines shall perish, saith the Lord
GOD.
9 Thus saith the LORD; For three transgressions of [z]Tyrus, and for four, I will not
turn away *the punishment* thereof; [a]because
they delivered up the whole captivity to
Edom, and remembered not [b]the brotherly
covenant:
10 [c]But I will send a fire on the wall of
Tyrus, which shall devour the palaces thereof.

A. M. cir. 3217
B. C. cir. 787
Ante U. C. 34
Amulii Sylvii,
R. Alban.,
cir. annum 10

11 Thus saith the LORD; For
three transgressions of [d]Edom,
and for four, I will not turn
away *the punishment* thereof;
because he did pursue [e]his brother [f]with the
sword, and [g]did cast off all pity, [h]and his
anger did tear perpetually, and he kept his
wrath for ever:
12 But [i]I will send a fire upon Teman,
which shall devour the palaces of Bozrah.
13 Thus saith the LORD; For three transgressions of [k]the children of Ammon, and
for four, I will not turn away *the punishment*
thereof; because they have [l]ripped [m]up the
women with child of Gilead, [n]that they might
enlarge their border:
14 But I will kindle a fire in the wall of
[o]Rabbah, and it shall devour the palaces
thereof, [p]with shouting in the day of battle,
with a tempest in the day of the whirlwind:
15 And [q]their king shall go into captivity,
he and his princes together, saith the LORD.

[s]2 Chron. xxviii. 18; Isa. xiv. 29; Jer. xlvii. 4, 5; Ezek. xxv. 15; Zeph. ii. 4——[t]Or, *carried them away with an entire captivity;* 2 Chron. xxi. 16, 17; Joel iii. 6——[u]Ver. 9——[v]Jer. xlvii. 1——[w]Zeph. ii. 4; Zech. ix. 5, 6——[x]Psa. lxxxi. 14——[y]Jer. xlvii. 4; Ezek. xxv. 16——[z]Isa. xxiii. 1; Jer. xlvii. 4; Ezek. xxvi., xxvii., xxviii.; Joel iii. 4, 5——[a]Ver. 6——[b]Heb. *the covenant of brethren;* 2 Sam. v. 11; 1 Kings v. 1; ix. 11-14——[c]Ver. 4, 7, &c.

[d]Isa. xxi. 11; xxxiv. 5; Jer. xlix. 8, &c.; Ezek. xxv. 12, 13, 14; xxxv. 2, &c.; Joel iii. 19; Obad. 1, &c.; Mal. i. 4——[e]Gen. xxvii. 41; Deut. xxiii. 7; Mal. i. 2——[f]2 Chron. xxiii. 17——[g]Heb. *corrupted his compassions*——[h]Ezek. xxxv. 5——[i]Obad. 9, 10——[k]Jer. xlix. 1, 2; Ezek. xxv. 2; Zeph. ii. 9——[l]Or, *divided the mountains*——[m]Hos. xiii. 16——[n]Jer. xlix. 1——[o]Deut. iii. 11; 2 Sam. xii. 26; Jer. xlix. 2; Ezek. xxv. 5——[p]Chap. ii. 2——[q]Jer. xlix. 3

which extends from south to north, between Libanus and Anti-Libanus.

The people of Syria shall go into captivity unto Kir] KIR is supposed to be the country of *Cyrene* in Albania, on the river *Cyrus*, which empties itself into the Caspian Sea. The fulfilment of this prophecy may be seen in 2 Kings xvi. 1-9.

Verse 6. *They carried away captive*] Gaza is well known to have been one of the five lordships of the Philistines; it lay on the coast of the Mediterranean Sea, near to Egypt. Erkon, Ashdod, and Askelon, were other signories of the same people, which are here equally threatened with Gaza. The *captivity* mentioned here may refer to *inroads* and *incursions* made by the Philistines in times of peace. See 2 Chron. xxi. 16. The *margin* reads, *an entire captivity.* They took *all* away; none of them afterwards returned.

Verse 9. *Tyrus*] See an ample description of this place, and of its desolation and final ruin, in the notes on Ezek. xxvi., xxvii., and xxviii.

The brotherly covenant] This possibly refers to the very friendly league made between Solomon and Hiram, king of Tyre, 1 Kings v. 12; but some contend that the brotherly covenant refers to the *consanguinity* between the *Jews* and *Edomites.* The Tyrians, in exercising cruelties upon these, did it, in effect, on the Jews, with whom they were connected by the most intimate ties of kindred; the two people having descended from the two brothers, Jacob and Esau. See *Calmet.*

Verse 10. *I will send a fire on the wall of Tyrus*] The destructive *fire* or *siege* by Nebuchadnezzar, which lasted *thirteen* years, and ended in the destruction of this ancient city; see on Ezekiel, chap. xxvi. 7-14, as above. It was finally ruined by *Alexander*, and is now only a place for a few poor fishermen to spread their nets upon.

Verse 11. *For three transgressions of Edom*] That the *Edomites* (notwithstanding what *Calmet* observes above of the *brotherly covenant*) were always implacable enemies of the Jews, is well known; but most probably that which the prophet has in view was the part they took in distressing the Jews when Jerusalem was besieged, and finally taken, by the Chaldeans. See Obad. 11-14; Ezek. xxv. 12; xxxv. 5; Psa. cxxxvii. 7.

Verse 12. *Teman—Bozrah.*] Principal cities of Idumea.

Verse 13. *The children of Ammon*] The country of the Ammonites lay to the east of Jordan, in the neighbourhood of Gilead. *Rabbah* was its capital.

Because they have ripped up] This refers to some barbarous transaction well known in the time of this prophet, but of which we have no distinct mention in the sacred historians.

Verse 14. *With shouting in the day of battle*] They shall be totally subdued. This was done by Nebuchadnezzar. See Jer. xxvii. 3, 6.

Verse 15. *Their king shall go into captivity*] Probably מלכם *malcham* should be *Milcom*, who was a chief god of the Ammonites; and the following words, *he and his princes*, may refer to the *body of his priesthood*. See 1 Kings xi. 33, and the notes there. All these countries were subdued by Nebuchadnezzar.

CHAPTER II

The prophet goes on to declare the judgments of God against Moab, 1–3; *against Judah,* 4, 5; *and then against Israel, the particular object of his mission. He enumerates some of their sins,* 6–8, *aggravated by God's distinguishing regard to Israel,* 9–12; *and they are in consequence threatened with dreadful punishments,* 13–16. *See* 2 Kings xv. 19, *and* xvii. 6.

A. M. cir. 3217
B. C. cir. 787
Ante U. C. 34
Amulii Sylvii, R. Alban., cir. annum 10

THUS saith the LORD; For
three transgressions of
[a]Moab, and for four, I will not
turn away *the punishment*
thereof; because he [b]burned the bones of the
king of Edom into lime:
2 But I will send a fire upon Moab, and it
shall devour the palaces of [c]Kirioth: and
Moab shall die with tumult, [d]with shouting,
and with the sound of the trumpet:
3 And I will cut off [e]the judge from the
midst thereof, and will slay all the princes
thereof with him, saith the LORD.
4 Thus saith the LORD; For three transgressions of Judah, and for four, I will not
turn away *the punishment* thereof; [f]because
they have despised the law of the LORD, and
have not kept his command-
ments, and [g]their lies caused
them to err, [h]after the which
their fathers have walked:

A. M. cir. 3217
B. C. cir. 787
Ante U. C. 34
Amulii Sylvii, R. Alban., cir. annum 10

5 [i]But I will send a fire upon Judah, and
it shall devour the palaces of Jerusalem.
6 Thus saith the LORD; For three transgressions of Israel, and for four, I will not
turn away *the punishment* thereof; because
[k]they sold the righteous for silver, and the
poor for a pair of shoes;
7 That pant after the dust of the earth on
the head of the poor, and [l]turn aside the way
of the meek: [m]and a man and his father will
go in unto the *same* [n]maid, [o]to profane my
holy name:
8 And they lay *themselves* down upon

[a]Isa. xv., xvi.; Jer. xlviii.; Ezek. xxv. 8; Zeph. ii. 8 — [b]2 Kings iii. 27 — [c]Jer. xlviii. 41 — [d]Chap. i. 14 — [e]Num. xxiv. 17; Jer. xlviii. 7 — [f]Lev. xxvi. 14, 15; Neh. i. 7; Dan. ix. 11 — [g]Isa. xxviii. 15; Jer. xvi. 19, 20; Rom. i. 25 — [h]Ezek. xx. 13, 16, 18, 24, 40 — [i]Jer. xvii. 27; Hos. viii. 14 — [k]Isa. xxix. 21; chap. viii. 6 — [l]Isa. x. 2; chap. v. 12 — [m]Ezek. xxii. 11 — [n]Or, *young woman* — [o]Lev. xx. 3; Ezek. xxxvi. 20; Rom. ii. 24

NOTES ON CHAP. II

Verse 1. *For three transgressions of Moab, and for four*] See an explanation of this form, chap. i. 2. The land of the Moabites lay to the east of the Dead Sea. For the origin of this people, see Gen. xix. 37.

He burned the bones of the king of Edom into lime] Possibly referring to some brutality; such as opening the grave of one of the Idumean kings, and calcining his bones. It is supposed by some to refer to the fact mentioned 2 Kings iii. 26, when the kings of Judah, Israel, and Idumea, joined together to destroy Moab. The king of it, despairing to save his city, took *seven hundred* men, and made a desperate sortie on the quarter where the king of Edom was; and, though not successful, took prisoner the son of the king of Edom; and, on their return into the city, offered him as a burnt-offering upon the wall, so as to terrify the besieging armies, and cause them to raise the siege. Others understand the son that was sacrificed to be the king of Moab's own son.

Verse 2. *The palaces of Kirioth*] This was one of the principal cities of the Moabites.

Moab shall die with tumult] All these expressions seem to refer to this city's being taken by *storm*, which was followed by a total slaughter of its inhabitants.

Verse 3. *I will cut off the judge*] It shall be so destroyed, that it shall never more have any *form of government*. The *judge* here, שופט *shophet*, may signify the chief magistrate. The chief magistrates of the Carthaginians were called *suffetes;* probably taken from the Hebrew JUDGES, שופטים *shophetim.*

Verse 4. *For three transgressions of Judah*] We may take the *three* and *four* here to any latitude; for this people lived in continual hostility to their God, from the days of *David* to the time of *Uzziah*, under whom Amos prophesied. Their iniquities are *summed* up under *three* general heads: 1. They despised, or *rejected the law of the Lord.* 2. They *kept not his statutes.* 3. They followed lies, were idolaters, and followed false prophets rather than those sent by Jehovah.

Verse 5. *I will send a fire upon Judah*] This *fire* was the war made upon the Jews by *Nebuchadnezzar*, which terminated with the sackage and burning of Jerusalem and its *palace* the *temple.*

Verses 6-8. *For three transgressions of Israel, &c.*] To be satisfied of the exceeding delinquency of this people, we have only to open the

A. M. cir. 3217
B. C. cir. 787
Ante U. C. 34
Amulii Sylvii,
R. Alban.,
cir. annum 10

clothes [p]laid to pledge [q]by every
altar, and they drink the wine
of [r]the condemned *in* the house
of their god.

9 Yet destroyed I the [s]Amorite before them,
[t]whose height *was* like the height of the
cedars, and he *was* strong as the oaks; yet I
[u]destroyed his fruit from above, and his roots
from beneath.

10 Also [v]I brought you up from the land of
Egypt, and [w]led you forty years through the
wilderness, to possess the land of the
Amorite.

11 And I raised up of your sons for prophets, and of your young men for [x]Nazarites.
Is it not even thus, O ye children of Israel?
saith the LORD.

12 But ye gave the Nazarites
wine to drink; and commanded
the prophets, [y]saying, Prophesy not.

13 [z]Behold, [a]I am pressed under you, as a
cart is pressed *that is* full of sheaves.

14 [b]Therefore the flight shall perish from
the swift, and the strong shall not strengthen
his force, [c]neither shall the mighty deliver
[d]himself.

15 Neither shall he stand that handleth the
bow; and *he that is* swift of foot shall not
deliver *himself:* [e]neither shall he that rideth
the horse deliver himself.

16 And *he that is* [f]courageous among the
mighty shall flee away naked in that day,
saith the LORD.

[p]Exod. xxii. 26——[q]Ezek. xxiii. 41; 1 Cor. viii. 10; x. 21——[r]Or, *such as have fined*, or *mulcted*——[s]Num. xxi. 24; Deut. ii. 31; Josh. xxiv. 8——[t]Num. xiii. 28, 32, 33——[u]Isa. v. 24; Mal. iv. 1——[v]Exod. xii. 51; Mic. vi. 4——[w]Deut. ii. 7; viii. 2——[x]Num. vi. 2; Judg. xiii. 5

[y]Isa. xxx. 10; Jer. xi. 21; chap. vii. 12, 13; Mic. ii. 6——[z]Isa. i. 14——[a]Or, *I will press your place, as a cart full of sheaves presseth*——[b]Chap. ix. 1, &c.; Jer. ix. 23——[c]Psa. xxxiii. 16——[d]Heb. *his soul*, or *life*——[e]Psa. xxxiii. 17——[f]Heb. *strong of his heart*

historical and prophetic books in any part; for the whole history of the Israelites is one tissue of transgression against God. Their crimes are enumerated under the following heads:—

1. Their judges were *mercenary* and *corrupt*. They took bribes to condemn the righteous; and even for articles of clothing, such as a *pair of shoes*, they condemned the poor man, and delivered him into the hands of his adversary.

2. They were unmerciful to the poor generally. *They pant after the dust of the earth on the head of the poor;* or, to put it on the head of the poor; or, they bruise the head of the poor against the dust of the earth. Howsoever the clause is understood, it shows them to have been general oppressors of the poor, showing them neither *justice* nor *mercy*.

3. They *turn aside the way of the meek*. They are peculiarly oppressive to the *weak* and *afflicted*.

4. They were licentious to the uttermost abomination; for in their idol feasts, where young women prostituted themselves publicly in honour of *Astarte*, the father and son entered into impure connections with the same female.

5. They were cruel in their oppressions of the poor; for the garments or beds which the poor had pledged they retained contrary to the law, Exod. xxii. 7-26, which required that such things should be restored before the setting of the sun.

6. They punished the people by unjust and oppressive fines, and served their tables with wine bought by such fines. Or it may be understood of their appropriating to themselves that wine which was allowed to criminals to mitigate their sufferings in the article of death; which was the excess of inhumanity and cruelty.

Verse 9. *Yet destroyed I the Amorite*] Here follow general heads of God's mercies to them, and the great things he had done for them. 1. Bringing them out of Egypt. 2. Miraculously sustaining them in the wilderness *forty* years. 3. Driving out the Canaanites before them, and giving them possession of the promised land. 4. Raising up prophets among them to declare the Divine will. 5. And forming the holy institution of the Nazarites among them, to show the spiritual nature of his holy religion, ver. 9-11.

Verse 12. *But ye gave the Nazarites wine*] This was expressly forbidden in the laws of their institution. See Num. vi. 1-3.

Prophesy not.] They would not worship God, and they would not hear the voice of his prophets.

Verse 13. *Behold, I am pressed under you*] The *marginal* reading is better: "Behold, I will press your place, as a cart full of sheaves presseth." I will bring over you the *wheel of destruction;* and it shall grind your *place*—your *city* and *temple*, as the wheel of a cart laden with sheaves presses down the ground, gravel, and stones over which it rolls.

Verse 14. *The flight shall perish from the swift*] The swiftest shall not be able to save himself from a swifter destruction. None, by might, by counsel, or by fleetness, shall be able to escape from the impending ruin. In a word, God has so fully determined to avenge the quarrel of his broken covenant, that all attempts to escape from his judgments shall be useless.

Verse 15. *Neither shall he that rideth the horse deliver himself.*] I believe all these sayings, from verse 13 to 16 inclusive, are proverbs, to show the inutility of all attempts, even in the best circumstances, to escape the doom now decreed, because the cup of their iniquity was full.

Verse 16. *Shall flee away naked*] In some cases the alarm shall be in the *night;* and even the most heroic shall start from his bed, and through terror not wait to put on his clothes.

CHAPTER III

This chapter begins with reproving the twelve tribes in general, 1, 2; *and then particularly the kingdom of Israel, whose capital was Samaria. The prophet assures them that, while they were at variance with God, it would be unreasonable in them to expect his presence or favour,* 3–8. *Other neighbouring nations are then called upon to take warning from the judgments about to be inflicted upon the house of Israel, which would be so general that only a small remnant should escape them,* 9–15. *The image used by the prophet on this occasion,* (see verse 12,) *and borrowed from his former calling, is very natural and significant, and not a little dignified by the inspired writer's lofty air and manner.*

A. M. cir. 3217
B. C. cir. 787
Ante U. C. 34
Amulii Sylvii,
R. Alban.,
cir. annum 10

HEAR this word that the
LORD hath spoken against
you, O children of Israel, against
the whole family which I
brought up from the land of Egypt, saying,
2 [a]You only have I known of all the families
of the earth: [b]therefore I will [c]punish you
for all your iniquities.
3 Can two walk together, except they be
agreed?
4 Will a lion roar in the forest, when he hath
no prey? will a young lion [d]cry
out of his den, if he have taken
nothing?
5 Can a bird fall in a snare
upon the earth, where no gin *is* for him? shall
one take up a snare from the earth, and have
taken nothing at all?
6 Shall a trumpet be blown in the city, and
the people [e]not be afraid? [f]shall there be
evil in a city, [g]and the LORD hath not done *it?*
7 Surely the Lord GOD will do nothing, but

[a]Deuteronomy vii. 6; x. 15; Psalm cxlvii. 19, 20 [b]See Daniel ix. 12; Matthew xi. 22; Luke xii. 47; Romans ii. 9; 1 Peter iv. 17——[c]Hebrew, *visit upon*

[d]Hebrew, *give forth his voice*——[e]Or, *not run together* [f]Isaiah xlv. 7——[g]Or, *and shall not the LORD do* somewhat?

NOTES ON CHAP. III

Verse 1. *Against the whole family*] That is, all, both the kingdoms of Israel and Judah. In this all the *twelve* tribes are included.

Verse 2. *You only have I known*] I have taken no other people to be my own people. I have *approved* of you, loved you, fed, sustained, and defended you; but because you have forsaken me, have become idolatrous and polluted, therefore *will I punish you.* And the punishment shall be in proportion to the privileges you have enjoyed, and the grace you have abused.

Verse 3. *Can two walk together*] While ye loved and served me, I dwelt in you and walked among you. Now ye are become alienated from me, your nature and mine are totally opposite. I am holy, ye are unholy. We are no longer *agreed,* and can no longer *walk together.* I can no longer hold communion with you. I must cast you out. The similes in this and the *three* following verses are all chosen to express the same thing, viz., that no calamities or judgments can fall upon any people but by the express will of God, on account of their iniquities; and that whatever his prophets have foretold, they have done it by direct revelation from their Maker; and that God has the highest and most cogent reason for inflicting the threatened calamities. This correctness of the prophets' predictions shows that they and I are in communion.

Verse 4. *Will a lion roar*] Should I threaten such a judgment without cause?

Verse 5. *Can a bird fall in a snare*] Can ye, as a sinful people, fall into calamities which I have not appointed?

Shall one *take up a snare—and have taken nothing*] Will the *snare be removed before it has caught the expected prey?*—shall I remove my judgments till they are fully accomplished? This is a curious passage, and deserves farther consideration. The original, literally translated, is nearly as follows: "Shall the trap arise from the ground; and catching, shall it not catch?" Here is a plain allusion to such traps as we employ to catch *rats, foxes,* &c. The jaws of the trap opening backward, press strongly upon a spring so as to keep it down; and a key passing over one jaw, and hooking on a table in the centre, the trap continues with expanded jaws, till any thing touch the table, when the key, by the motion of the table, being loosened, the spring recovers all its elastic power, and throws up the jaws of the trap, and their serrated edges either close in each other, or on the prey that has moved the table of the trap. Will then the jaws of such a trap suddenly spring up from the ground, on which before they were lying flat, and catch nothing? Shall they let the prey that was within them escape? Certainly not. So my trap is laid for these offenders; and when it springs up, (and they themselves will soon by their transgressions free the key,) shall not the whole family of Israel be inclosed in it? Most certainly they shall. This is a singular and very remarkable passage, and, when properly understood, is beautifully expressive.

Verse 6. *Shall a trumpet be blown*] The sign of alarm and invasion.

And the people not be afraid?] Not take the alarm, and provide for their defence and safety?

Shall there be evil in a city] Shall there be any public calamity on the wicked, that is not an effect of my displeasure? The word does not mean *moral* evil, but punishment for sin; calamities falling on the workers of iniquity. *Natural evil* is the punishment of *moral evil:* God sends the former when the latter is persisted in.

A. M. cir. 3217
B. C. cir. 787
Ante U. C. 34
Amulii Sylvii,
R. Alban.,
cir. annum 10

[h]he revealeth his secret unto his
servants the prophets.
8 [i]The lion hath roared, who
will not fear? the Lord GOD
hath spoken, [k]who can but prophesy?
9 Publish in the palaces at Ashdod, and in
the palaces in the land of Egypt, and say,
Assemble yourselves upon the mountains of
Samaria, and behold the great tumults in the
midst thereof, and the [l]oppressed in the midst
thereof.
10 For they [m]know not to do right, saith
the LORD, who store up violence and [n]robbery
in their palaces.
11 Therefore thus saith the Lord GOD; [o]An
adversary *there shall be* even round about the
land; and he shall bring down thy strength
from thee, and thy palaces shall be spoiled.
12 Thus saith the LORD; As
the shepherd [p]taketh out of the
mouth of the lion two legs, or a
piece of an ear; so shall the
children of Israel be taken out that dwell in
Samaria in the corner of a bed, and [q]in
Damascus *in* a couch.
13 Hear ye, and testify in the house of
Jacob, saith the Lord GOD, the God of
hosts.
14 That in the day that I shall [r]visit the
transgressions of Israel upon him I will also
visit the altars of Beth-el: and the horns of the
altar shall be cut off, and fall to the ground.
15 And I will smite [s]the winter house with
[t]the summer house; and [u]the houses of ivory
shall perish, and the great houses shall have
an end, saith the LORD.

[h]Gen. vi. 13; xviii. 17; Psa. xxv. 14; John xv. 15 —— [i]Chap. i. 2 —— [k]Acts iv. 20; v. 20, 29; 1 Cor. ix. 16 —— [l]Or, *oppressions* —— [m]Jer. iv. 22 —— [n]Or, *spoil*

[o]2 Kings xvii. 3, 6; xviii. 9, 10, 11 —— [p]Heb. *delivereth* —— [q]Or, *on the bed's feet* —— [r]Or, *punish Israel for* —— [s]Jer. xxxvi. 22 —— [t]Judg. iii. 20 —— [u]1 Kings xxii. 39

Verse 7. *Surely the Lord God will do nothing*] In reference to the punishment, correction, or blessing of his people—

But he revealeth his secret unto his servants the prophets.] They are in strict correspondence with him, and he shows them *things to come*. Such *secrets* of God are revealed to them, that they may inform the people; that, by repentance and conversion, they may avoid the evil, and, by walking closely with God, secure the continuance of his favour.

Verse 8. *The lion hath roared*] God hath sent forth a terrible alarm, *Who will not fear?* Can any hear such denunciations of Divine wrath and not tremble?

The Lord God hath spoken] And those only who are in communion with him have heard the speech. *Who can but prophesy?* Who can help proclaiming at large the judgment threatened against the nation?

But I think נבא *naba*, here, is to be taken in its natural and ideal signification, to *pray, supplicate*, or *deprecate vengeance*. The Lord hath spoken of punishment—who can help *supplicating* his mercy, that his judgments may be averted?

Verse 9. *Publish in the palaces*] The housetops or flat roofs were the places from which public declarations were made. See on Isa. xxi. 1, and on Matt. x. 27. See whether in those places there be not *tumults, oppressions*, and *rapine* sufficient to excite my wrath against them.

Verse 10. *For they know not to do right*] So we may naturally say that they who are doing *wrong*, and to their own prejudice and ruin, must certainly be ignorant of what is *right*, and what is their own interest. But we say again, "There are none so blind as those who will not see." *Their eyes*, saith the Lord, *they have closed*.

Verse 11. *An adversary, round about the land*] Ye shall not be able to escape; wherever ye turn, ye shall meet a foe.

Verse 12. *As the shepherd taketh out of the mouth of the lion*] Scarcely any of you shall escape; and those that do shall do so with extreme difficulty, just as a shepherd, of a whole sheep carried away by a lion, can recover no more than *two* of its *legs*, or a piece of its *ear*, just enough to prove by the *marks* on those parts, that they belonged to a sheep which *was his own*.

So shall the children of Israel be taken out] Those of them that escape these judgments shall escape with as great difficulty, and be of as *little worth*, as the *two legs* and *piece of an ear* that shall be snatched out of the lion's mouth. We know that when the Babylonians carried away the people into Chaldea they left behind only a few, and those the *refuse of the land*.

In the corner of a bed] As the *corner* is the most honourable place in the East, and a *couch in the corner of a room* is the place of the *greatest distinction;* so the words in the text may mean, that even the *metropolitan cities*, which are in the *corner*—in the most honourable place—of the land, whether *Samaria* in *Israel*, or *Damascus* in *Syria*, shall not escape these judgments; and if any of the distinguished persons who dwell in them escape, it must be with as great difficulty as the fragments above-mentioned have been recovered from a lion. The passage is obscure. Mr. *Harmer* has taken great pains to illustrate it; but I fear with but little success. A general sense is all we can arrive at.

Verse 13. *Hear ye*] This is an address to the prophet.

Verse 14. *In the day that I shall visit*] When Josiah made a reformation in the land he destroyed *idolatry*, pulled down the temples and altars that had been consecrated to idol worship, and even burnt the bones of the priests of Baal and the golden calves upon their own altars. See 2 Kings xxiii. 15, 16, &c.

Verse 15. *I will smite the winter house with*

the summer house] I will not only destroy the *poor habitations* and *villages* in the country, but I will destroy those of the *nobility* and *gentry;* as well as the *lofty palaces* in the fortified cities in which they dwell in the *winter season*, as those *light* and *elegant seats* in which they spend the *summer season*. Dr. *Shaw* observes that "the hills and valleys round about Algiers are all over beautified with gardens and *country seats*, whither the inhabitants of *better fashion* retire during the *heats of the summer season*. They are *little white houses*, shaded with a variety of *fruit trees* and *evergreens*, which beside shade and retirement, afford a *gay* and *delightful prospect toward the sea*. The *gardens* are all well stocked with *melons*, fruits, and pot herbs of all kinds; and (which is chiefly regarded in these *hot countries*) each of them enjoys a great command of *water*."

And the houses of ivory] Those remarkable for their *magnificence* and their *ornaments*, not built of *ivory*, but in which *ivory* vessels, *ornaments*, and *inlaying* abounded. Thus, then, the *winter houses* and the *summer houses*, the *great houses* and the *houses of uncommon splendour*, shall all perish. There should be a total desolation in the land. No kind of house should be a refuge, and no kind of habitation should be spared. Ahab had at Samaria a house that was called the *ivory house*, 1 Kings xxii. 39. This may be particularly referred to in this place. We cannot suppose that a house constructed *entirely* of *ivory* can be intended.

CHAPTER IV

Israel reproved for their oppression, 1–3; *idolatry*, 4, 5; *and for their impenitence under the chastising hand of God*, 6–11. *The omniscience and uncontrollable power of God*, 12, 13.

A. M. cir. 3217
B. C. cir. 787
Ante U. C. 34
Amulii Sylvii, R. Alban., cir. annum 10

HEAR this word, ye [a]kine of
Bashan, that *are* in the
mountain of Samaria, which
oppress the poor, which crush
the needy, which say to their masters, Bring,
and let us drink.
2 [b]The Lord God hath sworn by his holiness, that, lo, the days shall come upon you,
that he will take you away [c]with hooks,
and your posterity with fishhooks.
3 And [d]ye shall go out at the
breaches, every *cow at that*
which is before her; and [e]ye shall cast *them*
into the palace, saith the Lord.
4 [f]Come to Beth-el, and transgress; at
[g]Gilgal multiply transgression; and
[h]bring your sacrifices every morning, [i]*and*

A. M. cir. 3217
B. C. cir. 787
Ante U. C. 34
Amulii Sylvii, R. Alban., cir. annum 10

[a]Psalm xxii. 12; Ezekiel xxxix. 18——[b]Psalm lxxxix. 35——[c]Jeremiah xvi. 16; Habakkuk i. 15——[d]Ezekiel xii. 5, 12

[e]Or, *ye shall cast away the things of the palace* [f]Ezek. xx. 39——[g]Hos. iv. 15; xii. 11; chap. v. 5 [h]Num. xxviii. 3, 4——[i]Deut. xiv. 28

NOTES ON CHAP. IV

Verse 1. *Hear this word, ye kine of Bashan*] Such an address was quite natural from the herdsman of Tekoa. *Bashan* was famous for the fertility of its soil, and its flocks and herds; and the prophet here represents the iniquitous, opulent, idle, lazy drones, whether men or women, under the idea of fatted bullocks, which were shortly to be led out to the slaughter.

Verse 2. *He will take you away with hooks*] Two modes of fishing are here alluded to: 1. Angling with rod, line, and baited hook. 2. That with the gaff, eel-spear, harpoon, or such like; the *first* used in catching *small fish*, by which the *common people* may be here represented; the *second*, for catching large fish, such as leave the sea, and come up the rivers to deposit their spawn; or such as are caught in the sea, as sharks, whales, dolphins, and even the hippopotamus, to which the more *powerful* and *opulent inhabitants* may be likened. But as the words in the text are generally *feminine*, it has been supposed that the prophecy is against the proud, powerful, voluptuous *women*. I rather think that the prophet speaks catachrestically; and means men of effeminate manners and idle lives. They are not the *bulls of Bashan*, but the *cows;* having little of the manly character remaining. Some understand the latter word as meaning a sort of *basket* or *wicker fish-nets*.

Verse 3. *And ye shall go out at the breaches*] Probably the metaphor is here kept up. They shall be caught by the *hooks*, or by the *nets;* and though they may make *breaches* in the latter by their flouncing when caught, they shall be taken out at these very breaches; and cast, not in the *palace*, but into a reservoir, to be kept awhile, and afterwards be taken out to be destroyed. *Samaria* itself is the *net;* your adversaries shall besiege it, and make *breaches* in its walls. At those *breaches* ye shall endeavour to *make your escape*, but ye shall be *caught* and led into *captivity*, where most of you shall be destroyed. See *Houbigant* on this passage.

Verse 4. *Come to Beth-el and transgress*] Spoken *ironically*. Go on to worship your calves at Beth-el; and *multiply* your *transgressions at Gilgal;* the very place where I *rolled away* the reproach of your fathers, by admitting them there into my covenant by circumcision. A place that should have ever been *sacred to me;* but you have now *desecrated* it by enormous idolatries. Let your *morning* and *evening*

A. M. cir. 3217
B. C. cir. 787
Ante U. C. 34
Amulii Sylvii, R. Alban., cir. annum 10

your tithes after [k]three years:
5 [l]And [m]offer a sacrifice of thanksgiving with leaven, and proclaim *and* publish [n]the free offerings: [o]for [p]this liketh you, O ye children of Israel, saith the Lord GOD.
6 And I also have given you cleanness of teeth in all your cities, and want of bread in all your places: [q]yet have ye not returned unto me, saith the LORD.
7 And also I have withholden the rain from you, when *there were* yet three months to the harvest: and I caused it to rain upon one city, and caused it not to rain upon another city: one piece was rained upon, and the piece whereupon it rained not withered.
8 So two *or* three cities wandered unto one city, to drink water; but they were not satisfied: [r]yet have ye not returned unto me, saith the LORD.
9 [s]I have smitten you with blasting and mildew: [t]when your gardens and your vineyards and your fig trees and your olive trees increased, [u]the palmerworm devoured *them:* yet have ye not returned unto me, saith the LORD.
10 I have sent among you the pestilence [v]after [w]the manner of Egypt: your young men have I slain with the sword, [x]and have taken away your horses; and I have made the stink of your camps to come up unto your nostrils: [y]yet have ye not returned unto me, saith the LORD.
11 I have overthrown *some* of you, as God overthrew [z]Sodom and Gomorrah, [a]and ye were as a firebrand plucked out of the burn-

[k]Hebrew, *three* years *of days*——[l]Leviticus vii. 13; xxiii. 17——[m]Hebrew, *offer by burning*——[n]Leviticus xxii. 18, 21; Deuteronomy xii. 6——[o]Psalm lxxxi. 12——[p]Hebrew, *so ye love*——[q]Isaiah xxvi. 11; Jeremiah v. 3; Hag. ii. 17; ver. 8, 9——[r]Ver. 6, 10, 11——[s]Deut. xxviii. 22; Hag. ii. 17——[t]Or, *the multitude of your gardens, &c., did the palmerworm,* &c.——[u]Joel i. 4; ii. 25——[v]Or, *in the way*——[w]Exod. ix. 3, 6; xii. 29; Deut. xxviii. 27, 60; Psa. lxxviii. 50——[x]Heb. *with the captivity of your horses;* 2 Kings xiii. 7——[y]Ver. 6——[z]Gen. xix. 24, 25; Isa. xiii. 19; Jer. xlix. 18——[a]Zech. iii. 2; Jude 23

sacrifices be offered still to your senseless gods; and continue to support your present vicious *priesthood* by the regular *triennial tithes* which should have been employed in my service; and,

Verse 5. *Offer a sacrifice of thanksgiving*] To the senseless *metal,* and the unfeeling *stock* and *stone* images, from which ye never did, and never could receive any help. Proceed yet farther, and bring *free-will offerings;* testify superabundant gratitude to your wooden and metallic gods, to whom ye are under such immense imaginary obligations! *Proclaim* and *publish* these offerings, and set forth the perfections of the objects of your worship; and see what they can do for you, when I, Jehovah, shall send *drought,* and *blasting,* and *famine,* and *pestilence,* and the *sword* among you.

Verse 6. *Cleanness of teeth*] Scarcity of bread, as immediately explained. Ye shall have no trouble in cleaning your teeth, for ye shall have nothing to eat.

Yet have ye not returned unto me, saith the Lord.] This reprehension is repeated *five* times in this chapter; and in it are strongly implied God's longsuffering, his various modes of fatherly chastisement, the ingratitude of the people, and their obstinate wickedness. The *famine* mentioned here is supposed to be that which is spoken of 2 Kings viii. 1; but it is most likely to have been that mentioned by Joel, chaps. i. and ii.

Verse 7. *When* there were *yet three months to the harvest*] St. Jerome says, from the end of April, when the *latter rain* falls, until harvest, there are *three* months, *May, June,* and *July,* in which no rain falls in Judea. The rain, therefore, that God had withheld from them, was that which was usual in the spring months, particularly in April.

I caused it to rain upon one city] To prove to them that this rain did not come *fortuitously* or of *necessity,* God was pleased to make these *most evident distinctions.* One city had rain, and could fill all its tanks or cisterns, while a neighbouring city had none. One *farm* or *field* was well watered, and abundant in its crops, while one contiguous to it had not a shower. In these instances a *particular providence* was most evident. "And yet, they did not return to the Lord."

Verse 9. *I have smitten you with blasting and mildew*] He sent *blasting* and *mildew* on the *crops,* and the *locust* on the *gardens, vineyards,* and *fields;* and this in such a way as to show it was a *Divine judgment.* They saw this; "yet they did not return to the Lord!"

Verse 10. *I have sent—the pestilence*] After the *blasting* and the *mildew,* the *pestilence* came; and it acted among them as one of the *plagues* of Egypt. Besides this, he had suffered their enemies to attack and prevail against them; alluding to the time in which the Syrians besieged Samaria, and reduced it to the most extreme necessity, when the head of an ass was sold for eighty pieces of silver, and the fourth part of a cab of dove's dung for five; and mothers ate the flesh of their children that had died through hunger, 2 Kings vi. 25. And the people were miraculously relieved by the total slaughter of the Syrians by the unseen hand of God, 2 Kings vii. 1, &c. And yet, after all those signal judgments, and singular mercies, "they did not return unto the Lord!"

Verse 11. *I have overthrown* some *of you*] In the destruction of your cities I have shown my judgments as signally as I did in the destruction of Sodom and Gomorrah; and those of you that did escape were as "brands plucked out of the fire;" if not *consumed,* yet *much*

A. M. cir. 3217
B. C. cir. 787
Ante U. C. 34
Amulii Sylvii,
R. Alban.,
cir. annum 10

ing: [b]yet have ye not returned unto me, saith the LORD.

12 Therefore thus will I do unto thee, O Israel: *and* because I will do this unto thee, [c]prepare to meet thy God, O Israel.

13 For, lo, he that formeth the mountains, and createth the [d]wind, [e]and declareth unto man what *is* his thought, [f]that maketh the morning darkness, [g]and treadeth upon the high places of the earth, [h]The LORD, The God of hosts, *is* his name.

[b]Ver. 6——[c]See Ezek. xiii. 5; xxii. 30; Luke xiv. 31, 32
[d]Or, *spirit*——[e]Psa. cxxxix. 2; Dan. ii. 28

[f]Ch. v. 8; viii. 9——[g]Deut. xxxii. 13; xxxiii. 29; Mic. i. 3
[h]Isa. xlvii. 4; Jer. x. 16; chap. v. 8; ix. 6

scorched. And as the judgment was evidently from my hand, so was the deliverance; "and yet ye have not returned unto me, saith the Lord."

Verse 12. *Therefore thus will I do unto thee*] I will continue my judgments, I will fight against you; and, because I am thus determined,—

Prepare to meet thy God, O Israel.] This is a military phrase, and is to be understood as a challenge to come out to battle. As if the Lord had said, I will attack you immediately. Throw yourselves into a posture of defence, summon your idols to your help: and try how far your strength, and that of your gods, will avail you against the unconquerable arm of the Lord of hosts! This verse has been often painfully misapplied by public teachers; it has no particular relation to *the day of judgment,* nor to the *hour of death.* These constructions are impositions on the text.

Verse 13. *He that formeth the mountains*] Here is a powerful description of the majesty of God. He formed the earth; he created the wind; he knows the inmost thoughts of the heart; he is the Creator of darkness and light; he steps from mountain to mountain, and has all things under his feet! Who is he who hath done and can do all these things? JEHOVAH ELOHIM TSEBAOTH, *that is his name.* 1. The self-existing, eternal, and independent Being. 2. The God who is in covenant with mankind. 3. The universal Commander of all the hosts of earth and heaven. This name is farther illustrated in the following chapter. These words are full of instruction, and may be a subject of profitable meditation to every serious mind.

CHAPTER V

This chapter opens with a tender and pathetic lamentation, in the style of a funeral song, over the house of Israel, 1, 2. *The prophet then glances at the awful threatenings denounced against them,* 3; *earnestly exhorting them to renounce their idols, and seek Jehovah, of whom he gives a very magnificent description,* 4–9. *He then reproves their injustice and oppression with great warmth and indignation; exhorts them again to repentance; and enforces his exhortation with the most awful threatenings, delivered with great majesty and authority, and in images full of beauty and grandeur,* 10–24. *The chapter concludes with observing that their idolatry was of long standing, that they increased the national guilt, by adding to the sins of their fathers; and that their punishment, therefore, should be great in proportion,* 25–27. *Formerly numbers of them were brought captive to Damascus,* 2 Kings x. 32, 33; *but now they must go beyond it to Assyria,* 2 Kings xv. 29; xvii. 6.

A. M. cir. 3217
B. C. cir. 787
Ante U. C. 34
Amulii Sylvii,
R. Alban.,
cir. annum 10

HEAR ye this word which I [a]take up against you, *even* a lamentation, O house of Israel.

2 The virgin of Israel is fallen; she shall no more rise: she is forsaken upon her land; *there is* none to raise her up.

3 For thus saith the Lord GOD; The city that went out *by* a thousand shall leave a hundred, and that which went forth *by* a hundred shall leave ten, to the house of Israel.

4 For thus saith the LORD unto the house of Israel, [b]Seek ye me, [c]and ye shall live:

5 But seek not [d]Beth-el, nor enter into Gilgal, and pass not to [e]Beer-sheba: for Gilgal

[a]Jer. vii. 29; Ezek. xix. 1; xxvii. 2——[b]2 Chron. xv. 2; Jer. xxix. 13; ver. 6

[c]Isaiah lv. 3——[d]Chapter iv. 4——[e]Chap. viii. 14

NOTES ON CHAP. V

Verse 1. *Hear ye this word*] Attend to this doleful song which I make for the house of Israel.

Verse 2. *The virgin of Israel*] The kingdom of Israel, or the *ten* tribes, which were carried into captivity; and are now totally lost in the nations of the earth.

Verse 3. *The city that went out* by *a thousand*] The city that could easily have furnished, on any emergency, a *thousand* fighting men, can now produce scarcely one *hundred—one* in *ten* of the former number; and now of the *hundred* scarcely *ten* remain: so reduced was Israel when Shalmaneser besieged and took Samaria, and carried the residue into captivity.

Verse 4. *Seek ye me, and ye shall live*] Cease your rebellion against me; return to me with all your heart; and though consigned to *death,* ye shall be rescued and *live.* Deplorable as your case is, it is not utterly desperate.

Verse 5. *But seek not Beth-el*] *There* was

A. M. cir. 3217
B. C. cir. 787
Ante U. C. 34
Amulii Sylvii,
R. Alban.,
cir. annum 10

shall surely go into captivity, and
[f]Beth-el shall come to naught.
6 [g]Seek the LORD, and ye shall
live; lest he break out like fire
in the house of Joseph and devour *it,* and
there be none to quench *it* in Beth-el.
7 Ye who [h]turn judgment to wormwood,
and leave off righteousness in the earth.
8 *Seek him* that maketh the [i]seven stars
and Orion, and turneth the shadow of death
into the morning, [k]and maketh the day dark
with night: that [l]calleth for the waters of the
sea, and poureth them out upon the face of
the earth: [m]The LORD *is* his name:
9 That strengtheneth the [n]spoiled against
the strong, so that the spoiled shall come
against the fortress.
10 [o]They hate him that rebuketh in the
gate, and they [p]abhor him that speaketh uprightly.

11 Forasmuch therefore as
your treading *is* upon the poor,
and ye take from him burdens of
wheat: [q]ye have built houses of
hewn stone, but ye shall not dwell in them;
ye have planted [r]pleasant vineyards, but ye
shall not drink wine of them.
12 For I know your manifold transgressions, and your mighty sins: [s]they afflict the
just, they take [t]a bribe, and they [u]turn aside
the poor in the gate *from their right.*
13 Therefore [v]the prudent shall keep silence
in that time; for it *is* an evil time.
14 Seek good, and not evil, that ye may
live: and so the LORD, the God of hosts,
shall be with you, [w]as ye have spoken.
15 [x]Hate the evil, and love the good, and
establish judgment in the gate: [y]it may be
that the LORD God of hosts will be gracious
unto the remnant of Joseph.

[f]Hosea iv. 15; x. 3——[g]Ver. 4——[h]Chap. vi. 12——[i]Job ix. 9; xxxviii. 31——[k]Psalm civ. 20——[l]Job xxxviii. 34; chap. ix. 6——[m]Chap. iv. 13——[n]Hebrew, *spoil*——[o]Isaiah xxix. 21——[p]1 Kings xxii. 8——[q]Deuteronomy xxviii. 30, 38, 39; Mic. vi. 15; Zephaniah i. 13; Haggai i. 6——[r]Hebrew, *vineyards of desire*——[s]Chap. ii. 26——[t]Or, *a ransom*——[u]Isaiah xxix. 21; chap. ii. 7——[v]Chap. vi. 10——[w]Micah iii. 11——[x]Psa. xxxiv. 14; xcvii. 10; Rom. xii. 9——[y]Exod. xxxii. 30; 2 Kings xix. 4; Joel ii. 14

one of Jeroboam's *golden calves,* and at *Gilgal* were *carved images;* both were places in which idolatry was triumphant. The prophet shows them that all hope from those quarters is utterly vain; for Gilgal shall go into captivity, and Beth-el be brought to naught. There is a play or paronomasia on the *letters* and *words* in this clause: הגלגל גלה יגלה ובית אל יהיה לאון *haggilgal galoh yigleh, ubeith el yiheyeh leaven.* "This Gilgal shall go captive into captivity; and Beth-el (the house of God) shall be for Beth-aven," (the house of iniquity.)

Verse 6. *Seek the Lord, and ye shall live*] Repeated from ver. 4.

In the house of Joseph] The Israelites of the *ten* tribes, of whom Ephraim and Manasseh, sons of Joseph, were the chief.

Verse 7. *Ye who turn judgment to wormwood*] Who pervert judgment; causing him who obtains his suit to mourn sorely over the *expenses* he has *incurred* in gaining his *right.*

Verse 8. *That maketh the seven stars and Orion*] Or, *Hyades* and *Arcturus, Kimah* and *Kesil.* See my notes on Job ix. 9, and xxxviii. 32, where the subject of this verse is largely considered.

Turneth the shadow of death into the morning] Who makes day and night, light and darkness.

Calleth for the waters of the sea] Raising them up by evaporation, and collecting them into clouds.

And poureth them out] Causing them to drop down in showers upon the face of the earth. Who has done this? JEHOVAH *is his name.*

Verse 9. *That strengtheneth the spoiled*] Who takes the part of the poor and oppressed against the oppressor; and, in the course of his providence, sets up the former, and depresses the latter.

Verse 10. *They hate him that rebuketh in the gate*] They cannot bear an upright *magistrate,* and will not have *righteous laws* executed.

Verse 11. *Your treading* is *upon the poor*] You tread them under your feet; they form the road on which ye walk; and yet it was by oppressing and improverishing them that ye gained your riches.

Ye take from him burdens of wheat] Ye will have his *bread* for doing him justice.

Verse 12. *I know your manifold transgressions*] I have marked the *multitude* of your *smaller crimes,* as well as your *mighty offences.* Among their *greater offences* were, 1. Their afflicting the righteous. 2. Taking bribes to blind their eyes in judgment. And, 3. Refusing to hear the poor, who had no money to give them.

Verse 13. *The prudent shall keep silence*] A wise man will consider that it is useless to complain. He can have no justice without bribes; and he has no money to give: consequently, in such *an evil time,* it is best to keep silence.

Verse 14. *Seek good, and not evil*] Is there a greater mystery in the world, than that a man, instead of seeking *good,* will seek *evil,* knowing that it is *evil?*

And so the Lord] As God is the Fountain of good, so they who seek the supreme good seek him: and they who seek shall find him; *for the Lord, the God of hosts, shall be with him.*

Verse 15. *Hate the evil, and love the good*] What *ruins* you, *avoid;* what *helps* you, *cleave* to. And as a proof that you take this advice,

A. M. cir. 3217
B. C. cir. 787
Ante U. C. 34
Amulii Sylvii,
R. Alban.,
cir. annum 10

16 Therefore the LORD, the
God of hosts, the Lord, saith
thus; Wailing *shall be* in all
streets; and they shall say in all
the highways, Alas! alas! and they shall call
the husbandman to mourning, and [z]such as
are skilful of lamentation to wailing.
17 And in all vineyards *shall be* wailing:
for [a]I will pass through thee, saith the LORD.
18 [b]Wo unto you that desire the day of the
LORD! to what end *is* it for you? [c]the day
of the LORD *is* darkness, and not light.
19 [d]As if a man did flee from a lion, and
a bear met him; or went into the house and
leaned his hand on the wall, and a serpent bit
him.
20 *Shall* not the day of the
LORD *be* darkness, and not
light? even very dark, and no
brightness in it?
21 [e]I hate, I despise your feast days, and
[f]I will not [g]smell in your solemn assemblies.
22 [h]Though ye offer me burnt-offerings and
your meat-offerings, I will not accept *them:*
neither will I regard the [i]peace-offerings of
your fat beasts.
23 Take thou away from me the noise of
thy songs; for I will not hear the melody of
thy viols.
24 [k]But let judgment [l]run down as waters,
and righteousness as a mighty stream.
25 [m]Have ye offered unto me sacrifices

[z]Jer. ix. 17——[a]Exod. xii. 2; Nah. i. 12——[b]Isa. v. 19; Jer. xvii. 15; Ezek. xii. 22, 27; 2 Pet. iii. 4——[c]Jer. xxx. 7; Joel ii. 2; Zeph. i. 15——[d]Jer. xlviii. 44 [e]Prov. xxi. 27; Isa. i. 11–16; Jer. vi. 20; Hos. viii. 13

[f]Lev. xxvi. 31——[g]Or, *smell your holy days*——[h]Isa. lxvi. 3; Mic. vi. 6, 7——[i]Or, *thank-offerings*——[k]Hos. vi. 6; Mic. vi. 8——[l]Heb. *roll*——[m]Deut. xxxii. 17; Josh xxiv. 14; Ezek. xx. 8, 16, 24; Acts vii. 42, 43; See Isa. xliii. 23

purify the *seats of justice;* and then expect God to be gracious to the *remnant of Joseph*—to the posterity of the ten tribes.

Verse 16. *They shall call the husbandman to mourning*] Because the crops have failed, and the ground has been tilled in vain.

Such as are skilful of lamentation] See the note on Jer. ix. 17.

Verse 17. *And in all vineyards* shall be *wailing*] The places where festivity especially used to prevail.

I will pass through thee] As I passed, by the ministry of the destroying angel, through Egypt, not to *spare*, but to *destroy*.

Verse 18. *Wo unto you that desire the day of the Lord*] The prophet had often denounced the coming of *God's day*, that is, of a *time of judgment;* and the unbelievers had said, "Let his day come, that we may see it." Now the prophet tells them that that day would be to them *darkness*—calamity, and *not light*—not prosperity.

Verse 19. *As if a man did flee from a lion, and a bear met him*] They shall go from one evil to another. He who escapes from the *lion's* mouth shall fall into the *bear's* paws:—

Incidit in Scyllam, cupiens vitare Charybdim.

The Israelites, under their king *Menahem*, wishing to avoid a civil war, called in *Pul*, king of *Assyria*, to help them. This led to a series of evils inflicted by the Syrian and Assyrian kings, till at last Israel was ravaged by *Shalmaneser*, and carried into captivity. Thus, in avoiding one evil they fell into another still more grievous.

Leaned his hand on a wall, and a serpent bit him.] Snakes and venomous animals are fond of taking up their lodging in *walls of houses*, where they can either find or make *holes;* and it is dangerous to sit near them or lean against them. In the East Indies they keep the faithful *mongose*, a species of *ichneumon*, in their houses, for the purpose of destroying the snakes that infest them.

Verse 21. *I hate, I despise your feast days*] I *abominate* those sacrificial festivals where there is no *piety;* and I *despise* them because they *pretend* to be what they are not. This may refer to the *three annual festivals* which were still observed in a certain way among the Israelites.

Verse 22. *The peace-offerings of your fat beasts.*] מריאיכם *merieychem* probably means *buffaloes;* and so *Bochart*.

Verse 23. *The noise of thy songs—the melody of thy viols.*] They had both *vocal* and *instrumental music* in those sacrificial festivals; and God hated the *noise* of the *one* and *shut* his *ears* against the *melody* of the *other*. In the *first* there was nothing but *noise*, because their *hearts* were not right with God; and in the *latter* there could be nothing but (זמרת *zimrath*) cutting and scraping, because there was *no heart*—no religious sense in the thing, and nearly as little in them that used it. See on chap. vi. 5.

Verse 24. *Let judgment run down*] Let the execution of justice be everywhere like the *showers* that fall upon the land to render it fertile; and let righteousness in *heart* and *life* be like a mighty river, or the Jordan, that shall wind its course through the whole nation, and carry every abomination into the Dead Sea. Let *justice* and *righteousness* prevail everywhere, and sweep their contraries out of the land.

Verse 25. *Have ye offered unto me sacrifices*] Some have been led to think that "during the *forty years* which the Israelites spent in the wilderness, between Egypt and the promised land, they did *not offer any sacrifices*, as in their circumstances it was impossible; they offered none because they had none." But such people must have forgotten that when the covenant was made at Sinai, there were *burnt-offerings* and *peace-offerings* of *oxen* sacrificed to the Lord, Exod. xxiv. 5; and at the setting up of the tabernacle the *twelve princes* of the *twelve tribes* offered each a *young bullock*, a *ram*, and a *lamb*, for a *burnt-offering;* a *kid*

A. M. cir. 3217
B. C. cir. 787
Ante U. C. 34
Amulii Sylvii,
R. Alban.,
cir. annum 10

and offerings in the wilderness
forty years, O house of
Israel?
26 But ye have borne [n]the
tabernacle [o]of your Moloch and Chiun
your images, the star of your god,
which ye made to your-
selves.
27 Therefore will I cause you
to go into captivity [p]beyond
Damascus, saith the LORD, [q]whose name *is*
The God of hosts.

[n]Or, *Siccuth your king*——[o]1 Kings xi. 33

[p]2 Kings xvii. 6——[q]Chap. iv. 13

for a *sin-offering;* two *oxen*, five *rams*, five *he-goats*, and five *lambs*, for a *peace-offering*, Num. vii. 12, &c.; which amounted to an immense number of victims offered in the course of the *twelve days* during which this *feast of the dedication* lasted. At the consecration of priests, *bullocks* and *rams* to a considerable number were offered, see Lev. viii. 1, &c.; but they were not offered so *regularly*, nor in *such abundance*, as they were after the settlement in the promised land. Learned men, therefore, have considered this verse as speaking thus: Did ye offer to me, during forty years in the wilderness, sacrifices in *such a way* as was *pleasing to me?* Ye did not; for your hearts were divided, and ye were generally in a spirit of insurrection or murmuring.

Verse 26. *But ye have borne*] The preceding verse spoke of their *fathers;* the present verse speaks of the *Israelites then existing*, who were so grievously addicted to idolatry, that they not only worshipped at stated public places the *idols* set up by *public authority*, but they *carried their gods about with them* everywhere.

The tabernacle of your Moloch] Probably a small portable shrine, with an image of their god in it, such as *Moloch;* and the *star* or *representative* of their god *Chiun*. For an ample exposition of this verse, see the note on Acts vii. 42; to which let me add, that from *Picart's* Religious Ceremonies, vol. iii. p. 199, we find that there was an idol named Choun worshipped among the *Peruvians* from the remotest antiquity.

Verse 27. *Will I cause you to go into captivity beyond Damascus*] That is, into *Assyria*, the way to which, from Judea, was by Damascus.

But St. *Stephen* says, Acts vii. 43, *beyond Babylon;* because the Holy Spirit that was in him chose to *extend* the meaning of the original text to that great and final captivity of the Jews in general, when Zedekiah, their last king, and the people of Judea, were carried into Mesopotamia, Armenia, and Media; see 2 Kings xvii. 7, 24. This captivity happened after the time of Amos.

CHAPTER VI

The prophet reproves his people for indulging themselves in luxurious ease, and forming alliances with their powerful idolatrous neighbours, 1. *He asks if* their *lands or* their *lot be better than their own,* 2, *that they should choose to worship the gods of the heathen, and forsake Jehovah. Then follows an amplification of the sin which the prophet reproves,* 3–6; *to which he annexes very awful threatenings, confirmed by the oath of Jehovah,* 7, 8. *He next particularly specifies the punishment of their sins by pestilence,* 9–11; *by famine, or a drought that should harden the earth so that it could not be tilled,* 12; *and by the sword of the Assyrians,* 14.

A. M. cir. 3217
B. C. cir. 787
Ante U. C. 34
Amulii Sylvii,
R. Alban.,
cir. annum 10

WO [a]to them *that* [b]*are* at
ease in Zion, and trust in
the mountain of Samaria, *which
are* named [c]chief[d] of the nations,
to whom the house of Israel
came!
2 [e]Pass ye unto [f]Calneh, and
see; and from thence go ye to

[a]Luke vi. 24——[b]Or, *are secure*——[c]Exod. xix. 5

[d]Or, *first-fruits*——[e]Jer. ii. 10——[f]Isa. x. 9; taken cir. 794

NOTES ON CHAP. VI

Verse 1. *Wo to them* that are *at ease in Zion*] For השאננים *hashshaanannim*, "who dwell at ease," it has been proposed to read השעננים *hashshaanannim*, "who confidently lean," the two words differing only in *one letter*, an ע *ain* for an א *aleph*. They leaned confidently on Zion; supposing that, notwithstanding their iniquities they should be saved for *Zion's sake*. Thus the former clause will agree better with the latter, "leaning upon Zion," and "trusting in the mountain of Samaria." Those *that are at ease* may mean those who have no concern about the threatened judgments, and who have no deep concern for the salvation of their own souls. *Houbigant* would read, "Wo to them who despise Zion, and trust in Samaria." So the *Septuagint*, reading שנאים *soneim*, *hating*, instead of שאננים *shaanannim*, being at *rest*, *tranquil*. *Calmet* first proposed this conjecture; *Houbigant* follows him.

Are *named chief*] *Newcome* renders, "That are named after the chief of the nations;" and observes, that the Hebrew word נקבי *nekubey* is an allusion to marking a name or character by *punctures*. See on Isa. xliv. 5. They call themselves not after their ancestors, but after the *chief of the idolatrous nations* with whom they intermarry contrary to the law.

Perhaps the words here rather refer to the *mountains* and their *temples*, than to the *people*. The *mountain* of *Zion*, and the *mountain* of *Samaria*, were considered the *chief* or **most**

A. M. cir. 3217
B. C. cir. 787
Ante U. C. 34
Amulii Sylvii,
R. Alban.,
cir. annum 10

[g]Hamath the great: then go down to [h]Gath of the Philistines: [i]*be they* better than these kingdoms? or their border greater than your border?

3 Ye that [k]put far away the [l]evil day, [m]and cause [n]the [o]seat of violence to come near;

4 That lie upon beds of ivory, and [p]stretch themselves upon their couches, and eat the lambs out of the flock, and the calves out of the midst of the stall;

5 [q]That [r]chant to the sound of the viol, *and* invent to themselves instruments of music, [s]like David;

6 That drink [t]wine in bowls, and anoint themselves with the chief ointments: [u]but they are not grieved for the [v]affliction of Joseph.

7 Therefore now shall they go captive with the first that go captive, and the banquet of them that stretched themselves shall be removed.

8 [w]The Lord GOD hath sworn by himself,

---

[g]2 Kings xviii. 34——[h]Joshua xi. 22; 1 Samuel v. 8; 2 Chronicles xxvi. 6——[i]Nahum iii. 8——[k]Ezekiel xii. 27——[l]Chap. v. 18; ix. 10——[m]Chap. v. 12; ver. 12——[n]Psalm xciv. 20——[o]Or, *habitation*——[p]Or, *abound with superfluities*——[q]Isaiah v. 12——[r]Or, *quaver*——[s]1 Chronicles xxiii. 5——[t]Or, *in bowls of wine*——[u]Genesis xxxvii. 25——[v]Heb. *breach*——[w]Jer. li. 14; Heb. vi. 13, 17

---

celebrated among the nations, as the two kingdoms to which they belonged were the most distinguished on the earth.

Verse 2. *Pass ye unto Calneh*] This is, says *Calmet*, the Ctesiphon on the river Tigris.

Hamath] The same as *Emesa. Hamath* was a city on the Orontes, in Syria.

Gath] A well-known town, and head of one of the *five* seignories of the Philistines.

Be they *better*] You have no more reason to expect exemption from the consequences of your sins than they had. *They* have been punished; so shall you. Why then will ye trust in their gods, that could not save their own cities?

Verse 3. *Ye that put far away the evil day*] Wo to you who will not consider the day of approaching vengeance; but continue in your iniquity, and harden your hearts. Ye bring your iniquities nearer, and still suppose your punishment to be at a greater distance.

Verse 4. *That lie upon beds of ivory*] The word הוי *hoi, wo,* is understood at the beginning of each of the *first, third, fourth, fifth,* and *sixth* verses. The *beds* mentioned here may be either *sofas to recline on at table*, or *beds to sleep on;* and these among the ancients were ornamented with ivory inlaid. They were called *lectos eburatos* by Plautus, *lectos eburnos* by Horace, "ivory beds." Probably those ornamented with *shells*, or *mother-of-pearl*, may be intended. Several works of this kind may be still seen in Palestine and other places. I have before me a cross brought from Jerusalem, incrusted all over with *mother-of-pearl*, and various figures chased on it.

There must have been a great deal of luxury and effeminacy among the Israelites at this time; and, consequently, abundance of riches. This was in the time of Jeroboam the second, when the kingdom had enjoyed a long peace. The description in the *fourth, fifth,* and *sixth* verses, is that of an Asiatic court even in the present day.

Verse 5. And *invent to themselves instruments of music, like David*] See the note on 1 Chron. xxiii. 5; and see especially the note on 2 Chron. xxix. 25. I believe that David was not authorized by the Lord to introduce that multitude of musical instruments into the Divine worship of which we read; and I am satisfied that his conduct in this respect is most solemnly reprehended by this prophet; and I farther believe that the use of such instruments of music, in the Christian Church, is *without* the *sanction* and *against* the *will* of God; that they are subversive of the spirit of true devotion, and that they are *sinful.* If there was a *wo to them* who *invented* instruments of music, as did David under the law, is there *no wo, no curse* to them who invent them, and introduce them into the worship of God in the Christian Church? I am an old man, and an old minister; and I here declare that I never knew them productive of any good in the worship of God; and have had reason to believe that they were productive of much evil. Music, *as a science,* I esteem and admire: but instruments of music *in the house of God* I abominate and abhor. This is the abuse of music; and here I register my protest against all such corruptions in the worship of the Author of Christianity. The late venerable and most eminent divine, the Rev. *John Wesley*, who was a *lover of music*, and an *elegant poet*, when asked his opinion of instruments of music being introduced into the chapels of the Methodists said, in his terse and powerful manner, "I have no objection to instruments of music in our chapels, provided they are neither HEARD nor SEEN." I say the same, though I think the expense of purchase had better be spared.

The word הפרטים *happoretim,* which we render *chant*, and the margin *quaver*, signifies to *dance*, to *skip*, &c. In the sight of such a text, fiddlers, drummers, waltzers, &c., may well tremble, who perform to excite detestable passions.

Verse 6. *That drink wine in bowls*] Perhaps the *costliness* of the *drinking vessels*, more than the *quantity* drank, is that which is here reprehended by the prophet. Drinking vessels of the most costly materials, and of the most exquisite workmanship, are still in use; and as to *precious ointments* and *perfumes* among the Jews, we have a proof that the contents of one small box was worth *three hundred denarii,* at least *seven pounds ten shillings* sterling. See the case in the Gospel, John xii. 5, and the note there.

Verse 7. *With the first that go captive*] The house of *Israel* shall be carried into captivity *before* the house of *Judah*.

Verse 8. *The Lord God hath sworn by him-*

A. M. cir. 3217
B. C. cir. 787
Ante U. C. 34
Amulii Sylvii,
R. Alban.,
cir. annum 10

saith the LORD the God of hosts,
I abhor [x]the excellency of Jacob,
and hate his palaces: therefore
will I deliver up the city with all
[y]that is therein.
9 And it shall come to pass, if there remain
ten men in one house, that they shall die.
10 And a man's uncle shall take him up, and
he that burneth him, to bring out the bones
out of the house, and shall say unto him that
is by the sides of the house, *Is there* yet *any*
with thee? and he shall say, No. Then shall
he say, [z]Hold thy tongue: [a]for [b]we may not
make mention of the name of the LORD.
11 For, behold, [c]the LORD commandeth, [d]and
he will smite the great house
with [e]breaches, and the little
house with clefts.
12 Shall horses run upon the
rock? will *one* plough *there* with oxen? for
[f]ye have turned judgment into gall, and the
fruit of righteousness into hemlock:
13 Ye which rejoice in a thing of naught,
which say, Have we not taken to us horns by
our own strength?
14 But, behold, [g]I will raise up against you
a nation, O house of Israel, saith the LORD
the God of hosts; and they shall afflict you
from the [h]entering in of Hamath unto the
[i]river of the wilderness.

A. M. cir. 3217
B. C. cir. 787
Ante U. C. 34
Amulii Sylvii,
R. Alban.,
cir. annum 10

---

[x]Psa. xlvii. 4; Ezek. xxiv. 21; chap. viii. 7——[y]Heb. *the fulness thereof*——[z]Chap. v. 13——[a]Chap. viii. 3 [b]Or, *they will not*, or *have not*

[c]Isa. lv. 11——[d]Chap. iii. 15——[e]Or, *droppings* [f]Hos. x. 4; chap. v. 7——[g]Jer. v. 15——[h]Num. xxxiv. 8; 1 Kings viii. 65——[i]Or, *valley*

---

self] בנפשו *benaphsho*, by his soul, his *being*, *existence*.

Verse 9. *Ten men—they shall die.*] ALL shall be cut off by the sword, or by captivity, or by famine.

Verse 10. *A man's uncle shall take him up*] Bp. *Newcome* says, this obscure verse seems to describe the effects of famine and pestilence during the siege of Samaria. The carcass shall be burnt; and the bones removed with no ceremony of funeral rites, and without the assistance of the nearest kinsman. Solitude shall reign in the house; and if one is left, he must be silent, (see chap. viii. 3,) and retired, lest he be plundered of his scanty provision! *Burning the body*, and then collecting the *ashes*, and putting them into an urn, was deemed the most honourable mode of burial.

Verse 11. *He will smite the great house with breaches*] The great and small shall equally suffer; no distinction shall be made; rich and poor shall fall together; death has received his commission, and he will spare none. *Horace* has a sentiment precisely like this, Carm. Lib. i., Od. iv., v. 13.

Pallida mors æquo pulsat pede pauperum TABERNAS,
Regumque TURRES.

With equal pace impartial fate
Knocks at the *palace* as the *cottage* gate.

But this may refer particularly to the houses of the poor in Eastern countries; their mud walls being frequently full of *clefts;* the earth of which they are built seldom adhering together because of its *sandiness*.

Verse 12. *Shall horses run upon the rock*] First, they *could not* do it, because they were *unshod;* for the shoeing of horses with *iron* was not then known. Secondly, If they did run on the rock, it would be *useless* to their owner, and *hurtful* to themselves. Thirdly, And it would be as useless to *plough on the rock with oxen;* for there it would be impossible to sow with any advantage. Fourthly, Just as useless and injurious would it be to put *gall* in the place of judgment, and hemlock in the place of righteousness. You have not only been labouring in vain for yourselves, but you have also been oppressive to others; and for both ye shall suffer.

Verse 13. *Ye which rejoice in a thing of naught*] In your idols: for an idol is nothing in the world.

Have we not taken to us horns] We have arrived to power and dignity by our strength. *Horns* were the symbols of *power* and *authority*. So *Horace:*—

Vina parant animos: tum pauper cornua sumet.

"Wine repairs our strength, and furnishes the poor with horns."

At such times they think themselves as great as the greatest.

Verse 14. *I will raise up against you a nation*] The *Assyrians* under *Pul*, *Tiglath-pileser*, and *Shalmaneser*, who subdued the Israelites at various times, and at last carried them away captive in the days of Hosea, the last king of Israel in Samaria.

From the entering in of Hamath (on the *north*) *unto the river of the wilderness.*] Besor, which empties itself into the sea, not far from Gaza, and was in the *southern* part of the tribe of Simeon.

CHAPTER VII

In this chapter God represents to Amos, by three several visions, the judgments he is about to bring on Israel. The first is a plague of locusts, *threatening to cut off the hopes of the harvest by attacking it in the time of the second growth; the first luxuriances of the crop being probably mowed for the king's horses,* 1–3. *The next vision threatens a judgment by* fire, *which would consume a great part,* 4–6; *and the third a total overthrow of Israel, levelling it as it were by a line,* 7–9. *The rest of the chapter is a denunciation of heavy judgments against Amaziah, priest of Beth-el, who had brought on accusation to the king against the prophet,* 10–17.

A. M. cir. 3217
B. C. cir. 787
Ante U. C. 34
Amulii Sylvii, R. Alban., cir. annum 10

THUS hath the Lord GOD showed unto me; and, behold, he formed [a]grasshoppers in the beginning of the shooting up of the latter growth; and, lo, *it was* the latter growth after the king's mowings.

2 And it came to pass, *that* when they had made an end of eating the grass of the land, then I said, O Lord GOD, forgive, I beseech thee: [b]by [c]whom shall Jacob arise? for he *is* small.

3 [d]The LORD repented for this: It shall not be, saith the LORD.

4 Thus hath the Lord GOD showed unto me: and, behold, the Lord GOD called to contend by fire, and it devoured the great deep, and did eat up a part.

5 Then said I, O Lord GOD, cease, I beseech thee: [e]by whom shall Jacob arise? for he *is* small.

A. M. cir. 3217
B. C. cir. 787
Ante U. C. 34
Amulii Sylvii, R. Alban., cir. annum 10

6 The LORD repented for this: This also shall not be, saith the Lord GOD.

7 Thus he showed me: and, behold, the Lord stood upon a wall *made* by a plumbline, with a plumbline in his hand.

8 And the LORD said unto me, Amos, what seest thou? And I said, A plumbline. Then said the Lord, Behold, [f]I will set a plumbline in the midst of my people Israel: [g]I will not again pass by them any more:

9 [h]And the high places of Isaac shall be desolate, and the sanctuaries of Israel shall be laid waste; and I will rise against [i]the house of Jeroboam with the sword.

10 Then Amaziah [k]the priest of Beth-

[a]Or, *green worms*——[b]Isaiah li. 19; verse 5——[c]Or, *who of* or *for Jacob shall stand?*——[d]Deuteronomy xxxii. 36; verse 6; Jonah iii. 10; James v. 16——[e]Verse 2, 3——[f]See 2 Kings xxi. 13; Isa. xxviii. 17; xxxiv. 11; Lamentations ii. 8——[g]Ch. viii. 2; Micah vii. 18——[h]Beer-sheba, Gen. xxvi. 25; xlvi. 1; chap. v. 5; viii. 14——[i]1 Kings xvi. 3——[k]1 Kings xii. 32

NOTES ON CHAP. VII

Verse 1. *Behold, he formed grasshoppers*] גבי *gobai* is generally understood here to signify *locusts*. See the notes on Joel i. and ii.

The shooting up of the latter growth] The *early crop* of grass had been already mowed and housed. The *second crop* or *rowing*, as it is called in some places, was not yet begun. By the *king's mowings* we may understand the *first crop*, a portion of which the king probably claimed as being the better hay; but the words may signify simply the *prime crop*, that which is the *best of the whole. Houbigant* thinks the *shearing of the king's sheep* is meant.

Verse 2. *By whom shall Jacob arise?*] The *locusts*, the symbols of the many enemies that had impoverished Jerusalem, having devoured much of the produce of the land, were proceeding, till, at the intercession of the prophet, they were removed. Then, seeing in the light of prophecy the nation in every sense brought low, he cries, "By whom shall Jacob arise? for he is small." *Calmet* justly remarks: "After the death of Jeroboam the second, the kingdom, so flourishing and powerful before, was reduced to such weakness that it was obliged to have recourse to strangers for support. *Menahem* applied to Pul, king of Assyria, whence arose the final misery of the state.

Verse 3. *The Lord repented*] Changed his purpose of destroying them by the locusts. See ver. 6.

Verse 4. *The Lord God called to contend by fire*] Permitted *war*, both *civil* and *foreign*, to harass the land, after the death of Jeroboam the second. These wars would have totally destroyed it, had not the prophet interceded.

It devoured the great deep, and did eat up a part.] We are here to understand the partially destructive wars which afterwards took place; for the Lord causes all these things to pass before the eyes of Amos in the vision of prophecy; and intimates that, at the intercession of his prophets, *total* ruin should be prevented.

Verse 7. *With a plumbline in his hand.*] This appears to be intended as an emblem of strict justice, and intimated that God would now visit them according to their iniquities.

Verse 8. *I will set a plumbline*] I will visit them by *justice* without any mixture of *mercy*.

Verse 9. *And the high places of Isaac shall be desolate*] Their total destruction is at hand. The *high place of Isaac* was *Beer-sheba*, where Isaac had built an altar to the Lord, Gen. xxvi. 25. This high place, which had been abused to idolatrous uses, was demolished by Josiah, king of Judah, as we read in 2 Kings xxiii. 8, for *he defiled all the high places from Geba to Beer-sheba.*

I will rise against the house of Jeroboam] The Lord had promised to Jehu, the ancestor of Jeroboam, that his family should sit on the throne of Israel to the *fourth generation.* Zechariah, the son of Jeroboam, was the *fourth* in order after Jehu; and on him the threatening in this verse fell; for he was murdered by Shallum after he had reigned six months, and in him the family became extinct. See 2 Kings x. 30, and xv. 8-10.

Verse 10. *Amaziah the priest of Beth-el*] The idolatrous priest who had been established by the king to maintain the worship of the golden calves which Jeroboam the elder had set up at this place.

A. M. cir. 3217
B. C. cir. 787
Ante U. C. 34
Amulii Sylvii,
R. Alban.,
cir. annum 10

el, sent to [l]Jeroboam king of
Israel, saying, Amos hath conspired against thee in the midst
of the house of Israel: the land
is not able to bear all his words.
11 For thus Amos saith, Jeroboam shall die
by the sword, and Israel shall surely be led
away captive out of their own land.
12 Also Amaziah said unto Amos, O thou
seer, go flee thee away into the land of Judah,
and there eat bread, and prophesy there:
13 But [m]prophesy not again any more at
Beth-el: [n]for it *is* the king's [o]chapel, and it
is the [p]king's court.
14 Then answered Amos, and said to Amaziah, I *was* no prophet, neither *was* I [q]a prophet's son; [r]but I *was* a herd-
man, and a gatherer of [s]syca-
more fruit:
15 And the LORD took me [t]as
I followed the flock, and the LORD said unto
me, Go, prophesy unto my people Israel.
16 Now therefore hear thou the word of
the LORD: Thou sayest, Prophesy not against
Israel, and [u]drop not *thy word* against the
house of Isaac.
17 [v]Therefore thus saith the LORD; [w]Thy
wife shall be a harlot in the city, and thy sons
and thy daughters shall fall by the sword, and
thy land shall be divided by line; and thou
shalt die in a polluted land: and Israel shall
surely go into captivity forth of his land.

A. M. cir. 3217
B. C. cir. 787
Ante U. C. 34
Amulii Sylvii,
R. Alban.,
cir. annum 10

[l]2 Kings xiv. 23——[m]Chapter ii. 12——[n]1 Kings xii. 32; xiii. 1——[o]Or, *sanctuary*——[p]Hebrew, *house of the kingdom*——[q]1 Kings xx. 35; 2 Kings ii. 5; iv. 38; vi. 1——[r]Chap. i. 1; Zechariah xiii. 5——[s]Or, *wild figs*——[t]Hebrew, *from behind*——[u]Ezekiel xxi. 2; Micah ii. 6——[v]See Jeremiah xxviii. 12; xxix. 21, 25, 31, 32——[w]Isa. xiii. 16; Lam. v. 11; Hos. iv. 13; Zech. ix. 2

Amos hath conspired against thee] This was truly a *lying* prophet; there is not one word of truth in this message which he sent to Jeroboam. Amos had not conspired against the king—had not said that Jeroboam should die by the sword—and had not said that Israel should be carried away captive, though this last was implied in God's threatenings, and afterwards delivered by this prophet; see ver. 17.

Verse 12. *O thou seer*] He pretends kindness to the prophet, and counsels him to go into Judea, and prophesy there and be safe, even in the time that he had accused him of *high treason* against Jeroboam. Hireling priests of this kind have ever been the great enemies of the true prophets of God; and when they could bring no charge of false doctrine or immorality against them, have accused them of conspiring against the government; and because they have preached against *sin*, have held them up as exciting insurrection among the people.

Verse 13. *But prophesy not—at Beth-el*] He must not speak against idolatry, because that was the king's religion; and he who speaks against the king's religion must be an enemy to the state. This was the doctrine held in England by popish James II. and his insidious Jesuit hireling priests, till God in his mercy put this pitiful tyrant down, and with him his false prophets, and the degrading superstition which they endeavoured to establish in these lands.

Verse 14. *I was no prophet*] I am an extraordinary messenger of God. I am not called to the prophetic office but for *this occasion*. I have no message to *Judah*, and therefore need not go there. I have a message to *Israel* alone, and I must faithfully deliver it.

For the account which Amos gives here of himself, see the *introduction*.

Verse 16. *Now therefore hear thou the word of the Lord*] While he was speaking in his own vindication, God seems to have inspired him with the awful prediction which he immediately delivers.

Verse 17. *Thy wife shall be a harlot*] As this was *the word of the Lord*, so it was fulfilled; but as we have no farther account of this idolatrous priest, so we cannot tell in what circumstances these threatenings were executed. 1. His wife was to be a public prostitute; she was probably such already privately in the temple, as the wife of an idolatrous priest. 2. His sons and daughters were to fall by the sword. 3. Their *inheritance* was to be taken by strangers. 4. And himself was to die a captive in a heathen land.

Israel shall surely go into captivity] He now declares fully what he had not declared before, though Amaziah had made it a subject of accusation. This particular was probably revealed at this instant, as well as those which concerned Amaziah and his family.

CHAPTER VIII

This chapter begins with a fourth vision denoting the certainty and nearness of the destruction of Israel, 1–3. *The prophet then proceeds to reprove their oppression and injustice,* 4–7. *Strong and beautiful figures, by which is represented the complete dissolution of the Israelitish polity,* 8–10. *The people threatened with a most awful judgment; a* FAMINE *of the word of God,* 11–14.

A. M. cir. 3217
B. C. cir. 787
Ante U. C. 34
Amulii Sylvii,
R. Alban.,
cir. annum 10

THUS hath the Lord GOD
showed unto me: and be-
hold a basket of summer fruit.
2 And he said, Amos, what
seest thou? And I said, A basket of summer
fruit. Then said the LORD unto me, [a]The
end is come upon my people of Israel; [b]I
will not again pass by them any more.
3 And [c]the songs of the temple [d]shall be
howlings in that day, saith the Lord GOD:
there shall be many dead bodies in every
place; [e]they shall cast *them* forth [f]with
silence.
4 Hear this, O ye that [g]swallow up the
needy, even to make the poor
of the land to fail,
5 Saying, When will the [h]new
moon be gone, that we may sell
corn? and [i]the Sabbath, that we may [k]set
forth wheat, [l]making the ephah small, and the
shekel great, and [m]falsifying the balances by
deceit?
6 That we may buy the poor for [n]silver,
and the needy for a pair of shoes; *yea,* and
sell the refuse of the wheat?
7 The LORD hath sworn by [o]the excellency
of Jacob, Surely [p]I will never forget any of
their works.

[a]Ezek. vii. 2——[b]Chap. vii. 8——[c]Chap. v. 23——[d]Heb. *shall howl*——[e]Chap. vi. 9, 10——[f]Heb. *be silent*——[g]Psa. xiv. 4; Prov. xxx. 14——[h]Or, *month*

[i]Neh. xiii. 15, 16——[k]Heb. *open*——[l]Mic. vi. 10, 11——[m]Heb. *perverting the balances of deceit;* Hos. xii. 7——[n]Chap. ii. 6——[o]Chap. vi. 8——[p]Hos. viii. 13; ix. 9

NOTES ON CHAP. VIII

Verse 1. *A basket of summer fruit.*] As summer fruit was not proper for *preserving*, but must be eaten as soon as gathered, so the Lord intimates by this symbol that the kingdom of Israel was now *ripe* for destruction, and that punishment must descend upon it without delay. Some think the prophet means the fruits at the end of *autumn*. And as *after the autumn* no fruit could be expected, so Israel's summer is gone by, her autumn is ended, and she shall yield no more fruit. Or, the autumn of her iniquity is come; the measure is filled up, and now she shall gather the *fruit* of her sin in the abundance of her punishment.

Verse 2. *A basket of summer fruit*] כלוב קיץ *kelub kayits; the end is come*—בא הקץ *ba hakkets:* here is a paronomasia or play upon the words *kayits, summer fruit,* and *kets, the end,* both coming from similar roots. See the note on Ezek. vii. 2, where there is a similar play on the same word.

I will not again pass by them any more.] I will be no longer their Guardian.

Verse 3. *The songs of the temple*] Instead of שירות *shiroth, songs, Houbigant* reads שורות *shoroth,* the *singing women;* and *Newcome* follows him: "And the singing women of the palace shall howl in that day." Instead of joyous songs, they shall have nothing but lamentation.

They shall cast them *forth with silence.*] Every place shall be filled with the dead, and a dreadful silence shall reign universally; the few that remain being afraid either to speak or complain, or even to chant a funeral dirge for the most respectable of the dead.

Verse 4. *Hear this, O ye that swallow up the needy*] Ye that *bruise* the poor; exact from them, and *tread them under foot.*

Verse 5. *When will the new moon be gone*] This was kept as a kind of *holy day,* not by Divine command, but by *custom.* The *Sabbath* was strictly holy; and yet so covetous were they that they grudged to give to God and their own souls this seventh portion of time! But bad and execrable as *they* were, they neither *set forth their corn,* nor *their wheat,* nor *any other kind of merchandise,* on the *Sabbath.* They were *saints* then, when compared to multitudes called *Christians,* who keep their shops either *partially* or *entirely open* on the Lord's day, and *buy* and *sell* without any scruples of conscience. Conscience! alas! they have *none;* it is seared as with a hot iron. The strong man armed, in them, is quiet, for all his goods are in peace.

Making the ephah small, and the shekel great] Giving *short measure,* and taking *full price;* or, buying with a *heavy weight,* and selling with one that was *light.*

Falsifying the balances] Having *one scale light,* and the *other weighty; one end* of the *beam long,* and the *other short.* A few months ago I detected a knave with such balances; with a slip of his finger along the beam he altered the *centre,* which made *three ounces short weight in every pound.* He did it so dexterously, that though I knew he was cheating, or, as the prophet expresses it, was *falsifying the balances by deceit,* it was some time before I could detect the fraud, and not till I had been several times cheated by this accomplished knave. So we find that though the knaves of ancient Israel are dead, they have left their successors behind them.

Verse 6. *That we may buy the poor for silver*] Buying their services for such a time, with just money enough to clear them from other creditors.

And the needy for a pair of shoes] See on chap. ii. 6.

And sell the refuse of the wheat?] Selling bad wheat and damaged flour to poor people as good, knowing that such cannot afford to prosecute them.

Verse 7. *By the excellency of Jacob*] By the *state of eminence* to which he had raised the descendants of Jacob; or, by the *excellent* ONE *of Jacob,* that is, HIMSELF. The meaning is: "As surely as I have raised you to such a state of eminence, so surely will I punish you in proportion to your advantages and your crimes."

A. M. cir. 3217
B. C. cir. 787
Ante U. C. 34
Amulii Sylvii, R. Alban., cir. annum 10

8 [q]Shall not the land tremble for this, and every one mourn that dwelleth therein? and it shall rise up wholly as a flood; and it shall be cast out and drowned, [r]as *by* the flood of Egypt.

9 And it shall come to pass in that day, saith the Lord God, [s]that I will cause the sun to go down at noon, and I will darken the earth in the clear day:

10 [t]And I will turn your feasts into mourning, and all your songs into lamentations; [u]and I will bring up sackcloth upon all loins, and baldness upon every head; [v]and I will make it as the mourning of an only *son,* and the end thereof as a bitter day.

11 Behold, the days come, saith the Lord God, that I will send a famine in the land, not a famine of bread, nor a thirst for water, but [w]of hearing the words of the Lord:

12 And they shall wander from sea to sea, and from the north even to the east, they shall run to and fro to seek the word of the Lord, and shall not find *it.*

13 In that day shall the fair virgins and young men faint for thirst.

14 They that [x]swear by [y]the sin of Samaria, and say, Thy god, O Dan, liveth; and, The [z]manner [a]of Beer-sheba liveth; even they shall fall, and never rise up again.

[q]Hos. iv. 3——[r]Chap. ix. 5——[s]Job v. 14; Isa. xiii. 10; lix. 9, 10; Jer. xv. 9; Mic. iii. 6——[t]Isa. i. 14; Tob. ii. 6——[u]Isa. xv. 2, 3; Jer. xlviii. 37; Ezek. vii. 18; xxvii. 31

[v]Jer. vi. 26; Zech. xii. 10——[w]1 Sam. iii. 1; Psa. lxxiv. 9; Ezek. vii. 26——[x]Hos. iv. 15——[y]Deut. ix. 2 [z]Heb. *way;* see Acts ix. 2; xviii. 25; xix. 9, 23; xxiv. 14——[a]Chap. v. 5

Verse 8. *Shall not the land tremble for this*] It is supposed that an *earthquake* is here intended, and that the *rising up* and *subsiding as a flood* refers to that *heaving motion* that takes place in an earthquake, and which the prophet here compares to the *overflowing* and *subsiding* of the *waters of the Nile.* But it may refer to commotions among the people.

Verse 9. *I will cause the sun to go down at noon*] This may either refer to that *darkness* which often precedes and accompanies *earthquakes,* or to an *eclipse.* Abp. *Usher* has shown that about eleven years after Amos prophesied there were two great *eclipses of the sun;* one at the *feast of tabernacles,* and the other some time before the *passover.* The prophet may refer to the darkness occasioned by those eclipses; yet I rather think the whole may refer to the *earthquake.*

Verse 10. *I will turn your feasts into mourning*] See on ver. 3.

A bitter day.] A time of grievous calamity.

Verse 11. *A famine in the land*] The most grievous of all famines, a famine of *the words of Jehovah;* a time in which no prophet should appear, no spiritual counsellor, no faithful reprover, none any longer who would point out the way of salvation, or would assure them of the mercy of God on their repentance and return to him. This is the severest of God's judgments on this side the worm that never dieth, and the fire that is never quenched.

Verse 12. *They shall wander from sea to sea*] From the Mediterranean to the Dead Sea or from west to east, and from north to south, *to seek the word of the Lord;* to find a prophet, or any person authorized by God to show them the end of their calamities. In this state they shall continue, because they have rejected Him who is the bread of life.

Verse 14. *By the sin of Samaria*] *Baal,* who was worshipped here.

Thy god, O Dan] The golden calf, or ox, the representative of the Egyptian god Apis, or Osiris.

The manner of Beer-sheba] The worship, or object of worship. Another of the golden calves which Jeroboam had set up there. The word דרך *derech, way,* is here taken for the *object* and *mode* of worship; see Acts xix. 9, where *way* is taken for the *creed* and *form* of Divine worship as practised by the followers of Christ, and by which they were distinguished from the Jews. See also Acts ix. 2.

CHAPTER IX

The first part of this chapter contains another vision, in which God is represented as declaring the final ruin of the kingdom of Israel, and the general dispersion of the people, 1–10. *The prophet then passes to the great blessedness of the people of God under the Gospel dispensation,* 11–15. *See* Acts xv. 15, 16.

A. M. cir. 3217
B. C. cir. 787
Ante U. C. 34
Amulii Sylvii, R. Alban., cir. annum 10

I SAW the Lord standing upon the altar: and he said, Smite the [a]lintel of the door, that the posts may shake: and [b]cut [c]them in the head, all of them; and I will slay the last of them with the sword: [d]he that fleeth of them shall not flee away, and he that escapeth of them shall not be delivered.

2 [e]Though they dig into hell, thence shall mine hand take them: [f]though they climb up to heaven, thence will I bring them down:

3 And though they hide themselves in the top of Carmel, I will search and take them out thence; and though they be hid from my sight in the bottom of the sea, thence will I command the serpent, and he shall bite them:

4 And though they go into captivity before their enemies, [g]thence will I command the sword, and it shall slay them: and [h]I will set mine eyes upon them for evil, and not for good.

5 And the Lord God of hosts *is* he that toucheth the land, and it shall [i]melt, [k]and all that dwell therein shall mourn: and it shall rise up wholly like a flood; and shall be drowned, *as by* the flood of Egypt.

6 *It is* he that buildeth his [l] [m] stories [n] in the heaven, and hath founded his [o]troop in the earth; he that [p]calleth for the waters of the sea, and poureth them out upon the face of the earth: [q]The Lord *is* his name.

7 *Are* ye not as children of the Ethiopians

[a]Or, *chapiter*, or *knop*——[b]Or, *wound them*——[c]Psa. lxviii. 21; Habakkuk iii. 13——[d]Chap. ii. 14——[e]Psa. cxxxix. 8, &c.——[f]Job xx. 6; Jeremiah li. 53; Obadiah 4——[g]Leviticus xxvi. 33; Deuteronomy xxviii. 65; Ezekiel v. 12——[h]Leviticus xvii. 10; Jeremiah xliv. 11 [i]Micah i. 4——[k]Chap. viii. 8——[l]Or, *spheres*——[m]Hebrew, *ascensions*——[n]Psalm civ. 3, 13——[o]Or, *bundle* [p]Chap. v. 8——[q]Chap. iv. 13

NOTES ON CHAP. IX

Verse 1. *I saw the Lord standing upon the altar*] As this is a continuation of the preceding prophecy, the *altar* here may be one of those either at *Dan* or *Beer-sheba.*

Smite the lintel] Either the piece of timber that *binds the wall above the door*, or the *upper part* of the *door frame*, in which the *cheeks*, or side posts, are inserted, and which corresponds to the threshold, or lower part of the door frame.

And cut them in the head] Let all the lintels of all the doors of all those temples be thus cut, as a sign that the whole shall be thrown down and totally demolished. Or this may refer to their *heads—chief men*, who were principals in these transgressions. Mark their temples, their priests, their prophets, and their princes, for destruction.

He that fleeth—shall not flee away] He shall be caught before he can get out of the reach of danger.

And he that escapeth (that makes good his flight) *shall not be delivered.*] Captivity, famine, or sword, shall reach him even there.

Verse 2. *Though they dig into hell*] Though they should get into the deepest caverns; *though they climb up to heaven*—get to the most inaccessible heights; I will drag them up from the one, and pull them down from the other.

Verse 3. *Though they hide themselves*] All these are metaphorical expressions, to show the impossibility of escape.

Verse 4. *I will set mine eyes upon them for evil*] I will use that very *providence* against them which before worked for their good. Should they look upward, they shall see nothing but the terrible lightning-like eye of a sin-avenging God.

Verse 5. *The Lord God of hosts* is *he*] So powerful is he that a touch of his hand shall *melt* or dissolve *the land*, and cause all its *inhabitants to mourn.* Here is still a reference to the *earthquake.* See the note, chap. viii. 8, where the same images are used.

Verse 6. *Buildeth his stories in the heaven*] There is here an allusion to large houses, where there are *cellars*, or places dug in the ground as *repositories* for corn; *middle apartments*, or stories, for the families to live in; and the *house-top* for persons to take the air upon. There may be here a reference to the *various systems* which God has formed in illimitable space, *transcending each other*, as the *planets* do in our solar system: and thus we find Solomon speaking when addressing the Most High: "The heavens and the heaven of heavens cannot contain thee, השמים ושמי השמים *hashshamayim ushemey hashshamayim*, 1 Kings viii. 27. Six *heavens* are necessarily implied in these *three* words. According to the *points*, the *first* and *third* are in the *dual* number, and the *second* is the *contracted form* of the plural. But how many more *spheres* may be intended who can tell? There may be millions of millions of *stellar systems* in unlimited space; and then what are all these to the VAST IMMENSITY *of God!*

Hath founded his troop in the earth] אגדתו *aguddatho*, from אגד *agad*, to *bind* or *gather together*, possibly meaning the *seas* and other *collections of waters* which he has *gathered together* and *bound* by his perpetual decree, that they cannot pass; yet when *he calleth for* these very *waters*, as in the *general deluge*, he "poureth them out upon the face of the earth."

The Lord is *his name.*] This points out his *infinite essence.* But what is that essence? and what is his nature? and what his immensity and eternity? What archangel can tell?

Verse 7. *Children of the Ethiopians*] Or *Cushites.* Cush was the son of Ham, Gen. x. 6; and his descendants inhabited a part of Arabia Petræa and Arabia Felix. All this stock was universally despised. See *Bochart.*

A. M. cir. 3217
B. C. cir. 787
Ante U. C. 34
Amulii Sylvii,
R. Alban.,
cir. annum 10

unto me, O children of Israel? saith the LORD. Have not I brought up Israel out of the land of Egypt? and the [r]Philistines from [s]Caphtor, and the Syrians from [t]Kir?

8 Behold, [u]the eyes of the Lord GOD *are* upon the sinful kingdom, and I [v]will destroy it from off the face of the earth; saving that I will not utterly destroy the house of Jacob, saith the LORD.

9 For, lo, I will command, and I will [w]sift the house of Israel among all nations, like as *corn* is sifted in a sieve, yet shall not the least [x]grain fall upon the earth.

A. M. cir. 3217
B. C. cir. 787
Ante U. C. 34
Amulii Sylvii,
R. Alban.,
cir. annum 10

10 All the sinners of my people shall die by the sword, [y]which say, The evil shall not overtake nor prevent us.

11 [z]In that day will I raise up the tabernacle of David that is fallen, and [a]close up the breaches thereof; and I will raise up his ruins, and I will build it as in the days of old:

12 [b]That they may possess the remnant of

[r]Jer. xlvii. 4——[s]Deut. ii. 23; Jer. xlvii. 4——[t]Ch. i. 5
[u]Ver. 4——[v]Jer. xxx. 11; xxxi. 35, 36; Obad. 16, 17

[w]Heb. *cause to move*——[x]Heb. *stone*——[y]Chap. vi. 3
[z]Acts xv. 16, 17——[a]Heb. *hedge*, or *wall*——[b]Obad. 19

The Philistines from Caphtor] The island of *Crete*, the people of which were the *Cherethim*. See 1 Sam. xxx. 14; Ezek. xxv. 16; Zeph. ii. 5.

The Syrians from Kir?] Perhaps a city of the *Medes*, Isa. xxii. 6. *Aram*, from whom Syria had its name, was the son of *Shem*, Gen. x. 22. Part of his descendants settled in this city, and part in *Aram Naharaim*, "Syria of the two rivers," viz., *Mesopotamia*, included between the *Tigris* and the *Euphrates*.

The meaning of the verse is this: Do not presume on my having brought you out of the land of Egypt and house of bondage, into a land flowing with milk and honey. I have brought other nations, and some of your neighbours, who are your enemies, from comparatively barren countries, into fruitful territories; such, for instance, as the *Philistines* from *Caphtor*, and the *Syrians* from *Kir*.

Verse 8. *The eyes of the Lord God* are *upon the sinful kingdom*] The kingdom of Israel, peculiarly sinful; and therefore to be signally destroyed by the Assyrians.

I will not utterly destroy the house of Jacob] The race shall not become extinct: I will reserve them as monuments of my *justice*, and finally of my *mercy*.

Verse 9. *I will sift the house of Israel among all nations*] I will disperse them over the face of the earth; and yet I will so order it that the *good* shall not be *lost;* for though they shall be mixed among distant nations, yet there shall be a general restoration of them to their own land.

The least grain] צרור *tseror*, little stone, pebble, or gravel. Not one of them, howsoever little or contemptible, when the time comes, shall be left behind. All shall be collected in Christ, and brought into their own land.

Verse 10. *All the sinners of my people*] Those who are the boldest and most incredulous; especially they who *despise* my warnings, and *say the evil day shall not overtake nor prevent us;* they shall die by the sword. It is no evidence of a man's safety that he is *presumptuously fearless*. There is a blessing to him who *trembles at God's word*.

Verse 11. *Will I raise up the tabernacle of David*] It is well known that the *kingdom of Israel*, the most profane and idolatrous, fell first, and that the *kingdom of Judah* continued long after, and enjoyed considerable prosperity under Hezekiah and Josiah. The remnant of the Israelites that were left by the Assyrians became united to the kingdom of Judah; and of the others, many afterwards joined them: but this comparatively short prosperity and respite, previously to the Babylonish captivity, could not be *that*, as *Calmet* justly observes, which is mentioned here. This could not be called *closing up the breaches, raising up the ruins, and building it as in the days of old;* nor has any state of this kind taken place since; and, consequently, the prophecy remains to be fulfilled. It must therefore refer to *their restoration under the Gospel*, when they shall receive the Lord Jesus as their Messiah, and be by him restored to their own land. See these words quoted by James, Acts xv. 17. Then indeed it is likely that they shall possess the *remnant of Edom*, and have the whole length and breadth of Immanuel's land, ver. 12. Nor can it be supposed that the victories gained by the *Asmoneans* could be that intended by the prophet, and which he describes in such lofty terms. These victories procured only a short respite, and a very imperfect re-establishment of the tabernacle of David; and could not warrant the terms of the prediction in these verses.

Verse 12. *That they may possess the remnant of Edom*] Bp. *Newcome* translates this clause as follows: "That the residue of men may seek Jehovah, and all the heathen who are called by my name. Here, instead of אדום *Edom*, he reads אדם *Adam, men* or *mankind*, which is the reading of the *Arabic*, and some MSS. of the *Syriac*, and of Acts xv. 17.

The Pachomian MS. of the *Septuagint* adds here, ὅπως ἐκζητήσωσι με, *that they may seek me*. And the *Arabic* has الرب *the Lord;* and instead of יירשו *yireshu*, "they shall possess," the learned bishop seems to have read ידרשו *yidreshu*, "they may seek;" and thus the text resembles the quotation by St. James, Acts xv. 17, "That the residue of men might seek after the Lord." It is strange that not one of the MSS. collated by *Kennicott* and *De Rossi*, nor any of my *own*, favours or countenances any of these alterations. I am of opinion, therefore, that we must dismiss all these conjectural emendations, and take the *Hebrew* text as we find it. That it speaks of the *conversion of the Jews* in Gospel times, we have the authority of the New Testament as above to prove; and if

A. M. cir. 3217 B. C. cir. 787 Ante U. C. 34 Amulii Sylvii, R. Alban., cir. annum 10

[c]Edom, and of all the heathen, [d]which are called by my name, saith the LORD that doeth this.

13 Behold [e]the days come, saith the LORD, that the ploughman shall overtake the reaper, and the treader of grapes him that [f]soweth seed; [g]and the mountains shall drop [h]sweet wine, and all the hills shall melt.

14 [i]And I will bring again the captivity of my people of Israel, and [k]they shall build the waste cities, and inhabit *them;* and they shall plant vineyards, and drink the wine thereof; they shall also make gardens, and eat the fruit of them.

15 And I will plant them upon their land, and [l]they shall no more be pulled up out of their land which I have given them, saith the LORD thy God.

---

[c]Num. xxiv. 18——[d]Heb. *upon whom my name is called*——[e]Lev. xxvi. 5——[f]Heb. *draweth forth*——[g]Joel iii. 18——[h]Or, *new wine*

[i]Jer. xxx. 3——[k]Isa. lxi. 4; lxv. 21; Ezek. xxxvi. 33-36——[l]Isa. lx. 21; Jer. xxxii. 41; Ezek. xxxiv. 28; Joel iii. 20

---

we cannot make the *words*, as they stand *there, entirely* to agree with the words here, the *subject* is not affected by it. The Jews shall *be converted and restored*, and this text in both covenants is a proof of it.

Verse 13. *The ploughman shall overtake the reaper*] All the seasons shall succeed in due and natural order: but the crops shall be so copious in the fields and in the vineyards, that a long time shall be employed in gathering and disposing of them; so that the seasons of *ploughing, sowing, gathering the grapes, treading the wine-press*, &c., *shall press on the heels of each other;* so *vast* will be the abundance, and so *long* the time necessary to *gather* and *cure* the *grain* and *fruits*. We are informed by travellers in the Holy Land, Barbary, &c., that the vintage at Aleppo lasts from the *fifteenth* of September to the middle of November; and that the sowing season begins at the close of October, and lasts through all November. Here, then, the ploughman, sower, grape-gatherer, and operator at the wine-press, not only succeed each other, but have parts of these operations *going on at the same time.* But great fertility in the land, abundance in the crops, and regularity of the seasons, seem to be the things which the prophet especially predicts. These are all *poetical* and *prophetical* images, by which happy *times* are pointed out.

Verse 14. *They shall plant vineyards, and drink the wine*] When threatened with *great evils*, chap. v. 11, it is said, "They shall plant pleasant vineyards but shall not drink the wine of them." *Previously* to their *restoration*, they shall labour for *others; after* their restoration, they shall labour for *themselves.*

Verse 15. *I will plant them upon their land*] They shall receive a permanent establishment there.

And they shall no more be pulled up] Most certainly this prophecy has never yet been fulfilled. They were *pulled out* by the *Assyrian captivity*, and by that of *Babylon*. Many were *planted in again*, and again *pulled out* by the *Roman conquest* and *captivity*, and were *never since planted in*, but are now *scattered* among all the nations of the earth. I conclude, as the word of God cannot fail, and this has not yet been fulfilled, it therefore follows that it will and must be fulfilled to the fulness of its spirit and intention. And this is established by the conclusion: "Saith the Lord thy God." He is JEHOVAH, and cannot fail; he is THY GOD, and will do it. He *can* do it, because he is JEHOVAH; and he *will* do it, because he is THY GOD. Amen.

THE BOOK

OF THE

PROPHET OBADIAH

Chronological Notes relative to this book, upon the supposition that it was written about five hundred and eighty-seven *years before the commencement of the Christian era*

Year from the Creation, according to Archbishop Usher, 3417.—Year of the Jewish era of the world, 3174. —Year since the Flood, 1761.—Year from the vocation of Abram, 1335.—Year from the foundation of Solomon's temple, 425. Year since the division of Solomon's monarchy into the kingdoms of Israel and Judah, 389.—Year of the era of Iphitus, 298.—Second year of the *forty-eighth* Olympiad.—Year from the building of Rome, according to the Varronian or generally received computation, 167.—Year from the building of Rome, according to the Fasti Consulares, 166.—Year from the building of Rome, according to Polybius the historian, 165.—Year from the building of Rome, according to Fabius Pictor, 161.—Year since the overthrow of the kingdom of Israel by Shalmaneser, king of Assyria, 135.—Year since the destruction of the kingdom of Judah by Nebuchadnezzar, king of Babylon, 2.—Year of the Julian Period, 4127.—Year of the era of Nabonassar, 161.—Year before the birth of Christ, 583.—Year before the vulgar era of Christ's nativity, 587.—Cycle of the Sun, 11.—Cycle of the Moon, 4.—Thirtieth year of Tarquinius Priscus, the fifth king of the Romans.—Thirty-ninth year of Cyaraxes or Cyaxares, the fourth king of Media.—Nineteenth year of Agasicles, king of Lacedæmon of the family of the Proclidæ.—Twenty-first year of Leon, king of Lacedæmon, of the family of the Eurysthenidæ.—Thirty-third year of Alyattes II., king of Lydia.—Sixteenth year of Æropas, the seventh king of Macedon.—Eighth year of Apries, king of Egypt; the same with the celebrated Pharaoh-hophrah.—Ninth year of Baal, king of the Tyrians.—Twentieth year of Nebuchadnezzar, king of Babylon.

OBADIAH

God is here represented as summoning the nations against Edom, and declaring that his strongholds should not save him, 1–4; *that not a remnant, not a gleaning, should be left of him,* 5; *that the enemy would search out his people, and totally subdue them; and that none of their allies should stand by them,* 6–9. *He then enlarges on their particular offence, and threatens them with a speedy recompense,* 10–16. *The Babylonians accordingly subdued the Edomites, and expelled them from Arabia Petræa, of which they never afterwards recovered possession. The remaining verses contain a prophecy of the restoration of the Jews from the Babylonish captivity, and of their victory over all their enemies,* 17–21. *Some commentators think that these last verses were fulfilled by the conquests of the Maccabees over the Edomites. See* 1 Macc. v. 3–5, 65, &c.

A. M. cir. 3417
B. C. cir. 587
Ol. XLVIII. 2
TarquiniiPrisci, R. Roman., cir. annum 30

THE vision of Obadiah. Thus saith the Lord GOD [a]concerning Edom; [b]We have heard a rumour from the LORD, and an ambassador is sent among the heathen, Arise ye, and let us rise up against her in battle.

[a]Isa. xxi. 11; xxxiv. 5; Ezek. xxv. 12, 13, 14; Joel iii. 19; Mal. i. 3——[b]Jer. xlix. 14, &c.

Who was this prophet? *where* born? of *what country?* at *what time* did he prophesy? *who* were his *parents? when* and *where* did he *die?* are questions which have been asked from the remotest antiquity; and which, to this day, have received no answer worthy of recording. There is a multitude of opinions concerning these points; and their *multitude* and *discrepancy* are the strongest proofs of their *uncertainty.* All that seems probable is, that, as he prophesied concerning the *destruction of Edom,* he flourished a little before, or a little after, the

A. M. cir. 3417
B. C. cir. 587
Ol. XLVIII. 2
TarquiniiPrisci,
R. Roman.,
cir. annum 30

2 Behold, I have made thee
small among the heathen: thou
art greatly despised.
3 The pride of thine heart hath
deceived thee, thou that dwellest in the clefts
[c]of the rock, whose habitation *is* high; [d]that
saith in his heart, Who shall bring me down
to the ground?
4 [e]Though thou exalt *thyself* as the eagle,
and though thou [f]set thy nest among the stars,
thence will I bring thee down, saith the LORD.
5 If [g]thieves came to thee, if robbers by
night, (how art thou cut off!) would they not
have stolen till they had
enough? if the grape-gatherers
came to thee, [h]would they not
leave [i]*some* grapes?

A. M. cir. 3417
B. C. cir. 587
Ol. XLVIII. 2
TarquiniiPrisci,
R. Roman.,
cir. annum 30

6 How are *the things* of Esau searched out!
how are his hidden things sought up!
7 All the men of thy confederacy have
brought thee *even* to the border: [k]the [l]men
that were at peace with thee have deceived
thee, *and* prevailed against thee; [m]*they
that eat* thy bread have laid a wound under
thee: [n]*there is* none understanding [o]in
him.

[c]2 Kings xiv. 7——[d]Isa. xiv. 13, 14, 15; Rev. xviii. 7——[e]Job xx. 6; Jer. xlix. 16; li. 53; Amos ix. 2——[f]Isa. xiv. 13; Nah. iii. 16; Hab. ii. 9——[g]Jer. xlix. 9

[h]Deut. xxiv. 21; Isa. xvii. 6; xxiv. 13——[i]Or, *gleanings*——[k]Heb. *the men of thy peace*——[l]Jer. xxxviii. 22——[m]Heb. the men *of thy bread*——[n]Isa. xix. 11, 12——[o]Or, *of it*

taking of Jerusalem by Nebuchadnezzar, which happened about *five hundred and eighty-eight* years before Christ; and the destruction of Idumea by the same monarch, which took place a short time after; probably between 588 B. C. and 575 B. C., in the interval of the *thirteen* years which Nebuchadnezzar employed in the siege of Tyre, which he undertook immediately after the capture of Jerusalem.

Obadiah foretells the subduction of the Idumeans by the Chaldeans, and finally by the Jews, whom they had used most cruelly when brought low by other enemies. These prophecies have been literally fulfilled for the Idumeans, as a nation, are totally extinct.

Whoever will be at the trouble to collate this short prophecy with the *forty-ninth* chapter of Jeremiah, will find a remarkable *similarity*, not only in the *sentiments* and *words*, but also in *whole verses*. In the above chapter Jeremiah predicts the destruction of the Idumeans. Whether he copied *Obadiah*, or *Obadiah* copied him, cannot be determined; but it would be very strange if two prophets, unacquainted with each other, should speak of the same event precisely in the same terms. See the parallel texts in the margin, and the notes on Jer. xlix. 1, &c.

NOTES ON THE BOOK OF OBADIAH

Verse 1. *We have heard a rumour*] See Jer. xlix. 14, where the same expressions are found. The prophet shows that the enemies of Idumea had confederated against it, and that Jehovah is now summoning them to march directly against it.

Verse 2. *I have made thee small among the heathen*] God ever attributes to *himself* the *rise and fall of nations*. If they be *great* and *prosperous*, it is by God's *providence;* if they be *low* and *depressed*, it is by his *justice*. Compared with the Assyrians, Chaldeans, Egyptians, Syrians, Arabs, and other neighbouring nations, the Idumeans were a small people.

Verse 3. *The pride of thine heart*] St. Jerome observes that all the southern part of Palestine, from Eleutheropolis to Petra and Aialath, was full of *caverns hewn out of the rocks*, and that the people had subterranean dwellings similar to ovens. Here they are said to *dwell in the clefts of the rock*, in reference to the caverns above mentioned. In these they conceived themselves to be *safe*, and thought that no power brought against them could dislodge them from those fastnesses. Some think that by סלע *sela, rock, Petra*, the capital of Idumea, is intended.

Verse 4. *Though thou exalt* thyself *as the eagle*] Though like this bird thou get into the *highest cliff of the highest rock*, it will not avail thee. To defend thee, when Jehovah has determined thy destruction, thy *deepest caves* and *highest rocks* will be equally useless. See Jer. xlix. 16.

Verse 5. *If thieves came to thee*] That is, if *thieves* entered thy dwellings, they would not have taken every thing; they would have laid hold on thy wealth; and carried off as much as they could escape with conveniently; if *grape-gatherers* entered thy vineyards, they would not have taken *every bunch;* some *gleanings* would have been left. But the Chaldeans have stripped thee bare; they *have searched out all thy hidden things*, ver. 6, they have left thee nothing. *How art thou cut off!* Thou art totally and irretrievably ruined! The prophet speaks of this desolation as if it had *already taken place*.

Verse 7. *All the men of thy confederacy*] The Chaldeans are here intended, to whom the Idumeans were attached, and whose agents they became in exercising cruelties upon the Jews.

Have brought thee even *to the border*] Have hemmed thee in on every side, and reduced thee to distress. Or, they have driven thee to thy border; cast thee out of thy own land into the hands of thine enemies.

The men that were at peace with thee] The men of *thy covenant*, with whom thou hadst made a *league*.

That eat *thy bread*] That professed to be thy *firmest friends*, have all joined together to destroy thee.

Have laid a wound] Placed a snare or trap *under thee*. See *Newcome*.

There is *none understanding in him*.] Private counsels and public plans are all in operation against thee; and yet thou art so foolish and infatuated as not to discern thy own danger.

A. M. cir. 3417 B. C. cir. 587 Ol. XLVIII. 2 TarquiniiPrisci, R. Roman., cir. annum 30

8 [p]Shall I not in that day,
saith the LORD, even destroy the
wise *men* out of Edom, and understanding out of the mount
of Esau?

9 And thy [q]mighty *men,* O [r]Teman, shall
be dismayed, to the end that every one of
the mount of Esau may be cut off by
slaughter.

10 For *thy* [s]violence against thy brother
Jacob shame shall cover thee, and [t]thou shalt
be cut off for ever.

11 In the day that thou stoodest on the other
side, in the day that the strangers [u]carried
away captive his forces, and foreigners entered into his gates, and [v]cast lots upon Jerusalem, even thou *wast* as one of them.

12 But [w]thou shouldest not have [x]looked
on [y]the day of thy brother in the day that he
became a stranger; neither shouldest thou have
[z]rejoiced over the children of Judah in the day
of their destruction; neither shouldest thou
have [a]spoken proudly in the day of distress.

13 Thou shouldest not have
entered into the gate of my people in the day of their calamity;
yea, thou shouldest not have
looked on their affliction in the day of their
calamity, nor have laid *hand* on their [b]sub-
stance in the day of their calamity.

14 Neither shouldest thou have stood in the
crossway, to cut off those of his that did escape; neither shouldest thou have [c]delivered
up those of his that did remain in the day of
distress.

15 [d]For the day of the LORD *is* near upon
all the heathen: [e]as thou hast done, it shall
be done unto thee: thy reward shall return
upon thine own head.

16 [f]For as ye have drunk upon my holy
mountain, *so* shall all the heathen drink continually, yea, they shall drink, and they shall
[g]swallow down, and they shall be as though
they had not been.

17 [h]But upon Mount Zion [i]shall be [k]de-
liverance, and [l]there shall be holiness; and the

[p]Job v. 12, 13; Isa. xxix. 14; Jer. xlix. 7——[q]Psa. lxxvi. 5; Amos ii. 16——[r]Jer. xlix. 7——[s]Gen. xxvii. 11; Psa. cxxxvii. 7; Ezek. xxv. 12; xxxv. 5; Amos i. 11——[t]Ezek. xxxv. 9; Mal. i. 4——[u]Or, *carried away his substance*——[v]Joel iii. 3; Nah. iii. 10——[w]Or, *do not behold, &c.*——[x]Psa. xxii. 17; liv. 7; lix. 10; Mic. iv. 11; vii. 10——[y]Psa. xxxvii. 13; cxxxvii. 7

[z]Job xxxi. 29; Mic. vii. 8; Prov. xvii. 5; xxiv. 17, 18——[a]Heb. *magnified thy mouth*——[b]Or, *forces*——[c]Or, *shut up;* Psa. xxxi. 8——[d]Ezek. xxx. 3; Joel iii. 14——[e]Ezek. xxxv. 15; Hab. ii. 8——[f]Jer. xxv. 28, 29; xlix. 12; Joel iii. 17; 1 Pet. iv. 17——[g]Or, *sup up*——[h]Joel ii. 32——[i]Amos ix. 8——[k]Or, *they that escape*——[l]Or, *it shall be holy;* Joel iii. 17

Verse 8. *Shall I not—destroy the wise* men] It appears, from Jer. xlix. 7, that the Edomites were remarkable for wisdom, counsel, and prudence. See on the above place.

Verse 9. *Thy mighty* men, *O Teman*] This was one of the strongest places in Idumea; and is put here, as in Amos i. 2, and elsewhere, for *Idumea* itself.

Mount of Esau] Mount *Seir.*

Verse 10. *For* thy *violence against thy brother Jacob*] By this term the *Israelites* in general are understood; for the *two* brothers,—*Jacob*, from whom sprang the *Jews*, and *Esau*, from whom sprang the *Idumeans* or *Edomites*,—are here put for the *whole people* or descendants of both. We need not look for particular cases of the *violence* of the Edomites against the Jews. *Esau*, their founder, was not more inimical to his brother *Jacob*, who deprived him of his birthright, than the *Edomites* uniformly were to the *Jews*. See 2 Chron. xxviii. 17, 18. They had even stimulated the Chaldeans, when they took Jerusalem, to destroy the temple, and level it with the ground. See Psa. cxxxvii. 7.

Verse 11. *Thou stoodest on the other side*] Thou not only didst not help thy brother when thou mightest, but thou didst assist his foes against him.

And cast lots] When the Chaldeans cast lots on the spoils of Jerusalem, thou didst come in for a share of the booty; "thou wast as one of them."

Verse 12. *Thou shouldest not have looked*] It shows a malevolent heart to rejoice in the miseries of those who have acted unkindly or wickedly towards us. The Edomites triumphed when they saw the judgments of God fall upon the Jews. This the Lord severely reprehends in verses 12-15. If a man have acted cruelly towards us, and God punish him for this cruelty, and we rejoice in it, we make his crime our own; and then, as we have done, so shall it be done unto us; see ver. 15. All these verses point out the part the Edomites took against the Jews when the Chaldeans besieged and took Jerusalem, destroyed the temple, and divided the spoils.

Verse 14. *Neither shouldest thou have stood in the crossway*] They are represented here as having stood in the *passes* and *defiles* to prevent the poor Jews from escaping from the Chaldeans. By *stopping these passes*, they threw the poor fugitives back into the teeth of their enemies. They had gone so far in this systematic cruelty as to deliver up the few that had taken refuge among them.

Verse 15. *The day of the Lord* is *near*] God will not associate thee with him in the judgments which he inflicts. *Thou* also art *guilty*, and shalt have *thy punishment* in due course with the other sinful nations.

Verse 16. *For as ye have drunk*] This address is to the *Jews*. As ye have been visited and punished upon my holy mountain in Jerusalem, so shall other nations be punished in their respective countries. See Jer. xlix. 12.

Verse 17. *But upon Mount Zion shall be de-*

A. M. cir. 3417
B. C. cir. 587
Ol. XLVIII. 2
TarquiniiPrisci,
R. Roman.,
cir. annum 30

house of Jacob shall possess their possessions.

18 And the house of Jacob [m]shall be a fire, and the house of Joseph a flame, and the house of Esau for stubble, and they shall kindle in them, and devour them; and there shall not be *any* remaining of the house of Esau; for the LORD hath spoken *it.*

19 And *they of* the south [n]shall possess the mount of Esau; [o]and *they of* the plain the Philistines: and they shall possess the fields of Ephraim, and the fields of Samaria: and Benjamin *shall possess* Gilead.

20 And the captivity of this host of the children of Israel *shall possess* that of the Canaanites, *even* [p]unto Zarephath; and the captivity of Jerusalem, [q]which *is* in Sepharad, [r]shall possess the cities of the south.

21 And [s]saviours shall come up on Mount Zion to judge the mount of Esau; and the [t]kingdom shall be the LORD'S.

---

[m]Isa. x. 17; Zech. xii. 6——[n]Amos ix. 12——[o]Zeph. ii. 7——[p]1 Kings xvii. 9, 10——[q]Or, shall possess *that which* is *in Sepharad*

[r]Jer. xxxii. 44——[s]1 Tim. iv. 16; James v. 20——[t]Psa. xxii. 28; Dan. ii. 44; vii. 14, 27; Zech. xiv. 9; Luke i. 33; Rev. xi. 15; xix. 6

---

liverance] Here is a promise of the return from the Babylonish captivity. They shall come to *Zion*, and there they shall *find safety;* and it is remarkable that after their return they were greatly befriended by the Persian kings, and by Alexander the Great and his successors; so that, whilst they ravaged the neighbouring nations, the Jews were unmolested. See *Calmet.*

And there shall be holiness] They shall return to God, separate themselves from their idols, and become a better people than they were when God permitted them to be carried into captivity.

The house of Jacob shall possess] They were restored to their former possessions. But this may refer also to their future restoration under the Gospel, when they shall be truly converted, and become holiness to the Lord; for *salvation* and *holiness* shall be the characteristics of *Zion*—the *Christian Church*, for ever.

Verse 18. *The house of Jacob shall be a fire*] After their return from captivity, the *Jews*, called here the *house of Jacob* and the *house of Joseph*, did break out as a flame upon the Idumeans; they reduced them into slavery; and obliged them to receive circumcision, and practise the rites of the Jewish religion. See 1 Macc. v. 3, &c.; 2 Macc. x. 15-23; and *Joseph.* Antiq., lib. xiii. c. 17.

There shall not be any *remaining*] As a *people* and a *nation* they shall be totally destroyed. This is the meaning; it does not signify that *every individual* shall be destroyed.

Verse 19. They of *the south*] The Jews who possessed the *southern* part of *Palestine*, should render themselves masters of the mountains of Idumea which were contiguous to them.

They of *the plain*] From Eleutheropolis to the Mediterranean Sea. In this and the following verse the prophet shows the different districts which should be occupied by the Israelites after their return from Babylon.

The fields of Samaria] Alexander the Great gave Samaria to the Jews; and John Hyrcanus subdued the same country after his wars with the Syrians. See *Josephus*, contra. App. lib. ii., and Antiq. lib. xiii., c. 18.

Benjamin shall possess *Gilead.*] *Edom* lay to the *south;* the *Philistines* to the *west; Ephraim* to the *north;* and *Gilead* to the *east.* Those who returned from Babylon were to extend themselves everywhere. See *Newcome;* and see, for the fulfilment, 1 Macc. v. 9, 35, 45; and ix. 35, 36.

Verse 20. *Zarephath*] Sarepta, a city of the Sidonians, 1 Kings xvii. 9. That is, they should possess the whole city of *Phœnicia*, called here that of the *Canaanites.*

Which is *in Sepharad*] This is a difficult word. Some think the *Bosphorus* is meant; others, *Spain;* others, *France;* others, the *Euphrates;* others, some district in *Chaldea;* for there was a city called *Siphora*, in *Mesopotamia*, above the division of the Euphrates. Dr. *Lightfoot* says it was a part of *Edom.* Those who were captives among the Canaanites should possess the country of the *Canaanites;* and those whom the *Edomites* had enslaved should possess the cities of their masters. See *Newcome* and *Lowth.*

Verse 21. *And saviours shall come up*] Certain persons whom God may choose to be *deliverers* of his people; such as *Zerubbabel, Ezra, Nehemiah*, and the *Maccabees.*

Some think these *saviours*, מושיעים *moshiim*, mean the *apostles* of our Lord. Several MSS. have מושעים *mushaim*, the *preserved;* those *that are saved*, i. e., they who were *delivered* from the captivity; and *those of Mount Zion* shall *judge*, that is, shall *execute judgment* on the Edomites. And as the Asmonean princes joined the *priesthood* to the *state*, it might be what the prophet means when he says, "the kingdom shall be the Lord's," the high priest having both the *civil* and *ecclesiastical power* in his own hands. And these actually were masters of Edom, and judged and *governed* the *mountain of Esau.* And thus this prophecy appears to have had a very literal fulfilment.

But if we take the whole as referring to the *times of the Gospel*, which I believe is not its *primary* sense, it may signify the conversion and restoration of the Jews, and that under JESUS CHRIST the original *theocracy* shall be restored; and thus, once more, in the promised land, it may be said,—

והיתה ליהוה המלוכה

hammeluchah laihovah vehayethah.

"And the kingdom shall belong to Jehovah."

INTRODUCTION TO THE BOOK

OF THE

PROPHET JONAH

JONAH, the son of Amittai, the *fifth* of the minor prophets, was a Galilean, a native of Gath-hepher, which is believed to be the same as Jotapata, celebrated for the siege which Josephus the historian there maintained against the Roman army, a little before the destruction of Jerusalem. Gath-hepher was situated in the land of Zebulon, where was the canton of Ophir or Hepher. St. Jerome places it *two* miles from Sepphoris, in the way towards Tiberias. Some rabbins are of opinion that Jonah was the widow of Sarepta's son, restored to life by Elijah.

What we know with certainty of Jonah is, that God having commanded him to go to Nineveh, and there proclaim that the cry of the inhabitants' sins was come up to heaven, and they were threatened with approaching ruin; instead of obeying these orders, he resolved to flee away, and go to Tarsus in Cilicia. For this purpose he embarked at Joppa; but the Lord having sent a violent tempest while he was upon the sea, the mariners, with great fear, cried each of them to his god. In the meantime Jonah slept in the hold; whereupon the pilot wakened him; and they who were in the ship cast lots to know how this tempest was occasioned. The lot falling upon Jonah, they asked him who he was, and what he had done to bring upon them such a storm? He told them he was a Hebrew; that he worshipped the God of heaven; was one of his prophets; and fled from his presence to avoid going to Nineveh, whither he was sent. They asked him what was to be done to secure them from shipwreck? He replied: Throw me into the sea, and the tempest will cease.

God prepared a great fish to swallow up Jonah. This fish, according to some, was a whale; or, as others say, the lamia, *canis carcharias*, or the sea-dog. The prophet continued in the fish *three* days and *three* nights. He cried unto the Lord, and the Lord heard him, and commanded the fish to cast him upon the shore, as it is believed, at the foot of a mountain which projects a great way into the sea, between Berytus and Tripoli. Others think it was upon the coast of Cilicia, *two* leagues north from Alexandretta.

After this the word of the Lord came a second time to Jonah, and directed him to go to Nineveh. When he came into the city, which was three days' journey in extent, about twenty-five leagues in circumference, Jonah walked up and down a whole day, crying out, "In forty days Nineveh shall be destroyed." The Ninevites believed his word; they appointed a public fast to be observed; and, from the meanest of the people to the greatest, covered themselves with sackcloth. The king of Nineveh, supposed to have been *Sardanapalus*, known in profane authors by the name of *Anacyndaraxa* or *Anabaxarus*, descended from his throne, and covered himself with sackcloth, and sat down upon ashes. God suffered himself to be moved with their repentance, and did not execute the sentence which he had pronounced against them.

Jonah was afflicted at this; and complained to God, saying, that he had always questioned whether, as being a God of clemency and mercy, he would not be flexible to their prayers.

After this, in all probability, Jonah returned from Nineveh into Judea.

The Greeks have for a long time expressed their veneration for Jonah. There was a church dedicated to this prophet in the sixth age.

We do not know when it was that Jonah foretold how Jeroboam II., king of Israel, should restore the kingdom of Samaria to its former extent, from the entrance of Hamath to the Dead Sea. Whether this was before or after his going to Nineveh, we cannot tell.

Our Saviour makes frequent mention of Jonah in the Gospels. He says that the Ninevites shall one day rise in judgment against the Jews, and condemn them, because they repented at the preaching of Jonah, and the Jews would not hearken to Him who was greater than Jonah. And when the Pharisees required a sign of him to prove his mission, he said he would give them no other than that of the prophet Jonah, that is to say, of his resurrection, which would complete all his miracles, and render the Jews inexcusable in their hardness of heart. For a discussion of the question concerning the *three days and three nights* which Jonah lay in the belly of the fish, see Matt. xii. 40, and the notes there. And for Oriental and Jewish *legends* and *fabulous relations* relative to the history of this prophet, see *Calmet* in his preface to this book.

That there are *difficulties* in this book every man must allow; and that learned men have differed greatly in their mode of interpreting the book, and explaining these difficulties, is well known. Some have considered it an *allegory;* referring entirely to Manasseh, and what was done *before, during,* and *after* the war with Esar-haddon, king of Assyria. Manasseh being taken prisoner by the Assyrians, and thrust into a *dungeon;* where, having lain *three days and three nights,* on his earnest prayer to God in the dungeon, he was delivered, &c. Others have thought, that instead of a *fish,* a *ship* is meant, which had the image of a *whale* on the *stern,* and might be called Κητος, or the *whale.* Others have thought that the whole of the account of Jonah's being swallowed by a great fish, his praying in its belly, and being cast on dry land, was a *dream* which he had while *fast asleep* in the ship. See chap. i. 5. And others state that the whole book is a *parable,* intending to point out God's *justice* and *mercy,* and how prevalent *repentance* is to turn aside the threatened stroke of Divine wrath.

There is a *fable,* most probably of Phœnician origin, which, bearing some similitude to the history of Jonah, may have been taken from this book. Laomedon, king of Troy, having displeased Neptune, to appease him, was required to expose his daughter *Hesione* to be devoured by a *sea-monster.* She was chained to a rock, and was awaiting her fate at the next flux of the tide. In the interim *Hercules* slew the sea-monster, and delivered the princess. To this *Lycophron,* in his *Cassandra,* ver. 33, &c., is supposed to allude:—

Τριεσπερου λεοντος, ὁν ποτε γναθοις
Τριτωνος ημαλαψε καρχαρος κυων.

"Of the lion the offspring of three nights, which the fierce dog of Triton swallowed down greedily."

The scholiasts explain this in the following manner: While the princess was standing chained to the rock, expecting the greedy dog (καρχαρος κυων, the *shark*) to come and devour her, Hercules stood by ready armed; and when the monster came forward with open mouth, he jumped directly down his throat, and spent *three days* in cutting and hacking his entrails; and afterwards *came out of the monster,* with the loss of all the hair on his head. *Cyril,* in his comment, says this was occasioned by the *incredible heat* of the *monster's stomach.*

This *fable* might have been easily taken from the *true history;* though some have been ready enough to intimate that the history of the prophet was taken from the *fable.*

The appeal made to the *main facts* of this history by our Lord, proves that we are to admit of no *allegorical* exposition of these facts. 1. There was such a person as Jonah. 2. He was swallowed by a sea-monster, in whose belly he was miraculously preserved three days and three nights. 3. This same prophet preached to the Ninevites; and they repented, and turned from their sins, under his ministry. This testimony puts an end to all mythological, allegorical, and hypothetical interpretations of those great facts. And in its literal sense alone, I undertake the interpretation of this book.

THE BOOK

OF THE

PROPHET JONAH

Chronological Notes relative to this Book, upon the supposition that the repentance of the Ninevites happened in the twenty-third year of the reign of Jehu, king of Israel

Year from the Creation, according to Archbishop Usher, 3142.—Year of the Julian Period, 3852.—Year since the Flood, 1486.—Year from the foundation of Solomon's temple, 150.—Year since the division of Solomon's monarchy into the kingdoms of Israel and Judah, 114.—Year before the *first* Olympiad, 86.—Year before the building of Rome, according to the Varronian computation, 109.—Year before the birth of Jesus Christ, 858.—Year before the vulgar era of Christ's nativity, 862.—Twelfth year of Charilaus, king of Lacedæmon, of the family of the Proclidæ.—Fifty-second year of Archelaus, king of Lacedæmon, of the family of the Eurysthenidæ.—Second year of Phereclus, perpetual archon of the Athenians.—Fourteenth year of Alladius Sylvius, king of the Albans.—Twenty-third year of Jehu, king of Israel.—Seventeenth year of Joash, king of Judah.

CHAPTER I

Jonah, sent to Nineveh, flees to Tarshish, 1–3. *He is overtaken by a great tempest,* 4–14; *thrown into the sea,* 15, 16; *and swallowed by a fish, in the belly of which he is miraculously preserved alive three days and three nights,* 17.

A. M. cir. 3142
B. C. cir. 862
Ante U. C. 109
Alladii Sylvii, R. Alban., cir. annum 14

NOW the word of the LORD
came unto [a]Jonah [b]the son
of Amittai, saying,
2 Arise, go to Nineveh, that
[c]great city, and cry against it;
for [d]their wickedness is come
up before me.
3 But Jonah [e]rose up to flee

[a]2 Kings xiv. 25——[b]Called, Matt. xii. 39, *Jonas*
[c]Gen. x. 11, 12; chap. iii. 2, 3; iv. 11
[d]Gen. xviii. 20, 21; Ezra ix. 6; James v. 4; Rev. xviii. 5
[e]Chap. iv. 2

NOTES ON CHAP. I

Verse 1. *Now the word of the Lord came unto Jonah*] All that is certainly known about this prophet has already been laid before the reader. He was of Gath-hepher, in the tribe of Zebulun, in lower Galilee, Josh. xix. 13; and he prophesied in the reigns of Jeroboam the Second, and Joash, kings of Israel. Jeroboam came to the throne *eight hundred and twenty-three* years before the Christian era, and reigned in Samaria *forty-one* years, 2 Kings xiv. 23-25. As a prophet, it is likely that he had but this one mission.

Verse 2. *Go to Nineveh*] This was the capital of the Assyrian empire, and one of the most *ancient* cities of the world, Gen. x. 10; and one of the *largest*, as it was *three days' journey in circumference*. Ancient writers represent it as *oblong;* being in length *one hundred and fifty* stadia, and *ninety* in breadth, the compass being *four hundred and eighty* stadia. Now as the *stadium* is allowed to have been equal to our *furlong*, eight of which make a mile, this amounts to *fifty-four* English miles: see on chap. iii. 3. But we must not suppose that all this *space* was covered with compact streets and buildings; it took in a considerable space of country, probably all the cultivated ground necessary to support all the inhabitants of that district. *Calmet* computes the measurement of the circumference to be equal to *twenty-five* French leagues. It is reported to have had walls *one hundred feet high*, and so *broad* that *three chariots* might run abreast upon them. It was situated on the *Tigris*, or a little to the *west*, or on the west *side* of that river. It was well peopled, and had at this time *one hundred and twenty thousand* persons in it reputed to be in a state of infancy, which on a moderate computation would make the whole number *six hundred thousand* persons. But some, supposing that persons not being able to distinguish their right hand from their left must mean *children under two years* of age, and reckoning *one* such child for every *twenty* persons from that age upwards, make the population amount to *two millions five hundred thousand.* Nor can this be considered an exaggerated estimate, when we know that London, not one-tenth of the size of ancient Nineveh, contains a population of upwards of *one million.* But calcula-

A. M. cir. 3142 B. C. cir. 862 Ante U. C. 109 Alladii Sylvii, R. Alban., cir. annum 14

unto [f]Tarshish from the presence of the LORD, and went down to [g]Joppa; and he found a ship going to Tarshish: so he paid the fare thereof, and went down into it, to go with them unto Tarshish [h]from the presence of the LORD.

4 But [i]the LORD [k]sent out a great wind into the sea, and there was a mighty tempest in the sea, so that the ship [l]was like to be broken.

5 Then the mariners were afraid, and cried every man unto his god, and [m]cast forth the wares that *were* in the ship into the sea, to lighten *it* of them. But Jonah was gone down [n]into the sides of ship; and he lay, and was fast asleep.

6 So the shipmaster came to him, and said unto him, What meanest thou, O sleeper? arise, [o]call upon thy God, [p]if so be that God will think upon us, that we perish not.

7 And they said every one to his fellow, Come, and let us [q]cast lots, that we may know for whose cause this evil *is* upon us. So they cast lots, and the lot fell upon Jonah.

8 Then said they unto him, [r]Tell us, we pray thee, for whose cause this evil *is* upon us; What *is* thine occupation? and whence comest thou? what *is* thy country? and of what people *art* thou?

9 And he said unto them, I *am* a Hebrew; and I fear [s]the LORD, the God of heaven,

[f]1 Kings x. 22——[g]Josh. xix. 46; 2 Chron. ii. 16; Acts ix. 36——[h]Gen. iv. 16; Job i. 12; ii. 7——[i]Psa. cvii. 25 [k]Heb. *cast forth*——[l]Heb. *thought to be broken*——[m]So Acts xxvii. 18, 19, 38

[n]1 Samuel xxiv. 3——[o]Psa. cvii. 28——[p]Joel ii. 14 [q]Joshua vii. 14, 16; 1 Samuel x. 20, 21; xiv. 41, 42: Prov. xvi. 33; Acts i. 26——[r]Joshua vii. 19; 1 Samuel xiv. 43——[s]Or, *JEHOVAH*

tions of this kind, relative to matters of such remote antiquity, are generally precarious, and not very useful: and ancient authors, though the only guides, are not always safe conductors. *Mosul* is generally supposed to be the same as the ancient *Nineveh.* It is in the province of Dearbekir, on the west bank of the Tigris.

Their wickedness is come up before me.] This is a *personification* of evil. It ascends from earth to heaven; and stands before the Supreme Judge, to bear witness against its own delinquency, and that of the persons whom it has seduced.

Verse 3. *To flee unto Tarshish*] Some say *Tartessus*, in Spain, near the straits of Gibralter; others, *Tarsus*, in *Cilicia;* and others, *Taprobana*, or the island of Ceylon, formerly called Taprobah; and *Tabrobavagh* in Sanscrit, to the present day.

And went down to Joppa] This place is celebrated as that where *Andromeda*, daughter of *Cepheus*, was chained to a rock, and exposed to be devoured by a sea-monster, from which she was delivered by the valour of Perseus. It is the nearest port to Jerusalem on that side of the Mediterranean.

And he found a ship] The Phœnicians carried on a considerable trade with *Tartessus*, Ezek. xxvii. 12; and it was probably in one of their ships that Jonah *embarked.*

He paid the fare thereof] He paid for his *passage.* This shows that there was *traffic* between the two places, and that each passenger paid a stated *fare.*

From the presence of the Lord.] He considered that God was peculiarly resident in Judea; and if he got out of that land, the Lord would most probably appoint another prophet to carry the message; for Jonah appears to have considered the enterprise as difficult and dangerous, and therefore wished to avoid it.

Verse 4. *A great wind*] They were overtaken with a *storm*, which appears from the sequel to have come by the immediate direction of God.

Like to be broken] They had nearly suffered *shipwreck.*

Verse 5. *Cried every man unto his god*] The *ship's crew* were all heathens; and, it is probable, heathens who had each a different object of religious worship.

Cast forth the wares] Threw the *lading overboard* to lighten the ship, hoping the better to *ride out* the storm.

Jonah was gone down] Most probably into the *hold* or *cabin* under the deck; or where they had berths for passengers in the sides of the ship; something in the manner of our *packets.*

Was fast asleep.] Probably quite exhausted and overcome with distress, which in many cases terminates in a deep sleep. So the disciples in the garden of Gethsemane.

Verse 6. *The shipmaster*] Either the *captain* or the *pilot.*

Arise, call upon thy God] He supposed that Jonah had *his* god, as well as they had *theirs;* and that, as the danger was imminent, every man should use the influence he had, as they were all equally involved in it.

Verse 7. *Come, and let us cast lots*] This was a very ancient mode of endeavouring to find out the mind of Divine Providence; and in this case it proves that they supposed the storm to have arisen on account of some hidden crime of some person *aboard.*

A philosopher being at sea in a violent storm, when the *crew* began to call earnestly to the gods for safety, he said, "Be silent, and cease your prayers; for should the gods know that *you* are here, we shall all be lost."

The lot fell upon Jonah.] In this case God *directed the lot.*

Verse 8. *Tell us—for whose cause*] A very gentle method of bringing the charge home to himself, and the several questions here asked gave the utmost latitude to make the best of his own case.

Verse 9. *I fear the Lord*] In this Jonah was *faithful.* He gave an honest testimony concern-

A. M. cir. 3142
B. C. cir. 862
Ante U. C. 109
Alladii Sylvii,
R. Alban.,
cir. annum 14

[t]which hath made the sea and the dry *land.*

10 Then were the men [u]exceedingly afraid, and said unto him, Why hast thou done this? For the men knew that he fled from the presence of the LORD, because he had told them.

11 Then said they unto him, What shall we do unto thee, that the sea [v]may be calm unto us? for the sea [w]wrought, [x]and was tempestuous.

12 And he said unto them, [y]Take me up, and cast me forth into the sea; so shall the sea be calm unto you: for I know that for my sake this great tempest *is* upon you.

13 Nevertheless the men [z]rowed hard to bring *it* to the land; [a]but they could not: for the sea wrought, and was tempestuous against them.

A. M. cir. 3142
B. C. cir. 862
Ante U. C. 109
Alladii Sylvii,
R. Alban.,
cir. annum 14

14 Wherefore they cried unto the LORD, and said, We beseech thee, O LORD, we beseech thee, let us not perish for this man's life, and [b]lay not upon us innocent blood: for thou, O LORD, [c]hast done as it pleased thee.

15 So they took up Jonah, and cast him forth into the sea: [d]and the sea [e]ceased from her raging.

16 Then the men [f]feared the LORD exceedingly, and [g]offered a sacrifice unto the LORD, and made vows.

17 Now the LORD had prepared a great fish to swallow up Jonah. And [h]Jonah was in the [i]belly of the fish three days and three nights.

---

[t]Psa. cxlvi. 6; Acts xvii. 24——[u]Heb. *with great fear* [v]Heb. *may be silent from us*——[w]Or, *grew more and more tempestuous*——[x]Heb. *went*——[y]John xi. 50——[z]Heb. *digged*——[a]Prov. xxi. 30——[b]Deut. xxi. 8

[c]Psa. cxv. 3——[d]Psa. lxxxix. 9; Luke viii. 24 [e]Heb. *stood*——[f]Mark iv. 41; Acts v. 11——[g]Heb. *sacrificed a sacrifice unto the LORD, and vowed vows* [h]Matt. xii. 40; xvi. 4; Luke xi. 30——[i]Heb. *bowels*

---

ing the God he served, which placed him before the eyes of the sailors as infinitely higher than the objects of their adoration; for the God of Jonah *was the God of heaven, who made the sea and the dry land,* and governed both. He also honestly told them that he was *fleeing from the presence of this God,* whose honourable call he had refused to obey. See ver. 10.

Verse 11. *What shall we do unto thee*] In these poor men there was an uncommon degree of *humanity* and *tender feeling.*

Verse 12. *I know that for my sake*] I am not worthy to live; *throw me overboard.* God will not quiet the storm till I am cast out of the ship. Here was deep compunction; and honest avowal of sin; and a justification of the displeasure which God had now manifested.

Verse 13. *The men rowed hard*] Were very unwilling to proceed to this extremity, and thought they would risk every thing rather than cast this disobedient prophet into the great deep.

Verse 14. *They cried unto the Lord*] Under a conviction that he was the self-existing Being, the Maker of the heavens and the earth, and the author of the present storm, they put up their prayers to him.

Let us not perish for this man's life] They were now about to *cast him overboard;* but seemed to call God to witness that it was with the utmost reluctance, and only in obedience to his command. There is a parallel passage in the *Argonautics,* which has been quoted to illustrate this:—

Πολλα δε μερμηριζον ενι φρεσι πευκαλιμησι,
Η μεν αποφθισωσι, και ιχθυσι κυρμα βαλωσιν
Αινολεχη Μηδειαν, αποτρεψωσι δ' Ερινυν.
Ver. 1171.

"And much they doubted, in their prudent minds,
Whether to kill and cast a prey to fishes
Wretched Medea, and avert their fate."

See *Newcome.*

Verse 16. *Offered a sacrifice*] The first perhaps ever offered on board a vessel since the ark floated on the waters of the great deluge; and it is most probable that these heathens, witnessing what was done, became sincere converts to the true God.

Verse 17. *Now the Lord had prepared a great fish*] דג גדול *dag gadol.* This could not have been a *whale,* for the throat of that animal can scarcely admit a man's leg; but it might have been a *shark,* which abounds in the Mediterranean, and whose mouth and stomach are exceedingly capacious. In several cases they have been known to swallow a man when thrown overboard. See the note on Matt. xii. 40, where the whole subject of this verse is considered at large. That *days and nights* do not, among the Hebrews, signify *complete* days and nights of *twenty-four* hours, see Esth. iv. 16, compared with chap. v. 1; Judg. xiv. 17, 18. Our Lord lay in the grave *one* natural day, and part of *two* others; and it is most likely that this was the precise time that Jonah was in the fish's belly.

CHAPTER II

This chapter (except the first verse and the last, which make a part of the narrative) contains a beautiful prayer or hymn, formed of those devout thoughts which Jonah had in the belly of the great fish, with a thanksgiving for his miraculous deliverance.

A. M. cir. 3142
B. C. cir. 862
Ante U. C. 109
Alladii Sylvii,
R. Alban.,
cir. annum 14

THEN Jonah prayed unto the
LORD his God out of the
fish's belly,
2 And said, I [a]cried [b]by rea-
son of mine affliction unto the LORD, [c]and
he heard me: out of the belly of [d]hell cried
I, *and* thou heardest my voice.
3 [e]For thou hadst cast me into the deep, in
the [f]midst of the seas; and the floods compassed me about: [g]all thy billows and thy
waves passed over me.
4 [h]Then I said, I am cast out of thy sight;
yet I will look again [i]toward thy holy temple.
5 The [k]waters compassed me about, *even*
to the soul: the depth closed me round about,
the weeds were wrapped about my head.
6 I went down to the [l]bottoms
of the mountains; the earth
with her bars *was* about me for
ever: yet hast thou brought
up my life [m]from [n]corruption, O LORD my
God.
7 When my soul fainted within me I remembered the LORD: [o]and my prayer came
in unto thee, into thine holy temple.
8 They that observe [p]lying vanities forsake
their own mercy.
9 But I will [q]sacrifice unto thee with the
voice of thanksgiving; I will pay *that* that I
have vowed. [r]Salvation *is* of the LORD.
10 And the LORD spake unto the fish, and
it vomited out Jonah upon the dry *land*.

A. M. cir. 3142
B. C. cir. 862
Ante U. C. 109
Alladii Sylvii,
R. Alban.,
cir. annum 14

---

[a]Psa. cxx. 1; cxxx. 1; cxlii. 1; Lam. iii. 55, 56——[b]Or, *out of mine affliction*——[c]Psa. lxv. 2——[d]Or, *the grave;* Isa. xiv. 9——[e]Psa. lxxxviii. 6——[f]Heb. *heart*——[g]Psa. xlii. 7——[h]Psa. xxxi. 22——[i]1 Kings viii. 38

[k]Psa. lxix. 1; Lam. iii. 54——[l]Heb. *cuttings off*——[m]Psa. xvi. 10——[n]Or, *the pit*——[o]Psa. xviii. 6——[p]2 Kings xvii. 15; Psa. xxxi. 6; Jer. x. 8; xvi. 19——[q]Psa. l. 14, 23; cxvi. 17, 18; Hos. xiv. 2; Heb. xiii. 15——[r]Psa. iii. 8

NOTES ON CHAP. II

Verse 1. *Then Jonah prayed—out of the fish's belly*] This verse makes the *first* of the *second* chapter in the Hebrew text.

It may be asked, "How could Jonah either pray or breathe in the stomach of the fish?" Very easily, if God so willed it. And let the reader keep this constantly in view; the whole is a *miracle*, from Jonah's being swallowed by the fish till he was cast ashore by the same animal. It was God that had *prepared the great fish*. It was the *Lord that spake to the fish, and caused it to vomit Jonah upon the dry land*. ALL is miracle.

Verse 2. *Out of the belly of hell*] Among the Hebrews שאול *sheol* means the *grave*, any *deep pit*, the *place of separate spirits*, &c. Here the prophet represents himself as in the *bottom of the sea;* for so *sheol* must be understood in this place.

Verse 3. *All thy billows and thy waves passed over me.*] This may be understood *literally;* while the fish, in whose belly he was, sought its pleasure or sustenance in the paths of the deep, the waves and billows of the sea were rolling above. This line seems borrowed from Psa. xlii. 7.

Verse 4. *I am cast out of thy sight*] See Psa. xxxi. 22.

Thy holy temple.] Then Jerusalem was not yet destroyed, for the *temple* was standing.

Verse 5. *The waters compassed me about even to the soul*] So as to seem to deprive me of life. I had no hope left.

The weeds were wrapped about my head.] This may be understood literally also. He found himself in the fish's stomach, together with *sea weeds*, and such like marine substances, which the fish had taken for its aliment.

Verse 6. *I went down to the bottoms of the mountains*] This also may be literally understood. The fish followed the slanting base of the mountains, till they terminated in a plain at the bottom of the great deep.

The earth with her bars] He represents himself as a prisoner in a dungeon, closed in with *bars* which he could not remove, and which at first appeared to *be for ever*, i. e., the place where his life must terminate.

Yet hast thou brought up my life] The substance of this poetic prayer was composed while in the fish's belly; but afterwards the prophet appears to have thrown it into its present poetic form, and to have added some circumstances, such as that before us; for he now speaks of his deliverance from this imminent danger of death. "Thou hast brought up my life from corruption."

Verse 7. *When my soul fainted*] When I had given up all hope of life.

My prayer came in unto thee] Here prayer is *personified*, and is represented as a *messenger* going from the *distressed*, and entering into the temple of God, and standing before him. This is a very fine and delicate image. This clause is one of those which I suppose the prophet to have added when he *penned* this prayer.

Verse 8. *They that observe lying vanities*] They that trust in idols, follow *vain predictions*, permit themselves to be influenced with *foolish fears*, so as to induce them to *leave the path of obvious duty, forsake their own mercy.* In leaving that God who is the *Fountain of mercy,* they abandon that *measure of mercy* which he had treasured up for them.

Verse 9. *But I will sacrifice unto thee*] I will make a sincere vow, which, as soon as my circumstances will permit, I will faithfully execute; and therefore he adds, "I will pay that which I have vowed."

Salvation is *of the Lord.*] All *deliverance* from *danger*, *preservation* of *life*, *recovery* from *sickness*, and *redemption* of the *soul* from the *power*, *guilt*, and *pollution* of sin, is from Jehovah. He *alone* is the *Saviour*, he *alone* is the *Deliverer;* for all *salvation* is *from the Lord.*

Verse 10. *And the Lord spake unto the fish*] That is, by his influence the fish swam to shore, and cast Jonah on the dry land. So the whole was a miracle from the beginning to the end; and we need not perplex ourselves to find out *literal* interpretations; such as, "When Jonah was thrown overboard he swam for his life, earnestly praying God to preserve him from drowning; and by his providence he was thrown into a *place of fish*—a *fishing cove*, where he was for a time *entangled among the weeds*, and hardly escaped with his life; and when safe, he composed this poetic prayer, in *metaphorical language*, which some have wrongly interpreted, by supposing that he was *swallowed by a fish;* when דג *dag* should have been understood, as a *place of fish*, or *fishing creek*," &c. Now I say the original has no such meaning in the Bible: and this gloss is plainly contrary to the *letter of the text;* to all *sober* and *rational modes of interpretation;* and to the express *purpose* for which God appears to have wrought this miracle, and to which *Jesus Christ* himself *applies* it. For as Jonah was intended for a *sign* to the Jews of the resurrection of Christ, they were to have the proof of this *semiosis*, in his lying as long in the *heart of the earth* as the prophet was in the *belly of the fish;* and all interpretations of this kind go to deny both the *sign* and the thing *signified.* Some men, because they cannot work a miracle themselves, can hardly be persuaded that God can do it.

The *text*, and the *use* made of it by Christ, most plainly teach us that the prophet was literally swallowed by a fish, by the order of God; and that by the Divine power he was *preserved alive*, for what is called *three days and three nights, in the stomach of the fish;* and at the conclusion of the above time that same fish was led by the unseen power of God to the shore, and there compelled to eject the prey that he could neither kill nor digest. And how easy is all this to the *almighty power* of the *Author* and *Sustainer* of *life*, who has a sovereign, omnipresent, and energetic sway in the heavens and in the earth. But foolish man will affect to be wise; though, in such cases, he appears as the recently born, stupid offspring of the wild ass. It is bad to follow *fancy*, where there is so much at stake. Both *ancients* and *moderns* have grievously trifled with this prophet's narrative; merely because they could not rationally account for the thing, and were unwilling (and why?) to allow any miraculous interference.

CHAPTER III

Jonah is sent again to Nineveh, a city of three days' journey, (being sixty miles in circumference, according to Diodorus Siculus,) 1–4. *The inhabitants, in consequence of the prophet's preaching, repent in dust and ashes,* 5–9. *God, seeing that they were deeply humbled on account of their sins, and that they turned away from all their iniquities, repents of the evil with which he had threatened them,* 10.

A. M. cir. 3142 B. C. cir. 862 Ante U. C. 109 Alladii Sylvii, R. Alban., cir. annum 14

AND the word of the Lord
came unto Jonah the second
time, saying,
2 Arise, go unto Nineveh, that
great city, and preach unto it
the preaching that I bid thee.
3 So Jonah arose, and went
unto Nineveh, according to the

A. M. cir. 3142 B. C. cir. 862 Ante U. C. 109 Alladii Sylvii, R. Alban., cir. annum 14

NOTES ON CHAP. III

Verse 1. *And the word of the Lord*] The same *oracle* as that before given; and which, from what he had felt and seen of the justice and mercy of the Lord, he was now prepared to obey.

Verse 2. *And preach unto it the preaching*] וקרא את הקריאה *vekera eth hakkeriah*, "And cry the cry that I bid thee." Be my herald, and faithfully deliver my message. The word κηρυξ in Greek answers to the Hebrew קורא *kore:* both signifying a *crier*, a *herald*, a *preacher;* one that *makes proclamation* with a *loud* and *earnest cry*. Such was John Baptist, Isa. xl. 3; such was Jesus Christ, John vii. 18-37; and such were all his apostles. And such earnestness becomes a ministry that has to do with immortal souls, asleep and dead in sin, hanging on the brink of perdition, and insensible of their state. The soft-speaking, gentle-toned, unmoved preacher, is never likely to awaken souls. As we preach, so the people hear; scarcely receiving any counsels that appear to have no importance by the *manner* in which they are *delivered*. But this earnestness is widely different from that noisy, blustering, screaming rant, that manifests more of the turbulence of disorderly passions, than of the real inspired influence of the Spirit of God.

Verse 3. *Nineveh was an exceeding great city, of three days' journey.*] See on chap. i. 2. *Strabo* says, lib. xvi., πολυ μειζων ην της Βαβυλωνος, "it was much larger than Babylon:" and Ninus, the builder, not only proposed to make it the *largest* city of the world, but the largest that *could be built by man.* See *Diodor.* Sic. Bib. l. ii. And as we find, from the lowest computation, that it was at least *fifty-four* or *sixty* English miles in circumference, it would take the prophet *three* days to walk round upon the walls, and announce from them the terrible

A. M. cir. 3142
B. C. cir. 862
Ante U. C. 109
Alladii Sylvii,
R. Alban.,
cir. annum 14

word of the LORD. Now Nineveh was an [a]exceeding great city, of three days' journey.

4 And Jonah began to enter into the city a day's journey, and [b]he cried, and said, Yet forty days, and Nineveh shall be overthrown.

5 So the people of Nineveh [c]believed God, and proclaimed a fast, and put on sackcloth, from the greatest of them even to the least of them.

6 For word came unto the king of Nineveh, and he arose from his throne, and he laid his robe from him, and covered *him* with sackcloth [d]and sat in ashes.

7 [e]And he caused *it* to be proclaimed and [f]published through Nineveh by the decree of the king and his [g]nobles, saying, Let neither man nor beast, herd nor flock, taste any thing: let them not feed, nor drink water:

8 But let man and beast be covered with sackcloth, and cry mightily unto God: yea, [h]let them turn every one from his evil way, and from the [i]violence that *is* in their hands.

9 [k]Who can tell *if* God will turn and repent, and turn away from his fierce anger, that we perish not?

10 [l]And God saw their works, that they turned from their evil way; and God repented of the evil, that he had said that he would do unto them; and he did *it* not.

A. M. cir. 3142
B. C. cir. 862
Ante U. C. 109
Alladii Sylvii,
R. Alban.,
cir. annum 14

---

[a]Heb. *of God;* so Gen. xxx. 8; Psa. xxxvi. 6; lxxx. 10——[b]See Deut. xviii. 62——[c]Matt. xii. 41; Luke xi. 32——[d]Job ii. 8——[e]2 Chron. xx. 3; Joel ii. 15——[f]Heb. *said*——[g]Heb. *great men*——[h]Isa. lviii. 6——[i]Isa. lix. 6——[k]2 Samuel xii. 22; Joel ii. 14——[l]Jer. xviii. 8; Amos vii. 3, 6

---

message, "Yet *forty* days, and Nineveh will be destroyed!"

Verse 4. *Yet forty days*] Both the *Septuagint* and *Arabic* read *three days.* Probably some early copyist of the *Septuagint,* from whom our modern editions are derived, mistook the Greek numerals *μ forty* for *γ three;* or put the *three* days' *journey* in preaching instead of the *forty days* mentioned in the denunciation. One of *Kennicott's* MSS., instead of ארבעים *arbaim, forty,* has שלשים *sheloshim, thirty:* but the Hebrew text is undoubtedly the true reading; and it is followed by *all* the ancient versions, the *Septuagint* and *Vulgate* excepted. Thus God gives them time to *think, reflect, take counsel,* and *return* to him. Had they only *three days' space,* the denunciation would have so completely confounded them, as to excite nothing but terror, and prevent repentance and conversion.

Verse 5. *The people of Nineveh believed God*] They had no doubt that the threatening would be fulfilled, unless their speedy conversion prevented it; but, though not expressed, they knew that the threatening was conditional. "The promises and threatenings of God, which are merely personal, either to any particular man or number of men, are always conditional, because the wisdom of God hath thought fit to make these depend on the behaviour of men."—Dr. S. Clarke's Sermons, vol. i.

Proclaimed a fast] And never was there one so general, so deep, and so effectual. Men and women, old and young, high and low, and even the cattle themselves, all kept such a fast as the total abstinence from food implies.

Verse 6. *Word came unto the king*] This, some think, was *Pul;* others, *Sardanapalus* his son, king of Assyria, who flourished in the reign of Jeroboam the Second: but it seems more probable that the monarch here alluded to was a king of Assyria contemporary with Joash, king of Judah. It was by the decree of the king that the fast was instituted, and became general.

Verse 8. *Let man and beast be covered*] This was done that every object which they beheld might deepen the impression already made, and cause them to mourn after a godly sort. *Virgil* tells us that the mourning for the death of Julius Cæsar was so general, that the *cattle* neither *ate* nor *drank:*—

Non ulli pastos illis egere diebus
Frigida, Daphni, boves ad flumina: nulla neque amnem
Libavit quadrupes, nec graminis attigit herbam.
Ecl. v. 24.

"The swains forgot their sheep, nor near the brink
Of running waters brought their herds to drink.
The thirsty cattle of themselves abstain'd,
From water, and their grassy fare disdain'd."
DRYDEN.

And that they sometimes *changed* or *reversed* the harness and ornaments of cattle, as indicative of mourning, we have a proof in Virgil's description of the funeral procession in honour of Pallas, slain by Turnus, *Æn.* xi. ver. 89.

Post bellator equus, positis insignibus, Æthon
It lacrymans, guttisque humectat grandibus ora.

"Stripp'd of his trappings, and his head declined,
Æthon, his generous warrior-horse, behind,
Moves with a solemn, slow, majestic pace;
And the big tears come rolling down his face."

Verse 9. *Who can tell* if *God will turn and repent*] There is at least a peradventure for our salvation. God *may* turn towards us, change his purpose, and save us alive. While there is life there is hope; God has no pleasure in the death of sinners; he is gracious and compassionate. Himself has prescribed repentance; if we repent, and turn to him from our iniquities, who knows then whether God will not turn, &c.

Verse 10. *And God saw their works*] They repented, and brought forth *fruits* meet for repentance; works which showed that they did most earnestly repent. He therefore changed his purpose, and the city was saved. The purpose was: If the Ninevites do not return from their evil ways, and the violence that is in their hands, within *forty* days, I will destroy the city. The Ninevites did return, &c., and therefore escaped the threatened judgment. Thus we see that the threatening was conditional.

CHAPTER IV

Jonah, dreading to be thought a false prophet, repines at God's mercy in sparing the Ninevites, whose destruction he seems to have expected, from his retiring to a place without the city about the close of the forty days. But how does he glorify that mercy which he intends to blame! And what an amiable picture does he give of the compassion of God! 1–5. *This attribute of the Deity is still farther illustrated by his tenderness and condescension to the prophet himself, who, with all his prophetic gifts, had much of human infirmity,* 6–11.

A. M. cir. 3142
B. C. cir. 862
Ante U. C. 109
Alladii Sylvii,
R. Alban.,
cir. annum 14

BUT it displeased Jonah exceedingly, and he was very angry.
2 And he prayed unto the
LORD, and said, I pray thee, O LORD, *was*
not this my saying, when I was yet in my
country? Therefore I [a]fled before unto Tarshish: for I knew that thou *art* a [b]gracious
God, and merciful, slow to anger, and of
great kindness, and repentest thee of the evil.
3 [c]Therefore now, O LORD, take, I beseech
thee, my life from me; for [d]*it*
is better for me to die than to
live.
4 Then said the LORD, [e]Doest
thou well to be angry?
5 So Jonah went out of the city, and sat on
the east side of the city, and there made him
a booth, and sat under it in the shadow, till
he might see what would become of the city.
6 And the Lord GOD prepared a [f]gourd,[g]
and made *it* to come up over Jonah, that it

A. M. cir. 3142
B. C. cir. 862
Ante U. C. 109
Alladii Sylvii,
R. Alban.,
cir. annum 14

---

[a]Chap. i. 3——[b]Exod. xxxiv. 6; Psa. lxxxvi. 5; Joel ii. 13
[c]1 Kings xix. 4——[d]Ver. 8

[e]Or, *Art thou greatly angry?*——[f]Or, *palmecrist*
[g]Heb. *Kikajon*

NOTES ON CHAP. IV

Verse 1. *But it displeased Jonah exceedingly*] This hasty, and indeed inconsiderate prophet, was vexed because his prediction was not fulfilled. He had more respect to his high sense of his own honour than he had to the goodness and mercy of God. He appeared to care little whether *six hundred and twenty thousand* persons were destroyed or not, so he might not pass for a deceiver, or one that denounced a falsity.

And he was very angry.] Because the prediction was not literally fulfilled; for he totally lost sight of the *condition.*

Verse 2. *I know that thou* art *a gracious God*] See the note on Exod. xxxiv. 6.

Verse 3. *Take, I beseech thee, my life from me*] קח נא את נפשי *kach na eth naphshi,* "Take, I beseech thee, even my soul." Do not let me survive this disgrace. Thou hast spared this city. I thought thou wouldst do so, because thou art *merciful* and *gracious;* and it was on this account that I refused to go at first, as I knew that thou mightest *change thy purpose,* though thou hadst commanded me to make an absolute denunciation of judgment. God has left this example on record to show that an inconsiderate man is not fit to be employed in his work; and he chose this one example that it might serve as an endless warning to his Church to employ no man in the work of the ministry that is not scripturally acquainted with God's justice and mercy.

Verse 4. *Doest thou well to be angry?*] ההיטב הרה לך *haheitib harah lac,* "Is anger good for thee?" No, anger is good for no man; but an angry preacher, minister, bishop, or prophet, is an abominable man. He who, in denouncing the word of God against sinners, joins his own *passions* with the Divine threatenings, is a cruel and bad man, and should not be an overseer in God's house. A *surly bishop,* a *peevish, passionate preacher,* will bring neither glory to God, nor good to man. Dr. Taylor renders the clause, "Art thou very much grieved?" A man may be very much grieved that a sinner is lost; but who but he who is of a fiendish nature will be grieved because God's mercy triumphs over judgment?

Verse 5. *So Jonah went out of the city*] I believe this refers to what had *already passed;* and I therefore agree with Bp. *Newcome,* who translates, "Now Jonah HAD gone out of the city, and HAD sat," &c.; for there are many instances where verbs in the preterite form have this force, the ו *vau* here turning the *future* into the *preterite.* And the passage is here to be understood thus: When he had delivered his message he left the city, and went and made himself a tent, or got under some shelter on the east side of the city, and there he was determined to remain till he should see what would become of the city. But when the *forty* days had expired, and he saw no evidence of the Divine wrath, he became angry, and expostulated with God as above. The *fifth* verse should be read in a parenthesis, or be considered as beginning the chapter.

Verse 6. *And the Lord God prepared a gourd*] I believe this should be rendered in the preterpluperfect tense. The Lord HAD prepared—this plant, קיקיון *kikayon.* It had in the course of God's providence been planted and grown up in that place, though perhaps not yet in full leaf;

A. M. cir. 3142 B. C. cir. 862 Ante U. C. 109 Alladii Sylvii, R. Alban., cir. annum 14

might be a shadow over his head, to deliver him from his grief. So Jonah [h]was exceeding glad of the gourd.

7 But God prepared a worm when the morning rose the next day, and it smote the gourd that it withered.

8 And it came to pass, when the sun did arise, that God prepared a [i]vehement east wind; and the sun beat upon the head of Jonah, that he fainted, and wished in himself to die, and said, [k]*It is* better for me to die than to live.

9 And God said to Jonah, [l]Doest thou well to be angry for the gourd? And he said, [m]I do well to be angry, *even* unto death.

10 Then said the LORD, Thou hast [n]had pity on the gourd, for the which thou hast not laboured, neither madest it grow; which [o]came up in a night, and perished in a night:

11 And should not I spare Nineveh, [p]that great city, wherein are more than sixscore thousand persons [q]that cannot discern between their right hand, and their left hand; and *also* much [r]cattle?

[h]Heb. *rejoiced with great joy*——[i]Or, *silent*——[k]Ver. 3——[l]Or, *Art thou greatly angry*——[m]Or, *I am greatly angry*

[n]Or, *spared*——[o]Heb. *was the son of the night*——[p]Ch. i. 2; iii. 2, 3——[q]Deut. i. 39——[r]Psa. xxxvi. 6; cxlv. 9

and Jonah made that his tent. And its thick branches and large leaves made it an ample shelter for him; and because it was such, he *rejoiced greatly* on the account. But what was the *kikayon?* The best judges say the *ricinus* or *palma Christi*, from which we get what is vulgarly called *castor oil*, is meant. It is a tree as large as the olive, has leaves which are like those of the vine, and is also quick of growth. This in all probability was the plant in question, which had been already planted, though it had not attained its proper growth, and was not then in full leaf. *Celsus*, in his *Hierobot.*, says it grows to the height of an olive tree; the trunk and branches are hollow like a kex, and the leaves sometimes as broad as the rim of a hat. It must be of a soft or spongy substance, for it is said to grow surprisingly fast. See *Taylor* under the root קיק, 1670. But it is evident there was something *supernatural* in the growth of this plant, for it is stated to have *come up in a night;* though the Chaldee understands the passage thus: "It was here last night, and is withered this night." In one night it might have blown and expanded its leaves considerably, though the plant had existed before, but not in full bloom till the time that Jonah required it for a shelter.

Verse 7. *But God prepared a worm*] By being eaten through the root, the plant, losing its nourishment, would soon wither; and this was the case in the present instance.

Verse 8. *A vehement east wind*] Which was of itself of a *parching, withering* nature; and the *sun*, in addition, made it intolerable. These winds are both scorching and suffocating in the East, for deserts of burning sand lay to the east or south-east; and the easterly winds often brought such a multitude of *minute particles of sand* on their wings, as to add greatly to the mischief. I believe these, and the sands they carry, are the cause of the *ophthalmia* which prevails so much both in Egypt and India.

Verse 9. *I do well to be angry*, even *unto death.*] Many persons suppose that the *gifts of prophecy* and *working miracles* are the highest that can be conferred on man; but they are widely mistaken, for the gifts *change not the heart*. Jonah had the gift of prophecy, but had not received that grace which destroys the *old man* and *creates the soul anew in Christ Jesus.* This is the *love* of which St. Paul speaks, which if a man have not, though he had the gift of prophecy, and could miraculously remove mountains, yet in the sight of God, and for any good himself might reap from it, it would be as sounding brass and a tinkling cymbal. Jonah was a prophet, and yet had all his old bad tempers about him, in a shameful predominancy. *Balaam* was of the same kind. So we find that God gave the *gift of prophecy* even to *graceless* men. But many of the prophets were sanctified in their nature before their call to the prophetic office, and were the most excellent of men.

Verse 10. *Which came up in a night*] St. Jerome, speaking of this plant, the *kikayon*, assigns to it an extraordinary rapidity of growth. It delights in a sandy soil, and in a few days what was a *plant* grows into a *large shrub.* But he does not appear to have meant the *ricinus;* this however is the most likely. The expressions *coming up in a night* and *perishing in a night* are only metaphorical to express *speedy growth* and *speedy decay;* and so, as we have seen, the Chaldee interprets it, די בליליא הדין הוה ובליליא אוחרנא אבד "which existed this night, but in the next night perished;" and this I am satisfied is the true import of the Hebrew phrase.

Verse 11. *And should not I spare Nineveh*] In ver. 10 it is said, *thou hast had pity* on the gourd, אתה חסת *attah* CHASTA; and here the Lord uses the same word, ואני לא אחום *veani lo* ACHUS, "And shall not *I have pity* upon Nineveh?" How much is the *city* better than the *shrub?* But besides this there are in it *one hundred and twenty thousand* persons! And shall I destroy them, rather than thy *shade* should be withered or thy *word* apparently fail? And besides, these persons are *young*, and have *not offended*, (for they knew not the difference between their *right hand and their left*,) and should not I feel *more pity* for those innocents than thou dost for the fine *flowering plant* which is withered in a night, being itself exceedingly *short-lived?* Add to all this, they have now turned from those sins which induced me to denounce judgment against them. And should I destroy *them* who are now *fasting* and *afflicting their souls;* and, covered with sackcloth, are lying in the dust before me, bewailing their offences and supplicating for mercy? Learn, then, from this, that it is the incorrigibly wicked on whom my judgments must fall, and against whom they are threatened. And know, that to that man will I look who is of a broken and contrite spirit, and who trembles at my word. Even the *dumb beasts* are objects of my compassion; I will spare *them* for the sake of their penitent owners; and remember with the rest, *That the Lord careth for oxen.*

The great number of *cattle* to which reference is here made were for the support of the inhabitants; and probably at this time the Ninevites gathered in their cattle from the champaign pasture, expecting that some foe coming to besiege them might seize upon them for their forage, while they within might suffer the lack of all things.

No doubt that ancient Nineveh was like ancient Babylon, of which *Quintus Curtius* says, the buildings were not close to the walls, there being the space of an acre left between them; and in several parts there were within the walls portions of cultivated land, that, if besieged, they might have provisions to sustain the inhabitants.

And I suppose this to be true of all large ancient cities. They were rather *cantons* or *districts* than cities such as now are, only all the different inhabitants had joined together to wall in the districts for the sake of mutual defence.

This last expostulation of God, it is to be hoped, produced its proper effect on the mind of this irritable prophet; and that he was fully convinced that in this, as in all other cases, God had done all things well.

From this short prophecy many useful lessons may be derived. The Ninevites were on the verge of destruction, but on their repentance were respited. They did not, however, continue under the influence of good resolutions. They relapsed, and about *one hundred and fifty* years afterwards, the Prophet *Nahum* was sent to predict the miraculous discomfiture of the Assyrian king under Sennacherib, an event which took place about 710 B. C.; and also the total destruction of Nineveh by Cyaxares and his allies, which happened about 606 B. C. Several of the ancients, by allegorizing this book, have made Jonah declare the *divinity, humanity, death,* and *resurrection* of Christ. These points may be found in the Gospel history, their true repository; but *fancy* can find them any where it pleases to seek them; but he who seeks not for them will never find them here. Jonah was a type of the resurrection of Christ; nothing farther seems revealed in this prophet relative to the mysteries of Christianity.

In conclusion: while I have done the best I could to illustrate the very difficult prophet through whose work the reader has just passed, I do not pretend to say I have removed every difficulty. I am satisfied only of one thing, that I have conscientiously endeavoured to do it, and believe that I have generally succeeded; but am still fearful that several are left behind, which, though they may be accounted for from the briefness of the narrative of a great transaction, in which so many surprising particulars are included, yet, for general apprehension, might appear to have required a more distinct and circumstantial statement. I have only to add, that as several of the facts are evidently *miraculous,* and by the prophet stated as such, others may be probably of the same kind. On this ground all difficulty is removed; for God *can* do what he *pleases.* As his power is *unlimited,* it can meet with no *impossibilities.* He who gave the *commission* to Jonah to go and *preach to the Ninevites, and prepared the great fish* to swallow the disobedient prophet, could maintain his life for *three days and three nights* in the belly of this marine monster; and cause it to *eject him* at the termination of the appointed time, on *any sea-coast* he might choose; and afterwards the Divine power could carry the deeply contrite and now faithful prophet over the intervening distance between that and Nineveh, be that distance greater or less. Whatever, therefore, cannot be accounted for on mere natural principles in this book, may be referred to this *supernatural* agency; and this, on the ostensible principle of the prophecy itself, is at once a mode of interpretation as easy as it is rational. God gave the commission; he raised the storm; he prepared the fish which swallowed the prophet; he caused it to cast him forth on the dry land; he gave him a fresh commission, carried him to the place of his destination, and miraculously produced the sheltering gourd, that came to perfection in a night and withered in a night. This God therefore performed the other facts for which we cannot naturally account, as he did those already specified. This concession, for the admission of which both common sense and reason plead, at once solves all the real or seeming difficulties to be found in *the Book of the Prophet Jonah.*

INTRODUCTION TO THE BOOK

OF THE

PROPHET MICAH

MICAH, the Morasthite, or of Moresa, a village near the city Eleutheropolis, in the southern part of Judah, is the *sixth* in order of the *twelve* minor prophets. He prophesied under Jotham, Ahaz, and Hezekiah, kings of Judah, for about *fifty* years. Some have confounded him with Micaiah, son of Imlah, who lived in the kingdom of the ten tribes, under the reign of Ahab.

The spurious Dorotheus says that Micah was buried in the burying-place of the Anakim, whose habitation had been at Hebron, and round about it. This prophet appeared almost at the same time with Isaiah, and has even borrowed some expressions from him. Compare Isa. ii. 2 with Mic. iv. 1, and Isa. xli. 15 with Mic. iv. 13.

The prophecy of Micah contains but *seven* chapters. He foretells the calamities of Samaria, which was taken by Shalmaneser, and reduced to a heap of stones. Afterwards he prophesies against Judah, and declares the troubles that Sennacherib should bring upon it under the reign of Hezekiah. Then he declaims against the iniquities of Samaria. He foretells the captivity of the *ten* tribes, and their return into their own country. The *third* chapter contains a pathetic invective against the princes of the house of Jacob, and the judges of the house of Israel; which seems levelled against the chief of the kingdom of Judah, the judges, the magistrates, the priests, the false prophets, &c. He upbraids them with their avarice, their injustice, and falsehood; and tells them they will be the occasion that Jerusalem shall be reduced to a heap of rubbish, and the mountain of the temple shall be as a forest. We are informed, Jer. xxvi. 18, 19, that this prophecy was pronounced in the reign of Hezekiah; and that it saved Jeremiah from death.

After these terrible denunciations, Micah speaks of the reign of the Messiah, and of the establishment of the Christian Church. And as the peaceable times which succeeded the return from the Babylonish captivity, and which were a figure of the reign of the Messiah, were disturbed by a tempest of a short continuance, Micah foretold it in such a manner as agrees very well with what Ezekiel says of the war of Gog against the Jews. Micah speaks in particular of the birth of the Messiah; that he was to be born at Bethlehem; and that his dominion was to extend to the utmost parts of the earth. He says that God should raise *seven* shepherds, who should reign by the sword over Assyria, and in the land of Nimrod; which Calmet explains of Darius, son of Hystaspes; and of the *seven* confederates that killed the magian, and who possessed the empire of the Persians, after the extinction of the family of Cyrus. The *fifth* chapter, from ver. 7 to the end, describes the flourishing estate of the Jews in their own country, from the reign of Darius, and after the Maccabees; yet in such a manner, that he mingles several things in it that can apply only to the Church of Jesus Christ.

The two last chapters of Micah contain, first, a long invective against the iniquities of Samaria: then he foretells the fall of Babylon; the re-establishment of the cities of Israel; the greatness of the country possessed by the Israelites; their happiness; the graces wherewith God will favour them; and all this in such lofty terms, that they chiefly agree with the Christian Church. St. Jerome says that Micah was buried at Morasthi, ten furlongs from Eleutheropolis; and Sozomenes says that his tomb was revealed to Zebennus, bishop of Eleutheropolis, under the reign of Theodosius the Great. He calls the place of his burial Beretsate, which is probably the same as Morasthi, ten furlongs from Eleutheropolis.

Bishop *Newcome* observes that Micah was of the kingdom of Judah, as he only makes mention of kings who reigned over that country. It is supposed that he prophesied farther on in the reign of Hezekiah than Hosea did; although chap. v. 5 was written before the captivity of the ten tribes, which happened in the *sixth* year of Hezekiah. It is plain from chap. i. 1, 5, 9, 12, 13, that he was sent both to Israel and Judah. Like Amos and Hosea, he reproves and threatens, with great spirit and energy, a corrupt people. See chap. ii. 1, 2, 3, 8, 9, 10; iii. 2, 3, 4, 6, 10–16; vii. 2, 3, 4. And, like Hosea, he inveighs against the princes and prophets with the highest indignation. See chap. iii. 5–7, 9–12; vii. 3. The reader will observe that these similar topics are treated of by each prophet with remarkable variety, and copiousness of expression.

Some of his prophecies are distinct and illustrious ones, as chap. ii. 12, 13; iii. 12; iv. 1–4, 10; v. 2, 3, 4; vi. 13; vii. 8, 9, 10.

We may justly admire the *elegance* of his diction:—

Chap. ii. 12.—"I will surely gather, O Jacob, all of thee:
I will surely assemble the residue of Israel.
I will put them together as sheep of Bozra,
As a flock in the midst of their fold:
They shall make a tumult from the multitude of men.
13.—He that forceth a passage is come up before them:
They have forced a passage, and have passed through the gate; and are gone forth by it:
And their King passeth before them, even Jehovah at the head of them."

Chap. iv. 1.—"But it shall come to pass, in the latter days,
That the mountain of the temple of Jehovah shall be
Established on the top of the mountains,
And it shall be exalted above the hills;
And the people shall flow into it:
2.—And many nations shall go, and shall say,
Come, and let us go up unto the mountain of Jehovah,
And unto the temple of the God of Jacob:
That he may teach us of his ways, and that we may walk in his paths.
For from Sion shall go forth a law,
And the word of Jehovah from Jerusalem.
3.—And he shall judge between many people,
And he shall convince strong nations afar off:
And they shall beat their swords into ploughshares,
And their spears into pruninghooks:
Nation shall not lift up sword against nation,
Neither shall they any longer learn war."

His *animation*, chap. i. 5, lines 3, 4:—

"What is the transgression of Jacob?—is it not that of Samaria?
And what are the high places of Judah?—are they not those of Jerusalem?"

Chap. iv. 9.—"And now why dost thou cry out loudly?
Is there no king in thee?
Hath thy counsellor perished?
For pangs have seized thee, as a woman in travail."

There are few beauties of composition of which examples may not be found in this prophet. For *sublimity* and *impressiveness* in several places, he is unrivalled. The *Lord's controversy*, chap. vi. 1–8, is equal to any thing even in the prophet Isaiah. It has a powerful effect on every attentive reader.

His *strength* of *expression*:—

Chap. i. 6.—"Therefore will I make Samaria a heap of the field, a place for the plantings of a vineyard:
And I will pour down her stones into the valley, and I will discover her foundations."
iii. 2.—"Ye who hate good and love evil:
Who pluck their skin from off them,
And their flesh from off their bones.
3.—Who have also eaten the flesh of my people,
And have flayed their skin from off them,
And have broken their bones;
And have divided them asunder, as flesh in the pot:
And as meat within the caldron."
vii. 1.—"Wo is me; for I am become
As the gatherers of late figs, as the gleaners of the vintage.
There is no cluster to eat:
My soul desireth the first-ripe fig.
2.—The good man is perished from the land,
And there is none upright among men.
All of them lie in wait for blood;
They hunt every man his brother for his destruction."

His *pathos*:—

Chap. i. 16.—"Make thee bald, and cut off thine hair for thy delicate children;
Enlarge thy baldness as the eagle;
For they are gone into captivity from thee."
ii. 4.—"In that day shall a proverb be taken up against you;
And a grievous lamentation shall be made:
Saying, 'We are utterly laid waste:
He hath changed the portion of my people:
How hath he departed from me,
To bring again him that divided our fields!' "

His *sublimity*:—

Chap. i. 2.—"Hear, O ye people, all of you:
Hearken, O land, and all that are therein.
And let the Lord Jehovah be witness against you;
Even the Lord from his holy temple.
3.—For, behold, Jehovah will go forth from his place:
And he will come down, and will tread upon the high places of the earth.
4.—And the mountains shall be molten under him;
And the valleys shall cleave asunder;
As wax before the fire,
As waters poured down a steep place."
Chap. vi. 1.—"Hear ye now what Jehovah saith:
Arise, contend thou before the mountains;
And let the hills hear thy voice."
vii. 15.—"The nations shall see, and shall be confounded because of their might:
They shall lay their hand upon their mouth; their ears shall be deaf.
7.—They shall lick the dust as the serpent;
As the creeping things upon the earth, they shall tremble from their close places:
Because of Jehovah our God, they shall stand in awe; and they shall fear because of thee."

THE BOOK

OF THE

PROPHET MICAH

Chronological Notes relative to this Book

Year from the Creation, according to Archbishop Usher, 3254.—Year of the Julian Period, 3964.—Year since the Flood, 1598.—Year from the vocation of Abram, 1171.—Year since the first celebration of the Olympic games in Elis by the Idæi Dactyli, 704.—Year from the destruction of Troy, according to the general computation of chronologers, 434.—Year since the commencement of the kingdom of Israel, by the Divine appointment of Saul to the regal dignity, 346.—Year from the foundation of Solomon's temple, 262.—Year since the division of Solomon's monarchy into the kingdoms of Israel and Judah, 226.—Year since the restoration of the Olympic games at Elis by Lycurgus, Iphitus, and Cleosthenes, 135.—Year from the foundation of the kingdom of Macedon by Caranus, 65.—Year from the foundation of the kingdom of Lydia by Ardysus, 49.—All before this reign concerning Lydia is entirely fabulous.—Year since the conquest of Corœbus at Olympia, usually called the first Olympiad, 27.—Third year of the *seventh* Olympiad.—Year before the building of Rome, according to the Varronian computation, 4.—Year from the building of Rome, according to Cato and the Fasti Consulares, 3.—Year from the building of Rome, according to Polybius the historian, 2.—Year before the building of Rome, according to Fabius Pictor, 2.—Year before the commencement of the era of Nabonassar, 2.—Year before the birth of Christ, 746.—Year before the vulgar era of Christ's nativity, 750.—Cycle of the Sun, 16.—Cycle of the Moon, 12.—Twenty-first year of Theopompus, king of Lacedæmon, of the family of the Proclidæ.—Twenty-seventh year of Polydorus, king of Lacedæmon, of the family of the Eurysthenidæ.—Twelfth year of Alyattes, king of Lydia.—Fifth year of Charops, the first decennial archon of the Athenians.—Fourth year of Romulus, the first king of the Romans.—Tenth year of Pekah, king of Israel.—Ninth year of Jothan, king of Judah.

CHAPTER I

The prophet begins with calling the attention of all people to the awful descent of Jehovah, coming to execute his judgments against the kingdoms of Israel and Judah, 1–5; *first against Samaria, whose fate the prophet laments in the dress of mourners, and with the doleful cries of the fox or ostrich,* 6–8; *and then against Jerusalem, which is threatened with the invasion of Sennacherib. Other cities of Judah are likewise threatened; and their danger represented to be so great as to oblige them to have recourse for protection even to their enemies the Philistines, from whom they desired at first to conceal their situation. But all resources are declared to be vain; Israel and Judah must go into captivity,* 9–16.

A. M. cir. 3254
B. C. cir. 750
A. U. C. cir. 4
Romuli,
R. Roman.,
cir. annum 4

THE word of the LORD that
came to [a]Micah the Morasthite in the days of Jotham,
Ahaz, *and* Hezekiah, kings of
Judah, [b]which he saw concerning Samaria and Jerusalem.
2 [c]Hear, all ye people;
[d]hearken, O earth, and [e]all

[a]Jer. xxvi. 18——[b]Amos i. 1——[c]Heb. *Hear, ye people, all of them*

[d]Deuteronomy xxxii. 1; Isa. i. 2——[e]Heb. *the fulness thereof*

NOTES ON CHAP. I

Verse 1. *The word of the Lord that came to Micah the Morasthite*] For all authentic particulars relative to this *prophet*, see the *preface*.

In the days of Jotham, Ahaz, and *Hezekiah*] These *three* kings reigned about threescore years; and Micah is supposed to have prophesied about *forty* or *fifty* years; but no more of his prophecies have reached posterity than what are contained in this book, nor is there any evidence that any more was written. His time appears to have been spent chiefly in *preaching* and *exhorting;* and he was directed to write

A. M. cir. 3254
B. C. cir. 750
A. U. C. cir. 4
Romuli,
R. Roman.,
cir. annum 4

that therein is: and let the Lord
GOD [f]be Witness against you,
the Lord from [g]his holy temple.
3 For, behold, [h]the LORD
cometh forth out of his [i]place, and will come
down, and tread upon the [k]high places of the
earth.
4 And [l]the mountains shall be molten under
him, and the valleys shall be cleft, as wax
before the fire, *and* as the waters *that are*
poured down [m]a steep place.
5 For the transgression of Jacob *is* all this,
and for the sins of the house of Israel. What
is the transgression of Jacob? *is it* not Samaria? and what *are* the high places of Judah?
are they not Jerusalem?

6 Therefore I will make Samaria [n]as a heap of the field,
and as plantings of a vineyard:
and I will pour down the stones
thereof into the valley, and I will [o]discover
the foundations thereof.
7 And all the graven images thereof shall
be beaten to pieces, and all the [p]hires thereof
shall be burned with the fire, and all the idols
thereof will I lay desolate: for she gathered
it of the hire of a harlot, and they shall return to the hire of a harlot.
8 Therefore [q]I will wail and howl, [r]I will
go stripped and naked: [s]I will make a wailing
like the dragons, and mourning as the [t]owls.
9 For [u]her wound *is* incurable; for [v]it is

[f]Psa. l. 7; Mal. iii. 5——[g]Psa. xi. 4; Jonah ii. 7; Hab. ii. 20——[h]Isa. xxvi. 21——[i]Psa. cxv. 3——[k]Deut. xxxii. 13; xxxiii. 29; Amos iv. 13——[l]Judg. v. 5; Psa. xcvii. 5; Isa. lxiv. 1, 2, 3; Amos ix. 5; Hab. iii. 6, 10——[m]Heb. *a descent*——[n]2 Kings xix. 25; chap. iii. 12

[o]Ezek. xiii. 14——[p]Hos. ii. 5, 12——[q]Isa. xxi. 3; xxii. 4; Jer. iv. 19——[r]Isa. xx. 2, 3, 4——[s]Job xxx. 29; Psa. cii. 6——[t]Heb. *daughters of the owl*——[u]Or, she is *grievously sick of her wounds*——[v]2 Kings xviii. 13; Isa. viii. 7, 8

those parts only that were calculated to profit succeeding generations.

Verse 2. *Hear, all ye people*] The very commencement of this prophecy supposes *preceding* exhortations and predictions.

Hearken, O earth] ארץ *arets*, here, should be translated *land*, the country of the Hebrews being only intended.

And let the Lord God be Witness] Let him who has sent me with this message be witness that I have delivered it faithfully; and be a witness against you, if you take not the warning.

The Lord from his holy temple.] The place where he still remains as your King, and your Judge; and where you profess to pay your devotions. The temple was yet standing, for Jerusalem was not taken for many years after this; and these prophecies were delivered before the captivity of the *ten* tribes, as Micah appears to have been sent both to Israel and to Judah. See ver. 5-9, 12, 13.

Verse 3. *For, behold, the Lord cometh forth*] See this clause, Amos iv. 13. He represents Jehovah as a mighty conqueror, issuing from his pavilion, stepping from mountain to mountain, which rush down and fill the valleys before him; a consuming fire accompanying him, that melts and confounds every hill and dale, and blends all in universal confusion. God is here represented as doing that *himself* which other conquerors do by the multitude of their hosts; levelling the mountains, filling some of the valleys, and digging for waters in others, and pouring them from hills and dales for the use of the conquering armies, by pipes and aqueducts.

And why is all this mighty movement? Verse 5. "For the transgression of Jacob *is* all this, and for the sins of the house of Israel."

Verse 5. *What* is *the transgression of Jacob?*] Is it not something extremely grievous? Is it not that of *Samaria?* Samaria and Jerusalem, the chief cities, are infected with *idolatry*. Each has its *high places*, and its *idol worship*, in opposition to the worship of the true God. That there was *idolatry* practised by the *elders of Israel*, even *in the temple* of Jehovah, see Ezek. viii. 1, &c. As the royal cities in both kingdoms gave the *example* of gross idolatry, no wonder that it spread through the whole land, both of Israel and Judah.

Verse 6. *I will make Samaria*] I will bring it to desolation: and, instead of being a royal city, it shall be a *place for vineyards. Newcome* observes, that Samaria was situated on a hill, the right soil for a vineyard.

I will discover the foundations thereof.] I will cause its walls and fortifications to be razed to the ground.

Verse 7. *All the hires thereof shall be burned*] Multitudes of women gave the money they gained by their public *prostitution* at the temples for the support of the priesthood, the ornamenting of the walls, altars, and images. So that these things, and perhaps several of the images themselves, were literally the *hire of the harlots:* and God threatens here to deliver all into the hands of enemies who should seize on this wealth, and literally spend it in the *same way* in which it was acquired; so that "to the hire of a harlot these things should return."

Verse 8. *I will make a wailing like the dragons*] *Newcome* translates:—

I will make a wailing like the foxes, (or jackals,)

And mourning like the daughters of the ostrich. This beast, the *jackal* or *shiagal*, we have often met with in the prophets. Travellers inform us that its *howlings* by night are most lamentable; and as to the *ostrich*, it is remarkable for its *fearful shrieking* and *agonizing groanings* after night. Dr. Shaw says he has often heard them groan as if they were in the greatest agonies.

Verse 9. *Her wound* is *incurable*] Nothing shall prevent their utter ruin, for they have filled up the measure of their iniquity.

A. M. cir. 3254
B. C. cir. 750
A. U. C. cir. 4
Romuli,
R. Roman.,
cir. annum 4

come unto Judah; he is come
unto the gate of my people, *even*
to Jerusalem.
10 [w]Declare ye *it* not at Gath,
weep ye not at all: in the house of [x]Aphrah
[y]roll thyself in the dust.
11 Pass ye away, [z]thou [a]inhabitant of
Saphir, having thy [b]shame naked: the inhabitant of [c]Zaanan came not forth in the
mourning of [d]Beth-ezel; he shall receive of
you his standing.
12 For the inhabitant of Maroth [e]waited
carefully for good: but [f]evil came down from
the LORD unto the gate of Jerusalem.
13 O thou inhabitant of [g]Lachish, bind the
chariot to the swift beast: she
is the beginning of the sin to
the daughter of Zion: for the
transgressions of Israel were
found in thee.
14 Therefore shalt thou [h]give presents [i]to
Moresheth-gath: the houses of [k]Achzib [l]*shall
be* a lie to the kings of Israel.
15 Yet will I bring an heir unto thee, O inhabitant of [m]Mareshah: [n]he shall come unto
[o]Adullam the glory of Israel.
16 Make thee [p]bald, and poll thee for thy
[q]delicate children; enlarge thy baldness as
the eagle; for they are gone into captivity
from thee.

[w]2 Sam. i. 20——[x]That is, *dust*——[y]Jer. vi. 26 [z]Or, *thou that dwellest fairly*——[a]Heb. *inhabitress* [b]Isa. xx. 4; xlvii. 2, 3; Jer. xiii. 22; Nah. iii. 5——[c]Or, *the country of flocks*——[d]Or, *a place near*——[e]Or, *was grieved*——[f]Amos iii. 6

[g]2 Kings xviii. 14, 17——[h]2 Sam. viii. 2; 2 Kings xviii. 14, 15, 16——[i]Or, *for*——[k]That is, *a lie*——[l]Josh. xv. 44 [m]Josh. xv. 44——[n]Or, *the glory of Israel shall come*, &c. [o]2 Chron. xi. 7——[p]Job i. 20; Isa. xv. 2; xxii. 12; Jer. vii. 29; xvi. 6; xlvii. 5; xlviii. 37——[q]Lam. iv. 5

He is come—even *to Jerusalem.*] The desolation and captivity of Israel shall first take place; that of Judah shall come after.

Verse 10. *Declare ye* it *not at Gath*] Do not let this prediction be known among the *Philistines*, else they will glory over you.

House of Aphrah] Or, *Beth-aphrah.* This place is mentioned Josh. xviii. 23, as in the tribe of Benjamin. There is a paronomasia, or play on words, here: בבית לעפרה עפר *bebeith leaphrah aphar*, "Roll thyself in the dust in the house of dust."

Verse 11. *Inhabitant of Saphir*] *Sapher, Sepphoris*, or *Sephora*, was the strongest place in Galilee.—*Calmet.* It was a city in the tribe of Judah, between Eleutheropolis and Ascalon.—*Houbigant.*

Zaanan] Another city in the tribe of Judah, Josh. xv. 13.

Beth-ezel] A place near Jerusalem, Zech. xiv. 5. Some think that Jerusalem itself is intended by this word.

Verse 12. *The inhabitant of Maroth*] There was a city of a similar name in the tribe of Judah, Josh. xv. 59.

Verse 13. *Inhabitant of Lachish*] This city was in the tribe of Judah, Josh. xv. 39, and was taken by Sennacherib when he was coming against Jerusalem, 2 Kings xviii. 13, &c., and it is supposed that he wished to reduce this city first, that, possessing it, he might prevent Hezekiah's receiving any help from Egypt.

She is *the beginning of the sin*] This seems to intimate that Lachish was the first city in Judah which received the idolatrous worship of Israel.

Verse 14. *Give presents to Moresheth-gath*] *Calmet* says that *Moresa* or *Morashti*, and *Achzib*, were cities not far from Gath. It is possible that when Ahaz found himself pressed by *Pekah*, king of Israel, he might have sent to these places for succour, that by their assistance he might *frustrate the hopes of the king of Israel;* and this may be the meaning of "The houses of Achzib shall be a lie to the kings of Israel." In these verses there are several instances of the *paronomasia.* See ver. 10, עפר *aphar, dust*, and עפרה *aphrah*, the name of the city. Ver. 11. צאנן *tsaanan, the city*, and יצאה *yatsah, to go out.* Ver. 13, לכיש *lachish, the city*, and רכש *rechesh, the swift beast.* Ver. 14, אכזיב *achzib, the city*, and אכזב *achzab, a lie.* Such paronomasias were reputed ornaments by the prophets. They occur in Isaiah with great effect. See Isa. v. 7.

Verse 15. *Yet will I bring an heir unto thee, O—Mareshah*] Here is another instance, הירש *haiyeresh, to bring an heir*, and מרשה *mareshah, the city*, the name of which signifies *heirship.* And so of the above proper names.

Adullam the glory of Israel.] This was a fenced city in the south of Judah (see 2 Chron. xi. 7) towards the Dead Sea.

There is much obscurity in the concluding verses of this chapter. They undoubtedly refer to the *captivity* of Israel, and to *circumstances* of *distress*, &c., which are not mentioned in any of the historical books, and therefore their reference and meaning can only be conjectured.

Verse 16. *Make thee bald*] *Cutting off the hair* was a sign of great distress, and was practised on the death of near relatives; see Amos viii. 10. The desolation should be so great that Israel should feel it to her utmost extent; and the *mourning* should be like that of a mother for the death of her most delicate children.

Enlarge thy baldness as the eagle] Referring to the *moulting* of this bird, when in casting its feathers and breeding new ones, it is very sickly, and its strength wholly exhausted.

They are gone into captivity] This is a prediction of the captivity by Shalmaneser. Samaria, the chief city, is called on to deplore it, as then fast approaching.

CHAPTER II

Here the prophet denounces a wo against the plotters of wickedness, the covetous and the oppressor, 1, 2. *God is represented as devising their ruin,* 3. *An Israelite is then introduced as a mourner, personating his people, and lamenting their fate,* 4. *Their total expulsion is now threatened on account of their very numerous offences,* 5–10. *Great infatuation of the people in favour of those pretenders to Divine inspiration who prophesied to them peace and plenty,* 11. *The chapter concludes with a gracious promise of the restoration of the posterity of Jacob from captivity; possibly alluding to their deliverance from the Chaldean yoke, an event which was about* two hundred *years in futurity at the delivery of this prophecy,* 12, 13.

A. M. cir. 3274
B. C. cir. 730
A. U. C. cir. 24
Romuli,
R. Roman.,
cir. annum 24

WO to them [a]that devise
iniquity, and [b]work evil
upon their beds! when the
morning is light, they practise
it, because [c]it is in the power of their hand.
2 And they covet [d]fields, and take *them* by
violence; and houses, and take *them* away:
so they [e]oppress a man and his house, even a
man and his heritage.
3 Therefore thus saith the LORD; Behold,
against [f]this family do I devise an evil, from
which ye shall not remove your necks; neither
shall ye go haughtily: [g]for this time *is* evil.
4 In that day shall *one* [h]take up a parable
against you, and [i]lament [k]with a doleful lamentation, *and* say, We be ut-
terly spoiled: [l]he hath changed
the portion of my people: how
hath he removed *it* from me!
[m]turning away he hath divided our fields.
5 Therefore thou shalt have none that shall
cast [n]a cord by lot in the congregation of the
LORD.
6 [o] [p]Prophesy [q]ye not, *say they to them that*
prophesy: they shall not prophesy to them,
that they shall not take shame.
7 O *thou that are* named the house of Jacob,
is the Spirit of the LORD [r]straitened? *are*
these his doings? do not my words do good
to him that walketh [s]uprightly?

A. M. cir. 3274
B. C. cir. 730
A. U. C. cir. 24
Romuli,
R. Roman.,
cir. annum 24

[a]Hos. vii. 6——[b]Psa. xxxvi. 4——[c]Gen. xxxi. 29——[d]Isa. v. 8——[e]Or, *defraud*——[f]Jer. viii. 3——[g]Amos v. 13; Eph. v. 16——[h]Hab. ii. 6——[i]2 Sam. i. 17——[k]Heb. *with a lamentation of lamentations*——[l]Ch. i. 15

[m]Or, *instead of restoring*——[n]Deut. xxxii. 8, 9——[o]Or, *Prophesy not as they prophesy*——[p]Heb. *drop,* &c.; Ezek. xxi. 2——[q]Isa. xxx. 10; Amos ii. 12; vii. 16——[r]Or, *shortened*——[s]Heb. *upright*

NOTES ON CHAP. II

Wo to them that devise iniquity] Who lay *schemes* and *plans* for transgressions; who make it their *study* to find out new modes of sinning; and make these things their *nocturnal* meditations, that, having fixed their plan, they may begin to execute it as soon as it is *light* in the *morning.*

Because it is in the power of their hand.] They think they *may* do whatever they have *power* and *opportunity* to do.

Verse 2. *They covet fields*] These are the rich and mighty in the land; and, like Ahab, they will take the vineyard or inheritance of any poor Naboth on which they may fix their covetous eye; so that they take away even the *heritage* of the poor.

Verse 3. *Against this family* (the Israelites) *do I devise an evil*] You have *devised* the evil of *plundering* the upright; I will devise the evil to you of *punishment* for your conduct; you shall have your *necks* brought under the yoke of servitude. Tiglath-pileser ruined this kingdom, and transported the people to Assyria, under the reign of Hezekiah, king of Judah; and Micah lived to see this catastrophe. See on ver. 9.

Verse 4. *Take up a parable against you*] Your wickedness and your punishment shall be subjects of common conversation; and a *funeral dirge* shall be composed and sung for you as for the *dead.* The *lamentation* is that which immediately follows: *We be utterly spoiled;* and ends, *Are these his doings?* ver. 7.

Verse 5. *None that shall cast a cord*] You will no more have your inheritance divided to you by lot, as it was to your fathers; ye shall neither have fields nor possessions of any kind.

Verse 6. *Prophesy ye not*] Do not predict any more evils—we have as many as we can bear. We are utterly ruined—shame and confusion cover our faces. The original is singular, and expressive of sorrow and sobbing. Literally, "Do not cause it to rain; they will cause it to rain; they cannot make it rain sooner than this; confusion shall not depart from us." To *rain,* often means to *preach,* to *prephesy;* Ezek. xx. 46, xxi. 2; Amos vii. 16; Deut. xxxii. 2; Job xxix. 22; Prov. v. 3, &c.

The last line Bp. *Newcome* translates, "*For* he shall not remove *from himself* reproaches;" and paraphrases, "The true prophet will subject himself to public disgrace by exercising his office."

Verse 7. *Is the Spirit of the Lord straitened?*] This is the complaint of the Israelites, and a part of the lamentation. Doth it not speak by other persons as well as by Micah? Doth it communicate to us such influences as it did formerly? Is it true that these evils are threatened by that Spirit? Are these his doings? To which Jehovah answers, "Do not my words do good to him that walketh uprightly?" No upright man need fear any word spoken by me: my words to such yield instruction and comfort; never dismay. Were ye upright, ye would not complain of the words of my prophets. The last clause may be translated, "Walking with him that is upright." The upright

A. M. cir. 3274
B. C. cir. 730
A. U. C. cir. 24
Romuli,
R. Roman.,
cir. annum 24

8 Even [t]of late my people is
risen up as an enemy: ye pull
off the robe [u]with the garment
from them that pass by securely
as men averse from war.
9 The [v]women of my people have ye cast
out from their pleasant houses; from their
children have ye taken away my glory for
ever.
10 Arise ye, and depart; for this *is* not *your*
[w]rest: because it is [x]polluted, it shall destroy
you, even with a sore destruction.
11 If a man [y]walking [z]in the spirit and
falsehood do lie, *saying,* I will prophesy unto
thee of wine and of strong
drink; he shall even be the prophet of this people.
12 [a]I will surely assemble, O
Jacob, all of thee; I will surely gather the
remnant of Israel; I will put them together
[b]as the sheep of Bozrah, as the flock in the
midst of their fold: they shall make great
noise by reason of *the multitude of* men.
13 The breaker is come up before them:
they have broken up, and have passed through
the gate, and are gone out by it: [c]and [d]their
king shall pass before them, [e]and the LORD
on the head of them.

[t]Heb. *yesterday*——[u]Heb. *over against a garment*——[v]Or, *wives*——[w]Deut. xii. 9——[x]Lev. xviii. 25, 28; Jeremiah iii. 2

[y]Or, *walk with the wind, and lie falsely*——[z]Ezek. xiii. 3——[a]Chap. iv. 6, 7——[b]Jer. xxxi. 10——[c]Ezek. xxxvi 37——[d]Hos. iii. 5——[e]Isa. lii. 12

man walks *by* the word; and the word walks *with* him who walks *by* it.

Verse 8. *My people is risen up as an enemy*] Ye are not only opposed to me, but ye are enemies to each other. Ye rob and spoil each other. Ye plunder the peaceable passenger; depriving him both of his *upper* and *under* garment; *ye pull off the robe* from those who, far from being spoilers themselves, *are averse from war.*

Verse 9. *The women of my people*] Ye are the cause of the women and their children being carried into captivity—separated from their pleasant habitations, and from my temple and ordinances—and from the blessings of the covenant, which it is my *glory* to give, and theirs to receive. These two verses may probably relate to the war made on Ahaz by Rezin, king of Syria, and Pekah, king of Israel. They fell suddenly upon the Jews; killed in one day *one hundred and twenty thousand,* and took *two hundred thousand* captive; and carried away much spoil. Thus, they *rose up against them as enemies,* when there was peace between the two kingdoms; spoiled them of their goods, carried away *men, women,* and *children,* till, at the remonstrances of the prophet *Oded,* they were released. See 2 Chron. xxviii. 6, &c. Micah lived in the days of Ahaz, and might have seen the barbarities which he here describes.

Verse 10. *Arise ye, and depart*] Prepare for your captivity; ye shall have no *resting* place here: the very *land is polluted* by your iniquities, and shall vomit you out, and it shall be *destroyed;* and the *destruction* of it shall be great and *sore.*

Some think this is an exhortation to the *godly,* to leave a land that was to be destroyed so speedily.

Verse 11. *If a man walking in the spirit and falsehood*] The meaning is: If a man who professes to be *Divinely inspired* do *lie,* by prophesying of plenty, &c., then such a person shall be *received* as a *true prophet* by this people. It not unfrequently happens that the Christless worldling, who has got into the priest's office for a maintenance, and who leaves the people undisturbed in their unregenerate state, is better received than the faithful pastor, who proclaims the justice of the Lord, and the necessity of repentance and forsaking sin, in order to their being made partakers of that holiness without which no man shall see God.

Verse 12. *I will surely assemble*] This is a promise of the restoration of Israel from captivity. He compares them to a flock of sheep rushing together to their fold, the *hoofs* of which make a *wonderful noise* or *clatter.* So when *one hundred* sheep run, *eight hundred* toes or divisions of these *bifid* animals make a clattering noise. This appears to be the image.

Verse 13. *The breaker is come up*] He who is to give them *deliverance,* and lead them out on the way of their return. He who takes down the *hurdles,* or makes *a gap* in the *wall* or *hedge,* to permit them to pass through. This may apply to those *human agents* that shall permit and order their return. And *Jehovah* being *at their head,* may refer to their final restoration, when the Lord Jesus shall become their leader, they having returned unto him as the shepherd and bishop of their souls; and they and the Gentiles forming one fold under one shepherd, to go no more out into captivity for ever. Lord, hasten the time!

CHAPTER III

In this chapter the prophet inveighs with great boldness and spirit against the princes and prophets of Judah; and foretells the destruction of Jerusalem as the consequence of their iniquity, 1–12. *The last verse was fulfilled to a certain extent by Nebuchadnezzar; but most fully and literally by the Romans under Titus. See* Josephus.

A. M. cir. 3294
B. C. cir. 710
A. U. C. cir. 44
NumæPompilii,
R. Roman.,
cir. annum 6

AND I said, Hear, I pray you,
O heads of Jacob, and ye
princes of the house of Israel;
[a]*Is it* not for you to know judgment?
2 Who hate the good, and love the evil;
who pluck off their skin from off them, and
their flesh from off their bones;
3 Who also [b]eat the flesh of my people,
and flay their skin from off them, and they
break their bones, and chop them in pieces, as
for the pot, and [c]as flesh within the caldron.
4 Then [d]shall they cry unto the LORD, but
he will not hear them; he will even hide his
face from them at that time, as they have behaved themselves ill in their doings.
5 Thus saith the LORD [e]concerning the prophets that make my people err, that [f]bite with
their teeth, and cry, Peace; and [g]he that putteth not into their mouths, they
even prepare war against him:
6 [h]Therefore night *shall be*
unto you, [i]that ye shall not have
a vision; and it shall be dark unto you, [k]that
ye shall not divine; [l]and the sun shall go
down over the prophets, and the day shall be
dark over them.
7 Then shall the seers be ashamed, and the
diviners confounded: yea, they shall all cover
their [m]lips; [n]for *there is* no answer of God.
8 But truly I am full of power by the Spirit
of the LORD, and of Judgment, and of might,
[o]to declare unto Jacob his transgression, and
to Israel his sin.
9 Hear this, I pray you, ye heads of the house
of Jacob, and princes of the house of Israel,
that abhor judgment, and pervert all equity.
10 [p]They build up Zion with [q]blood,

A. M. cir. 3294
B. C. cir. 710
A. U. C. cir. 44
NumæPompilii,
R. Roman.,
cir. annum 6

[a]Jer. v. 4, 5——[b]Psa. xiv. 4——[c]Ezek. xi. 3, 7——[d]Psa. xviii. 41; Prov. i. 28; Isa. i. 15; Ezek. viii. 18; Zech. vii. 13——[e]Isa. lvi. 10, 11; Ezek. xiii. 10; xxii. 25——[f]Chap. ii. 11; Matt. xii. 15——[g]Ezek. xiii. 18, 19——[h]Isa. viii. 20, 22; Ezek. xiii. 23, 24; Zech. xiii. 4——[i]Heb. *from a vision*——[k]Heb. *from divining*——[l]Amos vii. 9——[m]Heb. *upper lip*——[n]Psa. lxxiv. 9; Amos viii. 11——[o]Isa. lviii. 1——[p]Jeremiah xxii. 13——[q]Ezekiel xxii. 27; Habakkuk ii. 12; Zeph. iii. 3

NOTES ON CHAP. III

Verse 1. *Hear—O heads of Jacob*] The metaphor of the *flock* is still carried on. The *chiefs of Jacob*, and the *princes of Israel*, instead of taking care of the *flocks*, defending them, and finding them pasture, oppressed them in various ways. They are like *wolves*, who *tear the skin of the sheep*, and the *flesh off their bones*. This applies to all unjust and oppressive rulers.

Suetonius tells us, in his Life of *Tiberius*, that when the governors of provinces wrote to the emperor, entreating him to increase the *tributes*, he wrote back: "It is the property of a good *shepherd* to *shear* his sheep, not to *skin* them." Præsidibus onerandas tributo provincias suadentibus rescripsit: BONI PASTORIS esse TONDERE pecus, non DEGLUBERE. This is a maxim which many rulers of the earth do not seem to understand.

Verse 4. *Then shall they cry*] When calamity comes upon these oppressors, they shall cry for deliverance: but *they shall not be heard;* because, in their unjust exactions upon the people, they went on ruthlessly, and would *not hear* the cry of the oppressed.

Verse 5. *That bite with their teeth*] That eat to the full; that are well provided for, and as long as they are so, prophesy smooth things, and cry, *Peace!* i. e., Ye shall have nothing but peace and prosperity. Whereas the true prophet, "who putteth not into their mouths," who makes no provision for their evil propensities, "they prepare war against him." קדשו עליו מלחמה *kiddeshu alaiv milchamah*, "They *sanctify a war* against him." They call on all to help them to put down a man who is speaking evil of the *Lord's people;* and predicting the destruction of *his temple*, and *Israel his inheritance.*

Verse 6. *Night* shall be *unto you*] Ye shall have no *spiritual light*, nor will God give you any revelation of his will.

The sun shall go down over the prophets] They prospered for a while, *causing the people to err;* but they shall also be carried into captivity, and then the sun of their prosperity shall go down for ever, and the very *day* that gives *light* and comfort to others, shall be *darkness* and calamity to them.

Verse 7. *Shall the seers be ashamed*] For the *false visions* of comfort and prosperity which they pretended to see.

And the diviners confounded] Who pretended to foretell future prosperity; for they themselves are now *thralled* in that very *captivity* which the true prophets foretold, and which the false prophets said should not happen.

Verse 8. *But—I am full of power*] Here is the character of the true prophet. *He is filled*, all his soul is occupied with *power*, כח *coach*, with heavenly energy; *by the Spirit of the Lord*, the fountain of all truth and might; *and of judgment*, which enables him to make a proper discernment between the precious and the vile; *and of might*, גבורה *geburah*, prevalent power, against which vice shall not be able to prevail, and before which iniquity shall not be able to stand: but all shall fall together, and be confounded.

Verse 9. *Hear this*] An appeal similar to that in ver. 1.

Verse 10. *They build up Zion with blood*] They might cry out loudly against that butchery practised by Pekah, king of Israel, and Pul coadjutor of Rezie, against the Jews. See on chap. ii. 9. But these were by no means clear themselves; for if they *strengthened the city*, or *decorated the temple*, it was by the produce of their *exactions* and *oppressions* of the people.

I do not know a text more applicable than

A. M. cir. 3294
B. C. cir. 710
A. U. C. cir. 44
NumæPompilii,
R. Roman.,
cir. annum 6

[r]and Jerusalem with iniquity.

11 [s]The heads thereof judge for reward, and [t]the priests thereof teach for hire, and the prophets thereof divine for money: [u]yet will they lean upon the LORD, [v]and say, *Is* not the LORD among us? none evil can come upon us.

12 Therefore shall Zion for your sake be [w]ploughed *as* a field; [x]and Jerusalem shall become heaps, and [y]the mountain of the house as the high places of the forest.

[r]Heb. *bloods*——[s]Isa. i. 23; Ezek. xxii. 12; Hos. iv. 18; chap. vii. 3——[t]Jer. vi. 13——[u]Isa. xlviii. 2; Jer. vii. 4; Rom. ii. 17——[v]Heb. *saying*——[w]Jer. xxvi. 18; chap. i. 6——[x]Psa. lxxix. 1——[y]Chap. iv. 2

this to *slave-dealers;* or to any who have *made their fortunes* by such *wrongs* as affect the *life* of man; especially the former, who by the gains of this diabolic traffic have *built houses,* &c.; for, following up the prophet's *metaphor,* the *timbers,* &c., are the *bones* of the hapless Africans; and the *mortar,* the blood of the defenceless progeny of Ham. What an account must all those who have any hand in or profit from this detestable, degrading, and inhuman traffic, give to Him who will shortly judge the quick and dead!

Verse 11. *The heads thereof judge for reward*] This does not apply to the *regular law officers,* who have their proper *salaries* for giving up their whole time and attention to the conscientious discharge of the duties of their office; but to those who take a *reward,* who take BRIBES, for the perversion of justice; who will decide in favour of those from whom they get the *greatest reward.*

The prophets—divine for money] These are evidently the false prophets; for none, professing to be sent by God, used any kind of *divination.*

Yet will they lean upon the Lord] They will prescribe fasts and public thanksgivings, while not one sin is repented of or forsaken, and not one public grievance is redressed.

Is *not the Lord among us?*] Here is his *temple,* here are his *ordinances,* and here are his *people.* Will he leave these? Yes, he will abandon the whole, because all are *polluted.*

Verse 12. *Therefore shall Zion—be ploughed* as *a field*] It shall undergo a variety of reverses and sackages, till at last *there shall not be one stone left on the top of another, that shall not be pulled down;* and then a *plough* shall be drawn along the site of the walls, to signify an irreparable and endless destruction. Of this ancient custom *Horace* speaks, *Odar.* lib. i., Od. 16, ver. 18.

Altis urbibus ultimæ
Stetere causæ cur perirent
Funditus, imprimeretque muris
Hostile aratrum exercitus insolens

"From hence proud cities date their utter falls;
When, insolent in ruin, o'er their walls
The wrathful soldier drags the hostile plough,
That haughty mark of total overthrow."

FRANCIS.

Thus did the *Romans* treat Jerusalem when it was taken by *Titus. Turnus Rufus,* or as he is called by St. Jerome, *Titus Arinius Rufus,* or *Terentius Rufus,* according to *Josephus,* caused a plough to be drawn over all the courts of the temple to signify that it should never be rebuilt, and the place only serve for *agricultural* purposes. See the note on Matt. xxiv. 2. Thus *Jerusalem became heaps,* an indiscriminate mass of ruins and rubbish; and *the mountain of the house,* Mount Moriah, on which the temple stood, became so much neglected after the total destruction of the temple, that it soon resembled the *high places of the forest.* What is said here may apply also, as before hinted, to the ruin of the temple by Nebuchadnezzar in the last year of the reign of Zedekiah, the last king of the Jews.

As the *Masoretes,* in their division of the Bible, reckon the *twelve minor prophets* but as *one book,* they mark this verse (*twelfth* of chap. iii.) the MIDDLE *verse* of these prophets.

CHAPTER IV

In the commencement of this chapter we have a glorious prophecy of the establishment and prosperity of the Messiah's kingdom; its peaceful character, increasing spiritual and political influence, ultimate universality, and everlasting duration, 1–4. *Then breaks in a chorus of his people declaring their peculiar happiness in being members of his kingdom,* 5. *The prophet resumes the subject; predicts the restoration and future prosperity of Israel,* 6–8; *and exhorts them not to be discouraged at their approaching captivity, as they should in due time not only be delivered from it, but likewise be victorious over all their enemies,* 9–13. *These last verses, which evidently contain a prediction of the final triumph of Christianity over every adversary, have been applied to the conquests of the Maccabees; but the character and beneficial results of their military exploits, as far as we have any account of them, correspond but in a very faint degree to the beautiful and highly wrought terms of the prophecy. The first* three *verses of this chapter are very similar to the commencement of the second chapter of Isaiah; and the* fourth, *for beauty of imagery and elegance of expression, is not unworthy of that prophet.*

A. M. cir. 3294
B. C. cir. 710
A. U. C. cir. 44
NumæPompilii,
R. Roman.,
cir. annum 6

BUT [a]in the last days it shall
come to pass, *that* the
mountain of the house of the
LORD shall be established in the
top of the mountains, and it shall be exalted
above the hills; and people shall flow unto it.
2 And many nations shall come, and say,
Come, and let us go up to the [b]mountain of
the LORD, and to the house of the God of
Jacob; and he will teach us of his ways, and
we will walk in his paths; for the law shall
go forth of Zion, and the word of the LORD
from Jerusalem.
3 And he shall judge among many people,
and rebuke strong nations afar off; and they
shall beat their swords into [c]ploughshares,
and their spears into [d]pruninghooks: nation
shall not lift up a sword against nation,
[e]neither shall they learn war any more.
4 [f]But they shall sit every man under his
vine and under his fig tree; and none shall
make *them* afraid: for the
mouth of the LORD of hosts hath
spoken *it*.

A. M. cir. 3294
B. C. cir. 710
A. U. C. cir. 44
NumæPompilii,
R. Roman.,
cir. annum 6

5 For [g]all people will walk
every one in the name of his god, and [h]we
will walk in the name of the LORD our God
for ever and ever.
6 In that day, saith the LORD, [i]will I assemble
her that halteth, [k]and I will gather her that
is driven out, and her that I have afflicted;
7 And I will make her that halted [l]a remnant,
and her that was cast far off a strong
nation: and the LORD [m]shall reign over them
in Mount Zion from henceforth, even for ever.
8 And thou, O tower of [n]the flock, the
stronghold of the daughter of Zion, unto thee
shall it come, even the first dominion; the
kingdom shall come to the daughter of Jerusalem.
9 Now why dost thou cry out aloud? [o]*is there*
no king in thee? is thy counsellor perished?

[a]Isa. ii. 2, &c.; Ezek. xvii. 22, 23——[b]Isa. xiv. 25——[c]Isa. ii. 4; Joel iii. 10——[d]Or, *scythes*——[e]Psa. lxxii. 7——[f]1 Kings iv. 25; Zech. iii. 10——[g]Jer. ii. 11——[h]Zech. x. 12——[i]Ezek. xxxiv. 16; Zeph. iii. 19

[k]Psa. cxlvii. 2; Ezek. xxxiv. 13; xxxvii. 21——[l]Chap. ii. 12; v. 3, 7, 8; vii. 18——[m]Isa. ix. 6; xxiv. 23; Dan. vii. 14, 27; Luke i. 33; Rev. xi. 15——[n]Or, *Edar;* Gen. xxxv. 21——[o]Jer. viii. 19

NOTES ON CHAP. IV

Verses 1-4. *But in the last days it shall come to pass*] These *four* verses contain, says Bp. *Newcome*, a prophecy that was to be fulfilled by the coming of the Messiah, when the Gentiles were to be admitted into covenant with God, and the apostles were to preach the Gospel, beginning at Jerusalem, Luke xxiv. 47; Acts ii. 14, &c.; when Christ was to be the spiritual Judge and King of many people, was to convince many nations of their errors and vices, and was to found a religion which had the strongest tendency to promote peace. Bp. *Lowth* thinks that "Micah took this passage from Isaiah;" or the Spirit may have inspired both prophets with this prediction; or both may have copied some *common original*, the words of a prophet well known at that time. The variations (few and of little importance) may be seen in the notes on the parallel passages, Isa. ii. 2, &c.; to which the reader is requested to refer.

Verse 4. *Under his vine and under his fig tree*] A proverbial expression, indicative of perfect peace, security, and rural comfort. See on Isa. ii. 1. This verse is an addition to the prophecy as it stands in Isaiah.

Verse 5. *Every one in the name of his god*] This shall be the state of the Gentile world; but after the captivity, the Jews walked in the name of Jehovah alone; and acknowledge no other object of religious worship to the present day.

Verse 6. *Will I assemble her that halteth—driven out—afflicted*] Under these epithets, the state of the Jews, who were to be gathered into the Christian Church, is pointed out. They *halted* between the true God and idols; they were *driven out* into captivity, because of this idolatry; and they were variously *afflicted*, because they would not return unto the Lord that bought them.

Verse 7. *Her that halted a remnant*] I will preserve them as a distinct people after their return from captivity, for the farther purposes of my grace and mercy.

And the Lord shall reign over them in Mount Zion] The *Chaldee* is remarkable here, and positively applies the words to the Messiah: "But thou, O Messiah, of Israel, who art hidden because of the sins of the congregation of Zion, the kingdom shall come unto thee."

Verse 8. *O tower of the flock*] I think the temple is meant, or Jerusalem; the place where the *flock*, the whole *congregation* of the people assembled to worship God. *Newcome* retains the Hebrew word עדר *eder*, a tower in or near *Beth-lehem*, Gen. xxxv. 21, or, as some think, a tower near the *sheep-gate* in Jerusalem. I believe Jerusalem, or the temple, or both, are meant; for these were considered *the stronghold of the daughter of Zion*, the fortress of the Jewish people.

Even the first dominion] What was this? The Divine *theocracy* under Jesus Christ; this former, this *first dominion*, was to be restored. Hence the angel called him *Immanuel*, God with us, ruling among us.

Verse 9. Is there *no king in thee?*] None. And why? Because thou hast rejected Jehovah thy king.

Is thy counsellor perished?] No: but thou hast rejected the words and advices of the prophets.

A. M. cir. 3294 B. C. cir. 710 A. U. C. cir. 44 NumæPompilii, R. Roman., cir. annum 6

for [p]pangs have taken thee as a
woman in travail.

10 Be in pain, and labour to
bring forth, O daughter of Zion,
like a woman in travail: for now shalt thou go
forth out of the city, and thou shalt dwell in the
field, and thou shalt go *even* to Babylon; there
shalt thou be delivered; there the LORD shall
redeem thee from the hand of thine enemies.

11 [q]Now also many nations are gathered
against thee, that say, Let her be defiled, and
let our eye [r]look upon Zion.

12 But they know not [s]the
thoughts of the LORD, neither
understand they his counsel: for
he shall gather them [t]as the
sheaves into the floor.

13 [u]Arise and thresh, O daughter of Zion:
for I will make thine horn iron, and I will
make thy hoofs brass: and thou shalt [v]beat
in pieces many people: [w]and I will consecrate their gain unto the LORD, and their
substance unto [x]the LORD of the whole
earth.

[p]Isa. xiii. 8; xxi. 3; Jer. xxx. 6; l. 43——[q]Lam. ii. 16——[r]Obad. 12; chap. vii. 10——[s]Isa. lv. 8; Rom. xi. 33

[t]Isa. xxi. 10——[u]Isa. xli. 15, 16; Jer. li. 33——[v]Dan. ii. 44——[w]Isa. xviii. 7; xxiii. 18; lx. 6, 9——[x]Zech. iv. 14; vi. 5

Pangs have taken thee] He is speaking of the desolations that should take place when the Chaldeans should come against the city; and hence he says, "Thou shalt go to Babylon;" ye shall be cast out of your own land, and sent slaves to a foreign country. He represents the people under the notion of a *woman in travail.*

Verse 10. *There shalt thou be delivered*] There God shall meet thee; and by redeeming thee from thy captivity, bringing thee back to thine own land, and finally converting thee unto himself, shall deliver thee from the *burden* of grief and wo which thou now bearest, and under which thou dost groan.

Verse 11. *Many nations are gathered against thee*] The Chaldeans, who were composed of many nations. And, we may add, all the surrounding nations were their enemies; and rejoiced when the Chaldean army had overthrown Jerusalem, destroyed the temple, and led the people away captive.

Let her be defiled] This was their cry and their wish: Let Jerusalem be laid as *low* as she can be, like a thing *defiled* and *cast away* with abhorrence; that *their eyes might look upon Zion* with scorn, contempt, and exultation.

Verse 12. *But they know not the thoughts of the Lord*] These think that God has utterly rejected his people, and they shall have a troublesome neighbour no more: but this is not his design; he will afflict them for a time; but these, the enemies of his people, he will gather as *sheaves* into the *threshing-floor*, there to be trodden, and the wheel to go over them. This is the *counsel*, the *purpose of God,* which these do not understand. The persons here referred to are not only the *Chaldeans* which were threshed by the *Persians* and *Medes;* but the Idumeans, Ammonites, Moabites, and Philistines, which the Jews afterwards subdued.

Verse 13. *Arise and thresh, O daughter of Zion*] This refers to the subject of the preceding verse. When God shall have *gathered together* all thy enemies, as into the *threshing-floor*, he will give thee *commission* and *power* to get a complete victory over them, and reduce them to servitude. And that thou mayest be able to do this, he will be on thy side as a powerful helper; here signified by the metaphors, *iron horns*, and *brazen hoofs.* Thou shalt have *power*, *authority*, and *unconquerable strength;* for thine enemies shall be no more against thee than the *corn* against *oxen* shod with *brass*, or a puny animal against the horn of a fierce *bull* tipped with *iron.*

I will consecrate their gain unto the Lord] What they have taken from thee in the way of spoil shall be restored; and again consecrated unto the service of him who will show himself to be *the Lord*, the Supreme Governor of the *whole earth.* Was not this prediction fulfilled when Cyrus gave the Jews permission to return to their own land, and gave them back the sacred vessels of the temple which Nebuchadnezzar had carried away? The Maccabees and their successors recovered much of the booty of which the neighbouring nations had deprived the Jews; and the *treasure* taken was devoted to Jehovah. The *first* verse of the next chapter should conclude this.

CHAPTER V

This chapter begins, according to the opinion of some commentators, with a prophecy concerning the siege of Jerusalem by Nebuchadnezzar, and the great indignities which Zedekiah should suffer from the Babylonians, 1. *We have next a most famous prediction concerning the birthplace of the Messiah, "whose goings forth have been from* of old, *from* EVERLASTING," 2. *See* Matt. ii. 6. *The Jews obstinately persisting in their opposition to the Messiah, God will therefore give them up into the hands of their enemies till the times of the Gentiles be fulfilled: and then all the posterity of Jacob, both* Israel *and* Judah, *shall be converted to the faith of our Lord Jesus Christ, and, along with the Gentiles, be brought into the large and peaceful pastures of this Great Shepherd of the sheep,* 3, 4. *After this illustrious prophecy, the prophet goes on to foretell the downfall of the Assyrians, by whom are meant the enemies of the Church in general, the* type *being probably put for the* antitype; *the miraculous discomfiture of the great Assyrian army in the reign of Sennacherib strongly shadowing forth the glorious and no less miraculous triumphs of Christianity in the latter times,* 5, 6. *See* Isa. xi. 16. *Some understand this prophecy of Antiochus and the seven famous Maccabees, with their eight royal successors, from Aristobulus to Antigonus; and it is not impossible that these people may be also intended, for we have often had occasion to remark that a prophecy of the Old Testament Scriptures has frequently more than one aspect. The* seventh *verse was fulfilled by the Jews spreading the knowledge of the true God during their captivity, and so paving the way for the Gospel; but will be more signally fulfilled after their conversion and restoration. See* Rom. xi. 12–15. *The remaining verses contain a prophecy of the final overthrow of all the enemies of pure and undefiled religion, and of the thorough purification of the Church of God from the corruptions of Antichrist,* 9–15.

A. M. cir. 3294
B. C. cir. 710
A. U. C. cir. 44
NumæPompilii, R. Roman., cir. annum 6

NOW gather thyself in troops,
O daughter of troops: he
hath laid siege against us: they
shall [a]smite the judge of Israel,
with a rod upon the cheek.
2 But thou, [b]Beth-lehem Ephratah, *though*
thou be little [c]among the [d]thousands of Judah,
yet out of thee shall he come forth unto me
that is to be [e]Ruler in Israel; [f]whose goings forth *have been* from of old, from
[g]everlasting.

3 Therefore will he give them
up, until the time *that* [h]she
which travaileth hath brought
forth: then [i]the remnant of his
brethren shall return unto the children of
Israel.
4 And he shall stand and [k]feed [l]in the
strength of the LORD, in the majesty of the
name of the LORD his God; and they shall
abide: for now [m]shall he be great unto the
ends of the earth.

[a]Lam. iii. 30; Matt. v. 39; xxvii. 30——[b]Matt. ii. 6; John vii. 42——[c]1 Sam. xxiii. 23——[d]Exod. xviii. 25——[e]Gen. xlix. 10; Isa. ix. 6——[f]Psa. xc. 2; Prov. viii. 22, 23; John i. 1

[g]Heb. *the days of eternity*——[h]Chap. iv. 10——[i]Chap. iv. 7——[k]Or, *rule*——[l]Isa. xl. 11; xlix. 10; Ezek. xxxiv. 23; chap. vii. 14——[m]Psa. lxxii. 8; Isa. lii. 13; Zech. ix. 10; Luke i. 32

NOTES ON CHAP. V

Verse 1. *O daughter of troops*] The Chaldeans, whose armies were composed of *troops* from various nations.

He (Nebuchadnezzar) *hath laid siege against us;* (Jerusalem;) *they shall smite the judge of Israel* (Zedekiah) *with a rod upon the cheek.*] They shall offer him the greatest *indignity.* They slew his sons before his face; and then put out his eyes, loaded him with chains, and carried him captive to Babylon.

Verse 2. *But thou, Beth-lehem Ephratah*] I have considered this subject in great detail in the *notes* on Matt. ii. 6, to which the reader will be pleased to refer. This verse should begin this chapter; the *first* verse belongs to the preceding chapter.

Beth-lehem Ephratah, to distinguish it from another Beth-lehem, which was in the tribe of *Zebulun,* Josh. xix. 15.

Thousands of Judah] The tribes were divided into small portions called *thousands;* as in our country certain divisions of counties are called *hundreds.*

Whose goings forth have been *from of old*] In every age, from the foundation of the world, there has been some manifestation of the Messiah. He was the hope, as he was the salvation, of the world, from the promise to Adam in paradise, to his manifestation in the flesh *four thousand* years after.

From everlasting] מימי עולם *miyemey olam,* "From the days of all time;" from time as it came out of eternity. That is, there was *no time* in which he has not been *going forth—coming* in various ways to save men. And he that *came forth* the moment that time had its birth, was *before that time* in which he began to *come forth* to save the souls that he had *created.* He was *before* all things. As he is the *Creator* of all things, so he is the *Eternal,* and *no part* of what was *created.* All *being* but God has been *created.* Whatever has *not been created* is God. But Jesus is the *Creator* of all things; therefore he is God; for he cannot be a *part* of his *own work.*

Verse 3. *Therefore will he give them up*] Jesus Christ shall give up the disobedient and rebellious Jews into the hands of all the nations of the earth, till *she who travaileth hath brought forth;* that is, till the Christian Church, represented Rev. xii. 1, under the notion of a *woman in travail,* shall have had the fulness of the Gentiles brought in. *Then the remnant of his brethren shall return;* the Jews also shall be converted unto the Lord; and thus *all Israel shall be saved,* according to Rom. xi. 26.

Unto the children of Israel.] Taking in *both families,* that of *Judah* and that of *Israel.* The remnant of the *ten tribes,* wherever they are, shall be brought in under Christ; and though now *lost* among the nations of the earth, they will then not only be brought in among the *fulness of the Gentiles,* but most probably be *distinguished* as *Jews.*

On this verse Abp. *Newcome* says, "The sense is, God will not fully vindicate and exalt his people, till the virgin mother shall have brought forth her Son; and till Judah and Israel, and all the true sons of Abraham among their brethren the Gentiles, be converted to Christianity.

Verse 4. *He shall stand and feed*] The *Messiah* shall *remain* with his followers, supporting and *governing them in the strength and majesty of the Lord,* with all the miraculous interferences of his power, and all the glories of his grace.

And they shall abide] After this the Jews shall no more go astray, but shall remain one people with the Gentiles, under the one Shepherd and Bishop of all souls.

Newcome translates, "They shall be converted," for instead of וישבו *veyashebu,* he reads וישובו *veyashubu,* which gives him the translation above. This is the reading of *three* MSS. of *Kennicott's* and *De Rossi's,* with the *Syriac, Chaldee,* and *Vulgate.*

For now shall he be great] The Messiah shall be *great,* as bringing salvation to the *ends*

A. M. cir. 3294
B. C. cir. 710
A. U. C. cir. 44
NumæPompilii,
R. Roman.,
cir. annum 6

5 And this *man* [n]shall be the
peace, when the Assyrian shall
come into our land: and when
he shall tread in our palaces,
then shall we raise against him seven shepherds, and eight [o]principal men.
6 And they shall [p]waste the land of Assyria
with the sword, and the land of [q]Nimrod [r]in
the entrances thereof: thus shall he [s]deliver
us from the Assyrian, when he cometh into our
land, and when he treadeth within our borders.
7 And [t]the remnant of Jacob shall be in the
midst of many people [u]as the dew from the
LORD, as the showers upon the grass, that
tarrieth not for man, nor waiteth for the sons
of men.
8 And the remnant of Jacob
shall be among the Gentiles in
the midst of many people as a
lion among the beasts of the for-
est, as a young lion among the flocks of [v]sheep:
who, if he go through, both treadeth down,
and teareth in pieces, and none can deliver.
9 Thine hand shall be lifted up upon thine
adversaries, and all thine enemies shall be
cut off.
10 [w]And it shall come to pass in that day,
saith the LORD, that I will cut off thy horses
out of the midst of thee, and I will destroy
thy chariots:
11 And I will cut off the cities of thy land,
and throw down all thy strongholds:

[n]Psa. lxxii. 7; Isa. ix. 6; Zech. ix. 10; Luke ii. 14; Eph. ii. 14——[o]Heb. *princes of men*——[p]Heb. *eat up* [q]Gen. x. 8, 10, 11

[r]Or, *with her own naked swords*——[s]Luke i. 71 [t]Ver. 3——[u]Deut. xxxii. 2; Psa. lxxii. 6; cx. 3——[v]Or, *goats*——[w]Zech. ix. 10

of the earth. All nations shall receive his religion, and he shall be universal King.

Verse 5. *And this* man *shall be the peace*] This clause should be joined to the preceding verse, as it finishes the prophecy concerning our blessed Lord, who is the *Author* and *Prince of Israel;* and shall finally give *peace* to all nations, by bringing them under his yoke.

When the Assyrian shall come] This is a new prophecy, and relates to the subversion of the Assyrian empire.

Then shall we raise against him seven shepherds] Supposed to mean the *seven Maccabees, Mattathias*, and his *five* sons, and *Hyrcanus*, the son of *Simon.*

Eight principal men.] Eight princes, the *Asmonean* race; beginning with *Aristobulus*, and ending with *Herod*, who was married to *Mariamne.—Sharpe.* Perhaps *seven* and *eight* are a definite for an indefinite number, as Eccl. xi. 2; Job v. 19. The prophet means the chiefs of the Medes and Babylonians, the prefects of different provinces who took Nineveh, whose number may have been what is here specified.—*Newcome.*

Calmet considers this as referring to the invasion of Judea by *Cambyses*, when the Lord raised up against him the *seven magi.* He of them who passed for king of the Persians was the *Smerdis* of *Herodotus*, the *Oropastes* of Trogus, and the *Artaxerxes* of Ezra. These magi were put to death by *seven Persian chiefs;* who, having delivered the empire from them, set one of themselves, *Darius*, the son of Hystaspes, upon the throne.

Verse 6. *The land of Nimrod*] Assyria, and Nineveh its capital; and Babylon, which was also built by Nimrod, who was its *first* king, Gen. x. 11, 12, in the *margin.*

In the entrances thereof] At its *posts* or *watergates;* for it was by rendering themselves masters of the Euphrates that the Medes and Persians took the city, according to the prediction of Jeremiah, chap. li. 32, 36.

Calmet thinks that this refers to the deliverance of the land from *Cambyses* by his death, and the insurrection of the *eight princes* mentioned above, who made themselves masters of the whole Babylonian empire, &c. Perhaps it is best to refer it to the invasion of Judea by *Nebuchadnezzar;* and the final destruction of the *Babylonish* empire by *Cyrus*, who took Babylon, slew Belshazzar, and possessed himself of the kingdom.

Verse 7. *The remnant of Jacob*] From the reign of *Darius Hystaspes* (*Ahasuerus*, husband of *Esther*) the Jews were greatly favoured. Those who continued in Persia and Chaldea were greatly honoured under the protection of *Mordecai* and *Esther.—Calmet.* But others consider this as applying to the *Maccabees.*

As a dew from the Lord] Even during their captivity many of the Jews were the means of *spreading the knowledge of the one true God;* see Dan. ii. 47; iii. 29; iv. 34; vi. 26. This may be *the dew from the Lord* mentioned here. When the Messiah appeared, the Gospel was preached by *them;* and it shall again be propagated by their future glorious restoration, Rom. xi. 12, 25.

The grass, that tarrieth not for man] Which *grass* springs up without the attention and culture of man; לאיש *leish*, even the *best* and *most skilful* of men.

Nor waiteth for the sons of men.] לבני אדם *libney adam*, for the *sons of Adam*, the first transgressor. The *dew* and the *showers* descend on the earth and water it, in order to render it fruitful; and the *grass* springs up independently either of the *worth* or *wickedness* of man. All comes through *God's bounty*, who causes his *sun* to shine on the *just* and the *unjust*, and his *rain* to descend on the *evil* and the *good.*

Verse 8. *As a lion*] In this and the following verse the victories of the Maccabees are supposed to be foretold.

Verse 9. *All thine enemies shall be cut off.*] The *Assyrians*, who had destroyed *Israel;* and the *Babylonians*, who had ruined *Judah.*

Verse 10. *I will cut off thy horses*] Thou shalt have no need of *cavalry* in thine armies; God will fight for you.

Verse 11. *I will—throw down all thy strong-*

A. M. cir. 3294 B. C. cir. 710 A. U. C. cir. 44 NumæPompilii, R. Roman., cir. annum 6

12 And I will cut off witchcrafts out of thine hand; and thou shalt have no *more* [x]soothsayers.

13 [y]Thy graven images also will I cut off, and thy [z]standing images out of the midst of thee; and thou shalt [a]no more worship the work of thine hands.

14 And I will pluck up thy groves out of the midst of thee: so will I destroy thy [b]cities.

15 And I will [c]execute vengeance in anger and fury upon the heathen, such as they have not heard.

[x]Isa. ii. 6——[y]Zech. xiii. 2——[z]Or, *statues*——[a]Isa. ii. 8——[b]Or, *enemies*——[c]Psa. cxlix. 7; ver. 8; 2 Thess. i. 8

holds] Thou shalt have no need of *fortified cities;* I will be thy defence.

Verse 12. *I will cut off witchcrafts*] Thou shalt seek help only in Jehovah thy God. They have had neither soothsayers, images, groves, nor high places, from the captivity to the present day.

Verse 13. *Thy graven images also will I cut off*] Thou shalt be no more an idolatrous people.

Verse 15. *I will execute vengeance—upon the heathen*] And he did so; for the empires of the *Assyrians, Chaldeans*, and others, the sworn enemies of the Jews, have long since been utterly destroyed.

CHAPTER VI

This chapter reproves and threatens. The manner of raising the attention by calling on man to urge his plea in the face of all nature, and on the inanimate creation to hear the expostulation of Jehovah with his people, is awakening and sublime. The words of Jehovah follow, 3–5. *And God's mercies having been set forth to his people, one of them is introduced, in a beautiful dramatic form, asking what his duty is towards a God so gracious,* 6, 7. *The answer follows in the words of the prophet,* 8; *who goes on to upbraid the people of his charge with their injustice and idolatry, to which he ascribes want of success in their lawful undertakings, and those heavy calamities which are now impending,* 9–15.

A. M. cir. 3294 B. C. cir. 710 A. U. C. cir. 44 NumæPompilii, R. Roman., cir. annum 6

HEAR ye now what the LORD saith; Arise, contend thou [a]before the mountains, and let the hills hear thy voice.

2 [b]Hear ye, O mountains, [c]the LORD's controversy, and ye strong foundations of the earth: for [d]the LORD hath a controversy with his people, and he will plead with Israel.

3 O my people, [e]what have I done unto thee? and wherein have I wearied thee? testify against me.

4 [f]For I brought thee up out of the land of Egypt, and redeemed thee out of the house of servants; and I sent before thee Moses, Aaron, and Miriam.

[a]Or, *with*——[b]Deut. xxxii. 1; Psalm l. 1, 4; Isa. i. 2——[c]Hos. xii. 2——[d]Isa. i. 18; v. 3, 4; xliii. 26; Hos. iv. 1——[e]Jer. ii. 5, 31——[f]Exod. xii. 51; xiv. 30; xx. 2; Deut. iv. 20; Amos ii. 10

NOTES ON CHAP. VI

Verse 1. *Arise, contend thou*] This chapter is a sort of *dialogue* between God and the people. GOD speaks the *five* first verses, and convicts the people of sin, righteousness, and judgment. The PEOPLE, convinced of their iniquity, deprecate God's judgments, in the *sixth* and *seventh* verses. In the *eighth* verse God prescribes the *way* in which they are to be *saved;* and then the *prophet*, by the command of God, goes on to remonstrate from the *ninth* verse to the end of the chapter.

Verse 2. *Hear ye, O mountains*] Micah, as God's advocate, summons this people into judgment, and makes an appeal to inanimate creation against them. He had spoken to the priests, to the princes, to the people. He had done every thing that was necessary to make them wise, and holy, and happy; they had uniformly disobeyed, and were ever ungrateful. It was not consistent with either the justice or mercy of God to permit them to go on without reprehension and punishment. He now calls them into judgment; and such was the nature of their crimes that, to heighten the effect, and show what reason he had to punish such a people, he appeals to *inanimate creation*. Their ingratitude and rebellion are sufficient to make the *mountains*, the *hills*, and the *strong foundations of the earth* to hear, tremble, and give judgment against them. This, then, is the *Lord's controversy* with his people, and thus he will plead with Israel.

Verse 3. *O my people, what have I done unto thee?*] They are called to show why God should not pronounce sentence upon them. This condescension is truly astonishing! God appears to humble himself to his creatures. You have acted basely, treacherously, and ungratefully to me; this had already been proved by the prophets. What *cause* have I given you for such conduct? I have required a *religious service* from you; but have I wearied you by a fatiguing round of difficult duties? If I have, now testify against me; and you shall be first heard, and your plea received, if it be reasonable and good. They are silent; and God proceeds, and states what he has done for them.

Verse 4. *I brought thee up out of the land*

A. M. cir. 3294 B. C. cir. 710 A. U. C. cir. 44 NumæPompilii, R. Roman., cir. annum 6

5 O my people, remember now what [g]Balak king of Moab consulted, and what Balaam the son of Beor answered him from [h]Shittim unto Gilgal; that ye may know [i]the righteousness of the LORD.

6 Wherewith shall I come before the LORD, *and* bow myself before the high God? shall I come before him with burnt-offerings, with calves [k]of a year old?

7 [l]Will the LORD be pleased with thousands of rams, *or* with ten thousands of [m]rivers of oil? [n]shall I give my first-born *for* my transgression, the fruit of my [o]body *for* the sin of my soul?

8 He hath [p]showed thee, O man, what *is* good; and what doth the LORD require of thee, but [q]to do justly, and to love mercy, and to [r]walk humbly with thy God?

[g]Num. xxii. 5; xxiii. 7; xxiv. 10, 11; Deut. xxiii. 4, 5; Josh. xxiv. 9, 10; Rev. ii. 14——[h]Num. xxv. 1; xxxiii. 49; Josh. iv. 19; v. 10——[i]Judg. v. 11——[k]Heb. *sons of a year?*——[l]Psa. l. 9; li. 16; Isa. i. 11——[m]Job xxix. 6——[n]2 Kings xvi. 3; xxi. 6; xxiii. 10; Jer. vii. 31; xix. 5; Ezek. xxiii. 37——[o]Heb. *belly*——[p]Deut. x. 12; 1 Sam. xv. 22; Hos. vi. 6; xii. 6——[q]Gen. xviii. 19; Isa. i. 17——[r]Heb. *humble* thyself *to walk*

of Egypt] Where you were *slaves*, and grievously oppressed; from all this I *redeemed* you. Was this a small benefit? *I sent before thee* MOSES, my chosen servant, and instructed him that he might be your *leader* and *lawgiver*. *I sent with* him AARON, that he might be your *priest*, and transact all spiritual matters between myself and you, in offerings, sacrifices, and atonements. I *sent* MIRIAM, to whom I gave the spirit of *prophecy*, that she might tell you things to come, and be the director of your *females*. To this sense the *Chaldee*, "I have sent *three* prophets before you; Moses, that he might teach you the tradition of judgments; Aaron, that he might make atonement for the people; and Miriam, that she might instruct the females."

Verse 5. *Remember now what Balak king of Moab consulted*] He sent for Balaam to *curse* your fathers; but by my influence he was obliged to *bless them*. See Num. xxii. and xxiii., and the notes there, where this subject is largely considered.

From Shittim unto Gilgal] From the encampment at Shittim, Num. xxv. 1, on the way to that of Gilgal, Josh. iv. 19. Balaam gave different answers in the interval between these places. We may suppose that the encampments of Israel advanced slowly to that part of Jordan which was opposite to Gilgal. The *Chaldee* has, "Were there not wonderful things done in your behalf from the valley of Shittim to the house of Gilgal?" See Josh. iii. 1; iv. 20. Thus there will be a reference to the miraculous passage over Jordan. See *Newcome*.

That ye may know the righteousness] The just, equitable, and merciful dealing of the Most High. Recollect *those* things, that ye may have a proper impression of *this*. There are many interpretations given of this rather obscure clause; what I have proposed seems to me the most *simple*.

This is the sum of the address; and here the case of the plaintiff terminates, the prisoners being called to show why the sentence of the law should not be pronounced. I make no apology for using any *forensic* terms, as the passages before us refer to a *case* brought into a *court* to be *judged*, and the terms in the original are all such as are proper for a *court of justice;* and the thing itself is called the *Lord's controversy*, ריב יהוה *rib Yehovah*, *Jehovah's suit at law*. And hence it is said, *He will plead*, litigate, *with Israel*.

Verse 6. *Wherewith shall I come before the Lord*] Now the people, as defendants, appear; but instead of vindicating themselves, or attempting to dispute what has been alleged against them, they seem at once to *plead guilty;* and now anxiously inquire how they shall appease the wrath of the Judge, how they shall make atonement for the sins already committed.

Bow myself before the high God] They wish to pray, and to make supplication to their Judge; but how shall they come before him? They have no right to come into his presence. Some *offering* must be brought; but of what *kind*, or of what *value?* Their sin is unprecedented, and usual methods of access will not avail. They are distracted in their minds, and make a variety of proposals to themselves, some *rational*, some *absurd* and *impossible*, and some even *sinful*.

Shall I come before him with burnt-offerings] This is *resonable*, and according to the *law;* but this will be insufficient.

Verse 7. *Will the Lord be pleased with thousands of rams*] These might be *procured*, though with difficulty; but conscience says, neither will these do.

With ten thousands of rivers of oil] This is *absurd* and *impossible;* but could even these be procured, could they all make atonement for such *guilt*, and *ingratitude*, and *rebellion?*

Shall I give my first-born for *my transgression*] This was *sinful and wicked;* but such offerings had been made by the *Phœnicians*, and their successors the *Carthaginians;* and this very custom was copied by the corrupt Israelites. See some cases of such offerings, 2 Kings iii. 27; Lev. xx. 27.

The fruit of my body for *the sin of my soul?*] This clause is an explanation of the former. Shall I make the first-born, the best and goodliest of my children, חטאת *chattath*, a SIN-OFFERING *for my soul?* And thus the original is used in a multitude of places.

When they had put all these questions to their reason and conscience, they found no satisfaction; their distraction is increased, and despair is about to take place, when Jehovah, the plaintiff, in his mercy interposes:

Verse 8. *He hath showed thee, O man, what is good*] All the modes of expiation which ye have proposed are, in the sight of God, unavailable; they cannot do away the *evil*, nor purify from the *guilt* of sin. He himself has shown thee what is *good;* that which is *profitable* to *thee*, and *pleasing* to himself. And what is *that?* Answer. Thou art—

A. M. cir. 3294
B. C. cir. 710
A. U. C. cir. 44
NumæPompilii,
R. Roman.,
cir. annum 6

9 The [s]LORD's voice crieth unto
the city, and [t]*the man of* wisdom
shall see thy name: hear ye the
rod, and who hath appointed it.
10 [u]Are there yet the treasures of wickedness in the house of the wicked, and the
[v]scant measure [w]*that is* abominable?

A. M. cir. 3294
B. C. cir. 710
A. U. C. cir. 44
NumæPompilii,
R. Roman.,
cir. annum 6

11 [x]Shall I count *them* pure
with the [y]wicked balances, and
with the bag of deceitful weights?
12 For the rich men thereof are full of vio-

---

[s]Deut. xv. 5; xxvi. 17; xxviii. 1, 2; xxx. 10——[t]Or, *thy name shall see that which is*——[u]Or, Is there *yet unto every man a house of the wicked,* &c.——[v]Hebrew, *measure of leanness;* Amos viii. 5——[w]Deuteronomy xxv. 13–16; Proverbs xi. 1; xx. 10, 23——[x]Or, *Shall I be pure with,* &c.——[y]Hos. xii. 7

I. *To do justly;* to give to all their due.

1. To *God* his due; thy *heart,* thy *body, soul,* and *spirit;* thy *wisdom, understanding, judgment.* "To love him with all thy heart, soul, mind, and strength, and thy neighbour as thyself." This is God's *due* and *right* from every man.

2. Thou art to give thy *neighbour* his due; to do to him as thou wouldst that he should do to thee, never working ill to him.

3. Thou art to give to *thyself* thy due; not to deprive thy soul of what God has provided for it; to keep thy body in temperance, sobriety, and chastity; avoiding all excesses, both in *action* and *passion.*

II. *Thou art to love mercy;* not only to do what *justice* requires, but also what *mercy, kindness, benevolence,* and *charity* require.

III. But how art thou to do this? Thou art to *walk humbly with thy God;* הצנע *hatsnea,* to *humble thyself* to walk. This implies to acknowledge thy iniquity, and submit to be saved by his free mercy, as thou hast already found that no kind of *offering* or *sacrifice* can avail. Without this humiliation of soul there never was, there never can be, any *walking with God;* for without his mercy no soul can be saved; and he must be THY *God* before thou canst *walk with him.* Many, when they hear the nature of sin pointed out, and the way of salvation made plain through the blood of the Lamb, have shut their eyes both against sin and the proper sacrifice for it, and parried all exhortation, threatening, &c., with this text: "God requires nothing of us but to do justly, love mercy, and walk humbly with him." Now I ask any man, Art thou willing to *stand* or *fall* by *this text?* And it would cost me neither much time nor much pains to show that on this ground no soul of man can be saved. Nor does God say that this *doing justly,* &c., shall *merit* eternal glory. No. He shows that in *this way* all men *should walk;* that this is *the duty of* EVERY *rational being:* but he well knows that no *fallen soul* can act thus without especial assistance from him, and that it is only the *regenerate man,* the man who has found redemption through the blood of the cross, and has God for HIS God, that can *thus act* and *walk. Salvation is of the mere mercy of God alone;* for by the *works of the law shall no flesh be justified.*

The manner of raising attention, says Bp. *Newcome,* on ver. 1, 2, by calling on man to urge his plea in the face of all nature, and on the inanimate creation to hear the expostulation of Jehovah with his people, is truly awakening and magnificent. The words of Jehovah follow in ver. 3, 4, 5. And God's mercies having been set before the people, one of them is introduced in a beautiful dramatic form; asking what his duty is towards so gracious a God, ver. 6, 7. The answer follows in the words of the prophet, ver. 8. Some think we have a sort of dialogue between *Balak* and *Balaam,* represented to us in the prophetical way. The *king of Moab* speaks, ver. 6. *Balaam* replies by another question in the two first hemistichs of ver. 7. The *king of Moab* rejoins in the remaining part of the verse; and *Balaam* replies, ver. 8. Bps. *Butler* and *Lowth* favour this. I cannot agree.

Verse 9. *The Lord's voice crieth unto the city*] No man is found to hear; but the *man of wisdom* will hear, תושיה *tushiyah;* a word frequent in the writings of Solomon and Job, signifying wisdom, wealth, substance, reason, essence, happiness; any thing that is complete; or that which is substantial, in opposition to vanity, emptiness, mere show, unsubstantiality. When God speaks, the *man of common sense,* who has any knowledge of God or his own soul, will *see* thy *name;* but instead of יראה *yireh, will see,* the *Septuagint, Syriac, Vulgate,* and *Arabic,* with *twelve* of *Kennicott's* and *De Rossi's* MSS., have read יראי *yirey, they that* FEAR. The *Vulgate* reads:—

Et salus erit timentibus nomen tuum.

"And thou shalt be salvation to them that fear thy name."

The *Septuagint*—Και σωσει φοβουμενους το ονομα αυτου.

And he shall save those who fear his name.—This the *Arabic* copies.

The *Targum* has, "And the teachers shall fear the name." That is, יהוה *Yehovah.*

The *French Bible* is very strange:—

Car ton nom voit comme il va de tout.

"For thy name sees how every thing goes."

The word תושיה *tushiyah,* mentioned above, which occasions all the difficulty, has been read with an ע *ain* by the *Vulgate* and *Septuagint,* as coming from the root ישע *yasha, to be saved;* and it is very likely that this was the *original* reading. The two last letters in the word, יה, might have been easily mistaken in the MS. for the letter ע, where I may suppose the word stood thus, תושע, *shall be saved;* and as several MSS. read יראי *yirey,* they who *fear,* instead of יראה *yireh,* he shall *see,* the whole clause might have been just what it appears in the *Vulgate* and *Septuagint.* It is also necessary to remark that the word in dispute has various forms in some MSS., which is a strong presumption against its authenticity. See *Kennicott* and *De Rossi.*

Verse 10. *Are there yet the treasures of wickedness*] Such as false balances and deceitful weights. See on Hos. xii. 7. This shows that they were not DOING JUSTLY. They did not *give to each his due.*

A. M. cir. 3294
B. C. cir. 710
A. U. C. cir. 44
NumæPompilii,
R. Roman.,
cir. annum 6

lence, and the inhabitants thereof have spoken lies, and [z]their tongue *is* deceitful in their mouth.

13 Therefore also will I [a]make *thee* sick in smiting thee, in making *thee* desolate because of thy sins.

14 [b]Thou shalt eat, but not be satisfied; and thy casting down *shall be* in the midst of thee; and thou shalt take hold, but shalt not deliver; and *that* which thou deliverest will I give up to the sword.

15 Thou shalt [c]sow, but thou shalt not reap; thou shalt tread the olives, but thou shalt not anoint thee with oil; and sweet wine, but shalt not drink wine.

A. M. cir. 3294
B. C. cir. 710
A. U. C. cir. 44
NumæPompilii,
R. Roman.,
cir. annum 6

16 For [d]the statutes of [e]Omri are [f]kept, and all the works of the house of [g]Ahab, and ye walk in their counsels; that I should make thee [h]a [i]desolation, and the inhabitants thereof a hissing: therefore ye shall bear the [k]reproach of my people.

[z]Jer. ix. 3, 5, 6, 8——[a]Lev. xxvi. 16; Psa. cvii. 17, 18
[b]Lev. xxvi. 26; Hos. iv. 10——[c]Deut. xxviii. 38, 39, 40; Amos v. 11; Zeph. i. 13; Hag. i. 6——[d]Or, *he doth much keep the*, &c.

[e]1 Kings xvi. 25, 26——[f]Hos. v. 11——[g]1 Kings xvi. 30, &c.; xxi. 25, 26; 2 Kings xxi. 3——[h]1 Kings ix. 8; Jer. xix. 8——[i]Or, *astonishment*——[k]Isa. xxv. 8; Jer. li. 51; Lam. v. 1

Verse 12. *For the rich men thereof are full of violence*] This shows that they did not *love mercy*.

The inhabitants thereof have spoken lies] This shows that they did not *humble themselves to walk with God*.

Verse 13. *Will I make* thee *sick in smiting thee*] Perhaps better, "I also am weary with smiting thee, in making thee desolate for thy sins." They were corrected, but to no purpose; they had stroke upon stroke, but were not amended.

Verse 14. *Thou shalt eat, but not be satisfied*] All thy possessions are cursed, because of thy sins; and thou hast no *real good* in all thy enjoyments.

And thy casting down] For וישחך *veyeshchacha*, "thy casting down," *Newcome*, by transposing the ח and ש, reads ויחשך *veyechshach*, "and it shall be dark;" and this is probably the true reading. The *Arabic* and *Septuagint* have read the same. "There shall be calamity in the midst of thee." It shall have its *seat* and *throne* among you.

Verse 15. *Thou shalt sow, but thou shalt not reap*] Thou shalt labour to amass property, but thou shalt not have God's blessing; and whatever thou collectest, thy enemies shall carry away. And at last carry thyself into captivity.

Verse 16. *The statutes of Omri are kept*] *Omri*, king of Israel, the father of Ahab, was one of the worst kings the Israelites ever had; and *Ahab* followed in his wicked father's steps. The *statutes* of those kings were the very grossest *idolatry*. *Jezebel*, wife of the latter, and daughter of *Ithobaal*, king of Tyre, had no fellow on earth. From her Shakespeare seems to have drawn the character of *Lady Macbeth;* a woman, like her prototype, mixed up of *tigress* and *fiend*, without *addition*. Omri, Ahab, and Jezebel, were the *models* followed by the Israelites in the days of this prophet.

The inhabitants thereof a hissing] לשרקה *lishrekah*, "for a *shriek;*" because those who should see them should be both *astonished* and *affrighted* at them.

There are few chapters in the prophets, or in the Bible, superior to this for genuine worth and importance. The structure is as elegant as it is impressive; and it is every way worthy of the Spirit of God.

CHAPTER VII

The prophet begins this chapter with lamenting the decay of piety and the growth of ungodliness, using a beautiful allegory to imply (as explained in verse 2) that the good man is as seldom to be met with as the early fig of best quality in the advanced season, or the cluster after the vintage, 1, 2. *He then reproves and threatens in terms so expressive of great calamities as to be applied in the New Testament to times of the hottest persecution*, 3–6. *See* Matt. x. 35, 36. *Notwithstanding which a Jew is immediately introduced declaring, in the name of his captive people, the strongest faith in the mercy of God the most submissive resignation to his will, and the firmest hope in his favour in future times, when they should triumph over their enemies*, 7–10. *The prophet upon this resumes the discourse, and predicts their great prosperity and increase*, 11, 12; *although the whole land of Israel must first be desolated on account of the great wickedness of its inhabitants*, 13. *The prophet intercedes in behalf of his people*, 14. *After which God is introduced promising, in very ample terms, their future restoration and prosperity*, 15–17. *And then, to conclude, a chorus of Jews is introduced, singing a beautiful hymn of thanksgiving, suggested by the gracious promises which precede*, 18–20.

A. M. cir. 3294
B. C. cir. 710
A. U. C. cir. 44
NumæPompilii,
R. Roman.,
cir. annum 6

WO is me! for I am as [a]when they have gathered the summer fruits, as [b]the grape-gleanings of the vintage: *there is* no cluster to eat: [c]my soul desireth the first-ripe fruit.

2 The [d]good [e]*man* is perished out of the earth: and *there is* none upright among men: they all lie in wait for blood; [f]they hunt every man his brother with a net.

3 That they may do evil with both hands earnestly, [g]the prince asketh, [h]and the judge *asketh* for a reward; and the great *man,* he uttereth [i]his mischievous desire: so they wrap it up.

4 The best of them [k]*is* as a brier: the most upright *is sharper* than a thorn hedge: the day of thy watchmen *and* thy visitation cometh; now shall be their perplexity.

5 [l]Trust ye not in a friend, put ye not confidence in a guide: keep the doors of thy mouth from her that lieth in thy bosom.

[a]Heb. *the gatherings of summer*——[b]Isa. xvii. 6; xxiv. 13——[c]Isa. xxviii. 4; Hos. ix. 10——[d]Psa. xii. 1; xiv. 1, 3; Isa. lvii. 1——[e]Or, *godly,* or *merciful*

[f]Hab. i. 15——[g]Hos. iv. 18——[h]Isa. i. 23; chap. iii. 11——[i]Heb. *the mischief of his soul*——[k]2 Sam. xxiii. 6, 7; Ezek. ii. 6; see Isa. lv. 13——[l]Jer. ix. 4

NOTES ON CHAP. VII

Verse 1. *Wo is me!* This is a continuation of the preceding discourse. And here the prophet points out the *small number* of the upright to be found in the land. He himself seemed to be the only person who was on God's side; and he considers himself as a *solitary grape*, which had escaped the general gathering. The word קיץ *kayits,* which is sometimes used for *summer,* and *summer fruits* in general, is here translated *late figs;* and may here, says Bishop *Newcome,* be opposed to the *early ripe fig* of superior quality. See on Hos. ix. 10, and Amos viii. 1, 2. He desired to see the *first-ripe fruit*—distinguished and eminent piety; but he found nothing but a very imperfect or spurious kind of godliness.

Verse 2. *The good* man *is perished out of the earth*] A similar sentiment may be found, Psa. xii. 1; Isa. lvii. 1. As the *early fig* of excellent flavour cannot be found in the advanced season of summer, or a *choice cluster of grapes* after vintage, so neither can the good and upright man be discovered by searching in Israel. This comparison, says Bp. *Newcome,* is beautifully implied.

They hunt every man his brother with a net.] This appears to be an allusion to the ancient mode of duel between the *retiarius* and *secutor.* The former had a *casting net,* which he endeavoured to throw over the head of his antagonist, that he might then despatch him with his short sword. The other parried the cast; and when the *retiarius* missed, he was obliged to *run* about the field to get time to *set his net in right order* for another throw. While he ran, the other *followed,* that he might despatch him before he should be able to recover the proper position of his net; and hence the latter was called *secutor,* the *pursuer,* as the other was called *retiarius,* or the *net man.* I have explained this before on Job, and other places; but because it is rarely noticed by commentators, I explain the allusion here once more. Abp. *Newcome,* by not attending to this, has translated איש את אחיהו יצודו חרם *ish eth achihu yatsudu cherem,* "They hunt every man his brother for his destruction;" though he put *net* in the *margin.*

Verse 3. *That they may do evil with both hands*] That is, earnestly, greedily, to the uttermost of their power. The *Vulgate* translates: Malum manuum suarum dicunt bonum; "The evil of their hands they call good."

The prince asketh] A bribe, to forward claims in his court.

The judge asketh *for a reward*] That he may decide the cause in favour of him who gives most money, whether the cause be *good* or *evil.* This was notoriously the case in our own country before the giving of *Magna Charta;* and hence that provision, Nulli vendemus justitiam aut rectum: "We will not sell justice to any man." And *this* was not the only *country* in which justice and judgment were put to sale.

The great man, *he uttereth his mischievous desire*] Such consider themselves *above law,* and they make no secret of their unjust determinations. *And so they wrap it up*—they all conjoin in doing evil in their several offices, and oppressing the poor; so our translators have interpreted the original ויעבתוה *vayeabtuha,* which the *versions* translate variously. *Newcome* has, "And they do abominably."

Verse 4. *The best of them* is *as a brier*] They are useless in themselves, and cannot be touched without *wounding* him that comes in contact with them. He alludes to the *thick thorn hedges,* still frequent in Palestine.

The day of thy watchmen] The day of vengeance, which the prophets have foreseen and proclaimed, is at hand. *Now shall be their perplexity;* no more *wrapping up,* all shall be *unfolded.* In that day every man will wish that he were different from what he is found to be; but he shall be judged for what he *is,* and for the deeds he *has done.*

Verse 5. *Trust ye not in a friend*] These times will be so evil, and the people so wicked, that all *bonds* will be *dissolved;* and even the most intimate will betray each other, when they can hope to serve themselves by it.

On this passage, in the year 1798, I find I have written as follows:—

"*Trust ye not in a friend.*—Several of those whom I have delighted to call by that name have deceived me.

"*Put ye not confidence in a guide.*—Had I followed some of these I should have gone to perdition.

"*Keep the door of thy mouth from her that lieth in thy bosom.*—My wife alone never deceived me."

It is now *twenty-seven* years since, and I find no cause to alter what I then wrote.

A. M. cir. 3294
B. C. cir. 710
A. U. C. cir. 44
NumæPompilii,
R. Roman.,
cir. annum 6

6 For [m]the son dishonoureth
the father, the daughter riseth up
[l]against her mother, the daughter-
in-law against her mother-in-
law; a man's enemies *are* the men of his own
house.
7 Therefore [n]I will look unto the LORD: I
will wait for the God of my salvation: my
God will hear me.
8 [o]Rejoice not against me, O mine enemy:
[p]when I fall, I shall arise; when I sit in darkness, [q]the LORD *shall be* a light unto me.
9 [r]I will bear the indignation of the LORD,
because I have sinned against him, until he
plead my cause, and execute judgment for
me: [s]he will bring me forth to the light, *and*
I shall behold his righteousness.
10 [t]Then *she that is* mine
enemy shall see *it*, and [u]shame
shall cover her which said unto
me, [v]Where is the LORD thy
God? [w]mine eyes shall behold her: now [x]shall
she be trodden down [y]as the mire of the
streets.
11 *In* the day that thy [z]walls are to be built,
in that day shall the decree be far removed.
12 *In* that day *also* [a]he shall come even to
thee from Assyria, [b]and *from* the fortified
cities, and from the fortress even to the river,
and from sea to sea, and *from* mountain to
mountain.
13 [c]Notwithstanding the land shall be desolate because of them that dwell therein,
[d]for the fruit of their doings.

---

[m]Ezek. xxii. 7; Matt. x. 21, 35, 36; Luke xii. 53; xxi. 16; 2 Tim. iii. 2, 3——[n]Isa. viii. 17——[o]Prov. xxiv. 17; Lam. iv. 21——[p]Psa. xxxvii. 24; Prov. xxiv. 16——[q]Psa. xxvii. 1——[r]Lam. iii. 39——[s]Psa. xxxvii. 6——[t]Or, *And thou wilt see her that is mine enemy, and cover her with shame*——[u]Psa. xxxv. 26——[v]Psa. xlii. 3, 10; lxxix. 10; cxv. 2; Joel ii. 17——[w]Chap. iv. 11——[x]Heb. *she shall be for a treading down*——[y]2 Sam. xxii. 43; Zech. x. 5——[z]Amos ix. 11, &c.——[a]Isa. xi. 16; xix. 23, &c.; xxvii. 13; Hos. xi. 11——[b]Or, *even to*——[c]Or, *After that it hath been*——[d]Jeremiah xxi. 14; chap. iii. 12

Verse 6. *For the son dishonoureth the father*] See the use our Lord has made of these words, where he quotes them, Matt. x. 21, 25, 36, and the notes there.

Verse 7. *Therefore I will look unto the Lord*] Because things are so, I will *trust* in the Lord more firmly, *wait* for him more patiently, and more *confidently* expect to be supported, defended, and saved.

Verse 8. *Rejoice not against me, O mine enemy*] The captive Israelites are introduced as speaking here and in the preceding verse. The *enemy* are the *Assyrians* and *Chaldeans;* the *fall* is their *idolatry* and consequent *captivity;* the *darkness*, the *calamities* they suffered in that captivity; their *rise* and *light*, their *restoration* and consequent *blessedness*.

To *rejoice over the fall or miseries of any man*, betrays a malignant spirit. I have known several instances where people professing to *hold a very pure and Christian creed*, having become unfaithful and fallen into sin, their opponents, who held a very impure and unchristian creed, have exulted with "Ha, ha! so would we have it!" and have shown their malignity more fully, by giving all possible *publicity* and *circulation* to such *accounts*. Perhaps in the sight of God this was worse than the poor wretch's *fall*, in which they exulted as having taken place in one who held a creed different from their own. But these *arose again* from their fall, while those *jesters at holiness* continued in the *gall of bitterness* and *bonds of inward corruption*.

Verse 9. *I will bear the indignation of the Lord*] The words of the penitent captives, acknowledging their sins and praying for mercy.

Until he plead my cause] And wo to the *slanderers*, when God undertakes to plead for the *fallen* who have *returned* to him with *deep compunction of heart*, seeking redemption in the blood of the cross.

Verse 10. *Then* she that is *mine enemy*] This may refer particularly to the *city of Babylon*.

Shall she be trodden down] Literally fulfilled in the sackage of that city by the Persians, and its consequent total ruin. It became as *mire;* its walls, formed of brick *kneaded with straw* and *baked in the sun*, becoming exposed to the *wet*, dissolved, so that a vestige of the city remains not, except a few bricks digged from under the rubbish, several pieces of which now lie before me, and show the perishing materials of which the *head* of this proud empire was composed.

Verse 11. In *the day that thy walls are to be built*] This refers to *Jerusalem;* the *decree*, to the purpose of God to deliver the people into captivity. "This shall be far removed." God having *purposed* their return, I cannot think, with some commentators, that this verse contains *threatenings* against Jerusalem, and not *promises*. See the *first* chapter of Haggai, where the subject is similar; and the restoration of Jerusalem is certainly what the prophet describes.

Verse 12. In *that day* also *he shall come*] Bp. *Newcome* translates:—

> "And in that day they shall come unto thee
> From Assyria and the fenced cities;
> And from Egypt even unto the river."

Calmet translates:—

> "They shall come to thee from Assyria even unto Egypt;
> And from Egypt even to the river; (Euphrates;)
> And from one sea to another, and from one mountain to another."

This, says he, gives an easy sense; whereas we cannot tell where to find those *fortified cities* spoken of by other *translators*. The

A. M. cir. 3294
B. C. cir. 710
A. U. C. cir. 44
NumæPompilii,
R. Roman.,
cir. annum 6

14 [e]Feed thy people with
thy rod, the flock of thine heritage, which dwell solitarily *in*
[f]the wood, in the midst of Car-
mel: let them feed *in* Bashan and Gilead, as
in the days of old.
15 [g]According to the days of thy coming
out of the land of Egypt will I show unto
him marvellous *things.*
16 The nations [h]shall see and be confounded
at all their might: [i]they shall lay *their*
hand upon *their* mouth, their ears shall be
deaf.
17 They shall lick the [k]dust like a serpent, [l]they shall move out of their holes like
[m]worms of the earth: [n]they shall be afraid of
the LORD our God, and shall
fear because of thee.
18 [o]Who *is* a God like unto
thee, that [p]pardoneth iniquity,
and passeth by the transgression of [q]the
remnant of his heritage? [r]he retaineth not
his anger for ever, because he delighteth *in*
mercy.
19 He will turn again, he will have compassion upon us; he will subdue our iniquities; and thou wilt cast all their sins into the
depths of the sea.
20 [s]Thou wilt perform the truth to Jacob,
and the mercy to Abraham, [t]which thou
hast sworn unto our fathers from the days
of old.

[e]Or, *Rule;* Psalm xxviii. 9; chap. v. 4——[f]Isaiah xxxvii. 24——[g]Psalm lxviii. 22; lxxviii. 12——[h]Isa. xxvi. 11——[i]Job xxi. 5; xxix. 9——[k]Psalm lxxii. 9; Isa. xlix. 23——[l]Psa. xviii. 45——[m]Or, *creeping things*

[n]Jeremiah xxxiii. 9——[o]Exodus xv. 11——[p]Exodus xxxiv. 6, 7; Jeremiah l. 20——[q]Chap. iv. 7; v. 3, 7, 8
[r]Psalm ciii. 9; Isa. lvii. 10; Jer. iii. 5——[s]Luke i. 72, 73
[t]Psalm cv. 9, 10

Israelites were to return from their captivity, and re-occupy their ancient country from Assyria to Egypt; that is, from the *river Euphrates* to the *river Nile;* and from the *Mediterranean Sea* to the *Ocean;* and from *Mount Libanus* to the *mountains of Arabia Petræa,* or Mount *Seir.* See Amos viii. 12. This prediction was literally fulfilled under the *Asmoneans.* The Jewish nation was greatly extended and very powerful under Herod, at the time that our Lord was born. See *Calmet.*

Verse 13. *Notwithstanding the land shall be desolate*] This should be translated in the preter tense, "Though the land HAD been desolate;" that is, the land of Israel had been desolate during the captivity, which captivity was the "fruit of the evil doings of them that had dwelt therein."

Verse 14. *Feed thy people with thy rod*] בשבטך *beshibtecha,* "with thy crook." The shepherd's crook is most certainly designed, as the word *flock* immediately following shows. No *rod* of *correction* or *affliction* is here intended; nor does the word mean such.

Solitarily] They have been long without a shepherd or spiritual governor.

In the midst of Carmel] Very fruitful in vines.

Bashan and Gilead] Proverbially fruitful in pasturages.

Verse 15. *According to the days*] This is the answer to the prophet's prayer; and God says he will protect, save, defend, and *work miracles for them* in their restoration, such as he wrought for their fathers in their return from Egypt to the promised land.

Verse 16. *The nations shall see and be confounded*] Whether the words in these verses (15, 16, and 17) be applied to the return from the Babylonish captivity, or to the prosperity of the Jews under the Maccabees, they may be understood as ultimately applicable to the final restoration of this people, and their lasting prosperity under the Gospel.

Verse 18. *Who is a God like unto thee, &c.*] Here is a challenge to all idol worshippers, and to all those who take false views of the true God, to show his like. See his characters; they are immediately subjoined.

1. *He pardoneth iniquity.* This is the prerogative of God alone; of that Being who alone has power to *save* or to *destroy.*

2. *He passeth by transgression.* He can heal *backsliding,* and restore them that are fallen.

3. *He retaineth not his anger for ever.* Though, justly displeased because of sin, he pours out his judgments upon the wicked; yet when they return to him, he shows "that he retaineth not his anger forever," but is indescribably ready to save them.

4. *He delighteth in mercy.* Judgment is his strange work: he is ever more ready *to save* than to *destroy.* Nothing can *please him better* than having the opportunity, from the return and repentance of the sinner, to show him that mercy without which he must perish everlastingly.

5. Because he is such a God—1. "He will turn again." His face has been long turned from us, because of our sins. 2. "He will have compassion upon us," pity our state, and feel for our sorrows. 3. "He will subdue our iniquities." Though they have been mighty, he will bring them down, and bruise them under our feet. 4. "He will cast all their sins into the depths of the sea." Will fully pardon them, and never more remember them against us. Instead of חטאתם *chattotham,* THEIR *sins,* five MSS. of *Kennicott's* and *De Rossi's,* with the *Septuagint, Syriac, Vulgate,* and *Arabic,* read חטאתינו *chattotheynu,* OUR *sins.* He will plunge them into eternal oblivion, never more to come into sight or remembrance; like a stone dropped into the "depths of the sea."

Verse 20. *Thou wilt perform the truth to Jacob*] The *promises* which he has made to Jacob and his posterity. Not one of them can ever fall to the ground. "And the mercy to Abraham, which thou hast sworn;" viz., that "in his Seed all the families of the earth should be blessed;" that the *Messiah* should come from ABRAHAM, *through* his son ISAAC, *by* JACOB and

DAVID; be a light to lighten the Gentiles, and the glory of his people Israel. And this *promise*, and this *oath*, God has most signally fulfilled by the *incarnation of Christ*, who was sent to bless us by turning away every one of us from his iniquities; and for this purpose he was delivered for our offences, and rose again for our justification; and repentance and remission of sins are preached in his name to all nations. The proclamation was *first* made at Jerusalem; and that the prophet refers to *this*, is evident from the use made of these words by Zacharias, the father of John the Baptist, when, under the *full afflatus of the Spirit of God*, he quoted this phophecy of Micah, as fulfilled in the *incarnation of Christ*, Luke i. 72, 73. The *Chaldee* paraphrases this last verse with spirit and propriety: "Thou wilt give the truth to Jacob his son, as thou hast promised by oath to him in Beth-el. And the mercy to Abraham and to his seed after him, as thou didst swear to him amidst the divisions. Thou wilt be mindful of us on account of the binding of Isaac, who was bound upon the altar before thee. And thou wilt do us that good, which, from the most ancient days, thou hast promised to our fathers by an oath." *Between the divisions*, refers to the covenant made between God and Abraham, Gen. xv. 9, 10, 11, 17, 18. Well might the prophet exult in his challenge to earth and hell. WHO IS A GOD LIKE UNTO THEE! Hell is speechless, earth is dumb. Infidels dare not open their mouths!!! Hallelujah! מי אל כמוך *mi El camocha!* JESUS is the mighty God and Saviour, pardoning iniquity, transgression, and sin, and saving to the uttermost all that come unto God through him. Blessed be God! Reader, lay this to heart.

INTRODUCTION TO THE BOOK

OF THE

PROPHET NAHUM

NAHUM, the *seventh* of the *twelve* minor prophets, was a native of Elkoshai, a little village of Galilee, whose ruins were still in being in the time of St. Jerome. However there are some who think that Elkoshai is rather the name of his father, and that the place of his birth was Bethabor, or Bethabara, beyond Jordan. They used to show the tomb of the prophet at a village called Beth-gabre, now called Gibbin, near Emmaus. The Chaldee calls him Nahum of Beth-koshi, or of Beth-kitsi; but the situation of this place is as much unknown as that of Elkoshai.

The particular circumstances of the life of Nahum are altogether unknown. His prophecy consists of *three* chapters, which make up but *one* discourse, wherein he foretells the destruction of Nineveh. He describes it in so lovely and pathetic a manner, that he seems to have been upon the spot to declare to the Ninevites the destruction of their city.

Opinions are divided as to the time in which he prophesied. Josephus will have it that he foretold the fall of Nineveh *one hundred and fifteen* years before it happened, which will bring the time of Nahum to that of King Ahaz. The Jews say that he prophesied under Manasseh. We are inclined to be of St. Jerome's opinion, that he foretold the destruction of Nineveh in the time of Hezekiah, and after the war of Sennacherib in Egypt, mentioned by Berosus. Nahum speaks plainly of the taking of No-Ammon, a city of Egypt; of the haughtiness of Rabshakeh; of the defeat of Sennacherib; and he speaks of them as things that were past. He supposes that the Jews were still in their own country, and that they there celebrated their festivals. He speaks of the captivity, and of the dispersion of the *ten* tribes. All these evidences convince us that Nahum cannot be placed before the *fifteenth* year of Hezekiah, since the expedition of Sennacherib against this prince was in the *fourteenth* year of his reign.

This prophet gives us a fine description of the destruction of Nineveh. He says that this city should be ruined by a deluge of waters, which should overflow it and demolish its walls.

Diodorus Siculus and *Athenæus* relate, that during the time this city was besieged by Belesis and by Arbaces, under Sardanapalus, the river Tigris swelled so as to overthrow twenty furlongs of the walls of Nineveh. But as the siege mentioned by Nahum was long after the taking of Nineveh under Sardanapalus, it must needs be that the same thing happened to Nineveh at the second and last siege, under Nebuchadnezzar and Astyages. Probably the besiegers at this second siege determined the course of the waters, and brought on the same fate to the city by the same means as at the first siege. And as the walls of those ancient cities were generally formed of *brick kneaded with straw* and *baked in the sun*, a *flood* of *waters* could easily effect their dissolution. *Babylon* was built in the same manner; and this is the reason why scarcely any vestiges of those cities are to be found. See on chap. iii. 14.

The time of the prophet's death is not known. The Greek meneologies and the Latin martyrologies place his festival on the first of December. *Petrus Natalis* places it on the twenty-fourth of the same month, which he says was the day of his death, without acquainting us whence he had learned this circumstance.

The conduct and imagery of this prophetical poem are truly admirable.

The exordium sets forth with grandeur the justice and power of God, tempered by lenity and goodness, chap. i. 1–8.

A sudden address to the Assyrians follows; and a prediction of their perplexity and overthrow, as devisers of evil against the true God, ver. 9–11. Jehovah himself then proclaims freedom to his people from the Assyrian yoke, and the destruction of the Assyrian idols, ver. 12–14. Upon which the prophet, in a most lively manner, turns the attention of Judah to the approach of the messenger who brings such glad tidings, and bids her celebrate her festivals and offer her thank-offerings, without fear of so powerful an adversary, ver. 15.

Chap. ii. In the next place Nineveh is called on to prepare for the approach of her enemies, as instruments in the hands of Jehovah; and the military array and muster of the Medes and Babylonians, their rapid approach to the city, the process of the siege, the capture of the place, the captivity, lamentation, and flight of the inhabitants, the sacking of the wealthy city, and the consequent desolation and terror, are described in the true spirit of Eastern poetry, and with many pathetic, vivid, and sublime images, ver. 1–10.

A grand and animated allegory succeeds this description, ver. 11, 12; which is explained and applied to the city of Nineveh in ver. 13.

Chap. iii. The prophet denounces a wo against Nineveh for her perfidy and violence, and strongly places before our eyes the number of her chariots and cavalry, her burnished arms, and the great and unrelenting slaughter which she spread around her, ver. 1–3.

He assigns her idolatries as one cause of her ignominious and unpitied fall, ver. 4–7.

He foretells that No-Ammon, (the Diospolis in the Delta,) her rival in populousness, confederacies, and situation, should share a like fate with herself, ver. 8–11; and beautifully illustrates the ease with which her strong holds should be taken, ver. 12, and her pusillanimity during the siege, ver. 13.

He pronounces that all her preparations, ver. 14, 15, her numbers, her opulence, her multitude of chief men, would be of no avail, ver. 15–17.

He foretells that her tributaries would desert her, ver. 18.

He concludes with a proper epiphonema; the topics of which are, the greatness and incurableness of her wound, and the just triumph of others over her on account of her extensive oppressions, ver. 19.

To sum up all with the decisive judgment of an eminent critic: "Not one of the minor prophets equals the sublimity, genius, and spirit of Nahum. Besides, his prophecy is a perfect poem. The *exordium* is exceedingly majestic. The *apparatus* for the destruction of Nineveh, and the description of that catastrophe, are painted in the most glowing colours, and are admirably clear and powerful." *Lowth*, Prælect. Heb. xxi., p. 282.

It must be farther observed, that this prophecy was highly interesting to the Jews; as the Assyrians had often ravaged their country, and I suppose had recently destroyed the kingdom of Israel. See *Calmet.*

THE BOOK

OF THE

PROPHET NAHUM

Chronological Notes relative to this Book, upon the supposition that it was written about seven hundred and thirteen *years before the commencement of the Christian era*

Year from the Creation, according to Archbishop Usher, 3291.—Year of the Julian Period, 4001.—Year since the Flood, 1635.—Year from the vocation of Abram, 1208.—Year since the first celebration of the Olympic games in Elis by the Idæi Dactyli, 741.—Year from the destruction of Troy, according to the general computation of chronologers, 471.—Year since the commencement of the kingdom of Israel, by the Divine appointment of Saul to the regal dignity, 383.—Year from the foundation of Solomon's temple, 299.—Year since the division of Solomon's monarchy into the kingdoms of Israel and Judah, 263.—Year since the restoration of the Olympic games at Elis by Lycurgus, Iphitus, and Cleosthenes, 172.—Year from the foundation of the kingdom of Macedon by Caranus, 102.—Year from the commencement of the reign of Ardysus over Lydia, 84.—Year since the conquest of Corœbus at Olympia, usually called the first Olympiad, 64.—Fourth year of the *sixteenth* Olympiad.—Year from the building of Rome, according to the Varronian computation, 41.—Year from the building of Rome, according to Cato and the Fasti Consulares, 40.—Year from the building of Rome, according to Polybius the historian, 39.—Year from the building of Rome, according to Fabius Pictor, 35.—Year of the era of Nabonassar, 35.—Year since the destruction of the kingdom of Israel by Shalmaneser, king of Assyria, 9.—Year before the birth of Christ, 709.—Year before the vulgar era of Christ's nativity, 713.—Cycle of the Sun, 25.—Cycle of the Moon, 11.—Eleventh year of Zeuxidamus, king of Lacedæmon, of the family of the Proclidæ.—Twelfth year of Eurycrates, king of Lacedæmon, of the family of the Eurysthenidæ.—Sixth year of Gyges, king of Lydia.—Tenth year of Hippomenes, decennial archon of the Athenians.—Second year of Cordiccas, governor of the Medes, according to some chronologers.—Seventeenth year of Perdiccas, king of Macedon.—Third year of Numa Pompilius, the second king of Rome.—Fourteenth year of Hezekiah, king of Judah.

CHAPTER I

This chapter opens the prophecy against the Assyrians and their metropolis with a very magnificent description of the infinite justice, tender compassion, and uncontrollable power of God, 1–8. *To this succeeds an address to the Assyrians; with a lively picture of their sudden overthrow, because of their evil device against Jerusalem,* 9–11. *Then appears Jehovah himself, proclaiming deliverance to his people from the Assyrian yoke, and the destruction of the Assyrian idols,* 12–14; *upon which the prophet, with great emphasis, directs the attention of Judah to the approach of the messenger who brings such glad tidings; and exultingly bids his people to celebrate their solemn feasts, and perform their vows, as a merciful Providence would not suffer these enemies of the Jewish state to prevail against them,* 15.

A. M. cir. 3291
B. C. cir. 713
Ol. cir. XVI. 4
NumæPompilii,
R. Roman.,
cir. annum 3

THE burden of [a]Nineveh.
The book of the vision of
Nahum the Elkoshite.
2 [b]God *is* [c]jealous, and [d]the
LORD revengeth; the LORD
revengeth, and [e]*is* furious;
the LORD will take vengeance
on his adversaries, and he

[a]Zech. ii. 13——[b]Or, *The LORD* is *a jealous God, and a Revenger*, &c.——[c]Ezod. xx. 5; xxxiv. 14; Deut. iv. 24; Josh. xxiv. 19——[d]Deut. xxxii. 35; Psa. xciv. 1; Isa. lix. 11——[e]Heb. *that hath fury*

NOTES ON CHAP. I

Verse 1. *The burden of Nineveh.*] משא *massa* not only signifies a *burden*, but also a thing *lifted up*, *pronounced*, or *proclaimed;* also a *message*. It is used by the prophets to signify the *revelation* which they have received from God to deliver to any particular people: the *oracle*—the *prophecy*. Here it signifies the *declaration* from God relative to the overthrow

A. M. cir. 3291
B. C. cir. 713
Ol. cir. XVI. 4
NumæPompilii,
R. Roman.,
cir. annum 3

reserveth *wrath* for his enemies.
3 The LORD *is* [f]slow to anger,
and [g]great in power, and will
not at all acquit *the wicked;* [h]the LORD
hath his way in the whirlwind and in the
storm, and the clouds *are* the dust of his
feet.
4 [i]He rebuketh the sea, and maketh it dry,
and drieth up all the rivers: [k]Bashan languisheth, and Carmel, and the flower of Lebanon languisheth.
5 [l]The mountains quake at him, and [m]the
hills melt, and [n]the earth is burned at his
presence; yea, the world, and
all that dwell therein.

A. M. cir. 3291
B. C. cir. 713
Ol. cir. XVI. 4
NumæPompilii,
R. Roman.,
cir. annum 3

6 Who can stand before his
indignation? and [o]who can [p]abide
in the fierceness of his anger? [q]his fury is
poured out like fire, and the rocks are thrown
down by him.
7 [r]The LORD *is* good, a [s]strong hold in the
day of trouble; and [t]he knoweth them that
trust in him.
8 [u]But with an overrunning flood he will
make an utter end of the place thereof, and
darkness shall pursue his enemies.
9 [v]What do ye imagine against the LORD?

[f]Exod. xxxiv. 6, 7; Neh. ix. 17; Psa. ciii. 8; Jonah iv. 2——[g]Job ix. 4——[h]Psa. xviii. 7, &c.; xcvii. 2; Hab. iii. 5, 11, 12——[i]Psa. cvi. 9; Isa. l. 2; Matt. viii. 26——[k]Isa. xxxiii. 9——[l]Psa. lxviii. 8——[m]Judg. v. 5; Psa. xcvii. 5; Mic. i. 4——[n]2 Pet. iii. 10——[o]Mal. iii. 2——[p]Heb. *stand up*——[q]Rev. xvi. 1——[r]1 Chron. xvi. 34; Psa. c. 5; Jer. xxxiii. 11; Lam. iii. 25——[s]Or, *strength*——[t]Psa. i. 6; 2 Tim. ii. 19——[u]Dan. ix. 26; xi. 10, 22, 40——[v]Psa. ii. 1

of Nineveh, and the *commission* of the prophet to deliver it.

As the Assyrians under Pul, Tiglath-pileser, and Shalmaneser, three of their kings, had been employed by a just God for the chastisement of his disobedient people; the end being now accomplished by them, God is about to *burn the rod* wherewith he corrected Israel; and Nineveh, the capital of the Assyrian empire, is to be destroyed. This prediction appears to have been accomplished a short time after this by Nebuchadnezzar and Cyaxares, the Ahasuerus of Scripture.

Nahum, נחום *Nachum,* signifies *comforter.* The name was very suitable, as he was sent to *comfort* the people, by showing them that God was about to destroy their adversaries.

Verse 2. *God* is *jealous*] For his own glory.

And—revengeth] His justice; by the destruction of his enemies.

And is *furious*] So powerful in the manifestations of his judgments, that nothing can stand before him.

He reserveth wrath] Though they seem to prosper for a time, and God appears to have passed by their crimes without notice, yet he *reserveth—treasureth* up—*wrath* for them, which shall burst forth in due time.

Verse 3. *The Lord* is *slow to anger*] He exercises much longsuffering towards his enemies, that this may lead them to repentance. And it is because of this longsuffering that vengeance is not speedily executed on every evil work.

Great in power] Able at all times to *save* or to *destroy.*

The Lord hath *his way in the whirlwind and in the storm*] These are the *effects* of his *power;* and when they appear unusual, they may be considered as the *immediate* effects of his power: and although he be *in them* to punish and destroy, he is in them to *direct* their *course,* to determine their *operations,* and to defend his followers from being injured by their violence. The pestilential wind which slew *one hundred and eighty-five thousand* of the Assyrians did not injure *one* Israelite. See 2 Kings xix. 35.

The clouds are *the dust of his feet.*] This is spoken in allusion to a *chariot and horses* going on with *extreme rapidity:* they are all *enveloped in a cloud of dust.* So Jehovah is represented as coming through the circuit of the heavens as rapidly as lightning; the *clouds* surrounding him as the *dust* does the chariot and horses.

Verse 4. *He rebuketh the sea*] The Red Sea, and the rivers: probably an allusion to the passage of the *Red Sea* and *Jordan.*

The description of the coming of Jehovah, from the third to the sixth verse, is dreadfully majestic. He is represented as controlling *universal nature.* The *sea* and the *rivers* are dried up; the *mountains* tremble, the *hills* melt, and the *earth* is burnt at his presence. *Bashan, Carmel,* and *Lebanon* are withered and languish: streams of *fire* are poured out, and the *rocks* are cast down to make him a passage. If, then, the *seas,* the *rivers,* the *mountains,* the *hills,* the *rocks,* and the *earth* itself, fail before Jehovah, or flee from his presence, how shall *Nineveh* and the *Assyrian empire* stand before him?

Verse 7. *The Lord* is *good*] In the midst of judgment he remembers mercy; and among the most dreadful denunciations of wrath he mingles promises of mercy. None that trust in him need be alarmed at these dreadful threatenings; they shall be discriminated in the day of wrath, for the *Lord knoweth them that trust in him.*

Verse 8. *But with an overrunning flood*] Bishop *Newcome* thinks this may refer to the manner in which Nineveh was taken. The *Euphrates* overflowed its banks, deluged a part of the city, and overturned *twenty* stadia of the wall; in consequence of which the desponding king burnt himself, and his palace, with his treasures.—*Diodor. Sic.*, Edit. Wessel., p. 140, lib. ii., s. 27.

Darkness shall pursue] Calamity. All kinds of calamity shall pursue them till they are destroyed.

Verse 9. *Affliction shall not rise up the second time.*] There shall be no need to *repeat the judgment;* with *one blow* God will make a full end of the business.

A. M. cir. 3291
B. C. cir. 713
Ol. cir. XVI. 4
NumæPompilii,
R. Roman.,
cir. annum 3

[w]he will make an utter end:
affliction shall not rise up the
second time.
10 For while *they be* folden
together [x]*as* thorns, [y]and while they are
drunken *as* drunkards, [z]they shall be devoured as stubble fully dry.
11 There is *one* come out of thee, [a]that
imagineth evil against the LORD, [b]a wicked
counsellor.
12 Thus saith the LORD; [c]Though *they be*
quiet, and likewise many, yet thus [d]shall they
be [e]cut down, when he shall [f]pass through.
Though I have afflicted thee, I will afflict thee
no more.
13 For now will I [g]break his
yoke from off thee, and will
burst thy bonds in sunder.
14 And the LORD hath given
a commandment concerning thee, *that* no
more of thy name be sown: out of the house
of thy gods will I cut off the graven image
and the molten image: [h]I will make thy
grave; for thou art vile.
15 Behold [i]upon the mountains the feet of
him that bringeth good tidings, that publisheth peace! O Judah, [k]keep thy solemn
feasts, perform thy vows: for [l]the [m]wicked
shall no more pass through thee; [n]he is
utterly cut off.

---

[w]1 Sam. iii. 12——[x]2 Sam. xxiii. 6, 7——[y]Chap. iii. 11——[z]Mal. iv. 1——[a]2 Kings xix. 22, 23——[b]Heb. *a counsellor of Belial*——[c]Or, *If* they would have been *at peace, so* should they have been *many, and so should they have been shorn, and he should have passed away*

[d]2 Kings xix. 35, 37——[e]Hebrew, *shorn*——[f]Isaiah viii. 8; Daniel xi. 10——[g]Jeremiah ii. 20; xxx. 8——[h]2 Kings xix. 37——[i]Isaiah lii. 7; Romans x. 15——[k]Hebrew, *feast*——[l]Hebrew, *Belial*——[m]Ver. 11, 12 [n]Ver. 14

Verse 10. *While* they be *folden together*] However united their counsels may be, they shall be as *drunken men*—perplexed and unsteady in all their resolutions; and before God's judgments they shall be as *dry thorns* before a devouring fire.

Verse 11. *Imagineth evil against the Lord*] Such were *Pul*, 2 Kings xv. 10; *Tiglath-pileser*, 2 Kings xv. 29; *Shalmaneser*, 2 Kings xvii. 6; and *Sennacherib*, 2 Kings xviii. 17, and xix. 23.

A wicked counsellor.] *Sennacherib* and *Rabshakeh.*

Verse 12. *Though* they be—*many*] *Sennacherib* invaded Judea with an army of nearly *two hundred thousand* men.

Thus shall they be cut down] The angel of the Lord (a suffocating wind) slew of them in one night *one hundred and eighty-five thousand*, 2 Kings xix. 35.

Verse 13. *Now will I break his yoke from off thee*] This refers to the *tribute* which the Jews were obliged to pay to the Assyrians, 2 Kings xvii. 14.

Verse 14. *No more of thy name be sown*] No more of you shall be carried away into *captivity*.

I will make thy grave; for thou art vile] I think this is an address to the Assyrians, and especially to *Sennacherib*. The text is no obscure intimation of the fact. The *house of his gods is to be his grave:* and we know that while he was worshipping in the house of his god *Nisroch*, his two sons, *Adrammelech* and *Sharezer*, smote him there that he died, 2 Kings xix. 37.

Verse 15. *Behold upon the mountains*] Borrowed probably from Isa. lii. 7, but applied here to the *messengers* who brought the *good tidings* of the *destruction of Nineveh*. Judah might then *keep her solemn feasts*, for the wicked Assyrian should *pass through the land no more;* being entirely cut off, and the imperial city razed to its foundations.

CHAPTER II

Nineveh is now called upon to prepare for the approach of her enemies, the instruments of Jehovah's vengeance, 1; *and the military array and muster, the very arms and dress, of the Medes and Babylonians in the reigns of Cyaxares and Nabopolassar; their rapid approach to the city; the process of the siege, and the inundation of the river; the capture of the place; the captivity, lamentation, and flight of the inhabitants; the sacking of this immense, wealthy, and exceedingly populous city; and the consequent desolation and terror, are all described in the pathetic, vivid, and sublime imagery of Hebrew poetry,* 2–10. *This description is succeeded by a very beautiful and expressive allegory,* 11–12; *which is immediately explained, and applied to the city of Nineveh,* 13. *It is thought by some commentators that the metropolitan city of the Assyrian empire is also intended by the tender and beautiful simile, in the* seventh *verse, of a great princess led captive, with her maids of honour attending her, bewailing her and their own condition, by beating their breasts, and by other expressions of sorrow.*

A. M. cir. 3291
B. C. cir. 713
Ol. cir. XVI. 4
NumæPompilii,
R. Roman.,
cir. annum 3

HE [a]that [b]dasheth in pieces is come up before thy face: [c]keep the munition, watch the way, make *thy* loins strong, fortify *thy* power mightily.

2 [d]For the LORD hath turned away [e]the excellency of Jacob, as the excellency of Israel: for [f]the emptiers have emptied them out, and marred their vine branches.

3 The shield of his mighty men is made [g]red, the valiant men *are* [h]in scarlet: the chariots *shall be* with [i]flaming torches in the day of his preparation, and the fir trees shall be terribly shaken.

4 The chariots shall rage in the streets, they shall jostle one against another in the broad ways: [k]they shall seem like torches, they shall run like the lightnings.

5 He shall recount his [l]worthies: they shall stumble in their walk; they shall make haste to the wall thereof, and the [m]defence shall be prepared.

6 The gates of the rivers shall be opened, and the palace shall be [n]dissolved.

7 And [o]Huzzab shall be [p]led away captive, she shall be brought up, and her maids shall lead *her* as with the voice of [q]doves, tabering upon their breasts.

8 But Nineveh *is* [r]of old like a pool of water: yet they shall flee away. Stand, stand, *shall they cry;* but none shall [s]look back.

[a]Or, *The disperser*, or *hammer*——[b]Jer. l. 23——[c]Jer. li. 11, 12; chap. iii. 14——[d]Isa. x. 12; Jer. xxxv. 29——[e]Or, *the pride of Jacob as the pride of Israel*——[f]Psa. lxxx. 12; Hos. x. 1——[g]Isa. lxiii. 2, 3——[h]Or, *dyed scarlet*——[i]Or, *fiery torches*

[k]Heb. *their show*——[l]Or, *gallants*——[m]Heb. *covering*, or *coverer*——[n]Or, *molten*——[o]Or, *that which was established*, or *there was a stand made*——[p]Or, *discovered*——[q]Isa. xxxviii. 14; lix. 11——[r]Or, *from the days that she hath been*——[s]Or, *cause* them *to turn*

NOTES ON CHAP. II

Verse 1. *He that dasheth in pieces*] Or *scattereth.* The Chaldeans and Medes.

Keep the munition] Guard the fenced places. From this to the end of the fifth verse, the *preparations* made at Nineveh to repel their enemies are described. The description is exceedingly picturesque.

Watch the way] By which the enemy is most likely to approach.

Make thy *loins strong*] Take *courage.*

Fortify thy *power*] Muster thy troops; call in all thy allies.

Verse 2. *For the Lord hath turned away*] Bishop *Newcome* reads, *for the Lord restoreth*, by a slight alteration in the text. I do not see that we gain much by this. The Lord *has* been opposed to Jacob, and the enemy has prevailed against him.

Emptied them out] Brought them from their own land into captivity. This was the *emptying!*

Verse 3. *The shield of his mighty men is made red*] These things may refer to the warlike preparations made by the Ninevites: they had *red shields*, and *scarlet* or *purple clothing;* their chariots were finely *decorated*, and proceeded with amazing rapidity.

The fir trees shall be terribly shaken.] This may refer to the *darts*, *arrows*, and *javelins*, flung with destructive power.

Verse 4. *The chariots shall rage*] Those of the *besiegers* and the *besieged*, meeting in the streets, producing universal confusion and carnage.

Verse 5. *He shall recount his worthies*] Muster up his most renowned warriors and heroes.

Shall make haste to the wall] Where they see the enemies making their most powerful attacks, in order to get possession of the city.

Verse 6. *The gates of the rivers shall be opened*] I have already referred to this, see the note on chap. i. 8; but it will be necessary to be *more particular.* The account given by *Diodorus Siculus*, lib. ii., is very surprising. He begins thus: Ην δ' αυτῳ λογιον παραδεδομενον εκ προγονων, κ. τ. λ.—"There was a prophecy received from their forefathers, that Nineveh should not be taken *till the river first became an enemy to the city.* It happened in the *third* year of the siege, that the Euphrates [query, *Tigris*] being swollen with continued rains, overflowed part of the city, and threw down *twenty* stadia of the wall. The king then imagining that the oracle was accomplished, and that *the river was now manifestly become an enemy to the city*, casting aside all hope of safety, and lest he should fall into the hands of the enemy, built a large funeral pyre in the palace, (εν τοις βασιλειοις,) and having collected all his gold and silver and royal vestments, together with his concubines and eunuchs, placed himself with them in a little apartment built in the pyre; burnt them, himself, and the palace together. When the death of the king (*Sardanapalus*) was announced by certain deserters, the enemy entered in by the breach which the waters had made, and took the city."

Thus the prophecy of Nahum was literally fulfilled: "the gates of the river were opened, and the palace dissolved," i. e., *burnt.*

Verse 7. *And Huzzab shall be led away captive*] Perhaps *Huzzab* means the *queen of Nineveh*, who had escaped the burning mentioned above by Diodorus. As there is no account of the *queen* being burnt, but only of the king, the concubines, and the eunuchs, we may, therefore, naturally conclude that the queen escaped; and is represented here as *brought up* and delivered to the conqueror; her maids at the same time bewailing her lot. Some think Huzzab signifies Nineveh itself.

Verse 8. *But Nineveh* is *of old like a pool of water*] מימי *mimey*, from days. Bp. *Newcome* translates the line thus: "And the waters of Nineveh are a pool of waters." There may be reference here to the fact given in the preceding note, the *overflowing of the river* by which the city was primarily destroyed.

Stand, stand] Consternation shall be at its utmost height, the people shall flee in all directions; and though *quarter* is offered, and they

A. M. cir. 3291
B. C. cir. 713
Ol. cir. XVI. 4
NumæPompilii,
R. Roman.,
cir. annum 3

9 Take ye the spoil of silver, take the spoil of gold: [t]for *there is* none end of the store *and* glory out of all the [u]pleasant furniture.

10 She is empty, and void, and waste: and the [v]heart melteth, and [w]the knees smite together, [x]and much pain *is* in all loins, and [y]the faces of them all gather blackness.

11 Where *is* the dwelling of [z]the lions, and the feeding place of the young lions, where the lion, *even* the old lion, walked, *and* the lions' whelp, and none made *them* afraid?

12 The lion did tear in pieces enough for his whelps, and strangled for his lionesses, and filled his holes with prey, and his dens with ravin.

13 [a]Behold, I *am* against thee, saith the LORD of hosts, and I will burn her chariots in the smoke, and the sword shall devour thy young lions: and I will cut off thy prey from the earth, and the voice of [b]thy messengers shall no more be heard.

[t]Or, *and* their *infinite store,* &c.——[u]Heb. *vessels of desire*——[v]Isa. xiii. 7, 8——[w]Dan. v. 6——[x]Jer. xxx. 9——[y]Joel ii. 6

[z]Job iv. 10, 11; Ezek. xix. 2–7——[a]Ezek. xxix. 3; xxxviii. 3; xxxix. 1; chap. iii. 5——[b]2 Kings xviii. 17, 19; xix. 9, 23

are assured of safety if they remain, yet not *one looketh back.*

Verse 9. *Take ye the spoil*] Though the king burnt his treasures, vestments, &c., he could not totally *destroy* the *silver* and the *gold.* Nor did he burn the *riches of the city;* these fell a prey to the conquerors; and there was *no end of the store* of *glorious* garments, and the most costly *vessels* and *furniture.*

Verse 10. *She is empty, and void, and waste*] The original is strongly emphatic: the words are of the *same sound;* and increase in their *length* as they point out *great, greater,* and *greatest* desolation.

בוקה ומבוקה ומבלקה

Bukah, umebukah, umebullakah.

She is *void, empty,* and *desolate.*

The faces of them all gather blackness.] This marks the diseased state into which the people had been brought by reason of *famine,* &c.; for, as Mr. *Ward* justly remarks, "*sickness* makes a great change in the countenance of the Hindoos; so that a person who was rather *fair* when in *health,* becomes nearly *black* by *sickness.*" This was a general case with the Asiatics.

Verse 11. *Where* is *the dwelling of the lions*] *Nineveh,* the habitation of *bold, strong,* and *ferocious* men.

The feeding place of the young lions] Whither her victorious and rapacious generals frequently *returned* to *consume* the produce of their success. Here they *walked* at large, and *none made them afraid.* Wheresoever they turned their arms they were victors; and all nations were afraid of them.

Verse 12. *The lion did tear*] This verse gives us a striking picture of the manner in which the Assyrian conquests and depredations were carried on. How many people were spoiled to enrich his *whelps*—his sons, princes, and *nobles!* How *many women* were *stripped* and *slain,* whose spoils went to decorate his *lionesses*—his *queen concubines* and *mistresses.* And they had even more than they could assume; *their holes and dens*—treasure-houses, palaces, and *wardrobes*—were filled *with ravin,* the riches which they got by the plunder of *towns, families,* and *individuals.* This is a very fine allegory, and admirably well supported.

Verse 13. *Behold, I* am *against thee*] Assyria, and Nineveh its capital. I will deal with you as you have dealt with others

The voice of thy messengers] Announcing thy splendid victories, and the vast spoils taken —*shall no more be heard*—thou and thy riches, and ill-got spoils, shall perish together.

CHAPTER III

The prophet denounces a wo against Nineveh for her perfidy and violence. He musters up before our eyes the number of her chariots and cavalry; points to her burnished arms, and to the great and unrelenting slaughter which she spreads around her, 1–3. *Because Nineveh is a city wholly given up to the grossest superstition, and is an instructress of other nations in her abominable rites, therefore she shall come to a most ignominious and unpitied end,* 3–7. *Her final ruin shall be similar to that of No, a famous city of Egypt,* 8–11. *The prophet then beautifully describes the great ease with which the strong holds of Nineveh should be taken,* 12, *and her judicial pusillanimity during the siege,* 13; *declares that all her preparation, her numbers, opulence, and chieftains, would be of no avail in the day of the Lord's vengeance,* 14–17; *and that her tributaries would desert her,* 18. *The whole concludes with stating the incurableness of her malady, and the dreadful destruction consequently awaiting her; and with introducing the nations which she had oppressed as exulting at her fall,* 19.

A. M. cir. 3291
B. C. cir. 713
Ol. cir. XVI. 4
NumæPompilii,
R. Roman.,
cir. annum 3

WO to the [a]bloody [b]city!
it *is* all full of lies *and*
robbery; the prey departeth not;
2 The noise of a whip, and [c]the
noise of the rattling of the wheels, and of the
prancing horses, and of the jumping chariots.
3 The horsemen lifteth up both [d]the bright
sword and the glittering spear: and *there is*
a multitude of slain, and a great number
of carcasses; and *there is* none end of
their corpses; they stumble upon their
corpses:
4 Because of the multitude of the whoredoms of the well-favoured harlot, [e]the mistress of witchcrafts, that selleth nations through her whoredoms, and families through her witchcrafts.
5 [f]Behold, I *am* against thee, saith the LORD
of hosts; and [g]I will discover thy skirts upon thy face, [h]and I will show the nations thy nakedness, and the kingdoms thy shame.
6 And I will cast abominable
filth upon thee, and [i]make thee
vile, and will set thee as [k]a gazing-stock.
7 And it shall come to pass, *that* all they
that look upon thee [l]shall flee from thee, and say, Nineveh is laid waste: [m]who will bemoan her? whence shall I seek comforters for thee?
8 [n]Art thou better than [o]populous[p] [q]No,
that was situate among the rivers, *that had* the waters round about it, whose rampart *was* the sea, *and* her wall *was* from the sea?
9 Ethiopia and Egypt *were* her strength,
and *it was* infinite; Put and Lubim were [r]thy helpers.
10 Yet *was* she carried away, she went into
captivity: [s]her young children also were dashed in pieces [t]at the top of all the streets: and they [u]cast lots for her honourable men, and

A. M. cir. 3291
B. C. cir. 713
Ol. cir. XVI. 4
NumæPompilii,
R. Roman.,
cir. annum 3

---

[a]Heb. *city of bloods*——[b]Ezek. xxii. 2, 3; xxiv. 6, 9; Hab. ii. 12——[c]Jer. xlvii. 3——[d]Heb. *the flame of the sword, and the lightning of the spear*——[e]Isa. xlvii. 9, 12; Rev. xviii. 2, 3——[f]Chap. ii. 13——[g]Isa. xlvii. 2, 3; Jer. xiii. 22, 26; Ezek. xvi. 37; Mic. i. 11——[h]Hab. ii. 16

[i]Mal. ii. 9——[k]Heb. x. 33——[l]Rev. xviii. 10
[m]Jer. xv. 5——[n]Amos vi. 2——[o]Or, *nourishing*
[p]Heb. *No Amon*——[q]Jer. xlvi. 25, 26; Ezek. xxx. 14–16
[r]Heb. *in thy help*——[s]Psa. cxxxvii. 9; Isa. xiii. 16; Hos. xiii. 16——[t]Lam. ii. 19——[u]Joel iii. 3; Obad. 11

NOTES ON CHAP. III

Verse 1. *Wo to the bloody city!*] Nineveh: the threatenings against which are continued in a strain of invective, astonishing for its richness, variety, and energy. One may hear and see the *whip crack*, the *horses prancing*, the *wheels rumbling*, the *chariots bounding* after the *galloping steeds;* the *reflection* from the *drawn* and highly *polished swords;* and the *hurled spears*, like *flashes* of *lightning*, dazzling the eyes; the *slain* lying in *heaps*, and *horses* and *chariots* stumbling over them! O what a picture, and a *true representation* of a battle, when one side is broken, and all the *cavalry* of the conqueror fall in upon them, *hewing* them down with their swords, and trampling them to pieces under the hoofs of their horses! O! infernal war! Yet sometimes thou art the scourge of the Lord.

Verse 4. *Because of the multitude of the whoredoms*] Above, the Ninevites were represented under the emblem of a *lion tearing all to pieces;* here they are represented under the emblem of a *beautiful harlot* or public *prostitute*, enticing all men to her, inducing the nations to become idolatrous; and, by thus perverting them, rendering them also objects of the Divine wrath.

Mistress of witchcrafts, that selleth nations through her whoredoms] Using every means to excite to idolatry; and being, by *menace* or *wiles*, successful in all.

Verse 5. *I will discover thy skirts upon thy face*] It was an ancient, though not a laudable custom, to strip prostitutes naked, or throw their clothes over their heads, and expose them to public view, and public execration. This verse alludes to such a custom.

Verse 6. *I will cast abominable filth upon thee*] I will set thee as a *gazing-stock*. This was a punishment precisely like our *pillory*. They put such women in the pillory as a *gazing-stock;* and then, *children* and *others* threw *mud, dirt*, and *filth* of all kinds at them.

Verse 7. *Who will bemoan her?*] In such cases, who pities the delinquent? She has been the occasion of ruin to multitudes, and now she is deservedly exposed and punished. And so it should be thought concerning Nineveh.

Verse 8. *Art thou better than populous No*] No-Ammon, or *Diospolis*, in the *Delta*, on one branch of the Nile. This is supposed to be the city mentioned by *Nahum;* and which had been lately destroyed, probably by the Chaldeans.

The waters round about it] Being situated in the *Delta*, it had the *fork* of two branches of the Nile to defend it by land; and its barrier or *wall* was the *sea*, the Mediterranean, into which these branches emptied themselves: so that this city, and the place it stood on, were wholly surrounded by the waters.

Verse 9. *Ethiopia and Egypt* were *her strength*] The land of *Cush*, not far from *Diospolis;* for it was in Arabia, on the *Red Sea*.

Put and Lubim] A part of Africa and Libya, which were all within reach of forming alliances with *No-Ammon* or *Diospolis*.

Verse 10. *They cast lots for her honourable men*] This refers still to the city called *populous No*. And the custom of *casting lots* among the commanders, for the prisoners which they had taken, is here referred to.

A. M. cir. 3291 B. C. cir. 713 Ol. cir. XVI. 4 NumæPompilii, R. Roman., cir. annum 3

all her great men were bound in chains.
11 Thou also shalt be [v]drunken: thou shalt be hid, thou also shalt seek strength because of the enemy.
12 All thy strong holds *shall be like* [w]fig trees with the first-ripe figs: if they be shaken, they shall even fall into the mouth of the eater.
13 Behold, [x]thy people in the midst of thee *are* women: the gates of thy land shall be set wide open unto thine enemies: the fire shall devour thy [y]bars.
14 Draw thee waters for the siege, [z]fortify thy strong holds: go into clay, and tread the mortar, make strong the brick-kiln.
15 There shall the fire devour thee; the sword shall cut thee off, it shall eat thee up like [a]the cankerworm: make thyself many as the cankerworm, make thyself many as the locusts.
16 Thou hast multiplied thy merchants above the stars of heaven: the cankerworm [b]spoileth, and fleeth away.
17 [c]Thy crowned *are* as the locusts, and thy captains as the great grasshoppers, which camp in the hedges in the cold day, *but* when the sun ariseth they flee away, and their place is not known where they *are*.
18 [d]Thy shepherds slumber, O [e]king of Assyria: thy [f]nobles shall dwell *in the dust:* thy people is [g]scattered upon the mountains, and no man gathereth *them*.
19 *There is* no [h]healing of thy bruise; [i]thy wound is grievous: [k]all that hear the bruit of thee shall clap the hands over thee: for upon whom hath not thy wickedness passed continually?

[v]Jer. xxv. 17, 27; chap. i. 10——[w]Rev. vi. 13——[x]Jer. l. 37; li. 30——[y]Psa. cxlvii. 13; Jer. li. 30——[z]Chap. ii. 1——[a]Joel i. 4——[b]Or, *spreadeth himself*——[c]Revelation ix. 7

[d]Exod. xv. 16; Psa. lxxvii. 6——[e]Jer. l. 18; Ezek. xxxi. 3, &c.——[f]Or, *valiant ones*——[g]1 Kings xxii. 17 [h]Heb. *wrinkling*——[i]Mic. i. 9——[k]Lam. ii. 15; Zeph. ii. 15; see Isa. xiv. 8, &c.

Great men were bound in chains] These were reserved to grace the *triumph* of the victor.

Verse 12. *Thy strong holds*] The effects of the consternation into which the Ninevites were cast by the assault on their city are here pointed out by a very expressive metaphor; the *first-ripe figs*, when at *full maturity*, fell from the tree with the *least shake;* and so, at the first *shake* or *consternation*, all the *fortresses* of Nineveh were abandoned; and the king, in despair, burnt himself and household in his own palace.

Verse 13. *Thy people*—are *women*] They lost all courage, and made no resistance. O verè Phrygiæ, neque enim Phryges: "Verily, ye are Phrygian women, not Phrygian men." So said *Numanus* to the *Trojans*. *Virg.*, *Æn.* ix.

Verse 14. *Draw thee waters for the siege*] The Tigris ran near to Nineveh, and here they are exhorted to lay in plenty of fresh water, lest the siege should last long, and lest the enemy should cut off this supply.

Go into clay, and tread the mortar] This refers to the manner of forming bricks anciently in those countries; they digged up the clay, kneaded it properly by *treading*, mixed it with straw or *coarse grass*, moulded the bricks, and dried them in the sun. I have now some of the identical bricks, that were brought from this country, lying before me, and they show all these appearances. They are compact and very hard, but wholly soluble in water. There were however others without *straw*, that seem to have been *burnt in a kiln* as ours are. I have also some fragments or *bats* of these from Babylon.

Verse 15. *Make thyself many as the cankerworm*] On the *locusts*, and their operations in their various *states*, see the notes on Joel ii. The multitudes, successive swarms, and devastation occasioned by locusts, is one of the most expressive similes that could be used to point out the successive armies and all-destroying influences of the enemies of Nineveh. The account of these destroyers from Dr. *Shaw*, inserted Joel ii., will fully illustrate the verses where allusion is made to locusts.

Verse 16. *Thou hast multiplied thy merchants*] Like Tyre, this city was a famous resort for merchants; but the multitudes which were there previously to the siege, like the locusts, took the alarm, and fled away.

Verse 17. *Thy crowned* are *as the locusts*] Thou hast numerous *princes* and numerous *commanders*.

Which camp in the hedges in the cold day] The locusts are said to *lie in shelter* about the *hedges* of fertile spots when the weather is *cold*, or during the *night;* but as soon as the *sun* shines out and is hot, they come out to their forage, or take to their wings.

Verse 18. *Thy shepherds slumber*] That is, the rulers and tributary princes, who, as *Herodotus* informs us, deserted Nineveh in the day of her distress, and came not forward to her succour.

Diodorus Siculus says, lib. ii., when the enemy shut up the king in the city, many nations revolted, each going over to the besiegers, for the sake of their liberty; that the king despatched messengers to all his subjects, requiring power from them to succour him; and that he thought himself able to endure the siege, and remained in expectation of armies which were to be raised throughout his empire, relying on the *oracle* that *the city would* not be taken *till the river became its enemy.* See the note on chap. ii. 6.

Verse 19. There is *no healing of thy bruise*] Thou shalt never be rebuilt.

All that hear the bruit of thee] The report or account.

Shall clap the hands] Shall exult in thy downfall.

For upon whom hath not thy wickedness passed] Thou hast been a *universal oppressor*, and therefore all nations rejoice at thy fall and utter desolation.

Bp. *Newton* makes some good remarks on the fall and total ruin of Nineveh.

"What probability was there that the capital city of a great kingdom, a city which was *sixty* miles in compass, a city which contained so many *thousand* inhabitants, a city which had walls a *hundred* feet high, and so thick that *three* chariots could go abreast upon them, and which had *one thousand five hundred* towers, of *two hundred* feet in height; what probability was there that such a city should ever be totally destroyed? And yet so totally was it destroyed that the place is hardly known where it was situated. What we may suppose helped to complete its ruin and devastation, was Nebuchadnezzar's enlarging and beautifying Babylon, soon after Nineveh was taken. From that time no mention is made of Nineveh by any of the sacred writers; and the most ancient of the heathen authors, who have occasion to say any thing about it, speak of it as a city that was once great and flourishing, but now destroyed and desolate. Great as it was formerly, so little of it is remaining, that authors are not agreed even about its situation. From the general suffrage of ancient historians and geographers, it appears to have been situated upon the Tigris, though others represent it as placed upon the Euphrates. *Bochart* has shown that *Herodotus*, *Diodorus Siculus*, and *Ammianus Marcellinus*, all *three* speak differently of it; sometimes as if situated on the Euphrates, sometimes as if on the Tigris; to reconcile whom he supposes that there were *two* Ninevehs; and Sir *John Marsham*, that there were *three;* the Syrian upon the Euphrates, the Assyrian on the Tigris, and a *third* built afterwards upon the Tigris by the Persians, who succeeded the Parthians in the empire of the East, in the *third* century, and were subdued by the Saracens in the *seventh* century after Christ. But whether this latter was built in the same place as the old Nineveh, is a question that cannot be decided.

"There is a city at this time called Mosul, situate upon the western side of the Tigris; and on the opposite eastern shore are ruins of great extent, which are said to be those of Nineveh.

"Dr. *Prideaux*, following *Thevenot*, observes that Mosul is situated on the west side of the Tigris, where was anciently only a suburb of the old Nineveh; for the city itself stood on the east side of the river, where are to be seen some of its ruins of great extent even to this day. Even the ruins of old Nineveh, as we may say, have been long ago ruined and destroyed; such an utter end hath been made of it, and such is the truth of the Divine predictions!

"These extraordinary circumstances may strike the reader more strongly by supposing only a parallel instance. Let us then suppose that a person should come in the name of a prophet, preaching repentance to the people of this kingdom, or otherwise denouncing the destruction of the capital city within a few years. 'With an overflowing flood will God make an utter end of the place thereof; he will make an utter end: its place may be sought, but it shall never be found.' I presume we should look upon such a prophet as a madman, and show no farther attention to his message than to deride and despise it. And yet such an event would not be more strange and incredible than the destruction and devastation of Nineveh; for Nineveh was much the larger, stronger, and older city of the two. And the Assyrian empire had subsisted and flourished more ages than any form of government in this country; so there is no objecting the instability of Eastern monarchies in this case. Let us then, since this event would not be more improbable and extraordinary than the other, suppose again, that things should succeed according to the prediction; that the floods should arise, and the enemies should come; the city should be overthrown and broken down, be taken and pillaged, and destroyed so totally that even the learned could not agree about the place where it was situated. What would be said or thought in such a case? Whoever of posterity should read and compare the prophecy and event together, must they not, by such an illustrious instance, be thoroughly convinced of the providence of God, and of the truth of his prophet, and be ready to acknowledge, 'Verily, this IS the word which the Lord hath spoken; verily, there IS a God who judgeth the earth?' "—See Bp. *Newton*, vol. i., dissert. 9.

THE BOOK

OF THE

PROPHET HABAKKUK

Chronological Notes relative to this Book, upon the supposition that it was written a little before the destruction of Jerusalem, about six hundred *years before the commencement of the Christian era.*

Year from the Creation, according to Archbishop Usher, 3404.—Year of the Julian Period, 4114.—Year since the Flood, 1748.—Year since the vocation of Abram, 1321.—Year from the foundation of Solomon's temple, 412.—Year since the division of Solomon's monarchy into the kingdoms of Israel and Judah, 376.—First year of the *forty-fifth* Olympiad.—Year since the destruction of the kingdom of Israel by Shalmaneser, king of Assyria, 121.—Year before the birth of Jesus Christ, 596.—Year before the vulgar era of Christ's nativity, 600.—Cycle of the Sun, 26.—Cycle of the Moon, 10.—Third year of Æropas, king of Macedon.—Twentieth year of Alyattes II., king of Lydia.—Twenty-sixth year of Cyaxares or Cyaraxes, king of Media.—Sixth year of Agasicles, king of Lacedæmon, of the family of the Proclidæ.—Eighth year of Leon, king of Lacedæmon, of the family of the Eurysthenidæ.—Seventh year of Nebuchadnezzar, king of Babylon.—Seventeenth year of Tarquinius Priscus, king of the Romans.—Eleventh year of Jehoiakim, king of Judah.

CHAPTER I

The prophet enters very abruptly on his subject, his spirit being greatly indignant at the rapid progress of vice and impiety, 1–4. *Upon which God is introduced threatening very awful and sudden judgments to be inflicted by the ministry of the Chaldeans,* 5–10. *The Babylonians attribute their wonderful successes to their idols,* 11. *The prophet then, making a sudden transition, expostulates with God (probably personating the Jews) for permitting a nation much more wicked than themselves, as they supposed, to oppress and devour them, as fishers and foulers do their prey,* 12–17.

A. M. cir. 3404
B. C. cir. 600
Ol. XLV. 1
TarquiniiPrisci,
R. Roman.,
cir. annum 17

THE [a]burden which Habakkuk the prophet did see.
2 O LORD, how long shall I
cry, [b]and thou wilt not hear!
even cry out unto thee *of* violence, and thou wilt not save!
3 Why dost thou show me
iniquity, and cause *me* to behold

[a]Zech. ix. 1; xii. 1; Mal. i. 1

[b]Lam. iii. 8

We know little of this prophet; for what we find in the *ancients* concerning him is evidently fabulous, as well as that which appears in the *Apocrypha*. He was probably of the tribe of *Simeon*, and a native of *Beth-zacar*. It is very likely that he lived after the destruction of Nineveh, as he speaks of the *Chaldeans*, but makes no mention of the *Assyrians*. And he appears also to have prophesied *before* the Jewish captivity, see chap. i. 5; ii. 1; iii. 2, 16-19; and therefore Abp. *Newcome* thinks he may be placed in the reign of Jehoiakim, between the years 606 B. C. and 598 B. C.

As a *poet*, Habakkuk holds a high rank among the Hebrew prophets. The beautiful connection between the parts of his prophecy, its diction, imagery, spirit, and sublimity, cannot be too much admired; and his hymn, chap. iii., is allowed by the best judges to be a masterpiece of its kind. See *Lowth's* Prælect. xxi., xxviii.

NOTES ON CHAP. I

Verse 1. *The burden*] המשא *hammassa* signifies not only the *burdensome* prophecy, but the prophecy or *revelation* itself which God presented to the *mind* of Habakkuk, and which he *saw*—clearly perceived, in the light of prophecy, and then faithfully declared, as this book shows. The word signifies an *oracle* or *revelation* in general; but chiefly, one relative to *future calamities*.

Verse 2. *O Lord, how long shall I cry*] The prophet feels himself strongly excited against the vices which he beheld; and which, it appears from this verse, he had often declaimed

A. M. cir. 3404
B. C. cir. 600
Ol. XLV. 1
TarquiniiPrisci, R. Roman., cir. annum 17

grievance? for spoiling and violence *are* before me: and there are *that* raise up strife and contention.

4 Therefore the law is slacked, and judgment doth never go forth: for the [c]wicked doth compass about the righteous; therefore [d]wrong judgment proceedeth.

5 [e]Behold ye among the heathen, and regard, and wonder marvellously: for *I* will work a work in your days, *which* ye will not believe, though it be told *you*.

6 For, lo, [f]I [g]raise up the Chaldeans, *that* bitter and hasty nation, which shall march through the [h]breadth of the land, to possess the dwellingplaces *that are* not theirs.

A. M. cir. 3404
B. C. cir. 600
Ol. XLV. 1
TarquiniiPrisci, R. Roman., cir. annum 17

7 They *are* terrible and dreadful: [i]their judgment and their dignity shall proceed of themselves.

8 Their horses also are swifter than the leopards, and are more [k]fierce than the [l]evening wolves: and their horsemen shall spread themselves, and their horsemen shall come from far; [m]they shall fly as the eagle *that* hasteth to eat.

9 They shall come all for violence: [n]their[o] faces shall sup up *as* the east wind, and they

[c]Job xxi. 7; Psa. xciv. 3, &c.; Jer. xii. 1——[d]Or, *wrested*——[e]Isa. xxix. 14; Acts xiii. 41——[f]Deut. xxviii. 49, 50; Jer. v. 15——[g]Fulfilled 2 Chron. xxxvi. 6 [h]Heb. *breadths*——[i]Or, *from them shall proceed the judgment of these, and the captivity of these*——[k]Heb. *sharp*——[l]Ezekiel xxii. 27; Jeremiah v. 6; Zephaniah iii. 3——[m]Jeremiah iv. 13——[n]Or, *the supping up of their faces*, &c., or *their faces shall look toward the east*——[o]Hebrew, *the opposition of their faces toward the east*

against, but in vain; the people continued in their vices, and God in his longsuffering.

Habakkuk begins his prophecy under a similar *feeling*, and nearly in similar *words*, as *Juvenal* did his Satires:—

Semper ego auditor tantum? Nunquamne reponam?
Vexatus toties rauci Theseide Codri?
Sat. i. 1.

"Shall I always be a hearer only? Shall I never reply? So often vexed?"

Of *violence*] The most unlawful and outrageous acts.

Verse 3. *And cause* me *to behold grievance*] עמל *amal*, labour, toil, distress, misery, &c., the common fruits of sin.

Verse 4. *The law is slacked*] They pay no attention to it; it has lost all its vigour, its restraining and correcting power; it is not executed; right *judgment* is never *pronounced;* and the *poor righteous man* complains in vain that he is grievously oppressed by the *wicked*, and by those in power and authority. That the utmost depravity prevailed in the land of Judah is evident from these verses; and can we wonder, then, that God poured out such signal judgments upon them? When *judgment doth not proceed* from the seat of judgment upon earth, it will infallibly *go forth* from the throne of judgment in heaven.

Verse 5. *Behold ye among the heathen*] Instead of בגוים *baggoyim*, among the *nations* or *heathen*, some critics think we should read בגדים *bogedim, transgressors;* and to the same purpose the *Septuagint*, *Syriac*, and *Arabic* have read; and thus it is quoted by St. *Paul*, Acts xiii. 41. But neither this, nor any tantamount reading, is found in any of the MSS. yet collated. *Newcome* translates, "See, ye transgressors, and behold a wonder, and perish."

I *will work a work in your days*] As he is speaking of the desolation that should be produced by the *Chaldeans*, it follows, as Bp. *Newcome* has justly observed, that the Chaldeans invaded Judah *whilst* those were living whom the prophet addressed.

Which *ye will not believe*] Nor did they, after all the declarations of various prophets. They still supposed that God would not give them up into the hands of their enemies, though they continued in their abominations!

It is evident that St. Paul, in the above place, *accommodates* this prediction to his own purpose. And possibly this sense might have been the intention of the Divine Spirit when he first spoke the words to the prophet; for, as God *works* in reference to *eternity*, so he *speaks* in reference to the same; and therefore there is an infinity of meaning in his WORD. These appear to be the words of God in answer to the prophet, in which he declares he will entirely ruin this wicked people by means of the Chaldeans.

Verse 6. That *bitter and hasty nation*] Cruel and oppressive in their disposition; and prompt and speedy in their assaults and conquests.

Verse 7. *Their judgment—shall proceed of themselves.*] By revolting from the Assyrians, they have become a great nation. Thus, their judgment and excellence were the result of their own valour. Other meanings are given to this passage.

Verse 8. *Their horses also are swifter than the leopards*] The Chaldean cavalry are proverbial for swiftness, courage, &c. In Jeremiah, chap. iv. 13, it is said, speaking of Nebuchadnezzar, "His chariots are as a whirlwind; his horses are swifter than eagles."

Oppian, speaking of the horses bred about the Euphrates, says, "They are by nature warhorses, and so intrepid that neither the sight nor the roaring of the lion appals them; and, besides, they are astonishingly fleet."

The *leopard*, of all quadrupeds, is allowed to be the *swiftest*.

The evening wolves] The wolf is remarkable for his quick sight. *Ælian* says, Οξυωτεστατον εστι ζωον, και μεντοι, και νυκτος και σεληνης ουκ ουσης ὁδε ὁρᾳ; "The wolf is a very fleet animal; and, besides, it can see by night, even when there is no moonlight." Some think the *hyæna* is meant: it is a swift, cruel, and untameable animal. The other prophets speak of the Chaldeans in the same way. See Deut. xxviii. 49; Jer. xlviii. 40; xlix. 22; Ezek. xvii. 5; Lam. iv. 19.

Verse 9. *Their faces shall sup up* as *the east*

A. M. cir. 3404
B. C. cir. 600
Ol. XLV. 1
TarquiniiPrisci,
R. Roman.,
cir. annum 17

shall gather the captivity as the
sand.
10 And they shall scoff at the
kings, and the princes shall be a
scorn unto them: they shall deride every
strong hold; for they shall heap dust, and
take it.
11 Then shall *his* mind change, and he
shall pass over, and offend, [p]*imputing* this his
power unto his god.
12 [q]*Art* thou not from everlasting, O LORD
my God, mine Holy One? we shall not die.
O LORD, [r]thou hast ordained them for judgment; and, O [s]mighty God, thou hast [t]estab-
lished them for correction.
13 [u]*Thou art* of purer eyes than to behold
evil, and canst not look on [v]iniquity: [w]where-
fore lookest thou upon them that deal treacherously, *and* holdest thy tongue
when the wicked devoureth *the*
man that is more righteous
than he?
14 And makest men as the fishes of the sea,
as the [x]creeping things, *that have* no ruler
over them?
15 They [y]take up all of them with the angle,
they catch them in their net, and gather them
in their [z]drag: therefore they rejoice and are
glad.
16 Therefore [a]they sacrifice unto their net,
and burn incense unto their drag; because by
them their portion *is* fat, and their meat,
[b]plenteous.[c]
17 Shall they therefore empty their net,
and not spare continually to slay the nations?

A. M. cir. 3404
B. C. cir. 600
Ol. XLV. 1
TarquiniiPrisci,
R. Roman.,
cir. annum 17

[p]Dan. v. 4——[q]Psa. xc. 2; xciii. 2; Lam. v. 19 [r]2 Kings xix. 25; Psa. xvii. 13; Isa. x. 5, 6, 7; Ezek. xxx. 25——[s]Heb. *rock;* Deut. xxxii. 4——[t]Heb. *founded* [u]Psa. v. 5

[v]Or, *grievance*——[w]Jer. xii. 1——[x]Or, *moving* [y]Jer. xvi. 16; Amos iv. 2——[z]Or, *flue net*——[a]Deut. viii. 17; Isa. x. 13; xxxvii. 24, 25——[b]Or, *dainty* [c]Heb. *fat*

wind] This may be an allusion to those *electrical winds* which prevail in that country. Mr. *Jackson*, in his overland journey from India, mentions his having bathed in the *Tigris*. On his coming out of the river one of those winds passed over him, and, in a moment, carried off every particle of *water* that was on his body and in his bathing dress. So, the Chaldeans shall leave no substance behind them; their *faces*, their bare *appearance*, is the proof that nothing good shall be left.

Shall gather the captivity as the sand.] They shall carry off innumerable captives.

Verse 10. *They shall scoff at the kings*] No power shall be able to stand before them. It will be only as *pastime* to them to take the strongest places. They will have no need to build formidable ramparts: by sweeping the *dust* together they shall make mounts sufficient to pass over the walls and take the city.

Verse 11. *Then shall* his *mind change*] This is thought to relate to the change which took place in Nebuchadnezzar, when "a beast's heart was given to him," and he was "driven from the dwellings of men." And this was because of his *offending*—his pride and arrogance; and his attributing all his success, &c., to his *idols*.

Verse 12. Art *thou not from everlasting*] The idols change, and their worshippers change and fail: but thou, Jehovah, art *eternal;* thou canst not change, and they who trust in thee are safe. Thou art infinite in thy mercy; therefore, "we shall not die," shall not be totally exterminated.

Thou hast ordained them for judgment] Thou hast raised up the Chaldeans to correct and punish us; but thou hast not given them a commission to destroy us totally.

Instead of לא נמות *lo namuth*, "we shall not die," *Houbigant* and other critics, with a little transposition of letters, read אל אמת *El emeth*, "God of truth;" and then the verse will stand thus: "Art thou not from everlasting, O Jehovah, my God, my Holy One? O Jehovah, GOD OF TRUTH, thou hast appointed them for judgment." But this emendation, however elegant, is not supported by any MS.; nor, indeed, by any of the ancient *versions*, though the *Chaldee* has something like it. The common reading makes a very good sense.

Verse 13. Thou art *of purer eyes*] Seeing thou art so pure, and canst not look on iniquity —it is so abominable—how canst thou bear with them who "deal treacherously, and hold thy tongue when the wicked devour the righteous?" All such questions are easily solved by a consideration of God's ineffable mercy, which leads him to *suffer long* and be kind. He has no pleasure in the death of a sinner.

Verse 14. *Makest men as the fishes of the sea*] Easily are we taken and destroyed. We have no *leader* to guide us, and no *power* to defend ourselves. Nebuchadnezzar is here represented as a fisherman, who is constantly casting his nets into the sea, and enclosing multitudes of fishes; and, being always successful, he sacrifices to his own net—attributes all his conquests to his own power and prudence; not considering that he is only like a *net* that, after having been used for a while, shall at last be thrown by as useless, or burnt in the fire.

Verse 16. *They sacrifice unto their net*] He had no God; he cared for none; and worshipped only his *armour* and *himself.* King *Mezentius*, one of the worst characters in the *Æneid* of *Virgil*, is represented as invoking his own *right hand* and his *spear* in battle. *Æn.* x. 773.

Dextra mihi Deus, et telum quod missile libro,
Nunc adsint.

"My strong right hand and sword, assert my
stroke.
Those only gods Mezentius will invoke."

DRYDEN.

And *Capaneus*, in *Statius*, gives us a more decisive proof of this *self-idolatry*. *Thebaid*, lib. x.

Ades, O mihi dextera tantum
Tu præses belli, et inevitabile Numen,
Te voco, te solum Superum contemptor adoro.

"Only thou, my right hand, be my aid; I contemn the gods, and adore thee as the chief in battle, and the irresistible deity." The poet tells us that, for his impiety, Jupiter slew him with thunder.

This was an ancient idolatry in this country, and has existed till within about a century. There are relics of it in different parts of Europe; for when military men *bind themselves* to accomplish any particular purpose, it is usual to *lay their hand* upon their sword: but formerly they *kissed* it, when swearing by it. With most heroes, the *sword* is both their *Bible* and their *God*. To the present day it is a custom among the *Hindoos* annually to *worship* the implements of their *trades*. See WARD.

Verse 17. *And not spare continually to slay the nations?*] They are running from conquest to conquest; burning, slaying, sacking, and slaughtering. Like the fishermen, who throw cast after cast while any fish are to be caught, so Nebuchadnezzar is destroying one nation after another. This last sentence explains the allegory of the *net*.

CHAPTER II

The prophet, waiting for a return to his expostulation, is answered by God that the time for the destruction of the Jewish polity by the Chaldeans is not only fixed in the Divine counsel, but is awfully near; and he is therefore commanded to write down the vision relative to this appalling subject in the most legible characters, and in the plainest language, that all who read it with attention (those just persons who exercise an unwavering faith in the declaration of God respecting the violent irruption of the merciless Babylonians) may flee from the impending vengeance, 1–4. *The fall of the Chaldeans, and of their ambitious monarch is then predicted,* 5–10; *and, by a strong and bold personification, the very stone and wood of those magnificent buildings, which the Babylonish king had raised by oppression and bloodshed, pronounce his wo, and in responsive taunts upbraid him,* 11, 12. *The prophet then beautifully sets forth the absolute impotence of every effort, however well conducted, which is not in concert with the Divine counsel: for though the wicked rage, and threaten the utter extermination of the people of God; yet when the* SET time *to favour Zion is come, the destroyers of God's heritage shall themselves be destroyed, and "the earth shall be filled with the knowledge of the glory of God, as the waters cover the sea,"* 13, 14. *See* Psa. cii. 13–16. *For the cup of idolatry which Babylon has given to many nations, she will receive of the Lord's hand the cup of fury by the insurrection of mighty enemies (the Medes and Persians) rushing like wild beasts to destroy her,* 15. *In the midst of this distress the prophet very opportunely asks in what the Babylonians had profited by their idols, exposes the absurdity of trusting in them, and calls upon the whole world to stand in awe of the everlasting Jehovah,* 16–19.

A. M. cir. 3404
B. C. cir. 600
Ol. cir. XLV. 1
TarquiniiPrisci, R. Roman., cir. annum 17

I WILL [a]stand upon my watch,
and set me upon the [b]tower,
[c]and will watch to see what he
will say [d]unto me, and what I
shall answer [e]when [f]I am
reproved.
2 And the LORD answered me,
and said, [g]Write the vision, and

A. M. cir. 3404
B. C. cir. 600
Ol. cir. XLV. 1
TarquiniiPrisci, R. Roman., cir. annum 17

[a]Isa. xxi. 8, 11——[b]Heb. *fenced place*——[c]Psa. lxxxv. 8
[d]Or, *in me*

[e]Or, *when I am argued with*——[f]Heb. *upon my reproof, or arguing*——[g]Isa. viii. 1; xxx. 8

NOTES ON CHAP. II

Verse 1. *I will stand upon my watch*] The prophets are always represented as *watchmen*, watching constantly for the comfort, safety, and welfare of the people; and watching also to receive information from the Lord: for the prophetic influence was not *always* with them, but was granted only at particular times, according to the will of God. When, in doubtful cases, they wished to know what God was about to do with the country, they retired from society and gave themselves to meditation and prayer, waiting thus upon God *to hear what he would say* IN *them*.

What he will say unto me] בי *bi*, IN *me*—in my understanding and heart.

And what I shall answer when I am reproved.] What I shall say to God *in behalf* of the people; and what the Lord shall command me to say *to the people*. Some translate, "And what he will answer for my conviction." Or, "what shall be answered to my pleading."

Verse 2. *Write the vision*] Carefully take down all that I shall say.

Make it *plain upon tables*] Write it in a full, plain, legible hand.

That he may run that readeth it.] That he who attentively peruses it may speed to save his life from the irruption of the Chaldeans, by which so many shall be cut off. The prophet does not mean that the words are to be made so plain, that a man *running by* may easily read them, and catch their meaning. This interpretation has been frequently given; and it has been incautiously applied to the whole of the Bible: "God's book is so plain, that he that runs may read;" but it is very foolish: God

A. M. cir. 3404 B. C. cir. 600 Ol. cir. XLV. 1 TarquiniiPrisci, R. Roman., cir. annum 17

make *it* plain upon tables, that
he may run that readeth it.
3 For [h]the vision *is* yet for
an appointed time, but at the
end it shall speak, and not lie: though it
tarry, wait for it; because it will [i]surely come,
it will not tarry.
4 Behold, his soul *which* is lifted up is not
upright in him: but the [k]just shall live by
his faith.
5 [l]Yea also, because he transgresseth by
wine, *he is* a proud man, neither keepeth at
home, who enlargeth his desire [m]as hell, and *is*
as death, and cannot be satisfied, but gathereth unto him all nations, and
heapeth unto him all people:
6 Shall not all these [n]take up a
parable against him, and a
taunting proverb against him, and say, [o]Wo
to him that increaseth *that which is* not his!
how long? and to him that ladeth himself
with thick clay!
7 Shall they not rise up suddenly that shall
bite thee, and awake that shall vex thee, and
thou shalt be for booties unto them?
8 [p]Because thou hast spoiled many nations,
all the remnant of the people shall spoil thee;
[q]because of men's [r]blood, and *for* the violence

[h]Dan. x. 14; xi. 27, 35——[i]Heb. x. 37——[k]John iii. 36; Rom. i. 17; Gal. iii. 11; Heb. x. 38——[l]Or, *How much more*

[m]Prov. xxvii. 20; xxx. 16——[n]Mic. ii. 4——[o]Or, *Ho, he*——[p]Isaiah xxxiii. 1——[q]Ver. 17——[r]Hebrew, *bloods*

never intends that his words shall be understood by the *careless*. He that *reads, studies, meditates*, and *prays*, shall understand every portion of this sacred book that relates immediately to his own salvation. But no *trifler* can understand it. If the contents of a *play-bill* were to be read as many read the *Bible*, they would know just as much of the *one* as they do of the *other*.

Verse 3. *The vision* is *yet for an appointed time*] The Chaldeans, who are to ruin Judea, shall *afterwards* be ruined themselves: but they must do this work *before* they receive their wages; therefore the vision is for an *appointed time. But at the end it shall speak*. When his work of devastation is done, his day of retribution shall take place.

Though it tarry] Though it appear to be long, do not be impatient; *it will surely come; it will not tarry* longer than the prescribed time, and this time is not far distant. Wait for it.

Verse 4. *Behold, his soul* which *is lifted up*] He that presumes on his safety without any special warrant from God, is a *proud man;* and whatever he may profess, or think of himself, his *mind is not upright in him*. But he that is *just by faith shall live*—he that *believes* what God hath said relative to the Chaldeans besieging Jerusalem, shall make his escape from the place, and consequently shall *save his life*. The words in the *New Testament* are accommodated to the *salvation* which *believers in Christ* shall possess. Indeed, the just—the true Christians, who believed in Jesus Christ's words relative to the destruction of Jerusalem, when they found the Romans coming against it, left the city, and escaped to *Pella* in Cœlesyria, and did *live*—their lives were saved: while the unbelieving Jews, to a man, either *perished* or were made *slaves*. One good sense is, He that believes the promises of God, and has found life through believing, shall live by his faith.

Verse 5. *Because he transgresseth by wine*] From the present translation, it is not easy to see either reason or meaning in the first clause of this verse. *Newcome* translates, "Moreover, as a mighty man transgresseth through wine, he is proud, and remaineth not at rest." *Houbigant* thus: "For he, though he be a despiser, and powerful, and proud, yet shall he not have rest."

Nebuchadnezzar is here represented in his usual character, *proud, haughty*, and *ambitious;* inebriated with his successes, and determined on more extensive conquests; and, like the *grave*, can never have enough: yet, after the subjugation of many peoples and nations, he shall be brought down, and become so despicable that he shall be a *proverb* of *reproach*, and be taunted and scorned by all those whom he had before enslaved.

And cannot be satisfied] When he has obtained all that is within his reach, he wishes for more; and becomes miserable, because any limits are opposed to his insatiable ambition. It is said of *Alexander:*—

Unus Pellæo juveni non sufficit orbis;
Æstuat infelix angusto limite mundi.
Juv. Sat. x. 168.

One world sufficed not Alexander's mind;
Coop'd up, he seem'd on earth and seas confined.

And the poet justly ridicules him, because at last the sarcophagus was found *too large* for his body!

Verse 6. *Shall not all these take up a parable against him*] His ambition, derangement, and the final destruction of his mighty empire by the Persians, shall form the foundation of many *sententious sayings* among the people. "He who towered so high, behold how *low* he is fallen!" "He made himself a god; behold, he herds with the *beasts* of the field!" "The disturber of the peace of the world is now a *handful of dust!*"

Verse 7. *Shall they not rise up suddenly*] Does not this refer to the *sudden* and *unexpected taking of Babylon by Cyrus*, whose troops entered into the city through the bed of the Euphrates, whose waters they had diverted by another channel; so that the Babylonians *knew nothing of the matter* till they *saw* the Persian soldiers *rise up as in a moment*, in the very heart of their city?

Verse 8. For *the violence of the land*] Or, *for the violence* done *to the land* of Judea, *and to the city* of Jerusalem.

A. M. cir. 3404
B. C. cir. 600
Ol. cir. XLV. 1
TarquiniiPrisci,
R. Roman.,
cir. annum 17

of the land, of the city, and of all that dwell therein.

9 Wo to him that [s]coveteth [t]an evil covetousness to his house, that he may [u]set his nest on high, that he may be delivered from the [v]power of evil!

10 Thou hast consulted shame to thy house by cutting off many people, and hast sinned *against* thy soul.

11 For the stone shall cry out of the wall, and the [w]beam out of the timber shall [x]answer it.

12 Wo to him that buildeth a town with [y]blood, [z]and stablisheth a city by iniquity!

13 Behold, *is it* not of the LORD of hosts [a]that the people shall labour in the very fire, and the people shall weary themselves [b]for very vanity?

A. M. cir. 3404
B. C. cir. 600
Ol. cir. XLV. 1
TarquiniiPrisci,
R. Roman.,
cir. annum 17

14 For the earth shall be filled [c]with the [d]knowledge of the glory of the LORD, as the waters cover the sea.

15 Wo unto him that giveth his neighbour drink, that puttest thy [e]bottle to *him*, and makest *him* drunken also, that thou mayest [f]look on their nakedness!

16 Thou art filled [g]with shame for glory: [h]drink thou also and let thy foreskin be uncovered: the cup of the LORD's right hand shall be turned unto thee, and shameful spewing *shall be* on thy glory.

17 For the violence of Lebanon shall cover thee, and the spoil of beasts, *which* made them afraid, [i]because of men's blood, and for the violence of the land, of the city, and of all that dwell therein.

---

[s]Jer. xxii. 13——[t]Or, *gaineth an evil gain*——[u]Jer. xlix. 16; Obad. 4——[v]Heb. *palm of the hand*——[w]Or, *piece*, or *fastening*——[x]Or, *witness against it*——[y]Jer. xxii. 13; Ezek. xxiv. 9; Mic. iii. 10; Nah. iii. 1

[z]Heb. *bloods*——[a]Jer. li. 58——[b]Or, *in vain*——[c]Or, *by knowing the glory of the LORD*——[d]Isa. xi. 9——[e]Hos. vii. 5——[f]Gen. ix. 22——[g]Or, *more with shame than with glory*——[h]Jer. xxv. 26, 27; li. 57——[i]Ver. 8

Verse 9. *An evil covetousness to his house*] Nebuchadnezzar wished to aggrandize his *family*, and make his *empire* permanent: but both *family* and *empire* were soon cut off by the death of his son Belshazzar, and the consequent destruction of the Chaldean empire.

Verse 10. *Hast sinned* against *thy soul.*] Thy *life* is forfeited by thy crimes.

Verse 11. *The stone shall cry out of the wall, and the beam out of the timber shall answer it.*] This appears to refer to the ancient mode of building walls; *two* or *three courses* of *stone*, and then *one course* of *timber*. See 1 Kings vi. 36: thus was the palace of Solomon built. The splendid and costly buildings of Babylon have been universally celebrated. But how were these buildings erected? By the *spoils* of conquered nations, and the expense of the *blood* of multitudes; therefore the *stones* and the *timber* are represented as calling out for vengeance against this ruthless conqueror.

Verse 12. *Wo to him that buildeth a town with blood*] At the expense of much slaughter. This is the answer of the *beam* to the *stone*. And these things will refer to the vast fortunes gained, and the buildings erected, by means of the *slave-trade;* where, to a considerate and humane mind, the *walls* appear as if composed of the *bones* of *negroes*, and *cemented* by their *blood!* But the towns or houses *established* by this *iniquity* soon come to ruin; and the fortunes made have, in most cases, become as chaff and dust before the whirlwind of God's indignation. But where are the dealers in the souls and bodies of men? Ask *him* who has them in his keeping. He can tell.

Verse 13. *The people shall labour in the very fire*] All these superb buildings shall be burnt down. See the parallel passage, Jer. li. 58, and the note there.

Shall weary themselves for very vanity?] For the gratification of the wishes of ambition, and in buildings which shall be brought to naught.

Verse 14. *For the earth shall be filled*] This is a singular and important verse. It may be *first* applied to *Babylon*. God's power and providence shall be widely displayed in the destruction of this city and empire, in the humiliation of Nebuchadnezzar, Dan. iv. 37, and in the captivity and restoration of his people. See *Newcome*, and see Isa. xi. 9.

Secondly. It may be applied to the *glorious days* of the *Messiah*. The *land of Judea* should by his preaching, and that of his disciples, be *filled with the knowledge of God*. God's great design fully discovered, and the scheme of salvation amply explained.

Thirdly. It may be applied to the *universal spread of the Gospel* over the habitable globe; when the fulness of the Gentiles should be brought in, and the Jews gathered in with that fulness. The *earth* cannot perish till every continent, island, and inhabitant, is illuminated with the light of the Gospel.

Verse 15. *Wo unto him that giveth his neighbour drink*] This has been considered as applying to *Pharaoh-hophra*, king of Egypt, who enticed his neighbours Jehoiachin and Zedekiah to rebel against Nebuchadnezzar, whereby the nakedness and imbecility of the poor Jews was soon discovered; for the Chaldeans soon took Jerusalem, and carried its kings, princes, and people, into captivity.

Verse 16. *The cup of the Lord's right hand*] Among the ancients, all drank out of the same cup; was passed from hand to hand, and each drank as much as he chose. The Chaldeans gave to the neighbouring nations *the cup of idolatry* and of *deceitful alliance;* and in return they received from the Lord the *cup of his fury*. So *Grotius*.

Verse 17. *For the violence of Lebanon*] Or, the violence done to *Lebanon;* to *men*, to *cattle*, to *Judea*, and to *Jerusalem*. See the note on the parallel place, ver. 8. This may be a threatening against *Egypt*, as the former was against *Chaldea*.

A. M. cir. 3404
B. C. cir. 600
Ol. cir. XLV. 1
Tarquinii Prisci,
R. Roman.,
cir. annum 17

18 [k]What profiteth the graven
image that the maker thereof
hath graven it; the molten image, and a [l]teacher of lies,
that [m]the maker of his work trusteth therein,
to make [n]dumb idols?
19 Wo unto him that saith to the wood,
Awake; to the dumb stone,
Arise, it shall teach! Behold, it
is laid over with gold and
silver, [o]and *there is* no breath
at all in the midst of it.
20 But [p]the LORD *is* in his holy temple:
[q]let [r]all the earth keep silence before him.

[k]Isa. xliv. 9, 10; xlvi. 2——[l]Jer. x. 8, 14; Zech. x. 2——[m]Heb. *the fashioner of his fashion*——[n]Psa. cxv. 5; 1 Cor. xii 2——[o]Psa. cxxxv. 17——[p]Psa. xi. 4——[q]Heb. *be silent all the earth before him*——[r]Zeph. i. 7; Zech. ii. 13

Verse 18. *What profiteth the graven image*] This is against idolatry in general, and every species of it, as well as against those princes, priests, and people who practise it, and encourage others to do the same. See on the parallel passages in the margin.

Dumb idols?] אלילים אלמים *elilim illemim*, "dumb nothings." This is exactly agreeable to St. Paul, 1 Cor. viii. 4, who says, "An idol is nothing in the world." What signify the idols worshipped by the Chaldeans, Tyrians, and Egyptians? They have not been able to save their worshippers.

Verse 19. *Wo unto him*] How foolish and contemptible to worship a thing *formed by the hand of man* out of *wood, stone, gold*, or *silver!* The meanest *brute* is superior to them all; it *breathes* and *lives*, but they have *no breath* in them. However, they are said above to be *teachers of lies;* that is, they appeared to give out *oracles:* but these were *lies;* and were not given by the *statue, but by the priest.*

Verse 20. *The Lord* is *in his holy temple*] Jehovah has his *temple*, the *place* where he is to be *worshipped;* but *there* there is no *image. Oracles*, however, are given forth; and every word of them is *truth*, and is fulfilled in its season. And this temple and its worship are *holy;* no *abomination* can be practised there, and every thing in it leads to *holiness* of heart and life.

Let all the earth keep silence before him.] Let all be dumb. Let none of them dare to open their mouths in the presence of Jehovah. He alone is Sovereign. He alone is the arbiter of life and death. Let all hear his commands with the deepest respect, obey them with the promptest diligence, and worship him with the most profound reverence. When an Asiatic sovereign goes to the mosque on any of the eastern festivals, such as the *Bairham*, the deepest *silence* reigns among all his retinue, viziers, foreign ambassadors, &c. They all bow respectfully before him; but no word is spoken, no sound uttered. It is to this species of reverence that the prophet alludes, and with this he concludes the *prophetic* part of this book. What God has threatened or promised, that he will fulfil. Let every soul bow before him, and submit to his authority.

CHAPTER III

The prophet, being apprized of the calamities which were to be brought on his country by the ministry of the Chaldeans, and the punishments which awaited the Chaldeans themselves, partly struck with terror, and partly revived with hope and confidence in the Divine mercy, beseeches God to hasten the redemption of his people, 1, 2. *Such a petition would naturally lead his thoughts to the astonishing deliverance which God vouchsafed to the same people of old; and the inference from it was obvious, that he could with the same ease deliver their posterity now. But, hurried on by the fire and impetuosity of his spirit, he disdains to wait the process of connecting these ideas, and bounds at once into the midst of his subject: "God came from Teman,"* &c., 3. *He goes on to describe the majesty and might which God displayed in conducting his people to the land of promise; selecting the most remarkable circumstances, and clothing them in the most lofty language. As he goes along, his fancy becomes more glowing, till at length he is transported to the scene of action, and becomes an eyewitness of the wonders he describes. "I beheld the tents of Cushan in affliction,"* 4–6. *After having touched on the principal circumstances of that deliverance which he celebrates, he returns to what passed before them in Egypt; his enthusiasm having led him to begin in the midst of his subject,* 7–15. *And at last he ends the hymn as he began it, with expressing his awe of the Divine judgments, and his firm trust in the mercy and goodness of God while under them; and that in terms of such singular beauty, elegance, and sublimity, as to form a very proper conclusion to this admirable piece of Divinely inspired composition,* 16–19. *It would seem from the title, and the note appended at the end, that it was set to music, and sung in the service of the temple.*

A. M. cir. 3404
B. C. cir. 600
Ol. cir. XLV. 1
Tarquinii Prisci,
R. Roman.,
cir. annum 17

A PRAYER of Habakkuk
the prophet [a]upon [b]Shi-
gionoth.
2 O LORD, I have heard [c]thy
speech, *and* was afraid: O LORD, [d]revive[e]
thy work in the midst of the years, in the
midst of the years make known: in wrath remember mercy.
3 God came from [f]Teman, [g]and the Holy
One from Mount Paran. Se-
lah. His glory covered the
heavens, and the earth was full
of his praise.

A. M. cir. 3404
B. C. cir. 600
Ol. cir. XLV. 1
Tarquinii Prisci,
R. Roman.,
cir. annum 17

4 And *his* brightness was as the light; he
had horns *coming* out of his hand: and there
was the hiding of his power.
5 [i]Before him went the pestilence, and [k]burn-
ing [l]coals went forth at his feet.

---

[a]Psalm vii. title——[b]Or, *according to variable songs,* or *tunes,* called in Hebrew, *Shigionoth*——[c]Hebrew, *thy report,* or *thy hearing*——[d]Or, *preserve alive*——[e]Psa. lxxxv. 6——[f]Or, *the south*——[g]Deuteronomy xxiii. 2; Judges v. 4; Psalm lxviii. 7——[h]Or, *bright beams out of his side*——[i]Nah. i. 3——[k]Or, *burning diseases;* Deuteronomy xxxii. 24——[l]Psa. xviii. 8, 12; Isa. vi. 6; xlvii. 14

NOTES ON CHAP. III

Verse 1. *A prayer of Habakkuk—upon Shigionoth.*] See the note on the *title* of Psa. vii., where the meaning of *Shiggaion* is given. The *Vulgate* has, *pro ignorantiis, for ignorances,* or sins committed in ignorance; and so it is understood by the *Chaldee.* The *Syriac* has nothing but merely, *A prayer of Habakkuk.* And the *septuagint,* instead of *Shigionoth,* have *μετα ῳδης, with a hymn,* which is copied by the *Arabic.*

I suspect that the *title* here given is of a *posterior* date to the prophecy. It appears to interrupt the connection between this and the termination of the preceding verse. See them together:—

Chap ii 20: "But the Lord is in his holy temple:
Be silent before him, all the earth.
iii. 1: O Lord, I have heard thy speech:
I have feared, O Lord, thy work.
As the years approach thou hast shown;
As the years approach thou makest known.
In wrath thou rememberest mercy."

The prophet may here refer to the *speech* which God had communicated to him, chap. i. 5-11, ii. 4-20, and the terror with which he was struck, because of the judgments denounced against Jerusalem. I have followed the version of Apb. *Newcome* in this *first* verse. The critical reader may consult his notes, and the *various readings* of *Kennicott* and *De Rossi.*

Verse 2. *In the midst of the years*] בקרב שנים *bekereb shanim,* "As the years approach." The nearer the time, the clearer and fuller is the prediction; and the signs of the times show that the complete fulfilment *is at hand.* But as the judgments will be heavy, (and they are not greater than we deserve,) yet, *Lord, in the midst of wrath*—infliction of punishment—*remember mercy,* and spare the souls that return unto thee with humiliation and prayer.

Verse 3. *God came from Teman*] Bp. *Lowth* observes: "This is a sudden burst of poetry, in the true spirit of the ode; the concealed connection being that God, who had formerly displayed such power in delivering the Israelites from Egyptian slavery, might succour their posterity in a like wonderful manner." Hence the prophet selects the most striking facts of that first deliverance; and to decorate and render them impressive, brings forth all the powers of his genius, in all the strength and elegance of his language. "What crowns the sublimity of this piece," says Bp. *Lowth,* "is the singular elegance of the close; and were it not that antiquity has here and there thrown its veil of obscurity over it, there could not be conceived a more perfect and masterly poem of its kind." See, for more particulars, his *twenty-eighth* Prelection.

I shall endeavour to show the *facts* in the *deliverance from Egypt,* to which the prophet refers.

Teman] This was a city, the capital of a province of Idumea, to the south of the land of Canaan. Num. xx. 21; Jer. xlix. 7.

Paran] Was a city which gave its name to a province in Arabia Petræa. Gen. xxi. 21; Deut. xxxiii. 2.

Selah] This word is not well known; probably it means a pause or alteration in the music. See it in the Psalms, and its explanation there.

His glory covered the heavens] His glory when he descended on Mount Sinai, and in the pillar of fire by night.

The earth was full of his praise.] All the land was astonished at the magnificence of his works in behalf of his people. Instead of *praise,* some translate *splendour.* The whole land was illuminated by his glory.

Verse 4. *He had horns* coming *out of his hand*] קרנים *karnayim, rays.* His *hand*—his *power*—was manifested in a particular place, by the sudden issuing out of pencils of rays, which diverged in coruscations of light, so as to illuminate the whole hemisphere. Yet "there was the hiding of his power." His Majesty could not be seen, nor any kind of image, because of the insufferable splendour. This may either refer to the *lightnings* on Mount *Sinai;* or to the *brightness* which occasionally proceeded from the *shechinah* or glory of God between the cherubim, over the mercy-seat. See *Capellus* and *Newcome.* If *lightnings* are intended, the *dense cloud* from which they proceeded may be meant by the "hiding of his power;" for when the lightnings burst forth, his power and energy became manifest.

Probably from this the *Jupiter Keraunos* or *Jupiter Brontes* of the heathens was borrowed; who is always represented with forked or zigzag lightnings in his hand.

Verse 5. *Before him went the pestilence*] This plague was several times inflicted on the disobedient Israelites in the wilderness; see Num. xi. 33, xiv. 37, xvi. 46; and was always the proof that the *just God* was then manifesting his *power among them.*

A. M. cir. 3404
B. C. cir. 600
Ol. cir. XLV. 1
Tarquinii Prisci,
R. Roman.,
cir. annum 17

6 He stood, and measured the
earth: he beheld, and drove
asunder the nations; [m]and the
[n]everlasting mountains were
scattered, the perpetual hills did bow: his
ways are [o]everlasting.
7 I saw the tents of [p]Cushan [q]in affliction:
and the curtains of the land of Midian did
tremble.
8 Was the LORD displeased against the
rivers? *was* thine anger
against the rivers? *was* thy
wrath against the sea, [r]that
thou didst ride upon thine
horses *and* [s]thy chariots of salvation?
9 Thy bow was made quite naked, *according*
to the oaths of the tribes, *even thy* word.
Selah. [t]Thou [u]didst cleave the earth with
rivers.

[m]Nah. i. 5——[n]Gen. xliv. 26——[o]Psa. cxxxix. 24 [p]Or, *Æthiopia*——[q]Or, *under affliction*, or *vanity* [r]Deut. xxxiii. 26, 27; Psa. lxviii. 4; civ. 3; ver. 15

[s]Or, *thy chariots* were *salvation*——[t]Or, *Thou didst cleave the rivers of the earth*——[u]Psalm lxxviii. 15, 16; cv. 41

Burning coals went forth at his feet.] *Newcome* translates, "And flashes of fire went forth after him." The disobedient Israelities were consumed by a *fire* that went out from Jehovah; see Lev. x. 2; Num. xi. 1, xvi. 35. And the burnt-offering was consumed by a fire which came out from before Jehovah, Lev. xi. 24.

Verse 6. *He stood, and measured the earth*] ארץ *erets, the land;* he divided the promised land among the *twelve tribes*. This is the allusion; and this the prophet had in his eye. God not only made a *general assignment* of the land to the Hebrews; but he even *divided it* into *such portions* as the different families required. Here were both *power* and *condescension*. When a conqueror had subdued a country, he divided it among his soldiers. Among the Romans, those among whom the conquered lands were divided were termed *beneficiarii;* and the lands *beneficia*, as being held on the beneficence of the sovereign.

He beheld, and drove asunder the nations] The nations of *Canaan*, the *Hittites, Hivites, Jebusites*, &c., and all who opposed his people. Even his *look* dispersed them.

The everlasting mountains were scattered] Or, *broken asunder*. This may refer to the *convulsions* on Mount Sinai; and to the earthquake which announced the descent of the Most High. See Exod. xix. 18. "God occupied the summit of the eternal Mount Sinai; and led his people over the eternal mountains of Arabia Petræa; and this sense is preferable to the figurative one, that his ways or doings are predetermined from everlasting."—*Newcome.* The epithets עד *ad*, and עולם *olam, eternal*, and *everlasting*, are applied to mountains and immense rocks, because no other parts of nature are less subject to *decay* or *change*, than these immense masses of earth and stone, and that almost indestructible stone, *granite*, out of which *Sinai* appears to be formed. A piece of the beautiful granite of this mountain now lies before me. This is a figurative description of the passage of the Israelites through the deserts of Arabia, over mountains, rocks, and through the trackless wilderness; *over* and *through* which God, by his power and providence, gave them a safe passage.

The following beautiful piece from the Fragments of Æschylus will illustrate the preceding description, and please the learned reader.

Χωριζε θνητων τον Θεον, και μη δοκει
Ομοιον αυτῳ σαρκινον καθεσταναι·
Ουκ οισθα δ' αυτον· ποτε μεν ὡς πυρ φαινεται
Απλαστον ὁρμῃ· ποτε δ' ὑδωρ, ποτε δε γνοφος.
Και θηρσιν αυτος γινεται παρεμφερης,
Ανεμῳ, νεφει τε, κᾳστραπῃ, βροντῃ, βροχῃ.
῾Υπηρετει δ' αυτῳ θαλασσα, και πετραι,
Και πασα πηγη, χ' ὑδατος συστηματα·
Τρεμει δ' ορη και γαια και πελωριος
Βυθος θαλασσης, κωρεων ὑψος μεγα,
Οταν επιβλεψῃ γοργον ομμα δεσποτου.

ÆSCHYLI *Fragm.*

Confound not God with man; nor madly deem
His form is mortal, and of flesh like thine.
Thou know'st him not. Sometimes like *fire* he
glows
In wrath severe; sometimes as *water* flows;
In brooding *darkness* now his power conceals
And then in *brutes* that mighty power reveals.
In *clouds* tempestuous we the Godhead find;
He mounts the *storm*, and rides the winged
wind;
In vivid *lightnings* flashes from on high;
In rattling *thunders* rends the lowering sky;
Fountains and *rivers, seas* and *floods* obey,
And *ocean's* deep abyss yields to his sway;
The *mountains* tremble, and the *hills* sink
down,
Crumbled to dust by the Almighty's frown.
When God unfolds the terrors of his eye,
All things with horror quake, and in confusion
lie.

J. B. B. CLARKE.

Verse 7. *I saw the tents of Cushan in affliction*] *Cush* is Arabia. The Arabians dwelt in *tents*, hence they were called *Scenitæ*. When the Lord appeared on *Mount Sinai*, the *Arabs* of the Red Sea abandoned their tents, being terror-struck; and the *Midianites* also were seized with fear. See the desolation wrought among this people by Phinehas, Num. xxxi. 1, &c., on account of their having enticed the Israelites to idolatry, Num. xxv. 1, &c. Either *Cush* and *Midian* lay contiguous to each other; or, these names are poetically used to express the *same place*.

Verse 8. *Was the Lord displeased against the rivers?*] *Floods;* here is a reference to the passage of the Red Sea. The Lord is represented as heading his troops, riding in his chariot, and commanding the sea to divide, that a free passage might be left for his army to pass over.

Verse 9. *Thy bow was made quite naked*] That is, it was *drawn out of its case;* as the *arrows* had their *quiver*, so the *bows* had their *cases*. A fine *oriental bow* and *bow-case*, with *quiver* and *arrows*, are now before me; they show with what propriety Jehovah is represented as taking his bow out of its case, in

A. M. cir. 3404
B. C. cir. 600
Ol. cir. XLV. 1
Tarquinii Prisci,
R. Roman.,
cir. annum 17

10 [v]The mountains saw thee,
and they trembled: the overflowing of the water passed
by: the deep uttered his voice,
and [w]lifted up his hands on high.
11 [x]The sun *and* moon stood still in their
habitations; [y]at the light of thine [z]arrows they
went, *and* at the shining of thy glittering spear.
12 Thou didst march through the land in
indignation, [a]thou didst thresh
the heathen in anger.
13 Thou wentest forth for the
salvation of thy people, *even* for
salvation with thine anointed; [b]thou woundedst the head out of the house of the wicked,
[c]by discovering the foundation unto the neck.
Selah.
14 Thou didst strike through with his staves

A. M. cir. 3404
B. C. cir. 600
Ol. cir. XLV. 1
Tarquinii Prisci,
R. Roman.,
cir. annum 17

[v]Exod. xix. 16, 18; Judg. v. 4, 5; Psa. lxviii. 8; lxxvii. 18; cxiv. 4——[w]Exod. xiv. 22; Josh. iii. 16——[x]Josh. x. 12, 13——[y]Or, *thine arrows walked in the light*, &c.

[z]Josh. x. 11; Psa. xviii. 14; lxxvii. 17, 18——[a]Jer. li. 33; Amos i. 3; Mic. iv. 13——[b]Josh. x. 24; xi. 8, 12; Psa. lxviii. 21——[c]Heb *making naked*

order to set his arrow upon the cord, to shoot at his enemies. It is not the *drawing out*, or *making bare* the *arrow*, that is mentioned here; but the taking the *bow out of its case* to prepare to shoot.

This verse appears to be an answer to the questions in the preceding: "Was the Lord displeased," &c. The answer is, All this was done "according to the oaths of the tribes;" the covenant of God, frequently repeated and renewed, which he made with the tribes, to give them the land of the Canaanites for their inheritance.

Thou didst cleave the earth with rivers.] Or, "Thou didst cleave the streams of the land." Or, "Thou cleavedst the dry land into rivers." This may be a reference to the passage of Jordan, and transactions at *Arnon* and the brook *Jabbok*. See Num. xxi. 13-15.

In this verse we have *Selah* again, which, as before, may signify a *pause*, or some alteration in the *music*.

Verse 10. *The mountains saw thee*] This is the continued answer to the questions in ver. 8. These are figures highly poetic, to show with what ease God accomplished the most arduous tasks in behalf of his people. As soon as the *mountains* saw him, they trembled, they were in *pangs*. When he appeared, the *sea* fled to right and left, to give him a passage. "It uttered its voice." The separation of the waters occasioned a terrible noise. "And it lifted up its hands on high." Its waters, being separated, stood in *heaps* on the right hand and left. These heaps or waves are poetically represented here as the *hands* of the *sea*.

Verse 11. *The sun* and *moon stood still*] This was at the prayer of Joshua, when he fought against the Amorites. See Josh. x. 11, 12, and the notes there.

At the light of thine arrows they went] I think we should translate,—

By *their* light, thine arrows went abroad;
By *their* brightness, the lightning of thy spear.

Calvin very justly remarks that the *arrows* and *spears* of the Israelites are called those *of God*, under whose auspices the people fought: the meaning is, that by the *continuation* of the *light of the sun and moon*, then stayed in their course, the Israelites *saw* how to continue the battle, till their enemies were all defeated.

Verse 12. *Thou didst march through the land*] This refers to the conquest of Canaan. God is represented as going at the head of his people as general-in-chief; and leading them on from conquest to conquest—which was the fact.

Thou didst thresh the heathen in anger.] Thou didst *tread them down*, as the oxen do the sheaves on the threshing-floor.

Verse 13. *Thou wentest forth for the salvation of thy people*] Their deliverance would not have been effected but through thy interference.

For salvation with thine anointed] That is, with *Joshua*, whom God had *anointed*, or solemnly *appointed* to fill the place of Moses, and lead the people into the promised land. If we read, with the common text, משיחך *meshichecha*, "thy anointed," the singular number, Joshua is undoubtedly meant, who was God's instrument to put the people in possession of Canaan: but if, with several MSS. and some copies of the *Septuagint*, we read משיחיך *meshicheycha*, "thy anointed ones," the *Israelites* must be intended. They are frequently called *God's anointed*, or *God's saints*. The sense is very far-fetched when applied to *Jesus Christ*.

Thou woundedst the head out of the house of the wicked] This alludes to the slaying of the *first-born* through all the land of Egypt. These were the *heads* of the *houses* or *families*.

By discovering the foundation unto the neck.] The general meaning of this clause is sufficiently plain: the government of these lands should be utterly subverted; the very foundations of it should be *razed*. But what means *unto the neck*, עד צואר *ad tsavvar?* Several critics read עד צור *ad tsur*, "Unto the ROCK," that on which the house is founded: and this very intelligible reading is obtained by the *omission* of a *single letter*, א *aleph*, from the word צואר. This conjecture has been adopted by *Newcome*, though unsupported either by *MS.* or *version*. But is the conjecture necessary? I think not: read the verse as it ought to be read, and all will be plain. "Thou hast wounded the head even unto the neck, in the house of the wicked, by laying bare the foundation." The whole head, neck, and all are cut off. There was no hope left to the Egyptians, because the *first-born* of every family was *cut off*, so that the very *foundation* was *laid bare*, no first-born being left to continue the *heirship* of families.

Verse 14. *Thou didst strike through*] The Hebrew will bear this sense: "Thou hast pierced amidst their tribes the head of their troops," referring to Pharaoh and his generals, who came like a *whirlwind* to fall upon the poor Israelites, when they appeared to be hemmed in by sea, and no place for their escape. If we follow the common reading, it seems to intimate that the troops of Pharaoh, in their confusion (for God shone out upon them from the cloud) fell foul of each other; and with

A. M. cir. 3404
B. C. cir. 600
Ol. cir. XLV. 1
Tarquinii Prisci,
R. Roman.,
cir. annum 17

the head of his villages: they
[d]came out as a whirlwind to
scatter me: their rejoicing
was as to devour the poor
secretly.
15 [e]Thou didst walk through the sea with
thine horses, *through* the [f]heap of great waters.
16 When I heard, [g]my belly trembled; my
lips quivered at the voice; rottenness entered
into my bones, and I trembled in myself, that
I might rest in the day of trouble: when he
cometh up unto the people, he will [h]invade
them with his troops.
17 Although the fig tree shall
not blossom, neither *shall* fruit
be in the vines; the labour of
the olive shall [i]fail, and the
fields shall yield no meat; the flock shall be
cut off from the fold, and *there shall be* no
herd in the stalls:
18 [k]Yet I will [l]rejoice in the LORD, I will
joy in the God of my salvation.
19 The Lord GOD *is* [m]my strength, and he
will make my feet [n]like hinds' *feet,* and he will
make me to [o]walk upon mine high places. To
the chief singer on my [p]stringed instruments.

A. M. cir. 3404
B. C. cir. 600
Ol. cir. XLV. 1
Tarquinii Prisci,
R. Roman.,
cir. annum 17

[d]Heb. *were tempestuous*——[e]Ver. 8; Psa. lxxvii. 19——[f]Or, *mud*——[g]Psa. cxix. 120; Jer. xxiii. 9——[h]Or, *cut them in pieces*——[i]Heb. *lie*——[k]Job xiii. 15

[l]Isa. xli. 16; lxi. 10——[m]Psa. xxvii. 1——[n]2 Sam. xxii. 34; Psa. xviii. 33——[o]Deut. xxxii. 13; xxxiii. 29——[p]Heb. *neginoth;* Psa. iv. title

their staves, or weapons, slew one another: but the *head of the villages* or *towns*, i. e., *Pharaoh*, was drowned with his army in the Red Sea.

Verse 15. *Thou didst walk through the sea*] There was no occasion to *hurry* across; all was safe, for God had divided the waters: and his *terrible cloud* had removed from *before*, and stood *behind* them, so that it was between them and the Egyptians. See Exod. xiv. 19, 20.

Verse 16. *When I heard, my belly trembled*] The prophet, having finished his account of the wonders done by Jehovah, in bringing their fathers from Egypt into the promised land, now returns to the desolate state of his countrymen, who are shortly to be led into captivity, and suffer the most grievous afflictions; and although he had a *sure word of prophecy* that they should be ultimately *delivered*, yet the thoughts of the evils they must previously endure filled his soul with terror and dismay; so that he wishes to be removed from earth before this tribulation should come, that his eyes might not behold the desolations of his country.

When he (Nebuchadnezzar) *cometh up unto the people,* (the Jews,) *he will invade them* (overpower and carry them away captive) *with his troops.*

Verse 17. *Although the fig tree shall not blossom*] תפרח *tiphrach*, "shall not flourish," shall *not put forth its young figs*, for the fig tree does *not blossom*. The *young figs appear* as soon as the *old ones* are *ripe*, as I have often had occasion to observe.

This verse most nervously paints the desolate state of the land of Judea during the captivity. In its hemistich form, it may be translated thus:—

For the fig tree shall not flourish,
And there shall be no fruit on the vines;
The fruit of the olive shall fail,
And the fields shall supply no food:
The flocks shall be cut off from the fold,
And no herds shall be found in the stalls:
Yet in Jehovah will I exult;
I will joy in the God of my salvation.

The *Vulgate* has:—

Yet I in the Lord will rejoice,
And will exult in Jesus my God.

The *Targum* countenances this version:—

ואנא במימרא דיי אבוע *veana bemeimra dayai abua*, "But in the WORD of the Lord will I rejoice," i. e., the *personal, substantial* Word of Jehovah.

These two verses give the finest display of *resignation* and *confidence* that I have ever met with. He saw that evil was at hand, and *unavoidable;* he *submitted* to the dispensation of God, whose Spirit enabled him to paint it in all its calamitous circumstances. He knew that God was merciful and gracious. He trusted to his promise, though all appearances were against its fulfilment; for he knew that the word of Jehovah could not fail, and therefore his confidence is unshaken.

No paraphrase can add any thing to this hymn, which is full of inexpressible *dignity* and *elegance*, leaving even its unparalleled *piety* out of the question.

Verse 19. *The Lord God* is *my strength*] This is an imitation, if not a quotation, from Psa. xviii. 32, 33, where see the notes.

Will make me to walk upon mine high places] This last verse is spoken in the person of the people, who seem to anticipate their restoration; and that they shall once more rejoice in the hills and mountains of Judea.

To the chief singer on my stringed instruments.] This line, which is evidently a *superscription*, leads me to suppose that when the prophet had completed his short ode, he folded it up, with the *above direction* to the master singer, or leader of the choir, to be sung in the temple service. Many of the *Psalms* are directed in the same way. "To the master singer;" or, "chief musician;" to be sung, according to their nature, on *different kinds* of instruments, or with particular *airs* or *tunes.*

Neginoth, נגינות which we translate *stringed instruments*, means such as were struck with a *plectrum*, or *excited* by some kind of *friction* or *pulsation;* as *violins* and *cymbals*, or *tambarines* are. I do not think that the line makes any part of the prophecy, but merely the *superscription* or *direction* of the work when it was finished. The ending will appear much more dignified, this line being separated from it.

THE BOOK

OF THE

PROPHET ZEPHANIAH

Chronological Notes relative to this Book, upon the supposition that it was written in the twelfth year of the reign of Josiah, king of Judah

Year from the Creation, according to Archbishop Usher, 3374.—Year of the Julian Period, 4084.—Year since the Flood, 1718.—Year from the vocation of Abram, 1291.—Year from the foundation of Solomon's temple, 382.—Year since the division of Solomon's monarchy into the kingdoms of Israel and Judah, 346. —Year since the conquest of Corœbus at Olympia, usually called the first Olympiad, 147.—Third year of the *thirty-seventh* Olympiad.—Year from the building of Rome, according to the Varronian computation, 124.—Year of the era of Nabonassar, 118.—Year since the destruction of the kingdom of Israel by Shalmaneser, king of Assyria, 92.—Year before the birth of Christ, 626.—Year before the vulgar era of Christ's nativity, 630.—Cycle of the Sun, 24.—Cycle of the Moon, 18.—Eighteenth year of Phraortes, king of Media. This monarch is supposed by some to have been the same with the Arphaxad of the Apocrypha. —Eleventh year of Philip I., king of Macedon.—Twenty-second year of Archidamus, king of Lacedæmon, of the family of the Proclidæ.—Fifteenth year of Eurycrates II., king of Lacedæmon, of the family of the Eurysthenidæ.—Twenty-ninth year of Cypselus, who had seized upon the government of Corinth.—Forty-second year of Psammitichus, king of Egypt, according to Helvicus.—Tenth year of Kiniladachus, king of Babylon, according to the same chronologer. This monarch was the immediate predecessor of Nabopolassar, the father of Nebuchadnezzar.—Second year of Sadyattes, king of Lydia.—Eleventh year of Ancus Martius, the fifth king of the Romans.—Twelfth year of Josiah, king of Judah.

CHAPTER I

This chapter begins with denouncing God's judgments against Judah and Jerusalem, 1–3. Idolaters, and sinners of several other denominations, are then particularly threatened; and their approaching visitation enlarged on, by the enumeration of several circumstances which tend greatly to heighten its terrors, 4–18.

A. M. cir. 3374
B. C. cir. 630
Olymp.
cir. XXXVII. 3
A. U. C. cir.
124

THE word of the LORD
which came unto Ze-
phaniah the son of Cushi, the
son of Gedaliah, the son of
Amariah, the son of Hizkiah,
in the days of Josiah the son
of Amon, king of Judah.
2 [a]I will utterly consume all

[a]Heb. *By taking away I will make an end*

NOTES ON CHAP. I

Verse 1. *The word of the Lord which came unto Zephaniah*] Though this prophet has given us so large a list of his ancestors, yet little concerning him is known, because we know nothing certain relative to the persons of the family whose names are here introduced. We have one *chronological note* which is of more value for the correct understanding of his prophecy than the other could have been, how circumstantially soever it had been delivered; viz., that he prophesied *in the days of Josiah, son of Amon, king of Judah;* and from the description which he gives of the *disorders* which prevailed in Judea in his time, it is evident that he must have prophesied *before* the reformation made by Josiah, which was in the *eighteenth* year of his reign. And as he predicts the *destruction of Nineveh*, chap. ii. 13, which, as *Calmet* remarks, could not have taken place before the *sixteenth* of Josiah, allowing with *Berosus twenty-one* years for the reign of Nabopolassar over the Chaldeans; we must, therefore, place this prophecy about the beginning of the reign of Josiah, or from B. C. 640 to B. C. 609. But see the chronological notes.

Verse 2. *I will utterly consume all* things]

A. M. cir. 3374
B. C. cir. 630
Olymp.
cir. XXXVII. 3
A. U. C. cir.
124

things from off [b]the land, saith
the LORD.
3 [c]I will consume man and
beast, I will consume the fowls
of the heaven, and the fishes of the sea, and
[d]the [e]Stumbling-blocks with the wicked; and
I will cut off man from off the land, saith the
LORD.
4 I will also stretch out mine hand upon
Judah, and upon all the inhabitants of Jerusalem; and [f]I will cut off the remnant of Baal
from this place, *and* the name of [g]the Chemarims with the priests;
5 And them [h]that worship the host of heaven upon the housetops: [i]and them that worship *and* [k]that swear [l]by the LORD, and that
swear [m]by Malcham:
6 And [n]them that are turned
back from the LORD; and *those*
that [o]have not sought the
LORD, nor inquired for him.
7 [p]Hold thy peace at the presence of the
Lord GOD: [q]for the day of the LORD *is* at
hand: for [r]the LORD hath prepared a sacrifice, he hath [s]bid his guests.
8 And it shall come to pass in the day of
the LORD's sacrifice, that I will [t]punish [u]the
princes, and the king's children, and all such
as are clothed with strange apparel.
9 In the same day also will I punish all
those that leap on the threshold, which fill
their masters' houses with violence and deceit.
10 And it shall come to pass in that day,
saith the LORD, *that there shall be* the noise

A. M. cir. 3374
B. C. cir. 630
Olymp.
cir. XXXVII. 3
A. U. C. cir.
124

[b]Heb. *the face of the land*——[c]Hos. iv. 3——[d]Ezek. vii. 19; xiv. 3, 4, 7; Matt. xiii. 41——[e]Or, *idols*——[f]Fulfilled, cir. 624; 2 Kings xxiii. 4, 5——[g]Hos. x. 5——[h]2 Kings xxiii. 12; Jer. xix. 13——[i]1 Kings xviii. 21; 2 Kings xvii. 33, 41——[k]Isa. xlviii. 1; Hos. iv. 15

[l]Or, *to the LORD*——[m]Josh. xxiii. 7; 1 Kings xi. 33——[n]Isa. i. 4; Jer. ii. 13, 17; xv. 6——[o]Hos. vii. 7——[p]Hab. ii. 20; Zech. ii. 13——[q]Isa. xiii. 6——[r]Isa. xxxiv. 6; Jer. lvi. 10; Ezek. xxxix. 17; Rev. xix. 17——[s]Heb. *sanctified*, or *prepared*——[t]Heb. *visit upon*——[u]Jer. xxxix. 6

All being now ripe for destruction, I will shortly bring a universal scourge upon the land. He speaks particularly of the idolaters.

Verse 3. *I will consume man and beast*] By *war*, and by *pestilence*. Even the *waters* shall be infected, and the *fish* destroyed; the *air* become contaminated, and the *fowls* die.

Verse 4. *I will cut off the remnant of Baal*] I think he refers here, partly at least, to the reformation which Josiah was to bring about. See the account, 2 Kings xxiii. 5.

The Chemarims] The *black-robed* priests of different idols. See the note on 2 Kings xxiii. 5. These were put down by Josiah.

Verse 5. *The host of heaven*] Sun, moon, planets, and stars. This worship was one of the most ancient and the most common of all species of idolatry; and it had a greater semblance of reason to recommend it. See 2 Kings xxiii. 5, 12; Jer. xix. 13, xxxii. 29.

That swear by the Lord, and that swear by Malcham] Associating the name of an *idol* with that of the Most High. For *Malcham*, see on Hos. iv. 15, and Amos v. 26.

Verse 6. *Them that are turned back*] Who have forsaken the true God, and become idolaters.

Nor inquired for him] Have not desired to know his will.

Verse 7. *Hold thy peace at the presence of the Lord God*] הס *has*, the same as *hush, hist*, among us. Remonstrances are *now* useless. You had time to acquaint yourselves with God; you would not: you cry now in vain; destruction is at the door.

The Lord hath prepared a sacrifice] A slaughter of the people.

He hath bid his guests] The Babylonians, to whom he has given a commission to destroy you. In all festivals sacrifices, 1. The victims were offered to God, and their blood poured out before the altar. 2. The people who were invited feasted upon the sacrifice. See on Isa. xxxiv. 6.

Verse 8. *I will punish the princes, and the king's children*] After the death of Josiah the kingdom of Judah saw no prosperity, and every reign terminated miserably; until at last King Zedekiah and the *king's children* were cruelly massacred at Riblah, when Nebuchadnezzar had taken Jerusalem.

Strange apparel] I really think this refers more to their embracing idolatrous customs and heathen usages, than to their *changing their dress*. They acquired *new habits*, as we would say; *customs*, that they used as they did their *clothing*—at all times, and in every thing.

Verse 9. *That leap on the threshold*] Or, *that leap over the threshold*. It is most probable that the *Philistines* are here meant. After the time that Dagon fell before the ark, and his hands were broken off on the threshold of his temple, his worshippers would no more set a foot upon the threshold, but stepped or leaped over it, when they entered into his temple. The *Chaldee* understands this of the Philistines, without giving this reason for it. Some understand it of haughtiness and pride: others think that *leaping on the threshold* refers to the customs of the Arabs, who used to ride into people's houses, and take away whatever they could carry; and that this is the reason why, in several parts of the East, they have their doors made very low, to prevent those depredators from entering. In this manner, we learn the *Persians* have frequently oppressed the poor *Armenians*, going on horseback into their houses, and taking whatever they thought proper. Mr. *Harmer* understands it in this way.

Verse 10. *A cry from the fish-gate*] This gate, which is mentioned Neh. iii. 3, was opposite to Joppa; and perhaps the way in which the news came of the irruption of the Chaldean army, the *great crashing from the hills*.

The second] Or *second* city, may here mean a part of Jerusalem, mentioned 2 Kings xxii. 14, 2 Chron. xxxiv. 22.

A. M. cir. 3374
B. C. cir. 630
Olymp.
cir. XXXVII. 3
A. U. C. cir.
124

of a cry from [v]the fish-gate, and a howling from the second, and a great crashing from the hills.

11 [w]Howl, ye inhabitants of Maktesh, for all the merchant people are cut down; all they that bear silver are cut off.

12 And it shall come to pass at that time, *that* I will search Jerusalem with candles, and punish the men that are [x]settled [y]on their lees: [z]that say in their heart, The LORD will not do good, neither will he do evil.

13 Therefore their goods shall become a booty, and their houses a desolation: they shall also build houses, but [a]not inhabit *them*; and they shall plant vineyards, but [b]not drink the wine thereof.

14 [c]The great day of the LORD *is* near, *it is* near, and hasteth greatly, *even* the voice of the day of the LORD: the mighty man shall cry there bitterly.

A. M. cir. 3374
B. C. cir. 630
Olymp.
cir. XXXVII. 3
A. U. C. cir.
124

15 [d]That day *is* a day of wrath, a day of trouble and distress, a day of wasteness and desolation, a day of darkness and gloominess, a day of clouds and thick darkness.

16 A day of [e]the trumpet and alarm against the fenced cities, and against the high towers.

17 And I will bring distress upon men, that they shall [f]walk like blind men, because they have sinned against the LORD: and [g]their blood shall be poured out as dust, and their flesh [h]as the dung.

18 [i]Neither their silver nor their gold shall be able to deliver them in the day of the LORD'S wrath; but the whole land shall be [k]devoured by the fire of his jealousy: for [l]he shall make even a speedy riddance of all them that dwell in the land.

[v]2 Chron. xxxiii. 14——[w]James v. 1——[x]Heb. *curded*, or *thickened*——[y]Jer. xlviii. 11; Amos vi. 1 [z]Psa. xciv. 7——[a]Deut. xxviii. 30, 39; Amos v. 11 [b]Mic. vi. 15——[c]Joel ii. 1, 11

[d]Isa. xxii. 5; Jer. xxx. 7; Joel ii. 2, 11; Amos v. 18; ver. 18——[e]Jer. iv. 19——[f]Deut. xxviii. 29; Isa. lix. 10 [g]Psa. lxxix. 3——[h]Psa. lxxxiii. 10; Jer. ix. 22; xvi. 4 [i]Prov. xi. 4; Ezek. vii. 19——[k]Ch. iii. 8——[l]Ver. 2, 3

Verse 11. *Maktesh*] *Calmet* says this signifies a *mortar*, or a *rock in form of a mortar*, and was the name of a quarter of Jerusalem where they hulled rice, corn, &c., according to St. Jerome. Some think the city of Jerusalem is meant, where the inhabitants should be beat and pounded to death as grain is pounded in a mortar.

Newcome translates it, the *lower* city, and considers it the *valley* in Jerusalem, which divided the *upper* from the *lower* city.

They that bear silver] The merchants, money-changers, usurers, rich men.

Verse 12. *I will search Jerusalem with candles*] I will make a universal and thorough search.

That are settled on their lees] Those who are *careless*, satisfied with the goods of this life; who trust in their riches, and are completely irreligious; who, while they acknowledge that there is a God, think, like the *Aristotelians*, that he is so supremely happy in the contemplation of his own excellences, that he feels it beneath his dignity to concern himself with the affairs of mortals.

Verse 13. *Their goods* (in which they trust) *shall become a booty*] To the Chaldeans. They shall have no profit of all their labours. *The houses they have built they shall not inhabit;* of the wine of the *vineyards they have planted*, they shall not drink. See Amos v. 11, where we find the same evils threatened.

Verse 14. *The great day of the Lord* is *near*] It commenced with the death of the good king Josiah, who was slain by Pharaoh-necho at Megiddo, and continued to the destruction of Jerusalem by Nebuchadnezzar.

Verse 15. *That day* is *a day of wrath*] See the parallel passages in the *margin*, and the notes there. From the *fourteenth* to the *sixteenth* verse inclusive there is a most beautiful amplification of the disasters that were coming on Jerusalem; the *invasion, incursion, attack, carnage, confusion, horrible din* occasioned by the *sound* of the *trumpet*, the *cries* of the *people*, and the *shrieks* and *groans* of the *dying*, are pointed out with great force and mighty effect.

Verse 17. *They shall walk like blind men*] Be in the most perplexing *doubt* and *uncertainty;* and while in this state, have their blood poured out by the sword of their enemies, and their flesh trodden under foot.

Verse 18. *Their silver nor their gold*] In which they trusted, and from which they expected happiness; these shall not profit them in this awful day. And God will bring this about speedily; and a *speedy riddance*—a universal desolation, shall in a short time take place in every part of the land.

CHAPTER II

The prophet, having declared the judgments which were ready to fall on his people, earnestly exhorts them to repentance, that these judgments may be averted, 1–3. He then foretells the fate of other neighbouring and hostile nations: the Philistines, 4–7; Moabites and Ammonites, 8–11; Ethiopians, 12; and Assyrians, 13. In the close of the chapter we have a prophecy against Nineveh. These predictions were accomplished chiefly by the conquests of Nebuchadnezzar.

A. M. cir. 3374
B. C. cir. 630
Olymp.
cir. XXXVII. 3
A. U. C. cir.
124

GATHER [a]yourselves together, yea, gather together, O nation [b]not desired;
2 Before the decree bring
forth, *before* the day pass [c]as the chaff, before
[d]the fierce anger of the LORD come upon you,
before the day of the LORD's anger come upon
you.
3 [e]Seek ye the LORD, [f]all ye meek of the
earth, which have wrought his judgment, seek
righteousness, seek meekness: [g]it may be ye
shall be hid in the day of the LORD's anger.
4 For [h]Gaza shall be forsaken, and Ashkelon a desolation: they shall drive out Ashdod
[i]at the noonday, and Ekron shall be rooted up.
5 Wo unto the inhabitants of [k]the sea-
coasts, the nation of the Cherethites; the
word of the LORD *is* against you; O [l]Canaan,
the land of the Philistines, I will even destroy
thee, that there shall be no inhabitant.
6 And the sea-coasts shall be
dwellings *and* cottages for
shepherds, [m]and folds for flocks.
7 And the coast shall be for [n]the remnant of
the house of Judah; they shall feed thereupon:
in the houses of Ashkelon shall they lie down
in the evening: [o]for the LORD their God shall
[p]visit them, and [q]turn away their captivity.
8 [r]I have heard the reproach of Moab, and
[s]the revilings of the children of Ammon,
whereby they have reproached my people, and
[t]magnified *themselves* against their border.
9 Therefore *as* I live, saith the LORD of
hosts, the God of Israel, Surely [u]Moab shall
be as Sodom, and [v]the children of Ammon as
Gomorrah, [w]*even* the breeding of nettles, and
salt-pits, and a perpetual desolation: [x]the

A. M. cir. 3374
B. C. cir. 630
Olymp.
cir. XXXVII. 3
A. U. C. cir.
124

---

[a]Joel ii. 16——[b]Or, *not desirous*——[c]Job xxi. 18; Psa. i. 4; Isa. xvii. 13; Hos. xiii. 3——[d]2 Kings xxiii. 26 [e]Psa. cv. 4; Amos v. 6——[f]Psa. lxxvi. 9——[g]Joel ii. 14; Amos v. 15; Jonah iii. 9——[h]Jer. xlvii. 4, 5; Ezek. xxv. 15; Amos i. 6, 7, 8; Zech. ix. 5, 6——[i]Jer. vi. 4; xv. 8 [k]Ezek. xxv. 16——[l]Josh. xiii. 3——[m]See Isa. xvii. 2 ver. 14

[n]Isa. xi. 11; Mic. iv. 7; v. 7, 8; Hag. i. 12; ii. 2; verse 9——[o]Or, *when*, &c.——[p]Exod. iv. 31; Luke i. 68 [q]Psa. cxxvi. 1; Jer. xxix. 14; chap. iii. 20——[r]Jer. xlviii. 27; Ezek. xxv. 8——[s]Ezek. xxv. 3, 6——[t]Jer. xlix. 1 [u]Isa. xv.; Jer. xlviii.; Ezek. xxv. 9; Amos ii. 1——[v]Amos i. 13——[w]Gen. xix. 25; Deut. xxix. 23; Isa. xiii. 19; xxxiv. 13; Jer. xlix. 18; l. 40——[x]Ver. 7

NOTES ON CHAP. II

Verse 1. *Gather yourselves*] Others, *sift yourselves. Separate* the *chaff* from the wheat, before the judgments of God fall upon you. *O nation not desired—unlovely*, not delighted in; hated because of your sin. The Israelites are addressed.

Verse 3. *Ye meek of the earth*] ענוי *anavey*, ye *oppressed* and *humbled* of the land.

It may be ye shall be hid] The sword has not a commission against you. Ask God, and he will be a refuge to you from the storm and from the tempest.

Verse 4. *Gaza shall be forsaken*] This prophecy is against the *Philistines*. They had been greatly harassed by the kings of Egypt; but were completely ruined by Nebuchadnezzar, who took all Phœnicia from the Egyptians; and about the time of his taking Tyre, devastated all the seignories of the Philistines. This ruin we have seen foretold by the other prophets, and have already remarked its exact fulfilment.

Verse 5. *The sea-coasts, the nation of the Cherethites*] The *sea-coasts* mean all the country lying on the Mediterranean coast from Egypt to Joppa and Gaza. The *Cherethites*—the *Cretans*, who were probably a colony of the Phœnicians. See on 1 Sam. xxx. 14, and Amos ix. 7.

Verse 6. *And the sea-coasts shall be dwellings*] *Newcome* considers רת *keroth* as a proper name, not *cottages* or *folds*. The *Septuagint* have Κρητη, *Crete*, and so has the *Syriac*. Abp. *Secker* notes, *Alibi non extat* כרת, *et forte notat patriam των* כרתים. "The word כרת is not found elsewhere, and probably it is the name of the country of the Cherethim."

Verse 7. *The coast shall be for the remnant*] Several devastations fell on the Philistines. Gaza was ruined by the army of Alexander the Great, and the *Maccabees* finally accomplished all that was predicted by the prophets against this invariably wicked people. They lost their polity, and were at last obliged to receive circumcision.

Verse 8. *I have heard the reproach of Moab*] God punished them for the cruel part they had taken in the persecutions of the Jews; for when they lay under the displeasure of God, these nations insulted them in the most provoking manner. See on Amos i. 13, and the parallel texts in the *margin*.

Verse 9. *The breeding of nettles*] That is, their land shall become desolate, and be a place for nettles, thorns, &c., to flourish in, for want of cultivation.

A. M. cir. 3374 B. C. cir. 630 Olymp. cir. XXXVII. 3 A. U. C. cir. 124

residue of my people shall
spoil them, and the remnant of
my people shall possess them.
10 This shall they have [y]for
their pride, because they have reproached and
magnified *themselves* against the people of the
LORD of hosts.
11 The LORD *will be* terrible unto them: for
he will [z]famish all the gods of the earth;
[a]and *men* shall worship him, every one from
his place, *even* all [b]the isles of the heathen.
12 [c]Ye Ethiopians also, ye *shall be* slain by
[d]my sword.
13 And he will stretch out his hand against
the north, and [e]destroy Assyria; and will make
Nineveh a desolation, *and* dry
like a wilderness.
14 And [f]flocks shall lie down
in the midst of her, all [g]the
beasts of the nations: both the [h]cormorant
[i]and the bittern shall lodge in the [k]upper
lintels of it; *their* voice shall sing in the
windows; desolation *shall be* in the thresholds: [l]for he shall uncover the [m]cedar work.
15 This *is* the rejoicing city [n]that dwelt
carelessly, [o]that said in her heart, I *am,* and
there is none beside me: how is she become
a desolation, a place for beasts to lie down in!
every one that passeth by her [p]shall hiss *and*
[q]wag his hand.

A. M. cir. 3374 B. C. cir. 630 Olymp. cir. XXXVII. 3 A. U. C. cir. 124

[y]Isa. xvi. 6; Jer. xlviii. 29——[z]Heb. *make lean* [a]Mal. i. 11; John iv. 21——[b]Gen. x. 5——[c]Isa. xviii. 1, xx. 4; Jer. xlvi. 9; Ezek. xxx. 9——[d]Psa. xvii. 13 [e]Isa. x. 12; Ezek. xxxi. 3; Nah. i. 2; ii. 10; iii. 15, 18 [f]Ver. 6

[g]Isa. xiii. 21, 22——[h]Or, *pelican*——[i]Isa. xxxiv. 11, 14——[k]Or, *knops*, or *chapiters*——[l]Or, *when he hath uncovered*——[m]Jer. xxii. 14——[n]Isa. xlvii. 8——[o]Rev. xviii. 7——[p]Job xxvii. 23; Lam. ii. 15; Ezek. xxvii. 36 [q]Nah. iii. 19

Verse 10. *Because they have reproached*] See on ver. 8.

Verse 11. *He will famish all the gods of the earth*] They shall have no more *sacrifices;* their worship shall be entirely destroyed. Idolaters supposed that their gods actually *fed* on the *fumes* and *spirituous* exhalations that arose from the burnt-offerings which they made unto their idols. It is in reference to this opinion that the Lord says, "He will famish all the gods of the land."

Verse 12. *Ye Ethiopians also*] Nebuchadnezzar subdued these. See Jer. xlvi. 2, 9; Ezek. xxx. 4, 10. See also on Amos ix. 17.

Verse 13. *He will—destroy Assyria*] He will overthrow the empire, and *Nineveh,* their metropolitan city. See on Jonah and Nahum.

Verse 14. *And flocks shall lie down in the midst of her*] Nineveh was so completely destroyed, that its situation is not at present even known. The present city of *Mossoul* is supposed to be in the *vicinity* of the place where this ancient city stood.

The cormorant קאת *kaath; and the bittern,* קפד *kippod.* These *Newcome* translates, "The pelican and the porcupine."

Their *voice shall sing in the windows*] The windows shall be all demolished; wild fowl shall build their nests in them, and shall be seen coming from their sills; and the fine *cedar* ceilings shall be exposed to the weather, and by and by crumble to dust. See the note on Isa. xxxiv. 11, 14, where nearly the same terms are used.

I have in another place introduced a remarkable couplet quoted by Sir *W. Jones* from a Persian poet, which speaks of desolation in nearly the same terms.

پرده داري ميكند در قصر قيصر عنكبوت
بومي نوبت ميزند بر كنيد افراسياب

"The spider holds the veil in the palace of Cæsar:
The owl stands sentinel in the watchtower of Afrasiab."

Verse 15. *This* is *the rejoicing city*] The city in which mirth, jocularity, and pleasure, reigned without interruption.

And *wag his hand*] Will point her out as a mark and monument of Divine displeasure.

CHAPTER III

The prophet reproves Jerusalem, and all her guides and rulers, for their obstinate perseverance in impiety, notwithstanding all the warnings and corrections which they had received from God, 1–7. *They are encouraged, however, after they shall have been chastised for their idolatry, and cured of it, to look for mercy and restoration,* 8–13; *and excited to hymns of joy at the glorious prospect,* 14–17. *After which the prophet concludes with large promises of favour and prosperity in the days of the Messiah,* 18–20. *We take this extensive view of the concluding verses of this chapter, because an apostle has expressly assured us that in* EVERY *prophetical book of the Old Testament Scriptures are contained predictions relative to the Gospel dispensation. See* Acts iii. 24.

A. M. cir. 3374
B. C. cir. 630
Olymp.
cir. XXXVII. 3
A. U. C. cir.
124

WO to [a]her [b]that is filthy and
polluted, to the oppressing
city!
2 She [c]obeyed not the voice;
she [d]received not [e]correction; she trusted not
in the LORD; she drew not near to her God.
3 [f]Her princes within her *are* roaring lions;
her judges *are* [g]evening wolves; they gnaw
not the bones till the morrow.
4 Her [h]prophets *are* light *and* treacherous persons: her priests have polluted the
sanctuary, they have done [i]violence to the
law.
5 [k]The just LORD [l]*is* in the midst thereof;
he will not do iniquity: [m]every morning doth
he bring his judgment to light, he faileth not:
but [n]the unjust knoweth no shame.
6 I have cut off the nations: their [o]towers
are desolate; I made their streets
waste, that none passeth by:
their cities are destroyed, so that
there is no man, that there is
none inhabitant.
7 [p]I said, Surely thou wilt fear me, thou
wilt receive instruction; so their dwelling
should not be cut off, howsoever I punished
them; but they rose early, *and* [q]corrupted all
their doings.
8 Therefore [r]wait ye upon me, saith the
LORD, until the day that I rise up to the prey:
for my determination *is* to [s]gather the nations,
that I may assemble the kingdoms, to pour
upon them mine indignation, *even* all my
fierce anger: for all the earth [t]shall be devoured with the fire of my jealousy.
9 For then will I turn to the people [u]a pure

A. M. cir. 3374
B. C. cir. 630
Olymp.
cir. XXXVII. 3
A. U. C. cir.
124

[a]Or, *gluttonous*——[b]Heb. *craw*——[c]Jer. xxii. 21——[d]Jer. v. 3——[e]Or, *instruction*——[f]Ezek. xxii. 27; Mic. iii. 9, 10, 11——[g]Hab. i. 8——[h]Jer. xxiii. 11, 32; Lam. ii. 14; Hos. ix. 7——[i]Ezek. xxii. 26——[k]Deut. xxxii. 4

[l]Ver. 15, 17; see Mic. iii. 11——[m]Heb. *morning by morning*——[n]Jer. iii. 3; vi. 15; viii. 12——[o]Or, *corners*——[p]So Jer. viii. 6——[q]Gen. vi. 12——[r]Psa. xxvii. 14; xxxvii. 34; Prov. xx. 22——[s]Joel iii. 2——[t]Chap. i. 18——[u]Isa. xix. 18

NOTES ON CHAP. III

Verse 1. *Wo to her that is filthy*] This is a denunciation of Divine judgment against Jerusalem.

Verse 2. *She obeyed not the voice*] Of conscience, of God, and of his prophets.

She received not correction] Did not profit by his chastisements; was uneasy and ill-tempered under her afflictions, and derived no manner of good from these chastisements.

She trusted not in the Lord] Did not consider him as the *Fountain* whence all help and salvation should come; and rather sought for support from *man* and *herself*, than from God.

She drew not near to her God.] Did not worship him; did not walk in his ways; did not make *prayer* and supplication to him.

Verse 3. *Her princes*—are *roaring lions*] Tearing all to pieces without shadow of law, except their own despotic power.

Her judges are *evening wolves*] Being a little afraid of the lion-like princes, they practise their unjust dealings from evening to morning, and take the *day* to find their rest.

They gnaw not the bones till the morrow.] They devour the flesh in the night, and gnaw the bones and extract the marrow afterwards. They use all violence and predatory oppression, like wild beasts; they shun the light, and turn day into night by their revellings.

Verse 4. *Her prophets* are *light* and *treacherous persons*] They have no *seriousness*, no *deep conviction* of the awful nature of their *office*, no *concern* for the *immortal souls* of the people. *Treacherous persons*—they betray the souls of the people for the sake of worldly *honour, pleasure*, and *profit*. Even in our own enlightened country we find prophets who prefer *hunting* the *hare* or the *fox*, and pursuing the *partridge* and *phesant*, to *visiting the sick*, and *going* after the *strayed, lost sheep* of the *house of Israel*. Poor souls! They know neither God nor themselves; and if they did visit the sick, they could not speak to them to exhortation, edification, or comfort. God never called them to his work; therefore they know nothing of it. But O, what an account have these *pleasure-taking false prophets* to render to the Shepherd of souls!

They have done violence to the law.] They have forced wrong constructions on it in order to excuse themselves, and lull the people into spiritual slumber. So we find that it was an ancient practice for men to wrest the Scriptures to their own destruction.

Verse 5. *The just Lord* is *in the midst thereof*] He sees, marks down, and will punish all these wickednesses.

Every morning doth he bring his judgment to light] The sense is, says Bp. *Newcome*, "Not a day passes but we see instances of his goodness to righteous men, and of his vengeance on the wicked."

Verse 6. *I have cut off the nations*] Syria, Israel, and those referred to, Isa. xxxvi. 18, 20. —*Newcome.*

Verse 7. *Surely thou wilt fear me*] After so many displays of my sovereign power and judgments.

But they rose early] And instead of returning to God, they practised every abomination. They were diligent to find out times and places for their iniquity. This is the worst state of man.

Verse 8. *Wait ye upon me*] Expect the fulfilment of all my promises and threatenings: I am God, and change not.

For all the earth] All the land of Judah.

Verse 9. *Will I turn to the people*] This promise must refer to the conversion of the Jews under the Gospel.

That they may all call] That the whole nation may invoke God by Christ, and serve him with *one consent;* not one unbeliever being found among them.

The *pure language*, שפה ברורה *saphah beru-*

A. M. cir. 3374
B. C. cir. 630
Olymp.
cir. XXXVII. 3
A. U. C. cir.
124

[v]language, that they may all
call upon the name of the LORD,
to serve him with one [w]consent.
10 [x]From beyond the rivers of
Ethiopia my suppliants, *even* the daughter of
my dispersed, shall bring mine offering.
11 In that day shall thou not be ashamed for
all thy doings, wherein thou hast transgressed
against me: for then I will take away out of
the midst of thee them that [y]rejoice in thy
pride, and thou shalt no more be haughty [z]be-
cause of my holy mountain.
12 I will also leave in the midst of thee [a]an
afflicted and poor people, and they shall trust
in the name of the LORD.
13 [b]The remnant of Israel [c]shall not do
iniquity, [d]nor speak lies; neither shall a deceitful tongue be
found in their mouth: for [e]they
shall feed and lie down, and none
shall make *them* afraid.
14 [f]Sing, O daughter of Zion: shout, O
Israel; be glad and rejoice with all the heart,
O daughter of Jerusalem.
15 The LORD hath taken away thy judgments,
he hath cast out thine enemy: [g]the King of
Israel, *even* the LORD, [h]*is* in the midst of thee:
thou shalt not see evil any more.
16 In that day [i]it shall be said to Jerusalem,
Fear thou not: *and to* Zion, [k]Let not thine
hand be [l]slack.
17 The LORD thy God [m]in the midst of thee

A. M. cir. 3374
B. C. cir. 630
Olymp.
cir. XXXVII. 3
A. U. C. cir.
124

[v]Heb. *lip*——[w]Heb. *shoulder*——[x]Psa. lxviii. 31; Isa. xviii. 1, 7; lx. 4, &c.; Mal. i. 11; Acts viii. 27——[y]Jer. vii. 4; Mic. iii. 11; Matt. iii. 9——[z]Heb. *in my holy*——[a]Isa. xiv. 32; Zech. xi. 11; Matt. v. 3; 1 Cor. i. 27, 28; James ii. 5——[b]Mic. iv. 7; chap. ii. 7

[c]Isa. lx. 21——[d]Isa. lxiii. 8; Rev. xiv. 5——[e]Ezek. xxxiv. 28; Mic. iv. 4; vii. 14——[f]Isa. xii. 6; liv. 1; Zech. ii. 10; ix. 9——[g]John i. 49——[h]Ver. 5, 17; Ezek. xlviii. 35; Rev. vii. 15; xxi. 3, 4——[i]Isa. xxxv. 3, 4——[k]Heb. xii. 12——[l]Or, *faint*——[m]Ver. 15

rah, may here mean the *form of religious worship.* They had been before *idolaters:* now God promises to restore his *pure worship* among them. The word has certainly this meaning in Psa. lxxxi. 6; where, as God is the speaker, the words should not be rendered, "I heard a language which I understood not;" but, "I heard a religious confession, which I approved not." See Isa. xix. 18; Hos. xiv. 3; and see Joel ii. 28, where a similar promise is found.

Verse 10. *From beyond the rivers of Ethiopia*] This may denote both *Africa* and the southern *Arabia. Bochart* thinks that *Arabia Chusæ*r is meant; and that the rivers are *Besor*, which flows into the *Mediterranean; Rhinocorura*, which flows into the Lake *Sirbonis; Trajanus Amnis*, which flows into the *Red Sea;* and the river *Corys. Calmet* thinks that these *rivers* mean the *Nile*, which by *seven mouths* falls into the Mediterranean. The Nile comes from *Ethiopia*, properly so called; and runs through all Egypt, and falls into the sea at that part of Arabia which the Scripture calls *Cush* or *Ethiopia.*

My dispersed] The Jews, scattered through different parts of the world. *Shall bring mine offering.* Shall acknowledge my mercy in sending them the *Messiah* to bless them, by turning every one of them away from their iniquities.

Verse 11. *Shalt thou not be ashamed*] Thy punishment shall cease, for God shall pardon thy sin.

For then I will take away out of the midst of thee] The wicked Jewish priests and scribes who blasphemed Christ, and would not come under his yoke.

Because of my holy mountain.] Thou wilt no more *boast in my temple*, but become *meek* and *lowly* in following him who is meek and lowly in heart, that ye may obtain rest to your souls.

Verse 12. *An afflicted and poor people*] In such a state will the Jews be found when they shall hear the universal call, and believe in Christ Jesus. Indeed, this is the *general state* of the Jews in the *present day;* except a *few* that are *called Jews*, who are *very rich;* and who believe just as much in the *God of Jacob*, as they do in *Jesus Christ.*

Verse 13. *The remnant of Israel shall not do iniquity*] O what a change! And then, how different shall they be from their *present selves!* Iniquity, lying, and deceit shall not be found among them! A Jew once said to me, "Tere are shome of you Christians who are making wonderful efforts to convert the Tshews (Jews.) *Ah, dere ish none but Gott Almighty dat can convert a Tshew.*" Truly I believe him. Only God can convert any man; and if there be a *peculiar difficulty* to convert any soul, that difficulty must lie in the *conversion* of the *Jew.*

Verse 14. *Sing, O daughter of Zion*] Here is not only a gracious prophetic promise of their restoration from captivity, but of their conversion to God through Christ.

Verse 15. *The King of Israel*, even *the Lord*, is *in the midst of thee*] They have never had a *king* since the death of Zedekiah, and never shall have one till they have the *King Messiah* to reign among them; and this promise refers to that event.

Verse 16. *Fear thou not*] Thou shalt have no more captivities nor national afflictions.

Let not thine hands be slack.] This may refer, *first*, to the rebuilding of the temple of God, after the return from Babylon; and, *secondly*, to their diligence and zeal in the Christian Church.

Verse 17. *The Lord thy God*] יהוה אלהיך *Yehovah Eloheycha*, "The self-existent and eternal Being, who is in covenant with you;" the character of God in reference to the Jews when standing in the nearest relation to them.

Is *mighty*] גבור *gibbor*, is the *prevailing One*, the *all-conquering Hero.* The character which is given to Christ, Isa. ix. 6: "His name shall be called אל גבור *El gibbor*, the prevailing Almighty God."

He will save] *Deliver* thee from all the

A. M. cir. 3374 B. C. cir. 630 Olymp. cir. XXXVII. 3 A. U. C. cir. 124

is mighty; he will save, [n]he will
rejoice over thee with joy; [o]he
will rest in his love, he will joy
over thee with singing.

18 I will gather *them that* [p]*are* sorrowful
for the solemn assembly, *who* are of thee, *to*
whom [q]the reproach of it *was* a burden.

19 Behold, at that time I will undo all that
afflict thee: and I will save her that [r]halteth,
and gather her that was driven
out; and [s]I will get them praise
and fame in every land [t]where
they have been put to shame.

20 At that time [u]will I bring you *again*,
even in the time that I gather you: for I will
make you a name and a praise among all people of the earth, when I turn back your captivity before your eyes, saith the LORD.

[n]Deut. xxx. 9; Isa. lxii. 5; lxv. 19; Jer. xxxii. 41——[o]Heb. *he will be silent*——[p]Lam. ii. 6——[q]Heb. *the burden upon it* was *reproach*——[r]Ezek. xxxiv. 16; Mic. iv. 6, 7——[s]Heb. *I will set them for a praise*——[t]Heb. *of their shame*——[u]Isa. xi. 12; xxvii. 12; lvi. 8; Ezek. xxviii. 25; xxxiv. 13; xxxvii. 21; Amos ix. 14

power from all the *guilt*, and from all the *pollution* of thy sins; and when thus *saved*, "he will rejoice over thee with joy," with peculiar gladness. "He will rest in his love,"—he will renew his love. He will show the same love to you that he did of old to *Abraham*, *Isaac*, and *Jacob*.

He will joy over thee with singing.] The conversion of the Jews will be a subject of peculiar delight and exultation to God himself! There will be a *more* than *ordinary joy* in heaven, when the Jews return to God through Christ. This event cannot be at a great distance; they are as *wretched* and as *ungodly* as they can well be. The *arms of Christians* are open to receive them; and *all things are now ready!*

Verse 18. *I will gather—sorrowful*] This may refer to those who, during the captivity, *mourned* for their former religious assemblies; and who were *reproached* by their enemies, because they could not enjoy their religious solemnities. See Psa. cxxxvii.: "By the rivers of Babylon, there we sat down; yea, we wept, when we remembered Zion. For there they that carried us away captive required of us a song," &c. This very circumstance may be the reference here.

Verse 19. *I will undo all that afflict thee*] They who have persecuted you shall be punished for it. It shows much malignity and baseness of mind, to afflict or reproach those who are lying under the chastising hand of God. This was the conduct of the Edomites, Moabites, and Ammonites, when the Jews were in adversity; and how severely did the Lord punish them for it! And he gave this as the *reason* for the severity of the punishment.

The first clause here is translated thus by Abp. *Newcome:* "Behold I will work with thee for thy sake at that time." The original is obscure; and it may bear the above sense.

I will save her that halteth] See Micah iv. 6, where there is a parallel place.

And gather her that was driven out] By captivity. The reference may be to renewing the covenant with the Jews, who were considered as an unfaithful spouse divorced by her husband. I will bring her back to my house.

I will get them praise and fame in every land] They shall become a great, a good, and a useful people. And as they are now a proverb of reproach, full of base wiles and degrading selfishness, they shall lose this character, and be totally changed; and they shall be as eminent for excellence, as they were before for baseness, in those countries where they had sojourned.

Verse 20. *At that time*] *First*, when the *seventy* years of the Babylonish captivity shall terminate. "I will bring you again" to your own land; and this restoration shall be a type of their redemption from sin and iniquity; and *at this time*, and at this only, will they have a *name* and *praise* among *all* the *people* of the *earth*, not only among the Jews, but the Gentiles.

Before your eyes] Some read *before* THEIR *eyes;* that is, the eyes of all people. On their conversion to Christianity, they shall become as eminent as they ever were in the most illustrious days of their history, Lord, hasten the conversion of Israel! Amen.

THE BOOK

OF THE

PROPHET HAGGAI

Chronological Notes relative to this book

Year from the Creation, according to Archbishop Usher, 3484.—Year of the Julian Period, 4194.—Year since the Flood, 1828.—Year from the vocation of Abram, 1301.—Year since the first celebration of the Olympic games in Elis by the Idæi Dactyli, 934.—Year since the foundation of the monarchy of the Israelites by the Divine appointment of Saul to the regal dignity, 576.—Year from the foundation of the temple, 492.—Year from the division of Solomon's monarchy into the kingdoms of Israel and Judah, 456.—Year since the re-establishment of the Olympic games at Elis by Lycurgus, Iphitus, and Cleosthenes, 365.—Year since the conquest of Corœbus at Olympia, usually called the first Olympiad, 257.—First year of the *sixty-fifth* Olympiad.—Year from the building of Rome, according to the Varronian or generally received computation, 234.—Year from the building of Rome, according to Cato and the Fasti Consulares, 233.—Year from the building of Rome, according to Polybius the historian, 232.—Year from the building of Rome, according to Fabius Pictor, 228.—Year of the era of Nabonassar, 228.—Year since the destruction of the kingdom of Israel by Shalmaneser, king of Assyria, 202.—Year since the destruction of the kingdom of Judah by Nebuchadnezzar, king of Babylon, 68.—Year since the destruction of the Chaldean empire by the Persians, 18.—Year before the birth of Christ, 516.—Year before the vulgar era of Christ's nativity, 520.—Cycle of the Sun, 22.—Cycle of the Moon, 14.—Second year of Darius I., king of Persia.—Twenty-eighth year of Amyntas, king of Macedon.—Seventh year of Demaratus, king of Lacedæmon, of the family of the Proclidæ.—Eleventh year of Cleomenes, king of Lacedæmon, of the family of the Eurysthenidæ.—Fifteenth year of Tarquinius Superbus, the last king of the Romans.—This was about twelve years before the abolition of the regal government of the Romans by the expulsion of the Tarquins.—Confucius, the celebrated Chinese philosopher, is supposed to have flourished about this time.

CHAPTER I

The prophet reproves the people, and particularly their ruler and high priest, for negligence and delay in rebuilding the temple; and tells them that their neglect was the cause of their having been visited with unfruitful seasons, and other marks of the Divine displeasure, 1–11. *He encourages them to set about the work, and on their doing so, promises that God will be with them,* 12–15.

A. M. 3484 B. C. 520 Ol. LXV. 1 Anno Tarquinii Superbi, R. Roman., 15

IN [a]the second year of Darius
the king, in the sixth month,
in the first day of the month,
came the word of the LORD [b]by
Haggai the prophet unto [c]Zerub-
babel the son of Shealtiel, [d]gov-

A. M. 3484 B. C. 520 Ol. LXV. 1 Anno Tarquinii Superbi, R. Roman., 15

[a]Ezra iv. 24; v. 1; Zechariah i. 1——[b]Hebrew *by the hand of Haggai*——[c]1 Chronicles iii. 17, 19; Ezra iii. 2; Matthew i. 12; Luke iii. 27——[d]Or, *captain*

We know nothing of the parentage of *Haggai.* He was probably born in Babylon during the captivity, and appears to have been the first prophet sent to the Jews after their return to their own land. He was sent particularly to encourage the Jews to proceed with the building of the temple, which had been interrupted for about *fourteen* years. *Cyrus,* who had published an edict empowering the Jews to return to Jerusalem and rebuild their city and temple, revoked this edict in the second year of his reign, through the evil advice of his courtiers and other enemies of the Jews. After his death *Cambyses* renewed the prohibition; but after the death of Cambyses, *Darius,* the son of *Hystaspes,* renewed the *permission;* and Haggai was sent to encourage his countrymen to proceed with the work. Darius came to the throne

A. M. 3484 B. C. 520 Ol. LXV. 1 Anno Tarquinii Superbi, R. Roman., 15

ernor of Judah, and to [e]Joshua
the son of Josedech, [f]the high
priest, saying,
2 Thus speaketh the LORD of
hosts, saying, This people say, The time is not
come, the time that the LORD's house should
be built.
3 Then came the word of the LORD [g]by
Haggai the prophet, saying,
4 [h]*Is it* time for you, O ye, to dwell in your
ceiled houses, and this house *lie* waste?
5 Now therefore thus saith the LORD of
hosts; [i]Consider [k]your ways.
6 Ye have [l]sown much, and bring in little;
ye eat, but ye have not enough; ye drink, but
ye are not filled with drink; ye clothe you,
but there is none warm; and [m]he that earneth wages, earneth wages *to put it* into a bag
[n]with holes.
7 Thus saith the LORD of
hosts; Consider your ways.
8 Go up to the mountain, and
bring wood, and build the house;
and I will take pleasure in it, and I will be
glorified, saith the LORD.
9 [o]Ye looked for much, and, lo, *it came*
to little; and when ye brought *it* home, [p]I
did [q]blow upon it. Why? saith the LORD
of hosts. Because of mine house that *is*
waste, and ye run every man unto his own
house.
10 Therefore [r]the heaven over you is stayed
from dew, and the earth is stayed *from* her
fruit.
11 And I [s]called for a drought upon the land,
and upon the mountains, and upon the corn,
and upon the new wine, and upon the oil, and
upon *that* which the ground bringeth forth,

[e]Ezra iii. 2; v. 2——[f]1 Chron. vi. 15——[g]Ezra v. 1 [h]2 Sam. vii. 2; Psa. cxxxii. 3, &c.——[i]*Set your heart on your ways*——[k]Lam. iii. 40; ver. 7——[l]Deut. xxviii. 38; Hos. iv. 10; Mic. vi. 14, 15; chap. ii. 16

[m]Zech. viii. 10——[n]Heb. *pierced through*——[o]Chap. ii. 16——[p]Chap. ii. 17——[q]Or, *blow it away*——[r]Lev. xxvi. 19; Deut. xxviii. 23; 1 Kings viii. 35——[s]1 Kings xvii. 1; 2 Kings viii. 1

about the year B. C. 521, and published his edict of permission for the Jews to rebuild the city and temple in the second year of his reign, which was the *sixteenth* of their return from Babylon.

NOTES ON CHAP. I

Verse 1. *In the sixth month*] Called *Elul* by the Hebrews. It was the *sixth* month of the ecclesiastical year, and the *last* of the *civil* year, and answered to a part of our *September*.

Zerubbabel the son of Shealtiel] Who was son of *Jeconiah*, king of Judah, and of the family of David, and exercised the post of a governor *among* the people, but not *over* them, for both he and they were under the Persian government; but they were permitted to have *Zerubbabel* for their own governor, and *Joshua* for their high priest; and these regulated all matters relative to their peculiar political and ecclesiastical government. But it appears from Ezra, v. 3, that *Tatnai*, the governor on this side the river, had them under his cognizance. None of their own governors was absolute. The Persians permitted them to live under their own laws and civil regulations; but they always considered them as a colony, over which they had a continual superintendence.

Joshua the son of Josedech] And son of Seraiah, who was high priest in the time of Zedekiah, and was carried into captivity by Nebuchadnezzar, 1 Chron. vi. 15. But Seraiah was slain at Riblah, by order of Nebuchadnezzar, 2 Kings xxv. 18-21.

Verse 2. *The time is not come*] They thought that the *seventy years* spoken of by Jeremiah were not yet completed, and it would be useless to attempt to rebuild until that period had arrived. But Abp. *Usher* has shown that from the commencement of the last siege of Jerusalem unto this time, precisely *sixty-nine* years had been completed.

Verse 4. Is it *time for you*] If the *time be not come* to rebuild the *temple*, it cannot be come for you to *build yourselves comfortable houses:* but ye are rebuilding your houses; why then do ye not rebuild the house of the Lord? The foundation of the temple had been laid *fourteen* years before, and some considerable progress made in the building; and it had been *lying waste* in that unfinished state to the present time.

Verse 5. *Consider your ways*] Is it fit that you should be building yourselves *elegant houses*, and neglect a *place* for the *worship* of that God who has restored you from captivity?

Verse 6. *Ye have sown much*] God will not bless you in any labour of your hands, unless you rebuild his temple and restore his worship. This verse contains a series of *proverbs;* no less than *five* in the compass of a few lines.

Verse 8. *Go up to the mountain, and bring wood*] Go to Lebanon, and get timber. In the second year of the return from the captivity, they had procured cedar trees from Lebanon, and brought them to Joppa, and had hired masons and carpenters from the Tyrians and Sidonians; but that labour had been nearly lost by the long suspension of the building. Ezra iii. 7.

Verse 9. *Ye looked for much*] Ye made great pretensions at first; but they are come to nothing. Ye did a little in the beginning; but so scantily and unwillingly that I could not but reject it.

Ye run every man unto his own house.] To rebuild and adorn it; and God's house is neglected!

Verse 10. *Therefore the heaven over you is stayed from dew*] It appears from the following verse that God had sent a drought upon the

A. M. 3484 B. C. 520 Ol. LXV. 1 Anno Tarquinii Superbi, R. Roman., 15

and upon men, and upon cattle,
and [t]upon all the labour of the
hands.
12 [u]Then Zerubbabel the son
of Shealtiel, and Joshua the son of Josedech,
the high priest, with all the remnant of the
people, obeyed the voice of the LORD their God,
and the words of Haggai the prophet, as the
LORD their God had sent him, and the people
did fear before the LORD.
13 Then spake Haggai the LORD'S messenger
in the LORD'S message unto the people,
saying, [v]I *am* with you, saith
the LORD.
14 And [w]the LORD stirred up
the spirit of Zerubbabel the son
of Shealtiel, [x]governor of Judah, and the
spirit of Joshua the son of Josedech, the high
priest, and the spirit of all the remnant of
the people: [y]and they came and did work in
the house of the LORD of hosts, their God.
15 In the four and twentieth day of the
sixth month, in the second year of Darius the
king.

A. M. 3484 B. C. 520 Ol. LXV. 1 Anno Tarquinii Superbi, R. Roman., 15

---

[t]Chap. ii. 17——[u]Ezra v. 2——[v]Matt. xxviii. 20; Romans viii. 31——[w]2 Chron. xxxvi. 22; Ezra i. 1——[x]Chap. ii. 21——[y]Ezra v. 2, 8

---

land, which threatened them with scarcity and famine.

Verse 12. *Then Zerubbabel*] The threatening of Haggai had its proper effect. The civil governor, the high priest, and the whole of the people, united together to do the work. When the authority of God is acknowledged, his words will be carefully obeyed.

Verse 13. *Then spake Haggai*] He was the *Lord's messenger*, and he came with the *Lord's message*, and consequently he came with *authority*. He is called מלאך יהוה *malach Yehovah, the angel of Jehovah*, just as the *pastors* of the seven Asiatic Churches are called ANGELS *of the Churches*, Rev. i. 2.

I am *with you, saith the Lord.*] Here was high encouragement. What may not a man do when God is his helper?

Verse 14. *And the Lord stirred up the spirit*] It is not only necessary that the *judgment* should be enlightened, but the *soul* must be *invigorated* by the Spirit of God, before any good work can be effectually done.

Verse 15. *In the four and twentieth day*] Haggai received his commission on the *first* day of this month and by the *twenty-fourth* day he had so completely succeeded that he had the satisfaction to see the whole people engaged heartily in the Lord's work; they left their own houses to build that of the Lord. Here was a *faithful reprover*, and he found *obedient ears;* and the Lord's work was done, for *the people had a mind to work.*

CHAPTER II

When this prophecy was uttered, about four *years before the temple was finished, and* sixty-eight *after the former one was destroyed, it appears that some old men among the Jews were greatly dispirited on account of its being so much inferior in magnificence to that of Solomon. Compare* Ezra iii. 12. *To raise the spirits of the people, and encourage them to proceed with the work, the prophet assures them that the glory of the second temple should be greater than that of the first, alluding perhaps to the glorious doctrines which should be preached in it by Jesus Christ and his apostles,* 1–9. *He then shows the people that the oblations brought by their priests could not sanctify them while they were unclean by their neglect of the temple; and to convince them that the difficult times they had experienced during that neglect proceeded from this cause, he promises fruitful seasons from that day forward,* 10–19. *The concluding verses contain a prediction of the mighty revolutions that should take place by the setting up of the kingdom of Christ under the type of Zerubbabel,* 20–23. *As the time which elapsed between the date of the prophecy and the dreadful concussion of nations is termed in verse* 6, A LITTLE WHILE, *the words may likewise have reference to some temporal revolutions then near, such as the commotions of Babylon in the reign of Darius, the Macedonian conquests in Persia, and the wars between the successors of Alexander; but the aspect of the prophecy is more directly to the amazing victories of the Romans, who, in the time of Haggai and Zechariah, were on the* VERY EVE *of their successful career, and in the lapse of a few centuries subjugated the whole habitable globe; and therefore, in a very good sense, God may be said by these people to have shaken "the heavens, and the earth, and the sea, and the dry land;" and thus to have prepared the way for the opening of the Gospel dispensation. See* Heb. xii. 25–29. *Others have referred this prophecy to the period of our Lord's second advent, to which there is no doubt it is also applicable; and when it will be in the most signal manner fulfilled. That the convulsion of the nations introducing this most stupendous event will be very great and terrible, is sufficiently plain from* Isaiah xxxiv., xxxv., *as well as from many other passages of holy writ.*

A. M. 3484 IN the seventh *month,* in the
B. C. 520 one and twentieth *day* of
Ol. LXV. 1 the month, came the word of the
Anno Tarquinii Superbi, R. Roman., 15 LORD [a]by the prophet Haggai,
saying,
2 Speak now to Zerubbabel the son of Shealtiel, governor of Judah, and to Joshua the son of Josedech, the high priest, and to the residue of the people, saying,
3 [b]Who *is* left among you that saw this house in her first glory and how do ye see it now? [c]*is it* not in your eyes in comparison of it as nothing?
4 Yet now, [d]be strong, O Zerubbabel, saith the LORD; and be strong, O Joshua, son of
Josedech, the high priest; and be A. M. 3484
strong, all ye people of the land, B. C. 520
saith the LORD, and work: for I Ol. LXV. 1
am with you, saith the LORD of Anno Tarquinii Superbi, R. Roman., 15
hosts:
5 [e]*According to* the word that I covenanted with you when ye came out of Egypt, so [f]my Spirit remaineth among you: [g]fear ye not.
6 For thus saith the LORD of hosts: [h]Yet once, it *is* a little while, and [i]I will shake the heavens, and the earth, and the sea, and the dry *land;*
7 And I will shake all nations, [k]and the Desire of all nations shall come; and I will fill this house with glory, saith the LORD of hosts.

---

[a]Heb. *by the hand of*——[b]Ezra iii. 12——[c]Zech. iv. 10
[d]Zech. viii. 9——[e]Exod. xxix. 45, 46

[f]Neh. ix. 20; Isa. lxiii. 11——[g]Isa. vii. 4——[h]Ver. 21; Heb. xii. 26——[i]Joel iii. 16——[k]Gen. xlix. 10; Mal. iii. 1

NOTES ON CHAP. II

Verse 1. *In the seventh* month] This was a *new* message, and intended to prevent discouragement, and excite them to greater diligence in their work.

Verse 3. *Who* is *left among you that saw this house in her first glory?*] Who of you has seen the *temple* built by *Solomon?* The foundation of the present house had been laid about *fifty-three* years after the destruction of the temple built by Solomon and though this prophecy was uttered *fifteen* years after the foundation of this second temple, yet there might still survive some of those who had seen the temple of Solomon.

Is it *not in your eyes*] Most certainly the Jews at this time had neither *men* nor *means* to make any such splendid building as that erected by Solomon. The *present* was as nothing when compared with the *former.*

Verse 4. *Yet now be strong*] Do not let this discourage you. The chief glory of the temple is not its splendid building, but my *presence;* and as *I covenanted to be with you* when ye came out of Egypt, so I will fulfil my covenant; for *my Spirit remaineth among you, fear not;* ver. 5. What is the most splendid cathedral, if God be not in it, influencing all by his presence and Spirit? But he will not be in it unless there be a messenger of the Lord there, and unless he deliver the Lord's message.

Verse 6. *Yet once, it* is *a little while, and I will shake the heavens*] When the law was given on Mount Sinai, there was an earthquake that shook the whole mountain, Exod. xix. 18. "The political or religious revolutions which were to be effected in the world, or both, are here," says Abp. *Newcome,* "referred to; compare ver. 21, 22; Matt. xxiv. 29; Heb. xii. 26-28. The political ones began in the overthrow of the Persian monarchy by Alexander, within two centuries after this prediction; and if the Messiah's kingdom be meant, which is my opinion, this was erected in somewhat more than five centuries after the second year of Darius; a short period of time when compared with that which elapsed from the creation to the giving of the law, or from the giving of the law to the coming of the Messiah's kingdom. It must be understood that the word אחת *achath, once,* has a clear sense, if understood of the *evangelical age;* for *many* political revolutions succeeded, as the conquest of Darius Codomanus, and the various fortunes of Alexander's successors; but only one great and final *religious revolution.*"—*Newcome.*

Verse 7. *And the Desire of all nations shall come*] The present Hebrew text is as follows: ובאו חמדת כל הגוים. This is a difficult place if understood of a *person:* but חמדת *chemdath, desire,* cannot well agree with באו *bau, they shall come.* It is true that some learned men suppose that חמדות *chemdoth, desirable things,* may have been the original reading: but this is supported by no MS., nor is באו found in the *singular* number in any. It is generally understood of the *desirable* or *valuable things* which the different nations should bring into the temple; and it is certain that many rich presents were brought into this temple. All are puzzled with it. But the principal difficulty lies in the verb ובאו *ubau, they shall come.* If we found ובאה חמדת *ubaa chemdath* in the singular, then it would read as in our text, *And the Desire of all nations shall come:* but no such reading appears in any MS.; nor is it *fairly* acknowledged, except by the *Vulgate,* which reads, Et veniet desideratus cunctis gentibus, "And that which is desired," or the desired Person, "shall come to all nations." In ver. 7 God says *he will shake* or stir up *all nations;* that these nations shall *bring their desirable things;* that the house shall be *filled with God's glory;* that the *silver* and *gold,* which these nations are represented as bringing by way of gifts, are *the Lord's;* and that the glory of this latter house shall exceed the former. Bp. *Chandler* labours to vindicate the present translation; but he makes rash assertions, and is abandoned by the Hebrew text. The בא *ba, to come,* is often used in the sense of *bring,* and that חמדת *chemdath, desire,* may be considered as the *plural* for חמדות, having the point *holem* instead of the ו *vau,* and thus mean *desirable things,* will not be denied by those who are acquainted with the

A. M. 3484
B. C. 520
Ol. LXV. 1
Anno Tarquinii Superbi,
R. Roman., 15

8 The silver *is* mine, and the gold *is* mine, saith the LORD of hosts.

9 [l]The glory of this latter house shall be greater than of the former, saith the LORD of hosts: and in this place will I give [m]peace, saith the LORD of hosts.

10 In the four and twentieth *day* of the ninth *month,* in the second year of Darius, came the word of the Lord by Haggai the prophet, saying,

11 Thus saith the LORD of hosts; [n]Ask now the priests *concerning* the law, saying,

12 If one bear holy flesh in the skirt of his garment, and with his skirt do touch bread, or pottage, or wine, or oil, or any meat, shall it be holy: And the priests answered and said, No.

13 Then said Haggai, If *one that is* [o]unclean by a dead body touch any of these, shall it be unclean? And the priests answered and said, It shall be unclean.

A. M. 3484
B. C. 520
Ol. LXV. 1
Anno Tarquinii Superbi,
R. Roman., 15

14 Then answered Haggai, and said, [p]So *is* this people, and so *is* this nation before me, saith the LORD; and so *is* every work of their hands; and that which they offer there *is* unclean.

15 And now, I pray you, [q]consider from this day and upward, from before a stone was laid upon a stone in the temple of the LORD:

16 Since those *days* were, [r]when *one* came to a heap of twenty *measures,* there were *but* ten: when *one* came to the press-fat for to draw out fifty *vessels* out of the press, there were *but* twenty.

17 [s]I smote you with blasting and with mildew and with hail [t]in all the labours of your hands; [u]yet ye *turned* not to me, saith the LORD.

---

[l]John i. 14——[m]Psa. lxxxv. 8, 9; Luke ii. 14; Eph. ii. 14——[n]Lev. x. 10, 11; Deut. xxxiii. 10; Mal. ii. 7 [o]Num. xix. 11——[p]Titus i. 15

[q]Chap. i. 5——[r]Chap. i. 6, 9; Zech. viii. 10——[s]Deut. xxviii. 22; 1 Kings viii. 37; chap. i. 9; Amos iv. 9 [t]Chap. i. 11——[u]Jer. v. 3; Amos iv. 6, 8, 9, 10, 11

---

genius and construction of the Hebrew language. Bp. *Chandler* thinks that בא, *he came,* cannot be used of *things,* but of *persons* only. Here he is widely mistaken, for it is used of *days* perpetually; and of the *ark,* 2 Sam. vi. 9; and of *mounts coming* against Jerusalem, Jer. xxxii. 24; and of *trees coming* to adorn the temple, Isa. lx. 13; and of *silver* and *gold coming* into the temple, Josh. vi. 19; and Jer. vi. 20, Why doth *incense come* to me? See Abp. *Secker's* notes. I cannot see how the words can apply to Jesus Christ, even if the construction were less embarrassed than it is; because I cannot see how he could be called THE DESIRE OF ALL NATIONS. The whole seems to be a metaphorical description of the *Church of Christ,* and of his filling it with all the excellences of the Gentile world, when the fulness of the Gentiles shall be brought in.

Verse 9. *And in this place will I give peace*] שלום *shalom, a peace-offering,* as well as *peace* itself; or *Jesus Christ,* who is called the *Prince of peace,* through whom *peace* is proclaimed between God and man, between man and his fellows; and through whom *peace* is established in the *disconsolate soul.* And at this temple this *peace* was first promulgated and proclaimed.

But it is said that *the glory of this latter house shall be greater than of the former.* Now this cannot be said because Jesus Christ made his *personal* appearance in that temple, or rather in that built by Herod; for, though we allow that Jesus Christ is *equal* with God, we do not grant that he is *greater.* Now the *first temple* was the *dwelling-place of God:* here he manifested his glory between the cherubim, and it was his *constant residence* for more than *four hundred* years. But the *glory of this latter house was greater* because under it the grand scheme of human salvation was exhibited, and the redemption price paid down for a lost world. As all probably applies to the *Christian Church,* the *real house of God,* its glory was most certainly *greater* than any glory which was ever possessed by that of the Jews. See on ver. 22, 23.

Verse 10. *In the four and twentieth* day *of the ninth* month] Three months after they had begun to rebuild the temple, Haggai is ordered to go and put *two questions* to the priests. 1. If one bear holy flesh in the skirt of his garment, and he touch any thing with his skirt, is that thing made holy? The priests answered, No! ver. 12. 2. If one has touched a *dead body,* and thereby become unclean, does he communicate his uncleanness to whatever he may *touch?* And the priests answered, YES! ver. 13.

Verse 14. *Then answered Haggai—So* is *this people*] As an *unclean* man communicates his uncleanness to every thing he touches, so are ye unclean; and whatever ye have hitherto done is polluted in the sight of God. For your neglect of my temple has made you unclean, as if you had contracted legal pollution by touching a dead body.

Verse 16. *Since those* days *were*] I have shown my displeasure against you, by sending *blasting* and *mildew;* and so poor have been your *crops* that a heap of corn which should have produced *twenty measures* produced only *ten;* and that quantity of *grapes* which in other years would have produced *fifty* measures, through their poverty, smallness, &c., produced only *twenty.* And this has been the case ever since the *first stone was laid in this temple;* for your hearts were not right with me, and therefore I blasted you in all the labours of your hands; and *yet ye have not* turned *to me,* ver. 17.

A. M. 3484
B. C. 520
Ol. LXV. 1
Anno Tarquinii Superbi,
R. Roman., 15

18 Consider now from this
day and upward, from the four
and twentieth day of the ninth
month, even from [v]the day that
the foundation of the LORD's temple was laid,
consider *it*.
19 [w]Is the seed yet in the barn? yea, as
yet the vine, and the fig tree, and the pomegranate,
and the olive tree, hath not brought
forth: from this day will I bless *you*.
20 And again the word of the LORD came
unto Haggai, in the four and twentieth day
of the month, saying,
21 Speak to Zerubbabel, [x]governor of Judah,
saying, [y]I will shake the heavens
and the earth;
22 And [z]I will overthrow the
throne of kingdoms, and I will
destroy the strength of the kingdoms of the
heathen; and [a]I will overthrow the chariots,
and those that ride in them; and the horses
and their riders shall come down, every one
by the sword of his brother.
23 In that day, saith the LORD of hosts,
will I take thee, O Zerubbabel, my servant,
the son of Shealtiel, saith the LORD, [b]and
will make thee as a signet: for [c]I have chosen
thee, saith the LORD of hosts.

[v]Ezek. viii. 9——[w]Zech. viii. 12——[x]Ch. i. 14——[y]Ver. 6, 7; Heb. xii. 26——[z]Dan. ii. 44; Matt. xxiv. 7

[a]Mic. v. 10; Zech. iv. 6; ix. 10——[b]Cant. viii. 6; Jer. xxii. 24; Ecclus. xlix. 11——[c]Isa. xlii. 1; xliii. 10

Verse 18. *Consider now from this day*] I will now change my conduct towards you: *from this day* that ye have begun heartily to rebuild my temple, and restore my worship, *I will bless you.* Whatever you *sow*, whatever you *plant*, shall be blessed; your land shall be fruitful, and ye shall have abundant crops of all sorts.

Verse 20. *Again the word of the Lord came*] This was a *second* communication in the same day.

Verse 21. *I will shake the heavens and the earth*] *Calmet* supposes that the invasion of *Cambyses*, and his death, are what the prophet has in view by this *shaking of the heavens and the earth:* but this invasion and defeat happened *three years before* they had begun to work at the temple; and how could it be made a matter of *interest* to Zerubbabel? *Calmet* answers this, by translating the words in the *past tense;* and shows that the fact was recalled to Zerubbabel's attention, to fix his confidence in God, &c. Bp. *Newcome* says we may well understand this and the *twenty-second* verse of the calamity undergone by Babylon in the reign of Darius; of the Macedonian conquests in Persia; and of the wars which the successors of Alexander waged against each other: others understand it of the Romans.

Verse 23. *In that day, saith the Lord*] Some think, says this same learned writer, that *Zerubbabel* is put here for his *people* and *posterity:* but it may well be said that the commotions foretold began in the rebellion of Babylon, which Darius besieged and took; and exercised great cruelties upon its inhabitants.—*Herod.* lib. iii., sec. 220. *Justin.* i. 10. *Prideaux* places this event in the *fifth* year of Darius; others, with more probability, in the *eighth* year. Compare Zech. ii. 9.

And will make thee as a signet] I will exalt thee to high dignity, power, and trust, of which the *seal* was the instrument or sign in those days. Thou shalt be under my peculiar care, and shalt be to me very precious. See Jer. xxii. 24; Cant. viii. 6; and see the notes on these two places.

For I have chosen thee] He had an important and difficult work to do, and it was necessary that he should be assured of God's especial care and protection during the whole.

ON the *three* last verses of this prophecy a sensible and pious correspondent sends me the following illustration, which I cheerfully insert. Though in many respects different from that given above, yet I believe that the kingdom of Christ is particularly designed in this prophecy.

"I think there is an apparent difficulty in this passage, because the wars of the Persians and Babylonians were not so interesting to the rising commonwealth of the Jews as many subsequent events of *less* note in the world, but which were more directly levelled at their own national prosperity; and yet neither the one nor the other could be termed 'a shaking of the heavens and the earth, and an overthrow of the throne of kingdoms.'

"I know not if the following view may be admitted as an explanation of this difficult passage. I take 'the shaking of the heavens and earth' here (as in ver. 6) to have a more distant and comprehensive meaning than can belong to Zerubbabel's time, or to his immediate posterity; and that it extends not only to the overthrow of kingdoms *then* existing, but of the future great monarchies of the world; and not excepting even the civil and ecclesiastical establishments of the Jews themselves. For I take 'the heavens,' in the prophetic language, uniformly to denote the true Church, and never the superstitions and idols of the nations.

"What, then, are we to understand by the *promise* made to Zerubbabel, 'I will make thee as a signet?' In the first place, the *restitution* of the religious and civil polity of the people of Israel, conformably to the promises afterwards given in the *four* first chapters of Zechariah. And, secondly, as the royal signet is the instrument by which kings give validity to laws, and thereby unity and consistence to their empire; so Jehovah, the God and King of Israel, condescends to promise he will employ *Zerubbabel* as his instrument of gathering and uniting the people again as a distinguished nation; and that such should be the *permanency* of their political existence, that, whilst other nations and mighty empires should be overthrown, and their very *name* blotted out under heaven, the Jews should ever remain a distinct people, even in the wreck of their own government, and the loss of all which rendered their religion splendid and attractive.

"In confirmation of this interpretation, I would refer to the threatening denounced against Jeconiah, (called Coniah, Jer. xxii.,) the *last* reigning king of Judah, and the progenitor of Zerubbabel. I apprehend I may be authorized to read Jer. xxii. 24 *thus:* 'As I live, saith the Lord, though Coniah, the son of Jehoiakim, king of Judah, *be the signet* upon my right hand, yet will I pluck thee thence, and I will give thee into the hand of them that seek thy life,' &c.

"If it be considered that the kings of Judah were in an *especial* and peculiar manner the delegates of Jehovah, governing in his name and by his authority, a peculiar propriety will appear in their being resembled to *signets*, or royal seals contained in rings. Compare Gen. xli. 42; Esth. iii. 10, 12, viii. 2, 8; Dan. vi. 7. And the promise to Zerubbabel will be equivalent to those which clearly predict the preservation of the Jewish people by the Divine command. see Zech. ii.; and the faithfulness of God to his covenant concerning the Messiah, who should be born of the seed of Abraham, and in the family of David, of whose throne he was the rightful Proprietor.

"According to this view, by the promise, 'In that day—I will make thee as a signet,' &c., must be understood, that the preservation of the Jews as a distinct people, *when all the great empires of the heathen were overthrown*, would *manifest* the honour now conferred on Zerubbabel as *the instrument of their restoration* after the Babylonish captivity. Thus the promise to Abraham, Gen. xii., 'I will make of thee a great nation—and in thee shall all families of the earth be blessed,' evidently referred to a very distant future period and the honour connected with it could not be enjoyed by Abraham during his mortal life."

M. A. B.

I think, however, that we have lived to see the spirit of this prophecy fulfilled. The earth *has been* shaken; another shaking, and time shall be swallowed up in eternity.

INTRODUCTION TO THE BOOK

OF THE

PROPHET ZECHARIAH

ZECHARIAH, the eleventh of the twelve minor prophets, was son of Berechiah, and grandson of Iddo. He returned from Babylon with Zerubbabel: and began to prophesy in the second year of the reign of Darius, son of Hystaspes, in the year of the world 3484; before Christ, 516; before the vulgar era, 520; in the eighth month of the holy year; and two months after Haggai had begun to prophesy.

These two prophets, with united zeal, encouraged at the same time the people to go on with the work of the temple, which had been discontinued for some years.

The time and place of the birth of Zechariah are unknown. Some will have him to have been born at Babylon, during the captivity; others think he was born at Jerusalem, before the tribes of Judah and Benjamin were carried away. Some maintain that he was a priest; but others affirm that he was no priest. Many say he was the immediate son of Iddo; others believe, with much more reason, that he was son of Berechiah, and grandson of Iddo.

He has been confounded with one Zechariah, the son of Barachiah, who lived in the time of Isaiah; and with Zechariah, the father of John the Baptist; which opinion is plainly incongruous. Lastly, he has been thought to be Zechariah the son of Barachiah, whom our Saviour mentions, and says he was killed between the temple and the altar; though no such thing is anywhere said of our prophet. A tomb is shown to this day at the foot of the Mount of Olives, which, it is pretended, belongs to the prophet Zechariah. *Dorotheus* maintains that he was buried in a place called Bethariah, one hundred and fifty furlongs from Jerusalem.

Zechariah is the longest and the most obscure of all the twelve minor prophets. His style is interrupted, and without connection. His prophecies concerning the Messiah are more particular and express than those of the other prophets. Some modern critics, as *Mede* and *Hammond*, have been of opinion that the *ninth*, *tenth*, and *eleventh* chapters of this prophet were written by Jeremiah; because in Matthew, chap. xxvii. 9, 10, under the name of Jeremiah, we find quoted Zechariah; (chap. xi. 12;) and as the aforesaid chapters make but one continued discourse, they concluded from thence that all three belonged to Jeremiah. But it is much more natural to suppose that, by some unlucky mistake, the name of Jeremiah has slipped into the text of St. Matthew instead of that of Zechariah.

The prophet Zechariah exactly foretold the siege of Babylon by Darius, son of Hystaspes. This prince laid siege to that rebellious city at the beginning of the *fifth* year of his reign, and reduced it at the end of *twenty* months. The prophets Isaiah and Jeremiah had foretold this calamity, and had admonished the Jews, that inhabited there to make their escape when they perceived the time draw nigh. Isaiah says to them, "Go ye forth to Babylon, flee from the Chaldeans; with a voice of singing declare ye, tell this, utter it even to the end of the earth; say ye, The Lord hath redeemed his servant Jacob." And Jeremiah says, "Remove out of the midst of Babylon, and go forth out of the land of the Chaldeans, and be as the he-goats before the flocks." And elsewhere, "Flee out of the midst of Babylon, and deliver every man his soul; be not cut off in her iniquity: for this is the time of the Lord's vengeance, He will render unto her a recompense." Lastly, Zechariah, a little before the time of her fall, writes thus to the Jews that were still in this city: "Ho, ho, come forth, and flee from the land of the north, saith the Lord; for I have spread you abroad as the four winds of heaven, saith the Lord. Deliver thyself, O Zion, that dwellest with the daughter of Babylon. For thus saith the Lord of hosts, after the glory hath he sent me unto the nations which spoiled you, for he that toucheth you, toucheth the apple of his eye. For, behold, I will shake mine hand upon them, and they shall be a spoil to their servants; and ye shall know that the Lord of hosts hath sent me."

It is probable that the Jews took advantage of these admonitions, and returned from Babylon into their country; or, at least, withdrew into a place of more security till the city was taken. We do not hear, either from the history or the prophecies, that they suffered any thing by this siege, or that Darius, son of Hystaspes, bore them any grudge for the revolt of Babylon; which seems to indicate that they had no part in it.

The Mohammedans do not distinguish between the prophet Zechariah, and Zachariah the father of John the Baptist. Some of them make him to be descended from David; and others, from Levi. By an anachronism that is still more insupportable, these confound Mary, the mother of Jesus Christ, with Mary or Miriam, the sister of Moses, which they derive even from the Koran itself.

The author of Tarik Montekhib relates that, when Jesus Christ was born of the virgin, the prophet Zechariah could not believe that a child could be born without a father; and that, declaring his sentiments upon this point, the Jews entertained a suspicion of him, and obliged him to betake himself to flight. He withdrew; and hid himself in a hollow oak, which the Jews sawed in two.

Such is the ignorance of the Mussulmans as regards the history both of the Old and New Testaments.

THE BOOK

OF THE

PROPHET ZECHARIAH

Chronological Notes relative to this Book

Year from the Creation, according to Archbishop Usher, 3484.—Year of the Julian Period, 4194.—Year of the Jewish era of the world, 3241.—Year from the Flood, 1828.—Year from the vocation of Abram, 1401.—Year since the first celebration of the Olympic games in Elis, by the Idæi Dactyli, 934.—Year since the destruction of Troy, according to the general account, 664.—Year since the foundation of the monarchy of the Israelites by the Divine appointment of Saul to the regal dignity, 576.—Year from the foundation of Solomon's temple, 492.—Year from the division of Solomon's monarchy into the kingdoms of Israel and Judah, 456.—Year since the re-establishment of the Olympic games in Elis by Lycurgus, Iphitus, and Cleosthenes, 365.—Year since the conquest of Corœbus at Olympia, usually called the first Olympiad, 257.—First year of the *sixty-fifth* Olympiad.—Year from the building of Rome, according to the Varronian or generally received computation, 234.—Year from the building of Rome, according to Cato and the Fasti Consulares, 233.—Year from the building of Rome, according to Polybius the historian, 232.—Year from the building of Rome, according to Fabius Pictor, 228.—Year of the era of Nabonassar, 228.—Year since the destruction of the kingdom of Israel by Shalmaneser, king of Assyria, 202.—Year since the destruction of the kingdom of Judah by Nebuchadnezzar, king of Babylon, 68.—Year since the destruction of the Chaldean empire by the Persians, 18.—Year before the birth of Christ, 516.—Year before the vulgar era of Christ's nativity, 520.—Cycle of the Sun, 22.—Cycle of the Moon, 14.—Second year of Darius I., king of Persia.—Twenty-eighth year of Amyntas, king of Macedon.—Seventh year of Demaratus, king of Lacedæmon, of the family of the Proclidæ.—Eleventh year of Cleomenes, king of Lacedæmon, of the family of the Eurysthenidæ.—Fifteenth year of Tarquinius Superbus, the last king of the Romans.—This was about twelve years before the commencement of the consular government. According to some chronologers this was the age of Confucius.

CHAPTER I

The prophet earnestly exhorts the people to repentance, that they may escape such punishments as had been inflicted on their fathers, 1–6. *The vision of the* horses, *with the signification,* 7–11. *The angel of the Lord successfully intercedes in behalf of Jerusalem,* 12–17. *The vision of the* four horns, *and of the* four carpenters, 18–21.

A. M. 3484 B. C. 520 Ol. LXV. 1 Anno Tarquinii Superbi, R. Roman., 15

IN the eighth month, [a]in the
second year of Darius, came
the word of the LORD [b]unto
Zechariah, the son of Berechiah,
the son of Iddo the prophet, saying,

A. M. 3484 B. C. 520 Ol. LXV. 1 Anno Tarquinii Superbi, R. Roman., 15

2 The LORD hath been [c]sore
displeased with your fathers.
3 Therefore say thou unto
them, Thus saith the LORD of
hosts; Turn [d]ye unto me, saith the LORD of

[a]Ezra iv. 24; Hag. i. 1——[b]Ezra v. 1; Matt. xxiii. 35
[c]Heb. *with displeasure*

[d]Jer. xxv. 5; xxxv. 15; Mic. vii. 19; Mal. iii. 7; Luke xv. 20; James iv. 8

NOTES ON CHAP. I

Verse 1. *In the eighth month, in the second year of Darius*] This was *Darius Hystaspes;* and from this date we find that Zechariah began to prophecy just *two months* after *Haggai.*

Son of Iddo] There are a number of various readings on this name, עדו *Iddo,* and עדוא *Iddo,* both in MSS. and in editions; but they are only different ways of writing the same name.

Verse 2. *The Lord hath been sore displeased with your fathers.*] For their ingratitude, idolatry, iniquity, and general rebellion.

Verse 3. *Turn ye unto me*] This shows that they had *power* to return, if they would but *use* it.

A. M. 3484
B. C. 520
Ol. LXV. 1
Anno Tarquinii Superbi,
R. Roman., 15

hosts, and I will turn unto you, saith the LORD of hosts.

4 Be ye not as your fathers, [e]unto whom the former prophets have cried, saying, Thus saith the LORD of hosts; [f]Turn ye now from your evil ways, and *from* your evil doings: but they did not hear, nor hearken unto me, saith the LORD.

5 Your fathers, where *are* they? and the prophets, do they live for ever?

6 But [g]my words and my statutes, which I commanded my servants the prophets, did they not [h]take hold of your fathers? and they returned and said, [i]Like as the LORD of hosts thought to do unto us, according to our ways, and according to our doings, so hath he dealt with us.

7 Upon the four and twentieth day of the eleventh month, which *is* the month Sebat, in the second year of Darius, came the word of the LORD unto Zechariah, the son of Berechiah, the son of Iddo the prophet, saying,

[e]2 Chron. xxxvi. 15, 16——[f]Isa. xxxi. 6; Jer. iii. 12; xviii. 11; Ezek. xviii. 30; Hos. xiv. 1——[g]Isa. lv. 1
[h]Or, *overtake*——[i]Lam. i. 18; ii. 17

And I will turn unto you] I will show you mercy and grant you salvation, if you will *use the grace I have already given you.* Men are *lost*, because they *turn not* unto God; but no man is lost because he had not *power* to return. God gives this, and he will require it.

Verse 5. *Your fathers, where* are *they?*] *Israel* has been destroyed and ruined in the bloody wars with the *Assyrians;* and *Judah*, in those with the *Chaldeans.*

The prophets, do they live for ever?] They also, who spoke unto your fathers, are dead; but their *predictions* remain; and the *events*, which have taken place according to those predictions, prove that God sent them.

Verse 6. *Did they not take hold of your fathers?*] Every thing happened according to the predictions, and they were obliged to acknowledge this; and yet they would not turn from their evil way.

Verse 7. *Upon the four and twentieth day of the eleventh month*] This revelation was given about *three months* after the former, and *two months* after they had recommenced the building of the temple.

Sebat] Answers to a part of our February. See Hag. ii. 18.

Verse 8. *I saw by night*] The time was emblematical of the affliction under which the Jews groaned.

A man] An angel in the form of a man: supposed to have been the *Lord Jesus;* who seems to have appeared often in this way, as a prelude to his incarnation; see Josh. v. 13; Ezek. i. 26; Dan. vii. 13, and x. 5. The same, probably, that appeared to Joshua with a drawn sword, as the *captain of the Lord's host.* Josh. v. 13-15.

A. M. 3484
B. C. 520
Ol. LXV. 1
Anno Tarquinii Superbi,
R. Roman., 15

8 I saw by night, and behold [k]a man riding upon a red horse, and he stood among the myrtle trees that *were* in the bottom; and behind him *were there* [l]red horses, [m]speckled, and white.

9 Then said I, O my lord, what *are* these? And the angel that talked with me said unto me, I will show thee what these *be*.

10 And the man that stood among the myrtle trees, answered and said, [n]These *are they* whom the LORD hath sent to walk to and fro through the earth.

11 [o]And they answered the angel of the LORD that stood among the myrtle trees, and said, We have walked to and fro through the earth, and, behold, all the earth sitteth still, and is at rest.

12 Then the angel of the LORD answered and said, [p]O LORD of hosts, how long wilt thou not have mercy on Jerusalem, and on the cities of Judah, against which thou hast had indignation [q]these threescore and ten years?

[k]Josh. v. 13; Rev. vi. 4——[l]Chap. vi. 2-7——[m]Or, *bay*——[n]Heb. i. 14——[o]Psa. ciii. 20, 21——[p]Psa. cii. 13; Rev. vi. 10——[q]Jer. xxv. 11, 12; Dan. ix. 2; ch. vii. 5

A red horse] An emblem of war and bloodshed.

Among the myrtle trees] This tree was an emblem of *peace;* intimating that all war was shortly to end. But some think these trees are emblematical of the true followers of Christ.

And behind him were there *red horses*] Probably pointing out the *different orders* of angels in the heavenly host, which are employed by Christ in the defence of his Church. The different *colours* may point out the *gradations* in power, authority, and excellence, of the angelic natures which are employed between Christ and men.

Verse 9. *O my lord, what* are *these*] The angel here mentioned was distinct from those mentioned in the *eighth* verse; he who talked with the prophet, ver. 13.

Verse 10. *The man that stood among the myrtle trees*] The angel of the Covenant, as above, ver. 11.

Whom the Lord hath sent] Who are constituted guardians of the land.

Verse 11. *All the earth sitteth still, and is at rest.*] There is general *peace* through the Persian empire, and other states connected with Judea; but the Jews are still in *affliction;* their city is not yet restored, nor their temple built.

Verse 12. *Then the angel of the Lord*] He who was among the myrtles—the Lord Jesus.

O Lord of hosts, how long] Jesus Christ was not only the "Lamb slain from the foundation of the world," but was always the sole *Mediator* and *intercessor* between God and man.

These threescore and ten years?] This cannot mean the duration of the captivity for that was nearly twenty years past. It must mean simply the time that had elapsed from the de-

A. M. 3484
B. C. 520
Ol. LXV. 1
Anno Tarquinii Superbi, R. Roman., 15

13 And the LORD answered the angel that talked with me *with* [r]good words, *and* comfortable words.

14 So the angel that communed with me said unto me, Cry thou, saying, Thus saith the LORD of hosts; I am [s]jealous for Jerusalem and for Zion with a great jealousy.

15 And I am very sore displeased with the heathen *that are* at ease: for [t]I was but a little displeased, and they helped forward the affliction.

16 Therefore thus saith the LORD; [u]I am returned to Jerusalem with mercies: my house shall be built in it, saith the LORD of hosts, and [v]a line shall be stretched forth upon Jerusalem.

17 Cry yet, saying, Thus saith the Lord of hosts; My cities through [w]prosperity shall yet be spread abroad; [x]and the LORD shall yet comfort Zion, and [y]shall yet choose Jerusalem.

18 Then lifted I up mine eyes, and saw, and behold four horns.

19 And I said unto the angel that talked with me, What *be* these: And he answered me, [z]These *are* the horns which have scattered Judah, Israel, and Jerusalem.

20 And the LORD showed me four carpenters.

21 Then said I, What come these to do? And he spake, saying, These *are* the horns which have scattered Judah, so that no man did lift up his head: but these are come to fray them, to cast out the horns of the Gentiles, which [a]lifted up *their* horn over the land of Judah to scatter it.

[r]Jer. xxix. 10——[s]Joel viii. 18; ch. viii. 2——[t]Isa. xlvii. 6——[u]Isa. xii. 1; ch. ii. 10; viii. 3——[v]Ch. ii. 1, 2

[w]Heb. *good*——[x]Isa. li. 3——[y]Isa. xiv. 1; ch. ii. 12; iii. 2——[z]Ezra iv. 1, 4, 7; v. 3——[a]Psa. lxxv. 4, 5

struction of the temple to the time in which the angel spoke. As the temple was destroyed in the *nineteenth* year of Nebuchadnezzar, and this vision took place in the *second* year of Darius, the term of *seventy* years was completed, or nearly so, between these two periods.

Verse 13. *The Lord answered the angel*] And the angel told the prophet that the answer was gracious and comfortable. This answer is given in the next verse.

Verse 14. *I am jealous for Jerusalem*] I have for them a strong affection; and indignation against their enemies.

Verse 15. *I was but a little displeased*] I was justly displeased with my people, and I gave their enemies a commission against them; but they carried this far beyond my design by oppression and cruelty; and now they shall suffer in their turn.

Verse 16. *I am returned to Jerusalem with mercies*] Before, he came to them in *judgments;* and the principal mercy is, the house of the Lord shall be rebuilt, and the ordinances of the Lord re-established.

And a line shall be stretched forth] The circuit shall be determined, and the city built according to the *line* marked out.

Verse 17. *My cities—shall yet be spread abroad*] The whole land of Judea shall be inhabited, and the ruined cities restored.

Verse 18. *And behold four horns.*] Denoting *four powers* by which the Jews had been oppressed; the *Assyrians, Persians, Chaldeans,* and *Egyptians.* Or these enemies may be termed *four,* in reference to the *four cardinal points of the heavens,* whence they came:—

1. NORTH. The Assyrians and Babylonians.
2. EAST. The Moabites and Ammonites.
3. SOUTH. The Egyptians.
4. WEST. The Philistines. See *Martin.*

Verse 20. *Four carpenters.*] Four other *powers,* who should defeat the powers intended by the *horns.* These are the same as the *four chariots* mentioned chap. vi. 1, 2, 3, 6, 7. The *first* was NABOPOLASSAR, father of Nebuchadnezzar, who overturned the empire of the *Assyrians.* The *second* was CYRUS, who destroyed the empire of the *Chaldeans.* The *third* was ALEXANDER *the Great,* who destroyed the empire of the *Persians.* And the *fourth* was PTOLEMY, who rendered himself master of *Egypt.* Some of these had already been cast down; the rest were to follow. *Calmet* gives this interpretation, and vindicates it at length.

Verse 21. *These are come to fray them*] To break, pound, and reduce them to powder. *Fray,* from the French, *frayer,* to *rub.* חרשים *charashim* signifies either *carpenters* or *smiths;* probably the latter are here intended, who came with *hammers, files,* and such like, to destroy these *horns,* which no doubt seemed to be of *iron.*

From a sensible correspondent I have received the following note:—

"The word we translate *carpenters,* חרשים *charashim,* is a root which, according to Mr. *Parkhurst,* denotes *silent thought* or *attention;* and in *kal* and *hiphil,* to *contrive, devise secretly,* or *in silence;* hence applied as a noun to an *artificer* of any kind, and to any work which disposes to silent attention. Thus, to *potters' ware,* Lev. vi. 28; Job ii. 8; and in many other places. So also to *ploughing,* Deut. xxii. 10; Prov. xx. 4, which requires constant attention to make 'the right-lined furrow.' Let it be remembered that in ancient times *such works* were more esteemed than the useless ones we have learned to admire. So again, in Gen. xxiv. 21, and elsewhere, it implies *to be silent,* as in deep thought or great attention.

"Now it is evident that the purport of this vision is the same with the gracious declarations which precede it, viz., to express the return of the protecting mercies of God to his people, delivering them from their enemies. I should therefore be inclined to render חרשים

charashim here, *watchers* or *inspectors*, in the sense which our translators have rendered the *Chaldee* עיר *ir, a watcher*, in the *fourth* chapter of Daniel, ver. 13; understanding thereby 'spirits of the heavens, which go forth from standing before the Lord of all the earth,' Zech. vi. 5, and are described in the first vision as 'sent to walk to and fro through the earth.' This gives to the whole narrative a sublime and important sense, affording us some glimpse of the Divine government by the ministration of angels, such as Jacob was favoured with in his vision at Beth-el, and which our Saviour himself informed Nathanael constituted part of the glory of his mediatorial kingdom."

M. A. B.

CHAPTER II

The vision with which this chapter opens, portended great increase and prosperity to Jerusalem. Accordingly Josephus tells us, (Wars v. iv. 2,) *that "the city, overflowing with inhabitants, extended beyond its walls," as predicted in the* fourth *verse, and acquired much glory during the time of the Maccabees; although these promises, and particularly the sublime image in the* fifth *verse, has certainly a still more pointed reference to the glory and prosperity of the Christian Church in the latter days,* 1–5. *See* Rev. xxi., xxii. *In consequence of these promises, the Jews, still inhabiting Babylon and the regions round about, are called upon to hasten home, that they might not be involved in the fate of their enemies, who were destined to fall a prey to the nations which they had formerly subdued; God's great love and zeal for his people moving him to glorify them by humbling all their adversaries,* 6–9. *The most gracious promises of God's presence with his Church, and her consequent increase and prosperity, set forth in the remaining verses,* 10–13, *were to a certain extent fulfilled in the great number of proselytes made to Judaism after the return from the captivity; but shall be more fully accomplished after the restoration of the Jews to the favour of God under the Gospel. "For if the casting away of the natural Israel be the reconciling of the world, what shall the receiving of them be but life from the dead?"*

A. M. cir. 3485
B. C. cir. 519
Ol. cir. LXV. 2
Tarquinii Superbi, R. Rom., cir. annum 16

I LIFTED up mine eyes again,
and looked, and behold [a]a
man with a measuring-line in his
hand.
2 Then said I, Whither goest thou? And
he said unto me, [b]To measure Jerusalem, to
see what *is* the breadth thereof, and what *is*
the length thereof.
3 And, behold, the angel that talked with me
went forth, and another angel went out to
meet him,
4 And said unto him, Run, speak to this
young man, saying, [c]Jerusalem shall be inhabited *as* towns without walls for the
multitude of men and cattle
therein:

A. M. cir. 3485
B. C. cir. 519
Ol. cir. LXV. 2
Tarquinii Superbi, R. Rom., cir. annum 16

5 For I, saith the LORD, will
be unto her [d]a wall of fire
round about, [e]and will be the glory in the
midst of her.
6 Ho, ho, *come forth,* and flee [f]from the
land of the north, saith the LORD: for I have
[g]spread you abroad as the four winds of the
heaven, saith the LORD.
7 [h]Deliver thyself, O Zion, that dwellest
with the daughter of Babylon.
8 For thus saith the LORD of hosts; after
the glory hath he sent me unto the nations

[a]Ezekiel xl. 3——[b]Revelation xi. 1; xxi. 15, 16——[c]Jeremiah xxxi. 27; Ezekiel xxxvi. 10, 11——[d]Isaiah xxvi. 1; chap. ix. 8——[e]Isaiah lx. 19; Rev. xxi. 23——[f]Isaiah xlviii. 20; lii. 11; Jeremiah i. 14; l. 8; li. 6, 45——[g]Deuteronomy xxviii. 64; Ezekiel xvii. 21——[h]Revelation xviii. 4

NOTES ON CHAP II

Verse 1. *A man with a measuring-line in his hand.*] Probably a representation of *Nehemiah*, who got a commission from *Artaxerxes Longimanus* to build up the walls of Jerusalem; for hitherto it had remained without being enclosed.

Verse 4. *Run, speak to this young man*] Nehemiah must have been a *young man* when he was ساقي *sakee*, or cup-bearer, to Artaxerxes.

As *towns without walls*] It shall be so numerously inhabited as not to be contained within its ancient limits. *Josephus*, speaking of this time, says, WARS v. iv. 2, "The city, overflowing with inhabitants, by degrees extended itself beyond its walls."

Verse 5. *I—will be unto her a wall of fire*] Her safety shall consist in my defence. I shall be as *fire* round about her. No adversary shall be permitted to touch her. Much of this must refer to the *New Jerusalem.*

Verse 6. *Flee from the land of the north*] From Chaldee, Persia, and Babylon, where several of the Jews still remained. See ver. 7.

Verse 8. *After the glory*] After your *glorious deliverance* from the different places of your dispersion; *He hath sent me unto the nations which spoiled you*, that *they* may fall under grievous calamities, and be punished in their turn. On *Babylon* a great calamity fell, when besieged and taken by the *Persians.*

The following note I received from a sensible and pious correspondent:—

5. "For I, saith the Lord, will be unto her a wall of fire round about, and will be the glory in the midst of her.

8. "For thus saith the Lord of hosts, who hath sent *me, the future glory* (or the glory

A. M. cir. 3485
B. C. cir. 519
Ol. cir. LXV. 2
Tarquinii Superbi, R. Rom., cir. annum 16

which spoiled you: for he that
[i]toucheth you toucheth the apple
of his eye.
9 For behold, I will [k]shake
mine hand upon them, and they shall be a
spoil to their servants: and [l]ye shall know
that the LORD of hosts hath sent me.
10 [m]Sing and rejoice, O daughter of Zion:
for lo, I come, and I [n]will dwell in the midst
of thee, saith the LORD.
11 [o]And many nations shall be joined to
the LORD [p]in that day, and shall
be [q]my people: and I will dwell
in the midst of thee, and [r]thou
shalt know that the LORD of
hosts hath sent me unto thee.

A. M. cir. 3485
B. C. cir. 519
Ol. cir. LXV. 2
Tarquinii Superbi, R. Rom., cir. annum 16

12 And the LORD shall [s]inherit Judah his
portion in the holy land, and [t]shall choose
Jerusalem again.
13 [u]Be silent, O all flesh, before the LORD:
for he is raised up [v]out of [w]his holy habitation.

---

[i]Deut. xxxii. 10; Psa. xvii. 8; 2 Thess. i. 6——[k]Isa. xi. 15; xix. 16——[l]Chap. iv. 9——[m]Isa. xii. 6; liv. 1; Zeph. iii. 14——[n]Lev. xxvi. 12; Ezek. xxxvii. 27; chap. viii. 3; John i. 14; 2 Cor. vi. 16——[o]Isa. ii. 2, 3; xlix. 22; lx. 3, &c.; chap. viii. 22, 23

[p]Chap. iii. 10——[q]Exod. xii. 49——[r]Ezek. xxxiii. 33; ver. 9——[s]Deut. xxxii. 9——[t]Chap. i. 17——[u]Hab. ii. 20; Zeph. i. 7——[v]Psa. lxviii. 5; Isa. lvii. 15——[w]Heb. *the habitation of his holiness;* Deuteronomy xxvi. 15; Isa. lxiii. 15

---

which is to come) unto the nations which spoiled you; for he that toucheth you toucheth the apple of his eye. Behold, I will shake mine hand upon them, and they shall be a spoil to their servants; and ye shall know that the Lord of hosts hath sent *me.* Sing and rejoice, O daughter of Zion; for lo, *I come,* and I will dwell in the midst of thee, saith the Lord. And *many* nations shall be joined to the Lord in that day, and shall be *my* people; and I will dwell in the midst of thee, and thou shalt know that the Lord of hosts hath *sent me* unto thee. And the Lord shall inherit Judah his portion in the holy land, and shall choose Jerusalem again.

"*If* in the *eighth* verse אחר כבוד may be rendered the *future,* or the *glory that is to come,* it will harmonize with the context as a prophecy of the Messiah, whereas in our English translation the words *after the glory* are unintelligible. And so the *Seventy.*

"It is evident the person speaking is distinguished from the Lord of hosts, as being *sent by him;* yet this person sent is also called Jehovah; and the nations who shall be joined to Jehovah in that day are called *his people;* and *he* (the person sent) will dwell in the midst of *thee,* (i. e., Zion,) and shall inherit Judah his portion, &c.

"In confirmation of my view of the *eighth* verse, I think Exod. xxxiii. may be compared with it. Moses besought God that he would show him *his glory;* upon which it was said to him, "Whilst my glory passeth by,' I will put thee in a cleft of the rock, and will cover thee with my hand *whilst I pass by;* and I will take away my hand, and thou shalt see my אחר *achar.* Now as this was a fulfilment of Moses's request, who entreated to behold the glory, it follows that this אחר was the Divine glory, which *alone he was capable of seeing.*

"'No man hath seen God at any time, the only begotten Son, (the Lord Jesus Christ,) which is in the bosom of the Father, *he hath declared him.*'"

M. A. B.

Toucheth the apple of his eye.] בבבת עינו *bebabath eyno, the babet of his eye.* This is a remarkable expression. Any person, by looking into the eye of another, will see his own image perfectly expressed, though in extreme minature, in the pupil. Does our English word *babbet* or *baby* come from this? And does not the expression mean that the eye of God is ever *on* his follower, and that his person is ever impressed on the eye, the notice, attention, providence, and mercy of God?

Verse 9. *I will shake mine hand upon them*] I will *threaten* first, and then stretch out my hand of *judgment* against them.

A spoil to their servants] To those whom they had formerly *subjected* to their sway. As the *Babylonians* to the Medes and Persians; and so of the rest in the subversion of empires.

Verse 10. *I will dwell in the midst of thee, saith the Lord*] This must chiefly refer to the *Christian church,* in which God ever dwells by the power of his Spirit, as he *had* done by the symbol of his presence in the first Jewish temple.

Verse 11. *Many nations shall be joined to the Lord*] This most certainly belongs to the *Christian church.* No *nation* or *people* ever became converts to the Jewish religion; but *whole nations* have embraced the faith of our Lord Jesus Christ.

Verse 12. *The Lord shall inherit Judah his portion in the holy land*] This is a promise of the final restoration of the Jews, and that they should be God's portion in their *own land.*

Verse 13. *Be silent, O all flesh*] Let all the nations of the world be astonished at this. God will *arise,* and deliver this ancient people, and bring them into the glorious liberty of the sons of God.

CHAPTER III

While the Jews were rebuilding their temple, their adversaries endeavoured to stop the work, Ezra v. *This vision is therefore calculated to give them the strongest encouragement that God, after plucking them as brands out of the fire (or captivity of Babylon,) would not now give them up, but would continue to prosper and favour them; and that notwithstanding the interruptions they should meet with, the work should be finished under the gracious superintendence of Providence; and their high priest, clothed in his pontifical robes, would soon officiate in the holy of holies,* 1–7. *The subject is then, by an easy transition, applied to a much greater future deliverance and restoration, of which Joshua and his companions, delivered now, are declared to be figures or types; for that the Messiah or Branch, the great high priest typified by Joshua, would be manifested; and, like the principal stone represented in the vision, become the chief corner stone of his Church; that the all-seeing eye of God would constantly guard it; and that by his atonement he would procure for it peace and pardon,* 8–10.

A. M. cir. 3485 B. C. cir. 519 Ol. cir. LXV. 2 Tarquinii Superbi, R. Rom., cir. annum 16

AND he showed me [a]Joshua
the high priest standing before the angel of the LORD, and
[b]Satan [c]standing at his right
hand [d]to resist him.
2 And the LORD said unto Satan, [e]The
LORD rebuke thee, O Satan; even the LORD
that [f]hath chosen Jerusalem rebuke thee: [g]*is*
not this a brand plucked out of the fire?
3 Now Joshua was clothed with [h]filthy garments, and stood before the angel.
4 And he answered and spake unto those
that stood before him, saying,
Take away the filthy garments
from him. And unto him he
said, Behold, I have caused thine
iniquity to pass from thee, [i]and I will clothe
thee with change of raiment.
5 And I said, Let them set a fair [k]mitre upon
his head. So they set a fair mitre upon his
head, and clothed him with garments. And
the angel of the LORD stood by.
6 And the angel of the LORD protested unto
Joshua, saying,

A. M. cir. 3485 B. C. cir. 519 Ol. cir. LXV. 2 Tarquinii Superbi, R. Rom., cir. annum 16

---

[a]Hag. i. 1——[b]Psa. cix. 6; Rev. xii. 10——[c]That is, *an adversary*——[d]Heb. *to be his adversary*——[e]Jude 9——[f]Chap. i. 17; Rom. viii. 33

[g]Amos iv. 11; Rom. xi. 5; Jude 23——[h]Isa. lxiv. 6——[i]Isa. lxi. 10; Rev. xix. 8; Luke xv. 22——[k]Exod. xxix. 6; chap. vi. 11

NOTES ON CHAP. III

Verse 1. *And he showed me Joshua the high priest*] The Angel of the Lord is the *Messiah*, as we have seen before; Joshua, the high priest, may here represent the *whole Jewish people;* and *Satan*, the grand *accuser* of the brethren. What the subject of dispute was, we perhaps learn from Jude 9. Michael and Satan disputed *about the body of Moses*. This could not refer to the *natural body* of the Jewish lawgiver, which had been dead about *one thousand* years; it must therefore refer to that *body of laws* given to the Jews by Moses, for the breach of which Satan, who was their *tempter* to disobedience, now comes forward as their *accuser;* that, exciting the justice of God against them, they may be all brought to perdition. There is a *paronomasia* here:—

Satan standing at his right hand to resist him.] שטן Satan signifies an *adversary.* לשטנו *lesiteno*, to be his adversary, or accuser.

Verse 2. Is *not this a brand plucked out of the fire?*] The Jews were *nearly destroyed* because of their sins; a remnant of them is yet left, and God is determined to preserve them. He has had mercy upon them, and forgiven them their sins. Wouldst thou have them destroyed? It is God that hath justified them; who art *thou* that condemnest them? *The Lord rebuke thee!* God confound thee for what thou hast done, and for what thou desirest farther to do! It is evident that Jude 9 relates to this circumstance—the very same *phraseology* which occurs here. See the notes on Jude 9, where the subject is largely considered. With difficulty has this remnant escaped, and God will not permit fresh evils to fall upon them, by which they might be totally consumed. This was Satan's design, who accuses the followers of God day and night. See Rev. xii. 10.

Verse 3. *Joshua was clothed with filthy garments*] The Jewish people were in a most forlorn, destitute, and to all human appearance despicable, condition; and besides all, they were sinful, and the priesthood defiled by idolatry; and nothing but the mercy of God could save them.

Verse 4. *Take away the filthy garments*] The Jews wore *sackcloth* in times of public calamity; probably the *filthy garments* refer to this. Let their clothing be changed. I have turned again their captivity; I will fully restore them, and blot out all their iniquities.

Verse 5. *A fair mitre upon his head*] To signify that he had renewed to him the office of the *high priesthood*, which had been defiled and profaned before. The *mitre* was the *bonnet* which the high priest put on his head when he entered into the sanctuary, Exod. xxviii. 4, &c.

Clothed him with garments] Referring to the vestments of the high priest. The true high priest, who is over the house of God, will establish his office among them, when they shall acknowledge him as their *Messiah*, and seek redemption in the blood of the sacrifice which he has offered for their sins; and not for theirs only, but for the sins of the whole world.

A. M. cir. 3485
B. C. cir. 519
Ol. cir. LXV. 2
Tarquinii Superbi, R. Rom.,
cir. annum 16

7 Thus saith the LORD of hosts; If thou wilt walk in my ways, and if thou wilt [l]keep my [m]charge, then thou shalt also [n]judge my house, and shalt also keep my courts, and I will give thee [o]places to walk among these that [p]stand by.

8 Hear now, O Joshua the high priest, thou and thy fellows that sit before thee: for they *are* [q]men [r]wondered at: for behold, I will bring forth [s]my servant The [t]BRANCH.

9 For behold the stone that I have laid before Joshua; [u]upon one stone *shall be* [v]seven eyes: behold, I will engrave the graving thereof, saith the LORD of hosts, and [w]I will remove the iniquity of that land in one day.

A. M. cir. 3485
B. C. cir. 519
Ol. cir. LXV. 2
Tarquinii Superbi, R. Rom.,
cir. annum 16

10 [x]In that day, saith the LORD of hosts, shall ye call every man his neighbour [y]under the vine and under the fig tree.

---

[l]Lev. viii. 35; 1 Kings ii. 3; Ezek. xliv. 16——[m]Or, *ordinance*——[n]Deut. xvii. 9; Mal. ii. 7——[o]Heb. *walks*——[p]Chap. iv. 14; vi. 5——[q]Psa. lxxi. 7; Isa. viii. 18; xx. 3——[r]Heb. *men of wonder*, or *sign*, as Ezek. xii. 11; xxiv. 24——[s]Isa. xlii. 1; xlix. 3, 5; lii. 13; liii. 11; Ezek. xxxiv. 23, 24——[t]Isa. iv. 2; xi. 1; Jer. xxiii. 5; xxxiii. 15; chap. vi. 12; Luke i. 78——[u]Psa. cxviii. 22; Isa. xxviii. 16——[v]Chap. iv. 10; Rev. v. 6——[w]Jer. xxxi. 34; l. 20; Mic. vii. 18, 19; chap. xiii. 1——[x]Chap. ii. 11; Isa. ii. 11; xxvi. 1; xxix. 28; lii. 6——[y]1 Kings iv. 25; Isa. xxxvi. 16; Mic. iv. 4

Verse 7. *If thou wilt walk in my ways*] If ye, Israelites, priests and people, now restored to your own land, will walk in my ways, &c., ye shall be a part of my family; and have *places*—mansions—in eternal glory, with all them that are sanctified.

Verse 8. *O Joshua—thou, and thy fellows*] Thy *countrymen*, who have now returned from your captivity, in a very *wonderful* manner. אנשי מופת *anshey mopheth, figurative men*, men whose office and ministration *prefigured* the Lord Jesus Christ; and therefore it is immediately added, "I will bring forth my servant The BRANCH." Abp. *Newcome* thinks this means *Zerubbabel*, so called because he was the grandson of Jehoiakim, or Jeconiah, king of Judah, Matt. i. 12, and heir to the throne of Judah. The *Chaldee* has, "My servant the Messiah." See the note on Isa. iv. 2. I think the word cannot apply to Zerubbabel, except as a *type* of Christ; in that sense it may be understood of him. See chap. vi. 11, 12.

Verse 9. *For behold the stone that I have laid*] Alluding no doubt to the *foundation stone* of the temple: but this represented *Christ Jesus:* "Behold, I lay in Zion for a foundation a STONE, a tried stone, a precious CORNER STONE, a SURE FOUNDATION," Isa. xxviii. 16. This means Christ, and none other; on him his whole Church rests, as a building does on its foundation.

Upon one stone shall be *seven eyes*] This is supposed to mean the *providence* of God, as under it all the work should be completed. There may be an allusion to the *seven counsellors*, which stood always about the persons of the Asiatics sovereigns; and those who were the governors of provinces were termed the *eyes of the king.* To this there is an allusion in Rev. i. 4. In Christ there is a plentitude of *wisdom, power, goodness, mercy, truth, love*, and *compassion*, to *direct, protect, save, uphold, purify, govern*, and *preserve* all the souls that trust in him.

I will engrave the graving thereof] This is an allusion to *engraving precious stones*, in which the ancients greatly excelled. *Heads, animals*, and *various devices* were the subjects of those engravings. But what was *this* engraving? Was it not the following words? I will remove the iniquity of that land in one day;" and was not this when Jesus Christ *expired upon the cross?* This was the grand, the only atonement, satisfaction, and sacrifice for the sins of the whole world. Does not our Lord refer to this place, John vi. 27? *Him hath God the Father sealed;* and on the inscription there was, "This is my beloved Son, in whom I am well pleased." See the note on the above passage.

Verse 10. *Shall ye call every man his neighbour*] See on Isa. xxxvi. 16. Every one shall be inviting and encouraging another to believe on the Lord Jesus Christ; and thus taste and see that God is good. See on Isaiah ii. 2, 3. And there shall be the utmost liberty to preach, believe on, and profess the faith of our Lord Jesus Christ.

CHAPTER IV

The prophet, overpowered by his last vision, is roused by the angel to behold another, 1; *intended also to assure the Jews of the success of Joshua and Zerubbabel in building the temple, and surmounting every obstacle in the way; till at length, by the good providence of God, it should be finished, amidst the joyful acclamations of the spectators,* 2–10. *The angel's explanation of the* golden candlestick, and *of the* two olive trees, 11–14.

A. M. cir. 3485
B. C. cir. 519
Ol. cir. LXV. 2
Tarquinii Superbi, R. Rom., cir. annum 16

AND [a]the angel that talked with me came again, and waked me, [b]as a man that is wakened out of his sleep,

2 And said unto me, What seest thou? And I said, I have looked, and behold [c]a candlestick all *of* gold, [d]with a bowl upon the top of it, [e]and his seven lamps thereon, and [f]seven pipes to the seven lamps, which *are* upon the top thereof.

3 [g]And two olive trees by it, one upon the right *side* of the bowl, and the other upon the left *side* thereof.

4 So I answered and spake to the angel that talked with me, saying, What *are* these, my lord?

5 Then the angel that talked with me answered and said unto me, Knowest thou not what these be? And I said, No, my lord.

A. M. cir. 3485
B. C. cir. 519
Ol. cir. LXV. 2
Tarquinii Superbi, R. Rom., cir. annum 16

6 Then he answered and spake unto me, saying, This *is* the word of the LORD unto Zerubbabel, saying, [h]Not by [i]might, nor by power, but by my Spirit, saith the LORD of hosts.

7 Who *art* thou, [k]O great mountain? before Zerubbabel *thou shalt become* a plain: and he shall bring forth [l]the headstone *thereof* [m]*with* shoutings, *crying,* Grace, grace, unto it.

8 Moreover, the word of the LORD came unto me, saying,

9 The hands of Zerubbabel [n]have laid the foundation of this house; his hands [o]shall also finish it; and [p]thou shalt know that the [q]LORD of hosts hath sent me unto you.

10 For who hath despised the day of [r]small

[a]Chap. ii. 3——[b]Dan. viii. 18——[c]Exod. xxv. 31; Rev. i. 12——[d]Heb. *with her bowl*——[e]Exod. xxv. 37; Rev. iv. 5——[f]Or, *seven several pipes to the lamps,* &c. [g]Ver. 11, 12; Rev. xi. 4

[h]Hos. i. 7——[i]Or, *army*——[k]Jer. li. 25; Matt. xxi. 21 [l]Psa. cxviii. 22——[m]Ezra iii. 11, 13——[n]Ezra iii. 10 [o]Ezra vi. 15——[p]Chap. ii. 9, 11; vi. 15——[q]Isa. xlviii. 15; chap. ii. 8——[r]Hag. ii. 3

NOTES ON CHAP. IV

Verse 1. *The angel—came again, and waked me*] Abp. *Newcome* considers this vision as represented on the same night, chap. i. 8, with the preceding ones. See the latter part of ver. 10, compared with chap. iii. 9. After some interval the prophet, overpowered with the vision which had been presented to him, was awakened from his prophetic trance as from a sleep.

Verse 2. *A candlestick all* of *gold*] This candlestick is formed in some measure after that of the *sanctuary,* Exod. xxv. 31, 32: but in that of the sanctuary there was no *bowl,* nor *seven pipes,* nor *seven lamps,* nor the *two olive trees.* The *two olive trees* were to supply the *bowl* with *oil;* the *bowl* was to communicate the oil to the *seven pipes;* and the *seven pipes* were to supply the *seven lamps.* In general, the *candlestick,* its *bowl, pipes, lamps,* and *olive trees,* are emblems of the pure service of God, and the grace and salvation to be enjoyed by his true worshippers. The *candlestick* may, however, represent the whole *Jewish state, ecclesiastical* and *civil;* the *oil,* producing the *light,* the *grace* and *mercy* of God; and the *two olive trees,* the source of *infinite* love, whence that grace proceeds. The *pipes* may signify all *means of grace;* and the *seven lamps,* the perfection and abundance of the *light* and salvation provided. Some may take them in the following way:—1. The *olive trees,* the Divine goodness, yield the *oil* from the *olive berry,* which is its fruit. 2. From each comes a pipe to convey the oil to the bowl. 3. This *oil* is collected in the *bowl,* which is supposed to represent Jesus, the great Mediator, through whom alone all grace and mercy descend to man. 4. The *seven pipes,* the various means of grace—reading, hearing, prayer, sacraments, &c.—through which Christ dispenses his grace and blessing to his followers. 5. The *seven lamps*—the Spirit of God in its plentitude of graces, gifts, and light, dispensed to the Christian Church.

Verse 6. *This* is *the word of the Lord unto Zerubbabel*] This prince was in a trying situation, and he needed especial encouragement from God; and here it is:

Not by might, (of thy own,) *nor by power,* (authority from others,) *but by my Spirit*—the providence, authority, power, and energy of the Most High. In this way shall my temple be built; in this way shall my Church be raised and preserved. No secular arm, no human prudence, no earthly policy, no suits at law, shall ever be used for the founding, extension, and preservation of my Church. But the spirit of the world says, "These are all *means* to which we must have recourse; otherwise the cause of God may be ruined." Satan, thou liest!

Verse 7. *O great mountain?*] The hinderances which were thrown in the way; the regal prohibition to discontinue the building of the temple.

Before Zerubbabel—a plain] The sovereign power of God shall remove them. March on, Zerubbabel; all shall be made plain and smooth before thee. I have given thee the work to do, and I will remove all hinderances out of thy way.

He shall bring forth the headstone] As he has laid the *foundation stone,* so shall he put on the headstone: as he has *begun* the building, so shall he *finish* it!

With *shoutings*] The universal acclamation of the people.

Grace, grace unto it.] How beautiful is this structure! May the favour of God ever rest upon it, and be manifested in it!

Verse 10. *Who hath despised the day of small things?*] The poverty, weakness, and un-

A. M. cir. 3485
B. C. cir. 519
Ol. cir. LXV. 2
Tarquinii Superbi, R. Rom., cir. annum 16

things? [s]for they shall rejoice, and
shall see the [t]plummet in the hand
of Zerubbabel *with* those seven;
[u]they *are* the eyes of the LORD,
which run to and fro through the whole earth.
11 Then answered I, and said unto him,
What *are* these [v]two olive trees upon the
right *side* of the candlestick, and upon the left
side thereof?
12 And I answered again, and said unto him,
What *be these* two olive branches
which, [w]through the two golden
pipes, [x]empty [y]the golden *oil* out
of themselves?
13 And he answered me and said, Knowest
thou not what these *be?* And I said, No, my
lord.
14 Then said he, [z]These *are* the two
[a]anointed ones, [b]that stand by [c]the LORD of
the whole earth.

[s]Or, *since the seven eyes of the LORD shall rejoice* — [t]Heb. *stone of tin* — [u]2 Chron. xvi. 9; Prov. xv. 3; chap. iii. 9 — [v]Ver. 3 — [w]Heb. *by the hand* — [x]Or, *empty out of themselves* oil into *the gold* — [y]Heb. *the gold* — [z]Rev. xi. 4 — [a]Heb. *sons of oil* — [b]Chap. iii. 7; Luke i. 19; [c]See Josh. iii. 11, 13; chap. vi. 5

befriended state of the Jews. It was said, "What do these feeble Jews?" "Will they build," &c.? No. But God will build by them, and perfect his building too.

And shall see the plummet in the hand of Zerubbabel] He is *master builder* under God, the *grand architect.*

Those seven—are *the eyes of the Lord*] Either referring to his particular and especial *providence;* or to those *ministering spirits,* whom he has employed in behalf of the Jews, to dispense the blessings of that providence. See the reading in the *margin.*

Verse 11. *What* are *these two olive trees*] See on ver. 2.

Verse 12. *What* be *these two olive branches*] That is, two *boughs* laden with *branches of olive berries.*

Verse 14. *These* are *the two anointed ones*] Joshua, the high priest; and Zerubbabel the governor. These are *anointed*—appointed by the Lord; and *stand by him,* the one to minister in the *ecclesiastical,* the other in the *civil* state.

Probably we may not be able to comprehend the whole of this hieroglyphical vision; for even the interpreting angel does not choose to answer the questions relative to this, which were put to him by the prophet. See ver. 4 and 11. But though the *particulars* are hard to be understood; yet the general meaning has, I hope, been given.

CHAPTER V

The vision of the large flying roll, with the angel's explanation, 1–4. *The vision of the ephah, and of the woman sitting on it, with the signification,* 5–11.

A. M. cir. 3485
B. C. cir. 519
Ol. cir. LXV. 2
Tarquinii Superbi, R. Rom., cir. annum 16

THEN I turned, and lifted up
mine eyes, and looked, and
behold a flying [a]roll.
2 And he said unto me, What
seest thou? And I answered, I see a flying
roll; the length thereof *is* twenty cubits, and
the breadth thereof ten cubits.
3 Then said he unto me, This *is* the [b]curse
that goeth forth over the face of the whole
earth: for [c]every one that stealeth shall be
cut off *as* on this side, according
it; and every one that sweareth
shall be cut off *as* on that side,
according to it.
4 I will bring it forth, saith the LORD of
hosts, and it shall enter into the house of the
thief, and into the house of [d]him that sweareth
falsely by my name: and it shall remain in the
midst of his house, and [e]shall consume it, with
the timber thereof, and the stones thereof.

[a]Ezek. ii. 9 — [b]Mal. iv. 6 — [c]Or, *every one of this* people *that stealeth holdeth* himself *guiltless, as it* doth — [d]Lev. xix. 12; chapter viii. 17; Mal. iii. 5 — [e]See Lev. xiv. 45

NOTES ON CHAP. V

Verse 1. *Behold a flying roll.*] This was *twenty cubits long,* and *ten cubits broad;* the prophet saw it expanded, and *flying.* Itself was the catalogue of the crimes of the people, and the punishment threatened by the Lord. Some think the crimes were those of the *Jews;* others, those of the *Chaldeans.* The *roll* is mentioned in allusion to those large rolls on which the Jews write the *Pentateuch.* One now lying before me is one hundred and fifty-three feet long, by twenty-one inches wide, written on fine brown Basle goat-skin; some time since brought from Jerusalem, supposed to be four hundred years old.

Verse 3. *Every one that stealeth—and every one that sweareth*] It seems that the roll was written both on the front and back: *stealing* and *swearing* are supposed to be two general heads of crimes; the former, comprising sins against men; the latter, sins against God. It is supposed that the roll contained the sins and punishments of the Chaldeans.

Verse 4. *Into the house of him*] Babylon, the house or city of Nebuchadnezzar, who was

A. M. cir. 3485
B. C. cir. 519
Ol. cir. LXV. 2
Tarquinii Superbi, R. Rom., cir. annum 16

5 Then the angel that talked with me went forth, and said unto me, Lift up now thine eyes, and see what *is* this that goeth forth.

6 And I said, What *is* it? And he said, This *is* an ephah that goeth forth. He said moreover, This *is* their resemblance through all the earth.

7 And, behold, there was lifted up a [f]talent of lead; and this *is* a woman that sitteth in the midst of the ephah.

8 And he said, This *is* wickedness. And he cast it into the midst of the ephah; and he cast the weight of lead upon the mouth thereof.

9 Then lifted I up mine eyes, and looked, and, behold, there came out two women, and the wind *was* in their wings; for they had wings like the wings of a stork: and they lifted up the ephah between the earth and the heaven.

10 Then said I to the angel that talked with me, Whither do these bear the ephah?

11 And he said unto me, [g]To build it a house in [h]the land of Shinar: and it shall be established, and set there upon her own base.

[f]Or, *weighty piece*

[g]Jer. xxix. 5, 28——[h]Gen. x. 10

a public *plunderer*, and a most glaring *idolater*.

Verse 6. *This* is *an ephah that goeth forth.*] This, among the Jews, was the ordinary measure of grain. The *woman* in the *ephah* is supposed to represent *Judea*, which shall be visited for its sins; the *talent of lead* on the *ephah*, within which the woman was enclosed, the *wrath* of God, bending down this culprit nation, in the measure of its sins; for the angel said, "This is wickedness;" that is, the *woman* represents the *mass of iniquity* of this nation.

Verse 9. *There came out two women*] As the *one woman* represented the *impiety* of the Jewish nation; so these *two* women who were to *carry the ephah*, in which the woman INIQUITY was shut up, under the *weight* of a *talent* of *lead*, may mean the desperate UNBELIEF of the Jews in rejecting the Messiah; and that IMPIETY, or universal *corruption* of manners, which was the consequence of their *unbelief*, and brought down the wrath of God upon them. The strong *wings*, like those of *a stork*, may point out the *power* and *swiftness* with which Judea was carried on to fill up the *measure* of her iniquity, and to meet the punishment which she deserved.

Between the earth and the heaven.] Sins against GOD and MAN; sins which *heaven* and *earth* contemplated with *horror*.

Or the *Babylonians* and *Romans* may be intended by the *two women* who carried the Jewish ephah to its final punishment. The *Chaldeans* ruined Judea *before* the advent of our Lord; the *Romans*, shortly *after*.

Verse 11. *To build it a house in the land of Shinar*] The land of *Shinar* means *Babylon*; and *Babylon* means *Rome*, in the Apocalypse. The *building the house* for the woman imprisoned in the ephah may signify, that there should be a *long captivity* under the *Romans*, as there was under that of *Shinar* or *Babylon*, by which *Rome* may here be represented. That *house* remains to the present day: the *Jewish woman* is still in the *ephah;* it is *set on its own base*—continues still as a *distinct nation;* and the *talent of lead*—God's displeasure—is still on the top. O Lord, save thy people, the remnant of Israel!

CHAPTER VI

The vision of the four chariots drawn by several sorts of horses, 1–8. The other vision in this chapter may refer in its primary sense to the establishment of the civil and religious polity of the Jews under Joshua and Zerubbabel; but relates, in a fuller sense, to the Messiah, and to that spiritual kingdom of which he was to be both king and high priest. In him all these types and figures were verified; in him all the promises are yea and amen, 9–15.

A. M. cir. 3485
B. C. cir. 519
Ol. cir. LXV. 2
Tarquinii Superbi, R. Rom., cir. annum 16

AND I turned, and lifted up mine eyes, and looked, and behold, there came four chariots out from between two mountains; and the mountains *were* mountains of brass.

2 In the first chariot *were* [a]red horses; and in the second chariot [b]black horses;

3 And in the third chariot [c]white horses; and in the fourth

[a]Chap. i. 8; Rev. vi. 4

[b]Rev. vi. 5——[c]Rev. vi. 2

NOTES ON CHAP. VI

Verse 1. *There came four chariots*] Four monarchies or empires. This is supposed to mean the same with the vision of the *four horns*, in chap. i.

Mountains of brass.] The strong barriers of God's purposes, which restrained those powers within the times and limits appointed by Jehovah.

Verse 2. *In the first chariot* were *red horses*] The empire of the Chaldeans, which overthrew the empire of the *Assyrians*.

A. M. cir. 3485 B. C. cir. 519 Ol. cir. LXV. 2 Tarquinii Superbi, R. Rom., cir. annum 16

chariot grisled and [d]bay horses.

4 Then I answered [e]and said unto the angel that talked with me, What *are* these, my lord?

5 And the angel answered and said unto me, [f]These *are* the four [g]spirits of the heavens, which go forth from [h]standing before the LORD of all the earth.

6 The black horses which *are* therein go forth into [i]the north country; and the white go forth after them; and the grisled go forth toward the south country.

7 And the bay went forth, and sought to go, that they might [k]walk to and fro through the earth: and he said, Get you hence, walk to and fro through the earth. So they walked to and fro through the earth.

8 Then cried he upon me, and spake unto me, saying, Behold, these that go toward the north country have quieted my [l]spirit in the north country.

9 And the word of the LORD came unto me, saying,

10 Take of *them of* the captivity, *even* of Heldai, of Tobijah, and of Jedaiah, which are come from Babylon, and come thou the same day, and go into the house of Josiah the son of Zephaniah;

11 Then take silver and gold, and make [m]crowns, and set *them* upon the head of Joshua the son of Josedech, the high priest;

[d]Or, *strong*——[e]Chap. v. 10——[f]Psa. civ. 4; Heb. i. 7, 14——[g]Or, *winds*——[h]1 Kings xxii. 19; Dan. vii. 10; chap iv. 14; Luke i. 19

[i]Jer. i. 14——[k]Gen. xiii. 17; chap. i. 10——[l]Judg. viii. 3; Eccles. x. 4——[m]Exod. xxiii. 36; xxix. 6; Lev. viii. 9; chap. iii. 5

The second chariot black horses] The empire of the *Persians*, founded by *Cyrus*, which destroyed the empire of the *Chaldeans*.

Verse 3. *The third chariot white horses*] The empire of the *Greeks*, founded by *Alexander the Great*, which destroyed the empire of the *Persians*.

The fourth chariot grisled and bay horses.] That is *party-coloured horses;* or with horses, some *grisled* and some *bay*. The empire of the Romans or of the Greeks. The Greeks *divided* after the death of Alexander; one part pointing out the *Lagidæ*, who attacked and subdued *Egypt;* and the other, the *seleucidæ*, who subdued Syria under Seleucus.

Verse 5. *The four spirits of the heavens*] Ministers of God's wrath against the sinful nations of the world.

Verse 6. *The black horses*] This refers to the *second chariot;* of the *first* the angel makes no mention, because the empire designed by it had ceased to exist. *This had red horses*, to show the *cruelty* of the Chaldeans towards the Jews, and the *carnage* they committed in the land of Judea.

The black] *Cyrus*, at the head of the *Persians* and *Medes*, bringing devastation and death among the Chaldeans, called the *north* in many parts of Scripture.

The white] *Alexander*, who was *splendid* in his victories, and *mild* towards all that he conquered

The grisled] The *Lagidæ* or *Ptolemies*, who founded an empire in Egypt; of these some were *good*, some *bad*, some *despotic*, some *moderate*, some *cruel*, and some *mild;* represented by the *party-coloured horses*.

Verse 7. *And the bay went forth*] The *Seleucidæ*, who conquered Syria and the upper provinces, and who wished to extend their conquests, and "sought to go, that they might walk to and fro throughout the earth," were of unbounded ambition, and sought *universal empire;* such as *Antiochus the Great*. "So they walked to and fro," did extend their conquests; and harassed many countries by their vexatious and almost continual wars. Some think the *Romans* are meant, who carried their conquests hither and thither, just as the Divine providence permitted them.

Verse 8. *Have quieted my spirit in the north country.*] They have fulfilled my judgments on *Assyria* and *Chaldea*. Nabopolassar and Cyrus first, against the Assyrians and Chaldeans; and Alexander next, against the Persians. On this vision Abp. *Newcome* remarks:—

The *black horses* seem to denote the *Persian* empire; which, by subduing the *Chaldeans*, and being about to inflict a second heavy chastisement on *Babylon*, *quieted God's spirit* with respect to *Chaldea;* a country always spoken of as lying to the *north* of the Jews.

The *white horses* seem to be the Macedonian empire; which, like the Persian, overcame *Chaldea*.

The *spotted bay horses* seem to be the *Roman* empire. This description suits it because it was governed by *kings*, *consuls*, *dictators*, and *emperors*. It penetrated *southward* to Egypt and Africa. The Roman empire is mentioned twice, ver. 6, 7, under each epithet given it, ver. 3.

Verse 10. *Take of* them of *the captivity*] The names that follow were probably those to whom the silver and golden vessels of the temple were intrusted; and who might have had *bullion* of silver and gold, for particular purposes, about the ornaments of the temple.

The house of Josiah] Probably an artificer in silver, gold, &c.

Verse 11. *Make crowns*] עטרות *ataroth;* but *seven* MSS. of *Kennicott's* and *De Rossi's*, and *one* ancient of my own, with the *Syriac* and *Chaldee*, have עטרת *atereth*, a *crown*, or *tiara*. And as *Joshua* the high priest is *alone* concerned here, I think *one crown* only is intended.

A. M. cir. 3485
B. C. cir. 519
Ol. cir. LXV. 2
Tarquinii Superbi, R. Rom., cir. annum 16

12 And speak unto him, saying, Thus speaketh the LORD of hosts, saying, Behold [n]the man whose name *is* The [o]BRANCH; and he shall [p]grow up out of his place, [q]and he shall build the temple of the LORD.

13 Even he shall build the temple of the LORD; and he [r]shall bear the glory, and shall sit and rule upon his throne; and [s]he shall be a priest upon his throne: and the counsel of peace shall be between them both.

14 And the crowns shall be to Helen, and to Tobijah, and to Jedaiah, and to Hen the son of Zephaniah, [t]for a memorial in the temple of the LORD.

15 And [u]they *that are* far off shall come and build in the temple of the LORD, and [v]ye shall know that the LORD of hosts hath sent me unto you. And *this* shall come to pass, if ye will diligently obey the voice of the LORD your God.

---

[n]See Luke i. 78; John i. 45——[o]Chap. iii. 8——[p]Or, *branch up from under him*——[q]Chap. iv. 9; Matt. xvi. 18; Eph. ii. 20, 21, 22; Heb. iii. 3

[r]Isa. xxii. 24——[s]Psa. cx. 4; Heb. iii. 1——[t]Exod. xii. 14; Mark xiv. 9——[u]Isa. lvii. 19; lx. 10; Eph. ii. 13, 19——[v]Chap. ii. 9; iv. 9

Verse 12. *Behold the man whose name* is *The BRANCH!*] I cannot think that *Zerubbabel* is here intended; indeed, he is not so much as mentioned in chap. iii. 8. *Joshua and his companions* are called אנשי מופת *anshey mopheth, figurative* or *typical men;* the crowning therefore of Joshua in this place, and calling him the BRANCH, was most probably in reference to that glorious person, the *Messiah*, of whom he was the *type* or *figure.* The *Chaldee* has, "whose name is my MESSIAH," or CHRIST.

And he shall grow up out of his place] That is, out of David's root, tribe, and family.

And he shall build the temple of the Lord.] This cannot refer to the building of the temple then in hand, for Zerubbabel was its builder: but to that temple, the Christian Church, that was typified by it; for Zerubbabel is not named here, and only *Joshua* or *Jesus* (the name is the same) is the person who is to be *crowned* and *to build this spiritual temple.*

Verse 13. *Even he shall build the temple*] *Joshua*, not *Zerubbabel.*

He shall bear the glory] Have all the honour of it; for none can do this but himself. The *Messiah* is still intended.

And shall sit and rule upon his throne] For the government of the Church shall be upon his shoulder.

And he shall be a priest upon his throne] He shall, as the great *high priest*, offer the only *available offering* and *atonement;* and so he shall be both *king* and *priest*, a *royal king* and a *royal priest;* for even the *priest* is here stated to *sit upon his throne.*

And the counsel of peace shall be between them both.] Whom? Zerubbabel and Joshua? Certainly not Zerubbabel, for he is not mentioned in all this prediction; but, as the *Messiah* is intended, the *counsel of peace*—the *purpose to establish peace* between heaven and earth, must be between the *Father* and the *Son.*

Verse 14. *And the crowns shall be*] One of my MSS. has אטרות *ataroth, crowns*, corrected into עטרת *atereth, crown;* and so the *Septuagint, Syriac*, and *Arabic.* The *Chaldee* has, "And praise shall be," &c. The meaning appears to be this, that the *crown* made for *Joshua* should be delivered to the persons mentioned here and in ver. 10, to be laid up in the temple of the Lord, as a *memorial* of this typical transaction.

Verse 15. *And they* that are *far off shall come*] The Gentiles shall come to the Saviour of the world; and *build*—become a part of this new temple; for they, as *living stones*, shall become a holy temple, a habitation of God through the Spirit.

Ye shall know that the Lord of hosts hath sent me] These predictions, relative to the *regal* and *sacerdotal offices* of the Messiah, shall be so circumstantially fulfilled, that ye, Jews, shall be obliged to acknowledge that the Lord of hosts hath sent me with this message.

And this *shall come to pass*] Your own temple shall be rebuilt, and God shall dwell among you now, *if ye will diligently obey the voice of Jehovah your God.*

CHAPTER VII

Some Jews being sent from those who remained at Babylon to inquire of the priests and prophets at Jerusalem whether they were still bound to observe those fasts which had been appointed on occasion of the destruction of Jerusalem, and kept during the captivity, the prophet is commanded to take this opportunity of enforcing upon them the weightier matters of the law, judgment *and* mercy, *that they might not incur such calamities as befell their fathers. He also intimates that in their former fasts they had regarded themselves more than God; and that they had rested too much on the performance of external rites, although the former prophets had largely insisted on the superior excellence of moral duties,* 1–14.

A. M. 3486
B. C. 518
Ol. LXV. 3
Anno Tarquinii Superbi, R. Roman., 17

AND it came to pass in the
fourth year of king Darius,
that the word of the LORD came
unto Zechariah in the fourth *day*
of the ninth month, *even in* Chisleu;
2 When they had sent unto the house of
God Sherezer and Regem-melech, and their
men, [a]to pray before the LORD,
3 *And* to [b]speak unto the priest which
were in the house of the LORD of hosts, and
to the prophets, saying, Should I weep in
[c]the fifth month, separating myself, as I have
done these so many years?
4 Then came the word of the LORD of hosts
unto me, saying,
5 Speak unto all the people of the land, and
to the priests, saying, When ye [d]fasted and
mourned in the fifth [e]and seventh *month,*
[f]even those seventy years, did ye at all fast
[g]unto me, *even* to me?
6 And when ye did eat, and when ye did
drink, [h]did not ye eat *for yourselves,* and
drink *for yourselves?*

7 [i]*Should ye* not *hear* the
words which the LORD hath
cried [k]by the former prophets,
when Jerusalem was inhabited
and in prosperity, and the cities thereof round
about her, when *men* inhabited [l]the south and
the plain?

A. M. 3486
B. C. 518
Ol. LXV. 3
Anno Tarquinii Superbi, R. Roman., 17

8 And the word of the LORD came unto
Zechariah, saying,
9 Thus speaketh the LORD of hosts, saying,
[m]Execute [n]true judgment, and show mercy
and compassions every man to his brother:
10 And [o]oppress not the widow, nor the fatherless, the stranger, nor the poor, [p]and let
none of you imagine evil against his brother in
your heart.
11 But they refused to hearken, and [q]pulled
[r]away the shoulder, and [s]stopped [t]their ears,
that they should not hear.
12 Yea, they made their [u]hearts *as* an adamant stone, [v]lest they should hear the law,
and the words which the LORD of hosts hath
sent in his [w]Spirit by the former prophets:

---

[a]Heb. *to entreat the face of the LORD;* 1 Sam. xiii. 12; chap. viii. 21——[b]Deut. xvii. 9, 10, 11; xxxiii. 10; Mal. ii. 7——[c]Jer. lii. 12; chap. viii. 19——[d]Isa. lviii. 5——[e]Jer. iv. 1; chap. viii. 19——[f]Chap. i. 12——[g]See Rom. xiv. 6——[h]Or, be *not ye they that,* &c.——[i]Or, Are *not* these *the words*——[k]Heb. *by the hand of,* &c.——[l]Jer. xvii. 26——[m]Isa. lviii. 6, 7; Jer. vii. 23; Mic. vi. 8; chap. viii. 16; Matt. xxiii. 23——[n]Heb *Judge judgment of truth*——[o]Exod. xxii. 21, 22; Deut. xxiv. 17; Isa. i. 17; Jer. v. 28——[p]Psa. xxxvi. 4; Mic. ii. 1; chap. viii. 17——[q]Neh. ix. 29; Jer. vii. 24; Hos. iv. 16——[r]Heb. *they gave a backsliding shoulder*——[s]Heb. *made heavy*——[t]Acts vii. 57——[u]Ezek. xi. 19; xxxvi. 26——[v]Neh. ix. 29, 30——[w]Heb. *by the hand of*

NOTES ON CHAP. VII

Verse 1. *The fourth year of King Darius*] Two years after they began to rebuild the temple, see chap. i. 1, A. M. 3486.

The ninth month, even *in Chisleu*] This answers to a part of our *November* and *December.* The names of the month appear only under and after the captivity.

Verse 2. *When they had sent—Sherezer and Regem-melech*] To inquire whether the fasts should be continued, which they had hitherto observed on account of their ruined temple; and the reason why they inquired was, that they were rebuilding that temple, and were likely to bring it to a joyful issue.

Verse 5. *When ye fasted and mourned in the fifth*—month] This they did in the remembrance of the *burning of the temple,* on the *tenth* day of that month; and on the *seventh month,* on the *third* of which month they observed a fast for the murder of Gedaliah, and the dispersion of the remnant of the people which were with him. See Jer. xli. 1, and 2 Kings xxv. 25.

Verse 6. *And when ye did eat*] They had not observed those fasts as they should have done. They deplored the loss of their temple, and its riches, &c.; but they did not *humble themselves* because of those iniquities which had brought the *displeasure* of God upon them, their temple, and their city.

Verse 7. *The words which the Lord hath cried by the former prophets*] נביאים הראשנים *nebiim harishonim*, is the title which the Jews give to *Joshua*, *Judges*, the two books of *Samuel*, and the two books of *Kings*.

The *latter prophets,* נביאים אחרונים *nebiim acharonim*, are *Isaiah*, *Jeremiah*, *Ezekiel*, and the *twelve minor prophets.*

The *hagiographa*, כתובים *kethubim*, holy writings, are the *Psalms*, *Proverbs*, *Job*. *Canticles*, *Ruth*, *Lamentations*, *Ecclesiastes*, *Esther*, *Daniel*, *Ezra*, *Nehemiah*, and the two books of *Chronicles*. But the above words, *the former prophets*, seem to apply to *Isaiah*, *Jeremiah*, and *Ezekiel*.

The south and the plain?] From Eleutheropolis to the sea, Obad. 19. The *south* was the wilderness and mountainous parts of Judea: and the *plain*, the plains of Jericho.

Verse 9. *Execute true judgment*] See the parallel texts in the margin.

Verse 10. *Evil against his brother in your heart.*] Do not indulge an *unfavourable opinion* of another: do not *envy* him; do not *harbour* an *unbrotherly feeling* towards him.

Verse 11. *Pulled away the shoulder*] From under the yoke of the law, like an unbroken or restive bullock in the plough.

Verse 12. *Made their hearts* as *an adamant stone*] שמיר *shamir* may mean the *granite*. This is the hardest stone with which the common people could be acquainted. Perhaps the *cor-*

A. M. 3486
B. C. 518
Ol. LXV. 3
Anno Tarquinii Superbi,
R. Roman., 17

[x]therefore came a great wrath
from the LORD of hosts.
13 Therefore it is come to
pass, *that* as he cried, and they
would not hear; so [y]they cried, and I would
not hear, saith the LORD of hosts.

[x]2 Chron. xxxvi. 16; Dan. ix. 11——[y]Prov. i. 24–28; Isa. i. 15; Jer. xi. 11; xiv. 12; Mic. iii. 4——[z]Deut. iv. 27;

undum, of which *emery* is a species, may be intended. *Bochart* thinks it means a stone used in *polishing* others. The same name, in Hebrew, applies to different stones.

Verse 14. *I scattered them with a whirlwind*]

A. M. 3486
B. C. 518
Ol. LXV. 3
Anno Tarquinii Superbi,
R. Roman., 17

14 But [z]I scattered them with
a whirlwind among all the nations
[a]whom they knew not. Thus
[b]the land was desolate after
them, that no man passed through nor returned:
for they laid [c]the [d]pleasant land desolate.

xxviii. 64; Ezek. xxxvi. 19; ch. ii. 6——[a]Deut. xxviii. 33——[b]Lev. xxvi. 22——[c]Dan. viii. 9——[d]Heb. *land of desire*

This refers to the swift victories and cruel conduct of the Chaldeans towards the Jews; they came upon them like a *whirlwind;* they were tossed to and fro, and up and down, everywhere scattered and confounded.

CHAPTER VIII

In this chapter God promises the continuance of his favour to those who are returned from the captivity; so that, upon the removal of his judgments, the fasts they had observed during the captivity may now be converted to so many occasions of rejoicing. He likewise promises in due time a general restoration of his people, and the enlargement of the Church by the accession of the Gentiles, 1–20. *The conclusion of the chapter intimates farther that the Jews, after their restoration, will be instrumental in converting many other nations,* 21–23. *Compare* Rom. xi. 15, 16.

A. M. 3486
B. C. 518
Ol. LXV. 3
Anno Tarquinii Superbi,
R. Roman., 17

AGAIN the word of the LORD
of hosts came *to me,* saying,
2 Thus saith the LORD of hosts;
[a]I was jealous for Zion with
great jealousy, and I was jealous for her with
great fury.
3 Thus saith the LORD; [b]I am returned
unto Zion, and [c]will dwell in the midst of Jerusalem:
and Jerusalem [d]shall be called A city
of truth: and [e]the mountain of the LORD of
hosts, [f]The holy mountain.
4 Thus saith the LORD of hosts; [g]There
shall yet old men and old women dwell in the
streets of Jerusalem, and every
man with his staff in his hand
[h]for very age.
5 And the streets of the city
shall be full of boys and girls playing in the
streets thereof.
6 Thus saith the LORD of hosts; If it be
[i]marvellous in the eyes of the remnant of this
people in these days, [k]should it also be marvellous
in mine eyes? saith the LORD of hosts.
7 Thus saith the LORD of hosts; Behold, [l]I
will save my people from the east country, and
from [m]the west country;

[a]Neh. i. 2; chap. i. 14——[b]Chap. i. 16——[c]Chap. ii. 10——[d]Isa. i. 21, 26——[e]Isa. ii. 2, 3——[f]Jer. xxxi. 23——[g]See 1 Sam. ii. 31; Isa. lxv. 20, 22; Lam. ii. 20, &c.; v. 11–14——[h]Heb. *for multitude of days*

[i]Or, *hard,* or *difficult*——[k]Gen. xviii. 14; Luke i. 37; xviii. 27; Rom. iv. 21——[l]Isa. xi. 11, 12; xliii. 5, 6; Ezek. xxxvii. 21; Amos ix. 14, 15——[m]Heb. *the country of the going down of the sun;* See Psa. l. 1; cxiii. 3; Mal. i. 11

NOTES ON CHAP. VIII

Verse 2. *I was jealous*] Some refer this to the *Jews* themselves. They were as the *spouse* of Jehovah: but they were *unfaithful,* and God punished them as an *injured husband* might be expected to punish an unfaithful wife. Others apply it to the *enemies of the Jews.* Though I gave them a commission to afflict you, yet they exceeded their commission: I will therefore deal with them in *fury—*in *vindictive justice.*

Verse 3. *I am returned unto Zion*] I have restored her from her captivity. I will dwell among them. The temple shall be rebuilt, and so shall Jerusalem; and instead of being false, unholy, and profligate, it shall be *the city of truth,* and *my holy mountain.* TRUTH *shall dwell in it.*

Verse 4. *There shall yet old men and old women*] In those happy times the followers of God shall live out all their days, and the *hoary head* be always found in the way of righteousness.

Verse 5. *The streets of the city shall be full of boys and girls*] The progeny shall be *numerous, healthy,* and *happy.* Their innocent gambols and useful exercises shall be a means of *health,* and a proof of *happiness.* To be healthy, children must have exercise. But they cannot take exercise, except in the way of play and diversion: *ergo,* such playfulness cannot be sinful. Let them be kept from evil words, lying, swearing, and scurrility; and all the rest may be innocent.

Verse 6. *If it be marvellous*] You may think that this is impossible, considering your present low condition: but suppose it be impossible in *your eyes,* should it be so in *mine? saith the Lord of hosts.*

Verse 7. *I will save my people from the east*

A. M. 3486
B. C. 518
Ol. LXV. 3
Anno Tarquinii
Superbi,
R. Roman., 17

8 And I will bring them, and they shall dwell in the midst of Jerusalem: [n]and they shall be my people, and I will be their God, [o]in truth and in righteousness.

9 Thus saith the LORD of hosts; [p]Let your hands be strong, ye that hear in these days these words by the mouth of [q]the prophets, which *were* in [r]the day *that* the foundation of the house of the LORD of hosts was laid, that the temple might be built.

10 For before these days [s]there was no [t]hire for man, nor any hire for beasts; [u]neither *was there any* peace to him that went out or came in because of the affliction: for I set all men every one against his neighbour.

11 But now I *will* not *be* unto the residue of this people as in the former days, saith the LORD of hosts.

12 [v]For the seed *shall be* [w]prosperous; the vine shall give her fruit, and [x]the ground shall give her increase, and [y]the heavens shall give their dew; and I will cause the remnant of this people to possess all these *things*.

13 And it shall come to pass, *that* as ye were [z]a curse among the heathen, O house of Judah, and house of Israel; so will I save you, and [a]ye shall be a blessing: fear not, *but* [b]let your hands be strong.

14 For thus saith the LORD of hosts; [c]As I thought to punish you, when your fathers provoked me to wrath, saith the LORD of hosts, [d]and I repented not:

15 So again have I thought in these days to do well unto Jerusalem and to the house of Judah: fear ye not.

16 These *are* the things that ye shall do; [e]Speak ye every man the truth to his neighbour; [f]execute the judgment of truth and peace in your gates:

17 [g]And let none of you imagine evil in your hearts against his neighbour; and [h]love no false oath: for all these *are things* that I hate, saith the LORD.

18 And the word of the LORD of hosts came unto me, saying,

19 Thus saith the LORD of hosts; [i]The fast of the fourth *month*, [k]and the fast of the fifth, [l]and the fast of the seventh, [m]and the fast of the tenth, shall be to the house of Judah [n]joy and gladness, and cheerful [o]feasts; [p]therefore love the truth and peace.

20 Thus saith the LORD of hosts; *It shall*

[n]Jer. xxx. 22; xxxi. 1, 33; ch. xiii. 9——[o]Jer. iv. 2 [p]Hag. ii. 4; ver. 18——[q]Ezra v. 1, 2——[r]Hag. ii. 18 [s]Or, *the hire of man became nothing*, &c.——[t]Hag. i. 6, 9, 10; ii. 16——[u]2 Chron. xv. 5——[v]Hos. ii. 21, 22; Joel ii. 22; Hag. ii. 19——[w]Heb. *of peace*——[x]Psa. lxvii. 6 [y]See Hag. i. 10——[z]Jer. xlii. 18——[a]Gen. xii. 2; Ruth iv. 11, 12; Isa. xix. 24, 25; Zeph. ii. 20; Hag. ii. 19

[b]Ver. 9——[c]Jer. xxxi. 28——[d]2 Chron. xxxvi. 16: chap. i. 6——[e]Chap. vii. 9; ver. 19; Eph. iv. 25 [f]Heb. *judge truth and the judgment of peace*——[g]Prov. iii. 29; chap. vii. 10——[h]Chap. v. 3, 4——[i]Jer. lii. 6, 7 [k]Jer. lii. 12, 13; chapter vii. 3, 5——[l]2 Kings xxv. 25; Jer. xli. 1, 2——[m]Jer. lii. 4——[n]Esth. viii. 17; Isa. xxxv. 10——[o]Or, *solemn*, or *set times*——[p]Ver. 16

country, and from the west] From every land in which any of them may be found. But these promises principally regard the Christian Church, or the bringing in the Jews with the fulness of the Gentiles.

Verse 9. *By the mouth of the prophets*] The day or time of the foundation was about *two years* before, as this discourse of the prophet was in the *fourth* year of Darius. After this God raised up prophets among them.

Verse 10. *For before these days there was no hire for man*] Previously to this, ye had no prosperity; ye had nothing but civil divisions and domestic broils. I abandoned you to your own *spirits*, and to your own *ways*.

Verse 12. *For the seed* shall be *prosperous*] Ye shall be a holy and peaceable people; and God will pour down his blessing on yourselves, your fields, and your vineyards.

Verse 13. *As ye were a curse*] Instead of being execrated among the people, ye shall be blessed; instead of being reproached, ye shall be commended. Ye shall be a *blessing* to all the nations round about. All these promises we may expect to be completely fulfilled when the Jews acknowledge their Messiah.

O house of Judah, and house of Israel] The restoration shall be complete, when both *Israel* and *Judah* are brought back.

Verse 16. *Speak ye every man the truth*] See chap. vii. 9, 10.

Verse 19. *The fast of the fourth* month] To commemorate the *taking of Jerusalem;* 2 Kings xxv. 3; Jer. xxxix. 2, and lii. 6, 7.

The fast of the fifth] In memory of the *ruin of the temple*, 2 Kings xxv. 8; Jer. lii. 12, 13.

The fast of the seventh] For the *murder of Gedaliah*, Jer. xli. 1-17.

The fast of the tenth] In commemoration of the *siege of Jerusalem*, which began on the *tenth* day of the *tenth* month; 2 Kings xxv. 1; Jer. lii. 4; Ezek. xxiv. 1, 2; and see on chap. vii. 3, 5.

Cheerful feasts] Ye shall find all your evils so completely redressed, that these *mournful fasts* shall be turned into *joyful feasts*.

Verse 20. *There shall come people*] Similar promises to those in Isa. ii. 3, and in Mic. iv. 1, 2. Many *Gentiles*, as well as *Jews*, will then be found devoting themselves to the Lord.

A. M. 3486
B. C. 518
Ol. LXV. 3
Anno Tarquinii Superbi,
R. Roman., 17

yet *come to pass,* that there shall
come people, and the inhabitants
of many cities:
21 And the inhabitants of one
city shall go to another, saying, [q]Let us [r]go
[s]speedily [t]to pray before the LORD, and to
seek the LORD of hosts: I will go also.
22 Yea, [u]many people and strong nations
shall come to seek the LORD of hosts in Jerusalem, and to pray before the
LORD.
23 Thus saith the LORD of
hosts; In those days *it shall*
come to pass, that ten men shall [v]take hold
out of all languages of the nations, even shall
take hold of the skirt of him that is a Jew,
saying, We will go with you: for we have
heard [w]*that* God *is* with you.

[q]Isa. ii. 3; Mic. iv. 1, 2——[r]Or, *continually*——[s]Hebrew, *going*——[t]Heb. *to entreat the face of the LORD;* chapter vii. 2——[u]Isaiah lx. 3, &c.; lxvi. 23——[v]Isaiah iii. 6; iv. 1——[w]1 Cor. xiv. 25

Verse 21. *I will go also.*] This is the answer of the person *invited.* It is a good work. We must have God for our friend. We cannot expect this unless we *seek* him: and as we know not what an hour may bring forth, let us go *speedily.*

Verse 22. *And strong nations*] This may refer to the conversion of the *Mohammedan* tribes; especially to those in the vicinity of Palestine. Perhaps even the *Egyptians,* inhabitants of *Arabia Petræa,* of *Syria,* &c.

Verse 23. *Ten men—shall take hold of the skirt of him that is a Jew*] The converts from among the Gentiles shall be to the Jews as *ten* to *one.* But *ten* may here signify a great number, without comparison. And from this scripture it appears as if the Jews, converted to God, should be the instruments of converting many *Gentiles.* See on Isa. iii. 6. *Catching hold of the skirt* is a gesture naturally used to entreat assistance and protection. This and the three foregoing verses, says Abp. *Newcome,* refer to the great accession of converts which the Jewish Church received between the captivity and the coming of Christ; to the number of *Christian* disciples which the Jewish preachers made, and to the future conversions of which the restoration of the Jews will be an eminent cause.

CHAPTER IX

Syria, Phœnicia, and Palestine, were conquered by Nebuchadnezzar, and afterwards by Alexander. Some apply the beginning of this chapter (1–7) *to the one event, and some to the other. The close of the* seventh *verse relates to the number of Philistines that should become proselytes to Judaism; (see* Joseph. *Antiq.* xiv. 15, 4;) *and the* eighth, *to the watchful providence of God over his temple in those troublesome times. From this the prophet passes on to that most eminent instance of God's goodness to his Church and people, the sending of the Messiah, with an account of the peaceable tendency and great extent of his kingdom,* 9, 10. *God then declares that he has ratified his covenant with his people, delivered them from their captivity, and restored them to favour,* 11, 12. *In consequence of this, victory over their enemies is promised them in large and lofty terms, with every other kind of prosperity,* 13–17. *Judas Maccabeus gained several advantages over the troops of Antiochus, who was of Grecian or Macedonian descent. But without excluding these events, it must be allowed that the terms of this prophecy are much too strong to be confined to them; their ultimate fulfilment must therefore be referred to Gospel times.*

A. M. cir. 3417
B. C. cir. 587
Ol. XLVIII. 2
TarquiniiPrisci, R. Roman., cir. annum 30

THE [a]burden of the word of
the LORD in the land of Hadrach, and [b]Damascus *shall be*
the rest thereof: when [c]the eyes
of man, as of all the tribes of
Israel, *shall be* toward the LORD.
2 And [d]Hamath also shall
border thereby; [e]Tyrus, and

[a]Jer. xxiii. 33——[b]Amos i. 3——[c]2 Chron. xx. 12; Psa. cxlv. 15 [d]Jer. xlix. 23——[e]Isa. xxiii.; Ezek. xxvi., xxvii., xxviii.; Amos i. 9

NOTES ON CHAP IX

Verse 1. *The burden of the word of the Lord*] The *oracle* contained in the word which Jehovah now speaks.

This is a prophecy against Syria, the Philistines, Tyre, and Sidon, which were to be subdued by Alexander the Great. After this the prophet speaks gloriously concerning the coming of Christ, and redemption by him.

Most learned men are of opinion that this and the succeeding chapters are not the work of *Zechariah,* but rather of *Jeremiah, Hosea,* or some one before the captivity. It is certain that chap. xi. 12, 13, is quoted Matt. xxvii. 9, 10, as the language of *Jeremiah* the prophet. The *first eight* chapters appear by the introductory parts to be the prophecies of *Zechariah:* they stand in connection with each other, are pertinent to the time when they were delivered, are uniform in style and manner, and constitute a regular whole; but the *six last* chapters are not expressly assigned to Zechariah, and are unconnected with those that precede:—the *three* first of them are unsuitable in many parts to the time when Zechariah lived; all of them

A. M. cir. 3417
B. C. cir. 587
Ol. XLVIII. 2
TarquiniiPrisci,
R. Roman.,
cir. annum 30

[f]Zidon, though it be very
[g]wise.
3 And Tyrus did build herself
a strong hold, and [h]heaped up
silver as the dust, and fine gold as the mire of
the streets.
4 Behold, [i]the LORD will cast her out, and
he will smite [k]her power in the sea; and she
shall be devoured with fire.
5 [l]Ashkelon shall see *it,* and fear; Gaza
also *shall see it,* and be very sorrowful, and
Ekron; for her expectation shall be ashamed;
and the king shall perish from
Gaza, and Ashkelon shall not be
inhabited.
6 And a bastard shall dwell
[m]in Ashdod, and I will cut off the pride of
the Philistines.
7 And I will take away his [n]blood out of
his mouth, and his abominations from between
his teeth: but he that remaineth, even he
shall be for our God, and he shall be as a
governor in Judah, and Ekron as a Jebusite.
8 And [o]I will encamp about mine house

[f]1 Kings xvii. 9; Ezekiel xxviii. 21; Obadiah 20 [g]Ezekiel xxviii. 3, &c.——[h]Job xvii. 16; Ezekiel xxviii. 4, 5——[i]Isaiah xxiii. 1——[k]Ezekiel xxvi. 1, 7

[l]Jeremiah xlvii. 1, 5; Zephaniah ii. 4——[m]Amos i. 8——[n]Hebrew, *bloods*——[o]Psalm xxxiv. 7; chapter ii. 5

have a more adorned and poetical turn of composition than the eight first chapters, and they manifestly break the unity of the prophetical book.

I conclude, from internal marks, that these three chapters, (ix., x., xi.,) were written much *earlier* than the time of Jeremiah, and before the captivity of the *ten tribes.* They seem to suit *Hosea's* age and manner; but whoever wrote them, their Divine authority is established by the two *quotations* from them, chap. ix. 9, and xi. 12, 13. See below.

The *twelfth, thirteenth,* and *fourteenth* chapters form a distinct prophecy, and were *written after the death of Josiah,* chap. xii. 11; but whether before or after the captivity, and by *what prophet,* is uncertain, although I incline to think that the author lived *before* the destruction of Jerusalem by the Babylonians. See on chap. xiii. 2-6. They are *twice* quoted in the New Testament, chap. xii. 10, and xiii. 7.—*Newcome.*

My own opinion is, that these chapters form not only a distinct *work,* but belong to a *different author.* If they do not belong to *Jeremiah,* they form a *thirteenth* book in the *minor prophets,* but the inspired writer is unknown.

The land of Hadrach] The valley of Damascus, or a place near to Damascus. Alexander the Great gained possession of Damascus, and took all its treasures; but it was without blood; the city was betrayed to him.

Damascus shall be *the rest thereof*] The principal part of this calamity shall fall on this city. God's anger *rests* on those whom he *punishes,* Ezek. v. 13, xvi. 42, xxiv. 13. And his rod, or his *arm, rests* upon his enemies, Psa. cxxv. 3; Isai. xxx. 23. See *Newcome.*

When the eye of man] *Newcome* translates thus:

"For the eye of Jehovah is *over* man,
And over all the tribes of Israel."

This is an easy sense, and is followed by the *versions.*

Verse 2. *And Hamath also shall border thereby*] *Hamath* on the river Orontes; and *Tyre* and *Sidon,* notwithstanding their political wisdom, address, and cunning, shall have a part in the punishment.

These prophecies are more suitable to the days of *Jeremiah* than to those of *Zechariah;* for there is no evidence—although Alexander did take Damascus, but *without bloodshed*—that it was destroyed from the times of Zechariah to the advent of our Lord. And as *Tyre* and *Sidon* were lately destroyed by Nebuchadnezzar, it is not likely that they could soon undergo another devastation.

Verse 3. *And Tyrus did build herself*] The rock on which Tyre was built was strongly *fortified;* and that she had abundance of *riches* has been already seen, Ezek. xxviii. 1, &c.

Verse 4. *Will smite her power in the sea*] See Ezek. xxvi. 17. Though Alexander did take Tyre, Sidon, Gaza, &c.; yet it seems that the prediction relative to their destruction was fulfilled by *Nebuchadnezzar.* See Amos i. 6-8; Zeph. ii. 4, 7.

Verse 5. *Ashkelon shall see* it, *and fear*] All these prophecies seem to have been fulfilled before the days of Zechariah; another evidence that these last chapters were not written by him.

Her expectation shall be ashamed] The expectation of being succoured by Tyre.

Verse 6. *A bastard shall dwell in Ashdod*] This character would suit Alexander very well, who most certainly was a *bastard;* for his mother Olympia said that Jupiter Ammon entered her apartment in the shape of a dragon, and begat Alexander! Could her husband Philip believe this? The word signifies a *stranger.*

Verse 7. *I will take away his blood out of his mouth*] The Philistines, when incorporated with the Israelites, shall abstain from *blood,* and every thing that is abominable.

And Ekron as a Jebusite.] As an inhabitant of Jerusalem. Many of the Philistines became proselytes to Judiasm; and particularly the cities of Gaza, and *Ashdod.* See *Joseph.* Antiq. lib. xiii., c. 15, s. 4.

Verse 8. *I will encamp about mine house*] This may apply to the conquests in Palestine by *Alexander,* who, coming with great wrath against Jerusalem, was met by *Jaddua* the high priest and his fellows in their sacred robes, who made intercession for the city and the temple; and, in consequence, Alexander spared *both,* which he had previously purposed to destroy. He showed the Jews also much favour, and remitted the tax every *seventh year,* be-

A. M. cir. 3417
B. C. cir. 587
Ol. XLVIII. 2
TarquiniiPrisci,
R. Roman.,
cir. annum 30

because of the army, because of
him that passeth by, and because
of him that returneth: and [p]no
oppressor shall pass through
them any more: for now [q]have I seen with
mine eyes.
9 [r]Rejoice greatly, O daughter of Zion;
shout, O daughter of Jerusalem: behold, [s]thy
King cometh unto thee: he *is* just, and
[t]having salvation; lowly, and riding upon an
ass, and upon a colt the foal of an ass.
10 And I [u]will cut off the chariot from
Ephraim, and the horse from Jerusalem, and
the battle bow shall be cut off: and he shall
speak [v]peace unto the heathen: and his dominion *shall be* [w]from sea *even*
to sea, and from the river *even*
to the ends of the earth.
11 As for thee also, [x]by the
blood of thy covenant I have sent forth thy
[y]prisoners out of the pit wherein *is* no water.
12 Turn you to the strong hold, [z]ye prisoners of hope: even to-day do I declare *that*
[a]I will render double unto thee;
13 When I have bent Judah for me, filled
the bow with Ephraim, and raised up thy sons,
O Zion, against thy sons, O Greece, and made
thee as the sword of a mighty man.
14 And the LORD shall be seen over them,
and [b]his arrow shall go forth as the lightning:

A. M. cir. 3417
B. C. cir. 587
Ol. XLVIII. 2
TarquiniiPrisci,
R. Roman.,
cir. annum 30

[p]Isa. lx. 18; Ezek. xxviii. 24——[q]Exod. iii. 7
[r]Isa. lxii. 11; ch. ii. 10; Matt. xxi. 5; John xii. 15
[s]Jer. xxiii. 5; xxx. 9; John i. 49; Luke xix. 38——[t]Or,
saving himself——[u]Hos. i. 7; ii. 18; Mic. v. 10; Hag. ii. 22

[v]Eph. ii. 14, 17——[w]Psa. lxxii. 8——[x]Or, *whose covenant* is *by blood;* Exod. xxiv. 8; Heb. x. 29; xiii. 20
[y]Isa. xlii. 7; li. 14; lxi. 1——[z]Isa. xlix. 9——[a]Isa. lxi. 7
[b]Psa. xviii. 14; lxxvii. 17; cxliv. 6

cause the *law* on that year forbade them to *cultivate* their ground. See this extraordinary account in *Joseph.* Antiq. lib. xi., c. 8, s. 5. Bishop *Newcome* translates: "I will encamp about my house with an army, so that none shall pass through or return."

Verse 9. *Rejoice greatly, O daughter of Zion*] See this prophecy explained on Matt. xxi. 5.

Behold, thy King cometh] Not *Zerubbabel*, for he was never *king;* nor have they had a *king*, except Jesus the Christ, from the days of Zedekiah to the present time.

He is *just*] The righteous One, and the Fountain of righteousness.

Having salvation] He alone can *save* from *sin*, *Satan*, *death*, and *hell.*

Lowly] Without *worldly pomp* or *splendour;* for neither his kingdom, nor that of his followers, is of *this world.*

Riding upon an ass] God had commanded the kings of Israel not to multiply *horses.* The kings who broke this command were miserable themselves, and scourgers to their people. Jesus came to *fulfil the law.* Had he in his title of *king* rode upon a *horse*, it would have been a *breach* of a positive command of God; therefore, he rode upon an *ass*, and thus fulfilled the *prophecy*, and kept the *precept* unbroken. Hence it is immediately added—

Verse 10. *I will cut off the chariot from Ephraim, and the horse from Jerusalem*] No wars shall be employed to spread the kingdom of the Messiah; for it shall be founded and established, "not by might nor by power, but by the Spirit of the Lord of hosts," chap. iv. 6.

Verse 11. *As for thee also* (Jerusalem) *by the blood of thy covenant*] The covenant made with Abraham, Isaac, Jacob, and the Israelites in general, and ratified by the *blood* of many victims; until the time should come in which the *Messiah* should shed his blood, as typified by the ancient sacrifices.

I have sent forth thy prisoners] Those who were under the arrest of God's judgments; the *human race*, fast bound in sin and misery, and who by the pitifulness of his tender mercy were loosed, he dying in their stead.

Verse 12. *Turn you to the strong hold*] Ye who *feel* your *sins*, and are *shut up* under a sense of your guilt, look up to him who was delivered for your offences, and rose again for your justification. Ye have *hope;* let that hope lead you to *faith*, and that faith to the *blood of the covenant;* and, through that *blood*, to GOD, the Father of all.

I will render double unto thee] Give thee an *abundance* of peace and salvation.

Verse 13. *When I have bent Judah*] Judah is the *bow*, and Ephraim is the *arrows;* and these are to be shot against the *Greeks.* I am inclined, with Bp. *Newcome*, to consider that the language of this prophecy is too strong to point out the only trifling advantage which the *Maccabees* gained over *Antiochus*, who was of *Macedonian descent;* and it is probable that these prophecies remain to be fulfilled against the present possessors of *Javan* or *Greece*, *Macedonia*, and a part of *Asia Minor.*

Verse 14. *The Lord shall be seen over them*] Shadowing and refreshing them, as the cloud did the camp in the wilderness.

His arrow shall go forth as the lightning] They shall be conquered in a way that will show that God fights for his followers.

The description here is very sublime; we have a good imitation of it in Nonnus:—

Και τοτε γαιαν ἁπασαν επεκλυσεν ὑετιος Ζευς,
Πυκνωσας νεφεεσσιν ὁλον πολον· ουρανιη γαρ
Βρονταιοις παταγοισι Διος μυκησατο σαλπιγξ.

NONN. DIONYS., lib. 6. ver. 229.

"When heaven's dread *trumpet*, sounding from on high,
Breaks forth in thunders through the darken'd sky;
The pregnant clouds to floods of rain give birth.
And stormy Jove o'erwhelms the solid earth."

J. B. B. C.

In these two verses there is a fine *image*, and an *allusion* to a particular fact, which have escaped the notice of every commentator. I

A. M. cir. 3417 B. C. cir. 587 Ol. XLVIII. 2 TarquiniiPrisci, R. Roman., cir. annum 30

and the Lord GOD shall blow
the trumpet, and shall go [c]with
whirlwinds of the south.
15 The LORD of hosts shall
defend them; and they shall devour, and
[d]subdue with sling-stones; and they shall
drink, *and* make a noise as through wine; and
they [e]shall be filled like bowls, *and* as [f]the
corners of the altar.

16 And the LORD their God
shall save them in that day as the
flock of his people: for [g]*they*
shall be as the stones of a crown,
[h]lifted up as an ensign upon his land.
17 For [i]how great *is* his goodness, and how
great *is* his beauty! [k]corn shall make the
young men [l]cheerful, and new wine the
maids.

---

[c]Isa. xxi. 1——[d]Or, *subdue the stones of the sling*——[e]Or, *shall fill both the bowls, &c.*——[f]Lev. iv. 18, 24; Deut. xii. 27

[g]Isa. lxii. 3; Mal. iii. 17——[h]Isa. xi.1 2——[i]Psa. xxxi. 19——[k]Joel iii. 18; Amos ix. 14——[l]Or, *grow*, or *speak*

---

must repeat the verses: 13: When I have *bent* Judah for me, *filled the bow* with Ephraim, and raised up thy sons, O Zion, against thy sons, O Greece, and made thee as the sword of a mighty man. 14: And the LORD shall be seen over them, and *his arrows shall go forth like lightning.* The reader will consult what is said on Hos. vii. 16, relative to the *oriental bow*, which resembles a ◯ in its quiescent state, and must be *recurved* in order to be strung. Here, *Judah* is represented as the *recurved bow; Ephraim*, as an *arrow* placed on the *string*, and then discharged against the Javanites or Greeks with the momentum of *lightning;* the *arrow kindling* in its course through the air, and thus becoming the bolt of death to them against whom it was directed.

Volat illud, et incandescit eundo,
Et quos non habuit, sub nubibus invenit ignes.

"It flies apace; and, *heating*, mounts on high,
Glows in its course, and *burns* along the sky."

Verse 15. *The Lord of hosts shall defend them*] He alone is the sure trust of his Church.

Subdue with sling-stones] This was an ancient and powerful *instrument* in the hands of the Hebrews. See the note on Judg. xx. 16.

They shall drink] After the victory gained as above, thy people shall hold a *feast*, and *drink and be filled with wine.* There is no intimation here that they shall *drink the blood of their enemies*, as some barbarous nations were accustomed to do. When they have gained the victory, they shall banquet abundantly on the spoils taken from the enemy.

As the corners of the altar.] They shall pour out libations of wine at the foot of the altar, as the priests were accustomed to pour out the blood of the victims.

Verse 16. *Shall save them in that day*] They are his *flock*, and he is their *Shepherd;* and, as his own, he shall save and defend them.

As *the stones of a crown*] אבני נזר מתנוססות *abney nezer mithnosesoth*, "crowned stones erecting themselves;" i. e., being *set up by themselves*, as *monuments* of some deliverance, they seem to be *lifting themselves up;* offering themselves to the *attention* of every passenger. It may however refer to *stones anointed with oil;* a sort of temporary *altars* set up to the Lord for a victory gained. The same word is used, Lev. xxi. 12: "Because the crown, נֵזֶר *nezer*, of the anointing oil of his God is upon him." Perhaps most of those *upright stones*, standing in *circles*, which pass for *druidical monuments*, were erected to commemorate victories, or to grace the tomb of an illustrious chief. These verses may refer to some final victory over the enemies of God's people.

Verse 17. *How great* is *his goodness*] In *himself* and towards *them.*

And how great is his beauty!] His *comeliness, holiness*, and *purity*, put *in* and upon them.

Corn shall make the young men cheerful] They shall be gladdened and strengthened by plenty of food; and they shall *speak aloud* of God's mercies in their *harvest home.*

And new wine the maids.] Who shall prepare the wine from an abundant vintage.

CHAPTER X

The promise of prosperity and plenty in the close of the preceding chapter leads the prophet to suggest, next, the means of obtaining them; supplication to Jehovah, and not to idols, whose worship had already proved a fertile source of calamities, 1–3. *The rest of the chapter (like the preceding) promises to the Jews a restoration to their own land under rulers and governors, victory over their enemies, and much increase and prosperity; and this in a manner so miraculous that it is described,* 4–12, *by allusions to the deliverance from Egypt.*

A. M. cir. 3417
B. C. cir. 587
Ol. XLVIII. 2
TarquiniiPrisci,
R. Roman.,
cir. annum 30

ASK ye [a]of the LORD [b]rain
[c]in the time of the latter
rain; *so* the LORD shall make
[d]bright clouds, and give them
showers of rain, to every one grass in the field.
2 For the [e]idols[f] have spoken vanity, and
the diviners have seen a lie, and have told
false dreams; they [g]comfort in vain: therefore they went their way as a flock, they [h]were
troubled, [i]because *there was* no shepherd.
3 Mine anger was kindled against the shepherds, [k]and I [l]punished the goats: for the
LORD of hosts [m]hath visited his flock the house
of Judah, and [n]hath made them as his goodly
horse in the battle.
4 Out of him came forth [o]the corner, out of
him [p]the nail, out of him the battle-bow, out
of him every oppressor together.
5 And they shall be as mighty *men,* which
[q]tread down *their enemies* in the mire of the
streets in the battle: and they
shall fight, because the LORD *is*
with them, and [r]the riders on
horses shall be confounded.

A. M. cir. 3417
B. C. cir. 587
Ol. XLVIII. 2
TarquiniiPrisci,
R. Roman.,
cir. annum 30

6 And I will strengthen the house of Judah,
and I will save the house of Joseph, and [s]I
will bring them again to place them; for I
[t]have mercy upon them: and they shall be
as though I had not cast them off: for I *am*
the LORD their God, and [u]will hear them.
7 And *they of* Ephraim shall be like a
mighty *man,* and their [v]heart shall rejoice as
through wine: yea, their children shall see
it, and be glad; their heart shall rejoice in
the LORD.
8 I will [w]hiss for them, and gather them;
for I have redeemed them: [x]and they shall
increase as they have increased.
9 And [y]I will sow them among the people: and they shall [z]remember me in far

---

[a]Jer. xiv. 22——[b]Deut. xi. 14——[c]Job. xxix. 23; Joel ii. 23——[d]Or, *lightnings;* Jer. x. 13——[e]Jer. x. 8; Heb. ii. 18——[f]Heb. *teraphim;* Judg. xvii. 5——[g]Job xiii. 4——[h]Or, *answered that,* &c.——[i]Ezek. xxxiv. 5 [k]Ezek. xxxiv. 16——[l]Heb. *visited upon*——[m]Luke i. 68 [n]Cant. i. 9

[o]Num. xxiv. 17; 1 Sam. xiv. 38; Isa. xix. 13——[p]Isa. xxii. 23——[q]Psa. xviii. 42——[r]Or, *they shall make the riders on horses ashamed*——[s]Jer. iii. 18; Ezek. xxxvii. 21 [t]Hos. i. 7——[u]Chap. xiii. 9——[v]Psa. civ. 15; chap. ix. 15——[w]Isa. v. 26——[x]Isa. xlix. 19; Ezek. xxxvi. 37 [y]Hos. ii. 23——[z]Deut. xxx. 1

NOTES ON CHAP. X

Verse 1. *Ask ye of the Lord rain*] Rain in the due seasons—1. To *impregnate* the *seed* when sown; and 2. To *fill the ear* near the time of *harvest*—was so essential to the fertility of the land, and the well-being of the people, that it stands well among the chief of God's mercies; and the promise of it here shows that God designs to ensure the prosperity promised, by using those means by which it was promoted.

Verse 2. *The idols have spoken vanity*] This is spoken of the *Jews*, and must refer to their idolatry practised before the captivity, for there were no *idols after.*

Therefore they went their way] They were like a *flock* that had no *shepherd,* shifting from place to place, and wandering about in the wilderness, seeking for pasture, wherever they might find it. Some think that the *idols* and *diviners* were those of the *Seleucidæ Greeks,* who excited their masters with promises of success against the Maccabees. Others think that the Babylonish captivity is foretold; for a *determined future* event is frequently spoken of by the prophets as *past.*

Verse 3. *Mine anger was kindled against the shepherds*] Bad kings and bad priests. *I will punish the goats;* these were the wicked *priests,* who were *shepherds* by their *office,* and *goats* by the *impurity* of their *lives.*

As his goodly horse in the battle.] The honourable *war horse,* or the *horse* that carried the general's equipage. In the unaccountable variation of interpreters on these chapters, this, among other things, is thought to be spoken of *Matthias,* and *Judas Maccabeus,* who assembled the people from all quarters, as a shepherd gathers his sheep together; and led them against the *sons of Greece,* the *Seleucidæ Greeks.* Others refer every thing here to times before the *captivity.*

Verse 4. *Out of him came forth the corner*] This is spoken of the tribe of Judah: all strength, counsel, and excellence came from that tribe. The *corner stone,* the *ornament* and *completion* of the building; *the nail,* by which the tents were fastened, and on which they hung their clothes, armour, &c.; *the battlebow,* the choicest archers.

Every oppressor together.] Those heroes and generals, by whom, under God, their foes should be totally routed. *Newcome* translates, "Every ruler together." Perhaps all this is spoken of the *Messiah.*

Verse 5. *They shall be as mighty* men] The Maccabees and their successors.

Riders on horses] The Macedonians, who opposed the Maccabees, and had much cavalry; whereas the Jews had none, and even few weapons of war; yet they overcame these horsemen.

Verse 6. *I will strengthen the house of Judah*] I doubt whether the *sixth, seventh, eighth,* and *ninth* verses are not to be understood of the future ingathering of the Jews in the times of the Gospel. See Jer. iii. 14; xxiii. 6; Hosea i. 2; vi. 11.

Verse 7. *Ephraim shall be like a mighty* man] This tribe was always distinguished for its valour.

Verse 8. *I will hiss for them*] אשרקה *eshrekah,* "I will shriek for them;" call them with such a *shrill strong voice,* that they shall *hear* me, and find that it is the voice of their redemption.

Verse 9. *I will sow them among the people*]

A. M. cir. 3417 B. C. cir. 587 Ol. XLVIII. 2 TarquiniiPrisci, R. Roman., cir. annum 30

countries; and they shall live
with their children, and turn
again.
10 [a]I will bring them again also
out of the land of Egypt, and gather them out
of Assyria; and I will bring them into the land
of Gilead and Lebanon; and [b]*place* shall
not be found for them.
11 [c]And he shall pass through the sea with
affliction, and shall smite the
waves in the sea, and all the deeps
of the river shall dry up: and
[d]the pride of Assyria shall be
brought down, and [e]the sceptre of Egypt
shall depart away.
12 And I will strengthen them in the LORD:
and [f]they shall walk up and down in his name,
saith the LORD.

[a]Isa. xi. 11, 16; Hos. xi. 11——[b]Isa. xlix. 20——[c]Isa. xi. 15, 16——[d]Isa. xiv. 25——[e]Ezek. xxx. 13——[f]Mic. iv. 5

Wherever they have been dispersed, my voice in the preaching of the Gospel shall reach them. *And they shall remember me*, and they and their children *shall turn again to the Lord*, through Messiah their King.

Verse 10. *Out of the land of Egypt*] I will bring them out of all the countries where they have been dispersed, and bring them back to their own land; and they shall be so numerous that they shall scarcely find there, in all its length and breadth, a sufficiency of room. If all the Jews that are now scattered over the face of the earth were gathered together, they would make a *mighty nation*. And God will gather them together. As a wonderful providence has preserved them in every place, so a wondrous providence will collect them from every place of their dispersion. When the *great call* comes, no one soul of them shall be left behind.

Verse 11. *And he shall pass through the sea*] Here is an allusion to the passage of the *Red Sea*, on their coming *out of Egypt*, and to their *crossing Jordan*, when they went into the *promised land;* the *waves* or waters of both were *dried up*, thrown from side to side, till all the people passed safely through. When they shall return from the various countries in which they now sojourn, God will work, if necessary, similar miracles to those which he formerly worked for their forefathers; and the people shall be glad to let them go, however much they may be profited by their operations in the state. Those that oppose, as *Assyria* and *Egypt* formerly did, shall be *brought down*, and their *sceptre broken*.

Verse 12. *I will strengthen them in the Lord*] I, the God of Israel, will strengthen them in the Lord—Jesus, *the Messiah;* and thus indeed the *Chaldee: I will strengthen them*, בימרא דיי *bemeymre dayai, in* or *by the* WORD *of Jehovah*, the same *personal Word* which we so often meet with in the *Chaldee* paraphrases or *Targum*.

They shall walk up and down in his name] In the name of the Messiah. *Saith the Lord*—GOD speaks here, not of himself, but concerning his *Christ*. The Jews shall have complete liberty; they shall appear everywhere as a part of the flock of Christ, and no difference be made between them and the converted Gentiles. They shall be all *one fold* under *one Shepherd* and Bishop of all souls.

CHAPTER XI

The commencement of this chapter relates to the destruction of Jerusalem and the Jewish polity, probably by the Babylonians; at least in the first instance, as the fourth *verse speaks of the people thus threatened as the prophet's charge,* 1–6. *The prophet then gives an account of the manner in which he discharged his office, and the little value that was put on his labours. And this he does by symbolical actions, a common mode of instruction with the ancient prophets,* 7–14. *After the prophet, on account of the unsuccessfulness of his labours, had broken the two crooks which were the true badges of his pastoral office, (to denote the annulling of God's covenant with them, and their consequent divisions and dispersions,) he is directed to take instruments calculated to hurt and destroy, perhaps an iron crook, scrip, and stones, to express by these symbols the judgments which God was about to inflict on them by wicked rulers and guides, who should first destroy the flock, and in the end be destroyed themselves,* 15–17. *Let us now view this prophecy in another light, as we are authorized to do by Scripture,* Matt. xxvii. 7. *In this view the prophet, in the person of the Messiah, sets forth the ungrateful returns made to him by the Jews, when he undertook the office of shepherd in guiding and governing them; how they rejected him, and valued him and his labours at the mean and contemptible price of thirty pieces of silver, the paltry sum for which Judas betrayed him. Upon which he threatens to destroy their city and temple; and to give them up to the hands of such guides and governors as should have no regard to their welfare.*

A. M. cir. 3417
B. C. cir. 587
Ol. XLVIII. 2
TarquiniiPrisci,
R. Roman.,
cir. annum 30

OPEN [a]thy doors, O Lebanon,
that the fire may devour thy
cedars.
2 Howl, fir tree; for the cedar
is fallen; because the [b]mighty is spoiled:
howl, O ye oaks of Bashan; [c]for [d]the forest
of the vintage is come down.
3 *There is* a voice of the howling of the
shepherds; for their glory is spoiled; a voice
of the roaring of young lions; for the pride of
Jordan is spoiled.
4 Thus saith the LORD my God; [e]feed the
flock of the slaughter;
5 Whose possessors slay them, and [f]hold
themselves not guilty: and they that sell
them [g]say, Blessed *be* the LORD; for I am
rich: and their own shepherds pity them
not.
6 For I will no more pity the inhabitants of
the land, saith the LORD: but lo,
I will [h]deliver the men every
one into his neighbour's hand,
and into the hand of his king:
and they shall smite the land, and out of their
hand I will not deliver *them*.
7 And I will [i]feed the flock of slaughter,
[k]*even* you, [l]O poor of the flock. And I took
unto me two staves; the one I called Beauty,
and the other I called [m]Bands; and I fed the
flock.
8 Three shepherds also I cut off [n]in one
month; and my soul [o]loathed them, and their
soul also abhorred me.
9 Then said I, I will not feed you: [p]that
that dieth, let it die: and that that is to be cut
off, let it be cut off; and let the rest eat
everyone the flesh [q]of another.
10 And I took my staff, *even* Beauty, and

A. M. cir. 3417
B. C. cir. 587
Ol. XLVIII. 2
TarquiniiPrisci,
R. Roman.,
cir. annum 30

[a]Chap. x. 10——[b]Or, *gallants*——[c]Isa. xxxii. 12
[d]Or, *the defenced forest*——[e]Ver. 7——[f]Jer. ii. 3; l. 7
[g]Deut. xxix. 19; Hos. xii. 8——[h]Heb. *make to be found*
[i]Ver. 4

[k]Or, *verily the poor*——[l]Zeph. iii. 12; Matt. xi. 5
[m]Or, *Binders*——[n]Hos. v. 7——[o]Heb. *was straitened for them*——[p]Jer. xv. 2; xliii. 11——[q]Heb. *of his fellow*, or *neighbour*

NOTES ON CHAP. XI

Verse 1. *Open thy doors, O Lebanon*] I will give Mr. *Joseph Mede's* note upon this verse:—

"That which moveth me more than the rest, is in chap. xi., which contains a prophecy of the destruction of Jerusalem, and a description of the wickedness of the inhabitants, for which God would give them to the sword, and have no more pity upon them. It is expounded of the destruction by *Titus;* but methinks such a prophecy was nothing seasonable for Zachary's time, (when the city yet for a great part lay in her ruins, and the temple had not yet recovered hers,) nor agreeable to the scope. *Zachary's* commission, who, together with his colleague *Haggai*, was sent to encourage the people, *lately returned* from captivity, to build their temple, and to instaurate their commonwealth. Was this a fit time to foretell the destruction of both, while they were yet but *a-building?* And by Zachary too, who was to encourage them? Would not this better befit the desolation by Nebuchadnezzar?" I really think so. See Mr. *J. Mede's* lxi. Epistle.

Lebanon signifies the temple, because built of materials principally brought from that place.

Verse 2. *Howl, fir tree*] This seems to point out the fall and destruction of all the mighty men.

Verse 3. *Young lions*] Princes and rulers. By *shepherds, kings* or *priests* may be intended.

Verse 4. *Feed the flock of the slaughter*] This people resemble a flock of sheep *fattened* for the shambles; *feed*, instruct, this people who are about to be *slaughtered*.

Verse 5. *Whose possessors*] Governors and false prophets, *slay them*, by leading them to those things that will bring them to destruction.

And they that sell them] Give them up to idolatry; and bless God, strange to tell, that they get *secular advantage* by the establishment of this *false religion*.

Verse 6. *For I will no more pity*] I have determined to deliver them into the hands of the Chaldeans.

Verse 7. *And I will feed the flock of slaughter*] I showed them what God had revealed to me relative to the evils coming upon the land; and I did this the more especially for the sake of *the poor of the flock*.

Two staves] Two *shepherd's crooks*. One I called *Beauty*—that probably by which they marked the sheep; dipping the end into *vermilion*, or some red liquid. And this was done when they were to *mark* every *tenth* sheep, as it came out of the field, when the *tithe* was to be set apart for the Lord.

The other I called Bands] Probably that with the *hook* or *crook* at the head of it, by which the shepherd was wont to catch the sheep by the horns or legs when he wished to bring any to hand.

And I fed the flock.] These two rods show the *beauty* and *union* of the people, while under God as their Shepherd. It was the *delight* of God to see them in a state of *peace* and *harmony*.

Verse 8. *Three shepherds also I cut off in one month*] Taking this *literally*, some think the *three shepherds* mean the *three* Maccabees, *Judas, Jonathan*, and *Simon;* others, the *three* wicked high priests, *Jason, Alcimus*, and *Menelaus;* others, the *three* last princes of the Asmonean race, *Alexander, Hyrcanus*, and *Antigonus*.

Perhaps *three orders* may be intended: 1. The *priesthood*. 2. The *dictatorship*, including the Scribes, Pharisees, &c. 3. The *magistracy*, the great sanhedrin, and the smaller councils. These were all annihilated by the Roman conquest.

Verse 9. *I will not feed you*] I shall instruct

A. M. cir. 3417
B. C. cir. 587
Ol. XLVIII. 2
TarquiniiPrisci,
R. Roman.,
cir. annum 30

cut it asunder, that I might
break my covenant which I had
made with all the people.
11 And it was broken in that
day: and [r]so [s]the poor of the flock that
waited upon me knew that it *was* the word
of the LORD.
12 And I said unto them, [t]If ye think good,
give *me* my price, and if not, forbear. So
they [u]weighed for my price thirty *pieces* of
silver.
13 And the LORD said unto me, Cast it unto
the [v]potter: a goodly price that I was prized
at of them. And I took the thirty *pieces* of
silver, and cast them to the potter in the house
of the LORD.
14 Then I cut asunder mine other staff, *even*
[w]Bands, that I might break the
brotherhood between Judah and
Israel.
15 And the LORD said unto me,
[x]Take unto thee yet the instruments of a foolish shepherd.
16 For lo, I will raise up a shepherd in
the land, *which* shall not visit those that be
[y]cut off, neither shall seek the young one, nor
heal that that is broken, nor [z]feed that that
standeth still: but he shall eat the flesh of the
fat, and tear their claws in pieces.
17 [a]Wo to the idol shepherd that leaveth the
flock! the sword *shall be* upon his arm,
and upon his right eye: his [b]arm shall be
clean dried up, and his right eye shall be utterly darkened.

A. M. cir. 3417
B. C. cir. 587
Ol. XLVIII. 2
TarquiniiPrisci,
R. Roman.,
cir. annum 30

[r]Or, *the poor of the flock*, &c., *certainly knew*——[s]Zeph. iii. 12; ver. 7——[t]*If* it be *good in your eyes*——[u]Matt. xxvi. 15; see Exod. xxi. 32

[v]Matt. xxvii. 9, 12——[w]Or, *Binders*——[x]Ezek. xxxiv. 2, 3, 4——[y]Or, *hidden*——[z]Or, *bear*——[a]Jer. xxiii. 1; Ezek. xxxiv. 2; John x. 12, 13——[b]Psa. x. 5

you no longer: some of you are appointed to death by *famine;* others, to be *cut off* by the *sword;* and others of you, to such *desparation* that ye shall *destroy one another.*

Verse 10. *I took my staff—Beauty, and cut it asunder*] And thus I showed that I determined no longer to preserve them in their *free* and *glorious* state. And thus I *brake my covenant with them*, which they had broken on their part already.

Verse 11. *So the poor of the flock*] The pious, who attended to my teaching, saw that this was the *word*—the *design*, of God.

Verse 12. *If ye think good, give* me *my price*] "Give me my hire." And we find they rated it contemptuously; *thirty* pieces of silver being the price of a slave, Exod. xxi. 32.

Verse 13. *And the Lord said unto me, Cast it unto the potter*] Jehovah calls the price of his prophet *his own price;* and commands that it should not be accepted, but given to a potter, to foreshadow the transaction related Matt. xxvii. 7.

"Earthen vessels were used in the temple; and we may suppose that some Levites were employed within the sacred precincts to furnish them. To these, the humblest of his ministers in the temple, God commands that the *degrading price* should be cast." This is the substance of the notes on these two verses, given by Abp. *Newcome.*

We may look at it in another light, *Give me my price!* הבו שכרי *habu sichri, bring my price,* or *give* him *my price;* that is, Give the money to Judas which you have agreed to give him; for he can neither betray me nor you crucify me, but my own permission. *But if not, forbear;* take time to consider this bloody business, and in time *forbear.* For though I *permit* you to do it, yet remember that the *permission* does not *necessitate* you to do it; and the salvation of the world may be effected without this *treachery* and *murder.*

See my notes on this place, Matt. xxvii. 9, where I have examined the evidence for the reading of "Zechariah the prophet," instead of "Jeremiah."

Verse 14. *That I might break the brotherhood*] I cannot, says *Newcome*, explain this passage, without supposing that the kingdom of Israel *subsisted* when the prophet wrote it; and that either the wars between Judah and Israel are referred to, (see 2 Kings xvi. 5,) or the captivity of the ten tribes, when the *brotherly connection* between these kingdoms ceased.

Verse 15. *The instruments of a foolish shepherd.*] Such as a *bag without bread*, a *scrip without measure*, and a *staff without a hook*, &c.; things that were needless or of no use; to point out to the Jewish pastors, who took no care of the flock, but devoured them, or ruled them with force and with cruelty.

Verse 16. *I will raise up a shepherd in the land*] Some wicked king; and *Newcome* supposes *Hoshea* may be meant. See 2 Kings xvii. 1, 2, and to such an abominable sovereign the prophecy may well apply.

Verse 17. *Wo to the idol shepherd*] רעי האליל *roi haelil*, "the worthless," or "good for nothing shepherd." The shepherd in name and office, but not performing the *work* of one. See John x. 11.

The sword shall be *upon his arm*] Punishment shall be executed upon the wicked Jews, and especially their wicked kings and priests. See ver. 16.

Arm—the secular power; *right eye*—the ecclesiastical state.

His arm shall be clean dried up] The secular power shall be broken, and become utterly inefficient.

His right eye shall be utterly darkened] Prophecy shall be restrained; and the whole state, ecclesiastical and civil, shall be so completely *eclipsed*, that none of their functions shall be performed. This may refer to the worthless and wicked governor mentioned in the preceding verse.

There are several things in this chapter that are very *obscure*, and we can hardly say what opinion is right; nor is it at all clear whether they refer to a very early or late period of the Jewish history.

CHAPTER XII

The first part of this chapter, with several passages in chap. xiv., *relates to an invasion that shall be made on the inhabitants of Judea and Jerusalem in the latter ages of the world, some time after the restoration and settlement of the Jews in their own land. It also describes, in very magnificent terms, the signal interposition of God in their favour. From this the prophet proceeds in the latter part of the chapter,* 10–14, *to describe the spiritual mercies of God in converting his people; and gives a very pathetic and affecting account of the deep sorrow of that people, when brought to a sense of their great sin in crucifying the Messiah, comparing it to the sorrow of a parent for his first-born and only son, or to the lamentations made for Josiah in the valley of Megiddon,* 2 Chron. xxxv. 24, 25. *A deep, retired sorrow, which will render the mourners for a season insensible to all the comforts and enjoyments of the most endearing society.*

A. M. cir. 3417
B. C. cir. 587
Ol. XLVIII. 2
TarquiniiPrisci, R. Roman., cir. annum 30

THE burden of the word of the LORD for Israel, saith the LORD, [a]which stretcheth forth the heavens, and layeth the foundation of the earth, and [b]formeth the spirit of man within him.

2 Behold, I will make Jerusalem [c]a cup of [d]trembling unto all the people round about, [e]when they shall be in the siege both against Judah *and* against Jerusalem.

3 [f]And in that day will I make Jerusalem [g]a burdensome stone for all people: all that burden themselves with it shall be cut in pieces, though all the people of the earth be gathered together against it.

4 In that day, saith the LORD, [h]I will smite every horse with astonishment, and his rider with madness: and I will open mine eyes upon the house of Judah, and will smite every horse of the people with blindness.

A. M. cir. 3417
B. C. cir. 587
Ol. XLVIII. 2
TarquiniiPrisci, R. Roman., cir. annum 30

5 And the governors of Judah shall say in their heart, [i]The inhabitants of Jerusalem *shall be* my strength in the LORD of hosts their God.

6 In that day will I make the governors of Judah [k]like a hearth of fire among the wood, and like a torch of fire in a sheaf; and they shall devour all the people round about, on the right hand and on the left: and Jerusalem shall be inhabited again in her own place, *even* in Jerusalem.

7 The LORD also shall save the tents of Judah first, that the glory of the house of David and the glory of the inhabitants of Jerusalem do not magnify *themselves* against Judah.

8 In that day shall the LORD defend the

[a]Isa. xlii. 5; xliv. 24; xlv. 12, 18; xlviii. 13——[b]Num. xvi. 22; Eccles. xii. 7; Isa. lvii. 16; Heb. xii. 9——[c]Isa. li. 17, 22, 23——[d]Or, *slumber*, or *poison*——[e]Or, *and also against Judah* shall he be *which shall be in siege against Jerusalem*——[f]Ver. 4, 6, 8, 9, 11; chap. xiii. 1; xiv. 4, 6, 8, 9, 13——[g]Matt. xxi. 44——[h]Psa. lxxvi. 6; Ezek. xxxviii. 4——[i]Or, There is *strength to me* and *to the inhabitants*, &c.; Joel iii. 16——[k]Obad. 18

NOTES ON CHAP. XII

Verse 1. *The burden of the word of the Lord*] This is a new prophecy. It is directed both to *Israel* and *Judah*, though *Israel* alone is mentioned in this verse.

Which stretcheth forth the heavens] See on Isa. xlii. 5.

Formeth the spirit of man within him.] Then it is not the *same substance* with his body. It is a SPIRIT within HIM.

Verse 2. *Jerusalem a cup of trembling*] The Babylonians, who captivated and ruined the Jews, shall in their turn be ruined.

I incline to think that what is spoken in this chapter about the *Jews* and *Jerusalem*, belongs to the "glory of the latter times."

Shall be in the siege] This may refer to some war against the Church of Christ, such as that mentioned Rev. xx. 9.

Verse 3. *A burdensome stone*] Probably referring to that *stone* which was thrown on the breast of a *culprit* adjudged to lose his life by *stoning*, by which the whole region of the thorax, *heart, lungs, liver,* &c., was broken to pieces.

Verse 4. *I will smite every horse*] Some apply this to the *wars* of the *Maccabees* with the *Syrians;* but it is more likely to be a prophecy not yet accomplished. The terms are too strong for such petty and evanescent victories as those of the Maccabees.

Verse 5. *The governors of Judah*] This supposes a *union* between the two kingdoms of Israel and Judah.

Verse 6. *Jerusalem shall be inhabited again*] This seems to refer to the future conversion of the Jews, and their "return to their own land."

Verse 7. *The Lord also shall save the tents of Judah first*] This, I suppose, refers to the same thing. The Gospel of Christ shall go from the *least* to the *greatest. Eminent men* are not the *first* that are called; the *poor* have the Gospel preached to them. And this is done in the wise providence of God, that the "glory of the house of David," &c., that secular influence may appear to have no hand in the matter; and that God does not send his Gospel to a *great man*, because he is *such.*

Verse 8. *He that is feeble among them—shall be as David*] Here is a marked *difference* between *Judaism* and *Christianity.* So clear, full, and efficient shall be the salvation of believers under the *Gospel*, that the *feeblest* among them

A. M. cir. 3417
B. C. cir. 587
Ol. XLVIII. 2
TarquiniiPrisci, R. Roman., cir. annum 30

inhabitants of Jerusalem; and [l]he that is [m]feeble [n]among them at that day shall be as David; and the house of David *shall be* as God, as the angel of the LORD before them.

9 And it shall come to pass in that day, *that* I will seek to [o]destroy all the nations that come against Jerusalem.

10 [p]And I will pour upon the house of David, and upon the inhabitants of Jerusalem, the spirit of grace and supplications: and they shall [q]look upon me whom they have pierced, and they shall mourn for him, [r]as one mourneth for *his* only *son,* and shall be in bitterness for him, as one that is in bitterness for *his* first-born.

A. M. cir. 3417
B. C. cir. 587
Ol. XLVIII. 2
TarquiniiPrisci, R. Roman., cir. annum 30

11 In that day shall there be a great [s]mourning in Jerusalem, [t]as the mourning of Hadadrimmon in the valley of Megiddon.

12 [u]And the land shall mourn, [v]every family apart; the family of the house of David apart, and their wives apart; the family of the house of [w]Nathan apart, and their wives apart;

13 The family of the house of Levi apart, and their wives apart; the family [x]of Shimei apart, and their wives apart;

14 All the families that remain, every family apart, and their wives apart.

[l]Joel iii. 10——[m]Or, *abject*——[n]Heb. *fallen*——[o]Hag. ii. 22; ver. 3——[p]Jer. xxxi. 9; l. 4; Ezek. xxxix. 29; Joel ii. 28——[q]John xix. 34, 37; Rev. i. 7——[r]Jer. vi. 26; Amos viii. 10

[s]Acts ii. 37——[t]2 Kings xxiii. 29; 2 Chron. xxxv. 24——[u]Matthew xxiv. 30; Revelation i. 7——[v]Hebrew, *families, families*——[w]2 Sam. v. 14; Luke iii. 31——[x]Or, *of Simeon,* as LXX.

shall be as strong, as full of courage, and as successful as David when he went against Goliath. The least in the kingdom of heaven was greater than John the Baptist.

And the house of David—as the angel of the Lord] The *family*, the *Church* of the *true David*, the *Lord Jesus*, shall be as the *angel* of the Lord; shall *stand in the Divine presence* like *Gabriel;* for Christ hath said, "Blessed are the pure in heart, for they shall see God." So "we all, with open face beholding as in a glass the glory of the Lord, are changed from glory into glory, as by the Spirit of the Lord." Thus the house of David, the *true Christians*, shall here walk *with*, *after*, and *before* God.

Verse 9. *I will seek to destroy all the nations*] When this time shall arrive, all nations that "will not receive the faith of our Lord Jesus" shall be destroyed, when the longsuffering of God shall no longer wait upon them. This seems to belong to a period yet very remote.

Verse 10. *I will pour upon the house of David*] This is the *way* in which the *Jews* themselves shall be brought into the *Christian Church*. 1. "They shall have the spirit of grace;" God will show them that he yet bears *favour* to them. 2. They shall be excited to *fervent* and continual *prayer* for the restoration of the Divine favour. 3. Christ shall be preached unto them; and they shall *look upon* and believe in him *whom they pierced*, whom they crucified at Jerusalem. 4. This shall produce deep and sincere repentance; they shall *mourn*, and be in bitterness of soul, to think that they had crucified the Lord of life and glory, and so long continued to contradict and blaspheme, since that time.

Verse 11. *A great mourning*] A universal repentance.

As the mourning of Hadadrimmon] They shall mourn as deeply for the crucified Christ as their forefathers did for the death of Josiah, who was slain at Hadadrimmon in the valley of Megiddon. See 2 Chron. xxxv. 24, 25.

Verse 12. *Every family apart*] The meaning of the word *apart*, which recurs here so often, may be this: Their sorrow shall be so deep and distressing, that every one will endeavour to avoid another, and vent his grief and distress of soul in *private*. And even *husbands* and *wives* shall separate from each other in this general mourning, as they were obliged to do by law in certain circumstances. See 1 Cor. vii. 5, and the note there.

CHAPTER XIII

After the humiliation and conversion of the Jews, foretold in the preceding chapter, they are here promised the full pardon of their sins, and a deliverance from idolatry and false prophets, 1–6. *Prophecy concerning the death of the Messiah, and the persecution of his disciples,* 7. *The remaining verses may refer to those Jewish converts to Christianity who survived the calamities which their country suffered from the Romans,* 8, 9.

A. M. cir. 3417
B. C. cir. 587
Ol. XLVIII. 2
TarquiniiPrisci,
R. Roman.,
cir. annum 30

IN [a]that day there shall be [b]a
fountain opened to the house
of David and to the inhabitants
of Jerusalem for sin and for [c]un-
cleanness.

2 And it shall come to pass in that day,
saith the LORD of hosts, *that* I will [d]cut off
the names of the idols out of the land, and they
shall no more be remembered: and also I
will cause [e]the prophets and the unclean
spirit to pass out of the land.

3 And it shall come to pass, *that* when any
shall yet prophesy, then his father and his mother that begat him shall say unto him, Thou
shalt not live; for thou speakest lies in the
name of the LORD: and his father and his mother that begat him [f]shall thrust
him through when he prophesieth.

A. M. cir. 3417
B. C. cir. 587
Ol. XLVIII. 2
TarquiniiPrisci,
R. Roman.,
cir. annum 30

4 And it shall come to pass in
that day, *that* [g]the prophets shall
be ashamed every one of his vision, when he
hath prophesied; neither shall they wear [h]a
[i]rough garment [k]to deceive:

5 [l]But he shall say, I *am* no prophet, I *am*
a husbandman; for man taught me to keep
cattle from my youth.

6 And *one* shall say unto him, What *are*
these wounds in thine hands? Then he shall
answer, *Those* with which I was wounded *in*
the house of my friends.

7 Awake, O sword, against [m]my Shepherd,
and against the man [n]*that is* my Fellow,

[a]Chap. xii. 3——[b]Heb. ix. 14; 1 Pet. i. 19; Rev. i. 5——[c]Heb. *separation for uncleanness*——[d]Exod. xxiii. 13; Josh. xxiii. 7; Psa. xvi. 4; Ezek. xxx. 13; Hos. ii. 17; Mic. v. 12, 13——[e]2 Pet. ii. 1

[f]Deut. xiii. 6, 8; xviii. 20——[g]Mic. iii. 6, 7——[h]2 Kings i. 8; Isa. xx. 2; Matt. iii. 4——[i]Heb. *a garment of hair*——[k]Heb. *to lie*——[l]Amos vii. 14——[m]Isa. xl. 11; Ezek. xxxiv. 23——[n]John x. 30; xiv. 10, 11; Phil. ii. 6

NOTES ON CHAP. XIII

Verse 1. *In that day there shall be a fountain opened*] This chapter is a *continuation* of the preceding, and should not have been separated from it.

A fountain] The source of mercy in Christ Jesus; perhaps referring to the death he should die, and the *piercing* of *his side*, when *blood and water issued out.*

To the house of David] To David's family, and *such like persons* as it included. See the history of David and his sons, and then learn *for whom* Christ shed his blood.

Inhabitants of Jerusalem] Such like persons as the Jews were in *every part of their history*, and in their *last* times, when they clamoured for the blood of Christ, and pursued him unto death! Learn from this also *for whom* Christ died! These were the *worst* of the human race; and if he died for *them*, none need *despair.* They *rejected, betrayed, crucified, slew*, and *blasphemed* Christ, and afterwards persecuted his followers. For these he died! Yes: and he tasted death for EVERY MAN.

For sin and for uncleanness.] For the removal of the *guilt* of sin, and for the *purification* of the soul from the uncleanness or pollution of sin.

Verse 2. *I will cut off the names of the idols*] There shall not only be no *idolatry*, but the very *names* of the *idols* shall be forgotten, or be held in such abhorrence that no person shall *mention* them. This prophecy seems to be ancient, and to have been delivered while idolatry had prevalence in Israel and Judah.

I will cause the prophets] All false teachers.

And the unclean spirit] That which leads to impurity, the spirit of *divination;* the lust of the flesh, and of the eye, and the pride of life. Satan shall have neither a *being in*, nor *power over*, the hearts of sincere believers in Christ.

Verse 3. *When any shall yet prophesy*] Falsely; such shall be the horror of such an evil, that there shall be no toleration of it. Itself, and they who practise it, shall be everywhere destroyed.

Verse 4. *Neither shall they wear a rough garment*] A *rough garment* made of *goats'* hair, *coarse* wool, or the *course pile* of the *camel*, was the ordinary garb of God's prophets. And the false prophets wore the same; for they pretended to the same gifts, and the same spirit, and therefore they wore the same kind of *garments.* John Baptist had a garment of this kind.

Verse 5. *But he shall say, I* am *no prophet*] This must be the case of a *false prophet* or diviner, who had been obliged to give up his infamous practice, and become even a *labourer* in the land. But having been known to be such, he is questioned by the people to see if he still were addicted in heart to the same practices. He declares he is *no prophet*, neither true nor false; that he is now a *husbandman*, and was brought up a *herdsman.*

Verse 6. *What are these wounds in thine hands?*] *Marks* which he had received in honour of his idols. But he shall excuse himself by stating that he had received these marks in his *own family;* when, most probably, they had been dedicated to some of those idols. See the note on Isa. xliv. 5. I do not think that these words are spoken at all concerning Jesus Christ. I have heard them quoted in this way; but I cannot hear such an application of them without horror. In quoting from the Old Testament in reference to the New, we cannot be too cautious. We may wound the truth instead of honouring it.

Verse 7. *Awake, O sword, against my Shepherd*] This is generally understood of Jesus Christ. The *sword* is that of Divine justice, which seemed to have been long *asleep*, and should long ago have struck either MAN, or his SUBSTITUTE, the *Messiah.* Jesus is here called God's *Shepherd*, because he had appointed him to *feed* and *govern*, as well as to *save*, the whole lost world. This is a prosopopœia, and

A. M. cir. 3417 B. C. cir. 587 Ol. XLVIII. 2 TarquiniiPrisci, R. Roman., cir. annum 30

saith the LORD of hosts: [o]smite
the Shepherd, and the sheep shall
be scattered: and I will turn
mine hand upon [p]the little ones.
8 And it shall come to pass, *that* in all the
land, saith the LORD, two parts therein shall
be cut off *and* die; [q]but the third shall be
left therein.

9 And I will bring the third
part [r]through the fire, and
will [s]refine them as silver is
refined, and will try them as
gold is tried: [t]they shall call on my name,
and I will hear them: [u]I will say, It *is* my
people; and they shall say, The LORD *is* my
God.

A. M. cir. 3417 B. C. cir. 587 Ol. XLVIII. 2 TarquiniiPrisci, R. Roman., cir. annum 30

[o]Matt. xxvi. 31; Mark xiv. 27——[p]Matt. xviii. 10, 14; Luke xii. 32——[q]Rom. xi. 5——[r]Isa. xlviii. 10 [s]1 Pet. i. 6, 7

[t]Psa. l. 15; xci. 15; chap. x. 6——[u]Psalm cxliv. 15; Jeremiah xxx. 22; Ezekiel xi. 20; Hosea ii. 23; chap. viii. 3

the address to the sword is very poetic. There is a fine passage in *Æschylus* to the same effect:—

Ξενος δε κληροις επινωμᾳ,
Χαλυβος Σκυθων αποικος,
Κτεανων χρηματοδαιτας
Πικρος, ωμοφρων σιδαρος,
Χθονα ναιειν διαπηλας
Ὁποσαν αν και φθιμενοισι κατεχειν,
Των μεγαλων πεδιων αμοιρους,
ÆSCHYL. *Sept. cont. Theb.* 733.

"The rude barbarian, from the mines
Of Scythia, o'er the lots presides;
Ruthless to each his share assigns,
And the contested realm divides:
To each allots no wider a domain
Than, on the cold earth as they lie,
Their breathless bodies occupy,
Regardless of an ampler reign:
Such narrow compass does the *sword*—
A cruel umpire—their high claims afford."
POTTER.

The man that is *my Fellow*] ועל גבר עמיתי *veal geber amithi*, "upon the strong man," or, "the hero that is *with* ME;" my neighbour. "The WORD was God, and the WORD was WITH God;" John i. 1. "I and my Father are ONE;" John x. 30.

Smite the Shepherd, and the sheep shall be scattered] This is quoted by our Lord, Matt. xxvi. 31, in relation to his disciples, who should be scattered on his crucifixion: and they were so; for every one, giving up all for lost, *went to his own house*.

And I will turn mine hand upon the little ones.] I will take care of the *little flock*, and preserve them from Jewish malice and Gentile persecution. And so this little flock was most wondrously preserved, and has been increasing from year to year from that time to the present day.

Verse 8. *Two parts therein shall be cut off*] In the war with the Romans.

But the third shall be left] Those who believe on the Lord Jesus Christ shall be preserved alive; and not one of these perished in the siege, or afterwards, by those wars.

Verse 9. *I will bring the third part through the fire*] The *Christian Church* shall endure a great fight of afflictions, by which they shall be refined—not consumed.

They shall call on my name] In this way shall they offer all their prayers and supplications to God.

I will say, It is *my people*] The Church that I have chosen in the place of the Jews who have filled up the measure of their iniquity.

And they shall say, The Lord is *my God*] And thus *communion* shall be established between me and them for ever. Thus there shall be a general restoration.

CHAPTER XIV

The commencement of this chapter relates to the destruction of Jerusalem by the Romans, and to the calamities consequent on that event. From this great Jewish tragedy the prophet immediately passes to the utter extermination of the enemies of Christianity in the latter days. God will display his power in behalf of his people in a manner so astonishing and miraculous, that even they themselves, and much more their enemies, shall be struck with terror, 4, 5. *The national prosperity of the Jews shall then be permanent and unmixed,* 6, 7; *and these people shall be made the instruments of converting many to the faith of the Messiah,* 8, 9. *The great increase and prosperity of the Christian Church, the New Jerusalem, is then described in terms accommodated to Jewish ideas; and the most signal vengeance denounced against all her enemies,* 10–19. *From that happy period God's name will be honoured in every thing, and his worship every where most reverently observe,* 20, 21.

A. M. cir. 3417
B. C. cir. 587
Ol. XLVIII. 2
TarquiniiPrisci, R. Roman., cir. annum 30

BEHOLD, [a]the day of the LORD cometh, and thy spoil shall be divided in the midst of thee.

2 For [b]I will gather all nations against Jerusalem to battle; and the city shall be taken, and [c]the houses rifled, and the women ravished; and half of the city shall go forth into captivity, and the residue of the people shall not be cut off from the city.

3 Then shall the LORD go forth, and fight against those nations, as when he fought in the day of battle.

4 And his feet shall stand in that day [d]upon the mount of Olives, which *is* before Jerusalem on the east, and the mount of Olives shall cleave in the midst thereof toward the east and toward the west, [e]*and there shall be* a very great valley; and half of the mountain shall remove toward the north, and half of it toward the south.

A. M. cir. 3417
B. C. cir. 587
Ol. XLVIII. 2
TarquiniiPrisci, R. Roman., cir. annum 30

5 And ye shall flee *to* the valley of [f]the mountains; [g]for the valley of the mountains shall reach unto Azal: yea, ye shall flee like as ye fled from before the [h]earthquake in the days of Uzziah king of Judah: [i]and the LORD my God shall come, *and* [k]all the saints with thee.

6 And it shall come to pass in that day, [l]*that* the light shall not be [m]clear, *nor* [n]dark:

7 But [o]it shall be [p]one day [q]which shall be known to the LORD, not day, nor night: but it shall come to pass, *that* at [r]evening time it shall be light.

8 And it shall be in that day, *that* living [s]waters shall go out from Jerusalem: half of

[a]Isaiah xiii. 9; Joel ii. 31; Acts ii. 20——[b]Joel iii. 2——[c]Isa. xiii. 16——[d]See Ezek. xi. 23——[e]Joel iii. 12, 14——[f]Or, *my mountains*——[g]Or, *when he shall touch the valley of the mountains to the place he separated* [h]Amos i. 1——[i]Matt. xvi. 27; xxiv. 30, 31; xxv. 31; Jude 14

[k]Joel iii. 11——[l]That is, it shall not be clear in some places, and dark in other places of the world——[m]Heb. *precious*——[n]Heb. *thickness*——[o]Or, *the days hall be one* [p]Rev. xxii. 5——[q]Matt. xxiv. 36——[r]Isa. xxx. 26; lx. 19, 20; Rev. xxi. 23——[s]Ezek. xlvii. 1; Joel iii. 18; Rev. xxii. 1

NOTES ON CHAP. XIV

Verse 1. *Behold, the day of the Lord cometh*] This appears to be a prediction of that war in which Jerusalem was finally destroyed, and the Jews scattered all over *the face of the earth;* and of the effects produced by it.

Verse 2. *I will gather all nations*] The *Romans*, whose armies were composed of all the nations of the world. In this verse there is a pitiful account given of the *horrible outrages* which should be committed during the siege of Jerusalem, and at its capture.

The residue of the people shall not be cut off] Many were preserved for *slaves*, and for *exhibition* in the provincial theatres.

Verse 3. *Then shall the Lord go forth, and fight against those nations*] Against the Romans, by means of the northern nations; who shall destroy the whole empire of this once mistress of the world. But this is an obscure place.

Verse 4. *And his feet shall stand*] He shall appear in full possession of the place, as a mighty conqueror.

And the mount of Olives shall cleave] God shall display his miraculous power as fully in the final restoration of the Jews, as he did when he divided the Red Sea that their forefathers might pass through dry-shod. Some refer this to the *destruction of the city by the Romans*. It was on the mount of Olives that *Titus* posted his army to batter Jerusalem. Here the *tenth* legion that came to him from Jericho was placed. JOSEPH. *De Bello*, lib. vi. c. 3. It was from *this mountain* that our Lord beheld Jerusalem, and predicted its future destruction, Luke xix. 41, with Matt. xxiv. 23; and it was from this mountain that he ascended to heaven, (Acts i. 12,) utterly leaving an ungrateful and condemned city.

And half of the mountain shall remove] I really think that these words refer to the *lines* of *circumvallation*, to intrenchments, redoubts, &c., which the Romans made while carrying on the siege of this city; and particularly the *lines* or *trenches* which the army made on Mount *Olivet* itself.

Verse 5. *Ye shall flee* to *the valley*] Some think this refers to the valley through which *Zedekiah* and others endeavoured to escape when Nebuchadnezzar pressed the siege of Jerusalem: but it appears to speak only of the *Jewish wars* of the *Romans*.

Azal] This, as a *place*, is not known. If a *place*, it was most probably *near* to Jerusalem; and had its *name* from that circumstance.

Verse 6. *The light shall not be clear,* nor *dark*] Metaphorically, there will be a *mixture* of *justice* and *mercy* in all this; or a *bright light and darkness*. *Mercy* shall triumph over *judgment*. There shall be *darkness*—distress, &c.; but there shall be more *light*—joy and prosperity—than *darkness*.

Verse 7. *At evening time it shall be light.*] At the *close* of this awful visitation, there shall be *light*. The light of the glorious Gospel shall go forth from Jerusalem; and next, from the Roman empire to every part of the earth.

Verse 8. *Living waters shall go out*] There shall be a wide diffusion of Divine knowledge, and of the plan of human salvation, which shall go out by apostles and preachers, first from Jerusalem, then to Syria, Asia Minor, Greece, Italy, the isles of the sea, Britain, &c.

The former sea, and—the hinder sea] The *Dead Sea* and the *Mediterranean;* see on Joel ii. 20. These are *metaphors*.

In summer] In time of *drought;* or in the countries where there was *no knowledge of God*, there shall these *waters* flow. The stream shall never cease; it shall run in *summer* as

A. M. cir. 3417
B. C. cir. 587
Ol. XLVIII. 2
TarquiniiPrisci,
R. Roman.,
cir. annum 30

them toward the [t]former sea, and half of them toward the hinder sea: in summer and in winter shall it be.

9 And the LORD shall be [u]King over all the earth: in that day shall there be [v]one LORD, and his name one.

10 All the land shall be [w]turned [x]as a plain from Geba to Rimmon south of Jerusalem; and it shall be lifted up, and [y]inhabited [z]in her place, from Benjamin's gate unto the place of the first gate, unto the corner gate, [a]and *from* the tower of Hananeel, unto the king's winepresses.

11 And *men* shall dwell in it, and there shall be [b]no more utter destruction; [c]but Jerusalem [d]shall be safely inhabited.

12 And this shall be the plague wherewith the LORD will smite all the people that have fought against Jerusalem; Their flesh shall consume away while they stand upon their feet, and their eyes shall consume away in their holes, and their tongue shall consume away in their mouth.

A. M. cir. 3417
B. C. cir. 587
Ol. XLVIII. 2
TarquiniiPrisci,
R. Roman.,
cir annum 30

13 And it shall come to pass in that day, *that* [e]a great tumult from the LORD shall be among them; and they shall lay hold every one on the hand of his neighbour, and [f]his hand shall rise up against the hand of his neighbour.

14 And [g]Judah also shall fight [h]at Jerusalem; [i]and the wealth of all the heathen round about shall be gathered together, gold, and silver, and apparel, in great abundance.

15 And [k]so shall be the plague of the horse, of the mule, of the camel, and of the ass, and of all the beasts that shall be in these tents, as this plague.

16 And it shall come to pass, *that* every one that is left of all the nations which came against Jerusalem shall even [l]go up from year to year

[t]Or, *eastern*, Joel ii. 20——[u]Dan. ii. 44; Rev. xi. 15——[v]Eph. iv. 5, 6——[w]Or, *compassed*——[x]Isa. xl. 4——[y]Chap. xii. 6——[z]Or, *shall abide*——[a]Neh. iii. 1; xii. 30; Jer. xxxi. 38——[b]Jer. xxxi. 40——[c]Jer. xxiii. 6——[d]Or, *shall abide*——[e]1 Sam. xiv. 15, 20——[f]Judg. vii. 22; 2 Chron. xx. 23; Ezek. xxxviii. 21——[g]Or, *thou also, O Judah, shalt*——[h]Or, *against*——[i]Ezek. xxxix. 10, 17, &c.——[k]Ver. 12——[l]Isa. lx. 6, 7, 9; lxvi. 23

well as *winter.* These are living waters—*perennial, incessant;* and waters that shall *preserve life.* See John vii. 37.

Verse 9. *And the Lord shall be King*] When this universal diffusion of Divine knowledge shall take place. Wherever it goes, the *laws of God* shall be *acknowledged;* and, consequently, he shall be King over the whole earth.

One Lord, and his name one.] There shall be in those blessed days, only *one religion,* and one *form of religion.* There shall not be *gods many,* and *lords many.* All *mankind* shall be of *one religion,* the essence of which is, "Thou shalt love the *Lord thy God* with all thy heart, soul, mind, and strength; and thy NEIGHBOUR as thyself."

Verse 10. *All the land shall be turned as a plain*] Or rather, "He shall encompass the whole land as a plain." He shall cast his defence all around it; from *Geba,* in Benjamin, north of Jerusalem, (Josh. xxi. 17,) to *Rimmon* in Judah, to the *south of Jerusalem,* Josh. xv. 32.

It shall be lifted up] The city shall be exhalted.

And inhabited in her place] Jerusalem, shall be rebuilt *in the very place* in which it originally stood. From *Benjamin's gate,* which was probably on the *north* side of Jerusalem, unto the *place of the first gate,* supposed to be that called the *old gate,* Neh. iii. 6, xii. 39, placed by *Lightfoot* towards the *southwest.*

Unto the corner gate] See 2 Kings xiv. 13.

The tower of Hananeel] This *tower* and the *corner gate* seem to be placed as *two extremities* of the city.

Unto the king's wine-presses] Near to the *king's gardens, southward.*—See *Newcome.*

Verse 11. *There shall be no more utter destruction*] After this final restoration of Jerusalem it shall never more be destroyed; but as this was the *first city* of the living God upon earth, so shall it be *the last;* it shall be *safely inhabited.* It shall see war no more.

Verse 12. *And this shall be the plague*] All her enemies shall be destroyed.

Their flesh shall consume away] These are the effects of *famine* which are described in this verse.

Verse 13. *A great tumult from the Lord*] Among those enemies of his Church, who shall engage and destroy each other.

Verse 14. *And Judah also shall fight*] They shall have little else to do than take the spoil, *the wealth of all the heathen round about;* gold, silver, and apparel.

Verse 15. *So shall be the plague of the horse, and the mule*] There shall be plagues on the *substance* of the enemies of the Church, as there were on the *cattle* and *goods* of the *Egyptians.*

Verse 16. *Shall even go up from year to year*] The Jews had *three* grand original festivals, which characterized different epochs in their history, viz.:—

1. The *feast* of the *passover,* in commemoration of their departure from Egypt.
2. The *feast* of *pentecost,* in commemoration of the giving of the law upon Mount Sinai.
3. The *feast* of *tabernacles,* in commemoration of their wandering forty years in the wilderness.

This last feast is very properly brought in here to point out the final restoration of the Jews, and their *establishment* in the light and liberty of the Gospel of Christ, after their *long wandering* in vice and error.

A. M. cir. 3417
B. C. cir. 587
Ol. XLVIII. 2
TarquiniiPrisci,
R. Roman.,
cir. annum 30

to worship the King, the LORD of hosts, and to keep [m]the feast of tabernacles.

17 [n]And it shall be, *that* whoso will not come up of *all* the families of the earth unto Jerusalem to worship the King, the LORD of hosts, even upon them shall be no rain.

18 And if the family of Egypt go not up, and come not, [o]that [p]*have* no *rain,* there shall be the plague wherewith the LORD will smite the heathen that come not up to keep the feast of tabernacles.

19 This shall be the [q]punishment of Egypt, and the punishment of all nations that come not up to keep the feast of tabernacles.

20 In that day shall there be upon the [r]bells of the horses, [s]HOLINESS UNTO THE LORD; and the pots in the LORD'S house shall be like the bowls before the altar.

21 Yea, every pot in Jerusalem and in Judah shall be holiness unto the LORD of hosts: and all they that sacrifice shall come and take of them, and seethe therein: and in that day there shall be no more the [t]Canaanite in [u]the house of the LORD of hosts.

[m]Lev. xxiii. 34, 43; Deut. xvi. 13, 16; Neh. viii. 14; Hos. xii. 9; John vii. 2——[n]Isa. lx. 12——[o]Heb. *upon whom* there is *not*

[p]Deut. xi. 10——[q]Or, *sin*——[r]Or, *bridles*——[s]Isa. xxiii. 18——[t]Isa. xxxv. 8; Job iii. 17; Rev. xxi. 27; xxii. 15——[u]Eph. ii. 19, 20, 21, 22

Verse 17. *Upon them shall be no rain.*] Those who do not worship God shall not have his blessing; and those who do not attend *Divine ordinances* cannot have the graces and blessings which God usually dispenses by them. On such slothful, idle Christians, *there shall be no rain!*

Verse 18. *If the family of Egypt*] This may allude to those Jews who, flying from the persecution of *Antiochus Epiphanes,* settled in Egypt, and built a temple at *Heliopolis,* under the direction of *Onias,* son of the high priest. *Joseph.* Antiq. lib. xiii., c. 6, and WAR, lib. vii., c. 36. If these do not rejoin their brethren, *they shall have no rain,* no interest in the favour of God.

Verse 19. *This shall be the punishment—of all nations that come not up*] God will have his public worship *established* everywhere, and those who do not worship him shall lie under his curse.

Verse 20. *Upon the bells of the horses*] They appear, formerly, to have had bells on horses, camels, &c., as we have now, to amuse the animals, and encourage them in their work. In some very fine Asiatic paintings now before me, I see *bells* both on *horses, mules,* and *camels;* little bells tied to their *legs,* and *larger* ones about their *necks,* particularly in the representation of a *caravan* passing through the valley of serpents, in the island of *Serendib,* now *Ceylon.* The margin reads *bridles.*

HOLINESS UNTO THE LORD] As the Gospel is a *holy* system, preaching *holiness* and producing *holiness* in those who believe, so all *without,* as well as *within,* shall bear this *impress;* and even a man's *labour* shall be begun and continued, and ended in the Lord; yea, and the *animals* he uses, and the *instruments* he works with, shall be all consecrated to God through Christ.

The pots] "The meanest utensil in the house of God, Neh. x. 29, shall be as the vessels of silver, and gold used in solemn sacrifice; they shall be *like the bowls before the altar.*"—See *Newcome.*

Verse 21. *Yea, every pot in Jerusalem*] "The utensils of the Jews shall be treated as *holy,* and the worshippers shall use them reverently. The idea of *preparing food* in them (*they that—seethe therein*) is taken from the custom of feasting after sacrifice. And no *trafficker* (see Ezek. xviii. 4) shall pollute the house of God, as was the custom when our blessed Lord cleansed the temple."—See *Newcome.* This is what is called the *Canaanite in the house of God.* The *Canaanite* is the *merchant;* and where such are tolerated in a place dedicated to Divine worship, *that* is not the house of the *Lord of hosts.* In *churches* and *chapels, collections* may be made for the *simple purpose* of *supporting* and *extending* the worship of Jehovah; but for no other purpose, especially on the Lord's day. *Amen.*

THE BOOK

OF THE

PROPHET MALACHI

Chronological Notes relative to this Book

Year from the Creation, according to Archbishop Usher, 3607.—Year from the vocation of Abram, 1524.—Year since the destruction of Troy, 787.—Year since the commencement of the kingdom of Israel by the Divine appointment of Saul to the regal dignity, 698.—Year from the division of Solomon's monarchy into the kingdoms of Israel and Judah, 578.—Fourth year of the *ninety-fifth* Olympiad.—Year from the building of Rome, according to the Varronian computation, 356.—Year before the vulgar era of Christ's nativity, 397.—Cycle of the Sun, 5.—Cycle of the Moon, 4.

CHAPTER I

This chapter begins with showing the great and free favour which God had manifested to the Israelites, above what he had done to the Edomites, who are threatened with farther marks of the Divine displeasure; alluding, perhaps, to the calamities which they suffered from Judas Maccabeus and John Hyrcanus, (see 1 Macc. v. 65, *and Joseph.* Antiq. xiii. 9,) 1–5. *God then reproaches his people, and especially their priests, for their ungrateful returns to his distinguished goodness,* 6. *They are particularly charged with sacrificing the refuse of beasts,* 7–9, *for which God threatens to reject them,* 10, *and choose other nations who will show more reverence to his name and worship,* 11–14.

A. M. cir. 3607
B. C. cir. 397
Ol. cir. XCV. 4
Urbis Conditæ
cir. annum
356

THE burden of the word of the
Lord to Israel [a]by Malachi.
2 [b]I have loved you, saith the
Lord. Yet ye say, Wherein
hast thou loved us? *Was* not Esau Jacob's
brother? saith the Lord: yet
[c]I loved Jacob,
3 And I hated Esau, and [d]laid
his mountains and his heritage
waste for the dragons of the wilderness.

A. M. cir. 3607
B. C. cir. 397
Ol. cir. XCV. 4
Urbis Conditæ
cir. annum
356

---

[a]Heb. *by the hand of Malachi*——[b]Deut. vii. 8; x. 15
[c]Rom. ix. 13

[d]Jer. xlix. 18; Ezek. xxxv. 3, 4, 7, 9, 14, 15; Obadiah 10, &c.

NOTES ON CHAP. I

Verse 1. *The burden of the word of the Lord to Israel by Malachi.*] This prophet is undoubtedly the *last* of the Jewish prophets. He lived after Zechariah and Haggai; for we find that the *temple*, which was begun in their time, was standing complete in his. See chap. iii. 10. Some have thought that he was contemporary with Nehemiah; indeed, several have supposed that *Malachi*, is no other than *Ezra* under the feigned name of *angel of the Lord*, or *my angel*. John the Baptist was the link that connected Malachi with Christ. According to Abp. *Usher* he flourished B. C. 416; but the authorized version, which we have followed in the margin, states this event to have happened *nineteen* years later. Both the Hebrew language and poetry had declined in his days.

Israel.—Here means the Jewish people in general.

Verse 2. Was *not Esau Jacob's brother?*] Have I not shown a greater *partiality* to the *Israelites* than I have to the *Edomites?*

I loved Jacob] My *love to Jacob* has been proved by giving him greater privileges and a better inheritance than what I have given to *Esau*.

Verse 3. *And I hated Esau*] I have shown him *less love;* Gen. xxix. 30, 31. I comparatively *hated* him by giving him an inferior lot. And now, I have not only laid waste the dwelling-place of the Edomites, by the incursions of their enemies; but (ver. 4) they shall remain the perpetual monuments of my vengeance. On the subject of *loving Jacob* and *hating Esau*, see the notes on Gen. xxvii., and Rom. ix. 13. Let it be remembered, 1. That there is not a word spoken here concerning the *eternal state* of either Jacob or Esau. 2. That what is spoken concerns merely their *earthly possessions*. And, 3. That it does not concern the *two brothers* at all, but the *posterity* of each.

A. M. cir. 3607
B. C. cir. 397
Ol. cir. XCV. 4
Urbis Conditæ cir. annum 356

4 Whereas Edom saith, We are impoverished, but we will return and build the desolate places; thus saith the LORD of hosts, They shall build, but I will throw down; and they shall call them, The border of wickedness, and, The people against whom the LORD hath indignation for ever.

5 And your eyes shall see, and ye shall say, [e]The LORD will be magnified [f]from [g]the border of Israel.

6 A son [h]honoureth *his* father, and a servant his master: [i]if then I *be* a father, where *is* mine honour? and if I *be* a master, where *is* my fear? saith the LORD of hosts unto you, O priests, that despise my name. [k]And ye say, Wherein have we despised thy name?

7 [l]Ye offer [m]polluted bread upon mine altar; and ye say, Wherein have we polluted thee? In that ye say, [n]The table of the LORD *is* contemptible.

8 And [o]if ye offer the blind [p]for sacrifice, *is it* not evil? and if ye offer the lame and sick, *is it* not evil? offer it now unto thy governor; will he be pleased with thee, or [q]accept thy person? saith the LORD of hosts.

9 And now, I pray you, Beseech [r]God that he will be gracious unto us: [s]this hath been [t]by your means: will he regard your persons? saith the LORD of hosts.

A. M. cir. 3607
B. C. cir. 397
Ol. cir. XCV. 4
Urbis Conditæ cir. annum 356

10 Who *is there* even among you that would shut the doors *for naught?* [u]neither do ye kindle *fire* on mine altar for naught. I have no pleasure in you, saith the LORD of hosts, [v]neither will I accept an offering at your hand.

11 For [w]from the rising of the sun even unto the going down of the same my name *shall be* great [x]among the Gentiles; [y]and in every place [z]incense *shall be* offered unto my name, and a pure offering; [a]for my name *shall be* great among the heathen, saith the LORD of hosts.

12 But ye have profaned it, in that ye say, [b]The table of the LORD *is* polluted; and the fruit thereof, *even* his meat, *is* contemptible.

13 Ye said also, Behold, what a weariness *is it!* [c]and ye have snuffed at it, saith the LORD of hosts; and ye brought *that which was* torn, and the lame, and the sick; thus ye brought an offering: [d]should I accept this of your hand? saith the LORD.

14 But cursed *be* [e]the deceiver, [f]which hath in his flock a male, and voweth, and sacrificeth unto the LORD a corrupt thing: for [g]I *am* a great King, saith the LORD of hosts, and my name *is* dreadful among the heathen.

---

[e]Psa. xxxv. 27——[f]Or, *upon*——[g]Heb. *from upon*——[h]Exod. xx. 12——[i]Luke vi. 46——[k]Chap. ii. 14, 17; iii. 7, 8, 13——[l]Or, *Bring unto*, &c.——[m]Deut. xv. 21——[n]Ezek. xli. 22; ver. 12——[o]Lev. xxii. 22; Deut. xv. 21; ver. 14——[p]Heb. *to sacrifice*——[q]Job xlii. 8——[r]Heb. *the face of God*——[s]Hos. xiii. 9——[t]Heb. *from your hand*

[u]1 Cor. ix. 13——[v]Isa. i. 11; Jer. vi. 20; Amos v. 21——[w]Psa. cxiii. 3; Isa. lix. 19——[x]Isa. lx. 3, 5——[y]John iv. 21, 23; 1 Tim. ii. 8——[z]Rev. viii. 3——[a]Isaiah lxvi. 19, 20——[b]Ver. 7——[c]Or, *whereas ye might have blown it away*——[d]Lev. xxii. 20, &c.——[e]Ver. 8——[f]Or, *in whose flock is*——[g]Psa. xlvii. 2; 1 Tim. vi. 15

Verse 4. *They shall build, but I will throw down*] We have already seen enough of the wickedness of the *Edomites* to justify the utmost severity of Divine justice against them. The *pulling down* predicted here was by Judas Maccabeus· see 1 Mac. v. 65; and by John Hyrcanus; see *Joseph.* Antiq., lib. xiii. c. 9. s. 1.

They shall call them, The border of wickedness] A wicked land. Among this people scarcely any trace of good could ever be noted.

Verse 5. *Your eyes*] Ye Israelites *shall see*, in your succeeding generations, that—

The Lord will be magnified] By his kindness *in* Israel, and his judgments *beyond.*

Verse 6. *A son honoureth* his *father*] I am your *Father*—where, then, is my honour? Where your filial obedience?

If I be *a master, where* is *my fear?*] The respect due to me.

Verse 7. *Ye offer polluted bread*] The priests, probably to ingratiate themselves with the people, took the refuse beasts, &c., and offered them to God; and thus the sacrificial ordinances were rendered *contemptible.*

Verse 8. *Offer it now unto thy governor*] פחת *pechath*, a word signifying a *lieutenant*, or *viceroy*, among the Chaldeans, Syrians, and Persians; for neither at this time, nor ever after, was there a *king* in Israel.

Verse 9. *Beseech God*] There were evident marks of God's displeasure in the land, and it was occasioned by these pollutions through the priests. And now he exhorts *them* to pray to God that they may be pardoned: for, if this practice be persisted in, God will not accept any offering made by them.

Verse 10. *Who* is—*among you*] From this we learn that there was not one sincere or honest priest among them. They were selfish and worldly; and so basely so, that not one of them would even kindle a fire on the hearth of the altar unless he were paid for it.

Verse 11. *From the rising of the sun*] The total abolition of the Mosaic sacrifices, and the establishment of a *spiritual* worship over the whole earth, is here foretold. The *incense* of praise, and the *pure offering* of the *Lamb without spot*, and through him a holy, loving heart, shall be presented everywhere *among the Gentiles;* and the Jews and their mock offerings shall be rejected.

Verse 12. *Ye have profaned it*] Ye have desecrated God's worship; is it any wonder that God should cast you off, and follow you with his judgments?

Verse 13. *Ye have snuffed at it*] A metaphor taken from cattle which do not like their *fodder*. They *blow strongly* through their nose upon it; and after this neither *they* nor *any other cattle* will eat it.

Ye brought that which was *torn, and the lame, and the sick*] There had never been such abominations in the Divine worship before. What was of no worth in itself, and what could not be used by its owner, was brought to God's altar, and offered for sacrifice! Was not the punishment of these wretches less than their crimes?

Verse 14. *Cursed* be *the deceiver*] Those who act thus, as they cannot elude God's *notice*, so neither shall they escape his *curse*.

And voweth, and sacrificeth—a corrupt thing] The history of Ananias and Sapphira, Acts v. 1, &c., is a complete comment on this. It was high time to break up this corrupt service; and after this time God does not appear to have paid any regard to it, for he sent them no other prophet.

CHAPTER II

The priests reproved for their unfaithfulness in their office, for which they are threatened to be deprived of their share of the sacrifice, (the shoulder,) and rewarded only with ignominy and ordure, 1–3. *The degeneracy of the order is then complained of, and they are again threatened,* 4–9. *The rest of the chapter reproves the people for marrying strange and idolatrous women; and multiplying divorces, with all their consequent distress, in order to make way for such illicit alliances,* 10–17. *See* Neh. x. 30, *and* xiii. 33, *&c.*

A. M. cir. 3607
B. C. cir. 397
Ol. cir. XCV. 4
Urbis Conditæ cir. annum 356

AND now, O ye priests, this
commandment *is* for you.
2 [a]If ye will not hear, and if
ye will not lay *it* to heart, to
give glory unto my name, saith the LORD of
hosts, I will even send a curse upon you, and
I will curse your blessings: yea, I have
[b]cursed them already, because ye do not lay
it to heart.
3 Behold, I will [c]corrupt your
seed, and [d]spread dung upon
your faces, *even* the dung of
your solemn feasts; and [e]*one*
shall [f]take you away with it.
4 And ye shall know that I have sent this
commandment unto you, that my covenant
might be with Levi, saith the LORD of hosts.
5 [g]My covenant was with him of life and

[a]Lev. xxvi. 14, &c.; Deut. xxviii. 15, &c.——[b]2 Pet. ii. 14——[c]Or, *reprove*——[d]Heb. *scatter*

[e]Or, *it shall take you away to it*——[f]1 Kings xiv. 10 [g]Num. xxv. 12; Ezek. xxxiv. 25; xxxvii. 26

NOTES ON CHAP. II

Verse 2. *If ye will not hear*] What I have spoken, *lay it to heart*, and let it sink down into your souls.

Give glory unto my name] That *honour* that is due to me as a *Father*, and that *fear* that belongs to me as a *Master*, chap. i. 6.

I will even send a curse upon you] I will dispense no more good.

I will curse your blessings] Even that which *ye have* already shall not profit you. When temporal blessings are not the means of leading us to God and heaven, they will infallibly lead us to hell. In speaking of the abuse of temporal blessings, one of our old poets, in his homely phrase, expresses himself thus,—

Thus God's best gifts, usurped by wicked ones,
To poison turn by their con-ta-gi-ons.

Yea, I have cursed them already] This may refer, generally, to *unfruitful seasons;* or, particularly, to a *dearth* that appears to have happened about this time. See Haggai i. 6-11.

Verse 3. *Behold, I will corrupt your seed*] So as to render it unfruitful. *Newcome* translates,—"I will take away from you the shoulder." This was the part that belonged to the priest, Lev. vii. 32; Deut. xviii. 3.

Spread dung upon your faces] Instead of *receiving* a sacrifice at your hands, I will throw your offerings back into your faces. Here God shows his *contempt* for *them* and their offerings.

Verse 4. *This commandment*] That in the *first* verse; to drive such priests from his presence and his service.

That my covenant might be with Levi] I gave the priesthood and the service of my altar to that tribe.

Verse 5. *My covenant was with him of life and peace*] These are the *two* grand blessings given to men by the NEW *Covenant*, which was shadowed by the OLD. To man, excluded from the favour of God, and sentenced to death because of sin, God gave ברית *berith*, a *covenant sacrifice*, and this secured *life*—exemption from the death deserved by transgressors; communication of that *inward spiritual life* given by Christ, and issuing in that *eternal life* promised to all his faithful disciples. And, as it secured *life*, so it gave *peace*, prosperity, and happiness; *peace* between God and man, between man and man, and between man and his own conscience.

A. M. cir. 3607 B. C. cir. 397 Ol. cir. XCV. 4 Urbis Conditæ cir. annum 356

peace; and I gave them to him
[h]for the fear wherewith he feared
me, and was afraid before my
name.

6 [i]The law of truth was in his mouth, and iniquity was not found in his lips: he walked with me in peace and equity, and did [k]turn many away from iniquity.

7 [l]For the priest's lips should keep knowledge, and they should seek the law at his mouth: [m]for he *is* the messenger of the LORD of hosts.

8 But ye are departed out of the way; ye [n]have caused many to [o]stumble at the law; [p]ye have corrupted the covenant of Levi, saith the LORD of hosts.

9 Therefore [q]have I also made you contemptible and base before all the people, according as ye have not kept my ways, but [r]have [s]been partial in the law.

10 [t]Have we not all one Father? [u]hath not one God created us? why do we deal treacherously every man against his brother, by profaning the covenant of our fathers?

11 Judah hath dealt treacherously, and an abomination is committed in Israel and in Jerusalem; for Judah hath profaned the holiness of the LORD which he [v]loved, [w]and hath married the daughter of a strange god.

12 The LORD will cut off the man that doeth this, [x]the master and the scholar, out of the tabernacles of Jacob, [y]and him that offereth an offering unto the LORD of hosts.

13 And this have ye done again, covering the altar of the LORD with tears, with weeping, and with crying out, insomuch that he regardeth not the offering any more, or receiveth *it* with good will at your hand.

14 Yet ye say, Wherefore? Because the LORD hath been witness between thee and [z]the wife of thy youth, against whom thou hast

[h]Deut. xxxiii. 8, 9——[i]Deut. xxxiii. 10——[k]Jer. xxiii. 22; James v 20——[l]Deut. xvii. 9, 10; xxiv. 8; Lev. x. 11; Ezra vii. 10; Jer. xviii. 18; Hag. ii. 11, 12 [m]Gal. iv. 14——[n]1 Sam. ii. 17; Jer. xviii. 15——[o]Or, *fall in the law*——[p]Neh. xiii. 29——[q]1 Sam. ii. 30

[r]Or, *lifted up the face against*——[s]Heb. *accepted faces* [t]1 Cor. viii. 6; Eph. iv. 6——[u]Gen. i. 27; Deut. iv. 32; Job xxxi. 15——[v]Or, *ought to love*——[w]Ezra ix. 1; x. 2; Neh. xiii. 23——[x]Or, *him that waketh and him that answereth*——[y]Neh. xiii. 28, 29——[z]Prov. v. 18

Verse 6. *The law of truth was in his mouth*] See the qualifications of Levi: 1. "He feared me;" he was my sincere worshipper. 2. "He was afraid;" he acted as in the presence of a *just* and holy God, and acted *conscientiously* in all that he did. 3. "My law of truth was ever in his mouth;" by this he directed his own conduct and that of others. 4. "No iniquity;" nothing contrary to justice and equity ever proceeded "from his lips." 5. "He walked with me in peace;" he lived in such a way as to keep up union with me. 6. "He did turn many away from iniquity;" by his upright administration, faithful exhortations, and pious walk, he became the instrument of converting many sinners. This character suits every genuine minister of God. And as the priest's *lips* should preserve knowledge, so the *people* should seek "the law at his mouth;" for he is the messenger of the Lord of hosts, ver. 7.

Verse 8. *But ye are departed out of the way*] Ye are become impure yourselves, and ye have led others into iniquity.

Verse 9. *Therefore have I also made you contemptible*] The people despised you because they saw that you acted contrary to your functions. This has happened repeatedly since, to several *classes of priests*. Not maintaining, by *purity of life* and *soundness of doctrine*, the dignity of the ministerial function, they became contemptible before the people; their meager preaching was disregarded, and their persons at last cast out as a general loathing to the universe! See what happened to the truly abominable priesthood of France and Rome, 1796-8. They were the *sole cause* of that *infidelity* that brought about the *revolution*. They are now partially restored; and are endeavouring to supply by *grimace, paltry superstition*, and *jesuitical cunning*, what they want in purity of morals, soundness of doctrine, and unction from God. They must mend, or look for another revolution. Mankind will no longer put up with the *chaff* of puerile and fanatical ceremonies in place of the *wheat* of God's word and worship.

Verse 10. *Have we not all one Father?*] From this to ver. 16 the prophet censures the *marriages* of *Israelites* with *strange women*, which the law had forbidden, Deut. vii. 3. And also *divorces*, which seem to have been multiplied for the purpose of contracting these prohibited marriages.—*Newcome*.

Why do we deal treacherously] Gain the affections of the daughter of a brother *Jew*, and then *profane the covenant of marriage*, held sacred among *our fathers*, by putting away this same wife and daughter! How wicked, cruel, and inhuman!

Verse 11. *Daughter of a strange god.*] Of a man who worships an idol.

Verse 12. *The master and the scholar*] He who teachers such doctrine, and he who follows this teaching, the Lord will cut off both the one and the other.

Verse 13. *Covering the altar of the Lord with tears*] Of the poor women who, being *divorced* by cruel husbands, come to the priests, and make an appeal to God at the altar; and ye do not speak against this glaring injustice.

Verse 14. *Ye say, Wherefore?*] Is the Lord angry with us? Because ye have been *witness* of the *contract* made between the parties; and

A. M. cir. 3607
B. C. cir. 397
Ol. cir. XCV. 4
Uebis Conditæ
cir. annum
356

dealt treacherously: [a]yet *is* she
thy companion, and the wife of
thy covenant.
15 And [b]did not he make one?
Yet had he the [c]residue of the Spirit. And
wherefore one? That he might seek [d]a [e]godly
seed. Therefore take heed to your spirit, and
let none deal [f]treacherously against the wife of
his youth.
16 For [g]the LORD, the God of Israel, saith
[h]that he hateth [i]putting away: for *one* covereth violence with his garment,
saith the LORD of hosts: therefore take heed to your spirit,
that ye deal not treacherously.
17 [k]Ye have wearied the LORD with your
words. Yet ye say, Wherein have we wearied
him? When ye say, Every one that doeth
evil *is* good in the sight of the LORD, and he
delighteth in them; or, Where *is* the God of
judgment?

A. M. cir. 3607
B. C. cir. 397
Ol. cir. XCV. 4
Urbis Conditæ
cir. annum
356

[a]Prov. ii. 17——[b]Matt. xix. 4, 5——[c]Or, *excellency*——[d]Heb. *a seed of God*——[e]Ezra ix. 2; 1 Cor. vii. 14——[f]Or, *unfaithfully*——[g]Deut. xxiv. 1; Matt. v. 32; xix. 8——[h]Or, *if he hate her, put* her *away*——[i]Heb. *to put away*——[k]Isa. xliii. 24; Amos ii. 13; chap. iii. 13, 14, 15

when the lawless husband divorced *his wife, the wife of his youth, his companion*, and the *wife of his covenant*, ye did not execute on him the discipline of the law. They kept their wives till they had *passed their youth*, and then put them away, that they might get *young ones* in their place.

Verse 15. *And did not he make one?*] ONE of *each kind*, Adam and Eve. *Yet had he the residue of the Spirit;* he could have made millions of pairs, and inspired them all with *living souls*. Then *wherefore one?* He made one pair from whom all the rest might proceed, that he might have a *holy offspring;* that children being a marked property of *one man* and *one woman*, proper care might be taken that they should be brought up in the discipline of the Lord. Perhaps the *holy* or *godly seed*, זרע אלהים *zera Elohim, a seed of God*, may refer to the MESSIAH. God would have the *whole human race* to spring from *one pair*, that Christ, springing from the *same family*, might in his sufferings taste death for every *man;* because he had that nature that was common to the *whole human race*. Had there been *several heads of families* in the beginning, Jesus must have been incarnated *from each of those heads*, else his death could have availed for those only who belonged to the *family* of which he was incarnated.

Take heed to your spirit] Scrutinize the motives which induce you to put away your wives.

Verse 16. *For the Lord—hateth putting away*] He abominates all such divorces, and *him* that makes them.

Covereth violence with his garment] And he also *notes* those who frame idle excuses to *cover* the *violence* they have done to the wives of their youth, by putting them away, and taking others in their place, whom they *now* happen to like better, when their own wives have been worn down in domestic services.

Verse 17. *Ye have wearied the Lord*] He has borne with you so long, and has been provoked so often, that he will bear it no longer. It is not fit that he should.

Every one that doeth evil] Ye say that it is *right* in the sight of the Lord to put away a wife, because she has no longer found favour in the sight of her husband. And because it has not been signally punished hitherto, ye blaspheme and cry out, "Where is the God of judgment?" Were he such as he is represented, would he not speak out? All these things show that this people were horribly corrupt. The priests were bad; the prophets were bad; the Levites were bad; and no wonder that the people were irreligious, profane, profligate, and cruel.

CHAPTER III

In allusion to the custom of sending pioneers to prepare the way for the march of an eastern monarch, the coming of Christ's forerunner is described, and then the coming of Christ himself, 1; *with the terrible judgments which were to accompany that event, in order to refine and purify his people and his priests,* 2–6. *The following verses reprehend them for withholding the legal tithes and offerings, with large promises in case of their repentance and amendments,* 7–12. *The prophet expostulates with the people for their hard and profane speeches against the conduct of Providence, and declares God will one day make a fearful and final distinction between the righteous and the wicked, whose different characters are in the mean time carefully recorded,* 13–18.

A. M. cir. 3607
B. C. cir. 397
Ol. cir. XCV. 4
Urbis Conditæ
cir. annum
356

BEHOLD, [a]I will send my
messenger, and he shall
[b]prepare the way before me: and
the LORD, whom ye seek, shall
suddenly come to his temple, [c]even the Messenger of the covenant, whom ye delight in:
behold, [d]he shall come, saith the LORD of hosts.
2 But who may abide [e]the day of his coming? and [f]who shall stand when he appeareth?
for [g]he *is* like a refiner's fire, and like fuller's
soap.
3 And [h]he shall sit *as* a refiner and purifier
of silver; and he shall purify the sons of Levi,
and purge them as gold and silver, that they
may [i]offer unto the LORD an offering in righteousness.
4 Then [k]shall the offering of Judah and Jerusalem be pleasant unto the LORD, as in the
days of old, and as in [l]former years.
5 And I will come near to you to judgment;
and I will be a swift witness
against the sorcerers, and against
the adulterers, [m]and against false
swearers, and against those that
[n]oppress the hireling in *his* wages, the
widow, and the fatherless, and that turn aside
the stranger *from his right*, and fear not me,
saith the LORD of hosts.
6 For I *am* the Lord, [o]I change not; [p]there-
fore ye sons of Jacob are not consumed.
7 Even from the days of [q]your fathers ye
are gone away from mine ordinances, and have
not kept *them*. [r]Return unto me, and I will
return unto you, saith the LORD of hosts.
[s]But ye said, Wherein shall we return?
8 Will a man rob God? Yet ye have robbed
me. But ye say, Wherein have we robbed
thee? [t]In tithes and offerings.
9 Ye *are* cursed with a curse: for ye have
robbed me, *even* this whole nation.

A. M. cir. 3607
B. C. cir. 397
Ol. cir. XCV. 4
Urbis Conditæ
cir. annum
356

[a]Matt. xi. 10; Mark i 2; Luke i. 76; vii. 27——[b]Isa. xl. 3——[c]Isa. lxiii 9——[d]Hag. ii. 7——[e]Chap. iv. 1
[f]Rev. vi. 17——[g]See Isa. iv. 4; Matt. iii. 10, 11, 12
[h]Isa. i. 25; Zech. xiii. 9——[i]1 Pet. ii. 5

[k]Chap. i. 11——[l]Or, *ancient*——[m]Zech. v. 4; James v. 4, 12——[n]Or, *defraud*——[o]Num. xxiii. 19; Rom. xi. 29; James i. 17——[p]Lam. iii. 22——[q]Acts vii. 51——[r]Zech. i. 3——[s]Chap. i. 6——[t]Neh. xiii. 10, 12

NOTES ON CHAP. III

Verse 1. *Behold, I will send my messenger*] מלאכי *Malachi*, the very name of the *prophet*. But this speaks of John the Baptist. I, the Messiah, the *Seed of God*, mentioned above, *will send my messenger*, John the Baptist.

He shall prepare the way] Be as a pioneer before me; a corrector of civil abuses, and a preacher of righteousness.

And the Lord, whom ye seek] The *Messiah*, whom ye expect, from the account given by the prophet Daniel, in his *seventy weeks*, chap. ix. 24.

Shall suddenly come to his temple] Shall soon be presented before the Lord in his temple; cleanse it from its defilement, and fill it with his teaching and his glory.

The Messenger of the covenant] He that comes to fulfil the great design, in reference to the covenant made with Abram, that *in his seed all the families of the earth should be blessed.* See the *parallel* texts in the margin, and the *notes* on them.

Verse 2. *But who may abide the day of his coming?*] Only they who shall believe on his name; for they that *will* not, shall be blinded, and the unbelieving nations shall be destroyed by the Romans.

Like fuller's soap] כברית *keborith*, from ברר *barar*, to *cleanse*, any thing that deterges. *Kali*, or *fern ashes*, or such things. I doubt whether the *composition* which we call *soap*, was known in ancient times.

Verse 3. *He shall sit* as *a refiner*] Alluding to the case of a refiner of metals, *sitting* at his fire; increasing it when he sees necessary, and watching the process of his work.

The sons of Levi] Those who minister in their stead under the NEW *covenant*, for the OLD Levitical institutions shall be abolished; yet, under the preaching of our Lord, a *great number of the priests became obedient to the faith*, Acts vi. 7; and, as to the others that did not believe, this great Refiner threw them as *dross* into the Roman fire, that consumed both Jerusalem and the temple.

Verse 5. *I will come near to you to judgment*] And what fearful *cases* does he get to judge! *Sorcerers, adulterers, false swearers, defrauders of the wages* of the *hireling, oppressors* of *widows* and *orphans*, and *perverters* of the *stranger* and such as *do not fear the Lord:* a horrible crew; and the land at that time was full of them. Several were converted under the preaching of Christ and his apostles, and the rest the Romans *destroyed* or carried into *captivity*.

Verse 6. *I* am *the Lord, I change not*] The new dispensation of grace and goodness, which is *now* about to be introduced, is not the effect of any *change* in my *counsels;* it is, on the contrary, the fulfilment of my everlasting purposes; as is also the throwing aside of the Mosaic ritual, which was only intended to *introduce* the great and glorious Gospel of my Son.

And because of this ancient covenant, ye Jews are not *totally consumed;* but ye are now, and shall be still, preserved as a distinct people—monuments both of my justice and mercy.

Verse 7. *Gone away from mine ordinances*] Never acting according to their spirit and design.

Return unto me] There is still space to repent.

Wherein shall we return?] Their consciences were *seared*, and they knew not that they were *sinners*.

Verse 8. *Will a man rob God?*] Here is one point on which ye are guilty; ye withhold the *tithes* and *offerings* from the temple of God, so that the Divine worship is neglected.

A. M. cir. 3607
B. C. cir. 397
Ol. cir. XCV. 4
Urbis Conditæ
cir. annum
356

10 [u]Bring ye all the tithes into [v]the storehouse, that there may be meat in mine house, and prove me now herewith, saith the LORD of hosts, if I will not open you the [w]windows of heaven, and [x]pour [y]you out a blessing, that *there shall* not *be room* enough *to receive it.*

11 And I will rebuke [z]the devourer for your sakes, and he shall not [a]destroy the fruits of your ground; neither shall your vine cast her fruit before the time in the field, saith the LORD of hosts.

12 And all nations shall call you blessed: for ye shall be [b]a delightsome land, saith the LORD of hosts.

13 [c]Your words have been stout against me, saith the LORD. Yet ye say, What have we spoken *so much* against thee?

14 [d]Ye have said, It *is* vain to serve God: and what profit *is it* that we have kept [e]his ordinance, and that we have walked [f]mournfully before the LORD of hosts?

A. M. cir. 3607
B. C. cir. 397
Ol. cir. XCV. 4
Urbis Conditæ
cir. annum
356

15 And now [g]we call the proud happy; yea, they that work wickedness [h]are set up; yea, *they that* [i]tempt God are even delivered.

16 Then they [k]that feared the LORD [l]spake often one to another: and the LORD hearkened, and heard *it,* and [m]a book of remembrance was written before him for them that feared the LORD, and that thought upon his name.

17 And [n]they shall be mine, saith the LORD of hosts, in that day when I make up my [o]jewels;[p] and [q]I will spare them, as a man spareth his own son that serveth him.

18 [r]Then shall ye return, and discern between the righteous and the wicked, between him that serveth God and him that serveth him not.

---

[u]Prov. iii. 9, 10——[v]1 Chron. xxxvi. 20; 2 Chron. xxxi. 11; Neh. x. 38; xvi. 12——[w]Gen. vii. 11; 2 Kings vii. 2——[x]Heb. *empty out*——[y]2 Chron. xxxi. 10 [z]Amos iv. 9——[a]Heb. *corrupt*——[b]Dan. viii. 9——[c]Ch. ii. 17——[d]Job xxi. 14, 15; xxii. 17; Psa. lxxiii. 12; Zeph. i. 12——[e]Heb. *his observation*——[f]Heb. *in black*

[g]Psa. lxxiii. 12; chap. ii. 17——[h]Heb. *are built* [i]Psa. xcv. 9——[k]Psa. lxvi. 16; chap. iv. 2——[l]Hebrews iii. 13——[m]Psa. lvi. 8; Isa. lxv. 6; Rev. xx. 12——[n]Exodus xix. 5; Deut. vii. 6; Psa. cxxxv. 4; Tit. ii. 14; 1 Peter ii. 9——[o]Or, *special treasure*——[p]Isa. lxii. 3 [q]Psalm ciii. 13——[r]Psa. lviii. 11

Verse 9. *Ye are cursed with a curse*] The whole nation is under my displeasure. The curse of God is upon you.

Verse 10. *Bring ye all the tithes*] They had so withheld these that the priests had not food enough to support life, and the sacred service was interrupted. See Neh. xiii. 10.

And prove me now herewith] What ye give to God shall never lessen your store. Give as ye *should,* and see whether I will not so increase your store by *opening the windows of heaven*—giving you *rain* and *fruitful seasons* —that your *barns* and *granaries* shall not be able to contain the abundance of your *harvests* and *vintage.*

Verse 11. *I will rebuke the devourer*] The *locusts,* &c., shall not come on your crops; and those that are in the country I will disperse and destroy.

Neither shall your vine cast her fruit] Every *blossom* shall bear *fruit,* and every *bunch of grapes* come to *maturity.*

Verse 12. *All nations shall call you blessed*] They shall see that a peculiar blessing of God rests upon you, and your *land shall be delightsome;* like *Paradise,* the *garden of the Lord.*

Verse 13. *Your words have been stout against me*] He speaks here to *open infidels* and *revilers.*

What have we spoken] They are ready either to deny the whole, or impudently to maintain and defend what they had spoken!

Verse 14. *Ye have said, It is vain to serve God*] They strove to destroy the Divine worship; they asserted that it was *vanity;* that, if they performed acts of worship, they should be nothing the better; and if they abstained, they should be nothing the worse. This was their teaching to the people.

Walked mournfully] Even *repentance* they have declared to be useless. This was a high pitch of ungodliness; but see what follows; behold the general *conclusions* of these reprobates—

Verse 15. *And now we call the proud happy*] Proud and insolent men are the only happy people, for they domineer everywhere, and none dares to resist them.

They that work wickedness are set up] The *humble* and *holy* are depressed and miserable; the *proud* and *wicked* are in places of *trust* and *profit.* Too often it is so.

They that *tempt God are even delivered.*] Even those who *despise* God, and *insult* his justice and providence, are preserved in and from dangers; while the *righteous* fall by them.

Verse 16. *They that feared the Lord*] There were a few godly in the land, who, hearing the language and seeing the profligacy of the rebels above, concluded that some signal mark of God's vengeance must fall upon them; they, therefore, as the corruption increased, cleaved the closer to their Maker. There are *three characteristics* given of this people, viz.:—

1. *They feared the Lord.* They had that reverence for Jehovah that caused them to depart from evil, and to keep his ordinances.

2. *They spake often one to another.* They kept up the communion of saints. By mutual exhortation they strengthened each other's hands in the Lord.

3. *They thought on his name.* His name was sacred to them; it was a fruitful source of profound and edifying *meditation.* The *name of God* is *God himself* in the plenitude of his power, omniscience, justice, goodness, mercy, and truth. What a source for thinking and contemplation! See how God treats such per-

sons: *The Lord hearkened* to their conversation, *heard* the meditations of their hearts; and so *approved* of the whole that *a book of remembrance was written before the Lord*—all their *names* were carefully *registered* in heaven. Here is an allusion to *records* kept by kings, Esth. vi. 1, of such as had performed signal services, and who should be the first to be rewarded.

Verse 17. *They shall be mine*] I will acknowledge them as *my subjects and followers;* in *the day*, especially, when I come to punish the wicked and reward the righteous.

When I make up my jewels] סגלה *segullah*, my *peculium*, my *proper treasure;* that which is *a man's own*, and *most prized* by him. Not *jewels;* for in no part of the Bible does the word *mean* a *gem* or *precious stone* of any kind. The interpretations frequently given of the word in this verse, comparing *saints* to *jewels*, are *forced* and *false*.

I will spare them] When I come to visit the wicked, I will take care of them. I will act towards them as a *tender father* would act towards his most *loving* and *obedient son*.

Verse 18. *Then shall ye return*] To your *senses*, when perhaps *too late;* and *discern*—see the difference which God makes, *between the righteous and the wicked*, which will be most *marked* and *awful*.

Between him that serveth God] Your obedience to whom, ye said, would be unprofitable to you.

And him that serveth him not.] Of whom ye said, his disobedience would be no prejudice to him. You will find the former received into the kingdom of glory; and the latter, with yourselves, thrust down into the bitter pains of an eternal death. Reader, ponder these things.

In the great day of the Lord, at least, if not long before, it will be fully discovered who have been the truly wise people; those who took up their cross and followed Christ; or those who satisfied the flesh, with its affections and desires, following a multitude to do evil.

CHAPTER IV

God's awful judgments on the wicked, 1. *Great blessedness of the righteous*, 2, 3. *The prophet then, with a solemnity becoming the last of the prophets, closes the Sacred Canon with enjoining the strict observance of the law till the forerunner already promised should appear, in the spirit of Elijah, to introduce the Messiah, and begin a new and everlasting dispensation*, 4–6.

A. M. cir. 3607
B. C. cir. 397
Ol. cir. XCV. 4
Urbis Conditæ cir. annum 356

FOR behold, [a]the day cometh, that shall burn as an oven; and all [b]the proud, yea, and all that do wickedly, shall be [c]stubble: and the day that cometh shall burn them up, saith the LORD of hosts, that it shall [d]leave them neither root nor branch.

2 But unto you that [e]fear my name shall the [f]Sun of righteousness arise with healing in his wings; and ye shall go forth, and grow up as calves of the stall.

3 [g]And ye shall tread down the wicked; for they shall be ashes under the soles of your

[a]Joel ii. 31; ch. iii. 2; 2 Pet. iii. 7——[b]Chap. iii. 18 [c]Obad. 18——[d]Amos ii. 9——[e]Chap. iii. 16

[f]Luke i. 78; Eph. v. 14; 2 Pet. i. 19; Rev. ii. 28——[g]2 Sam. xxviii. 43; Mic. vii. 10; Zech. x. 5

NOTES ON CHAP. IV

Verse 1. *Behold, the day cometh, that shall burn as an oven*] The destruction of Jerusalem by the Romans.

And all the proud] This is in reference to ver. 15 of the preceding chapter.

The day that cometh shall burn them up] Either by famine, by sword, or by captivity. All those rebels shall be destroyed.

It shall leave them neither root nor branch.] A proverbial expression for total destruction. Neither *man* nor *child* shall escape.

Verse 2. *You that fear my name*] The persons mentioned in the *sixteenth* verse of the preceding chapter; ye that look for redemption through the Messiah.

The Sun of righteousness] The Lord Jesus, the promised Messiah; the Hope of Israel.

With healing in his wings] As the *sun*, by the rays of *light* and *heat*, revives, cheers, and fructifies the whole creation, giving, through God, *light* and *life* everywhere; so Jesus Christ, by the influences of his *grace* and *Spirit*, shall quicken, awaken, enlighten, warm, invigorate, heal, purify, and refine every soul that believes in him; and, by his *wings* or *rays*, diffuse these blessings from one end of heaven to another; everywhere invigorating the *seeds* of *righteousness*, and *withering* and *drying up* the *seeds of sin*. The *rays* of this *Sun* are the *truths* of his *Gospel*, and the *influences* of his *Spirit*. And at present these are universally diffused.

And ye shall go forth] Ye who believe on his name shall go forth out of Jerusalem when the Romans shall come up against it. After Cestius Gallus had blockaded the city for some days, he suddenly raised the siege. The Christians who were then in it, knowing, by seeing Jerusalem encompassed with armies, that the day of its destruction was come, when their Lord commanded them to flee into the mountains, took this opportunity to escape from Jerusalem, and go to Pella, in Cœlesyria; so that no Christian life fell in the siege and destruction of this city.

But these words are of more general application and meaning; "ye shall go forth" in all the occupations of life, but particularly in the means of grace; and—

Grow up as calves of the stall] Full of health, of life, and spirits; satisfied and happy.

Verse 3. *Ye shall tread down*] This may be the commission given to the Romans: Tread down the wicked people, tread down the wicked place; set it on fire, and let the *ashes* be trodden down under your feet.

A. M. cir. 3607
B. C. cir. 397
Ol. cir. XCV. 4
Urbis Conditæ
cir. annum
356

feet in the day that I shall do
this, saith the LORD of hosts.
4 Remember ye the [h]law of
Moses my servant, which I com-
manded unto him [i]in Horeb for all Israel, *with*
[k]the statutes and judgments.
5 Behold, I will send you [l]Elijah the prophet [m]before the coming of the
great and dreadful day of the
LORD:
6 And [n]he shall turn the heart
of the fathers to the children, and the heart of
the children to their fathers, lest I come and
[o]smite the earth with [p]a curse.

[h]Exod. xx. 3, &c.——[i]Deut. iv. 10——[k]Psa. cxlvii. 19
[l]Matt. xi. 14; xvii. 11; Mark ix. 11; Luke i. 17

[m]Joel ii. 31——[n]Ecclus. xlviii. 10——[o]Zech. xiv. 12
[p]Zech. v. 3

Verse 4. *Remember ye the law of Moses*] Where all these things are predicted. The *Septuagint, Arabic,* and *Coptic,* place this verse the last.

Verse 5. *Behold, I will send you Elijah the prophet*] This is meant alone of John the Baptist, as we learn from Luke i. 17, (where see the note,) in whose spirit and power he came.

Verse 6. *And he shall turn* (convert) *the heart of the fathers* (עַל *al,* WITH) *the children*] Or, together with the children; both old and young. *Lest I come, and,* finding them unconverted, *smite the land with a curse,* חרם *cherem, utter extinction.* So we find that, had the Jews turned to God, and received the Messiah at the preaching of John the Baptist and that of Christ and his apostles, the awful חרם *cherem* of final excision and execration would not have been executed upon them. However, they filled up the cup of their iniquity, and were *reprobated,* and the Gentiles *elected* in their stead. Thus, the last was first, and the first was last. Glory to God for his unspeakable gift!

There are *three* remarkable *predictions* in this chapter:—1. The advent of John Baptist, in the spirit and authority of Elijah. 2. The manifestation of Christ in the flesh, under the emblem of the Sun of righteousness. 3. The final destruction of Jerusalem, represented under the emblem of a burning oven, consuming every thing cast into it. These three prophecies, relating to the most important facts that have ever taken place in the history of the world, announced here nearly *four hundred* years before their occurrence, have been most circumstantially fulfilled.

In most of the Masoretic Bibles the *fifth* verse is repeated after the *sixth*—"Behold, I send unto you Elijah the prophet, before the great and terrible day of Jehovah come;" for the Jews do not like to let their sacred book end with a *curse;* and hence, in reading, they immediately subjoin the above verse, or else the *fourth*—"Remembering ye the law of Moses my servant."

In one of my oldest MSS. the *fifth* verse is *repeated,* and written at full length: "Behold, I send you Elijah the prophet, before the coming of the great and dreadful day of the Lord." In another, only these words are added: "Behold, I will send you Elijah." It is on this ground that the Jews expect the reappearance of Elijah the prophet; and at their marriage-feast always set a chair and knife and fork for this prophet, whom they suppose to be invisibly present. But we have already seen that John the Baptist, the forerunner of our Lord, was the person designed; for he came in the spirit and power of Elijah, (see on chap. iii. 1,) and has fulfilled this prophetic promise. John is come, and the Lord Jesus has come also; he has shed his blood for the salvation of a lost world; he has ascended on high; he has sent forth his Holy Spirit; he has commissioned his ministers to proclaim to all mankind redemption in his blood; and he is ever present with them, and is filling the earth with righteousness and true holiness. Hallelujah! The kingdoms of this world are about to become the kingdoms of God and our Lord Jesus! And now, having just arrived at the end of my race in this work, and seeing the wonderful extension of the work of God in the earth, my heart prays:—

O Jesus, ride on, till all are subdued,
Thy mercy make known, and sprinkle thy blood;
Display thy salvation, and teach the new song,
To every nation, and people, and tongue!

In most MSS. and *printed Masoretic Bibles* there are only *three* chapters in this prophet, the *fourth* being joined to the *third,* making it *twenty-four* verses.

In the Jewish reckonings the *Twelve Minor Prophets* make but one book; hence there is no Masoretic note found at the end of any of the preceding prophets, with accounts of its *verses, sections,* &c.; but, at the end of *Malachi* we find the following table, which, though it gives the number of verses in each prophet, yet gives the *total sum, middle verse,* and *sections,* at the end of Malachi, thereby showing that they consider the whole *twelve* as constituting but *one book.*

MASORETIC NOTES

On the Twelve Minor Prophets

Hosea has - - - - -	197 verses.
Joel- - - - - - - -	73
Amos - - - - - - - -	146
Obadiah - - - - - -	21
Jonah - - - - - -	48
Micah - - - - - - -	105
Nahum - - - - - -	57
Zephaniah - - - - -	53
Habakkuk - - - - -	56
Haggai - - - - - -	38
Zechariah - - - - -	211
Malachi - - - - - -	55

The sum of all the verses of the Twelve Minor Prophets is 1060

The middle verse is Micah, chap. iii. ver. 12.

Number of Sections, 21.

TO GOD THE FATHER, SON, AND HOLY GHOST, BE ETERNAL PRAISES. AMEN.

I have this day completed this Commentary, on which I have laboured *above thirty* years; and which, when I began, I never expected to live long enough to finish. May it be a means of securing glory to God in the highest, and peace and good will among men upon earth! Amen, Amen. ADAM CLARKE.

Heydon Hall, Middlesex,
Monday, March 28, A. D. 1825.

AN

EPITOME OF THE JEWISH HISTORY

FROM THE

TIME OF NEHEMIAH AND MALACHI TO THE BIRTH OF CHRIST

FILLING UP THE CHASM BETWEEN

THE OLD AND NEW TESTAMENTS

As many have wished to see an epitome of the Jewish history, from the days of the prophet Malachi to the advent of Christ, in order to connect the history of the Old and New Testaments, I have prepared the following, which, in such a work as this, is as much as should be expected.

On all hands *Malachi* is allowed to have been the *last* prophet under the Old Testament; and he flourished about *four hundred and nine* years before the coming of Christ, according to the commonly received chronology; and *Nehemiah*, who was contemporary with him, was the last of those civil governors appointed by God himself. His last act of reformation is fixed by Prideaux, B. C. 409; soon after which it is supposed that he died, as at this time he could not be less than *seventy* years of age. For the administration of affairs in his times and in those of Ezra, whom he succeeded in the government of Judea, the reader is referred to the notes on Ezra, Nehemiah, and Daniel.

We have seen, in the book of Nehemiah, that, on the return of the Jews from the Chaldean captivity, many of them brought strange wives and a spurious offspring with them, and refusing to put them away, were banished by Nehemiah, and went and settled in Samaria. Among those exiles there was a son of Jehoiada, the high priest, named *Manasseh*, who had married the daughter of Sanballat the Horonite, and put himself under the protection of his father-in-law, who was governor of the place. After the death of Nehemiah, Sanballat obtained a grant from Darius to build a temple on Mount *Gerizim*, near Samaria, of which he made *Manasseh*, his son-in-law, high priest. This temple was begun to be built B. C. 408.

From the building of this temple, *Samaria* became the refuge of all refractory Jews: and though by this means the old superstition of the land was reformed to the worship of the God of *Israel*, they of *Jerusalem* would never consider the *Samaritan Jews* otherwise than *apostates*. On the other hand, the *Samaritans* maintained that Mount *Gerizim* was the only proper place for the worship of God. This people rejected all traditions, and adhered only to the written word contained in the five books of *Moses*.

Nehemiah's death was also attended with a change of the *Jewish* government at *Jerusalem*. *Judea* had no longer a governor of its own. It was united to the *prefecture* of *Syria;* the rulers of which committed the administration of both *civil* and *ecclesiastical* affairs to the high priest for the time being.

By this means the high priesthood became an office under the *heathen;* and towards the latter end of *Artaxerxes Mnemon's* reign, B. C. 405, who succeeded his father *Darius Nothus*, B. C. 423, the office was conferred by the governor of *Syria* and *Phœnicia*. For *Bagoses*, the governor, took upon himself to displace *Johanan* the high priest, in favour of the said priest's brother *Joshua;* which nomination, though it did not take place, (for *Johanan* slew his brother *Joshua* in the inner court of the temple, as he endeavoured by force to usurp the high-priest's office by virtue of the governor's commission, B. C. 366,) was attended with this bad consequence—that *Bagoses*, hearing of the murder, came in great wrath to *Jerusalem*, and laid a heavy fine upon the nation, which lasted *seven* years, or during the whole of his government.

Artaxerxes Mnemon died B. C. 359, with grief at the brutality of his son *Ochus*, who had so terrified his eldest brother *Ariaspes*, that he poisoned himself, and had his younger brother *Harpates* assassinated. So that *Ochus* succeeded to the dignity and empire of his father.

In the third year of *Ochus*, about 356 before *Christ*, *Alexander the Great* was born at *Pella* in *Macedonia*. *Ochus*, having reigned *twenty-one* years, was poisoned by his favourite *Bagoas*, in hopes of getting the whole government into his own hands, and to put the crown on the head of *Arses*, his youngest son, whom he also poisoned soon after, and raised *Codomannus*, a distant relation of the late king, to the throne. This new king took the name of *Darius;* and when *Bagoas* had also prepared a poisonous draught for *him*, he obliged *Bagoas* to drink it himself; by which means he saved his own life, and punished the traitor.

It was about the year B. C. 336 that *Alexander the Great* succeeded to the kingdom of *Macedon*, on the death of his father *Philip*, who was slain by the noble Macedonian *Pausanias*, as he celebrated the marriage of his daughter with *Alexander*, king of *Epirus*, before he set out upon the *Grecian* expedition against *Persia*, being chosen *captain-general* of the united forces of *Greece*.

Alexander also succeeded to that command by a new election. In one campaign he overran all *Asia Minor;* vanquished *Darius* in two battles; took his mother, wife, and children prisoners; and subdued all *Syria* as far as *Tyre*, B. C. 332.

During the siege of *Tyre*, he demanded the submission of the neighbouring provinces of *Galilee*, *Samaria*, and *Judea*. The two former submitted to him; but *Judea* would not renounce their allegiance to *Darius* so long as he lived. This brought upon them the wrath of the conqueror; who, having taken *Tyre*, by carrying a bank from the continent through the sea to the island on which the city stood, and burned it down to the ground, destroyed and slew all the inhabitants in a barbarous manner, both in the sackage of the town, and afterwards in cold blood; and then marched to Jerusalem to wreak his vengeance upon the Jews. Upon his approach, and the report of his having crucified *two thousand* of the *Tyrian* prisoners, the high priest *Jaddua* and all the city were under dreadful apprehensions. They had nothing but God's protection to depend upon. They fasted and prayed: and God in a vision directed the high priest to go in his pontifical robes, attended by the high priests in their proper habits, and all the people in white garments, and meet *Alexander* out of the city.

As soon as *Alexander* saw this procession moving towards him, and the high priest in the front, he was overawed, drew near, bowed down, and saluted him in a religious manner; alleging that he did so in regard to that God whose priest he was; adding, moreover, that the high priest so habited had appeared to him in a dream at *Dio* in *Macedonia*, assuring him of success against the *Persians*.

Jaddua conducted him into the city; and, having offered sacrifices in the temple, showed him the prophecies of *Daniel*, concerning the overthrow of the *Persian* empire by a *Grecian* king.

Alexander was well satisfied with his reception at *Jerusalem;* and at his departure granted the *Jews* a *toleration* of their religion, and an exemption from tribute every *seventh* year. And the *Jews* were so well pleased with the conqueror's behaviour, that, upon his signifying that he would receive as many of them as would enlist into his service, great multitudes entered under his banner, and followed him in his other expeditions.

The *Samaritans* met him with great pomp and parade, as he left *Jerusalem*, and invited him to their city. But *Alexander* deferred both the invitation, and petition for certain privileges, till his return from *Egypt;* and left his favourite *Andromachus* governor of *Syria* and *Palestine*.

Andromachus, coming some time after to *Samaria* upon business, was burned to death in his house, as it was thought on purpose, by the *Samaritans*, in revenge of the slight which they apprehended *Alexander* had shown them. But as soon as *Alexander* heard it, he caused those to be put to death who had acted any part in the murder, banished all the other inhabitants from *Samaria*, planted therein a colony of *Macedonians*, and gave the residue to the *Jews*.

Upon the ruin of the *Persians*, *Alexander* had erected the *Grecian* or *Macedonian* monarchy. But coming to *Babylon*, after the conquest of the most part of the then known world, he gave himself up so much to drunkenness and gluttony, that he soon put an end to his life, B. C. 323.

Here it cannot be amiss to observe, that *Alexander* was of a bold and enterprising spirit; but more full of fire than discretion. His actions, though successful, were furious and extravagantly rash. His few virtues were obscured with more and greater vices. *Vainglory* was his predominant passion; and the fables of the ancient *Greek* heroes were the only *charts* by which he steered his conduct. His dragging *Balis* round *Gaza*, his expedition into *India*, his drunken procession through *Caramania*, and taking to himself the name of the son of *Jupiter*, are so many vouchers of this assertion. And, were all his actions duly considered and estimated, he would be properly characterized the great *cut-throat* of the age in which he lived; as all they are who delight in bloodshed, and will forfeit ALL to obtain *universal monarchy;* whereas those only are the true *heroes* who most benefit the world, by promoting the peace and welfare of mankind. In a righteous cause, or a just defence of a man's country, all actions of valour are worthy of praise; but in *all other* cases *victory* and *conquest* are no more than *murder* and *robbery*. Therefore *Alexander's* heroism is to be avoided, and not to be followed, as the surest way to honour and glory.

Alexander was no sooner dead, than *Ptolemy Soter* seized upon *Egypt;* and having in vain endeavoured to gain *Syria, Phœnicia*, and *Judea* from *Laomedon*, whom *Alexander* had appointed governor instead of *Andromachus*, who was burnt, invaded them by sea and land, took *Laomedon* prisoner, and got possession of those provinces also, except *Judea;* which, upon the account of their allegiance to the surviving governor, refusing to yield, felt the severity of the conqueror; for, understanding that the *Jews* would not so much as defend themselves on the *Sabbath day*, he stormed *Jerusalem*, took it without resistance on that day, and carried above *one hundred thousand* of them captives into *Egypt*.

From this time we may date the *Jews'* subjection to the kings of *Egypt*. And it was in the *fifth* year of this *Ptolemy's* reign that *Onias* the *Jewish* high priest died, and was succeeded by his son *Simon the Just*, on whom an eulogium may be found in Ecclus. l. 1, &c., B. C. 292.

Simon the Just was high priest *nine* years, and is supposed to have completed the canon of the Old Testament by adding the books of *Ezra, Nehemiah, Esther, Malachi*, and the two books of *Chronicles*, with the aid and assistance of the great synagogue. He was succeeded by his brother *Eleazar*, his son *Onias* being a minor, B. C. 291.

Ptolemy Soter was succeeded by his son *Ptolemy Philadelphus*, B. C. 285, who completed the college or *museum* of learned men, and the famous library at *Alexandria* in *Egypt*, which was begun by his father, and contained *seven hundred thousand* volumes, and placed in that library an authentic translation of the book of the *law*. This translation was finished under the inspection of *Eleazar* the high priest, and is called the *Septuagint*, on account of the joint labour of *seventy-two* translators employed in it, B. C. 254.

Ptolemy Philadelphus died in the *thirty-ninth* year of his reign, and in the *sixty-third* of his age, B. C. 247. He was a learned prince, and a great patron of learning; so that men of learning flocked to his court from all parts, and partook of his favour and bounty. Among these were the poets *Theocritus, Callimachus, Lycophron*, and *Aratus*, and *Manetho*, the *Egyptian* historian.

B. C. 247, *Ptolemy Euergetes* succeeded his father *Ptolemy* in *Egypt*. He found *Onias*, the son of *Simon the Just*, in the *pontificate* at *Jerusalem*, who was very old, weak, inconsiderate, and covetous. And *Euergetes*, perceiving that the high priest had for many years kept back the annual tribute, sent one *Athenion*, an officer at court, to *Jerusalem*, to demand it, being a very large sum, with threats of sending an army to dispossess them of the country upon refusal.

This demand and threatening threw the whole nation into great confusion; and one *Joseph*, the high priest's nephew by his sister's side, rebuked his uncle sharply for his injustice and ill management of the public interest, proposed *Onias's* journey to *Alexandria*, as the best expedient, and, upon his uncle's refusal, offered to go in person to pacify the king's wrath, which was accepted by the high priest, and approved by the people, B. C. 226.

Joseph all this time had entertained *Athenion* in a most elegant manner at his own house, and at his departure loaded him with such valuable gifts, that when he arrived at *Alexandria*, he found the king prepared much in his favour to receive him, and made himself more acceptable by informing him concerning the revenues of *Cœlesyria* and *Phœnicia*, whose value he had inquired more perfectly from their *farmers*, with whom he had traveled to court part of the way; and was thereupon admitted the king's *receiver general* of *Cœlesyria, Phœnicia, Judea*, and *Samaria*. He immediately satisfied the king for his uncle's arrears with *five hundred* talents he borrowed at *Alexandria* on the credit of his new office, which he enjoyed *twenty-two* years, though he met with great opposition at his first collecting, till he had brought some of the ringleaders to exemplary punishment.

B. C. 221. All things were again composed at *Jerusalem;* and *Philopater* having succeeded his father *Ptolemy Euergetes* in *Egypt*, and defeated the army of *Antiochus the Great*, he in the *fifth* year of his reign took the tour of *Jerusalem* while he visited his conquests. But this was very unfortunate for the *Jews*. For *Philopater* being led by a vain curiosity to enter into the *sanctuary* and the *holy of holies* on the great day of *expiation*, B. C. 217, where no one but the high priest was allowed to enter, he was opposed by the deprecations and lamentations of the people; and when he would still advance beyond the inner *court*, he was seized with such a terror and consternation, that he was obliged to be carried back in a manner half dead. He recovered; but when he left the city, he vowed revenge. And accordingly, he was no sooner returned to *Alexandria* than he deprived the *Jews* of all their rights and privileges; ordered them to be stigmatized with a burn representing an *ivy leaf*, under pain of death, in honour of his god *Bacchus;* and excluded all persons from his presence that would not sacrifice to the god he worshipped. Then he commanded as many *Jews* as he could seize in *Egypt* to be brought and shut up in the *Hippodrome*, or place for horse-races, at *Alexandria*, to be destroyed by *elephants*. But God turned the wild beasts upon those that came to see the dreadful massacre, by which numbers of the spectators were slain; and so terrified the king and his subjects with other tokens of his displeasure and power, that *Philopater* immediately not only released the *Jews* from the *Hippodrome*, but restored the whole nation to their privileges, reversed every decree against them, and put those *Jews* to death who for fear of persecution had apostatized from their religion.

Ptolemy Philopater was succeeded, B. C. 204, by his son *Ptolemy Epiphanes*, then only five years old. This minority gave *Antiochus the Great* an opportunity to regain *Cœlesyria* and *Palestine:* in which expedition the *Jews* had shown so much favour to *Antiochus*, that he granted them many favours, a liberty to live according to their own laws and religion, a prohibition to strangers to enter within the *sept* of the temple, &c. But as soon as *Ptolemy* was marriageable, he made peace with him, and gave him his daughter, with *Cœlesyria* and *Palestine* for her portion. On this occasion *Joseph*, who had been *Ptolemy's* receiver general in those provinces, and displaced by *Antiochus*, was restored.

Ptolemy in a short time had a son; and it being customary on such occasions for all the great officers of state to congratulate the king and queen, and to carry them presents, *Joseph*, whose age would not permit him to take so long a journey, sent his son *Hyrcanus*, B. C. 187, who, upon an unlimited credit given him by his father, when he was arrived at *Alexandria*, borrowed a *thousand talents*, or *two hundred thousand pounds* sterling, with which, buying a hundred beautiful boys for the king, and as many beautiful young maids for the queen, at the price of a talent per head, and presenting them each with a talent in their hands, and disposing of the remaining sum among the courtiers and great officers, he so obliged the king and queen, and all the court, that he found it easy to supplant his father, and obtained the king's commission for collecting the royal revenues in all the country beyond *Jordan*.

Hyrcanus, having thus abused his trust, went with a strong guard to execute his office; and being met by his brothers, killed two of them. He came to *Jerusalem;* but his father would not admit him to his presence, and he was shunned by every body. Upon the death of his father, which happened soon after, he endeavoured by force of arms to oust his brethren from the *paternal* estate. This disturbed the peace of Jerusalem for a while; till at last his brothers, being assisted by the high priest and the generality of the people, drove him over *Jordan*, where he lived in a strong castle, till he fell upon his own sword and killed himself to avoid the punishment with which *Antiochus Epiphanes*, upon his succeeding to the throne of *Syria*, threatened him. B. C. 175.

Antiochus the Great being slain by the inhabitants of *Elymais*, as he attempted by night to plunder the temple of *Jupiter Belus*, thereby to pay the *Romans* according to his agreement, his son *Seleucus Philopater* succeeded him in the provinces of *Syria, Judea*, &c., and resided at *Antioch*.

Seleucus, at his first advancement to the dominion of these provinces, continued his father's favours to the *Jews;* but being afterwards informed by one *Simon* a *Benjamite* that there was great treasure in the temple, he sent one *Heliodorus* to seize it, and to bring all the riches he could find therein to *Antioch*. *Heliodorus* attempted to execute this commission; but he was so terrified at the sight of an armed host of angels that appeared to defend the entrance of the sacred treasury, that he fell speechless to the ground; nor did he recover till the high priest interceded to God for him.

This same *Heliodorus* poisoned his sovereign *Seleucus*, hoping to obtain the kingdom; but his design was frustrated by *Eumenes*, king of *Pergamus*, and his brother *Attalus*, who set *Antiochus Epiphanes*, another son of *Antiochus the Great*, on the throne of *Syria*.

Epiphanes, at his accession to the throne, finding himself hard pressed by the *Romans*, endeavoured to raise their heavy tribute by all manner of exactions. Amongst other means he deposed the good and pious high priest, *Onias*, and sold the pontificate to his brother *Jason* for the yearly sum of *three hundred and sixty* talents; and afterwards he deposed *Jason*, and sold it to his brother *Menelaus* for *three hundred* talents more, B. C. 174.

Menelaus, having invaded the pontificate by these unjust means, and finding himself straitened to raise the annual payment according to contract, by the means of *Lysimachus*, another of his brothers, he robbed the temple of many gold vessels, which, being turned into money, he paid to the king; and bribed *Andronicus*, the governor of *Antioch*, to murder his brother *Onias*, lest at any time he should stand in his way. It is true that at the instance of the people *Andronicus* was seized and executed for his villany and murder, and *Lysimachus* was put to death by the mob at *Jerusalem;* yet *Menelaus* found means by bribery, not only to acquit himself, but to obtain sentence against, and even the execution of, the *three* delegates that went from *Jerusalem* to prosecute him in the name of the *sanhedrin*.

But while *Antiochus* was engaged in the *Egyptian* war, *Jason* on a false report that the king was dead, marched with a thousand men, surprised the city of *Jerusalem*, drove *Menelaus* into the castle, and cruelly put to the sword and to other kinds of death all those that he thought were his adversaries.

Immediately the news of this revolution and massacre reached *Antiochus*, he hastened to reduce the *Jews* to their obedience; and in his way, being informed that the inhabitants of *Jerusalem* had made great rejoicings at the report of his death, he was so provoked, that, taking the city by storm, B. C. 170, he slew *forty thousand* persons, and sold as many more for slaves to the neighbouring nations. He entered the *holy of holies*, sacrificed a sow upon the altar of burnt-offerings, and caused the broth or liquor thereof to be sprinkled all over the temple. He plundered the temple of as much gold and furniture as amounted to *eight hundred* talents of gold. Then, returning to *Antioch*, he made one *Philip*, a most barbarous and cruel man, governor of *Judea; Andronicus*, as bad a man, governor of *Samaria;* and continued *Menelaus*, the worst of all, in the pontificate. And, as if this was not sufficient to satisfy his rage, he not long after sent an army of *two and twenty thousand* men, under *Apollonius* his general, with commission to put all the men of *Jerusalem* to the sword, and to make slaves of the women and children; which was rigorously executed on a Sabbath day, so that none escaped but such as could hide themselves in caves, or reach the mountains by flight.

This cruelty soon after pursued the *Jews*, wherever dispersed: for by a *general* decree to oblige all people in his dominions to conform to the religion of the king, one *Athenæus*, a *Grecian* idolater, was pitched upon to receive and instruct all the *Jews* that would turn idolaters, and to punish with the most cruel deaths those who refused. It was at this time that the temple was dedicated to *Jupiter Olympius;* the books of the law were burned; and women, accused of having their children circumcised, were led about the streets with these children tied about their necks, and then both together cast headlong over the steepest part of the wall, B. C. 167; for many of them chose rather to die than to renounce their God; as the holy zeal and religious fortitude of the very aged and pious *Eleazar*, a chief doctor of the law, and of the heroine *Salomona* and her seven sons, do testify; whom neither the instruments of death could terrify, nor the allurements of the tyrant could persuade, to forfeit their interest with the Almighty, either by idolatry or dissimulation.

Matthias, great grandson of *Asmonæus*, and a priest of the first course, retired with his five sons, *John, Simon, Judas, Eleazar*, and *Jonathan*, from the persecution at *Jerusalem*, to a little place called *Modin*, in the tribe of *Dan*. But as soon as they were discovered, *Antiochus* sent one *Appelles* to that place, to oblige all the inhabitants, on pain of death, to turn idolaters. This officer delivered his commission by endeavouring to persuade *Matthias* to embrace idolatry, tendering to him the king's favour, and promising him great riches; which the good priest not only scornfully rejected, but slew the first *Jew* that dared to approach the idolatrous altar; and then, turning upon the king's commissioner, he despatched him and all his attendants, with the assistance of his sons and those that were with them. After this he put himself at the head of as many *Jews* as he could collect; and, having broken down the idols and the altars of the heathens, retired with them into the mountains. Here, as he took measures for their defence, he was joined by a numerous party of *Assidæans;* a valiant people, who practised great hardships and mortifications, and were resolved to lay down their lives for the recovery of the temple. By these, and the accession of great numbers of other *Jews, Matthias* found himself in a capacity to take the field; but as their mistaken notion about resting on the *Sabbath day* had been one great cause of their being surprised by their enemies, and brought many great misfortunes upon them, because they would not defend themselves on that day from their enemies, he caused it to be unanimously agreed and decreed, that it was lawful, and that they might defend themselves, and repel force by force, on the Sabbath day, should they be attacked.

After this decree had passed, with the approbation of the priests and elders, *Matthias* left his lurking-places, marched round the cities of *Judah*, pulled down the *heathen* altars, restored the true worship and circumcision, and cut off both the apostates and persecutors that fell in his way, till death summoned him to immortality, in the *hundred and forty-seventh* year of his age.

When he found death approaching, he exhorted his five sons to persevere in the cause of God, as he had begun; and he appointed his son *Judas* his successor in the command of the army; and *Simon* to be their counsellor, B. C. 166. He was buried at *Modin* with great lamentation of all *Israel*.

Judas, who had signalized himself on former occasions for his great valour, was distinguished by the title *Maccabeus;* and having taken the command of his people upon him, he prosecuted the good work of reformation begun by his father, and took all the measures he was able, by fortifying towns, building castles, and placing strong garrisons, to maintain the liberty and religion of his country against all opposition.

Apollonius was sent by *Antiochus* to march an army of *Samaritans* against him; but he was killed, and his troops defeated and entirely routed, after a great slaughter, by our young general, who, finding *Apollonius's* sword among the spoils, took it for his own use, and generally fought with it ever after.

This news having reached *Cœlosyria, Seron*, deputy-governor of that province, marched with all the forces he could collect to revenge the death of *Apollonius;* but he met with the same fate.

Antiochus was so enraged at these defeats, that he immediately ordered *forty thousand* foot, *seven thousand* horse, and a great number of auxiliaries, made up of the neighbouring nations and apostate *Jews*, to march against *Judea*, under the command of *Ptolemy Macron, Nicanor*, and *Gorgias, three* eminent commanders, B. C. 162.

Upon their advancing as far as *Emmaus*, about *seven* miles from *Jerusalem, Judas*, who may be suppoesd at that time besieging or at least blocking up *Jerusalem*, then in the hands of the heathen, retired to *Mizpeh*. Here the whole army addressed themselves to God. *Judas* exhorted them most pathetically to fight for their *religion, laws*, and *liberties;* but at last, giving those leave to withdraw from his army that had built houses, or betrothed wives within the year, or that were in any degree fearful, he presently found himself at the head of no more than *three thousand* men.

However, he was resolved to give the enemy battle. In the mean time God ordained him an easy victory; for while *Gorgias* was detached with *five thousand* foot and *one thousand* horse to surprise his little army by night, *Judas*, being informed of the design, marched by another way, fell upon the camp in the absence of *Gorgias*, killed *three thousand* men, put the rest to flight, and seized the camp. *Gorgias*, not finding the *Jews* in their camp, proceeded to the mountains, supposing they were fled thither for safety. But not meeting with them there, he was much surprised in his return at what had happened in his absence; and his army, hearing that *Judas* waited to give them a warm reception in the plains, flung down their arms and fled. *Judas* in the pursuit killed *six thousand* more, and wounded and maimed most of the rest. This victory opened to him the gates of *Jerusalem*, where he and his army celebrated the next day, which was a *Sabbath*, with great devotion and thanksgiving.

Timotheus and *Bacchides*, governors or lieutenants under *Antiochus*, marched immediately to the assistance of *Gorgias;* but they fell a sacrifice to the valour and conduct of *Judas*, who, by the spoils taken from the enemy, was enabled the better to carry on the war.

This defeat was succeeded by another of *Lysias*, the governor of all the country beyond the *Euphrates*. He had penetrated as far as *Bethzura*, a strong fortress about *twenty* miles from *Jerusalem*, threatening to destroy the country with an army of *sixty thousand* foot and *five thousand* horse. But he was defeated also by *Judas* with *ten thousand* men only.

This victory gave him some respite; and accordingly he restored the temple to the true worship of God, removed all the profanations, built an altar of *unhewn stones*, and replaced the furniture that *Antiochus* had carried away, out of the gold and other rich spoils taken in this war. Thus he dedicated the temple again, and ordained that a feast of *dedication* should be kept *annually*, in commemoration thereof for ever, about the 20th of *November*.

His next care was to subdue the fortress on Mount *Acra*, which *Apollonius* had erected to command the temple; and being yet in the power of the heathens, gave them great opportunities to annoy the *Jews* that went to worship in the temple. But not having men enough to spare to form a blockade, he silenced it by another fortification, which he erected on the mountain of the temple.

When this revolt and success of the *Jews* reached *Antiochus*, in his expedition into *Persia*, he threatened utterly to destroy the whole nation, and to make *Jerusalem* the common place of burial to all the *Jews*. But God visited him with a sudden and sore disease. He at first was afflicted with grievous torments in his bowels; his *privy parts* were ulcerated and filled with an innumerable quantity of vermin; and the *smell* was so offensive that he became nauseous to himself and all about him. Then his mind was so tormented with direful spectres and apparitions of evil spirits, and the remorse of his wicked life and profanations gnawed him so grievously, that he at last acknowledged the justice of God in his punishment, and offered up many vows and promises of a full reparation in case he recovered. But God would not hear him; therefore, when his body was almost half consumed with abominable ulcers, he died under the most horrid torments of body and mind, in the twelfth year of his reign.

Judas Maccabeus began now to consider how the government should be fixed, and therefore, in a general assembly held at *Maspha*, he revived the ancient order, and appointed rulers over thousands, hundreds, fifties, and tens. And it is also probable that he constituted the high court of *sanhedrin*, in which was a settled *Nasi*, president or prince, who was the high priest for the time being; an *Abbethdin*, or father of the house of judgment, who was the president's *deputy;* and a *Chacan*, or *the wise man*, who was *sub-deputy*. The other members were called *elders* or *senators*, men of untainted birth, good learning, and profound knowledge in the law, both priests and laymen. And they in particular were empowered to decide all *private* difficult controversies, all *religious* affairs, and all important matters of *state*.

This was properly the senate or great council of the nation, which grew into great power under the administration of the *Asmonean* princes, and was in great authority in the days of our Saviour's ministry.

Lysias, who had been so shamefully routed by *Judas*, having the care of *Antiochus's* son, who was called *Antiochus Eupater*, and only *nine* years old, set him on the throne, and seized the government and tuition of the young king into his own hands, and immediately combined with the neighbouring *Idumeans* and other nations, enemies to *Judah*, to unite in an attempt utterly to destroy and extirpate the whole race of *Israel*.

When *Judas* was informed of this confederacy, he resolved to prevent their intentions, and to carry the war into *Idumea*. Thus he entered their country by *Acrabatene*, a canton of *Judea*, near the southern extremity of the *Dead Sea*, and slew there *twenty thousand* of them. Then falling upon the children of *Bean*, another tribe of the *Idumeans*, he killed *twenty thousand* more, routed their army, and took their strong holds. Hence passing over *Jordan* into the land of the *Ammonites*, he defeated them in several engagements, slew great numbers of them, and took the city *Jahazah*, at the foot of Mount *Gilead*, near the brook *Jazah;* and so returned home.

After his return into *Judea*, one *Timotheus*, a governor in those parts, pretended to follow him with a numerous army. But *Judas* fell upon him; and having overthrown him with a very great slaughter, pursued him to the city *Gazara*, in the tribe of *Ephraim*, which he took; and he slew both *Timotheus* and his brother *Chereas*, governor of that city, and *Apollophanes*, another great captain of the *Syrian* forces.

This success stirred up the jealousy of the heathen nations about *Gilead*, who fell upon the *Jews* in the land of *Tob;* and, having slain *one thousand*, took their goods, carried their wives and children captives, and drove the residue to seek for refuge and security in the strong fortress *Dathema*, in *Gilead*. But *Timotheus*, the son of him slain at *Gazara*, shut them up with a great army, and besieged them, while the inhabitants of *Tyre*, *Sidon*, and *Ptolemais*, were contriving to cut off all the *Jews* that lived in *Galilee*.

Judas, in this critical juncture, by the advice of the *sanhedrin*, dividing his army into *three* parts, he and his brother *Jonathan* marched with *eight thousand* men to the relief of the *Gileadites;* his brother marched with *three thousand* into *Galilee;* and his brother *Joseph* was left with the command of the remainder to protect *Jerusalem* and the country round, and to remain wholly on the *defensive*, till *Judas* and *Simon* should return.

In their march to *Gilead*, *Judas* and *Jonathan* attacked *Bossora*, a town of the *Edomites*, slew all the males, plundered it, released a great number of *Jews* reserved to be put to death as soon as *Dathema* should be taken, and burned the city. When they arrived before *Dathema*, which was by a forced march in the night, the brothers gave *Timotheus* so sudden and violent an assault, that they put his army to flight, and slew *eight thousand* in the pursuit. And wherever he came and found any *Jews* oppressed or imprisoned, he released them in the same manner as he did at *Bossora*.

At the same time *Simon* defeated the enemy several times in *Galilee*, drove them out of the country, and pursued them with very great slaughter to the gates of *Ptolemais*. But *Joseph*, contrary to his orders, *leaving Jerusalem*, was put to flight by *Gorgias*, governor of *Syria*, and lost *two thousand* men in that ill-projected expedition, against *Jamnia*, a seaport on the *Mediterranean*.

Lysias by this time had assembled an army of *eight hundred thousand* men, *eighty* elephants, and all the horse of the kingdom, and marched in person against the *Hebrew* conqueror. *Judas* met him at the siege of *Bethzuna*, gave him battle, slew *eleven thousand* foot, *one thousand six hundred* horse, and put the rest to flight.

This victory was happily attended with a peace between *Judas* and *Lysias*, in the name of the young king; by which the heathen decree of uniformity made by *Epiphanes* was rescinded, and the *Jews* permitted to live according to their own laws.

However, this peace was soon broke by the people of *Joppa* and *Jamnia;* but *Judas* was no sooner informed that they had cruelly treated and murdered the *Jews* that lived amongst them, but he fell upon *Joppa* by night, burned their shipping, and put all to the sword that had escaped the fire; and he set fire to the haven of *Jamnia*, and burned all the ships in it.

Timotheus also, who had fled before this conqueror, was discontented with the peace, and gathered an army of *one hundred and twenty thousand* foot, and *two thousand five hundred* horse, in order to oppress the *Jews* in *Gilead*. But when the news of this armament reached *Judas*, he marched against him; and after he had defeated a strong party of wandering *Arabs*, and made peace with them; taken the city *Caspis*, which was *Heshbon* in the tribe of *Reuben;* slain the inhabitants; destroyed the place; taken *Caraca* also, and put its garrison of *ten thousand* men to the sword, he came up with *Timotheus* near *Raphon* on the river *Jabbok*, gave him battle, slew *thirty thousand* of his men, took him prisoner, pursued the remainder of his army to *Carnion* in *Arabia;* took that city also, and slew *twenty-five thousand* more of *Timotheus's* forces; but gave him his life and liberty, on the promise that he would release all the *Jewish* captives throughout his dominions.

As he returned to *Jerusalem* he stormed the strong city of *Ephron*, well garrisoned by *Lysias*, put *twenty-five thousand* people to the sword; plundered it, and razed it to the ground; because the people refused to grant him a passage through it. This campaign was concluded with a day of thanksgiving in the temple at *Jerusalem*.

Thus *Judas*, finding himself disengaged from the treaty of peace by these hostilities, carried the war into the south of *Idumea;* dismantled *Hebron*, the metropolis thereof; passed into the land of the *Philistines*, took *Azotus* or *Ashdod*, destroyed their idols, plundered their country, and returned to *Judea*, to reduce the fortress of *Acra*, which was still in the hands of the king of *Syria*, and was very troublesome in time of war to those that resorted to the temple.

Judas prepared for a regular siege; but *Antiochus*, being informed of its distress, marched to its relief with an army of *one hundred and ten thousand* foot, *twenty thousand* horse, *thirty-two* elephants with castles on their backs full of archers, and *three hundred* armed chariots of war. In his way through *Idumea*, he laid siege to *Bethzura*, which at last was forced to surrender, after *Judas*, who had marched to its relief, had killed *four thousand* of the enemy by surprise in the night; lost his brother *Eleazar* in battle, crushed to death by an elephant that he had stabbed; and was forced to retreat and shut himself and his friends up in the temple.

The king and *Lysias* were both present in this army of the *Syrians;* and would have compelled *Judas* to surrender, had not *Philip*, whom *Epiphanes* had upon his death-bed appointed guardian of his son, taken this opportunity of their absence to seize upon *Antioch*, and to take upon him the government of the *Syrian* empire.

Upon this news *Lysias* struck up a peace immediately with *Judas*, upon honourable and advantageous terms to the *Jewish* nation. But though it was ratified by oath, *Eupater* ordered the fortifications of the temple to be demolished.

It was in this war that *Menelaus*, the wicked high priest, fell into disgrace with *Lysias*, while he was prompting the heathen barbarity to destroy his own people: for being accused and convicted of being the author and fomentor of this *Jewish* expedition, *Lysias* ordered him to be carried to *Berrhœa*, a town in *Syria;* and there to be cast into a high tower of *ashes*, in which there was a wheel which continually stirred up and raised the ashes about the criminal, till he was suffocated, and died. This was a punishment among the *Persians* for criminals in high life. This wicked high priest was succeeded at the promotion of *Antiochus Eupater*, by one *Alcimus*, a man altogether as wicked as his immediate predecessor.

Eupater returned home, and by an easy battle killed the usurper *Philip*, and quelled the insurrection in his favour. But it was not so with *Demetrius*, the son of *Seleucus Philopater*, who, being now come to maturity, claimed the kingdom in right of his father, elder brother to *Epiphanes*.

Demetrius had been sent to *Rome*, as a hostage, in exchange for his uncle *Antiochus Epiphanes*, in the very year that his father died. *Antiochus*, returning in the very nick of time, was declared king, in prejudice to the right of *Demetrius*. And though *Demetrius* had often solicited the assistance of the *Roman* senate, under whom he was educated, to restore him to his kingdom, reasons of state swayed with them rather to confirm *Eupater*, a *minor*, in the government, than to assert the right of one of a mature understanding. Yet, though he failed in this application, *Demetrius* resolved to throw himself upon Providence. To which end, leaving *Rome incog.*, *Demetrius* got safe to *Tripolis*, in *Syria;* where he gave out that he was sent, and would be supported by the *Romans*, to take possession of his father's kingdom. This stratagem had its desired effect; every one deserted from *Eupater* to *Demetrius;* and the very soldiers seized on *Eupater* and *Lysias*, and would have delivered them into his hands. But *Demetrius* thought it more politic not to see them; and having ordered them to be put to death, was presently settled in the possession of the whole kingdom.

During this interval the *Jews* enjoyed a profound peace, but having refused to acknowledge *Alcimus* their high priest because he had *apostatized* in the time of the persecution, *Alcimus* addressed the new king, *Demetrius*, implored his protection against *Judas Maccabeus*, and so exasperated him against the whole body of his party by false representations, that *Demetrius* ordered *Bacchides* to march an army into *Judea*, and to confirm *Alcimus* in the pontificate.

Alcimus was also commissioned with *Bacchides* to carry on the war in *Judea*, who upon the promise of a safe conduct, having got the scribes and doctors of the law into their power, put *sixty* of them to death in one day. *Bacchides* left him in possession with some forces for his support; with which he committed many murders, and did much mischief; and at last obtained another army from *Demetrius*, under the command of *Nicanor*, to destroy *Judas;* to disperse his followers, and the more effectually to support the said *Alcimus* in his post of high priest.

Nicanor, who had experienced the valour of *Judas*, proposed a compromise: but *Alcimus*, expecting more advantage to himself by a war, beat the king off it; so that *Nicanor* was obliged to execute the first order. The war was carried on with various success, till *Nicanor* was slain in a pitched battle near a village called *Bethoron;* and his whole army of *thirty-five thousand* men, casting down their arms, were to a man cut off in the flight.

This victory was followed with a day of thanksgiving, which was established to be continued every year under the name of the *anniversary* day of solemn thanksgiving.

Judas, observing that the *Syrians* paid no regard to any treaties, thought that, by making a league with the *Romans*, his nation would be much better secured against such a perfidious people. Therefore he sent *Jason* and *Eupolemus* to *Rome*, who soon obtained the ratification of a league of mutual defence between them, and a letter to *Demetrius*, requiring him, upon the peril of having war denounced against him, to desist from giving the Jews any more uneasiness and trouble.

This, however, proved of no service. For while this league was negotiating, *Demetrius* sent *Bacchides* and *Alcimus* a second time into *Judea* with a numerous army to revenge the defeat and death of *Nicanor*. At this time *Judas* had no more than *three thousand* men to oppose them; and of these all but *eight hundred* deserted their general, at the report of the number and strength of their enemies. Yet *Judas* refused to yield up the cause of God; and being followed by that handful of brave men, he charged and broke the right wing, where *Bacchides* commanded in person, and pursued them as far as the mountains of *Azotus;* and must have gained a complete victory, had not his little army been followed and encompassed by the *left* wing. But being surrounded with an exceeding great force, the *Jews* sold their lives at a dear rate; *Judas* was killed, and then such as survived him were forced to flee away.

His body was carried off by his brothers *Simon* and *Jonathan*, and buried in the sepulchres of his ancestors, at *Modin*, with great funeral honour, as he deserved.

Bacchides, after his success, seized on the whole country, and used the adherents of the *Maccabees* so inhumanly, that *Jonathan* was necessitated to retire at the head of his distressed countrymen to the Wilderness of *Tekoa*. This little army encamped with a morass on one side, and the river *Jordan* on the other. *Bacchides* pursued them; secured the pass of their encampment; and, though he attacked them on the *Sabbath day*, he lost a *thousand* men in the assault, before the *Maccabees* broke; and then, being overpowered by numbers, they threw themselves into the river, and escaped by swimming to the other side, without being pursued.

About this time (B. C. 160) *Alcimus*, the wicked pontiff, died suddenly of a palsy; and *Demetrius*, having received the *senatorian* letter from *Rome*, commanding him to desist from vexing the *Jews*, recalled *Bacchides;* so that *Jonathan* found himself in a condition to bring his affairs into better order. But this state of rest lasted only for two years; for the malcontents invited *Bacchides* to return with his army, under a promise to support his enterprise, and to seize *Jonathan*. But before this association could take place, *Jonathan* had information of it, took *fifty* of the principal conspirators, and put them to death. And when *Bacchides* arrived with his great army, *Jonathan* and his brother *Simon* gave him such uneasiness, and so artfully distressed and harassed his army, without giving him any pitched battle, that *Bacchides* grew weary of his undertaking, put several of those that invited him to that expedition to death, and at last made peace with the *Maccabees*, restored all his prisoners, and swore never more to *molest* the *Jews*, B. C. 158.

When *Jonathan* found himself in quiet possession of *Judea*, and that there was no more to fear from *Bacchides*, he punished the apostate *Jews* with death, reformed the Church and state, and rebuilt the walls about the temple and city of *Jerusalem*. And soon after, the high priesthood having been vacant seven years, he put on the *pontifical* robe, at the nomination of *Alexander*, who, by the assistance of the *Roman* senate, and the management of one *Heraclides*, claimed the crown of *Syria* in right of his pretended father *Antiochus Epiphanes*.

Jonathan, though *Demetrius* made him more advantageous offers, suspected that these promises were not real, but only to serve the present purpose, and accepted *Alexander's* proposals; which was so acceptable to the new king, that when he had beaten and slain *Demetrius*, and made himself master of the whole *Syrian* monarchy, he invited *Jonathan* to his marriage with *Cleopatra*, daughter of *Ptolemy*, king of *Egypt;* and, besides great personal honours, conferred on him the post of *general* of all his forces in *Judea*, and chief sewer of his household, B. C. 153.

However, this prosperity was soon disturbed by *Apollonius*, governor of *Cœlosyria*, who, taking part with *Demetrius*, the son of *Demetrius* the late king, who had concealed himself with his brother *Antiochus* in *Crete*, during the late troubles, was now landed in *Cilicia* with an army of mercenaries, and had marched with an army as far as *Jamnia*, challenging *Jonathan* to give him battle. *Jonathan* marched out with a body of *ten thousand* men; took *Joppa* in sight of the enemy; gave *Apollonius* battle, beat him, and pursued his broken forces to *Azotus*, where he destroyed *eight thousand* men, the temple of *Dagon*, and the city, with fire and sword, which engaged *Alexander's* affections so much, that he gave him the golden *buckle*, (a distinguished mark of the royal family of *Persia*,) and the city and *territories* of *Ecron*.

After this succeeded a surprising revolution in *Syria*. *Alex-*

ander had called to his assistance his father-in-law *Ptolemy Philometer*, who, suspecting that his son *Alexander* had conspired his death, carried off his daughter *Cleopatra;* gave her to *Demetrius, Alexander's* competitor; then, turning his arms upon *Alexander*, settled *Demetrius* upon the throne of his ancestors; and, after gaining a complete victory, forced him to flee into *Arabia*, where *Zabdiel*, the king of the country, cut off his head, and sent it to *Ptolemy*, B. C. 146.

This *Demetrius* took the style of *Nicanor*, or Conqueror; and though he summoned *Jonathan* to appear before him to answer certain accusations, the high priest found means to gain his favour; and not only a confirmation of former, but a grant of additional privileges; which, with the promise to withdraw the heathen garrison from *Acra*, so recommended him to *Jonathan*, that, when *Demetrius* was in danger of being murdered by the inhabitants of *Antioch*, he marched *three thousand* men to the king's assistance, burned a great part of the city, slew *one hundred thousand* of the inhabitants with fire and sword, and obliged the rest to throw themselves upon the king's mercy. Yet this service, and his promise also, was presently forgot by *Demetrius*, when he thought the storm was blown over; and, he would, on the contrary, have certainly obliged him, under pain of military execution, to pay the usual taxes and tribute paid by his predecessors, had he not been prevented by the treason of a discontented courtier, whose name was *Tryphon*.

Tryphon (B. C. 144) at first declared for, and set *Antiochus Theos*, the son of the late *Alexander*, on the throne of *Syria*, after he had vanquished *Demetrius*, and forced him to retire into *Seleucia*. *Jonathan*, for his own interest, declared for the new king; by which he obtained a confirmation of the pontificate, &c., and his brother *Simon* was made commander of all his forces from *Tyre* to *Egypt*.

As soon as *Demetrius* heard of *Jonathan's* revolt, he marched to chastise him for it; but it turned to his loss; for he was repulsed twice, and lost *Gaza*, with all the country as far as *Damascus*, and *Joppa* in the land of the *Philistines*.

Tryphon intended now to pull off the mask; but not daring to attempt so foul a crime till *Jonathan* could be removed, prevailed with him to disband his army, and to accompany him with *one thousand* men only to *Ptolemais;* where he was no sooner entered, but his men were put to the sword, and *Jonathan* put under an arrest. Then, marching his army into *Judea*, he proposed to restore him, on condition of *one hundred* talents; and that his two sons should be given for hostages of their father's fidelity. *Jonathan* was persuaded to comply with this demand: but the villain not only caused them and their father to be put to death, but having also murdered *Antiochus* privately, he assumed the title of king of *Syria*.

Simon (B. C. 143,) hearing that his brother was murdered, and buried at *Bascama*, in *Gilead*, sent and brought him thence, and buried him under a curious monument of white wrought and polished marble, at *Modin*. And after he was admitted governor in his stead, he offered his service to *Demetrius*, then at *Laodicea;* who, on condition that the *Jews* would assist him in the recovery of his crown, conceded to him the high priesthood and principality, and granted the people many privileges.

But *Demetrius* being about this time persuaded to head the *Elymæan, Parthian*, and *Bactrian* revolters against *Mithridates*, king of *Parthia*, *Simon* applied himself to fortifying his cities; and reduced the fortress of *Acra;* which he not only took, but even levelled the mount on which it was built.

Mithridates (B. C. 141) vanquished *Demetrius;* and after he had taken him prisoner, gave him his daughter *Rhodaguna* in marriage; which so exasperated his wife *Cleopatra*, then shut up in *Seleucia*, that she offered herself and the kingdom to *Antiochus*, his brother, B. C. 139, then in *Crete*. *Antiochus* accepted the proposal; and upon his landing in *Syria* with an army of mercenaries, he was so strengthened with deserters from *Tryphon's* forces, that he drove him into *Apamea*, near the mouth of the *Orontes*, and took him and put him to death.

Thus *Antiochus* became possessed of his father's throne; though not without the assistance of *Simon*, whom he had promised to reward with many new privileges. But he no sooner found himself delivered from all opposition, than he forgot his promises; and, on the contrary, demanded the restoring of *Joppa* and *Gazara*, &c., or a *thousand* talents in lieu of them.

Simon refused to comply; and *Antiochus* sent *Cendebeus* with an army to force him. *Simon*, now very old, attended by his sons *Judas* and *John Hyrcanus*, put him to flight at the first onset, and killed a great number of the enemy in the pursuit. After this, *Simon*, and his sons *Judas* and *Mattathias*, B. C. 135, being perfidiously murdered by *Ptolemy*, *Simon's* son-in-law, whom he had made governor of the *plains of Jericho*, at an entertainment prepared for them in the castle of *Jericho*, with a design to usurp the government of *Judea* to himself, sent a party to *Gazara* to seize *John Hyrcanus* also. But he was informed, and so prepared to receive them, that he despatched the intended murderers; and hastening to *Jerusalem*, secured both the city and the temple, where he was declared his father's successor in the pontificate and principality of the *Jews*.

Antiochus thought to serve himself of these distractions and accordingly marched a large army into *Judea;* and after he had driven *Hyrcanus* into *Jerusalem*, obliged him to accept of a peace upon the hard terms of delivering up their arms, dismantling *Jerusalem*, paying a tribute for *Joppa*, &c., held by the *Jews* out of *Judea*, and *five hundred* talents to buy off the rebuilding of *Acra*.

Hyrcanus accompanied *Antiochus* to the *Parthian* war, in which he signalized himself with great renown. He returned home at the end of the year. But *Antiochus*, who chose to winter in the *East*, was with his whole army destroyed in one night by the natives, who, taking the advantage of their separate quarters all over the country, rose on them, and cut their throats in cold blood: so that *Antiochus* himself was slain, and out of *four hundred thousand* persons, of which his army consisted, scarce a man escaped to carry home the news of this massacre.

Phraortes, the king of *Parthia*, having suffered much by this invasion of *Antiochus*, endeavoured to get quit of him by sending his prisoner *Demetrius Nicanor* into *Syria*, to recover his own kingdom; so that when the news came of *Antiochus's* death, he was without more delay reinstated on the throne. But his tyrannical proceedings presently raised him up a new pretender to the crown, (B. C. 127,) one *Alexander Zabina*, the pretended son of *Alexander Balas*, who, by the assistance of *Ptolemy Physcon*, king of *Egypt*, defeated him in the field; and, taking him prisoner in *Tyre*, put him to death.

Zabina being raised to the throne of *Syria* by the king of *Egypt*, *Ptolemy* expected that he should hold it in homage from him; and, upon his refusal, gave his daughter *Tryphæna* to *Antiochus Gryphus*, the son of *Nicanor*, whom he made king of *Syria*, and pursued *Zabina* till he got him into his hands, and put him to death.

Hyrcanus, in the midst of these revolutions, shook off the *Syrian* yoke. He built the famous tower of *Baris* upon a steep rock. He took several cities on the borders of *Judea*, amongst which was *Shechem*, the chief seat of the *Samaritans*, (B. C. 130,) and destroyed the temple on Mount *Gerizim*. He extended his conquests over the *Idumeans*, (B. C. 129,) who were prevailed on to embrace the *Jewish* religion; so that from this time they exchanged the name of *Idumeans* or *Edomites* for that of *Jews*. He renewed the alliance with the senate of *Rome*, and obtained greater privileges and advantages than his nation ever had before; and concluded his military operations with the siege and utter destruction of *Samaria*, under the conduct of his sons *Aristobulus* and *Antigonus*.

After these great actions, *Hyrcanus* enjoyed full quiet from all foreign wars; and had nothing to trouble him at home, but the false insinuations of the Pharisee *Eleazar*, who declared that his mother was a captive taken in the wars, and that, therefore, he was incapable of holding the high priesthood. *Hyrcanus* had been educated in this sect: but one *Jonathan*, an intimate friend of his, and a *Sadducee*, took this opportunity to draw him over to his own sect; which he effected so sincerely, that *Hyrcanus* renounced the Pharisees for ever, abrogated their traditional constitutions, and made it penal for any one to observe them. Yet he was an excellent governor; and, dying in the *thirtieth* year of his administration, left *five* sons: but the high priesthood and sovereignty he left to *Judas Aristobulus*, his eldest son, B. C. 107.

Aristobulus (B. C. 107) was the first since the captivity that put on the diadem, and assumed the title of *king:* but he was of that suspicious and cruel disposition, that he cast his own mother into prison, and starved her to death, imprisoned all his brethren except *Antigonus*, whom at last he ordered to be murdered in a fit of jealousy, B. C. 106: of which, however, he repented, and gave up the ghost in great anxiety of mind, after a reign of no more than *one* year; though in that time *Antigonus* had reduced the *Itureans* to his *obedience*, and forced them to conform to the religion of the *Jews*. At this time *Pompey* and *Cicero* were born.

Alexander Jannæus, his *third* brother, was released from his confinement by *Salome*, *Aristobulus's* widow. The like favour was also extended to his two other brothers. But as soon as *Jannæus* was settled on the throne, he put one of them to death under a suspicion of treason, and he took *Absalom* the younger into his favour.

This *Alexander* (B. C. 105) attempted to extend his dominions by new conquests. But in his attempts against *Ptolemais* and *Ptolemy Lathyrus*, who came to the assistance of *Zoilus* and the *Gazæans*, he lost a fine army, and was reduced to sue for protection from *Cleopatra*, who had seized upon *Egypt*, and obliged her son *Lathyrus* to be contented with the island of *Crete*.

Cleopatra, at first, was inclined to take advantage of *Alexander's* misfortunes, and to seize upon him and his dominions; but *Ananias*, one of her generals, by birth a *Jew*, and a relation to *Alexander*, dissuaded her from so unjust a design, and obtained her protection for him.

Nevertheless *Alexander's* martial spirit sought out new employments. His country being clear of foreign forces, he attacked and took *Gadara* and *Amathus* in *Syria*. But being followed by *Theodorus*, prince of *Philadelphia*, who had laid up his treasure at *Amathus*, he lost his plunder, *ten thousand* men, and all his baggage, B. C. 101.

This did not deter him from attempting the reduction of *Gaza;* which, however, he could not have taken, had it not been treacherously surrendered to him by *Lysimachus*, the governor's brother. Here *Alexander*, ordering his soldiers to kill, plunder, and destroy, was the author of a sad scene of barbarity, and reduced that ancient and famous city to ruin and desolation.

After his return from this carnage, he was grossly insulted by a mob at home, while he was offering the usual sacrifices on the *feast of tabernacles*. But he made the people pay dearly for it; for he fell upon them with his soldiers, and slew *six thousand*. And from this time he took into his pay *six thousand* mercenaries from *Pisidia* and *Cilicia*, who always attended his person, and kept off the people while he officiated.

B. C. 101. All being again quieted at home, *Alexander* marched against the *Moabites* and *Ammonites*, and made them tributaries. In his return he took possession of *Amathus*, which *Theodorus* had evacuated; but he lost most of his army, and was very near losing his own life in an ambuscade which *Thedus*, an *Arabian* king, had laid for him near *Gadara*. This raised fresh discontents among his subjects, and new troubles at home, which were attended with the most unheard-of barbarities. They were not able to overpower him; but his wickedness had so provoked them that nothing but his blood could satisfy them; and at length, being assisted by *Demetrius Euchærus*, king of *Damascus*, they entirely routed him, so that he was forced to consult his own safety by fleeing to the mountains.

His misfortune was the cause of *six thousand* of his rebel subjects deserting him; which, when *Demetrius* perceived, he withdrew, and left the revolters to fight their own battle. After this separation *Alexander* gained several advantages; and at last, having cut the major part off in a decisive battle, he took *eight hundred* of the rebels in *Bethome*, whom he carried to *Jerusalem;* and having first killed their wives and children before their faces, he ordered them all to be crucified in one day, before him and his wives and concubines, whom he had invited to a feast at the place of execution. Then, resolving to revenge himself on the king of *Damascus*, he made war on him for three years successively, and took several places; when, returning home, he was received with great respect by his subjects.

His next expedition was against the castle of *Ragaba*, in the country of the *Gerasens*, where he was seized with a quartan ague, which proved his death, B. C. 79. His queen *Alexandra*, by his own advice, concealed it till the castle was taken; and then, carrying him to *Jerusalem*, she gave his body to the leaders of the Pharisees, to be disposed of as they should think proper; and told them, as her husband had appointed her regent during the minority of her children, she would do nothing in the administration without their advice and help.

This address to the Pharisees so much gained their esteem that they not only settled the queen dowager in the government, but were very lavish in their encomiums on her deceased husband, whom they honoured with more than ordinary pomp and solemnity at his funeral.

The Pharisees having now the management of the queen regent, and of *Hyrcanus* and *Aristobulus*, her sons by *Alexander*, had all the laws against Pharisaism repealed and abolished, recalled all the exiles, and demanded justice against those that had advised the crucifixion of the *eight hundred rebels*.

The queen made her eldest son, *Hyrcanus*, high priest. But *Aristobulus* was not contented to live a private life; and therefore, as soon as his mother seemed to decline, he meditated in what manner he might usurp the sovereignty from his brother, at her decease; and he had taken such measures beforehand, that upon the death of his mother he found himself strong enough to attempt the crown, though *Alexandra* had declared *Hyrcanus* her successor. The two armies met in the plains of *Jericho;* but *Hyrcanus*, being deserted by most of his forces, was obliged to resign his crown and pontificate to *Aristobulus*, and promise to live peaceably upon his private fortune.

This resignation was a subject of great discontent to some of *Hyrcanus's* courtiers, among whom was *Antipater*, father to *Herod the Great*, who persuaded *Hyrcanus* to fly to *Aretas*, king of *Arabia*, who, on certain conditions, supplied him with *fifty thousand* men, with which *Hyrcanus* entered *Judea*, and gained a complete victory over *Aristobulus*. But while he besieged him in the temple, *Aristobulus*, with the promise of a large sum of money, engaged *Pompey*, the general of the *Roman* army, then before *Damascus*, to oblige *Aretas* to withdraw his forces; but *Aristobulus*, though he was for the present delivered from his brother's rage, prevaricated so with *Pompey*, that he at last confined *Aristobulus* in chains, took *Jerusalem* sword in hand, retrenched the dignity and power of the principality, destroyed the fortifications, ordered an annual tribute to be paid to the *Romans*, and restored *Hyrcanus* to the pontificate, and made him prince of the country, but would not permit him to wear the diadem.

Pompey, having thus settled the government of *Judea*, returned in his way to *Rome* with *Aristobulus*, his sons *Alexander* and *Antigonus*, and two of his daughters, to adorn his triumph.

Alexander found means to escape, by the way, and about three years after arrived in *Judea*, and raised some disturbance; but he was defeated in all his attempts by *Gabinius*, the *Roman* governor in *Syria*, who, after this, coming to *Jerusalem*, confirmed *Hyrcanus* in the high priesthood, but removed the civil administration from the *sanhedrin* into five courts of justice of his own erecting, according to the number of five provinces, into which he had divided the whole land.

When *Aristobulus* had lain five years prisoner at *Rome*, he with his son escaped into *Judea*, and endeavoured to raise fresh trouble; but Gabinius soon took them again; and being remanded to *Rome*, the father was kept close confined, but the children were released.

It was about this time, B. C. 48, that the civil war between *Pompey* and *Cæsar* broke out; and when *Aristobulus* was on the point of setting out, by *Cæsar's* interest, to take the command of an army in order to secure *Judea* from *Pompey's* attempts, he was poisoned by some of *Pompey's* party.

When *Cæsar* was returned from the *Alexandrian* war, he was much solicited to depose *Hyrcanus* in favour of *Antigonus*, the surviving son of *Aristobulus;* but *Cæsar* not only confirmed *Hyrcanus* in the high priesthood and principality of Judea, and to his family in a perpetual succession, but he abolished the form of government lately set up by *Gabinius*, restored it to its ancient form, and appointed *Antipater* procurator of *Judea* under him.

Antipater, who was a man of great penetration, made his son *Phasael* governor of the country about *Jerusalem*, and his son *Herod* governor of *Galilee*.

Soon after this appointment, *Herod*, who was of a very boisterous temper, having seized upon one *Hezekiah*, a ringleader of a gang of thieves, and some of his men that infested his territories, he put them to death. This was presently looked upon as a breach of duty to the *sanhedrin*, before whom he was summoned to appear. But lest the sentence of that court should pass upon him, he fled to *Sextus Cæsar*, the *Roman* prefect of *Syria* at *Damascus;* and, with a large sum of money, obtained of him the government of *Cœlesyria*. He afterwards raised an army, marched into *Judea*, and would have revenged the indignity which he said the *sanhedrin* and high priest had cast upon him, had not his father and brother prevailed with him to retire for the present.

While *Julius Cæsar* lived, the *Jews* enjoyed great privileges; but his untimely death, B. C. 44, by the villanous and ungrateful hand of *Brutus*, *Cassius*, &c., in the senate house, as he was preparing for an expedition against the *Parthians* to revenge his country's wrong, delivered them up as a prey to every hungry general of *Rome*. *Cassius* immediately seized upon *Syria*, and exacted above *seven hundred* talents of silver from the *Jews;* and the envy and villany of *Malicus*, who was a *natural Jew*, and the next in office under *Antipater*, an *Idumean*, rent the state into horrid factions. *Malicus* bribed the high priest's butler to poison his friend *Antipater*, to make way for himself to be the next in person to *Hyrcanus*. *Herod*, making sure of *Cassius*, by obtaining his leave and assistance to revenge his father's death, took the first opportunity to have him murdered by the *Roman* garrison at *Tyre*.

The friends of *Malicus*, having engaged the high priest and *Felix* the *Roman* general at *Jerusalem* on their side, resolved to revenge his death on the sons of *Antipater*. All *Jerusalem* was in an uproar; *Herod* was sick at *Damascus;* so that the whole power and fury of the assailants fell upon *Phasael*, who defended himself very strenuously, and drove the tumultuous party out of the city. As soon as *Herod* was able, the two brothers presently quelled the faction; and had not *Hyrcanus* made his peace by giving *Herod* his granddaughter *Mariamne* in marriage, they certainly would have shown their resentment of the priest's behaviour with more severity.

Again, this faction was not so totally extinguished but that several principal persons of the Jewish nation, upon the defeat of *Brutus* and *Cassius*, accused *Phasael* and *Herod* to the conqueror, *Mark Anthony*, of usurping the government from *Hyrcanus*. But the brothers had so much interest with the conqueror that he rejected the complaints of the deputies, made them both tetrarchs, and committed all the affairs of Judea to their administration; and to oblige the *Jews* to obey his decision in this affair, he retained fifteen of the deputies as hostages for the people's fidelity, and would have put them to death had not *Herod* begged their lives.

The *Jews*, however, when *Anthony* arrived at *Tyre*, sent *one thousand* deputies with the like accusations, which he, looking upon as a daring insult, ordered his soldiers to fall upon them, so that some were killed and many wounded. But upon *Herod's* going to *Jerusalem* the citizens revenged this affront in the same manner upon his retinue; the news whereof so enraged *Anthony*, that he ordered the fifteen hostages to be immediately put to death, and threatened severe revenge against the whole faction. But after that *Mark Anthony* was returned to *Rome*, the *Parthians*, at the solicitation of *Antigonus*, the son of *Aristobulus*, who had promised them a reward of a thousand talents and eight hundred of the most beautiful women in the country, to set him on the throne of Judea, entered that country, and being joined by the factious and discontented Jews, (B. C. 37,) took *Jerusalem* without resistance, took *Phasael* and *Hyrcanus*, and put them in chains; but *Herod* escaped under the cover of night and deposited his mother, sister, wife, and his wife's mother, with several other relations and friends, in the impregnable fortress *Massada*, near the lake *Asphaltites*, under the care of his brother *Joseph*, who was obliged to go to *Rome* to seek protection and relief.

In the mean time *Antigonus* remained in possession of all the country, and was declared king of *Judea*. The *Parthians* delivered *Hyrcanus* and *Phasael* to *Antigonus;* upon which *Phasael*, being so closely handcuffed and ironed that he foresaw his ignominious death approaching, dashed his own brains out against the wall of the prison. *Antigonus* cut off the ears of *Hyrcanus*, to incapacitate him from the high priesthood, and returned him again to the *Parthians*, who left him at *Seleucia*, in their return to the East.

Herod on this occasion served himself so well on the friendship which had been between his father and himself with the *Roman* general, *Mark Anthony*, and the promise of a round sum of money, that he in seven days' time obtained a senatorial decree, constituting him king of *Judea*, and declaring *Antigonus* an enemy to the *Roman* state. He immediately left *Rome*, landed at *Ptolemais*, raised forces, and being aided with *Roman* auxiliaries, by order of the senate, he reduced the greater part of the country, took *Joppa*, relieved *Massada*, stormed the castle of *Ressa*, and must have taken *Jerusalem* also, had not the *Roman* commanders who were directed to assist him been bribed by *Antigonus*, and treacherously obstructed his success. But when *Herod* perceived their collusion, he, for the present, satisfied himself with the reduction of *Galilee;* and hearing of *Anthony's* besieging *Samosata* on the *Euphrates*, went in person to him to represent the ill treatment he had met with from the generals, *Ventidius* and *Silo*, whom he had commanded to serve him.

Upon his departure, *Herod* left the command of his forces to his brother *Joseph*, with charge to remain upon the defensive. But Joseph, contrary to orders, attempting to reduce *Jericho*, was slain, and most of his men were cut to pieces. And thus *Herod* again lost *Galilee* and *Idumea*.

Mark Anthony granted all he requested; and though at first the army which *Anthony* had spared him was roughly handled, and he himself wounded as he approached *Jerusalem* to revenge his brother's death, he afterwards slew *Pappus*, *Antigonus's* general, and entirely defeated his army; and in the next campaign, after a siege of several months, *Herod*, assisted by *Socius*, the *Roman* general, took it by storm. The soldiers expecting the spoils of the city as their due, and being exasperated by the long resistance of the citizens, spared neither men, women, nor children, and would certainly have utterly destroyed every thing and person with rapine and devastation, death and slaughter, had not *Herod* redeemed them with a large sum of money.

Antigonus surrendered himself to *Socius*, who carried him in chains to *Anthony;* and he for a good sum of money was bribed to put him to death, that in him the *Asmonæan* family, which had lasted *one hundred and twenty-nine* years, might be extinct.

By this event *Herod* found himself once more in full power, and at liberty to revenge himself upon his enemies. He began his reign with the execution of all the members of the great *Sanhedrin* except *Pollio* and *Sameas*, who are also called *Hillel* and *Shammai*. Then he raised one *Ananel*, born of the pontifical family at *Babylon*, to the place of *high priest;* but *Mark Anthony*, at the intercession of *Cleopatra*, queen of Egypt, who was solicited thereto by *Alexandra*, *Mariamne's* mother, and the entreaties of his own beloved *Mariamne* in behalf of her young brother, prevailed with him to annul this nomination, and to prefer *Aristobulus* to the pontificate. But as *Hyrcanus* was yet alive, and the *Jews*, in the place of his exile, paid him all the honours and reverence due to their king and high priest, *Herod*, under a pretence of gratitude and friendship to that author of all his fortunes, prevailed with the old prince to desire it, and with *Phraortes*, king of *Parthia*, to permit his return to *Jerusalem*, with an intention to cut him off at a proper opportunity; which he soon after did on a pretence of his holding treasonable correspondence with *Malchus*, king of *Arabia*. But in the mean time *Alexandra*, valuing herself upon the interest she had with *Cleopatra*, laid a scheme to obtain the regal dignity for her son *Aristobulus*, by the same means that she had got him the pontificate. But this intrigue ended in the death of *Aristobulus*, and her own close confinement at first, and afterwards in her own and her daughter *Mariamne's* death; though this tragic scene was at several times acted under disguise. *Aristobulus* was drowned at *Jericho*, as it were accidentally, B. C. 29, in a fit of jealousy; *Mariamne* was adjudged to die, and *Alexandra* was ordered for execution, B. C. 28, on a supposition that she wished his death; which unjust sentence pursued his very innocent children *Alexander* and *Aristobulus*, for expressing their dislike of their father's cruelty to their mother *Mariamne*. But it is very probable that he himself had fallen a sacrifice to *Octavius* after the battle, and the total loss of *Mark Anthony* at *Actium*, (fought B. C. 31,) had he not hastened to the conqueror at *Rhodes*, and in an artful speech appeased him, and with a promise to support his faction in those parts, obtained from him a confirmation of his royal dignity.

The cruelties, however, which he exercised to his own flesh and blood filled his mind with agonies of remorse, which brought him into a languishing condition; and what helped to increase his disorder was the conspiracy of *Antipater*, his eldest son by *Doris*, born to him whilst he was a private man. But *Herod* having discovered the plot, accused him thereof before *Quintilius Varus*, the *Roman* governor of *Syria*, and put him to death also; which occasioned that remarkable exclamation of the Emperor *Octavius*, that "it was better to be *Herod's* hog than his son."

The great pleasure that *Herod* took (B. C. 25) in obliging his protector *Octavianus*, and the dread he had of being dethroned for his cruelties, prompted him to compliment him with the names of two new cities, the one to be built on the spot where *Samaria* stood before *Hyrcanus* destroyed it, (B. C. 22,) which he called *Sebaste*, the Greek word for *Augustus*, the other was *Cæsarea*, once called the *Tower of Straton*, on the sea-coast of *Phœnicia*. After this he built a theatre and amphitheatre in the very city of *Jerusalem*, to celebrate games and exhibit shows in honour of *Augustus;* set up an image of an eagle, the *Roman* ensign, over one of the gates of the temple; and at last carried his flattery so far as idolatrously to build a temple of white marble in memory of the favours he had received from *Octavianus Augustus*.

These advances to idolatry were the foundation of a conspiracy of ten men, who bound themselves with an oath to assassinate him in the very theatre. But being informed thereof in time, *Herod* seized the conspirators, and put them to death with the most exquisite torments; and to ingratiate himself with the *Jews*, he formed a design to rebuild the temple, (B. C. 17,) which now, after it had stood five hundred years, and suffered much from its enemies, was fallen much into decay. He was two years in providing materials; and it was so far advanced that Divine service was performed in it nine years and a half more, though a great number of labourers and artificers were continued to finish the outworks till several years after our Saviour's ascension; for when *Gessius Florus* was appointed governor of *Judea*, he discharged *eighteen thousand* workmen from the temple at one time. And here it should be observed that these, for want of employment, began those mutinies and seditions which at last drew on the destruction both of the temple and *Jerusalem*, in A. D. 70.

Thus I have finished that brief connection of the affairs of the *Jews* from the death of *Nehemiah* and conclusion of the Old Testament, to the coming of *Christ*, where the New Testament begins, which from the creation of the world, according to the most exact computation, is the year 4000.

The general state of the heathen world was in profound peace under the *Roman* emperor, *Augustus*, to whom all the known parts of the earth were in subjection when Christ was born. This glorious event took place in the year of the Julian Period 4709, and the fifth before the vulgar era of Christ commonly noted A. D., Anno Domini, or the year of our Lord. See the learned *Dr. Prideaux's* connected History of the Old and New Testaments.

I need not add here the years from the birth of Christ to the end of the New Testament History, as these are regularly brought down in a *Table of Remarkable Eras*, immediately succeeding the Acts of the Apostles, and terminating at A. D. 100.

For the desolation that took place when the temple was taken and destroyed, see the notes on Matt. xxiv. 31.

The general history of the Jews, especially from the destruction of their temple, A. D. 70, to the end of the *sixteenth* century, has been written by Mr. *Basnage*, entitled, "Histoire des Juifs, depuis Jesus Christ, jusqu à present; pour servir de continuation à l'Histoire de Joseph;" the *best edition* of which was printed at the Hague, 1716, 12mo., in *fifteen* vols. The *first* edition was translated into English by T. Taylor, A. M., Lond. 1708, fol.; but the author has greatly enlarged and corrected his work in the Hague edition above mentioned. The *learning* and *research* manifested in this work are amazing; and on the subject nothing better, nothing more accurate and satisfactory, can be well expected. This work I heartily recommend to all my readers.

For the *state* of the Jews in different nations of the earth, the Itinerary of *Rabbi Benjamin*, a native of Tudela, in the kingdom of Navarre, has been referred to; first translated from *Hebrew* into *Latin* by *B. A. Montanus*, and printed at Antwerp, in 1575, and much better by *Constantine L'Empereur*, and printed at Leyden, 12mo., with the Hebrew text and notes, 1633. This work has gone through *many* editions among the Jews, in Hebrew and in German. It has also been translated into *French* by *Baratier*, with many learned notes, Amsterdam, 1734.

But all the preceding translations have been totally eclipsed by that of the Rev. *B. Gerrans*, lecturer of St. Catherine Coleman, and second master of Queen Elizabeth's free grammar school, St. Olave, Southwark, with a Dissertation and Notes, 12mo., Lond. 1784. If we can believe *Rab. Benjamin*, (who it appears flourished in A. D. 1160,) he travelled over the whole world, and found the Jews in general in a most *flourishing* state, and living under their own laws in many places. But the work is a wretched imposition, too hastily credited by some learned men; written with a view of keeping up the credit of the Jewish people, and with the tacit design to show that *the Messiah is not yet come*, and that the *sceptre has not departed from Judah, nor a lawgiver from between his feet;* but he is at such variance with himself, and with the whole geography of the globe, that, as Mr. *Gerrans* properly observes, no *map* could possibly be made of his travels. "Reduce," says he, "the universe to its primeval chaos; confound Asia with Africa; north with south, and heat with cold; make cities provinces, and provinces cities; people uncultivated deserts with free and independent Jews, and depopulate the most flourishing kingdoms; make rivers run when and where you please, and call them by any names but the right one; take Arabia upon your back, and carry it to the north of Babylon; turn the north pole south, or any other way you please; make a new ecliptic line, and place it in the most whimsical and eccentric position which the most hobby-horsical imagination can possibly conceive or describe; and such a *map* will best suit such an *author*." What therefore this author says of his travels and discoveries is worthy of no regard; and it is a doubt with me (if this person ever existed) whether he ever travelled beyond the limits of the kingdom of Navarre, or passed the boundaries of the city of Tudela. I mention these works, the *first* in the way of strong recommendation; the *second*, to put the reader on his guard against imposition; at the same time recommending these *outcasts of Israel* to his most earnest commiseration and prayers, that the God of all grace may speedily call them to eternal glory by Christ Jesus, that all Israel may be saved; and that through all their dispersions they may be soon found singing the song of Moses and the Lamb! Amen, Amen.

CONCLUSION

In my *general preface* prefixed to the book of *Genesis*, I gave a succinct account of the *plan* I pursued in preparing this work for the press; but as this plan became necessarily *extended*, and led to much farther reading, examination, and discussion, I judge it necessary, now that the work is concluded, to give my readers a general *summary* of the whole, that they may be in possession of my mode of proceeding, and be enabled more fully to comprehend the *reasons* why the work has been *so long* in passing through the press. [This refers only to the *first* edition.]

My education and habits from early youth led me to read and study the Bible, not as a *text-book* to confirm the articles of a *preconceived creed*, but as a *revelation from God to man*, (of his will and purposes in reference to the origin and designation of his human offspring,) which it was the duty of all the inhabitants of the earth deeply to study, and earnestly to endeavour to understand, as it concerned their peace and happiness, and the perfection of their being in reference to both worlds.

Conscious that translators in general must have had a *particular creed*, in reference to which they would naturally consider every text, and this reference, however honestly intended, might lead them to glosses not always fairly deducible from the original words, I sat down with a heart as free from bias and sectarian feeling as possible, and carefully read over, cautiously weighed, and literally translated every word, *Hebrew* and *Chaldee*, in the Old Testament. And as I saw that it was possible, even while assisted by the best *translations* and best *lexicographers*, to mistake the import of a Hebrew term, and considering that the *cognate Asiatic languages* would be helps of great importance in such an inquiry, I collated every verse where I was apprehensive of any difficulty with the *Chaldee*, *Syriac*, *Arabic*, and *Persian*, and the *Æthiopic* in the Polyglot *translation*, as far as the sacred writings are extant in these languages; and I did this with a constant reference to the *various readings* collected by *Houbigant*, *H. Michaelis*, *Kennicott*, and *De Rossi*, and to the best editions of the *Septuagint* and *Vulgate*, which are the earliest translations of the Hebrew text that have reached our times.

Nor have I been satisfied with these collections of various readings; I have examined and collated several ancient *Hebrew* MSS., which preceding scholars had never seen, with many ancient MSS. of the *Vulgate* equally unknown to Biblical critics. This work required much time and great pains, and necessarily occasioned much delay; and no wonder, when I have often, on my plan, been obliged to employ as much time in visiting many sources and sailing down their streams, in order to ascertain a genuine reading, or fix the sense of a disputed verse, as would have been sufficient for some of my contemporaries to pass whole sheets of their work through the press. Had I not followed this method, which to me appeared absolutely necessary, I should have completed my work, such as it would have been, in less than one half of the time.

These previous readings, collations, and translations, produced an immense number of notes and observations on all parts of the Old Testament, which, by the advice and entreaty of several learned and judicious friends, I was induced to extend in the form of a *perpetual comment* on every book in the Bible. This being ultimately revised and completed as far as the book of *Judges*, which formed, in my purpose, the boundary of my proceedings on the Hebrew Scriptures, I was induced to commit it to press.

Though my friends in general wished me to go forward with the *Old Testament*, yet, as several of them were apprehensive, from the infirm state of my health at that time, that I might not live long enough to finish the whole, they advised me strongly to omit for the present the Old Testament, and begin with the New. This was in conformity with my own feelings on the subject; having wished simply to add the *four Gospels* and *Acts of the Apostles* to the *five books of Moses* and the books of *Joshua* and *Judges;* as these two parcels of Divine revelation, carefully illustrated, would give a full view of the *origin* and *final settlement* of the *Church* of the *Old Covenant*, and the commencement and completion of *that* of the *New*. And thus I proceeded:—

After having literally translated every word of the *New Testament*, that last best gift of God to man; comparing the whole with all the *ancient versions*, and the most important of the *modern;* collating all with the *various readings* collected by *Stephens*, *Courcel*, *Fell*, *Gherard of Maestricht*, *Bengel*, *Mill*, *Wetstein*, and *Griesbach;* actually examining many MSS., either cursorily or not at all examined by *them;* illustrating the whole by quotations from ancient authors, *rabbinical*,

Grecian, *Roman*, and *Asiatic;* I exceeded my previous design, and brought down the work to the end of the *Apocalypse;* and passed the whole through the press.

I should mention here a *previous* work, (without which any man must be ill qualified to undertake the illustration of the New Testament,) viz., a careful examination of the *Septuagint*. In *this* the phraseology of the New Testament is contained, and from this the import of that phraseology is alone to be derived. This I read carefully over to the end of the book of Psalms, in the edition of Dr. *Grabe*, from the *Codex Alexandrinus;* collating it occasionally with editions taken from the *Vatican* MS., and particularly that printed by *Field*, at Cambridge, 1665, 18mo., with the Parænetic preface of the learned Bishop Pearson. Without this previous work, who did ever yet properly comprehend the *idiom* and *phraseology* of the Greek Testament? Now, all these are parts of my labour which common readers cannot conceive; and which none can properly appreciate, as to the pains, difficulty, and time which must be expended, who have not themselves trodden this almost unfrequented path.

When the New Testament was thus prepared and finished at press, I was induced, though with great reluctance, to recommence the Old. I was already nearly worn down by my previous work, connected with other works and duties which I could not omit; and though I had gone through the most important parts of the sacred records, yet I could easily foresee that I had an ocean of difficulties to wade through in those parts that remained. The *Historical Books* alone, in their *chronology*, *arrangement of facts*, *concise* and often *obscure phraseology*, presented not a few; the books of *Solomon*, and those of the *major* and *minor prophets*, a *multitude*. Notwithstanding all these, I hope I may say that, having obtained help of God, I am come with some success to the conclusion; having aimed at nothing, throughout the whole, but the *glory of God* and the *good of men*.

But still something remains to be said concerning the *modus operandi*, or *particular plan of proceeding*. In prosecuting this work I was led to attend, in the *first* instance, more to *words* than to *things*, in order to find their true ideal meaning; together with those different shades of *acceptation* to which they became subject, either in the circumstances of the speakers and those who were addressed, or in their application to matters which use, peculiarity of place and situation, and the lapse of time, had produced. It was my invariable plan to ascertain first, the *literal meaning* of every word and phrase; and where there was a *spiritual* meaning, or reference, to see how it was founded on the literal sense. He who assumes his spiritual meanings first, is never likely to interpret the words of God either to his own credit or to the profit of his readers; but in this track commentator has followed commentator, so that, in many cases, instead of a careful display of *God's words* and the *objects* of his providence and mercy, we have tissues of *strange doctrines*, *human creeds*, and *confessions of faith*. As I have said in another place, I speak not against *compilations* of this kind; but let them be founded on the words of God, first properly understood.

As I proceeded in my work I met with other difficulties. I soon perceived an almost continual reference to the *literature*, *arts*, and *sciences* of the *Ancient World*, and of the *Asiatic* nations in particular; and was therefore obliged to make these my particular study, having found a thousand passages which I could neither illustrate nor explain, without some general knowledge at least of their *jurisprudence*, *astronomy*, *architecture*, *chemistry*, *chirurgery*, *medicine*, *metallurgy*, *pneumatics*, &c., with their *military tactics*, and the *arts* and *trades* (as well *ornamental* as *necessary*) which are carried on in common life.

In the course of all this labour I have also paid particular attention to those *facts* mentioned in the sacred writings which have been the subjects of *animadversion* or *ridicule* by *free-thinkers* and *infidels* of all classes and in all times: and I hope I may say that no such passage is either designedly *passed by* or *superficially* considered; that the strongest objections are fairly produced and met; that all such parts of these Divine writings are, in consequence, exhibited in their own lustre; and that the truth of the doctrine of our salvation has had as many *triumphs* as it has had *attacks* from the rudest and most formidable of its antagonists; and on all such disputed points I humbly hope that the reader will never consult these volumes in vain. And if those grand doctrines which constitute what by some is called *orthodoxy;* that prove that God is loving to every man; that from his innate, infinite, and eternal goodness, he *wills* and has made *provision* for the salvation of *every human soul;* be found to be those which alone have stood the rigid test of all the above sifting and examination; it was not because these were sought for beyond all others, and the Scriptures *bent* in that way in order to favour them; but because these doctrines are essentially contained in, and established by, the ORACLES OF GOD.

I may add, that these doctrines and all those connected with them, (such as the defection and sinfulness of man; the incarnation and sacrificial death of Christ; his infinite, unoriginated, and eternal Deity; justification by faith in his blood; and the complete sanctification of the soul by the inspiration of the Holy Spirit,) have not only been shown to be *the doctrines* of the sacred records, but have also been subjected to the strongest test of logical examination; and, in the notes, are supported by arguments, many of them new, applied in such a way as has not been done before in any similar or theological work.

In this arduous labour I have had no assistants; not even a single week's help from an *amanuensis;* no person to look for common-places, or refer to an ancient author; to find out the place and transcribe a passage of Greek, Latin, or any other language, which my memory had generally recalled, or to verify a quotation; the help excepted which I received in the *chronological* department from my nephew. I have laboured *alone* for nearly *twenty-five years previously* to the work being sent to press; and *fifteen* years have been employed in bringing it through the press to the public; and thus about *forty years* of my life have been consumed; and from this the reader will at once perceive that the work, *well* or *ill* executed, has not been done in a *careless* or *precipitate* manner; nor have any means within my reach been neglected to make it in every respect, as far as possible, what the title-page promises,—A HELP TO A BETTER UNDERSTANDING OF THE SACRED WRITINGS.

Thus, through the merciful help of God, my labour in this field terminates; a labour, which were it yet to commence, with the knowledge I now have of its difficulty, and my, in many respects, *inadequate means*, millions, even of the gold of Ophir, and all the honours that can come from man, could not induce me to undertake. Now that it is finished, I regret not the labour; I have had the testimony of many learned, pious, and judicious friends relative to the execution and usefulness of the work. It has been admitted into the very *highest ranks* of society, and has lodged in the cottages of the poor. It has been the means of doing good to the *simple of heart;* and the *wise man* and the *scribe*, the *learned* and the *philosopher*, according to their own generous acknowledgments, have not consulted its pages in vain.

For these, and all his other mercies to the writer and reader, may God, the Fountain of all good, be eternally praised!

ADAM CLARKE.

Eastcott, April 17, 1826.

A TABLE

Of the several places of the OLD TESTAMENT *cited in the* NEW, *which are taken from the Hebrew or Septuagint, from both, or from neither*

In this Table, O stands for the *Old Testament;* H, for *Hebrew;* G, for the *Greek* version or *Septuagint;* and N, for *neither,* or *doubtful.*

MATTHEW

Chap.	Ver.		
i.	23.	from Isa. vii. 14.	O
ii.	6.	from Mic. v. 2.	N
	15.	from Hos. xi. 1.	H
	18.	from Jer. xxxi. 15.	H
	23.	from Judg. xiii. 5.	N
iii.	3.	from Isa. xl. 3.	G
iv.	4.	from Deut. viii. 3.	G
	6.	from Psa. xci. 11, 12.	N
	7.	from Deut. vi. 16.	G
	10.	from Deut. vi. 13.	N
	15, 16.	from Isa. ix. 1, 2.	N
v.	21.	from Exod. xx. 13; Lev. xxiv. 21.	N
	31.	from Deut. xxiv. 1.	O
	33.	from Num. xxx. 2.	N
	38.	from Exod. xxi. 24.	O
	43.	from Lev. xix. 18.	N
viii.	17.	from Isa. liii. 4.	H
ix.	13.	from Hos. vi. 6.	H
xi.	10.	from Mal. iii. 1.	H and N
	14.	from Mal. iv. 5.	H
xii.	4.	from 1 Sam. xxi. 6.	O
	5.	from Num. xxviii. 9.	O
	18, &c.,	from Isa. xlii. 1.	G and N
xiii.	14.	from Isa. vi. 9, 20.	G
	35.	from Psa. lxxviii. 2.	G and N
xv.	4.	from Exod. xx. 12, xxi. 17.	O
	8, 9.	from Isa. xxix. 13.	G
xix.	4.	from Gen. i. 27.	O
	5.	from Gen. ii. 24.	O
	7.	from Deut. xxiv. 1.	O
xxi.	5.	from Zech. ix. 9.	N
	9.	from Psa. cxviii. 25, 26.	O
	13.	from Isa. lvi. 7, partim. from Jer. vii. 11, partim.	N
	16.	from Psa. viii. 2.	O
	42.	from Psa. cxviii. 22, 23.	O
xxii.	24.	from Deut. xxv. 5.	O
	32.	from Exod. iii. 6.	O
	37.	from Deut. vi. 5.	N
	39.	from Lev. xix. 18.	O
	44.	from Psa. cx. 1.	O
xxiv.	15.	from Dan. xii. 11.	G
	29.	from Isa. xiii. 10.	N
xxvii.	9, 10.	from Zech. xi. 13.	O and N
	35.	from Psa. xxii. 18.	O
	46.	from Psa. xxii. 1.	O

MARK

Chap.	Ver.		
i.	2.	from Mal. iii. 1.	O
	3.	from Isa. xl. 3.	O
ii.	26.	from 1 Sam. xxii. 6.	N
iv.	12.	from Isa. vi. 9.	O
vii.	6.	from Isa. xxix. 13.	O
x.	8.	from Gen. ii. 24.	O
xi.	9, 10.	from Psa. cxviii. 22, 23.	O
	17.	from Isa. lvi. 7: Jer. vii. 11.	O
xii.	10, 11.	from Psa. cxviii. 22, 23	O
	19.	from Deut. xxv. 5.	O
xii.	26.	from Exod. iii. 6.	O
	29, 30.	from Deut. vi. 4, 5.	O
	31.	from Lev. xix. 18.	O
	36.	from Psa. cx. 1.	O
xiii.	14.	from Dan. xii. 11.	O
xiv.	27.	from Zech. xiii. 7.	H and N
xv.	28.	from Isa. liii. 12.	O
	34.	from Psa. xxii. 1.	O

LUKE

Chap.	Ver.		
ii.	23.	from Exod. xiii. 2; Num. viii. 17.	N
	24.	from Lev. xii. 8.	O
	34.	from Isa. viii. 14.	N
iv.	4.	from Deut. viii. 3.	O
	8.	from Deut. vi. 13.	O
	10, 11.	from Psa. xci. 11, 12.	O
	12.	from Deut. vi. 16.	O
	18, 19.	from Isa. lxi. 1, 2.	G and N
vi.	4.	from 1 Sam. xxi. 6.	O
vii.	27.	from Mal. iii. 1.	O
x.	27.	from Deut. vi. 5; Lev. xix. 18.	O
xix.	46.	from Isa. lvi. 7; Jer. vii. 11.	O
xx.	17.	from Psa. cxviii. 22.	O
	37.	from Exod. iii. 6.	O
	42, 43.	from Psa. cx. 1.	O
xxii.	37.	from Isa. liii. 12.	O

JOHN

Chap.	Ver.		
i.	23.	from Isa. xl. 3.	O
ii.	17.	from Psa. lxix. 9.	O
vii.	42.	partim from Mic. v. 2, partim.	O
		from 1 Sam. xvi. 1, partim.	O
viii.	5.	from Lev. xx. 10.	O
	17.	from Deut. xvii. 6.	O
x.	34.	from Psa. lxxxii. 6.	O
xii.	15.	from Zech. ix. 9.	O
	38.	from Psa. liii. 1.	O
	40.	from Isa. vi. 10.	N
xiii.	18.	from Psa. xli. 9.	N
xix.	24.	from Psa. xxii. 18.	O
	28, 29.	from Psa. lxix. 21.	O
	36.	from Exod. xii. 46.	N
	37.	from Zech. xii. 10.	H

ACTS

Chap.	Ver.		
i.	20.	partim from Psa. lxix. 26, partim.	N
		from Psa. cix. 8, partim.	N
ii.	17, &c.	from Joel ii. 28, &c.	G
	25, &c.	from Psa. xvi. 8, &c.	G
	34, 35.	from Psa. cx. 1.	O
iii.	22.	from Deut. xviii. 15, 18, 19.	N
	25.	from Gen. xxii. 18.	N
iv.	25, 26.	from Psa. ii. 1, 2.	O

Chap. Ver.

vii. 42, 43. from Amos v. 25, 26, 27. N
49, 50. from Isa. lxvi. 1, 2. O
viii. 32, 33. from Isa. liii. 7, 8. G
xiii. 33. from Psa. ii. 7. O
34. from Isa. lv. 3. O
xiii. 35. from Psa. xvi. 10. O
41. from Hab. i. 5. G
47. from Isa. xlix. 6. O
xv. 16, 17. from Amos ix. 11, 12. G
xxiii. 5. from Exod. ii. 28. O
xxviii. 26, 27. from Isa. vi. 9, 10. O

ROMANS

i. 17. from Hab. ii. 4. O
iii. 4. from Psa. li. 4. G
10, 11, 12. from Psa. xiv. 1, 2, 3. N
13. from Psa. v. 10; Psa. cxl. 4.
14. from Psa. x. 7.
15. from Prov. i. 16.
16, 17. from Isa. lix. 7, 8.
18. from Psa. xxxvi. 12. } from Psa. xiv. 1, 2, 3, juxta, lxx. G
iv. 3. from Gen. xv. 6. O
17. from Gen. xvii. 5. O
18. from Gen. xv. 5. O
viii. 36. from Psa. xliv. 23. O
ix. 9. from Gen. xviii. 10. O
12. from Gen. xxv. 23. O
13. from Matt. i. 2. O
15. from Exod. xxxiii. 9. O
17. from Exod. ix. 16. H
25. from Hos. ii. 23. O
26. from Hos. i. 10. O
27, 28. from Isa. x. 22, 23. O
29. from Isa. i. 9. O
33. from Isa. viii. 14, and xxviii. 16 H
5. from Lev. xviii. 5. O
6. from Deut. xxx. 12. O
8. from Deut. xxx. 14. O
11. from Isa. xxviii. 16. G
13. from Joel ii. 32. O
15. from Isa. lii. 7. H
16. from Isa. liii. 1. O
18. from Psa. xix. 5. O
19. from Deut. xxxii. 21. O
x. 20, 21. from Isa. lxv. 1, 2. O
xi. 3. from 1 Kings xix. 10. O
4. from 1 Kings xix. 18. H
8. from Isa. xxix. 9, vi. 9. N
9, 10. from Psa. lxix. 23, 24. G
26. from Isa. lix. 20. N
27. from Isa. xxvii. 9. N
34. from Isa. xl. 13. O
35. from Job xli. 2 or 10. H
xii. 19. from Deut. xxxii. 35. H
20. from Prov. xxv. 21, 22. O
xiv. 11. from Isa. xlv. 23. N
xv. 3. from Psa. lxix. 10. O
9. from Psa. xviii. 50. O
10. from Deut. xxxii. 43. O
11. from Psa. cxvii. 1. O
12. from Isa. xi. 10. O
21. from Isa. lii. 15. O

1 CORINTHIANS

i. 19. from Isa. xxix. 14. G and N
31. from Jer. ix. 24. O
ii. 9. from Isa. lxiv. 4. N
16. from Isa. xl. 13. O
iii. 19. from Job v. 13. H
20. from Psa. xciv. 11. N
vi. 16. from Gen. ii. 24. O
ix. 9. from Deut. xxv. 4. O
x. 7. from Exod. xxxii. 6. O
26. from Psa. xxiv. 1. O

Chap. Ver.

xiv. 21. from Isa. xxviii. 11, 12. N
xv. 45. from Gen. ii. 7. O
54. from Isa. xxv. 8. H

2 CORINTHIANS

iv. 13. from Psa. cxvi. 10. O
vi. 2. from Isa. xlix. 8. O
16. from Lev. xxvi. 11, 12; Ezek. xxxvii. 27. O
vi. 17. from Isa. lii. 11. O
18. from Jer. xxxi. 1, 9. O
viii. 15. from Exod. xvi. 18. O
ix. 9. from Psa. cxii. 9. O
xiii. 1. from Deut. xvii. 6. O

GALATIANS

iii. 8. from Gen. xii. 3, xviii. 18. O
10. from Deut. xxvii. 26 O
11. from Hab. ii. 4. O
12. from Lev. xviii. 5. O
13. from Deut. xxi. 23. O
16. from Gen. xvii. 7. O
iv. 22. from Gen. xvi. 15, 21. O
27. from Isa. liv. 1. O
30. from Gen. xxi. 10. O

EPHESIANS

iv. 8. from Psa. lxviii. 19. N
v. 31. from Gen. ii. 24. O
vi. 2, 3. from Exod. xx. 12; Deut. v. 16. G

1 TIMOTHY

v. 18. from Deut. xxv. 4. O

HEBREWS

i. 5. from Psa. ii. 7; 2 Sam. vii. 14. O
6. from Psa. xcvii. 7. G
7. from Psa. civ. 4. O
8, 9. from Psa. xlv. 6, 7. O
10–12. from Psa. cii. 25–27. O
13. from Psa. cx. 1. O
ii. 6–8. from Psa. viii. 4–6. O
12. from Psa. xxii. 22. O
13. from 2 Sam. xxii. 3, and Isa. viii. 18. O
iii. 7–11. from Psa. xcv. 7–11. O
iv. 4. from Gen. ii. 2. O
v. 5. from Psa. ii. 7. O
6. from Psa. cx. 4. O
vi. 14. from Gen. xxii. 17. O
vii. 1. from Gen. xiv. 18. O
17. from Psa. cx. 4. O
viii. 5. from Exod. xxv. 40. O
8–12. from Jer. xxxi. 31–34. N
ix. 20. from Exod. xxiv. 8. O
x. 5–7. from Psa. xl. 6–8. G
16, 17. from Jer. xxxi. 32, 34. O
30. from Deut. xxxii. 35, 36. O
37, 38. from Hab. ii. 3, 4. G and N
xi. 5. from Gen. v. 24. G
18. from Gen. xxi. 12. O
22. from Gen. xlvii. 31. G
xii. 5, 6. from Prov. iii. 11, 12. O
16. from Gen. xxv. 33. O
18. from Exod. xix. 16. O
20. from Exod. xix. 19. O
26. from Hag. ii. 6. O
29. from Deut. iv. 24. O
xii. 5. from Deut. xxxi. 6, 8, and Josh. i. 5. O
6. from Psa. cxviii. 6. O

JAMES

i. 12. from Job v. 17. N
ii. 8. from Lev. xix. 18. O
23. partim from Gen. xv. 16, partim. O
from 2 Chron. xx. 7, partim. O

Chap.	Ver.		
iv.	5.	from Gen. vi. 3, 5.	N
	6.	from Prov. iii. 34.	G

1 PETER

i.	16.	from Lev. xi. 44.	O
	25.	from Isa. xl. 6, 7.	G
ii.	6.	from Isa. xxviii. 16.	O
	7.	from Psa. cxviii. 22; Isa. viii. 14.	O
	22.	from Isa. liii. 9.	O
ii.	24, 25.	from Isa. liii. 5, 6.	O
iii.	6.	from Gen. xviii. 12.	O
	10–12.	from Psa. xxxiv. 12–16.	O
iv.	18.	from Prov. xi. 31.	N
v.	5.	from Prov. iii. 34.	O

2 PETER

ii.	22.	from Prov. xxvi. 11.	O
iii.	8.	from Psa. xc. 4.	O
	9.	from Ezek. xxxiii. 11.	O

JUDE

	9.	from Zech. iii. 2.	H

APOCALYPSE

Chap.	Ver.		
i.	7.	from Zech. xii. 10.	H
ii.	23.	from Psa. vii. 10.	O
	27.	from Psa. ii. 10.	O
iii.	7.	from Isa. xxii. 22.	O
	19.	from Prov. iii. 12.	O
iv.	8.	from Isa. vi. 3.	O
v.	5.	from Gen. xlix. 9.	O
	11.	from Dan. vii. 10.	O
vi.	14.	from Isa. xxxiv. 4.	O
	16.	from Isa. ii. 19; Hos. x. 8.	O
vii.	3.	from Ezek. ix. 4.	O
vii.	17.	from Isa. xxv. 8.	O
x.	5.	from Dan. xii. 7.	O
	9.	from Ezek. iii. 3.	O
xi.	4.	from Zech. iv. 3.	O
xii.	5.	from Psa. ii. 9.	O
xiii.	10.	from Gen. ix. 6.	O
xiv.	5.	from Psa. xxxii. 2.	O
	8.	from Psa. xxi. 9.	O
	10.	from Psa. lxxv. 8.	O
xv.	4.	from Jer. x. 7.	O
	8.	from Exod. xl. 34.	O
xviii.	2.	from Isa. xiii. 21, 22.	O
	4.	from Isa. xlviii. 20; Jer. l. 8.	O
	6.	from Psa. cxxxvii. 8.	O
	7.	from Isa. xlvii. 7, 8.	O
	11.	from Ezek. xxvii. 35, 36.	O
	17, &c.	from Ezek. xxix. 29, &c.	O
	21.	from Jer. li. 64.	O
	23.	from Jer. xxv. 10.	O
xix.	13.	from Isa. lxiii. 2, 3.	O
xx.	8.	from Ezek. xxxviii. 2; xxxix. 1.	O
xxi.	1.	from Isa. lxv. 17.	O
	4.	from Isa. xxv. 8.	O
	15.	from Ezek. xl. 3.	O
	23.	from Isa. lx. 19.	O
	25.	from Isa. lx. 20.	O
	27.	from Isa. xxxv. 8.	O
xxii.	5.	from Isa. lx. 19, 20.	O

18 H. 27 G. 47 N. Plerumque O.; i. e., 200, aut eo circiter.

The above table was printed by Mr. E. Leigh, for his *Critica Sacra*. I have made a few corrections and additions.—A. C.

TABLE I

Of passages collected from the Old Testament, *as a testimony to the* New; *not indeed in the same words, but having the same meaning*

Chap. Ver.

GENESIS

i. 1. By faith we know that the worlds were made. Heb. xi. 3.
The heavens were of old. 2 Pet. iii. 5.
27. Adam was first formed. 1 Tim. ii. 13.
ii. 22. But the man is not of the woman. 1 Cor. xi. 8.
iii. 4. But the serpent deceived Eve by his subtilty. 2 Cor. xi. 3.
6. Adam was not deceived. 1 Tim. ii. 14.
iv. 4. By faith Abel offered unto God a more excellent sacrifice than Cain. Heb. xi. 4.
8. From the blood of righteous Abel. Matt. xxiii. 35.
Not as Cain, who was of that wicked one. 1 John iii. 12.
Wo to them, for they have gone in the way of Cain. Jude 12.
v. 24. By faith Enoch was translated. Heb. xi. 5.
vi. 12. When once the longsuffering of God waited. 1 Pet. iii. 20.
13. By faith Noah was warned. Heb. xi. 7.
22. Noah, the eighth person, a preacher of righteousness. 2 Pet. ii. 5.
vii. 4. For as the days that were before the flood. Matt. xxiv. 32.
ix. 6. All they that take the sword shall perish by the sword. Matt. xxvi. 52; Rev. xiii. 10.
xii. 4. By faith Abraham, when he was called. Heb. xi. 8.
xiv. 18. For this Melchisedek. Heb. vii. 1.
xvi. 15. Abraham had two sons, the one by a bondmaid. Gal. iv. 22.
xvii. 11. And gave him the covenant of circumcision. Acts vii. 8; Rom. iv. 11.
xviii. 10. By faith Sarah herself received strength. Heb. xi. 11.
12. As Sarah obeyed Abraham. 1 Pet. iii. 6.
xix. 25. And the cities of Sodom and Gomorrah. 2 Pet. ii. 6.
As Sodom and Gomorrah. Jude 7.
26. Remember Lot's wife. Luke xvii. 32.
For as it was in the days of Lot, they ate, they drank, they bought. Luke xvii. 27.
xxi. 1. Abraham had a son by the free-woman. Gal. iv. 22.
xxii. 1. By faith, Abraham, when he was tried. Heb. xi. 17.
9. Abraham offered his son upon the altar. James ii. 21.
xxii. 16. As he spoke unto our fathers. Luke i. 55.

Chap. Ver.

xxv. 22. Rebecca also conceived by one, our father Isaac. Rom. ix. 10.

31. Lest there be a fornicator or profane person, as was Esau, who for one mess of pottage sold his birthright. Heb. xii. 16.

xxvii. 28. By faith he blessed them concerning things to come. Heb. xi. 20.

xlviii. 15. By faith, Jacob when he was dying. Heb. xi. 21.

xlix. 10. Of whom Moses wrote in the law. John i. 45.

l. 24. By faith, Joseph, when he died. Heb. xi. 22.

EXODUS

ii. 2. By faith, Moses, when he was born. Heb. xi. 23.

11. By faith, Moses, when he was come to years. Heb. xi. 24.

Moses, seeing one of them suffering wrong. Acts vii. 24.

iii. 2. And when forty years were expired. Acts vii. 30.

xii. 11. Through faith he kept the passover. Heb. xi. 28.

xix. 22. They were baptized unto Moses in the cloud. 1 Cor. x. 2.

By faith they passed through the Red Sea. Heb. xi. 29.

xvi. 15. Our fathers ate manna in the wilderness. John vi. 49.

He gave them bread from heaven. John vi. 31.

They did all eat that spiritual meat. 1 Cor. x. 3.

xvii. 6. For they drank of that spiritual rock which followed them. 1 Cor. x. 4.

xix. 6. A holy nation, a peculiar people. 1 Pet. ii. 9.

12. And if a beast touch the mountain. Heb. xii. 20.

16. Ye are not come unto the mountain. Heb. xii. 18.

xxiv. 8. When Moses had spoken every precept. Heb. ix. 19.

xxvi. 1. For there was a tabernacle made, the first. Heb. ix. 2.

xxxii. 6. Be not ye idolaters, as were some of them. 1 Cor. x. 7.

xl. 4. Wherein was the candlestick. Heb. ix. 2.

LEVITICUS

xii. 3. Ye on the Sabbath circumcise a man. John vii. 22.

When eight days were fulfilled. Luke ii. 21.

4. When the days of their purification. Luke ii. 22.

6. And to offer a sacrifice according to the law. Luke ii. 24.

xiv. 4. Bring the gift which Moses hath commanded. Matt. viii. 4; Mark i. 44.

xvi. 14. If the blood of bulls and goats. Heb. ix. 13.

17. The whole multitude of the people were without worshipping. Luke i. 10.

xix. 15. Not with respect to persons. James ii. 1.

17. If thy brother sin against thee. Matt. xviii. 15; Luke xvii. 3.

xx. 10. Moses in the law commanded such to be stoned. John viii. 5.

Chap. Ver.

NUMBERS

viii. 16. Every male that openeth the womb. Luke ii. 23.

ix. 18. All our fathers were under the cloud. 1 Cor. x. 1.

xi. 7. He gave them bread from heaven to eat. John vi. 31.

xii. 7. Moses was faithful in all his house. Heb. iii. 2.

xiv. 37. Whose carcasses fell in the wilderness. Heb. iii. 17.

xvi. 1. They have perished in the gainsaying of Korah. Jude 11.

xix. 3. For the bodies of the beasts whose blood is brought. Heb. xiii. 12.

xx. 10. They drank of that spiritual rock that followed them. 1 Cor. x. 4.

xxi. 5. Neither let us tempt Christ. 1 Cor. x. 9.

9. As Moses lifted up the serpent in the wilderness. John iii. 14.

xxii. 23. The dumb ass speaking with a man's voice. 2 Pet. ii. 16.

39. Following the way of Balaam. 2 Pet. ii. 15; Jude 11.

xxiv. 14. They hold the doctrine of Balaam, who taught Balak. Rev. ii. 14.

xxv. 6. Let us not commit adultery as some of them. 1 Cor. x. 8.

xxvi. 64. Whose bodies fell in the wilderness. 1 Cor. x. 5.

xxviii. 8. The priests profane the Sabbath in the temple. Matt. xii. 5.

DEUTERONOMY

i. 16, 17. Have not respect of persons. James ii. 1, 9.

x. 17. For there is no respect of persons with God. Rom. ii. 11; Acts x. 34; Col. iii. 25; Ephes. vi. 9.

xvii. 6. He that despised Moses' law. Heb. x. 28.

xviii. 1. Do ye not know that they who minister in holy things. 1 Cor. ix. 13.

xxiv. 1. Whosoever shall put away his wife. Matt. v. 31, xix. 7; Mark x. 4.

JOSHUA

ii. 1. Likewise Rahab the harlot. James ii. 25.

vi. 20. By faith the walls of Jericho fell down. Heb. xi. 30.

By faith, Rahab the harlot. Heb. xi. 31.

1 SAMUEL

xxi. 6. Do ye not know what David did when he was hungry. Matt. xii. 3; Mark ii. 25; Luke vi. 4.

1 KINGS

ii. 10. Let me speak freely concerning the patriarch David. Acts ii. 29, xiii. 36.

x. 1. The queen of the south. Matt. xii. 42; Luke xi. 31.

xvii. 1. The heavens were shut for the space of three years. Luke iv. 25.

Elijah was a man of like passions with us. James v. 17.

2 KINGS

iv. 29. Salute no man by the way. Luke x. 4.

v. 13. Many lepers were in Israel. Luke iv. 27.

Chap. Ver.

1 CHRONICLES

xxiii. 13. But no man receiveth this honour to himself, but he that was called, as was Aaron. Heb. v. 4.

JOB

i. 21. For we brought nothing into this world. 1 Tim. vi. 7.
v. 17. Blessed is the man that endureth temptation. James i. 12.
xxxiv. 19. For God is no respecter of persons. Acts x. 34.

PSALMS

xli. 10. But the Son of man goeth. Matt. xxvi. 24; Mark xiv. 21; Luke xxii. 22.
cxxxii. 5. David desired to find a tabernacle for the God of Jacob. Acts vii. 46.

PROVERBS

xi. 31. If the righteous scarcely be saved. 1 Pet. iv. 18.
xvii. 27. Let every one be swift to hear. James i. 19.
xx. 9. If we say we have no sin. 1 John i. 8.
xxiv. 13. Have not the faith, with respect of persons. James ii. 1.
xxv. 6. Sit not down in the chief seat. Luke xiv. 8.

ISAIAH

viii. 14. Behold this is set for the fall and rising again. Luke ii. 34.
xiii. 10. After the tribulation of those days, the sun shall be darkened. Matt. xxiv. 29; Mark xiii. 24.

Chap. Ver.

xli. 8. He hath holpen his servant Israel. Luke i. 54.
liv. 1. Blessed are the barren. Luke xxiii. 29.
lviii. 7. I was hungry and ye gave me meat. Matt. xxv. 35.
lxiii. 2. Clothed with a garment dipped in blood. Rev. xix. 13.

JEREMIAH

ii. 21. A man that was a householder. Matt. xxi. 33; Mark xii. 1; Luke xx. 9.
xviii. 6. Shall the thing formed say to him who formeth it. Rom. ix. 20.

EZEKIEL

xii. 21. Where is the promise of his coming. 2 Pet. iii. 4.
xviii. 7. I was hungry and ye gave me meat. Matt. xxv. 35.
xxxix. 2. And when the thousand years shall be finished. Rev. xx. 7.

DANIEL

vii. 10. And thousands of thousands. Rev. v. 11.
xii. 7. And the angel which I saw standing on the sea. Rev. x. 5.

JOEL

iii. 15. The sun shall be darkened. Matt. xxiv. 29; Mark xiii. 24.

MICAH

ii. 10. Here we have no continuing city. Heb. xiii. 14.
iv. 7. He shall reign over the house of Jacob. Luke i. 33.

TABLE II

Of passages collected from the Old Testament, *as a testimony to the* New; *not indeed in the same words, but having the same meaning*

Chap Ver.

GENESIS

i. 27. He made them male and female. Matt. xix. 4.
ii. 2. And God rested the seventh day. Heb. iv. 4.
7. And the first man Adam was. 1 Cor. xv. 47.
24. Therefore shall a man leave father and mother. Matt. xix. 5; Mark x. 7; 1 Cor. vi. 16; Eph. v. 31.
And they two shall be one flesh. Matt. xix. 5; Mark x. 7; 1 Cor. vi. 16; Eph. v. 31.
xii. 1, 5, 6. Go out of thy country. Acts vii. 3.
In thy seed shall all the kindreds of the earth be blessed. Acts iii. 25.
xv. 5. So shall be thy seed. Rom. iv. 18.
6. And Abraham believed. Rom. iv. 18; James ii. 23; Gal. iii. 6.
13, 16. Thy seed shall sojourn. Acts vii. 6.
xvii. 4. Thou shalt be a father of many nations. Rom. iv. 17.
xviii. 10. I will return, according to the time of life. Rom. ix. 9.
xxi. 10. Cast out the bondwoman and her son. Gal. iv. 30.
In Isaac shall thy seed be called. Rom. ix. 7.

Chap. Ver.

xxii. 17. In blessing will I bless thee. Heb. vi. 14.
18. In thy seed shall all nations of the earth be blessed. Gal. iii. 8; Acts iii. 25.
xxv. 23. The elder shall serve the younger. Rom. ix. 12.

EXODUS

iii. 6. I am the God of Abraham. Matt. xxii. 32; Mark xii. 26; Luke xx. 37; Acts vii. 32.
ix. 16. For this cause have I raised thee up. Rom. ix. 17.
xii. 46. A bone of him shall not be broken. John xix. 36.
xiii. 2. Every male that openeth the womb. Luke ii. 23.
xvi. 18. He that gathered much had nothing over. 2 Cor. viii. 15.
xx. 12. Honour thy father and mother. Matt. xv. 4; Eph. vi. 2.
13. Thou shalt not kill. Matt. v. 21.
14. Thou shalt not commit adultery. Matt. v. 27.
15. Thou shalt not steal, &c. Rom. xiii. 9.
17. Thou shalt not covet. Rom. vii. 7.

Chap. Ver.

xxi. 17. He that curseth his father or mother. Matt. xv. 4; Mark vii. 10.
24. Eye for eye, tooth for tooth. Matt. v. 38.
xxii. 28. Thou shalt not speak evil of the ruler of thy people. Acts xxiii. 5.
xxiv. 8. Behold the blood of the covenant. Heb. ix. 20; xiii. 20; 1 Pet. i. 2.
xxv. 40. Look that thou make all after the pattern. Heb. viii. 5; Acts vii. 44.
xxxii. 1. Make us gods that may go before us. Acts vii. 40.
xxxiii. 19. I will be gracious to whom I will be gracious. Rom. ix. 15.
xxxiv. 33. Moses put a veil on his face. 2 Cor. iii. 13.

LEVITICUS

xi. 44. Ye shall be holy, for I am holy. 1 Thess. iv. 7; 1 Pet. i. 15, 16.
xviii. 5. Which if a man do, he shall live in them. Luke x. 28; Rom. x. 5.
xix. 12. Ye shall not swear by my name falsely. Matt. v. 33; James v. 12.
18. Thou shalt love thy neighbour as thyself. Matt. v. 43; xxii. 39; Gal. v. 14; James ii. 8.
xx. 9. Every one that curseth father or mother. Matt. xv. 4.
xxiv. 20. Eye for eye, tooth for tooth. Matt. v. 38.
xxvi. 11. I will dwell among you. 2 Cor. vi. 16.

NUMBERS

ix. 12. Nor break any bone of it. John xix. 36.

DEUTERONOMY

iv. 24. The Lord thy God is a consuming fire. Heb. xii. 29.
v. 16. Honour thy father and thy mother. Matt. xv. 4; Mark vii. 13; Eph. vi. 2.
17. Thou shalt not kill. Matt. v. 21.
18. Thou shalt not commit adultery. Luke xviii. 20.
19. Thou shalt not steal. Luke xviii. 20; Rom. xiii. 9.
20. Thou shalt not bear false witness. Luke xviii. 20; Rom. xiii. 9.
21. Thou shalt not covet. Rom. vii. 7.
vi. 4. Hear, O Israel, the Lord our God is one Lord. Mark xii. 29.
5. Thou shalt love the Lord. Matt. xxii. 37; Mark xii. 30; Luke x. 27.
13. Thou shalt fear the Lord thy God, and serve him. Matt. iv. 10; Luke iv. 8.
16. Ye shall not tempt the Lord your God. Matt. iv. 7; Luke iv. 12.
viii. 3. Man doth not live by bread only. Matt. iv. 4; Luke iv. 4.
x. 17. God accepteth not persons. Acts x. 34; Rom. ii. 11; Gal. ii. 6; Eph. vi. 9; 1 Pet. i. 17.
xviii. 15. A prophet shall the Lord raise up unto thee. John i. 45; Acts iii. 22, vii. 37.
xix. 15. At the mouth of two witnesses. Matt. xviii. 16; John viii. 17; 2 Cor. xiii. 1; 1 Tim. v. 19; Heb. x. 28.
21. An eye for an eye, tooth for tooth, hand for hand. Matt. v. 38.
xxi. 23. He that is hanged is accursed. Gal. iii. 13.
xxv. 4. Thou shalt not muzzle the ox. 1 Cor. ix. 9; 1 Tim. v. 18.
5. If a man's brother die. Matt. xxii. 24; Mark xii. 19; Luke xx. 28.

Chap. Ver.

xxvii. 26. Cursed is he who confirmeth not all the words of this law. Gal. iii. 10.
xxx. 12. Who shall go up for us to heaven. Rom. x. 6, &c.
14. But the word is very nigh unto thee. Rom. x. 6, &c.
xxxii. 21. I will move them to jealousy. Rom. x. 19.
35. To me belong vengeance and recompense. Rom. xii. 19; Heb. x. 30.

JOSHUA

i. 5. I will not fail thee. Heb. xiii. 5.

2 SAMUEL

vii. 14. I will be his father. Heb. i. 5.

1 KINGS

xix. 10. They have slain thy prophets. Rom. xi. 3.
18. I have left me seven thousand in Israel. Rom. xi. 4.

JOB

v. 13. He taketh the wise in their own craftiness. 1 Cor. iii. 19.

PSALMS

ii. 1. Why do the heathen rage. Acts iv. 25.
7. Thou art my Son, this day have I begotten thee. Acts xiii. 33; Heb. i. 5; v. 3.
9. Thou shalt break them with a rod of iron. Rev. ii. 27, xii. 5, xix. 15.
iv. 4. Stand in awe and sin not. Eph. iv. 26.
v. 9. Their throat is an open sepulchre. Luke xi. 44; Rom. iii. 13.
vi. 8. Depart from me, ye workers of iniquity. Matt. vii. 23, xxv. 41; Luke xiii. 27.
viii. 2. Out of the mouths of babes and sucklings. Matt. xi. 25, xxi. 16; 1 Cor. i. 27.
4. What is man that thou art mindful of him. Heb. ii. 6.
6. Thou hast put all things under his feet. 1 Cor. xv. 27; Heb. ii. 8.
x. 7. His mouth is full of cursing. Rom. iii. 14.
xiv. 3. There is none that doeth good. Rom. iii. 10.
xvi. 8. I have set the Lord always before me. Acts ii. 25.
10. Thou wilt not suffer thy holy one to see corruption. Acts ii. 31, xiii. 35.
xviii. 2. My God, in whom I will trust. Heb. ii. 13.
49. I will give thanks unto thee among the heathen. Rom. xv. 9.
xix. 4. Their line is gone out through all the earth. Rom. x. 18.
xxi. 1. My God, my God, why hast thou forsaken me? Matt. xxvii. 46; Mark xv. 34.
18. They part my garments among them. Luke xxiii. 34; John xix. 23, 24.
22. I will declare thy name to my brethren. Heb. ii. 12.
xxiv. 1. The earth is the Lord's. 1 Cor. x. 26, 28.
xxxi. 5. Into thy hand I commit my spirit. Luke xxiii. 46; Acts vii. 59.
xxxiv. 12. What man is he that desireth life. 1 Pet. iii. 10.

Chap. Ver.

xxxv. 19. They hated me without a cause. John xv. 25.

xl. 6. Sacrifice and offering thou didst not desire. Matt. xii. 7; Heb. x. 5.

xli. 9. He who did eat of my bread. John xiii. 18.

xliv. 22. For thy sake are we killed all the day. Rom. viii. 36.

xlv. 6. Thy throne, O God, is for ever and ever. Heb. i. 8.

li. 4. That thou mightest be justified when thou speakest. Rom. iii. 4.

lv. 22. Cast thy burden upon the Lord. 1 Pet. v. 7.

lxii. 12. Thou renderest to every man according. Matt. xvi. 27; Rom. ii. 6; 1 Cor. iii. 8.

lxviii. 18. Thou hast ascended on high, and led captivity captive. Eph. iv. 8.

lxix. 9. The zeal of thy house hath eaten me up. John ii. 17.

The reproaches of them that reproach thee. Rom. xv. 3.

22. Let their table become a snare. Rom. xi. 9, 10.

25. Let their habitation be desolate. Acts i. 20.

lxxviii. 2. I will open my mouth in parables. Matt. xiii. 35.

24. He gave them bread from heaven. John vi. 31; 1 Cor. x. 3.

lxxxii. 6. I have said, Ye are gods. John x. 34.

lxxxix. 20. I have found David my servant. Acts xiii. 22.

xci. 11. He will give his angels charge concerning thee. Matt. iv. 6; Luke iv. 10.

xciv. 11. The Lord knoweth the thoughts of man. 1 Cor. iii. 20.

xcv. 7. To-day, if ye will hear his voice. Heb. iii. 7, iv. 7.

11. Unto whom I sware in my wrath. Heb. iv. 3.

cii. 25. Thou, Lord, in the beginning hast laid. Heb. i. 10.

civ. 4. Who maketh his angels spirits. Heb. i. 7.

cix. 8. His bishopric let another take. Acts. i. 20.

cx. 1. The Lord said unto my lord. Matt. xxii. 44; Mark xii. 42; Acts ii. 34; 1 Cor. xv. 25.

Until I make thine enemies thy footstool. 1 Cor. xv. 25.

4. Thou art a priest for ever. Heb. v. 6, vii. 17, 21.

The Lord hath sworn, and will not repent. Heb. vii. 17.

cxii. 9. He hath dispersed abroad. 2 Cor. ix. 9.

cxvi. 10. I believed; therefore have I spoken. 2 Cor. iv. 13.

11. I said in my haste, All men are liars. Rom. iii. 4.

cxvii. 1. Praise the Lord, all ye nations. Rom. xv. 11.

cxviii. 6. The Lord is on my side. Heb. xiii. 6.

22. The stone which the builders rejected. Matt. xxi. 42; Mark xii. 10; Luke xx. 17; Acts iv. 11; 1 Pet. ii. 4, 7.

25, 26. Save now, I beseech thee,—Blessed is he that cometh. Matt. xxi. 9.

cxxxii. 11. Of the fruit of thy body. Luke i. 69; Acts ii. 30.

cxl. 3. Adder's poison is under their lips. Rom. iii. 13.

PROVERBS

Chap. Ver.

iii. 7. Be not wise in thine own eyes. Rom. xii. 16.

11. My son, despise not the chastening of the Lord. Heb. xii. 5.

12. For whom the Lord loveth he chasteneth. Rev. iii. 19.

x. 12. Love covereth all sins. 1 Pet. iv. 8.

xvii. 15. Whoso rewardeth evil for good. 1 Thess. v. 15; 1 Pet. iii. 9.

xx. 20. Whoso curseth his father. Matt. xv. 4.

xxv. 21. If thine enemy be hungry, give him bread. Matt. v. 44; Rom. xii. 20.

xxvi. 11. As a dog returneth to his vomit. 2 Pet. ii. 22.

ISAIAH

i. 9. Except the Lord had left us a very small remnant. Rom. ix. 29.

v. 1, &c. My well beloved hath a vineyard. Matt. xxi. 33; Mark xii. 1; Luke xx. 9.

vi. 3. Holy, holy, holy. Rev. iv. 8.

9. Hear ye indeed, but understand not. Matt. xiii. 14; Mark iv. 12; Luke viii. 10; John xii. 40; Acts xxviii. 26; Rom. xi. 8.

vii. 14. Behold, a virgin shall conceive. Matt. i. 23; Luke i. 31.

viii. 18. Behold, I and the children. Heb. ii. 13.

ix. 1. The land of Zebulun and the land of Naphtali. Matt. iv. 16.

x. 22. Yet a remnant of them shall return. Rom. ix. 27.

xi. 4. With the breath of his lips shall he slay the wicked. 2 Thess. ii. 8; Rev. i. 16.

xxi. 9. Babylon is fallen, is fallen. Rev. xiv. 8, xviii. 2.

xxii. 13. Let us eat and drink, for to-morrow we die. 1 Cor. xv. 32.

22. He shall open, and none shall shut. Rev. iii. 7.

xxv. 8. The Lord will wipe away tears from all faces. Rev. vii. 17.

xxviii. 11. For with stammering lips and another tongue. 1 Cor. xiv. 21.

16. Behold, I lay in Zion for a foundation. Matt. xxi. 42; Acts iv. 11; Rom. ix. 33; Eph. ii. 20; 1 Pet. ii. 6–8.

xxix. 13. This people draw near me with their mouth. Matt. xv. 8, 9; Mark vii. 6.

14. The wisdom of their wise shall perish. 1 Cor. i. 19.

xxxiii. 18. Where is the wise, where is the receiver? 1 Cor. i. 20.

xl. 3. The voice of him that crieth in the wilderness. Matt. iii. 3; Mark i. 3; Luke iii. 4; John i. 23.

6. All flesh is grass. James i. 10; 1 Pet. i. 24.

13. Who hath directed the Spirit of the Lord. Rom. xi. 34; 1 Cor. ii. 16.

xli. 4. I the Lord the first, and with the last. Rev. i. 17.

xlii. 1. Behold my servant whom I uphold Matt. xii. 18.

xliii. 19. Behold, I will do a new thing. 2 Cor. v. 17; Rev. xxi. 5.

xliv. 6. I am the first, and I am the last. Rev. xxii. 13.

xlv. 9. Shall the clay say to him that fashioneth it. Rom. ix. 20.

23. Unto me every knee shall bow. Rom. xiv. 11; Phil. ii. 10.

xlix. 6. I will give thee for a light to the Gentiles. Luke ii. 32; Acts xiii. 47, xxvi. 8.

Chap. Ver.

8. In an acceptable time have I heard thee. 2 Cor. vi. 2.

10. They shall not hunger nor thirst. Rev. vii. 16.

l. 6. I hid not my face from shame and spitting. Matt. xxvi. 67, xxvii. 26.

lii. 7. How beautiful upon the mountains. Rom. x. 15.

5. My name continually every day is blasphemed. Rom. ii. 24.

11. Depart ye, depart ye, touch no unclean thing. 2 Cor. vi. 17; Rev. xviii. 4.

15. For that which had not been told them. Rom. xv. 21.

liii. 1. Who hath believed our report? John xii. 38; Rom. x. 16.

4. Surely he hath borne our griefs. Matt. viii. 17.

5. He was bruised for our iniquities. Rom. iv. 25; 1 Cor. xv. 3; 1 Pet. ii. 24.

7. He is brought as a lamb to the slaughter. Acts viii. 32.

9. He did no violence, neither was deceit found in his mouth. 1 Pet. ii. 22.

12. He was numbered with the transgressors. Mark xv. 28; Luke xxii. 37.

liv. 1. Sing, O barren, thou that didst not bear. Gal. iv. 27.

13. All thy children shall be taught of the Lord. John vi. 45; 1 Cor. ii. 10.

lv. 1. Ho, every one that thirsteth. John iv. 14, vii. 37; Rev. xxi. 6, xxii. 17.

3. I will give you the sure mercies of David. Acts xiii. 34.

lvi. 7. For my house shall be called a house of prayer. Matt. xxi. 13; Mark xi. 17; Luke xix. 46.

lix. 7. Wasting and destruction are in their paths. Rom. iii. 15.

17. He put on righteousness as a breastplate. Eph. vi. 14, 17; 1 Thess. v. 8.

20. The Redeemer shall come to Zion. Rom. xi. 26.

lx. 11. Thy gates shall be open continually. Rev. xxi. 25.

19. The sun shall be no more thy light. Rev. xxi. 23, xxii. 5.

lxi. 1. The Spirit of the Lord is upon me. Luke iv. 18.

lxii. 11. Say ye to the daughter of Zion. Matt. xxi. 5; John xii. 15.

lxiv. 4. Men have not seen nor perceived by the ear. 1 Cor. ii. 9.

lxv. 1. I am sought of them that asked not for me. Rom. ix. 24–26, x. 20; Eph. ii. 13.

2. I have spread out my hands all the day. Rom. x. 21.

17. I create new heavens and a new earth. 2 Pet. iii. 13; Rev. xxi. 1.

lxvi. 1. Heaven is my throne. Acts vii. 48, 49, xvii. 24.

24. Their worm shall not die, neither shall their fire. Mark ix. 44–48.

JEREMIAH

vii. 11. Is this house become a den of robbers. Matt. xxi. 13; Luke xix. 46.

ix. 24. But let him that glorieth glory in this. 1 Cor. i. 31; 2 Cor. x. 17.

x. 7. Who would not fear thee, O king of nations! Rev. xv. 4.

xvii. 10. I the Lord search the heart and try the reins. Rom. viii. 27; Rev. ii. 23.

xxxi. 9. I will be a father to Israel. 2 Cor. vi. 18; Rev. xxi. 7.

Chap. Ver.

15. A voice was heard in Ramah. Matt. ii. 17, 18.

31. Behold, the days come—that I will make a new covenant. Heb. viii. 8, x. 10.

li. 8. Babylon is suddenly fallen. Rev. xiv. 8, xviii. 2.

EZEKIEL

iii. 1–3. Eat this roll. Rev. x. 9.

xx. 11, 13, 21. Which if a man do he shall even live in them. Rom. x. 5; Gal. iii. 12.

xxxii. 8. All the bright lights of heaven will I make dark. Matt. xxiv. 29.

xxxvi. 23. I will sanctify my great name which was profaned. Rom. ii. 24.

DANIEL

ix. 27. The overspreading of abominations. Matt. xxiv. 15; Mark xiii. 14; Luke xxi. 20.

HOSEA

i. 10. In the place where it was said unto them. Rom. ix. 26.

ii. 23. I will say unto them that were not my people. Rom. ix. 25; 1 Pet. ii. 10.

vi. 6. For I desired mercy, and not sacrifice. Matt. ix. 13; xii. 7.

x. 8. They shall say unto the mountains, Cover us. Luke xxiii. 30; Rev. vi. 16, ix. 6.

xi. 1. I called my son out of Egypt. Matt. ii. 15.

xiii. 14. O death, I will be thy plagues. 1 Cor. xv. 54, 55.

JOEL

ii. 28. It shall come to pass in the last days. Acts ii. 17.

32. Whosoever shall call on the name of the Lord. Rom. x. 13.

AMOS

v. 25. Have ye offered to me sacrifices. Acts vii. 42.

vi. 1. Wo to them that are at ease in Zion. Luke vi. 24.

ix. 11. I will raise up the tabernacle of David. Acts xv. 16, 17.

JONAH

i. 17. Jonah was in the belly of the fish three days and three nights. Matt. xii. 40, xvi. 4; Luke xi. 30.

iii. 4–9. The people of Nineveh repented. Matt. xii. 41; Luke xi. 32.

MICAH

v. 2. Thou, Beth-lehem Ephratah. Matt. ii. 6; John vii. 42.

vii. 6. The son dishonoureth his father. Matt. x. 21, 35, 36; Luke xii. 53, xxi. 16.

NAHUM

i. 15. Behold upon the mountains the feet. Rom. x. 15.

HABAKKUK

i. 5. Behold ye among the heathen—and wonder. Acts xiii. 41.

Chap. Ver.

ii. 4. But the just shall live by faith. John iii. 36; Rom. i. 17; Gal. iii. 11; Heb. x. 38.

HAGGAI

ii. 6. I will shake the heavens and the earth. Heb. xii. 26.

ZECHARIAH

viii. 16. Speak every man truth to his neighbour. Eph. iv. 25.

ix. 9. Behold thy King cometh. Matt. xxi. 5; John xii. 15.

xi. 11, 12. So they weighed for my price thirty pieces of silver. Matt. xxvi. 15, xxvii. 9, 10.

Chap. Ver.

xii. 10. They shall look upon me whom they have pierced. John xix. 34, 37; Rev. i. 7.

xiii. 7. I will smite the Shepherd. Matt. xxvi. 31; Mark xiv. 27.

MALACHI

i. 2, 3. I loved Jacob, and hated Esau. Rom. ix. 13.

iii. 1. Behold, I send my messenger. Matt. xi. 10; Mark i. 2; Luke i. 76, vii. 27.

iv. 5. Behold, I will send you Elijah the prophet. Matt. xi. 14, xvii. 11; Mark ix. 11; Luke i. 17.

6. He shall turn the hearts of the fathers to the children. Luke i. 17.

GENERAL INDEX

TO THE

NOTES ON THE OLD TESTAMENT

N. B. *In principio* refers to the observations at the *beginning*, and *in fine* to those at the *end*, of the chapter.

A

AARON, why called "God's holy one," Deut. xxxiii. 8.

Abana, a river of Damascus; reasons for believing that the river known in the time of Elisha by this name is a branch of the Barrady, 2 Kings v. 12.

Abarim, mountains of, Dr. Shaw's description of the, Num. xxvii. 12. The fortieth station of the Israelites in the wilderness, Num. xxxiii. 47.

Abed-nego, derivation of the name, Dan. i. 7. How it should be pronounced, *ibid.*

Aben Ezra, account of this commentator, General Preface, p. 2.

Abenim, אבנים, why weights were originally so named by the Hebrews, Lev. xx. 36.

Abib, constituted the first month of the Jewish ecclesiastical year, Exod. xii. 2.

Abijah, battle of, with Jeroboam, great discordances in the versions respecting the number of the combatants and of the slain, 2 Chron. xiii. 3. The number of men engaged and slain, probably only a tenth part of that stated in the present copies of the Hebrew, *ibid.*

Ablutions, before offering sacrifice to the gods, evidently borrowed by the heathens from the Jewish purifications, Exod. xix. 10.

Abner, observations on David's lamentation over, 2 Sam. iii. 33.

Aboras, where this river is situated, Ezek. i. 1.

Abrabanel or *Abarbanel*, (*Rabbi Isaac*) account of this commentator, General Preface, p. 2.

Abraham, import of the name, Gen. xii. 2; xiv. 13; xvii. 5. In what it differs from Abram, Gen. xii. 2. Extreme trifling of rabbins and others upon this name, Gen. xvii. 5. Reasons for believing that the *righteous man* spoken of in the forty first chapter of Isaiah refers to Abraham rather than to Cyrus, Isa. xli. 2. Character of Abraham, Gen. xxv., *in fine.*

Abraham's bosom, lying in, and *to recline next to Abraham in the kingdom of heaven,* images by which the state of the blessed is represented, Isa. lxvi. 24. A similar imagery employed by heathen writers, *ibid.*

Abrech, אברך, rendered *bow the knee*, of doubtful signification, Gen. xli. 43.

Absalom, David's very pathetic lamentation on the death of, 2 Sam. xviii. 33. In what order the words were probably pronounced, *ibid.*

Absalom's hair, substance of Bochart's dissertation on the weight of, 2 Sam. xiv. *in fine.* The reasoning of this great Hebrew critic not conclusive, and another mode proposed of removing the difficulties which exist in the present Hebrew text upon this subject, *ibid.*

Abu Thaher, a chief of the Carmathians, singular anecdote respecting, Gen. xxxiv. 24.

Abyssinia, list of the monarchs of, from Maqueda, queen of Saba, to the nativity, 1 Kings x., *in fine.*

Acacia Nilotica, some account of the, Exod. xxv. 5. Supposed by some to be the Shittim wood of Scripture, *ibid.*

Acanthum vulgare, a species of thistle extremely prolific, Gen. iii. 18. Calculation of the number of individuals that could proceed from a single plant in four years, *ibid.*

Acarus sanguisugus, description of this animal, Exod. viii. 16.

Achad, אחד, probable reason why the Jews, assembled in synagogue, so frequently repeat, and loudly vociferate, this word, whenever that very celebrated passage in the Pentateuch relative to the unity of the Divine Being occurs in the Sabbath readings, Deut. vi. 4.

Achan, inquiry whether the sons and daughters of this man were stoned to death and burnt as well as their father, Josh. vii. 25.

Achashdarpeney, אחשדרפני, import of this word, Ezra viii. 36; Esth. iii. 12; Dan. iii. 2.

Achmetha, the same with Ecbatana, Ezra vi. 2.

Adad, a Syrian idol, supposed to have been the same with Jupiter and the sun, Isa. lxvi. 17. Meaning of the name, according to Macrobius, *ibid.* The appellation of this idol formed a part of the name of some Syrian kings, *ibid.*

Adam, meaning of this word, Gen. i. 26. The names given by Adam to the animals, a strong proof of the original perfection and excellence of man, Gen. ii. 20.

Additions in the versions to the commonly received Hebrew text, Gen. iv. 8; xlvi. 20; Num. x. 6; Judg. iv. 9; Neh. vii. 69. Esth. ii. 20; Psa. xiv. 3, *et in fine;* xxxviii. 20; cxlviii. 8; Prov. iv., *in fine;* xii. 11; xix. 22; xxii. 1.

Adjuration, most solemn form of, in use among all nations, Deut. iv. 26.

Adonai, אדני, its derivation and import, Gen. xv. 8; Psa. xcvii. 1.

Adonis, situation of this river, 1 Kings v. 9. Probable origin of the fable concerning, Ezek. viii. 14.

Adoration, origin of the word, 1 Kings xix. 18; Job xxxi. 26; Hos. xiii. 2. The kings of Persia never admitted any to their presence without first requiring the act of prostration, called *adoration*, Isa. xlix. 23. Very remarkable example of adoration as related by Harmer, *ibid.*

Adrammelech, an object of idolatrous worship among the Sepharvites, 2 Kings xvii. 31, *et in fine.* Meaning of the name, *ibid.* Represented, according to Jarchi, under the form of a mule, 2 Kings xvii. 31.

Adullam, where situated, Mic. i. 15.

Adultery, anciently punished by burning, Gen. xxxviii. 24. Derivation of the word, according to Minshieu, *ibid.* How the crime of adultery was punished among the Chaldeans, Persians, and Romans, Prov. vi. 33; Ezek. xxiii. 25.

Adulteresses, punishment of, among the ancient Germans, Hos. ii. 3.

Adytum, Αδυτον, definition of this word by Hesychius, Isa. xlv. 19.

Æge or *Ægea*, the usual burying-place of the ancient Macedonian kings, Dan. viii. 5.

Ægeadæ, the people that inhabited Æge or Ægea, Dan. viii. 5.

Ælian, remark of, how common angelic appearances are to be distinguished from those of the gods, Ezek. i. 7.

Ænigma, see *Enigma.*

Aeroliths, Izarn's table respecting, showing the places and times in which these substances fell, and the testimonies by which these facts are supported, Josh. x. 11. Chemical analyses of two aeroliths by Fourcroy and Vauquelin, *ibid.* Hypotheses by which the falling of stones from the atmosphere have been accounted for, *ibid.*

Æschylus, citation of a very beautiful passage from this poet respecting the omnipotence of the Divinity, Hab. iii. 6.

Æthiopians, conjecture concerning their origin, Gen. x. 6.

Æthiopic version, account of the, General Preface, p. 21.

Æthon, one of the horses of the sun, according to the pagan mythology, meaning of the name, 2 Kings ii. 11.

Afghans, singular and very interesting remark of Sir William Jones respecting the probable origin of this people, 2 Kings xvii. 6.

Afrasiab, an ancient king, when and where he flourished, Job xviii. 15.

Agate, some account of this precious stone, Exod. xxviii. 17.

Antiochus Epiphanes, this Syrian monarch supposed by Martin to be the Gog of Ezekiel, Ezek. xxxviii. 2.

Anubis, a city of Egypt, why also called Cynopolis, Exod. xi. 7.

Anubis Latrator, why this Egyptian idol was so named, Exod. xi. 7.

Apalim, עפלים, rendered *emerods*, probably mean *hemorrhoids*, 1 Sam. v. 8.

Apicius, an individual immensely rich, Esth. iii. 9. His tragical end, *ibid.*

Apis, an object of Egyptian idolatry, Gen. xliii. 32; Deut. iv. 17. Thought to have been posterior to the time of Joseph, *ibid.* The molten calf of Aaron supposed by some to have been an exact resemblance of this Egyptian idol, Exod. xxxii. 4. For what purpose a white bull was occasionally sacrificed to Apis by the Egyptians, Lev. xvi. 10.

Apocryphal writings, that St. Paul quoted from the, according to the opinion of some, utterly incredible, Isa. lxiv. 4.

Apollo, whence this heathen divinity had his name, according to Plutarch, Exod. iii. *in fine.* Worshipped under the form of a crow by the ancient Egyptians, Exod. viii. 26. Whence the fable of Apollo or the sun being seated in a blazing chariot, drawn by horses which breathed and snorted fire, originated, according to some, 2 Kings ii. 11.

Απομυιος, why this epithet was applied to Jupiter, Exod. viii. 24.

Aponius, a commentator on Solomon's Song, General Preface, p. 4.

Aquila, a translator of the Hebrew Scriptures into Greek, General Preface, p. 21.

Arabic version of the Old Testament, some account of the, General Preface, p. 22; Isa. lxvi., *in fine.*

Arabon, ערבון, rendered *pledge*, inquiry into its import, Gen. xxxviii. 17.

Arabs, their independent condition from the remotest antiquity, an irrefragable proof of the Divine origin of the Pentateuch, Gen. xvi. 12. Dr. Shaw's account of the manner in which the Arabs entertain strangers, Judg. vi. 19. Volney's description of their personal appearance, Job v. 5. Various tribes of Arabs, Isa. xlii. 11.

Aram Naharaim, the same with Mesopotamia, Amos ix. 7.

Arbiter bibendi, among the Romans, who were the, Esth. i. 8.

Arbor infelix, the tree on which criminals were hanged so named among the Romans, Josh. viii. 29; Esth. vii. 8.

Archimedes, how this celebrated mathematician destroyed the Roman fleet, and thus prolonged for a short time the political existence of Syracuse, Eccles. ix. 14.

Architecture of the temple, Dr. Delaney's remarks on the Divine original of the, 1 Chron. xxviii. 19.

Arcturus, import of the Hebrew word so translated very uncertain, Job ix. 9.

Ardsheer Diraz Dest, the same with Artaxerxes Longimanus, Ezra i. 1.

Argonautics, citation of a passage from the, which bears a close analogy to a part of the history of Jonah, Jonah i. 14.

Ariel, conjecture why Jerusalem was so named, Isa. xxix. 1.

Ariopharnes, king of Thrace, anecdote respecting, 1 Kings iii. 25.

Aristotle, Works of, said to contain four hundred and forty-five thousand two hundred and seventy verses; in what sense we are to understand this statement, Introduction to Ezra.

Ark of Noah, its tonnage according to Arbuthnot, Gen. vi. 15. Shown to have been sufficiently capacious to contain every species of animal, with food for twelve months, *ibid.* Dr. Lightfoot's calculation of its draught of water, Gen. viii. 4.

Ark, in which were deposited the two tables of stone, its construction and dimensions, Exod. xxv. 10. Why the ark is called *the footstool of God*, Isa. lx. 13.

Arks of the heathens, some account respecting the, Exod. xxv., *in fine.*

Armour, burning of, as an offering made to the god supposed to be the giver of victory, a custom among some heathen nations, Isa. ix. 4. The Romans used it as an emblem of peace, *ibid.* Description of a medal struck by Vespasian illustrative of this ancient custom, *ibid.*

Arpach, ארפח, import of this memorial symbol of the rabbins, Masoretic Notes at the end of Numbers.

Arrack, made of the juice of the date or palm tree, Psa. xcii. 12.

Arrows, customary among the heathens to represent any judgment from the gods under the notion of, Deut. xxxii. 23. Arrows, round the heads of which inflammable matter was rolled and then ignited, were used by the ancients, and shot into towns to set them on fire, and were discharged among the towers and wood-works of besiegers, Psa. lxxvi. 3.

Arsenal, for the temple, provided by David, according to Josephus, 2 Kings xi. 10.

Arvad or *Arad*, where situated, Ezek. xxvii. 8.

Asa, king of Judah, his very magnificent funeral, 2 Chron. xvi. 14.

Asaph, a very celebrated musician who flourished in the time of David, Psa. l., *in principio.* Twelve of the Psalms in the sacred canon, which bear the name of Asaph, thought by some to have been written by him, *ibid.* The style of David and Asaph compared, *ibid.*

Ashchenaz, where situated, Jer. li. 27.

Asher, why so named, Gen. xxx. 13.

Asherah, אשרה, rendered *grove*, more probably signifies an idol of some description; perhaps the same with the Venus of the pagan mythology, 2 Kings xxi., *in fine.*

Ashes upon the head, a sign of sorrow and great distress among many nations, 1 Sam. iv. 12.

Ashima, an ancient object of idolatrous worship, 2 Kings xvii., *in fine.*

Ashtoreth, an idol of the Sidonians, 1 Kings xi. 5; 2 Kings xxiii. 13.

Ashummed Jugg, of the Hindoos, particular description of the, with an explanation of the mystic ceremonies, as given by the commentators upon their original scriptures, Lev. xvi. 10. A very close copy of the Jewish scape-goat, *ibid.*

Asiatic bow, description of the, Psa. lxxviii. 57. Figure of its form in its quiescent state, and when ready to discharge the arrow or missile, *ibid.*; Zech. ix. 14.

Asiatic idols, description of several in the author's possession, Ezek. i. 10.

Asiatic proverbs, collection of, Prov. xxxi. *in. fine.*

Asmoneans, observations on the motto said to have been upon their ensigns, Exod. xv. 11.

Asnapper, very uncertain who, Ezra iv. 10.

Asp, a very small serpent peculiar to Egypt and Libya, Psa. xci. 13. No remedy for the bite of an asp, *ibid.* Singular effect of the venom upon the animal system, *ibid.* Why Cleopatra, the celebrated queen of Egypt, chose to die by the bite of this animal, *ibid.*

Asphaltites, Lake of, exceedingly salt, Josh. xv. 62.

Ass's head, in the Holy of Holies, probable origin of the story of the heathens, that the Jews had a figure of this description to which they paid religious worship, 2 Kings xvii., *in fine.*

Assembly of Divines, account of their notes upon the Scriptures, General Preface, p. 7.

Assyrians, their origin, Gen. xxv. 18. The same people with the Babylonians, according to Herodotus and Strabo, Isa. xlv. 25.

Astrology, Judicial, demonstrated to be vain, unfounded, absurd, and wicked, 1 Sam. vi., *in fine.*

Asuppim, the house of, why so named, 1 Chron. xxvi. 15.

Asyla, of the Greeks and Romans, for what purpose erected, Num. xxxv. 11.

Atlas, fable of, whence it originated, Job xxvi. 11.

Atmosphere, enumeration of some of the great benefits derived from the, Job xxviii., *in fine.* Calculation of its pressure upon the whole terraqueous globe, 1 Sam. ii., *in fine;* Job xxxviii., *in fine.* Observations on its refractive nature, 2 Kings xx., *in fine.* In what sense the atmosphere may be termed the *belt* or *girdle* of the earth, *ibid.*

Atonement or *expiation* for sin, tradition concerning, strongly and universally retained among the heathens, 2 Kings xvii., *in fine.*

Attic moneys, tables of the, Exod. xxxvi. 24.

Augustine, some account of this celebrated commentator, General Preface, p. 4.

Aur, אור, generally translated *light*, has various imports in different parts of the Old Testament, Gen. i. 3.

Aurum Reginæ or *Queen Gold*, what, Esth. ii. 18.

Authorized version, detailed account of the, General Preface, p. 14, &c.

Autumnal rains, in the East, Dr. Shaw's account of the, with their accompaniments, Psa. cxxxv. 7.

Avarice, very nervous saying of an English poet concerning, Jer. xvii. 11.

Aven or *On*, the famous Heliopolis, Ezek. xxx. 17.

Aven, Plain of, the same with Baal-Bek, according to Calmet, Amos i. 5.

Avites, very uncertain who these people were, 2 Kings xvii., *in fine.* Conjecture of Grotius respecting them, *ibid.*

Ayal, איל, Dr. Shaw's opinion relative to the meaning of this Hebrew word, Deut. xii. 15.

Azariah, import of this name, Dan. i. 7.

Azubah, wife of Caleb, why so named, according to the Targum, 1 Chron. ii. 18.

B

Baal, what this term imports, Judg. ii. 11.
Baal-bek, the ancient Aven or Heliopolis, Amos i. 5.
Baal-hatturim, (*Rabbi Jacob*) account of this commentator, General Preface, p. 2.
Baal-peor, probably the Priapus of the Moabites, and worshipped with the same obscene and abominable rites, Num. xxiii. 28; Deut. iii. 29.
Baal-zebub, the god of Ekron, why so named, Exod. iii. 24; 2 Kings i. 2.
Baal-zephon, probably an idol temple, Exod. xiv. 2.
Babel, derivation and import of this name, Gen. xi. 9.
Babel, tower of, heathen testimonies concerning, Gen. xi. 4. Various conjectures relative to the purpose for which this tower was built, Gen. xi. 9.
Babet or *Baby*, conjecture respecting the origin of this word, Zech. ii. 8.
Babylon, its great naval power before the time of Cyrus, Isa. xliii. 14. Semiramis, the foundress of this part of the Babylonian greatness, *ibid.* Manner of the taking of Babylon by Cyrus, Isa. xxi. 1, xliv. 27, xlv. 2; Jer. l. 24. Policy of the Persian monarchs in destroying the naval importance of Babylon, Isa. xliii. 14. Some particulars of the greatness of Babylon, Isa. xiii. 19, xlv. 2. Notation of the several steps by which the remarkable prophecies against this great city were ultimately accomplished in its total ruin, *ibid.* The annihilation of its walls accounted for, *ibid.* Deliverance from Babylon a frequent figure in the prophetical writings for the deliverance of the people of God from the power of evil under the Gospel dispensation, Isa. xl. 6–8.
Babylonian embassy to Hezekiah, observations on the, 2 Kings xxi., *in fine.*
Babylonians, singular custom among these people of selling all their marriageable virgins by public auction, Gen. xxix. 20. In what the dress of this people consisted, according to Herodotus, Dan. iii. 21.
Babylonish robes, some account of the, Josh. vii. 21.
Bacchus, some portions of the fable concerning, very similar to what is related of Moses, Exod. iv. 17. This idol worshipped under the form of a goat by the ancient Egyptians, Exod. viii. 26.
Backbite and *Backbiter*, words of Anglo-Saxon origin, Psa. xv. 3. Intended to convey the treble sense of *knavishness, cowardice*, and *brutality*, *ibid.*
Bacon's (*Friar*) method of restoring and strengthening the natural heat, 1 Kings i., *in fine.*
Badad, בדד, import of this word when employed by the Jews as a memorial symbol, Masoretic notes at the end of Numbers.
Badgers' skins, the Hebrew words so translated of very uncertain import, Exod. xxv. 5.
Baeshah, באשה, various conjectures respecting the meaning of this word, Job xxxi. 40.
Ba gad, בא גד, import of this phrase when employed by the Jews as a memorial symbol, Masoretic Notes at the end of Leviticus.
Baking in the East, manner of, with an account of the instruments employed in the process, Lev. ii. 7.
Balaam, character of this prophet of the Most High God, Num. xxiv., *in fine.* Observations on his famous prophecy concerning a star to spring out of Jacob, Num. xxiv. 6.
Balance, trial by the, a species of ordeal among the Hindoos, Num. v., *in fine.*
Banditti, hordes of, frequent in Arabia to the present day, Job i. 15.
Banner, giving the, very ingenious illustration of, by Mr. Harmer, Psa. lx. 4, *et in fine.*
Barach, ברך, generally rendered *to bless*, very extensive import of the original word, Gen. ii. 3; 1 Kings xxi. 9.
Barbary, Dr. Shaw's account of the chocolate-coloured pottage made by the inhabitants of, Gen. xxv. 29.
Bards, among the ancient Druids, who, Num. xxi. 27.
Barley harvest, time of its commencement in Palestine, Ruth i. 22.
Barrady, Maundrell's account of this river, 2 Kings v. 12.
Barrows or *Tumuli*, in England, what, 2 Sam. xviii. 17.
Bars of the pit, what probably meant by this phrase among the ancients, Job xvii. 16.
Batanim, בטנים, its import uncertain, Gen. xliii. 11.
Bath, some account of this Hebrew measure of capacity, Exod. xvi. 16; Ezra vii. 22.
Battering-ram, description of the, Ezek. v. 2. This machine unknown in the time of Homer, *ibid.*
Battle, trial by, when and where supposed to have had its origin, Num. v., *in fine.*
Baxter, (*Richard*) a commentator on the New Testament, General Preface, p. 7.
Beards, held in high respect in the East, the possessor considering it his greatest ornament, often swearing by it, and in matters of great importance pledging it, 2 Sam. x. 4; Song v. 13; Isa. vii. 20. Never cut off but in mourning or as a mark of slavery, *ibid.*; Jer. xli. 5. Considered by the Turks a great affront to take a man by his beard, unless it be to kiss it, Isa. vii. 20. Beards of the Macedonians ordered by Alexander to be shaved off, and the singular reason given by this king for the mandate, 2 Sam. ii. 16.
Bedaui or *Beduui*, a people of Arabia, Isa. xlii. 11.
Bede, account of this commentator, General Preface, p. 4.
Bedolach, בדלח, translated *bdellium*, Bochart's opinion respecting the meaning of this word, Gen. ii. 12.
Bedouin, Volney's description of the, Job v. 5.
Beds of ivory, what, Amos vi. 4.
Beech tree, juice of the, used for drink in the northern parts of Europe, Job xxx. 4.
Bees, Homer's very nervous description of a great swarm of, Psa. cxviii. 12.
Behemah, בהמה, translated *cattle*, import of the term, Gen. i. 24.
Behemoth, various conjectures respecting the animal intended by this name in Scripture, Job xl. 15. Reasons for supposing it to have been a species now extinct, perhaps the mammoth, *ibid.*
Belial, its derivation and import, Deut. xiii. 13, xv. 9.
Belibbo, בלבו, import of this memorial symbol of the rabbins, Masoretic Notes at the end of Exodus.
Bellerophon, son of Glaucus, king of Ephyra, story of, supposed to be a fabulous formation from the Scripture account of David's adultery with Bathsheba, and his murder of Uriah, 2 Sam. xi. 14.
Bells on horses, camels, &c., account of the, Zech. xiv. 20.
Belt, the chief ornament of a soldier, and highly prized in all ancient nations, 2 Sam. xviii. 11. Considered a rich present from one chieftain to another, *ibid.*
Ben, בן, *a son*, whence derived, Ruth iv. 11; Psalm cxxvii. 1.
Beneficiarii, among the Romans, who, Hab. iii. 6.
Bene-jaakan, the twenty-seventh station of the Israelites in the wilderness, Num. xxxiii. 31.
Beney adam, בני אדם, and *beney ish*, בני איש, very remarkable distinction between, Psa. lxii. 9.
Bengel, (*John Albert*) author of an edition of the Greek Testament, with various readings and critical notes, General Preface, p. 10.
Benjamin, why so named, Gen. xxxv. 18. Remarks upon the provisions set before this patriarch by Joseph being much greater than what were set before each of his brethren, Gen. xliii. 34.
Benjamite messenger, remarks upon his very laconic relation of the discomfiture of the Israelites by the Philistines, and of the taking of the ark of God, 1 Sam. iv. 17.
Benson, (*Dr.*) a commentator on different portions of the New Testament, General Preface, p. 8.
Bereshith, the first book of the Hebrew Scriptures, whence so named, Preface to the Book of Genesis.
Berith, ברית, rendered *covenant*, what it imports, Gen. vi. 18; Lev. xxvi. 15.
Beryl, account of this precious stone, Exod. xxviii. 17; Ezek. x. 9.
Bethany, why so named, Isa. x. 30.
Beth-el, meaning of this name, Gen. xxviii. 19.
Beth-jesimoth, the forty-second and last station of the Israelites in the wilderness, where situated, Num. xxxiii. 49.
Bethron, why probably so named, Song ii. 17.
Beth-shean, the same that was afterwards called *Scythopolis*, Josh. xvii. 11.
Beth-shemesh, various conjectures concerning the number of the inhabitants of, who were smitten for looking into the ark, 1 Sam. vi. 19. The words חמשים אלף איש *chameshim, elaph ish, fifty thousand men*, which stand in our present Hebrew copies, most probably an interpolation, *ibid.*
Bethyllia or *consecrated stones*, remarks upon the, Gen. xxviii. 18; Job xxxi. 1; Isa. lvii. 6.
Bey of Tunis, his manner of living, as mentioned by Pococke, Neh. iv. 18.
Beza, (*Theodore*) account of this commentator, General Preface, p 8.
Bezer, one of the cities of refuge, import of the name, Josh. xx. 7.
Bibliotheca Magna Rabbinica of Bartolocci, account of this great work, General Preface, p. 3.
Bildad, the Shuhite, who, Job ii. 11.
Bipens, a military weapon of the ancients, Eph. vi. 13.
Birds, thoughts on the wonderful structure of their wings and feathers, Gen. i. 22.
Birth-days, keeping of, a custom of very remote antiquity, Gen. xl. 20.

Bishebuah, בשבעה, a Jewish memorial symbol, Masoretic Notes at the end of Deuteronomy.
Bishop, remarkable saying of a, Job xix. 15.
Bitter waters of jealousy, rabbinical notion how a Jewess, suspected of adultery, could be said, in drinking these waters, to drink the very *words* of the execration written by the priest, Num. v. 23.
Blair's affecting picture of the death of a wicked man, Job xxvii. 8.
Blayney, (*Rev. Dr.*) translator of the Prophet Jeremiah, with notes, General Preface, p. 10.
Blasphemy of Shelomith's son, very doubtful in what it consisted, Lev. xxiv. 16, &c.
Blemishes, curious rabbinical enumeration of the, which disabled a Jew from entering into the priest's office, Lev. xxii. 20.
Blessings and curses of the law, observations on the mode in which these were pronounced, and the arrangement of the tribes for this purpose on Mounts Gerizim and Ebal, Deut. xxvii. 26.
Blood, prohibition of the eating of, one of the seven Noahic precepts, Gen. ix. 4. Philosophical reasons for the prohibition, *ibid.* The eating of blood forbidden by the law of Moses, Lev. iii. 17, xvii. 10–14. Dr. Hunter's theory of the vitality of the blood, Lev. xvii. 11.
Blotting out of the book of God, what meant by this phrase, Exod. xxxii. 32.
Board, account of the, borne by the criminal in China, to which the accusation is affixed, Job xxxi. 36.
Boccore, Dr. Shaw's account of this species of fig, Isa. xxviii. 4.
Bochart, (*Samuel*) author of a very accurate work on the geography of the sacred writings, General Preface, p. 9.
Bochim, why probably so named, Judg. iii. 5.
Bodies of the illustrious dead, how treated, according to Virgil, 2 Chron. xvi., *in fine*.
Bolled, import of this word, Exod. ix. 31.
Bones, enumeration of the, in the human body, Job xxxiii. 19.
Bonny, inhabitants of, mode in which these people construct their dwellings, Deut. xx. 5.
Book of Life and *Book of Death*, among the Chinese, what, Exod. xxxii. 32. See also Ezek. ix. 1.
Book of the Wars of the Lord, Dr. Lightfoot's opinion concerning the, Num. xxi. 14.
Booths or *sheds*, erected in the East by the keepers of the vineyards, to cover them from the scorching sun while watching the ripening grapes, made of the lightest and most worthless materials, Job xxvii. 18.
Boruwlaski, (*Count*) some account of this famous Polish dwarf, 1 Sam. xvii., *in fine*.
Bosom, the place where the Asiatics carry every thing precious or valuable, Job xxiii. 12.
Bottles of the ancients ordinarily made of goat's skin, Gen. xxi. 14; 2 Sam. xvi. 1. Description of one in the author's possession, 2 Sam. xvii. 28; Job xxxii. 19.
Bow, the grand weapon of our English ancestors, 2 Sam. viii. 18.
Bow, song of the, remarks upon its great excellences, 2 Sam. i., *in fine*. Dr. Kennicott's Latin version, *ibid.*
Bow of the Asiatics, description of the, Psa. lxxviii. 57. Figure of its form in its quiescent state, and when ready to discharge the missile, *ibid.*; Hos. vii. 16, Zech. ix. 14. General dimensions of the Persian bows, according to Xenophon, Isa. xiii. 18.
Bowing the body, manner of, in Eastern countries, Exod. iv. 31. The Jewish custom in this respect described, *ibid.*
Brain, contained in the cranium, and enveloped with the dura and pia mater, the golden bowl of Scripture, Eccles. xii. 6. Why so named, *ibid.*
Branches, feast of, for what purpose instituted, Exod. xxiii. 14.
Brass, a factitious metal known from very remote antiquity, Exod. xxv. 3; Psa. xviii. 34. How made, *ibid.*; Job xxviii. 2.
Breaking the jaws of the wicked, a metaphor taken from hunting, Job xxix. 17.
Breastplate of judgment, why so named, Exod. xxviii. 15. Its description and ornaments, *ibid.* Breastplates, something like that of the Jewish high priest, formerly worn by the president of the courts of justice in Egypt, Exod. xxviii. 30.
Bribery, ordinance against, in Magna Charta, Exod. xxiii. 8, 1 Sam. viii. 3; Mic. vii. 9. Some account of the intolerable abuses which prevailed in this country before the publication of the great charter, *ibid.*
Bricks, dimensions of the, commonly used by the ancients in building, according to Palladius, Ezek. v. 1. Manner of their formation, Isa. ix. 9, xiii. 19, xxx. 13; Nah. iii. 14.
Brimstone, used by the ancients in their superstitious purifications, Job xviii. 15. This illustrated by quotations from Pliny, Ovid, and Servius, *ibid.*
British army, descending scale of commanders in a, Num. ii., *in fine*. Ascending scale of ranks which every officer must pass through, *ibid.*
British constitution, great advantages of the, pointed out, 1 Sam. viii., *in fine*. Shown to be much more excellent than even the constitution of the kingdom of Israel, in the reign of David, 2 Sam. v., *in fine*.
Broidered coat, what, Exod. xxviii. 4.
Bruce's opinion respecting the situation of Ezion-geber, Tarshish, and Ophir, 1 Kings ix., *in fine*. His account of Solomon's voyage to Ophir, 1 Kings x., *in fine*. His description of the manner in which the rain-clouds are frequently collected together in Abyssinia, 1 Kings xviii. 44.
Brundusium, import of this name in the ancient language of that country, Isa. v. 1.
Brydone, (*Mr. Patrick*) his argument against the Mosaic account of the creation, drawn from the eruptions of Mount Ætna, and the formation of the different lavas, considered, Gen. i., *in fine*.
Bubastis, a city in which the Egyptians were accustomed to hold their principal annual feast in honour of Diana, Exod. x. 9.
Budhoo, priests of, manner of their dancing, jumping, &c., when making offerings to their demon gods, 1 Kings xviii. 26. Priests of this idol shave their heads close to the skin, Ezek. xliv. 20.
Buildings, Eastern, description of the walls, &c., of the, Isa. ix. 9, xiii. 19, xxx. 13.
Bul, an ancient Hebrew month, answering to a part of our October and November, 1 Kings vi. 38. This name supposed to be of Chaldean origin, 1 Kings vi. 1.
Burdensome stone, what probably meant by this expression, Zech. xii. 3.
Burkitt, (*Rev. William*) author of a very useful commentary on the New Testament, General Preface, p. 8.
Burkius, (*Phil. David*) author of notes on the twelve minor prophets, General Preface, p. 10.
Burns, (*Charles*) extraordinary stature of this man, 1 Sam. xvii., *in fine*.
Burnt-offerings, have been common among almost all the people of the earth, Lev. i. 4.
Burying in towns, churches, and chapels, observations on the great impropriety of, Lev. xi. 8.

C

Cab, see *Kab*.
Cables, made by the Egyptians of the leaves of the flag, Job viii. 11.
Cabod, כבוד, a memorial symbol of the rabbins, Masoretic notes at the end of Deuteronomy.
Caduceus, the, or rod of Mercury, evidently borrowed from the Scripture account of the rod of Moses, Exod. iv. 17.
Cœli enarrant, first six verses of this Psalm from an old English manuscript, Psa. xix. 3.
Cœlius Antipater, an accredited historian who lived before the time of Pliny, Isa. ii. 13–16. This writer assures us that he had seen a merchant who had made a voyage from Gades to Ethiopia, *ibid.*
Cain, import of this name, Gen. iv. 1.
Cairns, what, Josh. vii. 26; 2 Sam. xviii. 17.
Calais, affecting history of the six citizens of, who presented themselves before Edward III., with ropes round their necks, and the keys of the town and castle in their hands, 1 Kings xx., *in fine*.
Calmet, (*Dom. Augustine*) a very celebrated commentator upon the whole Scriptures, General Preface, page 5. His enumeration of the different ways in which a Hebrew might lose his liberty, Exod. xxi. 2.
Calneh, the same with Ctesiphon, according to Calmet, Amos iv. 2.
Caloric, or *natural heat*, when accumulated in any particular part, will diffuse itself to all bodies with which it comes in contact, till their temperature be equal, 2 Kings iv. 35.
Calves of gold, set up by Jeroboam, remarks concerning the, 1 Kings xii. 28, 29.
Calvin, (*John*) a commentator on all the prophets and the evangelists, General Preface, p. 6.
Cambyses, king of Persia, the Gog of Ezekiel, according to Calmet, Ezek. xxxviii. 2.
Camel, Volney's description of the, Job v. 5.
Campbell, (*Dr.*) author of a treatise on the evangelists, General Preface, p. 8.
Canaan, land of, its superficial contents, Num. xviii. 21. What proportion of the promised land belonged to the Levites, *ibid.*
Canaanites, where those people, particularly so named, were situated, Josh. iii. 10.
Candle or *lamp*, often used as the emblem of prosperity and posterity, Job xxi. 17.
Candlestick, golden, of the temple or tabernacle, description of the, Exod. xxv. 31.

Candlesticks in the heathen temples, bearing a great number of lamps, Exod. xxv., *in fine.*
Canoes, formerly wholly constructed from the papyrus, Isa. xviii. 1, 2.
Cantate Domino, great similarity between this psalm and the Magnificat, or Song of the Blessed Virgin, Psa. xcviii., *in fine.* List of the most striking parallels, *ibid.*
Canticles, book of, carefully transcribed from a manuscript of the fourteenth century in the editor's possession, Introduction to Solomon's Song, *in fine.*
Cape of Good Hope, passage round the, known to the ancients, Isa. ii. 13–16. This navigation recovered by the Portuguese, after it had been lost for many centuries, *ibid.*
Caphtor, the island of Crete, Amos ix. 7.
Cappadocians, from whom descended, Gen. x. 2.
Caraba, description of the, Isa. xxv. 6.
Caravans in the East, some account of the, Song vi. 4. Manner in which the hadgees or pilgrims are conducted by these conveyances in their travels by night, *ibid.*
Carbuncle, account of this precious stone, Exod. xxviii. 17.
Carduus vulgatissimus, a species of thistle amazingly prolific, Gen. iii. 18.
Carmel, altar on this mount mentioned by Tacitus and Suetonius, which Vespasian went to consult, 1 Kings xviii. 30.
Carmelites, religious order of the, different opinions respecting the time of the foundation of this order, Josh. xix. 26.
Carolina sylvestris, a species of thistle amazingly prolific, Gen. iii. 18.
Caryl, (*J.*) a commentator on the book of Job, General Preface, p. 7.
Casiphia, generally supposed to be the same with the *Caspian mountains,* Ezra viii. 17.
Cassiopeia, form of the constellation of, resembled by Aratus to a key, Isa. xxii. 22.
Cassiterides, the same with the islands of Scilly and Cornwall, Isa. ii. 13–16.
Castor oil, whence obtained, Jonah iv. 6.
Castrametation of the ancient Israelites, Scheuchzer's remarks on the, Num. ii., *in fine.*
Cataneans, from whom supposed to be descended, Gen. xxv. 2.
Cato's directions in the construction of threshing-floors, 1 Sam. xxiii., *in fine.*
Cattle, mischievous, customary among the Romans to twist hay about the horns of, that people seeing it might shun them, Exod. xxi. 28.
Causes, two supreme, coeternal, and independent, according to the magian theology, Isa. xlv. 7.
Caves, vast capacity of, in the East, according to Strabo and Pococke, 1 Sam. xxiv. 3; Isa. ii. 19–21.
Cedar of Lebanon, Gabriel Sionita's description of the, Num. xxiv. 6. Some curious particulars concerning this tree related by De la Roque, which he learned from the Maronites of Mount Libanus, *ibid.* Maundrell's description of the cedars he found growing on Mount Lebanus in 1697, *ibid.* Psa. xcii. 12.
Cedreans, their origin, Gen. xxv. 13.
Ceeneth, כנת, various conjectures respecting the meaning of this word, Ezra iv. 11.
Celibacy has no countenance in the sacred oracles, Gen. ii. 18, 24.
Cemarim, an order of idolatrous priests in Judea in the time of Josiah, 2 Kings xxiii. 5. Why Christian ministers have been called *cemarim* by the Jews, *ibid.*
Census of the children of Israel, in the second year after their departure from Egypt, compared with another census of the same people made thirty-eight years afterwards, Num. i. 46. Curious observation of Ainsworth on the number of families in the twelve tribes at the second census, Num. xxvi. 51.
Centurion, derivation and import of this word, Gen. xxxvi. 15.
Cerastes, whence this animal has its name, Gen. xlix. 17.
Chacameyah, חכמיה, rendered *wise men,* Porphyry's definition of the original term, Gen. xli. 8.
Chag, חג, Parkhurst's definition of this word, Lev. vii., *in fine.* Its import among the Jews when used as a memorial symbol, Masoretic notes at the end of Deuteronomy.
Chairs, never used in Persia but at the coronation of their kings, Isa. lii. 2. Eastern chairs always so high as to make a footstool necessary, *ibid.*
Chalal, חלל, a word very improperly rendered in our version, Ezek. xxi. 14. Its genuine import, *ibid.*
Chaldaic version, account of, the General Preface, p. 21.
Chaldeans, from whom these people probably had their name, Gen. xi. 34; Isa. xxiii. 13. Some account of the ancient condition of this people, Isa. xxiii. 13.
Chalil, חליל, a wind-instrument, 1 Sam. x. 5.
Champion, whence derived, and what its import, 1 Sam. xvii. 4.
Chance, inquiry into the derivation and meaning of this word, 1 Sam. vi. 9.
Chaos, notions of the heathens concerning this divinity probably borrowed from the Mosaic account of the creation, Gen. i. 2.
Chaplets, wearing of, at banquets, customary among the ancient Jews, Greeks, and Romans, Isa. xlviii. 1.
Chappelow, a commentator on the book of Job, General Preface, p. 7.
Chapters, division of the Holy Scriptures into, by whom effected, Introduction to Ezra. Instances of the very injudicious division of the chapters of holy writ, Isa. iv. 1, ix. 7, xiii., *in principio;* xv., *in principio;* xxvii., *in principio.*
Charashim, חרשים, rendered *carpenters,* inquiry into the true import of this word, Zech. i. 21.
Charetummim, חרטמים, import of this word, Gen. xli. 8; Exod. vii. 11.
Chariot, emblematical of Jehovah, remarks upon the, Ezek. i. Observations on it by the continuator of the Historical Discourses of Saurin, Ezek. x., *in fine.*
Charming of serpents and other animals, how this was professed to be done by ancients and moderns, Psa. lviii. 4, *et in fine.*
Chasdim, the same with the Chaldeans, Isa. xxiii. 13.
Chatath, חטאת, and *Chatah,* חטאה, commonly translated *sin,* import of these words, Gen. iv. 7.
Chebar, Chaborus, or *Aboras,* where this river is situated, Ezek. i. 1.
Chelekeca, חלקך, import of this word when used as a memorial symbol, Masoretic notes at the end of Numbers.
Chemosh, the grand idol of the Ammonites, Ruth i. 15; Jer. xlviii. 7.
Cherem, חרם, what it imports, Lev. xxvii. 21, 28, 29. The Jews had a most horrible form of excommunication called by this name, Num. xxii. 6.
Cherethites, who, 1 Sam. xxx. 14; Ezek. xxv. 16; Amos ix. 7; Zeph. ii. 5.
Chersydrus, a very venomous reptile, Num. xxi. 6.
Cherubim, various opinions concerning the, Gen. iii. 24. How represented, *ibid.;* Exod. xxv. 18, xxxvi. 8; Psa. xviii. 10. Improperly written *cherubims,* Gen. iii. 24; Exod. xxv. 18; Ezek. x. 20.
Chevy Chase, quotation from this old national ballad respecting the slaying of Sir Hugh Montgomery, 1 Kings xxii. 34.
Chical, see *Jackal.*
Chickpea, Dr. Shaw's account of the, 2 Kings vi. 25.
Children, among many ancient nations, considered the property of their parents, who had a right to dispose of them for the payment of their debts, 2 Kings iv. 1. Carrying of children astride upon the hip, with the arm round their body, a general custom in the East, according to Chardin, Isa. lx. 4. Children formerly sometimes employed to despatch captives, Judg. viii. 21. Considered disgraceful to fall by the hand of a child, *ibid.*
Chiliarch, its import, Gen. xxxvi. 15.
Chilmad, possibly *Chalmadora* on the Euphrates, Ezek. xxvii. 23.
Chimah and *Chesil,* Dr. Hales' reasons for the supposition that by these terms the constellations Taurus and Scorpio are intended, Job ix., *in fine.*
Chinese chronology of ancient events of a very extravagant and fabulous complexion, Isa. lxv. 22.
Chinnereth, sea of, where situated, Num. xxxiv. 11.
Chiromancy, upon what the doctrine of, is built as its Scripture foundation, according to John Taisnier, Job xxxvii. 7.
Chittim, the island of Cyprus, according to Josephus, Jer. ii. 10. Bochart's conjecture, *ibid.* Other conjectures, Isa. xxiii. 1; Ezek. xxvii. 6.
Choheleth, or *The Royal Preacher,* some account of this work, as given by the late Rev. John Wesley, Introduction to Ecclesiastes.
Chomesh, חמש, rendered *the fifth rib,* what it properly imports, 2 Sam. xx. 10.
Choun, an idol worshipped among the Peruvians from the remotest antiquity, Amos v. 26.
Christ, of the same import with *Messiah,* Exod. xxix. 7.
Chronicle, remarks on the, which was read to Ahasuerus, Esth. vi. 1.
Chronicles, books of, this portion of holy writ variously named in the versions, Preface to Chronicles. The author or authors of the Chronicles not known, *ibid.* Reasons for the supposition that Ezra was the compiler, *ibid.* Jerome's opinion of these books, *ibid.*
Chronological list of the prophets of the Old Testament from Adam to Malachi, Introduction to Isaiah. Chronological list of the *sixteen* prophets whose writings are preserved, *ibid.*

Crocodile, a sacred animal among the Egyptians, Exod. i. 11. Number and curious disposition of its scales, Job xii. 21. Eyes of the crocodile among the Egyptians, the emblem of the morning, Job xli. 18. Amazing strength of this animal in its tail, Job xli. 19. Particular description of the crocodile, Job xli., *passim*. This animal supposed to be the leviathan of Scripture, *ibid*.
Crooked serpent, various conjectures respecting the meaning of this phrase, Job xxvi. 13.
Cross, curious extract from a Saxon's homily relative to the canonical times of signing the body with the mark of the cross, Psa. cxix. 164.
Cross, trial by the, a species of ordeal frequent in the middle ages, Num. v., *in fine*.
Crown taken from the king of the Ammonites, valuation of the, 2 Sam. xii. 20.
Crusaders, instance of their horrible cruelties, as related in the Gasta Dei per Francos, Psa. lx., *in fine*.
Crystal, some account of this mineral, Job xxviii. 17.
Cubians, where these people were situated, according to Ptolemy, Ezek. xxx. 5.
Cud, derivation and import of the term, Lev. xi. 3. Philosophical observations relative to the faculty which certain animals possess of chewing the cud, *ibid*.
Cudworth, (*Dr.*) his excellent remarks on the ark, table of shewbread, &c., Exod. xxv. 23.
Cumean sibyl, Virgil's description of the seat of the, Isa. xlv. 19.
Cup, its metaphorical import in Scripture, Psa. xi. 6, cxvi. 13. This metaphor similarly employed among the heathens, as shown by a quotation from Homer, *ibid*.
Cup of consolation, its literal and metaphorical acceptation, Jer. xvi. 8.
Cup of trembling, probably an allusion to the ancient method of taking off criminals by a cup of poison, Isa. li. 17.
Cup of the wrath of Jehovah, a very bold, highly poetical, and sublime image, frequently employed by the sacred writers, Isa. i. 22, li. 21. Whence this figure is taken, Isa. i. 22.
Cupel, a sort of instrument used in the purification of silver, Prov. xvii. 3. Its description and use, Psa. xii. 6; Jer. vi. 27.
Cupid and Psyche, an ancient allegory by which marriage is happily illustrated, Gen. ii. 24.
Customs and usages of universal prevalence, enumeration of, from which the derivation of mankind from one common stock is demonstrable, Gen. x., *in fine*.
Cutheans, who, 2 Kings xvii. 24.
Cutting off the hair, a sign of great distress, and practised on the death of near relatives, Isa. xv. 2; Amos viii. 10; Mic. i. 16.
Cuttings of the flesh, common among the heathens in their religious rites, Lev. xix. 28; Deut. xiv. 1; Jer. xvi. 16.
Cymbal, description of this ancient musical instrument, Isa. xviii. 1.
Cynopolis, why this city was so named, Exod. xi. 7.
Cyrus, why so partial to the Jews, according to Josephus, Ezra i. 1. A *golden eagle*, *αετος χρυσους*, the ensign of Cyrus, according to Xenophon, Isa. xlvi. 11. This Persian monarch very probably named by Isaiah עיט *aeit*, or *the eagle*, from this circumstance, *ibid*. Pliny's account of the wealth taken by Cyrus in Asia, Isa. xlv. 3. Manner of the death of Cyrus as related by Herodotus, *ibid*.; Ezek. xxxv. 6. Vast extent of his empire, Ezra i. 2; Esth. i. 1. Xenophon's list of the nations conquered by Cyrus, Isa. xlv. 1. The *righteous man* mentioned by Isaiah to be understood of *Abraham*, and not of this monarch, Isa. xli. 2.

D

Dabar Yehovah, דבר יהוה, import of this phrase, Lev. xxvi. 15.
Dædalus and Icarus, fable of, moralized by a Roman poet, Prov. xxv. 7.
Dagon, description of this idol of the Philistines by Diodorus Siculus, Judg. xvi. 23. A quotation from Horace, which seems to have an allusion to the image of Dagon, *ibid*.; 1 Sam. v. 4. This idol supposed to have been the same with Dirceto, Attergatis, the Venus of Askelon, and the Moon, 1 Sam. v. 2.
Daman-Israel, account of this animal, Prov. xxx. 24.
Damascenes, excessive superstition of the, according to the Midrash, Isa. xvii. 1.
Damascus, the capital of the ancient kingdom of Syria, Amos i. 3.
Damme, (*Thomas*) extraordinary longevity of this man, Psa. xc., *in fine*.
Dan, why this patriarch was so named, Gen. xxx. 6.
Daniel, sketch of the life and character of this prophet, Introduction to Daniel, p. 560. Chronological arrangement of the events recorded in his book, *ibid*., pp. 562, 563.
Daphne, Ovid's description of the beauties of, Song iv. 7.
D'Arvieux's account of the costly ornaments of the Arabian ladies, Song i. 10.
Date, or *palm tree*, its description and various uses, Psa. xcii. 12.
Date wine, see *Palm wine*.
Daughters given in marriage according to their seniority, a very ancient custom, still observed among the Hindoos, Gen. xxix. 26.
David, number of the children born to this prince in Jerusalem, according to the Hebrew text, 2 Sam. v. 14–16. Number according to the Septuagint version, *ibid*. Our English version, which states that David houghed all the chariot horses of Hadadezer, shown not to contain the sense of the original, 2 Sam. viii. 4. Dr. Delaney's enumeration of the wars which David righteously undertook, and gloriously terminated, in the first nineteen or twenty years of his reign, 2 Sam. x. 19. The account of David's adultery with Bath-sheba, and his murder of Uriah (as recorded in the Old Testament) an illustrious proof of the truth of Divine revelation, 2 Sam. xi., *in fine*. Dr. Kennicott's remarks upon the Song which David composed when God had delivered him out of the hand of all his enemies, 2 Sam. xxii., *in fine*. A peculiarly sublime passage of this Song pointed out, where sense and sound are astonishingly combined, 2 Sam. xxii. 11; Psa. xviii. 10. L. De Dieu's judicious observations on the Scripture statement that the kingdom of David shall be perpetual, 2 Sam. xxiii., *in fine*. The tomb of David said to have been ransacked by Hyrcanus, the high priest, when besieged by Antiochus, and three thousand talents taken from it, to induce Antiochus to raise the siege, 1 Kings ii. 10. Dr. Kennicott's criticism on that part of the sacred text containing an account of David's dying charge relative to Shimei, 1 Kings ii., *in fine*. Calculation of the equivalent in British standard to the hundred thousand talents of gold and to the million talents of silver that were prepared by David for the temple, 2 Chron. x., *in fine*. In what sense those scriptures are to be understood which state David to have been *a man after God's own heart*, 1 Sam. xiii. 14. Sketch of the life and character of David, book of Psalms, *in fine*.
Day, Jewish division of the, Exod. xii. 6. Natural division of the day for necessary refreshment, Eccles. x. 17.
Days of the creation, supposed to typify the *chiliads* of the world which are to elapse before the commencement of the rest that remains for the people of God, Gen. i. 16.
Days of restraint, why this name was given to certain holy days ordained by the law, Isa. i. 13.
Daysman, what intended by this term in our courts of jurisprudence, Job ix. 30.
Dead, methods of honouring the, among the ancients, Gen. l. 26. Customary in ancient times to deposit gold, silver, and precious stones with the more illustrious dead, 1 Kings ii. 10. Raising the bodies of the dead, and scattering their bones about, formerly the highest expression of hatred and contempt, Jer. viii. 1.
Dead Sea, description of its waters, Gen. xix. 25.
Death, fine saying of Seneca relative to, Job iii. 9.
Death, image of, why hung up by Domitian in his dining-room, Isa. xxii. 13. Impious epigram of Martial on this image, *ibid*.
Death of the righteous, import of this phrase in the time of Moses, Num. xxiii. 10.
Debash, דבש, rendered *honey*, what it properly imports, Gen. xliii. 11.
Decalogue, controversy whether this was written on the first tables, Exod. xxxiv. 1.
Dedication, feast of the, why instituted, Exod. xxiii. 14.
Defunct, frequent repetition of the name of the, common in lamentations, 2 Sam. xix. 4.
Delhi, remarkable Persian couplet above the hall of audience in the imperial palace at, Neh. ii. 8.
Delaney's character of David, 1 Chron. xxix., *in fine*.
Delphic oracle, description of the, by Diodorus and Strabo, Isa. xlv. 19. Cicero's account of the answers generally given by the, *ibid*.
Demosthenes, passage in, admired by Longinus for the sublimity of its sentiment, as well as the harmony of its numbers, Isa. xliv. 22.
Desmond, countess of, extraordinary longevity of the, Psa. xc., *in fine*.
Desolation, very nervously described by a Persian poet, Job xviii. 15; Isa. xiii. 22; Zeph. ii. 14.
Destinies, or *Fatal Sisters*, fable of the, Job vii. 6.

Decvæux's analysis of the book of Ecclesiastes, Introduction to Ecclesiastes.
Deus judicium, Montgomery's poetical version of the principal passages in this Psalm, Psa. lxxii., *in fine*.
Deus misereatur, an ancient opinion of the Christian Church that the triple mention of אלהים *Elohim, God*, in the close of this Psalm, has a reference to the Holy Trinity, Psa. lxvii. 7.
Deuteronomy, the last book of the Pentateuch, why so named, Preface to Deuteronomy.
Devil, whence this word is derived, Job i. 6. The name of this apostate spirit nearly the same in most European languages, Psa. cix. 6.
Dew, thoughts on the manner of its production, Deut. xxxii. 2; Job xxxviii. 28.
Diadem of the earth, a most elegant expression to show the progress of the sun through the twelve signs of the zodiac in a natural year, Psa. lxv. 11.
Dial of Ahaz, observations on the nature and structure of the, with a diagram of its supposed form, 2 Kings xx., *in fine*.
Diamond, some account of this precious substance, Exod. xxviii. 17.
Diana of Ephesus, image of, supposed to have been an aerolith bearing some rude resemblance to the human form, Josh. x. 11.
Dibon-gad, the thirty-eighth station of the Israelites in the wilderness, where supposed to be situated, Num. xxxiii. 45.
Didymus, import of this name, Gen. xxv. 24.
Dinah, why so named, Gen. xxx. 21.
Diodorus Siculus, his account of the funeral ceremonies of the Egyptians, Gen. l. 2.
Diospolis, or *Thebes*, the No of Jeremiah. See chap. xlvi. 25. See also Ezek. xxx. 14.
Dipsas, mortal effects of the bite of the, as described by Lucan, Num. xxi. 6.
Diseases, charming away of, how professed to be done by ancients and moderns, Psa. lviii. 4, *et in fine*.
Divination by arrows, manner of, among the Arabs, Ezek. xxi. 21.
Divination by cups, of very remote antiquity, Gen. xliv. 5.
Divination by serpents, common among the ancients, Deut. xviii. 10.
Divine Being, some observations on the manner of approaching the, in prayer, Exod. ix. 29.
Divinity of Christ demonstrated, Psa. xlv. 8; Isa. vii. 15, ix. 7; Mic. v. 2, vii. 20; Zech. ii. 8, xiii. 7.
Divorcement, form of a bill of, among the Jews, Deut. xxiv. 3.
Dixit insipiens, remarks on six verses supposed to be cited by St. Paul from this Psalm, but which do not exist in the present copies of the common Hebrew text; Psa. xiv. 3, *et in fine*.
Dodd, (Rev. Dr. William) author of a very excellent commentary on the Scriptures, General Preface, p. 9.
Doddridge, (Dr. Philip) account of this commentator, General Preface, p. 8.
Dogs, remarks upon the howlings of, Exod. xi. 7.
Domesday book, account of, 2 Sam. xxiv. 8. At present in a state of great preservation in the Chapter House, Westminster, *ibid*.
Domine, Dominus noster, the whole of this Psalm given at full length from an ancient manuscript, Psa. viii., *in fine*.
Domitian, account of the expulsion of the Jews from Rome by this emperor, Psa. cix. 11.
Doors of the courts and houses in Palestine made very low to prevent the Arabs, who seldom leave the backs of their horses, from riding into the courts and houses, and spoiling the goods, Prov. xvii. 19.
Dophkah, the eighth station of the Israelites in the wilderness, Num. xxxiii. 12.
Dothan, where supposed to have been situated, 2 Kings vi. 13.
Dove's dung, the Hebrew word so rendered probably means a kind of pulse, 2 Kings vi. 25. Dove's dung of great value in the East for its power in producing cucumbers, melons, &c., *ibid*.
Dowry, to give a, for a wife, a custom very frequent among all ancient nations, Gen. xxix. 20. The Tartars and Turks still buy their wives, *ibid*.
Drag, an instrument used in threshing, Isa. xxviii. 27, 28. Its description, *ibid*.
Dragon-well at Jerusalem, why probably so named, Neh. ii. 13.
Dream, ineffectual working of the imagination in a, figuratively employed by sacred and profane writers, Isa. xxix. 7. Citation of instances from Virgil and Lucretius, *ibid*.
Dreams, enumeration of their causes, Gen. xli., *in fine*, 1 Kings iii. 5; Jer. xxiii. 27. Gregory Nyssen's theory respecting dreams, 1 Kings iii. 5. Joseph's dream of the eleven stars bowing down to him, supposed by Vallancy to have reference to the signs of the zodiac, Gen. xlix., *in fine*. Discourse on Nebuchadnezzar's dream of the metallic image, Dan. ii., *in fine*.
Dress of an English beau in the fourteenth century, as described by Dr. Henry, Lev. xix. 19. Curious extract against luxury in dress, taken from a sermon composed in the fourteenth century, *ibid*.
Drinking, regulations respecting, among the ancient Greeks and Romans, in their entertainments, Esth. i. 8.
Druids, Pliny's account of their great veneration for the oak and misletoe, Gen. xxi. 33.
Drunkenness, Herbert's nervous description of the baleful effects of, xxiii. 33.
Drusius, (John) account of this commentator, General Preface, p. 6.
Dudaim, דודאים, import of this word extremely uncertain, Gen. xxx. 14.
Duelling, when the general practice of, is supposed to have taken place, Num. v., *in fine*. Account of the duel between Dioxippus the Athenian, and Horatus a Macedonian, as given by Quintus Curtius, 2 Sam. xxiii. 21. Description of the ancient mode of duel between the retiarius and secutor, Mic. vii. 2. Observations on the practice of duelling in this country, Hos. iv. 2.
Duke, derivation and import of this word, Gen. xxxvi. 15.
Dung of the ox and cow in a dried state a common fuel in the East, Isa. xxvii. 11; Ezek. v. 12.
Dura, plain of, uncertain where situated, Dan. iii. 1.
Durandus, his account of the manner of constructing the *pallium* or *pall*, 1 Kings xix., *in fine*.
Dust, throwing of, into the air, a mark among the ancients of the greatest contempt, 2 Sam. xvi. 13.
Dyrbeans, anecdote concerning these people, Lev. vi. 3.

E

Eagle, esteemed by the heathens as a bird sacred to Jupiter, and thought by them to be employed in carrying the souls of departed heroes, kings, &c., into the celestial regions, Exod. xix. 4. Whence this fable probably originated, *ibid*. The eagle was the Roman ensign, Deut. xxviii. 49. A golden eagle was the ensign of Cyrus, according to Xenophon, Isa. xlvi. 11. The eagle proverbial among ancients and moderns for its strong and clear sight, Job xxxix. 27–29. Some eagles stated to have attained a very great age, Psa. ciii. 5. A very current opinion among the ancients that the eagle moults in his old age, and renews his feathers, and with them his youth, Isa. xl. 31.
Ear, boring of the, an ancient custom in the East, Exod. xxi. 6.
Earing, whence derived, and its ancient and modern acceptations, Gen. xlv. 6.
Ear-rings, formerly worn as amulets and charms, Gen. xxxv. 4. The Ishmaelites or Arabs had probably a crescent in each ear-ring, Judg. viii. 21.
Earth, rotation round its axis the cause of the regular succession of day and night, Gen. i. 4; Psa. xix. 5. Its superficial and solid contents, Psa. viii. 3. Its spheroidal figure, Gen. i. 10. What to be understood by the *pillars* or *compressors* of the earth, 1 Sam. ii., *in fine*.
Earth, two mules' burden of, inquiry into what Naaman meant by this phrase, 2 Kings v. 17.
Earth and water, annual offering of, to the Persian monarchs, and its signification, Neh. ii. 3.
Earthen jars, vessels in which the people of the East keep their corn and meal to preserve them from insects, 1 Kings xvii. 12.
Earthquakes, description of, with their accompaniments, 1 Kings xix. 11.
Eastern bow, description of the, Psa. lxxviii. 57. Its figure, and what named by the Greeks when in a quiescent state, and when ready to discharge the missile, *ibid.*; Hos. vii. 16; Zech. ix. 14.
Eastern divan, in what its furniture chiefly consists, Isa. xxxviii. 2.
East Indian ink, readily discharged from the paper by the application of a wet sponge, Num. v. 23.
Ebronah, the thirtieth station of the Israelites in the wilderness, Num. xxxiii. 34.
Eden, its derivation and import, Gen. ii. 8.
Edge-tools of the ancients commonly made of stones and flints, Josh. v. 2.
Edicts of the Persian monarchs could not be formally repealed; but new edicts could be issued by which the preceding might be counteracted, Esth. viii. 8.

Eve, meaning of the word, Gen. iii. 20. This name contains in itself a prophecy of the redemption of the world by Jesus Christ, *ibid.*
Events, enumeration of the different methods of recording, among the ancients, Jer. xvii. 1.
Evermore, import of this term, Exod. xv. 18; Psa. xvi. 11.
Evil report, fine personification of, by Virgil, 2 Sam. xiii. 30.
Execrations against those who should rebuild those cities which had been destroyed in war, the revival of whose power and influence was dreaded, frequent in ancient history, Josh. vi., *in fine*. Some examples produced, *ibid.* Pouring execrations on an enemy previously to battle, an ancient custom, Num. xxii. 6; Psa. lxxxiii. 15.
Exodus, the second book of the Old Testament Scriptures, whence so named, Preface to Exodus.
Expeditions of the ancient Eastern monarchs, manner of the, Isa. xl. 3.
Expiation, feast of, why instituted, Exod. xxiii. 14.
Expounding of the Scriptures, manner of, among the Jews, Neh. viii., *in fine.*
Ezekiel, Archbishop Newcome's historical sketch of the times in which this prophet lived, Introduction to Ezekiel. Character of Ezekiel as a poet drawn up by this great prelate, *ibid.* Chronological table of the prophecies of Ezekiel from Calmet, *ibid.* Plan and description of Ezekiel's temple, Ezek. xlviii., *in fine.*
Ezer kenegedo, עזר כנגדו, translated *helpmeet*, inquiry into the import of these words, Gen. ii. 18.
Ezion-gaber, the thirty-first station of the Israelites in the wilderness, some account of, Num. xxxiii. 35.
Ezra, biographical sketch of, by Prideaux, Introduction to Ezra.
Ezra, book of, very remarkable passage said to have been originally contained in this portion of holy writ, which the Jews are accused by Justin Martyr of erasing through their enmity to the Christians, Ezra x., *in fine.*

F

Fable of Dædalus and Icarus, with its moral as given by a Roman poet, Prov. xxv. 7.
Face or *Forehead*, why the first part of the body whence the sweat begins to issue, Gen. iii. 19.
Face, covering of the, a sign of mourning, 2 Sam. xix. 4. When a criminal was ordered to have his face covered, it was a sign among the Persians and Romans of his being devoted to death, Esth. vii. 8.
Falarica, see *Phalarica.*
Falcon, natural history of the, Job xxxix. 26.
False witnesses, laws of the Hebrews, Romans, and English against, Deut. xix. 19.
Falsity diffused through the nature of man, Psa. cxvi. 11. This idea finely expressed by Herbert, *ibid.* Remarkable Italian proverb to the same effect, *ibid.*
Fame, fine personification of, by Virgil, 2 Sam. xiii. 30.
Family religion, maintenance of, indispensable, Gen. xviii., *in fine*, xix., *in fine;* Deut. iv. 9, vi. 7.
Famines that were decreed to take place before the coming of the Messiah, according to the Targum, Ruth i. 1.
Father, probably a name of office in Egypt, Gen. xlv. 8. Certain officers of state among the Phœnicians, Persians, Arabians, and Romans, addressed by this title, *ibid.* Among the Jews, *father* was the title of preceptor, and *son*, that of disciple or scholar, Prov. i. 8.
Favouritism has often brought prosperous nations to the brink of ruin, Eccles. x. 5.
Feasts, three principal, of the Jews, which, Zech. xiv. 16.
Federal act formed by Joshua with the people of Israel, a little before his death, outline of Saurin's excellent dissertation on the, Josh. xxiv., *in fine.*
Felling of trees, directions of Vitruvius respecting, 1 Kings v. 6.
Ferdinand IV., king of Naples and the Sicilies, institute of this monarch relative to mournings for the dead, Gen. l. 7.
Ferdoosy, remarks on the famous epic poem written by this man, Esth. vi. 1.
Festivals, Jewish, some account of the, Exod. xxiii. 14.
Figs, Eastern, Dr. Shaw's account of the, Isa. xxviii. 4. Citation from Pliny relative to the medical properties of the fig, with Philemon Holland's translation, Isa. xxxviii. 21.
Filigree silver-work, Asiatics greatly excel in this kind of production, Prov. xxv. 11. Instances which have come under the author's inspection, *ibid.*
Final perseverance of the saints, doctrine of the, considered, Deut. vii. 12; 2 Sam. vii. 15; Ezek. xviii. 24.
Fine linen of Egypt, observations upon the, Gen. xli. 42.
Finger-mountain, the highest of the mountains of Ararat, where some have supposed the ark of Noah to have rested, Gen. viii. 4.
Fire, among the Hebrews and many other ancient nations, a very significant emblem of the Deity, Exod. iii. 2. This element the offspring of Ormusd, according to the modern Parsees, *ibid.* Deified among the Egyptians, Exod. xii., *in fine.*
Fire-cross, of the ancient Highlanders, what, Judg. xix. 29; 1 Sam. xi., *in fine.*
Fire consuming the thorns, a beautiful metaphor used by sacred and profane writers, Psa. cxviii. 12.
Fire-ordeal, among the Persians, account of the, Num. v., *in fine.*
Fire of God, import of this Hebraism, Job i. 16.
First-born, observations on the import of this term in various parts of the Scripture, Exod. xii. 29.
First-born, redemption of the, one of the rites still practised among the Jews, Num. xviii. 16. How this rite was performed, *ibid.*
First-fruits offered to God not only by the Hebrews, but several quotations from ancient writers to show that the heathens also offered them to their idols, Exod. xxii. 29.
Fishes, their amazing fecundity instanced in the tench, carp, and cod, Gen. i. 20.
Flag, Hasselquist's description of the, Job viii. 11. Ropes made of its leaves by the Egyptians, *ibid.*
Flail or *Staff*, account of this instrument used in threshing, Isa. xxviii. 27, 28.
Flesh, preservation of, by potting, common in Asiatic countries, Gen. xlv. 23.
Flint, our ancestors had their arrow and spear-heads of this substance, Josh. v. 2.
Flocks, why great care was necessary in driving them, among the ancients, Isa. xl. 11.
Flogging, system of, among the British, considered, Deut. xxv. 3. Saying of a Mandarin on this subject, *ibid.*
Flour of parched barley, according to Mr. Jones, the chief provision of the Moors in their journeys, 2 Sam. xvii. 28.
Flux and reflux of the ocean, phenomena and cause of the, Job xxxviii. 11; Psa. civ. 9.
Footstool, a necessary appendage to a throne, Isa. lii. 2, lx. 13.
Formido or *Terror*, among the ancients, what, Isa. xxiv. 17, 18.
Forty, Ainsworth's observations upon the very frequent occurrence of this number in Scripture, Deut. xxv. 3.
Forty days, a remarkable period in Scripture, Gen. vii. 4; Deut. xxv. 3.
Forty years, which are stated to have elapsed from the commencement of Absalom's rebellion to his departure for Hebron, most manifestly a corruption of the sacred text, 2 Sam. xv. 7.
Fosse-street, some account of, Job xxiii. 11.
Foxes, formerly a custom in Rome to let loose a number of, in the circus, with lighted flambeaux on their backs, that the people might be amused in seeing these animals run about till roasted to death by the flames with which they were enveloped, Judg. xv., *in fine*. Origin of this custom as given by Ovid, and by Serrarius and Bochart, *ibid.*
Frankincense, description of this resinous substance, Exod. xxx. 34.
Fray, whence this word is derived, Zech. i. 21.
Free agency of man demonstrated, Deut. v. 29, xi. 26, xxx. 15.
Freemen forbidden by Diocletian and Maximian to be sold on account of debt, 2 Kings iv. 1.
Friend, Cicero's definition of a genuine, Psa. xxix. 7.
Frogs, according to Bryant, a sacred animal among the Egyptians, Exod. xii., *in fine.*, xx. 4.
Froissart's account of the six citizens of Calais, who came to Edward III. with ropes round their necks, and the keys of the town and castle in their hands, 1 Kings xx., *in fine.*
Fuel, great scarcity of, in most parts of the East, Isa. xxvii. 11.
Funeral banquets to commemorate the dead, and comfort the surviving relatives, common among the ancients, Jer. xvi. 8.
Funeral ceremonies among the ancient Egyptians, account of the by Diodorus Siculus, Gen. l. 2.
Fur, how this Latin word has been applied by the ancient Romans, Psa. lxxxvi. 16.

G

Gad, why so named, Gen. xxx. 11.
Gad, perhaps an object of idolatrous worship among the ancient Israelites, Isa. lxv. 11.
Gal, גל, import of this term, Gen. xxxi. 46.
Galbanum, description of this plant, Exod. xxx. 34.
Gall, anciently supposed to be that in which the poison of serpents consists, Job xx. 16.
Galvanism, method of decomposing water by, Job xxxviii. 26.

Gam, גֵּד, import of this Jewish memorial symbol, Masoretic notes at the end of Genesis.

Gammadims, various conjectures respecting the import of the Hebrew term so translated, Ezek. xxvii. 11.

Gaon, (*Rabbi Saadias*) account of this commentator, General Preface, p. 3.

Gaphrith, גָּפְרִית, rendered *brimstone*, of very uncertain etymology, Gen. xix. 24.

Gardens encompassing Damascus, Maundrell's description of the, Isa. i. 30.

Garments, presents of, by Asiatic sovereigns to ambassadors and persons of distinction, very frequent, Gen. xlv. 22. Description of the garments appertaining to the Jewish priesthood, Exod. xxviii. Customary in the East to pull off the upper garments in times of great mourning, Exod. xxxiii. 5.

Garments, transparent, of the ancient Greeks and Romans, Isa. iii. 23. These garments called by the Romans *multitiæ* and *Coæ*, and why, *ibid*.

Garvanços, Dr. Shaw's account of this plant, 2 Kings vi. 25.

Gate, the place of judgment in the East, Judg. v. 11; Job v. 4; xxix. 7; Isa. xxix. 21.

Gates of many Eastern cities closed at sunset, and on no consideration opened till the following morning, Neh. vii. 3. Gates in Priam's palace covered with plates of brass, 1 Kings iv. 13.

Gat phe, גֵּט פֶּה, import of this memorial symbol of the rabbins, Masoretic notes at the end of Leviticus.

Gava, גָּרַע, the authorized version frequently inaccurate in the rendering of this word, Gen. xxv. 8. What the original term properly imports, *ibid*.

Gaza, why so named, and where situated, Judg. xvi. 1.

Gebal, where situated, Ezek. xxvii. 9.

Gehenna, why this word is used by our Saviour for the place of punishment of the wicked in a future state, Isa. xxx. 33.

Genealogical lists contained in the Old Testament Scriptures of essential service in the cause of Divine revelation, Gen. xxxvi., *in fine*.

Generation, various lengths of a, among the ancients, Gen. xv. 16.

Genesis, the first book of the Old Testament Scriptures, whence so named, Preface to Genesis. General Observations on the great importance of this book, Gen. l., *in fine*.

Genista, or *common furze*, exceedingly prolific, Gen. iii. 18.

Genius, extraordinary, of some men, reflections concerning the, Exod. xxviii. 3; xxxi. 6.

Gentiles very probably borrowed their first sacrificial rites from the patriarchs, Num. xix. 2.

Gentoo laws, very interesting extract from Mr. Halhed's code of, relative to the Ashummed Jugg, Lev. xvi. 10.

Gentoos, remarkable law among these people respecting marriage, Gen. xxix. 25.

Georgium Sidus, or *Herschel*, periodic and sidereal revolutions, distances from the sun and earth, diameter, volume, density, and hourly orbital motion, of this primary planet, Gen. i. 1.

Gerizim, some account of this mount, Deut. xxvii. 4.

Gershom, why so named, Exod. ii. 22; xviii. 3.

Ghost, its derivation and import, Gen. xxv. 8. To GIVE UP *the ghost*, an act properly attributable to Jesus Christ alone, *ibid*.

Giants, seven Hebrew words rendered thus in our English Bibles, Gen. vi. 4. Fable of the giants, Job xxvi. 5.

Gibborim, גִּבֹּרִים, rendered *mighty men*, what it properly signifies, Gen. vi. 4.

Giblites, an ancient people famous for their knowledge in ship-building, 1 Kings v. 18; Psa. lxxxiii. 7.

Gibyle, where situated, Psa. lxxxiii. 7.

Gideon, principle which impelled him to slay Zebah and Zalmunna illustrated by a quotation from Virgil, Judg. viii. 18. Character of Gideon, Judg. viii., *in fine*.

Gifts, rabbinical enumeration of the, presented to the priests, Num. xviii. 20.

Gigantic stature, account of persons of, in modern times, Num. xiii. 33.

Gilgal, a place of great celebrity in the Jewish history, Josh. iv. 19.

Gill, (*Dr. John*) author of a very diffuse commentary on the Old and New Testaments, General Preface, p. 8.

Girba or *Caraba*, description of the, Isa. xxv. 6.

Girding up of the loins, what meant by this phrase among the ancients, Jer. i. 17.

Girdle, a very general and expensive article of dress in the East, Prov. xxxi. 24. The girdle so essential a part of a soldier's accoutrement, being the last he put on to make himself ready for action, that *to be girdled* anciently imported "to be *completely* armed, and ready for battle," Isa. v. 27.

Girgashites, where these people were situated, Josh. iii. 10.

Gitagovinda, or *the songs of Jayadeva*, given at full length. See the Song of Solomon, *in fine*.

Glass, manufacture of, known to the ancients, Deut. xxxiii. 19; Josh. xi. 8.

Glean, whence derived, Ruth ii. 2. Formerly a custom in England and Ireland for the poor to collect the straggling ears of corn after the reapers, *ibid*. Present law of England with respect to gleaning, *ibid*.

Glowing sandy plain, its deceptive appearance at a distance, Isa. xxxv. 7. Dr. Hyde's explanation and derivation of the original term so translated, *ibid*.

Goadby, author of a work entitled, "An Illustration of the Sacred Writings," General Preface, p. 9.

Goat, an object of religious veneration in Egypt, 2 Chron. xi. 15. Why a symbol of the Grecian or Macedonian power, Dan. viii. 5.

Goat's hair of Asia Minor, Syria, Cilicia, and Phrygia, description of the, Exod. xxv. 4.

Goat's skin used in Barbary for the carrying of meal, figs, and raisins, Deut. xxviii. 5. All sorts of things, both dry and liquid in Eastern countries, generally carried in a goat's or kid's skin, *ibid*.

God, derivation and import of the term, Gen. i. 1, iii. 22. A notion prevalent among the ancient Jews and heathens that if any man saw God or his representative angel, he must surely die, Judg. vi. 29, xiii. 22. The Hebrew original of Esther, (as it has come down to us,) remarkable for not containing the name of *God* or *Lord*, Esth. ii., *in fine*. This circumstance not true of the Septuagint version of this book, *ibid*.

God the only ruler of princes, in what sense this phrase is to be taken, 1 Sam. xxiv. 7.

God be gracious unto thee, my son! a usual form of salutation in the East from the aged and superiors to the younger and inferiors, Gen. xliii. 29.

God make thee as fruitful as Ephraim, and multiply thee as Manasseh! a form of salutation still in use, Gen. xlviii. 20.

God make thee as Sarah and Rebecca! a salutation still in use, Gen. xlviii. 20.

Gods, carrying of the, to battle, customary among most nations, 2 Sam. v. 21. Whence this custom probably originated, Jer. xlviii. 7.

Goel, גֹּאֵל, import of this term, Gen. xlviii. 16; Ruth ii. 20. Applicable to our Lord Jesus Christ in a most eminent sense, *ibid*.

Gog, various conjectures concerning the person or people intended by this name, Isa. lxiii., *in principio*. Ezek. xxxviii. 2.

Golan, one of the cities of refuge, import of the name, Josh. xx. 7.

Gold, four Hebrew words so translated, Exod. xxv. 3; Job xxviii. 16, 17, 19. Calculation of the value of the gold, in British standard, which came to Solomon in one year, independently of what the chapmen and merchants brought him, 2 Chron. x., *in fine*.

Gold of Parvaim, various conjectures respecting the meaning of the Hebrew words so translated, 2 Chron. ii. 6.

Gold chain, in several nations, the emblem of civil authority, Gen. xli. 42; Prov. lxxiii. 6; Prov. i. 9.

Golden Psalm, the meaning of, see on Psa. xvi. 1, and in title of Psa. lx.

Golden age, idea of the renewal of the, among the ancient Greeks and Romans, Isa. xi. 6–8. Citations from Ferdusi and Ibn Onein upon the same subject, *ibid*.

Golden bowl, what meant by this phrase, Eccles. vii. 6.

Golden Fleece, probable origin of the fable of the, Exod. xxv. 5.

Golden image of Nebuchadnezzar, calculation of its weight of gold, upon the supposition of its having been a circular column of solid gold, Dan. iii. 1. Highly probable that it was only gilt, or covered with thin plates of gold, *ibid*. Not likely that this image was in the human form, *ibid*.

Goliath of Gath, his extraordinary stature reduced to English measure, 1 Sam. xvii. 4. Description of his armour, 1 Sam. xvii. 4–6. Probable weight of his panoply, 1 Sam. xvii. 7.

Gomed, גֹּמֶד, rendered *cubit*, of very doubtful signification, Judg. iii. 16.

Good shepherd, qualifications of a, Ezek. xxxiv. 6.

Good, (*Mr. Mason*) his reasons for the supposition that Moses was the writer of the book of Job, Preface to Job.

Gopher wood, different opinions concerning the, Gen. vi. 14. The same with the cypress, according to Bochart, *ibid*.

Goshen, conjecture of Jerome and others why this land was so named, Gen. xlv. 10.

Gourd kind, fruits of the, in much request in the East, Isa i. 8.

Grain formerly separated from the husk, in Palestine, by the feet of the oxen trampling among the sheaves, or by bringing a rough-shod wheel over them, Prov. xx. 26.

Granite, its component parts, Psa. cv. 41.

Grapes, bunches of, grew to an extraordinary size in the promised land, Num. xiii. 23.

Grave the appointed house for the whole human family, a most solemn truth well expressed in several quotations from poets, ancient and modern, 1 Kings ii. 2; Job iii. 19, xxx. 23.

Great fish that swallowed up Jonah could not have been a whale, and why, Jonah i. 17. That it was a shark, not an improbable conjecture, *ibid.* Strange trifling of ancient and modern commentators relative to this subject, Jonah ii. 10.

Great lights, the sun and moon so called in Scripture, not according to their bulk or solid contents, but from the proportion of light they shed on the earth, Gen. i. 16.

Great sea, a term in Scripture for the Mediterranean, Dan. vii. 4.

Greaves of brass or *iron*, account of this species of armour among the ancients, 1 Sam. xvii. 6.

Greek cities declared free by the Romans, and the rapture of the inhabitants on the occasion, as related by Livy, Psa. cxxvi. 1.

Greeks, from whom supposed to be descended, Gen. x. 2; Joel iii. 6.

Gregory the Great, account of this Catholic commentator, General Preface, p. 4.

Grief, excessive, its strong effect upon the mental faculty, Lev. x. 3. Remarkable saying of Seneca on this subject, *ibid.* Passage in the Psalms in which deep-seated grief is surprisingly expressed in the very *sound* of the words, Psa. lxxxi. 13.

Grinding of corn, manner of doing this in the East, Exod. xi. 5.

Grot between Aleppo and Bir capacious enough, according to Tavernier, to hold near three thousand horse, Isa. ii. 19–21. Maundrell's account of several grots of vast capacity, *ibid.*

Grotius, (Hugo) or *Hugh le Groot*, a celebrated commentator upon the whole Scriptures, General Preface, p. 6.

Groves, plantations of, about idol temples, for the purpose of obscene worship, Deut. xvi. 21; Isa. i. 29, 30.

Grounds and Reasons of the Christian Religion, a Deistical work so entitled, arguments of its author purporting to show that the promise of the Messiah is not to be gathered from the seventh chapter of the second book of Samuel, stated and refuted, 2 Sam. vii., *in fine.*

H

Habakkuk, some account of this prophet, Hab. i., *in principio.* His style as a poet, *ibid.*

Habergeon, or *Hauberk*, description of the, Exod. xxxix. 43. Probable derivation of the word, Neh. iv. 16.

Hachammah, החמה, a rabbinical memorial symbol, Masoretic notes at the end of Deuteronomy.

Hades, image of, sometimes employed in ancient poetry, Isa. v. 13, 14, xiii., *in principio.* Beautiful personification of, Hos. xiii. 14.

Hafiz, remarkable couplet in this author something similar to a passage in the Psalms, Psa. xxvii. 9.

Hagar, Abram's handmaid, import of her name, Gen. xvi. 1.

Hagarites, tribes of Nomade or Scenite Arabs, 1 Chron. v. 10.

Haggai, some account of this prophet, Hag. i., *in principio.*

Hagiographa, what books of holy writ were known among the Jews by this name, Zech. vii. 7.

Hail, general supposition respecting the mode of its formation, Exod. ix. 18; Job xxxviii. 22.

Hail-storms, account of several in England and elsewhere, Exod. ix. 18; Josh. x. 11.

Haime, (John) a preacher among the Wesleyan Methodists, singular anecdote respecting, 2 Sam. vii., *in fine.*

Hair, much used in divination among the ancients, and for purposes of superstition among the Greeks, Lev. xix. 27; Num. vi. 18. Tearing the hair a mark of deep affliction and distress, Josh. vii. 6; 1 Sam. iv. 12; Job i. 20; Jer. xvi. 6.

Halimus, a species of plant, where found, Job xxx. 4.

Ham, Dr. Hales' remarks on the political condition of the descendants of, Gen. ix., *in fine.*

Haman the Agagite, remarks on his offer of paying out of his own private property into the exchequer of the Persian monarch the enormous sum of ten thousand talents of silver, to prevent any deficiency accruing to the revenue in consequence of the execution of the projected massacre of the Jews, Esth. iii. 9.

Hamath, probably the famous city of Emessa, 2 Sam. viii. 9; Amos vi. 2.

Hammond, (Dr. Henry) account of this commentator, General Preface, p. 7.

Hananiah, import of the name, Dan. i. 7.

Hand in the clouds, all the appearances of God thus represented in a very ancient manuscript of the Septuagint, Dan. x. 10.

Hand placed on the head, a mark of deep sorrow occasioned by utter desolation, Jer. ii. 37.

Handmills formerly in use among the ancients, and still used in many parts of the East, Deut. xxiv. 6.

Hands, stretching out of the, and lifting them up to heaven, in frequent use among the ancients, Exod. ix. 29. This practice of antiquity illustrated by quotations from Homer and Virgil, *ibid.* See also 1 Kings viii. 22.

Handwriting on the wall of Belshazzar's palace, conjecture why it could not be read by the wise men of Babylon, Dan. v. 8. Exhibition of the writing in the ancient Hebrew characters, in which it is thought to have been originally written, Dan. v. 25.

Hanger, origin of this word, Gen. xxvii. 3.

Hanging up by the hand, very probably a mode of punishment in former times, Lam. v. 12.

Hannah, import of the name, 1 Sam. i. 2. Dr. Hales' observations on her prophetic song, 1 Sam. ii. 1. Exhibition of the whole of this hymn in hemistich or poetic lines, *ibid.*

Hannets, הנץ, a rabbinical memorial symbol, Masoretic notes at the end of Deuteronomy.

Hanno the Carthaginian, remarkable among the ancients for having sailed round the Cape of Good Hope, Isa. ii. 13–16.

Haphtorah, see *Sections of the Law and Prophets.*

Haradah, the twentieth station of the Israelites in the wilderness, Num. xxxiii. 24.

Hardening of Pharaoh's heart, inquiry into the import of this phrase, Exod. iv. 21. When properly understood, gives not the least countenance to the doctrine of unconditional election and reprobation, *ibid.* Exod. ix. 15, *et in fine.*

Hardicanute, quotation from the old ballad of, relative to predatory excursions, Job v., *in fine.*

Hardy, publisher of a Greek Testament with notes, General Preface, p. 7.

Hareth, an eminent Arabian poet, Psa. lx., *in principio.*

Harlot, conjectures respecting the origin of this word, Gen. xxxiv. 31.

Harmer, (Rev. Mr.) author of a very useful work, entitled "Observations on various Passages of Scripture," General Preface, p. 9.

Harpocrates, the god of silence, represented with his finger compressing his upper lip, Job xxi. 5.

Hart, reason assigned by Ælian, Appian, Nicander, and Pliny, why this animal more than any other thirsts for the waters, Psa. xlii., *in fine.* Ridiculous assertion of several of the primitive fathers relative to this animal, *ibid.*

Harvest-field, Homer's description of the labours of a, as represented by Vulcan on one compartment of the shield which he made for Achilles, Ruth ii. 5.

Harvest-home, probable origin of this custom, Exod. xxii. 29.

Hashem, השם, possibly the name of some Egyptian deity, Lev. xxiv. 10.

Hashmonah, the twenty-fifth station of the Israelites in the wilderness, conjecture respecting, Num. xxxiii. 29.

Hassan Sabat, anecdote respecting, Gen. xxxiv. 24.

Hawk, the flight of this bird wonderfully swift, Job xxxix. 26. Instances produced, *ibid.* From the swiftness of this bird the Egyptians, in their hieroglyphics, made it the emblem of the wind, *ibid.*

Hayemim, הימם, rendered *mules*, numerous conjectures respecting its import, Gen. xxxvi. 24.

Hazeroth, the thirteenth station of the Israelites in the wilderness, where situated, according to Dr. Shaw, Num. xxxiii. 17.

Head, covering of the, the attitude not only of a mourner, but of a culprit, 2 Sam. xv. 30.

Head, lifting up of the, inquiry into the import of this phrase, Gen. xl. 20.

Head, putting dust upon the, a mark of deep affliction and distress, Josh. vii. 6.

Heathen rites, enumeration of, which greatly resemble those contained in the Jewish worship, Exod. xxv., *in fine;* xxvii. *in fine.*

Hebrew manuscripts, account of, formerly in the possession of the Rev. Cornelius Schulting, a Protestant minister at Amsterdam, Isa. lxvi., *in fine.*

Hebrew moneys, table of the, Exod. xxxviii. 24.

J

Jabbok, from whom this brook took its name, according to Calmet, Gen. xxv. 2.

Jabesh-gilead, remarks of a literary friend upon the inhabitants of this place taking the bodies of Saul and his sons from the wall of Beth-shan, and burning them in Jabesh, 1 Chron. x., *in fine*.

Jabez, great discordances in the versions in their rendering of the sacred text relative to this man, 1 Chron. iv. 9. Observations on the prayer of Jabez, 1 Chron. iv., *in fine*.

Jackal or *Shiagal*, howlings of the, by night most lamentable, Mic. i. 8. Hasselquist's account of this animal, Isa. i. 8.

Jacob, why so named, Gen. xxv. 26. Dr. Kennicott's remarks relative to the time spent by this patriarch in the service of his father-in-law Laban in Mesopotamia, Gen. xxxi., *in fine*. Character of this patriarch, Gen. xlix., *in fine*.

Jaddua, stratagem of, by which Jerusalem was prevented from being destroyed by Alexander, Eccles. ix. 14; Zech. ix. 8.

Jael, thoughts on her conduct towards Sisera, Judg. iv., *in fine*.

Jah, יה, a name of God, inquiry into its import, Exod. xv. 2.

Jamaica, remarkable phenomena occasioned by an earthquake in this island, Psa. xviii. 15.

Jami Jemsheed or *The Cup of Jemsheed*, traditions concerning, Gen. xliv. 5.

Jao, Ιαω, evidently a corruption of Jehovah, frequent on Egyptian monuments, Exod. iii. 15.

Japheth, remarkable coincidence between the name of this son of Noah and the political condition of his posterity, Gen. ix., *in fine*. Japheth supposed to have been the same with the *Japetus* of the Greeks, Gen. x. 2.

Jarchi or *Isaaki*, *(Rabbi Solomon)* account of this commentator, General Preface, p. 2.

Jarmain or *Mishnical Doctors*, some account of the, Introduction to Ezra.

Jasher, *book of*, possibly the same with the *book of the wars of the Lord* mentioned by Moses, Num. xxi. 14.

Jasper, some account of this precious stone, Exod. xxviii. 17.

Java, eldest son of the emperor of, who was reigning in 1648, remarkable for having six fingers on each hand, and six toes on each foot, 2 Sam. xxi. 20.

Jayadeva, *Songs of*, given at full length. See Song of Solomon, *in fine*.

Jebusites, the ancient inhabitants of Jerusalem, Josh. iii. 10.

Jehoram, king of Judah, remarks on the writing said to have been sent to him from Elijah the prophet, 2 Chron. xxi. 12.

Jehovah, observations upon this appellative of the Divine Being, Exod. vi. 3, ix. 1, xxxiv. 6.

Jehu, inquiry into the import of the original words rendered *top of the stairs*, where Jehu was proclaimed king, 2 Kings ix. 13. Character of this prince, 2 Kings x., *in fine*.

Jenkins, *(Henry)* his great age, Job xiv. 5; Psa. xc., *in fine*.

Jeopardy, a word of French origin, derived from the exclamation of a disappointed gamester, Judg. v. 18.

Jephthah, *vow of*, inquiry into the meaning of the Hebrew text respecting the, Judg. xi. 31, *et in fine*.

Jeremiah, some account of this prophet, Introduction to Jeremiah. His character as a writer, *ibid*. Chronological tables of his prophecies, as drawn up by Drs. Blayney and Dahler, *ibid*. Remarks on a supposed interpolation in the *tenth* chapter of this prophet, Jer. x. 11.

Jericho, observations on the curse pronounced against this city by Joshua, Josh. vi. 26, and on its rebuilding by Hiel, 1 Kings xvi. 34.

Jeroboam I., king of Israel, his invention of a political religion, something similar to that contained in the law of Moses, 1 Kings xii. 28–33.

Jerome, account of this celebrated commentator, General Preface, p. 4.

Jerusalem, conjecture concerning the derivation of this name, Josh. x. 1. Surrounded by hills and mountains, Psa. cxxv. 2.

Jeshurun, its derivation and import, Deut. xxxii. 15; Isa. xliv. 2. Conjecture of Grotius respecting it, Isa. xliv. 2.

Jether the Ishmaelite, why so named, according to the Targum, 1 Chron. ii. 17.

Jew, remarkable saying of a, to the author, Zeph. iii. 13.

Jewels of the feet, nostrils, &c., Isa. ii. 17.

Jewish rolls, description of the, Jer. xxxvi. 2.

Jews, particular description of their very gross idolatries previously to the Babylonish captivity, Ezek. viii., *passim*. Dr. Blayney's observations on the six deportations of these people in the reign of Nebuchadnezzar, Jer. lii. 28–30. Circumstantial history of the Jews from the taking of Jerusalem by the Babylonians to their retreat into Egypt, Jer. xl.–xliv. Great favour shown to the Jews by Alexander and the Ptolemies, Isa. xix., *in principio*. This the means in the hand of God of diffusing the knowledge of the true God among heathen nations, and preparing them for the reception of Christianity, Isa. xxiv. 14. Citations from Juvenal and Seneca to show that the Jews were despised by the heathens for observing the Sabbath, Lam. i. 7. Remarkable custom among the ancient Jews in behalf of one capitally convicted, as related in the Mishna and the Gemara of Babylon, Isa. liii. 8. Prophetic penitential confession and supplication of the Israelites in their present state of dispersion, Isa. lxiii. 7, &c. Brief sketch of the history of the Jews from the Babylonish captivity as given by Dr. Taylor, Esth. x., *in fine*. Bp. Newton's observations on their wonderful preservation as a distinct people for so many ages, Jer. xlvi., *in fine*.

Jezebel, reflections on the very tragical end of this wicked woman, 2 Kings ix. 37.

Jezreel, import of the name, Hos. i. 4.

Jichta or *Equus hemionus*, natural history of the, Job xxxix. 5.

Joachan ben Zachai, parable of this rabbi very similar to that of our Lord relative to the wise and foolish virgins, Isa. lxv. 11.

Joash, curious circumstance mentioned by the Targum, relative to the coronation of, 2 Chron. xxiii. 21.

Job, reasons advanced to show that this man lived posterior to the promulgation of the law, Job i., *in fine*, ix., *in fine*. Sketch of his character, Job xlii., *in fine*.

Job, *book of*, its character, and various opinions respecting the writer. See the Preface, and chap. xlii., *in fine*. Very remarkable prophecy in this book relative to the redemption of the world by Jesus Christ, and the general resurrection, Job xix. 25, *et in fine*.

Jonah, some account of this prophet, Introduction to Jonah. Fable of Laomedon, king of Troy, and his daughter Hesione, supposed to be founded upon the story of Jonah being swallowed by a great fish, *ibid*.

Jonathan ben Uzziel's curious reason for the command given by Pharaoh to the Egyptian women to destroy all the male children of the Hebrews, Exod. i. 16.

Joppa, where situated, Jonah i. 3.

Jordan, some account of this celebrated river of Israel, Num. xxxiv. 12. Description of its source as given by Josephus, Josh. i. 2. When it overflows its banks, and the reason assigned, Josh. iii. 15.

Joseph, why so named, Gen. xxx. 24. Extravagant notions of the Mohammedans with respect to the comeliness of this patriarch, Gen. xxxix. 7, xlix. 22. Dr. Delaney's remarks on Joseph's bowing himself, with his face to the earth before his dying father, Gen. xlviii. The Doctor's strong encomium of Joseph on this account very reprehensible, *ibid*. Strictures on the moral and political conduct of Joseph, Gen. l., *in fine*. History of this patriarch by Justin, the Roman historian, *ibid*.

Josephus, a celebrated Jewish historian and commentator, account of, General Preface, p. 2.

Joshua, brief sketch of his character, Josh. xxiv., *in fine* See also the Preface to Joshua.

Josiah, king of Judah, very remarkable prophecy concerning, 1 Kings xiii. 2, 3.

Jotbathah, the twenty-ninth station of the Israelites in the wilderness, Num. xxxiii. 33.

Jotham, *parable of*, the oldest and best fable or apologue in the world, Judg. ix. 8. Its most excellent moral pointed out, and illustrated by a quotation from Shakspeare, Judg. ix. 14.

Jove, or *Jupiter*, a corruption of Jehovah, Exod. iii. 15.

Jubilate Deo, a Psalm which has long made a part of the public worship of the established church, Psa. c., *in fine*. The Anglo-Saxon and Anglo-Scottish versions of this Divine ode given at full length, *ibid*.

Jubilee, institution of the year of, Lev. xxv. 8, &c. Conjecture relative to the derivation of the word *jubilee*, Lev. xxv. 11. Typical import of this institution, according to Parkhurst, *ibid*. Calmet's thoughts on the very great advantages which the Jewish people derived from this Divine ordinance, Lev. xxv., *in fine*.

Judah, why so named, Gen. xxix. 35. Illustrious prophecy concerning the Messiah, who was to spring from this patriarch, Gen. xlix. 8–12.

Judah, *kingdom of*, its north and south boundaries, 2 Chron. xix. 4.

Judas, whence this Asmonean prince is said to have obtained his surname of Maccabeus, Exod. xv. 11.

Judea, Harmer's observations on the fertility of the land of, Deut. viii. 8. Judea sometimes called *The Mountain*, and why, Isa. v. 1.

K

Knives of rock, stone, or *flint,* common among the ancients, Josh. v. 2.
Koheleth, derivation and import of this word, Eccles. i. 1.
Korah and his company, probable allusion in the book of Job to the destruction of, Job xx. 26, 27, 28.
Koran, for what excellences it possesses it is principally indebted to the sacred Scriptures, Exod. xx., *in fine;* Num. iii. 1; Deut. xxxiv., *in fine.* The Mohammedans never write the Koran upon vellum or skin of any kind, Ezek. xliv. 17. Copies of the Koran frequently highly illuminated, Psa. lx., *in principio.* Citation of a beautiful passage from the Koran, which is said to have been the means of converting Labid, an Arabian poet, to Mohammedanism, Isa. viii. 21.
Korban, import of this word, Lev. i. 2.
Κρασπεδον, a term importing rather the *fringe,* than the *hem* of a Jewish garment, Num. xvi. 38.
Krebsius, (*Jo Tobias*) an eminent Biblical critic, General Preface, p. 12.
Kumund, a sort of running loop among the Persians, for what purpose employed, Job xix. 6.
Kurtuk Dumnik, Frazer's account of the, Judg. ix., *in fine.*
Kupke, a great Biblical critic, General Preface, p. 12.

L

Lachrymatories or *Urnæ Lachrymales,* small vials so named, into which it was customary among the ancient Greeks and Romans to put the tears shed for the death of any person, and offer them upon the tomb of the deceased, Psa. lvi. 8. Of what materials these lachrymatories were constructed, *ibid.* Account of one in the author's possession, *ibid.*
Lad, a word supposed to be of Hebrew origin, Gen. xxxvii. 2.
Ladder of Jacob, very probably an emblem of the providence of God, by which he watches over and regulates all terrestrial things, Gen. xxviii. 12.
Lahatim, להטים, rendered *enchantments,* what the probable import of this term, Exod. vii. 11.
Lake below the wine-press, what, Isa. v. 2.
Lambs, immense number of, annually slain in Jerusalem at the feast of the passover, in the time of Cestius, the Roman general, Num. xxix. 12.
Lamech's speech to his wives, as it stands in the Hebrew original, probably the oldest piece of poetry in the world, Gen. iv. 23. Inquiry into the cause of this remarkable speech, *ibid.*
Lamentations, very noisy among the Asiatics, Gen. xlv. 2.
Lamentations of Jeremiah, Hebrew names of this portion of the sacred canon, Introduction to the Lamentations. Its appellation in the Septuagint version, *ibid.* Singular opinion of Herman Van der Hardt, relative to this poem, *ibid.* Its very technical character, *ibid.* Observations of Drs. Lowth, Smith, and Blayney, on the peculiar style of this composition, *ibid.*
Lamp, to raise up a, to a person, what intended by this phrase both in sacred and profane history, 2 Sam. xiv. 7.
Lamps first introduced into the pagan temples by the Egyptians, Exod. xxv., *in fine.*
Lampsacus, singular preservation of this city by Anaximenes, Eccles. ix. 14.
Lance, usual in Arab camps for every man to have his lance stuck in the ground beside him, that he may be ready for action in a moment, 1 Sam. xxvi. 12.
Land, measurement of, by the ancients by lines or cords of a certain length, in a similar way to that by the *chain* among us, and the *schœnus* or *cord* among the Egyptians, Deut. iii. 4.
Land of promise, some account of the, Num. xxxiv. 13.
Landmarks of the ancients, in what they generally consisted, Deut. xix. 14; Job xxiv. 2. Held very sacred among the Romans, and at last deified, Deut. xix. 14; Prov. xxii. 28. A passage from Ovid in illustration of this circumstance, Prov. xxii. 28.
Land-torrents, which make a sudden appearance, and as suddenly vanish, allusion to, Job vi. 15.
Lapide, (*Cornelius à*) account of this voluminous commentator, General Preface, p. 5.
Lapis lazuli, its component parts, Job xxxviii. 38.
Lass, supposed to be a contraction of *ladess,* an old English word for a *girl* or *young woman,* Gen. xxxvii. 2.
Latter days, a phrase in Scripture generally importing the times of the Messiah, Isa. ii. 2; Dan. ii. 28.
Leaping on or *over the threshold,* what probably meant by this expression, Zeph. i. 9. Harmer's conjecture, *ibid.*
Leasing, derivation and meaning of this old English word, Psa. iv. 2, lv. 6.
Leb, לב, and לבב, *Lebab,* what these words import when employed by the Jews as memorial symbols, Masoretic notes at the end of Numbers and Deuteronomy.
Lebeid, quotation of several sentiments from the poem of, very similar to some in the book of Job, Job xxxi. 21. This poem contained in the *Moallakat,* Psa. lx., *in principio.*
Lecha, לך, import of this Jewish memorial symbol, Masoretic notes at the end of Genesis.
Lectisternium, Jerome's account of this pagan festival of antiquity, Isa. lxv. 11.
Leech, the ancient English word for a physician, Isa. iii. 7.
Lemuel's description of a virtuous wife. Prov. xxxi. 10–31.
Lentulus, the augur, the immense wealth this man is said to have possessed, Esth. iii. 9.
Leopard, proverbial among the ancients for its swiftness, Hab. i. 8.
Leper, an emblem of the wretched state of man by the fall, according to Dr. Lightfoot, as contradistinguished from the NAZARITE, an emblem of man in his state of innocence, Num. vi. 2.
Leprosy, Maundrell's account of the appearance of several persons whom he saw infected with this disorder in Palestine, Lev. xiii. 2. This malady a most expressive emblem of the pollution of the soul of man by sin, Lev. xiii., *in fine,* xiv. *in fine.*
Lethe, among the ancient mythologists, what, Psa. lxxxviii. 12.
Letters, alphabetic, when and by whom invented, Exod. xxxi., *in fine.*
Letters, sent to chiefs and governors in the East, always carefully folded up, and put in costly silken bags, and these carefully sealed, Neh. vi. 5. An *open* letter sent by Sanballat to Nehemiah a mark of contempt, *ibid.*
Levi, import of the name, Gen. xxix. 34. Conjectures why the posterity of this patriarch were appointed to the service of the sanctuary, Num. iii. 12. Very beautiful paronomasia on the name of Levi, Num. xviii. 2.
Levi ben Gershom, (*Rabbi*) account of this commentator, General Preface, p. 3.
Leviathan, supposed to be the crocodile, Job xli. 1; Isa. xxviii. 1. This hypothesis not without its difficulties, Job xli., *in fine.* Not impossible that the animal described in Scripture under this name is now wholly extinct, *ibid.*
Leviticus, the third book of the Pentateuch, why so named, Preface to Leviticus.
Lex, derivation and import of the word, Exod. xii. 49.
Lex talionis, earliest account we have of the, Exod. xxi. 24. Constituted a part of the Twelve Tables so famous in antiquity, *ibid.*
Libations of water, wine, milk, honey, and *blood,* frequent among the Greeks and Romans, 1 Sam. vii. 6; 2 Sam. xxiii. 16. The term libation sometimes synonymous with *covenant,* Isa. xxx. 1.
Libnah, the sixteenth station of the Israelites in the wilderness, uncertain where situated, Num. xxxiii. 20.
Lick, supposed to be of Hebrew origin, Prov. ii. 16.
Lie, definition of a, Gen. xx. 12.
Life, unreasonable attachment to, strongly ridiculed by the heathen poets, Gen. xxv. 8. Probable origin of the phrase, "I put my life in my hands," Judg. xii. 3. Its import, Psa. cxix. 109.
Light, inquiry into its production on the first day of the creation, Gen. i. 3. Its immense diffusion and extreme velocity, *ibid.* 1 Kings viii. 27; Job xxxviii. 26.
Lightfoot, (*Dr. John*) a very learned commentator on the whole Scriptures, General Preface, p. 7.
Lignum infelix, the tree on which criminals were hanged so named among the Romans, Josh. viii. 29.
Ligure, account of this precious stone, Exod. xxviii. 17.
Limercece, a species of food, how prepared, 2 Sam. xvii. 28.
Linen yarn, the import of the Hebrew word thus rendered extremely uncertain, 1 Kings x. 28.
Lines in the writings of prose authors, as well as of poets, termed *verses* by the ancients, Introduction to Ezra.
Lion, Homer's beautiful description of the great courage and fierceness of this animal after a long abstinence from food, Isa. xxxi. 4. Five Hebrew words rendered *lion* in our version, with an inquiry into the particular import of each, Job iv. 11.
Lion, the standard of Judah, Gen. xlix. 8.
Lion of God, an ancient appellation for a *hero,* a figure still employed in the same sense by the Arabians and Persians, Isa. xxxiii. 7.
Liverpool, great storm of hail near this town, Exod. ix. 17.
Living waters, what meant by this phrase among the ancients, Gen. xxvi. 19; Lev. xiv. 5; Psa. xxxvi. 9; Zech. xiv. 9.

Lo, לא, the Hebrews had a peculiar way of joining this particle to a noun, to signify in a strong manner a total negation of the thing expressed by the noun, Isa. x. 15. Several examples produced, *ibid.*

Loadstone, probably known in the East long before its discovery by the Europeans, Job xxviii. 18.

Lo-ammi, son of Hosea, meaning of the name, Hos. i. 9.

Locke, account of this commentator, General Preface, p. 8.

Locusts, description of the, Exod. x. 4. Volney's account of their terrible devastations in Syria, Egypt, and Persia, *ibid.* Dr. Shaw's relation of most formidable swarms of these insects in Barbary which came under his immediate observation, *ibid.;* Joel i. 12, ii. 2. Curious remark of an Arabic writer with respect to the similitude of the locust to ten different kinds of animals, Joel ii. 4. Relation by Livy and Augustine of a pestilence occasioned by an immense swarm of locusts, Joel ii. 20.

Log, some account of this Hebrew measure of capacity, Exod. xvi. 16.

Long, (*Dr.*) his ingenious experiment to ascertain the superficial proportion of land and water on the whole terraqueous globe, Gen. i. 10, vii. 11; Job xxviii. 25.

Longevity, some instances of, among the moderns, Psa. xc., *in fine.*

Longinus, (*Dionysius*) his remarkable criticism upon passages in the first chapter of Genesis, Gen. i. 3; Preface to Job.

Lord, its derivation and import, Gen. ii. 4.

Lord's day, or *Christian Sabbath*, should be kept strictly holy, Amos viii. 5.

Lord's prayer, as it stands in the present authorized version, exhibits the best specimen of our ancient language now in use, Preface to Job.

Lo-ruhamah, import of the name, Hos. i. 6.

Lost property, laws relative to the finding of, among the Hebrews, Romans, and others, Lev. vi. 3.

Lot, meaning and use of the, Num. xxxvi. 55. Manner of casting lots in the case of the scape-goat, Lev. xvi. 8, 9. How the land of Canaan was divided to the Israelites by lot, Josh. xiv. 2, xviii. 11.

Lo techsar, לא תחסר, import of these words when used as a memorial symbol, Masoretic notes at the end of Deuteronomy.

Louis de Dieu, account of this commentator, General Preface, p. 5.

Louis XIV., motto on the brass ordnance of, Judg. xiv. 3.

Love of God, Deut. vi. 5, x. 12, xi. 1.

Love of neighbour, Scripture precept concerning, Lev. xix. 18.

Lowth, (*Dr.*) a very celebrated commentator on portions of the Old Testament Scriptures, General Preface, pp. 8, 10.

Lu, לו, import of this Hebrew interjection when used as a memorial symbol, Masoretic notes at the end of Numbers.

Lucan's description of the splendour of the apartments of Cleopatra, queen of Egypt, Ezek. xxviii. 14.

Lud, the same with Lydia, Ezek. xxvii. 10.

Luther, (*Martin*) character of, 2 Kings xii. 6.

Luxury, formerly the characteristic of the Eastern princes, and particularly of the Persians, Esth. i. 4.

Lying, excellent advice of a genuine Christian poet against, Josh. ii., *in fine.* Saying of Diphilus upon this subject not defensible upon Christian principles, 1 Sam. xxi. 2.

Lyranus, or *Nicholas de Lyra*, account of this commentator, General Preface, p. 3.

M

Maachah, mother of Asa, king of Judah, inquiry into the nature of the idolatry patronized by this woman, 1 Kings xv. 13.

Mabul, מבול, a word applied only to the general deluge, Gen. vi. 17. Its derivation, Gen. vii. 11.

Maccabees, very fanciful rabbinical derivation of the name of this people, Psa. xxi. 15.

Machpelah, cave at, the first public burying-place mentioned in history, Gen. xlix. 29.

Macknight, (*Dr.*) author of a translation of the Epistles, with notes, General Preface, p. 8.

Maedi, a tribe of Arabs, whence so named, Isa. xlii. 11.

Magian religion, great principle of the, Isa. xlv. 7.

Magnet, reasons for believing that this stone was known in the East long before its discovery by the Europeans, Job xxviii. 18.

Magnitudes, *bulks*, or *volumes* of the sun, moon, and planets, compared with that of the earth, Gen. i. 1.

Magog, conjecture where situated, Ezek. xxviii. 2.

Maher-shalal-hash-baz, meaning of the name, Isa. viii. 1.

Maimonides, or *Rabbi Moses ben Maimon*, account of this commentator, General Preface, p. 3.

Major hostia, or *chief sacrifice*, what so considered by the pagans, according to Livy, Lev. i. 2.

Makheloth, the twenty-first station of the Israelites in the wilderness, Num. xxxiii. 25.

Malachi, some account of this prophet, Mal. i., *in principio.*

Maldonat, (*John*) a commentator on particular parts of the Old and New Testaments, General Preface, p. 5.

Manasseh, why so named, Gen. xli. 51.

Mandrakes, some account of these plants, Gen. xxx. 14.

Manes, or *ghosts of the dead*, or *spirits presiding over the dead*, formerly supposed to have their habitation in the centre of the earth, or in the deepest pits or caverns, Job xxviii. 11. A quotation from Ovid to this effect, *ibid.* Several captives have sometimes, in time of war, been sacrificed to the manes of the departed hero, 2 Chron. xvi., *in fine.*

Manifesto of the Duke of Brunswick, reflections on this document, 2 Kings xviii. 17; Isa. xxxvii. 9.

Manna, why so named, Exod. xvi. 15.

Manners of the ancients and moderns compared, 2 Sam. iii., *in fine.*

Mantes, or *bald locusts*, Dr. Shaw's account of the, Joel ii. 2.

Mantle or *pallium*, the peculiar garb of a Hebrew prophet, 1 Kings xix. 19; 2 Kings ii. 8. Probably dressed with the hair on, *ibid.* A sort of mantle was the habit of the Greek philosophers, 1 Kings xix., *in fine.*

Marah, the fourth station of the Israelites in the wilderness, where supposed to be situated, Num. xxxiii. 8.

Marble, temple built of large blocks of white marble, beautifully polished, according to Josephus, 1 Chron. xxix. 2.

Mareshah, *Maresheth*, or *Marasthi*, a place famous for being the birth-place of the prophet Micah, and for a battle fought near it between Asa, king of Judah, and Zerah, king of the Æthiopians, Josh. xv. 44.

Mark, variety of opinions respecting that which God set upon Cain, Gen. iv. 15.

Marks indelibly printed on the hands and other parts of the body, both by ancients and moderns, Isa. xliv. 5, xlvi. 16.

Maroth, מראת, rendered *looking-glasses* in our version, signifies polished metallic surfaces of any description, Exod. xxxviii. 8.

Marriage, a very solemn contract among the ancients, Gen. xxix. 22. Reason for believing that sacrifices were offered and libations poured out on such an occasion, *ibid.* Customary in the East, according to Sir John Chardin, for youths that were never married always to marry virgins, and widowers, however young, to marry widows, Isa. lxii. 5. Remarkable law among the Gentoos respecting marriage, Gen. xxix. 26. Customary in ancient times for a king or great man to promise his daughter in marriage to him who should take a city, kill an enemy, &c., Josh. xv. 16.

Marriage ceremonies among the Romans, Song v. 5.

Marrow, in what manner this substance is contained in the bones, Prov. iii. 8. The solidity and strength of the bone occasioned by the marrow which is diffused through it, *ibid.* This circumstance illustrated by an easy experiment, *ibid.*

Mars, periodic and sidereal revolutions, semimajor axis of orbit in English miles, perigeal and apogeal distances, diameter, relative volume or bulk, time of rotation, inclination of axis to orbit, mass or attractive power compared with that of the earth, (from which the density or specific gravity is easily deducible,) and mean hourly orbitical motion, of this primary planet, Gen. i. 1.

Marseilles, ancient inhabitants of, when afflicted with any pestilence, sacrificed one of their citizens to appease the wrath of the divinity, Lev. xvi. 10.

Martin, (*David*) translator of the Scriptures into French, with notes, General Preface, p. 7.

Maschil or *Maskil*, why this title is given to several of the Psalms, Psa. xxxii., *in principio.*

Mashal, what, among the Hebrews, Isa. vi. 10, xiv. 4, xxviii. 20, xxix. 17.

Mask, definition of a composition so named, Introduction to Solomon's Song.

Masoretes, account of these eminent Jewish commentators, General Preface, p. 2.

Masoretic punctuations, critical observations on the, Isa. lxvi., *in fine.*

Massa, משא, rendered *burden*, inquiry into the meaning of this word, Nah. i. 1; Hab. i. 1; Zech. ix. 1.

Masses, or *attractive powers*, of the sun, moon, and primary planets, compared with that of the earth, Gen. i. 1.

N

Net, description of that species of combat among the Romans, in which one of the combatants was armed with a sword and shield, and the other with a trident and net, Job xix. 6.

Newcome, (*Dr.*) translator of the minor prophets, with critical notes, General Preface, p. 10.

New moon, feast of the, when celebrated, Exod. xxiii. 14; Psa. lxxxi. 3. Method adopted by the ancient Jews of ascertaining the day of the new moon, Psa. lxxxi. 3.

New song, meaning of this phrase illustrated by two quotations from Virgil, Psa. cxlix. 1.

New-year's-day, a time of festivity in all civilized nations, Num. xxix. 1.

Nibhaz, an object of idolatrous worship among the Avites, 2 Kings xvii., *in fine*. According to the rabbins, was in the shape of a dog, much like the Anubis of the Egyptians, *ibid.* Conjecture respecting the derivation of the name, *ibid.* Jurieu's ingenious idea upon this subject, *ibid.*

Night, very philosophical saying of Servius respecting, in his comment upon a passage in the fourth Æneid, Job vii. 2.

Nile, overflowing of the, of essential service in the fertilization of Egypt, Gen. xli. 25, 31; Isa. xviii. 2. Pliny's scale of the different heights to which the waters of the Nile ascend, with the consequent degrees of plenty and dearth, *ibid.* The Nile an object of religious worship among the ancient Egyptians, Exod. vii. 15; viii. 26. Great salubrity and peculiar pleasantness of its waters, Exod. vii. 18. Abounds with incredible numbers of all sorts of fish, according to Diodorus, Isa. xix. 8.

Nilus, a name given to Bacchus, by Diodorus and Macrobius, on account of his being said to have been exposed on the Nile, Exod. iv. 17.

Nimbus. A practice among many nations to represent those men to whom they attributed extraordinary sanctity, and whom they supposed to have had familiar intercourse with the Deity, with a lucid *nimbus* or *glory* round their heads, Exod. xxxiv. 29.

Nimrod, probably the same with Ninus, Gen. x. 11.

Nineveh, some account of this very celebrated city of antiquity, Jonah i. 2, iii. 3. Bishop Newton's remarks upon the fall and irretrievable ruin of Nineveh, Nah. iii., *in fine.*

Ninyas, son of Ninus and Semiramis, supposed by Dr. Shuckford to be the same with Chedorlaomer, Gen. xiv. 1.

Nissah, נסה, rendered *tempt*, what it properly imports, Gen. xxii. 1.

Noah, whence this name is probably derived, Gen. v. 29.

No-Ammon, the Diospolis of the Greeks, Nah. iii. 8.

Nominative case often used for the *vocative* by the ancient Greeks, especially in the Attic dialect of their language, Psa. xlv. 6.

Νομος, its derivation and import, Exod. xii. 49.

Nonnus the poet, quoted Zech. ix. 14. See notes.

Noonday, the time allotted by the heathens for the worshipping of demons, Psa. xci. 6.

Noph, the same which was afterwards named Memphis, and now Cairo, Ezek. xxx. 13; Jer. ii. 16, xlvii. 14.

Northern army, why this name is given to immense swarms of locusts, Joel ii. 20.

Norwich, ancient city of, formerly stood some miles from the modern city so named, Josh. xvi., *in fine.*

Nose or *nostrils*, considered by the ancients the seat of anger, Psa. xviii. 8.

Nose, cutting off the, a frequent punishment of adulterers among the Persians and Chaldeans, Ezek. xxiii. 25. Adulteresses formerly thus treated by the Egyptians, *ibid.*

Nose-ring, or jewel for the nose, of very frequent use in the East, Gen. xxiv. 22; Prov. xxv. 12; Isa. iii. 21.

Nova Zembla, extraordinary instance of refraction of the solar light in this island in the sixteenth century, 2 Kings xx., *in fine.*

Novus, not unfrequently synonymous with *magnus mirandus*, Psa. cxlix. 1.

Numanus, remarkable saying of, to the Trojans, as related by Virgil, Nah. iii. 13.

Numbers, the fourth book of the Pentateuch, why so named, Preface to Numbers.

Numbers in the sacred Scriptures often erroneous, and why, 2 Sam. x. 18.

Nuptial crown, among the Greeks and Romans, what, Song iii. 11.

O

Oak, a sacred tree among the ancient Greeks and Romans, Gen. xxi. 23; the Druids had their feasts and sacrifices under it, *ibid.* Why this tree was named *robur* by the Romans, Hos. iv. 13. Accounted one of the most long-lived of all the trees of the forest, Isa. lxv. 22.

Oath, inquiry into the spirit and essence of an, Gen. xxiv. 9 Deut. vi., *in fine.*

Obadiah, some account of this prophet, Obad., *in principio.*

Obed, the father of Jesse, why so named, Ruth iv. 17.

Obed-edom, very curious and whimsical rabbinical account of the mode in which God is said to have blessed this Gittite, while the ark remained in his house, 1 Chron. xiii. 14.

Oboth, אבות, what this term imports, Lev. xix. 31.

Oboth, אבת, the thirty-sixth station of the Israelites in the wilderness, Num. xxxiii. 43.

Ode, what is generally understood by this term, Introduction to the Song of Solomon. Isaiah's prophetic ode on the destruction of Babylon by the Medes and Persians, and the deliverance of Judah from captivity, a composition of supreme and singular excellence, standing unrivalled among all the monuments of classic antiquity, Isa. xiii., *in principio.*

Oded, remarks on the beautiful speech of this prophet to the Israelites, 2 Chron. xxviii. 9.

Offerings, Jewish, general account of the, Lev. vii., *in fine.* The reference in which they all stood to the great sacrifice offered by Christ, *ibid.*

Og, king of Bashan, remarks upon his very great stature, Deut. iii. 11. Extreme trifling of the rabbins upon this subject, *ibid.*

Oil, anointing with, an ancient method of installation to particular offices, Exod. xxix. 7.

Oil, holy anointing, its component parts, and the quantity of each ingredient, Exod. xxx. 21.

Oil, trial by boiling, a species of ordeal among the Hindoos, Num. v., *in fine.*

Olam, עולם, inquiry into its general import, Gen. xiii. 15, xvii. 7, 8, xxi. 33; Exod. xii. 14; Num. xxv. 13; 2 Kings v. 27; Eccles. iii. 11, 12, xii. 15; Mic. v. 2; Hab. iii. 6.

Olam haba, עולם הבא, *the world to come*, a phrase applied by the Jews to the days of the Messiah, Heb. ii. 5.

Old age, great reverence paid to, by the ancient and modern Egyptians, Gen. xlviii. 12; by the ancient Romans, *ibid.*; and even to this day by the Mohammedans, *ibid.* Bacon's grand secret for the strengthening of the natural heat in aged persons, Ruth iv. 16; 1 Kings i., *in fine.*

Olives, mount of, Zech. xiv. 4.

Omer, some account of this Hebrew measure of capacity, Exod. xvi. 16.

Omniscience of God, thoughts concerning the, Gen. xvi. 15.

On or *Aven*, the famous Heliopolis, Ezek. xxx. 17.

Only Son, Christ the, see on Psa. xxii. 20.

Onycha, account of this perfume, Exod. xxx. 34.

Onyx, the name of a precious stone, whence it has its name, Gen. ii. 12; Exod. xxv. 7; Job xxviii. 16. The Hebrew word so translated of uncertain import, Exod. xxviii. 17.

Opal, its component parts, Job xxxviii. 38.

Opes, riches, whence derived, Gen. xxxiii. 19.

Ophel, a part of Mount Sion, rising higher than the rest, Isa. xxxii. 14.

Ophiamanteia of the Greeks, what, Lev. xix. 26.

Ophir, situation of, utterly unknown, 1 Kings ix. 28. Dr. Jubb's conjecture, Isa. ii. 13–16.

Ophthalmia, how generally caused in Egypt, Deut. xxviii. 24.

Optic nerve, account of the, Eccles. xii. 3.

Oracles of the heathens expressed in such dubious language as to appear to be fulfilled in whatever way the events might happen, 1 Kings xxii. 15. Some examples produced, *ibid.* The pagan oracles generally delivered their answers from some deep and obscure cavern, Isa. xlv. 19.

Orange garden of the emir of Beroot, Maundrell's description of the, Isa. i. 30.

Orbits, mean hourly motions of the primary planets in their, Gen. i. 1. Inclination of the axes of rotation of the earth, moon, Mars, Jupiter, and Saturn to the planes of their orbits, Gen. i. 1. Angles with the semidiameters of the orbits of the satellites of Jupiter, Saturn, and Herschel subtend, as seen from the earth, when the radii vectores of their primaries are equal to one half of the latera transversa, or principal diameters of the eclipses in which they move round the sun, *ibid.*

Ordeal, trial by, some account of the, Num. v., *in fine.* Why called *Judicium Dei*, "The judgment of God," *ibid.* Supposed to have taken its origin from the waters of jealousy, *ibid.*

Oreb, a prince of the Midianites, import of his name, Judg. vii. 25.

Origen, account of this commentator, General Preface, p. 3. Specimens of his very fanciful interpretation of Scripture, Exod. i., *in fine.* Num. xii. 14. His thoughts on the miracle of the fleece, dew, and dry ground, Judg. vi., *in fine.* Origen's account of a dispute he had with some of the Jews relative to a passage in Isaiah, Isa. liii. 8.

P

Philo Judæus, account of this Jewish commentator, General Preface, p. 2.

Philosopher, anecdote of a, Jer. v. 1. Remarkable saying of a philosopher when at sea in a violent storm, Jonah i. 7.

Φιλοσοφος, probable origin of this word, Gen. xli. 8.

Phlegon, one of the horses of the sun, according to the pagan mythology, what the name signifies, 2 Kings ii. 11.

Phoceans, remarkable imprecation of the, when resolved to leave their country, and never to revisit it, Jer. li. 64.

Phocylides, citation of a very remarkable passage from this poet, Jer. ix. 24.

Phosphorescence of the sea in certain states of the weather, Job xli. 32.

Phrygians, Bochart's conjecture concerning their origin, Gen. x. 2.

Phut, a people of Africa, Ezek. xxvii. 10.

Phylacteries, particular account of the, Exod. xiii. 9.

Pibeseth, probably the same with Bubastum, or Bubaste, Ezek. xxx. 17.

Pihahiroth, the third station of the Israelites in the wilderness, what supposed to be its present appellation, Num. xxxiii. 7.

Pikudim, פקדים, its derivation and import, Lev. xxvi. 15.

Pilgash, פלגש, rendered *concubine*, inquiry into its import, Gen. xxii. 24, xxxiv. 31.

Pilgrim, a word of French or Latin origin, Gen. xlvii. 9.

Pilkington's reasons for the supposition that from the 12th to the 31st verse of the first book of Samuel is an interpolation of some rabbin, 1 Sam. xvii., *in fine*.

Pillar of a cloud in the wilderness, observations concerning the, Exod. xiii. 21, xiv. 20.

Pillar of salt into which Lot's wife was changed, various opinions and legends concerning the, Gen. xix. 26.

Pillars of heaven, what intended by this strongly figurative expression, Job xxvi. 11.

Pindar's elegant ridicule of the work of the statuary, when set in competition with his own poetry, Isa. xlvi. 3.

Pinna magna, a species of muscle found on the shores of the Mediterrenean, 1 Chron. xv. 27; Prov. xxxi. 22. Description of a pair of gloves which the author has seen made of this very rich stuff, *ibid*.

Piscator, (*John*) author of a comment on the whole Scriptures, General Preface, p. 6.

Pitcher broken at the fountain, what meant by this phrase, Eccles. xii. 6.

Pitfall or *fovea*, among the ancients, what, Psa. vii. 15, lvii. 6; Isa. xxiv. 17, 18; Ezek. xix. 4.

Plagues of Egypt, times of their happening, according to Archbishop Usher, Exod. vii. 17. Critical observations on these Divine judgments, Exod. vii., *et seq.* Seven of these plagues more largely described in the Samaritan copies than in the Hebrew, Exod. xi., *in fine*. Translation of the *eleventh* chapter of Exodus from the Samaritan text ranged in collateral columns with that in our common version, to show the great additions in the former, *ibid*. General observations on the ten plagues of Egypt, Exod. xii., *in fine*.

Plane tree, conjectures why this tree was so named, Gen. xxv. 37.

Planets, primary and secondary, tables of their revolutions, distances, &c., Gen. i. 1. To prevent mistake, it will be proper to observe that the least and greatest distances of the planets and satellites from the earth, contained in these tables, are their perigeal and apogeal distances when the radii vectores of the planets are equal to the semimajor axes of their orbits, the earth being in every case assumed to be at its mean distance from the sun. But on account of the eccentricities of the planetary orbits, the distances of the planets from the earth, when in *perigee* and *apogee*, are very variable. The nearest possible approaches of the inferior planets Mercury and Venus to the earth (viz., when the inferior conjunction of each takes place in the higher apsis) are, respectively, 52,376,602 and 27,339,176 English miles. The greatest possible distances of these planets from the earth (viz., when the superior conjunction of each is made in the aphelion) are, respectively, 138,620,495 and 163,667,549 English miles. The perigeal distances of Mars, Jupiter, Saturn, and Herschel (when the opposition of each to the sun takes place in the lower apsis or perihelion) are respectively, 35,357,826, 376,944,330, 766,223,200, and 1,642,663,450 English miles. The greatest possible apogeal distances of these planets (viz., when the conjunction of each with the sun is in the higher apsis) are, respectively, 255,709,508, 616,586,248, 1,056,059,684 and 2,002,487,006 English miles. In these calculations the eccentricities of the orbits of the planets, in English miles, have been assumed as follows:—that of Mercury, 7,598,601; Venus, 471,320; the Earth, 1,604,800; Mars, 13,665,466; Jupiter, 24,346,964; Saturn, 50,988,386; and Herschel, 85,035,892.

Plant of renown, observations on the Hebrew words thus rendered, Ezek. xxxiv. 29.

Platforms common on the houses of the East, Judg. iii. 20.

Plato, republic of, thoughts concerning the, Deut. xxxiv., *in fine*.

Pledge of the beard, in the East, the most secure of all pledges, which the owner will redeem at the hazard of his life, 2 Sam. x. 4.

Pleiades, Hebrew word so translated of very uncertain import, Job ix. 9, xxxviii. 31.

Ploughing the foundations of cities, a custom among ancient conquerors to signify an *irreparable and total destruction*, Mic. iii. 12.

Ploughing with one's heifer, or *ploughing in another man's ground*, what meant by this phrase among the ancient Jews, Greeks, and Romans, Judg. xiv. 18.

Ploughing iniquity and reaping the same, a proverbial mode of expression, illustrated by quotations from sacred and profane writers, Job iv. 8.

Plutarch's account of a man who, aiming a blow at his enemy's life, cut open an imposthume, which, by a salutary discharge, saved his life, Prov. xxvii. 5.

Poetic compositions, titles of, among the Asiatics, frequently bore no resemblance to the subjects, Psa. xxii., *in principio*. Many examples produced, *ibid*.

Poetry in use among all nations from the remotest antiquity, Exod. xv. 1. Its advantages pointed out, *ibid.;* Deut. xxxi. 19. Character of the Hebrew poetry; and its great superiority, in many respects, over that of any other nation, Isa. ii. 13–16.

Poison, trial by, a species of ordeal among the Hindoos, Num. v., *in fine*.

Poison of serpents supposed by the ancients to consist in their gall, which is thought to be copiously exuded when these animals are enraged, Job xx. 16.

Polygamy tolerated under the Mosaic dispensation, 2 Sam. v. 13. Shown to be unnatural, and what could not have entered into the original design of God, *ibid.;* Mal. ii. 14, 15.

Polytheism, in some of its branches, so utterly contemptible, that it became an object of ridicule among the more serious heathens, Psa. cxv. 4. Quotation of a remarkable passage from Juvenal to this effect, *ibid*.

Poole, (*Matthew*) account of this commentator, General Preface, pp. 7, 11.

Pools, Maundrell's description of the supposed remains of those made by Solomon for the reception and preservation of the waters of a spring, Isa. i. 30.

Popilius, remarkable anecdote concerning this Roman legate, Dan. xi. 30.

Porte, the, why the Ottoman court was probably so named, Isa. xxix. 21.

Postdiluvian patriarchs, table of the great discrepances in the Hebrew, Samaritan, and Septuagint copies, with respect to the times they are stated to have lived before their sons' birth, Gen. v. 3.

Potters' wheel, description of the, Jer. xviii. 3.

Præster, terrible effects of the bite of the, as described by Lucan, Num. xxi. 6.

Prayer, observations on, Psa. lxxxviii. 2. Citation of a very remarkable passage from the Iliad upon this subject, *ibid*.

Prayers to angels and departed saints, examination of a passage in the Psalms which the Romanists allege in favour of, Psa. cxxxviii. 1.

Preaching from a text, probable origin of, Neh. viii., *in fine*.

Precession of the equinoxes, quantity of the, in 4138 years, Job ix., *in fine*. The precession caused by a very slow revolution of the celestial poles around the poles of the ecliptic, Psa. xix. 5. See *Equinoctial points, precession of the*.

Predestination, unconditional, to eternal life and to eternal death, cannot be supported by the example of God's dealings with Jacob and Esau, or their posterity, Gen. xxv. 23, xxvii. 28–40, *et in fine;* xxix. 31; Mal. i. 3.

Presents to the great indispensable in Eastern countries, Isa. lvii. 9. When accepted by the superior, a certain pledge of favour, Gen. xxxiii. 10. Offered with very great ceremony, Judg. iii. 18. Numerous examples in Homer and other ancient writers of presents of arms and clothing made by warriors to each other in token of friendship, 1 Sam. xviii. 4.

Prevent, acceptation of this term among our English ancestors, Psa. xxi. 3. Whence derived, *ibid*.

Pride ever makes its possessor unhappy, Esth. v. 13. Examples produced, *ibid*.

Prideaux's account of the monies of different nations, Exod. xxxix. 24.

Priesthood, Jewish and pagan, none eligible to the, that had any sort of blemish, Lev. xxi. 17–21.

Q

R

Raiment, shaking of the, what it imported among the ancient Jews, Neh. v. 13.
Rain, how produced, Gen. ii. 6; Exod. ix. 27; Job xxxvi. 27; Eccles. i. 7. Rain, according to St. Jerome, never falls in Judea in the time of harvest, 1 Sam. xii. 17. Times of the *former* and *latter* rain, Jer. iii. 3, v. 24.
Rainbow, origin and nature of the, Gen. ix. 13. Reasons for believing that this phenomenon was of as frequent occurrence *before* as *after* the flood, *ibid.* Quotations from Homer and Virgil to show that both the Greeks and Romans considered the rainbow as a Divine token or portent, Gen. ix. 17.
Rakesh, רקש, rendered *dromedaries,* probably means *post-horse,* 1 Kings iv. 28.
Rakia, רקיע, translated *firmament,* proper meaning of the term, Gen. i. 6.
Ram, a sacred animal among the Egyptians, Exod. viii. 26. Eusebius's reasons for this, *ibid.* Rams with *red* or *violet-coloured* fleeces often mentioned by ancient writers, Exod. xxv. 5.
Rameses, the same with *Goshen,* Gen. xlvi. 28, 34, xlvii. 23.
Ramoth, one of the cities of refuge, import of the name, Josh. xx. 7.
Ranges for pots, description of an Arabian custom to which this expression has an allusion, Lev. xi. 35.
Rape of the Sabine women, substance of Livy's account of the, Judg. xxi., *in fine.*
Raphelius, (*G.*) an eminent Biblical critic, General Preface, p. 12.
Rash judgments, doubly pernicious, 2 Sam. vi. 22.
Rashim, ראשים, a degree of civil distinction among the Hebrews, Josh. xxiii. 2.
Ravens, arguments to show that Elijah was not fed by these birds, as stated in our English version, but that the Hebrew word ערבים *orbim,* is probably the name of a people that lived in or near Arabia, 1 Kings xvii., *in fine.*
Rebellion against the state, act of, defined, Judg. iii., *in fine;* Ezra iv. 19.
Rechabites, short sketch of their history, Jer. xxxv. 2.
Red heifer, remarks upon several curious particulars respecting the ordinance of the, Num. xix. 2.
Red Sea, conjecture why so named, Exod. x. 19; Num. xxiii. 10. Description of its two gulfs, *ibid.* Observations upon the miraculous separation of its waters in the time of Moses, Exod. xiv. 21, *et in fine.* The sixth station of the Israelites in the wilderness was in the vicinity of this sea, Num. xxxiii. 10. Manifest allusion, in the book of Job, to the miraculous passage of the Israelites through the Red Sea, Job xxvi. 12.
Redeemer of blood, who, among the Jews, Num. xxxv. 19.
Redemption of the first-born, a rite still practised among the Jews, Num. xviii. 16. How performed, according to Leo of Modena, *ibid.*
Refraction, observations on the nature of, 2 Kings xx., *in fine.* Extraordinary refraction of the rays of light in Nova Zembla in the year 1596, *ibid.*
Rehoboam, Houbigant's conjecture relative to the age of this prince at the commencement of his reign over Judah, 2 Chron. xii. 13.
Religion, in its pure state, the strongest bulwark of the state, 1 Chron. xxvi., *in fine.* Definition of true religion, Gen. ix. 20; Prov. i. 7.
Remes, רמש, translated *creeping thing,* inquiry into its import, Gen. i. 24.
Remigius of Auxerre, a commentator on the twelve minor prophets, General Preface, p. 4.
Rending the clothes, a mark of deep affliction and distress among the ancients, Josh. vii. 6; 1 Sam. iv. 12; Ezra ix. 3; Job i. 20, ii. 12; Jer. xvi. 6.
Renominatus, derivation and import of this Latin term, Gen. vi. 4.
Rephaim, valley of, celebrated for its plentiful harvest, Isa. xvii. 5. Used poetically for any fruitful country, *ibid.*
Rephidim, the tenth station of the Israelites in the wilderness, Num. xxxiii. 14.
Reprobation, unconditional, doctrine of, demonstrated to be a lie against all the attributes of Deity, Psa. cxlv. 9; Jer. xviii. 6.
Responsive songs, frequent among the ancient Jews, Isa. vi. 3, xxvii. 2, xl. 9.
Restitution, doctrine of, Gen. xlii., *in fine.*
Resurrection of the dead, doctrine of the, a popular and common doctrine among the Jews long before the advent of our Lord, Isa. xxvi. 19, xlv. 8.
Retiarius, among the Romans, who, Job xix. 6; Mic. vii. 2.
Reuben, import of the name, Gen. xxix. 32.
Revelation of God, particular explanation of the various terms employed to point out different properties of the, Lev. xxvi. 15; Psa. cxix., *in principio.*
Reverend, and *most reverend,* observations on these ecclesiastical titles, Psa. cxi. 9.
Revolutions, periodic and *sidereal,* of the sun, moon, and planets, Gen. i. 1. Periodic and synodic revolutions of the satellites of Jupiter, Saturn, and the Georgium Sidus, *ibid.*
Riblah, where this ancient city was situated, Jer. xxxix. 5.
Rice, method practised by the ancients of sowing this grain, Eccles. xi. 1; Isa. xxxii. 20.
Rice, trial by, a species of ordeal among the Hindoos, Num. v., *in fine.*
Riches, instances of immense, possessed by some of the ancients, Esth. iii. 9.
Ricinus or *Palma Christi,* account of the, as given by Celsus, Jonah iv. 6.
Ricknild or *Icknild-street,* where situated, Job xxiii. 11.
Riddles or *enigmas,* customary among the ancient Greeks to propose such at entertainments, and to give a recompense to those who found them out, Judg. xiv. 14. Examples of Greek enigmas, with their solutions, *ibid.* From what the English word *riddle* is derived, Ezek. xvii. 2.
Ridorus, (*C. Cæcilius*) immense wealth of this individual, Esth. iii. 9.
Righteous and *righteousness,* true etymology of these words, Psa. xii. 8. Their import, *ibid.*
Rimmon, a Syrian idol, possibly the same with the Remphan of the New Testament, 2 Kings v. 26. Supposed by Selden to be the same with Elion, a god of the Phœnicians, *ibid.* Other suppositions, *ibid.*
Rimmon-parez, the fifteenth station of the Israelites in the wilderness, Num. xxxiii. 19.
Ring of Saturn, its perigeal and apogeal distances, diameter, time of rotation, and inclination of axis to the orbit of the planet, Gen. i. 1.
Rings of gold, ensigns of civil power among the ancients, Psa. lxxiii. 6.
Rissah, the seventeenth station of the Israelites in the wilderness, Num. xxxiii. 21.
Rithmah, the fourteenth station of the Israelites in the wilderness, where situated, and why so named, Num. xxxiii. 18.
River of the pool, see *Pallacopas.*
Robe of the Jewish high priest, description of the, Exod. xxviii. 4, 31.
Rock in Horeb, some account of the, Exod. xvii. 6; Psa. cv. 41. Its present appearance, *ibid.*
Rock of a sword, meaning of this phrase, Deut. viii. 8.
Rolls of the Jews, how made, and in what manner written upon, Jer. xxxvi. 2; Ezek. ii. 9, 10.
Roman moneys, table of the, Exod. xxxviii. 24.
Rome, Ovid's account of the ceremonies used in laying the foundations of the walls of the city of, Neh. xii. 27.
Ropes of great strength made in Ireland of the fibres of bog-wood, or the larger roots of the fir, Judg. xvi. 7. Ropes made of the leaves of the flag by the Egyptians, Job viii. 11.
Rotations of the sun, moon, and planets, in what times performed, Gen. i. 1.
Rough garments of the ancient prophets, some account of the, Zech. xiii. 4.
Royal river, see *Naharmalca.*
Ruach, רוח, various opinions concerning the meaning of this word, Gen. i. 2; Eccles. iii. 21.
Ruby, some account of the oriental, Job xxviii. 18. Its component parts, Job xxxviii. 38.
Rushn Achter's extraordinary fortune as expressed in a Persian couplet, Eccles. iv. 15.
Ruth, book of, uncertain by whom written, Preface to Ruth. Sum of its history, *ibid.*
Rutty, (*Dr. John*) extract from his Spiritual Diary, Introduction to the Psalms.

S

Saady, beautiful couplet in this poet, in which the work of total desolation is most forcibly expressed, Job xviii. 15.
Saba, reservoir of, description of this stupendous work of antiquity, Isa. i. 30. By whom supposed to have been constructed, *ibid.*
Sabbath, observations on the institution of the, Gen. ii. 3. Rigorous observances of this day by the ancient Jews, Exod. xvi. 29.
Sabbatus, Houbigant's excellent observations on the remarkable fulfilment of the prophecy that the land of Israel should enjoy her Sabbaths in a state of desolation which the Israelites had profaned in the time of their prosperity, Lev. xxvi. 34.

Sabbatical year, reasons for its institution, according to Calmet, Exod. xxiii. 11.
Sabeans, from whom descended, Gen. xxv. 3. In the opinion of Bruce, a distinct people from the Ethiopians, 1 Kings x. 1.
Sabeism, in what this idolatrous system of religion consisted, Job xxxi. 26.
Sabine women, account of the rape of the, Judg. xxi., *in fine.*
Sacceans, from whom thought to have descended, Gen. xxv. 2.
Sack, שׂק, a word that has passed into a great number of languages, Job xvi. 15.
Sackbut, why this musical instrument was probably so named, Dan. iii. 5.
Sacred hieroglyphics, explanation of the, Introduction to Isaiah.
Sacrifices, design of the, under the Mosaic economy, *twofold*, Gen. ix. 20. No genuine religion could ever possibly exist without sacrifice *actually offered* or *implied*, *ibid.*
Sakar, שכר, the same with the date or palm wine, according to Theodoret and Chrysostom, Isa. v. 11, xxiv. 9.
Salam, sacredness of this word of salutation among the Arabs, Gen xxxvii. 4; 1 Sam. x. 4.
Salisbury, ancient city of, was not situated where the modern city of the same name now stands, Josh. xvi., *in fine.*
Salonius, bishop of Vienna, account of this commentator, General Preface, p. 4.
Salsaria, salsolo, or *saltwort*, an extensive genus of plants, Job xxx. 4.
Salt, an essential ingredient in all offerings, Jewish or pagan, Lev. ii. 13.
Salt, sowing a place with, a custom in different nations to express permanent desolation and abhorrence, Josh. ix. 45. Some examples produced, *ibid.*
Salt Sea, where situated, Gen. xix. 45; Num. xxxiv. 3.
Salutation, various forms of, Gen. xxix. 6, xxxvii. 4, xliii. 29, xlviii. 20; 1 Sam. x. 4.
Samaria, slight sketch of its history, 1 Kings xvi. 24. Its modern appellation, Isa. xxviii. 1.
Samaritan text, some account of the, General Preface, p. 20.
Samaritan version, character of the, General Preface, p. 20.
Samaritans, their present condition, according to Baron Sylvestre de Lacy, 2 Kings xvii. 27.
Samiel, a pestilential east wind, 1 Kings xx., *in fine.*
Samson, why probably so named, Judg. xiii. 24. Sketch of his character, Judg. xvi., *in fine.*
Samuel, derivation and import of the name, 1 Sam. i. 28. Sketch of the character of this prophet, 1 Sam. xxv., *in fine.*
Samuel, books of, very uncertain by whom written, Preface to 1 Samuel. Calmet's conjecture concerning, *ibid.* Several reasons advanced to show that the twenty-first chapter of the second book of Samuel, as it stands in the Hebrew, is in a state of great corruption, 2 Sam. xxi., *in fine.*
Sanctification, Scripture doctrine of, Exod. xiii. 2.
Sanctuary, a part of the tabernacle, why so named, Exod. xxv. 8. Its typical import, *ibid.*
Sandal tree, some account of the, Num. xxiv. 6.
Santeer, an Egyptian instrument of music, probably the same with the *psaltery*, Dan. iii. 5. Dr. Russel's description of it, *ibid.*
Sapphire, description of this precious stone, Exod. xxiv. 10; Job xxviii. 16; Ezek. i. 26.
Saracens, memorable defeat of the, by the Spaniards, Ezek. xxxix. 9.
Sarah, wife of Abraham, import of her name, Gen. xvii. 5. In what this name possibly differs from Sarai, *ibid.*
Sarbal, סרבל, rendered *hat*, what its real import, Dan. iii. 21.
Sarcasm, remarkable example of this figure of speech, Ezek. xxxv. 6.
Sard, some account of this precious stone, Job xxviii. 16.
Sardius, description of this precious stone, Exod. xxviii. 17.
Sardonyx, account of this precious stone, Job xxviii. 16.
Sarepta or *Zarephath*, its present condition according to Maundrell, 1 Kings xvii. 9.
Saris, סריס, import of this word, Gen. xxxviii. 36.
Satan, שטן, *Σατανας*, meaning of this word, 1 Kings v. 4, xi. 14; Job i. 6, 7. Not found in the plural number in the originals of the Old and New Testaments, and the reason assigned, Job i. 6. Observations on the permission given to this great adversary to tempt man, Job xiii., *in fine.*
Satellites of Jupiter, Saturn, and *Herschel* or the *Georgium Sidus*, tables of their motions, distances, &c., Gen. i. 1. Radii of the orbits of these satellites in parts of the ecliptic, as seen from the earth, when their primaries are at their mean distances from, and in quartile aspect with, the sun, Gen. i. 1. See *Orbit.*
Saturn, periodic and sidereal revolutions, semimajor axis of orbit in English miles, mean perigeal and apogeal distances, diameter, proportional bulk, time of rotation, inclination of axis to orbit, mass, and mean hourly orbitical motion, of this primary planet, Gen. i. 1.
Saul, his tragical end, with a sketch of his character, 1 Sam. xxxi. The appearance of Samuel to this king after the prophet's death shown to have been wholly independent of the incantations of the witch of Endor, 1 Sam. xxviii. 14.
Saul's malady, Dr. Scheuchzer's theory respecting, 1 Sam. xvi. 14.
Saurin's singular apostrophe to Louis XIV., when treating of the banishment of the Protestants from France by the revocation of the edict of Nantz, 2 Sam. ii. 5.
Sauromates, from whom descended, according to Calmet, Gen. x. 3.
Scale, Ainsworth's conjecture concerning the derivation of this word, Gen. xx. 16.
Scape-goat, ceremonies concerning the, and its very expressive typical import, Lev. xvi.
Scaurus, (*M.*) valuation of his furniture which was burnt at Tusculum, Esth. iii. 9.
Sceptre, swearing by the, usual among the ancients, Num. xvii. 8. Quotations from Homer and Virgil illustrative of the form of this oath, *ibid.*
Sceptre of gold worn by the ancient princes of Persia, Esth. v. 2. Citation from Xenophon in illustration of this, *ibid.*
Scheuchzer, (*Dr. I. James*) author of an elaborate work on the natural history of the Bible, General Preface, p. 9.
Sciences and arts, the late amazing and extraordinarily rapid discoveries and improvements in every department of the, shown to be not the effect of *chance*, but the result of a most gracious *providence* of God in behalf of his intelligent offspring, Exod. xxviii. 3.
Schism in religion defined, Josh. xxii., *in fine.*
Schoettgenius, (*Christian*) author of Horæ Hebraicæ et Talmudicæ in Universum Novum Testamentum, General Preface, p. 7.
Schultens, (*Albert*) a commentator on the book of Job, General Preface, p. 7.
Scinocephalus, an animal peculiarly sacred to the ancient Egyptians, 2 Kings xvii., *in fine.* Of what it was reputed hieroglyphical, and for what purpose kept in their temples, *ibid.*
Scoffers, manner in which they turned into ridicule the warnings of God by his prophets, Isa. xxviii. 9.
Scorpion, a military weapon among the Romans, why so named, 1 Kings xii. 11.
Scotch woman, remarkable anecdote of a, Job xxxiv. 28.
Scott, (*Rev. T.*) author of a very useful commentary on the Scriptures, General Preface, p. 9.
Scriptures, how divided by the Jews, Zech. vii. 7.
Scythians, whence they had their origin, Gen. x. 2. The Gog of Ezekiel, according to Houbigant, Ezek. xxxviii. 2.
Seah, what this Hebrew measure contained, according to Bishop Cumberland, Gen. xviii. 6. See also Exod. xvi. 16.
Sealing up transgression in a bag, what meant by this expression among the ancients, Job xiv. 17.
Seals, for sealing clay, frequent in the East, Job xxxviii. 13. Description of six of these seals in the author's possession, *ibid.*
Seasons of the year, time of their commencement, according to the Copts, Gen. vii. 22.
Sebaste, the ancient Samaria, Isa. xxviii. 1. *Maundrell's* account of its situation, *ibid.*
Secondary planets, revolutions, distances, magnitudes, &c., of the, Gen. i. 1.
Sectarian marks of the ancients and moderns, some account of the, Lev. xix. 28. More largely explained, Deut. xxxii. 5; Isa. xliv. 5, xlvi. 16; Ezek. ix. 4.
Sections of the law, table of the, as read in the different Jewish synagogues for every Sabbath of the year; in which are incorporated the *haphtaroth* or *sections of the prophets*, as they are appointed to be read in the synagogues of the Portuguese and Italian, and the German and Dutch Jews, Deut. xxxiv., *in fine.* To determine the order of the reading the *pareshioth* and *haphtaroth* for any given Jewish year, the following tables, inserted at the end of the notes on Deuteronomy, have been carefully constructed:—I. A perpetual table, showing, through the course of thirteen lunar cycles (which embrace every possible variation) the day of the week with which the Jewish year begins and on which the passover is held; as also the lengths of the months

T

Tahapanes or *Tahpanhes*, a city of Egypt, the same with Daphne, Jer. ii. 16, xliii. 7. According to Jerome, the place where Jeremiah was stoned to death, Jer. xliii. 7.
Tahath, the twenty-second station of the Israelites in the wilderness, Num. xxxiii. 26.
Taisnier, author of a famous work on chiromancy, Job xxxvii. 7.
Tale, its derivation and import, Exod. v. 8.
Talent of gold among the Hebrews, what was its value, Exod. xxxviii. 24. Valuation of the Babylonish talent of gold and silver, *ibid.* Calculation of the value, in British standard, of the 120 talents of gold which the queen of Sheba gave to King Solomon, 2 Chron. x., *in fine.* Valuation of the *six hundred and sixty-six* talents of gold that came to Solomon in one year, 1 Kings x. 14; 2 Chron. ix., *in fine.*
Talmud of Babylon, account of the, General Preface, p. 2.
Talmud of Jerusalem, account of the, General Preface, p. 2.
Tambellit, Sir John Chardin's account of the, Gen. xlii. 25.
Tammuz, see *Thammuz.*
Tancred, banner of, what, Psa. lx., *in fine.*
Tanneenim, תנינם, translated *whales*, inquiry into the import of this word, Gen. i. 21.
Tarah, the twenty-third station of the Israelites in the wilderness, Num. xxxiii. 27.
Targets of beaten gold, calculation of the value of the *two hundred* which Solomon put in the house of the forest of Lebanon, 2 Chron. x., *in fine.*
Targum on the two books of Chronicles, attributed to R. Joseph the Blind, account of the, General Preface, p. 2; Preface to the two books of Chronicles.
Targum, or *Chaldee paraphrase* on Solomon's Song, given at full length, Song of Solomon, *in fine.*
Targum ascribed to Jonathan ben Uzziel, account of the General Preface, p. 2.
Targum Yerushlemey, account of the, General Preface, p. 1.
Tarrentes, Vinisauf's account of, Exod. viii. 16.
Tarshish, the place to which Jonah attempted to flee, various conjectures where situated, Jonah i. 3. Dr. Jubb's reason for thinking that to go to *Tarshish* and to *Ophir* is one and the same thing, Isa. ii. 13–16.
Tartak, an object of idolatrous worship among the Avites, 2 Kings xvii., *in fine.* Whence the name is probably derived, according to Parkhurst, *ibid.* What the *emblem* of this idol, according to the Jews, *ibid.*
Tartan, the name of an *office*, and not a *person*, according to Calmet, 2 Kings xviii. 17.
Tartars or *Tatars*, their origin, Gen. x. 2.
Tartarus or *hell*, opinion of the ancients respecting, Job xxvi. 6.
Tatian, author of a Harmony of the Four Gospels, General Preface, p. 3.
Tatnai's letter to Darius, remarks on, Ezra v., *in fine.*
Tau, the last letter of the Hebrew alphabet, why probably so named, Psa. lxxviii. 41. Its form on the ancient Samaritan coins still extant, Ezek. ix. 4.
Taylor, *(Dr.)* remarkable reply of, to his persecutors, Job xix. 22.
Tebeth, תבה, rendered *ark*, what it properly signifies, Gen. vi. 14.
Teeth, description of the, Eccles. xii. 4. Names and uses of the three kinds of, in the human subject, *ibid.*
Tehaphnehes, Tahpanhes, or *Tahapanes*, the same with the Pelusian Daphne, Ezek. xxx. 18. See *Tahapanes.*
Telesm, corruptly called *talisman*, whence derived, and what it signifies, Num. xxxiii. 41; 1 Sam. vi., *in fine.* Description and reported virtues of several telesms, 1 Sam. vi., *in fine.*
Temple, Dr. Delaney's remarks on the Divine original of the architecture of the, 1 Chron. xxviii. 18. Reflections on the spoliation of the temple by Titus, Exod. xxv. 31.
Temple of Solomon, dimensions of the, in English measure, 1 Kings vi. 2. Reason why neither hammer, axe, nor any tool of iron, was suffered to be heard in the temple during the time of its building, 1 Kings vi. 7. Its description and history, according to Calmet and Josephus, 1 Kings vi., *in fine.*
Temple of Diana at Ephesus, some account of this celebrated edifice, 1 Kings vi., *in fine.*
Tent, portable, a necessary part of a traveller's baggage in countries subject to violent tempests, Isa. iv. 6.
Tents, feast of, a pagan festival of antiquity, in imitation of the Jewish feast of tabernacles, Lev. xxiii. 34.
Teraphim, various opinions concerning the, Gen. xxxi. 19; 1 Sam. xviii. 13; Isa. ii. 8.
Terebinth tree, the אלה, *ellah* of Isaiah, according to Celsius, Isa. i. 29, 30.
Terminus, see *Landmark.*
Terror or *formido*, description of the, used by the ancients in hunting, Isa. xxiv. 17, 18.
Tertullian, quotation of a remarkable passage from, to show that the heathens borrowed many of their religious rites from the Hebrews, Exod. xxvii., *in fine.* Quotation from a work against the heretic Marcion, attributed to Tertullian, respecting Gideon's three hundred men who were victorious over the Midianites, Judg. vii. 20.
Thammuz or *Tammuz*, probably the same with Adonis, Ezek. viii. 3. Meaning of the name, Ezek. viii. 14.
Tharafah, an eminent Arabic poet, Psa. lx., *in principio.*
T'heb, anecdote of a prince who was required to pronounce this word, Judg. xii. 6.
Thebais, mountains of the desert of, described, Deut. xxxii. 10.
Thebes, city of, the *No* of Jeremiah, see chap. xlvi. 25. Whence the fable respecting the manner of its being built probably originated, 2 Chron. xxxiv.
Theocracy, the political state of the Jews, before the reign of Saul, Judg. iii. 10; 1 Sam. viii. 5.
Theodotion, a translator of the Hebrew Scriptures into Greek, some account of, General Preface, p. 21.
Theodulus of Cœlesyria, a commentator on the Epistle to the Romans, General Preface, p. 4.
Theophilus of Antioch, a commentator on the Four Gospels, General Preface, p. 4.
Theophylact, account of this commentator, General Preface, p. 4.
Θεος, several citations from the Septuagint in which this word with the article prefixed has the import of Θεε, *O God*, Psa. xlv. 8.
Thomas, import of this name, Gen. xxv. 24.
Thracians, from whom descended, Gen. x. 2.
Three, a mystical number in Scripture, according to Ainsworth, Gen. xxii. 4.
Three and four times, a mode of expression among the ancients, denoting *abundance and excess*, Amos i. 3. Several examples produced, *ibid.*
Threshing, different ways of, in use among the Hebrews, and the manner of performing them, Isa. xxviii. 27, 28.
Threshing-floors, Cato's directions in the construction of, 1 Sam. xxiii., *in fine.* How to be constructed, according to Columella, *ibid.*
Throne, description of a, by Athenæus, Isa. lii. 2.
Throne of Solomon, curious account of the, extracted from a Persian manuscript, 2 Chron. x., *in fine.*
Thunder and lightning, according to the pagans, the mode by which Jupiter testified his approbation of the sacrifices offered to him, Lev. ix. 23.
Thunder clap, how caused by the lightning, Job xxxviii. 26. Illustrated by an easy experiment on the air pump, *ibid.*
Thunder cloud, rule by which its distance from the spectator of the lightning issuing from it is calculated, Job xxxvii. 4.
Thyrsus of Bacchus, fable of the, evidently borrowed from the story of the rod of Moses, Exod. iv. 17.
Tiberius Cæsar, remarkable saying of, Mic. iii. 1.
Tides, phenomena and cause of the, Job xxxviii. 11.
Tiglath-pileser, king of Assyria, supposed by Prideaux to have been the same with Arbaces, called by Ælian Thilgamus, and by Usher Ninus junior, 2 Kings xv. 29.
Tigris, account of a very remarkable overflowing of this river, Introduction to Nahum. See chap. ii. 6.
Time, אדן *idden*, and מועד *moad*, thus rendered in our common version, the prophetic symbol for *a year*, Dan. iv. 16, vii. 25, xii. 8.
Tin, method adopted in Cornwall of purifying this metal from all its dross, Jer. xxiii. 29.
Tippoo Sultan, description of a seal of, in the author's possession, Esth. iii. 9.
Tirshatha, probably the name of an office, Ezra ii. 63; Neh. viii. 9.
Titans, fable of the, Job xxvi. 5; Hesiod's description of Jupiter fighting against the Titans, one of the grandest things in all pagan antiquity, Psa. xviii. 7.
Tithes, disquisition concerning, Gen. xxviii., *in fine;* Ezek. xliv. 28.
Tithing the sheep, manner of, among the Jews, Ezek. xx. 37; Zech. xi. 7.
Titles given to the sovereigns and great men of the East extremely pompous, Job xxxii., *in fine.* Some examples produced, *ibid.*
Titus, triumphal arch of, particular description of the devices and inscription on the, Exod. xxv. 31.
Tobh, תוב, generally translated *good*, inquiry into its import, Gen. i. 10.
Toga prætexta, description of this Roman vestment, Gen. xxxvii. 3.

Toga virilis or *toga pura*, account of the, Gen. xxxvii. 3.

Togarmah, what people possibly meant by this name, Ezek. xxvii. 14.

Togatus, why this word is employed in speaking of a Roman, 1 Kings xix., *in fine*.

Tohoo, תֹהוּ, and *bohoo*, בֹהוּ, translated "without form and void," inquiry into the import of these words, Gen. i. 2. The names of the Syrian and Egyptian gods Theuth and Baü, probably borrowed from these terms, *ibid*.

Toleration, unlimited, in religious matters, should be allowed under the Christian dispensation, and why, Num. xv. 14.

Tombs of the dead very sacred among the ancients, Neh. ii. 5.

Toozuki Teemour, beautiful saying in the, quoted, Deut. xxxii. 24; Lam. iii. 12.

Topaz, description of this precious stone, Exod. xxviii. 17; Job xxviii. 18, 19. Where found in abundance, according to Diodorus Siculus, Job xxviii. 19.

Toph, תֹף, its import, Exod. xv. 20; 1 Sam. x. 5; Job xxi. 12; Psa. lxxxi. 2.

Tophet, Jerome's account of, 2 Kings xxiii. 10. Derivation of the name, according to the rabbins, *ibid*. Farther description, Isa. xxx. 33.

Torah, תּרה, its derivation and import, Exod. xii. 49; Lev. xxvi. 15.

Toston, (*Peter*) extraordinary longevity of this man, Psa. xc., *in fine*.

Transpositions in the Hebrew text, some instances of, Isa. vii. 4, viii. 12; Jer. xxiv. 1.

Trap to catch rats, foxes, &c., particular description of the, Amos iii. 5.

Treading of cattle, a method employed by the ancients in separating the corn from the ear, Isa. xxviii. 27, 28.

Tread-mill, in this country, the revival of an ancient employment for slaves, Isa. xlvii. 2.

Tree, accounted by the Jews as accursed and polluted, on which a malefactor had been executed, or on which he had been hanged after having been put to death by stoning, Isa. xv. 19.

Tree of the knowledge of good and evil, observations concerning the, Gen. ii. 9.

Tree of life, observations on the, Gen. ii. 9, iii. 19.

Trees, remarkable longevity of some species, Isa. lxv. 22. Extravagant notions of the Chinese respecting what they call the immortal tree, *ibid*. Trees in very ancient times frequently served for the temples of the gods, Judg. iii. 7.

Trefoil, this herb said to have been the means of fully convincing the learned Erasmus of the truth of the doctrine of the Trinity, Eccles. iii. 14.

Tremellius, author of a Latin version of the Hebrew Bible, with critical notes, General Preface, p. 6.

Trial by jury, one of the greatest ornaments of the British constitution, Gen. xxxvii. 36.

Trinity, doctrine of the, shown to be a doctrine of Scripture, Gen. i. 1, 26; Deut. vi. 4; Isa. xlviii. 16.

Troglodytes, who, Isa. ii. 13–16.

Troy, calamities of, described by Virgil under imagery similar to what Jeremiah employs in narrating the miseries of Jerusalem, Lam. i. 20.

Trumpets, feast of, why so named, and when celebrated, Exod. xxiii. 14.

Tryphon, human beings sacrificed to, in several cities of Egypt, according to Plutarch, Exod. xii., *in fine*.

Tsach, צַח, a memorial symbol of the rabbins, Masoretic notes at the end of Leviticus.

Tsahar, צֹהַר, rendered *window*, of very doubtful signification, Gen. vi. 16.

Tsal, צֵל, literally importing to *overspread* or *overshadow*, how metaphorically applied, Num. xiv. 9.

Tse, צֵא, import of this word among the Jews, when employed as a memorial symbol, Masoretic notes at the end of Genesis.

Tseba, צְבָא, host or army, inquiry into the meaning of the original term, Gen. ii. 1.

Tsebi, צְבִי, Dr. Shaw's opinion relative to the meaning of this Hebrew word, Deut. xii. 15.

Tsidekah or *Tsidekath*, צְדָקָת, its derivation and import, Lev. xxvi. 15. A beautiful paronomasia on this word, Isa. v. 7.

Tug, a species of cord among the Irish, how manufactured and for what purposes employed, Judg. xvi. 7.

Tumeet, a species of food, how prepared, 2 Sam. xvii. 28.

Tumuli or *barrows*, in England, what, 2 Sam. xviii. 17. To make the tumulus still more elevated and conspicuous, a pillar or some other ornament was often erected upon it, Isa. liii. 9.

Turkish couch, description of a, Song iii. 10.

Tutelar deity, among heathen nations, every city said to have a, Jer. ii. 28. The tutelary saints of the Romanists a copy of this pagan superstition, *ibid*.

Twilight, how caused, 2 Kings xx., *in fine*; Job xxxviii. 12; Prov. iv. 18.

Tympanum, description of this musical instrument, Gen. xxxi. 27.

Typhon, the evil demon, worshipped among the Egyptians, Num. xix. 2. Formerly customary to sacrifice red bulls to appease this divinity, *ibid*.

Tyre, some account of this celebrated city of antiquity, and its great vicissitudes of fortune, Josh. xix. 29; Ezek. xxv., xxvi., xxvii.; Isa. xxiii. Why called *the daughter of Tarshish*, Isa. xxiii. 10.

U

Ugab, עוּגָב, rendered *organ*, what it imports, Gen. iv. 21; Job xxi. 12; xxx. 31.

Ulai, the same with the Euläeus, a river which divided Shushan or Susiana, from Elymais, Dan. viii. 2.

Ulaloo or *Ullaloo*, the funeral song of the Irish, Isa. lii. 5.

Umbilical cord, the medium by which the fetus receives its nourishment while in the womb of its mother, Prov. iii. 8; Song vii. 2; Ezek. xvi. 4.

Ungodly, definition of this word, Psa. i. 1. In what it differs in import from *sinner* and *scornful*, *ibid*.

Unicorn, what animal probably intended by the Hebrew word so translated, Num. xxiii. 22; Deut. xxxiii. 17; Job xxxix. 9. The animal like a horse, with one long rich curled horn growing out of his forehead, commonly called the *unicorn*, shown to be wholly fabulous, Job xxxix. 9. Very curious passage in an old Psalter respecting this animal, Psa. xxii. 21.

Uniformity of worship, absolute necessity of, under the Mosaic economy, Deut. xii. 14. Why not so necessary under the Christian dispensation, *ibid*.

Uninterrupted succession, boasted of in the Romish Church, a mere fable, Ezek. xxxiv. 23, 24.

Universe, thoughts on the vast immensity of the, 1 Kings viii. 27; Amos ix. 6.

Upper garments, customary in the East to pull off the, in times of deep mourning, Exod. xxxiii. 5.

Ur, account of this very ancient city of Chaldea, Gen. xi. 31. Its primitive inhabitants generally supposed to have been *ignicolists*, *ibid*.

Urim and Thummim, various conjectures concerning, Exod. xxviii. 30. Inquiry into the mode of consultation by, *ibid.*; Josh. vii. 14; 1 Sam. xxviii. 6.

Urnæ Lachrymales, see *Lachrymatories*.

Urns containing the ashes and half-calcined bones of the dead, of frequent occurrence in barrows or tumuli in this country, 2 Chron. xvi., *in fine*; Jer. xxxiv. 2.

Usury, observations concerning, Exod. xxii. 25; Psa. xv. 5. The Jews remarkable for usury and usurious contracts, *ibid*.

Uxor, why a married woman was so called among the Romans, Song v. 5.

Uz, the country of Job, where probably situated, Preface to the book of Job, and chap. i. 1.

V

Valerianus, how this Roman emperor was treated by Sapor, king of Persia, Isa. li. 23.

Vallancy, (*General*) his ingenious hypothesis that the twelve patriarchs are resembled to the twelve signs of the zodiac, Gen. xlix., *in fine*. The asterism belonging to each patriarch, *ibid*.

Valley of vision, what meant by this expression, Isa. xxii., *in principio*.

Van of the ancients, what, Isa. xxx. 28.

Vasco de Gama, a celebrated Portuguese navigator, who recovered the passage round the Cape of Good Hope after it had been intermitted and lost for many centuries, Isa. ii. 13–16.

Vates and *poeta*, synonymous terms among the Romans, Gen. xx. 7.

Veeheyeh, וְאָהְיָה, import of this memorial symbol of the rabbins, Masoretic notes, end of Leviticus.

Vegetable creation, astonishing power with which God has endued its different species to multiply themselves, instanced in the elm, Gen. i. 12.

Veil of the Eastern women, description of the, Song iv. 1.

Veil of the tabernacle, description of the, Exod. xxvi. 31. Its great costliness, *ibid*.

Veil on the face of Moses, its typical import, Exod. xxxiv. 32.

Veil to shade the court, of what form, Isa. xl. 22.

Whit or *wid*, derivation and import of this old English word, 1 Sam. iii. 18.

Whitby, (*Dr.*) a very able commentator on the New Testament, General Preface, p. 8.

White asses or *ass colts*, riding upon, anciently the privilege of persons of high rank, Gen. xlix. 8.

Whoredom, the idolatries of the Jews very frequently so termed in the prophetical writings, 1 Chron. v. 25; Ezek. xvi. 23.

Wild ass, natural history of the, Job xxxix. 5–8.

Wild grapes, the Hebrew word so translated, in the opinion of Hasselquist, means the *solanum incanum* or *hoary nightshade*, known to the Arabs by the name of *aneb el dib*, Isa. v. 2.

Will, observations on the freedom of the, Psa. cx. 3; Prov. i. 10.

Wind-mills, an invention posterior to that of *water-mills* Isa. xlvii. 2.

Wine, anciently the expressed juice of the grape, without fermentation, Gen. xl. 11. Method adopted by the inhabitants of the East in cooling their wines, Prov. xxv. 13. How the ancients preserved their wine, Song ii. 4. The wines of Egypt, according to Hasselquist, not the produce of its own vineyards, Isa. v. 2. Account of the *mixed wine* of the ancient Greeks and Romans, Isa. i. 22. Observations on the mode of the treatment of wines, Isa. xxv. 6.

Wine-presses in Persia, how formed, according to Chardin, Isa. v. 2.

Wing, an emblem of protection, Ruth iii. 9.

Winged cymbal, the same with the Egyptian sistrum, according to Bochart, Isa. xviii. 1.

Winnowing of grain, how formerly effected, Ruth iii. 2; Psa. i. 4. Nearly the same with that practised in various parts of England and Ireland before the invention of the winnowing machine, *ibid.*

Wisdom of Solomon, the sacred historian's resemblanee of the extraordinary greatness of the, to the *sand on the seashore*, very beautifully illustrated by Lord Bacon, 1 Kings iv. 29.

Witches, consideration of the question whether the persons thus denominated only *pretended* to have, or *actually possessed*, the power commonly attributed to them, Exod. xxii. 18.

Withresd, king of Kent, singular anecdote respecting, 2 Chron. ii. 11.

Wives of the conquered king the property of the conqueror, 2 Sam. xvi. 21.

Wizard, derivation and import of this word, Lev. xix. 31; Deut. xviii. 11. Wizard usually considered the masculine of *witch*, *ibid.*

Wolf, remarkable for its fierceness and quick sight, Hab. i. 8. Why the tribe of Benjamin was resembled to this animal, Gen. xlix. 27.

Wolf grapes, the same with the *solanum incanum* or *hoary nightshade*, Isa. v. 2.

Woman, inquiry into the derivation of the term, Gen. ii. 23. To be slain by a woman considered by the ancients a mark of great disgrace, Judg. ix. 54.

Women employed in Eastern countries in grinding the corn, Exod. xi. 5; Isa. xlvii. 2. Women, among the ancients, generally kept houses of entertainment, or in other words, were tavern-keepers, Josh. ii. 1. Several quotations from ancient writers in attestation of this circumstance, *ibid.* Women formerly employed in the tabernacle service, Exod. xxxviii. 8; 1 Sam. ii. 22. The announcing and celebrating of great events formerly performed by women, Isa. xl. 9.

Word, citations from the Targums in which מימרא *meimra* or *word*, is evidently used *personally*, Gen. xv. 1, xxvi. 5, xxxi. 3; Exod. iv. 12; Judg. i. 19; 1 Chron. v. 22, vii. 21, ix. 20, xvi. 2, xxi. 13, 15; 2 Chron. ii. 1, xiv. 11, xv. 2, xvii. 3, xx. 17, 20, 29, 37, xxi. 14, xxv. 7, xxvi. 16, xxviii. 3, xxxii. 8, 16, 21, 31, xxxiii. 13, 17, 18, xxxvi. 33; Job xlii. 10; Psa. xxiii. 4, lv. 16, lxviii. 16; Isa. xlv. 22.

World, this word sometimes used for *land* or *country*, Isa. xiii. 11, xxiv. 14.

Worlds, thoughts respecting the plurality of, Deut. x. 14; 1 Kings viii. 27.

Wormwood, figurative import of this word in Scripture, Deut. xxix. 18; Lam. iii. 15. A man grievously afflicted termed by an Arabic poet *a pounder of wormwood*, *ibid.*

Wotteth, its derivation and import, Gen. xxxix. 8.

Writing on the Egyptian papyrus, mode of, in ancient times, Num. ix. 1. Transpositions, errors of very easy occurrence, *ibid.* Account of the different modes of writing in the time of Job, Job xix. 23.

X

Xerxes, immense wealth of this Persian monarch, Dan. xi. 3. His prodigious armament against Greece, *ibid.*

Xylophoria, a Jewish feast, for what purpose instituted, Exod. xxiii. 14; Neh. x. 34.

Y

Yad, יד, a Jewish memorial symbol, Masoretic notes at the end of Joshua.

Yagid, יגיד, a Jewish memorial symbol, Masoretic notes at the end of Deuteronomy.

Yam, ים, rendered *sea*, its general import, Num. xxxiv. 6; Deut. xxxiii. 23; Josh. i. 4. Generally rendered in the Septuagint by *θαλασσα*, Num. xxxiv. 6.

Year, length of a *tropical* or *natural*, according to the computation of modern astronomers, Gen. i. 14.

Year of release, institution of the, Deut. xv. 1. The whole book of Deuteronomy appointed to be read at this time, Deut. xxxi. 10, 11. This precept appears to have been very little attended to by the Jews, *ibid.*

Yechaveh, יחוה, and *yehegeh*, יהגה, import of these Jewish memorial symbols, Masoretic notes at the end of Exodus and Leviticus.

Yenachilam, ינחילם, import of this Jewish memorial symbol, Masoretic notes at the end of Deuteronomy.

Yideonim, ידענים, why *witches* were so denominated by the ancients, Lev. xix. 31; Deut. xviii. 11.

Yisadecha, יסעדך, import of this memorial symbol of the rabbins, Masoretic notes at the end of Exodus.

Yobelim, יובלים, improperly rendered *rams' horns*, Josh. vi. 4.

Youth of both sexes in Eastern countries marriageable at a very early age, 2 Kings xvi. 2.

Z

Zabii, singular instance of superstition among the, Exod. xxiii. 19.

Zahab, זהב, its derivation and import, Job xxviii. 17.

Zalmonah, the thirty-fourth station of the Israelites in the wilderness, where probably situated, and why so named, Num. xxxiii. 41.

Zamarenians, from whom probably descended, Gen. xxv. 2.

Zamzummim, some account of this ancient people, Deut. ii. 20.

Zaphnath-paaneah, import of this word very uncertain, Gen. xli. 45. Probably an Egyptian epithet, *ibid.*

Zarah, import of the name, Gen. xxxviii. 30.

Zarephath, the same with *Sarepta* of the Sidonians, 1 Kings xvii. 9.

Zebulun, why so named, Gen. xxx. 20.

Zechariah, some account of this prophet, Introduction to Zechariah.

Zeeb, a prince of the Midianites, import of his name, Judg. vii. 25.

Zeh, זה, import of this word among the Jews, when used as a memorial symbol, Masoretic notes at the end of Genesis.

Zelgaphoth, a pestilential east wind, suddenly killing those who are exposed to it, 1 Kings xx., *in fine.* Highly probable that a wind of this description, and not a *wall*, as stated in our translation, occasioned the death of the twenty-seven thousand Syrians in the time of Ben-hadad, *ibid.*

Zelophehad's daughters, peculiar case of, Num. xxvii. 1. Solemn trifling of some commentators relative to the mysterious imports of their names, Num. xxvii. 7.

Zeradusht, *Zerdust*, or *Zeratusht*, see *Zoroaster*.

Zidon, where situated, Ezek. xxvii. 8.

Zif, a Hebrew month answering to a part of our April and May, 1 Kings vi. 38. This name supposed to have been borrowed from the Chaldeans, and to be an evidence that the books of Kings were written after the Babylonish captivity, 1 Kings vi. 1.

Zikenim, זקנים, a degree of civil distinction among the Hebrews, Josh. xxiii. 2.

Zimerah, זמרה, probably a kind of musical instrument, Psa. lxxxi. 2.

Zin, wilderness of, the thirty-second station of the Israelites in the wilderness, some account of, Num. xxxiii. 36.

Zion, capture of this very celebrated fortress of the Jebusites by David, 2 Sam. v. 7. Dr. Kennicott's translation of the Hebrew text which contains the account, *ibid.*

Ziph, where situated, Psa. liv., *in principio.*

Zoan, the same with *Tanis*, Ezek. xxx. 14.

Zodiac, signs of the, known in Egypt and Chaldea in the time of Joseph, Gen. xlix., *in fine.* Very elegant allusion in the book of Psalms to the twelve signs of the zodiac, Psa. lxv. 11.

Zohair, an eminent Arabic poet, Psa. lx., *in principio*.
Zonah, זונה, commonly rendered *harlot*, what it properly imports, Gen. xxxviii. 15, 21. Distinction between זונה *zonah* and קדשה, *kedeshah*, both indifferently rendered *harlot* in our versions, Gen. xxxviii. 21.
Zophar the Naamathite, who, Job ii. 11.
Zoroaster or *Zeradusht*, traditions concerning, Exod. iii. 2. Character of the institutes attributed to him, Deut. xxxiv., *in fine*. In what sense we are to understand the tradition that the works of Zoroaster, which are in prose, contain *two millions* of verses, Introduction to Ezra. Zoroaster supposed by some to be a confused picture of the prophet Daniel, Introduction to Daniel.
Zuleekha, the name of Potiphar's wife, according to the Asiatics, Gen. xxxix. 6. Remarkable anecdote concerning this woman, as related in the Koran, *ibid*.
Zumeet, a kind of food, how prepared, 2 Sam. xvii. 28.
Zuzim, a people of antiquity, possibly the same with the Zamzummim, Gen. xiv. 5; Deut. ii. 20.